INGENIX®

AF685968

Coders' Desk Reference *for* Procedures

2010

Notice

Coders' Desk Reference for Procedures is designed to be an authoritative source of information about coding and reimbursement issues. Every effort has been made to verify accuracy and all information is believed reliable at the time of publication. Absolute accuracy cannot be guaranteed, however. This publication is made available with the understanding that the publisher is not engaged in rendering legal or other services that require a professional license. If you identify a correction or wish to share information, please email the Ingenix customer service department at customerservice@ingenix.com or fax us at 801.982.4033.

American Medical Association Notice

Fee schedules, relative value units, conversion factors and/or related components are not assigned by the AMA, are not part of CPT, and the AMA is not recommending their use. The AMA does not directly or indirectly practice medicine or dispense medical services. The AMA assumes no liability for data contained or not contained herein.

CPT is a registered trademark of the American Medical Association.

Copyright

Made in the USA.

ISBN 978-1-60151-290-1

Acknowledgments

The following staff contributed to the development and/or production of this book:

Steven Woodward, *Product Manager*
Karen Schmidt, BSN, *Technical Director*
Stacy Perry, Manager, *Desktop Publishing*
Lisa Singley, *Project Manager*
LaJuana Green, RHIA, CCS, *Clinical/Technical Editor*
Nannette Orme, CPC, CEMC, PCS, *Clinical/Technical Editor*
Tracy Betzler, *Desktop Publishing Specialist*
Hope M. Dunn, *Desktop Publishing Specialist*
Toni Stewart, *Desktop Publishing Specialist*
Kimberli Turner, *Editor*

Clinical/Technical Editors

Nannette Orme, CPC, CEMC, PCS

Ms. Orme has more than 10 years of experience in the health care profession. She has extensive background in CPT, HCPCS, and ICD-9-CM coding. She recently served several years as a consultant with PricewaterhouseCoopers. Her areas of expertise include physician audits and education, compliance and HIPAA legislation, litigation support for Medicare self-disclosure cases, hospital chargemaster maintenance, and emergency department coding. Ms. Orme has presented at national professional conferences and contributed articles for several professional publications. She is a member of the American Academy of Professional Coders and the Utah Medical Group Management Association (UMGMA).

Our Commitment to Accuracy

Ingenix is committed to producing accurate and reliable materials. To report corrections, please visit www.ingenixonline.com/accuracy or email accuracy@ingenix.com. You can also reach customer service by calling 1.800.INGENIX (464.3649), option 1.

Contents

Introduction

Coding is a complicated business. It's not enough to have a current copy of a CPT® book. Medical coders also need dictionaries and specialty texts if they are to accurately translate physicians' operative reports or patient charts into CPT codes.

That's why Ingenix originally developed *Coders' Desk Reference*—now known as *Coders' Desk Reference for Procedures*—to provide a resource with answers to CPT coding questions. We polled the medical reimbursement community and our technical staff to determine the issues causing bottlenecks in a coder's workload.

We know that experienced coders are frustrated by limited definitions accompanying many CPT codes. Beginning coders need guidelines on the use of CPT codes and basic information about medical and reimbursement issues. Everyone requires up-to-date information about the anticipated changes in procedural coding.

Coders' Desk Reference for Procedures (CDR) answers the questions of both experienced and novice medical coders. Coders, physicians, registered nurses, physician assistants, and physical therapists contributed to the technical information contained in CDR. The result is a compendium of answers to a wide variety of CPT coding questions.

Since the first release of CDR in 1995, coders' corrections, suggestions, and tips have been incorporated into every printing, making this book as informative and useful as possible. Changes reflecting the dynamic world of coding are ongoing, and Ingenix encourages input for inclusion in future editions of the book. Information in CDR has been updated to reflect 2010 CPT codes.

Format

CDR is divided into convenient sections for easy use, with each section organized in alphabetic or numeric order. Simply access the section by thumbing through the convenient tabbing system to find the specific item of interest.

Using CPT Codes

For the new coder, and even for the veteran, this chapter provides an overview of the CPT book: what it is and how best to use this coding system for identifying procedures.

Using CPT Modifiers

Modifiers augment CPT codes to the satisfaction of private and government payers. Ingenix coding experts interpret CPT modifiers and identify their advantage in reimbursement.

Using E/M Codes

Although some of the most commonly used codes by physicians of all specialties, evaluation and management (E/M) codes are amongst the least understood. These codes, introduced in the 1992 CPT book, were designed to increase accuracy and consistency in the reporting of non-procedural encounters. This section includes a listing of the categories and subcategories of E/M codes, as well as a glossary of terms relating to E/M services.

Reimbursement Terms

In order to get reimbursed in a timely manner, it is important to have a clear understanding of the terminology used by major insurers and the federal government. This section includes up-to-date terminology that will help coders have a better understanding of the complex reimbursement climate.

Abbreviations, Acronyms, and Symbols

The medical profession has its own shorthand for documentation. Here, acronyms, abbreviations, and symbols commonly seen on operative reports or medical charts are listed for easy reference.

Prefixes and Suffixes

The uniquely efficient language of medicine is based on prefixes and suffixes attached to root words to modify the meaning. Medical prefixes and suffixes evolved from the Greek and Latin used by pioneering physicians.

Procedural Eponyms

What is the Mitrofanoff operation? What is the Binet test? Eponyms honor the developer of a procedure or test, but do little to clarify what the procedure is. Editors have researched the procedural eponyms found in the index of the CPT book and provide simplified explanations of what the procedures are, along with applicable CPT codes.

Surgical Terms

Operative reports contain words and phrases that not only communicate the importance and urgency of surgery, but they communicate the techniques as well. CDR's glossary of surgical terms includes the terms most commonly used in operative reports to describe techniques and tools.

Anatomy Charts

Illustrations are included by body system with additional plates showing the planes of the body and Rule of Nines for burns.

CPT Lay Descriptions

The lay descriptions contained in the *Coders' Desk Reference for Procedures* are written to provide a common or generally accepted method of accomplishing the service indicated by the CPT code description. In cases where more than one procedure or method is reported by a single code, one example of those methods or procedures may be given in the lay description. No lay description in this product is intended to give an absolute, required method of performing the service described in the CPT code. Reflecting the full spectrum of variations in technology and of professional techniques would be impossible in a book this size. Ordered numerically, each CPT code is followed by a detailed description of the procedure that code represents.

Coders' Desk Reference for Procedures was developed to help providers comply with the emerging standards by which medical services are coded, reported, and paid. Remember that *Coders' Desk Reference for Procedures* is a post-treatment medical reference and, as such, it is inappropriate to use this manual to select medical treatment.

Using CPT® Codes

The codes of the *Physicians' Current Procedural Terminology* (CPT) book constitute procedural and medical service components. The CPT book is in its fourth edition with revisions occurring every year.

The CPT coding system was selected as one of the National Code Sets mandatory for use to facilitate electronic transactions, including health claims, enrollments, eligibility, payment/remittance, and referral authorization. CPT codes are divided into three categories to enhance the use of the CPT system by practicing physicians, managed care and other payer organizations, and researchers. Category I codes refer to the accustomed five-digit numerical system. Category II codes are a set of optional tracking codes, developed principally for performance measurement. The CPT Category III codes are temporary codes to identify new and emerging technologies.

History of CPT

The CPT book is a standardized system of five-digit codes and descriptive terms used to report medical services and procedures performed by physicians. The system was developed and is updated and published annually by the AMA. CPT codes communicate to payers, and in some instances other providers and even patients, the procedures and services performed during a medical encounter.

The AMA published the first edition of the CPT book in 1966 as a companion piece to its Current Medical Terminology (CMT), a manual of preferred medical nomenclature, then in its third edition. The first edition of CPT (5 x 7 inches, 163 pages) contained a listing of four-digit codes and brief descriptions to report a full range of medical procedures and services. Each code was cross-referenced to then-available diagnostic codes: the *Standard Nomenclature of Diseases and Operations* (SNDO) and the *International Classification of Diseases, Adapted* (ICDA).

Editors of the first edition cited a variety of sources in developing the work, including the Social Security Administration, the Blue Shield Manual of Statistical Requirements, and the Relative Value Studies of the California Medical Society. The four-digit codes do not approximate those of today's CPT. The task of modifying them to the present format was reserved for the editors of the second edition, published in 1970.

The 1970 edition of the CPT book marks the genesis of the coding manual familiar to today's medical office workers. Many of the 1970 edition's five-digit codes and expanded descriptions in this work remain unchanged. The number of coded procedures far exceeds those available to users of the first edition and guidelines to the various sections appear for the first time. The second edition was developed with assistance from a handful of members of medical professional societies, a practice that would evolve into more than the 100-member CPT Advisory Committee, and representatives from 18 organizations comprising the Health Care Professionals Advisory Committee (HCPAC) currently listed in CPT 2010.

The third edition of the CPT book published in 1973 offered new features, such as alphabetic modifiers and starred procedures marked by an asterisk. Deleted codes (but not new codes) could be found in an appendix. This edition also saw the medical codes moved to the front of the code listings, a benchmark that would stand for almost 20 years until the introduction of the evaluation and management (E/M) codes in 1992.

The fourth edition of the CPT book was originally published in 1977. This edition began the custom of significant yearly revisions, usually concentrated on a limited number of sections. Since then, medical office coders have made an annual ritual of anticipating the code changes and the related effects on coding and billing habits for their practices.

The CPT Book Conventions

The CPT book is self-referencing. Its introductory material provides information about its rules, format, and guidelines. The introduction to the CPT book should be carefully studied at least once by medical coders and reviewed annually for changes. Classes and correspondence courses teach medical coding and several introductory coding books convey the CPT book fundamentals. Additionally, the AMA and private consultants sponsor coding seminars to discuss changes and methods to implement these changes into regular coding practice.

The heart of this chapter is a glossary of the CPT book terminology. Consult these listings as needed to solve procedural coding problems. However, a brief primer to conventions, rules, and anomalies is presented below.

The six major sections of Category 1 codes in the CPT book are:

- Evaluation and Management (E/M)
- Anesthesiology
- Surgery

- Radiology (including nuclear medicine and diagnostic ultrasound)
- Pathology and Laboratory
- Medicine

A common misconception about the CPT book is that its organization serves to arrange procedural codes according to the major medical specialties that can report them. This is simply not the case. Any qualified physician can render any service or procedure listed by code. A physician's advanced medical training dictates the types of services and procedures customarily performed. Many physicians, particularly those in primary care, can in the course of a day perform work coded from all six sections.

The CPT book is, however, primarily a reference for physicians' work; only a very small code set can be reported by non-physicians (e.g., chiropractors, physician assistants, nurse practitioners, physical or occupational therapists, speech and language therapists, dieticians or nutritionists, pharmacists). The rest of the codes report the physicians' work or, in some instances, the work of others under close physician supervision. Payers almost universally assume a physician performs the work coded. Non-physician work and coding must be clearly negotiated in advance with all involved payers.

Although required by almost all third-party payers, the existence of a CPT procedure code does not in any way guarantee payment when the work is performed. Insurance plans vary widely in reimbursement.

Format

The printed format is designed to save a great deal of space while still making a great deal of sense. A key to interpreting this space-saving scheme involves the use of the semicolon (;).

A main code is typically a single-sentence description, constructed so that pertinent adjunct information follows the semicolon. The following indented codes appear only as brief adjunct information. An important coding axiom is that an indented code always includes the common portion of the preceding main code description as it appears up to and including the semicolon.

25500 Closed treatment of radial shaft fracture; without manipulation

25505   with manipulation

The complete description of code 25505 is: Closed treatment of radial shaft fracture; with manipulation. Although 25505 appears under 25500, it stands alone to describe a treatment requiring manipulation.

Symbols and Appendix B

Symbols alert users to changes or other attributes of a code. The symbols appear in the left margin, just in front of the code number, as shown here:

●	A closed black circle designates a new code. This symbol will display in black in the standard edition of CPT.
▲	A black triangle indicates a code description has been changed or altered. This symbol will display in black in the standard edition of CPT.
✚	A black ✚ symbol indicates an add-on code, which is reported secondarily in addition to the primary procedure.
⊙	A black bulls eye identifies codes in which moderate (conscious) sedation anesthesia would not be reported separately when performed during the same session by the same provider.
⚡	A black lightning bolt denotes codes for vaccines that are pending FDA approval.

These symbols may have a bearing on assignment of codes for a practice.

Modifiers

Code modifiers were introduced to the CPT book more than 25 years ago to flag a service that is altered in some way from the stated description. The basic definition of the coded service remains intact. Modifiers more precisely convey the nature of the service or procedure. Modifiers are two-digit codes and those commonly used in a practice become second nature. They may or may not affect the level of reimbursement.

Modifiers can indicate:

- A service or procedure represents only a professional or a technical component
- A service or procedure was performed by more than one physician
- Only part of a service was performed
- An adjunct service was performed
- A bilateral service was performed
- A service or procedure was provided more than once
- Unusual events occurred
- A procedure or service was altered in some way

Consult Appendix A of the CPT book for a listing with full descriptions of modifiers. Additionally, individual sections of the CPT book may contain special instructions for the use of modifiers to codes in that particular section. See the Modifiers chapter of this book for further discussion.

Glossary of Terms

Use the following glossary of terms to troubleshoot and solve CPT code-related claims problems. Other chapters of this book will be useful for modifier-related and E/M problems. And, as stated earlier, the CPT book introduction and introductory material at the section heads can help coders sort out problem areas.

Add-on Code—CPT code representing a procedure performed in addition to the primary procedure and designated with a ✚ in the CPT book. Add-on codes are never reported as stand-alone services but are reported secondarily in addition to the primary procedure.

Alphabetic Reference Index—The coding process begins with a careful examination of the medical record to determine primary and secondary procedures, as well as any modifying or extenuating circumstances. The alphabetic index is the starting point of all CPT coding. Do not select codes solely on the basis of information in the index—it is only a reference to the full listing of codes. The alphabetic index is not a substitute for the main text. You must refer to the main text to ensure appropriate code selection.

Anesthesia 00100–01999, 99100–99140—The Anesthesia section includes codes to report "general, regional, supplementation of local anesthesia, or other supportive services." See the anesthesia chapter in this book for code-to-code crosswalks.

Appendixes—Thirteen appendixes appear toward the back of the CPT book. Appendix A is a listing of modifiers and their descriptions. Appendix B is a listing of additions, deletions, and revisions that were accomplished to compile the current edition. Appendix C is a series of clinical examples for E/M codes. Appendix D is a summary of add-on codes. Appendix E is a summary of CPT codes exempt from modifier 51. Appendix F is a summary of CPT codes exempt from modifier 63. Appendix G is a summary of the CPT codes that include moderate (conscious) sedation. Appendix H is a listing of performance measures for category II codes. Appendix I contains the genetic testing code modifiers. Appendix J identifies the nerves associated with electrodiagnostic testing of sensory, motor, and mixed nerves. Appendix K identifies the vaccine codes listed in the CPT book that are awaiting FDA approval. Appendix L identifies the vascular families. Appendix M supplies a crosswalk to newly deleted CPT codes.

Bilateral Procedure—Modifier 50 is used in those instances where a bilateral code for the same operative session is unavailable. The second (or bilateral) procedure is identified by the primary procedure code along with the modifier. An anatomical counterpart must exist for the procedure. See the Modifiers chapter of this book for more information.

Category Codes— The main section of CPT codes are considered Category I. Category I CPT codes describe a procedure or service identified with a five-digit CPT code and descriptor nomenclature. Category II CPT codes are a set of codes used for supplemental tracking and performance measurements. Primarily these codes are used to report quality measures when participating in Medicare's Physician Quality Reporting Initiative. For more information about PQRI, see the CMS website at http://www.cms.hhs.gov/pqri/.

Category III codes facilitate data collection for new services and procedures to substantiate usage and clinical efficacy. Category III codes are used to track new and emerging technologies.

Code Changes—To keep up with the dynamic nature of medicine, the AMA revises and publishes the CPT book on an annual basis. Appendix B consists of a summary of additions, deletions, and revisions to the current edition. These changes are indicated in the CPT book as follows:

●	New codes—New codes are identified by a blackened circle. This symbol will display in black in the standard edition of CPT.
●14301	**Adjacent tissue transfer or rearrangement, any area; defect 30.1 sq cm to 60.0 sq cm**
▲	Revised codes—Revised codes are identified by a blackened triangle. This symbol will display in black in the standard edition of CPT.
▲21015	**Radical resection of tumor (eg, malignant neoplasm), soft tissue of face or scalp; less than 2 cm**
( )	Deleted codes—Deleted codes are identified by parentheses. **(14300 has been deleted. To report, see 14301, 14302)**

Code Ranges—Whenever more than one code applies to a given entry in the index, all applicable codes are listed. If two or more nonsequential codes apply, they are separated by a comma. For example:

Rhytidectomy
Forehead 15824, 15826

If two or more sequential codes apply, a hyphen is used. For example:

Angiography
Renal 75722-75724

Conscious Sedation—This icon ⊙ identifies procedures that include moderate (conscious) sedation anesthesia. Moderate (conscious) sedation codes should not be reported with these procedures.

Consultations—This term defines times when a treating physician asks the advice or opinion of another physician. A consulting physician has a wide degree of latitude in providing services, but does not assume care or provide treatment plans. The E/M code range 99241–99255 reports consultation services and the E/M chapter of this book can be consulted for more information.

Correct Coding Initiative—Centers for Medicare and Medicaid Services (CMS) correct coding initiative (CCI) provides edits that determine the appropriateness of CPT code combinations in billing for Medicare claims. The edits are designed to detect "fragmentation," or separate coding of the component parts of a procedure.

Cross-reference—The following reference appears in CPT to direct coders to additional material:

- See—this directs the user to refer to the term listed after the word "see."

Evaluation and Management (E/M) —This series of codes provides a means to classify and report the extent of a physician's involvement for a full range of common physician/patient encounters.

E/M codes describe the intensity of a medical encounter as measured by the risks and complexities associated with the diagnosis and medical decision making. The more detailed the components and the more complex the diagnosis and treatment plan, the more valuable the E/M service.

The simplest, most basic treatment constitutes what many refer to as level 1 in treatment. Higher levels are assigned consequential to the complexity of services and diagnoses. See the E/M chapter in this book for more information about this series of codes.

Global Surgery Package—This denotes a normal surgical procedure with no complications that includes all of the elements needed to perform the procedure. Fragmentation, or "unbundling," refers to providers who may intentionally or accidentally charge separately for procedures included in the global package for that given surgical procedure.

Guidelines—Guidelines appear at the beginning of each of the six major sections of CPT. The guidelines define items that are necessary to interpret and report the procedures and services contained in that section.

Incidental Procedures—An incidental procedure is generally minor and considered an integral part of the primary procedure. Incidental procedures are not separately reimbursable and are included in the primary charge.

Indented Code Description—Indented code descriptions include all words up to the semicolon of the main description preceding it. See also Format.

Main Terms, Listing in Index—Procedures are listed in the CPT book index by:

- Procedure or service (endoscopy or splint)
- Organ or other anatomic site (tibia or colon)
- Condition (abscess or entropion)
- Key synonyms
- Key eponyms (disease or procedure named after a person, e.g., Mohs technique)
- Abbreviations such as MRI for magnetic resonance imaging

Medicine Services—The CPT book's Medicine section is found at the end of the book. Among the many diagnostic and therapeutic services included under medicine are immunizations, injections, specialty specific codes, and special services. The guidelines begin with instructions on billing multiple procedures. Coders are instructed to report each procedure separately. Note that the word "procedures" may include medical and/or evaluation and management services.

Modifiers, CPT—CPT modifiers show that a service was altered from the stated description without actually changing the basic definition of the service. The CPT Modifiers chapter of this book explains how modifiers are used and which modifiers affect reimbursement. For example, modifier 27 Multiple Outpatient Hospital E/M Encounters on the Same Date, identifies hospital resources used in relation to separate and distinct E/M encounters performed by physicians in multiple outpatient settings on the same date.

Outpatient Services—This term usually refers to physician office, clinical, and hospital outpatient department settings. The E/M code range 99201–99215 reports services in these settings. See the E/M chapter of this book for more information.

Parenthetical—A parenthetical phrase is one enclosed by parentheses ( ). Information specific to a given code may be included as a parenthetical phrase following the code. These constitute directions to the coder and should be followed. Read all of the rules, guidelines, and general information in each section and subsection.

Pathology and Laboratory—The Pathology and Laboratory section of the CPT book is divided into 18 subsections. Many procedures are performed by various methods and coders must know the methodology used. In many instances, identification of method is the key to appropriate coding.

Pathology and Laboratory services are provided by pathologists or technologists under supervision of a physician. If the pathologist must review a test result and/or render an opinion, the appropriate code should be selected and modifier 26 attached to indicate that only a professional component was provided.

Radiology—Reporting radiological procedures involves two components: the technical and the professional. The technical component is that part of the procedure specific to the equipment, including the services of a technician. The professional component is specific to the physician's evaluation of the images. CPT coding and nomenclature in the radiology section is under constant review in an effort to reflect current standards of service for this broad specialty.

Separate Procedures—Separate procedures are defined in the CPT book as services that are "commonly carried out as an integral component of a total service or procedure." These services are noted in the CPT book with the parenthetical phrase (separate procedure) at the end of the description. When this phrase appears before the semicolon, all indented descriptions that follow are covered by it.

To reduce fragmented billing, review pertinent surgical codes that include the notation (separate procedure), and apply these guidelines:

- Code separate procedures only when the procedure is performed alone rather than in conjunction with related procedures.
- When a procedure that is ordinarily a component of a larger procedure is performed alone for a specific purpose, you can list it by itself or as a multiple procedure with modifier 51 and/or 59 attached. In other words, it is unrelated to the other procedure performed in a multiple setting. The operative report and associated ICD-9-CM code must be clear and specific to substantiate a separate procedure in conjunction with another major surgical procedure.

Subterms—A main term may be followed by a series of indented terms that modify the main term. Subterms affect the selection of appropriate codes.

Surgery—The Surgery section of CPT includes two types of procedures: therapeutic and diagnostic. To select CPT surgical codes that accurately reflect the service performed, read surgical code descriptions carefully and remember that modifiers may have a significant impact on reimbursement. See the lay description chapter of the *Coders' Desk Reference* for general explanations of procedures.

Surgical Package Procedures—The CPT book defines a surgical package in terms of a normal, uncomplicated performance of specific surgical services, with the assumption that on average, all surgical procedures of a given type are similar with respect to skill level, duration, and length of normal follow-up care. The majority of CPT surgical codes are package services; they include related minor procedures and normal follow-up. Reimbursement for package procedures includes the actual surgical service, local infiltration, metacarpal, metatarsal, and digital block or local anesthesia (when used), and an allowance for normal postoperative care. One related E/M encounter provided after the decision for surgery has been made is also normally included. See also Unbundling and Separate Procedures.

Unbundling—Unbundling a code is similar to coding an incidental procedure but usually involves less subtle fragmenting of a bill. Never divide the components of a procedure when one code covers all of the components. Examples of minor procedures always included in the primary surgical package include the following:

- Local infiltration of medication
- Closure of surgically created wounds, minor debridement, and wound culture
- Exploration of operative area
- Lysis of moderate amounts of adhesion and fulguration of bleeding points
- Application of dressings
- Application of splints with musculoskeletal procedures

Unlisted Procedure or Service—Codes have been designated to report services or procedures that are not found in the CPT book. These codes usually end in the number 99. When an unlisted procedure code is used, a manual review by the payer is necessary. Documentation, such as operative notes and a cover letter, should be submitted with the claim. The provider should establish the fee for an unlisted procedure. It may help the payer if the provider relates the service's value to a procedure of similar value and worth.

Using CPT® Modifiers

Modifiers allow coders to indicate that a service was altered in some way from the stated CPT description without actually changing the basic definition of the service. Modifiers are considered an essential component of accurate coding. Some modifiers impact reimbursement and others identify special circumstances. Modifiers can indicate the following:

- A service or procedure represents only a professional or technical component
- A service or procedure was performed by more than one physician
- Only part of a service was performed
- An adjunctive service was performed
- A bilateral procedure was performed
- A service or procedure was provided more than once
- Unusual events occurred
- A procedure or service was altered in some way

Physical status modifiers, P1-P6, specifically used for anesthesia services, are not discussed in this chapter. HCPCS modifiers, beginning with an alpha character, may be appended to CPT codes in specific circumstances. HCPCS modifiers are not discussed in this chapter.

22 Increased Procedural Services

Modifier 22 is not appropriate for CPT codes with the term "simple" as part of the code description. Rather, modifier 22 is used to indicate that a procedure was complicated, complex, difficult, or took significantly more time than usually required by the provider to complete the procedure. Documentation should be provided with the billing and kept in the medical record when this modifier is used. When modifier 22 is used, an operative report should always be attached to the claim.

The fee reported for modifier 22 should be the usual and customary amount for the procedure plus an additional amount for the unusual circumstances. If modifier 22 is appended to a code that is not the primary code, and modifier 51 has been appended, modifier 22 should be paid in addition to the cut contract rate paid for the code.

Modifier 22 often produces an automatic review or audit by payers. If the operative report attached to the claim does not indicate appropriate use of the modifier, the increase in payment will be denied. Periodic orientation for all involved in the coding process is important from both a legal and reimbursement perspective.

Because modifier 22 is often used when complications are encountered during surgical procedures, medical necessity is substantiated by additional diagnostic codes that identify the complication. These diagnostic codes should reflect the operative condition and the complication(s) encountered during the surgery.

23 Unusual Anesthesia

This modifier is used by anesthesiologists to indicate that this procedure is normally performed under local or regional block but due to unusual circumstances, general anesthesia is needed. This modifier is not appropriate for use with codes that include the term "without anesthesia" in the descriptor, or for procedures normally performed under general anesthesia.

24 Unrelated Evaluation and Management Service by the Same Physician During a Postoperative Period

This modifier reports that an unrelated E/M service was provided by the surgeon within the global period. Use of this modifier needs to be correlated to a diagnosis code that is unrelated to the surgical diagnosis code.

25 Significant, Separately Identifiable Evaluation and Management Service by the Same Physician on the Same Day of the Procedure or Other Service

This modifier indicates that on the same day a procedure or service identified by a CPT code is performed, the patient's condition required a significant, separately identifiable E/M code beyond the usual level of service required for the procedure. In addition, the modifier denotes that the patient's condition required services that were above and beyond the usual preoperative and postoperative care associated with the actual procedure performed.

This modifier is not appropriate with an E/M code that has a minimum level of service. Assign the proper E/M code and amount as appropriate for service rendered. Most payers will allow payment for significant E/M services on the day of a procedure. Performance of a procedure includes an evaluation of the patient as it relates to that procedure or service code. When the patient's condition causes the evaluation to exceed that usual level of service, the appropriate E/M code is listed and appended with modifier 25.

Paper documentation does not need to accompany the claim, but the medical record must clearly identify relevant criteria for separate reporting of an E/M service in addition to the procedure/service code.

Note: Modifier 25 has been approved for hospital outpatient use.

26 Professional Component

Modifier 26 identifies the physician's component of a two-component service. Do not use this modifier with procedures that are either 100 percent technical or 100 percent professional. It is only used on procedures having both components, such as x-rays or pathology codes; and it results in payment being made for only the professional component of the service. Using modifier 26 also alerts payers to expect a separate claim from the facility for the technical component.

27 Multiple Outpatient Hospital E/M Encounters on the Same Date

Modifier 27 gives physicians the means for reporting the use of hospital resources when providing E/M services in multiple outpatient settings on the same date.

Note: Modifier 27 has been approved for hospital outpatient use.

32 Mandated Services

Modifier 32 identifies services that are mandated by Medicare, a peer review organization, a state, local, or government agency, and private payers. Reimbursement may be made at 100 percent of the allowable amount for the service or procedure (such as consultations and related diagnostic services). Deductibles or co-payments may also be waived by the payer. Keep in mind, however, that not all payers cover services when they are mandated, and often expect the government agency to pay for the service (e.g., an examination to determine abuse, disability, or confirm rape).

47 Anesthesia By Surgeon

Modifier 47 identifies that the surgeon administered regional or general anesthesia. The most common use of this modifier is for a Bier block, which is not identified with its own code. The claim should identify the time spent administering the block. The charge for anesthesia by a surgeon is usually based on time increments instead of a percentage of the total charge for the surgical service. Reimbursement policies for these situations vary dramatically. The predominant attitude of most payers is that a physician should perform the role of the operating surgeon or the anesthesiologist, but not both. Contact payers for specific instructions.

50 Bilateral Procedure

Modifier 50 identifies an identical procedure performed bilaterally during a single operative session. Depending upon payer rules, you will either have to (1) list the procedure twice and append modifier 50 to the second procedure, or (2) only list the code once with the bilateral modifier appended.

Do not use modifier 50 when a code description specifically states that the procedure is bilateral, such as code 58700 *Salpingectomy, complete or partial, unilateral or bilateral (separate procedure)*. Also, modifier 50 should not be used on procedures where the organ is considered to be midline, such as the bladder, uterus, esophagus, or nasal septum.

Note: Medicare and many national payers are moving toward the single line entry to identify a bilateral situation. However, careful monitoring will ensure correct reimbursement for both sides. Some payers allow 100 percent for each side if a separate incision is involved. Payers that do not allow 100 percent for the second side usually allow from 50 to 75 percent. Because of the varying allowances, monitor your reimbursement to determine the percentage allowed for the second side.

Note: Modifier 50 has been approved for hospital outpatient use.

51 Multiple Procedures

Modifier 51 designates multiple procedures that are rendered at the same operative session or on the same day. CPT states that modifier 51 should be used when a combination of surgical services, medical services, or surgical and medical services are provided. Modifier 51 is not used with E/M services. It is applicable when multiple related procedures are performed and there is no single inclusive code available. List the primary procedure first on the electronic billing format or claim form, then attach modifier 51 to each secondary procedure code.

The following guidelines make good billing and coding practice for modifier 51:

- List the procedure code with the highest value first when billing Medicare and commercial payers.
- List additional procedures by descending value.
- Clearly state in your operative reports which procedures were accomplished through separate incisions and which were done through the same incision.
- Do not combine charges when coding multiple, unrelated procedures. List each procedure separately on the claim form and indicate each charge.

- If a comprehensive procedure has a single CPT code, report that code rather than "unbundling" or listing the individual components.

Note: This modifier should not be appended to designated "add-on" codes.

52 Reduced Services

Modifier 52 identifies situations where the physician elects to reduce or eliminate a portion of a service or procedure. Cover letters or operative reports are not necessary when modifier 52 is used since these claims are not usually sent to medical review. Cover letters and operative reports may even impede claims processing. However, physicians may find it helpful to provide the payer with an explanation of the reduced fee compared to the usual fee. The reduction in charge reflects the reduction or elimination of a portion of the service.

Note: For hospital outpatient reporting of a previously scheduled procedure or service that is reduced or canceled due to extenuating circumstances or those that threaten the well being of the patient prior to or after administration of anesthesia, see modifiers 73 and 74.

Note: Modifier 52 has been approved for hospital outpatient and discontinued radiology use.

53 Discontinued Procedure

Modifier 53 is used to denote a surgical or diagnostic procedure terminated by the physician because of concerns about the procedure's impact on the patient's well being. Add modifier 53 to the code for the discontinued procedure. This code can only be used if the procedure was discontinued after anesthesia was administered and/or the patient was prepped in the operating suite.

Note: This modifier is not used to report the elective cancellation of a procedure prior to the patient's anesthesia induction and/or surgical preparation in the operating suite. For outpatient hospital/ambulatory surgery center (ASC) reporting of a previously scheduled procedure or service that is reduced or canceled due to extenuating circumstances or those that threaten the well being of the patient prior to or after anesthesia, see modifiers 73 and 74.

54 Surgical Care Only

Modifier 54 is used when one physician performs a surgical procedure and another provides preoperative and/or postoperative management. The surgeon who performs the procedure reports modifier 54. Both physicians need to determine what percentage of the overall fee each will bill for their individual services (e.g., 70 percent for the surgery and 30 percent for the postoperative care). Do not bill more than 100 percent for the service provided. CMS identifies the percentage assigned in the intraoperative column in the Medicare Reimbursement Table.

55 Postoperative Management Only

Modifier 55 is used when one physician provides postoperative management after another physician has performed the surgical procedure. The physician providing postoperative management bills the surgical procedure code at the percentage agreed upon (see modifier 54) with modifier 55 attached. CMS identifies the percentage assigned in the postoperative column in the Medicare Reimbursement Table.

56 Preoperative Management Only

Modifier 56 identifies the physician providing preoperative care during the preoperative time clause established by the payer but not performed in the actual surgery. Use this modifier only with codes from the Surgery and Medicine sections of the CPT book. It does not appear in guidelines of the E/M codes. CMS identifies the percentage assigned in the intraoperative column in the Medicare Reimbursement Table.

57 Decision for Surgery

Modifier 57 identifies an E/M service that resulted in the initial decision to perform surgery. Because the CPT book does not designate whether the surgery decided upon is major or minor, diagnostic or therapeutic, use modifier 57 to identify when the decision for any surgery is made.

The prevailing industry standard is to use modifier 25 for minor procedures and modifier 57 on major procedures. CMS identifies minor as having 10 or less follow-up days and major as having 90 follow-up days assigned. Providers are more likely to use modifier 25 to identify that a significant, separately reportable E/M service was provided on the same day a minor procedure was performed.

58 Staged or Related Procedure or Service by the Same Physician During the Postoperative Period

When reporting modifier 58, the physician may need to indicate that the procedure or service was one of the following: 1) planned prospectively at the time of the original procedure, or staged; 2) more extensive than the original procedure; or 3) for therapy following a diagnostic surgical procedure. Do not use this modifier to report the treatment of a problem that requires a return to the operating room (see modifier 78). Modifier 58 is included in the guidelines for Surgery services.

Note the following about modifier 58:

- The existence of CPT modifier 58 does not negate the global fee concept; therefore, services that are included in CPT as multiple sessions are otherwise defined as including multiple services or events may not be billed with this modifier.

- Modifier 58 should not alter the amount charged or paid for subsequent unrelated or staged procedures that are performed during the postoperative period of a previous procedure.

Note: Modifier 58 has been approved for hospital outpatient use.

59 Distinct Procedural Service

Sometimes, a physician is required to report modifier 59 to indicate that a procedure or service is distinct from other services performed on the same day. Modifier 59 is used to identify procedures that are not normally reported together, but are appropriate under the circumstances. According to the CPT book, "This may represent a different session or patient encounter, different procedure or surgery, different site or organ system, separate incision/excision, separate lesion, or separate injury (or area of injury in extensive injuries) not ordinarily encountered or performed on the same day by the same physician."

Note: Modifier 59 has been approved for hospital outpatient use.

62 Two Surgeons

Modifier 62 indicates that the skills of two or more surgeons (sometimes with different skills) are required to manage a specific surgical procedure. Multiple-surgeon procedures may be related or unrelated. When the procedures are unrelated, identify the separate services performed by each surgeon. List multiple related procedures as though one physician performed all procedures and add modifier 62. The surgeons should agree on charges, procedure codes, and reimbursement percentage splits prior to submission. Because of many variables, it is imperative you coordinate the physicians' billing, and submit complete and detailed documentation.

Note: If a co-surgeon assists in performing additional procedures during the same surgical session, those are reported using separate procedure codes with modifier 80 or 82, as appropriate.

63 Procedure Performed on Infants less than 4 kg

Modifier 63 is appended to codes in the 20000–69999 range, unless specifically designated otherwise, to denote procedures performed on infants and neonates presently weighing up to 4 kg. The patient's size increases the complexity and physician work for these procedures.

66 Surgical Team

Modifier 66 identifies complex procedures that require concomitant services. Several physicians, from the same or different specialties, other highly skilled and specially trained personnel, and different types of complex equipment may be used in the surgery. Team surgery is usually confined to organ transplants and re-transplants. Identify these circumstances for team surgery by listing all procedures as though performed by one physician and add modifier 66 to each procedure code used. The surgeons should agree on charges, procedure codes, and reimbursement splits prior to claims submission. Because of many variables, carefully coordinate the physicians' billing and submit complete and detailed documentation. Also, include a cover letter explaining the reimbursement distribution for each member of the team. The total of charges for all procedures performed may be increased up to 50 percent for team surgery. The reimbursement is divided among the surgeons, contingent upon actual fees, complexity of procedures, and medical review.

73 Discontinued Outpatient Hospital/Ambulatory Surgery Center (ASC) Procedure Prior to the Administration of Anesthesia

Modifier 73 identifies those situations when a physician may cancel a surgical or diagnostic procedure subsequent to the patient's surgical prep (including sedation — when provided — and being taken to the room where the procedure is to be performed) but prior to the administration of anesthesia (local, regional block(s) or general). The physician may cancel a surgical or diagnostic procedure due to extenuating circumstances or those that threaten the well being of the patient. Under these circumstances, the intended service that is prepared for but canceled can be reported by its usual procedure number and the addition of modifier 73.

Note: The elective cancellation of a service prior to the administration of anesthesia and/or surgical preparation of the patient should not be reported. For physician reporting of a discontinued procedure, see modifier 53.

Note: Modifier 73 has been approved for hospital outpatient use.

74 Discontinued Outpatient Hospital/Ambulatory Surgery Center (ASC) Procedure After Administration of Anesthesia

Modifier 74 identifies those situations when a physician may terminate a surgical or diagnostic procedure after the administration of anesthesia (local, regional block(s) or general) or after the procedure

Using CPT® Modifiers

was started (incision made, intubation started, scope inserted, etc.) due to extenuating circumstances or those that threaten the well being of the patient. Under these circumstances, the procedure started but terminated can be reported by its usual procedure number and the addition of modifier 74.

Note: The elective cancellation of a service prior to the administration of anesthesia and/or surgical prep of the patient should not be reported. For physicians reporting a discontinued procedure, see modifier 53.

Note: Modifier 74 has been approved for hospital outpatient use.

76 Repeat Procedure or Service By Same Physician

Modifier 76 indicates that the exact procedure had to be repeated by the same physician. Use this modifier to identify a procedure or service that was repeated subsequent to the original procedure or service. This distinguishes the procedure or service from either a duplicate service or billing error. Payers may require additional documentation to establish medical necessity. Modifier 76 is easily misused, so note the following applications of other modifiers:

- A staged or related procedure or service by the same physician during the postoperative period is reported with modifier 58.
- A return to the operating room for a related procedure or service during the postoperative period is reported with modifier 78.
- An unrelated procedure or service by the same physician during the postoperative period is reported with modifier 79.

Note: Modifier 76 has been approved for hospital outpatient use.

77 Repeat Procedure by Another Physician

Modifier 77 indicates that a service or procedure performed by one physician was repeated by another physician. This modifier is usually used during the postoperative period of the procedure or service. The second physician adds the modifier to the procedure or service code used by the first physician.

It is appropriate to use modifier 22 when the procedure is unusually complicated, or modifier 52 when only a portion of the procedure or service is repeated. The ICD-9-CM diagnostic codes must substantiate the medical necessity of repeating the procedure. Because payers often require additional documentation to establish medical necessity, it is advisable to submit the operative report with a cover letter.

Note: Modifier 77 has been approved for hospital outpatient use.

78 Unplanned Return to the Operating/Procedure Room by the Same Physician Following Initial Procedure for a Related Procedure During the Postoperative Period

Modifier 78 is used to report related procedures performed in the operating room within the assigned postoperative period of a surgical procedure. Do not use modifier 78 for repeat procedures performed on the same day, rather, append modifier 76.

Note: Modifier 78 has been approved for hospital outpatient use.

79 Unrelated Procedure or Service by the Same Physician During the Postoperative Period

Modifier 79 was added to notify payers that the procedure was performed during a postoperative period of another procedure but is not related to that surgery. The diagnostic codes must document the medical necessity of the service, so the ICD-9-CM codes are usually different for this service from those reported with the initial procedure. Do not use modifier 79 to report staged or related procedures or services performed by the same physician during the assigned postoperative period of a procedure.

Note: Modifier 79 has been approved for hospital outpatient use.

80 Assistant Surgeon

Modifier 80 identifies surgical assistant services and is applied to the surgical procedure code. Assisting physicians usually charge 16 to 30 percent of their normal fee for performing the surgery alone. Be aware that payers may use the surgeon's contract rate to figure the assistant's percentage, and usually will not pay a resident for an assistant surgeon fee.

81 Minimum Assistant Surgeon

Modifier 81 identifies minimal surgical assistant service when assistance is required for a short time. Minimal assistant surgeons usually charge from 10 to 15 percent for their services. Be aware that not all payers will allow this modifier to be used for that purpose. Always bill for non-physician assistants at surgery as instructed by the payer.

82 Assistant Surgeon (when qualified resident surgeon not available)

Modifier 82 identifies situations when a qualified resident is unavailable to assist in surgery and another physician must be brought in to assist. The documentation should indicate why a qualified resident was unable to assist in surgery. Assisting physicians usually charge 16 to 30 percent of their normal fee. Be aware that modifier 80 is used more frequently than modifier 82 by surgeon assistants. Bill according to the payer rules for assistant surgery modifiers.

90 Reference (Outside) Laboratory

Modifier 90 identifies laboratory procedures performed by a party other than the treating or reporting physician. HMOs and private payers may allow a fee for a blood draw (arterial and/or venous) and a fee for transport to an outside facility. Use 99000 to report this type of service—not modifier 90.

91 Repeat Clinical Diagnostic Laboratory Test

Modifier 91 identifies tests repeated on the same day for the same patient to obtain multiple results. Do not use this modifier, however, for tests rerun to confirm initial results or due to testing problems.

Note: Modifier 91 has been approved for hospital outpatient use.

92 Alternative Laboratory Platform Testing

Modifier 92 identifies testing that is performed utilizing a kit or transportable instrument that consists in part or entirely of a one-time use, disposable analytical chamber. The test is designed to be hand-carried or transported to the patient's location for immediate test administration at that site; it does not require permanent dedicated space. Examples of codes that might be appropriate for submission with modifier 92 include those for HIV testing (86701–86703).

99 Multiple Modifiers

Modifier 99 identifies circumstances when two or more modifiers are necessary to delineate a service. Append modifier 99 to the procedure code and list all appropriate modifiers as subsequent line items.

Genetic Testing Modifiers

Genetic testing code modifiers for use with CPT and HCPCS Level II codes are to be used when reporting molecular laboratory procedures related to genetic testing. The AMA says the modifiers "provide diagnostic granularity of service to enable providers to submit complete and precise genetic testing information without altering test descriptors."

These modifiers are sorted by mutation. The numeric digit indicates the disease category and the alphabetic digit denotes the gene type. In CPT, these modifiers impact the molecular diagnostic (83890–83913) and molecular cytogenetic (88230–88299) codes.

Neoplasia (Solid Tumor, Excluding Sarcoma and Lymphoma)

0A BRCA1 (Hereditary breast/ovarian cancer)

0B BRCA2 (Hereditary breast cancer)

0C Neurofibromin (Neurofibromatosis, type 1)

0D Merlin (Neurofibromatosis, type 2)

0E c-RET (Multiple endocrine neoplasia, types 2A/B, familial medullary thyroid carcinoma)

0F VHL (Von Hippel Lindau disease, renal carcinoma)

0G SDHD (Hereditary paraganglioma)

0H SDHB (Hereditary paraganglioma)

0I ERRB2, commonly called Her-2/neu

0J MLH1 (HNPCC, mismatch repair genes)

0K MSH2, MSH6, or PMS2 (HNPCC, mismatch repair genes)

0L APC (Hereditary polyposis coli)

0M Rb (Retinoblastoma)

0N TP53, commonly called p53

0O PTEN (Cowden's syndrome)

0P KIT, also called CD117 (Gastrointestinal stromal tumor)

0Z Solid tumor gene, not otherwise specified

Neoplasia (Sarcoma)

1A WT1 or WT2 (Wilm's tumor)

1B PAX3, PAX7, or FOX01A (Alveolar rhabdomyosarcoma)

1C FLI1, ERG, ETV1, or EWSR1 (Ewing's sarcoma, desmoplastic round cell)

1D DDIT3 or FUS (Myxoid liposarcoma)

1E NR4A3, RBF56, or TCF12 (Myxoid chondrosarcoma)

1F SSX1, SSX2, or SYT (Synovial sarcoma)

1G MYCN (Neuroblastoma)

1H COL1A1 or PDGFB (Dermatofibrosarcoma protuberans)

1I TFE3 or ASPSCR1 (Alveolar soft parts sarcoma)

1J JAZF1 or JJAZ1 (Endometrial stromal sarcoma)

1Z Sarcoma gene, not otherwise specified

Neoplasia (Lymphoid/Hematopoietic)

2A RUNX1 or CBFA2T1, commonly called AML1 or ETO, genes associated with t(8;21) AML1–also ETO (Acute myelogenous leukemia)

2B BCR or ABL1, genes associated with t(9;22) (Chronic myelogenous or acute leukemia)_ BCR—also ABL (Chronic myeloid, acute lymphoid leukemia)

Using CPT® Modifiers

2C PBX1 or TCF3, genes associated with t(1;19) (Acute lymphoblastic leukemia)CGF1

2D CBFB or MYH11, genes associated with inv16 (Acute myelogenous leukemia) CBF beta (Leukemia)

2E MML (Acute leukemia)

2F PML or RARA, genes associated with t(15;17) (Acute promyelocytic leukemia) PML/RAR alpha (Promyelocytic leukemia)

2G ETV6, commonly called TEL, gene associated with t(12;21) (Acute leukemia)TEL (Leukemia)

2H BCL2 (B cell lymphoma, follicle center cell origin) bcl-2 (Lymphoma)

2I CCND1, commonly called BCL1, cyclin D1 (Mantle cell lymphoma, myeloma) bcl-1 (Lymphoma)

2J MYC (Burkitt lymphoma) c-myc (Lymphoma)

2K IgH (Lymphoma/leukemia)

2L IGK (Lymphoma/leukemia)

2M TRB, T cell receptor beta (Lymphoma/leukemia)

2N TRG, T cell receptor gamma (Lymphoma/leukemia)

2O SIL or TAL1 (T cell leukemia)

2T BCL6 (B cell lymphoma)

2Q API1 or MALT1 (MALT lymphoma)

2R NPM or ALK, genes associated with t(2;5) (Anaplastic large cell lymphoma)

2S FLT3 (Acute myelogenous leukemia)

2Z Lymphoid/hematopoietic neoplasia, not otherwise specified

Non-neoplastic Hematology/Coagulation

3A F5, commonly called Factor V (Leiden, others) (Hypercoagulable state)

3B FACC (Fanconi anemia)

3C FACD (Fanconi anemia)

3D HBB, beta globin (Thalassemia, sickle cell anemia, other hemoglobinopathies)

3E HBA, commonly called alpha globin (Thalassemia)

3F MTHFR (Elevated homocystinemia)

3G F2, commonly called prothrombin (20210, others) (Hypercoagulable state) Prothrombin (Factor II, 20210A) (Hypercoagulable state)

3H F8, commonly called Factor VIII (Hemophilia A/VWF)

3I F9, commonly called Factor IX (Hemophilia B)

3K F13, commonly called Factor XIII (Bleeding or hypercoagulable state) beta globin

3Z Non-neoplastic hematology/coagulation, not otherwise specified

Histocompatibility/Blood Typing/Identity/Microsatellite

4A HLA-A

4B HLA-B

4C HLA-C

4D HLA-D

4E HLA-DR

4F HLA-DQ

4G HLA-DP

4H Kell

4I Fingerprint for engraftment (post-allogeneic progenitor cell transplant)

4J Fingerprint for donor allelotype (allogeneic transplant)

4K Fingerprint for recipient allelotype (allogeneic transplant)

4L Fingerprint for leukocyte chimerism (allogeneic solid organ transplant)

4M Fingerprint for maternal versus fetal origin

4N Microsatellite instability

4O Microsatellite loss (loss of heterozygosity)

4Z Histocompatibility/blood typing, not otherwise specified

Neurologic, Non-neoplastic

5A ASPA, commonly called Aspartoacylase A (Canavan disease)

5B FMR-1 (Fragile X, FRAXA, syndrome)

5C FRDA, commonly called Frataxin (Friedreich ataxia)

5D HD, commonly called Huntington (Huntington's disease)

5E GABRA5, NIPA1, UBE3A, or ANCR GABRA (Prader Willi-Angelman syndrome)

5F GJB2, commonly called Connexin-26 (Hereditary hearing loss) Connexin-32 (GJB2) (Hereditary deafness)

5G GJB1, commonly called Connexin-32 (X-linked Charcot-Marie-Tooth disease)

5H SNRPN (Prader Willi-Angelman syndrome)

5I SCA1, commonly called Ataxin-1 (Spinocerebellar ataxia, type 1)

5J SCA2, commonly called Ataxin-2 (Spinocerebellar ataxia, type 2)

5K MJD, commonly called Ataxin-3 (Spinocerebellar ataxia, type 3, Machado-Joseph disease)

5L CACNA1A (Spinocerebellar ataxia, type 6)

5M ATXN7 Ataxin-7 (Spinocerebellar ataxia, type 7)

5N PMP-22 (Charcot-Marie-Tooth disease, type 1A)

5O MECP2 (Rett syndrome)

5Z Neurologic, non-neoplastic, not otherwise specified

Muscular, Non-neoplastic

6A DMD, commonly called dystrophin (Duchenne/Becker muscular dystrophy)

6B DMPK (Myotonic dystrophy, type 1)

6C ZNF-9 (Myotonic dystrophy, type 2)

6D SMN1/SMN2 (Autosomal recessive spinal muscular atrophy)

6E MTTK, commonly called tRNAlys (Myotonic epilepsy, MERRF)

6F MTTL1, commonly called tRNAleu (Mitochondrial encephalomyopathy, MELAS)

6Z Muscular, not otherwise specified

Metabolic, Other

7A APOE, commonly called apolipoprotein E (Cardiovascular disease, Alzheimer's disease)

7B NPC1 or NPC2, commonly called sphingomyelin phosphodiesterase (Niemann-Pick disease)

7C GBA, commonly called acid beta glucosidase (Gaucher disease)

7D HFE (Hemochromatosis)

7E HEXA, commonly called hexosaminidase A (Tay-Sachs disease)

7F ACADM (medium chain acyl CoA dehydrogenase deficiency)

7Z Metabolic, other, not otherwise specified

Metabolic, Transport

8A CFTR (Cystic fibrosis)

8B PRSS1 (Hereditary pancreatitis)

8C Long QT syndrome, KCN (Jervell and Lange-Nielsen syndromes, types 1, 2, 5, and 6) and SCN (Brugada syndrome, SIDS and type 3)

8Z Metabolic, transport, not otherwise specified

Metabolic-Pharmacogenetics

9A TPMT, commonly called thiopurine methyltransferase (patients on antimetabolite therapy)

9B CYP2 genes, commonly called cytochrome p450 (drug metabolism)

9C ABCB1, commonly called MDR1 or p-glycoprotein (drug transport)

9D NAT2 (drug metabolism)

9L Metabolic-pharmacogenetics, not otherwise specified

Dysmorphology

9M FGFR-1 (Pfeiffer and Kallmann syndromes)

9N FGFR2 (Crouzon, Jackson-Weiss, Apert, Saethre-Chotzen syndromes)

9O FGFR3 (Achondroplasia, hypochondroplasia, thanatophoric dysplasia, types I and II, Crouzon syndrome with acanthosis nigricans, Muencke syndromes)

9P TWIST (Saethre-Chotzen syndrome)

9Q DGCR, commonly called CATCH-22 (DiGeorge and 22q11 deletion syndromes)

9Z Dysmorphology, not otherwise specified

Using E/M Codes

The medical community relies on evaluation and management (E/M) codes for patient care and reimbursement, yet the codes cause more of an uproar than any other code set. E/M codes are difficult to understand. Coders and physicians have grappled over the complex guidelines defining the use of E/M codes since their inception. In 1997, E/M documentation guidelines were revised by the AMA, which holds the copyright to the CPT book, and the Centers for Medicare and Medicaid Services (CMS). Providers may use either the 1995 or 1997 guidelines, depending upon which set is more advantageous.

The jointly developed E/M framework is available from the CMS website, http://www.cms.hhs.gov/MLNEdWebGuide/25_EMDOC.asp.

Categories and Subcategories of Service

Office or Other Outpatient Services

New Patient 99201–99205

Established Patient 99211–99215

Hospital Observation Services

Observation Care Discharge Services 99217

Initial Observation Care 99218–99220

Hospital Inpatient Services

Initial Hospital Care 99221–99223

Subsequent Hospital Care 99231–99233

Observation or Inpatient Care Services (Including Admission and Discharge Services) 99234–99236

Hospital Discharge Services 99238–99239

Consultations

Office or Other Outpatient Consultations 99241–99245

Inpatient Consultations 99251–99255

Emergency Department Services

New or Established Patient 99281–99285

Other Emergency Services 99288

Critical Care Services

99291–99292

Nursing Facility Services

Initial Nursing Facility Care 99304–99306

Subsequent Nursing Facility Care 99307–99310

Nursing Facility Discharge Services 99315–99316

Other Nursing Facility Services 99318

Domiciliary, Rest Home (e.g., Boarding Home) or Custodial Care Services

New Patient 99324–99328

Established Patient 99334–99337

Domiciliary, Rest Home (e.g., Assisted Living Facility), or Home Care Plan Oversight Services

99339-99340

Home Services

New Patient 99341–99345

Established Patient 99347–99350

Prolonged Services

Prolonged Physician Service With Direct (Face-to-Face) Patient Contact 99354–99357

Prolonged Physician Service Without Direct (Face-to-Face) Patient Contact 99358–99359

Physician Standby Services 99360

Case Management Services

Anticoagulant Management 99363–99364

Medical Team Conferences 99366–99368

Care Plan Oversight Services

99374–99380

Preventive Medicine Services

New Patient 99381–99387

Established Patient 99391–99397

Individual Counseling 99401–99404

Behavior Change Interventions, Individual 99406–99409

Group Counseling 99411–99412

Other Preventive Services 99420–99429

Non-Face-to-Face Physician Services

Telephone Services 99441–99443

On-Line Medical Evaluation 99444

Special E/M Services

Basic Life and/or Disability Evaluation Services 99450

Work Related or Medical Disability Evaluation Services 99455–99456

Newborn Care Services

Initial/Subsequent Hospital Care 99460-99463

Delivery/Birthing Room Attendance and Resuscitation Services 99464-99465

Inpatient Neonatal Intensive Care Services and Pediatric and Neonatal Critical Care Services

Pediatric Critical Care Patient Transport	99466-99467
Inpatient Neonatal and Pediatric Critical Care	99468-99476
Initial and Continuing Intensive Care Services	99477-99480

Other E/M Services

99499

Glossary of E/M Coding Terms

Behavior change interventions—These codes (99406-99409) report individual intervention services for patients who exhibit behaviors (e.g., tobacco use, substance abuse, obesity) that may often be considered illnesses in and of themselves. These codes may be reported when the intervention is performed prior to the behavior resulting in illness or may be performed as a component of the treatment for conditions related to or worsened by the behavior. Services reported by these codes include assessing the readiness for and barriers to behavioral change, advising changes in behavior, suggesting specific actions and motivational counseling, and arranging for specific services and follow-up.

Care plan oversight services—These codes report the services of a physician providing ongoing review and revision of a patient's care plan involving complex or multidisciplinary care modalities. Only one physician may report this code per patient per 30-day period and only if 15 minutes or more are spent during the 30 days. Also, low intensity and infrequent supervision services are not reported separately.

Case management services—These codes report the care a physician or other qualified health care professional coordinates with an interdisciplinary team of physicians or health professionals/agencies without a patient encounter. Documentation must spell out the services each team member renders to the care plan.

Chief complaint—The chief complaint is a concise statement describing the symptom, problem, condition, diagnosis, or other factor for the patient encounter. The chief complaint is often written in the patient's words. The medical record should clearly reflect the chief complaint.

Components—Three key components—history, examination, and medical decision making—appear in the descriptors for office and other outpatient services, hospital observation services, hospital inpatient services, consultations, emergency department services, nursing facility services, domiciliary care services, and home services. Refer to CPT 2009 for E/M services and instructions for selecting a level of service.

The descriptors for the levels of E/M services recognize a total of seven components, including the three key components, used in defining the levels of E/M services. These components are as follows:

- History
- Examination
- Medical decision making
- Counseling
- Coordination of care
- Nature of presenting problem
- Time

Concurrent care—Concurrent care describes similar services provided to the same patient on the same day by more than one physician. No special reporting is required for concurrent care. The diagnosis codes and physician specialties should mesh.

Consultations—The CPT book provides two subcategories of consultations: (1) Office or Other Outpatient Consultations, and (2) Initial Inpatient Consultations. If counseling dominates the encounter, time determines the correct code.

The general rules and requirements of a consultation are as listed below:

- Requests for consultation must come from an attending physician or other appropriate source, and the necessity for this service must be documented in the patient's record. Include the name of the requesting physician on the CMS-1500 form or electronic billing.
- A consultation initiated by the patient or a family member and not requested by a physician should not be reported with consultation codes. Use the appropriate office visit code.
- A consultation mandated by a third-party payer should be reported with modifier 32.
- The consultant may initiate diagnostic and/or therapeutic services, such as writing orders or prescriptions and initiating treatment plans.
- The opinion rendered and services ordered or performed must be documented in the patient's medical record and a report of this information communicated to the requesting entity.
- Report separately any identifiable procedure or service performed on, or subsequent to, the date of the initial consultation.
- When the consultant assumes responsibility for the management of any or all of the patient's care subsequent to the initial consultation, consult codes are no longer appropriate. Depending on

the location, identify the correct subsequent or established patient codes.

Contributory components—Counseling, coordination of care, and the nature of the presenting problem are not major considerations in most encounters and, thus, provide contributory information to the code selection process. The exception arises when counseling or coordination of care dominates the encounter (more than 50 percent of the time spent). In these cases, time determines the proper code. Documentation of the exact amount of time spent substantiates the selected code. For office encounters, count only the time spent face-to-face with the patient and/or family; for hospital or other inpatient encounters, count the time spent in the patient's unit or on the patient's floor, but be sure the time spent and counted is directed at caring only for one patient. The time assigned to each code is an average and varies by physician.

Coordination of care—This is one of the contributory factors in determining E/M service levels. Care coordinated with other providers or agencies without a patient encounter on that day is reported using the case management codes.

When coordination of care dominates (more than 50 percent) the physician/patient and/or family visit, time is considered the key or controlling factor to qualify for a particular level of E/M services.

Counseling—A discussion between the physician and the patient and/or family concerning one or more of the following areas as designated by the American Medical Association:

- Diagnostic results, impression, and/or recommended diagnostic studies
- Prognosis
- Risks and benefits of management (treatment) options
- Instructions for management (treatment) and/or follow-up
- Importance of compliance with chosen management (treatment) options
- Risk factor reduction
- Patient and family education

When counseling dominates (more than 50 percent) the physician/patient and/or family encounter, time is considered the key or controlling factor to qualify for a particular level of E/M services.

Critical care services—Critical care is not specific to a location such as an ICU or CCU. Critical care is determined by the patient's critically ill or critically injured condition requiring this type of physician care. Routine visits to a stabilized patient in an ICU are not critical care. General guidelines for critical care are as follows:

- Critical care codes include evaluation and management of the critically ill or injured patient, requiring constant attendance of the physician.
- AMA and CMS have assigned procedures that should not be reported separately.
- Care provided to a patient who is not critically ill or critically injured but happens to be in a critical care unit should be identified using subsequent hospital care codes or inpatient consultation codes as appropriate.
- Although critical care typically requires interpretation of multiple physiologic parameters and/or application of advanced technology, critical care may be provided in life-threatening situations when these elements are not present.
- Critical care codes identify the total duration of time spent by a physician on a given date, even if the time is not continuous. Code 99291 reports the first hour of critical care and is used only once per date. Code 99292 reports each additional 30 minutes of critical care per date.
- Critical care of less than 15 minutes beyond the first hour or less than 15 minutes beyond the final 30 minutes should not be reported.
- Refer to the CPT book for examples of correct reporting of critical care services.

Documentation—The following basic principles of documentation apply to all types of medical and surgical services in all settings:

1. The medical record should be complete and legible.
2. The documentation of each patient encounter should include or provide reference to the reason for the encounter and, as appropriate:
   - Relevant history, examination findings, and prior diagnostic test results
   - Assessment, clinical impression, or diagnosis
   - Plan for care
3. Date and legible identity of the observer must be in the medical record.
4. If not specifically documented, the rationale for ordering diagnostic and other ancillary services should be easily inferred.
5. Past and present diagnoses should be accessible to the treating and/or consulting physician.
6. Appropriate health risk factors should be identified.
7. The patient's progress, response to, and changes in treatment, and revision of diagnosis should be documented.

8. The CPT and ICD-9-CM codes reported on the health insurance claim form or billing statement should be supported by the documentation in the medical record.

Domiciliary, rest home, or custodial care services—These codes report care given to patients residing in a long-term care facility that provides room and board, as well as other personal assistance services that do not include a medical component.

Emergency department services—Emergency Department (ED) service codes do not differentiate between new and established patients and are used by hospital based and non-hospital based physicians.

Time is not a descriptive component for the emergency department levels of E/M services since services are on a variable basis and usually involve multiple encounters with several patients over extended periods of time.

Associated with ED services is 99288 Physician direction of emergency medical systems (EMS) emergency care, advanced life support. The physician must be located in the ED or critical care department, be in two-way voice communication with the ambulance or rescue personnel outside the hospital, and direct the performance of necessary medical procedures.

Established patient—This patient has received professional services within the past three years from the physician, or another physician of the same specialty who belongs to the same group practice.

Examination component guidelines—History, physical examination, and medical decision-making are considered key to selecting the correct level of E/M codes. Four levels characterize the examination component, as follows:

- Problem focused—A limited exam of the affected body area or organ system.
- Expanded problem focused—A limited exam of the affected body area or organ system and other symptomatic or related organ system(s).
- Detailed—An extended exam of the affected body area and other symptomatic or related organ system(s).
- Comprehensive—A general multi-system exam or a complete exam of a single organ system. The comprehensive exam performed as part of the preventive medicine evaluation and management service is multi-system, but its extent is based on age and risk factors identified.

Examinations—CPT recognizes the following organ systems:

- ENT (Ears, nose, mouth, and throat)
- Eyes
- Cardiovascular
- Respiratory
- Gastrointestinal
- Genitourinary
- Musculoskeletal
- Skin
- Neurological
- Psychiatric
- Hematologic/lymphatic/immunologic

In addition, CPT recognizes the following body areas:

- Head, including the face
- Neck
- Chest, including breasts and axillae
- Abdomen
- Genitalia, groin, buttocks
- Back
- Each extremity

History component guidelines—History, examination, and medical decision-making are considered key to selecting the correct level of E/M codes. Four levels characterize the history component, as follows:

- Problem focused: Chief complaint; brief history of present illness or problem.
- Expanded problem focused: Chief complaint; brief history or present illness; problem-pertinent system review.
- Detailed: Chief complaint; extended history of present illness; problem-pertinent system review extended to include a review of a limited number of additional systems; pertinent past, family, and/or social history directly related to the patient's problems.
- Comprehensive: Chief complaint; extended history of present illness; review of systems related to present illness/problems and a review of all additional body systems; detailed past, family, and social history.

Each category is comprised of two to four of the following elements:

Chief complaint (CC);
History of present illness (HPI);
Review of systems (ROS); and
Past, family, and/or social history (PFSH).

The documentation guidelines supplement the information found in CPT and are summarized as follows:

- The chief complaint, review of systems, and the past, family, and/or social history may be included as separate elements of the history. Or, this information may be included in the description of the history of the present illness.
- The comprehensive history obtained as part of the preventive medicine evaluation and management service is not problem-oriented and does not involve a chief complaint or present illness. It does, however, include a comprehensive system review and comprehensive or interval past, family, and social history as well as a comprehensive assessment/history of pertinent risk factors.
- A review of systems and/or past, family, and/or social history obtained during an earlier encounter does not need to be re-recorded if there is evidence that the physician reviewed and updated the previous information. This may occur when a physician updates his or her own record, or in an institutional setting or group practice where many physicians use a common record. The review and update may be documented by describing any new review of systems and/or past, family, and/or social history information. Or, the documentation may note no change in the information since the date and location of the earlier review of systems and/or past, family and/or social history.
- The review of systems and/or past, family, and/or social history may be recorded by ancillary staff or on a form completed by the patient. To document that the physician reviewed the information, there must be a notation supplementing or confirming the information recorded by others.
- If the physician cannot obtain a history from the patient or other source, the record should describe the patient's condition or other circumstance that precludes obtaining a history.
- The medical record should clearly reflect the chief complaint.
- To qualify for a brief history of the present illness, the medical record should describe one to three elements of the present illness.
- To qualify for an extended history of the present illness, the medical record should describe four or more elements of the present illness or associated comorbidities.
- To qualify for a problem–pertinent review of systems, the patient's positive responses and pertinent negatives for the system related to the problem should be documented.
- To qualify for an expanded review of systems, the patient's positive responses and pertinent negative responses for two or more systems should be documented.

History of present illness (HPI)—The HPI describes the patient's history of present illness from the first sign and/or symptom to the present condition. The description of the developing illness or injury includes location, quality, severity, timing, context, modifying factors, and associated signs and symptoms significantly related to the present problem.

Brief and extended HPIs are distinguished by the amount of detail needed to accurately characterize the clinical problem.

- A brief HPI consists of one to three elements of the HPI.
- An extended HPI consists of at least four elements of the HPI.

Home services—These are services and care provided at the patient's home. Home services to new patients (99341-99345) and those for established patients (99347-99350) include typical times the physician may spend with the patient and/or family.

Hospital discharge services—These codes vary depending upon the patient's hospital status. Code 99217 is reported when a patient is discharged from "observation status" on a day other than the initial date of "observation status." Services include final exam of the patient, discussion of the hospital stay, instructions for continuing care, and preparation of the discharge records. Use 99234-99236 to report services to a patient designated as "observation status" or "inpatient status" and discharged on the same date. Codes 99238-99239 apply to all services provided to a patient on the date of discharge when other than the initial date of inpatient status. Use 99238 for 30 minutes or less, and 99239 for more than 30 minutes. Use Subsequent Hospital Care codes (99231-99233) for reporting concurrent care provided on discharge day by another physician.

Hospital inpatient services—These codes (99221-99239) report admission to a hospital setting, follow-up care provided in a hospital setting, and hospital discharge day management. For inpatient care, the time component includes not only face-to-face time with the patient but also the physician's time spent in the patient's unit or on the patient's floor. This time may include family counseling or discussing the patient's condition with the family; establishing and reviewing the patient's record; documenting within the chart; and communicating with other health care professionals such as other physicians, nursing staff, respiratory therapists, and so on.

Hospital observation services—These codes (99217-99220, 99234-99236) report E/M services provided to patients designated or admitted as observation status in a hospital. It is not necessary that the patient be located in an observation area designated by the hospital to use these codes; however, whenever a patient is placed in a separately designated observation area of the hospital or emergency department, these codes should be used:

- Observation care discharge services: Use 99217 only if discharge from observation status occurs on a date other than the initial date of observation status. The code includes final examination of the patient, discussion of the hospital stay, instructions for continuing care, and preparation of discharge records.
- Observation or inpatient care services (99234–99236) are used to report observation or inpatient hospital care services provided to patients admitted and discharged on the same date of service.

Level of E/M services—The level of E/M service is dependent on two or three key components—history, physical exam, and medical decision-making. Other components considered contributory to the level of E/M service are counseling, coordination of care, nature of presenting problem, and time.

Medical decision-making—This term is one of three key components necessary in determining the correct level of E/M services, as it describes the complexity of establishing a diagnosis and/or selecting management options, as measured by:

- The number of possible diagnoses and/or the number of management options that must be considered
- The amount and/or complexity of medical records, diagnostic tests, and/or other information that must be obtained, reviewed, and analyzed
- The risk of significant complications, morbidity and/or mortality, as well as comorbidities, associated with the patient's presenting problem, the diagnostic procedure, and/or the possible management options.

The CPT book lists four types of medical decision making, as described here:

- Straightforward: Minimal risk of complications and/or morbidity or mortality; minimal or no complexity of the data to be reviewed; and a minimal number of diagnoses or management options.
- Low complexity: Low risk, limited complexity of the data to be reviewed, and a limited number of diagnoses or management options.
- Moderate complexity: Moderate risk, moderate complexity of the data to be reviewed, and multiple diagnoses.
- High complexity: High risk, extensive complexity of data to be reviewed, and an extensive number of diagnoses.

The medical decision-making component guidelines are summarized as follows:

- An assessment, clinical impression, or diagnosis should be documented for each encounter. This information may be explicitly stated or implied in documented decisions regarding management plans and/or further evaluation.
- The initiation of or changes in treatment should be documented. Treatment includes a wide range of management options including patient instruction, nursing instructions, therapies, and medications.
- If referrals are made, consultations requested, or advice sought, the record should indicate who receives the advice, who requests the advice, and where the referral or consultation is made.
- If a diagnostic service (test or procedure) is ordered, planned, scheduled, or performed at the time of the E/M encounter, the type of service (e.g., lab or x-ray) should be documented.
- The review of lab, radiology, and/or other diagnostic tests should be documented. The review may be documented by initialing and dating the report containing the test results.
- A decision to obtain old records or decisions to obtain additional history from the family, caretaker, or other source to supplement that obtained from the patient should be documented.
- Relevant findings from the review of old records and/or the receipt of additional history from the family, caretaker, or other sources should be documented. If there is no relevant information beyond that already obtained, that fact should be documented.
- The results of discussion of laboratory, radiology, or other diagnostic test with the physician who performed or interpreted the study should be documented.
- Comorbidities, underlying disease, or other factors that increase the complexity of medical decision making by increasing the risk of complications, morbidity, and/or mortality should be documented.
- The direct visualization and independent interpretation of an image, tracing, or specimen previously or subsequently interpreted by another physician should be documented.

- If a surgical or invasive diagnostic procedure is prescribed, planned, or scheduled at the time of the E/M encounter, the type of procedure (e.g., laparoscopy) should be documented.
- If a surgical or invasive diagnostic procedure is performed at the time of the E/M encounter, the specific procedure should be documented.
- The referral for or decision to perform a surgical or invasive diagnostic procedure on an urgent basis should be documented or implied.

Medical team conferences—These codes (99366–99368) report face-to-face participation by no less than three qualified health care professionals from different disciplines or specialties. Each participant must have performed a face-to-face evaluation or treatment of the patient within the past 60 days. Code selection is determined by the participation of physician vs. nonphysician health care provider as well as the presence or absence of the patient and/or family. Only one individual from the same specialty may report a code from this range for the same encounter. Team conferences must last a minimum of 30 minutes in order to be reported; those lasting fewer than 30 minutes are not reported separately.

New patient—This patient has not received any professional services within the past three years from the physician or another physician of the same specialty who belongs to the same group practice.

Nursing facility services—These E/M services have been grouped into four subcategories: Comprehensive Nursing Facility Assessments (99304-99306), Subsequent Nursing Facility Care (99307-99310), Nursing Facility Discharge Services (99315-99316), and Other Nursing Facility Services (99318). Report other services, such as medical psychotherapy, separately when provided in addition to E/M services. The discharge service subcategory reports the time spent by a physician for the final nursing facility discharge of a patient, such as the final exam and a discussion of the nursing facility stay. The annual nursing facility evaluation and assessment of a patient (99318) includes completion of assessment tools, protocols, and patient–specific treatment plan.

Office or other outpatient services—Use these codes (99201-99215) to report the services for most patients' encounters. Multiple office or outpatient visits provided on the same calendar date are billable if medically necessary. Support the claim with documentation.

On-line medical evaluation—Use this code (99444) to report a physician response via the Internet to a patient's on-line inquiry. This code reports a non-face-to-face encounter and includes all related phone calls, orders for lab work, and provision of prescriptions related to the on-line encounter. Each physician may report this code only once during a seven-day period for the same episode of care. The encounter must be stored permanently, either via electronic means or in hard copy. If this on-line encounter relates to an E/M service provided by the physician within the previous seven days, it is considered covered by the original E/M service. Likewise, if the on-line encounter relates to a procedure performed by the physician and occurs within the postoperative period, it is considered covered by the previously reported procedure code(s).

Past, family and/or social history (PFSH)—The PFSH provides information relevant to the patient's past illnesses and treatments, the patient's family, and an age–appropriate review of the patient's past and current activities.

- **Past history**—A review of the patient's past experiences with illnesses, injuries, and treatments that includes significant information as designated by the AMA:
  - Allergies
  - Operations
  - Injuries/trauma
  - Pregnancy history
  - Growth and development history
  - Immunization history
  - Behavioral/functional history
  - Other relevant past history
- **Family history**—A review of medical events in the patient's family that includes significant information as designated by the AMA:
  - Cardiovascular disease: stroke, myocardial infarction or other cardiovascular illness
  - Cancer
  - Alcohol/tobacco/drug abuse
  - Domestic violence, child abuse
  - Lipid disorders
  - Hereditary disorders
  - Other relevant family history
- **Social history**—An age–appropriate review of past and current activities that includes significant information as designated by the AMA:

  Status of immediate and extended family
  - Marital status
  - Employment status
  - Occupational history
  - Tobacco/alcohol/drug abuse
  - Education
  - Housing/source of drinking water

- Other relevant social factors

Other relevant social factors consist of a review of three areas:

- Past history (the patient's past experiences with illnesses, operations, injuries, and treatments)
- Family history (a review of medical events in the patient's family, including diseases that may be hereditary or place the patient at risk)
- Social history (an age–appropriate review of past and current activities)

A pertinent PFSH is a review of the history area directly related to the problem identified in the HPI.

- At least one specific item from any of the three history areas must be documented for a pertinent PFSH.

A complete PFSH is a review of two or all three of the PFSH history areas, depending on the category of the E/M service. A review of three history areas is required for services that by their nature include a comprehensive assessment or reassessment of the patient. A review of two of the three history areas is sufficient for other services.

Patient transport—Patient transport codes report the physician's direct face-to-face contact with a critically ill patient during transport between facilities.

Place of Service—The E/M code section is divided into subsections by type and place of service. Keep the following in mind when coding each service setting:

- A patient is considered an outpatient at a health care facility until formal inpatient admission occurs.
- Consultation codes are linked to location.
- Admission to a hospital or nursing facility includes evaluation and management services provided elsewhere (e.g., office or emergency department) by the admitting physician on the same day.

Presenting problem—A disease, condition, illness, injury, symptom, sign, finding, complaint, or other reason for an encounter, with or without the physician establishing a diagnosis at the time of the encounter. E/M codes recognize five types of presenting problems, defined as follows:

- Minimal: A problem that may not require the presence of the physician, but service is provided under the physician's supervision.
- Self-limited or minor: A problem that runs a definite and prescribed course, is transient in nature, and is not likely to permanently alter the patient's health status OR has a good prognosis with management/compliance.
- Low severity: A problem where the risk of morbidity without treatment is low; there is little risk of mortality without treatment; full recovery without functional impairment is expected.
- Moderate severity: A problem where the risk of morbidity without treatment is moderate; there is moderate risk of mortality without treatment; uncertain prognosis OR increased probability of prolonged functional impairment.
- High severity: A problem where the risk of morbidity without treatment is high to extreme; there is a moderate to high risk of mortality without treatment OR high probability of severe, prolonged functional impairment.

Prolonged services—This section of E/M codes includes three service categories, as described here:

- Prolonged physician service with direct face-to-face patient contact: These codes report services involving direct patient contact beyond the usual service, with separate codes for office or outpatient encounters (99354 and 99355) and for inpatient encounters (99356 and 99357). Prolonged physician services are reportable in addition to other physician services, including any level of E/M service. The codes report the total duration of face-to-face time spent by the physician on a given date, even if the time is not continuous.
- Prolonged physician service without face-to-face direct patient contact: These prolonged physician services without direct patient contact may include review of extensive records and tests, and communication (other than telephone calls, 99441–99443) with other professionals and/or the patient and family. These are beyond the usual services and include both inpatient and outpatient settings. Report these services in addition to other services provided, including any level of E/M service. Use 99358 to report the first hour and 99359 for each additional 30-minute period. All aspects of time reporting are the same as explained above for direct patient contact services.
- Physician standby services: Code 99360 identifies when a physician is requested by another physician to be on standby, and the standby physician has no direct patient contact. The standby physician may not provide services to other patients or be proctoring another physician for the time to be reportable. Also, if the standby physician ultimately provides services subject to a

surgical package, the standby is not separately reportable. This code reports cumulative standby time by date or service. Less than 30 minutes is not reportable, and a full 30 minutes must be spent for each unit of service reported. For example, "25 minutes" is not reportable, and "50 minutes" is reported as one unit (99360 x 1).

Review of systems—The physician asks a series of questions to identify the signs and/or symptoms the patient is experiencing or has experienced. The review of system (ROS) is divided into three types, as follows:

- Problem pertinent: Questions directly relating to the present illness
- Extended: Questions relating to the present illness and a limited number of additional systems
- Complete: Questions relating to the present illness and all additional body systems

For purposes of ROS, the following systems are recognized

- Constitutional symptoms (e.g., fever, weight loss)
- Eyes
- Ears, nose, throat, mouth
- Cardiovascular
- Respiratory
- Gastrointestinal
- Genitourinary
- Musculoskeletal
- Integumentary (skin and/or breast)
- Neurological
- Psychiatric
- Endocrine
- Hematologic/lymphatic
- Allergic/immunologic

A problem–pertinent ROS inquires about the system directly related to the problem identified in the HPI:

- The patient's positive responses and pertinent negatives for the system related to the problem should be documented.

An extended ROS inquires about the system directly related to the problem(s) identified in the HPI and a limited number of additional systems:

- The patient's positive responses and pertinent negatives for two or more systems should be documented.

A complete ROS inquires about the system(s) directly related to the problem(s) identified in the HPI plus all additional body systems:

- At least 10 organ systems must be reviewed. These systems with positive or pertinent negative responses must be individually documented. For the remaining systems, a notation indicating all other systems are negative is permissible. In the absence of such a notation, at least 10 systems must be individually documented.

Service components—The seven components used in defining levels of E/M are as follows:

- History
- Examination
- Medical decision making
- Counseling
- Coordination of care
- Nature of presenting problem
- Time

The three components of history, examination, and medical decision making are key to selecting the correct level of E/M codes. In most cases, all three components must be addressed in the documentation. However, in established, subsequent, and follow-up categories, only two of the three must be met or exceeded for a given code.

The key components (history, exam, decision making) must meet or exceed the stated requirements to qualify for a particular level of E/M service for the following new or initial patient categories and subcategories:

- Office or other outpatient services, new patient
- Initial observation care
- Initial hospital care
- Observation or inpatient care (same admission and discharge date)
- Office or other outpatient consultations
- Initial inpatient consultations
- Emergency department services
- Initial nursing facility care
- Other nursing facility services
- Domiciliary, rest home, or custodial care services, new patient
- Home services, new patient

Two of the three key components (history, exam, decision making) must meet or exceed the stated requirements to qualify for a particular level of E/M service for the following established or follow-up patient categories and subcategories:

- Office or other outpatient services, established patient
- Subsequent hospital care

- Subsequent nursing facility care
- Domiciliary, rest home, or custodial care services, established patient
- Home services, established patient

Service levels—E/M services within subcategories are arranged in levels, each with the same basic format:

- A unique code
- Place and/or type of service
- What is included in the service
- The nature of the presenting problem
- Time spent

Special E/M services—This series of codes reports physician evaluations to establish baseline information for insurance certification and/or work–related or medical disability.

Standby services—See Prolonged services: Physician standby services.

Subsequent nursing facility care—See Nursing facility services.

Time—Adding time in CPT 1992 was done to assist physicians in selecting the most appropriate level of E/M services. The time frames are based on data on the amount of time and work associated with typical E/M services as obtained from surveys of practicing physicians. Subsequently, specific times expressed in the visit code descriptors are averages and represent a range of time that may be higher or lower depending on actual clinical circumstances.

Time, however, is not a descriptive component for the emergency department levels of E/M services since these services are typically provided on a variable intensity basis, often involving multiple encounters with several patients over an extended period of time. It is often difficult for physicians to provide accurate estimates of the time spent face-to-face with the patient.

Diagnosis or Management Options

The number of possible diagnoses and/or the number of management options a physician must consider is based on the number and types of problems addressed during the encounter, the complexity of establishing a diagnosis, and the management decisions that are made by the physician.

Generally, decision making with respect to a diagnosed problem is easier than that for an identified but undiagnosed problem. The number and type of diagnostic tests employed may be an indicator of the number of possible diagnoses. Problems that are improving or resolving are less complex than those that are worsening or failing to change as expected. The need to seek advice from others is another indicator of complexity of diagnostic or management problems. Document the information, as noted in the following:

- For each encounter, an assessment, clinical impression, or diagnosis should be documented. It may be explicitly stated or implied in documented decisions regarding management plans and/or further evaluation.
- For a presenting problem with an established diagnosis, the record should reflect whether the problem is: a) improved, well controlled, resolving, or resolved; or b) not adequately controlled, worsening, or failing to change as expected.
- For a presenting problem without an established diagnosis, the assessment or clinical impression may be stated in the form of differential diagnoses or as a "possible," "probable," or "rule out" diagnosis.
- In the absence of a definitive diagnosis, documented signs and symptoms are reported.
- The initiation of, or changes in, treatment should be documented. Treatment includes a wide range of management options including patient instruction, nursing instructions, therapies, and medications.
- If referrals are made, consultations requested, or advice sought, the record should indicate to whom or where the referral or consultation is made or from whom the advice is sought.

Amount and/or Complexity of Data to Review

The amount and complexity of data to be reviewed is based on the types of diagnostic testing ordered or reviewed. A decision to obtain and review old medical records and/or obtain history from sources other than the patient increases the amount of complexity of data to be reviewed.

Discussion of contradictory or unexpected test results with the physician who performed or interpreted the test is an indication of the complexity of data being reviewed. On occasion the physician who ordered a test may personally review the image, tracing, or specimen to supplement information from the physician who prepared the test report or interpretation; this is another indication of the complexity of data being reviewed.

For additional information, review the section "Medical Decision Making."

Assessing Risk

The risk of significant complications, morbidity, and/or mortality is based on the risks associated with the presenting problem, the diagnostic procedure, and the possible management options:

- Comorbidities/underlying disease or other factors that increase the complexity of medical decision making by increasing the risk of complications, morbidity, and/or mortality should be documented.
- If a surgical or invasive diagnostic procedure is ordered, planned, or scheduled at the time of the E/M encounter, the type of procedure (e.g., laparoscopy) should be documented.
- If a surgical or invasive diagnostic procedure is performed at the time of the E/M encounter, the specific procedure should be documented. The referral for or decision to perform a surgical or invasive diagnostic procedure on an urgent basis should be documented or implied.

The accompanying table may be used to help determine whether the risk of significant complications, morbidity, and/or mortality is minimal, low, moderate, or high. Since risk is complex and not readily quantifiable, the table includes common clinical examples rather than absolute measures of risk. Keep in mind the following:

- The assessment of risk of the presenting problem is based on the risk related to the disease process anticipated between the present encounter and the next one.
- The assessment of risk of selecting diagnostic procedures and management options is based on the risk during and immediately following any procedures or treatment.
- The highest level of risk in any one category (presenting problem, diagnostic procedure, or management options) determines the overall risk.

Level of Risk	Presenting Problem	Diagnostic Procedure(s) Ordered	Management Options Selected
Minimal	• One self-limited or minor problem, e.g., cold, insect bite, tinea corporis	• Laboratory tests requiring venipuncture • Chest x-rays • EKG/EEG • Urinalysis • Ultrasound, e.g., echocardiography • KOH prep	• Rest • Gargles • Elastic bandages • Superficial dressings
Low	• Two or more self-limited or minor problems • One stable chronic illness, e.g., well controlled hypertension, Type II diabetes, cataract, BPH • Acute uncomplicated illness or injury, e.g., cystitis, allergic rhinitis, simple sprain	• Physiologic tests not under stress, e.g., pulmonary function tests • Non-cardiovascular imaging studies with contrast, e.g., barium enema • Superficial needle biopsies • Clinical laboratory tests requiring arterial puncture • Skin biopsies	• Over-the-counter drugs • Minor surgery with no identified risk factors • Physical therapy • Occupational therapy • IV fluids without additives
Moderate	• One or more chronic illnesses with mild exacerbation, progression, or side effects of treatment • Two or more stable chronic illnesses • Undiagnosed new problem with uncertain prognosis, e.g., lump in breast • Acute illness with systemic symptoms, e.g., pyelonephritis, pneumonitis, colitis • Acute complicated injury, e.g., head injury with brief loss of consciousness	• Physiologic tests under stress, e.g., cardiac stress test, fetal contraction stress test • Diagnostic endoscopies with no identified risk factors • Deep needle or incisional biopsy • Cardiovascular imaging studies with contrast and no identified risk factors, e.g., arteriogram, cardiac catheterization • Obtain fluid from body cavity, e.g., lumbar puncture, thoracentesis, culdocentesis • Minor surgery with identified risk factors	• Elective major surgery (open, percutaneous or endoscopic) with no identified risk factors • Prescription drug management • Therapeutic nuclear medicine • IV fluids with additives • Closed treatment of fracture or dislocation without manipulation

Level of Risk	Presenting Problem	Diagnostic Procedure(s) Ordered	Management Options Selected
High	• One or more chronic illnesses with severe exacerbation, progression, or side effects of treatment • Acute or chronic illnesses or injuries that pose a threat to life or bodily function, e.g., multiple trauma, acute MI, pulmonary embolus, severe respiratory distress, progressive severe rheumatoid arthritis, psychiatric illness with potential threat to self or others, peritonitis, acute renal failure • An abrupt change in neurologic status, e.g., seizure, TIA, weakness, sensory loss	• Cardiovascular imaging studies with contrast with identified risk factors • Cardiac electrophysiological tests • Diagnostic endoscopies with identified risk factors • Discography	• Elective major surgery (open, percutaneous or endoscopic) with identified risk factors • Emergency major surgery (open, percutaneous or endoscopic) • Parenteral controlled substances • Drug therapy requiring intensive monitoring for toxicity • Decision not to resuscitate or to de-escalate care because of poor prognosis

Reimbursement Terms

An increasingly complex reimbursement climate means new terminology develops every year. The following glossary includes terms not only used when coding, it includes terms used by major insurers and the federal government.

AAPA. American Academy of Physician Assistants.

AAPCC. Adjusted average per capita cost. Estimated average cost of Medicare benefits for an individual, based upon criteria including age, sex, institutional status, Medicaid, disability, and end-stage renal failure.

AAPPO. American Association of Preferred Provider Organizations.

abstractor. Person who selects and extracts specific data from the medical record and enters the information into computer files.

accrual. Amount of money set aside to cover a health care benefit plan's expenses based upon estimates using a combination of data, including the claims system and the plan's prior history.

ACLS. Advanced cardiac life support. Certification for health care professionals who have achieved proficiency in providing emergent care of cardiac and respiratory systems and medication management.

ACMCS. American College of Medical Coding Specialists.

ACR. Adjusted community rate, calculation of what premium the plan charges to provide Medicare-covered benefits for greater frequency of use by participants

activities of daily living. Self-care activities often used to determine a patient's level of function such as bathing, dressing, using a toilet, transferring in and out of bed or a chair, continence, eating, and walking.

actuarial assumptions. Characteristics used in calculating the risks and costs of a plan, including age, sex, and occupation of enrollees; location; utilization rates; and service costs.

adjudication. Processing and review of a submitted claim resulting in payment, partial payment, or denial. In relationship to judicial hearings, it is the process of hearing and settling a case through an objective, judicial procedure.

admission. Formal acceptance of a patient by a health care facility.

ADS. Alternative delivery system. Any health care delivery system other than traditional fee-for-service.

adverse selection. In health care contracting, the risk of enrolling members who are sicker than assumed and who will utilize expensive services more frequently.

age restriction. In health care contracting, limitation of benefits when a patient reaches a certain age.

age/sex rating. In health care contracting, structuring capitation payments based on members' ages and genders.

aggregate amount. Contracted maximum for which a member is insured for any single event in a health plan.

AHA. American Hospital Association. Health care industry association that represents the concerns of institutional providers. The AHA hosts the National Uniform Billing Committee (NUBC), which has a formal consultative role under HIPAA. The AHA also publishes ICD-9-CM Coding Clinic.

AHIMA. American Health Information Management Association. Association of health information management professionals that offers professional and educational services, providing these certifications: RHIA, RHIT, CCS, and CCS-P.

"Al-Anon, Alateen". Alcoholic support groups.

ALOS. Average length of stay. Utilization benchmark average compiled from the actual number of inpatient days calculated using factors such as geographical location and diagnosis.

AMA. American Medical Association. Professional organization for physicians. The AMA is the secretariat of the National Uniform Claim Committee (NUCC), which has a formal consultative role under HIPAA. The AMA also maintains the Current Procedural Terminology (CPT) coding system.

ambulatory surgery. Surgical procedure in which the patient is admitted, treated, and released on the same day.

AMCRA. American Managed Care Review Association.

American Academy of Professional Coders. National organization for coders and billers offering certification based upon physician-, facility- or payer-specific guidelines, providing CPC, CPC-H, CPC-P and CIRCC, as well as a variety of specialty credentials.

American College of Medical Coding Specialists. National organization for coders, billers, and payers offering certification based upon physician-, facility-, or payer-specific guidelines, providing PCS, FCS, and CSP credentials and education.

AMLOS. Arithmetic mean length of stay. Average number of days patients within a given DRG stay in the hospital. The AMLOS is used to determine payment for outlier cases and to predict occupancy rates.

ANA. American Nursing Association.

AOA. American Osteopathic Association.

AP-DRG. All patient diagnosis-related group. 3M HIS made revisions and adjustments to the DRG system, now referred to as the All Patient DRGs. Early features of AP-DRGs included MDC 24, specifically devoted to HIV, and restructuring of the major diagnostic categories governing newborns.

APA. American Psychiatric Association.

APG. Ambulatory patient group. Reimbursement methodology developed for the Centers for Medicare and Medicaid Services.

appeal. Specific request made to a payer for reconsideration of a denial or adverse coverage or payment decision and potential restriction of benefit reimbursement.

appropriateness of care. Proper setting of medical care that best meets the patient's care or diagnosis, as defined by a health care plan or other legal entity.

APR. Average payment rate. Amount of money CMS could pay an HMO for services provided to Medicare recipients under a risk contract.

ART. Accredited record technician. Former AHIMA certification describing medical records practitioners; now known as a registered health information technician (RHIT).

AS. Associate of Science.

ASN. Associate of Science, Nursing.

ASO. Administrative services only. Contractual agreement between a self-funded plan and an insurance company in which the insurance company assumes no risk and provides administrative services only.

assignment. In medical reimbursement, the arrangement in which the provider submits the claim on behalf of the patient and is reimbursed directly by the patient's plan. By doing so, the provider agrees to accept what the plan pays.

assignment of benefits. Authorization from the patient allowing the third-party payer to pay the provider directly for medical services. Under Medicare, an assignment is an agreement by the hospital or physician to accept Medicare's payment as the full payment and not to bill the patient for any amounts over the allowance amount, except for deductible and/or coinsurance amounts or noncovered services.

at risk. In medical reimbursement, a type of contract between Medicare and a payer or a payer and a provider in which the payer (in the case of Medicare) and the provider (in the case of the payer contracts) gets paid a set amount for care of a patient base. If costs exceed the amount the payer or provider were paid, the patients still receive care during the term of the contract.

attained age. In medical reimbursement, the age of the member as of the last birthday.

auditor. Professional who evaluates a provider's utilization, quality of care, or level of reimbursement.

AWP. *1)* Average wholesale price. Pharmaceutical price based on common data that is included in a pharmacy provider contract. **2)** Any willing provider. Describing statutes requiring a provider network to accept any provider who meets the network's usual selection criteria.

backlog. In medical reimbursement, the queue of claims that have not been adjudicated.

balance billing. Arrangement prohibited in Medicare regulations and some payer contracts whereby a provider bills the patient for charges not reimbursed by the payer.

basic coverage. Insurance providing coverage for hospital care.

basic health services. Defined set of benefits all federally qualified HMOs must offer enrollees.

board certification. Certification in a particular specialty based on the physician's demonstration of expertise and experience.

boarder. Individual who receives lodging, such as a parent, caregiver, or other family member, who is not a patient but may wish or need to be near the patient.

boarder baby. *1)* Newborn that remains in the nursery following discharge because the mother is still hospitalized. **2)** Premature infant who no longer needs intensive care but who remains for observation or to reach developmental milestones.

book of business. Payer's list of clients and contracts.

BSN. Bachelor of Science, Nursing.

bundled. *1)* Gathering of several types of health insurance policies under a single payer. **2)** Inclusive grouping of codes related to a procedure when submitting a claim.

business coalition. Employers who form a cooperative to purchase health care less expensively.

cafeteria plan. Employer's offer of various services of many payers as separate elements in a health care plan.

Cap. *1)* Capitation. *2)* Contract maximum.

capitation. Contractual agreement whereby the provider is paid a fixed amount for treating enrolled patients regardless of utilization.

care unit. Specific department or facility within a hospital or long-term care facility designed and staffed for treating a particular type of patient.

carrier. Insurer or health plan that may underwrite, administer, or sell a range of health benefit programs.

carve-out. Medical benefits for a specific type of care considered covered by separate guidelines or not covered by the payer.

case management. Ongoing review of cases by professionals to assure the most appropriate utilization of services

case manager. Medical professional (usually a nurse or social worker) who reviews cases every few days to determine necessity of care and to advise providers on payers' utilization restrictions. Certifies ongoing care.

case mix index. Sum of all DRG relative weights, divided by the number of Medicare cases.

catastrophic case management. Method of reviewing ongoing cases in which the patient sustains catastrophic or extremely costly medical problems.

catchment area. Geographical area from which a health care organization draws its members.

CC. Complication or comorbid condition.

CCU. Coronary care unit. Facility dedicated to patients suffering from heart attack, stroke, or other serious cardiopulmonary problems.

CDC. Centers for Disease Control and Prevention.

census. In medical reimbursement, number and demographics of patients or members

certification. Approval by a payer's case manager to continue care for a given number of days or visits.

cherry picking. In medical reimbursement, the practice of enrolling only healthy individuals and excluding those with existing problems.

chief complaint. In medical documentation, the presenting problem bringing the patient to the health encounter.

churning. *1)* Performance-based reimbursement system emphasizing provider productivity. *2)* When a provider sees a patient more than medically necessary with the intent of generating more revenue.

CLA. Certified laboratory assistant.

claim. Statement of services rendered requesting payment from an insurance company or a government entity.

claim lag. Time incurred between the date of a claim and its submission or payment. c. manual. Administrative guidelines used by claims processors to adjudicate claims according to company policy and procedure.

claim manual. Administrative guidelines used by claims processors to adjudicate claims according to company policy and procedure.

claims manager. Payer's manager who oversees the employee who processes routine claims.

claims reviewer. Payer employee who reviews claims like an auditor, looking at coding, prior authority, contract violations, etc.

CLIA. Clinical Laboratory Improvement Amendments. Requirements set in 1988, CLIA imposes varying levels of federal regulations on clinical procedures. Few laboratories, including those in physician offices, are exempt. Adopted by Medicare and Medicaid, CLIA regulations redefine laboratory testing in regard to laboratory certification and accreditation, proficiency testing, quality assurance, personnel standards, and program administration.

closed claim. Claim for which all apparent benefits have been paid.

closed panel. Arrangement in which a managed care organization contracts providers on an exclusive basis, restricting the providers from seeing patients enrolled in other payers' plans.

closed treatment. Realignment of a fracture or dislocation without surgically opening the skin to reach the site. Treatment methods employed include with or without manipulation, and with or without traction.

CMA. Certified medical assistant.

CMI. Case mix index. Sum of all DRG relative weights, divided by the number of Medicare cases. A low CMI may denote DRG assignments that do not adequately reflect the resources used to treat Medicare patients.

CMP. Competitive medical plan. Federal designation allowing plans to obtain eligibility to receive a Medicare risk contract without having to qualify as an HMO.

CMS. Centers for Medicare and Medicaid Services. Federal agency that administers the public health programs.

CMS-1500. Universal form used to file professional claims.

CMT. Certified medical transcriptionist.

COA. Certificate of authority. State license to operate as an HMO.

COB. Coordination of benefits. In health care contracting, method of integrating benefits payable when there is more than one group insurance plan so that the insured's benefits and the payment of insurance benefits from all sources do not exceed 100 percent of the allowed medical expenses.

COBRA. Consolidated Omnibus Reconciliation Act. Federal law that allows and requires past employees to be covered under company health insurance plans for a set premium, allowing individuals to remain insured when their current plan or position has been terminated.

coder. Professional who translates documented, written diagnoses and procedures into numeric and alphanumeric codes.

coding conventions. Each space, typeface, indentation, and punctuation mark determining how ICD-9-CM codes are interpreted. These conventions were developed to help match correct codes to the diagnoses that are encountered.

coinsurance. Percentage of allowanced charges that a beneficiary must pay toward cost of care.

commercial carriers. For-profit insurance companies issuing health coverage.

common working file. System of local databases containing total beneficiary histories developed by CMS to improve Medicare claims processing. Medicare fiscal intermediaries and carriers interact with these databases to obtain data on eligibility, utilization, Medicare secondary payer (MSP), and other detailed claims information. The CWF is authorized to deny payment on claims on a prepayment basis. There are nine CWF regionally based sectors.

community rating. Methodology of state and federal governments that requires qualified HMOs to request the same amount of money for each member in a plan.

comorbidity. Preexisting condition that causes an increase in length of stay by at least one day in approximately 75 percent of cases. Used in DRG reimbursement.

comparative performance report. Report that provides an annual comparison of a physician's services and procedures with those of another physician in the same specialty and geographic area.

complex repair. Surgical closure of a wound requiring more than layered closure of the deeper subcutaneous tissue and fascia (i.e., debridement, scar excision, placement of stents or retention sutures, and sometimes site preparation or undermining that creates the defect requiring complex closure).

complication. Condition arising after the beginning of observation and treatment that modifies the course of the patient's illness or the medical care required, or an undesired result or misadventure in medical care.

component code. In CCI, the code following the comprehensive code that cannot be charged to Medicare when the comprehensive code is charged.

component coding. Coding a service that represents only a portion of the entire service provided, meant to standardize the reporting of interventional radiology services. Component coding allows a physician, regardless of specialty, to specifically identify and report those aspects of the service he or she provided, whether the procedural component, the radiological component, or both.

comprehensive codes. Code behind which component codes fall.

consultation. Advice or an opinion regarding diagnosis and treatment of a patient rendered by a medical professional at the request of the primary care provider.

continuity of coverage. In health care contracting, transfer of benefits from one plan to another without a lapse of coverage.

conversion. In health care contracting, shifting of a member under a group contract to an individual contract in accordance with contract terms and occurring with a change in employer benefits or when the covered person leaves the group.

conversion factor. *1)* Dollar value for each relative value unit. When this dollar amount is multiplied by the total relative value units, it yields the reimbursement rate for the service. **2)** National multiplier that converts the geographically adjusted relative value units into Medicare fee schedule dollar amounts that applies to all services paid under the MFS.

coordinated care. In health care contracting, system of health care delivery that influences utilization, quality of care, and cost of services. Managed care integrates financing and management with an employed or contracted organized provider network that delivers services to an enrolled population.

copayment. Cost-sharing arrangement in which a covered person pays a specified portion of allowed charges. In relation to Medicare, the copayment designates the specific dollar amount that the patient must pay and coinsurance designates the percentage of allowed charges.

correct coding initiative. Official list of codes from the Centers for Medicare and Medicaid Services' (CMS) National Correct Coding Policy Manual for Part B Medicare Carriers that identifies services considered an integral part of a comprehensive code or mutually exclusive of it.

corridor deductible. Fixed out-of-pocket amount the member must pay before benefits are available.

COT. *1)* Chain of trust. In health care contracting, pattern of agreements that extend protection of health care data. Each covered entity that shares health care data with a second entity must require the second entity to provide protections comparable to those provided by the covered entity. The second entity, in turn, must require any other entities with which it shares the data to satisfy the same requirements. *2)* Certified ophthalmic technician.

COTA. Certified occupational therapy assistant.

counseling. Discussion with a patient and/or family concerning one or more of the following areas: diagnostic results, impressions, and/or recommended diagnostic studies; prognosis; risks and benefits of management (treatment) options; instructions for management (treatment) and/or follow-up; importance of compliance with chosen management (treatment) options; risk factor reduction; and patient and family education.

covered charges. Charges for medical care and supplies that are medically necessary and met coverage and program guidelines.

covered person. Any person entitled to benefits under the policy, whether a member or dependent.

CPR. Computerized patient record. Computer application that allows all or most elements of a patient's medical record to be stored in a computerized database.

credentialing. *1)* Reviewing the medical degrees, licensure, malpractice, and any disciplinary record of medical providers for panel and quality assurance purposes and to grant hospital privileges. *2)* Coding certification.

critical care. Treatment of critically ill patients in a variety of medical emergencies that requires the constant attendance of the physician (e.g., cardiac arrest, shock, bleeding, respiratory failure, postoperative complications, critically ill neonate).

CRNA. Certified registered nurse anesthetist. Nurse trained and specializing in the administration of anesthesia.

crosswalk. Cross-referencing of CPT codes with ICD-9-CM, anesthesia, dental, or HCPCS Level II codes.

CRT. Certified respiratory therapist.

CSO. Clinical service organization. Health care organization developed by academic medical centers to integrate medical school, faculty practice plan, and hospital.

CST. Certified surgical technologist.

cutback. Reduction of the amount or type of insurance for a member who attains a specified age or condition (e.g., age 65, retirement).

daily benefit. Specified maximum benefit payable for room and board charges at a hospital.

database. Electronic store of utilization information used by payers to pay claims, negotiate contracts, and track utilization and cost of services.

date of service. Day the encounter or procedure is performed or the day a supply is issued.

DAW. Dispense as written. Notation from a physician to a pharmacist requesting that the brand name medication be given in lieu of a generic medication.

days per thousand. Standard unit of measurement of utilization determined by calculating the number of hospital days used in a year for each 1,000 covered lives.

DC. *1)* Doctor of chiropractic medicine. *2)* Discontinue. *3)* Direct current.

decapitation. Inadequate capitation.

deductible. Predetermined dollar amount of covered billed charges that the patient must pay toward the cost of care.

direct claim payment. Method where members deal directly with the payer rather than submitting claims through the employer.

direct contract model. Plan that contracts directly with individual private practice physicians rather than through an intermediary.

discharge plan. Treatment plan by the provider for continued patient care after discharge that may include home care, the services of case managers or other health care providers, or transfer to another facility.

discharge status. Disposition of the patient at discharge (e.g., left against medical advice, discharged home, transferred to an acute care hospital, expired).

discharge transfer. Discharge of a patient from one facility to another.

disposition of patient. Description of the patient's status and destination at discharge (e.g., discharged to home) used for data and quality assurance purposes.

DME. Durable medical equipment. Medical equipment that can withstand repeated use, is not disposable, is used to serve a medical purpose, is generally not useful to a person in the absence of a sickness or injury, and is appropriate for use in the home. Examples of durable medical equipment include hospital beds, wheelchairs, and oxygen equipment.

DO. Doctor of osteopathy.

DOS. Date of service. In health care contracting, day the encounter or procedure is performed or the day a supply is issued.

DPM. Doctor of podiatric medicine.

DRG. Diagnosis related group. Method CMS uses to pay hospitals for Medicare recipients based on a statistical system of classifying any inpatient stay into one of several hundred groups. It is a classification scheme whose patient types are defined by patients' diagnoses or procedures and, in some cases, by the patient's age or discharge status. Each DRG is intended to be medically meaningful and would ordinarily require approximately equal resource consumption as measured by length of stay and cost.

drug formulary. List of prescription medications preferred for use by a health plan and dispensed through participating pharmacies to covered persons.

DSM-IV. Diagnostic and Statistical Manual of Mental Disorders, Fourth Edition. Manual used by mental health workers as the diagnostic coding system for substance abuse and mental health patients

dual option. Offering of an HMO and traditional plan by one carrier.

DUR. Drug utilization review. Review to assure prescribed medications are medically necessary and appropriate.

E code. ICD-9-CM diagnosis code that describes the circumstance that caused an injury, not the nature of the injury. E codes are used to classify external causes of injury, poisoning, or other adverse effects. An E code should not be used as a principal diagnosis because the intermediary will reject the claim.

E/M. Evaluation and management services. Assessment, counseling, and other services provided to a patient and reported through CPT codes.

E/M service components. Key components in determining the correct level of E/M codes are history, examination, and medical decision-making.

EAP. Employee assistance program. Services designed to help employees, their family members, and employers find solutions for workplace and personal problems that affect morale, productivity, or financial issues such as workplace stress, family/marital concerns, legal or financial problems, elder care, child care, substance abuse, emotional/stress issues, and other daily living concerns.

EdD. Doctor of education.

EDI. Electronic data interchange. Transference of claims, certifications, quality assurance reviews, and utilization data via computer in X12 format. May refer to any electronic exchange of formatted data.

EHO. Emerging healthcare organizations. Hospitals and other providers that are emerging or affiliating.

elective admission. Admission made at the discretion of the patient and facility based on available resources.

ELOS. Estimated length of stay. Average number of days of hospitalization required for a given illness or procedure, based on prior histories of patients who have been hospitalized for the same illness or procedure.

emergency admission. Admission in which the patient requires immediate medical or psychiatric attention because of life-threatening, severe, and potentially disabling conditions.

emergency department. Organized hospital-based facility for the provision of unscheduled episodic services to patients who present for immediate medical attention. The facility must be available 24 hours a day.

emergency outpatient. Patient admitted for diagnosis and treatment of a condition requiring immediate attention but who will not stay at that facility or be transferred to another.

EMT. Emergency medical technician.

EMT-P. Paramedic.

encoder. Computer application that assists in the assignment of a diagnosis or procedure code and may also assign reimbursement categories and values.

encounter. Direct personal contact between a patient and a physician, or other person who is authorized by state licensure law and, if applicable, by hospital staff bylaws, to order or furnish hospital services for diagnosis or treatment of the patient.

enrollee. In medical reimbursement, person who subscribes to a specific health plan.

enrollment. Number of lives covered by the plan.

EOB. Explanation of benefits. Statement mailed to the member and provider explaining claim adjudication and payment.

episode of care. One or more health care services received during a period of relatively continuous care by a hospital or health care provider.

EPO. Exclusive provider organization. In health care contracting, an organization similar to an HMO, but the member must remain within the provider network to receive benefits. EPOs are regulated under insurance statutes rather than HMO legislation.

ERISA. Employee Retirement Income Security Act of 1974, Public Law 93-406. Mandates reporting, disclosure of grievance and appeals requirements, and fiduciary standards for private group life and health plans, and preempts state benefit mandates and premium tax laws for self-funded group health plans.

established patient. *1)* Patient who has received professional services in a face-to-face setting within the last three years from the same physician or another physician of the same specialty who belongs to the same group practice. *2)* For OPPS hosptials, patient who has been registered as an inpatient or outpatient in a hospital's provider-based clinic or emergency department within the past three years.

exclusions. Services excluded from a plan's coverage by the employer or payer because of risk or cost.

experience rating. In medical reimbursement, designation of a group's previous claims history to help determine premium rates.

extramural birth. Infant born outside of a sterile environment.

facility. Place of patient care, including inpatient and outpatient, acute or long term.

facility of payment. Contractual relationship that permits the payer to pay someone other than the member or provider.

fact-oriented V codes. Codes that do not describe a problem or a service; they simply state a fact. These generally do not serve as an outpatient primary or inpatient principal diagnosis.

FAR. Federal acquisition regulations. Regulations of the federal government's acquisition of services.

FDA. Food and Drug Administration. Federal agency responsible for protecting public health by substantiating the safety, efficacy, and security of human and veterinary drugs, biological products, medical devices, national food supply, cosmetics, and items that give off radiation.

Federal Register. Government publication listing changes in regulations and federally mandated standards, including coding standards such as HCPCS Level II and ICD-9-CM.

federally qualified HMO. HMO that meets CMS guidelines for Medicare reimbursement.

fee schedule. List of codes and related services with pre-established billing amounts by a provider, or payment amounts by a payer that could be percentages of billed charges, flat rates, or maximum allowable amounts established by third-party payers. Medicare fee schedules apply to clinical laboratory, radiology, and durable medical equipment services.

FEHBARS. Federal Employee Health Benefits Acquisition Regulations. Federal regulations for acquisition of health services used by government agencies and subcontractors.

FEHBP. Federal Employee Health Benefits Program. Provides health plans to federal workers.

FFS. Fee for service. *1)* Payment for services, usually physician services, on a service-by-service basis rather than an alternative payment system like capitation. Fee-for-service arrangements may be discounted or undiscounted rates. *2)* Situation in which the payer pays full charges for medical services.

formulary. List of prescription medications preferred for use by the health plan and dispensed through participating pharmacies to covered persons.

FPP. Faculty practice plan. Group practice developed around a teaching program or medical school.

fraternal insurance. Cooperative plan provided to members of an association or fraternal group.

FTE. Full time employee. Accounting equivalent of one full time employee that includes wages, benefits, and other costs.

gatekeeper. Primary care physician in a health care system in which a member's care must be provided by a primary care physician unless the physician refers the member to a specialist or approves the care provided by a specialist.

GHAA. Group Health Association of America. HMO trade organization.

global surgery package. Surgical procedure with without complications that includes all of the elements needed to perform the procedure and routine follow-up care.

GMLOS. Geometric mean length of stay. Statistically adjusted value for all cases for a given diagnosis-related group, allowing for the outliers, transfer cases, and negative outlier cases that would normally skew the data. The GMLOS is used to determine payment only for transfer cases (i.e., the per diem rate).

government mandates. Services mandated by state or federal law such as the correct use of ICD-9-CM codes.

grace period. Set number of days past the due date of a premium payment during which medical coverage may not be canceled and the premium payment may be made, or after employment termination. It varies by health plan contract and state law but is generally 30 to 60 days.

group model. HMO that contracts with a group of providers.

group practice. Group of providers that shares facilities, resources, and staff, and who may represent a single unit in a managed care network.

grouper. Computer application that assigns diagnosis-related groups (DRGs).

guidelines. Information appearing at the beginning of each of the six major sections of the CPT book. They also may appear at the beginning of subsections and code ranges. The information contained in the guidelines provides definitions, explanations of terms, and factors relevant to the section.

HCPCS. Healthcare Common Procedure Coding System. *HCPCS Level I.* Healthcare Common Procedure Coding System Level I. Numeric coding system used by physicians, facility outpatient departments, and ambulatory surgery centers (ASC) to code ambulatory, laboratory, radiology, and other diagnostic services for Medicare billing. This coding system contains only the American Medical Association's Physicians' Current Procedural Terminology (CPT) codes. The AMA updates codes annually. *HCPCS Level II.* Healthcare Common Procedure Coding System Level II. National coding system, developed by CMS, that contains alphanumeric codes for physician and nonphysician services not included in the CPT coding system. HCPCS Level II covers such things as ambulance services, durable medical equipment, and orthotic and prosthetic devices. *HCPCS modifiers.* Two-character code (AA-ZZ) that identifies circumstances that alter or enhance the description of a service or supply. They are recognized by carriers nationally and are updated annually by CMS.

HCPCS modifiers. Two-character code (AA-ZZ) that identifies circumstances that alter or enhance the description of a service or supply. They are recognized by carriers nationally and are updated annually by CMS.

HHS. Health and Human Services. Cabinet department that oversees the operating divisions of the federal government responsible for health and welfare. HHS oversees the Centers for Medicare and Medicaid Services, Food and Drug Administration, Public Health Service, and other such entities.

HIAA. Health Insurance Association of America. Trade organization for payers.

hierarchy. Rank or order of codes. Numerical hierarchy plays a key role in ICD-9-CM coding because each digit beyond three adds more detail.

HMO. Health maintenance organization. Medical health insurance coverage that pays claims based on a provider cost, per diem, or charge basis. Hospitals contract with an HMO to provide care at a contractually reduced price. HMO members pay a set monthly amount for coverage and are treated without additional cost, except for a copayment or deductible amount, payable by the patient. Like all managed care organizations, HMOs use a variety of mechanisms to control costs, including utilization management, discounted provider fee schedules, and financial incentives. HMOs use primary care physicians as gatekeepers and tend to emphasize preventive care.

hold harmless. Contractual clause stating that if either party is held liable for malpractice, the other party is absolved.

home health. Palliative and therapeutic care and assistance in the activities of daily life to home bound Medicare and private plan members.

hospice. Organization that furnishes inpatient, outpatient, and home health care for the terminally ill. Hospices emphasize support and counseling services for terminally ill people and their families, pain relief, and symptom management. When the Medicare beneficiary chooses hospice benefits, all other Medicare benefits are discontinued, except physician services and treatment of conditions not related to the terminal illness.

hospital admission plan. Used to facilitate admission to the hospital and to assure prompt payment to the hospital.

IBNR. Incurred but not reported. Amount of money the payer's plan accrues to forestall unknown medical expenses.

ICD-10. International Classification of Diseases, Tenth Revision. Classification of diseases by alphanumeric code, used by the World Health Organization.

ICD-10-CM. International Classification of Diseases, Tenth Edition, Clinical Modification. Diagnostic coding system developed to replace ICD-9-CM in the United States. It is a clinical modification of the World Health Organization's ICD-10, already in use in much of the world, and used for mortality reporting in the United States. The implementation date for ICD-10-CM has been set for October 1, 2013.

ICD-9-CM. International Classification of Diseases, Ninth Edition, Clinical Modification. Clinical modification of the international statistical coding system used to report, compile, and compare health care data, using numeric and alphanumeric codes to help plan, deliver, reimburse, and quantify medical care in the United States.

ICF. *1)* International Classification of Functioning, Disability, and Health. World Health Organization coding system for reporting an individual's capacity to cope in situations that are the consequence of disease. The classification identifies functional limits set by the severity of the disease, without identifying the disease itself. Code examples include d550, to report the ability to open bottles and cans, use eating implements, and consume meals in a culturally accepted way; or the ability to walk, reported for different distances with codes in the d450 category of ICF. The United States has not adopted ICF for use. However, it is under investigation at the National Center for Health Statistics as a reporting mechanism for the future. *2)* Intermediate care facility. Health care facility that furnishes services to patients who do not require the degree of care provided by a hospital or skilled nursing facility or a step-down facility for patients who are leaving the hospital but who cannot be discharged to home because of continuing medical needs.

immediate maternity. Coverage provided for pregnancies that began prior to the date the member became insured.

in plan. Services chosen from a network provider.

incontestable clause. Provision in a policy that prohibits the plan from disputing coverage for certain conditions after a specified period of time.

inpatient hospitalization. Period in which a patient is housed in a single hospital usually without interruption.

inpatient reimbursement. Payment to hospital for the costs incurred to treat a patient.

insurance carrier. Insurer or health plan that may underwrite, administer, or sell a range of health benefit programs.

intermediate repair. *1)* Surgical closure of a wound requiring closure of one or more of the deeper subcutaneous tissue and non-muscle fascia layers in addition to suturing the skin. *2)* Contaminated wounds with single layer closure that need extensive cleaning or foreign body removal.

internal skeletal fixation. Repair involving wires, pins, screws, and/or plates placed through or within the fractured area to stabilize and immobilize the injury.

IPA. Individual practice association. Organization made up of providers who, along with the rest of a group, contract with payers at a discounted fee-for-service or capitated rate.

IPO. Individual practice organization. Organization made up of providers who, along with the rest of a group, contract with payers at a discounted fee-for-service or capitated rate.

IS. Information services. Administrators of the computer systems used by payers and providers.

JCAHO. Joint Commission on Accreditation of Healthcare Organizations. Organization that accredits health care organizations. In the future, the JCAHO may play a role in certifying these organizations' compliance with the HIPAA A/S requirements. Previously known as the Joint Commission for the Accreditation of Hospitals.

JD. Doctor of jurisprudence.

key components. Three components of history, examination, and medical decision making are considered the keys to selecting the correct level of E/M codes. In most cases, all three components must be addressed in the documentation. However, in established, subsequent, and follow-up categories, only two of the three must be met or exceeded for a given code.

lag study. Report used by plan managers to determine how long claims are pending and how much is paid out each month.

lapse. Terminated policy.

late effect. Abnormality, dysfunction, or other residual condition produced after the acute phase of an illness, injury, or disease is over. There is no time limit on when late effects can appear.

LCSW. Licensed clinical social worker.

limiting charge. Maximum amount a nonparticipating physician or provider can charge for services to a Medicare patient.

limits. In medical reimbursement, ceiling for benefits payable under a plan

line of business. Different health plans offered by a larger insurer or insurance broker as a product line.

lives. Unit of measurement used by plans to determine the number of people covered. Calculated by multiplying the number of members by 2.5.

local medical review policy. Carrier-specific policy applied in the absence of a national coverage policy to make local Medicare coverage decisions, including the development of a draft policy based on a review of medical literature, an understanding of local practice, and the solicitation of comments from the medical community and Carrier Advisory Committee.

long-term care facility. Nursing home or, more specifically, a facility offering extended, nonacute care to a resident patient whose illness does not require acute care.

loss ratio. Ratio between the cost to deliver medical care and the amount of money taken in by the plan.

LPN. Licensed practical nurse.

LVN. *1)* Licensed visiting nurse. *2)* Licensed vocational nurse.

MA. *1)* Master of arts degree. *2)* Medical assistant. *3)* Mental age.

MAC. Maximum allowable charge. Amount set by the insurer as the highest amount that can be charged for a particular medical service or by a pharmacy vendor.

malingering. Feigning of illness, as the result of intentional deceit or as the result of mental illness.

managed health care. *1)* Managing active cases to ensure care is the most appropriate, efficient, and effective. *2)* System of health care meant to manage overall cost. *3)* Method of health care whereby contracted physicians participate in managing health care costs.

mandated benefits. Services mandated by state or federal law such as in cases of child abuse or rape, not necessarily covered by insurers.

maximum allowable charge. Amount set by the insurer as the highest amount that can be charged for a particular medical service or by a pharmacy vendor.

MCE. Medical care evaluation.

MCO. Managed care organization. Generic term for various health benefit plans that provide coverage for health care services in conjunction with management and review of services provided to ensure that services are medically necessary and appropriate.

MD. Medical doctor.

MDC. Major diagnostic category. Dividing all possible principal diagnoses into mutually exclusive categories. These broad classifications of ICD-9-CM diagnoses are typically grouped by organ system.

ME. Medical examiner.

MEd. Master of education.

Medicaid. Joint federal and state program that covers medical expenses for people with low incomes and limited resources who meet the criteria. The benefits for recipients vary from state to state.

medical consultation. Advice or an opinion rendered by a physician at the request of the primary care provider.

medical meaningfulness. Patients in the same DRG can be expected to evoke a set of clinical responses that result in a similar pattern of resource use.

Medicare. Federally funded program authorized as part of the Social Security Act that provides for health care services for people age 65 or older, people with disabilities, and people with end-stage renal disease (ESRD).

Medicare Fee Schedule. Fee schedule based upon physician work, expense, and malpractice designed to slow the rise in cost for services and standardize payment to physicians regardless of specialty or location of service with geographic adjustments.

Medicare Part A. Hospital insurance coverage that includes hospital, nursing home, hospice, home health, and other inpatient care. Claims are submitted to intermediaries for reimbursement.

Medicare Part B. Supplemental medical insurance coverage that includes outpatient hospital care, physician and other qualified professional care. Claims from providers or suppliers other than a hospital are submitted to carriers for reimbursement. Hospital outpatient claims are submitted to their FI.

Medicare secondary payer. Specified circumstance when other third-party payers have the primary responsibility for payment of services and Medicare is the secondary payer. Medicare is secondary to workers' compensation and automobile, medical no-fault, and liability insurance, EGHPs, LGHPs, and certain employer health plans covering aged and disabled beneficiaries. The MSP program prohibits Medicare payment for items or services if payment has been made or can reasonably be expected to be made by another payer, as described above.

Medicare supplement. Private insurance coverage that pays the Medicare deductible and copayments and may also pay the costs of services not covered by Medicare.

Medigap policy. Health insurance or other health benefit plan offered by a private company to those entitled to Medicare benefits. The policy covers charges not payable by Medicare because of deductibles, coinsurance amounts, or other Medicare-imposed limitations.

member. In medical reimbursement, subscriber of a health plan.

member months. In medical reimbursement, total of months each member was covered.

member services. In health care contracting, the payer department that works as a patient advocate to solve problems and may take claims appeals to a final committee after all other processes have been exhausted.

mental health substance abuse. Payer term for services rendered to members for emotional problems or chemical dependency.

MeSH. Medical staff-hospital organization.

MET. Multiple employer trust. Group of employers that join together to purchase health insurance using a self-funded approach to lower costs by the broadening membership pool to prevent an adverse selection.

MEWA. Multiple employer welfare association. Group of employers that join together to purchase health insurance using a self-funded approach to lower costs by the broadening membership pool to prevent an adverse selection.

MHA. Master of health administration.

minor procedure. Self-limited procedure, usually with an assignment of 0 or 10 follow-up days by payers. A minor procedure may be considered by many payers to be part of the global package for a primary surgical service and cannot be billed separately from the primary procedure.

MIS. Management information system. Hardware and software facilitating claims management.

mixed model. HMO that includes both an open panel and closed panel option.

MLP. Midlevel practitioners. Professionals such as nurse practitioners, nurse midwives, physical therapists, physician assistants, and others who provide medical care but do so with physician input.

MLT. Medical laboratory technician.

modality. *1)* Form of imaging. These include x-ray, fluoroscopy, ultrasound, nuclear medicine, duplex Doppler, CT, and MRI. *2)* Any physical agent applied to produce therapeutic changes to biologic tissue; includes but is not limited to thermal, acoustic, light, mechanical, or electric energy.

modifier. Two-character code attached to a HCPCS code as a suffix to identify circumstances that alter or enhance the description of a service or supply.

morbidity rate. In health care contracting, an actuarial term describing predicted medical expense rate.

MPH. Master of public health. Advanced degree.

MSA. Medical savings account.

MSN. Master of science in nursing.

MSW. Master's in social work.

MT. Medical technologist.

multiple birth. Two or more infants delivered at the same time.

multiple employer group. Group of employers who contract together to subscribe to a plan, broadening the risk pool and saving money. Different from a multiple employer trust.

NA. Nurse assistant.

NAHMOR. National Association of HMO Regulators.

NAIC. National Association of Insurance Commissioners. Organization of state insurance regulators.

national coverage policy. Statement of Medicare coverage decisions that applies to all practitioners in states and regions. These policies indicate whether and under what circumstances procedures, services, and supplies are covered.

NBICU. Newborn intensive care unit. Special care unit for premature and seriously ill infants.

NCHS. National Center for Health Statistics. Division of the Centers for Disease Control and Prevention that compiles statistical information used to guide actions and policies to improve the public health of U.S. citizens. The NCHS maintains the ICD-9-CM coding system.

NCQA. National Committee for Quality Assurance. Organization that accredits managed care plans, or HMOs. In the future, the NCQA may play a role in certifying these organizations' compliance with the HIPAA A/S requirements.

ND. Doctor of naturopathy.

NEC. Not elsewhere classifiable. Condition or diagnosis that is not provided with its own specified code in ICD-9-CM, but included in a more broadly defined code for other specified conditions.

neonatal period. Period of an infant's life from birth to the age of 27 days, 23 hours, and 59 minutes.

network model. Plan that contracts with multiple groups of providers, or networks, to provide care.

new patient. Patient who is receiving face-to-face care from a provider or another physician of the same specialty who belongs to the same group practice for the first time in three years. For OPPS hospitals, a patient who has not been registered as an inpatient or outpatient, including off-campus provider based clinic or emergency department, of the hospital within the past three years.

newborn admission. Infant born in the facility.

normal delivery. Baby delivered without complication.

NOS. Not otherwise specified. Condition or diagnosis remains ill defined and is unspecified without the necessary information for selecting a more specific code.

NP. *1)* Nurse practitioner. *2)* Neuropsychiatry.

OB. Obstetrician.

observation patient. Patient who needs to be monitored and assessed for inpatient admission or referral to another site for care

occupational therapy. Training, education, and assistance intended to assist a person who is recovering from a serious illness or injury perform the activities of daily life.

OL. Outlier threshold. Component that figures in the reimbursement calculation for a DRG.

open enrollment period. Time during which subscribers in a health benefit program have an opportunity to re-enroll or select an alternative health plan being offered to them, usually without evidence of insurability or waiting periods.

open panel. Arrangement in which a managed care organization that contracts with providers on an exclusive basis is still seeking providers.

OPL. Other party liability. In coordination of benefits, the decision that the other plan is the primary plan.

orthotic. Use of a mechanical orthopedic device that compensates for, supports, corrects, or prevents deformities.

OTR. Occupational therapist registered.

out of plan. In health care contracting, services of a provider who is not a member of the preferred provider network.

out of service area. In health care contracting, medical care received out of the geographic area that may or may not be covered, depending on the plan.

outlier. Case classified to a specific DRG but with exceptionally high costs compared with other cases classified to the same DRG. The fiscal intermediary makes a payment in addition to the original DRG amount for these situations. A cost outlier is paid an amount in excess of the cut-off threshold for a given DRG. The day outlier no longer applies.

outpatient. Patient who receives care without being admitted for inpatient or residential care.

outpatient visit. Encounter in a recognized outpatient facility.

overutilization. Services rendered by providers more frequently than usual.

PA. *1)* Physician assistant. Medical professional who receives additional training and can assess, treat, and prescribe medications under a physician's review. *2)* Posteroanterior. *3)* Pulmonary artery.

paneled. In health care contracting, provider contracted with an HMO.

par provider. Provider who is participating in the health plan or Medicare program.

partial disability. Congenital or acquired inability to perform part of one's job.

partial hospitalization. Situation in which the patient only stays part of each day over a long period. Cardiac, rehabilitation, and chronic pain patients, for example, could use this service.

partial payment. Payment to a provider or member with the expectation that other payments will be made before the claim is closed.

PAS norms. Based on a professional activity study performed regularly by the Commission on Professional and Hospital Activities and broken out by average length of stay (ALOS) by region.

PBM. Prescription benefit managers. HMO staff who monitor amount and use of drugs prescribed.

PCP. Primary care physician. Physician who makes an initial diagnosis and referral and retains control over the patient and utilization of services both in and outside of the plan.

pediatric patient. Patient usually younger than 14 years of age.

peer review. Evaluation of the quality of the total health care provided by medical staff with equivalent training, such as physician-to-physician or nurse-to-nurse evaluation.

PEPM. Per employee per month.

PEPP. Payment error prevention program. Program to help reduce Medicare PPS inpatient hospital payment errors.

per diem reimbursement. In health care contracting, reimbursement to an institution based on a set rate per day rather than on a charge-by-charge basis.

percutaneous skeletal fixation. Treatment that is neither open nor closed. In this procedure, the injury site is not directly visualized. Instead, fixation devices (pins, screws) are placed to stabilize the dislocation using x-ray guidance.

perinatal death. Stillborn births and neonatal deaths.

PharmD. Doctor of pharmacy.

PhD. Doctor of philosophy.

PHO. Physician-hospital organization.

physician assistant. Medical professional who receives additional training and can assess, treat, and prescribe medications under a physician's review.

PIN. Physician identification number.

plan manager. Payer employee managing all of the contracts and contract negotiations for one or more specific plans.

PMPM. Per member per month.

PMPY. Per member per year.

pooling. Health payers' practice of combining risk.

POS. Point of service. Health benefit plan allowing the covered person to choose to receive a service from a participating or nonparticipating provider, with different benefit levels associated with the use of participating providers.

posting date. Date a charge is posted to a patient account by the provider, frequently not the same as the actual date of service, but usually within five days of the actual date of service.

PPA. Preferred provider arrangement. Similar to a PPO.

PPS. Prospective payment system. Reimbursement methodology that uses predetermined rates for each type of discharge, procedure, service, or item based on a standard type of case. For hospital inpatients, the Medicare PPS system of DRGs was implemented in 1983 to hold down the rising cost of health care. For hospital outpatients, OPPS has been based on ambulatory payment classifications effective August 1, 2000. For skilled nursing facilities, it is based on the RUGs-III system, and for home health it is based on the HHRGs.

precert. Preferred provider organization. Program that establishes contracts with providers of medical care. Usually the benefit contract provides significantly better benefits and lower member cost for services received from preferred providers, encouraging covered persons to use these providers, who may be reimbursed on a discounted basis.

precertification. Preadmission certification. Approval in advance of a procedure or hospital stay by a payer employee, who considers the diagnosis, the planned treatment, and expected length of stay.

preexisting condition. Symptom that causes a person to seek diagnosis, care, or treatment for which medical advice or treatment was recommended or received by a physician within a certain time period before the effective date of medical insurance coverage. The preexisting condition waiting period is the time the beneficiary must wait after buying health insurance before coverage begins for a condition that existed before coverage was obtained.

premature delivery. Infant delivered with time of gestation less than 37 weeks.

presenting problem. Disease, condition, illness, injury, symptom, sign, finding, complaint, or other reason for the patient encounter

primary care. Basic or general health care, traditionally provided by family practice, pediatrics, and internal medicine practitioners.

primary diagnosis. Current, most significant reason for the services or procedures provided.

principal diagnosis. Condition established after study to be chiefly responsible for occasioning the admission of the patient to the hospital for care.

principal procedure. Procedure performed for definitive treatment rather than for diagnostic or exploratory purposes, or that was necessary to treat a complication. Usually related to the principal diagnosis.

PRO. Peer review organization. Organization that contracts with CMS to conduct preadmission, preprocedure, and postdischarge medical reviews and determine medical necessity, appropriateness, and quality of certain inpatient and outpatient surgical procedures for which payment may be made in whole or in part under the Medicare program.

problem-oriented V codes. ICD-9-CM codes that identify circumstances that could affect the patient in the future but are neither a current illness nor an injury. Use these codes to describe an existing circumstance or problem that may influence future medical care.

professional association plans. Plan provided by a professional association that affords self-employed professionals (e.g., physicians, CPAs, lawyers) less expensive coverage.

provider. All-inclusive, generic term for people or institutions that provide health care. The provider may be a physician, hospital, pharmacy, other facility, or other health care provider.

PT. Physical therapy.

PTA. Physical therapy assistant.

PTMPY. Per thousand members per year.

QA. Quality assurance. Monitoring and maintenance of established standards of quality for patient care.

QM. Quality management. Monitoring and maintenance of established standards of quality.

RBRVS. Resource-based relative value scale. Fee schedule introduced by CMS to reimburse physician Medicare fees based on the amount of time and resources expended in treating patients with adjustments for overhead costs and geographical differences.

reasonable and customary. Fees charged for medical services that are considered normal, common, and in line with the prevailing fees in the provider's geographical area.

referral. Approval from the primary care physician to see a specialist or receive certain services. May be required for coverage purposes before a patient receives care from anyone except the primary physician.

regional medical center. Hospital that provides comprehensive services to a large regional area but that may not be a tertiary care facility. Largely used in the west where facilities may serve hundreds of square miles.

rehabilitation. Restoration of physical and mental functions to allow the usual daily activities of life.

reimbursement. Payment of actual charges or allowable incurred as a result of accident or illness.

reinsurance. Insurance purchased by an HMO, insurance company, or self-funded employer from another insurance company to protect itself against all or part of the losses that may be incurred in the process of honoring the claims of its participating providers, policy holders, or employees and covered dependents.

relative weight. Assigned weight that is intended to reflect the relative resource consumption associated with each DRG. The higher the relative weight, the greater the payment to the hospital. The relative weights are calculated by CMS and published in the final prospective payment system rule.

review committee. Multidisciplinary committee that considers denied cases being appealed, catastrophic cases, or fee-for-service cases.

RHIA. Registered health information administrator. Accreditation for medical record administrators, previously known as a registered records administrator (RRA), through AHIMA.

RHIT. Registered health information technician. Accreditation for medical records practitioners, previously known as accredited records technician (ART), through AHIMA.

risk contract. Contract between Medicare and a payer or a payer and a provider in which the payer (in the case of Medicare) and the provider (in the case of the payer contracts) receive a set amount for care of a patient base. If costs exceed the amount the payer or provider was paid, the patients still receive care during the term of the contract.

risk factor reduction. Reduction of risk in the pool of members of a health plan.

risk manager. Person charged with keeping financial risk low, including malpractice cases.

risk pool. Pool of people who will be in the insured group, their medical and mental histories, other factors such as age, and their predicted health.

RN. Registered nurse.

RPh. Registered pharmacist.

RPT. Registered physical therapist.

RRA. Registered records administrator.

RRT. Registered respiratory therapist.

rush charge. Charge for expeditious test results.

RVS. Relative value study. Guide that shows the relationship between the time, resources, competency, experience, severity, and other factors necessary to perform procedures that is multiplied by a dollar conversion factor to determine a monetary value for the procedure.

RVU. Relative value unit. Value assigned a procedure based on difficulty and time consumed. Used for computing reimbursement under a relative value study.

sanction. Imposition of penalties or exclusion of a provider for fraud or infractions such as an inappropriate use of services, providing procedures that may harm the patient, or applying inferior techniques.

schedule. Listing of amounts payable for specific procedures.

second opinion. Medical opinion obtained from another health care professional, relevant to clinical evaluation, before the performance of a medical service or surgical procedure. Includes patient education regarding treatment alternatives and/or to determine medical necessity.

secondary insurer. In a COB arrangement, the insurer that reimburses for benefits pending after payment by the primary insurer.

self-funded plan. Plan where the risk is assumed by the employer rather than the insurer. The employer generally pays claims directly from a general fund account that may be managed by a third party.

self-insured. Individual or organization that assumes the financial risk of paying for health care.

self-pay patients. Patients who pay for medical care out-of-pocket.

separate procedures. Services commonly carried out as a fundamental part of a total service, and as such usually do not warrant a separate identification. They are noted in the CPT book with the parenthetical phrase (separate procedure) at the end of the description, and are payable only when they are performed alone.

service date. Date a charge is incurred for a service.

service plan. *1)* Plan that has contracts with providers but is not a managed care plan. *2)* Another name for Blue Cross/Blue Shield plans.

service-oriented V codes. ICD-9-CM codes that identify or define examinations, aftercare, ancillary services, or therapy. Use these V codes to describe the patient who is not currently ill but seeks medical services for some specific purpose such as follow-up visits. You can also use this type of V code as a primary diagnosis for outpatient services when the patient has no symptoms that can be coded and screening services are provided.

shadow pricing. Setting rates just below a competitor's rates. Maximizes profits but raises medical costs.

short-stay patients. In medical reimbursement, inpatients admitted for 48 hours or less, or outpatients who stay 24 hours or less.

sick baby. Infant with medical complications not resulting from premature birth.

simple repair. Surgical closure of a superficial wound, requiring single layer suturing of the skin (epidermis, dermis, or subcutaneous tissue).

skeletal traction. Applying a pulling force directly on the long axis of bones by inserted wires or pins and using weights and pulleys to keep the bone in proper alignment.

skin traction. Application of a pulling force to a limb accomplished by a device fixed to felt dressings or strappings on the body surface.

small subscriber group aggregate. Aggregate of professional associations, small business, or other entities formed to be considered a single, large subscriber group.

SNF. Skilled nursing facility. Institution or a distinct part of an institution that is primarily engaged in providing skilled nursing care and related services for residents who require medical or nursing care; or rehabilitation services for the rehabilitation of injured, disabled, or sick persons. A SNF may be a part of a hospital or a separate entity, such as a nursing home. In order for a patient to be transferred between a hospital and a SNF, the transferring facility must complete a written transfer statement. A swing-bed hospital provides skilled nursing care and related services similar to those of a SNF.

specimen. Tissue cells or sample of fluid taken for analysis, pathologic examination, and diagnosis.

SSN. Social security number.

staff model. HMO that employs its own providers.

standard anesthesia formula. Reimbursement formula that consists of base units plus time units plus modifying units (e.g., physical status and qualifying circumstances) plus other allowed unit/charges that is multiplied by a conversion factor.

stat charge. Charge for expeditious test results.

state insurance commission. State group that approves insurance certificates for each state and regulates the industry based on statutes.

steering. Providing financial incentives to plan members to use the managed care provider panel.

stop loss. In health care contracting, a form of reinsurance that protects health insurance above a certain limit and minimizes risks for providers.

subrogation. Recovery of monies or benefits from a third party who is liable for the payment.

subsidiary codes. Services that are not included as part of the primary procedure but that are not performed alone and may be identified as each additional, or list-in-addition-to services. Phrases that help identify subsidiary codes include, but are not limited to: each additional, list in addition to, and done at time of other major procedure

substantial comorbidity. Preexisting condition that will, because of its presence with a specific principal diagnosis, cause an increase in the length of stay by at least one day in approximately 75 percent of the cases.

substantial complication. Condition that arises during the hospital stay that prolongs the length of stay by at least one day in approximately 75 percent of the cases.

subtraction. Removal of an overlying structure to better visualize the structure in question by imposing one x-ray on top of another.

supplemental health services. Optional services that a health plan may cover or provide.

surgical package. Normal, uncomplicated performance of specific surgical services, with the assumption that, on average, all surgical procedures of a given type are similar with respect to skill level, duration, and length of normal follow-up care.

swing bed. Bed used for acute or long-term care, depending on the patient's need and the hospital's level of occupancy. Swing beds typically are available in small and rural hospitals. A swing-bed patient may be admitted and discharged from acute care and readmitted to a swing bed to receive skilled or intermediate levels of care. At times, the patient may remain in the same bed while changes occur in his or her care, charges, and payment.

TCC. Transitional care center. Facility used in lieu of an extended care facility or before discharge to an extended care facility.

technical component. Portion of a health care service that identifies the provision of the equipment, supplies, technical personnel, and costs attendant to the performance of the procedure other than the professional services.

TEFRA. Tax Equity and Fiscal Responsibility Act. Protects the rights of full-time employees to remain on the company's health plan to age 69.

tertiary care facility. Hospital providing specialty care to patients referred from other hospitals because of the severity of their injuries or illnesses.

therapeutic. Act meant to alleviate a medical or mental condition.

therapeutic procedure. Treatment of a pathological or traumatic condition through the use of activities performed to treat or heal the cause or to effect change through the application of clinical skills or services that attempt to improve function.

third-party payer. Public or private organization that pays for or underwrites coverage for health care expenses for another entity, usually an employer (e.g., Blue Cross, Blue Shield, Medicare, Medicaid, commercial insurers).

three-digit diagnostic codes. Codes used only when no fourth or fifth digit is available. There are only about 100 codes at the highest level of specificity in the three-digit form. Most payers, including Medicare, do not accept three-digit codes when higher levels of specificity exist.

time limit. In health care contracting, a set number of days in which a claim can be filed according to the payer or state insurance commission.

TPA. *1)* Third-party administrator. Firm that performs administrative functions for a self-funded plan but assumes no risk. *2)* Trading partner agreement. Agreement between the provider and the receiver of the claim transmission detailing the electronic data interchange requirements between the parties. For purposes of HIPAA, a trading partner agreement may not include any agreement to use the codes, segments, or transactions published in an implementation guide in a manner different from that prescribed in the applicable guide. The agreement does not need to be formal. It may take the form of a manual, bulletin, or memorandum.

TPL. Third party liability. Payer liable for the cost of an illness or injury, such as auto or homeowner insurer.

TQM. Total quality management. Concept that quality is an organic part of a plan's service and a provider's care and can be quantified and constantly improved.

transfer. Transfer between hospitals occurs when a patient is admitted to a hospital, discharged, and subsequently admitted to another hospital for additional treatment once the patient's condition has stabilized or a diagnosis has been established.

treatment plan. Plan of care established by the provider outlining specific deficits and planned treatment that may be submitted to the case manager when seeking certification for a plan member.

triage. Medical screening of patients to determine priority of treatment based on severity of illness or injury and resources at hand.

triple option. Offering of an HMO, indemnity plan, and preferred provider organization by one insurance firm.

UB-04. Uniform institutional claim form developed by the NUBC that was implemented in May 2007.

UB-92. Common paper claim form used by facilities to bill for services.

UCR. Usual, customary, and reasonable. Fees charged for medical services that are considered normal, common, and in line with the prevailing fees in a given geographical area.

unbundling. Separately packaging costs or services that might otherwise be billed together including billing separately for health care services that should be combined according to the industry standards or commonly accepted coding practices.

underwriting. Evaluating and determining the financial risk a member or member group will have on an insurer.

unlisted procedure. Procedural descriptions used when the overall procedure and outcome of the procedure are not adequately described by an existing procedure code. Such codes are used as a last resort and only when there is not a more appropriate procedure code.

unspecified. Term in ICD-9-CM that indicates more information is necessary to code the term to further specificity. In these cases, the fourth digit of the code is always 9.

upcoding. Practice of billing a code that represents a higher reimbursement than the code for the procedure actually performed.

UPIN. Unique physician identification number. Number unique to each physician, assigned by CMS, to identify physicians and suppliers who provide medical services or supplies to Medicare beneficiaries. It is a six-character, alphanumeric identification number designed to track payment and utilization information for individual physicians. The attending physician and operating physician identification numbers are required when billing for Medicare services.

URAC. Utilization Review Accreditation Commission. Accrediting body of case management.

urgent admission. Admission in which the patient requires immediate attention for treatment of a physical or psychiatric problem.

USP. United States pharmacopoeia.

USPHS. United States Public Health Service.

utilization review. Formal assessment of the medical necessity, efficiency, and/or appropriateness of health care services and treatment plans on a prospective, concurrent, or retrospective basis.

utilization review nurse. Nurse who evaluates cases for appropriateness of care and length of service and can plan discharge and services needed after discharge.

V code. Part of ICD-9-CM codes, V codes describe circumstances that influence a patient's health status and identify reasons for medical encounters resulting from circumstances other than a disease or injury already classified in the main part of ICD-9-CM.

weighting. Assigning more worth to a fee based on the number of times it is charged, weighting the resource-based relative value fees for an area.

well-baby care. Medical services, immunizations, and regular provider visits considered routine for an infant.

withhold. Percentage of payment to providers held by HMO until cost of referral or services has been determined. If the provider goes over the amount determined appropriate, the HMO keeps that amount.

workers' compensation. State-governed system designated to administer and regulate the provision and cost of medical treatment and wage losses arising from a worker's job-related injury or disease, regardless of who is at fault. In exchange, the employer is protected from being sued.

wraparound plan. Insurance or health plan coverage for copays and deductibles not covered under a member's base plan.

Clinical Abbreviations, Acronyms, & Symbols

The acronyms, abbreviations, and symbols used by health care providers speed communications. The following list includes the most often seen acronyms, abbreviations, and symbols. In some cases, abbreviations have more than one meaning. Multiple interpretations are separated by a slash (/). Abbreviations of Latin phrases are punctuated.

Abbreviation	Meaning
@	at
<	less than
>	greater than
A	**1)** assessment **2)** blood type
a (ante)	before
a fib	atrial fibrillation
a flutter	atrial flutter
A&P	auscultation and percussion
a.a.	of each
a.c.	before eating
a.d.	**1)** right ear **2)** to, up to
a.m.	morning
a.s.	left ear
a.u.	each ear, both ears
A/G	albumin-globulin ratio
A2	aortic second sound
AA	Alcoholics Anonymous
AAHP	American Association of Health Plans
AAL	anterior axillary line
AAMT	American Association for Medical Transcription
AAROM	active assistive range of motion
ab	abortion
AB	blood type
abd	abdomen
ABE	acute bacterial endocarditis
ABG	arterial blood gas
abn.	abnormal
ABO	referring to ABO incompatibility
abs. fev.	without fever
ACD	absolute cardiac dullness
ACE	1) adrenal cortical extract 2) angiotensin converting enzyme
ACL	anterior cruciate ligament
ACLS	advanced cardiac life support
ACP	acid phosphatase
acq.	acquired
ACR	adjusted community rating
ACSW	Academy of Certified Social Workers
ACTH	adrenocorticotropic hormone
ACVD	acute cardiovascular disease
ad lib	as desired, at pleasure
ad. lib.	as desired
ADA	**1)** American Dental Association **2)** Americans with Disabilities Act
ADH	antidiuretic hormone
ADL	activities of daily living
adm	admission, admit
ADM	alcohol, drug, or mental disorder
ADP	adenosine diphosphate
ADS	alternative delivery system
AE	above the elbow
AF	atrial fibrillation
AFB	acid fast bacilli
AGA	appropriate (average) for gestational age
AgNO3	silver nitrate
AHC	alternative health care
AI	aortic insufficiency
AICD	automatic implant cardioverter defibrillator
AID	**1)** acute infectious disease **2)** artificial insemination donor
AIDS	acquired immunodeficiency syndrome
AIH	artificial insemination by husband
AK	above the knee
AKA	above knee amputation
ALA	aminolevulinic acid
alb. (albus)	white
alk. phos.	alkaline phosphatase
ALL	acute lymphocytic leukemia
ALOS	average length of stay
ALP	alkaline phosphatase
ALS	advanced life support
ALT	alanine aminotransferase
ama	against medical advice
amb	ambulate
AMI	acute myocardial infarction
AML	acute myelogenous leukemia
AMML	acute myelomonocytic leukemia
AMP	**1)** adenosine monophosphate **2)** ampule
ANS	autonomic nervous system
ANSI	American National Standards Institute
ANSI/HISB	ANSI Health Information Standards Board
ant	anterior
AOD	arterial occlusive disease
AODM	adult onset diabetes mellitus
AP	**1)** antepartum **2)** anterior-posterior
Ap	apical
A-P	anterior posterior
APC	ambulatory payment classification
APM	arterial pressure monitoring
approx	approximately
appy.	appendectomy
APT	admissions per thousand
aq.	water (aqua)

ARC	AIDS-related complex
ARD	acute respiratory disease
ARDS	adult respiratory distress syndrome
ARF	**1)** acute renal failure **2)** acute respiratory failure
AROM	**1)** active range of motion **2)** artificial rupture of membranes
art.	artery, arterial
AS	**1)** aortic stenosis **2)** arteriosclerosis
ASAP	as soon as possible
ASC	ambulatory surgery center
ASCVD	arteriosclerotic cardiovascular disease
ASCX12N	American Standard Committee standard for claims and reimbursement
ASD	atrial septal defect
ASHD	arteriosclerotic heart disease
ASO	administrative services only
ASR	age/sex rate
Asst	assistance (min= minimal; mod= moderate)
AST	aspartate aminotransferase
ATP	adenosine triphosphate
AUR	ambulatory utilization review
AV	atrioventricular
A-V	arteriovenous
AVF	arteriovenous fistula
AWP	average wholesale price
ax	auxiliary
AZT	azidothymidine
B&B	bowel and bladder
b.i.d.	two times a day
b.i.n.	twice a night
b.i.s.	twice
Ba	barium
bal.	bath
BB	blow bottles
BBB	bundle branch block
BCC	basal cell carcinoma
BCP	birth control pill
BE	**1)** barium enema **2)** below the elbow
BI	**1)** bowel impaction **2)** brain injury
bib.	drink
BICROS	bilateral routing of signals
BK	below the knee
BKA	below knee amputation
BLS	basic life support
BM	bowel movement
BMR	basal metabolic rate
BMT	bone marrow transplant
BO	body order
BOW	bag of water
BP	blood pressure
BPD	bronchopulmonary dysplasia
BPH	benign prostatic hypertrophy
Br	breastfeeding
BrC	breast care
BRM	biological response modifier
BRP	**1)** bathroom, private **2)** bathroom privileges
BS	**1)** bachelor of surgery **2)** bowel sounds **3)** breath sounds
BSA	body surface area
BSC	bedside commode
BSD	bedside drainage
BUN	blood urea nitrogen
BUR	back-up rate (ventilator)
BUS	Bartholin urethra Skene's
bx	biopsy
C	**1)** centigrade **2)** cervical vertebrae **3)** complements
c̄	with
C&S	culture and sensitivity
c.m.	tomorrow morning
c.n.	tomorrow night
c/m	counts per minute
c/o	complaints of
C/S	cesarean section
Ca	**1)** calcium **2)** cancer
CA	cancer
CABG	coronary artery bypass graft
CAC	certified alcoholism counselor
CAD	coronary artery disease
Cap	capitation
CAPD	continuous ambulatory peritoneal dialysis
caps.(capsula)	capsule
CAT	computerized axial tomography
cath	catheterize
CBC	complete blood count
CBR	complete bedrest
cc	chief complaint
C-collar	cervical collar
CCPD	continuous cycling peritoneal dialysis
CCU	coronary care unit
CDC	Centers for Disease Control and Prevention
CDH	congenital dislocation of hip
CE	cardiac enlargement
CEA	carcinoembryonic antigen
CF	cystic fibrosis
CH,Chol	cholesterol
CHD	**1)** congenital heart disease **2)** congestive heart disease
CHF	congestive heart failure
chgd	changed
chr.	chronic
CI	confidence interval
CIS	carcinoma in situ
Cl	chloride
cl liqs	clear liquids
CLC	creative living center
CLD	**1)** chronic liver disease **2)** chronic lung disease
CLL	chronic lymphatic leukemia
cm	centimeter
cm2	square centimeters
CMC	carpometacarpal
CMG	cystometrogram

CMHC community mental health center
CML chronic myelogenous leukemia
CMP competitive medical plan
CMRI cardiac magnetic resonance imaging
CMS **1)** Centers for Medicare and Medicaid Services **2)** circulation motion sensation
CMS-1500 universal paper billing form developed by CMS
CMV cytomegalovirus
cn cranial nerves
CNM certified nurse midwife
CNP continuous negative airway pressure
CNS central nervous system
co cardiac output
CO2 carbon dioxide
COC certificate of coverage
COLD chronic obstructive lung disease
CON certificate of need
conc. concentration
cont. continue
COPD chronic obstructive pulmonary disease
CP cerebral palsy
CPAP continuous positive airway pressure
CPB cardiopulmonary bypass
CPD cephalopelvic disproportion
CPHA Commission on Professional and Hospital Activities
CPK creatine phosphokinase
CPM continuous passive motion
CPR **1)** cardiopulmonary resuscitation **2)** computer-based patient record
CPT chest physical therapy
CQI continuous quality improvement
CR **1)** carrier replacement **2)** creatine
CRC community rating by class
CRF chronic renal failure
CRH corticotropic releasing hormone
crit. hematocrit
CROS contralateral routing of signals
CRP C-reactive protein
CS central service
CSF cerebrospinal fluid
CT **1)** carpal tunnel syndrome **2)** computerized or computed tomography **3)** corneal thickness
CTLSO cervical-thoracic-lumbar-sacral-orthosis
CTZ chemoreceptor trigger zone
cu cubic
CV cardiovascular
CVA **1)** cerebral vascular accident **2)** cerebrovascular accident **3)** costovertebral angle
CVD **1)** cardiovascular disease **2)** cerebrovascular disease
CVI chronic venous insufficiency
CVL central venous line
CVMS clean voided midstream urine
CVP central venous pressure
CVU cerebrovascular unit
CW closed ward
CXR chest x-ray
CXy chest x-ray
cysto cystoscopy
D **1)** day **2)** diopter
D&C dilation and curettage
D/C **1)** discharge **2)** discontinue
D/R dayroom
D/W dextrose in water
DAW dispense as written
dc **1)** discontinue **2)** doctor of chiropractic medicine
DC **1)** doctor of chiropractic medicine **2)** dual choice
DCI duplicate coverage inquiry
DC'd **1)** discharged **2)** discontinued
DCR dacryocystorhinostomy
DD down drain
DDST Denver developmental screening test
DE dose equivalent
decem ten
decub. **1)** decubitus ulcer **2)** lying down
def. deficient, deficiency
del delivery
dep. dependent
det. let it be given
DEXA dual energy x-ray absorptiometry
dexter right
dextra right
DHEA dehydroepiandrosterone
DHT dihydrotestosterone
DIC disseminated intravascular coagulopathy
DIF direct immunofluorescence
dim. divide in half
disp disposition
DJD degenerative joint disease
DKA diabetic ketoacidosis
DM diabetes mellitus
DMD Duchenne muscular dystrophy
DME durable medical equipment
DNA deoxyribonucleic acid
DNP do not publish
DNR do not resuscitate
DNS do not show
DO doctor of osteopathy
DOA dead on arrival
DOB date of birth
doc. **1)** doctor **2)** document
DOE dyspnea on exertion
DOS date of service
DPR drug price review
DPT diphtheria-pertussis-tetanus
DR delivery room
Dr doctor
dr. dram
Dsg dressing
DSS dioctyl sulfosuccinate
DTRs deep tendon reflexes

DTs	delirium tremens
DUE	drug use evaluation
duo	two
duodecim.	twelve
dur. dolor.	while pain lasts
DVT	deep vein thrombosis
dx	diagnosis
DX	diagnosis code
dz	disease
e.m.p.	as directed
E/M	evaluation and management
ead.	the same
EAP	employee assistance program
EBL	estimated blood loss
EBV	Epstein-Barr virus
ECCE	extracapsular cataract extraction
ECF	**1)** extended care facility **2)** extracellular fluid
ECG	electrocardiogram
ECHO	**1)** echocardiogram **2)** enterocytopathogenic human orphan virus
ECMO	extracorporeal membrane oxygenation
ECT	**1)** electro-convulsive therapy **2)** emission computerized tomography
ectopic	ectopic pregnancy (OB)
ED	**1)** effective dose **2)** emergency department
EDC	**1)** estimated date of confinement **2)** expected date of confinement
EDI	electronic data interchange
EEG	electroencephalogram
EENT	eye, ear, nose, and throat
EGA	estimated gestational age
EGD	esophagus, stomach, and duodenum
EKG	electrocardiogram
EMG	electromyogram
en	**1)** clyster **2)** enema
en bloc	in total
ENG	electronystagmogram
eng.	engorged
ENT	ear, nose, and throat
EO	elbow orthosis
EOG	electrooculography
EOI	evidence of insurability
EOM	**1)** end of month **2)** extraocular motion **3)** extraocular muscles
EOMB	explanation of Medicare benefits
EOMI	extraocular motion intact
EOP	external occipital protuberance
EOY	end of year
Epis.	episiotomy
EPO	epoetin alfa
EPS	electrophysiologic stimulation
EPSDT	early periodic screening, diagnosis and treatment
ER	emergency room
ERC	endoscopic retrograde cholangiography
ERCP	endoscopic retrograde cholangiopancreatography
ERG	electroretinogram
ESR	erythrocyte sedimentation rate
ESRD	end stage renal disease
EST	electroshock therapy
ESWL	extracorporeal shockwave lithotripsy
et	and
ET	endotracheal
ETG	episode treatment group
ETOH	alcohol
EVR	evoked visual response
Ex	examination
exc	excise
ext.	extremity
extr.	extract
F	**1)** Fahrenheit **2)** female
F (on OB)	firm
f.m.	make a mixture
F/U	follow-up
FAS	fetal alcohol syndrome
FB	foreign body
FB (fb)	fingerbreadths
FBR	foreign body removal
FBS	fasting blood sugar
FDP	fibrin degradation products
Fe	**1)** female **2)** iron
FEV	forced expiratory volume
FFP	fresh frozen plasma
FH	family history
FHR	fetal heart rate
FHT	fetal heart tone
FI	firm one finger down from umbilicus
fl	fluid
fluro	fluoroscopy
FM	face mask
FME	full-mouth extraction
FMG	fine mesh gauze
FNP	family nurse practitioner
FOD	free of disease
fort.	strong (fortis)
FP	**1)** family planning **2)** family practitioner
FR	**1)** family relationship **2)** Federal Register
FRAT	free radical assay test
FSA	flexible spending account
FSE	fetal scalp electrode
FSH	follicle stimulating hormone
FTND	full term normal delivery
FTSG	full thickness skin graft
FTT	failure to thrive
FUO	fever of unknown origin
FVC	forced vital capacity
fx	fracture
fxBB	fracture, both bones
G	gram
GA	gastric analysis
gav.	gavage

GB	gallbladder
GDM	gestational diabetes mellitus
GFR	glomerular filtration rate
GH	growth hormone
GI	gastrointestinal
GIFT	gamete intrafallopian transfer
GLC	gas liquid chromatography
Gly. supp.	glycerin suppository
GMP	guanosine monophosphate
GNID	gram-negative intracellular diplococcic
GnRH	gonadotropin-releasing hormone
GP	general practitioner
gr.	grain
grav	number of pregnancies
GS	general surgeon
GSR	galvanic skin response
gsw	gunshot wound
gt.	drop
gtt.	drops
GU	genitourinary
Gu	guaiac
GxT	graded exercise test
gyn	gynecology
H	Hertel measurement
h (hora)	hour
H&P	history and physical
h.d.	at bedtime
H.O.	house officer
h.s.	at bedtime
H2O	water
H2O2	hydrogen peroxide
HA	***1)*** headache ***2)*** hearing aide
HAA	hepatitis antigen
HAAb	hepatitis antibody A
HaAg	hepatitis antigen A
HAI	hemaglutination test
HAV	hepatitis A virus
HB	***1)*** headbox ***2)*** hepatitis B
HBcAg	hepatitis antigen B
HBD	hydroxybutyric dehydrogenase
HBO	hyperbaric oxygen
HbO2	oxyhemoglobin
HBP	high blood pressure
HBsAb	hepatitis surface antibody B
HBsAg	hepatitis antigen B
HBV	***1)*** hepatitis B vaccine ***2)*** hepatitis B virus
HCG	human chorionic gonadotropin
HCl	hydrochloric acid
Hct	hematocrit
Hctz	hydrochlorothiazide
HCVD	hypertensive cardiovascular disease
HD	hip disarticulation
HDL	high-density lipoproteins
HEDIS	Health Plan Employer Data and Information Set
HEENT	head, eyes, ears, nose, and throat
Hg	hemoglobin
Hgb	hemoglobin
HGH	human growth hormone
HH	hard of hearing
HHA	home health agency
HIAA	hydroxyindoleacetic acid
Hib	hemophilus influenzae vaccine
HIV	human immunodeficiency virus
HLV	herpes-like virus
HMD	hyaline membrane disease
HMS	hepatosplenomegaly
HNAD	hyperosmolar nonacidotic diabetes
HOB	head of bed
hor. decub.	at bedtime
HORF	high output renal failure
HPF	high power field
HPG	human pituitary gonadotropin
HPI	history of present illness
HPL	human placental lactogen
HPs	***1)*** Hanta virus pulmonary syndrome ***2)*** hot packs
HPV	human papilloma virus
HR	***1)*** Harrington rod ***2)*** heart rate ***3)*** hour
HRT	hormone replacement therapy
hrt.	heart
HS	heelstick
HSA	health service agreement
HSBG	heelstick blood gas
HSG	hysterosalpingogram
HSP	health service plan
HSV	herpes simplex virus
ht.	height
HTLV/III	human T-cell lymphotropic virus /three
HTN	hypertension
HVA	homovanillic acid
Hx	history
hypo	hypodermic injection
I& D	incision and drainage
I& O	intake and output
IA	intra-arterial
IAB	intra-aortic balloon
IABC	intra-aortic balloon counterpulsation
IABP	***1)*** intra-arterial blood pressure ***2)*** intra-aortic balloon pump
IBNR	incurred but not reported
IBS	irritable bowel syndrome
IBW	ideal body weight
IC	infant care
ICCE	intracapsular cataract extraction
ICH	intracranial/cerebral hemorrhage
ICP	intracranial pressure
ICS	intercostal space
ICSH	interstitial cell stimulating hormone
ICU	intensive care unit
ID	infective dose
Id31	radioactive iodine
IDDM	insulin dependent diabetes mellitus
IDH	isocitric dehydrogenase
IDM	infant of diabetic mother

Ig immunoglobulin, gamma
IH infectious hepatitis
II icteric index
IM **1)** infectious mononucleosis **2)** internal medicine **3)** intramuscular
IMC intermediate care
IME independent medical evaluation
IMO integrated multiple option
IMV intermittent mandatory ventilation
inc. incision
indep independent
INF **1)** inferior **2)** infusion
INH inhalation solution
INJ injection
instill instillation
IOL intraocular lens
IOP intraocular pressure
IP **1)** interphalangeal **2)** intraperitoneal
IPA individual practice association
IPD intermittent peritoneal dialysis
IPPB intermittent positive pressure breathing
IQ intelligence quotient
IRDS idiopathic respiratory distress syndrome
ISC infant servo-control
ISG immune serum globulin
IT intrathecal administration
ITP idiopathic thrombocytopenia purpura
IU international units
IUD intrauterine device
IV intravenous
IVC **1)** inferior vena cava **2)** intravenous cholangiogram
IVF in vitro fertilization
IVH intraventricular hemorrhage
IVP intravenous pyelogram
JODM juvenile onset diabetes mellitus
JVD jugular venous distention
JVP jugular venous pressure
K potassium
Kcal kilocalorie
KCl potassium chloride
kg kilogram
KJ knee jerk
KO **1)** keep open **2)** knee orthosis
KUB kidneys, ureters, bladder
KVO keep vein open
L&A light and accommodation
L&W living and well
LA left atrium
LAD left anterior descending
LAP leucine aminopeptidase
lap. **1)** laparoscopy **2)** laparotomy
LAT lateral
LAV lymphadenopathy associated virus
LAVH laparoscopic assisted vaginal hysterectomy
LB legbag
LBB left bundle branch
LBBB left bundle branch block
LBP lower back pain
LD lethal dose
LDH lactate dehydrogenase
LDL low-density lipoproteins
LE **1)** lower extremity 2) lupus erythematosus
LEEP loop electrocautery excision procedure
LGA large for gestational age
LH luteinizing hormone
LHF left heart failure
LHR leukocyte histamine release
Li lithium
lido lidocaine
liq. solution (liquor)
LKS liver, kidneys, spleen
LLETZ large loop excision of transformation zone of cervix of uterus
LLL left lower lobe
LLQ left lower quadrant
LMD local medical doctor
LML left medio-lateral position
LMN lower motor neuron
LMP last menstrual period
LMS **1)** lateral medullary syndrome **2)** left main stem **3)** leiomyosarcoma
LMT left mentum transverse position
LOA leave of absence
LOC **1)** level of consciousness **2)** loss of consciousness
LOM limitation of motion
LOP left occiput posterior position
LOS length of stay
LOT left occiput transverse position
LP lumbar puncture
LPM liters per minute
LR **1)** lactated Ringer's **2)** log roll
LS fusion lumbar sacral fusion
LSA left sacrum anterior position
LSB left sternal border
LSO lumbar sacral orthosis
LT left
LTC long term care
lul left upper lobe
luq left upper quadrant
LV left ventricle
lymphs lymphocytes
lytes electrolytes
M **1)** male **2)** manifest refraction
M1 mitral first sound
M2 mitral second sound
MA1 volume respirator
MAC **1)** maximum allowable charge **2)** monitored anesthesia care **3)** Medicare Administrative Contractor
MAD monoamine oxidase (inhibitor)
man. prim. first thing in the morning
MAP mean arterial pressure
MASER microwave amplification by stimulated emission of radiation

MAST	military antishock trousers
MBC	**1)** maximum breathing capacity **2)** minimum bactericidal concentration
MBD	minimal brain dysfunction
mcg	microgram
MCH	mean corpuscular hemoglobin
MCHC	mean corpuscular hemoglobin concentration
MCL	midclavicular line
MCP	metacarpophalangeal
MCR	modified community rating
MCT	mediastinal chest tube
MCV	mean corpuscular volume
MD	**1)** manic depression **2)** medical doctor **3)** muscular dystrophy **4)** myocardial disease
MDC	major diagnostic category
MDD	manic-depressive disorder
Mec	meconium
MED	minimal effective dose
med/surg	medical, surgical
meds	medications
mEq	milliequivalent
mEq/1	milliequivalent per liter
MFD	minimum fatal dose
MFT	muscle function test
Mg	magnesium
mg	milligram
MH/CD	mental health/chemical dependency
MH/SA	mental health/substance abuse
MHC	mental health clinic
MI	myocardial infarction
min	minimum, minimal, minute
misc.	miscellaneous
ML	midline
ml	milliliter
MLC	midline catheter
mm	millimeter
mmHg	millimeters of mercury
MMPI	Minnesota Multiphasic Personality Inventory
MMRV	measles, mumps, rubella vaccine
MOM	milk of magnesia
mono	**1)** monocyte **2)** mononucleosis
mor. dict.	in the manner directed
MPD	maximum permissible dose
MR	mitral regurgitation
MRA	magnetic resonance angiography
MRI	magnetic resonance imaging
mRNA	messenger RNA
MS	**1)** morphine sulfate **2)** multiple sclerosis
MSHJ	medical staff hospital joint venture
MSLT	multiple sleep latency testing
MSO	management service organization
MSS	medical social services
MSW	master's in social work
MTD	right eardrum
MTM	Metamucil

MTP	metatarsophalangeal
MTS	left eardrum
multip.	multipara
MVP	mitral valve prolapse
MWS	Mickey-Wilson syndrome
N	nitrogen
N&V	nausea and vomiting
n.p.o.	nothing by mouth
N2O	nitrous oxide
Na	sodium
NaCl	sodium chloride (salt)
NAD	no appreciable disease
NAT	nonaccidental trauma
NB	newborn
NBICU	newborn intensive care unit
NBT	nitroblue tetrazolium
NCA	neurocirculatory asthenia
NCHS	National Center for Health Statistics
NCPDP	National Council of Prescription Drug Programs
NCPR	no cardiopulmonary resuscitation
NCQA	National Committee on Quality Assurance
NCR	no cardiac resuscitation
NCV	nerve conduction velocity
NCVHS	National Committee on Vital Health Statistics
NDC	national drug code
NEC	**1)** necrotizing enterocolitis **2)** not elsewhere classified
neg.	negative
NF	national formulary
NG	nasogastric
NGU	nongonococcal urethritis
NIDDM	non-insulin dependent diabetes mellitus
NJ	nasojejunal
NKA	no known allergies
NKMA	no known medical allergies
NNR	new and nonofficial remedies
noc.	night
Non-par	non-participating provider
NOS	not otherwise specified
novem.	nine
NP	**1)** neuropsychiatry **2)** nurse practitioner
NPA	**1)** national prescription audit **2)** non-par approved
NP-CPAP	nasopharyngeal continuous positive airway pressure
NPI	National provider identifier
NPN	**1)** non-par not approved **2)** nonprotein nitrogen
NPRM	notice of proposed rule making
npt	normal pressure and temperature
NS	**1)** normal saline **2)** not significant
NSAID	nonsteroidal anti-inflammatory drug
NSD	nominal standard dose
NSR	normal sinus rhythm

NST	nonstress test
NSVB	normal spontaneous vaginal bleeding
NSVD	normal spontaneous vaginal delivery
NT	**1)** nasotracheal **2)** nontender
NTE	neutral thermal environment
NTP	normal temperature and pressure
nyd	not yet diagnosed
O	**1)** blood type **2)** oxygen
o	no information
O&P	ova and parasites
o.d.	right eye
o.m.	**1)** every morning **2)** otitis media
o.n.	every night
o.s.	left eye
o.u.	each eye, both eyes
O2	oxygen
OA	**1)** open access **2)** osteoarthritis
OAG	open angle glaucoma
OB	obstetrician
OB-GYN	obstetrics and gynecology
OC	**1)** office call **2)** open crib **3)** oral contraceptive
OCT	**1)** ornithine carbamyl transferase **2)** oxytocin challenge test
octo.	eight
OFC	occipitofrontal circumference
oint	ointment
OJ	orange juice
omn. hor.	every hour
OMS	oromaxillary surgery
OMT	osteopathic manipulation therapy
ONH	optic nerve head
OOA	out-of-area
OOB	out of bed
OOPs	out-of-pocket costs/expenses
OPD	outpatient department
OPG	oculoplethysmography
ophth	ophthalmology
OPV	oral polio vaccine
OR	operating room
ORIF	open reduction internal fixation
oris	mouth
ortho.	orthopedics
os	mouth
OSA	obstructive sleep apnea
OST	oxytocin stress test
OT	occupational therapy
OTC	over-the-counter
OTD	organ tolerance dose
OTH	other routes of administration
ov.	**1)** office visit **2)** ovum
OW	open ward
oz.	ounce
P	**1)** after **2)** phosphorus **3)** plan **4)** pulse
P& A	percussion and auscultation
P&T	pharmacy and therapeutics
p.c.	after eating
p.m.	after noon
p.p.	near point of visual accommodation
p.r.	**1)** for point of visual accommodation **2)** through the rectum
p.r.n.	as needed for
p/o	by mouth
P+PD	percussion & postural drainage
P2	pulmonic 2nd sound
PA	**1)** physician assistant **2)** posteroanterior **3)** pulmonary artery
PAB	premature atrial beats
PAC	**1)** pre-admission certification **2)** premature atrial contraction
PACU	post anesthesia care unit
PAD	pulmonary artery diastolic
PAH	para-aminohippurate
PAP	**1)** Papanicolaou test or smear **2)** pulmonary artery pressure
Par	participating provider
PAR	**1)** parenteral **2)** post anesthesia recovery
para	**1)** along side of **2)** number of pregnancies, as para 1, 2, 3, etc.
PARR	post anesthesia recovery room
part. vic.	in divided doses
PAT	paroxysmal atrial tachycardia
path	**1)** pathology **2)** physicians at teaching hospitals
PBI	protein-bound iodine
PC	packed cells
PCA	patient controlled analgesia
PCD	polycystic disease
PCG	phonocardiogram
PCN	**1)** penicillin **2)** primary care network
PCP	primary care physician
PCPM	per contract per month
PCR	**1)** physician contingency reserve **2)** polymerase chain reaction
PCTA	percutaneous transluminal angioplasty
PCV	packed cell volume
PCW	pulmonary capillary wedge
PD	**1)** Parkinson's disease **2)** postural drainage
PDA	patent ductus arteriosus
PE	**1)** physical examination **2)** practice expense **3)** pulmonary edema **4)** pulmonary embolism
PEC	pre-existing condition
Peds	pediatrics
PEG	pneumoencephalogram
PEN	parenteral and enteral nutrition
PENS	percutaneous electrical nerve stimulation
PERRLA	pupils equal, regular, reactive to light and accommodation
PET	positron emission tomography
PFC	persistent fetal circulation
PFT	pulmonary function test
PG	prostaglandin
PH	past history

pH potential of hydrogen
PHO physician-hospital organization
PI present illness
PICC peripherally inserted central catheter
PID pelvic inflammatory disease
pk. pack
PKU phenylketonuria
PMG primary medical group
PMHx past medical history
PMI point of maximum intensity
PMN polymorphonuclear neutrophil leukocytes
PMPM per member per month
PMPY per member per year
PMS premenstrual syndrome
PNC premature nodal contraction
PND **1)** paroxysmal nocturnal dyspnea **2)** post nasal drip
PNS peripheral nervous system
PO **1)** (per os) by mouth **2)** postoperative
POD postoperative day
polys polymorphonuclear neutrophil leukocytes
POR problem oriented record
pos. positive
post or PM postmortem exam or autopsy
post. cib. after meals
PP postprandial
PPD **1)** percussion and postural drainage **2)** purified protein derivative
PPH postpartum hemorrhage
PPP protamine paracoagulation
pr per return
PRBC packed red blood cells
preg pregnant
PREs progressive resistive exercises
previa placenta previa
primip primipara
PROM premature rupture of membranes
PSA prostate specific antigen
PSP phenolsulfonphthalein
PsyD doctor of psychology
Pt **1)** patient **2)** prothrombin time
PT **1)** physical therapy **2)** prothrombin time
PTA **1)** percutaneous transluminal angioplasty **2)** prior to admission
PTB patellar tendon bearing (cast)
PTCA percutaneous transluminal coronary angioplasty
PTH parathyroid hormone
PTT partial thromboplastin time
PUD peptic ulcer disease
pulv. powder
PVC premature ventricular contraction
PVD premature ventricular depolarization
PVL paraventricular leukomalacia
Px prognosis
PZI protamine zinc insulin
Q. every
q.2h every two hours
q.a.m. every morning
q.d. every day
q.h. every hour
q.h.s. every night
q.i.d. four times daily
q.n. every night
q.o.d. every other day
q.q.h. every four hours
QA quality assurance
QM quality management
qns quantity not sufficient
qs quantity sufficient
quattour four
quicdecem fifteen
quinque five
quotid daily
R **1)** respiration **2)** right atrium
r roentgen units (x-rays)
R&C reasonable and customary
R,R,& E round, regular, and equal
R/O rule out
RA rheumatoid arthritis
RATx radiation therapy
RBB right bundle branch
RBBB right bundle branch block
RBC red blood cell
RBOW ruptured bag of water
RBRVS resource based relative value scale
RCD relative cardiac dullness
RDS respiratory distress syndrome
REM rapid eye movement
RESA radial cryosurgical ablation
resp respiration, respiratory
Retro retrospective rate derivation
rev. revise, revision
Rh Rhesus
Rh neg Rhesus factor negative
RHD rheumatic heart disease
RHF right heart failure
RIA radioimmunoassay
RL Ringer's lactate
RLE right lower extremity
RLF retrolental fibroplasia
RLL right lower lobe
rlq right lower quadrant
RMA right mentum anterior position
RMC rating method code
RML right middle lobe
RMP right mentum posterior position
RMT right mentum transverse position
RN registered nurse
RNA ribonucleic acid
ROA right occiput anterior position
ROM range of motion
ROP right occiput posterior position
ROS review of systems
RPG retrograde pyelogram

RPR	venereal disease report
RR	recovery room
RRR	regular rate and rhythm
RS	reducing substances
RSV	respiratory syncytial virus
RT	***1)*** recreational therapist ***2)*** respiratory therapist ***3)*** resting tracing ***4)*** right
RTC	return to clinic
RUL	right upper lobe
ruq	right upper quadrant
RV	right ventricle
Rx	take (prescription; treatment)
RxN	reaction
s̄	without
S& A	sugar and acetone
s.c.	subcutaneous
s.l.	under the tongue, sublingual
S.O.S.	if necessary (si opus sit)
S/P	status post
SAH	subarachnoid hemorrhage
SALT	serum alanine aminotransferase
SAST	serum aspartate aminotransferase
SB	sinus bradycardia
SBFT	small bowel follow through
S-C disease	sickle cell hemoglobin-c disease
SCI	spinal cord injury
SCR	standard class rate
sed rate	sedimentation rate of erythrocytes
SEM	systolic ejection murmur
Seno supp	Senokot suppository
septem	seven
sex	six
SG	Swan-Ganz
SGA	small for gestational age
SGOT	serum glutamic oxaloacetic acid
SH	social history
SHBG	sex hormone binding globulin
SIADH	syndrome of inappropriate antidiuretic hormone
SIC	standard industry code
SIDS	sudden infant death syndrome
Sig.	write on label (Rx) or let it be labeled
Sig. S. (Signa)	mark or write
sine	without
SISI	short increment sensitivity index
SLE	systemic lupus erythematosus
SMO	slip made out
SNF	skilled nursing facility
SNS	sympathetic nervous system
SOAP	subjective objective assessment plan
SOB	shortness of breath
sol.	solution
SOP	standard operation procedure
SPD	summary plan description
SpGr	specific gravity
SQ	***1)*** status quo ***2)*** subcutaneous
SROM	spontaneous rupture of membranes
ss	half
SSE	soap suds enema
ST	sinus tachycardia
staph	staphylococcus
stat	immediately
STD	sexually transmitted disease
STH	somatotrophic hormone
strep	streptococcus
STS	serology test for syphilis
STSG	split thickness skin graft
STU	skin test unit
subcu	subcutaneous
subind.	immediately after
supp	suppository
Sv	scalp vein
SVC	service
SVCS	superior vena cava syndrome
Sx	***1)*** sign ***2)*** symptom
T	***1)*** temperature ***2)*** tender ***3)*** thoracic vertebrae
T&A	tonsils and adenoids
T&C	type and crossmatch
t.d.s.	three times a day
t.i.d.	three times daily
T3	triiodothyronine
T4	thyroxine
TA	***1)*** tension by applanation ***2)*** transactional analysis
tab.	tablet (tabella)
TAH	total abdominal hysterectomy
Tap/H2O/E	tap water enema
TAT	***1)*** tetanus antitoxin ***2)*** turnaround time
TB	tuberculosis
Tb	tubercule bacillus
TBA	to be arranged
TBG	***1)*** thyroid binding globulin ***2)*** thyroxine
TBI	total body irradiation
TBSA	total body surface area
TC&DB	turn, cough, and deep breathe
Td	tetanus
temp	temperature
TENS	transcutaneous electrical nerve stimulation
TEVAP	transurethral electrovaporization of prostate
TFT	transfer factor test
THA	total hip arthroplasty
Thal	thalassemia
THC	tetrahydrocannabinol
TI	tricuspid insufficiency
TIA	transient ischemic attack
TIBC	total iron binding capacity
tinct	tincture
TKA	total knee arthroplasty
TM	tympanic membrane
TMJ	temporomandibular joint
TNS	transcutaneous nerve stimulator or stimulation
TO	telephone order
TOA	tubo-ovarian abscess

TORCH toxoplasmosis, other (includes syphilis), rubella, cytomegalovirus, and herpes virus
TP total protein
TPAL term pregnancies, premature infants, abortions, living children
TPN total parenteral nutrition
TPR temperature, pulse, respiration
Tr ***1)*** tinctura, tincture ***2)*** trace
TRAM transverse rectus abdominis musculocutaneous
trans transverse
tres three
TRF thyrotropin releasing factor
TRH thyrotropin releasing hormone
tRNA transfer ribonucleic acid
Ts tension by Schiotz
TSA tumor specific antigen
TSD Tay-Sachs disease
TSE testicular self-exam
TSH thyroid stimulating hormone
TSS toxic shock syndrome
TTN transient tachypnea of newborn
TULIP transurethral ultrasound guided laser induced prostate
TUR transurethral resection
TURP transurethral resection of prostate
TWE tap water enema
Tx treatment
U unit
U&C usual and customary
U/A urinalysis
UAC umbilical artery catheter or catheterization
UC unit clerk
UCHD usual childhood diseases
UCR usual, customary, and reasonable
UE upper extremity
UFR uroflowmetry
UGI upper gastrointestinal
UM ***1)*** unit manager ***2)*** utilization management
UMN upper motor neuron
ung. ointment
unus. one
UPP urethra pressure profile
UR utilization review
ur. Urine
URI upper respiratory infection
URN utilization review nurse
US ***1)*** ultrasound ***2)*** unstable spine
ut dict. as directed
UTI urinary tract infection
UV ultraviolet light
UVC umbilical vein catheter
V Fib ventricular fibrillation
V tach ventricular tachycardia
VA Veterans Administration
Va visual acuity
VBAC vaginal birth after cesarean
VC vena cava
VCG vectorcardiogram
VD venereal disease
VDH valvular disease of the heart
VDRL venereal disease research laboratory
VE voluntary effort
VEP visual evoked potential
VF ***1)*** ventricular fibrillation ***2)*** visual field
VIP vasoactive intestinal peptide
Vit vitamin (followed by specific letter)
VO verbal order
VO2 maximum oxygen consumption
VP ***1)*** vasopressin ***2)*** voiding pressure
VPC ventricular premature contraction
VPRC volume of packed red cells
VS ***1)*** vesicular sound ***2)*** vital signs
VSD ventricular septal defect
vv veins
w/HSBH warmed heelstick blood gas
WAK wearable artificial kidney
WB whole blood
WBC white blood count
WC wheelchair
WCC well child care
WD well developed
W-D wet to dry (dressings)
WLS wet lung syndrome
WN well nourished
WNL within normal limits
Wt weight
x except
XM cross match
Y-O year-old
YTD year-to-date
ZIFT zygote intrafallopian transfer

Prefixes & Suffixes

The uniquely efficient language of medicine is possible thanks to the prefixes and suffixes attached to roots. Changing prefixes and suffixes allows subtle and overt changes in meaning of the terms.

Prefixes are one half of the medical language equation and are attached to the beginning of words. For example, the prefix "eu-," meaning good or well, combined with the Greek word for death, "thanatos," produces euthanasia — a good death.

Suffixes are the other half of the equation These are attached to the ends of words. The following prefixes and suffixes are paired with their meanings.

a-	without, away from, not
ab-	from, away from, absent
acro-	extremity, top, highest point
ad-	toward, adherence to, or increase
adeno-	relating to a gland
adip-	relating to fat
aero-	relating to gas or air
-agra	severe pain
-algia	pain
all-	another, other, or different
allo-	difference or divergence from the norm
ambi-	***1)*** both sides ***2)*** about or around
an-	without, away from, not
angi-	relating to a vessel
aniso-	dissimilar, unequal, or asymmetrical
ankylo-	bent, crooked, or two parts growing together
ante-	in front of, before
antero-	before, front, anterior
anti-	in opposition to, against
antro-	relating to a chamber or cavity
arch-	beginning, first, principal
archo-	relating to the rectum or anus
arterio-	relating to an artery
arthro-	relating to a joint
-ase	denoting an enzyme
astro-	star-like or shaped
atelo-	incomplete or imperfect
auto-	relating to the self
axio-	relating to an axis
balano-	relating to the glans penis or glans clitoridis
baro-	relating to weight or heaviness
basi-	relating to the base or foundation
bi-	double, twice, two
-blast	incomplete cellular development
blasto-	relating to an early, formative, or primitive stage of a cell or embryonic element or layer
blenn-	relating to mucus
blepharo-	relating to the eyelid
brachi-	relating to the arm
brachy-	short
brady-	slow or prolonged
broncho-	relating to the trachea
cac-	diseased or bad
cardio-	relating to the heart
carpo-	relating to the wrist
cata-	down from, down, according to
celo-	***1)*** tumor or hernia ***2)*** cavity
-centesis	puncture
-cephal	relating to the head
cervico-	relating to the neck or neck of an organ
cheilo-	relating to the lip
chole-	relating to the gallbladder
-cle	small or little
cleido-	relating to the clavicle
cyst-	relating to the urinary bladder or a cyst
-cyte	having to do with cells
cyto-	in relation to a cell
dacry-	pertaining to the lacrimal glands
-dactyl	relating to the fingers or toes
dactyl-	relating to the fingers or toes
demi-	half the amount
-desis	binding or fusion
desmo-	relating to ligaments
deuter-	secondary or second
dextro-	meaning on or to the right
dorsi-	relating to the back
dys-	painful, bad, disordered, difficult
echo-	reverberating sound
ecto-	external, outside
-ectomy	excision, removal
ectro-	congenital absence of something
endo-	within, internal
entero-	relating to the intestines
epi-	on, upon, in addition to
eu-	well, healthy, good, normal
exo-	outside of, without
-ferous	produces, causes, or brings about
fibro-	relating to fibers or fibrous tissue
-fuge	drive out or expel
galacto-	relating to milk
gastro-	relating to the stomach and abdominal region
-genic	production, causation, generation
genito-	relating to reproduction
gono-	relating to the genitals, offspring, origination
-gram	drawn, written, and recorded
-graphic	written or drawn
gyn-	relating to the female gender
hema-	relating to blood
hemi-	half
hepato-	relating to the liver
histo-	relating to tissue

homeo- indicates resemblance or likeness
hydro- relating to fluid, water, or hydrogen
hyper- excessive, above, exaggerated
hypo- below, less than, under
hyster- relating to either the womb or hysteria
-ia state of being, condition (abnormal)
-iasis condition
idio- distinct or individual characteristics
ileo- relating to the ileum (part of the small intestine)
ilio- relating to the pelvis
infra- inferior to, beneath, under
irid- relating to the iris
ischio- relating to the hip
iso- equal
-it is inflammation
jejuno- relating to the jejunum (part of the small intestine)
juxta- next to, near
karyo- relating to the nucleus of a cell
kerato- relating to the cornea or horny tissue
laparo- **1)** flank, loins **2)** operations through the abdominal wall
laryngo- relating to the larynx
lien- relating to the spleen
lip- relating to fat
lith- relating to a hard or calcified substance
lumbo- relating to the loin region
-lysis release, free, reduction of
macro- oversized, large
mal- bad, poor, ill
melano- dark or black in color
meningo- relating to membranes covering the brain and spine
mesio- **1)** Toward the middle **2)** Secondary
meta- indicates a change
-metry scientific measurement
mis- bad, improper
my- relating to muscle
myc- relating to fungus
myelo- relating to bone marrow or the spinal cord
narco- indicates insensate condition or numbness
necro- indicates death or dead tissue
nephr- relating to the kidney
noci- relating to injury or pain
nycto- relating to darkness or night
odont- relating to the teeth
-odynia indicates pain or discomfort
-oid indicates likeness or resemblance
oligo- indicates few or small
-ology study of
-oma tumor
omo- relating to the shoulder
omphalo- relating to the navel
onco- relating to a mass, tumor, or swelling
onycho- relating to the finger- or toenails
oophor- relating to the ovaries
opistho- indicates behind or backwards
orchi- relating to the testicles
-orraphy suturing
oscheo- relating to the scrotum
-oscopy to examine
-osis condition, process
osteo- having to do with bone
-ostomy indicates a surgically created artificial opening
oto- relating to the ear
-otomy indicates a cutting
pachy- indicates heavy, large, or thick
-pagus indicates fixed or joined together
pali- repetition, back again, recurring
panto- indicates the whole or all
para- indicates near, similar, beside, or past
-pathic indicates a feeling, diseased condition, or therapy
patho- indicates sensitivity, feeling, or suffering
ped- relating to the foot
-penia indicates a deficiency, less than normal
peri- about, around, or in the vicinity
pero- indicates being maimed or deformed
-pexy fixation
phaco- relating to the lens of the eye
phago- relating to eating and ingestion
pharyngo- relating to the pharynx
-philia inordinate love of or craving for something
phlebo- relating to the vein
-phobia abnormal fear of or aversion to
phreno- **1)** relating to the diaphragm **2)** head or mind
pimel- relating to fat
-plasty indicates surgically formed or molded
platy- indicates wide or broad
-plegia indicates a stroke or paralysis
pleio- more, additional
pleur- relating to the side or ribs
pneum- relating to respiration, air, the lungs
pod- relating to the feet
-poietic indicates producing or making
poly- indicates much or many
-praxis indicates activity, action, condition, or use
procto- relating to the rectum and/or anus
proso- indicates toward the front, anterior, forward
pseudo- indicates false or imagined
pulmo- relating to the lungs and respiration
pyelo- relating to the pelvis
pygo- relating to the buttocks or rump
pyle- relating to an opening/orifice of the portal vein
pyloro- relating to the pylorus (the stomach opening into the duodenum)
pyo- relating to pus
pyreto- indicates a fever, heat
rachi- relating to the spine

recto-	meaning straight or relating to the rectum
retro-	indicates behind, backward, in a reverse direction
-rhage	indicates bleeding or other fluid discharge
-rhaphy	indicates a suture or seam joining two structures
rheo-	indicates a flow or stream of fluid
rhino-	relating to the nose
-rrhagia	indicates an abnormal or excessive fluid discharge
-rrhexis	splitting or breaking
sacro-	relating to the sacrum (base of the vertebral column)
salpingo-	relating to the fallopian or eustachian tubes
sarco-	relating to flesh
scapho-	indicates deformed condition, shaped like a boat
scapulo-	relating to the shoulder
schisto-	***1)*** indicates cleft or split ***2)*** Fissure
scoto-	***1)*** relating to darkness ***2)*** Visual field gap
sial-	relating to saliva
sinistro-	on or to the left
somato-	relating to the body
-spasm	contraction
spheno-	relating to the sphenoid bone at the base of the skull
sphygmo-	relating to the pulse
splanch-	***1)*** relating to the intestines ***2)*** viscera
steato-	relating to fat
stetho-	relating to the chest
stomato-	relating to the mouth
sym-	indicates together with, along with, beside
syn-	indicates being joined together
tachy-	indicates swift or fast
tarso-	***1)*** relating to the foot ***2)*** margin of the eyelid
-taxy	arrangement, grouping
teleo-	indicates complete or perfectly formed
teno-	relating to tendons
terato-	indicates being seriously deformed, especially a fetus
thalamo-	relating to the thalamus (origin of nerves in the brain)
thanato-	relating to death
thoraco-	relating to the chest
thrombo-	relating to blood clots
thymo-	relating to the thymus
toco-	relating to birth
-tomy	indicates a cutting
trachelo-	relating to the neck
trichi-	***1)*** relating to hair ***2)*** hair-like shape
-trophy	relating to food or nutrition
-tropic	indicates an affinity for or turning toward
-tropism	responding to an external stimulus
tympano-	relating to the eardrum
typhlo-	***1)*** relating to the cecum ***2)*** relating to blindness
vaso-	relating to blood vessels
ventro-	***1)*** relating to the abdomen ***2)*** anterior surface of the body
vesico-	relating to the bladder
viscero-	relating to the abdominal organs
xeno-	relating to a foreign substance
xero-	indicates a dry condition

Procedural Eponyms

The medical custom of honoring a popular procedure's originator by name may prove to be problematic for the coder, who may have no trouble coding a Marshall-Marchetti but be faced with choosing one of the many Campbell procedures.

The following list includes many of the procedures described by eponym in the CPT book.

Addam Operation

26040 Fasciotomy, palmar (eg, Dupuytren's contracture); percutaneous

26045 Fasciotomy, palmar (eg, Dupuytren's contracture); open, partial

Procedure releases a Dupuytren's contracture.

Adson test

95870 Needle electromyography; limited study of muscles in one extremity or non-limb (axial) muscles (unilateral or bilateral), other than thoracic paraspinal, cranial nerve supplied muscles, or sphincters

Test provides a physiological assessment for thoracic outlet syndrome.

Albarran test

89235 Water load test

Test screens for colibacilluria, a bacteria found in the intestine.

Alexander's operation

58400 Uterine suspension, with or without shortening of round ligaments, with or without shortening of sacrouterine ligaments; (separate procedure)

58410 Uterine suspension, with or without shortening of round ligaments, with or without shortening of sacrouterine ligaments; with presacral sympathectomy

Uteral displacement is repaired by shortening round ligaments.

Altemeier procedure

45130 Excision of rectal procidentia, with anastomosis; perineal approach

Procedure removes a rectal prolapse through a perineal approach (45130), or through a combined abdominal and perineal approach (45135).

Amussat's operation

44025 Colotomy, for exploration, biopsy(s), or foreign body removal

Long transverse incision is made to expose the colon.

Anderson tibial lengthening

27715 Osteoplasty, tibia and fibula, lengthening or shortening

Tibia is severed and screws are affixed to plates supporting the bone across the gap in this technique to lengthen the patient's leg.

Aries-Pitanguy mammaplasty

19318 Reduction mammaplasty

Procedure reduces breast size.

Babcock operation

37700 Ligation and division of long saphenous vein at saphenofemoral junction, or distal interruptions

Varicose veins are eliminated using a long probe and tying the end of the vein to it to draw out the vein by invagination.

Baldy-Webster operation

58400 Uterine suspension, with or without shortening of round ligaments, with or without shortening of sacrouterine ligaments; (separate procedure)

Ligaments may be used to correct displacement of the uterus.

Barany caloric test

92533 Caloric vestibular test, each irrigation (binaural, bithermal stimulation constitutes four tests)

Extent of nystagmus is determined by irrigating the external auditory meatus with either hot or cold water.

Bardenheuer operation

37616 Ligation, major artery (eg, post-traumatic, rupture); chest

Arterial fistula in the chest is repaired by ligation and sutures.

Barkan's operation

65820 Goniotomy

Technique corrects glaucoma by opening Schlemm's canal.

Barker operation

28120 Partial excision (craterization, saucerization, sequestrectomy, or diaphysectomy) bone (eg, osteomyelitis or bossing); talus or calcaneus

Process involves incision of the dorsal area of the foot.

Barr procedure

27691 Transfer or transplant of single tendon (with muscle redirection or rerouting);

deep (eg, anterior tibial or posterior tibial through interosseous space, flexor digitorum longus, flexor hallucis longus, or peroneal tendon to midfoot or hindfoot)

Procedure corrects talipes equinovarus that may result from polio, and includes the anterior transfer of the tibialis posterior tendon.

Barsky's procedure

26580 Repair cleft hand

Cleft hand is repaired by closing the cleft, bringing the ring and index fingers closer together, and correcting webbing between the fingers.

Bassett's operation

56630 Vulvectomy, radical, partial

56631 Vulvectomy, radical, partial; with unilateral inguinofemoral lymphadenectomy

56632 Vulvectomy, radical, partial; with bilateral inguinofemoral lymphadenectomy

56633 Vulvectomy, radical, complete

56634 Vulvectomy, radical, complete; with unilateral inguinofemoral lymphadenectomy

56637 Vulvectomy, radical, complete; with bilateral inguinofemoral lymphadenectomy

56640 Vulvectomy, radical, complete, with inguinofemoral, iliac, and pelvic lymphadenectomy

Dissection of the inguinal glands for a radical resection of the vulva.

Batch-Spittler-McFaddin operation

27598 Disarticulation at knee

Leg is severed at the knee joint, which offers an alternative to severing a long bone.

Battle's operation

44950 Appendectomy;

44960 Appendectomy; for ruptured appendix with abscess or generalized peritonitis

Rectus muscle is temporarily retracted in this appendectomy.

Bender-Gestalt test

96101 Psychological testing (includes psychodiagnostic assessment of emotionality, intellectual abilities, personality and psychopathology, eg, MMPI, Rorschach, WAIS), per hour of the psychologist's or physician's time, both face-to-face time with the patient and time interpreting test results and preparing the report

96102 Psychological testing (includes psychodiagnostic assessment of emotionality, intellectual abilities, personality and psychopathology, eg, MMPI and WAIS), with qualified health care professional interpretation and report, administered by technician, per hour of technician time, face-to-face

96103 Psychological testing (includes psychodiagnostic assessment of emotionality, intellectual abilities, personality and psychopathology, eg, MMPI), administered by a computer, with qualified health care professional interpretation and report

Psychological test gauges perceptual-motor coordination to assess personality dynamics, review organic brain impairment, and measure neurological maturity.

Benedict test for dextrose

81005 Urinalysis; qualitative or semiquantitative, except immunoassays

Test using sodium or potassium citrate and sodium carbonate in a reagent determines dextrose content of urine.

Bevan's operation

54640 Orchiopexy, inguinal approach, with or without hernia repair

Procedure brings an undescended testicle down into the scrotum.

Biesenberger mammaplasty

19318 Reduction mammaplasty

Reduction procedure uses transposition of the nipple with excision of the side of the mammary gland and rotation of the remaining glandular pedicle to form a skin brassiere.

Billroth operation

43631 Gastrectomy, partial, distal; with gastroduodenostomy

Anastomosis of the stomach to the duodenum or jejunum.

Binet test

96101 Psychological testing (includes psychodiagnostic assessment of emotionality, intellectual abilities, personality and psychopathology, eg, MMPI, Rorschach, WAIS), per hour of the psychologist's or physician's time, both face-to-face time with the patient and time interpreting test results and preparing the report

96102 Psychological testing (includes psychodiagnostic assessment of emotionality, intellectual abilities, personality and psychopathology, eg, MMPI and WAIS), with qualified health care professional interpretation and report, administered by technician, per hour of technician time, face-to-face

96103 Psychological testing (includes psychodiagnostic assessment of emotionality, intellectual abilities, personality and psychopathology, eg, MMPI), administered by a computer, with qualified health care professional interpretation and report

Test gauges mental capacity among children and youth using a standard series of questions gauged on the capacity of normal intellect among the same age groups.

Bohler reduction

28405 Closed treatment of calcaneal fracture; with manipulation

Traction method treats a closed fracture of the heel bone.

Bristow procedure

23460 Capsulorrhaphy, anterior, any type; with bone block

Anterior capsulorrhaphy prevents chronic separation of the shoulder. In this procedure, the bone block is affixed to the anterior glenoid rim with a screw.

Brock's operation

33470 Valvotomy, pulmonary valve, closed heart; transventricular

33471 Valvotomy, pulmonary valve, closed heart; via pulmonary artery

33472 Valvotomy, pulmonary valve, open heart; with inflow occlusion

33474 Valvotomy, pulmonary valve, open heart; with cardiopulmonary bypass

33476 Right ventricular resection for infundibular stenosis, with or without commissurotomy

Valvulotome passed through the wall of the right ventricle into the pulmonary artery assists in the relief of pulmonary valvular stenosis.

Browne's operation

54324 One stage distal hypospadias repair (with or without chordee or circumcision); with urethroplasty by local skin flaps (eg, flip-flap, prepucial flap)

Hypospadias is repaired with a strip of epithelium left on the top of the penis to form a top of the urethra. Margins of the incision are used to form the bottom.

Burgess amputation

27880 Amputation, leg, through tibia and fibula;

Long posterior flap is preserved to cover the incision to amputate the leg below the knee.

Burrow's operation

14000 Adjacent tissue transfer or rearrangement, trunk; defect 10 sq cm or less

Triangles of skin at the base of the pedicle of a skin flap are excised to achieve advancement.

Callander knee disarticulation

27598 Disarticulation at knee

Patella is removed and the long anterior and posterior skin flaps of the tibia are retained to enhance healing.

Carpue's operation

30400 Rhinoplasty, primary; lateral and alar cartilages and/or elevation of nasal tip

Nose is repaired by folding a flap from the forehead and pedicle at the root of the nose around the area to be repaired.

Chiari osteotomy

27156 Osteotomy, iliac, acetabular or innominate bone; with femoral osteotomy and with open reduction of hip

Top of the femur is altered to correct a dislocated hip caused by congenital conditions or cerebral palsy. A plate and screws are often used.

Cotting's operation

11765 Wedge excision of skin of nail fold (eg, for ingrown toenail)

Physician removes part of the toe and the ingrown part of the toenail.

Dana rhizotomy

63185 Laminectomy with rhizotomy; one or two segments

Posterior nerve roots of the spine are severed to relieve chronic pain or spasms.

Dandy ventriculocisternostomy

62200 Ventriculocisternostomy, third ventricle;

Operation establishes an opening from the third ventricle to the interpeduncular cistern.

Daviel's operation

66830 Removal of secondary membranous cataract (opacified posterior lens capsule and/or anterior hyaloid) with corneo-scleral section, with or without iridectomy (iridocapsulotomy, iridocapsulectomy)

Lens is extracted through a corneal incision.

Day test

82270 Blood, occult, by peroxidase activity (eg, guaiac), qualitative; feces, consecutive collected specimens with single determination, for colorectal neoplasm screening (ie, patient was provided three cards or single triple card for consecutive collection)

Test determines presence of blood in the feces.

Delorme pericardiectomy

33030 Pericardiectomy, subtotal or complete; without cardiopulmonary bypass

Method excises a diseased pericardium constricting the ventricle.

Denonvillier's operation

14060 Adjacent tissue transfer or rearrangement, eyelids, nose, ears and/or lips; defect 10 sq cm or less

Defective nasal ala is corrected using a triangular flap from the opposite side of the nose.

Dunn arthrodesis

28725 Arthrodesis; subtalar

Procedure fuses talus in the foot.

Dupuy-Dutemp reconstruction

67971 Reconstruction of eyelid, full thickness by transfer of tarsoconjunctival flap from opposing eyelid; up to two-thirds of eyelid, one stage or first stage

Skin from the opposing lid is used to reconstruct the other eyelid.

Dwyer instrumentation technique

22845 Anterior instrumentation; 2 to 3 vertebral segments

22846 Anterior instrumentation; 4 to 7 vertebral segments

22847 Anterior instrumentation; 8 or more vertebral segments

Anterior procedure using rods and attachments to straighten the spine.

Eggers procedure

27100 Transfer external oblique muscle to greater trochanter including fascial or tendon extension (graft)

Hamstring muscles of the knee and thigh area are transferred to a new position on the femoral condyle.

Emmet's operation

56800 Plastic repair of introitus

56810 Perineoplasty, repair of perineum, nonobstetrical (separate procedure)

Procedure involves: **1)** *Repair of perineum;* **2)** *Repair of the cervix uteri.*

Everbusch's operation

67904 Repair of blepharoptosis; (tarso) levator resection or advancement, external approach

Elevating the levator muscle corrects ptosis of the upper eyelid.

Farnsworth-Munsell color test

92283 Color vision examination, extended, eg, anomaloscope or equivalent

Test evaluates problems in depth perception.

Farr test

82784 Gammaglobulin; IgA, IgD, IgG, IgM, each

82785 Gammaglobulin; IgE

Antibody reacts to radioactive antigen and precipitates, leaving a free antigen in solution. Radio markers tag the suspected antigen.

Frazier-Spiller procedure

61450 Craniectomy, subtemporal, for section, compression, or decompression of sensory root of gasserian ganglion

Sensory root of the gasserian ganglion is compressed or decompressed to relieve trigeminal neuralgia.

Frickman proctopexy

45550 Proctopexy (eg, for prolapse); with sigmoid resection, abdominal approach

To correct rectal prolapse, rectum is sutured to the anterior presacral fascia and attached to the sigmoid colon, which has been shortened to help suspend the rectum.

Frost Suture

67875 Temporary closure of eyelids by suture (eg, Frost suture)

Temporary sutures of the eyelid.

Fukala's operation

66840 Removal of lens material; aspiration technique, one or more stages

Physician removes the lens of the eye to treat near-sightedness.

Gil-Vernet pyelotomy

50120 Pyelotomy; with exploration

Calyces and renal pelvis of the kidney are explored.

Gonin's operation

67107 Repair of retinal detachment; scleral buckling (such as lamellar scleral dissection, imbrication or encircling procedure), with or without implant, with or without cryotherapy, photocoagulation, and drainage of subretinal fluid

Thermocautery of the fissure of a detached retina is performed through an incision in the sclera.

Graefe's operation

66830 Removal of secondary membranous cataract (opacified posterior lens capsule and/or anterior hyaloid) with corneo-scleral section, with or without iridectomy (iridocapsulotomy, iridocapsulectomy)

Cataracts are corrected by removing the lens, lacerating the capsule, and performing an iridectomy via the sclera.

Grice arthrodesis

28725 Arthrodesis; subtalar

Bone graft is planted in the lateral part of the subtalar joint.

Gritti amputation

27598 Disarticulation at knee

Leg is amputated through the knee, and kneecap is used as the flap over the wound.

Guthrie test

84030 Phenylalanine (PKU), blood

Bacterial inhibition assay measures serum phenylalanine; and is in widespread use for detection of phenylketonuria in newborn.

Halsted mastectomy

19305 Mastectomy, radical, including pectoral muscles, axillary lymph nodes

Radical mastectomy includes removal of the breast along with pectoral minor muscle.

Ham test

85475 Hemolysin, acid

Test checks for acidified serum.

Harii Procedure

25430 Insertion of vascular pedicle into carpal bone (eg, Hori procedure)

Procedure involves complex repair of an injury that affects the dorsal skin, subcutaneous fat, including the nerves and blood vessels and the covering immediately adjacent to the tendon.

Hartley-Krause

61450 Craniectomy, subtemporal, for section, compression, or decompression of sensory root of gasserian ganglion

Gasserian ganglion is removed to relieve trigeminal neuralgia.

Heaf test

86580 Skin test; tuberculosis, intradermal

Test checks for tuberculin antibodies.

Heine's operation

66700 Ciliary body destruction; diathermy

Ciliary body is destroyed to relieve glaucoma.

Hibbs' fusion

22841 Internal spinal fixation by wiring of spinous processes

Physician fractures the spinous processes and presses each tip downward to rest in the fractured area of the process below it.

Hicks-Pitney test

85730 Thromboplastin time, partial (PTT); plasma or whole blood

Thromboplastin generation test measures the efficiency of plasma in forming thromboplastin.

Holten test

82575 Creatinine; clearance

Creatines are used to test renal efficiency.

Holter monitor procedure

93235 Electrocardiographic monitoring for 24 hours by continuous computerized monitoring and non-continuous recording, and real-time data analysis utilizing a device capable of producing intermittent full-sized waveform tracings, possibly patient activated; includes monitoring and real-time data analysis with report, physician review and interpretation

Patient wears a portable instrument to chart long-term behavior of the heart.

Howard test

52005 Cystourethroscopy, with ureteral catheterization, with or without irrigation, instillation, or ureteropyelography, exclusive of radiologic service;

Both ureters are catheterized and urine is collected from each kidney to test renal function.

Huggins' orchiectomy

54520 Orchiectomy, simple (including subcapsular), with or without testicular prosthesis, scrotal or inguinal approach

Testes removed due to prostate cancer, among other diagnoses.

Hummelsheim operation

67340 Strabismus surgery involving exploration and/or repair of detached extraocular muscle(s) (List separately in addition to code for primary procedure)

Correction of strabismus by adjusting the eye muscles.

Ishihara test

92283 Color vision examination, extended, eg, anomaloscope or equivalent

Color blindness test uses plates painted with dots depicting various figures.

Jannetta decompression

61458 Craniectomy, suboccipital; for exploration or decompression of cranial nerves

Microsurgery relieves pressure on the cranial nerves.

Keen laminectomy

63198 Laminectomy with cordotomy with section of both spinothalamic tracts, two stages within 14 days; cervical

Physician removes sections of the posterior branches of spinal nerves to affected muscles and spinal accessory nerves to correct torticollis.

Keitzer test

51772 Urethral pressure profile studies (UPP) (urethral closure pressure profile), any technique

Sound is used to test the pressure of an external stream of urine.

Killian operation

31070 Sinusotomy frontal; external, simple (trephine operation)

Wall of the frontal sinus is excised to remove diseased tissue and create an opening through the nose.

Knapp's operation

66160 Fistulization of sclera for glaucoma; sclerectomy with punch or scissors, with iridectomy

Peripheral opening in the capsule is formed behind the iris to remedy a cataract.

Koop inguinal orchiopexy

54640 Orchiopexy, inguinal approach, with or without hernia repair

Undescended testicle is retrieved from the abdomen via an inguinal approach.

Korte-Ballance anastomosis

64868 Anastomosis; facial-hypoglossal

Facial and hypoglossal nerves are joined.

Krause decompression

61450 Craniectomy, subtemporal, for section, compression, or decompression of sensory root of gasserian ganglion

Gasserian ganglion is excised to relieve trigeminal neuralgia.

Krimer's palatoplasty

14040 Adjacent tissue transfer or rearrangement, forehead, cheeks, chin, mouth, neck, axillae, genitalia, hands and/or feet; defect 10 sq cm or less

Physician sutures mucoperiosteal flaps from each side of the palatal cleft at the medial line.

Lambrinudi arthrodesis

28730 Arthrodesis, midtarsal or tarsometatarsal, multiple or transverse;

Triple fusion prevents the foot drop that may result from polio.

Landboldt's operation

67971 Reconstruction of eyelid, full thickness by transfer of tarsoconjunctival flap from opposing eyelid; up to two-thirds of eyelid, one stage or first stage

67973 Reconstruction of eyelid, full thickness by transfer of tarsoconjunctival flap from opposing eyelid; total eyelid, lower, one stage or first stage

67974 Reconstruction of eyelid, full thickness by transfer of tarsoconjunctival flap from opposing eyelid; total eyelid, upper, one stage or first stage

67975 Reconstruction of eyelid, full thickness by transfer of tarsoconjunctival flap from opposing eyelid; second stage

Double pedicle or flap of eyelid skin is taken from the upper lid to form a lower eyelid.

Lane's operation

44150 Colectomy, total, abdominal, without proctectomy; with ileostomy or ileoproctostomy

Fecal production is halted by dividing the ileum near the cecum to close the distal portion of the colon. The proximal end of the colon is anastomosized with the upper part of the rectum or lower part of the sigmoid.

Laroyenne operation

57010 Colpotomy; with drainage of pelvic abscess

Douglas pouch is punctured to evacuate pus and to facilitate drainage.

Lempert's fenestration

69820 Fenestration semicircular canal

Small window is drilled in the lateral semicircular canal and a skin flap is placed over the fistula to remedy otosclerosis.

Leriche sympathectomy

64809 Sympathectomy, thoracolumbar

Procedure involves sympathetic denervation.

Longmire anastomosis

47765 Anastomosis, of intrahepatic ducts and gastrointestinal tract

Biliary obstruction is corrected with an intrahepatic cholangiojejunostomy and partial hepatectomy.

Lorenz's operation

27258 Open treatment of spontaneous hip dislocation (developmental, including congenital or pathological), replacement of femoral head in acetabulum (including tenotomy, etc.);

Chronic dislocation of the hip is corrected by tying the head of the femur to the acetabulum to develop a socket.

Lowsley's operation

54380 Plastic operation on penis for epispadias distal to external sphincter;

Simple epispadias is corrected by closing the glandular cleft urethra, splitting the glans, and burying the repaired urethra deep into the soft tissue.

Luschka proctectomy

45111 Proctectomy; partial resection of rectum, transabdominal approach

Technique used to resect the rectum.

MacEwen hernia repair

49505 Repair initial inguinal hernia, age 5 years or over; reducible

Hernia sack is used to construct a closing ring in this radical cure of a hernia.

Madlener operation

58600 Ligation or transection of fallopian tube(s), abdominal or vaginal approach, unilateral or bilateral

In this sterilization method, a clamp crushes the middle portion of fallopian tube, which is then shut by suture.

Manchester colporrhaphy

58400 Uterine suspension, with or without shortening of round ligaments, with or without shortening of sacrouterine ligaments; (separate procedure)

Procedure attempts to preserve the uterus following prolapse by amputating the vaginal portion of the cervix, shortening the cardinal ligaments, and performing a colpoperineorrhaphy posteriorly.

Mantoux test

86580 Skin test; tuberculosis, intradermal

Standard test checks for tuberculosis.

Maydl colostomy

45563 Exploration, repair, and presacral drainage for rectal injury; with colostomy

Procedure in which colon is drawn out through the wound and maintained in position by a glass rod until adhesions have formed.

Mayo hernia repair

49585 Repair umbilical hernia, age 5 years or over; reducible

Physician excises a hernia mass and overlaps the space with abdominal muscles.

McDonald cerclage

57700 Cerclage of uterine cervix, nonobstetrical

Opening of cervix is decreased via sutures around the bottom of the cervix

McIndoe vaginal construction

57291 Construction of artificial vagina; without graft

Physician constructs an artificial vagina without using a graft.

Meller's excision

68530 Removal of foreign body or dacryolith, lacrimal passages

Physician removes a tear sac obstructing the lacrimal passages.

Mikulicz resection

44320 Colostomy or skin level cecostomy;

44322 Colostomy or skin level cecostomy; with multiple biopsies (eg, for congenital megacolon) (separate procedure)

Procedure is done in stages and includes exteriorizing a section of intestine, usually the colon, resecting the exteriorized loop, and eliminating the fecal fistula by crushing the spur between the two barrels of the anastomosis. The fecal fistula is closed.

Miles' colectomy

44155 Colectomy, total, abdominal, with proctectomy; with ileostomy

Lower sigmoid colon and rectum are removed for treatment of cancer. Physician removes the pelvic colon, mesocolon, and adjacent lymph nodes and establishes a permanent colostomy.

Millin-Read

57288 Sling operation for stress incontinence (eg, fascia or synthetic)

Suprapubic approach is used in the procedure to remedy stress incontinence.

Mitrofanoff operation

50845 Cutaneous appendico-vesicostomy

Appendix is connected to the bladder and skin as an opening for urine.

Mosenthal test

81002 Urinalysis, by dip stick or tablet reagent for bilirubin, glucose, hemoglobin, ketones, leukocytes, nitrite, pH, protein, specific gravity, urobilinogen, any number of these constituents; non-automated, without microscopy

Urine test for kidney function that is taken while the patient prescribes to a general diet.

Procedural Eponyms

Moynihan test

74246 Radiological examination, gastrointestinal tract, upper, air contrast, with specific high density barium, effervescent agent, with or without glucagon; with or without delayed films, without KUB

Radiological test determines hourglass stomach, a condition marked by the inability of the stomach muscles to contract, consequently resulting in digestive problems.

Naffziger operation

61330 Decompression of orbit only, transcranial approach

Lateral and superior orbital walls are removed to decompress the orbit in cases of severe malignant exophthalmos.

Noble intestinal plication

44680 Intestinal plication (separate procedure)

Procedure involves suturing the intestine.

Patey's mastectomy

19307 Mastectomy, modified radical, including axillary lymph nodes, with or without pectoralis minor muscle, but excluding pectoralis major muscle

Modified radical mastectomy includes removal of the breast and axillary lymph nodes with preservation of the pectoralis major muscle.

Patterson's test

84525 Urea nitrogen; semiquantitative (eg, reagent strip test)

Test using blood and a reagent detects urea. Blood turns green if positive.

Pean's amputation

27290 Interpelviabdominal amputation (hindquarter amputation)

Arteries and veins are ligated during each step to amputate the hip joint.

Pemberton osteotomy

27147 Osteotomy, iliac, acetabular or innominate bone; with open reduction of hip

Osteotomy is performed to position triradiate cartilage as a hinge for rotating the acetabular roof in cases of dysplasia of the hip in children.

Polya anastomosis

43632 Gastrectomy, partial, distal; with gastrojejunostomy

Anastomosis of the transected stomach to the side of the jejunum following gastrectomy.

Porter-Silber test

82528 Corticosterone

Test to determine corticosterone, a mineral important in sodium retention.

Prentice orchiopexy

54640 Orchiopexy, inguinal approach, with or without hernia repair

Inguinal incision is made to move undescended testicles to the scrotum.

Regnoli's excision

41140 Glossectomy; complete or total, with or without tracheostomy, without radical neck dissection

Partial or total surgical excision of the tongue.

Rehfuss' test

91055 Gastric intubation, washings, and preparing slides for cytology (separate procedure)

Gastric secretion is determined by drawing specimens of digestion every 15 minutes after eating.

Reinsch test

83015 Heavy metal (eg, arsenic, barium, beryllium, bismuth, antimony, mercury); screen

Test determines level of heavy metals in body tissue.

Ridell sinusotomy

31080 Sinusotomy frontal; obliterative, without osteoplastic flap, coronal incision (includes ablation)

Physician destroys frontal sinus to eliminate tumors.

Salter osteotomy

27146 Osteotomy, iliac, acetabular or innominate bone;

Innominate bone of the hip is cut, removed, and repositioned to repair a congenital dislocation, subluxation, or deformity.

Shirodkar procedure

57700 Cerclage of uterine cervix, nonobstetrical

Nonabsorbent suture material is used for a cerclage involving purse-string suture of an incompetent cervical os.

Smith-Robinson arthrodesis

22808 Arthrodesis, anterior, for spinal deformity, with or without cast; 2 to 3 vertebral segments

Fusion procedure requires an anterior approach to remove cervical disks and use of a bone graft fashioned to replace the disks.

Stoffel rhizotomy

63185 Laminectomy with rhizotomy; one or two segments

Nerve roots are sectioned to relieve pain or spastic paralysis.

Taarnhoj procedure

61450 Craniectomy, subtemporal, for section, compression, or decompression of sensory root of gasserian ganglion

The skull is opened at the temporal region and the gasserian ganglion nerve root is sectioned, decompressed, or compressed, depending on the patient's complaint.

Touroff ligation

37615 Ligation, major artery (eg, post-traumatic, rupture); neck

Neck is incised and an artery or a vein, damaged or ruptured by trauma, is isolated and tied off with sutures.

Tzank smear

87207 Smear, primary source with interpretation; special stain for inclusion bodies or parasites (eg, malaria, coccidia, microsporidia, trypanosomes, herpes viruses)

Test determines if there are altered epithelial cells (Tzank cells) in the fluid of the bullae of pemphigus vulgaris.

Valentine's test

81020 Urinalysis; two or three glass test

Another term for the three glass test which uses three vials of the same stream of urine to determine contents of the anterior urethra, bladder, ureters, and seminal vesicles.

Van Den Bergh test

82247 Bilirubin; total

Test involves comparing serum or plasma to bilirubin.

Van Slyke method

82131 Amino acids; single, quantitative, each specimen

Test checks for amino-acid nitrogen.

Walsh modified radical prostatectomy

55810 Prostatectomy, perineal radical;

Radical prostatectomy resects the rectum and surrounding tissue.

Wasserman test

86592 Syphilis test; qualitative (eg, VDRL, RPR, ART)

Wasserman is the original test for syphilis.

Wertheim hysterectomy

58210 Radical abdominal hysterectomy, with bilateral total pelvic lymphadenectomy and para-aortic lymph node sampling (biopsy), with or without removal of tube(s), with or without removal of ovary(s)

Radical operation for uterine carcinoma includes excising a portion of the vagina and lymph nodes.

Westergren test

85652 Sedimentation rate, erythrocyte; automated

Test determines the sedimentation rate of red blood cells in fluid blood by mixing venous blood with an aqueous solution of sodium citrate and allowing it to stand for measured periods of time.

Wheeler Procedure

68820 Discission of secondary membranous cataract (opacified posterior lens capsule and/or anterior hyaloid); stab incision technique (Ziegler or Wheeler knife)

Procedure is to correct entropion with secondary membranous cataract.

Whipple Procedure

48150 Pancreatectomy, proximal subtotal with total duodenectomy, partial gastrectomy, choledochoenterostomy and gastrojejunostomy (Whipple-type procedure); with pancreatojejunostomy

Procedure removes pancreas and gastric structures.

Whitehead hemorrhoidectomy

46260 Hemorrhoidectomy, internal and external, complex or extensive;

Two circular incisions above and below hemorrhoidal veins pull down normal mucosa for suturing to anal skin.

Whitman astragalectomy

28130 Talectomy (astragalectomy)

Physician removes cartilage of the talus.

Surgical Terms

A special language is spoken in the surgical suite and written in the charts documenting procedures performed there. The following list includes many of the medical terms heard most often in the operating room.

ablation. Removal or destruction of tissue by cutting, electrical energy, chemical substances, or excessive heat application.

abrasion. Removal of layers of the skin occurring as a superficial injury, or a procedure for removal of problematic skin or skin lesions.

achalasia. Failure of the smooth muscles within the gastrointestinal tract to relax at points of junction; most commonly referring to the esophagogastric sphincter's failure to relax when swallowing.

acromioplasty. Repair of the part of the shoulder blade that connects to the deltoid muscles and clavicle.

advance. Move away from the starting point.

allograft. Graft from one individual to another of the same species.

amputation. Removal of all or part of a limb or digit through the shaft or body of a bone.

analysis. Study of body fluid, tissue, section, or parts.

anastomosis. Surgically created connection between ducts, blood vessels, or bowel segments to allow flow from one to the other.

aneurysm. Circumscribed dilation or outpouching of an artery wall, often containing blood clots and connecting directly with the lumen of the artery.

angioplasty. Reconstruction or repair of a diseased or damaged blood vessel.

antibody. Immunoglobulin or protective protein encoded within its building block sequence to interact only with its specific antigen.

antigen. Substance inducing sensitivity or triggering an immune response and the production of antibodies.

antrum. Chamber or cavity, typically with a small opening.

appliance. Device providing function to a body part.

arthrocentesis. Puncture and aspiration of fluid from a joint for diagnostic or therapeutic purposes or injection of anesthetics or corticosteroids.

arthrodesis. Surgical fixation or fusion of a joint to reduce pain and improve stability, performed openly or arthroscopically.

arthroplasty. Surgical reconstruction of a joint to improve function and reduce pain; may involve partial or total joint replacement.

arthroscopy. Use of an endoscope to examine the interior of a joint (diagnostic) or to perform surgery on joint structures (therapeutic).

arthrotomy. Surgical incision into a joint that may include exploration, drainage, or removal of a foreign body.

articulate. Comprised of separate segments joined together, allowing for movement of each part on the other.

aspiration. Drawing fluid out by suction.

assay. Test of purity.

astragalectomy. Surgical removal of the astragalus (talus), the bone that forms the ankle joint by articulating with the tibia and fibula.

augmentation. Add to or increase the substance of a body site, usually performed as plastic reconstructive measures. Augmentation may involve the use of an implant or prosthesis, especially within soft tissue or grafting procedures, such as bone tissue.

autograft. Any tissue harvested from one anatomical site of a person and grafted to another anatomical site of the same person. Most commonly, blood vessels, skin, tendons, fascia, and bone are used as autografts.

avulse. Tear away from, whether in an accidental injury or as a surgical procedure.

benign. Mild or nonmalignant in nature.

biofeedback. Process by which a person learns to influence autonomic or involuntary nervous system responses and physiologic responses normally regulated voluntarily, but whose control has been affected by trauma or disease.

biometry. Statistical analysis of biological data.

biopsy. Tissue or fluid removed for diagnostic purposes through analysis of the cells in the biopsy material.

blood type. Classification of blood by group.

bougie. Probe used to dilate or calibrate a body part.

brachytherapy. Form of radiation therapy in which radioactive pellets or seeds are implanted directly into the tissue being treated to deliver their dose of radiation in a more directed fashion. Brachytherapy provides radiation to the prescribed body area while minimizing exposure to normal tissue.

bridge. Connection between two parts of an organ or body part.

brush. Tool used to gather cell samples or clean a body part.

burr. Specialized surgical drill used to shape or make holes in bones or gain access into the cranium.

bursa. Cavity or sac containing fluid that occurs between articulating surfaces and serves to reduce friction from moving parts.

bypass. Auxiliary or diverted route to maintain continuous flow.

C-arm. Portable x-ray fluoroscopy machine often used in surgery.

calculus. Abnormal, stone-like concretion of calcium, cholesterol, mineral salts, or other substances that forms in any part of the body.

cannula. Tube inserted into a blood vessel, duct, or body cavity to facilitate passage.

capsulorrhaphy. Suturing or repair of a joint capsule.

capsulotomy. Incision of a joint capsule.

cast. Rigid encasement or dressing molded to the body from a substance that hardens upon drying to hold a body part immobile during the healing period; a model or reproduction made from an impression or mold.

catheter. Flexible tube inserted into an area of the body for introducing or withdrawing fluid.

cauterize. Heat or chemicals used to burn or cut.

celiotomy. Incision into the abdominal cavity.

cement. Any substance that solidly bonds two objects or surfaces together.

centesis. Puncture.

cephalad. Toward the head.

cerclage. Looping or encircling an organ or tissue with wire or ligature for positional support.

chemodenervation. Chemical destruction of nerves. A substance, for example, Botox, is used to temporarily inhibit the transfer of chemicals at the presynaptic membrane, blocking the neuromuscular junctions.

chemosurgery. Application of chemical agents to destroy tissue, originally referring to the in situ chemical fixation of premalignant or malignant lesions to facilitate surgical excision.

chemotherapy. Treatment of disease, especially cancerous conditions, using chemical agents.

chisel. Instrument for cutting or planing bone.

chondral. Relating to cartilage.

chromotubation. Injection of a medication or saline solution into the uterine cavity and fallopian tubes to verify patency of the tubes.

cicatricial. Of or relating to scarring. c. entropion. Scarring that results in inversion of the eyelid, causing the lid margin to rest against and irritate the eyeball. c. lagophthalmos. Scarring that results in an eye that cannot be completely closed. c. pemphigoid. Autoimmune disease causing blisters on the skin, often accompanied by itching and/or burning and resulting in scarring.

ciliary. Pertaining to the eyelid, eyelashes, or specific structures of the eyeball. c. block. Increase in intraocular pressure that is accompanied by a shallow anterior chamber and forward displacement of the iris and lens. c. body. Structure of the eye that produces the aqueous humor within the anterior chamber that nourishes the lens and cornea. The ciliary body is part of the uvea and connects anteriorly to the root of the iris and posteriorly to the choroid at the ora serrata retinae. It is divided into the pars plana and the pars plicata.

circumcise. Circular cutting around the genitals to remove the prepuce or foreskin.

clamp. Tool used to grip, compress, join, or fasten body parts.

closure. Repairing an incision or wound by suture or other means.

clysis. Fluids injected into the body.

coctolabile. Capable of being destroyed or altered when boiled.

comminuted. Fracture type in which the bone is splintered or crushed.

commissure. Juncture where two corresponding parts come together, especially referring to the union site of adjacent heart valve cusps.

complex. Composite or collection of related things, such as symptoms, anatomical parts, or surgical procedures.

condyle. Rounded end of a bone that forms an articulation.

conization. Excision of a cone-shaped piece of tissue.

constriction. Narrowed or squeezed portion of a tubular or luminal structure, such as a duct, vessel, or tube (e.g., esophagus). The narrowing can be a defect that is occurring naturally, or one that is surgically induced for therapeutic reasons.

contour. Act of shaping along desired lines.

corpectomy. Removal of the body of a bone, such as a vertebra.

correct. Body part modification.

craterization. Excision of a portion of bone creating a crater-like depression to facilitate drainage from infected areas of bone.

cross match. Test used to match the compatibility of a donor's blood or organ to the recipient.

crus. *1)*. Any body part resembling a leg. *2)*. Lower part of the leg.

cryotherapy. Any surgical procedure that uses intense cold for treatment.

culture. Growth of microorganisms in a medium conducive to their development.

curettage. Removal of tissue by scraping.

cutaneous. Relating to the skin.

cystotomy. Surgical incision into the gallbladder or urinary bladder.

debridement. Removal of dead or contaminated tissue and foreign matter from a wound.

decompress. To relieve pressure.

decubitus. Patient lying on the side.

dehiscence. Complication of healing in which the surgical wound ruptures or bursts open, superficially or through multiple layers.

deligation. Closure by tying up; sutures, ligatures.

depressor. Tool used to push body tissue out of the way.

dermabrasion. Cosmetic procedure that smooths out flaws and disfigured skin and promotes the growth of a new layer of skin cells by removing the outer layer of skin by mechanical or chemical means such as fine sandpaper, wire brushes, and caustic substances.

destruction. Ablation or eradication of a structure or tissue.

detection. Search for presence of a tissue or material.

diagnostic. Aid in diagnosis.

dialysis. Artificial filtering of the blood to remove contaminating waste elements and restore normal balance.

diaphysis. Central shaft of a long bone.

diathermy. Applying heat to body tissues by various methods for therapeutic treatment or surgical purposes to coagulate and seal tissue.

dilation. Artificial increase in the diameter of an opening or lumen made by medication or by instrumentation.

dilution. Concentration reduction of a mixture or solution by adding more fluid.

disarticulation. Removal of a limb through a joint.

discectomy. Surgical excision of an intervertebral disk.

dislocation. Displacement of a bone in relation to its neighboring tissue, especially a joint.

dissection. Separating by cutting tissue or body structures apart.

distention. Enlarged or expanded due to pressure from inside.

diversion. Rechanneling of body fluid through another conduit.

diverticulum. Pouch or sac in the walls of an organ or canal.

division. Separating into two or more parts.

donor. Person from whom tissues or organs are removed for transplantation.

dorsum. Back side or back part of the body or individual anatomical structure.

dosimetry. Component in the administration of radiation oncology therapy in which a radiation dose is calculated to a specific site, including implant or beam orientation and exposure, isodose strengths, tissue inhomogeneities, and volume.

drain. Device that creates a channel to allow fluid from a cavity, wound, or infected area to exit the body.

drill. Making a hole in a bone or hard tissue.

dynamic. Manifesting motion in response to force.

echography. Radiographic imaging that uses sound waves reflected off the different densities of anatomic structures to create images.

ectopic. *1)*. Fertilized ovum that implants and develops outside the uterus. The ovum may implant itself in different sites, such as the fallopian tube, the ovary, the abdomen, or the cervix. *2)*. Organ or other structure that is aberrant or out of place.

edentulous. Loss of all or some of the natural teeth.

electrocautery. Division or cutting of tissue using high-frequency electrical current to produce heat, which destroys cells.

elevator. Tool for lifting tissues or bone.

elution. Separation of one solid from another, usually by washing.

embolism. Obstruction of a blood vessel resulting from a clot or foreign substance.

endoscopy. Visual inspection of the body using a fiberoptic scope.

enterostomy. Surgically created opening into the intestine through the abdominal wall.

epiphysis. End of a long bone.

epithelize. Formation of epithelial cells over a surface.

escharotomy. Surgical incision into the scab or crust resulting from a severe burn in order to relieve constriction and allow blood flow to the distal unburned tissue.

esophagoscopy. Internal visual inspection of the esophagus through the use of an endoscope placed down the throat.

evacuation. Removal or purging of waste material.

evisceration. Removal of contents of a cavity.

examination. Comprehensive visual and tactile screening and specific testing leading to diagnosis or, as appropriate, to a referral to another practitioner.

exchange. Substitution of one thing for another.

excise. Remove or cut out.

exenteration. Surgical removal of the entire contents of a body cavity, such as the pelvis or orbit.

exfoliate. Skin falling off in layers.

exploration. Examination for diagnostic purposes.

exposure. In surgery, to display, reveal, or make accessible.

expression. In surgery, the squeezing out of tissue.

exteriorize. In surgery, to expose an organ temporarily for observation.

external fixation. Rods and pins connected in a lattice to secure bone.

extract. Condensed medication.

fascia. Fibrous sheet or band of tissue that envelops organs, muscles, and groupings of muscles.

fasciotomy. Incision or transection of fascial tissue.

fenestration. Presence of small openings from piercing or perforations.

fibrosis. Formation of fibrous tissue as part of the restorative process.

filiform. Probe with woven-thread end.

fissure. Deep furrow, groove, or cleft in tissue structures.

fistula. Abnormal tube-like passage between two body cavities or organs or from an organ to the outside surface.

fistulization. Creation of a communication between two structures that were not previously connected.

fit. Attack of acute symptoms.

fixate. Hold, secure, or fasten in position.

fixation. Act or condition of being attached, secured, fastened, or held in position.

flap. Mass of flesh and skin partially excised from its location but retaining its blood supply that is moved to another site to repair adjacent or distant defects.

fluoroscopy. Radiology technique that allows visual examination of part of the body or a function of an organ using a device that projects an x-ray image on a fluorescent screen.

follow-up. Visits or treatment following a procedure.

forceps. Tool used for grasping or compressing tissue.

fossa. Indentation or shallow depression.

fragment. Small piece broken off a larger whole; to divide into pieces.

free graft. Unattached piece of skin and tissue moved to another part of the body and sutured into place to repair a defect.

frozen section. Group of similar cells that have been frozen and thinly sliced according to specifications to preserve the tissue for diagnostic or histochemistry studies.

fulgurate. Destruction by electric current.

furuncle. Inflamed, painful cyst or nodule on the skin caused by bacteria, often staphylococcus, entering along the hair follicle.

fusion. Union of adjacent tissues, especially bone.

Gigli saw. Saw made of thin, flexible wire with teeth along the edge used for cutting bones (e.g., craniotomy).

graft. Tissue implant from another part of the body or another person.

guillotine. Instrument used for severing tonsils from their attachments.

halo. Tool for stabilizing the head and spine.

harvest. Removal of cells or tissue from their native site to be used as a graft or transplant to another part of the donor's body or placed into another person.

hematoma. Tumor-like collection of blood in some part of the body caused by a break in a blood vessel wall, usually as a result of trauma.

hemilaminectomy. Excision of a portion of the vertebral lamina.

hemiphalangectomy. Excision of part of the phalanx.

hemostasis. Interruption of blood flow or the cessation or arrest of bleeding.

hemostat. Tool for clamping vessels and arresting hemorrhaging.

hernia. Protrusion of a body structure through tissue.

hidradenitis. Infection or inflammation of a sweat gland and is usually treated by incision and drainage.

homograft. Graft from one individual to another of the same species.

hyperthermia. Body temperature rising above 99 degrees Fahrenheit. This elevated temperature can be the result of illness or artificially created as a therapy.

hypertrophic. Enlarged or overgrown from an increase in cell size of the affected tissue.

hypophysectomy. Destruction of the pituitary gland.

hypothermia. Therapeutic lack of heat.

identification. Recognition of body part or tissue.

imaging. Radiologic means of producing pictures for clinical study of the internal structures and functions of the body, such as x-ray, ultrasound, magnetic resonance, or positron emission tomography.

imbrication. Overlapping of tissues during closure.

immunotherapy. Therapeutic use of serum or gamma globulin.

implant. Material or device inserted or placed within the body for therapeutic, reconstructive, or diagnostic purposes.

impression. Mold of a body part to be used as a pattern in making a replacement part, prosthesis, or stabilizing device for that area of the body.

in situ. Located in the natural position or contained within the origin site, not spread into neighboring tissue.

incise. To cut open or into.

incubation. Culture cultivation under controlled conditions.

infusion. Introduction of a therapeutic fluid, other than blood, into the bloodstream.

inguinal. Within the groin region.

inject. Introduction into body tissues.

innervate. Supplying a stimulus or energy to nerve fibers connected to a part.

inseminate. Inject with semen.

insert. To put into.

instillation. Administering a liquid slowly over time, drop by drop.

instrumentation. Use of a tool for therapeutic reasons.

insufflation. Blowing air or gas into a body cavity.

interpretation. Professional health care provider's review of data with a written or verbal opinion.

interstitial. Within the small spaces or gaps occurring in tissue or organs.

intracavitary. Within a body cavity.

intubate. Insertion of a tube into a body canal or organ.

inversion. Turning inward, inside out, or upside down.

irrigate. Washing out, lavage.

kinetics. Motion or movement.

laminectomy. Removal or excision of the posterior arch of a vertebra to provide additional space for the nerves and widen the spinal canal.

lance. Incise with a lancet.

lancet. Pointed surgical knife.

laparoscopy. Direct visualization of the peritoneal cavity, outer fallopian tubes, uterus, and ovaries utilizing a laparoscope, a thin, flexible fiberoptic tube.

laparotomy. Incision through the flank or abdomen for therapeutic or diagnostic purposes.

laryngoscopy. Examination of the larynx with an endoscope.

laser. Concentrated light used to cut or seal tissue.

lateral. To/on the side.

lavage. Washing.

lesion. Area of damaged tissue that has lost continuity or function, due to disease or trauma. Lesions may be located on internal structures such as the brain, nerves, or kidneys, or visible on the skin.

ligation. Tying off a blood vessel or duct with a suture or a soft, thin wire.

limited. Bounded.

lingual. Surface of the tooth closest to the tongue or relating to the tongue and its surrounding areas.

lithotripsy. Destruction of calcified substances in the gallbladder or urinary system by smashing the concretion into small particles to be washed out. This may be done by surgical or noninvasive methods, such as ultrasound.

localization. Limitation to one area.

lysis. Destruction, breakdown, dissolution, or decomposition of cells or substances by a specific catalyzing agent.

manipulate. Treatment by hand.

manometric. Pertaining to pressure, as measured in a meter.

marsupialization. Creation of a pouch in surgical treatment of a cyst in which one wall is resected and the remaining cut edges are sutured to adjacent tissue creating an open pouch of the previously enclosed cyst.

mastectomy. Surgical removal of one or both breasts.

mastotomy. Incision of the breast, often performed for exploration of suspicious tissue or for drainage of an abscess.

meatus. Opening or passage into the body.

metatarsectomy. Excision or resection of a metatarsal bone in the foot between the tarsal and phalangeal bones.

microdissection. Dissection of tissue using a microscope.

microrepair. Repair of tissue at a level that requires using a microscope.

modification. Changing of tissues.

monitoring. Recording of events; keep track, regulate, or control patient activities and record findings.

motility. Capability of independent, spontaneous movement.

myotomy. Surgical cutting of a muscle to gain access to underlying tissues or for therapeutic reasons.

necropsy. Autopsy or postmortem examination performed in order to ascertain the cause of death or the changes caused by disease.

necrosis. Death of cells or tissue within a living organ or structure.

nephrotic. Degeneration of renal epithelium.

neurectomy. Excision of all or a portion of a nerve.

neurotomy. Dissection of a nerve.

obliterate. Get rid or do away with completely.

observation. Perception of events.

obturate. To occlude or close off an opening.

obturator. Prosthesis used to close an acquired or congenital opening in the palate that aids in speech and chewing.

occlusion. Constriction, closure, or blockage of a passage.

open fracture. Exposed break in a bone, always considered compound due to its high risk of infection from the open wound leading to the fracture. Broken bone ends may protrude through the skin and contaminants or foreign bodies are often embedded in the tissues.

orchiectomy. Surgical removal of one or both testicles via a scrotal or groin incision, indicated in cases of cancer, traumatic injury, and sex reassignment surgery.

osteomyelitis. Inflammation of bone that may remain localized or spread to the marrow, cortex, or periosteum, in response to an infecting organism, usually bacterial and pyogenic.

osteophytes. Bony outgrowth.

osteoplasty. Plastic surgery of a bone.

osteoporotic. Porous condition of bones from a loss of bone mass or density.

osteotome. Tool used for cutting bone.

osteotomy. Surgical cutting of a bone.

packing. Material placed into a cavity or wound, such as gels, gauze, pads, and sponges.

palpate. Examination by feeling with the hand.

paring. Cutting away an edge or a surface.

paronychia. Infection of nail structures.

pedicle. Stem-like, narrow base or stalk attached to a new growth.

peduncle. Connecting structures of the brain.

penetrate. Pierce.

percutaneous. Through the skin.

periosteum. Double-layered connective membrane on the outer surface of bone.

photocoagulation. Application of an intense laser beam of light to disrupt tissue and condense protein material to a residual mass, used especially for treating ocular conditions.

pilonidal. Containing a tuft of hair.

pinning. Bone fastening.

plethysmography. Recording of the volume changes in an organ or body part, particularly related to the amount of blood circulating through it.

pleurodesis. Injection of a sclerosing agent into the pleural space for creating adhesions between the parietal and the visceral pleura to treat a collapsed lung caused by air trapped in the pleural cavity, or severe cases of pleural effusion.

plication. Surgical technique involving folding, tucking, or pleating to reduce the size of a hollow structure or organ.

portable. Movable.

probing. Exploration using a slender, often flexible rod.

procedure. Diagnostic or therapeutic service provided for the care and treatment of a patient, usually conforming to a specific set of steps or instructions.

process. Anatomical projection or prominence on a bone.

prone. Lying face downward.

prophylaxis. Intervention or protective therapy intended to prevent a disease.

prosthesis. Man-made substitute for a missing body part.

prostrate. Recline on one's front.

pump. Forcing gas or liquid from a body part.

puncture. Creating a hole.

pyelotomy. Incision or opening made into the renal pelvis.

radical. Extensive surgery.

radiograph. Image made by an x-ray.

radiopaque dye. Medium injected into the body that is impenetrable by x-rays.

ream. Shape or enlarge a hole.

recess. Small empty cavity in a body part.

reconstruct. Tissue rebuilding.

reduce. Restoration to normal position or alignment.

reduction. Correction of a fracture, dislocation, or hernia to the correct place and alignment, manually or by surgery.

refer. Recommendation to another source.

regulation. Directive, order, ruling, or law put forth by an executive authority granted such powers by law.

reimplant. Reinsert or reattach tissue.

reinforce. Enhancement of strength.

reinnervation. Restoration of nerve function.

release. Disconnection of a tendon or ligament.

reoperation. Repeat performance of operation.

repair. Surgical closure of a wound. The wound may be a result of injury/trauma or it may be a surgically created defect. Repairs are divided into three categories: simple, intermediate, and complex.

replacement. Insertion of new tissue or material in place of old one.

reposition. Placement of an organ or structure into another position or return of an organ or structure to its original position.

resect. Cutting out or removing a portion or all of a bone, organ, or other structure.

reservoir. Space or body cavity for storage of liquid.

response. Reaction to stimulus.

retraction. Act of holding tissue or a structure back away from its normal position or the field of interest.

revascularize. Restoring blood flow or blood supply to a body part.

revision. Reordering or rearrangement of tissue to suit a particular need or function.

rod. Straight, slim, cylindrical metal instrument for therapeutics.

rongeur. Sharp-edged instrument with a scoop-tip used to cut through tissue and bone.

routine. Normal activity.

sclerose. To become hard or firm and indurated from increased formation of connective tissue or disease.

section. Process of cutting a division or segment out of a part.

selective. Separation.

sequestrectomy. Surgical excision of a nonviable piece of bone that has become walled off, or sequestered, away from living bone during necrosis.

seton. Finely spun thread or other fine material for leading the passage of wider instruments through a fistula, canal, or sinus tract.

sever. Separate completely.

shunt. Surgically created passage between blood vessels or other natural passages, such as an arteriovenous anastomosis, to divert or bypass blood flow from the normal channel.

sialolith. Calculus, stone, or concretion within the salivary ducts or glands.

sigmoidoscopy. Endoscopic examination of the entire rectum and sigmoid colon, often including a portion of the descending colon and usually performed with a flexible fiberoptic scope in conjunction with a surgical procedure.

smear. Specimen for study that is spread out across a glass slide.

snare. Wire used as a loop to excise a polyp or lesion.

sound. Long, slender tool with a type of curved, flat probe at the end for dilating strictures or detecting foreign bodies.

spatulate. Cut the open end of a tubular structure with a lengthwise incision and open the end out further for greater opening size in an anastomosis.

speculum. Tool used to enlarge the opening of any canal or cavity.

spiculum. Small, needle-like body or spike.

steal. Diversion of blood to another channel.

stenosis. Narrowing or constriction of a passage.

stent. Tube to provide support in a body cavity or lumen.

stereotaxis. Three-dimensional method for precisely locating structures.

stoma. Opening created in the abdominal wall from an internal organ or structure for diversion of waste elimination, drainage, and access.

strapping. Application of overlapping strips of tape or bandaging to put pressure on the affected area.

stricture. Narrowing of an anatomical structure.

subluxation. Partial or complete dislocation.

suction. Vacuum evacuation of fluid or tissue.

supine. Lying on the back.

suppression. Holding back, putting in check, or inhibiting an act, function, thought, or desire.

suppurative. Forming pus.

survival. Continued life.

suspension. Fixation of an organ for support; temporary state of cessation of an activity, process, or experience.

suture. Stitching technique employed in wound closure.

symphysis. Joint that unifies two opposed bones by a junction of bony surfaces to a plate of fibrocartilage.

synchondrosis. Two bones joined by hyaline cartilage or fibrocartilage. Typically, the bones fuse as they mature.

synovia. Clear fluid lubricant of joints, bursae, and tendon sheaths, secreted by the synovial membrane.

talectomy. Surgical removal of the astragalus (talus), the bone that forms the ankle joint by articulating with the tibia and fibula. Indications include trauma, congenital abnormalities, severe fractures, chronic infection, or tumors.

tap. Withdraw fluid through a needle or trocar.

technique. Manner of performance.

teletherapy. External beam radiotherapy or other treatment applied from a source maintained at a distance away from the body.

tenodesis. Stabilization of a joint by anchoring tendons.

tenolysis. Release of a tendon from adhesions.

therapeutic. Act meant to alleviate a medical or mental condition.

thoracentesis. Surgical puncture of the chest cavity with a specialized needle or hollow tubing to aspirate fluid from within the pleural space for diagnostic or therapeutic reasons.

thoracotomy. Surgical procedure for opening the chest wall in order to access the lungs, esophagus, trachea, aorta, heart, and diaphragm.

thrombectomy. Removal of a clot (thrombus) from a blood vessel utilizing various methods.

tomograph. Method of precise x-ray.

tracheostomy. Formation of a tracheal opening on the neck surface with tube insertion to allow for respiration in cases of obstruction or decreased patency. A tracheostomy may be planned or performed on an emergency basis for temporary or long-term use.

traction. Drawing out or holding tension on an area by applying a direct therapeutic pulling force.

tractor. Instrument for pulling an organ.

transcatheter. Procedure or treatment performed via a catheter.

transection. Transverse dissection; to cut across a long axis; cross section.

transfer. Transfer between hospitals occurs when a patient is admitted to a hospital, discharged, and subsequently admitted to another hospital for additional treatment once the patient's condition has stabilized or a diagnosis has been established.

transplant. Insertion of an organ or tissue from one person or site into another.

transposition. Removal or exchange from one side to another; change of position from one place to another.

treatment. Management of patient.

trephine. *1)*. Specialized round saw for cutting circular holes in bone, especially the skull. *2)*.

Instrument that removes small disc-shaped buttons of corneal tissue for transplanting.

trocar. Cannula or a sharp pointed instrument used to puncture and aspirate fluid from cavities.

tube. Long, hollow cylindrical instrument or body structure.

ultrasound. Imaging using ultra-high sound frequency bounced off body structures.

undiversion. Restoration of continuity, flow, or passage through the normal channel.

urachus. Embryonic tube connecting the urinary bladder to the umbilicus during development of the fetus that normally closes before birth, generally in the fourth or fifth month of gestation.

ureostomy. Connection of the ureter to a stoma on the abdominal skin.

ureterocele. Saccular formation of the lower part of the ureter, protruding into the bladder.

ureteropyelogram. Radiologic study of the renal pelvis and the ureter.

valve. Fold or membrane within a body canal or passageway that prevents backflow of fluids running through it.

varices. Enlarged, dilated, or twisted, turning veins.

vasectomy. Surgical procedure involving the removal of all or part of the vas deferens, usually performed for sterilization or in conjunction with a prostatectomy.

vestigal. Remains or remnant of a structure occurring in the fetal stage of growth.

vomer. Flat bone that forms the lower, posterior portion of the nasal septum.

xenograft. Tissue that is nonhuman and harvested from one species and grafted to another. Pigskin is the most common xenograft for human skin and is applied to a wound as a temporary closure until a permanent option is performed.

Rule of Nines for Burns

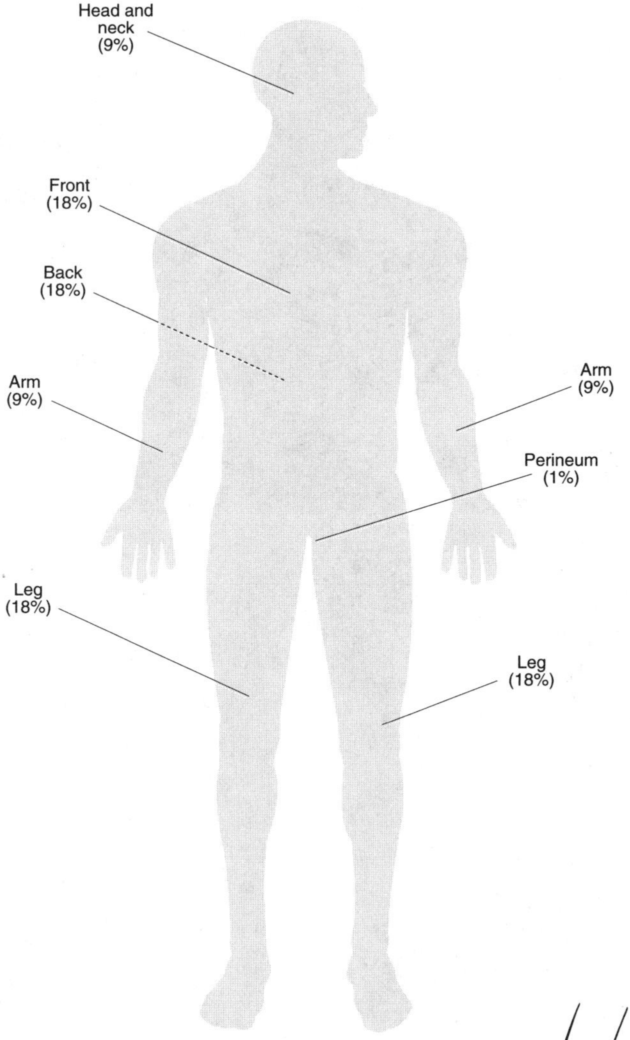

First-degree burns involve surface layers only and tissue destruction is minimal.

Second-degree burns damage deeper epidermal layers and upper layers of the dermis; damage to sweat glands, hair follicles, and sebaceous glands may occur.

Third-degree burns include destruction of both epidermis and dermis and tissue death extends below the hair follicles and sweat glands.

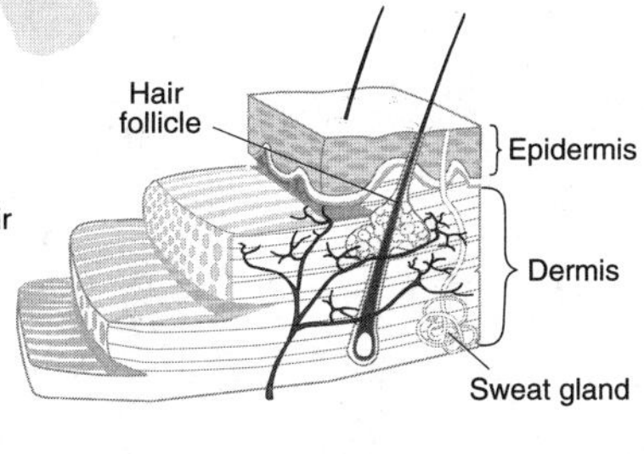

Skeletal System

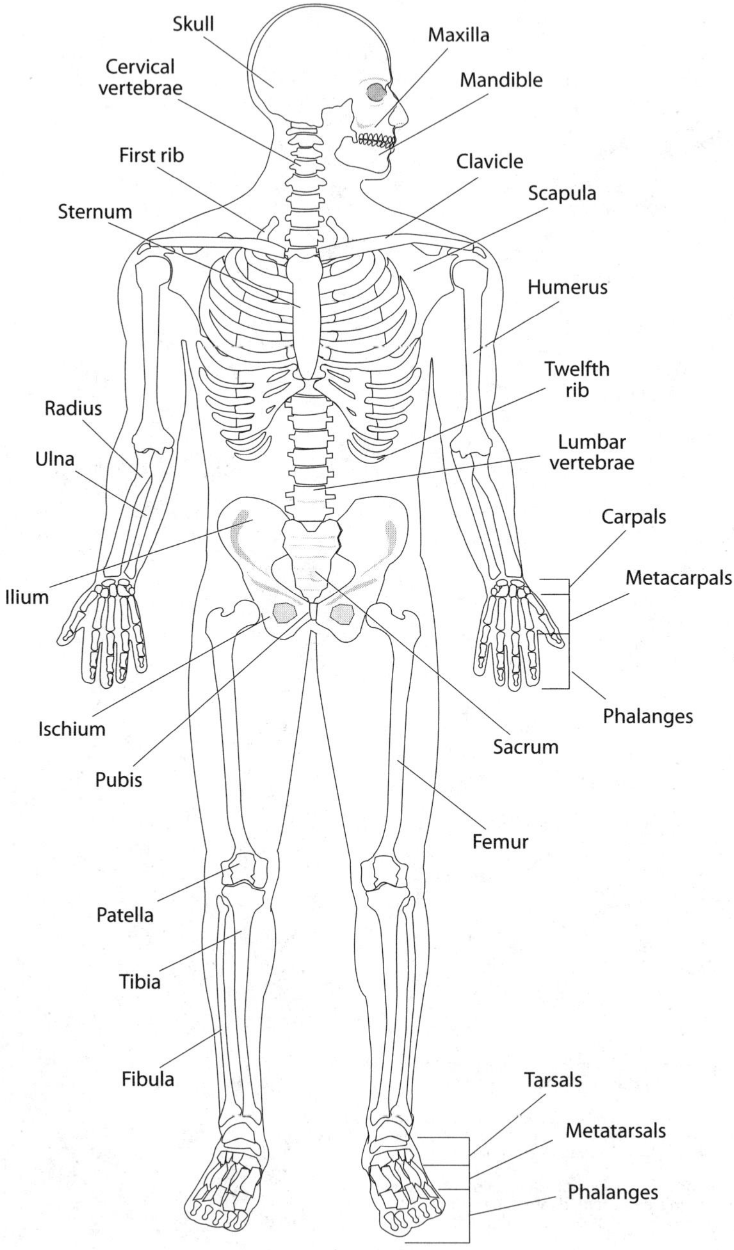

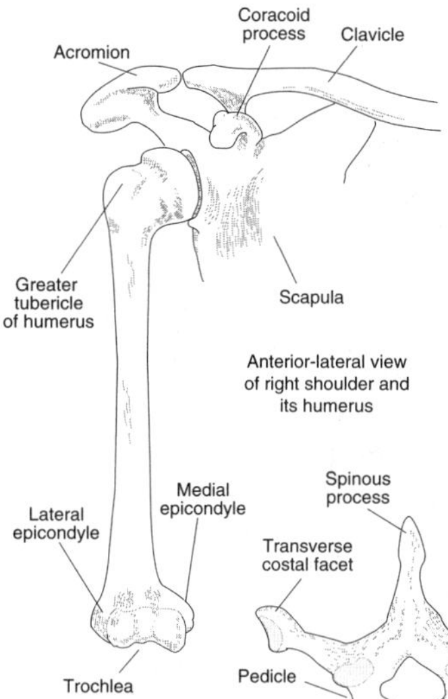

Anterior-lateral view of right shoulder and its humerus

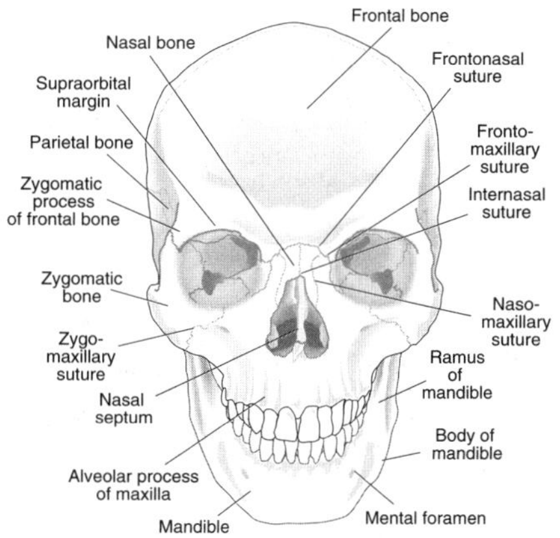

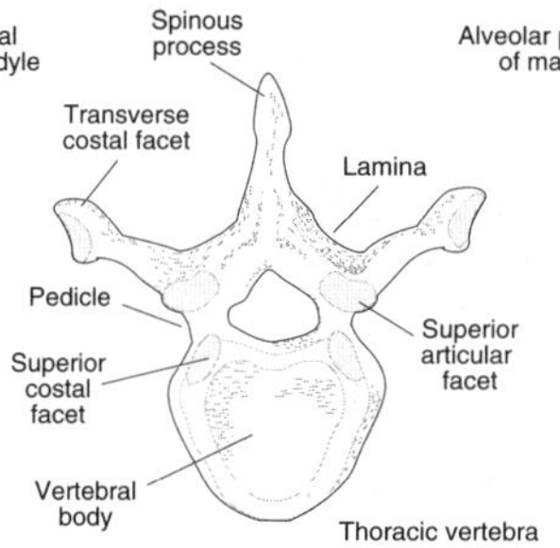

Thoracic vertebra (superior view)

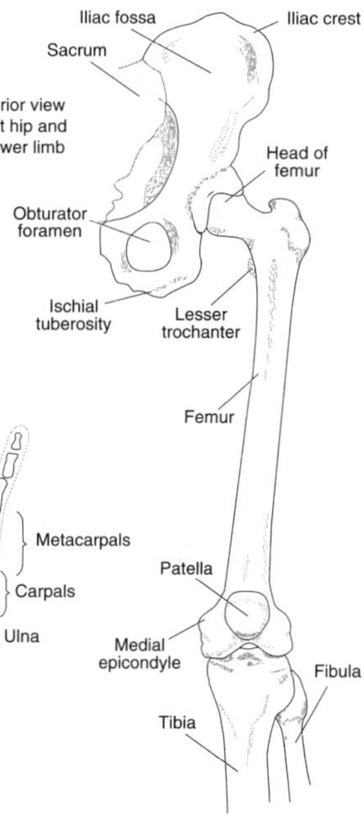

Anterior view of left hip and its lower limb

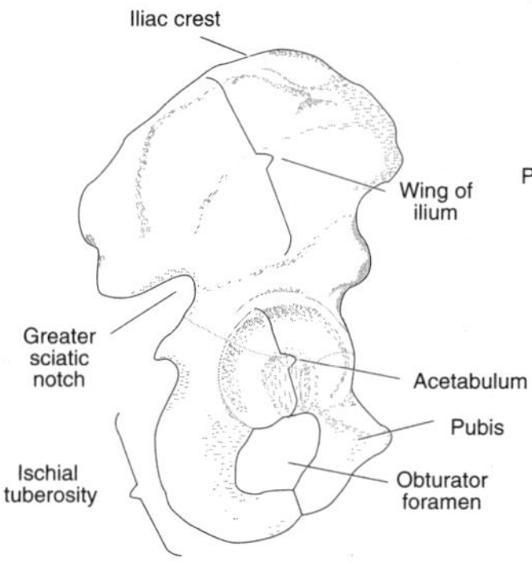

Lateral view of right hip socket

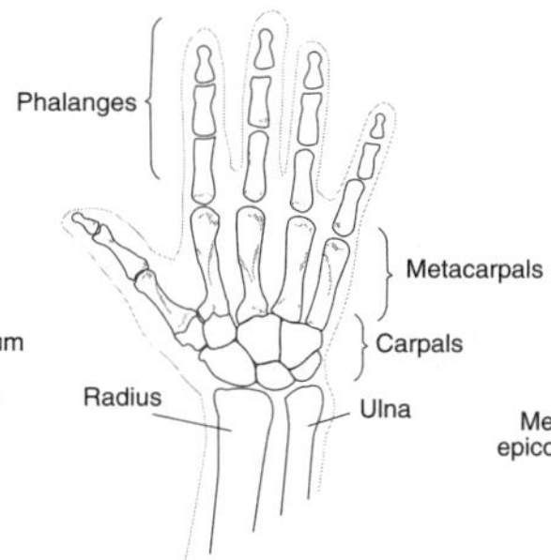

Dorsal view of right hand and wrist

Lymphatic System

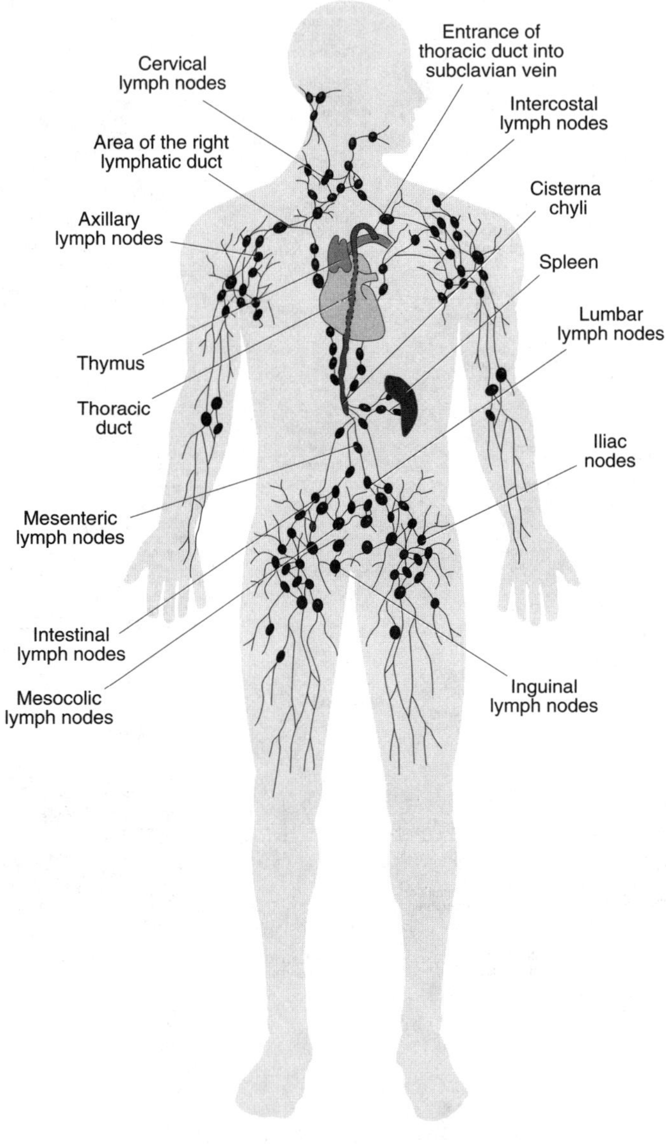

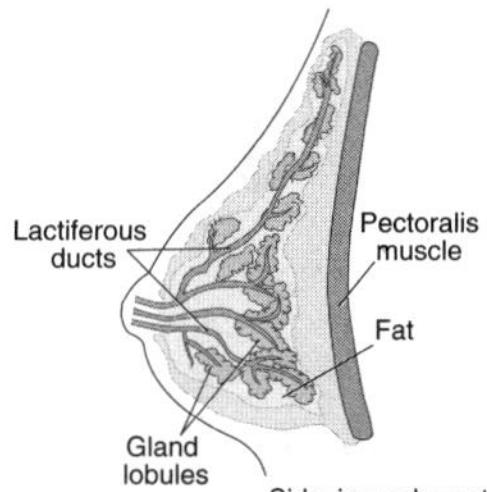

Sideview schematic of female breast

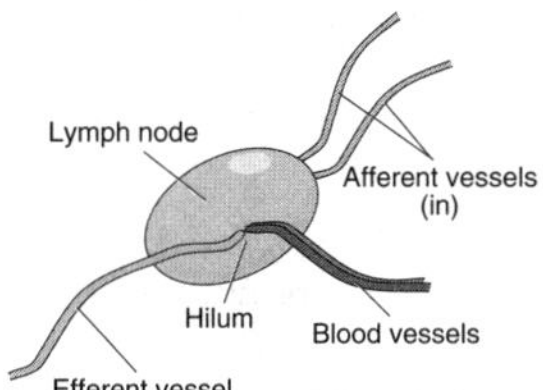

Schematic of lymph node

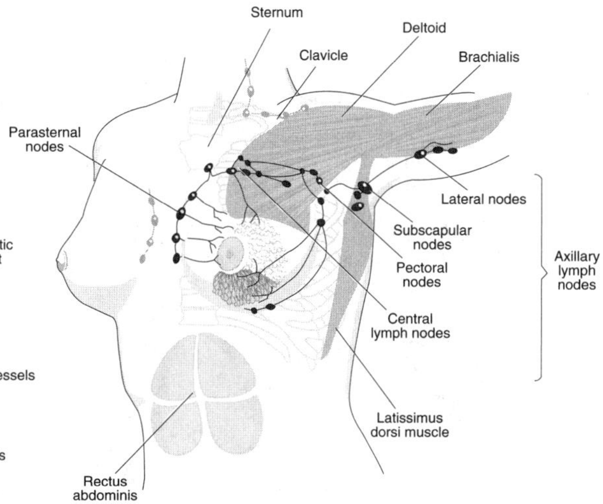

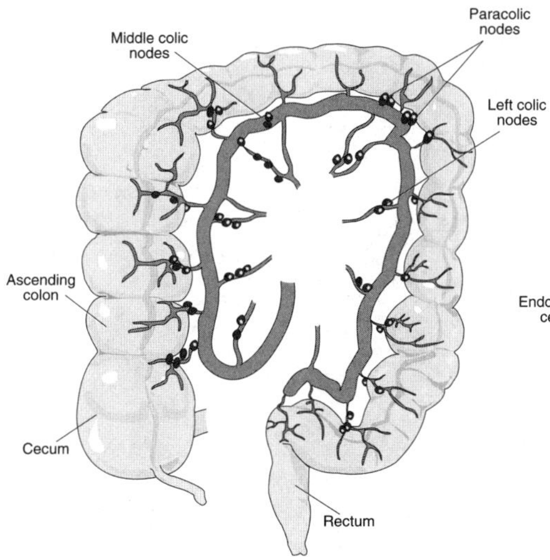

Lymphatic drainage of the colon follows blood supply

Schematic of lymphatic capillaries

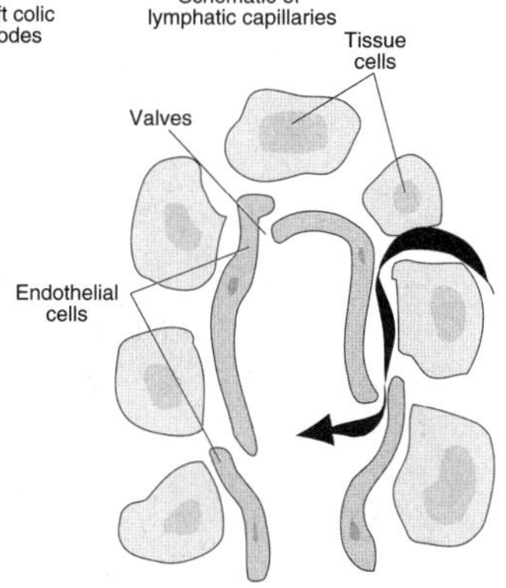

Fluids and particles can enter the capillary through overlapping valves

Endocrine System

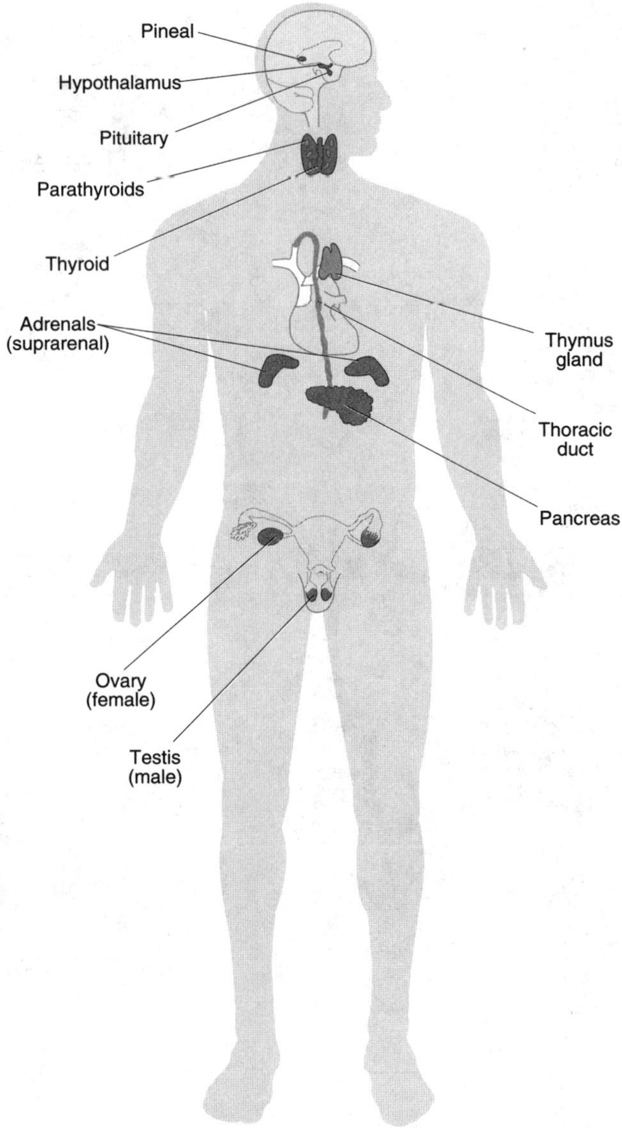

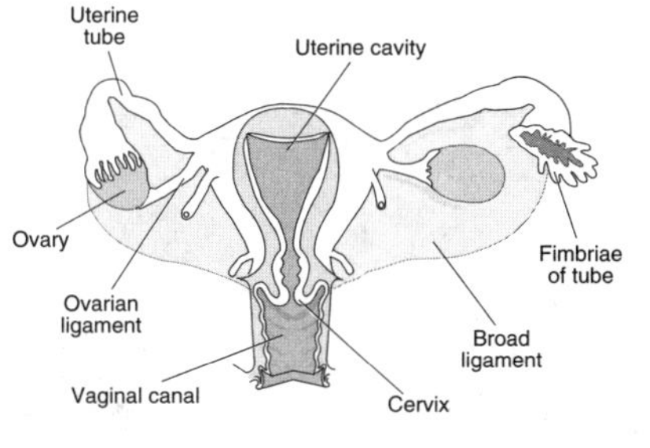

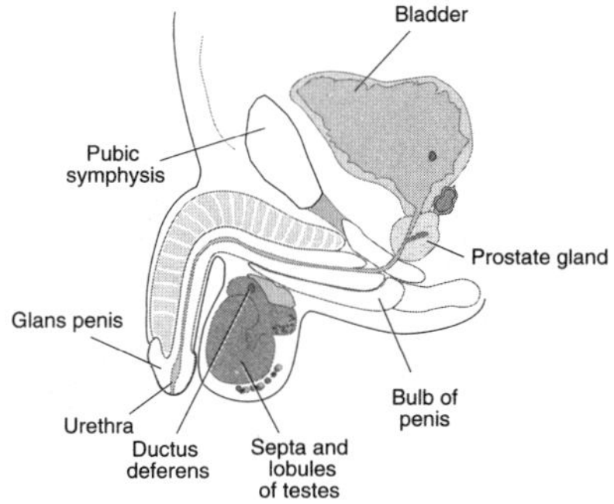

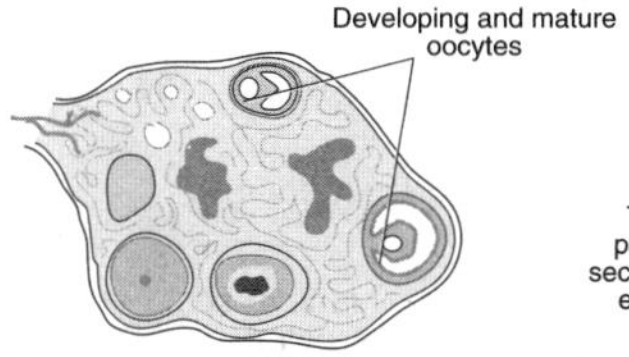

Cross section of ovary showing development of egg (oocyte)

The placenta is considered part of the endocrine system, secreting chorionic gonadotropin, estrogen, progesterone, and somatomammotropin

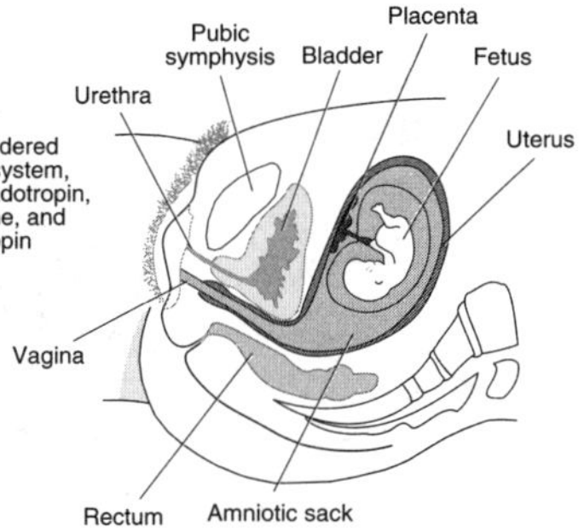

The thyroid gland governs body metabolism

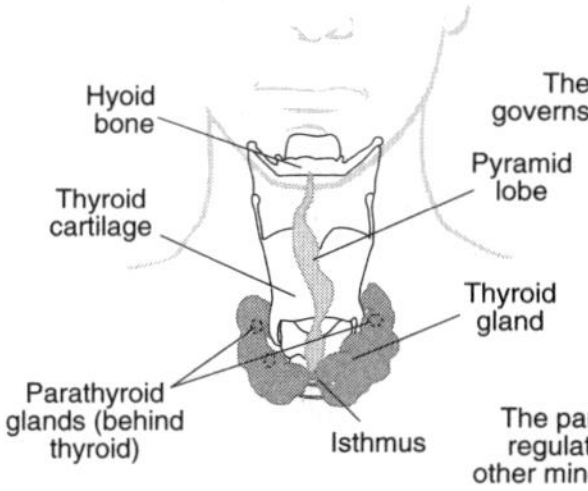

The parathyroid glands regulates calcium and other minerals and vitamins

The pancreas secretes insulin and glucagon, which regulate glucose, lipid and protein metabolism

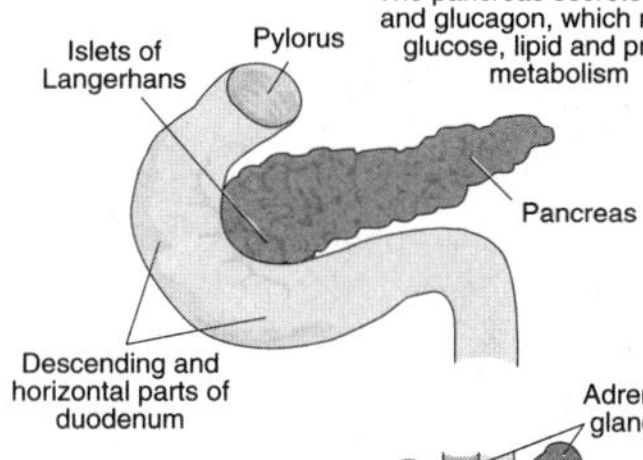

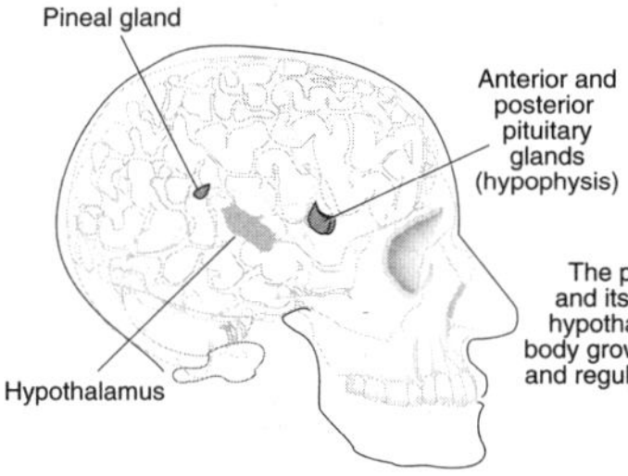

The pituitary gland and its controller, the hypothalamus, control body growth and stimulate and regulate other glands

The adrenal glands (or suprarenal glands) govern numerous metabolic functions and are closely associated with the kidneys

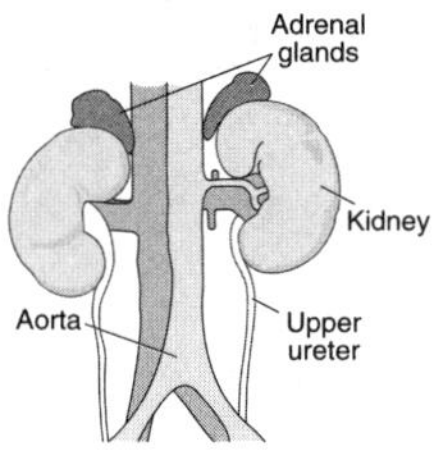

Digestive Tract

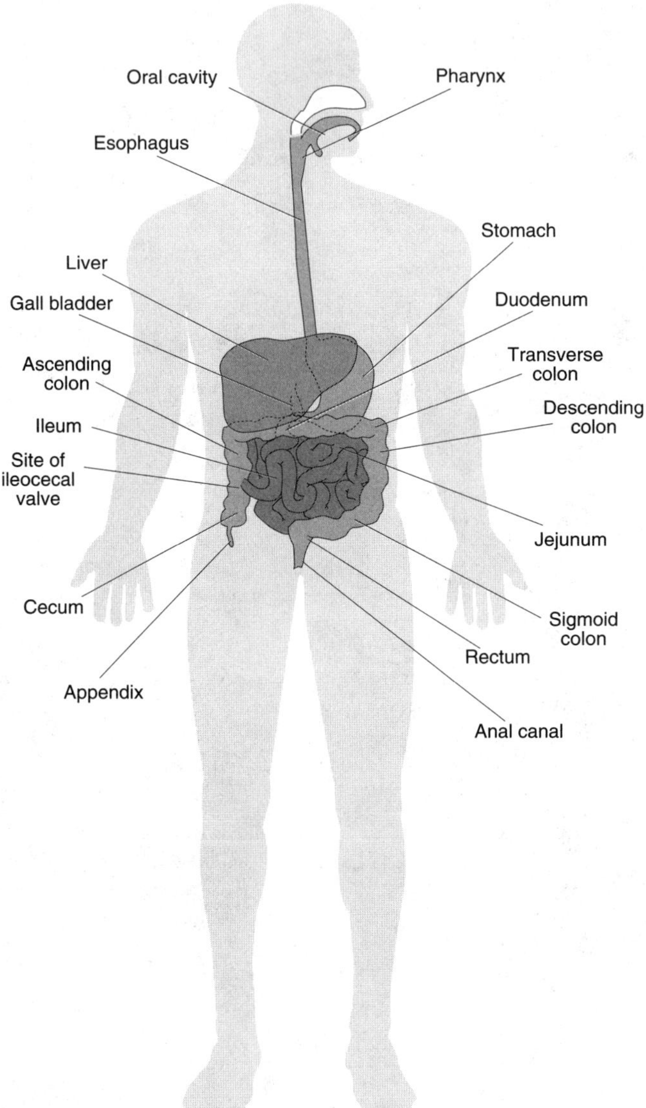

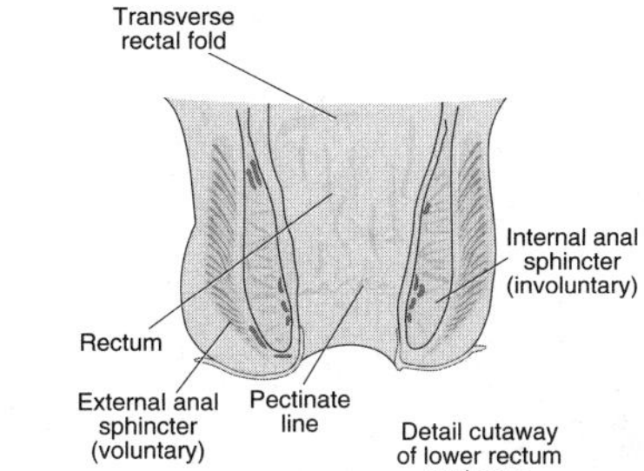

Detail cutaway of lower rectum and anus

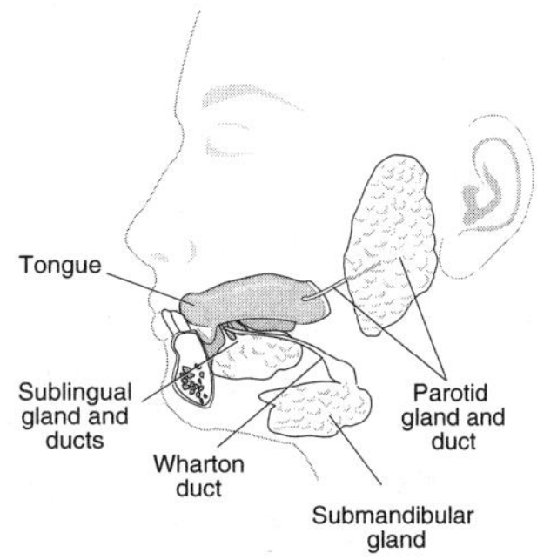

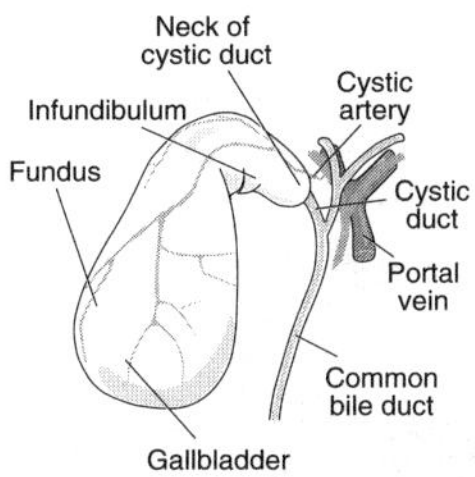

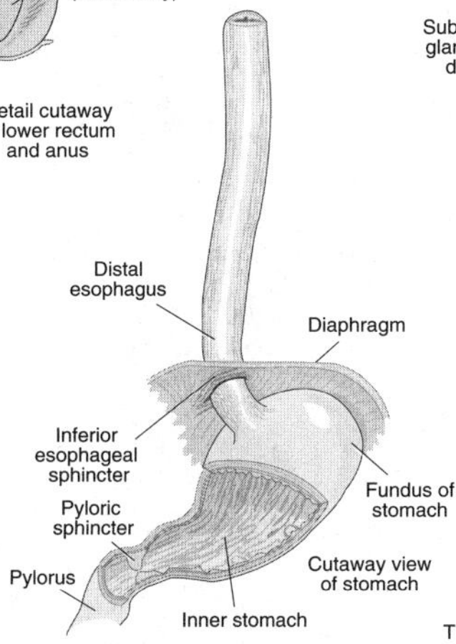

Cutaway view of stomach

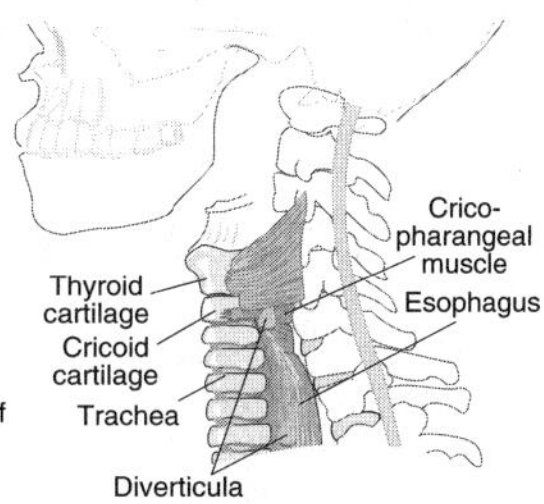

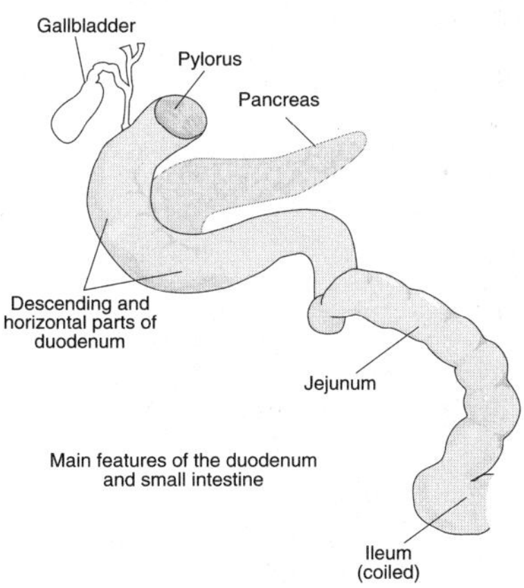

Main features of the duodenum and small intestine

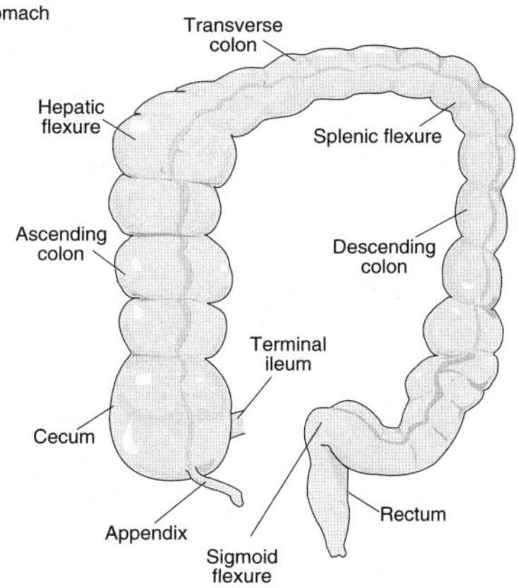

Nervous System

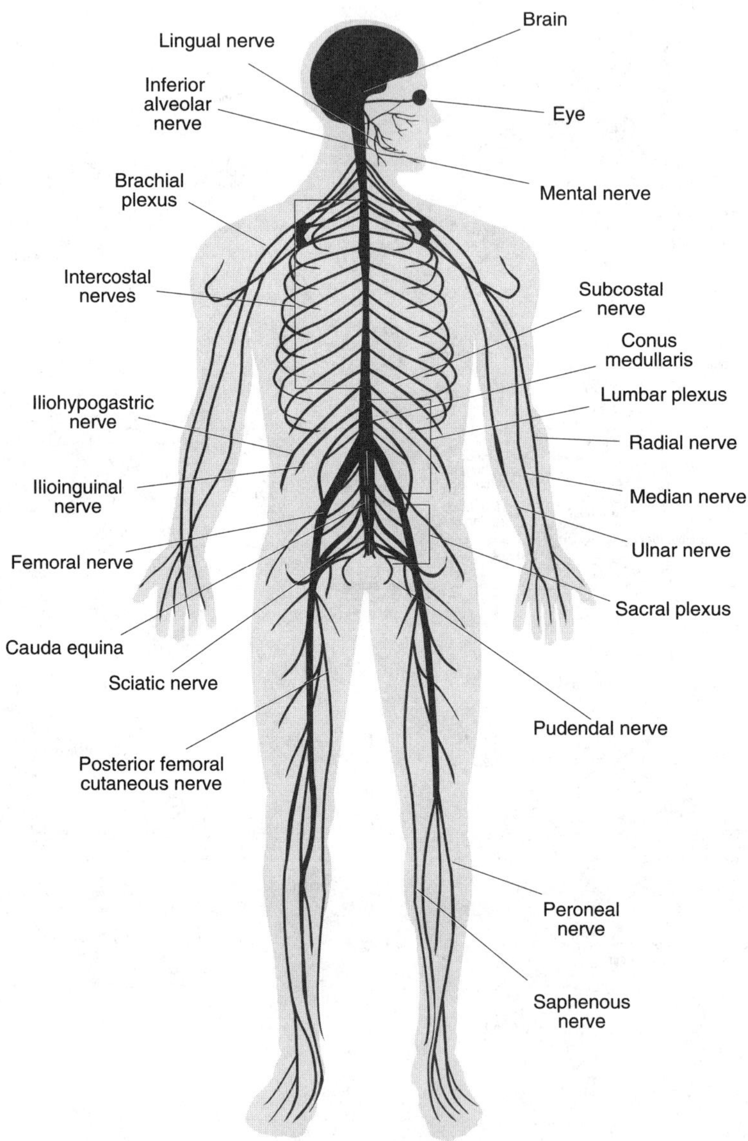

Anatomy Charts

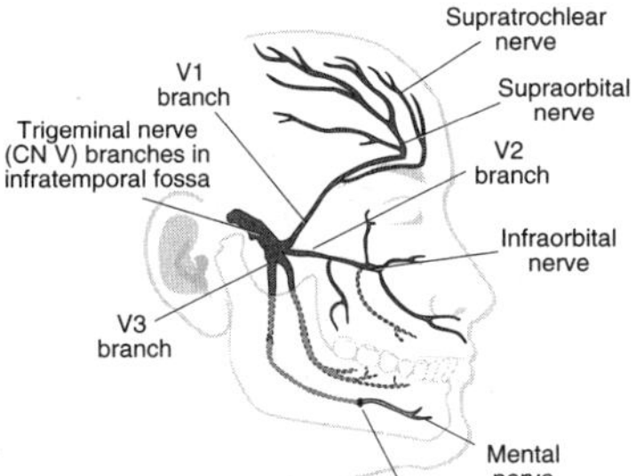

Branches of the trigeminal nerve

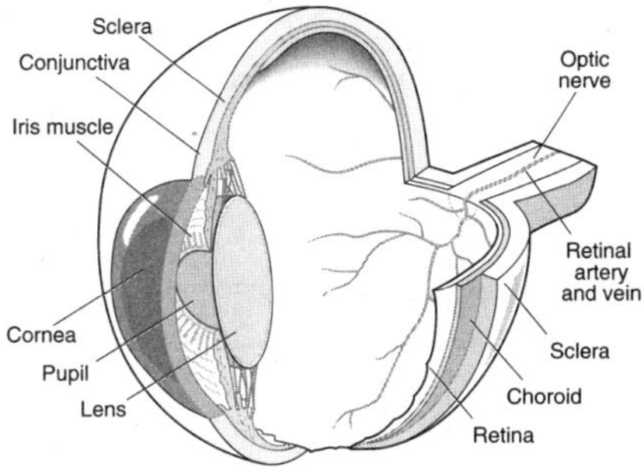

Anterior and posterior chambers of the eye

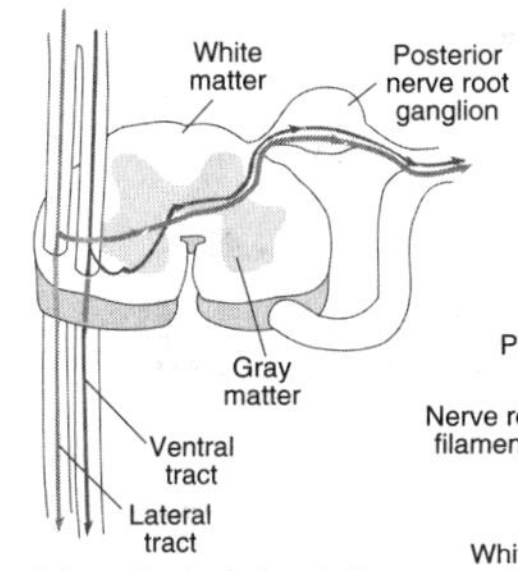

Schematic of spinal cord slice showing simplified sensory tracts and nerve roots

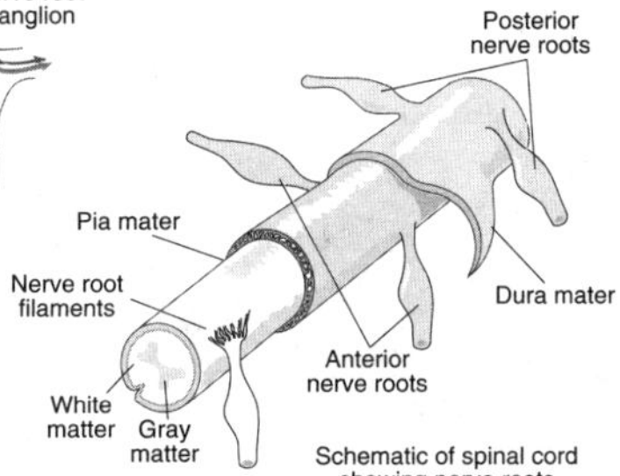

Schematic of spinal cord showing nerve roots

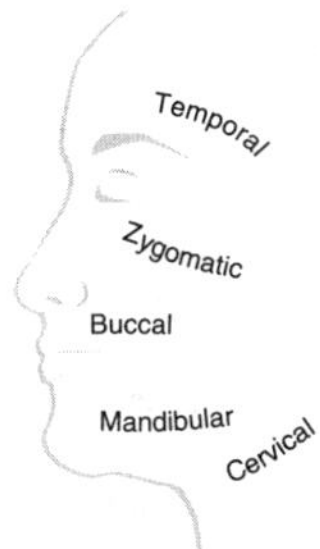

The main branches of the facial nerve (CN VII)

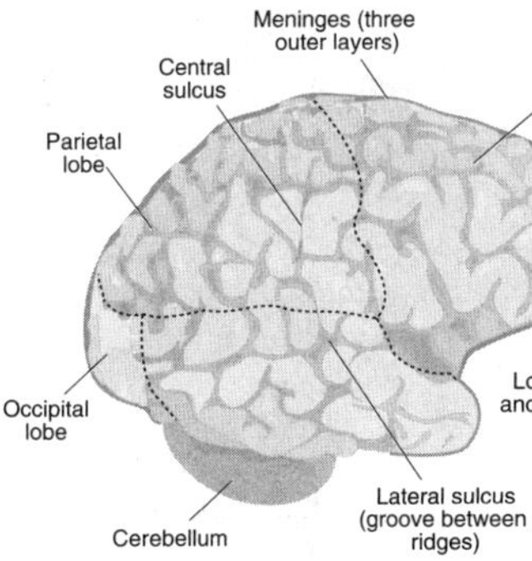

Lobes of the brain and surface features

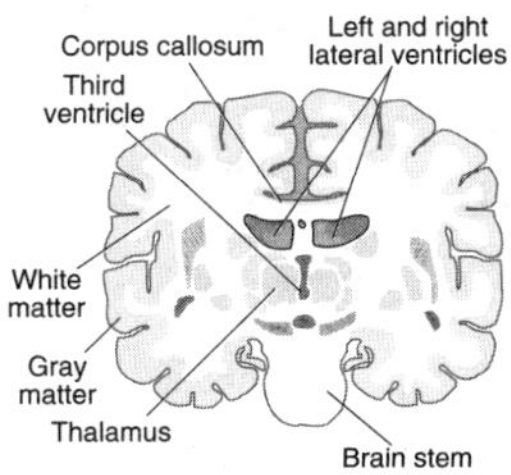

Frontal section of the brain

Circulatory System: Arterial

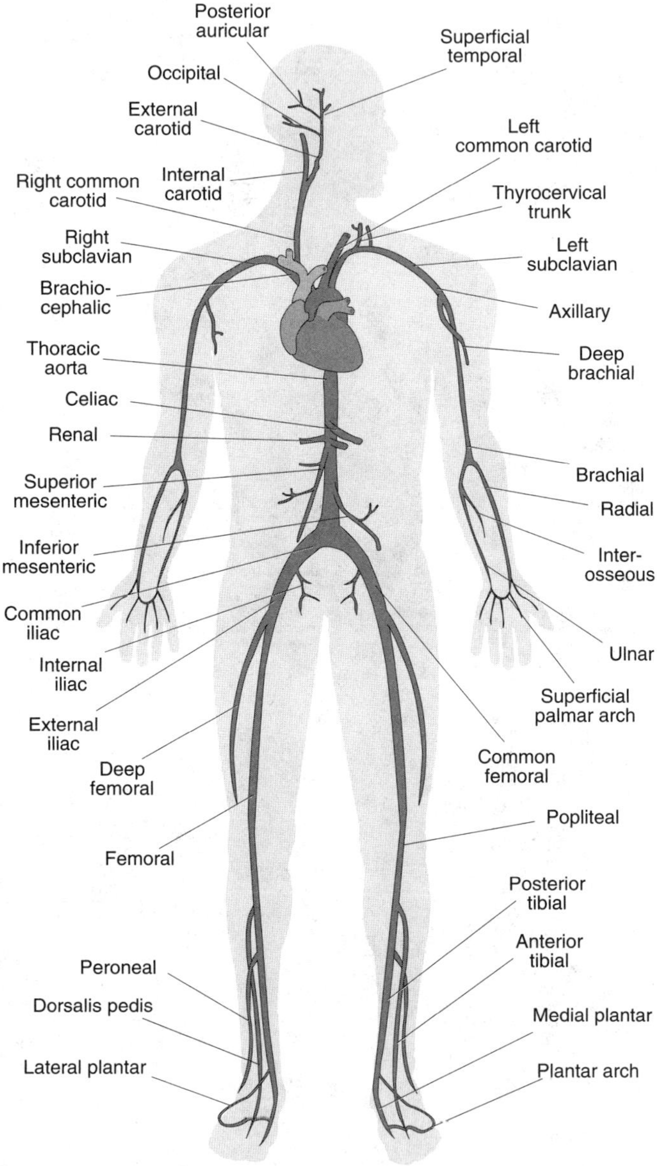

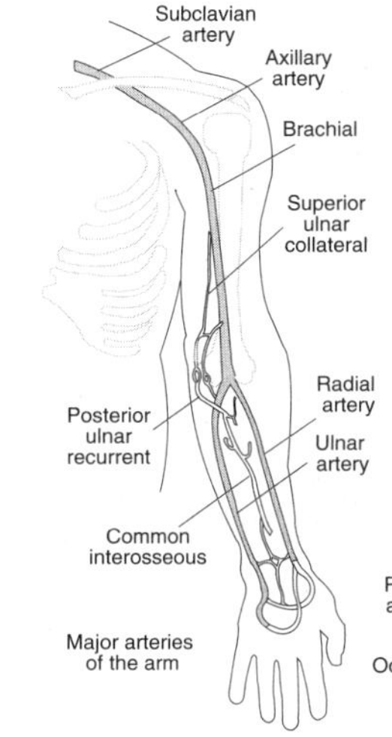

Major arteries of the arm

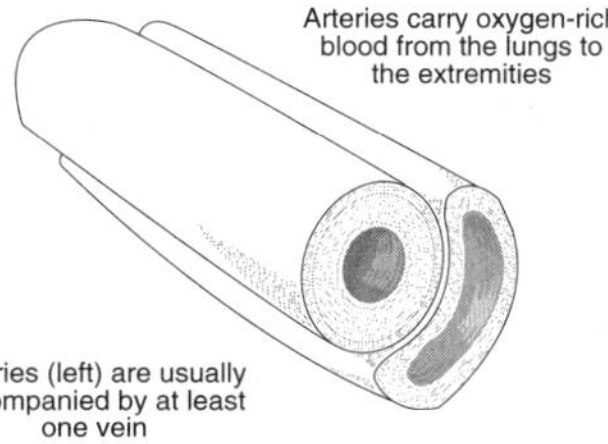

Arteries carry oxygen-rich blood from the lungs to the extremities

Arteries (left) are usually accompanied by at least one vein

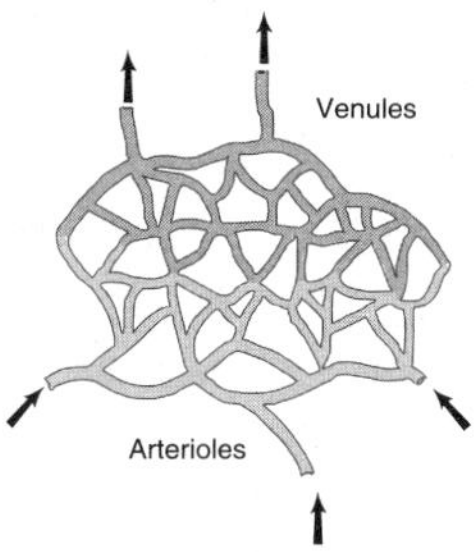

Schematic of a capillary bed containing arterioles, the smallest type of artery

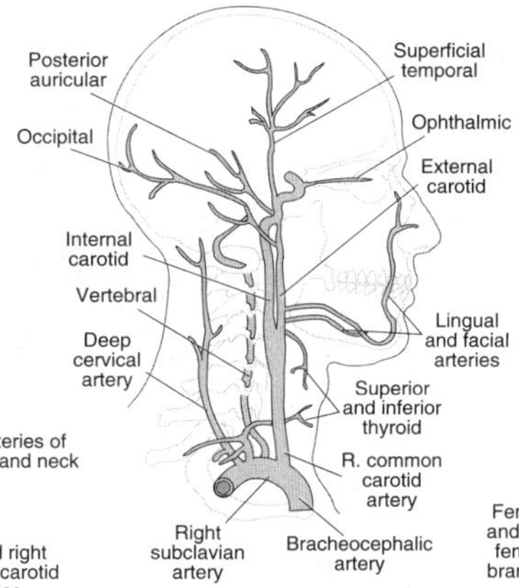

Major arteries of the head and neck

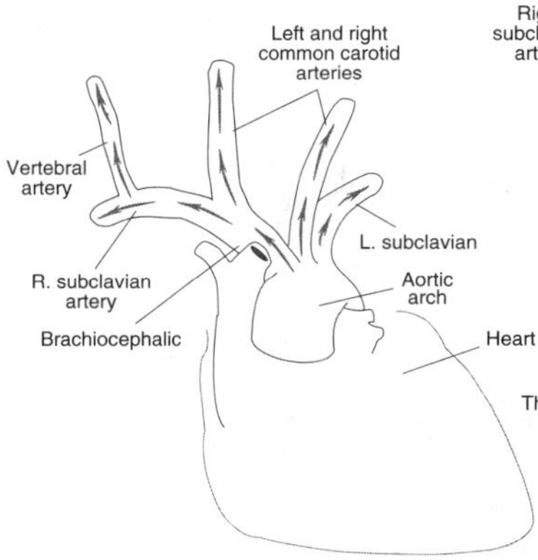

The great vessels

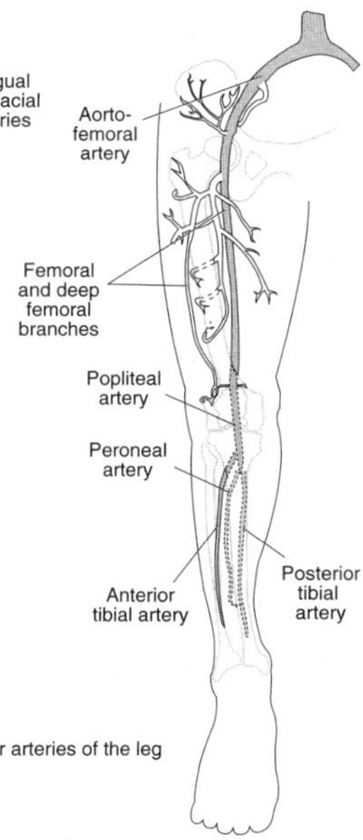

Major arteries of the leg

Anatomy Charts

Circulatory System: Venous

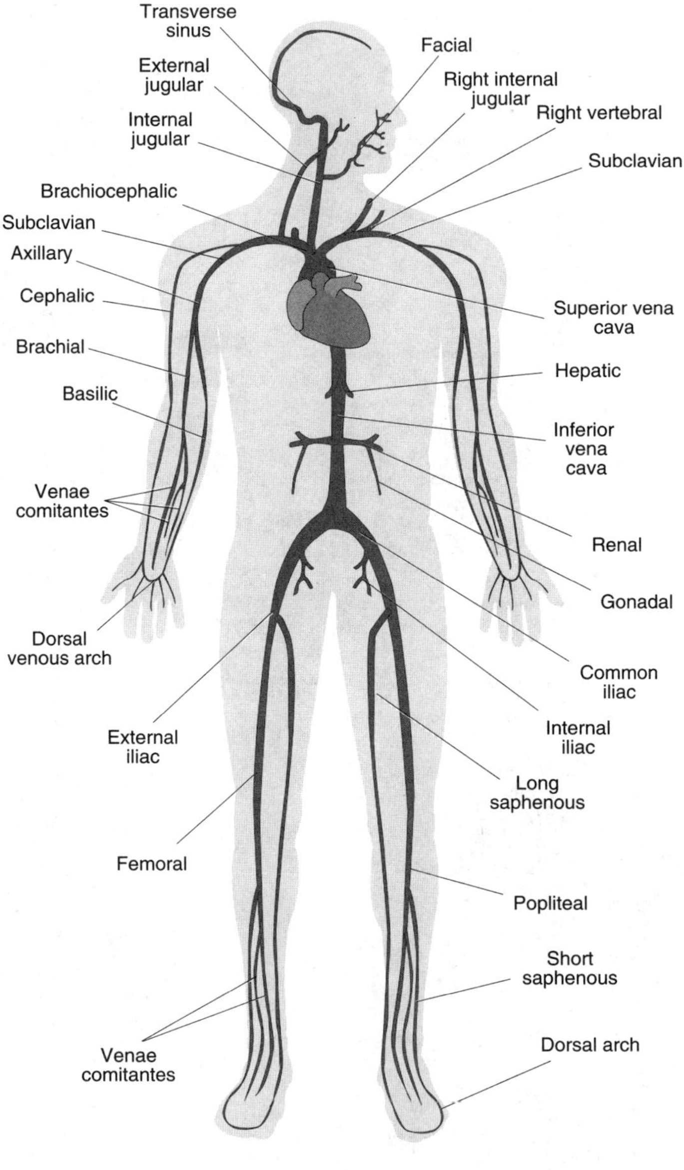

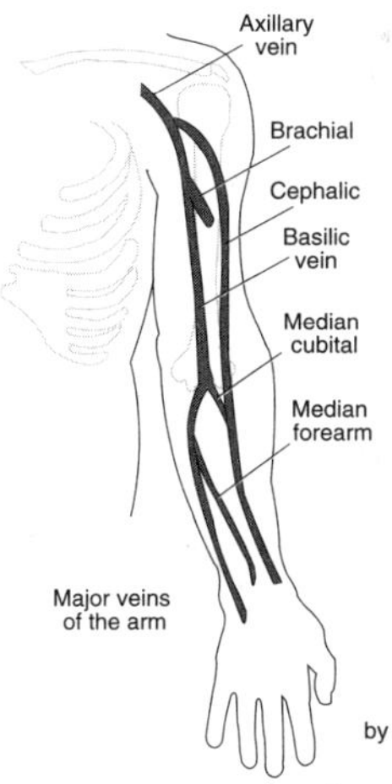

Major veins of the arm

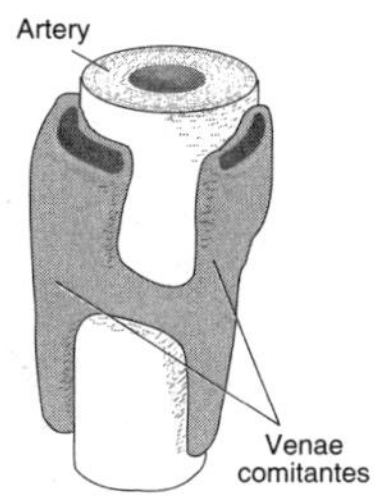

Arteries are typically accompanied by paired veins known as "venae comitantes"

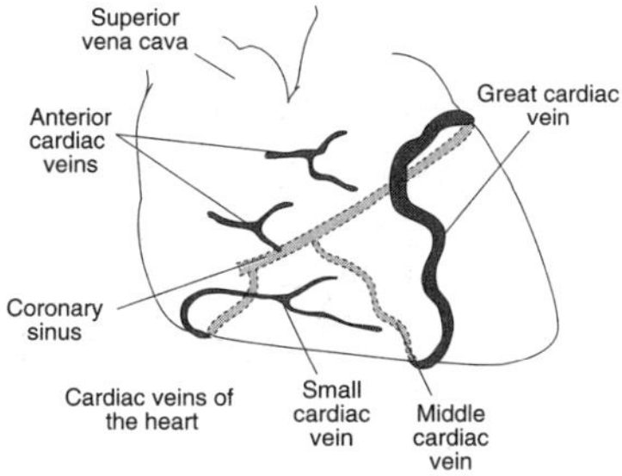

Cardiac veins of the heart

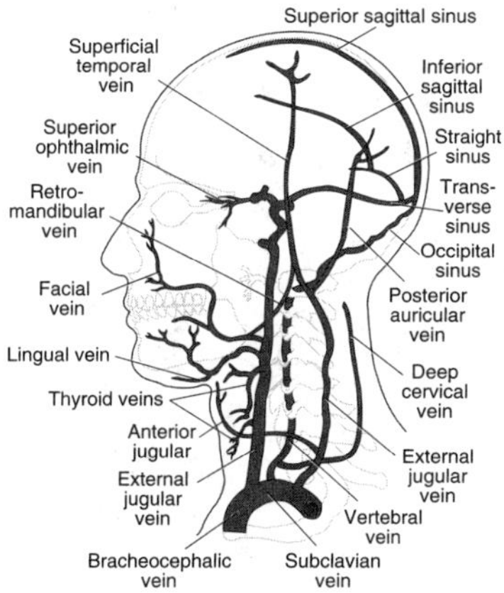

Venous blood flow is assisted by valves in the lumen of the vessels

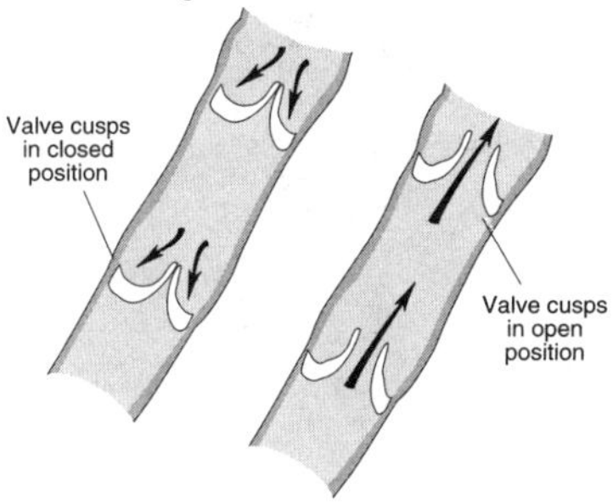

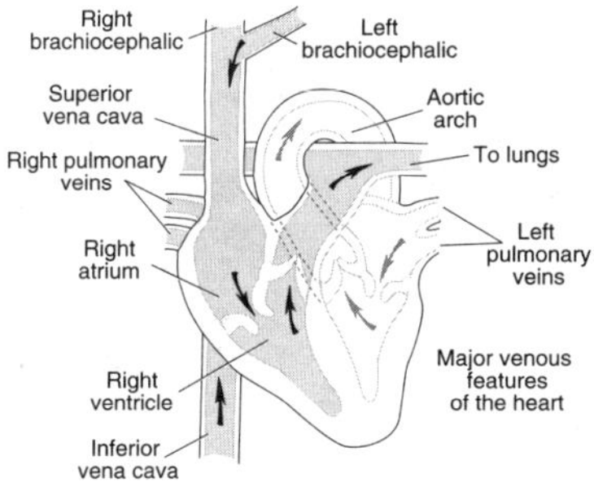

Major venous features of the heart

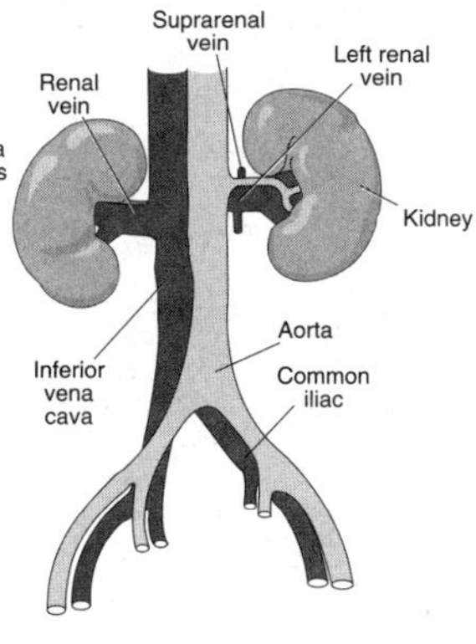

The inferior vena cava and its main tributaries

Urogenital Tract

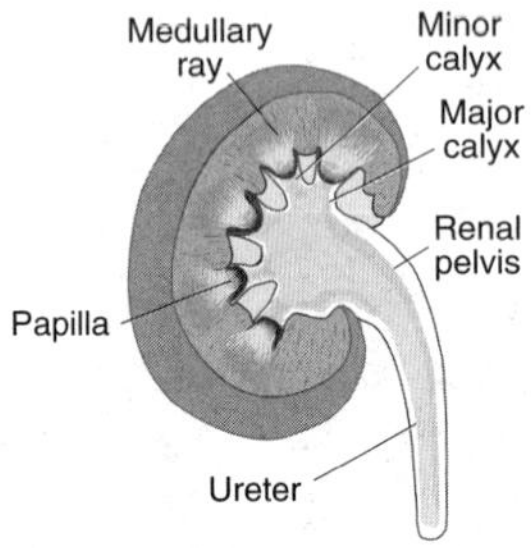

Cutaway detail of right kidney

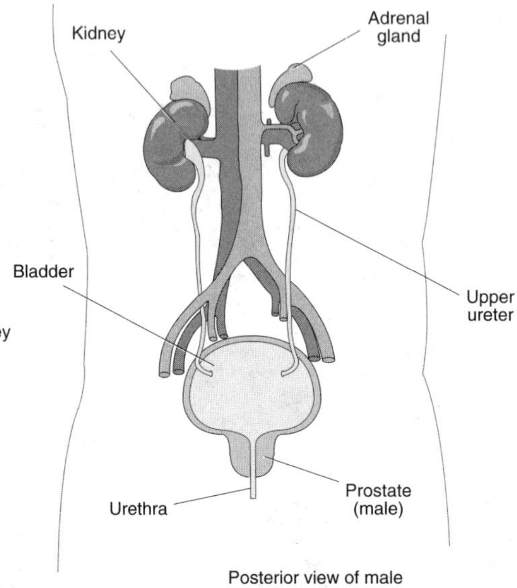

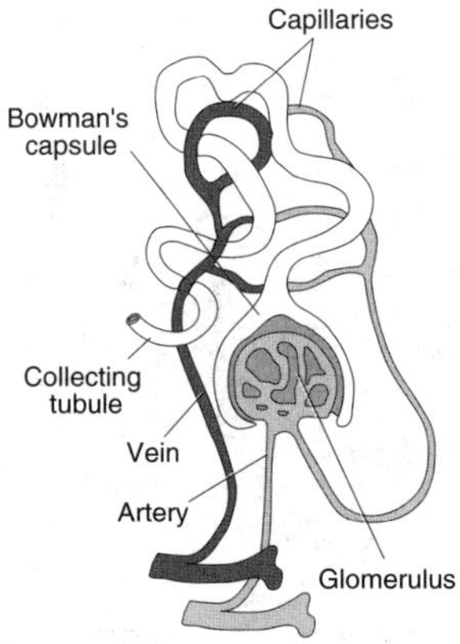

Schematic of nephron, the tiny filtering mechanism of the kidney

Posterior view of male bladder and prostate

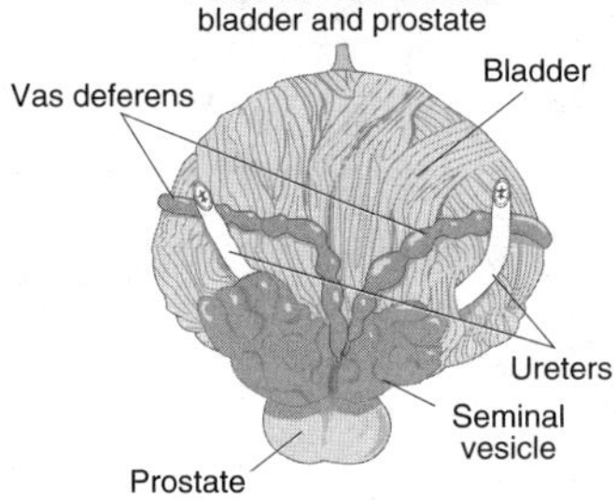

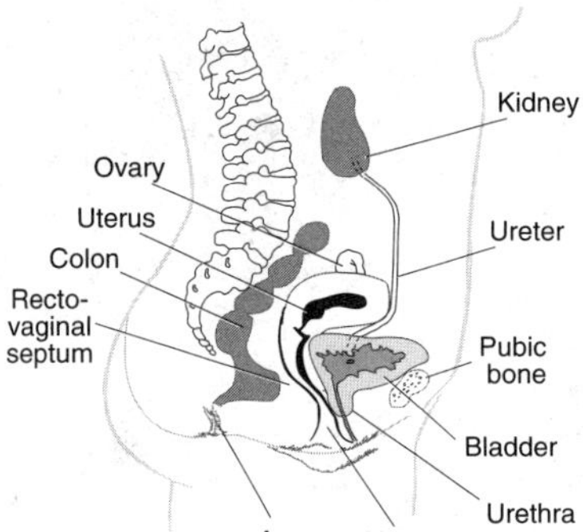

Sideview schematic of female urogenital system

Posterior view showing location of kidneys and ureters

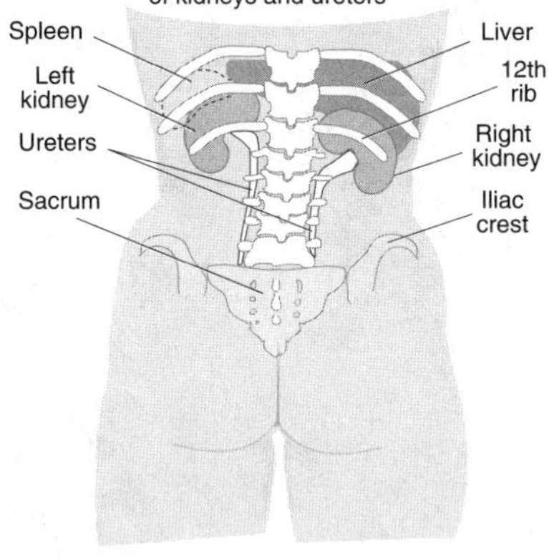

Anatomy Charts

Respiratory System

The bronchi (dark below) branch further into bronchioles and then into alveolar sacs where venous blood is aerated

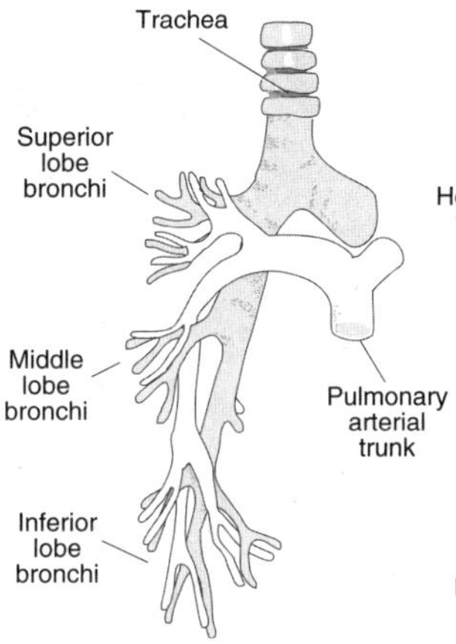

The pulmonary arteries (white above) deliver venous blood to the lungs where it is oxygenated and converted into arterial blood

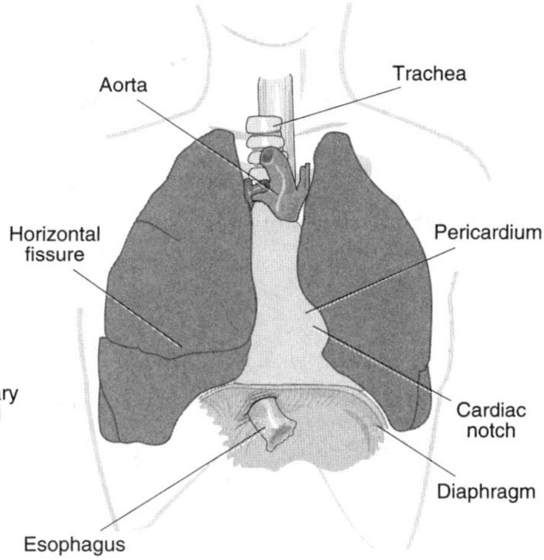

The right lung is larger and heavier than its counterpart due to space lost to the bulge of the heart at the cardiac notch

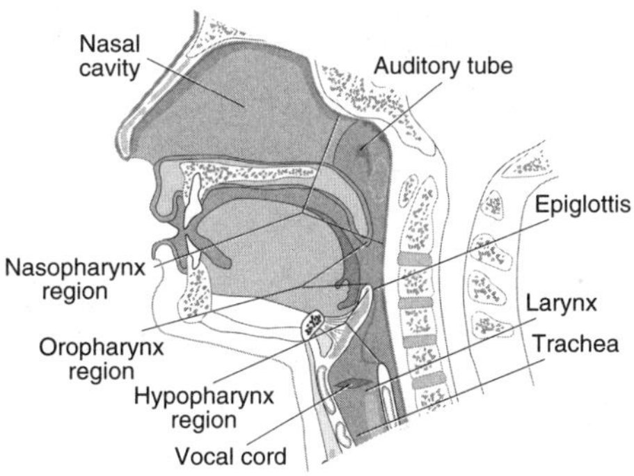

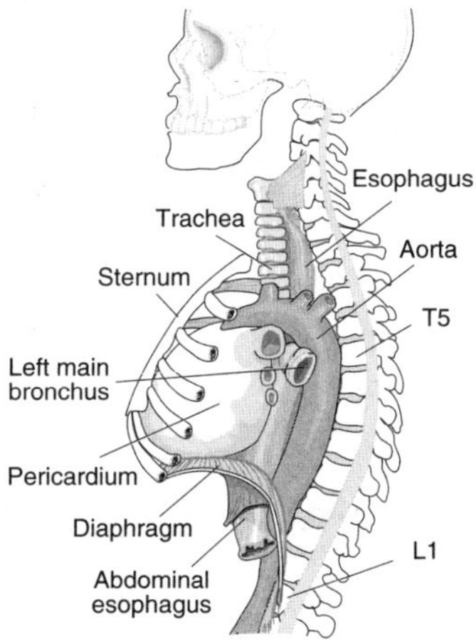

Body Planes and Movements

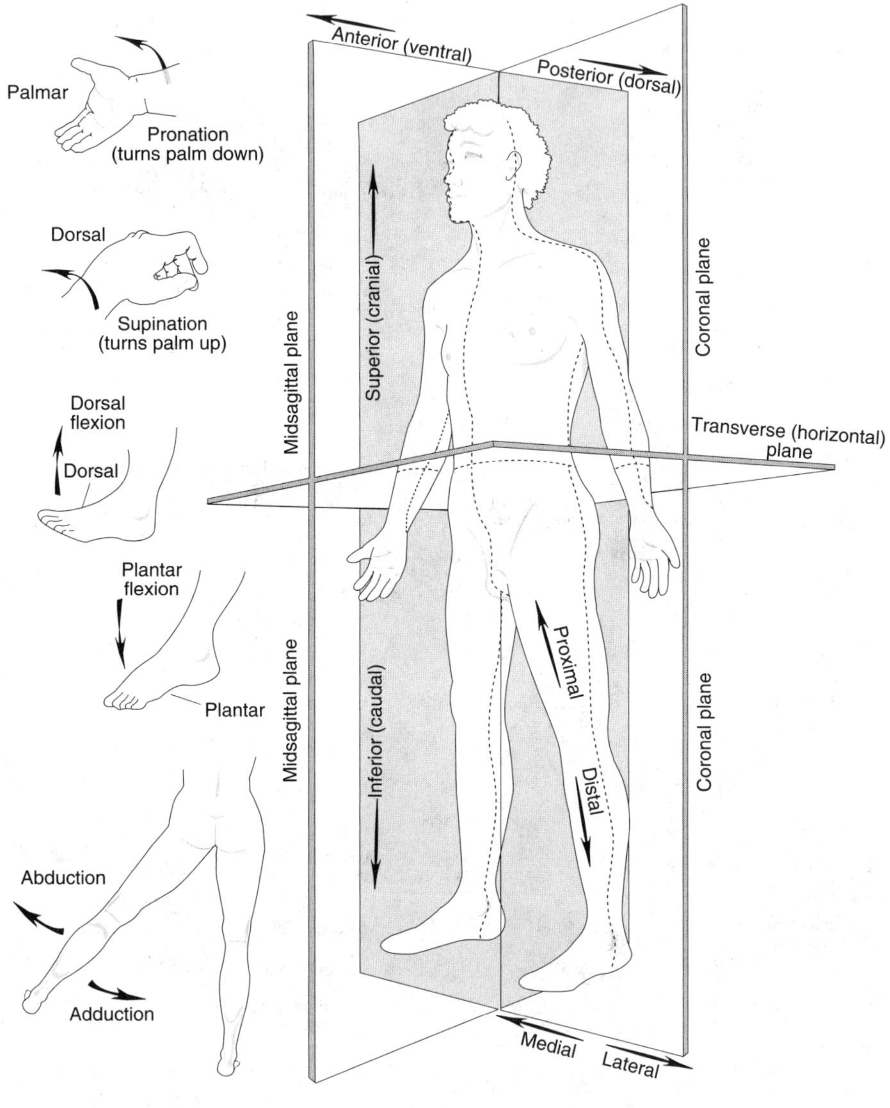

CPT® Lay Descriptions

CPT descriptions are written for people with medical training but may not offer the details needed to choose a code based on a patient's chart or an operative report. The following overview of the procedures listed in CPT describes the most common methods of each in general terms. Where possible, descriptions are in lay terms for coders' use. Key words used in the operative report are included to facilitate coding.

Unlisted procedures are excluded from this chapter. Be aware insurance payers usually review unlisted procedure codes manually, increasing processing time and the need for documentation.

Because some consecutive codes describe similar procedures, their descriptions have been combined under one heading, which indicates the range of codes described. If a satisfactory code description cannot be matched with the patient's chart, consult the physician.

Integumentary

10021-10022

Fine needle aspiration (FNA) is a percutaneous procedure that uses a fine gauge needle (often 22 or 25 gauge) and a syringe to sample fluid from a cyst or remove clusters of cells from a solid mass. First, the skin is cleansed. If a lump can be felt, the radiologist or surgeon guides a needle into the area by palpating the lump. If the lump is non-palpable, the FNA procedure is performed under image guidance using fluoroscopy, ultrasound, or computed tomography (CT), with the patient positioned according to the area of concern. In fluoroscopic guidance, intermittent fluoroscopy guides the advancement of the needle.
Ultrasonography-guided aspiration biopsy involves inserting an aspiration catheter needle device through the accessory channel port of the echoendoscope; the needle is placed into the area to be sampled under endoscopic ultrasonographic guidance. After the needle is placed into the region of the lesion, a vacuum is created and multiple in and out needle motions are performed. Several needle insertions are usually required to ensure that an adequate tissue sample is taken. CT image guidance allows computer-assisted targeting of the area to be sampled. At the completion of the procedure, the needle is withdrawn and a small bandage is placed over the area. Report 10021 if fine needle aspiration is performed without imaging guidance. Report 10022 if imaging guidance is used to assist in locating the lump.

10040

The physician makes a small incision through the skin overlying a lesion, or multiple lesions, such as comedones (blackheads), cysts, or pustules for acne surgery. The skin over the lesion is removed. The lesion is opened with a surgical instrument and the fluid is drained for secondary healing. The lesion may be removed or marsupialized by exteriorizing the cyst and making a pouch where it used to be enclosed. No sutures are needed. Do not bill a benign lesion excision code (11400-11446) and chemical exfoliation for acne (17360) on same date of service with 10040.

10060-10061

The physician makes a small incision through the skin overlying an abscess for incision and drainage (e.g., carbuncle, cyst, furuncle, paronychia, hidradenitis). The abscess or cyst is opened with a surgical instrument, allowing the contents to drain. The lesion may be curetted and irrigated. The physician leaves the surgical wound open to allow for continued drainage. For complicated or multiple cysts in 10061, the physician may place a Penrose latex drain or gauze strip packing to allow continued drainage. Complicated cysts may require later surgical closure. Report 10060 for incision and drainage of a simple or single abscess.

10080-10081

Pilonidal cysts are entrapped epithelial tissue located in the sacrococcygeal region above the buttocks. These cysts may produce fluid or exudate into the cystic lining and are usually associated with ingrown hair. An incision is made to allow drainage of cystic fluid or exudate. Curettage is performed to remove the cystic epithelial lining. The wound heals secondarily relying on local wound care. Report 10081 if the procedure is more complicated and requires excision of tissue, primary closure, and/or Z-plasty.

10120-10121

The physician removes a foreign body embedded in subcutaneous tissue. The physician makes a simple incision in the skin overlying the foreign body. The foreign body is retrieved using hemostats or forceps. The skin may be sutured or allowed to heal secondarily. Report 10121 if the procedure is more complicated, requiring dissection of underlying tissues.

10140

The physician makes an incision in the skin to decompress and drain a hematoma, seroma, or other collection of fluid. A hemostat bluntly penetrates the fluid pockets, allowing the fluid to evacuate. A latex drain or gauze packing may be placed into the incision site. This will allow the escape of any fluids that may continue to enter the pocket. A pressure dressing may be placed over the region. Any drain or packing is removed within 48 hours. The incision can be closed primarily or may be left to granulate without closure.

10160
The physician performs a puncture aspiration of an abscess, hematoma, bulla, or cyst. The palpable collection of fluid is located subcutaneously. The physician cleanses the overlying skin and introduces a large bore needle on a syringe into the fluid space. The fluid is aspirated into the syringe, decompressing the fluid space. A pressure dressing may be placed over the site.

10180
This procedure treats an infected postoperative wound. A more complex than usual incision and drainage procedure is necessary to remove the fluid and allow the surgical wound to heal. The physician first removes the surgical sutures or staples and/or makes additional incisions into the skin. The wound is drained of infected fluid. Any necrotic tissue is removed from the surgical site and the wound is irrigated. The wound may be sutured closed or packed open with gauze to allow additional drainage. If closed, the surgical site may have suction or latex drains placed into the wound. If packed open, the wound may be sutured again during a later procedure.

11000-11001
The physician surgically removes extensive diseased or infected skin. The skin may be of an eczematous nature possessing erythema, vesicles, and scales. Bacteria or fungus may be causing the skin infection. Wet compresses are used initially to remove scaly skin. Abrasive techniques may be employed to remove remaining scales. A scalpel may be used to decompress vesicles and excise dead skin. After debridement, topical lubricants and antibiotic preparations are placed on the skin. Report 11000 for up to 10 percent of the body surface. Report 11001 once for each additional 10 percent of the body surface, or part thereof, in addition to the primary procedure.

11004-11006
Debridement is carried out for a severe type of tissue infection that causes gangrenous changes, systemic disease, and tissue death. These types of infections are caused by virulent strains of bacteria, such as "flesh-eating" streptococcus, and affect the skin, subcutaneous fat, muscle tissue, and muscle fascia. Surgery is performed immediately upon diagnosis to open and drain the infected area, excise the dead or necrotic tissue. Report 11004 for surgical debridement of necrotic soft tissue in the external genitalia and perineum; 11005 for the abdominal wall, with or without surgical closure of the abdominal fascia; and 11006 for both areas, with or without surgical closure of the abdominal fascia.

11008
The physician removes prosthetic material or mesh previously placed in the abdominal wall. This may be done due to the presence of a chronic infection, a necrotizing soft tissue infection, or a recurrent mesh infection. Surgery is performed immediately after diagnosis and usually under general anesthesia. The skin is incised and the tissue dissected exposing the prosthetic material. Debridement of the tissue adjacent to or incorporated in the mesh may be performed with instruments or irrigation. Unincorporated or infected areas of the mesh are excised and removed with any remaining areas of infection or necrotic tissue. Incorporated mesh that is not infected may be left in the wound. The area is irrigated and the wound is sutured.

11010-11012
The physician surgically removes foreign matter and contaminated or devitalized skin and other tissue in and around the site of a fracture or dislocation. This debridement is done in preparation for treating the fracture. Debridement reported with this service includes prolonged cleansing of the wound, removal of all foreign or dead tissue material using forceps, scissors, scalpel, or other instruments, exploration of all injured soft tissue—including tendons, ligaments, and nerves, as well as irrigation of all layers of tissue. Contamination of a wound by foreign matter is usually associated with open fractures, although this type of debridement may be performed with open or closed fractures and/or dislocations and is done to reduce swelling and bleeding, and to leave behind viable tissue. Report 11010 for skin and subcutaneous tissue debridement; 11011 for skin, subcutaneous tissue, muscle fascia, and muscle layers; and 11012 for debridement of skin, subcutaneous tissue, muscle fascia, muscle, and bone.

11040-11042
The physician surgically removes necrotic or dead skin. The physician uses a scalpel or dermatome to remove a superficial layer of affected skin. The epidermal layer is removed with the underlying dermis remaining intact. The partial thickness of skin is excised until viable, bleeding tissue is encountered. A topical antibiotic is placed on the wound. A gauze dressing or an occlusive dressing may be placed over the surgical site. Report 11040 for partial thickness debridement; 11041 for full thickness and 11042 if debridement includes subcutaneous tissue.

11043-11044
The physician surgically removes necrotic skin, underlying tissue, and muscle. The physician uses a scalpel to excise the affected tissue into the muscle layer. The dissection is continued until viable, bleeding tissue is encountered. Depending on wound size, closure may be immediate or delayed. The wound may be packed open with gauze and require immediate or

delayed reconstruction. Report 11044 if bone is also debrided.

11055-11057
The physician removes a benign hyperkeratotic skin lesion such as a corn or callus by cutting, clipping, or paring. Report 11055 when one lesion is removed; 11056 when two to four lesions are removed; and 11057 when more than four lesions are removed.

11100-11101
The physician removes a biopsy sample of skin, subcutaneous tissue, and/or mucous membrane for histologic study under a microscope. A single lesion is biopsied in 11100. Report 11101 for each separate lesion biopsied in addition to the primary procedure. Some normal tissue adjacent to the diseased tissue is also removed for comparison purposes. The excision site may be closed simply or may be allowed to granulate without closure.

11200-11201
The physician removes skin tag lesions. Skin tags are common benign tumors found on many body regions, most frequently around the axillae, inguinal area, head, and neck. The physician uses sharp excision with scissors or scalpel, chemical cautery, electrical cautery, ligature strangulation, or any combination of these methods. Report 11200 for up to 15 lesions and 11201 for each additional 10 lesions, or part thereof, beyond the initial 15.

11300-11303
The physician removes a single, elevated epidermal or dermal lesion from the trunk, arm, or legs by shave excision. Local anesthesia is injected beneath the lesion. A scalpel blade is placed against the skin adjacent to the lesion and the physician uses a horizontal slicing motion to excise the lesion from its base. The wound does not require suturing and bleeding is controlled by chemical or electrical cauterization. Report 11300 for a lesion diameter 0.5 cm or less; 11301 for 0.6 cm to 1 cm; 11302 for 1.1 cm to 2 cm; and 11303 for lesions greater than 2 cm.

11305-11308
The physician removes a single, elevated epidermal or dermal lesion from the scalp, neck, hands, feet, or genitalia by shave excision. Local anesthesia is injected beneath the lesion. A scalpel blade is placed against the skin adjacent to the lesion and the physician uses a horizontal slicing motion to excise the lesion from its base. The wound does not require suturing and bleeding is controlled by chemical or electrical cauterization. Report 11305 for a lesion diameter 0.5 cm or less; 11306 for 0.6 cm to 1 cm; 11307 for 1.1 cm to 2 cm; and 11308 for lesions greater than 2 cm.

11310-11313
The physician removes a single, elevated epidermal or dermal lesion from the face, ears, eyelids, lips, nose, or mucous membrane by shave excision. Local anesthesia is injected beneath the lesion. A scalpel blade is placed against the skin adjacent to the lesion and the physician uses a horizontal slicing motion to excise the lesion from its base. The wound does not require suturing and bleeding is controlled by chemical or electrical cauterization. Report 11310 for a lesion diameter 0.5 cm or less; 11311 for 0.6 cm to 1 cm; 11312 for 1.1 cm to 2 cm; and 11313 for lesions greater than 2 cm.

11400-11406
The physician excises a benign (noncancerous) lesion, including the margins, except a skin tag, on the trunk, arms, or legs. After administering a local anesthetic, the physician makes a full-thickness incision through the dermis with a scalpel, usually in an elliptical shape around and under the lesion, and removes it. The physician may suture the wound simply. Complex or layered closure is reported separately, if required. Report 11400 for an excised diameter 0.5 cm or less; 11401 for 0.6 cm to 1 cm; 11402 for 1.1 cm to 2 cm; 11403 for 2.1 cm to 3 cm; 11404 for 3.1 cm to 4 cm; and 11406 if the excised diameter is greater than 4 cm.

11420-11426
The physician excises a benign (noncancerous) lesion, including the margins, except a skin tag, on the scalp, neck, hands, feet, and genitalia. After administering a local anesthetic, the physician makes a full-thickness incision through the dermis with a scalpel, usually in an elliptical shape around and under the lesion, and removes it. The physician may suture the wound simply. Complex or layered closure is reported separately, if required. Report 11420 for an excised diameter 0.5 cm or less; 11421 for 0.6 cm to 1 cm; 11422 for 1.1 cm to 2 cm; 11423 for 2.1 cm to 3 cm; 11424 for 3.1 cm to 4 cm; and 11426 if the excised diameter is greater than 4 cm.

11440-11446
The physician removes a benign (noncancerous) lesion, except a skin tag, including the margins, from the eyelids, ears, face, lips, nose, or mucous membrane. After administering a local anesthetic, the physician makes a full-thickness incision through the dermis with a scalpel, usually in an elliptical shape around and under the lesion, and removes it. The physician may suture the wound simply. Complex or layered closure is reported separately, if required. Report 11440 for an excised diameter 0.5 cm or less; 11441 for 0.6 cm to 1 cm; 11442 for 1.1 cm to 2 cm; 11443 for 2.1 cm to 3 cm; 11444 for 3.1 cm to 4 cm; and 11446 if the excised diameter is greater than 4 cm.

11450-11451
Hidradenitis is a chronic suppurative disease that produces scarring of the skin and subcutaneous tissue. Clinically visible are at least two blackheads with several surface openings, subcutaneous communication, and subsequent abscess formation in the axillary region. The abscesses lead to extensive

scarring of the dermis. The physician performs a wide excision of the abscess. The excision site is left open to heal by granulation or may be sutured simply or in layers for 11450. Report 11451 if complex repair requires local pedicle flap coverage or skin grafting.

11462-11463
Hidradenitis is a chronic suppurative disease that produces scarring of the skin and subcutaneous tissue. Clinically visible are at least two blackheads with several surface openings, subcutaneous communication, and subsequent abscess formation in the inguinal region. The abscesses lead to extensive scarring of the dermis. The physician performs a wide excision of the abscess. The excision site is left open to heal by granulation or may be sutured simply or in layers for 11462. Report 11463 if complex repair requires local pedicle flap coverage or skin graft.

11470-11471
Hidradenitis is a chronic suppurative disease that produces scarring of the skin and subcutaneous tissue. Clinically visible are at least two blackheads with several surface openings, subcutaneous communication, and subsequent abscess formation in the perianal, perineal, or umbilical regions. The abscesses lead to extensive scarring of the dermis. The physician performs a wide excision of the abscess. The excision site is left open to heal by granulation or may be sutured simply or in layers for 11470. Report 11471 if complex repair requires local pedicle flap coverage or skin graft.

11600-11606
The physician removes a malignant lesion, including the margins, from the trunk, arms, or legs. After administering a local anesthetic, the physician makes a full-thickness incision through the skin, usually in an elliptical shape around and under the lesion. The lesion and a rim of normal tissue are removed. The skin incision is sutured simply. Complex or layered closure is reported separately, if required. Immediate reconstruction with local flaps may be necessary and is also reported separately. Report 11600 for an excised diameter 0.5 cm or less; 11601 for 0.6 cm to 1 cm; 11602 for 1.1 cm to 2 cm; 11603 for 2.1 cm to 3 cm; 11604 for 3.1 cm to 4 cm; and 11606 if the excised diameter is greater than 4 cm.

11620-11626
The physician removes a malignant lesion, including the margins, from the scalp, neck, hands, feet, or genitalia. After administering a local anesthetic, the physician makes a full-thickness incision through the skin, usually in an elliptical shape around and under the lesion. The lesion and a rim of normal tissue are removed. The skin incision is sutured simply. Complex or layered closure is reported separately, if required. Immediate reconstruction with local flaps may be necessary and is also reported separately. Report 11620 for an excised diameter 0.5 cm or less; 11621 for 0.6 cm to 1 cm; 11622 for 1.1 cm to 2 cm; 11623 for 2.1 cm to 3 cm; 11624 for 3.1 cm to 4 cm; and 11626 if the excised diameter is greater than 4 cm.

11640-11646
The physician removes a malignant lesion, including the margins, from the face, ears, eyelids, nose, or lips. After administering a local anesthetic, the physician makes a full-thickness incision through the skin, usually in an elliptical shape around and under the lesion. The lesion and a rim of normal tissue are removed. The skin incision is sutured simply. Complex or layered closure is reported separately, if required. Immediate reconstruction with local flaps may be necessary and is also reported separately. Report 11640 for an excised diameter 0.5 cm or less; 11641 for 0.6 cm to 1 cm; 11642 for 1.1 cm to 2 cm; 11643 for 2.1 cm to 3 cm; 11644 for 3.1 cm to 4 cm; and 11646 if the excised diameter is greater than 4 cm.

11719
A physician trims a fingernail or toenail usually with scissors, nail cutters, or other instruments. This code is used when the nails are not defective from nutritional or metabolic abnormalities. It is used for one or more nails.

11720-11721
The physician debrides fingernails or toenails, including tops and exposed undersides, by any method. The cleaning is performed manually with cleaning solutions, abrasive materials, and tools. The nails are shortened and shaped. Report 11720 for one to five nails and 11721 for six or more.

11730-11732
The physician avulses a nail plate partially or completely. A digital nerve block is used to numb the top of the digit. The physician bluntly dissects the nail plate from the nail bed. Any bleeding is cauterized. The digit is bandaged. Report 11730 if only one nail plate is removed. Report 11732 for each additional nail plate removed.

11740
The physician evacuates blood from a hematoma located beneath a fingernail or toenail. The physician uses an electrocautery needle to pierce the nail plate so a hematoma can drain. Pressure may be applied to the nail bed to force the blood from beneath the nail plate. A loose dressing is applied so the area can continue to drain.

11750-11752
The physician removes all or part of a fingernail or toenail, including the nail plate and matrix. In 11750, the physician bluntly dissects the nail plate away from the nail bed. The germ matrix is destroyed using electrocautery or excision. Bleeding is stopped with electrocautery and the wound is dressed. In 11752, the tuft of the distal phalanx is removed.

11755
The physician removes a portion of the nail unit for a biopsy sample. Sections may be taken from the hard nail itself, the nail bed, lateral skin, or underlying soft tissue. The specimen is excised by clippers or with a scalpel.

11760
The physician repairs a damaged nail bed. The physician removes the damaged and surrounding nail from the nail bed. The nail bed is sutured into correct position. Bleeding is controlled through electrocautery and the wound is dressed.

11762
The physician repairs a damaged nail bed using a skin graft. The physician cleans the nail bed and prepares it for the graft. The graft is obtained and sutured into place. Hemostasis is achieved and a dressing is applied.

11765
The physician excises a wedge of restrictive skin in the nail fold to free an ingrown nail. The physician performs a wedge excision of the skin overlapping the lateral nail. The nail is examined and trimmed to encourage straight growth. The wound is dressed.

11770-11772
A pilonidal cyst or sinus is entrapped epithelial tissue located in the sacrococcygeal region above the buttocks. These lesions are usually associated with ingrown hair. A sinus cavity is present and may have a fluid-producing cystic lining. With a small or simple sinus in 11770, the physician uses a scalpel to completely excise the involved tissue. The wound is sutured in a single layer. In 11771, the extensive sinus is superficial to the underlying fascia but has subcutaneous extensions. The physician uses a scalpel to completely excise the lesion. The wound may be sutured in several layers. In 11772, the sinus is more complicated and has many subcutaneous extensions. The physician uses a scalpel to completely excise the involved tissue. Local soft tissue flaps (i.e., Z-plasty) may be required for closure of a large defect or the wound may be left open to heal by granulation.

11900-11901
The physician uses a syringe to inject a pharmacologic agent underneath or into seven or fewer skin lesions in 11900 and more than seven lesions in 11901. The lesions may be any healed skin lesions including post-laceration and post-surgical scar bands. The physician may inject steroids or anesthetics (not pre-operative local anesthetic) into these lesions.

11920-11922
The physician introduces insoluble opaque pigment into color defects of the skin. A marking pen is used first to outline the area to be tattooed. The dye is injected into the skin with a pneumatic tattooing instrument to create an artificially pigmented area that approximates the appearance of normal skin tissue. Report 11920 for a tattoo area of 6 sq cm or less, 11921 for 6.1 sq cm to 20 sq cm, and 11922 for each additional 20 sq cm or part thereof.

11950-11954
The physician uses an injectable dermal implant to correct small soft tissue deformities. This technique is used to treat facial wrinkles, post-surgical defects, and acne scars. The injectable filling material can be autologous fat, synthetic surgical compound, or a commercially produced collagen preparation. The physician uses a syringe to inject the selected material into the dermis of the skin. The injection will augment the dermal layer and alleviate the soft tissue depression. Report 11950 for an injection of 1 cc or less; 11951 for 1.1 cc to 5 cc; 11952 for 5.1 cc to 10 cc; and 11954 for an injection of more than 10 cc.

11960
The physician uses a tissue expander to stretch skin and soft tissue prior to definitive reconstruction on tissue other than breast. These expanders are balloon-type devices that stretch the skin and enhance epithelial and collagen expansion and reduce or eliminate the need for skin grafts during reconstruction. The physician makes an incision into the skin. The subcutaneous layer is identified. Blunt dissection is used to separate the skin and subcutaneous layers. The tissue expander is placed into the prepared site. The wound is sutured. The expander is inflated. During the post-operative visits, greater volume is placed into the expander stretching the skin. The expander remains in place until the final reconstruction is performed.

11970
The physician removes a subcutaneous tissue expander and places a permanent prosthesis for final reconstruction. The tissue expander is deflated. The physician uses a scalpel to make an incision. Blunt dissection is used to remove the tissue expander. The permanent prosthesis is placed into the recipient bed. The prosthesis may be an autologous graft or commercially prepared synthetic material. The graft prosthesis may require stabilization with sutures, wires, or screws. The incision is closed with sutures.

11971
The physician removes a subcutaneous tissue expander without placing a prosthesis or performing final reconstruction. Initially, the tissue expander is deflated. The physician uses a scalpel to make an incision. Blunt dissection is used to remove the tissue expander. A surgical drain may be placed in the wound. The incision is closed with sutures.

11975
The physician makes a small incision in the skin on the inside of the upper arm of a female patient and, using a trocar, inserts implantable contraceptive capsules subdermally. The trocar is a sharp-tipped metal tube

through which the capsules are passed. The incision is closed.

11976
The physician makes a small incision in the skin on the inside of the upper arm of a female patient and removes contraceptive capsules previously implanted subdermally. The incision is closed.

11977
The physician makes a small incision in the skin on the inside of the upper arm of a female patient and removes contraceptive capsules previously implanted subdermally. New capsules are inserted in their place or into a new site. The incision is closed.

11980
Biodegradable time-release medication pellets are implanted subcutaneously for the slow delivery of hormones. The physician makes a small incision in the skin with a scalpel. A trocar and cannula are inserted into the incised area. Hormone pellets are inserted through the cannula and the cannula is withdrawn. Pressure is applied to the incised area until any bleeding is stopped, and the incision is closed with Steri-strips. The time-release medication is typically used for women who require hormone replacement therapy during menopause. One method is to implant pellets of testosterone and/or estradiol (taken in conjunction with progesterone) into the fatty tissue of the buttocks. New pellets may be inserted whenever symptoms recur, usually in six to nine months.

11981
A non-biodegradable drug delivery implant is inserted to deliver a therapeutic dose of the drug continuously at a predetermined rate of release. One such system works via a semipermeable membrane at one end of the subcutaneous cylinder that permits the entrance of fluid; the drug is delivered from a port at the other end of the cylinder at a controlled rate appropriate to the specific therapeutic agent. The physician injects local anesthesia and makes a small incision in the skin with a scalpel to insert the miniature drug-containing titanium, surgical grade stainless steel or polymeric cylinder, which is held in place with sutures tied by a knot or secured by a single running stitch. The wound is closed with sutures. Various types of medications for different indications may be administered via a non-biodegradable drug delivery implant system that may come in other forms.

11982
A non-biodegradable drug delivery implant that delivers a therapeutic dose of the drug continuously at a predetermined rate of release is removed. One such system works via a semipermeable membrane at one end of the subcutaneous cylinder that permits the entrance of fluid; the drug is delivered from a port at the other end of the cylinder at a controlled rate appropriate to the specific therapeutic agent. The physician injects local anesthesia and makes a small incision in the skin with a scalpel to remove a previously implanted miniature drug-containing titanium, surgical grade stainless steel or polymeric cylinder. The wound is closed with sutures. Various types of medications for different indications may be administered via a non-biodegradable drug delivery implant system that may come in other forms.

11983
A non-biodegradable drug delivery implant that delivers a therapeutic dose of the drug continuously at a predetermined rate of release is removed with reinsertion of a new one. One such system works via a semipermeable membrane at one end of the subcutaneous cylinder that permits the entrance of fluid; the drug is delivered from a port at the other end of the cylinder at a controlled rate appropriate to the specific therapeutic agent. The physician injects local anesthesia and makes a small incision in the skin with a scalpel to remove a previously implanted miniature drug-containing titanium, surgical grade stainless steel or polymeric cylinder. A replacement cylinder is inserted and held in place with sutures tied by a knot or secured by a single running stitch. The wound is closed with sutures. Various types of medications for different indications may be administered as a non-biodegradable drug delivery implant system that may come in other forms.

12001-12007
The physician sutures superficial lacerations of the scalp, neck, axillae, external genitalia, trunk, or extremities. A local anesthetic is injected around the laceration and the wound is cleansed, explored, and often irrigated with a saline solution. The physician performs a simple, one-layer repair of the epidermis, dermis, or subcutaneous tissues with sutures. With multiple wounds of the same complexity and in the same anatomical area, the length of all wounds sutured is summed and reported as one total length. Report 12001 for a total length of 2.5 cm or less; 12002 for 2.6 cm to 7.5 cm; 12004 for 7.6 cm to 12.5 cm; 12005 for 12.6 cm to 20 cm; 12006 for 20.1 cm to 30 cm; and 12007 if the total length is greater than 30 cm.

12011-12018
The physician sutures superficial lacerations of the face, ears, eyelids, nose, lips, and/or mucous membranes. A local anesthetic is injected around the laceration and the wound is cleansed, explored, and often irrigated with a saline solution. The physician performs a simple, one-layer repair of the epidermis, dermis, or subcutaneous tissue with sutures. With multiple wounds of the same complexity and in the same anatomical area, the length of all wounds sutured is summed and reported as one total length. Report 12011 for a total length of 2.5 cm or less; 12013 for 2.6 cm to 5 cm; 12014 for 5.1 cm to 7.5 cm; 12015 for 7.6 cm to 12.5 cm; 12016 for 12.6 cm to 20 cm;

12017 for 20.1 cm to 30 cm; and 12018 if the total length is greater than 30 cm.

12020-12021
There has been a breakdown of the healing skin either before or after suture removal. The skin margins have opened. The physician cleanses the wound with irrigation and antimicrobial solutions. The skin margins may be trimmed to initiate bleeding surfaces. Report 12020 if the wound is sutured in a single layer. Report 12021 if the wound is left open and packed with gauze strips due to the presence of infection. This allows infection to drain from the wound and the skin closure will be delayed until the infection is resolved.

12031-12037
The physician performs an intermediate repair of a laceration of the scalp, axillae, trunk, and/or extremities (except hands and feet) using layered closure. A local anesthetic is injected around the laceration, and the wound is cleansed, explored, and often irrigated with a saline solution. Due to deeper or more complex lacerations, deep subcutaneous or layered suturing techniques are required. The physician closes tissue layers under the skin with dissolvable sutures before suturing the skin. Extensive cleaning or removal of foreign matter from a heavily contaminated wound that is closed with a single layer may also be reported as an intermediate repair. With multiple wounds of the same complexity and in the same anatomical area, the length of all wounds sutured is summed and reported as one total length. Report 12031 for a total length of 2.5 cm or less; 12032 for 2.6 cm to 7.5 cm; 12034 for 7.6 cm to 12.5 cm; 12035 for 12.6 cm to 20 cm; 12036 for 20.1 cm to 30 cm; and 12037 if the total length is greater than 30 cm.

12041-12047
The physician performs an intermediate repair of a laceration of the neck, hands, feet, and/or external genitalia using layered closure. A local anesthetic is injected around the laceration, and the wound is cleansed, explored, and often irrigated with a saline solution. Due to deeper or more complex lacerations, deep subcutaneous or layered suturing techniques are required. The physician closes tissue layers under the skin with dissolvable sutures before suturing the skin. Extensive cleaning or removal of foreign matter from a heavily contaminated wound that is closed with a single layer may also be reported as an intermediate repair. With multiple wounds of the same complexity and in the same anatomical area, the length of all wounds sutured is summed and reported as one total length. Report 12041 for a total length of 2.5 cm or less; 12042 for 2.6 cm to 7.5 cm; 12044 for 7.6 cm to 12.5 cm; 12045 for 12.6 cm to 20 cm; 12046 for 20.1 cm to 30 cm; and 12047 if the total length is greater than 30 cm.

12051-12057
The physician performs an intermediate repair of a laceration of the face, ears, eyelids, nose, lips, and/or mucous membranes using layered closure. A local anesthetic is injected around the laceration, and the wound is cleansed, explored, and often irrigated with a saline solution. Due to deeper or more complex lacerations, deep subcutaneous or layered suturing techniques are required. The physician closes tissue layers under the skin with dissolvable sutures before suturing the skin. Extensive cleaning or removal of foreign matter from a heavily contaminated wound that is closed with a single layer may also be reported as an intermediate repair. With multiple wounds of the same complexity and in the same anatomical area, the length of all wounds sutured is summed and reported as one total length. Report 12051 for a total length of 2.5 cm or less; 12052 for 2.6 cm to 5 cm; 12053 for 5.1 cm to 7.5 cm; 12054 for 7.6 cm to 12.5 cm; 12055 for 12.6 cm to 20 cm; 12056 for 20.1 cm to 30 cm; and 12057 if the total length is greater than 30 cm.

13100-13102
The physician repairs complex wounds of the trunk. The physician performs complex, layered suturing of torn, crushed, or deeply lacerated tissue. The physician debrides the wound by removing foreign material or damaged tissue. Irrigation of the wound is performed and antimicrobial solutions are used to decontaminate and cleanse the wound. The physician may trim skin margins with a scalpel or scissors to allow for proper closure. The wound is closed in layers. The physician may perform scar revision, which creates a complex defect requiring repair. Stents or retention sutures may also be used in complex repair of a wound. Reconstructive procedures, such as utilization of local flaps, may be required and are reported separately. Report 13100 for wounds 1.1 cm to 2.5 cm; 13101 for 2.6 cm to 7.5 cm; and 13102 for each additional 5 cm or less.

13120-13122
The physician repairs complex wounds of the scalp, arms, and/or legs. The physician performs complex, layered suturing of torn, crushed, or deeply lacerated tissue. The physician debrides the wound by removing foreign material or damaged tissue. Irrigation of the wound is performed and antimicrobial solutions are used to decontaminate and cleanse the wound. The physician may trim skin margins with a scalpel or scissors to allow for proper closure. The wound is closed in layers. The physician may perform scar revision, which creates a complex defect requiring repair. Stents or retention sutures may also be used in complex repair of a wound. Reconstructive procedures, such as utilization of local flaps, may be required and are reported separately. Report 13120 for wounds 1.1 cm to 2.5 cm; 13121 for 2.6 cm to 7.5 cm; and 13122 for each additional 5 cm or less.

13131-13133
The physician repairs complex wounds of the forehead, cheeks, chin, mouth, neck, axillae, genitalia, hands, and/or feet. The physician performs complex, layered suturing of torn, crushed, or deeply lacerated tissue. The physician debrides the wound by removing foreign material or damaged tissue. Irrigation of the wound is performed and antimicrobial solutions are used to decontaminate and cleanse the wound. The physician may trim skin margins with a scalpel or scissors to allow for proper closure. The wound is closed in layers. The physician may perform scar revision, which creates a complex defect requiring repair. Stents or retention sutures may also be used in complex repair of a wound. Reconstructive procedures, such as utilization of local flaps, may be required and are reported separately. Report 13131 for wounds 1.1 cm to 2.5 cm; 13132 for 2.6 cm to 7.5 cm; and 13133 for each additional 5 cm or less.

13150-13153
The physician repairs complex wounds of the eyelids, nose, ears, and/or lips. The physician performs complex, layered suturing of torn, crushed, or deeply lacerated tissue. The physician debrides the wound by removing foreign material or damaged tissue. Irrigation of the wound is performed and antimicrobial solutions are used to decontaminate and cleanse the wound. The physician may trim skin margins with a scalpel or scissors to allow for proper closure. The wound is closed in layers. The physician may perform scar revision, which creates a complex defect requiring repair. Stents or retention sutures may also be used in complex repair of a wound. Reconstructive procedures, such as utilization of local flaps, may be required and are reported separately. Report 13150 for wounds 1 cm or less; 13151 for 1.1 cm to 2.5 cm; 13152 for 2.6 cm to 7.5 cm; and 13153 for each additional 5 cm or less.

13160
The physician secondarily repairs a surgical skin closure after an infectious breakdown of the healing skin. After resolution of the infection, the wound is now ready for closure. The physician uses a scalpel to excise granulation and scar tissue. Skin margins are trimmed to bleeding edges. The wound is sutured in several layers.

14000-14001
The physician transfers or rearranges adjacent tissue to repair traumatic or surgical wounds of the trunk. This includes, but is not limited to, such rearrangement procedures as Z-plasty, W-plasty, ZY-plasty, or tissue transfers such as rotational or advancement flaps. Report 14000 for defects that are 10 sq cm or less and 14001 for defects that are 10.1 sq cm to 30 sq cm.

14020-14021
The physician transfers or rearranges adjacent tissue to repair traumatic or surgical wounds of the scalp, arms, and/or legs. This includes, but is not limited to, such rearrangement procedures as Z-plasty, W-plasty, ZY-plasty, or tissue transfers such as rotational or advancement flaps. Report 14020 for defects that are 10 sq cm or less and 14021 for defects that are 10.1 sq cm to 30 sq cm.

14040-14041
The physician transfers or rearranges adjacent tissue to repair traumatic or surgical wounds on the forehead, cheeks, chin, mouth, neck, axillae, genitalia, hands, and/or feet. This includes, but is not limited to, such rearrangement procedures as Z-plasty, W-plasty, ZY-plasty, or tissue transfers such as rotational flaps or advancement flaps. Report 14040 for defects that are 10 sq cm or less and 14041 for defects that are 10.1 sq cm to 30 sq cm.

14060-14061
The physician transfers or rearranges adjacent tissue to repair traumatic or surgical wounds of the eyelids, nose, ears, and/or lips. This includes, but is not limited to, such rearrangement procedures as Z-plasty, W-plasty, ZY-plasty, or tissue transfers such as rotational flaps or advancement flaps. Report 14060 for defects that are 10 sq cm or less and 14061 for defects that are 10.1 sq cm to 30 sq cm.

14301-14302
The physician transfers or rearranges adjacent tissue of any area to repair traumatic or surgical wounds. This includes, but is not limited to, such rearrangement procedures as Z-plasty, W-plasty, ZY-plasty, or tissue transfers such as rotational flaps or advancement flaps. Report 14301 for defects 30.1 sq cm to 60 sq cm. Report 14302 for each additional 30 sq cm or part thereof.

14350
The physician creates a filleted finger or toe flap to repair a large deficit on the hand or foot. The physician makes a bilateral longitudinal incision and dissects the tissue away from the donor site, protecting vascular integrity. The recipient site is prepared and the flap is rotated into place. Excess tissue is excised and the wound is sutured in layers.

15002-15003
The physician prepares tissue to receive a free skin graft needed to close or repair a defect. Skin, subcutaneous tissue, scars, burn eschar, and lesions are excised to provide a healthy, vascular tissue bed (where new vessels have been formed) onto which a skin graft will be placed. Alternatively, the physician may prepare tissue by incising or excising a scar contracture that is causing excessive tightening of the skin. Simple debridement of granulations or of recent avulsion is included. Report 15002 for the first 100 sq cm or 1 percent of body area of infants and children for grafts of the trunk arms and legs. Report 15003 for each additional 100 sq cm (or part thereof) of graft area or

each additional 1 percent of surface body area in infants and children within the same areas.

15004-15005

The physician prepares tissue to receive a free skin graft needed to close or repair a defect. Skin, subcutaneous tissue, scars, burn eschar, and lesions are excised to provide a healthy, vascular tissue bed (where new vessels have been formed) onto which a skin graft will be placed. Alternatively, the physician may prepare tissue by incising or excising a scar contracture that is causing excessive tightening of the skin. Simple debridement of granulations or of recent avulsion is included. Report 15004 for the first 100 sq cm or 1 percent of body area in infants and children of the face, scalp, eyelids, mouth, neck, ears, orbits, genitalia, hands, and/or feet. Report 15005 for each additional 100 sq cm (or part thereof) or each additional 1 percent of body area in infants and children.

15040

The physician harvests skin (keratinocytes and dermal tissue), 100 sq cm or less, to use for a tissue cultured skin autograft. The donor site is first injected with epinephrine solution to control blood loss and aid the skin harvesting technique. Skin is harvested by taking a split-thickness graft with a dermatome, up to 100 sq cm, and the donor site is dressed. This code reports only the skin harvesting to be used for tissue-cultured autograft. Later, skin cells will be isolated from the outer layer (epidermis) and inner layer (dermis) and placed in a nutrient solution that stimulates exponential division of the harvested skin cells. Using this tissue culture technique, even a smaller biopsy of skin will provide large populations of skin cells that are stored in liquid nitrogen until needed for grafting. The cells are combined with a fabric made from collagen and the outer surface is exposed to the air to stimulate development of an epidermal barrier. Once the epidermal barrier has developed, the cultured skin autograft may be used for grafting.

15050

The physician obtains one or more pinch grafts to cover a 2 cm or less open area, such as an ulcer of the toe or fingertip. The physician incises the skin to obtain a split thickness skin graft. The donor site is closed. The recipient site is cleaned and prepared. The graft is sewn into place.

15100-15101

The physician takes a split-thickness skin autograft from one area of the body and grafts it to an area needing repair. This procedure is performed when direct wound closure or adjacent tissue transfer is not possible. The physician harvests a split-thickness skin graft with a dermatome. The epidermis or top layer of skin is taken, along with a small portion of the dermis or bottom layer of the skin. This graft is applied to the recipient area on the trunk, arms, or legs. Report 15100 for the first 100 sq cm or less in adults or 1 percent of the total body area of infants and children. Report 15101 for each additional 100 sq cm or each additional 1 percent of the total body area in infants and children.

15110-15111

The physician takes an epidermal autograft from one area of the body and grafts it to an area needing repair. This procedure is performed when direct wound closure or adjacent tissue transfer is not possible. The physician harvests an epidermal skin graft with a dermatome. The epidermal autograft should be as thin as possible: 0.05 mm (0.002 inches) to 0.13 mm (0.005 inches). Only the epidermis or top layer of skin is taken. The dermis or bottom layer of the skin is left behind and will regenerate new skin. The epidermal autograft is sutured or stapled to the recipient area on the trunk, arms, or legs. Report 15110 for the first 100 sq cm or less in adults or children age 10 or older or 1 percent of the total body surface area of infants and children younger than age 10. Report 15111 for each additional 100 sq cm or part thereof in adults or each additional 1 percent of the total body area or part thereof in infants and children.

15115-15116

The physician takes an epidermal autograft from one area of the body and grafts it to an area needing repair. This procedure is performed when direct wound closure or adjacent tissue transfer is not possible. The physician harvests an epidermal skin graft with a dermatome. The epidermal autograft should be as thin as possible: 0.05 mm (0.002 inches) to 0.13 mm (0.005 inches). Only the epidermis or top layer of skin is taken. The dermis or bottom layer of the skin is left behind and will regenerate new skin. The epidermal autograft is sutured or stapled onto the recipient area on the face, scalp, eyelids, neck, ears, orbits, mouth, genitalia, hands, feet, and/or multiple digits. Report 15115 for the first 100 sq cm or less in adults or children age 10 or older or 1 percent of the total body surface area in infants and children younger than age 10. Report 15116 for each additional 100 sq cm or part thereof in adults or each additional 1 percent of the total body area or part thereof in infants and children.

15120-15121

The physician takes a split-thickness skin autograft from one area of the body and grafts it to an area needing repair. This procedure is performed when direct wound closure or adjacent tissue transfer is not possible. The physician harvests a split-thickness skin graft with a dermatome. The epidermis or top layer of skin is taken, along with a small portion of the dermis or bottom layer of the skin. This graft is sutured or stapled onto the recipient area of the face, scalp, eyelids, neck, ears, orbits, mouth, genitalia, hands, feet, and/or multiple digits. Report 15120 for the first 100 sq cm or less in adults or children age 10 or over or 1 percent of the total body area of infants and children younger than age 10. Report 15121 for each additional 100 sq cm and each additional 1 percent of total body area of infants and children.

15130-15131

The physician takes a dermal autograft from one area of the body and grafts it to an area needing repair. This procedure is performed when direct wound closure or adjacent tissue transfer is not possible. A dermal skin graft is harvested by first raising a split-thickness skin graft 0.010 to 0.015 inches in depth with a dermatome, but not removing it. The dermatome is adjusted to remove the desired graft and a second pass is made over the newly created donor site at that depth to remove a dermal layer autograft. The dermal autograft is sutured or stapled onto the recipient area on the trunk, arms, or legs. Report 15130 for the first 100 sq cm or less in adults or children age 10 or older or 1 percent of the total body surface area in infants and children younger than age 10. Report 15131 for each additional 100 sq cm or part thereof in adults or each additional 1 percent of the total body area or part thereof in infants and children.

15135-15136

The physician takes a dermal autograft from one area of the body and grafts it to an area needing repair. This procedure is performed when direct wound closure or adjacent tissue transfer is not possible. A dermal skin graft is harvested by first raising a split-thickness skin graft 0.010 to 0.015 inches in depth with a dermatome, but not removing it. The dermatome is adjusted to remove the desired graft and a second pass is made over the newly created donor site at that depth to remove a dermal layer autograft. The dermal autograft is sutured or stapled onto the recipient area on the face, scalp, eyelids, neck, ears, orbits, mouth, genitalia, hands, feet, and/or multiple digits. Report 15135 for the first 100 sq cm or less in adults or children age 10 or older or 1 percent of the total body surface area in infants and children younger than age 10. Report 15136 for each additional 100 sq cm or part thereof in adults or each additional 1 percent of the total body area or part thereof in infants and children.

15150-15152

The physician takes a previously prepared, tissue-cultured epidermal autograft from the transport medium and grafts it to an area needing repair on the trunk, arms, or legs. The autograft is applied and secured to the recipient bed with sutures, staples, or fibrin sealant, and a dressing is applied to the site. The tissue-cultured autograft was previously prepared, in a separate procedure, by harvesting skin (keratinocytes and dermal tissue) from the patient and placing the cells in a nutrient solution to stimulate exponential division of the harvested skin cells. The cultured skin cells are stored in liquid nitrogen until needed for grafting. The cells are combined with a fabric made from collagen, and the outer surface is exposed to the air to stimulate development of an epidermal barrier. Once the epidermal barrier has developed, the cultured skin autograft is used for grafting. These codes report the grafting procedure. Report 15150 for the first 25 sq cm or less of graft area on the trunk, arms, or legs. Report 15151 for an additional 1 sq cm to 75 sq cm of graft area. Report 15152 for each additional 100 sq cm of graft area in adults and children age 10 or older or each additional 1 percent of total body surface area or part thereof in infants and children younger than age 10.

15155-15157

The physician takes a previously prepared, tissue cultured epidermal autograft from the transport medium and grafts it to an area needing repair on the face, scalp, eyelids, mouth, neck, ears, orbits, genitalia, hands, feet, and/or multiple digits. The autograft is applied and secured to the recipient bed with sutures, staples, or fibrin sealant, and a dressing is applied to the site. The tissue cultured autograft was previously prepared, in a separate procedure, by harvesting skin (keratinocytes and dermal tissue) from the patient and placing the cells in a nutrient solution to stimulate exponential division of the harvested skin cells. The cultured skin cells are stored in liquid nitrogen until needed for grafting. The cells are combined with a fabric made from collagen, and the outer surface is exposed to the air to stimulate development of an epidermal barrier. Once the epidermal barrier has developed, the cultured skin autograft is used for grafting. These codes report the grafting procedure. Report 15155 for the first 25 sq cm or less of graft area. Report 15156 for an additional 1 sq cm to 75 sq cm of graft area. Report 15157 for each additional 100 sq cm of graft area in adults and children age 10 or older or each additional 1 percent of total body surface area or part thereof in infants and children younger than age 10.

15170-15171

The physician applies an acellular dermal replacement graft to a wound on the trunk, arms, or legs. The acellular replacement is removed from its solution, applied to the prepared graft area, and secured to the recipient bed with sutures, staples, or fibrin sealant. A net dressing is applied over the site and covered with gauze dressings. Acellular dermal replacement is a temporary skin substitute that covers excised wounds until skin grafts can be placed. Acellular dermal replacement products typically consist of a bilaminate with a dermal section of porous lattice fibers made from a biologic substance such as bovine cartilage and an epidermal section of a synthetic substance such as silicone. This type of skin substitute interacts with the body to promote wound healing. In addition, skin substitutes help control the moisture loss that occurs with a full-thickness or deep partial-thickness dermal injury. Skin substitutes also serve as a template to generate neodermis, a dermal-like tissue that readily accepts a thin epidermal autograft applied in a subsequent surgical procedure. Report 15170 for the first 100 sq cm or less in adults or children age 10 or older or 1 percent of the total body surface area in infants and children younger than age 10. Report 15171 for each additional 100 sq cm or part thereof in adults or each additional 1 percent of the total body area or part thereof in infants and children.

15175-15176

The physician applies an acellular dermal replacement graft to a wound on the face, scalp, eyelids, neck, ears, orbits, mouth, genitalia, hands, feet, and/or multiple digits. The acellular replacement is removed from its solution, applied to the prepared graft area, and secured to the recipient bed with sutures, staples, or fibrin sealant. A net dressing is applied over the site and covered with gauze dressings. Acellular dermal replacement is a skin substitute that covers excised wounds until skin autografts can be placed. Acellular dermal replacement products typically consist of a bilaminate with a dermal section of porous lattice fibers made from a biologic substance such as bovine cartilage and an epidermal section of a synthetic substance such as silicone. This type of skin substitute interacts with the body to promote wound healing. In addition, skin substitutes help control the moisture loss that occurs with a full-thickness or deep partial-thickness dermal injury. Skin substitutes also serve as a template to generate neodermis, a dermal-like tissue that readily accepts a thin epidermal autograft applied in a subsequent surgical procedure. Report 15175 for the first 100 sq cm or less in adults or children age 10 or older or 1 percent of the total body surface area in infants and children younger than age 10. Report 15176 for each additional 100 sq cm in adults or each additional 1 percent or part thereof of the total body area in infants and children.

15200-15201

The physician harvests a full-thickness skin graft with a scalpel from one area of the body and grafts it to an area needing repair. A full-thickness skin graft consists of both the superficial and deeper layers of skin (epidermis and dermis). The resulting surgical wound at the donor site is closed by lifting the remaining skin edges and placing sutures to close directly. Fat is removed from the graft, which is sutured onto the recipient bed to cover a defect of the trunk of no more than 20 sq cm. Report 15201 for each additional 20 sq cm or part thereof.

15220-15221

The physician harvests a full-thickness skin graft with a scalpel from one area of the body and grafts it to an area needing repair. A full-thickness skin graft consists of both the superficial and deeper layers of skin (epidermis and dermis). The resulting surgical wound at the donor site is closed by lifting the remaining skin edges and placing sutures for direct closure. Fat is removed from the graft, which is sutured onto the recipient bed to cover a defect of the scalp, arms, and/or legs of no more than 20 sq cm. Report 15221 for each additional 20 sq cm or part thereof.

15240-15241

The physician harvests a full-thickness skin graft with a scalpel from one area of the body and grafts it to an area needing repair. A full-thickness skin graft consists of both the superficial and deeper layers of skin (epidermis and dermis). The resulting surgical wound at the donor site is closed by lifting the remaining skin edges and placing sutures for direct closure. Fat is removed from the graft, which is sutured onto the recipient bed to cover a defect of the forehead, cheeks, chin, mouth, neck, axillae, genitalia, hands, and/or feet of 20 sq cm or less. Report 15241 for each additional 20 sq cm or part thereof.

15260-15261

The physician harvests a full-thickness skin graft with a scalpel from one area of the body and grafts it to an area needing repair. A full-thickness skin graft consists of both the superficial and deeper layers of skin (epidermis and dermis). The resulting surgical wound at the donor site is closed by lifting the remaining skin edges and placing sutures for direct closure. Fat is removed from the graft, which is sutured onto the recipient bed to cover a defect of the nose, ears, eyelids, and/or lips of up to 20 sq cm. Report 15261 for each additional 20 sq cm or part thereof.

15300-15301

The physician applies a skin allograft for temporary wound closure to a wound on the trunk, arms, or legs. A skin allograft is used as a temporary measure to close the wound and provide a barrier against infection and fluid loss, reduce pain, and promote healing of underlying tissues until a permanent graft can be applied. The allograft is obtained from the skin bank and fashioned to fit the size and contours of the previously prepared wound bed on the trunk, arms, or legs. The skin allograft is placed over the wound and sutured or stapled into place. Report 15300 for the first 100 sq cm or less in adults or children age 10 or older or 1 percent of the total body surface area in infants and children younger than age 10. Report 15301 for each additional 100 sq cm in adults or each additional 1 percent of the total body area of infants and children.

15320-15321

The physician applies a skin allograft for temporary wound closure to a wound on the face, scalp, eyelids, mouth, neck, ears, orbits, genitalia, hands, feet, and/or multiple digits. A skin allograft is used as a temporary measure to close the wound and provide a barrier against infection and fluid loss, reduce pain, and promote healing of underlying tissues until a permanent graft can be applied. The allograft is obtained from the skin bank and fashioned to fit the size and contours of the previously prepared wound bed. The skin allograft is placed over the wound and sutured or stapled into place, dressed with low adhering dressing and absorbent dressing reinforcement, and secured with net dressing. Report 15320 for the first 100 sq cm or less in adults or children age 10 or older or 1 percent of the total body surface area in infants and children younger than age 10. Report 15321 for each additional 100 sq cm or each additional 1 percent of the total body area of infants and children.

15330-15331

The physician applies an acellular dermal allograft to a wound of the trunk, arms, or legs. An acellular dermal allograft is a chemically treated, cadaver-harvested allograft that has been processed to remove all epidermal antigenic cellular components, rendering the graft immunologically inert while preserving the dermal matrix. The dermal allograft is fashioned to fit the size and contours of the previously prepared wound bed, once healthy viable tissue has been exposed. The graft is placed over the wound and sutured or stapled into place. In a separately reportable procedure, the dermal allograft is covered with a local skin flap or a split-thickness autograft. The wound is dressed. Report 15330 for the first 100 sq cm or less in adults and children age 10 or older or 1 percent of the total body surface area in infants and children younger than age 10. Report 15331 for each additional 100 sq cm in adults or each additional 1 percent of the total body surface area in infants and children.

15335-15336

The physician applies an acellular dermal allograft to a wound of the face, scalp, eyelids, mouth, neck, ears, orbits, genitalia, hands, feet, and/or multiple digits. An acellular dermal allograft is a chemically treated, cadaver-harvested allograft that has been processed to remove all epidermal antigenic cellular components, rendering the graft immunologically inert while preserving the dermal matrix. The dermal allograft is fashioned to fit the size and contours of the previously prepared wound bed, once healthy, viable tissue has been exposed. The graft is placed over the wound and sutured or stapled into place. In a separately reportable procedure, the dermal allograft is covered with a local skin flap or a split-thickness autograft may be applied over the acellular dermal allograft. The wound is dressed. Report 15335 for the first 100 sq cm or less in adults and children age 10 or older or 1 percent of the total body surface area in infants and children younger than age 10. Report 15336 for each additional 100 sq cm in adults or each additional 1 percent of the total body surface area in infants and children.

15340-15341

The physician applies a tissue cultured allogeneic skin substitute to a wound. The skin substitute is fenestrated, placed onto the wound site, and secured with interrupted sutures. Using this type of graft requires only minimal site preparation and debridement, which are not reported separately. Allogeneic skin substitutes may be temporary or permanent. Temporary skin substitutes are used on fresh, partial thickness wounds and are left until healed. Temporary skin substitutes have an outer epidermal barrier made of a thin silicon film and an inner dermal layer of human-derived fibroblast products, such as collagen, fibronectin, and glycosaminoglycan, or collagen bonded onto nylon filament weave. The dermal layer provides an adherent protective dressing that supports infiltration and proliferation of new matrix cells in normal tissue alignment. Permanent skin substitutes have a bioactive dermal layer, composed of a collagen and fibroblast or collagen and glycosaminoglycan matrix that incorporates itself with neodermis growth or biodegrades as neodermis is formed. The outer, epidermal layer may also be biologic, derived from human epidermis (e.g., neonatal male foreskin) or a thin silicone elastomer, which is later replaced with epidermal autografts. Report 15340 for the application of a tissue cultured allogeneic skin substitute up to 25 sq cm. Report 15341 for the application of each additional 25 sq cm or part thereof.

15360-15361

The physician applies a tissue cultured allogeneic dermal substitute to a wound on the trunk, arms, or legs. The skin substitute is applied to the previously prepared wound site, secured with interrupted sutures or surgical staples, and covered with gauze and bulky protective dressings. Allogeneic dermal substitutes act as a permanent dermal transplant that incorporates itself with neodermis growth. Graft tissue is harvested from a living person (e.g., neonatal male foreskin) or a cadaver and processed by a tissue bank. The epithelial layer of the allograft material is removed and the dermis is treated to yield a cryopreserved, lyophilized allodermis for grafting. There is no protective epidermal component with allogeneic dermal substitutes, which require the application of separate epithelial autografts. Report 15360 for the first 100 sq cm or less in adults or children age 10 or older or 1 percent of body area of infants and children younger than age 10. Report 15361 for each additional 100 sq cm in adults or each additional 1 percent of body area of infants and children.

15365-15366

The physician applies a tissue cultured allogeneic dermal substitute to a wound on the face, scalp, eyelids, mouth, neck, ears, orbits, genitalia, hands, feet, and/or multiple digits. The skin substitute is applied to the previously prepared wound site, secured with interrupted sutures or surgical staples, and covered with gauze and bulky protective dressings. Allogeneic dermal substitutes act as a permanent dermal transplant that incorporates itself with neodermis growth. Graft tissue is harvested from a living person (e.g., neonatal male foreskin) or a cadaver and processed by a tissue bank. The epithelial layer of the allograft material is removed and the dermis is treated to yield a cryopreserved, lyophilized allodermis for grafting. There is no protective epidermal component with allogeneic dermal substitutes, which require the application of separate epithelial autografts. Report 15365 for the first 100 sq cm or less in adults or children age 10 or older or 1 percent of body area of infants and children younger than age 10. Report 15366 for each additional 100 sq cm in adults or each additional 1 percent of body area in infants and children.

15400-15401

The physician applies a xenograft to cover a wound on the patient. Xenograft dermal (skin) tissue is harvested from a non-human species (usually porcine) and used to cover a skin defect in humans. The physician covers the recipient site with this temporary resurfacing material to maintain viability of the tissue underneath the wound until a future transplant of appropriate skin graft material can be done. This procedure is often performed on burn patients when autografting is not feasible. Report 15400 for the first 100 sq cm or less in adults or children age 10 or older or 1 percent of body area of infants and children younger than age 10. Report 15401 for each additional 100 sq cm in adults or each additional 1 percent of body area in infants and children.

15420-15421

The physician applies a xenograft to cover a wound on the face, scalp, eyelids, neck, ears, orbits, mouth, genitalia, hands, feet, and/or multiple digits. Xenograft dermal (skin) tissue is harvested from a non-human species (usually porcine) and used to cover a skin defect in humans. The physician covers the recipient site with this temporary resurfacing material to maintain viability of the tissue underneath the wound until a future transplant of appropriate skin graft material can be done. This procedure is often performed on burn patients when autografting is not feasible. Report 15420 for the first 100 sq cm or less in adults or children age 10 or older or 1 percent of body area in infants and children younger than age 10. Report 15421 for each additional 100 sq cm in adults or each additional 1 percent of body area in infants and children.

15430-15431

The physician implants an acellular xenograft to reconstruct a soft tissue defect. Acellular xenograft implants are used to fill soft tissue voids following surgical or traumatic injuries, to reconstruct acquired or congenital defects of the skin and soft tissues, to reconstruct the pelvic floor, and to augment tissue for cosmetic enhancement. Other uses of acellular xenograft implants are being tested. The physician prepares the recipient site. The acellular xenograft implant is fashioned to conform to the defect and implanted. Report 15430 for the first 100 sq cm or less in adults or children age 10 or older or 1 percent of body area in infants and children younger than age 10. Report 15431 for each additional 100 sq cm in adults or each additional 1 percent of body area in infants and children.

15570-15576

The physician forms a direct or tubed pedicle flap to reconstruct traumatic defects. A pedicle flap of full-thickness skin and subcutaneous tissue that retains its supporting blood vessels is developed in the donor area. A tubed pedicle flap maintains two vascular ends and the cut edges of the raised flap are sutured together to form a tube. The flap may be rotated or transferred to the defect area and sutured to the recipient bed in layers. The physician closes the harvest region in layers or covers it with a split-thickness skin graft. Repairs to the donor area using skin grafts or flaps are reported separately. Other exposed regions, including portions of the pedicle, may also be covered with a split-thickness skin graft. Once the recipient site has healed, a second surgery will detach the pedicle and return the unused flap to its anatomic location. Report 15570 for a pedicle flap on the trunk; 15572 for the scalp, arms, or legs; 15574 for the forehead, cheeks, chin, mouth, neck, axillae, genitalia, hands, or feet; and 15576 if the pedicle flap is applied to the eyelids, nose, ears, lips, or intraoral area.

15600-15630

The physician sections the direct or tubed pedicle flap several weeks following reconstruction of traumatic defects. Blood flow is now established in the recipient area. The unused portion of the flap is detached and prepared for reinsertion into its original anatomic site. Previous skin grafts are removed from the donor beds. The returned flap is sutured in layers to the harvest site. Any exposed subcutaneous tissue is closed primarily or covered with a split-thickness skin graft. Report 15600 if performed at the trunk; 15610 for the scalp, arms, or legs; 15620 for the forehead, cheeks, chin, neck, axillae, genitalia, hands, or feet; and 15630 if performed on the eyelids, nose, ears, or lips.

15650

A previously placed pedicle flap has been in position long enough to receive a good blood supply from the recipient area. As an intermediate step, the physician releases the flap from its donor attachment and moves it completely to a new location. This same tissue may be moved further along the body in a similar manner at a later date. This is known as walking the flap or walk up procedure.

15731

The physician forms a vascular pedicle flap from the forehead to correct an adjacent defect of the nose, forehead, temple, or scalp. The physician determines the best site for creation of the flap, marks the area, and verifies the location of the supratrochlear or supraorbital artery via Doppler. A flap with an artery along its long axis is called an axial flap. A paramedian flap is an axial flap with origins along the midline of the forehead and is commonly used in nasal reconstructive surgery following excision of a malignancy. The physician cuts and undermines the skin and subcutaneous tissue, taking care to preserve vascular flow to the flap tissue. The thickness of the flap may be reduced, depending on the thickness of the defect at the recipient site. The flap is rotated or advanced to the defect site and secured with sutures. The donor site is closed directly.

15732-15738
The physician repairs a defect area using a muscle, muscle and skin, or a fascia and skin flap. The physician rotates the prepared flap from the donor area to the site needing repair, suturing the flap in place. The donor area is closed primarily with sutures. If a skin graft or flap is used to repair the donor site, it is considered an additional procedure and is reported separately. Report 15732 for a muscle, myocutaneous, or fasciocutaneous flap of the head and neck; 15734 if performed on the trunk; 15736 if performed on an upper extremity; and 15738 if performed on a lower extremity.

15740-15750
The physician forms an island pedicle flap. A defect is being covered by elevation of a flap of skin and subcutaneous tissue. The flap is rotated into a nearby but not immediately adjacent defect. Often this flap will be transferred through a tunnel underneath the skin and sutured into its new position. The donor site is closed directly. Report 15750 if the pedicle is neurovascular, containing nerve and blood vessel elements.

15756
The physician implants a free muscle or myocutaneous flap with microvascular anastomosis. With the patient under general anesthesia, the physician prepares and irrigates the wound. The muscle or myocutaneous flap is removed from the donor site and prepared. The physician inserts the flap and uses half-mattress sutures to secure the section. Using microscopy, the physician joins the vessels, uniting the flap tissue to the site. Before all are joined, the physician may inject fluorescein dye in the vascular system and check the area for fluorescence under an ultraviolet light. Adjustments and corrections to the vascular connections are made and the physician sutures the skin. A light dressing is applied and, in many cases, the flap is splinted to help prevent shrinkage. The donor site is sutured and covered with a light dressing.

15757
The physician implants a free skin flap with microvascular anastomosis. With the patient under general anesthesia, the physician prepares and irrigates the wound. The new skin is removed from the donor site and prepared. The physician inserts the new skin and uses half-mattress sutures to secure the section. Using microscopy, the physician joins the vessels and nerves uniting the new skin to the site. Before all are joined, the physician may inject fluorescein dye in the vascular system and check the area for fluorescence under an ultraviolet light. Adjustments and corrections to the vascular connections are made, and the physician sutures the skin. Light dressing is applied; and, in many cases, the flap is splinted to help prevent shrinkage. The donor site is sutured and covered with a light dressing.

15758
The physician implants a free fascial flap with microvascular anastomosis. With the patient under general anesthesia, the physician prepares and irrigates the wound. The new fascia is removed from the donor site and prepared. The physician inserts the new fascia and uses sutures to secure the section. Using microscopy, the physician joins the vessels and nerves uniting the new fascia to the site. Before all are joined, the physician may inject fluorescein dye in the vascular system and check the area for fluorescence under an ultraviolet light. Adjustments and corrections to the vascular connections are made and the physician sutures the skin. A light dressing is applied and, in many cases, the flap is splinted to help prevent shrinkage. The donor site is sutured and covered with a light dressing.

15760
The physician takes a full-thickness composite graft of more than one tissue type, such as a mixture of cartilage, from the external ear or nasal ala area, with a scalpel. This type of graft is used on defects that need both skin and structural support to ensure survival of the graft with minimal scarring and contraction, and to maintain the continuity of the local flesh. The graft tissue is "assembled" into the recipient bed and primary closure is done on the donor area with layered sutures.

15770
The physician takes a graft composed of derma, fat, and fascia to repair and blend in defects left behind by atrophy, surgical excisions, or other fleshy defects, much like a composite graft. The derma-fat-fascia graft may be a continuous piece of all three of these layers, individual sections done layer by layer, or graft pieces laid in the recipient bed as combinations, such as a fascia-fat layer, followed by a dermal layer. The graft is used on defects much like a composite graft to maintain support for the continuity of the local flesh. The graft is laid in the recipient area so as to fill and blend in pockets of defects to restore the surrounding area to normal positioning and to maintain the continuity of the local flesh.

15775-15776

The physician performs a punch graft for hair transplant. The physician uses a punch tool to remove a small segment of scalp containing hair and hair follicles. This is transferred and inset into a non-hair bearing area. Report 15775 for one to 15 punch grafts and 15776 for more than 15 punch grafts.

15780-15783

The physician performs dermabrasion of the total face in 15780 for conditions such as acne scarring, fine wrinkling, rhytids, and general keratosis. The physician uses a powered rotary instrument to sand down or smooth scarred or wrinkled areas. The physician lowers raised lesions or thins thickened tissue to regenerate skin with a smoother appearance. Report 15781 for a dermabrasion performed on one segment of the face; 15782 for regional dermabrasion, other than the face; and 15783 for a superficial dermabrasion on any site.

15786-15787

The physician uses abrasive techniques to smooth down or remove an isolated lesion such as a scar or skin thickening secondary to sun damage. Report 15786 for a single lesion and 15787 for each additional four lesions or less.

15788-15793

The physician performs a chemical peel of the epidermal or dermal layers of the skin. The physician uses chemical agents, such as glycolic acid or phenol, to remove fine wrinkles or areas of abnormal pigmentation. The treatment is localized to surface layers of facial skin only in 15788. Report 15789 for a chemical facial peel of the deeper dermal layer; 15792 for an epidermal chemical peel other than facial; and 15793 for a dermal chemical peel other than facial.

15819

The physician removes excess skin from the neck area. The physician marks the area to be removed. The skin is incised and the excess tissue is resected. The skin is reapproximated and sutured in layers.

15820-15821

The physician performs a blepharoplasty of the lower eyelid. Through an incision beneath the eyelash line, the physician dissects the skin of the lower eyelid to the subcutaneous/muscle fascial layers. The skin is pulled tight and excess skin is excised. Muscle fascia may be sutured to support sagging muscles. In 15821, orbital fat, or an extensive herniated fat pad, is removed from the tissues. The incision is closed with layers.

15822-15823

The physician performs a blepharoplasty of the upper eyelid. Through an incision usually in the crease of the upper eyelid, the physician dissects the skin of the upper eyelid to the subcutaneous/muscle fascial layers. The skin is pulled tight and redundant skin is excised. Muscle fascia may be sutured to support sagging muscles. In 15823, orbital fat may be removed from the tissues as well as excessive redundant skin that mechanically weighs down the eyelid, obstructing the visual field. The incision is closed with layers.

15824, 15826

The physician performs a rhytidectomy of the forehead. The physician excises a portion of skin in order to eliminate wrinkles in the forehead. Most commonly an incision is made in the hairline and a subcutaneous dissection is carried down to the level of the eyebrow. The excess skin is removed and the forehead is elevated and sutured into the new position. Incisions are repaired in layers. Report 15826 if the rhytidectomy is done to reduce glabellar frown lines, the vertical furrows in the forehead area between the eyebrows caused by the corrugator and procerus muscles that may be debulked before incisions in the eyebrows are closed.

15825

The physician performs a rhytidectomy of the neck. The physician makes an incision usually in front of the ear. Tension is increased in the facial muscles by freeing the superficial musculoaponeurotic system (SMAS) (facial muscles are interlinked by the SMAS). The physician trims and tightens the SMAS by securing it with sutures to tissues in front of the ear. An additional incision below the chin is necessary to correct the platysma muscle. The physician makes an incision through the platysma muscle, creating a flap, which is moved up and back. The muscle is tightened, trimmed, and secured with layered sutures. The skin incisions are closed with layered sutures.

15828-15829

The physician makes an incision in a crease or wrinkle of the cheek, chin, or neck to perform a rhytidectomy. Tension is increased by removing excess skin and fat. An additional incision in front of the ear may be necessary. Tension is increased in the facial muscles by freeing the superficial musculoaponeurotic system (SMAS) (facial muscles are interlinked by the SMAS). The physician trims and tightens the SMAS by securing it with sutures to tissues in front of the ear. Report 15829 for a SMAS flap.

15830-15839

The physician removes excessive skin and subcutaneous tissue (including lipectomy). In 15830, the physician makes an incision traversing the abdomen below the belly button in a horizontal fashion. Excessive skin and subcutaneous tissue are elevated off the abdominal wall and excess tissue and fat are excised. The flaps are brought together and sutured in at least three layers. The physician may also suture the rectus abdominis muscles together in the midline to reinforce the area. Report 15832 for removal of excess skin and subcutaneous tissue on the thigh; 15833 for the leg; 15834 for the hip; 15835 for the buttock; 15836 for the arm; 15837 for the forearm or hand; 15838 for the submental fat pad (inferior to the chin); and 15839 for any other area.

15840-15845
The physician harvests a graft for facial nerve paralysis. The physician removes connective tissue (fascia) from a predetermined location of the body (often fascia lata from the leg). This graft is transplanted to the face and sutured into place underneath the skin in order to partially suspend or reanimate previously paralyzed areas of the face. Report 15841 if a free muscle graft is used; 15842 if a free muscle flap by microsurgical technique is used; and 15845 if a regional muscle transfer is performed.

15847
The physician excises excess skin, usually the result of significant weight loss in the patient, while preserving the position of the umbilicus. A wide transverse incision is made in the lower abdomen. The physician dissects fat and skin free from underlying muscle and fascia from the site of the incision to the ribs. The umbilicus is dissected free from the skin, but remains attached by a stalk to the abdomen. The physician uses sutures or staples to plicate and tighten the rectus sheath. The dissected skin is stretched back over the abdomen and excess skin and fat are excised. An incision is made in the skin to accommodate the umbilicus, which is sutured in place. The skin is closed in layers and a temporary drain may be placed.

15850-15851
The physician who completed the surgery on the patient now removes sutures on that patient with the aid of sedation or general anesthesia. Report 15851 for removal of sutures by another surgeon under anesthesia (not local).

15852
The physician changes a dressing on a wound other than a burn while the patient is under sedation or general anesthesia. This is commonly done for severe crush injuries where serial tissue debridement is required and also for certain types of infection.

15860
The physician injects a dye such as fluorescein or methylene blue to test the viability of blood vessels in a flap or graft. The agent is injected intravenously.

15876-15879
The physician performs a lipectomy of the head and neck in 15876. The physician makes small incisions inside the mouth or in the skin of the chin overlying an area of fat deposits. A liposuction cannula is inserted through the incision and the physician moves the cannula through the fat deposits, creating tunnels and removing excess deposits. A separate incision behind the ear may be necessary to remove additional fat deposits. The incisions are closed simply. Report 15877 for a lipectomy of the trunk; 15878 if liposuction is done on an upper extremity; and 15879 for lower extremity.

15920-15922
The physician excises a coccygeal pressure ulcer with coccygectomy. The patient is positioned prone (face down) and the physician makes a 15 cm elliptical incision over the coccyx (tailbone), removing the strip of skin that contains the pressure sore. After freeing the coccyx from the surrounding soft tissues, it is separated from the sacrum and removed. The soft tissue is brought back together and the wound is closed with sutures. Report 15922 if the wound is closed using a skin flap from the groin or other donor site. The flap is sutured in place and covered with mesh petroleum gauze and loose bandages.

15931-15933
The physician excises a sacral pressure ulcer. The patient is positioned prone (face down) and the physician makes an elliptical incision over the sacrum, removing the strip of skin that contains the pressure sore. The wound is irrigated and the soft tissue is brought back together and closed with sutures. Report 15933 if bone below the wound is removed before the soft tissue is brought back together and closed.

15934-15935
The physician excises a sacral pressure ulcer. The patient is positioned prone (face down) and the physician makes a 15 cm elliptical incision over the sacrum, removing the strip of skin that contains the pressure sore. The wound is irrigated and closed using a skin flap from the groin or other donor site. The flap is sutured in place and covered with mesh petroleum gauze and loose bandages. Report 15935 if bone below the wound is removed before the wound is repaired with a skin flap.

15936-15937
The physician excises a sacral ulcer to prepare for muscle or myocutaneous flap or skin graft closure. The physician makes an incision around the pressure sore that lies over the sacrum. The infected wound is removed and the area is irrigated. The space that remains is filled with a muscle flap graft, usually taken from the latissimus dorsi muscle and the overlying skin. The donor site is prepared and the incision is made for the appropriate size of graft to be taken. Once the portion of the muscle is removed, the overlying skin is removed and the wound is sutured closed. The graft is sutured in place and a soft dressing is applied. Report 15937 if the underlying bone is removed before the wound is repaired with the flap or graft.

15940-15941
The physician excises an ischial pressure ulcer. An incision is made around the wound over the ischial tuberosity to remove the infected pressure sore. The remaining healthy tissues are irrigated, the wound is closed with sutures, and a soft dressing is applied.

Report 15941 if a portion of bone from the ischium is removed before the wound is sutured closed.

15944-15945

The physician excises an ischial pressure ulcer, with skin flap closure. An incision is made around the wound over the ischial tuberosity in order to remove the infected pressure sore. The infected tissue is removed; however, the wound is large enough to require a flap of skin from another part of the body, such as the groin area at the front of the hip, to completely close the area. The physician makes an appropriate size flap from the donor area and sutures it in place following the removal of the infected tissue. The donor site is sutured closed and soft dressings are used to cover the wounds. Report 15945 if a portion of bone from the ischium is removed before the wound is closed with the flap.

15946

The physician excises an ischial pressure ulcer and performs an ostectomy to prepare for muscle or myocutaneous flap or skin graft closure. The infected wound is removed with part of the ischial bone and the area is irrigated. The space that remains is filled with a muscle flap graft, usually taken from the latissimus dorsi muscle and the overlying skin. The donor site is prepared and the incision is made for the appropriate size of graft to be taken. Once the portion of the muscle is removed, the overlying skin is removed and the wound is sutured closed. The graft is sutured in place and a soft dressing is applied.

15950-15951

The physician excises a trochanteric pressure ulcer, with primary suture closure. The physician makes an elliptical shaped incision around the wound, which is located over the outer hip bone. The infected pressure ulcer is removed and the wound is irrigated. The soft tissues are brought back together and closed with sutures. A soft dressing is applied. Report 15951 if a portion of the underlying bone is also removed because of the extent of the infection.

15952-15953

The physician excises a trochanteric pressure ulcer with skin flap closure. An incision is made around the wound over the trochanter (outer hip bone) in order to remove the infected pressure sore. The infected tissue is removed; however, the wound is large enough to require a graft of skin from another part of the body to completely close the area. Two common skin flap donor sites are the scapular region (upper back over the shoulder blade) and the groin area at the front of the hip. The physician takes an appropriate size graft from the donor area and sutures it in place following removal of the infected tissue. The donor site is sutured closed and soft dressings are used to cover the wounds. Report 15953 if a portion of the underlying bone is also removed before skin grafting.

15956-15958

The physician excises a trochanteric pressure ulcer to prepare for muscle or myocutaneous flap or skin graft closure. The physician makes an incision around the pressure sore that lies over the trochanter (outer hip bone). The wound may be of substantial size where muscle and skin grafting are necessary to fill the space left by the removal of the infected tissues. The infected wound is removed and the area is irrigated. The space that remains is filled with a muscle flap graft, usually taken from the latissimus dorsi muscle and the overlying skin. The donor site is prepared and the incision is made for the appropriate size of graft to be taken. Once the portion of the muscle is removed, the overlying skin is removed and the wound is sutured closed. The graft is sutured in place and a soft dressing is applied. Report 15958 if a portion of the trochanter is also removed.

16000

The physician treats a first-degree burn. The physician performs a simple cleaning and applies an ointment or a dressing.

16020-16030

The physician applies dressing material(s) and/or debrides a partial-thickness burn of blisters and nonviable or nonadherent tissue, initial or subsequent. The physician removes devitalized tissue or tissue that is contaminated by bacteria, foreign material, dead cells, or a crust. The wound is cleansed and a dressing is applied. Report 16020 for treatment of a small burn area, less than 5 percent of total body surface area; 16025 for a medium-sized area, 5 to 10 percent of total body surface area, such as the whole face or a whole extremity; and 16030 for a large burn area, greater than 10 percent of total body surface area, such as more than one extremity.

16035-16036

The physician performs an escharotomy. Eschar is a leathery slough produced by thermal burns. The physician makes an incision through the area of eschar and undermines it. With adequate incision of the eschar, the physician achieves release of movement for the underlying tissue. Report 16035 for the initial incision and 16036 for each additional incision.

17000-17003

The physician destroys or excises premalignant lesions using a laser, electrosurgery, cryosurgery, chemical treatment, or surgical curettement. Local anesthesia is included. Report 17000 when one lesion is destroyed and 17003 when two to 14 lesions are destroyed.

17004

The physician excises or destroys premalignant lesions using a laser, electrosurgery, cryosurgery, chemical treatment, or surgical curettement. Local anesthesia is included. This code reports destruction of 15 or more lesions during the same surgical session.

17106-17108

The physician destroys a collection of abnormal proliferative blood vessels within the skin. To complete this procedure, the physician usually applies a laser treatment in a technique similar to painting the skin. This destroys the vessels, creating scar tissue that eventually fades. No incision is made and no tissue is removed. Report 17106 if the treated area totals less than 10 sq cm; 17107 for 10 sq cm to 50 sq cm; and 17108 for more than 50 sq cm.

17110-17111

The physician uses a laser, electrosurgery, cryosurgery, chemical treatment, or surgical curettement to obliterate or vaporize benign lesions other than skin tags or cutaneous vascular proliferative lesions. Report 17110 for 14 lesions or less and 17111 for 15 or more lesions.

17250

The physician destroys a form of exuberant or excessive healing tissue known as granulation tissue or proud flesh. The physician destroys the tissue by applying chemicals such as silver nitrate.

17260-17266

The physician destroys a malignant lesion of the trunk, arms, and legs. Destruction may be accomplished by using a laser or electrocautery to burn the lesion, cryotherapy to freeze the lesion, chemicals to destroy the lesion, or surgical curettement to remove the lesion. Report 17260 for a lesion diameter 0.5 cm or less; 17261 for 0.6 cm to 1 cm; 17262 for 1.1 cm to 2 cm; 17263 for 2.1 cm to 3 cm; 17264 for 3.1 cm to 4 cm; and 17266 if the lesion diameter is greater than 4 cm.

17270-17276

The physician destroys a malignant lesion of the scalp, neck, hands, feet, or genitalia. Destruction may be accomplished by using a laser or electrocautery to burn the lesion, cryotherapy to freeze the lesion, chemicals to destroy the lesion, or surgical curettement to remove the lesion. Report 17270 for a lesion diameter 0.5 cm or less; 17271 for 0.6 cm to 1 cm; 17272 for 1.1 cm to 2 cm; 17273 for 2.1 cm to 3 cm; 17274 for 3.1 cm to 4 cm; and 17276 if the lesion diameter is greater than 4 cm.

17280-17286

The physician destroys a malignant lesion of the face, ears, eyelids, nose, lips, or mucous membranes. Destruction may be accomplished by using a laser or electrocautery to burn the lesion, cryotherapy to freeze the lesion, chemicals to destroy the lesion, or surgical curettement to remove the lesion. Report 17280 for a lesion diameter 0.5 cm or less; 17281 for 0.6 cm to 1 cm; 17282 for 1.1 cm to 2 cm; 17283 for 2.1 cm to 3 cm; 17284 for 3.1 cm to 4 cm; and 17286 if the lesion diameter is greater than 4 cm.

17311-17315

The physician performs chemosurgery using Mohs micrographic technique. The physician places a chemical agent on the lesion prior to excision. This chemical acts as a tissue fixative. The lesion is excised via serial tangential cuts, allowing the physician to more closely assess wound margins and the extent of the defect being excised. Report 17311 for first stage, fresh tissue, up to five specimens of the head, neck, hands, feet, genitalia, or any location with surgery directly involving muscle, cartilage, bone, tendon, major nerves, or vessels and 17312 for each additional stage, fixed or fresh tissue, up to five specimens. Report 17313 for first stage, fixed or fresh tissue, up to five specimens of the trunk, arms, or legs and 17314 for additional stages, each stage, up to five specimens. Report 17315 in addition to the code for the primary procedure for each additional block after the first 5 tissue blocks, any stage.

17340

The physician performs cryotherapy for acne. The physician freezes the area of acne with a chemical such as liquid nitrogen by applying a soaked cotton tip to the lesion for a short period of time. This leads to scabbing and healing.

17360

The physician destroys the area of acne with a chemical exfoliator such as acne paste or acid by touching a soaked cotton tip applicator to the lesion for a short period of time (commonly 30 seconds). This leads to formation of eschar and healing.

17380

The physician uses electrolysis to remove hair. This code is used to report a 30-minute session. The physician inserts the electroneedle into the hair follicle and applies electrical current, killing the follicle. The electroneedle is removed.

19000-19001

The physician punctures with a syringe needle the skin of the breast overlying a cyst. The needle is inserted into the cyst and fluid is evacuated into the syringe, thus reducing the size of the cyst. The physician withdraws the needle and applies pressure to the puncture wound to stop the bleeding. Report 19001 for aspiration of each additional cyst of the breast.

19020

The physician makes an incision in the skin of the breast over the site of an abscess or suspicious tissue for exploration or drainage. The infected cavity is accessed and specimens for culture are taken before the cavity is irrigated with warm saline solution. Bleeding vessels may be tied or cauterized. If no abscess or suspicious tissue is found, the wound is closed with sutures. In the case of an abscess, the wound is usually loosely packed with gauze to promote free drainage rather than being closed with sutures.

19030
The physician performs an injection procedure for mammary ductogram or galactogram. A cannula or needle is inserted into the duct of the breast. Contrast media is introduced into the breast duct for the purpose of radiographic study. A dissecting microscope may be used to aid in placing the cannula. The needle or cannula is removed once the study has been completed.

19100
The physician inserts a large gauge needle through the skin of the breast and into the suspect breast tissue. The needle is removed along with a core of breast tissue. Pressure is applied to the puncture site to stop any bleeding.

19101
The physician removes tissue for biopsy. The physician makes an incision in the skin of the breast near the site of the suspect mass. The mass is identified and a sample of the lesion is removed. This specimen is often examined immediately. If the lesion is benign, the incision is repaired with layered closure. If malignant, the incision may be closed pending a separate, more extensive surgical session, or a more extensive surgery may occur immediately, in which case this code would not be reported.

19102-19103
The physician performs a breast biopsy with image guidance using a percutaneous needle core in 19102, and an automated vacuum assisted or rotating biopsy device, in 19103. In 19102, under image guidance, the physician inserts a large gauge (e.g., 14 gauge), hollow core biopsy needle through the skin of the breast and into the suspicious breast tissue. The physician takes five or more cores of tissue to obtain a sufficient amount of tissue for diagnosis. In 19103, under image guidance, an automated vacuum assisted or rotating biopsy device is inserted through the skin into the suspicious breast tissue and a core of suspect tissue is removed for biopsy. The needle or automated vacuum assisted or rotating biopsy device is withdrawn. Pressure and bandages are applied to the puncture site.

19105
The physician uses cryotherapy to obliterate a fibroadenoma of the breast. The patient's skin is cleansed and the ablation site is anesthetized. Ultrasound is used to locate the tumor. A cryoprobe is inserted through a small incision and placed within the fibroadenoma under ultrasound. The device initiates ice ball formation. The cryoprobe is warmed before removal from the breast. This code reports treatment of one fibroadenoma.

19110
The physician makes an incision at the edge of the areola near the site of a suspect duct for nipple exploration, with or without excision of a solitary lactiferous duct or a papilloma lactiferous duct. The duct is dissected from surrounding tissue and examined. Surrounding ducts and tissue are also examined. The suspect duct may be excised. Bleeding vessels are controlled with electrocautery or ligated with sutures. The incision is sutured in layered closure and a light pressure dressing is applied.

19112
The physician makes an incision around the abnormal opening of a lactiferous duct fistula on the skin. The fistula is dissected down to the duct. The duct, fistula, and skin opening are all excised. The remaining portion of the duct may be ligated. The wound is irrigated with warm sterile saline and closed in layers.

19120
The physician excises breast tissue for biopsy. The physician makes an incision in the skin of the breast overlying the site of the mass. Skin and tissue are dissected from the site of the defective tissue. The lesion is removed without attention to obtaining clean margins. Bleeding vessels are controlled with electrocautery or ligated with sutures. A drain may be inserted into the wound. The incision is sutured in layered closure and a light pressure dressing is applied.

19125-19126
The physician uses radiologic markers to identify breast tissue to be excised for biopsy. The physician makes an incision in the skin of the breast over the site of the lesion marked for excision by preoperative placement of a radiological marker. The lesion and marker are excised, without attention to obtaining clean margins. Bleeding vessels are controlled with electrocautery or ligated with sutures. A drain may be inserted into the wound. The incision is sutured in layered closure and a light dressing is applied. Report 19126 for each additional lesion identified by a pre-operative marker and removed during the same surgical session.

19260
The physician excises a chest wall tumor, including ribs. An incision in the skin of the chest overlying the site of the tumor is made. The tumor and surrounding tissue are excised. The tissue removed includes at least one adjacent rib above and below the tumor site and all intervening intercostal muscles. It may also include an en bloc resection of muscles, including the pectoralis minor or major, the serratus anterior, or the latissimus dorsi. The physician ligates or cauterizes bleeding vessels. A chest tube may be placed to re-expand the lung. The incision is repaired with layered closure and a pressure dressing is applied to the wound.

19271-19272
The physician excises a chest wall tumor, involving ribs, with plastic reconstruction. The physician makes an incision in the skin of the chest overlying the tumor. The tumor and surrounding tissue are excised and

includes at least one adjacent rib above and below the tumor site and all intervening intercostal muscles. It may also include an en bloc resection of muscles, including the pectoralis minor or major, the serratus anterior, or the latissimus dorsi. In 19272, lymphatic tissue lying in the mediastinum is also removed. The physician ligates or cauterizes bleeding vessels. A chest tube may be placed to re-expand the lung. Plastic reconstruction is done and may involve rib grafts and/or a myocutaneous flap. A pressure dressing is applied to the wound.

19290-19291
Placement of a needle localization wire into a breast lesion is performed to assist in operative identification of the suspect tissue. The physician punctures the skin overlying a breast mass and inserts a needle threaded with a guide wire. Using radiological guidance to facilitate placement, the physician inserts the wire into the mass. Sometimes dye is also injected into the suspect tissue. The wire will help identify a nonpalpable mass that is to be removed from the patient during a separate operative session. Report 19291 for each additional lesion localization wire placed.

19295
The physician places a metallic clip prior to a breast biopsy or aspiration. Using image guidance, the physician places a metallic clip adjacent to a breast lesion to mark the site for a separately reportable breast biopsy or aspiration.

19296-19297
A remote single or multichannel afterloading expandable catheter for interstitial radiotherapy treatment is placed in the breast following partial mastectomy. A catheter is placed at a later date, separate from the lumpectomy surgery in 19296, and concurrently with the lumpectomy in 19297. This is a single catheter with an expandable balloon tip that holds the radioactive seed or treatment source, which is loaded and removed for each session. The catheter can be single or multichannel, depending on the treatment delivery requirements. During the lumpectomy surgery, an uninflated balloon catheter is inserted into the recently created tumor cavity and positioned under imaging with a portion of the catheter remaining outside of the body. If a separate procedure is done after surgery, a small incision is first made and the uninflated balloon catheter is guided into position under imaging. After correct placement is determined, the balloon is inflated with saline to fit snugly into the lumpectomy cavity, and the breast is bandaged. The catheter remains until radiotherapy treatment sessions are complete.

19298
Using imaging guidance, at the time of a partial mastectomy, or subsequent to a partial mastectomy having been performed, remote afterloading catheters are placed into the breast for interstitial radiotherapy application. The lumpectomy site is identified. A template with pre-drilled holes that function as coordinates for catheter placement around the surgical area may be applied for imaging. Brachytherapy needles are first inserted into the chosen coordinates. The brachytherapy catheters are fed into position through the needles, which are removed. A catheter button is positioned to hold each catheter in place and imaging confirms their position. These remain in place until the actual loading of the radioactive material for treatment. This code reports only the placement of the catheters.

19300
The physician performs a mastectomy for gynecomastia on a male patient. The physician makes a circular incision in the skin of the breast at the edge of the areola or in the inframammary fold. Extraneous fat and breast tissue are dissected from the pectoral fascia and removed. Bleeding vessels are ligated with sutures or cauterized. The incision is sutured in layered closure and a dressing is applied.

19301-19302
The physician excises a breast tumor and a margin of normal tissue. The physician performs a partial mastectomy by making an incision through the skin and fascia over a breast malignancy and clamping any lymphatic and blood vessels. The physician excises the mass along with a margin or rim of healthy tissue. This procedure is often referred to as a segmental mastectomy or a quadrantectomy, but is also called a lumpectomy. In 19302, an axillary lymphadenectomy is also performed. The lymph nodes between the pectoralis major and the pectoralis minor muscles and the nodes in the axilla are removed through a separate incision. A drainage tube may be placed through a separate stab incision to enhance drainage from the wound or lymphatic system. The incision is repaired with layered closure and a dressing is applied.

19303
The physician removes all subcutaneous breast tissue, with or without nipple and skin. The physician performs a simple, complete mastectomy. The physician makes an elliptical incision around the breast that includes the tail of Spence, the extension of mammary tissue into the axillary region. The breast tissue is dissected from the pectoral fascia and sternum. The breast tissue is removed, along with a portion of skin, including the nipple. In a modification of the simple mastectomy, skin and nipple may be spared, but all subcutaneous breast tissue is removed. The physician ligates any bleeding vessels. A closed wound drainage catheter may be inserted and the edges of skin are approximated, sutured, and a dressing is applied.

19304
The physician performs a subcutaneous mastectomy. The physician makes an incision in the inframammary

crease. The breast is dissected from the pectoral fascia and from the skin. The breast tissue is removed, but the skin and pectoral fascia remain. The physician may ligate any bleeding vessels. The nipple and areola may be examined by a pathologist and retained if free of disease. If no prosthesis is to be inserted, a closed wound suction catheter may be inserted. The wound is closed and a light pressure dressing is applied.

19305
The physician performs a radical mastectomy. The physician makes an elliptical incision that includes the nipple and the tail of Spence, the extension of mammary tissue into the axillary region. The breast, along with the overlying skin, the pectoralis major and minor muscles, and the lymph nodes in the axilla, are removed as a single specimen. Bleeding vessels are ligated or electrocauterized. In large-breasted patients, adequate skin may be available for primary closure. Patients with insufficient skin for coverage may require skin grafts or myocutaneous flaps. If no prosthesis is to be inserted, a closed wound suction catheter may be inserted. The wound is closed and a pressure dressing is applied.

19306
The physician performs a radical Urban-type mastectomy. The physician makes an elliptical incision that includes the nipple and the tail of Spence, the extension of mammary tissue into the axillary region. The breast tissue, skin, and pectoral muscles are removed. All tissue within the parameters of the sternum, the rectus fascia, the latissimus dorsi muscle, and the clavicle are removed, including the axillary and internal mammary lymph nodes. Bleeding vessels are ligated or electrocauterized. In large-breasted patients, adequate skin may be available for primary closure. Patients with insufficient skin for coverage may require skin grafts or myocutaneous flaps. If no prosthesis is to be inserted, a closed wound suction catheter may be inserted. The wound is closed and a pressure dressing is applied.

19307
The physician performs a modified radical mastectomy. The physician makes an elliptical incision that includes the nipple and the tail of Spence, the extension of mammary tissue into the axillary region. The breast tissue and skin are dissected from the pectoral fascia and removed from the pectoral muscle. The pectoralis minor muscle may also be resected to facilitate the axillary dissection, but the pectoralis major muscle is left intact. Bleeding vessels are ligated or electrocauterized. The breast tissue and axillary tissue, including lymph nodes, are removed en bloc and the wound is irrigated. Adequate skin is usually available for primary closure. Patients with insufficient skin for coverage may require skin grafts or myocutaneous flaps. If no prosthesis is to be inserted, a closed wound suction catheter may be inserted. The wound is closed and a pressure dressing is applied.

19316
The physician performs a breast lift, or mastopexy, relocating the nipple and areola to a higher position and removing excess skin below the nipple and above the lower breast crease. The physician makes a skin incision above the nipple, in the location to which the nipple will be elevated. Another skin incision is made around the circumference of the nipple. Two skin incisions are made from the circular cut above the nipple to the fold beneath the breast, one on either side of the nipple, forming a keyhole shaped skin incision. This skin is cut away from the breast tissue and removed. The physician elevates the breast to its new position and closes the incision, excising any redundant skin in the fold beneath the breast. The incision is repaired with layered closure.

19318
The physician reduces the size of the breast, removing wedges of skin and breast tissue from a female patient. The physician makes a circular skin incision above the nipple, in the position to which the nipple will be elevated. Another skin incision is made around the circumference of the nipple. Two incisions are made from the circular cut above the nipple to the fold beneath the breast, one on either side of the nipple, creating a keyhole shaped skin and breast incision. Wedges of skin and breast tissue are removed until the desired size is achieved. Bleeding vessels may be ligated or cauterized. The physician elevates the nipple and its pedicle of subcutaneous tissue to its new position and sutures the nipple pedicle with layered closure. The remaining incision is repaired with layered closure.

19324
The physician increases the size of the breast without using a prosthesis or implant by rearranging existing fat and mammary tissue of the patient. The physician makes a skin incision in the fold beneath the breast or in a circular cut around the areola. This skin is cut away from the breast tissue and the breast tissue is rearranged. The physician may excise redundant skin to augment the breast's appearance. The incisions are repaired with layered closure.

19325
The physician increases the size of the breast by inserting a prosthesis or implant. The physician makes an incision in the fold under the breast and dissects the breast tissue and muscle layer free from the chest wall to accommodate a prosthesis positioned under the muscle. As an alternative, the prosthesis may also be positioned between the muscle and the existing breast tissue or skin. The incision is repaired with layered closure.

19328

A breast implant or prosthesis that is still intact is removed. The physician makes an incision in the fold under the breast, around the nipple, or at the site of an existing mastectomy incision and dissects muscle, fat, and breast tissue from the existing implant. The intact implant is removed. Any infection is irrigated. The physician repairs the incision with layered closure.

19330

A breast implant or prosthesis that is leaking or defective is removed. The physician makes an incision in the fold under the breast or around the nipple and dissects muscle, fat, and breast tissue from the existing implant. The leaking implant material is removed, checking surrounding tissue closely for adhesions or deposits of the material that have infiltrated beyond the capsule. The implant material and any affected tissue are excised. The physician repairs the incision with layered closure.

19340

The physician performs an immediate breast prosthesis insertion following surgery. The physician dissects the breast tissue and muscle layer free from the chest wall to accommodate a prosthesis positioned under the muscle in a patient who has just undergone mastopexy, mastectomy, or a reconstructive process during this same surgical session. The same surgical skin incisions are most often used. As an alternative, the prosthesis may also be positioned between the muscle and the existing breast tissue or skin. The incision is repaired with layered closure.

19342

The physician inserts a breast prosthesis after a patient has had previous breast surgery. Delayed insertion is done at a later time, usually after the wound has healed, and may be several months after the original surgery. The physician makes an incision in the fold under the breast or along a previous surgical incision and dissects the tissue and muscle layer free from the chest wall to accommodate a prosthesis positioned under the muscle. As an alternative, the prosthesis may also be positioned between the muscle and the existing breast tissue or skin. The incision is repaired with layered closure.

19350

The nipple and areola are reconstructed. The physician excises graft skin, usually from the inner thigh, behind the ear, or a section excised from the patient's existing areola. The donor site is repaired with sutures. To create a new nipple, the physician excises the lower section of tissue from the patient's existing nipple or removes tissue from the ear or labia. This donor site is repaired with sutures. A thin, circular layer of surface skin is removed from the breast at the site of the graft. The areola skin graft is positioned and sutured to the breast and the nipple graft is sutured to a small, circular incision in the areola's center.

19355

Inverted nipples are corrected by making two or more radial incisions in the areola and elevating the inverted nipple into an everted position. Ductal channels and fibrous bands may be transected to accomplish this. Tissue may be removed. The nipple is secured with sutures and incisions in the areola are closed.

19357

The physician performs breast reconstruction with a tissue expander, immediate or delayed. The physician makes an incision in the skin of a patient who has undergone a mastectomy. A pocket is created using an existing chest wall muscle and an expandable implant is placed into it at the site of the mastectomy. In some cases, the implant's button-shaped portal may be brought out through the skin so it is accessible by needle. Usually, the portal remains beneath the surface of the skin. The physician injects saline into the access portal to expand the implant until it has stretched the surrounding tissue to a size slightly larger than the patient's existing breast. In some cases, the expander remains a permanent prosthesis and small amount of fluid is aspirated until it duplicates the size of the existing breast. In other cases, a second surgery (reported separately) excises the implant and replaces it with a permanent breast prosthesis.

19361

The physician performs breast reconstruction with a latissimus dorsi flap. The physician transfers skin and muscle from the patient's back to the breast area to correct defects created from a previous modified radical or radical mastectomy. The physician makes a skin incision in the back and dissects a portion of the latissimus muscle and the overlying skin from surrounding structures. The muscle-skin flap remains attached to a main artery. In preparation for the transfer, the mastectomy scar is excised. The muscle flap is rotated to the front of the chest through a tunnel under the armpit so that it extends through to the mastectomy incision. The incision in the back is repaired with layered closure. The physician adjusts the flap for the most aesthetic appearance and secures it with sutures to the chest wall, adjacent muscles, and skin. The incision is repaired with sutures.

19364

The physician excises a free flap of skin, fat, and muscle from another site on the patient for use in the reconstruction of the breast following a modified radical or radical mastectomy. The free flap is excised with careful dissection of vascular channels, commonly from the thigh or buttocks, and the operative wound is sutured in a layered repair. In preparation for the graft, the mastectomy scar is excised with blood vessels preserved. The free flap is transferred to the mastectomy site and microvascular anastomosis is done to provide the graft with a viable blood supply. The physician adjusts the flap for the most aesthetic appearance and secures it with sutures to the chest wall, adjacent muscles, and skin. If the free flap does not have sufficient fat, a breast implant may be required. The chest incision is repaired with sutures.

19366
The physician excises skin, fat, and/or muscle from another site on the patient for use in the reconstruction of the breast following a modified radical or radical mastectomy. The tissue is excised and the operative wound is sutured in a layered repair. In preparation for the graft, any mastectomy scar is excised. The tissue is transferred to the mastectomy site. The physician adjusts the flap for the most aesthetic appearance and secures it with sutures to the chest wall, adjacent muscles, and skin. An operating microscope may be employed. If the tissue does not have sufficient bulk, a breast implant may be required. The chest incision is repaired with sutures.

19367-19369
The physician performs a transverse rectus abdominis myocutaneous flap (TRAM) procedure for breast reconstruction. The physician first designs then cuts a skin island flap on the lower abdominal wall. A superior skin and fat flap is elevated off the rectus abdominis muscle. A transverse incision is made in the rectus sheath and the muscle is divided and elevated, keeping the superior epigastric arteries intact for blood supply. Once the muscle is elevated, the physician makes an incision through the chest skin. This is also elevated, creating a pocket for the muscle flap. A connecting tunnel is made between the elevated chest skin and the inferiorly positioned flap. The flap is passed superiorly under the tunnel of tissue, placed into its new position, and sutured, after contouring a breast. The abdominal wall is closed by reapproximating the remaining anterior rectus muscle to the remaining lateral muscle and sheath. Skin edges are brought together and sutured in layers. Suction drains are also placed. Report 19368 if microvascular anastomosis for connecting blood vessels is used. Report 19369 if the muscle/skin complex has two pedicles or both sides of the rectus abdominis are elevated (bilateral or hemiflaps).

19370
An open periprosthetic capsulotomy on the breast is done by making an incision in the skin of the breast, at the site of a mastectomy scar, in the skin fold beneath the breast, or around the nipple. The physician uses a cautery knife to cut into the area of fibrous scarring associated with a breast implant. Incisions are made into the scar (contracted capsule) to cut around its circumference and enlarge the pocket in which the prosthesis is placed. Loosening the capsule relieves pain and tightness caused by the contracture. No tissue is removed. The incision is repaired with layered closure.

19371
The physician performs a periprosthetic capsulectomy on the breast. An incision in the skin of the breast at the site of a mastectomy scar, in the skin fold beneath the breast, or around the nipple is made. The physician uses a cautery knife to cut into the area of fibrous scarring associated with a breast implant. The contracted capsule is excised from the breast tissue and the prosthesis is removed. The incision is repaired with layered closure.

19380
Revision is done on a reconstructed breast, usually to correct a problem with asymmetry. The physician makes an incision in the breast skin along the areola or at the fold under the breast or in prior surgical incisions. Tissue therein may be rearranged or secured with sutures to revise the shape of the reconstructed breast. An existing breast prosthesis may be replaced with a prosthesis of a different configuration. Excess skin or tissue from the reconstructed breast may be removed. Once the breast has been revised to its desired shape, the physician repairs the incision with layered closure.

19396
The physician creates a custom breast implant model or moulage that closely resembles the remaining breast configuration of a mastectomy patient. From this a custom breast implant will be created.

Musculoskeletal

20000-20005
The physician makes an incision through skin directly over an abscessed area. The abscess cavity is explored, debrided, and drained. For a deep or complicated abscess procedure in 20005, the physician may evaluate the underlying muscle, fascia, and/or bone. Depending on the appearance of the area, the physician may remove dead bone and/or place a drain or packing after copious irrigation of the area.

20100-20103
The physician explores a penetrating wound in the operating room, such as a gunshot or stab wound, to help identify damaged structures. Nerve, organ, and blood vessel integrity is assessed. The wound may be enlarged to help assess the damage. Debridement, removal of foreign bodies, and ligation or coagulation of minor blood vessels in the subcutaneous tissues, fascia, and muscle are also included in this range of codes. Damaged tissues are debrided and repaired when possible. The wound is closed (if clean) or packed open if contaminated by the penetrating body. Report 20100 for exploration of a neck wound. Report 20101 for exploration of a chest wound. Report 20102 for exploration of an abdomen, flank, or back wound. Report 20103 for exploration of a wound to an extremity.

20150

Excision of the epiphyseal bar is a procedure performed to treat a partial epiphyseal arrest in a patient with significant remaining growth in a long bone, such as the femur, tibia, or fibula. This is caused, in many cases, by an injury or infection involving the epiphyseal plate (growth plate). The patient is placed in the supine position and a tourniquet is applied to the proximal thigh and raised to the appropriate pressure. For excision of the distal femur or proximal tibia, the knee is extended on a radiolucent operating table with the intention of resecting two rectangular areas, one on the medial side and one on the lateral side of the bone. Under fluoroscopic image intensification, a stab wound incision is made laterally or medially at the level of the growth plate. On one side at a time, an osteotome is driven to a depth of 1 cm into the growth plate and rotated 180 degrees to create an opening in the epiphysis. An oval curette is directed through the hole to a depth of about one-third the width of the growth plate. The physician sweeps the curette across the growth plate to remove the rectangular area. If an excision of the epiphyseal bar of the proximal tibia or fibula is performed, the peroneal nerve must be protected. The proximal growth plate of the fibula is approached through an incision anterior to the fibula and exposed anteriorly by subcutaneous blunt dissection. The growth plate is identified by subperiosteal elevation and a rectangular area is removed with a curette. The tourniquet is released and hemostasis is achieved. A piece of autogenous fat from the subcutaneous tissue (though the same incision) or an inert substance may be interpositioned in the cavity allowing growth to continue in the epiphysis. The wound is closed with sutures and the wound is wrapped with a compressive dressing to reduce the formation of a hematoma. The limb is placed in a knee immobilizer.

20200-20205

The physician secures a sample of tissue from a muscle for biopsy. The physician incises the overlying skin and bluntly dissects to the suspect muscle. The muscle tissue is obtained. Bleeding is controlled and the wound is sutured in layers. Report 20200 if the muscle site sampled is superficial and 20205 if the muscle site sampled is deep.

20206

The physician removes a sample of muscle tissue using a percutaneous needle. The physician applies a local anesthetic to the skin. The physician uses a bore needle to pierce the skin, fascia, and muscle, obtaining a sample of muscle tissue. The needle is withdrawn. No repair is usually necessary. Radiologic supervision, if necessary, is reported separately.

20220-20225

The physician usually performs a biopsy on bone to confirm a suspected growth, disease, or infection. The physician normally uses local anesthesia; however, general anesthesia may be used. The physician places a large needle into the spinous process or other superficial bone to obtain the sample in 20220. For sampling a deeper lying bone, such as a vertebra in 20225, an exploring needle is passed through a larger needle to the desired depth and a piece of tissue is removed for testing. Different approaches are taken for vertebral biopsies, based on differing levels of vertebrae. The top three cervical vertebrae are approached from a pharyngeal or anterior approach. The lower four cervical vertebrae are approached from a lateral direction. Thoracic and lumbar vertebra are approached from behind and to the right to avoid major arteries. Radiographs are sometimes used to confirm the placement of the needle.

20240-20245

The physician performs an open biopsy on bone to confirm a suspected growth, disease, or infection. With the patient under general anesthesia, and placed in the appropriate position, the physician makes an incision overlying the biopsy site and carries it down through the tissue to the level of the bone being biopsied. A piece of bone tissue is removed and sent for examination. The wound is sutured closed and the patient is moved to the recovery area. Report 20240 if the biopsy is of a superficial bone such as the ribs, ilium, sternum, or spinous process; report 20245 if the bone biopsied lies deep, such as the femur or ischium.

20250-20251

This procedure is used to confirm a suspected growth, disease, or infection of a vertebral body. The patient is placed in a prone position. A midline incision is made overlying the vertebra to be biopsied. The incision is carried down and the fascia is incised. Paravertebral muscles are retracted and the vertebral area to be biopsied is identified. A piece of tissue is excised or a needle is used to extract a sample of tissue for evaluation. The paravertebral muscles are replaced in their anatomical position and the incision is closed in layers. Report 20250 for thoracic vertebral biopsy and 20251 for lumbar or cervical vertebral biopsy.

20500

A physician injects a sinus tract (a canal or passage leading to an abscess) with a therapeutic agent such as Betadine, to act as a chemical irritant or antibiotic to clear the infection in an abscess or a cyst. X-rays are reported separately.

20501

The physician injects a sinus tract (a canal or passage leading to an abscess) with a radiopaque agent, to determine the existence, nature, or size of an abscess or a cyst. X-rays are reported separately.

20520-20525

The physician removes a foreign body in a muscle or tendon sheath. The physician incises the skin and dissects to the muscle or sheath. The foreign body is isolated by palpation or radiographic imagery (separately reported) and removed. The incision may be closed if clean or packed if contaminated by the object. Report 20520 if the removal is simple; report 20525 if the foreign object lies deep or requires a complicated procedure to remove it.

20526
A physician administers a single therapeutic injection of corticosteroid or anesthetic, 4 cm proximal to the wrist crease between the tendons of the radial flexor and the long palmar muscles on the lateral side of the forearm. This procedure is performed for therapeutic relief of the persistent symptoms of carpal tunnel syndrome.

20550-20551
The physician injects a therapeutic agent into a single tendon sheath, or ligament, aponeurosis such as the plantar fascia in 20550 and into a single tendon origin/ insertion site in 20551. The physician identifies the injection site by palpation or radiographs (reported separately) and marks the injection site. The needle is inserted and the medicine is injected. After withdrawing the needle, the patient is monitored for reactions to the therapeutic agent.

20552-20553
The physician injects a therapeutic agent into a single or multiple trigger points of one or two muscles in 20552 and into a single or multiple trigger points for three or more muscles in 20553. Trigger points are focal, discrete spots of hypersensitive irritability identified within bands of muscle. These points cause local or referred pain. Trigger points may be formed by acute or repetitive trauma to the muscle tissue, which puts too much stress on the fibers. The physician identifies the trigger point injection site by palpation or radiographic imaging and marks the injection site. The needle is inserted and the medicine is injected into the trigger point. The injection may be done under separately reportable image guidance. After withdrawing the needle, the patient is monitored for reactions to the therapeutic agent. The injection procedure is repeated at the other trigger points for multiple sites.

20555
Interstitial radioelement application is a form of brachytherapy (treatment involving the placement of radioactive isotopes for internal radiation) in which the applicators are placed directly within the tissues of the body. The physician places needles or catheters into muscle and/or soft tissue close to the tumor bed for subsequent interstitial radioelement application to treat such tumors as soft tissue sarcoma. If the tumor bed is close to bone or neurovascular structures, materials such as gel-foam may be inserted between the catheters and the critical structures. Catheters may be secured to muscle with absorbable sutures. The radioactive isotopes, such as iridium-192, may be introduced directly after the needle or catheter insertion or on a subsequent visit. The isotopes are contained within tiny seeds (sources) that are left in place to deliver radiation over a period of weeks or months. They do not cause any harm after becoming inert. This method provides radiation to the prescribed body area while minimizing exposure to normal tissue.

20600-20610
After administering a local anesthetic, the physician inserts a needle through the skin and into a joint or bursa. A fluid sample may be removed from the joint or a fluid may be injected for lavage or drug therapy. The needle is withdrawn and pressure is applied to stop any bleeding. Report 20600 for arthrocentesis of a small joint or bursa, such as of the fingers or toes; 20605 for an intermediate joint or bursa, such as the wrist, elbow, ankle, olecranon bursa, or temporomandibular or acromioclavicular area. Report 20610 for a major joint or bursa injection or aspiration, such as of the shoulder, hip, knee joint, or subacromial bursa.

20612
The physician aspirates and/or injects a ganglion cyst. After administering a local anesthetic, the physician inserts a needle through the skin and into the ganglion cyst. A ganglion cyst is a benign mass consisting of a thin capsule containing clear, mucinous fluid arising from an aponeurosis or tendon sheath, such as on the back of the wrist or foot. A fluid sample may be withdrawn from the cyst or a medicinal substance may be injected for therapy. The needle is withdrawn and pressure is applied to stop any bleeding.

20615
After administering a local anesthetic, the physician inserts a needle through the skin and into a bone cyst. A fluid sample is removed from the cyst and medication injected for lavage or drug therapy. The needle is withdrawn and pressure is applied to stop any bleeding.

20650
The physician makes a small skin incision laterally or medially over the affected bone. A Steinmann pin is drilled transversely through the bone so that an end protrudes through the skin from either side. An apparatus with a weight is attached to the pin, providing a traction force to reduce (reposition) and align the fracture as a temporary measure to stabilize it until the fracture itself can be addressed.

20660
The physician applies cranial tongs, a caliper, or a stereotactic frame to stabilize an injured cervical spine for radiography, a stretch test, surgery, or spinal realignment. The physician places the patient supine with the head supported just over the end of the table. The physician applies Betadine solution with sponges

to the hair above the ears. The physician separates or removes hair 1 cm above the ears slightly posterior to the midlateral line. A local anesthetic is injected into the areas selected for pin insertion. Tongs are held in the appropriate position while both skull pins are inserted simultaneously, keeping the tongs equidistant from the skull on either side. The pins are advanced until the indicator button on one pin protrudes 2 to 3 mm. Lock nuts are applied and the pins are checked every two to three hours for proper tightness.

20661-20663
The physician applies a cranial halo to stabilize an injured cervical spine for radiography, traction, or to facilitate surgery in 20661. The physician places the patient supine (lying on the back) with the head supported just over the end of the stretcher. Skin and scalp are sterilized with a povidone-iodine solution. The halo is positioned about the patient's head below the area of greatest skull diameter. A local anesthetic is injected into the areas selected for frame pin insertion. The anterior pins are inserted first, followed by the posterior pins. Two diagonally opposed pins are tightened simultaneously until all four engage the skin and bone. Using a torque screwdriver, all are tightened and secured with nuts or set screws before attachment to a traction setup or to a halo vest or cast. Report 20662 for application of a pelvic halo and 20663 for a femoral halo. These procedures include removal of the halo.

20664
The physician places a cranial halo on the skull of a child whose skull is unusually thin because of a congenital or developmental problem. With the patient under general anesthesia, the physician sterilizes the skin and scalp with a povidone-iodine solution. The halo is positioned on the patient's head with six or more pins, which are advanced until firm, but not to the tension allowed by a normal skull. Diagonally opposed pins are tightened simultaneously. All are secured with nuts. This code includes the removal of the halo.

20665
The physician removes tongs or a halo applied by another physician. Maintaining alignment of the cervical spine, the physician unscrews the frame pins from the skull and removes the tongs or halo. Bone wax may be applied to the wounds to promote healing of the skull. Dressing may be applied to the skin wounds and the skin may be sutured.

20670
The physician makes a small incision overlying the site of the implant. The implant is located. The physician removes the implant by pulling or unscrewing it. The incision is closed with sutures and/or Steri-strips.

20680
The physician makes an incision overlying the site of the implant. Deep dissection is carried down to visualize the implant, which is usually below the muscle level and within bone. The physician uses instruments to remove the implant from the bone. The incision is repaired in layers using sutures, staples, and/or Steri-strips.

20690-20692
The physician applies an external fixation system to help a fracture or joint injury heal. This procedure is performed in addition to a coded treatment of fracture or joint injury unless listed as part of the basic procedure. This procedure uses an external fixator to stabilize an injury such as a simple fracture. One or more pins or wires may be used. Small stab incisions are made in the skin and a drill is used to make a hole into the bone. Each pin or wire is inserted into the bone through the drill holes and secured to an external fixation device. This holds the fracture or joint in a stable position. Report 20690 if uniplane fixation is applied and 20692 if multiplane fixation is applied.

20693
The physician performs adjustment or revision of external fixation to allow for healing that may be hindered due to the development of neurovascular problems, infections, loosening of pins, or failure of the bone fracture to heal. The physician places the patient under anesthesia. Additional pins, wires, rings, or bars may be needed or existing ones moved. The physician drills a hole through the bone and inserts the pin or other fixation instrument, which is attached to external frame devices.

20694
The physician removes the external fixation frame and pulls pins out manually while the patient is under anesthesia. Incisions are closed with sutures and Steri-strips.

20696-20697
Using stereotactic computer-assisted adjustment, such as a spatial frame, the physician applies a unilateral external fixation system with pins or wires in more than one plane (multiplane) to help a fracture or joint injury heal. This procedure is performed in addition to a reported treatment of fracture or joint injury unless listed as part of the basic procedure. This procedure uses an external fixator to stabilize an injury such as a simple fracture. Small stab incisions are made in the skin, and a drill is used to make a hole into the bone. Each pin or wire is inserted into the bone through the drill holes and secured to an external fixation device. This holds the fracture or joint in a stable position. Report 20696 for the application, including imaging, initial and subsequent alignments, assessments, and computations of adjustment schedules. Report 20697 for the removal and replacement of each strut.

20802
The physician replants an arm following a complete amputation. The physician reattaches the upper extremity at a level between the elbow and shoulder. With the patient under anesthesia, the physician identifies the severed neurovascular structures, muscles, bone, and tendons. Each tissue is systematically reattached using sutures, wires, plates, or other fixation devices. Dead tissue is debrided. The skin is joined and closed with sutures after thorough cleaning and irrigation.

20805
The physician reattaches a severed forearm at a level between the wrist and the elbow. With the patient under anesthesia, the physician identifies each structure that has been cut or separated. The nerves, blood vessels, tendons, and bone are each reattached using sutures, wires, plates, or other fixation devices. Dead tissue is debrided. The skin is joined and closed with sutures after thorough cleaning and irrigation.

20808
The physician reattaches a hand that has been completely severed from the forearm between the wrist and the fingers. With the patient under anesthesia, the physician identifies the nerves, blood vessels, tendons, and bones. Each structure is reattached in a systematic fashion with debridement of dead tissue. Sutures, wires, plates, or other devices may be used. Copious irrigation is required. The overlying soft tissues and skin are joined with sutures in layers.

20816
The physician reattaches one of the four fingers, excluding the thumb, which has been completely severed from the hand at or near its articulation with its specific metacarpal bone. With the patient under anesthesia, the physician identifies the nerves, tendons, blood vessels, and bones. Dead tissue is debrided and the wound is irrigated. Each tissue is systematically reattached using sutures, wires, plates, or other devices. Skin is joined and sutured closed.

20822
The physician reattaches one of the four fingers, excluding the thumb, which has been completely severed from the hand at a level between the fingertip and the attachment of the finger to the hand itself. With the patient under anesthesia, the physician identifies severed structures, including nerves, blood vessels, tendons, and bones. Dead tissue is debrided and the wound is irrigated. Each tissue is systematically reattached using sutures, wires, plates, or other devices. Skin is joined in layers with sutures.

20824
The physician reattaches the thumb that has been completely severed from the hand at the attachment of the thumb to the hand itself. With the patient under anesthesia, the physician identifies severed structures, including nerves, blood vessels, tendons, and bones. Dead tissue is debrided and the wound is irrigated. Each tissue is systematically reattached using sutures, wires, plates, or other devices. Skin is joined in layers with sutures.

20827
The physician reattaches a thumb that has been completely severed from the hand at a point distal to where the thumb attaches to the hand. With the patient under anesthesia, the physician identifies severed tissues, including nerves, blood vessels, tendons, and bones. Dead tissue is debrided and the wound is irrigated. Each tissue is systematically reattached using sutures, wires, plates, or other devices. Skin is joined in layers with sutures.

20838
The physician reattaches a foot that has been completely amputated at or near the ankle. With the patient under anesthesia, the physician identifies severed structures, including blood vessels, nerves, tendons, and bones. Dead tissue is debrided and the wound is irrigated. Each tissue is reattached using sutures, wires, plates, pins, or other devices. Skin is joined in layers with sutures.

20900-20902
Bone grafts offer physicians excellent building blocks when repairing skeletal problems. The physician makes an incision overlying the rib, ilium, fibula, or other site from which the autograft will be harvested. Fascia and muscles are incised and retracted. A knife, chisel, cutter, or saw may be used to obtain the bone graft, which will be prepared as needed for implantation. Cancellous bone chips may be obtained, as well. The incision is closed with sutures. Report 20900 if the graft is small. Report 20902 if the graft is larger than a dowel or a button.

20910
The physician takes a cartilage graft from the rib for later use in reconstructing areas of the lower face such as the temporomandibular joint (TMJ). The physician makes a small incision in the skin through the pectoralis muscle and dissects adjacent tissues away near the sternum. The rib is exposed where the bone and cartilage meet. The cartilage is removed. After the cartilage is harvested, the donor site is closed with layered sutures.

20912
The physician takes a cartilage graft from the nasal septum for later use in an autologous reconstructive procedure. For instance, harvested nasal cartilage is often used as a spreader graft or as a nasal alar batten graft to repair a dysfunctional or collapsed internal nasal valve. Usually under local anesthesia and through a small internal incision (6-8 mm), the physician harvests a piece of septal cartilage from within the nose for later grafting. Graft sizes vary and can be 1-3 mm

thick, from 4-8 mm wide, and up to 35 mm in length. A generous amount of cartilage must be maintained to continue functioning as nasal support.

20920
The physician harvests fascia lata by making a small incision over the lateral aspect of the lower thigh. A stripper instrument is advanced upward underneath the fascia as the physician maintains downward pressure on the cut end of fascia lata. Once the desired graft length is obtained, the cutting mechanism on the stripper is used to release the fascia from above. The stripper and graft are removed together and the wound is sutured. A compressive dressing is also applied.

20922
Fascia lata is a thick band of connective tissue lying underneath the skin of the thigh. It is also called the external investing fascia. To obtain a portion to use for a graft, the physician incises skin and subcutaneous tissue, elevates the flap off the fascia lata. The amount of connective tissue is acquired by incising and elevating the fascia of the thigh musculature. A small strip or patch may be obtained in this manner. The wound is closed primarily.

20924
The physician decides on a donor site and makes a cut down to the desired tendon. The tendon is severed and one end held with a hemostat. Dissection is carried to the muscular origin and the tendon is removed. A pressure dressing is applied.

20926
The physician obtains a paratenon, fat, or dermis graft. The physician incises the skin and retracts the skin flap to expose the underlying connective tissue. The tissue is incised to the required layer. The graft is lifted and implanted in the recipient site in a separately reportable procedure. The donor site is sutured in layers.

20930-20931
The physician obtains a bone graft from a cadaver donor that is frozen or freeze dried until used. The physician prepares and inserts the allograft in a separately reportable spinal procedure. In 20930, the allograft is prepared as cancellous chips (morselized). In 20931, the allograft is prepared in a bicortical or tricortical shape for structural use.

20936
During a vertebral fusion or other spinal procedure, the physician may use bone fragments taken from the vertebral bodies adjacent to the affected disc, from the spinous process, or laminar fragment. Some of these may have been removed during the surgery or as part of the surgical approach. Local grafts prevent extra morbidity caused by obtaining an iliac or a tibial graft and lessen the possibility of cadaver-borne transmittable diseases. When grafts are harvested, they are obtained through the use of power tools or chisels. The grafts may be morselized, carved into pegs, or shaped as bars.

20937-20938
Bone grafts offer physicians excellent building blocks when repairing vertebral problems. The physician makes an incision over the ilium, fibula, or other site from which the autograft will be obtained. Fascia and muscles are incised and retracted. A knife, chisel, cutter, or saw may be used to obtain the autograft, which will be prepared as needed for implantation in the spine. In 20937, cancellous bone chips (morselized) are obtained. In 20938, structural bicortical or tricortical grafts are obtained. The incision is closed with sutures.

20950
The physician inserts an interstitial fluid pressure monitoring device into a muscle compartment using a wick catheter, needle, or other method. The physician checks the monitoring device for escalation of pressure, which indicates developing compartment syndrome and tissue ischemia. Once the data has been gathered, the catheter or needle is removed.

20955-20962
The physician takes a bone graft from the fibula in 20955 for later reconstruction of another area. The physician makes an incision in the skin overlying the fibula. The bone is isolated and dissected away from adjacent structures with the small blood vessels that supply blood to the bone attached. The bone is grafted to the recipient area to eliminate a defect. The small blood vessels are sutured to blood vessels at the recipient site to provide blood flow to the grafted bone. After the graft is complete, the skin incision is closed with layered sutures. Report 20956 if the iliac crest bone is removed; 20957 if metatarsal bone is removed; and 20962 if other than fibula, iliac crest, or metatarsal bone is used for the graft.

20969
The physician makes an incision in the skin overlying the area of harvest from a bone other than the iliac crest, metatarsal, or great toe. The physician includes a portion of the overlying skin to be removed along with bone. The skin remains viable by being supplied with blood from vessels coming from the bone. The bone is isolated and dissected away from adjacent structures with the small blood vessels that supply blood to the bone still attached. This allows the surgeon to reconstruct a defect of bone and skin using a grafted osteocutaneous flap.

20970-20973
The physician harvests a portion of the iliac crest along with overlying skin. The physician makes an incision in the skin overlying the iliac crest. The bone is isolated and dissected away from adjacent structures with the small blood vessels that supply blood to the bone still attached. In this case, the surgeon usually includes the

deep circumflex iliac artery. The wound is closed, suction drains placed, and a pressure dressing is applied. Report 20972 if the procedure is performed at the metatarsal. Report 20973 if the procedure is performed on the great toe with web space.

20974-20975
The physician performs electrical stimulation of bone. The physician places electrodes over the skin surface along the region of a fracture or defect and administers a low voltage current. This is a non-surgical technique used to stimulate bone healing. Report 20975 if invasive.

20979
A rehabilitation specialist or physical therapist applies low-intensity ultrasound to a bone by placing a transducer on the skin to stimulate bone healing.

20982
Percutaneous radiofrequency ablation of bone tumors may be done as a safe and effective alternative or adjunct to radiation/chemotherapy for metastatic bone cancer lesions and as an effective alternative/adjunct to surgical treatment for benign, but painful, osteoid osteomas. Tumors are destroyed using heat energy, basically "cooking" tumors through a needle. This procedure is performed with the patient under conscious sedation or general anesthesia. The patient is connected to an electrical circuit by placing grounding pads on the thighs. A tiny needle-electrode with an insulated shaft, and an uninsulated tip is inserted through the skin, directly into the tumor. Ultrasound, CT scan, or MRI may be used to guide the needle. This code includes CT guidance. The appropriate amount of wattage and current are sent through the needle from a generator. Active ablation is done for about 10 to 15 minutes. The energy leads to cell death and coagulation, resulting in a sphere of dead tissue after every treatment session. A small margin of normal tissue next to tumors is also burned, to try to leave no single tumor cell behind.

20985
Imageless computer-assisted surgery (CAS) is an adjunct process used in conjunction with certain orthopaedic procedures. Using such tools as markers, reference frames, intraoperative sensing, and computer workstations, imageless computer-assisted navigational procedures increase visualization of the surgical field and aid in precise navigation with minimally invasive approaches. Imageless navigation uses angles and measurements (kinematics) for anatomy determination. Through direct imageless applications, landmarks are established on a universal limb model. This application requires touch-pointing the anatomic landmarks, which are then registered in the computer for use in accurate navigation and measurement in relation to any bone or instrument movement as the surgery is performed. This application provides a way to establish coordinates as an aid for precisely locating anatomical structures in open or percutaneous procedures without the use of preoperative or intraoperative images. Code 20985 is reported in addition to the procedure code when the physician uses an imageless system to help determine coordinates.

21010
The physician makes an incision into the temporomandibular joint (TMJ). The physician may use several incisional patterns, including the preauricular approach, making an incision through the skin anterior to the contour of the ear. The physician may also approach the TMJ through an incision inside or behind the ear. The physician dissects the tissue layers away until the TMJ is exposed and the joint can be incised. The skin incision is closed with sutures.

21011-21014
The physician removes a soft tissue tumor from the subcutaneous tissues (21011-21012) or the subfascial tissues (21013-21014) of the face or scalp, not involving bone. An incision is made over the tumor and dissection exposes it. The tumor and any adjacent tissue that may be affected are excised. Large resections may be needed. The type of tumor determines the extent of the tumor margin resection area. Muscle or fascia may need to be repaired and drains may be placed. The surgical wound may be repaired with layers of sutures, staples, or Steri-strips. Report 21011 (subcutaneous) or 21013 (subfascial) for excision of tumors whose resected area is less than 2 cm; report 21012 (subcutaneous) or 21014 (subfascial) for excision of tumors 2 cm or greater.

21015-21016
The physician performs a radical resection of a malignant soft tissue tumor from the face or scalp, not involving bone. An incision is made over the tumor and dissection exposes it. The tumor and any adjacent tissue that may be affected by the spread of the neoplasm are excised. Large resections may be needed. The type and stage of the lesion determines the extent of the tumor margin resection area. Muscle or fascia may need to be repaired and drains may be placed. The surgical wound is repaired by intermediate or complex closure, adjacent tissue transfer, or graft. Report 21015 for excision of tumors whose resected area is less than 2 cm and 21016 for excision of tumors 2 cm or greater.

21025
The physician removes infected or dead bone tissue from the mandible. This procedure can be performed intraorally through the mucosa or extraorally through a skin incision. If only a small amount of bone is affected, the physician may saucerize the area by grinding the dead bone away with drills or osteotomes. Healthy bone and the continuity of the mandible are left intact. Antibiotic-impregnated acrylic beads may be implanted into the surgical site to stop infection after the removal of bone. These beads are removed at a later

time. Extensive bone removal in large sections or blocks may require a separate bone harvesting/grafting procedure to repair continuity defects. The incisions are closed simply.

21026
The physician removes dead or infected bone from facial bones. A transoral incision in the maxillary buccal vestibule is the most frequent approach. Facial incisions would only be used for large lesions or for additional surgical access. The physician reflects the overlying mucosa, exposing the dead bone. Drills, saws, and osteotomes are used to remove the bone. The transoral incisions are closed in a single layer. Any cutaneous incision is closed in layers.

21029
The physician removes a benign tumor from a facial bone by contouring the excess bone down to the appropriate structure. A transoral incision is made in the maxillary buccal vestibule. The physician reflects the overlying mucosa, exposing the excessive bone. Rotary burs, files, and osteotomes are used to remove this bone. The transoral incision is closed in a single layer.

21030
The physician removes a cyst or benign tumor from the maxilla (upper jaw) or the zygoma (arched cheekbone) by enucleation and/or curettage, not requiring osteotomy. Using an intraoral approach, the physician incises and reflects a mucosal flap of tissue inside the mouth overlying the tumor. In an extraoral approach, the physician approaches the defect through an external skin incision. The tumor is identified and removed from the maxilla or zygoma by scraping with a curette or by cutting the tumor out in such a way as to leave it intact and remove it whole. The mucosal flap is sutured primarily or the subcutaneous tissues and skin incisions on the face are closed with layered sutures.

21031
The physician removes a benign outgrowth of bone (torus mandibularis) most commonly from the lingual (tongue) side of the mandible. Using an intraoral approach, the physician makes an incision in the mucosa overlying the outgrowth of bone and reflects the tissue. The excess bone is removed with a drill or osteotome. The mucosal incision is closed with sutures.

21032
The physician excises a torus palatinus (a bony protuberance), usually found at the junction of the intermaxillary and transverse palatine structures, by making an incision through the mucosa overlying the protuberance. The torus is exposed. Drills, osteotomes, or files are used to remove and contour the bone. The tissue is sutured directly over the bone. Some soft tissue may be excised prior to closure for adaptation over the newly contoured bone.

21034
The physician excises a malignant tumor from the maxilla (upper jaw) or the zygoma (arched cheekbone). Incisions include transoral (e.g., maxillary buccal vestibular) and facial (e.g., Weber-Ferguson). The bony mass is excised with the use of drills, saws, and osteotomes. The tumor is removed to "free margins" as determined with intraoperative tissue specimens sent to the pathologist for immediate microscopic examination. The physician may remove teeth and overlying mucosa. Some surgical defects may require immediate soft tissue reconstruction (e.g., myocutaneous flaps). Transoral incisions are closed in a single layer and facial incisions are closed in layers. Intraoral surgical splints may be used.

21040
The physician removes a cyst or benign tumor from the mandible by enucleation and/or curettage, not requiring osteotomy. Using an intraoral approach, the physician incises and reflects a mucosal flap of tissue inside the mouth overlying the tumor. In an extraoral approach, the physician approaches the defect through an external skin incision. The tumor is identified and removed from the mandible by scraping with a curette or by cutting the tumor out in such a way as to leave it intact and remove it whole. The mucosal flap is sutured primarily or subcutaneous tissue and skin incisions on the face are closed with layered sutures.

21044
The physician removes a malignant tumor from the mandible. Through an intraoral and/or extraoral approach, the physician isolates and dissects the mandibular tumor. The tumor and surrounding tissues are removed. The tissues are closed with layered sutures or may be packed and left open. A separately reportable reconstructive procedure, such as bone harvesting, may be necessary.

21045
The physician removes a malignant tumor from the mandible in a radical resection. An intraoral and/or extraoral approach is used to reach the site of the tumor. The tumor and surrounding tissues are removed. Resection or removal of a part or all of the mandible is performed. Immediate or delayed reconstruction with bone grafts, tissue rearrangement, flaps, or prosthetic devices is sometimes required. The skin incisions are closed with layered sutures.

21046-21047
The physician excises a cyst or benign tumor from the mandible (lower jaw) by intraoral osteotomy in 21046 and by extraoral osteotomy and partial mandibulectomy in 21047. For the intraoral approach, the physician incises and reflects a mucosal flap of tissue inside the mouth overlying the tumor to reach

Musculoskeletal

the bone. In an extraoral approach, the physician approaches the defect through an external skin incision and dissects down through the tissue layers to reach the tumor. The tumor is identified and removed along with overlying bone by cutting into the mandible using a drill or osteotome. Additional bone removal from the mandible is done in 21047 to excise the tumor fully. With large tumors, the surgical wounds may be packed and sutured or reconstructive procedures such as harvesting of bone for grafting may be needed, depending on the size of the surgical wound. The mucosal flap is sutured primarily or the subcutaneous tissues and skin incisions on the face are closed with layered sutures.

21048-21049
The physician excises a cyst or benign tumor from the maxilla (upper jaw) by intraoral osteotomy in 21048 and by extraoral osteotomy and partial maxillectomy in 21049. For the intraoral approach, the physician incises and reflects a mucosal flap of tissue inside the mouth overlying the tumor to reach the bone. In an extraoral approach, the physician approaches the defect through an external skin incision and dissects down through the tissue layers to reach the tumor. The tumor is identified and removed along with overlying bone by cutting into the maxilla using a drill or osteotome. Additional bone removal from the maxilla is done in 21049 to excise the tumor fully. With large tumors, the surgical wounds may be packed and sutured or reconstructive procedures, such as harvesting of bone for grafting, may be needed, depending on the size of the surgical wound. The mucosal flap is sutured primarily or the subcutaneous tissues and skin incisions on the face are closed with layered sutures.

21050
The physician removes the condyle of the mandible, the posterior, rounded projection on the angled branch of the jaw that articulates with the temporal bone. An incision is usually made in the skin anterior to the contour of the ear. The physician dissects the tissue layers until the condyle is exposed. The condyle is cut with drills or saws from the mandible and removed. An additional incision just under the angle of the mandible may be required. The area can be reconstructed with bone and cartilage, or a prosthetic condyle may be inserted. The skin incision is closed with layered sutures and a pressure dressing may be applied.

21060
The physician removes part or all of the meniscus (articular disc) of the temporomandibular joint. An incision is usually made in the skin anterior to the contour of the ear. The physician dissects the tissue layers until the meniscus is exposed. The meniscus is clamped and removed. The joint may be left without a disc or the disc may be replaced with tissue grafted from other areas of the body or with an artificial disc. The skin incision is closed with layered sutures and a pressure dressing may be applied.

21070
The physician removes the diseased or fractured coronoid process of the mandible, the anterior projection on the angled branch of the jaw to which the temporal muscle is attached. The physician makes an incision intraorally along the external oblique ridge of the mandible. The tissue is reflected from the bone, exposing the coronoid process. Using drills and/or osteotomes, the coronoid process is clamped and sectioned from the mandible. The muscle attachments are cut from the coronoid process and will retract, forming scar tissue. The coronoid process is removed. The mucosal incision is closed primarily.

21073
With the patient under general anesthesia or monitored anesthesia care (MAC), the physician applies a downward pressure on the posterior teeth while pushing the mandible back over the articular eminence and returning it to its correct position. No incisions are made and no intermaxillary fixation is used.

21076
The physician fabricates a custom obturator prosthesis to separate the mouth from other structures of the face and skull while performing surgery or allowing facial injuries to heal. The physician identifies the extent of the patient's injuries and determines the type of prosthesis that is required. Impressions of the mouth are taken to make models. A custom obturator prosthesis for that particular patient is prepared from the models.

21077
The physician fabricates a custom orbital prosthesis for the orbit of the eye for the purpose of protecting surrounding structures while surgery is performed or for the healing of facial and skull injuries. The physician identifies the extent of the patient's injuries or disease to determine the exact nature of the required prosthesis. Impressions of the orbit of the eye are taken and used to make models. A custom prosthesis for the particular patient is made from the models.

21079-21080
The physician fabricates an obturator prosthesis to provide a separation between the mouth and the surgical site and/or protect the surgical site while assisting the patient's ability to talk and chew. Impressions are made of the mouth. The impressions are used to make models from which a custom obturator prosthesis is fabricated. The physician makes an interim or temporary obturator prosthesis in 21079 and a definitive obturator prosthesis in 21080, which separates the nasal and sinus complex from the mouth.

21081
The physician fabricates a prosthesis used in a mandibular resection procedure. Impressions are made

of the mandible. The impression is fashioned into a cast model, which the physician uses to construct an external prosthetic device.

21082
The physician fabricates a prosthesis used to augment the palate. Impressions are made of the maxilla and palate. The impression is fashioned into a cast model. The prosthesis is fabricated from this cast.

21083
The physician fabricates a palatal lift prosthesis for the patient who requires the prosthesis to maintain velopharyngeal competence. Impressions are made of the maxilla and palate. The impression is fashioned into a cast model. A customized prosthesis is fabricated from this cast.

21084
The physician fabricates a prosthesis used to aid speech. An impression is made of the affected area and the physician customizes a prosthetic device from a cast model of the impression.

21085
The physician fabricates a splint used in an oral surgical procedure. An impression is made of the area and the physician customizes the splint from the cast model of the impression. These splints may be used in orthognathic reconstructive jaw surgery (repositioning of jaws), for repair of traumatic injuries, or in ablative tumor surgery with or without jaw resection.

21086
The physician designs and prepares a prosthesis for the auricle (pinna or external ear). An impression is taken, from which a cast is made, and the prosthesis is fabricated from this mold. The mold is shaped and honed to fit.

21087
The physician makes a nasal prosthesis after resection of part or all of the nose. A full-face impression or moulage is taken before or after removal of the nose. A stone cast of the patient's face is made from the moulage. Presurgical photographs of the patient are also used as a guide. A customized nasal prosthesis is fabricated on the face cast. The prosthesis is made of latex and is painted to match the color of the patient's skin. This artificial nose is placed and maintained with skin adhesive glue.

21088
The physician makes a facial prosthesis after resection of part or all of the face. A full-face impression or moulage is taken before or after removal of the affected facial area. A stone cast of the patient's face is made from the moulage. Presurgical photographs of the patient are also used as a guide. A customized prosthesis is fabricated on the face cast. The prosthesis is made of latex and is painted to match the color of the patient's skin. This artificial face is placed and maintained with skin adhesive glue.

21100
The physician places the halo for maxillofacial fixation over the patient's head and tightens four screws into place. The halo is connected to interdental fixation, which has the jaws wired together. Arch bars, ivy loops, or other wires are attached to the teeth and wired together. For edentulous patients (without teeth), or partially edentulous patients, dentures or splints may be wired to the jaws first and wired together to provide intermaxillary fixation. Orthodontic appliances may also be used.

21110
The physician applies interdental fixation to wire the jaws together for conditions other than a fracture or dislocation. Arch bars, ivy loops, or other wires are attached to the teeth and wired together. For edentulous patients (without teeth), or partially edentulous patients, dentures or splints may be wired to the jaws first and wired together to provide intermaxillary fixation. Orthodontic appliances may also be used.

21116
The physician injects a radiopaque dye into the temporomandibular joint. The physician or radiologist threads a small catheter into the temporomandibular joint by inserting a needle through the skin and into the superior and/or inferior joint spaces. Dye is injected. Separately reported radiographs are taken to study the soft tissue anatomy of the joint, such as the articular disc or ligaments.

21120-21123
The physician places an implant or a graft onto the chin to augment or enlarge it. Various materials can be used, including tissue grafted from the patient's own body or taken from a tissue bank. Prosthetic devices may also be used. This procedure is most commonly performed from an intraoral approach. The physician makes an incision in the mandibular labial vestibule inside the lower lip. The mucosa is reflected from the chin and the implanted material placed between the mucosa and the bone. A skin incision may also be made under the chin. The implant may be secured to the bone using wires or screws or may be left to be held in place by the surrounding tissue. The mucosa is sutured simply. Report 21121 if a sliding osteotomy is performed to correct the chin; 21122 if two or more osteotomies are performed; and 21123 if interpositional bone grafts are used for the genioplasty.

21125
The physician uses prosthetic material to augment the body or angle of the mandible. The physician may use an intraoral approach or may make skin incisions extraorally below the body or angle of the mandible. The physician dissects tissues away and the bone of the

body or angle is exposed. A synthetic material is placed on the mandible to augment the contours. The material is secured with screws or wires. The incisions are sutured simply.

21127
The physician uses a bone graft to augment the body or angle of the mandible. The physician harvests bone from another site on the patient's body, most commonly the rib, hip, or skull, and repairs the surgically created wound of the harvest site. The physician may use an intraoral approach or skin incisions. The physician dissects adjacent structures away and the body or angle of the mandible is exposed. The graft is placed on an area of the body or angle to augment the contours. The graft may also be placed between portions of bone of the body or angle (interpositional grafting). The graft is secured with screws or wires. The intraoral incisions are sutured simply. The extraoral incisions are closed with layered sutures.

21137
The physician performs surgery on the forehead to correct a skeletal deformity. With the patient under anesthesia, the physician makes an incision in the hairline to expose the forehead of the skull. The deformity in the bone is identified and fully exposed. The physician uses a variety of surgical instruments to reshape the bone to make it follow a more normal contour. The wound is irrigated and closed in layers.

21138
The physician performs surgery on the forehead to correct a skeletal deformity using the application of prostheses or bone grafts to obtain a more normal contour. With the patient under anesthesia, the physician makes an incision in the hairline to expose the forehead of the skull. The deformity in the bone is identified and fully exposed. The physician uses a variety of surgical instruments to reshape the bone to make it follow a more normal contour. Prostheses may be applied and/or autografts may be harvested and applied as part of the procedure. The wounds are irrigated and closed in layers.

21139
The physician corrects a skeletal deformity of the frontal sinus or repairs the anterior frontal sinus wall. An incision is made at the forehead hairline or the eyebrows. The forehead is exposed directly over the frontal sinus wall. The deformity or deficit is identified. Soft tissue is debrided. The physician reshapes the anterior wall of the sinus. If the wall is prominent or badly misshapen, the physician elevates it from the forehead and resets it in the appropriate anatomic and cosmetic position. Fixation devices such as wires may be required to maintain the repaired wall. The wound is irrigated and closed in layers. A soft dressing is applied.

21141-21143
The physician performs a LeFort I osteotomy to repair congenital malformations or acquired deformities of the facial bones, without using a bone graft. With the patient under anesthesia, the physician makes a horizontal cut through the maxillary sinuses and nasal septum through an intraoral incision, and into the pterygoid fissure. Surgical instruments are used to complete the separation of the maxilla from the skull base. The maxilla is down-fractured to mobilize it and can be moved into the proper predetermined position. If segmental surgery in the maxilla was necessary, the mobilized segments are held in position by a template secured to the upper teeth. Maxillary malpositioning is corrected and the maxilla is wired to the mandible, which is positioned as a whole unit. Rigid fixation of the maxilla is achieved with miniplates or intermaxillary wires. The operative site is irrigated with antibiotic solution and the oral mucosa is closed as needed. Report 21141 if a single piece segment if repositioned; 21142 for lower maxillary midface reconstruction with two piece segmental movement; and 21143 if multiple piece (three or more) osteotomies are performed.

21145-21147
The physician performs a LeFort I osteotomy and bone grafts to repair congenital malformations or acquired deformities of the facial bones. With the patient under anesthesia, the physician makes a horizontal cut through the maxillary sinuses and nasal septum through an intraoral incision and into the pterygoid fissure. Surgical instruments are used to complete the separation of the maxilla from the skull base. The maxilla is down-fractured to mobilize it for movement into the proper predetermined position. If segmental surgery in the maxilla was necessary, the mobilized segments are held in position by a template secured to the upper teeth. Maxillary malpositioning is corrected. Cranial or iliac bone grafts are placed and the donor site repaired. The maxilla is wired to the mandible, which is positioned as a whole unit. Rigid fixation of the maxilla is achieved with miniplates or intermaxillary wires. The operative site is irrigated with antibiotic solution and the oral mucosa is closed as needed. Report 21145 if a single piece segment is repositioned; 21146 for lower maxillary midface reconstruction with two piece segmental movement; and 21147 if multiple piece (three or more) segmental osteotomies are performed.

21150
The physician reconstructs the midface to correct developmental or acquired skeletal deformities. The physician may use a variety of incisions, including a bicoronal scalp flap, lower eyelid, and transoral incisions. Through these incisions, the nasofrontal junction, inferior orbital rims, and maxilla are exposed. Osteotomies of the pyramidal nasoorbitomaxillary midface (LeFort II) are performed with saws, burs, or

Musculoskeletal

osteotomes. The midface is down-fractured from the stable bone. The physician removes excess bone at fracture sites to accommodate anterior intrusion (superior repositioning) of the midface. The midface is reduced in the desired position with wires, plates, and/or screws. The transoral incision is closed in a single layer. Lower eyelid and scalp incisions are closed in layers. Intermaxillary fixation may be applied.

21151

The physician reconstructs the midface to correct developmental or acquired skeletal deformities. The physician may use a variety of incisions, including a bicoronal scalp flap, lower eyelid, and transoral incisions. Through these incisions, the physician exposes the nasofrontal junction, inferior orbital rims, and maxilla. Osteotomies of the pyramidal midface (LeFort II) are performed with saws, burs, or osteotomes. The midfacial segment is down-fractured from the stable bone and rotated or advanced with precise measurement into a new position. The physician reduces the midface with wires, plates, and/or screws. The physician harvests bone grafts from the patient's hip, rib, or skull and closes the surgically created wound. The interpositional bone grafts are placed between the bony interfaces of the repositioned nasoorbitomaxillary midface. The transoral incisions are closed in a single layer. Lower eyelid and scalp incisions are closed in layers. Intermaxillary fixation may be applied.

21154

The physician reconstructs the midface to correct developmental or acquired skeletal deformities. The physician uses a variety of incisions, including a bicoronal scalp flap, lower eyelid, and transoral incisions. Complete separation of the midface from the cranial base is necessary. Surgical fractures are made through the zygomas, orbits, and bones of the nasofrontal region. Osteotomies of the complete midface (LeFort III) are performed with saws, burs, or osteotomes. The midface is down-fractured from the stable cranial bone and placed with precise measurement into presurgically determined position. The physician reduces the midface with wires, plates, and/or screws. The physician harvests bone grafts from the patient's hip, rib, or skull, and closes the surgically created wound. The interpositional bone grafts are placed between the bony interfaces of the midface. The transoral incisions are closed in a single layer. Lower eyelid and scalp incisions are closed in layers. Intermaxillary fixation may be applied.

21155

The physician reconstructs both the midface and the maxilla to correct developmental or acquired skeletal deformities. The physician uses a variety of incisions, including a bicoronal scalp flap, lower eyelid, and transoral incisions. Complete separation of the midface (LeFort III) from the cranial base is necessary. Additionally, horizontal down-fracture of the maxilla is necessary to correct alignment of the teeth. Surgical fractures are made through the zygomas, orbits, and bones of the nasofrontal region with saws, burs, or osteotomes. The physician also makes a horizontal osteotomy, separating the maxilla from the midface. The midface is down-fractured from the stable cranial base and the maxilla is down-fractured from the midface segment. Both the midface and the maxilla are placed into new positions and reduced with wires, plates, and/or screws. The physician harvests bone grafts from the patient's hip, rib, or skull, and closes the surgically created wound. The interpositional bone grafts are placed between the bony interfaces of the maxilla and the midface. The transoral incisions are closed in a single layer. Lower eyelid and scalp incisions are closed in layers. Intermaxillary fixation may be applied.

21159

The physician reconstructs the midface with the forehead to correct developmental or acquired skeletal deformities. Surgical fractures are made through the zygomas, frontal bone, and orbits. Complete separation of the midface with the frontal bone from the cranial base is necessary. The physician uses a variety of incisions, including a bicoronal scalp flap, eyelid, and transoral incisions. Osteotomies of the complete midface (LeFort III) together with the frontal bone are performed with saws, burs, or osteotomes. The midface with the frontal bone is down-fractured from the stable cranial base. The midface and frontal bone are placed with precise measurement into new positions and reduced with wires, plates, and/or screws. The physician harvests bone grafts from the patient's hip, rib, or skull and closes the surgically created wound. The interpositional bone grafts are placed between the bony interfaces of the newly positioned midface and forehead segment. The transoral incisions are closed in a single layer. Eyelid and scalp incisions are closed in layers. Intermaxillary fixation may be applied.

21160

The physician reconstructs both the midface with the forehead and the maxilla to correct developmental or acquired skeletal deformities. Complete separation of the midface with the frontal bone from the cranial base is necessary along with horizontal down-fracture of the maxilla from the midface. Surgical fractures are made through the zygomas, frontal bone, and orbits. The physician uses a variety of incisions, including a bicoronal scalp flap, eyelid, and transoral incisions. Osteotomies of the complete midface (LeFort III) together with the frontal bone and also the lower maxilla from the midface are performed with saws, burs, or osteotomes. The midface and frontal bones are down-fractured from the stable cranial base and the maxilla is horizontally down-fractured from the midface. The midface with the frontal bone and the maxilla are placed into new positions and reduced with wires, plates, and/or screws. The physician harvests bone grafts from the patient's hip, rib, or skull and closes the surgically created wound. The interpositional bone grafts are placed between the bony interfaces of the maxilla and the midface segment. The transoral incisions are closed in a single layer. Eyelid and scalp incisions are closed in layers. Intermaxillary fixation may be applied.

21172
The physician performs reconstructive surgery on the lower forehead and superior-lateral orbit of the eye to correct skeletal abnormalities, with or without grafts. The physician may use a variety of incisions, including through the eyelids and scalp, to obtain access to the site. The soft tissues are dissected as needed to expose the bones. The physician performs osteotomies of the forehead and orbit as needed. The bones are manipulated and realigned to the desired position. The physician may obtain bone grafts from the patient's hip, rib, or skull that can be placed to augment the forehead and orbit reconstruction. The bones are held in place with the use of wires, plates, or screws. The wounds are irrigated and each closed in layers.

21175
The physician performs reconstructive surgery on the lower forehead and both superior lateral orbital rims to correct skeletal abnormalities of the cranium, with or without grafts. The physician utilizes a variety of incisions about the eyes, forehead, and scalp to gain access to these bones. The soft tissues are dissected as needed to expose the bones. Several osteotomies of the forehead and orbits are made so that the deformity can be corrected. The bones are manipulated, contoured, and shifted as needed to place them in the desired positions. The physician may obtain bone grafts from the patient's hip, rib, or skull that can be placed to augment the reconstruction. Various internal fixation devices are employed to hold the reduction rigidly in place, such as wires, pins, plates, or screws. The wounds are irrigated and closed in layers.

21179-21180
The physician performs reconstructive surgery of the forehead and the supraorbital rims of both eyes to correct skeletal deformities of the cranium. With the patient under anesthesia, the physician uses any of a variety of incisions about the eyes, forehead, and scalp to gain access to these bones. The soft tissues are dissected as needed to expose the bones. Osteotomies of the bones are performed in multiple places to facilitate manipulating the bones into the desired position. The bones are shaped as needed. In 21179, the physician utilizes allografts or synthetic prosthetic material to augment the reconstruction. In 21180, the physician employs autografts, harvested from the patient's hip, rib, or skull. Pins, wires, plates, and screws are used to hold the bones and graft in rigid reduction. The wounds are irrigated and closed in layers.

21181
The physician performs surgery to correct distortion expansion or deformity of a cranial bone caused by a benign extracranial lesion. The physician utilizes any of a variety of incisions to access the site. The incisions are carried deep to the bone and the tumor is identified and exposed. The physician uses surgical instruments to debride, reshape, and contour the cranial bone to conform to its normal anatomic position and profile. The bone and wounds are irrigated and closed in layers.

21182-21184
The physician performs reconstructive surgery of the cranial bones including the orbit walls and rims, forehead, and nasoethmoid complex following the excision of benign tumors from within and without the cranium. The physician utilizes a variety of incisions through the mouth, eyelids, and scalp to gain access to these bones. The incisions are carried deep, soft tissues are reflected, and the bones are individually identified and exposed. Osteotomies are performed as needed to surgically fracture and manipulate the bones into their desired and acceptable positions. This may require advancement of the forehead. Bone grafts are harvested from a site such as the hip, skull, or ribs. Multiple grafts may be required to augment and stabilize the reconstructed cranial bones following tumor removal. Internal fixation devices such as wires, plates, and screws are used to hold the reduction securely in place. The incisions are all irrigated and closed in layers. Report 21182 if the total area of bone grafting is less than 40 sq cm; 21183 if the total area of bone grafting is greater than 40 sq cm but less than 80 sq cm; and 21184 if the total area of bone grafting is greater than 80 sq cm.

21188
The physician reconstructs the midface to correct developmental or traumatic skeletal deformities. Reconstruction includes both osteotomies and bone grafts. The physician may use a variety of incisions, including a bicoronal scalp flap, eyelid, and transoral incisions. Through the incisions, the physician performs osteotomies as necessary of the midface with saws, burs, or osteotomes. The osteotomies performed here do not follow the standard LeFort surgical fracture lines. The midfacial bones are down-fractured from the stable cranial base. The midface is placed with precise measurement into a new position. Bone grafts are harvested from the patient's hip, rib, or skull and the surgically created wound is closed. The interpositional bone grafts are placed between the bony interfaces of the repositioned maxilla and midface. Internal fixation devices such as wires, plates, and screws are used to hold the reduction securely in place. The transoral incisions are closed in a single layer. Eyelid and scalp

incisions are closed in layers. Intermaxillary fixation may be applied.

21193-21194

The physician reconstructs the ramus of the mandible using various osteotomies (bone cuts) to correct mandibular deformities. Vertical, horizontal, L, inverted L, and C osteotomies are used. The type of osteotomy refers to the shape and direction of the bone cuts. The physician makes a skin incision below the angle of the mandible. Vertical ramus and horizontal osteotomies may also be accomplished from an intraoral approach. The tissue is dissected to the mandible and the bone of the mandibular ramus is exposed. Bone cuts are made in various shapes according to necessity using drills, saws, or osteotomes. The physician moves part of the separated mandible into a new position. The osteotomy cuts are securely reduced with wires, screws, or plates. The incision is sutured. No bone grafts are used in 21193. Report 21194 if bone grafts are taken from another site on the patient's body, such as the rib, hip, or skull, and used to aid reconstruction and healing of the mandible.

21195-21196

The physician reconstructs the mandibular ramus to lengthen, set back, or rotate the mandible. Using an intraoral approach, the physician makes an incision overlying the external oblique ridge, through the mucosa near the second mandibular molars. The mandibular ramus is exposed by reflecting the tissue from both sides of the ramus. Drills, saws, and/or osteotomes are used to cut the mandible along the inside, top, and outside surfaces of the bone, but not completely through. The physician uses osteotomes and/or other instruments to pry the mandible apart along the bone cuts in a sagittal plane. Once separated, the physician moves the mandible into the desired position and holds the bone in reduction using wires. No rigid internal fixation devices are used in 21195. In 21196, screws or plates are placed in or on the bone. The physician may also make small 0.5 cm skin incisions near the mandibular angle, through which instruments place the plates or screws. The mucosal and skin incisions are sutured closed.

21198-21199

The physician performs an osteotomy on a segment of the mandible to correct a localized deformity. The teeth are moved within a segment or block of bone. Using an intraoral approach, the physician makes an incision in the mucosa to expose the segment of bone to be moved. Drills, saws, and/or osteotomes are used to cut a section of the alveolar bone. These cuts do not extend through the mandible, but include only a segment above the inferior border. The segment is moved into the desired position and held in reduction with wires, screws, or plates. The segment may also be held in place by a preformed acrylic interocclusal splint. The mucosa is sutured simply. Report 21198 when a segmental osteotomy of the mandible is performed. Report 21199 when a segmental osteotomy of the mandible is performed and the genioglossus (primary tongue muscle) is advanced.

21206

The physician performs an osteotomy on a segment of the maxilla to correct a localized deformity. The teeth are moved within a segment or block of bone. Using a circumvestibular incision, the physician exposes the segment of bone to be moved. Drills, saws, and/or osteotomes are used to cut a section of the alveolar bone. These cuts do not extend through the maxilla, but include only a segment. The segment is moved into the desired position and held in reduction with wires, screws, or plates. The segment may also be held in place by a preformed acrylic interocclusal splint. The mucosa is sutured simply and intermaxillary fixation may be placed.

21208

The physician augments the facial bones with implanted grafts or prosthetic devices, altering the contours of the face. The physician may use an intraoral approach or other incisions to access the operative site. The tissue is dissected, exposing the bone for augmentation. A bone graft is taken from another part of the body, such as the hip, rib, or skull, and grafted onto the facial bone to contour the face. Other materials such as prosthetic implants or donor bone may also be used. The implant is secured to the bone using screws, wires, or plates. The mucosa is sutured simply.

21209

The physician removes protrusions of excess or misshaped facial bone to reduce the contours of the face. The physician may use an intraoral approach or other incisions to access the operative site. The tissue is dissected, exposing the bone for reduction. A reciprocation saw or drill is used to cut and remove the bone, reducing its contours. The mucosal incision is sutured simply.

21210

The physician reconstructs the nasal, maxillary, or malar area bones with a bone graft to correct defects due to injury, infection, or tumor resection. The procedure may also be performed to augment atrophic or thin bone, or to aid in healing fractures. The physician harvests bone from the patient's hip, rib, or skull. Incisions are made overlying the harvest site. Tissues are dissected away to the desired bone. The physician removes the bone as needed for grafting to the defect area. After the bone is harvested, the donor site is repaired in layers. Access incisions are made to the recipient site and the area of bony defect is exposed. The graft is placed to repair the defect and may be held in place with wires, plates, or screws. The access sites are irrigated and sutured closed.

21215
The physician reconstructs the mandible with a bone graft to correct defects due to injury, infection, or tumor resection. The procedure may also be performed to augment atrophic or thin mandibles, or to aid in healing fractures. The physician harvests bone from another site on the patient's body, most commonly the rib, hip, or skull, and repairs the surgically created wound. The physician makes facial skin incisions to expose the mandible and place the graft from the donor site. Occasionally, intraoral incisions are used. The graft is held firmly positioned with wires, plates, or screws. The incisions are sutured with a layered closure.

21230-21235
The physician reconstructs an area of the face, chin, nose, or ear with a cartilage graft harvested from the ribs. The physician makes a small incision near the sternum through the pectoralis muscle exposing the rib where the bone and cartilage meet. Cartilage is removed from the area and the donor site is closed directly. The physician may make lower eyelid incisions to expose the defect area of the face or nose. Recipient sites of the chin or the ear may also be prepared for the rib cartilage graft. The graft is placed and held in place with wires, plates, or screws. The incisions are sutured with a layered closure. Report 21235 if ear cartilage is harvested for a graft to the nose or ear.

21240
The physician repairs or reconstructs the temporomandibular joint. An incision is made through the skin anterior to the contour of the ear or within the ear. The tissues are dissected and the joint is exposed. Once the joint is exposed, a variety of repairs may be performed. The articular disc may be repositioned or the ligaments may be repaired or shortened. The condylar head may be smoothed or recontoured, or the articular disc may be removed. If removed, tissue may be taken from another part of the body to replace the articular disc. The tissue may be fascia from nearby muscles such as the temporalis muscle, cartilage from the ear, dermis, or other tissues. The incisions are closed directly.

21242
The physician repairs or reconstructs the temporomandibular joint with a donor graft. An incision is made through the skin anterior to the contour of the ear or within the ear. The tissues are dissected and the joint is exposed. Once the joint is exposed, a variety of repairs may be performed. Donor tissue (allograft material) is used to replace the articular disc or other parts of the joint. The incisions are closed directly.

21243
The physician partially or totally replaces the diseased or injured temporomandibular joint with a prosthetic joint. An incision is made through the skin anterior to the contour of the ear or within the ear. An additional skin incision just beneath the angle of the mandible may also be necessary. An artificial fossa can be placed above the condyle and secured with screws. If the condyle needs replacement, it is removed and a prosthetic condyle is secured to the remaining condylar neck, typically using screws. Both the fossa and the condyle may need to be replaced. The incisions are closed directly.

21244
The physician reconstructs the mandible by inserting a bone plate with posts that extend through the lower border of the mandible and into the mouth. The posts can be used to retain dentures in an atrophic or thin mandible. The physician makes an incision through the skin under the chin and dissects the tissues to the bone. Holes are drilled upward through the bone and into the mouth. The posts of the plate are placed through the holes and into the mouth. The plate is secured extraorally to the mandible with screws and the incision is closed with layered sutures.

21245-21246
The physician places a metal framework between the mucosa and the bone of the maxilla or mandible. The metal framework has posts that extend vertically and protrude through the mucosa into the mouth. The posts are used to retain an upper denture in the maxilla or lower denture in the mandible when teeth are missing. Intraoral surgery is performed in one or two sessions. The physician makes an incision along the crest of the edentulous area (without teeth) and exposes as much of the bone as possible. If performed in two sessions, the physician makes impressions of the exposed bone and sutures the mucosa closed. The impression is used to make models for custom framework. At the second surgical session, the physician removes the sutures and again exposes the bone. The metal framework, with the attached posts, is placed on the bone. The mucosa and periosteum are sutured over the framework and around the protruding posts. Scarring, which occurs with healing, keeps the framework in place. If performed in one session, a CT scan is used to make a plastic model of the mandible or maxilla from which the framework and posts are fabricated. A single surgical session is used to insert the framework as described above. Incisions are closed simply with sutures. Report 21245 for partial reconstruction. Report 21246 for complete reconstruction.

21247
The physician reconstructs the mandibular condyle of the temporomandibular joint (TMJ) using bone and cartilage taken from the rib. The physician harvests the rib by making a small incision through the pectoralis major muscle and dissecting through the tissue to the rib. Part of the rib and the cartilage near the sternum

are removed. The donor site is closed with layered sutures. The physician makes incisions through the skin anterior to the contour of the ear and dissects tissue to the TMJ site. Another incision is often made beneath the angle of the mandible and the tissue is dissected to the bone. The bone is exposed superiorly as far as possible. The rib graft is inserted through the lower incision with the cartilaginous end placed upward into the joint, replacing the condyle. Through both incisions, the rib is manipulated into the proper position and secured to the mandible using plates, screws, or wires. The incisions are closed with layered sutures.

21248-21249

The physician places metal implants into the bone of the maxilla or mandible. Metal posts attached to the implants protrude through the mucosa into the mouth. Artificial teeth or dentures are attached to the roots to replace missing teeth. These implants may be cylindrical or thin blades. The physician makes incisions through the mucosa to expose the bone using an intraoral approach. Precision holes are drilled in the bone where the implants are to be placed. With blade style implants, the posts are already attached to the implant and the mucosa is sutured simply around the post. With cylindrical implants, the mucosa is sutured over the top of the implant and is allowed to heal while buried under the mucosa. The incisions are closed simply. A second procedure is performed three to eight months later. The implant is exposed again and the abutment connectors are attached. Report 21248 for partial reconstruction. Report 21249 for complete reconstruction.

21255

The physician reconstructs the zygomatic arch and glenoid fossa. Bone and cartilage grafts are used in reconstruction. The physician harvests bone grafts from the patient's hip, rib, or skull and closes the surgically created wound. Costal cartilage grafts are most frequently used. The physician makes a hemicoronal incision with a preauricular (in front of the ear) extension. The tissues are reflected to access the zygomatic arch of the cheekbone and the glenoid fossa (depression of the temporal bone at the base of the arch where the mandible articulates). The grafts are placed and the reconstructed arch and fossa are stabilized with internal fixation of sutures, wires, plates, and/or screws. The incision is closed in layers.

21256

The physician increases both the size of the bone structure and outline of the bony orbit. The physician uses a variety of incisions to access the surgical site including bicoronal, lower eyelid, eyebrow, and maxillary vestibular incisions. Cuts are made in the orbital rims using drills or saws. The bone is advanced [illegible] desired positions and secured with wires, plates, [illegible]/or screws. The physician harvests bone from the patient's hip, rib, or skull and closes the surgically created graft donor site. These bone grafts are fashioned by the physician to augment bone or replace congenitally absent bone. The grafts are secured with wires, plates, and/or screws. Incisions through skin are repaired with a layered closure. Intraoral incisions are closed in a single layer.

21260

The physician moves the orbits closer to one another. The physician uses a variety of incisions to access the surgical sites including bicoronal, lower eyelid, eyebrow, and maxillary vestibular incisions. The reconstruction techniques for repositioning of the orbits center around the nasoorbital area and include reconstruction of the nose and the maxilla. Strategic cuts are made around the orbits with drills or saws. Bony cuts are made in the nasal and ethmoid bones and portions of these bones are removed. The bony orbits are realigned to desired positions and secured with wires, plates, and/or screws. The physician harvests bone from the patient's hip, rib, or skull and closes the surgically created graft donor site. These bone grafts are fashioned by the physician to augment bone, filling in the spaces left by the repositioning, and to maintain the medial positions of the orbits. Small, separate bone grafts may be placed directly on bony step defects. Large grafts are secured with wires, plates, and/or screws. Incisions through skin are repaired with a layered closure. Intraoral incisions are closed in a single layer.

21261

The physician moves the orbits closer to one another. For severe cases, a combined intra- and extracranial approach is used. The physician uses a variety of incisions to access the surgical site including bicoronal, lower eyelid, eyebrow, and maxillary vestibular incisions. To gain complete access to the orbits, a frontal craniotomy is performed, temporarily removing a portion of the frontal bone, retracting the brain, and making orbital osteotomy cuts from the inside of the skull. Cuts are made to release the bony orbits of the eye so they may be positioned closer together, using drills or saws. Bony cuts are made in the nasal and ethmoid bones and portions of these bones are removed. The bony orbits are realigned to desired positions and secured with wires, plates, and/or screws. The physician harvests bone from the patient's hip, rib, or skull and closes the surgically created graft donor site. These bone grafts are fashioned by the physician to augment bone, filling in the spaces left by the repositioning, and to maintain the medial positions of the orbits. Small, separate bone grafts may be fashioned by the physician and placed directly on bony step defects. Large grafts are secured with wires, plates, and/or screws. The frontal bone is again placed in its anatomic location and secured with wires, plates, and/ or screws. Incisions through skin are repaired with a layered closure. Intraoral incisions are closed in a single layer.

21263

The physician moves the orbits closer to one another and advances the frontal bone to increase forehead contours. The physician uses a variety of incisions to access the surgical site including bicoronal, lower eyelid, eyebrow, and maxillary vestibular incisions. To gain complete access to the orbits, a frontal craniotomy is performed, temporarily removing a portion of the frontal bone, retracting the brain, and making orbital cuts from the inside of the skull. Cuts are made to release the bony orbits of the eye so they may be positioned closer together, using drills or saws. Bony cuts are made in the nasal and ethmoidal bones and portions of these bones are removed. The bony orbits are realigned and the frontal bone of the forehead is advanced and repositioned into the desired location and secured with wires, plates, and/or screws. The physician harvests bone from the patient's hip, rib, or skull and closes the surgically created graft donor site. These bone grafts are fashioned by the physician to augment bone, filling in the spaces left by the repositioning, and to maintain the medial positions of the orbits. Small, separate bone grafts may be placed directly on bony step defects. Large grafts are fixated with wires, plates, and/or screws. Incisions through skin are repaired with a layered closure. Intraoral incisions are closed in a single layer.

21267

The physician moves the positioning of an orbit on one side. The physician uses a variety of incisions to access the surgical site including coronal, lower eyelid, eyebrow, and maxillary vestibular incisions. Cuts are made in the orbital rims using drills or saws. The bony orbit is realigned to the desired position and secured with wires, plates, and/or screws. The physician harvests bone from the patient's hip, rib, or skull and closes the surgically created graft donor site. These bone grafts are fashioned by the physician to augment bone, replace congenitally absent bone, and recontour facial shapes while maintaining the new position of the orbit. Small separate bone grafts may be placed directly on bony step defects. Large grafts are fashioned and secured with wires, plates, and/or screws. Incisions through skin are repaired with a layered closure. Intraoral incisions are closed in a single layer.

21268

The physician moves the positioning of an orbit on one side. The physician uses a variety of incisions to access the surgical site including coronal, lower eyelid, eyebrow, and maxillary vestibular incisions. To gain complete access to the orbit, a frontal craniotomy is performed, temporarily removing a portion of the frontal bone, retracting the brain, and making cuts from the inside of the skull. Cuts are made in the orbital rims using drills and saws. The bony orbit is realigned to the desired position and secured with wires, plates, and/or screws. The physician harvests bone from the patient's hip, rib, or skull and closes the surgically created graft donor site. These bone grafts are fashioned by the physician to augment bone, replace congenitally absent bone, and recontour facial shapes while maintaining the new position of the orbit. Small, separate bone grafts may be placed directly on bony step defects. Large grafts are secured with wires, plates, and/or screws. The frontal bone is replaced in its anatomic location and secured with wires, plates, and/ or screws. Incisions through skin are repaired with a layered closure. Intraoral incisions are closed in a single layer.

21270

The physician augments the malar (cheek) prominence with prosthetic material. Incisions are made through the lower eyelids and maxillary buccal vestibule to expose the malar defect. The prosthetic implant is positioned and fixated on the malar prominence with wires, plates, and/or screws. The eyelid incisions are closed in layers. The oral vestibular incision is closed in a single layer.

21275

The physician performs a second procedure to continue corrections of skeletal deformities of the orbits and face. The physician uses a variety of incisions to access the surgical site including bicoronal, lower eyelid, eyebrow, and maxillary vestibular incisions. Revision cuts are made using drills and saws. Bone is realigned to the desired positions and secured again with wires, plates, and/or screws. The physician may harvest bone from the patient's hip, rib, or skull and close the surgically created graft donor site. Bone grafts are fashioned by the physician and secured with wires, plates, and/or screws, if necessary. Incisions through skin are repaired with a layered closure. Intraoral incisions are closed in a single layer.

21280

The physician reattaches the medial canthal ligament. The medial canthal ligament is attached medially to nasal-orbital bones and laterally to the orbital fascia, the upper eyelid, and the lower eyelid. The ligament is isolated through a bicoronal incision or through skin incisions placed beside the ligament. After locating the ligament, stainless steel suture or wire is placed through the ligament. A hole is made in the nasal bones on the opposite side with a drill or awl. The suture or wire is passed under the nasal complex to the opposite side through the bony hole. The suture or wire is ligated to the bone. Any incisions are repaired with a layered closure.

21282

The physician reattaches the lateral canthal ligament to correct soft tissue structures of the lateral aspect of the eye and eyelids. The lateral canthal ligament is attached laterally to the orbital aspect of the zygoma and medially to the orbital fascia, the upper eyelid, and the lower eyelid. The ligament is isolated through a horizontal skin incision placed beside the ligament. After locating the ligament, the physician places stainless steel suture or wire through the ligament. A hole is made in the zygoma with a drill. The physician passes the suture or wire through the bony hole. The suture or wire is ligated to the bone. Skin incisions are repaired with a layered closure.

21295-21296

The physician reduces the size of the masseter muscle and bone when the muscle has become hypertrophic (overly enlarged). The physician makes skin incisions in the neck just beneath the angle of the mandible. The tissues are dissected to expose the masseter muscle and mandible. The physician removes appropriate amounts of muscle and may use drills, saws, or osteotomes to remove bone in the area of the angle to produce the desired contour. The incision is repaired with a layered closure and pressure dressings are placed on the site. Report 21295 for an extraoral approach. Report 21296 for an intraoral approach.

21310

The physician treats a stable, non-displaced nasal fracture. No physical manipulation of the nasal bones or stabilization from splints is necessary. Treatment includes external agents (i.e., ice therapy) and prescribing pharmacologic agents.

21315

The physician treats a displaced nasal fracture by manipulating the fractured bones. The physician places nasal elevators or forceps into the nose and realigns the nasal bones. After the bones are realigned, they are stable and require no additional stabilization with splints.

21320

The physician treats a displaced nasal fracture by manipulating the nasal bones. The physician places nasal elevators or forceps into the nose and realigns the nasal bones. After the bones are realigned, they remain slightly mobile and require additional stabilization with splints. External splinting may consist of a cast taped to the reduced nose. Internal splinting consists of supporting the nasal septum by splints or packing with gauze strips.

21325

The physician treats a displaced nasal fracture. After unsatisfactory results with closed manipulation of the fractured bones, the physician performs open treatment. Open reduction allows the physician to visualize the fracture. Lacerations may be present, allowing direct visualization. Incisions are made inside the nose to expose the nasal septum and portions of the nasal bones. The physician realigns the fractured es using nasal elevators and forceps. It may be ry to remove small segments of bone for adequate realignment. Intranasal incisions are closed in a single layer. Any lacerated skin areas are closed in layers. After the bones are realigned, they remain slightly mobile and require additional stabilization with splints. External splinting may consist of a cast taped to the reduced nose. Internal splinting consists of supporting the nasal septum by splints or packing with gauze strips.

21330

The physician treats a displaced nasal fracture. After unsatisfactory results with closed manipulation of the fractured bones, the physician performs open treatment. Open reduction allows the physician to visualize the fracture. Lacerations may be present, allowing direct visualization. Incisions are made inside the nose to expose the nasal septum and portions of the nasal bones. Additionally, bicoronal or other local skin incisions may be used to expose the fractured nasal bones. The physician realigns the fractured bones using nasal elevators and forceps. The bones are fixed in reduction with wires, plates, and/or screws. Intranasal incisions are closed in a single layer. Lacerations and other skin incisions are repaired with layered closure.

21335

The physician makes an incision to treat a displaced nasal fracture and also repair the fractured nasal septum. Open treatment is necessary after unsatisfactory results with closed manipulation of the fractured bones and allows the physician to visualize the fractures. Lacerations overlying the fractures may allow direct visualization. Incisions may be made inside the nose to expose the nasal septum and portions of the nasal bones. Additionally, bicoronal and other local skin incisions may be used to expose the fractured nasal bones. The nasal septum is exposed and portions of the fractured cartilaginous and bony septum are removed. The physician realigns the nasal bones using nasal elevators and forceps. Transseptal sutures are placed to prevent formation of a septal hematoma. Intranasal incisions are closed in a single layer. Lacerations and other skin incisions are repaired with layered closure. After the bones are realigned, they remain slightly mobile and require additional stabilization with splints. External splinting may consist of a cast taped to the reduced nose. Internal splinting consists of supporting the nasal septum by splints or packing with gauze strips.

21336

The physician makes an incision to repair a nasal septal fracture. Open treatment is necessary after unsatisfactory results with closed manipulation of the fractured septum and allows the physician to visualize the septal fracture. Incisions are made inside the nose. The nasal septum is exposed and portions of the fractured cartilaginous and bony septum are removed. Transseptal sutures are placed to prevent formation of a septal hematoma. Intranasal incisions are closed in single layers. Stabilization such as internal splinting may be used to support the septum during healing. Internal splinting consists of supporting the nasal septum by splints or packing with gauze strips.

21337
The physician repairs a fracture of the nasal septum. No intranasal incisions are made. The physician uses nasal elevators and forceps to realign the septal fracture. Transseptal sutures are placed to prevent formation of a septal hematoma. Internal splints or packing with gauze strips may be used for stabilization to support the septum during healing.

21338-21339
The physician repairs fractures of the nasoethmoid region, which includes nasal and ethmoid bones and the medial wall of the orbit. Lacerations may be present allowing direct visualization. The physician may use bicoronal, local skin, and lower eyelid incisions to expose the fractured bones. The medial canthal ligaments are examined and, if detached, are repaired in a separately reportable procedure with transnasal stainless steel sutures or wire. The physician realigns the fractured bones and holds them in rigid reduction with internal wires, plates, and/or screws. Any lacerated skin areas are repaired and other skin incisions are closed in layers. No external fixation is employed in 21338. Report 21339 if external pin fixation is used to support grossly depressed fractures.

21340
The physician repairs fractures of the nasoethmoid region with percutaneous (through the skin) approaches. Percutaneous pins or screws are placed into stable bone and attached to external support such as splints, headcaps, or wire fixation to aid in reduction of the fractures. If the medial canthal ligaments are detached, they are repaired through a percutaneous approach with awls or K-wires and transnasal stainless steel sutures or wire. Injuries of the nasolacrimal complex are repaired using non-resorbable sutures and polyethylene tubing.

21343
The physician realigns a depressed frontal bone fracture overlying the frontal sinus. This fracture does not involve injury to the nasofrontal duct drainage of the frontal sinus. The physician may access the frontal bone with a bicoronal incision or local skin incisions overlying the fracture. Sinus mucosa may be removed. The bone is realigned and stabilized with wires, plates, and/or screws. The incisions are repaired with a layered closure.

21344
The physician realigns a complicated frontal bone fracture and obliterates the frontal sinus. This fracture injures the duct drainage of the frontal sinus and requires obliteration of the nasofrontal duct to prevent postoperative sinus complications. The physician may access the frontal bone with a bicoronal incision or local skin incisions overlying the fracture. Sinus mucosa is removed from the frontal sinus. If the posterior wall of the sinus is fractured, the bony wall may be removed, thus cranializing the sinus. The nasofrontal duct is plugged (i.e., bone) and obliterating material (i.e., fat, muscle) is placed into the sinus cavity. The frontal bone is realigned and stabilized with wires, plates, and/or screws. The incisions are repaired with a layered closure.

21345
The physician realigns a pyramidal fracture (LeFort II type) of the nasal and maxillary complex without making incisions. The fractured bones are realigned without internal fixation. Intermaxillary fixation is used to realign the fracture. Arch bars are placed onto the patient's upper and lower dental arches with individual wire ligatures around the teeth to provide interdental fixation. The proper occlusion is maintained by securing the maxillary and mandibular arch bars together. For edentulous patients, a splint or the patient's dentures can be modified to provide the necessary fixation.

21346
The physician realigns a pyramidal (LeFort II type) midface fracture of the nasomaxillary complex. An incision is made through the maxillary buccal vestibule (cheek side) to expose the bony maxilla. The nasomaxillary complex is manipulated, realigning the fracture. The physician uses wires, plates, and/or screws to stabilize the fracture. The mucosal incision is closed in a single layer. Intermaxillary fixation may be applied.

21347
The physician realigns a complex pyramidal (LeFort II type) midface fracture of the nasomaxillary complex using more than one site of open access. Multiple incisions are made to expose the fracture sites. These incisions include the bicoronal scalp flap, lower eyelid, and transoral incisions. The nasomaxillary complex is manipulated, realigning the fractured bones. The fracture is stabilized with wires, plates, and/or screws. The transoral incision is closed in a single layer. The scalp and lower eyelid incisions are repaired with a layered closure. Intermaxillary fixation may be applied.

21348
The physician realigns a complex pyramidal (LeFort II type) midface fracture of the nasomaxillary complex with bone grafting. Access incisions may include the bicoronal scalp flap, lower eyelid, and/or transoral incisions. The pyramidal fracture is exposed and the complex is manipulated, realigning the fractured bones. Comminution of bone (e.g., nasofrontal region, orbital floors) requires bone grafting of these areas. The physician uses wires, plates, and/or screws to stabilize the fracture. Through a separate incision, the physician

Musculoskeletal

may harvest a bone graft from the patient's hip, rib, or skull and close the surgically created wound. The physician reconstructs areas of bony defect. The transoral incision is closed in a single layer. The scalp and lower eyelid incisions are repaired with a layered closure. Intermaxillary fixation may be used to additionally stabilize the fracture.

21355
The physician percutaneously reduces a fracture of the malar or cheek area, including the zygomatic arch. A stab incision is made through the skin overlying the fracture area. Without soft tissue dissection, an instrument (e.g., bone hook, Carroll-Girard screw) is inserted and used to lift, manipulate, and reduce the fracture. The stab incision is closed in a single layer.

21356
The physician reduces a depressed fracture of the zygomatic arch through an indirect approach. No internal fixation is used. A facial incision (e.g., Gillies approach) is made in the scalp extending beneath the temporalis fascia. An instrument is inserted through the incision, following underneath the fascia, and taken to the middle surface of the zygomatic arch. The instrument is swept along the arch upwardly and outwardly to reduce the fracture back into proper position. A transoral incision (e.g., Keen approach) may also be used, made in the posterior buccal sulcus. An elevator instrument is inserted through the incision and taken to the medial surface of the zygomatic arch, avoiding damage to branches of the facial nerve passing beside the arch. The arch is lifted laterally to its correct anatomic position. The facial incision is closed in layers. The transoral incision is closed in a single layer.

21360
The physician reduces a fracture of the malar complex. No internal fixation is used. The physician makes facial incisions through the scalp, eyebrow, and/or lower eyelid. A transoral incision is also made through the maxillary buccal vestibule. The fracture sites are exposed. Instruments may be inserted into the bone (e.g., Carroll-Girard screw) or beneath the complex to lift the fracture. The fractured malar complex is reduced manually. The facial incisions are closed in layers. The transoral incision is closed in a single layer.

21365
The physician reduces a complicated fracture of the malar area. Internal fixation is necessary for fracture stability. The physician makes multiple incisions to expose and explore the fracture. Facial incisions are made through the scalp, eyebrow, and/or lower eyelid. A transoral incision is made though the maxillary buccal vestibule. Instruments may be inserted into the bone (e.g., Carroll-Girard screw) or beneath the complex to lift the fracture. The fractured malar complex is reduced and fixated with wires, plates, and/or screws. The facial incisions are closed in layers. The transoral incision is closed in a single layer.

21366
The physician reduces a complicated fracture of the malar area. Bone grafting is necessary to reconstruct bony defects (e.g., orbital floor, anterior maxillary wall) and internal fixation is necessary for fracture stability. The physician makes multiple incisions to expose and explore the fracture. Facial incisions are made through the scalp, eyebrow, and/or lower eyelid. A transoral incision is made though the maxillary buccal vestibule. Instruments may be inserted into the bone (e.g., Carroll-Girard screw) or beneath the malar complex to lift the fracture. The fractured complex is reduced and fixated with wires, plates, and/or screws. Through a separate incision, the physician harvests a bone graft from the patient's hip, rib, or skull and closes the surgically created wound. The graft is placed on the malar defect area and may be stabilized with sutures, wires, plates, and/or screws. The facial incisions are closed in layers. The transoral incision is closed in a single layer.

21385
The physician repairs a blowout fracture of the orbital floor. A maxillary vestibular incision is made on the side of the orbital fracture. In the maxillary bone, a window opening is made into the maxillary sinus, using a drill and bone forceps. The orbital floor is visualized from inside the maxillary sinus. The fractured orbital floor is realigned and supported from inside the maxillary sinus with lubricated gauze packing or a ballooned catheter. The physician sutures the end portion of the gauze or catheter to the maxillary mucosa. Most of the intraoral incision is sutured in a single layer. The exposed gauze or catheter remains in place and is removed after adequate healing.

21386
The physician repairs a blowout fracture of the orbital floor. Lower eyelid incisions are made in the subtarsal skin crease along the inferior orbital margin with a lateral extension to expose and explore this fracture. This allows the physician to inspect the floor, infraorbital rim, and medial/lateral orbital walls. The physician realigns the fractured orbital floor by gentle manipulation. The realigned orbital floor is stable or the fracture is very small, not requiring an implant or bone graft. The lower eyelid incision is closed in layers.

21387
The physician repairs a blowout fracture of the orbital floor with a combined periorbital and maxillary sinus approach. The physician makes both lower eyelid skin incisions and intraoral incisions to expose and explore this fracture. A lower eyelid incision allows the physician to inspect the infraorbital rim and floor. Additionally, the orbital floor is visualized from inside the maxillary sinus by a maxillary vestibular incision above the tooth apices on the side of the fracture. The physician realigns the fractured orbital floor by manipulation from either access. The realigned orbital

floor may be supported from inside the maxillary sinus with lubricated gauze packing or a ballooned catheter. The physician sutures the end portion of the gauze or catheter to the maxillary mucosa. Most of the intraoral incision is sutured in a single layer. The lower eyelid incision is closed in layers. The exposed gauze or catheter remains in place intraorally and is removed after adequate healing.

21390
The physician repairs a blowout fracture of the orbital floor using lower eyelid incisions made in the subtarsal skin crease along the inferior orbital margin with a lateral extension. This allows the physician to inspect the floor, infraorbital rim, and medial/lateral orbital walls. The physician elevates the orbital soft tissue from the bone, exposing the fracture. Small fragments of fractured bone may be removed and the remaining fractured bone is realigned by gentle manipulation. A bony hole remains in the orbital floor, requiring an implant to prevent orbital soft tissue from entering the maxillary sinus below. The physician fashions an alloplastic implant material to cover the hole. The physician places the implant over the bony hole. The lower eyelid incision is closed in layers.

21395
The physician repairs a blowout fracture of the orbital floor using lower eyelid incisions made in the subtarsal skin crease along the inferior orbital margin with a lateral extension. This allows the physician to inspect the floor, infraorbital rim, and medial/lateral orbital walls. The physician elevates the orbital soft tissue from the bone, exposing the fracture. Small fragments of fractured bone may be removed and the remaining fractured bone is realigned by gentle manipulation. A bony hole remains in the orbital floor and will require a graft to prevent orbital soft tissue from entering the maxillary sinus below. The physician harvests bone from the patient's hip, rib, or skull, and closes the surgically created graft donor site. The harvested bone is fashioned to cover the hole. The physician places the bone graft over the bony hole and may secure it to the infraorbital rim with wire or sutures. The lower eyelid incision is repaired with a layered closure.

21400
The physician treats a fracture of the orbit, other than a floor blowout fracture. Incisions and bony manipulation are not necessary. This is a non-displaced or minimally displaced fracture of the orbital rims or walls that can be identified on x-ray.

21401
Thc physician treats a fracture of the orbit, other than a floor blowout fracture. No incisions are necessary. This is a minimally displaced fracture of the orbital rims or walls that can be identified on x-ray. The physician realigns the fracture bones by using manual manipulation or with bone hooks and Carroll-Girard screws. The realigned bones are stable and no internal fixation is necessary.

21406
The physician openly treats a fracture of the orbit, other than a floor blowout fracture. This is a displaced fracture of the orbital rims or walls that can be identified on x-ray. The physician makes periorbital incisions to expose the fracture site. The fractured bones are realigned and may be stabilized with wires, plates, and/or screws. No sizable bony holes that would require coverage remain in the orbit. The incisions are closed in layers.

21407
The physician openly treats a fracture of the orbit, other than a floor blowout fracture. This is a displaced fracture of the orbital rims or walls that can be identified on x-ray. The physician makes periorbital incisions to expose the fracture site. The fractured bones are realigned and may be stabilized with wires, plates, and/or screws. After realignment, bony holes remain in the orbit that require coverage to prevent orbital soft tissue from entering into these holes. These holes are usually found in the medial or lateral walls of the orbit. An alloplastic implant is selected, shaped, and placed over the bony hole. The incisions are closed in layers.

21408
The physician openly treats a fracture of the orbit, other than a floor blowout fracture. This is a displaced fracture of the orbital rims or walls that can be identified on x-ray. The physician makes periorbital incisions to expose the fracture site. The fractured bones are realigned and may be stabilized with wires, plates, and/or screws. After realignment, bony holes remain in the orbit, requiring coverage to prevent orbital soft tissue from entering these holes. The holes are usually found in the medial or lateral walls of the orbit. The physician harvests bone from the patient's hip, rib, or skull, and closes the surgically created graft donor site. The bone graft is shaped and placed over the bony hole. The incisions are closed in layers.

21421
The physician treats a palatal or maxillary fracture (LeFort I type) by applying interdental (intermaxillary) fixation for stabilization. No incisions are made with this technique. Intermaxillary fixation is used to realign the fracture. Arch bars are placed onto the patient's upper and lower dental arches with individual wire ligatures around the teeth. The fracture reduction is maintained in proper occlusion by securing the maxillary and mandibular arch bars together. For edentulous patients, a custom-made acrylic splint or the patient's dentures can be modified to provide the necessary interdental fixation.

21422

The physician uses open treatment to reposition and stabilize a palatal or maxillary fracture (LeFort I type). Transoral incisions are made in the maxillary buccal (cheek) vestibule to expose the maxillary fracture. The fracture is repositioned and stabilized with plates, screws, and/or wires. The transoral mucosal incision is closed in a single layer. A customized acrylic palatal splint may be wired to the maxillary teeth to stabilize the palatal fracture. Intermaxillary fixation may be applied.

21423

The physician repositions and stabilizes a complicated palatal or maxillary fracture (LeFort I type). Transoral incisions are made in the maxillary buccal vestibule to expose the maxillary fracture. Additional lower eyelid or other skin incisions may be necessary to assist in repair of the fracture. The maxilla is repositioned and stabilized with plates, screws, and/or wires. The infraorbital nerve may need to be repositioned. The anterior maxillary walls may need bone grafting to support the infraorbital nerve. The transoral mucosal incision is closed in a single layer. Any skin or eyelid incisions are closed in layers. A customized acrylic palatal splint may be wired to the maxillary teeth to stabilize a palatal fracture. Intermaxillary fixation may be applied.

21431

The physician treats a craniofacial separation (LeFort III type) without surgically opening the fracture but with the use of interdental wiring of denture or splint. The physician uses surgical instruments intranasally and intraorally to reduce the separation. Intermaxillary (interdental) wire fixation is used to realign the fracture. A custom-made acrylic splint or the patient's dentures are wired to the jaw to provide for the necessary fixation. Arch bars are placed onto the patient's upper and lower dental arches with individual wire ligatures around the teeth. The fracture reduction is maintained in proper occlusion by securing the maxillary and mandibular arch bars together for immobilization until healing is complete.

21432-21436

The physician performs surgery to openly treat a craniofacial separation (LeFort III type). The physician uses any of a variety of incisions, including intraoral and lateral eyebrow incisions. Surgical instruments are utilized to reduce the separation. The physician uses wire, plates, and screws to hold the bones in their acceptable anatomic positions for healing. The wounds are irrigated and closed in layers. Report 21433 if the procedure is complicated (comminuted or involving the cranial nerve), requiring multiple incisions to be made for more than one site of open access. Report 21435 if the procedure is complicated, utilizing internal and/or external fixation techniques such as transosseous wiring, pins, or miniplates at the fracture site, or cranial vault fixation such as head caps or halo frames with suspension wires. Report 21436 if the procedure is complicated, using multiple surgical approaches and internal fixation of the fracture bones, together with bone grafts, taken from a separate donor site on the patient.

21440

The physician stabilizes and repairs a fracture of the mandibular or maxillary alveolar bone without making incisions. The physician moves the fractured bone into the desired position manually. The fracture is stabilized by wiring both the involved teeth and adjacent stable teeth to an arch bar. Another technique utilizes dental composite bonding of both involved and stable teeth to a heavy, stainless steel wire. A customized acrylic splint may be used to stabilize the teeth. Intermaxillary fixation may also be applied.

21445

The physician stabilizes and reduces a fracture of the mandibular or maxillary alveolar bone from an incisional access site. Intraoral incisions are made in the buccal vestibule to expose the fracture. The physician moves the fractured bone into the desired position manually. The fracture is stabilized by wiring both the involved teeth and adjacent stable teeth to an arch bar. A customized acrylic splint may be used to stabilize the teeth. The fractured alveolar bone may be reduced by wires, plates, and/or screws. Intermaxillary fixation may also be applied. The intraoral incision is closed in a single layer.

21450-21451

The physician treats a mandibular fracture with no direct manipulation or stabilization in 21450. Close observation, a soft diet, or other restrictions of activity are examples of treatment. The physician repositions a mandibular fracture with some manipulation in 21451. The physician moves the fractured bone back into the desired position manually. No incisions are made with this technique.

21452

The physician treats a mandibular fracture percutaneously by applying external fixation. The physician makes 0.5 cm stab incisions in the skin at several points near the inferior border of the mandible on both sides of the fracture. Without soft tissue dissection, holes are drilled and threaded rods or pins are screwed into the holes and used to manipulate and reduce the fracture. A metal or acrylic bar is connected to the protruding posts in a horizontal fashion, stabilizing the fracture.

21453

The physician treats a mandibular fracture by applying interdental or intermaxillary fixation (wiring the jaws together) for stabilization. No incisions are made with this technique. The physician wires arch bars to the upper and lower dental arches with individual wire ligatures around the teeth or uses other wiring techniques to provide the intermaxillary fixation. Edentulous patients (without teeth) may have dentures or custom-made acrylic splints wired to the jaws first. The jaws are wired together to provide intermaxillary fixation.

21454
The physician treats a mandibular fracture through incisions and by applying external fixation. An intraoral approach may be used or a skin incision may be made overlying the area. The tissue is dissected to the bone and the fracture is exposed and repositioned directly. The fracture may also be approached through traumatic lacerations. Once the fracture is moved to the desired position, the physician makes 0.5 cm incisions in the skin at several points near the inferior border of the mandible on both sides of the fracture. Holes are drilled into the mandible and threaded rods or pins are screwed into the holes. A metal or acrylic bar is connected to the protruding posts in a horizontal fashion, stabilizing the fracture. Intermaxillary fixation may be placed.

21461-21462
The physician repositions and stabilizes a mandibular fracture. Incisions are made in the skin overlying the fractured area or intraorally through the mucosa. The tissue is dissected to the bone and the fracture exposed. The fracture is repositioned and the bones stabilized with plates, screws, or wires. The incisions are closed with sutures. Intermaxillary fixation is not applied in 21461. In 21462, intermaxillary or interdental fixation is applied. Arch bars are placed onto the patient's upper and lower dental arches with individual wire ligatures around the teeth and the jaws are wired together.

21465
The physician openly repositions and/or stabilizes a fracture of the mandibular condyle. An incision is made through the skin anterior to the contour of the ear or through the ear. An intraoral approach is used on occasion. The tissues are dissected to the temporomandibular joint and the fractured condyle is exposed. Depending on the location of the fracture, a second skin incision below the angle of the mandible may be necessary to move the fracture to the desired position. The fractured condyle is repositioned, manually or with instruments. The fracture is stabilized with wires, screws, or plates, or may be left without internal fixation. The incision is closed with layered sutures. Intermaxillary fixation may be placed.

21470
The physician openly repositions and/or stabilizes a complicated fracture of the mandible. Multiple incisions are made through the skin and/or the intraoral mucosa to approach and treat the fracture. Once in proper position, the fractured bones are held in rigid reduction with internal fixation of wires, screws, or plates, and the mandible is immobilized with interdental (intermaxillary) fixation. The mucosal incisions are sutured simply and the skin incisions are closed with layered sutures. The physician wires arch bars to the upper and lower dental arches with individual wire ligatures around the teeth or uses other wiring techniques. Edentulous patients (without teeth) may have dentures or custom-made acrylic splints wired to the jaws first. The jaws are wired together to provide interdental fixation.

21480
The physician repositions a dislocation of the temporomandibular joint. No incisions are made and no intermaxillary fixation is used. The physician corrects the dislocation manually to rearticulate the joint.

21485
The physician repositions a dislocation of the temporomandibular joint. This is a complicated dislocation that may be recurrent and requires immobilization. The physician corrects the dislocation manually to rearticulate the joint. Intermaxillary fixation is applied. The physician wires arch bars to the upper and lower dental arches with individual wire ligatures around the teeth or uses other wiring and splinting techniques and the jaws are wired together.

21490
The physician surgically repositions a dislocation of the temporomandibular joint. The physician exposes the joint by making an incision anterior to the contour of the ear or through the ear. Tissues are dissected to expose the joint. The condyle and disc are moved into normal position using instruments. The ligaments may be repaired. The incision is closed with layered sutures.

21495
The physician treats a fracture of the hyoid bone by open surgery. The physician obtains x-rays (reported separately) that demonstrate a fracture of the hyoid bone, leaving it in an unstable or unsatisfactory position. With the patient under anesthesia, the physician makes an incision in the neck overlying the hyoid bone. Tissues are dissected deep to the bone and the fracture is identified. The physician manipulates the fracture fragments into position and may use internal fixation devices to hold the fracture in reduction. The wound is irrigated and closed in layers.

21497
The physician treats conditions other than fractures, such as temporomandibular dislocations, by applying intermaxillary fixation (wiring the jaws together) for immobilization. No incisions are made with this technique; however, the physician may have already surgically reduced the dislocation. The physician may wire arch bars to the teeth or use other wiring techniques to provide the interdental fixation. For edentulous patients (without teeth), dentures or

custom made acrylic splints are wired to the jaws. The jaws are wired together.

21501-21502
The physician performs surgery to remove or drain an abscess or hematoma from the deep soft tissues of the neck or thorax. With proper anesthesia administered, the physician makes an incision overlying the site of the abscess or hematoma of the neck or thorax. Dissection is carried down through the deep subcutaneous tissues and may be continued into the fascia or muscle to expose the abscess or hematoma. The incision may be extended if the mass is larger than expected. The abscess or hematoma is incised and the contents are drained. The area is irrigated and the incision is repaired in layers with sutures, staples, and/or Steri-strips; closed with drains in place; or simply left open to further facilitate drainage of infection. Report 21502 if a partial rib ostectomy is performed during this procedure.

21510
The physician incises the bone cortex of infected bone in the thorax to treat an abscess or osteomyelitis. The physician makes an incision over the affected area. Dissection is carried down through the soft tissues to expose the bone. The periosteum is split and reflected from the bone overlying the infected area. A curette may be used to scrape away the abscess or infected portion down to healthy bony tissue or drill holes may be made through the cortex into the medullary canal in a window outline around the infected or abscessed bone. The area is drained and debrided of infected bony and soft tissue. The physician irrigates the area with antibiotic solution, the periosteum is closed over the bone, and the soft tissues are sutured closed; or the wound is packed and left open, allowing the area to drain. Secondary closure is performed approximately three weeks later. Dressings are changed daily.

21550
The physician performs a biopsy of the soft tissues of the neck or thorax. With proper anesthesia administered, the physician identifies the mass through palpation and x-ray (reported separately), if needed. An incision is made over the site and dissection is taken down to the subcutaneous fat or further into the fascia or muscle to reach the lesion. A portion of the tissue mass is excised and submitted for pathology. The area is irrigated and the incision is closed with layered sutures.

21552-21556
The physician removes a tumor from the soft tissue of the neck or anterior thorax (chest) that is located in the subcutaneous tissue in 21552 or 21555 and in the deep soft tissue, below the fascial plane or within the muscle, in 21554 or 21556. With the proper anesthesia administered, the physician makes an incision in the skin overlying the mass and dissects down to the tumor. The extent of the tumor is identified and a dissection is undertaken all the way around the tumor. A portion of neighboring soft tissue may also be removed to ensure adequate removal of all tumor tissue. A drain may be inserted and the incision is repaired with layers of sutures, staples, or Steri-strips. Report 21555 for excision of subcutaneous tumors whose resected area is less than 3 cm and 21552 for excision of subcutaneous tumors 3 cm or greater. Report 21556 for excision of subfascial or intramuscular tumors whose resected area is less than 5 cm and 21554 for excision of subfascial or intramuscular tumors 5 cm or greater.

21557-21558
The physician performs a radical resection of a malignant soft tissue tumor from the neck or anterior thorax, not involving bone. An incision is made over the tumor and dissection exposes it. The tumor and any adjacent tissue that may be affected by the spread of the neoplasm are excised. Large resections may be needed. The type and stage of the lesion determines the extent of the tumor margin resection area. Muscle or fascia may need to be repaired and drains may be placed. The surgical wound is repaired by intermediate or complex closure, adjacent tissue transfer, or graft. Report 21557 for excision of tumors whose resected area is less than 5 cm and 21558 for excision of tumors 5 cm or greater.

21600
The physician removes part of one rib. With the patient under anesthesia, the physician makes an incision in the skin of the chest overlying the rib. The tissues are dissected deep to the rib itself. The rib is identified. The physician removes the desired part of the rib using a saw and other instruments. The remaining pieces of the rib and the wound itself are irrigated and debrided. The incision is sutured in layers.

21610
The physician resects the costovertebral joint. The physician makes a posterior incision overlying the joint. The tissues are dissected from the joint and the transverse process is cut from the vertebral body. The physician removes all or a portion of the adjacent rib. The incision is sutured in layers.

21615-21616
The physician performs surgery to remove the first rib and/or an extraneous cervical rib. With the patient under anesthesia, an incision is made in the skin just above the clavicle on the affected side and carried deep to the rib. The rib is identified and the attached soft tissues are dissected from the bone. The physician excises the rib using a saw and other surgical instruments. The rib is freed from its articulation and removed. The wound is irrigated and closed in layers. A dressing is applied. Report 21616 if a sympathetic nerve pathway is cut during the procedure.

21620
The physician removes a portion of the sternum from the chest. With the patient under anesthesia, the physician makes an incision in the skin overlying the sternum. This is carried deep through the subcutaneous tissues to the bone. The sternum is identified and the attached soft tissues are dissected from the bone. The physician marks the portion of the sternum to be removed. The bone is cut in the appropriate places using a saw and other surgical instruments. The remaining portion of the bone is irrigated and smoothed as needed. The wound is closed in layers and a dressing is applied.

21627
The physician performs a debridement of the sternum. With the patient under anesthesia, the physician makes an incision in the skin overlying the sternum. The incision is carried deep to the bone. The sternum is debrided as warranted using any of a variety of hand or powered surgical instruments. Irrigation is used so that debridement can be completed as extensively as indicated. The wound may be loosely packed and a dressing applied or it may be closed in layers and a dressing applied.

21630-21632
The physician removes most or all of the sternum from the chest. With the patient under anesthesia, the physician makes a long incision overlying the sternum and anterior chest. This is carried deep to the bone. Dissection is performed around the sternum. Ribs are disarticulated as needed and thorough debridement is accomplished. Using saws and other surgical instruments, the physician removes the bone. Internal fixation devices (reported separately) are often needed to support the ribs and chest wall. The wound is irrigated and closed in layers. Report 21632 if a mediastinal lymphadenectomy is performed during the procedure.

21685
The hyoid bone is a small C-shaped bone in the neck above the Adam's apple, or thyroid cartilage, with muscles of the tongue and throat attached to it. Hyoid myotomy and suspension is done to open the oro-hypopharyngeal airway for correcting breathing in sleep apnea. It involves repositioning and fixating the hyoid bone to improve the airway. A submental incision is made to expose the hyoid bone in the neck. The muscles below the hyoid are transected and separated to expose a small, isolated, mid-portion of the hyoid bone. Strips of fascia lata (bands of fibrous tissue), nonresorbable suture, or other strong materials are wrapped around the body of the hyoid and used to pull it forward and secure it to the inferior mandibular border. An alternative method pulls the hyoid downward to the voicebox cartilage for thyro-hyoid suspension, and secures it there.

21700-21705
The physician performs a surgical procedure where the scalenus anticus muscle is divided, usually for the purpose of treating thoracic outlet syndrome. With the patient under anesthesia, the physician makes an incision overlying the scalene muscle. This incision is carried deep to the muscle. The muscle is exposed and identified. A discission of the muscle is performed in line of the fibers. This relieves the pressure on the neurovascular structures. The wound is irrigated and closed in layers. Report 21700 if the procedure does not include resection of the cervical rib. Report 21705 if resection of the cervical rib is performed during the procedure.

21720-21725
Torticollis is a dysfunction of the neck with congenital or traumatic onset. The head becomes inclined toward the affected side and the face toward the opposite side. The physician makes an incision 5 cm long above and parallel to the medial end of the collarbone to access the tendons of the sternocleidomastoid muscle. A blunt instrument is placed behind the tendons to protect vital structures in the neck. The muscle's tendons attach just behind the ear and to the collarbone. The physician splits the tendons further up the muscle to release the restriction. The physician probes the wound to identify remaining tight muscles or fascia, which are cut until full motion is obtained. The physician closes the incision with sutures and Steri-strips. A cervical collar is applied for six weeks in 21720 and a cast is applied to hold the neck in place in 21725.

21740
The physician performs surgery on the anterior chest to correct pectus excavatum (a depression in the chest wall) or pectus carinatum (a forward projection of the chest wall). With the patient under anesthesia, the physician makes an incision overlying the anterior sternum. This is carried deep to the bone. The costal cartilages are exposed and deformed rib ends are freed from their sternal attachments. The sternum is mobilized and restored to its normal position. Internal fixation devices are employed to hold the sternum in corrected alignment. The physician irrigates the wound and closes it in layers with sutures.

21742-21743
The physician performs a Nuss procedure, also known as minimally invasive repair of pectus excavatum (MIRPE), without thoracoscopy in 21742 and with thoracoscopy in 21743. Pectus excavatum is a depression of the sternum and chest, giving a sunken appearance. The chest is first marked at strategic points and the length of a curved steel bar, called the Lorenz pectus bar, to be inserted into the sternum is measured and shaped to fit the individual's chest. Midaxillary line incisions are made on the right and left side aligned with the deepest depression point. A skin tunnel is raised from the incisions and another small lateral

Musculoskeletal

incision is made for insertion of a thoracoscope. The skin incisions are elevated and a long introducer instrument is inserted through the right intercostal space at the top of the pectus ridge and slowly advanced across the anterior mediastinal space with videoscopic guidance. The sternum is forcefully lifted as the introducer is passed to the other side. Once behind the sternum, the tip is pushed through the intercostal space at the top of the pectus ridge on the left side and brought out through that skin incision. Umbilical tape is pulled through the tunnel and used to guide the prepared bar. The bar is inserted with the convex curve facing posteriorly and rotated with a flipping instrument until the convex curve faces anteriorly. The bar can be pulled back out and bent in a more ideal curvature for correction as many times as needed. Usually only one bar is placed. With the bar in position, a stabilizing bar is sutured around the pectus bar and to the muscle. Sutures are placed in the lateral chest wall musculature as well as one other fixation point to the side of the sternum around one rib and the pectus bar. Wounds are closed and the patient is extubated while deeply anesthetized and kept well sedated for a few days with pain management therapy.

21750

The physician performs surgery on the sternum bone to put the bone back together following previous surgical separation. With the patient under anesthesia, the physician makes an incision overlying the sternum. The incision is carried deep to the bone and the separated pieces are identified. The physician may debride soft tissue or bone. The bony fragments are manipulated back together and held in place. The physician uses wire or other internal fixation devices to maintain the bone in appropriate position. The wound is irrigated and closed in layers.

21800

Closed treatment of an uncomplicated rib fracture is performed. The rib fracture may be diagnosed by examination alone or with separately reportable x-rays. If the fracture is nondisplaced and stable, closed treatment is initiated. Closed treatment involves management of the rib fracture directed at protecting the underlying lung and ensuring adequate oxygenation and ventilation, evaluation to exclude complications, pain control, patient education, and routine follow-up. Braces or splints are not used as they restrict normal chest expansion and can lead to pulmonary complications. The patient's activity is modified while the fracture heals.

21805

The physician performs surgery on a fractured rib without the need for any internal or external fixation devices. With the patient under anesthesia, the physician makes an incision overlying the fractured rib. This is carried deep to the bone. The fracture is found and the pieces are identified. Dead tissue is debrided as needed. The physician manipulates the fracture fragments into an acceptable position and alignment. The wound is irrigated and closed in layers.

21810

The physician treats a rib fracture that results in a so-called "flail chest" using external fixation devices. A flail chest inhibits proper pulmonary function. With the patient under anesthesia, the physician makes an incision overlying the fractured rib. The physician identifies the rib involved. Using external fixation and other devices such as pins, screws, and sandbags, the physician stabilizes the rib fracture and the chest wall. The wound is closed with layered sutures.

21820

Separately reportable x-rays are used to identify if a fracture of the sternum is present. If the fracture is non-displaced and stable, closed treatment is initiated. Braces or splints are not used. The patient's activity is modified while the fracture heals.

21825

The physician performs an open surgical reduction of a sternum fracture. The patient is positioned supine on the operating table. A longitudinal incision is made along the midportion of the sternum. Dissection exposes the fractured sternum. The surgeon reduces the fracture. If fixation is needed to keep the fracture stable, the physician drills holes on either side of the fracture. Wire is passed through the holes and around the fracture and the wire ends are twisted together to immobilize the fracture. The incision is repaired in layers with sutures, staples, or Steri-strips.

21920-21925

The physician performs a biopsy of the soft tissues of the back or flank. The patient is positioned lying on the side or prone. With proper anesthesia administered, an incision is made over the biopsy area. Dissection is carried down within the superficial soft tissue layers in 21920, usually the subcutaneous fat to the uppermost fascial layer. In 21925, dissection is taken down deep within the soft tissue, such as into the fascial layer or within the muscle. A portion of the tissue is excised and submitted for pathology. The area is irrigated and the incision is closed with layered sutures, staples, or Steri-strips.

21930-21933

The physician removes a tumor from the soft tissue of the back or flank that is located in the subcutaneous tissue in 21930-21931 and in the deep soft tissue, below the fascial plane or within the muscle, in 21932-21933. The patient is positioned lying on the side or prone. With the proper anesthesia administered, the physician makes an incision in the skin overlying the mass and dissects down to the tumor. The extent of the tumor is identified and a dissection is undertaken all the way around the tumor. A portion of neighboring soft tissue may also be removed to ensure adequate removal of all tumor tissue. A drain may be inserted and the incision is repaired with layers of sutures, staples, or Steri-strips. Report 21930 for excision of subcutaneous tumors whose resected area is less than 3 cm and 21931 for excision of subcutaneous tumors 3 cm or greater. Report 21932 for excision of subfascial or intramuscular tumors whose resected area is less than 5 cm and 21933 for excision of subfascial or intramuscular tumors 5 cm or greater.

21935-21936

The physician performs a radical resection of a malignant soft tissue tumor from the back or flank, not involving bone. An incision is made over the tumor and dissection exposes it. The tumor and any adjacent tissue that may be affected by the spread of the neoplasm are excised. Large resections may be needed. The type and stage of the lesion determines the extent of the tumor margin resection area. Muscle or fascia may need to be repaired and drains may be placed. The surgical wound is repaired by intermediate or complex closure, adjacent tissue transfer, or graft. Report 21935 for excision of tumors whose resected area is less than 5 cm and 21936 for excision of tumors 5 cm or greater.

22010-22015

The physician performs an open incision and drainage of a deep abscess of the posterior spine. Once a paraspinal soft tissue abscess or a lumbar psoas muscle abscess is identified by MRI or CT scan, an aspiration biopsy may be performed prior to open surgical drainage. The extent of the surgery depends on the size of the abscess and the area affected. The deep fascia is incised and the wound opened, irrigated, and debrided. Necrotic tissue and debris are removed and the cavity is irrigated with antibiotic solution. The wound is closed in layers and a drain or wound vacuum device may be placed. Report 22010 for incision and drainage of a deep abscess in the cervical, thoracic, or cervicothoracic region of the posterior spine and 22015 for the lumbar, sacral, or lumbosacral region.

22100-22103

The physician removes spurs, other growths, or bone disease by partial resection of a posterior vertebral component such as the spinous process, lamina, or facet. The patient is placed prone and an incision is made overlying the affected vertebra and taken down to the level of the fascia. The fascia is incised and the paravertebral muscles are retracted. The physician removes the affected part of the spinous process, lamina, or facet. Paravertebral muscles are repositioned and the tissue and skin is closed with layered sutures. Report 22100 for a cervical vertebral segment; 22101 for a thoracic vertebral segment; and 22102 for a lumbar vertebral segment. Report 22103 for each additional segment in conjunction with the code for the primary procedure.

22110-22116

The physician removes spurs, other growths, or bone disease by partial resection of a vertebral body. With the patient stabilized by a halo or cranial tongs, the physician makes an anterior incision to reach the vertebral body. Lower cervical vertebrae are approached above the clavicle, dividing the superficial muscles and fascia and retracting the trachea, esophagus, and thyroid medially. After blunt division of the deep fascia and paravertebral muscles, the anterior aspect of the cervical spine is exposed. The bony lesion is identified and excised from the affected vertebral body. Once the lesion is removed, a drain is placed and the incision is closed in layered sutures. The halo or tongs are attached to a body jacket to assure stabilization of the spine. Report 22110 for a cervical segment; 22112 for a thoracic segment; and 22114 for a lumbar vertebral segment. Report 22116 for each additional segment in conjunction with the code for the primary procedure.

22206-22208

Three-column spinal osteotomy is performed to correct moderate to severe spinal deformities that result in limited flexibility. Also known as pedicle subtraction osteotomy, it involves cutting and removing one or more portions of the vertebral segment in order to prepare for spinal realignment. The three columns consist of the anterior (anterior two-thirds of the vertebral body), the middle (posterior third of the vertebral body and the pedicle), and the posterior (articular facets, lamina, and spinous process). Using a posterior or posterolateral approach, the surgeon excises all posterior elements at the site of the correction, including the pedicles and the adjacent facet joints (inferior and superior). The physician then removes a posterior wedge of cancellous bone from the vertebral body to achieve the desired correction. The entire posterior and lateral vertebral body walls may also be removed. The osteotomy is closed by extending the patient's position on the operative frame or through instrumentation compression. Report 22206 if the procedure is performed on a thoracic vertebral segment and 22207 if the segment is lumbar. Report 22208 for each additional vertebral segment in conjunction with the code for the primary procedure.

22210-22216

Spinal osteotomy is performed to correct spinal deformities, such as severe cervical kyphosis occurring with rheumatoid arthritis that makes it difficult to properly elevate the chin off the chest. For a cervical posterior osteotomy, the patient is placed in the prone position with a supporting chest pad and the head resting on a frame or in a sitting position with the head supported by a halo and traction with the arms resting on the table. A posterior midline incision is made over the cervicothoracic junction. The physician exposes the spinous processes from C5 to T1. The muscles and ligamentous attachments are stripped from the spinous process at the desired level and dissection continues subperiosteally. The posterior elements of C7, the spinous process and laminae, are removed as are the articulating inferior half of C6 and upper portion of T1. The osteotomy continues with lateral resections of bone that are beveled toward each other so the opposing surfaces are parallel after extension. Assuring the absence of any nerve root compression, the forward parts of the vertebrae are fractured. The gap closes posteriorly as the lateral masses meet. The muscles are reattached and the wound is closed with layered sutures over a suction drain. The angle of the neck is adjusted and stabilized using the halo and a halo vest. Report 22212 if a similar osteotomy procedure is performed on a thoracic vertebral segment and 22214 if the segment is lumbar. Report 22216 for each additional vertebral segment in conjunction with the code for the primary procedure. If bone grafts and/or spinal instrumentation are needed to maintain the spine in the straightened position, report them separately in addition to the definitive procedure.

22220-22226

Spinal osteotomy is performed to correct spinal deformities. In this procedure, the physician uses an anterior approach to reach the involved vertebrae. For a cervical vertebral segment in 22220, an incision is made through the neck, avoiding the esophagus, trachea, and thyroid. For a thoracic vertebral segment in 22222, an incision is made through the chest, with possible detachment of the clavicle, costal cartilage, and manubrium. For a lumbar vertebral segment in 22224, an incision is made through the tenth rib, into the chest cavity with rib spreaders, and dissection of abdominal contents away from the diaphragm. Retractors separate the intervertebral muscles. A marker is inserted in the affected vertebral segment and the location is confirmed by separately reportable x-ray. With a rongeur, the physician cleans out the intervertebral disc space between the concerned vertebral bone and its neighboring vertebrae. An osteotomy of the single vertebral segment is carried out by removing a wedge of bone from the middle portion of the vertebral body. The spine is extended to achieve correction and separately reportable bone grafts and/or spinal instrumentation may need to be placed to maintain the spine in the straightened position. The muscles are reattached and the wound is closed with layered sutures. Report 22226 for each additional vertebral segment in conjunction with the code for the primary procedure.

22305-22310

Closed treatment of a vertebral process fracture is only indicated if the spine is stable and the type of fracture does not require intervention. In the case of the cervical spine, the physician initially immobilizes the patient's neck and spine with sandbags or a cervical collar, as necessary. Report 22305 if the fracture is located in the vertebral process. Report 22310 if the fracture is located in the vertebral body and casting or bracing is applied without any prerequisite manipulation.

22315

Following dislocation or traumatic or pathological fracture of the vertebrae, the physician decompresses the spine into proper alignment and immobilizes the vertebrae. The fracture or dislocation may be realigned by manual manipulation of the spine. If traction is employed, the patient is placed supine with a halo or tongs affixed to the skull. General anesthesia may be administered. Traction is applied to the feet and the halo or tongs, decompressing the vertebrae. As the traction is increased in stages, the physician assures that there is no additional neurological deficit. Traction is removed when the desired correction of the spine is accomplished. The patient is immobilized with bracing or casting, such as a halo cast.

22318-22319

The physician performs open treatment and/or reduction of an odontoid fracture and/or dislocation, including the os odontoideum. The os odontoideum (dens) is the tooth-like process located on the second cervical vertebra in the neck. The patient is placed in a supine position and the fracture or dislocation is reduced with skeletal traction. The physician makes an anterior 6 to 7 cm transverse skin incision at the level of the C5-6 disc space. Dissection is carried down to the odontoid process by longitudinally splitting the muscle and by blunt careful dissection of the space between the carotid, trachea, and esophagus. A retractor is placed and the anterior longitudinal ligament is incised. The superior thyroid artery may be ligated. Using imaging intensification, internal fixation is applied to hold the fracture in proper reduction. Guidewires are inserted into an area of the dens and screws are placed over the wires. No grafting is done in 22318. In 22319, bone grafts are placed to stabilize the fracture or dislocation. When the procedure is completed, a drain may be placed and the wound is closed with layered sutures.

22325-22328

The physician performs open treatment and/or reduction of a vertebral fracture or dislocation from a posterior approach. The patient is placed prone and the skin, fascia, and paravertebral muscles are incised and retracted to expose the fractured vertebra or dislocated segment. The proper rod (e.g., Harrington, Edwards) is selected and anatomic or C-shaped hooks are placed on vertebrae above and below the injury. The rod is inserted in the hooks and the spine is aligned. If fusion is desired, the physician may place separately reportable grafts between the vertebrae or place sleeves on the rod and position them to stabilize the injured vertebrae. The incision is closed by layered sutures. Report 22325 if the site is lumbar; 22326 if the site is cervical; and 22327 if the site is thoracic. Report 22328 for each additional fractured vertebra or dislocated segment in conjunction with the code for the primary procedure.

22505
Spinal manipulation under anesthesia (SMUA) is performed mostly by osteopaths although orthopedists may also use it to treat spinal dysfunction and alleviate neck and back pain. The induction of anesthesia reduces muscle tone and the natural reflex actions so that the spine can be manipulated more effectively to restore joint function and reduce pain. The manipulations are carried out so as to break up fibrotic adhesions of the soft tissues in and around to the spinal joints. SMUA is usually followed by a week of daily rehabilitative manipulation to maintain joint mobility and prevent re-adhesion of the fibrotic tissue.

22520-22522
Percutaneous vertebroplasty is performed by a one- or two-sided injection of a vertebral body. A local anesthetic is administered. In a separately reportable procedure, the radiologist uses imaging techniques, such as CT scanning and fluoroscopy, to guide percutaneous placement of the needle during the procedure and to monitor the injection procedure. Sterile biomaterial such as methyl methacrylate is injected from one side or both sides into the damaged vertebral body and acts as a bone cement to reinforce the fractured or collapsed vertebra. The procedure does not restore the original shape to the vertebra, but it does stabilize the bone, preventing further fracture or collapse. Following the procedure, the patient may experience significant, almost immediate, pain relief. Report 22520 for percutaneous vertebroplasty of one vertebral body at the thoracic level; 22521 for percutaneous vertebroplasty of one vertebral body at the lumbar level; and 22522 for each additional thoracic or lumbar vertebral body treated.

22523-22525
The physician performs a percutaneous kyphoplasty, a modification of the percutaneous vertebroplasty, to reduce the pain associated with osteoporotic vertebral compression fractures. This procedure has the added advantage of restoring vertebral body. The procedure is performed under separately reported x-ray. The patient is placed in a prone, slightly flexed position. A 5 mm to 7 mm incision is made and small cannulas are inserted into the vertebral body from both sides. Balloon catheters, called "tamps," are inserted into the vertebra and inflated. The tamps create a void in the soft trabecular bone and restore vertebral alignment. The balloon is removed and bone cement is injected into the cavity. Report 22523 when the procedure is performed in the thoracic spine; 22524 when the procedure is performed in the lumbar spine; and 22525 for each additional vertebral body.

22526-22527
Percutaneous intradiscal annuloplasty is a minimally invasive technique performed under fluoroscopic guidance to treat small tears in the annulus without an associated disc protrusion. The most common technique is intradiscal electrothermal therapy (IDET). In IDET, the physician advances a needle into the disc using x-ray image guidance. The appropriate treatment catheter is selected and inserted through the needle. Once the catheter is in position, the temperature of the heating portion of the catheter is increased gradually, raising the temperature of the affected site. The increased heat contracts and thickens the collagen disc wall, which may result in contracture and closure of the tears in the annulus. The physician may perform the procedure on one (unilateral) or both sides of the disc. Report 22526 when a single disc is treated and 22527 for one or more additional discs.

22532-22534
Arthrodesis is performed by lateral extracavitary approach. A midline incision is made in the area of the fractured segment and inferiorly curved out to the lateral plane. The paraspinous muscles are exposed, lifted off the spinous processes, and divided and lifted off the ribs. Imaging must be used to identify the targeted interspace. The corresponding rib is dissected from the intercostal muscles and resected in one piece from the curve to the costovertebral connection. The appropriate transverse process and part of the facet and pedicle are removed with a drill from the lateral aspect. The dura and the vertebral body are exposed from the dorsolateral view. Further posterior and lateral access to the vertebral body is gained by gently retracting the nerve root and surrounding structures. A minimal discectomy is now done to prepare the interspace by removing the damaged tissue with curettes and rongeurs. Cartilage is scraped, bone is decorticated, and the arthrodesis is accomplished by tapping bone graft material into the vertebral endplates. A drain is placed and closure is done in layers. Report 22532 for thoracic arthrodesis; 22533 for lumbar arthrodesis; and 22534 for each additional thoracic or lumbar vertebral segment done by lateral extracavitary approach.

22548
Spinal arthrodesis, or fusion, may be done for conditions of herniated disc, degenerative, traumatic, and/or congenital lesions, or to stabilize fractures or dislocations of the spine. Skull tong traction is applied. Avoiding the esophagus, pharynx, or esophageal nerve, the physician may incise the back of the throat, but most often enters from the outside of the neck, left of the throat to reach the C1-C2 (atlas-axis) vertebrae. Retractors separate the intervertebral muscles. A drill is inserted in the affected vertebrae and the location confirmed by x-ray. The physician incises a trough in the front of the vertebrae with a drill or saw. The physician cleans out the intervertebral disc spaces with a rongeur and removes the cartilaginous plates above

and below the vertebrae to be fused. The odontoid process (dens), the tooth-like projection located on the second cervical vertebra in the neck, may be excised. The physician obtains and packs separately reportable grafts of iliac or other donor bone into the spaces and trims them. Traction is gradually decreased to maintain the graft in its bed. The fascia is sutured. A drain is placed in the incision and the incision is sutured.

22554-22585
Spinal arthrodesis, or fusion, may be done for conditions of herniated disc, degenerative, traumatic, and/or congenital lesions, or to stabilize fractures or dislocations of the spine. Skull tong traction is applied. The physician uses an anterior approach to reach the damaged vertebrae. For cervical vertebrae in 22554, an incision is made through the neck, avoiding the esophagus, trachea, and thyroid. Retractors separate the intervertebral muscles. A drill is inserted in the affected vertebrae and the location is confirmed by separately reportable x-ray. The physician incises a trough in the front of the vertebrae with a drill or saw. The physician cleans out the intervertebral disc spaces with a rongeur and removes the cartilaginous plates above and below the vertebrae to be fused. The physician obtains and packs separately reportable grafts of iliac or other donor bone into the spaces and trims them. Traction is gradually decreased to maintain the graft in its bed. The fascia is sutured. A drain is placed and the incision is sutured. Report 22556 if the spinal arthrodesis site is thoracic. Report 22558 if the spinal arthrodesis site is lumbar. Report 22585 for each additional interspace treated in conjunction with the code for the primary procedure.

22590
Spinal arthrodesis, or fusion, may be done for conditions of herniated disc, degenerative, traumatic, and/or congenital lesions, or to stabilize fractures or dislocations of the spine. The patient is placed in a Stryker frame with a previously applied halo vest. The physician incises the skin from the occiput to the C3 vertebra, opens the fascia, and retracts the paravertebral muscles. A horizontal hole is drilled in the occiput using a burr. A second hole is drilled in the base of C2. The physician places wires through these holes. A third wire is placed around the ring of C1. Separately reportable bone grafts are obtained from the iliac crest or other donor bone. They are prepared, positioned, and tied in place using the wires. The retractors are removed and the incision is closed over a drain.

22595
Spinal arthrodesis, or fusion, may be done for conditions of herniated disc, degenerative, traumatic, and/or congenital lesions, or to stabilize fractures or dislocations of the spine. The patient is placed in a Stryker frame with a previously applied halo vest. The physician makes an incision from the occiput to the fourth or fifth vertebra. The physician exposes the posterior arch of the atlas (C1) and laminae of the axis (C2) and removes all soft tissue from bony surfaces. The upper arch of C1 is exposed and a wire loop is brought from below upward under the arch of the atlas and sutured. The physician passes the free ends through the loop, grasping the arch of C1. A graft taken from the iliac crest or other donor bone is placed against the lamina of the C2 and the arch of C1 beneath the wire. The physician passes one end of the wire through the spinous process of C2 and twists it securely into place. The retractors are removed and the incision is closed over a drain.

22600-22614
Spinal arthrodesis, or fusion, may be done for conditions of herniated disc, degenerative, traumatic, and/or congenital lesions, or to stabilize fractures or dislocations of the spine. The physician makes an incision overlying the vertebrae and separates the fascia and the supraspinous ligaments in line with the incision. The physician prepares the vertebrae and lifts ligaments and muscles out of the way. A chisel elevator is used to strip away the capsules of the lateral articulations and the articular cartilage and cortical bone is excised. Separately reportable chips are cut from the fossa below the lateral articulations and from the laminae, or fragments of the spinous process are taken and used to fill the interlaminal space and the gap left by the articular cartilage removal. Additional bone grafts are taken from the ilium or other donor bone and are used to join the laminae. The periosteum, ligaments, and paravertebral muscles are sutured to secure the bone grafting. The skin and subcutaneous tissues are closed with sutures, as well. Report 22600 for cervical arthrodesis; 22610 for thoracic arthrodesis; 22612 for lumbar arthrodesis; and 22614 for each additional vertebral segment in conjunction with the code for the primary procedure.

22630-22632
Spinal arthrodesis, or fusion, may be done for conditions of herniated disc, degenerative, traumatic, and/or congenital lesions, or to stabilize fractures or dislocations of the spine. The physician makes an incision overlying the lumbar vertebrae and separates the fascia and the supraspinous ligaments in line with the incision. The physician prepares the vertebrae and lifts ligaments and muscles out of the way. A chisel elevator is used to strip away the capsules of the lateral articulations and the articular cartilage and cortical bone is excised. Separately reportable chips are cut from the fossa below the lateral articulations and from the laminae, or fragments of the spinous process are taken and used to fill the interlaminal space and the gap left by the articular cartilage removal. Part of the lamina may be removed on one side and/or part of the disc may be removed to facilitate preparation of the interspace for fusion. Additional bone grafts are taken from the ilium or other donor bone and are used to

bridge the laminae. The periosteum, ligaments, and paravertebral muscles are sutured to secure the bone grafting. The skin and subcutaneous tissues are closed with sutures as well. Report 22632 for each additional interspace in conjunction with the code for the primary procedure.

22800-22804
Spinal arthrodesis, or fusion, is done here to correct a spinal deformity. The patient is placed prone. A midline posterior incision is made overlying the affected vertebrae. The fascia and the paravertebral muscles are incised and retracted. The physician uses a curette and rongeur to clean interspinous ligaments. One of several techniques may be used. In one, the spinous processes are split and removed and a curette is used to cut into the lateral articulations. Thin pieces of separately reportable iliac or other donor bone graft are placed in these slots. Grafts are obtained, prepared, and packed on both sides of the spinal curve, with more bone chips on the concave sides. Separately reportable instrumentation may be affixed to the spine. The incision is closed with layered sutures. A cast may be applied to stabilize the spine. Report 22800 for fusion of up to six vertebral segments; 22802 for fusion of seven to 12 vertebral segments; and 22804 for 13 or more vertebral segments.

22808-22812
Spinal arthrodesis, or fusion, is done here to correct a spinal deformity. An anterior approach is used. In the case of affected thoracolumbar vertebrae, the dissection is carried out through the abdominal muscles to the tenth rib, which is resected to allow access to the vertebrae in back. Dissection continues until the vertebral bodies are exposed. The physician cleans out the intervertebral disc spaces and removes the cartilaginous plates above and below the vertebrae to be fused. The physician obtains and packs separately reportable grafts of iliac or other donor bone into the spaces. Separately reportable instrumentation may be affixed to the spine. A drainage tube may be placed and the surgical wound is sutured closed. A cast may be applied to stabilize the spine. Report 22808 if two to three vertebral segments are fused; 22810 if four to seven vertebral segments are fused; and 22812 if eight or more vertebral segments are fused.

22818-22819
The physician performs this procedure for spinal deformities of kyphosis, a hunchback type increase in the convex curvature of the thoracic spine. The patient is placed prone. The physician makes a posterior midline incision, superior to the spinal abnormality, and dissects the periosteum of the normal vertebrae above and down into the lamina of the affected vertebrae, until the foramina are exposed on both sides of the spine. The nerve, artery, and vein within the foramina are divided, exposing the dural sac. The sac is dissected and the dura is closed with suture, leaving the sac remnant. Dissection is continued around the affected vertebral bodies and the intervertebral disc of the vertebra at the apex of the kyphosis is removed first, followed by the vertebra. Just enough vertebrae are removed to correct the kyphosis. The sac remnant that was left is used to cover the site of the resected vertebrae. Removed vertebral bodies are morselized and used for bone grafting. Rod instrumentation is applied and segmental wires are used to hold the rod in place. The wound is irrigated and closed with layered sutures over suction drains. A body jacket is applied. Report 22818 if a single or two-segment kyphectomy is performed. Report 22819 if a three or more segments kyphectomy is performed.

22830
The physician explores an existing fusion to diagnose and correct problems. The patient is placed in various positions depending on how the original fusion was performed (e.g., anterior, posterior, posterolateral). The physician makes an incision overlying the fused vertebrae. Fascia and paravertebral muscles are incised and retracted. The physician explores previous instrumentation, grafts, and wires; any or all may be partially replaced or adjusted during the exploration. When the exploration is complete, the fascia and vertebral muscles are repaired and returned to their anatomical positions. The incision is closed with layered sutures.

22840
The physician uses spinal instrumentation to correct a defect of the spine caused by disease, trauma, or congenital anomaly and to stabilize the spine to reduce risks of neurological damage or nonfusion after arthrodesis. Non-segmental instrumentation is a construct placed with fixation at either end only and not in the intervening levels. The physician makes a midline incision in the skin, fascia, and paravertebral muscles over the affected vertebrae. Upper and lower hooks or screws are introduced into the vertebral pedicles. A rod fashioned to fit the spinal contours is anchored to the screws or hooks. To achieve correction, distraction is applied with an instrument to increase the distance between the hooks at each end of the rod, which is secured in position. Another method of securing the rod is to use wires passed under prepared lamina and tightened around the rods. The minimal wiring inherent in this procedure should not be reported with 22841. The wound is closed with layered sutures. These Harrington rod instrumentation techniques have become outdated and are being replaced by more rigid, segmental fixation methods.

22841
Internal spinal fixation by wiring the spinous processes, also called Drummond wiring, is done with wires attached to a button that gives the needed purchase at the base of the spinous process and has a hole in its surface for the wire coming from the

Musculoskeletal

opposite direction to pass through. The spine is exposed in the standard manner and a hook is used to grasp the upper and lower pedicle of the selected fusion levels. Using an awl or a clamp, the physician makes a hole in the base of each involved spinous process and passes two button wire implants in opposite directions through the bony hole, making sure that each wire also passes through the hole in the opposite button, and pulls the buttons snugly to the base of the spinous process. The buttons are tamped into place. In some cases, only one button wire is passed from the convex to the concave side. A contoured distraction rod is inserted into the open loops of the wire implants and the hooks at the top and bottom and secured. Distraction is applied for correction, which is maintained by tightening the wires. Further distraction may be applied to the rod and a clamp placed to prevent loss of the correction. The laminae and transverse processes lateral to the buttons may be decorticated before closure of the wound.

22842-22844
Segmental instrumentation is a construct placed with fixation not only at either end but also at the levels between. The physician makes a midline incision in the skin, fascia, and paravertebral muscles over the affected vertebrae. Multiple hooks or screws are introduced into the vertebral pedicles where fixation is needed. Dual rods, such as Harrington distraction and compression rods, are anchored to the screws or hooks. Distraction is the force that produces kyphosis and compression corrects kyphosis, the abnormal hunchback curvature of the spine. To achieve correction, the compression assembly is tightened in place before distraction is applied and secured in position. The wound is closed with layered sutures. The Harrington rod instrumentation techniques are being replaced by three-dimensional correction techniques where rods can be bent along the length and applied at any level, in rotation, with distraction and compression applied between segments. Report 22842 for fixation of three to six vertebral segments; 22843 for seven to 12 vertebral segments; and 22844 for 13 or more vertebral segments.

22845-22847
Anterior instrumentation is reserved for flexible lumbar or thoracolumbar scoliotic curves. Several methods and types are available (e.g., Dwyer, Zielke, Scottish Rite) but all are based on a rod or cable fixated through large-headed, slotted, or cannulated screws. A thoracic or general surgeon assists for the intraoperative exposure, mainly thoracoabdominal or abdominal retroperitoneal. A hole is made in the vertebral body on the lateral side as posteriorly as possible. The screw is inserted across the midportion of the vertebra to the opposite cortex in a slight posteroanterior angle. A flexible threaded rod or cable is inserted in the angled screw heads. The spine is derotated and the rod is locked into its straighter position with nuts. The wound is closed in a routine manner. Report 22845 for two to three vertebral segments; 22846 for four to seven vertebral segments; and 22847 for eight or more vertebral segments.

22848
The physician joins axial connectors, such as the tail end of spinal instrumentation devices, to a rod configured to fit along the flat of the sacrum and impacted longitudinally between the cornices of the ilium just above the greater sciatic notch. The rod is driven through the ilium and negates the need for anterior instrumentation. This procedure, usually called the "Galveston technique," often accompanies a procedure for scoliosis, myelomeningocele, or paralytic spinal defects where sacral fixation is not desirable.

22849
This code describes the procedures used following failure of devices such as wires, screws, cables, plates, or rods used in spinal fixation. The patient is placed in the position dictated by the failure. The physician makes a midline incision overlying the damaged section. The fascia, paravertebral muscles, and ligaments are retracted. A number of reparative techniques may be used, depending on the device and point of failure. In most cases, the device must be replaced. The physician closes the muscles, fascia, and skin with layered sutures.

22850
Previously applied posterior spinal nonsegmental instrumentation is removed. Instrumentation is sometimes removed when correction is complete and stable, when the patient is a growing juvenile, or when the instrumentation causes complications, such as infection or pain. The patient is placed prone. The physician makes an incision overlying the affected area through the skin, fascia, and paravertebral muscles. Collagen is removed. The instrumentation is exposed and the superior hook or screw is loosened. Using forceps, the upper and lower hooks are disconnected from the vertebra and the hardware is removed.

22851
This procedure is performed to replace a vertebral body or partial vertebral body resected due to destruction by disease, trauma, or other processes. Once the vertebral body has been removed by a separately identifiable procedure, a hole is cored out of the vertebral bodies above and below the removed vertebrae to secure a biomechanical device (ceramic block, metal/synthetic cage, threaded bone dowel, methylmethacrylate) into the resulting vertebral defect or interspace. The physician selects the biomechanical device best suited to the location and type of deformity being corrected. For example, to correct a deformity caused by a malignancy, the physician may elect to inject methylmethacrylate into the area and allow it to dry to replace the excised vertebral body. Screws, wires,

or plates may be used to secure the device. Muscles are allowed to fall back into place and the wound is closed over a drain with layered sutures.

22852
Previously applied posterior spinal segmental instrumentation is removed. Instrumentation is sometimes removed when correction is complete and stable, when the patient is a growing juvenile, or when the instrumentation causes complications, such as infection or pain. The patient is placed prone. The physician makes a midline incision overlying the affected area through the skin, fascia, and paravertebral muscles. Collagen is removed. The instrumentation is exposed. Using forceps, the superior hook is loosened. The superior, inferior, and all segmental hooks between are disconnected from the vertebrae. The hardware is removed. The incision is closed with layered sutures.

22855
Previously applied anterior spinal instrumentation is removed. Instrumentation is sometimes removed when correction is complete and stable, when the patient is a growing juvenile, or when the instrumentation causes complications, such as infection or pain. The patient is placed supine for the removal of anterior spinal fixation devices. The physician makes an abdominal retroperitoneal or thoracic incision to reach the affected area. Collagen is removed. The instrumentation is exposed and the superior hook or screw is loosened. Using forceps, the superior hook or screw is disconnected from the vertebra, as are the inferior and all segmental hooks or screws. The hardware is removed. The incision is closed with layered sutures.

22856-22857
Total disc arthroplasty is performed to replace a severely damaged or diseased intervertebral disc, most often caused by degenerative disc disease. The physician uses an anterior approach to reach the damaged cervical vertebrae in 22856 by making an incision through the neck, avoiding the esophagus, trachea, and thyroid. In 22857, the physician uses an anterior approach to reach the damaged lumbar vertebrae by making an incision through the abdomen. Some implants require only minimal access, approximately 7 cm long, for a mini-retroperitoneal approach. Retractors separate the intervertebral muscles. The affected intervertebral disc location is confirmed by separately reportable x-ray. The physician cleans out the intervertebral disc space with a rongeur, removing the cartilaginous material to be replaced in preparation for inserting the implant. Preparation may include discectomy, osteophytectomy for nerve root or spinal cord decompression, and/or microdissection. One type of implant for total disc replacement has two endplates made of a metal alloy and a convex weight-bearing surface made of ultra high molecular weight polyethylene. The endplates are inserted in a collapsed form and seated into the vertebral bodies above and below the interspace. Minimal distraction is applied to open the intervertebral space, and the polyethylene disc material is snap-fitted into the lower endplate. With the disc assembly complete, the wound is closed, and a drain may be placed. Each of these codes reports a single interspace and includes fluoroscopy when performed.

22861-22862
The physician revises an artificial disc prosthesis placed during a previous disc arthroplasty through anterior approach. The prosthesis may be migrating from a lack of fixation and require components to be replaced or adjusted. The physician approaches the cervical vertebrae in 22861 by making an incision through the neck, avoiding the esophagus, trachea, and thyroid. The lumbar vertebrae (22862) are approached by making an incision through the abdomen. Retractors separate the intervertebral muscles. The implant is located, the area is explored, and any adhesions are freed. Distraction is applied to open the intervertebral space. The arthroplastic disc is removed, and the endplates of the vertebral body are reshaped and prepped for reinsertion. New height, depth, and width dimensions may also be taken with the vertebral body distracted in cases where another, more appropriately sized disc prosthesis is required. The components are reinserted, and the fascia and vertebral muscles are repaired and returned to their anatomical positions. The incision is closed. Each of these codes reports a single interspace and includes fluoroscopy when performed.

22864-22865
The physician removes an artificial disc prosthesis placed during a previous disc arthroplasty by anterior approach. The physician approaches the cervical vertebrae in 22864 by making an incision through the neck, avoiding the esophagus, trachea, and thyroid. The lumbar vertebrae (22865) are approached by making an incision through the abdomen. Retractors separate the intervertebral muscles. The implant is located and any adhesions are freed. Distraction is applied to open the intervertebral space, and the implant is removed. The area is explored and debrided. When the procedure is complete, the fascia and vertebral muscles are repaired and returned to their anatomical positions, drains are placed, and the wound is closed. Each of these codes reports a single vertebral interspace and includes fluoroscopy when performed.

22900-22903
The physician removes a tumor from the soft tissue of the abdominal wall that is located in the subcutaneous tissue in 22902-22903 and in the deep soft tissue, below the fascial plane or within the muscle, in 22900-22901. The patient is positioned supine on the operating table. With the proper anesthesia administered, the physician makes an incision in the skin overlying the mass and dissects down to the

tumor. The extent of the tumor is identified and a dissection is undertaken all the way around the tumor. A portion of neighboring soft tissue may also be removed to ensure adequate removal of all tumor tissue. A drain may be inserted and the incision is repaired with layers of sutures, staples, or Steri-strips. Report 22902 for excision of subcutaneous tumors whose resected area is less than 3 cm and 22903 for excision of subcutaneous tumors 3 cm or greater. Report 22900 for excision of subfascial or intramuscular tumors whose resected area is less than 5 cm and 22901 for excision of subfascial or intramuscular tumors 5 cm or greater.

22904-22905

The physician performs a radical resection of a malignant soft tissue tumor from the abdominal wall, not involving bone. An incision is made over the tumor and dissection exposes it. The tumor and any adjacent tissue that may be affected by the spread of the neoplasm are excised. Large resections may be needed. The type and stage of the lesion determines the extent of the tumor margin resection area. Muscle or fascia may need to be repaired and drains may be placed. The surgical wound is repaired by intermediate or complex closure, adjacent tissue transfer, or graft. Report 22904 for excision of tumors whose resected area is less than 5 cm, and 22905 for excision of tumors 5 cm or greater.

23000

The physician removes subdeltoid calcareous deposits by making a small incision over the deltoid muscle to expose the rotator cuff tendons. The raised area over the calcium deposits is incised in line with the axis of the fibers and the calcareous deposits are removed. A large cavity is made in the tendon with a curette to remove all damaged tissue. The opening is closed with side-to-side sutures. Once the tendon is repaired, the skin incision is closed and a soft dressing is applied.

23020

Capsular contracture release is not commonly performed unless the shoulder is fixed in marked internal rotation and adduction. In this position, the arm is unable to move away from the body. The physician makes an incision at the front of the shoulder where the deltoid meets the pectoral muscle. The subscapularis tendon is removed from the glenoid rim. The anterior capsule is left intact. The pectoralis major tendon is severed from its attachment on the humerus. The skin incision is closed and a soft dressing is applied. The arm is positioned in abduction (arm elevated out to the side of the body).

23030-23031

The physician drains a deep abscess or hematoma in 23030 or an infected bursa in 23031 from the shoulder area. The physician makes an incision in the shoulder overlying the site of the abscess, hematoma, or bursa to be incised. Dissection is carried down through the deep subcutaneous tissues and may be continued into the fascia or muscle to expose the abscess or hematoma. The incision may be extended if the mass is larger than expected. When the infected bursa, abscess, or hematoma is identified, it is incised and the contents are drained. The area is irrigated and the incision is repaired in layers with sutures, staples, and/or Steri-strips; closed with drains in place; or simply left open to further facilitate drainage of infection.

23035

The physician incises bone cortex in the shoulder area to treat a bone abscess or osteomyelitis. The physician makes an incision over the affected area of the shoulder. Dissection is carried down through the soft tissues to expose the bone. The periosteum is split and reflected from the bone overlying the infected area. A curette may be used to scrape away the abscess or infected portion down to healthy bony tissue or drill holes may be made through the cortex into the medullary canal in a window outline around the infected or abscessed bone. The area is drained and debrided of infected bony and soft tissue. The physician irrigates the area with antibiotic solution, the periosteum is closed over the bone, and the soft tissues are sutured closed; or the wound is packed and left open, allowing the area to drain. Secondary closure is performed approximately three weeks later. Dressings are changed daily. A splint may be applied to limit shoulder movement.

23040-23044

The physician performs an arthrotomy of the glenohumeral joint in 23040 or the acromioclavicular or sternoclavicular joint in 23044 that includes exploration, drainage, or removal of any foreign body. An incision is made over the joint to be exposed. The soft tissues are dissected away and the joint capsule is exposed and incised. The joint space is explored, any necrotic tissue is removed, and infection or abnormal fluid is drained. If a foreign body is present (e.g., bullet, nail, gravel), it is exposed and removed. The wound is irrigated with antibiotic solution. The physician may leave the wound packed open with daily dressing changes to allow for further drainage and secondary healing by granulation. If the incision is repaired, drain tubes may be inserted and the incision is repaired in layers with sutures, staples, and/or Steri-strips. A splint may be applied to limit shoulder motion.

23065-23066

The physician performs a biopsy of the soft tissues of the shoulder area. With proper anesthesia administered, an incision is made over the biopsy area. Dissection is carried down within the superficial soft tissue layers in 23065, usually the subcutaneous fat to the uppermost fascial layer. In 23066, dissection is taken down deep within the soft tissue, such as into the fascial layer or within the muscle. A portion of the tissue is excised and submitted for pathology. The area is irrigated and the incision is closed with layered sutures, staples, or Steri-strips.

23071-23076

The physician removes a tumor from the soft tissue of the shoulder area that is located in the subcutaneous tissue in 23071 and 23075 and in the deep soft tissue, below the fascial plane or within the muscle, in 23073 and 23076. With the proper anesthesia administered, the physician makes an incision in the skin overlying the mass and dissects down to the tumor. The extent of the tumor is identified and a dissection is undertaken all the way around the tumor. A portion of neighboring soft tissue may also be removed to ensure adequate removal of all tumor tissue. A drain may be inserted and the incision is repaired with layers of sutures, staples, or Steri-strips. Report 23075 for excision of subcutaneous tumors whose resected area is less than 3 cm and 23071 for excision of subcutaneous tumors 3 cm or greater. Report 23076 for excision of subfascial or intramuscular tumors whose resected area is less than 5 cm and 23073 for excision of subfascial or intramuscular tumors 5 cm or greater.

23077-23078

The physician performs a radical resection of a malignant soft tissue tumor from the shoulder area, not involving bone. An incision is made over the tumor and dissection exposes it. The tumor and any adjacent tissue that may be affected by the spread of the neoplasm are excised. Large resections may be needed. The type and stage of the lesion determines the extent of the tumor margin resection area. Muscle or fascia may need to be repaired and drains may be placed. The surgical wound is repaired by intermediate or complex closure, adjacent tissue transfer, or graft. Report 23077 for excision of tumors whose resected area is less than 5 cm and 23078 for excision of tumors 5 cm or greater.

23100

The physician performs an arthrotomy and biopsy of the glenohumeral joint. An incision is made over the shoulder joint and carried down through the soft tissues to gain access into the glenohumeral joint. A biopsy sample of the joint tissue is removed and saved for testing. The wound is repaired in layered sutures.

23101

The physician makes an incision into the acromioclavicular or sternoclavicular joint to remove torn cartilage and take a tissue sample. An incision is made through the skin and the underlying muscle is divided to gain access to the joint capsule. Once the capsule is penetrated, any torn cartilage is identified and removed. A tissue specimen is removed for biopsy. The joint is irrigated, the capsule is closed, and the soft tissues are sutured in layers. A soft dressing is applied.

23105-23106

The physician performs an arthrotomy and synovectomy of the glenohumeral joint, with or without biopsy. With the patient lying on one side and the arm suspended in traction, the physician makes an incision overlying the shoulder. The joint capsule is exposed by dissecting down through the soft tissues and freeing and reflecting the muscles. The joint capsule is incised to expose the synovium. Motorized resectors are used to remove the synovium, the inner membrane of the articular capsule that lines the joint cavity. A sample of the tissue for biopsy may also be removed. Following completion of the synovectomy, the shoulder is irrigated, a drain tube may be placed, and the incision is closed in layers with sutures, staples, or Steri-strips. Report 23106 if the procedure is done on the sternoclavicular joint.

23107

The physician performs an arthrotomy of the glenohumeral joint with joint exploration and removal of any loose or foreign bodies. An incision is made over the glenohumeral joint. The soft tissues are dissected away and the joint capsule is exposed and incised. The joint space is explored and any loose or foreign body (e.g., free cartilage, bone fragments, gravel) is exposed and removed. The wound is irrigated with antibiotic solution. The physician may leave the wound packed open with daily dressing changes to allow for further drainage and secondary healing by granulation. If the incision is repaired, drain tubes may be inserted and the incision is repaired in layers with sutures, staples, and/or Steri-strips. A splint may be applied to limit shoulder motion.

23120-23125

Removal of the clavicle (collar bone) is successfully performed without significant loss of function to the upper extremity for such problems as old, chronic, or acute unreduced dislocations. An incision is made horizontally along the portion of the bone to be removed. The skin is reflected, the bone is cleared of soft tissue attachments, and divided with an osteotome or bone-cutting rongeurs. For a partial resection, the remaining end of the clavicle is rounded and smoothed to eliminate the rough edge. If the medial end of the clavicle is removed, the clavicle may be stabilized to the first rib and the sternocleidomastoid may be detached. The periosteum and soft tissues are plicated and sutured over the raw end of the clavicle. The wound is closed and a soft dressing is applied. Report 23120 for a partial claviculectomy and 23125 for total claviculectomy.

23130

A partial acromioplasty or acromionectomy, with or without coracoacromial ligament release, is done. This procedure is also commonly performed during repair to the rotator cuff in an effort to increase the space below the acromion where the cuff tendons traverse toward their insertion on the humerus. An incision is made overlying the area. Dissection is carried down to the acromion. Acromioplasty involves the division of the acromioclavicular ligament followed by the use of a burr to cut away the under surface of the acromion. During acromionectomy, the distal portion of the acromion is removed. The coracoacromial ligament, a wide, strong band spanning between the acromion and the coracoid process of the scapula, may also be released. The joint is irrigated and the incisions are closed with sutures or Steri-strips.

23140-23146

A bone cyst or benign tumor of the clavicle or scapula is removed. The physician makes an incision overlying the cyst or tumor. The skin and underlying soft tissues are reflected to expose the periosteum, which is separated from the bone. Curettes or osteotomes are used to scrape or cut the lesion from the bone. Once the benign tumor or cyst is removed and healthy bone tissue is present, the periosteum is repositioned and the incision is repaired in layers. If the bone defect created requires a graft for repair, the physician obtains the necessary size bone graft from a separate donor site on the patient and packs it into the site where the tumor or bone cyst was removed or uses a bone bank allograft. Report 23145 if an autograft is obtained and 23146 if an allograft is used.

23150-23156

A bone cyst or benign tumor of the proximal humerus is removed. The physician makes an incision in the upper arm overlying the cyst or tumor. The skin and underlying soft tissues are reflected to expose the periosteum, which is separated from the bone. Curettes or osteotomes are used to scrape or cut the lesion from the bone. Once the benign tumor or cyst is removed and healthy bone tissue is present, the periosteum is repositioned and the incision is repaired in layers. If the bone defect created requires a graft for repair, the physician obtains the necessary size bone graft from a separate donor site on the patient and packs it into the site where the tumor or bone cyst was removed or uses a bone bank allograft. Report 23155 if the procedure is done with an autograft and 23156 if an allograft is used.

23170-23174

The physician removes infected portions of the clavicle in 23170 due to a bone abscess or osteomyelitis. This infection often leaves open sinus tracts in the bone that require removal. The physician makes an incision overlying the sequestered area of bone in the clavicle. Once the skin and soft tissues are reflected, a small window is cut into the bone to gain access to the sequestrum, or necrosed piece of bone that has become separated from sound bone. All purulent material and scarred or necrotic tissue are removed. The remaining space is filled with surrounding soft tissues or free tissue transfer. The area is irrigated and an antibiotic solution is used to prevent further infection. The wound is closed loosely over drains if possible. The arm is positioned in a sling or splint and protected to prevent fracture of the clavicle. Report 23172 if the sequestrectomy is performed on the scapula and 23174 if this procedure is performed on the humeral head to the surgical neck.

23180-23184

The physician performs a partial excision of the clavicle in 23180 to remove infected bone. An incision is made over the infected part of the clavicle and the underlying soft tissues are divided to expose the bone. The periosteum is reflected and the infected portion of bone is removed and irrigated. The excavation of bone may excise a crater-like piece, leave a small saucer-like shelf depression in the bone, or may remove a portion of the shaft (diaphysis) of a long bone. If a significant portion of bone is removed, the physician may use bone graft material to fill the cavity left in the bone. The periosteum is closed over the bone, the soft tissues are sutured closed, and a soft dressing is applied. Report 23182 for partial excision of the scapula and 23184 for partial excision of the proximal humerus.

23190

The physician removes a portion of the scapula (shoulder blade). An oblique skin incision is made across the scapula and the underlying trapezius muscle is reflected to expose the superior medial angle. The portion of the scapula is removed and the remaining border is smoothed to prevent trauma to the surrounding tissues. A portion of the supraspinatus and levator scapulae tendons are resected and sutured to the trapezius muscle and remaining border of the scapula. The wound is irrigated and the incision is sutured. A soft dressing is applied.

23195

The physician performs a resection of the humeral head. An incision is made over the joint in the upper arm and the underlying muscles are divided to expose the bone. The joint capsule is incised and tendons are removed from the bone. The physician makes a horizontal cut through the humerus just distal to the head and removes the bone. Separately reportable hemiarthroplasty to replace the proximal humeral bone with an implant for attaching the tendons and reconstructing the joint usually follows.

23200-23210

The physician performs a radical resection of a tumor of the clavicle bone in 23200. Either end may be resected or the bone may be excised. An incision is made horizontally along the portion of the bone with the tumor to be removed. The skin and soft tissues are reflected. The acromioclavicular and/or sternoclavicular ligaments may need to be divided to free the bone from the joint at either respective end. The bone is cleared of soft tissue attachments, such as the platysma and pectoral muscles, and the diseased bone is resected with an osteotome or bone-cutting rongeurs, along with any soft tissues involved with the tumor. If the tumor is removed from one end, the remaining end of the clavicle is rounded and smoothed to eliminate the rough edge. The periosteum and soft tissues are plicated and sutured over the raw end of the clavicle. The wound is closed and a soft dressing is applied. Report 23210 if a similar procedure is performed on the scapula.

23220
The physician performs a radical resection of a tumor of the proximal humerus. Removal of the proximal portion of the humerus is often performed for aggressive benign lesions and low-grade malignancies. A longitudinal incision is made from the acromioclavicular joint to the lateral border of the biceps tendon. The underlying muscles are divided to expose the bone. The joint capsule is incised and tendons are removed from the bone at the level of the proximal joint. The humerus is divided by a horizontal cut a few centimeters distal to the tumor site. A portion of the remaining medullary bone is taken for testing. The proximal portion of the bone is removed, along with any soft tissues involved with the tumor. Reconstructive alternatives following resection include reconstruction with flail shoulder, with passive spacer, with arthrodesis, and with arthroplasty.

23330
The physician removes a foreign body of the shoulder. The physician makes a small incision over the foreign body and reflects the skin to expose it. The foreign body is removed, the wound is irrigated, and the skin is closed with sutures or Steri-strips.

23331-23332
The physician removes a foreign body from deep within the shoulder, such as an artificial shoulder joint. A long incision is made overlying the shoulder. The physician dissects through each layer of tissue down to the bones in the shoulder. The shoulder joint is exposed. The physician may debride any inflamed synovial or other scar tissues. The foreign body is removed from within the joint and from inside the humerus bone. The physician irrigates the joint with antibiotic solution. The wound is closed in layers unless there is infection present. If infection is present, the wound is left open to drain. Report 23332 if complicated, including "total shoulder."

23350
This procedure is commonly used in the diagnosis of a rotator cuff tear. The patient is positioned supine on the x-ray table. The skin and deep tissues lateral to the coracoid process are injected with a local anesthetic. A no. 20 spinal needle 7.5 cm long is inserted into the joint at the same location and the position is checked by separately reportable x-ray. From 15 ml to 20 ml of a suitable contrast medium is injected; resistance is felt when the joint is full. The shoulder is taken through a full range of motion and separately reportable x-rays are taken to see if there is leakage of the substance to other parts of the joint and a proper diagnosis is made.

23395-23397
In the case of bicipital syndrome with rotator cuff pathology, the biceps tendon has become detached from the shoulder. The physician makes an anterior superior approach to the shoulder and splits and reflects the deltoid muscle. An acromioplasty is performed and the coracoacromial ligament is excised. The long head of the biceps tendon is identified and reattached to the humerus by tenodesis procedure. The rotator cuff is repaired prior to closure of the incisions. A soft dressing and sling are applied for two weeks. If the rotator cuff is repaired, an abduction pillow is used for four to six weeks. Report 23397 if multiple muscle transfers are performed during the procedure.

23400
Sprengel's deformity is a congenital deformity where the scapula is positioned higher in the thoracic region than normal. The physician makes an incision beginning 1 cm superior to the middle of the scapular spine continuing medially along the spine to the medial portion of the bone and inferiorly to the inferior angle of the scapula. The deep fascia is reflected to expose the insertion of the trapezius on the scapular spine. It is reflected along with the supraspinatus muscle. The rhomboid major and minor and levator scapula muscles are also reflected to release the scapula from its abnormal position. If the upper portion of the bone is abnormally shaped, a portion of it may be removed. Once the scapula is normally positioned to match the opposite side, the muscles are reattached to the bone in their new orientation. A portion of the trapezius may now form a flap or may require a portion to be excised in order to take up slack in the muscle. The incision is closed with sutures and a Velpeau bandage is applied for two weeks.

23405-23406
This procedure may be performed if closed manipulation under anesthesia is unsuccessful to gain adequate motion of the shoulder. An incision along the anterior deltoid and pectoral region is made and the skin is reflected to expose the underlying muscles. The subscapularis tendon is removed from the glenoid rim of the scapula. The physician may also release portions of the pectoral muscle fibers to gain further motion of the shoulder. The incision is closed with sutures and the arm is passively placed in abduction. Report 23406 if a tenotomy is performed on multiple tendons through the same incision.

23410-23412
The physician repairs a ruptured rotator cuff. A longitudinal incision is made along the anterior portion of the shoulder and the skin is reflected. The deltoid fibers and the underlying tissues are divided. The coracoacromial ligament is divided and the

supraspinatus tendon is detached by a transverse incision along the greater tuberosity. The distal frayed edges of the tendon are removed. A trench is chiseled into the humeral bone along the level of the anatomical neck of the humerus. The supraspinatus tendon flap is buried in it. The flap is fixed with sutures tied to the tendon and passed through holes drilled in the bone. The repair is completed with side-to-side sutures of the supraspinatus to the adjacent subscapularis and infraspinatus tendons. The incision is closed and a soft dressing is applied. Protected motion in a specific progression of exercises is followed. Report 23410 if the repair is done for an acute rupture of the musculotendinous cuff and 23412 if chronic.

23415

The physician performs a coracoacromial ligament release, with or without acromioplasty. The patient is positioned on the side with the affected side up. The physician makes an incision centered over the acromioclavicular joint. The soft tissues are reflected and the ligament between the coracoid and the acromion is released. The physician may perform an acromioplasty where the underside of the acromion is reduced to allow more room for the rotator cuff tendons. Acromioplasty involves the division of the acromioclavicular ligament followed by the use of a burr to cut away the under surface of the acromion. During acromionectomy, the distal portion of the acromion is removed. Following completion, the joint is irrigated and the incisions are closed with sutures or Steri-strips.

23420

The most common approach to reconstruct a complete rotator cuff avulsion tear of the shoulder is an anterior approach through an incision over the acromioclavicular joint. If the infraspinatus is to be shifted, a second incision is made along the scapular spine posteriorly, detaching a portion of the posterior deltoid if necessary. The margins of the tear are freshened and a non-absorbable suture closes the longitudinal portion of the tear. A portion of the articular cartilage on the underside of the humeral head is removed. The raw edges of the torn tendon are brought into contact with raw bone and the ends of the sutures are passed through holes drilled through the greater tuberosity and tied over its lateral aspect. The physician performs an acromioplasty. Acromioplasty involves the division of the acromioclavicular ligament followed by the use of a burr to cut away the under surface of the acromion. During acromionectomy, the distal portion of the acromion is removed. Once the reconstruction is complete, the incision is closed and the arm may be positioned in an abduction splint or pillow for protection.

23430

Tenodesis is performed on the long tendon of the biceps. The long head of the biceps tendon may become frayed and ruptured in chronic impingement syndrome, bicipital tenosynovitis, or degenerative conditions of the shoulder. Complete ruptures may leave a frayed proximal segment attached to the supraglenoid tubercle, which may become trapped between the humeral head and glenoid. In this case, the remaining stump of the tendon can be removed by a motorized shaver. A simultaneous subacromial decompression may be performed. Debridement of the frayed portion of the tendon may be performed.

23440

The long tendon of the biceps is resected or transplanted. The long head of the biceps tendon is an important stabilizer of the humeral head. When the proximal end of the tendon is detached from the glenoid, it is rolled or knotted, sutured, and inserted through a keyhole-shaped opening in the cortex of the humerus in the floor of the bicipital groove. This is performed through a longitudinal incision at the anterior aspect of the shoulder. Once proper fixation is obtained, the incision is closed and the arm is supported in a sling. Active elbow flexion and shoulder elevation are limited until proper fixation and healing are complete.

23450-23455

An anterior capsulorrhaphy is performed on the shoulder in a Putti-Platt or Magnuson type operation. An anterior incision is made at the deltopectoral-pectoral interval. The coracoid process is identified and the tendon of the biceps (short head) is at times incised distal to the coracoid for exposure. The anterior capsule is visualized through a small transverse incision of the subscapularis tendon, which is tagged for identification and removed from its attachment on the capsule. The quality and laxity of the capsule are assessed and the joint is explored for damage to the labrum or glenoid. The joint is irrigated to remove any loose bodies. If there is no other abnormal laxity, the capsule is advanced superiorly and attached to the labrum with sutures. An appropriate amount of slack is taken up to provide stability within the joint. Once the capsule is reattached, the subscapularis tendon is reapproximated but not tightened and repaired. A subcutaneous drain is placed and the wound is closed. Report 23455 if a Bankart type operation with labral repair is done.

23460-23462

An anterior capsulorrhaphy of any type with bone block is performed on the shoulder. If there is significant damage to the glenoid where more than one third of the glenoid is deficient, a bone block procedure is performed to increase the surface area of the glenoid. The patient is placed in a lateral position or modified beach chair position. A horizontal or vertical incision is placed inferior to the scapular spine, allowing a bone graft to be taken from the scapular spine if necessary. An additional incision is made at the lateral border of the acromion and carried posteriorly to the axillary crease. The deltoid is split to expose the infraspinatus and teres minor tendons. The capsule is exposed and incised with a T-shaped cut. The capsule is reattached to the glenoid through drill holes or by means of suture anchors taking up slack on the inferior portion of the capsule. The capsular repair may be reinforced using the infraspinatus tendon if the local tissue is felt to be insufficient. The bone block is placed on the posterior inferior portion of the glenoid fossa and fixated with a screw. This bone fragment is usually obtained from the spine of the scapula through a posterior incision. Report 23462 if the procedure is performed with coracoid process transfer.

23465
A posterior capsulorrhaphy of the glenohumeral joint is done with or without bone block. The patient is placed in a lateral position or modified beach chair position. A horizontal or vertical incision is placed inferior to the scapular spine, allowing a bone graft to be taken from the scapular spine if necessary. An additional incision is made at the lateral border of the acromion and carried posteriorly to the axillary crease. The deltoid is split to expose the infraspinatus and teres minor tendons. The capsule is exposed and incised with a T-shaped cut. The capsule is reattached to the glenohumeral joint through drill holes or by means of suture anchors taking up slack on the inferior portion of the capsule. The capsular repair may be reinforced using the infraspinatus tendon if the local tissue is felt to be insufficient. When a bone block is used, it is placed at the posterior inferior quadrant of the glenohumeral joint to increase the articulation surface of the glenoid. This technique is rarely used. Once the incision is closed, the arm is placed in an Orthoplast splint with the arm in external rotation for the first six weeks. Motion is protected.

23466
A capsulorrhaphy of the glenohumeral joint for any type multidirectional instability is done. The surgical approach may differ from patient to patient depending upon the patient's history. The incision is determined by the side of most significant instability. A separately reportable arthroscopic examination of the shoulder should be performed first to fully determine the extent of damage to the joint and the appropriate surgical approach. An anterior H-plasty is commonly used to tighten the capsule. In some cases, both medial and lateral capsular incisions may be required to provide sufficient capsular tension.

23470
Hemiarthroplasty is performed on the glenohumeral joint. A long curved incision is made from the superior aspect of the acromion along the deltopectoral interval to the deltoid insertion. The deltoid is retracted laterally and the pectoralis medially. The fascia between the pectoralis and the clavicle is divided and the subacromial space is freed with a gloved finger or periosteal elevator. The coracoacromial ligament is freed and often an acromioplasty is performed to allow for freedom of movement after surgery. The subscapularis tendon is tagged and removed from the capsule. The anterior joint capsule is divided and the glenohumeral joint is dislocated by further external rotation and extension of the arm. The joint is explored and all loose bodies are removed. The humeral head is removed with a reciprocating saw or osteotome. A trial prosthesis is placed along the proximal humerus as a guide for proper inclination of the osteotomy. A horizontal cut (osteotomy) is made as previously determined and a large curette is used to open the medullary canal for placement of the stem of the prosthesis. The canal is enlarged with a reamer to the appropriate size. The prosthesis is positioned in proper rotational alignment to articulate with the glenoid. Any remaining osteophytes (bone spurs) are removed. The joint is irrigated. The prosthesis is reduced into the glenoid and the subscapularis tendon is sutured in place with multiple interrupted non-absorbable sutures with the shoulder in neutral position. The deltopectoral interval is closed loosely over drainage tubes. The arm is placed in a sling and swathe bandage.

23472
A total shoulder replacement is done for the glenohumeral joint. A long curved incision is made from the superior aspect of the acromion along the deltopectoral interval to the deltoid insertion. The deltoid is retracted laterally and pectoralis medially. The fascia between the pectoralis and the clavicle is divided and the subacromial space is freed with a gloved finger or periosteal elevator. The coracoacromial ligament is freed and often an acromioplasty is performed to allow for freedom of movement after surgery. The subscapularis tendon is tagged and removed from the capsule. The anterior joint capsule is divided and the glenohumeral joint is dislocated by further external rotation and extension of the arm. The joint is explored and all loose bodies are removed. The humeral head is removed with a reciprocating saw or osteotome. In addition, a prosthetic device is placed proximally at the glenoid to articulate with the prosthetic humeral head. Prior to placement of the humeral prosthesis, the joint is opened to fully expose the glenoid surface. The surface cartilage of the glenoid is removed. A power drill is used to cut a slot into the glenoid the exact size of the holding device of the glenoid component. Small curettes are used to remove cancellous bone from the base of the coracoid bone. With a bur, articular cartilage is removed from the surface of the glenoid. A trial glenoid component is used to properly prepare the bone and fit the prosthesis. Once the glenoid preparation is complete, the glenoid vault is drilled and filled with polymethylmethacrylate (bone cement). The glenoid component is pushed into place and held until the

Musculoskeletal

cement is cured. Prior to final insertion of the humeral component, an anterior acromioplasty and acromioclavicular arthroplasty are performed, if necessary. If large rotator cuff tears are found, they are repaired at this time. The joint is brought through a full range of motion and fully irrigated. The subscapularis tendon is repaired to stabilize the joint; however, the joint capsule is not usually resutured. Drains are placed and the deltopectoral interval is sutured closed. The arm is placed in a sling and swathe.

23480

The physician performs an osteotomy (bone cut) of the clavicle. The physician makes an incision in the skin overlying the clavicle. Tissue is dissected down to the bone. Using a surgical saw or other sharp instrument, the physician cuts through the bone. Surgical screws, a metal plate, or wires may secure the cut bone in the correct position. The wound is irrigated and the skin is closed in layers.

23485

The physician performs an osteotomy (bone cut) of the clavicle that is not healing or has healed in an unacceptable position. The physician makes an incision in the skin overlying the clavicle. Tissue is dissected down to the bone. Using a surgical saw or other sharp instrument, the physician cuts through the bone. Surgical screws, a metal plate, or wires may secure the cut bone in the correct position. The physician harvests a bone graft from the patient through a separate incision. The physician repairs the surgically created graft donor site. The graft is placed in the clavicle. Surgical screws, plates, or other hardware secure the bone graft. The incision is closed in layers.

23490-23491

The physician performs a preventative nailing, plating, pinning, or wiring of the clavicle to the coracoid process in order to gain better fixation and prevent further dislocation of the acromioclavicular joint. Access to the joint is obtained through a lateral incision over the acromion process. The skin and soft tissues are reflected. The screw or other fixation device of choice is positioned and may be checked by separately reportable x-ray. The procedure may be accomplished with the use of methylmethacrylate, which can be injected into a weak or defective bone area and hardens to act like a bone cement. The incision is closed with sutures and movement is restricted for four to six weeks. The hardware is removed when stability is determined. Report 23491 for similar prophylactic treatment of the proximal humerus.

23500-23505

The physician treats a fracture of the clavicle bone without surgery or manipulation. Separately reportable x-rays confirm the stable position of the fractured pieces. No manipulation is required. The physician may apply a clavicle brace, tape, or splint until the fracture heals. In 23505, the fracture is displaced and manipulation is required. A local anesthetic may be given. The physician pushes or pulls on the bony pieces or manipulates the shoulder in such a way to properly align the fracture. The physician may apply a clavicle brace, tape, or splint until the fracture heals.

23515

The physician treats a fracture of the clavicle with open surgery. The physician makes an incision overlying the fractured area of the clavicle. Tissue is dissected down to the bone and the fracture is identified. The physician debrides any nonviable tissues. Any tissue that has become lodged between the fracture pieces is removed. The physician may apply screws, wires, or plates to secure the fracture. The wound is irrigated and the incision is closed. A splint or brace may also be applied on the outside of the clavicle or shoulder.

23520-23525

The physician treats a dislocation of the joint between the sternum and the clavicle (sternoclavicular) without making incisions and without any manipulation in 23520. The physician applies a splint or brace to hold the joint in place until it has healed. In 23525, manipulation is required. Anesthesia may be necessary. The physician pushes, pulls, or moves the arm and chest to restore the joint to correct position and alignment. After manipulation, the patient is placed in a brace or splint.

23530-23532

The physician treats a chronic or acute dislocation of the sternoclavicular joint. The physician makes an incision overlying the joint between the clavicle and sternum where the dislocation has occurred. The tissues are dissected down to the joint and the dislocation is visualized. The physician may debride the area before realigning the joint back to proper position. In 23532, the physician harvests a fascial graft from the patient through a separate incision. The physician repairs the surgically created graft donor site. The fascial graft is attached to the bones in the sternoclavicular joint, preventing recurrent dislocation. Fixation may be applied. The joint is irrigated and the incision is closed in layers. A splint or brace may be applied to the outside of the body.

23540-23545

The physician treats a dislocation of the acromioclavicular joint (between the acromion process of the scapula and the clavicle). In 23540, no manipulation is required and the physician places the affected shoulder and arm in a sling or other brace. In 23545, manipulation is necessary to correct the dislocation. Anesthesia may be needed. The physician manipulates the joint by pushing or pulling on the shoulder and arm to align the bones. The physician applies a sling or other brace.

23550-23552
The physician treats an acute or chronic dislocation of the acromioclavicular joint (between the acromion process of the scapula and the clavicle). An incision is made overlying the shoulder at the articulation of the acromion of the scapula and the end of the clavicle. Dissection is carried through the tissues to the joint. Any nonviable tissue is removed. The bones are identified and the dislocation is visualized. The physician uses a heavy nonabsorbable suture, a wire, or screws to secure the two bones in their proper joint alignment. In 23552, the physician harvests a fascial graft from the patient through a separate incision. The physician repairs the surgically created graft donor site. The fascial graft is a strong piece of connective tissue that is attached to the bones in the acromioclavicular joint, preventing recurrent dislocation. When the joint is restored, the wound is irrigated and the incision is closed in layers. A dressing is applied. A sling or brace is applied to the shoulder and arm.

23570
The physician treats a fracture of the scapula bone without surgery or any type of manipulation. Separately reportable x-rays confirm the stable position of the fractured pieces. The physician places the shoulder in a sling or other brace until the fracture heals.

23575
The physician treats a fracture of the scapula bone without any incisions. Separately reportable x-rays confirm the nature of the fracture and the displacement of the pieces. The physician manipulates (pushes, pulls, or moves) the scapula and arm to align the fractured pieces. Separately reportable serial x-rays may be necessary while the manipulation is performed to confirm alignment. The physician may apply traction devices to the body to maintain satisfactory fracture reduction. A brace, splint, or cast may be applied to hold the bones in the correct position until they are healed.

23585
The physician treats a fracture of the scapula with open surgery. The physician makes an incision overlying the area of the fractured scapula and dissects the tissues down to the bone to visualize the fracture. Nonviable tissues or those between the fragments are debrided. The physician places the fragments back together in their correct anatomic position manually or with instruments. Internal fixation devices such as screws, metal plates, sutures, or wire may be applied to secure the bones. The wound is irrigated and the incisions are closed in layers with sutures.

23600-23605
Separately reportable x-rays confirm a stable, non-displaced proximal humeral fracture. No manipulation or open reduction is required in 23600. The arm is positioned in a sling and protected from movement to allow adequate healing. In 23605, the physician manipulates (pushes, pulls, or moves) the upper arm in the shoulder area to align the fractured pieces. Separately reportable serial x-rays may be necessary while the manipulation is performed to confirm alignment. The physician may apply traction devices to the body to maintain satisfactory fracture reduction. A brace, splint, or cast may be applied to hold the bones in the correct position until they are healed.

23615-23616
The physician performs open treatment of a proximal humeral (surgical or anatomical neck) fracture. An incision is made anteromedially extending posteriorly along the acromion to the lateral half of the spine of the scapula. The deltoid is detached from the exposed portion of the spine of the scapula. The deltoid is reflected down to expose the joint capsule and the humerus. The fractured portion of the proximal humerus (surgical or anatomical neck) is identified and the fracture is aligned. If the tuberosity is involved, it may also be repaired. Internal fixation may be used to stabilize the fracture site. Once the fracture is stabilized, the wound is irrigated. The deltoid is repositioned and sutured in place. The skin is sutured and the wound is covered with a soft dressing. The arm is positioned in a sling and movement is restricted to allow for proper healing. Report 23616 when the fracture cannot be repaired and a prosthetic proximal humeral replacement is necessary.

23620-23625
Separately reportable x-rays determine a stable, non-displaced greater humeral tuberosity fracture. The arm is positioned in a sling and motion of the shoulder is protected to prevent pull of the muscles that attach to the bone of the upper arm. Report 23625 if the fracture is displaced and manipulation is required. A local anesthetic may be given. The physician pushes or pulls on the bony pieces or manipulates them in such a way to properly align the fracture.

23630
The physician performs open treatment of a greater humeral tuberosity fracture. An anterior longitudinal incision is made and the underlying deltoid fibers are divided to expose the fracture site. Often this injury will include damage to the rotator cuff tendons requiring repair of the soft tissues in addition to the fracture site. The soft tissues are reflected to expose the bone and any loose bodies are removed. The fracture may be stabilized by internal fixation and the soft tissues are reattached by suture. The skin incision is closed and a soft dressing is applied. The arm is placed in a sling and movement is restricted to allow for adequate healing.

23650-23655
The physician performs closed treatment of a shoulder dislocation by manipulation. The most common form

of shoulder dislocation is the traumatic anterior inferior dislocation. A closed manipulation requires the patient to be positioned to allow the arm to hang forward. The physician applies gentle traction to distract the joint and manually relocates the glenohumeral joint back into position. Report 23655 if the manipulation treatment requires anesthesia.

23660
The physician performs open treatment of an acute shoulder dislocation. A posterior dislocation would be more likely to require an open reduction procedure than an anterior dislocation. The shoulder is approached through a deltopectoral incision. The joint is inspected and the head of the humerus is reduced into its proper position. The subscapularis tendon is attached to the head of the humerus with sutures or screws. If there is significant posterior translation, the posterior capsule is tightened. The incision is closed and the arm is immobilized in 20 degrees of external rotation.

23665
The physician performs closed reduction of a shoulder dislocation with greater humeral tuberosity fracture. With the patient positioned prone and the arm hanging toward the floor, manual distraction is attempted. If not successful, the physician may hang a five-pound weight from the arm in an attempt to reduce the shoulder into place. Once shoulder reduction is obtained, a neurovascular examination is performed and treatment of the humeral tuberosity fracture is addressed. The arm is immobilized for three to six weeks.

23670
The physician performs open reduction of a shoulder dislocation with greater humeral tuberosity fracture. The physician may enter the shoulder anteriorly through a deltopectoral approach or superiorly through a deltoid splitting approach. The soft tissues are reflected and the fracture is observed. Once the dislocated joint is reduced into proper position, the repair of the humeral tuberosity fracture is addressed. Larger fragments may be stabilized with screws, wire sutures, staples, or other internal fixation measures. These fragments usually require later removal of the fixation device to allow full motion of the shoulder. If the fragment is small, it can be removed and the tendons of the rotator cuff advanced and attached to the defect in the bone. Once the fracture is stable, the incision is closed and the arm is protected in a sling for four to six weeks.

23675
The physician performs closed reduction of a shoulder dislocation with surgical or anatomical neck fracture. With the patient positioned prone and the arm hanging toward the floor, manual distraction is attempted. If not successful, the physician may hang a five-pound weight from the arm in an attempt to reduce the shoulder into place. Once shoulder reduction is obtained, a neurovascular examination is performed and treatment of the humeral surgical or anatomical neck fracture is addressed. The arm is immobilized for three to six weeks.

23680
The physician performs open reduction of a shoulder dislocation with surgical or anatomical neck fracture. The physician may enter the shoulder anteriorly through a deltopectoral approach or superiorly through a deltoid splitting approach. The soft tissues are reflected and the fracture is observed. Once the dislocated joint is reduced into proper position, the repair of the humeral surgical or anatomical neck fracture is addressed. Larger fragments may be stabilized with screws, wire sutures, staples, or other internal fixation measures. These fragments usually require later removal of the fixation device to allow full motion of the shoulder. An intramedullary rod may be placed through the shaft of the bone as well. Once the fracture is stable, the incision is closed and the arm is protected in a sling for four to six weeks.

23700
Manipulation of the shoulder under anesthesia may be necessary to regain the loss of motion that occurs in the case of frozen shoulder or following a surgical procedure. The patient is positioned supine and given general anesthesia. Following full evaluation, the physician manipulates the shoulder to achieve the appropriate range of motion. A fixation apparatus may also be applied.

23800-23802
The physician performs arthrodesis of the glenohumeral joint. The shoulder is positioned in what is considered the most functional position, slightly abducted to the side with forward elevation. A dorsolateral semicircular incision is made across the glenohumeral joint and carried distally at the midpoint. The articular cartilage is removed from the head of the humerus (ball) and the glenoid cavity (socket). The head is split and a wedge of bone is removed. This wedge is where the acromion will rest when the arm is positioned in abduction. At this point, bone grafting or plate fixation may be added to the procedure to stabilize the glenohumeral joint. If a plate is used, a second procedure will be needed to remove the hardware. Cast application or external fixation may be used in a number of ways. Report 23802 if an autogenous graft is used.

23900
The physician performs a forequarter interthoracoscapular amputation. The physician incises the skin overlying the shoulder and dissects the disease-free soft tissue away from the bone to create a skin flap to cover the wound. The clavicle is disarticulated from the sternum and the chest wall is freed from muscular attachments to the arm. The

quarter section is removed and the wound is sutured in layers. If enough disease-free tissue is not available for primary closure, the wound is packed closed with gauze.

23920-23921

The physician disarticulates the shoulder. The physician incises the skin overlying the shoulder. The rotator cuff is incised, freeing the arm of ligamentous and muscular attachments. The arm is removed and the wound is sutured in layers. Report 23920 for the first amputation. Report 23921 for a secondary closure of the wound or scar revision.

23930-23931

The physician drains a deep abscess or hematoma in 23930 or an infected bursa in 23931 from within the upper arm or elbow area. With proper anesthesia administered, the physician makes an incision in the upper arm or elbow overlying the site of the abscess, hematoma, or bursa to be incised. Dissection is carried down through the deep subcutaneous tissues and may be continued into the fascia or muscle to expose the abscess or hematoma. The incision may be extended if the mass is larger than expected. When the infected bursa, abscess, or hematoma is identified, it is incised and the contents are drained. The area is irrigated and the incision is repaired in layers with sutures, staples, and/or Steri-strips; closed with drains in place; or simply left open to further facilitate drainage of infection.

23935

The physician incises the bone cortex of infected bone in the humerus or elbow to treat an abscess or osteomyelitis. The physician makes an incision over the affected area. Dissection is carried down through the soft tissues to expose the bone. The periosteum is split and reflected from the bone overlying the infected area. A curette may be used to scrape away the abscess or infected portion down to healthy bony tissue or drill holes may be made through the cortex into the medullary canal in a window outline around the infected or abscessed bone. The area is drained and debrided of infected bony and soft tissue. The physician irrigates the area with antibiotic solution, the periosteum is closed over the bone, and the soft tissues are sutured closed; or the wound is packed and left open, allowing the area to drain. Secondary closure is performed approximately three weeks later. Dressings are changed daily. A splint may be applied to limit elbow movement.

24000

The physician performs an arthrotomy on the elbow that includes exploration, drainage, or removal of any foreign body. A longitudinal incision over the part of the elbow to be exposed (e.g., the anterior, posterior, medial, or lateral aspect) is made. The soft tissues are dissected away and the joint capsule is exposed and incised. The joint is explored, any necrotic tissue is removed, and infection or abnormal fluid is drained. If a foreign body is present (e.g., bullet, nail, gravel), it is exposed and removed. The wound is irrigated with antibiotic solution. The physician may leave the wound packed open with daily dressing changes to allow for further drainage and secondary healing by granulation. If the incision is repaired, drain tubes may be inserted and the incision is repaired in layers with sutures, staples, and/or Steri-strips. A splint may be applied to limit elbow motion.

24006

The physician performs an arthrotomy of the elbow with capsular excision for release. The physician makes an incision over the anterior part of the elbow. Dissection exposes the joint capsule. The radial nerve is identified and protected. The anterior elbow joint capsule is incised and portions of it are removed. By excising the capsule, any scarring limiting elbow motion is minimal. Additional incisions (e.g., medial elbow incision) are made if other parts of the capsule are also to be excised. The physician repairs the incision in layers with sutures, staples, and/or Steri-strips. The elbow is placed in a posterior splint.

24065-24066

The physician performs a biopsy of the soft tissues of the upper arm or elbow area. With proper anesthesia administered, an incision is made over the biopsy area. Dissection is carried down within the superficial soft tissue layers in 24065, usually the subcutaneous fat to the uppermost fascial layer. In 24066, dissection is taken down deep within the soft tissue, such as into the fascial layer or within the muscle. A portion of the tissue is excised and submitted for pathology. The area is irrigated and the incision is closed with layered sutures, staples, or Steri-strips.

24071-24076

The physician removes a tumor from the soft tissue of the upper arm or elbow area that is located in the subcutaneous tissue in 24071and 24075 and in the deep soft tissue, below the fascial plane or within the muscle, in 24073 and 24076. With the proper anesthesia administered, the physician makes an incision in the skin overlying the mass and dissects down to the tumor. The extent of the tumor is identified and a dissection is undertaken all the way around the tumor. A portion of neighboring soft tissue may also be removed to ensure adequate removal of all tumor tissue. A drain may be inserted and the incision is repaired with layers of sutures, staples, or Steri-strips. Report 24075 for excision of subcutaneous tumors whose resected area is less than 3 cm and 24071 for excision of subcutaneous tumors 3 cm or greater. Report 24076 for excision of subfascial or intramuscular tumors whose resected area is less than 5 cm and 24073 for excision of subfascial or intramuscular tumors 5 cm or greater.

24077-24079

The physician performs a radical resection of a malignant soft tissue tumor from the upper arm or elbow area, not involving bone. An incision is made over the tumor and dissection exposes it. The tumor and any adjacent tissue that may be affected by the spread of the neoplasm are excised. Large resections may be needed. The type and stage of the lesion determines the extent of the tumor margin resection area. Muscle or fascia may need to be repaired and drains may be placed. The surgical wound is repaired by intermediate or complex closure, adjacent tissue transfer, or graft. The arm may be placed in a posterior splint. Report 24077 for excision of tumors whose resected area is less than 5 cm and 24079 for excision of tumors 5 cm or greater.

24100-24101

The physician makes a long, straight, lateral incision to access the elbow joint and perform an arthrotomy. The physician may also use a medial, anterior, or posterior approach. The joint capsule is exposed by dissecting down through the soft tissues and freeing and reflecting the common origin of the extensor muscles. The joint capsule is incised to expose the synovium, which lies within the joint capsule. A small portion of the synovium is excised for biopsy in 24100. In 24101, additional dissection is carried out to further explore the joint cavity. Any loose or foreign bodies (e.g., free cartilage, bone chips, gravel) are removed and a biopsy may be taken. The physician irrigates the joint. The physician may leave the wound packed open with daily dressing changes to allow for further drainage and secondary healing by granulation. A drain tube may be placed and the incision repaired in layers with sutures, staples, and/or Steri-strips. A splint may be applied to limit elbow movement.

24102

The physician makes a long, straight, lateral incision over the elbow to perform an arthrotomy and remove the synovium. The physician may also use a medial, anterior, or posterior approach. The joint capsule is exposed by dissecting down through the soft tissues and freeing and reflecting the common origin of the extensor muscles. The joint capsule is incised to expose the synovium, the inner membrane of the articular capsule that lines the joint cavity. The inflamed or enlarged synovium is dissected away from the capsule and the bones and removed. Motorized shavers may be used. A drain tube may be placed and the incision is repaired in layers with sutures, staples, and/or Steri-strips. A splint may be applied to limit elbow movement.

24105

The physician excises the olecranon bursa by making a longitudinal incision along the posteromedial border of the elbow and dissecting down to expose the bursa, the fluid filled sac that lubricates the joint against friction. The bursa is excised. The surrounding tissue is examined for any sign of infection. The wound is irrigated and the incision is repaired in layers with sutures, staples, and/or Steri-strips.

24110-24116

A bone cyst or benign tumor of the humerus is removed. The physician makes an incision in the upper arm overlying the cyst or tumor. The skin and underlying soft tissues are reflected to expose the periosteum, which is separated from the bone. Curettes or osteotomes are used to scrape or cut the lesion from the bone. Once the benign tumor or cyst is removed and healthy bone tissue is present, the periosteum is repositioned and the incision is repaired in layers. If the bone defect created requires a graft for repair, the physician obtains the necessary size bone graft from a separate donor site on the patient and packs it into the site where the tumor or bone cyst was removed, or uses a bone bank allograft. Report 24115 if the procedure is done with an autograft and 24116 if an allograft is used.

24120-24126

The physician uses excision or curettage to remove a bone cyst or benign tumor of the head or neck of the radius or olecranon process in 24120. The physician makes a longitudinal incision along the lateral aspect of the elbow. A posterior incision may also be made to access the olecranon process. To expose the radial head and/or neck, the common origin of the extensor muscles is reflected and the joint capsule is incised. The bone cyst or tumor is identified and the periosteum is separated from the bone. Curettes or osteotomes are used to scrape or cut the lesion from the bone. Once the benign tumor or cyst is removed and healthy bone tissue is present, the periosteum is repositioned and the incision is repaired in layers, including the joint capsule, if incised. If the bone defect created requires a graft for repair, the physician obtains the necessary size bone graft from a separate donor site on the patient and packs it into the site where the tumor or bone cyst was removed or uses a bone bank allograft. Report 24125 if an autograft is obtained and 24126 if an allograft is used.

24130

The radial head is excised in this procedure. The physician makes a longitudinal incision along the lateral aspect of the elbow. The elbow joint is exposed by freeing and reflecting the common origin of the extensor muscles. The joint capsule is incised and the radial head is exposed. The physician uses a bone-cutting saw to excise the radial head. The capsule is closed with sutures and the incision is repaired in layers with sutures, staples, and/or Steri-strips.

24134-24138

The physician removes infected portions of bone, due to a bone abscess or osteomyelitis, from the shaft or distal humerus in 24134, from the radial head or neck in 24136, and from the olecranon process in 24138. This infection often leaves open sinus tracts in the bone that require removal. The physician makes an incision overlying the sequestered area of bone, which includes incising the capsule if the elbow joint is involved. Once the skin and soft tissues are reflected, a small window is cut into the bone to gain access to the sequestrum, or necrosed piece of bone that has become separated from sound bone. All purulent material and scarred or necrotic tissue are removed. The remaining space is filled with surrounding soft tissues or free tissue transfer. The area is irrigated and an antibiotic solution is used to prevent further infection. The wound is closed loosely over drains if possible or may be packed open with dressings. The patient may be placed in a splint to limit elbow motion.

24140-24147

The physician performs a partial excision of the humerus in 24140, the radial head or neck in 24145, or the olecranon process in 24147 to remove infected bone. An incision is made over the infected part of the bone and the underlying soft tissues are divided to expose the bone. The elbow joint capsule may be incised if necessary. The periosteum is reflected and the infected portion of bone is removed and irrigated. The excavation of bone may excise a crater-like piece, leave a small saucer-like shelf depression in the bone, or may remove a portion of the shaft (diaphysis) of a long bone. If a significant portion of bone is removed, the physician may use bone graft material to fill the cavity left in the bone. The periosteum is closed over the bone, the soft tissues are sutured closed, and a soft dressing is applied. A long splint may be applied to limit elbow motion.

24149

The physician radically resects the elbow joint capsule, undesirable soft tissue and bone, and releases a contracture of a muscle or tendon. With the patient under anesthesia, the physician makes a long longitudinal incision overlying the elbow. Depending on the extent of the excess bone to be removed or the severity of the contracture, additional incisions may be required. The incision is continued deep to the elbow joint capsule itself. Nerves, vessels, and tendons are retracted. The capsule is fully exposed. A thorough debridement is undertaken to excise unwanted soft tissue. The overgrown and excess bone is isolated and excised. The capsule is resected. The contracture of the elbow involving muscle, tendon, scar tissue, or soft tissue is identified and explored. The physician releases the offending tissue to allow full elbow range of motion. The wound or wounds are irrigated and closed in layers. A dressing is applied.

24150

The physician performs a radical resection of a tumor of the shaft or distal humerus. The physician makes an incision overlying the involved area of bone, dissecting down to expose the tumor site. The involved vessels and nerves are protected. Proximate muscles are detached extraperiosteally by sharp dissection, and the tumor is excised, including the immediately surrounding bone and any involved soft tissue. The wound is closed with layered sutures.

24152

The physician performs a radical resection of a tumor of the radial head or neck. The physician makes an anterolateral incision overlying the elbow or forearm. Dissection exposes the radial head or neck. The radial vessels and nerve are protected. The tumor is excised, including the radial head or neck. The physician selects the level of the radius to be divided. The physician uses a bone saw to divide the bone at the appropriate level. The muscles are detached by sharp dissection. Radical resection may also include removal of surrounding soft tissues such as muscles, fascia, and vessels. The wound is closed with layered sutures.

24155

An elbow joint arthrectomy is performed to remove the joint by resection of the distal humerus and the proximal radius and ulna. The physician makes a longitudinal incision along the lateral elbow. Dissection is carried down through the joint capsule to expose the distal humerus and the proximal radius and ulna. The physician selects the level at which the bones are to be resected. The physician uses a bone saw to divide the bones at the appropriate level. The physician preserves the surrounding muscle attachments to maintain some support and function for moving the elbow. However, gross instability of the elbow is present. The incision is repaired in layers using staples, sutures, and/or Steri-strips.

24160-24164

The physician makes an incision overlying the elbow joint implant. The incision may be made on the medial, lateral, or posterior portion of the elbow. In 24164, the incision may be made along the lateral elbow to expose the radial head. Dissection exposes the implant (e.g., pin, wire, screw). The physician uses instruments to remove the implant from the bone. The incision is repaired with sutures and/or Steri-strips.

24200-24201

The physician removes a foreign body of the upper arm or elbow area. If the foreign body is a result of trauma, an open wound may already exist. The physician may make a separate incision or access the foreign body through the open wound. Location of the foreign body may be determined prior to surgery by separately reportable x-rays. A subcutaneous foreign body is located between the skin and muscle layer in 24200. The foreign body is deep and may be within muscle in 24201. More extensive dissection and a larger incision may be necessary for a deep foreign body. Once the foreign body is visualized, it is removed. The physician may also debride any surrounding damaged soft tissue.

The wound is irrigated. Drains may be placed in the wound and the incision repaired in layers with sutures, staples, and/or Steri-strips. A splint may be applied to limit elbow motion.

24220
Elbow arthrography provides information about the capsule size, the synovial lining, the articular surfaces of the joints, and detects loose bodies and capsular leaks. The patient is positioned sitting or supine (lying face up) with the elbow flexed at 90 degrees. One of two injection sites may be used, a lateral or posterior approach. The contrast medium is injected. A fluoroscope is used to study the elbow. No incisions are made. This code reports the injection only. The radiological exam is reported separately.

24300
Manipulation of the elbow under anesthesia may be necessary to gain the loss of motion following a surgical procedure or due to scar tissue. Following the induction of general anesthesia, the physician evaluates the elbow. The elbow is manipulated by stretching, rotation, and other maneuvers to gain the appropriate range of motion.

24301
The physician performs a muscle or tendon transfer of the upper arm or elbow. An example is transfer of the latissimus dorsi muscle. This transfer restores active elbow flexion by transferring the origin and belly of the latissimus dorsi to the arm and anchoring the origin near the radial head. The patient is placed side lying with the affected side up. An incision is made starting at the loin and extending up to the axilla and distally along the medial aspect of the arm to the anterior elbow. The physician cuts free the origin of the latissimus dorsi. The muscle itself is cut free from the underlying abdominal muscles. The origin of the latissimus dorsi muscle is sutured to the biceps tendon and the periosteal tissues about the radial tuberosity. The incision is repaired in layers with sutures, staples, and/or Steri-strips.

24305
The physician lengthens a tendon of the upper arm or elbow. An anterior curvilinear incision is made, for example, over the anterior elbow to lengthen the biceps tendon. Dissection exposes the distal biceps tendon. The biceps tendon is divided by Z-plasty and stretched into extension, causing it to stretch and release to a lengthened position. If the elbow joint capsule is thickened, the physician may elect to excise this part of the capsule and any fibrous bands or bone spurs in the anterior part of the elbow joint. A drain is inserted into the wound and the incision is repaired in layers using sutures, staples, and/or Steri-strips. The elbow is placed in a splint or cast in an extended position.

24310
For tenotomy of the distal biceps tendon, an incision is made over the anterior elbow to expose the biceps tendon. The tendon is cut all the way through so as to release the flexion contracture. No repair of the tendon is made. The incision is repaired with sutures. The elbow may be placed in a splint to keep it in as much extension as possible.

24320
A Seddon-Brookes type upper arm tenoplasty with muscle transfer restores elbow flexion by prolonging the tendon of the pectoralis major muscle with the long head of the biceps brachii. The physician makes an incision from the deltopectoral groove to the midportion of the upper arm. The pectoralis major tendon is exposed through dissection, detached from its insertion, and mobilized from the chest wall toward the clavicle. The tendon of the long head of the biceps is exposed and severed from its origin and withdrawn into the wound. The long head of the biceps is dissected from the short head. An L-shaped incision is made over the anterior aspect of the elbow. The long head of the biceps is divided and freed distally to its attachment on the radius. The biceps tendon and muscle are withdrawn through the distal L-shaped incision. Through the proximal incision, the tendon and muscle belly of the long head of the biceps is passed through two slits in the tendon of the pectoralis major and looped on itself so that its proximal tendon is brought into the distal L-shaped incision. The end of the proximal tendon is sutured through a slit in the distal tendon and the tendon of the pectoralis major is sutured to the long head of the biceps at their junction. The incisions are repaired in layers using sutures, staples, and/or Steri-strips. A posterior plaster splint is applied with the elbow in flexion.

24330-24331
To perform a Steindler-type advancement for flexor-plasty of the elbow, the physician transfers the common origin of the pronator teres, flexor carpi radialis, palmaris longus, flexor digitorum sublimis, and flexor carpi ulnaris from the medial epicondyle of the humerus proximally and laterally onto the anterior surface of the humerus so that it performs elbow flexion rather than forearm pronation. This is done when the biceps brachii and brachialis are paralyzed. The physician makes a curved longitudinal incision over the medial side of the elbow extending over the medial condyle area and along the pronator teres. The ulnar nerve is identified and retracted for protection. The common origin of the pronator teres, flexor carpi radialis, palmaris longus, flexor digitorum sublimis, and flexor carpi ulnaris is detached as a whole from the medial epicondyle. These muscles are freed up for about 4 cm. A fascia lata graft is taken from the lateral thigh and one end is sutured to the common origin to extend it, while the other end is advanced and attached 5 cm up the lateral side of the humerus. A cast is

applied with the elbow in flexion. In 24331, an anterior transfer of the triceps (extensor advancement) is performed in conjunction with elbow flexor-plasty. A posterolateral incision is made over the lower upper arm. The triceps tendon is exposed and divided at its insertion, dissected from the back of the lower humerus, and brought around to the lateral side. An anterolateral curvilinear incision is made to expose the radial tuberosity. Another 4 cm long fascia lata graft is harvested and attached to the triceps tendon to extend it for advancement. The other end of the fascia lata graft is attached to the tuberosity of the radius. This creates added elbow flexibility. A cast is applied with the elbow in flexion.

24332
Tenolysis involves transection of adhesions that have formed between the tendon and its surrounding tissues. Beginning proximally along the supracondylar ridge and ending near the subcutaneous border of the ulna, the physician makes a deep dissection to the anterior aspect of the capsule. The triceps tendon is retracted posteriorly to expose the olecranon fossa and tenolysis of the triceps and posterior capsulectomy is performed. Tenolysis should be performed under a local anesthetic so that full release can be confirmed. If, however, general or regional anesthesia is used, the physician may check the adequacy of the removal of all adhesions by manually pulling the tendons.

24340
The physician treats a rupture of a distal biceps tendon by reattachment of the biceps tendon to the radius, direct reimplantation, or inserting a loop of fascia lata graft around the proximal radius. Reattachment of the biceps tendon to the radius is described. The patient is placed supine. The physician makes an anterior lateral incision on the lower upper arm, extending transversely across the antecubital fossa. The torn biceps tendon is identified and the tear is minimally debrided. Two Bunnell sutures are placed in the torn end. A second incision is made over the dorsal aspect of the proximal forearm to expose the radial tuberosity. The physician uses a high-speed burr to evacuate a 5 mm to 7 mm defect in the radial tuberosity. Three holes are drilled through this window to the opposite side of the tuberosity. The physician places sutures through the holes and places the tendon into the window in the tuberosity. The sutures are pulled tight and secured. The incisions are repaired in layers with drains inserted. The elbow is placed in a splint in 90 degrees of flexion and full supination.

24341
The physician repairs one of the muscles or tendons in the upper arm or elbow, not including those of the rotator cuff. With the patient under general anesthesia, the physician makes an incision directly overlying the torn muscles or tendon. The incision is carried deep through the subcutaneous tissue. The extent of the tear is ascertained through debridement and exploration. The physician repairs the tissue using appropriate fixation devices such as sutures, wires, or screws. Additional incisions are often required when a tendon is completely ruptured. When the repair is complete, the incision is closed in layers. Use this code to report both the initial, primary repair done near the time of injury or a secondary repair, done sometime after the incident of injury or following a previous surgical repair.

24342
The physician performs reinsertion of a distal ruptured biceps or triceps tendon. For the triceps tendon, a posterior longitudinal incision is made to expose the tendinous portion of the triceps. Drill holes are made in the olecranon. Sutures from the triceps tendon are passed through the drill holes, pulled tight, and secured. The physician may harvest a fascia graft from the forearm. The proximal attachment of the fascia graft is left attached to the epicondyle. The distal part is detached, raised, and sutured to the distal triceps for reinforcement. The incision is repaired in layers with sutures, staples, and/or Steri-strips. The arm is immobilized in less than 90 degrees of flexion.

24343
The lateral collateral ligament (LCL) is the ligament of the elbow along the outer aspect that connects the distal end of the humerus to the proximal end of the ulna and provides lateral stability to the joint. Injury to the LCL can lead to elbow dislocation. Anterior-posterior and lateral x-rays of the elbow are taken and reported separately. The physician administers a local anesthetic block, makes an incision, and dissects down to the damaged lateral collateral ligament. If the ligament has been pulled from its attachment on the bone, the ligament is reattached with large sutures or a metal bone staple. More than one incision may be necessary. The damaged collateral ligament is repaired with local tissue that can be used to restore its functionality. For mid-ligament tears, the ends of the ligament are sewed together to repair ligament continuity.

24344
The lateral collateral ligament (LCL) of the elbow is reconstructed with a tendon graft. The LCL is the ligament along the outer aspect of the elbow that connects the distal end of the humerus to the proximal end of the ulna. It provides lateral stability to the joint and injury to the LCL can lead to elbow dislocation. Anterior-posterior and lateral x-rays of the elbow are taken and reported separately. The physician administers a local anesthetic block, makes an incision, and dissects to the damaged lateral collateral ligament. The palmaris longus tendon is usually used for the graft. The physician makes a transverse proximal wrist crease incision directly over the tendon, divides it, and holds it taut. A second transverse incision is made

about 8 cm above the first incision on the forearm to again identify the tendon. The graft segment is divided and withdrawn. Alternatively, a tendon stripper can be used. The tendon is grafted to the lateral collateral ligament to restore functionality. The wound is closed and a dressing applied. The hand and wrist may be put in a plaster cast, splint, or bandage, depending on which tendons were involved.

24345

The medial collateral ligament (MCL) is posterior to the axis of elbow flexion and primarily serves as the medial stabilizer of the flexed elbow joint. X-rays (reported separately) are taken to identify abnormally wide joint space on the medial side. An MRI (reported separately) may be taken to show focal discontinuity of the ligament and joint fluid extravasation. Repair of a freshly torn medial collateral ligament usually requires the surgeon to make an incision through the skin over the area where the tear in the ligament has occurred. If the ligament has been pulled from its attachment on the bone, the ligament is reattached with large sutures or a metal bone staple. More than one incision may be necessary. The damaged ligament is repaired with local tissue that can be used to restore its functionality. For mid-ligament tears, the ends of the ligament are sewed together to repair ligament continuity. The procedure is normally performed under general anesthesia or with a local block.

24346

The medial collateral ligament (MCL) is posterior to the axis of elbow flexion and primarily serves as the medial stabilizer of the flexed elbow joint. X-rays (reported separately) are taken to identify abnormally wide joint space on the medial side. An MRI (reported separately) may be taken to show focal discontinuity of the ligament and joint fluid extravasation. The palmaris longus tendon is the most commonly used tendon graft for the elbow. The procedure is normally performed under general anesthesia. The physician makes a transverse proximal wrist crease incision directly over the tendon, divides it, and holds it taut. A second transverse incision is made about 8 cm above the first incision on the forearm to again identify the tendon. The graft segment is divided and withdrawn. Alternatively, a tendon stripper can be used. The tendon is grafted to the medial collateral ligament to restore functionality. The wound is closed and a dressing applied. The hand and wrist may be put in a plaster cast, splint, or bandage, depending on which tendons were involved.

24357

The physician performs a percutaneous (through the skin) lateral or medial tenotomy for tennis elbow, golfer's elbow, or epicondylitis. Following administration of a local anesthetic, the physician advances an 18- or 20-guage needle through the abnormal region of the tendon. The tip of the needle is drawn back and forth to repeatedly perforate (fenestrate) the tendinotic tissue in multiple locations. Any calcifications or spurs are mechanically fragmented and the bony surface of the apex and epicondylar face are abraded to stimulate new blood vessels. The fenestrated tendon is then infiltrated with a corticosteroid/bupivacaine solution.

24358-24359

The physician performs open tenotomy (cutting or release) to treat lateral epicondylitis (tennis elbow) or medial epicondylitis (golfer's elbow. An incision is made over the lateral epicondyle of the humerus. In 24358, the physician removes (debrides) damaged soft tissue or bone. In 24359, the physician also repairs or reattaches the affected tendon. The incision is repaired in layers with sutures, staples, and/or Steri-strips. The arm is placed in a sling.

24360

The physician performs a membrane arthroplasty of the elbow. A longitudinal incision is made over the lateral elbow. All soft tissue is dissected from the distal humerus. The elbow is dislocated. Osteophytes and articular cartilage are removed from the distal humerus so that a smooth, rounded surface remains. Articular cartilage is left intact on the proximal ulna and radius. The physician uses a motorized dermatome to remove a thin split-thickness skin graft from the patient's lower abdomen. Small drill holes are made in the distal end of the humerus. The graft is sutured into place over the distal end of the humerus with the dermal surface placed against the bone and the fat facing the new joint space. The elbow joint is reduced (realigned). The physician repairs the incision in layers using sutures, staples, and/or Steri-strips. The elbow is placed in a posterior splint in 90 degrees of flexion.

24361

The physician performs an arthroplasty of the elbow with distal humeral prosthetic replacement. The physician makes a 10 cm longitudinal incision over the medial aspect of the elbow. The ulnar nerve is identified and retracted to protect it from injury. The joint capsule is excised and the radius and ulna are separated from the humerus. A Kirschner wire is drilled into the trochlea (distal humerus) along the axis of the joint. Using an osteotome, high speed burr, or saw, the physician trims and remodels the distal end of the humerus. A prosthesis is fitted to the distal humerus and hammered into place. The ulna and radius are reduced to the prosthesis. If the radial head is severely deformed or arthritic, the physician may resect (remove) it. Other adjustments may be made, such as sculpting the semilunar notch or olecranon. Sculpting allows better articulation with the prosthesis and better elbow motion. The flexor origins are reattached to the epicondyle. The physician repairs the incision in layers with sutures, staples, and/or

Steri-strips. A long arm cast or splint is applied with the elbow in 90 degrees of flexion.

24362
The physician performs an arthroplasty of the elbow with an implant and fascia lata ligament reconstruction. The physician makes a 10 cm longitudinal incision over the medial aspect of the elbow. The ulnar nerve is identified and retracted to protect it from injury. The joint capsule is excised and the radius and ulna are separated from the humerus. A Kirschner wire is drilled into the trochlea (distal humerus) along the axis of the joint. Using an osteotome, high speed burr, or saw, the physician trims and remodels the distal end of the humerus. A prosthesis is fitted to the distal humerus and hammered into place. The ulna and radius are reduced to the prosthesis. If the radial head is severely deformed or arthritic, the physician may resect (remove) it. Other adjustments may be made, such as sculpting the semilunar notch or olecranon. Sculpting allows better articulation with the prosthesis and better elbow motion. The flexor origins are reattached to the epicondyle. For the fascia lata ligament reconstruction, an additional incision may be necessary on the posterior aspect of the elbow and forearm. The radial head and olecranon are exposed. Through an incision on the lateral side of the thigh, a long rectangle of fascia lata is removed. The fascia is folded in half crosswise and the folded edge is anchored to the anterior part of the capsule with sutures. The distal half is sutured in place over the trochlear notch. A fold of the same fascia is inserted between the radial head and ulna and fixed with sutures. The capsule is sutured closed. The incisions are repaired in layers with sutures, staples, and/or Steri-strips. A long arm cast or splint immobilizes the elbow at 90 degrees of flexion.

24363
The physician performs a total elbow arthroplasty with distal humerus and proximal ulnar prosthetic replacement. The patient is placed supine with the affected arm on the chest and a sandbag beneath the shoulder. Different types of prosthetic implants are available. Selection depends on capsuloligamentous structures, muscular integrity, and the amount of bone remaining at the elbow joint. A technique for a semiconstrained (two to three part) hinged prosthesis is described. The physician makes a straight, midline, posterior incision. The ulnar nerve is identified and retracted for protection. The triceps mechanism is elevated from the olecranon. The collateral ligaments are preserved. A portion of the olecranon is cut and removed to allow implantation of the ulnar stem. The distal humerus is prepared by removing cancellous bone with a curette. The physician uses a rasp to open and contour the humeral and ulnar medullary canals for insertion of the prosthetic stems. Cement is inserted into the ulnar and humeral medullary canals with a cement gun or syringe. The elbow is flexed and the prosthesis is inserted into the humeral and ulnar medullary canals at the same time. The elbow joint is fully extended while the cement hardens. The triceps mechanism is sutured back to fascia. The ulnar nerve is positioned anterior to the elbow. The physician inserts drain tubes. The incision is repaired in layers with sutures, staples, and/or Steri-strips. A posterior splint is applied to the elbow in 90 degrees of flexion.

24365
The physician performs an arthroplasty on the radial head by making a 5 cm to 6 cm longitudinal incision along the lateral aspect of the elbow. The elbow joint is exposed by freeing and reflecting the common origin of the extensor muscles. The joint capsule is incised and the radial head is exposed. The physician uses a bone cutting saw to excise the radial head. The capsule is closed with sutures and the incision is repaired in layers with sutures, staples, and/or Steri-strips.

24366
The physician performs an arthroplasty on the radial head with an implant. The patient is positioned supine or lateral (lying on one side) with the affected elbow up. The physician makes an incision beginning just above the lateral epicondyle and extending distally approximately 6 cm across the joint. Dissection exposes the capsule, which is incised. The annular ligament is incised transversely so that the neck of the radius can be osteotomized. A burr or rasp is used to prepare the medullary canal of the radius to accept the implant. The implant is inserted into the medullary canal of the radius and positioned into contact with the capitellum. The annular ligament is reattached. A suction drain is inserted. The physician repairs the incision in layers using sutures, staples, and/or Steri-strips. The arm may be placed in a posterior elbow splint at 90 degrees of flexion.

24400
The physician performs an osteotomy of the humerus with or without internal fixation. The physician makes a longitudinal incision overlying the involved portion of the shaft of the humerus to expose the affected part of the bone. An osteotomy is made through the humerus, usually in a wedge shape. This allows the bone to be realigned. The physician may apply plates and screws to hold the bone together in the correct position (internal fixation). The incision is repaired in layers with sutures, staples, and/or Steri-strips. The arm may be placed in a cast or splint for immobilization.

24410
The physician performs multiple osteotomies with realignment on an intramedullary rod of the humeral shaft. This is done to treat the deformities of osteogenesis imperfecta. The physician makes a longitudinal incision through the skin, fascia, and muscle to expose the shaft of the bone subperiosteally. Osteotomies are made through the proximal and distal

Musculoskeletal

metaphyses; the shaft is removed and studied to determine how many osteotomies must be made to thread the segments onto the intramedullary rod. Additional osteotomies, usually three or four, are performed to correct the alignment. The fragments are shifted and rotated to facilitate aligning them end to end on the straight nail. Autografts may be added if the cortex is thin. The intramedullary nail is inserted so that the ends extend into the canals at the distal and proximal ends. The periosteum is sutured over the bone and the wound is closed and dressed.

24420
The physician performs osteoplasty of the humerus for shortening or lengthening. An incision is made through the skin, fascia, and muscle in the upper arm over the humeral shaft. Vessels and nerves are exposed and retracted. Dissection continues to expose the shaft of the humerus. An osteotomy is made at the determined point on the humerus. The physician removes a wedge of bone. To shorten the humeral shaft, a plate is attached to the distal segment with screws. Reduction forceps are used to hold and compress the osteotomy while the plate is attached to the proximal fragment with screws. To lengthen the bone, the segments are retracted, usually 2 mm to 3 mm, and fixed at that distance with plates and screws. X-rays (reported separately) are used to check rotational alignment of the segments. Drain tubes are inserted, the incision is repaired in layers with sutures, staples, and/or Steri-strips, and the arm is immobilized.

24430-24435
The physician repairs a nonunion or malunion of the humerus without using a graft in 24430 and with an iliac or other autograft in 24435. The physician exposes the nonunion or malunion of the humerus by making a 10 cm to 15 cm longitudinal incision through the skin, fascia, and muscle over the fracture site. With a reciprocating saw, the bone is divided through the nonunion. The fragments are aligned. A compression plate is centered over the fracture and screws are inserted. In 24435, a bone graft is needed to help heal the fracture due to bone loss. Autogenous iliac bone is typically used, but proximal tibia grafts may also be used. Both require a separate incision and wound closure of the harvest site. The physician uses an osteotome to harvest strips of bone, which are placed around the ends of the humeral fracture in addition to the compression plate for internal fixation. The incision is repaired in layers with sutures, staples, and/or Steri-strips. The limb is immobilized.

24470
The physician performs a hemiepiphyseal arrest. Angular deformities are typically a complication of fractures of the lateral condylar physis. The most common deformity is cubitus valgus. To treat cubitus valgus, the physician makes a longitudinal posterior incision along the distal humerus. The humerus is exposed. If a nonunion exists from a previous condylar physeal fracture, it may be approached from the same incision and the ends are denuded and a local bone graft is applied. The physician applies a cancellous screw to provide fixation and compression across the nonunion. An osteotomy is performed across the distal humerus, correcting both the angulation and realigning the longitudinal axis of the humerus with that of the forearm. The osteotomy is secured with screws. The physician repairs the incision in layers with sutures, staples, and/or Steri-strips. The elbow is immobilized in a splint or brace.

24495
The physician performs a decompression fasciotomy in the forearm with exploration of the brachial artery. The physician makes a longitudinal incision on the anterior forearm, from just lateral and proximal to the biceps tendon distal toward the radial styloid, excising the deep fascia, and exposing the brachioradialis laterally and the biceps and brachialis medially, to decompress the compartment. The brachial artery is explored proximally to identify the origin of decreased circulation. The fascial incision remains open. The skin incision may be left open or closed.

24498
The physician applies prophylactic treatment to prevent fracture. A longitudinal incision is made through the skin, fascia, and muscle along the humerus to expose the worrisome area. Pins or a plate and screws are used to stabilize the bone. If defects in the bone do not allow for good internal fixation, methylmethacrylate, a bone cementing substance when hard, may be used to fill in the gaps. Wiring may also be wrapped around the bone to provide additional fixation. An intramedullary nail may also be inserted through the canal of the humerus to provide internal stabilization. The incisions are repaired in layers with sutures, staples, and/or Steri-strips.

24500-24505
The physician performs closed treatment of a humeral shaft fracture. In 24500, the segments are determined to be aligned and stable and no manipulation of the bone fragments is necessary. Treatment involves immobilization, using one of several methods, of the elbow and possibly of the glenohumeral joint for several weeks until union is established. In 24505, the physician must first manually coerce the fractured bone into alignment. Skeletal traction may also be applied in 24505.

24515
The physician repairs a humeral shaft fracture openly with a plate or screws, with or without cerclage. A lateral or anterolateral incision is made overlying the fracture site. The fracture is reduced by manipulation and bone reduction forceps. A compression plate with screws secures and compresses the fragments. Cerclage wiring might be used to facilitate fixation of the

fracture. One or more wires may be placed around the humerus, over the fracture site. The incision is closed with sutures, staples, and/or Steri-strips.

24516

The physician repairs a humeral shaft fracture with insertion of an intramedullary implant, with or without cerclage and/or locking screws. A straight lateral incision is made through the skin, fascia, and muscles to expose the fracture site. If there are multiple fragments or if there is a long spiral fracture, cerclage wires may be wrapped around the bone to hold the fragments in place. Using a guide rod to direct a reamer and rod, an intramedullary nail is placed within the humeral shaft. The nail may be locked in place proximally and distally with locking screws. The wound is irrigated, a drain may be inserted, and the wound is closed in layers.

24530-24535

Closed treatment of a supracondylar or transcondylar fracture, which may have an extending fracture line between the condyles, is indicated when the fragments are not separated and appear stable. No manipulation is required in 24530. Supracondylar fractures in the adult are usually treated with a caption splint or hanging arm cast. Transcondylar fractures may be treated conservatively with a hanging arm cast and elbow immobilization. In 24535, manipulation is necessary to realign the fracture into proper reduction. Skin or skeletal traction may also be applied. Pins, wires, or tongs are inserted into the bone for skeletal traction through a small incision without opening the fracture. A weight and pulley system is attached to exert a constant force of traction and keep the fractured bones in alignment.

24538

The physician performs percutaneous skeletal fixation of a supracondylar or transcondylar humeral fracture, which may have an extending fracture line between the condyles. The elbow is prepared and draped. The fracture is reduced by applying longitudinal traction and manipulating the fracture into alignment. Pins are inserted through the condyles and metaphysis diagonally, avoiding the ulnar nerve to hold the fractured pieces stable. The pins are clipped and bent beneath the skin. The incision is closed with layered sutures and the arm is immobilized.

24545-24546

In 24545, the physician performs open treatment of a supracondylar or transcondylar humeral fracture that does not have an extending fracture line present between the condyles. In 24546, the humeral condylar fracture has an extending fracture line between the condyles that may create a third fracture piece. The physician makes a posterior incision from midline of the arm to just distal to the olecranon, exposing the olecranon, triceps tendon, and distal humerus. The ulnar nerve is isolated and retracted. Preserving as much soft tissue attachment as possible, the physician exposes and assembles the fragments, reducing the condyles and fixing the fragments with screws, pins, or plates as may be needed to hold the condyles firmly reduced to the metaphysis. The joint is irrigated and the wounds are closed with drain placement if needed.

24560-24565

The physician repairs a humeral medial or lateral epicondylar fracture without incision or manipulation in 24560. Closed treatment of a humeral epicondylar fracture is indicated when the fragments are not separated and appear stable. No manipulation is required. No incisions are made. The arm is placed in a posterior elbow splint at 90 degrees of flexion. Report 24565 if manipulation is required to reduce the fracture into position.

24566

The physician fixates a humeral medial or lateral epicondylar fracture percutaneously. The physician uses separately reportable fluoroscopy to realign the fracture by manipulation first. Once the bone is realigned, the physician fixates the pieces to the humeral shaft by driving percutaneous wires through the pieces and into the shaft.

24575

The physician openly treats a fracture of the medial or lateral epicondyle of the humerus. The physician makes an incision in the skin overlying the fractured epicondyle. This is carried deep through the fascia to the bone. Fracture fragments are identified and manipulated into the appropriate anatomic position. The epicondyle may be immobilized in place using internal fixation devices such as plates, screws, or wires if needed. The wound is irrigated and closed in layers.

24576-24577

The physician repairs a humeral medial or lateral condylar fracture without incision or manipulation in 24576. Closed treatment of a humeral condylar fracture is indicated when the fragments are not separated and appear stable. No manipulation is required. No incisions are made. The arm is placed in a posterior elbow splint at 90 degrees of flexion. Report 24577 if manipulation is required to reduce the fracture into position.

24579

The physician openly repairs a humeral condylar fracture, medial or lateral. The physician makes an incision exposing the posterior elbow. Skin and subcutaneous tissue are reflected to expose the olecranon and triceps tendon. The ulnar nerve is retracted. The condyles are reduced and may be temporarily fixed with internal fixation devices such as wires, or screws may be placed across the major fragments. Small fragments may require excision. The incision is closed with sutures and the elbow is immobilized in a posterior elbow splint.

24582
The physician fixates a humeral medial or lateral condylar fracture percutaneously by manipulating the fracture in a closed fashion and inserting pins through the skin and bones to maintain appropriate position. Separately reportable x-rays, including fluoroscopic views, are obtained to ascertain the extent of the fracture. The physician manipulates the arm, elbow, and forearm in such a way to restore the fractured pieces to the acceptable position. The physician places pins through the skin and into the bones to immobilize the reduction until healing is complete.

24586-24587
The physician openly treats a periarticular fracture (distal humerus and proximal ulna and/or proximal radius) and/or dislocation of the elbow. The physician may make more than one incision depending on the extent of the fractures and/or dislocation. If there is a dislocation, it is reduced (realigned) first. The fractures are reduced and secured with plates, screws, pins, wires, or a combination of these. The physician may place a pin through the olecranon for skeletal traction in a patient with multiple injuries to temporarily stabilize the fracture and/or dislocation. In 24587, if joint surface congruity cannot be restored, the physician performs a total elbow arthroplasty. For elbow arthroplasty, the physician makes a straight, midline, posterior incision. The ulnar nerve is identified and retracted for protection. The triceps mechanism is elevated from the olecranon. The collateral ligaments are preserved. A portion of the olecranon is cut and removed to allow implantation of the ulnar stem. The distal humerus is prepared by removing cancellous bone with a curette. The physician uses a rasp to open and contour the humeral and ulnar medullary canals for insertion of the prosthetic stems. Cement is inserted into the ulnar and humeral medullary canals with a cement gun or syringe. The elbow is flexed and the prosthesis is inserted into the humeral and ulnar medullary canals at the same time. The elbow joint is fully extended while the cement hardens. The triceps mechanism is sutured back to fascia. The ulnar nerve is positioned anterior to the elbow. Arthroplasty may be performed in conjunction with some internal fixation for fracture reduction and stabilization.

24600-24605
The physician performs closed treatment of an elbow dislocation when there are no fractures. The forearm typically dislocates posteriorly. The physician manually reduces (realigns) the dislocation with pressure to the area. The elbow is placed in a posterior elbow splint or elbow brace at 90 degrees of flexion with the forearm supinated. The procedure is performed without anesthesia in 24600 or with anesthesia in 24605.

24615
To openly treat an acute or chronic elbow dislocation, the physician may use the Osborne-Cotterill technique of dislocation treatment. The physician makes a longitudinal incision over the lateral aspect of the elbow. The physician dissects the elbow posterior to the lateral collateral ligament. Any bone fragments are removed. The physician roughens the bone at the lateral epicondyle and lateral side of the capitellum. The physician uses an awl to make one or two transverse holes through the lateral condyle close to the articular surface of the humerus. Sutures are passed through these holes and through the posterolateral part of the capsule. The capsule is fixed to the bone as tightly as possible. The incision is repaired in layers. A long arm cast or splint is applied with the elbow in 40 degrees of flexion for approximately four weeks.

24620
The physician treats a Monteggia type fracture dislocation at the elbow (fracture of the proximal end of the ulna with dislocation of the radial head) by manipulation. No incisions are made. The physician manually realigns the radial head back into position. If alignment of the ulnar fracture is not adequate, the physician may also manually align this fracture. Once satisfactory and stable reduction (realignment) is achieved, the elbow is placed in a posterior splint or cast. The elbow is immobilized at 120 degrees of flexion to prevent recurrent dislocation of the radial head.

24635
The physician openly treats a Monteggia type fracture dislocation at the elbow (fracture of the proximal end of the ulna with dislocation of the radial head), with or without internal fixation. The physician makes a longitudinal incision along the lateral aspect of the elbow. Dissection exposes the radial head and proximal ulna. The physician determines the status of the annular ligament. If the ligament is intact, the physician incises it so the radial head can be reduced. The ligament is repaired with nonabsorbable sutures. More commonly, the ligament is torn or avulsed, requiring reconstruction. If so, a strip of fascia 1.3 cm wide and 11 cm long is dissected from the muscles of the forearm. If the ulnar fracture is stable, no internal fixation is required. If the fracture is unstable, internal fixation is typically applied. A compression plate or an intramedullary nail may be utilized for internal fixation. The new annular ligament (fascial strip) is sutured about the radial neck. The incision is repaired in layers with sutures, staples, and/or Steri-strips. The elbow is placed in a posterior splint or cast at 120 degrees of flexion, preventing redislocation of the radial head.

24640
The physician performs closed treatment of nursemaid elbow in a child with manipulation. To realign a

subluxated (partially dislocated) radial head, the physician supinates the forearm (palm upward) while flexing the elbow. No incisions are made. If stability of the radial head is questionable, a cast or splint is applied with the elbow in 90 degrees of flexion.

24650-24655
The physician performs closed treatment of a radial head or neck fracture without manipulation in 24650 and with manipulation in 24655. In 24650, the radial fracture is determined to be stable and nondisplaced and can be splinted or braced without requiring manipulation. In 24655, the physician performs manual manipulation to realign the fractured bone by applying pressure. No incisions are made. The arm is placed in a posterior elbow splint or brace.

24665-24666
The physician performs open treatment of a radial head or neck fracture, with or without internal fixation or radial head excision in 24665 and with radial head prosthetic replacement in 24666. The physician makes an incision along the posterolateral aspect of the elbow. The common origin of the extensor muscles is reflected and the joint capsule is incised, exposing the radial head and neck. All loose particles of bone are removed, the elbow joint is irrigated, and the fractured fragments are reduced. In 24665, the physician may need to remove the radial head to achieve good reduction and screws or other internal fixation devices may be employed to stabilize the fracture. In 24666, the physician uses a bone cutting saw to excise the radial head and replaces it with a prosthesis before repairing the capsule and the incision in layers with sutures, staples, and/or Steri-strips. A posterior elbow splint is applied with the elbow at 90 degrees of flexion.

24670-24675
The physician performs closed treatment of an olecranon or coronoid process fracture. No manipulation is required in 24670. In 24675, mild or slight separation of the fragments requires manipulation. The physician manually manipulates the area, reducing the proximal end ulnar fracture. No incisions are made. The arm may be placed in a posterior elbow splint at 90 degrees of flexion.

24685
The physician openly treats a fracture of the olecranon or coronoid process (proximal end of the ulna). The physician makes a 10 cm incision along the posterolateral border of the elbow. Dissection exposes the fracture. If the fracture is not comminuted, a figure-of-eight wire loop stabilizes the fracture. The physician drills a hole from side to side in the distal fragment. Wire is passed through the drill hole in the distal fragment and through the triceps aponeurosis. This creates a figure-of-eight loop. The wire is pulled tight and twisted. If the fracture is more distal, a medullary pin or screw may be used as well. If medullary fixation is used, the pin or screw is inserted through the olecranon and into the medullary canal of the ulna. The physician repairs the incision in layers with sutures, staples, and/or Steri-strips.

24800-24802
The physician performs an arthrodesis of the elbow joint and makes a posterior longitudinal or posterolateral incision. If the physician does not use a bone graft, the triceps tendon is split and released from the olecranon. The joint capsule is incised to expose the radial head and neck and the radial head is excised. A posterior and anterior synovectomy is performed. The physician trims the olecranon into a triangular shape with a saw. A triangular hole is created through the lower end of the humerus and the olecranon is inserted through this triangular hole. The physician places a bone screw obliquely through the humerus and into the ulna. The triceps tendon is repaired with sutures. The physician repairs the incision in layers and the elbow is immobilized in a long arm cast. If a bone graft is used, the physician prepares a bed for the graft in the posterior surface of the lower humerus. A cleft is formed in the upper part of the tip of the olecranon. If local autograft bone is used, it is harvested from the surrounding healthy bone and no separate incision is required. The autograft is fitted into the olecranon cleft and humeral bed. If allograft (donor) bone is used, it is fitted in the same manner. In 24802, an autogenous graft is harvested from the patient's upper tibia or iliac crest with an osteotome. The physician repairs the surgically created graft donor site. One or two screws are inserted through the graft and into the humerus to make it secure. Bone chips are packed into the humeral-ulnar joint. The physician repairs the incision in layers with sutures. A long arm cast is applied with the elbow in approximately 90 degrees of flexion.

24900
The physician amputates the arm through the humerus. The physician makes an incision distal to the intended level of bone section, and fashions anterior and posterior skin flaps. The brachial artery and vein are identified, double ligated, and divided just proximal to the level of bone section. Nerves are also divided proximal to the site to ensure retraction to the end of the stump. Muscles are sectioned slightly distal to the stump. The humerus is divided and the end is smoothed. The triceps muscle is flapped over the end of the bone and sutured into the anterior fascia. The wound is closed over a drain tube with suction and the fascia and skin flaps are closed.

24920
The physician amputates the arm through the humerus using an open, circular technique. The physician makes an incision distal to the intended level of bone section in a circular manner to the fascia and fashions anterior and posterior skin flaps. The brachial artery and vein are identified, double ligated, and divided just proximal to the level of bone section. Nerves are also

divided proximal to the site to ensure retraction to the end of the stump. Muscles are sectioned slightly distal to the stump. The humerus is divided and the end is smoothed. The triceps muscle is flapped over the end of the bone and sutured into the anterior fascia. The wound is closed over a drain tube with suction and the fascia and skin flaps are closed.

24925
The physician performs a secondary closure or scar revision of an existing amputation. The physician excises the granulation and scar tissues and remodels the soft tissues to close over the amputation again. Arteries and veins are identified, ligated, and divided, as necessary, as well as nerves. The wound is closed over a drain tube with suction and the fascia and skin flaps are closed.

24930
The physician re-amputates the arm through the humerus. The physician makes an incision distal to the intended level of bone section and fashions anterior and posterior skin flaps. The brachial artery and vein are identified, double ligated, and divided just proximal to the level of bone section. Nerves are also divided proximal to the site to ensure retraction to the end of the stump. Muscles are sectioned slightly distal to the stump. The humerus is divided again and the end is smoothed. The triceps muscle is flapped over the end of the bone and sutured into the anterior fascia. The wound is closed over a drain tube with suction and the fascia and skin flaps are closed.

24931
The physician amputates the arm through the humerus bone and places a surgical implant in the arm. The physician makes an incision in a circular fashion around the arm distal to the level of the planned amputation of the humerus. The vessels and nerves are identified, divided, and ligated. The humerus bone is divided in two, completing the amputation. The physician spares the skin, soft tissue, and muscle needed to close the amputation incision. Any of a variety of implants, such as rods, are utilized to maintain the length of the arm or to replace a portion of the amputated humerus. Fixation devices are used. The incision is irrigated. Retained muscle flaps are closed over exposed bone. The wound is closed in layers and a soft dressing is applied.

24935
The physician elongates a stump of an upper extremity. First, the physician obtains the bone graft. The physician incises the skin over the area where the bone graft is to be obtained (usually the iliac crest). The tissue is dissected away from the bone and the graft is harvested. The wound is sutured in layers. The skin overlying the stump is incised to expose the bony stump. The graft is pinned or plated to the existing bone. The tissues are replaced around the bone and the wound is sutured in layers.

24940
Cineplasty is an outdated procedure performed for upper arm amputation to create a muscle motor that acts on an inserted pin to provide the energy for prosthetic action or movement. A muscle tunnel is created into a muscle such as the flexors and extensors of the forearm biceps, the triceps, and pectoralis major. The muscle must be one that functions voluntarily, delicately, and forcibly enough to exert energy over a good range. A skin-lined tube is created within the muscle tunnel that can, after healing, accept a pin for prosthesis being inserted and removed at will. Contraction of the muscle causes displacement of the tunnel and the pin and provides the motor energy for prosthetic action. This has been replaced by technological advances that use myoelectrical sensors attached to the skin.

25000
The physician incises the extensor tendon sheath over the wrist. The physician incises the skin just proximal to the anatomic snuffbox. The tissues are dissected and the extensor retinaculum of the first extensor compartment is identified and incised. The incision is sutured in layers.

25001
The physician incises the flexor tendon sheath over the wrist. The physician makes a radial incision. The tissues are dissected to the tendon sheath. The compartment is identified and incised. When incising the flexor carpi radialis (FCR), the tendon sheath is opened proximal to distal. The fibro-osseous tunnel is released along the ulnar border of the trapezium. The incision is closed with layered sutures.

25020-25023
The physician performs a decompression fasciotomy of the forearm and/or wrist extensor or flexor compartment without debridement in 25020 and with debridement of any nonviable tissue, including muscles and nerves in 25023. The physician makes an incision over the flexor or extensor compartment of the forearm. This is carried deep to the fascia and the fascia itself is incised and released. In 25020, the skin is sutured closed, if possible. In 25023, the physician explores the compartment and debrides any nonviable tissue that may include muscle, nerve, or fascia. The wound is irrigated and typically left open. Closure is accomplished during a later, separately reportable procedure.

25024-25025
The physician performs a decompression fasciotomy of the forearm and/or wrist extensor and flexor compartment without debridement in 25024 and with debridement of any nonviable tissue, including muscles and nerves in 25025. A decompression fasciotomy of the forearm for compartment syndrome is described here. An anterior curvilinear incision for volar fasciotomy is made beginning on the ulnar side of

the forearm, crossing the elbow crease at an angle to reach the radial side, curving back to the ulnar side, and while continuing toward the palm, the incision is centered where it crosses the wrist flexion crease, and extends into the palm medially along the crease. The superficial volar compartment is released along its length, to free the fascia over the compartment muscles. Muscles and nerves are retracted to expose the flexor digitorum profundus in the deep compartment. If its overlying fascia is tight, it too is incised. Report 25025 if any nonviable tissue that may include muscle, nerve, or fascia is found and requires debridement. The dorsal compartments are checked and/or pressure measurements are taken. The volar fasciotomy usually sufficiently decompresses the dorsal musculature also. If the dorsal compartments still require release, an incision is made beginning distal to the lateral epicondyle and extending about 10 cm distally. The subcutaneous tissue is undermined and the fascia is released over the extensor retinaculum. A dressing and a long arm splint are applied to hold the elbow in flexion. The arm is elevated and wound closure is usually done at five days.

25028-25031

The physician drains a deep abscess or hematoma in 25028 or an infected bursa in 25031 from the forearm and/or wrist. The physician makes an incision in the forearm or wrist overlying the site of the abscess, hematoma, or bursa. Dissection is carried down through the deep subcutaneous tissues and may be continued into the fascia or muscle to expose the abscess or hematoma. The incision may be extended if the mass is larger than expected. When the infected bursa, abscess, or hematoma is identified, it is incised and the contents are drained. The area is irrigated and the incision is repaired in layers with sutures, staples, and/or Steri-strips; closed with drains in place; or simply left open to further facilitate drainage of infection.

25035

The physician incises the bone cortex of infected bone in the forearm and/or wrist to treat an abscess or osteomyelitis. The physician makes an incision over the affected area. Dissection is carried down through the soft tissues to expose the bone. The periosteum is split and reflected from the bone overlying the infected area. A curette may be used to scrape away the abscess or infected portion down to healthy bony tissue or drill holes may be made through the cortex into the medullary canal in a window outline around the infected or abscessed bone. The area is drained and debrided of infected bony and soft tissue. The physician irrigates the area with antibiotic solution, the periosteum is closed over the bone, and the soft tissues are sutured closed; or the wound is packed and left open, allowing the area to drain. Secondary closure is performed approximately three weeks later. Dressings are changed daily. A splint may be applied to limit wrist motion.

25040

The physician performs an arthrotomy of a radiocarpal or midcarpal joint that includes exploration, drainage, or removal of any foreign body. An incision is made over the joint to be exposed. The soft tissues are dissected away and the joint capsule is exposed and incised. The joint space is explored, any necrotic tissue is removed, and infection or abnormal fluid is drained. If a foreign body is present (e.g., bullet, nail, gravel), it is exposed and removed. The wound is irrigated with antibiotic solution. The physician may leave the wound packed open with daily dressing changes to allow for further drainage and secondary healing by granulation. If the incision is repaired, drain tubes may be inserted and the incision is repaired in layers with sutures, staples, and/or Steri-strips.

25065-25066

The physician performs a biopsy of the soft tissues of the forearm and/or wrist. With proper anesthesia administered, an incision is made over the biopsy area. Dissection is carried down within the superficial soft tissue layers in 25065, usually the subcutaneous fat to the uppermost fascial layer. In 25066, dissection is taken down deep within the soft tissue, such as into the fascial layer or within the muscle. A portion of the tissue is excised and submitted for pathology. The area is irrigated and the incision is closed with layered sutures, staples, or Steri-strips. If the wrist is involved, a splint may be applied to limit motion.

25071-25076

The physician removes a tumor from the soft tissue of the forearm and/or wrist area that is located in the subcutaneous tissue in 25071and 25075 and in the deep soft tissue, below the fascial plane or within the muscle, in 25073 and 25076. With the proper anesthesia administered, the physician makes an incision in the skin overlying the mass and dissects down to the tumor. The extent of the tumor is identified and a dissection is undertaken all the way around the tumor. A portion of neighboring soft tissue may also be removed to ensure adequate removal of all tumor tissue. A drain may be inserted and the incision is repaired with layers of sutures, staples, or Steri-strips. Report 25075 for excision of subcutaneous tumors whose resected area is less than 3 cm and 25071 for excision of subcutaneous tumors 3 cm or greater. Report 25076 for excision of subfascial or intramuscular tumors whose resected area is less than 3 cm and 25073 for excision of subfascial or intramuscular tumors 3 cm or greater.

25077-25078

The physician performs a radical resection of a malignant soft tissue tumor from the forearm and/or wrist area, not involving bone. An incision is made over the tumor and dissection exposes it. The tumor

Musculoskeletal

and any adjacent tissue that may be affected by the spread of the neoplasm are excised. Large resections may be needed. The type and stage of the lesion determines the extent of the tumor margin resection area. Muscle or fascia may need to be repaired and drains may be placed. The surgical wound is repaired by intermediate or complex closure, adjacent tissue transfer, or graft. If the wrist is involved, a splint may be applied to limit motion. Report 25077 for excision of tumors whose resected area is less than 3 cm and 25078 for excision of tumors 3 cm or greater.

25085
The physician performs a capsulotomy of the wrist. The physician makes an incision overlying the wrist joint. The tissues are dissected to the joint capsule. The physician makes an incision in the capsule, allowing better joint movement. The incision is closed in layers with sutures.

25100-25101
The physician makes a longitudinal incision over the part of the wrist to be exposed (e.g., anterior, posterior, medial, or lateral aspect) to access the wrist joint and perform an arthrotomy. The soft tissues are dissected away to expose the joint capsule, which is incised to expose the synovium lying within the capsule. A small portion of the synovium is excised for biopsy in 25100. In 25101, additional dissection is carried out to further explore the joint cavity. Any loose or foreign bodies (e.g., free cartilage, bone chips, gravel) are removed and a biopsy may be taken. The physician irrigates the joint. The physician may leave the wound packed open with daily dressing changes to allow for further drainage and secondary healing by granulation. A drain tube may be placed and the incision repaired in layers with sutures, staples, and/or Steri-strips. A splint may be applied to limit wrist movement.

25105
The physician makes a longitudinal incision over the part of the wrist to be exposed (e.g., anterior, posterior, medial, or lateral aspect) to perform an arthrotomy and remove the synovium. The joint capsule is exposed by dissecting down through the soft tissues and freeing and reflecting the muscles. The joint capsule is incised to expose the synovium, the inner membrane of the articular capsule that lines the joint cavity. The inflamed or enlarged synovium is dissected away from the capsule and the bones and removed. A drain tube may be placed and the incision is repaired in layers with sutures, staples, and/or Steri-strips. A splint may be applied to limit wrist movement.

25107
The physician performs a distal radioulnar arthrotomy for repair of a triangular cartilage complex. The physician incises the skin over the wrist and dissects down through the soft tissues to expose the joint and locate the triangular cartilage complex. The defect is identified and debrided or sutured to return to a correct anatomic state. The wound is repaired in layers with sutures, staples, and/or Steri-strips. A splint may be applied to limit wrist movement.

25109
The physician excises a flexor or extensor tendon of the wrist or forearm. The physician incises the overlying skin and dissects the tendon. The tendon is freed and resected. The operative incision is closed in sutured layers.

25110
The physician makes an incision overlying the affected tendon in the volar or dorsal aspect (flexor or extensor tendons) of the forearm and/or wrist. Dissection exposes the affected tendon. The lesion is excised or shelled out, leaving normal tissue intact. If incised, the tendon sheath is closed. The incision is repaired in layers with sutures, staples, and/or Steri-strips.

25111-25112
The physician removes a ganglion from the wrist in 25111 or a recurrent ganglion in 25112. An incision is made overlying the ganglion. The tissues are dissected around the ganglion, freeing it from surrounding tissue. (Scar tissue may be removed in 25112.) The physician may dissect deep within the wrist joint in order to excise all of the ganglion. The ganglion is removed. The joint or muscle tissue may be repaired in 25112. The physician irrigates the wound with antibiotic solution and closes the wound in layers.

25115-25116
Radical excision is removal of all diseased and/or inflamed tissue and may include removal of a portion of surrounding normal tissue. The physician excises the bursa, synovia of the wrist, or forearm tendon sheaths of the flexors in 25115 and extensors in 25116. The physician makes a longitudinal incision over the volar aspect of the distal forearm and wrist. Dissection exposes the flexor tendons of the wrist. The physician excises the bursa and any inflamed and hypertrophied tissues from around the tendons. The tendons are left intact, allowing them to glide better during wrist movement. In 25116, the physician may perform a transposition of the dorsal retinaculum if enough tissue is removed from the wrist extensors. A transposition makes a smooth gliding surface no longer present between the extensor tendons and carpal bones of the wrist. The dorsal retinaculum is incised in the mid-line, tucked underneath the extensor tendons, and closed with sutures. The incisions are repaired in layers with sutures, staples, and/or Steri-strips. The wrist may be placed in a splint.

25118-25119
The physician performs a synovectomy of the extensor tendon sheath in the wrist. The physician makes a curved, longitudinal incision over the back of the wrist, radial to the ulna. A longitudinal incision is made through the deep fascia and the extensor retinaculum,

entering the involved compartment. Hypertrophic synovium is removed from each extensor tendon sheath. If an area of a tendon appears frayed to the point of possible rupture, it may be sutured to an adjacent extensor tendon above and below the damaged area. After completing the tenosynovectomy, the physician evaluates the wrist. If synovitis is present, the joint is opened and a wrist synovectomy is performed. The dorsal retinaculum is sutured back into place, deep to the exterior tendons. Closure is performed after a drain is placed. The wrist is held in a neutral position, the fingers in extension. Report 25119 if resection of the distal ulna is performed as part of the procedure.

25120-25126

A bone cyst or benign tumor of the radius or ulna, excluding the head, neck, or olecranon process, is removed. The physician makes an incision in the forearm overlying the cyst or tumor. The skin and underlying soft tissues are reflected to expose the periosteum, which is separated from the bone. Curettes or osteotomes are used to scrape or cut the lesion from the bone. Once the benign tumor or cyst is removed and healthy bone tissue is present, the periosteum is repositioned and the incision is repaired in layers. If the bone defect created requires a graft for repair, the physician obtains the necessary size bone graft from a separate donor site on the patient and packs it into the site where the tumor or bone cyst was removed or uses a bone bank allograft. Report 25125 if the procedure is done with an autograft and 25126 if an allograft is used.

25130-25136

A bone cyst or benign tumor of the carpal bones is removed. The physician makes an incision in the wrist overlying the cyst or tumor. The skin and underlying soft tissues are reflected to expose the periosteum, which is separated from the bone. Curettes or osteotomes are used to scrape or cut the lesion from the bone. Once the benign tumor or cyst is removed and healthy bone tissue is present, the periosteum is repositioned and the incision is repaired in layers. If the bone defect created requires a graft for repair, the physician obtains the necessary size bone graft from a separate donor site on the patient and packs it into the site where the tumor or bone cyst was removed or uses a bone bank allograft. Report 25135 if the procedure is done with an autograft and 25136 if an allograft is used.

25145

The physician removes infected portions of bone from the forearm and/or wrist. The physician makes an incision overlying the sequestered area of bone, which includes incising the capsule if the wrist joint is involved. Once the skin and soft tissues are reflected, a small window is cut into the bone to gain access to the sequestrum, or necrosed piece of bone that has become separated from sound bone. All purulent material and scarred or necrotic tissue are removed. The remaining space is filled with surrounding soft tissues or free tissue transfer. The area is irrigated and an antibiotic solution is applied. The wound is closed loosely over drains or may be packed open with dressings. The patient may be placed in a posterior elbow splint or wrist splint to limit motion.

25150-25151

The physician performs a partial excision of the ulna in 25150 or the radius in 25151 to remove infected bone. An incision is made over the infected part of the bone and the underlying soft tissues are divided to expose the bone. The periosteum is reflected and the infected portion of bone is removed and irrigated. The excavation of bone may excise a crater-like piece, leave a small saucer-like shelf depression in the bone, or may remove a portion of the shaft (diaphysis) of a long bone. If a significant portion of bone is removed, the physician may fill the cavity in a separately reported grafting procedure The periosteum is closed over the bone, the soft tissues are sutured closed, and a soft dressing is applied to the elbow or a wrist splint may be used to limit elbow and/or wrist motion.

25170

The physician performs a radical resection of a tumor of the radius or ulna. The physician makes a skin incision along the lateral, anterior, or dorsal aspect of the forearm, depending on the area of resection. Resection of the proximal ulna is described. The physician makes a longitudinal posterior incision, dissecting down to expose the tumor site. The triceps insertion is detached from the ulna. The physician uses a bone saw to make an osteotomy cut in the ulna and the tumor is excised, including the immediate surrounding bone and any involved soft tissue. If much of the proximal ulna is removed, the radius may be dislocated posteriorly so that the radial neck articulates with the trochlea and the triceps tendon is sutured to the radial head. Drains are inserted and the incision is repaired in layers. A posterior splint is applied. No bone graft is used. Similar technique may be used for the radius.

25210

The physician removes one of the eight carpal bones of the wrist. An incision is made in the wrist overlying the carpal bone to be removed. The tissues are dissected down to the bone. The physician identifies the bone visually and dissects it free of the surrounding structures. Some ligaments may be reattached to other bones. The carpal bone is excised. The physician cleans the wound with antibiotic solution. The wound is repaired in layers.

25215

The physician removes all four bones in the proximal row of the carpal bones of the wrist. An incision is made overlying the wrist. The physician carries the incision down to the carpal bone. The physician identifies the two rows of carpal bones. The physician removes all four bones in the proximal row one by one while preserving tendons, nerves, and blood vessels. Each of the bones is dissected free and removed. Ligaments may need to be reattached to other bones. The physician irrigates the wound with antibiotic solution. The wound is closed in layers.

25230
The physician performs a radial styloidectomy by making a bayonet-shaped incision along the radial aspect of the wrist. The radial artery and nerve are exposed. The joint capsule is incised to expose the radial styloid. The physician uses a thin osteotome or thin oscillating saw blade to cut the radial styloid perpendicular to the long axis of the radius. The incision is repaired in layers with sutures, staples, and/or Steri-strips. The wrist is placed in an anterior splint.

25240
The distal ulna is partially or completely excised. The physician makes a medial longitudinal incision to expose the distal ulna. The ulna is located subcutaneously and does not require much dissection. The periosteum is incised and reflected to expose the distal ulna. Drill holes are made through the ulna 2.5 cm above the distal head. The physician uses bone-biting forceps to complete the division of the bone and remove the fragment. To stabilize the free end of the ulna, the physician reefs (overlaps) the periosteal envelope and ligament. The incision is repaired in layers with sutures, staples, and/or Steri-strips. Immobilization of the wrist is usually not necessary.

25246
The physician injects contrast material into the wrist joint for arthrography. The physician inserts a needle into the wrist and aspirates joint fluid for culture. Contrast material is injected into the wrist and the wrist is manipulated to distribute the dye. As the dye fades, a second injection may be made.

25248
The physician removes a deeply implanted foreign body from the forearm or wrist. The physician incises the site and dissects down to reach the area where the foreign object is embedded. Exploration of the site is done. Separately reportable x-rays may be taken to locate the object. All parts of the object are removed. The wound is sutured in layers.

25250
The physician removes a prosthesis from the wrist. An incision is made overlying the wrist. The physician extends the incision deep to the wrist joint, opening the joint. The physician identifies the artificial joint piece that has failed. Using hand and powered instruments, the physician removes the prosthesis. The joint and incision both are irrigated with antibiotic solution and repaired in layers. If infection is present, the incision is left open to drain temporarily.

25251
The physician performs a complicated removal of all of the parts of a wrist joint prosthesis, including total wrist. An incision is made overlying the wrist. The physician may use the previous wrist surgery incision. The physician extends the incision down to the wrist joint by dividing and dissecting tissues. Some tissue may require debridement. The joint is entered through an arthrotomy cut. The physician identifies the pieces of artificial joint. Each piece is dissected free from the bone. Any loose pieces are removed. The joint is explored. The physician may smooth or debride the ends of the exposed bone. Any nonviable soft tissue and synovium is removed. The joint is irrigated with antibiotic solution. If infection is present, the joint and incision are left open for temporary drainage. Otherwise, the incisions are repaired in layers.

25259
Manipulation of the wrist under anesthesia may be necessary to gain the loss of motion following a surgical procedure or due to scar tissue. Following the induction of general anesthesia, the physician evaluates the wrist. The wrist is manipulated by stretching, rotation, and other maneuvers to gain the appropriate range of motion.

25260-25263
The physician repairs a flexor tendon or muscle of the forearm and/or wrist. The repair is done to restore continuity for normal function by reapproximating the severed ends. Primary tendon repairs can be performed when a clean wound is presented close to the time of injury that can be satisfactorily stabilized for a good end result-such as wounds inflicted with a sharp edge. Secondary tendon repairs are those that must wait because of complicated wounds or those that are performed again after an unsatisfactory first repair. The physician identifies the tendon or muscle by extending the original laceration or making new incisions. The ends of the severed tendon are identified and repaired at the level of separation. The ends are reapproximated using the suture configuration of choice from several different stitching techniques. If the injury occurs in the area of carpal tunnel, at the wrist flexion crease, complete or partial release of the transverse carpal ligament may be necessary. The flexor profundus and sublimis tendons are repaired with attention to proper orientation and location in the carpal tunnel. After the ends are properly matched and sutured, nerves and vessels are repaired as needed. The wound is closed and the limb is immobilized in a posterior splint at approximately 45 degrees of flexion. Involved fingers are held in passive flexion by an elastic band attached at the wrist level and at the fingernail by a wire. Report 25260 for a primary repair, one performed within the first 12-24 hours of injury where tendons are involved.

Report 25263 for a secondary repair, one performed 10 or more days out from the injury or a subsequent repair done when the first procedure failed to restore function. Use these codes once for each tendon or muscle repaired.

25265
The physician performs a secondary repair of a flexor tendon or muscle of the forearm and/or wrist with a free graft. A secondary tendon repair is one performed 10 or more days out from the injury because of complicated wounds that would compromise immediate repair or one performed again after the first procedure failed to restore function. When the flexor tendons in the forearm and wrist area have become tightly contracted, a graft is necessary to bring the ends together. The palmaris longus is the graft of choice. The physician first approaches the involved flexor muscle or tendon through a zigzag incision on the palmar surface of the wrist or forearm, depending on the area of the tendon in need of grafting. The possibly scarred flexor tendon is freed and brought out through the incision, preserving as much healthy sheath as possible. The free graft is obtained by making a transverse incision in the volar wrist, dividing the palmaris longus tendon at its insertion, and while holding tension on the graft at its distal end with a clamp, advancing a tendon stripper into the proximal forearm. The proximal end is mobilized and the graft is withdrawn. Likewise, another incision may be made more proximally in the forearm, the tendon divided, and the segment withdrawn. The transverse skin incision is closed. The tendon graft is threaded through the forearm using a tendon passer. The tendon ends must be attached to the graft under the right tension. The junctures are secured using a monofilament wire and several possible suturing techniques. The wound is closed and dressed. A dorsal splint is applied maintaining wrist flexion to protect repair.

25270-25272
The physician repairs an extensor tendon or muscle of the forearm and/or wrist. The repair is done to restore continuity for normal function by reapproximating the severed ends. Primary tendon repairs can be performed when a clean wound is presented close to the time of injury that can be satisfactorily stabilized for a good end result, such as wounds inflicted with a sharp edge. Secondary tendon repairs are those that must wait because of complicated wounds or those that are performed again after an unsatisfactory first repair. The physician identifies the tendon or muscle by extending the original laceration or making new incisions. The ends of the severed tendon are identified and repaired at the level of separation. The ends are reapproximated using the suture configuration of choice from several different stitching techniques. Tendons in the dorsal wrist area are retained by the dorsal carpal ligament (extensor retinaculum) and are encased in fibro-osseous canals. They tend to get stuck in their canals as they heal; therefore, release of the sutured area may be necessary by excising a portion of the overlying carpal ligament. Many extensor tendons in the dorsal forearm are covered by their respective muscles and must be sutured, since sutures placed in muscle tend to pull out of the tissue. The wound is closed and the wrist is immobilized with a volar splint, in moderate or full extension. Report 25270 for a primary repair, one performed within the first 12-24 hours of injury. Report 25272 for a secondary repair, one performed 10 or more days out from the injury or a subsequent repair done when the first procedure failed to restore function. Use these codes once for each tendon or muscle repaired.

25274
The physician performs a secondary repair of an extensor tendon or muscle of the forearm and/or wrist with a free graft. A secondary tendon repair is one performed 10 or more days out from the injury because of complicated wounds that would compromise immediate repair or one performed again after the first procedure failed to restore function. When the extensor tendons in the forearm and wrist area have become tightly contracted or a segment of tendon has been lost, a graft is necessary to bring the ends together. The palmaris longus is the graft of choice. The physician first approaches the involved extensor muscle or tendon through an incision on the dorsal surface of the wrist or forearm, depending on the area of the tendon in need of grafting. The possibly scarred tendon is freed and the ends brought out through the incision for repair. The free graft is obtained by making a transverse incision in the volar wrist, dividing the palmaris longus tendon at its insertion, and while holding tension on the graft at its distal end with a clamp, advancing a tendon stripper into the proximal forearm. The proximal end is mobilized and the graft is withdrawn. Likewise, another incision may be made more proximally in the forearm, the tendon divided, and the segment withdrawn. The transverse skin incision is closed. The tendon graft is threaded through the forearm using a tendon passer. The tendon ends must be attached to the graft under the right tension. The junctures are secured using a monofilament wire and several possible suturing techniques. The wound is closed and the wrist is immobilized with a volar splint, in moderate or full extension.

25275
The physician repairs an extensor tendon sheath of the forearm and/or wrist with a free graft. This is done for extensor carpi ulnaris (ECU) subluxation. The ECU passes through a groove at the distal end of the ulna and is covered by a ligament. The ECU is the only wrist extensor that lies in its own retaining fibro-osseous sheath tunnel. Disruption of this compartment sheath is what allows the extensor carpi ulnaris to sublux. An incision is made and the underlying tissues are

dissected to reach the sheath disruption of the ECU tendon. If the fibro-osseous sheath has ruptured so that the sheath lies under the ECU tendon on its ulnar groove, the sheath is sutured together directly over the tendon. When the fibro-osseous sheath has ruptured so that the sheath lies superficial to the tendon, the sheath is reconstructed with a piece of the extensor retinaculum, the fibrous sheet, or band of fascia overlying the extensor tendons. The subcutaneous tissues and skin are closed and a dressing is applied.

25280

The physician lengthens or shortens a flexor or extensor tendon of the forearm and/or wrist. For lengthening, the physician makes an incision in the forearm and down through the tissues to identify the affected tendon. The physician may make a series of small, equal-depth cuts spaced on opposite sides of the tendon to allow it to stretch without tearing through. An elongated Z incision may be cut in the tendon and the ends of the long half of each section are sewn together or an oblique incision is made across the tendon and the ends are slid apart until the pointed tips meet, which are sutured together. Several methods are also used to shorten a tendon that has become too long to function properly. A Z incision may be made in the tendon and the two short sides of the Z brought together and reapproximated. The tendon can be doubled over on itself with a small fold and sutured. A wedge-shaped piece may be excised and the two ends sutured. The soft tissue is closed in layers and a bandage is applied.

25290

The physician performs an open tenotomy on a flexor or extensor tendon of the forearm and/or wrist. An incision is made in the wrist or forearm over the site where the tendon to be cut may be accessed. The subcutaneous tissues and fascia are dissected to reach the target tendon. The usual method is to cut into the tendon so as to allow it to expand and heal as a longer tendon, thereby releasing a contracture caused by the tendon. The tissue layers and skin are closed and a dressing is applied.

25295

Tenolysis of a flexor or extensor tendon is indicated in the case of extrinsic extensor or flexor tendon tightness. In the case of flexor tightness, the physician approaches the involved flexor system through a zigzag incision that is long enough to uncover the length of the flexor. The physician excises all limiting adhesions, whether the excess scarring is located proximally in the forearm and/or distally in the wrist. The tendon involved is released of motion-limiting adhesions. The retinacular pulley system is preserved. During the procedure, the patient's active motion is re-evaluated. To achieve this, a local anesthesia is supplemented by an intravenous analgesic-tranquilizer combination drug. After tissue closure, the physician applies a splint over the dressing. These must be applied in a manner that allows continued flexion to maintain the tendon's gliding action through the lysed scars. The above techniques are the same for extrinsic extensors, except there is no critical annular pulley system to preserve, although the sagittal bands must be protected.

25300-25301

The physician performs a tenodesis at the wrist. In 25300, the physician exposes the flexor tendons of the fingers at the wrist level. The terminal phalangeal flexors to be fixated (usually all four) are identified in the depths of the wound. A window is made in the anterior surface of the distal radius proximal to the wrist. A similar second window is made more proximally. A criss-cross type of suture is passed through all four flexor digitorum profundi tendons side-by-side. The tendons are transected proximal to this suture. The tendons are drawn into the more distal window in the radius, through the medullary canal, out the proximal window, and sutured back to themselves. The tension on the tenodesis is adjusted so that with the wrist in extension, the fingers naturally flex into the palm, closing the hand as desired. Tenodesis of the finger flexors can give an enhanced natural grip action using wrist extension for those with impaired control of movement. All open soft tissues are sutured in layers. The wrist is immobilized in five to 10 degrees of extension with the metacarpophalangeal joints flexed and the interphalangeal joints extended. Report 25301 if the extensors of the fingers are fixated to bone at the wrist.

25310-25312

The physician performs a flexor or extensor tendon transplantation or transfer in the forearm and wrist. The physician exposes the tendon to be transferred by making a longitudinal incision near its insertion. The insertion is released from near its bony attachment for transfer to the involved tendon. The tendon may not be released, but rather only the central portion. Through a separate incision, the physician exposes the involved tendon. A tunnel is prepared around or through the arm between the transferred and involved tendon. This tunnel must permit a straight line of pull between the two tendons. The transferred tendon is passed through the tunnel. A small, longitudinal hole is created in the involved tendon. The distal end of the transferred tendon is passed through the involved tendon and sutured to that tendon. After these procedures are complete, all wounds are closed with sutures. Report 25312 if the procedure is performed with tendon grafts, each tendon.

25315-25316

The physician performs a flexor origin slide in the forearm or wrist for conditions such as cerebral palsy. The physician makes a longitudinal incision from within a few centimeters proximal to the medial epicondyle, distally through the middle of the forearm.

The ulnar nerve, median nerve, and brachial artery are identified and tagged. A periosteal elevator is inserted between the brachialis and the common flexor-pronator origin from the medial epicondyle. The elevator is brought out between the numeral and ulnar heads of the flexor carpi ulnaris on the anterior side of the elbow. The origin of the flexors is dissected using a scalpel to detach the muscle subperiosteally. The origins of the pronator teres, flexor carpi radialis, palmaris longus, and the numeral head of the flexor carpi ulnaris are released. The physician dissects the origins of the flexor digitorum superficialis. The ulnar head of the flexor carpi ulnaris is detached subperiosteally. The physician brings together the detached muscles from the proximal and ulnar sides at the interosseous space on the proximal side. Neurolysis of the median and ulnar nerves is performed. The muscles are slid distally the desired amount and are fixed in several places to periosteum and subcutaneous tissue. The ulnar nerve is transposed over the medial epicondyle. The wound is closed in layers. The elbow joint is maintained at 90 degrees, the wrist and fingers in extension, the forearm in supination. Report 25316 if this procedure is performed with a tendon transfer.

25320

The physician performs an open capsulorrhaphy or reconstruction of the wrist by any method (capsulodesis, ligament repair, tendon transfer, or graft), including synovectomy, capsulotomy, and open reduction to stem carpal instability. The wrist and finger extensors are retracted laterally and medially. The capsule is longitudinally cut over the involved carpus for exposure. If dislocation was present prior to surgery, this is reduced. The necessary fixation is carried out (i.e., Kirchner wires, screws). Carpal instability may result from dislocation of carpal bones and any number of ligamentous injuries that require reduction and repair, involving the joint capsule. Scapholunate dissociation and instability is one of the most common injuries. Dorsal intercarpal ligament capsulodesis may be performed to reduce the scapholunate gap. A flap of dorsal intercarpal ligament is elevated off the trapezoid and left attached to the triquetrum. The scaphoid inherently tends to sublux in the palmar direction in a flexed posture with dorsal rotational subluxation of the posterior pole. The scaphoid is brought out of its flexed position by applying dorsal pressure to the posterior pole and the scapholunate gap is reduced. The ligamentous flap is rotated down, stretched, and attached to the distal pole of the scaphoid. A flap of wrist capsule may also be created that is left attached to the radius and inserted into the distal pole of the scaphoid to tether it in chronic conditions.

25332

The physician performs an arthroplasty of the wrist. The physician makes a straight, dorsal, longitudinal incision centered over the wrist from the middle of the third metacarpal proximally. Skin and subcutaneous tissues are elevated off the fascia and retinaculum. The retinaculum over the fourth dorsal compartment is incised longitudinally and elevated medially and laterally. The extensor pollicis longus is freed, retracted radially, and left in the rerouted position at the end of the procedure. A longitudinal incision is made in the capsule. A capsular periosteal flap is elevated through the dorsal radioulnar ligaments. The distal radius is excised, as is the distal ulna if it is dislocated or severely involved. A cut is made through the hamate, capitate, trapezoid, and distal scapho-trapezoid area. The carpus is removed. The medullary canal of the radius is reamed. A fine awl is used to penetrate the base of the capitate and the shaft of the third metacarpal. The medullary canal of this bone is reamed. If using a double-stemmed component, an additional canal is prepared in the second metacarpal. Appropriate short canals are prepared in the carpal bones. With the wrist in 10 to 20 degree extension, the capsular-periosteal sleeves are repaired over the prosthesis. The extensor retinaculum may be used to reinforce the capsule, or may be repaired anatomically. The skin is closed over a deep and a superficial suction drain.

25335

The physician performs a centralization of the wrist on the ulna for conditions including radial club hand. The physician makes two incisions. A transverse incision is made over the end of the ulna to remove excess skin and fatty tissue and to expose the distal ulna. A Z-plasty incision may be needed on the radial surface of the distal forearm and wrist to give extra length to the tight skin on this side. The physician next incises the capsule, flexes the elbow, and reduces the carpus over the ulna. Insertions of the flexor carpi radialis and brachioradialis are cut. The distal end of the ulna is shaved to flatten its surface, and a Kirschner wire is drilled through the capitate and through the base of the third metacarpal. The second wire is removed and the ulnar wire is driven through the hole it created. The distal ulnocarpal capsule is pulled proximally over the ulna and sutured with nonabsorbable suture. The extensor carpi ulnaris is advanced distally over the fifth metacarpal tightly. The flexor carpi ulnaris is sutured with the extensor carpi ulnaris. The two incisions are closed. The wrist is placed in a neutral position, and a bulky dressing is applied.

25337

Restoring stability to a wrist with an unstable distal ulna or distal radioulnar joint may require just a few procedures, or it may dictate many procedures. In all cases, the physician must expose the distal radioulnar joint by making a curvilinear incision on the dorsal wrist starting proximal to the ulnar styloid and extending it dorsally, over the ulnar styloid to the carpus. The proximal and ulnar half of the extensor retinaculum is reflected radially. The extensor digiti

Musculoskeletal

minimi is retracted, revealing the styloid notch of the radius and the triangular fibrocartilage complex (TFC). The capsule is sharply detached from the radius exposing the ulnar head. If a styloid fracture is found, two drill holes are made proximally from the fracture to exit facing the radius. A wire is passed around or through the styloid using similar drill holes, and the two free ends of the wire are passed proximally through the fracture site into the previously drilled holes in the proximal shaft. The wire is twisted, compressing the styloid to the shaft. If the triangular fibrocartilaginous complex is avulsed from styloid, an intraosseous wiring as described above may be used to restore distal radioulnar stability. If the TFC is not avulsed, an intraosseous wire with a 24-gauge, or larger, should be used. The capsule is sutured closed, and the skin is closed in layers. Over the dressing, a long-arm cast is applied with the elbow flexed, the forearm in zero degree extension, and the wrist in neutral.

25350-25355

The physician performs an osteotomy (bone cut) of the radius. An incision is made in the forearm overlying the distal third area of the radius in 25350 or the middle or proximal third in 25355. The physician performs dissection through the tissue layers and down to the bone. The periosteum is removed from the bone site where the osteotomy will be made. The physician cuts through the radius. The physician realigns the bone to the desired position. Metal plates and screws are typically applied to stabilize the bone. The wound is irrigated with antibiotic solution and repaired in layers. A cast or splint may be applied to further stabilize and support the bone.

25360-25365

The physician performs an osteotomy of the ulna in 25360 or of both the ulna and radius in 25365. The physician makes a longitudinal incision along the medial border of the forearm to expose the affected part of the ulna. Two separate incisions may be necessary in 25365. An osteotomy (bone cut) is made through the ulna, usually in a wedge shape. This allows the bone to be realigned. The physician applies plates and screws to hold the osteotomy together in the correct position. The incisions are repaired in layers with sutures, staples and/or Steri-strips. The arm may be placed in a splint for immobilization.

25370-25375

The physician treats the radius or ulna in 25370 or both in 25375. A longitudinal incision is made to expose the shaft of the bone. Two separate incisions may be necessary in 25375. The physician makes an osteotomy (bone cut) through the proximal and distal ends of the bone shaft. The bone shaft is removed from the wound. The physician studies the bone shaft to determine how many times it must be osteotomized so that its segments can be threaded onto a medullary nail. The osteotomies are made, and each fragment placed end to end on the medullary nail. Because the cortex of the ulna and radius are very thin, a bone graft is usually added. This may be harvested from the surrounding area, or a separate incision may be needed. A separate incision would be made over the iliac crest, bone harvested, and the incision closed. The medullary nail is inserted into place. The periosteum is sutured into place. The physician repairs the incision in layers with sutures, staples, and/or Steri-strips. The arm is immobilized in a cast.

25390, 25392

The physician shortens the radius or ulna in 25390 and shortens both in 25392. An incision is made on the anterior aspect of the distal forearm. Any exposed arteries are retracted. The physician continues dissection to expose the distal shaft of the radius and/or ulna. Based on preoperative x-rays, an osteotomy is made at the distal end of the radius and/or ulna. A more proximal osteotomy is made which shortens the radius and/or ulna usually by 2 mm to 3 mm. The physician removes the bone fragment. A plate is attached to the distal segment with screws. Reduction forceps hold and compress the osteotomy while the plate is attached to the proximal fragment with screws. Separately reportable x-rays are used to check radioulnar length. Drain tubes are inserted. The physician repairs the incision in layers with sutures, staples, and/or Steri-strips. However, the forearm fascia is left open to minimize the chances of compartment syndrome. The forearm is placed in a splint.

25391, 25393

The radius or ulna of the forearm is lengthened with an autograft in 25391 and both are lengthened with an autograft in 25393. One bone is often bowed due to the shortened and hypoplastic development of the other, as in congenital pseudoarthrosis. The forearm is incised and the overlying tissue is dissected to reach the bone. A few centimeters of bone may need to be resected to remove the deformity, taking care to preserve the epiphysis is the case of growing children. Surrounding abnormal tissues are also resected. The newly created defect is bridged with a vascularized bone graft from the patient, often taken from the fibula. The autograft is fixed to the bone of the radius and/or ulna with an intramedullary K-wire and may be proximally supported by placing another K-wire. Vascular anastomosis is completed between the artery of the graft and the ulnar or radial artery and the graft vein and the basilic vein. The wound is closed. A skin island that was preserved with the vascularized autograft may also be incorporated in the wound closure. A cast is applied to the forearm.

25394

The physician shortens a carpal bone. The physician makes the incision over the area of the carpal bone. Dissection is carried down to the level of the carpal bone and an osteotomy is done. The bone is shortened. The amount of bone removed is dependent on the condition treated. The incision is closed with sutures.

25400-25405

The physician exposes a nonunion or malunion of the radius or ulna by making a 10 cm to 15 cm longitudinal incision over the fracture site. With a reciprocating saw, each bone is divided through the nonunion. The fragments are aligned. A compression plate is centered over the fracture and screws are inserted. In 25405, a bone graft is needed to help heal the nonunion due to loss of bone. For example, if the nonunion is old, approximately 0.6 cm to 1.3 cm of bone is resected from the ends of the fragments. Autogenous iliac bone is typically used. Bone from the upper tibia may also be used. This requires an incision over the site of harvest. The physician uses an osteotome to harvest strips of bone. These strips are placed around the ends of the fracture along with the compression plate for internal fixation. The incision is repaired in layers with sutures, staples, and/or Steri-strips. However, the deep fascial layer is not closed because of the potential to develop compartment syndrome. A long arm cast is applied with the elbow at 90 degrees of flexion.

25415-25420

The physician exposes the nonunions through two 10 cm to 15 cm longitudinal incisions One incision is made on the lateral aspect and one on the medial aspect of the forearm. With a reciprocating saw, the physician divides each bone through the nonunion. The fragments are aligned. The physician centers a compression plate over the fracture and inserts screws. In 25420, a bone graft is needed to help bone healing of the nonunion due to loss of bone. For example, if the nonunion is old, approximately 0.6 cm to 1.3 cm of bone is resected from the ends of the fragments. Autogenous iliac bone graft is typically used. The physician makes an incision over the iliac crest. Once the bone is exposed, an osteotome is used to harvest strips of bone. These strips are placed around the ends of the fracture. Internal fixation with a compression plate is the same as for 25415. The incision are repaired in layers with sutures, staples, and/or Steri-strips. However, the deep fascial layer is not closed because of the potential to develop compartment syndrome. A long arm cast is applied with the elbow in 90 degrees of flexion.

25425-25426

The physician repairs a defect of the radius or ulna in 25425 or of both the radius and ulna in 25426. The physician makes a longitudinal incision along the forearm. An anterior approach is made for the radius, medial for the ulna, or two incision for both. The defect is exposed through dissection. To harvest the bone graft, the physician makes a separate incision over the iliac crest. Bone from the upper tibia may also be used. The bone is exposed, and the physician uses an osteotome to harvest strips of bone. These bone strips are used to fill the defect. A screw or wire wrapped around the defect holds the bone graft in place. The incision is repaired in layers with sutures, staples, and/or Steri-strips. However, the deep fascial layer is not closed because of the potential to develop compartment syndrome. The arm may be placed in a long arm cast with the elbow at 90 degrees of flexion.

25430

The physician makes an incision over the dorsal aspect of the distal forearm and wrist. The dorsal tendons that cover the fourth compartment are identified and the anterior interosseous artery and vein are identified and isolated. Using magnification the distal artery and vein are ligated. After radiological confirmation the skin over the lunate is incised. Dissection is completed through the lunate capsule. A small hole is drilled into the cancellous portion of the lunate bone. The distal ends of the ligated artery and vein are inserted into the lunate opening and secured with nylon sutures. The capsule is closed and the skin is closed in layers.

25431

Nonunion of the carpal bone refers to fractures that still allow free movement of bone ends more than six months after the injury and the start of treatment. In the case of a complex nonunion, the physician may take a graft from the medial aspect of the ulna and reinsert it into the prepared carpal site. Intravenous anesthesia is administered. An autogenous iliac bone graft is typically used for repair, which is obtained through an incision over the iliac crest. Once the bone is exposed, an osteotome is used to harvest strips of bone. These strips are placed between the carpal bones of the fracture through a 2 centimeter incision made at the base of the involved metacarpus. The physician centers a compression plate over the fracture and inserts screws. Lunate fractures require a short-arm spica cast or splint with thumb immobilization. Fractures of the pisiform can be immobilized with a volar splint. Injuries to the triquetrum are best treated with a sugar tong splint. Treatment of a hamate fracture involves a short-arm cast with the fourth and fifth metacarpophalangeal joints held in flexion.

25440

The physician performs this procedure when a scaphoid fracture has not healed and particularly if nonunion is accompanied by displacement of the fracture. The physician makes a 4 cm to 5 cm longitudinal incision along the radial border of the flexor carpi radialis tendon to expose the fracture site. The capsule is divided longitudinally, and the underlying ligaments are retracted. An egg-shaped cavity is created in the fracture fragments. A cancellous bone graft is obtained and the graft is jammed between the fragments as they are distracted. The physician uses internal fixation such as a Kirschner wires to affix the bones if instability exists. If a radial styloidectomy is performed, the physician makes an incision on the radial wrist at the base of the thumb. Radial styloid bone is removed. The physician closes the incision(s) with sutures.

25441
The physician performs an arthroplasty on the wrist to relieve function-limiting wrist pain. The physician makes a T-shaped incision overlying the dorsal wrist. The capsule and synovium are incised and elevated. The distal end of the radius and the proximal carpal row are excised to accommodate the implant. The medullary canal of the third metacarpal is exposed and an awl is placed into the canal for reaming. The awl is removed and the prosthetic awl is impacted into the base of the carpus and third metacarpal shaft. The medullary canal of the radius is reamed and implanted with the prosthesis. Cement is injected into the medullary canal of the third metacarpal after previously inserting a small cancellous bone plug. The distal component is impacted home first. The proximal component is generally not cemented and is impacted only. The capsule is repaired over the prosthesis with strong sutures. A suction drain is placed beneath the capsule. The retinaculum is repaired over all of the extensor tendons. The skin is sutured closed, and the wrist is immobilized.

25442
The physician performs this arthroplasty to decrease ulnar bone overgrowth following resection of the distal ulna. The physician makes a dorsal ulnar longitudinal incision overlying the ulnar head. The extensor retinaculum is incised. The neck of the ulna is subperiosteally exposed and the ulnar head is resected at the neck. The cut edge of the ulna is smoothed and medullary canal reamed to accept the stem of the implant. The implant is tested and two drill holes are made 2 cm from the resected bone. The physician stabilizes the distal ulna by attaching the base of the sixth dorsal compartment retinaculum to the interosseous membrane with sutures. The distal end of the ulna is pressed volarly and is sutured tightly into the soft tissue on the radial side with the radial itself. The wound is closed with sutures over a drain. A conforming dressing is applied.

25443
The physician performs an arthroplasty with prosthetic replacement of the scaphoid. The physician makes a straight, longitudinal, or curvilinear incision over the anatomic snuff-box (superficial to the scaphoid), the "V" between your thumb and index finger. The capsule is incised longitudinally. The scaphoid is removed maintaining ligament stability. If a defect is found in the distal capsule, this is closed with a nonabsorbable suture. A hole is made in the proximal joint surface of the trapezium for insertion of the prosthetic stem. An implant is inserted. The implant is stabilized with sutures through drill holes in the lunate and radial styloid. The implant is also stabilized with a K-wire passed through the implant into an adjacent carpal bone or the radius. The capsule is closed, followed by skin closure. A compression dressing is applied.

25444
The physician performs an arthroplasty with prosthetic replacement of the lunate. The physician makes a straight, longitudinal or transverse incision over the dorsum of the wrist ulnar to Lister's tubercle of the radius. The fourth dorsal compartment is opened and the radiocarpal joint capsule is transversely cut. The scapholunate and lunate-triquetral interosseous ligaments are cut. The lunate is removed. If a defect in the volar ligamentous capsule is found, it is repaired. A hole is made in the middle of the triquetrum to accept the prosthetic stem. The implant is fixed to the carpus and radius with a K-wire. An absorbable suture may be placed through the scaphoid and prosthesis to increase stability. The distal capsule flap is sutured to the radius with nonabsorbable sutures. The wounds are closed and a bulky compression dressing is applied.

25445
The physician performs an arthroplasty with prosthetic replacement of the trapezium. The physician makes a straight, longitudinal cut from the middle of the thumb metacarpal to the radial styloid. The capsule is split longitudinally from the metacarpal to the scaphoid. The capsule and periosteum are elevated off the trapezium. The radial portion of the trapezoid is removed. The base of the first metacarpal is squared off. A triangular hole is made in the base of the metacarpal, and the canal is made to accept the implant stem. The size of the implant should be slightly smaller than a tight fit. The capsule is repaired and reinforced by suturing slips of the abductor pollicis and flexor carpi radialis muscles to the capsule. A K-wire is placed through the implant and into the trapezoid or capitate to stabilize the position for six weeks. The skin is closed, leaving the wire protruding through incision, and a bulky dressing is applied to keep the thumb abducted.

25446
The physician performs a total wrist arthroplasty. The physician makes a straight, dorsal, longitudinal incision centered over the wrist from the middle of the third metacarpal proximally. The skin and subcutaneous tissues are elevated off the underlying fascia and retinaculum. The retinaculum over the fourth dorsal compartment is incised longitudinally and elevated. The extensor pollicis longus is freed and retracted radically. A longitudinal incision is made in the capsule overlying the distal radius. Ulnarly, a capsular periosteal flap is elevated through the dorsal radioulnar ligaments. Radially, the subperiosteal dissection continues to the radial styloid beneath the first dorsal compartment. The distal radius is excised,

as is the distal ulna if it is dislocated or severely involved. A cut, made to match the shape of the prosthesis of choice, is made through the hamate, capitate, trapezoid, and distal scaphotrapezoid area. The carpus is removed. The medullary canal of the radius is reamed. A fine awl is used to penetrate the base of the capitate and the shaft of the third metacarpal. The medullary canal of this bone is reamed. If using a double-stemmed component, an additional canal is prepared in the second metacarpal. The component is inserted into the canals. Appropriate short canals are prepared in the carpal bases. The metallic components are inserted. The prosthetic polyethylene ball is placed on the trunnion and motion is tested. When desired motion is achieved, cement is mixed and injected into the medullary canals. The capsular-periosteal tissues are repaired over the prosthesis. The extensor retinaculum may be used to reinforce the capsule. The skin is closed over a deep and a superficial suction drain.

25447

The physician performs an interposition arthroplasty of the intercarpal or carpometacarpal joints. The physician makes a zigzag incision over the proximal one third of the first metacarpal and extends it along the first wrist extensor compartment. The metacarpal joint is vertically incised to release the capsule from the base of the metacarpal. The joint is completely dislocated to expose the metacarpal end. The physician resects the metacarpal based perpendicular to its long axis. The base is shaped to allow the insertion of a metacarpal prosthesis. The medullary canal of the metacarpal is reamed to accept the prosthetic stem. The stem is inserted and the base of the prosthesis is seated on the flat surface of the trapezium bone. A Kirschner wire is inserted through the first metacarpal and into the carpus to ensure alignment. The capsule and wounds are sutured closed. This procedure may be referred to as a ligament reconstruction tendon interposition (LRTI) or a Burton LRTI.

25449

The physician revises an arthroplasty, including removal of an implant in the wrist joint. The physician makes an incision over the wrist, reduces the joint if it is not already dislocated, and removes the device from the radius and the one or two metacarpals in which it was implanted. If necessary, a new device is placed into the wrist. The skin is closed in layers and a bulky dressing is applied.

25450-25455

The physician makes an incision overlying the distal forearm and along the medial (ulna) or lateral (radius) aspect in 25450 or both in 25455. The distal epiphyseal plate is located here. Dissection exposes the epiphyseal plate. The physician may elect to use a curette to scrape out the epiphysis (growth plate). A staple may be placed through the epiphyseal plate instead. Either procedure arrests further growth of that particular bone. The physician repairs the incision in layers with sutures, staples, and/or Steri-strips.

25490-25492

The physician applies prophylactic treatment. The physician treats the radius in 25490. A longitudinal incision is made along the forearm. Dissection exposes the affected part of the radius. In 25491, the ulna is treated. A longitudinal incision is required along the medial aspect of the ulna. In 25492, both the radius and ulna are treated, which may require two separate incisions. Pins or a plate with screws are used to stabilize the bone. If there are defects in the bone, such that the internal fixation does not provide good purchase with the bone, methylmethacrylate (cement) is used to fill in the gaps. Wiring (cerclage) may also wrapped around the bone to provide additional fixation. The physician may also insert an intramedullary nail through the canal of the radius to provide internal stabilization. This is usually inserted through the distal end of the radius. The incisions are repaired in layers with sutures, staples, and/or Steri-strips.

25500-25505

The physician treats a radial shaft fracture without manipulation in 25500 or with manipulation in 25505. No incisions are made. If manipulation is required (25505), anesthesia may be necessary to relax the muscles. With the elbow at 90 degrees of flexion, the physician uses a combination of traction and countertraction while the radius is reduced. The patient may be placed in a long arm cast. The cast is removed after approximately 18 days and a functional brace is applied, allowing wrist and elbow movement, but limited pronation and supination.

25515

The physician treats a radial shaft fracture. If internal fixation is required, the physician may use plate and screw fixation or a medullary nail. A plate and screw fixation is described. If the fracture is in the lower half of the radius, an anterior forearm incision is made. If the fracture is in the upper half of the radius, a posterior forearm incision is made. Dissection exposes the fractured fragments. The physician uses bone-holding forceps to reduce the fracture. A plate of appropriate length is selected and centered over the fracture. Plates with five or six holes are usually required. The screws are inserted. The incision is repaired in layers. The deep fascia is not closed because of the potential of developing compartment syndrome. Depending on the rigidity of the fixation, a cast or splint may be applied.

25520

The physician treats a radial shaft fracture and a dislocation of the distal radio-ulnar joint. No incisions are made. The physician may reduce the fracture and

Musculoskeletal

dislocation by manipulation with traction force. A long arm cast is applied to immobilize the elbow and wrist.

25525
The physician makes a 5 to 6 inch longitudinal incision over the anterior aspect of the forearm and centered over the fracture. Dissection exposes the pronator quadratus muscle, which is freed from the radius. The physician reduces the fracture with bone-holding forceps. A plate of appropriate length may be selected and centered over the fracture. The screws are inserted. The pronator quadratus muscle is reattached. The incision is repaired in layers with sutures, staples, and/or Steri-strips. The deep fascia is not closed. The physician places the arm in a cast. The physician may also apply percutaneous skeletal fixation. Kirschner wires are inserted through small stab incisions through the radius and into the ulna to stabilize the radius.

25526
The physician treats a radial shaft fracture via an open approach, using internal fixation when required. This procedure includes repair of the triangular fibrocartilage complex. After the affected hand is suspended in finger traps, the physician reduces the fracture and confirms the reduction radiographically. Under separately reportable radiographic guidance, a Kirschner wire is inserted from the tip of the radial styloid obliquely across the fracture site. A second pin is inserted in a slightly more longitudinal direction. Finger traps are removed and the pins are cut off approximately 2 cm above the skin and bent at right angles. If tears are present in the fibrocartilage complex, they are repaired with sutures. Skin incisions may be made to prevent skin tethering. A dressing and splint are applied.

25530-25535
The physician treats an ulnar shaft fracture without manipulation in 25530 or with manipulation in 25535. No incisions are made. If manipulation is required, the physician uses a combination of traction and countertraction with manual manipulation of the fracture. The patient is placed in a long arm cast with the elbow at 90 degrees of flexion. A functional splint or brace is applied.

25545
The physician makes an incision along the subcutaneous border of the ulna, exposing the shaft fracture. The physician reduces the fracture with bone-holding forceps. If internal fixation is required, a plate of appropriate length is selected and centered over the fracture. The screws are inserted. Only the subcutaneous tissue is closed. The skin incision is repaired with sutures, staples, and/or Steri-strips. Depending on the rigidity of the fixation, a cast or splint may be applied.

25560-25565
For undisplaced and stable fractures, the physician immobilizes the elbow and wrist with a long arm cast. Separately reportable x-rays are taken to confirm that displacement does not occur. In 25565, the fractures are displaced and manual reduction is required. Analgesia or a certain degree of sedation may be necessary. The physician uses a combination of traction and manual manipulation to reduce the fractures. A long arm cast immobilizes the elbow and wrist.

25574-25575
When both the radius and ulna are fractured, the physician exposes and reduces both fractures prior to fixation. Separate incisions along the forearm may be needed to expose the fracture. In 25574, only one fracture is stabilized, requiring only one incision. The other fracture is stable and does not require fixation. In 25575, both radial and ulnar fractures require fixation, usually requiring separate incisions. Once the fracture site is exposed and reduced, internal fixation is applied. A plate of appropriate length is selected and centered over the fracture. The physician inserts the screws. The incisions are repaired in layers with sutures, staples, and/or Steri-strips. The deep fascia is not closed, preventing the development of compartment syndrome. Depending upon the rigidity of the fixation, a cast or splint may be applied.

25600-25605
The physician treats a distal radial fracture. A Colles' fracture is a fracture of the distal radius with dorsal displacement. A Smith fracture is palmar displacement of the distal radius. The ulnar styloid is usually fractured. If good alignment and correct angulation of the distal radial articular surface is present, the physician immobilizes the wrist and forearm in a cast or splint until the fracture or epiphyseal separation is stable. In 25605, manipulation is required to reduce an unstable and/or displaced fracture or epiphyseal separation. For either 25600 or 25605, closed treatment of the ulnar styloid may be performed. Analgesia or sedation may be necessary to achieve reduction. The physician uses a combination of longitudinal distraction of the fracture and manipulation of the distal fragment to achieve reduction. The wrist and forearm are placed in a cast or splint until the fracture or epiphyseal separation is stable.

25606
The physician treats a fracture of the distal radius. The physician first manipulates the area to reduce the fracture. The physician applies a combination of traction on the wrist and manipulation of the distal radius to reduce the fracture. An assistant maintains the reduction. Using a drill, the physician inserts two Kirschner wires percutaneously (directly through the skin) through the radial styloid, across the fracture, and into the opposite metaphyseal cortex of the ulna. The

Kirschner wires are cut off just beneath the skin. The arm is immobilized in a cast. The wires are removed in six weeks. If there is a severely comminuted fracture of the distal radius that is not suitable for percutaneous Kirschner wire stabilization alone, the physician may apply a traction cast or an Ace-Colles external fixator. For application of a traction cast, the fracture or separation is first reduced and a Steinmann pin is inserted transversely through the proximal elbow. A second pin is inserted transversely through the bases of the second and third metacarpals. A plaster cast is applied above and below the elbow and incorporates the two pins. The pins and cast are left in place for approximately eight weeks. With an external fixator, the fracture or separation is first reduced by manipulation and traction. The external fixator is applied to the forearm and wrist to stabilize the fracture or separation.

25607-25609
The physician makes a 7.5 cm longitudinal incision along the anterolateral aspect of the distal forearm. The physician exposes the fracture by dissecting between the planes of muscles and tendons of the lateral wrist area while protecting the median nerve. The pronator quadratus muscle is severed from the radius. The physician reduces the fracture or separation. A small T-plate is fixed to the proximal fragment with one or two screws. Usually no screw is inserted through the distal part of the plate since it acts as a buttress and helps hold the fracture in reduction. Direct visualization and separately reportable x-rays are used to confirm correct reduction and restoration of the joint surface. The pronator quadratus is replaced at its origin on the radius. The incision is repaired in layers using sutures, staples, and/or Steri-strips. The arm is immobilized in a cast. Report 25607 for open treatment of the fracture with internal fixation; 25608 for fracture repair in which two fragments of bone in the joint receive internal fixation; and 25609 for fracture repair in which three or more fragments of bone in the joint receive internal fixation.

25622-25624
The physician treats a scaphoid fracture of the wrist without open surgery or manual manipulation in 25622. Separately reportable x-rays confirm the position and alignment of the bone. In 25624, manipulation of the bone is required. The patient may require anesthesia. The physician manipulates the area by pushing on the wrist bones, particularly the scaphoid. The physician also pulls on the fingers and forearm, moving the fractured area back into position. Separately reportable x-rays confirm alignment. In both 25662 and 25624, a cast is placed on the wrist and forearm with a thumb spica to hold the fracture in position.

25628
The physician treats a fracture of the wrist scaphoid bone. An incision is made over the scaphoid bone. The physician extends the incision down to the bone and the fracture is identified. Soft tissue is debrided as necessary. The physician places the bone fragments in their correct anatomical position. Typically, screws are applied to hold the pieces together. The physician irrigates the wound and closes it in layers. A cast or splint is applied to provide additional support of the area.

25630-25635
The physician performs closed treatment of a fracture of the carpal bone, reported for each bone treated. Triquetrum fractures are usually nondisplaced and respond well to casting or splinting for six weeks. Capitate fractures are generally treated by conservative casting, immobilizing the wrist and thumb. Hamate fractures are accompanied by fractures at the base of the ulnar metacarpal, and become asymptomatic after a four to six week-period of immobilization. Lunate fractures are similarly treated by immobilization. Report 25630 if no manipulation is performed; report 25635 if manipulation is performed, each bone.

25645
The physician performs open treatment of a fracture of the carpal bone. Only some carpal bones are treated with open procedures. For hook of the hamate fractures, the physician makes an incision over the ulnar aspect of the wrist. The fracture is reduced and fixed with Kirschner wires, or the hook is excised. The tissue is closed in layers and a compression dressing is applied. Trapezium fractures are often treated with open surgery and may require secondary surgery to treat symptoms of pain. Capitate fractures—especially if associated with scaphoid fractures—are often treated with reduction and internal fixation via Kirschner wires. In cases in which Lunate fractures do not respond well to immobilization, the physician may elect open treatment. An incision is made over the lunate to excise avulsed fragments. The soft tissue is closed in layers and a compression dressing is applied.

25650
The physician treats an ulnar styloid fracture with a cast or splint. No manual manipulation and no incisions are required.

25651
The physician performs percutaneous skeletal fixation of an ulnar styloid fracture. Following fixation of the ulnar styloid fragment, the remaining depressed articular fragments are elevated and reduced with traction, direct pressure, or with use of a small incision and application of pointed reduction clamps.

25652
If closed reduction of the ulnar styloid fracture is not possible, the physician extends an incision down to the

Musculoskeletal

bone and identifies the fracture. Soft tissue is debrided as necessary. The physician places the bone fragments in their correct anatomical position. The wound is irrigated and closed in layers. A cast or splint is applied to provide additional support.

25660
The physician repairs the dislocation of radiocarpal or intercarpal bones with manipulation. Sustained traction is held while the physician applies force to reduce the dislocated bone(s) into the proper anatomical position. Immobilization post-reduction depends on the physician's preference.

25670
The physician performs an open treatment of radiocarpal or intercarpal dislocation, one or more bones. The physician makes a dorsal incision overlying the wrist, and the dislocation is reduced. If involved ligaments are torn, they are repaired to stabilize the reduction. The physician may use the overlying capsule to reinforce the stabilization. The soft tissue is closed in layers and a compression dressing is applied.

25671
Percutaneous pinning is commonly performed at 10 days from injury. The physician may use fluoroscopic guidance to perform an initial closed reduction and to insert pins from the radial styloid to the ulnar cortex of the radius for percutaneous fixation.

25675
The physician performs a closed treatment of distal radioulnar dislocation with manipulation. The physician reduces the dislocation by pronation (if the ulna is involved) and supination (if the ulna is dorsal). The arm is immobilized.

25676
The physician performs an open treatment a distal radioulnar dislocation, acute or chronic. For a locked dislocation or incongruous reduction, the physician opens the joint for reduction, and repairs the triangular fibrocartilage (TFC)/ulnar collateral ligament complex (UCLC), stabilizing the repair with Kirschner wires. The physician incises the dorsum of the wrist on the ulnar side. The proximal and ulnar half of the extensor retinaculum is raised radially. The extensor digiti minimi is retracted to reveal the TFC. The capsule is detached from the radius and reflected ulnar. After the dislocated joint is reduced, the TFC lesion may be repaired or reconstructed using a local or grafted tissue from the retinaculum, extensor carpi ulnaris, or flexor carpiulnaris. Kirschner wires may be used to stabilize the repair, after which the overlying soft tissue is sutured closed and a bulky dressing is applied.

25680
The physician performs closed treatment of a trans-scaphoperilunar type of fracture dislocation using manipulation. After being placed in continual traction for five to 10 minutes, the patient's hand is dorsiflexed while maintaining traction. While stabilizing the lunate volar, gradual palmar flexion reduces the capitate. The wrist is immobilized in a dorsal plaster thumb spica splint at 30 degrees volar flexion. Usually, if the scaphoid is properly reduced (visualized via separately reportable radiographs), the midcarpal joint is adequately reduced as well.

25685
The physician performs open treatment of trans-scaphoperilunar type of fracture dislocation. The physician makes a longitudinal, volar incision overlying the wrist, radial to the flexor carpi radialis tendon. This muscle is retracted toward the ulnar side, and the wrist joint is opened exposing the scaphoid fracture. After the fracture is reduced, Kirschner wires are drilled into the scaphoid to hold the reduction. If fixation of the scaphoid adequately stabilizes the midcarpal joint, no further fixation is required. If separately reportable radiographs visualize even the slightest tendency of volar subluxation, or rotary instability of the lunate, the volar incision must be extended and occasionally, a dorsal incision must be made. In such cases, additional Kirschner wires should be introduced to stabilize the capitate-lunate joint. If this operation is performed within two to three weeks of injury, bone grafting is not used. If open reduction is delayed for more than three weeks post-surgery, bone grafting (reported separately) may be used. Capsular and skin closure is performed.

25690
The physician treats a lunate dislocation with manipulation. During sustained traction, the physician applies force to reduce the dislocated lunate. Immobilization post reduction depends on the physician's preference.

25695
The physician performs an open lunate dislocation. The physician makes both dorsal and volar incisions over the wrist. Through the dorsal longitudinal incision, the extensor tendons are retracted. The proximal pole of the scaphoid is retracted to expose the capitate. Through the volar longitudinal incision, the flexor tendons and median nerve are retracted to the radial side exposing a tear in the volar capsule and ligaments. The dislocated lunate is reduced through the volar approach by manually pushing it back between the capitate and radius while an assistant applies axial traction through the hand. The physician repairs the capsular-ligamentous complex tear with nonabsorbable sutures. On the dorsal side, the physician reduces the proximal pole of the capitate into the distal concavity of the lunate. The proximal pole of the scaphoid is reduced. Kirschner wires are drilled into the scaphoid, lunate, and capitate for stabilization. The physician repairs the dorsal ligamentous complex. The skin is closed.

25800-25810

The physician performs fusion of the wrist joint, including the radiocarpal, intercarpal and/or carpometacarpal joints. The physician exposes the wrist through a dorsal, longitudinal incision. A dorsal tenosynovectomy is performed, and the wrist capsule is elevated exposing the radiocarpal joint. The physician excises the distal ulna and performs a synovectomy of the radiocarpal joint. The radial collateral ligament is released from the radial styloid. The cartilage and sclerotic bond is removed from the distal radius and proximal carpal row. Using an awl, the physician makes a channel in the medullary canal of the radius, through which a Steinmann pin is used for internal fixation. The pin is drilled through the carpus to exit between the second and third, or between the third and fourth metacarpal, depending on alignment between the carpus and the radius. One or two small staples, or an obliquely-placed Kirschner, may be used to provide additional fixation on the radiocarpal joint. The position of the wrist can be varied only five to 10 degrees by adjusting the direction of the pin as it is driven into the radius. A drain is placed in the subcutaneous and prior to skin closure. A milky compression dressing is applied, and the wrist is splinted in the desired position of fusion. Report 25800 if performed without bone graft. Report 25805 if performed with sliding graft. Report 25810 if performed with iliac or other autograft.

25820-25825

The physician performs intercarpal or radiocarpal fusion. The physician makes a curved dorsal incision from the bases of the second and third metacarpal to the tubercle. The wrist joint capsule is opened via a longitudinal incision centered over the capitate-lunate joint. The dorsal three-quarters of the capitate, lunate, and scaphoid bones are removed. Approximately 25 degrees of wrist dorsiflexion will lock the graft in place. If the graft needs further stabilization, crossed Kirschner wires may be used for fixation. The skin is closed in layers. A long-arm cast is placed for six weeks followed by a short-arm gauntlet for an additional six weeks. Report 25820 if a graft is not used. Report 25825 if a fitted circular or rectangular corticocancellous graft from the iliac crest is removed and precisely shaped to fit the recipient. This graft is fit into the proximal row carpal area that has been removed.

25830

The physician performs fusion of the distal radioulnar joint and resection of the ulna, sometimes using a bone graft. The physician makes a dorsal, curvilinear incision over the distal radioulnar joint. The extensor retinaculum is reflected, uncovering the extensor carpi ulnaris and extensor digiti minimi tendons. The capsule is cut and reflected, exposing the ulnar head. A small lamina spreader may be used to view the sigmoid notch of the radius. The periosteum is stripped from the ulna just proximal to the articular surface. The dorsal radioulnar ligaments are stripped sharply. If the distal ulna has been removed, or part of the distal ulna is missing, the remaining portion is decorticated. The radius is prepared by making a notch in the ulnar aspect where the distal ulna can be slotted. The ulna is manually compressed into the notch, holding the forearm in 10-15 degree pronation. The physician drives a Kirschner wire from the ulna into the radius and two compression screws from the outer aspect of the ulna through both cortices of the radius. The extensor retinaculum is reconstructed and the skin is closed.

25900

In elective below-elbow amputations, the physician cuts the soft tissue flaps distal to the intended level of bone amputation. The physician dissects the superficial veins and cuts them at the level of the amputation. Cutaneous nerves are cut proximal to the level of the amputation. The dorsal and volar antebrachial fascia is cut, and, depending on the level of amputation, the tendons or muscle bellies are divided after the radial and ulnar vessels are severed. Muscle bellies are incised just distal to the planned level of bony resection. Nerves are cut through a separate incision, and brought under the muscle. The anterior and posterior interosseous vessels should be ligated or coagulated with electrocautery. An incision in the periosteum is carried out sharply and circumferentially. The bone is transected at the desired level at this time and the specimen is removed. The bone ends are smoothed with a rasp. Closure is accomplished after hemostasis is obtained following tourniquet release. The skin flaps can be fashioned, and subcutaneous tissue and skin are closed in separate layers. A drain is sometimes placed. The stump is dressed and wrapped with an elastic bandage applied more firmly distally than proximally.

25905

The physician performs a guillotine amputation. Just distal to the level of intended bone section, the physician incises the skin in a circular manner down to the deep fascia and allows it to retract. The muscles at the edge of the retracted skin are divided. All vessels encountered are ligated and divided. All major nerves are divided at a proximal level so that they retract proximal to the end of the stump. The physician sections the bone at the ends of the retracted muscles. The bone end is covered by the distal muscle bulk, and the skin is stretched over the stump and sutured closed. The stump is covered with a compressive dressing to control post-surgical edema.

25907

The physician performs secondary closure or scar revision after the stump has granulated or healed by a scar. In this procedure, no additional bone is sectioned. The physician resects the scar and granulation tissue from the end of the stump. Skin flaps are fashioned as close as possible to the thick scar surrounding the granulating wound. The dense layer of scar tissue is excised from over the end of the bone. Additional muscle may be removed as well. The skin flaps are pulled over the end of the stump and connected with nonabsorbable sutures. A temporary drain or suction tubes may also be used.

25909

The physician performs a reamputation. A reamputation may be necessary at a proximal level to reach healthy tissue. The physician cuts the soft tissue flaps distal to the intended level of bone amputation. The physician dissects the superficial veins and cuts them at the level of the amputation. Cutaneous nerves are cut proximal to the level of the amputation. The dorsal and volar antebrachial fascia is cut, and, depending on the level of amputation, the tendons or muscle bellies are divided after the radial and ulnar vessels are severed. Muscle bellies are incised just distal to the planned level of bony resection. Nerves are cut through a separate incision, and brought under the muscle. The anterior and posterior interosseous vessels should be ligated or coagulated with electrocautery. An incision in the periosteum is carried out sharply and circumferentially. The bone is transected at the desired level at this time and the specimen is removed. The bone ends are smoothed with a rasp. Closure is accomplished after hemostasis is obtained following tourniquet release. The skin flaps can be fashioned and subcutaneous tissue and skin are closed.

25915

The physician performs the Krukenberg procedure, a forearm amputation. The physician longitudinally splits the stump into radial and ulnar rays by making a dorsal, longitudinal incision toward the ulnar aspect of the forearm. Also, a volar, longitudinal incision is made toward the radial aspect of the forearm. The muscles left or transferred to the radial side of the forearm are the radial wrist extensors and flexors, the flexors of the index and long fingers, the index and long finger extensors, the pronator teres, the palmaris longus, and the brachioradialis. The remaining muscles are left or inserted on the ulnar side of the forearm. On occasion, some muscles need resection to reduce bulk, but the pronator teres must be preserved. The interosseous membrane is freed along its ulnar border. Skin closure is performed, ensuring the tactile skin is placed over the contact surfaces between the radius and ulna.

25920-25924

The physician disarticulates (amputates) the hand from the forearm through the wrist. The physician makes a long, palmar flap and a short, dorsal flap at a level distal to the radioulnar joint. These flaps are pulled back proximally and all veins are ligated. The physician cuts the superficial branch of the radial nerve and the dorsal sensory branch of the ulnar nerve. The lateral and medial antebrachial cutaneous nerves are cut. The radial and ulnar blood vessels are severed proximate to the wrist. The median nerve is cut while traction is applied. The flexor and extensor tendons are pulled distally and cut. The physician makes a transverse, dorsal incision of the dorsal radiocarpal ligament to view the radiocarpal joint. Circumferential dissection of the radiocarpal capsular and ligamentous attachments are carried out. The amputated specimen is removed. The styloid processes are rounded off, and the skin flaps are closed in two layers of subcutaneous tissue and skin. A soft dressing is applied distal to proximal. Report 25920 if an amputation through the wrist is performed. Report 25922 if a secondary closure or scar revision is performed on the stump. Report 25924 if a re-amputation is performed. All use a similar technique.

25927-25931

The physician amputates the fingers. The physician makes circumferential incisions around each digit excluding the thumb. These incisions are carried out at the mid-proximophalangeal level. The extensor digitorum communis of each digit (also the extensor indicis proprius of the index and the extensor digiti minimi of the little) are transected at the metacarpal bases. Individually, each metacarpal bone is transected and elevated from its soft tissue bed. The lumbricals and dorsal interossei are sectioned. Identified blood vessels are ligated. Nerves are ligated and transected. The flexor tendons are transected and allowed to retract in the palm. The volar plate, ligaments, and palmar fascia at this level are all cut and amputated digits are removed. The open periosteal tubes are closed. The soft tissue flaps are drawn over the end of the stump, and interrupted sutures are used. A soft dressing is applied. Report 25927 if an amputation is performed. Report 25929 if a secondary closure or scar revision is performed. Report 25931 if a re-amputation is performed. All use a similar technique.

26010-26011

The physician drains an abscess located in a finger. In 26010, the physician lances an abscess located in the cutaneous tissue of a finger. In 26011, the abscess just reaches deep subcutaneous tissue and requires debridement and irrigation. The wound may be left open to drain.

26020

The physician drains fluid located in a tendon sheath located in a finger or in the palm. The physician incises the skin above the affected sheath and dissects to the tendon sheath. The sheath is lanced and drained. An irrigation catheter may be placed and the wound is irrigated for up to 48 hours. The incision is sutured in layers.

26025-26030

The physician drains a palmar bursa or multiple bursas located on the ulnar or radial side of the palm. The physician incises the skin over the bursa and dissects to the bursa. The bursa is lanced and irrigated with a catheter. The catheter is removed and the incision is sutured in layers. Report 26025 for a single bursa, report 26030 for multiple and/or complicated bursas.

26034
The physician incises the bone cortex of infected bone in the hand or finger to treat an abscess or osteomyelitis. The physician makes an incision over the affected area. Dissection is carried down through the soft tissues to expose the bone. The periosteum is split and reflected from the bone overlying the infected area. A curette may be used to scrape away the abscess or infected portion down to healthy bony tissue or drill holes may be made through the cortex into the medullary canal in a window outline around the infected or abscessed bone. The area is drained and debrided of infected bony and soft tissue. The physician irrigates the area with antibiotic solution, the periosteum is closed over the bone, and the soft tissues are sutured closed; or the wound is packed and left open, allowing the area to drain. Secondary closure is performed approximately three weeks later. Dressings are changed daily. A splint may be applied to limit movement.

26035
The physician decompresses fingers and/or a hand damaged due to an injection injury. The physician incises the skin overlying the entry point of the injection injury. The tissue is dissected to the fascial or periosteal layers and injected material is removed. If the injected material has followed the periosteum or fascia proximally, the incision length is increased until all the injected material is removed. The wound is irrigated and sutured in layers.

26037
The physician decompresses the hand fascia. The physician incises the skin overlying the affected fascia. The fascia is incised and the underlying tissues are irrigated. The incision is sutured in layers.

26040-26045
The physician incises the palmar fascia to release a Dupuytren's contracture. A Dupuytren's contracture is a shortening of the palmar fascia resulting in flexion deformity of a finger. In 26040, the physician makes a stab wound through the subcutaneous to the palmar fascia, which is incised. In 26045, the subcutaneous tissue is incised and retracted to expose the palmar fascia. The palmar fascia is incised to relieve tension and allow the hand to extend correctly. The operative wound is sutured in layers.

26055
The physician makes an incision in a tendon sheath to release tension in the tendon. (For example, this procedure would be performed to relieve trigger finger.) The physician incises the skin overlying the tendon and dissects to the tendon sheath The sheath is incised lengthwise. The incision is sutured in layers.

26060
The physician incises a tendon at the subcutaneous level. The physician incises the overlying skin. The tendon is severed through the subcutaneous tissue. The incision is sutured in layers. Report each digit separately.

26070-26080
The physician performs an arthrotomy of a carpometacarpal joint in 26070, a metacarpophalangeal joint in 26075, or an interphalangeal joint in 26080 that includes exploration, drainage, or removal of any loose or foreign body. An incision is made over the joint to be exposed. The soft tissues are dissected away and the joint capsule is exposed and incised. The joint space is explored, any necrotic tissue is removed, and infection or abnormal fluid is drained. If a foreign body is present (e.g., bullet, nail, gravel), it is exposed and removed. The wound is irrigated with antibiotic solution. The physician may leave the wound packed open with daily dressing changes to allow for drainage and secondary healing by granulation. If the incision is repaired, drain tubes may be inserted and the incision closed in layers with sutures, staples, and/or Steri-strips. Report 26075 and 26080 once for each specified joint.

26100-26110
The physician performs an arthrotomy of a carpometacarpal joint in 26100, a metacarpophalangeal joint in 26105, or an interphalangeal joint in 26110 with biopsy. An incision is made over the joint to be exposed. The soft tissues are dissected away and the joint capsule is exposed and incised. The joint space is explored and a biopsy sample, such as from the synovial membrane, or fluid is removed. The wound is irrigated and may be left open with daily dressing changes to allow for secondary healing. If the incision is repaired, drain tubes may be inserted and the incision closed in layers with sutures, staples, and/or Steri-strips. Report codes 26100-26110 once for each specified joint.

26111-26116
The physician removes a tumor or vascular malformation from the soft tissue of the hand or finger that is located in the subcutaneous tissue in 26111 and 26115 and in the deep soft tissue below the fascial plane, or within the muscle, in 26113 or 26116. With the proper anesthesia administered, the physician makes an incision in the skin overlying the mass and dissects down to the tumor or malformation. The extent of the tumor is identified and a dissection is undertaken all the way around the tumor. The blood vessels are ligated and the defective tissue of the vascular malformation is excised. A portion of neighboring soft tissue may also be removed to ensure

adequate removal of all tumor tissue. A drain may be inserted, and the incision is repaired with layers of sutures, staples, or Steri-strips. Report 26115 for excision of subcutaneous tumors whose resected area is less than 1.5 cm and 26111 for excision of subcutaneous tumors 1.5 cm or greater. Report 26116 for excision of subfascial or intramuscular tumors whose resected area is less than 1.5 cm and 26113 for excision of subfascial or intramuscular tumors 1.5 cm or greater.

26117-26118
The physician removes a malignant soft tissue tumor from the hand or finger, not involving bone. An incision is made over the tumor and dissection exposes it. The tumor and any adjacent tissue that may be affected by the spread of the neoplasm are excised. Large resections may be needed. The type and stage of the lesion determines the extent of the tumor margin resection area. Muscle or fascia may need to be repaired and drains may be placed. The surgical wound is repaired by intermediate or complex closure, adjacent tissue transfer, or graft. Report 26117 for excision of tumors whose resected area is less than 3 cm, and 26118 for excision of tumors 3 cm or greater.

26121-26125
The physician removes the palmar fascia. The physician incises the overlying skin and subcutaneous tissue. The palmar fascia is exposed and resected. Tendon sheaths are freed. The incision is sutured in layers if possible. Z-plasties are performed or skin grafts are obtained to close the wound if necessary. In 26121, the palmar fascia is removed. In 26123, part of the palmar fascia is removed and flexor tendons at proximal interphalangeal joints are released. Use 26125 to report additional digits.

26130
The physician removes the synovial membrane from the carpometacarpal joint. The physician incises the skin overlying the affected joint. The joint capsule is exposed by dissecting down through the soft tissues and freeing and reflecting the muscles. The joint capsule is incised to expose the synovium, the inner membrane of the articular capsule that lines the joint cavity. The inflamed or enlarged synovium is dissected away from the capsule and the bones and removed. A drain tube may be placed and the incision is repaired in layers with sutures, staples, and/or Steri-strips. A splint may be applied to limit movement.

26135
The physician removes the synovial membrane from the metacarpophalangeal joint, releases intrinsic musculature, and reconstructs the extensor hood. The physician incises the skin overlying the affected joint and dissects down through the soft tissues to the joint capsule. The joint capsule is incised and the synovium, the inner membrane of the articular capsule that lines the joint cavity, is removed. Intrinsic muscle contractions are released by exposing the extensor aponeurosis and incising the fibers at their insertion down into the tendon with a parallel incision, while preserving the transverse fibers. The adequacy of the dissection is tested and adjusted before the remaining flap part of the extensor hood is resected. The incision is closed with running sutures and a plaster splint is applied to hold the metacarpophalangeal joints in extension but allow full movement of the interphalangeal joints. Report each finger separately.

26140
The physician removes the synovial membrane from the proximal interphalangeal joint and reconstructs the extensor tendon. The physician makes a midlateral incision overlying the proximal interphalangeal joint, severs the attachment of the transverse retinacular ligament, and elevates the extensor hood. The collateral ligament and central tendon are identified and the joint is entered. The synovium, the inner membrane of the articular capsule that lines the joint cavity, is removed. The transverse retinacular ligament is relocated and the extensor tendons over the dorsum of the finger are repaired as needed and reattached to the joint. The incision is sutured in layers. Report each finger separately.

26145
The physician removes the synovial membrane from a flexor tendon sheath (tenosynovectomy) at the palm or finger. The physician incises the skin of the affected finger on the palmar side in a zigzag fashion and exposes the flexor tendon sheath. Taking care not to damage neurovascular bundles, the sheath is excised, except for a small area in the middle of the phalanx sections. The synovium is removed as much as possible and the incision is closed with interrupted sutures. A compression dressing and supportive wrist splint are applied.

26160
The physician excises a lesion of the tendon sheath or joint capsule in the hand or finger, such as a cyst or ganglion. The physician incises the overlying skin and dissects to locate the affected area. The lesion, cyst, or ganglion is identified and excised from the tendon sheath or joint capsule. The incision is sutured in layers.

26170-26180
The physician excises a flexor or extensor tendon in the hand or finger. Included in these codes are flexor tendons extending from the palm of the hand to the fingertips, essential to grasping motion, and extensor tendons stretching from the wrist along the back of the hand to the fingertips, essential to opening the hand. The physician incises the overlying skin and dissects to the flexor or extensor tendon. The tendon is freed and resected. The incision is sutured in layers. Report 26170 for each flexor or extensor tendon of the hand

and 26180 for each flexor or extensor tendon of the finger.

26185
This procedure is rarely performed, but may be necessary in cases of sesamoid fracture or when performing a metacarpal-sesamoid synostosis. The physician makes a midlateral incision over the metacarpophalangeal joint of the thumb on the radial side. The radial side of the extensor apparatus is opened, and the radial carpal ligament is dissected. The opponens pollicis muscle is separated from its attachment to the metacarpal neck. The metacarpophalangeal joint is opened through incision. In the case of a fracture, the fractured bone is exposed and removed. In a synostosis, the lateral sesamoid bone is exposed, its cartilage is removed along with the cortex of the first metacarpal neck. Drill holes are placed in the metacarpal neck and a wire suture is passed around the sesamoid bone. The capsule and overlying tissue are sutured closed.

26200-26205
A bone cyst or benign tumor of the metacarpal bones is removed. The physician makes an incision in the hand overlying the cyst or tumor. The skin and underlying soft tissues are reflected to expose the periosteum, which is separated from the bone. Curettes or osteotomes are used to scrape or cut the lesion from the bone. Once the benign tumor or cyst is removed and healthy bone tissue is present, the periosteum is repositioned and the incision is repaired in layers. If the bone defect created requires a graft for repair, the physician may obtain the necessary size bone graft from a separate donor site on the patient and pack it into the site where the tumor or bone cyst was removed. Report 26205 if an autograft is obtained.

26210-26215
A bone cyst or benign tumor of the proximal, middle, or distal phalanx of the finger is removed. The physician makes an incision in the finger overlying the cyst or tumor. The skin and underlying soft tissues are reflected to expose the periosteum, which is separated from the bone. Curettes or osteotomes are used to scrape or cut the lesion from the bone. Once the benign tumor or cyst is removed and healthy bone tissue is present, the periosteum is repositioned and the incision is repaired in layers. If the bone defect created requires a graft for repair, the physician may obtain the necessary size bone graft from a separate donor site on the patient and pack it into the site where the tumor or bone cyst was removed. Report 26215 if an autograph is obtained.

26230-26236
The physician performs a partial excision of a metacarpal bone in 26230, the proximal or middle phalanx of a finger in 26235, or the distal phalanx of a finger in 26236 to remove infected bone. An incision is made over the infected part of the hand or finger and the underlying soft tissues are divided to expose the bone. The periosteum is reflected and the infected portion of bone is removed and irrigated. The excavation of bone may excise a crater-like piece, leave a small saucer-like shelf depression in the bone, or may remove a portion of the shaft (diaphysis) of a long bone. If a significant portion of bone is removed, the physician may use bone graft material to fill the cavity left in the bone. The periosteum is closed over the bone, the soft tissues are sutured closed, and a soft dressing is applied.

26250-26262
The physician performs a radical resection of a tumor. The physician incises the overlying skin and dissects to determine the extent of invasion. The bone and surrounding tissues are resected. If a graft is needed for reconstruction, it is obtained from the distal radius or iliac crest. Skin is approximated over the surgical defect and sutured in layers. In 26250, a tumor of the metacarpal bone is excised. In 26260, a tumor of the proximal or middle phalanx of a finger is excised. In 26262, a tumor of the distal phalanx of a finger is excised.

26320
The physician removes a previously placed implant from a finger or hand. The physician incises the overlying skin and dissects to the implant. The implant is removed and the incision is sutured in layers.

26340
Manipulation of the finger joint under anesthesia may be necessary to regain the loss of motion following a surgical procedure or due to scar tissue. Following the induction of general anesthesia, the physician evaluates the finger. The finger is manipulated by stretching, rotation, and other maneuvers to gain the appropriate range of motion.

26350-26352
The physician repairs or advances a single tendon not located in "no man's land." "No man's land" is located between the A1 pulley and the insertion of the superficialis tendon. The physician incises the skin overlying the proximal or distal phalanx and dissects to the tendon. The tendon is repaired with sutures or advanced to improve joint function. Primary repair is done immediately after injury. Secondary repair is done sometime after the incident of injury or following a previous surgical repair. If a graft is needed for secondary repair, it is obtained from the palmaris longus tendon or from the foot. The incision is sutured in layers. Report 26350 for each primary or secondary tendon repair without autograft. Report 26352 for each secondary tendon repair with autograft.

26356-26358
The physician repairs or advances a single flexor tendon located in "no man's land." "No man's land" is located between the A1 pulley and the insertion of the

superficialis tendon. The physician incises the skin overlying the medial phalanx and dissects to the tendon. The tendon is repaired with sutures or advanced and sutured to improve joint function. Primary repair is done immediately after injury. Secondary repair is done sometime after the incident of injury or following a previous surgical repair. If a graft is needed for secondary repair, it is obtained from the palmaris longus tendon or from the foot. The incision is sutured in layers. Report 26356 for each primary flexor tendon repair or advancement without a free graft. Report 26357 for each secondary flexor tendon repair or advancement without a free graft and 26358 for each secondary tendon repair with a free graft (includes harvesting the graft).

26370-26373
The physician repairs or advances the profundus flexor tendon; the superficialis tendon is intact. The physician incises the skin overlying the damaged tendon. The tendon is repaired with sutures or advanced to improve joint function. Primary repair is done immediately after injury. Secondary repair is done sometime after the incident of injury or following a previous surgical repair. If a graft is needed for secondary repair, it is obtained from the palmaris longus tendon or from the foot. The incision is sutured in layers. Report 26370 for each primary tendon repair without graft. Report 26372 for each secondary tendon repair with free graft. Report 26373 for each secondary tendon repair without free graft.

26390
The physician excises a flexor tendon in a finger or hand and implants a synthetic rod for delayed tendon graft. The physician incises the overlying skin and dissects to the tendon. The tendon is freed. The proximal and distal ends are severed and the tendon is removed. The physician implants a synthetic rod so the surrounding tissue will form a natural tube for a tendon graft. The incision is closed. This code is reported once for each rod that is implanted.

26392
The physician removes a synthetic rod used to create a natural location for a tube graft and inserts a flexor tendon graft. The physician incises the overlying skin and dissects to the rod. The rod is removed. A graft is obtained from the palmaris longus tendon or from the foot and inserted in the new position. The proximal and distal ends are sutured into place and the incision is sutured in layers. This code is reported once for each rod that is removed and replaced by a tendon graft.

26410-26412
The physician repairs or advances a single extensor tendon located in the hand. The physician incises the skin overlying the tendon. The tendon is repaired with sutures or advanced to improve joint function. Primary repair is done immediately after injury. Secondary repair is done sometime after the incident of injury or following a previous surgical repair. If a graft is needed for secondary repair, it is obtained from the palmaris longus tendon or from the foot. The incision is sutured in layers. Report 26410 for each primary or secondary tendon repair without free graft. Report 26412 for each secondary tendon repair with free graft.

26415
The physician excises an extensor tendon in a finger or hand and implants a synthetic rod for delayed tendon graft. The physician incises the overlying skin and dissects to the tendon. The tendon is freed. The proximal and distal ends are severed and the tendon is removed. The physician implants a synthetic rod so the surrounding tissue will form a natural tube for a tendon graft. The incision is closed. This code is reported once for each rod that is implanted.

26416
The physician removes a synthetic rod used to create a natural location for a tube graft and inserts an extensor tendon graft. The physician incises the overlying skin and dissects to the rod. The rod is removed. A graft is obtained from the palmaris longus tendon or from the foot and inserted in the new position. The proximal and distal ends are sutured into place and the incision is sutured in layers. This code is reported once for each rod that is removed and replaced by a tendon graft.

26418-26420
The physician repairs or advances a single extensor tendon located in the finger. The physician incises the skin overlying the tendon. The tendon is repaired with sutures or advanced to improve joint function. Primary repair is done immediately after injury. Secondary repair is done sometime after the incident of injury or following a previous surgical repair. If a graft is needed for secondary repair, it is obtained from the palmaris longus tendon or from the foot. The incision is sutured in layers. Report 26418 for each primary or secondary tendon repair without free graft. Report 26420 for each secondary tendon repair with free graft.

26426-26428
The physician repairs a Boutonniere, or buttonhole, deformity of the central slip extensor tendon with a soft tissue procedure that reconstructs the central slip using the lateral band in 26426 or a free tendon graft in 26428. In this deformity, the tendons are imbalanced due to synovitis in the proximal interphalangeal (PIP) joint that causes a stretching of the central slip and subluxation of the lateral bands, which become tight from the swollen joint pressure and act as flexors to the PIP joint. This causes hyperextension deformities in the distal interphalangeal and metacarpophalangeal joints. The physician makes a dorsal, longitudinal incision over the proximal interphalangeal joint to the distal IP joint. The displaced lateral bands are mobilized and a tenotomy is done on the two lateral tendons next to the distal IP joint. The functionality of the central tendon must be restored. The lateral bands

are aligned with the central tendon and used as local tissue to reconstruct the central slip. Report 26428 if a separate free tendon graft must be harvested to repair the central slip. A synovectomy is done. Tendon balance must be assured before the proximal IP joint is fixed in extension. The finger is later placed in a dynamic extension splint after removal of the fixation wire.

26432
The physician repairs the distal insertion extensor tendon without incising the skin. The physician uses a splint to pin the finger in an extended position. If extensive damage occurred during injury, pins may be used to stabilize the joint.

26433-26434
The physician repairs the distal insertion of an extensor tendon (mallet finger), using a graft if necessary. The physician incises the overlying skin and dissects to the damaged tendon. The tendon is repaired with sutures to improve joint function. If a graft is needed for repair, it is obtained from the palmaris longus tendon or from the foot. The incision is sutured in layers. Primary repair is done immediately after injury. Secondary repair is done sometime after the incident of injury or following a previous surgical repair. Report 26433 for primary or secondary repair without a graft and 26434 for primary or secondary repair requiring a graft.

26437
The physician realigns an extensor tendon in the hand. The physician incises the overlying skin and dissects to the damaged tendon. The tendon is realigned to correct finger position. The incision is sutured in layers. Report each tendon separately.

26440-26442
The physician removes scar tissue to release a flexor tendon in a finger or the palm. The physician incises the overlying tissue and dissects to the affected tendon. The scar tissue is debrided and removed, freeing the tendon. The incision is sutured in layers. In 26440 repair is limited to the palm or finger. In 26442, repair extends to the hand and finger. Report each tendon separately.

26445-26449
The physician removes scar tissue to release an extensor tendon in a finger or the dorsum of hand. The physician incises the overlying tissue and dissects to the affected tendon. The scar tissue is debrided and removed, freeing the tendon. The incision is sutured in layers. In 26445 repair is limited to the hand or finger. In 26449, repair extends to the finger, including forearm. Report each tendon separately.

26450-26455
The physician incises a flexor tendon. The physician incises the overlying skin and dissects to the flexor tendon. The tendon is incised. The incision is sutured in layers. In 26450, the tendon is located in the palm. In 26455, the tendon is located in a finger. Report each tendon separately.

26460
The physician incises an extensor tendon in a hand or finger. The physician incises the overlying skin and dissects to the extensor tendon. The tendon is incised. The incision is sutured in layers. Report each tendon separately.

26471-26474
The physician sutures the tendon to the proximal or distal interphalangeal joint for stabilization. The physician incises the overlying skin and dissects to the joint. The tendon is incised and sutured over the joint space, providing joint stabilization. The incision is sutured in layers. In 26471, the proximal joint is stabilized. In 26474, the distal joint is stabilized. Report each tendon separately.

26476
The physician lengthens an extensor tendon in a hand or a finger. The physician incises the overlying skin and dissects to the tendon. The physician performs step cuts to lengthen the tendon. The incision is sutured in layers. Report each tendon separately.

26477
The physician shortens an extensor tendon in a hand or a finger. The physician incises the overlying skin and dissects to the tendon. The physician removes a section of the tendon and sutures the ends back together, shortening the tendon. The incision is sutured in layers. Report each tendon separately.

26478
The physician lengthens a flexor tendon in a hand or a finger. The physician incises the overlying skin and dissects to the tendon. The physician performs step cuts to lengthen the tendon. The incision is sutured in layers. Report each tendon separately.

26479
The physician shortens a flexor tendon in the hand or finger. The physician incises the overlying skin and dissects to the tendon. The physician removes a section of the tendon and sutures the ends back together, shortening the tendon. The incision is sutured in layers. Report each tendon separately.

26480-26489
The physician transfers or transplants a tendon; a free tendon graft may be used if necessary. The physician incises the overlying skin and dissects to the tendon to be moved. The tendon is freed, transferred and sutured into place. If a free tendon graft is used, it is obtained from the palmaris longus tendon or from the foot. The incision is sutured in layers. For transfer or transplant of a carpometacarpal or dorsum of hand tendon without a free graft report 26480 for each tendon; report 26483 if a free graft is used. For transfer or transplant of a palmar tendon without a free graft,

report 26485 for each tendon; report 26489 if a free tendon graft is used.

26490-26494
The physician transfers the superficialis tendon to restore palmar abduction to the thumb. The physician incises the overlying skin and dissects to the superficialis tendon. The tendon is freed and transferred to restore function. If a graft is used, the graft is obtained from the palmaris longus or the abductor digiti minimi. The graft is approximated and sutured into place. The incision is sutured in layers. Report 26490 if no graft is used. Report 26492 if a graft is used. Report each tendon separately. In 26494 the hypothenar muscle is transferred. The muscle tendon is resected from its distal attachment, transferred to the site and sutured into place.

26496
The physician performs this procedure when opposition of the thumb is lost because of median nerve paralysis. Methods described using this code include (1) attaching the extensor pollicis brevis to the extensor carpi ulnaris around the ulnar border of the wrist; (2) attaching the extensor carpi radialis longus to the extensor pollicis longus around the ulnar border of the wrist; (3) attaching the extensor indicis proprius tendon, with a small portion of the extensor hood, to the flexor pollicis longus tendon just distal to the metacarpophalangeal (MP) joint; (4) attachment of the extensor digiti minimi around the ulnar border of the wrist to the thumb MP joint; (5) attachment of the extensor indicis proprius with a small portion of the extensor hood around the ulnar border of the wrist to the thumb MP joint; (6) transfer of the adductor pollicis to the tendon of the superficial head of the flexor pollicis brevis; (7) attachment of the flexor pollicis longus around the ulnar aspect of the flexor carpi ulnaris into the abductor pollicis brevis of the interphalangeal joint.

26497-26498
The physician transfers a tendon to restore intrinsic function to the fingers. The physician incises the overlying skin and dissects to the affected tendon. The tendon is freed, transferred and sutured into place to restore function to the flexor digitorum profundus. The incision is sutured in layers. In 26497, intrinsic function is restored to the ring and small finger. In 26498, intrinsic function is restored to all four fingers.

26499
The physician corrects a claw finger. The superficialis technique involves splitting the flexor digitorum superficialis of the long finger into four slips. One slip is passed through the lumbrical canal of each finger to be inserted into the radial lateral band of the dorsal apparatus. This slip is sutured with the wrist in 30 degrees palmar flexion, the MP joints in 80 to 90 degree flexion, and the interphalangeal joints in full extension. In the dorsal approach, the tendon slips of the extensor carpi radialis brevis are passed superficial to the dorsal carpal ligament, through the intermetacarpal spaces, through the lumbrical canal volar to the deep transverse metacarpal ligament. The tendon is attached to the radial lateral bands of the long, ring and little fingers, and the ulnar lateral band of the index finger. A modification of the latter procedure involves detaching the extensor carpi radialis longus at its insertion and passing it deep to the brachioradialis to the volar sides of the forearm proximate to the wrist. The grafts of the plantaris or palmaris tendons are used. The lateral bands are identified through dorsoradial incisions over the proximal phalanx (except the index finger, which has the ulnar lateral band exposed). The tendon slips are directed through the carpal tunnel volar to the deep transverse metacarpal ligament and into the lateral bands. The tendons are sutured with the wrist dorsiflexed 45 degrees, the MP joints are flexed 70 degrees, and the interphalangeal joints are fixed at zero degrees. Incisions are closed.

26500-26502
The physician reconstructs a tendon pulley. The physician incises the overlying skin and dissects to the damaged pulley located in the A1 position or the distal interphalangeal joint position. In 26500, the tendon pulley is reconstructed using neighboring tissue. In 26502, the physician obtains a fascial graft for reconstruction.

26508
The physician incises the thenar muscle to release, for example, thumb contracture. The physician incises the overlying skin and dissects to the thenar muscle. The scarred muscle tissue is incised to release contracture. The incision is sutured in layers.

26510
The physician performs a cross intrinsic transfer to restore anatomic position and intrinsic function to the fingers. The physician incises the overlying skin and dissects to the affected tendons. The ulnar tendon is resected and transferred to the radial side of the joint, where it is sutured into place. The incision is sutured in layers.

26516-26518
The physician performs a capsulodesis to stabilize the metacarpophalangeal joint. The physician incises the overlying the skin and dissects to the MP joint. The capsule of the joint is sutured to the proximal and distal bones to stabilize the joint. The incision is sutured in layers. In 26516 one digit is repaired. In 26517 two digits are repaired. In 26518 three or four digits are repaired.

26520-26525
The physician removes or incises the joint capsule to release contracture and restore function. The physician incises the overlying the skin and dissects to the

metacarpophalangeal joint. The capsule of the joint is incised or resected and removed. The incision is sutured in layers. In 26520, the capsulectomy or capsulotomy is performed on the metacarpophalangeal joint. In 26525 the capsulectomy or capsulotomy is performed on the interphalangeal joint. Report each joint separately.

26530-26531
The physician performs an arthroplasty on the metacarpophalangeal joint. The physician incises the overlying the skin and dissects to the MP joint. In 26530 the joint is reconstructed using neighboring tissue. In 26531, a prosthetic joint is used to replace the diseased joint. Report each joint separately. Report each tendon separately.

26535-26536
The physician performs an arthroplasty on the interphalangeal joint. The physician incises the overlying the skin and dissects to the I-P joint. In 26535 the joint is reconstructed using neighboring tissue. In 26536, a prosthetic joint is used to replace the diseased joint. Report each joint separately.

26540-26542
The physician performs a primary repair on a collateral ligament of a metacarpophalangeal joint, possibly using a graft or advancement. The physician incises the overlying the skin and dissects to the MP joint. In 26540, the ligament is repaired with sutures. In 26541, a palmaris longus tendon or fascial graft is obtained. The graft is sutured into place. In 26542, an adductor tendon is advanced and sutured into place to stabilize the joint. The incision is sutured in layers.

26545
The physician uses a graft to repair a collateral ligament of an interphalangeal joint. The physician incises the overlying the skin and dissects to the I-P joint. A palmaris longus tendon or fascial graft is obtained and sutured into place. to stabilize the joint. The incision is sutured in layers. Report each joint separately.

26546
The physician performs this procedure to promote healing of a fractured phalanx or metacarpal that fails to heal. The physician makes an incision overlying the dorsal aspect of the fracture of the digit. The extensor mechanism is retracted and the fracture is exposed. Surgical resection of the nonunion itself may be performed. If this resection takes place, fibrous tissue must be removed until there are freshened fracture ends. If a resultant gap produces unacceptable shortening. Fixation such as Kirschner wires or pins, or AO plates is applied. The physician closes the incision with sutures.

26548
The physician repairs a volar plate of an interphalangeal joint. The physician incises the overlying the skin and dissects to the I-P joint. The plate of the joint is sutured to the proximal and distal bones to stabilize the joint. The incision is sutured in layers.

26550
The physician replaces all or part of a thumb with the index finger. The extent of an index finger used is determined by the size of the defect. The physician harvests the index finger with its tendons, blood vessels, and nerves intact and transfers the digit to the thenar eminence. If the thenar eminence must be created, the physician will transfer the index metacarpal along with the digit. If the index metacarpal is not needed, it is removed to provide space for function. The tendons are sutured to the new digit to provide abduction function. The skin is reapproximated and sutured in layers.

26551
The physician performs this procedure to provide functional thumb reconstruction in cases of traumatic thumb amputation and congenital absence of the thumb. Two surgical teams are employed, one at the hand and the other at the foot. One physician makes a linear incision over the dorsal aspect of the foot, traveling from proximal to distal, aiming toward the great toe. This incision stops at the base of the toe and a circular incision is made around the toe. The medial and lateral dorsal foot flaps are raised. The first dorsal metatarsal artery (FDMA) and deep peroneal nerve (DPN) are identified and exposed proximally to the dorsalis pedis artery (DPA). The portion of the DPA that passes to the plantar side of the foot is ligated. On the plantar surface, the flexor hallucis longus (FHL) is identified along with the plantar digital nerves and arteries on either side. The physician dissects into the web space between the great and second toes where the first plantar metatarsal artery (FPMA) is divided, as are vessels to the second toe. The DPN is split and the fibers to the great toe are divided. On the plantar surface, the digital nerves are divided. The FHL is divided through a separate incision in the midfoot, and is pulled into the distal wound. The tourniquet is released and adequate circulation is confirmed. The great toe is perfused for 20 minutes prior to completion of the dissection and transfer to the hand. The second surgical team begins preparing the hand soon after toe dissection begins. The physician on this team make a radially based palmar thumb skin flap. The dorsal incision extends into the wrist area where the cephalic vein, superficial radial nerve, dorsal dominant branch of the radial artery, and extensor tendons are identified. A transverse incision is made over the volar wrist to allow identification of the flexor pollicis longus (FPL). The thumb metacarpal or phalanx is cut squarely at a right angle to two vertically placed interosseous compression wires and longitudinally placed K-wire, which helps hold the digit in extension. Extensor tendon and flexor tendon repairs are performed. The abductor and adductor tendons are repaired to the

Musculoskeletal

extensor mechanism. The vascular repairs are completed using standard microvascular techniques. The superficial radial nerve and DPN are joined dorsally, and the digital nerve repairs are completed volarly. The skin is closed with drains. If a skin graft is necessary, it is placed dorsally over the area of the dorsal veins. The donor site is closed by removal of the metatarsal condyles and suturing of the volar plate and sesamoids to the distal metatarsal.

26553-26554

The physician sometimes uses this procedure in cases of traumatic thumb amputation or congenital absence. Two surgical teams are used to complete the transfer. The first team makes a linear incision over the dorsal aspect of the foot, lateral to the dorsalis pedis artery (DPA), traveling from proximal to distal, aiming toward the second toe. Depending on the joint used, the physician may save skin for a graft. The physician harvests two veins in the foot, the dorsalis pedis and metatarsal arteries, the deep peroneal nerve branch, and the extensor tendon to the second toe, and performs an osteotomy at the joint needed. Digital nerves are harvested from the plantar surface. The second team prepares for the toe by making an incision over the wrists where the cephalic vein, superficial radial nerve, dorsal dominant branch of the radial artery, and the flexor pollicis longus (FPL). The thumb metacarpal or phalanx is cut squarely at a right angle to its long axis after appropriate measurement. If the toe is being transferred to a different finger position, the vein, superficial nerve, digital artery, and extensor tendon are all dissected. To attach the toes to the needed position, the physician affixes the bones by crossed Kirschner wires. The flexor muscles are attached to those of the toe. The digital nerves are repaired, and the palmar wounds are closed. The extensor tendons are attached, followed by the approximation of the dorsal sensory nerves, followed by vascular anastomoses. Incisions are closed using sutures. Report 26554 if more than one toe must be transferred because of finger/thumb deficit.

26555

The physician removes a digit, including the metacarpal bone, to improve hand function following trauma or disease. The physician incises the skin overlying the damaged bone. The bone, tendons, nerves, and muscles are removed. The remaining fingers are reapproximated and sutured to provide correct positioning. The skin is reapproximated and sutured in layers.

26556

The physician performs this procedure if finger joint function is absent, disturbed, or destroyed because of congenital malformation, trauma, or disease. The graft may be an autograft or allograft. Techniques include (1) toe proximal interphalangeal joint (PIPJ) transfer for finger metacarpophalangeal joint (MPJ) and PIPJ reconstruction; (2) metatarsophalangeal (MTPJ) transfer for MPJ or trapeziometacarpal (TMJ) reconstruction; (3) PIPJ or digital interphalangeal joint (DIPJ) "finger bank" transfer. If performing the toe PIPJ transfer for finger PIPJ reconstruction, the physician will engage two teams to prepare the donor and recipient sites simultaneously. One physician makes a longitudinal dorsal incision overlying the toe. The dorsalis pedis and first dorsal metatarsal arteries are dissected, as are dorsal veins. The tibial-side digital artery is divided distally at the level of the DIPJ. The fibular side artery is ligated. The extensor mechanism is cut proximally and distally and the joint is isolated by distal disarticulation through the DIPJ and proximal osteotomy through the first phalanx. The second team prepares the hand by excising the involved PIPJ and dissecting a suitable artery. The toe joint is transferred and stabilized with an intraosseous wire and longitudinal Kirschner wire. The extensor mechanism from the toe is attached to that of the finger. The artery from the toe is attached to that of the finger. At least two veins from the foot are sutured to veins of the hand. The foot wound is closed. The hand wound is also sutured closed. If performing the toe MTPJ transfer for MPJ reconstruction, the physician makes a curved incision to expose the finger joint. The ulnar side of the extensor hood is incised and retracted, and the joint is resected. The radial artery and the cephalic vein are identified through a separate incision. A small branch of the superficial radial nerve is dissected at the wrist level to be sutured to the nerve of the transplanted joint. The donor site is prepared by dissection of the great saphenous vein and first dorsal metatarsal artery. The terminal branch of the deep peroneal nerve is dissected. The toe graft is turned 180 degrees around its longitudinal axis, from dorsal to volar, and attached to the finger. The physician uses a Kirschner wire and anastomoses the vessels. The extensor mechanism is sutured and the skin is closed. The donor site is filled with the finger joint or by bone graft.

26560-26562

The physician repairs a syndactyly (web finger) using skin flaps and grafts. The physician incises the skin of the web for digital release and the underlying tissues are freed. In 26560, the repair is accomplished with skin flaps from the incision area. In 26561, the physician obtains grafts to provide skin coverage. In 26562, the syndactyly is complex and involves the phalangeal bones and fingernails. When possible, the bones are separated. Bone grafts are obtained when necessary for reconstruction. When reconstruction is complete, the skin is reapproximated and sutured in layers.

26565-26567

The physician performs an osteotomy to correct the metacarpal or phalanx. The physician incises the skin and dissects to the bone. The bone is incised and removed. The incision is sutured in layers. In 26565 a metacarpal is corrected, in 26567, a phalanx of the finger is corrected.

26568
The physician performs an osteoplasty to lengthen a metacarpal or phalanx. The physician incises the skin and dissects to the defective bone. The periosteum is incised and pulled away from the bone. The bone is cut and the proximal and distal ends are distanced. The periosteum is laid over the bone, and the incision is sutured in layers. The hand is splinted in anatomic position until bone callous is formed.

26580
The physician repairs a cleft hand. A cleft hand is a malformation where the division between the fingers extends into the metacarpus. The middle digits may be absent and remaining digits are abnormally large. The physician incises the overlying skin and dissects to the deformity. The tissues are brought together with sutures, and the tendons are approximated to produce tensor and extensor function. Following correction of the metacarpus, the skin is reapproximated, reduced, and sutured in layers.

26587
The physician reconstructs the hand by removing a polydactylous (extra) digit where the digit contains both soft tissue and bone. Excision of a digit containing soft tissue only is reported using 11200. The physician incises the skin at the base of the supernumerary digit. The bone is cut and the digit is resected. The skin is reapproximated, reduced, and sutured in layers.

26590
The physician corrects macrodactylia, which is an abnormal largeness of the fingers. The physician incises and retracts the skin to expose the underlying tissue. Reduction is accomplished by removing excess connective tissue and bone if necessary. The tissues are reanastomosed and secured with sutures. The incisions are sutured in layers.

26591
The physician repairs the intrinsic muscles of the hand to restore intrinsic function. The physician incises the overlying skin and dissects to the damaged muscle. The integrity of the tendons and muscles are tested. Defects are corrected to restore function. The incision is sutured in layers. When reporting this procedure, indicate which intrinsic muscle was repaired (interossei or lumbricales). Report each muscle separately.

26593
The physician releases the intrinsic muscles of the hand to restore intrinsic function. The physician incises the overlying skin and dissects to the contracted muscle. The intrinsic muscle is incised to release contracture. The incision is sutured in layers. When reporting this procedure, indicate which intrinsic muscle was released (interossei or lumbricals). If microsurgery is used, report using modifier -20 or 09920. Report each muscle separately.

26596
The physician excises a constricting ring of finger using multiple Z-plasties. The physician cuts the restricted skin in z shaped incisions. The Z flaps are reapproximated, increasing skin surface area without using grafts. The flaps are sutured closed.

26600-26605
The physician treats a metacarpal fracture with or without manipulation. The physician uses an x-ray to determine the location and severity of the fracture. In 26600, the fracture does not require realignment. In 26605, the proximal and distal ends of the fracture are not in correct anatomical position, and the physician reduces the fracture to correct alignment. The bones are splinted in anatomic position. Report each bone separately.

26607
The physician treats a metacarpal fracture with manipulation and external fixation. The physician uses a separately reportable x-ray to determine the location and severity of the fracture. The physician reduces the fracture to correct alignment of the proximal and distal ends of the bone. External fixation is placed to stabilize the fracture. The bones are splinted in anatomic position. Report each bone separately.

26608
The physician fixates a metacarpal fracture using a percutaneously placed wire. The physician uses an x-ray to determine the location and severity of the fracture. The physician reduces the fracture to correct alignment of the proximal and distal ends of the bone. The physician drills a wire through the metacarpophalangeal joint, through the fracture, and into the proximal bone. The drill entry point dressed and the hand is splinted.

26615
The physician performs open correction of a metacarpal fracture. Internal fixation may be used. The physician uses an x-ray to determine the location and severity of the fracture. The physician incises the overlying skin to expose the fracture. A wire or plate may be placed for internal fixation. The incision is sutured in layers and the hand is splinted.

26641-26645
The physician manipulates a carpometacarpal dislocation or fracture dislocation of the thumb to restore anatomical position. The physician determines the dislocated position of the bone. The bone is relocated to correct anatomical position using external manipulation, and the hand is splinted. Report 26641 for dislocation without fracture, report 26645 for dislocation including fracture (Bennett fracture).

26650
The physician manipulates a carpometacarpal fracture dislocation of the thumb to restore anatomical position and secures the bone with a wire. The physician determines the dislocated position of the bone. The bone is relocated to correct anatomical position using external manipulation. The physician drills a wire through the metacarpophalangeal joint, through the fracture, and into the proximal bone. The drill entry point is dressed and the hand is splinted.

26665
The physician performs open reduction of a carpometacarpal fracture dislocation of the thumb. The physician uses an x-ray to determine the position and severity of the defect. The physician incises the overlying skin to expose the fracture and the bones are reapproximated. A wire or plate may be placed for internal fixation. The incision is sutured in layers and the hand is splinted.

26670-26675
The physician treats a carpometacarpal (other than the thumb) dislocation using manipulation; anesthesia may be used if necessary. The physician determines the dislocated position of the bone. The physician uses external manipulation to relocate the bone. In 26670, dislocation is minor and no anesthesia is needed. In 26675, dislocation is major and anesthesia is required.

26676
The physician manipulates a carpometacarpal dislocation (other than the thumb) to restore anatomical position and secures the bone with a wire. The physician determines the dislocated position of the bone. The bone is relocated to the correct anatomical position using external manipulation. The physician drills a wire through the carpometacarpal joint. The drill entry point is dressed and the hand is splinted.

26685-26686
The physician performs open reduction of a carpometacarpal dislocation on a joint other than the thumb. The physician uses a separately reportable x-ray to determine the position and severity of the defect. The physician incises the overlying skin to expose the dislocation. A wire or plates may be placed for internal fixation. The incision is sutured in layers and the hand is splinted. Report 26685 for each joint that is repaired simply. Report 26686 for complex or multiple dislocations, or when delayed treatment of the dislocation is performed.

26700-26705
The physician treats a metacarpophalangeal dislocation using manipulation; anesthesia may be used if necessary. The physician determines the dislocated position of the bone. The physician uses external manipulation to relocate the bone. In 26700, dislocation is minor and no anesthesia is needed. In 26705, dislocation is major and anesthesia is required.

26706
The physician manipulates a metacarpophalangeal dislocation to restore anatomical position and secures the bone with a wire. The physician determines the dislocated position of the bone. The bone is relocated to correct anatomical position using external manipulation. The physician drills a wire into the metacarpophalangeal joint, through the fracture, and into the proximal bone. The drill entry point dressed and the hand is splinted.

26715
The physician performs open reduction of a metacarpophalangeal fracture dislocation. The physician uses an x-ray to determine the position and severity of the defect. An incision is made on the overlying skin to expose the fracture and the bones are reapproximated. A wire or plate may be placed for internal fixation. The incision is sutured in layers and the hand is splinted.

26720-26725
The physician treats a phalangeal shaft fracture of the proximal or middle phalanx, finger, or thumb with or without manipulation. In 26720, no manipulation is necessary. In 26725, the physician manipulates the bones to restore anatomical position. The hand is splinted for stabilization.

26727
The physician treats a phalangeal shaft fracture of the proximal or middle phalanx, finger, or thumb with manipulation and secures it with a wire. The physician drills a wire into the tip of the finger bone, through the fracture, and into the proximal bone. The drill entry point dressed and the hand is splinted.

26735
The physician performs open correction of a phalangeal shaft fracture. The physician uses an x-ray to determine the position and severity of the defect. The physician incises the overlying skin to expose the fracture and the bones are reapproximated. A wire or plate may be placed for internal fixation. The incision is sutured in layers and the hand is splinted.

26740-26742
The physician treats an articular fracture involving a metacarpophalangeal or interphalangeal joint with or without manipulation. In 26740, no manipulation is necessary. In 26742, the physician manipulates the bones to restore anatomical position. The hand is splinted for stabilization.

26746
The physician performs open reduction of an articular fracture involving a metacarpophalangeal or interphalangeal joint. The physician uses an x-ray to determine the position and severity of the defect. An incision is made on the overlying skin to expose the fracture and the bones are reapproximated. A wire or

plate may be placed for internal fixation. The incision is sutured in layers and the hand is splinted.

26750-26755
The physician treats distal phalangeal fracture of the finger or thumb with or without manipulation. In 26750, no manipulation is necessary. In 26755, the physician manipulates the bones to restore anatomical position. The hand is splinted for stabilization.

26756
The physician treats a distal phalangeal fracture of the finger or thumb with manipulation and secures it with a wire. The physician drills a wire into the tip of the finger bone, through the fracture, and into the proximal bone. The drill entry point dressed and the hand is splinted.

26765
The physician performs open reduction of a distal phalangeal fracture of the finger or thumb. The physician uses an x-ray to determine the position and severity of the defect. An incision is made on the overlying skin to expose the fracture and the bones are reapproximated. A wire or plate may be placed for internal fixation. The incision is sutured in layers and the hand is splinted.

26770-26775
The physician treats an interphalangeal joint dislocation using manipulation; anesthesia may be used if necessary. The physician determines the dislocated position of the bone and uses external manipulation to relocate the bone. In 26770, dislocation is minor and no anesthesia is needed. In 26775, dislocation is major and anesthesia is required.

26776
The physician manipulates an interphalangeal joint dislocation to restore anatomical position and secures the bone with a wire. The physician determines the dislocated position of the bone. The bone is relocated to correct anatomical position using external manipulation. The physician drills a wire through the interphalangeal joint for stabilization and the hand is splinted.

26785
The physician performs open correction of an interphalangeal joint dislocation. The physician uses an x-ray to determine the position and severity of the defect. An incision is made on the overlying skin to expose the dislocated joint and the bones are reapproximated. A wire may be placed for internal fixation. The incision is sutured in layers and the hand is splinted.

26820
The physician fuses the thumb in opposition. The physician incises the overlying skin and dissects to the metacarpophalangeal joint. A bone graft is obtained from the distal radius or iliac crest and placed to secure the joint. A wire is placed through the joint until fusion is complete. The incision is sutured in layers and the thumb is splinted for stabilization.

26841-26844
The physician fuses the carpometacarpal joint of a finger or the thumb. Internal or external fixation may be used. The physician incises the overlying skin and dissects to the carpometacarpal joint. The joint is fixated with a wire, screws, or plates. The incision is sutured in layers and the hand is splinted. If a graft is obtained, the physician harvests bone from the distal radius or iliac crest. The graft is interposed between the two bones to prevent movement and a wire is placed through the joint until fusion is complete. In 26841, the thumb is treated; report 26842 if an autograft is obtained and used. In 26843, a finger joint is treated; report 26844 if an autograft is obtained and used. The incision is sutured in layers and the hand is splinted.

26850-26852
The physician fuses a metacarpophalangeal joint. Internal or external fixation may be used. The physician incises the overlying skin and dissects to the metacarpophalangeal joint. The physician may use a wire to stabilize the joint until fusion is complete. Report 26852 if an autograft is obtained and used. Bone is harvested from the distal radius or iliac crest and interposed between the two bones to prevent movement. The incision is sutured in layers and the hand is splinted.

26860-26863
The physician fuses an interphalangeal joint. Internal or external fixation may be used. The physician incises the overlying skin and dissects to the interphalangeal joint. The physician may use a wire to stabilize the joint until fusion is complete. Report 26861 for each additional interphalangeal joint. Report 26862 if an autograft is obtained and used. A graft is harvested from the distal radius or iliac crest and interposed between the bones to prevent movement. Report 26863 for autografts on each additional interphalangeal joints. The incision is sutured in layers and the hand is splinted.

26910
The physician amputates a metacarpal bone including a finger or the thumb. An interosseous transfer may be performed. The physician incises the overlying skin and dissects to the defective metacarpal bone. The bone is freed of all muscular and vascular attachments and removed. Tissues that are no longer necessary for anatomical function are removed. Interossei muscles may be transferred to adjacent metacarpals to retain intrinsic muscle function. Soft tissue structures are returned to anatomic position; the skin is reapproximated, reduced and sutured in layers.

26951-26952
The physician amputates a finger or thumb, primary or secondary to injury. Neurectomies are performed. The overlying skin is incised and the tissues are dissected to the bone. The bone is removed. The vessels and nerves are ligated using microsurgical techniques. Primary amputation is removal of the digit following an acute injury or infection. Secondary amputation occurs when earlier attempts to preserve the digit have failed. In 26951, the wound is approximated, reduced, and sutured in layers. In 26952, local advancement flaps are necessary for closure.

26990-26991
The physician drains a deep abscess or hematoma in 26990 or an infected bursa in 26991 from the pelvis or hip joint area. The physician makes an incision overlying the site of the abscess, hematoma, or bursa. Dissection is carried through the deep subcutaneous tissues and may be continued into the fascia or muscle to expose the abscess or hematoma. The incision may be extended if the mass is larger than expected. When the infected bursa, abscess, or hematoma is identified, it is incised and the contents are drained. The area is irrigated and the incision is repaired in layers with sutures, staples, and/or Steri-strips; closed with drains in place; or simply left open to further facilitate drainage of infection.

26992
The physician incises the bone cortex of infected bone in the pelvis and/or hip joint to treat an abscess or osteomyelitis. The physician makes an incision over the affected area. Dissection is carried through the soft tissues to expose the bone. The periosteum is split and reflected from the bone overlying the infected area. A curette may be used to scrape away the abscess or infected portion to healthy bony tissue or drill holes may be made through the cortex into the medullary canal in a window outline around the infected or abscessed bone. The area is drained and debrided of infected bony and soft tissue. The physician irrigates the area with antibiotic solution, the periosteum is closed over the bone, and the soft tissues are sutured closed; or the wound is packed and left open, allowing the area to drain. Secondary closure is performed approximately three weeks later. Dressings are changed daily.

27000
The physician makes a small incision approximately 0.5 inches long over the origin of the adductor muscles. Dissection is carried to the adductor tendon. The physician uses a small blade to release (free by incision) the tendon. The incision is repaired in layers with sutures and Steri-strips. A spica cast is applied for three to four weeks to keep the hip in abduction.

27001-27003
The physician performs a tenotomy of the adductor of the hip. An incision is made starting at the pubis and extending approximately 5 cm along the inner thigh, in line with the V adductor longus muscle. The tendinous origins of the adductor muscles are identified and separated to allow lengthening. In 27003, the adductor muscles are separated from each other and the obturator nerve is located. The anterior and posterior branches of the nerve are removed. To perform a tenotomy, the tendinous origins of the adductor muscles are divided. The physician repairs the incision in layers. A cast may be applied for three to six weeks to hold the hip in abduction.

27005
The physician makes a 10 cm to 15 cm incision overlying the anterior iliofemoral area. The iliacus muscle and femoral nerve are identified and separated. The iliacus muscle and psoas tendon are separated. The psoas tendon is transferred superiorly and sutured to the anterior capsule of the hip joint. The iliacus muscle is also sutured to the capsule. The incision is repaired in layers.

27006
The patient is placed in a lateral position. A transverse incision is made starting just below the anterosuperior iliac spine and extending to just above the greater trochanter. The gluteus medius and minimus are tenotomized. To perform a tenotomy, the tendinous origins of the abductor muscles are separated. The incision is repaired in layers over a suction drain.

27025-27027
The physician performs a fasciotomy of any type in 27025, treating a swollen area of the hip or thigh. In 27027, the physician performs a unilateral decompression fasciotomy of the pelvic compartments (including gluteus medius-minimus, gluteus maximus, iliopsoas, and/or tensor fascia lata muscle) to treat compartment syndrome. Swelling applies pressure to the neurovascular tissues and muscles and may result in tissue death and loss of limb. One or more incisions are made over the affected area. The fascial planes are dissected out and separated to release pressure caused by swelling. The wounds are left open for approximately 72 hours and repaired in layers with sutures and/or staples.

27030
The physician performs an arthrotomy of the hip to drain infection. An incision is made over the hip. The soft tissues are dissected away, the joint capsule is exposed and incised, and the infection or abnormal fluid is drained. The wound is irrigated with antibiotic solution. The physician may pack the wound and leave it open with daily dressing changes to allow for further drainage and secondary healing by granulation tissue. If the incision is repaired, drain tubes may be inserted and the incision closed in layers with sutures, staples, and/or Steri-strips.

27033
The physician performs an arthrotomy of the hip that includes exploration or removal of any loose or foreign body. An incision is made over the hip, the soft tissues are dissected away, and the joint capsule is exposed and incised. The joint space is explored and any necrotic tissue is removed. If a loose or foreign body is present (e.g., bone fragment, free cartilage, bullet, gravel), it is exposed and removed. The wound is irrigated with antibiotic solution. The physician may leave the wound open with daily dressing changes to allow for secondary healing or drainage. If the incision is repaired, drain tubes may be inserted and the incision closed in layers with sutures, staples, and/or Steri-strips.

27035
The physician makes an incision overlying a nerve of the hip joint. The physician uses a posterior approach to the sciatic or an anterior approach to its branches (the femoral or obturator nerves). The physician dissects the tissue to locate and isolate the nerve. The nerve is cut and the incision repaired in layers.

27036
The physician performs surgery on the hip joint capsule. An incision is made over the hip. Sharp and blunt dissection is utilized to continue deep through the fascia to the hip capsule. The capsule itself is incised. The physician removes all or part of the capsule. Excess bone in and around the capsule is identified, exposed, and removed. To accomplish this, the physician releases some or all of the hip flexor muscle. After the capsule and the excess bone have been removed, the muscles are repaired as warranted. The wound is closed in layers. A drain may be left in the hip joint.

27040-27041
The physician performs a biopsy to evaluate soft tissue. The area for biopsy is in the subcutaneous tissue between the muscle and skin layers in 27040. The suspect area is deeper and may be within muscle in 27041. An incision is made to expose the area. A tumor is typically surrounded by a capsule. The physician makes an incision through the capsule, removing a portion of the tumor for biopsy. The incision is repaired in layers using sutures, staples, and/or Steri-strips.

27043-27048
The physician removes a tumor from the soft tissue of the pelvis and hip area that is located in the subcutaneous tissue in 27043 and 27047 and in the deep soft tissue, below the fascial plane, or within the muscle in 27045 and 27048. With the proper anesthesia administered, the physician makes an incision in the skin overlying the mass and dissects to the tumor. The extent of the tumor is identified and a dissection is undertaken all the way around the tumor. A portion of neighboring soft tissue may also be removed to ensure adequate removal of all tumor tissue. A drain may be inserted and the incision is repaired with layers of sutures, staples, or Steri-strips. Report 27047 for excision of a subcutaneous tumor whose resected area is less than 3 cm and 27043 for excision of a subcutaneous tumor 3 cm or greater. Report 27048 for excision of a subfascial or intramuscular tumor whose resected area is less than 5 cm and 27045 for excision of a subfascial or intramuscular tumor 5 cm or greater.

27049, 27059
The physician removes a malignant soft tissue tumor from the pelvis and hip area, not involving bone. An incision is made over the tumor and dissection exposes it. The tumor and any adjacent tissue that may be affected by the spread of the neoplasm are excised. Large resections may be needed. The type and stage of the lesion determines the extent of the tumor margin resection area. Muscle or fascia may need to be repaired and drains may be placed. The surgical wound is repaired by intermediate or complex closure, adjacent tissue transfer, or graft. Report 27049 if the resection area is less than 5 cm. Report 27059 if the resection area is 5 cm or greater.

27050-27052
The physician performs an arthrotomy of the sacroiliac joint in 27050 and the hip joint in 27052 with a biopsy. An incision is made over the joint to be incised. The soft tissues are dissected away and the joint capsule is exposed and incised. A tissue sample is removed for biopsy and the wound is irrigated. The incision is closed in layers with sutures, staples, and/or Steri-strips.

27054
The physician makes an incision over the hip joint to be exposed and performs an arthrotomy to remove the synovium. The joint capsule is exposed by dissecting through the soft tissues and freeing and reflecting the muscles. The joint capsule is incised to expose the synovium, the inner membrane of the articular capsule that lines the joint cavity. The inflamed or enlarged synovium is dissected away from the capsule and the bones and removed. A drain tube may be placed and the incision is repaired in layers with sutures, staples, and/or Steri-strips.

27057
The physician performs a unilateral decompression fasciotomy of the pelvic compartments (including gluteus medius-minimus, gluteus maximus, iliopsoas, and/or tensor fascia lata muscle) to treat compartment syndrome. Swelling applies pressure to the neurovascular tissues and muscles and may result in tissue death and loss of limb. One or more incisions are made over the affected area. The fascial planes are dissected out and separated to release pressure caused by swelling, and nonviable muscle is debrided. The

Musculoskeletal

wounds are left open for approximately 72 hours and repaired in layers with sutures and/or staples.

27060-27062
The physician makes an incision overlying the ischial tuberosity at the base of the buttock. Dissection exposes the ischial bursa in 27060. For excision of a trochanteric bursa in 27062, an incision is made over the lateral aspect of the hip. The infected or calcified bursa is dissected out from the surrounding tissue and removed. The incision is repaired in layers using sutures, staples, and/or Steri-strips.

27065
The physician excises a bone cyst or benign tumor from superficial bone in the pelvic and hip area (the wing of the ilium, symphysis pubis, or greater trochanter of the femur). An incision is made overlying the area to expose the superficial bone cyst or benign tumor. Dissection is carried down to the cyst or tumor. The lining of the bone (periosteum) is also incised to further expose the cyst or tumor. The physician may make a few cuts above and below the lesion for removal or may remove it with a curette, depending on the position and location of the cyst or tumor. If the cyst or tumor is large enough to weaken the integrity of the bone, a bone autograft may be necessary. Bone chips are harvested from the surrounding cancellous (spongy) bone and are packed into place where the cyst or tumor was removed The incision is repaired in layers using sutures, staples, and/or Steri-strips.

27066-27067
The physician excises a bone cyst or benign tumor from deep bone in the pelvic and hip area. The physician makes an incision overlying the area, exposing the deep bone cyst or benign tumor. Further soft tissue dissection is required. The lining of the bone (periosteum) is also incised to further expose the cyst or tumor. The physician may make a few cuts above and below the area for removal or may remove it with a curette, depending on the position and location of the cyst or tumor. If the cyst or tumor was large enough to weaken the integrity of the bone, a bone autograft may be necessary. Bone chips are harvested from the surrounding cancellous (spongy) bone and are packed into place where the cyst or tumor was removed. In 27067, a separate incision is required to harvest bone from the patient's iliac crest or other donor site. Both cortical and cancellous bone is acquired for bone grafting and the donor site is repaired. The bone graft is placed and the incision is repaired in layers using sutures, staples, and/or Steri-strips.

27070-27071
The physician performs a partial excision of superficial bone in the pelvis and hip area in 27070 (wing of the ilium, symphysis pubis) and of deeper bone in 27071 to remove infected bone. An incision is made over the infected area and the underlying soft tissues are divided to expose it. The periosteum is reflected and the infected portion of bone is removed and irrigated. The excavation of bone may excise a crater-like piece or leave a small saucer-like shelf depression in the bone. If a significant portion of bone is removed, the physician may use bone graft material to fill the cavity left in the bone. The periosteum is closed over the bone, the soft tissues are sutured closed, and a soft dressing is applied.

27075
The physician performs a radical resection (excision) of a tumor. The patient is positioned for a lithotomy with the buttock elevated. For resection of a tumor of the pubis and/or ischium, an incision is made from the pubic tubercle to the ischial tuberosity. The adductor and obturator muscles are detached from the pubis and ischium. Additional dissection is carried down to better expose the pubis and ischium. The remaining muscles and ligaments are released (freed by incision) while the pudendal and genital nerves and vessels are protected. The bone(s) is separated and cut with bone-cutting forceps and an osteotome or saw. The bone segments are removed. A separate incision is made to resect the ilium. The portion of the ilium needing resection is dissected out by releasing muscles, tendons, and ligaments. The incisions are repaired in layers.

27076
The physician performs a radical resection (excision) of a tumor. The patient is placed in a lateral decubitus (lying on the side) position. The physician makes an incision from the posterior crest of the ilium to the symphysis pubis. A vertical extension of this incision is made, extending into the proximal thigh. The physician carries dissection down, while protecting the femoral artery, vein, and nerve. The physician uses a saw to divide (separate) the ilium and the pubic bone. Any remaining soft tissue is released (freed by incision) from the segment of bone to be removed. The inguinal ligament is reattached to the iliopsoas tendon to prevent a hernia. The incision is repaired in layers over a suction drain.

27077
The physician performs a radical resection (excision) of a tumor of the innominate bone in which the bone is removed in total. The patient is placed in a supine position with the involved side elevated. The physician makes an incision extending from the posterosuperior iliac spine, along the iliac crest, to the symphysis pubis. A vertical incision is made extending into the upper thigh. The abdominal muscles are detached. All muscles that attach to the innominate bone are divided and detached. Vessels and nerves are also separated and/or ligated. The hip joint capsule is incised. The sacroiliac joint is exposed and divided with an osteotome. The innominate bone is removed. The incision is repaired in layers.

27078
The physician performs a radical resection (excision) of a tumor of the ischial tuberosity and greater trochanter of the femur. The patient is positioned prone to access the ischial tuberosity and a lateral decubitus position to access the greater trochanter. The physician makes an incision overlying the involved bone and dissects through the deep layers. The ischial tuberosity or greater trochanter is exposed and resected. The wound is closed in layers with sutures.

27080
The physician makes a 15 cm vertical incision over the coccyx. The coccyx is freed from surrounding soft tissue and disarticulated from the sacrum (separated from the joint). The incision is repaired in layers using sutures, staples, and/or Steri-strips. If infection is present, the physician may pack the wound with gauze, allowing the wound to heal by granulation tissue from within.

27086-27087
The physician makes an incision overlying the site of the foreign body in the pelvis or hip. The foreign body is removed from the subcutaneous tissue in 27086. Deeper dissection is required in 27087 and more attention may be given to possibly damaged vessels and/or nerves. The physician irrigates the wound. The incision is repaired with sutures, staples, and/or Steri-strips.

27090
The patient is placed in a lateral decubitus position (lying on the side). The physician may access the prosthesis through the previous hip surgery incision. The physician exposes and incises the hip joint capsule. The hip is manually dislocated. Any scar tissue is removed. The physician disimpacts the femoral prosthesis, removing cement as needed. The physician repairs the incision in layers with sutures.

27091
The patient is placed in a lateral decubitus position (lying on the side). The physician may access the prosthesis through the previous hip surgery incision. Any scar tissue is resected. The physician exposes and incises the hip joint capsule. The hip is manually dislocated. Methylmethacrylate (cement) is removed from the upper portion of the stem. The physician removes the stem with forceful blows. The physician removes any cement. The physician may make a bone window in the femoral cortex to remove additional cement. If there is bony ingrowth, flexible osteotomes may be used to remove the bone, allowing further stem retraction. The physician removes cement from the border of the implant with chisels and gouges. The physician removes the acetabular components with instruments. Any remaining loose cement is removed with a large curette or other instrument. A spacer of methylmethacrylate formed into a cube shape may be inserted into the space between the femur and tibia. The spacer prevents the soft tissues from compressing the joint space. The spacer is secured until another prosthesis is inserted. Drains may be placed. The wound may be left open for healing or the incision is repaired in layers.

27093-27095
The physician may apply skin traction to increase the space between the femoral head and acetabulum. Using a fluoroscope, the physician places a metallic marker over the femoral neck. The point is marked on the skin with ink. The femoral artery is palpated and marked on the skin as well, avoiding inadvertent puncture. The physician inserts a needle (1 1/2" for children, 3 1/2" for adults) and passes it into the capsule (located by fluoroscope). The synovial fluid is aspirated for a culture check. After aspiration, a contrast agent is injected into the hip joint and the needle is removed. X-rays are taken with the hip in neutral, external, and internal rotation for children and adults. The frog leg position is also taken for children. A second set of x-rays may be taken following the hip movements. The procedure is performed without anesthesia in 27093 and with anesthesia in 27095.

27096
The physician injects the sacroiliac joint, the articulation between the sacrum and ilium in the pelvis. The physician draws contrast, an anesthetic and/or steroid into a syringe. Through a posterior approach a needle (syringe attached) is inserted into the sacroiliac joint. The physician pushes on the syringe to deliver its content into the joint. The needle is withdrawn. CT or fluoroscopic guidance is used to guide the sacroiliac injection.

27097
The hamstring tendon is a fibrous connective tissue extension that attaches the (hamstrings) muscles to bone. The hamstrings include the semitendinous, semimembranous, and biceps femoris; they flex and extend the thigh. The hamstrings origins are in the ischium or femur and the insertions are in the tibia and fibula. The physician makes an incision overlying the hamstring origin. Muscle and fascia is exposed. The physician makes multiple cuts in muscle fascia. The incision is repaired in layers.

27098
The patient is placed in the lithotomy position with the buttocks at the end of the operating table, and the legs in pelvic stirrups. The physician makes an incision starting just superior to the adductor longus tendon, and extending posteriorly in a straight line to the ischial tuberosity. The adductor longus tendon is severed from its origin on the pubic ramus. Next, the physician releases by incision the origins of the pubic adductor brevis, gracilis, and adductor magnus tendons. The physician grasps the freed ends of the tendons with a clamp, holding them along the side of the ischial tuberosity. The ends of the tendons are

Musculoskeletal

sutured to the tuberosity with nonabsorbable sutures. The incision is repaired in layers. A spica cast may also be applied for three weeks.

27100
The physician performs a muscle transfer, substituting the external oblique muscle for a paralyzed abductor of the hip. An incision is made starting at the pubic tubercle and extending along the crest of the ilium to its mid-point. Two incisions are made in the aponeurosis of the external oblique, freeing it from its medial and lateral origins. An aponeurosis connects a muscle with the parts it moves. The cut edges of the external oblique are folded under and sutured together to form a cone-shaped structure. The physician makes a 6 cm lateral incision over the greater trochanter. Two holes are drilled through the greater trochanter, 1 cm in diameter. A subcutaneous tunnel is made extending proximally across the ilium. The cone-shaped external oblique muscle is passed distally through the tunnel. While the hip is held in wide abduction, the end of the muscle (which serves as a tendon) is passed through the holes in the trochanter, and sutured firmly to itself. When desired, a strong tensor fascia latae tendon may be transferred posteriorly on the iliac crest as well. The incision is repaired in layers. A spica cast is applied for four weeks.

27105
The physician makes an incision overlying the paraspinal muscle. The muscle is detached from its insertion point. The muscle is transferred and reattached to the hip. The incision is repaired in layers with sutures.

27110
The physician performs a transfer of the iliopsoas for weakened or paralyzed gluteus minimus and medius muscles. An incision is made along the anterior two-thirds of the iliac crest and extending distally along the inner border of the sartorius muscle to the middle of the thigh. Dissection is carried down to the deep fascia. The iliac crest is exposed. If there is a hip flexion contracture, the physician may release both of these at the same time by incision. Next, the femoral nerve is identified and moved from the surgical area. The abdominal muscles are detached from the anterior two-thirds of the iliac crest. The lesser trochanter is identified and detached from the femur along with the insertion portion of the iliopsoas tendon. Using blunt and sharp dissection, the iliacus muscle is detached from the pelvis. The physician makes an oval hole through the iliac wing and passes the iliopsoas tendon and the iliacus muscle through the hole. The greater trochanter is exposed through dissection. Using an awl and burr, a hole is made through the greater trochanter, through which the iliopsoas tendon is passed. Several strong sutures are used to anchor the tendon securely to the greater trochanter. The iliacus muscle is sutured to the ilium, and the abdominal muscles to the iliac crest. The incision is repaired in layers. A spica cast is applied for three to four weeks, holding the hip in full abduction, extension, and neutral rotation.

27111
The physician makes an incision beginning lateral and posterior to the anterosuperior iliac spine. The incision extends anteriorly and distally, crossing the tensor fascia latae. The periosteum along the crest of the ilium is incised, reflecting the tensor fascia latae and gluteal muscles. The physician also reflects the attachment of the abdominal muscles until the iliacus is exposed. The anterosuperior iliac spine is resected along with the origin of the sartorius muscle. This muscle is reflected distally. The physician identifies the femoral nerve and vessels. The nerve and vessels are retracted to identify the apex of the lesser trochanter. The physician uses an osteotome to divide or separate the trochanter. The tensor fascia latae is divided halfway between its origin and insertion, so that a trough can be cut in the wing of the ilium. The physician will lay the iliopsoas in the trough. The iliopsoas is transferred laterally, determining its position on the femur. The thigh is held in full abduction during the transfer so that the iliopsoas has powerful tension. A small window is cut on the femur at this site, and the lesser trochanter is anchored to it. The vastus lateralis is sutured to the edge of the iliopsoas tendon and the iliacus muscle to the psoas. The tensor fascia latae is repaired and the anterosuperior spine is anchored back to the ilium. The incision is repaired in layers. A spica cast is applied with the hip in internal rotation, slight flexion, and full abduction for four weeks.

27120
Acetabuloplasty redirects the inclination of the acetabular roof by an osteotomy of the ilium. The Pemberton acetabuloplasty is described as follows: The patient is placed in a supine position. Using an anterior iliofemoral approach, the physician carries dissection down to expose the hip joint capsule and sciatic notch. The capsule is incised. Using a curved osteotome, a bone cut is made through the lateral cortex of the ilium. Another cut is made through the medial cortex of the ilium. After completing the osteotomy, a wide, curved osteotome is inserted into the front part of the osteotomy and used to lever the distal fragment distally, until the front edges are 2.5 cm to 3 cm apart. A wedge of bone is removed from the iliac crest and placed in the osteotomy made earlier in the ilium. The wedge is driven firmly into place. If necessary, the graft may be secured with pins. The hip is repositioned and the capsule is tightened with sutures. The incision is repaired in layers. A spica cast is applied from the nipple line to the toes on the affected side and to above the knee on the opposite side. The cast is worn for approximately three months.

27122

The physician incises the hip joint capsule to expose the femoral head, neck, and acetabular rim. These components are removed. The physician uses a curette to remove any remaining necrotic or infected bone. The physician drains any intrapelvic abscesses. Drains are inserted. The incision is repaired in layers with sutures, staples, and/or Steri-strips. The hip is immobilized in a cast or with traction.

27125

The physician makes a posterolateral incision over the hip with the patient in a lateral decubitus position. The fascia lata is incised and the muscles around the hip joint are retracted to visualize the capsule. The physician incises the capsule, exposing the femoral neck. The femoral neck is removed with a reciprocating saw. The excised femoral head is measured with a caliper to determine the appropriate size for replacement. The physician prepares the femoral by enlarging the canal with a rasp. The stem is secured into the femoral shaft. The stem is inserted and pounded into place with an impactor. The physician repositions the femoral stem prosthesis. Hip motion and stability are evaluated. The capsule is closed and the incision repaired in layers.

27130

The physician makes an incision along the posterior aspect of the hip with the patient in a lateral decubitus position. The short external rotator muscles are released by incision from their insertion on the femur, exposing the joint capsule. The physician incises the capsule. The hip is dislocated posteriorly. The physician removes the femoral head with a reciprocating saw. The physician removes any osteophytes around the rim of the acetabulum with an osteotome. The acetabulum is reamed out with a power reamer, exposing both subchondral and cancellous bone. The acetabular component is inserted. The femoral canal is prepared using a hand or power reamer. The physician prepares the femoral shaft by enlarging the canal with a rasp. The stem is secured into the femoral shaft. The stem is inserted and pounded into place with an impactor. The physician repositions the femoral stem prosthesis. The physician may augment the area with an autograft or allograft. The graft may be donor bone or harvested from the removed femoral head. The physician places the bone graft into the canal and/or acetabulum. The hip is repositioned. The external rotator muscles are reattached. The incision is repaired in layers with suction drains.

27132

The physician performs a conversion of a previous hip surgery to total hip replacement. Total hip replacement is replacement of both the femoral head and acetabulum. The physician may access the area through the previous hip surgery incision, extending it to allow adequate exposure of the hip joint. Muscles are reflected as well. The physician removes any hardware (internal fixation). The physician incises the capsule. The hip is dislocated. The physician removes the femoral head with a reciprocating saw. Next, the acetabulum is prepared. The physician removes any osteophytes around the rim of the acetabulum with an osteotome. The acetabulum is reamed out with a power reamer, exposing both subchondral and cancellous bone. The acetabular component is inserted. The femoral canal is prepared using a hand or power reamer. The excised femoral head is measured with a caliper to determine the appropriate size for replacement. The physician prepares the femoral shaft by enlarging the canal with a rasp. The physician selects the type of stem to be used. The stem is secured into the femoral shaft. The stem is inserted and pounded into place with an impactor. The physician reduces the femoral stem prosthesis. The physician may augment the area with an autograft or allograft. The graft may be harvested from the resected femoral head (autograft). Donor bone (allograft) may be used instead. The hip is reduced. Any reflected muscles are reattached. The incision is repaired in layers with suction drains.

27134

The physician revises a total hip arthroplasty. With the patient in a lateral decubitus position, the physician may access the hip through the previous hip surgery incision. Muscles are reflected. A trochanteric osteotomy may be performed with an oscillating saw. The physician incises the hip joint capsule. Any scar tissue is removed. The physician manually dislocates the hip. Cement is removed from the upper portion of the femoral stem with a motorized or hand instrument. The stem may be removed. If the stem has fractured, the physician may drill a hole in the femoral shaft so that an instrument may remove the broken portion. The physician removes scar tissue and cement from around the acetabular component with chisels and gouges. The acetabular component is removed from its bed. The physician reconstructs the acetabulum with cement or screws and bone graft. The new femoral stem is inserted into the femoral shaft. The physician may augment the area with an autograft or allograft. The physician reduces the hip and closes the capsule. The greater trochanter is wired into place. Suction drains may be placed in the wound. The incision is repaired in layers with sutures, staples, and/or Steri-strips.

27137

The physician revises a total hip arthroplasty. With the patient in a lateral decubitus position, the physician accesses the acetabular component through a previous hip surgery incision. Muscles are reflected. The physician may perform an osteotomy of the greater trochanter with an oscillating saw. The capsule is incised and the hip manually dislocated. Any scar

Musculoskeletal

tissue is removed from around the acetabulum. The physician removes cement from around the acetabular component with chisels and gouges. The acetabulum is levered out from its bed. The acetabulum may need to be reamed out in preparation for the new component. The physician reconstructs the acetabulum with or without cement. If the acetabulum is reconstructed without cement, the component is usually inserted and fixed with screws. Prior to the acetabulum placement, the physician may harvest a bone graft from the patient's iliac crest and close the surgically created graft donor site. Donor bone (allograft) may be used instead. If cement is used, it secures the new component in the acetabular bed. Once the cement has dried, the hip is reduced and the capsule closed. The physician may place suction drains in the wound. The incision is repaired in layers with sutures, staples, and/or Steri-strips.

27138
With the patient in a lateral decubitus position, the physician may access the femoral component through the previous hip surgery incision. Muscles are reflected. The physician may perform an osteotomy of the greater trochanter. The hip joint capsule is exposed and incised. The physician dislocates the hip joint. If cement was used on the previous arthroplasty, the physician uses a motorized or hand instrument to remove it from around the upper portion of the femoral stem. If loose enough, the stem is removed with forceful blows. If the stem cannot be removed, additional cement may need to be removed from the femoral shaft, so the stem can be extracted. The physician may place cement in the femoral shaft and insert the new femoral component. If the revision is cementless, donor bone (allograft) may be inserted as needed into the femoral shaft between the cortex and femoral component. The hip is reduced. The physician reattaches the greater trochanter with wires. The incision is repaired in layers with sutures, staples, and/or Steri-strips.

27140
The physician makes a longitudinal incision over the greater trochanter with the patient in a lateral decubitus position. The physician detaches the greater trochanter with a Gigli saw or osteotome. The physician may reposition the trochanter more lateral, or more distal and lateral. Repositioning increases the abductor lever arm and/or tightens the abductor musculature. The physician drills holes to secure the trochanter to the femur with wire. The incision is repaired in layers.

27146
For a Salter innominate osteotomy, the patient is placed supine. The adductor muscles are released by a subcutaneous tenotomy. The physician makes a small incision approximately 0.5 inch long over the origin of the adductor muscles. Dissection is carried down to the adductor tendon. The physician uses a small blade to release (free by incision) the tendon. The physician makes an incision from the middle of the iliac crest to the inguinal area. The rectus femoris is released from its attachment by incision. The physician exposes and incises the joint capsule. If the ligamentous teres is hypertrophied, it is excised. If the femoral head remains unstable, an osteotomy of the innominate bone is performed. The hip is allowed to dislocate. The physician makes an osteotomy cut on the innominate bone using a Gigli saw. The osteotomy extends from the sciatic notch to the anteroinferior spine. The physician may harvest a separately reportable full thickness bone graft from the anterior part of the iliac crest and close the surgically created graft donor site. The graft is trimmed to the shape of the wedge and inserted into the osteotomy. A Kirschner wire is drilled through the ilium, bone graft, and into the lower fragment. Another wire is placed parallel to the first. Joint stability is reevaluated. Any released muscles are reattached. The capsule is closed with sutures, giving added stability to the reduction. The incision is repaired in layers. A single spica cast is applied.

27147
For a Salter innominate osteotomy, the patient is placed supine. The adductor muscles are released by a subcutaneous tenotomy. The physician makes a small incision approximately 0.5 inch long over the origin of the adductor muscles. Dissection is carried down to the adductor tendon. The physician uses a small blade to release the tendon. The physician makes an incision from the middle of the iliac crest to the inguinal area. The rectus femoris is released from its attachment by incision. The physician exposes and incises the joint capsule. If the ligamentous teres is hypertrophied, it is excised. The physician reduces the femoral head into the acetabulum. If the femoral head remains unstable, an osteotomy of the innominate bone is performed. The hip is allowed to dislocate. The physician makes an osteotomy cut on the innominate bone using a Gigli saw. The osteotomy extends from the sciatic notch to the anteroinferior spine. The physician may harvest a separately reportable full thickness bone graft from the anterior part of the iliac crest and close the surgically created graft donor site. The graft is trimmed to the shape of the wedge and inserted into the osteotomy. A Kirschner wire is drilled through the ilium, bone graft, and into the lower fragment. Another wire is placed parallel to the first. The femoral head is reduced again into the acetabulum. Any released muscles are reattached. The capsule is closed with sutures, giving added stability to the reduction. The incision is repaired in layers. A single spica cast is applied for eight to 10 weeks.

27151-27156
The patient is placed in a supine position. The physician makes an incision from the middle of the iliac crest to the inguinal area. The rectus femoris is

released from its attachment by incision. The physician exposes and incises the joint capsule. If the ligamentous teres is hypertrophied, it is excised. The physician reduces the femoral head into the acetabulum. If the femoral head remains unstable, an osteotomy of the innominate bone is performed. The hip is allowed to dislocate. The physician makes an osteotomy cut on the innominate bone using a Gigli saw. The osteotomy extends from the sciatic notch to the anteroinferior spine. The physician harvests a separately reportable full thickness bone graft from the anterior part of the iliac crest and closes the surgically created graft donor site. The graft is trimmed to the shape of the wedge and inserted into the osteotomy. A Kirschner wire is drilled through the ilium, bone graft, and into the lower fragment. Another wire is placed parallel to the first. For femoral osteotomy, a lateral incision is made from the greater trochanter, extending down the leg 8 cm to 12 cm. Dissection exposes the lateral femur. Transverse and longitudinal orientation lines are made on the femoral cortex with an osteotome. The physician makes an osteotomy cut at the transverse line in a transverse or oblique direction. Another cut is made at an angle so that a wedge of bone can be removed to complete the correction. The rectus femoris is reattached to its insertion point. In 27156, the hip is reduced as well. A side plate is secured to the femur with bone screws. The incision is repaired in layers. A one and one-half spica cast is applied for eight to 12 weeks.

27158

The patient is placed in a supine position. The physician releases the adductor muscles by subcutaneous tenotomy. The physician makes a small incision over the origin of the adductor muscles. Dissection is carried down to the adductor tendon. The physician uses a small blade to release (free by incision) the tendon. The physician makes an incision from the middle of the iliac crest to the middle of the inguinal ligament. The head of the rectus femoris muscle is released. Dissection exposes the hip joint capsule, which is incised in a T-shaped fashion. The periosteum is stripped from the medial surface of the ilium to the sciatic notch. The ilium is divided or cut with a Gigli saw in a straight line from the sciatic notch to the anteroinferior spine. A full-thickness bone graft is removed from the iliac crest and trimmed to the shape of a wedge. The physician closes the surgically created graft donor site. This allows the acetabulum together with the pubis and ischium to be rotated as a unit. The bone graft is inserted into the osteotomy. Two Kirschner wires are drilled parallel to each other through the ilium and bone graft for fixation. The femoral head is reduced into the acetabulum. The capsule is repaired and tightened with sutures to add stability to the joint. The incision is repaired in layers. The same procedure is performed on the other side. Both hips are placed in spica casts.

27161

With the patient in a lateral position, the physician makes an incision extending from the anterosuperior iliac spine, over and to a point 10 cm below the greater trochanter. The fascia lata and gluteal muscles are divided or separated. Dissection exposes the hip joint. The physician incises the capsule. The physician makes two osteotomy cuts in the femoral neck. The size of the osteotomies is determined by separately reportable x-ray prior to surgery. A Steinmann pin may be drilled into the femoral neck before the osteotomy is completed to control the position of the proximal femur. The cut wedge of bone is removed. The physician inserts several 5 mm Steinmann pins through the femoral neck and across the osteotomy site and epiphyseal plate to prevent further slipping. The capsule is closed. The incision is repaired in layers.

27165

The physician exposes the lateral aspect of the proximal femur by making a lateral longitudinal incision. The femur is divided or separated with an osteotome at a level slightly above the lesser trochanter. The physician places the extremity in the corrected position. A rigid internal fixation device, such as a plate and screws, may stabilize the area. External fixation may be applied instead. The incision is repaired in layers with sutures, staples, and/or Steri-strips. A spica cast is applied for eight to 12 weeks.

27170

The physician makes an incision over the affected area. The physician harvests bone from the patient's iliac crest and closes the surgically created graft donor site. Bone chips are packed around the non-union fracture site. An allograft (donor bone) may be used instead. The nonunion site may be stabilized with internal fixation. The incisions are repaired in layers with sutures, staples, and/or Steri-strips.

27175-27176

Separately reportable x-rays are taken to determine the position of the slipped femoral epiphysis. The physician may apply skin traction in 27175 with the limb in internal rotation for three to four days. Gradual improvement is accomplished without reduction. In 27176, the physician makes a small stab incision. Use of a fluoroscope determines the correct site for inserting pins through the lateral femoral cortex, femoral neck, and into the epiphysis to stabilize the slip. The small stab incision is closed with sutures. The patient is placed on crutches for four to six weeks.

27177

The physician makes an anterior iliofemoral incision with the patient in a supine position. Dissection exposes the capsule of the hip. The physician incises the capsule, retracting it to expose the femoral neck and epiphysis. A square window is made in the anterior surface of the femoral neck. Under separately reportable x-ray, the physician inserts a hollow mill through the window and drills across the epiphyseal plate and into the epiphysis. The tunnel is enlarged with a curette. The physician makes a separate incision over the ilium and removes sections of bone from the outer surface of the ilium. The bone sections are sandwiched together, placed in the tunnel, and driven across the epiphyseal plate into the epiphysis. If the physician uses single or multiple pinning rather than a bone graft, an incision is made overlying the greater trochanter and upper femur. The physician exposes the intertrochanteric area. Under separately reportable x-ray, the physician inserts a guide pin through the femur, femoral neck, and into the femoral head. One or two pins are inserted parallel to the guide pin. The guide pin is removed and the incision repaired in layers. The physician may place the limb in skin traction.

27178
The physician treats a slipped femoral epiphysis by manipulating the area. Following manipulation by the physician, the reduction is confirmed with separately reportable x-ray. The epiphysis is secured with Knowles pins or cannulated hip screws. An incision is made overlying the greater trochanter and upper femur. The physician exposes the intertrochanteric area. Under separately reportable x-ray, the physician inserts a guide pin through the femur, femoral neck, and into the femoral head. One or two 3/16 inch Knowles pins are inserted parallel to the guide pin. The guide pin is removed and the incision repaired in layers. The physician may place the limb in skin traction.

27179
With the patient in a supine position, the physician makes an anterior iliofemoral incision. Dissection exposes the capsule, which is incised and retracted. Retraction of the capsule exposes the femoral neck and the slipped epiphysis. To correct the deformity, the physician resects a wedge of bone from the anterosuperior aspect of the femoral neck with an osteotome. A single Knowles pin is drilled into the epiphysis. The physician uses the pin to rotate the epiphysis into its normal position and to hold it into place as well. The edges of the osteotomy are brought together. The physician makes a short, lateral skin incision just below the greater trochanter. Under separately reportable x-ray, the physician inserts three Knowles pins through the incision, the trochanter, and into the neck and epiphysis. The single Knowles pin is removed from the epiphysis and the incision repaired in layers. If fixation is secure, the limb may be placed in balanced suspension. Otherwise, a cast is applied from the nipple line to the toes on the affected side.

27181
With the patient in a supine position, the physician makes an anterior iliofemoral incision. Dissection is carried down to the hip joint capsule. The capsule is incised and retracted, exposing the femoral neck and epiphysis. A single Knowles pin is drilled into the epiphysis to control its position later. The physician resects a wedge of bone (osteotomy) from the anterosuperior part of the femoral neck. The physician fractures the posterior cortex of the femoral neck. The Knowles pin is used to rotate the epiphysis into its normal position in the acetabulum. The physician rotates the thigh internally to oppose the osteotomy surfaces. A short, lateral skin incision is made just below the greater trochanter. Under separately reportable x-ray, the physician inserts three Knowles pins through the incision, the trochanter, and into the femoral neck and epiphysis. The single Knowles pin is removed and the incision repaired in layers. Depending on how secure the fixation is, the physician may place the extremity in a balanced suspension or apply a cast from the nipple line to the toes on the affected side.

27185
Epiphyseal arrest is performed to arrest or stop growth of the greater trochanter growth plate. The patient is placed in a side-lying position. The physician makes a straight incision over the greater trochanter. Dissection exposes the area. The physician uses a curette to scrape out the growth plate. Screw(s) or staples are placed through the greater trochanter, across the growth plate, and into the femur. The incision is repaired in layers.

27187
The patient is placed supine or in a side-lying position, depending on the area for treatment. The physician may make tiny incisions to insert pins under roentgenographic control. The physician may need to perform an open procedure. In an open procedure an incision is made and dissection carried down to the femoral neck or proximal femur. The internal fixation (nailing, plating with screws, or cerclage with wires wrapped around the femur) is applied. The physician may use cement (methylmethacrylate) as needed to secure the fixation or strengthen the bone. The incision is repaired in layers.

27193
The physician treats a pelvic ring fracture or dislocation. The displacement or dislocation is less than 1 cm. No manipulation is required. Treatment typically is bed rest and crutches.

27194
The physician performs manual manipulation to reduce the fracture, dislocation, or subluxation of the pelvic ring. Vigorous manipulation may be necessary. The patient may require greater sedation. Anesthesia is required for placement of skeletal traction through the distal femur or proximal tibia. Separately reportable x-rays may be used to verify position of the reduced fracture, dislocation, or subluxation.

27200

For closed treatment of a coccygeal fracture, the physician will prescribe bed rest to alleviate symptoms. Sitting on a rubber ring may also lessen symptoms. Closed manual manipulation may be performed as well.

27202

The patient is positioned prone. The physician makes a vertical incision in the gluteal fold. Dissection is carried down to the coccyx. The fractured portion is removed or internal fixation is applied. The incision is repaired in layers.

27215

The physician performs open treatment of iliac spine(s), tuberosity avulsion, or iliac wing fracture(s) by making an incision overlying the site of injury. Dissection exposes the avulsion and/or fracture. For an avulsion, a screw(s) is drilled through the bone fragment, reattaching the tendon and bone fragment to the original positions. The physician stabilizes an iliac wing fracture with a plate and screws across the fracture. The incision is repaired in layers. Suction drains may be applied. This code reports unilateral treatment for fracture patterns of the pelvic bone that do not disrupt the pelvic ring and includes internal fixation when performed.

27216

The physician performs unilateral percutaneous skeletal fixation of a posterior pelvic bone fracture (including ipsilateral ilium, sacroiliac joint, and/or sacrum) for fracture patterns that disrupt the pelvic ring. With the patient in a supine position, the physician inserts two to three pins through the skin and into the iliac crest. The pins are directed at specific angles. The physician attaches pin holders to each ring and curved ring segments to pin holders. The physician uses the rings to gently reduce (reposition) an unstable pelvic fracture or dislocation, if needed. Frame clamps are attached to the rings and tightened to secure fixation. The frame is left in place for approximately eight to 12 weeks.

27217

The physician performs unilateral open treatment of an anterior pelvic bone fracture or dislocation (includes the pubic symphysis and/or ipsilateral superior/inferior rami). With the patient in a supine position, the physician makes a curvilinear, transverse incision above the superior pubic ramus. Dissection exposes the pubic symphysis and/or rami. The separation (fracture and/or dislocation) may be reduced by the physician by applying manual ilium-to-ilium compression. For internal fixation, a plate is applied with screws directed into the bone. The incision is repaired in layers with suction drains. This code is reported for fracture patterns that disrupt the pelvic ring and includes internal fixation when performed.

27218

The physician performs unilateral open treatment of a posterior pelvic bone fracture or dislocation (includes ipsilateral ilium, sacroiliac joint, and/or sacrum). With the patient in a supine position, the physician makes an incision along the anterior iliac crest. The iliacus muscle is dissected and reflected medially with the abdominal contents to expose the injury. If needed, the physician manipulates the pelvis and leg to reduce (reposition) the fracture or dislocation. Compression plates and screws achieve internal fixation. In other approaches, reconstruction plates, transiliac rod fixators, or screws alone may be used for internal fixation of the ilium, sacroiliac joint, and/or sacrum. The incision is repaired in layers with suction drains. This code reports treatment for fracture patterns that disrupt the pelvic ring and include internal fixation when performed.

27220-27222

Closed treatment of an acetabulum fracture may be indicated when a fracture is non-displaced, bone is osteoporotic, or when only a minor portion of the acetabulum is involved. The patient may be placed in skin (Bucks) traction for eight to 12 weeks. The physician performs closed reduction (repositioning) with manipulation in 27222. General anesthesia is usually required. The physician may apply skeletal traction, placing a Kirschner wire or Steinmann pin through the tibia by the tibial tuberosity. Weight is attached to provide a traction force. While traction force is applied along the axis of the leg, a lateral traction force is applied to the proximal thigh. The physician manipulates the leg through abduction and internal rotation, and adduction. Typically, skeletal traction is continued for eight to 12 weeks.

27226

For a posterior wall fracture, the patient is placed in a lateral position. The incision extends from the greater trochanter to within 6 cm of the posterosuperior iliac spine. For an anterior wall fracture, the physician approaches the fracture through the ilioinguinal area. The patient is positioned supine. The physician makes an incision just above the symphysis pubis and extends it laterally to the iliac crest. For an anterior wall fracture, skeletal traction may be applied during the procedure. In both cases, extensive dissection of muscles and fascia is required to expose the fracture site. The joint is debrided of any free fragments. The fractured fragments are reduced. For a posterior wall fracture, internal fixation is achieved by using screws and a plate across the posterior wall to buttress the fragments. For an anterior wall fracture, internal fixation is usually achieved with the use of a two screw technique. The incision is repaired in layers using sutures, staples, and/or Steri-strips. Closed suction drainage is used.

27227
A transverse fracture involves both the anterior column and posterior column of the acetabulum. For transverse fractures, an approach as for a posterior wall fracture (see 27226) can often be used. If the fracture is more complex, different approaches may be used, providing exposure to both the anterior and posterior columns without making two separate incisions. Internal fixation is accomplished using screws and plate(s) techniques (see 27226). The incision is repaired in layers using sutures, staples, and/or Steri-strips. Closed suction drainage is used.

27228
The patient is placed supine. The physician makes an incision beginning at the upper portion of the symphysis pubis, extending upwards along the iliac crest, and ending at its most superior aspect. The origins of the abdominal muscles and iliacus are elevated from the iliac crest. Dissection is carried down through the inguinal canal, protecting vessels and nerves. The physician treats the anterior column fracture first by reducing the fragments and securing fixation with lag screws. The physician uses pointed reduction forceps to reduce (reposition) the fracture. The fracture is stabilized with a combination of lag screw and plate fixation. There may be an associated T-fracture which has a transverse pattern with a vertical split extending through the obturator ring. For a T-fracture, the physician makes a posterior incision with the patient in a prone (face down) position. At times, the two column fracture and T-fracture can be treated from a posterior approach. An anterior approach may be necessary, in which the patient is turned from prone to supine. All incisions are repaired in layers. Postoperative immobilization or traction is only necessary if satisfactory reduction and fixation are not achieved.

27230-27232
The physician treats a non-displaced, stable fracture of the femur. No manual manipulation is necessary in 27230. Manipulation is required in 27232 to treat a displaced fracture. The physician manually flexes the hip while applying manual traction force and internally rotating and abducting the hip. The patient may be placed in a supine position and Buck's (skin) traction applied. A splint may be applied to stabilize the fracture for three to six weeks. Skeletal traction may be necessary as well. A Steinmann pin or Kirschner wire is inserted through the tibia near the tibial tuberosity. A weight is attached. Traction may be continued for approximately six weeks.

27235
The physician performs percutaneous skeletal fixation of the proximal end of a femoral neck fracture. The physician makes a small stab incision (1 cm to 2 cm) overlying the lateral aspect of the thigh and just below the greater trochanter. A pin is drilled at approximately a 45 degree angle through the cortex and neck and into the femoral head. Two to five additional pins are inserted parallel to the first pin. Final x-rays are taken to confirm positions. The physician may close the stab incision made for each pin with a single suture.

27236
The physician directly exposes the femoral fracture for treatment. The patient is placed in a supine position or slightly rolled up onto the other side. A 15 cm incision is made over the lateral hip. The fascia lata is split and the vastus lateralis muscle is detached from the femur. The physician exposes the femoral neck and head. A small periosteal elevator or Kirschner wire is used to reduce (reposition) the fracture. The physician places guide pins through the bone and across the fracture. The guide pins help determine correct screw length. The physician may use cannulated screws or compression hip screws and a plate to achieve internal fixation. In some cases due to the risk of subsequent non-union or avascular necrosis, the physician may replace the femoral head with a femoral prosthesis. The femoral canal is reamed out. A prosthesis of the proper size and length is selected and inserted into the femoral canal. The physician reduces the prosthesis into the acetabulum. The incision is repaired in layers with sutures, staples, and/or Steri-strips.

27238-27240
For a non-displaced, stable fracture in 27238, the physician applies a spica cast or brace. Manual manipulation is necessary to align fragments in 27240. The physician applies skeletal traction using a tibial pin. A Steinmann pin is inserted transversely across the upper tibia. With the thigh supported in slings, weight is applied to create the traction force. Traction remains in place for approximately 12 weeks, after which a spica cast may be applied. If skeletal traction is not necessary, a form of Russell's skin traction is placed on the lower leg. This type of traction is a foam boot with an attached weight providing the traction force.

27244
The physician makes an incision over the upper lateral thigh, exposing the fracture area through tissue dissection. The patient is in a lateral decubitus (lying on the side) position or may be placed in traction on a table. The fracture is reduced. Placement of an interfragmentary screw may achieve initial stability. A plate is inserted and screws stabilize the fragments. If additional fixation is needed, the physician may apply cerclage wiring, placing a wire around the fractured bones. The incision is repaired in layers with sutures, staples, and/or Steri-strips.

27245
The patient is placed in a supine position, or slightly rolled up onto the opposite side. The physician makes an incision over the posterolateral aspect of the hip. The fascia lata is divided or separated. The vastus lateralis muscle is detached from its origin site. The

physician will place the intramedullary nail into the canal medial to the tip of the greater trochanter. Both the proximal and distal canals are reamed in preparation for placement of the intramedullary nail. The physician reduces the fracture with bone-holding forceps or cerclage wires (wires wrapped around the fragments), or both. The intramedullary nail, is placed through the proximal fragment, into the canal, and driven into the shaft of the femur. The physician inserts a nail or screw into the femoral head by drilling a tunnel from the lateral cortex, passing through a hole in the intramedullary nail, and into the femoral head. The triflange nail is driven through the tunnel, through the hole in the intramedullary nail and into the femoral head. The physician may elect to place cerclage wires for added stability. The vastus lateralis muscle is reattached and the fascia lata repaired as well. The incision is repaired in layers with sutures, staples, and/or Steri-strips.

27246-27248
In 27246, the physician treats a greater trochanteric fracture without manipulation. The fracture is not displaced and may be treated with skin traction while in wide abduction. Other treatments include a spica cast applied for six weeks or protected weight bearing with crutches for four to six weeks. In 27248, the fracture may be displaced and may require internal fixation. The physician makes a straight, lateral skin incision overlying the greater trochanter. Dissection is carried to visualize the fragment. The physician may apply bone screws, pegs, or wire loops to secure the fragment. The incision is repaired in layers with sutures, staples, and/or Steri-strips. Toe touch weight bearing with crutches is allowed for three to four weeks, followed by partial weight bearing for another three to four weeks.

27250-27252
The physician treats a hip dislocation without anesthesia in 27250 or with anesthesia in 27252. Two types of closed reduction techniques are used depending on the type of dislocation: the Stimson maneuver and the Allis maneuver. General or spinal anesthesia is applied. The Stimson maneuver is a procedure for posterior dislocations. The patient is positioned prone (face down) with the lower limbs hanging from the end of the table. Stabilizing pressure is placed on the sacrum. The physician holds the knee and ankle flexed to ninety degrees and applies gentle downward pressure to the leg, just below the knee. The Allis maneuver is a procedure for anterior dislocations. The patient is positioned supine. The pelvis is stabilized and lateral traction force is applied to the inside of the thigh. The physician applies longitudinal traction in line with the axis of the femur, and gently abducts and internally rotates the femur to achieve reduction. Other techniques similar to those described above may also be used. After reduction, light skin traction may be applied.

27253
The physician performs open treatment of a hip dislocation. The physician makes an incision along the posterior aspect of the hip. The gluteus maximus muscle is split. The physician exposes the hip joint, allowing manual reduction of the dislocated hip. Reduction is accomplished without traumatizing the articular cartilage. The incision is repaired in layers with sutures, staples, and/or Steri-strips.

27254
The physician treats a traumatic hip dislocation. The physician makes an incision along the posterior aspect of the hip. The gluteus maximus muscle is split and the hip joint exposed. Fractures of the acetabulum and femoral head are visualized. If the fractures remain stable and the joint surface congruent when reduced, no internal fixation is required. If the fractures are not stable after reduction of the dislocation, internal fixation is applied. Cancellous bone screws or Kirschner wires may stabilize the fractures. The incision is repaired in layers with sutures, staples, and/or Steri-strips. The limb may be placed in skeletal or skin traction following the reduction. External fixation is applied if there is significant soft tissue trauma around the hip.

27256-27257
The physician treats a spontaneous hip dislocation. For an infant patient (age birth to six months) a Pavlik harness is applied. The harness is a dynamic flexion abduction orthosis. The harness consists of a chest strap, two shoulder straps, and two stirrups. The physician applies the harness with the child in a supine position. The harness holds the hip in 90 to 110 degrees of flexion, and moderate abduction. Skin traction may also be applied to infants of six to 18 months of age. A mechanical pulley is attached to the patient's leg with ace wraps securing the material to the skin. Weight is attached to the other end of the pulley to apply the traction force to the hip, allowing a gentle reduction of the hip dislocation. The hip is maintained in approximately 30 to 40 degrees of flexion. Traction time varies from two to six weeks. A splint or hip spica cast is applied to hold the hips in abduction. In an older patient, reduction may be possible by applying skin traction to the affected lower extremity. The procedure is performed without anesthesia in 27256 or with anesthesia in 27257.

27258
The physician performs open treatment of a spontaneous hip dislocation. The physician first performs an adductor tenotomy. The physician makes a small incision approximately 0.5 inch long over the origin of the adductor muscles. Dissection is carried down to the adductor tendon. The physician uses a small blade to release (free by incision) the tendon. The physician makes an incision from the middle of the iliac crest to a point midway between the

Musculoskeletal

anterosuperior iliac spine and the midline of the pelvis. Dissection exposes the capsule. The iliac epiphysis is detached from the ilium. The sartorius and rectus femoris tendons are divided or separated. The physician makes a T-shaped incision in the capsule. The entrance to the acetabulum is enlarged with sequential incisions in the labrum, which surrounds the acetabulum. This allows the femoral head to be reduced. Once the reduction is concentric and stable, the capsule is tightened and closed with sutures, stabilizing the hip joint. The rectus femoris and sartorius tendons are sutured to their origins. The iliac epiphysis is also reattached. The incision is repaired in layers. A double hip spica cast is applied with the hip in 90 degrees of flexion and 40 to 55 degrees of abduction.

27259
The physician first performs an adductor tenotomy (see 27000). The physician makes an incision from the middle of the iliac crest to a point midway between the anterosuperior iliac spine and the midline of the pelvis. Dissection exposes the capsule. The iliac epiphysis is detached from the ilium. The sartorius and rectus femoris tendons are separated. The physician makes a T-shaped incision in the capsule. The entrance to the acetabulum is enlarged with sequential incisions in the labrum which surrounds the acetabulum. This allows the femoral head to be reduced. Once the reduction is concentric and stable, the capsule is tightened and closed with sutures, stabilizing the hip joint. The rectus femoris and sartorius tendons are sutured to their origins. The iliac epiphysis is also reattached. Femoral shaft shortening is performed as well. The physician makes both an anterior ilioinguinal and a straight lateral incision from the tip of the greater trochanter to the distal third of the femoral shaft. Open reduction is performed through the ilioinguinal incision. The femoral shaft is exposed through the lateral incision. A lag screw is inserted into the femoral neck. Once the bone cut is made at the appropriate distance below the first cut and angled to allow varus and derotation of the femur, the cut segment is removed. A side plate with screws secures the two segments. The incisions are repaired in layers. A spica cast is applied with the extremity in neutral rotation and slight flexion and abduction.

27265-27266
The physician treats a post hip arthroplasty dislocation with manual manipulation. Distal manipulative traction is applied to the leg, reducing the dislocation. No anesthesia is necessary in 27265. Regional or general anesthesia is required in 27266.

27267-27268
The physician treats a closed fracture of the femoral head. No incision is made and the surgeon does not expose the bone. No manual manipulation is necessary in 27267. In 27268, manipulation, or manual correction of the bone to its correct anatomical position, is required. General anesthesia may be necessary and Buck's (skin) or other forms of traction may be utilized.

27269
The physician directly exposes the femoral head fracture for treatment. After determining the position and severity of the defect by x-ray, the physician incises the overlying skin and muscle to expose the hip joint. Fractures of the femoral head are visualized. If the fractures remain stable and the joint surface congruent when reduced, no internal fixation is required. If the fractures are not stable after reduction of the dislocation, internal fixation is applied. The incision is repaired in layers with sutures, staples, and/or Steri-strips. The limb may be placed in skeletal or skin traction.

27275
The patient is administered general anesthesia. If manipulation is performed to increase motion, the physician applies gradual pressure in the desired direction. The gradual pressure releases adhesions or scar tissue, increasing motion. Manipulation of the hip joint is a closed procedure, requiring no incision.

27280
The physician makes an incision along the posterior two-thirds of the iliac crest, continuing curved around the posterosuperior spine. The soft tissues are reflected to expose the ilium. A rectangular bone window is cut and removed from the ilium. The physician removes cartilage from the sacral surface of the joint, as well as from the joint surface of the block of bone. The physician replaces the block of bone and countersinks it so that its cancellous surface contacts the cancellous bone of the sacrum. The edges of the bone window are osteotomized and the fragments turned inward to secure the block and promote bone formation. The incision is repaired in layers using sutures. The physician may place the patient in a trunk and pelvic cast or brace.

27282
The physician makes an incision overlying the symphysis pubis. Dissection is carried down to the joint. Soft tissue between bone is excised. The physician may harvest a bone graft from the patient through a separate incision or from surrounding bone. The physician closes the surgically created graft donor site. Internal fixation is applied to the fusion with screws and/or plates. The incision is repaired in layers.

27284
To perform an intra-articular arthrodesis, the physician makes an anterior iliofemoral incision. The sartorius and rectus femoris muscles are detached from their origins. The iliopsoas is reflected from the front of the hip joint. The physician dislocates the hip anteriorly. Cartilage is removed from the femoral head and

acetabulum down to bleeding cancellous bone. The physician packs the space between the surfaces of the femoral head and acetabulum with cancellous autogenous bone grafts. An example of the position in which the hip may be fused is: 30 degrees of flexion, 0 to 5 degrees of adduction, and 10 degrees of external rotation. The physician may use compression screws to increase the stability of the fusion. The sartorius and rectus femoris muscles are reattached. The screws are placed through the femoral head and into the supra-acetabular area of the ilium. The incision is repaired in layers with suction drains. The limb may be placed in a single spica cast or in balanced suspension.

27286

To perform an intra-articular arthrodesis, the physician makes an anterior iliofemoral incision. The sartorius and rectus femoris muscles are detached from their origins. The iliopsoas is reflected from the front of the hip joint. The physician dislocates the hip anteriorly. Cartilage is removed from the femoral head and acetabulum down to bleeding cancellous bone. The physician packs the space between the surfaces of the femoral head and acetabulum with cancellous autogenous bone grafts. The physician harvests a bone graft from the patient's iliac wing and crest and closes the surgically created graft donor site. The graft is positioned so it spans the anterior aspect of the hip from the pubic ramus to the femoral neck. The graft is secured with cancellous lag screws. The arthrodesis is performed so that the hip is in 10 degrees of external rotation, 0 to 5 degrees of adduction, and 30 degrees of flexion. A subtrochanteric osteotomy (bone cut) is made just below the lesser trochanter. The sartorius and rectus femoris muscles are reattached and the iliopsoas muscle is repositioned. The incision is repaired in layers with suction drains. A one and one-half spica cast is applied.

27290

The patient is placed in a lateral (on the side) position with the operative side up. There are three parts to this procedure including, anterior, perineal, and posterior. Each part requires a separate incision for exposure, dissection, and development of skin flaps. The physician separates the nerves and ligates the vessels. Vessels are ligated anteriorly and posteriorly; the sciatic nerve is cut high and tied. The pelvic ring, extending from the symphysis pubis to the attachment of the ilium to the sacrum, is sectioned and removed. Some muscle is retained, such as the gluteus maximus part of the skin flaps. The flaps are closed with interrupted sutures over drains. The drains are removed in 48 to 72 hours.

27295

The physician makes an anterior racquet-shaped incision beginning at the anterosuperior iliac spine and curving distally and medially. The incision extends to a point on the medial aspect of the thigh, 5 cm below the origin of the adductor muscles. The femoral artery and vein are ligated. The femoral nerve is divided. The physician continues the incision around the posterior aspect of the thigh to 5 cm below the ischial tuberosity and laterally to the base of the greater trochanter. All muscles around the hip are detached. The physician detaches the gluteal muscles, reflecting the muscle mass proximally for later use as a flap. The sciatic nerve is ligated and separated. The physician incises the hip joint capsule and ligamentum teres to complete the disarticulation. The gluteal flap is brought around the wound and sutured. The physician places a drain in the inferior part of the incision. The edges of skin are closed with nonabsorbable sutures.

27301

The physician drains an abscess, a hematoma, or a bursa from deep within the thigh or knee region. The physician makes an incision in the thigh or knee overlying the site of the abscess, hematoma, or bursa to be incised. Dissection is carried through the deep subcutaneous tissues and may be continued into the fascia or muscle to expose the abscess, hematoma, or bursa. The incision may be extended if the mass is larger than expected. When the bursa, abscess, or hematoma is identified, it is incised and the contents are drained. The area is irrigated and the incision is repaired in layers with sutures, staples, and/or Steri-strips; closed with drains in place; or simply left open to further facilitate drainage of infection.

27303

The physician incises the bone cortex of infected bone in the femur or knee to treat an abscess or osteomyelitis. The physician makes an incision over the affected area. Dissection is carried through the soft tissues to expose the bone. The periosteum is split and reflected from the bone overlying the infected area. A curette may be used to scrape away the abscess or infected portion down to healthy bony tissue or drill holes may be made through the cortex into the medullary canal in a window outline around the infected or abscessed bone. The area is drained and debrided of infected bony and soft tissue. The physician irrigates the area with antibiotic solution, the periosteum is closed over the bone, and the soft tissues are sutured closed; or the wound is packed and left open, allowing the area to drain. Secondary closure is performed approximately three weeks later. Dressings are changed daily. A splint may be applied to limit knee movement.

27305

For release of the iliotibial band, the patient is placed in a lateral decubitus position. The physician exposes the iliotibial tract through a 4 cm lateral, longitudinal incision just above the femoral condyle. The physician incises the iliotibial tract, fascia lata, and intramuscular septum transversely 2.5 cm above the patella. In severe contractures, the physician may remove a segment of the iliotibial tract and septum. The incision is closed in layers with sutures, staples, and/or Steri-strips.

27306-27307
The physician performs a percutaneous tenotomy (cut) of the adductor or hamstring muscle. The physician palpates the tendon to be released. A small incision is made to access the tendon. The physician's thumb presses on the tendon to create tension. The physician uses an 11-blade to make a cut through the tendon, releasing it. More than one tendon is released in 27307. The incision is closed with sutures.

27310
The physician performs an arthrotomy on the knee that includes exploration, drainage, or removal of any foreign body. An incision is made over the knee. The soft tissues are dissected away and the joint capsule is exposed and incised. The patella may be moved laterally for better exposure. The compartments are explored, any necrotic tissue is removed, and infection or abnormal fluid is drained. If a foreign body is present (e.g., bullet, nail, gravel), it is exposed and removed. The wound is irrigated with antibiotic solution. The physician may leave the wound packed open temporarily to allow for drainage in the case of any purulent exudate. If the incision is repaired, drain tubes may be inserted and the incision is closed in layers with sutures, staples, and/or Steri-strips.

27323-27324
The physician performs a biopsy of the soft tissues of the thigh or knee area. With proper anesthesia administered, an incision is made over the biopsy area. Dissection is carried down within the superficial soft tissue layers in 27323, usually the subcutaneous fat to the uppermost fascial layer. In 27324, dissection is taken deep within the soft tissue, such as into the fascial layer or within the muscle. A portion of the tissue is excised and submitted for pathology. The area is irrigated and the incision is closed with layered sutures, staples, or Steri-strips.

27325
The physician performs an incisional resection of a segment of a nerve. The physician makes a transverse incision over the hamstring muscle. The fascia is divided to expose the nerves that supply the muscle. The appropriate nerve branch is identified by stimulating it with an electrical current or gently pressing it with forceps. Once this is accomplished, the nerve is divided and removed from the muscle, resolving the clonus or spasm. The incision is repaired in layers.

27326
The physician performs an incisional resection of a segment of a nerve. The physician makes a transverse incision over the distal portion of the popliteal (back of the knee) fossa. The fascia is divided to expose the tibial nerve. The appropriate nerve branch is identified by stimulating it with an electrical current or gently pressing it with forceps. Once this is accomplished, the nerve is divided and removed from the muscle, resolving the clonus or spasm. The incision is repaired in layers.

27327-27328, 27337-27339
The physician removes a tumor from the soft tissue of the thigh or knee area that is located in the subcutaneous tissue in 27327 and 27337 and in the deep soft tissue, below the fascial plane, or within the muscle in 27328 and 27339. With the proper anesthesia administered, the physician makes an incision in the skin overlying the mass and dissects to the tumor. The extent of the tumor is identified and a dissection is undertaken all the way around the tumor. A portion of neighboring soft tissue may also be removed to ensure adequate removal of all tumor tissue. A drain may be inserted and the incision is repaired with layers of sutures, staples, or Steri-strips. Report 27327 for excision of a subcutaneous tumor whose resected area is less than 3 cm, and 27337 for excision of a subcutaneous tumor that is 3 cm or greater. Report 27328 for excision of a subfascial or intramuscular tumor whose resected area is less than 5 cm, and 27339 for excision of a subfascial or intramuscular tumor that is 5 cm or greater.

27329, 27364
The physician performs a radical resection (excision) of a malignant soft tissue tumor from the thigh or knee area, not involving bone. An incision is made over the tumor and dissection exposes it. The tumor and any adjacent tissue that may be affected by the spread of the neoplasm are excised. Large resections may be needed. The type and stage of the lesion determines the extent of the tumor margin resection area. Muscle or fascia may need to be repaired and drains may be placed. The surgical wound is repaired by intermediate or complex closure, adjacent tissue transfer, or graft. Report 27329 for a resection area of less than 5 cm, and 27364 for a resection area 5 cm or greater.

27330-27331
The physician usually makes an anteromedial incision to gain adequate exposure of the knee joint. The patella is shifted to the side to examine the area. Each compartment of the knee joint is visually examined. The physician may need to make an additional incision to further explore other areas of the knee joint. If there is suspicion that synovium may be diseased, a tissue biopsy is taken. Any loose bodies or foreign bodies are removed in 27331. Incisions are closed with sutures, staples, and/or Steri-strips. A temporary drain may be placed.

27332-27333
The physician makes an incision along the anteromedial or anterolateral aspect of the knee, depending on which cartilage is torn (medial or lateral in 27332 or both in 27333). Dissection is carried down

to the cartilage. The patella is shifted aside and the knee joint exposed. The torn cartilage is removed and the roughened edges are smoothed. A partial synovectomy and release or excision (partial or total) of plica may be performed. Plica is a fold, pleat, band, or shelf of synovial tissue (e.g., transverse suprapatellar, medial suprapatellar, mediopatellar and infrapatellar). The chondral surface of the patella may be debrided as well. A temporary drain may be applied. The incision is repaired in layers with sutures, staples, and/or Steri-strips.

27334-27335
The physician makes an anteromedial incision for anterior synovectomy. Once the knee joint is accessed, proliferative, diseased synovium is removed. If posterior synovectomy is required, the physician will position the patient prone and make an "s" shaped incision along the popliteal (back of the knee) area. Both anterior and posterior synovectomy is performed in 27335. Dissection exposes the knee joint. Diseased synovium is removed. Incisions are closed with sutures, staples, and/or Steri-strips. A temporary drain may be applied.

27337-27339
These are resequenced codes. Please see 27327-27328 for the lay description.

27340
The physician makes a small incision over the upper portion of the patella. The bursal sac is located in fat in front of the patella. Dissection is carried down to the area of infection or inflammation. The bursa is removed. The incision is repaired in layers with sutures and Steri-strips.

27345
A Bakers cyst is located in the popliteal space (back of the knee). The physician makes a popliteal incision, carrying dissection to expose the semimembranosus tendon. The cyst is typically located around this tendon. The cyst is excised from the tendon. The incision is repaired in layers with sutures.

27347
The physician excises a lesion of the meniscus or capsule of the knee. Types of lesions treated include a cyst or ganglion (fluid-filled sac). Lesions may be located in the meniscus—the cartilage between the knee joint—(following an injury), or on the capsule, the fibrous covering over the joint space. Through an incision over the knee the physician dissects the tissues to the level of the cyst or ganglion. The lesion is excised, and the wound is closed with layered sutures.

27350
Patellectomy is removal of the patella. A hemipatellectomy or partial patellectomy is removal of cartilage from the patella or removal of a portion of the bone. A transverse "u" shaped incision is made over the anterior aspect of the knee joint just below the patella. The patella is excised from the tissue surrounding it (capsule, quadriceps, and patellar tendons). The physician takes the upper part of the capsule and quadriceps tendon medially and distally so that they overlap the lower part of the capsule. The physician sutures the capsule and tendon in place. Incisions are repaired with sutures, staples, and/or Steri-strips.

27355-27358
A bone cyst or benign tumor of the femur is removed. The physician makes an incision in the thigh overlying the cyst or tumor. The skin and underlying soft tissues are reflected to expose the periosteum, which is separated from the bone. Curettes or osteotomes are used to scrape or cut the lesion from the bone. Once the benign tumor or cyst is removed and healthy bone tissue is present, the periosteum is repositioned and the incision is repaired in layers. If the bone defect created requires a graft for repair, the physician obtains the necessary size bone graft from a separate donor site on the patient and packs it into the site where the tumor or bone cyst was removed or uses a bone bank allograft. Report 27356 if an allograft is used and 27357 if an autograft is obtained. Report 27358 if internal fixation is applied for more stability, such as bone screws, compression plates, or an intramedullary nail.

27360
The physician performs a partial excision of the femur, proximal tibia, and/or fibula to remove infected bone. An incision is made over the infected part of the bone and the underlying soft tissues are divided to expose it. The periosteum is reflected and the infected portion of bone is removed and irrigated. The excavation of bone may excise a crater-like piece, leave a small saucer-like shelf depression in the bone, or may remove a portion of the shaft (diaphysis) of a long bone. If a significant portion of bone is removed, the physician may use bone graft material to fill the cavity left in the bone. The periosteum is closed over the bone, the soft tissues are sutured closed, and a soft dressing is applied.

27364
This is a resequenced code. Please see 27329 for the lay description.

27365
The physician makes an incision overlying a tumor of the femur or knee. Adequate exposure is accomplished. Resection is performed including adjacent periosteum and muscle, a cuff of normal bone both proximal and distal to the lesion, and skin and soft tissues as necessary. For a malignant neoplasm of the femur or knee, additional bone and/or soft tissue may need to be removed, thus compromising the stability or integrity of the femur or knee joint. Separately reportable procedures, such as reconstruction of ligaments and/or tendons, reattachment of muscles, placement of donor bone

graft, and use of an external fixator may be necessary as well. The incision is repaired in layers.

27370
The patient is placed supine (lying on the back) on an x-ray table with the knee flexed over a small pillow. A skin anesthetic may be applied. The physician passes a 20-gauge needle into the femoropatellar space. Air and a single or double contrast agent is injected into the space. After the injection is complete, the patient is asked to move the knee to produce an even coating of the joint structures. Multiple roentgenographic views are taken of the knee.

27372
The physician removes a foreign body (i.e., nail, piece of wood) in the thigh or knee. For a foreign body in the thigh, an incision is made overlying the object. Tissue is dissected around the object. The physician may need to suture damaged muscle or other soft tissues. The wound is irrigated with antibiotic solution. The incision will typically be closed, unless an infection is present, in which case it will be left open temporarily to drain.

27380-27381
An incision is made from the upper portion of the patella and extending to a point just medial to the lower part of the tibial tuberosity. The patellar tendon is exposed, and all scar tissue removed. The ruptured ends of the tendon are debrided. Sutures are passed through the ruptured ends to bring them together. A fascia lata graft may be used for reinforcement of the suture line by being incorporated in both ends of the ruptures in a figure "8" fashion. Another technique for reinforcement is to sever the semitendinosus tendon, and make transverse drill holes through the distal third of the patella and transversely through the tibial tuberosity. The semitendinosus tendon is looped through the drill holes and sewn back onto itself at the tibial tubercle. In 27381, the repair is augmented with tissues (tendon or fascia) from surrounding areas or allograft tissue. The incision is closed with sutures and staples or Steri-strips.

27385-27386
The physician makes an incision over the site of injury. Dissection is carried down to the ruptured muscle. The torn ends are debrided so that healthy muscle tissue can be accurately opposed. Nonabsorbable sutures are placed close together around the circumference of the muscle. In 27386, the repair may be reinforced by using strips of fascia lata tissue. The physician makes an incision over the fascia lata in order to obtain the needed tissue. The fascia lata strips are interwoven with sutures around the ruptured muscle. Incisions are repaired with sutures and staples or Steri-strips.

27390-27392
The patient is positioned prone (lying face down). The physician makes a 7 to 10 cm, longitudinal incision beginning just above the popliteal crease and extending upward. Dissection exposes the hamstring tendons. The tendon sheath is divided and the tendon is incised transversely at two levels, 3 cm apart. The physician flexes the hip while the knee remains extended, causing the tendon to lengthen. The tendon sheath is closed. In 27391, two or three tendons are lengthened on the same leg. In 27392, the same technique is performed on both legs. The incision is repaired in layers.

27393-27395
The patient is positioned prone (lying face down). The physician makes a 7 to 10 cm, longitudinal incision beginning just above the popliteal crease and extending upward. Dissection exposes the hamstring tendons. The tendon sheath is divided and the tendon is incised transversely at two levels, 3 cm apart. The physician flexes the hip while the knee remains extended, causing the tendon to lengthen. The tendon sheath is closed. In 27394, two or three tendons are lengthened on the same leg. In 27395, the same technique is performed on both legs. The incision is repaired in layers.

27396-27397
The physician performs transplant or transfer of a single thigh tendon in 27396 and performs multiple transplants or transfers in 27397, using redirection or rerouting of muscle. The incisions are closed in layers.

27400
The physician makes a curvilinear incision over the biceps femoris tendon, extending just above the fibular head. The peroneal nerve is retracted so that the biceps tendon is exposed. This tendon is divided and repositioned on the lateral femoral condyle where it is anchored firmly. A similar incision is made on the medial side of the knee to expose the semimembranosus, semitendinosus, and gracilis tendons. The tendons are each divided and anchored firmly to the medial femoral condyle. The incisions are repaired in layers.

27403
With the knee in 60 degrees of flexion, the physician makes a vertical incision on the medial or lateral joint line area, depending on which meniscus needs repair. The meniscus is exposed and the edges of the tear are debrided with a small curette or scalpel. A rasp abrades the debrided edges of the tear, creating an increased inflammatory healing response. Sutures are placed through the tear in the meniscus every 3 mm to 4 mm. The incision is repaired with sutures and Steri-strips.

27405-27409
For a primary collateral repair (27405), the physician makes an incision on the lateral or medial aspect of the knee, depending on which ligament is torn (medial collateral or lateral collateral). Sutures may be used to tie the torn ends together. If the attachment of the

ligament to the bone is torn away, a screw may be used for fixation. For a cruciate ligament primary repair (27407), an incision is made to gain access into the knee joint (the physician may use the arthroscope for part of the procedure). Screws and/or sutures are used to reattach the torn end to the bone. Both collateral and cruciate ligaments are repaired in 27409. Incisions are closed with sutures, staples, and/or Steri-strips. A temporary drain may be applied.

27412
Autologous chondrocyte implantation is performed to treat knee defects caused by damage to the hyaline cartilage. Some of the patient's own cartilage is collected and placed in an ex vivo culture to produce more articular cartilage cells. An initial arthroscopy is done with a biopsy to harvest normal cartilage from a minor load-bearing area within the knee. The chondrocytes are sent to the laboratory where they are isolated from the cartilage matrix and cultured for three to four weeks to increase the number of viable cells. The cells are returned in suspension for surgical implantation. A knee arthrotomy is done with any necessary debridement of the surgical field. A periosteal flap graft is next created as a patch. A gel-like medium containing the cultured chondrocytes is placed into the defect area and the periosteal graft is sutured around the periphery to cover the chondrocytes.

27415
An osteochondral allograft is a type of bone/cartilage transplant that treats defects of the knee from disabling cartilage injury or disease, such as osteochondritis dissecans. Arthroscopic imaging, x-rays, and/or MRI is done to determine the size and type of lesion. Donor tissue from a tissue bank is used fresh. For open transplantation, the surgeon exposes the defect area by cutting to the bone and retracting the soft tissue. The defect is excised, and the margins are squared off and abraded to reach healthy, bleeding, subchondral bone. Using coring reamers, the graft is sized out of the donor material and press-fit into the defect like a type of bone plug. Supplementary fixation may be used by inserting biodegradable pins. The incision is closed. When a mosaic technique is used, cylindrical grafts are taken from the donor material and placed in corresponding cylindrical holes of the same depth and diameter made in the recipient area.

27416
The physician performs a mosaicplasty of the knee, in which cylindrical "plugs" of cartilage and underlying bone are taken from non-weightbearing areas and repositioned to damaged areas. Each plug is a few millimeters in diameter; when multiple cartilage plugs are positioned into the defective area the result is a mosaic-tile appearance. The physician makes an incision over the area of cartilage damage. A coring tool is utilized to form a round hole, sized to fit the plug, in the bone at the damaged area. The physician harvests the plug of normal cartilage, along with the underlying bone. The harvested plugs are implanted into the hole created in the damaged area.

27418
A lateral parapatellar incision is made extending from the top of the patella to the tibial tubercle. Small osteotomes or an oscillating saw is used to free a 6 cm to 8 cm block of bone, which includes the tibial tubercle near its upper end. A small bony platform is made on the medial side of the long bone block. The block is elevated anteriorly and its upper end is swung up onto the platform, while the lower end pivots. Cancellous bone is removed from the lower end of the block in order to improve the cosmetic appearance. Two bone screws secure the block. Incisions are closed with sutures, staples, or Steri-strips. By elevating the tibial tubercle, forces are decreased on the underneath surface of the patella.

27420
An incision is made on the anteromedial aspect of the knee beginning above the patella and ending 1.3 cm below the tibial tuberosity. The area where the patellar tendon inserts into the tibial tuberosity is resected, including a thin piece of bone 1.3 cm square. The patellar tendon is pulled medially and distally on the tibia and a site is selected for reattachment. At the site, an "I" shaped incision is made and the patellar tendon is secured here temporarily with sutures. Next, the insertion of the vastus medialis muscle is transformed laterally and distally and sutured in place. After the alignment of the patella has been checked, the patellar tendon is anchored into the tibia with a staple. The incision is closed with sutures, staples, or Steri-strips.

27422
An anteromedial incision is made parallel to the quadriceps tendon and the patella. Dissection is carried down to the vastus medialis muscle/tendon to the site where it attaches to the patella. An incision is made along the vastus medialis tendon parallel to the patella. The tendon is overlapped and sutured, pulling the patella more medially and allowing for improved patellar alignment. Tissue layers are closed with sutures. The incision is closed with sutures and Steri-strips.

27424
Patellectomy is removal of the patella. A transverse U-shaped incision is made over the anterior aspect of the knee just below the patella. The skin edges are retracted, and the incision is carried through the quadriceps expansion at the level of the distal third of the patella. The patella is excised from the capsule, quadriceps, and patellar tendons. The proximal part of the capsule and quadriceps tendon are taken medially and distally so that they overlap the distal part of the capsule by 1.3 cm and sutured in place. The insertion

Musculoskeletal

of the vastus medialis is freed and transferred distally and laterally. Incisions are closed in layers with sutures.

27425
The physician performs an open lateral retinacular release. Lateral retinacular release is done when too much lateral tension on the patella from tightness of the lateral retinaculum causes patellar misalignment, not allowing correct movement. This can be associated with articular cartilage lesions and idiopathic chondromalacia. The physician makes an incision to access the lateral patellofemoral and the lateral patellotibial ligaments. These tight lateral ligaments that are holding the patella out of alignment, are released, detaching the patella from the soft tissue structures, including the lateral retinaculum, muscle fibers, and joint capsule.

27427-27429
The physician performs an extra-articular and/or intra-articular ligamentous reconstruction procedure of the knee. To perform a lateral extra-articular augmentation in 27427, the physician makes an incision over the distal iliotibial band. The band is incised, elevated, and secured to the distal femur with a cancellous screw and washer. In 27428, the physician makes an anteromedial incision to access the knee joint. The torn ligament (collateral or cruciate) is identified. The ligament is reattached at its torn end. If reattachment is not possible, the physician will obtain a graft (such as a tendon) harvested from the patient or a donor graft, and attach it to the original location of the ligament. In 27429, both extra- and intra-articular ligamentous reconstruction are performed. A temporary drain is applied and incisions are repaired in layers with sutures, staples, and/or Steri-strips.

27430
The physician corrects a shortened or fibrotic quadriceps muscle. An anterior longitudinal incision is made from the upper one third of the thigh to the lower part of the patella. Deep fascia is divided and the rectus femoris muscle is separated from the vastus medialis and lateralis muscles. The vastus intermedius muscle is excised because it is usually scarred and is binding the posterior surface of the rectus femoris and patella to the femur. If the vastus medialis and lateralis muscles are badly scarred, subcutaneous tissue and fat are interposed between them and the rectus. If these muscles are relatively normal, they are sutured to the rectus at the lower one third of the thigh. Layers and incisions are closed with sutures and staples or Steri-strips.

27435
The physician corrects severe flexion contractures of the knee that cannot be corrected by more conservative means. The patient is positioned prone and a curvilinear incision (approximately 15 cm long) is made over the popliteal (back of the knee) space. The medial and lateral aspects of the joint capsule are exposed by dissecting through subcutaneous tissue and deep fascia. The common peroneal nerve and popliteal vessels and nerves are retracted. The medial and lateral portions of the capsule are divided, allowing the knee to be completely extended. The subcutaneous tissue and skin incisions are repaired in layers.

27437-27438
The physician makes a medial patellar incision, exposing the underneath surface (subchondral bone) of the patella. Abrasion arthroplasty or a smoothing of the bone surface is performed to encourage growth of new cartilage. If cancellous bone is exposed and abrasion arthroplasty would not be effective, the physician may place a prosthesis (also called hemiarthroplasty) on the back side of the patella in 27438. The underneath side of the patella is smoothed to make room for the prosthesis. The physician secures the prosthesis with screws or glue. The prosthesis sits in the trochlear groove in the position where the patella slides up and down when the knee bends and straightens. The incision is repaired in layers with sutures, staples, and/or Steri-strips.

27440
The physician replaces the damaged or degenerated tibial portion of the knee joint. The physician makes a medial incision along the patella. Dissection exposes the knee joint and tibial plateau. The menisci and anterior cruciate ligament are removed. The physician may also need to release other soft tissues around the knee to correct contractures and restore range of motion. The physician makes a bone cut through the tibial plateau using a cutting-alignment jig. Peg holes are made on the remaining tibial plateau and the tibial component is placed into position. Screws and/or glue secure the component. The incision is repaired in layers with sutures, staples, and/or Steri-strips.

27441
The physician replaces the damaged or degenerated cartilage of the tibial component of the knee joint. The physician makes a medial incision along the patella. Dissection exposes the knee joint and tibial plateau. The menisci and anterior cruciate ligament are removed. The physician may also need to release other soft tissues around the knee to correct contractures and restore range of motion. If the synovium around the knee joint is diseased, the physician may remove it as well. Any osteophytes (bony outgrowths) interfering with motion may be removed. The physician makes a bone cut through the tibial plateau using a cutting-alignment jig to achieve correct alignment. Peg holes are made on the remaining tibial plateau and the tibial component is placed into position. Screws and/or glue secure the tibial component. The incision is repaired in layers with sutures, staples, and/or Steri-strips.

27442-27443
The physician replaces the damaged or degenerated cartilage of the femoral condyles or tibial plateau. The physician makes a medial incision along the patella and carries dissection to expose the knee joint. If the femoral condyles are replaced, the physician uses a cutting-alignment jig to determine proper alignment of the bone cut and resects or cuts the distal femur. Additional smaller cuts may be made on the femur for rotational alignment. The physician may need to release soft tissues around the knee to correct contractures and restore range of motion. If the tibial plateau is replaced, the physician first removes the menisci and other soft tissue as needed. A cutting alignment jig is used to determine proper alignment of the tibial bone cut. Once the bone cuts are made, peg holes are also made into the bone. The prosthesis is placed into position and secured with screws and/or glue. In 27443, debridement and synovectomy are also performed. Any osteophytes interfering with range of motion are debrided and removed. The physician will also remove any diseased synovium present around the knee joint. The incision is repaired in layers with sutures, staples, and/or Steri-strips.

27445
The physician exposes the knee joint by making a straight longitudinal incision directly over the knee. Bone cuts are made to resect the anterior and posterior femoral condyles. A tibial cutting guide is used to remove a minimal amount of bone from the proximal tibia. A template is placed on the cut tibial surface and an osteotome is used to remove a square of bone from the tibial surface as outlined by the hole in the tibial template. The stem of the tibial component is placed into the hole and the femoral component is placed on the distal femur. Two polyethylene bushings are inserted into the femoral component and joined to the tibial component with the metal axle. The patellar component is applied by making a cut along the articular surface, making a peg hole, and inserting the component. If the patella does not track properly, a separately reportable lateral retinacular release is performed. All components are cemented into place. The joint is irrigated. The incision is closed in layers and placement of temporary suction drainage tubes.

27446
The physician replaces one diseased or damaged compartment of the knee, including the femoral condyle and tibial plateau on the same side. A medial incision is made along the patella and dissection exposes the knee joint. The physician prepares the selected compartment for arthroplasty by removing the meniscus. Other soft tissue around the compartment may also need to be released. Using a cutting-alignment jig, the physician makes bone cuts on the femoral condyle and tibial plateau of the compartment being replaced. The other compartment is left intact. Peg holes are made into the bone and the femoral and tibial components are placed into position. The components are secured with screws and/or glue. The incision is repaired in layers with sutures, staples, and/or Steri-strips.

27447
The physician replaces severely damaged or worn cartilage of the knee joint. A midline incision is made over the knee. Dissection exposes the knee joint. The physician may release soft tissues and/or ligaments in order to correct deformities and improve range of motion. The physician uses a cutting-alignment jig placed on the upper tibia to remove the tibial joint surface (both medial and lateral compartments) by making a bone cut. A cutting-alignment jig is also used on the femoral condyles to make the appropriate bone cut. Depending on the integrity of the joint surface of the patella, the physician may also make a bone cut to remove damaged cartilage. If the joint surface is healthy, it is left intact. Peg holes are usually made, and the components of the prosthesis are placed into position on the tibia, femur, and, if needed, the patella. The components are secured with glue and/or bone screws. The incision is repaired in layers with sutures, staples, and/or Steri-strips.

27448-27450
The physician performs an osteotomy of the femur. A medial or lateral incision is made to approach the femur. After the femur is exposed, a Kirschner wire is placed where a blade-plate is to be inserted. The physician inserts the blade of the plate at the determined angle an osteotomy (bone cut) that is performed transversely. The physician may use a nail plate and screws for internal fixation in 27450. Alignment of the knee now allows weight bearing to occur on the healthier compartment of the knee joint. The incision is repaired in layers with sutures, staples, and/or Steri-strips.

27454
The physician exposes the shaft of the femur with a long, longitudinal, lateral incision. An osteotomy (bone cut) is made through the proximal and distal ends of the femur. The femoral shaft is removed. Osteotomies are made (three or four) on the shaft, and the fragments are threaded end-to-end and aligned on a nail. If the cortex of the bone is very thin, the physician may need to add a separately reportable bone graft. The nail is inserted into the proximal and distal ends of the femur. The periosteum (bone lining) is sutured over the bone and the incision is repaired in layers.

27455
The physician removes a wedge of bone from the upper tibia below the growth plate. To correct the tibial varum (bow-legs) in an eight-year-old child, for example, a 3 cm to 4 cm lateral incision is made over the fibula. An oblique osteotomy of the fibula is performed. An anterolateral incision is made to gain access to the upper tibia. A Steinmann pin is inserted

through the midshaft of the tibia, parallel to the ankle joint, and another pin is inserted through the upper tibia parallel to the knee joint. The pins are used as guides to make a bony wedge cut (osteotomy) using a bone saw and chisel. The bone ends are approximated, correcting the deformity. The physician may use an AO five-hole compression plate or staples for internal fixation. The excised bone wedge may be used as a bone graft to fill in any defects. The incisions are closed, and the leg placed in a cast with the knee in 30 to 45 degrees of flexion.

27457
The physician performs an osteotomy of the proximal tibia to remove loading forces from damaged cartilage and bone. The load is transferred to normal cartilage and bone of the opposite knee compartment. For a valgus osteotomy (bone cut), the physician makes an incision over the lateral proximal tibia. For a varus osteotomy, the incision is made medially. Dissection is carried down to the bone. For a valgus osteotomy, the fibular head is removed with an oscillating saw. The osteotomy is made approximately 2 cm below the joint line. The degree of correction has been calculated before surgery with x-ray films. The physician uses an oscillating saw to cut a wedge of bone at the determined angle, three-quarters of the width through the tibia. The cut wedge is removed and an osteotome completes the bone cut. The cut edges of the osteotomy are brought together and secured with a staple. The incision is repaired in layers with sutures, staples, and/or Steri-strips.

27465-27468
Femoral shortening or lengthening techniques equalize leg lengths or treat malunions of the femur. The physician shortens the femur in 27465. An incision is made to expose the tip of the greater trochanter. The femoral canal is reamed and prepared for the insertion of an intramedullary nail. Next the femur is exposed through a lateral longitudinal incision at the middle third of the thigh. Two bone cuts are made to remove a length of bone. After the cut segment is removed, the bone ends are approximated, and the intramedullary nail is inserted into the femoral canal. Plates and screws may be used for fixation if the intramedullary nail is contraindicated, as in osteomyelitis or a deformity that precludes the use of a nail. The leg is placed in a Thomas splint. For femoral lengthening in 27466, two puncture wounds are made laterally in the distal and proximal femur. Two holes at each end are drilled in the bone, and a screw is inserted in each drill hole. The physician makes a lateral longitudinal incision 6 cm to 8 cm long to expose the femur. At the osteotomy site, an oscillating saw cuts through the femur. The Wagner distraction apparatus is attached to the two sets of screws, so that the apparatus is 1 cm to 2 cm lateral to the thigh. The incision is repaired in layers. The device is distracted up to 5 mm to 6 mm immediately. The apparatus is operated by a knob. Lengthening is about 1.5 mm or 1 cm per week. Both lengthening and shortening are performed in 27468. When the appearance of the femur is normal and the medullary has been reestablished, the plate and screws are removed.

27470-27472
The physician repairs a nonunion or malunion of the femur. The physician makes a lateral incision to expose the femur. If there is no distortion of the intramedullary canal, intramedullary nailing is performed for fixation of the nonunion. If failed internal fixation is present, the physician removes the plates and screws. If there is malalignment of the medullary canal, a compression plate and screws are used for repair. In 27472, there is a loss of bone. The physician harvests bone with an osteotome from the iliac crest or from the femur itself and closes the surgically created donor site. Copious amounts of bone are placed around the nonunion site. The incision is repaired in layers and a temporary drain is applied.

27475-27479
The physician performs epiphysiodesis to achieve complete arrest of the longitudinal growth at the physis (growth plate) of the longer limb. A 5 cm to 7 cm longitudinal incision is made along the lower femur, beginning just above the joint line. The distal femur physis is exposed. Osteotomes excise a rectangular piece of bone from the epiphyseal plate. The growth plate is drilled in anterior, posterior, and distal directions. A curette is used to remove the growth plate. The physician harvests bone from the patient's hip or femur and closes the surgically created graft donor site. The separately reportable cancellous bone graft is packed into the defect created by the removal of the growth plate. The rectangular piece of bone is reinserted into its original bed and securely seated with a mallet. The arrest procedure is the same whether performed on the medial or lateral side. The periosteum and incision are repaired in layers. In 27477, the same procedure is performed for the proximal tibial and fibular epiphyseal growth plates. In 27479, a combination of distal femur and proximal tibia and fibula epiphyseal arrest is performed.

27485
The physician performs hemiepiphyseal arrest on the distal femur or proximal tibia or fibula. For genu valgus, arrest of the medial femoral physis and/or proximal tibia is performed to realign the knee joint. A 5 cm to 7 cm, longitudinal incision is made along the lower femur, beginning just above the joint line. The distal femur physis is exposed. Osteotomes excise a rectangular piece of bone from the epiphyseal plate. The growth plate is drilled in anterior, posterior, and distal directions. A curette is used to remove the growth plate. The physician harvests bone from the patient's hip or femur and closes the surgically created graft donor site. The separately reportable cancellous

bone graft is packed into the defect created by the removal of the growth plate. The rectangular piece of bone is reinserted into its original bed and securely seated with a mallet. The periosteum and incision are repaired in layers.

27486-27487
The physician performs a revision of a total knee arthroplasty. Typically, previous skin incisions are incorporated to expose the knee. One or both (femoral and tibial) components are removed as determined by the physician. In order to remove the components, an osteotome or saw may be used to loosen the cement or bone so that the prosthesis can be topped out with a mallet. If any cement is present, it is removed in order to protect and preserve as much bone as possible. Bone cuts are made to accommodate the new prosthesis. If significant bone defects are present on the femur, tibia, or both, a bone graft may be needed. An allograft (donor bone) may be packed into the defect. The components of the new prosthesis are placed into position and may be cemented for fixation. The femoral and tibial component are revised in 27487. The incision is repaired with sutures, staples, and/or Steri-strips.

27488
The physician inserts a temporary spacer into the knee joint. To remove the knee prosthesis, the physician makes an incision directly over the original incision line. The prosthesis is exposed. An osteotome or saw may loosen the cement or bone around the components, so that they may be tapped out with a mallet. The cement is removed a piece at a time to protect and preserve as much bone as possible. Once the prosthesis is removed, there is an open space where the knee prosthesis was between the femur and tibia. A spacer of methylmethacrylate formed into a cube shape may be inserted into the space between the femur and tibia. The spacer prevents the soft tissues from compressing the joint space. The spacer is secured until another prosthesis is inserted. The incision is repaired in layers.

27495
The physician applies a prophylactic treatment to the femur. Methylmethacrylate may be applied to an area of resection because of malignancy. Fixation (nailing, pinning, plating, or wiring) and a prophylactic treatment may be an alternative to bone grafting.

27496-27497
The physician performs a decompression fasciotomy on one compartment of the thigh and/or knee. A longitudinal incision is made over the affected compartment. Dissection is carried through the fascial layers to the muscle compartments. An incision may also be made through the intramuscular septum to release pressure. If any necrotic tissue is present, it is debrided. Debridement of nonviable muscle and/or nerve is performed in addition in 27497. The incision may be left open for two to five days and repaired in layers with sutures.

27498
The physician performs a decompression fasciotomy on multiple compartments of the thigh and/or knee. One incision may be used to gain access to one or two compartments of the thigh. If not, a longitudinal incision is made over each compartment. Once the incision is made, dissection is carried through the fascial layers to the muscle compartments. An incision may also be made through the intramuscular septum to release pressure. The incision may be left open for two to five days and repaired in layers with sutures.

27499
The physician performs a decompression fasciotomy of multiple compartments of the thigh and/or knee, and debrides any nonviable tissue. The physician makes one or more extensive longitudinal incisions over the involved compartments. The incisions are carried deep to the fascia of each compartment. These fascia are incised to expose the compartments and relieve the pressures. A thorough exploration is undertaken and the physician debrides any nonviable tissue. This would typically be muscle, but it may also include other tissues within the compartment. The incisions are normally left open for several days before secondary closure is accomplished.

27500
The physician treats a femoral shaft fracture without manipulation. The fractured segments are aligned and stable. Treatment may be with a molded long leg cast, cast brace, or spica cast for several weeks until union is established.

27501
The physician treats a supracondylar or transcondylar femoral fracture without manipulation. The fractured segments are aligned and stable and no manipulation is required. If there is an intercondylar extension of the fracture such as a "T" or "Y" fracture extending into the joint, the intra-articular relationships of the knee must be reestablished. Treatment may be with a molded long leg cast, cast brace, or spica cast for several weeks until union is established.

27502
Closed reduction of the fracture is required by manual reduction by the physician or in conjunction with skin or skeletal traction. If skin traction is used, the leg is placed in full extension and bandages and straps are encircled around the leg starting at the foot and extending to the thigh. Weight is added to provide the traction force. The best application of skin traction is to temporarily provide comfort and support to the fractured limb until a definitive form of therapy is available. For skeletal traction, a pin is placed transversely through the proximal tibia with the knee in slight flexion. Traction weight is 15 to 20 pounds,

Musculoskeletal

and thereafter may be reduced gradually. If the physician is concerned about accurate reduction, a second pin may be placed through the distal femur, permitting early movement of the knee. Traction can maintain position until bone healing is well established. If traction is not needed, the extremity is placed in a spica cast or cast brace.

27503
The physician may reduce a displaced fracture manually without the use of skin or skeletal traction. If the intra-articular relationships of the knee cannot be reestablished manually, traction is generally not as effective as skeletal traction, but can be used by wrapping circular wraps around the lower extremity and attaching weight. Skeletal traction is more commonly used by placing a pin through the proximal tibia with the thigh, knee, and leg supported in suspension with some knee flexion. Traction weight of 15 to 20 pounds is applied and thereafter reduced gradually. The physician may need to perform manipulative reduction while in traction if accurate reduction cannot be obtained by traction alone. Traction is used to maintain position until bone healing is well established, or a cast or cast brace may be applied after the fracture becomes stable.

27506
With the patient in a lateral or supine (lying on the back) position, the physician makes a straight lateral incision to expose the fracture site. If there are large butterfly-type fragments or there is a long spiral fracture, cerclage wires may be wrapped around the bone to hold the fragments in place. The intramedullary nail is put into place by making a 4 cm to 6 cm incision over the tip of the greater trochanter. The trochanteric fossa is exposed. A drill hole is made into the center of the femoral canal. A reaming guide is used to ream out the intramedullary canal to the desired length, making room for the implant or nail. A nail-driving guide is inserted, and the nail is driven into place with a hammer. If it is a comminuted fracture, the physician may use interlocking screws to provide better fixation. One or two screws are placed proximally and/or distally through the femur and intramedullary implant. This technique helps secure rotator stability. The interlocking screws may be removed after six to eight weeks.

27507
With the patient in a supine (lying on the back) or lateral decubitus (lying on the side) position, the physician makes a lateral or anterolateral incision. The fracture is reduced by manipulation and bone reduction forceps. A compression plate with screws and/or leg screws secure and compress the fragments. The physician may elect to use cerclage wiring in conjunction with plates or screws in order to facilitate fixation of the fracture. The wire is placed around the femur, over the fracture site. One or more wires may be used. The incision is closed with sutures, staples, and/or Steri-strips.

27508
Closed treatment of a femoral fracture of the distal end of the medial or lateral condyle is indicated if the intra-articular relationships of the knee are intact and stable, as found upon x-ray. If the fracture does not need reduction, skeletal traction is not required. A spica cast brace is used until bony union is secure.

27509
Percutaneous skeletal fixation can be used for internal fixation in nonunions, malunions, and open or closed fractures of the distal femur area. Fixation pins are introduced through stab wounds (small incision over the bone). A small hole is drilled and a pin placed across the fracture line to hold it in place. Two, three, or more pins may be used. The ends of the pins are cut off beneath the skin, and the small incision closed with suture or Steri-strips. The pins are left in place approximately three to six weeks, and removed.

27510
Closed treatment of femoral fracture of the distal end of the medial or lateral condyle is indicated if the intra-articular relationships of the knee are intact and stable upon x-ray. If reduction of the fracture is required, skeletal traction is most commonly used. A pin is placed through the proximal tibia and the leg is supported in suspension with some knee flexion. Traction weight is 15 to 20 pounds initially, and thereafter may be reduced gradually. If reduction cannot be obtained by traction alone, the physician may manually reduce the fracture under anesthesia. The physician may use a second pin through the distal femur to aid in accurate reduction and permit early movement in the knee. Traction can be used to maintain position until bone healing is well established.

27511
The physician performs open treatment of a femoral supracondylar or transcondylar fracture. An incision is made along the medial or lateral femoral condyle area to expose the fracture site. The fragments are manually reduced and internal fixation is typically accomplished using a buttress blade plate or screw-plate with screws. The incision is closed.

27513
The physician performs open treatment of a femoral supracondylar or transcondylar fracture with intercondylar extension. Since this type of fracture includes a fracture line extending into the joint, it is important to secure accurate articular surface restoration and to retain the reduction. An incision is made over the medial or lateral femoral condyle to expose the fracture site. The fracture is reduced. Cancellous bone screws or bolts may be used to secure the condyle fracture, and a blade-plate with screws for

the supracondylar fracture. The physician may repair only the condyles, leaving the patient in skeletal traction for treatment of the supracondylar portion of the fracture.

27514
The physician performs open treatment of a fracture of the lateral or medial distal end of the femur. A curvilinear incision is made along the lateral or medial distal end of the femur, exposing the fracture site. The physician reduces the fracture, ensuring restoration of the articular surface of the knee joint and of the patellofemoral groove. After reduction, if the fracture is stable, no internal fixation is used. However, with this type of fracture internal fixation is typically used. A dynamic condylar screw system or an angled blade-plate with screws may achieve internal fixation of the fracture. The incision is closed with sutures, staples, and/or Steri-strips, or left open for secondary closure.

27516-27517
An abduction type separation is caused by a blow to the lateral side of the distal femur. There may typically be a fracture in conjunction with the epiphyseal separation. If alignment and stability are adequate, a single hip spica cast is used with the knee immobilized in extension. In 27517, closed reduction is attempted first in a more problematic fracture or separation such as in a hyperextension injury. If this is unsuccessful, the physician may insert a Steinmann pin in the femur above the fracture or separation, and another pin in the proximal third of the tibia. Gentle skeletal traction is applied to disengage the fragments while the physician reduces the displacement. A hip spica cast is applied with the knee in 45 to 60 degrees of flexion. In three to four weeks, the cast and pins are removed and an above-knee cast is applied.

27519
The physician performs open treatment of a distal femoral epiphyseal separation. The physician makes an anteromedial or anterolateral, longitudinal incision to expose the epiphysis on the distal femoral condyle area. The articular surface of the epiphysis is examined. The physician may use a Knowles pin placed into the displaced epiphyseal fragment, and use it as a handle to guide the displaced fragment back into position. Additional threaded pins or screws are directed transversely across the epiphysis or across the metaphysis as needed to complete fixation. The incision is closed with sutures and placed in a splint or long leg brace. If there is an open wound associated with the injury, the wound is irrigated and debrided.

27520
Closed treatment of a patellar fracture is indicated when there is 2 mm or less displacement, separation, or step off. X-ray determines any displacement. The leg is placed in a long leg cast or splint to keep the knee immobilized for three to six weeks.

27524
A vertical midline incision is made beginning 5 cm above the patella and ending at the midportion of the patellar tendon. The patellar fracture is identified and the knee joint is irrigated and inspected for any loose fragments. Clotted blood is removed from the fracture surfaces. The physician may use two types of treatment, depending on the type of fracture. The physician may place tension band wiring through drill holes made in the fragments to hold them together. Other fractures require screw fixation placed perpendicular to the fractured surfaces. If the patellar fracture is so severely fragmented that internal fixation or tension band wiring cannot be used, partial or complete removal of the patella is performed by the physician. If only a partial patellectomy is performed, the patellar tendon is reattached to the remaining patella with sutures and wire. Dissection and/or soft tissue repair of surrounding tissues may be necessary. Incisions are closed with sutures, staples, and/or Steri-strips.

27530-27532
Closed treatment of a tibial plateau fracture is indicated when the fractured segments are stable, in good alignment, and the tibial joint surface is congruent. The physician may need to perform a manual reduction in 27532 to realign the fractured segments. The physician may also use skeletal traction such as Kirschner wire. A wire is placed through the tibia and a traction bow is applied, reducing or realigning the fractured segments.

27535-27536
The physician makes a vertical incision on the side of the patella overlying the medial or lateral tibial plateau to correct a unicondylar (27535) fracture. A bicondylar fracture (27536) is treated by making both a medial and a lateral parapatellar incision. The incision extends downward to the upper portion of the tibia. If reduction is needed to realign the joint surfaces, the physician may use an AO distracter, an external device anchored with screws in the tibia and medial femoral condyle to distract the fractured fragments, allowing them to realign. Instead of a distracter, the physician may use a bone punch to raise fragments. Kirschner wires may be applied to provide provisional fixation of the fragments. A plate, such as a "T" or "L" plate, is fitted to the contour of the bone. Screws are inserted to secure fixation and to compress the fragments so that healing may occur. The incision is closed with sutures, staples, and/or Steri-strips.

27538
There are three types of fractures of the intercondylar spine and tibial tuberosity. Types I and II of the intercondylar spine and Type I of the tibial tuberosity are typically treated in a closed reduction. If the fragment appears stable and is not displaced, no manipulation for reduction is needed. If the fragment is displaced, reduction may be achieved by extending the

knee. The knee may also be aspirated. A splint or a locked, long-leg knee brace may be used for four to six weeks.

27540
The physician performs open treatment of an intercondylar spine and/or tuberosity fracture of the knee. If adequate closed reduction of the fragment cannot be achieved, an open procedure is needed to ensure normal knee range of motion and function. Open treatment is typically performed for Type III intercondylar spine fracture and Types II and III tibial tuberosity fracture. The physician makes an anteromedial incision to expose the knee, and the fragments are identified. For the intercondylar spine fracture, the fragment is reduced by placing the knee in full extension. Two holes are drilled through the tibial epiphysis. A wire or nonabsorbable suture is passed through the lowest portion of the anterior cruciate ligament and through the drill holes and tied together. The knee is flexed and extended so the reduction is stable. For a tibial tuberosity fracture, the fragment is reduced by extending the knee. Two small pins or a bone screw are placed through the fragment to hold it in place. The incision is closed. A splint or brace is applied for four to six weeks.

27550-27552
Radiographic evaluation is performed to help determine the direction of knee dislocation. Minor instabilities can be reduced without anesthesia by applying manual longitudinal traction (27550). If secondary restraints (ligaments) were damaged, anesthesia may be required in order to reduce the dislocation (27552). The knee is usually aspirated, and placed in a posterior splint for support. The physician may do further tests to evaluate ligamentous, capsular, meniscal, and vascular integrity. The knee is usually placed in a splint or immobilizer.

27556-27557
In an open knee dislocation there is considerable soft tissue trauma. The physician may debride the injury and explore the popliteal space for arterial evaluation and/or repair. If the joint is unstable after the dislocation is reduced, the physician may decide to use internal fixation for a period of time. Two transfixion pins drilled across the joint can provide good stability against recurrent dislocation. The wound may be left open to allow for drainage and treatment of infection. In 27557, primary ligamentous repair is performed at the same time, or at a later date after certification of popliteal artery flow, or after artery repair. The torn ligaments are reattached with screws, staples, and/or sutures. The incision or wound is closed or left open temporarily depending on the size of the wound, or if an infection is present.

27558
In an open knee dislocation, there will be considerable soft tissue trauma. The physician may need to debride the injury and explore the popliteal space for arterial evaluation and/or repair. If the joint is unstable after the dislocation is reduced, the physician may apply internal fixation for a period of time. Two transfixion pins drilled across the joint can provide good stability against recurrent dislocation. Those ligaments not able to be repaired directly may need augmentation or reconstruction. Typically the posterior cruciate ligament and sometimes the anterior cruciate ligament will be reconstructed by drilling bone tunnels in the tibia and femur, and passing donor ligament grafts through the tunnels and into the knee joint to take the place of the torn ligaments. The incision or wound is closed or left open temporarily depending on the size of the wound, or if an infection is present.

27560-27562
When the patella dislocates, it typically moves to the lateral side of the knee and off of the femoral condyles. Frequently the physician is able to gently extend the knee, causing the patella to move back into its normal position without administering anesthesia (27560). If the patient is in pain and guarding excessively, the physician may use anesthesia (27562) to relax the patient so the patella can be realigned. An x-ray may be taken to check the position of the patella. A splint or brace may be applied to give the patella additional support.

27566
If there is significant damage to the patella, such as an osteochondral fracture, or severe cartilage breakdown associated with a patellar dislocation, a partial or total patellectomy may need to be performed with this procedure. A medial longitudinal patellar incision is made to expose the patella and medial retinaculum. If the patella is still dislocated, it is reduced at this time. If significant damage has occurred to the patella as noted above, the physician may remove a portion or all of it. This is done by incising the tendon that encases the patella and using a saw and osteotome to resect the damaged portion of the patella. The tendon sheath is closed with sutures. To repair the patellar dislocation, the physician places the sutures in the medial retinaculum to tighten it down, which in turn keeps the patella or the tendon sheath from moving out from the trochlear groove. The incision is closed with sutures, staples, and/or Steri-strips.

27570
The physician increases range of knee motion limited by adhesions or scar tissue. After general anesthesia is administered, the physician bends the knee and applies gradual pressure until the desired range of motion for the knee is achieved. Traction or other fixation devices may be applied.

27580
The physician makes a long incision along the inside of the patella. The patella is reflected laterally to expose the knee joint. Bone cuts are made to flatten out the

joint surfaces of the femur and tibia. A U-shaped groove is made on the underneath side of the patella and a corresponding one on the femur. The patella is placed into the femoral groove and secured with screws. The physician makes an incision overlying the iliac crest, harvests a graft, and closes the surgically created graft donor site. The bone graft is placed between the joint surfaces. An external fixator compresses the joint surfaces. The knee is typically fused in 10 to 15 degrees of flexion. The incision is closed with sutures, staples, and/or Steri-strips.

27590-27591
The physician makes incisions so that equal anterior and posterior flaps are fashioned. Dissection is carried down to the femur. Arteries and veins are doubly ligated and transected. The sciatic nerve is divided. A Gigli saw is used to section the femur and bevel the cut ends. The anterior and posterior myofascial flaps are sutured together and secured to the lower end of the femur through drill holes. Incisions are closed in layers and a temporary drain is applied. For fitting (27591) an immediate postoperative prosthesis (IPOP), a rigid dressing is applied at the time of amputation. A closed-end stump sock is placed over the dressings. Felt pads are used over bony prominences to evenly distribute the pressure. An elastic, plaster cast is applied over the amputation site. A belt suspension apparatus may be incorporated into the cast. If immediate weight bearing is planned, an end-plate is wrapped into the lower portion of the cast to allow attachment of a temporary prosthesis.

27592
An open amputation is one in which the skin is not closed over the end of the stump, but is rather followed by a secondary closure (reamputation, scar revision) at a later date. The purpose of this type of amputation is to prevent or eliminate infection so that final closure of the stump may be carried out without breakdown of the wound. This procedure is usually used in severe traumatic wounds with extensive destruction of tissue. Just below the intended bone section, the physician makes a circular incision to the deep fascia. Muscles and nerves are divided and all vessels ligated. The bone is sectioned, and the wound is dressed. Skin traction is applied by covering the stump with a stockinette which is glued to the skin. The free end of the stockinette is split into 4 tails and tied together over the stump. A rope is attached to the stockinette and traction of 3 to 5 pounds is applied in order to gradually stretch the skin over the stump, while the stump is healed by a sear. This may take two to three weeks or more. The stump is dressed at intervals while continuing the traction.

27594
The physician performs secondary closure or scar revision after the stump has granulated or healed by a sear. In this procedure, no additional bone is sectioned. The physician resects the scar and granulation tissue from the end of the stump. Skin flaps are fashioned as close as possible to the thick scar surrounding the granulating wound. The dense layer of scar tissue is excised from over the end of the bone. Additional muscle may be removed as well. The skin flaps are pulled over the end of the stump and connected with nonabsorbable sutures. A temporary drain or suction tubes may also be used.

27596
After the stump has granulated or healed by sear, the physician performs secondary closure or scar revision. This procedure will usually be performed 2 to 3 weeks or more after the initial open amputation was completed. Additional bone is sectioned, usually at a more proximal or higher level. Skin flaps are fashioned and pulled over the stump and closed with nonabsorbable sutures. A temporary drain or suction tubes are used as well.

27598
The physician performs disarticulation at the knee, which is a disjoining but not removal of bone above the knee. Equal anterior and posterior incisions are made around the knee. The patellar tendon is sectioned close to where it attaches to the tibial tubercle. The tendons surrounding the knee are divided from their insertions on the tibia. The same is done with the cruciate ligaments. Arteries and veins are ligated and nerves are divided. The patella is removed. A saw is used to remove the femoral condyles 1.5 cm above the level of the knee joint. The patellar tendon is pulled into the intercondylar notch and sutured to the remaining portions of the cruciate ligaments. The hamstring tendons are sutured to the patellar tendon. A temporary drain is placed in the knee joint and the incision is closed in layers.

27600-27602
The physician performs a decompression fasciotomy on the compartments of the leg to reduce high pressure within those compartments. The physician treats the anterior or lateral compartments of the leg in 27600, the posterior compartments in 27601, or the anterior and/or lateral and posterior compartments in 27602. The physician makes incisions overlying the compartments measured at dangerous levels. The incisions are carried deep to the respective fascia. The physician makes long incisions in the fascia to relieve the pressure. The fascial and skin incisions are left open. Any nonviable tissue is removed.

27603-27604
The physician drains an abscess or hematoma in 27603 or an infected bursa in 27604 from deep within the leg or ankle. The physician makes an incision in the leg or ankle overlying the site of the abscess, hematoma, or bursa to be incised. Dissection is carried through the deep subcutaneous tissues and may be continued into the fascia or muscle to expose the abscess or hematoma. The incision may be extended if the mass is

larger than expected. When the infected bursa, abscess, or hematoma is identified, it is incised and the contents are drained. The area is irrigated and the incision is repaired in layers with sutures, staples, and/or Steri-strips; closed with drains in place; or simply left open to further facilitate drainage of infection.

27605-27606
The physician performs a percutaneous tenotomy of the Achilles tendon. The physician infiltrates the skin and Achilles tendon with a local anesthetic about 1 cm above the insertion into the calcaneus. A knife blade or tenotome held vertically is inserted through the skin and subcutaneous tissue into the Achilles tendon. The blade is turned medially and laterally and swept back forth, creating a nick in the tendon, until the foot can be dorsiflexed at the ankle. Pressure is applied over the incision for about five minutes. A dressing and long leg cast is applied with the ankle in ten degree dorsiflexion and the knee in maximal extension. Report 27605 if performed with local anesthesia; report 27606 if general anesthesia is required.

27607
The physician incises infected bone in the tibia, fibula, or ankle to treat a bone abscess or osteomyelitis. The physician makes an incision over the affected area. Dissection is carried through the soft tissues to expose the bone. The periosteum is split and reflected from the bone overlying the infected area. A curette may be used to scrape away the abscess or infected portion to healthy bony tissue or drill holes may be made through the cortex into the medullary canal in a window outline around the infected or abscessed bone. The area is drained and debrided of infected bony and soft tissue. The physician irrigates the area with antibiotic solution, the periosteum is closed over the bone, and the soft tissues are sutured closed; or the wound is packed and left open, allowing the area to drain. Secondary closure is performed approximately three weeks later. Dressings are changed daily. A splint may be applied to limit ankle movement.

27610
The physician performs an arthrotomy of the ankle that includes exploration, drainage, or removal of any foreign body. An incision is made over the ankle area to be exposed. The soft tissues are dissected away and the joint capsule is exposed and incised. The joint space is explored, any necrotic tissue is removed, and infection or abnormal fluid is drained. If a foreign body is present (e.g., bullet, nail, gravel), it is exposed and removed. The wound is irrigated with antibiotic solution. The physician may leave the wound packed open with daily dressing changes to allow for further drainage or secondary healing by granulation. If the incision is repaired, drain tubes may be inserted and the incision is closed in layers with sutures, staples, and/or Steri-strips.

27612
The physician performs an arthrotomy on the ankle for posterior capsular release, with or without Achilles tendon lengthening by making an incision along the Achilles tendon and retracting the muscles to expose the posterior ankle capsule. The capsule is incised to increase dorsiflexion. If the Achilles tendon is lengthened, the physician notches the tendon at the medial and lateral aspects to release contracture. The wound is sutured in layers.

27613-27614
The physician performs a biopsy of the soft tissues of the leg or ankle area. With proper anesthesia administered, an incision is made over the biopsy area. Dissection is carried down within the superficial soft tissue layers in 27613, usually the subcutaneous fat to the uppermost fascial layer. In 27614, dissection is taken deep within the soft tissue, such as into the fascial layer or within the muscle. A portion of the tissue is excised and submitted for pathology. The area is irrigated and the incision is closed with layered sutures, staples, or Steri-strips.

27615-27616
The physician performs a radical resection (excision) of a malignant soft tissue tumor from the leg or ankle area, not involving bone. An incision is made over the tumor and dissection exposes it. The tumor and any adjacent tissue that may be affected by the spread of the neoplasm are excised. Large resections may be needed. The type and stage of the lesion determines the extent of the tumor margin resection area. Muscle or fascia may need to be repaired and drains may be placed. The surgical wound is repaired by intermediate or complex closure, adjacent tissue transfer, or graft. Report 27615 for a resected area that is less than 5 cm, and 27616 for a resected area that is 5 cm or greater.

27618-27619, 27632-27634
The physician removes a tumor from the soft tissue of the leg or ankle area that is located in the subcutaneous tissue in 27618 and 27632 and in the deep soft tissue, below the fascial plane, or within the muscle in 27619 and 27634. With the proper anesthesia administered, the physician makes an incision in the skin overlying the mass and dissects to the tumor. The extent of the tumor is identified and a dissection is undertaken all the way around the tumor. A portion of neighboring soft tissue may also be removed to ensure adequate removal of all tumor tissue. A drain may be inserted and the incision is repaired with layers of sutures, staples, or Steri-strips. Report 27618 for excision of a subcutaneous tumor whose resected area is less than 3 cm, and 27632 for a resected area 3 cm or greater. Report 27619 for excision of a subfascial or intramuscular tumor whose resected area is less than 5 cm, and 27634 for a resected area 5 cm or greater.

27620
The physician performs an arthrotomy of the ankle that includes exploration, drainage, or removal of any foreign body. An incision is made over the ankle area to be exposed. The soft tissues are dissected away and the joint capsule is exposed and incised. The joint space is explored, any necrotic tissue is removed, and infection or abnormal fluid is drained. If a foreign body is present (e.g., bullet, nail, gravel), it is exposed and removed. The wound is irrigated with antibiotic solution. The physician may leave the wound packed open with daily dressing changes to allow for further drainage or secondary healing by granulation. If the incision is repaired, drain tubes may be inserted and the incision is closed in layers with sutures, staples, and/or Steri-strips.

27625
The physician performs an arthrotomy of the ankle and removes the synovium. An incision is made over the ankle. The soft tissues are dissected away and the joint capsule is exposed. An incision is made through the capsule and into the joint. The synovium is removed through the incision. The wound is irrigated with antibiotic solution the incision is closed in layers with sutures, staples, and/or Steri-strips.

27626
To correct thickening of the synovium, the physician makes an incision over the tendon and exposes the tendon sheath. The synovium is the lining that bathes the joint in fluid. The physician removes the affected sheath from the tendon and the joint space is opened and the synovium is removed. The wound is irrigated and closed with sutures.

27630
The physician makes an incision over the site of the lesion on the tendon sheath or capsule. Dissection exposes the tendon or capsule. The tissues are dissected around the lesion, freeing it from surrounding tissue and the lesion is excised. The operative site is irrigated with antibiotic solution and the wound closed with layered sutures.

27632-27634
These are resequenced codes. Please see 27618-27619 for the lay description.

27635-27638
A bone cyst or benign tumor of the tibia or fibula is removed. The physician makes an incision in the lower leg overlying the cyst or tumor. The skin and underlying soft tissues are reflected to expose the periosteum, which is separated from the bone. Curettes or osteotomes are used to scrape or cut the lesion from the bone. Once the benign tumor or cyst is removed and healthy bone tissue is present, the periosteum is repositioned and the incision is repaired in layers. If the bone defect created requires a graft for repair, the physician obtains the necessary size bone graft from a separate donor site on the patient and packs it into the site where the tumor or bone cyst was removed or uses a bone bank allograft. Report 27637 if an autograft is obtained and 27638 if an allograft is used.

27640-27641
The physician performs a partial excision of the tibia in 27640 or the fibula in 27641 to remove infected bone. An incision is made over the affected part of the bone and the underlying soft tissues are divided to expose it. The periosteum is reflected and the infected portion of bone is removed and irrigated. The excavation of bone may excise a crater-like piece, leave a small saucer-like shelf depression in the bone, or may remove a portion of the shaft (diaphysis) of a long bone. If a significant portion of bone is removed, the physician may use bone graft material to fill the cavity left in the bone. The periosteum is closed over the bone, the soft tissues are sutured closed, and a soft dressing is applied.

27645-27647
The physician removes a tumor with radical resection. The physician incises the overlying skin and dissects to the bone, freeing the involved bone from muscular attachments and the tissue bed. The area affected by tumor is removed, and the wound is sutured in layers. Report 27645 if the tumor is located in the tibia. Report 27646 if the tumor is located in the fibula. Report 27647 if the tumor is located on the talus or calcaneus.

27648
The physician injects radiopaque fluid into the ankle for arthrography. The physician inserts a needle into the ankle joint and aspirates if necessary. Opaque contrast solution is injected into the ankle, and the needle is removed. A separately reportable arthrogram is taken of the ankle.

27650-27652
The physician repairs a ruptured Achilles tendon. An incision is made overlying the tendon. The physician extends the incision through the tissues to the tendon. The physician identifies the tear and debrides any rough edges. In 27652, the physician harvests a fascial graft from the patient through a separate incision. The physician repairs the surgically created graft donor site. The graft is incorporated into the repair of the tendon and secured to the area with fixation (e.g., screw). The tendon is repaired, typically with a heavy nonabsorbable suture. The wound is irrigated with antibiotic solution and closed in layers. A cast, splint, or brace may be applied.

27654
The physician repairs a secondarily torn Achilles tendon. An incision is made overlying the tendon. The physician extends the incision deep to the tendon. The tear or rupture is identified. Because the repair is secondary, significant scar tissue may be debrided. Any nonviable tissue is also removed. A graft may be

harvested from the patient through a separate incision. The physician repairs the surgically created graft donor site and the tendon with a suture or with both the graft and suture. The graft may be secured to the area of repair with a screw. The physician irrigates the wound with antibiotic solution. The wound is closed in layers. A cast or splint may be applied.

27656
The physician repairs a fascial defect of the leg. The physician incises the skin overlying the defect. If underlying muscles are herniated through the fascial defect, they are pulled to their correct anatomical position and secured with sutures. The wound is sutured in layers.

27658-27659
An incision is made overlying the damaged flexor tendon in the leg. The physician extends the incision deep to the tendon. The tear or rupture is identified. If the repair is secondary, significant scar tissue may be debrided, and a graft may be necessary. Any nonviable tissue is also removed. The physician repairs the tendon with sutures or by placing a graft and suturing. The graft may be secured to the area of repair with a screw. The physician irrigates the wound with antibiotic solution. The wound is closed in layers. A cast or splint may be applied. Primary repair is done immediately after injury. Secondary repair is done sometime after the incident of injury or following a previous surgical repair. Report 27658 for a primary repair without graft and 27659 for a secondary repair, with or without a graft.

27664-27665
The physician makes a midline, longitudinal incision to expose the damaged extensor tendon in the leg. The surgical site is irrigated and the torn ends of the tendon are realigned to provide for better attachment and brought together and sutured. The tendon may be attached to the retinaculum around the knee. If the repair is secondary, significant scar tissue may be debrided, and a graft may be necessary. Any nonviable tissue is also removed. The physician repairs the tendon with sutures or by placing a graft and suturing. The graft may be secured to the area of repair with a screw. The physician irrigates the wound with antibiotic solution. The wound is closed in layers. A cast or splint may be applied. Primary repair is done immediately after injury. Secondary repair is done sometime after the incident of injury or following a previous surgical repair. Report 27664 for a primary repair without graft and 27665 for a secondary repair, with or without a graft.

27675
The physician makes a longitudinal curved incision that extends from the distal end of the fibula, over the lateral border of the foot to the cuboid bone. A posterior skin flap is elevated at the lateral malleolus, using the deep fascia with its base attached to the tip of the lateral malleolus. The peroneal tendons and sheaths are identified and placed in their appropriate anatomic position and secured in place with sutures or drill holes and suture anchors. The incision is sutured in layers.

27676
A longitudinal lateral ankle incision is made and a groove created in the posterior aspect of the fibular malleolus (fibular osteotomy). The peroneal tendons are placed in the groove and held in place with a thick osteoperiosteal flap from the surface of the malleolus that is swung posteriorly over the tendons or with a wedge of bone cut from the lateral malleolus that is displaced posteriorly over the tendons. The wound is irrigated and sutured in layers. A short leg case is usually applied and modified to walking cast once the stitches are removed.

27680-27681
The physician corrects a tightened or adhesed tendon sheath in the leg or ankle by making a longitudinal incision over the restricted tendon. Skin is retracted and scar tissue is removed. The physician dissects the tendon with a sharp instrument to free it from the bone. The wound is sutured and dressed with compression bandages. Report 27680 if the procedure is performed on a single tendon. Report 27681 if multiple tendons, requiring separate incisions, are freed from tightened or adhesed tendon sheaths.

27685-27686
The physician makes three incisions on the lateral side of the foot centered over the sinus tarsi. The physician exposes the extensor digitorum brevis tendon, and reflects it distally to expose the anterior part of the talocalcaneal joint. The calcaneocuboid joint is identified and all tight surrounding structures are released. A second incision is made on the medial side of the foot centered over the prominent head of the talus. The physician releases all tight structures on the medial and dorsal aspects of the head of the talus and the navicular. The anterior part of the talus is freed from its attachments to the navicular and calcaneus. If the peroneal, and extensor hallucis longus and extensor digitorum longus tendons remain contracted the physician lengthens them by Z-plasty. A third incision is made on the medial side of the Achilles tendon, lengthened by Z-plasty. The physician inserts a Steinmann pin through the navicular and into the neck of the talus to maintain the reduction. The wound is closed in layers and a long-leg cast with the knee flexed and the foot in proper position. The Steinmann pins are removed in eight weeks.

27687
The physician performs a gastrocnemius recession. To lengthen the gastrocnemius muscle using the Strayer procedure, the physician makes a posterior longitudinal incision 10 cm to 15 cm long overlying the middle of the calf. The medial sural nerve is retracted and the incision is deepened to the fascia to

expose the gastrocnemius. This muscle is dissected bluntly from the underlying soleus muscle to their common tendon at the calcaneus. A probe or clamp is inserted deep to the gastrocnemius and its tendon is severed. The physician dorsiflexes the foot until there is a 2 cm to 2.5 cm gap between the two tendon segments. The two muscle bellies are dissected from their fascial attachments proximally to the popliteal fossa. The physician passes a finger from side-to-side beneath the muscle to completely separate the gastrocnemius from the soleus. The proximal part of the tendon is sutured to the soleus with fine interrupted silk sutures. The wound is closed.

27690-27692
Because this procedure involves transfer or transplant of a single tendon from a number of different sites on the foot, the exact procedure will differ depending on the specific tendon involved. When transfer of the anterior tibial tendon is performed, an anterior lower-leg incision is made and the tendon extracted and passed posteriorly through the interosseous membrane to the calcaneus. A posterior heel incision is made and the tendon end is fixed to the calcaneus and/or Achilles tendon. The wound is closed in layers over a drain with a subcutaneous layer closed so that the skin can be brought together under minimal tension. The patient is placed into a dressing incorporating plaster splints.

27695-27696
The collateral ligament is two-part ligament that stabilizes the medial side of the ankle. The physician makes a curved incision across the inside of the ankle. The skin is reflected to expose the torn ligament. Holes are drilled diagonally across the talus and two non-absorbable sutures are placed through these holes and the ligament. Report 27696 if a similar procedure is performed to attach the ligament to the medial malleolus, which requires the placement of a screw through the fibula to the tibia. The wound is closed and dressed. The leg is immobilized in a long leg cast with the knee flexed to 30-45 degrees for four weeks followed by a walking cast for four weeks.

27698
This procedure reports a secondary repair of a disrupted collateral ligament of the ankle. Secondary repair is done sometime after the incident of injury or following a previous surgical repair. There are several techniques, including Watson-Jones, Evan and Chrisman-Snook. In a Watson-Jones repair, an ankle incision is made and the peroneus brevis tendon divided and mobilized. It is passed through drill holes in the talus and fibular malleolus to reconstruct both the calcaneofibular and anterior talofibular ligaments (lateral collateral ligament). An Evans procedure involves mobilizing the peroneus brevis tendon and passing it through a drill hole in the lateral fibular malleolus to reconstruct the collateral ligament. A Chrisman-Snook procedure involves dividing the peroneus brevis tendon and using it in the repair of the collateral ligament.

27700-27703
The physician performs arthroplasty to correct joint problems caused by arthritis. Three portal incisions are made at the front and sides of the ankle. Joint surfaces are smoothed and scar tissues are removed from the joint. If excessive damage is noted, the physician replaces damaged parts of the ankle with a prosthesis and reports 27702. Report 27703 if a loose component must be revised.

27704
The physician removes an implant. The preexisting skin incision is opened and the tibial and talus components are removed with accompanying cement. Bone grafts are placed in the resulting defect and the ankle is secured with compression or screws. The wound is sutured and a cast is applied for up to 12 weeks.

27705-27709
The physician performs an osteotomy (bone cut) of the tibia in 27705, of the fibula in 27707, or of both in 27709. An incision is made in the skin overlying the osteotomy site. Separate incisions may be necessary to access both tibia and fibula in 27709. The physician dissects the tissues down to the bone. The bone is exposed. The physician makes a cut through the tibia, fibula, or both in the desired location and plane. The bone is aligned to the proper position. Fixation, such as screws or plates may be applied to maintain position. The physician irrigates the area with antibiotic solution and closes it in layers. A splint, cast, or brace may be applied.

27712
The physician makes an incision along the shaft of the limb, exposing the bone. Another incision is made through the periosteum to expose the entire shaft. The physician cuts through the proximal and distal ends of the bone, temporarily removes the shaft, and makes three or four cuts through the shaft. These segments are threaded onto a medullary nail and shifted as necessary to alignment. Bone grafts are added if the cortex is extremely thin. The shaft is placed back into position with the medullary nail extending into the bone at either end. The periosteum is sutured over the bone and the wound is closed with sutures. The extremity is immobilized by cast until healed.

27715
The patient is placed prone and an incision is made over the distal lateral fibula. The physician places two screws 1.5 cm apart through fibula to the tibia, securing the fibula during the procedure. The fibula is cut above the screws. Incisions are made at the top and bottom of the tibia, and Schanz screws are placed parallel to the plane of the knee outside the leg.

Another incision is made at the front of the tibia, making a transverse cut through the bone. The Achilles tendon may be lengthened. An external distraction device is attached to the screws and the distance increased by 1.5 cm per day or 10 cm per week. After the desired length is achieved, a shortened or lengthened metal plate and screws are attached, with possible bone grafting. The wound is closed.

27720-27722
To correct nonunion of the tibia in 27720, the physician makes an incision on the medial aspect of the tibia through the periosteum. The bone is divided by transverse cuts and the pieces are manually rotated into position and stabilized with a metal plate and screws. In 27722, the physician makes an anteromedial incision and fibrous tissue is removed from the site. The ends of the fragments are roughened and the distal segment is hollowed out. A rectangular window is cut into the bone just above the site, cancellous bone is removed, and placed around the fixation site. The wound is closed, dressed and a cast is applied.

27724
The physician repairs a tibia fracture that has not healed or has healed in malalignment. An incision is made in the skin overlying the tibial fracture site. The incision is extended to the bone. The physician identifies the fracture or malunion. Any scar tissue is debrided from around and between the fracture pieces so that the clean edges of bone can be approximated. A bone graft is harvested through a separate incision from the patient's ilium or from another bone. The physician repairs the surgically created graft donor site. The graft is placed at the fractúre site and the fracture is manipulated into the desired position and alignment. The physician applies fixation, such as screws, plates, wires, or rods to stabilize the fracture. The wound is irrigated with antibiotic solution and closed in layers. A splint, brace, or cast may be applied.

27725
The physician repairs a fracture of the tibia that has not healed or has healed in malalignment. An incision is made in the skin overlying the fracture site. The physician extends the incision deep to the bone. The fracture or malunion is identified. Any scar tissue is debrided from around and between the fracture pieces. An osteotomy of the bone is performed if needed to correct the malalignment. Using the adjacent fibula as a strut, the fibula is attached to the tibia with fixation, such as plates, screws, or wires. This attachment allows the fibula to heal to the tibia in a synostosis. The physician irrigates the wound with antibiotic solution and closes it in layers. A brace, cast, or splint may be applied.

27726
Nonunion of a fracture is the absence of healing between fractured bone parts, while in malunion some healing occurs but the fracture fragments are in poor alignment. The physician repairs a nonunion or malunion of the fibula utilizing internal fixation. The physician exposes the nonunion or malunion by making an incision through the skin, fascia, and muscle over the fracture site. Intervening scar tissue may be removed and the bone is divided. The fragments are aligned and an internal fixation device is inserted. The incision is repaired in layers with sutures, staples, and/or Steri-strips. The limb is immobilized.

27727
Congenital Anterolateral Bowing of the Tibia is a rare condition that is present in 1 in 250,000 live births. The affected leg is bowed forwards, and usually shortened. By age 2, the bowed tibia fractures spontaneously, and does not heal. However, before the fracture occurs, the physician may place the affected leg in a thermoplastic brace to protect it. Once the fracture occurs, it does not heal, and forms a pseudarthrosis (non-union). Surgical repair using fibula graft or using the Ilizarov technique of repair is often used.

27730-27742
The physician performs epiphyseal arrest on the distal tibia (lower leg toward the ankle). The physician makes a 2 cm incision over the physis on the deformed side of the bone. A 1 square cm bone block is removed from the physeal line. A curette is used to roughen the remaining walls of the block site. The block is rotated and replaced in its original space. The wound is closed with sutures. Report 27732 if performed on the distal fibula; report 27734 if performed on both the distal tibia and fibula (two bones of the lower leg); report 27740 if performed on both ends of the bones; and report 27742 if performed on the distal femur.

27745
Preventive nailing of a bone may be performed if a surgeon feels that a bone is not stable on its own despite the lack of a true fracture site. An incision is made to reflect the soft tissues and the periosteum is divided to expose the bone. The bone is plated or pinned as necessary. the soft tissues are repositioned and skin is closed with sutures. Often weight-bearing is progressed as with normal fractures or internal fixation procedures.

27750
The physician treats a fracture of the tibial shaft without open surgery or any manipulation of the bones. Separately reportable x-rays confirm a fracture of the tibial shaft with or without a simultaneous fibular fracture. The position and alignment of the fracture fragments are stable. The physician applies a cast or brace to maintain the stability of the fragments.

27752
The physician treats a tibial shaft fracture without surgery but with manipulation of the bones. Separately reportable x-rays confirm a fracture of the tibial shaft

with or without a simultaneous fibular fracture. Using anesthesia, and with the use of skeletal traction as required, the physician manipulates the fracture. Manipulation is accomplished by pushing, pulling, rotating, or otherwise maneuvering the bones so they are properly aligned. Separately reportable x-rays confirm proper alignment. Skeletal traction may not be removed and a cast or brace may be applied to the leg to maintain stability of the bone.

27756
The physician treats a fracture of the tibia shaft by placing pins or screws through the skin and into the bone. Separately reportable x-rays confirm that the fracture, with or without an associated fibular fracture, can be treated without any long incisions or exposure of the bone. The physician makes small stab wounds in the skin overlying the fracture. Using separately reportable fluoroscopic x-ray as needed, the physician inserts the pins or screws through the small incisions and through the fractured pieces. The pins or screws hold the fractured pieces together. The wounds are irrigated with antibiotic solution and the skin is closed. A dressing is applied. The leg is placed in a cast, splint, or brace.

27758
The physician repairs a fracture of the shaft of the tibia using internal fixation devices. An incision is made overlying the fracture area of the tibia. The physician extends the incision deep to the bone, identifying and exposing the fracture. Tissue is debrided as needed. The physician manipulates the pieces of bone together under direct visualization. Fixation devices, such as plates and screws or cerclage wires, are applied to hold the fracture in the desired position. The wound is irrigated with antibiotic solution. The physician may close the wound in layers or the wound may be left open to drain.

27759
The physician makes an incision over the proximal tibia. The tissue is dissected. The physician carries the incision to the bone. Separately reportable fluoroscopic x-ray may be used throughout the rest of the procedure to confirm stabilization of the fracture. The physician drills a hole in the proximal tibia and places a long guidewire into the marrow canal of the bone. This guide wire is threaded distally in the canal and across the fracture site to the distal tibia. Bone reamers are sequentially placed over the guide wire in even larger sizes to ream the inside of the bone. Reaming is continued until the desired size is reached. The physician chooses the correct size rod to be implanted in the canal. The physician inserts the rod into the proximal tibia over the guide wire and drives it through the intramedullary canal to the distal tibia. The guide wire is removed. The incision is irrigated with antibiotic solution and the skin is closed in layers. A splint or brace may be applied to the leg.

27760
The physician treats a fracture of the medial malleolus of the ankle without surgery or any manipulation of the bones. Separately reportable x-rays confirm the fracture is in an acceptable position. A cast or brace is placed on the leg to hold the fragments in place.

27762
The physician treats a fractured medial malleolus without open surgery but with manipulation of the fracture. Separately reportable x-rays confirm the fracture is in an unacceptable position. Using anesthesia as needed, the physician manipulates the fracture by pushing, pulling, or maneuvering the fracture into the desired position. Traction may be used to aid in the manipulation or for stabilization. A cast or brace is applied to the leg.

27766
The physician makes an incision overlying the medial malleolus near the ankle. The incision is extended through the tissue and deep to the bone. The fractured medial malleolus is identified. The physician places the fractured pieces of bone into proper position and alignment. The physician applies bone fixation devices, such as screws or pins, to secure the fractured pieces. The wound is irrigated with antibiotic solution and closed in layers. A splint, cast, or brace is applied to the leg.

27767-27768
In 27767, the physician treats a fracture of the posterior malleolus of the ankle without open surgery or any manipulation of the bones. Separately reportable x-rays confirm the fracture is in an acceptable position. A cast or brace is placed on the leg to hold the fragments in place. In 27768, the physician treats a fractured posterior malleolus without open surgery but with manipulation of the fracture. Using anesthesia as needed, the physician manipulates the fracture by pushing, pulling, or maneuvering the fracture into the desired position. Traction may be used to aid in the manipulation or for stabilization. A cast or brace is applied to the leg.

27769
The physician performs open treatment of a posterior malleolus fracture. The physician makes an incision overlying the posterior malleolus near the ankle. The incision is extended through the tissue and deep to the bone. The fractured posterior malleolus is identified. The physician places the fractured pieces of bone into proper position and alignment. The physician may apply bone fixation devices, such as screws or pins, to secure the fractured pieces. The wound is irrigated with antibiotic solution and closed in layers. A splint, cast, or brace is applied to the leg.

27780-27781
The physician treats a fracture of the fibula without open surgery or any manipulation of the bony

fragments in 27780. Separately reportable x-rays are obtained that confirm a stable fracture of the proximal fibula or shaft. The physician applies a cast or brace to the leg to secure the fracture while it heals. In 27781, separately reportable x-rays confirm a fracture that is unstable and requires manipulation. Using anesthesia as needed, the physician pushes, pulls, or maneuvers the leg until the fracture is in the proper position and alignment. A cast or brace is placed on the leg to hold the fracture in place while it heals.

27784
The physician makes an incision in the skin of the leg overlying the fractured area of the fibula. The tissues are dissected deep to the bone and the fracture is identified. Any nonviable tissue is debrided. The physician places the bony fragments into their correct position and alignment. Fixation devices, such as plates, screws, or wires may be applied to maintain the fracture reduction. With the fracture stabilized, the physician irrigates the wound with antibiotic solution. The wound is closed in layers. A cast, splint, or brace may be applied to the leg.

27786-27788
The physician treats a fracture of the distal fibula (also known as the lateral malleolus) without open surgery or any manipulation of the bones in 27786. Separately reportable x-rays confirm the fracture of the distal fibula with the bony fragments in stable position. The physician applies a cast or brace to hold the fracture in place until it heals. In 27788, separately reportable x-rays confirm a fracture that is unstable and requires manipulation. Using anesthesia as needed, the physician pushes, pulls, or maneuvers the leg until the fracture is in the proper position and alignment. A cast or brace is placed on the leg to hold the fracture in place while it heals.

27792
The physician makes an incision in the skin of the leg overlying the fractured area of the distal fibula. The tissues are dissected deep to the bone and the fracture is identified. Any nonviable tissue is debrided. The physician places the bony fragments into their correct position and alignment. Fixation devices, such as plates, screws, or wires, may be applied to maintain the fracture reduction. With the fracture stabilized, the physician irrigates the wound with antibiotic solution. The wound is closed in layers. A cast, splint, or brace may be applied to the leg.

27808-27810
The physician treats a bimalleolar fracture of the ankle without open surgery or any manipulation of the fractured pieces in 27808. A bimalleolar fracture may include the lateral and medial malleoli, the lateral and posterior malleoli, or the medial and posterior malleoli. Separately reportable x-rays confirm the fracture of the malleoli with the bony fragments in stable position. The physician applies a cast or brace to hold the fracture in place until it heals. In 27810, separately reportable x-rays confirm fractures of the malleoli that are unstable and require manipulation. Using anesthesia as needed, the physician pushes, pulls, or maneuvers the foot, ankle, and leg until the fracture is in the proper position and alignment. A cast or brace is placed on the leg to hold the fracture in place while it heals.

27814
The physician performs open treatment of a bimalleolar ankle fracture. The fracture may consist of the lateral and medial malleoli, the lateral and posterior malleoli, or the medial and posterior malleoli. The physician makes incisions on each side of the ankle overlying the fractures. Each incision is carried deep through the soft tissues and to the bone. The fractures are identified by exposing the fragments. Nonviable tissue and any intervening tissue between the ends of the fractured pieces are debrided. Each malleolus fracture is placed into its correct position one at a time. Bony fixation devices, such as metal plates, screws, wires, or pins, may be applied to stabilize the fractures. When the fractures are stabilized, the skin incisions are irrigated with antibiotic solution and closed in layers. A cast or brace may be applied to the leg.

27816-27818
The physician treats a fracture of the ankle involving all three of the malleoli (medial, lateral, and posterior) without open surgery or any manipulation of the fractured pieces in 27816. Separately reportable x-rays confirm the fracture of the malleolus of the ankle with the bony fragments in stable position. The physician applies a cast or brace to hold the fracture in place until it heals. In 27818, separately reportable x-rays confirm trimalleolar ankle fracture that is unstable and requires manipulation. Using anesthesia as needed, the physician pushes, pulls, or maneuvers the foot, ankle, and leg until the fracture is in the proper position and alignment. A cast or brace is placed on the leg to hold the fracture in place while it heals.

27822-27823
The physician makes at least two separate incisions in the skin overlying the trimalleolar fracture. This fracture involves all three malleoli: medial, lateral, and posterior. The incisions are carried deep to the bones and the extent of each fracture is identified. Any nonviable or intervening tissue is dissected and debrided as needed. One at a time, the physician restores the fractured pieces to their correct positions. Using bony fixation devices, such as pins, plates, or screws, the physician repairs the fractures of the lateral and medial malleolus. The posterior malleolus (lip) fracture is left in position without applying fixation devices in 27822. In 27823, the posterior malleolus (lip) fracture is also repositioned to its correct position and secured similarly. Another incision may be required to obtain adequate fixation of all three

fractures. The wounds are irrigated with antibiotic solution and closed in layers. A cast or brace is applied to the foot and leg.

27824-27825
The physician treats a fracture of the distal tibia extending into the ankle joint without open surgery or any manipulation of the fractured pieces. Separately reportable x-rays confirm the fracture of the distal tibia extending into the ankle joint (e.g., pilon or tibial plafond) with the bony fragments in stable position. Using anesthesia as needed, the physician applies a cast or brace to the foot and leg to hold the fracture in place until it heals. In 27825, separately reportable x-rays confirm a distal tibia fracture (e.g., pilon or tibial plafond) that is unstable and requires manipulation. Using anesthesia as needed, the physician pushes, pulls, or maneuvers the foot, ankle, and leg until the fracture is in the proper position and alignment. Traction may be applied. A cast or brace is applied to the foot and leg.

27826-27828
The physician treats a fracture of the distal tibia with fixation of the fibula only in 27826, the tibia only in 27827, or both in 27828. The physician makes an incision overlying the ankle to treat a fracture of the distal tibia, extending into the ankle joint (pilon or tibial plafond fracture). The incision is carried to the bone. Often, two or more incisions are necessary in 27828. Any nonviable tissues are dissected and debrided. The fracture pieces are placed in appropriate position. Using the fibula bone as a strut or splint, the physician may apply fixation devices such as screws or plates to stabilize the fracture. No fixation devices are applied to the tibia in 27826. In 27827, the physician applies fixation to the tibia to stabilize the fractured pieces. In 27828, fixation is applied to both the tibia and fibula. The wound is irrigated with antibiotic solution and closed in layers. A cast, brace, or splint is applied.

27829
The physician makes an incision in the skin overlying the ankle. The tissues are dissected to the distal joint between the tibia and fibula. Nonviable tissues are debrided as needed. The physician places the tibia and fibula in the correct position to reduce or realign the disruption. Fixation devices, such as screws, are applied as needed to hold the joint (also known as a syndesmosis) in the correct position. The wound is irrigated and closed in layers. A cast or brace may be applied to the leg.

27830-27831
The physician treats a dislocation of the proximal joint (near the knee) between the tibia and fibula without the use of anesthesia in 27830 or with anesthesia in 27831. Separately reportable x-rays are obtained that confirm the dislocation. No open surgery or extensive manipulation is necessary in 27830. Anesthesia is necessary in 27831 to perform manipulation of the leg and correctly aligning the bones. The physician applies a brace or splint to the leg and knee to hold the bones in appropriate position while healing takes place.

27832
The physician makes an incision overlying the joint between the tibia and fibula and near the knee to reposition a dislocation of these two bones. Tissue is dissected to the joint and the joint is exposed. The physician identifies the dislocation and treats it one of several ways. The area may be treated by holding the joint together with fixation devices such as screws, pins, or wires. The physician may excise or remove a piece of the proximal fibula. The physician irrigates the wound and closes it in layers. A brace or splint may be applied to protect the joint and maintain its position until it heals.

27840-27842
The physician treats a dislocation of the ankle joint without anesthesia in 27840. Separately reportable x-rays confirm that the ankle joint requires no manipulation or open surgery. A cast or brace is applied to stabilize the dislocation. In 27842, anesthesia is required to perform manipulation of the dislocated ankle joint. Percutaneous skeletal fixation, such as pins, may be applied. The physician makes small incisions in the skin and inserts the pins through the skin and into the bones of the ankle joint. No open incisions are necessary. When the ankle joint is stabilized, the physician applies a cast or brace.

27846-27848
The physician treats a dislocation of the ankle joint with open surgery. An incision is made overlying the ankle joint and is extended deep to the joint. More than one incision may be necessary in 27848. Tissues are dissected around the joint. The joint may need to be surgically opened to restore it in the appropriate position. Percutaneous skeletal fixation may be applied to stabilize the dislocation. If applied, the physician makes small incisions in the skin and inserts the pins through the skin and into the bones. No repair or internal fixation is necessary in 27846. In 27848, bony fixation devices, such as screws, plates, or wires are necessary. External fixation devices may also be applied on the outside of the ankle to maintain joint position. The physician irrigates the joint and wound and closes the wound in layers. A brace, splint, or cast is applied to maintain the relocated joint.

27860
The physician performs manipulation of the ankle with the patient under general anesthesia. The physician pushes, pulls, and maneuvers the foot, ankle, and leg to treat a stiff ankle. The physician may apply traction devices to the ankle to help perform the manipulations. Traction is removed.

Musculoskeletal

27870

The physician performs surgery on the ankle to fuse the ankle joint. The physician makes two or more incisions overlying the ankle joint, exposing the joint. The incisions are individually extended deep to the joint. The physician opens the joint through an arthrotomy incision. Tissue is dissected and debrided as necessary. The surfaces of the joint are prepared so that they can be fused together. Preparation includes debriding and smoothing so that an intimate fit can be accomplished. Numerous methods can be used to fuse the joint, including screws, plates, or external fixation devices. The physician irrigates the joint and closes the arthrotomy. The incisions are the irrigated and closed in layers. A cast or brace is applied to hold the newly fused joint in place until the bones heal together.

27871

The periosteum is stripped from the anteroposterior fibula, the lateral talus, and the calcaneus. The distal portion of the fibula is removed about 1.5 centimeters above the level of the distal tibia and the dissection is carried over the anterior distal tibia to the medial malleolus. The physician makes an incision along the tibia and the periosteum is stripped distally to the level of the calcaneus. Using a saw, the physician cuts through the neck of talus to mobilize and remove the talus as one large fragment or morselized fragments. With the talus gone, the calcaneus can be seen. The distal end of the tibia is removed perpendicular to the long axis of the tibia. The physician uses a saw to remove the dorsal calcaneus and to create a flat surface for the arthrodesis. The two flat surfaces of the distal tibia and dorsal calcaneus are brought together to establish a varus/valgus and dorsiflexion/ plantar flexion alignment. A cut is made along the anterior tibia parallel to the cut made in the neck of the talus which creates a flat surface for apposing the neck of the talus. The bone surfaces are deeply scaled to prepare for internal fixation. Kirschner wires are used to place the tibia and calcaneus in apposition. Using an anterior cruciate guide, a pin is guided form the calcaneus across the fusion site to the anterior cortex of the tibia. Once satisfactory fixation has been achieved, cannulated screws are placed through the neck of the talus into the tibia. The wound is closed over a drain and a dressing incorporating plaster splints is applied. Marcaine is instilled through the drain tube into the wound.

27880

The physician performs an amputation of the leg below the knee. The physician makes an incision in the skin of the leg at the level where the amputation is to take place. The incision is carried completely around the leg. The tissue is dissected to the bones. The large arteries, veins, and nerves are identified and tied off prior to being cut. Tissue is further debrided as needed. The tibia and fibula are identified. The physician surgically cuts the bones, completing the amputation. The wound is irrigated and closed in layers, including the skin. A soft dressing is placed over the stump.

27881

The physician performs an amputation of the leg below the knee and the fitting technique for an artificial leg. The physician makes an incision in the skin of the leg at the level where the amputation will be performed. The incision is extended completely around the leg. The tissue is dissected to the bones. The large arteries, veins, and nerves are identified and tied off prior to being cut. Tissue is further debrided as needed. The physician surgically cuts the tibia and fibula individually to complete the amputation. The wound is irrigated with antibiotic solution. The wound and skin are closed in layers. The remaining stump is fitted with a cast to prepare it for eventual placement of an artificial leg.

27882

The physician places a pneumatic tourniquet on the thigh. The limb is measured for optimal stump length and marks are made to facilitate skin flap preparation. Progressive incisions are made through soft tissues, and nerves and vessels are ligated. The tibia and fibula are bisected with a circular saw, rounded, and smoothed. The calf muscles are brought forward over the ends of the tibia and fibula and attached to the connective tissue on the front of the stump. The tourniquet is released and bleeding points are electrocoagulated. A drainage tube is placed deep in the muscle flap and the skin flaps are closed and sutured. A soft dressing is applied, followed by a rigid dressing in preparation for prosthetic devices fabrication.

27884

The physician performs an amputation of the leg below the knee as part of a secondary closure of a wound or to revise a scar. The physician makes the necessary incisions on the leg where the amputation is to be performed. Open wounds are debrided as necessary. Scars are excised. The physician dissects the tissue around the tibia and fibula. The tibia and fibula are surgically cut to complete the amputation. The wounds are irrigated with antibiotic solution and closed in layers. Any previous wounds left open are also irrigated and closed. Any scars that may cause problems with the use of an artificial leg are excised and revised. The stump may be placed in a soft dressing.

27886

The physician performs an amputation on the leg below the knee in a patient who has already undergone amputation. The physician identifies the additional area of the remaining stump requiring amputation. An incision is made in the skin at the appropriate site and extended laterally and medially around the leg. The tissue is dissected to the bones. The large arteries, veins, and nerves are identified and tied off prior to being cut. Tissue is further debrided as needed. The physician surgically cuts the tibia and fibula individually to complete the reamputation. The wound is irrigated with antibiotic solution. The wound and skin may be closed in layers. If infection is present, the incision may be temporarily left open to drain.

27888
The physician performs an amputation of the foot near the ankle while leaving much of the soft tissue of the heel intact. The physician makes a long incision in the skin overlying the ankle at about the level of the medial and lateral malleoli. The incision is carried deep to the ankle joint. The talus bone is removed from the joint and the incision is carried to the heel bone (calcaneus). The soft tissues of the bottom of the heel are kept with the leg. The skin on the bottom of the foot is cut to complete the amputation of the foot. The major arteries, veins, and nerves are identified and ligated. The wound is irrigated with antibiotic solution and may be closed in layers. If infection of the foot is present, this operation is performed in two stages. The amputation is performed and later the soft tissues and skin are repaired and closed. A soft dressing is applied.

27889
The physician performs an amputation of the ankle directly through the joint with removal of the foot. An incision is made overlying the ankle joint. The incision is carried around the ankle and deep to the joint. The tissues are dissected and the major arteries, veins, and nerves are identified and individually ligated. The ankle joint is opened through an arthrotomy incision and the foot is dislocated from the ankle joint and removed. Tissue is debrided as necessary. Muscles and tendons are attached to the remaining tibia and fibula bones as appropriate. The wound is irrigated with antibiotic solution and may be closed in layers. If infection is present, the incision is temporarily left open to drain. A soft dressing, cast, or splint may be applied.

27892
The physician performs surgery on the anterior and/or lateral compartments of the leg reducing high pressure within the compartments. The physician makes incisions in the skin overlying the respective compartments. Multiple incisions may be required. The incisions are extended deep to the muscle fascia. Long incisions are made in the fascia to relieve the pressure. The muscles are examined and any nonviable muscle or nerve tissue is debrided and removed. The physician may also debride and remove nonviable muscle tissue from within the compartments. The incisions in the fascia and skin are left open.

27893
The physician performs surgery on the posterior compartments of the leg to reduce high pressure within the compartments. The physician also removes muscle tissue from within the compartments that has become nonviable because of the high pressures. The physician makes incisions in the skin overlying the posterior compartments of the leg. Several incisions may be required. These are extended deep to the muscle fascia. Long incisions are made in the fascia the full length of the compartments. The underlying muscles are examined. Any and all nonviable muscle and nerve tissue is debrided and removed. The fascia and skin incisions are left open.

27894
The physician performs surgery on all the compartments of the leg to reduce high pressures within the compartments. Muscle and nerve tissue that has become nonviable because of the high pressures is debrided. The physician makes multiple incisions in the skin overlying the respective compartments of the leg. These incisions are carried deep to the muscle fascia. Long incisions are made in the fascia the full length of the muscles. The muscles in each compartment are examined. Any nonviable muscle or nerve tissue is debrided. The incisions in the skin and the fascia are left open.

28001
The physician performs this procedure to correct bursa, fluid-filled sacks that reduce friction. The physician makes an incision over the bursa. Soft tissues are retracted and an incision is made in the bursa to drain fluid. An antibiotic is often injected to clear the infection. The incision is sutured and dressed.

28002-28003
An incision is made through skin and fascia to expose the infection. The infected tissue is removed, and the bursal sac may be removed or simply incised and drained. If the wound is large, the physician may leave the incision open after irrigating the area, treating it with antibiotic, and packing it with petroleum gauze. The wound heals from inside. Report 28003 if more than one incision is necessary.

28005
The physician incises the bone cortex of infected bone in the foot to treat an abscess or osteomyelitis. The physician makes an incision over the affected area. Dissection is carried through the soft tissues to expose the bone. The periosteum is split and reflected from the bone overlying the infected area. A curette may be used to scrape away the abscess or infected portion to healthy bony tissue or drill holes may be made through the cortex into the medullary canal in a window outline around the infected or abscessed bone. The area is drained and debrided of infected bony and soft tissue. The physician irrigates the area with antibiotic solution, the periosteum is closed over the bone, and the soft tissues are sutured closed; or the wound is packed and left open, allowing the area to drain. Secondary closure is performed approximately three weeks later. Dressings are changed daily. A splint may be applied to limit movement.

Musculoskeletal

28008

There are two common techniques used in fasciotomies of the foot and/or toes. For flexion contracture of the toe, a plantar incision is made. A transverse division of the fibrotic and contracted cord of plantar fascia in the foot and/or toe is performed through one or more incisions. A percutaneous procedure may be performed instead which involves making a stab incision over the center of the plantar fascia where it attaches to the calcaneus. The plantar fascia is transversely divided.

28010-28011

This procedure is performed to correct mallet or hammer toe. The physician makes a small incision at the crease of the toe where the tendon is restricted. The tendon is released from the bone and the toe is straightened. The incision is sutured and dressing applied. Report 28011 if more than one toe is being straightened.

28020-28024

The physician performs an arthrotomy of an intertarsal or tarsometatarsal joint in 28020, a metatarsophalangeal joint in 28022, or an interphalangeal joint in 28024 that includes exploration, drainage, or removal of any loose or foreign body. An incision is made over the joint to be exposed. The soft tissues are dissected away and the joint capsule is exposed and incised. The joint space is explored, any necrotic tissue is removed, and infection or abnormal fluid is drained. If a foreign body is present (e.g., bullet, nail, gravel), it is exposed and removed. The wound is irrigated with antibiotic solution. The physician may leave the wound packed open with daily dressing changes to allow for drainage and secondary healing by granulation. If the incision is repaired, drain tubes may be inserted and the incision is closed in layers with sutures, staples, and/or Steri-strips.

28035

The physician releases the tarsal tunnel, decompressing the posterior tibial nerve. The tarsal tunnel is located on the inside of the ankle. A curved incision is made along the inner ankle, behind the medial malleolus. Dissection exposes the flexor retinaculum. The retinaculum is released along the tunnel. The posterior tibial nerve is identified by blunt dissection and traced as it courses down through the tarsal tunnel. Three branches of the posterior tibial nerve are also traced at the point. Once the posterior tibial nerve and its terminal branches are released, the nerve is inspected to see if any other constrictions are present. The incision is closed layers without closing the retinaculum.

28039-28045

The physician removes a tumor from the soft tissue of the foot or toe that is located in the subcutaneous tissue in 28039 and 28043 and in the deep soft tissue, below the fascial plane, or within the muscle in 28041 and 28045. With the proper anesthesia administered, the physician makes an incision in the skin overlying the mass and dissects down to the tumor. The extent of the tumor is identified and a dissection is undertaken all the way around the tumor. A portion of neighboring soft tissue may also be removed to ensure adequate removal of all tumor tissue. A drain may be inserted and the incision is repaired with layers of sutures, staples, or Steri-strips. Report 28043 for excision of a subcutaneous tumor whose resected area is less than 1.5 cm and 28039 for a resected area that is 1.5 cm or greater. Report 28045 for excision of a subfascial or intramuscular tumor whose resected area is less than 1.5 cm and 28041 for a resected area 1.5 cm or greater.

28046-28047

The physician performs a radical resection (excision) of a malignant soft tissue tumor from the foot or toe, not involving bone. An incision is made over the tumor and dissection exposes it. The tumor and any adjacent tissue that may be affected by the spread of the neoplasm are excised. Large resections may be needed. The type and stage of the lesion determines the extent of the tumor margin resection area. Muscle or fascia may need to be repaired and drains may be placed. The surgical wound is repaired by intermediate or complex closure, adjacent tissue transfer, or graft. Report 28046 for a resected area of less than 3 cm, and 28047 for a resected area 3 cm or greater.

28050-28054

Arthrotomy is performed to determine the type and extent of a growth. The physician makes the incision at the joint line and opens the skin to remove a part of the growth. The incision is often left open to allow for pathology confirmation of the growth's composition and allow for synovectomy if malignant. Once complete, the wound is sutured closed. Report 28050 for an intertarsal or tarsometatarsal joint; report 28052 for metatarsophalangeal joint; and report 28054 for an interphalangeal joint.

28055

The patient lies in the supine position and is placed under general anesthesia. A physician, using loupe magnification, marks the dorsal side of the affected web space, including both metatarsal heads and metatarsophalangeal joints. The physician makes a straight dorsal skin incision midline in the intermetatarsal space beginning at the metatarsal heads and extending to the terminal skin fold of the web space. A blade is used to deepen the incision through subcutaneous tissue to the level of the interosseous fascia. The layer is split to expose the transverse metatarsal ligament, which is also divided. The physician uses a laminar to spread the metatarsal heads and the nerve is dissected out in the web space to its bifurcation. The inflamed bursal tissue is removed, though the plantar fat pad generally is left intact. The physician dissects the nerve 3 cm and cleanly divides at its proximal point. The wound is irrigated. The subcutaneous tissue and skin are sutured and a compression dressing is used to protect the wound.

28060-28062

Heel pain originates deep within the foot, directly on the heel bone or within the foot's connective tissues, called the fascia. Pain can result when these tissues become irritated or inflamed, or when small spurs grow on the heel bone. Prior to surgery a tourniquet is applied to the ankle. The surgeon makes a longitudinal incision inside the heel and the fat that has filled the wound is separated with a key elevator. The medial third of the plantar fascia is identified using right angle retractors under direct vision. Report 28062 when the medial third of the plantar fascia is incised and a 1-centimeter segment is removed. The tourniquet is released and the skin closed with nonabsorbable sutures. A dressing and a removable walking boot are applied. The sutures are removed in about three weeks and weightbearing is increased; though the radical procedure increases postoperative recovery period.

28070-28072

The physician makes an incision on the top of the foot over the small bones of the foot in front of the ankle. The skin is reflected to expose the tendons. They are divided and the soft tissue reflected to expose the bones. The synovium is the lining between the bones that becomes thickened and inflamed with some disease processes. The synovium is removed by careful dissection. The bones are allowed back into their original position and the skin is closed with sutures. Report 28072 if the area of incision is further toward the toes, between the long bones of the foot and the phalanges (toes).

28080

Surgery for Morton's neuroma involves removal of the fibrous nerve growth from between the toes. The physician places a tourniquet at the ankle and a small incision is made on the top of the foot between the third and fourth metatarsal bones. The soft tissue is reflected in the web space and the bones are separated. Pressure is applied to the bottom of the foot under the web space causing the neuroma to protrude upward. The neuroma is removed and the nerve trunk is cut to prevent regrowth. The tourniquet is removed and the incision is closed with sutures.

28086-28088

A synovectomy is performed to relieve pain in the active stages of disease before joint destruction. For this procedure description the flexor hallucis longus (FHL) tendon was used as the example. The patient is placed in a supine position with a tourniquet placed around the ankle. The physician makes a 5-centimeter incision behind the medial malleolus and toward the navicular. The neurovascular bundle is retracted, revealing the FHL in its fibro-osseous sheath. The reticulum is released to the level of the sustentaculum tali and the tendon is inspected. A tenosynovectomy is performed and the tenosynovial tissue is debrided. Any nodules are excised and longitudinal tears are repaired. The FHL is released until the retinaculum no longer prohibits its motion. The distal soft tissue is approximated and the skin is sutured closed. A below-knee splint or cast is applied. This procedure will vary depending upon which tendon is affected. Use 28088 when affected tendon is the extensor tendon.

28090-28092

The physician makes an incision through the skin on the foot to expose a portion of the tendon requiring removal and suturing ends together, or a portion of the joint capsule or lining of the joint may be removed from the foot. The lesion, usually a cyst or benign ganglion growth, is excised or removed from the tissue surrounding the tendon. Every effort is made not to disrupt the tendon itself. The incision is closed and a soft dressing is applied. Report 28092 if the lesion is located in the toes. Report each toe separately.

28100-28103

A bone cyst or benign tumor of the talus or calcaneus is removed. The physician makes an incision in the ankle or heel overlying the cyst or tumor. The skin and underlying soft tissues are reflected to expose the periosteum, which is separated from the bone. Curettes or osteotomes are used to scrape or cut the lesion from the bone. Once the benign tumor or cyst is removed and healthy bone tissue is present, the periosteum is repositioned and the incision is repaired in layers. If the bone defect created requires a graft for repair, the physician obtains the necessary size bone graft from a separate donor site on the patient (usually the iliac crest) and packs it into the site where the tumor or bone cyst was removed or uses a bone bank allograft. Report 28102 if an autograft is obtained and 28103 if an allograft is used.

28104-28107

A bone cyst or benign tumor of the tarsal or metatarsal is removed. The physician makes an incision in the foot overlying the cyst or tumor. The skin and underlying soft tissues are reflected to expose the periosteum, which is separated from the bone. Curettes or osteotomes are used to scrape or cut the lesion from the bone. Once the benign tumor or cyst is removed and healthy bone tissue is present, the periosteum is repositioned and the incision is repaired in layers. If the bone defect created requires a graft for repair, the physician obtains the necessary size bone graft from a separate donor site on the patient (usually the iliac crest) and packs it into the site where the tumor or bone cyst was removed or uses a bone bank allograft. Report 28106 if an autograft is obtained and 28107 if an allograft is used.

28108
A bone cyst or benign tumor of the phalanges of the foot is removed. The physician makes an incision in the affected toe overlying the cyst or tumor. The skin and underlying soft tissues are reflected to expose the periosteum, which is separated from the bone. Curettes or osteotomes are used to scrape or cut the lesion from the bone. Once the benign tumor or cyst is removed and healthy bone tissue is present, the periosteum is repositioned and the incision is repaired in layers.

28110
The physician makes a lateral incision over the distal third of the fifth metatarsal bone to expose the metatarsal head. An osteotome is used to remove the lateral extension of the bone (bunionette). The cut is made along the shaft of the bone. The wound is irrigated and the soft tissues are sutured. Soft dressing is applied and weight bearing is allowed as tolerated.

28111-28114
The patient is placed under regional anesthesia and an ankle tourniquet is applied. The physician incises the first metatarsophalangeal joint and inserts a Weitlaner retractor into the wound to remove the joint capsule as well as any proliferative synovial tissue. The physician detaches the adductor hallucis tendon from the base of the phalanx and cuts the metatarsal head and base with an osteotome. A longitudinal incision is made in the second and fourth dorsal web spaces, which exposes the base of the phalanx for excision with a bone cutter. The same is done for all the lesser toes. The physician uses blunt dissection to strip the plantar structures that are around the metatarsal head and places them on the plantar aspect of the foot. The fat pad is returned to its position under the metatarsal heads. If an arthrodesis is performed, the physician drives Steinmann pins through the tip of the toe and back across to the site of the arthrodesis. The skin is sutured closed and a dressing applied. Report 28111 for a complete excision of the first metatarsal head. Report 28112 for the excision of the second, third, or fourth metatarsal heads and 28113 for the fifth metatarsal head. Report 28114 when using a Clayton type procedure in the approach to the metatarsal heads. The physician makes an incision over the metatarsal heads that curves to overlie the first metatarsophalangeal joint. The exposed extensor tendons are retracted or, if contracted, cut in the line of the incision. The physician opens the incision by depressing the toes and the bases of the proximal phalanges, thus, delivering the heads into the wound. The metatarsal heads are dissected free with partial excision of the proximal phalanges, excluding the first metatarsal. Only the subcutaneous tissue and skin are sutured. If the extensor tendon has been cut, it is resutured.

28116
A tarsal coalition is an abnormal fusion of the tarsal bones or small bones of the foot near the ankle. A common procedure is for the physician to reproduce the division of the calcaneus and the navicular. An incision is made on the dorsal aspect of the foot. The soft tissues and tendons are reflected to expose the bones. An osteotome is used to divide the calcaneus and the navicular. The ends of the bones are smoothed for better articulation or movement of the joint. The wound is irrigated and sutured closed.

28118
A mid-thigh tourniquet is placed on the leg to control bleeding. The physician makes a longitudinal incision on the lateral side of the ankle behind the ankle bone. The peroneal tendons are protected and the plantar fascia is reflected to expose the calcaneus. A crescent shaped cut is made into the bone with a motor saw using a curved blade. The bottom of the heel bone is shifted backward to correct the deformity. The bone fragments are secured in place with a staple or wire. A short leg case is applied for six weeks. At that time the staple or wire is removed and full weight bearing is allowed.

28119
The physician applies a tourniquet to the ankle. The medial third of the plantar fascia is incised and, through the incision, the abductor hallucis muscle is elevated and a portion of the deep fascia of the abductor hallucis released, if required. To excise the spur, a key elevator is placed forward and back of the spur and the spur is transected with an osteotome. The cut spur is removed using a rongeur and the bone edges smoothed. Thrombin or bone wax can be packed at the cut edge of the bone. In some cases, part of the flexor digitorum brevis must be removed for a calcaneal spur that is deeply embedded. Once the spur is removed, the margins are smoothed with a bone rasp. The wound is irrigated and a dressing is applied.

28120-28124
The physician performs a partial excision of the talus or calcaneus in 28120, a tarsal or metatarsal bone in 28122, or the phalanx of a toe in 28124 to remove infected bone or bony prominence. An incision is made over the affected part of the foot, ankle, heel, or toe and the underlying soft tissues are divided to expose the bone. The periosteum is reflected and the infected portion of bone is removed and irrigated. The excavation of bone may excise a crater-like piece, leave a small saucer-like shelf depression in the bone, or may remove a portion of the shaft (diaphysis) of a long bone. If a significant portion of bone is removed, the physician may use bone graft material to fill the cavity left in the bone. The periosteum is closed over the bone, the soft tissues are sutured closed, and a soft dressing is applied. A short leg cast may be applied to keep the foot and ankle in position.

28126
This procedure is often performed in conjunction with other separately reportable procedures in an effort to

correct alignment of the toes. A dorsal longitudinal incision is made on top of the foot where the toe joins the foot. The soft tissues are reflected to expose the bone. A wedge of bone is cut out of and removed from the proximal phalanx. The remaining portions of the bone are approximated to realign the toe. The bones are held in this position by a Kirschner wire that is drilled and placed through the end of the bone. The wound is sutured and the foot is elevated for 72 hours. After that time the patient is allowed to bear weight as tolerated in a wood soled shoe.

28130

The physician performs surgery on the astragalus, the bone that articulates with the fibula and tibia to form the ankle joint. The physician makes a curved incision overlying the lateral part of the ankle. The incision is carried down to the joint capsule of the subtalar and talonavicular joints. The capsule is excised and the surrounding ligaments are divided. The talus is removed. If further correction is needed, the physician may elect to excise the navicular bone in a procedure to be reported separately. The calcaneus is usually placed in the ankle mortise and held in place by inserting a Kirschner wire through the heel into the tibia. The incision is closed in layers.

28140

The physician makes an incision on the dorsal aspect of the foot over the affected metatarsal. With the patient under anesthesia, the physician dissects to the metatarsal bone. The affected part of the metatarsal is cut with a bone saw on either end and removed. The incision is closed in layers with sutures, staples, and Steri-strips.

28150

The physician removes a single phalanx of a toe. An incision is made over the involved toe. This is carried deep through the fascia to the bone. The specific phalanx is identified. Using blunt and sharp dissection, the phalanx is isolated and exposed. The physician removes the bone as indicated. The wound is irrigated and the tissues are closed in layers to include the skin. Code for each phalanx removed.

28153

The physician resects the condyle of the distal end of the phalanx, amputating the toe. The physician makes a curvilinear incision to fashion "fish-mouth" skin flaps side-to-side or dorsally to plantarly. The amputation can be done as a disarticulation or by resecting through the bone. If the head of the toe is disarticulated, the capsular ligaments are severed and the distal phalanx is removed. The capsule is approximated with sutures. If the bone is resected, a power saw is used to transect the proximal phalanx. A drain may be used. The skin flaps are approximated with sutures and a compression dressing is applied. Report each toe separately.

28160

The physician removes a part of the phalanges or interphalangeal joint for problems including trauma, infection, tumors, and gangrene resulting from diabetes. The physician makes an oblique incision over the toe and dissection exposes the affected bone. Using a small bone cutter, the physician excises the involved bone that may include the interphalangeal joint. Any angular areas of bone are rounded to relieve internal and external pressure. Sutures are used to close the incision and skin flaps without tension.

28171-28175

The physician performs a radical resection (excision) of a tumor. Radical tumor removal involves complete removal of the affected tarsal bone (28171), including the navicular, cuboid, or any of the three cuneiform bones, and the soft tissues that surround it. This is performed in order to prevent spreading of the tumor to adjacent tissues. If it is determined that the foot is going to be spared from amputation, the affected bone and soft tissues would be removed through a dorsal incision at the front of the ankle. The skin and tendons are reflected and the bone is identified. The capsule is released and the bone is removed in one piece. Tissue samples are taken to determine the extent of tumor growth and need of soft tissue removal. Once complete, the wound is closed with sutures and dressing and cast are applied. Report 28173 if the tumor resection is performed on the metatarsal bone(s) in which case an incision is made longitudinally over the affected metatarsal bone(s). Report 28175 if the tumor resection involves the phalanges of the toe (proximal, middle, or distal).

28190-28193

Subcutaneous refers to something under the skin. An incision is made through the skin and it is reflected to expose the foreign body. It is removed and the wound is irrigated and the wound is closed. A dressing is applied and aftercare may include antibiotic injection into the wound and orally. Weight bearing is allowed as the wound heals. Report 28192 if the foreign body lies deeper in the foot. Report 28193 if repair of torn tendon, nerves, and blood supply is required.

28200-28202

If the tendon has ruptured, surgery may be required to repair the ruptured tendon or to replace it with a tendon graft. Usually, another tendon in the foot, such as the tendon that bends the four lesser toes is used as a tendon graft to replace the function of the posterior tibial tendon. In cases of a fixed flatfoot, the physician may perform a fusion (or arthrodesis) of the foot that requires the removal of a joint between two bones and the two bones on either side of the joint are allowed to grow together. This type of operation is used to stop pain from joints or to realign the bones. Several joints must be fused to control the flatfoot after a posterior tibial tendon rupture. Report 28022 if a free graft is used for the repair. The patient may be placed in a cast for six to eight weeks.

28208-28210
A dorsal incision is made on top of the foot over the injured extensor tendon. The skin is reflected and the ends of the tendon are exposed. They are cleaned for easier attachment. The ends are brought together and sutured. The wound is closed and a soft dressing and cast are applied for 3 weeks. Report 28210 if secondary with free graft, each tendon.

28220-28222
The patient is in a supine position and general anesthesia is administered. A tourniquet is placed on the thigh to create a bloodless field desirable for the procedure. An incision is made over the flexor hallucis longus (FHL); a procedure often used to alleviate the pain associated with "dancer's tendonitis." The deep fascia is divided and the surgeon retracts the neurovascular bundle. The fascia is opened and the surgeon frees the tendon from any surrounding adhesions. The tendon is retracted and inspected for tears that should be debrided or repaired. The wound is irrigated and closed in layers with catgut. A plaster cast or splint is applied. Report 28222 when the procedure is performed on multiple tendons.

28225-28226
The patient is in a supine position and general anesthesia is administered. A tourniquet is placed on the thigh to create a bloodless field desirable for the procedure. The foot and great toe is placed in a dorsiflex position to simplify finding of the proximal and distal ends of the extensor hallucis longus. An incision is made over the dorsal aspect of the first metatarsal. The fascia is opened and the physician frees the tendon from the any surrounding adhesions. The tendon is retracted and inspected for tears that should be debrided or repaired. The wound is irrigated and closed in layers with catgut A short-leg compression dressing incorporating plaster splints is applied. Report 28226 when the procedure is performed on multiple tendons.

28230
A small incision is made on the back of the ankle and a sharp blade knife is inserted into the Achilles tendon and rotated medially and laterally. The foot is forced into dorsiflexion to stretch the tendon to the appropriate length. Direct pressure is applied to control bleeding. A suture is made in the incision and a dressing is applied.

28232-28234
This procedure is often done for repair of hammer toe. A small incision is made on the crease of the toe on the bottom of the foot. The skin is reflected and the tendon is exposed. The tendon is released from its attachment site allowing the toe to extend. This is usually is accompanied by other procedures. The incision is closed with sutures and a soft dressing is applied. Report 28234 if the incision is made on the dorsal toe and the extensor tendon is released.

28238
The physician advances the posterior tibial tendon with excision of the accessory navicular bone. The physician makes a longitudinal skin incision on the medial side of the foot from the tip of the medial malleolus to the medial cuneiform. Dissection exposes the posterior tibialis tendon. The accessory navicular is identified and removed with sharp dissection. The physician detaches the distal portion of the posterior tibialis tendon and drills a hole through the navicular. The tendon is passed through the drill hole and sutured back to itself or to surrounding periosteal tissue. Wounds are sutured closed.

28240
A dorsal incision is made over the first metatarsal bone extending to the middle of the big toe. The skin is reflected to expose the underlying soft tissues. The abductor hallucis muscle is identified and its distal insertion is removed from the bone of the big toe. This allows the toe to move back out into proper alignment. The incision is closed with sutures and a soft dressing is applied. The patient can bear weight while using a wood soled shoe.

28250
A longitudinal incision is made on the medial side of the heel and is carried distally to the other side of the heel in order to expose the underlying soft tissues. The superficial and deep layers of the plantar fascia are separated from the muscle and fat by blunt dissection. This allows for freedom of movement of the fascia and releases the scar tissue. Once sufficient movement is obtained, the incision is sutured and a soft dressing is applied. Weight bearing is allowed as the wound heals.

28260-28262
This procedure is often performed in an effort to correct club foot deformity. A medial incision is made on the inner ankle to expose the underlying tissues. The skin and tendons are reflected to expose the joint capsule of the talonavicular joint. The joint capsule is cut by sharp dissection to release the deformity of the mid foot. Several releases can be made from this approach. A particular order is followed in order to obtain the appropriate amount of release. The incision is closed with sutures and a cast is applied. Report 28261 if tendon lengthening is also performed. Report 28262 when posterior, medial, and subtalar soft tissue contractures are released to correct severe clubfoot deformity. The patient is placed supine and a posteromedial skin incision is made. The tibialis posterior, flexor digitorum longus, and flexor hallucis longus are identified and mobilized. The contracted tendons are lengthened. The talonavicular and talotibial joint capsules are incised. The joint capsules are cut by sharp dissection to release the deformity.

Bones are placed in correct alignment and secured with a single Kirschner wire.

28264-28272

Two straight incisions are made, one between the first and second metatarsals and the second in line with the fourth metatarsal. The tendons and nerve bundles are reflected to expose the intermetatarsal space. The ligament there is divided by careful dissection. The dorsal capsule of the first tarsometatarsal joint is divided. The second tarsometatarsal joint is identified and divided. Similar incisions are made at the bases of other metatarsals. When sufficient motion is gained the bleeding is controlled and the incisions are closed with sutures. A series of short leg casts are applied for 8-12 weeks. Report 28270 if the joint capsule released is that between the tarsal and the toe. Report 28272 if the joint capsule released is that between the small bones of the toe.

28280

This procedure is performed when there is a deformity of the foot where toes are missing and a large gap exists between the toes present. A dorsal incision is made along the web space extending to the ends of both toes. The skin is reflected and the alignment of the bones are corrected with osteotomies of the base of the proximal phalanx. The toes are approximated and the incisions closed bringing the toes together and eliminating the gap between them. This produces an artificial syndactylism or webbing of the toes. A soft dressing is applied and weight bearing is allowed in two to three weeks.

28285

Hammertoe describes an abnormal flexion posture of the proximal interphalangeal joint of one of the lesser toes. Conservative treatment is usually unsuccessful. The physician makes an elliptical incision over the proximal interphalangeal joint 5 mm to 6 mm wide. A portion of the extensor tendon and joint capsule under the skin is removed. The collateral ligaments are cut to allow the toe to be flexed to 90 degrees. The head and neck of the proximal phalanx are removed with a small power blade saw and the ends of the bones are smoothed. The toe is checked for ROM and the extensor tendon is reattached and the incision is closed with sutures.

28286

An elliptical shaped incision is made in the skin under the fifth toe. The soft tissues are reflected to expose the underlying structures. The proximal phalanx is removed leaving a space between the base of the metatarsal and the distal phalanx. The deep tissues and skin incisions are closed with sutures.

28288

The physician surgically removes a portion of a metatarsal head of the foot. A separate incision is made for each involved bone in the dorsal aspect of the foot. The tendons are retracted and preserved. The incision is carried deep to the particular metatarsal head. The bony spurs or prominences are excised from the head using appropriate surgical instruments. The physician debrides and smooths the remaining bone. The wound is irrigated and closed in layers. Code for each metatarsal head removed.

28289

The physician corrects a hallux rigidus deformity and performs a cheilectomy. Hallux rigidus is a condition caused by degenerative (DJD) arthritic changes at the first metatarsophalangeal joint; the condition causes pain, limited range of motion, and dorsiflexion. In the context of this procedure a cheilectomy refers to excision of part of the lip of the first metatarsophalangeal joint. The podiatrist makes a dorsal incision over the first metatarsophalangeal joint. The extensor hallucis longus tendon is retracted, and the joint capsule is entered. Osteophytes and part of the metatarsal head are excised. Bony irregularities may be removed using a chisel, and edges smoothed with a rasp. When adequate dorsiflexion (60-80 degrees) is obtained the capsule is closed, the tendon is returned to its correct anatomical position, and the skin is closed with sutures.

28290

The physician surgically corrects a bunion of the foot using a Silver-type procedure. The physician makes an incision over the top of the foot between the first and second toes. The incision is carried deep to the head of the first metatarsal bone. The physician releases (frees) the structure of the lateral joint realigning the toe. A second incision is made over the medial aspect (inside) of the big toe and carried deep to the bone. The offending bony spur, known as a bunion, is removed from the head of the first metatarsal bone. The sesamoid bones, which lie underneath this bone, are examined removed as needed. The incisions are irrigated and closed in layers.

28292

The physician surgically corrects a bunion of the foot using a Keller, McBride, or Mayo type procedure. The physician makes an incision along the medial aspect (inside) of the big toe. The incision is carried deep to the metatarsophalangeal joint. In a Keller procedure, the median eminence and one-third of the base of the proximal phalanx are resected. This is followed by repair of the plantar plate and stabilization with a longitudinal K-wire. In a McBride procedure, the adductor tendon and transverse metatarsal ligament are released through an incision made between the first and second toe. Following the release of the contractured lateral structures, the subluxated first MP joint is reduced and the median eminence is excised. The medial capsule of the first MP joint is imbricated through a medial arthrotomy incision. In a Mayo procedure, the first metatarsal head and its articular cartilage are removed and the remaining bone is restructured. Excision of a medial exostosis is performed. The external joint capsule is configured so that it can be used as cartilage between the metatarsal bone and the base of the first proximal phalanx. Fixation devices may hold the bone fragments in position. The wound is closed in layers after thorough irrigation.

28293
The physician treats a bunion of the foot by removing the joint of the big toe and replacing it with an artificial implant. The physician makes an incision over the big toe where it joins the foot. The incision is carried deep to the joint (first metatarsal phalanges joint). An incision is made in the joint capsule and it is exposed. The physician removes (resects) the surfaces of the bones in the joint. The sesamoid bones of the foot are examined and removed as necessary. The bones are placed in proper alignment and debrided further as needed. An artificial implant is placed in the joint and fixed to the bones. The incision is irrigated and closed in layers.

28294
The physician treats a bunion of the foot with tendon transplants. The physician makes an incision over the top of the foot between the first and second toes. The incision is carried deep to the metatarsophalangeal joint. The extensor tendon of the big toe is identified and cut to restore the toe to its correct alignment. The extensor tendon is reattached (transplanted) to the head of the metatarsal bone. Other tendons may also be cut and reattached until correct anatomical alignment is achieved. Any contracted structures are released as needed. The sesamoid bones are examined and removed as necessary. A second incision is typically made over the inside of the big toe. This incision is carried deep to the bony eminence, or bunion, which is surgically removed. The proximal phalanx and metatarsal bone are fused. The incisions are irrigated and closed in layers.

28296
The physician treats a bunion of the foot with an osteotomy, a cut in the first metatarsal bone. The physician makes an incision in the skin over the top of the foot at the base of the big toe. Depending on the particular osteotomy to be performed, the incision may be made over the medial (inside) of the foot; or two separate incisions may be made. The incision is carried deep to the bone. Tissue is dissected and debrided as needed. The bony eminence, or bunion, is removed from the first metatarsal head. The physician cuts through the bone, performing the desired osteotomy. The pieces of bone are realigned to their correct position. Fixation devices may hold the bone fragments in position. The wound is closed in layers after thorough irrigation.

28297
The physician treats a bunion of the foot using a Lapidus-type procedure in which the joint between the first metatarsal bone and first cuneiform bone is fused. The physician makes an incision in the skin between the first and second toes on the top of the foot. The incision is extended deep to the first metatarsophalangeal joint. The physician releases the contracted structures of the lateral joint. A second incision is made in the top of the foot over the first metatarsocuneiform joint. The joint capsule is exposed and opened. The articular cartilage of the joint is removed. The ends of the bones are fashioned so they fit intimately together. The joint and bones of the big toe are manipulated into alignment. Fixation devices are needed to fuse the metatarsal and cuneiform bones. Prior to closing the incisions, the sesamoid bones are examined and removed as needed. The wounds are irrigated and closed in layers.

28298
The physician treats a bunion of the foot using a phalanx osteotomy (Akin procedure). This procedure consists of a removal of a bony wedge from the base for the proximal phalanx. A medial based wedge (0.3-0.4 mm) is cut allowing reorientation of bone while leaving the lateral cortex intact. The medial eminence is excised. Fixation is usually accomplished by crossed K-wires, pins, or screws. The wound is closed in layers after irrigation.

28299
The physician treats a severe hallux valgus (bunion) deformity of the foot by double osteotomy. The physician makes an incision over the first metatarsal. Various methods of double osteotomy may be performed. In a distal Austin double osteotomy, the soft tissue is corrected and a V-osteotomy is made through the metatarsal head and neck that is displaced laterally to replace the metatarsal head over sesamoids. K wire fixation is used and a cast is applied.

28300-28302
The physician performs an osteotomy of the calcaneus with or without internal fixation in 28300. An incision is made on the lateral aspect of the foot. The sural nerve is exposed and retracted. The calcaneus is exposed by stripping off the peroneal sheath from the calcaneus. A saw blade is used to make an oblique cut in the calcaneus. Another cut is made to free a 4 mm to 8 mm wedge of bone. The physician gently manipulates and closes the osteotomy site, stabilizing the site with a screw, staple, or Steinmann pin, if necessary. The incision is closed in layers and a plaster splint (reported separately) is applied. Report 28302 if this procedure is performed on the talus.

28304-28305
The physician makes an incision over the base of the first metatarsal, and over the second and third metatarsals depending on the extent and type of

plantar flexion deformity. The physician retracts the tendons and incises the periosteum to expose the metatarsal. A sagittal saw is used to remove a wedge of bone. Samples screws, or Kirschner wires are used for fixation. After the immediate postoperative dressing, a short leg case is applied and worn for six to eight weeks. Report 28305 when a bone graft is necessary due to the segmental bone loss. For this procedure, the physician debrides the metatarsal joint and a bone graft from the iliac crest graft is shaped and placed between the prepared surfaces of the proximal phalanx and the first metatarsal. Steinmann pins are centered on the phalangeal articular surface and driven distally, crossing the interphalangeal joint and exiting at the tip of the toe. The physician uses a lamina spreader to place the bone graft and drives Steinmann pins across the bone graft into the metatarsal metaphysis until they penetrate the metatarsal cortex. The pins are severed at their tips of the tie, leaving a short extension to aid in later pin removal. The tissue and skin are sutured closed.

28306-28308

A dorsomedial incision is made over the big toe and the skin and soft tissues are reflected. In many cases this procedure is performed in an effort to correct the poor alignment of the big toe. In addition to removal of the medial eminence, a cut is made through the metatarsal shaft and a portion of the bone is removed in order to correct the alignment of the bone. Wires are used to reattach the bone in its corrected alignment. Sutures are used to close the incision. Weight bearing is protected for several weeks. Report 28307 if a bone graft is used to correct the alignment of the first metatarsal shaft and attached with wire or screws. Report 28308 if the procedure is performed on other metatarsal bones.

28309

The physician treats a patient with a high arch (pes cavus) by performing osteotomies (bone cuts) on the metatarsal bones of the foot. Two or more incisions are made on the dorsal surface (top) of the foot over the metatarsal bones. The incisions are carried deep to the bones. Tissue is dissected and debrided as needed. The physician makes cuts through the metatarsal bones one at a time. The bones are each manipulated in such a way that the angles are changed. The manipulation allows the high arch to be shifted to an appropriate position. Multiple fixation devices such as screws, plates, or pins are applied to hold the bones in their new positions. The incisions are irrigated and closed in layers.

28310-28312

A medial incision is made on the proximal phalanx or first digit of the big toe. The periosteum is divided from the bone and a wedge section of bone is removed. The toe is properly aligned and a screw is place through the bone to maintain alignment. The incision is closed with sutures. Weight bearing is allowed in six weeks at that time the screw is commonly removed. Report 28312 when procedure is performed on any other phalanges of any toe.

28313

In this procedure the correction of the toe deformity is made by releasing soft tissues and possibly involving tendon transfers. It does not include cutting or realigning the shafts of the bones. An incision is made on top of the toe to be operated on. The involved tendons are identified and released and reattached at another portion of the bone and the joint capsule may be released to decrease the abnormal pull on the joint. Once proper alignment is obtained, the incisions are closed and a soft dressing is applied. Weight bearing is protected and gradually progressed.

28315

The sesamoid bone is a small bone that lies under the metatarsal heads of each toe. This procedure involves the removal of that bone. A dorsal incision is made between the first and second metatarsal bones proximal to the web space. The soft tissues are reflected in order to separate the two metatarsal heads. The inter-sesamoid ligament is released and the sesamoid bone is removed with small Kocher clamp or forceps. The soft tissues are replaced and the incision is closed with sutures. Weight bearing is permitted as the wound heals.

28320

Nonunion or malunion of the talus may result from trauma. Fractures are rare but may unite in malposition. The treatment of choice depends upon the portion of bone involved. If the top if the talus (articular surface) is involved, the treatment of choice is to fuse the talus to the tibia with bone grafting and casting. The same can be done for malunion of the calcaneus. In this case the calcaneus may be fused to the talus.

28322

An incision is made on the dorsum of the foot parallel with the shaft of the affected bones. The old fracture is exposed and divided with an osteotome. A small portion of the bone must be removed to produce a nonunion or division between the bone surfaces. The bones alignment is corrected and stabilized with a medullary pin. The incision is closed with sutures and a cast is applied. At three weeks the medullary pin is removed and a walking boot is applied. A felt pad is placed under the metatarsal region to maintain proper alignment.

28340-28341

Macrodactyly is the overgrowth of one or several adjacent digits of a hand or foot. The physician generally stages the surgery to control blood supply. In the first stage, reported using 28340, the physician removes the distal half of the middle phalanx and the tip of the remaining shaft is shaped to a pencil point. The articular surface of the distal phalanx is reamed to create a receptacle, which is fitted over the end of the middle phalanx. Kirschner wires are used to hold the position. An incision is made across the digit at the mid phalanx level and carried down to the midsagittal line. The soft tissue (up to 20 percent) is excised over the dorsum. A hump is created with the plantar tissue. In the second stage, reported using 28341, the physician performs the underlying bony work following the excision of soft tissue over the dorsum. Kirschner wire is used to stabilize the digit and the extensor tendon is shortened while the flexor tendon is left alone. Epiphysiodesis of the bones is performed during growth.

28344
This is a congenital anomaly where an extra toe is present. Correction is obtained by surgical removal of the accessory digit. An oval shaped incision is made at the base of the toe to be removed. The underlying tendons are drawn distally and divided. The joint capsule of the metatarsophalangeal joint is incised and the joint is disarticulated and the toe is removed. If x-rays reveal any development of an extra metatarsal bone, the incision is continued proximally and the bone is also removed. The incision is closed and a soft dressing is applied.

28345
The physician surgically corrects the congenital deformity of webbed skin between the toes of the foot. Separately reportable x-rays are obtained of the foot and toes to ensure that no extra bones are present. The physician operates on one web space at a time. The skin is incised between each toe and the excess tissue is removed. A thorough debridement is performed, including the removal of any extraneous subcutaneous or nonviable tissues. Skin grafts may be required depending on the extent of the webbing removed and the debridement performed. The incisions are individually closed in layers to ensure proper skin coverage of the toes. A soft dressing is typically applied.

28360
Cleft foot (lobster foot) is an anomaly in which a single cleft or division extends proximally into the foot, sometimes even as far as the midfoot. Generally one or more toes are missing and often their metatarsals are absent. The goal is to improve function of the foot. A V-shaped incision is made at the cleft and the skin of the opposing surfaces within the cleft is removed, but the dorsal and plantar skin flaps are left to close the cleft when sutured together. Any bone or joint deformity is corrected at the time of surgery. This may include capsulotomies and osteotomies of any retained metatarsals and phalanges. If pin fixation is required the pins and short leg cast are removed at six weeks.

28400
The physician treats a fracture of the calcaneus bone without open surgery or manipulation of the bone. Separately reportable x-rays confirm a fracture of the calcaneus bone with the fracture fragments in acceptable position. The physician places the foot and leg in a cast, brace, or splint to provide protection while the bone heels.

28405
The physician treats a fracture of the calcaneus without open surgery but with manipulation of the fracture pieces. Separately reportable x-rays confirm a fractured calcaneus with the fracture pieces in an unacceptable position. The physician pushes and otherwise maneuvers the fracture fragments into the proper position. No incisions are required.

28406
The physician treats a fracture of the calcaneus without open surgery but with the use of manipulation and pins placed through the skin and into the bone. With the patient under anesthesia, the physician pushes and otherwise maneuvers the fracture fragments into the proper position. Through small holes in the skin, the physician places pins that are driven into the pieces of the bone in appropriate places to hold the fracture in position for healing. X-rays (separately reported) are used to help guide the pins correctly. With the fracture reduced, the physician places the foot and leg in a cast, splint, or brace.

28415
The physician performs surgery on a fracture of the calcaneus bone. An incision is made in the skin overlying the fractured area of the calcaneus. The incision is extended deep to the bone. Tissues are dissected and debrided as required. The fracture fragments are identified. The physician places the bony pieces in their correct position. Fixation devices may be applied on the inside adjacent to the bone. The incision is irrigated and closed in layers.

28420
The physician treats a fracture of the calcaneus with open surgery and the use of bone graft. The physician makes an incision in the skin overlying the fractured calcaneus. Tissues are dissected and debrided as needed as the incision is carried down to the bone. The fracture is identified and exposed. Through a separate incision, the physician obtains a bone graft from the patient's ilium and closes the surgically created graft donor site. The fractured pieces are placed in appropriate position and the bone graft is placed in and around the fracture site. Fixation devices are applied to hold the fracture and graft in the correct position. The wound is irrigated and closed in layers.

28430
The physician treats a fracture of the talus bone in the ankle without performing open surgery or any

manipulation of the fracture. X rays (reported separately) confirm a fracture of the talus bone with the fractured pieces in an acceptable position. The physician applies a cast, brace, or splint to protect the ankle and keep the fracture positioned correctly. No incisions are required.

28435
The physician treats a fracture of the talus bone of the ankle without performing open surgery but with manipulation of the fracture. X rays (separately reported) confirm a fracture of the talus bone with the fractured pieces in an unacceptable position. With the patient under anesthesia (separately reported), the physician pushes, pulls, or otherwise maneuvers the foot, ankle, and leg to restore the fracture to a satisfactory position.

28436
The physician treats a fracture of the talus bone of the ankle without open surgery but with the use of manipulation and pins placed through small holes in the skin and into the bone. With the patient under anesthesia, the physician pushes, pulls, or otherwise maneuvers the foot, ankle, and leg to restore the fracture to a satisfactory position. Surgical pins are placed through the skin and guided into the talus bone. The pins help manipulate the fracture pieces and hold them in the proper place. Screws may also be applied. X-rays (separately reported) are obtained to confirm the correct placement of the fixation and the fracture.

28445
The physician treats a fracture of the talus bone of the ankle with open surgery. An incision is made in the skin overlying the fractured talus. This is extended deep to the talus bone. Tissues are dissected and debrided as needed. The fracture is identified and exposed. Any intervening tissue between the fractured pieces is removed. The physician reduces (realigns) the fracture, placing the pieces back into satisfactory position. Fixation devices are applied as needed to hold the fragments in place internally. The wound is irrigated and closed.

28446
After the size and type of lesions are determined radiographically, the physician performs an open osteochondral autograft on the talus (ankle bone). The physician exposes the defect area by cutting to the bone and retracting the soft tissue. The defect is excised and the margins are squared off and abraded to reach healthy, bleeding, subchondral bone. Using coring reamers, an osteochondral graft is harvested from a non-load bearing region of articular cartilage and implanted into the damaged joint location. Supplementary fixation may be used by inserting biodegradable pins. The incision is closed.

28450
The physician treats a fracture of one of the tarsal bones, other than the calcaneus or the talus without performing open surgery or any manipulation. X-rays (separately reported) confirm a fracture of the navicular, cuboid, or one of the three cuneiforms, with the fragments in acceptable position. The physician applies a cast, brace, or splint to the foot and leg to protect the fracture and hold it in the appropriate position.

28455
The physician treats a fracture of one of the tarsal bones other than the talus or calcaneus without performing open surgery but with manipulation of the fracture. Separately reportable x-rays confirm a fracture of the navicular, cuboid, or one of the cuneiform bones with the fracture fragments in an unacceptable position. With the patient under anesthesia as needed, the physician pushes, pulls, or otherwise maneuvers the foot, ankle, or leg to restore the bony pieces to a satisfactory position.

28456
The physician treats a fracture of one of the tarsal bones other than the talus or calcaneus without open surgery but with the aid of manipulation and pins placed through skin and into the bone. The physician pushes, pulls, or otherwise maneuvers the foot, ankle, or leg to restore the fracture of the navicular, cuboid, or one of the cuneiforms to a satisfactory position. Pins or screws are placed through small holes in the skin and guided into the bone. X-rays (separately reported) are used to help manipulate the fracture as needed. A cast, brace or splint is applied.

28465
The physician treats a fracture of one of the tarsal bones, other than the talus or calcaneus, with open surgery. The physician makes an incision in the skin of the foot overlying the particular fracture of the navicular, cuboid, or one of the three cuneiform bones. Tissue is dissected and debrided deep to the bone. The fracture is identified and exposed. The physician places the fracture fragments in their correct position. Any intervening or nonviable tissue is removed. Fixation devices such as screws, plates, pins, or wires are applied as needed to hold the fracture properly. The incision is irrigated and closed in layers.

28470
The physician treats a fracture of one of the five metatarsal bones without open surgery or any manipulation of the fracture. X-rays (separately reported) confirm a fracture of a metatarsal bone of the foot with the fracture fragments in acceptable position and alignment. The physician places the foot, ankle, and leg in a cast, splint, or brace as needed.

28475
The physician treats a fracture of one of the five metatarsal bones in the foot without performing open surgery but with manipulation of the fracture. X-rays (separately reported) confirm a fracture of the metatarsal bone with the bony pieces in an unacceptable position. The physician pushes, pulls, or other maneuvers the foot to restore the fracture fragments to a satisfactory position and alignment. X-rays (separately reportable) confirm desired results. The foot and leg are placed in a cast or brace.

28476
The physician treats a fracture of one of the five metatarsal bones without performing open surgery but with the use of manipulation and fixation pins that are placed through skin and into the bone. The physician pushes, pulls, or otherwise maneuvers the foot, toes, or ankle to restore the fractured bone to its proper position. Fixation pins, wires, or screw are inserted through small holes in the skin and guided into the fracture pieces. X-rays (separately reported) are often used to aid in the proper placement of the fixation and to ensure that the fracture is in satisfactory position.

28485
The physician treats a fracture of one of the five metatarsals with open surgery. An incision is made overlying the particular metatarsal fracture. The tissues are dissected and debrided as needed. The fracture is identified and exposed. Any tissue between the fracture pieces is removed. The fracture fragments are reduced (realigned) to their correct position. Fixation devices are applied as needed to hold the fracture in place. The wound is irrigated and closed in layers.

28490
The physician treat as a fracture of the big toe involving one or both of the bones without any open surgery or manipulation of the bones. X-rays (separately reported) confirm a fracture or fractures of the bones in the big toe with the fragments in an acceptable position for healing. The physician places a cast, sling, or brace on the toe and foot as needed.

28495
The physician treats a fracture of the big toe involving one or both of the bones without open surgery, but with manipulation of the fracture. X-rays (reported separately) of the big toe confirm a fracture or fracture of the bones in the big toe in an unacceptable position. With the patient under anesthesia as required, the physician pulls or pushes on the toe and foot to restore the bony pieces to their proper place. X-rays (separately reported) are taken to ensure that the fracture is aligned correctly. A cast, splint, or brace is placed on the toe and foot.

28496
The physician treats a fracture of the big toe involving one or both of the bones without open surgery but with pin fixation through the skin and manipulation of the fractures. The physician pushes, pulls, or otherwise maneuvers the toe and foot to place the fracture pieces in their appropriate position. Fixation devices such as pins or wires are inserted through small holds in the skin and guided into the bone. The fixation is used to manipulate the fracture further into proper position and to hold bones in the right place. X-rays (separately reported) are used to confirm the desired placement and fracture alignment.

28505
The physician treats a fracture of the big toe involving one or both of the bones with open surgery. An incision is made in the skin overlying the big toe. The tissues are dissected and debrided down to the bones. The fracture or fractures are identified and exposed. The physician places the fracture fragments into their proper position removing any intervening tissue. Fixation devices such as pins screws, wires, or plates are applied to hold the bony pieces together as required. The wound is irrigated and closed in layers. A cast, splint, or brace may be applied to the toe and foot.

28510
The physician treats a fracture of one of the four toes other than the big toe. No open surgery or manipulation of the toe or foot is required. X-rays (reported separately) of the toe confirm a fracture or fractures of the bones where the fragments are in an acceptable position. The physician applies a splint, brace, or cast to the toe and foot.

28515
The physician treats a fracture of one of the four toes other than the big toes involving one or more of the bones in the toe without performing open surgery but with manipulation of the toe and foot. X-rays (reported separately) confirm a fracture or fractures of the toe with the bony pieces in unacceptable positions for correct healing. The physician pulls or pushes on the toe or foot in such a way as to restore the bones to their correct alignment. X-rays (reported separately) are taken to confirm the desired result. A splint, cast or brace may be applied.

28525
The physician treats a fracture of one of the four toes, other than the big toe, with open surgery and fixation devices as needed. An incision is made in the skin overlying the fractured toe. The tissues are dissected to identify and expose the fracture or fractures. The physician places the fracture fragments into their correct position. Fixation devices are applied as needed to hold the bony pieces together. This may include pins, wires, or screws. The wound is irrigated and closed in layers.

28530
The physician treats a fracture of a sesamoid bone in the foot without performing any open surgery. X-rays (separately reported) confirm a fracture of the sesamoid bone. The physician places the foot and ankle in a splint, brace, or cast to protect the bone while it heals.

28531
The physician treats a fracture of a sesamoid bone in the foot by open surgery. An incision is made in the foot over the fractured sesamoid bone. The incision is carried deep to the bone, tissue is dissected, and tissue is debrided to expose the fracture. The physician may apply a fixation device to hold the fracture together. The bone may be excised if it is nonviable. The wound is irrigated and closed in layers.

28540
The physician reduces a tarsal bone dislocation, other than talotarsal, without requiring anesthesia. Separately reportable x-rays are obtained of the foot to demonstrate a tarsal bone dislocation in such a position that the physician can return it to the correct position without the need for anesthesia. The physician manipulates the involved bones to restore normal anatomy and function. Separately reportable x-rays are again obtained to note the desired outcome. A cast or brace is applied as indicated.

28545
The physician reduces a tarsal bone dislocation, other than talotarsal, with the use of anesthesia. Separately reportable x-rays are obtained of the foot to demonstrate a tarsal bone dislocation which will require anesthesia to reduce. General or regional anesthesia is employed. Without any surgical incision, the physician manipulates the involved bones so as to return them to the appropriate anatomic position. Separately reportable x-rays are obtained to confirm the adequacy of the reduction. A cast or brace is applied.

28546
The physician treats dislocation of a bone in the foot, other than talotarsal, with manipulation and percutaneous skeletal fixation. The physician performs this procedure on the joints of the mid-foot with the patient soothed by general anesthesia or a nerve block. The physician manually reduces the dislocation between the tarsal bones. Radiographs or fluoroscopy (reported separately) are typically used to confirm proper alignment and position. To stabilize the dislocation, small stab incisions are made, and holes are drilled through the bone. Pins are inserted through the drill holes and cross the affected joint(s) to maintain the reduction. The pins are cut just below the surface of the skin.

28555
The physician performs open treatment of a dislocation of the tarsal bone, sometimes using internal fixation. With the patient under anesthesia, the physician makes an incision and dissects down to the dislocated tarsal bones that are located in the mid-foot. The physician reduces the dislocation. To stabilize the dislocation, the physician may elect Kirschner wires placed through drill holes in the adjacent bone or bone screws. The incision is closed in layers with sutures and Steri-strips. A cast may be applied.

28570-28575
The physician treats talotarsal joint dislocation without surgery. The physician may use separately reportable x-rays to identify dislocation and congruency of joint surfaces. The physician manipulates the bones back into position. A short leg cast is applied with the foot in a plantar flexed position. Report 28570 if the manipulation is performed without anesthesia. Report 28575 if anesthesia is required to perform the procedure.

28576
The physician repairs the dislocation of a joint of the foot with percutaneous skeletal fixation, with manipulation. The physician performs this procedure with the patient soothed by general anesthesia or a spinal block. The physician manually reduces the dislocation between the talus and tarsal bones and uses separately reportable x-ray or fluoroscopy to confirm alignment and position. To stabilize the dislocation, small stab incisions are made and holes are drilled through the bones. Pins are inserted through the drill holes that cross the affected joint(s) and maintain the reduction. The pins are cut just below the surface of the skin.

28585
The physician treats a talotarsal joint dislocation, sometimes using internal fixation. This dislocation involves the talonavicular joint. Open treatment is required in cases where closed reduction was unsuccessful, or where the dislocation is unstable. An incision is made over the dorsal part of the foot and dissection exposes the talonavicular joint dislocation. The physician reduces the dislocation. The physician may elect to use Kirschner wires or screws that are placed through drilled holes in the talus and navicular to hold them in place. The incision is closed in layers with sutures and Steri-strips.

28600-28605
The patient is positioned supine on the table. The physician manually manipulates the foot in an effort to reposition the tarsal and metatarsal bones into proper alignment. Report 28600 if no anesthesia is required; however, pain medication may be given orally if needed. Report 28605 if performed with patient under general or regional anesthesia.

28606
With the patient under anesthesia, the foot is manually manipulated to correct the dislocation of the

tarsometatarsal joint. A small stab incision is made over the tarsal bone and a small pin or screw is inserted to stabilize the affected tarsal and metatarsal bones. The incision is closed with one to two sutures and a cast is applied.

28615
The physician performs open treatment of a tarsometatarsal joint dislocation. A dorsal incision is made over the dislocated bones. The soft tissues are reflected to expose the joint. The joint is properly aligned and stabilized with screws, plates, or wire fixation. The incision is closed with sutures and a cast is applied. Weight bearing is allowed at six weeks. At that time the physician may remove the metal fixation.

28630-28635
The patient is placed supine on the table. The physician manually manipulates the foot in order to reduce the dislocation of the metatarsophalangeal joint (joint between the long bone of the foot and the toe). Report 28630, if this is performed without anesthesia. Report 28635 if performed under general anesthesia.

28636
With the patient under anesthesia, the foot is manually manipulated to correct the dislocation of the long bone of the foot and the toe. A small stab incision is made over the metatarsal bone and a small pin or screw is inserted to stabilize the two bones. The incision is closed with one to two sutures and a cast is applied.

28645
The physician performs open treatment of a metatarsophalangeal joint dislocation. A dorsal incision is made over the dislocated bones. The soft tissues are reflected to expose the joint. The joint is properly aligned and stabilized with screws, plates, or wire fixation. The incision is closed with sutures and a cast is applied. Weight bearing is allowed at six weeks. At that time the physician removes the metal fixation.

28660
The physician reduces a dislocation of an interphalangeal joint of a toe without the need of anesthesia. Separately reportable x-rays are obtained which identify the specific dislocation. The physician manipulates the toe without performing surgery to reduce the dislocation. Post reduction x-rays are obtained.

28665
The physician reduces a dislocation of an interphalangeal joint of a toe with the use of anesthesia. Separately reportable x-rays are obtained to identify the specific dislocation. A local or regional anesthetic is employed. The physician manipulates the toe to reduce the dislocation. Separately reportable x-rays are obtained to confirm that appropriate position has been accomplished.

28666
The physician reduces the dislocation of an interphalangeal joint of a toe with the use of percutaneous fixation. Separately reportable x-rays are obtained to demonstrate the dislocated joint. Anesthesia is typically employed. The physician inserts metal pins or wires directly through the sterilized skin of the toe and into the affected phalanges. The toe is manipulated with the help of these fixation devices to reduce the dislocation. Separately reportable x-rays are obtained to ensure that the joint is again anatomically correct. The pins or wires may be removed or retained for later removal.

28675
The physician reduces a dislocation of the interphalangeal joint of a toe by surgically opening the joint. Separately reportable x-rays are obtained to determine the extent of the dislocation. The patient is taken to the operating room and anesthesia is utilized. The physician makes a longitudinal incision over the dislocated bones. The incision is continued deep to the joint. The capsule is identified and opened. The physician identifies the dislocation and reduces it. This may require the use of internal fixation devices to complete the reduction and/or hold it in place. The wound is irrigated and closed in layers. A dressing is applied.

28705
The physician fuses several joints in and around the ankle. It can be performed in one operation or in two separate surgeries. In either case, the physician makes at least one incision around the ankle. Incisions are continued deep to the ankle mortise itself and to the following joints: the talocalcaneal, the talonavicular, and the calcaneocuboid. The capsule of each joint is opened, explored, and debrided. Osteotomies are performed so that viable bone is available on each side of the joints. The physician utilizes a variety of internal fixation devices such as pins, wires, plates, or screws to connect the bones together across each joint. This allows the bones to fuse together as they heal. Because of the extensive nature of the surgery, and the time required for healing, the surgery is frequently performed in two stages. Incisions are irrigated and closed as usual. A cast is applied until the fusion is solidly healed.

28715
The physician fuses the talonavicular, the calcaneocuboid, and the subtalar (talocalcaneal) joints. The physician makes incisions on each side of the foot. These are carried deep to the joints. Tendons are reflected and protected. Each joint is identified. Soft tissues are debrided. The capsules are opened and the joints visualized. Surgical curettes are used to remove the articular cartilage of the joints one at a time so that viable bone is exposed. The physician uses any of a variety of surgical fixation devices including screws,

plates, or wires to connect the bones of each individual joint together. The incisions are irrigated and closed in layers. A cast is applied and continued until all three joints are solidly fused.

28725
The physician fuses the subtalar (talocalcaneal) joint. An incision is made over the lateral ankle and foot. The physician extends this incision deep to the subtalar joint. Tendons and nerves are retracted and protected. Soft tissues are debrided. The joint capsule is incised and the joint is debrided as necessary. Surgical instruments including curettes are utilized to remove the articular cartilage of the joint. Fixation devices such as screws, pins, or wires are employed to maintain fixation of the talus. The incision is closed in layers. A cast is typically applied.

28730
The physician performs surgery on the foot in which more than one of the midtarsal or tarsometatarsal joints are fused. The physician makes one or more incisions over the dorsal aspect of the foot in the skin overlying the affected joints. The incisions are continued deep through the subcutaneous tissue. Nerves and tendons are retracted. The physician identifies the specific problem joints of the tarsals and metatarsals, performing capsulotomies. The joints are entered, explored, and debrided. The physician utilizes any of a variety of friction devices to hold each joint in its fused position. The wounds are irrigated and closed in layers.

28735
The physician performs surgery on the foot in which more than one of the midtarsal or tarsometatarsal joints are fused. The metatarsals are also osteotomized to correct for a flat foot deformity. The physician makes one or more incisions in the dorsal skin of the foot overlying the affected joints and metatarsals. The incisions are continued deep to the particular joints. Nerves and tendons are retracted. The shafts of the metatarsals that will undergo osteotomy are isolated and debrided. The physician performs capsulotomy on each joint to be fused. The metatarsals are cut and realigned in a plantar flexion position to correct flatfoot deformity. The joints, debrided of their articular cartilage, are fashioned for a close fit. The physician utilizes any of a variety of fixation devices such as wires, plates, pins, or screws to hold the metatarsal and the joints in alignment. The incisions are irrigated and closed in layers.

28737
The physician fuses the navicular and cuneiform bones of the foot and advances distally with the posterior tibial tendon the calcaneonavicular, navicular cuneiform and cuneiform metatarsal ligaments. An incision is made over the medial aspect of the foot. This is carried to the tendon and ligaments. The physician creates an osteoperiosteal flap incorporating the tibial tendon and the ligaments. The navicular-cuneiform and metatarsal-cuneiform joints are opened. The surfaces of the joints are denuded of their articular cartilage. The physician utilizes fixation devices such as screws, pins, wires, or plates to hold the joints in position. The flap of ligaments and tendon together is passed forward beneath the anterior tibia and transplanted to the first cuneiform bone and the base of the first metatarsal bone. Friction devices are employed to hold the flap. The incision is irrigated and closed in layers.

28740
The physician fuses one of the midtarsal or tarsometatarsal joints of the foot. Separately reportable x-rays are used to determine the particular joint to be fused. The physician makes an incision in the skin directly overlying the joint. Tendons and nerves are retracted and a capsulotomy is performed. The physician removes the articular cartilage of the bones on both sides of the joint. The bony surfaces are fashioned for a close fit. Any of a variety of fixation devices are used to hold the bones in proper alignment. The wound is irrigated and debrided. The incision is closed in layers.

28750
The physician fuses the joint between the great toe and the first metatarsal bone. A longitudinal incision is made on the dorsal surface of the first toe. It is deepened through the subcutaneous tissue and fascia to the first metatarsophalangeal joint. The nerves and tendons are retracted. A capsulotomy is performed. The physician makes parallel cuts of the metatarsal with a saw or osteotome. The two cuts are placed together in the desired alignment and position. Fixation devices hold the bones in position. The wound is irrigated and closed in layers.

28755
The physician fuses the interphalangeal joint on the great toe. An incision is made over the dorsal aspect of the toe directly overlying the joint. The incision is continued deep to the joint. A capsulotomy is performed. Parallel cuts are made on the two phalanges that constitute the joint. The physician places the cut bones together. Pins or screws hold the bones in the correct alignment. The wound is irrigated and closed.

28760
The physician performs a Jones type procedure. The physician fuses the interphalangeal joint of the great toe and transfers the extensor hallucis longus tendon from its insertion on the phalanges to the first metatarsal bone. An incision is on the dorsal aspect of the great toe and distal first metatarsal. It is continued deep to the extensor hallucis longus tendon. The physician fuses the interphalangeal joint. Fixation devices hold the fusion in place for healing. The neck of the first metatarsal bone is identified dorsally. The extensor hallucis longus tendon is identified dorsally. The extensor hallucis longus tendon is attached to the

metatarsal using any of a variety of fixation devices. The incision is irrigated and closed in layers.

28800
The physician amputates the foot across the midtarsal region. The physician makes the incision so that skin flaps are made dorsally and plantarly. The skin is refracted and the dissection is carried down through the soft tissue. The tendons are severed and allowed to retract. The dorsal and plantar ligaments of the calcaneocuboid and talonavicular joints are released so that the foot can be removed. The physician may also perform a percutaneous Achilles tenotomy (reported separately) to prevent flexion contracture. Skin flaps are closed and a soft compression dressing is applied.

28805
The physician amputates the foot across the transmetatarsal region. The physician makes the incision so that skin flaps are made dorsally and plantarly. The skin is refracted and the dissection is carried down through the soft tissue. The tendons are severed and allowed to retract. The dorsal and plantar ligaments are released so that the foot can be removed. The physician may also perform a percutaneous Achilles tenotomy (reported separately) to prevent flexion contracture. Skin flaps are closed and a soft compression dressing is applied.

28810
The physician performs an amputation of a metatarsal bone and its attached toe. An incision is made dorsally over the involved metatarsal and toe. This is carried deep to the tarsometatarsal joint. The joint and capsule are identified. A capsulotomy is performed and the metatarsal is disarticulated from the other toes. The incision is continued around the toe itself. Tendons are retracted or removed as indicated. The metatarsal bone and the toe are completely dissected free from the foot and removed. The wound is irrigated and debrided. It is closed in layers. A dressing and a cast or a brace are applied.

28820
The physician performs an amputation of a toe at the metatarsophalangeal joint. An incision is made over and around the affected toe where the toe joins the foot. The physician continues the incision deep to the metatarsophalangeal joint. The capsule is identified and a capsulotomy is performed. The proximal phalanx bone is disarticulated from the metatarsal bone. The joint is debrided. The tendon and soft tissues are excised for closure and skin coverage. The toe is excised free from the foot. The wound is irrigated and closed in layers. A dressing and firm-soled shoe are applied.

28825
The physician performs an amputation of a portion of a toe at the level of an interphalangeal joint. An incision is made over the involved toe. It is carried deep to the planned interphalangeal joint amputation site. Skin is preserved around the toe for closure. The physician extends the incision deep to the joint capsule. A capsulotomy is performed and the joint is disarticulated. Debridement is performed. The soft tissues are excised and prepared for the amputation. The desired portion of toe to include the disarticulated bone is excised free. The wound is irrigated and closed in layers. A dressing and post-operative shoe are applied.

28890
The physician treats plantar fasciitis with extracorporeal shock wave therapy (ESWT). This condition is the result of inflammation of the connective tissue from the base of the toes, extending across the arch of the foot, and inserting into the heel bone. When associated with a heel spur, it may also be referred to as "heel spur syndrome." When the condition fails to respond to a more conservative treatment regimen, including exercise, anti-inflammatories, physical therapy modalities, and orthotic devices, ESWT may be indicated. ESWT is the administration of high intensity sound waves at the rate of two or three times per second, from outside of the body. Treatment is provided on an outpatient basis and takes about 30 minutes to perform. Local anesthesia may be provided.

29000
The physician constructs this body cast to provide a foundation for a halo in which the cervical spine must be stabilized. This involves use of a torso body cast to which the halo is attached. Casting material is applied tightly, beginning at the pelvis and extending up the torso to the upper chest. Extenders from the halo (which is already inserted around the head) can be attached to the body cast. This holds the halo very securely. An alternative is to use a prefabricated torso/chest brace that is placed on the upper torso. The previously applied halo is attached.

29010-29015
The physician applies a Risser jacket, a method of correction for a scoliotic curve. The physician places the patient face up on a canvas strap tied to a rectangular frame. A stockinette is stretched over the patient from the head to the knees. A metallic half-circle carrying a moveable jack with a metal plate to be directed toward the apex of the angulation of the ribs is suspended beneath the frame. The rib angulation area is protected by a heave piece of felt covered with a contoured square piece of plaster that rests on the plate. The jack is turned so that it presses the plate in a direction on the rib angulation that corrects the scoliotic curvature. A second jack may be applied to correct a double primary curve or a secondary lumbar curve. The cast is applied in sections while traction is applied to the head with a hatter and the pelvis with a pelvic belt attached to the plaster

girdle. The casting begins with a well-molded neck and shoulder section and finishes with incorporating the trunk. Separately reportable spinal instrumentation largely eliminates the use of the Risser jacket. Report 29015 if this jacket includes the head.

29020-29025
The physician applies a turnbuckle jacket to treat scoliotic curves. The physician places the patient face up on a horizontal canvas strap attached to a rectangular frame. Traction is applied by pulling distally on the pelvis on the convex side of the scoliotic curve and the head is pulled toward the concave side. All bony prominences are padded well and two or three layers of felt are placed under the proposed location of the anterior hinge. A body cast is applied extending from the neck to above the knee on the convex side of the curve. Metal hinges are placed in the front and back of the cast toward the convex side of the curve. The cast is allowed to dry for three to five days, cut at the level of the hinges on the concave side forward and back to the hinges. Turnbuckle lugs are inserted into these cuts. A turnbuckle is attached to these edges. From the opposite side of the cast, the physician removes a large elliptical window between the hinges. The turnbuckle is turned each morning. When x-rays (reported separately) indicate the hinges are on the convex side of the curve, no further correction may be obtained by traction. The sides of the cast are reinforced with plaster and wood strips. The turnbuckle and lugs are removed. A large window is cut in the cast over the area of fusion. Report 29020 for application of the jacket. Report 29025 if the head is included in the jacket.

29035-29046
The physician applies a body cast, shoulder to hips. The physician applies two layers of stockinette to the patient's torso (armpits to hips), adding cotton and felt padding over bony prominences. Fiberglass or plaster cast is applied over the stockinette to create a rigid cast. Report 29035 for application of the cast. Report 29040 if the cast includes the head, Minerva type. Report 29044 if the cast includes one thigh. Report 29046 if the cast includes both thighs.

29049-29085
The physician applies a figure-of-eight cast to maintain shoulder retraction while a clavicle fracture heals. A cast method is seldom used; shoulder retraction is maintained with a figure-of-eight shoulder strap. Report 29049 for the cast itself. Report 29055 if the cast includes a shoulder spica. Report 29058 if the cast includes a plaster Velpeau. Report 29065 if the cast is constructed from shoulder to hand. Report 29075 if the cast is constructed from the elbow to finger. Report 29085 if the cast is constructed over the hand and lower forearm.

29086
The hand is placed in the functioning position, with the thumb opposed. The physician extends a synthetic stockinette from the proximal interphalangeal (PIP) joints of the hand to the wrist joint and cuts a hole for the thumb. The physician covers the gap at the thumb metacarpophalangeal (MCP) joint by splitting the thumb tube to extend it proximal to the MCP joint. Synthetic cast padding is wrapped to cover the cast area two to three layers thick, with extra layers at the proximal wrist to protect the wrist joint during flexion and extension. The physician uses 1-inch or 2-inch casting tape to wrap the hand and thumb in a thumb spica. The wrapping starts with one full around the metacarpals and wrapping the tape around the thumb and hand in a figure-eight pattern, alternating the direction of the wrap around the thumb. The free ends of the stockinette are tucked under the second layer of wrap.

29105
The physician applies a splint from the shoulder to the hand. A long arm posterior splint is used to immobilize a number of injuries around the elbow and forearm. A cotton bandage is wrapped around the forearm from the midpalm region to midarm. Plaster strips or fiberglass splints are applied along the back of the arm and forearm, maintain the elbows and wrist in the desired position.

29125-29126
The physician applies a splint from the forearm to the hand. A short arm splint is used to immobilize the wrist. Cotton padding is applied from midforearm to the midpalm region. Plaster strips or fiberglass splint material are applied along the palm side of the hand, extending to midforearm, maintain the wrist in the desired position. An Ace wrap is applied by the physician to hold the splint material in position. Report 29125 if the splint is static, keeping the wrist totally immobilized. Report 29126 if the splint is dynamic, allowing some movement.

29130-29131
The physician applies a finger splint. This type of splint is applied to immobilize the digits. A twin layer of cotton padding is applied by the physician to the digit, covering the last to joints of that digit. Plaster casting or fiberglass splint material is applied to the finger from just beyond the knuckle to the tip of the finger. Usually the finger is immobilized in a straight position. Report 29130 if the splint applied is static for full immobilization. Report 29131 if the splint applied is dynamic for some movement.

29200-29280
The physician or a medical professional under the physician's direction performs strapping with tape on a patient of any age. In 29200, this technique was once more frequently used to compress the thorax offering some support and to limit deep inhalation following

Musculoskeletal

fracture. This support does not promote healing, but provides palliative relief. A thoracic elastic or canvas binder is more commonly used. Report 29240 if the strapping is applied to the shoulder; report 29260 if strapping is applied to the elbow or wrist; and report 29280 if strapping is applied to the hand or finger.

29305-29325
The physician applies a hip spica cast. The hip spica cast is ideal for patients of all ages who may have hip problems ranging from fractures to dislocations. The physician applies cast padding to the lower torso and hips and extends this down the affected leg in 29305. It may extend below the knee depending on the physician's preference and the extent of hip immobilization desired. The hip is placed at the desired angle and casting material is placed over the padding material and allowed to dry. Report 29325 if the physician applies a one and one-half spica or a cast that envelopes both legs.

29345-29355
The physician applies a cast from the thigh to the toes. The physician places the ankle and knee at the desired angle. Cast padding is applied from the toes to the upper portion of the thigh. Casting material is moistened and applied in an overlapping pattern from the toes to the upper thigh and allowed to harden. Report 29355 if the cast is a walker or ambulatory type.

29358
The physician applies a long leg cast brace for a fracture. Code with caution: this cast is rarely applied, having been replaced by a pre-fabricated long leg brace. The physician places a metal or plastic support (with or without a hinge) on either side of the knee. Casting material is applied over the supports to hold them in place. The cast allows the knee to bend and straighten while stabilizing the knee during side-to-side movement.

29365
The physician applies a cylinder cast from thigh to ankle. This cast is used for fractures of the femur that extend into the knee joint. The knee is positioned at the desired angle. The cast and material are applied and allowed to dry.

29405-29425
The physician applies a cast below the knee to the toes. The physician positions the ankle at the desired angle. Cast padding is applied from the toes to just below the knees. Casting material is moistened and applied to the leg in an overlapping fashion and allowed to dry. Report 29425 if the cast is a walking or ambulatory type.

29435
The physician applies the patellar tendon bearing (PTB) cast for tibial shaft fractures. The cast is constructed to transfer weight to the upper tibia rather than the shaft of the tibia. The physician applies the casting material so that a shelf is formed under the tibial tuberosity/patellar tendon to bear the load of the cast. The foot is also included as part of the cast.

29440
The physician adds a walker to a previously applied cast. Lower extremity casts may be modified for walking with the addition of a walker. There are two types of walkers available: (1) those made of hard rubber and incorporated into the cast and (2) those applied over the cast like a shoe or boot. If the rubber walker is used, it must be secured to the cast with additional plaster.

29445
The physician applies a rigid total contact leg cast. The rigid total contact leg cast is applied to feet and legs demonstrating venous stasis ulcers. Of primary importance in applying this cast is even distribution of contact of the cast over the foot, ankle, and lower leg. The method and cast material used varies with the applicator. Sometimes wound dressing must be applied over the ulcers prior to application of the cast. The cast begins at the foot and extends to just below the knee.

29450
The physician applies a clubfoot cast with molding or manipulation. The cast may be long or short. If applying a cast to the right foot, the physician uses the left hand to grasp the right heel of the patient, placing the thumb over the talar prominence. The physician's right hand grasps the forefoot. The thumb and index finger hold the metatarsophalangeal joint of the great toe and longitudinal traction is exerted on the forefoot. At the same time, gentle pressure is exerted over the head of the talus. After one to two minutes of traction, the foot elongates. It is held in this corrected position while a cast made of fast-setting plaster is applied by a second person over layers of sheet cotton. The cast may be applied only to the foot and connected to the leg in separate parts or the cast may be applied at one time. If applied to the left foot, the physician uses the right hand to grasp the heel.

29505
The physician applies a long leg splint from thigh to the ankle or toes. A long leg posterior splint is used to immobilize a number of injuries around the knee or ankle. The physician wraps cotton bandaging around the involved leg from the upper thigh to the ankle or toes. Plaster strips or fiberglass splint material are applied along the posterior aspect of the leg from the upper thigh to the ankle or toes. After the splint material dries, it is secured into place by an Ace wrap.

29515
The physician applies a short leg splint from calf to foot. A short leg splint is used to immobilize the ankle. The physician wraps cotton bandaging from just below the knee to the toes. Plaster strips or fiberglass splinting

material are applied to the posterior of the calf, around the heel, and along the bottom of the foot to the toes. The splint material is allowed to dry. The splint is secured into place with an Ace wrap.

29520-29550

The physician or medical professional uses tape to strap a lower extremity. In 29520, taping of the hip for immobilization is rarely used because of the hip muscles' superior strength to that of the tape. A hip spica taping procedure may be used to hold analgesic packs in place and to offer mild support to injured hip adductor s or flexors. The patient stands with all weight on the unaffected leg. Six inch Ace wrap is usually used. The end of the wrap begins at the upper part of the thigh and immediately encircles the upper thigh and groin, crossing the starting point. When the starting end is reached the roll is taken completely around the waist and fixed firmly above the iliac crest. The wrap is carried around the thigh at groin level and up again around the waist. The end is secured with tape. Report 29520 if the site taped is the hip. Report 29530 if the site taped is the knee. Report 29540 if the site taped is the ankle and/or foot. Report 29550 if the site taped is the toes.

29580

The physician applies an Unna boot to the leg or foot of a patient. An Unna boot is typically used to treat or prevent venostasis dermatitis or ulcers of the lower leg or foot. It is also used to control postoperative edema like that resulting from an amputation. The physician prepares this semirigid dressing by first making a paste of zinc oxide, gelatin, and glycerin. This is applied to the skin of the leg. A spiral or figure eight bandage is wrapped evenly over the leg. Paste is reapplied and further bandages are applied in the same fashion until the desired rigidity is obtained. Elastic bandages are often added to the dressings for reinforcement. The dressing is typically replaced at least once a week or more often as needed.

29581

A health care practitioner applies a multilayer venous wound compression device to the area of the leg below the knee. Compression therapy is often used in the treatment of extensive venous ulcers. The device may consist of a multilayer bandaging system composed only of elastic bandages, or may be paired with a knitted, tubular, open-toed, and heelless elastic knee-length compression garment. In one method, after wound debridement and dressing, cotton gauze and cotton crepe bandages are applied to the lower leg. Next, a positioner is placed over the bandages and adjusted to the desired position. The compression device is slipped over the positioner, adjusted to assure appropriate placement, and the positioner removed.

29590

The physician applies Denis-Browne splint strapping to an infant to correct equinovarus deformity. It is performed on infants no later than two to three weeks after birth. The deformed foot is taped to foot plates attached to a crossbar that is no wider than the infant's pelvis. The foot is retaped weekly to maintain a snug fit. This method involves three phases. Phase One requires at least five to six weeks and consists of progressive external rotation and abduction of the foot. The foot is maintained in this for about five months. Phase Two consists of placing the foot in an open-toed shoe on the bar in the corrected position for an additional six months or until the infant begins walking. Phase Three consists of wearing the shoe and bar at night and a below-knee brace during the day. The day brace has a 90 degree plantar flexion stop and a spring dorsiflexion assist. This is continued for as long as necessary and usually for a minimum of 2 to 3 years.

29700-29715

The physician removes or bivalves a cast. These codes are used to remove a cast or to simply cut it in half for the purpose of using one half the cast as a splint or for intermittent immobilization. A manual cast saw is used to make two cuts in the cast. One cut is extended along the medial edge of the cast. The second cut is extended along the lateral edge of the cast. These cuts are started proximally and are extended distally. Once the cuts are made, the cast may be removed. The front and back portion of the cast may be applied and secured using an Ace bandage intermittently for immobilization. Only one half may be Ace wrapped for splinting purposes. Report 29700 if the cast is a gauntlet, boot or body cast. Report 29705 if a full arm or full leg cast is removed. Report 29710 if a shoulder cast or hip spica, Minerva or Risser jacket is removed. Report 29715 if a turnbuckle jacket is removed.

29720

The physician repairs a spica, body cast, or jacket due to normal wear and tear, revision of the cast or jacket, or the cutting of a window to check the status of a wound, incision, or other area. Additional casting material is applied in the normal manner.

29730

The physician chooses this procedure to check the status of a wound that is underneath the cast or to visualize an area under the cast where infection may exist. A cast saw is used to cut a section in the cast. This is removed to create a window. Once the status is determined, the physician may reinsert the section and hold it in place with casting material.

29740-29750

The physician wedges a cast. X-rays (reported separately) of a casted, fractured extremity may show slight malalignment. Wedging of the cast may correct this malalignment without having to remove the cast. The bony deformities identified by the physician and the necessary direction and amount of correction is decided. The necessary cut is made in the cast using a

Musculoskeletal

cast saw. A wedge of plastic or wood is wedged into the cast cut to redirect the pressure of the cast on the fracture site to correct the bony deformity. Report 29740 if the wedge is placed in a cast. Report 29750 if the cast wedge is placed in a cast that has been applied for correction of clubfoot deformity.

29800
The physician inserts an arthroscope into the temporomandibular joint to examine the joint space(s). The physician may lavage or wash the joint. The physician makes a 0.5 cm vertical incision anterior to the contour of the ear. The arthroscope is inserted into the joint through the incision. A needle is placed into the joint in front of the arthroscope to allow the saline from the arthroscope to flow out of the joint. An instrument may also be inserted through the arthroscope for biopsy of the synovium (lining of the joint). The arthroscope and outflow needle are removed and the incision is closed with simple sutures.

29804
The physician inserts two arthroscopic cannulas into the temporomandibular joint. The physician introduces an arthroscope into one cannula to view the joint and operative field. Through the other arthroscopic cannula, small instruments are inserted and used to surgically repair the joint. The physician makes a 0.5 cm vertical incision anterior to the contour of the ear. The arthroscope is inserted through the incision into the joint. A second arthroscopic cannula is inserted into the joint through which instruments are inserted to repair the joint. A biopsy of the synovium (lining of the joint) may be performed. The arthroscopes are removed and the incisions are closed with layered sutures.

29805
A general anesthetic is commonly administered for shoulder arthroscopic procedures. Two to four small poke hole incisions are made above the joint and fluid is introduced into the joint space to provide a better view. A band is placed to restrict blood flow. A small incision is made on one side of the joint and the arthroscope is inserted. The inside of the joint may be viewed through the eyepiece or the image can be reproduced on a screen. A cannula may be introduced to take a synovial biopsy. Once the biopsy is completed, the physician irrigates the joint until it is clear of blood and loose particles. A long acting local anesthetic may be injected into the joint to help with post-operative pain. The joint is irrigated and suture or Steri-strip closes the incisions. The area is covered with a dressing and a sling or shoulder immobilizer is applied.

29806
The patient is positioned side-lying with arm suspended using a weight and a pulley system. An anesthetic is administered. Two to four small poke hole incisions are made around the shoulder joint to allow access to all areas of the shoulder joint. A solution is pumped through one of these incisions and into the joint to expand the joint for better visualization and to cleanse the joint. The arthroscope is inserted through a hole allowing the physician to perform a diagnostic arthroscopic exam by visualizing the shoulder joint. The corticoid process is identified and the tendon of the biceps (short head) is at times incised distal to corticoid for exposure. The anterior capsule is visualized through a small transverse incision of the subscapularis tendon which is tagged for identification and removed from its attachment on the capsule. The quality and laxity of the capsule are assessed and the joint is explored for damage to the labrum or glenoid. The joint is irrigated to remove any loose bodies. If there is no other abnormal laxity, the capsule is advance superiorly and attached to the labrum with sutures. An appropriate amount of slack is taken up to provide stability within the joint. Once the capsule is reattached, the subscapularis tendon is reapproximated but not tightened and repaired. A long acting local anesthetic may be injected into the joint to help with post-operative pain. The joint is irrigated and suture or Steri-strip closes the incisions. The area is covered with a dressing and a sling or shoulder immobilizer is applied.

29807
SLAP lesions are injuries to the labrum that extend from anterior to the biceps tendon to posterior to the biceps tendon. For a SLAP lesion repair, the physician makes three incisions: one for the arthroscope, a second for the suture hook, and a third for a cannula. The surgeon prepares the bony bed with a small ball burr and drills or punches a hole at the cartilage bone junction of the superior labrum. A hook is passed through the anterior superior portal and the inside limb is grasped with a suture retrieval forceps. The physician sets an anchor into the drill hole by mounting the suture anchor on the inserter and sliding it down the suture. The physician closes the loop with a slipknot that is tied and tightened outside the cannula. A knot pusher secures the knot under arthroscopic control. A long acting local anesthetic may be injected into the joint to help with post-operative pain. The joint is irrigated and suture or Steri-strip closes the incisions. The area is covered with a dressing and a sling or shoulder immobilizer is applied.

29819
To remove loose bodies, such as floating cartilage, the physician visualizes the foreign bodies and removes them with instruments passed through the portal holes. For a synovectomy, the physician makes several half-inch incisions to allow arthroscopic investigation of any problems associated with the synovium. Through the arthroscope, the physician removes the synovium from inside the shoulder joint using cutting tools and arthroscopic suction equipment. A long acting local anesthetic may be injected into the joint to

help with post-operative pain. The joint is irrigated and suture or Steri-strip closes the incisions. The area is covered with a dressing and a sling or shoulder immobilizer is applied.

29820-29821
The patient is positioned side-lying with arm suspended using a weight and a pulley system. An anesthetic is administered. Two to four small poke hole (port) incisions are made around the shoulder joint to allow access to all areas of the shoulder joint. A solution is pumped through one of these incisions and into the joint to expand the joint for better visualization and to cleanse the joint. The arthroscope is inserted through a hole allowing the physician to perform a diagnostic arthroscopic exam by visualizing the shoulder joint. The synovium is removed with a motorized synovial resector inserted through a port. The instruments are removed and a long acting local anesthetic may be injected into the joint to help with post-operative pain. The joint is irrigated and suture or Steri-strip closes the incisions. The area is covered with a dressing and a sling or shoulder immobilizer is applied. Report 29820 for a partial synovectomy and 29821 for a complete synovectomy.

29822-29823
The patient is positioned side-lying with arm suspended using a weight and a pulley system. An anesthetic is administered. Two to four small poke hole (port) incisions are made around the shoulder joint to allow access to all areas of the shoulder joint. A solution is pumped through one of these incisions and into the joint to expand the joint for better visualization and to cleanse the joint. The arthroscope is inserted through a hole allowing the physician to perform a diagnostic arthroscopic exam by visualizing the shoulder joint. A long acting local anesthetic may be injected into the joint to help with post-operative pain. The joint is irrigated and suture or Steri-strip closes the incisions. The area is covered with a dressing and a sling or shoulder immobilizer is applied. Report 29822 if the arthroscopic surgery is performed with limited debridement and 29823 if the procedure includes extensive debridement.

29824
The physician makes two to four small poke hole incisions around the shoulder joint to allow access to all areas of the joint. A solution is pumped through one of these incisions and into the joint to expand the joint for better visualization and to cleanse the joint. The arthroscope is inserted through a hole allowing the physician to perform a diagnostic arthroscopic exam by visualizing the shoulder joint. The physician may shell the bone out of its periosteal lining, including the distal articular surface, when using arthroscopic guidance. A long acting local anesthetic may be injected into the joint to help with post-operative pain. The joint is irrigated and suture or Steri-strip closes the incisions. The area is covered with a dressing and a sling or shoulder immobilizer is applied.

29825
The physician makes two to four small poke hole incisions around the shoulder joint to allow access to all areas of the joint. A solution is pumped through one of these incisions and into the joint to expand the joint for better visualization and to cleanse the joint. The arthroscope is inserted through a hole allowing the physician to perform a diagnostic arthroscopic exam by visualizing the shoulder joint. The physician may shell the bone out of its periosteal lining, including the distal articular surface, when using arthroscopic guidance. The physician lyses and resects adhesions, with or without manipulation. A long acting local anesthetic may be injected into the joint to help with post-operative pain. The joint is irrigated and suture or Steri-strip closes the incisions. The area is covered with a dressing and a sling or shoulder immobilizer is applied.

29826
The physician makes two to four small poke hole incisions around the shoulder joint to allow access to all areas of the joint. A solution is pumped through one of these incisions and into the joint to expand the joint for better visualization and to cleanse the joint. The subacromial space is decompressed and a partial acromioplasty, with or without coracoacromial release, is performed. The patient is seated with the torso raised and a sheet placed on the medial border of the affected scapula. Anterior, lateral, and posterior arthroscopic portals are established and a cannula is inserted through the anterior and lateral portals to accommodate the inflow and instrumentation. The arthroscope is inserted into the posterior portal, where it is driven into the subacromial space for visualization of the subacromial joint. A limited bursectomy is performed using a full radius shaver and, if necessary, the physician clears the undersurface of the antero-lateral acromion of soft tissue using intra-articular cautery. The acromial ligament may be released. A long acting local anesthetic may be injected into the joint to help with post-operative pain. The joint is irrigated and suture or Steri-strip closes the incisions. The area is covered with a dressing and a sling or shoulder immobilizer is applied.

29827
The physician performs a surgical arthroscopy of the shoulder to repair a torn rotator cuff. The patient is positioned side-lying with the arm suspended. Small poke hole incisions are made around the shoulder through which the arthroscopic instruments are inserted. A solution is pumped through one of these incisions to cleanse and expand the joint for better visualization. The physician first performs a diagnostic arthroscopic exam to assess the joint. A limited bursectomy may be performed with a subacromial

Musculoskeletal

decompression in which the undersurface of the antero-lateral acromion is cleared of soft tissue, if necessary. A small skin incision may be made laterally incorporating one of the portholes to facilitate the arthroscopic repair. The deltoid muscle is split from its acromion attachment about 5 cm and the tendon edge is debrided and mobilized. A transverse bony trough 3 to 4 mm is made and tunnels are drilled through the bone trough to the lateral cortex of the greater tuberosity. The tendon edge is brought into the trough with permanent sutures and anchor sutures are placed. Sutures are placed into the bone and brought through the tendon. A hemostat is placed on the cuff to retract the tendon and take tension off the sutures. The anchor sutures are tied down, followed by the sutures to the bony trough. The free ends of the sutures are passed through the tunnels and tied over a bony bridge. The longitudinal portions of the tear are closed with absorbable suture and a range of motion check is done on the arm. The deltoid splits, subcutaneous tissue, and skin are closed and the arm is placed in a sling to maintain abduction.

29828

The physician performs arthroscopic biceps tenodesis. With the patient under appropriate anesthesia, standard arthroscopic portals are established. A monofilament suture is passed through an 18-gauge needle placed into the biceps tendon, and an arthroscopic suture instrument is utilized to retrieve the suture. The physician uses an arthroscopic basket to release the tendon from its origin, and the arthroscopic equipment is transferred to the subacromial space. Using the arthroscopic basket, the physician identifies and opens the tendon sheath. Electrocautery may be used to clean the surrounding tissues. A probe is utilized to free the tendon, which is extracted through one of the arthroscopic portals. The tendon is then pulled into a humeral socket that has been drilled at the top of the bicipital groove. Under arthroscopic control, it is fixed using a bioabsorbable interference screw. Instrumentation is removed and the arthroscopic portals are closed with sutures.

29830-29838

The physician performs elbow arthroscopy with the patient in a supine position. General anesthesia is preferred. The physician makes 1 cm portal incisions to insert the arthroscope into the elbow joint space. The five most commonly used portals are the lateral, anterolateral, anteromedial, posterolateral, and straight positions. The physician places the arthroscope into the elbow joint and examines the humeral-ulnar and radial-ulnar joints. The elbow is flexed and extended, and pronated and supinated to allow visualization and examination of all joint spaces and surfaces. If there is evidence of synovial proliferation or inflammation indicating disease, the physician uses an instrument to obtain a small piece of synovium for biopsy. In 29830, the physician performs a diagnostic arthroscopy. In 29834, the physician examines all parts of the elbow joint with the arthroscope. Any loose bodies (e.g., small pieces of cartilage from chondral injuries) or foreign bodies (e.g., bullet or nail) are removed by identifying them through the arthroscope and using another portal incision to remove the object. In 29835, the physician may also perform a partial synovectomy, where in 29836 the physician may perform a complete synovectomy. In 29837, the physician perform a limited debridement. In 29838, the physician uses the arthroscope to examine all parts of the elbow joint. Debridement is performed on proliferative cartilage, a degenerative joint, or roughened or frayed articular cartilage. The physician uses instruments through the arthroscope to cut and remove inflamed and proliferated synovium and to clean and smooth the articular joint surfaces of the elbow. Extensive debridement includes all joints of the elbow. The portal incisions are closed with sutures or Steri-strips.

29840-29845

The physician performs wrist arthroscopy. The joint is distended using finger traps on the index and long fingers that are attached to a 10 pound weight pulley. Counter traction is applied to the arm with a second 10 lb pulley. The joint is injected with lidocaine and epinephrine to distend the capsule. A wrap is applied to the forearm to prevent extravasation of fluid. Portal incisions are made. The scope is inserted. The physician inspects the wrist joint. The wrist is manipulated to allow visualization of all joint spaces and surfaces. In 29840, a diagnostic arthroscopy is performed A synovial biopsy may also be obtained. In 29843, an infection is treated using lavage and drainage. Irrigation fluid is directed into each compartment of the wrist joint using the arthroscope for visualization. Lavage is continued until the fluid is clear. A motorized suction cutter may be used to remove encrusted fluid (exudate) and any fibrinous clots. Drains are placed as needed. The portal incisions are closed with sutures or Steri-strips. In 29844, the synovial membrane lining the joint capsule is partially removed and in 29845 it is completely removed. This is accomplished by use of a motorized, suction cutting resector. The joint is irrigated and all instruments are removed. Drains are placed as needed. The portal incisions are closed with sutures or Steri-strips.

29846

The physician performs surgical wrist arthroscopy with excision and/or repair of the triangular fibrocartilage and/or joint debridement. The joint is distended using finger traps on the index and long fingers that are attached to a 10 pound weight pulley. Counter traction is applied to the arm with a second 10 lb pulley. The joint is injected with lidocaine and epinephrine to distend the capsule. A wrap is applied to the forearm to prevent extravasation of fluid. Portal incisions are made. The scope is inserted. The physician inspects the wrist joint. The wrist is manipulated to allow visualization of all joint spaces and surfaces. The joint is debrided, which involves removing any inflamed or devitalized tissue. The articular surfaces are cleaned and smoothed. Tears present in the triangular fibrocartilage are sutured or the cartilage is removed with instruments placed through the arthroscope. The joint is irrigated and all instruments are removed. The portal incisions are closed with sutures or Steri-strips.

29847
The physician performs surgical wrist arthroscopy with internal fixation for a fracture or joint instability. The joint is distended using finger traps on the index and long fingers that are attached to a 10 pound weight pulley. Counter traction is applied to the arm with a second 10 lb pulley. The joint is injected with lidocaine and epinephrine to distend the capsule. A wrap is applied to the forearm to prevent extravasation of fluid. Portal incisions are made. The scope is inserted. The physician inspects the wrist joint. The wrist is manipulated to allow visualization of all joint spaces and surfaces. The site of the fracture or instability is identified. The physician uses instruments placed through the arthroscope to manipulate the fracture or unstable area into proper alignment. Internal fixation, consisting of wires, pins, and/or screws, is applied. The joint is irrigated and all instruments are removed. The portal incisions are closed with sutures or Steri-strips.

29848
The patient is placed supine with the arm positioned on a hand table. Endoscopic release may be accomplished by a one or two portal technique. In a single portal technique, a small, 1 1/2 cm, horizontal incision is made at the wrist. Using a two portal technique, two small incisions are made, one in the palm and one at the wrist. The palmar skin, underlying cushioning fat, protective fascia, and muscle are not cut. The endoscope is introduced underneath the transverse carpal ligament. The endoscope allows the physician to view the procedure on a monitor. A blade attached to the arthroscope is used to incise the transverse carpal ligament from the inside of the carpal tunnel. The instruments are removed and the portal(s) closed with sutures or Steri-strips. A splint may be applied.

29850-29851
The physician makes 1 cm long portal incisions on either side of the patellar tendon for arthroscopic access into the knee joint. The knee joint is examined with the arthroscope and the fracture site is identified. Any loose bodies are removed and the physician may debride the knee joint. If the fracture is not displaced (29850) and appears stable, no fixation is needed. If the fracture is not stable (29851), the physician may reduce the fracture by manipulating it into place and applying one or more screws for adequate fixation. An additional incision may be made for better access in applying fixation. Incisions are closed with sutures and staples and/or Steri-strips. A temporary drain may be applied. A post-op brace or splint may be used.

29855-29856
The physician treats a unicondylar (29855) or bicondylar (29856) tibial fracture. The physician makes 1 cm long incisions on either side of the patellar tendon to access the knee joint and insert the arthroscope. The knee may be irrigated free of blood. The knee joint is examined with the arthroscope and, if possible, the fracture fragments are identified. A calibrated hole probe can be used to palpate the bone fragments and to measure their size and displacement. An osteotome or probe can sometimes be used in conjunction with the arthroscope to reduce the fracture fragments. If not, an additional incision is made 3 to 4 cm below the joint line. An impactor is used to elevate the fragment. The fracture may be stabilized with cancellous screws. Incisions are closed with sutures and Steri-strips.

29860
The physician performs an arthroscopy for diagnostic purposes with the patient supine, or in a side-lying position. The hip is abducted and distracted with enough force to allow adequate visualization through the arthroscope. Once joint distraction has been verified radiologically, a needle is inserted with fluoroscopic guidance into the joint to create a portal just superior to the greater trochanter. Using the Seldinger technique, a wire is introduced through the needle. A small skin incision is made, a trocar is placed over the wire, and it is advanced to the hip capsule where the sharpened end is used to break through the hip capsule and into the joint. An arthroscope is placed over the trocar into the joint. Using the same technique, a second (anterolateral) port is established to aid in the examination of the joint structures and to pass instruments. The joint is examined and a portion of synovium may be removed for biopsy. The instruments are removed. A temporary drain may be placed, and the incisions are closed with Steri-strips and/or sutures.

29861
The physician performs an arthroscopy for removal of a loose or foreign body with the patient in a supine, or lateral (side-lying) position. The hip is abducted and distracted with enough force to allow adequate visualization through the arthroscope. Once joint distraction has been verified radiologically, the hip is prepped and draped; a needle is inserted (avoiding neurovascular structures), by use of fluoroscopic guidance, into the joint to create a portal just superior to the greater trochanter. Using the Seldinger technique a wire is introduced through the needle. A small skin incision is made, a trocar is placed over the wire, and is advanced to the hip capsule where the sharpened end is used to break through the hip capsule and into the joint. A fiberoptic arthroscope especially designed for

Musculoskeletal

hip arthroscopy is placed over the trocar into the joint. Using the same technique, a second (anterolateral) port is established to aid in the examination of the joint structures, and to pass instruments. The joint is examined. Small loose bodies can be suctioned or irrigated from the joint. Larger loose bodies are divided into smaller pieces, or shaved, and grasped by a clamp and removed. The instruments are removed. A temporary drain may be placed, and the incisions are closed with Steri-strips and/or sutures.

29862
The physician performs an arthroscopy to remove a lesion of the articular cartilage, and/or to resect the labrum with the patient in a supine, or side-lying position. The hip is abducted and distracted with enough force to allow adequate visualization through the arthroscope. Once joint distraction has been verified radiologically, a needle is inserted with fluoroscopic guidance into the joint to create a portal just superior to the greater trochanter. Using the Seldinger technique, a wire is introduced through the needle. A small skin incision is made, a trocar is placed over the wire, and it is advanced to the hip capsule where the sharpened end is used to break through the hip capsule and into the joint. A fiberoptic arthroscope is placed over the trocar into the joint. Using the same technique, a second (anterolateral) port is established to aid in the examination of the joint structures and to pass instruments. If a third port is necessary, it is usually placed close to the anterolateral port. The joint is examined. The articular cartilage is debrided/shaved, or an abrasion arthroplasty is performed until bleeding bone is reached. The joint is irrigated. A resection of the labrum (acetabular lip) may be performed. The instruments are removed. A temporary drain may be placed, and the incisions are closed with Steri-strips and/or sutures.

29863
The physician performs an arthroscopy with a synovectomy with the patient in a supine, or sidelying position. The hip is abducted and distracted with enough force to allow adequate visualization through the arthroscope. Once joint distraction has been verified radiologically, a needle is inserted with fluoroscopic guidance into the joint to create a portal just superior to the greater trochanter. Using the Seldinger technique, a wire is introduced through the needle. A small skin incision is made, a trocar is placed over the wire, and it is advanced to the hip capsule where the sharpened end is used to break through the hip capsule and into the joint. An arthroscope is placed over the trocar into the joint. Using the same technique, a second (anterolateral) port is established to aid in the examination of the joint structures, and to pass instruments. If a third port is necessary, it is usually placed close to the anterolateral port. The joint is examined. Using an instrument passed through the anterolateral port, perilabial, ligamentum teres, and inferior capsule synovium may be excised and removed. The instruments are removed. A temporary drain may be placed, and the incisions are closed with Steri-strips and/or sutures.

29866-29867
An osteochondral graft is a bone/cartilage transplant that treats defects of the knee from disabling cartilage injury or disease, such as osteochondritis dissecans. Arthroscopic osteochondral grafting using the mosaicplasty technique is described here. Multiple cylindrical grafts are placed in corresponding size cylindrical holes made in the recipient area—instead of using one larger bone plug. Portals for inserting the instruments are chosen to ensure perpendicular access to the recipient site. Detached cartilage is excised, the margins squared off, and the subchondral bone is abraded to healthy, bleeding tissue. The number and size of grafts needed is determined. In 29866, a tubular chisel is used to harvest cylindrical osteochondral grafts down to the desired level, perpendicular to the cartilage surface, from the patient. Grafts are harvested from the non-weight bearing patellofemoral area, medial or lateral femoral trochlear rim, or the intercondylar notch periphery. The grafts are ejected from the chisel. A guide tube is put in place and the recipient hole is drilled to the desired depth with a graduated bit, replaced with a tapered dilator, and the graft is inserted and tamped into place. This is repeated until all grafts have been placed. Report 29867 when fresh donor tissue from a tissue bank is used instead of harvested from the patient.

29868
A previously removed meniscus, the fibrocartilaginous support of the knee joint, is replaced with a cadaver donor meniscus, medial or lateral. Imaging is done to size-match the graft to the recipient knee. The arthroscope and a tibial guide are placed through portal holes. The remaining native meniscal cartilage is removed, including resectioning the native horns. Pins are placed at posterior and anterior horn locations, suture tunnels are drilled over the pins, and sutures are passed. The anterior portal is widened, and both the anterior and posterior sutures are brought out together. The graft is brought in through the widened incision, or a necessary arthrotomy, and sutures are placed through each horn of the implant. The posterior and anterior horn sutures are drawn out through the tibial tunnel and secured to the tibial bone. Meniscal repair techniques are used to suture the graft securely to the capsule placing knots directly over the capsule. Routine closure is performed. Other techniques may employ separate bone plugs attached to the horns to insert the graft or a common bone attached to both horns on the graft inserted into a receiving slot in the tibia.

29870
The physician performs a diagnostic arthroscopy of the knee. Portal incisions of 1 cm in length are made on either side of the patellar tendon for arthroscopic access into the knee joint. With the use of the arthroscope and a probe, each compartment of the knee is examined for pathology. This includes examination of the patellar-articular surface, medial and lateral meniscus, cruciate ligaments, and joint surfaces. Additional portal incisions may be made to better access some compartments. If there is suspicion of a primary disease of the synovium, a biopsy is performed. A temporary drain may be applied. Incisions are closed with sutures and Steri-strips.

29871
The physician makes 1 cm long portal incisions on either side of the patellar tendon to arthroscopically access the knee joint. Lavage is accomplished with a minimum of 4 liters of a physiologic solution. The irrigation solution is directed into each compartment while visualizing through the arthroscope. Lavage is continued until the outflow is clear. A motorized suction cutter is used to remove encrusted fluid (exudate) and any fibrinous clots. Drains are placed as needed and incisions are closed with sutures and Steri-strips. The drains are removed after 48 to 78 hours.

29873
The physician performs a knee arthroscopy with lateral release. Lateral retinacular release is done when too much lateral tension on the patella from tightness of the lateral retinaculum causes patellar misalignment, not allowing correct movement. This can be associated with articular cartilage lesions and idiopathic chondromalacia. The physician makes 1 cm long portal incisions on either side of the patellar tendon to arthroscopically access the knee joint. The instruments are inserted and the knee is assessed. The release is done at the end of the arthroscopy. The tight lateral ligaments, including the lateral patellofemoral and the lateral patellotibial ligament, are released detaching the patella from the soft tissue structures, including the lateral retinaculum, muscle fibers, and joint capsule.

29874
The physician makes 1 cm long portal incisions on either side of the patellar tendon for arthroscopic access into the knee joint. A thorough exam is made of each compartment in the knee. Additional portal incisions may be made to gain better access to the knee compartments. Any loose bodies (fragments of cartilage or bone) encountered are removed through the portal incisions. Small loose bodies can be suctioned or irrigated from the joint. Larger loose bodies are grasped by a clamp and removed. Very large loose bodies may require enlargement of a portal or division with an arthroscopic scissor before removal. A temporary drain may be applied and incisions are closed with sutures and Steri-strips.

29875-29876
The physician performs an arthroscopic synovectomy. The physician makes 1 cm long portal incisions on either side of the patellar tendon for arthroscopic access into the joint. Proliferative, diseased synovium is removed with a motorized, suction, cutting resector. If the plica located along the medial side of the patella is inflamed, it may require removal. Removal is accomplished by dividing and excising the plica. The synovectomy is limited in 29875. For a more extensive synovectomy (29876), up to six portal incisions may be made to access all of the involved compartments of the knee. A temporary drain may be applied and incisions are closed with sutures and Steri-strips.

29877
The physician makes 1 cm long portal incisions on either side of the patellar tendon for arthroscopic access into the knee joint. Lesions in the articular cartilage are identified by the arthroscope and the use of a probe. Additional portal incisions may be made to provide better access to the cartilage lesions. Debridement of the unstable hyaline cartilage or partially fragmented cartilage is accomplished with a motorized suction cutter. This smoothes the roughened or damaged cartilage. Any loose bodies are removed. After debridement, the joint is flushed. A temporary drain may be applied, and incisions are closed with sutures and Steri-strips.

29879
The physician makes 1 cm long portal incisions on either side of the patellar tendon for arthroscopic access into the knee joint. Lesions of the articular cartilage are identified by the arthroscope and the use of a probe. Additional portal incisions may be made to provide better access to the lesions. Debridement of the unstable or fragmented cartilage is accomplished with a motorized suction cutter. The cartilage is smoothed down to the layer of subchondral bone which promotes bleeding and regeneration of cartilage. Any loose bodies are removed. The physician may also drill holes into the subchondral bone or create tiny fractures (microfractures) to further promote cartilage regeneration. The joint is flushed. A temporary drain may be applied. Incisions are closed with sutures and Steri-strips.

29880-29881
The physician makes 1 cm long portal incisions on either side of the patellar tendon for arthroscopic access into the knee joint. Once the meniscal tear is identified, additional portal incisions may be made to provide easier access to the area. There may be a tear on both the medial and lateral meniscus (29880) or on only the medial or the lateral meniscus (29881). The procedure is the same for medial or lateral meniscal tears. Angled scissors, a motorized cutter, or punch

forceps remove torn fragments. The remaining intact meniscus is trimmed and contoured. A temporary drain may be applied and the incisions closed with sutures and Steri-strips.

29882-29883
The physician makes 1 cm long portal incisions on either side of the patellar tendon for arthroscopic access into the knee joint. The meniscal tear(s) is identified through the arthroscope. There may be a tear on only the medial or the lateral meniscus (29882) or both may be torn (29883). Depending on the site of the tear, other portal incisions may be made to gain better access. Angled scissors, motorized cutters, and punch forceps are used to debride the tear margins and break the surface of the adjacent synovium in preparation for repair. A 3 cm to 4 cm incision is made along the medial or lateral joint line, depending on which meniscus is torn. A cannula passes sutures through the meniscal tear and out through the joint line incision. A temporary drain may be applied. Subcutaneous layers are sutured and skin closure is with Steri-strips. Typically, a hinged knee brace is applied after surgery.

29884
The physician makes 1 cm long portal incisions for arthroscopic access into and around the knee joint. A blunt trocar, a knife, scissors, or a mechanical shaver may remove any adhesions limiting range of knee motion. If a manipulation is performed, the physician will remove the arthroscope and apply gradual, progressive pressure to bend or straighten the knee. Manipulation helps the knee regain range of motion. A drain may be applied. Incisions are closed with sutures and Steri-strips.

29885
The physician makes a 1 cm long portal incision on either side of the patellar tendon. The defect is visualized through the arthroscope. Any loose bodies are removed with grasping instruments. A motorized suction cutter is used to debride the disrupted hyaline cartilage. Drill holes 2 cm in depth are made into the lesion, penetrating the vascular bone at the base of the defect. This promotes bleeding and subsequent healing of the lesion. The donor harvests bone from the patient's hip, rib, or skull and closes the surgically created donor site. The bone is sized to fit the defect. The physician determines if a screw is needed for internal fixation. If so, a screw is placed. A temporary drain may be applied. The incisions are closed with sutures and Steri-strips.

29886
The physician makes a 1 cm long portal incision on either side of the patellar tendon. The defect is visualized through the arthroscope. A motorized suction cutter is used to debride the disrupted hyaline cartilage. Drill holes 2 cm in depth are made into the lesion in order to penetrate the vascular bone at the base of the defect. This promotes bleeding and subsequent healing of the lesion. The incisions are closed with sutures and Steri-strips. A temporary drain may be applied.

29887
The physician makes a portal incision 1 cm long on either side of the patellar tendon. The defect is visualized through the arthroscope. A motorized suction cutter debrides the disrupted hyaline cartilage. Drill holes 2 cm in depth are made into the lesion in order to penetrate the vascular bone at the base of the defect. This promotes bleeding and subsequent healing of the lesion. Internal fixation is accomplished by placing a screw into the lesion. The incisions are closed with sutures and Steri-strips. A temporary drain may be applied.

29888-29889
The physician makes a portal incision 1 cm long on either side of the inferior patella for arthroscopic access into the knee joint. If the ligament is intact but torn away from its bony attachment, the physician may reattach the ligament with a screw. If the ligament is nonfunctional, it is removed with the arthroscope. For an anterior cruciate ligament reconstruction (29888), a 5 cm to 12 cm incision is made on the anterior lower patella and upper tibia. A tunnel is drilled through the tibia into the knee joint. A second tunnel is drilled from inside the knee joint, through the femur. With the aid of the arthroscope for visualization, a new ligament graft is placed in the tibial tunnel and positioned inside the knee joint. The bony ends of the ligament are placed in the tibial and femoral tunnels. The ligament is secured with interference screws in both tunnels. For a posterior cruciate ligament reconstruction (29889), an additional 3 cm to 5 cm incision is made along the medial aspect of the knee joint to allow for proper location of the femoral tunnel. Incisions are closed with staples or Steri-strips. A temporary drain may be inserted.

29891
The physician performs an arthroscopy to excise an osteochondral defect, including drilling of the talus and/or tibia. The patient is placed supine with the hip and upper part of the leg elevated, rotated slightly forward, and with the lower part of the leg, ankle and foot resting on a cushioned platform. The ankle joint is distended to allow access for the first port. Distraction is usually not performed. The skin is superficially anterolateral incised. The tissues and tendons are separated to the joint capsule by a clamp, and a blunt trocar is inserted into the joint. The arthroscope in placed over the trocar, and advanced into the joint. A second anteromedial portal is established for further examination and for instrument passage. The joint is examined and any loose bodies are removed. The osteochondral defect of the talus and/or tibia is excised and the sides of the crater are contoured. Multiple

holes may be drilled in the bone to promote vascularization. The joint is irrigated, and the instruments are removed. A temporary drain may be placed, and the incisions are closed with Steri-strips and/or sutures.

29892
The physician performs an arthroscopy to aid in the repair of a large osteochondritis dissecans lesion, talar dome fracture, or tibial plafond fracture. The patient is placed supine with the hip and upper part of the leg elevated, rotated slightly forward, and with the lower part of the leg, ankle, and foot resting on a cushioned platform. The ankle joint is distended to allow access for the first port. The skin is superficially incised. The tissues and tendons are separated to the joint capsule by a clamp, and a blunt trocar is inserted into the joint. The arthroscope is placed over the trocar and advanced into the joint. A second anteromedial portal is established for further examination and for instrument passage. The joint is examined, and any loose bodies are removed. A large osteochondritis dissecans lesion is excised, and the sides of the crater are contoured; a talar dome or tibial plafond fracture is treated. Internal fixation may be applied at the fracture site. A temporary drain may be placed, and the incisions are closed with Steri-strips and/or sutures.

29893
The physician performs a plantar fasciotomy using an endoscope. The patient is placed prone. After administering a local anesthetic, the physician makes a small incision to create a passage for the endoscope. Other incisions are made as needed for additional instruments. One or more transverse divisions of the contracted and fibrotic cord(s) of plantar fascia in the foot are performed for therapeutic release. The instruments are removed and the wound closed with simple or layered sutures.

29894
The physician performs arthroscopy on an ankle joint to remove a loose body or foreign body from the joint. After induction of anesthesia in the operating room, the physician makes two to four 0.5 cm incisions around the ankle. Using arthroscopic instruments, the physician enters the ankle through these small incisions. The offending loose body or foreign body is identified. Instruments are introduced through the portal incisions and utilized to remove the foreign body. The joint is examined through the arthroscope and irrigated. The skin portals are closed and a dressing is applied.

29895
The physician performs arthroscopy on an ankle joint to remove the synovial lining of the joint. With the patient soothed by general anesthesia, the physician makes two to four 0.5 cm skin incisions around the ankle. The physician introduces the arthroscope into the ankle and conducts an exam. The offending synovial tissue is identified. Additional instruments are placed through the incisions. Using the arthroscope, the physician uses these instruments to excise the synovium. The joint is irrigated and the skin portals are closed. A dressing is applied.

29897
The physician performs arthroscopy on the ankle joint to minimally debride the joint. With the patient under general anesthesia, the physician makes two to four 0.5 cm skin incisions around the ankle joint. The arthroscope is introduced into the ankle joint and an examination is performed. The physician identifies areas of the joint where debridement is required. Additional surgical instruments are placed through the skin portals and into the joint. These are used to debride frayed, nonviable, or extraneous tissue. The ankle is irrigated and the skin incisions are closed. A dressing is applied.

29898
The physician performs arthroscopy on the ankle joint to extensively debride the joint. With the patient under general anesthesia, the physician makes two to four 0.5 cm skin incisions around the ankle joint. The arthroscope is introduced into the joint and the physician conducts an examination. Frayed cartilage, redundant synovium, defects in the articular surfaces, or bony abnormalities are identified. Additional arthroscopic instruments are placed into the joint through the skin incisions. These are used to extensively debride, excise, smooth, and/or wash out the offending tissues. A thorough irrigation is undertaken. The skin incisions are closed and a dressing is applied.

29899
The physician performs an arthroscopic arthrodesis of the ankle to fuse the joint in cases of severe degenerative or inflammatory arthritis. The patient is supine of the table with the ankle hanging off the table and a leg holder applied for positioning. Traction is applied and three small poke hole incisions are made around the ankle for portals through which the arthroscopic instruments are inserted. In the medial compartment, a full-radius resector is used to remove the soft tissue and expose the medial malleolus, medial side of the talus, and the talar dome. The articular cartilage is removed from the medial malleolus and talus around to the side of the ankle and as far posteriorly as is visible. The avascular subchondral bone is removed the same way starting laterally. The posterior tissues are removed next. After debridement of the articular cartilage and subchondral bone, a guide pin is placed through the fibula at an angle and a similar guide pin is placed through the tibia. Pin position is confirmed. The pins are backed out slightly while the joint is reduced and traction is removed. Joint reduction is checked. Guide pins are advanced into the talus under fluoroscopy and cancellous screws

are passed over the pins. The joint is held in position while the screws are secured. Parallel medial screws are placed, one in the talus dome apex and the other behind and parallel to the first. X-rays are taken to confirm adequate reduction and fixation. The incisions are closed and a drain is placed.

29900

The metacarpophalangeal joints consist of the convex heads of the metacarpals articulating with the concave bases of the proximal phalanges. The metacarpophalangeal joint of interest is placed for easy access and an injection of local anesthetic is administered. Incisions for portals are made in the respective metacarpal to allow the arthroscope and surgical instruments to be introduced into the joint. The arthroscope is inserted through a portal into the joint, and the surgical equipment is passed through a second portal. A third portal may have been made for pumping fluid in to expand the joint space for clearer visualization. A needle is inserted through the trocar and twisted to cut out the tissue segment for biopsy. The biopsy needle, trocar, and arthroscope are removed. The site is cleansed and a pressure bandage is applied.

29901

The metacarpophalangeal joints consist of the convex heads of the metacarpals articulating with the concave bases of the proximal phalanges. The metacarpophalangeal joint of interest is placed for easy access and an injection of local anesthetic is administered. Incisions for portals are made in the respective metacarpal to allow the arthroscope and surgical instruments to be introduced into the joint. The arthroscope is inserted through a portal into the joint, and the surgical equipment is passed through a second portal. A third portal may have been made for pumping fluid in to expand the joint space for clearer visualization. Arthroscopic debridement is carried out over the surface of the lesion. The physician must avoid debridement of the adjacent joint surface, so as to avoid possible ankylosis. Closure of the wound includes a re-approximation of the attachment of adductor tendon to the dorsal extensor hood.

29902

The physician makes an incision along the midlateral aspect of the thumb, curves the incision over the MP joint, and extends the incision to the EPL tendon. The Stener lesion can be seen as a mass of tissue proximal to the adductor aponeurosis. A Stener lesion occurs when a torn distal edge of ulnar collateral ligament displaces superficially and proximally to the adductor aponeurosis. The ruptured end of ligament is no longer in contact with its area of insertion of the phalanx. A longitudinal incision is made through the aponeurosis volar to the edge of the EPL, leaving a rim of tissue on the tendon to be used for later closure. The adductor tendon is retracted volarly and the dorsal capsule is reflected to permit a clear view of the joint and the inside portion of the collateral ligament. The physician assesses the injury (i.e., ligament rupture at the insertion into the phalanx). The ulnar collateral ligament flap is partially dissected and mobilized off the metacarpal and the volar edge of the proximal phalange is debrided of soft tissue. The physician drills two parallel holes distally and dorsally to exit on the far side of the cortex. Sutures are passed through the distal ligament and pulled through the drill holes and tied over a padded button. Closure of the wound includes a re-approximation of the attachment of adductor tendon to the dorsal extensor hood.

29904-29907

The physician performs arthroscopy on the subtalar joint (the joint of the foot located at the meeting point of the talus and the calcaneus, or heel bone). After induction of anesthesia, the physician makes two to four 0.5 cm incisions around the ankle. Using arthroscopic instruments, the physician enters the ankle through these small incisions. In 29904, instruments are introduced through the portal incisions and utilized to remove loose or foreign bodies. In 29905, the physician removes the synovial lining of the joint using arthroscopic tools. The offending synovial tissue is identified and additional instruments are placed through the portals. Using the arthroscope, the physician uses these instruments to excise the synovium. In 29906, the physician debrides the joint. The physician identifies areas of the joint where debridement is required. Additional surgical instruments are placed through the skin portals and into the joint. These are used to debride frayed, nonviable, or extraneous tissue. In 29907, the physician performs arthrodesis (fusion) of the subtalar joint using arthroscopic equipment. Morcellized bone grafting and internal screw fixation may be utilized. Following each of these procedures, the joint is examined through the arthroscope and irrigated. The skin portals are closed and a dressing is applied.

Respiratory

30000-30020

The physician makes an incision to decompress and drain a collection of pus or blood in the nasal mucosa for 30000 or septal mucosa for 30020. A hemostat bluntly penetrates the pockets and allows the fluid to evacuate. Once decompressed, a small latex drain may be placed into the incision site. This allows an escape for any fluids that may continue to enter the pocket. If a drain is used, it is removed within 48 hours. The nasal cavity may be packed with gauze or Telfa to provide pressure against the mucosa and assist decompression after drainage. The incision may be closed primarily or may be left to granulate without closure.

30100
The physician removes mucosa from inside the nose for biopsy. This biopsy is performed when the mucosa is suspicious for disease. Some normal tissue adjacent to the diseased mucosa is also removed during the biopsy. This allows the pathologist to compare diseased versus nondiseased tissues. The excision site may be closed primarily with sutures or may be allowed to granulate without closure.

30110
The physician removes a polyp from inside the nose. Nasal polyps may obstruct both the airway passages and sinus drainage ducts in the nose. The area is approached intranasally. Topical vasoconstrictive agents are applied to the nasal mucosa. Local anesthesia is injected underneath and around the polyp. A scalpel or biting forceps excise the polyp. Small polyps may leave mucosal defects that do not require closure. With larger defects, the mucosa is closed with sutures in a single layer. The physician may place Telfa to pack the nasal cavity during the first 24 hours.

30115
The physician removes complicated nasal polyps in a hospital setting. Nasal polyps may obstruct both the airway passages and sinus drainage ducts in the nose. The area is approached intranasally. Topical vasoconstrictive agents are applied to the nasal mucosa. Local anesthesia is injected underneath and around the polyp. Large polyps are removed with a wire snare stretching the polyp base; the snare or a scalpel can be used to detach the polyp from its mucosal base. A scalpel or biting forceps excise smaller polyps. Small polyps may leave mucosal defects that do not require closure. With larger defects, the mucosa is closed with sutures in a single layer. The physician may place Telfa to pack the nasal cavity during the first 24 hours.

30117-30118
The physician removes or destroys intranasal soft tissue lesions using techniques such as cryosurgery, chemical application, or laser surgery. The lesion is approached intranasally in 30117 or through skin incisions externally in the lateral ala in 30118. The physician performs a lateral rhinotomy by retracting the lateral ala to expose the internal nose. Cryosurgery will freeze and kill soft tissue lesions. Laser surgery will vaporize and emulsify the lesions. Chemical application of topical vasoconstrictive agents and local anesthesia cauterizes vessels and limits post-surgical hemorrhage. No post-operative wound closure or intranasal packing is necessary.

30120
The physician surgically removes diseased tissue caused by rhinophyma from the external nasal tip. Local anesthesia is injected into the nasal tip. The excess tissue is removed by carving and recontouring hyperplastic tissue from the area. Scalpels, dermabrasion (planing with fine sandpaper or wire brushes), and lasers are common methods of removing this excess tissue. A thin layer of epithelium is maintained over the nasal cartilages to ensure adequate healing. Separately reportable skin grafting may be necessary for very large lesions.

30124-30125
The physician removes a dermoid (developmental) cyst of the nose that may be associated with the soft tissue only in 30124 or may extend into bone and/or cartilage in 30125. If associated with the nasal bone, the usual location is at the bone-cartilage junction. Dependent on the size and location, the cyst may be removed using skin or intranasal incisions. A fistula opening may be present and its tract would be excised. Commonly, an incision is made overlying the cyst in the nasal skin. The cyst is removed from its cavity using curettes. The defect size dictates post-removal cavity packing and/or separately reportable reconstruction. Incisions may be closed in single and layers.

30130
The physician removes a part of or the entire inferior nasal turbinate located on the lateral wall of the nose. The turbinate is primarily removed in cases of hypertrophy that obstruct the nasal airway. The physician places topical vasoconstrictive drugs on the turbinate to shrink the blood vessels. A mucosal incision is made around the base of the turbinate. The physician fractures the bony turbinate from the lateral nasal wall with a chisel or drill. The turbinate is excised. Electrocautery may control bleeding. The nasal mucosa is sutured in single layers. The nasal cavity may be packed with gauze.

30140
The physician removes a part of or all of the inferior turbinate bone through a submucous incision. The physician places vasoconstrictive drugs on the turbinate to shrink the blood vessels. A full thickness incision is made over the anterior-inferior surface of the turbinate and continued deep to bone. The physician lifts the mucoperiosteum with an elevator to expose the bony turbinate. A chisel or forceps is used to remove portions of the bony turbinate. Electrocautery may control bleeding. The turbinate mucosa is closed in a single layer.

30150-30160
The physician resects a portion of the nose in 30150 or the total nose in 30160, leaving a surgical defect. The extent of the resection is determined by the extent of the tumor or trauma. A full thickness incision is made through the external nose. All diseased or damaged soft tissue is excised to clear margins. Underlying bone or cartilage may be removed. Exposed bone or cartilage is covered with mucosal flaps or separately reportable skin grafts.

30200

The physician injects a pharmacologic agent (i.e., steroids, sclerosing agents) into the submucosal tissue overlying the nasal turbinate. The inferior nasal turbinate is most commonly involved. Enlarged turbinates obstruct airflow through the nasal cavity. Turbinates with allergic hypertrophy or hypertrophy compensating for septal deviation may benefit from therapy.

30210

The physician displaces mucopurulent secretions (pus and mucous) from sinuses by gravity replacement with a second liquid. This therapy is effective for the ethmoid and sphenoid sinuses. While lying supine, the patient's head is hyperextended. The nose is filled with isotonic saline solution. The physician closes one nostril and applies suction to the other nostril. The patient repeats vowels or words (phonates), elevating the soft palate and creating negative pressure. While the patient is phonating, the physician suctions the nostril. The saline solution enters the sinus, displacing the secretions of the sinuses. The secretions are suctioned from the nostril.

30220

The physician uses an alloplastic button to obturate (close) a nasal septal opening. This procedure is performed as an option to surgical reconstruction of the septum such as grafting. The commercially available alloplastic button is made of silicone rubber. The physician inserts the button into the septal perforation securing it with transseptal sutures.

30300-30310

The physician removes a foreign body from the inside of the nasal cavity, in the office for 30300 or under general anesthesia for 30310. Foreign bodies are defined as objects not normally found in the body. An object may be embedded in normal tissue as a result of some type of trauma. Topical vasoconstrictive agents and local anesthesia are applied to the nasal mucosa. A small incision may be necessary to access the foreign body. Blunt dissection and retrieval of the object is performed with hemostats or forceps. Sutures may close the mucosa in a single layer if the size of the dissection requires.

30320

The physician removes a foreign body from deep within the nasal cavity, accessing the area with a lateral rhinotomy surgical approach. This foreign body is located in an area of difficult access and requires complex surgery to remove it. Foreign bodies are defined as objects not normally found in the body. The object may be embedded in normal tissue as a result of some type of trauma. Topical vasoconstrictive agents and local anesthesia are applied to the nasal mucosa. A full-thickness skin incision is made from the nostril extending along the nasal alar rim and continuing superiorly. The incision can extend to the medial aspect of the eyebrow if necessary. The lateral aspect of the nose is retracted, exposing the bony structures beneath the soft tissue. Blunt dissection and retrieval of the object is performed with hemostats or forceps. The surgical wound is closed in layers.

30400

The physician performs surgery to reshape the external nose. No surgery to the nasal septum is necessary. The physician may perform surgery open (external skin incisions) or closed (intranasal incisions). Topical vasoconstrictive agents are applied to shrink the blood vessels and local anesthesia is injected into the nasal mucosa. After incisions are made, dissections expose the external nasal cartilaginous and bony skeleton. The cartilages may be reshaped with files. Fat may be removed from the subcutaneous regions. Incisions are closed in single layers. Steri-strip tape is used to support cartilaginous surgery of the nasal tip.

30410

The physician performs surgery to reshape the external nose. No surgery to the nasal septum is necessary. This surgery can be performed open (external skin incisions) or closed (intranasal incisions). Topical vasoconstrictive agents are applied to shrink the blood vessels and local anesthesia is injected in the nasal mucosa. After incisions are made, dissections expose the external nasal cartilaginous and bony skeleton. The cartilages may be reshaped by trimming or may be augmented by grafting. Local grafts from adjacent nasal bones and cartilage are not reported separately. The physician may reshape the dorsum with files. The physician fractures the lateral nasal bones with chisels. Fat may be removed from the subcutaneous regions. Incisions are closed in single layers. Steri-strip tape is used to support cartilaginous surgery of the nasal tip. An external splint or cast supports changes in bone position.

30420

The physician performs surgery to reshape the external and internal nose. The nasal septum internally supports the shape of the external nasal appearance. The physician reshapes a fractured or deformed septum. Rhinoplasties can be performed open (external skin incisions) or closed (intranasal incisions). Topical vasoconstrictive agents are applied to shrink the blood vessels and local anesthesia is injected into the nasal mucosa. After incisions are made, dissections expose the external nasal cartilaginous and bony skeleton. The cartilages may be reshaped by trimming or may be augmented by grafting. Local grafts from adjacent nasal bones and cartilage are not reported separately. The physician may reshape the dorsum with files. Fat may be removed from the subcutaneous regions. A vertical incision is made in the septal mucosa and the mucoperichondrium is elevated from the septal cartilage. Septal cartilage may be removed or grafted. The physician fractures the lateral nasal bones with chisels and manually repositions them in the desired positions. Incisions are closed in single layers. Steri-strip tape is used to support cartilaginous surgery of the nasal tip. An external splint or cast supports changes in bone position.

30430
The physician performs a second surgery to reshape the external nose and correct unfavorable results from the initial rhinoplasty. Secondary rhinoplasties can be performed open (external skin incisions) or closed (intranasal incisions). Topical vasoconstrictive agents are applied to shrink the blood vessels and local anesthesia is injected in the nasal mucosa. After incisions are made, dissections expose the external nasal cartilaginous and bony skeleton. The cartilages and nasal tip may be reduced by trimming or may be augmented by grafting. The bony dorsum may receive grafts. Local grafts from adjacent nasal bones and cartilage are not reported separately. Incisions are closed in single layers. Steri-strip tape is used to support cartilaginous surgery of the nasal tip.

30435
The physician performs a second surgery to reshape the external nose and correct unfavorable results from the initial rhinoplasty. Secondary rhinoplasties can be performed open (external skin incisions) or closed (intranasal incisions). Topical vasoconstrictive agents are applied to shrink the blood vessels and local anesthesia is injected in the nasal mucosa. After incisions are made, dissections expose the external nasal cartilaginous and bony skeleton. The physician refractures the lateral nasal bones with chisels and manually repositions them in the desired positions. The bony dorsum may receive grafts. Local grafts from adjacent nasal bones and cartilage are not reported separately. Incisions are closed in single layers. Steri-strip tape is used to support cartilaginous surgery of the nasal tip. An external splint or cast supports changes in bone position.

30450
The physician performs a second surgery to reshape the external nose and correct unfavorable results from the initial rhinoplasty. Secondary rhinoplasties can be performed open (external skin incisions) or closed (intranasal incisions). Topical vasoconstrictive agents are applied to shrink the blood vessels and local anesthesia is injected in the nasal mucosa. After incisions are made, dissections expose the external nasal cartilaginous and bony skeleton. The cartilages and nasal tip may be reduced by trimming or augmented by grafting. The bony dorsum may receive grafts as well. Local grafts from adjacent nasal bones and cartilage are not reported separately. The physician refractures the lateral nasal bones with chisels and manually repositions them in the desired position. Incisions are closed in single layers. Steri-strip tape is used to support cartilaginous surgery of the nasal tip. An external splint or cast supports changes in bone position.

30460
The physician reshapes the external nose and corrects secondary developmental cleft lip and/or palate deformities. Rhinoplasties can be performed open (external skin incisions) or closed (intranasal incisions). Topical vasoconstrictive agents are applied to shrink the blood vessels and local anesthesia is injected in the nasal mucosa. After incisions are made, dissections expose the external nasal cartilaginous and bony skeleton. The cartilages and nasal tip may be reduced by trimming or may be augmented by grafting. Local grafts from adjacent nasal bones and cartilage are not reported separately. Incisions are closed in single layers. Steri-strip tape supports cartilaginous surgery of the nasal tip.

30462
The physician reshapes the external and internal nose and corrects developmental cleft lip and/or palate deformities. Deflection of the nasal septum can cause airway obstruction and affect both support and appearance of the external nasal cartilages. Rhinoplasties can be performed open (external skin incisions) or closed (intranasal incisions). Topical vasoconstrictive agents are applied to shrink the blood vessels and local anesthesia is injected in the nasal mucosa. After incisions are made, dissections expose the external nasal cartilaginous and bony skeleton. The cartilages and nasal tip may be reduced by trimming or may be augmented by grafting. The physician makes a vertical incision in the septal mucosa and elevates the mucoperichondrium from the septal cartilage. Septal cartilage may be removed or grafted. The nasal dorsum may be a graft recipient. Local grafts from adjacent nasal bones and cartilage are not reported separately. The physician fractures the lateral nasal bones with chisels and manipulates the bones into the desired positions. Incisions are closed in single layers. Steri-strip tape supports cartilaginous surgery of the nasal tip. An external splint or cast supports changes in bone position.

30465
The physician repairs a nasal vestibular stenosis using a variety of techniques. Separately reportable cartilage (e.g., auricular composite) graft may be used to support the cartilaginous skeleton and vestibular soft tissue scarring. In one external approach the physician makes an incision in the upper lateral cartilage, in another approach a "V" shaped cut may be made. In either case the incision is followed by an osteotomy of the medial aspect of the nasal bones. A spreader graft is placed to widen the nasal vestibule. The incision is closed or closed in a V-Y manner (lengthens the columella) with suture.

30520
The physician reshapes the nasal septum, correcting airway obstruction. Topical vasoconstrictive agents are applied to shrink the blood vessels and local anesthesia is injected in the nasal mucosa. The physician makes a vertical incision in the septal mucosa and elevates the mucoperichondrium from the septal cartilage. The deviated portion of the bony and cartilaginous septum is excised or augmented by grafting. Local grafts from adjacent nasal bones and cartilage are not reported separately. If the cartilaginous septum remains bowed, partial or full-thickness incisions are made in the cartilage to straighten the septum. Excess cartilage is excised from the bone-cartilage junction. Incisions are closed in single layers. Transseptal sutures are placed. Septal splints may support the septum during healing.

30540
The physician reconstructs the congenitally or acquired absent openings between the nasal cavity and the pharynx (throat). Topical vasoconstrictive agents are applied, and local anesthesia is injected in the nasal mucosa. A mastoid curette or scalpel is placed in the nose and passed to the closure along the floor of the nose. The physician gently punctures the closure to create an opening in the nasopharynx. Sequential rubber tubes of increasing size are placed through the new opening. Once the new opening is dilated to the desired diameter, the rubber tubes are sutured to the nasal columella. The tubes remain for a three- to eight-week healing period to ensure patency of the new posterior nares after removal.

30545
The physician reconstructs the congenitally or acquired absent openings between the nasal cavity and the pharynx (throat). Topical vasoconstrictive agents are applied to the nasal mucosa. Local anesthesia is injected in the nasal mucosa and maxilla. A midpalatal incision is made extending posterior to the nasopalatine foramen to the soft palate. The mucoperiosteum is elevated, exposing the hard palate. Using drills and chisels, the physician creates bony windows at the posterior hard palate, removing bony obstructions between the nasal floor and the pharynx. The physician places rubber tubes along the nasal floor through the new openings into the nasopharynx. The rubber tubes are sutured to the nasal columella. The palatal incision is closed in a single layer. The rubber tubes remain for a three- to eight-week healing period to ensure patency of the new posterior nares after removal.

30560
The physician removes mucosal scarring which blocks the passage of air in the nose. Nasal synechiae are formed when two bleeding mucosal surfaces contact forming scar tissue and eventual fibrosis. These patients are unable to breathe through the nose. The physician makes an intranasal approach to the synechia. Topical vasoconstrictive agents are applied and local anesthesia is injected in the nasal mucosa. An attempt to minimize intra- and postoperative mucosal bleeding is made. A scalpel is used to excise the mucosal tissue. Mucosal edges are sutured with resorbable sutures. Postoperative gauze packing or splints may be used to absorb hemorrhage until mucosal healing occurs. Long term splinting may be necessary to prevent reformation of the synechiae.

30580
The physician closes an opening between the mouth and the maxillary sinus. The communication is through the maxillary bone and this tract is lined with epithelium. Local anesthesia is injected into the mucosa. The physician uses a scalpel to excise the epithelized tract. An incision is made into the palatal mucosa and a local mucosal flap is developed. The flap is sutured in layers, covering the oromaxillary tract. Careful postoperative instructions are given to limit sinus pressure by not allowing nose blowing which would reopen the tract and impair healing.

30600
The physician closes an opening between the mouth and nasal cavity. The communication is through the maxillary hard palate and the tract is lined with epithelium. Local anesthesia is injected into the mucosa. The physician uses a scalpel to excise the epithelized tract. An incision is made into the palatal mucosa and a local mucosal flap is developed. The flap is sutured in layers, covering the oronasal tract.

30620
The physician removes diseased intranasal mucosa and replaces it with a separately reportable split thickness graft. The surgery is performed on one nasal side. A lateral rhinotomy is made to expose the intranasal mucosa. The diseased mucosal tissue is excised from the septum, nasal floor, and anterior aspect of the inferior turbinate. A split thickness graft is sutured to the recipient bed, covering the exposed cartilage and submucosal surfaces. Gauze packing and splints are placed in the grafted nasal cavity.

30630
The physician repairs perforations in the nasal septum. Topical vasoconstrictive agents are applied and local anesthesia is injected into the nasal mucosa. The physician creates local mucoperichondrial flaps on either side of the perforation with a scalpel. Each flap is designed only exposing one side of the septal cartilage while retaining mucosal coverage of the septal cartilage on the opposite side. The flaps are sutured in a single layer to cover the perforation. Larger defects may require the use of separately reportable autogenous grafts (i.e., muscle fascia) in addition to local flaps. Transseptal sutures and septal stents support the septal mucosa and maintain the new position of the flaps.

30801-30802
The physician uses electrocautery, tissue volume reduction, and/or radiofrequency ablation to reduce inflammation or remove excessive mucosa from the soft tissue of the inferior nasal turbinates unilaterally or bilaterally. Ablation procedures may be performed superficially in 30801 or deep in the mucosa (intramural) in 30802. Topical vasoconstrictive agents are applied to the nasal mucosa. Excessive or hypertrophied mucosa is cauterized or ablated and may be excised. Postoperative bleeding is minimal and there is typically no need for intranasal packing.

30901-30903
To control a less serious nosebleed in 30901, the physician applies electrical or chemical coagulation or packing materials to the anterior (front) section of the nose. Only limited electrical or chemical coagulation is used. To control a less responsive nosebleed in 30903, the physician uses extensive electrical coagulation or extensive packing in the anterior (front) section of the nose.

30905-30906
To control bleeding that is coming from the posterior (back) of the nose (nasopharynx), the physician places extensive packing into the nasal cavity through the back of the throat. Extensive electrical coagulation may be required. The patient may return (e.g., 30906) if the bleeding recurs.

30915
When nasal packing fails to control nasal hemorrhage, the physician administers a local anesthetic and makes an incision along the side of the nose near the inner canthus of the eye to expose the ethmoid arteries. The periosteum (periorbitum) is elevated. The anterior ethmoid artery is identified in the suture line between the frontal and ethmoid bones. The posterior ethmoid artery is located entering the posterior medial wall near the orbital apex. A clip or suture completes the ligation. The incision is repaired with a layered closure.

30920
When nasal packing proves inadequate to stop nasal hemorrhage, the physician makes an incision in the mucous membrane under the upper lip. The incision above the canine tooth on the side of the hemorrhage is commonly referred to as a Caldwell-Luc approach. An opening is created through the bone into the normal maxillary sinus. Through an operating microscope, the physician locates and incises the posterior wall of the maxillary sinus. Through this incision, The maxillary artery is isolated and ligated with sutures or a clip. The posterior maxillary sinus wall is repaired. The incision is repaired with a layered closure.

30930
The physician fractures a portion of the inferior turbinate bone to reposition the nasal turbinate. This procedure is performed on a hypertrophied (enlarged) inferior turbinate obstructing the nasal airway. With repositioning, the hypertrophied turbinate should shrink in size, allowing normal airflow. Topical vasoconstrictive drugs are placed on the turbinate to shrink the blood vessels. Commonly, the physician uses a blunt instrument to out-fracture the turbinate. This can be performed with or without incisions. If visualization is necessary, the physician makes a full thickness incision over the anterior-inferior surface of the turbinate and continues it deep to bone. An elevator lifts the mucoperiosteum, exposing the bony turbinate. The physician fractures the bony turbinate with a chisel. Electrocautery may control bleeding. The turbinate mucosa is closed in a single layer.

31000-31002
The physician irrigates infected sinuses through cannulas. Topical vasoconstrictive agents are applied. The maxillary sinus is entered in 31000 through the natural ostium or opening in the middle meatus of the nasal cavity or through an antral puncture beneath the inferior nasal turbinate. The sphenoid sinus is entered in 31002 through the sphenoethmoidal recess in the superior nasal cavity. A flexible cannula is inserted into these openings and the sinuses are irrigated with saline solutions. These lavages will reduce inflammation and remove purulent (pus) discharge in the sinuses.

31020
The physician surgically creates an opening from the nasal cavity into the maxillary sinus to allow adequate sinus drainage. An antral "window" is made in the inferior meatus or by enlargement of the natural ostium in the middle meatus. Topical vasoconstrictive agents are applied to the nasal mucosa. Local anesthesia is injected into the nasal mucosa. A trocar is used to create an opening into the desired antral window location. The opening is enlarged with biting forceps. The maxillary sinus can be inspected and irrigated with direct visualization. A temporary irrigation catheter may be placed into the sinus and secured with sutures to the nose. The nasal cavity may be packed for 24 to 48 hours if excessive bleeding occurs during the procedure.

31030-31032
The physician creates several maxillary sinus openings to allow adequate sinus drainage for treatment of irreversible maxillary sinus disease. An intraoral incision is made in the labial mucosa, exposing the canine fossa. The canine fossa is perforated with a trocar and biting forceps increase the opening into the maxillary sinus. Sinus mucosa is removed with curettes. A second opening is made from the nasal cavity into the inferior meatus. Topical vasoconstrictive agents are applied to the nasal mucosa and local anesthesia is injected. A trocar perforates an opening into the inferior meatus. The opening is enlarged with biting forceps. An antrochoanal polyp is present in 31032 within both the maxillary sinus and nasal cavity.

The mucosa adjacent to the natural ostium is removed with the polyps. The intraoral incision is repaired in a single layer.

31040

The physician opens the pterygopalatine space to access the nerves or blood vessels located within the fossa. An intraoral incision is made in the maxillary buccal vestibule. An opening is made in the anterior maxillary wall with drills and chisels. Electrocautery of the sinus membrane of the posterior maxillary wall is performed to control bleeding. Chisels create an opening in the posterior maxillary wall. This bone is removed, providing an entrance into the pterygopalatine space. Fat is abundant and protects the fossa's vidian nerve, the sphenopalatine ganglion, and the branches of the internal maxillary artery. These structures are dissected free from fat and may be ligated and sectioned. The intraoral incision is closed in a single layer.

31050-31051

The physician enters the diseased sphenoid sinus. While open, biopsies may be taken of the sphenoidal masses. The sinus mucosa or mucosal polyps are removed in 31051. Due to its location deep within the skull, the sphenoid sinus surgery is accessed through structures overlying the sinus. Most commonly, an intraoral incision is made in the maxillary labial vestibule. The nasal septal cartilage is dissected from the nasal floor and is detached from the anterior nasal spine. The anterior cartilaginous septum is displaced and dissection continues to the bony nasal septum. The physician uses rongeurs to remove the bony septum, exposing the sphenoid region. The anterior wall of the sphenoid sinus is also removed with rongeurs. The physician uses an operating microscope to remove sinus contents. The nasal midline is reestablished and the cartilage is reattached to the nasal spine. Transseptal sutures are placed. The intraoral incision is closed in a single layer. The nose is packed and external nasal dressings may be placed.

31070

The physician uses a trephine to access the frontal sinus in 31070. In 31071, frontal sinusotomy is accomplished with an intranasal approach accessed through the agger nasi bone cells for drainage. The frontal sinus opening is obstructed by sinus disease, not allowing the sinus to drain into the nose. A small skin incision is made beneath the unshaven medial eyebrow. The dissection is carried to the frontal bone overlying the frontal sinus. The physician uses a round burr to make an opening into the sinus cavity. Tissue for culture may be taken at this time. The sinus is irrigated with saline solutions. Two irrigation catheters are placed into the sinus through the bony opening. The wound is closed in layers. The catheters are sutured to the skin. The exposed catheters are used to irrigate the sinus and are removed once the sinus inflammation subsides and the irrigation fluid starts to exit through the nose.

31075

The physician makes an external skin incision in the medial orbit to access the frontal sinus. The curvilinear incision is made beneath the eyebrow along the medial orbit extending to the superior aspect of the orbit. The dissection continues to the bone. The physician uses a drill and forceps to create an opening into the frontal sinus and, if needed, the ethmoid sinus. Pathologic and/or diseased tissue membrane is removed with curettes. The inferior wall of the sinus can be removed, increasing the drainage from the sinus into the nose. The wound is closed in layers.

31080-31081

The physician removes the frontal sinus mucosa and places material into the sinus cavity to prevent regrowth of the sinus mucosa. To access the frontal sinus through a brow incision in 31080, a full thickness incision is made from the superior aspect of one eyebrow, extending through the nasofrontal junction to the opposite eyebrow. A bicoronal flap may access the frontal sinus in 31081. After the physician exposes the sinus, the frontal bone overlying the frontal sinus is removed with drills, saws, and chisels. The contents of the exposed sinus are removed with curettes and burrs. The nasofrontal duct is obstructed with an alloplastic or autogenous material (bone). The sinus cavity is obliterated with autologous fat harvested from the abdomen or buttocks. The removed frontal bone is returned and secured with wires, plates, and/or screws. Incisions are repaired in layers.

31084-31085

The physician removes the frontal sinus mucosa and places material into the sinus cavity to prevent regrowth of the sinus mucosa. In the frontal sinus access, an osteoplastic flap is used. The periosteum of the excised frontal bone is preserved. When the frontal sinus is accessed by brow incision in 31084, an incision is made from the superior aspect of one eyebrow, extending through the nasofrontal junction to the opposite eyebrow. A bicoronal flap accesses the frontal sinus in 31085. Dissection is carried to the periosteal layer. A template is made from a radiograph outlining the frontal sinus. The template is placed over the frontal sinus and the periosteum is excised around the template. The physician removes the frontal bone, with attached periosteum overlying the frontal sinus, using drills, saws, and chisels. The contents of the exposed sinus are removed with curettes and burrs. The nasofrontal duct is obstructed with an alloplastic (synthetic) or autogenous material (i.e., bone). The sinus cavity is obliterated with autologous fat harvested from the abdomen or buttocks. The frontal bone flap is returned and secured with sutures, wires, plates, and/or screws. The incisions are repaired in layers.

31086-31087

The physician enters the frontal sinus to remove pathologic lesions and diseased sinus mucosa. In the frontal sinus access, an osteoplastic flap is used in which the periosteum of the excised frontal bone is preserved. When the frontal sinus is accessed by brow incision in 31086, an incision is made from the superior aspect of one eyebrow, extending through the nasofrontal junction to the opposite eyebrow. A bicoronal flap accesses the frontal sinus in 31087. Dissection is carried to the periosteal layer. A template is made from a radiograph outlining the frontal sinus. The template is placed over the frontal sinus and the periosteum is excised around the template. The physician removes the frontal bone with attached periosteum overlying the frontal sinus using drills, saws, and chisels. The contents of the exposed sinus are removed with curettes and burrs. No obliteration of the sinus is necessary. The frontal bone flap is returned and secured with sutures, wires, plates, and/or screws. The incisions are repaired in layers.

31090

The physician enters three or more sinuses to remove diseased sinus contents using multiple approaches. Sinus disease may involve any of the maxillary, ethmoid, sphenoid, and/or frontal sinuses. The physician uses multiple approaches to the sinus including, intraoral, intranasal, skin and/or bicoronal incisions. Once the sinus is accessed, the physician removes its contents with curettes. Incisions are repaired in both single and layers, depending on the access.

31200

The physician removes diseased tissue from the ethmoid sinuses. The physician accesses the ethmoid sinuses through the nose. Topical vasoconstrictive agents are placed on the nasal mucosa to shrink the blood vessels. Local anesthesia is injected into the nasal mucosa. The physician retracts the middle turbinate anteriorly, exposing the sinus opening. A small curette may be advanced into the anterior ethmoid cells. The physician uses the curette to remove any diseased tissue of the anterior sinus, and allows the sinus to drain.

31201

The physician removes diseased tissue from the anterior and posterior ethmoid sinuses. The physician accesses the ethmoid sinuses through the nose. Topical vasoconstrictive drugs are placed on the nasal mucosa. Local anesthesia is injected into the nasal mucosa. The physician retracts the middle turbinate anteriorly, exposing the sinus opening. A small curette is used to remove the uncinate process in the bone. The physician may advance the curette into the anterior ethmoid cells. The physician uses blunt forceps to open posterior bony cells. Curettes remove diseased tissue and allow postoperative drainage of both the anterior and posterior ethmoid sinuses.

31205

The physician removes diseased tissue of the ethmoid sinuses. A curvilinear incision is made between the nasal dorsum and the medial canthus of the eye. Dissection is carried to the medial orbital bone. A bony window is made through the lamina papyracea bone, exposing the lateral ethmoid sinus. The physician removes all diseased tissue. The nasal cavity is penetrated through the medial ethmoid region. Nasal gauze packing is placed through the extranasal incision. The external skin incision is repaired with a layered closure.

31225

The physician removes a portion of or all of the diseased maxilla. Incisions may be intraoral or may include skin incisions such as the Weber-Ferguson approach. Dissection is continued to expose and isolate the planned bony excision. The physician uses drills, saws, and chisels to fracture the maxilla from the midface. The fractured maxilla and adjacent tissue are loosened and removed to "free margins" as determined with intraoperative tissue specimens sent to the pathologist for immediate microscopic examination. All sinus mucosa is removed. Exposed bone may be covered with a separately reportable split thickness skin graft. A splint may be placed to obturate (block) the mouth from the surgical area. All skin incisions are repaired with a layered closure.

31230

The physician removes the maxilla, eye, and orbital soft tissue. Incisions may be intraoral or may include skin incisions such as a modified Weber-Ferguson incision that includes incision in the upper eyelid. Dissection is continued to expose and isolate the planned bony excision. The physician uses drills, saws, and chisels to fracture the maxilla from the midface. The fractured maxilla and adjacent tissue are loosened and removed to "free margins" as determined with intraoperative tissue specimens sent to the pathologist for immediate microscopic examination. The upper eyelid incision is dissected to the periosteum of the superior orbit. The maxilla is retracted downward, so the physician can visualize the optic nerve and blood vessels. The optic nerve is severed and the vessels are ligated. The maxilla, adjacent soft tissue, and orbital contents are removed in one specimen. All sinus mucosa is removed. Exposed bone is covered with a separately reportable split thickness skin graft. A splint may be placed to obturate (block) the mouth from the surgical area. All skin incisions are repaired with a layered closure.

31231

The physician uses an endoscope for a diagnostic evaluation of the nose. An endoscope has a rigid fiberoptic telescope that allows the physician both increased visualization and magnification of internal anatomy. Topical vasoconstrictive agents are applied to the nasal mucosa and nerve blocks with local anesthesia are performed. The endoscope is placed into the nose and a thorough inspection of internal nasal structures is accomplished. No surgical procedure is performed.

31233

The physician uses an endoscope for a diagnostic evaluation of the nose and the maxillary sinus. An endoscope has a rigid fiberoptic telescope that allows the physician both increased visualization and magnification of internal anatomy. Topical vasoconstrictive agents are applied to the nasal mucosa and nerve blocks with local anesthesia are performed. The endoscope is placed into the nose and a thorough inspection of the internal nasal structures is accomplished. A trocar puncture is made directly into the inferior meatus area of the nose or after a mucosal incision into the canine fossa of the maxilla. The endoscope is placed into the maxillary sinus for evaluation. The intraoral mucosa may be closed in a single layer. The nasal puncture wound does not require closure. No other procedure is performed on the sinus at this time.

31235

The physician uses an endoscope for a diagnostic evaluation of the nose and the sphenoid sinus. An endoscope has a rigid fiberoptic telescope that allows the physician both increased visualization and magnification of internal anatomy. Topical vasoconstrictive agents are applied to the nasal mucosa and nerve blocks with local anesthesia are performed. The endoscope is placed into the nose and a thorough inspection of the internal nasal structures is accomplished. Access to the sphenoid sinus is accomplished by a trocar puncture made directly into the sphenoid sinus after negotiation through the ethmoids or by cannulation of the sphenoid drainage system that enters the sphenoethmoidal recess. The endoscope is placed into the sphenoid sinus for evaluation. The sphenoidal puncture wound does not require closure. No other procedure is performed on the sinus at this time.

31237

The physician uses an endoscope for a diagnostic evaluation of the nose. An endoscope has a rigid fiberoptic telescope that allows the physician both increased visualization and magnification of internal anatomy. Topical vasoconstrictive agents are applied to the nasal mucosa and nerve blocks with local anesthesia are performed. The endoscope is placed into the nose and a thorough inspection of the internal nasal structures is accomplished. Any identified lesions can be removed by intranasal instruments placed parallel to the endoscope. Scalpels, forceps, snares, and other instruments are used to remove diseased mucosa or lesions from the internal nose. The nose may be packed if excessive bleeding occurs.

31238

The physician uses an endoscope for a diagnostic evaluation of the bleeding nose. An endoscope has a rigid fiberoptic telescope that allows the physician both increased visualization and magnification of internal anatomy. Topical vasoconstrictive agents are applied to the nasal mucosa and nerve blocks with local anesthesia are performed. The endoscope is placed into the nose and a thorough inspection of the internal nasal structures is accomplished. Any bleeding sources are identified. Electrocautery instruments or lasers are placed parallel to the endoscope and are used to stop internal nasal bleeding.

31239

The physician uses an endoscope to visually and surgically assist during a dacryocystorhinostomy. When the lacrimal system is obstructed and excessive tearing is a problem for the patient, a dacryocystorhinostomy is performed. In this procedure, the new lacrimal drainage system is surgically created from the lower eyelid into the nose. An endoscope allows the physician both increased visualization and magnification of the internal anatomy. Topical vasoconstrictive agents are applied to the nasal mucosa and nerve blocks with local anesthesia are performed. The endoscope is placed into the nose. The nasolacrimal duct and other lacrimal structures are visualized. Endoscopy may aid in location of structures or enhance intranasal procedures like osteotomies and internal splinting with Teflon tubes.

31240

The physician uses an endoscope for an intranasal evaluation and surgical resection of a concha bullosa, an intranasal cyst has caused distention (stretching or swelling) of the turbinate bone. This swelling is called a concha bullosa. An endoscope has a rigid fiberoptic telescope that allow the physician both increased visualization and magnification of internal anatomy. Topical vasoconstrictive agents are applied to the nasal mucosa and nerve blocks with local anesthesia are performed. The endoscope is placed into the nose and thorough inspection of internal nasal structures is accomplished. A scalpel or biting forceps are introduced parallel to the endoscope and are used to excise the concha bullosa. Electrocautery may be used for hemostasis. The nasal cavity may be packed with Telfa or gauze for 24 to 48 hours.

31254-31255

The physician uses an endoscope for surgical resection of the anterior or posterior ethmoidectomy. Disease of the anterior ethmoid sinus may block maxillary sinus drainage. An endoscope allows both increased visualization and magnification of internal anatomy. Topical vasoconstrictive agents are applied to the nasal mucosa and nerve blocks with local anesthesia are performed. The endoscope is placed into the nose and a thorough inspection of internal nasal structures is accomplished. A scalpel or biting forceps is introduced parallel to the endoscope and is used to remove diseased tissues. Polyps may be excised. Electrocautery may be used for hemostasis. The nasal cavity may be packed with Telfa or gauze for 24 to 48 hours. Report 31255 if a total ethmoidectomy is performed.

31256-31267
The physician uses an endoscope for surgical resection of the maxillary sinus. Topical vasoconstrictive agents are applied to the nasal mucosa and nerve blocks with local anesthesia are performed. The endoscope is placed into the nose and a thorough inspection of internal nasal structures is accomplished. A scalpel or biting forceps is introduced parallel to the endoscope and is used to remove diseased tissues. Polyps may be excised. An antrostomy is performed in 31256, creating an opening for drainage from the maxillary sinus. Additionally, in 31267, the maxillary sinus may be opened and the mucosa removed. In either case, electrocautery may be used for hemostasis. The nasal cavity may be packed with Telfa or gauze for 24 to 48 hours.

31276
The physician uses an endoscope for surgical resection of the frontal sinus. Topical vasoconstrictive agents are applied to the nasal mucosa and nerve blocks with local anesthesia are performed. The endoscope is placed into the nose and a thorough inspection of the internal nasal structures is accomplished. A scalpel or biting forceps is introduced parallel to the endoscope and is used to remove diseased tissues from the frontal sinus. Polyps are removed. An antrostomy is sometimes performed, creating an opening for drainage from the maxillary sinus. Electrocautery may be used for hemostasis. The nasal cavity may be packed with Telfa or gauze for 24 to 48 hours.

31287-31288
The physician uses an endoscope for surgical access of the sphenoid sinus. The sphenoid can be explored with direct access or through the posterior ethmoid sinus. The isolated access to the sphenoid sinus is through dilation of the sphenoid ostium. The middle turbinate may be fractured or partially removed for access. The ostium is cannulated and dilated. The physician uses forceps or a sphenoid punch to open the sinus cavity. Additionally, diseased mucosa or tissue is removed in 31288. The nose may be packed if excessive bleeding occurs.

31290-31291
The physician uses an endoscope for surgical access and repair of cerebrospinal fluid leaks in ethmoid and sphenoid sinuses. Topical vasoconstrictive agents and local anesthesia are applied to the nasal mucosa. The endoscope is placed into the nose. The middle turbinate may be fractured to provide access. In 31290, the ethmoid sinus is entered through the ethmoid bulla. In 31291, the sphenoid sinus can be explored through the posterior ethmoid sinus or through direct access. If accessed through the ethmoid sinus, the sphenoid ostium is cannulated and dilated. The physician uses forceps or a sphenoid punch to open the sinus cavity. Once the sinus cavity is entered, the cerebrospinal fluid leak is isolated. Local mucosal or muscle flaps may be developed to plug the defect. Autologous fat, muscle or fascia lata may also be used to seal the leak.

31292-31293
The physician uses an endoscope for surgical access to decompress the orbit. Decompression may occur through one orbital wall in 31292 or through two orbital walls in 31293. The inferior orbital wall is approached through a canine fossa puncture into the maxillary sinus. The inferior orbital wall is the roof of the maxillary sinus. Forceps remove orbital bone while preserving the orbital periosteum. This allows orbital contents to herniate into the maxillary sinus. The medial orbital wall can be approached through the ethmoid sinuses. The ethmoids are may be opened through the maxillary sinus or by a separate intranasal ethmoid approach. The medial wall of the orbit is the lateral wall of the ethmoids. Bone is removed from this region, also allowing orbital contents to herniate into the ethmoid regions. The nose may be packed if excessive bleeding occurs.

31294
The physician uses an endoscope for surgical access to decompress the optic nerve in the posterior orbit. The optic nerve sends transmissions that provide the sense of sight. This nerve enters the posterior cone through the optic foramen (orbital apex). The orbital apex may be approached through the sphenoid sinus. The sphenoid sinus may be explored through the posterior ethmoid sinus or directly. The middle turbinate may be fractured or partially removed to provide access. Isolated access to the sinus is through cannulation and dilation of the sphenoid ostium. The physician uses a forceps or a sphenoid punch to gain entry into the sinus cavity. Bone is removed from the lateral portion of the sinus, decompressing the optic nerve. The nose may be packed if excessive bleeding occurs.

31300
A laryngocele is an air-filled dilation of the laryngeal ventricle that connects with the laryngeal cavity. The physician first performs a tracheostomy on the patient. Using a horizontal neck incision, the physician exposes the larynx and performs a thyrotomy and laryngofissure, opening the larynx at the midline of the thyroid cartilage. The laryngocele or tumor is isolated, dissected, and excised. A cordectomy, the excision of all or part of the vocal cord, may also be performed. The incision is repaired in sutured layers.

Respiratory

31320

The physician first performs a tracheostomy on the patient. Using a horizontal neck incision, the physician exposes the larynx and performs a thyrotomy and laryngofissure, opening the larynx at the midline of the thyroid cartilage. The larynx is explored, but no other procedure is performed. The incision is repaired in sutured layers.

31360-31365

The physician removes the larynx in 31360, and removes the larynx and surrounding tissues in 31365. First, a tracheostomy is performed. The physician makes a low collar or midline cervical incision for 31360 or a horizontal neck incision for 31365. The strap muscles of the neck and thyroid isthmus are cut. Part or all of the hyoid bone is removed. The trachea and inferior pharyngeal constrictor muscles are transected. By cutting the hypopharyngeal walls, the larynx is freed and removed. Resected tissues may include part of the esophagus and base of the tongue for 31360. In 31365, an extensive dissection may include removal of the sternocleidomastoid muscle, the submandibular salivary gland, the internal jugular vein and the lymph nodes of the lateral neck, under the chin and mandible, and the supraclavicular nodes. Any reconstruction performed at this time is separately reported. When either excision is completed, the incision is sutured in layers.

31367-31368

The surgeon removes the larynx in 31367, and the larynx and surrounding tissues in 31368. First, a tracheostomy is performed. The physician approaches the larynx through the thyroid cartilage for 31367 or a horizontal neck incision for 31368. The epiglottis, false vocal cords, mucosal lining of the ventricles, part or all of the hyoid bone, and superior part of the laryngeal cartilage are removed in 31367. In 31368, an extensive dissection may include removal of the sternocleidomastoid muscle, the submandibular salivary gland, the internal jugular vein and the lymph nodes of the lateral neck, under the chin and mandible, and the supraclavicular nodes. Any reconstruction performed at this time is separately reported. When either excision is completed, the incision is sutured in layers.

31370-31382

The physician removes a portion of the larynx. First, a tracheostomy is performed. The physician makes a low collar or midline cervical incision. The strap muscles of the neck are retracted and a midline incision of the perichondrium is made, exposing the larynx. The laryngeal cartilage is incised. In 31370, a horizontal incision is made above or below the affected area, and the diseased tissue is excised. The airway is reconstructed above to the pharynx or below to the trachea. In 31375, the vocal cord and adjacent cartilage is resected. In 31380, incision are a made into both halves of the thyroid cartilage, and the anterior part of the thyroid cartilage and the affected portions of both vocal cords are excised. In 31382, the area of resection also includes part or all of the arytenoid. In each instance, the pharynx is closed by suturing the perichondrium and strap muscles. The incision is sutured in layers.

31390

The physician removes the larynx and pharynx. First, a tracheostomy is performed. The physician approaches the pharynx and larynx through a horizontal neck incision. The epiglottis, false vocal cords, mucosal lining of the ventricles, part or all of the hyoid bone, pharynx, and superior part of the laryngeal cartilage are removed. Extensive dissection may include removal of the sternocleidomastoid muscle, the submandibular salivary gland, the internal jugular vein and the lymph nodes of the lateral neck, under the chin and mandible, and the supraclavicular nodes. When either excision is completed, the incision is sutured in layers.

31395

The physician removes the larynx and pharynx and performs reconstruction with available tissues. First, a tracheostomy is performed. The physician approaches the pharynx and larynx through a horizontal neck incision. The epiglottis, false vocal cords, mucosal lining of the ventricles, part or all of the hyoid bone, pharynx, and superior part of the laryngeal cartilage are removed. Extensive dissection may include removal of the sternocleidomastoid muscle, the submandibular salivary gland, the internal jugular vein and the lymph nodes of the lateral neck, under the chin and mandible, and the supraclavicular nodes. Reconstruction of the pharyngeal area can be achieved in a number of ways; one of the most common is the myocutaneous flap reconstruction using the pectoralis major muscle and its overlying skin. The flap is rotated and inserted through a previously created tunnel between the clavicle and overlying skin. The flap is sutured into place to reconstruct the pharynx. The incision is sutured in layers.

31400

The physician secures the arytenoid process. First, a tracheostomy is performed. The physician exposes and transects the inferior pharyngeal constrictor muscle and continues dissection to reach the arytenoid cartilage. In an arytenoidopexy, the arytenoid cartilage is tacked against the thyroid ala to lateralize the arytenoid. In an arytenoidectomy, the arytenoid cartilage is resected and removed. The incision is closed with layered sutures.

31420

The physician excises all or part of the epiglottis, the cartilage that protects the entrance to the larynx. The physician uses an intra-oral approach to access and remove the epiglottis or lesions involving the tip of the epiglottis. If the affected area is minor, no sutures are needed. If the area involve most or all of the epiglottis, the remaining tissues are sutured together.

31500
The physician places an endotracheal tube to provide air passage in emergency situations. The patient is ventilated with a mask and bag and positioned by extending the neck anteriorly and the head posteriorly. The physician places the laryngoscope into the patient's mouth and advances the blade toward the epiglottis until the vocal cords are visible. An endotracheal tube is inserted between the vocal cords and advanced to the proper position. The cuff of the endotracheal tube is inflated.

31502
The physician removes the indwelling tracheotomy tube and replaces it with a new one. The procedure is performed before healing sufficient to form a fistula tract has taken place; usually a few days within placement of the original tube.

31505-31513
The physician administers a topical anesthetic to the oral cavity, pharynx, and larynx and positions the patient's head and laryngoscopic mirror so as to view the larynx through the reflection. The interior of the larynx is examined for diagnostic purposes in 31505. In 31510, suspect tissue or a lesion may be stained for identification and a biopsy of the tissue is taken. In 31511, a foreign body is identified and withdrawn by grasping it with forceps. In 31512, a lesion is identified and excised. In 31513, an injection is given into the vocal cords.

31515
The physician uses an aspirator to remove excess saliva or semi-solid foreign material from the larynx. After applying topical anesthesia to the oral cavity and pharynx, the physician inserts the laryngoscope through the patient's mouth. An aspirator is fed through the laryngoscope and the larynx is cleared of saliva and semi-solid foreign material. If a tracheoscopy is performed, a bronchoscope is inserted through the laryngoscope for microscopic visualization of the trachea and bronchi. No other procedure is performed.

31520-31525
The physician places a rigid laryngoscope to examine the patient's larynx. The physician administers a topical anesthetic to the oral cavity, pharynx, and larynx and inserts the laryngoscope through the patient's mouth. The interior of the larynx of a newborn is examined in 31520 and of a patient other than a newborn in 31525. If a tracheoscopy is performed, a bronchoscope is inserted through the laryngoscope for visualization of the trachea and bronchi. No other procedure is performed at this time.

31526
The physician uses an operating microscope or telescope to examine the interior of the larynx. After administering a topical anesthetic to the oral cavity, pharynx, and larynx, the physician inserts the laryngoscope into the patient's mouth and examines the larynx. If a tracheoscopy is performed, a bronchoscope is inserted through the laryngoscope for microscopic visualization of the trachea and bronchi. No other procedure is performed at this time.

31527
The physician administers a topical anesthetic to the oral cavity, pharynx, and larynx and inserts the laryngoscope through the patient's mouth. The interior of the larynx is examined. An obturator is an object that is used to close an opening. A wire is threaded through a cannulated needle which has been placed into the larynx. The end of the wire is grasped with forceps and drawn out through the laryngoscope. The wire is drawn through the obturator and threaded through another needle in the supraglottic space. The external ends of the wire are knotted over a stent.

31528-31529
The physician dilates the tracheobronchial stenosis. The physician administers a topical or general anesthetic and inserts the laryngoscope into the patient's mouth. The interior of the larynx is examined. The physician manipulates the laryngoscope to dilate areas of the tracheobronchial stenosis. Use 31529 to report subsequent dilations. If a tracheoscopy is performed, a bronchoscope is inserted through the laryngoscope for visualization of the trachea and bronchi.

31530-31531
The physician performs a direct, operative laryngoscopy to remove a foreign body. A topical anesthetic is administered to the oral cavity, pharynx, and larynx and the laryngoscope is inserted into the patient's mouth. The interior of the larynx is examined. In 31530, the foreign body is located, grasped with biopsy forceps and withdrawn. In 31531, the physician uses a microscope or telescope to locate and remove the foreign body.

31535-31536
The physician performs a direct, operative laryngoscopy with biopsy. A topical anesthetic is administered to the oral cavity, pharynx, and larynx and the laryngoscope is inserted into the patient's mouth. The interior of the larynx is examined. In 31535, a lesion is biopsied with a sharp basket or cup forceps. Sometimes staining with toluidine blue is used to delineate the biopsy site. In 31536, the physician uses an operating microscope or a telescope to isolate and biopsy the lesions. This is usually done for smaller lesions.

31540-31541
The physician performs a direct operative laryngoscopy with excision of tumor and/or stripping of the vocal cords or epiglottis. A topical anesthetic is administered

to the oral cavity, pharynx, and larynx and the laryngoscope is inserted into the patient's mouth. The interior of the larynx is examined and a laryngeal tumor may be isolated, dissected, and excised. The vocal cords or epiglottis may also be removed using stripping forceps. An operating microscope or a telescope is used in 31541. This is usually done for smaller lesions.

31545-31546

The physician removes a non-neoplastic lesion(s) of the vocal cords. Non-neoplastic lesions include nodules, polyps, and cysts. The physician administers a topical anesthetic to the oral cavity, pharynx, and larynx and inserts the laryngoscope into the patient's mouth. The interior of the larynx is examined. A solution of saline and adrenaline is infused beneath the surface of the vocal fold to better define the lesion(s) and to protect the deeper vocal tissue from injury. The vocal lesion(s) is identified and isolated. Lesions are decorticated rather than excised using a submucosal (subepithelial) technique. This technique disturbs only the superficial tissue layers while preserving the surface membrane. Mucosal incisions are made on the superior (ventricular) surface of the lesion(s). The lesion(s) is removed with gentle dissection and or suction. If there is sufficient redundant mucosa following removal of the lesion(s), a local tissue flap is created by trimming and redraping the mucosa over the vocal fold (31545). If there is not sufficient mucosa to form a local flap, a mucosal tissue autograft is harvested and applied (31546). Since these procedures require the use of high magnification and specially designed micro-instruments, an operating microscope or telescope is included and should not be reported separately.

31560-31561

The physician performs a direct, operative laryngoscopy with removal of the arytenoid cartilage. A topical anesthetic is administered to the oral cavity, pharynx, and larynx and the laryngoscope is inserted into the patient's mouth. The interior of the larynx is examined and the arytenoid cartilage is exposed by excising the overlying mucosa. The arytenoid is dissected from its muscular attachments and removed. An operating microscope or a telescope is used in 31561.

31570-31571

The physician performs a direct laryngoscopy with therapeutic injection into the vocal cords. The physician injects the vocal cords with a therapeutic substance such as glycerin, sesame oil, Gelfoam, or Teflon paste (Polytef). Injury to the larynx may result in a permanently damaged voice. An injection with a therapeutic substance into an affected vocal cord can augment its size and help bring it into apposition with the other vocal cord, creating a more complete glottic closure. The injected material hardens and retains its shape for improvement in voice quality. A Teflon paste injection is used when a permanent augmentation is desired. A glycerin, sesame oil, or Gelfoam injection is used to create a temporary augmentation until a permanent solution to an incomplete glottic closure is found. The physician administers a topical anesthetic to the oral cavity, pharynx, and larynx and inserts the laryngoscope into the patient's mouth. The interior of the larynx is examined and the physician injects the vocal cord at one to three sites with the selected therapeutic substance. No other procedure is performed. An operating microscope or a telescope is used in 31571.

31575-31576

The physician administers a topical anesthetic to the oral cavity, pharynx, and larynx and uses a nasal or oral approach to insert a flexible fiberoptic laryngoscope. The interior of the larynx is examined in 31575. Additionally, in 31576, a lesion is biopsied with a sharp basket or cup forceps. Sometimes staining with toluidine blue is used to delineate the biopsy site.

31577-31578

The physician removes a foreign body from the larynx. The physician administers a topical anesthetic to the oral cavity, pharynx, and larynx and uses a nasal or intraoral approach to insert a flexible fiberoptic laryngoscope. The interior of the larynx is examined in 31577, the foreign body is located, grasped with biopsy forceps and withdrawn. In 31578, the physician locates and excises the lesion.

31579

The physician examines the larynx and vocal cord function. The patient is prepared with a nasal spray containing topical decongestant and anesthetic. The physician passes a flexible laryngoscope through the patient's nose into the pharynx and larynx, which are examined. The stroboscope responds to the fundamental frequency of the vibrating vocal cords, allowing the physician to see vocal cord function. No other procedure is performed.

31580-31582

The physician excises a laryngeal web, a congenital malformation of the larynx. The physician first performs a tracheostomy on the patient. Using a horizontal neck incision, the physician exposes the laryngeal web. In 31580, the web lies between the vocal cords. The physician excises the web and inserts a laryngeal keel, or spacer, between the vocal cords. The laryngotomy incision is closed. During a separate operative session after the larynx has had time to heal, the physician reenters the operative site through the same incision and removes the keel. The incision is repaired in sutured layers. In 31582, the stenosis, or web, involves the arytenoid cartilages. The physician excises the affected area in the posterior glottis. A rib graft is obtained and sewn to provide posterior stability to the larynx and adjacent trachea. The incision is sutured in layers.

31584
The physician reduces a fractured larynx to its anatomical position. The physician first performs a low tracheostomy on the patient to secure the airway and prevent extravasation of air into the surrounding tissues. Using a horizontal neck incision, the physician exposes the thyroid cartilage and repairs the mucosal defects. The thyroid cartilage is stabilized with wire stents. The incision is repaired in sutured layers.

31587-31588
The physician restores a cricoid split. (A cricoid split is a break in the circular cartilage of the larynx.) The physician first performs a low tracheostomy on the patient. Using a horizontal neck incision, the physician exposes the cricoid split and restores it to its normal anatomical position (reduction). The cartilage is affixed with wire. A stent may be placed to maintain cricotracheal continuity. The incision is repaired in sutured layers. Report 31588 for laryngoplasty, not otherwise specified.

31590
The physician restores innervation to the larynx using a neuromuscular pedicle (flap). The physician makes a horizontal neck incision and dissects the strap muscles of the anterior neck. The descending branch of the hypoglossal nerve is located. The nerve and the muscle are rotated to the larynx and secured with sutures. The incision is sutured in layers.

31595
The physician severs the laryngeal nerve. The recurrent laryngeal nerve controls the action of the vocal cords. The physician makes a vertical incision and retracts the strap muscles and dissects the tissue until the nerve is exposed and identified. The physician severs the recurrent laryngeal nerve prior to its point of branching. The incision is repaired in sutured layers.

31600-31610
The physician creates a tracheostomy. The physician makes a horizontal neck incision and dissects the muscles to expose the trachea. The thyroid isthmus is cut if necessary. The trachea is incised and an airway is inserted. After bleeding is controlled, a stoma is created by suturing the skin to the tissue layers. In 31600, the tracheostomy is a planned procedure. In 31601 it is performed on patients aged under two years. In 31603, it is performed under emergency conditions, transtracheal. In 31605, it is performed under emergency conditions, cricothyroid membrane. In 31610, skin flaps are used to create a more permanent stoma.

31611
The physician constructs a tracheal esophageal fistula for vocalization. The physician makes a horizontal neck incision and dissects the tissues between the tracheostoma and the esophagus. The esophagus is incised and a laryngeal speech prosthesis is inserted between the esophagus and the trachea, creating a fistula. The prosthesis, called a voice button or a Blom-Singer prosthesis, is a one-way valve enabling the patient to phonate. The physician closes the incision around the prosthesis.

31612
The physician punctures the trachea with a needle to aspirate secretions or inject a therapeutic agent. The physician palpates the site and inserts a hollow point needle. Secretions are aspirated or a therapeutic agent is injected. The needle is removed.

31613-31614
The physician revises a tracheal stoma. The physician incises the stoma area and resects redundant scar tissue or a poorly healing wound. The skin is re-anastomosed and sewn to the stoma in sutured layers. Report 31613 for performance of a simple revision and 31614 if a complex procedure is performed with flap rotation.

31615
The physician views the airway using a bronchoscope placed through an existing tracheostomy. The physician examines the conducting airways. The bronchoscope is removed.

31620
Endobronchial ultrasound (EBUS) is performed during a diagnostic or therapeutic bronchoscopy. The physician uses ultrasound to view the structure of the tracheobronchial wall. Ultrasound creates pictures by bouncing sound waves through interior body structures, which reflect back to a receiving unit at varying speeds as the waves pass through different densities of tissue. The sound waves are converted to electrical pulses displayed in picture form on screen. Through a channel of the bronchoscope, the physician passes a transducer or ultrasound probe within a flexible sheath, usually equipped with a balloon tip, down to the target area and views the inside of the trachea or bronchus during the primary procedure using the images created by EBUS.

31622-31624
The physician views the airway using a flexible fiberoptic or rigid bronchoscope that is introduced through the nasal or oral cavity. The airway is anesthetized. The bronchoscope is inserted and advanced through the nasal or oral cavity, past the larynx to inspect the bronchus. In 31622, after diagnostic visualization of the bronchus, cell washings may be obtained through the bronchoscope. In 31623, sample lung tissue is obtained with brushings or protected brushing through the scope. In 31624, the bronchoscopy includes bronchial alveolar lavage, which allows lung tissue to be sampled by irrigating with saline followed by suctioning the fluid. The

Respiratory

bronchoscope is removed. These codes include fluoroscopic guidance, when performed.

31625
The physician views the airway using a flexible fiberoptic or rigid bronchoscope that is introduced through the nasal or oral cavity. The airway is anesthetized. The bronchoscope is inserted and advanced through the nasal or oral cavity, past the larynx to inspect the bronchus, including fluoroscopic guidance, if used. After diagnostic visualization of the bronchus, a sample of bronchial or endobronchial tissue is removed for study. More than one site may be biopsied. Bleeding is assessed and controlled, and the bronchoscope is removed.

31626
The physician views the airway using a flexible fiberoptic or rigid bronchoscope that is introduced through the nasal or oral cavity. The airway is anesthetized. The bronchoscope is inserted and advanced through the nasal or oral cavity, past the larynx to inspect the bronchus, including fluoroscopic guidance, if used. After diagnostic visualization of the bronchus, one or more fiducial markers are placed.

31627
The physician views the airway using a flexible fiberoptic or rigid bronchoscope that is introduced through the nasal or oral cavity. The airway is anesthetized. The bronchoscope is inserted and advanced through the nasal or oral cavity, past the larynx to inspect the bronchus, including fluoroscopic guidance, if used. This code reports the use of computer-assisted, image-guided navigation, and includes 3D reconstruction.

31628-31629
The physician views the airway using a flexible fiberoptic or rigid bronchoscope that is introduced through the nasal or oral cavity. The airway is anesthetized. The bronchoscope is inserted and advanced through the nasal or oral cavity, past the larynx to inspect the bronchus, including fluoroscopic guidance, if used. After diagnostic visualization of the bronchus, the physician passes closed biopsy forceps (31628) through a channel in the bronchoscope and through the bronchial wall to obtain one or more lung tissue samples from a single lobe. Alternately, the physician passes a needle (31629) through a channel in the bronchoscope and through the bronchial wall to obtain one or more aspiration biopsies of the trachea, main stem, and/or lobar bronchi. Bleeding is assessed and controlled, and the bronchoscope is removed.

31630
The physician performs tracheal/bronchial dilation or closed fracture reduction using a flexible fiberoptic or rigid bronchoscope introduced through the nasal or oral cavity. The physician uses the views obtained through the bronchoscope to identify any narrowing or fracture of the trachea or bronchus. The physician introduces a wire through the narrowed or fractured part of the airway and removes the bronchoscope. A series of dilators or stents are passed over the wire to open the airway until sufficient dilation or closed reduction of the stricture or fracture is accomplished. This may be done with or without fluoroscopic guidance.

31631
The physician places a tracheal stent or stents using a flexible fiberoptic or rigid bronchoscope introduced through the nasal or oral cavity, using local anesthesia of the patient's airway. The physician uses the views obtained through the bronchoscope to identify any narrowing or area of the trachea that requires stenting for support. The physician introduces a wire through the narrowed part of the trachea and removes the bronchoscope. If dilation is first required, a series of dilators are passed over the wire to open the airway until sufficient tracheal/bronchial dilation is accomplished. A stent is passed over the wire to the target area in the trachea and positioned in place to maintain an open airway. This may be done with or without fluoroscopic guidance.

31632-31633
The physician views the airway using a flexible fiberoptic or rigid bronchoscope that is introduced through the nasal or oral cavity. The airway is anesthetized. The bronchoscope is inserted. It is advanced through the larynx to the bronchus. Fluoroscopy (x-ray) may be used to assist with navigation of the bronchoscope tip to the abnormal tissue to be biopsied. Code 31632 is an add-on code to be used with 31628, in which the physician passes closed biopsy forceps through a channel in the bronchoscope, through the bronchial wall, and obtains tissue samples in one lobe. Report 31632 for each additional lobe in which this is done. Code 31633 is an add-on code to be used with 31629, in which a needle is passed through a channel in the bronchoscope, into the trachea, main stem, and/or a lobe of the bronchus, and an aspiration biopsy is obtained. Report 31633 for each additional lobe in which this is done.

31635
The physician views the airway using a flexible fiberoptic or rigid bronchoscope introduced through the nasal or oral cavity, using local anesthesia of the patient's airway. The physician uses the views obtained through the bronchoscope to locate the foreign body within the airway. The physician passes a snare, basket, or biopsy forceps through a channel in the bronchoscope to grasp the foreign body. The bronchoscope and foreign body are removed. This may be done with or without fluoroscopic guidance.

31636-31638
A rigid or flexible bronchoscopy is performed, with or without fluoroscopic guidance, to place a bronchial

stent. The type of stent used, as well as the level of patency vs. obstruction in the airway, will vary the placement technique. Initial assessment with the bronchoscope is done to determine the lesion's size and location. If fluoroscopy is used, the distal target position for stent placement is marked with a radiopaque object, such as a treated paperclip taped to the chest. If the airway is near completely occluded, a flexible tipped guidewire is placed through the bronchoscope, a balloon catheter is fed over the guidewire, and initial dilation is done. With the bronchoscope removed and the wire still in place, the stent, such as woven mesh or single wire stent with polyurethane covering, is passed over the guidewire by a stent catheter just past the obstruction. The stent is deployed by slowly sliding the plastic sheath covering back until it is snugly fitted. Report 31636 for the initial bronchial stent placement, 31637 for each additional major bronchus stented, and 31638 for the revision of a stent inserted in a previous session.

31640

The physician views the airway using a flexible fiberoptic or rigid bronchoscope introduced through the nasal or oral cavity, using local anesthesia of the patient's airway. The physician uses the views obtained through the bronchoscope to identify the tumor from within the airway. The physician may use fluoroscopy (x-ray) to assist with navigation of the bronchoscope tip to the abnormal tissue. The physician passes forceps through channels in the bronchoscope to grasp and excise the tumor. The bronchoscope is removed. This may be done with or without fluoroscopic guidance.

31641

The physician views the airway using a bronchoscope introduced through the nasal or oral cavity, using local anesthesia of the patient's airway. The physician uses the views obtained through the bronchoscope to identify the tumor and/or area of stenosis from within the airway. Fluoroscopy (x-ray) may be used to assist with navigation of the bronchoscope tip to the abnormal tissue and is included when performed. The physician passes a laser or freezing (cryo) probe through a channel in the bronchoscope to destroy the tumor or any areas of stenosis. The bronchoscope is removed.

31643

The physician views the airway using a bronchoscope with a fiberoptic camera and operating device. The airway is anesthetized and the bronchoscope is introduced through the nasal or oral cavity and advanced through the bronchus. A catheter is inserted through the bronchoscope into a lung cavity and is placed at the site where, in a separately reportable procedure, intracavitary radioelements will be applied. This code includes the use of fluoroscopic guidance, when performed.

31645-31646

The physician views the airway using a bronchoscope introduced through the nasal or oral cavity, using local anesthesia of the patient's airway. The physician uses the views obtained through the bronchoscope to identify the closest approach to the fluid collection or abscess from within the airway. The physician may use fluoroscopy (x-ray) to assist with navigation of the bronchoscope tip to the fluid collection or abscess. The physician passes a catheter through a channel in the bronchoscope and aspirates the tracheobronchial tree. Alternately, the physician passes a needle through a channel in the bronchoscope into the fluid collection and aspirates fluid through the needle. The bronchoscope is removed. Report 31645 for the initial treatment only. Report 31646 for any subsequent aspiration procedures. These codes include the use of fluoroscopic guidance, when performed.

31656

The physician views the airway using a bronchoscope introduced through the nasal or oral cavity, using local anesthesia of the patient's airway. The physician uses the views obtained through the bronchoscope to identify the bronchial segment to be studied. The physician may use fluoroscopy (x-ray) to assist with navigation of the bronchoscope tip. The physician passes a needle or catheter through a channel in the bronchoscope into the bronchial segment and injects the contrast material for bronchography. The bronchoscope is removed. This code includes the use of fluoroscopic guidance, when performed.

31715

The physician injects contrast material for a bronchography into the trachea, just below the voice box. The physician palpates the laryngeal structures and identifies the tracheal rings. The physician inserts a needle into the trachea. After verifying placement, the physician injects the contrast material for a bronchography (reported separately).

31717

The physician catheterizes the trachea to obtain a bronchial brush biopsy. The physician inserts a needle through the cricoid cartilage or the trachea. A catheter is passed over the needle and a brush is placed through the catheter to obtain bronchial tissue. A bronchoscope may be used to guide the brush. The brush is withdrawn through the catheter and both are removed. The incision may be closed with sutures.

31720-31725

The physician aspirates sputum from the lungs using a nasal tracheal catheter. The physician passes a suction catheter through the nose into the trachea. Saline may be used to liquefy secretions. The secretions are removed with suction and the catheter is removed. Report 31725 if a tracheobronchial approach with fiberscope is used at bedside.

31730
The physician introduces a needle wire dilator/stent into the trachea to relieve a subglottic stenosis. The physician places a needle through the cricoid membrane or trachea. A wire is passed through the needle and the needle is removed. A series of dilators or stents are passed over the wire to open the trachea. When sufficient dilation is gained, a stent or indwelling tube for oxygen therapy is left in place to maintain patency.

31750
The physician performs an anterior cervical incision and dissects surrounding tissues and muscles to expose the trachea. An airway is inserted and the trachea is incised. Surgical repair of the trachea is undertaken. End-to-end anastomosis of the trachea may be performed. For satisfactory reconstruction, it may be necessary for the physician to surgically repair the trachea using splints constructed from rib or costal cartilage to patch the length of the trachea. Once repair is achieved, the airway is removed and the incisions are closed.

31755
The physician performs an anterior cervical incision and dissects surrounding tissues and muscles to expose the trachea and pharynx. An airway may be inserted and the trachea and pharynx are incised. The physician incises the trachea and pharynx in such a way as to create an opening from the trachea to the pharynx. The physician may implant a device like the Singer-Blom prosthesis between the trachea and pharynx. The purpose of the prosthesis is to produce speech in a previously laryngectomized patient. Once repair is achieved, the airway, if inserted, is removed and the incisions are closed.

31760
The physician makes an incision in the thorax and approaches the trachea by opening the rib cage. An airway is inserted and the trachea is incised. Surgical repair of the trachea is undertaken. End-to-end anastomosis of the trachea may be performed. For satisfactory reconstruction, it may be necessary for the physician to surgically repair the trachea using splints constructed from rib or costal cartilage to patch the length of the trachea. Once repair is achieved, the airway is removed and the incisions are closed.

31766
The physician reconstructs the carina. The carina is the junction of the trachea and the bronchi. The physician uses a midline sternotomy or a lateral thoracotomy approach to access the carina. The carina is located and repaired primarily if possible. More extensive damage may be repaired with a Silastic stent or an autograft. A chest tube is inserted, and the wound is sutured in layers.

31770-31775
The physician repairs a bronchus. The physician makes a lateral thoracotomy incision to access the bronchus. An autograft or Silastic stent may be used to repair the bronchus in 31770. A chest tube is inserted and the wound is sutured in layers. Report 31775 if an excision stenosis and anastomosis are performed with this procedure.

31780
The physician excises a tracheal stenosis and re-anastomoses the trachea. The physician makes a horizontal neck incision to access the stenosis. The trachea is incised and the stenosis is resected. The proximal and distal portions of the trachea are brought together and closed with sutures. The wound is sutured in layers.

31781
The physician excises a tracheal stenosis and re-anastomoses the trachea. The physician makes a cervicothoracic incision to access the stenosis. The trachea is incised and the stenosis is resected. The proximal and distal portions of the trachea are brought together and closed with sutures. The wound is sutured in layers.

31785
The physician excises a tracheal tumor or carcinoma. The physician makes a horizontal neck incision to access the mass. The trachea is incised and the mass is resected. If necessary, the proximal and distal portions of the trachea are brought together and closed with sutures. The wound is sutured in layers.

31786
The physician excises a tracheal tumor or carcinoma. The physician makes a thoracic approach to access the mass. The trachea is incised and the mass is resected. If necessary, the proximal and distal portions of the trachea are brought together and closed with sutures. The wound is sutured in layers.

31800-31805
The physician closes a wound or injury of the cervical trachea in 31800 or the intrathoracic trachea in 31805. The physician debrides the wound and closes the trachea with sutures. The tissues are sutured in layers.

31820-31825
The physician closes a tracheostomy or fistula. The physician excises the scarred tissue forming the tracheostomy or fistula. If the trachea has healed, it is closed with sutures. The remaining tissues of the tracheostomy or fistula are pulled together and the wound is sutured in layers. Report 31820 if the tracheostomy or fistula is closed without plastic repair; report 31825 if the tracheostomy or fistula is closed with plastic repair of the skin made to hide the repair.

31830
The physician revises a tracheostomy scar. The physician incises the skin around the tracheostomy scar and removes the scarred tissues. The incision is sutured in layers, leaving a less noticeable scar.

32035
The physician removes the purulent fluid of an empyema by creating a drainage wound in the chest. Using a scalpel, an incision is made through the skin of the chest and the incision is deepened to expose a portion of a rib. To enter the chest cavity, a short segment of the exposed rib is removed using rib cutters. The resulting defect in the chest wall allows for the continuous release of pus from the empyema (abscess in the chest cavity).

32036
The physician removes the purulent fluid of an empyema (abscess in the chest cavity) by creating a drainage wound in the chest. Using a scalpel, an incision is made through the skin of the chest and the incision is deepened to expose a portion of a rib. To create a drainage site, a short segment of the rib is removed using rib cutters. The resulting defect in the chest wall allows for the continuous release of pus from the empyema. To ensure that the drainage wound stays open, a flap is created in the skin and subcutaneous tissues.

32095
The physician removes a sample of tissue from the lung or the pleura (the tissue covering the inside surface of the chest cavity or the surface of the lung). Using a scalpel, the skin between two ribs is incised and the tissues separated to expose the inside of the chest cavity. A representative sample of tissue is removed using a biopsy needle or by cutting with a scalpel or scissors. The surgical wound created is closed by suturing.

32100
The physician opens the chest cavity widely to directly visualize and assess the organs and structures in the chest and/or to obtain tissue for study and analysis. Using a scalpel the surgeon makes a long incision around the side of the chest between two of the ribs. The incision is carried through all the tissue layers into the chest cavity. Rib spreaders are inserted into the wound and the ribs are spread apart exposing the lung, the heart, and other structures. The area of the chest cavity is explored by pushing aside the deflated lung with a gloved hand and large gauze sponges. Tissue can be sampled by using a biopsy needle or by grasping tissue and cutting it with a scalpel or scissors. After the removal of the instruments and gauze sponges the incision is closed in layers of sutures. A chest tube(s) may be used to provide drainage for the chest cavity. Alternately, the chest cavity can be opened and the operation performed through a vertical incision in the center of the chest through the sternum. The skin incision is carried down to the sternum bone and a saw is used to split the sternum. With the sternum split in half, the chest is entered by spreading the sternum apart with a set of rib spreaders. When the procedure is complete, the wound is closed by using wires to bring the two halves of the sternum together and the skin is closed over the sternum by suturing.

32110
The physician opens the chest cavity widely to directly visualize and assess the organs and structures in the chest and to control bleeding and/or repair injury to the lung. Using a scalpel, the surgeon makes a long incision around the side of the chest between two of the ribs. The incision is carried through all the tissue layers into the chest cavity. Rib spreaders are inserted into the wound and the ribs are spread apart exposing the lung, the heart and other structures. The area of the chest cavity is explored by pushing aside the deflated lung with a gloved hand and large gauze sponges. The site of the injury is identified and repaired. After the removal of the instruments and gauze sponges the incision is closed in layers of sutures. A chest tube(s) may be used to provide drainage for the chest cavity. Alternately, the chest cavity can be opened and the operation performed through a vertical incision in the center of the chest through the sternum. The skin incision is carried down to the sternum bone and a saw is used to split the sternum. With the sternum split in half the chest is entered by spreading the sternum apart with a set of rib spreaders. When the procedure is complete the wound is closed by using wires to bring the two halves of the sternum together and the skin closed over the sternum by suturing.

32120
The physician opens the chest cavity widely to directly visualize and assess the organs and structures in the chest after recent surgery in the chest. Using a scalpel, the surgeon makes a long incision around the side of the chest between two of the ribs. The incision is carried through all the tissue layers into the chest cavity. Rib spreaders are inserted into the wound and the ribs are spread apart exposing the lung, the heart, and other structures. The area of the chest cavity is explored by pushing aside the deflated lung with a gloved hand and large gauze sponges. Repairs can be made as indicated and discovered while exploring the chest cavity. After the removal of the instruments and gauze sponges, the incision is closed in layers of sutures. A chest tube(s) may be used to provide drainage for the chest cavity. Alternately, the chest cavity can be opened and the operation performed through a vertical incision in the center of the chest through the sternum. The skin incision is carried down to the sternum bone and a saw is used to split the sternum. With the sternum split in half, the chest is entered by spreading the sternum apart with a set of rib spreaders. When the procedure is complete, the wound is closed by using wires to bring the two halves of the

sternum together and the skin is closed over the sternum by suturing.

32124
The physician opens the chest cavity widely to directly visualize and separate the surface of the lung which has become adherent to the inside surface of the chest cavity. Using a scalpel, the surgeon makes a long incision around the side of the chest between two of the ribs. The incision is carried through all the tissue layers into the chest cavity. Rib spreaders are inserted into the wound and the ribs are spread apart exposing the lung. Using a gloved hand and a large moist gauze sponge the surgeon manually divides the tissues attaching the lung to the wall of the chest cavity. After the procedure is completed, the instruments and gauze sponges are removed and the incision is closed in layers of sutures. A chest tube(s) may be used to provide drainage for the chest cavity. Alternately, the chest cavity can be opened and the operation performed through a vertical incision in the center of the chest through the sternum. The skin incision is carried down to the sternum bone and a saw is used to split the sternum. With the sternum split in half, the chest is entered by spreading the sternum apart with a set of rib spreaders. When the procedure is complete, the wound is closed by using wires to bring the two halves of the sternum together and the skin is closed over the sternum by suturing.

32140
The physician opens the chest cavity widely to remove one or more lung cysts. Using a scalpel, the surgeon makes a long incision around the side of the chest between two of the ribs. The incision is carried through all the tissue layers into the chest cavity. Rib spreaders are inserted into the wound and the ribs are spread apart exposing the lung. Space is made in the chest by packing the uninvolved lung away from the operative field by using large moist gauze sponges. In order to perform the procedure the pleural surface may require an operative procedure such as pneumonolysis (separation of the surface of the lung which has become adherent to the inside surface of the chest cavity). The lung cyst is located and removed by sharp and blunt dissection of the tissues. After the procedure is completed, the instruments and gauze sponges are removed and the incision is closed in layers of sutures. A chest tube(s) may be used to provide drainage for the chest cavity. Alternately, the chest cavity can be opened and the operation performed through a vertical incision in the center of the chest through the sternum. The skin incision is carried down to the sternum bone and a saw is used to split the sternum. With the sternum split in half, the chest is entered by spreading the sternum apart with a set of rib spreaders. When the procedure is complete, the wound is closed by using wires to bring the two halves of the sternum together and the skin is closed over the sternum by suturing.

32141
The physician opens the chest cavity widely to remove one or more lung bullae (large non-functional air sacs). Using a scalpel, the surgeon makes a long incision around the side of the chest between two of the ribs. The incision is carried through all the tissue layers into the chest cavity. Rib spreaders are inserted into the wound and the ribs are spread apart exposing the lung. Space is made in the chest by packing the uninvolved lung away from the operative field by using large moist gauze sponges. In order to perform the procedure the pleural surface may require an operative procedure such as pneumonolysis (separation of the surface of the lung which has become adherent to the inside surface of the chest cavity). The lung bullae is located and removed by sharp and blunt dissection of the tissues and often by folding and suturing of the tissues (plication). After the procedure is completed, the instruments and gauze sponges are removed and the incision is closed in layers of sutures. A chest tube(s) may be used to provide drainage for the chest cavity. Alternately, the chest cavity can be opened and the operation performed through a vertical incision in the center of the chest through the sternum. The skin incision is carried down to the sternum bone and a saw is used to split the sternum. With the sternum split in half, the chest is entered by spreading the sternum apart with a set of rib spreaders. When the procedure is complete, the wound is closed by using wires to bring the two halves of the sternum together and the skin is closed over the sternum by suturing.

32150
The physician opens the chest cavity widely to remove a foreign body or fibrin deposit (thick insoluble protein deposit formed after the clotting of blood) in the pleura (the membranous tissues investing the lungs and lining the thoracic cavity). Using a scalpel, the surgeon makes a long incision around the side of the chest between two of the ribs. The incision is carried through all the tissue layers into the chest cavity. Rib spreaders are inserted into the wound and the ribs are spread apart exposing the lung. Space is made in the chest by packing the uninvolved lung away from the operative field by using large moist gauze sponges. The foreign body or fibrin deposit is located and removed by sharp and blunt dissection. After the procedure is completed, the instruments and gauze sponges are removed and the incision is closed in layers of sutures. A chest tube(s) may be used to provide drainage for the chest cavity. Alternately, the chest cavity can be opened and the operation performed through a vertical incision in the center of the chest through the sternum. The skin incision is carried down to the sternum bone and a saw is used to split the sternum. With the sternum split in half, the chest is entered by spreading the sternum apart with a set of rib spreaders. When the procedure is complete, the wound is closed by using wires to bring the two halves of the sternum together and the skin is closed over the sternum by suturing.

32151
The physician opens the chest cavity widely to remove a foreign body in the lung. Using a scalpel, the surgeon makes a long incision around the side of the chest between two of the ribs. The incision is carried through all the tissue layers into the chest cavity. Rib spreaders are inserted into the wound and the ribs are spread apart exposing the lung. Space is made in the chest by packing the uninvolved lung away from the operative field by using large moist gauze sponges. The foreign body is located and removed by sharp and blunt dissection. After the procedure is completed, the instruments and gauze sponges are removed and the incision is closed in layers of sutures. A chest tube(s) may be used to provide drainage for the chest cavity. Alternately, the chest cavity can be opened and the operation performed through a vertical incision in the center of the chest through the sternum. The skin incision is carried down to the sternum bone and a saw is used to split the sternum. With the sternum split in half, the chest is entered by spreading the sternum apart with a set of rib spreaders. When the procedure is complete, the wound is closed by using wires to bring the two halves of the sternum together and the skin is closed over the sternum by suturing.

32160
The physician opens the chest cavity widely to perform direct manual cardiac massage in the treatment of a cardiac arrest. Using a scalpel, the surgeon makes a long incision around the side of the chest between two of the ribs. The incision is carried through all the tissue layers into the chest cavity. Rib spreaders are inserted into the wound and the ribs are spread apart exposing the lung. Space is made in the chest by packing the uninvolved lung away from the operative field by using large moist gauze sponges. The heart is exposed and squeezed rhythmically to mimic cardiac contractions thus pumping blood through the body. The heart may be directly contra-shocked to produce spontaneous heart beats. After the procedure is completed, the instruments and gauze sponges are removed and the incision is closed in layers of sutures. A chest tube(s) may be used to provide drainage for the chest cavity. Alternately, the chest cavity can be opened and the operation performed through a vertical incision in the center of the chest through the sternum. The skin incision is carried down to the sternum bone and a saw is used to split the sternum. With the sternum split in half, the chest is entered by spreading the sternum apart with a set of rib spreaders. When the procedure is complete, the wound is closed by using wires to bring the two halves of the sternum together and the skin is closed over the sternum by suturing.

32200
The physician treats an abscess or cyst in the lung by draining the pus or fluid directly through the chest wall. Using a scalpel, the skin between two ribs is incised and the tissues separated to expose the inside of the chest cavity. The lung is cut with scissors or a scalpel down to the abscess or the cyst. The abscess or cyst is opened and the fluid is allowed to drain through the wound created in the lung and the chest wall. A rubber drainage tube may be left in place to maintain or facilitate drainage. The incision is not sutured closed. The outside incision is dressed with bulky gauze dressing to absorb the drainage.

32201
The physician performs a pneumonostomy with percutaneous drainage of an abscess or cyst. The physician may create a small incision in the skin between two ribs proximal to the abscess or cyst in order to ease placement of drainage instruments through the skin into the lung (percutaneous). The physician uses a CAT scan or ultrasound to guide the placement of a drainage needle or trocar into the abscess or cyst. The physician advances the drainage needle or trocar through the chest wall into the lung to gain access to the abscess or cyst. The fluid is allowed to drain. Once the abscess or cyst is drained, a drainage catheter may be placed. Sutures may be placed to secure the drainage catheter in place. The operative site is cleaned and bandaged. For radiological supervision and interpretation, see 75989.

32215
The physician treats repeat pneumothorax by producing adhesions between the surface of the lung and the inside surface of the chest cavity. To create the adhesions, a chemical solution is injected into the chest cavity and allowed to circulate over the surface of the lung and the inside surface of the chest cavity. The physicians injects the solution by passing a tube into the chest cavity. The physician passes a trocar over the top of a rib and punctures through the chest tissues between the ribs and enters the pleural cavity. With the end of the trocar in the chest cavity, the physician advances the plastic tube into the chest cavity. The sharp instrument is removed leaving one end of the plastic catheter in place within the chest cavity. A syringe is attached to the outside end of the catheter and fluid is injected into the chest cavity. The fluid selected is design to cause the formation of adhesive scar tissue between the surface of the lung and the inside surface of the chest cavity. Once the lung is stuck to the chest wall it can no longer collapse and allow the formation of a pneumothorax.

32220-32225
The physician removes a constricting membrane or layer of tissue from the surface of the lung (decortication) in order to permit the lung to fully expand. The physician opens the chest cavity widely. Using a scalpel, the surgeon makes a long incision around the side of the chest between two of the ribs. The incision is carried through all the tissue layers into the chest cavity. Rib spreaders are inserted into the wound and the ribs are spread apart exposing the lung.

The constricting membrane is stripped off the surface of the lung. In 32225, only a portion of the lung surface is removed. The chest wall incision is sutured closed in layers. A chest tube(s) may be used to provide drainage for the chest cavity. Alternately, the chest cavity can be opened by a vertical incision in the front of the chest through the sternum. The skin incision is carried down to the sternum bone and a saw is used to split the sternum. With the sternum split in half, the chest is entered by spreading the sternum apart with a set of rib spreaders. When the procedure is complete, the wound is closed by using wires to bring the two halves of the sternum together and the skin is closed by suturing.

32310

The physician removes the membranous tissue lining the inside surface of the chest cavity (the parietal pleura). The physician opens the chest cavity widely to gain access to the inside surface of the chest. Using a scalpel, the surgeon makes a long incision around the side of the chest between two of the ribs. The incision is carried through all the tissue layers into the chest cavity. Rib spreaders are inserted into the wound and the ribs are spread apart exposing the lung. The parietal pleura is stripped from the inside surface of the chest. The chest wall incision is sutured closed in layers. A chest tube(s) may be used to provide drainage for the chest cavity. Alternately, the chest cavity can be opened and the operation performed through a vertical incision in the center of the chest through the sternum. The skin incision is carried down to the sternum bone and a saw is used to split the sternum. With the sternum split in half, the chest is entered by spreading the sternum apart with a set of rib spreaders. When the procedure is complete, the wound is closed by using wires to bring the two halves of the sternum together and the skin is closed over the sternum by suturing.

32320

The physician removes a constricting membrane or layer of tissue from a portion of the surface of the lung (decortication) in order to permit the lung to fully expand and also removes the membranous tissue lining the inside surface of the chest cavity (the parietal pleura). The physician opens the chest cavity widely. Using a scalpel, the surgeon makes a long incision around the side of the chest between two of the ribs. The incision is carried through all the tissue layers into the chest cavity. Rib spreaders are inserted into the wound and the ribs are spread apart exposing the lung. The constricting membrane is stripped off the surface of the lung. The parietal pleura is stripped from the inside surface of the chest. The chest wall incision is sutured closed in layers. A chest tube(s) may be used to provide drainage for the chest cavity. Alternately, the chest cavity can be opened and the operation performed through a vertical incision in the center of the chest through the sternum. The skin incision is carried down to the sternum bone and a saw is used to split the sternum. With the sternum split in half, the chest is entered by spreading the sternum apart with a set of rib spreaders. When the procedure is complete, the wound is closed by using wires to bring the two halves of the sternum together and the skin is closed over the sternum by suturing.

32400

The physician obtains a sample of the lining of the lung and/or the lining of the inside of the chest cavity by needle biopsy. Using a pleural biopsy needle, the physician passes the needle over the top of a rib, punctures through the chest tissues between two ribs, enters the pleural cavity and slightly punctures the surface of the lung. With the end of the needle in the chest cavity, the physician withdraws a piece of tissue. The needle is withdrawn and the puncture site covered with a bandage. The procedure is often done under radiological guidance to assure more precise placement of the needle.

32402

The physician removes a sample of tissue from the pleura (the tissue covering the inside surface of the chest cavity or the surface of the lung). A small opening is created in the chest. The skin between two ribs is incised and the tissues separated to create a small opening in the chest. Under direct vision through this opening, a representative sample of tissue is removed using a biopsy needle or by cutting the tissue with a scalpel or scissors. The surgical wound created is closed by suturing.

32405

The physician obtains a sample of the lung or the mediastinum (the tissues in the center of the chest between the two lung cavities) by puncturing through the space between two of the ribs with a needle. The procedure is often done under radiological guidance to assure more precise placement of the needle. Using a biopsy needle, the physician passes the needle over the top of a rib, punctures through the chest tissues, enters the pleural cavity, and punctures into the area of concern in the lung or the mediastinum. With the end of the needle in the chest cavity, the physician withdraws a piece of tissue. The needle is withdrawn and the puncture site covered with a bandage.

32420

The physician removes a collection of fluid in a lung by puncturing through the space between the ribs and entering the lung. Using an aspirating needle attached to a syringe, the physician passes the needle over the top of a rib, punctures through the chest tissues, enters the pleural cavity, and directs the needle into the fluid area of the lung. With the end of the needle in the fluid cavity within the lung, the physician withdraws the fluid by pulling back on the plunger of the syringe.

32421
The physician removes fluid from the chest cavity by puncturing through the space between the ribs. Using an aspirating needle attached to a syringe, the physician passes the needle over the top of a rib, punctures through the chest tissues, and enters the pleural cavity. Separately reportable imaging guidance may be used. With the end of the needle in the chest cavity, the physician withdraws the fluid from the chest cavity by pulling back on the plunger of the syringe.

32422
The physician removes fluid from the chest cavity by puncturing through the space between the ribs. To enter the chest cavity, the physician passes a small trocar or needle over the top of a rib, punctures through the chest tissues between the ribs, and enters the pleural cavity. Separately reportable image guidance may be used. The physician advances the catheter over the needle or small trocar into the chest cavity. The sharp instrument is removed leaving one end of the plastic catheter in place within the chest cavity. A syringe is attached to the outside end of the catheter and fluid is removed from the chest cavity by pulling back on the plunger of the syringe. The outside end of the tube may be connected to a water seal system to prevent air from being sucked into the chest cavity and to allow continuous or intermittent removal of fluid.

32440
The physician removes one lung in its entirety. The physician opens the chest cavity widely to gain access to the lung to be removed. Using a scalpel, the surgeon makes a long incision around the side of the chest between two of the ribs. The incision is carried through all the tissue layers into the chest cavity. Rib spreaders are inserted into the wound and the ribs are spread apart exposing the lung, heart, and other structures. The root of the lung is found by pushing aside the deflated lung with a gloved hand and large moist gauze sponges. Within the root of the lung, the blood vessels and bronchial tubes are clamped, tied off, and cut. The lung is removed through the wide chest incision. After the removal of the instruments and gauze sponges, the chest incision is sutured closed in layers. A chest tube(s) may be used to provide drainage for the chest cavity. Alternately, the chest cavity can be opened and the operation performed through a vertical incision in the center of the chest through the sternum. The skin incision is carried down to the sternum bone and a saw is used to split the sternum. With the sternum split in half, the chest is entered by spreading the sternum apart with a set of rib spreaders. When the procedure is complete, the wound is closed by using wires to bring the two halves of the sternum together and the skin is closed over the sternum by suturing.

32442
The physician removes one lung in its entirety. The physician opens the chest cavity widely to gain access to the lung to be removed. Using a scalpel, the surgeon makes a long incision around the side of the chest between two of the ribs. The incision is carried through all the tissue layers into the chest cavity. Rib spreaders are inserted into the wound and the ribs are spread apart exposing the lung, heart, and other structures. The root of the lung is found by pushing aside the deflated lung with a gloved hand and large moist gauze sponges. Within the root of the lung, the blood vessels and bronchial tubes are clamped, tied off, and cut. The lung and a segment of the trachea are removed through the wide chest incision. The trachea is sutured to the main bronchial tube of the remaining lung in the other half of the chest. After the removal of the instruments and gauze sponges, the chest incision is sutured closed in layers. A chest tube(s) may be used to provide drainage for the chest cavity. Alternately, the chest cavity can be opened and the operation performed through a vertical incision in the center of the chest through the sternum. The skin incision is carried down to the sternum bone and a saw is used to split the sternum. With the sternum split in half, the chest is entered by spreading the sternum apart with a set of rib spreaders. When the procedure is complete, the wound is closed by using wires to bring the two halves of the sternum together and the skin is closed over the sternum by suturing.

32445
The physician removes one lung in its entirety and the pleural membranes covering the lung and the inside surface of the chest cavity (the parietal pleura). The physician opens the chest cavity widely to gain access to the lung to be removed. Using a scalpel, the surgeon makes a long incision around the side of the chest between two of the ribs. The incision is carried through all the tissue layers down to the membrane lining the chest cavity. Rib spreaders are inserted into the wound and the ribs are spread apart, taking care to preserve the integrity of the chest lining. Holding a gauze sponge, the surgeon strips away the lining inside the chest all the way around to the root of the lung. This creates a sac of the parietal pleura that contains the lung. Within the root of the lung, the blood vessels and bronchial tubes are clamped, tied off, and cut. The lung and the pleural tissues of the inside of the chest wall are removed through the wide chest incision. After the removal of the instruments and gauze sponges, the chest incision is sutured closed in layers. A chest tube(s) may be used to provide drainage for the chest cavity.

32480-32482
The physician removes a single lobe of one lung in 32480 and two lobes of one lung in 32482. In 32480 the physician opens the chest cavity widely to gain access to the lung to be removed. Using a scalpel, the surgeon makes a long incision around the side of the chest between two of the ribs. The incision is carried through all the tissue layers into the chest cavity. Rib

spreaders are inserted into the wound and the ribs are spread apart exposing the lung. The lobe(s) to be removed is identified and isolated in the operative field by pushing aside the deflated lung with a gloved hand and large moist gauze sponges. Within the lobe(s) of the lung, the main blood vessels and bronchial tubes are clamped, tied off, and cut. The lobe(s) is removed through the wide chest incision. After the removal of the instruments and gauze sponges, the chest incision is sutured closed in layers. A chest tube(s) may be used to provide drainage for the chest cavity. Alternately, the chest cavity can be opened and the operation performed through a vertical incision in the center of the chest through the sternum. The skin incision is carried down to the sternum bone and a saw is used to split the sternum. With the sternum split in half, the chest is entered by spreading the sternum apart with a set of rib spreaders. When the procedure is complete, the wound is closed by using wires to bring the two halves of the sternum together and the skin is closed over the sternum by suturing.

32484

The physician removes a segment of a lobe of one lung. The physician opens the chest cavity widely to gain access to the lung to be removed. Using a scalpel, the surgeon makes a long incision around the side of the chest between two of the ribs. The incision is carried through all the tissue layers into the chest cavity. Rib spreaders are inserted into the wound and the ribs are spread apart exposing the lung. The segment to be removed is identified and isolated in the operative field by pushing aside the deflated lung with a gloved hand and large moist gauze sponges. Within the segment of the lung, the main blood vessels and bronchial tubes are clamped, tied off, and cut. The segment is removed through the wide chest incision. After the removal of the instruments and gauze sponges, the chest incision is sutured closed in layers. A chest tube(s) may be used to provide drainage for the chest cavity. Alternately, the chest cavity can be opened and the operation performed through a vertical incision in the center of the chest through the sternum. The skin incision is carried down to the sternum bone and a saw is used to split the sternum. With the sternum split in half, the chest is entered by spreading the sternum apart with a set of rib spreaders. When the procedure is complete, the wound is closed by using wires to bring the two halves of the sternum together and the skin is closed over the sternum by suturing.

32486

The physician removes a portion (lobectomy, bilobectomy or segmentectomy) of one lung and repairs a bronchial tube that has been partially resected. The physician opens the chest cavity widely to gain access to the lung to be removed. Using a scalpel, the surgeon makes a long incision around the side of the chest between two of the ribs. The incision is carried through all the tissue layers into the chest cavity. Rib spreaders are inserted into the wound and the ribs are spread apart exposing the lung. The portion of lung to be removed is identified and isolated in the operative field by pushing aside the deflated lung with a gloved hand and large moist gauze sponges. Within the lung, main blood vessels and bronchial tubes are clamped, tied off, and cut. The resected part of the lung is removed through the wide chest incision. The segment of diseased or damaged bronchial tube is removed. The healthy end of the smaller bronchial tube in the remaining lobe is sutured to the main bronchial tube in the root of the lung. After the removal of the instruments and gauze sponges, the chest incision is sutured closed in layers. A chest tube(s) may be used to provide drainage for the chest cavity. Alternately, the chest cavity can be opened and the operation performed through a vertical incision in the center of the chest through the sternum. The skin incision is carried down to the sternum bone and a saw is used to split the sternum. With the sternum split in half, the chest is entered by spreading the sternum apart with a set of rib spreaders. When the procedure is complete, the wound is closed by using wires to bring the two halves of the sternum together and the skin is closed over the sternum by suturing.

32488

The physician removes the remaining portion(s) of a lung from a prior partial lung removal. The physician opens the chest cavity widely to gain access to the lung to be removed. Using a scalpel, the surgeon makes a long incision around the side of the chest between two of the ribs. The incision is carried through all the tissue layers into the chest cavity. Rib spreaders are inserted into the wound and the ribs are spread apart exposing the lung. The remaining portion of lung is isolated in the operative field by pushing aside the deflated lung with a gloved hand and large moist gauze sponges. Within the root of the lung, the blood vessels and bronchial tubes are clamped, tied off, and cut. The lung is removed through the wide chest incision. After the removal of the instruments and gauze sponges, the chest incision is sutured closed in layers. A chest tube(s) may be used to provide drainage for the chest cavity. Alternately, the chest cavity can be opened and the operation performed through a vertical incision in the center of the chest through the sternum. The skin incision is carried down to the sternum bone and a saw is used to split the sternum. With the sternum split in half, the chest is entered by spreading the sternum apart with a set of rib spreaders. When the procedure is complete, the wound is closed by using wires to bring the two halves of the sternum together and the skin is closed over the sternum by suturing.

32491

The physician removes part of an emphysematous lung. The physician opens the chest cavity widely to gain access to the lung to be removed. The physician makes a long incision around the side of the chest between two of the ribs, or the physician may use an incision through the center of the sternum. The incision is carried through all the tissue layers into the chest cavity, and rib spreaders are used to expose the lung. The lung tissue to be removed is identified and isolated in the operative field by pushing aside the deflated lung with a gloved hand and large moist gauze sponges. The lung tissue may be further isolated using a row of staples. The tissue is excised and instruments and gauze sponges are removed. The chest incision is sutured closed in layers (sternal wires are used if the chest was entered through a midline sternal incision). A chest tube(s) may be used to provide drainage for the chest cavity.

32500
The physician removes a wedge-shaped portion(s) of a lobe(s) of one or both lungs. The physician opens the chest cavity widely to gain access to the lung to be removed. Using a scalpel, the surgeon makes a long incision around the side of the chest between two of the ribs. The incision is carried through all the tissue layers into the chest cavity. Rib spreaders are inserted into the wound and the ribs are spread apart exposing the lung. The area to be removed is identified and isolated in the operative field by pushing aside the deflated lung with a gloved hand and large moist gauze sponges. The healthy portions of the lung surrounding the area(s) to be removed are clamped with clamps and the portion is removed by cutting the lung tissue isolated by the clamps. Sutures or surgical clips are used to repair the cut portion of the remaining lung tissue. After the removal of the instruments and gauze sponges, the chest incision is sutured closed in layers. A chest tube(s) may be used to provide drainage for the chest cavity. In another technique, the chest cavity can be opened and the operation performed through a vertical incision in the center of the chest through the sternum. The skin incision is carried down to the sternum bone and a saw is used to split the sternum. With the sternum split in half, the chest is entered by using a set of rib spreaders to separate the sternum. When the procedure is complete, wires are used to bring the halves of the sternum together. The skin is closed over the sternum by suturing.

32501
During lobectomy or segmentectomy, the physician repairs part of a bronchus. After removing the lobes or lobe segments (see codes 32480, 32482, 32484 for procedure description), the segment of diseased or damaged bronchial tube is repaired and sutured to the main bronchial tube in the root of the lung. The remaining instruments and gauze sponges are removed from the chest cavity. The chest incision is sutured closed in layers (sternal wires are used if the chest was entered through a midline sternal incision). A chest tube(s) may be used to provide drainage for the chest cavity. List this code separately in addition to the primary procedure.

32503-32504
The physician removes a tumor from the apex of the lung, such as a Pancoast tumor, as well as a portion of the chest wall. The patient may be intubated with a double lumen endotracheal tube to verify correct positioning and to evaluate endobronchial disease. The chest cavity is entered using an anterior or posterior incision. The posterior incision is made along the outline of the scapula, entering the pleural space at the third or fourth intercostal space. In some cases, an anterior transcervical approach is used. The necessary extended en bloc resection of the chest wall includes posterior portions of the first three ribs, part of the upper thoracic vertebrae (including the transverse process), the intercostal nerves, the lower trunk of the brachial plexus, the stellate ganglion, a section of the dorsal sympathetic ganglion, and the portion of the involved lung. For tumors that are situated peripherally, the apical segment of the upper lobe of the lung is separated from the remaining superior lobe by using a GIA-75 stapler. The apex of the lung is left attached to the chest wall. The first through third, fourth, or fifth ribs are sectioned anteriorly. The subclavian artery is sharply dissected from the surrounding structures. A subperiosteal dissection is performed around the first rib, which is transected, and the subclavian vessels are mobilized superiorly. If preoperative magnetic resonance imaging demonstrated vessel involvement, an initial anterior approach is performed to dissect or graft the vessels. The ribs are disarticulated and the tumor, along with the involved chest wall, is gradually mobilized. Next, the segmental vessels are identified, doubly ligated, and transected. The parietal pleura are bluntly dissected along the anterior border of the spinal column. The tumor and the involved chest wall that has remained attached to the inferior trunk of the brachial plexus is excised, using caution to spare the T1 nerve root as it crosses beneath the angle of the first rib to join the C8 nerve root. If a tumor has invaded the vertebral bodies, the subclavian artery, or the C8 to T1 nerve routes, a multidisciplinary approach may be necessary. At the completion of the procedure, two large chest tubes are placed: one at the apex of the chest to drain any residual air and the other to drain fluids. Report 32504 when chest wall reconstruction is performed.

32540
The physician removes an empyema (an abscess in the chest cavity between the lung and the chest wall) in its entirety, including the pleural membranes surrounding the abscess. The physician opens the chest cavity to gain access to the abscess. Using a scalpel, the surgeon makes an incision around the side of the chest between two of the ribs. The incision is carried through all the tissue layers down to the membrane lining the chest cavity. Rib spreaders are inserted into the wound and the ribs are spread apart exposing the tissues, taking

Respiratory

care to preserve the integrity of the chest lining. Holding a gauze sponge, the surgeon strips away the lining adherent to the chest wall and the abscess and carries this all the way around the abscess. This creates a sac that contains the abscess. The intact mass is shelled out through the chest incision. After the removal of the instruments and gauze sponges, the chest incision is sutured closed in layers leaving a drainage tube or the wound is partially closed to allow drainage.

32550
The physician inserts a tunneled, indwelling pleural catheter to aid quality of life and long-term management of malignant effusion. The catheter allows drainage on an outpatient or home basis and consists of flexible rubber tubing with a safety drainage valve to provide access to the pleural cavity and prevent air and fluid entering. A polyester cuff secures the catheter in place and helps prevent infection. Under conscious sedation with local anesthesia, and using separately reportable ultrasonic and/or fluoroscopic guidance, the physician inserts the catheter percutaneously through a small incision in the anterior axillary area. The pleural catheter is threaded over a guidewire to access the pleural cavity, tunneled under the skin along the chest wall, and brought out that side in the lower chest. After placement, the patient may drain pleural fluid at home periodically into vacuum bottles by connecting the matching drainage line access tip to the valve.

32551
The physician removes fluid and/or air from the chest cavity by puncturing through the space between the ribs. To enter the chest cavity, the physician passes a trocar over the top of a rib, punctures through the chest tissues between the ribs, and enters the pleural cavity. Separately reportable imaging guidance may be used. With the end of the trocar in the chest cavity, the physician advances the plastic tube into the chest cavity. The sharp trocar is removed leaving one end of the plastic catheter in place within the chest cavity. A large syringe is attached to the outside end of the catheter and the fluid (blood or pus) is removed from the chest cavity by pulling back on the plunger of the syringe. The outside end of the tube may be connected to a water seal system to prevent air from being sucked into the chest cavity and to allow continuous or intermittent removal of air or fluid.

32552
The physician removes a previously placed, indwelling tunneled pleural catheter with cuff. Following administration of local anesthesia along the subcutaneous catheter tunnel, blunt dissection is used to release the cuff and the catheter is meticulously withdrawn. Conscious sedation may be required.

32553
The physician places one or more interstitial devices such as gold seeds (fiducial markers) for radiation therapy guidance or a dosimeter to gauge the amount of radiation received. Implanted percutaneously in and/or around an intrathoracic soft tissue tumor, these act as radiographic landmarks to define the position of the target lesion. Under CT or other image guidance, the physician injects a small capsule or seed into the intrathoracic tissue using a needle injection device. Allowing for precision in targeting radiation and/or for measuring the radiation doses received, an injected fiducial marker is visible by ultrasound and fluoroscopy and permits accurate triangulation of the tissue to be treated. An injected capsule dosimeter relays radiation dose information so that the clinical team can monitor for any deviation between the radiation plan and the actual radiation received.

32560
The physician instills an agent for pleurodesis (such as talc for recurrent or persistent pneumothorax) into the chest cavity via chest tube or catheter by puncturing through the space between the ribs. To enter the chest cavity, the physician passes a trocar over the top of a rib, punctures through the chest tissues, and enters the pleural cavity. With the end of the trocar in the chest cavity, the physician advances the plastic tube into the chest cavity. The sharp instrument is removed leaving one end of the plastic catheter in place within the chest cavity. A syringe is attached to the outside end of the catheter and the agent is injected into the chest cavity. The agent selected is designed to cause adhesion of the surface of the lung to the inside surface of the chest cavity.

32561-32562
The physician instills a fibrinolytic agent (one that breaks up fibrinous adhesions) into the chest cavity via a chest tube or catheter by puncturing through the space between the ribs. To enter the chest cavity, the physician passes a trocar over the top of a rib, punctures through the chest tissues, and enters the pleural cavity. With the end of the trocar in the chest cavity, the physician advances the plastic tube into the chest cavity. The sharp instrument is removed, leaving one end of the plastic catheter in place within the chest cavity. A syringe is attached to the outside end of the catheter and a fibrinolytic agent, such as a saline mixture with Streptokinase or urokinase, is injected into the chest cavity. The agent selected is designed to break up multiloculated pleural effusions and facilitate adequate drainage. Report 32561 for the first day of instillation and 32562 for each subsequent day.

32601
The physician examines the inside of the chest cavity through a rigid or flexible fiberoptic endoscope. The procedure can be done under local or general anesthesia. The surgeon makes a small incision between two ribs and by blunt dissection and the use of a trocar enters the thoracic cavity. The endoscope is passed through the trocar and into the chest cavity. The

lung is usually partially collapsed by instilling air into the chest through the trocar, or if general anesthesia is used, the lung may be collapsed through a double lumen endotracheal tube inserted through the mouth into the trachea. The contents of the chest cavity are examined by direct visualization and/or the use of a video camera. Still photographs may be taken as part of the procedure. At the conclusion of the procedure, the endoscope and the trocar are removed. A chest tube for drainage and re-expansion of the lung is usually inserted through the wound used for the thoracoscopy.

32602

The physician examines the inside of the chest cavity through a rigid or flexible fiberoptic endoscope and takes a sample(s) of tissue. The procedure can be done under local or general anesthesia. The surgeon makes a small incision between two ribs and by blunt dissection and the use of a trocar enters the thoracic cavity. The endoscope is passed through the trocar and into the chest cavity. The lung is usually partially collapsed by instilling air into the chest through the trocar or, if general anesthesia is used, the lung may be collapsed through a double lumen endotracheal tube inserted through the mouth into the trachea. The contents of the chest cavity are examined by direct visualization and/or the use of a video camera. Still photographs may be taken as part of the procedure. The tissue selected for biopsy is identified and a biopsy taken using a device through the endoscope or the insertion of an instrument through a second incision in the chest. At the conclusion of the procedure, the endoscope and the trocar are removed. A chest tube for drainage and re-expansion of the lung is usually inserted through the wound used for the thoracoscopy.

32603-32604

The physician examines the inside of the pericardial sac through a rigid or flexible fiberoptic endoscope. The procedure can be done under local or general anesthesia. The physician makes a small incision between two ribs and by blunt dissection and the use of a trocar enters the thoracic cavity. The endoscope is passed through the trocar and into the chest cavity. The lung is usually partially collapsed by instilling air into the chest through the trocar or, if general anesthesia is used, the lung may be collapsed through a double lumen endotracheal tube inserted through the mouth into the trachea. The endoscope is advanced to and into the pericardial sac as the physician views the structures and the anatomy of the area through the scope. The contents of the pericardial sac are examined by direct visualization and/or the use of a video camera. Still photographs may be taken as part of the procedure. At the conclusion of the procedure the endoscope and the trocar are withdrawn. A chest tube for drainage and re-expansion of the lung is usually inserted through the wound used for the thoracoscopy. In 32604, the tissue selected for biopsy is identified and the biopsy is taken using a device inserted through the endoscope.

32605-32606

The physician examines the inside of the mediastinal space, through a rigid or flexible fiberoptic endoscope. The procedure can be done under local or general anesthesia. The physician makes a small incision between two ribs and by blunt dissection and the use of a trocar enters the thoracic cavity. The endoscope is passed through the trocar and into the chest cavity. The lung is usually partially collapsed by instilling air into the chest through the trocar or, if general anesthesia is used, the lung may be collapsed through a special double lumen endotracheal tube inserted through the mouth into the trachea. As the physician views the structures and the anatomy of the area through the endoscope, the endoscope is advanced into the mediastinum (area inside the center of the chest cavity between the lungs). The contents of the mediastinal space are examined by direct visualization and/or by the use of a video camera. Still photographs may be taken as part of the procedure. In 32606, the tissue selected for biopsy is identified and a biopsy taken using a device inserted through the endoscope. At the conclusion of the procedure, the endoscope and the trocar are withdrawn. A chest tube for drainage and re-expansion of the lung is usually inserted through the wound used for the thoracoscopy.

32650

The physician examines the inside of the chest cavity through a rigid or flexible fiberoptic endoscope and induces adhesion of the surface of the lung to the inside surface of the chest cavity. The procedure can be done under local or general anesthesia. The physician makes a small incision between two ribs and by blunt dissection and the use of a trocar enters the thoracic cavity. The endoscope is passed through the trocar and into the chest cavity. The lung is usually partially collapsed by instilling air into the chest through the trocar or, if general anesthesia is used, the lung may be collapsed through a double lumen endotracheal tube inserted through the mouth into the trachea. The contents of the chest cavity are examined by direct visualization and/or by the use of a video camera. Still photographs may be taken as part of the procedure. A second trocar and instruments may be inserted into the chest cavity through a second wound in the chest. Adhesion may be induced in one of two ways: by abrading the surfaces of the lung and the inside of the chest cavity or by the instillation of chemicals into the chest cavity that bath the surfaces of the lung and the inside of the chest cavity. Most commonly, a chemical solution is instilled into the chest through the endoscope or second puncture site. At the conclusion of the procedure, the endoscope and the trocar are removed. A chest tube for drainage and re-expansion of the lung is usually inserted through the wound used for the thoracoscopy.

32651-32652

The physician examines the inside of the chest cavity through a rigid or flexible fiberoptic endoscope and removes a portion of the tissue covering the surface of the lung. The procedure can be done under local or general anesthesia. The physician makes a small incision between two ribs and by blunt dissection and the use of a trocar enters the thoracic cavity. The endoscope is passed through the trocar and into the chest cavity. The lung is usually partially collapsed by instilling air into the chest through the trocar or, if general anesthesia is used, the lung may be collapsed through a double lumen endotracheal tube inserted through the mouth into the trachea. The contents of the chest cavity are examined by direct visualization and/or by the use of a video camera. Still photographs may be taken as part of the procedure. A second and/or third trocar and instruments may be inserted into the chest cavity through a second and/or third wound in the chest. Under direct visualization through the endoscope, the physician strips away the membranous tissues covering a portion of the lung (or all of the lung ins 32652) using instruments inserted into the chest through the secondary sites. Code 32652 includes intrapleural pneumonolysis in which the physician divides the tissues attaching the lung to the wall of the chest cavity. At the conclusion of the procedure, the endoscope and the trocar are removed. A chest tube for drainage and re-expansion of the lung is usually inserted through the wound used for the thoracoscopy.

32653

The physician examines the inside of the chest cavity through a rigid or flexible fiberoptic endoscope and removes a foreign body or a fibrin deposit (the thick tissue much like remains of a blood clot). The procedure can be done under local or general anesthesia. The surgeon makes a small incision between two ribs and by blunt dissection and the use of a trocar enters the thoracic cavity. The endoscope is passed through the trocar and into the chest cavity. The lung is usually partially collapsed by instilling air into the chest through the trocar or, if general anesthesia is used, the lung may be collapsed through a double lumen endotracheal tube inserted through the mouth into the trachea. The contents of the chest cavity are examined by direct visualization and/or by the use of a video camera. Still photographs may be taken as part of the procedure. A second and/or third trocar and instruments may be inserted into the chest cavity through a second and/or third wound in the chest. The foreign body or fibrin deposit is located and removed using instruments through the scope or the secondary sites. At the conclusion of the procedure, the endoscope and the trocar are removed. A chest tube for drainage and re-expansion of the lung is usually inserted through the wound used for the thoracoscopy.

32654

The physician examines the inside of the chest cavity through a rigid or flexible fiberoptic endoscope and controls bleeding from a wound to the chest. The procedure can be done under local or general anesthesia. The physician makes a small incision between two ribs and by blunt dissection and the use of a trocar enters the thoracic cavity. The endoscope is passed through the trocar and into the chest cavity. The lung is usually partially collapsed by instilling air into the chest through the trocar or, if general anesthesia is used, the lung may be collapsed through a double lumen endotracheal tube inserted through the mouth into the trachea. The contents of the chest cavity are examined by direct visualization and/or by the use of a video camera. Still photographs may be taken as part of the procedure. A second and/or third trocar and instruments may be inserted into the chest cavity through a second and/or third wound in the chest. Under direct visualization through the endoscope, the physician manipulates the instruments inserted through the secondary sites and localizes the site of the bleeding. The hemorrhage is controlled by clipping or cauterizing the damaged blood vessel. At the conclusion of the procedure, the endoscope and the trocar(s) are removed. A chest tube for drainage and re-expansion of the lung is usually inserted through the wound used for the thoracoscopy.

32655

The physician examines the inside of the chest cavity through a rigid or flexible fiberoptic endoscope and removes one or more lung bullae (large non-functional air sacs). The physician makes a small incision between two ribs and by blunt dissection and the use of a trocar enters the thoracic cavity. The endoscope is passed through the trocar and into the chest cavity. The lung is usually partially collapsed by instilling air into the chest through the trocar or the lung may be collapsed through a double lumen endotracheal tube inserted through the mouth into the trachea. The contents of the chest cavity are examined by direct visualization and/or by the use of a video camera. Still photographs may be taken as part of the procedure. A second and/or third trocar and instruments may be inserted into the chest cavity through a second and/or third wound in the chest. Under direct visualization through the endoscope, the physician manipulates the instruments inserted through the secondary sites and localizes the bullae. The bulla(e) is removed by sharp and blunt dissection of the tissues which often requires folding and suturing of the tissues (plication). In order to perform the procedure, the pleural surface may require an operative procedure such as pneumonolysis (separation of the surface of the lung which has become adherent to the inside surface of the chest cavity). At the conclusion of the procedure, the endoscope and the trocar(s) are removed. A chest tube for drainage and re-expansion of the lung is usually inserted through the wound used for the thoracoscopy.

32656
The physician examines the inside of the chest cavity through a rigid or flexible fiberoptic endoscope and removes the inside lining of the chest cavity (the parietal pleura). The physician makes a small incision between two ribs and by blunt dissection and the use of a trocar enters the thoracic cavity. The endoscope is passed through the trocar and into the chest cavity. The lung is usually partially collapsed by instilling air into the chest through the trocar or the lung may be collapsed through a double lumen endotracheal tube inserted through the mouth into the trachea. The contents of the chest cavity are examined by direct visualization and/or by the use of a video camera. Still photographs may be taken as part of the procedure. A second and/or third trocar and instruments may be inserted into the chest cavity through a second and/or third wound in the chest. Under direct visualization through the endoscope the physician manipulates the instruments inserted through the secondary sites and strips away the parietal pleura from the inside surface of the chest. At the conclusion of the procedure, the endoscope and the trocar(s) are removed. A chest tube for drainage and re-expansion of the lung is usually inserted through the wound used for the thoracoscopy.

32657
The physician removes a wedge-shaped portion of a lobe of one or both lungs through a rigid or flexible fiberoptic endoscope. The physician makes a small incision between two ribs and by blunt dissection and the use of a trocar enters the thoracic cavity. The endoscope is passed through the trocar and into the chest cavity. The lung is usually partially collapsed by instilling air into the chest through the trocar or the lung may be collapsed through a double lumen endotracheal tube inserted through the mouth into the trachea. The contents of the chest cavity are examined by direct visualization and/or by the use of a video camera. Still photographs may be taken as part of the procedure. A second and/or third trocar and instruments may be inserted into the chest cavity through a second and/or third incision in the chest. Under direct visualization through the endoscope, the physician manipulates the instruments inserted through the secondary sites; and clamps the healthy portions of the lung surrounding the area to be removed. With clamps in place, the portion of lung is removed by cutting the lung tissue isolated by the clamps. The cut portions of the remaining lung tissue are repaired by suturing or clipping with surgical clips. At the conclusion of the procedure, the endoscope and the trocar(s) are removed. A chest tube for drainage and re-expansion of the lung is usually inserted through the wound initially created for the horoscope insertion.

32658
The physician examines the inside of the pericardial sac through a rigid or flexible fiberoptic endoscope and removes a blood clot or foreign body. The procedure can be done under local or general anesthesia. The physician makes a small incision between two ribs and by blunt dissection and the use of a trocar enters the thoracic cavity. The endoscope is passed through the trocar and into the chest cavity. The lung is usually partially collapsed by instilling air into the chest through the trocar or, if general anesthesia is used, the lung may be collapsed through a double lumen endotracheal tube inserted through the mouth into the trachea. The endoscope is advanced to and into the pericardial sac as the physician views the structures and the anatomy of the area through the scope. The contents of the pericardial sac are examined by direct visualization and/or by the use of a video camera. Still photographs may be taken as part of the procedure. The clot and/or foreign body is identified and removed using a device through the endoscope or using a second instrument introduced into the area through a second insertion site in the chest. At the conclusion of the procedure, the endoscope and the trocar are withdrawn. A chest tube for drainage and re-expansion of the lung is usually inserted through the wound used for the thoracoscopy.

32659
The physician operates on the pericardial sac (the sac surrounding the heart) through a rigid or flexible fiberoptic endoscope and creates a hole in the pericardial sac for drainage. The procedure can be done under local or general anesthesia. The physician makes a small incision between two ribs and by blunt dissection and the use of a trocar enters the thoracic cavity. The endoscope is passed through the trocar and into the chest cavity. The lung is usually partially collapsed by instilling air into the chest through the trocar or, if general anesthesia is used, the lung may be collapsed through a double lumen endotracheal tube inserted through the mouth into the trachea. The endoscope is advanced to and into the pericardial sac as the physician views the structures and the anatomy of the area through the scope. The contents of the pericardial sac are examined by direct visualization and/or by the use of a video camera. Still photographs may be taken as part of the procedure. Using an instrument introduced through the endoscope or through a second wound in the chest, the physician creates an opening in the pericardial sac to allow constant drainage from the sac. The drainage opening is made by the creation of a window (a flap) in the pericardium or by resecting (cutting away) a portion of the pericardium. At the conclusion of the procedure, the endoscope and the trocar are withdrawn. A chest tube for drainage and re-expansion of the lung is usually inserted through the wound used for the thoracoscopy.

32660
The physician removes the pericardial sac through a rigid or flexible fiberoptic endoscope. The physician

makes a small incision between two ribs and by blunt dissection and the use of a trocar enters the thoracic cavity. The endoscope is passed through the trocar and into the chest cavity. The lung is usually partially collapsed by instilling air into the chest through the trocar or the lung may be collapsed through a double lumen endotracheal tube inserted through the mouth into the trachea. The endoscope is advanced to and into the pericardial sac as the physician views the structures and the anatomy of the area through the scope. The contents of the pericardial sac are examined by direct visualization and/or by the use of a video camera. Still photographs may be taken as part of the procedure. Using instruments introduced through a second and/or third wound in the chest, and manipulated by direct vision through the endoscope, the physician removes the pericardial sac. At the conclusion of the procedure, the endoscope and the trocar are withdrawn. A chest tube for drainage and re-expansion of the lung is usually inserted through the wound used for the thoracoscopy.

32661

The physician examines the inside of the pericardial sac through a rigid or flexible fiberoptic endoscope and removes a cyst, tumor, or mass lesion inside the pericardial sac. The procedure can be performed under local or general anesthesia. The physician makes a small incision between two ribs and by blunt dissection and the use of a trocar enters the thoracic cavity. The endoscope is passed through the trocar and into the chest cavity. The lung is usually partially collapsed by instilling air into the chest through the trocar or, if general anesthesia is used, the lung may be collapsed through a double lumen endotracheal tube inserted through the mouth into the trachea. The endoscope is advanced to and into the pericardial sac as the physician views the structures and the anatomy of the area through the scope. The contents of the pericardial sac are examined by direct visualization and/or by the use of a video camera. Still photographs may be taken as part of the procedure. The cyst, tumor, or mass is identified and removed using instruments guided through the endoscope or by using instruments introduced into the area through a second and/or third insertion site in the chest. At the conclusion of the procedure, the endoscope and the trocar are withdrawn. A chest tube for drainage and re-expansion of the lung is usually inserted through the wound initially created for the horoscope insertion.

32662

The physician removes a cyst, tumor, or mass from the mediastinum through a rigid or flexible fiberoptic endoscope. The procedure can be done under local or general anesthesia. The physician makes a small incision between two ribs and by blunt dissection and the use of a trocar enters the thoracic cavity. The endoscope is passed through the trocar and into the chest cavity. The lung is usually partially collapsed by instilling air into the chest through the trocar or, if general anesthesia is used, the lung may be collapsed through a double lumen endotracheal tube inserted through the mouth into the trachea. As the physician views the structures and the anatomy of the area through the endoscope, the endoscope is advanced to and into the mediastinum (area inside the center of the chest cavity between the lungs). The contents of the mediastinal space are examined by direct visualization and/or by the use of a video camera. Still photographs may be taken as part of the procedure. The cyst, tumor, or mass is identified and removed using instruments guided through the endoscope or by using instruments introduced into the area through a second and/or third insertion site in the chest. At the conclusion of the procedure, the endoscope and the trocar are withdrawn. A chest tube for drainage and re-expansion of the lung is usually inserted through the wound used for the thoracoscopy.

32663

The physician removes all or a segmental portion of a lobe of one lung through a rigid or flexible fiberoptic endoscope. The physician makes a small incision between two ribs and by blunt dissection and the use of a trocar enters the thoracic cavity. The endoscope is passed through the trocar and into the chest cavity. The lung is usually partially collapsed by instilling air into the chest through the trocar or the lung may be collapsed through a double lumen endotracheal tube inserted through the mouth into the trachea. The contents of the chest cavity are examined by direct visualization and/or by the use of a video camera. Still photographs may be taken as part of the procedure. Additional instruments may be inserted into the chest cavity through a second and/or third wound in the chest. Under direct visualization through the endoscope, the physician manipulates the instruments inserted through the secondary sites and clamps the blood vessels and bronchial tubes going to the area of lung to be removed. With the clamps in place the portion of lung is removed by dividing the vessel and bronchial tubes isolated by the clamps. Any cut portions of the remaining lung tissue are repaired by suturing or clipping with surgical clips. At the conclusion of the procedure, the endoscope and the trocar(s) are removed. A chest tube for drainage and re-expansion of the lung is usually inserted through the wound used for the thoracoscopy.

32664

The physician performs a sympathectomy inside of the chest cavity through a rigid or flexible fiberoptic endoscope. The procedure can be done under local or general anesthesia. The physician makes a small incision between two ribs and by blunt dissection and the use of a trocar enters the thoracic cavity. The endoscope is passed through the trocar and into the chest cavity. The lung is usually partially collapsed by instilling air into the chest through the trocar or, if general anesthesia is used, the lung may be collapsed through a double lumen endotracheal tube inserted through the mouth into the trachea. The contents of the chest cavity are examined by direct visualization and/or by the use of a video camera. Still photographs may be taken as part of the procedure. A second and/or third trocar and instruments may be inserted into the chest cavity through a second and/or third wound in the chest. Under direct visualization through the endoscope, the physician manipulates the instruments inserted through the secondary sites and localizes and isolates a portion of the sympathetic nerves as they course deeply through the chest. The sympathectomy is accomplished by clipping and/or cutting the nerves. At the conclusion of the procedure, the endoscope and the trocar(s) are removed. A chest tube for drainage and re-expansion of the lung is usually inserted through the wound used for the thoracoscopy.

32665
The physician repairs a diseased and malfunctioning esophagus by operating through a series of several ports through the chest wall, guided under direct visualization through an endoscope introduced into the chest cavity. The physician makes a small incision between two ribs and by blunt dissection and the use of a trocar enters the thoracic cavity. The endoscope is passed through the trocar and into the chest cavity. The lung is usually partially collapsed by instilling air into the chest through the trocar or the lung may be collapsed through a double lumen endotracheal tube inserted through the mouth into the trachea. The contents of the chest cavity are examined by direct visualization and/or by the use of a video camera. Still photographs may be taken as part of the procedure. Several other trocars and instruments are inserted into the chest cavity through a series of similar puncture wounds placed at various locations in the chest. A second fiberoptic endoscope is passed through the mouth and guided into the esophagus just above the stomach to assist in the procedure. Under direct visualization through the chest endoscope, the physician manipulates the instruments inserted through the secondary chest sites and operates on the esophagus just above its junction with the stomach. The esophagus is presented to the physician by flexing the tip of the scope inside the esophagus. The outer longitudinal muscle of the esophagus is identified, and cut in a longitudinal fashion and the incision is carried down through the circular muscle layer of the esophagus. The length of the incision is carried onto the surface of the stomach about one centimeter. The depth of the incision in the esophageal wall is down to but not through the mucosal tissues lining the inside of the esophagus. Care is taken not to enter the inside of the esophagus. The incision relaxes the esophagus just above the stomach and allows food to more easily enter the stomach in those patients who have difficulty swallowing due to disease in this area of the esophagus. At the conclusion of the procedure, the endoscope and the trocar(s) are removed. A chest tube for drainage and re-expansion of the lung is usually inserted through the wound used for the thoracoscopy.

32800
The physician repairs a hernia of the chest wall that allows the bulging of the lung through a defect in the chest wall. The physician makes an incision through the skin overlying the defect and carries the incision down to the inside lining of the chest cavity. The defect is repaired by the folding and suturing of tissues or the rotation of muscle and/or thick fibrous tissue flaps over the area and suturing of the flap over the defect. Alternately, the defect can be covered by a synthetic mesh material which is sutured in place. The incision is closed in layers of sutures.

32810
The physician treats a draining empyema (accumulation of pus in the chest cavity) by resecting a rib, irrigating the empyema space with an antibiotic solution intermittently over an extended period of time, and closing of the empyema space in six to eight weeks. This code reports the closure portion only.

32815
The physician repairs a major bronchial fistula (an abnormal passageway between the remaining end of a bronchial tube and the chest that occurs sometimes after the removal of a lung or portion of a lung). The physician enters the chest cavity through a vertical incision made in the middle of the front of the chest. The incision is carried down to the sternum which is split in order to enter the chest cavity at the root of the lung near the center of the chest. The fistula exposure often requires the resection of one or two of the upper ribs. The end of the bronchial tube is located and the stump of the bronchial tube is reamputated and the inside lining of the bronchial tube is treated with silver nitrate to destroy the mucus forming cells lining the bronchus. The stump is sutured or stapled. The chest defect created is repaired and the sternum closed using wire sutures and the skin closed in layers of sutures. A chest tube may be inserted into the chest cavity for drainage.

32820
The physician repairs and reconstructs the chest wall following a major disfiguring injury to the chest (e.g. a shotgun blast). Using prosthetic materials, muscle and skin flaps and possibly skin grafts, the surgeon repairs a large defect(s) in the chest wall. This may require the use of one or more stages to finish the reconstruction.

32850
The physician performs a donor pneumonectomy(ies) for transplant from a cadaver donor. In cases where the donor has been declared brain dead, adequate functioning of the heart, lungs, and circulatory system are maintained prior to removal of the organ. During

surgical removal of the lung(s), the donor may be placed on a cardiopulmonary bypass machine to maintain perfusion to the organs. The physician makes a long, mid-line vertical incision through all the layers of the skin down to the sternum bone. The sternum is split and the chest cavity entered. Each lung is removed in one block by dividing the trachea and the major arteries and veins that carry blood to and from the heart. The lung(s) is preserved for transplantation into the recipient. The organ(s) remains under refrigeration, specially packed in a sealable container with some preserving solution and kept on ice in a suitable carrier.

32851
The physician performs a single lung transplantation of the recipient patient. The physician makes a long, mid-line vertical incision through all the layers of the skin down to the sternum bone. The sternum is split and the chest cavity entered. The patient's original lung is deflated and the root of the lung isolated and the major arteries and veins that carry blood to and from the heart are identified and divided. The main bronchial tube to that lung is severed and the lung removed. The donor lung is placed in the chest cavity and its bronchial tube and arteries and veins sutured to the patients where the former lung was attached. Circulation and functioning of the donor lung is assured and the chest is closed. The sternum is closed using wire sutures and the skin closed in layers of sutures. A chest tube(s) is inserted into the chest cavity for drainage. During the procedure the patient's oxygenation and circulation is maintained by the patient's own heart and other lung.

32852
The physician performs a single lung transplantation of the recipient patient. The physician makes a long, mid-line vertical incision through all the layers of the skin down to the sternum bone. The sternum is split and the chest cavity entered. During the transplantation of the lung, the patient is placed on a cardiopulmonary bypass machine to maintain circulation to the organs. The patient's original lung is deflated and the root of the lung isolated and the major arteries and veins that carry blood to and from the heart are identified and divided. The main bronchial tube to that lung is severed and the lung removed. The donor lung is placed in the chest cavity and its bronchial tube and arteries and veins sutured to the site where the former lung was attached. Circulation and functioning of the donor lung is assured and the chest is closed. The sternum is closed using wire sutures and the skin closed in layers of sutures. A chest tube(s) is inserted into the chest cavity for drainage.

32853
The physician performs a double lung transplantation of the recipient patient. The physician makes a long, midline vertical incision through all the layers of the skin down to the sternum bone. The sternum is split and the chest cavity entered. The patient's original lungs are deflated sequentially and the root of the lung isolated and the major arteries and veins that carry blood to and from the heart are identified and divided. The tracheal tube to the lungs is severed and the lungs removed. The donor lungs are placed in the chest cavity as a single unit or one at a time. The tracheal tube and arteries and veins sutured to the site where the former lungs were attached. Circulation and functioning of the donor lungs are assured and the chest is closed. The sternum is closed using wire sutures and the skin closed in layers of sutures. Chest tubes are inserted into the chest cavities for drainage.

32854
The physician performs a double lung transplantation of the recipient patient. The surgeon makes a long, midline vertical incision through all the layers of the skin down to the sternum bone. The sternum is split and the chest cavity entered. During the transplantation of the lungs, the patient is placed on a cardiopulmonary bypass machine to maintain circulation to the organs. The patient's original lungs are deflated and the root of the lung isolated and the major arteries and veins that carry blood to and from the heart are identified and divided. The tracheal tube to the lungs is severed and the lungs removed. The donor lungs are placed in the chest cavity as a single unit or one at a time. The tracheal tube and arteries and veins sutured to the site where the former lungs were attached. Circulation and functioning of the donor lungs are assured and the chest is closed. The sternum is closed using wire sutures and the skin closed in layers of sutures. Chest tubes are inserted into the chest cavities for drainage.

32855-32856
The physician performs a standard backbench preparation of one or both lungs following procurement from a cadaver donor. Backbench or back table preparation refers to procedures performed on the donor organs following procurement to prepare the donor organs for transplant. Both lungs are removed or the heart and lungs are removed en bloc. If the heart and lungs are removed en bloc, back table separation of the heart and lungs is performed. The lungs are inspected following procurement to identify any injury or abnormality not noted prior to procurement. The physician prepares the lungs by dissecting free any residual soft tissue. Attention is focused on the pulmonary venous/atrial cuff, pulmonary artery, and bronchus. The pulmonary venous/atrial cuff is inspected and any residual tissue removed. The pulmonary artery, which was divided at its bifurcation, is inspected and any residual tissue removed. The aorta, which was divided distal to the innominate artery, is inspected and residual tissue removed. When all residual soft tissue has been removed and the vessels prepared, the lung(s) is ready for transplant. Report

32855 for backbench preparation of one lung (unilateral). Report 32856 for backbench preparation of both lungs (bilateral).

32900
The physician resects a rib(s) without entering the chest cavity. The surgeon make an incision in the skin overlying the rib to be removed and carries that incision through the tissues down to the rib. The tissues are dissected away from the rib taking care not to puncture through the pleural membrane on the inside surface of the rib. This avoids the egress of air into the chest cavity. With the tissue removed from the surface of the rib, the rib is cut at two places and the intervening section removed. The resulting defect may be covered by the use of muscle flaps grafted to the area. The remaining tissues and skin are closed by suturing in layers.

32905
The physician performs a thoracoplasty which is the removal of the skeletal support of a portion of the chest to treat chronic thoracic empyema (accumulation of pus in the chest cavity) when there is insufficient lung tissue to fill the chest space. The procedure is carried out primarily on the upper chest. An incision is made through the skin down to the ribs. The Schede operation consists of the extensive unroofing of an empyema space by resecting the overlying ribs and portions of membrane lining the chest cavity (parietal pleural peel). The muscles in the area are partially closed over gauze packing and the skin partially closed by suturing in layers. As the packing is withdrawn in stages a few days later, it is hoped that freshly granulation tissue fills in the space formerly occupied by the empyema. The original Schede type operation is rarely performed but several modifications are currently done.

32906
The physician closes a bronchopleural fistula and performs a thoracoplasty which is the removal of the skeletal support of a portion of the chest to treat chronic thoracic empyema (accumulation of pus in the chest cavity) when there is insufficient lung tissue to fill the chest space. The procedure is carried out primarily on the upper chest. An incision is made through the skin down to the ribs. The Schede operation consists of the extensive unroofing of an empyema space by resecting the overlying ribs and portions of membrane lining the chest cavity (parietal pleural peel). The bronchopleural fistula (an abnormal passageway between the remaining end of a bronchial tube that occurs sometimes after the removal of a lung or portion of a lung) is identified and resected, then closed by suturing. Closure of the fistula sometimes requires muscle flap grafts taken from outside the chest cavity. After the repair of the fistula, the muscles in the area are partially closed over gauze packing and the skin partially closed by suturing in layers. As the packing is withdrawn in stages a few days later, it is hoped that freshly granulation tissue fills in the space formerly occupied by the empyema. The original Schede type operation is rarely performed but several modifications are currently done.

32940
The physician opens the chest cavity and separates the surface of the lung, which has become adherent to the inside surface of the chest cavity. Using a scalpel, the surgeon makes an incision around the side of the chest between two of the ribs. The incision is carried through all the tissue layers down to the tissue lining the chest cavity. Rib spreaders are inserted into the wound and the ribs are spread apart exposing the membrane lining the chest cavity (the parietal pleura). The surgeon separates the tissue between the periosteal membrane adherent to the inside surface of the lung and the parietal pleural membrane. This allows the movement of the lung within the chest cavity. The area or space created is packed or filled and the incision is closed in layers of sutures.

32960
The physician partially collapses a lung by injecting air into the chest cavity by puncturing through the space between the ribs. Using a needle attached to a syringe the physician passes the needle over the top of a rib and punctures through the chest tissues and enters the pleural cavity. With the end of the needle in the chest cavity, the physician injects air into the chest cavity to create a partial collapse of one lung, most commonly used to treat tuberculosis. A small plastic tube may be passed through the chest and left in place for repeated injections of air.

32997
The physician performs total lavage on one lung. The physician views the airway using a fiberoptic or rigid bronchoscopy. The airway is anesthetized and the bronchoscope is introduced through the nasal or oral cavity and advanced to the lungs. Saline is introduced through the bronchoscope and the lung tissue is washed or bathed. The saline is removed by suction and the solution containing the cells that have been obtained in the procedure may be sent to pathology to diagnosis certain diseases, such as cancer. The procedure also may be performed to treat specific diseases or injuries.

32998
In a minimally invasive procedure, the physician uses the heat created from high-frequency radio waves to destroy one or more tumors in the lung, pleura, or chest wall. A small incision is made in the skin of the chest and the lesion is accessed by inserting between the ribs an ablation probe connected to a radiofrequency generator. Under CT guidance that is reported separately, the ablation probe is advanced into the lesion of the lung, pleura, or chest wall. Treatment with the heat probe usually takes several minutes and

may include repositioning the probe within the lesion so that overlapping ablations treat the entire tumor. The incision is closed with sutures. This process may be repeated for multiple lesions within the same lung.

Cardiovascular

33010-33011

The physician drains fluid from the pericardial space. The physician may perform this procedure using anatomic landmarks or under fluoroscopic or echocardiographic (ultrasound) guidance (separately reported). The physician places a long needle below the sternum and directs it into the pericardial space. When pericardial fluid is aspirated, the physician may advance a guidewire through the needle into the pericardial space and exchange the needle over the guidewire for a drainage catheter. The physician removes as much pericardial fluid as is required, removes the needle or catheter, and dresses the wound. Report 33011 for each subsequent pericardiocentesis.

33015

The physician drains fluid from the pericardial space. The physician may perform this procedure using anatomic landmarks or under fluoroscopic or echocardiographic (ultrasound) guidance (separately reported). The physician places a long needle below the sternum and directs it into the pericardial space. When pericardial fluid flows back through the needle, the physician passes a guidewire through the needle into the pericardial space. The physician exchanges the needle over the wire for an indwelling drainage catheter. The physician attaches the catheter to a drainage bag, sutures the indwelling catheter into place on the chest wall, and dresses the wound.

33020

The physician removes a clot or foreign body from the pericardial space. The physician performs a midline sternotomy, incising skin, fascia, and the sternum. The pericardium is incised and the clot or foreign body is removed. The pericardium is repaired loosely, leaving gaps for blood and fluid to drain into the pleural space. The sternum is reanastomosed with sternal wires and the skin is sutured in layers.

33025

The physician gains access to the pericardium through an incision through the sternum (median sternotomy), the subxiphoid space or the chest wall (lateral thoracotomy). The physician makes an incision in the pericardium and creates an opening in the pericardium large enough to allow drainage of pericardial fluid into the pleural space. The physician closes the sternal or chest wall incision and dresses the wound. The physician may leave chest tubes and/or a mediastinal drainage tube in place following the procedure.

33030-33031

The physician gains access to the pericardium through an incision through the sternum (median sternotomy). The physician cuts away most or all of the pericardial tissue while the heart is still beating (without cardiopulmonary bypass), taking care to leave the phrenic nerves intact. The physician closes the sternal or chest wall incision and dresses the wound. The physician may leave chest tubes and/or a mediastinal drainage tube in place following the procedure. Report 33031 if the procedure is performed with a cardiopulmonary bypass.

33050

The physician gains access to the pericardium through an incision through the sternum (median sternotomy) or the chest wall (lateral thoracotomy). The physician places cardiopulmonary bypass catheters (usually through incisions in the right atrial appendage and aorta or femoral artery). The physician stops the heart by infusing cardioplegia solution into the coronary circulation. The physician cuts away the pericardial cyst or tumor while the heart is still. The physician takes the patient off cardiopulmonary bypass, closes the surgical incisions and dresses the sternal or chest wall wound. The physician may leave chest tubes and/ or a mediastinal drainage tube in place following the procedure.

33120

Cardiopulmonary bypass is employed. Venous tubes are placed in both caval veins. The part of the heart that is opened depends on where the tumor is located. Every effort is made to avoid making an incision in any ventricular wall. After the heart is opened. The tumor is resected with a margin of normal heart tissue. Any problems created by this resection (damage to heart valves, holes in the walls between heart chambers or the outside of the heart, injury to coronary arteries) are repaired. All holes in the heart are closed. Cardiopulmonary bypass is stopped when heart function returns.

33130

Cardiopulmonary bypass is only required if a significant portion of the heart or major vessel must be removed with the tumor to get a margin of normal tissue around the tumor. The tumor and surrounding normal tissue are removed. Defects created in the heart, coronary arteries or major vessels are repaired.

33140-33141

The physician performs transmyocardial laser revascularization to restore the flow of blood and oxygen to the heart. Varying approaches may be employed. The procedure is frequently performed on the beating heart, although cardiopulmonary bypass may be initiated. In the beating heart: Using a scalpel the physician makes a 10 centimeters to 15 centimeters incision on the left side of the chest between the ribs and exposes the surface of the heart. The area of ischemia (in still vital tissue) is identified. A laser is inserted through the chest opening and is fired (between heartbeats) through the filled left ventricle. Between 10 channels to 40 channels (small holes) are created to encourage new capillary growth in the area. As the channels are created pressure is applied to each to help close the openings. When the procedure is completed the laser is removed and the wound is closed with layered sutures. If cardiopulmonary bypass was initiated it is discontinued, the patient is rewarmed, and the heartbeat is restored. Report 33140 if the transmyocardial laser revascularization is performed alone. Report 33141 when it is performed at the time of another open cardiac procedure.

33202

The physician places one or more electrical leads on the outside of the heart (epicardial electrodes) by open chest incision. The incision can be in the middle of the chest (midline sternotomy), a vertical incision just below the ribcage (subxiphoid), or between the ribs on the left side of the body (thoracotomy). The chest cavity is opened. After the heart is exposed, electrodes are affixed to the appropriate areas of the heart muscle. The electrodes are tested and then tunneled under the coastal margin to the upper abdomen to a pulse generator or to the infraclavicular area if the generator is in that area. The physician closes the incision in layered sutures.

33203

The physician places electrical leads on the outside of the heart (epicardial electrodes) using an endoscopic approach. Three trocars are placed in the left anterior chest wall and the left lung is collapsed. A small incision is made in the chest (thoracostomy) and a 12 mm trocar is placed. The thoracoscope (endoscope) is inserted. Two additional trocars are placed under thoracoscopic visualization in the inframammary anterolateral region. Under thoracoscopic guidance, the pericardium is grasped and incised. The lateral trocar is removed and the incision enlarged to allow passage of the epicardial electrode placement device and the electrodes through the intercostal space. The electrodes are placed intrapericardially. The pericardium is approximated with a single stitch to hold the electrodes in place. The electrodes are tested and then tunneled under the costal margin to the upper abdomen to a pulse generator or over the ribs to the infraclavicular area if the generator is in that area. The thoracoscope is removed and a thoracostomy tube is placed at this site. The lung is expanded and the incisions closed in layered suture.

33206-33211

Access to the central caval veins is obtained through the subclavian vein or jugular vein. The vein is penetrated with a large needle and a wire is passed through it. A fluoroscope (separately reported) is used to guide the wire into the right atrium. A pocket for the pacemaker generator is created and the wire is tested. The wire is connected to the generator and the generator is closed in its pocket. Report 33207 if the guide and pacemaker wires are placed in the right ventricle; report 33208 if elements of 33206 and 33207 are combined; report 33210 or 33211 if the pacemaker generator is not implanted but temporarily placed outside the body and a transvenous single chamber cardiac electrode or pacemaker catheter (33210) or transvenous dual chamber (33211) electrode(s) are placed are inserted or replaced.

33212-33214

A single or dual chamber pacemaker pulse generator is inserted or replaced. If this is an initial insertion, a pocket for the pacemaker generator is created either subcutaneously in the subclavicular region or underneath the abdominal muscles just below the ribcage. The generator is inserted into the pocket. If the generator is being replaced, the old pacemaker generator pocket is opened and the old generator removed in a separately reportable procedure. The new generator is then placed into the existing pocket. The pacer wire(s) is tested and connected to the generator. The pocket is closed. Report 33212 if inserting or replacing a single chamber (atrial or ventricular) pacemaker pulse generator and 33213 for a dual chamber (atrial and ventricular). In 33214, a single chamber system is converted to a dual chamber system. The existing pacemaker generator pocket is opened and the single chamber generator removed. The dual chamber generator is then placed into the existing pocket. The existing pacer wire is tested and connected to the generator. A second lead is placed and tested. The pocket is closed.

33215

A previously placed transvenous right atrial or right ventricular electrode is repositioned. This is done when the system does not function due to improper placement of the electrode wire itself. The generator is removed and the wire is tested to ensure that the wire is not defective, but simply in the wrong place. It is reattached to the generator in its new position and tested again.

33216-33217

The physician inserts a single transvenous electrode in 33216 and two transvenous electrodes in 33217 when there is a problem with the electrode wire of a permanent pacemaker or cardioverter-defibrillator. The generator is removed and the wire is first tested. When the wire is found defective, another transvenous electrode is inserted. Access to the central caval veins is obtained through the subclavian vein or jugular vein. The vein is penetrated with a large needle and a wire is passed through it. Fluoroscopy (separately reported) is used to guide the wire into position. The wire is connected to the generator and testing is done again.

33218-33220
In 33218, the pacemaker or cardioverter/defibrillator pocket is opened and the generator is removed. The electrode wire is tested. Repairs are performed. The wire is retested and reconnected to the generator. The generator is placed back in its pocket and the pocket is closed. Report 33220 if the pacemaker or cardioverter-defibrillator is a dual chamber model with two electrodes.

33222-33223
This procedure is performed for patient comfort, impending exposure of the generator through the skin or complications from the original generator placement (e.g., infection, bleeding). The pocket is opened. The generator is removed and the pocket is assessed. If it can be reused, it is revised. If not, a new pocket is formed somewhere within the reach of the pacemaker wires. The wires are brought through a new subcutaneous tunnel into the new pocket and connected to a new or the old generator. The old pocket is closed and the generator is placed in the new pocket, which is closed. If the old pocket is to be used, the generator is simply reinserted and the pocket closed. Report 33222 when a pacemaker pocket is revised or relocated. Report 33223 when a cardioverter-defibrillator pocket is revised.

33224
If biventricular pacing is required, an additional electrode is placed in the left ventricle. With the pacemaker or pacing cardioverter-defibrillator already in place, the physician gains access transvenously through the subclavian or jugular vein. A fluoroscope may be used for guidance and a pacing electrode is inserted in the ventricular chamber of the heart, usually in the coronary sinus tributary. The generator pocket may be revised and/or the generator removed, inserted, or replaced. The electrode is connected to the generator and the pocket is closed.

33225
If biventricular pacing is required, an additional electrode is placed in the left ventricle. During insertion of a pacing cardioverter-defibrillator or pacemaker pulse generator, the physician gains access transvenously through the subclavian or jugular vein. A fluoroscope may be used for guidance and a pacing electrode is inserted in the ventricular chamber of the heart, usually in the coronary sinus tributary. The electrode is connected to the generator and the generator pocket is closed.

33226
The physician gains access transvenously through the subclavian or jugular vein. A fluoroscope may be used for guidance and the pacing electrode that is already in place in the ventricular chamber of the heart, usually in the coronary sinus tributary, is repositioned. The generator pocket may be revised and/or the generator removed, inserted, or replaced. The electrode is connected to the generator and the pocket is closed.

33233
In 33233, only the pulse generator is removed. The pacemaker generator pocket is opened. The generator is disconnected from the wire(s) and removed. The wire(s) are left in place in the pocket and the pocket is closed or a new pacemaker generator is inserted. If a new pacemaker is inserted, it is reported separately.

33234-33235
In 33234 and 33235, only the transvenous electrode(s) are removed. In 33234, the generator pocket is opened and the wire is disconnected from the generator. The wire is dissected from the scar tissue that has formed around it. Once the wire is completely freed, it is twisted in a direction opposite to that used for insertion (counter clockwise). The wire is withdrawn. Bleeding from the tracts leading to the vein is controlled with sutures. A new wire may be placed, but is reported separately. Report 33235 for a dual lead system (removal of two wires).

33236-33237
Code 33236 reports the removal of a single lead epicardial pacemaker system and electrodes. The old pacemaker pocket is opened and the generator is removed. The old wires are cut and the incision is closed. The old chest incision is opened. The wires are pulled into the chest and they are followed onto the heart surface. The electrodes are detached from the heart. The chest incision is closed. Report 33237 if a dual lead epicardial system is being removed.

33238
The physician removes a transvenous electrode(s) by thoracotomy. Prior to this procedure, the pacemaker pocket was opened, the generator removed, and the wires cut. The right chest is opened and the superior caval vein is dissected out. Tourniquets are placed around the vein above and below the planned site of opening. The tourniquets are tightened and a hole is made in the caval vein. The cut ends of the wires are pulled out through the hole in the caval vein. The ends of the wires that are still in the heart are twisted counterclockwise until they are free and are withdrawn through the caval vein. The hole in the caval vein is closed and the tourniquets released. The chest is closed.

33240
This operation is done only when defibrillator electrodes are already in place. The previous pocket is opened or a new pocket is created for the defibrillator generator. AICD pulse generators are implanted subcutaneously usually in an infraclavicular or abdominal pocket. The electrodes are tested. The electrodes are connected to the defibrillator and it is placed in the pocket. The pocket is closed.

33241
In 33241, only the AICD pulse generator is removed. The subcutaneous generator pocket is opened and the generator is removed. The electrodes are detached from the generator and the electrodes are placed in the pocket. The pocket is closed or a new cardioverter-defibrillator generator is inserted.

33243
In 33243, only the electrodes are removed. The generator pocket is opened and the electrode wires are disconnected. The old chest incision is opened and the electrodes are dissected out and removed. The chest incision is closed.

33244
Code 33244 reports removal of electrodes only by transvenous extraction, which is currently the most common technique for removing AICD electrodes since most cardioverter-defibrillator electrodes are now placed transvenously. The generator pocket is opened and the wire is disconnected from the generator. The wire is dissected from the scar tissue that has formed around it. Once the wire is completely freed, it is twisted in a direction opposite to that used for insertion (counter clockwise). The wire is withdrawn. Bleeding from the tracts leading to the vein is controlled with sutures. A new wire may be placed, but is reported separately.

33249
The physician inserts a pulse generator with transvenous electrode placement. Transvenous placement is currently the most common technique for placing implantable cardioverter-defibrillator (ICD) electrodes. An ICD is a device designed to administer an electric shock to control cardiac arrhythmias and restore a normal heartbeat. Local anesthesia is administered. An incision is made in the infraclavicular area. The subcutaneous tissue is opened and a pocket is created for the pulse generator. Transvenous electrode placement is performed under separately reportable fluoroscopic guidance. The electrode catheter is advanced through the superior vena cava into the heart and placed in the appropriate site in the right ventricle (single chamber system) or in the right ventricle and atrium (dual chamber system). Multiple leads may be required for both single and dual chamber systems. Once all leads are placed, they are tested and connected to the pulse generator that is placed in the previously prepared pocket. All incisions are closed.

33250
Cardiopulmonary bypass is usually required. The heart is exposed through the sternum. A mapping grid of electrodes is placed over the surface of the beating heart. The location of the arrhythmia source is determined. The source is destroyed using electrical current, freezing, or cutting. Any bleeding is controlled with sutures. The chest is closed.

33251
Cardiopulmonary bypass is required. The heart is exposed through the sternum. A mapping grid of electrodes is placed over the surface of the beating heart. The right atrium is opened and a long cut is made around the tricuspid valve until the cut on the outside of the heart is seen. Any other focuses of the arrhythmia are destroyed with electrical current or freezing. The right atrium is closed. Cardiopulmonary bypass is discontinued when heart function returns.

33254-33256
The physician performs operative ablation and reconstruction of the atria to treat atrial fibrillation. Atrial fibrillation is rapid, randomized muscle contraction of the atrial myocardium causing an irregular, rapid heart rate. In a maze procedure, the physician seeks to permanently interrupt aberrant electrical conduction within the atria to restore normal sinus rhythm. The physician performs a midline sternotomy, incising the skin, fascia, muscles, and sternum. The pericardium is incised. For a limited operative ablation and reconstruction (33254), also referred to as a modified maze procedure, an incision is made into the left or right atrium. A combination of surgical incision and/or energy sources such as heat, microwave, laser, ultrasound, or cryoprobe is used to create lesions that will heal into scars that disrupt conduction. In 33255 and 33256, an extensive operative ablation and reconstruction is performed. In an extensive procedure, the right and/or left atrial tissue and/or atrial septum is treated as described in 33254, and additional operative ablation involving the atrioventricular annulus is performed. In any of these procedures, the left atrial appendage may be excised or isolated. In 33256, lines are placed for cardiopulmonary bypass. When cardiopulmonary bypass is achieved, an extensive ablation and reconstruction procedure is performed. The atrial incision lines are reanastomosed. The pericardium is repaired loosely, leaving gaps for blood and fluid to drain into the pleural space. The sternum is reanastomosed with sternal wires and the skin is sutured in layers.

33257-33259
Concurrently with other cardiac procedures, the physician performs operative tissue ablation and reconstruction of the atria to treat atrial fibrillation. Atrial fibrillation is rapid, randomized muscle contraction of the atrial myocardium causing an irregular, rapid heart rate. In this procedure, the physician seeks to permanently interrupt aberrant electrical conduction within the atria to restore normal sinus rhythm. The physician performs a midline sternotomy, incising the skin, fascia, muscles, and sternum. The pericardium is incised. For a limited operative tissue ablation and reconstruction of atria (33257), also referred to as a modified maze procedure, an incision is made into the left or right

Cardiovascular

atrium. A combination of surgical incision and/or energy sources, such as heat, microwave, laser, ultrasound, or cryoprobe, is used to create lesions that will heal into scars that disrupt conduction. In 33258 and 33259, an extensive operative tissue ablation and reconstruction of the atria is performed. In these extensive procedures, the right and/or left atrial tissue and/or atrial septum is treated as described in 33257, and additional operative ablation involving the atrioventricular annulus is performed. In any of these procedures, the left atrial appendage may be excised or isolated. In 33259, lines are placed for cardiopulmonary bypass. When cardiopulmonary bypass is achieved, an extensive tissue ablation and atria reconstruction procedure is performed. The atrial incision lines are reanastomosed. The pericardium is repaired loosely, leaving gaps for blood and fluid to drain into the pleural space. The sternum is reanastomosed with sternal wires and the skin is sutured in layers.

33261

Following initiation of cardiopulmonary bypass, the physician exposes the heart through the sternum. A mapping grid of electrodes is placed over the surface of the beating heart. The location of the arrhythmia source is determined. The source is destroyed using electrical current, freezing or cutting, though not in the tricuspid valve. Any bleeding is controlled with sutures. The chest is closed.

33265-33266

The physician performs endoscopic operative ablation and reconstruction of the atria to treat atrial fibrillation. Atrial fibrillation is rapid, randomized muscle contraction of the atrial myocardium causing an irregular, rapid heart rate. In a maze procedure, the physician seeks to permanently interrupt aberrant electrical conduction within the atria to restore normal sinus rhythm. Through multiple endoscopic incisions in the chest, the physician accesses and visualizes the outer (epicardial) surface of the heart. For a limited or modified maze procedure performed endoscopically (33265), the pulmonary veins or other anatomically defined triggers are isolated in the left or right atrium and a heat, microwave, laser, ultrasound, or cryoprobe is used to create lesions from the outside of the left atrium that will heal into scars that disrupt conduction. In 33266, the right and/or left atrial tissue and/or atrial septum is treated as described in 33265, and additional operative ablation involving the atrioventricular annulus is performed. In either of these procedures, the left atrial appendage may be excised or isolated. Once sufficient interruption of electrical conduction has been accomplished, the endoscope is removed and access incisions are sutured in layers.

33282-33284

The physician implants or removes an electronic device that is capable of recording heart rates and rhythms for over one year. In 33282, the physician uses a scalpel to make an incision and dissects down to the level of subcutaneous tissue located over the left pectoral or mammary area. A cardiac event (loop) recorder is implanted into the subcutaneous tissue. Electrodes that sense heart activity are located on the surface of the event recorder, making it unnecessary to place transvenous leads. The recorder continuously monitors the heart's electrical activity in a "loop" with new ECG information replacing old information. If symptoms occur the patient uses an external hand-held device to freeze a record of the event. In 33284, the physician removes the event recorder when sufficient information regarding the heart's activities has been obtained or when the batteries run out by incising down to the level of the recorder and removing it. In either surgery the incision is closed with sutures. This type of recorder is capable of storing many separate events. When appropriate a "programmer" is used by the physician to retrieve the information that can be displayed, stored or printed.

33300-33305

The physician gains access to the heart using an incision through the sternum (median sternotomy) or the left anterior chest wall (thoracotomy). A pericardial window may be created if the diagnosis of penetrating cardiac trauma is not confirmed. Once penetrating trauma has been confirmed, the pericardial sac is incised and clotted blood and fluid removed. The entire heart is inspected and wound site(s) identified. Small lacerations are repaired with sutures and reinforced with Teflon felt pledges to anchor the sutures. Lacerations to small coronary vessels are ligated. Lacerations to larger coronary vessels are repaired. Large myocardial wounds may require synthetic grafting to cover the wound. The surgical incision is closed. Chest tubes and/or a mediastinal drainage tube may be left in place following the procedure. Report 33300 when the procedure is performed without cardiopulmonary bypass; report 33305 when cardiopulmonary bypass is required.

33310-33315

The physician exposes the heart via the sternum. The foreign body is located by feeling the heart. If possible, the object is removed from the surface of the heart. If necessary, a hole is made in one of the ventricles or atria to remove the object or thrombus lodged there. The holes are closed with sutures and small reinforcing patches of Teflon felt. Report 33310 if cardiopulmonary bypass is not initiated; report 33315 if cardiopulmonary bypass is initiated.

33320-33322

The physician gains access to the mediastinum through an incision through the sternum (median sternotomy) or the chest wall (lateral thoracotomy). The physician repairs the aorta or great vessels while the heart is still beating. The physician closes the surgical incisions and

Cardiovascular

dresses the sternal or chest wall wound. The physician may leave chest tubes and/or a mediastinal drainage tube in place following the procedure. Report 33321 if performed with a shunt bypass; report 33322 if performed with a cardiopulmonary bypass.

33330
The physician gains access to the mediastinum through an incision through the sternum (median sternotomy) or the chest wall (lateral thoracotomy). The physician sews in the aortic or great vessel graft while the heart is still beating. The physician closes the surgical incisions and dresses the sternal or chest wall wound. The physician may leave chest tubes and/or a mediastinal drainage tube in place following the procedure.

33332
The physician gains access to the mediastinum through an incision through the sternum (median sternotomy) or the chest wall (lateral thoracotomy). The physician uses purse string incisions to place a shunt (bypass) catheter around the abnormal area of the vessel to be repaired. The physician sews in the aortic or great vessel graft while the heart is still beating. The physician removes the bypass catheter, closes the surgical incisions and dresses the sternal or chest wall wound. The physician may leave chest tubes and/or a mediastinal drainage tube in place following the procedure.

33335
The physician gains access to the mediastinum through an incision through the sternum (median sternotomy) or the chest wall (lateral thoracotomy). The physician places cardiopulmonary bypass catheters usually through incisions in the right atrial appendage and aorta or femoral artery. The physician stops the heart by infusing cardioplegia solution into the coronary circulation. The physician sews in the aortic or great vessel graft while the heart is still. The physician takes the patient off cardiopulmonary bypass, closes the surgical incisions and dresses the sternal or chest wall wound. The physician may leave chest tubes and/or a mediastinal drainage tube in place following the procedure.

33400
Cardiopulmonary bypass is initiated. The aorta is clamped from above the heart and a cold preserving solution is pumped through the heart. The aorta is opened near the valve. The spaces where the heart valve leaflets meet have been fused by inflammation and scarring in diseases requiring this operation. The scars between the leaflets are cut with a knife. The aorta is closed and the clamp is removed. Cardiopulmonary bypass is discontinued when heart function returns.

33401
This operation is of historical interest only. The following vessels are clamped or occluded with tourniquets: the superior caval vein, the inferior caval vein, and the aorta. The aorta is quickly opened above the heart and the scar tissue between the valve leaflets are cut with a knife. The aorta is quickly closed and the clamps removed. The operation (except for opening and closing) must be done in no more than five minutes to prevent brain damage.

33403
Cardiopulmonary bypass is initiated. A purse string is placed in the left ventricular apex. The purse string is reinforced with small patches of Teflon felt. An incision is made in the center of the purse string. Blunt dilators are passed through the hole and across the aortic valve. Progressively larger dilators are inserted until the valve is wide open. The dilators break the scar tissues that are cut in an open aortic valvoplasty. The valve leaflets are frequently damaged to the point that the valve must be replaced. After the valve is fully dilated, the purse string is tied off. Cardiopulmonary bypass is discontinued when heart function returns.

33404
Cardiopulmonary bypass is required. A hole is made in the tip of the left ventricle and another is made in the aorta above the coronary arteries. The conduit is oriented so that the valve in it will only let blood flow out of the heart, but not back in. One end of the conduit is sewn to the hole in the tip of the heart. The other end is sewn to the hole in the aorta. Air is removed from the heart and from the conduit. Cardiopulmonary bypass is discontinued when heart function returns.

33405
Cardiopulmonary bypass is initiated. A clamp is placed on the aorta well above the heart. A cold preserving solution is pumped into the coronary arteries to stop the heart. The aorta is opened just above the aortic valve. The valve leaflets are cut out and the annulus of the valve (ring of tissue where the valve leaflets normally attach to the aorta) is cleaned of calcium. The valve annulus size is measured and an appropriate artificial valve is selected. The artificial valve is sewn to the valve annulus. The aorta is closed and the clamp is taken off. Cardiopulmonary bypass is discontinued when heart function returns.

33406
Cardiopulmonary bypass is initiated. A clamp is placed on the aorta well above the heart. A cold preserving solution is pumped into the coronary arteries to stop the heart. The aorta is opened just above the aortic valve. The valve leaflets are cut out and the annulus of the valve (ring of tissue where the valve leaflets normally attach to the aorta) is cleaned of calcium. At this point an allograft is selected. The tissue valve is trimmed so that it can be sewn to the valve annulus. The aorta above the graft valve is trimmed so that the valve cusps can be suspended when the graft is in place. By doing so, the coronary arteries are not

obstructed by the graft. The new valve is sewn in place. The valve annulus size is measured and an appropriate artificial valve is selected. The artificial valve is sewn to the valve annulus. The aorta is closed and the clamp is taken off. Cardiopulmonary bypass is discontinued when heart function returns.

33410
Cardiopulmonary bypass is initiated. A clamp is placed on the aorta and above the heart. A cold preserving solution is pumped into the coronary arteries to stop the heart. The aorta is opened just above the aortic valve. The valve leaflets are cut out and the annulus of the valve (ring of tissue where the valve leaflets normally attach to the aorta) is cleaned of calcium. The valve annulus size is measured and an appropriate stentless tissue valve is selected, (the stentless valve is unique because unlike other valves it has no rigid external frame or sewing ring) and sutured directly into the aortic wall. The aorta is closed and the clamp is taken off. Cardiopulmonary bypass is discontinued when heart function returns. The wound is closed with layered sutures.

33411
Cardiopulmonary bypass is initiated. A clamp is placed on the aorta well above the heart. A cold preserving solution is pumped into the coronary arteries to stop the heart. The aorta is opened just above the aortic valve. The valve leaflets are cut out and the annulus of the valve (ring of tissue where the valve leaflets normally attach to the aorta) is cleaned of calcium. At this point a homograft or a xenograft is selected. The tissue valve is trimmed so that it can be sewn to the valve annulus. The aorta above the graft valve is trimmed so that the valve cusps can be suspended when the graft is in place and so the coronary arteries are not obstructed by the graft. When the valve is sized, it must be greater than or equal to 19 mm on a normal sized adult. If a smaller valve is inserted, the heart will slowly fail. To enlarge the valve, the aorta is cut longitudinally toward the heart and through the commissure (connecting point where two valve leaflets meet on the aortic wall) between the non-coronary leaflet (no coronary is near this leaflet) and the left coronary leaflet (leaflet near the left coronary artery) and across the valve annulus for a variable distance. The cut may need to extend onto the roof of the left atrium and onto the anterior leaflet of the mitral valve. The end of the cut is determined by the point at which the aortic root will accommodate at least a 19 mm valve. The anterior mitral leaflet, left atrial roof and the aorta are repaired with patches. The new valve is sewn in place. The aorta is closed and the clamp is taken off. Cardiopulmonary bypass is discontinued when heart function returns.

33412
Cardiopulmonary bypass is initiated. A clamp is placed on the aorta well above the heart. A cold preserving solution is pumped into the coronary arteries to stop the heart. The aorta is opened just above the aortic valve. The valve leaflets are cut out and the annulus of the valve (ring of tissue where the valve leaflets normally attach to the aorta) is cleaned of calcium. At this point a homograft or a xenograft is selected. The tissue valve is trimmed so that it can be sewn to the valve annulus. The aorta above the graft valve is trimmed so that the valve cusps can be suspended when the graft is in place and so the coronary arteries are not obstructed by the graft. When the valve is sized, it must be greater than or equal to 19 mm on a normal sized adult. If a smaller valve is inserted, the heart will slowly fail. The aorta is incised longitudinally toward a point just to the left of the right coronary artery. The cut is carried across the annulus and for a variable distance onto the right ventricular infundibulum. A triangular patch of pericardium or Dacron (a gusset, for example) is used to close the incision in the right ventricle and aorta and to enlarge the aortic annulus. The new valve is sewn in place. The aorta is closed and the clamp is taken off. Cardiopulmonary bypass is discontinued when heart function returns.

33413
Cardiopulmonary bypass is initiated. The aorta and pulmonary artery are separated and the main pulmonary trunk is completely cleaned off. After the heart is stopped, the pulmonary trunk is detached from the branching point of the left and right pulmonary arteries. It is taken off the heart with a small lip of heart muscle. Care is taken when the muscle of interventricular septum is cut. It is possible to damage a large branch of the left anterior descending coronary artery when this muscle is cut. The aorta is opened above the valve. The coronary arteries are detached from the aorta with a surrounding "button" of aortic wall. Next, the aortic valve and its annulus are removed from the heart. A length of the ascending aorta is also removed. The pulmonary artery is sewn to the heart in the aortic position. The commissures and cusps of the pulmonary valve are lined up to be in the same positions as their aortic counterparts were before the aortic valve was removed. The open end of the pulmonary artery is sewn to the ascending aorta. The coronary arteries are re-implanted on the pulmonary artery in positions similar to their positions on the aorta. The pulmonary valve and artery from an organ donor are sewn into the pulmonary position.

33414
The physician enlarges the aortic outflow track using what known as a Konno procedure. The physician performs a midline sternotomy, incising the skin, fascia, muscles, and sternum. The pericardium is incised and lines are placed for cardiopulmonary bypass. When bypass is established, the right ventricle is incised and the aortic outflow track is enlarged by incising the septum. Two patches are applied; the first

is placed from the septum to the aortic annulus, enlarging the track. The second patch is placed from the base of the first patch at the septum, closing the right ventricle. The pericardium is repaired loosely, leaving gaps for blood and fluid to drain into the pleural space. The sternum is reanastomosed with sternal wires and the skin is sutured in layers.

33415-33416
Cardiopulmonary bypass is initiated. The aorta is opened and the left ventricular outflow tract is assessed below the valve. There is usually a clearly definable ring or shelf below the valve. This is taken off with a tool designed for the purpose. Usually, the left ventricular septal muscle is thickened. A trough of muscle tissue is cut out of the left ventricular septal muscle. The aorta is closed. Cardiopulmonary bypass is discontinued when heart function returns. Report 33416 if there is no ring of subvalvular tissue to remove.

33417
Cardiopulmonary bypass is required. A piece of pericardium or Dacron is prepared. The aorta is clamped beyond the area of narrowing. The heart is stopped with a cold preserving solution. The aorta is opened longitudinally across the area of narrowing. The aorta is closed with a patch sewn onto the incision of the aorta. The clamp is released. Cardiopulmonary bypass is discontinued when heart function returns.

33420
The left chest is opened. The pericardium is opened. A gloved finger is used to invert the left atrial appendage into the left atrium. The finger is placed across the mitral valve. Blunt tearing is used to open the areas between the leaflets, which have been obliterated by scar tissue and inflammation. The finger is removed and the chest is closed.

33422
Cardiopulmonary bypass is initiated. The left atrium is opened from the right side. The mitral valve is exposed. The scar tissue between the lateral ends of the valve leaflets is divided sharply. The left atrium is closed. Cardiopulmonary bypass is discontinued when heart function returns.

33425-33427
This operation is done to improve the ability of the mitral valve to close completely when the ventricle contracts. It is done in patients whose mitral valve has lost the ability to close normally. In almost all cases, this is the result of a mitral valve prolapse in which the mitral leaflets and the cords that tether them on the ventricle have become elongated. Cardiopulmonary bypass is initiated. The left atrium is opened and the mitral valve is exposed. Redundant leaflet tissue is excised and defects in the valve leaflets are closed with sutures. The cords are also shortened with sutures. Valve closure is assessed after the repair. The left atrium is closed and cardiopulmonary bypass is discontinued when heart function returns. Report 33426 if the mitral valve diameter is enlarged requiring placement of a prosthetic ring. Report 33427 if a more extensive repair, including transfer of cords from the posterior leaflet to the anterior leaflet, is performed. A prosthetic ring may be required with extensive reconstruction.

33430
Cardiopulmonary bypass is initiated. The left atrium is opened and the mitral valve is exposed. All leaflet tissue and its attached cords are cut out. Sutures are placed in the mitral annulus. The annulus is sized and an appropriate artificial valve is selected (either a totally mechanical valve or a valve with plastic supports and tissue leaflets). The sutures are passed through the sewing ring of the annulus and the sutures are tied down so the sewing ring is rightly adherent to the annulus. The left atrium is closed. Cardiopulmonary bypass is discontinued when heart function returns.

33460
Cardiopulmonary bypass is initiated. The right atrium is opened and the tricuspid valve is exposed. The valve tissue and its cords are completely excised. The right atrium is closed. Cardiopulmonary bypass is discontinued when heart function returns.

33463-33464
Cardiopulmonary bypass is initiated with venous uptake tubes in both of the caval veins. The right atrium is opened valvuloplasty of the tricuspid valve almost always requires nothing more than reducing the diameter of the tricuspid valve. A double purse string of sutures is place around the circumference of the valve and tightened to reduce the valve diameter. The right atrium is closed. Report 33464 if a stiff ring is used to the reduce the valve's diameter rather than purse strings.

33465
Cardiopulmonary bypass is initiated with venous uptake tubes in both caval veins. The right atrium is opened and the tricuspid valve leaflets are excised. A valve of an appropriate diameter is selected (usually it is a tissue/plastic valve, although a metal valve can also be used). Sutures are placed around the tricuspid valve annulus circumference. They are brought through the sewing ring of the valve. The valve is seated so that the sewing ring is resting on the annulus. The sutures are tied tightly. The right atrium is closed. Cardiopulmonary bypass is discontinued when heart function returns.

33468
In this anomaly, the tricuspid valve annulus is displaced onto the right ventricle, the right ventricle becomes atrophied and the valve leaflets become tethered to the wall of the ventricle. Cardiopulmonary bypass is initiated with venous uptake tubes in both caval veins. The right atrium is opened. The valve is

detached from the ventricular wall around its circumference. The edge of the cut valve is sewn circumferentially around the lone port by the true junction of the right atrium and right ventricle. The right atrium is closed. Cardiopulmonary bypass is discontinued when heart function returns.

33470-33471
Cardiopulmonary bypass is not required. The heart is exposed through the sternum. A U-stitch reinforced with small patches of Teflon felt is placed in the right ventricular outflow tract muscle. A hole is made in the center of this U-stitch. Dilators are passed through the hole and across the valve. Gradually larger dilators are passed until the valve opening is large enough. The last dilator is removed and the U-stitch is tied to stop any bleeding. The chest is closed. In this operation, the valve is dilated from below. Report 33471 if the U-stitch is placed in the pulmonary artery and the valve is dilated from above.

33472-33474
The heart is exposed through the sternum. Tourniquets are placed around the superior and inferior caval veins. These are tightened. A hole is made in the pulmonary artery and the pulmonary valve is cut opened through this hole. The hole in the pulmonary artery is closed and the tourniquets are released. Report 33474 if cardiopulmonary bypass with two venous uptake tubes is used.

33475
Cardiopulmonary bypass is initiated with venous uptake tubes in both caval veins. The pulmonary artery is opened and the pulmonary valve leaflets are cut out. Stitches are placed around the circumference of the pulmonary annulus and the valve is sized. An appropriate artificial valve is selected. The stitches are passed through the sewing ring of the valve. The sewing ring is seated against the valve annulus and the stitches are tied. The hole in the pulmonary artery is closed. Cardiopulmonary bypass is discontinued when heart function returns.

33476-33478
Cardiopulmonary bypass is initiated. The right ventricular infundibular muscle is opened and the obstructing muscle bands are cut out. The valve may also need to be opened. If so, the valve is cut open. The hole in the right ventricle is closed with a patch of pericardium. Cardiopulmonary bypass is discontinued when heart function returns. Report 33478 if the operation if performed with a gusset, with or without commissurotomy or infundibular resection.

33496
This procedure is typically performed to repair a normal artificial prosthetic valve that is malfunctioning due to leakage around the valve sewing ring or when a normal prosthetic valve is impeded by blood clot or growth of surrounding tissue (pannus) into the functioning part of the valve. The exposes the heart through the sternum. Cardiopulmonary bypass is initiated. The prosthetic valve is exposed (this is most likely a prosthetic valve in the aortic or mitral position) and the valve is repaired. Cardiopulmonary bypass is discontinued when heart function returns. The incision is closed: the bones with wires or sutures, the soft tissues with sutures.

33500-33501
Cardiopulmonary bypass is initiated. The site of the fistula has been previously determined by cardiac catheterization. The venous end of the fistula is ligated with sutures. Cardiopulmonary bypass is often discontinued. If the fistula is to a cardiac chamber, that chamber is opened and the chamber end of the fistula is closed with a stitch. Report 33501 if cardiopulmonary bypass is not used.

33502
The physician ligates an anomalous coronary artery arising from the pulmonary artery. Ligation of the anomalous coronary artery has a poor prognosis and may be performed as a temporary measure prior to creation of a double coronary artery system during a subsequent surgical intervention. The anomalous coronary artery is exposed at the site of origin in the pulmonary artery. A suture is placed around the artery and it is ligated.

33503-33504
The physician repairs an anomalous coronary artery arising from the pulmonary artery using a graft. The anomalous coronary artery is identified and detached. The subsequent hole in the pulmonary artery is sutured closed. An opening is made in the side of the aorta and the free end of the coronary artery is anastomosed to the aorta. Report 33504 if cardiopulmonary bypass is required. This procedure will most always require the cardiopulmonary bypass.

33505
The physician repairs an anomalous coronary artery arising from the pulmonary artery by construction of an intrapulmonary artery tunnel. Cardiopulmonary bypass is required. This operation is done in cases where the anomalous coronary artery is located far from the aorta on the left lateral side of the pulmonary artery. Openings are made in the aorta and the pulmonary artery at the level of the anomalous coronary artery where the vessels touch each other. The two open areas are sewn together to create a direct aortopulmonary opening. A flap of pulmonary artery wall is created with the anomalous coronary artery at one end. The flap is fashioned into a tunnel with the flap as one side of the tunnel, the back wall of the pulmonary artery as the other side of the tunnel, the hole between the aorta and pulmonary artery as one end, and the anomalous coronary artery as the other end. In this way, blood from the aorta is diverted into the anomalous coronary artery. The hole in the

pulmonary artery is closed. Cardiopulmonary bypass is discontinued when heart function returns.

33506

The physician repairs an anomalous coronary artery arising from the pulmonary artery by translocation from the pulmonary artery to the aorta. The anomalous coronary artery arising from the pulmonary artery is detached. The subsequent hole in the pulmonary artery is closed with stitches. An opening is created in the side of the aorta and the coronary artery is anastomosed into the opening. Cardiopulmonary bypass is almost always required for this operation.

33507

The physician repairs an anomalous coronary artery by unroofing or translocation. Common anomalies repaired using this technique include anomalous right coronary artery arising from the left coronary sinus, anomalous left coronary artery arising from the right coronary sinus, and anomalous coronary artery arising from a single ostia. Cardiopulmonary bypass is almost always required. The physician detaches the posterior commissure of the aortic valve. Unroofing of the intramural segment of the coronary artery is accomplished by excision of a triangular portion of the internal aortic wall. The coronary arteries are excised as a single disc and divided into two cuffs. An arterial switch is performed. The posterior commissure of the aortic valve is resuspended to a pericardial patch used to reconstruct the pulmonary artery sinus.

33508

A surgical vascular endoscopy is done that includes video-assisted harvesting of a vein for a coronary artery bypass. The physician makes a portal incision above the saphenous vein. The endoscope is inserted into the incision and visualization occurs on a video monitor. CO2 gas is insufflated through the endoscope and dissection is made to the vein. A cannula is inserted and a portion of the vein to be removed is released from the surrounding structures. The vein is tied off above and below the portion of the vein to be removed. The vein is removed through the harvesting cannula. The endoscope is removed and the incision is closed with sutures and Steri-strips. The portion of the vein removed is prepared for use in cardiac bypass surgery.

33510-33516

Cardiopulmonary bypass is initiated with a single, two-stage venous uptake tube. Saphenous vein is harvested from either leg. Vein may also be taken from the arm, the back of the leg, or from a cadaver. A clamp is placed on the aorta above the heart. Cold preserving solution is pumped through the coronary arteries to stop the heart. A point is chosen on the diseased coronary (arteries) beyond the area of disease and a longitudinal incision is cut in it. The proximal part (the part nearest the thigh) of the vein is trimmed to the same length as the cut in the coronary artery and is cleaned off. The end of the vein is sewn to the side of the coronary artery. A 3 mm to 6 mm hole is punched in the ascending aorta and the other end of the vein graft is sewn to this hole. The clamp on the aorta is released. Cardiopulmonary bypass is discontinued when heart function returns. Report 33511 if two coronary venous grafts are needed; report 33512 if three are needed; report 33513 if four are performed; report 33514 if five are performed; report 33516 if six or more are performed.

33517-33523

The physician initiates cardiopulmonary bypass with a single, two-stage venous uptake tube. The physician harvests saphenous vein from the legs. Other vein grafts may be obtained from the arms, backs of the legs, or cadavers (organ donors.) These sources are inferior to the saphenous vein. Arterial grafts may be obtained from the internal mammary artery (along the lateral side of the breastbone), the gastroepiploic artery (from the abdomen), the inferior epigastric artery (from the abdominal wall), or the radial artery (from the nondominant hand). The most commonly used vessel is the internal mammary artery. It is left connected at one end to the subclavian artery from which it arises. Report 33517 for a single vein graft, 33518 if two venous grafts are performed, 33519 if three venous grafts are performed, 33521 if four venous grafts are performed, 33522 if five venous grafts are performed, and 33523 if six or more venous grafts are performed.

33530

For descriptions of the actual therapeutic procedure to be performed, please see the description of that procedure. The breast bone must be split again. Because the heart is invariably tightly adherent to the underside of the sternum in a redo operation, a vibrating saw is used to cut through it. After the sternum is cut, its halves are gently retracted while the tissues stuck to its under surface are cut down. Once the sternum can be opened, the heart is exposed by cutting any chest tissues that have stuck to it since the last operation. It is usually necessary to initiate cardiopulmonary bypass before the heart is completely cleaned off.

33533-33536

Cardiopulmonary bypass is initiated with a single, two-stage venous uptake tube. Arterial grafts may be obtained from the internal mammary artery (along the lateral side of the breast bone), the gastroepiploic artery (from the abdomen), the inferior epigastric artery (from the abdominal wall), or the radial artery (from the non-dominant hand). The most commonly used vessel is the internal mammary artery. It is left connected at one end to the arm artery from which it arises. Report 33534 if two arterial grafts are placed; report 33535 if three are placed; report 33536 if four or more are placed.

33542

This operation is almost always done in conjunction with coronary artery bypass grafting. Prior to placing the bypass grafts, the aneurysm is opened and any clot is removed from the ventricle. The aneurysm is opened widely and excised or opened, but not excised. The hole created by opening the aneurysm is closed with sutures directly or with a patch of Gortex, for example, or Dacron sewn into the hole. All stitches are placed in healthy (not aneurysm) heart tissue and care is taken to avoid the coronary arteries.

33545

This operation is always done in conjunction with coronary artery bypass grafting. The heart muscle involved in the infarction extends from the septum onto the surface of the heart. The heart is opened through this dead muscle and all dead muscle on the surface of the heart is cut out as is all the dead muscle in the septum. The septum is reconstructed by sewing in a patch of Gortex, for example, or Dacron. The surface of the heart is closed directly with sutures or with a patch sewn over the hole.

33548

The physician performs a surgical ventricular restoration (SVR) procedure to treat congestive heart failure subsequent to a myocardial infarction that has caused scarring or aneurysm of the left ventricle resulting in an enlarged rounded heart. SVR restores the heart to a more normal size and shape thereby improving function. Cardiopulmonary bypass is initiated. The ventricle is collapsed. A small incision is made in the bottom of the left ventricle through the scar tissue. The heart is opened and the area between the scar and the good heart muscle is identified. Using a plastic model of the heart selected based on the body surface area of the patient, the physician reshapes the heart. Rather than closing the defect, the physician sutures a patch over the defect to restore the normal spherical shape of the heart.

33572

This operation is only done when a coronary artery is so full of disease along its length that a good site for sewing on the bypass graft cannot be found. Coronary artery bypass grafts are almost always done along with the end arterectomy. The coronary artery to be cleaned out is opened along its length for a distance greater than that usually opened for a bypass alone, sometimes along its length. The plaque within the artery is separated from the outer layer of the arterial wall with a tool designed for the purpose. The plaque is removed from as much of the artery as is possible. A bypass graft is usually sewn to part of the hole left in the coronary. The rest of the hole is closed directly with suture or a patch of opened vein graft is laid over the open artery and sewn to the coronary artery wall to close the hole.

33600-33602

Cardiopulmonary bypass is initiated. The appropriate heart chamber (right atrium for the tricuspid valve; left atrium for the mitral valve) is opened and the valve is assessed. The hole in the leaflet is cleaned of any infection. If it can be closed directly without distorting the valve significantly, suture alone is used. If the hole is large, it is closed with a patch made of pericardium. The open heart chamber is closed and cardiopulmonary bypass is discontinued when heart function returns. Report 33602 if the pulmonary artery or aorta are opened to gain access to the valve.

33606

The heart is exposed by dividing the breast bone longitudinally. Mechanical, extra corporeal circulation is established and the heart is stopped (cardiopulmonary bypass). The pulmonary artery is cut just before it divides into right and left branches. The pulmonary artery end is connected to the side of the ascending aorta. A piece of Dacron graft is used to construct this connection. This allows the single ventricle to pump blood to the body.

33608

Mechanical, extra corporeal circulation is established and the heart is stopped (cardiopulmonary bypass). A hole is made in the pulmonary artery. This last hole is enlarged to cross any areas of narrowing. A cadaver ascending aorta is trimmed to the right length. A tube of artery or Dacron is sewn to the valve end of the cadaver aorta. The cadaver artery is connected to the hole in the pulmonary artery. The tube of aorta or Dacron is sewn to the hole in the ventricle to close the hole and allow blood to flow through the new valved tube that now connects the ventricle to the pulmonary artery.

33610

The heart is exposed by dividing the breast bone longitudinally. Mechanical, extra corporeal circulation is established and the heart is stopped (cardiopulmonary bypass). The heart is opened and the hole in the wall between the two ventricles is enlarged so that blood will flow freely across it. A baffle is placed to direct blood that flows across the enlarged ventricular septal defect out the aorta.

33611-33612

Cardiopulmonary bypass is initiated. A hole is made in the right ventricle free wall. This exposes the hole between the right and left ventricles. A patch of pericardium or Dacron is sewn in place to block the hole and directs blood ejected from the left ventricle (i.e. blood coming from the lungs) out the aorta. If the pulmonary artery is of adequate size, blood will flow from the right ventricle to the lungs. If it is inadequate or if the valve does not open, a conduit containing a valve (natural or artificial) is sewn to the hole in the right ventricle free wall. The far end of the conduit is attached to the pulmonary artery. This will allow blood to be pumped from the right ventricle to the lungs. Report 33612 if the obstructing muscles bundles in the outflow part of the right ventricle are excised when the heart is open.

33615

The right pulmonary artery (or left in situs inverses) is exposed from the main pulmonary trunk to the hilum of the lung. The superior vena cava is detached from the right atrium. The atrial hole is closed. A hole is made in the top part of the pulmonary artery and the cut end of the superior vena cava is connected to the hole in the pulmonary artery. Pulmonary blood flow comes directly from the venous system and bypasses the heart. Later the process is completed by performing a Fontan operation.

33617

This operation is usually considered to be the second stage of a Glen Repair. Cardiopulmonary bypass with or without circulatory arrest is required. In this operation blood flow is directed from the inferior caval vein, through a tunnel created inside the right atrium to the pulmonary artery. All systemic venous return is diverted away from the heart and directly into the pulmonary circulation. The right atrium is widely opened. A large patch of pericardium or Dacron is used in for one wall of the "tunnel." The lateral wall of the right atrium forms the other half of the "tunnel." The tunnel leads from the inferior caval vein, where it joins the right atrium, to the undersurface of the pulmonary artery. The "mouth" of the tunnel is connected to a hole on the undersurface of the pulmonary artery. Previously, or at the same time, the superior caval vein will already have been directly connected to the upper surface of the pulmonary artery.

33619

Cardiopulmonary bypass and circulatory arrest are required. After the bypass pump is turned off the small aorta is opened on the inner surface of its arch up to the point where the aortic diameter becomes "normal." The pulmonary artery is removed and its connection to the branched pulmonary artery is closed with a patch. A large, rectangular patch of pericardium is used to enlarge the small aorta. The pulmonary valve becomes the systemic arterial valve of the heart and is encircled by the large patch that becomes shaped like a tube as it is sewn along either side of the small ascending aorta and arch that have been opened longitudinally. The coronary arteries are small and still originate in the root of the abnormal aorta.

33641

Cardiopulmonary bypass is necessary. Two venous tubes are placed for the bypass machine—one draining the superior caval vein and the one draining the inferior caval vein. The right atrium is isolated by the putting tourniquets around the superior vena cava and inferior vena cava and their corresponding tubes. The right atrium is opened and the size and location of the arterial septal defect are assessed. If it is small enough or if the atrial septal tissue is sufficiently redundant, the defect is closed primarily with suture. If not, a patch of pericardium or Dacron is sewn to the edge of the defect to close it.

33645

The right atrium is opened and the size and location of the congenital sinus venosus defect is assessed. If it is small enough or if the atrial septal tissue is sufficiently redundant, the defect is closed primarily with suture. If not, a patch of pericardium or Dacron is sewn to the edge of the defect to close it. Care is taken to place the patch so that all pulmonary veins remain patent and there is no obstruction of the superior vena cava, right ventricle, or pulmonary veins by the patch.

33647

Cardiopulmonary bypass is established with the venous uptake tubes in both the superior and inferior caval veins. A hole in the right atrium or, if needed, a hole in one of the ventricles is made. The hole in the ventricle is made in the area of scar (if the ventricular septal defect is due to ischemia) or in the anterior part of the right ventricle (if the ventricular septal defect is congenital). All dead heart muscles is cut out (in ischemic ventricular septal defect) and the ventricular septal defect is closed with a patch of Dacron or pericardium. The hole in the atrium or ventricle is closed. Cardiopulmonary bypass is discontinued when heart function is restored.

33660

Cardiopulmonary bypass is established using venous uptake tubes in both the superior and inferior caval veins. The right atrium is opened. A radially oriented cleft or division in the anterior leaflet of the mitral valve is closed with interrupted sutures. Care is taken to assure that the valve closes properly after it is repaired. There is a line of denser valve tissue marking the anatomic line between the two AV valves. The ventricular septal defect is obliterated by sewing this line to the top of the septal muscle. The arterial septal defect is closed with a patch of Dacron or pericardium. The right atrium is closed and cardiopulmonary bypass is discontinued after heart function is restored.

33665

Cardiopulmonary bypass is established with the venous uptake tubes in both the superior and inferior caval veins. A hole in the right atrium or, if needed, a hole in one of the ventricles is made. The hole in the ventricle is made in the area of scar tissue (if the ventricular septal defect is due to ischemia) or in the anterior part of the right ventricle (if the ventricular septal defect is congenital). The AV valve anatomy can be highly variable, ranging from normal mitral and tricuspid anatomy with a subvalvular ventricular septal defect to grossly abnormal AV valve leaflet with two separate valves present separated by a line of tissue. The AV valves are repaired. Repair is all that is done if valvular competence can be restored to the left AV valve. If not, the valve is replaced with a mechanical valve on a tissue valve.

33670

Cardiopulmonary pulmonary bypass is established using venous uptake tubes in both the superior and inferior caval veins. The right atrium is opened. A radially oriented cleft or division in the anterior leaflet of the mitral value is closed with the interrupted sutures. Care is taken to assure that the valve closes properly after it is repaired. There is a raphe or line of denser value tissue marking the anatomic line between the two AR values. The ventricular septal defect is obliterated by sewing this line to the top of the septal muscle. The atrial septal defect is closed with a patch of Dacron or pericardium. The right atrium is closed and cardiopulmonary pulmonary bypass discontinued after heart function is restored. An opening in the right atrium is made. The competency of the single AV valve is assessed as is the imaginary line where the plane extending upward from the ventricular septal defect intersects the AV valve. The AV valve leaflets are divided along this line. The ventricular septal defect patch is placed. The valve leaflets are resuspended by sewing them to the ventricular septal defect patch. The competency of the valves is assessed. The atrial septal defect is closed with a patch sewn to the top of the ventricular septal defect patch or an extension of the ventricular septal defect patch is used to close the atrial septal defect (single patch technique). The hole in the right atrium is closed. Cardiopulmonary bypass is discontinued when cardiac function has returned.

33675

The physician repairs multiple defects in the tissue separating the right and left ventricles of the heart in an open heart procedure. Cardiopulmonary bypass is established with tubes in both the caval veins. The ventricular septal defects can almost always be accessed and repaired through an incision in the right atrium. Each ventricular septal defect is usually repaired with a patch of Dacron or pericardium, but may be closed using only sutures. The septal defects may be repaired with a pair of patches, one in each ventricle. After the ventricular septal defects are repaired, the access incision in the right atrium is closed with sutures. Cardiopulmonary bypass is discontinued when heart function returns. The chest incision is repaired.

33676

The physician repairs multiple defects in the tissue separating the right and left ventricles of the heart, and surgically releases fused leaflets within the pulmonary valve or resects the anterosuperior portion of the right ventricle (infundibulum). The heart is accessed through a midline sternal incision. Cardiopulmonary bypass is established with tubes in both the caval veins. The septal and ventricular defects can almost always be accessed and repaired through an incision in the right atrium, and the pulmonary valve is usually accessed through an incision in the pulmonary artery. Each ventricular septal defect is usually repaired with a patch of Dacron or pericardium, but may be closed using only sutures. The septal defects alternately may be repaired with a pair of patches, applied on each side of the septum. Fused pulmonary valve leaflets are incised and any abnormal tethering of the leaflets to the arterial wall is released. For infundibular resection, obstructions within the right ventricle are excised and the ventricle repaired. After repairs are complete, the access incision in the right atrium is closed with sutures. Cardiopulmonary bypass is discontinued when heart function returns. The chest incision is repaired.

33677

The physician repairs multiple defects in the tissue separating the right and left ventricles of the heart, removes a previously placed band from the pulmonary artery, and may place a gusset. The heart is accessed through a midline sternal incision. The physician gains access to the mediastinum through an incision through the sternum (median sternotomy). The physician places cardiopulmonary bypass catheters through incisions in the low inferior vena cava, the superior vena cava, and aorta or femoral artery. The physician stops the heart by infusing cardioplegia solution into the coronary circulation. The septal defects can almost always be accessed and repaired through an incision in the right atrium, and the pulmonary valve is usually accessed through an incision in the pulmonary artery. Each ventricular septal defect is usually repaired with a patch of Dacron or pericardium, but may be closed using only sutures. The septal defects alternately may be repaired with a pair of patches applied on each side of the septum. The physician removes the pulmonary artery band (placed during a previous surgery) and dilates the pulmonary artery to normal size. A triangular patch (gusset) may be sutured into the incised pulmonary artery to enlarge its circumference. The physician closes the cardiac incisions, takes the patient off cardiopulmonary bypass, closes the remaining surgical incisions, and dresses the sternal or chest wall wound. The physician may leave chest tubes and/or a mediastinal drainage tube in place following the procedure.

33681

The physician repairs a solitary defect in the tissue separating the right and left ventricles of the heart in an open heart procedure. Cardiopulmonary bypass is established with tubes in both the caval veins. The ventricular septal defect can almost always be accessed and repaired through an incision in the right atrium, except in the case of a supracristal ventricular septal defect, in which the ventricle is higher in the outflow part of the right ventricle. This type of ventricular septal defect is most often accessed and repaired through an incision in the pulmonary artery. All types of ventricular septal defects can be accessed and repaired through an incision in the muscle of the right ventricle, but this causes more damage and is avoided if possible. The ventricular septal defect is usually repaired with a patch of Dacron or pericardium, but may be closed using only sutures. After the ventricular septal defect is closed, the hole that has been created in the right atrium, right ventricle, or pulmonary artery is closed. The chest incision is repaired. Cardiopulmonary bypass is discontinued when heart function returns.

33684
The physician repairs a solitary defect in the tissue separating the right and left ventricles of the heart in an open heart procedure in conjunction with a pulmonary valvotomy or infundibular resection. Cardiopulmonary bypass is established with venous uptake tubes in both the caval veins. Prior to surgery, it is established by echocardiography, cardiac catheterization, or both that the diameter of the tricuspid valve is large enough to permit a normal cardiac output. If not, the operation is combined with a modified Blalock-Taussig shunt. The right ventricle or pulmonary artery is opened. Through either opening, the infundibular muscle blocking blood flow to the pulmonary artery can be cut out and cuts can be made in the pulmonary valve to reduce the restriction to blood flow that it presents. A singular ventricular septal defect is closed through either of these incisions, if possible. If it is not possible to close the ventricular septal defect with the exposure thus provided, the right atrium is opened and the ventricular septal defect closed. A patch is almost always used. All holes in the heart are closed. Cardiopulmonary bypass is discontinued when heart function is restored.

33688
The physician repairs a solitary defect in the tissue separating the right and left ventricles of the heart in an open heart procedure in conjunction with removal of a previously placed pulmonary artery (PA) band. The patient is prepared for cardiopulmonary bypass, but it is not established yet. The previously placed pulmonary artery band is dissected out and removed. Stenosis at the site of the pulmonary artery band is assessed before and after band removal with a pressure transducer connected to a needle probe that measures any pressure drop across the area of narrowing. Cardiopulmonary bypass is then established and the ventricular septal defect is repaired. If pulmonary artery pressures proximal to the band site remain high after band removal and ventricular septal defect closure or if the surgeon feels the residual stenosis is too tight, cardiopulmonary bypass is restarted. The surgeon then removes the stenosed segment of pulmonary artery followed by a primary repair or the surgeon makes an incision in the pulmonary artery across the area of narrowing and closes the defect with a patch graft.

Heart function is restored and cardiopulmonary bypass is discontinued.

33690
Cardiopulmonary bypass is not required. The pulmonary artery is exposed through a median sternotomy or left thoracotomy. A band of heavy Dacron suture or tape is place around the base of the pulmonary artery. Once the PA pressure distal to the band is less than half of the systemic pressure and the patients arterial saturation is greater than 70 percent, the band is tight enough, but not too tight. The incision is closed.

33692
Repair of this defect assumes that the pulmonary artery annulus and right ventricular outflow tract are of adequate size to permit normal pulmonary blood flow. Cardiopulmonary bypass is required.

33694
In this defect the pulmonary valve annulus and/or the right ventricular infundibulum are too small to allow normal pulmonary blood flow. The ventricular septal defect is closed. Cardiopulmonary bypass is required. A longitudinal incision is made in the PA and carried proximally across the pulmonary valve annulus and onto the muscles of the right ventricular outflow tract. Infundibular muscle is removed if necessary. The defect is closed with a patch of pericardium. Cardiopulmonary bypass is discontinued when heart function returns.

33697
The physician completely repairs tetralogy of Fallot with pulmonary atresia, including construction of a conduit from the right ventricle to the pulmonary artery and closure of the ventricular septal defect. Cardiopulmonary bypass is required. A hole is made in the right ventricle and any muscular obstruction in the outflow tract of the right ventricle is removed. The pulmonary artery or its branches are opened longitudinally until normal-sized vessels are encountered. The ventricular septal defect is closed. An aortic graft from an organ donor is trimmed to form a patch over the opened pulmonary artery. Any excess artery from the donor graft or a patch of pericardium or Dacron is sewn to the graft below the valve to use as a secondary patch for closing the hole in the right ventricle. The graft valve becomes the new pulmonary valve. After the patches and graft are sewn in place and heart function returns, cardiopulmonary bypass is stopped.

33702-33710
Cardiopulmonary bypass is required. After the heart is stopped, the aorta is opened and the fistula is identified. It is closed with a patch of pericardium. Any aorta valve incompetence is repaired by shortening the redundant valve leaflet diameter with stitches that reef in its free edge. The hole in the aorta is closed. Report

Cardiovascular

33710 if the sinus of Valsalva fistula is closed through the right atrium or through as incision in the aorta.

33720
Cardiopulmonary bypass is required. The aorta is opened after the heart has stopped. Thrombus (clot) in the aneurysm is removed. The neck of the aneurysm is closed with stitches. The aortic valve is usually incompetent. If the aortic annulus is sufficiently dilated by the aneurysm the aortic valve may need to be replaced with a mechanical aortic valve, a bio-mechanical valve or a tissue valve from an organ donor. After the valve is repaired or replaced, the aorta is closed. Cardiopulmonary bypass is discontinued after heart function returns.

33722
The physician closes a previously formed aortic-left ventricular tunnel. The physician performs a midline sternotomy, incising the skin, fascia, muscles, and sternum. The pericardium is incised and lines are placed for cardiopulmonary bypass. When bypass is established, the tunnel is isolated and ligated. The cardiac incision is closed. The pericardium is repaired loosely, leaving gaps for blood and fluid to drain into the pleural space. The sternum is reanastomosed with sternal wires and the skin is sutured in layers.

33724
The physician repairs an isolated partial anomalous venous return (scimitar syndrome) using one of two open techniques. Scimitar syndrome describes a congenital condition in which an aberrant vessel connects the pulmonary vein in the right lung to the inferior vena cava. It can be diagnosed in infancy through adulthood, and symptoms occurring in infancy suggest a more severe form of the disease. Scimitar syndrome is so named because the aberrant vein casts a shadow shaped like a curved Turkish sword, a scimitar, upon x-ray. A midline sternotomy is performed. In one technique, a long pericardial patch graft is used to divert the anomalous pulmonary venous drainage from the inferior vena cava into the left atrium. In the second technique, the anomalous pulmonary vein is divided off the inferior vena cava and reimplanted into the posterior wall of the right atrium. A short pericardial baffle is used to divert flow to the left atrium through an atrial septal defect. Grafts may be required to enlarge remaining vessels. In some cases, a separately reported right pneumonectomy is performed.

33726
The physician gains access to the heart through a midline sternotomy. The physician places cardiopulmonary bypass catheters usually through incisions in the right atrial appendage and aorta or femoral artery. The physician stops the heart by infusing cardioplegia solution into the coronary circulation. Either atria may be incised for exploration to locate and better visualize the defect. The blocked pulmonary vein is opened along its length. The inner layer of the artery is removed. The outer layer of the artery is closed with suture directly or with a patch of pericardium, saphenous vein, or Dacron.

33730
The physician performs a complete repair of total anomalous pulmonary venous return (TAPVR), a rare congenital defect in which all four pulmonary veins do not connect normally to the left atrium, but rather drain to the right atrium by way of an abnormal connection. Via a midline sternotomy, the physician exposes the heart. Cardiopulmonary bypass is initiated. The abnormal veins are rerouted to the left atrium, most often by connecting them directly to the back wall of the atrium. Any abnormal routes for pulmonary venous drainage are tied off, and any existing atrial septal defect is closed. The heart is restarted, cardiopulmonary bypass is discontinued, and the sternotomy is closed.

33732
This lesion is frequently considered to be related to TAPVR, but it is distinctly different. In this anomaly, there is a wall subdividing the left atrium between the pulmonary veins and the mitral valve. This restricts blood flow to the left ventricle and therefore to the rest of the body. Cardiopulmonary bypass is readied. The left atrium is opened and the membrane is cut out. The left atrium is closed. Cardiopulmonary bypass is discontinued when heart function returns.

33735
This procedure is of historical interest only. The procedure requires a median sternal opening or a right chest opening. A purse string is placed in the right atrial appendage and the appendage is opened in the middle of the purse string. A finger or a dilating tool is passed through the hole in the atrium and the wall between the right and left atria is torn open. The dilating instrument is removed and the purse string is tied to stop the bleeding.

33736-33737
This procedure is largely of historical interest. In most pediatric cardiac surgery centers, it has been supplanted by balloon dilation of a naturally occurring hole in the wall between the atrial chambers. No incision is needed for balloon dilation. Operative septostomy/septectomy requires cardiopulmonary bypass with venous uptake tubes in both caval veins. The right atrium is opened and the thin part of the wall between the right and left atria is cut out or opened widely. The goal is to allow free mixing of the blood from the right and left atria. Cardiopulmonary bypass is discontinued when heart function returns. Report 33737 if tourniquets are placed around the caval veins and the patient is placed head down so no air entering the right atrium crosses the wall between the right and left atria.

33750
In its unmodified form, this operation involves dividing the left subclavian artery, tying off the end of the artery going to the arm, and creating a connection between the end of this artery coming from the heart and the side of the pulmonary artery. The difficulty with this operation is making the connection to the pulmonary artery exactly the right size to supply adequate, but not excessive blood flow to the lungs. Instead, a modified version of the operation is usually performed. The artery to the arm is not divided. Instead, one end of a 3 mm to 5 mm diameter tube of Gortex is sewn to the side of the artery to the arm and the other end is sewn to the side of the pulmonary artery. The size of the tube determines the amount of blood flow to the lungs. Cardiopulmonary bypass is not required. The ductus arteriosus (a connection between the aorta and pulmonary artery that has been supplying blood to the lungs, but usually closes at birth) is tied off.

33755
This procedure requires cardiopulmonary bypass. It is designed to allow adequate blood flow to the lungs. After cardiopulmonary bypass is initiated, the aorta is occluded above the heart. Holes are made in parts of the aorta and pulmonary artery that are next to each other. The holes are sewn together. It is difficult to accurately control the diameter of the resulting connection and the resulting flow of blood into the lungs. Cardiopulmonary bypass is discontinued when heart function returns. The ductus arteriosus (a connection between the aorta and pulmonary artery that has been supplying blood to the lungs, but usually closes at birth) is tied off.

33762
The operation is performed through the left side of the chest. Cardiopulmonary bypass is not required. One end of a 3 mm to 5 mm diameter tube made of PTFE (e.g., Gortex) is sewn to the side of the descending aorta and the other end is sewn to some part of the pulmonary artery. The ductus arteriosus (a connection between the aorta and pulmonary artery that has been supplying blood to the lungs, but usually closes at birth) is tied off.

33764
The operation is done ether through an incision in the middle of the breast bone or through an incision in the left chest. Cardiopulmonary bypass is usually not required. One end of a 3 mm to 5 mm diameter tube made of Gortex is sewn to the side of the ascending aorta and the other end is sewn to some part of the pulmonary artery. The ductus arteriosus (a connection between the aorta and pulmonary artery that has been supplying blood to the lungs, but usually closes at birth) is tied off.

33766
This operation is performed when there is an irreparable obstruction to blood flow through the right side of the heart. It is usually done as a prelude to a bidirectional or bilateral Glen procedure, which is usually a prelude to a Fontan procedure. Cardiopulmonary bypass is usually required. The right (or the persistent left) superior caval vein is occluded and its connection with the heart is divided. The heart end of the superior caval vein is closed. The free end of the superior caval vein is sewn to the side of the corresponding pulmonary artery. It is assumed that the corresponding pulmonary artery is isolated from the opposite lung congenitally or surgically. The goal is to permit blood to flow directly from the superior caval vein to the lungs, thereby bypassing the right side of the heart.

33767
For this procedure, it is assumed that all the pulmonary arteries from both lungs communicate freely. Cardiopulmonary bypass is required. Circulatory arrest and deep cooling of the body are usually employed. The main pulmonary artery is often tied off. The superior caval vein is detached from its connection to the right atrium. The hole left in the right atrium is closed with sutures. The free end of the superior caval vein is sewn to a hole in the side of the pulmonary artery. In this way, blood can flow to the lungs without passing through the right side of the heart. This operation is usually done as a prelude to a Fontan procedure.

33768
A cavopulmonary anastomosis of an anomalous left superior vena cava is performed in conjunction with separately reportable repair of other cardiac anomalies (e.g., bidirectional Glenn procedure, modified Fontan procedure, outflow tract augmentation). Cavopulmonary anastomosis is required when a left superior vena cava is present. The left superior vena cava is dissected free. The left superior vena cava is divided and anastomosed in end-to-side fashion to the left pulmonary artery.

33770
The physician gains access to the mediastinum through an incision through the sternum (median sternotomy). The physician places cardiopulmonary bypass catheters usually through incisions in the right atrial appendage and aorta or femoral artery. The physician stops the heart by infusing cardioplegia solution into the coronary circulation. The physician applies a large Dacron patch to direct oxygenated blood from the left ventricle through the large ventricular septal defect into the aortic valve and ascending aorta. The physician ligates the proximal main pulmonary artery or oversews the pulmonic valve. The physician places a fabric conduit or a human cadaveric homograft to direct unoxygenated blood from the right ventricle to

the branch pulmonary arteries. The physician may place a bioprosthetic valve in the pulmonary outflow conduit if the pulmonary vascular resistance is elevated. The physician closes the cardiac incisions, takes the patient off cardiopulmonary bypass, closes the remaining surgical incisions and dresses the sternal or chest wall wound. The physician may leave chest tubes and/or a mediastinal drainage tube in place following the procedure.

33771

The physician gains access to the mediastinum through an incision through the sternum (median sternotomy). The physician places cardiopulmonary bypass catheters usually through incisions in the right atrial appendage and aorta or femoral artery. The physician stops the heart by infusing cardioplegia solution into the coronary circulation. The physician enlarges the ventricular septal defect anteriorly to avoid damage to the conduction bundles. The physician applies a large Dacron patch to form a tunnel from the left ventricle through the large ventricular septal defect into the aortic valve and ascending aorta. The physician ligates the proximal main pulmonary artery or oversews the pulmonic valve. The physician places a fabric conduit to direct right ventricular flow to the pulmonary artery. The physician may place a bioprosthetic valve in the pulmonary outflow conduit if the pulmonary vascular resistance is elevated. The physician closes the cardiac incisions, takes the patient off cardiopulmonary bypass, closes the remaining surgical incisions and dresses the sternal or chest wall wound. The physician may leave chest tubes and/or a mediastinal drainage tube in place following the procedure.

33774

The physician gains access to the mediastinum through an incision through the sternum (median sternotomy). The physician places cardiopulmonary bypass catheters through incisions in the low inferior vena cava, the superior vena cava, and aorta or femoral artery. The physician stops the heart by infusing cardioplegia solution into the coronary circulation. The physician excises the interatrial septum. The physician sews baffle material (pericardium or Dacron) to direct blood from the pulmonary veins to the right ventricle and the systemic venous drainage to the left ventricle. The physician may enlarge the pulmonary venous chamber with a woven Dacron or pericardial patch. The physician closes the cardiac incisions, takes the patient off cardiopulmonary bypass, closes the remaining surgical incisions and dresses the sternal or chest wall wound. The physician may leave chest tubes and/or a mediastinal drainage tube in place following the procedure.

33775

The physician gains access to the mediastinum through an incision through the sternum (median sternotomy). The physician places cardiopulmonary bypass catheters through incisions in the low inferior vena cava, the superior vena cava, and aorta or femoral artery. The physician stops the heart by infusing cardioplegia solution into the coronary circulation. The physician removes the pulmonary artery band (placed during a previous surgery) and dilates the pulmonary artery to normal size. If this is not possible, the physician removes the pulmonary band and constricted area of pulmonary artery, and applies a woven Dacron patch over the hole. The physician excises the interatrial septum. The physician sews baffle material (pericardium or Dacron) to direct blood from the pulmonary veins to the right ventricle and the systemic venous drainage to the left ventricle. The physician may enlarge the pulmonary venous chamber with a woven Dacron or pericardial patch. The physician closes the cardiac incisions, takes the patient off cardiopulmonary bypass, closes the remaining surgical incisions and dresses the sternal or chest wall wound. The physician may leave chest tubes and/or a mediastinal drainage tube in place following the procedure.

33776

The physician gains access to the mediastinum through an incision through the sternum (median sternotomy). The physician places cardiopulmonary bypass catheters through incisions in the low inferior vena cava, the superior vena cava, and aorta or femoral artery. The physician stops the heart by infusing cardioplegia solution into the coronary circulation. The physician closes the ventricular septal defect, usually with a Dacron patch. The physician excises the interatrial septum. The physician sews baffle material (pericardium or Dacron) to direct blood from the pulmonary veins to the right ventricle and the systemic venous drainage to the left ventricle. The physician may enlarge the pulmonary venous chamber with a woven Dacron or pericardial patch. The physician closes the cardiac incisions, takes the patient off cardiopulmonary bypass, closes the remaining surgical incisions and dresses the sternal or chest wall wound. The physician may leave chest tubes and/or a mediastinal drainage tube in place following the procedure.

33777

The physician gains access to the mediastinum through an incision through the sternum (median sternotomy). The physician places cardiopulmonary bypass catheters (through incisions in the low inferior vena cava, the superior vena cava, and aorta or femoral artery). The physician stops the heart by infusing cardioplegia solution into the coronary circulation. The physician makes an incision in the right ventricular outflow tract, resects the fibrous muscular tissue causing the subpulmonic obstruction, and sews the ventriculotomy closed. The physician excises the interatrial septum. The physician sews baffle material (pericardium or Dacron) to direct blood from the pulmonary veins to the right ventricle and the systemic venous drainage to the left ventricle. The physician may enlarge the pulmonary venous chamber with a woven Dacron or pericardial patch. The physician closes the cardiac incisions, takes the patient off cardiopulmonary bypass, closes the remaining surgical incisions and dresses the sternal or chest wall wound. The physician may leave chest tubes and/or a mediastinal drainage tube in place following the procedure.

33778

The physician gains access to the mediastinum through an incision through the sternum (median sternotomy). The physician places cardiopulmonary bypass catheters through incisions in the low inferior vena cava, the superior vena cava, and aorta or femoral artery. The physician stops the heart by infusing cardioplegia solution into the coronary circulation. The physician removes the coronary ostia from the aortic root and sews them into the root of the pulmonary trunk. The pulmonary trunk and aortic root are each transected and interchanged to direct blood from the pulmonary veins through the left ventricle to the aorta, and the systemic venous drainage to the pulmonary trunk via the right ventricle. The physician closes the cardiac incisions, takes the patient off cardiopulmonary bypass, closes the remaining surgical incisions and dresses the sternal or chest wall wound. The physician may leave chest tubes and/or a mediastinal drainage tube in place following the procedure.

33779

The physician gains access to the mediastinum through an incision through the sternum (median sternotomy). The physician places cardiopulmonary bypass catheters through incisions in the low inferior vena cava, the superior vena cava, and aorta or femoral artery. The physician stops the heart by infusing cardioplegia solution into the coronary circulation. The physician removes the pulmonary artery band placed during a previous surgery and dilates the pulmonary artery to normal size. If this is not possible, the physician removes the pulmonary band and constricted area of pulmonary artery, and applies a woven Dacron patch over the hole. The physician removes the coronary ostia from the aortic root and sews them into the root of the pulmonary trunk. The pulmonary trunk and aortic root are each transected and interchanged to direct blood from the pulmonary veins through the left ventricle to the aorta, and the systemic venous drainage to the pulmonary trunk via the right ventricle. The physician closes the cardiac incisions, takes the patient off cardiopulmonary bypass, closes the remaining surgical incisions and dresses the sternal or chest wall wound. The physician may leave chest tubes and/or a mediastinal drainage tube in place following the procedure.

33780

The physician gains access to the mediastinum through an incision through the sternum (median sternotomy). The physician places cardiopulmonary bypass catheters through incisions in the low inferior vena cava, the superior vena cava, and aorta or femoral artery. The physician stops the heart by infusing cardioplegia solution into the coronary circulation. The physician removes the coronary ostia from the aortic root and sews them into the root of the pulmonary trunk. The pulmonary trunk and aortic root are each transected and interchanged to direct blood from the pulmonary veins through the left ventricle to the aorta, and the systemic venous drainage to the pulmonary trunk via the right ventricle. The physician closes the ventricular septal defect, usually with a Dacron patch. The physician closes the cardiac incisions, takes the patient off cardiopulmonary bypass, closes the remaining surgical incisions and dresses the sternal or chest wall wound. The physician may leave chest tubes and/or a mediastinal drainage tube in place following the procedure.

33781

The physician gains access to the mediastinum through an incision through the sternum (median sternotomy). The physician places cardiopulmonary bypass catheters through incisions in the low inferior vena cava, the superior vena cava, and aorta or femoral artery. The physician stops the heart by infusing cardioplegia solution into the coronary circulation. The physician removes the coronary ostia from the aortic root and sews them into the root of the pulmonary trunk. The pulmonary trunk and aortic root are each transected and interchanged to direct blood from the pulmonary veins through the left ventricle to the aorta, and the systemic venous drainage to the pulmonary trunk via the right ventricle. The physician makes an incision in the right ventricular outflow tract, resects the fibrous muscular tissue causing the subpulmonic obstruction, and sews the ventriculotomy closed. The physician closes the cardiac incisions, takes the patient off cardiopulmonary bypass, closes the remaining surgical incisions and dresses the sternal or chest wall wound. The physician may leave chest tubes and/or a mediastinal drainage tube in place following the procedure.

33782-33783

The physician repairs anomalies of ventriculoarterial connection, ventricular septal defect (VSD), and pulmonary outflow tract obstruction (stenosis) in the Nikaidoh procedure. A median sternotomy incision is made and cardiopulmonary bypass is initiated. The physician may harvest a piece of pericardium to be used in the reconstruction of the right ventricular outflow tract, and mobilizes the branch pulmonary arteries. The physician harvests the aortic root from the right ventricle, with coronary arteries attached. The outlet septum is divided and the physician excises the pulmonary valve. The left ventricular outflow tract is reconstructed with the posteriorly translocated aortic root and the VSD patch. Using the pericardial patch, the physician reconstructs the right ventricular outflow tract. Report 33782 if no reimplantation of the coronary ostium is performed and 33783 if the physician reimplants one or both coronary ostia.

33786
The physician gains access to the mediastinum through an incision through the sternum (median sternotomy). The physician places cardiopulmonary bypass catheters usually through incisions in the right atrial appendage and aorta or femoral artery. The physician stops the heart by infusing cardioplegia solution into the coronary circulation. The physician applies a large Dacron patch to direct oxygenated blood from the left ventricle through the large ventricular septal defect into the aortic valve and ascending aorta. The physician ligates the proximal main pulmonary artery or oversews the pulmonic valve. The physician places a fabric conduit or a human cadaveric homograft to direct unoxygenated blood from the right ventricle to the branch pulmonary arteries after removing them from their origin(s) at the truncal vessel. The physician sews a pericardial patch in place to close the defect(s) in the truncal vessel. The physician may place a bioprosthetic valve in the pulmonary outflow conduit if the pulmonary vascular resistance is elevated. The physician closes the cardiac incisions, takes the patient off cardiopulmonary bypass, closes the remaining surgical incisions and dresses the sternal or chest wall wound. The physician may leave chest tubes and/or a mediastinal drainage tube in place following the procedure.

33788
The physician gains access to the mediastinum through an incision through the sternum (median sternotomy). The physician places cardiopulmonary bypass catheters usually through incisions in the right atrial appendage and aorta or femoral artery. The physician stops the heart by infusing cardioplegia solution into the coronary circulation. The physician identifies the coronary artery anomaly and reattaches the unperfused pulmonary artery to the pulmonic outflow tract, directly or using Dacron graft. The physician ligates the patent ductus arteriosus, if present. The physician closes the cardiac incisions, takes the patient off cardiopulmonary bypass, closes the remaining surgical incisions and dresses the sternal or chest wall wound. The physician may leave chest tubes and/or a mediastinal drainage tube in place following the procedure.

33800
The physician performs a right lateral thoracotomy or, sometimes, a midline sternotomy and identifies the ascending aorta. The physician isolates and removes the thymus to allow the ascending aorta to be mobilized and pulled forward. The physician sutures the adventitia of the ascending aorta and base of the innominate artery to the periosteum of the posterior aspect of the sternum or anterior rib. The physician may perform a similar operation on descending aorta, depending upon the site of tracheomalacia. The physician closes the thoracotomy or sternotomy, leaving chest or mediastinal tubes in place.

33802-33803
The physician gains access to the mediastinum through an incision through the left chest (posterolateral thoracotomy). The physician identifies the two aortic arches and occludes the smaller left arch with vascular clamps. The physician divides the arch and oversews and possibly ligates the divided ends. The physician dissects away the stumps of the divided left arch and frees them from their mediastinal attachments. The physician attaches traction sutures to the ligated stumps and to the endothoracic fascia anteriorly and posteriorly to minimize obstruction to the esophagus and trachea. The physician closes the remaining surgical incisions and dresses the chest wall wound. The physician may leave a chest tube and/or a mediastinal drainage tube in place following the procedure. Report 33803 if the procedure includes reanastomosis.

33813
Cardiopulmonary bypass is almost always required if the defect is in the wall between the right and left ventricle. If the hole is above the aortic and pulmonary valves, it may be possible to avoid cardiopulmonary bypass if the connection can be isolated and controlled with side-biting clamps on both the aorta and pulmonary artery.

33814
The physician gains access to the mediastinum through an incision through the sternum (median sternotomy). The physician places cardiopulmonary bypass catheters through incisions in the low inferior vena cava, the superior vena cava, and high aorta or femoral artery. The physician stops the heart by infusing cardioplegia solution into the coronary circulation. The physician cross-clamps the aorta, places sump suction in the left atrium to obtain a bloodless surgical field. The physician exposes the aortopulmonary septal defect by cutting through the ascending aorta or main pulmonary artery. The physician closes the defect with a Dacron fabric patch, closes the aortic or pulmonary arterial incision, takes the patient off cardiopulmonary bypass, closes the remaining surgical incisions and dresses the sternal wound. The physician may leave chest tubes and/or a mediastinal drainage tube in place following the procedure.

33820
The physician gains access to the mediastinum through an incision through the posterolateral left chest wall (posterolateral thoracotomy). The physician dissects

through the posterior chest wall musculature to expose the superior mediastinum. The physician dissects away the tissues surrounding the ductus and passes several heavy ligatures around the ductus and ties it off (ligation). The physician closes the surgical incisions and dresses the chest wall wound. The physician may leave chest tubes and/or a mediastinal drainage tube in place following the procedure.

33822-33824

The physician gains access to the mediastinum through an incision through the posterolateral left chest wall (posterolateral thoracotomy). The physician dissects through the posterior chest wall musculature to expose the superior mediastinum. The physician dissects away the tissues surrounding the ductus and passes several heavy ligatures around the ductus and ties it off (ligation) at each end. The physician occludes the ductus with vascular clamps and divides the ductus with scissors. The physician closes the aortic end with suture, then closes the pulmonary stump. The physician removes the vascular clamps, sutures the pleura closed, closes the remaining surgical incisions and dresses the chest wall wound. The physician may leave chest tubes and/or a mediastinal drainage tube in place following the procedure. Report 33824 if the patient is 18 years and older.

33840-33845

The physician gains access to the mediastinum through an incision through the posterolateral left chest wall (posterolateral thoracotomy). The physician dissects through the posterior chest wall musculature to expose the superior mediastinum, clamping and ligating large collateral vessels as they are encountered. The physician dissects away the tissues surrounding the aorta. The physician clamps the aorta on either side of the coarctation and ties off and divides the ligamentum arteriosum (or patent ductus arteriosus, if present). The physician excises the stricture sutures the two ends of the aorta to each other. The physician closes the mediastinal pleura and chest and dresses the chest wall wound. The physician may leave chest tubes and/or a mediastinal drainage tube in place following the procedure. Report 33845 if a graft is placed.

33851

The physician gains access to the mediastinum through an incision through the posterolateral left chest wall (posterolateral thoracotomy). The physician dissects through the posterior chest wall musculature to expose the superior mediastinum, clamping and ligating large collateral vessels as they are encountered. The physician dissects away the tissues surrounding the aorta. The physician clamps the aorta on either side of the coarctation and ties off and divides the ligamentum arteriosum (or patent ductus arteriosus, if present). The physician opens the aorta with a longitudinal incision that extends along the subclavian artery above and for a distance distally. The physician excises any extra tissue at the stricture site and sews in the left subclavian artery or a Dacron patch graft to attach and enlarge the aorta at the longitudinal incision. The physician closes the mediastinal pleura and chest and dresses the chest wall wound. The physician may leave chest tubes and/or a mediastinal drainage tube in place following the procedure.

33852

The physician surgically attaches the ascending and descending parts of the aorta, where normal connection is too small or interrupted entirely. The physician gains access to the mediastinum through an incision through the sternum (midline sternotomy). The physician clamps the aorta and left carotid artery to allow completion of the end-to-side attachment of a Dacron mesh graft to the ascending aorta. The physician cross-clamps the graft and releases the proximal clamp and the left carotid artery clamp. The physician uses end-to-side attachment to secure the distal graft to the descending aorta. The physician closes the mediastinal pleura and chest and dresses the chest wall wound. The physician may leave chest tubes and/or a mediastinal drainage tube in place following the procedure.

33853

The physician surgically attaches the ascending and descending parts of the aorta, where normal connection is too small or interrupted entirely. The physician gains access to the mediastinum through an incision through the sternum (midline sternotomy). The physician places cardiopulmonary bypass catheters (through incisions in the low inferior vena cava, the superior vena cava, and high aorta or femoral artery). The physician stops the heart by infusing cardioplegia solution into the coronary circulation. The physician clamps the aorta and left carotid artery to allow completion of the end-to-side attachment of a Dacron mesh graft to the ascending aorta. The physician cross-clamps the graft and releases the proximal clamp and the left carotid artery clamp. The physician uses end-to-side attachment to secure the distal graft to the descending aorta. The physician takes the patient off cardiopulmonary bypass, closes the mediastinal pleura and chest and dresses the chest wall wound. The physician may leave chest tubes and/or a mediastinal drainage tube in place following the procedure.

33860-33863

Cardiopulmonary bypass is required. Deep cooling of the body and circulatory arrest are often required, especially if the transverse arch of the aorta must be replaced. After circulatory arrest or if a cross-clamp can be placed on the aorta before its first branch, the aneurysm is opened. The hole in the aneurysm is lengthened along the aorta until the end of the aneurysm is reached. The aorta is divided at this point. A double layer of felt strips is placed circumferentially around the inner and outer circumference of the normal aorta with the aortic wall sandwiched in between. A Dacron tube graft is sewn to this end of the aorta and its felt layers. The aortic root where the aorta emerges from the heart is assessed. This area is where the aortic valve is located. If the valve closes normally, the aortic root size is reduced using stitches that also sew a double layer of felt to the aorta as previously described. This can only be done if the coronary arteries (which arise in this area) are not involved in the aneurysm. The open end of the Dacron tube is sewn to the prepared aortic root. If the valve does not close normally, it is replaced or repaired with stitches that reduce the length of its valve leaflets. The operation otherwise proceeds as it does when the valve closes normally. Report 33861 if coronary arteries must be cut out of the aneurysm; report 33863 if the end of the Dacron tube sewn to the aortic root contains an artificial valve and the patient's valve is removed.

33864

The surgeon repairs an aneurysm (an abnormally widened or weakened section of an artery) located in the thoracic aorta. The aorta is the largest artery in the body, extending from the heart through the chest and down into the abdomen. After induction of general anesthesia, the surgeon accesses the operative field via median sternotomy. Cardiopulmonary bypass is initiated. The coronary ostia are identified, detached from the aorta using dissecting scissors, and mobilized. After exposing the aneurysm site and clamping the artery above and below the aneurysm, the physician makes an incision into the aneurysm and removes any plaque deposits or clotted blood. The arterial section that is affected by the aneurysm is replaced with a synthetic graft. One end of the graft is attached to the arterial wall just above the beginning point of the aneurysm, while the other continues down through the artery to a point below the end of the aneurysm. The proximal coronary arteries are implanted into the aortic vascular graft. The physician performs a valve-sparing aortic root remodeling in which the dilated aortic root is replaced with a Dacron tube (graft), and the native aortic valve is integrated within the graft. The patient is taken off cardiopulmonary bypass and incisions are repaired. This procedure may be referred to as a David or Yacoub procedure in the operative note.

33870

This operation requires cardiopulmonary bypass. The patient's body temperature is lowered to 18-21 degrees centigrade and the bypass pump is stopped. The aneurysm is opened along its length and a patch of aortic wall containing the openings of the arteries to the head and arms is cut out. Each of these vessels will have been surrounded by tourniquets that were tightened before the bypass pump was stopped. The hole in the aneurysm is lengthened along the aorta until the end of the aneurysm is reached. The aorta is divided at this point. A double layer of felt strips is placed circumferentially around the inner and outer circumference of the normal aorta with the aortic wall sandwiched between. A Dacron tube graft is sewn to this end of the aorta and its felt layers. The aortic root where the aorta emerges from the heart is assessed. This area is where the aortic valve is located. If the valve closes normally, the aortic root size is reduced using stitches that also sew a double layer of felt to the aorta as previously described. The patch of aorta containing the openings for the vessels to the head and arms is sewn to a hole made in the top of the graft where it arches over.

33875-33877

A segment of the intrathoracic descending aorta is replaced with a tube of Dacron. This is done through an incision in the left chest cavity. The great concern in performing this operation is possible damage to the spinal cord. Preserving the spinal cord can be accomplished using a cardiopulmonary bypass circuit from above the aneurysm to below it, using deep cooling of the body and stopping the bypass machine, using perfusion of one or more spinal artery branches with blood pumped through it or using the "clamp and go" method in which no effort, except a speedy operation, is used to preserve the spinal cord. No matter what spinal cord preservation method is chosen, clamps are placed across the aorta above and below the aneurysm. The aneurysm is cut out and the ends of any small branches are closed with sutures. One end of a Dacron tube graft is sewn to the end of the aorta above the aneurysm and the other end of the graft is sewn to the aorta below the aneurysm. The clamps on the aorta are released. Report 33877 if aorta is exposed through the left chest.

33880-33881

The physician repairs the descending thoracic aorta by placing an endoprosthesis from within the artery. Endovascular repair may be performed for an aneurysm, pseudoaneurysm, dissection, penetrating ulcer, intramural hematoma, or traumatic disruption. The defect in the descending thoracic aorta is identified using aortography. The endoprosthesis, contained inside a holding device, is introduced into the artery under fluoroscopy and positioned at the target zone area of repair. Extension prostheses may be required to the level of the celiac artery origin. When the endoprosthesis is in position, it is deployed within the artery at the target site in the descending thoracic aorta, covering the origin of the left subclavian artery in 33880. A balloon angioplasty may be necessary to achieve proper positioning and functioning of the endoprosthesis. The placement position is confirmed, the catheter is removed, and the arteriotomy site is closed. Report 33880 when the repair covers the left subclavian artery origin and 33881 when the repair does not cover the left subclavian artery origin.

33883-33884

A leak, called an endoleak, may occur at the proximal fixation sites of a grafted descending thoracic aorta defect through the body of the graft or from patent arteries within the defect and may require endovascular repair. A proximal extension prosthesis is placed endovascularly to repair an endoleak in a grafted descending thoracic aortic aneurysm, pseudoaneurysm, dissection, penetrating ulcer, intramural hematoma, or traumatic disruption. The target site is identified by aortography and the proper extension prosthesis is selected. Under fluoroscopy, the extension prosthesis, contained inside a long plastic holding capsule, is threaded through the arteries to the site of the leak. Once the extension prosthesis is in place, the holding capsule is removed. The extension prosthesis, activated by heat, expands like a spring and becomes anchored to the artery wall at the site of the endoleak. If full expansion of the prosthesis does not occur automatically, a balloon catheter is threaded to the graft site and inflated within the endovascular prosthesis until full expansion is achieved. The placement position is confirmed, the catheter is removed, and the arteriotomy site is closed. Report 33883 for an initial proximal extension and 33884 for each additional proximal extension.

33886

A leak, called an endoleak, may occur at the distal fixation sites of a previously grafted descending thoracic aorta defect through the body of the graft or from patent arteries within the defect and may require endovascular repair. One or more distal extension prosthesis modules are placed endovascularly to the level of the celiac artery to repair an endoleak in a previously grafted descending thoracic aortic aneurysm, pseudoaneurysm, dissection, penetrating ulcer, intramural hematoma, or traumatic disruption. The target site is identified by aortography and the proper extension prosthesis is selected. Under fluoroscopy, the extension prosthesis, contained inside a long plastic holding capsule, is threaded through the arteries to the site of the leak. Once the extension prosthesis is in place, the holding capsule is removed. The extension prosthesis, activated by heat, expands like a spring and becomes anchored to the artery wall at the site of the endoleak. If full expansion of the prosthesis does not occur automatically, a balloon catheter is threaded to the graft site and inflated within the endovascular prosthesis until full expansion is achieved. The placement position is confirmed, the catheter is removed, and the arteriotomy site is closed. This code is reported only once regardless of the number of extension modules deployed.

33889

The physician performs a unilateral open subclavian to carotid artery transposition in conjunction with endovascular repair of the descending aorta. The physician performs a 2 to 3 cm supraclavicular incision to gain access to the carotid and subclavian arteries. The clavicular section of the sternocleidomastoid muscle is partially divided exposing the phrenic nerve, which is identified and avoided. The physician clears the adventitia of the chosen translocation site in the wall of the common carotid artery. The section of artery where the aneurysm occurs is isolated and dissected from adjacent structures. Vessel clamps are affixed above and below the defect. The repair is accomplished by excising the segment containing the aneurysm. The vessel ends are sutured in an end-to-end fashion. Next, the subclavian artery is transposed and anastomosed to the common carotid artery in an end-to-side fashion. Vessel clamps are removed and the incision is closed with layered sutures.

33891

The physician performs a transcervical retropharyngeal carotid-to-carotid bypass graft with other than vein in conjunction with endovascular repair of the descending thoracic aorta. Through incisions in the neck, the physician isolates and dissects the common carotid arteries, separating them from adjacent critical structures. The physician creates a bypass around a section of carotid artery that is damaged or blocked using a synthetic vein graft and one of two methods of repair. After vessel clamps have been affixed above and below the damaged area, the ends of the synthetic vein graft are sutured into the side of the carotid arterial wall (end-to-side). In the second method, the carotid artery may be cut above the damaged area and sutured to one end of a synthetic vein graft, which is sutured to the side of the carotid artery on the opposite side of the neck (end-to-end). In either case, the blocked or damaged section of artery is not removed. When the clamps are removed, the synthetic vein graft forms a new path through which blood can easily bypass the blocked or damaged area. After the graft procedure is completed, the skin incisions are repaired with layered sutures.

33910-33915

This operation is only done for patients who are in extremis following a pulmonary artery embolism (i.e., a blood clot originating in one of the large veins in the leg breaks loose and travels into the heart via the caval vein where it obstructs blood flow to the lungs). Survival is low. If cardiopulmonary bypass is used, the physician opens the right atrium widely. If cardiopulmonary bypass is not used, the right atrium is opened through a hole in the middle of a purse string. The clot is "milked" out of the pulmonary artery into the right atrium and out the hole. Report 33910 if cardiopulmonary bypass is required and the right atrium is opened widely. Report 33910 if cardiopulmonary bypass is initiated. Report 33915 if cardiopulmonary bypass is not initiated.

33916-33917
Cardiopulmonary bypass is required. Only the main and branch pulmonary arteries can be treated. The blocked arteries are opened along their lengths. The inner layer of the of each artery is removed. The outer layer of each artery is closed with suture directly or with a patch of pericardium, saphenous vein or Dacron. Report 33917 when a pulmonary stenosis is repaired by reconstruction with a patch or graft.

33920
Cardiopulmonary bypass is required. A hole is made in the right ventricle and any muscular obstruction in the outflow tract of the right ventricle is removed. The pulmonary artery or its branches are opened longitudinally until normal-sized vessels are encountered. The ventricular septal defect is closed. An aortic graft from an organ donor is trimmed to form a patch over the opened pulmonary artery. Any excess artery from the donor graft or a patch of pericardium or Dacron is sewn to the graft below the valve to use as a secondary patch for closing the hole in the right ventricle. The graft valve becomes the new pulmonary valve. After the patches and graft are sewn in place, cardiopulmonary bypass is stopped when heart function returns.

33922
Cardiopulmonary bypass is required. After it is started, cuts are made all the way across the pulmonary artery just above and just below the part of the artery containing the disease. The pulmonary artery is closed directly or is closed using a piece of the pulmonary artery or a piece of the aorta from an organ donor that is placed as an interposition graft.

33924
During a separately reportable congenital heart procedure, the physician ligates and takes down a previously formed systemic-to-pulmonary artery shunt. The shunt is ligated and the systemic arteries are returned to their correct anatomic position.

33925-33926
The physician repairs pulmonary artery arborization anomalies (i.e., stenosis of unbranched and intrapulmonary arteries) by unifocalization, a surgical technique in which the various sources of pulmonary blood supply can be perfused from a single source. In patients with pulmonary atresia or with a ventricular septal defect (VSD), the pulmonary blood supply often comes from multiple sources, particularly major aortopulmonary collateral arteries (MAPCA), which often arise from the aorta and its direct branches. Unifocalization, which may be performed as a single operation or as a staged procedure, interrupts the extracardiac sources of pulmonary arterial blood flow; restores segmental, lobar, and pulmonary arterial confluence; replaces missing central pulmonary arterial branches; and creates a central, accessible source of pulmonary arterial blood flow. The physician accesses the mediastinum through an extended median sternotomy or a bilateral transsternal thoracotomy. The major aortopulmonary collateral arteries are identified, mobilized, and dissected, using a variety of techniques, from the upper descending aorta, the aortic arch, brachiocephalic vessels, or coronary arteries, and anastomosed to the native pulmonary artery. Ligation of the collateral arteries at their origin is performed to achieve controlled perfusion. As each artery is ligated, desaturation is assessed by pulse oximetry. If desaturation approaches a compromising level, the surgeon may proceed with cardiopulmonary bypass at this point. Report 33925 when the procedure is performed without cardiopulmonary bypass and 33926 when it is performed with cardiopulmonary bypass.

33930
The physician performs a donor cardiectomy-pneumonectomy by removing the heart and lung from a donor cadaver for transplantation. This is usually performed when other organs such as the liver, kidneys, intestines, or pancreas are also acquired from the organ donor. The chest cavity is accessed and cold preserving solutions are infused into the aorta and pulmonary arteries. After enough solution has been given, the heart and lungs are removed by transection, en bloc. This includes the aorta well above the heart, the right atrium, the atrial septum, and the left atrium—completely and as close to the patient's spine (or as posteriorly) as possible. The heart/lung block is preserved for transplantation into the recipient. The organ remains under refrigeration, specially packed in a sealable container with some preserving solution and kept on ice in a suitable carrier.

33933
The physician performs a standard backbench preparation of the heart and lungs following procurement from a cadaver donor. Backbench or back table preparation refers to procedures performed on the donor organs following procurement to prepare the donor organs for transplant. The heart and lungs are removed en bloc. The heart and lungs are inspected following procurement to identify any injury or abnormality not noted prior to procurement. The physician prepares the heart and lungs by dissecting free any residual soft tissue. Attention is focused on the aorta, superior vena cava, inferior vena cava, and the trachea. The aorta, which was divided at the aortic arch, is inspected and residual tissue removed. The superior vena cava is inspected and residual tissue removed. The inferior vena cava is inspected to assure adequate length has been preserved. Any residual tissue is removed from the inferior vena cava. The trachea, which was divided as far above the carina as possible, is inspected and residual tissue removed. When all residual soft tissue has been removed and the vessels prepared, the heart and lungs are ready for transplant.

33935
The patient is placed on cardiopulmonary bypass and the heart and lungs are removed. The donor's organs are placed by sewing the left atrium of the donor to the left atrium of the recipient's first, and sewing together their atrial septums and their right atrium. The donor aorta is trimmed to an appropriate length and sewn to the ascending aorta of the recipient.
Immunosuppressive drugs may be given to the patient before, during and after the operation.
Cardiopulmonary bypass is discontinued when the donor's heart function returns.

33940
The physician performs a donor cardiectomy by removing the heart from a donor cadaver for transplantation. This is usually performed when other organs such as the liver, kidneys, intestines, or pancreas are also acquired from the organ donor. The chest cavity is accessed and cold preserving solutions are infused into the aorta and pulmonary arteries. After enough solution has been given, the heart and lungs are removed by transection, en bloc. This includes the aorta well above the heart, the right atrium, the atrial septum, and the left atrium—completely and as close to the patient's spine (or as posteriorly) as possible. The heart/lung block is preserved for transplantation into the recipient. The organ remains under refrigeration, specially packed in a sealable container with some preserving solution and kept on ice in a suitable carrier.

33944
The physician performs a standard backbench preparation of the heart following procurement from a cadaver donor. Backbench or back table preparation refers to procedures performed on the donor organs following procurement to prepare the donor organs for transplant. The heart is removed or the heart and lungs are removed en bloc. If the heart and lungs are removed en bloc, back table separation of the heart and lungs is performed. The heart is inspected following procurement to identify any injury or abnormality not noted prior to procurement. The physician prepares the heart by dissecting free any residual soft tissue. Attention is focused on the aorta, superior vena cava, inferior vena cava, and the left atrium. The aorta, which was divided at the aortic arch, is inspected and residual tissue removed. The superior vena cava is inspected and residual tissue removed. The inferior vena cava is inspected to assure adequate length has been preserved. Any residual tissue is removed. The left atrium is inspected and residual tissue removed. When all residual soft tissue has been removed and the vessels prepared, the heart is ready for transplant.

33945
The patient is placed on cardiopulmonary bypass. Cardiac transplantation may be performed by one of two techniques: total orthotopic heart replacement or heterotopic implantation. A total orthotopic heart replacement involves excising the ventricles, atrial appendages, and most of the coronary sinus from the donor heart. The recipient heart is opened. The atria, aorta, and pulmonary artery of the recipient heart are anastomosed to the donor heart. The sinoatrial nodes of both the donor and recipient heart are left intact. In a heterotopic implantation, the donor's organs are placed by sewing the left atrium of the donor heart to the left atrium of the recipient and sewing together the atrial septums and the right atrium. The donor aorta is trimmed to an appropriate length and sewn to the ascending aorta of the recipient. Immunosuppressive drugs may be given to the patient before, during, and after the operation. Cardiopulmonary bypass is discontinued when the donor heart begins functioning in the recipient.

33960
This operation is rarely done solely for pulmonary insufficiency (ECMD.) It can be done for right of left ventricular failure or both. Cardiopulmonary bypass is required. For right ventricular failure, a pump uptake tube is placed in the right ventricular apex. A pump delivery tube is placed in the pulmonary artery. The pump is turned on and the patient is weaned off of cardiopulmonary bypass. For left ventricular failure, the pump uptake tube is placed in one of the pulmonary veins or in the left ventricle apex. The arterial delivery tube is placed in the aorta. The pump is turned on and the patient is removed from cardiopulmonary bypass. Use 33960 for the initial 24 hours.

33961
This procedure involves maintaining the functioning of the external pumps, assessing the recovery of the patient's heart muscle, maintaining the patient's level of blood thinners, and assessing the need for emergency placement of an implantable ventricular assist device, a total artificial heart, or a donor heart transplant. Use 33961 for each additional 24-hour time period. Use 33961 in conjunction with 33960.

33967
An intra-aortic balloon catheter, usually with a 40 cc volume capacity, is inserted into the femoral artery and advanced under fluoroscopy to the distal portion of the aortic arch. After correct placement of the intra-aortic balloon assist device (IAB) in the descending aorta with its tip at the distal aortic arch, the balloon is connected to a drive console. The console consists of a pressurized gas reservoir, a monitor for ECG and pressure wave recording, adjustments for inflation/deflation timing, triggering selection switches, and battery back-up power sources. Helium or carbon dioxide is used for inflation. Inflation and deflation are synchronized to the patient's cardiac cycle. Inflation at the onset of diastole results in proximal and distal displacement of blood volume in the aorta. Deflation occurs just prior to the onset of systole. Once the patient's cardiac

performance improves, weaning from the intra-aortic balloon catheter pump (IABP) begins by gradually decreasing the balloon augmentation ratio under control of hemodynamic stability.

33968
The physician removes an intra-aortic balloon assist device (IABP). In a previous separately reportable procedure an IABP was inserted. When the patient is stabilized they are weaned off of the IAPB. The pump is turned off and the IABP catheter with the attached balloon is withdrawn from the femoral artery. Pressure is placed over the wound in the groin for a specified period of time. A light dressing is applied. The patient may be placed at bed rest and observed for several hours to avoid problems that could arise from bleeding or a hematoma at the puncture site.

33970
This operation is done to help support the function of the left ventricle of the heart. The left or right femoral artery is exposed in the groin. After the vessel is occluded above and below the proposed insertion site, the artery is opened transversely. The end of a small tube of Gortex may be sewn to the side of the artery, although this is only done sometimes. Tip of the balloon catheter is inserted into the artery (or Gortex tube). The clamp occluding the artery upstream is released and the balloon catheter is advanced to femoral artery and into the aorta above the level of the kidney arteries, but not beyond the left arm artery. It is connected to a pump and the pump is turned on. The pump inflates and deflates the balloon during each heartbeat cycle.

33971
The previously placed balloon pump is withdrawn and the artery is occluded above and below the hole. If a Gortex sleeve has been used, it is simply tied off and no other repair is needed. If the balloon was directly introduced into the artery, the hole is sewn shut. If sewing the hole shut narrows the artery significantly, the hole can be patched with a piece of saphenous vein or Dacron. If the arterial diameter has been damaged, the segment of artery containing the hole can be removed and the artery replaced with an interposition graft of saphenous vein or Dacron tube.

33973
The procedure is done when 1) the femoral arteries cannot be readily exposed in the operating room because of patient positioning; 2) the arteries are occluded by atherosclerosis or trauma; 3) there will be a need to reopen the patient's chest soon. A balloon placed in this fashion must be removed in the operating room and his chest must be reopened. A purse string is placed in the aorta. A hole is made in the aorta in the middle of the purse string. The balloon is inserted through this hole until it lies beyond the left arm artery but above the kidney arteries. The purse string is tightened with a tourniquet. The chest incision is not closed. The balloon is driven by a pump outside the patient.

33974
The physician removes an ascending aortic intra-aortic balloon assist device during performance of a primary procedure. If the sternum is open, the physician removes the aortic balloon while tightening purse-string sutures around the hole. When hemostasis is assured, the pericardium is repaired loosely with or without graft, leaving gaps for blood and fluid to drain into the plural space. The sternum is reanastomosed with sternal wires and the skin is sutured in layers. If the sternum is closed, a Dacron-tube graft (reported separately) is used as a vehicle for balloon removal. As the balloon is removed, the Dacron-tube graft tightens around the aortic incision to create aortic hemostasis.

33975-33976
Cardiopulmonary bypass is required. For right ventricular failure, a pump uptake tube is placed in the right ventricular apex. A pump delivery tube is placed in the pulmonary artery. The pump is turned on and the patient is weaned off cardiopulmonary bypass. For left ventricular failure, the pump uptake tube is placed in one of the pulmonary veins or in the left ventricle apex. The arterial delivery tube is placed in the aorta. The pump is turned on and the patient is removed from cardiopulmonary bypass. The implanted pump is placed in a pocket formed in the upper abdominal wall, but outside the abdominal cavity. Tubes for the pump drive are brought out through separate incisions in the skin. The pump is started and the patient is weaned off cardiopulmonary bypass. The device is removed when the patient's ventricle recovers, a total artificial heart is placed or the patient undergoes heart transplantation. Report 33976 if biventricular support is needed.

33977-33978
Cardiopulmonary bypass is required. The pump is stopped. All the tubes are removed and any holes in the heart or vessels are closed. The device is removed from the patient's body. Cardiopulmonary bypass is discontinued when the patient's heart function returns. An intra-aortic balloon pump is often required to allow discontinuation of bypass. All wounds are closed. Report 33978 if biventricular support is needed.

33979-33980
The physician makes a midline incision extending from the sternal notch to the umbilicus. Sternotomy is performed prior to creation of the pocket. The preperitoneal fat is dissected from the undersurface of the rectus sheath using low-power cautery. Superiorly the dissection is carried to the undersurface of the diaphragm until the apex of the heart can be palpated just lateral to the inferior phrenic artery and vein and carried well back into the retroperitoneum. The preperitoneal space is opened to allow room for the device outflow valve and graft conduit. The muscular

attachment of the right hemidiaphragm to the medial edge of the sternum is divided to allow room for the graft. A small incision is made and a tunneling device is passed subcutaneously inferiorly around the umbilicus, and into the pocket through the rectus sheath at its most inferior aspect. The tunneler is screwed onto the end of the drive line, which is pulled back through the tunnel to the skin. The drive line is not attached to the skin. Cardiopulmonary bypass is instituted using standard aortic and dual stage venous cannulae. The apex of the left ventricle is elevated. The physician cores out a piece of ventricle and places the apical cuff sutures. An apical vent is passed into the left ventricle. Pledgeted 2-0 Ethibond sutures are placed circumferentially partial thickness into the myocardium and passed through the sewing ring of the apical cuff. Once the apical cuff is secure, a cruciate incision in the diaphragm opposite the ventricular apex is made just lateral to the inferior phrenic vessels, and the inflow cannula is brought into the chest. The inflow cannula is inserted through the apical cuff until the sintered titanium surface is within the cuff. The Dacron tie of the inflow cuff is secured and an additional plastic band and Dacron tie are used to reinforce the connection and flatten out the silicone cuff. Blood is allowed to passively fill the device and exit via the outflow valve. A partial occluding clamp is placed on the right lateral aspect of the ascending aorta and a longitudinal aortotomy is performed. The periaortic adventitia is left in place and a strip of pericardium is incorporated into the anastomosis. The apex and heel of the anastomosis are reinforced with interrupted 4-0 Prolene pledgeted horizontal mattress stitches. Inotropic support is started before separating from bypass and activating the LVAD. The device is switched to automatic mode after the cessation of cardiopulmonary bypass. Transesophageal echocardiography is used to ensure adequate ventricular decompression and a bubble study is performed to rule out a patent foramen ovale. A thermodilution cardiac output is performed and compared to the output from the LVAD. In the presence of severe coagulopathy, the chest may need to be packed open. The device is removed (33980) when the patient's ventricle recovers, an artificial heart is placed, or the patient undergoes heart transplantation.

33981

The physician replaces the blood pump component of an extracorporeal ventricular assist device (VAD). The previously implanted pump, which was placed in a pocket formed in the upper abdominal wall (but outside the abdominal cavity), is removed. Pump replacement includes removal of the existing pump, insertion of a new pump, connection, de-airing, and new pump initiation. Report 33981 for one or more pumps; this code reports pump replacement of single or biventricular VAD systems.

33982-33983

The physician replaces the blood pump component of an implantable, intracorporeal, single ventricle VAD (ventricular assist device). This may be accomplished without cardiopulmonary bypass (33982) or with cardiopulmonary bypass (33983). Pump replacement includes removal of the existing pump, insertion of a new pump, connection, de-airing, and new pump initiation.

34001

To remove a blood clot in the carotid, subclavian, or innominate artery, the physician makes an incision in the skin of the neck usually in front of the sternocleidomastoid muscle over the site of the clot, or immediately above it. The artery is isolated and dissected from critical structures. The artery may be clamped above and below the clot and incised. The physician removes the blood clot and sutures the artery. The clamps are removed. If a catheter is required, it is threaded past the clot and a small balloon at its tip is inflated. The catheter is withdrawn, capturing and retrieving the clot. The physician may make several passes to remove all of the clot. The blood vessel is repaired with sutures and the skin incision is repaired with a layered closure.

34051

The physician exposes the innominate or subclavian artery by making an incision in the anterior chest (midline sternotomy or lateral thoracotomy). The physician identifies the embolus or thrombus and occludes the artery proximal to the clot. The physician makes a small incision in the artery proximal to the clot. The physician withdraws the clot by passing a Fogarty balloon catheter beyond the clot, inflating, and withdrawing the balloon. The physician establishes proof of patency by injecting contrast in the artery under fluoroscope. The physician sutures the arteriotomy closed, removes the vascular clamp or tie, and closes the chest wall the embolus or thrombus and occludes the artery proximal to the clot. The physician makes a small incision in the artery proximal to the clot. The physician withdraws the clot using ring forceps, or by passing a Fogarty balloon catheter beyond the clot, inflating, and withdrawing the balloon. The physician establishes proof of patency by injecting contrast in the artery under fluoroscope. The physician sutures the arteriotomy closed, removes the vascular clamp or tie, and closes the chest wall. The physician may establish proof of patency by injecting contrast in the artery under fluoroscope. The physician sutures the arteriotomy closed, removes the vascular clamp or tie, and closes the chest wall wound. The physician may leave chest tubes and/or a mediastinal drainage tube in place following the procedure.

34101

To remove a blood clot in the axillary, brachial, innominate, or subclavian artery, the physician makes an incision in the skin of the arm at the site of the blood clot or above it. The artery is isolated and dissected from critical structures. The artery may be clamped above and below the clot, and incised. The physician removes the blood clot and repairs the artery. The clamps are removed. If a catheter is required, it is threaded past the clot and a small balloon at its tip is inflated. The catheter is withdrawn, capturing and retrieving the clot. The physician may make several passes to remove all of the clot. The blood vessel is repaired with sutures and the skin incision is repaired with a layered closure.

34111

To remove a blood clot in the radial or ulnar artery, the physician makes an incision in the skin of the arm, over the site of the clot or immediately above it. The artery is isolated and dissected from adjacent critical structures. The artery may be clamped above and below the clot, and incised. The physician removes the blood clot and repairs the artery. The clamps are removed. If a catheter is required, it is threaded past the clot and a small balloon at its tip is inflated. The catheter is withdrawn, capturing and retrieving the clot. The physician may make several passes to remove all of the clot. The blood vessel is repaired with sutures and the skin incision is repaired with a layered closure.

34151

To remove a blood clot in the renal, celiac, mesentery, aortoiliac artery, the physician makes an incision in the skin of the abdomen over the site of the clot or immediately above or below it. The vein is isolated and dissected from adjacent critical structures. The artery may be clamped above and below the clot and incised. The physician removes the blood clot. The clamps are removed. If a catheter is required, it is threaded past the clot and a small balloon at its tip is inflated. The catheter is withdrawn, capturing and retrieving the clot. The physician may make several passes to remove all of the clot. The blood vessel is repaired with sutures and the skin incision is repaired with a layered closure.

34201

To remove a blood clot in the femoropopliteal or aortoiliac artery, the physician makes an incision in the skin of the leg over the femoral artery. The artery is isolated and dissected from adjacent critical structures. The artery may be clamped above and below the clot and incised. The physician removes the blood clot and repairs the vessel. The clamps are removed. If a catheter is required, it is threaded past the clot and a small balloon at its tip is inflated. The catheter is withdrawn, capturing and retrieving the clot. The physician may make several passes to remove all of the clot. The blood vessel is repaired with sutures and the skin incision is repaired with a layered closure.

34203

To remove a blood clot in the popliteal-tibio-peroneal artery, the physician makes an incision in the skin of the leg over the femoral or popliteal artery. The artery is isolated and dissected from adjacent critical structures. The artery may be clamped above and below the clot and incised. The physician removes the blood clot. The clamps are removed. If a catheter is required, it is threaded past the clot and a small balloon at its tip is inflated. The catheter is withdrawn, capturing and retrieving the clot. The physician may make several passes to remove all of the clot. The blood vessel is repaired with sutures and the skin incision is repaired with a layered closure.

34401

The physician exposes the vena cava by making an abdominal incision. The physician identifies the thrombus by venogram and may perform a contralateral femoral venogram to rule out inferior vena caval involvement. The physician makes an incision in the vena cava. The physician withdraws the clot by passing a Fogarty balloon catheter beyond the clot, inflating, and withdrawing the balloon. The physician may attempt to reduce the risk of pulmonary embolism by increasing intrathoracic pressure in a ventilated patient. The physician may establish proof of patency by repeat venography. The physician sutures the venotomy closed and closes the wound.

34421

To remove a blood clot in the vena cava, iliac, or femoropopliteal vein, the physician makes an incision in the skin of the upper leg over the site of the clot or immediately above or below it. The vein is isolated and dissected from adjacent critical structures. The vein may be clamped above and below the clot and incised. The physician removes the blood clot. The clamps are removed. If a catheter is required, it is threaded past the clot and a small balloon at its tip is inflated. The catheter is withdrawn, capturing and retrieving the clot. The physician may make several passes to remove all of the clot. The blood vessel is repaired with sutures and the skin incision is repaired with a layered closure.

34451

The physician exposes the common femoral, superficial femoral, and saphenous veins by making an inguinal incision. The physician identifies the thrombus by venogram and may perform a contralateral femoral venogram to rule out inferior vena caval involvement. The physician makes an incision in the distal common femoral vein. The physician withdraws the proximal clot by passing a Fogarty balloon catheter beyond the clot, inflating, and withdrawing the balloon. The physician may attempt to reduce the risk of pulmonary embolism by increasing intrathoracic pressure in a ventilated patient or asking the patient to perform a Valsalva maneuver if the procedure is performed under local anesthesia. The physician cuts down and introduces a Fogarty catheter via the popliteal vein, advancing the catheter toward the femoral vein while extruding thrombus through the femoral venotomy. The physician may establish proof of patency by repeat venography. The physician sutures the venotomy closed and closes the inguinal wound.

34471
To remove a blood clot in the subclavian vein, the physician makes an incision in the skin of the neck over the site of the clot or immediately above or below it. The vein is isolated and dissected from adjacent critical structures. The vein may be clamped above and below the clot and incised. The physician removes the blood clot. The clamps are removed. If a catheter is required, it is threaded past the clot and a small balloon at its tip is inflated. The catheter is withdrawn, capturing and retrieving the clot. The physician may make several passes to remove all of the clot. The blood vessel is repaired with sutures and the skin incision is repaired with a layered closure.

34490
To remove a blood clot in the axillary and subclavian vein, the physician makes an incision in the skin of the arm over the site of the clot or immediately above or below it. The vein is isolated and dissected from adjacent critical structures. The vein may be clamped above and below the clot and incised. The physician removes the blood clot. The clamps are removed. If a catheter is required, it is threaded past the clot and a small balloon at its tip is inflated. The catheter is withdrawn, capturing and retrieving the clot. The physician may make several passes to remove all of the clot. The blood vessel is repaired with sutures and the skin incision is repaired with a layered closure.

34501
The physician makes an incision in the skin overlying the site of the incompetent valve. The femoral vein is isolated and dissected from adjacent critical structures. The physician affixes vessel clamps above and below the malfunctioning valve. The physician opens the vein and repairs the valve leaflets by suture plication (tacking the excess valve material). The vein is repaired with sutures. The clamps are removed and the skin incision is repaired with a layered closure.

34502
The physician exposes the inferior vena cava by making an incision in the anterior abdomen. The physician clamps the vena cava proximally and sutures any defects closed. The physician may replace or bypass abnormal vena caval tissue with synthetic graft material. The physician may inject intravenous contrast under fluoroscope to demonstrate appropriate flow. The physician unclamps the vena cava and closes the abdominal wall incision. The physician may leave a surgical drain in place.

34510
The physician makes an incision in the skin overlying the site of the malfunctioning valve. The vein is isolated and dissected from adjacent critical structures. The physician affixes vessel clamps above and below the vein and excises the section of vein containing the malfunctioning valve. A section of harvested vein containing functional valves is sutured end-to-end to the vein. The clamps are removed and the skin incision is repaired with a layered closure.

34520
The physician makes an incision in the skin overlying the site of the incompetent valve. The incompetent vein is isolated and dissected from adjacent critical structures. The physician affixes vessel clamps above and below the vein. The divided section of incompetent vein is connected to a nearby vein with functioning valves, placing competent values above the incompetent vein. Both the vein and the skin incision are closed with sutures.

34530
The physician makes an incision in the skin overlying the site of the greater saphenous vein just below the knee. The vein is isolated and dissected from adjacent critical structures. The physician affixes vessel clamps above and below the incision site. The dissected section of saphenous vein is connected to the popliteal vein in an end-to-side anastomosis. The other end of the saphenous vein is closed with sutures. Once the saphenous vein and the popliteal vein are connected, the clamps are removed and the skin incision is repaired with layered closure.

34800
Endovascular repair of an infrarenal abdominal aortic aneurysm or dissection requires both a vascular surgeon and a radiologist. An incision is made over the femoral artery, which is normally used for access, and a guidewire is threaded into the blood vessel. A catheter with a stent-transporting tip is advanced over the guidewire into the vessel. The catheter carries the aortic tube prosthesis, approximately 6 inches long and contained inside a holding capsule, through the arterial tree to the site of the aortic infrarenal aneurysm. Once the stent is in proper position, the holding capsule is removed and the stent is deployed, expanding like a spring to anchor itself to normal walls of the aorta above and below the aneurysm. The device serves as a substitute channel for blood flow. If full expansion of the prosthesis does not occur, or leaks are present, a balloon catheter is threaded to the graft site and inflated within the prosthesis until full expansion is achieved and leaking is stopped. The catheter/ guidewire is removed and the arteriotomy site is closed. The aneurysm, excluded from the blood flow, typically shrinks over time.

34802-34803
Endovascular repair of an infrarenal abdominal aortic aneurysm or dissection requires both a vascular surgeon and a radiologist. An incision is made to access each femoral artery, normally used for access, and a guidewire is threaded into the blood vessel. A catheter

with a stent-transporting tip is advanced over the guidewire into the vessel. The catheter carries a synthetic endograft stent device, contained inside a plastic holding capsule, through the arterial tree to the site of the aneurysm. In 34802, the stent device is a modular bifurcated prosthesis with one docking limb, used when the aneurysm extends beyond the aorta into the iliac arteries, or not enough healthy aorta exists below the aneurysm. The modular bifurcated prosthesis has separate components: the main stent body with one open, short limb and one continuous, longer limb and a separate docking limb. The main component is deployed from its holding capsule after being positioned within the aorta so that the longer limb extends into one of the two iliac arteries. Through the opposite femoral artery, the separate docking limb is similarly brought into position at the aorto-iliac junction and attached to the main piece through the contralateral iliac. The docking limb is locked into the receiving short limb. Report 34803 when both legs of the modular bifurcated prosthesis are docking limbs.

34804

Endovascular repair of an infrarenal abdominal aortic aneurysm or dissection requires both a vascular surgeon and a radiologist. Bilateral guidewire/catheter placement in the access vessels is required in placing bifurcated prostheses. Gaining the necessary access usually requires an actual dissection for arterial exposure of at least one femoral or iliac artery (not the aneurysm) to allow for insertion of the endovascular device. A catheter with a stent-transporting tip is advanced over a guidewire into the vessel. The catheter carries a unibody bifurcated prosthesis, contained inside a plastic holding capsule, through the arterial tree to the site of the aneurysm. This two-legged device is shaped like an upside-down Y, similar to the modular bifurcated prostheses, except it is all in one piece—the limbs are not docking components. The device is deployed from its holding capsule after contralateral position confirmation within the aorta so that the limbs extend down into the two iliac arteries. After checking for full deployment and any leaks, the instruments are removed and the access site is repaired.

34805

Endovascular repair of an infrarenal abdominal aortic aneurysm or dissection requires the skills of both a vascular surgeon and a radiologist. General anesthesia is typically used. In endovascular repair, a small incision is made in the groin over one femoral artery or both femoral arteries through which the endovascular devices are inserted. If contralateral femoral access is necessary, a percutaneous sheath may be placed. Under separately reported fluoroscopy, an aorta-uni-iliac or aorto-unifemoral prosthetic graft device contained inside a plastic holding capsule is threaded through the arteries to the site of the infrarenal aneurysm. The endograft is deployed by slowly removing the holding capsule away from the endograft, with continual monitoring of the exact positioning. Once the prosthesis is in place, the holding capsule is removed. Balloon angioplasty is performed at the ends of the prosthesis to expand and seat the graft. Stents are also deployed within the body of the endograft to maintain expansion forces. The aorta-uni-iliac or aorto-unifemoral prosthetic endograft is supported along its length by a series of metal rings sutured to the graft and is held in place by the radial force applied by the rings to the patient's aorta. Once in place, the arteriotomy site is closed.

34806

The physician performs transcatheter placement of a wireless, physiologic sensor in the aneurysmal sac during the endovascular repair of an aneurysm of a major vessel, typically the aorta. In endovascular repair, a small incision is made in the groin over one femoral artery or both femoral arteries through which the endovascular devices are inserted. If contralateral femoral access is necessary, a percutaneous sheath may be placed. A capsule containing a permanent pressure sensor is deployed into the aorta at the site of the aneurysm. Under fluoroscopy, a prosthetic graft device contained inside a plastic holding capsule is threaded through the arteries to the site of the aneurysm. The endograft is deployed by slowly removing the holding capsule from the endograft, with continual monitoring of the exact positioning. Once the prosthesis is in place, the holding capsule is removed. The sensor is now wedged between the aorta wall and the wall of the endovascular graft. Balloon angioplasty is performed at the ends of the prosthesis to expand and seal the graft. Stents are also deployed within the body of the endograft to maintain expansion forces. The prosthetic endograft is supported along its entire length by a series of metal rings sutured to the graft and is held in place by the radial force applied by the rings to the patient's aorta. The pressure sensor is tested and calibrated before the arteriotomy site is closed. This code reports the placement of the pressure sensor as a code secondary to the primary repair and includes radiological supervision and interpretation, instrument calibration, and collection of pressure data.

34808

Endovascular placement of an iliac artery occlusion device is performed during separately reportable repair of an abdominal aortic aneurysm and/or endovascular graft procedure. As part of the repair, the iliac artery is occluded. Under separately reportable fluoroscopy, an iliac artery occlusion device is threaded through the arteries and placed distal to the aneurysm. When the aneurysmal repair is complete, the endovascular occlusion device may be left in the artery. Catheters and devices used for access and to deploy the occlusion device are removed and any bleeding controlled.

34812

The physician makes an incision in the groin area to expose the femoral artery on one side to facilitate the delivery of an endovascular prosthesis. The patient is placed supine and a skin incision is made in the groin. Hemostasis of vessels is achieved. The underlying subcutaneous layers and muscles are incised to reach the artery and reflected out of the way. The femoral artery is exposed in preparation for delivering an endovascular prosthesis and its sheath is opened with tape placed about it.

34813

During separately reportable endovascular repair of an aortic aneurysm, a diseased or damaged femoral artery is repaired by placing a prosthetic femoral-femoral graft. Through incisions in the skin of the upper thighs, the physician isolates and dissects a section of the affected femoral artery. Once vessel clamps have been affixed above and below the area of damaged vessel to be anastomosed, the femoral artery is cut above and below the diseased or damaged area and the new distal and proximal ends are sutured to the ends of the prosthetic graft, which now replaces the section of diseased or damaged artery. When the clamps are removed, the blood flows unobstructed through the femoral artery. After the graft is complete, the skin incisions are repaired with layered closures.

34820

The physician makes an abdominal or retroperitoneal incision to expose the iliac artery on one side to facilitate the delivery of an endovascular prosthesis or to perform temporary iliac artery occlusion during a procedure for endovascular therapy. The patient is placed supine and the buttocks are elevated. An incision is made parallel with and just above the inguinal ligament. The incision is in the middle third of a proximally curved line extending from the anterior superior iliac spine to the pubic symphysis. Hemostasis of vessels is achieved and the aponeuroses of the external and internal oblique and the transverses muscles are incised parallel to the inguinal ligament. The structures are reflected upward and medially, the transversalis fascia is opened, and the retroperitoneal space is entered. The iliac artery is exposed in preparation for delivering an endovascular prosthesis and its sheath is opened with tape placed about it. If the artery has been exposed for the purpose of placing a temporary occlusion device, the clamp is placed.

34825-34826

A leak, called an endoleak, may occur at fixation sites of a grafted aneurysm through the body of the graft or from patent arteries within the aneurysm sac and may require endovascular reparation. An extension prosthesis is placed endovascularly to repair an infrarenal abdominal aortic or iliac aneurysm, pseudoaneurysm, or dissection. Using separately reportable aortography, the target site is identified. The proper extension prosthesis is selected. Under separately reportable fluoroscopy, the extension prosthesis, contained inside a long plastic holding capsule, is threaded through the arteries to the site of the leak. Once the extension prosthesis is in place, the holding capsule is removed. The extension prosthesis, activated by heat, expands like a spring and becomes anchored to the artery wall at the site of the endoleak. If full expansion of the prosthesis does not occur automatically, a balloon catheter is threaded to the graft site and inflated within the endovascular prosthesis until full expansion is achieved. The catheter is removed and the arteriotomy site is closed. Report 34825 for placement of an extension prosthesis in the initial vessel and 34826 for placement of an extension prosthesis in each additional vessel.

34830-34832

An attempted endovascular repair of an aortic aneurysm originating below the renal arteries (infrarenal) fails necessitating open repair of the aneurysm as well as repair of any trauma associated with the endovascular attempt. An incision is made in the abdomen from just below the diaphragm to the umbilicus. The aorta is exposed, the aneurysm identified, and the aorta and other arteries inspected for injury resulting from the failed endovascular procedure. Repair of the aneurysm is accomplished by temporarily clamping the aorta both above and below the aneurysm. It is usually possible to place the upper clamp just below the origins of the renal arteries so that the kidneys continue to receive blood flow throughout the operation. Blood flow to the legs is interrupted while the aorta is clamped. The aneurysm is opened lengthwise and any thrombi (blood clots) removed. The aneurysm wall is not removed. The aorta is cut above and below the aneurysm and a prosthetic graft made of synthetic material is sutured in place between the two ends. The aneurysm wall is wrapped around the synthetic graft. The clamps are removed allowing blood to flow through the graft and into the vessels of the lower extremities. The surgical wound is closed. Repair using a tube prosthesis is reported with 34830; repair with an aorto-bi-iliac prosthesis is reported with 34831; and repair with an aorto-bifemoral prosthesis is reported with 34832.

34833

A conduit is created for the delivery of an aortic or iliac endovascular prosthesis by open iliac artery exposure via transabdominal or retroperitoneal incision. A skin incision is made parallel with and just above the inguinal ligament. The skin is incised and the retroperitoneal space is entered to access the iliac artery. Bowels, blood vessels, and other soft tissue is mobilized from the area to give clear access to the iliac artery. With adequate exposure, loops are passed around the vessel proximally and distally. Anticoagulation is achieved and vascular clamps are applied. An arteriotomy is made for creation of the conduit, which is formed by placing a tubular piece of bypass graft material that has been fashioned into the right size onto the iliac artery and suturing it together. The conduit is clamped and the vascular clamps are removed from the iliac artery. Additional sutures are placed as needed. Through the newly created conduit, endovascular repair by deployment of an aortic or iliac prosthesis may be undertaken. After the repair is complete, the conduit may be closed in one of two ways. The open end of the conduit may be sewn to the distal external iliac artery, and thereby left in place as a channel for external iliac bypass graft, or it may be cut close to the iliac artery and simply oversewn with sutures. This code reports the creation of the conduit, not the endovascular repair.

34834

Open brachial artery exposure via arm incision is done to assist in the deployment of an aortic or iliac endovascular prosthesis. An incision is made in the skin of the upper arm and nerves, blood vessels, and other soft tissue are mobilized from the area to give clear access to the brachial artery. With adequate exposure, loops are passed around the vessel proximally and distally. Anticoagulation is achieved and vascular clamps are alternately applied and removed as needed for introduction of guidewires, sheaths, and catheters through the brachial artery for accomplishing deployment of an aortic or iliac endovascular prosthesis. After the endovascular repair has been completed, the opening remaining in the brachial artery is closed with fine sutures after irrigation and trimming of the edges has been done. Hemostasis is achieved and the wound is irrigated and closed. This code reports the open brachial artery exposure, not the endovascular repair.

34900

An iliac artery aneurysm, pseudoaneurysm, vascular malformation, or trauma injury is repaired by placing a graft from within the artery. A leak, called an endoleak, may occur at fixation sites of a grafted aneurysm through the body of the graft or from patent arteries within the aneurysm sac and may require endovascular reparation. The aneurysm, injury site, or malformation is identified using angiography. The endograft, contained inside a holding device, is introduced into the artery under fluoroscopy and positioned at the target zone area of repair. This may need to be done by open access exposure of the artery or by threading guidewires and catheters through to the site. Once the endograft is in place, it is deployed within the artery at the aneurysm site. Balloon angioplasties and other stent deployments necessary to position the graft or ensure proper functioning are part of this procedure. The graft position is confirmed, any endoleaks are identified, and the status of runoff vessels is evaluated for any related stenosis, dissection, thrombosis, or embolism.

35001-35002

The physician makes an incision in the neck in front of the sternocleidomastoid muscle. The section of the carotid or subclavian artery (35001) or the ruptured section (35002) is isolated and dissected from adjacent critical structures. Vessel clamps are affixed above and below the defect. The repair may be accomplished by removing the segment of artery containing the aneurysm and suturing the exposed ends of the vessel in an end-to-end fashion or the aneurysm may be bypassed with a venous or synthetic graft. If a large section is removed, a harvested or synthetic graft is inserted into the defect, or a patch may be sutured into place to open the diameter of the vessel. The skin incision is repaired with a layered closure.

35005

The physician makes an incision in the skin overlying the neck. The enlarged or blocked section of the vertebral artery is isolated and dissected from muscles and adjacent critical structures. A portion of a cervical vertebra may be removed to access the defect. Vessel clamps are affixed above and below the defect, which may be repaired or removed. The repair may be accomplished by removing the segment of artery containing the aneurysm and suturing the exposed ends of the vessel in an end-to-end fashion or the aneurysm may be bypassed with a venous or synthetic graft. If a large section is removed, a harvested or synthetic graft is inserted into the defect. Instead of a complete graft, a patch may be sutured into place to open the diameter of the vessel. Once the vessel is repaired, the clamps are removed. The skin incision is repaired with a layered closure.

35011-35013

The physician makes an incision in the skin of the arm or axilla. The enlarged or blocked section of the axillary or brachial artery (35011) or the ruptured section (35013) is isolated and dissected from adjacent critical structures. Vessel clamps are affixed above and below the defect, which may be repaired or removed. The repair may be accomplished by removing the segment of artery containing the aneurysm and suturing the exposed ends of the vessel in an end-to-end fashion or the aneurysm may be bypassed with a venous or synthetic graft. If a large section is removed, a harvested or synthetic graft is inserted into the defect. Instead of a complete graft, a patch may be sutured into place to open the diameter of the vessel. Once the vessel is repaired, the clamps are removed. The skin incision is repaired with a layered closure.

35021

The physician exposes the innominate or subclavian artery by median sternotomy or lateral thoracotomy. The physician anticoagulates the patient with heparin, clamps the aortic arch widely around the origin of the innominate artery, and clamps the right common carotid and right subclavian arteries. The physician excises the aneurysmal tissue. The physician may use a woven Dacron patch graft or harvested vein to repair the aneurysmal artery. The physician unclamps the aorta, as well as the right common carotid and right subclavian arteries. The physician closes the sternotomy or thoracotomy, leaving a chest tube in place.

35022

The physician exposes the innominate or subclavian artery by median sternotomy or lateral thoracotomy. The physician clamps the aortic arch widely around the origin of the innominate artery, and clamps the right common carotid and right subclavian arteries. The physician excises the ruptured aneurysmal tissue. The physician may use a woven Dacron patch graft or harvested vein to repair the aneurysmal artery. The physician unclamps the aorta, as well as the right common carotid and right subclavian arteries. The physician closes the sternotomy or thoracotomy, leaving a chest tube in place.

35045

The physician makes an incision in the skin overlying the arm. The enlarged or blocked section of the radial or ulnar artery is isolated and dissected from adjacent critical structures. Vessel clamps are affixed above and below the defect, which may be repaired or removed. The repair may be accomplished by removing the segment of artery containing the aneurysm and suturing the exposed ends of the vessel in an end-to-end fashion or the aneurysm may be bypassed with a venous or synthetic graft. If a large section is removed, a harvested or synthetic graft is inserted into the defect. Instead of a complete graft, a patch may be sutured into place to open the diameter of the vessel. Once the vessel is repaired, the clamps are removed. The skin incision is repaired with a layered closure.

35081

The physician exposes the abdominal aorta using a transperitoneal approach, placing a long incision in the mid abdomen. The physician retracts the transverse colon and small bowel to allow dissection and exposure of the aorta. The physician places an umbilical tape or rubber catheter around the aorta proximal to the aneurysm. The physician exposes the iliac arteries and achieves control of blood flow with umbilical tape or rubber catheters. The physician anticoagulates the patient and cross-clamps the iliac arteries and proximal aorta. The physician opens and clears the aneurysm, controls collateral bleeding from the lumbar arteries with suture, and sutures a Y-shaped knitted Dacron graft to the proximal aorta. The physician sutures the distal ends of the graft to the iliac arteries. The physician may anastomose the inferior mesenteric arteries and any aberrant or accessory renal arteries to the Dacron graft. The physician sutures the remaining aneurysmal shell around the graft and closes the retroperitoneum. The physician closes the abdominal wound, leaving drains in place.

35082

The physician quickly exposes the abdominal aorta using a transperitoneal approach, placing a long incision in the mid abdomen. The physician retracts the transverse colon and small bowel to allow dissection and exposure of the aorta. The physician quickly achieves control of bleeding by pushing the liver aside and compressing the aorta manually against the spine. The physician resuscitates the patient with fluids and blood products if necessary, cross-clamps the aorta proximal to the dissection. The physician exposes the iliac arteries and achieves control of blood flow with umbilical tape or rubber catheters. The physician anticoagulates the patient (if bleeding is controlled) and cross-clamps the iliac arteries and proximal aorta. The physician opens and clears the aneurysm, controls collateral bleeding from the lumbar arteries with suture, and sutures a Y-shaped knitted Dacron graft to the proximal aorta. The physician sutures the distal ends of the graft to the iliac arteries. The physician sutures the remaining aneurysmal shell around the graft and closes the retroperitoneum. The physician closes the abdominal wound, leaving drains in place.

35091

The physician exposes the abdominal aorta using a transperitoneal approach, placing a long incision in the midabdomen. The physician retracts the transverse colon and small bowel to allow dissection and exposure of the aorta. The physician places an umbilical tape or rubber catheter around the aorta proximal to the aneurysm. The physician exposes the iliac arteries and achieves control of blood flow with umbilical tape or rubber catheters. The physician anticoagulates the patient and cross-clamps the iliac arteries and proximal aorta. The physician opens and clears the aneurysm, controls collateral bleeding from the lumbar arteries with suture, and sutures a Y-shaped knitted Dacron graft to the proximal aorta. The physician sutures the distal ends of the graft to the iliac arteries. The physician may anastomose the inferior mesenteric arteries and any aberrant or accessory renal arteries to the Dacron graft. The physician sutures the remaining aneurysmal shell around the graft and closes the retroperitoneum. The physician closes the abdominal wound, leaving drains in place.

35092

The physician quickly exposes the abdominal aorta using a transperitoneal approach, placing a long incision in the midabdomen. The physician retracts the transverse colon and small bowel to allow dissection and exposure of the aorta. The physician quickly achieves control of bleeding by pushing the liver aside and compressing the aorta manually against the spine. The physician resuscitates the patient with fluids and blood products if necessary, then cross-clamps the aorta proximal to the dissection. The physician exposes the iliac arteries and achieves control of blood flow with umbilical tape or rubber catheters. The physician anticoagulates the patient (if bleeding is controlled) and cross-clamps the iliac arteries and proximal aorta. The physician opens and clears the aneurysm, controls collateral bleeding from the lumbar arteries with suture, then sutures a Y-shaped knitted Dacron graft to the proximal aorta. The physician sutures the distal ends of the graft to the iliac arteries. The physician may anastomose the celiac, inferior mesenteric, and/or renal arteries to the Dacron graft. The physician sutures the remaining aneurysmal shell around the graft and closes the retroperitoneum. The physician closes the abdominal wound, leaving drains in place.

35102
The physician exposes the abdominal aorta using a transperitoneal approach, placing a long incision in the mid abdomen. The physician retracts the transverse colon and small bowel to allow dissection and exposure of the aorta. The physician places an umbilical tape or rubber catheter around the aorta proximal to the aneurysm. The physician exposes the iliac arteries and achieves control of blood flow with umbilical tape or rubber catheters. The physician anticoagulates the patient and cross-clamps the iliac arteries and proximal aorta. The physician opens and clears the aneurysm, controls collateral bleeding from the lumbar arteries with suture, then sutures a Y-shaped knitted Dacron graft to the proximal aorta. The physician sutures the distal ends of the graft to the iliac arteries. The physician may anastomose grafts from other involved iliac vessels (common, hypogastric, external) to the Dacron graft. The physician sutures the remaining aneurysmal shell around the graft and closes the retroperitoneum. The physician closes the abdominal wound, leaving drains in place.

35103
The physician quickly exposes the abdominal aorta using a transperitoneal approach, placing a long incision in the mid abdomen. The physician retracts the transverse colon and small bowel to allow dissection and exposure of the aorta. The physician quickly achieves control of bleeding by pushing the liver aside and compressing the aorta manually against the spine. The physician resuscitates the patient with fluids and blood products if necessary, then cross-clamps the aorta proximal to the dissection. The physician exposes the iliac arteries and achieves control of blood flow with umbilical tape or rubber catheters. The physician anticoagulates the patient (if bleeding is controlled) and cross-clamps the iliac arteries and proximal aorta. The physician opens and clears the aneurysm, controls collateral bleeding from the lumbar arteries with suture, then sutures a Y-shaped knitted Dacron graft to the proximal aorta. The physician sutures the distal ends of the graft to the iliac arteries. The physician may anastomose the celiac, inferior mesenteric, and/or renal arteries to the Dacron graft. The physician sutures the remaining aneurysmal shell around the graft and closes the retroperitoneum. The physician closes the abdominal wound, leaving drains in place.

35111
The physician exposes the splenic artery using an abdominal incision. If the aneurysm involves the proximal or distal (hilar) splenic artery, the physician may repair the aneurysm using harvested venous material or synthetic graft material or simply tie off the diseased artery and vein. If the aneurysm involves the middle splenic artery, which is surrounded by pancreatic tissue, the surgeon may tie off the artery to avoid dissection of the pancreas. The physician closes the abdominal wound, leaving drains in place.

35112
The physician quickly exposes the splenic artery using an abdominal incision, and gains control of bleeding by clamping the proximal splenic artery. If the aneurysm involves the proximal or distal (hilar) splenic artery, the physician may repair the aneurysm (using harvested venous material or synthetic graft material) or simply tie off the diseased artery and vein. If the aneurysm involves the middle splenic artery, which is surrounded by pancreatic tissue, the surgeon may tie off the artery to avoid dissection of the pancreas. The physician closes the abdominal wound, leaving drains in place.

35121
The physician exposes the involved hepatic, celiac, renal, or mesenteric artery using an abdominal incision, retracting and dissecting past large and small bowel. If the aneurysm involves an artery whose vascular distribution has adequate collaterals (the common hepatic artery, for example), the physician may simply tie off the diseased artery. Otherwise, the physician repairs the aneurysm, often using harvested vein graft, harvested internal iliac artery graft, or synthetic graft material. The physician closes the abdominal wound, leaving drains in place.

35122
The physician quickly exposes the involved hepatic, celiac, renal, or mesenteric artery using an abdominal incision, retracting and dissecting past large and small bowel. The physician controls bleeding by clamping or compressing the involved artery proximal to the rupture. If the aneurysm involves an artery whose vascular distribution has adequate collaterals (the common hepatic artery, for example), the physician may simply tie off the diseased artery. Otherwise, the physician repairs the aneurysm, often using harvested vein graft, harvested internal iliac artery graft, or synthetic graft material. The physician closes the abdominal wound, leaving drains in place.

35131

The physician exposes the involved iliac arterial branch(es) using a low abdominal incision. The physician repairs the aneurysm, clamping off the affected artery proximally and distally, replacing the affected arterial segment with harvested venous material or synthetic graft material such as Dacron mesh. The physician confirms arterial patency with a Doppler probe or by angiography. The physician closes the abdominal wound, leaving drains in place.

35132

The physician quickly exposes the involved iliac arterial branch(es) using a low abdominal incision. The physician gains control of bleeding by clamping or compressing the proximal segment of the affected artery. The physician repairs the aneurysm, clamping off the affected artery proximally and distally, replacing the affected arterial segment with harvested venous material or synthetic graft material such as Dacron mesh. The physician confirms arterial patency with a Doppler probe or by angiography. The physician closes the abdominal wound, leaving drains in place.

35141-35142

The physician makes an incision in the skin of the leg. The enlarged or blocked section of the femoral artery (35141) or ruptured section (35142) is isolated and dissected from adjacent critical structures. Vessel clamps are affixed above and below the defect, which may be repaired or removed. The repair may be accomplished by removing the segment of artery containing the aneurysm and suturing the exposed ends of the vessel in an end-to-end fashion or the aneurysm may be bypassed with a venous or synthetic graft. If a large section is removed, a harvested or synthetic graft is inserted into the defect. Instead of a complete graft, a patch may be sutured into place to open the diameter of the vessel. Once the vessel is repaired, the clamps are removed. The skin incision is repaired with a layered closure.

35151-35152

The physician makes an incision in the skin over the leg. The enlarged or blocked section of the popliteal artery (35151) or the ruptured section (35152) is isolated and dissected from adjacent critical structures. Vessel clamps are affixed above and below the defect, which may be repaired or removed. The repair may be accomplished by removing the segment of artery containing the aneurysm and suturing the exposed ends of the vessel in an end-to-end fashion or the aneurysm may be bypassed with a venous or synthetic graft. If a large section is removed, a harvested or synthetic graft is inserted into the defect. Instead of a complete graft, a patch may be sutured into place to open the diameter of the vessel. Once the vessel is repaired, the clamps are removed. The skin incision is repaired with a layered closure.

35180

The physician makes an incision in the skin of the head or neck over the site of the unnatural opening, a congenital fistula, that exists between an artery and vein. The fistula is isolated and dissected from adjacent critical structures, and vessel clamps are applied to the vein and the artery. The walls of the artery and vein creating the fistula are each sutured closed. A graft or patch graft may be required to complete the repair. The fistula is tied off, or it may be excised. Once the fistula has been eliminated, the clamps are removed and the skin incision is repaired with a layered closure.

35182

The physician exposes the congenital arteriovenous fistula by choosing an incision appropriate to the fistula site. The physician examines the fistulous connection and repairs it by ligation (tying it off), if possible. The physician may repair the fistula by clamping the connection from both sides, dividing the connection with scissors, and closing each side with suture. The physician may sew in synthetic graft material or vein material harvested from the patient to enlarge the arterial or venous lumen. The physician may confirm vessel patency with Doppler probe or angiography prior to closing the wound. The physician may leave surgical drains in place.

35184

The physician makes an incision in the skin of an extremity over the site of the unnatural opening, a congenital fistula, that exists between an artery and vein. The fistula is isolated and dissected from adjacent critical structures, and vessel clamps are applied to the vein and the artery. The walls of the artery and vein creating the fistula are each sutured closed. A graft or patch graft may be required to complete the repair. The fistula is tied off, or it may be excised. Once the fistula has been eliminated, the clamps are removed and the skin incision is repaired with a layered closure.

35188-35189

The physician makes an incision in the skin of the head or neck over the site of the unnatural opening, a fistula, created through trauma. The fistula connects an artery to a vein. The fistula is isolated and dissected from adjacent critical structures, and vessel clamps are applied to the vein and the artery. The walls of the artery and vein creating the fistula are each repaired and closed. A graft or patch graft may be required to complete the repair. The fistula is tied off or excised. Once the fistula has been eliminated, the clamps are removed and the skin incision is repaired with a layered closure. Report 35189 if either fistula is in the thorax or abdomen.

35190

The physician makes an incision in the skin of an extremity at the site of the unnatural opening, a fistula, created through trauma. It connects an artery to a vein. The fistula is isolated and dissected from adjacent critical structures, and vessel clamps are applied to the vein and the artery. The walls of the artery and vein creating the fistula are each repaired and closed. A graft or patch graft may be required to complete the repair. The fistula is tied off or excised. Once the fistula has been eliminated, the clamps are removed and the skin incision is repaired with a layered closure.

35201
The physician makes an incision in the skin of the neck over the site of an injured blood vessel. The vessel is isolated and dissected from adjacent critical structures, and vessel clamps are applied. The edges of the injured vessel may be trimmed to ease repair. A patch graft may be sutured over the defect or the hole in the vessel may be repaired with sutures. The clamps are removed and the skin incision is repaired with a layered closure.

35206
The physician makes an incision in the skin of an upper extremity over the site of an injured blood vessel. The vessel is isolated and dissected from adjacent critical structures, and vessel clamps are applied. The edges of the injured vessel may be trimmed to ease repair. A patch graft may be sutured over the defect or the hole in the vessel may be repaired with sutures. The clamps are removed and the skin incision is repaired with a layered closure.

35207
The physician makes an incision in the skin of the hand or finger over the site of an injured blood vessel. The vessel is isolated and dissected from adjacent critical structures, and vessel clamps are applied. The edges of the injured vessel may be trimmed to ease repair. A patch graft may be sutured over the defect or the hole in the vessel may be repaired with sutures. The clamps are removed and the skin incision is repaired with a layered closure.

35211
The physician exposes the abnormal blood vessel (arterial or venous) by choosing a thoracic incision appropriate to the involved vessel. The physician places cardiopulmonary bypass catheters (through incisions in the low inferior vena cava, the superior vena cava, and high aorta or femoral artery). The physician stops the heart by infusing cardioplegia solution into the coronary circulation. The physician examines the abnormal vessel and repairs it by ligation (tying it off), if possible. The physician may repair the vessel by clamping it proximally and distally to the defect, and suturing the defect closed. The physician may repair the vessel by sewing in synthetic graft material or vein material harvested from the patient in order to enlarge the lumen of the repaired vessel (patch graft). The physician confirms vessel patency with Doppler probe or angiography prior to taking the patient off cardiopulmonary bypass and closing the wound. The physician leaves chest and, possibly, mediastinal drains in place.

35216
The physician exposes the abnormal blood vessel (arterial or venous) by choosing a thoracic incision appropriate to the involved vessel. The physician examines the abnormal vessel and repairs it by ligation if possible. The physician may repair the vessel by clamping it proximally and distally to the defect, and suturing the defect closed. The physician may repair the vessel by sewing in synthetic graft material or vein material harvested from the patient in order to enlarge the lumen of the repaired vessel (patch graft). The physician confirms vessel patency with Doppler probe or angiography prior to closing the wound. The physician leaves chest and, possibly, mediastinal drains in place. If repair is accomplished with a venous bypass (rather than patch) graft, use 35246. If repair is accomplished with a synthetic bypass (rather than patch) graft, use 35276.

35221
The physician exposes the abnormal blood vessel (arterial or venous) by choosing an abdominal incision appropriate to the involved vessel. The physician examines the abnormal vessel and repairs it by ligation (tying it off), if possible. The physician may repair the vessel by clamping it proximally and distally to the defect, and suturing the defect closed. The physician confirms vessel patency with Doppler probe or angiography prior to closing the wound. The physician leaves surgical drains in place.

35226
The physician makes an incision in the skin of a lower extremity over the site of an injured blood vessel. The vessel is isolated and dissected from adjacent critical structures, and vessel clamps are applied. The edges of the injured vessel may be trimmed to ease repair. A patch graft may be sutured over the defect or the hole in the vessel may be repaired with sutures. The clamps are removed and the skin incision is repaired with a layered closure.

35231
The physician makes an incision in the skin in the neck over the site of an injured blood vessel. The vessel is isolated and dissected from adjacent critical structures, and vessel clamps are applied. The defect is too extensive to repair directly, so the physician removes a short length of vein. The physician repairs the injured vessel with a length of vein harvested from another site in the body or with cadaver vein. The vein is sutured end-to-end to the vessel, replacing the excised portion, or is used as a patch to repair a large hole in the side of the vessel. A patch graft may be sutured over any remaining the defect. The clamps are removed and the skin incision is repaired with a layered closure.

35236
The physician makes an incision in the skin of an upper extremity over the site of an injured blood vessel. The vessel is isolated and dissected from

adjacent critical structures, and vessel clamps are applied. The defect is too extensive to repair directly, so the physician removes a short length of vein. The physician repairs the injured vessel with a length of vein harvested from another site in the body or with cadaver vein. The vein is sutured end-to-end to the vessel, replacing the excised portion, or is used as a patch to repair a large hole in the side of the vessel. A patch graft may be sutured over any remaining defect. The clamps are removed and the skin incision is repaired with a layered closure.

35241
The physician exposes the abnormal blood vessel (arterial or venous) by choosing a thoracic incision appropriate to the involved vessel. The physician places cardiopulmonary bypass catheters through incisions in the low inferior vena cava, the superior vena cava, and high aorta or femoral artery. The physician stops the heart by infusing cardioplegia solution into the coronary circulation. The physician examines the abnormal vessel and repairs it by clamping proximally and distally to the defect, and sewing in venous graft material harvested from the patient in order to bypass the abnormal area of the vessel (bypass graft). The physician confirms vessel patency with Doppler probe or angiography prior to taking the patient off cardiopulmonary bypass and closing the wound. The physician leaves chest and, possibly, mediastinal drains in place. If repair is accomplished with a venous patch (rather than bypass) graft, use 35211. If repair is accomplished with a synthetic bypass (rather than venous bypass) graft, use 35271.

35246
The physician exposes the abnormal blood vessel (arterial or venous) by choosing a thoracic incision appropriate to the involved vessel. The physician examines the abnormal vessel and repairs it by clamping proximally and distally to the defect, and sewing in vein material harvested from the patient in order to bypass the abnormal portion of the repaired vessel (bypass graft). The physician confirms vessel patency with Doppler probe or angiography prior to closing the wound. The physician leaves chest and, possibly, mediastinal drains in place. If repair is accomplished with a venous patch (rather than bypass) graft, use 35216. If repair is accomplished with a synthetic bypass (rather than venous bypass) graft, use 35276.

35251
The physician exposes the abnormal blood vessel (arterial or venous) by choosing an abdominal incision appropriate to the involved vessel. The physician examines the abnormal vessel and repairs it by clamping proximally and distally to the defect, and sewing in vein material harvested from the patient in order to bypass the abnormal area of the diseased vessel (bypass graft). The physician confirms vessel patency with Doppler probe or angiography prior to closing the wound. The physician leaves surgical drains in place. If repair is accomplished with a venous patch (rather than bypass) graft, use 35221. If repair is accomplished with a synthetic bypass (rather than patch) graft, use 35281.

35256
The physician makes an incision in the skin of a lower extremity over the site of an injured blood vessel. The vessel is isolated and dissected from adjacent critical structures, and vessel clamps are applied. The defect is too extensive to repair directly, so the physician removes a short length of vein. The physician repairs the injured vessel with a length of vein harvested from another site in the body or with cadaver vein. The vein is sutured end-to-end to the vessel, replacing the excised portion, or is used as a patch to repair a large hole in the side of the vessel. A patch graft may be sutured over any remaining defect. The clamps are removed and the skin incision is repaired with a layered closure.

35261
The physician makes an incision in the skin of the neck over the site of an injured blood vessel. The vessel is isolated and dissected from adjacent critical structures, and vessel clamps are applied. The defect is too extensive to repair directly, so the physician removes a short length of vein. The physician repairs the injured vessel with a length of synthetic graft material. The synthetic vein is sutured end-to-end to the vessel, replacing the excised portion. A patch graft may be sutured over any remaining defect. The clamps are removed and the skin incision is repaired with a layered closure.

35266
The physician makes an incision in the skin of an upper extremity over the site of an injured blood vessel. The vessel is isolated and dissected from adjacent critical structures, and vessel clamps are applied. The defect is too extensive to repair directly, so the physician removes a short length of vein. The physician repairs the injured vessel with a length of synthetic graft material. The synthetic vein is sutured end-to-end to the vessel, replacing the excised portion. A patch graft may be sutured over any remaining defect. The clamps are removed and the skin incision is repaired with a layered closure.

35271
The physician exposes the abnormal blood vessel (arterial or venous) by choosing a thoracic incision appropriate to the involved vessel. The physician places cardiopulmonary bypass catheters (through incisions in the low inferior vena cava, the superior vena cava, and high aorta or femoral artery). The physician stops the heart by infusing cardioplegia solution into the coronary circulation. The physician

examines the abnormal vessel and repairs it by clamping proximally and distally to the defect, and sewing in synthetic graft material in order to bypass the abnormal area of the vessel (bypass graft). The physician confirms vessel patency with Doppler probe or angiography prior to taking the patient off cardiopulmonary bypass and closing the wound. The physician leaves chest and, possibly, mediastinal drains in place. If repair is accomplished with a venous patch (rather than bypass) graft, use 35211. If repair is accomplished with a venous bypass (rather than synthetic bypass) graft, use 35241.

35276

The physician exposes the abnormal blood vessel (arterial or venous) by choosing a thoracic incision appropriate to the involved vessel. The physician examines the abnormal vessel and repairs it by clamping proximally and distally to the defect, and sewing in synthetic graft material in order to bypass the abnormal portion of the repaired vessel (bypass graft). The physician confirms vessel patency with Doppler probe or angiography prior to closing the wound. The physician leaves chest and, possibly, mediastinal drains in place. If repair is accomplished with a venous patch (rather than bypass) graft, use 35216. If repair is accomplished with a venous bypass (rather than synthetic bypass) graft, use 35246.

35281

The physician exposes the abnormal blood vessel (arterial or venous) by choosing an abdominal incision appropriate to the involved vessel. The physician examines the abnormal vessel and repairs it by clamping proximally and distally to the defect, and sewing in synthetic graft material in order to bypass the abnormal area of the diseased vessel (bypass graft). The physician confirms vessel patency with Doppler probe or angiography prior to closing the wound. The physician leaves surgical drains in place. If repair is accomplished with a venous patch (rather than bypass) graft, use 35221. If repair is accomplished with a venous bypass (rather than synthetic bypass) graft, use 35251.

35286

The physician makes an incision in the skin of a lower extremity over the site of an injured blood vessel. The vessel is isolated and dissected from adjacent critical structures, and vessel clamps are applied. The defect is too extensive to repair directly, so the physician removes a short length of vein. The physician repairs the injured vessel with a length of synthetic graft material. The synthetic vein is sutured end-to-end to the vessel, replacing the excised portion. A patch graft may be sutured over any remaining defect. The clamps are removed and the skin incision is repaired with a layered closure.

35301

The physician makes an incision in the skin of the neck over the site of plaque or abnormal lining of the carotid, vertebral, or subclavian artery. The vessel is isolated and dissected from adjacent critical structures and vessel clamps are applied. A temporary vascular shunt may be placed, bypassing the area and allowing blood supply to continue uninterrupted during the procedure. The vessel is incised. Using a blunt, spatula-like tool, the plaque and the vessel lining are separated from the artery and removed. The edge of the normal artery lining may be sutured to the artery wall to prevent separation when blood flow resumes. After the plaque and lining are removed, a patch graft taken from another portion of the patient's body, a cadaver, or a synthetic source may be applied and sutured to the vessel. This enlarges the diameter of the artery. The vessel clamps are removed and the skin incision is repaired with layered closure.

35302-35304

The physician makes an incision in the skin of the leg over the site of a blood clot, plaque, or abnormal lining of the superficial femoral (35302), popliteal (35303), or tibioperoneal trunk (35304) arteries. The vessels are isolated and dissected from adjacent critical structures and vessel clamps are applied. The vessels are incised. Using a blunt, spatula-like tool, the plaque and the vessel lining are separated from the arteries and removed. The edge of the normal artery linings may be sutured to the artery walls to prevent separation when blood flow resumes. After the plaque and lining are removed, patch grafts taken from another portion of the patient's body, a cadaver, or a synthetic source may be applied and sutured to the vessels. This enlarges the diameter of the arteries. The vessel clamps are removed and the skin incision is repaired with layered closure.

35305

A thromboendarterectomy is performed on a tibial or peroneal artery. The physician makes an incision in the skin over the site of plaque or abnormal lining of a tibial or peroneal artery. The vessel is isolated and dissected from adjacent critical structures and vessel clamps are applied. The vessel is incised. Using a blunt, spatula-like tool, the plaque and the vessel lining are separated from the artery and removed. The edge of the normal artery lining may be sutured to the artery wall to prevent separation when blood flow resumes. After the plaque and lining are removed, a patch graft taken from another portion of the patient's body, a cadaver, or a synthetic source may be applied and sutured to the vessel. This enlarges the diameter of the artery. The vessel clamps are removed and the skin incision is repaired with layered closure. Report 35305 for thromboendarterectomy of the initial tibial or peroneal vessel.

35306
An additional thromboendarterectomy is performed on a tibial or peroneal artery. The physician makes an incision in the skin over the site of plaque or abnormal lining of an additional tibial or peroneal artery during a surgical session in which one tibial or peroneal artery has already been treated. The additional vessel is isolated and dissected from adjacent critical structures and vessel clamps are applied. The vessel is incised. Using a blunt, spatula-like tool, the plaque and the vessel lining are separated from the artery and removed. The edge of the normal artery lining may be sutured to the artery wall to prevent separation when blood flow resumes. After the plaque and lining are removed, a patch graft taken from another portion of the patient's body, a cadaver, or a synthetic source may be applied and sutured to the vessel. This enlarges the diameter of the artery. The vessel clamps are removed and the skin incision is repaired with layered closure.

35311
The physician exposes the innominate or subclavian artery by median sternotomy or lateral thoracotomy. The physician clamps the aortic arch widely around the origin of the diseased artery, then clamps the distal end of the diseased artery. After making a longitudinal incision in the diseased artery, the physician uses a spatula to remove the atherosclerotic material. The physician may tack (suture) down the inner layer of the artery with a few 6-0 sutures before closing the artery with suture. A woven Dacron patch graft or harvested vein may be used to enlarge the arterial lumen (patch graft). The physician unclamps the aorta, as well as the distal arterial clamp, and closes the sternotomy or thoracotomy, leaving a chest tube in place.

35321
The physician makes an incision in the skin of the axilla or arm over the site of a blood clot, plaque, or abnormal lining of the axillary or brachial artery. The vessel is isolated and dissected from adjacent critical structures and vessel clamps are applied. The vessel is incised. Using a blunt, spatula-like tool, the plaque and the vessel lining are separated from the artery and removed. The edge of the normal artery lining may be sutured to the artery wall to prevent separation when blood flow resumes. After the plaque and lining are removed, a patch graft taken from another portion of the patient's body, a cadaver, or a synthetic source may be applied and sutured to the vessel. This enlarges the diameter of the artery. The vessel clamps are removed and the skin incision is repaired with layered closure.

35331
The physician exposes the abdominal aorta using a transperitoneal approach, placing a long incision in the mid abdomen. The physician retracts the transverse colon and small bowel to allow dissection and exposure of the aorta. The physician exposes the iliac arteries and achieves control of blood flow with umbilical tape or rubber catheters placed proximal to the diseased area. The physician anticoagulates the patient and cross-clamps the iliac arteries and proximal aorta. A longitudinal incision down the affected portion of abdominal aorta allows the physician to use a spatula to remove the atherosclerotic material. The physician may tack (suture) down the inner layer of the aorta with small sutures. A woven Dacron patch graft or harvested vein may be used to enlarge the aortic lumen (patch graft). The physician sutures the aorta closed, closes the retroperitoneum, and closes the abdominal wound, leaving drains in place.

35341
The physician exposes the involved mesenteric, celiac, or renal artery using an abdominal incision, retracting and dissecting past large and small bowel. The physician clamps the aorta to isolate the involved vessel, places a longitudinal incision down the affected vessel, and uses a spatula to remove the atherosclerotic material. If there is significant stenosis at the arterial takeoff, the physician may open the aorta and remove the atherosclerotic material from within the aorta before suturing the aorta and diseased artery closed. The physician may use harvested vein to enlarge the arterial lumen (patch graft). The physician may perform arteriography or use a Doppler probe to establish patency of the vessel, before closing the abdominal wound, leaving drains in place.

35351
The physician exposes the involved iliac artery using an abdominal incision, retracting and dissecting past large and small bowel. The physician clamps the aorta to isolate the involved vessel, places a longitudinal incision down the affected vessel, and uses a spatula to remove the atherosclerotic material. If there is significant stenosis at the arterial takeoff, the physician may open the aorta and remove the atherosclerotic material from within the aorta before suturing the aorta and diseased artery closed. The physician may use harvested vein to enlarge the arterial lumen (patch graft). The physician may perform arteriography or use a Doppler probe to establish patency of the vessel before closing the abdominal wound, leaving drains in place.

35355
The physician exposes the involved iliac artery using abdominal and femoral incisions, retracting and dissecting past large and small bowel. The physician exposes the femoral artery via the femoral incision. The physician clamps the aorta to isolate the involved vessel, places a longitudinal incision down the involved vessel, and uses a spatula to remove the atherosclerotic material. If there is significant stenosis at the arterial takeoff, the physician may open the aorta and remove the atherosclerotic material from within the aorta before suturing the aorta and diseased artery closed. The physician may use harvested vein to enlarge the

arterial lumen (patch graft). The physician may perform arteriography or use a Doppler probe to establish patency of the vessel before closing the abdominal and femoral wounds, leaving drains in place.

35361
The physician exposes the involved iliac artery using an abdominal incision, retracting and dissecting past large and small bowel. The physician clamps the proximal aorta above the diseased area, places a longitudinal incision down the distal aorta and affected iliac artery, and uses a spatula to remove the atherosclerotic material before suturing the aorta and iliac artery closed. The physician may use harvested vein to enlarge the aortic or arterial lumen (patch graft). The physician may perform arteriography or use a Doppler probe to establish patency of the vessel before closing the abdominal wound, leaving drains in place.

35363
The physician exposes the involved abdominal aorta and iliac artery using an abdominal incision, retracting and dissecting past large and small bowel. The physician exposes the involved femoral artery via a femoral incision and dissection. The physician clamps the proximal aorta above the diseased area, places a longitudinal incision down the distal aorta and affected iliac artery, and uses a spatula to remove the atherosclerotic material before suturing the aorta and iliac artery closed. The physician places a longitudinal incision down the femoral artery and uses a spatula to remove any atherosclerotic material before sewing the femoral artery closed. The physician may use harvested vein to enlarge the aortic or arterial lumen (patch graft). The physician may perform arteriography or use a Doppler probe to establish patency of the vessel. The physician closes the femoral and abdominal wounds, leaving drains in place.

35371-35372
The physician makes an incision in the skin over the leg at the site of a blood clot, plaque, or abnormal lining of the common femoral artery (35371) or the deep (profunda) femoral artery (35372). The vessel is isolated and dissected from adjacent critical structures and vessel clamps are applied. The vessel is incised. Using a blunt, spatula-like tool, the plaque and the vessel lining are separated from the artery and removed. The edge of the normal artery lining may be sutured to the artery wall to prevent separation when blood flow resumes. After the plaque and lining are removed, a patch graft taken from another portion of the patient's body, a cadaver, or a synthetic source may be applied and sutured to the vessel. This enlarges the diameter of the artery. The vessel clamps are removed and the skin incision is repaired with layered closure.

35390
The physician makes an incision in the skin of the neck over the site of plaque or abnormal lining of the carotid, vertebral, or subclavian artery. The vessel is isolated and dissected from adjacent critical structures, and vessel clamps are applied. A temporary vascular shunt may be placed, bypassing the area and allowing blood supply to continue uninterrupted during the procedure. The vessel is incised. Using a blunt, spatula-like tool, the plaque and the vessel lining are separated from the artery and removed. The edge of the normal artery lining may be sutured to the artery wall to prevent separation when blood flow resumes. After the plaque and lining are removed, a patch graft taken from another portion of the patient's body, a cadaver, or a synthetic source may be applied and sutured to the vessel. This enlarges the diameter of the artery. The vessel clamps are removed and the skin incision is repaired with a layered closure. Use 35390 in conjunction with 35301.

35400
The purpose of this procedure is to use an endoscope to look inside a blood vessel. The physician places an introducer sheath in the vessel to be examined, using percutaneous puncture or a cutdown technique. The physician places an angioscopy catheter through the introducer sheath into the vessel to be examined. The physician advances the angioscope through the vessel, clearing the view with injections of saline. Once the inside of the vessel has been examined, the angioscope and sheath are withdrawn. Vessel hemostasis is achieved using sutures or manual pressure.

35450-35460
The physician makes an incision in the skin overlying the femoral artery. The artery is dissected from adjacent critical structures, and vessel clamps are applied. The physician may nick the artery to create an opening into which a catheter with a balloon attached is inserted into the vessel and threaded. The catheter is fed into the narrowed portion of the aorta, where its balloon is inflated in the narrowed area. The blood vessel is stretched to a larger diameter, allowing a more normal outflow of blood through the area. Several inflations may be performed along the narrowed area. The catheter is slowly withdrawn after deflation. Occasionally, the opening in the artery is repaired with sutures. The skin incision is repaired with a layered closure. Report 35450 if performed on the renal or another visceral artery; report 35452 if performed on the aortic artery; report 35454 if performed on the iliac artery; report 35456 if performed on the femoral-popliteal artery; report 35458 if performed on the brachiocephalic trunk or branches; report 35459 if performed on the tibioperoneal trunk and branches; and report 35460 if venous.

35470-35476

The physician isolates the femoral artery or (on occasion) the popliteal artery and inserts a large needle through the skin and into the artery. A guidance wire is threaded through the needle into the artery. The needle is removed. A catheter with a balloon attached follows the wire into the artery. The wire is removed. The catheter is fed through the arterial system and into the narrowed portion of the tibioperoneal trunk and, if necessary, one of its branches. There, the balloon is inflated. The blood vessel is stretched to a larger diameter, allowing a more normal outflow of blood through the area. Several inflations may be performed along the narrowed area. The catheter is slowly withdrawn after deflation. Pressure is applied to the puncture site to stop the bleeding after the catheter is removed. Report 35470 if tibioperoneal trunk or branches are treated; report 35471 if renal or visceral; report 35472 if aortic; report 35473 if iliac; report 35474 if femoral popliteal; report 35475 if brachiocephalic trunk or branches; report 35476 if venous.

35480-35485

The physician creates a femoral cutdown incision to expose one of the femoral arteries. The physician punctures the femoral artery with a large needle and passes a guidewire via the needle into the femoral artery. The physician removes the needle while leaving the guidewire in place, enlarges the arterial opening slightly with a blade, then slides an introducer sheath over the guidewire into the arterial lumen. The physician slides a guidewire through the atherectomy catheter or device, and inserts the guidewire/ atherectomy catheter combination through the introducer sheath into the aorta. The physician fluoroscopically positions the atherectomy device at the aortic stenosis and activates the device to remove the stenotic tissue. The physician rechecks the diameter of the lesion by angiography. The physician may perform several passes with the atherectomy device. The physician removes the atherectomy catheter, guidewire, and introducer sheath, closing the femoral arteriotomy with suture. The physician closes the femoral cutdown incision with suture. Report 35480 if the occlusion is in the renal or other visceral artery; report 35481 if it is located in the aortic artery; report 35482 if it is located in the iliac artery; report 35483 if it is located in the femoral-popliteal artery; report 35484 if it is located in the brachiocephalic trunk or branches; and report 35485 if located in the tibioperoneal trunk and branches.

35490-35495

The physician punctures the femoral artery with a large needle and passes a guidewire via the needle into the femoral artery. The physician removes the needle while leaving the guidewire in place, enlarges the arterial opening slightly with a blade, then slides an introducer sheath over the guidewire into the arterial lumen. The physician slides a guidewire through the atherectomy catheter or device, and inserts the guidewire/ atherectomy catheter combination through the introducer sheath up the aorta and out into the involved renal or other visceral artery. The physician fluoroscopically positions the atherectomy device at the arterial stenosis and activates the device to remove the stenotic tissue. The physician rechecks the diameter of the lesion by angiography. The physician may perform several passes with the atherectomy device. The physician removes the atherectomy catheter, guidewire, and introducer sheath, compressing the femoral artery manually until hemostasis is achieved. Report 35490 if performed in the renal or other visceral artery; report 35491 if performed in the aortic artery; report 35492 if performed in the iliac artery; report 35493 if performed in the femoral-popliteal artery; report 35494 if performed in the brachiocephalic trunk or branches; report 35495 if performed in the tibioperoneal trunk and branches.

35500

The physician harvests a vein from an upper extremity (arm) to use for a planned bypass procedure on a lower extremity vessel (leg) or coronary artery. An incision is made over the site on the arm. Tissue is dissected to the vein. The portion of the vein to be removed is released from the surrounding structures, and is tied off above and below the portion of vein to be removed. The vein is removed. The wound is closed with layered sutures. The portion of vein removed is prepared for use in a separately reportable bypass graft procedure of a leg vessel or coronary artery.

35501

The physician bypasses a blocked segment of common carotid artery to a segment of internal carotid artery on the same side of the neck. Through an incision in the skin of the neck in front of the sternocleidomastoid muscle, the physician isolates and dissects the common carotid artery, separating it from adjacent structures. After vessel clamps are affixed above and below the defect, the physician creates a bypass around the defective section of common carotid artery. The common carotid artery may be cut through below the damaged area and sutured to one end of the harvest vein (end-to-end), which is then sutured to the internal carotid artery beyond the affected area. As an alternative, the ends of the harvested vein are sutured into the side of the common carotid arterial wall and to the side of the internal carotid arterial wall (end-to-side). Either method results in a bypass of the damaged area. When the clamps are removed, the section of vein graft forms a new path through which blood can easily bypass the blocked area. The defective common carotid artery is not removed. After the graft is complete, the skin incision is repaired with layered closure.

35506
The physician bypasses a segment of blocked common carotid or subclavian artery. Through an incision in the skin at the side of the neck, the physician isolates and dissects the subclavian and common carotid arteries, separating them from adjacent critical structures. In this procedure, a blocked common carotid arterial flow may be bypassed to the subclavian artery, or a blocked subclavian arterial flow may be bypassed to the common carotid artery. To create a bypass around a section of artery that is damaged or blocked, the physician uses a harvested vein and one of two methods of repair. After vessel clamps have been affixed above and below the damaged area, the graft is sewn to the side of the two arteries (end-to-side) or cut ends may be sewn (end-to-end). The graft is attached above the portion of blocked artery. The blocked portion of artery is not removed. When the clamps are removed in either case, the section of vein graft forms a new path through which blood can easily bypass the blocked area. After the graft is complete, the skin incision is repaired with layered closure.

35508
Through an incision in the skin of the neck, the physician isolates and dissects the vertebral and carotid arteries, separating them from adjacent critical structures. The physician creates a bypass around a section of vertebral artery that is damaged or blocked, using a harvested vein and one of two methods of repair. After vessel clamps have been affixed above and below the damaged area, the graft is sewn to the side of the carotid artery and sewn to the side of the vertebral artery beyond the affected area (end-to-side) or sewn over the cut end of the vertebral artery after dividing it beyond the affected area (end-to-end). The damaged or blocked section of the vertebral artery is not removed. When the clamps are removed, the section of vein graft forms a new path through which blood can easily bypass the blocked area. After the graft is complete, the skin incision is repaired with a layered closure.

35509
The physician performs a vein bypass graft from one carotid to the contralateral carotid. Through incisions in the skin of the neck, the physician isolates and dissects the carotid arteries, separating them from adjacent critical structures. The physician creates a bypass around a section of carotid artery that is damaged or blocked, using a harvested vein and one of two methods of repair. After vessel clamps have been affixed above and below the damaged area, the ends of the vein graft are sutured into the side of the carotid arterial wall (end-to-side). In the second method, the carotid artery may be cut through above the damaged area and sutured to one end of a harvested vein, which is sutured to the side of the carotid artery on the opposite side of the neck (end-to-end). In either case, the blocked or damaged section of artery is not removed. When the clamps are removed, the section of vein graft forms a new path through which blood can easily bypass the blocked or damaged area. After the graft is complete, the skin incisions are repaired with layered closures.

35510
Through an incision in the skin at the side of the neck, the physician dissects down to the common carotid artery, separating soft tissue and adjacent critical structures. Soft tissue must be cleared for several centimeters. Dissection through the skin and soft tissue at the distal anastomosis site of this bypass graft is also done over the brachial artery in the arm. Next, a tunnel is made from the carotid through the axilla and down the arm to the brachial artery site. To create a bypass graft around the section of brachial artery that is damaged or blocked, the physician uses a harvested vein, usually the greater saphenous. After vascular clamps have been affixed above and below the anastomosis area on the carotid artery, the proximal arteriotomy is carried out and the harvested vein is sutured to the carotid artery. When this is completed and checked for hemorrhaging, the arterial clamps are removed. The vein graft is tunneled through the prepared space to the brachial artery and the distal arteriotomy and anastomosis are carried out in the same manner. The clamps are removed, additional sutures may be placed for complete hemostasis, and the patency of the graft is checked. The incisions are closed and the appropriate pulses are checked again before dressings are applied.

35511
Through incisions in the skin at the base of the neck, the physician isolates and dissects the subclavian arteries, separating them from adjacent critical structures. The physician creates a bypass around a section of subclavian artery that is damaged or blocked, using a harvested vein and one of two methods of repair after vessel clamps have been affixed above and below the defect. In the first method of repair the ends of the vein graft are sutured into the sides of the walls of the two subclavian arteries, resulting in a bypass of the damaged area. In the second method, the subclavian artery may be cut through beyond the damaged area and sutured to one end of a harvested vein, which is sutured to the subclavian artery on the opposite side of the neck. In either case, the blocked or damaged portion of the artery is not removed. When the clamps are removed, the section of vein graft forms a new path through which blood can easily bypass the blocked area. After the graft is complete, the skin incisions are repaired with a layered closure.

35512
Through an incision in the skin at the base of the neck, the physician dissects down to the subclavian artery just above the clavicle, separating soft tissue and adjacent critical structures. Soft tissue must be cleared

for several centimeters. Dissection through the skin and soft tissue at the distal anastomosis site for this bypass graft is also done over the brachial artery in the arm. Next, a tunnel is made from the subclavian, under the clavicle, through the axilla, and down the arm to the brachial artery site. To create a bypass graft around the section of brachial artery that is damaged or blocked, the physician uses a harvested vein, usually the greater saphenous. After vascular clamps have been affixed above and below the anastomosis area on the subclavian artery, the proximal arteriotomy is carried out and the harvested vein is sutured to the subclavian artery. When this is completed and checked for hemorrhaging, the arterial clamps are removed. The vein graft is tunneled through the prepared space to the brachial artery and the distal arteriotomy and anastomosis are carried out in the same manner. The clamps are removed, additional sutures may be placed for complete hemostasis, and the patency of the graft is checked. The incisions are closed and the appropriate pulses are checked again before dressings are applied.

35515

Through an incision in the skin of the neck, the physician isolates and dissects the vertebral and subclavian arteries, separating them from adjacent critical structures. The physician creates a bypass around a section of vertebral artery that is damaged or blocked, using a harvested vein and one of two methods of repair. Once vessel clamps are affixed above and below the defect, the ends of the harvested vein are sutured into the sides of the subclavian and vertebral arterial walls resulting in a bypass of the damaged area (end-to-side). In the second method, the vertebral artery can be cut through above the damaged area and sutured to one end of a harvested vein (end-to-end). The remaining end is sutured to the subclavian artery. In either case, the blocked or damaged vertebral artery is not removed. When the clamps are removed, the section of vein graft forms a new path through which blood can easily bypass the blocked area. After the graft is complete, the skin incision is repaired with a layered closure.

35516

Through an incision in the skin at the base of the neck and axilla, the physician isolates and dissects the subclavian and axillary arteries, separating them from adjacent critical structures. The physician creates a bypass around a section of subclavian artery that is damaged or blocked, using a harvested vein and one of two methods of repair. Once vessel clamps have been affixed above and below the defect, the ends of the harvested vein are sutured into the sides of the subclavian and axillary arterial walls resulting in a bypass of the damaged area (end-to-side). In the second method, the subclavian artery may be cut through before the damaged area and sutured to one end of a harvested vein, which is sutured to the axillary artery (end-to-end). The blocked or damaged portion of the subclavian artery is not removed. When the clamps are removed, the section of vein graft forms a new path through which blood can easily bypass the blocked area. After the graft is complete, the skin incisions are repaired with a layered closure.

35518

The physician makes an incision in the skin of both axillae. The physician creates a bypass around a section of axillary or subclavian artery that is damaged or blocked, using a harvested vein and one of two methods of repair. Once vessel clamps have been affixed above and below the defect, the ends of the harvested vein are sutured into the sides of the two axillary arterial walls, resulting in a bypass of the damaged area. In the second method, the axillary artery may be cut through beyond the damaged area and sutured to one end of a harvested vein, which is passed across the front of the chest under the skin and sutured to the side of the opposite axillary artery. The blocked or damaged portion of the axillary or subclavian artery is not removed. When the clamps are removed, the section of vein graft forms a new path through which blood can easily bypass the blocked area. After the graft is complete, the skin incisions are repaired with layered closures.

35521

The physician makes incisions in the skin of the axilla and upper thigh. The axillary and femoral arteries are isolated and dissected from adjacent critical structures. The physician creates a bypass around a section of lower aorta or iliac artery that is damaged or blocked using a harvested vein and one of two methods of repair. Once vessel clamps have been affixed above and below the areas of anastomosis, the harvested vein is sutured to an incision in the side of the axillary artery and passed through a subcutaneous tunnel on the side of the body and to the upper thigh. The harvested vein is sutured to the femoral artery (common, deep, or superficial) in an end-to-side or end-to-end fashion. The blocked or damaged portion of lower aorta or iliac artery is not removed. When the clamps are removed, the section of vein graft forms a new path through which blood can easily bypass the blocked area. After the graft is complete, the skin incisions are repaired with layered closures.

35522

Through an incision in the skin of the chest wall, the physician dissects down to the axillary artery just below the clavicle, separating soft tissue and adjacent critical structures. Soft tissue must be cleared for several centimeters. Dissection through the skin and soft tissue at the distal anastomosis site for this bypass graft is also done over the brachial artery in the arm near the elbow. Next, a tunnel is made from the exposed axillary, through the axilla and down the arm to the brachial artery site. To create a bypass graft around the section of brachial artery that is damaged or blocked, the physician uses a harvested vein, usually the greater saphenous. After vascular clamps have been affixed above and below the anastomosis area on the axillary artery, the proximal arteriotomy is carried out and the harvested vein is sutured to the axillary artery. When this is completed and checked for hemorrhaging, the arterial clamps are removed. The vein graft is tunneled through the prepared space to the brachial artery and the distal arteriotomy and anastomosis are carried out in the same manner. The clamps are removed, additional sutures may be placed for complete hemostasis, and the patency of the graft is checked. The incisions are closed and the appropriate pulses are checked again before dressings are applied.

35523

The physician performs a brachial-ulnar or –radial bypass graft. Through an incision in the skin of the upper arm, the physician dissects down to the brachial artery at a site above the diseased or damaged portion of the artery. Soft tissue and adjacent critical structures are separated. Soft tissue must be cleared for several centimeters. Dissection through the skin and soft tissue at the distal anastomosis site for this bypass graft is also done over the radial or ulnar artery. A tunnel is made from the exposed proximal brachial site down the arm to the radial or ulnar artery site. To create a bypass graft around the section of the artery that is damaged or blocked, the physician uses a harvested vein, usually the greater saphenous. After vascular clamps have been affixed above and below the proximal anastomosis area on the brachial artery, arteriotomy is carried out and the harvested vein is sutured to the artery. When this is completed and checked for hemorrhaging, the arterial clamps are removed. The vein graft is tunneled through the prepared space to the distal site on the radial or ulnar artery and arteriotomy and anastomosis are carried out again in the same manner. The clamps are removed, additional sutures may be placed for complete hemostasis, and the patency of the graft is checked. The incisions are closed and the appropriate pulses are checked again before dressings are applied.

35525

Through an incision in the skin of the upper arm, the physician dissects down to the brachial artery at a site above the diseased or damaged portion of the artery, usually in the mid to distal part, and separates soft tissue and adjacent critical structures. Soft tissue must be cleared for several centimeters. Dissection through the skin and soft tissue at the distal anastomosis site for this bypass graft is also done over the distal brachial artery in the arm, most often below the elbow. Next, a tunnel is made from the exposed proximal brachial site, down the arm to the distal brachial artery site. To create a bypass graft around the section of the artery that is damaged or blocked, the physician uses a harvested vein, usually the greater saphenous. After vascular clamps have been affixed above and below the proximal anastomosis area on the brachial artery, arteriotomy is carried out and the harvested vein is sutured to the brachial artery. When this is completed and checked for hemorrhaging, the arterial clamps are removed. The vein graft is tunneled through the prepared space to the distal site on the brachial artery and arteriotomy and anastomosis are carried out again in the same manner. The clamps are removed, additional sutures may be placed for complete hemostasis, and the patency of the graft is checked. The incisions are closed and the appropriate pulses are checked again before dressings are applied.

35526

The physician exposes the aorta by median sternotomy and exposes the carotid or subclavian artery extending this incision in the appropriate direction. The physician clamps the middle part of the right anterolateral aspect of the anterior ascending aorta with a J clamp. The physician makes a 2 cm to 3 cm longitudinal incision in the clamped portion of the aorta and sews the venous graft to the aortic incision. The physician clamps the vein and releases the aortic clamp to assess the anastomosis for leaks. The physician clamps the distal end of the diseased artery (carotid or subclavian). The physician makes a longitudinal incision in the diseased artery, distal to the blockage, and sews the venous graft to the arterial incision. The physician may also use harvested vein to enlarge the arterial lumen (patch graft). The physician removes the clamp from the vein graft. The physician may perform arteriography or use a Doppler probe to establish patency of the graft. The physician closes the sternotomy or thoracotomy, leaving a chest tube in place.

35531

The physician exposes the involved mesenteric or celiac artery using an upper midline abdominal incision, retracting and dissecting past large and small bowel. The physician exposes the distal thoracic aorta, administers heparin for anti coagulation, and clamps the aorta both proximal and distal to the celiac axis origin. The physician cuts out an elliptical disk of aortic wall from the anterior surface of the aorta. The physician exposes the involved vessel (mesenteric or celiac artery) and divides it proximal to the occlusion, closing off the proximal stump with suture. The physician sews a venous graft from the clamped aorta to the undiseased distal artery. The physician may use harvested vein to enlarge the arterial lumen (patch graft). The physician may perform arteriography or use a Doppler probe to establish patency of the graft. The physician closes the abdominal wound, leaving drains in place.

35533

Through incisions in the skin of the axilla and both upper thighs, the physician creates a bypass using a harvested vein around a section of lower aorta that is damaged or blocked. Once vessel clamps have been affixed above and below the area of anastomosis, the harvested vein is sutured to the side of the axillary artery and passed through a subcutaneous tunnel to the upper thigh, where it is sutured end-to-end or end-to-side to the femoral artery. A second harvested vein is sutured end-to-side to the femoral artery or to the vein graft descending from the axilla where it joins the femoral artery, and is passed through another subcutaneous tunnel to the opposite thigh, where it is sutured end-to-end or end-to-side to the femoral artery. When the clamps are removed, the two grafted vein limbs form a new path through which blood can easily bypass the blocked area. The section of blocked or damaged lower aorta is not removed. After the graft is complete, the incisions are repaired with layered closures.

35535

The physician performs hepatorenal bypass graft. With the patient placed supine, a right subcostal (beneath the ribs) incision is made and extended through the subcutaneous tissue, fat, and muscle. The abdominal cavity is entered, the stomach is retracted, and the lesser omentum is entered. The physician locates the common hepatic, proper hepatic, and gastroduodenal arteries. These are dissected and encircled with Silastic vessel loops. After the physician mobilizes the right renal vein, the right renal artery is exposed, dissected, and encircled with Silastic vessel loops. The physician harvests a greater saphenous vein segment and forms a proximal end-to-end anastomosis to the common hepatic artery. Distal anastomosis is then performed with the renal artery in either a side-to-side or end-to-end fashion. Bleeding is controlled and Doppler or duplex is performed to verify revascularization. After the graft is complete, the incisions are repaired with layered closure.

35536

The physician performs a bilateral subcostal incision from the right midrectus position extending into the left flank, and dissects past bowel and pancreas to expose the splenic vein. The physician exposes the splenic artery by careful dissection. The physician exposes the left renal artery by dissecting through the posterior parietal peritoneum, partially clamps it, and excises an ellipse of renal artery at its upper border. The physician performs end-to-side anastomosis of vein graft material from the splenic artery to the renal artery. The physician removes the clamps and assesses the anastomotic sites for leaks. The physician may perform Doppler studies or arteriography to establish patency of the graft. The physician closes the abdominal wound, leaving drains in place.

35537-35538

The physician exposes the involved abdominal aorta and iliac arteries using an abdominal incision, retracting and dissecting past large and small bowel. The physician partially clamps the aorta above the diseased area and places a longitudinal incision down the clamped portion of the aorta. The physician sews in a (two) venous graft(s), clamps the graft(s), and removes the aortic clamp to assess the anastomosis(es) for leaks. The physician clamps the iliac artery(ies) distal to the stenosis and incises and attaches the distal venous graft to the iliac artery(ies). The physician may also use harvested vein to enlarge the aortic or arterial lumen (patch graft). The physician may perform arteriography or use a Doppler probe to establish patency of the graft. The physician closes the abdominal wound, leaving drains in place. A bypass graft to a single iliac artery is performed in 35537; both iliac arteries are bypassed in 35538.

35539-35540

The physician makes an incision in the skin of the abdomen over a section of damaged or blocked lower aorta. The artery is isolated and dissected. Through a separate skin incision in the upper thigh, the femoral artery is isolated and dissected from adjacent critical structures. The physician creates a bypass around the damaged or blocked lower aorta using a harvested vein. Once vessel clamps have been affixed above the defect, the lower aorta may be cut through or tied off with sutures above the damaged or blocked area and sutured to one end of the harvested vein in an end-to-end or side-to-side fashion. In 35539, the graft to one femoral artery is passed through a tunnel on the inside of the upper thigh and sutured to the femoral artery. In 35540, a bifemoral bypass is accomplished and a second harvested vein is placed in a similar fashion to the second side. When the clamps are removed, the two grafted vein limbs form a new path through which blood can easily bypass the blocked area. The blocked or damaged portion of artery is not removed. After the graft is complete, the skin incisions are repaired with layered closures.

35548

The physician makes an incision in the skin of the abdomen over a section of damaged or blocked lower aorta. The artery is isolated and dissected from adjacent critical structures. Through a separate skin incision in the upper thigh, the femoral artery is isolated and dissected from adjacent critical structures. The physician creates a bypass around the damaged or blocked artery using a harvested vein. Once vessel clamps have been affixed above the defect, the lower aorta may be cut through or tied off with sutures above the damaged area and sutured to one end of the harvested vein. The vein graft is sutured to the iliac artery. A second vein is sutured to the iliac artery and the other end is passed through a tunnel on the inside of the upper thigh and sutured to a point on the femoral artery. When clamps are removed, the grafted vein forms a new path through which blood can easily bypass the blocked area. After the graft is complete, the skin incisions are repaired with layered closures.

35549
The physician makes an incision in the skin of the abdomen over a section of damaged or blocked lower aorta. The artery is isolated and dissected from adjacent critical structures. Through a separate skin incision in the upper thigh, the femoral artery is isolated and dissected from adjacent critical structures. The physician creates a bypass around the damaged section using a harvested vein. Once vessel clamps are affixed above the defect, the lower aorta is cut through or tied off with sutures above the damaged or blocked area and sutured to one end of the harvested vein. The free end of the harvested vein is sutured to the iliac artery. A second vein is sutured in place to join the aorta to the opposite iliac artery. Another vein is sutured to the iliac artery and passed through tunnels into the upper thigh where it is sutured to the femoral artery in the upper thigh. When the clamps are removed, the two grafted vein limbs form a new path through which blood can easily bypass the blocked area. After the grafts are complete, the skin incisions are repaired with layered closures. This procedure is repeated on the other side.

35551
The physician makes an incision in the skin of the abdomen over a section of damaged or blocked lower aorta. The artery is isolated and dissected from adjacent critical structures. Through a separate skin incision in the upper thigh, the femoral artery is isolated and dissected, and through a third skin incision behind the knee, the popliteal artery is isolated and dissected. The physician creates a bypass around the damaged artery that supplies the femoral-popliteal artery, using a harvested vein. Once vessel clamps have been affixed above the defect, the lower aortic artery is cut through or tied off with sutures above the damaged area and sutured to one end of the harvested vein. The graft is passed through a tunnel on the inside of the upper thigh and sutured to a point on the femoral artery. A third vein graft is sutured to the femoral artery and passed through a tunnel, where it is joined to the popliteal artery. It is also sutured. When the clamps are removed, the grafted vein forms a new path through which blood can easily bypass the blocked area. After the graft is complete, the skin incisions are repaired with layered closures.

35556
Through incisions in the skin of the leg overlying the femoral and popliteal arteries, the physician isolates and dissects a section of artery that is damaged or blocked. The physician creates a bypass around the superficial femoral artery, using a harvested vein and one of two methods of repair. Once vessel clamps have been affixed above and below the defect, the superficial femoral artery may be cut through above the damaged or blocked area and sutured to one end of a harvested vein. The vein is passed through a tunnel down the thigh muscles and behind the knee and sutured to the popliteal artery. In the second method, the ends of the harvested vein are sutured into the side of the femoral and popliteal arterial walls, resulting in a bypass of the damaged area. When the clamps are removed, the section of vein forms a new path through which blood can easily bypass the blocked area. The blocked or damaged portion of artery is not removed. After the graft is complete, the skin incisions are repaired with layered closures.

35558
Through incisions in the skin of the upper thighs, the physician isolates and dissects a section of the femoral arteries. The physician creates a bypass using a harvested vein. Once vessel clamps have been affixed above and below the area of anastomosis, the femoral artery may be cut through below the damaged area and sutured to one end of a harvested vein, which is sutured to the femoral artery in the opposite leg, resulting in a bypass of the damaged or blocked area. When the clamps are removed, the section of vein forms a new path through which blood can easily bypass the blocked area. The blocked or damaged portion of the artery is not removed. After the graft is complete, the skin incisions are repaired with layered closures.

35560
The physician exposes the involved abdominal aorta and renal artery using an abdominal incision, retracting and dissecting past large and small bowel. The physician partially clamps the aorta below the renal takeoff and places a small longitudinal incision down the clamped portion of the aorta. The physician sutures in a venous graft, clamps the graft and removes the aortic clamp to assess the anastomosis for leaks. The physician clamps the renal artery distal to the stenosis, incises the renal artery and attaches the distal venous graft to the distal renal artery. The physician may also use harvested vein to enlarge the renal arterial lumen (patch graft). The physician may perform arteriography or use a Doppler probe to establish patency of the graft. The physician closes the abdominal wound, leaving drains in place.

35563
The physician exposes the iliac arteries using an abdominal incision, retracting and dissecting past large and small bowel. The physician partially clamps the patent (non-diseased) iliac artery and places a longitudinal incision down the clamped portion of the aorta. The physician sews in a venous graft, clamps the graft and removes the iliac clamp to assess the anastomosis for leaks. The physician clamps the diseased iliac artery distal to the stenosis, places a distal incision and attaches the distal venous graft to the diseased iliac artery. The physician may also use harvested vein to enlarge the aortic or arterial lumen (patch graft). The physician may perform arteriography or use a Doppler probe to establish patency of the graft.

The physician closes the abdominal wound, leaving drains in place.

35565

Through incisions in the skin of the lower abdomen overlying the iliac artery and in the skin of the upper thigh overlying the femoral artery, the physician isolates and dissects a section of common iliac artery. The physician creates a bypass around the iliac artery, using a harvested vein and one of two methods of repair. Once vessel clamps have been affixed above and below the defect, the iliac artery may be cut or tied off with sutures above the damaged area and sutured to one end of a harvested vein. The graft is passed through a tunnel on the inside of the upper thigh and is sutured to the side of the femoral artery. In the second method, the end of the harvested vein is sutured to the side of the iliac artery. Either method results in a bypass of the damaged area. When the clamps are removed, the section of vein forms a new path through which blood can easily bypass the blocked area. After the graft is complete, the skin incisions are repaired with layered closures.

35566

Through incisions in the skin of the leg overlying the superficial femoral artery, the physician isolates and dissects sections of the femoral and anterior tibial, posterior tibial, or peroneal arteries. The physician creates a bypass around the affected artery using a harvested vein. Once vessel clamps have been affixed above and below the defect, the superficial femoral artery may be cut through above the damaged area and sutured to one end of a harvested vein, which is passed through an intramuscular tunnel and sutured to the anterior tibial, posterior tibial, peroneal, or other distal vessel. In the second method, the ends of the harvested vein are sutured to the side of the femoral artery and anterior tibial, posterior tibial, peroneal, or other distal vessel wall, resulting in a bypass of the damaged area. When the clamps are removed, the section of vein forms a new path through which blood can easily bypass the blocked area. The blocked or damaged portion of artery is left in place and not removed. After the graft is complete, the skin incisions are repaired with layered closures.

35570

The physician performs tibial-tibial, peroneal-tibial, or tibioperoneal trunk-tibial bypass graft. Through incisions in the skin of the leg overlying the affected tibial, peroneal, or tibioperoneal trunk artery, the physician isolates and dissects a section of arteries from adjacent critical structures. The physician creates a bypass around the affected artery using a harvested vein and one of two methods of repair. Once vessel clamps have been affixed above and below the defect, the artery may be cut through above the damaged area and sutured to one end of a harvested vein, which is sutured to the targeted tibial artery. In the second method, the ends of the harvested vein are sutured to the side of the bypassed artery and tibial vessel wall, resulting in a bypass of the damaged area. When the clamps are removed, the section of vein forms a new path through which blood can bypass the blocked area. The blocked or damaged portion of artery is left in place and not removed. After the graft is complete, the skin incisions are repaired with layered closures.

35571

Through incisions in the skin of the leg overlying the popliteal arteries, the physician isolates and dissects a section of arteries from adjacent critical structures. The physician creates a bypass around the artery, using a harvested vein and one of two methods of repair. Once vessel clamps have been affixed above and below the defect, the popliteal artery may be cut through above the damaged area and sutured to one end of a harvested vein, which is sutured to the tibial, peroneal, or other distal artery. In the second method, the ends of the harvested vein are sutured into the side of the popliteal and the tibial or peroneal arterial wall resulting in a bypass of the damaged area. When the clamps are removed, the section of vein forms a new path through which blood can easily bypass the blocked area. After the graft is complete, the incisions are repaired with layered closures.

35572

The physician harvests one segment of the femoropopliteal vein for a vascular reconstructive procedure. The leg is prepared circumferentially to make the leg accessible and provide optimal access. A single incision or multiple incisions can be made to harvest the vein. The vein is first located through an approximately 10 cm incision and dissected. The skin is cut over the course of the vein. If multiple incisions are made, the index finger is used to continue dissection along the anterior surface of the vein, with the incisions made about 2 to 4 cm from the last incision and the physician's finger underneath, or an external vein stripper is used with incisions made where the stripper meets resistance again. Branches of the vein are ligated. Dissection can begin at the proximal or distal end. The length of vein needed is estimated based on its intended purpose and the desired length is mobilized and divided at both ends. The vein is placed in a prepared solution of blood and saline at room temperature and prepared with diluted blood placed to flush the vein. A vascular device is applied, the vein is gently distended, and uncontrolled branches are closed. The vein is returned to the solution until used.

35583

Through an incision in the skin of the leg overlying the greater saphenous vein, the physician isolates and dissects the greater saphenous vein from adjacent critical structures from the upper thigh to the level of the knee. Vessel clamps are affixed above and below

Cardiovascular

the site of the anastomosis to the femoral and popliteal arteries. All side branches of the saphenous vein are tied off. The vessel's valves are destroyed. The upper end of the saphenous vein is divided and sutured into the femoral artery end-to-end or end-to-side. The lower end is divided and sutured into the popliteal artery end-to-end or end-to-side. The clamps are removed, and blood flows backward toward the feet, as if the vein were an artery. When the procedure is complete, the skin incision is repaired with a layered closure.

35585
Through an incision in the skin of the leg overlying the greater saphenous vein, the physician isolates and dissects the greater saphenous vein from adjacent critical structures. Vessel clamps are affixed above and below the site of anastomosis in the femoral artery and the distal artery. All side branches of the Saphenous are tied off. The vessel's valves are destroyed. The upper end of the saphenous vein is divided and sutured end-to-end or end-to-side in the femoral artery above the blockage. The lower end is divided and sutured end-to-end or end-to-side to the anterior tibial, posterior tibial, or peroneal artery below the blockage. The clamps are removed, and blood flows backward toward the feet, as if the vein were an artery. When the procedure is complete, the skin incision is repaired with a layered closure.

35587
Through an incision in the skin of the leg overlying the greater saphenous vein from the knee to the ankle, the physician isolates and dissects the greater Saphenous vein from adjacent critical structures along its length. Vessel clamps are affixed above and below the site of anastomosis on the popliteal and distal arteries. All side branches of the saphenous vein are tied off. The vessel's valves are destroyed. The upper end of the saphenous vein is divided and sutured into the popliteal-tibial artery. The lower end is divided and sutured into the peroneal artery. The clamps are removed, and blood flows backward through the vein toward the feet, as if it were an artery. When the procedure is complete, the incision is repaired with a layered closure.

35600
The physician harvests an artery from an upper extremity (arm) to use for a planned bypass procedure on a coronary artery. An incision is made over the site on the arm. Tissue is dissected to the artery. The portion of the artery to be removed is released from the surrounding structures and is tied off above and below the portion of artery to be removed. The artery is removed. The wound is closed with layered sutures. The portion of artery removed is prepared for use in a bypass graft procedure on a coronary artery (reported separately).

35601
Through an incision in the skin of the neck in front of the sternocleidomastoid muscle, the physician isolates and dissects the common carotid and internal carotid arteries, separating them from adjacent critical structures. The physician creates a bypass around the section of common carotid artery that is damaged or blocked, using a synthetic vein graft and one of two methods of repair involving the internal carotid artery on the same side of the neck. After vessel clamps have been affixed above and below the damaged area, the common carotid artery may be cut through below the damaged area and sutured to one end of the synthetic vein (end-to-end), which is sutured to the internal carotid artery beyond the affected area. In the second method, the ends of the synthetic vein are sutured into the side of the common carotid arterial wall and the internal carotid arterial wall (end-to-side). Either method results in a bypass of the damaged area. When the clamps are removed, the section of synthetic graft forms a new path through which blood can easily bypass the blocked area. The damaged or blocked carotid artery is not removed. After the graft is complete, the skin incision is repaired with layered closure.

35606
Through an incision in the skin at the side of the neck, the physician isolates and dissects the subclavian and carotid arteries, separating them from adjacent critical structures. To create a bypass around a section of subclavian artery that is damaged or blocked, the physician uses a synthetic vein and one of two methods of repair. After vessel clamps have been affixed above and below the damaged area, the graft is sewn to the side of the carotid artery and sewn to the side of the subclavian artery beyond the affected area (end-to-side) or sewn to the cut end of the subclavian artery after dividing it beyond the affected area (end-to-end). The damaged or blocked portion of the subclavian artery is not removed. When the clamps are removed in either case, the section of synthetic graft vein forms a new path through which blood can easily bypass the blocked area. After the graft is complete, the skin incision is repaired with a layered closure.

35612
Through incisions in the skin at the base of the neck, the physician isolates and dissects the subclavian arteries, separating them from adjacent critical structures. The physician creates a bypass around a section of subclavian artery that is damaged or blocked, using a synthetic vein and one of two methods of repair. Once vessel clamps have been affixed above and below the defect, the ends of the synthetic vein graft are sutured into the sides of the walls of the two subclavian arteries, resulting in a bypass of the damaged area. In the second method, the subclavian artery may be cut through beyond the damaged area and sutured to one end of a synthetic

vein, which is sutured to the subclavian artery on the opposite side of the neck. In either case, the blocked or damaged portion of the artery is not removed. When the clamps are removed, the section of synthetic vein graft forms a new path through which blood can easily bypass the blocked area. After the graft is complete, the skin incisions are repaired with a layered closure.

35616

Through an incision in the skin at the base of the neck and axilla, the physician isolates and dissects the subclavian and axillary arteries, separating them from adjacent critical structures. The physician creates a bypass around a section of subclavian artery that is damaged or blocked, using a synthetic vein and one of two methods of repair. Once vessel clamps have been affixed above and below the defect, the ends of the synthetic vein are sutured into the sides of the subclavian and axillary arterial walls resulting in a bypass of the damaged area (end-to-side). In the second method, the subclavian artery may be cut through before the damaged area and sutured to one end of a synthetic vein, which is sutured to the axillary artery (end-to-end). The blocked or damaged portion of the subclavian artery is not removed. When the clamps are removed, the section of synthetic vein graft forms a new path through which blood can easily bypass the blocked area. After the graft is complete, the skin incisions are repaired with a layered closure.

35621

The physician makes incisions in the skin of the axilla and upper thigh. The artery is isolated and dissected from adjacent critical structures. The physician creates a bypass around a section of lower aorta or iliac artery that is damaged or blocked using a synthetic vein and one of two methods of repair. Once vessel clamps have been affixed above and below the areas of anastomosis, the synthetic vein is sutured to an incision in the side of the axillary artery and passed through a subcutaneous tunnel on the side of the body and to the upper thigh. The synthetic vein is sutured to the femoral artery (common, deep, or superficial) in an end-to-side or end-to-end fashion. The blocked or damaged portion of lower aorta or iliac artery is not removed. When the clamps are removed, the section of synthetic vein graft forms a new path through which blood can easily bypass the blocked area. After the graft is complete, the skin incisions are repaired with layered closures.

35623

The physician makes incisions in the skin of the axilla and behind the knee or in the lower leg. The artery is isolated and dissected from adjacent critical structures. The physician creates a bypass around a section of lower aorta or iliac artery that is damaged or blocked using a synthetic vein and one of two methods of repair. Once vessel clamps have been affixed above and below the areas of anastomosis, the synthetic vein is sutured to an incision in the side of the axillary artery and passed through a subcutaneous tunnel on the side of the body and behind the knee or upper thigh. The synthetic vein is sutured to the popliteal or tibial artery in an end-to-side or end-to-end fashion. The blocked or damaged portion of lower aorta or iliac artery is not removed. When the clamps are removed, the section of synthetic vein graft forms a new path through which blood can easily bypass the blocked area. After the graft is complete, the skin incisions are repaired with layered closures.

35626

The physician exposes the aorta by median sternotomy and exposes the carotid or subclavian artery extending this incision in the appropriate direction. The physician clamps the middle part of the right anterolateral aspect of the anterior ascending aorta with a J clamp. The physician makes a 2-3 centimeter longitudinal incision in the clamped portion of the aorta and sews the arterial or synthetic graft to the aortic incision. The physician clamps the graft and releases the aortic clamp to assess the anastomosis for leaks. The physician clamps the distal end of the diseased artery (carotid or subclavian). The physician makes a longitudinal incision in the diseased artery, distal to the blockage, and sews the graft to the arterial incision. The physician may also use graft material to enlarge the arterial lumen (patch graft). The physician removes the clamp from the graft. The physician may perform arteriography or use a Doppler probe to establish patency of the graft. The physician closes the sternotomy or thoracotomy, leaving a chest tube in place.

35631

The physician exposes the involved mesenteric or celiac artery using an upper midline abdominal incision, retracting and dissecting past large and small bowel. The physician exposes the distal thoracic aorta, administers heparin for anticoagulation, and clamps the aorta both proximal and distal to the celiac axis origin. The physician cuts out an elliptical disk of aortic wall from the anterior surface of the aorta. The physician exposes the involved vessel (mesenteric or celiac artery) and divides it proximal to the occlusion, closing off the proximal stump with suture. The physician sews a synthetic or arterial graft from the clamped aorta to the undiseased distal artery. The physician may use graft material to enlarge the arterial lumen (patch graft). The physician may perform arteriography or use a Doppler probe to establish patency of the graft. The physician closes the abdominal wound, leaving drains in place.

35632-35634

The physician performs ilio-celiac (35632), ilio-mesenteric (35633), or iliorenal (35634) bypass using a synthetic graft. Through a midline abdominal incision, the physician retracts the intestines and

Cardiovascular

exposes the common iliac artery and the involved vessel (celiac, mesenteric, or renal artery). The common iliac artery is clamped proximally and distally. The physician makes an oval incision on the anterolateral aspect of the common iliac artery, temporarily releases the distal clamp, and administers heparin for anticoagulation. A synthetic graft is attached to the common iliac artery at the site of the arteriotomy and sutured in place. An end-to-end anastomosis of the synthetic graft to the disease-free portion of the celiac, mesenteric, or renal artery is created. The physician may perform arteriography or Doppler to establish patency of the graft. The physician closes the abdominal wound, leaving drains in place.

35636
The physician performs a bilateral subcostal incision from the right midrectus position extending into the left flank, and dissects past bowel and pancreas to expose the splenic vein. The physician exposes the splenic artery by careful dissection. The physician exposes the left renal artery by dissecting through the posterior parietal peritoneum, partially clamps it, and excises an ellipse of renal artery at its upper border. The physician performs an end-to-side anastomosis of synthetic or arterial graft material from the splenic artery to the renal artery. The physician removes the clamps and assesses the anastomotic sites for leaks. The physician may perform Doppler studies or arteriography to establish patency of the graft. The physician closes the abdominal wound, leaving drains in place.

35637-35638
The physician makes an incision in the abdominal wall and separates the muscles to expose the internal organs, which are checked for any undetected disease. The physician next locates the aorta and iliac arteries and isolates the obstruction by clamping the vessels. An artificial graft, commonly of polyester or polytetrafluoroethylene, is made ready. Synthetic grafts are preferred in aortoiliac bypass since they more closely match the luminal dimensions of the replaced arteries. The graft is sewn into place, with one end anastomosed to the aorta and the other end to the iliac artery. An artificial bypass graft to a single iliac artery is performed in 35637; both iliac arteries are bypassed in 35638.The physician removes the clamps, blood flows freely, and the physician assesses the anastomotic sites for leaks. The physician may perform Doppler studies or arteriography to establish patency of the graft. The abdominal wound is closed in layers.

35642
Through an incision in the skin of the neck, the physician isolates and dissects the vertebral and carotid arteries, separating them from adjacent critical structures. The physician creates a bypass around a section of vertebral artery that is damaged or blocked, using a synthetic vein and one of two methods of repair. After vessel clamps have been affixed above and below the damaged area, the synthetic graft is sewn to the side of the carotid artery and sewn to the side of the vertebral artery beyond the affected area (end-to-side) or sewn to the cut end of the vertebral artery after dividing it beyond the affected area (end-to-end). The damaged or blocked section of the vertebral artery is not removed. When the clamps are removed, the section of synthetic vein graft forms a new path through which blood can easily bypass the blocked area. After the graft is complete, the skin incision is repaired with a layered closure.

35645
Through an incision in the skin of the neck, the physician isolates and dissects the vertebral and subclavian arteries, separating them from adjacent critical structures. The physician creates a bypass around a section of vertebral artery that is damaged or blocked, using a synthetic vein and one of two methods of repair. Once vessel clamps are affixed above and below the defect, the ends of the synthetic vein are sutured into the sides of the subclavian and vertebral arterial walls resulting in a bypass of the damaged area (end-to-side). In the second method, the vertebral artery can be cut through above the damaged area and sutured to one end of a synthetic vein (end-to-end). The remaining end is sutured to the subclavian artery. In either case, the blocked or damaged vertebral artery is not removed. When the clamps are removed, the section of synthetic vein graft forms a new path through which blood can easily bypass the blocked area. After the graft is complete, the skin incision is repaired with a layered closure.

35646-35647
The physician makes an incision in the skin of the abdomen over a section of damaged or blocked lower aorta. The artery is isolated and dissected. Through a separate skin incision in the upper thigh, the femoral artery is isolated and dissected from adjacent critical structures. The physician creates a bypass around the damage or blocked lower aorta using a synthetic vein. Once vessel clamps have been affixed above the defect, the lower aorta may be cut through or tied off with sutures above the damaged or blocked area and sutured to one end of the synthetic vein in an end-to-end or side-to-side fashion. The graft to one femoral artery is passed through a tunnel on the inside of the upper thigh and sutured to the femoral artery. A second synthetic vein is placed in a similar fashion to the second side. When the clamps are removed, the two grafted synthetic vein limbs form a new path through which blood can easily bypass the blocked area. The blocked or damaged portion of artery is not removed. After the graft is complete, the skin incisions are repaired with layered closure.

35650
The physician makes an incision in the skin of both axillae. The physician creates a bypass around a section of axillary or subclavian artery that is damaged or blocked, using a synthetic vein and one of two methods of repair. Once vessel clamps have been affixed above and below the defect, the ends of the synthetic vein are sutured into the sides of the two axillary arterial walls, resulting in a bypass of the damaged area. In the second method, the axillary artery may be cut through beyond the damaged area and sutured to one end of a synthetic vein, which is passed across the front of the chest under the skin and sutured to the side of the opposite axillary artery. The blocked or damaged portion of the axillary or subclavian artery is not removed. When the clamps are removed, the section of synthetic vein graft forms a new path through which blood can easily bypass the blocked area. After the graft is complete, the skin incisions are repaired with layered closures.

35651
The physician makes an incision in the skin of the abdomen over a section of damaged or blocked lower aorta. The artery is isolated and dissected from adjacent critical structures. Through a separate skin incision in the upper thigh, the femoral artery is isolated and dissected and through a third skin incision behind the knee, the popliteal artery is isolated and dissected. The physician creates a bypass around the damaged artery that supplies the femoral-popliteal artery, using a synthetic vein. Once vessel clamps have been affixed above the defect, the lower aortic artery is cut through or tied off with sutures above the damaged area and sutured to one end of the synthetic vein. The graft is passed through a tunnel on the inside of the upper thigh and sutured to a point on the femoral artery. A third vein graft is sutured to the femoral artery and passed through a tunnel, where it is joined to the popliteal artery. It is also sutured. When the clamps are removed, the grafted synthetic vein forms a new path through which blood can easily bypass the blocked area. After the graft is complete, the skin incisions are repaired with layered closures.

35654
Through an incision in the skin of the axilla and both upper thighs, the physician creates a bypass around a section of lower aorta that is damaged or blocked, using a synthetic graft. Once vessel clamps have been affixed above and below the defect, the synthetic graft is sutured to the side of the axillary artery and passed through a subcutaneous tunnel to the upper thigh where it is sutured end-to-end or end-to-side to the femoral artery. A second synthetic graft is sutured end-to-side to the femoral artery and passed through another subcutaneous tunnel to the opposite thigh where it is sutured end-to-end or end-to-side to the femoral artery. The section of blocked artery is not removed. When the clamps are removed, the two synthetic grafted limbs form a new path through which blood can easily bypass the blocked area. After the graft is complete, the skin incisions are repaired with layered closures.

35656
Through incisions in the skin of the leg overlying the femoral and popliteal arteries, the physician isolates and dissects a section of artery that is damaged or blocked. The physician creates a bypass around the superficial femoral artery, using a synthetic vein and one of two methods of repair. Once vessel clamps have been affixed above and below the defect, the superficial femoral artery may be cut through above the damaged or blocked area and sutured to one end of a synthetic vein, which is passed through a tunnel down the thigh muscles to behind the knee and sutured to the popliteal artery. In the second method, the ends of the synthetic vein are sutured into the side of the femoral and popliteal arterial walls, resulting in a bypass of the damaged area. When the clamps are removed, the section of synthetic vein forms a new path through which blood can easily bypass the blocked area. The blocked or damaged portion of artery is not removed. After the graft is complete, the skin incisions are repaired with layered closures.

35661
Through incisions in the skin of the upper thighs, the physician isolates and dissects a section of the femoral arteries. The physician creates a bypass using a synthetic vein. Once vessel clamps have been affixed above and below the area of anastomosis, the femoral artery may be cut through below the damaged area and sutured to one end of a synthetic vein, which is sutured to the femoral artery in the opposite leg, resulting in a bypass of the damaged or blocked area. When the clamps are removed, the section of synthetic vein forms a new path through which blood can easily bypass the blocked area. The blocked or damaged portion of the artery is not removed. After the graft is complete, the skin incisions are repaired with layered closures.

35663
The physician exposes the iliac arteries using an abdominal incision, retracting and dissecting past large and small bowel. The physician partially clamps the patent (non-diseased) iliac artery and places a longitudinal incision down the clamped portion of the aorta. The physician sews in a synthetic or arterial graft, clamps the graft and removes the iliac clamp to assess patency of the anastomosis. The physician clamps the diseased iliac artery distal to the stenosis, places a distal incision and attaches the distal graft to the diseased iliac artery. The physician may also use graft material to enlarge the aortic or arterial lumen (patch graft). The physician may perform arteriography or use a Doppler probe to establish patency of the graft. The physician closes the abdominal wound, leaving drains in place.

35665
Through incisions in the skin of the lower abdomen overlying the iliac artery, and in the skin of the upper thigh overlying the femoral artery, the physician isolates and dissects a section of common iliac artery. The physician creates a bypass around the iliac artery, using a synthetic vein and one of two methods of repair. Once vessel clamps have been affixed above and below the defect, the iliac artery may be cut or tied off with sutures above the damaged area and sutured to one end of a synthetic vein. The graft is passed through a tunnel on the inside of the upper thigh and is sutured to the side of the femoral artery. In the second method, the end of the synthetic vein is sutured to the side of the iliac artery. Either method results in a bypass of the damaged area. When the clamps are removed, the section of synthetic vein forms a new path through which blood can easily bypass the blocked area. After the graft is complete, the skin incisions are repaired with layered closures.

35666
Through incisions in the skin of the leg overlying the superficial femoral artery, the physician isolates and dissects sections of the femoral and anterior tibial, posterior tibial or peroneal arteries. The physician creates a bypass around the affected artery using a synthetic vein. Once vessel clamps have been affixed above and below the defect, the superficial femoral artery may be cut through above the damaged area and sutured to one end of a synthetic vein, which is passed through an intramuscular tunnel and sutured to the anterior tibial, posterior tibial, peroneal, or other distal vessel. In the second method, the ends of the synthetic vein are sutured to the side of the femoral artery and anterior tibial, posterior tibial, peroneal, or other distal vessel wall, resulting in a bypass of the damaged area. When the clamps are removed, the section of synthetic vein forms a new path through which blood can easily bypass the blocked area. The blocked or damaged portion of artery is left in place and not removed. After the graft is complete, the skin incisions are repaired with layered closures.

35671
Through incisions in the skin of the leg overlying the popliteal arteries, the physician isolates and dissects a section of artery from adjacent critical structures. The physician creates a bypass around the artery, using a synthetic vein and one of two methods of repair. Once vessel clamps have been affixed above and below the defect, the popliteal artery may be cut through above the damaged area and sutured to one end of a synthetic vein, which is sutured to the tibial, peroneal, or other distal artery. In the second method, the ends of the synthetic vein are sutured into the side of the popliteal and the tibial or peroneal arterial wall resulting in a bypass of the damaged area. When the clamps are removed, the section of synthetic vein forms a new path through which blood can easily bypass the blocked area. After the graft is complete, the incision is repaired with layered closures.

35681-35683
In 35681 the physician constructs a composite graft from donor and synthetic materials. One common composite would involve the reconfiguring of a harvested vein into a length of larger diameter graft material. The harvested vein would be split lengthwise and wrapped in a spiral and sutured around a larger diameter mandrill. This length of composite graft would be used to complete the primary procedure. In 35682 a graft is constructed using tissue acquired from two veins at separate locations in the patient's body for the transplantation. In 35863 a graft is constructed using three or more segments of vein from two or more locations in the patient's body. In all three procedures veins are harvested by making an incision over the site where the vein will be removed. Tissues are dissected down to the vein and the vein is released from surrounding tissues. The vein is tied off above and below the area of vein that is to be removed. The vein is removed. The wound is closed with layered sutures. The portion of vein(s) removed is prepared for use in a separately reportable bypass graft procedure.

35685
The physician places a vein patch or cuff at a distal arterial anastomosis site during a bypass graft, synthetic conduit procedure of the lower extremity. The physician harvests the vein to be used for the vein patch from a previously chosen site. The vein patch is positioned and anastomosed between the distal portion of the synthetic vein graft and the native artery, end-to-end or side-to-end. The physician returns to the bypass graft surgery having performed this additional procedure.

35686
The physician creates a fistula between an artery and vein during a lower extremity bypass procedure. The physician harvests the vein to be used for creation of the fistula from a previously chosen site. The vein is anastomosed between the tibial or peroneal artery and a vein at or beyond the distal bypass anastomosis site. The physician returns to the bypass graft surgery having performed this adjuvant (additional) procedure.

35691
The physician performs a supraclavicular incision and exposes the vertebral and carotid arteries by careful dissection. The physician clears the adventitia of the chosen translocation site in the posterolateral wall of the common carotid artery. The physician anticoagulates the patient with heparin and divides the vertebral artery above the stenotic area. The physician ligates the proximal vertebral stump with suture and makes a small arteriotomy in the common carotid arterial wall with an aortic punch. The physician attaches the vertebral artery using an end-to-side anastomosis to the carotid artery. The physician may

perform arteriography or use a Doppler probe to establish patency of the graft. The physician closes the supraclavicular wound, leaving a drain in place.

35693
The physician performs a supraclavicular incision and exposes the vertebral and subclavian arteries by careful dissection. The physician clears the adventitia of the chosen translocation site in the subclavian artery lateral to the thyrocervical trunk. The physician anticoagulates the patient with heparin and divides the vertebral artery above the stenotic area. The physician ligates the proximal vertebral stump with suture and makes a small arteriotomy in the subclavian artery wall with an aortic punch. The physician attaches the vertebral artery using an end-to-side anastomosis to the subclavian artery. The physician may perform arteriography or use a Doppler probe to establish patency of the graft. The physician closes the supraclavicular wound, leaving a drain in place.

35694
The physician performs a supraclavicular incision and exposes the carotid and subclavian arteries by careful dissection. The physician clears the adventitia of the chosen translocation site in the posterolateral wall of the common carotid artery. The physician anticoagulates the patient's blood with heparin and divides the subclavian artery distal to the stenotic area. The physician ligates the proximal subclavian stump with suture and makes a small arteriotomy in the common carotid artery wall with an aortic punch. The physician attaches the subclavian artery using an end-to-side anastomosis to the carotid artery. The physician may perform arteriography or use a Doppler probe to establish patency of the graft. The physician closes the supraclavicular wound, leaving a drain in place.

35695
The physician performs a supraclavicular incision and exposes the carotid and subclavian arteries by careful dissection. The physician clears the adventitia of the chosen translocation site in the subclavian artery lateral to the thyrocervical trunk. The physician anticoagulates the patient's blood with heparin and divides the carotid artery above the stenotic area. The physician ligates the proximal carotid stump with suture and makes a small arteriotomy in the subclavian artery wall with an aortic punch. The physician attaches the carotid artery using an end-to-side anastomosis to the subclavian artery. The physician may perform arteriography or use a Doppler probe to establish patency of the graft. The physician closes the supraclavicular wound, leaving a drain in place.

35697
A reimplantation of a visceral artery to an infrarenal aortic prosthesis, each artery, is done in addition to the primary procedure of an open aortic aneurysm repair (35081). This surgery is performed when a visceral artery, such as the inferior mesenteric, has been determined not to supply sufficient blood flow to vital organs, after repair of the aortic aneurysm. After the aortic prosthesis has been placed and blood flow is re-established through the aorta, the physician dissects soft tissue from around the origin of the visceral artery in the aorta where it exits. A small button-shaped patch of aortic tissue is removed from this site. Next, a clamp is placed on the aortic prosthesis at the intended site for reimplantation and a hole is cut the size of the button patch, which is anastomosed to the recipient hole in the prosthesis. The suturing is tested by removing the clamps and placing any additional sutures for complete hemostasis.

35700
This code is only used with other codes to identify the reoperation aspect of this procedure, which usually requires more effort when performed again. Through incisions in the skin of the leg, overlying the affected artery, the physician isolates the graft. The physician makes an incision in the proximal portion of the graft and passes a Fogarty balloon catheter through the graft to clear and straighten it. If an arteriograph indicates the graft must be replaced, the physician makes a second incision distal to the inguinal incision, releases the graft, and places vein clamps above and below the stricture. The physician replaces the graft by suturing the ends of a new graft to the side of the arteries to form a bypass of the damaged area. The clamps are removed. After the stricture is controlled or the graft is otherwise complete, the incisions are repaired with layered closures.

35701
Through an incision in the skin overlying the carotid artery and in front of the sternocleidomastoid muscle, the physician dissects out around the carotid artery, freeing it so it can be examined. The artery is freed from any surrounding scar tissue that may be compressing it. Finding no perforations or other signs of injury, the physician repairs the skin incision with a layered closure.

35721
Through an incision in the skin overlying the femoral artery, the physician dissects around the sartorius and/or adductor longus muscles as necessary to access the femoral artery. The physician dissects out around the femoral artery, freeing it so it can be examined. The artery is freed from any surrounding scar tissue that may be compressing it. Finding no perforations or other signs of injury, the physician repairs the skin incision with a layered closure.

35741
Through an incision in the skin overlying the popliteal artery, the physician dissects around the popliteal vein and other critical structures as necessary to access the popliteal artery. The physician dissects out around the popliteal artery, freeing it so it can be examined. The

artery is freed from any surrounding scar tissue that may be compressing it. Finding no perforations or other signs of injury, the physician repairs the skin incision with a layered closure.

35761
Through an incision in the skin overlying the vessel to be examined, the physician dissects around any muscle, vessels, and/or other structures as necessary to access the vessel. The physician dissects out around the vessel, freeing it so it can be examined. The artery is freed from any surrounding scar tissue that may be compressing it. Finding no perforations or other signs of injury, the physician repairs the skin incision with a layered closure.

35800
Through an incision in the neck over the affected area, the physician isolates the vessel and explores it for postoperative complications such as hemorrhage, thrombosis, or infection. The physician dissects any adjacent critical structures as necessary to access the vessel. The complication is identified and corrected. A hemorrhage is controlled by ligation or suture repair of the artery. Thrombosis requires opening of the artery and the removal of the clot. Any infection is drained, and sometimes a temporary tube is placed so the infection can continue to drain. The physician sutures the skin incision with a layered closure once the postsurgical complication has been treated.

35820
The physician reopens the original incision site and inspects the operative area for active bleeding, hematoma, thrombus, and exudate. The physician removes or debrides any observed hematoma, thrombus, and infected tissues. The physician looks for and corrects any active bleeding sites using electrocautery or ligation of bleeding vessels. The physician may leave an infected wound open, but generally closes the incision, leaving drains and chest tubes in place.

35840
The physician reopens the original incision site and inspects the operative area for active bleeding, hematoma, thrombus, and exudate. The physician removes or debrides any observed hematoma, thrombus, and infected tissues. The physician looks for and corrects any active bleeding sites using electrocautery or ligation of bleeding vessels. The physician may leave an infected wound open, but generally closes the incision, leaving drains in place.

35860
Through an incision in the extremity over the affected area, the physician isolates the vessel and explores it for postoperative complications such as hemorrhage, thrombosis, or infection. The physician dissects any adjacent critical structures as necessary to access the vessel. The complication is identified and corrected. A hemorrhage is controlled by ligation or suture repair of the artery. Thrombosis requires opening of the artery and the removal of the clot. Any infection is drained, and sometimes a temporary tube is placed so the infection can continue to drain. The physician sutures the skin incision with a layered closure once the postsurgical complication has been treated.

35870
The physician opens the abdomen under antibiotic cover and exposes the graft-enteric fistula site by careful dissection (most often aortic/Dacron anastomosis with a fistulous connection to the duodenum). The physician disconnects the fistula and repairs the enteric defect using two layers of suture. The physician examines the vascular prosthesis, removes the prosthesis and sews in appropriate new bypass grafts if there is obvious graft infection. If there is no obvious infection, the physician repairs the graft with local sutures. The physician closes the wound, leaving drains in place.

35875-35876
Through an incision in the skin overlying the arterial or venous graft, the physician isolates the site of the thrombus. The physician dissects any muscle, overlying vessel, and/or adjacent critical structures to access the graft. To excise the thrombus from the graft, the blood vessel is clamped above and below the thrombus, an incision is made into the vessel or graft and the thrombus is removed. The graft or vessel is sutured at the site of the thrombectomy and the clamps are removed. To remove the thrombus with a catheter, the physician makes an incision in the vessel above or below the graft and threads the catheter past the thrombus. A balloon or tool at the tip of the catheter is inflated or extended. The physician withdraws the catheter, repeating as necessary, to capture and retrieve all of the thrombus. The blood vessel is repaired with sutures. After either procedure, the skin incision is repaired with a layered closure. In 35876, the thrombotic graft is removed, the graft site is repaired with sutures, and, avoiding the repair site, a new graft is sutured into place on the vessel. The skin incision is repaired with a layered closure.

35879-35881
The physician revises a lower extremity arterial bypass with vein-patch angioplasty or segmental vein interposition. A previous lower-extremity arterial bypass graft requires open revision due to graft-threatening stenosis. The physician makes an incision in a lower extremity over the site of a previous arterial bypass graft. Dissection is carried down to the graft. In 35879, angioplasty of the stenosed area is performed by excising the area of stenosis and using a patch of vein to close the created wound. In 35881, a segment of vein is excised from another area. The area of stenosis is excised and the vein segment is positioned between the two ends of the graft and

anastomosed in an end to end fashion. A thrombectomy is not performed. The wound is closed with layered sutures.

35883-35884
An open revision of the femoral anastomosis of a synthetic arterial bypass graft in the groin is performed using a nonautogenous (Dacron, ePTFE, bovine pericardium) patch graft (35883) or an autogenous vein patch graft (35884). This procedure is performed due to formation of an anastomotic aneurysm in the femoral artery. This occurs due to a defect in the anastomosis. Through an incision in the skin of the upper thigh, the physician isolates and dissects the anastomotic aneurysm. An arteriotomy is performed and the aneurysm excised. A patch graft is placed.

35901
Through an incision in the skin of the neck overlying the graft, the physician dissects around any muscle, vessels, or other structures to access the graft site. The physician dissects around the vessel, and applies vessel clamps above and below the graft. The physician excises above and below the existing infected graft. The blood vessel is repaired with sutures. A catheter may be left in place to help drain infection. The skin is loosely closed. If the excised graft is replaced with a new graft, report the appropriate revascularization code.

35903
Through an incision in the skin of the extremity overlying the graft, the physician dissects around any muscle, vessels or other structures to access the graft site. The physician dissects around the vessel, and applies vessel clamps above and below the graft. The physician excises above and below the existing infected graft. The blood vessel is repaired with sutures. A catheter may be left in place to help drain infection. The skin is loosely closed. If the excised graft is replaced with a new graft, report the appropriate revascularization code.

35905
Through an incision in the skin of the thorax overlying the graft, the physician dissects around any muscle, vessels or other structures to access the graft site. The physician dissects around the vessel, and applies vessel clamps above and below the graft. The physician excises above and below the existing infected graft. The blood vessel is repaired with sutures. A catheter may be left in place to help drain infection. The skin is loosely closed. If the excised graft is replaced with a new graft, report the appropriate revascularization code.

35907
Through an incision in the skin of the abdomen overlying the graft, the physician dissects around any muscle, vessels or other structures to access the graft site. The physician dissects around the vessel, and applies vessel clamps above and below the graft. The physician excises above and below the existing infected graft. The blood vessel is repaired with sutures. A catheter may be left in place to help drain infection. The skin is loosely closed. If the excised graft is replaced with a new graft, report the appropriate revascularization code.

36000-36005
In 36000, the physician places a needle or a catheter through a puncture in the skin and into a peripheral vein. In 36002, the physician injects a pseudoaneurysm (a pulsatile hematoma with a fibrous capsule) and maintains persistent communication with the adjacent vessel. The vessel wall does not heal and blood flows back and forth between the vessel and hematoma during the cardiac cycle. Under ultrasound control, the physician advances a 22-gauge needle into the lumen of the pseudoaneurysm and injects Thrombin to cause thrombosis of the pseudoaneurysm. In 36005, an opaque substance is injected through the catheter for venography. Once the procedure is complete, the catheter is removed and pressure is applied to stop bleeding at the injection site.

36010
The physician punctures a distal vein (typically antecubital, internal jugular, subclavian, or femoral) with a large needle and passes a guidewire via the needle into the punctured vein. The physician removes the needle while leaving the guidewire in place, and enlarges the skin opening slightly with a blade. The physician may slide an introducer sheath over the guidewire into the venous lumen, or may slide the catheter directly into the venous lumen without using an introducer sheath. If using an introducer sheath, the physician inserts the catheter into the vein through an O-ring in the introducer sheath (this prevents blood from leaking around the catheter) into the superior or inferior vena cava. The physician may check the catheter position with fluoroscope or with an x-ray.

36011-36012
Through a puncture through the skin, the physician passes a needle into the vein and threads a guidewire through the needle into the vein. The needle is removed and the wire is passed to the desired location in the venous system. A catheter follows the wire into the selected point in the vein and the wire is removed. A first order branch from the vena cava (36011) is any initial vessel draining directly into the vena cava (e.g., renal vein or jugular vein). A second order branch of the vena cava (36012) is any vein draining into a first order branch (e.g., left adrenal, petrosal sinus). Contrast material for venography is injected into the catheter that has traveled to an area upstream of the site under investigation. Once the procedure is complete, the catheter is removed, and pressure applied to stop bleeding at the injection site.

36013
The physician punctures a distal vein (typically antecubital, internal jugular, subclavian, or femoral)

with a large needle and passes a guidewire via the needle into the punctured vein. The physician removes the needle while leaving the guidewire in place, and enlarges the skin opening slightly with a blade. The physician slides an introducer sheath over the guidewire into the venous lumen. The physician inserts the catheter into the vein through an O-ring in the introducer sheath (this prevents blood from leaking around the catheter) and advances the catheter into the right heart or main pulmonary artery, using fluoroscopic guidance or while measuring pressures through the catheter lumen to ensure that the catheter tip is in the desired place. The physician may use the catheter to inject contrast material to perform venography or pulmonary arteriography.

36014

The physician punctures a distal vein (typically antecubital, internal jugular, subclavian, or femoral) with a large needle and passes a guidewire via the needle into the punctured vein. The physician removes the needle while leaving the guidewire in place, and enlarges the skin opening slightly with a blade. The physician slides an introducer sheath over the guidewire into the venous lumen. The physician inserts the catheter into the vein through an O-ring in the introducer sheath (this prevents blood from leaking around the catheter) and advances the catheter into one of the main pulmonary arteries (right or left) using fluoroscopic guidance and possibly measuring pressures through the catheter lumen to ensure that the catheter tip is in the desired place. The physician may use the catheter to inject contrast material to perform venography or pulmonary arteriography.

36015

The physician punctures a distal vein (typically antecubital, internal jugular, subclavian, or femoral) with a large needle and passes a guidewire via the needle into the punctured vein. The physician removes the needle while leaving the guidewire in place, and enlarges the skin opening slightly with a blade. The physician slides an introducer sheath over the guidewire into the venous lumen. The physician inserts the catheter into the vein through an O-ring in the introducer sheath (this prevents blood from leaking around the catheter) and advances the catheter into one of the segmental or subsegmental pulmonary arteries using fluoroscopic guidance and possibly measuring pressures through the catheter lumen to ensure that the catheter tip is in the desired place. The physician may use the catheter to inject contrast material to perform venography or pulmonary arteriography.

36100-36120

Through the skin of the neck (for the carotid or vertebral artery in 36100) or through the skin of the arm (into the brachial artery and upstream to the aortic arch in 36120) the physician inserts a needle into the underlying artery. A guidewire is threaded through the needle into the artery, and the needle is removed. A catheter follows the wire into the artery. The wire is removed. Contrast material is injected through the catheter into the artery for arteriography. Once either procedure is complete, the catheter is removed, and pressure applied to the puncture site to stop bleeding.

36140

Through a puncture in the skin over an extremity artery, the physician injects a needle into that artery and threads a guidewire through it. The needle is removed. A catheter follows the wire into the artery, and the wire is removed. Contrast material for arteriography is injected into the catheter placed upstream of the site under investigation. Once the procedure is complete, the catheter is removed, and pressure applied to stop bleeding at the injection site.

36147-36148

The physician inserts a needle or catheter into an arteriovenous (AV) shunt via a puncture in the skin overlying the artificial fistula or graft of a dialysis patient. The catheter is guided into the fistula and vessel to an area upstream of the site under investigation, and contrast material is injected into it. Once the procedure is complete, the catheter is removed from the shunt. Report 36147 for the initial access; this code includes shunt access, contrast injections, and all radiographic imaging deemed necessary from the arterial anastomosis and adjacent artery through the entire venous outflow (inferior and superior vena cava included). Report 36148 for each additional access made for therapeutic intervention.

36160

The physician punctures the left lumbar area, typically just above a rib, to direct a large needle into the aorta. When pulsatile red blood is obtained through the needle, indicating successful aortic puncture, the physician passes a guidewire via the needle into the punctured aorta. The physician removes the needle while leaving the guidewire in place, and enlarges the skin opening slightly with a blade. The physician slides a catheter over the guidewire into the aortic lumen and secures the catheter in place with suture.

36200

The physician punctures a distal artery (typically femoral, brachial, radial, or axillary) with a large needle and passes a guidewire via the needle into the punctured artery. The physician removes the needle while leaving the guidewire in place, and enlarges the skin opening slightly with a blade. The physician slides an introducer sheath over the guidewire into the arterial lumen. The physician inserts a catheter into the artery through an O-ring in the introducer sheath (this prevents blood from leaking around the catheter) and advances the catheter into the aorta. The physician may use the catheter to inject contrast material to perform aortography, measure aortic pressures, or to administer medication.

36215-36216
The physician passes a needle into the skin into an extremity artery, usually in the upper thigh. A guidewire is threaded through the needle into the vessel. The needle is removed. The wire is threaded into the aorta and up to the thoracic aorta where it is manipulated into a branch off the aortic arch. A catheter follows the wire into a first order thoracic or brachiocephalic artery. The wire is removed. The catheter may pass through the first order vessel into a second order thoracic or brachiocephalic artery. Contrast material for arteriography is injected into the catheter that has been guided to an area upstream of the site under investigation. In 36215, the catheter remains in a first order artery. In 36216, the catheter travels further to a second order artery. Upon completion, the catheter is removed, and pressure applied to stop bleeding at the puncture site.

36217-36218
The physician punctures the skin and underlying artery with a needle and threads a guidance wire through the needle into the artery. The needle is removed. The guidewire is manipulated into the specific artery. A catheter follows the wire into a first order thoracic or brachiocephalic artery. The catheter passes through the first order vessel into the second order thoracic or brachiocephalic artery. The catheter continues to a third order vessel. Contrast material for arteriography is injected into the catheter that has been guided to the site under investigation. Once the procedure is complete, the catheter is removed, and pressure applied to stop bleeding at the injection site. Use 36218 for an additional second order, third order, and beyond, thoracic or brachiocephalic branch, within a vascular family. Used 36218 in addition to 36216 or 36217.

36245-36246
The physician inserts a needle through the skin and into an underlying artery, usually a lower extremity artery, and threads a guidewire through the needle and into the artery. The needle is removed. The wire is threaded into the specific vessel. A catheter follows the wire into the artery branch. The wire is removed. Contrast material for arteriography is injected into the catheter that has been guided to the site under investigation. In 36245, the catheter remains in a first order artery. In 36246, the catheter travels farther, to a second order artery. Once the procedure is complete, the catheter is removed, and pressure applied to stop bleeding at the injection site.

36247-36248
The physician inserts a needle through the skin and into an underlying artery. A guidewire is threaded through the needle into the artery and the needle is removed. The guidewire is manipulated into the specific artery. A catheter follows the wire into the third order abdominal, pelvic, or lower extremity artery branch. Contrast material for arteriography is injected into the catheter that has been guided to the site under investigation. Once the procedure is complete, the catheter is removed, and pressure applied at the injection site. Report 36247 for a placement in the initial third order or more selective abdominal, pelvic, or lower extremity artery branch, within a vascular family. Report 36248 for any additional second order, third order, and beyond, abdominal, pelvic, or lower extremity artery branch, within a vascular family. Use 36248 in addition to 36246 or 36247.

36260
The physician performs an upper abdominal incision and exposes the hepatic artery. The physician punctures the hepatic artery with a large needle and passes a guidewire via the needle into the punctured artery. The physician removes the needle while leaving the guidewire in place. The physician slides the infusion catheter over the guidewire into the arterial lumen. The physician secures the catheter with suture and closes the abdominal wound around the proximal end of the infusion catheter. The physician may use the catheter to administer chemotherapeutic medication.

36261
The physician performs an upper abdominal incision and exposes the hepatic artery, locating the previously implanted infusion catheter. The physician may unkink the catheter or replace it over a wire. The physician secures the catheter with suture and closes the abdominal wound around the proximal end of the infusion catheter. The physician may use the catheter to administer chemotherapeutic medication.

36262
The physician performs an upper abdominal incision and exposes the hepatic artery while dissecting free the previously implanted infusion catheter. The physician removes the catheter, and may repair the arteriotomy with suture. The physician closes the abdominal wound, and may leave a drain in place.

36400
A needle is inserted through the skin to puncture the femoral or jugular vein of a child younger than age three. The needle is inserted into the vein and used for the withdrawal of blood for diagnostic study or for the therapeutic infusion of intravenous medication. A soft flexible catheter may be placed for prolonged therapy. Once the procedure is complete, the needle or catheter is withdrawn and pressure is applied over the puncture site to control bleeding. Use this code for venipuncture necessitating a physician's skill, not when routine venipuncture is performed.

36405-36406
A needle is inserted through the skin to puncture a vein of a child younger than age three. In 36405, the

scalp vein is punctured and in 36406, a vein other than the femoral, jugular, or scalp vein is used. The needle is inserted into the vein and used for the withdrawal of blood or for the therapeutic infusion of intravenous medication. A soft flexible catheter may be placed for prolonged therapy. Once the procedure is complete, the needle or catheter is withdrawn and pressure is applied over the puncture site to control bleeding. Use this code for venipuncture necessitating a physician's skill, not when routine venipuncture is performed.

36410
A needle is inserted through the skin to puncture a vein of a person three years of age or older. The needle is inserted into the vein and used for the withdrawal of blood for diagnostic study or for the therapeutic infusion of intravenous medication. A soft flexible catheter may be placed for prolonged therapy. Once the procedure is complete, the needle or catheter is withdrawn and pressure is applied over the puncture site to control bleeding. Use this code for venipuncture necessitating a physician's skill, not when routine venipuncture is performed.

36415-36416
A needle is inserted into the skin over a vein to puncture the blood vessel and withdraw blood for venous collection in 36415. In 36416, a prick is made into the finger, heel, or ear and capillary blood that pools at the puncture site is collected in a pipette. In either case, the blood is used for diagnostic study and no catheter is placed.

36420-36425
The physician makes an incision in the skin directly over the vessel and dissects the area surrounding the vein. A needle is passed into the vein for the withdrawal of blood or for the infusion of intravenous medication of a patient under 12 months of age (in 36420) or over 12 months of age (in 36425). A catheter may be left behind. Once the procedure is complete, the incision is repaired with a layered closure.

36430
The physician transfuses blood or blood components to a patient. The physician establishes venous access with a needle and catheter and transfuses the blood products.

36440
The physician performs a push transfusion on a child two years old and under. The physician calculates the amount of blood to be transfused and slowly injects it into the patient using a needle or existing catheter.

36450-36455
The physician performs an exchange transfusion on a newborn. The physician calculates the blood volume to be transfused. A needle is placed in an artery or in an existing arterial catheter. The patient's blood is removed and replaced simultaneously to maintain blood pressure. Report 36455 if the child is other than a newborn.

36460
The physician performs a blood transfusion to a fetus. The physician uses separately reportable ultrasound guidance to locate the umbilical vein. A needle is directed through the abdominal wall into the amniotic cavity. The umbilical vein is pierced and fetal blood is exchanged with transfused blood. The needle is withdrawn and the fetus is observed under separately reportable ultrasound.

36468
The physician inserts a tiny needle through the skin and directly into the tiny, distended veins in the arms, legs, or trunk. A solution (hypertonic saline and other solutions) is injected into these veins. The solution causes the walls of the veins to become inflamed, collapse, and stick together so the veins close.

36469
The physician inserts a tiny needle through the skin and directly into the tiny, distended veins in the face. A solution (hypertonic saline and other solutions) is injected into these veins. The solution causes the walls of the veins to become inflamed, collapse, and stick together so the veins close.

36470-36471
The physician injects a sclerosing solution into veins of the leg. The physician inserts a tiny needle through the skin and directly into any single vein (in 36470) or multiple veins of the same leg (in 36471). A solution (hypertonic saline and other solutions) is injected into these veins. The patient stands while the injection is given. The leg is elevated thereafter, and wrapped in an elastic dressing. The solution causes the walls of the veins to become inflamed, collapse, and stick together so the veins close.

36475-36476
The physician uses percutaneous, radiofrequency, endovenous ablation therapy to treat venous incompetence in an extremity vein. Radiofrequency energy is used to heat the vein and seal the vein closed. The most common site of treatment is the greater saphenous vein. The procedure includes any imaging guidance and monitoring. The leg is prepared and draped and a local anesthetic is applied to the puncture site. A needle is inserted into the access site. A guidewire is placed into the vessel using ultrasound guidance. An introducer sheath is placed over the guidewire and the guidewire is removed. The radiofrequency ablation catheter system is introduced and the tip is advanced to the site of the venous incompetence under ultrasound guidance. A local anesthetic agent is injected into the tissues surrounding the vein within its fascial sheath. The anesthetic is injected along the course of the vein. Ultrasonography is used to position the catheter tip at the level of the

terminal valve and the catheter electrodes are deployed. The electrodes should be just distal to the valve cusps of the terminal valve. Radiofrequency energy is applied until the thermocouple temperature rises to 80° to 85°C and remains at this temperature for 10 to 15 seconds. Once this temperature is reached, the catheter tip is slowly withdrawn until it reaches the introducer sheath in the distal vein. The console automatically shuts off. The ablation catheter and introducer sheath are removed and pressure is applied to the puncture site. Report 36475 for the first vein treated in a single extremity and 36476 for each additional vein treated through a separate access site in the same extremity.

36478-36479

The physician uses percutaneous, laser, endovenous ablation therapy to treat venous incompetence in an extremity vein. Laser energy is used to heat the vein and seal the vein closed. The most common site of treatment is the greater saphenous vein. The procedure includes any imaging guidance and monitoring. The leg is prepared and draped and a local anesthetic is applied to the puncture site. A needle is inserted into the access site. A guidewire is placed into the vessel using ultrasound guidance. An introducer sheath is placed over the guidewire and the guidewire is removed. The laser ablation catheter system is introduced and the tip is advanced to the site of the venous incompetence under ultrasound guidance. A local anesthetic agent is injected into the tissues surrounding the vein within its fascial sheath. The anesthetic is injected along the course of the vein. Ultrasonography is used to position the catheter tip at the level of the terminal valve and laser energy is applied via a laser fiber along the length of the vein as the catheter is slowly withdrawn. When the laser catheter tip reaches the introducer sheath in the distal vein, the laser energy is terminated. The ablation catheter and introducer sheath are removed and pressure is applied at the puncture site. Report 36478 for the first vein treated in a single extremity and 36479 for each additional vein treated through a separate access site in the same extremity.

36481

The physician numbs the right lateral abdominal wall with local anesthetic. The physician places a large needle through the skin into the liver, maneuvering the needle through the liver into the intrahepatic portal vein, injecting contrast under fluoroscope for localization. The physician places a wire through the needle, retrograde into the portal vein. The physician removes the wire over the needle, and advances a catheter over the wire, through the skin and liver into the portal vein. The physician secures the catheter with suture. Alternative methods include placing a catheter via the internal jugular vein or using a transsplenic approach.

36500

The physician inserts a needle through the skin and into a peripheral vein. A guidewire is threaded through the needle into the vessel. The needle is removed. The wire is manipulated into the vein draining from the organ to be sampled. The catheter follows the guidewire into the vein. Once the catheter has been placed, the guidewire is removed and the blood sample obtained. The catheter is removed and pressure is applied to the puncture site to stop the flow of blood.

36510

The physician catheterizes the umbilical vein for diagnostic or therapeutic purposes. The physician cleanses the umbilical cord stump and locates the umbilical vein. A catheter is inserted in the vein for reasons including blood sampling or administering medication.

36511-36513

Therapeutic apheresis is the removal of some specific circulating blood component, cells or plasma solute, that is directly responsible for a disease process. Cells and plasma components may also be mobilized from other tissue storage during apheresis, such as from the spleen and lymph nodes, for enhanced clearance of the undesired element. The patient is prepared much the same as giving a regular blood donation. Whole blood is drawn out of one arm and into an instrument called a separator, which uses a microprocessing technique to draw the blood, anticoagulate it, and separate the component to be removed by centrifugal spinning, filtration, or column adsorption with the help of computerized calibration. The cells to be removed are collected while the remainder of the blood is recombined and returned to the patient through a tube and needle in the other arm. Report 36511 for white blood cell isolation and removal (leukapheresis or lymphocytapheresis), 36512 for red blood cell removal, and 36513 for removal of platelets.

36514-36516

Therapeutic apheresis is the removal of some specific circulating blood component, cells or plasma solute, that is directly responsible for a disease process. Cells and plasma components may also be mobilized from other tissue storage during apheresis, such the from the spleen and lymph nodes, for enhanced clearance of the undesired element. The patient is prepared much the same as giving a regular blood donation. Whole blood is drawn out of one arm and into an instrument called a separator, which uses a microprocessing technique to draw the blood, anticoagulate it, and separate the component to be removed by centrifugal spinning, filtration, or column adsorption with the help of computerized calibration. Plasmapheresis, reported with 36514 is the isolation of the plasma from the blood. Plasma exchange isolates, discards, and replaces the plasma with a substitute fluid, like albumin. Plasma exchange is nonspecific since the plasma is discarded on the basis that toxins and antibodies accumulate in the plasma. The best method requires treating a disorder by removing the offending abnormal plasma component selectively. Apheresis for plasma with extracorporeal immunoadsorption and reinfusion of the patient's plasma may be done, reported with 36515. This procedure uses Protein A columns to specifically remove circulating immune complexes. Report 36516 for extracorporeal selective adsorption or selective filtration, such as dextran sulfate cellulose columns to selectively remove low-density lipoproteins, with plasma reinfusion.

36522

The physician draws a patient's blood and exposes the blood to light to eliminate destructive elements. The physician establishes venous access or attaches the machine to an existing central venous catheter line. The blood is removed and cycled through the pheresis machine where it is exposed to therapeutic wavelengths of light. The conditioned blood is returned to the patient through a catheter and a needle inserted in the vein.

36555-36556

A central venous access device (CVAD) or catheter is one in which the tip terminates in the subclavian, brachiocephalic, or iliac vein; the superior or inferior vena cava; or the right atrium. A centrally inserted CVAD has an entry site in the inferior vena cava or the jugular, subclavian, or femoral vein. For insertion of a non-tunneled, centrally inserted CVAD, the site over the access vein (e.g., subclavian, jugular) is injected with local anesthesia and punctured with a needle. A guidewire is inserted. The central venous catheter is placed over the guidewire. Ultrasound guidance may be used to gain venous access and/or fluoroscopy to check the positioning of the catheter tip. The catheter is secured into position and dressed. Non-tunneled catheters are percutaneously inserted for short term (five to seven days) use; to infuse medications, fluids, blood products, and parenteral nutrition; and to take blood draws. Report 36555 for insertion for children younger than five years of age and 36556 for a patient five years of age or older.

36557-36558

A central venous access device (CVAD) or catheter is one in which the tip terminates in the subclavian, brachiocephalic, or iliac vein; the superior or inferior vena cava; or the right atrium. A centrally inserted CVAD has an entry site in the inferior vena cava or the jugular, subclavian, or femoral vein. A tunneled catheter has an entrance site at a distance from its entrance into the vascular system; they are "tunneled" through the skin and subcutaneous tissue to a great vein. For insertion of a tunneled, centrally inserted CVAD, without subcutaneous port or pump, standard preparations are made and the site over the access vein (e.g., subclavian, jugular) is injected with local anesthesia and punctured with a needle or accessed by cutdown approach. A guidewire is inserted. A subcutaneous tunnel is created using a blunt pair of forceps or sharp tunneling tools, over the clavicle from the anterior chest wall to the venotomy site, which is dilated to the right size. The catheter is passed through this tunnel over the guidewire and into the target vein. Ultrasound guidance may be used to gain venous access and/or fluoroscopy to check the positioning of the catheter tip. The catheter is secured into position and any incisions are sutured. Report 36557 for insertion for children younger than five years of age and 36558 for a patient five years of age or older.

36560-36563

For insertion of a tunneled, centrally inserted CVAD, with subcutaneous port/pump, the site over the access vein (e.g., subclavian, jugular) is injected with local anesthesia and punctured with a needle or accessed by cutdown approach. A guidewire is inserted. A subcutaneous tunnel is created using a blunt pair of forceps or sharp tunneling tools, over the clavicle, from the anterior chest wall to the venotomy site, which is dilated to the right size. The catheter is passed through this tunnel over the guidewire and into the target vein. The subcutaneous pocket for the port/pump is created with an incision through the skin overlying the second rib, a few centimeters from the midline. Blunt dissection and cautery are used to create the pocket in the chest wall and the port/pump is placed. The catheter is connected to the port/pump and checked by injection. Ultrasound guidance may be used to gain venous access and/or fluoroscopy to check the positioning of the catheter tip. The catheter and port/pump are secured into position and any incisions are sutured. Report 36560 for insertion with a port for children younger than five years of age and 36561 for a patient five years of age or older. Report 36563 for insertion with a pump.

36565

For insertion of a tunneled, centrally inserted CVAD, requiring two catheters via two separate venous access sites, without subcutaneous port/pump, the sites of access (e.g., subclavian, jugular vein) for each catheter are injected with local anesthesia and two punctures are made with a needle or cutdown approach. Guidewires are inserted. Two subcutaneous tunnels are created using a blunt pair of forceps or sharp tunneling tools, over the clavicle, from the anterior chest wall to the venotomy sites, which are dilated to the right size. The catheters are each passed through their tunnel, over the guidewires, and into their venotomy sites. Ultrasound guidance may be used to gain venous access and/or fluoroscopy to check the positioning of the catheter tip. The catheters are secured into position and any incisions are sutured.

36566
For insertion of a tunneled, centrally inserted CVAD, requiring two catheters via two separate venous access sites, with subcutaneous ports, the sites of access (e.g., subclavian, jugular vein) for each catheter are injected with local anesthesia and two punctures are made with a needle or cutdown approach. Guidewires are inserted. Two subcutaneous tunnels are created using a blunt pair of forceps or sharp tunneling tools, over the clavicle, from the anterior chest wall to the venotomy sites, which are dilated to the right size. The catheters are each passed through their tunnel over the guidewires and into their venotomy sites. Two subcutaneous pockets for the ports are created with incisions through the skin in the chest wall, a few centimeters from the midline. Blunt dissection and cautery are used to create the pockets in the chest wall and the ports are placed. The catheters are connected to their respective ports and checked by injection. Ultrasound guidance may be used to gain venous access and/or fluoroscopy to check the positioning of the catheter tip. The catheters and ports are secured into position and any incisions are sutured.

36568-36569
A central venous access device or catheter is one in which the tip terminates in the subclavian, brachiocephalic, or iliac vein; the superior or inferior vena cava; or the right atrium. A peripherally inserted central venous catheter (PICC) has an entry site in the basilic or cephalic vein in the arm and is threaded into the superior vena cava above the right atrium. PICC lines are used for antibiotic therapy, chemotherapy, total parenteral nutrition, lab work, pain medications, blood transfusions, and hydration the same as a central line. For insertion of a (non-tunneled), peripherally inserted central venous catheter, without subcutaneous port or pump, the access vein (basilic or cephalic) is injected with local anesthesia and punctured with a needle. A guidewire is inserted. The central venous catheter is placed over the guidewire. Ultrasound guidance may be used to gain venous access and/or fluoroscopy to check the positioning of the catheter tip. The catheter is secured into position, and dressed. Report 36568 for insertion for children younger than five years of age and 36569 for a patient five years of age or older.

36570-36571
A central venous access device or catheter is one in which the tip terminates in the subclavian, brachiocephalic, or iliac vein; the superior or inferior vena cava; or the right atrium. A peripherally inserted central venous catheter (PICC) has an entry site in the basilic or cephalic vein in the arm and is threaded into the superior vena cava above the right atrium. PICC lines are used for antibiotic therapy, chemotherapy, total parenteral nutrition, lab work, pain medications, blood transfusions, and hydration the same as a central line. For insertion of a peripherally inserted central venous catheter with a subcutaneous port, the site over the access vein (basilic or cephalic) is injected with local anesthesia and punctured with a needle. A guidewire is inserted. The central venous catheter is placed over the guidewire and fed through the vein in the arm into the superior vena cava. The port may be placed in the chest in a subcutaneous pocket created through an incision in the chest wall, or placed in the arm through a small incision just above or halfway between the elbow crease and the shoulder on the inside of the arm. The port is attached to the catheter and checked. Ultrasound guidance may be used to gain venous access and/or fluoroscopy to check the positioning of the catheter tip. The catheter and port are secured into position and incisions are closed and dressed. Report 36570 for insertion for children younger than five years of age and 36571 for a patient five years of age or older.

36575
This code reports repair of a central venous access device (CVAD) that has external catheters with the access ports outside the body, and no subcutaneous ports or pumps, whether centrally or peripherally inserted, tunneled or non-tunneled. The repair is done on the catheter that is placed without any replacement of components. A Hickman catheter is an example of a tunneled CVAD with an external port.

36576
The physician repairs a central venous access device (CVAD) that has an internal access port/pump in a subcutaneous pocket that is connected to the catheter, whether centrally or peripherally inserted. The repair is done on the device as it is placed within the patient, without any replacement of components, catheter, or subcutaneous port/pump.

36578
The catheter only of a central venous access device with a subcutaneous port or pump is replaced, whether centrally or peripherally inserted. Local anesthesia is given and the subcutaneous pocket over the port is incised. The catheter is disconnected. A guidewire is placed through the existing catheter, which is removed over the guidewire. A new central venous catheter of correct length is placed into position and connected to the port/pump device that has not been removed or replaced. The connection with the new catheter is checked, as well as the catheter and port secured, and the wound is dressed.

36580
A non-tunneled, centrally inserted central venous catheter, without subcutaneous port or pump, is replaced through the same venous access site. Local anesthesia is given. A guidewire is first passed through the existing central line catheter and the catheter is removed. A new central venous catheter is placed back into position over the guidewire, secured into position, and dressed.

36581

A tunneled, centrally inserted central venous catheter, without subcutaneous port or pump is replaced. Local anesthesia is given and the sutures securing the cuff of the indwelling catheter are freed from the skin. A guidewire is next placed through the existing catheter, which is removed, and a new central venous catheter is inserted into the tunneled position over the guidewire. The new catheter is secured into position and the wound is dressed.

36582-36583

A tunneled, centrally inserted central venous catheter, along with a subcutaneous port (36582) or pump (36583) device is replaced. Local anesthesia is given and the subcutaneous pocket over the port/pump device is incised. The pump/port is dissected free and tested. The catheter is disconnected and the pump/port device is removed from its pocket. A guidewire is placed over the existing catheter, which is removed, and a new central venous catheter is threaded into position over the guidewire. A new pump/port device is inserted into the subcutaneous pocket and the catheter is connected. The connection is checked with an injection. The new pump/port is secured into the pocket, incisions are closed, and the wound is dressed.

36584

A peripherally inserted central venous catheter (PICC), without subcutaneous port or pump, is replaced through the same venous access site. Local anesthesia is given and the sutures securing the cuff of the catheter with external port are freed from the skin and it is partially withdrawn. A sheath is placed over the nonfunctioning catheter and it is completely withdrawn. A guidewire is inserted into the access site through the sheath and advanced. A new catheter of correct length is placed over the guidewire and the sheath and guidewire are removed. The catheter is fastened in position and the wound is dressed.

36585

A peripherally inserted central venous catheter (PICC), along with a subcutaneous port, is replaced through the same venous access site. Local anesthesia is given, the skin over the subcutaneous pocket is incised, and the port is dissected free. A sheath is placed over the nonfunctioning catheter and it is completely withdrawn. A guidewire is inserted into the access site through the sheath and advanced. A new catheter of correct length is placed over the guidewire and the sheath and guidewire are removed. The catheter is fastened in position and the wound is dressed.

36589

A tunneled central venous catheter without subcutaneous port or pump is removed. Local anesthesia is given and the sutures securing the cuff of the tunneled catheter's external port are freed from the skin. A guidewire is next placed through the catheter, which is withdrawn over the guidewire. After the guidewire is removed, the wound is dressed.

36590

A tunneled central venous access device, both catheter and subcutaneous port or pump, is removed. Local anesthesia is given and the subcutaneous pocket over the port/pump device is incised and the pump/port is dissected free. The catheter is disconnected and the pump/port device is removed from its pocket. A guidewire is placed over the existing catheter, which is withdrawn over the guidewire, and the guidewire is removed. The incisions are closed and the wound is dressed.

36591

The physician obtains a blood specimen from a previously placed, completely implantable venous access device. Completely implanted devices are those that have access through a subcutaneous port (e.g., Port-A-Cath, Infusaport). An implantable access device requires a percutaneous noncoring needle to accomplish the blood draw. The skin is cleansed with alcohol or iodine solution. The needle is placed into the port. Heparin is withdrawn. A second needle is inserted and the blood specimen obtained. The port is flushed with heparin solution.

36592

The physician obtains a blood specimen from an established central venous or peripheral venous catheter. A central venous catheter (CVC) is one that is inserted through the skin into central veins, such as the femoral, internal jugular, or subclavian veins. Peripheral catheters include those inserted in the arm veins (basilic or cephalic), such as a PICC line, saline lock, or heparin lock. In order to clear the catheter of any material that could contaminate the sample and affect the test results, a specific volume of infusing fluid and blood must be discarded before a blood specimen is obtained; this volume will vary depending on the type of catheter utilized. With a central venous catheter, a three-way stopcock is attached to the catheter's hub and two syringes attached to the stopcock. Using one syringe, the catheter is flushed with normal saline. A specific amount of blood is aspirated into the same syringe used for the saline flush and discarded. The blood sample is then withdrawn using the other syringe and placed into an appropriate tube for laboratory analysis. If using a peripheral venous catheter, a specific amount of blood is also aspirated and discarded before the blood sample is drawn.

36593

To remove a clot from an implanted vascular access device or catheter, the physician injects a thrombolytic agent (e.g., Streptokinase) into the catheter to dissolve the clot. The patient is observed for any abnormal signs of bleeding.

36595

Pericatheter obstructive material such as a fibrin sheath is removed from around a central venous device via separate venous access. Central venous catheters often fail because of the accumulation of an obstructing thrombus or fibrin sheath around the tip of the catheter. The catheter is first checked that it can aspirate and flush forward. The pericatheter material is identified by contrast material injection. Generally, a right femoral vein access is used. A guidewire followed by an angiographic catheter are advanced into the superior vena cava and exchanged for a loop snare with its catheter, which are advanced cephalad along the length of the central venous catheter beyond the ports. The loop snare is tightly closed about the central venous catheter to encircle it and slowly pulled down and off the tip of the catheter, stripping off the pericatheter obstructive material. This is repeated a few times and the catheter is rechecked for infusion and injection ability of the ports. A contrast study is done again to identify any fibrin and the process may be repeated until the fibrin sheath is completely removed.

36596

Intraluminal obstructive material, such as a thrombus or fibrin sheath, is removed from inside a central venous device through the lumen of the device. This does not require a separate access incision. The central venous catheter is first checked that it can aspirate and flush forward. The obstructing material is disrupted and removed mechanically by using an angioplasty balloon or other catheter introduced into the central venous catheter through its entry site on the skin. The catheter is checked for unimpeded, restored flow and the process may be repeated until the central venous catheter is cleared.

36597

A previously placed central venous catheter needs to be repositioned. It is possible for a catheter position to change significantly after the procedure is completed. Catheter position change and tip migration occur most often with subclavian venous access in women and obese patients, because the soft tissues of the chest wall move inferiorly with standing and often cause the catheter to get pulled back. When a catheter tip is incorrectly placed, it can increase the risks of thrombosis, fibrin sheath formation, perforation of the vein, and even arrhythmias. Fluoroscopy is used to check the positioning of the catheter tip and guide it to its correct position. Local anesthesia is given, and the sutures securing the cuff of the catheter may be freed from the skin. The catheter is partially withdrawn, and a sheath may be placed over the catheter at the existing venous access site. A guidewire is inserted through the catheter and advanced. The central venous catheter is maneuvered back into correct position and monitored with fluoroscopy to view correct placement of the tip.

36598

A previously placed central venous access device is evaluated for complications that may be interfering with its proper functioning or the ability to draw blood from the catheter. Complications may include the presence of a fibrin sheath around the end of the catheter, migration of the catheter tip, patency of the tubing, kinking, fracture, or leaks. A small amount of contrast agent is injected into the catheter and the central venous access device is examined under fluoroscopy as the flow is evaluated. Images are documented and a radiological report is prepared.

36600

The physician inserts a needle through the skin and punctures the artery to withdraw blood for testing. No catheter is left in the artery. Pressure is applied to the puncture site to stop the flow of blood.

36620-36625

The physician accesses, in most cases, the ulnar or radial artery to insert a cannula, or tube-shaped portal. In 36620, the physician inserts a needle through the skin to puncture the artery and inserts a cannula. In 36625, the physician makes an incision in the skin overlying the artery and dissects the surrounding tissue to access it. The artery is sometimes nicked with a thin-bladed scalpel before the physician inserts the cannula. This cannula acts as a portal for sampling, monitoring or transfusion. Once the procedure is complete, the cannula is removed. In an open procedure, the opening in the artery may be sutured and the incision repaired with a layered closure. Pressure is applied to the puncture if a percutaneous approach is used.

36640

The physician accesses the artery supplying the area to be treated. To insert a cannula, or tube-shaped portal for prolonged infusion therapy, the physician makes an incision above the artery and dissects the surrounding tissue to access it. The artery is sometimes nicked with a thin-bladed scalpel before the physician inserts the catheter. The catheter may be advanced to a site immediately upstream of the site to be treated. This catheter acts as a portal for the infusion of chemotherapy drugs and will remain in place until chemotherapy is completed. The catheter is removed, the hole in the artery is repaired, and the incision is repaired with a layered closure.

36660

The physician catheterizes an umbilical artery in a newborn for diagnostic or therapeutic purposes. The physician prepares the umbilical artery and passes a catheter sheath inside the lumen for arterial access. The catheter is attached to a pressure line that maintains patency of the arterial lumen. The access is used for diagnostic or therapeutic purposes, allowing the drawing of blood for tests or instillation of medication.

36680
The physician inserts a hollow needle through the skin and through the muscle tissue to puncture the bone marrow cavity, usually in the tibia or femur, of a patient whose vessels otherwise seem inaccessible. This needle is used as a method of infusing fluids into the blood vessels in the bone marrow.

36800
The physician isolates two veins, usually in the nondominant forearm, and inserts a needle through the skin and into each vessel. A guidance wire may be threaded through the needle into each vessel. The needle is removed. An end of a single cannula is inserted into each puncture, and any guidance wire removed. The cannula remains external, and may be left in place for several days. (This hemodialysis cannula is used to remove blood from the vein, route it through the dialysis machine, then reinfuse it.)

36810
The physician isolates an artery and a vein, usually in the nondominant forearm, and inserts a needle through the skin and into each vessel. A guidewire may be threaded through the needle into each vessel. The needle is removed. An end of a single cannula is inserted into each puncture, and any guidance wire removed. The Scribner cannula remains external, and may be left in place for several days. (This hemodialysis cannula is used to remove blood from the vessel, route it through the dialysis machine, then reinfuse it.)

36815
The physician repositions an external cannula or removes it, followed by closure of the insertion site using sutures on the vessels or skin as necessary. The cannula forms a ready connection between the artery and vein, or vein and vein, for hemodialysis or another purpose.

36818-36819
A vascular surgeon creates a connection between an artery and a vein for a vascular access site in patients with end stage renal disease that require hemodialysis. In 36819, the surgeon dissects down to the basilic vein on the medial side of the upper arm and mobilizes the vein. A subcutaneous tunnel on the anterior side of the arm is created, and the mobilized basilic vein is transposed to this tunnel and anastomosed to the brachial artery. Report 36818 if a similar arteriovenous connection is made in the upper arm by anastomosing the cephalic vein to the brachial artery.

36820
The physician creates a connection between an artery or vein, using a forearm vein in the arm—inverted end to end. The physician dissects down to the vein and artery. The subfascial plane is identified and elevated laterally to the flexor carpi radialis (FCR) and medially to the brachioradialis (BR). The plane between the BR and FCR is dissected and the perforating vessels are identified and cauterized. The pedicle is followed to the antecubital fossa. The tourniquet is released, and the vessels are further cleaned of their adventitia under loupe visualization. Using microvascular techniques, a suture for the arterial anastomosis is performed and closure is completed. Suction drains are placed in the neck. If a Doppler is to be used for postoperative assessment, a suture is placed to mark the pedicle site. A splint is fabricated and secured to the arm with an elastic bandage.

36821
Through an incision, usually in the skin over an artery in the nondominant wrist or antecubital fossa, the physician isolates a desired section of artery and neighboring vein. Vessel clamps are placed on the vein and adjacent artery. The vein is dissected free, divided, and the downstream portion of the vein is sutured to an opening created in the adjacent artery, usually in an end-to-side fashion, allowing blood to flow both down the artery and into the vein. Large branches of the vein may be tied off to cause flow down a single vein. The skin incision is repaired with a layered closure. This arteriovenous anastomosis will allow an increased blood flow through the vein, usually for hemodialysis.

36822
The physician inserts cannula(s) to provide prolonged extracorporeal circulation for cardiopulmonary insufficiency. A small incision is made along the right side of the neck. A single or double lumen cannula is inserted into a large vein in the neck and passed into the right atrium. This cannula carries blood that is low in oxygen and high in carbon dioxide into the extracorporeal membrane oxygenation (ECMO) circuit. In venovenous ECMO, if a double lumen cannula was inserted, blood that has passed through the membrane oxygenator that is now high in oxygen and low in carbon dioxide (oxygenated blood) will be rewarmed and returned via the same cannula. If a single lumen cannula is used a second cannula is inserted into a second vein (venovenous ECMO) or a main artery (venoarterial ECMO), usually the femoral but in children the carotid may be used. This second cannula passes from the ECMO circuit carrying oxygenated, rewarmed blood back to the vein or artery.

36823
The physician inserts arterial and venous cannula(s) for isolated extracorporeal circulation to an extremity to provide regional perfusion chemotherapy (RPC) with or without hyperthermia. The external iliac, common femoral, or subclavian artery and vein are isolated depending on the site of the tumor. A cannula is inserted into the selected artery and vein to isolate blood flow to and from the extremity. The blood flow from the isolated extremity is connected to a perfusion pump where the blood is oxygenated. The blood may be heated to between 40°-40.5° C (104°-105° F). One or more high dose chemotherapy agents are injected

and perfused over an hour or more with flow rates monitored and adjusted to minimize leakage into the systemic circulation. The combination of heat and the chemotherapy agent act to destroy the cancer cells. After completion of the perfusion procedure, the cannula(s) are removed and the artery and vein repaired.

36825-36830
The physician creates an arteriovenous fistula by other than direct anastomosis. The physician makes an incision in the skin over an artery and vein, and the vein and artery are dissected free. A vessel clamp is affixed to each. A length of harvested vein from the patient is used for an autogenous graft in 36825 and is sutured to the incised artery and vein, usually in an end-to-side fashion. The graft is passed in a superficial subcutaneous tunnel that is created bluntly and connects the arterial and venous sites. The clamps are removed, allowing the blood to flow through the graft, creating an arteriovenous fistula. The skin incision is repaired with a layered closure. Report 36830 if a nonautogenous graft, such as biological collagen or a thermoplastic graft, is used.

36831
The physician removes a blood clot from a surgically created connection between an artery and a vein (arteriovenous fistula). The procedure involves making an incision over the site of an existing fistula. The fistula is isolated and dissected free. Vessel clamps are affixed above and below the fistula. The blood clot is removed, the clamps are taken off, and the incision is repaired by layered sutures. The procedure may involve a vein acquired from the patient or the construction of a synthetic graft.

36832-36833
In 36832, the physician makes an incision at the site of an already existing artificial fistula between an artery and a vein. The fistula is dissected free. Vessel clamps are affixed above and below the fistula, which is incised. Revisions are made to the fistula at its juncture to the vein and/or artery and may require creating a new anastomosis with a graft obtained from a separate site or created with synthetic material. After the repair has been made, the fistula is sutured, the clamps removed, and the skin incision repaired with a layered closure. Report 36833 when the physician removes a blood clot at the fistula site in addition to revising the existing arteriovenous fistula.

36835
Through an incision in the skin overlying a large vein or artery of a child, the physician dissects the vessel that will receive a synthetic shunt. The vessel may be clamped. The vessel is nicked, and a needle threads a guidance wire into the vein or artery. The shunt follows, and the wire is removed. The physician sutures the synthetic shunt end-to-end, or end-to-side, to the vein or artery. The shunt is most often used for access in hemodialysis.

36838
A DRIL procedure, distal revascularization and interval ligation, is done to treat Steal syndrome occurring in patients with a permanent indwelling access site in the arm for hemodialysis. In Steal syndrome, the hand becomes cold and painful, due to ischemia because the hemodialysis access is taking the arm's blood supply. The DRIL procedure restores blood flow to the hand and preserves the access site. It is a two-step procedure. The surgeon first creates a bypass graft around the access site, using a harvested vein conduit, usually the greater saphenous. An incision is made in the upper arm for the proximal anastomosis, which is placed above the dialysis access site, nearer to the axilla. Soft tissue is dissected to expose the brachial artery. An incision is also made lower in the arm for the site of the distal anastomosis, which is placed below the dialysis access site, down in the forearm. A tunnel is created from one site to the other and the graft is completed using the harvested vein. This is the revascularization portion of the procedure and allows a good flow of blood around the access site. The second part of the procedure is the ligation. The brachial artery is tied off at a point between the dialysis access and the distal anastomosis site of the bypass graft. Now the arterial blood flow being pumped from the heart runs through the bypass, supplying the hand with oxygen before entering the access site. The incisions are closed and pulses are checked for good perfusion before applying dressings.

36860-36861
To remove a blood clot lodged in a previously placed cannula, the physician may inject a solution containing enzymes into the cannula to dissolve the clot (in 36860) or the physician may, after injecting a solution containing enzymes, insert a balloon catheter (in 36861) into the cannula to retrieve a clot there. The balloon is inserted and inflated beyond the clot. The catheter is slowly pulled out, capturing and retrieving the clot. Once the clot is dissolved or retrieved, the catheter is removed and the cannula is left in place.

36870
Under separately reportable radiologic guidance, a percutaneously placed catheter is advanced to the site of a thrombus or clot that has formed in a previously created connection between an artery and a vein, (arteriovenous fistula). The catheter is inserted into the clot and the clot is fragmented. Injection of urokinase may be required to dissolve the clot or percutaneous pharmacomechanical thrombolysis may be performed. Pharmacomechanical thrombolysis involves both injection of urokinase and mechanical fragmentation of the clot. Suction is applied and the clot fragments are removed through the catheter. The catheter is removed and pressure is applied at the insertion site.

37140
The physician performs portacaval venous anastomosis. The physician places a long right thoracoabdominal incision and exposes the liver. The physician exposes the inferior vena cava and portal vein through careful dissection. The physician places a plastic sling around the portal vein and ties it closed, just proximal to its bifurcation. The physician clamps and divides the portal vein. The physician applies a partial exclusion vascular clamp to the front of the vena cava and removes a small oval of tissue from the vena cava to allow end-to-side anastomosis of portal vein to the inferior vena cava. The physician removes the clamps and checks for appropriate flow without anastomotic leakage. The physician closes the incision, leaving a chest tube in place (but no abdominal drains, as this may lead to protein loss from postoperative drainage of ascites).

37145
The physician performs an abdominal incision and exposes the left renal vein and inferior vena cava. The physician transects the left renal vein and attaches it to the portal circulation by sewing the vena caval end to the portal vein, the superior mesenteric vein, or the splenic vein. Alternatively, the physician may divide the portal vein and attach its splanchnic end to the end of the transected renal vein. The physician assesses patency of the anastomosis and may measure venous pressures before closing the abdomen.

37160
The physician performs an upper midline vertical abdominal incision and retracts the transverse colon in a cephalad direction. The physician exposes the anterior surface of the inferior vena cava and frees the posterior surface of the superior mesenteric vein after careful dissection through the root of the transverse mesocolon. The physician isolates a long segment of the superior mesenteric vein with ties and partially occludes the inferior vena cava. The physician removes an ellipse of tissue from the inferior vena cava and performs and end-to-side anastomosis of Dacron graft to the inferior vena cava. The physician occludes the superior mesenteric vein, cuts an ellipse from its anterior surface, and sews the end of the Dacron graft to the side of the superior mesenteric vein. The physician assesses patency of the anastomosis and may measure venous pressures before closing the abdomen.

37180
The physician performs a bilateral subcostal incision from the right midrectus position extending into the left flank, and dissects past bowel and pancreas to expose the splenic vein. The physician dissects the splenic vein free, ligating the splenic vein toward the left and using the central (right) end of the vein for the anastomosis. The physician exposes the left renal vein by dissecting through the posterior parietal peritoneum. The physician exposes the left renal vein, partially clamps it, and excises an ellipse of renal vein at its upper border. The physician performs and end-to-side anastomosis of the splenic vein to the renal vein, using harvested vein graft material if extension is required. The physician removes the clamps. The physician may measure superior mesenteric (portal), renal, and splenic venous pressures. The physician may perform venography to establish patency of the graft. The physician closes the abdominal wound.

37181
The physician performs a bilateral subcostal incision from the right midrectus position extending into the left flank, and dissects past bowel and pancreas to expose the splenic vein. The physician dissects the splenic vein free, ligating or clipping any vessels in continuity to the vein. The physician exposes the left renal vein by dissecting through the posterior parietal peritoneum. The physician exposes the left renal vein, partially clamps it, and excises an ellipse of renal vein at its upper border. The physician performs and end-to-side anastomosis of the splenic vein to the renal vein, using harvested vein graft material if extension is required. The physician removes the clamps and divides the coronary (right gastric) vein, left gastric vein, and gastroepiploic veins. The physician may measure superior mesenteric (portal), renal, and splenic venous pressures. The physician may perform venography to establish patency of the graft. The physician closes the abdominal wound.

37182-37183
A transvenous intrahepatic portosystemic shunt (TIPS) is inserted in 37182 and replaced in 37183. Shunts are placed percutaneously to manage the complications of portal hypertension and control variceal bleeding and ascites. Once the patient is under general anesthesia or conscious sedation, the right internal jugular vein is accessed and a catheter is placed into the right hepatic vein. Catheter placement is verified with separately reportable venography. A Colapinto needle is advanced through the catheter into the wall of the right hepatic vein to access the right portal vein. A guidewire and catheter are advanced along this route into the portal vein and venography is performed again to verify placement. A self-expanding metallic stent is deployed through the catheter and dilated to the desired diameter where it bridges the portal and hepatic veins, using an angioplastic balloon. Postplacement venography and pressure measurements confirm adequate position and flow through the TIPS. The balloon, catheter, and other endoscopic tools are removed and pressure is applied to the insertion site, which may require suture. In 37183, the existing shunt is collapsed and removed through the catheter before a new one is inserted and dilated.

37184-37185
The physician treats an acute noncoronary arterial occlusion with a combination of thrombolytic drugs

and percutaneous mechanical thrombectomy. The devices used for mechanical thrombectomy include those that fragment the thrombus with or without removal of the clot, as well as those that come into contact with the wall of the vessel. For the procedure using the Trellis device, the artery is cannulated to gain access and 5,000 units of heparin are administered. Angiography is performed to confirm the occluded arteries. A hydrophilic wire is passed across the occlusion, followed by passing of the Trellis device over a stiff exchange length wire. The distal and proximal balloons are inflated in the artery on either side of a treatment zone containing infusion to isolate the treatment zone and to sustain the fluid concentration that is infused. One milligram of tissue plasminogen activator (TPA) is infused into the treatment zone. The Turbo Trellis is run at 4,000 rpm for five minutes. After the proximal balloon is deflated, small clots are removed via the integral aspiration port to prevent embolization. Fluoroscopic guidance services and injections administered during the course of the procedure are included in the service. Separately reportable procedures include other percutaneous interventions such as stent placement and diagnostic studies. Report 37184 for the first vessel and 37185 for the second and subsequent vessels in the same vascular family.

37186

The physician performs a secondary thrombectomy of a noncoronary arterial occlusion. Prior to or after a percutaneous intervention is performed, such as by balloon angioplasty or placement of a stent, the transcatheter removal of small sections of the thrombus or embolism is performed using suction, a snare basket, or a mechanical thrombectomy device under fluoroscopic guidance. Thrombolytic injections may also be used during the procedure.

37187-37188

The physician performs a percutaneous transluminal mechanical venous thrombectomy. A catheter sheath is inserted through a small incision in the vein, most commonly a groin incision in the femoral vein or an incision below the knee in the popliteal vein. Contrast is injected through the sheath and a separately reportable venography is performed to visualize the area of the vein being treated. Fluoroscopic guidance may be used. A guidewire is inserted through the sheath and advanced past the clot. A catheter is passed over the wire to the blocked area. A device at the tip of the catheter, a mechanical tool or a high-velocity liquid jet, is used to break the clot. A thrombolytic agent may be injected. When the procedure is completed, all instruments are removed and a compression bandage is applied. Report 37187 for the initial treatment. Report 37188 for repeat treatment on a subsequent day during the course of thrombolytic therapy.

37195

The physician remedies a stroke-causing blood clot obstructing blood flow to the brain. The physician infuses a thrombolytic ("clot-busting") drug through an intravenous catheter to help dissolve the clot and restore normal blood flow to the brain.

37200

A needle is inserted through the skin and into a blood vessel, and a guidewire is threaded through the needle into the vessel. The needle is removed. A catheter is threaded into the vessel, and the wire extracted. The catheter equipped with a biopsy instrument travels to the area to be sampled. The instrument extracts for biopsy tissue affixed to the vessel wall. Pressure is applied over the puncture site to stop bleeding after the catheter is removed. This procedure may also be performed through a skin incision with direct exposure of the access vessel.

37201-37202

A needle is inserted through the skin and into a blood vessel, and a guidewire is threaded through the needle into the vessel. The needle is removed. A catheter equipped with an infusion tip is threaded into the vessel, and the wire extracted. In 37201, the catheter travels to the point of a blood clot and drugs are infused until the clot is dissolved. In 37202, the catheter travels to the point of vasospasms and drugs are infused to reduce the spasms. Pressure is applied over the puncture site to stop the bleeding after the catheter is removed. This procedure may also be performed through a skin incision with direct exposure of the access vessel.

37203

A needle is inserted through the skin and into a blood vessel, and a guidewire is threaded through the needle into the vessel. The needle is removed. A catheter is threaded into the vessel, and the wire extracted. The catheter equipped with a grasping instrument travels to the site of the foreign body. The instrument grasps the foreign body, typically a fractured catheter, and retrieves it. Pressure is applied over the puncture site to stop bleeding after the catheter is removed. This procedure may also be performed through a skin incision with direct exposure of the access vessel.

37204

A needle is inserted through the skin and into a blood vessel, and a guidewire is threaded through the needle into the vessel. The needle is removed. A catheter is threaded into the vessel, and the wire extracted. The catheter travels to the point of the malformation and beads or another vessel-blocking device are released. The beads or other devise block the vessel. The catheter is removed and pressure is applied over the puncture site to stop bleeding.

37205-37206
The physician places an intravascular stent(s) percutaneously through a catheter into a blood vessel other than a coronary, carotid, or vertebral vessel. A guidewire is threaded through the needle into the blood vessel and the needle is removed. A catheter with a stent-transporting tip is threaded over the guidewire into the vessel, and the wire is extracted. The catheter travels to the point where the vessel needs additional support. The compressed stent(s) is passed from the catheter out into the vessel, where it deploys, expanding to support the vessel walls. The catheter is removed and pressure is applied over the puncture site. Code 37205 is used for a stent(s) placed in the initial vessel and 37206 is reported for each additional blood vessel traveled by the catheter where a stent(s) is placed.

37207-37208
The physician makes an incision in the skin overlying the vessel to be catheterized. The vessel is dissected, and nicked with a small blade. A catheter with a stent-transporting tip is threaded into the vessel. The catheter travels to the point where the vessel needs additional support, and the compressed stent(s) is passed from the catheter into the vessel, where it expands to support the vessel walls. The catheter is removed and the vessel may be repaired. The skin incision is repaired with a layered closure. This procedure may be done in one vessel (37207) or may be repeated in multiple vessels (37208). Use 37208 for each additional vessel.

37209
The physician exchanges a previously placed intravascular catheter during thrombolytic therapy. The physician sterilizes the exposed intravascular catheter and surrounding skin, generally with iodine solution. A guidewire is inserted through the catheter into the vessel and manipulated into position. The existing catheter is pulled out over the guidewire and a new catheter is placed over the wire into the final resting position. Contrast material is injected to verify positioning of both the guidewire and catheter placement before the new catheter is secured into position. The wire is removed, the catheter is secured with a new dressing applied, and thrombolytic therapy is resumed.

37210
In an endovascular procedure using angiographic guidance, the physician occludes branches of the uterine arteries to block the blood supply to uterine fibroid tumors. Through an incision in the left femoral artery, the physician advances a catheter containing granules of polyvinyl alcohol (PVA) to the branches of the contralateral (right) uterine artery adjacent to the fibroid tumors. PVA granules are released into these branches and they effectively block blood flow to the fibroid tumors. The catheter is retracted and the femoral incision treated with compression or sutured. This procedure is repeated from the right femoral artery advancing the catheter to the contralateral (left) uterine artery.

37215-37216
The physician places an intravascular stent percutaneously through a catheter into the cervical carotid artery. A needle is inserted through the skin into the access blood vessel, usually the brachial or femoral artery. A guidewire is threaded through the needle into the cervical carotid artery and the needle is removed. Long sheaths or guiding catheters are advanced into the stenosed cervical carotid artery. A filter protection device may be inserted distal to the stenosis to capture emboli. After filter opening, predilation of the stenosis with angioplasty balloons may be performed. A catheter with a stent-transporting tip is threaded over the guidewire into the vessel, and the wire is extracted. The catheter travels to the point where the vessel needs additional support. The compressed stent is passed from the catheter out into the vessel, where it deploys, expanding to support the vessel walls. The catheter is removed and pressure is applied over the puncture site. Report 37215 when stenting is performed with a filter protection device (distal embolic protection) and 37216 when stenting is performed without a filter protection device.

37250-37251
Intravascular ultrasound may be used during diagnostic evaluation of the noncoronary artery or vein It may also be used both before and after a therapeutic intervention upon a noncoronary artery or vein to assess patency and integrity of the vessel. A needle is inserted through the skin and into a blood vessel. A guide wire is threaded through the needle into a noncoronary blood vessel. The needle is removed. An intravascular ultrasound catheter is placed over the guide wire. The ultrasound catheter is used to obtain images from inside the vessel to assess area and extent of disease prior to interventional therapy as well as adequacy of therapy after interventional therapy. Code 37250 is reported for the initial vessel. In 37251, the physician advances the ultrasound catheter into additional vessels to assess patency and structure. The catheter and guide wire are removed, and pressure is applied over the puncture site to stop bleeding.

37500
Subfascial endoscopic perforator surgery (SEPS) is performed as a minimally invasive way to treat patients with chronic venous insufficiency (CVI) of the lower extremities. Incompetent calf perforator veins are ligated in this procedure. Perforator veins are an irregular group of veins growing as tributaries of the greater saphenous vein, which connect between it and other veins in the lower leg. They are considered incompetent when the direction of blood flow within the perforator vein changes upon applying distal

pressure. SEP is carried out under regional or general anesthesia. A rollover tourniquet technique is used to exsanguinate the leg and a single stab incision is made over the medial aspect of the calf through which the operating telescope is inserted. The subfascial plane is created with blunt dissection and maintained open by insufflating with carbon dioxide gas at low pressure. The perforators are identified and ligated, or transected, with a 5 mm ultrasonic scalpel. Patients may be given elastic stockings to wear for the next two weeks.

37565

Through an incision in the skin at side of neck in front of the sternocleidomastoid muscle, the physician isolates and dissects the internal jugular vein, separating it from critical structures. Using a vascular clip or ligature, the blood flow is reduced and the vein is ligated. Once the vein has been tied off, the skin incision is repaired with a layered closure.

37600

Through an incision in the skin at the side of neck in front of the sternocleidomastoid muscle, the physician isolates and dissects the external carotid artery, separating it from critical structures. Using a vascular clip or ligature, the blood flow is reduced and the artery is ligated. Once the artery has been tied off, the skin incision is repaired with a layered closure.

37605-37606

Through an incision in the skin at the side of neck, the physician isolates and dissects the internal or common carotid artery, separating it from critical structures. After vessel clamps have been affixed above and below the injured or affected artery, the physician sutures the artery to permanently stop the flow of blood through it (37605). The physician may apply a gradual occluding clamp (37606) to assess the effect of a ligation prior to complete occlusion (37605). Once the artery has been ligated or the occluding clamp has been placed, the vessel clamp is removed and the skin incision is repaired with a layered closure.

37607

The physician exposes the arteriovenous fistula by careful dissection. The physician isolates the fistula with ties or clamps. The physician may tie the arteriovenous fistula off completely (ligation) with suture, or the physician may partially obstruct (banding) the lumen of the fistula with a broader band in order to reduce flow. The physician closes the skin incision.

37609

Through an incision in the skin in front of the ear, the physician isolates and dissects the temporal artery, separating it from critical structures. Using a vascular clip or ligature, the artery is ligated or tissue samples are taken for biopsy. Once the artery has been tied off, the skin incision is repaired with a layered closure.

37615

Through an incision in the skin in the side of neck, usually in front of the sternocleidomastoid muscle, the physician isolates and dissects the ruptured or otherwise traumatized vessel, separating it from critical structures. Using a vascular clip or ligature, the vessel is ligated with sutures. Once the vessel has been tied off, the skin incision is repaired with a layered closure.

37616

The physician performs an incision of the chest wall (thoracotomy or median sternotomy) to best expose the involved artery. The physician identifies the injured artery and quickly clamps it to reduce blood loss. The physician ties off the artery completely (ligation), proximal and distal to the site of injury. The physician closes the chest, leaving chest tubes in place.

37617

The physician performs an abdominal incision to best expose the involved artery. The physician identifies the injured artery and quickly clamps it to reduce blood loss. The physician ties off the artery completely (ligation), proximal and distal to the site of injury. The physician closes the abdomen, leaving drains in place.

37618

Through an incision the skin of an extremity, usually over the damaged or traumatized vessel, the physician isolates and dissects the vessel, separating it from critical structures. Using a vascular clip or ligature, the vessel is ligated with sutures or vascular clips. Once the vessel has been tied off, the skin incision is repaired with a layered closure.

37620

The physician performs an upper midline abdominal incision and dissects to expose the inferior vena cava. The physician interrupts vena caval flow by tying the cava off with suture, folding it (plication), or clipping it. The physician closes the abdomen, leaving drains in place. The physician may place an intravascular umbrella device using a percutaneous (venous) approach. The physician places a needle in the femoral (or internal jugular) vein, advances a guidewire through the needle, removes the needle over the wire, and advances an introducer sheath over the wire into the femoral vein. The physician advances the umbrella device through the introducer sheath into the inferior vena cava under fluoroscopic guidance. The physician removes the introducer sheath and compresses the femoral vein manually until hemostasis is achieved.

37650

Through a small incision in the skin of the upper leg overlying the femoral vein, the physician isolates and dissects the femoral vein from other critical structures. After affixing vessel clamps, the physician ligates the vein or inserts a catheter into the femoral vein. A guidewire may be inserted prior to the catheter, then removed. Through the catheter, the physician places an occluding device (one that blocks blood flow) in the vein. The catheter is removed and the skin incision is repaired with a layered closure.

37660
The physician performs a lower midline abdominal incision and dissects to expose the common iliac vein. The physician interrupts common iliac venous flow by tying the common iliac vein off with suture. The physician closes the abdomen, leaving drains in place.

37700
Through multiple small incisions in the skin of the upper thigh and along the femoral vein or its branches lower in the thigh, the physician isolates and separates the saphenous vein at the point it joins the femoral vein or at several points farther down the leg. The physician affixes vessel clamps and ligates sections of the saphenous vein along the leg as necessary. Once the ligations are completed, each skin incision is repaired with a layered closure.

37718-37722
The physician makes a skin incision in the upper thigh or upper leg exposing the short saphenous vein (37718) or the long saphenous veins (37722). Additional skin incisions are made at the knee and the ankle and along the leg as necessary. A long wire is threaded through the length of the vein and brought out at the ankle. The vein is tied to the end of the wire and the wire is pulled out along with the vein. Once the vein has been removed, the skin incisions are repaired with layered closures. The leg is wrapped with an elastic pressure dressing postoperatively.

37735
The physician makes a skin incision in the upper thigh and the upper leg exposing the long and short saphenous veins. Additional skin incisions are made at the ankle and along the leg as necessary. A long wire is passed through the length of the vein and brought out at the ankle. Each vein is tied to the end of the wire and the vein is pulled out along with the wire. The physician uses a scalpel to remove the skin ulcer from the leg. The ulcer site is covered with a piece of skin that has been shaved from another part of the patient's body. Veins that connect superficial veins with deep veins may be tied off. The tough, fibrous envelope containing the muscle of the leg is split and removed at points where the superficial and deep veins connect. The skin incisions are repaired with layered closures. The leg is wrapped with an elastic pressure dressing postoperatively.

37760-37761
The physician performs a radical (Linton type) subfascial ligation (tying) of the perforator veins in 37760 and an open subfascial perforator vein ligation in 37761. Through incisions along the course of the saphenous vein, the veins connecting the deep and superficial veins of the leg are isolated. They are ligated, isolating the two systems along the course of the leg. The incisions may be sutured or covered with skin grafts taken from another part of the patient's body. Code 37760 includes skin grafts, when performed, and code 37761 includes the use of ultrasonic guidance, when performed. Both codes report a procedure involving one leg.

37765-37766
Stab phlebectomy for varicose veins is an ambulatory procedure that permits removal of nearly any incompetent vein below the saphenofemoral and saphenopopliteal junction. The varicose veins are identified with an indelible marking pen while the patient is standing. The patient is placed supine for further marking. Diluted lidocaine is injected into the tissues in large volumes until the perivenous tissues are engorged and distended with the anesthetic. Regional nerve blocks may be used for extensive areas. Tiny stab incisions are made with a scalpel or 18-gauge needle. The varicose vein is dissected with the phlebectomy hook. The vein is undermined along its course, all fibroadipose attachments to the vein are freed, and the vein is grasped with the hook and removed with mosquito forceps. Hemostasis is achieved by applying local compression to the veins already removed. The varicose vein is progressively extracted from one stab incision to the next. No skin closure is needed. Bandages are applied. Large pads are placed along the site of vein removal and covered with an inelastic bandage, followed by a second bandage of highly elastic material. Report 37765 when 10 to 20 stab incisions are made and 37766 when more than 20 are reported.

37780
The physician makes an incision in the skin overlying the short saphenous vein at its junction with the saphenopopliteal vein at the knee. The vessels are dissected and ties are placed around the short saphenous vein which is divided between the ties. Once the ties are in place and the vein has been divided, the skin incision is repaired with a layered closure.

37785
The physician ligates, divides, and/or excises varicose vein cluster(s) in one leg. The physician makes small incisions in the skin over localized areas of superficial varicose veins along the leg. These veins are isolated and dissected free of neighboring tissue, tied with sutures and divided, or stripped out bluntly. Pressure is applied over the site to stop bleeding. All incisions are repaired with a layered closure. The legs are wrapped in an elastic pressure dressing postoperatively.

37788-37790
Through an incision in the skin near the base of the penis, the physician isolates the penile artery and separates it from critical structures. In 37788, a neighboring artery in the groin or lower abdomen is

also isolated and dissected and a vessel clamp applied. The end of the neighboring artery is sewn into the penile artery in an end-to-side fashion, or a piece of harvested vein may be used to connect the two arteries to establish an adequate blood flow to the penis. The clamps are removed and incision is repaired with a layered closure. In 37790, through an inguinoscrotal incision, lateral to the root of the penis, and along the spermatic cord, the physician exposes the suspensory ligaments and detaches them from the pubic bone, The physician incises the superficial layer of Buck's fascia, exposing and suture-ligating each leaking vein. A segment of deep dorsal vein is dissected, ligated at both ends, and resected. The physician reattaches the suspensory ligaments and when the procedure is complete, closes the skin incision with a layered closure.

Hemic/Lymphatic

38100-38102

The physician makes a midline incision and dissects tissue around the spleen. The short stomach vessels are doubly ligated and cut. The splenic recess is dissected and the splenic artery and vein are divided and cut individually. The physician removes the spleen. A drain may be placed and the wound is irrigated. The incision is closed with sutures or staples and a dry dressing is applied. Report 38101 if performing a partial splenectomy; report 38102 if performing a total splenectomy in conjunction with another procedure.

38115

The physician makes an upper midline incision and dissects around the spleen until it is exposed. Lacerations are sutured. The damaged segment of the spleen is resected and removed and the edges are sutured. The wound is irrigated and the incision is closed using sutures or staples and a dry dressing.

38120

The physician performs a laparoscopic splenectomy. The patient is placed in a right lateral decubitus position, left arm over the head. With the patient under anesthesia, the physician makes a small incision in the abdominal wall and inserts a trocar just below or above the umbilicus. The physician insufflates the abdominal cavity and places the laparoscope through the umbilical incision. Additional small incisions are performed and trocars are placed into the peritoneal space to be used as ports for instruments, video camera (the camera allows the physician to operate both by viewing through the laparoscope and on a video monitor), and/or an additional light source. Dissection is carried down to the level of the spleen with care taken to identify tail of the pancreas. Electrocautery is used to divide ligaments and the spleen is mobilized. Short gastric vessels may be transected to gain additional exposure. The splenic vessels are transected and the spleen is excised using instruments to ensure hemostasis. The freed spleen is isolated and pouched. Pieces of the spleen are suctioned from the pouch through a trocar. The laparoscope and trocars are removed. The incisions are closed with sutures.

38200

The physician makes an incision in the left lower axilla. An 18 or 20 gauge sheath catheter is inserted into the middle of the soft sponge-like tissue of the spleen. The splenic vein is visualized and the catheter is placed. Around 2 cc to 3 cc of dye are injected per second totaling 15 cc to 20 cc of radiopaque dye. X-rays are taken every second for 12 seconds. The catheter is removed and the incision is covered with a dressing.

38204

This code is used to report the management involved in carrying out a donor search to locate a suitably matched donor for a transplant patient and to physically acquire the hematopoietic progenitor cells for the recipient's transplant.

38205-38206

Hematopoietic progenitor cells, or stem cells, harvested for transplantation are used to regenerate bone marrow and immune systems destroyed by chemotherapy and/or radiation therapy. These progenitor cells are not only acquired from bone marrow, but are also found in peripheral blood, collected by apheresis. For stem cell harvesting from peripheral blood by apheresis, the donor is often given a hematopoietic growth factor to mobilize progenitor cells into the blood stream. The patient is prepared much the same as giving a regular blood donation. Whole blood is drawn out of one arm and into an instrument called a cell separator. A column in the separator sorts out the desired cells from the other cells with the help of computerized calibration. The stem cells are collected while the remainder of the blood is returned to the donor through a tube and needle in the other arm. More than one collection session may be required to acquire the amount needed for transplanting. Blood-derived progenitor cells may also be harvested from placental and umbilical cord blood after delivery for transplantation to the neonate later in life or to others. Report 38205 when the cells are collected from a donor for transplantation to another person and 38206 when the cells are harvested from the patient. Report the appropriate code for each collection done.

38207

Progenitor cells (stem cells) harvested from umbilical cord and placental blood after delivery are cryopreserved and kept for transplantation to the neonate later in life or to other recipients. Peripheral blood progenitor cells can also be frozen with ease as well as marrow. The cells are preserved in a cryoprotectant solution generally containing dimethyl sulfoxide (DMSO), hydroxyethyl starch (HES), and a plasma protein such as human serum albumin. Salt solutions are used to dilute DMSO or adjust the cell concentration before freezing. The solution with the suspended cells is cooled at 1-3 degrees Celsius per minute and stored at -80 C or colder. The concentration of cells being frozen, the source and amount of plasma protein used, and the cooling technique used may vary. The cryopreserved cells are stored in bags or vials constructed of cryogenic-tolerant plastic and kept in most laboratories below -120 C in electrical freezers or nitrogen in the vapor or liquid phase. The ultra-low storage temperature is based on the possible progressive growth of ice crystals at warmer temperatures. Storage may be done at warmer temperatures up to -80 C for short-term storage for use within a few weeks or months of harvest, in conjunction with cryoprotectant solution.

38208
A previously frozen harvest of hematopoietic progenitor stem cells is thawed, without washing. A 37 C water bath filled with water is used to thaw the cells rapidly in order to melt the intracellular ice crystals quickly and stop the melting and refreezing of larger crystals. Because small ice crystals store more free surface energy than larger ice crystals, when they are released by thawing, they move to a lower energy state by fusing and forming larger ice crystals. To conquer this phenomenon, the volume and temperature of the thawing liquid must be adequate without allowing the cells to reach a temperature above 37 C where they will suffer heat damage. Cells are removed from the warm bath right when the last of the ice thaws and are infused or processed further immediately.

38209
Previously prepared hematopoietic progenitor cells (HPC) are thawed and washed to remove most of the dimethyl sulfoxide (DMSO) used in the cryoprotectant solution for initial freezing and to decrease the amount of cellular debris and hemoglobin in the infusate, which leads to clumping and trapping of the progenitor cells. A 37-degree Celsius water bath filled with water is used to thaw the cells rapidly in order to melt the intracellular ice crystals quickly and stop the melting and refreezing of larger crystals. Because small ice crystals store more free surface energy than larger ice crystals, when they are released by thawing, they move to a lower energy state by fusing and forming larger ice crystals. To conquer this phenomenon, the volume and temperature of the thawing liquid must be adequate without allowing the cells to reach a temperature above 37 C where they will suffer heat damage. The thawed solution is diluted slowly at room temperature with five to 10 volumes of a selected diluent, usually buffered saline with a macromolecular substance such as sorbitol or Dextran 40 added. This is especially true in thawing umbilical cord blood to retain all possible HPCs. Thawed cord blood is diluted with a buffer of Dextran 40 and albumin then centrifuged and resuspended in the same protein-containing medium. This dilution washing method improves post-thaw viability of the cells and helps to prevent osmotic shock by bringing the cells down from their hyperosmolar state in the postthaw solution.

38210
Specific cell depletion of a harvested preparation of hematopoietic progenitor cells (HPC) is sometimes needed to decrease the volume of the component or to remove certain cell populations for a particular transplant indication. T-cells within the HPC infusate are removed to help reduce the incidence and severity of chronic and acute graft vs. host disease in the recipient of cells from an allogeneic donor. More than one depletion technique may be employed, including physical and antibody-based methods such as elutriation, in which heavier constituents are made to settle out of a solution and separated from lighter elements; agglutination, in which antigen-bearing cells are made to clump together in a solution in the presence of specific antibodies (agglutinins); or complement-mediated killing. CD34+ cell enrichment technique have been recently developed in which T cells are nonspecifically separated along with other CD34- (antigen-negative) cells from the positive population. This is achieved by identifying the CD34 glycoprotein marker found on hematopoietic stem and progenitor cells and separating them from all the other negative cell population, which will include T-cells. The CD34+ cell enrichment technique can be successfully done after thawing, using the same techniques as prefreeze separation.

38211
Specific cell depletion of a harvested preparation of hematopoietic progenitor cells (HPC) is sometimes needed to decrease the volume of the component or to remove certain cell populations for a particular transplant indication. Tumor cells must be removed from autogenous harvests so the patient is not reinfused with more of his or her own cancer cells. For the removal of greater numbers of tumor cells from the harvest, combination purging techniques of cell enrichment and depletion may be employed. The recently developed CD34+ cell enrichment technique in which tumor cells are nonspecifically separated along with other CD34- (antigen-negative) cells from the positive population is employed first. The CD34 glycoprotein marker found on hematopoietic stem and progenitor cells is identified, separating them from all of the other negative cell population, which will include tumor cells. This is followed by a depletion technique for additional removal such as elutriation, in which heavier constituents are made to settle out of a solution and separated from lighter elements; centrifugation over gradients; or incubation with chemotherapeutic agents. Cell enrichment alone probably purges a number of cells about the same as a depletion technique alone, although reducing the number of tumor cells below assay detection.

38212-38213
Specific cell depletion of a harvested preparation of hematopoietic progenitor cells (HPC) is sometimes needed to decrease the volume of the component or to remove certain cell populations for a particular transplant indication. The removal of red blood cells is especially important for ABO-incompatible allogeneic donor transplantation and in cryopreserved harvests, particularly marrow. Mature blood cells do not survive the freezing process. Red cells become lysed stroma with free hemoglobin released into the solution when thawed. Damaged granulocytes and platelets also create cellular debris that further contribute to clumping in the infusate. Large quantities of mature blood cells requires freezing in large volumes which puts the patient at toxicity risk due to the corresponding large quantities of cryoprotectant used. Red cells in 38212 and platelets in 38213 are removed by centrifugation in blood transfer packs, cell washers, or apheresis devices. Peripheral blood-derived HPCs already collected by apheresis contain minimal amounts of blood cells and normally do not require this extra processing. Marrow collections, however, are processed before cryofreezing for removal of red blood cells, commonly with apheresis devices.

38214-38215
Excessive volume or cell content of harvested component can be a risk to the recipient and can complicate further processing techniques. Plasma removal is commonly done to deplete the volume of infusion given to a small patient and to reduce the isoagglutinins for allogeneic transplants for a red cell incompatible donor. Plasma volume depletion also reduces the amount of cryoprotectant used in freezing as well as the fat cell quantity in marrow harvests to alleviate respiratory difficulties. Plasma can be removed by centrifugation. Report 38214 if volume is reduced by depleting or removing the plasma. Report 38215 if the concentration of mononuclear cells or buffy coat layer of white blood cells (the leukocytes or granulocytes) within the blood plasma is reduced. This is also done with centrifugation, often by apheresis devices to enrich the mononuclear cell fraction, reducing granulocytes and reducing the storage volume with increased stem cell.

38220
Bone marrow samples are usually taken from the pelvic bone or sternum. The skin over the bone is first cleaned with an antiseptic solution. A local anesthetic is injected and the physician inserts a needle, known as a University of Illinois needle, beneath the skin and rotates it until the needle penetrates the cortex. At least half a teaspoon of marrow is sucked out of the bone by a syringe attached to the needle. If more marrow is needed, the needle is repositioned slightly, a new syringe is attached, and a second sample is taken. The samples are transferred from the syringes to slides and sent to a laboratory for analysis.

38221
Bone marrow samples are usually taken from the pelvic bone or sternum. The skin over the bone is first cleaned with an antiseptic solution. A local anesthetic is injected and the needle is inserted, rotated to the right, to the left, withdrawn, and reinserted at a different angle. This procedure is repeated until a small chip is separated from the bone marrow. The needle is again removed, and a piece of fine wire threaded through its tip transfers the specimen onto gauze. Samples contain bone marrow of which the structure has not been disturbed or destroyed. The bone must be decalcified overnight before it can be properly stained and examined.

38230
This procedure is for the removal of donor bone marrow. The physician places a large bore needle into the marrow cavity of the sternum, iliac crest, or ribs. The bone marrow is aspirated with a large syringe and placed in a container. The puncture wound is covered with a dressing.

38240-38242
This procedure is for the implantation of donor bone marrow or blood-derived peripheral stem cells. The recipient's immune system is first suppressed using radiation or chemotherapy. The harvested bone marrow or peripheral blood stem cells are injected into the recipient by intravenous drip therapy in a sterile environment. Report 38240 if the transplanted cells came from a donor other than the patient and 38241 if the transplant material is autologous and came from the patient. Leukemia patients who show molecular or clinical evidence of relapse after transplantation are infused with additional lymphocytes collected from their donor to help boost the graft vs. leukemia effect. Report 38242 if the patient receives an infusion of lymphocytes.

38300-38305
The physician performs this procedure to drain inflamed lymph nodes. The physician makes an incision over the affected lymph node and the abscess or infection is drained. The wound is irrigated and closed with sutures or Steri-strips. Report 38305 if the procedure is extensive.

38308
This procedure is performed to correct lymphangiomas, which are primarily found in the neck. The physician makes an incision over the site of the tumor. The tissue, muscles, nerves, and blood vessels are dissected away from the tumor. The tumor is removed. The incision is closed with sutures, wound drains are placed, and a dressing is applied.

38380-38382
The thoracic duct is sutured or ligated to correct chylothorax, the presence of lymphatic fluid within the pleural or lung space caused by a tear or injury to the

thoracic duct. The thoracic duct is a tubular structure, approximately 2-3 mm in diameter that originates in the cisterna chyli, which lies above of the second lumbar vertebral body. It ascends on the right, anterior to the vertebral bodies, entering the chest through the aortic hiatus. At the fourth or fifth thoracic vertebra, it crosses to the left and empties into the left jugulosubclavian venous junction. Tears or injury can occur in any segment (cervical, thoracic, abdominal) and the approach is dependent on the site of leak. An incision is made in the left neck, right or left chest, or abdomen. The involved compartment is drained of all effluent and the leak identified. The duct is ligated a few centimeters below the leak and also a few centimeters above it. Dry gauze is placed at the site of the leak to ensure that the ligation has completely sealed the leak. When it has been determined that the leak is completely sealed the gauze is removed and glue or other sealant is applied to the area. If the leak is repaired by thoracotomy, chest tubes are placed. Incisions are closed. Report 38380 for cervical; 38381 for thoracic; or 38382 for abdominal approach.

38500-38530
The physician performs a biopsy on or removes one or more superficial lymph nodes. The physician makes a small incision through the skin overlying the lymph node. The tissue is dissected to the node. A small piece of the node and surrounding tissue is removed, or the node may be removed. The incision is repaired with a layered closure. Report 38505 if a needle is used; report 38510 if deep cervical nodes are biopsied; report 38520 if deep cervical nodes with excision scalene fat pads are checked; report 38525 if deep axillary nodes are biopsied; and report 38530 if internal mammary nodes are biopsied.

38542
The physician makes an incision over one of three jugular groups and retracts tissue. The nodes are isolated and excised. The incision is closed by sutures.

38550-38555
The physician removes a cystic hygroma, also called a lymphangioma, from the neck or axilla. A cystic hygroma is a congenital anomaly typically found in the neck or axilla, sometimes extending into the head or chest. Cystic hygromas may be diagnosed during fetal ultrasound or evident at birth. The majority are evident by age 2. Rarely, they are diagnosed into adulthood. Because cystic hygromas can be very large and can extend into multiple areas of the head, neck, and chest, the location and size of the incision will vary. A surgical incision is made in the area of the cyst. If the hygroma does not involve deeper neurovascular structures, the physician dissects away the surrounding tissue and exposes the sac. The sac is excised. The incision is closed and a dry, sterile dressing applied. A larger cystic hygroma may not have a defined capsule and may wrap around blood vessels, nerves, and muscles. In that case, the surgeon dissects the tissue around these vital structures before removing the cystic hygroma. Cystic hygromas may be removed in part or in full depending on whether excision would compromise nerves or blood vessels. If the entire cystic hygroma cannot be excised, the surgeon may cauterize the part remaining. Report 38550 for excision of a cystic hygroma without deep neurovascular dissection; report 38555 when deep neurovascular dissection is required.

38562-38564
The physician makes a midline abdominal incision just below the navel. The surrounding tissue, nerves, and blood vessels are dissected away, and the pelvic and/or para-aortic lymph nodes are visualized. The nodes are removed. The wound is closed with sutures or staples. Report 38564 if retroperitoneal lymphadenectomy is performed.

38570
The physician performs laparoscopic retroperitoneal lymph node biopsies. The physician places a trocar at the umbilicus into the abdominal or retroperitoneal space and insufflates the peritoneal or retroperitoneal space. The laparoscope is placed through the umbilical trocar and additional trocars are placed into the peritoneal or retroperitoneal space. The lymph nodes are identified, dissected free of surrounding structures and sampled for further separately reported analysis. The trocars are removed and the incisions are closed.

38571
The surgeon performs laparoscopic bilateral pelvic lymphadenectomy. The surgeon places a trocar at the umbilicus into the abdominal or retroperitoneal space and insufflates the peritoneal or retroperitoneal space. The laparoscope is placed through the umbilical trocar and additional trocars are placed into the abdominal or retroperitoneal space. The iliac vessels are identified and the lymph nodes are dissected from the surrounding structures and removed. The trocars are removed and the incisions are closed.

38572
The physician performs laparoscopic bilateral pelvic lymphadenectomy and peri-aortic lymph node sampling. The physician places a trocar at the umbilicus and insufflates the abdominal or retroperitoneal cavity. The laparoscope is placed through the umbilical port and additional trocars are placed into the peritoneal or retroperitoneal space. The iliac vessels are identified and the lymph nodes are dissected from the vessels and surrounded structures and removed. Dissection is continued onto the aorta and peri-aortic nodes are sampled. The trocars are removed and the incisions are closed.

38700
The physician makes a curved incision beginning below the ear curving down to the top of the hyoid bone and continuing toward the chin. The tissues are

dissected and the targeted structures are exposed. The submental and submandibular lymph nodes are removed along with the submandibular gland and surrounding tissues. The incision is sutured with drain if necessary.

38720
The physician makes a large curved incision starting at the ear, going down the neck, and continuing to the chin. Incision may also be made starting at the original incision and continuing down the neck. The skin flaps are folded back and held in place with retractors. The tissue, lymph tissue, blood vessels, nerves, and muscles targeted for removal are dissected away and removed. The incision is closed with sutures.

38724
This lymph-removal procedure is performed to preserve the spinal accessory nerve, jugular vein, and the sternocleidomastoid muscles. The physician makes a large curved incision starting at the ear, going down the neck, and continuing to the chin. Other incisions may be made down the neck from the original incision. Skin and tissue are retracted and the physician removes the lymph nodes The incision is closed with sutures, including wound drains connected to suction. A tracheotomy may be performed.

38740-38745
The physician makes a diagonal incision across the lower axilla, exposing the axillary vein. The fatty tissue, lymph nodes, and vessels beneath the vein are dissected free. A drain is placed and connected to suction. The tissue and skin is closed with sutures. Report 38745 if a complete procedure is performed.

38746
The physician makes a large vertical chest incision over the sternum. The tissues are dissected away the sternum is exposed. The chest cavity is entered through the sternum, which is split and retracted. Lymph nodes near the lungs, around the heart, and behind the trachea are removed. The area is irrigated, the retractors are removed, and the incision is closed with sutures or staples.

38747
The physician makes a midline abdominal incision. The abdominal contents are exposed, allowing the physician to locate the lymph nodes. Each lymph node grouping, with or without para-aortic and vena caval nodes, is dissected away from the surrounding tissue, nerves, and blood vessels, and removed. The incision is closed with sutures or staples.

38760-38765
The physician makes an incision across the groin area. The surrounding tissue, nerves, and blood vessels are dissected away, and the inguinal and femoral lymph nodes are visualized. The nodes are removed by group. The wound is closed with sutures or staples. Report 38765 if performing pelvic lymphadenectomy concurrently.

38770
The physician makes a low abdominal vertical incision. The surrounding tissue, nerves, and blood vessels are dissected away, and the pelvic lymph nodes are visualized. The nodes are removed by group. The wound is closed with sutures or staples.

38780
The physician makes a large midline abdominal incision. The surrounding tissue, nerves, and blood vessels are dissected away, and the lymph nodes are visualized. The nodes are removed by group. Some surrounding tissues may also be removed. The wound is closed with sutures or staples.

38790
Vital blue dye is injected into the subcutaneous tissues for outlining of skin lymphatics. As soon as the lymphatic vessels are visualized by their blue color, the radiologist makes a small longitudinal incision over the area. Exposure of the lymph vessel is accomplished, the vessel is made taut, and it is cannulated with a 27 or 30 gauge needle with a fine catheter attached. A small amount of dye is injected to ensure correct placement, and the needle is advanced 2 to 3 mm into the vessel. The needle and catheter are secured. Dye is injected with a 10 cc syringe. X-rays are made and repeated 24 hours later. The physician removes the needle and closes the incision with sutures.

38792
The physician injects dye or contrast material into the patient to identify the sentinel lymph node. As soon as the node is visualized, the radiologist makes a small longitudinal incision over the area. The node is exposed and cannulated with a 27- or 30-gauge needle attached to a fine catheter. A small amount of dye is injected to ensure correct placement, and the needle is advanced 2 to 3 mm into the node. The needle and catheter are secured. Dye is injected with a 10 cc syringe. X-rays are taken and repeated 24 hours later. The physician removes the needle and closes the incision by suture.

38794
Exposure of the lymph vessel is accomplished, the vessel is made taut, and it is cannulated with a 27 or 30 gauge needle with a find catheter attached. The needle and catheter are secured. Medication is injected. The physician removes the needle and closes the incision with sutures.

Mediastinum and Diaphragm

39000-39010
The physician makes an incision low in the front of the neck, pulling back the sternomastoid muscles and the cranial vessels to the side and drawing the trachea and thyroid to the center. The space behind the esophagus is exposed. The foreign body is removed, biopsy of any abnormal mass performed, and Penrose drains are placed. The incision is closed with sutures or staples. Report 39010 if using a transthoracic approach.

39200
The physician makes an incision from in front of the axilla just below the nipple line. The incision extends below the tip of the shoulder blade and ascends to halfway between the spinal column and the shoulder blade. The physician exposes the rib cage, retracting muscles. A rib spreader is used to ease access to the thoracic cavity. The cyst is located and removed. The rib spreader is removed, and the wound is closed with sutures or staples.

39220
The physician makes an incision from in front of the axilla just below the nipple line. The incision extends below the tip of the shoulder blade and ascends to halfway between the spinal column and the shoulder blade. The physician exposes the rib cage by cutting through the muscles. The chest cavity is entered between the ribs by using a rib spreader. The tumor is located and dissected from the surrounding tissue. The wound is closed using sutures or staples.

39400
The physician makes a small incision in the notch above the sternum. The mediastinoscope is inserted and the explorations are carried out between the trachea and the major vessels. The mediastinal lymph nodes, thymus, and thyroid are visualized, and biopsy is performed through the mediastinoscope. The scope is removed, and the incision is closed with sutures or Steri-strips.

39501
The physician makes an abdominal or chest incision and exposes a tear in the diaphragm. The tear is repaired with nonabsorbable sutures. Occasionally the tear may be so extensive that an artificial patch is used to repair defects or reinforce sutures. The incision is closed with sutures or staples, and a dressing is applied.

39502
The physician makes an incision across the abdomen. The herniated stomach is returned to its appropriate position in the abdomen, and the hernia sac is cut away and removed. The enlarged opening in the diaphragm through which the esophagus passes is narrowed by placing sutures in the two pillars connecting the spinal column and diaphragm. Reforming the stomach, cutting the vagus nerve or altering the size of the stomach-intestinal opening may be performed as well. Drains are placed, and the wound is sutured closed.

39503
The physician makes an incision across the abdomen. The herniated stomach is returned to its appropriate position in the abdomen, and the hernia sac is cut away and removed. The enlarged opening in the diaphragm through which the esophagus passes is narrowed by placing sutures in the two pillars connecting the spinal column and diaphragm. Reforming the stomach, cutting the vagus nerve or altering the size of the stomach-intestinal opening may be performed as well. Drains are placed, and the wound is sutured closed.

39520-39531
The physician makes an incision across the chest. Tissues are dissected and the esophagus, diaphragm, and upper part of the stomach are exposed. The physician creates a segment of intra-abdominal esophagus held in place by a support of folds or tucks in the stomach surrounds about 280 degrees of the distal esophagus. The incision is closed with sutures or staples. Report 39530 if thoracoabdominal; report 39531 if thoracoabdominal with dilation of stricture.

39540-39541
This procedure is performed to repair a massive injury in the diaphragm allowing organs to protrude into the chest cavity. The physician makes an incision the chest or abdomen. The abdominal contents are drawn back into the abdomen, and the hole in the diaphragm is exposed. The opening is closed with sutures or by insertion of a patch. The tear is repaired with nonabsorbable sutures. The incision is closed with sutures or staples. Report 39541 if the hernia is chronic.

39545
The physician makes an incision across the chest or abdomen. The abdominal contents are drawn back into the abdomen, and the diaphragm is exposed. The connective tissue is used to stitch folds or tucks into the diaphragm to restore it to its original position. The incision is closed with sutures or staples.

39560
The surgeon removes all or part of the diaphragm, the large muscle separating the chest and abdominal cavities. The patient is taken to the operating room, the abdomen and/or chest are surgically opened, and the operation is preformed. This code involves a simple repair using sutures.

39561
The surgeon removes all or part of the diaphragm, the large muscle separating the chest and abdominal cavities. The patient is taken to the operating room, the abdomen and/or chest are surgically opened, and the operation is performed. This code involves a complex

repair using muscle or synthetic material for patching some of the area.

Digestive

40490
The physician performs a biopsy of a lesion on the lip. An incision is made in the lip and a portion of the lesion together with some normal tissue is removed. The surgical wound is closed directly.

40500
The physician removes the diseased vermilion border of the lip. The mucosa from the skin to the labial mucosa is separated from the underlying muscle and removed. The remaining labial mucosa is advanced and sutured to the skin, covering the exposed muscle and forming a new vermilion.

40510
The physician removes a portion of the lip using a transverse wedge technique. Incisions are made perpendicularly through the skin and mucosa and a wedge of the lip with surrounding tissue is removed. The physician extends the incisions below the surgical wound and advances the tissue flaps. The incisions are sutured primarily.

40520
The physician removes a portion of the lip using a "V" incision technique. A "V" cut is made around the portion of lip to be removed and the lip and surrounding tissue are removed. The surgical wound is closed primarily.

40525
The physician removes a full thickness portion of the lip with local flap reconstruction. A "V" incision may be made around the lesion and through the full thickness of the lip. The lesion and surrounding tissues are removed. A local skin flap is incised and advanced to the site of the surgical wound and sutured into place with layered closure.

40527
The physician removes a full thickness portion of the lip with a cross lip flap reconstruction. A "V" incision may be made around the lesion and through the full thickness of the lip. The lesion and surrounding tissues are removed. A skin flap from the upper lip is incised and cross advanced to the surgical site of the lower lip. The flap is sutured with layered closure.

40530
The physician performs a lip resection of more than one fourth without reconstruction. An incision may be made through the midline of the lip and extended over the portion of the lip to be removed. The tumor and surrounding tissues are removed. The oral cavity is closed primarily, and the lip and surrounding structures are closed with layered sutures.

40650
The physician repairs a full thickness laceration of the lip. The tissues of the vermilion are closed with layered sutures.

40652-40654
The physician repairs a laceration extending through the full thickness of the lip. In 40652, a laceration or surgically created wound of up to one-half the vertical height of the lip is closed with layered sutures and in 40654, a wound of more than one-half the vertical height of the lip is repaired.

40700
The physician surgically corrects a partial or complete unilateral developmental cleft lip/nasal deformity. A cleft lip may range in appearance as a "notch" in the upper lip to a complete separation running into the nose. The cleft margins are incised on either side from the mouth toward the nostril and through the full-thickness layers of mucosa, muscle, and skin. The vermilion border of the cleft lip is turned downward to restore the normal shape of the lip and the muscle and skin are brought together to close the cleft separation and preserve muscle function. The nasal deformity often caused by the cleft lip may be repaired. The physician closes the prepared margins in layers from the intraoral mucosa through the muscle with final closure of the skin.

40701
The physician surgically corrects a bilateral developmental cleft lip/nasal deformity in one operation. A cleft lip may range in appearance as a "notch" in the upper lip to a complete separation running into the nose. The cleft margins are incised on either side from the mouth toward the nostril and through the full-thickness layers of mucosa, muscle, and skin on both sides of the face. The vermilion border of the cleft lip is turned downward to restore the normal shape of the lip and the muscle and skin are brought together to close the cleft separations on each side and preserve muscle function. The nasal deformity often caused by the cleft lip may be repaired. The physician closes the prepared margins in layers from the intraoral mucosa through the muscle with final closure of the skin.

40702
The physician performs one stage of two surgeries to correct a bilateral cleft lip/nasal deformity. This may be necessary because of the severity or the vascular compromise of the deformity. Typically, the cleft lip is repaired first and nasal deformities are repaired in a second surgical session. A cleft lip may range in appearance as a "notch" in the upper lip to a complete separation running into the nose. The cleft margins are incised on either side from the mouth toward the nostril and through the full-thickness layers of mucosa, muscle, and skin on both sides of the face. The vermilion border of the cleft lip is turned downward to

restore the normal shape of the lip and the muscle and skin are brought together to close the cleft separations on each side and preserve muscle function. The prepared margins are closed in layers from the intraoral mucosa through the muscle with final closure of the skin. The second surgery is performed after adequate healing of the first surgical site.

40720
The physician performs a secondary cleft lip/nasal deformity repair after unfavorable results from a first surgical correction. This failure may be due to scar contracture (permanent shortening), wound dehiscence (splitting), or infection. The cleft margins are recreated to define clean edges for the defect through full-thickness layers of mucosa, muscle, and skin. The prepared margins are again closed in layers from the intraoral mucosa through muscle with final closure of the skin.

40761
The physician performs a complicated cleft lip/nasal deformity repair using pedicle flaps from the lower lip. This is necessary because of inadequate quantity or quality of upper lip soft tissue. A cleft lip may range in appearance as a "notch" in the upper lip to a complete separation running into the nose. The cleft margins are incised on either side from the mouth toward the nostril and through the full-thickness layers of mucosa, muscle, and skin. The vermilion border of the cleft lip is turned downward to restore the normal shape of the lip and the muscle and skin are brought together to close the cleft separation and preserve muscle function. A pedicle flap is designed from the lower lip based on blood supply. The flap is created with a full-thickness incision and rotated on its pedicle to the desired location. The flap is sutured in layers to the recipient tissue location. The prepared cleft margins are closed in layers from the intraoral mucosa through muscle with final closure of the skin.

40800-40801
The physician drains an abscess, a cyst, or a hematoma within the vestibule of the mouth. The vestibule consists of the mucosal and submucosal tissue of the lips and cheeks within the oral cavity, not including the dentoalveolar structures. The physician makes an incision in the tissue overlying the abscess, cyst, or hematoma. Tissues are dissected and the fluid is drained. Complicated drainage for larger lesions or drainage requiring multiple incisions is done in 40801. The physician may place a drain to facilitate healing. If a drain is placed, it is later removed.

40804-40805
The physician removes a foreign body embedded in the vestibule of the mouth. The vestibule consists of the mucosal and submucosal tissue of the lips and cheeks within the oral cavity, not including the dentoalveolar structures. The physician may simply grasp the object with an instrument and remove it or incisions may be made to free the object and remove it. Complicated removal of a large foreign body or one that is difficult to access is done in 40805. Closure of the wound may be needed.

40806
The physician performs a frenotomy by incising the labial frenum. The labial frenum is a connecting fold of mucous membrane that joins the lip to the gums at the inside midcenter. This procedure is often performed to release tension on the frenum and surrounding tissues. The frenum is simply incised and not removed.

40808
The physician performs a biopsy on a lesion in the vestibule of the mouth. The vestibule consists of the mucosal and submucosal tissue of the lips and cheeks within the oral cavity, not including the dentoalveolar structures. The physician makes an incision in the area of the vestibule to be biopsied and removes a portion of the lesion and some surrounding tissue. The incision is closed simply.

40810-40812
The physician removes a lesion in the vestibule of the mouth. The vestibule consists of the mucosal and submucosal tissue of the lips and cheeks within the oral cavity, not including the dentoalveolar structures. The physician makes an incision around the lesion and through submucosal tissue, removing the lesion. No repair of the wound is done in 40810. Simple repair of the wound is done in 40812, such as a sutured closure.

40814
The physician removes a lesion in the vestibule of the mouth with complex repair. The vestibule consists of the mucosal and submucosal tissue of the lips and cheeks within the oral cavity, not including the dentoalveolar structures. An incision is made around the lesion and through submucosal tissue, removing the lesion. Complex repair of the surgical wound left after excision of the lesion is required. This may include advancement of tissue flaps, rearrangement of tissue, or complex suturing techniques.

40816
The physician removes a lesion in the vestibule of the mouth. The vestibule consists of the mucosal and submucosal tissue of the lips and cheeks within the oral cavity, not including the dentoalveolar structures. An incision is made around the lesion and through the submucosal tissue, removing the lesion, along with the excision of underlying muscle as well. Complex repair of the surgical wound is required after excision of the lesion. This may include advancement of tissue flaps, rearrangement of tissue, or complex suturing techniques.

40818
The physician harvests mucosa from the vestibule to be used as a graft elsewhere in the mouth. The vestibule consists of the mucosal and submucosal tissue of the

lips and cheeks within the oral cavity, not including the dentoalveolar structures. A retractor is used to hold the mucosa to be grafted. The physician uses a scalpel to make an incision through the mucosa, usually in an elliptical shape. The physician grasps the mucosa with an instrument and the scalpel is used to cut just beneath the mucosa, freeing it from the underlying tissues. Any remaining fat or muscle attached to the mucosa is removed and the donor tissue is ready for grafting to another part of the mouth. The surgical wound is closed directly.

40819
The physician removes the labial or buccal frenum. The buccal frenum is a band of mucosal membrane that connects the alveolar (dental) ridge to the cheek and separates the lip vestibule from the cheek vestibule. The labial frenum is a connecting fold of mucous membrane that joins the lip to the gums at the inside midcenter. Incisions are made around the frenum and through the mucosa and submucosa. The underlying muscle is removed as well. The excision may extend to the interincisal papilla. The mucosa is closed simply, or the physician may rearrange the tissue as in a Z-plasty technique.

40820
The physician destroys a lesion or a scar in the vestibule of the mouth without excising it. Destruction may be accomplished by using a laser or electrocautery to burn the lesion, cryotherapy to freeze the lesion, or chemicals to destroy the lesion.

40830-40831
The physician sutures a laceration of the vestibule of the mouth measuring 2.5 cm or less in length. The physician performs a simple closure without submucosal sutures or tissue rearrangement in 40830. Extensive tissue damage or crushing, requiring complex closure, such as retention sutures, or the closure of a laceration more than 2.5 cm is done in 40831.

40840-40844
The surgeon performs a vestibuloplasty and deepens the vestibule of the mouth by any series of surgical procedures for the purpose of increasing the height of the alveolar ridge, allowing a complete denture to be worn. The vestibule refers to the mucosal and submucosal tissue of the inner lips and cheeks, the part of the oral cavity outside of the dentoalveolar structures. This procedure may be performed in several ways. The surgeon may rearrange the patient's own tissue or the submucosal tissue may be dissected and freed from the bone. The mucosa is moved deeper into the vestibule. Soft tissues may also be grafted into the mouth. An anterior procedure is performed in 40840; a one-sided procedure is done on the posterior portion of the mouth in 40842; and a posterior procedure is done on both sides of the mouth in 40843. Report 40844 when this procedure is done over the arch of the mouth.

40845
The surgeon performs a vestibuloplasty and deepens the vestibule of the mouth by any series of surgical procedures for the purpose of increasing the height of the alveolar ridge, allowing a complete denture to be worn. The vestibule refers to the mucosal and submucosal tissue of the inner lips and cheeks, the part of the oral cavity outside of the dentoalveolar structures. This procedure is performed for complex cases, such as those in which the physician must lower muscle attachments to provide enough space for deepening the vestibule. Soft tissue grafting from other areas of the body into the mouth is often required. Hypertrophied and hyperplastic tissue may need to be trimmed and soft tissue revised by dissecting it from the alveolar ridge and rearranging its attachment.

41000-41009
The physician makes a small intraoral incision through the mucosa of the tongue or floor of the mouth overlying an abscess, cyst, or hematoma and drains the fluid. The incision and drainage site of the cyst, hematoma, or abscess is on the tongue (lingual) in 41000. In 41005, the lesion is located superficially under the tongue (sublingual) and in 41006, the sublingual lesion is deep to the supramylohyoid muscle. The physician dissects through the anterior floor of the mouth into the supramylohyoid muscle to drain an abscess in the submental space in 41007. In 41008, the physician incises through the mucosa of the floor of the mouth to the supramylohyoid muscle and carries the dissection deeper into the tissue to reach the submandibular space. In 41009, the physician dissects down through the mucosa in the posterior floor of the mouth and into the masticator space, containing the ramus, the posterior part of the mandible, and the masticator muscles to drain the abscess.

41010
The physician makes an incision in the lingual frenum, freeing the tongue and allowing greater range of motion. The lingual frenum is the connecting fold or membrane under the tongue that attaches it to the floor of the mouth. Sutures may be placed. The frenum is simply incised and not removed.

41015-41018
The physician drains an abscess, a cyst, or a hematoma from the floor of the mouth by making an extraoral incision in the skin below the inferior border of the mandible and dissecting through the tissue to reach the affected space. In 41015, the physician dissects through the supramylohyoid muscle and submental space into the sublingual space below the tongue to drain the abscess. In 41016, dissection is taken to the supramylohyoid muscle to drain an abscess in the submental space. In 41017, the physician makes an incision under the angle of the mandible, or between

Digestive

the angle and the chin, and below the inferior border of the mandible. Dissection is limited to the submandibular space. In 41018, an incision is made just below the angle of the ramus of the mandible, the posterior part of the mandible, and into the masticator space containing the masticator muscles to drain the abscess, cyst, or hematoma. A drain may be placed to facilitate healing, which is later removed.

41019
The physician places needles, catheters, or other devices into the head and/or neck region for subsequent interstitial radioelement application. The route of insertion may be under the skin (percutaneous), through the mouth (transoral), or through the nose (transnasal). The radioactive isotopes that are introduced subsequently, such as iridium-192, are contained within tiny seeds that are left in place to deliver radiation over a period of time. They do not cause any harm after becoming inert. This method provides radiation to the prescribed body area while minimizing exposure to normal tissue.

41100-41105
The physician performs an excisional biopsy on a lesion in the anterior two-thirds of the tongue in 41100 or the posterior one-third of the tongue in 41105. The physician makes an incision around the lesion, usually in an elliptical shape, which typically includes the diseased tissue and part normal tissue. Incisions are carried beneath the tissue sample and the specimen is removed. The surgical wound is usually sutured simply.

41108
The physician performs an excisional biopsy on a lesion of the floor of the mouth. An incision is made around the lesion, usually in an elliptical shape, which typically includes the diseased tissue and part normal tissue. Incisions are carried beneath the tissue sample and the specimen is removed. The surgical wound is usually sutured simply.

41110
The physician removes a lesion in any area of the tongue. Incisions are made in an elliptical shape completely around and under the lesion. The lesion is excised. Due to the small size of the lesion, no suturing or closure of the surgical wound is necessary.

41112-41113
The physician removes a lesion in the anterior two-thirds of the tongue in 41112 or the posterior one-third in 41113. Incisions are made in the tissue completely around and under the lesion, typically in an elliptical shape, and the lesion is excised. The surgical wound is sutured closed.

41114
The physician removes a lesion in any area of the tongue with a local flap for closure. Incisions are made in the tissue completely around and under the lesion, usually in an elliptical shape, and the lesion is excised. A flap of mucosa from another part of the tongue is incised, moved, and sutured to repair the surgical wound. The donor site is closed with sutures.

41115
The physician removes a tight or short lingual frenum to free the tongue and allow greater range of motion. The lingual frenum is the connecting fold or membrane under the tongue that attaches it to the floor of the mouth. The physician makes incisions in the frenum both near the tongue and near the mandible, which ultimately connect as they move posteriorly. The frenum is excised. The surgical wound may be sutured.

41116
The physician excises a lesion from the floor of the mouth. The physician makes incisions in the tissue completely around and under the lesion, usually in an elliptical shape, and the lesion is excised with some surrounding normal tissue as well. The surgical wound is typically sutured simply.

41120-41130
The physician removes less than one half of the tongue in 41120 or one half of the diseased, often malignant, tongue in 41130. The physician makes incisions around the portion of the tongue to be removed and extends the incisions through the thickness of the tongue. Scalpels, scissors, electrocautery, or lasers may be used. The diseased portion is removed. After obtaining good hemostasis (controlled bleeding), the tongue is sutured closed to repair the surgical wound. Tissue grafting to close the wound is rarely needed.

41135
The physician removes a part of the diseased, and often malignant, tongue and performs a unilateral radical neck dissection. The physician makes incisions in the tissue around the portion of the tongue to be removed and extends the incisions through the thickness of the tongue. Scalpels, scissors, electrocautery, or lasers may be used. The diseased portion is removed. After obtaining good hemostasis (controlled bleeding), the tongue is sutured to repair the surgical wound. Tissue grafting to close the wound is rarely needed. Radical neck dissection is also done to remove lymph nodes, muscles, blood vessels, and other tissue from one side of the neck.

41140-41145
The physician removes the entire tongue, with or without a tracheostomy. The physician makes incisions through the thickness of the tongue. Scalpels, scissors, electrocautery, or lasers may be used. The tongue is removed. A tracheostomy may be performed. An incision is made in the front of the neck below the larynx. The physician dissects the tissues down to the trachea. An incision is made through the tracheal wall and an artificial airway is inserted, which extends out of the neck. The patient breathes through this airway.

No radical neck dissection is performed in 41140. Report 41145 if a unilateral radical neck dissection is also performed to remove lymph nodes, muscles, blood vessels, and other tissues from one side of the neck.

41150-41155
The physician removes part or all of the diseased or cancerous tongue and resects the mandible and the tissue of the floor of the mouth. The physician uses incisions both extraorally in the skin and intraorally through the mucosa. The physician removes the tongue by making incisions through the thickness of the tongue. Scalpels, scissors, electrocautery, or lasers may be used. The affected tissue of the mouth floor is removed with a scalpel and the diseased portion of the mandible is also accessed and resected. After removal of the diseased section, continuity of the mandible is reestablished. This is done with metal plates initially and bone grafting at a later time, or with immediate bone grafting. Skin or mucosal grafting may also be needed. The skin and mucosal incisions are repaired with layered sutures. No neck dissection is performed in 41150. Report 41155 if in addition, a radical neck dissection is performed and lymph nodes, muscles, blood vessels, and other tissue are removed from one side of the neck. Report 41153 if a glossectomy with resection of the floor of the mouth is done and lymph nodes and other soft tissue are removed from between the floor of the mouth and the hyoid bone for a suprahyoid neck dissection, without mandible resection.

41250-41251
The physician sutures a laceration measuring 2.5 cm or less of the mouth floor and/or anterior two-thirds of the tongue in 41250 or a laceration in the posterior one-third of the tongue in 41251. This is done simply without tissue rearrangement.

41252
The physician sutures a laceration of the mouth floor or portion of the tongue measuring 2.6 cm or more or requiring complex closure techniques. These may include tissue rearrangement, extensive submucosal suturing, debridement of grossly contaminated lacerations, or repair of through-and-through lacerations.

41500
The physician applies K-wire (Kirschner wire) for temporary fixation of the tongue. The K-wire is threaded through one side of the mandible, through the tongue, and through the opposite side of the mandible.

41510
The physician makes an incision in the commissure (corner) of the mouth. The tongue is sutured to the lip in the area previously incised to enlarge the mouth. The tongue is later sectioned from the mouth in a second surgical session.

41512
Moderate to severe obstructive sleep apnea (OSA) is often associated with collapse of the pharyngeal airway on multiple levels, including tongue base obstruction. The physician treats OSA with a tongue base suspension suture. A titanium screw is initially placed in the inner mandibular cortex. A permanent suture is placed through the posterior tongue base and secured anteriorly around the screw. This procedure is intended to support the pharynx and lessen collapse, partially reducing the respiratory severity of OSA.

41520
The physician performs a frenoplasty and surgically alters the frenum by rearranging the tissue, usually with a Z-plasty technique. The lingual frenum is the connecting fold or membrane under the tongue that attaches it to the floor of the mouth. An incision in the shape of a "Z" is made through the frenum and the tissues are reapproximated in a different position and sutured.

41530
Using radiofrequency, the physician ablates submucosal tissues with temperatures in the 60°C to 90°C range. The physician may perform the submucosal radiofrequency tissue volume reduction (RFTVR) of tongue base on one or more sites. RFTVR uses low levels of radiofrequency energy to create targeted coagulative submucosal lesions. When these necrotic lesions in the soft tissue heal, scar formation and retraction of tissue occur, thus producing an overall reduction in tissue volume. Code 41530 is reported per session.

41800
The physician drains an abscess, cyst, or hematoma from dentoalveolar structures. The physician may make gingival incisions to provide drainage. An artificial drain may be placed and removed at a later time. On occasion, drainage may be obtained by probing the gingival sulcus.

41805
The physician removes a foreign body embedded in the soft tissue of the dental alveolus (gingival or alveolar mucosa). The physician may simply grasp the object with an instrument and remove it. If the object is further embedded, incisions may be made in the mucosa near the object to remove it. Sutures may be necessary.

41806
The physician removes a foreign body embedded in the bone of dentoalveolar structures. The physician may simply grasp the object with an instrument and remove it. If the object is further embedded, mucosal incisions may be made to reach the foreign body in the bone,

Digestive

which is removed, possibly with drills or osteotomes as necessary. The incision is sutured simply.

41820
The physician excises or trims hypertrophic (overgrown) gingiva to normal contours. The physician excises the overgrown gingiva using a scalpel, electrocautery, or a laser. Periodontal dressing or packing is often placed. Use this code for each quadrant of the mouth where gingivectomy is performed.

41821
The physician removes a small piece of gingiva from the back or top of a tooth. A scalpel, a laser, or electrocautery is used to excise the tissue and establish normal gingival contours around the tooth. A periodontal dressing may be applied.

41822
The physician excises fibrous soft tissue overlying the tuberosities of dentoalveolar structures, reducing the size of the tuberosity. The physician makes wedged or elliptically shaped incisions through the soft tissue of the tuberosity. The tissue is removed and the surgical wound is sutured directly.

41823
The physician removes the osseous tissue from the tuberosities of dentoalveolar structures, producing more favorable bone contours. The physician makes an incision through the mucosa of the tuberosity and exposes the underlying bone. Drills, osteotomes, or files are used to remove and contour the bone. The tissue is sutured directly over the bone. Some soft tissue may be excised prior to closure for adaptation over the newly contoured bone.

41825-41826
The physician removes a lesion or tumor of the dentoalveolar structures. If the lesion is within the mucosa, the physician makes incisions around the lesion and dissects it away from adjacent structures. If the lesion is within the bone, the mucosa is incised and the underlying bone exposed. The lesion is removed from the bone and the incision closed with layered sutures. No repair is done in 41825 and simple repair of the surgical wound is done in 41826.

41827
The physician removes a lesion or tumor of the dentoalveolar structures. If the lesion is within the mucosa, the physician makes incisions around the lesion and dissects it away from adjacent structures. If the lesion is within the bone, the mucosa is incised and the underlying bone exposed. The lesion is removed from the bone. The resultant surgical wound is closed with complex repair techniques, such as tissue rearrangement with flaps, tissue grafting, or complex suturing.

41828
The physician excises hyperplastic or excessive mucosa from the alveolus. Incisions are made in the hyperplastic tissue, separating it from the normal mucosa. The excessive tissue is removed. The resultant defect may be directly sutured or left to heal without suturing. With large amounts of excess tissue, more than one surgical session may be required to eliminate all of the tissue. Use this code for each specified quadrant excised.

41830
The physician removes a portion of the alveolus. Incisions are made through the mucosa to expose the alveolar bone. Curettes, drills, or osteotomes are used to remove the diseased alveolar bone or sequestrum. The mucosa may be sutured directly over the surgical wound, or it may be packed and allowed to heal secondarily.

41850
The physician destroys a lesion of the dentoalveolar structures without excision. The physician may use different techniques of lesion destruction. Electrocautery may be used to burn the lesion, cryotherapy to freeze the lesion, or chemical injections to destroy the lesion. A laser which produces high-intensity light may be used to destroy the lesion. No suturing is required and the resultant surgical wound is left to heal secondarily.

41870
The physician takes mucosa from one area of the mouth and grafts it around the teeth to repair areas of gingival recession. The physician uses a scalpel to remove a small piece of mucosa, usually from the hard palate. After preparing the recipient site, the physician sutures the graft in the area of gingival recession.

41872
The physician alters the contours of the gums by performing gingivoplasty. Areas of gingiva may be excised or incisions may be made through the gingiva to create a gingival flap. The flap may be sutured in a different position, trimmed, or both. Any incisions made are closed with sutures.

41874
The physician alters the contours of the alveolus by selectively performing alveoloplasty to remove sharp areas or undercuts of alveolar bone. The physician makes incisions in the mucosa overlying the alveolus, exposing the alveolar bone. Drills, osteotomes, or files are used to contour the bone. The mucosa is sutured in place over the contoured bone.

42000
The physician drains an abscess of the palate or uvula. The abscess is opened with a surgical instrument and the fluid is drained. The wound is allowed to heal without closure.

42100
The physician performs a biopsy on a lesion of the palate or uvula. An incision is made in the tissue, usually in an elliptical shape and typically including part diseased and part normal tissue. Incisions are made beneath the tissue and the specimen is removed. The surgical wound is closed with sutures.

42104-42107
The physician removes a lesion of the palate or uvula. Incisions are made completely around and under a lesion, typically in an elliptical shape, removing the lesion. Due to the small size of the lesion, no suturing or closure of the surgical wound is necessary in 42104. Removal of larger lesions requires simple closure in 42106 or local flap closure in 42107.

42120
The physician resects the palate or area of a lesion. The physician excises the lesion and any adjacent tissue where the lesion may have spread. The surgical wound is repaired by intermediate or complex closure, adjacent tissue transfer, or graft.

42140
The physician removes the uvula with a full-thickness incision. Electrocautery may be used to control hemorrhage. Sutures may be used to close the mucosa in a single layer.

42145
The physician removes elongated and excessive tissues of the uvula, soft palate, and pharynx. Incisions are made in the soft palate mucosa and a wedge of mucosa is excised. Excessive submucosal tissue is removed and the uvula is partially excised. The midline at the uvula is sutured first. The physician closes the remaining mucosa in a single layer, reapproximating the soft palate and thus increasing the diameter of the oropharynx.

42160
The physician destroys a lesion of the palate or uvula. Destruction may be accomplished by using a laser or electrocautery to burn the lesion, cryotherapy to freeze the lesion, or chemicals to destroy the lesion.

42180-42182
The physician repairs a laceration of the palate measuring 2 cm or less in length in 42180 and more than 2 cm or complex in 42182. The physician sutures the wound in a simple closure without submucosal sutures or tissue rearrangement for 42180. The physician sutures a laceration greater than 2 cm or one that requires complex closure, such as tissue rearrangement, submucosal sutures, or extensive cleaning due to tissue damage or crushing in 42182.

42200
The physician repairs the developmental cleft opening of the palate. The cleft size and location will dictate the type of repair to be performed. The physician closes the opening between the oral and nasal cavities with a partition of soft tissue. Typically, incisions are made in the palatal mucosa adjacent to the alveolar (tooth-bearing) bone. The mucosa is elevated and loosened from the bony palate. The margins of the cleft are incised and dissected to develop mucosal and muscular layers. These incised midline margins are closed in layers, thus closing the communication between the oral and nasal cavities.

42205
The physician repairs the developmental cleft opening of the palate which extends through the alveolar ridge (tooth-bearing region) of the maxilla. The cleft size and location will dictate the type of repair performed. The physician closes the opening between the oral and nasal cavities with a partition of soft tissue. Closure of the alveolar ridge will benefit development of both the maxilla and the teeth. Typically, incisions are made in the palatal mucosa adjacent to the alveolar bone. The mucosa is elevated and loosened from the bony palate. The midline margins of the cleft are incised and dissected to develop mucosal and muscular layers. The physician closes the midline margins in layers.

42210
The physician repairs the developmental cleft opening of the palate and reconstructs the alveolar ridge (tooth-bearing region) of the maxilla. The cleft size and location will dictate the type of repair performed. The physician closes the opening between the oral and nasal cavities with a partition of soft tissue. Bony reconstruction of the alveolar ridge can stabilize maxillary segments, benefit development of the teeth, and aid dental rehabilitation of chewing functions. Typically, incisions are made in the palatal mucosa adjacent to the alveolar bone. The mucosa is elevated and loosened from the bony palate. The midline margins of the cleft mucosa and gingiva are incised and dissected to develop mucosal and muscular layers. Through a separate incision, the physician harvests bone from the hip or skull and closes the surgically created wound. The bone is placed in the alveolar cleft, reestablishing normal contours of the maxilla. The physician closes all midline incisions in layers and gingival incisions in a single layer.

42215
The physician revises previous repairs of the cleft palate. Wound dehiscence (splitting), infection, or scarring after initial surgeries could cause oral/nasal recommunication, developmental growth restrictions, or velopharyngeal incompetence. The defect will dictate the repair to be performed. Typically, incisions are made in the palatal mucosa adjacent to the alveolar (tooth-bearing) bone. The mucosa is elevated and loosened from the bony palate. The previous midline incisions are excised and dissected to develop mucosal and muscular layers. The physician resutures all

midline incisions in layers and gingival incisions are closed in a single layer.

42220
The physician revises the previous cleft palate incisions to lengthen the soft palate. Wound dehiscence (splitting), infection, or scarring after initial surgeries could cause developmental growth restrictions or velopharyngeal incompetence. The defect will dictate the repair performed. Typically, the soft palate lengthening is accomplished with the use of mucosal advancement flaps. Incisions are made in the palatal mucosa adjacent to the alveolar (tooth-bearing) bone. The mucosa is elevated and loosened from the bony palate. The pedicle flaps utilizing posterior palatine blood supply are developed and sutured to increase the anterior-posterior length of the soft palate. The physician sutures all remaining midline incisions in layers.

42225
The physician revises previous cleft palate incisions with pharyngeal flap techniques. Through the soft palate, a midline incision is made to expose the posterior pharyngeal wall. The physician incises a flap from the posterior pharyngeal wall through the mucosa, submucosa, and muscle. This flap is sutured to the soft palate. Revision of previous surgical incisions may be necessary. All remaining midline incisions are sutured in layers.

42226
The physician uses both advancement flaps and pharyngeal flaps to lengthen the soft palate. Typically, the soft palate lengthening is accomplished with the use of mucosal advancement flaps. Correction of velopharyngeal incompetence is accomplished by pharyngeal flap techniques. A midline incision through the soft palate is made to expose the posterior pharyngeal wall. The physician incises a flap from the posterior pharyngeal wall through mucosa, submucosa, and muscle. This flap is sutured to the soft palate. Advancement flaps utilizing posterior palatine blood vessels are used to lengthen the soft palate by suturing techniques that increase the anterior-posterior length of the soft palate. All remaining midline incisions are sutured in layers.

42227
The physician uses mucosal island flaps to lengthen the soft palate. Incisions are made in the palatal mucosa adjacent to the alveolar (tooth-bearing) bone. The mucosa is elevated and loosened from the bony palate. Advancement flaps utilizing posterior palatine blood vessels are used to lengthen the soft palate by suturing techniques that increase the anterior-posterior length of the soft palate. All remaining incisions are sutured in layers.

42235
The physician repairs the hard palate by closing the communication between the oral and nasal cavities. A combination of mucosal and mucoperiosteal flaps are used to repair the defect. The margins of the defect are incised and dissected to develop mucosal, muscular, and mucoperiosteal layers. The mucoperiosteum of the vomer (nasal septum) is elevated and sutured to the mucoperiosteum of the hard palate. This closes the communication between the oral and nasal cavities. Incisions are made in the palatal mucosa adjacent to the alveolar (tooth-bearing) bone. The mucosa is elevated and loosened from the bony palate. The palatal mucosa is closed in layers.

42260
The physician repairs a fistula communication from the nasal or sinus regions to the nasolabial region of the midface. The repair is dependent on the size of the fistular tract. For small defects, an excision of the epithelized tract is made from source to skin surface. This wound is sutured in layers. In larger defects, a nasolabial flap may be necessary after excision of the fistula. A nasolabial flap is designed, incised, and rotated to the defect region. The flap is sutured over the defect in layers.

42280
The physician takes impressions of the maxilla. A palatal prosthesis is customized from the cast model of the impression.

42281
The physician inserts a palatal prosthesis prepared by an outside laboratory. The prosthesis is retained by pins and augments the palate.

42300-42305
The physician drains an abscess of the parotid gland. An incision is made intraorally through the tissue overlying the gland. The physician dissects through the tissue overlying the abscess. The abscess is opened with a surgical instrument and the fluid is drained. Report 42305 if the excision is complicated.

42310
The physician drains an abscess of the submaxillary (submandibular) or sublingual gland. An incision is made intraorally through the tissue overlying the gland. The physician dissects through the tissue overlying the abscess. The abscess is opened with a surgical instrument and the fluid is drained.

42320
The physician drains an abscess of the submaxillary (submandibular) salivary gland. An incision is made extraorally through the skin overlying the gland. The physician dissects through the tissue overlying the abscess. The abscess is opened with a surgical instrument and the fluid is drained. A drain may be placed.

42330
The physician makes an incision in the submandibular, sublingual, or parotid ducts to remove a sialolith (a stone). An incision is made intraorally in the mucosa overlying the duct and tissue is dissected to reach the duct. The physician removes the stone in a simple sialolithotomy. The incision is usually not closed.

42335
The physician makes an incision in the submandibular duct to remove a complicated sialolith (a stone). An incision is made intraorally in the mucosa overlying the duct and tissue is dissected to reach the duct. A large stone and portion of surrounding tissue must be removed. The incision is usually not closed.

42340
The physician makes an incision in the parotid gland to remove a sialolith (a stone). An incision is made extraorally in the skin overlying the gland and dissected to reach the stone or the intraoral mucosa overlying the duct is incised. Tissue is dissected to the gland. The physician removes the stone. The incision is closed with layered sutures.

42400-42405
The physician performs a needle biopsy in 42400 or an incisional biopsy in 42405 of a salivary gland. For a needle biopsy, a needle is inserted through the skin overlying the salivary gland. The physician takes a tissue sample from the gland and withdraws the needle. For an incisional biopsy, an incision is made in the skin overlying the salivary gland. Tissues are dissected to the gland. An incision is made in the tissue of the gland and a small piece of the gland is removed. The surgical wound is sutured.

42408
The physician removes a sublingual salivary cyst. An incision is made intraorally in the floor of the mouth overlying the cyst. The physician removes the cyst.

42409
The physician incises and removes the mucosa overlying a cyst on the floor of the mouth. The roof of the cyst is removed and the remaining sides of the cyst wall are sutured to the mucosa, creating a pouch. The saliva drains through the pouch. The pouch shrinks in size to a small opening in the floor of the mouth. Saliva from the sublingual gland flows through this opening.

42410-42426
The physician excises a portion or all of the parotid gland with or without facial nerve preservation and unilateral neck dissection. The physician makes a preauricular incision with a curved cervical extension to the midpoint of the mandible. The anterior and posterior skin flaps are retracted and the tissues are retracted to expose the parotid gland, leaving the fascia over the gland intact. In 42410, the main trunk of the facial nerve is visualized and the lateral (superficial) lobe of the parotid gland is freed and excised. In 42415, the facial nerve is identified and the lateral lobe is lifted off the branches of the nerve using dissection. A nerve stimulator may be used to test nerve integrity. In 42420, the facial nerve is identified and the lateral lobe is lifted off the branches of the nerve using dissection. A nerve stimulator is used to test nerve integrity. The nerve is retracted so the deep parotid gland can be removed without damaging the facial nerve. The nerve stimulator is used often to ensure nerve integrity. In 42425, the physician removes the gland without capsule disruption, sacrificing the facial nerve. In 42426, the physician removes the gland without capsule disruption, sacrificing the facial nerve. The incision is extended inferiorly to dissect the unilateral neck for lymph node excision.

42440
The physician removes a diseased, infected, blocked, or injured submandibular gland. The physician makes an incision in the skin of the neck below the inferior border of the mandible and near the angle of the mandible. The underlying tissues are dissected to the submandibular gland. The gland is exposed, freed from the surrounding tissue, and removed. The incision is closed with sutures.

42450
The physician removes a diseased, infected, blocked, or injured sublingual gland. The physician makes an intraoral incision in the mucosa overlying the gland. Tissues are dissected down to the gland. The gland is exposed, freed from surrounding tissue, and removed. The incision is closed with sutures.

42500-42505
The physician repairs a salivary duct by inserting a hollow plastic or silicone tube into the duct. The tube is threaded through the duct. The duct is allowed to heal and may be sutured around the tube. In 42505, repair of the duct is complex and may be delayed. The tube is later removed and patency is restored.

42507
The physician makes an intraoral incision overlying the parotid duct. The path of the duct is diverted into a new position and sutured to the mucosa so that the opening of the duct is in a different location. To bypass a blockage, the duct may be cut behind the blockage and repositioned so that saliva can flow freely into the mouth. This procedure is performed on both parotid ducts.

42508
The physician makes an intraoral incision overlying the parotid duct. The path of the duct is diverted into a new position and sutured to the mucosa so that the opening of the duct is in a different location. To bypass a blockage, the duct may be cut behind the blockage and repositioned so that saliva can flow freely into the mouth. This procedure is performed on both parotid ducts. The physician also removes a submandibular

gland. The physician makes an incision in the skin of the neck below the inferior border of the mandible. The underlying tissues are dissected to the submandibular gland. The gland is exposed, freed from the surrounding tissue, and removed. The incision is closed with sutures.

42509
The physician makes an intraoral incision overlying the parotid duct. The path of the duct is diverted into a new position and sutured to the mucosa so that the opening of the duct is in a different location. To bypass a blockage, the duct may be cut behind the blockage and repositioned so that saliva can flow freely into the mouth. This procedure is performed on both parotid ducts. The physician also removes both submandibular glands. The physician makes an incision in the skin of the neck below the inferior border of the mandible. The underlying tissues are dissected to the submandibular gland. The gland is exposed, freed from the surrounding tissue, and removed. The incision is closed with sutures. The mucosal incisions are closed directly.

42510
The physician makes an intraoral incision overlying the parotid duct. The path of the duct is diverted into a new position and sutured to the mucosa so that the opening of the duct is in a different location. To bypass a blockage, the duct may be cut behind the blockage and repositioned so that saliva can flow freely into the mouth. This procedure is performed on both parotid ducts. The physician ligates both submandibular ducts. An incision may be made over the duct. Suture material is tied around the ducts to stop the flow of saliva. The mucosal incisions are closed directly.

42550
The physician inserts a small catheter into the duct of a salivary gland. A radiopaque dye (a dye which projects white on x-rays) is injected into the duct. The duct is filled with the dye back to and including the gland, if possible. A separately reported x-ray is taken. The x-ray shows the duct and gland filled with the dye, demonstrating the structure, blockages or disease affecting the structure.

42600
The physician closes a salivary fistula. The physician makes an incision around the fistula and excises the fistula down to the level of the duct. After excision of the fistula, the incision is closed directly.

42650
The physician inserts a probe into the salivary duct to dilate a narrowed section. The physician repeats the procedure with progressively larger probes until the desired amount of dilation is achieved.

42660
The physician introduces a catheter and dilates or expands the salivary duct. A radiopaque dye may be injected into the duct to outline the structure of the duct and any disease process. The catheter is removed.

42665
The physician makes an intraoral incision overlying a salivary duct and dissects to the layer of the duct. The duct is ligated (tied) and the incision is closed.

42700
The physician drains an abscess near or on a tonsil. The patient is given a topical anesthetic or placed under general anesthesia. Using an intraoral approach with a mouth gag, the physician incises the mucus membrane of the abscess. The abscess cavity is opened with angulated closed forceps or hemostat. The wound is irrigated and left open.

42720
The physician drains an abscess located on or near the pharynx. Retropharyngeal indicates the abscess is located on the back of the pharynx; parapharyngeal indicates the abscess is near the pharynx. The patient is given a topical anesthetic or placed under general anesthesia. Though an intraoral approach, the physician locates the abscess using a diagnostic needle puncture and aspiration at the point of maximal fluctuation on the pharynx. The physician incises the mucus membrane to open the abscess. The pus is evacuated using suction and sponging.

42725
The physician drains an abscess located on or near the pharynx. The patient is placed under general anesthesia. The physician makes an incision beneath the angle of the jaw and carries out a blunt dissection to locate and isolate the abscess. The physician incises the mucus membrane of the abscess. The pus is evacuated; a gauze or rubber drain may be inserted into the abscess cavity. The incision is repaired in sutured layers.

42800-42802
The physician obtains a biopsy of the oropharynx or hypopharynx. After the airway is secured with an endotracheal tube, a mouth gag is placed. The physician obtains a tissue sample through an incisional or snare technique. Bleeding is controlled through electrocautery, the wound is not closed. In 42800, tissue in the oropharynx is biopsied. In 42802, tissue in the hypopharynx is biopsied. If the lesion is deep in the hypopharynx, an operating laryngoscope is used to visualize the area.

42804-42806
The physician obtains a biopsy of the oropharynx or hypopharynx. After the airway is secured with an endotracheal tube, a mouth gag is placed. The physician obtains a tissue sample through an incisional or snare technique. Bleeding is controlled through electrocautery, the wound is not closed. In 42804, tissue with a visible in the nasopharynx is biopsied. In 42806, tissue in the nasopharynx is biopsied to survey

for an unknown primary lesion. If the lesion is deep in the nasopharynx, an operating laryngoscope is used to visualize the area.

42808
The physician removes or destroys a lesion of the pharynx. The physician uses an intraoral approach to excise or destroy the lesion. Destruction may be accomplished using a laser, cryosurgery, or electrocoagulation to cause the tissue to coagulate. Methods of excision may include avulsion or curettage.

42809
The physician removes a foreign body from the pharynx. The physician uses an intraoral approach with the aid of a tongue blade to visualize the foreign body. The foreign body is grasped with forceps and removed.

42810
The physician removes a branchial cleft cyst or vestige that is confined to the skin and subcutaneous tissues of the neck. A branchial cleft is an abnormal embryological remnant that resembles gills. The physician makes a horizontal neck incision just below the jaw line to access and remove the cyst or vestige. The incision is repaired in sutured layers.

42815
The physician removes a branchial cleft cyst or vestige that has extended beyond the skin and subcutaneous tissue. A branchial cleft is an abnormal embryological remnant that resembles gills. The physician makes one or two horizontal neck incisions just below the jaw line. The cyst or vestige is dissected from the surrounding muscle and fascia. If a fistula is present, a surrounding elliptical skin excision is performed. Any ducts of the cyst are dissected and traced to a pharyngeal communication. The cyst, vestige, and ducts are removed. A tissue drain is placed and the wound is sutured in layers.

42820-42821
The physician removes the tonsils and adenoids. The physician accesses the tonsils and adenoids in an intraoral approach. First, the physician removes the tonsils by grasping the tonsil with a tonsil clamp and dissecting the capsule of the tonsil. The tonsil is removed. Bleeding vessels are clamped and tied. Bleeding may also be controlled using silver nitrate and gauze packing. Using a mirror or nasopharyngoscope for visualization, the physician uses an adenotome or a curette and basket punch to excise the adenoids. Alternate surgical techniques for a tonsillectomy and adenoidectomy include electrocautery, laser surgery, and cryogenic surgery. Report 42820 if the patient is under 12 years. For patients 12 years or older, report 42821.

42825-42826
The physician removes the tonsils. The tonsillectomy can be the first the patient has undergone, or a secondary procedure to remove tonsil regrowth since the primary procedure. The physician accesses the tonsils in an intraoral approach. First, the physician removes the tonsils by grasping the tonsil with a tonsil clamp and dissecting the capsule of the tonsil. The tonsil is removed. Bleeding vessels are clamped and tied. Bleeding may also be controlled using silver nitrate and gauze packing. Alternate surgical techniques for a tonsillectomy include electrocautery, laser surgery, and cryogenic surgery. Report 42825 if the patient is under 12 years. For patients 12 years or older, report 42826.

42830-42836
The physician removes the adenoids. Using an intraoral approach and a mirror or nasopharyngoscope for visualization, the physician uses an adenotome or a curette and basket punch to excise the adenoids. Alternate surgical techniques for an adenoidectomy include electrocautery, laser surgery, and cryogenic surgery. For adenoidectomy performed as a primary procedure (the initial removal of the adenoid), report 42830 for patients under 12 years; report 42831 for patients 12 years and older. When performed as a secondary procedure (secondary procedure to remove adenoid tissue that has grown back since an initial adenoidectomy), report 42835 if the patient is under 12 years; report 42836 for patients 12 years and older.

42842-42845
The physician removes the tonsils, tonsillar pillars, and/or the retromolar trigone, along with any affected area of the maxilla or mandible involved in the tumor. First, the physician performs a tracheostomy. The involved tissue is resected. In addition to the above areas, radical resection may include a hemiglossectomy or a total glossectomy, as well as a full neck dissection. In 42842, the wound is so extensive that it is packed open and grafted at a later session. In 42844, the wound is less extensive and can be closed primarily with sutured layers. In 42845, a flap is rotated from the chest. If the wound included a resection of the mandible or maxilla, a fibular bone graft or a metal plate may be used to reconstruct the jaw.

42860
The physician removes portions of the tonsils not excised during primary resection or that have developed polyps. The physician cauterizes and/or snares the affected tissue. No closure is required.

42870
The physician removes or destroys the lingual tonsils. Because the abscessed tonsils may restrict the airway passage, the physician is present during intubation in case an emergency airway is needed. The physician uses an endotracheal tube or an operating laryngoscope with jet ventilation to ventilate the patient. Using an intraoral approach, the physician uses a laser to destroy the lingual tonsils.

Digestive

42890
The physician removes the affected portion of the pharyngeal wall. The physician makes a vertical incision in the neck and retracts the strap muscles. The affected area of the pharynx is excised and the pharyngeal walls are reapproximated and closed with sutures. The incision is sutured in layers. Occasionally, the area removed includes part of the thyroid ala, hyoid bone, and wall of the pyriform fossa. Procedures include: anterior transhyoid pharyngotomy, lateral pharyngotomy, and median labiomandibular glossotomy. Reconstructive surgery is required for closure.

42892
The physician removes the affected portion of the pharyngeal wall or pyriform sinus. The physician makes a vertical incision and retracts the strap muscles. The mucosa of the upper pyriform sinus and the affected portion of the pharynx are excised. The lateral and posterior pharyngeal walls are reapproximated and closed with sutures. The incision is sutured in layers.

42894
The physician removes the affected portion of the pharyngeal wall or pyriform sinus. The physician makes a vertical incision and retracts the strap muscles. The mucosa of the upper pyriform sinus and the affected portion of the pharynx are excised. Myocutaneous or fasciocutaneous flap reconstruction of the pharyngeal area may be achieved using the pectoralis major muscle and its overlying skin. The flap is rotated and inserted through a previously created tunnel between the clavicle and overlying skin and sutured into place to reconstruct the pharynx. Alternately, free muscle, skin, or fascial flap closure with microvascular anastomosis may be performed. The flaps used in reconstruction are separately reportable. The incisions are sutured in layers.

42900
The physician locates and sutures a wound or injury to the pharynx. The physician uses an intraoral or transhyoid approach, depending on the location and extent of the wound. For an intraoral approach, the physician uses a mirror for visualization. For a transhyoid approach, the physician makes a horizontal incision directly below the jaw line. The physician sutures the wound. If a transhyoid approach is used, the incision is sutured in layers.

42950
A variety of techniques may be used for pharyngeal reconstruction including skin grafts, tongue flaps, regional cutaneous flaps and microvascular free-tissue transfer. Skin grafts are commonly harvested from the forehead, deltopectoral, nape of the neck, and pectoralis major. Reconstruction is performed when direct wound closure or reapproximation is not possible.

42953
The physician repairs a tear at the pharyngeal esophageal junction. After the airway is secured, the physician makes a horizontal neck incision and retracts superficial tissues to expose the pharyngeal esophageal junction. The defect is identified, irrigated to reduce infection, and sutured in layers.

42955
The physician creates an opening to the pharynx for long term feeding. The physician makes a horizontal incision below the jaw line to create a communication between the pharyngeal lumen and the exterior of the patient's neck. The incision is sutured to create an opening for placement of a feeding tube.

42960-42962
The physician controls bleeding of the oropharynx. Primary hemorrhaging occurs within 24 hours after surgery; secondary hemorrhaging occurs 24 hours to two weeks after tonsillectomy. In 42960 and 42961, hemorrhaging is controlled using methods such as clot evacuation and applying pressure with sponges, electrocautery, or application of vasoconstrictor solutions such as tannic acid, silver nitrate, and epinephrine. Cellulose sponges that expand when placed in the tonsillar cavity may be used. Report 42961 when extensive bleeding requires hospitalization. In 42962, surgery is required to control hemorrhaging. Surgical intervention methods include suture ligation of bleeding vessels. In cases of profuse bleeding, emergency ligation of the external carotid artery may be performed. The tonsillar pillars may be approximated with sutures to control post-tonsillectomy bleeding.

42970-42972
The physician controls bleeding of the nasopharynx. Primary hemorrhaging occurs within 24 hours after surgery; secondary hemorrhaging occurs 24 hours to two weeks after adenoidectomy. In 42970 and 42971 hemorrhaging is controlled using methods such as clot evacuation and application of vasoconstrictor solutions such as tannic acid, silver nitrate, and epinephrine; electrocautery, and posterior or anterior nasal packing. Report 42971 when extensive bleeding requires hospitalization. In 42972, surgery is required to control hemorrhaging. Surgical intervention methods include ligation of ethmoidal arteries using silver clips and/or electrocautery. The physician may use a nasal or intraoral approach for secondary surgery.

43020
The physician makes an incision in the esophagus to remove a foreign body from it. The physician makes a horizontal or oblique incision in the lateral neck and into the esophagus, using forceps to grasp and extract the foreign body. The incision is closed with sutured layers.

43030
The physician incises the cricopharyngeal muscle, also known as the upper esophageal sphincter (UES). The physician makes a lateral neck incision to expose the UES, and a second lateral incision through the UES. The incision is repaired with sutured layers.

43045
The physician makes an incision in the esophagus to remove a foreign body. For a thoracic approach, the physician incises and dissects the left posterior chest wall to access the esophagus. The physician incises the esophagus and uses forceps to grasp and remove the foreign body. The esophageal incision is closed with sutures. The left posterior chest wall is closed with sutured layers.

43100
The physician removes a lesion in the esophagus. The physician makes a horizontal or oblique incision of the lateral neck. Next, the physician makes an incision in the esophagus and excises the lesion. The remaining esophageal borders are sutured together. The incision is sutured in layers.

43101
The physician removes a lesion in the esophagus. For a thoracic approach, the physician incises and dissects the left posterior chest wall to access the esophagus. For an abdominal approach, the physician makes an upper midline abdominal incision to access the esophagus transhiatally. The physician excises the lesion. The remaining esophageal borders are sutured together. The incision is closed with sutured layers.

43107
The physician removes most or all of the esophagus and attaches the stomach to the pharynx or cervical esophagus. The physician gains access to the esophagus through two incisions: an oblique cervical incision and a horizontal upper midline abdominal incision. The physician divides the esophagus at the cervical level (for an esophagogastrostomy) or at its origin at the pharynx (for a pharyngogastrostomy). The esophagus is removed through the abdominal incision and divided from the stomach. The stomach is pulled through the posterior mediastinum and anastomosed to the pharynx or the remaining cervical esophagus. If the stomach is used as the esophageal conduit, a pyloroplasty may be performed to open the pyloric sphincter. The incisions are repaired in sutured layers.

43108
The physician removes most or all of the esophagus and uses a bowel or colon graft for reconstruction. The physician gains access to the esophagus through two incisions: an oblique cervical incision and a horizontal upper midline abdominal incision. The physician divides the esophagus at the cervical level (for an esophagogastrostomy) or at its origin at the pharynx (for a pharyngogastrostomy). The esophagus is removed through the abdominal incision and divided from the stomach. A portion of the colon or small bowel is excised and freed of attachments, taking care to preserve its major vascular supply. Gastrointestinal continuity is reestablished by securing the distal and proximal bowel margins. Finally, the excised portion of the colon or bowel is attached to the pharynx or cervical esophagus and the stomach. This anastomosis creates a usable esophagus. If the stomach is used as the esophageal conduit, a pyloroplasty may be performed to open the pyloric sphincter. The incisions are repaired in sutured layers.

43112
The physician removes the esophagus through abdominal, chest and neck incisions and replaces the esophagus with stomach. The physician makes a midline abdominal incision. Next the stomach is dissected free of surrounding structures and the esophagus is mobilized as it passes through the diaphragm to the stomach. The physician makes an incision in the right chest between the ribs and exposes the esophagus. The esophagus is mobilized under direct vision in the chest from the diaphragm to the neck. Next, a longitudinal incision is made in the left or right neck and the esophagus is identified and mobilized in the neck. The esophagus is divided at its junction with the stomach and in the neck and the esophagus is removed. The stomach is pulled through the middle of the chest into the neck and the stomach is connected to the stump of the esophagus in the neck. The incisions are closed.

43113
The physician removes the esophagus through abdominal, chest and neck incisions and replaces the esophagus with colon or small bowel. The physician makes a midline abdominal incision. The stomach is dissected free of surrounding structures and the esophagus is mobilized as it passes through the diagram to the stomach. The physician makes an incision in the right chest between the ribs and exposes the esophagus. The esophagus is mobilized under direct vision in the chest from the diaphragm to the neck. The esophagus is divided at its junction with the stomach and in the neck and the esophagus is removed. The physician selects an appropriate segment of colon or small bowel. The bowel is divided proximal and distal to this segment and the bowel ends are reapproximated. The selected segment of colon or small bowel is pulled through the middle section of the chest and connected to the stump of the esophagus in the neck and to the stomach in the abdomen. The incisions are closed.

43116
The physician removes the affected portion of the esophagus and replaces it with a graft from the large or small intestine. The physician gains access to the esophagus through an oblique cervical incision. The

physician resects the affected portion of the cervical esophagus. Next, the physician obtains a graft from the large or small intestine. To do this, the physician makes a midline abdominal incision and frees a portion of the large or small intestine of muscular and vascular attachments. The intestine is resected and interposed to reestablish gastrointestinal continuity in the cervical esophagus. Microsurgical techniques are used to create a new blood supply for the graft. The distal and proximal portions of the remaining intestine are reconnected (anastomosis).

43117
The physician removes the distal esophagus and possibly the proximal stomach through abdominal and chest incisions and replaces the esophagus with the remaining stomach. The physician makes a midline abdominal incision. The stomach is dissected free of surrounding structures and the esophagus is mobilized as it passes through the diaphragm to the stomach. The esophagus is divided at its connection to the stomach or the stomach may be divided near its middle portion. Next, a right chest incision is made between the ribs to expose the esophagus. The distal esophagus is mobilized under direct vision and divided above its diseased segment. The distal esophagus and attached proximal stomach are them removed. The remaining stomach is pulled into the chest and connected to the stump of the proximal esophagus. Drains are placed into the chest near the new anastomosis and the incisions are closed.

43118
The physician removes the distal esophagus and possibly proximal stomach through abdominal and chest incisions and replaces the esophagus with colon or small bowel. The physician makes a midline abdominal incision. The stomach is dissected free of surrounding structures and the esophagus is mobilized as it passes through the diaphragm to the stomach. The esophagus is divided at its connection to the stomach or the stomach may be divided near its middle portion. An appropriate segment of colon or small bowel is selected and the bowel is divided proximal and distal to this segment and the bowel ends re- approximated. One end of the selected bowel segment is connected to the remaining stomach and the other end is placed through the diaphragm into the chest. A right chest incision is made between the ribs to expose the esophagus. The distal esophagus is mobilized under direct vision and divided above its diseased segment. The distal esophagus and attached proximal stomach are removed. The remaining end of the segment of colon or small bowel that has been attached to the stomach is pulled into the chest and connected to the stump of the proximal esophagus. Drains are placed into the chest near the new anastomosis and the incisions are closed.

43121
The physician removes the affected part of the esophagus and proximal stomach and reattaches the remaining stomach to the esophageal stump. The physician accesses the esophagus through a right posterolateral thoracotomy; no abdominal incision is made. The physician resects the affected portion of the distal esophagus and sometimes a portion of the proximal stomach. The resected area is removed. The stomach or gastric remnant is pulled into the thorax and sutured to the esophageal stump. If the stomach is used as the esophageal conduit, a pyloroplasty may be performed to open the pyloric sphincter. The incision is sutured in layers.

43122
The physician removes the distal esophagus and possibly proximal stomach through a combined abdominal and chest incision and replaces the esophagus with the remaining stomach. The physician makes a midline abdominal incision. The stomach is dissected free of surrounding structures and the esophagus is mobilized as it passes through the diaphragm to the stomach. The esophagus is divided proximally above the diseased area and distally at its junction with the stomach or the middle portion of the stomach may be divided. The distal esophagus and attached proximal stomach are removed. The remaining stomach is connected to the stump of the esophagus. The incision is closed.

43123
The physician removes the distal esophagus and possibly the proximal stomach through a combined abdominal and chest incision and replaces the esophagus with colon or small bowel. The physician makes a midline abdominal incision that may extend onto the chest between the ribs. The stomach is dissected free of surrounding structures and the esophagus is mobilized as it passes through the diaphragm to the stomach. The esophagus is divided proximally above the diseased area and distally at its junction with the stomach or the middle portion of the stomach may be divided. The distal esophagus and attached stomach are removed. An appropriate segment of colon or small bowel is selected. The bowel is divided proximal and distal to the segment and the bowel ends are re- approximated. The selected segment of bowel is connected proximally to the remaining esophageal stump and distally to the remaining stomach. The incision is closed.

43124
The physician removes the esophagus with no attempt to reconstruct the esophagus. The physician first creates a permanent tracheoplasty. The physician accesses the esophagus through an oblique cervical incision, a thoracotomy, and/or a midline abdominal incision and resects the affected portion of the esophagus. The esophageal stump is sutured to the

cervical incision, creating a connection from the exterior of the neck to the esophageal lumen to provide drainage of saliva and mucus. The incisions are closed with sutured layers.

43130-43135
The physician removes a diverticulum from the hypopharynx or esophagus. A diverticulum is pouch that occurs normally or because of a defect in the muscular membrane. In 43130 (cervical approach), the physician makes a lateral incision in the neck. In 43135 (thoracic approach), the physician incises and dissects the left posterior chest wall. The physician may dissect or incise the cricopharyngeus muscle to expose the diverticulum. The physician clamps the diverticulum and closes using sutures or staples. The incision is closed with sutured layers.

43200-43202
The physician views the esophagus. The physician introduces a rigid esophagoscope through the patient's mouth and into the esophagus under general anesthesia or a flexible esophagoscope under topical anesthesia with sedation. The physician views the esophagus and may take a specimen collection of cells by brushing or washing and aspirating the esophageal lining. Report 43201 if the physician also injects any substance into a specific area through the scope while viewing the esophagus. In 43202, bite biopsy forceps are used to obtain samples of the esophageal mucosa that appear abnormal.

43204-43205
The physician views the esophagus and identifies and treats varices. Varices are dilated, enlarged, and tortuous veins. The physician passes a rigid or flexible esophagoscope through the patient's mouth and into the esophagus to identify the varices. In 43204, the physician passes a sclerotherapy needle through the scope, and injects the varices with an agent that causes fibrosis (scarring). The result over time is obliteration of the varices. In 43205, the physician uses a suction tip to lift the varix and places a rubber band around the base of the varix.

43215
The physician locates and removes a foreign body from the esophagus. The physician passes a rigid or flexible esophagoscope through the patient's mouth and into the esophagus. The foreign body is located. It may be suctioned or grasped with forceps and retracted through the scope. An alternative technique is to pass a balloon beyond the foreign body. The balloon is inflated and withdrawn, capturing the foreign body.

43216-43217
The physician uses an esophagoscope to remove tumors, polyps, or lesions from the esophagus. The physician passes a rigid or flexible esophagoscope through the patient's mouth and into the esophagus and locates the lesion. In 43216, the base of the lesion is electrocoagulated and severed using biopsy forceps or bipolar cautery. In 43217, a snare loop is placed around the base of the lesion and closed (the tissue is electrocoagulated and severed as the loop is closed). The severed tissue is withdrawn through the scope. If the lesion is removed using laser therapy, electrocoagulation, or injection of toxic agents, report 43228.

43219
The physician examines the esophagus and places a plastic tube or stent. This procedure usually follows dilation for an obstruction. The physician passes a rigid or flexible esophagoscope through the patient's mouth and into the esophagus. A guidewire is placed through the scope, and the stent or plastic tube is advanced over the guidewire. The position of the stent is confirmed with the scope.

43220
The physician stretches esophageal tissue. The physician uses an esophagoscope to place a balloon and dilate the esophagus. The physician passes a rigid or flexible esophagoscope through the patient's mouth and into the esophagus. The balloon is advanced through the scope. A guidewire may be used. After entering the obstructed region, the balloon is briefly inflated several times.

43226
The physician stretches esophageal tissue. The physician passes a rigid or flexible esophagoscope through the patient's mouth and into the esophagus. A guidewire is placed through the scope and the scope is removed. A dilator is passed over the guidewire. This may be repeated several times using progressively larger dilators.

43227
The physician controls esophageal bleeding. The physician passes a rigid or flexible esophagoscope through the patient's mouth and into the esophagus. Control of bleeding may be achieved using several endoscopic methods including laser therapy, electrocoagulation, rubber band ligation, and injection of the bleeding vessel with sclerosants, ethanol, or adrenaline.

43228
The physician removes tumors, polyps, or lesions from the esophagus. The physician passes a rigid or flexible esophagoscope through the patient's mouth and into the esophagus and locates the lesion. The lesion is destroyed using laser therapy, electrocoagulation, or injection of toxic agents. If the lesion is destroyed using hot biopsy forceps, bipolar cautery report 43216 instead. If destroyed using snare technique, report 43217 instead.

43231
The physician views the esophagus and performs an endoscopic ultrasound examination. The physician

Digestive

passes a rigid or flexible esophagoscope through the patient's mouth and into the esophagus. The esophagus is examined and the area of interest is identified. The esophagoscope is removed and replaced with an echoendoscope or an ultrasound probe is passed through the already placed esophagoscope. The echoendoscope or ultrasound probe is fitted with a water-filled balloon near the tip; the tip contains a transducer that picks-up the ultrasound frequency and relays it to a processor, outside of the body. The water-filled tip is positioned in the esophagus, against the esophageal wall next to the area of interest. The area is scanned and an ultrasound image is projected through the processor to a monitor in real-time. When the ultrasound examination is complete the echoendoscope, or esophagoscope and ultrasound probe is removed.

43232
The physician views the esophagus and performs a transendoscopic ultrasound-guided intramural or transmural fine needle aspiration/biopsy. The physician passes a rigid or flexible esophagoscope through the patients' mouth and into the esophagus. The esophagus is examined and the area of interest is identified. The esophagoscope may be removed. A radial scanning echoendoscope is inserted and ultrasound scanning is performed, or an ultrasound probe is passed through the already placed esophagoscope. The site for a fine needle aspiration biopsy is determined. If a radial scanning echoendoscope is used it is removed and is replaced with a curvilinear array echoendoscope. The echoendoscope or ultrasound probe is fitted with a water-filled balloon near the tip; the tip contains a transducer that picks-up the ultrasound frequency and relays it to a processor, outside of the body. The water-filled tip is positioned in the esophagus, against the esophageal wall next to the predetermined fine needle aspiration (FNA) biopsy site. The area is scanned and an ultrasound image is projected through the processor to a monitor in real-time. A FNA needle is passed through the scope to the biopsy site and the needle is inserted through the wall of the esophagus to the lesion, or other structure, such as a lymph node. The area is biopsied. When the FNA is complete the echoendoscope, or esophagoscope and ultrasound probe is removed.

43234
The physician examines the upper gastrointestinal tract. The physician passes an endoscope through the patient's mouth into the esophagus. The esophagus, stomach, duodenum, and sometimes the jejunum are viewed.

43235-43236
The physician examines the upper gastrointestinal tract for diagnostic purposes. The physician passes an endoscope through the patient's mouth into the esophagus. The esophagus, stomach, duodenum, and sometimes the jejunum are viewed to determine if bleeding, tumors, erosions, ulcers, or other abnormalities are present. In 43235, specimens may be obtained by brushing or washing the esophageal lining with saline, followed by aspiration. Report 43236 if the physician injects any substance into the submucosa through the scope while viewing the upper gastrointestinal tract.

43237-43238
The physician performs an esophagogastroduodenoscopy (EGD) with a concomitant ultrasound examination for diagnostic purposes. The patient is prepped for an upper gastrointestinal exam, and the scope is advanced through the mouth into the stomach and duodenum or jejunum. An examination is carried out to determine if any bleeding, tumors, erosions, ulcers, or other abnormalities are present. Code 43237 is reported when the endoscope exam is followed by insertion of an echoendoscope for an ultrasound exam limited to the esophagus. Code 43238 is reported when the echoendoscope is inserted followed the EGD examination and an ultrasound examination is carried out, including transmural fine needle aspiration biopsy of the esophagus. Using real-time ultrasonic imaging guidance, the physician inserts a 22-gauge needle through the scope to the biopsy site and tissue is removed. Several passes may be made for an adequate specimen before the scope is removed.

43239
The physician examines the upper gastrointestinal tract for diagnostic purposes. The physician passes an endoscope through the patient's mouth into the esophagus. The esophagus, stomach, duodenum, and sometimes the jejunum are viewed to determine if bleeding, tumors, erosions, ulcers, or other abnormalities are present. In 43239, single or multiple tissue samples are obtained for biopsy specimens using bite forceps through the endoscope.

43240
The physician examines the upper gastrointestinal tract and performs transmural drainage of a pseudocyst. The physician passes an endoscope through the patient's mouth into the esophagus. The esophagus, stomach, duodenum and sometimes the jejunum are examined. The site for drainage of the pseudocyst is identified. A needle is passed through the scope to the site and the needle is inserted through the small intestinal wall into the pancreatic pseudocyst. The pseudocyst is drained. The endoscope is removed.

43241
The physician examines the upper gastrointestinal tract and places a tube or catheter. The physician passes an endoscope through the patient's mouth into the esophagus. The esophagus, stomach, duodenum, and sometimes the jejunum are viewed. The physician

places a tube or catheter through the endoscope. The endoscope is removed.

43242
The physician examines the upper gastrointestinal tract and performs transendoscopic ultrasound-guided intramural or transmural fine needle aspiration/biopsy. The physician passes an endoscope through the patient's mouth into the esophagus. The esophagus, stomach, duodenum, and sometimes the jejunum are viewed. The endoscope may be removed. A radial scanning echoendoscope is inserted and ultrasound scanning is performed to examine the esophagus, stomach, and the duodenum and/or jejunum; or an ultrasound probe is passed through the already placed endoscope. The site for a fine needle aspiration biopsy is determined. If a radial scanning echoendoscope is used, it is removed and replaced with a curvilinear array echoendoscope. The echoendoscope or ultrasound probe is fitted with a water-filled balloon near the tip; the tip contains a transducer that picks up the ultrasound frequency and relays it to a processor, outside of the body. The water-filled tip is positioned in the esophagus, stomach, or small intestine against the tissue wall next to the predetermined fine needle aspiration (FNA) biopsy site. The area is scanned and an ultrasound image is projected through the processor to a monitor in real-time. The needle is passed through the scope to the biopsy site and a biopsy is taken of the tissue or the needle is inserted through the wall of the esophagus, stomach, or small intestine and into a lesion or other structure, such as a lymph node. The area is biopsied. When the FNA/biopsy is complete, the instruments are removed.

43243-43244
The physician examines the upper gastrointestinal tract to identify and treat esophageal and/or gastric varices. Varices are dilated, enlarged, and twisted (tortuous) veins. The physician passes an endoscope through the patient's mouth into the esophagus. The entire esophagus, stomach, duodenum and sometimes the jejunum are viewed. The physician identifies the varices. In 43243, the physician passes a sclerotherapy needle through the scope, and injects the varices with an agent that causes fibrosis (scarring). The result is obliteration of the varices. In 43244, the physician uses a suction tip to lift the varix. The physician places a rubber band around the base of the varix.

43245
The physician uses an endoscope to examine the upper gastrointestinal tract to locate an obstruction. The physician passes an endoscope through the patient's mouth into the esophagus. The esophagus, stomach, duodenum, and sometimes the jejunum are viewed. If the gastric outlet (pylorus) is obstructed, the physician dilates it using various methods, such as a balloon, guide wire, or bogie. If balloon dilation is performed, the balloon is inflated briefly several time to enlarge the gastric outlet. When the dilation is complete, the balloon and endoscope are removed.

43246
The physician uses an endoscope to examine the upper gastrointestinal tract to guide placement of a gastrostomy tube. The physician passes an endoscope through the patient's mouth into the esophagus. The esophagus, stomach, duodenum, and sometimes the jejunum are viewed. The endoscope is used to guide the placement of a percutaneous gastrostomy tube. The tube is inserted through an incision of the abdomen. When in place, the tube connects the gastric lumen with the exterior abdominal wall.

43247
The physician uses an endoscope to examine the upper gastrointestinal tract to locate and remove a foreign body. The physician passes an endoscope through the patient's mouth into the esophagus. The esophagus, stomach, duodenum and sometimes the jejunum are viewed. The foreign body is located. It may be suctioned, or grasped with forceps and retracted through the endoscope.

43248
The physician uses an endoscope to examine and dilate a portion of the upper gastrointestinal tract. The physician passes an endoscope through the patient's mouth into the esophagus. The esophagus, stomach, duodenum and sometimes the jejunum are viewed. A guidewire is placed through the endoscope and the scope is removed. A dilator is passed into the esophagus over the guidewire. This may be repeated several times using progressively larger dilators.

43249
The physician visualizes the esophagus, stomach and proximal small bowel with an endoscope and dilates an esophageal stricture. The physician inserts the endoscope through the mouth into the esophagus. The endoscope is advanced under direct vision through the esophagus into the stomach. The stomach is visualized and the endoscope is advanced into and through the duodenum and into the proximal jejunum if possible. The endoscope is withdrawn. If an esophageal stricture is present a balloon on a catheter is advanced through the endoscope and through the stricture. The balloon is inflated to correct volume, pressure, and duration according to the package insert. The endoscope is removed.

43250-43251
The physician uses an endoscope to examine the upper gastrointestinal tract and locate and remove tumors, polyps, or other lesions. The physician passes an endoscope through the patient's mouth into the esophagus. The esophagus, stomach, duodenum, and sometimes the jejunum are viewed to locate the lesion. Report 43250, when the base of the lesion is electrocoagulated and severed using biopsy forceps or

Digestive

bipolar cautery. Report 43251 when a snare loop is placed around the base of the lesion and closed (the tissue is electrocoagulated and severed as the loop is closed). The severed tissue is withdrawn through the endoscope. The endoscope is removed.

43255
The physician uses an endoscope to access and control bleeding of the upper gastrointestinal tract. The physician passes an endoscope through the patient's mouth and into the esophagus. Control of bleeding may be achieved using several endoscopic methods including laser therapy, electrocoagulation, rubber band ligation, and injection of the bleeding vessel with sclerosants, ethanol, or adrenaline. The endoscope is removed.

43256
The physician uses an endoscope to examine the upper gastrointestinal tract and performs a transendoscopic stent placement. The physician passes an endoscope through the patient's mouth into the esophagus. The esophagus, stomach, duodenum, and sometimes the jejunum are viewed. The endoscope is placed at the site of an obstruction or stricture, the necessary stent length is determined and predilation of the obstruction or stenosis may be performed. The stent (endoprosthesis) is introduced into the site of the obstruction. Using a commercial delivery system a plastic covering over the stent is removed and the stent self-deploys, shoring-up the walls at a specific site in the esophagus or proximal small intestine. When necessary, a balloon catheter is placed into the stent and gently inflated to more fully deploy the stent. The delivery system and endoscope are removed.

43257
The physician uses thermal energy to the muscle of the lower esophageal sphincter and/or gastric cardia to treat gastroesophageal reflux disease. The physician performs an esophagogastroduodenoscopy (EGD) with a concomitant ultrasound examination for diagnostic purposes. The patient is prepped for an upper gastrointestinal exam, and the scope is advanced through the mouth into the stomach and duodenum or jejunum. An examination is carried out to determine if any bleeding, tumors, erosions, ulcers, or other abnormalities are present. Radiofrequency energy is applied through the scope equipment to apply heat to the muscle of the lower esophageal sphincter and/or the gastric cardia to treat gastroesophageal reflux disease (GERD). The heat is applied by electrodes placed in the esophageal tissue at multiple points above and below the squamocolumnar junction. Thermal lesions are created at the gastroesophageal junction that is thought to ablate the nerve pathways responsible for relaxing the sphincter and allowing reflux to occur. The thermal lesions are also thought to produce a "tightened" effect due to collagen contraction.

43258
The physician uses an endoscope to locate and remove tumors, polyps, or lesions from the upper gastrointestinal tract. The physician passes an endoscope through the patient's mouth into the esophagus. The esophagus, stomach, duodenum and sometimes the jejunum are viewed to locate the lesion. The lesion is destroyed using laser therapy, electrocoagulation, or injection of toxic agents. The endoscope is removed.

43259
The physician uses an endoscope to examine the upper gastrointestinal tract and performs an endoscopic ultrasound examination of the esophagus, stomach, and the duodenum and/or jejunum. The physician passes an endoscope through the patient's mouth into the esophagus. The esophagus, stomach, duodenum, and sometimes the jejunum, are viewed. The endoscope may be removed and a radial scanning echoendoscope inserted; or an ultrasound probe is passed through the already placed endoscope and an ultrasound examination is performed, including the esophagus, stomach, and the duodenum and/or jejunum. The echoendoscope or ultrasound probe is fitted with a water-filled balloon near the tip, which contains a transducer that picks-up the ultrasound frequency and relays it to a processor, outside of the body, where the internal images can be viewed on screen. When the ultrasound scanning is completed, the instruments are removed.

43260-43273
The physician performs an endoscopic retrograde cholangiopancreatography (ERCP) for diagnostic or therapeutic reasons, depending on the code. The physician passes the endoscope through the patient's oropharynx, esophagus, stomach, and into the small intestine. The ampulla of Vater is cannulated and filled with contrast. The common bile duct and the whole biliary tract, including the gallbladder, are visualized. Report 43261 if performed with biopsy; report 43262 if performed with sphincterotomy/papillotomy; report 43263 if performed with a pressure measurement of sphincter of Oddi; report 43264 if performed with an endoscopic retrograde removal of stones from biliary and/or pancreatic ducts; report 43265 if performed with an endoscopic retrograde destruction, lithotripsy of stones; report 43267 if performed with an endoscopic retrograde insertion of nasobiliary or nasopancreatic drainage tube; report 43268 if performed with an endoscopic retrograde insertion of tube or stent into bile or pancreatic duct; report 43269 if performed with an endoscopic retrograde removal of foreign body and/or change of tube or stent; report 43271 if performed with an endoscopic retrograde balloon dilation of ampulla, biliary, and/or pancreatic ducts; and report 43272 if performed with an ablation of tumors, polyps, or other lesions not amenable to removal by hot biopsy forceps, bipolar cautery, or snare

technique. An additional code (43273) is assigned if the physician performs endoscopic cannulation of papilla with direct visualization of the pancreatic and/or common bile duct(s).

43279
The physician performs laparoscopic esophagomyotomy (Heller myotomy), often for treatment of achalasia. Achalasia (a motility disorder of the esophagus) is caused by degeneration of the nerves in the esophageal wall and results in an absence of the typical wave-like motion of the esophagus and lack of relaxation of the lower esophagus. The physician makes several small incisions in the abdominal wall through which a video camera and laparoscopic instruments are inserted. An incision of the esophageal muscle is made using specialized laparoscopic instruments. To prevent reflux, a part of the upper stomach is then wrapped around the lower portion of the esophagus. Laparoscopic instruments are removed, and the small incisions are sutured. A swallowing study is typically obtained prior to discharge.

43280
The physician performs an esophagogastric fundoplasty using a laparoscope. With the patient under anesthesia, the physician places a trocar at the umbilicus into the abdomen and insufflates the abdominal cavity. The physician places a laparoscope through the umbilical incision and additional trocars are placed into the peritoneal space. Additional instruments are introduced through the trocars. The physician identifies the fundus and the esophagus and resects them. The fundus is wrapped around the lower end of the esophagus, which is rejoined to the stomach with sutures. The trocars are removed and the incisions are closed with sutures.

43281-43282
The physician repairs a paraesophageal hernia using a laparoscope and may also perform a fundoplasty when indicated. With the patient under anesthesia and in a supine position, the physician places laparoscopic ports in the upper abdomen, through which the appropriate surgical instruments are inserted. With the left lateral segment of the liver retracted, the hiatus is exposed. The physician reduces the herniated stomach into the abdomen and dissects the hernia sac and gastroesophageal fat pad using a combination of sharp and blunt dissection. If a fundoplasty is indicated, the physician identifies the fundus and the esophagus and resects them. The fundus is wrapped around the lower end of the esophagus, which is rejoined to the stomach with sutures. The instruments and trocars are removed and the incisions are closed with sutures. Report 43281 for a procedure performed without the implantation of mesh and 43282 for one requiring mesh implantation.

43300-43305
The physician repairs a defect in the esophagus using plastic repair or reconstruction. The physician makes a lateral neck incision to access the esophagus. The defect is identified and repaired. In 43305, the physician also transects the tracheoesophageal fistula. The physician closes the tracheal opening and repairs the esophagus. The incision is sutured in layers.

43310-43312
The physician repairs a defect in the esophagus using plastic repair or reconstruction. The physician makes a thoracic incision to access the esophagus. In 43310, the defect is identified and repaired. In 43312, the physician also transects the tracheoesophageal fistula. The physician closes the tracheal opening and repairs the esophagus. The incision is sutured in layers.

43313-43314
The patient is placed in the supine position with the left shoulder elevated and the head extended. A cervical incision is made along the anterior margin of the left sternocleidomastoid muscle, which is retracted laterally. The sternothyroid and sternohyoid muscles are divided, as well as for the branches of the ansa hypoglossi. The inferior pole of the thyroid gland is mobilized and retracted anteriorly. A dissection plane between the trachea and esophagus at the inlet of the thorax can be approached, entered, and dissected. The tracheal and esophageal defects are closed primarily. If the defect is large, a pedicle muscle patch is required to replace the tracheal defect (43314). A denervated and vascularized muscle pedicle is sutured to loose areolar tissue adjacent to the trachea on the opposite side. The esophagus is closed in two layers. The trachea is closed in one layer, with sufficient sutures to make an airtight closure.

43320
The physician performs a plastic repair of the lower esophagus where it joins the upper area (cardia) of the stomach. The physician may also transect the vagus nerve and/or enlarge the pylorus, the distal portion of the stomach. The physician accesses the esophagus through an upper abdominal or lateral thoracic incision. The diseased portion of the esophagus is resected. An anastomosis between the esophageal stump and the cardiac portion of the stomach is created. If the lesion is secondary to acid reflux, a vagotomy may be performed. The anterior and posterior trunks of the vagus nerve are transected to decrease acid production. If the gastric outlet area is decreased, a pyloroplasty may be performed to enlarge the pylorus. The incision is repaired in sutured layers.

43324
The physician mobilizes the lower end of the esophagus and folds the fundus of the stomach around it. The physician accesses the lower esophagus through an upper abdominal incision. The fundus of the stomach is moved up and wrapped around the terminal 3 cm to 4 cm of the esophagus and sutured into place. The lower esophageal sphincter passes through a short tunnel of stomach muscle, which

Digestive

prevents reflux through the sphincter. When performed for hiatal hernia, this procedure may include a sutured tightening of the junction of the diaphragmatic crura behind the esophagus.

43325
The physician pulls up part of the gastric fundus to cover the affected distal esophagus. A bougie (dilating instrument) is placed in the distal esophagus to maintain the esophageal opening. The physician accesses the esophagus and stomach through a transverse abdominal incision. The physician picks up the stomach 1 cm below the gastroesophageal (GE) junction and attaches it 1 cm above the GE junction. This fundic patch is sutured to the esophagus. Next, a Nissen fundoplication is performed by wrapping the rest of the fundus around the esophagus and suturing it into place. The incision is sutured in layers.

43326
The distal portion of the esophagus is lengthened by constructing a tube made of the stomach wall. The physician accesses the esophagus and stomach through a lateral thoracotomy. A bougie (dilating instrument) is passed through the esophagus into the stomach so the bougie spans the gastroesophageal junction. The stomach is divided along the bougie with a GIA stapler, forming a gastric tube which effectively lengthens the esophagus. The fundus of the stomach is dissected, wrapped around the distal esophagus and gastric tube, and sutured into place. The incision is sutured in layers.

43330-43331
The esophagus is repaired using a fundic flap. The physician accesses the esophagus through an upper abdominal or a thoracic incision. For an abdominal approach, report 43330. For a thoracic approach, report 43331. The physician makes an incision into the muscular layers of the distal esophagus and cardia of the stomach (myotomy), leaving a gastric fundic flap. The flap is pulled along the esophagus, and sutured onto the margins of the myotomy. Repair of a hiatal hernia is performed by restoring the herniated portion of the stomach back to the abdomen, then narrowing the hiatal opening of the diaphragm by suturing the left and right crura together. All incisions are sutured in layers.

43340-43341
The physician removes the affected esophagus and stomach, using the remaining stomach and jejunum to restore gastrointestinal continuity. The physician accesses the esophagus and stomach through an upper abdominal or a thoracic incision. For an abdominal approach, report 43340. For a thoracic approach, report 43341. The physician resects the affected part of the esophagus. The stomach is advanced through the hiatus and sutured to the esophageal remnant. The antral portion of the stomach is excised, and the proximal jejunum is sutured to the gastric remnant. The distal end of the duodenum is anastomosed to the jejunum; the proximal end of the duodenum is sutured closed to form a blind pouch. The incision is sutured in layers.

43350-43352
The physician connects the esophagus to the exterior of the body, creating a fistula for drainage. In 43350, the physician makes an upper midline abdominal incision to access the esophagus. In 43351, the physician uses a lateral thoracotomy to access the esophagus. In 43352, access is gained through a cervical incision. The physician makes an incision in the esophagus, or uses the esophageal stump as an opening. The proximal limb of the esophagus is exteriorized and sutured into place, creating a connection from the exterior of the body to the esophageal lumen for mucus drainage. The incision is sutured in layers.

43360-43361
The physician repairs the esophagus and other gastronomic structures for a number of reasons. The physician uses a thoracoabdominal approach as a continuous incision or separate thoracic and abdominal incisions. The stomach is mobilized and repositioned in the chest in the original esophageal bed and sutured to the esophageal stump. The incision and esophageal stoma are closed. A jejunostomy tube is left in place. Report 43361 if performed with colon interposition or small bowel reconstruction, including bowel mobilization, preparation, and/or anastomosis.

43400
The physician accesses the esophagus through a midline abdominal or thoracic incision, and makes a longitudinal incision in the esophagus. The physician locates the varices (tortuous, dilated veins) and ligates them with sutures. The esophagotomy is closed with sutures. The incision is sutured in layers.

43401
The physician uses a stapler to transect and repair the esophagus to remove esophageal varices. Varices are twisted, tortuous veins. The physician accesses the esophagus and stomach through an abdominal or thoracic incision. A stapler, placed through an incision in the anterior wall of the stomach, is directed upward into the esophagus. The stapler is positioned to transect the area around the varices. When the stapler is fired, the esophagus is simultaneously transected and re-anastomosed. The stapler is removed, and the incision in the stomach is repaired. The incision is sutured in layers.

43405
The physician ligates or staples the esophagus to promote healing of a preexisting esophageal perforation. The physician makes a midline upper abdominal incision and retracts the soft tissues to expose the gastroesophageal junction. the physician staples or ligates the junction of the stomach and

Digestive

esophagus. A gastrostomy is created for feeding. The distal end of the esophagus may be exteriorized as a mucus fistula. The incision is sutured in layers.

43410-43415
The physician sutures a wound or injury to the esophagus. The physician accesses the esophagus through a lateral neck, midline abdominal, or thoracic incision. For a cervical approach, report 43410. For a thoracic or transabdominal approach, report 43415. The physician exposes the affected segment of the esophagus, which is repaired by suturing. The incision is sutured in layers.

43420-43425
The physician closes an opening in the esophagus and returns it to its natural position. The physician accesses the defect through an oblique cervical incision along the border of the sternocleidomastoid muscle, a midline abdominal incision, or a thoracic incision. For a cervical approach, report 43420. For a thoracic or transabdominal approach, report 43425. The physician closes the opening with sutures and repositions the esophagus to its normal anatomical position. The incision is sutured in layers.

43450
The physician dilates the esophagus using an unguided dilator. The physician passes a dilator into the patient's throat down into the esophagus until the end of the dilator passes the stricture. A stricture is a decrease in the esophagus opening as a result of cicatricial (scar) contraction or a deposit of abnormal tissue. The dilator is withdrawn after it passes the stricture. This may be repeated several times to dilate the esophagus to an acceptable size.

43453
The physician dilates the esophagus by passing dilators over a guidewire. The physician uses a fluoroscope to place a guidewire into the patient's throat, down the esophagus, and into the stomach. A series of olive-shaped metal dilators (Eder-Puestow) are passed over the guidewire and withdrawn. The process is repeated until the esophagus is dilated to an acceptable size.

43456
The physician dilates the esophagus using a dilator that passes from the stomach through the esophagus. The physician uses a fluoroscope to place a guidewire into the patient's throat, down the esophagus, and into the stomach. A dilator is inserted through a gastrostomy tube and attached to the guidewire. Tension on the oral end of the wire pulls the dilator into the distal esophagus. The process is repeated until the esophagus is dilated to an acceptable size.

43458
The physician uses a balloon to dilate the esophagus which is constricted due to achalasia. In achalasia, the smooth muscles of the gastrointestinal tract fail to relax in response to normal stimulus. The physician uses a fluoroscope to place the balloon at the gastroesophageal junction. The balloon is inflated and deflated several times until the esophagus is dilated to an acceptable size. It is possible to use a guidewire to place the balloon.

43460
The physician inserts a multilumen tube into the esophagus through which a balloon is passed for the tamponade of bleeding esophageal varices. The balloon is inflated to exert pressure on the varices to stop bleeding. The balloon is left inflated so coagulation can occur before the physician proceeds with definitive treatment.

43496
The physician makes an abdominal incision to gain access to the omentum. The greater omentum is reflected to reveal the underlying small intestine. The jejunum is identified and removed. The remaining jejunum is reattached and the omentum is replaced. The free section of jejunum is transferred to another site with anastomosis of its vessels to another structure. Most commonly, the free transfer of a short segment of jejunum occurs between the pharynx and esophagus with microvascular anastomosis of jejunal vessels to the external carotid artery branches and the jugular vein. Portions of the pharynx and/or esophagus have already been resected with removal of cervical esophageal and hypopharyngeal carcinoma. Operative sites are sutured closed.

43500-43510
The physician performs a gastrostomy and explores gastric area, removes a foreign body or corrects a mucosal defect. The physician makes a midline epigastric incision and retracts the skin and underlying tissues laterally. The stomach is incised and explored. In 43500, a foreign body is removed. In 43501, a bleeding ulcer is identified and bleeding is controlled with electrocautery or ligation of vessels, and the mucosa is drawn over the ulcer and sutured. In 43502, an esophagogastric laceration is identified and bleeding is controlled with electrocautery or ligation of vessels, and the mucosa is drawn over the defect and sutured. In 43510, the physician introduces dilators into the esophagus from the stomach to increase the diameter of the esophagus. When dilation is complete, a stent is placed and secured with sutures to maintain to patency. After exploration or repair, the stomach is sutured in layers, the soft tissues are returned to anatomical position, and the incision is sutured in layers.

43520
The physician incises the pyloric muscle. The physician makes a small subcostal incision over the pyloric olive. The peritoneum is incised, the tissues are retracted, and the pylorus is identified. The serosa is incised and the tension of the pyloric muscle is released

with longitudinal incisions. The peritoneum is sutured closed and the operative site is sutured in layers.

43600

The physician obtains a biopsy of the stomach through an endoscope, capsule or tube. The physician anesthetizes the oropharynx and sedates the patient. An endoscope, capsule or tube is passed into the stomach and the stomach mucosa is biopsied. The physician uses a capsule or tube for biopsy of a random location. An endoscope is used for biopsy of a specific lesion.

43605

The physician makes a midline abdominal incision. The peritoneum is incised and tissues are retracted to identify the anterior surface of the stomach. An incision is made in the stomach and the physician explores the mucosa to obtain biopsies. Once biopsies are acquired, the stomach incision is closed with sutures or staples. The peritoneum is sutured closed and the abdominal incision is closed using layered sutures.

43610

The physician performs a local excision of an ulcer or benign tumor of the stomach. The physician makes a midline abdominal incision. Next, the stomach is dissected free of surrounding structures and the area of the tumor identified. The tumor is excised with a normal margin of stomach around the tumor. The defect created in the stomach is closed with sutures or a stapling device. The incision is closed.

43611

The physician performs a local excision of a malignant tumor of the stomach. The physician makes a midline abdominal incision. Next, the stomach is dissected free of surrounding structures and the area of the tumor identified. The tumor is excised with a normal margin of stomach around the tumor. The defect created in the stomach is closed with sutures or a stapling device. The incision is closed.

43620-43621

The physician removes the stomach and approximates a limb of small bowel to the esophagus by performing an esophagoenterostomy in 43620 or a Roux-en-Y esophagojejunostomy in 43621. The physician makes a midline abdominal incision. The stomach is dissected free of surrounding structures and its blood supply is divided. The stomach is divided at the gastroesophageal junction and at the gastroduodenal junction and removed. In 43620, the remaining duodenal end of the intestine is simply mobilized to the end of the esophagus and connected. In 43621, a measured limb of Roux, or limb of small intestine, is created by dividing the upper jejunum. The distal part of the now divided upper jejunum, the limb in continuity with the ileum, is brought up and anastomosed to the esophagus. The proximal end of the divided jejunum, the segment containing the duodenum, must be connected back into the limb of small bowel farther down from the esophageal anastomosis. This maintains continuity for the duodenal section, which was sealed upon removal of the stomach, but which is also receiving bile from the liver and gallbladder as well as pancreatic juice.

43622

The physician removes the stomach and forms a pouch of small bowel and approximates this to the esophagus. The physician makes a midline abdominal incision. Next, the stomach is dissected free of surrounding structures and its blood supply divided. The stomach is divided at the gastroesophageal junction and the gastroduodenal junction removed. The proximal jejunum is divided and the distal end of bowel is folded upon itself and approximated in such a way to form a pouch. The pouch is connected to the esophagus. The divided proximal jejunum is connected to the limb of small bowel distal to the esophageal anastomosis to restore intestinal continuity. The incisions are closed.

43631

The physician removes the distal stomach and approximates the proximal stomach to the duodenum. The physician makes a midline abdominal incision. The distal stomach (antrum) is dissected free from surrounding structures and the blood supply to the antrum is divided. Next, the gastroduodenal junction is divided and the stomach is divided in its middle portion removing the antrum. An anastomosis is made between the proximal stomach and the duodenum with staples or sutures. The incision is closed.

43632

The physician removes the distal stomach and approximates the proximal stomach to the jejunum. The physician makes a midline abdominal incision. The distal stomach (antrum) is dissected free from surrounding structures and the blood supply to the antrum is divided. Next, the gastroduodenal junction is divided and the stomach is divided in its middle portion removing the antrum. An anastomosis is made between the proximal stomach and the jejunum with staples or sutures. The incision is closed.

43633

The physician removes the distal stomach (antrum) and performs an anastomosis between the proximal stomach and a Roux-en-Y limb of jejunum. The physician makes a midline abdominal incision. Next, the distal stomach is dissected free of surrounding structures and the blood supply to the antrum is divided. The gastroduodenal junction and the middle portion of the stomach are divided and the antrum is removed. The vagus nerves, as they pass from the esophagus onto the stomach, are usually divided. The proximal jejunum is divided and the distal limb of jejunum is connected to the proximal stomach. The proximal jejunum is connected to the limb of jejunum distal to the gastrojejunostomy to restore intestinal continuity. The incisions are closed.

43634
The physician removes the distal stomach (antrum) and performs an anastomosis between the stomach and a pouch formed of jejunum. The physician makes a midline abdominal incision. The distal stomach is dissected free of surrounding structures and the blood supply to the antrum is divided. The gastroduodenal junction and the middle portion of the stomach are divided and the antrum is removed. The vagus nerves, as they pass from the esophagus onto the stomach, are usually divided. The proximal jejunum is divided and the distal end is folded upon itself and approximated in such a way to form a pouch. The pouch is connected to the proximal stomach and the proximal end of the divided jejunum is connected to the jejunal limb distal to the pouch anastomosis to establish intestinal continuity. The incision is closed.

43635
The physician performs this with a separately reportable partial distal gastrectomy and repairs the stomach and severs vagus nerves. The physician uses a midline abdominal approach. The distal stomach (antrum) is dissected free and the blood supply to the antrum divided. The distal stomach is removed and the proximal stomach is sutured to the duodenum. Truncal vagotomy is performed by severing both right and left vagus nerves just below the diaphragm.

43640-43641
The physician severs the vagus nerves and widens the pyloric canal, with or without making an incision in the stomach. The physician uses a midline upper abdominal incision to expose the muscular band surrounding the distal opening of the stomach. A longitudinal incision is made in the pylorus. The incision is closed with a single full thickness suture layer. The two branches of the vagus nerve are exposed and a truncal vagotomy is performed by severing both right and left vagus nerves. A gastrostomy may be created by inserting a tube from the stomach to the external surface of the abdominal wall. Report 43641 if performed with a parietal cell procedure.

43644
The physician performs a laparoscopic gastric bypass for morbid obesity by partitioning the stomach and performing a small bowel division with anastomosis to the proximal stomach (Roux-en-Y gastroenterostomy). This bypasses the majority of the stomach. The physician places a trocar though an incision above the umbilicus and insufflates the abdominal cavity. The laparoscope and additional trocars are placed through small portal incisions. The stomach is mobilized and the proximal stomach is divided with a stapling device along the lesser curvature, leaving only a small proximal pouch in continuity with the esophagus. A short limb of the proximal small bowel (150 cm or less) is divided and the distal end of the short intestinal limb is brought up and anastomosed to the proximal gastric pouch. The other end of the divided bowel is connected back into the small bowel distal to the short limb's gastric anastomosis to restore intestinal continuity. The instruments are removed.

43645
The physician performs a laparoscopic gastric bypass with small intestine reconstruction to limit absorption. This procedure is done to combine gastric restriction of intake with limited intestinal absorption. In one method used, the physician places a trocar though an incision above the umbilicus and insufflates the abdominal cavity. The laparoscope and additional trocars are placed through small portal incisions. The stomach is mobilized and the distal half is resected along a line from the lesser to greater curvature, leaving a "pouch" of stomach, which is connected directly to the final, distal section of small intestine. The bypassed duodenum, jejunum, and upper part of the divided ileum—the segment in connection with the gallbladder and pancreas, or the biliopancreatic loop—is anastomosed back to the common distal segment of the small intestine. This leaves a short common channel where food coming through the shortened alimentary tract combines with digestive juices from the much longer biliary tract before entering the colon. The instruments are removed.

43647-43648
The physician performs a laparoscopic placement of gastric neurostimulator electrodes. The physician makes an incision and places a trocar at the umbilicus to insufflate the abdomen. The laparoscope is placed through the umbilical port and additional trocars are placed into the abdominal cavity. The antrum of the stomach is identified and the physician secures two electrodes into the muscle of the pyloric antrum. The electrodes are connected to a neurostimulator that has been secured in a subcutaneous pocket in the abdomen in a separately reportable procedure. The physician removes the laparoscope and tools from the abdomen, which is deflated and repaired with sutures. Report 43647 if electrodes are placed or if existing electrodes are removed and replaced with new ones. Report 43648 for the revision or removal of the electrodes.

43651
The physician performs laparoscopic truncal vagotomy. The physician places a trocar through an incision above the umbilicus and insufflates the abdominal cavity. The laparoscope is placed through the supraumbilical port and additional trocars are placed into the abdominal cavity. The fascial anterior to the esophagus is incised and the distal esophagus is mobilized. The anterior and posterior vagal nerve trunks are identified and divided. The physician removes a small segment of each nerve. The trocars are removed and the incisions are closed.

43652
The physician performs laparoscopic selective or highly selective vagotomy. The physician places a trocar though an incision above the umbilicus and insufflates the abdominal cavity. The laparoscope is placed through the supraumbilical port and additional trocars are placed into the abdominal cavity. The distal esophagus is mobilized and the anterior and posterior vagal nerve trunks are identified. The main nerve trunks are followed down onto the stomach and the branches from the nerves to the proximal half of the stomach are divided. The trocars are removed and the incisions are closed.

43653
Using a laparoscope, the physician constructs a temporary or permanent gastrostomy for feeding. With the patient under anesthesia, the physician places a trocar at the umbilicus into the abdomen and insufflates the abdominal cavity. The physician places a laparoscope through the umbilical incision. An additional trocar is inserted through the abdominal wall into the intra-abdominal cavity at a previously determined site where the gastrostomy will reside. The gastrostomy tube is pulled through the trocar from outside the abdomen into the intra-abdominal cavity. The physician identifies the stomach and introduces instruments to open the organ and create a viable receptacle for the tube. The tip of the gastrostomy tube is inserted into the stomach, and the tube is clamped off on the outside of the body and sutured into place on the stomach. Additional sutures are placed in the abdominal wall to hold the gastrostomy tube in place and to secure the tube. The trocars are removed and the incisions are closed with staples or sutures.

43752
The physician places a naso- or orogastric tube. The patient is placed in an upright position. The physician checks the nostrils for obstruction and selects the nostril for tube insertion. The physician may swab the nostril and spray the oropharynx with medication to numb the nasal passage and suppress the gag reflex. Next, the physician lubricates the tube, elevates the tip of the nose, and introduces the nasogastric tube into the nostril. The tube is advanced and the position of the tube is checked using fluoroscopy to ensure it is aligned to enter the oropharynx. As the patient swallows, the physician advances the tube through the pharynx, esophagus, and into the stomach. Air is injected into the tube (at the nose) while the physician listens with a stethoscope positioned at the stomach for the air to come out of the tube. Gastric contents are aspirated. These precautions are performed to ensure the tube is positioned in the stomach. The nasogastric tube is taped to the nostril. If the tube is fitted with a balloon (at the end of the tube in the stomach), it is inflated to hold the tube in place. This code includes the fluoroscopic guidance, image documentation, and report.

43760
The physician changes a gastrostomy tube via percutaneous approach. No imaging or endoscopic guidance is utilized. If the old gastrostomy tube has been placed endoscopically, the physician must remove it by snaring and pulling it out through the mouth. A new tube is placed percutaneously through the abdominal wall via the existing tract. A small incision is made through the skin and fascia. A large bore needle with suture attached is passed through the incision into the lumen of the stomach. The needle is snared and the needle and suture are removed via the mouth. The gastrostomy tube is connected to the suture and passed through the mouth into the stomach and out the abdominal wall. The gastrostomy tube is sutured to the skin.

43761
The physician repositions a nasogastric or orogastric feeding tube through the duodenum for enteric nutrition. Under separately reportable fluoroscopic guidance, the physician passes the feeding tube through the stomach into the distal duodenum.

43770
The physician performs a laparoscopic gastric restrictive procedure in which an adjustable gastric restrictive device, such as a gastric band with subcutaneous port components, is inserted. This is a gastric restrictive procedure for treatment of morbid obesity that does not permanently alter the gastrointestinal tract. The physician places a trocar though an incision, generally above the umbilicus, and insufflates the abdominal cavity. The laparoscope and additional trocars are placed through small portal incisions. The silicone gastric band is introduced into the peritoneal cavity via a trocar and is placed and secured around the upper stomach to form a smaller stomach pouch with a narrowed outlet. A small port, or reservoir, is placed under the skin at the time of surgery and connected to the silicone band by tubing to facilitate postoperative adjustments of the outlet size by the addition or removal of saline via the port. The instruments are removed and the incisions are closed.

43771
The physician performs laparoscopic revision of an adjustable gastric restrictive device. This revision is most often performed for slippage of the device or for dilation of the gastric pouch. The physician places a trocar though an incision, generally above the umbilicus, and insufflates the abdominal cavity. The laparoscope and additional trocars are placed through small portal incisions. Saline is removed from the gastric restrictive device and the device is repositioned around the upper stomach. Saline is slowly reintroduced through the existing port to secure the device position. Once the device is in place, the instruments are removed and the incisions are closed.

This code reports revision of the device component only.

43772-43773

The physician performs laparoscopic removal of an adjustable gastric restrictive device component. The physician places a trocar though an incision, generally above the umbilicus, and insufflates the abdominal cavity. The laparoscope and additional trocars are placed through small portal incisions. Saline is removed from the gastric restrictive device and the component is removed. Once the device component has been removed, the instruments are withdrawn and the incisions are closed. Report 43772 for removal of an adjustable gastric restrictive device component only. Report 43773 for removal and replacement of an adjustable gastric restrictive device component only.

43774

The physician performs laparoscopic removal of an adjustable gastric restrictive device and subcutaneous port components. The physician places a trocar though an incision, generally above the umbilicus, and insufflates the abdominal cavity. The laparoscope and additional trocars are placed through small portal incisions. Saline is removed from the gastric device and the device is removed. Once the device has been removed, the subcutaneous port components are removed. The instruments are withdrawn and the incisions are closed.

43775

The physician performs a laparoscopic sleeve gastrectomy (LSG), a gastric restrictive procedure for the treatment of morbid obesity. Following appropriate anesthesia, the physician begins the longitudinal gastrectomy by placing a trocar though an incision, generally above the umbilicus, and insufflating the abdominal cavity. The laparoscope and additional trocars are placed through small portal incisions. The physician divides the greater curvature of the stomach from the left crus of the diaphragm to a point distal to the pylorus. The short gastric vessels are coagulated and gastric staplers are used. A gastric tube (sleeve) is formed and the remaining 80 percent of the stomach is excised. The instruments are removed and the incisions are closed.

43800

The physician repairs the pylorus. The physician makes an upper abdominal incision through skin, fascia, and muscles to expose the pylorus, a muscular band surrounding the distal opening of the stomach. A longitudinal incision is made in the pylorus. The incision is closed with a single full thickness suture layer.

43810

The physician performs a gastroduodenostomy. The physician uses an upper midline epigastric incision through fascia and muscle. The distal end of the greater curvature of the stomach is removed. The duodenum is mobilized and connected to the greater curvature. The anastomosis is closed with interrupted stitches and the abdominal incision is closed.

43820-43825

The physician performs a gastrojejunostomy to create a direct passage between the stomach and jejunum. The physician makes an upper abdominal incision to expose the stomach and small intestine. The distal portion of the stomach is resected and the jejunum is anastomosed to the gastric stump. The duodenal stump is closed. The vagal nerves are preserved. Report 43825 if a vagotomy is also performed.

43830-43831

The physician constructs a temporary or permanent gastrostomy for instillation of nutrients. After making a midline incision in the upper abdomen, the physician chooses a gastrostomy site on the middle anterior surface of the stomach. Stay sutures are placed and a small stab wound is made between purse string sutures. A gastrostomy tube is inserted and the purse string sutures are tied. The gastrostomy tube is withdrawn through a stab wound in the abdominal wall and stay sutures are placed in the posterior fascia. The abdominal incision is closed. Report 43831 if performed to facilitate feeding a neonate.

43832

The physician constructs a permanent gastrostomy for instillation of nutrients. After a small midline upper abdominal incision, the physician creates a flap with its base at the greater curvature of the stomach. The flap is converted into a tube by closure of the stomach incision. The tube is brought through the skin surface via a stab wound or tunnel. The end of the tube is everted slightly and sutured to the skin. The abdominal incision is closed with sutures.

43840

The physician repairs an ulcer, wound, or injury to the stomach or duodenum. The ulcer or wound is exposed by the physician via a midline upper abdominal incision or a transverse supraumbilical incision through skin, fascia, and muscle. The perforation is sutured closed and the peritoneal cavity is irrigated and suctioned to remove contamination. The abdominal fascia and peritoneum are closed in one layer. The skin and subcutaneous layers are not closed unless the perforation is less than two hours old.

43842-43843

The physician alters the stomach's size to help stem morbid obesity. The physician exposes the lesser curvature of the stomach via a midline abdominal incision through skin, fascia, and muscles. In 43842, double row of staples is placed in the upper portion of the stomach to create a small stoma. A small strip of mesh or a Silastic ring is wrapped around the stoma and stapled to itself. Report 43843 if the technique used is other than the vertical-banded gastroplasty, and allows for staples restricting other parts of the stomach.

43845
A partial gastrectomy with pylorus-preserving duodenoileostomy and ileoileostomy is done to combine gastric restriction with limited intestinal absorption for weight loss. This procedure is called a biliopancreatic diversion with duodenal switch. The stomach is resected along the greater curvature, leaving the pyloric valve intact with the remaining stomach that maintains its functionality. A portion of the duodenum is also left within the food track to preserve the pylorus/duodenum pathway. The duodenum is divided near the pyloric valve. The small intestine is also divided. The distal end of the small intestine in continuity with the large intestine is brought up and anastomosed to the short duodenal segment on the stomach. The other end of the small intestine—the duodenal segment in connection with the gallbladder and pancreas, or the biliopancreatic loop—is attached to the newly anastomosed other limb further down near the large intestine. This forms a 75 to 100 cm "common loop" where the contents of both these segments channel together before dumping into the large intestine.

43846
The physician performs a gastric bypass for morbid obesity by partitioning the stomach and performing a small bowel division and anastomosis to the proximal stomach (Roux-en-Y gastrojejunostomy). This bypasses the majority of the stomach. The physician makes a midline abdominal incision. The stomach is mobilized and the proximal stomach is divided with a stapling device along the lesser curvature, leaving only a small proximal pouch in continuity with the esophagus. A short limb of the proximal small bowel (150 cm or less) is divided and the distal end of the short intestinal limb is brought up and anastomosed to the proximal gastric pouch. The other end of the divided bowel is connected back into the small bowel distal to the short limb's gastric anastomosis to restore intestinal continuity. The incision is closed.

43847
The physician partitions the stomach and performs a small intestine anastomosis to the proximal stomach (Roux-en-Y gastrojejunostomy) in order to bypass the majority of the stomach. The physician makes a midline abdominal incision. Next, the stomach is mobilized and the proximal stomach is divided with a stapling device leaving only a small proximal pouch in continuity with the esophagus. The small intestine is reconstructed so that it is partially bypassed to limit the amount of area available for absorption of nutrients. The incision is closed.

43848
The physician uses an open technique to revise a failed gastric restrictive procedure for morbid obesity. Indications for revision include stomal stenosis, stomal dilation, non-emptying gastric pouch, gastroesophageal reflux, staple dehiscence, intragastric foreign body, gastric fistula, gastroesophageal fistula, failure to maintain weight loss, breakdown of staple continuity, and restored gastric continuity. This code is not used to report revision of an adjustable gastric restrictive device. Revision techniques vary depending on the technique used in initial gastric restrictive procedure (i.e., gastroplasty, partial gastrectomy, gastric bypass) and the nature of the gastric restrictive failure. Types of revision include gastroplasty, conversion of a gastroplasty to a gastric bypass, and revision of a gastric bypass. The physician makes a midline abdominal incision. Next, the stomach and previous anastomoses are dissected free of surrounding structures. This can involve painstaking lysis of adhesions between the liver, stomach, distal esophagus, colon, and/or spleen. The physician performs the required revision. If a gastroplasty is performed, a double row of staples is placed in the upper portion of the stomach to create a small stoma. A small strip of mesh or a Silastic ring is wrapped around the stoma and stapled to itself. A partial gastrectomy involves resecting the stomach along the greater curvature and leaving the pyloric valve intact with the remaining stomach to maintain functionality. If a gastric bypass is performed, the stomach is partitioned, the small bowel divided, and the small bowel is reanastomosed to the proximal stomach.

43850-43855
The physician revises and constructs an anastomoses between the stomach and the duodenum. The physician exposes the stomach and small intestine via a midline upper abdominal incision through skin, muscles, and fascia. The connection between the stomach and duodenum (gastroduodenostomy) is severed and the duodenal stump is closed. An 8 cm to 10 cm segment of the jejunum is reversed and anastomosed to the distal end of the stomach. The excised duodenum and segment of jejunum are connected to the jejunum. The abdominal incision is closed. Report 43855 if a vagotomy is performed in conjunction with this procedure.

43860-43865
The physician revises an anastomoses between the stomach and the jejunum. The physician exposes the stomach and small intestine via a midline upper abdominal incision through skin, muscles, and fascia. About 8 cm to 10 cm of the jejunum limb is divided, reversed and connected to the distal end of the stomach. The short reversed segment is connected to the jejunum and the remnant of jejunum and duodenum are anastomosed to the long segment of jejunum. A partial gastrectomy or intestine resection may be performed. The abdominal incision is closed. Report 43865 if a vagotomy is performed in conjunction with this procedure.

43870
The physician closes a gastrostomy no longer needed. The physician enters through previous gastrostomy. The stomach is dissected free of the abdominal wall. The stomach gastrostomy site is closed with sutures. The abdominal incision is closed with layered sutures.

43880
The physician closes a gastrocolic fistula. The physician exposes stomach and colon via a midline abdominal incision through skin, fascia, and muscle. The fistula is excised and the bowel mobilized. The fistula is located and resected. The abdominal incision is closed.

43881-43882
The physician performs placement of gastric neurostimulator electrodes in an open procedure. Through a laparotomy, the physician enters the abdominal cavity. The antrum of the stomach is identified and the physician secures two electrodes to the muscle of the pyloric antrum. The electrodes are connected to a neurostimulator that has been secured in a subcutaneous pocket in the abdomen in a separately reportable procedure. The physician closes the laparotomy with layered sutures. Report 43881 if electrodes are placed or if existing electrodes are removed and replaced with new ones. Report 43882 for the revision or removal of the electrodes.

43886
The physician performs an open revision of the subcutaneous port component used in a gastric restrictive procedure for the treatment of morbid obesity. The subcutaneous port is the access point for infusing saline into the gastric band to adjust the band for optimal performance. The physician makes an incision through the old scar near the original port. Dissection is carried down to the port. The sutures adhering the port to the fascia may be removed so that necessary repairs and revisions can be made. The port is secured to the fascia with sutures. The incision is closed with sutures.

43887-43888
The physician performs an open removal or a removal and replacement of the subcutaneous port component used in a gastric restrictive procedure for the treatment of morbid obesity. The subcutaneous port is the access point for infusing saline into the gastric band to adjust the band for optimal performance. The physician makes an incision through the old scar near the original port. Dissection is carried down to the port and the sutures adhering the port to the fascia are removed. The physician severs the tubing connected to the port. In 43887, the subcutaneous port is removed. In 43888, the original subcutaneous port is removed and replaced with a new port to which the tubing is reattached. The replacement port is secured to the fascia with sutures. The incision is closed with sutures.

44005
The physician frees intestinal adhesions. The physician enters the abdomen through a midline abdominal incision. The bowel is freed from its attachments to itself, the abdominal wall and/or other abdominal organs. The abdominal incision is closed.

44010
The physician opens the duodenum, explores the segment, collects tissue samples for biopsy, or removes a foreign body. The physician exposes the proximal duodenum via a midline upper abdominal incision through skin, fascia, and muscles. The duodenum is incised in a longitudinal fashion and the area of concern is exposed. The physician may choose during exploration to excise tissues, biopsy, or remove foreign bodies. The duodenum is closed with transverse interrupted sutures. The abdominal incision is closed.

44015
The physician places a tube in the jejunum for feeding during a separately reportable operation. The physician makes an abdominal incision. A section of proximal jejunum is selected and a tube is placed in the jejunum and brought out through the abdominal wall. This segment of jejunum is securely tacked to the inside of the abdominal wall. The incision is closed.

44020
The physician makes an incision in the small intestine (enterotomy) for biopsy, exploration or foreign body removal. The physician makes an abdominal incision. Next, the selected segment of small intestine is mobilized and incised to expose the area of interest. A biopsy is taken or a foreign body is removed. The enterotomy is closed with staples or sutures. The abdominal incision is closed.

44021
The physician places a tube in the small bowel for decompression. The physician makes an abdominal incision. Next, the small bowel is dissected free of surrounding structures. The proximal small bowel is incised (enterotomy) and a tube is threaded through the small bowel. The proximal end of the tube is brought out through the abdominal wall. The bowel is tacked to the inside of the abdominal wall where the tube goes through. The abdominal incision is closed.

44025
The physician makes an incision in the colon (colotomy) through which the colon is explored for biopsy or foreign body removal. The physician makes an abdominal incision. Next, the selected segment of colon is mobilized and a colotomy is made in the area of interest. The colon is explored and biopsy performed or foreign body removed. The colotomy is closed with staples or sutures. The abdominal incision is closed.

44050-44055

The physician reduces a volvulus, intussusception or internal hernia through an abdominal incision. The physician makes an abdominal incision. Next, the abdomen is explored and the twisted segment of bowel (volvulus), telescoped segment of bowel (intussusception) or internal hernia is manually reduced. The bowel is inspected to ensure viability. The incision is closed. Report 44055 if the problem is corrected by lysis of duodenal bands or reduction of midgut volvulus.

44100

The physician performs a peroral biopsy of the small intestine with a capsule. The physician places a biopsy capsule attached to a tube through the mouth and directs it into the small intestine usually with fluoroscopy. The capsule blade is fired by placing suction on the tube and a biopsy obtained. The tube and capsule are withdrawn.

44110

The physician removes one or more lesions in the small or large intestine through an incision in the colon (colotomy) or small intestine (enterotomy) without bowel resection. The physician makes an abdominal incision. Next, the segment of small intestine or colon containing the lesions is mobilized. An incision is made in the small intestine or colon and the lesions are removed. The enterotomy or colotomy is closed with staples or sutures. The abdominal incision is closed.

44111

The physician removes one or more lesions in the small or large intestine through multiple incisions in the colon (colotomy) or small intestine (enterotomy) without bowel resection. The physician makes an abdominal incision. Next, the segments of small intestine or colon containing lesions are mobilized. Incisions are made in the small intestine or colon and the lesions are removed. The enterotomies or colotomies are closed with staples or sutures. The abdominal incision is closed.

44120

The physician resects a segment of small intestine and performs an anastomosis between the remaining bowel ends. The physician makes an abdominal incision. Next, the selected segment of small bowel is isolated and divided proximally and distally to the remaining bowel and removed. The remaining bowel ends are reapproximated using staples or sutures. The incision is closed.

44121

The physician resects one or more segments of small intestine and performs an anastomosis between the remaining intestinal ends. The physician makes an abdominal incision. Next, the selected segments of small intestine are isolated and divided proximally and distally to the remaining intestine and removed. The remaining intestinal ends are reapproximated using staples or sutures. The incision is closed.

44125

The physician resects a segment of small bowel and brings the proximal end of bowel through the abdominal wall onto the skin as a stoma. The physician makes an abdominal incision. Next, the selected segment of small bowel is isolated and divided proximally and distally to the remaining bowel and removed. The proximal end of the remaining small bowel is brought through a separate incision in the abdominal wall onto the skin as a stoma. The initial incision is closed.

44126-44128

The physician resects a segment of small intestine and may perform tapering to fit the area of anastomosis. The physician makes an abdominal incision. The selected segment of small intestine is isolated and divided proximally and distally to the remaining bowel and removed. An end-to-end anastomosis of the proximal rectum to the distal and canal is performed. The remaining bowel ends are reapproximated using staples or sutures. The incision is closed. Report 44126 for a single resection and anastomosis. Report 44127 when tapering (gradually narrowing toward one end) of the bowel is performed with the resection and anastomosis. Report 44128 for each additional resection and anastomosis beyond the first one.

44130

The physician performs a small bowel anastomosis and may bring one end of small bowel through the abdominal wall onto the skin as a stoma. The physician makes an abdominal incision. A segment of small bowel may be resected. Next, a small bowel anastomosis is performed with staples or sutures. An end or loop of small bowel may be brought through a separate incision in the abdominal wall onto the skin as a stoma. The initial incision is closed.

44132-44133

The physician performs an open donor enterectomy from a cadaver donor in 44132 and an open partial enterectomy from a living donor in 44133. With the cadaver or living donor supine on the operating room table, the physician performs a midline abdominal incision. Tissue is incised and muscles are separated down to the level of the small intestine. In 44132, the small intestine can be mobilized and excised from the cadaver, as needed. In 44133, only a portion of the small intestine can be excised from the living donor and the bowel ends are anastomosed to restore continuity. Any bleeding is controlled, the area is irrigated, and the incision is closed with layered sutures. The acquired intestine is preserved for transplantation into the recipient, who may be hundreds of miles away. The organ remains under refrigeration, specially packed in a sealable container with some preserving solution and kept on ice in a suitable carrier.

44135-44136
The physician performs an intestinal allotransplantation. The patient is placed supine on the operating room table. After adequate preparation, the physician performs a midline abdominal incision, tissue is incised, and muscles are separated down to the level of the small intestine. The area of small intestine to be transplanted is located. An incision is made through the intestine, the area is examined, and the free intestinal edges are debrided or excised in order to accept the intestinal transplant. The previously excised small intestinal allograft, from a cadaver (44135) or partially excised small intestinal allograft, from a living donor (44136) are removed from the maintenance solution, and irrigated. The allograft is sized and is anastomosed first to one free end of the patient's small intestine and then the opposite end of the patient's small intestine. Any bleeding is controlled, the area is irrigated, and the small bowel is anatomically positioned in the abdominal cavity. The wound is closed with layered sutures over a drain. A dressing is applied.

44137
The physician removes a previously transplanted intestinal allograft due to complications such as infection or rejection. The physician makes an abdominal incision. The intestinal allograft is isolated and resected at sites distal and proximal to the anastomosis sites of the previously placed intestinal graft. The distal and proximal ends of the remaining intestine are reapproximated using staples or sutures. The incision is closed.

44139
The physician mobilizes the splenic flexure in conjunction with a partial colon resection. The physician makes an abdominal incision. The attachments between the splenic flexure of the colon and the lateral abdominal wall and spleen are dissected free and taken down to mobilize the colon. This is done to mobilize adequate length of colon in conjunction with a partial colon resection. At the completion of the procedure the abdominal incision is closed.

44140
The physician resects a segment of colon and performs an anastomosis between the remaining ends of colon. The physician makes an abdominal incision. Next, the selected segment of colon is isolated and divided proximally and distally to the remaining colon and removed. The remaining ends of colon are reapproximated with staples or sutures. The incision is closed.

44141
The physician resects a segment of colon and brings the proximal end of colon through the abdominal wall onto the skin as a colostomy. The physician makes an abdominal incision. Next, the selected segment of colon is isolated and divided proximally and distally to the remaining colon and removed. The proximal end of colon is brought through a separate incision on the abdominal wall and onto the skin as a colostomy. Alternately, the remaining bowel ends may be reapproximated and a loop of colon proximal to the anastomosis brought through a separate incision on the abdominal wall onto the skin as a loop colostomy. The initial incision is closed.

44143
The physician resects a segment of colon and brings the proximal end of colon through the abdominal wall onto the skin as a colostomy. The physician makes an abdominal incision. Next, the selected segment of colon is isolated and divided proximally and distally to the remaining colon and removed. The proximal end of colon is brought through a separate incision on the abdominal wall onto the skin as a colostomy. The distal end of colon is closed with staples or sutures and left in the abdomen. The initial incision is closed.

44144
The physician resects a segment of colon. The proximal and distal ends of colon are brought through the abdominal wall onto the skin as a colostomy and mucus fistula. The physician makes an abdominal incision. Next, the selected segment of colon is isolated and divided proximally and distally to the remaining colon and removed. The proximal end of colon or terminal ileum and the distal end of colon are brought through separate incisions on the abdominal wall onto the skin as an ileostomy or colostomy and mucus fistula. The initial abdominal incision is closed.

44145
The physician resects a segment of distal colon or rectum and performs a low colorectal anastomosis in the pelvis. The physician makes an abdominal incision. Next, the distal colon and rectum are mobilized and the selected segment divided proximally and distally to the remaining colon. An anastomosis is created between the proximal colon and remaining rectum in the pelvis with staples or sutures. The incision is closed.

44146
The physician resects a segment of distal colon or rectum and performs a low colorectal anastomosis in the pelvis and creates a proximal colostomy. The physician makes an abdominal incision. Next, the distal colon and rectum are mobilized and the selected segment of diseased colon and/or rectal tissue is removed. The new ends are brought together and an anastomosis is done between the colon and the rectum low in the pelvis with staples or sutures

Digestive

(coloproctostomy). A loop of colon above the newly sutured anastomosis is brought out through a separate incision in the abdominal wall and fixed there so the colon will empty through this artificial opening in the skin as a colostomy, usually temporary, to divert the fecal stream while the anastomosis heals. The initial incision is closed.

44147
The physician removes a segment of colon through a combined abdominal and transanal approach and reapproximates the remaining ends of the colon. The physician makes an abdominal incision. The distal colon and rectum are mobilized also by using a transanal approach. The segment of the colon to be eliminated is divided at the appropriate distal and proximal points and the remaining ends are anastomosed. The abdominal and transanal incisions are closed.

44150
The physician removes the entire colon and performs an ileostomy or an anastomosis between the ileum and rectum. The physician makes an abdominal incision. Next, the colon is mobilized and the colorectal junction and terminal ileum is divided. The colon is removed. The terminal ileum is approximated to the rectum or brought out through a separate incision on the abdominal wall onto the skin as an ileostomy. The initial incision is closed.

44151
The physician removes the entire colon and creates a reservoir of distal ileum (Kock pouch). The reservoir is brought out through the abdominal wall as a continent stoma. The physician makes an abdominal incision. Next, the colon is mobilized. The colorectal junction and terminal ileum is divided and the colon removed. The distal ileum is folded upon itself and approximated to form a pouch and valve. The distal end of the pouch is brought through a separate incision on the abdominal wall onto the skin as a continent ileostomy. The initial incision is closed.

44155
The physician removes the entire colon and rectum and brings the terminal ileum out through the abdominal wall onto the skin as an ileostomy. The physician makes an abdominal incision. Next, the colon and rectum are mobilized, the proximal rectum and distal ileum are divided, and the colon and proximal rectum are removed. The distal rectum is mobilized and removed through a perineal approach. The terminal ileum is brought out through a separate incision on the abdominal wall onto the skin as an ileostomy. The abdominal and perineal incisions are closed.

44156
The physician removes the entire colon and rectum and creates a pouch from the terminal ileum (Kock pouch) that is brought out through the abdominal wall as a continent ileostomy. The physician makes an abdominal incision. Next, the colon and rectum are mobilized, the proximal rectum and distal ileum are divided, and the colon and proximal rectum are removed. The distal rectum is mobilized and removed through a perineal approach. The terminal ileum is folded upon itself and approximated to form a pouch with a valve. The end of the pouch is brought out through a separate abdominal incision onto the skin as a continent ileostomy. The abdominal and perineal incisions are closed.

44157-44158
The physician removes the entire colon and rectum, strips the mucosa from the distal rectum, and performs an anastomosis between the terminal ileum and anus. The physician makes an abdominal incision. Next, the colon and rectum are mobilized. The mucosa of the distal rectum is stripped from a perineal approach. In 44157, the terminal ileum and rectum are divided and the colon is removed. The terminal ileum is pulled through the remaining muscular cuff of the rectum and approximated to the anus with sutures. A loop of ileum may be brought out through the abdominal wall onto the skin as an ileostomy proximal to the anastomosis. In 44158, the terminal ileum is folded upon itself and approximated in order to form a pouch. The pouch is pulled through the remaining muscular tube of the rectum and approximated to the anus with sutures. A loop of ileum may be brought out through a separate incision on the abdominal wall onto the skin as an ileostomy proximal to the anastomosis.

44160
The physician makes an abdominal incision and removes a segment of the colon and terminal ileum and performs an anastomosis between the remaining ileum and colon. The physician makes an abdominal incision. Next, the selected segment of colon and terminal ileum are isolated and divided proximal and distal to the remaining bowel and removed. An anastomosis is created between the distal ileum and remaining colon with staples or sutures. The incision is closed.

44180
The physician performs laparoscopic enterolysis to free intestinal adhesions. With the patient under anesthesia, the physician places a trocar at the umbilicus into the abdominal or retroperitoneal space and insufflates the abdominal cavity. The physician places a laparoscope through the umbilical incision and additional trocars are placed into the abdomen. Intestinal adhesions are identified and instruments are passed through to dissect and remove the adhesions. The trocars are removed and the incisions are closed with sutures.

44186
The physician constructs a jejunostomy using a laparoscope. With the patient under anesthesia, the

physician places a trocar at the umbilicus into the abdomen and insufflates the abdominal cavity. The physician places a laparoscope through the umbilical incision and additional trocars are placed into the peritoneal space. Additional instruments are introduced through the trocars. The physician identifies the jejunum and resects it, re-routing it to an opening created in the skin. An ostomy is created in the skin. The trocars are removed and the incisions are closed with sutures.

44187

The physician constructs a non-tube ileostomy or jejunostomy using a laparoscope. With the patient under general anesthesia, the physician places a trocar at the umbilicus into the abdomen and insufflates the abdominal cavity. The physician places a laparoscope through the umbilical incision. Additional trocars are placed through which the specialized surgical instruments are inserted. Next, the selected segment of jejunum or ileum is isolated. A loop or end of the selected segment of bowel is located and grasped. The skin and fat are excised, the fascia is opened, and the loop is exteriorized through a previously defined ileostomy or jejunostomy site. The laparoscope is removed, the ports are closed with incisions, and the stoma is matured.

44188

The physician constructs a colostomy or skin level cecostomy using a laparoscope. With the patient under general anesthesia, the physician places a trocar at the umbilicus into the abdomen and insufflates the abdominal cavity. The physician places a laparoscope through the umbilical incision. Additional trocars are placed, through which the specialized surgical instruments are inserted. The selected segment of colon or cecum is isolated. The physician brings a loop, end of colon, or cecum onto the skin as a stoma (colostomy or cecostomy) through a small incision in the abdominal wall. The laparoscope is removed, the ports are closed with incisions, and the stoma is matured.

44202-44203

The physician performs a laparoscopic single resection and anastomosis of the small intestine. With the patient under general anesthesia, a urinary catheter is inserted and the patient is placed in a supine or Trendelenburg position on the operating table. A 15-mmHg carbon dioxide pneumoperitoneum is established with a laparoscopic port placed through the umbilicus. The laparoscope is positioned in the abdominal cavity and a diagnostic laparoscopy is performed. The remaining laparoscopic ports are placed under direct vision. The transverse colon is located and maintained in upward traction. The ligament of Treitz is identified and the small intestine is run. The targeted section of small intestine is marked and suspended with traction sutures through the mesentery. The peritoneum overlying the mesentery is scored and the segment of small intestine marked for resection is devascularized. The bowel is divided proximal and distal to the segment with a stapler. The segment is brought out through an enlarged trocar site. The divided bowel ends are anastomosed with staples and inspected. The mesentery is closed with interrupted sutures. The trocars and laparoscope are removed and the incisions are closed with sutures. Report 44203 for each additional small intestine resection and anastomosis beyond the first.

44204-44205

With the patient under general anesthesia, a urinary catheter is inserted and the patient is placed supine or in a Trendelenburg position on the operating table. A 15-mmHg carbon dioxide pneumoperitoneum is established with a laparoscopic port placed through the umbilicus using a direct open technique; the laparoscope is positioned in the abdominal cavity and a diagnostic laparoscopy is performed. The remaining laparoscopic ports are placed under direct vision. The physician incises peritoneum along both sides to mobilize the colon. The greater omentum and colon are separated by incision to mobilize the hepatic and splenic flexures. The colon is mobilized centrally onto its mesentery and the mesenteric vessels are divided intracorporeally using titanium clips. The colon is divided with an endoscopic stapler, and the specimen is removed through an enlarged trocar site. If the procedure is being performed for malignancy, a wound protector is used. In 44204, the divided bowel ends are anastomosed and inspected. In 44205, for the ileocolostomy with removal of terminal ileum, the abdomen is deflated and the laparoscope and trocar incisions are closed. The segment of terminal ileum and cecum is removed and an anastomosis is done between the remaining ileum and colon and brought out through the trocar site to an opening created in the skin. The abdomen is deflated and the laparoscope and trocar incisions are closed.

44206-44207

The physician performs a laparoscopic partial colectomy with end colostomy and closure of the distal segment (Hartmann type) in 44206 and with anastomosis and coloproctostomy in 44207. With the patient under general anesthesia, a urinary catheter is inserted and the patient is positioned supine. Carbon dioxide gas is used to insufflate the abdomen through a laparoscopic port placed through the umbilicus. A 10 to 12 mm cannula is used to facilitate insertion of the laparoscope into the abdominal cavity. Cannulae are inserted in the right middle quadrant, the suprapubic area, and in the left middle quadrant to allow instrument access to the surgical site. The laparoscope is placed through the left cannula for mobilization of the colon. The physician dissects along the peritoneum to mobilize the colon. Once mobilized, the laparoscope is placed in the suprapubic cannula and the omentum is dissected using electrocautery and vascular clips. A 4 to 6 cm transverse incision is made at the appropriate cannula site depending on the portion of the resection. The colon is exteriorized and the distal segment is resected. In 44206, the new proximal end of the colon is brought through an opening made in the abdominal wall and anastomosed so as to exit onto the skin for a colostomy and the remaining distal end is closed off. In 44207, after the distal segment of diseased colon and/or rectal tissue is resected, the new ends are brought together and an anastomosis is done between the colon and the rectum low in the pelvis with staples or sutures (coloproctostomy). The abdominal cavity is inspected through the laparoscope for hemostasis and irrigated. The instruments are removed and the remaining abdominal wounds are closed.

44208

The physician performs a laparoscopic partial colectomy with anastomosis and coloproctostomy, with a colostomy. With the patient under general anesthesia, a urinary catheter is inserted and the patient is positioned supine. Carbon dioxide gas is used to insufflate the abdomen through a laparoscopic port placed through the umbilicus. A 10 12 mm cannula is used to facilitate insertion of the laparoscope into the abdominal cavity. Cannulae are inserted in the right middle quadrant, the suprapubic area, and in the left middle quadrant to allow instrument access to the surgical site. The laparoscope is placed through the left cannula for mobilization of the colon. The physician dissects along the peritoneum to mobilize the colon. Once mobilized, the laparoscope is placed in the suprapubic cannula and the omentum is dissected using electrocautery and vascular clips. A 4 to 6 cm transverse incision is made at the appropriate cannula site depending on the portion of the resection. The distal segment of diseased colon and/or rectal tissue is resected and the new ends are brought together and an anastomosis is done between the colon and the rectum low in the pelvis with staples or sutures (coloproctostomy). A loop of colon above the newly sutured anastomosis is brought out through a separate incision in the abdominal wall and fixed there so the colon will empty through this artificial opening in the skin as a colostomy, usually temporary, to divert the fecal stream while the anastomosis heals.

44210

The physician performs a laparoscopic total colectomy with ileostomy or ileoproctostomy. With the patient under general anesthesia, a urinary catheter is inserted and the patient is positioned supine. Carbon dioxide gas is used to insufflate the abdomen through a laparoscopic port placed through the umbilicus. A 10 to 12 mm cannula is used to facilitate insertion of the laparoscope into the abdominal cavity. Cannulae are inserted in the right middle quadrant, the suprapubic area, and in the left middle quadrant to allow instrument access to the surgical site. The laparoscope is placed through the left cannula for mobilization of the colon. The physician dissects along the peritoneum to mobilize the colon. Once mobilized, the laparoscope is placed in the suprapubic cannula and the omentum is dissected using electrocautery and vascular clips. A 4 to 6 cm transverse incision is made at the appropriate cannula site depending on the portion of the resection. After the colon has been mobilized, the colorectal junction and the terminal ileum are divided. The whole colon is removed. The terminal ileum is approximated to the rectum and the ends anastomosed together or it is brought out through a separate incision on the abdominal wall and sutured as an ileostomy artificial opening onto the skin.

44211

The physician performs a laparoscopic total colectomy with proctectomy with ileoanal anastomosis and creation of an ileal reservoir, with loop ileostomy, with or without rectal mucosectomy. With the patient under general anesthesia, a urinary catheter is inserted and the patient is positioned supine. Carbon dioxide gas is used to insufflate the abdomen through a laparoscopic port placed through the umbilicus. A 10 to 12 mm cannula is used to facilitate insertion of the laparoscope into the abdominal cavity. Cannulae are inserted in the right middle quadrant, the suprapubic area, and in the left middle quadrant to allow instrument access to the surgical site. The laparoscope is placed through the left cannula for mobilization of the colon. The physician dissects along the peritoneum to mobilize the colon. Once mobilized, the laparoscope is placed in the suprapubic cannula and the omentum is dissected using electrocautery and vascular clips. A 4 to 6 cm transverse incision is made at the appropriate cannula site depending on the portion of the resection. After the colon and rectum have been mobilized, they are removed. The mucosa of the remaining distal rectum may be stripped. The terminal ileum is folded upon itself and approximated in order to form a pouch and the terminal ileum is pulled through the remaining muscular tube of the rectum and approximated to the anus with sutures. A loop of ileum above the newly sutured ileoanal anastomosis is brought out through a separate incision in the abdominal wall and fixed there so the ileum will empty through this artificial opening in the skin as an ileostomy, usually temporary, to divert the fecal stream while the anastomosis heals.

44212

The physician performs a laparoscopic total colectomy with proctectomy, with ileostomy. With the patient under general anesthesia, a urinary catheter is inserted and the patient is positioned supine. Carbon dioxide gas is used to insufflate the abdomen through a laparoscopic port placed through the umbilicus. A 10 to 12 mm cannula is used to facilitate insertion of the laparoscope into the abdominal cavity. Cannulae are inserted in the right middle quadrant, the suprapubic area, and in the left middle quadrant to allow instrument access to the surgical site. The laparoscope is placed through the left cannula for mobilization of the colon. The physician dissects along the peritoneum to mobilize the colon. Once mobilized, the laparoscope is placed in the suprapubic cannula and the omentum is dissected using electrocautery and vascular clips. A 4 to 6 cm transverse incision is made at the appropriate cannula site depending on the portion of the resection. After the colon and rectum have been mobilized, they are removed. The terminal ileum is brought out through a separate incision on the abdominal wall and sutured as an ileostomy artificial opening onto the skin.

44213
The physician mobilizes the splenic flexure via a laparoscopic approach in conjunction with a separately reportable partial colon resection. With the patient under general anesthesia, a urinary catheter is inserted and the patient is placed supine or in a Trendelenburg position on the operating table. A 15-mmHg carbon dioxide pneumoperitoneum is established with a laparoscopic port placed through the umbilicus using a direct open technique. The laparoscope is positioned in the abdominal cavity and a diagnostic laparoscopy is performed. The remaining laparoscopic ports are placed under direct vision. The attachments between the splenic flexure of the colon and the lateral abdominal wall and spleen are dissected free and taken down in order to mobilize an adequate length of colon in conjunction with a partial colon resection. At the completion of the procedure, the abdomen is deflated and the laparoscope and trocar incisions are closed.

44227
The physician takes down (closes) a previously created enterostomy (stoma) of the large or small intestine using a laparoscope. With the patient under general anesthesia, the physician places a trocar at the umbilicus into the abdomen and insufflates the abdominal cavity. The physician places a laparoscope through the umbilical incision. Additional trocars are placed, through which the specialized surgical instruments are inserted. The stoma is mobilized and taken down from the abdominal wall. The stoma is resected and the bowel ends are reapproximated with staples or sutures. The laparoscope is removed, the ports are closed with incisions, and the stoma is matured.

44300
The physician places a tube in the small bowel for feeding or into the cecum for decompression via an open approach. The physician makes an abdominal incision. Next, a segment of proximal small bowel or the cecum is isolated. A tube is placed into the small bowel or cecum and brought out through the abdominal wall. The incision is closed.

44310
The physician brings a loop or end of jejunum or ileum through the abdominal wall onto the skin as a stoma. The physician makes an abdominal incision. Next, the selected segment of jejunum or ileum is isolated. A loop or end of the selected segment of bowel is secured through a separate incision on the abdominal wall onto the skin as a stoma. The initial incision is closed. This stoma is created for purposes other than enteral feeding.

44312
The physician revises an ileostomy through an incision around the stoma with release of scar tissue. The physician makes and incision around the ileostomy site. Next, the stoma is dissected free of the surrounding abdominal wall and constricting scar tissue is released. The stoma is reapproximated to the skin or the distal end of the stoma may be transected. Additional ileum may be pulled through the abdominal wall and approximated to the skin as a revised ileostomy.

44314
The physician revises an ileostomy by forming a new stoma site. The physician makes an abdominal incision. Next, the previous ileostomy is completely taken down. The distal ileum is brought through a new incision on the abdominal wall onto the skin as an ileostomy at a new site. The initial incision and former stoma site are closed.

44316
The physician forms a reservoir of distal ileum (Kock pouch) and brings it through the abdominal wall onto the skin as a continent ileostomy. The physician makes an abdominal incision. Next, the distal ileum is folded upon itself and approximated in such a way to form a pouch with a valve. The end of the pouch is brought through a separate incision on the abdominal wall onto the skin as a continent ileostomy. The initial incision is closed.

44320
The physician performs a colostomy or skin level cecostomy. An abdominal incision is made and the peritoneum is entered, followed by a thorough exploratory exam of abdominal organs and tissues, including lysis of any adhesions. The small bowel is mobilized and isolated out of the way. The distal bowel is measured for the appropriate length for pouch creation. A proximal point from the distal end is separated from its blood supply to be made into a pouch nipple valve. The pouch is fashioned into the right configuration and secured in place. The nipple valve component is intussuscepted and secured in place. The pouch end of colon (or cecum) is brought out through a separate incision on the abdominal wall onto the skin as a stoma (cecostomy or colostomy) and secured in place with a pouch nipple to mucocutaneous tissue anastomosis. The abdomen is irrigated, a final inspection is made, and a closed-system suction drain may be placed. The abdominal wall skin is closed and dressed and a pouch

intubation catheter is placed into the nipple valve and pouch.

44322
The physician performs multiple biopsies of the colon wall and brings a loop of colon or cecum through the abdominal wall onto the skin as a stoma. The physician makes an abdominal incision. Next, multiple biopsies are obtained along the length of the colon wall. A loop of colon or cecum is brought through a separate incision on the abdominal wall onto the skin as a stoma (colostomy or cecostomy). The initial incision is closed.

44340
The physician revises a colostomy through an incision around the stoma site with release of scar tissue. The physician makes an incision around the stoma site. Next, the stoma is dissected free of the surrounding abdominal wall and constricting scar tissue is released. The stoma is reapproximated to the skin or the distal stoma is transected and additional colon pulled through the abdominal wall and approximated to the skin as a revised colostomy.

44345
The physician revises a colostomy by forming a new stoma site. The physician makes an abdominal incision. Next, the previous colostomy is completely taken down. The distal end of colon is brought through a separate incision on the abdominal wall onto the skin at a new site as a revised colostomy The initial incision and previous stoma site are closed.

44346
The physician performs a colostomy revision and repairs a paracolostomy hernia. The physician makes an abdominal incision. Next, the previous colostomy site is taken down. The hernia at the former colostomy site is repaired. The end of colon is brought through a separate incision on the abdominal wall at a new site and onto the skin as a revised colostomy. The initial incision and previous stoma site are closed.

44360
The physician performs endoscopy of the proximal small bowel and may obtain brushings or washings. The physician places an endoscope through the mouth and advances it into the small intestine. An abdominal incision may be made to mobilize the small bowel and assist in running the bowel over the endoscope. The lumen of the small bowel is examined and brushings or washings may be obtained of suspicious areas. The endoscope is withdrawn at the completion of the procedure. If an incision was made, it is closed.

44361
The physician performs endoscopy of the proximal small bowel and obtains biopsies. The physician places an endoscope through the mouth and advances it into the small intestine. An abdominal incision may be made to mobilize the small bowel and assist in running the bowel over the endoscope. The lumen of the small bowel is examined and biopsies are obtained of suspicious areas. The endoscope is withdrawn at the completion of the procedure. If an incision was made, it is closed.

44363
The physician performs endoscopy of the proximal small bowel and removes a foreign body. The physician places an endoscope through the mouth and advances it into the small intestine, An abdominal incision may be made to mobilize the small bowel and assist in running the bowel over the endoscope. The bowel lumen is examined and the foreign body located. A snare or forceps is advanced through the endoscope and the foreign body grasped and removed. The endoscope is withdrawn at the completion of the procedure. If an incision was made, it is closed.

44364
The physician performs endoscopy of the proximal small bowel and removes a tumor or polyp by snare technique. The physician places an endoscope through the mouth and advances it into the small intestine. An abdominal incision may be made to mobilize the small bowel and assist in running the bowel over the endoscope. The bowel lumen is examined and the polyp or tumor is located and removed with a snare placed through the endoscope. The endoscope is withdrawn at the completion of the procedure. If an incision was made it is closed.

44365
The physician performs endoscopy of the proximal small bowel and removes a tumor or polyp with hot biopsy forceps or cautery. The physician places an endoscope through the mouth and advances it into the small intestine. An abdominal incision may be made to mobilize the small bowel and assist in running the bowel over the endoscope. The bowel lumen is examined and the polyp or tumor is located and removed with hot biopsy forceps or cautery placed through the endoscope. The endoscope is withdrawn at the completion of the procedure. If an incision was made, it is closed.

44366
The physician performs endoscopy of the proximal small bowel and controls an area of bleeding. The physician places an endoscope through the mouth and advances it into the small intestine. An abdominal incision may be made to mobilize the small bowel and assist in running the bowel over the endoscope. The bowel lumen is examined and the area of bleeding is identified and controlled. The endoscope is withdrawn at the completion of the procedure. If an incision was made, it is closed.

44369
The physician performs endoscopy of the proximal small bowel and ablates a tumor or polyp or other

lesion. The physician places an endoscope through the mouth and advances it into the small intestine. An abdominal incision may be made to mobilize the small bowel and assist in running the bowel over the endoscope. The bowel lumen is examined and the tumor, polyp, or other lesion is identified and ablated. The endoscope is withdrawn at the completion of the procedure. If an incision was made it is closed.

44370
The physician uses an endoscope to examine the proximal small intestine and performs a transendoscopic placement of a stent in the small intestine. The physician places an endoscope through the mouth and advances it into the small intestine. The lumen of the entire small intestine is visualized. The endoscope is placed at the site of an obstruction or stricture, the necessary stent length is determined and predilation of the obstruction or stenosis may be performed. The stent (endoprosthesis) is introduced into the site of the obstruction. Using a commercial delivery system, a plastic covering over the stent is removed and the stent self-deploys, shoring-up the walls at a specific site in the small intestine beyond the second portion of duodenum, not including the ileum. When necessary, a balloon catheter is placed into the stent and gently inflated to more fully deploy the stent. The delivery system and endoscope are removed.

44372
The physician performs endoscopy of the proximal small bowel and places a percutaneous jejunostomy tube. The physician places an endoscope into the mouth and advances it into the small intestine. The bowel lumen is visualized and transilluminated through the abdominal skin. A needle is placed through the skin into the lumen of the jejunum under visualization of the endoscope. A wire is threaded through the needle into the bowel lumen. The needle is removed. A jejunostomy tube is placed over the wire, through the skin, into the jejunum, and secured into place. The endoscope is withdrawn.

44373
The physician performs endoscopy of the proximal small bowel and converts a percutaneous gastrostomy tube to a percutaneous jejunostomy tube. The physician places an endoscope into the mouth and advances it into the stomach. A jejunostomy tube is advanced through the previously placed gastrostomy tube. The jejunostomy tube is grasped with a snare or forceps placed through the endoscope and advanced with the endoscope into the proximal jejunum. The endoscope is withdrawn.

44376
The physician performs endoscopy of the small bowel and may obtain brushings or washings. The physician places the endoscope into the mouth and advances it into the small intestine. An abdominal incision may be made to mobilize the small bowel and assist in running the bowel over the endoscope. The lumen of the small bowel is visualized and brushings or washings may be obtained. The endoscope is withdrawn at the completion of the procedure. If an incision was made, it is closed.

44377
The physician performs endoscopy of the entire small bowel and performs biopsies. The physician places the endoscope into the mouth and advances it into the small intestine. An abdominal incision may be made to mobilize the small bowel and assist in running the bowel over the endoscope. The lumen of the small bowel is visualized and biopsies are performed. The endoscope is withdrawn at the completion of the procedure. If an incision was made, it is closed.

44378
The physician performs endoscopy of the small intestine, which may include the ileum, and controls an area of bleeding. The physician places the endoscope into the mouth and advances it into the small intestine. The lumen of the small intestine is visualized and any area of bleeding is controlled using various methods, such as cautery, injection, or laser. In some cases, a separately reportable abdominal incision is made to mobilize the small intestine and assist in running the intestine over the endoscope. The endoscope is withdrawn at the completion of the procedure.

44379
The physician uses an endoscope to examine the small intestine and performs transendoscopic placement of a stent in the small intestine. The physician performs endoscopy of the small bowel and places a transendoscopic stent. The physician places an endoscope into the mouth and advances it into the small intestine. The lumen of the small intestine is visualized. The endoscope is placed at the site of an obstruction or stricture and the necessary stent length is determined. The stent (endoprosthesis) is introduced into the site of the obstruction. Using a commercial delivery system, a plastic covering over the stent is removed and the stent self-deploys, shoring-up the walls at a specific site in the small intestine beyond the second portion of the duodenum, including the ileum. When necessary, a balloon catheter is placed into the stent and gently inflated to more fully deploy the stent. The delivery system and endoscope are removed.

44380
The physician performs endoscopy through an ileostomy and may obtain brushings or washings. The physician places the endoscope into the ileostomy and advances the endoscope into the small intestine. The small bowel lumen is visualized and brushings or washings may be obtained. The endoscope is withdrawn at the completion of the procedure.

44382
The physician performs endoscopy through an ileostomy and obtains material for biopsies. The physician places the endoscope into the ileostomy and advances the endoscope into the small intestine. The small bowel lumen is visualized and biopsies are obtained. The endoscope is withdrawn at the completion of the procedure.

44383
The physician uses an endoscope through an ileostomy to view the ileum and places a transendoscopic stent. The physician places an endoscope into the mouth and advances it into the small intestine. The lumen of the ileum is visualized The endoscope is removed. The endoscope is placed at the site of an obstruction or stricture and the necessary stent length is determined. The stent (endoprosthesis) is introduced into the site of the obstruction. Using a commercial delivery system, a plastic covering over the stent is removed and the stent self-deploys, shoring-up the walls at a specific site in the ileum. When necessary, a balloon catheter is placed into the stent and gently inflated to more fully deploy the stent. The delivery system and endoscope are removed.

44385
The physician performs endoscopy of an intestinal pouch and may obtain brushings or washings. The physician places the endoscope into the pouch, through the anus, or abdominal wall stoma. The lumen of the pouch is visualized and brushings or washings may be obtained. The endoscope is removed at the completion of the procedure.

44386
The physician performs endoscopy of an intestinal pouch and obtains biopsies. The physician places the endoscope into the pouch through the anus or abdominal wall stoma. The lumen of the pouch is visualized and biopsies are obtained. The endoscope is removed at the completion of the procedure.

44388
The physician performs colonoscopy through an abdominal wall colostomy and may obtain brushings or washings. The physician places the endoscope into the colostomy and advances the endoscope into the colon. The lumen of the colon is visualized and brushings or washings may be obtained. The endoscope is withdrawn at the completion of the procedure.

44389
The physician performs colonoscopy through an abdominal wall colostomy and obtains biopsies. The physician places the endoscope into the colostomy and advances the endoscope into the colon. The lumen of the colon is visualized and biopsies are obtained. The endoscope is withdrawn at the completion of the procedure.

44390
The physician performs colonoscopy through an abdominal wall colostomy and removes a foreign body. The physician places the endoscope into the colostomy and advances the endoscope into the colon. The lumen of the colon is visualized. The foreign body is isolated and grasped with a snare or forceps (placed through the endoscope) and removed. The endoscope in withdrawn at the completion of the procedure.

44391
The physician performs colonoscopy through an abdominal wall colostomy and controls an area of bleeding. The physician places the endoscope into the colostomy and advances the endoscope into the colon. The lumen of the colon is visualized and the area of bleeding is identified and controlled. The endoscope is withdrawn at the completion of the procedure.

44392
The physician performs colonoscopy through an abdominal wall colostomy and removes a tumor, polyp, or other lesion with hot biopsy forceps or cautery. The physician places the endoscope into the colostomy and advances the endoscope into the colon. The lumen of the colon is visualized and the tumor, polyp, or lesion is identified and removed with hot biopsy forceps or cautery. The endoscope is withdrawn at the completion of the procedure.

44393
The physician performs colonoscopy through an abdominal wall colostomy and performs ablation of a tumor, polyp, or other lesion. The physician places the endoscope into the colostomy and advances the endoscope into the colon. The lumen of the colon is visualized and the tumor, polyp, or other lesion is identified and ablated. The endoscope is withdrawn at the completion of the procedure.

44394
The physician performs colonoscopy through an abdominal wall colostomy and removes a tumor, polyp or other lesion with a snare. The physician places the endoscope into the colostomy and advances the endoscope into the colon. The lumen of the colon is visualized and the tumor, polyp or other lesion is identified and removed with a snare placed through the endoscope. The endoscope is withdrawn at the completion of the procedure.

44397
The physician uses a colonoscope to examine the colon through an abdominal wall colostomy and places a transendoscopic stent. The physician places the endoscope into the colostomy and advances the endoscope into the colon. The lumen of the colon is visualized. The endoscope is placed at the site of an obstruction or stricture and the necessary stent length is determined. The stent (endoprosthesis) is introduced into the site of the obstruction. Using a commercial

delivery system, a plastic covering over the stent is removed and the stent self-deploys, shoring-up the walls at a specific site in the large intestine. When necessary, a balloon catheter is placed into the stent and gently inflated to more fully deploy the stent. The delivery system and colonoscope are removed.

44500
A long, Miller-Abbott style gastrointestinal tube with a mercury-filled balloon at the bottom is introduced, usually nasally, and used to clear gastrointestinal strictures. The patient is seated lower than the person performing the procedure and the dilator is placed in the posterior pharynx. The patient swallows and the tube and balloon are carried into the small intestine. The balloon is inflated and withdrawn until resistance is encountered. The balloon is partially deflated, withdrawn a little more, and re-inflated. This process is repeated several times to achieve dilation of the stricture. This procedure may be done without fluoroscopy or with fluoroscopy by instilling a diluted contrast into the balloon.

44602
The physician performs suture closure of a single small bowel perforation. The physician makes an abdominal incision. Next, the abdomen is explored and the small bowel perforation is identified and repaired with sutures. The incision is closed.

44603
The physician performs suture closure of multiple small bowel perforations. The physician makes an abdominal incision. Next, the abdomen is explored and the small bowel perforations are identified and repaired with sutures. The incision is closed.

44604
The physician performs suture closure of a colon perforation. The physician makes an abdominal incision. Next, the abdomen is explored and the colon perforation is identified and repaired with sutures. The incision is closed.

44605
The physician performs suture closure of a colon perforation and forms a colostomy proximal to the repair. The physician makes an abdominal incision. Next, the abdomen is explored and the colon perforation identified and repaired with sutures. A loop or end of colon proximal to the repair is brought out through a separate incision on the abdominal wall onto the skin as a colostomy. The initial incision is closed.

44615
The physician performs an abdominal incision to gain access to the site of an intestinal narrowing (stricture). Once identified, the intestinal stricture is incised (enterotomy) in a longitudinal manner. The physician may find it necessary or prudent to dilate the stenotic intestine to complete proper repair. The intestine is repaired or sutured. The two divided portions of the incised intestine may be reapproximated after one segment is drawn into the other (invagination) end to end (enterorrhaphy). The abdominal incision is sutured or stapled closed.

44620
The physician takes down and closes an enterostomy (stoma) of the small intestine or colon. The physician makes an incision around the stoma or a separate abdominal incision may be made. Next, the stoma is mobilized and taken down from the abdominal wall and the stoma is closed. The abdominal incisions are closed.

44625
The physician takes down an enterostomy (stoma) of small intestine or colon, other than colorectal. The stoma is resected and an anastomosis between the bowel ends is completed. The physician makes an incision around the stoma or a separate abdominal incision may be made. Next, the stoma is mobilized and taken down from the abdominal wall. The stoma is resected and the bowel ends are reapproximated with staples or sutures. The abdominal incisions are closed. Report 44625 if with resection and anastomosis other than colorectal.

44626
A surgeon closes a previously-existing enterostomy, or a surgically created opening, in the large or small intestine. This code includes both resection of the intestine and a colorectal anastomosis, or a reconnection of the colon and rectum.

44640
The physician takes down and closes an intestinal cutaneous fistula. The physician makes an abdominal incision. Next, the bowel is mobilized and the fistula is identified and taken down from the abdominal wall and skin. The segment of bowel containing the fistula is resected and the bowel ends reapproximated with staples or sutures. The abdominal wall incisions are closed.

44650
The physician closes a connection (fistula) between loops of small bowel or between the small bowel and colon. The physician makes an abdominal incision. Next, the enteroenteric or enterocolic fistula is identified and divided. The ends of the fistula may be closed with sutures or the segments of bowel involved with the fistula may be resected and the bowel ends reapproximated in order to completely remove the involved areas. The incision is closed.

44660
The physician closes a connection between the small bowel and bladder (enterovesical fistula). The physician makes an abdominal incision. Next, the enterovesical fistula is identified and divided. The ends of the fistula are closed with sutures. The incision is closed.

Digestive

44661
The physician closes a connection between the small or large intestine and bladder (enterovesical fistula) by resecting a portion of the intestine or bladder. The physician makes an abdominal incision. Next, the enterovesical fistula is identified and divided. The connection of the fistula to the bladder is resected and the bladder is closed with sutures. The segment of intestine containing the fistula is resected and the ends are reapproximated. The incision is closed.

44680
The physician folds the intestine upon itself and attaches the edges with sutures for anchoring purposes. The physician makes an abdominal incision. Next, the bowel is folded upon itself and the edges are plicated with sutures without making an anastomosis to anchor the bowel in place. The incision is closed.

44700
Prior to implementing radiation therapy, the physician uses mesh, other prosthesis, or native tissue (bladder or omentum) to lift and fix the small intestine away from the site of radiation therapy. An abdominal incision is made. If mesh or other prosthetic material is used, it is sutured into place. If native tissue is used, a sling is fashioned and sutured into place. The incision sutured closed.

44701
The patient's colon is flushed during a surgical procedure. A Foley catheter is inserted into the cecum through which the irrigation is performed. A noncrushing bowel clamp is placed across the terminal ilium to prevent the lavage fluid from flowing into the small intestine. An intravenous infusion set is connected to the catheter and a clear, corrugated scavenger tube is inserted in the distal bowel and secured in place. A closed irrigation system is created by securing a large bag to the free end of the tube, draped over the patient to the side. The colon is lavaged with warm, isotonic saline solution for 15 to 30 minutes until the flow through the tube is seen to be clear.

44715
The physician performs a standard backbench preparation of an intestine allograft requiring mobilizing and fashioning of the superior mesenteric artery and vein. Backbench or back table preparation refers to procedures performed on the intestine allograft to prepare the allograft for transplant. Removal of the small intestine graft requires careful dissection of the superior mesenteric artery (SMA) and superior mesenteric vein (SMV). Backbench or back table preparation of the SMA or SMV is required when the pedicles are too short. When a cadaver donor is used, the SMA and/or SMV are lengthened using free vascular grafts from the iliac or carotid arteries and veins that were procured from the cadaver. The physician performs the grafting procedure prior to transplantation of the intestine allograft.

44720
The physician performs a backbench preparation of an intestine allograft requiring venous anastomosis. Backbench or back table preparation refers to procedures performed on the intestine allograft to prepare the allograft for transplant. The physician procures venous grafts from the iliac or carotid veins of the cadaver. The physician applies the venous grafts to one of more venous sites on the intestine. Report 44720 for each venous anastomosis.

44721
The physician performs a backbench preparation of an intestine allograft requiring arterial anastomosis. Backbench or back table preparation refers to procedures performed on the intestine allograft to prepare the allograft for transplant. The physician procures arterial grafts from the iliac or carotid arteries of the cadaver. The physician applies the arterial grafts to one of more arterial sites on the intestine. Report 44721 for each arterial anastomosis.

44800
The physician excises a Meckel's diverticulum or an omphalomesenteric duct. The physician makes an abdominal incision. Next, the Meckel's diverticulum in the terminal ileum or the omphalomesenteric duct connecting the terminal ileum to the umbilicus is identified. The Meckel's diverticulum or omphalomesenteric duct is excised and the defect in the ileum is closed with sutures or staples or the segment of ileum may be excised and reapproximated. The incision is closed.

44820
The physician excises a lesion in the mesentery. The physician makes an abdominal incision. Next, the lesion in the mesentery is identified. The lesion is removed by shelling it out of the mesentery, resecting a portion of the mesentery with the lesion, or resecting a segment of bowel and mesentery to include the lesion with reapproximation of the bowel. The incision is closed.

44850
The physician repairs a defect in the mesentery with sutures. The physician makes an abdominal incision. Next, the mesenteric defect is identified and closed with sutures. The incision is closed.

44900
The physician drains an appendiceal abscess. The physician makes an abdominal incision. Next, the abscess near the appendix is identified and incised and drained. A drain may be left in the abscess cavity. The abdominal wall incision is closed and the skin incision may be left open to heal secondarily.

44901
The physician performs percutaneous drainage of an appendiceal abscess. The physician may create a small incision in the skin proximal to the appendiceal abscess to ease placement of drainage instruments through the skin. The physician uses a CAT scan or ultrasound to guide placement of a drainage needle or trocar into the appendiceal abscess. The physician advances the drainage needle or trocar through the abdominal wall into the peritoneum to gain access to the abscess cavity. The fluid is allowed to drain. Once drained, a catheter may be placed. Sutures may be secured to hold the drainage catheter in place. The operative site is subsequently cleaned and bandaged. For radiological supervision and interpretation, see 75989.

44950
The physician removes the appendix. The physician makes an abdominal incision. Next, the appendix is identified and mobilized, its blood supply is divided and the appendix is transected and removed. The incision is closed.

44955
The physician removes the appendix at the time of another major procedure. The physician identifies and mobilizes the appendix during a major procedure for which an incision has been made. The blood supply to the appendix is divided and the appendix is transected and removed. The incision is closed.

44960
The physician removes a perforated appendix. The physician makes an abdominal incision. The appendix is identified and mobilized, its blood supply is divided, and the appendix is transected and removed. The abscess cavity is debrided and irrigated. The incision is closed.

44970
The physician performs a laparoscopic appendectomy. The physician places a trocar at the umbilicus and insufflates the abdomen. The laparoscope is placed through the umbilical port and additional trocars are placed into the abdominal cavity. The appendix is identified, dissected from surrounding structures and its blood supply divided. The appendix is transected with staples or suture and removed. The trocars are removed and the incisions are closed.

45000
The physician drains a pelvic abscess through the rectum. The physician identifies the area of abscess through the rectum by palpation or preoperative localizing studies. Next, a transanal incision is made through the rectum into the abscess cavity and the abscess is irrigated and drained. The incision is left open to drain.

45005
The physician drains a submucosal rectal abscess. The physician identifies the area of abscess in the rectum. Next, a transanal incision is made through the rectal lining into the abscess cavity and the abscess is drained. The incision is left open to drain.

45020
The physician drains an abscess above the pelvic floor or behind the rectum through the rectum. The physician identifies the area of abscess by palpation or preoperative localizing studies. Next, a transanal incision is made through the rectum into the abscess cavity and the abscess is drained. The incision is left open to drain.

45100
The physician performs a biopsy of the rectal wall using a transanal approach. The physician performs an incisional biopsy or a suction biopsy of the low rectal wall. The biopsy may be closed with sutures.

45108
The physician removes a muscle tumor or a section of muscle from the anorectum. The physician identifies the anorectal muscle tumor or area of interest. A transanal incision is made through the rectal wall and the tumor or identified area of muscle is excised. The incision is closed by approximating the muscle edges and closing the incision in the rectal lining.

45110
The physician removes the entire rectum and anus and forms a colostomy. The physician makes an abdominal incision. The proximal rectum is mobilized within the abdomen to the level of the sphincter muscles and the colon is divided above the pelvic brim. An incision is made around the anus from a perineal approach and the anus and distal rectum are dissected free of surrounding structures and the anus and rectum are removed. The proximal end of colon is brought out through a separate incision on the abdominal wall as a colostomy. The abdominal and perineal incisions are closed.

45111
The physician removes the proximal rectum. The physician makes an abdominal incision. The distal colon and rectum are mobilized and divided proximal and distal to the segment of interest. The colon and distal rectum may be reapproximated or the proximal end of colon may be brought out through a separate incision on the abdominal wall as a colostomy and the remaining rectum closed with staples or sutures. The initial incision is closed.

45112
The physician removes the rectum and performs an anastomosis between the colon and the anus. The physician makes an abdominal incision. The distal colon and rectum are mobilized within the abdomen to the level of the sphincter muscles. The colon is divided

above the pelvic brim and the rectum at the level of the sphincter muscles and removed. The mucosa may be stripped from the remaining distal rectum from a perineal approach. The distal colon is pulled through the sphincter complex and approximated to the anus with sutures. The incision is closed.

45113

The physician removes the proximal rectum, strips the mucosa from the distal rectum and performs an anastomosis between an ileal pouch and the anus. The physician makes an abdominal incision. The distal colon and rectum are mobilized within the abdomen to the level of the sphincter muscles. The colon is divided above the pelvic brim and the rectum is divided above the sphincter muscles and removed. The mucosa of the distal rectum is stripped from a perineal approach. The distal ileum is folded upon itself and approximated in order to form a reservoir. The ileal pouch is pulled through the remaining muscular cuff of distal rectum and sutured to the anus. A loop ileostomy may be formed proximal to the anastomosis. The incision is closed.

45114

The physician removes a portion of the rectum through combined abdominal and transsacral approaches. The physician makes an abdominal incision. The proximal rectum and distal colon are mobilized and the colon is divided above the pelvic brim. An incision is made posteriorly at the junction of the sacrum and coccyx. The coccyx is excised. Dissection is continued posteriorly to further mobilize the rectum. The rectum is divided distally and the excised segment is removed. The distal end of colon is approximated to the remaining rectal stump with sutures or staples. The incisions are closed.

45116

The physician removes a portion of the rectum through a transsacral approach. The physician makes a posterior incision at the junction of the sacrum and coccyx. The coccyx is excised. Dissection is continued posteriorly and the rectum and distal colon are mobilized. The rectum is transected proximally and distally and a portion of the rectum is removed. The distal end of colon is approximated to the remaining rectal stump with sutures or staples. The incision is closed.

45119

The physician surgically removes the rectum. The physician makes an abdominal incision, and the distal part of the diseased colon and rectum are mobilized down to the level of the anal sphincter muscles. The rectum is incised at the level of the sphincter muscles while the colon is incised above the pelvic brim where it is disease free. The diseased colon and rectum are removed. The free end of the distal colon is brought through the sphincter complex and approximated with the anus to form a colo-anal anastomosis. The distal colon is folded and sutured in such a way as to create a colonic reservoir pouch. The physician may elect to bring a loop or end of the colon through a separate abdominal incision to create a stoma (enterostomy). The incisions are sutured closed.

45120

The physician removes or bypasses the diseased rectal segment and performs an anastomosis of the colon and anus. The physician makes an abdominal incision. The rectum and distal colon are mobilized and the colon is divided just proximal to the diseased rectal segment. The rectal segment may be removed and the distal colon pulled through the sphincter complex and approximated to the anus with sutures from a perineal approach. Alternatively, the distal colon may be pulled down and approximated to the anus with sutures, bypassing the diseased rectal segment with a combined longitudinal anastomosis between the colon and the diseased rectal segment. The incision is closed.

45121

The physician removes the rectum and part or all of the colon, and performs an anastomosis of the remaining colon or ileum and anus. The physician makes an abdominal incision. Multiple biopsies are taken of the colon wall to determine the level of disease. The involved rectum and colon are mobilized and removed. The remaining segment of colon or ileum is pulled through the sphincter complex and approximated to the anus with sutures from a perineal approach. Alternatively, the colon or ileum may be pulled down and approximated to the anus with sutures, bypassing a small remaining rectal segment with a combined longitudinal anastomosis to the rectal segment. The incision is closed.

45123

The physician removes a portion of the rectum through a perineal approach. The physician makes an incision around the anus. Dissection is continued around the anus to mobilize the anus and distal rectum. The anus and distal rectum are removed. A proximal colostomy may be formed. The incision is closed.

45126

The physician removes pelvic organs, with or without a colostomy, due to cancer of the colon and rectum. The physician makes an abdominal incision. The distal colon and rectum are mobilized and divided proximal and distal to the segment of interest. The pelvic organs are dissected free of surrounding structures and removed. The colon and rectum may be reapproximated or the proximal end of the colon may be brought out through a separate incision on the abdominal wall as a colostomy and the remaining rectum closed with staples or sutures. The initial incision is closed. In males the procedure may include removal of the prostate and bladder. In a female, the procedure may include removal of the bladder and also the uterus, cervix, fallopian tubes, and/or ovaries depending upon the extent of the disease.

45130
The physician removes a rectal prolapse through a perineal approach. The physician prolapses the rectum and colon through the anus. A circular incision is made through the distal rectum at the anorectal junction. The mesentery and blood supply to the prolapsed rectum is divided and the segment is telescoped out through the anus. The proximal rectum or colon is divided and the prolapsed segment is removed. The proximal end of rectum or colon is approximated to the anus with sutures or staples.

45135
The physician removes a rectal prolapse through a combined abdominal and perineal approach. The physician makes an abdominal incision. The proximal colon and rectum are mobilized. The rectum and colon are prolapsed through the anus. A circular incision is made through the distal rectum at the anorectal junction from a perineal approach. The mesentery and blood supply to the prolapsed rectum is divided and the segment is telescoped out through the anus. The proximal rectum or colon is divided and the prolapsed segment is removed. The proximal end of rectum or colon is approximated the anus with sutures or staples. The incision is closed.

45136
The physician excises an ileoanal reservoir and creates an ileostomy. The physician makes an abdominal incision. Dissection is carried down to the site of the ileoanal reservoir. The reservoir is excised at the level where the ileum was previously anastomosed to the anus. The anus is closed. The loose end of the ileum may be trimmed. A disk of skin is excised from the abdominal wall and the terminal ileum is brought out through the split rectus muscle and the opening in the abdomen to form a stoma on the abdominal wall. An anastomosis is performed via the transanal approach and the full thickness of the ileum is sutured to the anal canal. Interrupted sutures complete the ileostomy construction.

45150
The physician performs division of a rectal stricture. The physician makes longitudinal incisions in the scar tissue in one or more places circumferentially around the strictured area of the rectal mucosa. A dilatation of the strictured area may be performed. In addition the internal anal sphincter may be incised as part of the procedure.

45160
The physician removes a rectal tumor through a transsacral or transcoccygeal approach. The physician makes an incision at the junction of the sacrum and coccyx. The coccyx is excised and dissection is continued posteriorly to mobilize the rectum. The tumor is identified, an incision is made in the rectum (proctotomy), and the tumor is excised. The rectum is closed with sutures or staples. The initial incision is closed.

45171-45172
The physician removes a rectal tumor through a transanal approach. The physician explores the anal canal and exposes the tumor. Report 45171 for a partial thickness excision (one that excludes the muscularis propria) and 45172 for a full thickness excision (including the muscularis propria). The defect in the rectum is closed with sutures.

45190
The physician performs destruction of a rectal tumor from a transanal approach. The physician explores the anal canal and exposes the tumor. The tumor is ablated by electrosurgery, laser, freezing (cryosurgery), or some other method.

45300
The physician performs rigid proctosigmoidoscopy and may obtain brushings or washings. The physician inserts the rigid proctosigmoidoscope into the anus and advances the scope. The sigmoid colon and rectal lumen are visualized and brushings or washings may be obtained. The proctosigmoidoscope is removed at the completion of the procedure.

45303
The physician performs rigid proctosigmoidoscopy and performs dilation of a rectal stricture. The physician inserts the rigid proctosigmoidoscope into the anus and advances the scope. The sigmoid colon and rectal lumen are visualized. The stricture is identified and dilated with a balloon or other device. The proctosigmoidoscope is removed at the completion of the procedure.

45305
The physician performs rigid proctosigmoidoscopy and obtains biopsies. The physician inserts the rigid proctosigmoidoscope into the anus and advances the scope. The sigmoid colon and rectal lumen are visualized and biopsies are obtained of suspicious areas. The proctosigmoidoscope is removed at the completion of the procedure.

45307
The physician performs rigid proctosigmoidoscopy and removes a foreign body. The physician inserts the rigid proctosigmoidoscope into the anus and advances the scope. The sigmoid colon and rectal lumen are visualized and the foreign body is identified. The foreign body is removed by a snare or forceps inserted through the scope. The proctosigmoidoscope is removed at the completion of the procedure.

45308
The physician performs rigid proctosigmoidoscopy and removes a tumor, polyp, or other lesion. The physician

inserts the rigid proctosigmoidoscope into the anus and advances the scope. The sigmoid colon and rectal lumen are visualized and the tumor, polyp or other lesion is identified and removed by hot biopsy forceps or cautery. The proctosigmoidoscope is removed at the completion of the procedure.

45309
The physician performs rigid proctosigmoidoscopy and removes a tumor, polyp, or other lesion. The physician inserts the rigid proctosigmoidoscope into the anus and advances the scope. The sigmoid colon and rectal lumen are visualized and the tumor, polyp or other lesion is identified and removed by snare technique. The proctosigmoidoscope is removed at the completion of the procedure.

45315
The physician performs rigid proctosigmoidoscopy and removes multiple tumors, polyps, or other lesions. The physician inserts the rigid proctosigmoidoscope into the anus and advances the scope. The sigmoid colon and rectal lumen are visualized and the tumors, polyps, or other lesions are identified and removed by hot biopsy forceps cautery or snare technique. The proctosigmoidoscope is removed at the completion of the procedure.

45317
The physician performs rigid proctosigmoidoscopy and controls an area of bleeding. The physician inserts the rigid proctosigmoidoscope into the anus and advances the scope. The sigmoid colon and rectal lumen are visualized and the area of bleeding is identified and controlled. The proctosigmoidoscope is removed at the completion of the procedure.

45320
The physician performs rigid proctosigmoidoscopy and ablation of a tumor polyp or other lesion. The physician inserts the proctosigmoidoscope into the anus and advances the scope. The lumen of the sigmoid colon and rectum is visualized and the tumor, polyp or other lesion is identified and ablation performed. The proctosigmoidoscope is removed at the completion of the procedure.

45321
The physician performs rigid proctosigmoidoscopy and decompresses a sigmoid volvulus. The physician inserts the proctosigmoidoscope into the anus and advances the scope. The lumen of the sigmoid colon and rectum is visualized. The proctosigmoidoscope is advanced into the volvulus, decompressing the volvulus as it passes through the bowel lumen. The proctosigmoidoscope is removed at the completion of the procedure.

45327
The physician uses a rigid proctosigmoidoscopy to examine the rectum and sigmoid colon and places a transendoscopic stent. The physician inserts the rigid proctosigmoidoscope into the anus and advances the scope. The sigmoid colon and rectal lumen are visualized. The endoscope is placed at the site of an obstruction or stricture and the necessary stent length is determined. The stent (endoprosthesis) is introduced into the site of the obstruction. Using a commercial delivery system, a plastic covering over the stent is removed and the stent self-deploys, shoring up the walls at a specific site in the sigmoid colon. When necessary, a balloon catheter is placed into the stent and gently inflated to more fully deploy the stent. The delivery system and endoscope are removed.

45330
The physician performs flexible sigmoidoscopy and may obtain brushings or washings. The physician inserts the sigmoidoscope into the anus and advances the scope into the sigmoid colon. The lumen of the sigmoid colon and rectum are visualized and brushings or washings may be obtained. The sigmoidoscope is withdrawn at the completion of the procedure.

45331
The physician performs flexible sigmoidoscopy and obtains biopsies. The physician inserts the sigmoidoscope into the anus and advances the scope into the sigmoid colon. The lumen of the sigmoid colon and rectum are visualized and biopsies are obtained with forceps placed through the scope. The sigmoidoscope is withdrawn at the completion of the procedure.

45332
The physician performs flexible sigmoidoscopy and removes a foreign body. The physician inserts the sigmoidoscope into the anus and advances the scope into the sigmoid colon. The lumen of the sigmoid colon and rectum are visualized. The foreign body is identified and removed with a snare or forceps placed through the sigmoidoscope. The sigmoidoscope is withdrawn at the completion of the procedure.

45333
The physician performs flexible sigmoidoscopy and removes a tumor, polyp, or other lesion. The physician inserts the sigmoidoscope into the anus and advances the scope into the sigmoid colon. The lumen of the sigmoid colon and rectum are visualized and the tumor, polyp, or other lesion is identified and removed with hot biopsy forceps or cautery. The sigmoidoscope is withdrawn at the completion of the procedure.

45334
The physician performs flexible sigmoidoscopy and controls an area of bleeding. The physician inserts the sigmoidoscope into the anus and advances the scope into the sigmoid colon. The lumen of the sigmoid colon and rectum are visualized and the area of bleeding is controlled. The sigmoidoscope is withdrawn at the completion of the procedure.

45335
The physician performs flexible sigmoidoscopy and injects a substance into the submucosa, directed at specific areas through the scope while viewing the colon. The physician inserts the sigmoidoscope into the anus and advances the scope into the sigmoid colon. The lumen of the sigmoid colon and rectum are visualized. Submucosal saline injections, for instance, may be done before polypectomy using snare and electrocautery to greatly enhance the effectiveness of resection for large sessile colorectal polyps.

45337
The physician performs flexible sigmoidoscopy and decompresses a sigmoid volvulus. The physician inserts the sigmoidoscope into the anus and advances the scope into the sigmoid colon. The lumen of the sigmoid colon and rectum are visualized. The sigmoidoscope is advanced into the volvulus decompressing the volvulus as the scope passes through the bowel lumen. The sigmoidoscope is removed at the completion of the procedure.

45338
The physician performs flexible sigmoidoscopy and removes tumors, polyps or other lesions. The physician inserts the sigmoidoscope into the anus and advances the scope into the sigmoid colon. The lumen of the sigmoid colon and rectum are visualized. The tumor, polyp, or other lesions are identified and removed by snare technique. The sigmoidoscope is withdrawn at the completion of the procedure.

45339
The physician performs flexible sigmoidoscopy and performs ablation of a tumor, polyp or other lesion. The physician inserts the sigmoidoscope into the anus and advances the scope into the sigmoid colon. The lumen of the sigmoid colon and rectum are visualized. The tumor, polyp or other lesions are identified and ablated by laser or other method. The sigmoidoscope is withdrawn at the completion of the procedure.

45340
The physician performs flexible sigmoidoscopy and dilates strictures by balloon catheter. The physician inserts the sigmoidoscope into the anus and advances the scope into the sigmoid colon. The lumen of the sigmoid colon and rectum are visualized. Areas of stenosis are identified and a balloon catheter is passed to the point of constriction and a little beyond. The balloon is inflated to the appropriate diameter and gradually withdrawn through the stenosed area, stretching the walls of the bowel at the strictured area.

45341
The physician uses a flexible sigmoidoscopy to examine the rectum and sigmoid colon and performs an endoscopic ultrasound examination. The physician inserts the sigmoidoscopy into the anus and advances the scope into the sigmoid colon. The lumen of the sigmoid colon and rectum are visualized. The sigmoidoscope is removed and replaced with an echoendoscope or an ultrasound probe is passed through the already placed sigmoidoscope. The echoendoscope or ultrasound probe is fitted with a water-filled balloon near the tip; the tip contains a transducer that picks-up the ultrasound frequency and relays it to a processor, outside of the body. The water-filled tip is positioned in the sigmoid colon, against the colon wall next to the area of interest. The area is scanned and an ultrasound image is projected through the processor to a monitor in real-time. When the ultrasound examination is complete the echoendoscope, or esophagoscope and ultrasound probe is removed.

45342
The physician uses a flexible sigmoidoscopy to examine the rectum and sigmoid colon and performs a transendoscopic ultrasound guided intramural or transmural fine needle aspiration/biopsy. The physician inserts the sigmoidoscopy into the anus and advances the scope into the sigmoid colon. The lumen of the sigmoid colon and rectum are visualized. The sigmoidoscope may be removed. A radial scanning echoendoscope is inserted and ultrasound scanning is performed, or an ultrasound probe is passed through the already placed endoscope. The site for a fine needle aspiration biopsy is determined. If a radial scanning echoendoscope is used it is removed and is replaced with a curvilinear array echoendoscope. The echoendoscope or ultrasound probe is fitted with a water-filled balloon near the tip; the tip contains a transducer that picks-up the ultrasound frequency and relays it to a processor, outside of the body. The water-filled tip is positioned in the sigmoid colon against the colon wall next to the predetermined fine needle aspiration (FNA) biopsy site. The area is scanned and an ultrasound image is projected through the processor to a monitor in real-time. A FNA needle is passed through the scope to the biopsy site and a biopsy is taken of the tissue or the needle is inserted through the wall of the tissue into the lesion, or other structure, such as a lymph node. The area is biopsied. When the FNA is complete the echoendoscope or sigmoidoscope and ultrasound probe is removed.

45345
The physician uses a flexible sigmoidoscope to examine the rectum and sigmoid colon and places a transendoscopic stent. The physician inserts the sigmoidoscopy into the anus and advances the scope into the sigmoid colon. The lumen of the sigmoid colon and rectum are visualized. The endoscope is placed at the site of an obstruction or stricture and the necessary stent length is determined. The stent (endoprosthesis) is introduced into the site of the obstruction. Using a commercial delivery system, a plastic covering over the stent is removed and the stent self-deploys, shoring-up the walls at a specific site in

the sigmoid colon. When necessary, a balloon catheter is placed into the stent and gently inflated to more fully deploy the stent. The delivery system and endoscope are removed.

45355
The physician performs colonoscopy through an incision in the colon (colotomy). The physician makes an abdominal incision. Next, the colon may be mobilized. An incision is made in the colon in the segment of interest and the colonoscope is inserted through the colotomy and advanced to visualize the lumen of the colon. At the completion of the procedure the colonoscope is removed and the colotomy is closed with sutures or staples. The abdominal incision is closed.

45378
The physician performs colonoscopy and may obtain brushings or washings or perform colon decompression. The physician inserts the colonoscope into the anus and advances the scope through the colon past the splenic flexure. The lumen of the colon and rectum is visualized. Brushings or washings may be obtained or decompression of the colon may be performed. The colonoscope is withdrawn at the completion of the procedure.

45379
The physician performs colonoscopy and removes a foreign body. The physician inserts the colonoscope into the anus and advances the scope through the colon past the splenic flexure. The lumen of the colon and rectum is visualized. The foreign body is identified and removed by forceps or snare placed through the colonoscope. The colonoscope is withdrawn at the completion of the procedure.

45380
The physician performs colonoscopy and obtains tissue samples. The physician inserts the colonoscope into the anus and advances the scope past the splenic flexure. The lumen of the colon and rectum is visualized and biopsies are obtained. The colonoscope is withdrawn at the completion of the procedure.

45381
The physician performs flexible colonoscopy of the proximal to splenic flexure and injects a substance into the submucosa, directed at specific areas through the scope while viewing the colon. The physician inserts the colonoscope into the anus and advances the scope as far as the splenic flexure of the colon. The lumen of the colon is visualized. Submucosal saline injections, for instance, may be done before polypectomy using snare and electrocautery to greatly enhance the effectiveness of resection for large sessile colorectal polyps.

45382
The physician performs colonoscopy and controls an area of bleeding. The physician inserts the colonoscope into the anus and advances the scope past the splenic flexure. The lumen of the colon and rectum is visualized and the area of bleeding is identified and controlled. The colonoscope is withdrawn at the completion of the procedure.

45383
The physician performs colonoscopy and performs ablation of a tumor, polyp, or other lesions. The physician inserts the colonoscope into the anus and advances the scope past the splenic flexure. The lumen of the colon and rectum is visualized. The tumor, polyp, or other lesions are identified and ablated by laser or other method. The colonoscope is withdrawn at the completion of the procedure.

45384
The physician performs colonoscopy and removes a tumor, polyp or other lesions. The physician inserts the colonoscope into the anus and advances the scope past the splenic flexure. The lumen of the colon and rectum is visualized. The tumor, polyp or other lesions are identified and removed by hot biopsy forceps, or cautery. The colonoscope is withdrawn at the completion of the procedure.

45385
The physician performs colonoscopy and removes a tumor, polyp, or other lesions. The physician inserts the colonoscope into the anus and advances the scope past the splenic flexure. The lumen of the colon and rectum is visualized. The tumor, polyp, or other lesions are identified and removed by snare technique. The colonoscope is withdrawn at the completion of the procedure.

45386
The physician performs flexible colonoscopy of the proximal to splenic flexure and dilates strictures by balloon catheter. The physician inserts the colonoscope into the anus and advances the scope as far as the splenic flexure of the colon. The lumen of the colon is visualized. Areas of stenosis are identified and a balloon catheter is passed to the point of constriction and a little beyond. The balloon is inflated to the appropriate diameter and gradually withdrawn through the stenosed area, stretching the walls of the bowel at the strictured area.

45387
The physician uses a colonoscope to examine the colon and place a transendoscopic stent. The physician inserts the flexible endoscope into the anus and advances the scope beyond the splenic flexure. The lumen of the colon is visualized. The endoscope is placed at the site of an obstruction or stricture and the necessary stent length is determined. If the area is partially occluded or obstructed, a balloon-tipped catheter is inserted through the scope and the balloon is inflated to dilate the area before stent placement. The stent (endoprosthesis) is introduced to the site of the

lesion by a stent-carrying catheter inserted through the scope. The plastic covering over the stent is removed and the stent self-deploys, shoring-up the walls at the target site in the colon, proximal to the splenic flexure. When necessary, a balloon catheter is placed into the stent and gently inflated to more fully deploy the stent. The delivery system and endoscope are removed.

45391

The physician uses a flexible colonoscope to examine the colon past the splenic flexure and perform an endoscopic ultrasound (EUS) examination. Ultrasound and endoscopic imaging techniques are combined in this diagnostic modality. A flexible fiberoptic endoscope equipped with an ultrasound transducer at the tip is inserted into the anus and the scope is advanced beyond the splenic flexure. The lumen of the colon is visualized and the probe tip is guided next to the area of concern. Sound waves are sent out from the transducer and reflect back to a receiving unit at varying speeds as they pass through different densities of tissue. The waves are converted to electrical pulses displayed as a picture on screen. Using ultrasound from the endoscope instead of transcutaneously shortens the distance between the source and the target lesion and produces greater clarity from high frequency, high-resolution sound waves that have a short penetration distance. EUS is currently the most accurate method of staging cancer within the gastrointestinal tract.

45392

The physician uses a colonoscope to examine the colon past the splenic flexure and perform a transendoscopic ultrasound guided intramural or transmural fine needle aspiration/biopsy(s). A flexible fiberoptic endoscope equipped with an ultrasound transducer at the tip is inserted into the anus and the scope is advanced beyond the splenic flexure. The lumen of the colon is visualized and the probe tip is guided next to the area of concern. Sound waves are sent out from the transducer and reflect back to a receiving unit at varying speeds as they pass through different densities of tissue. The waves are converted to electrical pulses displayed as a picture on screen. A FNA needle is passed through the scope to the site of the lesion, lymph node, or tumor and a fine needle aspiration/biopsy(s) is taken of the abnormal tissue or fluid within the colon wall or through the intestinal wall. The instruments are removed.

45395-45397

With the patient under general anesthesia, the physician places a trocar at the umbilicus into the abdomen and insufflates the abdominal cavity. The physician places a laparoscope through the umbilical incision and additional trocars are placed, through which the surgical instruments are inserted. The physician mobilizes the sigmoid colon, tractions it upward, and incises the right pelvic peritoneum. Dissection and ligation are carried out on the inferior mesenteric artery and inferior mesenteric vein. The dissection is carried into the retrorectal space by using cautery scissors. The peritoneum is incised on both sides of the rectum and also anteriorly at the pouch of Douglas, and the mesorectum is mobilized off the sacrum. The physician frees the rectum from the posterior vaginal wall or the prostate and seminal vesicles. After the rectum is totally mobilized, a loop of sigmoid colon is brought through the small incision in a lower quadrant port, where it may be transected outside the body. The distal part is sutured shut and returned to the cavity and the stoma is matured. The specimen is removed en bloc during the perineal phase of the resection performed in a conventional fashion. The laparoscopic instruments are removed and the incisions are sutured. In 45397, the free end of the distal colon is brought through the sphincter complex and approximated with the anus to form a colo-anal anastomosis. The distal colon is folded and sutured in such a way as to create a colonic reservoir pouch. The physician may elect to bring a loop or end of the colon through a separate abdominal incision to create a stoma (diverting enterostomy).

45400-45402

The physician performs a laparoscopic proctopexy (or rectopexy) for correction of rectal prolapse. With the patient under general anesthesia, the physician places trocars into the abdomen and insufflates the abdominal cavity. Using a laparoscope, the physician completely mobilizes the rectum down to the pelvic floor and attaches the rectum to the sacrum using polypropylene mesh. The mesh is initially stapled to the sacral hollow and sutured on both sides of the rectum. The trocars are removed and the incisions are closed with sutures. In 45402, a laparoscopic sigmoid resection is performed in conjunction with the proctopexy. Using a laparoscope, the physician mobilizes the sigmoid colon and rectum. The redundant segment of sigmoid colon and rectum are excised and an anastomosis is created between the remaining bowel ends with sutures or staples. Following laparoscopic proctopexy as described above, the trocars are removed and the incision closed with sutures.

45500

The physician performs proctoplasty for an area of stenosis. The physician makes a longitudinal incision through the scar tissue at the anorectal junction or may completely excise the scar tissue to an area of normal mucosa. The surrounding perianal skin is undermined and mobilized in one of several possible fashions as a flap. The flap is approximated to the normal mucosa at the edges of the incised or excised scar, thus closing the wound.

45505

The physician performs proctoplasty for an area of prolapse of rectal mucosa (ectropion). The physician makes a circular incision just proximal to the prolapsing mucosa and mobilizes the redundant mucosa. An incision is made out onto the perianal skin to form a flap of skin on the right and left sides of the anus adjacent to the mobilized mucosa. The mucosa is excised and the flaps of skin are advanced into the anal canal. The mucosal edges are reapproximated in their normal anatomic position with sutures. The skin incisions are closed completing the procedure.

45520
The physician performs sclerotherapy for rectal prolapse. The physician identifies the anorectal ring. Sclerosing solution is injected into the submucosa of the rectum circumferentially just above the anorectal ring.

45540
The physician approximates the rectum to the sacrum (proctopexy) for rectal prolapse. The physician makes an abdominal incision. The rectum is completely mobilized from the sacrum and placed in upward tension to remove any redundancy. The rectum is reapproximated to the sacrum with sutures or a mesh may be wrapped around the rectum and attached to the sacrum. The incision is closed.

45541
Through a perineal approach, the physician approximates the rectum to the sacrum (proctopexy) for rectal prolapse. The physician makes a transverse incision between the anus and coccyx. Dissection is continued through the levator muscles to mobilize the rectum from the sacrum. The rectum is placed on upward tension to remove the redundancy and approximated to the sacrum with sutures or with a mesh wrapped around the rectum and secured to the sacrum. The incision is closed.

45550
The physician approximates the rectum to the sacrum and performs a sigmoid colon resection. The physician makes an abdominal incision. The sigmoid colon and rectum are mobilized. The redundant segment of sigmoid colon and rectum is excised and an anastomosis is created between the remaining bowel ends with sutures or staples. The rectum is approximated to the sacrum with sutures. The incision is closed.

45560
The physician repairs a rectocele, a herniation of the rectum against the vaginal wall. The physician makes an incision in the mucosa of the posterior vaginal wall over the rectocele. The rectocele is dissected free of surrounding structures and the levator muscles are identified. The rectum is plicated to surrounding fascia with multiple sutures and the levator muscles are reapproximated. The vaginal mucosa is excised and the incision is closed.

45562
The physician explores, repairs, and drains a rectal injury. The physician makes an abdominal incision. The rectal injury is explored and repaired with sutures if possible. An incision is made between the coccyx and anus and drains are placed in the presacral space. The abdominal incision is closed.

45563
The physician explores, repairs, and drains a rectal injury and performs a proximal colostomy. The physician makes an abdominal incision. The rectal injury is explored and repaired with sutures. A loop or end of sigmoid colon is brought through a separate incision on the abdominal wall as a colostomy. An incision is made between the sacrum and anus and drains are placed in the presacral space. The abdominal incision is closed.

45800
The physician closes a connection between the rectum and the bladder (rectovesical fistula). The physician makes an abdominal incision. The sigmoid colon and rectum are mobilized and the connection between the rectum and bladder is identified and divided. The fistulous openings in the rectum and bladder are debrided and closed with sutures.

45805
The physician closes a connection between the rectum and bladder (rectovesical fistula) and performs a proximal colostomy. The physician makes an abdominal incision. The sigmoid colon and rectum are mobilized and the connection between the rectum and bladder is identified and divided. The fistulous openings in the rectum and bladder are debrided and closed. The involved segment of colon or rectum may be excised. A loop or end of sigmoid colon proximal to the involved area is brought out through a separate incision on the abdominal wall as a colostomy. The abdominal incision is closed.

45820
The physician closes a rectourethral fistula. The physician makes an abdominal incision. The rectum is dissected from the prostate and the fistula is identified and divided. The fistulous opening in the rectum is closed with sutures and the opening in the urethra may be closed or left open. A pedicle of omentum is usually mobilized and placed between the areas of repair. The incision is closed. As an alternate method an incision may be made between the anus and urethra from a perineal approach and dissection continued between the rectum and urethra. The fistula is identified and divided and the openings in the rectum and urethra are closed. The incision is closed.

45825
The physician closes a rectourethral fistula and forms a proximal colostomy. The physician makes an abdominal incision. The rectum is dissected from the

prostate and the fistula is identified and divided. The fistulous opening in the rectum is closed with sutures and the opening in the urethra may be closed or left open. A pedicle of omentum is usually mobilized and placed between the areas of repair. A loop or end of proximal colon is brought through a separate incision on the abdominal wall as a colostomy. The initial incision is closed.

45900
The physician reduces a rectal prolapse (procidentia) to a patient under general anesthesia. The physician performs a manual reduction of an incarcerated rectal prolapse by pushing the prolapsed segment into the anus under the relaxation of anesthesia.

45905
The physician dilates the anal sphincter under anesthesia. The physician performs dilation of the anal sphincter digitally or with a dilating instrument under the relaxation of anesthesia.

45910
The physician dilates a rectal stricture under anesthesia. The physician performs dilation of a rectal stricture digitally or with a dilating instrument under the relaxation of anesthesia.

45915
The physician removes a foreign body or fecal impaction under anesthesia. The physician performs removal of a foreign body or fecal impaction manually or with an instrument under the relaxation of anesthesia.

45990
The physician performs a diagnostic anorectal exam. The patient is placed under general, spinal or epidural anesthesia. The physician examines the external perineal area. A pelvic examination is performed when appropriate. A digital rectal exam is performed. An anoscope is inserted into the rectum. The anal canal and distal rectum are visualized. The anoscope is removed and a rigid proctosigmoidoscope is inserted into the anus and advanced. The sigmoid colon and rectal lumen are visualized. The proctosigmoidoscope is removed.

46020
The physician makes an incision in the anal opening. A suture is passed and the seton is securely tied using a rubber band, or similar technique. A nylon suture is threaded around the sphincter and tied loosely. An elastic band is secured to the suture and a safety pin is attached. The pin is taped to the patient's thigh and the patient is instructed to adjust the amount of pull to produce minimal discomfort until the seton cuts through.

46030
The physician removes an anal seton or other marker. The physician identifies the seton stitch or other marker at the anal verge. The seton is divided and removed. The external anal sphincter at the level of the seton may be divided.

46040
The physician drains an perirectal or ischiorectal abscess. The physician identifies the location of the abscess. The perianal skin over the abscess is incised and the abscess cavity is opened and drained. The incision is packed open for continued drainage.

46045
The physician drains a perirectal abscess in the intramural, intramuscular, or submucosal position. The physician identifies the location of the abscess in relation to the sphincter muscles. The perianal skin or rectal mucosa over the abscess is incised. Dissection is carried through muscle if necessary and the abscess cavity is opened and drained. The incision is packed open for continued drainage.

46050
The physician drains a superficial perianal abscess. The physician identifies the location of the abscess. The perianal skin over the abscess is incised and the abscess cavity is opened and drained. The incision is packed open for continued drainage.

46060
The physician drains an ischiorectal or intramural perirectal abscess with fistulectomy or fistulotomy and may place a seton. The physician identifies the location of the abscess and the internal and external openings of the anal fistula in relation to the sphincter muscles. An incision is made in the perianal skin over the abscess and the abscess cavity is opened and drained. The mucosa, skin, and internal sphincter muscle overlying the fistula is incised and the fistula is completely unroofed or may be excised. If the fistula goes beneath the external sphincter muscle a stitch (seton) may be placed through the fistula tract to allow drainage and preserve continence. The incision is left open to drain and the abscess cavity is packed open for continued drainage.

46070
The physician incises a congenital anal septum. The physician identifies the anal opening and septum in the infant. The septum is sharply incised.

46080
The physician divides the anal sphincter. The patient is placed in jackknife or lithotomy position. The physician performs digital and instrumental dilation of the anus with exposure of the patient's anal canal. A small incision is made between the muscle layers of the anus and internal muscle is divided without opening the lining of the anus.

46083
The physician performs incision of a thrombosed external hemorrhoid. The physician identifies the

thrombosed external hemorrhoid. An incision is made in the skin over the hemorrhoid and the thrombus is removed. The incision is left open for continued drainage.

46200
The physician excises a fissure (fissurectomy) and may perform a sphincterotomy. The physician identifies the anal fissure and the internal sphincter muscle by palpation. An incision is made around the fissure, dissecting it free of underlying sphincter muscle, and the fissure is excised. The internal sphincter muscle may be incised, usually in a lateral position away from the fissure. The incision is usually left open to allow drainage.

46220
The physician performs excision of a single external anal papilla or skin tag. The physician identifies the anal skin tag or papilla, which is usually associated with the external edge of a fissure or fistula. An incision is made around the skin tag or papilla and the lesion is dissected from the underlying sphincter muscle and removed. The incision is closed with sutures or may be left partially open to drain.

46221
The physician performs hemorrhoidectomy by tying off (ligating) an internal hemorrhoid. The physician identifies the internal hemorrhoid. The hemorrhoid is ligated at its base with a rubber band. The hemorrhoid tissue is allowed to slough over time.

46230
The physician performs an excision of multiple external anal papillae or tags. Papillae are often associated with the external edge of an anal fissure or fistula. Once the physician has identified the external tags or papillae, incisions are made around the lesions. The lesions are dissected from the underlying sphincter muscle and removed. The incisions are closed with sutures or may be left partially open to drain.

46250
The physician performs an excision of external hemorrhoids. The physician identifies the external hemorrhoids. Incisions are made around the hemorrhoids and the lesions are dissected from the underlying sphincter muscle and removed. The incisions are closed with sutures.

46255
The physician performs excision of a single column or group of internal and external hemorrhoids. The physician explores the anal canal and identifies the hemorrhoid column. An incision is made in the rectal mucosa around the hemorrhoids and the lesions are dissected from the underlying sphincter muscles and removed. The incisions are closed with sutures.

46257
The physician performs excision of a single column or group of internal and external hemorrhoids and an associated fissure. The physician explores the anal canal and identifies the hemorrhoid column and the fissure. An incision is made in the rectal mucosa around the hemorrhoids and the lesions are dissected from the underlying sphincter muscles and removed. An incision is made around the fissure and the fissure is dissected from the underlying sphincter muscles and excised. The incisions are closed with sutures.

46258
The physician performs excision of a single column or group of internal and external hemorrhoids with associated fistulectomy and possible fissurectomy. The physician explores the anal canal and identifies the hemorrhoid column and the fistula. If the fistula is in the same plane as the hemorrhoid, a single incision is made in the mucosa around the lesions and the lesions are dissected from the underlying sphincter muscles and removed. If the lesions are in different planes, separate incisions are used to excise the lesions. If a fissure is present, it may be excised in a similar manner. The incisions are closed with sutures.

46260
The physician performs excision of two or more columns or groups of internal and external hemorrhoids. The physician explores the anal canal and identifies the hemorrhoid columns. Incisions are made in the rectal mucosa around the hemorrhoid columns. The lesions are dissected from the underlying sphincter muscles and removed. The incisions are closed with sutures.

46261
The physician performs excision of two or more columns or groups of internal and external hemorrhoids and an associated fissure. The physician explores the anal canal and identifies the hemorrhoid columns and the fissure. Incisions are made in the rectal mucosa around the hemorrhoid columns and around the fissure. The lesions are dissected from the underlying sphincter muscles and removed. The incisions are closed with sutures.

46262
The physician performs excision of two or more columns or groups of internal and external hemorrhoids with an associated fistulectomy and possible fissurectomy. The physician explores the anal canal and identifies the hemorrhoid columns and the fistula. Incisions are made in the rectal mucosa around the hemorrhoid columns and around the fistula. The lesions are dissected from the underlying sphincter muscles and removed. If a fissure is present, it may be excised in a similar manner. The incisions are closed with sutures.

46270
The physician excises or incises a subcutaneous anal fistula. The physician explores the anal canal and identifies the location of the fistula in relation to the sphincter muscles. The skin and subcutaneous tissue overlying the fistula is excised or incised to open the fistula tract. The incision is usually left open to allow continued drainage.

46275
The physician excises or incises an intersphincteric anal fistula. The physician explores the anal canal and identifies the location of the fistula in relation to the sphincter muscles. The skin, subcutaneous tissue, and internal sphincter muscle overlying the fistula are excised or incised to open the fistula tract. If the external sphincter is involved, a portion of the external sphincter may also be safely incised. The incision is usually left open to allow continued drainage.

46280
The physician excises or incises a transsphincteric, suprasphincteric, extrasphincteric, or multiple anal fistula. The physician explores the anal canal and identifies the location of the fistula in relation to the sphincter muscles. The tissue overlying the fistula or fistulas is excised or incised to open the fistula tract. If the external sphincter or the puborectal muscular sling is involved, only a portion of the muscle is incised to open the fistula. A permanent suture is placed through the remainder of the fistula tract (seton) in order to allow drainage and preserve continence. The incisions are usually left open to allow continued drainage. This code includes the seton placement, when performed.

46285
The physician performs a second stage excision or incision of an anal fistula. The physician explores the anal canal and identifies the location of the fistula in relation to the sphincter muscles. Usually the fistula tract has been partially opened and a seton may be in place. The remainder of the fistula tract is excised or incised and a seton if present is removed. The incision is usually left open to allow continued drainage.

46288
The physician excises an anal fistula and closes the defect with a rectal advancement flap. The physician explores the anal canal and identifies the location of the fistula in relation to the sphincter muscles. The fistula tract is excised. An incision is made onto the perianal skin and a wedge of skin and subcutaneous tissue is mobilized and advanced into the defect created by the excision of the fistula. The incisions are closed with sutures.

46320
The physician performs an excision of an external hemorrhoid that has become clotted with blood (thrombosed). Following appropriate anesthesia, the physician exposes the thrombosed external hemorrhoid. The hemorrhoid is completely excised with a scalpel. The site of the excision may be closed or left open to allow continued drainage.

46500
The physician performs sclerotherapy of internal hemorrhoids. The physician explores the anal canal and identifies the hemorrhoid columns. Sclerosing solution is injected into the submucosa of the rectal wall under the hemorrhoid columns.

46505
The physician utilizes chemodenervation (the use of chemical agents, including neurotoxins) to provide selective weakening of certain muscles or muscle groups by causing a neuromuscular blockade. Chemodenervation works by introducing a substance used to block the transfer of chemicals at the presynaptic membrane. Botulinum toxin type A (BTX-A, Botox®) is the most common substance used. To treat chronic anal fissures, the physician injects BTX-A into the internal anal sphincter. This permits chemical denervation of the anal sphincter and promotes healing of the fissure.

46600
The physician performs anoscopy and may obtain brushings or washings. The physician inserts the anoscope into the anus and advances the scope. The anal canal and distal rectal mucosa are visualized and brushings or washings may be obtained. The anoscope is withdrawn at the completion of the procedure.

46604
The physician performs anoscopy and performs anal dilation. The physician inserts the anoscope into the anus and advances the scope. The anal canal and distal rectal mucosa are visualized. Dilation of the anal sphincter or a distal stricture is performed with the anoscope, digitally, or by some other instrument. The anoscope is withdrawn at the completion of the procedure.

46606
The physician performs anoscopy and obtains tissue samples. The physician inserts the anoscope into the anus and advances the scope. The anal canal and distal rectal mucosa are visualized and tissue samples are obtained. The anoscope is withdrawn at the completion of the procedure.

46608
The physician performs anoscopy and removes a foreign body. The physician inserts the anoscope into the anus and advances the scope. The anal canal and distal rectal mucosa are visualized. The foreign body is identified and removed with a snare or forceps placed through the anoscope. The anoscope is withdrawn at the completion of the procedure.

46610
The physician performs anoscopy and removes a single tumor, polyp, or other lesion. The physician inserts the anoscope into the anus and advances the scope. The anal canal and distal rectal mucosa are visualized. The tumor, polyp, or other lesion is identified and removed by hot biopsy forceps or cautery. The anoscope is withdrawn at the completion of the procedure.

46611
The physician performs anoscopy and removes a single tumor, polyp, or other lesion. The physician inserts the anoscope into the anus and advances the scope. The anal canal and distal rectal mucosa are visualized. The tumor, polyp, or other lesion is identified and removed by snare technique. The anoscope is withdrawn at the completion of the procedure.

46612
The physician performs anoscopy and removes multiple tumors, polyps, or other lesions. The physician inserts the anoscope into the anus and advances the scope. The tumors, polyps or other lesions are identified and removed by hot biopsy forceps, cautery, or snare technique. The anoscope is removed at the completion of the procedure.

46614
The physician performs anoscopy and controls an area of bleeding. The physician inserts the anoscope into the anus and advances the scope. The anal canal and distal rectal mucosa are visualized. The area of bleeding is identified and controlled. The anoscope is withdrawn at the completion of the procedure.

46615
The physician performs anoscopy and performs ablation of a tumor, polyp, or other lesions. The physician inserts the anoscope into the anus and advances the scope. The anal canal and distal rectal mucosa are visualized. The tumor, polyp, or other lesions are identified and ablation of the lesions is performed. The anoscope is withdrawn at the completion of the procedure.

46700
The physician performs anoplasty for an anal stricture in an adult. The physician explores the anal canal and identifies the stricture. An incision is made in the scar of the stricture and a portion of the stricture is excised. Incisions are extended onto the perianal skin and subcutaneous tissue and skin flaps are mobilized and advanced into the defects created by the scar excision. The flaps are sutured to the surrounding skin and anoderm thus closing the defect.

46705
The physician performs anoplasty for an anal stricture in an infant. The physician explores the anal canal and identifies the stricture. An incision is made in the scar of the stricture and a portion of the stricture is excised. Incisions are extended onto the perianal skin and subcutaneous tissue and skin flaps are mobilized and advanced into the defects created by the scar excision. The flaps are sutured to the surrounding skin and anoderm thus closing the defect.

46706-46707
The physician repairs an anal fistula using fibrin glue (46706). Fibrin glue is made with human fibrinogen pooled from the plasma of long-term donors under control methods that avoid passing infection to the recipient. The glue is composed of two components, usually applied through double lumen catheters to guide the component injections separately to the tissue and must be applied at a temperature of 37 C. The fistula is localized and cannulated and then prepped for the glue. The margins and canal of the fistula are de-epithelialized with electrocoagulation and/or roughening the fistulous canal with a brush. Some bleeding actually improves the adhesion of the fibrin clot. The gluing is done so as to completely fill the defect and around the borders of the fistula, sealing it with a clot. Fibrin glue only works on tissue capable of local regeneration for wound healing since the glue does not actually function as a seal or a plug, but provides the substrate for fibroblasts to move in. After about four weeks, the glued surface is replaced by scar tissue and the fibrin glue totally decomposes. Mechanical stress must be avoided while this stage is developing. In 46707, the physician treats an anorectal fistula or artificial communication from the anus or rectum to the skin with a porcine small intestine submucosa (SIS) plug. The patient is in a prone position. Using a sterile probe, the physician identifies the primary fistula opening by advancing the probe through the secondary fistula opening. The fistula is irrigated. The fistula plug is introduced through the internal (primary) fistula opening and threaded into the fistula until the internal opening is occluded. The plug is trimmed flush with the mucosal wall of the anus or colon and also trimmed flush at the secondary site. Each end of the plug is secured with resorbable sutures.

46710-46712
The physician repairs an ileoanal pouch fistula or sinus by pouch advancement using a transperineal or combined transperineal and transabdominal approach. An ileoanal pouch is created as a place for the storage of stool in patients that have had their large intestines removed due to disease. The pouch is connected to the anus, allowing the patient to have a bowel movement into the anus rather than needing a colostomy bag. If a drainage tract (fistula or sinus) erodes from an ileoanal pouch to the perineal area or into the vagina, it can be repaired by dissecting the tract from its external origin, the skin of the perineum or the lining of the vagina, to its source at the ileoanal pouch, and closing the tissues. In 46710, the tract is dissected (removed) and closed starting in the perineal area. In 46712, the tract is dissected (removed) using an approach that combines

dissection starting in the perineal area moving toward the pouch along with an incision in the lower abdominal wall that allows access to the ileoanal pouch internally. In both cases, any damage done to the pouch is repaired (pouch advancement).

46715

The physician performs an incision to open a low imperforate anus ("cutback" procedure). The physician exposes the perineum and identifies the fistulous opening to the imperforate anus. An incision is made through the fistula into the anus onto the skin thus opening the anus. The anus is usually dilated with Hegar dilators. The incision is usually left open to heal.

46716

The physician transposes an ectopic anal orifice. The imperforate anus has usually been previously incised and opened. The physician makes an incision around the anus. Dissection is continued circumferentially around the distal rectum. Next, a cruciate incision is made over the usual site of the anus and an opening is created through the subcutaneous tissue and what remains of the external sphincter. The rectum is tunneled down through the new orifice and sutured to the new location. The incision at the previous anal site is closed.

46730

The physician repairs a high imperforate anus through a perineal or sacroperineal approach. The physician makes an incision at the usual site of the anus. Dissection is continued through the external sphincter. The puborectalis muscle is identified and dissection is carried through the muscle to identify and mobilize the rectal stump. The rectal stump is pulled through the sphincter complex, opened, and sutured to the sphincter and skin creating an anal opening. Alternately, a posterior midline sacral incision may be made initially. Dissection is carried superiorly, the puborectalis muscle is identified and a tract is formed through the puborectalis sling to the new anal opening. A perineal incision is made and the rectal stump mobilized and pulled through the sphincter complex onto the skin as described above.

46735

The physician repairs an imperforate anus by combined transabdominal and sacroperineal approaches. The physician makes a posterior midline incision on the sacrum and removes the coccyx. The puborectalis muscle is identified and a tract is made through the puborectalis sling to the future anal site. Next, the physician makes an abdominal incision and mobilizes the distal colon and rectum. The rectum is divided and the mucosa is striped from the distal rectum. An incision is made in the bottom of the rectal muscle pouch and the proximal rectum or colon is pulled through the muscular floor and puborectalis sling to the new anal site. A skin incision is made at the new anal site and the end of the colon is sutured to the sphincter muscles and skin creating a new anus. The incisions are closed.

46740

The physician repairs a high imperforate anus with a urethral or vaginal fistula through a perineal or sacroperineal approach. The physician makes an incision at the usual site of the anus. Dissection is continued through the external sphincter. The puborectalis muscle is identified and dissection is carried through the muscle to identify and mobilize the rectal stump. The urethral or vaginal fistula is identified, divided, and closed with sutures. The rectal stump is pulled through the sphincter complex, opened and sutured to the sphincter muscles and skin creating a new anal orifice. A posterior midline sacral incision may be made initially. Dissection is carried superiorly, the puborectalis muscle is identified and a tract is formed through the puborectalis sling to the new anal opening. A perineal incision is made at the site of the new anal opening. The rectal stump is mobilized, the fistula identified and divided, and the rectum pulled through the sphincter complex onto the skin as described above.

46742

The physician repairs an imperforate anus with a urethral or vaginal fistula by combined transabdominal and sacroperineal approaches. The physician makes a posterior midline incision on the sacrum and removes the coccyx. The puborectalis muscle is identified and a tract is developed through the puborectalis sling to the future anal site. Next, the physician makes an abdominal incision and mobilizes the distal colon and rectum. The rectum is divided, the mucosa is stripped from the distal rectum and the urethral or vaginal fistula is identified and closed with sutures. An incision is made in the bottom of the rectal muscle pouch and the proximal rectum or colon is pulled through the muscular floor and puborectalis sling to the new anal site. A skin incision is made at the new anal site end of the colon is sutured to the sphincter muscles and skin creating a new anus. The incisions are closed.

46744

The physician repairs a cloacal anomaly. The patient is placed in a lithotomy position. The physician makes a small incision in the perineum. The bladder, urethra, and vagina are dissected free of each other. A new rectum is formed by interposing muscle posterior to the rectum. The incision is closed with sutures.

46746

The physician repairs a cloacal anomaly. The physician makes a small incision, using a combined abdominal and sacroperineal approach. The bladder, urethra, and vagina are dissected free of each other. A new rectum is formed by interposing muscle posterior to the rectum. The incision is closed.

46748
The physician corrects a congenital anomaly of the cloaca. A cloacal anomaly usually involves a single opening on the anterior perineum for the urethra, vagina, and rectum. The physician enters the pelvic cavity through an incision in the lower abdomen and makes a second incision in the perineum from the clitoris to the anal area. The surgeon creates separate openings and divides membranes for the urethra, vagina, and rectum by using intestinal grafts, pedicle flaps, and free skin grafts.

46750
The physician performs anal sphincteroplasty for prolapse or incontinence in an adult. The physician makes a transverse incision anterior to the anus. Dissection is carried through subcutaneous tissues to expose the anal canal. The external anal sphincter muscle is dissected from the internal sphincter in the anterior plane and divided in the midline. The ends of the external sphincter are wrapped around the anal canal in an overlapping fashion and approximated with sutures. The incision is closed.

46751
The physician performs anal sphincteroplasty for prolapse or incontinence in a child. The physician makes a transverse incision anterior to the anus. Dissection is carried through the subcutaneous tissues to expose the anal canal. The external anal sphincter muscle is dissected from the internal sphincter and divided in the midline. The ends of the external sphincter are wrapped around the anal canal in an overlapping fashion and approximated with sutures. The incision is closed.

46753
The physician places a wire, suture, or muscular graft around the anus for rectal prolapse or incontinence (Thiersch procedure). The physician makes incisions on opposite sides of the anus in the lateral perianal subcutaneous tissue. A wire, suture or muscular graft mobilized from the thigh is wrapped around the anus in the subcutaneous space and secured in place. The incisions are closed.

46754
The physician removes a wire or suture that has been placed around the anal canal for rectal prolapse or incontinence. The physician makes incisions in the lateral perianal subcutaneous tissue. The wire or suture that is encircling the anus is identified, divided and removed. The incisions are closed.

46760
The physician performs an anal sphincteroplasty with a muscular graft for incontinence in an adult. The physician makes a transverse incision anterior to the anus. Dissection is carried through subcutaneous tissue to expose the anal canal and the remaining external sphincter muscle is dissected from the internal sphincter. A muscle from the thigh is mobilized and tunneled to the perineum. The muscle is wrapped around the anal canal and approximated with sutures. The incisions are closed.

46761
The physician performs sphincteroplasty with levator muscle imbrication for incontinence in an adult (Park repair). The physician makes a transverse incision anterior to the anus. Dissection is carried through the subcutaneous tissue to expose the anal canal. The external sphincter muscle is dissected from the internal sphincter and dissection is continued between the sphincters to expose the puborectalis muscle (levator). The edges of the puborectalis muscle are imbricated around the anal canal with sutures. The external sphincter muscle is imbricated around the anal canal with sutures. The incision is closed.

46762
The physician makes a midline abdominal incision. The physician dissects the perineum overlying the rectal orifice. The external anal sphincter muscle is mobilized along with its fibrotic ends. Surgical repair of the defective sphincter is performed with the implantation of an artificial sphincter. The external sphincter muscle may be wrapped around the anal canal and approximated without tension. The surgeon may find it necessary to approximate the levator ani muscle to restore the anorectal angle to normal; the puborectalis and external sphincter muscles are also tightened with sutures. This procedure lengthens the anal canal. Once implantation of the artificial sphincter is complete and the sphincter is reconstructed, the perineum is closed.

46900-46916
The physician performs destruction of anal lesions with chemicals in 46900. The physician exposes the perianal skin and identifies the lesions. The lesions are painted with destructive chemicals. In 46910, the physician performs destruction of anal lesions with electrodesiccation. The physician exposes the perianal skin and identifies the lesions. The lesions are destroyed with cautery. In 46916, the physician performs destruction of anal lesions with cryosurgery. The physician exposes the perianal skin and identifies the lesions. The lesions are frozen and destroyed, usually with liquid nitrogen.

46917-46922
The physician performs destruction of anal lesions with laser therapy in 46917. The physician exposes the perianal skin and identifies the lesions. The lesions are destroyed by laser ablation or laser excision. In 46922, the physician performs destruction of anal lesions by excision. The physician exposes the perianal skin and identifies the lesions. The lesions are surgically excised. The incisions are closed.

46924
The physician performs destruction of extensive anal lesions. The physician exposes the perianal skin and identifies the lesions. An extensive destruction of the lesions is performed by various methods, such as laser surgery, electrosurgery, cryosurgery, or chemosurgery.

46930
The physician destroys internal hemorrhoids using various forms of thermal energy. The physician explores the anal canal and identifies the hemorrhoid columns. The hemorrhoids may be destroyed by clamping and cauterization, by employing high-frequency radio waves (radiofrequency), or by infrared or laser coagulation, which causes the hemorrhoidal tissue to harden, deteriorate, and form scar tissue as the area heals. The hemorrhoidal remnants may be removed.

46940-46942
The physician performs an initial (46940) or subsequent (46942) curettage or cautery of an anal fissure with dilation of the anal sphincter. The physician exposes the perianal area and identifies the fissure. The fissure is debrided with curettage or cautery. The anal sphincter is manually dilated.

46945-46946
The physician performs ligation (tying off) of internal hemorrhoids using methods other than rubber bands. The physician explores the anal canal and identifies the hemorrhoid column(s). Report 46945 for ligation of a single hemorrhoid column or group and 46946 for ligation of two or more columns or groups.

46947
The physician performs a stapled hemorrhoidopexy for prolapsing internal hemorrhoids. After having fleet enemas or oral preparation for cleansing the colon, the patient is sedated and given local or spinal anesthesia. A circular anal dilator is inserted that reduces the prolapsed anal tissue. The center obturator piece is removed and the prolapsed mucosa falls into the dilator lumen. An anoscope is inserted through the dilator that pushes the mucosa back against the rectal wall for 270 degrees of rotation. The other tissue protrudes through a window in the scope through which a purse string suture is made, containing only mucous membrane. The anoscope is rotated until a purse-string suture is completed around the anal circumference. A circular stapler is positioned proximal to the suture. The ends are tied externally. With traction on the purse string suture, the prolapsed mucosa is brought into the casing of the circular stapler, which is fired to release two staggered rows of staples while a circular knife removes a column of redundant mucosa from the upper anal canal. The staple line is examined and instruments are removed.

47000-47001
The physician takes tissue from the liver for examination. In 47000, the physician uses separately reportable ultrasound guidance to place a hollow bore needle between the ribs on the patient's right side. The liver biopsy is sent for pathology for separately reportable activity. Report 47001 when the liver biopsy is performed during an open procedure.

47010
The physician incises the liver to drain an abscess or a cyst, sometimes taking one or two stages. The physician exposes the liver via an upper midline incision. The cyst is incised and suctioned with care to not contaminate the abdomen with purulent matter. Cultures and pathology are sent in a separately reported activity. The incision is closed.

47011
The physician performs a hepatotomy for percutaneous drainage of abscess or cyst, one or two stages. The physician may create a small incision in the skin proximal to the liver abscess or cyst to ease placement of drainage instruments through the skin (percutaneous). The physician uses a CAT scan or ultrasound to guide placement of a drainage needle or trocar into the liver abscess or cyst. The physician advances the drainage needle or trocar through the abdominal wall into the peritoneum to gain access to the abscess or cystic cavity. The procedure sometimes requires multiple stages. The fluid is allowed to drain. Once drained, a catheter may be placed. Sutures may be secured to hold the drainage catheter in place. The operative site is subsequently cleaned and bandaged. For radiological supervision and interpretation, see 75989.

47015
The physician performs aspiration or injection of liver parasitic cysts or abscesses. The physician makes an abdominal incision. The liver is mobilized and the parasitic cysts or abscesses are identified. The remaining abdominal contents are packed off with sponges for protection. The cysts are aspirated with a needle and syringe or unroofed and aspirated and may be injected with a hypertonic solution. The abdominal incision is closed.

47100
The physician takes a wedge-shaped section of liver tissue for biopsy. The physician exposes the abdomen via an upper abdominal incision through skin, fascia, and muscle. Interrupted mattress sutures are placed on the edge of the liver lobe. A pie-shaped wedge of the liver is resected and sent for pathology in a separately reportable activity. Electrocautery is used to obtain hemostasis of the liver edge. The abdominal incision is closed with layered sutures.

47120-47130

The physician removes a section of liver, or lobectomy. The physician exposes the liver via an upper midline incision through skin, fascia, and muscle. The fibrous connections of the liver to the diaphragm are divided and the portal structures are controlled. The portal and hepatic vessels associated with the affected lobe are divided. The portal structures are clamped. The liver parenchyma is divided by pressure or coagulation hemostasis. The portal clamp is removed and hemostasis is assured before the abdomen is closed with sutures. Report 47120 if a partial lobectomy is performed; report 47122 if a trisegmentectomy is performed; report 47125 if a total left lobectomy is performed; and report 47130 if a total right lobectomy is performed.

47133

The physician performs a donor hepatectomy by removing the liver from a cadaver donor for transplantation into another recipient. The physician accesses the liver, which is mobilized from its attachments. The blood supply and bile ducts to the liver are dissected free and isolated. The liver is removed with its attached blood vessels and bile ducts and perfused with a cold preservation solution and removed from the operative field. The liver is preserved for transplantation into the recipient. The organ remains under refrigeration, specially packed in a sealable container with some preserving solution and kept on ice in a suitable carrier.

47135

The physician performs partial or whole liver transplantation to the normal anatomic position of the liver in a patient of any age. The physician makes an abdominal incision. The diseased liver tissue is removed, hemostasis is achieved, and the liver bed is dried and prepared for the donor tissue. The donor liver is placed in the prepared liver bed. Anastomoses are created between the donor hepatic vessels and the appropriate recipient vessels. The donor bile duct is approximated to the recipient bile duct or to a limb of small bowel for drainage. Drains are placed and the abdominal incision is closed.

47136

The physician performs a partial or whole liver transplantation into a patient of any age to a position other than the normal anatomic position of the liver. The physician makes an abdominal incision. The donor liver is placed in an acceptable position in the upper abdominal cavity that is not the normal liver bed location. Anastomoses are created between the donor hepatic vessels and the appropriate recipient vessels. The donor bile duct is approximated to the recipient bile duct or to a limb of small bowel for drainage. Drains are placed and the abdominal incision is closed.

47140

Surgeons remove the left lateral portion only (segments II and III) of the liver from a living donor, who is oftentimes a parent of compatible blood type donating to an infant or young child. Bilateral subcostal incisions are made to the xiphoid and the peritoneum is entered. The liver is exposed and mobilized. The left hepatic vein is exposed, adhesions are removed, and the porta hepatis is encircled with a drain. The left hepatic artery is dissected free and looped. The gastrohepatic ligament is transected and any aberrant left hepatic arteries within it are dissected to the left gastric artery. The left lateral segment of the liver is now reflected forward and ligaments are dissected away. The left portal vein is dissected and encircled. The left bile duct is identified and the left hepatic duct is transected, along with any multiple bile ducts within the liver, while preserving blood supply to the main bile duct. Ultrasound is used to locate the left and middle hepatic veins and the left hepatic vein is dissected and encircled. The liver's resection lines are marked with cautery. Vessels and bile ducts within this area are sutured and divided. The liver is resected and hemostasis maintained with a laser coagulator. Clamps are applied to the left hepatic artery, hepatic vein, and portal vein. The left lateral segment is removed and perfused with preservative solution for transplant. The clamped vessels and the left bile duct are sutured. The liver is checked for complete hemostasis and any bile leaks before closing. The tissue is preserved for transplantation into the recipient. The organ remains under refrigeration, packed in a sealable container with some preserving solution and kept on ice in a suitable carrier.

47141

Surgeons remove the whole left lobe (segments II, III, and IV) of the liver from a living donor, who is oftentimes a parent of compatible blood type donating to an infant or young child. Bilateral subcostal incisions are made to the xiphoid and the peritoneum is entered. The liver is exposed and mobilized. The left hepatic vein is exposed, adhesions are removed, and the porta hepatis is encircled with a drain. The left hepatic artery is dissected free and looped. The gastrohepatic ligament is transected and any aberrant left hepatic arteries within it are dissected to the left gastric artery. The left lateral segment of the liver is now reflected forward and ligaments are dissected away. The left portal vein is dissected and encircled. The left bile duct is identified. A cholecystectomy and cholangiogram are performed with catheter insertion into the cystic duct. The left hepatic duct is transected, along with any multiple bile ducts within the liver, while preserving blood supply to the main bile duct. Ultrasound is used to locate the left and middle hepatic veins, which are dissected and encircled. The liver's resection lines are marked with cautery. Vessels and bile ducts within this area are sutured and divided. The liver is resected and hemostasis is maintained with a laser coagulator.

Clamps are applied to the left hepatic artery, hepatic vein, and portal vein. The total left lobe of the liver is removed and perfused with preservative solution for transplant. The clamped vessels and the left bile duct are sutured. The liver is checked for complete hemostasis and any bile leaks before closing. A final cholangiogram is performed, the catheter is removed, and the cystic duct is sutured. The tissue is preserved for transplantation into the recipient. The organ remains under refrigeration, packed in a sealable container with some preserving solution and kept on ice in a suitable carrier.

47142

Surgeons remove the whole right lobe (segments V, VI, VII, and VIII) of the liver from a living donor, who is oftentimes a parent of compatible blood type donating to an infant or young child. Bilateral subcostal incisions are made to the xiphoid and the peritoneum is entered. The liver is exposed and mobilized. Ligaments on the right are divided and dissection is continued to the inferior vena cava. Adhesions are removed and the porta hepatis is encircled with a drain. The right hepatic artery is dissected free and looped. A cholecystectomy and cholangiogram are performed with catheter insertion into the cystic duct. The right portal vein is dissected and encircled. The right bile ducts are identified. The right hepatic duct is transected within the liver parenchyma, along with any multiple bile ducts, while preserving blood supply to the main bile duct. The caudate lobe must be mobilized from the inferior vena cava. All accessory hepatic veins are ligated and ultrasound is used to locate the right and middle hepatic veins. The right hepatic vein is dissected and encircled. The liver's resection lines are marked with cautery. Vessels and bile ducts within this area are sutured and divided, maintaining the veins from segments V and VIII, and the liver is resected. Hemostasis is maintained with a laser coagulator. Clamps are applied to the right hepatic artery, hepatic vein, and portal vein. The right lobe of the liver is removed and perfused with preservative solution for transplant. The clamped vessels and the right bile duct are sutured. The liver is checked for complete hemostasis and any bile leaks before closing. A final cholangiogram is performed, the catheter is removed, and the cystic duct is sutured. The tissue is preserved for transplantation into the recipient. The organ remains under refrigeration, packed in a sealable container with some preserving solution and kept on ice in a suitable carrier.

47143

The physician performs a standard backbench preparation of cadaver donor whole liver graft without trisegment or lobe split prior to allotransplantation. Backbench or back table preparation refers to procedures performed on the donor organ following procurement to prepare the donor organ for transplant. After removal from the body, the liver is flushed with a preserving solution and packed. The superfluous tissues that accompany the liver when it is removed en bloc are removed. If the gallbladder has been removed with the liver, it is dissected free. Next, any necessary vascular reconstruction procedures are performed with the arteries being the most common sites of reconstruction. The goal of the physician is to provide a single common inflow vessel of sufficient length so that only one anastomosis is required in the recipient. Arterial grafting is performed using previously procured iliac artery grafts as required to accomplish this goal. Other vessels, including the vena cava and portal vein, are prepared and grafting performed as needed. All vessels and grafts are tested for patency and integrity by flushing with preservation solution. Next, the common bile duct is inspected and residual tissue removed. Following liver preparation, the internal iliac arteries and veins are prepared for use as arterial and venous grafts in the recipient. When all residual tissue has been removed, vascular grafting performed as needed, and the common bile duct prepared, the liver is ready for transplant.

47144

The physician performs a standard backbench preparation of cadaver donor whole liver graft with trisegment split of whole liver graft into two partial liver grafts prior to allotransplantation. Backbench or back table preparation refers to procedures performed on the donor organ following procurement to prepare the donor organ for transplant. After removal from the body, the liver is flushed with a preserving solution and packed. The superfluous tissues that accompany the liver when it is removed en bloc are removed. If the gallbladder has been removed with the liver, it is dissected free. In split liver transplants, the liver can be split prior to procurement (in situ) or during the back table preparation (ex situ). If an ex situ split is required, it is performed at this time. A trisegment split involves dividing the liver through the falciform ligament to create a small left lateral segment graft for a child and a large extended right lobe graft for an adult. Next, any necessary vascular reconstruction procedures are performed, with the arteries being the most common sites of reconstruction. The goal of the physician is to construct a single common inflow vessel of sufficient length in the donor liver segments so that only one anastomosis is required in the recipient. Arterial grafting is performed using previously procured iliac artery grafts as required to accomplish this goal. Other vessels, including the vena cava and portal vein, are prepared and venous grafting performed as needed. All vessels and grafts are tested for patency and integrity by flushing with preservation solution. Next, the common bile duct is inspected and residual tissue removed. Following liver preparation, the internal iliac arteries and veins are prepared for use as arterial and venous grafts in the recipient. When all residual tissue has been removed, vascular grafting

Digestive

performed as needed, and the common bile duct prepared, the liver segments are ready for transplant.

47145
The physician performs a standard backbench preparation of cadaver donor whole liver graft with lobe split of whole liver graft into two partial liver grafts prior to allotransplantation. Backbench or back table preparation refers to procedures performed on the donor organ following procurement to prepare the donor organ for transplant. After removal from the body, the liver is flushed with a preserving solution and packed. The superfluous tissues that accompany the liver when it is removed en bloc are removed. If the gallbladder has been removed with the liver, it is dissected free. In split liver transplants, the liver can be split prior to procurement (in situ) or during the back table preparation (ex situ). If an ex situ split is required, it is performed at this time. A lobe split involves dividing the liver through the main portal fissure and gallbladder bed to create right and left lobe grafts. Next, any necessary vascular reconstruction procedures are performed, with the arteries being the most common sites of reconstruction. The goal of the physician is to construct a single common inflow vessel of sufficient length in the two donor liver lobes so that only one anastomosis is required in the recipient. Arterial grafting is performed using previously procured iliac artery grafts as required to accomplish this goal. Other vessels, including the vena cava and portal vein, are prepared and venous grafting performed as needed. All vessels and grafts are tested for patency and integrity by flushing with preservation solution. Next, the common bile duct is inspected and residual tissue removed. Following liver preparation, the internal iliac arteries and veins are prepared for use as arterial and venous grafts in the recipient. When all residual tissue has been removed, vascular grafting performed as needed, and the common bile duct prepared, the two liver lobes are ready for transplant.

47146
The physician performs venous anastomosis during a backbench reconstruction of cadaver or living donor liver graft prior to allotransplantation. Previously procured iliac vein grafts from the liver donor are anastomosed to the veins of the donor liver as required. Multiple grafts may be required depending on anatomical variations found in the liver donor. Code 47146 is reported for each venous graft performed.

47147
The physician performs arterial anastomosis during a backbench reconstruction of cadaver or living donor liver graft prior to allotransplantation. Previously procured iliac artery grafts from the liver donor are anastomosed to the arteries of the donor liver as required. Multiple grafts may be required depending on anatomical variations found in the liver donor. Code 47147 is reported for each artery graft performed.

47300
The physician creates a pouch with the lining of a cyst on the liver. The physician exposes the liver via an upper midline abdominal incision through skin, fascia, and muscles. The cyst is incised and suctioned with care not to contaminate the abdomen. Electrocautery is used to resect the cyst wall to allow open drainage into the abdomen. The abdominal incision is closed with sutures.

47350-47362
The physician sutures a liver wound to control the bleeding or repair damage. In 47350, the physician exposes the liver via an upper midline abdominal incision. The abdomen is packed to control bleeding. The patient is stabilized hemodynamically. The liver is systematically exposed with pressure on bleeding points. The liver tissue is divided to expose the points of bleeding and the bleeding is controlled by ligation of bleeding vessels. The abdominal incision is closed. Report 47360 if the procedure requires a complex suture of liver wound or injury, with or without hepatic artery ligation; report 47361 if procedure requires an exploration of a hepatic wound, extensive debridement, coagulation and/or suture, with or without packing of the liver; and report 47362 if the procedure is a re-exploration of hepatic wound for removal of packing.

47370-47371
The physician places a laparoscope via a small periumbilical port or through a small incision in the right upper quadrant, and an additional port is placed in the right upper quadrant under direct vision. Adhesions are lysed and ligamentous attachments divided to mobilize the liver. The physician examines all the parietal and visceral peritoneal surfaces, the lesser sac, the omentum, and the viscera. The gastrohepatic omentum is opened for inspection of the caudate lobe, followed by sequential laparoscopic ultrasonographic examination of all eight liver segments using an ultrasonic probe. Radiofrequency ablation is performed using a 15-gauge needle with a retractable curved electrode placed percutaneously into the abdomen at the place overlying the area of interest under direct vision. The needle is directed into the center of the lesion under real-time ultrasound guidance, tines are deployed and alternating current is delivered to ablate the tumor. Upon completion of ablation, the probe tract is cauterized and the needle withdrawn. Report 47371 if ablation is accomplished using a cool-tipped multiple probe electrode.

47380
The physician performs radiofrequency ablation of a liver tumor via an open laparotomy. Grounding pads are placed on the patient's legs. The physician performs a midline laparotomy. Dissection is carried down to the liver. Under direct visualization, a needle-electrode, with an insulated shaft and an uninsulated distal tip, is

inserted into the tumor. Each treatment session has about 10 to 15 minutes of active ablation. The energy at the needle tip causes ionic agitation and frictional heat in the surrounding tissue, which, when hot enough, leads to cell death and coagulative necrosis. This results in a 3 to 5.5 cm sphere of dead tissue per treatment session. In large tumors, the physician may create more than one sphere next to each other to try to turn the tumor edges in three dimensions. A small margin of normal tissue next to the tumor is also burned, as a precaution to destroy all tumor cells. The tumor cells are not removed, but are gradually replaced by fibrosis and scar tissue. One method uses a needle-within-a-needle electrode system with an inner needle that expands once placed into the tumor.

47381
The physician performs cryosurgical ablation of a liver tumor. The physician performs a laparotomy. Dissection is carrier down to the liver. Cryosurgical probes are inserted into the liver tumor. The cryosurgical probes rapidly freeze (liquid nitrogen at -196°C or nitrous oxide at -89.5°C) the area being treated, the liver tissue is slowly thawed, and repeated cycles of freezing and thawing are immediately performed. Cryogen may also be applied directly into or on to the tumor by probe, direct application, spraying, or by pouring. The incision is closed with layered sutures.

47382
Intravenous sedation is administered and grounding pads are placed on the patient's legs. A needle-electrode, with an insulated shaft and an uninsulated distal tip, is inserted through the skin and directly into the tumor. Ultrasound, CT scan, or MRI guide the needles to the correct spot and monitor treatment. Each treatment session has about 10 to 15 minutes of active ablation. The energy at the needle tip causes ionic agitation and frictional heat in the surrounding tissue, which, when hot enough, leads to cell death and coagulative necrosis. This results in a 3 to 5.5 cm sphere of dead tissue per treatment session. In large tumors, the physician may create more than one sphere next to each other to try to turn the tumor edges in three dimensions. A small margin of normal tissue next to the tumor is also burned, as a precaution to destroy all tumor cells. The tumor cells are not removed, but are gradually replaced by fibrosis and scar tissue. One method uses a needle-within-a-needle electrode system with an inner needle that expands once placed into the tumor.

47400
The physician makes a midline abdominal incision. The physician makes an incision into the hepatic duct and surgically creates an artificial opening. The physician performs exploration, drainage, or removal of calculus from the hepatic duct. The hepatic duct is closed primarily or around a tube for continued drainage. If a drainage tube is placed, a separate incision is made in the abdominal wall through which the drainage tube is positioned. The abdominal incisions are closed.

47420-47425
The physician explores the common bile duct, removing calculus, draining purulent matter, and/or constructing a new duct. The physician exposes the common bile duct within the portal triad through a subcostal or upper midline incision. The common bile duct is incised, explored, and drained. The common bile duct is closed with interrupted sutures primarily or around a drainage tube (choledochostomy). If placed, the drainage tube is brought out through the skin at a site separate from the incision. The abdominal incision is closed. Report 47425 if this procedure performed with transduodenal sphincterotomy or sphincteroplasty.

47460
The physician performs a transduodenal sphincterotomy or sphincteroplasty and may repair the duodenal sphincter or remove a stone, as needed. The physician exposes the second portion of the duodenum via a subcostal or upper midline incision through skin, fascia, and muscle. The duodenum is opened using a longitudinal incision. The ampulla of Vater is identified and an incision is made in the ampulla at the two o'clock position. The common bile duct mucosa may be reapproximated to the duodenal mucosa and the duodenum transversely closed with interrupted sutures. Stones may be removed. The abdominal incision is closed.

47480
The physician performs a cholecystotomy or cholecystostomy with exploration, drainage, or removal of calculus. The physician exposes the gallbladder through a subcostal or upper midline incision. The gallbladder is incised, explored, and may be drained. Calculi may be removed. The gallbladder is closed with interrupted sutures primarily or around a drainage tube. If placed, the drainage tube is brought out through the skin at a site separate from the incision. The abdominal incision is closed.

47490
The physician inserts a tube into the gallbladder to allow drainage through the skin. The physician uses ultrasound guidance, separately reportable, to place a subcostal drainage tube into the gallbladder. The physician places a needle between the ribs into the gallbladder. The needle position is checked by aspiration. A guidewire is passed through the needle. A catheter is passed over the wire into the biliary tree. The wire is removed and the tube is left in place.

47500
The physician injects a radiographic medium for diagnostic purposes. Using separately reportable

computerized tomography or fluoroscopy guidance, the physician places a needle between the ribs into the lumen of the common bile duct. The needle position is checked by aspiration. Radiographic dye is injected. The needle is removed.

47505
The physician injects a radiographic medium through an existing catheter for diagnostic purposes. The physician injects a radiographic medium into the gallbladder via an existing tube while visualizing the liver under separately reportable fluoroscopy.

47510
The physician introduces a catheter into the liver to drain fluid. Using separately reportable computerized tomography or fluoroscopy guidance, the physician places a needle between the ribs into the lumen of the biliary tree. The needle position is checked by aspiration. A guidewire is passed through the needle. A catheter is passed over the wire into the biliary tree. The wire is removed and the catheter is left in place.

47511
The physician introduces a stent into a liver duct to open a stricture. Using separately reportable computerized tomography or fluoroscopy guidance, the physician places a needle between the ribs into the common bile duct across the stricture. A balloon catheter and stent is placed across the stricture. The stent is employed and the balloon and wire are removed. The stent and catheter remain in place and the catheter is sutured to the skin.

47525
The physician changes a drainage catheter in the liver. Under fluoroscopic guidance (reported separately), the physician passes a wire through the original catheter. A new catheter is passed over the guidewire. The new catheter is sutured to the skin.

47530
The physician revises or reinserts a tube to the liver. Under fluoroscopic guidance (reported separately), the physician passes a wire through the original catheter. The old catheter is removed. A new catheter is passed over the guidewire and sutured to the skin.

47550
The physician performs a biliary endoscopy during the same surgical session as other biliary procedures. The physician advances an endoscope through the previously made abdominal incision. With the endoscope the physician is able to directly visualize portions of the biliary tract, which may be filled with contrast medium for identifying the common bile duct, biliary tree and gall bladder (including areas of abnormality, stricture, or obstruction) under separately reportable fluoroscopy.

47552
The physician makes a small incision in the abdominal wall. The physician advances an endoscope through an opening in the abdominal wall or through a T-tube inserted through the abdominal wall into the common bile duct. With the endoscope, the physician is able to directly visualize portions of the biliary tract, which may be filled with contrast medium for identifying the common bile duct, biliary tree, and gall bladder (including areas of abnormality, stricture, or obstruction) under separately reportable fluoroscopy. The physician may collect specimens by brushing and/or washing (separate procedure). The endoscope is removed. The T-tube is withdrawn and the defect in the common bile duct is sutûred closed. The tract, peritoneum, and abdominal wall are closed with layered sutures.

47553
The physician makes a small incision in the abdomen. The physician advances an endoscope through an opening in the abdominal wall or through a T-tube inserted through the abdominal wall into the common bile duct. With the endoscope, the physician is able to directly visualize portions of the biliary tract, which may be filled with contrast medium for identifying the common bile duct, biliary tree, and gallbladder (including areas of abnormality, stricture, or obstruction) under separately reportable fluoroscopy. The physician advances biopsy forceps along the tract or T-tube to obtain single or multiple biopsies under direct endoscopic visualization or with the use of fluoroscopy. The endoscope is removed. The T-tube is withdrawn and the defect in the common bile duct is sutured closed. The tract, peritoneum, and abdominal wall are closed using a layered technique.

47554
The physician makes a small incision in the abdomen. The physician advances an endoscope through an opening in the abdominal wall or through a T-tube inserted through the abdominal wall into the common bile duct. With the endoscope, the physician is able to directly visualize portions of the biliary tract, which may be filled with contrast medium for identifying the common bile duct, biliary tree, and gallbladder (including areas of abnormality, stricture, or obstruction) under separately reportable fluoroscopy. Calculi are identified and removed. The endoscope is removed. The T-tube is withdrawn and the defect in the common bile duct is sutured closed. The tract, peritoneum, and abdominal wall are closed using a layered technique.

47555
The physician makes a small incision in the abdomen. The physician advances an endoscope through an opening in the abdominal wall or through a T-tube inserted through the abdominal wall into the common bile duct. With the endoscope, the physician is able to

directly visualize portions of the biliary tract, which may be filled with contrast medium for identifying the common bile duct, biliary tree, and gallbladder (including areas of abnormality, stricture, or obstruction) under fluoroscopy. The physician advances a balloon-tipped catheter through the tract or T-tube so that it is above the site of the duct stricture, inflates the balloon and draws it back through the site of stricture to achieve dilation. This procedure may be repeated until optimal dilation is obtained. The endoscope is removed and the tract, peritoneum, and abdominal wall are approximated. The endoscope is removed. The T-tube is withdrawn and the common bile duct is sutured closed. The abdomen is sutured closed.

47556
The physician makes a small incision in the abdomen. The physician advances an endoscope through an opening in the abdominal wall or through a T-tube inserted through the abdominal wall into the common bile duct. With the endoscope, the physician is able to directly visualize portions of the biliary tract, which may be filled with contrast medium for identifying the common bile duct, biliary tree, and gallbladder (including areas of abnormality, stricture, or obstruction) under separately reportable fluoroscopy. The physician advances a balloon-tipped catheter through the tract or T-tube so that it is above the site of duct stricture, inflates the balloon and draws it back through the site of stricture to achieve dilation. This procedure may be repeated until optimal dilation is obtained. The physician places a stent to prevent future stricture. The endoscope is removed. The T-tube is withdrawn and the defect in the common bile duct is sutured closed. The abdomen is sutured closed.

47560
The physician examines the peritoneal cavity and performs a contrast study of the bile ducts through the liver with the laparoscope. The physician places a trocar through a small abdominal incision and insufflates the abdominal cavity. The laparoscope is placed through the port and additional trocars are placed. The peritoneal cavity is examined. A contrast study of the bile ducts is obtained by placing a needle through the liver into an intrahepatic bile duct under fluoroscopy and injecting dye. The trocars are removed and the incisions are closed.

47561
The physician examines the peritoneal cavity, performs a contrast study of the bile ducts through the liver and obtains tissue samples with the laparoscope. The physician places a trocar through a small abdominal incision and insufflates the abdominal cavity. The laparoscope is placed through the port and additional trocars are placed. The peritoneal cavity is examined. A contrast study of the bile ducts is obtained by placing a needle through the liver into an intrahepatic bile duct under fluoroscopy and injecting dye. Tissue samples are obtained of one or more intra-abdominal structures. The trocars are removed and the incisions are closed.

47562
The physician removes the gallbladder through a laparoscope. The physician makes a 1.0-centimeter infraumbilical incision through which a trocar is inserted. Pneumoperitoneum is achieved by insufflating the abdominal cavity with carbon dioxide. A fiberoptic laparoscope fitted with a camera and light source is inserted through the trocar. Other incisions are made on right side of the abdomen and in the subxiphoid area to allow other instruments or an additional light source to be passed into the abdomen. The tip of the gallbladder is mobilized and placed in traction. The Hartmann's pouch (junction of the cystic duct and gallbladder neck) is identified. Tissue is dissected free from around the area for exposure of Calot's triangle (formed by the cystic artery, and cystic and common bile ducts). Clips are applied to the proximal area of the cystic duct and artery (close to the gallbladder) and the cystic duct and artery are cut. The gallbladder is dissected from the liver bed and removed through a trocar site. Any loose stones that have dropped into the abdominal cavity are retrieved with forceps. The intraabdominal cavity is irrigated. The trocars are removed and the incisions are closed.

47563
The physician removes the gallbladder and performs a contrast study of the bile ducts through the laparoscope. The physician places a trocar at the umbilicus and insufflates the abdominal cavity. The laparoscope is placed through the umbilical port and additional trocars are placed into the abdominal cavity. The gallbladder is mobilized and placed on traction. The neck of the gallbladder and cystic duct are dissected from surrounding structures. A contrast study of the bile ducts is obtained through the cystic duct. The cystic duct and artery are divided. The gallbladder is dissected from the liver bed and removed through a trocar site. The trocars are removed and the incisions are closed.

47564
The physician removes the gallbladder and performs a common bile duct exploration through the laparoscope. The physician places a trocar at the umbilicus and insufflates the abdominal cavity. The laparoscope is placed through the umbilical port and additional trocars are placed into the abdominal cavity. The gallbladder is mobilized and placed on traction. The neck of the gallbladder and cystic duct are dissected from surrounding structures. A contrast study of the bile ducts is usually obtained through the cystic duct. The common bile duct may be explored with a small choledochoscope through the cystic duct or a separate incision may be made in the common bile

duct. The common duct is visualized with a choledochoscope and stones may be extracted from the duct with a variety of instruments. If an incision was made in the common bile duct this is usually closed with sutures over a T-tube that is brought out through the abdominal wall. The cystic duct and artery are divided. The gallbladder is removed through a trocar site. A drain is usually placed below the liver and brought out through the abdominal wall. The trocars are removed and the incisions are closed.

Digestive

47570
Through the laparoscope the physician performs an anastomosis between the gallbladder and small bowel (cholecystoenterostomy). The physician places a trocar at the umbilicus and insufflates the abdominal cavity. The laparoscope is placed through the umbilical port and additional trocars are placed into the abdominal cavity. The gallbladder and a proximal loop of small bowel are identified and mobilized. An anastomosis is created between the gallbladder and loop or limb of proximal small bowel with staples or sutures. The trocars are removed and the incisions are closed.

47600-47605
The physician removes the gallbladder. The physician exposes the liver and gallbladder via a right subcostal incision. The cystic duct and cystic artery are ligated and the gallbladder is removed using electrocautery. The incision is closed with layered sutures. Report 47605 if this is performed with a cholangiography.

47610-47620
The physician removes the gallbladder and explores the common duct. The physician exposes the liver and gallbladder via a right subcostal incision. The cystic duct and cystic artery are ligated and the gallbladder removed using electrocautery. The common bile duct is exposed in the portal triad, incised, and the stones removed. The common bile duct is closed and the abdominal incision is closed with sutures. Report 47612 if this procedure is performed with choledochoenterostomy, establishment of communication between the intestine and the common bile duct; report 47620 if this procedure is performed with transduodenal sphincterotomy or sphincteroplasty, with or without cholangiography.

47630
The physician removes a stone from the biliary duct, percutaneous. Approximately two weeks after placement of a choledochostomy, the physician removes the choledochostomy tube (T-tube) and places a choledochoscope through the choledochostomy tract. The biliary tree, liver, and ampulla are visualized. Using a basket or snare through the choledochoscope and with fluoroscopy guidance (reported separately), the stones are removed.

47700
The physician explores a congenital atresia of the bile ducts without making a repair, with or without liver biopsy, with or without cholangiography. The physician uses an upper midline abdominal incision to expose the liver, gall bladder, and bile ducts. Inspection and evaluation of the gallbladder, common bile ducts, and duodenum is carried out to determine the status of the bile ducts. A tissue sample may be removed. Cholangiography may be performed. A biliary drainage tube may be placed.

47701
The physician performs a portoenterostomy, a procedure in which the jejunum is connected to the bile ducts and other portal structures of the liver and gallbladder. The physician exposes the liver and gallbladder via an upper midline or subcostal incision. The bile ducts are connected to the small bowel for drainage by anastomosing a Roux-en-Y hook of jejunum to the divided extravascular portal structures. The abdominal incision is closed.

47711
The physician performs excision of an extrahepatic bile duct tumor and reconstructs bile duct drainage. The physician makes an abdominal incision and explores the abdomen. The bile duct is dissected from surrounding structures and the tumor is identified and mobilized. The tumor is excised with a margin of normal bile duct tissue proximal and distal to the tumor. An anastomosis is usually created between the proximal end of the bile duct and a loop of small bowel to allow biliary drainage. The distal end of the bile duct is oversewn. The incision is closed.

47712
The physician performs excision of an intrahepatic bile duct tumor and reconstructs bile duct drainage. The physician makes an abdominal incision and explores the abdomen. The distal bile duct is isolated. The tumor is identified and dissection is continued proximally along the bile duct into the parenchyma of the liver beyond the tumor onto the left and right hepatic ducts. The tumor is excised with a normal margin of bile duct or hepatic duct proximal and distal to the tumor. An anastomosis is created between the proximal bile duct or left and right hepatic ducts and a limb of small bowel to allow biliary drainage. The distal end of the bile duct is oversewn. The incision is closed.

47715
The physician excises a cyst in the common bile duct. The physician exposes the liver and gallbladder via an upper midline or subcostal incision made through skin, fascia, and muscle. The cyst is exposed and excised and the defect of the biliary system is repaired. The abdominal incision is closed with layered sutures.

47720-47741
The physician performs a cholecystoenterostomy, in which a communication is made between the gallbladder and an artificial anus or fistula in the abdominal wall. The physician exposes the liver and gallbladder via an upper midline or subcostal incision. The cyst is opened and connected to the small intestine for drainage. The abdominal incision is closed. Report 47721 if this procedure is performed with gastroenterostomy; report 47740 if this procedure is performed with Roux-en-Y; and report 47741 if this procedure is performed with Roux-en-Y with gastroenterostomy.

47760
The physician performs an anastomosis between an extrahepatic biliary duct and the small bowel. The physician makes an abdominal incision and explores the abdomen. The extrahepatic biliary duct is divided and anastomosis is formed between an extrahepatic biliary duct and the small bowel with sutures or staples (end-to-side). The incision is closed in layers.

47765
The physician performs an anastomosis between an intrahepatic biliary duct and the small bowel. The physician makes an abdominal incision and explores the abdomen. The intrahepatic biliary duct is divided and anastomosis is formed between an intrahepatic biliary duct and the small bowel with sutures or staples (end-to-side). The incision is closed in layers.

47780
The physician performs an anastomosis between a limb of small bowel (Roux-en-Y) and the gallbladder and stomach. The physician makes an abdominal incision and explores the abdomen. The proximal small bowel is divided and anastomoses are formed between the distal limb of jejunum and the gallbladder and the stomach with sutures or staples. The proximal end of bowel is approximated to the limb of jejunum distal to the gallbladder and stomach anastomoses. This procedure is usually performed for a mass obstructing the bile duct and stomach. The incision is closed.

47785
The physician performs an anastomosis between a limb of small bowel (Roux-en-Y) and the intrahepatic biliary ducts. The physician makes an abdominal incision. The bile duct is isolated and dissection is carried proximally along the duct into the liver parenchyma exposing the intrahepatic biliary ducts. The bile duct is divided or excised. The proximal small bowel is divided and an anastomosis is created between the distal limb of jejunum and the intrahepatic biliary ducts with sutures. The distal bile duct is oversewn. The proximal end of bowel is approximated to the limb of jejunum distal to the bile duct anastomosis. The incision is closed.

47800
The physician reconstructs the biliary ducts through anastomosis. The physician exposes the liver and gallbladder via an upper midline or subcostal incision made via skin, fascia, and muscle. The abnormal biliary tree is excised and the resected ends are reconnected. The incision is closed with layered sutures.

47801
The physician inserts a stent into the bile duct. The physician makes a small incision overlying the bile duct. Using an endoscope or percutaneous choledochostomy tube, a catheter and stent are placed to bridge a narrowing in the common bile duct. The scope or tube is removed and the incision closed.

47802
The physician establishes a communication between the hepatic ducts and the intestine. The physician exposes the liver and gallbladder via an upper midline or subcostal incision. A Silastic tube is connected between the biliary tree and the intestine for drainage of biliary obstruction. The abdominal incision is closed.

47900
The physician performs suture closure of a biliary duct injury. The physician makes an abdominal incision. The bile duct is dissected from surrounding structures and the injury of the duct is identified. The duct injury is closed with sutures. A drain is usually placed and brought out through the abdominal wall. The incision is closed.

48000
The physician places peripancreatic drains for pancreatitis and performs cholecystostomy, gastrostomy and jejunostomy. The physician makes an abdominal incision. The pancreas is exposed, necrotic pancreatic tissue may be debrided and drains are placed around the pancreas. The gallbladder is identified and a tube is sutured into the gallbladder and brought out through the abdominal wall. An incision is made in the anterior gastric wall and a tube is sutured into the stomach and brought out through the anterior abdominal wall. An incision is made in a proximal segment of jejunum and a tube is sutured into the jejunum and brought out through the anterior abdominal wall. The abdominal incision is closed.

48001
The physician makes an upper transverse abdominal incision. The transverse colon and small intestines are retracted to reveal the underlying pancreas. Necrotic pancreatic tissue may be resected. Drains are placed circumferentially around the pancreas. The anterior gastric wall is incised and a drainage tube is inserted, sutured secure, and anchored through the abdominal wall. The jejunum is incised and a drainage tube is inserted, sutured, secured, and anchored through the abdominal wall. The gallbladder is located, incised,

Digestive

and a drainage tube is placed in it with the caudal end being drawn through a separate abdominal incision. The upper transverse abdominal incision is closed with sutures.

48020

The physician removes a stone from the pancreas. The physician exposes the pancreas via an upper midline incision through skin, fascia, and muscle. The pancreatic duct is opened and calculus removed. The pancreatic duct is connected directly to the small bowel for drainage. The abdominal incision is closed.

48100

The physician obtains a biopsy of the pancreas. The physician makes a midline epigastric incision and retracts the skin and underlying tissues laterally. The physician approaches the pancreas through the lesser sac of the omental bursa. The pancreas is palpated, the lesion is identified, and a biopsy is obtained by various methods, such as fine needle aspiration or needle core or wedge biopsy. Bleeding is controlled and the lesser sac is closed. Tissues are reapproximated to the anatomical position and the incision is sutured in layers.

48102

The physician removes tissue from the pancreas. The physician passes the biopsy needle through the skin of the upper abdomen under separately reportable computerized tomography guidance. The pancreatic lesion is removed and the specimen is sent for pathology for examination (reported separately).

48105

The physician performs resection and debridement of the pancreas for necrotizing pancreatitis. The physician makes an abdominal incision. The pancreas is exposed and necrotic areas of the pancreas and peripancreatic tissue are debrided. Drains are usually placed around the pancreas. The incision is closed.

48120

The physician excises a lesion of the pancreas. The physician makes a midline epigastric incision and retracts the skin and underlying tissues laterally. The physician approaches the pancreas through the lesser sac of the omental bursa or the through the transverse mesocolon. The pancreas is palpated, the lesion is identified and excised. Bleeding is controlled, and the lesser sac is closed. Tissues are reapproximated to anatomical position, and the incision is sutured in layers.

48140-48145

The physician removes the distal portion of the pancreas, with or without removing the spleen and jejunum. The physician makes a midline epigastric incision and retracts the skin and underlying tissues laterally. The physician approaches the pancreas through the lesser sac of the omental bursa or the through the transverse mesocolon. The pancreas is identified and freed from attachments. If the blood supply to the distal pancreas also supplies the spleen, the spleen is sacrificed in the resection. The pancreas is transected, and the distal portion is removed, with or without the spleen. In 48140, the pancreatic duct is not obstructed, permitting free drainage of pancreatic enzymes. In 48145, the duct flow is obstructed and a jejunal loop is brought up to create a fistula for enzyme flow to the digestive tract. Bleeding is controlled, and the lesser sac is closed. Tissues are reapproximated to anatomical position, and the incision is sutured in layers.

48146

The physician performs a near-total pancreatectomy. The physician makes an abdominal incision. The pancreas is exposed and the body and tail of the pancreas are mobilized. The pancreas is transected at the junction of the head and body of the pancreas over the superior mesenteric vessels. The distal pancreas is removed. Frequently the spleen is removed with the distal pancreas. The end of the proximal pancreas is closed with staples or sutures. Drains are usually placed in the pancreatic bed. The incision is closed.

48148

The physician excises the ampulla of Vater, a saccular dilation of liver and/or pancreas. The physician exposes the duodenum and pancreas via an upper midline abdominal incision. The duodenum is opened with a longitudinal incision. The ampulla of Vater is exposed and the abnormality is excised. The common bile duct and duodenal mucosa are re-approximated as needed. The duodenum is closed with transverse interrupted sutures. The abdominal incision is closed.

48150

The physician performs excision of the proximal pancreas, duodenum, distal bile duct and distal stomach with reconstruction (Whipple procedure) but with pancreatojejunostomy. The physician makes an abdominal incision and explores the abdomen. The duodenum, proximal pancreas, and bile duct are mobilized. The distal bile duct, distal stomach, and distal duodenum are divided. The pancreas is transected at the junction of the head and body and the pancreatic head, duodenum, distal stomach, and distal bile duct are removed en bloc. The anatomy is reconstructed by performing sequential anastomoses between the proximal jejunum and the distal bile duct and distal stomach. The edge of the remaining distal pancreas is closed with sutures or staples. The incision is closed.

48152

The physician performs excision of the proximal pancreas, duodenum, distal bile duct and distal stomach with reconstruction (Whipple procedure) but without pancreatojejunostomy. The physician makes an abdominal incision and explores the abdomen. The duodenum, proximal pancreas, and bile duct are mobilized. The distal bile duct, distal stomach, and distal duodenum are divided. The pancreas is transected at the junction of the head and body and the pancreatic head, duodenum, distal stomach, and distal bile duct are removed en bloc. The anatomy is reconstructed by performing sequential anastomoses between the proximal jejunum and the distal bile duct and distal stomach. The edge of the remaining distal pancreas is closed with sutures or staples. The incision is closed.

48153

The physician performs excision of the proximal pancreas, duodenum, and distal bile duct with reconstruction (pylorus preserving Whipple procedure). The physician makes an abdominal incision and explores the abdomen. The duodenum, proximal pancreas, and bile duct are mobilized. The distal bile duct and distal duodenum are divided. The proximal duodenum is divided just distal to the pylorus. The pancreas is transected at the junction of the head and body and the proximal pancreas, duodenum and distal bile duct are removed en bloc. The anatomy is reconstructed by performing sequential anastomoses between the proximal jejunum and the remaining pancreatic tail, distal bile duct and pylorus. The incision is closed.

48154

The physician performs excision of the proximal pancreas, duodenum and distal bile duct with reconstruction but without pancreatojejunostomy. The physician makes an abdominal incision and explores the abdomen. The duodenum, proximal pancreas and bile duct are mobilized. The distal bile duct and distal duodenum are divided. The proximal duodenum is divided just distal to the pylorus. The pancreas is transected at the junction of the head and body and the proximal pancreas, duodenum, and distal bile duct are removed en block. The anatomy is reconstructed by performing sequential anastomoses between the proximal jejunum and the distal bile duct and the pylorus. The edge of the remaining distal pancreas is closed with sutures or staples and no anastomosis is performed to the pancreas. The incision is closed.

48155-48160

The physician removes all or part of the pancreas. The physician makes a midline epigastric incision and retracts the skin and underlying tissues laterally. The physician approaches the pancreas through the lesser sac of the omental bursa or the through the transverse mesocolon. The pancreas is identified and freed from attachments. In 48155, the pancreas is removed. In 48160, all or part of the pancreas is removed and pancreatic islet cells are transplanted into the abdominal tissue. Blood vessels are ligated and the affected pancreas is removed. Bleeding is controlled, and the lesser sac is closed. Tissues are reapproximated to anatomical position, and the incision is sutured in layers.

48400

The physician performs a contrast study of the pancreatic duct. The physician makes an abdominal incision. The pancreas is exposed and may be mobilized by dissecting it from its retroperitoneal attachments. A separately reported pancreatogram may be obtained by injecting contrast into the common bile duct thus filling the pancreatic duct in a retrograde fashion and a radiograph obtained. Alternately, the duodenum may be opened and the pancreatic duct injected directly, or the tail of the pancreas may be transected and the pancreatic duct injected directly with contrast and a radiograph obtained. The duodenum is closed or the pancreatic tail is sutured closed. The incision is closed.

48500

The physician marsupializes a pancreatic cyst. The physician approaches the pancreas through a midline abdominal incision and retracts the skin and underlying tissues laterally. The physician approaches the pancreas through the lesser sac of the omental bursa or the through the transverse mesocolon. The cyst is located, and the anterior cyst wall is incised. The cut edges of the cyst are sutured to the skin edges establishing a pouch of what was formally an enclosed cyst. The remainder of the operative site is sutured in layers.

48510

The physician externally drains a pancreatic cyst. The physician approaches the pancreas through a midline abdominal incision. The physician locates the cyst through an incision and approaches the pancreas through the lesser sac of the omental bursa or the through the transverse mesocolon. Once the drain is placed, the adjacent tissues are returned to anatomic position and the operative site is sutured in layers.

48511

The physician performs percutaneous drainage of a pseudocyst of the pancreas. The physician may create a small incision in the flank, or abdomen proximal to the pancreatic pseudocyst in order to ease placement of drainage instruments through the skin into the pseudocyst for drainage of the pseudocyst to an external fluid collection system. The physician uses a CAT scan or ultrasound to guide placement of a drainage needle or trocar into the pseudocyst. The physician advances the drainage needle or trocar through the skin into the pseudocyst. The pseudocyst is allowed to drain. Once the pseudocyst is drained, a drainage catheter may be placed. Sutures may be placed to secure the drainage catheter in place. The operative site is cleaned and bandaged. For radiological supervision and interpretation, see 75989.

Digestive

48520
The physician creates an internal anastomosis of a pancreatic cyst to a portion of the gastrointestinal tract. The physician approaches the pancreas through a midline abdominal incision and retracts the skin and underlying tissues laterally. The physician approaches the pancreas through the lesser sac of the omental bursa or the through the transverse mesocolon. The cyst is located. The physician approximates the stomach wall or a loop of duodenum or jejunum and incises it. The anterior cyst wall is incised and the cyst edges are approximated with the cut edges of the gastrointestinal tract and sutured. The cyst is decompressed through the drainage tract. The surrounding tissues are returned to anatomic position and the operative site is sutured in layers.

48540
The physician creates a Roux-en-Y anastomosis to drain enzymes from the pancreatic duct. The physician approaches the pancreas through a midline abdominal incision and retracts the skin and underlying tissues laterally. The physician approaches the pancreas through the lesser sac of the omental bursa or the through the transverse mesocolon. The physician divides a loop of small intestine (usually the jejunum) and implants the distal end into the stomach or duodenum. The proximal end is anastomosed distal to the first anastomosis to prevent reflux. The pancreatic duct is fistulized to the proximal end to create a drain to the gastrointestinal tract for pancreatic enzymes. The surrounding tissues are returned to anatomic position and the operative site is sutured in layers.

48545
The physician repairs a pancreatic injury (pancreatorrhaphy). The physician makes an abdominal incision and the abdomen is explored. The pancreas is exposed and the pancreatic injury is identified and repaired with sutures. A peripancreatic drain is usually placed. The incision is closed.

48547
The physician performs duodenal exclusion and gastrojejunostomy for a pancreatic injury. The physician makes an abdominal incision and explores the abdomen. The pancreas is exposed and an injury in the duodenum or pancreas may be closed with sutures. An incision is made in the stomach (gastrotomy). The natural opening from the stomach to the duodenum is closed with sutures or staples. A limb of proximal small bowel is brought up to the stomach and an anastomosis is performed (gastrojejunostomy) at the site of the gastrotomy. The abdominal incision is closed.

48548
The physician creates a pancreaticojejunostomy to drain pancreatic enzymes through a side-to-side anastomosis. The physician makes a midline epigastric incision and retracts the skin and underlying tissues laterally. The physician approaches the pancreas through the lesser sac of the omental bursa or through the transverse mesocolon. A jejunal loop is brought up to create a fistula for enzyme flow to the digestive tract. Bleeding is controlled and the lesser sac is closed. Tissues are reapproximated to the anatomical position and the incision is sutured in layers.

48550
The physician performs a donor pancreatectomy by removing the pancreas with or without a segment of the duodenum from an organ donor. The physician makes an abdominal incision to access the pancreas and duodenum, which are mobilized and dissected free from their retroperitoneal attachments. The segments of mesenteric and splenic arteries and portal vein supplying the pancreas and duodenum are divided. The pancreas is removed en bloc with its vascular supply. Usually a segment of duodenum is also removed en bloc with the pancreas. The donor tissue is preserved for transplantation into the recipient, who may be hundreds of miles away. The organ remains under refrigeration, packed in a sealable container with some preserving solution and kept on ice in a suitable carrier.

48551
The physician performs a standard backbench preparation of a cadaver donor pancreas. Backbench or back table preparation refers to procedures performed on the donor organ following procurement to prepare the donor organ for transplant. In a separately reportable procedure, the physician removes the pancreas in conjunction with the thoracic organs, liver, and spleen from a cadaver donor. One pair of donor iliac arteries and vein are also procured for use in back table reconstruction procedures. Backbench procedures on the pancreas are accomplished at very cold temperatures to prevent the organ from deteriorating. Considerable back table preparation is required to prepare the pancreas for the transplant procedure. First, the pancreas is separated from the thoracic organs and liver. The spleen is removed by tying the individual vessels with 2-0 silk ligatures. The surrounding soft tissues are dissected from the pancreas allograft. The duodenal segment of bowel attached to the head of the pancreas is mobilized and shortened to allow for transplantation. The bile duct is ligated. Since the pancreas receives blood flow from two arteries, the superior mesenteric artery and the splenic artery, the arteries must be combined into one to allow anastomosis of the blood vessels in the transplant recipient. The physician performs a bypass graft from the previously procured iliac artery. The bypass graft consists of Y-graft arterial anastomoses of the internal iliac artery to the splenic artery and the external iliac artery to the superior mesenteric artery.

48552
The physician performs a backbench venous reconstruction of a cadaver donor pancreas allograft. Backbench or back table refers to procedures performed on the donor organ following procurement to prepare the donor organ for transplant. Backbench procedures on the pancreas are accomplished at very cold temperatures to prevent the organ from deteriorating. The physician dissects the portal vein. Venous anastomosis of the portal vein is required when there is not sufficient length or when there are anatomic variations in the donor organ. Previously procured iliac vein segments are fashioned and anastomosed as required to provide for systemic and portal drainage. More than one anastomosis may be required to accomplish this. Code 48552 is reported for each anastomosis.

48554
The physician performs pancreas transplantation. The physician makes an abdominal incision. The iliac arteries and veins in the pelvis are exposed and isolated. An anastomosis is usually performed between the artery and vein supplying the pancreas to the iliac artery and vein on one side of the pelvis. An additional anastomosis is usually performed between the attached duodenal segment and the bladder. The incision is closed.

48556
The physician removes a transplanted pancreas graft. The physician makes an abdominal incision. The pancreatic graft is mobilized. The vascular supply to the pancreatic graft is isolated, ligated and divided. The anastomosis between the duodenum and bladder is taken down and the defect in the bladder is closed with sutures. The incision is closed.

49000
To explore the intra-abdominal organs and structures, the physician makes a large incision extending from just above the pubic hairline to the rib cage. The abdominal cavity is opened for a systematic examination of all organs. The physician may take tissue samples of any or all intra-abdominal organs for diagnosis. The incision is closed with sutures.

49002
The physician reopens the incision of a recent laparotomy before the incision has fully healed to control bleeding, remove packing, or drain a postoperative infection.

49010
The physician explores the retroperitoneum and may obtain sample tissue for separately reportable diagnostic testing. The physician may approach the retroperitoneum through a flank or an abdominal incision. The surface of the retroperitoneum is inspected and any area of interest of the retroperitoneum may be opened and the retroperitoneum explored. Tissues may be sampled. The incision is closed.

49020-49021
In 49020, the physician makes an open abdominal or flank incision (laparotomy) to gain access to the peritoneal cavity. The peritoneum is explored and the abscess or isolated area of peritoneal inflammation is identified. The abscess is incised and drained, and inflamed peritoneal tissue may be excised. The abscess and surrounding peritoneal cavity may be irrigated. A drain may be placed whereby a separate abdominal incision is made and the drain is drawn through it and sutured in place. The physician may completely reapproximate the abdominal incision or leave a portion of the incision open to allow for further drainage. In 49021, to avoid exposure of the abdominal cavity, the physician makes a small skin incision in the abdomen or flank. Percutaneous needle aspiration and closed catheter drainage using computer tomographic (CT) or ultrasound guidance is performed. A needle, guidewire, or pigtail catheter is placed within the abscess. Specimens taken during these procedures are typically sent to microbiology for identification and to determine antibiotic suitability. If a drain is placed, it is removed at a later date. These procedures do not apply to abscess of the appendix.

49040
The physician drains a subdiaphragmatic or subphrenic abscess. The physician makes an abdominal incision and the abdomen is explored. The abscess beneath the diaphragm is identified and the abscess cavity is opened and drained. Irrigation of the cavity is usually performed. A drain is usually placed into the abscess cavity and brought out through the abdominal wall. The incision is closed. The superficial portion of the incision may be packed open to allow drainage.

49041
The physician performs percutaneous drainage of a subdiaphragmatic or subphrenic abscess. The physician may create a small incision in the flank, thorax or abdomen proximal to an abscess located beneath the diaphragm (subdiaphragmatic/subphrenic) in order to ease placement of drainage instruments through the skin into the subphrenic abscess for drainage of fluid. The physician uses a CAT scan or ultrasound to guide placement of a drainage needle or trocar into the subphrenic abscess. The physician advances the drainage needle or trocar through the skin into the abscess. The abscess is allowed to drain. Once emptied, a drainage catheter may be placed. Sutures may be placed to secure the drainage catheter in place. The operative site is cleaned and bandaged. For radiological supervision and interpretation, see 75989.

Digestive

49060
The physician drains a retroperitoneal abscess. The physician makes an abdominal or flank incision. The abscess is identified and the retroperitoneal space is entered. The abscess cavity is opened and drained. Irrigation of the cavity is usually performed. A drain is usually placed in the abscess cavity and brought out through the abdominal wall. The incision is closed. The superficial portion of the incision may be packed open to allow drainage.

49061
The physician performs a percutaneous drainage of a retroperitoneal abscess. The physician may create a small incision in the skin between two ribs proximal to the abscess or in the flank in order to ease placement of drainage instruments through the skin into the retroperitoneal space. The physician uses a CAT scan or ultrasound to guide placement of a drainage needle or trocar into the retroperitoneal abscess. The physician advances the drainage needle or trocar through the skin to gain access to the abscess. The fluid is allowed to drain. Once the abscess is drained, a drainage catheter may be placed. Sutures may be placed to secure the drainage catheter in place. The operative site is cleaned and bandaged. For radiological supervision and interpretation, see 75989.

49062
The physician drains a lymphocele to the peritoneal cavity. The physician creates an opening in a lymphatic swelling or cavity (lymphocele) located outside the abdominopelvic walls to drain the material contained within to a cavity of the peritoneum. Irrigation of the lymphocele is performed. The incision is sutured closed. For radiological supervision and interpretation, see 75989.

49080-49081
The physician withdraws fluid from the abdominal cavity (paracentesis) or performs infusion and drainage of fluid from the abdominal cavity (peritoneal lavage). The physician inserts a needle or catheter into the abdominal cavity and withdraws and drains fluid for diagnostic or therapeutic purposes. Alternately, the physician may insert a needle or catheter into the abdominal cavity and infuse and subsequently withdraw fluid for diagnostic or therapeutic purposes. The needle or catheter is removed at the completion of the procedure. In 49081, this is done subsequent to a previous peritoneocentesis procedure.

49180
Using radiological supervision, the physician locates the mass within or immediately outside the peritoneal lining of the abdominal cavity. A biopsy needle is passed into the mass, a tissue sample is removed, and the needle is withdrawn. This may be repeated several times. No incision is necessary.

49203-49205
The physician removes or destroys intraabdominal tumors, cysts, or endometriomas (displaced endometrial tissue) or primary or secondary mesenteric, peritoneal, or retroperitoneal tumors. The physician makes a large incision extending from just above the pubic hairline to the rib cage. The growths are removed using a laser, electric cautery, or a scalpel. The incision is closed with sutures. Report 49203 when the diameter of the largest tumor is 5 cm or smaller, 49204 when the diameter is 5.1 to 10 cm, and 49205 when the diameter is larger than 10 cm.

49215
The physician performs resection of a presacral or sacrococcygeal tumor. The physician makes an abdominal incision and explores the abdomen. The tumor is identified and the rectum is mobilized from the sacrum to expose the tumor. The tumor is dissected free of surrounding structures and removed. Alternately, the tumor may be approached posteriorly through an incision between the sacrum and coccyx. The coccyx is removed, the rectum is mobilized from the sacrum and the tumor is dissected from surrounding structures and removed. A portion of the sacrum may be excised en bloc with the tumor. The incision is closed.

49220
The physician performs a staging laparotomy for Hodgkin's disease or lymphoma. The physician makes an abdominal incision and the abdomen is explored. The spleen is mobilized, divided from its vascular supply and removed. Needle or wedge tissue samples are obtained from the left and right lobes of the liver for separately reportable analyses. Abdominal and retroperitoneal lymph nodes are identified and sampled. A bone marrow biopsy may be obtained. The ovaries may be plicated out of a planned radiation field. The incision is closed.

49250
The physician performs excision of the umbilicus. The physician makes an incision around the umbilicus and dissects the umbilicus from surrounding subcutaneous tissue. The umbilical arteries and vein, the urachal remnant, and the omphalomesenteric remnant identified and divided. The umbilicus is removed. The fascial defect is closed and the umbilicus is reconstructed with small skin flaps.

49255
The physician performs resection of the omentum or epiploectomy. The physician makes an abdominal incision and the abdomen is explored. The omentum is mobilized from the stomach and colon, divided from its blood supply and removed. One or more epiploica of the colon may be removed. The incision is closed.

49320
The physician makes a 1.0-centimeter incision in the umbilicus through which the abdomen is inflated and a fiberoptic laparoscope is inserted. Other incisions are also made through which trocars can be passed into the abdominal cavity to deliver instruments, a video camera, and when needed an additional light source. The physician manipulates the tools so that the pelvic organs, peritoneum, abdomen, and omentum can be viewed through the laparoscope and/or video monitor. Biopsy from any or all of the areas observed are obtained by brushing the surface and collecting the cells or by washing (bathing) the area with a saline solution, and suctioning out the cell rich solution. When the procedure is complete, the laparoscope, instruments, and light source are removed and the incisions are closed with sutures. If biopsy of pelvic organs is performed, the physician may also insert an instrument through the vagina to grasp the cervix and pass another instrument through the cervix, into the uterus to manipulate the uterus.

49321
The physician makes a 1.0-centimeter incision in the umbilicus through which the abdomen is inflated and a fiberoptic laparoscope is inserted. Other incisions are also made through which trocars can be passed into the abdominal cavity to deliver instruments, a video camera, and when needed an additional light source. The physician manipulates the tools so that the pelvic organs, peritoneum, abdomen and omentum can be viewed through the laparoscope and/or video monitor. Biopsy from any or all of the areas observed are obtained by grasping a sample with a biopsy forceps that is capable of "biting off" small pieces of tissue. When the procedure is complete, the laparoscope, instruments, and light source are removed and the incisions are closed with sutures. If biopsy of pelvic organs is performed, the physician may also insert an instrument through the vagina to grasp the cervix and pass another instrument through the cervix, into the uterus to manipulate the uterus.

49322
The physician makes a 1.0-centimeter incision in the umbilicus through which the abdomen is inflated and a fiberoptic laparoscope is inserted. A second incision is made directly below the umbilicus, just above the pubic hairline, through which a trocar can be passed into the abdominal cavity to deliver instruments. The physician manipulates the tools to view the pelvic organs through the laparoscope. An additional incision may be needed for a second light source. Once the biopsy site is viewed through the laparoscope, a 5.0-centimeter incision is made just above the site. Through this incision, the physician uses an aspirating probe to aspirate a cavity or cyst or to collect fluid for culture. The instruments are removed and the incisions are sutured.

49323
The physician drains a lymphocele to the peritoneal cavity. With the patient under anesthesia, the physician places a trocar at the umbilicus into the abdominal or retroperitoneal space and insufflates the abdominal cavity. The physician places a laparoscope through the umbilical incision and additional trocars are placed into the abdomen. The lymphocele is identified and instruments are passed through to open and drain the lymphocele. The trocars are removed and the incisions are closed with sutures.

49324-49325
A permanent intraperitoneal catheter is inserted laparoscopically for continuous drug infusion, such as insulin, morphine, or chemotherapeutic agents. The physician makes a 1 cm incision in the umbilicus through which the abdomen is inflated and a fiberoptic laparoscope is inserted. Other incisions are also made through which trocars can be passed into the abdominal cavity to deliver additional instruments. The physician manipulates the tools so that the pelvic organs, peritoneum, abdomen, and omentum can be viewed through the laparoscope and/or video monitor. If the physician is inserting a totally implantable, intraperitoneal drug delivery system, the pump reservoir is secured into a surgically prepared pocket in the subcutaneous fat of the lower or mid-left abdomen. The infusion line catheter from the pump is placed inside the peritoneal cavity with the tip free moving. If the physician is revising an intraperitoneal catheter, the catheter is inspected and freed of occlusion or blockage. When either procedure is complete, the laparoscope and other instruments are removed and the incisions are closed with sutures. Report 49324 for insertion of an intraperitoneal cannula or catheter and 49325 for its revision.

49326
Omentum is a strong and highly vascularized serous membrane in the abdomen. The physician makes a 1 cm incision in the umbilicus through which the abdomen is inflated and a fiberoptic laparoscope is inserted. Other incisions are also made through which trocars can be passed into the abdominal cavity to deliver instruments, a video camera, and, when needed, an additional light source. The physician manipulates the tools so the pelvic organs, peritoneum, abdomen, and omentum can be viewed through the laparoscope and/or video monitor. The physician isolates the omentum at the stomach and intestine and may cut, suture, or plicate omental tissue to achieve the desired effect. When the procedure is complete, the laparoscope, instruments, and light source are removed and the incisions are closed with sutures.

49400
The physician injects air contrast into the peritoneal cavity. The physician inserts a needle or catheter into the peritoneal cavity and injects air as a diagnostic

Digestive

procedure. An x-ray is usually obtained to define the pattern of air in the abdomen. The needle or catheter is removed at the completion of the procedure.

49402
The physician removes a foreign body from the abdominal cavity. The physician makes an abdominal incision and explores the abdominal cavity. The foreign body is identified and removed. The incision is closed.

49411
The physician places one or more interstitial devices such as gold seeds (fiducial markers) for radiation therapy guidance or a dosimeter to gauge the amount of radiation received. Implanted percutaneously in and/or around an intra-abdominal, intra-pelvic (excluding prostate), and/or retroperitoneal soft tissue tumor, these act as radiographic landmarks to define the position of the target lesion. Under CT or other image guidance, the physician injects a small capsule or seed into the targeted tissue using a needle injection device. Allowing for precision in targeting radiation and/or for measuring the radiation doses received, an injected fiducial marker is visible by ultrasound and fluoroscopy and permits accurate triangulation of the tissue to be treated. An injected capsule dosimeter relays radiation dose information so that the clinical team can monitor for any deviation between the radiation plan and the actual radiation received.

49419
A permanent intraperitoneal catheter with the reservoir is inserted subcutaneously for continuous drug infusion, such as insulin, morphine, or chemotherapeutic agents. In the case of a totally implantable, intraperitoneal insulin delivery system, the pump reservoir is inserted under general or local anesthesia into a surgically prepared pocket in the subcutaneous fat of the lower or mid-left abdomen. The infusion line catheter from the pump is placed inside the peritoneal cavity with the tip free moving.

49420
The physician places a temporary intraperitoneal catheter for drainage or dialysis. The physician makes a small abdominal incision, opens the peritoneum, the double-layered sac covering the internal organs and lining the abdominopelvic walls, and inserts the catheter into the cavity. The proximal end of the catheter is tunneled subcutaneously away from the initial incision and brought out through the skin. The incision is closed. Alternately, the physician may percutaneously insert the catheter over a wire placed through a needle inserted into the peritoneal cavity.

49421
The physician places a permanent intraperitoneal catheter for drainage or dialysis. The physician makes a small abdominal incision, opens the peritoneum and inserts the catheter into the abdominal cavity. The proximal end of the catheter is tunneled subcutaneously away from the initial incision and brought out through the skin. The incision is closed.

49422
The physician performs removal of an intraperitoneal catheter. The physician makes an incision over the insertion site of the catheter. The catheter is dissected free of surrounding scar tissue, transected and removed from the peritoneal insertion site and skin exit site. The incision at the insertion site of the catheter is closed. The skin exit site is left open to allow drainage.

49423
The physician exchanges a previously placed drainage catheter. The physician locates the drainage catheter and removes sutures that may be holding it in place. The drainage catheter is removed. With the use of fluoroscopy the physician places a new drainage catheter, and the physician may elect to use a catheter guidewire to assist in this maneuver. Once placed and found to be patent, the new drainage catheter may be sutured in place. For radiological supervision and interpretation, see 75984.

49424
The physician injects a radio-contrast dye through a previously placed catheter to determine the existence, nature, or size of an abscess or cyst. Once the radio-contrast dye is placed, the operative site is examined under direct fluoroscopy or with radiographic studies. The contrast dye may be aspirated and/or irrigated from the cyst or abscess. For radiological supervision and interpretation, see 76080.

49425
The physician places a peritoneal-venous shunt. The physician makes a small lateral upper abdominal incision. Dissection is carried through the abdominal wall layers, the peritoneum is entered and the peritoneal end of the catheter is inserted into the peritoneal cavity and sutured into place. A subcutaneous tunnel is created from the abdominal incision up to the neck and the catheter is pulled through the tunnel into the neck. A counter incision is made in the neck over the internal jugular vein and the venous end of the catheter is inserted into the jugular vein. The incisions are closed.

49426
The physician performs revision of a peritoneal-venous shunt. The physician may remove the shunt by incisions over the venous and peritoneal insertion sites with a subcutaneous tunnel is created from the abdominal incision up to the neck and the catheter is pulled through the tunnel into the neck. A counter incision is made in the neck over the internal jugular vein and the venous end of the catheter is inserted into the jugular vein. Alternately, the physician may make an incision over the dysfunctional end of the shunt and replace that portion of the shunt and insert it back into

the peritoneal cavity or jugular vein. The incisions are closed.

49427
The physician injects contrast into a peritoneo-venous shunt. The physician injects contrast material through the skin into the reservoir of the peritoneo-venous shunt. Radiography is used to visualize the flow of contrast through the shunt into the peritoneal and venous ends for evaluation.

49428
The physician performs ligation of a previously placed peritoneo-venous shunt. The physician makes an incision over the path of the shunt. The shunt tubing under the incision is isolated and ligated with sutures. The incision is closed.

49429
The physician performs removal of a peritoneal venous shunt. An incision is made over the abdominal insertion site of the shunt. The shunt is dissected from surrounding scar tissue and removed from the abdominal cavity. The fascia and peritoneum of the abdominal insertion site is closed. Usually the venous end of the catheter can be removed by placing traction on the shunt through the abdominal incision and pulling it through the subcutaneous tunnel. If necessary a second incision is made over the venous insertion site and the catheter removed from the jugular vein. The incisions are closed.

49435
A permanent, subcutaneous intraperitoneal catheter is lengthened with an extension and brought to the surface of the skin during the primary procedure in which a catheter/cannula is established. In the primary procedure, the physician makes a small abdominal incision, opens the peritoneum, and establishes the cannula. In 49435, the physician fits an extension to the cannula and tunnels subcutaneously to accommodate the extension. The physician makes a separate incision in the chest as an exit site for the extension. The extension is brought out through the skin and may be attached to the drug delivery system. The operative incision is closed.

49436
A previously implanted, permanent subcutaneous intraperitoneal catheter is brought to the surface of the skin. The physician makes a small abdominal incision, opens the peritoneum, and locates the end of the existing intraperitoneal cannula. An extension may be fitted to the existing cannula. The physician makes a separate incision as an exit site for the cannula. The cannula is brought out through the skin and may be attached to the drug delivery system. The operative incision is closed.

49440
The physician inserts a gastrostomy tube via percutaneous (under the skin) approach using fluoroscopic guidance. Percutaneous image-guided gastrostomy or enterostomy procedures may be indicated for patients who have an impaired swallowing mechanism, mechanical obstruction of the upper GI tract due to malignancy, or those with aberrant upper GI anatomy. Following administration of any necessary sedation, nasogastric or orogastric intubation is performed under fluoroscopic guidance and the stomach is insufflated. The skin and subcutaneous tissues overlying the stomach are anesthetized with lidocaine. Using a subcostal (below the ribs) approach and fluoroscopic guidance, the physician inserts a 7 cm, 18-gauge needle in the area of the horizontal portion of the greater curvature. A guidewire is then passed through the needle and the needle is withdrawn. A dilator is introduced over the wire and the tract is dilated. The physician places a self-retaining loop catheter into the stomach and injects a small amount of contrast material in order to confirm placement. A loop-locking suture is tied and nasogastric or orogastric tubes are removed. Antiseptic ointment and sterile dressings are applied. This code includes image documentation and report.

49441
The physician inserts a duodenostomy or jejunostomy tube via percutaneous (under the skin) approach using fluoroscopic guidance. Percutaneous image-guided gastrostomy or enterostomy procedures may be indicated for patients who have an impaired swallowing mechanism, mechanical obstruction of the upper GI tract due to malignancy, or those with aberrant upper GI anatomy. Particularly in patients who have undergone gastrectomy or gastric pull-up, the jejunum or duodenum is often a viable site for percutaneous feeding tube placement. Following administration of any necessary sedation and contrast materials, the physician identifies a suitable site for puncture of the duodenum or jejunum and a needle is inserted percutaneously. When the contrast material can be aspirated from the needle, a guidewire is inserted under fluoroscopic guidance. The tract is dilated and an appropriate catheter is inserted and secured to the skin with a stoma device. Nasogastric or orogastric tubes are removed. Antiseptic ointment and sterile dressings are applied. This code includes image documentation and report.

49442
The physician inserts a cecostomy or other colonic tube via percutaneous (under the skin) approach using fluoroscopic guidance. Following identification of the gallbladder, liver, and urinary bladder by ultrasound, the physician inserts a silicone catheter into the rectum and a retention balloon is filled with air. The abdomen is prepared and draped in sterile fashion and appropriate anesthesia is administered. The colon is inflated with air via the rectal catheter and the physician assesses the position of the cecum to determine the appropriate tract site. The physician

makes a small incision in the skin and inserts a puncture needle through the skin and soft tissues. Under fluoroscopic guidance, the needle is advanced into the cecum and contrast is injected to confirm the needle's position. Still using fluoroscopic guidance, a guidewire is advanced through the needle and positions the retention sutures. The physician removes the needle and clamps the sutures. A dilator is introduced over the wire, followed by an appropriately sized catheter. The catheter is locked and the physician confirms placement with contrast. The locked portion of the catheter is pulled against the cecum's anterior wall, where the retention sutures are anchored. Antiseptic ointment and sterile dressings are applied. This code includes image documentation and report.

49446
The physician converts a gastrostomy tube to a gastrojejunostomy tube via percutaneous (under the skin) approach using fluoroscopic guidance. Following administration of any necessary sedation and contrast materials, the physician advances a jejunostomy tube through the previously placed gastrostomy tube into the proximal jejunum. This code includes contrast injections, image documentation, and report.

49450
The physician replaces an existing gastrostomy, cecostomy, or other colonic tube via percutaneous (under the skin) approach using fluoroscopic guidance and contrast monitoring. The existing tube is removed and the replacement is placed percutaneously via the existing tract. Contrast injection allows for correct positioning to be visualized with fluoroscopic images displayed on a screen. In order for this code to be reported, the new tube must be placed via the existing percutaneous access site. This procedure includes contrast injection, image documentation, and report.

49451
The physician replaces an existing duodenostomy or jejunostomy tube via percutaneous (under the skin) approach using fluoroscopic guidance and contrast monitoring. The existing tube is removed and the replacement is placed percutaneously through the abdominal wall via the existing tract. Contrast injection allows for correct positioning to be visualized with fluoroscopic images displayed on a screen. In order for this code to be reported, the new tube must be placed via the existing percutaneous access site. This procedure includes contrast injection, image documentation, and report.

49452
The physician replaces an existing gastrojejunostomy tube via percutaneous (under the skin) approach using fluoroscopic guidance and contrast monitoring. The existing tube is removed and the replacement is placed percutaneously through the abdominal wall via the existing tract. Contrast injection allows for correct positioning to be visualized with fluoroscopic images displayed on a screen. In order for this code to be reported, the new tube must be placed via the existing percutaneous access site. This procedure includes contrast injection, image documentation, and report.

49460
The physician mechanically removes obstructive material from an existing tube (gastrostomy, duodenostomy, jejunostomy, gastrojejunostomy, or cecostomy) by any method. Fluoroscopic guidance and contrast imaging may be utilized. This procedure includes image documentation and report.

49465
The physician injects contrast via a percutaneous approach for the radiological evaluation of existing tubes (gastrostomy, duodenostomy, jejunostomy, gastrojejunostomy, or cecostomy). Image documentation and report are included in this procedure.

49491-49492
The physician repairs an initial, reducible, inguinal hernia in a preterm infant (less than 37 weeks gestation at birth), performed up to 50 weeks postconceptual age, with or without hydrocelectomy. The physician dissects in the preperitoneal plane to present the hernia ring. The physician applies manual pressure to the inguinal region from outside while trying to dissect the hernia sac to reduce the hernia. If that fails, which can occur when there is a discrepancy in size of the hernia compared to its contents, the physician enlarges the hernia ring by an electrocautery incision in a ventral direction. The incision is made in a ventromedial direction for medial hernias and a ventrolateral direction for lateral hernias. The hernia is reduced using pleural insufflation of carbon dioxide. If a hydrocele is present, it is incised and drained. The hernia defect is repaired by suture and reinforced by staples or mesh. Report 49492 if, in the case of an incarcerated or strangulated hernia, the physician empties the contents of the hernia sac, places the contents in the lower abdomen, and repairs the hernia defect by suture.

49495-49496
The physician repairs an initial, reducible, inguinal hernia in a full-term infant under age 6 months, or a preterm infant over 50 weeks postconceptual age and under 6 months at the time of surgery, with or without hydrocelectomy. The physician dissects in the preperitoneal plane to present the hernia ring. The physician applies manual pressure to the inguinal region from outside while trying to dissect the hernia sac to reduce the hernia. If that fails, which can occur when there is a discrepancy in size of the hernia compared to its contents, the physician enlarges the hernia ring by an electrocautery incision in a ventral direction. The incision is made in a ventromedial direction for medial hernias and a ventrolateral direction for lateral hernias. The hernia is reduced

using pleural insufflation of carbon dioxide. If a hydrocele is present, it is incised and drained. The hernia defect is repaired by suture and reinforced by staples or mesh. Report 49496 if, in the case of an incarcerated or strangulated hernia, the physician empties the contents of the hernia sac, places the contents in the lower abdomen, and repairs the hernia defect by suture.

49500
The physician repairs an inguinal hernia in a child between six months and 5 years of age. The physician makes a groin incision. The hernia sac is identified and dissected free of surrounding structures. The hernia sac is ligated and resected. If a hydrocele is present it is incised and drained. The groin incision is closed.

49501
The physician repairs an incarcerated inguinal hernia in a child between six months and 5 years of age. The physician makes a groin incision. The hernia sac is identified and dissected free of surrounding structures. The hernia sac is opened and the contents of the sac are examined. If the hernia contents are viable the hernia is reduced and the sac ligated and resected. If a hydrocele is present it is incised and drained. The groin incision is closed.

49505
The physician repairs an inguinal hernia in a patient age 5 or over. The physician makes a groin incision. The hernia sac is identified and dissected free from surrounding structures. The hernia sac is ligated and resected. The groin incision is closed.

49507
The physician repairs an incarcerated inguinal hernia in a patient over the age of 5 years. The physician makes a groin incision. The hernia sac is identified and dissected free from surrounding structures. The hernia sac is opened and the contents of the sac are examined. If the contents of the hernia are viable the hernia is reduced and the hernia sac is ligated and resected. The groin incision is closed.

49520
The physician repairs a recurrent inguinal hernia. The physician makes a groin incision. Dissection is continued through scar tissue and the spermatic cord and the hernia sac are identified and dissected from surrounding structures. The hernia sac may be ligated and resected. The incision is closed.

49521
The physician repairs an incarcerated recurrent inguinal hernia. The physician makes a groin incision. Dissection is continued through scar tissue and the spermatic cord and hernia sac is identified and dissected from surrounding structures. The hernia sac is opened and the contents of the sac are examined. If the contents of the hernia are viable the hernia is reduced and the hernia sac may be ligated and resected. The incision is closed.

49525
The physician repairs a sliding inguinal hernia. The physician makes a groin incision. The hernia sac is identified and dissected from surrounding structures. The hernia sac is opened and the abdominal viscera attached to the sac are dissected away from the sac if possible. The hernia contents are reduced and the hernia sac is closed and a portion of the sac may be resected. The incision is closed.

49540
The physician repairs a lumbar hernia. The physician makes an incision posteriorly over the hernia. The hernia sac is identified and dissected from surrounding structures to expose the fascial defect. The hernia is reduced and the hernia sac may be resected. The fascial defect is closed with sutures. The incision is closed.

49550
The physician repairs a femoral hernia. The physician makes a femoral or groin incision. The hernia sac is identified and dissected from surrounding structures. The femoral defect is closed with a prosthetic patch or sutures by plicating the fascia and muscles to cover the defect. The incision is closed.

49553
The physician repairs an incarcerated femoral hernia. The physician makes a groin or femoral incision. The hernia sac is identified and dissected from surrounding structures. The hernia sac is opened and the contents of the sac are examined. If the contents of the hernia are viable the hernia is reduced and the hernia sac is closed and may be resected. The femoral defect is closed with sutures by plicating the fascia and muscles to cover the defect. The incision is closed.

49555
The physician repairs a recurrent femoral hernia. The physician makes a groin or femoral incision. Dissection is continued through scar tissue and the hernia sac is identified and dissected from surrounding structures. The hernia sac is reduced and may be resected. The femoral defect is closed with sutures by plicating the fascia and muscles to cover the defect. The incision is closed.

49557
The physician repairs an incarcerated recurrent femoral hernia. The physician makes a groin or femoral incision. Dissection is continued through scar tissue and the hernia sac is identified and dissected from surrounding structures. The hernia sac is opened and the contents of the sac are examined. If the hernia contents are viable the hernia is reduced and the hernia sac is closed and may be resected. The femoral defect is closed with sutures by plicating fascia and muscle to cover the defect. The incision is closed.

49560
The physician repairs an incisional or ventral hernia. The physician makes an incision over the hernia. Dissection is continued through scar tissue and the hernia sac is identified and dissected from surrounding structures. The fascial defect is identified circumferentially. The hernia is reduced and the hernia sac may be resected. The hernia defect is closed with sutures. The incision is closed.

49561
The physician repairs an incarcerated incisional hernia. The physician makes an incision over the hernia. Dissection is continued through scar tissue and the hernia sac is identified and dissected from surrounding structures. The fascial defect is identified circumferentially. The hernia sac is opened and the contents of the hernia sac are examined. If the contents of the hernia sac are viable the hernia is reduced and the hernia sac is closed and may be resected. The hernia defect is closed with sutures. The incision is closed.

49565
The physician repairs a recurrent incisional or ventral hernia. The physician makes an incision over the hernia. Dissection is continued through scar tissue and the hernia sac is identified and dissected from surrounding structures. The fascial defect is identified circumferentially. The hernia is reduced and the sac may be resected. The hernia defect is closed with sutures. The incision is closed.

49566
The physician repairs an incarcerated recurrent incisional hernia. The physician makes an incision over the hernia. Dissection is continued through scar tissue and the hernia sac is identified and dissected from surrounding structures. The fascial defect is identified circumferentially. The hernia sac is opened and the contents of the sac are examined. If the contents of the hernia sac are viable the hernia is reduced and the hernia sac is closed and may be resected. The hernia defect is closed with sutures. The incision is closed.

49568
The physician implants mesh for an open incisional or ventral hernia repair or for closure of debridement for a necrotizing soft tissue infection. The defect is closed with mesh or some other prosthetic material. The incision is closed.

49570
The physician repairs an epigastric hernia. The physician makes an incision over the hernia. The hernia sac is identified and dissected from surrounding structures. The fascial defect is identified circumferentially. The hernia is reduced and the hernia sac may be resected. The hernia defect is closed with sutures. The incision is closed.

49572
The physician repairs an incarcerated epigastric hernia. The physician makes an incision over the hernia. The hernia sac is identified and dissected from surrounding structures. The fascial defect is identified circumferentially. The hernia sac is opened and the contents of the sac are examined. If the contents of the hernia are viable the hernia is reduced and the hernia sac may be resected. The hernia defect is closed with sutures. The incision is closed.

49580
The physician repairs an umbilical hernia in a child under 5 years of age. The physician makes an umbilical incision. The hernia sac and fascial defect are identified and dissected from surrounding structures. The hernia sac is reduced and may be resected. The hernia defect is closed with sutures. The incision is closed.

49582
The physician repairs an incarcerated umbilical hernia in a child under 5 years of age. The physician makes an umbilical incision. The hernia sac and fascial defect are identified and dissected from surrounding structures. The hernia sac is opened and the contents of the sac are examined. If the contents of the hernia sac are viable the hernia is reduced and the hernia sac may be resected. The hernia defect is closed with sutures. The incision is closed.

49585
The physician repairs an umbilical hernia in a patient over 5 years of age. The physician makes an umbilical incision. The hernia sac and fascial defect are identified and dissected from surrounding structures. The hernia is reduced and the hernia sac may be resected. The hernia defect is closed with sutures. The incision is closed.

49587
The physician repairs an incarcerated umbilical hernia in a patient over 5 years of age. The physician makes an umbilical incision. The hernia sac and fascial defect are identified and dissected from surrounding structures. The hernia sac is opened and the contents of the sac are examined. If the contents of the hernia sac are viable the hernia is reduced and the hernia sac may be resected. The hernia defect is closed with sutures. The incision is closed.

49590
The physician repairs a spigelian hernia. The physician makes an incision over the hernia. The hernia sac and fascial defect are identified and dissected from surrounding structures. The hernia is reduced and the hernia sac may be resected. The hernia defect is closed with a prosthetic patch or by plicating layers of muscle and fascia over the defect with sutures. The incision is closed.

49600
The physician repairs a small omphalocele. The physician identifies the omphalocele and dissects the peritoneal sac from the umbilicus and the abdominal wall defect. The peritoneal sac is reduced and the abdominal wall defect is closed with sutures. The umbilicus is reconstructed and the skin is loosely closed.

49605
The physician repairs a large omphalocele or gastroschisis. The peritoneal sac of the omphalocele is dissected from the umbilicus and surrounding structures and reduced or the herniated contents of the gastroschisis are reduced into the abdominal cavity if possible. The abdominal wall defect is identified. If possible the abdominal wall defect is closed with sutures and the umbilicus is reconstructed. If the defect is too large or if the herniated contents cannot be reduced a prosthetic material is used to create a patch or silo that is sutured over the defect to close the defect and accommodate the herniated contents.

49606
The physician removes a previously placed prosthesis and closes an omphalocele or gastroschisis. The physician removes the previously placed prosthetic material covering the abdominal wall defect. The herniated contents are reduced and the edges of the defect are identified. The abdominal wall defect is closed with sutures. The umbilicus is reconstructed with skin flaps if possible. The remainder of the skin incision is usually left open to allow drainage.

49610
The physician performs the first stage of an omphalocele repair (Gross type operation). The physician identifies the omphalocele. Skin flaps are widely mobilized around the omphalocele and the skin flaps are closed over the intact omphalocele with sutures. The abdominal wall defect is not addressed.

49611
The physician performs the second stage of an omphalocele repair (Gross type operation). The physician makes an incision in the previously closed skin over the omphalocele. Skin flaps are mobilized off the omphalocele and the peritoneal sac of the omphalocele is dissected from the abdominal wall defect. The abdominal wall defect is closed with sutures. The skin flaps are closed over the repair thus closing the incision.

49650-49651
The physician performs laparoscopic repair of an initial (49650) or recurrent (49651) inguinal hernia. The physician places a trocar at the umbilicus and insufflates the abdominal or retroperitoneal cavity. The laparoscope is placed through the umbilical port and additional trocars are placed into the peritoneal or retroperitoneal space. The hernia sac is identified and reduced into the abdominal cavity. A sheet of mesh is placed into the abdominal or retroperitoneal cavity and stapled into place on the pubis and abdominal wall covering the hernial defect. The trocars are removed, and the incisions are closed.

49652-49653
The physician performs laparoscopic repair of a ventral, lateral ventral (spigelian), umbilical, or epigastric hernia. Code 49652 reports repair of a reducible hernia; 49653 reports repair of a hernia that is incarcerated or strangulated. The physician places a trocar at the umbilicus and insufflates the abdominal or retroperitoneal cavity. The laparoscope is placed through the umbilical port and additional trocars are placed into the peritoneal or retroperitoneal space. The hernia sac is identified and reduced into the abdominal cavity. A sheet of mesh is often placed into the abdominal or retroperitoneal cavity and stapled into place on the pubis and abdominal wall covering the hernial defect. The trocars are removed, and the incisions are closed. These codes include the insertion of mesh, when performed.

49654-49657
The physician performs laparoscopic repair of an incisional hernia. The physician places a trocar at the umbilicus and insufflates the abdominal or retroperitoneal cavity. The laparoscope is placed through the umbilical port, and additional trocars are placed into the peritoneal or retroperitoneal space. The hernia sac is identified and reduced into the abdominal cavity. A sheet of mesh is often placed into the abdominal or retroperitoneal cavity and stapled into place on the pubis and abdominal wall covering the hernial defect. The trocars are removed, and the incisions are closed. Report code 49654 for repair of an initial reducible hernia and 49656 if the reducible hernia is recurrent. Report code 49655 for an initial incarcerated or strangulated hernia and 49657 if recurrent. These codes include the insertion of mesh, when performed.

49900
The physician performs a secondary closure of the abdominal wall for dehiscence or evisceration. The physician completely opens the former incision and removes the remaining sutures. Necrotic fascia is debrided to viable tissue. Any eviscerated abdominal contents are reduced into the abdominal cavity. The abdominal wall is closed with sutures.

49904-49906
The physician mobilizes an omental flap for reconstruction of a defect. The surgical recipient site of the flap is prepared. An upper abdominal transverse or midline incision is made. A laparotomy and manual exploration of the abdominal cavity is done first and the omentum and transverse colon are delivered from the cavity. The omentum is dissected from the transverse colon from left to right and small vessels are

ligated. When completely separated from the transverse colon, the omentum is dissected from the stomach with careful clamping, division, and ligation of vessels. The omentum is fully mobilized and pedicled on the right or left gastroepiploic vessel, depending on the purpose. More incisions and tunneling may be necessary to bring the flap into its new location to fill a defect. The flap may be used as a pedicled transposition flap or a free microvascular transfer flap. Report 49904 when the flap is transpositioned to repair an extra-abdominal defect, such as chest wounds after radiation and mastectomy or lower extremity trauma wounds. Report 49905 when the omental flap is repositioned to repair a defect intra-abdominally. Report 49906 when the omentum is used as a free vascularized transfer flap to repair defects such as hemifacial atrophy. Microvascular anastomosis is performed to maintain blood flow to the omental flap. The abdominal incision is closed. If a separate split-thickness skin graft is required for omental coverage, it is done immediately and applied directly over the omentum and a dressing is applied.

Urinary

50010

The physician examines the kidney and renal pelvis. To access the kidney, the physician makes an incision in the skin of the flank, cuts the muscles, fat, and fibrous membranes (fascia) overlying the kidney, and sometimes removes a portion of the eleventh or twelfth rib. The physician clears away the fatty tissue surrounding the kidney, explores the area, and performs a layered closure.

50020

The physician drains an infection (abscess) on the kidney or on the surrounding renal tissue in an open procedure. To access the renal or perirenal abscess, the physician makes a small incision in the skin of the flank, cuts the muscles, fat, and fibrous membranes (fascia) overlying the kidney, and sometimes removes a portion of the eleventh or twelfth rib. After exploring the abscess cavity, the physician irrigates the site, inserts multiple drain tubes through separate stab wounds, and sutures the drain tube ends to the skin. The physician packs the wound with gauze and sutures the fascia and muscles. The skin and subcutaneous tissue are usually left open to prevent formation of a secondary body wall abscess. The drainage catheters are later removed.

50021

The physician performs a percutaneous drainage of a perirenal or renal infection (abscess). The physician may create a small incision in the skin between two ribs proximal to the abscess or in the flank in order to ease placement of drainage instruments through the skin into an abscess located within the kidney or immediately adjacent to it. The physician uses a CAT scan or ultrasound to guide placement of a drainage needle or trocar into the abscess. The physician advances the drainage needle or trocar through the skin to gain access to the abscess. The fluid is allowed to drain. Once the abscess is drained a drainage catheter may be placed. Sutures may be placed to secure the drainage catheter in place. The operative site is cleaned and bandaged. For radiological supervision and interpretation, see 75989.

50040

The physician creates an opening from the kidney to the exterior of the body by making an incision in the kidney. To access the kidney, the physician makes an incision in the skin of the flank, cuts the muscles, fat, and fibrous membranes (fascia) overlying the kidney, and sometimes removes a portion of the eleventh or twelfth rib. Using an incision to open the renal pelvis (pyelotomy), the physician passes a curved clamp into the renal pelvis, a middle or lower minor calyx, and the cortex of the kidney. The physician inserts a catheter tip through the same path as the clamp, and passes the tube through a stab incision in the skin of the flank. After suturing the incisions, the physician inserts a drain tube, bringing it out through a separate stab incision, and performs a layered closure.

50045

The physician makes a small incision in the kidney to explore the interior of the kidney. To access the kidney, the physician makes an incision in the skin of the flank, cuts the muscles, fat, and fibrous membranes (fascia) overlying the kidney, and sometimes removes a portion of the eleventh or twelfth rib. The physician makes an incision in the kidney (nephrotomy) and sometimes places fine traction sutures at the edges of the incision. After exploration, the physician sutures the incision, inserts a drain tube, bringing it out through a separate stab incision, and performs a layered closure.

50060-50070

The physician removes a kidney stone (calculus) by making an incision in the kidney. To access the calculus, the physician makes an incision in the skin of the flank, cuts the muscles, fat, and fibrous membranes (fascia) overlying the kidney, and sometimes removes a portion of the eleventh or twelfth rib. The physician isolates the calculus and removes it through an incision. After examining the kidney for other defects, the physician sutures the incision, inserts a drain tube, bringing it out through a separate stab incision, and performs a layered closure. Simple removal of the calculus by nephrotomy is reported with 50060. Report 50065 when a previous surgery on the kidney complicates the procedure. Report 50070 if the procedure is complicated because of a congenital kidney abnormality, wherein the physician usually repairs any calyces that are obstructed or abnormally narrowed.

50075

The physician removes a stone that fills the calyces and renal pelvis (staghorn calculus) by making incisions in the kidney and renal pelvis. To access the staghorn calculus, the physician makes an incision in the skin of the flank, cuts the muscles, fat, and fibrous membranes (fascia) overlying the kidney, and sometimes removes a portion of the twelfth rib. After isolating the staghorn calculus, the physician makes an incision in the renal pelvis (pyelotomy) and may make an incision in the kidney (nephrotomy). The physician removes the staghorn calculus, irrigates the area, and examines the kidney for other defects. After closing the incisions, the physician inserts a drain tube and performs a layered closure.

50080-50081

The physician creates a percutaneous passageway to remove kidney stones (calculi). The physician makes a small incision in the skin of the back, inserts a large needle, and radiologically guides it toward the kidney or renal pelvis. After passing a guidewire through the needle, the physician dilates the passageway by inserting and removing tubes with increasingly larger diameters. The physician inserts an endoscope over the guidewire and passes an instrument through the endoscope to crush or extract calculi. The physician may pass a ureteral stent from the pelvis into the bladder. The physician removes the guidewire and allows the passageway to seal on its own, or inserts a nephrostomy or pyelostomy tube before removing the guidewire. Report 50080 for removal of calculi measuring up to 2 cm; use 50081 for removal of calculi measuring more than 2 cm.

50100

The physician corrects an obstruction by cutting across or repositioning renal vessels that deviate from proper anatomical placement. To access the kidney, the physician makes an incision in the skin of the flank, cuts the muscles, fat, and fibrous membranes (fascia) overlying the kidney, and sometimes removes a portion of the twelfth rib. After repositioning the aberrant vessels to a more functional anatomic placement, the physician performs a layered closure.

50120

The physician makes an incision in the renal pelvis to explore the calyces and renal pelvis. To access the kidney, the physician makes an incision in the skin of the flank, cuts the muscles, fat, and fibrous membranes (fascia) overlying the kidney, and sometimes removes a portion of the eleventh or twelfth rib. The physician makes an incision in the renal pelvis (pyelotomy). The physician may place fine traction sutures at the edges of the pyelotomy while exploring the calyces and renal pelvis. After closing the pyelotomy, the physician inserts a drain tube, bringing it out through a separate stab incision, and performs a layered closure.

50125

The physician makes an incision in the renal pelvis to insert a pyelostomy tube for drainage. To access the kidney, the physician makes an incision in the skin of the flank, cuts the muscles, fat, and fibrous membranes (fascia) overlying the kidney, and sometimes removes a portion of the eleventh or twelfth rib. After exposing the renal pelvis, the physician makes an incision in the renal pelvis (pyelotomy). The physician inserts the tip of a catheter into the renal pelvis and passes the tube out through a stab incision in the skin of the flank. The physician performs a layered closure.

50130

The physician removes stones (calculi) or an insoluble mass (coagulum) from the renal pelvis by making an incision into the renal pelvis. To access the kidney, the physician makes an incision in the skin of the flank, cuts the muscles, fat, and fibrous membranes (fascia) overlying the kidney, and sometimes removes a portion of the eleventh or twelfth rib. The physician makes an incision in the renal pelvis (pyelotomy) to isolate and remove the calculus. The physician irrigates the area and examines the renal pelvis for other defects. The physician inserts a drain tube, bringing it out through a separate stab incision, and performs a layered closure.

50135

The physician makes an incision in the renal pelvis of a kidney complicated by a congenital abnormality or a previous surgery. To access the kidney, the physician makes an incision in the skin of the flank, cuts the muscles, fat, and fibrous membranes (fascia) overlying the kidney, and sometimes removes a portion of the eleventh or twelfth rib. The physician makes an incision in the renal pelvis (pyelotomy) and explores the calyces and renal pelvis. The physician may place fine traction sutures at the edges of the pyelotomy while exploring the calyces and renal pelvis or repairing defects. After closing the pyelotomy and nephrotomy, the physician inserts a drain tube, bringing it out through a separate stab incision, and performs a layered closure.

50200

The physician extracts a plug of biopsy tissue from the kidney by inserting a needle or trocar in the skin of the back. Using radiologic or ultrasonic guidance, the physician advances the instrument into the suspect tissue of the kidney. With the instrument's cutting sheath, the physician traps a specimen of renal tissue and removes the instrument. After repeating the process several times, the physician applies pressure to the puncture wound.

50205

The physician excises a specimen of biopsy tissue from the kidney through an incision. To access the kidney, the physician makes an incision in the skin of the flank and cuts the muscles, fat, and fibrous membranes (fascia) overlying the kidney. After excising a specimen of the diseased or damaged renal tissue, the physician sutures the incision and performs a layered closure.

50220-50225
The physician removes the kidney and upper portion of the ureter. To access the kidney and ureter, the physician usually makes an incision in the skin of the flank, cuts the muscles, fat, and fibrous membranes (fascia) overlying the kidney, and sometimes removes a portion of the eleventh or twelfth rib. After mobilizing the kidney and ureter, the physician clamps, ligates, and severs the upper ureter and major renal blood vessels (renal pedicle). The physician removes the kidney and upper ureter, but does not remove the adrenal gland, surrounding fatty tissue, or Gerota's fascia. After controlling bleeding, the physician irrigates the site with normal saline and places a drain tube, bringing it out through a separate stab incision in the skin. The physician removes the clamps and performs a layered closure. Report 50225 when a previous surgery on the kidney and/or ureter complicates the procedure.

50230
The physician removes the kidney, surrounding fat, Gerota's fascia, adrenal gland, periaortic lymph nodes, and upper ureter. To access the kidney and upper ureter, the physician usually makes an incision in the skin of the chest (transthoracic approach) or flank. After mobilizing the kidney and ureter, the physician clamps, ligates, and severs the upper ureter and major renal blood vessels (renal pedicle). The physician removes the kidney, upper ureter, neural and vascular structures at the apex of the renal pelvis, surrounding fat, Gerota's fascia, adrenal gland, and involved renal lymph nodes. The physician irrigates the site, places a drain tube, removes the clamps, and performs a layered closure. In a transthoracic approach, the lung is re-expanded and the chest tube left in.

50234
The physician removes the kidney, ureter, and small cuff of the bladder through one excision. To access the kidney and ureter, the physician usually makes an incision in the skin of the flank, cuts the muscles, fat, and fibrous membranes (fascia) overlying the kidney, and sometimes removes a portion of the eleventh or twelfth rib. After mobilizing the kidney, ureter, and bladder, the physician clamps, ligates, and severs the ureter, major renal blood vessels (renal pedicle), and a small cuff of the bladder. The physician pulls the kidney, ureter, and bladder cuff upward through the flank incision. The physician does not remove the adrenal gland, surrounding fatty tissue, or Gerota's fascia. After controlling bleeding, the physician irrigates the site with normal saline and places a drain tube, bringing it out through a separate stab incision in the skin. The physician sutures and catheterizes the bladder, removes the clamps, and performs a layered closure.

50236
The physician removes the kidney, ureter, and small cuff of the bladder through two incisions. To access the kidney and upper ureter, the physician usually makes an incision in the skin of the flank, cuts the muscles, fat, and fibrous membranes (fascia) overlying the kidney, and sometimes removes a portion of the eleventh or twelfth rib. After mobilizing the kidney and ureter, the physician isolates, clamps, ligates, and severs the upper ureter and major renal blood vessels (renal pedicle) and removes the kidney. The physician does not remove the adrenal gland, surrounding fatty tissue, or Gerota's fascia. After controlling bleeding, the physician irrigates the site with normal saline and places a drain tube, bringing it out through a separate stab incision in the skin. To access the lower ureter and bladder, the physician makes an incision in the skin of the abdomen. After mobilizing the bladder, the physician removes the lower ureter and a small cuff of the bladder. The physician sutures and catheterizes the bladder. After placing a drain tube behind the bladder, the physician removes the clamps and performs a layered closure.

50240
The physician removes a portion of the kidney. To access the kidney and ureter, the physician usually makes an incision in the skin of the flank, cuts the muscles, fat, and fibrous membranes (fascia) overlying the kidney, and sometimes removes a portion of the eleventh or twelfth rib. After mobilizing the kidney and the major renal blood vessels (renal pedicle), the physician clamps the renal vessels, and sometimes induces hypothermia of the kidney with iced saline slush. The physician excises a wedge containing the diseased or damaged kidney tissue. After clamping and ligating the exposed arteries and veins, the physician inserts a drain tube, bringing it out through a separate stab incision in the skin, removes the clamps, and performs a layered closure.

50250
The physician performs cryosurgical ablation of one or more renal mass lesions. The physician performs a laparotomy. Dissection is carried down to the kidney. Intraoperative ultrasound may be used to identify the lesion. Cryosurgical probes are inserted into the kidney lesion. The cryosurgical probe delivers cryogen, a coolant, at subfreezing temperatures to freeze the lesion. The renal tissue is slowly thawed. A minimum of two cycles of freezing and thawing are performed. This is repeated for each lesion. When all lesions have been treated, the incision is closed with layered sutures.

50280-50290
The physician excises a cyst on the kidney or in the surrounding renal tissue. To access the kidney, the physician makes an incision in the skin of the flank, cuts the muscles, fat, and fibrous membranes (fascia)

Urinary

overlying the kidney, and sometimes removes a portion of the twelfth rib. After clearing away the fatty tissue surrounding the kidney, the physician excises the cyst from the renal surface. The physician destroys tiny vessels bordering the cyst with high-frequency electric current (fulguration) to minimize the need for sutures. If the cyst requires a deep excision, the physician usually sutures the renal tissue. The physician inserts a drain tube, bringing it out through a separate stab incision in the skin, and performs a layered closure. 50280 reports excision of a cyst (or cysts) on the kidney; 50290 reports excision of a cyst (or cysts) in the tissue surrounding the kidney.

50300
The physician performs a donor nephrectomy by removing the kidney and upper ureter from a cadaver for transplantation. To access the kidney and upper ureter, the physician usually makes a midline incision in the skin from the xiphoid process to the symphysis pubis. After cutting the muscles, fat, and fibrous membranes (fascia) overlying the kidney, the physician uses clamps, ties, suture ligatures, and electrocoagulation to control bleeding. Before clamping the major renal blood vessels (renal pedicle), the physician administers heparin sodium to prevent intravascular clotting. The physician dissects and removes the kidney, renal vessels, and ureter, usually removing sections of the inferior vena cava and aorta with both kidneys. The donor kidney is preserved for transplantation into the recipient. The organ remains under refrigeration, packed in a sealable container with some preserving solution and kept on ice in a suitable carrier.

50320
The physician performs an open donor nephrectomy from a living donor by removing one kidney and upper ureter for transplantation. To access the kidney, the physician usually makes an incision in the skin of the flank, cuts the muscles, fat, and fibrous membranes (fascia) overlying the kidney, and sometimes removes a portion of the eleventh or twelfth rib. After mobilizing the kidney and ureter, the physician administers an anticlogging agent. The physician clamps, ligates, and severs the upper ureter and major renal blood vessels (renal pedicle), and removes the kidney and upper ureter. The physician administers medication to reverse the effects of the anticlogging agent. After controlling bleeding, the physician irrigates the site, places a drain tube, and performs a layered closure. The donor kidney is preserved for transplantation into the recipient. The organ remains under refrigeration, packed in a sealable container with some preserving solution and kept on ice in a suitable carrier.

50323
The surgeon prepares a donor kidney from a cadaver prior to transplantation. Back table prep time is about an hour. The kidney and necessary vital structures removed en bloc usually contain some of the inferior vena cava, a cuff of aorta, perinephric tissue, the adrenal gland, and muscle, as well as some damaged blood vessels. The renal vein is dissected and the gonadal and adrenal veins are isolated and separated with ligatures. The renal artery is dissected from surrounding tissue along with the aortic patch. The adrenal gland, excess perinephric fat, and other tissue attachments are removed from the graft, taking care to leave fibrofatty tissue around the ureter to ensure its blood supply. The aortic patch, renal vein, and ureter are further repaired and/or modified to fit the recipient.

50325
The physician performs a standard backbench preparation of the kidney following procurement from a living donor. Backbench or back table preparation refers to procedures performed on the donor organ following procurement to prepare the donor organ for transplant. In a separately reportable procedure, the physician removes the kidney and upper ureter from a living donor. The kidney is flushed with a cold electrolyte solution to rinse any remaining donor blood from the kidney and lower its temperature. When the kidney is procured from a living donor, only minimal backbench preparation is required because most of the dissection is performed in situ during the nephrectomy. During the backbench preparation any excess perinephric fat and other tissue attachments are removed from the graft, taking care to leave fibrofatty tissue around the ureter to ensure its blood supply. Further separation of the renal artery or arteries from the renal veins is performed. The arterial and venous separation prevents the technical inconvenience of side-by-side anastomosis in the recipient. To reduce the risk of postoperative complications, the transplant ureter is shortened as needed leaving the vascularized periureteral fat intact. When all residual soft tissue has been removed and the blood vessels and ureters prepared, the kidney is ready for transplant.

50327
The surgeon reconstructs a donor kidney from a cadaver or living donor prior to transplantation with a venous anastomosis. This procedure consists of performing venoplasties on the donor kidney to extend the renal vein before grafting. The inferior vena cava is used from a cadaver donor. When the donor organ comes from a living donor, a cuff of the inferior vena cava attached to the renal vein is used. When the donor organ comes from a cadaveric source, the external iliac vein is also routinely procured and prepared for venous grafting to extend the renal vein for the recipient. The vessels are tested for patency by flushing with a preservation solution.

50328
The surgeon performs arterial anastomosis reconstruction of a donor kidney from a cadaver or living donor prior to transplantation. The allograft is

prepared with multiple renal arteries. When the donor organ comes from a cadaveric source, the aortic patch removed with the specimen is used for creating a viable renal artery graft for transplantation. Donor iliac arteries are routinely procured from cadaveric donors to be prepared and used as arterial grafting material. The segmental renal artery may also be anastomosed to the inferior epigastric artery when an aortic patch is not available, such as when the donor kidney is from a living donor. The vessels are tested for patency by flushing with a preservation solution.

50329
The physician performs a standard backbench reconstruction of the ureter following renal allograft procurement from a cadaver or living donor. Backbench or back table preparation refers to procedures performed on the donor organ following procurement to prepare the donor organ for transplant. In a separately reportable procedure, the physician removes the kidney en bloc from a cadaver donor or the kidney and upper ureter from a living donor. The kidney is flushed with a cold electrolyte solution to rinse any remaining donor blood from the kidney and lower its temperature. After preparing the kidney and blood vessels in a separately reportable procedure, the physician turns his attention to any required ureteral anastomosis. Ureteral anastomosis is generally required when anatomic variations are present in the donor organ. Anatomic variations for kidney donors include multiple ureters. When two or more ureters are present, the ureters may be separately implanted into the bladder or a side-to-side anastomosis of the ureters may be performed during the backbench preparation prior to implantation into the bladder. Code 50329 is reported when side-to-side anastomosis is performed and is reported for each anastomosis.

50340
The physician removes the kidney and the upper portion of the ureter in a patient who is to receive a kidney transplant. To access the kidney and ureter, the physician usually makes an incision in the skin of the flank, cuts the muscles, fat, and fibrous membranes (fascia) overlying the kidney, and sometimes removes a portion of the eleventh or twelfth rib. After mobilizing the kidney and ureter, the physician clamps, ligates, and severs the upper ureter and major renal blood vessels (renal pedicle). The physician removes the kidney and upper ureter, but does not remove the adrenal gland, surrounding fatty tissue, or Gerota's fascia. After controlling bleeding, the physician irrigates the site with normal saline and places a drain tube, bringing it out through a separate stab incision in the skin. The physician performs a layered closure.

50360
The physician surgically implants a human kidney and ureter from a living donor or cadaver into a transplant patient, without performing a concurrent nephrectomy on the recipient. To access the transplant site, the physician usually makes a curved, right or left lower quadrant incision in the skin. After cutting the muscles, fat, and fibrous membranes (fascia), the physician controls bleeding with clamps, ties, and electrocoagulation. The physician surgically connects the renal vein and artery of the donor kidney to the recipient's clamped and dissected internal iliac vein and hypogastric artery. After removing the clamps, the physician checks for leakage, bleeding, and insufficient blood supply. To implant the donor ureter, the physician makes an incision into the bladder and passes the ureter through the bladder. The physician sutures the ureter as well as the opening in the bladder (cystotomy). The physician performs a layered closure. The drain tube may be left in.

50365
The physician implants a donor kidney and upper ureter after removing the recipient's kidney and upper ureter. To access the recipient's kidney and ureter, the physician usually makes an incision in the skin of the flank, cuts the muscles, fat, and fibrous membranes (fascia) overlying the kidney, and sometimes removes a portion of the eleventh or twelfth rib. The physician clamps, ligates, and severs the upper ureter and major renal blood vessels (renal pedicle), and removes the kidney and upper ureter. To implant the donor kidney and upper ureter, the physician usually makes a curved lower quadrant incision in the skin. The physician surgically connects the renal vein and artery of the donor kidney to the recipient's clamped and dissected internal iliac vein and hypogastric artery. After incising the bladder, the physician passes the donor ureter through the bladder and sutures the ureter and opening in the bladder (cystotomy). The physician performs a layered closure. The drain tube may be left in.

50370
The physician removes a transplanted donor kidney from the recipient. To access the rejected kidney, the physician usually reopens the original kidney transplant incision, and cuts the muscles, fat, and fibrous membranes (fascia) overlying the kidney. After mobilizing the kidney, the physician clamps, ligates, and severs the major renal blood vessels (renal pedicle). The physician removes the rejected kidney. After controlling bleeding, the physician irrigates the site with normal saline. The physician may place a drain tube, bringing it out through a separate stab incision in the skin. After removing the clamps, the physician performs a layered closure.

50380
The physician moves the kidney from its original anatomic site and revascularizes the kidney by connecting the renal and iliac vessels to a new site. To access the transplant site, the physician usually makes a midline transabdominal incision in the skin and cuts

the muscles, fat, and fibrous membranes (fascia). After exposing the kidney, the physician clamps, ligates, and severs the renal vessels, keeping the ureter intact. The physician flushes the kidney with cold, anticoagulant electrolyte solution, and surgically connects the renal vessels to another appropriate arterial and venous site. The physician removes the clamps and checks for leakage, bleeding, and infarction. After placing a drain tube and bringing it out through a separate stab incision in the skin, the physician removes the clamps and performs a layered closure.

50382-50384
The physician percutaneously removes an internally dwelling ureteral stent through the renal pelvis in 50384. With the patient under moderate sedation, a long, thin needle is advanced into the renal calyx under imaging guidance and the position is confirmed with contrast and fluoroscopy. A guidewire is threaded over the needle into the renal pelvis, the needle is removed, and a sheath placed over the guidewire. A snare device is threaded through the sheath into position, the indwelling stent is grasped, and pulled out partially through the sheath until the proximal end is outside the ureter. A guidewire is threaded through the stent, which is guided completely out. In 50382, the physician replaces the indwelling ureteral stent after removal of the old stent. The guidewire is left in place, the length of the old stent is noted, and the replacement stent is advanced into the ureter until the distal end is in the bladder and the distal loop is deployed. Stent position is confirmed with the proximal loop in the renal pelvis. The instruments are removed.

50385-50386
Using snare or capture, the physician removes (50386) or removes and replaces (50385) an internally dwelling ureteral stent (a thin, flexible tube that is inserted into the ureter to assist in the drainage of urine from the kidney). In one method, under appropriate sedation and sonographic guidance, a rigid biopsy forceps is introduced through the urethra, advanced to the urinary bladder, and the stent is grasped and removed. These codes are appropriate only when the procedure is performed via a transurethral approach, without the use of cystoscopy. Radiological supervision and interpretation is included and should not be reported separately.

50387
The physician removes and replaces an externally accessible transnephric ureteral stent under fluoroscopic guidance. A transnephric ureteral stent is one that is placed through the wall of the flank into the renal pelvis and down into the ureter to keep the ureter open. Contrast may be injected at the entry site to assess anatomy and positioning. The suture holding the pigtail in place is cut and a guidewire is threaded through the stent lumen until it exits the distal end. The original stent is removed over the guidewire. Diameter and length are noted for a new stent, which is threaded over the guidewire until the distal end forms within the bladder. Fluoroscopy is used to assess the proximal position of formation within the renal pelvis. After position is verified, the guidewire is removed and the suture is put in position to hold the pigtail in place. Contrast may be injected to check position and function. Final adjustments are made for patient comfort, and the catheter may be sutured to the skin, capped, or a drainage bag may be attached.

50389
The physician removes an indwelling nephrostomy tube under fluoroscopic guidance that was previously placed concurrently with an indwelling ureteral stent. Nephrostomy tube removal may be done to avoid displacement of the stent. Contrast may first be injected through the indwelling catheter tube to verify placement and functioning of the stent. The suture holding the pigtail in place is cut and a guidewire is threaded through the nephrostomy tube under fluoroscopy, making certain that the pigtail or suture do not hook the stent and that the stent remains in proper position. The nephrostomy tube is pulled out over the guidewire, stent position is checked again, and the access site is dressed.

50390
The physician inserts a needle through the skin to inject or drain fluid from the renal pelvis or a renal cyst. The physician usually inserts a long, thin needle in the skin of the back. Using radiologic guidance, the physician advances the needle toward the renal pelvis or renal cyst and injects or drains fluid.

50391
The physician instills a therapeutic agent, such as an anticarcinogenic or an antifungal, through the tube of an established opening between the skin and kidney (nephrostomy), renal pelvis (pyelostomy), or ureter (ureterostomy). This type of intracavitary topical therapy is reliably done through a tube left in place following a previous surgery. After inserting a guidewire, an endoscope or flexible delivery catheter is passed through the tube into the kidney, renal pelvis, or ureter. To better view renal and ureteric structures, the physician may flush (irrigate) or introduce by drops (instillate) a saline solution. The physician introduces the therapeutic agent to the target area. After examination, the physician removes the instruments and reinserts the nephrostomy, pyelostomy, or ureterostomy tube or allows the surgical passageway to seal on its own.

50392
The physician inserts a catheter or intracatheter into the renal pelvis for drainage of urine and/or an injection. The physician usually inserts a long, thin needle with a removable probe in the skin of the back. Using radiologic guidance, the physician advances the

needle toward the renal pelvis. When urine flows back through the needle, the physician advances a catheter over the needle, and withdraws the needle.

50393
The physician inserts a catheter or stent through the renal pelvis into the ureter for drainage of urine and/or an injection. The physician usually inserts a long, thin needle with a removable probe in the skin of the back. The physician advances the needle toward the renal pelvis and into the ureter. When urine flows back through the needle, the physician advances a catheter over the needle. The physician removes the needle and leaves the catheter in place for drainage and/or injection.

50394
The physician injects a contrast agent through a tube or indwelling catheter into the renal pelvis to study the kidney and renal collecting system. The physician determines immediate allergic response to the contrast agent by injecting a small initial dose of contrast material through an existing pyelostomy or nephrostomy tube or indwelling ureteral catheter. If no allergic response occurs, a large quantity of contrast material is injected into the renal pelvis. The radiologist produces a representation of the kidney, renal pelvis, and/or ureter with an x-ray.

50395
The physician inserts a guide into the renal pelvis and/or ureter to establish a passageway between the skin and kidney. To create the percutaneous passageway, the physician makes a small incision in the skin of the back, inserts a large needle, and ultrasonographically guides it toward the kidney. After passing a guidewire through the needle through the kidney into the renal pelvis, the physician removes the needle by passing it backward over the guidewire. The physician enlarges (dilates) the guidewire passageway by inserting and removing tubes with increasingly larger diameters. When the passageway is sufficiently dilated, the physician passes a nephrostomy tube over the guidewire, removes the guidewire, and sutures the tube to the skin.

50396
The physician connects an indwelling ureteral catheter or existing pyelostomy or nephrostomy tube to a manometer line to measure pressure and flow in the kidneys and ureters. The physician connects a ureteral catheter or pyelostomy or nephrostomy tube to a manometer line filled with fluid. The physician inserts a bladder catheter that may be irrigated. The physician measures intrarenal and/or extrarenal pressure. After discontinuing perfusion of fluid, the physician aspirates residual fluid from the kidney and disconnects the manometer line. The physician may remove the ureteral catheter or pyelostomy or nephrostomy tube and dress the wound.

50398
The physician changes a nephrostomy or pyelostomy tube. To remove the existing tube, the physician takes out the sutures securing the tube to the skin. The physician inserts a guidewire through the tube and passes the tube back over the guidewire. The physician passes a new tube over the guidewire, removes the guidewire, and sutures the tube to the skin.

50400-50405
The physician uses plastic surgery to correct an obstruction or defect in the renal pelvis or ureteropelvic junction. To access the renal pelvis and ureter, the physician usually makes an incision in the skin of the flank. The physician incises, trims, and shapes the renal pelvis and ureter, using absorbable sutures or soft rubber drains for traction. The physician usually inserts a slender tube into the renal pelvis to provide support during healing. In Foley Y-pyeloplasty, the physician advances a Y-shaped flap of the renal pelvis into a vertical incision in the upper ureter. The physician may surgically fixate (nephropexy) a floating or mobile kidney, and/or establish an opening between the kidney (nephrostomy) or renal pelvis (pyelostomy) and the exterior of the body. The physician places a drain tube, bringing it out through a separate stab incision in the skin, and performs a layered closure. Report 50405 if a congenital abnormality, secondary pyeloplasty, solitary kidney, or calycoplasty complicates the procedure.

50500
The physician uses sutures to surgically fixate a wound or injury of the kidney. To access the kidney, the physician makes an incision in the skin of the flank, cuts the muscles, fat, and fibrous membranes (fascia) overlying the kidney, and sometimes removes a portion of the eleventh or twelfth rib. After using sutures to close or surgically fixate a kidney wound or injury, the physician places a drain tube, bringing it out through a separate stab incision in the skin, and performs a layered closure.

50520
The physician closes a fistula that is an abnormal opening between the skin and the kidney (nephrocutaneous) or the renal pelvis (pyelocutaneous). After excising the fistula, the physician sutures the clean percutaneous tissues together to create a smooth surface.

50525-50526
The physician closes a fistula that is an abnormal opening between the kidney and an organ of the digestive, respiratory, urogenital, or endocrine system. In 50525, the physician usually makes an incision in the abdomen, cuts the muscles, fat, and fibrous membranes (fascia) overlying the kidney to access the fistula. In 50526, the physician makes an incision in the skin of the chest, opens the chest cavity, collapses the lung, and separates the leaves of the diaphragm to

expose the kidney. After excising the fistula, the physician sutures the clean tissues together to create a smooth surface. The physician places a drain tube, bringing it out through a separate stab incision in the skin, and performs a layered closure. In 50526, the physician inserts a chest tube to re-expand the lung.

50540
The physician divides an abnormal union of the kidneys to correct a horseshoe kidney. To access the horseshoe kidney, the physician usually makes an incision in the skin of the lower abdomen and cuts the muscles, fat, and fibrous membranes (fascia) overlying the kidney. After incising the union and placing two rows of sutures to control bleeding, the physician usually performs pyeloplasty or another plastic procedure on one or both sides of the divided kidney. After completion of repair, the physician may rotate the kidney to effect drainage. The physician irrigates the site with normal saline, places a drain tube, bringing it out through a separate stab incision in the skin, and performs a layered closure.

50541-50542
The physician performs a laparoscopic surgical ablation of renal cysts in 50541 or a renal mass lesion in 50542 through the abdomen or back. With the abdominal approach, an umbilical port is created by placing a trocar at the level of the umbilicus. The abdominal wall is insufflated. The laparoscope is placed through the umbilical port and additional trocars are placed into the abdominal cavity. In the back approach, the trocar is placed at the back proximate to the retroperitoneal space near to the kidney with additional ports placed nearby for appropriate access to the operative site. The physician uses the laparoscope fitted with a fiberoptic camera and/or an operating instrument. The renal cysts or lesions are visualized through the scope and are ablated by fulguration or another method that can be utilized endoscopically, such as cryotherapy or radiofrequency thermal coagulation. The instruments are removed and the abdominal or back incisions are closed by staples or sutures.

50543
The physician performs a laparoscopic partial nephrectomy to treat small renal lesions or tumors. With an abdominal approach, an umbilical port is created by placing a trocar at the level of the umbilicus. The abdominal wall is insufflated. The laparoscope is placed through the umbilical port and additional trocars are placed into the abdominal cavity. In a back approach, the trocar is placed at the back proximate to the retroperitoneal space near to the kidney with additional ports placed nearby for appropriate access to the operative site. The physician uses the laparoscope fitted with a fiberoptic camera for direct vision and/or an operating instrument. Direct vision and the use of laparoscopic ultrasonography allow the physician to identify the tumors and assess the appropriate surgical margin that should be allowed. The diseased kidney tissue is removed with emphasis on hemostasis. Methods such as electrocautery, argon beam coagulator, topical agents, and microwave thermotherapy may be employed to help reduce bleeding during resection. Retrieval pouches used in endoscopic surgery allow removal of the tumor specimen without spilling. The instruments are removed and the abdominal or back incisions are closed by staples or sutures.

50544
The physician performs a laparoscopic pyeloplasty to correct an obstruction or defect in the renal pelvis or ureteropelvic junction through the abdomen or back. With the abdominal approach, an umbilical port is created by placing a trocar at the level of the umbilicus. The abdominal wall is insufflated. The laparoscope is placed through the umbilical port and additional trocars are placed into the abdominal cavity. In the back approach, the trocar is placed at the back proximate to the retroperitoneal space near to the kidney with additional ports placed nearby for appropriate access to the operative site. The physician uses the laparoscope fitted with a fiberoptic camera and/or an operating instrument. The physician incises, trims, and/or shapes the renal pelvis and ureter using absorbable sutures or soft rubber drains for traction. A tube is usually inserted to promote healing. The instruments are removed and abdominal or back incisions are closed by staples or sutures.

50545
The physician performs a radical nephrectomy, including removal of Gerota's fascia and surrounding fatty tissue, regional lymph nodes, and the adrenal gland through a laparoscope. The physician makes a 1 centimeter periumbilical incision and inserts a trocar. The abdominal cavity is insufflated with carbon dioxide. A fiberoptic laparoscope fitted with a camera and light source is inserted through the trocar. Other incisions (ports) are made in the abdomen or flank to allow other instruments or an additional light source to be passed into the abdomen or retroperitoneum. The colon is mobilized, and the laparoscope is advanced to the operative site. The ureter is transected at the ureterovesical junction. The physician clamps, ligates, and severs the renal vein and renal artery. The Gerota's fascia is dissected to expose the upper pole of the kidney. The adrenal gland is visualized. Clips are placed on the suprarenal vein and adrenal arteries (diaphragmatic [inferior phrenic], aortic, and renal) which are cut. Any lymph nodes in the surrounding area are excised and removed. The kidney, adrenal gland, renal (Gerota's) fascia, and surrounding fat are dissected free; they are bagged and removed through an enlarged port site. The instruments are removed. The incisions are closed with staples or suture.

50546

The physician removes the kidney and a portion of the ureter through a laparoscope. The physician makes a 1 cm periumbilical incision and inserts a trocar. The abdominal cavity is insufflated with carbon dioxide. A fiberoptic laparoscope fitted with a camera and light source is inserted through the trocar. Other incisions (ports) are made in the abdomen or flank to allow other instruments or an additional light source to be passed into the abdomen or retroperitoneum. The colon is mobilized and the laparoscope is advanced to the operative site. The physician mobilizes the kidney and clamps, ligates, and severs part of the ureter and major renal blood vessels (renal pedicle). The kidney and upper ureter are bagged and brought through one of the port sites (e.g., periumbilical) that has been slightly enlarged. The instruments are removed, and the small abdominal or flank incisions are closed with staples or suture.

50547

The physician performs a donor nephrectomy from a living donor by removing the kidney and upper portion of the ureter laparoscopically through the abdomen or back. With the abdominal approach, an umbilical port is created by placing a trocar at the level of the umbilicus. The abdominal wall is insufflated. The laparoscope is placed through the umbilical port and additional trocars are placed into the abdominal cavity. In the back approach, the trocar is placed at the back proximate to the retroperitoneal space near the kidney with additional ports placed nearby for appropriate access to the operative site. The physician uses the laparoscope fitted with a fiberoptic camera and/or operating instruments to explore the area. After mobilization of the kidney and ureter, an anti-clotting agent is administered. The physician clamps, ligates, and severs the upper ureter and major renal blood vessels (renal pedicle), and removes the kidney and upper ureter. The physician administers medication to reverse the effects of the anti-clotting agent. The small abdominal or back incisions are closed by staple or suture in the usual fashion. The donor kidney is preserved for transplantation into the recipient. The organ remains under refrigeration, packed in a sealable container with some preserving solution and kept on ice in a suitable carrier.

50548

The physician removes the kidney and all of the ureter through a laparoscope. The physician makes a 1.0-centimeter periumbilical incision and inserts a trocar. The abdominal cavity is insufflated with carbon dioxide. A fiberoptic laparoscope fitted with a camera and light source is inserted through the trocar. Other incisions (ports) are made in the abdomen or flank to allow other instruments or an additional light source to be passed into the abdomen or retroperitoneum. The colon is mobilized and the laparoscope is advanced to the operative site. The physician mobilizes the kidney and clamps, ligates, and severs the all of the ureter at the ureterovesical junction and major renal blood vessels (renal pedicle). The kidney and ureter are bagged and brought through one of the port sites (e.g., periumbilical) that has been slightly enlarged. The instruments are removed, and the small abdominal or flank incisions are closed with staple or suture.

50551

The physician examines the kidney and ureter with an endoscope passed through an established opening between the skin and kidney (nephrostomy) or renal pelvis (pyelostomy). After inserting a guidewire, the physician removes the nephrostomy or pyelostomy tube and passes the endoscope through the opening into the kidney or renal pelvis. To better view renal and ureteric structures, the physician may flush (irrigate) or introduce by drops (instillate) a saline solution. The physician may introduce contrast medium for radiologic study of the renal pelvis and ureter (ureteropyelogram). After examination, the physician removes the endoscope and guidewire and reinserts the nephrostomy tube or allows the surgical passageway to seal on its own.

50553

The physician examines the kidney and ureter with an endoscope passed through an established opening between the skin and kidney (nephrostomy) or renal pelvis (pyelostomy), and inserts a catheter into the ureter. After inserting a guidewire, the physician removes the nephrostomy or pyelostomy tube and passes the endoscope through the opening into the kidney or renal pelvis. To better view renal and ureteric structures, the physician may flush (irrigate) or introduce by drops (instillate) a saline solution. The physician may introduce contrast medium for radiologic study of the renal pelvis and ureter (ureteropyelogram). After examination, the physician passes a thin tube through the endoscope into the ureter. The physician may insert a balloon catheter to dilate a ureteral constriction. The physician reinserts the nephrostomy tube or allows the passageway to seal on its own.

50555

The physician examines the kidney and ureter with an endoscope passed through an established opening between the skin and kidney (nephrostomy) or renal pelvis (pyelostomy), and biopsies renal tissue. After inserting a guidewire, the physician removes the nephrostomy or pyelostomy tube and passes the endoscope through the opening into the kidney or renal pelvis. To better view renal and ureteric structures, the physician may flush (irrigate) or introduce by drops (instillate) a saline solution. The physician may introduce contrast medium for radiologic study of the renal pelvis and ureter (ureteropyelogram). After examination, the physician passes a cutting instrument through the endoscope into the suspect renal tissue and takes a biopsy specimen. The physician removes the endoscope and reinserts the nephrostomy or pyelostomy tube or allows the passageway to seal on its own.

50557
The physician examines the kidney and ureter with an endoscope passed through an established opening between the skin and kidney (nephrostomy) or renal pelvis (pyelostomy), and removes renal lesions by electric current (fulguration) or incision. After inserting a guidewire, the physician removes the nephrostomy or pyelostomy tube and passes the endoscope through the opening into the kidney or renal pelvis. To better view renal and ureteric structures, the physician may flush (irrigate) or introduce by drops (instillate) a saline solution. The physician may introduce contrast medium for radiologic study of the renal pelvis and ureter (ureteropyelogram). After examination, the physician passes through the endoscope an instrument that destroys lesions with electric current or incises lesions. The physician may insert a cutting instrument to biopsy renal tissue. The physician removes the endoscope and reinserts the nephrostomy/pyelostomy tube or allows the passageway to seal on its own.

50561
The physician examines the kidney and ureter with an endoscope passed through an established opening between the skin and kidney (nephrostomy) or renal pelvis (pyelostomy), and removes a foreign body or calculus. After inserting a guidewire, the physician removes the nephrostomy or pyelostomy tube and passes the endoscope through the opening into the kidney or renal pelvis. To better view renal and ureteric structures, the physician may flush (irrigate) or introduce by drops (instillate) a saline solution. The physician may introduce contrast medium for radiologic study of the renal pelvis and ureter (ureteropyelogram). After examination, the physician passes an instrument through the endoscope to remove a foreign body or calculus. The physician removes the endoscope and reinserts the nephrostomy tube or allows the surgical passageway to seal on its own.

50562
The physician examines the kidney and ureter with an endoscope passed through an established opening between the skin and kidney (nephrostomy) or renal pelvis (pyelostomy) and removes a foreign body or calculus. After inserting a guidewire, the physician removes the nephrostomy or pyelostomy tube and passes the endoscope through the opening into the kidney or renal pelvis. To better view renal and ureteric structures, the physician may flush (irrigate) or introduce by drops (instillate) a saline solution. The physician may introduce contrast medium for radiologic study of the renal pelvis and ureter (ureteropyelogram). After examination, the physician passes an instrument through the endoscope to resect a tumor. The tumor may be removed by cold-cup biopsy forceps with the bulk of the tumor being grasped and removed in piecemeal fashion until the base is reached. A cutting loop may be used to remove the tumor to the base, or the tumor may be ablated with YAG laser energy. The physician removes the endoscope and other instruments and reinserts the nephrostomy tube or allows the surgical passageway to seal on its own.

50570
The physician examines the kidney and ureter with an endoscope passed through an incision in the kidney (nephrotomy) or renal pelvis (pyelotomy). After accessing the renal and ureteric structures with an incision in the skin of the flank, the physician incises the kidney or renal pelvis and guides the endoscope through the incision. To better view renal and ureteric structures, the physician may flush (irrigate) or introduce by drops (instillate) a saline solution. The physician may introduce contrast medium for radiologic study of the renal pelvis and ureter (ureteropyelogram). After examination, the physician sutures the incision, inserts a drain tube, and performs a layered closure.

50572
The physician examines the kidney and ureter with an endoscope passed through an incision in the kidney (nephrotomy) or renal pelvis (pyelotomy), and inserts a catheter into the ureter. After accessing the renal and ureteric structures with an incision in the skin of the flank, the physician incises the kidney or renal pelvis and guides the endoscope through the incision. To better view renal and ureteric structures, the physician may flush (irrigate) or introduce by drops (instillate) a saline solution. The physician may introduce contrast medium for radiologic study of the renal pelvis and ureter (ureteropyelogram). After examination, the physician passes a thin tube through the endoscope into the ureter, and may insert a balloon catheter to dilate a ureteral constriction. The physician sutures the incisions, inserts a drain tube, and performs a layered closure.

50574
The physician examines the kidney and ureter with an endoscope passed through an incision in the kidney (nephrotomy) or renal pelvis (pyelotomy), and biopsies renal tissue. After accessing the renal and ureteric structures with an incision in the skin of the flank, the physician incises the kidney or renal pelvis and guides the endoscope through the incision. To better view renal and ureteric structures, the physician may flush (irrigate) or introduce by drops (instillate) a saline solution. The physician may introduce contrast medium for radiologic study of the renal pelvis and ureter (ureteropyelogram). After examination, the physician passes a cutting instrument through the endoscope into the suspect renal tissue and takes a biopsy specimen. The physician removes the

endoscope, sutures the incision, inserts a drain tube, and performs a layered closure.

50575

The physician examines the kidney and ureter with an endoscope passed through an incision in the kidney (nephrotomy) or renal pelvis (pyelotomy), and dilates ureter and ureteropelvic junction. After accessing the renal and ureteric structures with an incision in the skin of the flank, the physician incises the kidney or renal pelvis and guides the endoscope through the incision. To better view renal and ureteric structures, the physician may flush (irrigate) or introduce by drops (instillate) a saline solution. The physician may introduce contrast medium for radiologic study of the renal pelvis and ureter (ureteropyelogram). For endopyelotomy, the physician places endoscope through the ureter and/or the pelvis, incises the pelvis, enlarges the ureteropelvic junction, and sutures the junction as in a Y-V pyeloplasty. The physician inserts the stent through the renal pelvis into the junction, sutures the incisions, inserts a drain tube, and performs a layered closure.

50576

The physician examines the kidney and ureter with an endoscope passed through an incision in the kidney (nephrotomy) or renal pelvis (pyelotomy), and removes renal lesions by electric current (fulguration) or incision. After accessing the renal and ureteric structures with an incision in the skin of the flank, the physician incises the kidney or renal pelvis and guides the endoscope through the incision. To better view renal and ureteric structures, the physician may flush (irrigate) or introduce by drops (instillate) a saline solution. The physician may introduce contrast medium for radiologic study of the renal pelvis and ureter (ureteropyelogram). After examination, the physician passes through the endoscope an instrument that destroys lesions by electric current or incision The physician may insert instrument to biopsy renal tissue. The physician removes the scope, sutures the incision, inserts a drain tube, and performs a layered closure.

50580

The physician examines the kidney and ureter with an endoscope passed through an incision in the kidney (nephrotomy) or renal pelvis (pyelotomy), and removes a foreign body or calculus. After accessing the renal and ureteric structures with an incision in the skin of the flank, the physician incises the kidney or renal pelvis and guides the endoscope through the incision. To better view renal and ureteric structures, the physician may flush (irrigate) or introduce by drops (instillate) a saline solution. The physician may introduce contrast medium for radiologic study of the renal pelvis and ureter (ureteropyelogram). After examination, the physician passes instruments through the endoscope to remove a foreign body or calculus, and may pass a stent through the ureter into the bladder. The physician sutures the incision, inserts a drain tube, and performs a layered closure.

50590

The physician pulverizes a kidney stone (renal calculus) by directing shock waves through a liquid medium. Two different methods are currently available to accomplish this procedure. The physician first uses radiological guidance to determine the location and size of the renal calculus. In the first method, the patient is immersed in a liquid medium (degassed, deionized water) with shock waves directed through the liquid to the kidney stone. In the second method, the one most often used, the patient is placed on a treatment table. A series of shock waves are directed through a water-cushion, or bellow that is placed against the patient's body at the location of the kidney stone. Each shock wave is directed to the stone for only a fraction of a second, and the procedure generally takes from 30 to 50 minutes. The treatment table is equipped with video x-ray so the physician can view the pulverization process. Over several days or weeks, the tiny stone fragments pass harmlessly though the patient's urinary system and are discharged during urination.

50592

The physician performs percutaneous radiofrequency ablation of one or more renal tumors. Using computerized tomography (CT), magnetic resonance imaging (MRI), or ultrasound guidance, the site for the electrode placement is identified. With the patient under moderate sedation, a small incision is made and an internally cooled radiofrequency needle electrode is introduced and placed into the renal tumor. Placement of the tip is confirmed with image guidance. Alternating current is applied as needed until correct core heat is reached in the electrode. The tumor tissue is heated to a specified temperature with monitoring done before and after each treatment, depending on the ablation device used, until sufficient time results in permanent cell damage and tumor necrosis. Overlapping tumor tissue is ablated in the same manner until all margins are satisfactory. Hemostasis is maintained after the electrode needle is withdrawn, the site is cleaned, and dressings are applied. The ablated tissue remains in place and is absorbed over time and replaced with scar tissue.

50593

The physician uses percutaneously placed cryotherapy probes to destroy tumors of the kidney. The patient is positioned for best exposure of the affected kidney. Separately reportable images are obtained using ultrasound, CT, or MRI to localize the tumor and determine the site for cryoprobe placement. After planning the skin entry site, the cryoprobe is placed in the lesion and the tip confirmed in position. Cycles of freezing and thawing are monitored to ensure encapsulation of the tumor tissue and a sufficient margin within the ice ball created by the cryotherapy. After the second active thaw cycle, the cryoprobes are removed if the ice ball is judged to cover the tumor tissue. If freezing was insufficient, the probes may be removed and repositioned or additional probes may be added and freezing is continued until the tumor and margin receive two complete cycles. The instruments are removed, the incision site closed, and dressings are applied.

50600
The physician makes an incision in the ureter (ureterotomy) for examination of the ureter or insertion of a drainage catheter (ureterostomy tube) between the ureter and skin. To access the ureter, the physician makes an incision in the skin of the flank, and cuts the muscles, fat, and fibrous membranes (fascia) overlying the ureter. The physician makes an incision in the ureter and sometimes places fine traction sutures at the edges of the incision. The physician examines the interior of the ureter or, if the incision is for drainage, the physician inserts a catheter tip into the ureter and passes the tube through a stab incision in the skin of the flank. The physician sutures the incision and performs a layered closure.

50605
The physician makes an incision in the ureter (ureterotomy) to insert a catheter (stent) in the ureter. To access the ureter, the physician makes an incision in the skin of the flank, and cuts the muscles, fat, and fibrous membranes (fascia) overlying the ureter. The physician makes an incision in the ureter and sometimes places fine traction sutures at the edges of the incision. The physician inserts a slender rod or catheter into the ureter, sutures the incision, and performs a layered closure.

50610-50630
The physician makes an incision in the ureter (ureterotomy) to remove a stone (calculus) from the ureter. To access the ureter, the physician makes an incision in the skin and cuts the muscles, fat, and fibrous membranes (fascia) overlying the ureter. For the upper or middle third of the ureter, the physician usually makes an incision in the skin of the flank; to access the lower third of the ureter, the physician usually makes a curved lower quadrant incision. The physician isolates the calculus and removes it through an incision in the ureter. After examining the ureter for other defects, the physician sutures the incision and performs a layered closure, inserting a drain tube through a stab incision in the skin. Report 50610 for calculus removal from the upper third of the ureter; 50620 for calculus removal from the middle third; and 50630 for calculus removal from the lower third.

50650
The physician removes the ureter and a small cuff of the bladder. To access the ureter, the physician usually makes a curved lower quadrant incision in the skin of the abdomen, and cuts the muscles, fat, and fibrous membranes (fascia) overlying the ureter. The physician mobilizes the bladder, dissects a small cuff of the bladder, and ligates and dissects the ureter. After removing the bladder cuff and lower ureter, the physician sutures and catheterizes the bladder. The physician places a drain tube behind the bladder and performs a layered closure.

50660
The physician removes a ureter that deviates from proper anatomical placement. To access the ureter, the physician makes an incision in the skin of the abdomen, perineum, and/or vagina. The physician cuts the muscles, fat, and fibrous membranes (fascia) overlying the ureter. After mobilizing the bladder and ureter, the physician ligates, dissects, and removes the ureter. The physician places a drain tube at the site of the incision and performs a layered closure.

50684
The physician injects a contrast agent through an opening between the skin and the ureter (ureterostomy) or via an indwelling catheter into the ureter and renal pelvis to study the renal collecting system. To determine immediate allergic response to the contrast agent, the physician injects a dose of contrast material through the ureterostomy or indwelling catheter into the ureter and renal pelvis, and takes an x-ray.

50686
The physician connects an indwelling ureteral catheter or existing ureterostomy to a manometer line to measure pressure and flow in the kidneys and ureters. The physician connects a ureteral catheter or ureterostomy to a manometer line filled with fluid. The physician inserts a bladder catheter that may be irrigated. The physician measures intrarenal and/or extra renal pressure. After discontinuing perfusion of fluid, the physician aspirates residual fluid from the kidney and disconnects the manometer line. The physician may remove the ureteral catheter or ureterostomy tube (if applicable) and dress the wound.

50688
The physician changes an ureterostomy tube or an externally accessible ureteral stent via an ileal conduit. To remove the existing tube, the physician takes out the sutures securing the tube to the skin. The physician inserts a guidewire through the tube and passes the tube back over the guidewire. The physician passes a new tube over the guidewire, removes the guidewire, and sutures the tube to the skin. To change an externally accessible ureteral stent via an ileal conduit, a guidewire is inserted through the ileal conduit. An ileal conduit is an isolated loop of ileum to which the ureter has been anastomosed at one end with the opposite end exiting through the skin and attached to an ostomy bag. The existing stent is retrieved and a new stent is placed. The guidewire is removed.

Urinary

50690
The physician injects a contrast agent through an existing ileal stoma into the renal pelvis or ureters to study the ileal conduit (where the ureters have been diverted into the ilium) or percutaneously or intravenously via a catheter to study the renal collecting system. To determine immediate allergic response to the contrast agent, the physician injects a small, initial dose of contrast material. If an allergic response is not evident, a larger amount of radiopaque dye is injected into the ureter and renal pelvis, and radiographic pictures are obtained for a ureteropyelogram or study of the ileal conduit diversion.

50700
The physician uses plastic surgery to correct an obstruction or defect in the ureter. To access the ureter, the physician makes an incision in the skin and cuts the muscles, fat, and fibrous membranes (fascia) overlying the ureter. For the upper or middle third of the ureter, the physician usually makes an incision in the skin of the flank; to access the lower third of the ureter, the physician usually makes a curved lower quadrant incision. The physician inserts a catheter into the ureter to the point of obstruction. The balloon is inflated, sometimes using repeated inflation with increasing diameter of the catheter. The physician incises, trims, and shapes the ureter, using absorbable sutures or soft rubber drains for traction. The physician may insert a slender tube into the ureter to provide support during healing. The physician places a drain tube, bringing it out through a separate stab incision in the skin, and performs a layered closure.

50715
The physician surgically frees the ureter from localized inflammatory disease of retroperitoneal fibrous tissue. To access the ureter, the physician makes a midline incision in the skin of the abdomen and cuts the muscles, fat, and fibrous membranes (fascia) overlying the ureter. The physician incises surrounding fibrotic tissue to free the ureter, and may use sutures to reposition the ureter away from obstructive fibrous tissue. The physician places a drain tube, bringing it out through a separate stab incision in the skin, and performs a layered closure.

50722
The physician surgically frees the ureter from ureteral obstruction caused by aberrant ovarian veins (ovarian vein syndrome). To access the ureter, the physician makes an incision in the skin above the pubic hairline, and cuts the muscles, fat, and fibrous membranes (fascia) overlying the ureter. The physician incises surrounding adhesions to free the ureter from the obstructing ovarian veins. The physician places a drain tube, bringing it out through a separate stab incision in the skin, and performs a layered closure.

50725
The physician divides and reconnects a ureter aberrantly positioned behind the vena cava. To access the ureter, the physician makes a midline incision in the skin of the abdomen, and cuts the muscles, fat, and fibrous membranes (fascia) overlying the ureter. The physician dissects the ureter on both sides of the vena cava, leaving the ureteric segment behind the vena cava in place. The physician connects (anastomosis) the distal end of the ureter to the upper ureter by fashioning a long, elliptical flap from the renal pelvis. The physician may alternatively dissect and connect the two ends of the vena cava, positioning the ureter in front. To provide support during healing, the physician may insert a slender tube into the renal pelvis. After wrapping the anastomosis with perinephric fat, the physician inserts a drain tube and performs a layered closure.

50727-50728
The physician revises any surgical opening (anastomosis) between the skin and ureter, bladder, or colon segment. The physician removes the sutures securing the anastomosis to the skin and revises the anastomosis. The physician may make a midline incision in the skin of the abdomen to access the urinary tract. In 50728, the physician repairs a defect in surrounding fibrous membranes (fascia), and/or a rupture (hernia) in ureteral tissues.

50740
The physician surgically connects the upper ureter and renal pelvis to allow for urinary drainage. To access the renal pelvis and ureter, the physician makes an incision in the skin of the flank, cuts the muscles, fat, and fibrous membranes (fascia) overlying the kidney, and sometimes removes a portion of the eleventh or twelfth rib. The physician ligates the renal pelvis and ureter at the point of blockage. After excising the obstructing part of the ureter or pelvis, the physician surgically connects (anastomosis) the two structures, bypassing the obstructing point. To provide support during healing, the physician may insert a slender tube into the renal pelvis. After wrapping the anastomosis with perinephric fat, the physician inserts a drain tube and performs a layered closure.

50750
The physician connects the upper ureter and a renal calyx to allow for urinary drainage. To access the renal calyces and ureter, the physician makes an incision in the skin of the flank, cuts the muscles, fat, and fibrous membranes (fascia) overlying the kidney, and sometimes removes a portion of the eleventh or twelfth rib. The physician ligates the appropriate renal arteries and performs a partial nephrectomy by removing a part of the kidney. The physician partially mobilizes the calyx and ureter, and places a nephrostomy tube and stent. After surgically joining (anastomosing) the calyx and ureter, the physician closes the renal pelvis and

wraps the anastomosis with perinephric fat. The physician inserts a drain tube and performs a layered closure.

50760
The physician divides and reconnects the ureter to bypass a defect or obstruction. To access the ureter, the physician makes an incision in the skin of the abdomen and cuts the muscles, fat, and fibrous membranes (fascia) overlying the ureter. For the upper or middle third of the ureter, the physician usually makes an incision in the skin of the flank; to access the lower third of the ureter, the physician usually makes a curved lower quadrant incision. The physician ligates and dissects the ureter at the point of blockage, and surgically rejoins (anastomosis) the two ends, bypassing the obstructing point. To provide support during healing, the physician may insert a slender tube into the ureter. The physician inserts a drain tube and performs a layered closure.

50770
The physician divides and connects a diseased or obstructed ureter to the other ureter. To access the ureters, the physician usually makes a midline incision in the skin of the abdomen, and cuts the muscles, fat, and fibrous membranes (fascia) overlying the ureters. The physician ligates and dissects the ureter at the point of disease or blockage, and surgically attaches (anastomosis) the end of the usable ureteric portion to the other ureter. To provide support during healing, the physician may insert a slender tube into the ureter. The physician inserts a drain tube and performs a layered closure.

50780-50785
The physician connects the lower ureter and bladder to allow for urinary drainage. The physician usually makes an incision in the skin of the abdomen. After dissecting the ureter at the point of disease or obstruction, the physician brings the ureter through a stab incision in the bladder and sutures the ureter to the bladder. To provide support during healing, the physician may insert a catheter into the ureter. The physician inserts a drain tube and performs a layered duplicated ureter to the bladder. Report 50780 if this procedure is used. Report 50782 if the physician attaches a duplicated ureter to the bladder. Report 50783 if the anastomosis requires extensive urethral reconstruction. Report 50785 if the anastomosis requires suturing the bladder and psoas, or by fashioning a long, elliptical flap from the bladder.

50800
The physician connects the ureter to a segment of intestine to divert urine flow. To access the ureter and intestine, the physician makes an incision in the skin of the abdomen and cuts the corresponding muscles, fat, and fibrous membranes (fascia). The physician dissects the ureter, makes small incisions in the intestine segment, and surgically connects (anastomosis) the ureter to the intestine. To provide support during healing, the physician may insert a slender tube into the ureter. The physician inserts a drain tube and performs a layered closure.

50810
The physician connects the ureters to a segment of sigmoid colon to create a bladder with an opening to the skin. To access the ureters and sigmoid colon, the physician makes a midline incision in the skin of the abdomen and cuts the corresponding muscles, fat, and fibrous membranes (fascia). After dissecting an isolated segment of sigmoid colon, the physician reconnects (anastomosis) the divided colon to restore bowel continuity. The sigmoid section is closed by sutures on one end. The physician dissects each ureter, makes small incisions in the sigmoid segment, and surgically connects each ureter to the sigmoid segment. To provide support during healing, the physician may insert a slender tube into each ureter. The physician fashions a bladder by closing the proximal end of the sigmoid segment, and brings the distal end through an incision in the skin of the abdomen to establish an opening (colostomy) for intermittent emptying of urine. The physician inserts a drain tube and performs a layered closure.

50815-50820
The physician connects the ureters to a segment of intestine to divert urine flow through an opening in the skin. To access the ureters and intestine, the physician makes a midline incision in the skin of the abdomen and cuts the corresponding muscles, fat, and fibrous membranes (fascia). After dissecting an isolated segment of intestine, the physician reconnects (anastomosis) the divided intestine to restore bowel continuity. The colon segment is closed by sutures on one end. The physician dissects each ureter, makes small incisions in the intestine segment, and surgically connects each ureter to the colon segment. To provide support during healing, the physician may insert a slender tube into each ureter. The physician closes the proximal end of the intestine segment and brings the distal end through an incision in the skin of the abdomen to establish an opening (stoma) for direct emptying of urine. The physician inserts a drain tube and performs a layered closure. Report 50820 if the physician dissects a segment of ileal colon to divert urine flow.

50825
The physician connects the ureter(s) to loops of intestine fashioned into a reservoir with a valve opening. To access the intestine and ureters, the physician makes a midline incision in the skin of the abdomen and cuts the corresponding muscles, fat, and fibrous membranes (fascia). After dissecting an isolated segment of intestine, the physician reconnects (anastomosis) the divided intestine to restore bowel continuity. After shaping the intestine segment into a

pouch, the physician dissects each ureter, makes small incisions in the intestine segment, and surgically connects each ureter to the intestine segment. To provide support during healing, the physician inserts a slender tube into each ureter, and closes the pouch. The physician brings part of the pouch out through an abdominal wall opening, or anastomosis the pouch to the male urethra. The physician inserts a drain tube and performs a layered closure.

50830
The physician restores continuity of a ureter through which urine flow was previously diverted. To access the ureter, the physician usually reopens the original ureteral diversion incision and cuts the corresponding muscles, fat, and fibrous membranes (fascia). The physician reverses the diversion by removing sutures connecting the ureter and colon, colon segment, and/ or skin. The physician closes the opening in the skin used for the diversionary anastomosis. To restore ureteral continuity, the physician reconnects the upper and lower ureter segments or connects the ureter to the other ureter (ureteroureterostomy), or reimplants the ureter into the bladder (ureteroneocystostomy). To provide support during healing, the physician inserts a slender tube into the ureter. The physician inserts a drain tube and performs a layered closure.

50840
The physician replaces part or all of the ureter with a segment of intestine. To access the ureters and intestine, the physician makes a midline incision in the skin of the abdomen and cuts the corresponding muscles, fat, and fibrous membranes (fascia). After dissecting an isolated segment of intestine, the physician reconnects (anastomosis) the divided intestine to restore bowel continuity. The physician dissects and removes the diseased or defective ureteral segment, replacing it with the intestine segment. To provide support during healing, the physician may insert a slender tube into the ureter. The physician inserts a drain tube and performs a layered closure.

50845
The physician connects a segment of cecum colon (vermiform appendix) to the bladder to directly divert urine flow through an opening in the skin (cutaneous appendico-vesicostomy). To access the bladder and cecum colon, the physician makes a midline incision in the skin of the abdomen and cuts the corresponding muscles, fat, and fibrous membranes (fascia). After dissecting vermiform appendix, the physician sutures the colon to restore bowel continuity. The physician makes an incision in the bladder and surgically connects the proximal end of the vermiform appendix to the bladder. The physician brings the distal end of vermiform appendix through an incision in the skin of the abdomen to establish an opening (stoma) for direct emptying of urine. The physician inserts a drain tube and performs a layered closure.

50860
The physician connects the ureter to the skin for urinary drainage. To access the ureter, the physician makes a midline incision in the skin of the abdomen and cuts the corresponding muscles, fat, and fibrous membranes (fascia). The physician ligates the distal ureter and brings the proximal end to the skin. The physician splits the end of the ureter and sutures it to the skin with a double Z-plasty to prevent the ureter from narrowing. To provide support during healing, the physician may insert a slender tube into the ureter. The physician inserts a drain tube and performs a layered closure.

50900
The physician sutures a wound or defect in the ureter. To access the ureter, the physician makes an incision in the skin and cuts the muscles, fat, and fibrous membranes (fascia) overlying the ureter. For the upper or middle third of the ureter, the physician usually makes an incision in the skin of the flank; to access the lower third of the ureter, the physician usually makes a curved lower quadrant incision. The physician uses sutures to close or surgically fixate a ureteral wound or defect. To provide support during healing, the physician may insert a slender tube into the ureter. The physician inserts a drain tube and performs a layered closure.

50920
The physician closes an abnormal opening (fistula) between the skin and the ureter (ureterocutaneous). After excising the fistula, the physician sutures the clean percutaneous tissues together to create a smooth surface.

50930
The physician closes an abnormal opening (fistula) between the ureter and an organ of the digestive, respiratory, urogenital, or endocrine system. To access the ureter, the physician makes a midline incision in the skin of the abdomen and cuts the corresponding muscles, fat, and fibrous membranes (fascia). After excising the fistula, the physician sutures the clean tissues together to create a smooth surface. The physician places a drain tube, bringing it out through a separate stab incision in the skin, and performs a layered closure.

50940
The physician removes a thread, wire, or constricting band (ligature) placed on the ureter during a previous operative session. To access the ureter, the physician usually reopens the incision used for the previous operative session. After removing the ligature(s) from the ureter, the physician places a drain tube, bringing it out through a separate stab incision in the skin, and performs a layered closure.

50945
The physician performs a laparoscopic surgical removal of a stone (calculus) lodged in the ureter (ureterolithotomy). In an abdominal approach, the physician creates an umbilical port by placing a trocar at the level of the umbilicus. The abdominal wall is insufflated. The laparoscope is placed through the umbilical port and additional trocars are placed into the abdominal cavity. In the back (flank) approach, the trocar is placed at the back proximate to the retroperitoneal space near the kidney with additional ports placed nearby for appropriate access to the operative site. The physician uses the laparoscope fitted with a fiberoptic camera and/or an operating instrument to isolate the calculus and remove it through an incision in the ureter. The ureter is surgically closed. The small abdominal or back (flank) incisions are closed with staples or sutures.

50947-50948
The physician repositions the ureter on the bladder (due to an obstruction of the ureterovesical junction), using a laparoscopic approach. A stent may be placed with a cystoscope. In both procedures the physician makes a 1 centimeter periumbilical incision and inserts a trocar. The abdominal cavity is insufflated with carbon dioxide. A fiberoptic laparoscope fitted with a camera and light source is inserted through the trocar. Other incisions (ports) are made in the abdomen to allow other instruments or an additional light source to be passed into the abdomen. The physician manipulates the tools so the ureter and bladder can be observed through the laparoscope. The physician transects the ureter above the point of obstruction, brings the ureter through a stab incision in the bladder, and sutures the ureter to the new site on the bladder. In 50947, the physician inserts a cystoscope and places a stent in the repositioned ureter to provide support of the ureter. In 50948, the ureter is repositioned without cystoscopy or stent placement. The instruments are removed. The incisions are closed with staples or suture.

50951
The physician examines renal and ureteral structures with an endoscope passed through an established opening between the skin and ureter (ureterostomy). The physician inserts a guidewire, removes the ureterostomy tube, and passes the endoscope into the kidney or renal pelvis. The physician may flush (irrigate) or introduce by drops (instillate) a saline solution to better view the renal and ureteral structures, and/or may introduce contrast medium for radiologic study of the renal pelvis and ureter (ureteropyelogram). The physician removes the endoscope and guidewire and reinserts the ureterostomy tube or allows the passageway to seal on its own.

50953
The physician examines renal and ureteral structures with an endoscope passed through an established opening between the skin and ureter (ureterostomy), and inserts a catheter into the ureter. The physician inserts a guidewire, removes the ureterostomy tube, and passes the endoscope into the kidney or renal pelvis. The physician may flush (irrigate) or introduce by drops (instillate) a saline solution to better view the renal and ureteral structures, and/or may introduce contrast medium for radiologic study of the renal pelvis and ureter (ureteropyelogram). The physician passes a thin tube through the endoscope into the ureter, and may insert a balloon catheter to dilate a ureteral constriction. The physician removes the endoscope and guidewire and reinserts the ureterostomy tube or allows the passageway to seal on its own.

50955
The physician examines renal and ureteral structures with an endoscope passed through an established opening between the skin and ureter (ureterostomy), and biopsies renal and/or ureteral tissue. The physician inserts a guidewire, removes the ureterostomy tube, and passes the endoscope into the kidney or renal pelvis. The physician may flush (irrigate) or introduce by drops (instillate) a saline solution to better view the renal and ureteral structures, and/or may introduce contrast medium for radiologic study of the renal pelvis and ureter (ureteropyelogram). The physician passes a cutting instrument through the endoscope into the suspect tissue and takes a biopsy specimen. The physician removes the endoscope and guidewire and reinserts the ureterostomy tube or allows the passageway to seal on its own.

50957
The physician examines renal and ureteral structures with an endoscope passed through an established opening between the skin and ureter (ureterostomy), and removes lesions by electric current (fulguration) or incision. The physician inserts a guidewire, removes the ureterostomy tube, and passes the endoscope into the kidney or renal pelvis. The physician may flush (irrigate) or introduce by drops (instillate) a saline solution to better view the renal and ureteral structures, and/or may introduce contrast medium for radiologic study of the renal pelvis and ureter (ureteropyelogram). The physician passes through the endoscope an instrument that destroys lesions by electric current or incision. The physician may insert an instrument to biopsy renal tissue. The physician removes the endoscope and guidewire and reinserts the ureterostomy tube or allows the passageway to seal on its own.

50961
The physician examines renal and ureteral structures with an endoscope passed through an established opening between the skin and ureter (ureterostomy),

and removes a foreign body or calculus. The physician inserts a guidewire, removes the ureterostomy tube, and passes the endoscope into the kidney or renal pelvis. The physician may flush (irrigate) or introduce by drops (instillate) a saline solution to better view the renal and ureteral structures, and/or may introduce contrast medium for radiologic study of the renal pelvis and ureter (ureteropyelogram). The physician passes an instrument through the endoscope to remove a foreign body or calculus. The physician removes the endoscope and guidewire and reinserts the ureterostomy tube or allows the passageway to seal on its own.

50970
The physician examines renal and ureteral structures with an endoscope passed through an incision in the ureter (ureterotomy). After accessing the ureter with an incision in the skin of the flank, the physician incises the ureter and guides the endoscope through the incision. The physician may flush (irrigate) or introduce by drops (instillate) a solution to better view the renal and ureteral structures, and/or may introduce contrast medium for radiologic study of the renal pelvis and ureter (ureteropyelogram). After examination, the physician sutures the incision, inserts a drain tube, and performs a layered closure.

50972
The physician examines renal and ureteral structures with an endoscope passed through an incision in the ureter (ureterotomy), and inserts a catheter into the ureter. After accessing the ureter with an incision in the skin of the flank, the physician incises the ureter and guides the endoscope through the incision. The physician may flush (irrigate) or introduce by drops (instillate) a solution to better view the renal and ureteral structures, and/or may introduce contrast medium for radiologic study of the renal pelvis and ureter (ureteropyelogram). To catheterize the ureter, the physician passes a thin tube through the endoscope into the ureter. The physician may insert a balloon catheter to dilate a ureteral constriction. The physician sutures the incision, inserts a drain tube, and performs a layered closure.

50974
The physician examines renal and ureteral structures with an endoscope passed through an incision in the ureter (ureterotomy), and biopsies ureteral and/or renal tissue. After accessing the ureter with an incision in the skin of the flank, the physician incises the ureter and guides the endoscope through the incision. The physician may flush (irrigate) or introduce by drops (instillate) a solution to better view the renal and ureteral structures, and/or may introduce contrast medium for radiologic study of the renal pelvis and ureter (ureteropyelogram). The physician passes a cutting instrument through the endoscope into the suspect tissue and take a biopsy specimen. The physician removes the endoscope, sutures the incision, inserts a drain tube, and performs a layered closure.

50976
The physician examines renal and ureteral structures with an endoscope passed through an incision in the ureter (ureterotomy), and removes renal or ureteral lesions by electric current (fulguration) or incision. After accessing the ureter with an incision in the skin of the flank, the physician incises the ureter and guides the endoscope through the incision. The physician may flush (irrigate) or introduce by drops (instillate) a solution to better view the renal and ureteral structures, and/or may introduce contrast medium for radiologic study of the renal pelvis and ureter (ureteropyelogram). The physician passes through the endoscope an instrument that destroys lesions with electric sparks or incises lesions. The physician may insert an instrument to biopsy renal tissue. The physician removes the endoscope, sutures the incision, inserts a drain tube, and performs a layered closure.

50980
The physician examines renal and ureteral structures with an endoscope passed through an incision in the ureter (ureterotomy), and removes a foreign body or stone (calculus). After accessing the ureter with an incision in the skin of the flank, the physician incises the ureter and guides the endoscope through the incision. The physician may flush (irrigate) or introduce by drops (instillate) a solution to better view the renal and ureteral structures, and/or may introduce contrast medium for radiologic study of the renal pelvis and ureter (ureteropyelogram). The physician passes an instrument through the endoscope to remove a foreign body or calculus, and may pass a stent through the ureter into the bladder. The physician removes the endoscope, sutures the incision, inserts a drain tube, and performs a layered closure.

51020-51030
The physician makes an incision (cystotomy) or creates an opening (cystostomy) into the bladder to destroy abnormal tissue. To access the bladder, the physician makes an incision in the skin of the lower abdomen and cuts the corresponding muscles, fat, fibrous membranes (fascia), and bladder wall. Report 51020 if the physician uses electric current (fulguration) or (usually with the aid of a radiation oncologist) inserts radioactive material to destroy a lesion on the bladder. Report 51030 if the physician uses cryosurgery to destroy the lesion. The bladder wall and lower abdomen is sutured closed. If a cystostomy is made, the cystostomy tube is sutured in place and the bladder and abdominal wall is closed.

51040
The physician creates an opening into the bladder (cystostomy) through an incision in the bladder (cystotomy). To access the bladder, the physician makes an incision in the skin of the lower abdomen

and cuts the corresponding muscles, fat, and fibrous membranes (fascia). The physician makes a small incision and inserts a catheter (cystostomy tube) into the bladder, passing the tube through a stab incision in the skin of the abdomen. After closing the cystotomy, the physician may insert a drain tube, bringing it out through a separate stab incision, and performs a layered closure with absorbable sutures.

51045
The physician makes an incision in the bladder to insert a catheter or slender tube (stent) into the ureter. To access the bladder and ureters, the physician makes a midline incision in the skin of the abdomen and cuts the corresponding muscles, fat, and fibrous membranes (fascia). The physician incises the bladder (cystotomy) and inserts a stent or catheter in the ureter. Insertion of a ureteral catheter requires that the physician bring the tube end out through the urethra or bladder incision. The physician inserts a drain tube and performs a layered closure.

51050
The physician makes an incision in the bladder to remove a calculus. To access the bladder, the physician makes an incision in the skin of the lower abdomen and cuts the corresponding muscles, fat, and fibrous membranes (fascia). The physician performs a cystotomy, isolates the calculus, and removes it. The bladder neck is not excised. After examining the bladder for other defects, the physician sutures the incision and performs a layered closure using absorbable sutures, inserting a drain tube through a stab incision in the skin.

51060
The physician makes an incision in the bladder to remove a calculus in the ureter. To access the bladder and ureters, the physician makes a midline incision in the skin of the abdomen and cuts the corresponding muscles, fat, and fibrous membranes (fascia). The physician isolates the calculus and removes it through incisions in the bladder (cystotomy) and ureter (ureterotomy). After examining the ureter for other defects, the physician inserts a ureteral catheter and sutures the incisions. The physician inserts a drain tube and performs a layered closure.

51065
The physician makes an incision in the bladder and inserts an instrument in the ureter to remove or destroy the calculus. To access the bladder and ureters, the physician makes a midline incision in the skin of the abdomen and cuts the corresponding muscles, fat, and fibrous membranes (fascia). After isolating the calculus, the physician makes an incision in the bladder (cystotomy). The physician inserts an instrument (e.g., a stone basket) through the bladder incision into the ureter to remove or destroy a ureteral calculus. After examining the ureter for other defects, the physician inserts a ureteral catheter and sutures the incision. The physician inserts a drain tube and performs a layered closure.

51080
The physician drains an infection (abscess) near the bladder. To access the bladder, the physician makes an incision in the skin of the lower abdomen and cuts the corresponding muscles, fat, and fibrous membranes (fascia). After exploring the abscess cavity, the physician irrigates the site, inserts multiple drain tubes through separate stab wounds, and sutures the drain tube ends to the skin. The physician inserts a urethral catheter and performs a layered closure.

51100-51102
In 51100, the physician inserts a needle through the skin into the bladder to withdraw urine. In 51101, the physician inserts a trocar or intracatheter through the skin into the bladder. In 51102, a suprapubic catheter is placed into the bladder. This procedure may also be performed after the abdomen has been surgically incised.

51500
The physician removes a cyst or dilated urachus (the remnant of bladder development that attaches from bladder to umbilicus). To access the urachus, the physician makes an incision in the skin of the lower abdomen through the umbilicus, and cuts the corresponding muscles, fat, and fibrous membranes (fascia). After isolating the urachus with a clamp, the physician excises the urachal cyst or sinus and a small cuff of the bladder. The physician sutures the bladder and removes the urachal tissue, leaving the navel intact. The physician may also repair a rupture (hernia) of tissue in the umbilicus. After inserting a drain tube and urethral catheter, the physician performs a layered closure.

51520
The physician removes part or all of the bladder neck. The physician makes an incision in the skin of the lower abdomen and cuts the corresponding muscles, fat, and fibrous membranes (fascia). Through this incision, the physician accesses the bladder neck and removes diseased or enlarged bladder neck tissue. The bladder is sutured and the abdominal wall is closed.

51525
The physician removes a diverticulum, a herniated defect of the bladder. To access the diverticulum, the physician makes an incision in the skin of the lower abdomen and cuts the corresponding muscles, fat, and fibrous membranes (fascia). The physician makes an incision in the bladder and may insert a ureteral stent if the diverticulum is close to the ureter. After dissecting the diverticulum from surrounding tissues and arteries, the physician excises the defective tissue and closes the remaining musculature and mucosa with absorbable sutures. This process may be repeated in other

diverticula. The incision is repaired with a layered closure.

51530
The physician makes an incision in the bladder to remove a tumor of the bladder. To access the bladder, the physician makes an incision in the skin of the lower abdomen and cuts the corresponding muscles, fat, and fibrous membranes (fascia). The bladder is incised (cystotomy). After removing the tumor and surrounding diseased vesical tissue, the physician inserts a drain tube and performs a layered closure.

51535
The physician makes an incision in the bladder to remove or repair a saccular dilation of the ureteral end (ureterocele) that protrudes into the bladder. To access the bladder and ureters, the physician makes a midline incision in the skin of the abdomen and cuts the corresponding muscles, fat, and fibrous membranes (fascia). The physician incises the bladder (cystotomy) and excises or fulgurates the ureterocele. After examining the ureter for other defects, the physician sutures the bladder incision and inserts a ureteral catheter. The physician inserts a drain tube and performs a layered closure.

51550-51555
The physician removes a portion of diseased or damaged bladder tissue. To access the bladder, the physician makes an incision in the skin above the pubic bone and cuts the corresponding muscles, fat, and fibrous membranes (fascia). The physician mobilizes the bladder and the major vesical blood vessels, and incises the bladder wall to access the diseased or damaged bladder tissue. After removing the tissue, the physician inserts catheters into the bladder and urethra and sutures the bladder tissues. The physician performs a layered closure and inserts a drain tube, bringing it out through a separate stab incision in the skin. Report 51550 if the cystectomy presents few complications; report 51555 if the procedure is complicated because of prior administration of radiation, a previous surgery, or difficult access to the diseased or damaged bladder tissue.

51565
The physician removes diseased or damaged bladder tissue close to the ureteral orifice, and reimplants ureter(s) into the bladder (ureteroneocystostomy). To access the bladder and ureters, the physician makes a midline incision in the skin of the abdomen and cuts the corresponding muscles, fat, and fibrous membranes (fascia). The physician mobilizes the bladder, ureter(s), and the major vesical blood vessels, and may incise the bladder wall to access the diseased or damaged bladder tissue. The physician removes the diseased or damaged bladder tissue, requiring removal of the ureteral orifice and/or ureteral division. The physician brings the cut end of the ureter through a stab wound in the bladder and sutures the ureter to the bladder. To provide support during healing, the physician inserts a ureteral catheter, bringing the tube end out through the urethra or bladder incision. The physician inserts a drain tube and performs a layered closure.

51570-51575
The physician removes the bladder (cystectomy). To access the bladder, the physician makes an incision in the skin of the lower abdomen and cuts the corresponding muscles, fat, and fibrous membranes (fascia). Report 51570 if the physician dissects and ties (ligates) the hypogastric and vesical vessels, and severs the bladder from the urethra, rectum, surrounding peritoneum, vas deferens, and prostate (if applicable). After removing the bladder and controlling bleeding, the physician inserts drain tubes and performs a layered closure. If the physician bilaterally removes the pelvic lymph nodes, report 51575.

51580
The physician removes the bladder (cystectomy) and connects the ureters to the skin or sigmoid colon. To access the bladder and ureters, the physician makes a midline incision in the skin of the abdomen and cuts the corresponding muscles, fat, and fibrous membranes (fascia). The physician dissects and ligates the hypogastric and vesical vessels, and severs the bladder from the ureters and urethra. Blunt dissection from adherent rectum, surrounding peritoneum, and vas deferens and prostate may be needed. After controlling bleeding, the physician diverts urine by implanting the ureters to the skin (ureterocutaneous transplant), or connecting (anastomosing) the ureters to the sigmoid colon (ureterosigmoidostomy). To provide support during healing, the physician inserts a slender tube into each ureter. After completing the urinary diversion procedure, the physician inserts drain tubes and performs a layered closure.

51585
The physician removes the bladder (cystectomy) and pelvic lymph nodes, and connects the ureters to the skin or sigmoid colon. To access the bladder and ureters, the physician makes a midline incision in the skin of the abdomen and cuts the corresponding muscles, fat, and fibrous membranes (fascia). The physician dissects and ligates the hypogastric and vesical vessels, and severs the bladder from the ureters and urethra. Blunt dissection from adherent rectum, surrounding peritoneum, and vas deferens and prostate may be needed. The physician also removes external iliac, hypogastric, and obturator lymph nodes. After controlling bleeding, the physician diverts urine by implanting the ureters to the skin (ureterocutaneous transplant), or connecting the ureters to the sigmoid colon (ureterosigmoidostomy). The physician also inserts a slender tube into each ureter for support. After completing the urinary diversion procedure, the

physician inserts drain tubes and performs a layered closure.

51590
The physician removes the bladder (cystectomy) and diverts urine by connecting the ureters to a ureteroileal conduit or sigmoid bladder with an opening into the skin. To access the bladder and ureters, the physician makes a midline incision in the skin of the abdomen and cuts the corresponding muscles, fat, and fibrous membranes (fascia). The physician dissects and ligates the hypogastric and vesical vessels, and severs the bladder from the ureters and urethra. Blunt dissection from adherent rectum, surrounding peritoneum, and vas deferens and prostate may be needed. After controlling bleeding, the physician diverts urine by connecting the ureters to a segment of ileal or sigmoid colon fashioned into a conduit or bladder, respectively, with an opening into the skin. To provide support during healing, the physician inserts a slender tube into each ureter. After completing the urinary diversion procedure, the physician inserts drain tubes and performs a layered closure.

51595
The physician removes the bladder (cystectomy) and pelvic lymph nodes, and diverts urine by connecting the ureters to a ureteroileal conduit or sigmoid bladder with an opening into the skin. To access the bladder and ureters, the physician makes a midline incision in the skin of the abdomen and cuts the corresponding muscles, fat, and fibrous membranes (fascia). The physician dissects and ligates the hypogastric and vesical vessels, and severs the bladder from the ureters and urethra. Blunt dissection from adherent rectum, surrounding peritoneum, and vas deferens and prostate may be needed. The physician also removes external iliac, hypogastric, and obturator lymph nodes. After controlling bleeding, the physician diverts urine by connecting the ureters to a segment of ileal or sigmoid colon fashioned into a conduit or bladder, with an opening into the skin. The physician inserts a slender tube into each ureter. After completing the urinary diversion procedure, the physician inserts drain tubes and performs a layered closure.

51596
The physician removes the bladder (cystectomy) and diverts urine by any method, using any bowel segment to create a new bladder. To access the bladder and ureters, the physician makes a midline incision in the skin of the abdomen and cuts the corresponding muscles, fat, and fibrous membranes (fascia). The physician dissects and ligates the hypogastric and vesical vessels, and severs the bladder from the urethra. Blunt dissection from adherent rectum, surrounding peritoneum, and vas deferens and prostate may be needed. After controlling bleeding, the physician diverts urine by connecting the ureters to a segment of large or small bowel fashioned into a bladder with an opening into the skin. To provide support during healing, the physician inserts a slender tube into each ureter. After completing the urinary diversion procedure, the physician inserts drain tubes and performs a layered closure.

51597
The physician removes the bladder, lower ureters, lymph nodes, urethra, prostate (if applicable), colon, and rectum, due to a vesical, prostatic, or urethral malignancy. To access the bladder and ureters, the physician makes a midline incision in the skin of the abdomen and cuts the corresponding muscles, fat, and fibrous membranes (fascia). The physician dissects and ligates the hypogastric and vesical vessels, and severs the bladder, urethra, lower ureters, lymph nodes, and prostate (if applicable) from surrounding structures. The physician removes the bladder and diverts urine flow by transplanting the ureters to the skin or colon. The vagina and uterus (if applicable) and/or rectum and part of the colon may be removed and an artificial abdominal opening in the skin surface created for waste (colostomy). After completing the urinary diversion procedure, the physician inserts drain tubes and performs a layered closure.

51600-51610
The physician injects a radiocontrast agent through a catheter inserted in the bladder to study the lower urinary tract. Using radiologic instruments, the physician produces an image of the bladder with x-rays (cystogram). Filling, voiding, and post-voiding x-rays are obtained. The catheter is partially or completely withdrawn and the urethra is studied by x-ray. Report 51605 if the physician inserts a chain in the bladder or through the urethra as part of the injection procedure for contrast x-rays of the bladder and urethra (chain urethrocystogram). Report 51610 if contrast material is injected through a urethral catheter or catheter-tipped syringe for x-rays of the urethra and bladder (retrograde urethrocystogram).

51700
The physician irrigates the bladder with saline solution that is flushed, injected, or introduced by drops (instillation) through a catheter. The physician initially places the catheter into the bladder and irrigates by hand until the bladder is free of clots or debris. A three-way Foley catheter may be inserted for continuous bladder irrigation.

51701-51703
The patient is catheterized with a non-indwelling bladder catheter (e.g., for residual urine) in 51701; simple catheterization with a temporary indwelling bladder catheter (Foley) is performed in 51702. The area is properly cleaned and sterilized. A water-soluble lubricant may be injected into the urethra before catheterization begins. The distal part of the catheter is coated with lubricant. In males, the penis is held perpendicular to the body and pulled up gently and

the catheter is steadily inserted about 8 inches until urine is noted. In females, the catheter is gently inserted until urine is noted. With an indwelling catheter, insertion continues into the bladder until the retention balloon can be inflated. The catheter is gently pulled until the retention balloon is snuggled against the neck of the bladder. The catheter is secured to the abdomen or thigh and the drainage bag is secured below bladder level. Report 51703 if a change in anatomy, such as enlarging of the prostate or a fractured catheter or balloon, complicate the catheterization process.

51705-51710
The physician changes a cystostomy tube. To remove the existing tube, the physician removes the sutures securing the tube to the skin. Report 51705 if the physician inserts a guidewire through the tube and passes the tube back over the guidewire. The physician passes a new tube over the guidewire, removes the guidewire, and sutures the tube to the skin. Report 51710 if complications such as infection, inflammation, hemorrhage, constriction, or dilation arise.

51715
The physician injects natural proteins or synthetic material into the urethra and bladder neck, helping to prevent urinary incontinence. Before the injection, an endoscope is placed through the urethra into the bladder. Using local anesthesia, the physician makes one to three injections into the transurethral submucous. The injections are made through the endoscope into the affected area. The procedure can also be performed through the lower abdomen.

51720
The physician introduces by drops (instillation) an anticarcinogenic agent into the bladder to treat a cancer. Prior to the instillation of the agent, a standard lavage is usually performed. The anticarcinogenic agent is introduced through a catheter and held in the bladder for a specified amount of time. This procedure may be used in conjunction with a cystostomy (51020) or with procedures such as cystectomy for the removal of a tumor.

51725-51729
A cystometrogram (a graphic record of urinary bladder pressure at different volumes) is used to distinguish bladder outlet obstruction from other voiding dysfunctions. For a simple cystometrogram (51725), the physician inserts a pressure catheter into the bladder and connects it to a manometer line filled with fluid to measure pressure and flow in the lower urinary tract. For a complex cystometrogram (51726), the physician typically uses a transurethral catheter to fill the bladder with water or gas while simultaneously obtaining rectal pressure. As the bladder is being filled, intravesical pressure is measured by a microtip transducer or fluid-filled catheter attached to the transducer. Code 51727 reports a complex cystometrogram performed in conjunction with a study for measuring urethral pressure. In one technique, the bladder is filled with fluid and the catheter withdrawn into the urethra while bladder sensations and volume are recorded. Urethral pressure changes are recorded as the patient follows specific instructions (Valsalva maneuver, cough). For voiding pressure studies performed in conjunction with a complex cystometrogram (51728), a transducer is placed into the bladder and the bladder is filled with fluid. The patient is instructed to attempt to void upon the feeling of bladder fullness, and recordings are taken of bladder sensation and volume at specific times. Report 51729 if complex cystometrogram is combined with both voiding pressure studies and urethral pressure profile studies.

51736-51741
For simple uroflowmetry (51736), the physician assesses the rate of emptying the bladder by stopwatch, recording the volume of urine per time. For complex uroflowmetry, (51741), the physician assesses the rate of emptying of the bladder by electronic equipment, recording the volume of urine per time.

51784
The physician places a pad in the anal or urethral sphincter and measures the electrical activity with the bladder filled and during emptying.

51785
The physician places a pad or needle in the anal or urethral sphincter and measures the electrical activity with the bladder filled and during emptying.

51792
The physician electrically stimulates the head of the penis. The physician measures the delay time for travel of stimulation through the pelvic nerves to the pudendal nerve.

51797
The physician conducts an intraabdominal voiding pressure study. In one method, the physician places a rectal catheter simultaneously with a urethral catheter in order to determine how much the patient strains while attempting to void. This measures both the amount of pressure generated and the subsequent urine flow.

51798
Residual urine and/or bladder capacity is measured by ultrasound after the patient has voided. A portable ultrasound scanner is used for this purpose. Operation of the scanner is done simply by directing the scanning head over the suprapubic area while the patient is lying down in the supine position. The software built in to the scanner calculates the post-void residual urine volume immediately and also does calculations for the bladder capacity based on the individual's bladder shape and not on fixed geometric formulas.

51800
The physician uses plastic surgery to correct an obstruction or defect in the bladder or vesical neck and urethra. The bladder is distended using a Foley catheter. To access the bladder, the physician makes an incision in the skin of the lower abdomen and cuts the corresponding muscles, fat, and fibrous membranes (fascia). The physician incises, trims, and shapes the bladder or vesical neck and urethra, using absorbable sutures or soft rubber drains for traction. The physician may insert a catheter through the urethra to provide support during healing. In anterior Y-plasty, the physician makes a Y-shaped flap of the bladder extending the vertical incision into the vesical neck. The vertical part of this incision is pulled up into the V-shaped incision, which becomes a straight line when sutured. The physician may remove a portion of the vesical neck. The physician places a drain tube, bringing it out through a separate stab incision in the skin, and performs a layered closure.

51820
The physician uses plastic surgery to correct a defect in the bladder and urethra, and reimplants one or both ureters into the bladder (ureteroneocystostomy). To access the bladder, urethra, and ureters, the physician makes a midline incision in the skin of the abdomen and cuts the corresponding muscles, fat, and fibrous membranes (fascia). The physician incises, trims, and shapes the bladder and urethra, using absorbable sutures or soft rubber drains for traction. The physician brings the cut end of one or both ureters through a stab wound in the bladder and sutures the ureter(s) to the bladder. To provide support during healing, the physician inserts a ureteral catheter, bringing the tube end out through the urethra or bladder incision. The physician inserts a drain tube and performs a layered closure.

51840-51841
The physician performs a vesicourethropexy or urethropexy in the Marshall-Marchetti-Krantz or Burch style. The physician makes a small horizontal incision in the abdomen above the symphysis pubis, which is the midline junction of the pubic bones at the front. The bladder is suspended by placing several sutures through the tissue surrounding the urethra and into the vaginal wall. The sutures are pulled tight so that the tissues are tacked to the symphysis pubis and the urethra is moved forward. The incision is closed by suturing. 51841 is used when the procedure is performed for the second time or if some other factor increases the time or level of complexity.

51845
The physician surgically suspends the bladder neck by suturing surrounding tissue to the fibrous membranes (fascia) of the abdomen in a female patient. After inserting a catheter through the urethra to visualize the bladder neck, the physician makes an incision in the vagina, extending it upward toward the base of the bladder. On both sides of the vesical neck, the physician passes a needle through a small incision in the skin above the pubic bone down through the vaginal incision. The physician threads the needle in the vagina and pulls the needle back through the suprapubic incision. Dacron tubing may be threaded onto the sutures to provide extra periurethral support. The physician repeats this process, using an endoscope to ensure proper placement of the suspending sutures. After placing sutures on both sides of the bladder neck, the physician uses moderate upward traction to tighten the bladder neck. The physician inserts a drain tube, bringing it out through a stab incision in the skin, and performs a layered closure.

51860-51865
The physician sutures a wound, injury, or rupture in the bladder. To access the bladder, urethra, and ureters, the physician makes an incision in the skin of the abdomen and cuts the corresponding muscles, fat, and fibrous membranes (fascia). To provide support during healing, the physician may insert a catheter through the urethra. The physician inserts a drain tube and performs a layered closure. Constant irrigation is provided to help prevent infection. Report 51865 if the procedure is complicated by a previous surgery, congenital defect, or other reason.

51880
The physician closes an artificial opening into the bladder (cystostomy). To access the cystostomy, the physician uses the original incision creating the cystostomy or makes an incision in the skin of the lower abdomen. After removing the sutures securing the cystostomy tube to the skin and bladder, the physician removes the cystostomy tube and sutures the bladder musculature to repair the opening. The physician places a drain tube, bringing it out through a separate stab incision in the skin, and performs a layered closure of the abdominal cystostomy incision.

51900
The physician closes a vesicovaginal fistula, which is an abnormal passage between the bladder and the vagina. This procedure is done through the abdomen. The fistula and surrounding scar tissue of the vaginal wall are usually excised. The physician makes an incision in the skin, muscle, and fascia of the abdomen. The bladder wall is opened and the bladder explored. The fistula is excised along with the surrounding tissue. The resulting defect is closed with sutures in multiple layers. In some cases, a pedicle graft of tissue may be sutured between the bladder and the vagina. A urethral or suprapubic catheter is left in the bladder to prevent distension of the bladder and tension to the sutured areas.

51920-51925
The physician excises an abnormal opening between the uterus and the bladder, then sutures the clean

tissues together closing the resulting defect and creating a smooth surface. In 51920, the procedure is done through the bladder with a small abdominal incision or during a laparotomy. In 51925, the physician completes the fistula closure and also removes the uterus through a small horizontal incision just above the pubic hairline. To remove the uterus, the supporting pedicles containing the tubes, ligaments, and arteries are clamped and cut free. The uterus and cervix are removed along with a narrow rim or cuff of vaginal lining. The vaginal defect may be left open for drainage. The abdominal incision is closed by suturing.

51940
The physician repairs a congenital defect in the front of the bladder wall, which is associated with lack of closure of the pubic bone at the symphysis pubis. The physician makes an incision around the exposed bladder and around the urethra to develop thick skin flaps. The physician brings the skin flaps together in the midline to close the roof of the urethra and allow the bladder and prostatic urethra to drop back beneath the bony pelvis (male patients), or lengthen the urethra (female patients). To invert the bladder and establish a functional vesical neck, the physician dissects the edge of the bladder from the rectus muscle, and divides the fibromuscular bar that unites the pubic bone to the bladder base. To support the urethra and bladder neck, the physician brings the muscles of the urogenital diaphragm toward the midline. The physician places drain tubes and performs a layered closure.

51960
The physician reconstructs or enlarges a bladder with a segment of intestine. To access the intestine and bladder, the physician makes a transverse or longitudinal incision on the lower abdomen and cuts the corresponding muscles, fat, and fibrous membranes (fascia). After dissecting an isolated segment of colonic intestine, the physician reconnects (anastomosis) the ileum end-to-end to the ascending colon, restoring continuity to the bowel. The dissected segment of colon is opened and the distal ends are sutured. An incision is made at the bladder dome, a portion of the top of the bladder is removed in preparation, and the colonic segment is sutured to the bladder. After controlling bleeding, the physician inserts a catheter and closes the abdomen in layers over the catheter for support.

51980
The physician connects the bladder to the skin (cutaneous vesicostomy) for direct urinary drainage. The Blocksom technique is usually performed on newborns. To access the bladder, the physician makes a suprapubic incision in the abdomen and cuts the corresponding muscles, fat, and fibrous membranes (fascia). After securing the bladder dome to the rectus fascia, the physician incises the bladder to create an opening that is sutured to a small incision in the skin. To support the opening during healing, the physician inserts a catheter or stent into the bladder. The physician inserts a drain tube and performs a layered closure. In adults, the Lapides technique passes a flap of bladder beneath the skin to replace a retracted section of abdominal skin. The abdominal skin is passed below the abdominal surface and sutured to the opening in the bladder, making a long-term tubular passage for urine. A catheter is placed through the stoma for two or three days.

51990
The physician treats stress incontinence in the male or female patient. The physician makes a 1 cm incision just below the umbilicus through which a fiberoptic laparoscope is inserted. A second incision is made on the left or right side of the abdomen and a second instrument is passed into the abdomen. The physician then manipulates the tools so that the pelvic organs can be observed through the laparoscope. The bladder is suspended by placing several sutures through the tissue surrounding the urethra and into support structures. The sutures are pulled tight so that the urethra is elevated and moved forward. The instruments are removed and incisions are closed with sutures.

51992
The physician inserts an instrument through the cervix into the uterus to manipulate the uterus. Next, the physician makes a 1 cm incision just below the umbilicus through which a fiberoptic laparoscope is inserted. A second incision is made and a second instrument is passed into the abdomen. The physician manipulates the tools so that the pelvic organs can be observed through the laparoscope. The physician places a sling under the junction of the urethra and bladder. The physician places a catheter in the bladder, makes an incision in the anterior wall of the vagina, and folds and tacks the tissues around the urethra. A sling is formed out of synthetic material or from fascia harvested from the sheath of the rectus abdominis muscle. The loop end of the sling is sutured around the junction of the urethra. An incision is made in the lower abdomen and the ends of the sling are grasped with a clamp and pulled into the incision and sutured to the rectus abdominis sheath. The instruments are removed and incisions are closed with sutures.

52000
The physician examines the urethra, bladder, and ureteric openings into the bladder with a cystourethroscope passed through the urethra and bladder. No other procedure is performed at this time. After examination, the physician removes the cystourethroscope.

52001
Using a rigid or flexible cystoscope, the physician removes clots and examines the urethra, bladder, and ureteric openings into the bladder. The cystoscope is

introduced into the meatus and the urethra is inspected before proceeding to the bladder. When the bladder is entered, the urine is evacuated using a syringe; the cystoscope is advanced further through the bladder and deflected upward. Following cystoscopic examination, and localization of the area of interest, the physician inserts a suction and irrigation probe with laser guide to evacuate multiple obstructing clots and to automatically remove any tissue from the operative site. The operative site is irrigated. Following completion of the procedure, the instrument is removed.

52005-52007
The physician passes the cystourethroscope through the urethra into the bladder. After insertion of a catheter into the ureter, the physician may flush (irrigate) or introduce by drops (instillate) a saline solution to better view structures, and/or may introduce contrast medium for radiologic study of the renal pelvis and ureter (ureteropyelogram, retrograde pyelogram). The physician removes the cystourethroscope. If a brush biopsy of the ureter or renal pelvis is also performed, report 52007.

52010
The physician examines the urinary collecting system with a cystourethroscope passed through the urethra and bladder, and inserts a catheter into the ejaculatory duct. The physician may flush (irrigate) or introduce by drops (instillate) a saline solution to better view structures, and may introduce contrast medium for radiologic study of ejaculatory duct (duct radiography). The physician removes the cystourethroscope.

52204
The physician examines the urinary collecting system with a cystourethroscope passed through the urethra and bladder, and extracts biopsy tissue from the bladder or urethra. To do so, the physician passes a cutting instrument through the endoscope to the suspect tissue and traps a specimen of tissue. Multiple samples may be collected. The physician removes the instrument and cystourethroscope.

52214
The physician examines the urinary collecting system with a cystourethroscope passed through the urethra and bladder, and destroys tissue of the trigone, bladder neck prostatic fossa, urethra, or periurethral glands. The physician passes through the endoscope an instrument that uses electric current to destroy lesions on the urethra, periurethral glands, bladder neck, depression below the prostate surface (prostatic fossa), and triangular area at the base of the bladder (trigone). The physician may employ endoscopic use of liquid nitrogen or carbon dioxide (cryosurgery) or lasers to destroy lesions. The physician removes the instruments and cystourethroscope.

52224
The physician examines the urinary collecting system with a cystourethroscope passed through the urethra and bladder, and uses electric current (fulguration) to destroy lesions smaller than 0.5 cm. The physician may also employ endoscopic use of liquid nitrogen or carbon dioxide (cryosurgery) or lasers to destroy lesions. The physician may insert an instrument to extract biopsy tissue from the bladder. The physician removes the instruments and cystourethroscope.

52234-52240
The physician examines the urinary collecting system with a cystourethroscope passed through the urethra and bladder, and removes tumors of the bladder by electric current (fulguration) or excision. The physician passes an instrument through the endoscope to destroy or remove tumors of the bladder by electric current (fulguration) or excision. The physician may also use liquid nitrogen or carbon dioxide (cryosurgery) or lasers to destroy lesions. The physician removes the instruments and cystourethroscope. For small tumor(s) that are 0.5 up to 2 cm in size, report 52234. For medium bladder tumor(s) that are 2 to 5 cm in size, report 52235. For large tumor(s) that are larger than 5 cm, report 52240.

52250
The physician examines the urinary collecting system with a cystourethroscope passed through the urethra and bladder, and inserts a radioactive substance. To release a radioactive substance, the physician passes an instrument through the endoscope. The physician may insert instruments through the endoscope to remove lesions or extract biopsy tissue from the bladder. The physician removes the instruments and cystourethroscope.

52260-52265
The physician examines the urinary collecting system with a cystourethroscope passed through the urethra and bladder and dilates the bladder with a balloon to relieve chronic inflammation of the bladder (interstitial cystitis). The physician removes the instrument and cystourethroscope. If general or spinal anesthesia is administered to the patient, use 52260. If the procedure is performed using local anesthesia, use 52265.

52270-52276
The physician examines the urinary collecting system with a cystourethroscope passed through the urethra and bladder. With a cutting instrument introduced through the cystourethroscope, the physician incises the inside of the urethral constriction. The physician removes the instrument and cystourethroscope. For incision of a female urethra, report 52270; for a male urethra, report 52275. If the physician incises the scar tissue or stricture within the urethra to open the lumen diameter while maintaining direct vision of the urethral lumen in either sex, report 52276.

Urinary

52277

The physician examines the urinary collecting system with a cystourethroscope passed through the urethra and bladder, and makes an incision (sphincterotomy) in the musculature of the urethral closure (urethral sphincter). The physician passes a cutting instrument through the cystourethroscope for resection of the external sphincter. After the sphincterectomy, the physician removes the instrument and cystourethroscope.

52281

The physician expands the diameter of the urethra. The physician examines the urinary collecting system with a cystourethroscope passed through the urethra and bladder and dilates a stricture. The physician inserts a balloon catheter to dilate a urethral stricture or stenosis. The physician may pass a cutting instrument through the cystourethroscope to make an incision (meatotomy) in the opening of the urethra or inject radiocontrast for radiologic study of the bladder. After dilation, the physician removes the instrument and cystourethroscope.

52282

The physician expands the diameter of the urethra. With the patient under anesthesia, the physician examines the urinary collection system with a cystourethroscope passed through the urethra and dilates a stricture. Using an instrument passed through the cystourethroscope, the physician inserts a permanent stent to dilate the urethral stricture or stenosis. After placing the stent, the physician removes the instruments and cystourethroscope.

52283

The physician treats a stricture with steroids. The physician examines the urinary collecting system with a cystourethroscope passed through the urethra and bladder, injecting material into a stricture. The physician passes an instrument through the cystourethroscope to inject the steroid into the urethral stricture. The physician removes the instrument and cystourethroscope.

52285

The physician passes a cystourethroscope through the urethra and bladder to treat female urethral syndrome. The physician may pass instruments through the cystourethroscope to incise the opening of the urethra (urethral meatotomy), dilate the urethra, incise the inside the urethra, treat septal fibrosis of the urethra and vagina, incise the bladder neck, or destroy polyps of the urethra in the bladder neck or trigone with electric current (fulguration). The physician removes the instruments and cystourethroscope.

52290

The physician examines the urinary collecting system with a cystourethroscope passed through the urethra and bladder, and makes an incision in the opening of the ureter(s) into the bladder (ureteral meatotomy). The physician passes the cystourethroscope through the urethra into the bladder, and inserts a cutting instrument through the cystourethroscope to incise the opening of one or both ureters into the bladder. The physician removes the instrument and cystourethroscope.

52300

The physician corrects an orthotopic (normally positioned) intravesical ureterocele(s). A ureterocele is a saccular dilation generally associated with single ureters. An orthotopic ureterocele is less common than an ectopic ureterocele, see 52301. The physician passes the cystourethroscope through the urethra into the bladder, and examines the urinary collecting system. An instrument is inserted through the cystourethroscope which allows the physician the excise the ureterocele or destroy the ureterocele with electric current (fulguration). The physician removes the instrument and the cystourethroscope. The physician usually performs this procedure with local anesthesia. When an open procedure is necessary it is chosen on the basis of the anatomical location of the ureteral meatus, the position of the ureterocele, and the impairment of renal function.

52301

An ectopic (abnormally positioned) ureterocele is a saccular dilation generally located, in part, at the bladder neck or in the urethra. This type of ureterocele most often involves the upper pole of duplicated ureters. An ectopic ureterocele is four times more common than an intravesical, or orthotopic, ureterocele (52300), and in females the ectopic ureterocele may prolapse through the urethra. The physician passes the cystourethroscope through the urethra into the bladder, and examines the urinary collecting system. An instrument is inserted through the cystourethroscope which allows the physician to excise the ureterocele with electric current (fulguration). The physician removes the instrument and the cystourethroscope.

52305

The physician corrects a diverticulum in the bladder. The physician examines the urinary collecting system with a cystourethroscope passed through the urethra and bladder, and removes a saccular opening of the bladder (diverticulum) by excision or fulguration. The physician removes the instrument and cystourethroscope.

52310-52315

The physician examines the urinary collecting system with a cystourethroscope passed through the urethra and bladder, and removes a foreign body, calculus, or ureteral stent from the urethra or bladder. The physician passes the cystourethroscope through the urethra into the bladder, and inserts an instrument through the cystourethroscope to extract a foreign body, calculus, or ureteral stent from the urethra or bladder. The physician removes the instrument and cystourethroscope. Report 52315 if the procedure is complicated due to previous surgery or the size or condition of the foreign body, calculus, or ureteral stent.

52317-52318
The physician uses ultrasound to smash a calculus. The physician examines the urinary collecting system with a cystourethroscope passed through the urethra and bladder to remove a foreign body. The physician inserts an instrument that generates shock waves through the cystourethroscope. The physician crushes the calculus in the bladder (litholapaxy) and washes out the fragments through a catheter. Post-shockwave fragments too large to be easily suctioned may require manual crushing. For a calculus smaller than 2.5 cm, report 52317. For a calculus larger than 2.5 cm, report 52318.

52320-52330
The physician examines the urinary collecting system with a cystourethroscope passed through the urethra and bladder, and removes, fragments, or manipulates a calculus in the ureter. The physician passes the cystourethroscope through the urethra into the bladder, and inserts an instrument through the cystourethroscope to extract, fragment, or manipulate a calculus in the ureter. The physician inserts a ureteral catheter and removes the cystourethroscope. Report 52320 if the physician uses a stone basket or other instrument to remove the calculus. Report 52325 if the physician uses ultrasound or electrohydraulics to fragment the calculus. Report 52327 if the physician uses a subureteric injection of implant material. Report 52330 if the physician uses an instrument to manipulate, not remove, the calculus.

52332
The physician examines the urinary collecting system with a cystourethroscope passed through the urethra and bladder, and inserts an indwelling catheter (stent) in the ureter. The physician passes the cystourethroscope through the urethra into the bladder, and inserts an instrument through the cystourethroscope to insert an indwelling stent in the ureter. The stent provides support of the ureter. The physician removes the instrument and cystourethroscope.

52334
The physician examines the urinary collecting system, and creates an opening through the kidney to the exterior of the body (nephrostomy) by inserting a guidewire through a cystourethroscope. After examining the urinary collecting system through a cystourethroscope inserted through the urethra into the bladder, the physician inserts a catheter through the cystourethroscope into the ureter. The physician passes a guidewire through the ureteral catheter into the kidney and through a small incision in the skin of the flank. The physician removes the cystourethroscope and enlarges (dilates) the percutaneous opening by passing tubes with increasingly larger diameters through the skin incision over the guidewire to the kidney. The physician passes a nephrostomy tube over the guide, removes the guide, and sutures the tube to the skin. The physician usually withdraws the ureteral catheter at the end of the procedure.

52341-52343
The physician treats a ureteral stricture by balloon dilation, laser, electrocautery, or incision through a cystourethroscope. Under direct vision, the physician passes a flexible or rigid cystourethroscope through the urethra into the bladder. A balloon catheter is placed into the ureteral stricture, and the balloon is gently inflated. After approximately five minutes, the balloon is deflated and removed. In laser treatment of a ureteral stricture, probes, in combination with laser fibers, are used to apply laser energy to the stricture. In electrocautery, heat is applied to eliminate the stricture. The ureteral stricture may be incised alone or in combination with balloon dilation, laser, or electrocautery to open the blocked ureter. Report 52341 when a ureteral stricture is treated, 52342 when a ureteropelvic junction stricture is treated, or 52343 when an intra-renal stricture is treated.

52344-52346
The physician treats a ureteral stricture by balloon dilation, laser, electrocautery, or incision through a cystourethroscope and ureteroscope. Under direct vision, the physician passes a flexible or rigid cystourethroscope through the urethra into the bladder and a ureteroscope into the ureter and examines the urinary collecting system. In balloon dilation, a balloon catheter is placed into the ureteral stricture, and the balloon is gently inflated. After approximately five minutes, the balloon is deflated and removed. In laser treatment of a ureteral stricture, probes, in combination with laser fibers, are used to apply laser energy to the stricture. In electrocautery, heat is applied to eliminate the stricture. Alternately, the ureteral stricture may be incised alone or in combination with balloon dilation, laser, or electrocautery to open the blocked ureter. Report 52344 when a ureteral stricture is treated, 52345 when a ureteropelvic junction stricture is treated, or 52346 when an intra-renal stricture is treated.

52351
The physician examines the urinary collecting system for diagnostic purposes with endoscopes passed through the urethra into the bladder (cystourethroscope), ureter (ureteroscope), and renal pelvis (pyeloscope). After examination, the physician removes the endoscopes.

52352-52353
The physician examines the urinary collecting system with endoscopes passed through the urethra into the bladder (cystourethroscope), ureter (ureteroscope), and renal pelvis (pyeloscope), and removes or manipulates a stone (calculus). To extract or manipulate a calculus, the physician passes a stone basket through an endoscope. The physician inserts a ureteral catheter and removes the endoscopes. Report 52352 if the physician passes a stone basket through an endoscope to extract or manipulate a calculus. Report 52353 if the physician passes an electro-hydraulic lithotriptor probe through an endoscope to pulverize a calculus.

52354
The physician examines the urinary collecting system with endoscopes passed through the urethra into the bladder (cystourethroscope), ureter (ureteroscope), and renal pelvis (pyeloscope), and takes a biopsy and/or uses electric current (fulguration) to destroy a ureteral or renal pelvic lesion. The physician may take a biopsy of suspect tissue and/or destroy a lesion with electric current. The physician removes required instruments and endoscopes.

52355
The physician examines the urinary collecting system with endoscopes passed through the urethra into the bladder (cystourethroscope), ureter (ureteroscope), and renal pelvis (pyeloscope), and excises a ureteral or renal pelvic tumor. The physician inserts a cutting instrument through the endoscope and excises the tumor. After flushing the area with saline solution, the physician may insert a ureteral stent. The physician removes the cutting instrument and endoscopes.

52400
The physician examines the urinary collecting system with a cystourethroscope passed through the urethra and bladder, and incises, excises, or uses electric current (fulguration) to correct defects of the bladder neck or the back of the urethra.

52402
Through the urethra, the physician performs a transurethral resection or a transurethral incision of the ejaculatory ducts (TUIED). The cystourethroscope is introduced into the meatus and the urethra is inspected. Instruments are inserted through the cystourethroscope to the region of the ejaculatory ducts. The seminal vesicles are compressed and the ejaculatory ducts are incised with a hook electrode or resected in one "bite" with a loop electrode. The seminal vesicles are again compressed. The area is observed through the scope and the instruments and cystourethroscope are removed.

52450
Through a cystourethroscope, the physician incises the capsule of the prostate gland and into but not through the true prostate to create a larger passage for urine. A small transurethral tissue sample from the prostate is often collected at the same time. The bladder is catheterized for the immediate postoperative period.

52500
The physician relieves an obstruction of the outlet of the bladder. After the scope is passed through the urethra, instruments are inserted through the cystourethroscope to the target region. The physician excises the tissue responsible for the obstruction of urine flow.

52601
After preliminary cystourethroscopy, the physician passes the resectoscope under direct vision up the urethra to the region of the prostate. Meatotomy, cutting to enlarge the opening of the urethra, and/or dilatation of the urethra may be necessary to allow the passage of the resectoscope. The prostate gland is removed in a systematic fashion by using a series of small cuts into the glandular tissue with an electrocautery knife. The resected tissue is removed and the area is keep clear by irrigation through the resectoscope. Bleeding is controlled by fulguration. A catheter is passed into the bladder and left in place for the postoperative period.

52630
The physician inserts an endoscope through the urethra to remove residual or regrowth obstructive tissue from a previous surgical procedure. After preliminary cystourethroscopy, the physician passes the resectoscope into the urethra to the prostate. Meatotomy, cutting to enlarge the external opening of the urethra, and dilatation of the urethra may be necessary to allow the passage of the resectoscope. The physician removes residual tissue of the prostate gland through a series of small cuts. The resected tissue is removed, and the area is kept clear by irrigation through the resectoscope. Bleeding is controlled by fulguration. A catheter is passed into the bladder and left in place. If the same physician removes residual obstructive tissue within the postoperative period of a related procedure, report this code with modifier 78 appended.

52640
Contracture of the bladder neck outlet usually results from scarring after a transurethral resection of the prostate gland. After preliminary cystourethroscopy, the physician passes the resectoscope under direct vision up the urethra to the region of the bladder neck contracture. Meatotomy, cutting to enlarge the opening of the urethra, and dilation of the urethra may be necessary to allow the passage of the resectoscope. The scar tissue is incised at one to three sites or resected, using a cutting electrocautery knife. The operative site is inspected for bleeding, which is controlled by fulguration. A catheter is passed into the bladder at the

end of the procedure and let in place for the postoperative period.

52647-52649

The physician uses a laser to coagulate, vaporize, or enucleate the prostate through an endoscope or resectoscope inserted through the urethra. Dilation of the urethra may be necessary to permit endoscope insertion. The entire prostate is treated. To accomplish this, vasectomy, meatotomy, cystourethroscopy, and internal urethrotomy may be necessary. If enucleation is utilized, the tissue is divided and removed in small pieces (morcellation). Once the laser treatment is complete, a urinary catheter is inserted. Report 52647 if prostatic tissue is coagulated, 52648 if it is vaporized, and 52649 if it is enucleated.

52700

The physician inserts an endoscope through the urethra to drain an abscess on or near the prostate. The physician passes a cystourethroscope through the penile urethra to the region of the prostate and identifies the area of the abscess. A needle is passed into the abscess and purulent matter is removed by aspiration. The cystourethroscope is removed.

53000-53010

The physician makes an external incision in the urethra or creates an opening between the urethra and the skin. The physician passes a sound into the urethra until it meets the obstructing stricture. A longitudinal incision is made directly over the sound. After the stricture is identified, the urethra is incised the length of the stricture so defects may be removed. The sound is removed and a catheter is passed through the urethra into the area of the incision and guided past it into the bladder. The urethra is repaired over the catheter, using sutures. Occasionally, the urethra is not repaired by suturing but is simply allowed to grow epithelial cells (epithelialize) around the catheter. In 53010, the physician meets the stricture in the perineal part of the urethra.

53020-53025

The physician makes an incision in the opening of the urethra (urethral meatus) using a small pointed knife and a meatotomy clamp. The meatus is opened on the ventral surface and the meatus may be dilated. Sutures may be required on the mucosa of the meatus. The physician often uses a hemostat to separate the tissue in the urethra prior to making his incision. Report 53020 if the patient is older than one year, or 53025 if the patient is younger than 1 year.

53040-53060

The physician drains an abscess in the urethra resulting from a urethral infection or traumatic injury. The physician makes an incision through the skin, subcutaneous tissue, and overlying layers of muscle, fat, and tissue (fascia) over the site of the abscess. By blunt or sharp dissection, the incision is carried into the abscess. Several drains are inserted and the incision is closed in layers. Report 53040 for drainage of a deep periurethral abscess. For an abscess or cyst in Skene's or paraurethral glands in the female, report 53060.

53080-53085

The physician drains urine that has passed out of the urethra (extravasation) into the perineal tissue. The physician makes an incision through the skin over the site. The incision is carried to the extravasation for drainage. Following drainage, the incision is closed with sutures. Report 53080 for uncomplicated extravasation and 53085 for complicated extravasation.

53200

Using an open approach, the physician excises a specimen of tissue from the urethra for biopsy. At the site to be analyzed, a portion of the suspect tissue is excised by blunt or sharp dissection. The incision is closed in layers.

53210-53220

The physician removes the urethra and creates an opening between the bladder and skin for drainage of urine. The physician makes a slightly curved, suprapubic (Cherney) incision down to the ureter and bladder. The bladder is opened and the urethral orifice is circumcised and usually tied off with sutures. Tumors of the urethra are removed by partial or complete urethrectomy or by electric current (fulguration). If the bladder has been opened, it is closed in two layers or more. Report 53210 for females; use 53215 for male-specific procedure. Report 53220 for removal of malignant tumor from the urethra.

53230-53235

The physician removes a urethral diverticulum. In a female patient, a longitudinal incision is made in the anterior vaginal wall and the urethral diverticulum is separated from the vaginal wall by a combination of blunt and sharp dissection. The urethra may be opened back to the orifice of the diverticulum in order to facilitate identification. A balloon catheter may be inserted and inflated. Once the diverticulum has been excised, the urethra is closed over a catheter and the vaginal wall is repaired with a layered closure. In a male patient, a cystourethroscope is inserted into the urethra and the diverticulum is excised through a transurethral incision. The physician may inject fluid or pass a balloon catheter into the diverticulum to allow it to be easily found and dissected. The diverticulum is isolated down to the neck and transected. The physician closes the urethra, leaving a catheter in the urethra. Report 53230 if performed on a female and 53235 if performed on a male.

53240

The physician repairs a urethral diverticulum by creating a pouch (marsupialization). In a female patient, a longitudinal incision is made in the anterior vaginal wall of the female and the borders of the urethral diverticulum are raised and sutured to create a pouch. The interior of the sac separates and gradually closes by granulation. The urethra is closed over a catheter and the vaginal wall is repaired with a layered closure. In a male patient, a cystourethroscope is inserted into the urethra and the diverticulum treated in the same manner, but through the perineum.

53250

The physician excises a bulbourethral gland. A bulbourethral gland is located on each side of the prostate gland near the external sphincter and is connected to the urethra with a one-inch duct. The gland secretes what becomes part of the seminal fluid. The physician completes this procedure through transurethral or segmental resection with end-to-end sutures (anastomosis).

53260-53275

The physician removes urethral polyps or caruncles in either sex, or in a female, removes Skene's glands or treats urethral prolapse. In a female, the physician separates the urethra from the vaginal wall. The urethra is incised. A circular excision is made around the lesion and the targeted tissue is resected. The urethra and vaginal mucosa are reattached in layers. In a male, the physician uses a transurethral approach to similarly excise the defect. Report 53260 if removing distal urethral polyps; 53265 if removing a urethral caruncle; 53270 if removing the Skene's glands; or 53275 if treating urethral prolapse.

53400-53405

The physician reconstructs the urethra in two stages. In the first stage (53400), the area of the stricture is identified by a catheter and urethrography and its location is marked with ink or dye. The incision is made over the stricture area and targeted tissue is removed. Otherwise, the stricture is opened widely and the normal skin of the male or female is sutured to the edge of the mucosa on each side. In those areas in which mucosa had to be removed, the skin is sutured edge-to-edge. Six to eight weeks are required for complete healing of this stage. In the second stage (53405), the physician makes parallel incisions around the defect and continues around the urethral opening both proximally and distally. The lateral skin edges are closed over an indwelling catheter to create a new urethra. The corpora and muscles are closed, respectively, becoming the new urethra structure.

53410

The physician reconstructs the urethra of a male patient. The area of the urethral stricture is identified by catheterization. The physician cuts over the stricture area through the skin, fascia, corpus, and urethra. When the stricture is so severe that the urethral lumen cannot be identified, the physician removes the area involved. Otherwise, the stricture is opened widely and the normal skin is sutured to the edge of the mucosa on each side. In those areas in which the mucosa had to be removed, the skin is sutured edge-to-edge.

53415

The physician repairs the urethra. The stricture of the male perineal urethra is opened through a midline perineal or transpubic incision extending from the base of the scrotum to the anal margins. The physician makes an incision into the normal urethra distal to the stricture and opens the stricture on its ventral surface. From here a wide-based skin flap is developed by a U-shaped incision in the scrotum and advanced until it can be approximated to the posterior angle of the perineal incision without tension. The ends of the proximal and distal urethra are connected (anastomosis) to the extremities of the scrotal incision and anchored to the midline of the urethral bed to provide a stable urethral roof. When the urethra stricture has been opened but not excised, the edges of the longitudinal incision in the scrotal flap are sutured to the edges of the urethral wall. The outer edges of the flap are sutured to the edges of the original perineal skin incision.

53420-53425

Urethroplasties are performed to open a stricture, repair trauma, or correct a prolapse. In the first stage, the physician identifies the injured area using a catheter or a urethrograph. The incision is made over the injury and carried through the skin, fat, and other tissues (fascia). If a urethral prolapse is involved, other incisions may be involved. The problem is repaired or excised and layered sutures are made to provide adequate support. A catheter is placed and left for at least six to 12 days. In the second stage, to close the urethra, the physician cuts around the urethral defect, using skin from the scrotal flap to make a urethra. The right size urethra must be constructed to allow a catheter and prevent obstructions. The physician pulls the loose skin around the urethra and closes the incisions. The first stage is 53420; report 53425 for the second stage.

53430

The physician uses perineal or vaginal tissue to reconstruct the female urethra. With the patient in the lithotomy position and a catheter in the urethra, the physician cuts an inverted U-shaped flap above the urethral meatus and extending on the anterior vaginal wall. This flap is undermined with sharp dissection and spreading of the scissors around the upper portion of the urethral meatus, leaving a strip attached. The flap is sutured into a tube shape, reconstructing the distal urethra. The vaginal wall on each side is brought together in several layers to cover the new urethra. Small submucosal vessels are cauterized and a drain may be placed for one to two days.

53431

In the Tenago, Leadbetter procedure, the physician elongates the urethra by using bladder musculature.

Continence is achieved due to contraction of the bladder musculature. The physician exposes the bladder through a suprapubic incision. The bladder is opened and the bladder neck incision is made 2 cm lateral to the urethra on each side. The musculature is drawn together in a tube and attached to the urethra. The urethral canal is closed in a two-layer technique. For the Tenago procedure, they are moved laterally.

53440-53442
The physician produces a mechanical obstruction in the urethra or at the bladder neck to put pressure on the muscles, which will prevent leakage but still allows the patient to force urine. A small midline scrotal or penile incision is made to introduce a sling composed of fascia or synthetic material. The sling is placed across the muscles surrounding the urethra and anchored. Three screws on each side of the pelvic bone secure the sling. Tension of the sling is adjusted to obtain a stress pressure optimal for the patient. With the procedure completed, the incision is closed with layered sutures. Report 53442 when the physician removes the previously placed sling or accesses the site again for revision of the sling.

53444
A urethral retention catheter is placed in the bladder and a midline lower abdominal incision is made to gain access to the space of Retzius. The bladder neck and urethra are exposed and the plane between the bladder neck and urethra is dissected and the urethrovaginal septum is dissected at the midline attachment at the distance required for accommodating the tandem cuff. Having freed the bladder neck, the physician measures its circumference and the tandem cuff is placed in position around the bladder neck and the tubing brought to the suprapubic area.

53445
The physician implants an artificial sphincter to stem urinary incontinence. In male patients for whom the incontinence is caused by anything other than prostatic surgery, the prosthesis is inserted through a subpubic incision. In female patients, the sphincter is inserted through a suprapubic incision. The space of Retzius (between the bladder and the pubis) is opened and the bladder neck is cut free, making space for the device. The bladder neck circumference is measured and a cuff of slightly larger size is chosen and sutured around the bladder neck. A space is created below the skin low in the scrotum, and the control pump passed into this position from the subpubic incision. The pressure balloon is placed in a pocket behind the rectus muscle on the same side as the control pump. The physician injects fluid into the pressure balloon. In females, the plane between the bladder neck and vagina is dissected to serve the same purpose as the scrotum.

53446
In female patients, the physician makes a midline lower abdominal incision to gain access to the space of Retzius. The artificial urinary sphincter is exposed and the plane between the bladder neck and vagina is dissected. The device is removed and the opening is closed using suture for the rectus fascia. The subcutaneous tissues are closed and staples are used for skin closure. In male patients, the urethral bulb is exposed and the bulbospongiosus muscles are left intact over the urethra. The strap of the prosthesis is grasped under the crus and the muscle and the procedure is repeated distally to grasp the second lateral strap. The same maneuvers are repeated on the opposite site. The proximal straps are untied, as are the lateral straps. The incision is closed and a Foley catheter remains for several days.

53447
The physician removes and replaces an artificial sphincter (including pump, reservoir, and cuff) used to stem urinary incontinence. In male patients for whom the incontinence is caused by anything other than prostatic surgery, the prosthesis is accessed through a subpubic incision. In female patients, the sphincter is accessed through a suprapubic incision. The sphincter and pump are examined, removed, and replaced. The bladder neck circumference is measured and a cuff of slightly larger size is chosen and positioned around the bladder neck. A space is created below the skin low in the scrotum and the control pump passed into this position from the subpubic incision. The pressure balloon is placed in a pocket behind the rectus muscle on the same side as the control pump. The physician injects fluid into the pressure balloon and the connections are permanently established. In females, the plane between the bladder neck and vagina is dissected.

53448
In females, the vagina is prepared preoperatively and a urethral retention catheter is placed in the bladder. The patient is administered general anesthesia and placed supine. The physician makes a midline lower abdominal incision to gain access to the space of Retzius. The artificial urinary sphincter is exposed and the plane between the bladder neck and vagina is dissected. The device is removed. The area is irrigated with antibiotics and the physician debrides the infected tissue. Antibiotics are again used to flush the area. The tubing of the balloon of the replacement device is brought into the suprapubic area through a separate stab incision laterally in the rectus fascia. The control pump is passed through the suprapubic area through a subcutaneous track into the subcutaneous tissue of the ipsilateral labium. The device is emptied of fluid and a Hypaque solution is injected into the pressure balloon, using a 14-gauge blunt needle. The device components are connected, the pressure balloon is aspirated until empty, and the Hypaque solution is re-injected. Connections are completed between the control pump and cuff and reinforced by suture. The device is activated. The opening is closed using suture for the

rectus fascia. The subcutaneous tissues are closed and staples are used for skin closure. In males, the patient is placed under general anesthesia in the lithotomy position. The urethral bulb is exposed and the bulbospongiosus muscles are left intact over the urethra. The strap of the prosthesis is grasped under the crus and the muscle and the procedure is repeated distally to grasp the second lateral strap. The same maneuvers are repeated on the opposite site. The proximal straps are untied, as are the lateral straps. The area is irrigated by antibiotic, and the infected tissue is debrided. The area is again flushed by antibiotic and the physician inserts the replacement pump using the same steps in the procedure for placement of the artificial sphincter described. The incision is closed and a Foley catheter is left indwelling for several days.

53449

The physician repairs an inability of an inflatable sphincter device to stem incontinence. In male patients the prosthesis is accessed through a subpubic incision. In female patients, the sphincter is accessed through a suprapubic incision. The space of Retzius (between the bladder and the pubis) is opened and the device is located. The physician checks the cuff and sutures around the bladder neck. The physician locates reservoir and checks for any malfunctions or abnormalities. The pressure balloon, usually located in a pocket behind the rectus muscle on the same side as the control pump, is evaluated for patency and function. Any necessary repairs are completed. The physician closes the incisions. The reservoir is filled and all connections are made. Several test inflations and deflations are performed during closure. The physician places a catheter in the bladder for about one day.

53450

The physician performs this surgery to open or reconstruct the urethra, improving voiding or allowing insertion of an instrument. The meatus, which may be congenitally small or narrowed as the result of infection, is opened and a mucosal flap is advanced and sutured to the glans.

53460

The physician widens the meatus to enhance voiding. The physician makes an incision on the ventral surface of the penis and skin is freed from the shaft. Fibrous tissue is removed. An erection is artificially induced to confirm all fibrous tissue has been removed.

53500

Transvaginal, secondary, open urethrolysis is performed in cases when voiding is obstructed due to excessive periurethral scarring caused by previous surgical repair of stress incontinence, procedures such as bladder neck suspension. Urethrolysis involves cutting obstructive adhesions or bands of fibrous tissue that have grown to fix the urethra to the pubic bone. An incision is made through the vagina. The adhering fibrous bands and periurethral scar tissue are visualized and dissected. Lysis and removal continues until the urethra is mobilized away from the surrounding fibrous tissue. Some correction to vaginal abnormalities may be accomplished before closure of the incision. Postsurgical cystourethroscopy is included in this procedure to examine the urethra following urethrolysis.

53502-53515

The physician repairs a urethral wound or injury, including the skin and even more traumatic wounds requiring more than a layered closure. Examples include debridement of cuts (lacerations) or tears (avulsion). Suturing of the urethra is done in layers to prevent later complications and fistula formations. The tissue can be constructed around a catheter. Report 53502 if the patient is female; 53505 if the patient is male; 53510 if the wound in either sex is perineal; or 53515 if repair involves the prostate.

53520

The physician closes a urethrostomy or urethrocutaneous fistula. An elliptical incision is made around the opening of the urocutaneous fistula and carried deeper into the supporting tissue toward the urethra. The entire tract is freed and excised unless it involves other important structures, such as the external sphincters. When the tract cannot be completely removed, the remaining part is cut. The defect of the urethra is closed in layers over a catheter.

53600-53605

When the physician examines the male patient, a soft rubbery urethral catheter is passed and the stricture is noted. If a stricture is found, a dilator is used. Report 53600 for the first visit and 53601 for subsequent visits. Report 53605 if spinal anesthesia is administered.

53620-53621

The physician uses fine tools to dilate the male urethra. A filiform (a small silk-like instrument with woven spiral tips, to which followers made of a similar material can be attached by a screw-like mechanism) is used when a stricture cannot be passed. With a filiform as a guide, the follower is passed through the urethra. Increasing sizes of followers are introduced, dilating the stricture. The filiform is manipulated up a lubricated urethra to the stricture. The physician attaches a follower to the filiform and the stricture is widened. Report 53621 if it is a subsequent procedure.

53660-53665

The physician uses dilators of increasing size to widen the female urethra. A suppository or instillation of a saline solution may be used. Report 53660 for initial dilation, and 53661 for subsequent dilation. Use 53665 if general or spinal anesthesia is administered for dilation of female urethral stricture.

Urinary

53850
The physician performs transurethral destruction of prostate tissue by microwave thermotherapy. The physician inserts an endoscope in the penile urethra, prior to endoscope placement the urethra may need to be dilated to allow instrument passage. After the endoscope is passed, a microwave thermotherapy stylet is inserted in the urethra and the diseased prostate is treated with electromagnetic radiation. The treated prostate is examined for evidence of bleeding which may be controlled with electrocoagulation. The endoscope and instruments are removed. A urinary catheter is inserted into the bladder and left in place postoperatively.

53852
The physician performs transurethral destruction of prostate tissue by radiofrequency thermotherapy. The physician inserts an endoscope in the penile urethra, prior to endoscope placement. The urethra may be dilated to allow instrument passage. After the endoscope is placed a radio frequency thermotherapy stylet is inserted in the urethra and the diseased prostate is treated with radiant energy. The treated prostate is examined for evidence of bleeding, which may be controlled with electrocoagulation. The endoscope and instruments are removed. A urinary catheter is inserted into the bladder and left in place postoperatively.

53855
A physician inserts a temporary urethral stent in a patient with prostatic urethral obstruction to improve voiding function. The stent system consists of a proximal balloon to prevent distal displacement, a urine port situated above the balloon, and the stent. Topical anesthesia is administered and the physician inserts the probe to locate the external sphincter. Once the external sphincter is located, a measurement is taken and the proper size stent selected. The stent device is mounted on a single-use insertion tool and standard catheter insertion technique is used to insert it. The proximal tip, balloon, and urine port are positioned in the bladder and the balloon is inflated with 5 cc of water. The insertion device is removed. A distal anchor mechanism is secured by sutures. A retrieval suture that extends to the meatus and deflates the balloon when pulled is also secured. The stent is typically left in place for up to 30 days.

Male/Female

54000-54001
The prepuce is the fold of penile skin commonly called the foreskin. The physician makes a cut or slit in the prepuce to relieve a constriction that prevents the retraction of the foreskin back over the head of the penis. A segment of foreskin on the dorsal or the side of the penis is crushed with forceps. Using scissors, the physician makes a cut through the crushed tissue and sutures the divided skin to control bleeding. The prepuce of a newborn is slit in 54000, while 54001 reports the slitting of the prepuce of any male other than a newborn.

54015
The physician drains a deep abscess or hematoma (pocket of blood) by incising penile tissue. After instilling a local anesthesia, the physician makes an incision through the skin and deeper tissues into the abscessed cavity. The urethra and the main arteries and nerves are avoided. Often a drain is left in place to assure adequate drainage.

54050-54055
The physician treats skin lesions of the penis by local application of a chemical (54050) or local electrodesiccation (54055) to kill the diseased tissue or organism. Using a cotton-tipped applicator soaked in the chemical or an electrodesiccator, the physician applies the treatment to the specific lesions only, taking care to avoid touching normal skin with the chemical or the electrodesiccator. Using either method, no tissue is removed and no closure is required.

54056-54057
The physician treats skin lesions of the penis by local application of liquid nitrogen or the use of a cryothermal instrument (54056) or by laser beam (54057) to kill the diseased tissue or the organism. Using a cotton-tipped applicator dipped in liquid nitrogen (-78 degrees Celsius), the physician freezes or burns with the laser only the specific lesions. No tissue is removed and no closure is required.

54060
The physician excises selected large lesions of the penis not removable by other methods. After adequate local anesthesia has been administered, the physician cuts out an elliptical piece of skin that includes the lesion and a rim of normal tissue. With a forceps or hemostat clamp, the physician grasps and elongates the involved skin containing the lesion, causing the tissue to tent. Using a scalpel or scissors, an ellipse of tissue containing the lesion is excised. The resulting defect is closed with sutures.

54065
The physician destroys extensive lesions of the penis using one or more of several methods. Extensive destruction generally means the procedure took more time or was more difficult than usual due to such factors as the size and number of lesions involved. The methods used by the physician include local application of a chemical, freezing, electrodesiccation, laser vaporization to kill the diseased tissue, or excision. Local anesthesia may be used for these procedures. The physician applies the method only to the specific lesions.

54100
The physician removes a portion of a skin lesion on the penis by punch biopsy or by excising a small portion of the lesion with scalpel or scissors. The resulting defect may require simple repair with sutures.

54105
The physician removes a portion of a penile mass by deep punch biopsy or by making an incision in the penis and dissecting tissues to the deep mass and excising a portion of the lesion. The incision may be repaired with layered sutures.

54110-54112
Peyronie's disease is an induration and severe curvature of the erect penis due to fibrosis of the cavernous sheaths. The physician corrects Peyronie's disease by excising abnormal fibrous tissue on the dorsal aspect of the penis. After an incision is made around the penis, the physician retracts the skin to expose the abnormal tissue on the underlying normal spongy tissue. Avoiding critical nerves and blood vessels, with the penis erect, the defective tissue is excised. The skin is closed by suturing. Report 54111 if a graft measuring 5 cm or less in length is required; report 54112 if a graft greater than 5 cm is required.

54115
The physician removes a foreign body from deep within the shaft of the penis by making an incision and dissecting the tissues. The foreign body, usually a penile implant, is localized and removed. The resulting defect is closed with layered sutures.

54120
The physician removes a portion of the penis due to disease or mutilating injury. The distal penis is enclosed in a rubber glove and a tourniquet is applied at the base of the penis. An incision is made completely around the penile shaft. The various structures of the penis are isolated and divided with care to leave enough of the urethra to form an opening for the passage of urine. The remaining tissues and skin are closed with layered sutures.

54125
The physician removes the penis due to disease or mutilating injury. The distal penis is enclosed in a rubber glove. An incision is made from above the penis and carried around the base of the penile shaft and down through the midline of the scrotum. The various structures of the penis are isolated and divided with care to leave enough of the urethra for drainage. The urethra is brought through the perineum below the scrotum and an opening is created for the passage of urine. The remaining tissue and skin are closed in layered sutures with drains placed in the scrotum and a catheter in the bladder.

54130
The physician removes the entire penis and surrounding lymph nodes to treat invasive cancer. The distal penis is enclosed in a rubber glove. An incision is made from above the base of the penis and carried around the base of the penile shaft and down through the midline of the scrotum. The various structures of the penis are isolated and divided with care to leave enough of the urethra for drainage. The urethra is brought through the perineum below the scrotum and an opening is created for the passage of urine. The remaining tissues and skin are closed in layered sutures with drains placed in the scrotum and a catheter in the bladder. The physician also removes the lymph nodes in the groin areas. An incision is made from the pubic bone to the lateral pelvic bone exposing the area for dissection. The fatty tissues bearing the lymph nodes are removed. The defect is covered by rotating one of the thigh muscles over the area and suturing it in place. The subcutaneous tissues and the skin are closed in layered sutures over drains placed in the region.

54135
The physician removes the entire penis and surrounding lymph nodes to treat invasive cancer. The distal penis is enclosed in a rubber glove. An incision is made from above the base of the penis and carried around the base of the penile shaft and down through the midline of the scrotum. The various structures of the penis are isolated and divided leaving enough of the urethra for drainage. The urethra is brought through the perineum below the scrotum and an opening is created for the passage of urine. The remaining tissues and skin are closed in layered sutures with drains placed in the scrotum and a catheter in the bladder. The physician also removes the lymph nodes in the groin areas. An incision is made from the pubic bone to the lateral pelvic bone exposing the area for dissection. The fatty tissues bearing the lymph nodes are removed. The defect is covered by rotating one of the thigh muscles over the area and suturing it in place. The subcutaneous tissues and the skin are closed in layered sutures over drains placed in the region. A lower midline abdominal incision is made and the pelvic cavity is entered and the lymph nodes deep in the pelvis are removed. The abdominal incision is also closed in layers of sutures.

54150
After the administration of a local anesthetic by injection(s), the physician removes the foreskin of the penis by clamping the foreskin in a plastic device and trimming the excess protruding skin. A segment of foreskin on the dorsal or the side of the penis is crushed with forceps. A cut is made through the crushed tissue with scissors, and the divided foreskin is fitted in a plastic bell-shaped clamp. The clamp crushes a ring of the foreskin and holds the skin edges together while the excess skin is trimmed from the top of the device. The clamp is left in place and simply falls off when healing has finished days later.

54160-54161
The physician removes the foreskin of the penis in the baby up to 28 days of age (54160) or in a male older than 28 days (54161) by excision of the skin. A segment of foreskin on the dorsal or the side of the penis is crushed with forceps. A cut is made through the crushed tissue with scissors, and the divided foreskin is pulled down over the head of the penis while the excess skin is trimmed from around the head of the penis. Bleeding is controlled by chemical cautery or suture ligatures. The skin edges created are sutured together with absorbable suture material.

54162
The physician retracts the foreskin, releases the preputial post-circumcision adhesions, and cleanses the glans in a patient who is under general anesthesia. If retraction of the foreskin reveals a fibrous ring, the physician places two vertical incisions directly over the fibrous ring and the transversely running fibrous bands are divided to expose the underlying Bucks' fascia. With the foreskin retracted, the defect is closed horizontally with interrupted sutures.

54163
A repeat circumcision may be performed if there is circumferential scarring of excessive residual skin or incomplete removal of the preputial skin during the initial circumcision. First, the skin at the base of the penis is cleansed with alcohol and allowed to dry. The physician uses an index finger to palpate the lateral side of the penis to determine the position of the root of the penis. With a tuberculin syringe and needle, the anesthetic is injected parallel to the root of the penis. While the penis is stabilized by gentle downward or ventral traction, the needle is inserted at the base of the penis and inserted beneath the skin surface. The anesthetic is injected and the needle withdrawn. An incision is made around the base of the foreskin, the foreskin is pulled back, and it is cut away from the penis. Stitches are usually used to close the skin edges.

54164
The physician performs an incision of the membrane that attaches the foreskin to the glans and shaft of the penis (frenulum). A dorsal penile nerve block is administered with a needle directed through the fascia of the symphysis pubis and into the frenum space where the anesthetic is deposited to block the dorsal nerves of the penis. A longitudinal incision is made ventrally though the outer layer of the prepuce. After retracting the prepuce, the physician extends the incision along the inner layer. Bleeding is controlled with an electrocoagulator. The resultant wound is closed.

54200-54205
Peyronie's disease is an induration and severe curvature of the erect penis due to fibrosis of the cavernous sheaths. The physician injects medication into the abnormal fibrous tissue of the penis to correct painful curvature of the penis caused by Peyronie's disease. In 54200, no incision is made. The medication is injected into the dorsal area of the penis through the skin. In 54205, the physician makes an incision in the dorsum of the penis and identifies the abnormal fibrous tissue. An injection is made directly into the abnormal fibrous tissue under direct visualization through the incision.

54220
The corpora cavernosa are the spongy bodies of the penis, the dual columns of erectile tissue that form the back and sides of the penis. In priapism, this spongy tissue is in a state of persistent erection. The physician treats priapism by irrigating the corpora cavernosa. After adequate local anesthesia, the physician passes a large bore needle into the body of the penis and aspirates a quantity of blood and irrigates the space with 20 ml to 30 ml of saline solution. This may be accompanied by injecting medication into the same region, repeating it several times to get the abnormal erection to resolve.

54230
The corpora cavernosa are the spongy bodies of the penis, the dual columns of erectile tissue that form the back and sides of the penis. The physician injects medication into the penis for x-ray studies to evaluate erectile dysfunction. After placing a constricting rubber band around the penis, the physician passes a needle into the body of the penis and aspirates a small quantity of blood. X-ray contrast medication is injected directly into the body of the penis. The constricting band is removed and x-rays are taken to demonstrate the function and integrity of the corpora cavernosa and the blood flow of the penis.

54231
Corpora cavernosa is the spongy tissue of the penis. The physician injects vasoactive drugs into the corpora cavernosa for studies to evaluate erectile dysfunction. A rubber band is placed around the base of the penis and the intracavernous pressure is measured using instrumentation. The physician evaluates the penis for leakage between the diastolic and the systolic pressures. A swift rate of decay between the two indicates arterial and/or venous insufficiency of the penis. After the test, the band is removed and the instrumentation removed.

54235
Corpora cavernosa is the spongy tissue of the penis. The physician injects medication into the penis to treat erectile dysfunction. After placing a constricting rubber band around the penis, the physician passes a needle into the body of the penis and aspirates a small quantity of blood. The selected medication is injected directly into the body of the penis. This produces an erection in most patients that may last from minutes to hours.

54240
A plethysmograph is an instrument that measures variations in the volume of an organ and in the amount of blood in it or passing through it. The physician measures the physiological potential of the penis to attain and maintain an erection using plethysmography. The volume change of the penis is measured in response to external stimuli.

54250
The physician monitors nighttime erections in impotent patients during rapid eye movement sleep. Testing can be performed in a sleep center or in the patient's home. During the test, the patient's penis is wired to a strain gauge monitor and recordings are made of the strength and duration of any erections occurring while the patient sleeps.

54300
The physician corrects and repairs chordee, which is the abnormal curvature of the penis. To assist in planning the surgery, an artificial erection may be produced by placing a band around the base of the penis and injecting saline into the body of the penis. The area of deformity is determined and by using a combination of incisions and excisions of abnormal fibrous tissue and sometimes normal tissue, the defect is corrected. Care is taken to dissect around nerves and blood vessels. Sometimes the urethra is dissected free of its position and retracted temporarily away from the operative site. The separate tissues of the penis are closed in layers with absorbable suture material. An artificial erection may again be produced to test and demonstrate the adequacy of the repair.

54304
The physician corrects and repairs chordee, which is the abnormal curvature of the penis. The physician also prepares the penis for correction of hypospadias, an abnormal opening of the urethra on the underside of the penis or on the perineum. To assist in planning the surgery, an artificial erection may be produced by placing a band around the base of the penis and injecting saline into the body of the penis. The area of deformity is determined and the defect is corrected using a combination of incisions and excisions of the prepuce (foreskin). Care is taken to dissect around the nerves and blood vessels. Often the foreskin is used in a free graft or a flap graft to cover the ventral skin defects created to correct the chordee. The separate tissues of the penis are closed in layers with absorbable suture material. An artificial erection may again be produced to test and demonstrate the adequacy of the repair. The urethral opening is left on the ventral shaft of the penis for repair during a later stage.

54308-54312
The physician completes the repair of chordee (abnormal curvature of the penis) and hypospadias (an abnormal opening of the urethra on the underside of the penis or on the perineum) by creating a urethral opening in the end of the penis. The urethra is dissected free of the surrounding tissues to mobilize it. A distal urethra, less than 3 cm in 54308 or greater than 3 cm in 54312, is formed from the prepuce (foreskin) and an opening is created at or near the tip of the head of the penis. Urine may be diverted by the use of a catheter in the bladder. The skin is closed with sutures.

54316
The physician completes the repair of chordee (abnormal curvature of the penis) and hypospadias (abnormal opening of the urethra on the underside of the penis or on the perineum) by creating a urethral opening in the end of the penis. The urethra is mobilized by dissecting it free from the surrounding tissues. A distal urethra is formed from skin obtained from a site other than the genitalia and sutured to the existing urethra and to an opening created at or near the tip of the head of the penis. Urine may be diverted using a catheter in the bladder. The skin and tissues are closed with fine absorbable sutures.

54318
The physician completes the repair of chordee (abnormal curvature of the penis) and hypospadias (an abnormal opening of the urethra on the underside of the penis or on the perineum) by separating the temporary attachments sutured between the penis and scrotum during a previous stage of the repair. Urine may be diverted using a catheter in the bladder. The skin is closed with fine sutures.

54322
The physician corrects and repairs a chordee, which is an abnormal curvature of the penis. The physician also prepares the penis for correction of hypospadias, an abnormal opening of the urethra on the underside of the penis or on the perineum. The physician corrects hypospadias in the distal penis at the base of the head of the penis in a one-stage procedure. An incision is made around the shaft of the penis next to the glans (head) and the skin is dissected from the penile shaft taking care to avoid injury to the urethra. An erection is artificially produced to evaluate any chordee before and after the correction. Any chordee present is corrected by excising the responsible fibrous band. A second incision is made in the groove on the under side of the glans. Skin in the area is pulled up to the glans and fashioned into an opening by suturing in the head of the penis. A circumcision, or excision of some foreskin, may be performed. The original incision around the penis is closed by suturing.

54324
In a one-stage procedure, the physician corrects hypospadias, which is an abnormal opening of the urethra on the underside of the penis, in the distal or end portion of the penile shaft. An incision is made from the head of the penis around the urethral opening. An erection is artificially produced to evaluate

the chordee before and after the correction. Any chordee present is corrected by excising the responsible fibrous band. A flap is created from the skin below the urethral opening and flipped up and over the opening of the urethra and sutured together forming a tube extension of the urethra. The foreskin is divided and sutured over the defect left by the flap on the ventral surface of the penis. A circumcision is usually the result of the procedure.

54326
In a one-stage procedure, the physician corrects hypospadias, which is an abnormal opening of the urethra on the underside of the penis, in the distal or end portion of the penile shaft. An incision is made on the ventral surface of the penis and around the urethral opening. An erection is artificially produced to evaluate any chordee before and after the correction. Any chordee present is corrected by excising the responsible fibrous band. The urethra is dissected free of the shaft to mobilize it. A flap of skin is created from the foreskin and sutured together to form a tube to be used as a segment of urethra. The foreskin is further divided and sutured over the defect left by the flap on the ventral surface of the penis. Foreskin excision (circumcision) may be part of this procedure.

54328
Hypospadias is an abnormal opening of the urethra on the underside of the penis or on the perineum. The physician corrects hypospadias in the distal or end portion of the penile shaft in a one-stage procedure. An incision is made on the ventral surface of the penis and around the urethral opening. An erection is artificially produced to evaluate the chordee before and after the correction. Any chordee present is corrected by excising the responsible fibrous band. The urethra is dissected free of the shaft to mobilize it. An island flap of skin is created from the foreskin and sutured together to form a tube to be used as a segment of urethra. This formed urethral tube flap is sutured in place between the urethral opening in the shaft of the penis and an opening created in the head of the penis. The foreskin is further divided and sutured over the defect left by the flap on the ventral surface of the penis. Foreskin removal (circumcision) may be part of this procedure.

54332
Hypospadias is an abnormal opening of the urethra on the underside of the penis or on the perineum. The physician corrects hypospadias in the base portion of the penis in a one-stage procedure. An incision is made on the ventral surface of the penis and around the urethral opening. An erection is artificially produced to evaluate the chordee before and after the correction. Chordee is corrected by excising the responsible fibrous band. Considerable dissection is required to mobilize the urethra. An island flap of skin is created from the foreskin and sutured together to form a tube to be used as a segment of urethra. This formed urethral tube flap is sutured in place between the urethral opening at the base of the shaft of the penis and an opening created in the head of the penis. The foreskin and skin overlying the shaft are further divided and dissected free and sutured over the defect left by the flap on the ventral surface of the penis. A circumcision is usually the result of the procedure.

54336
Hypospadias is an abnormal opening of the urethra on the underside of the penis or on the perineum. The physician corrects hypospadias in the perineal portion of the penis in a one-stage procedure. An incision is made on the ventral surface of the penis and around the urethral opening. An erection is artificially produced to evaluate the chordee before and after the correction. Any chordee present is corrected by excising the responsible fibrous band. Considerable dissection is required to mobilize the urethra in preparation for repair of the hypospadias. An island flap of skin is created from the foreskin and sutured together to form a tube to be used as a segment of urethra. This formed urethral tube flap is sutured in place between the urethral opening at the base of the scrotum in the perineum and an opening created in the head of the penis. The foreskin and skin overlying the shaft are further divided and dissected free and sutured over the defect left by the flap and dissections on the ventral surface of the penis. Circumcision is usually the result of the procedure.

54340
Hypospadias is an abnormal opening of the urethra on the underside of the penis or on the perineum. The physician repairs a fistula, stricture, and/or diverticula resulting from a former hypospadias repair. The fistula (abnormal passage) or diverticula (pouch or sac) is identified and excised, often using microsurgical techniques. The defect in the urethra is repaired by suturing and the skin is also closed with sutures. A stricture (narrowing) is corrected by dilating the area with dilating catheters or by incision and suture closure.

54344
Hypospadias is an abnormal opening of the urethra on the underside of the penis or on the perineum. The physician repairs a fistula, diverticula, and/or stricture resulting from a former hypospadias repair. The fistula (abnormal passage) or diverticula (pouch or sac) is identified and excised, often using microsurgical techniques. The defect in the urethra is repaired by closure with a free patch graft or flap graft. The skin defect is closed by simple suturing or by the use of a flap skin graft. A stricture (narrowing) is corrected by dilating the area with dilating catheters or by incision and suture repair.

54348
Hypospadias is an abnormal opening of the urethra on the underside of the penis or on the perineum. The physician repairs a fistula, diverticula, and/or stricture resulting from a former hypospadias repair. The fistula (abnormal passage) or diverticula (pouch or sac) is identified and excised, often using microsurgical techniques. The defect in the urethra is repaired by closure with a free patch graft or a flap graft that both require extensive dissection, mobilization of tissues, and the creation of complicated grafts such as a tube graft. The skin defect is closed by simple suturing or by use of a flap skin graft. A stricture (narrowing) is corrected by dilating the area with dilating catheters or by incision and suture repair. The urine may be diverted through a catheter left in the bladder. The catheter can be passed through the urethra or placed directly in the bladder through the lower abdominal wall just above the pubic bone.

54352
Hypospadias is an abnormal opening of the urethra on the underside of the penis or on the perineum. The physician repairs severe, disabling complications from former hypospadias repairs. Often using microsurgical techniques and considerable excision of scarred and damaged tissues, the deformities and malfunctions of the urethra and penis are corrected. Two or three stages may be necessary to complete this complicated task. A new urethral segment is created with a free patch graft, a flap graft, or by the use of a tube graft. Extensive dissection and mobilization of tissues are generally required to complete the process. Skin defects are closed using flap or free skin grafts. Any strictures (narrowing of hollow structures) are corrected by dilating the area with dilating catheters or by incision and suture repair. Urine may be diverted through a catheter left in the bladder. The catheter can be passed through the urethra or placed in the bladder through an incision in the lower abdominal wall just above the pubic bone.

54360
The physician corrects an abnormal curvature of the penis using a series of excisions of tissue on the side of the penis. To assist in planning the surgery, an erection may be artificially produced by placing a band around the base of the penis and injecting saline into the body of the penis. The area of deformity is determined and using a combination of incisions and excisions of tissue, the defect is corrected. An incision is made in the skin of the penis just proximal to the glans (head of the penis) and the skin is pulled to the base of the penis, exposing the underlying tissues. Further dissection is done to expose the thick connective tissue on one side of the shaft. A series of parallel excisions are made and the resulting defects are closed by suturing. The separate tissues and the skin of the penis are closed in a layered fashion with absorbable suture material. An erection may again be induced to test the adequacy of the repair.

54380
The physician corrects epispadias, which is the congenital absence of the upper wall of the urethra. The urethra has its opening anywhere on the top surface of the penis. A closed urethra is created by reapproximating the tissues, and by using skin grafts, tube grafts, free tissue grafts, or a combination of techniques depending on the extent of the defect.

54385
The physician corrects epispadias and associated urinary incontinence in one or more stages. Epispadias with incontinence is the congenital absence of the upper wall of the urethra and the lack of function of the muscles that control the bladder neck. Through an incision in the lower abdomen, the surgeon reconstructs the bladder neck and reimplants the ureters from the kidneys away from the bladder neck outlet. A closed urethra is created by reapproximating the tissues and by using skin grafts, tube grafts, free tissue grafts, or a combination of techniques depending on the extent of the defect.

54390
The physician corrects epispadias and exstrophy of the bladder in stages. Epispadias is the congenital absence of the upper wall of the urethra. Bladder exstrophy is the turning inside out of the bladder so that the bladder is open directly to the outside and as such, urine does not collect in the bladder but simply drains without any control to the outside onto the lower abdomen. The first stage is to close the bladder through incisions in the lower abdomen. The surgeon frees the bladder from the abdominal wall and proceeds to close the bladder and reimplant the ureters from the kidneys away from the bladder neck outlet. In the second stage, a closed urethra is created by reapproximating the tissues and by using skin grafts, tube grafts, free tissue grafts, or a combination of techniques depending on the extent of the defect. In the following stages, the physician reconstructs the bladder neck to provide urinary control and, if necessary, does additional surgery on the penis and urethra.

54400-54401
The physician inserts a semi-rigid penile prosthesis in 54400, which is a hinged or malleable device, or a self-contained inflatable penile prosthesis in 54401, which is a one piece, paired hydraulic device that allows fluid to be pumped from one portion of the device to another. A transverse incision is made just above the penis over the pubic bone. With care to avoid important nerves and blood vessels, dissection is carried down to the erectile tissues at the base of the penis. Incisions are made in the thick fibrous membranes surrounding the two main erectile tissues to allow the insertion of dilators to create space for the

prostheses. The paired prosthetic devices are inserted one at a time into the two erectile tissue compartments down the length of the penis. The incisions and tissues are closed by suturing. The operation can also be done in similar fashion using an incision just below the scrotum in the perineum to enter the erectile tissue or in the upper scrotum at the base of the penis.

54405
The physician inserts an inflatable penile prosthesis made of three components-the reservoir, the pump, and two inflatable cylinders. A transverse incision is made at the base of the penis in the upper scrotum. With care to avoid the urethra and important nerves and blood vessels, dissection is carried down to the erectile tissues at the base of the penis. The thick fibrous membranes surrounding the two main erectile tissues are incised and dilators are inserted to create space for the prostheses. Two prosthetic devices are inserted into the two erectile tissue compartments down the length of the penis. A pouch is made in one side of the scrotum, and the pump mechanism and tubing are inserted into the space created. Using an index finger, the surgeon creates a tunnel from the pump to the space behind the pubic bone. The reservoir is placed behind the pubic bone with tubing running from it through the tunnel to the pump in the scrotum. The incisions and tissues are closed by suturing. The operation can also be done in similar fashion using an incision just below the scrotum in the perineum to enter the erectile tissue and in the area above the pubic bone to gain access to place the reservoir.

54406
The patient is taken to the operating room, placed in a supine or lithotomy position, and the physician makes an incision using the same penoscrotal or infrapubic approach as the original procedure to remove the multi-component, inflatable penile prosthesis. The physician makes an incision into the corpus cavernosum and the prosthesis is withdrawn. The corporotomy is closed by suture. The subcutaneous tissue is closed by suture and a dressing is applied to the incision. The bladder is emptied with a catheter. An indwelling urethral catheter, if used, is removed on the first postoperative day.

54408
Under general anesthesia, the patient is placed in a supine or lithotomy position and the physician makes an incision using the same penoscrotal or infrapubic approach as the original procedure to repair the previously placed multi-component, inflatable penile prosthesis. The physician makes an incision into the corpus cavernosum to inspect the previously placed prosthesis. Repairs are made. The corporotomy is closed by suture. The subcutaneous tissue is closed by suture and a dressing is applied to the incision. The bladder is emptied with a catheter. An indwelling urethral catheter, if used, is removed on the first postoperative day.

54410
Under general anesthesia, the patient is placed in a supine or lithotomy position and the physician makes an incision using the same penoscrotal or infrapubic approach as the original procedure to remove the previously placed multi-component, inflatable penile prosthesis and to insert a replacement during the same operative session. The physician makes an incision into the corpus cavernosum and the prosthesis is withdrawn. The replacement prosthesis is brought through the glans and the deflated cylinder is drawn into the distal corporal body for insertion into the crus of the penis. The corporotomy is closed and the cylinders are inflated and deflated several times to check the flow of the fluid to and from the cylinders. The reservoir is brought through the external inguinal ring and the bladder is emptied by catheter. The existing subfascial pocket in used to place the reservoir, as well as the pump/activator mechanism, which is placed in the existing scrotal pocket. Sutures are placed to prevent upward migration, the tubing is filled with fluid, and the physician makes the connections between the tubing of the pump and reservoir and the tubing of the pump and cylinders. Before the wound is closed, the prosthesis is cycled to check proper functioning. The corporotomy is closed by suture. The subcutaneous tissue is closed by suture and a dressing is applied to the incision. The bladder is emptied with a catheter. An indwelling urethral catheter, if used, is removed on the first postoperative day.

54411
The physician removes and replaces a multi-component inflatable penile prosthesis and irrigates and debrides infected tissue. The patient is taken to the operating room and placed under general anesthesia. The physician makes an incision using the same penoscrotal or infrapubic approach as the original procedure. The physician makes an incision into the corpus cavernosum and the prosthesis is withdrawn. Any infected tissue is debrided and irrigated with an antibiotic solution. The replacement prosthesis is brought through the glans and the deflated cylinder is drawn into the distal corporal body for insertion into the crus of the penis. The corporotomy is closed and the cylinders are inflated and deflated several times to check the flow of the fluid to and from the cylinders. The reservoir is brought through the external inguinal ring and the bladder is emptied by catheter. The existing subfascial pocket is used to place the reservoir, as well as the pump/activator mechanism, which is placed in the existing scrotal pocket. Any infected tissue is debrided and irrigated with an antibiotic solution. Sutures are placed to prevent upward migration, the tubing is filled with fluid, and the physician makes the connections between the tubing of the pump and reservoir and the tubing of the pump

and cylinders. Before the wound is closed, the prosthesis is cycled to check proper functioning. The corporotomy is closed by suture. The subcutaneous tissue is closed by suture and a dressing is applied to the incision. The bladder is emptied with a catheter. An indwelling urethral catheter, if used, is removed on the first postoperative day.

54415

The physician makes an incision using the same approach (i.e., penoscrotal or distal penile) as the original procedure to remove the non-inflatable or self-contained inflatable penile prosthesis in a patient who is under general anesthesia. An incision is made into the corpus cavernosum, the corporal tissue is dissected, and the prosthesis is removed from the corporal body. The wound is irrigated with antibiotics, and the corporotomy is closed by suture. The subcutaneous tissue is closed by suture and a dressing is applied to the incision. The bladder is emptied with a catheter.

54416

Under general anesthesia, the patient is placed in a supine or lithotomy position and the physician makes an incision using the same approach (i.e., penoscrotal or distal penile) as the original procedure to remove the non-inflatable (semi-rigid)or self-contained inflatable penile prosthesis and to insert a replacement prosthesis. An incision is made into the corpus cavernosum, the corporal tissue is dissected, and the prosthesis is removed from the corporal body. The wound is irrigated with antibiotics and the replacement prosthesis is advanced to the mid-glans and introduced into the corporal space. Once implanted, the wound is again irrigated with antibiotics, and the corporotomy is closed by suture. The subcutaneous tissue is closed by suture and a dressing is applied to the incision. The bladder is emptied with a catheter. An indwelling urethral catheter, if used, is removed on the first postoperative day.

54417

The physician removes and replaces a non-inflatable (semi-rigid) or inflatable (self-contained) penile prosthesis, and irrigates and debrides infected tissue. The physician makes an incision using the same intrapubic, penoscrotal, or distal penile approach as the original procedure to remove the prosthesis and to insert a replacement non-inflatable or inflatable penile prosthesis at the same operative session. Using corporal incisions, the physician is able to remove the prosthesis. A colposcopy may be performed to ensure all fibrous elements are excised, and a replacement prosthesis is implanted. Any infected tissue is debrided and irrigated with an antibiotic solution. The corporotomy is closed by suture. The subcutaneous tissue is closed by suture and a dressing is applied to the incision. The bladder is emptied with a catheter. An indwelling urethral catheter, if used, is removed on the first postoperative day.

54420

The physician treats priapism, an abnormally sustained erection, by creating a shunt for the diversion of blood from the penis to the femoral vein. An incision is made in the groin area of the thigh and the saphenous vein is cut and dissected free of its attachments creating a mobile segment about 10 cm long. A second incision is made at the base of the penis and the saphenous vein is tunneled through the subcutaneous tissues to the base of the penis. A 1 cm in diameter piece of the thick fibrous tissue of the corpus cavernosum (erectile tissue) is excised and the free end of the saphenous vein is sutured to the defect. The erection resolves as blood flows from the penis to the femoral vein through this saphenous vein segment. The incisions are closed by suturing. The procedure is sometimes repeated on the opposite side.

54430

The physician treats priapism, an abnormally sustained erection, by creating a shunt for the diversion of blood from one region of the penis to an adjacent region. With a catheter in the urethra into the bladder, an incision is made in the side of the penis. Dissection is carried to the thick fibrous tissues surrounding one of the corpus cavernosum (erectile tissue) and to the corpus spongiosum, which is the erectile tissue around the urethra. Oval discs of the fibrous tissue are excised from the adjacent surfaces of these two structures. The excisional defects are sutured together creating a shunt (passageway) for the flow of blood from the engorged corpus cavernosum to the corpus spongiosum thus relieving the erection. The tissues and the skin are sutured closed. The procedure is sometimes repeated on the opposite side.

54435

The physician treats priapism, an abnormally sustained erection, by creating a shunt for the diversion of blood from the one region of the penis to an adjacent region. With adequate local anesthesia, the head of the penis is punctured with a biopsy needle and advanced into the tip of the corpus cavernosum (erectile tissue). A portion of tissue from the head of the penis to the corpus cavernosum is removed as if taking a biopsy. This creates a passageway for blood trapped in the cavernosum to escape through the circulation to the head of the penis. The procedure is repeated to the opposite corpus cavernosum. The two puncture sites in the head of the penis are closed by suturing.

54440

The physician repairs an injury of the penis using one or more of plastic surgery techniques. The repair may require skin grafts, tissue grafts, urethral repair, extensive debridement, microsurgical repairs, or any combination.

54450
The physician treats adhesions between the uncircumcised foreskin and the head of the penis that prevent the retraction of the foreskin. Adhesions are broken by stretching the foreskin back over the head of the penis onto the shaft or by inserting a clamp between the foreskin and the head of the penis and spreading the jaws of the clamp.

54500
The physician obtains a sample of testicular tissue by needle biopsy. While the testis is held firmly with the scrotal skin stretched tightly over the testis and the epididymis positioned away from the biopsy site, a biopsy needle is inserted into the testis at the area of concern. The needle biopsy sheath is advanced over the needle and twisted to shear off the enclosed sample and withdrawn with the sample enclosed. The scrotal wound may be closed by suturing.

54505
The physician obtains a sample of testicular tissue by direct incisional biopsy. The procedure is done under local or regional anesthesia. While the testis is held firmly with the scrotal skin stretched tightly over the testis and the epididymis positioned away from the biopsy site, a small incision is made through the skin of the scrotum. The underlying tissues are incised and dissected to expose the testis. The testis is stabilized by two sutures and an ellipse of tissue is removed between the two sutures. The incisions are closed by suturing.

54512
The physician excises an extraparenchymal lesion of the testis. The physician makes an inguinal incision, incising the skin and subcutaneous fat. The testicle is delivered through the incision, the tunica vaginalis is opened, and the lesion is excised. The incision is closed with suture.

54520
An incision is made in one side of the scrotum and the tissues are separated to expose the spermatic cord. The spermatic cord is opened and the individual bundles making up the cord are cross-clamped, cut, and secured with nonabsorbable suture material. The testis is removed through the scrotal incision. If the patient so chooses, and if no contraindications are present, a prosthetic testis is inserted into the scrotum before the wound is closed in layers by suturing. An alternative method uses an incision in the groin. The testis is pulled through the incision after cutting and tying the cord in a fashion similar to the scrotal approach.

54522
The physician performs a partial excision of one testis or both testes. The surgeon makes a longitudinal incision midline in the scrotum to expose the testis. The tunica vaginalis is incised, and the testicular vessels and vas deferens are identified, clamped separately, and divided. The cords are ligated at a level slightly above the area of infection, abscess, neoplasm, or trauma and the spermatic cord is isolated for manipulation of the testicle. The testis is delivered to the wound and dissected below the ligated cords. The wound is closed by suture and a pressure dressing and scrotal supporter are applied.

54530
The physician performs a radical orchiectomy by removing en bloc the contents of half of the scrotum. An incision is made in the inguinal area from the pubic bone toward the lateral pelvic bone. The incision made deep into the tissues and the spermatic cord is dissected free and cross-clamped. The testis and all its associated structures are pushed up from the scrotum into the incision and removed. Packing is placed in the empty scrotum. When the spermatic cord is opened and the individual bundles making up the cord are cross-clamped, cut, and secured with nonabsorbable suture material, care is taken to avoid important nerves and vessels in the area. The packing is removed and bleeding controlled. A prosthetic testis may be placed in the scrotum before the incision is closed in layers by suturing. This procedure results in complete removal of the testis.

54535
The physician performs a radical orchiectomy by removing en bloc the entire contents of half of the scrotum and also explores the inside of the abdomen for evidence of tumor spread. An incision is made in the inguinal area from the pubic bone toward the lateral pelvic bone. The incision made deep into the tissues and the spermatic cord is dissected free and cross-clamped. The testis and all its associated structures are pushed up from the scrotum and delivered into the incision and removed. Packing is placed in the empty scrotum. Care is taken to avoid important nerves and vessels in the area, when the spermatic cord is opened and the individual bundles making up the cord are cross-clamped, cut and secured with nonabsorbable suture material. This results in complete removal of the testis. The packing is removed and bleeding controlled. A prosthetic testis may be placed in the scrotum before the incision is closed in layers by suturing. A midline incision is made from the upper to the lower abdomen and the abdominal cavity is entered. The back wall of the abdomen is exposed and the lymph nodes are checked for spread of tumor. Some may be removed and/or biopsied and the abdominal wound is closed in layers by suturing.

54550
The physician searches for a testis that failed to descend into the scrotum during development. An incision is made in the scrotum or the inguinal area from the pubic bone to the upper lateral pelvic area in the skin fold made by the thigh and the lower abdomen. The tissues are separated by dissection to

find the testis in the area. No other procedure is performed. The incision is closed in layers by suturing.

54560
The physician searches the abdominal cavity for a testis that failed to descend in to the scrotum during development. An incision is made in the inguinal area from the pubic bone to the upper lateral pelvic area or in the skin fold made by the thigh and the lower abdomen. The tissues are separated by dissection and the incision is extended into the abdominal cavity. No other procedure is performed at this time. The incision is closed in layers by suturing.

54600
The physician treats a torsion of the testis, which is a twisting of the testis upon itself so that its blood supply is compromised. The physician makes an incision in the scrotum and exposes the twisted testis. The testis and spermatic cord is untwisted to restore blood flow to the organ. If the testis is viable, the surgeon anchors the testis to the inside wall of the scrotum with three or more sutures. The incision is closed in layers by suturing. Because the problem that allowed the testis to twist may affect the other testis (contralateral testis), a second procedure is commonly performed to anchor it in similar fashion.

54620
The physician makes an incision in the scrotum and exposes the testis on side opposite to the one that had previously been twisted. The surgeon anchors the testis to the inside wall of the scrotum with three or more sutures to prevent the twisting of the cord and the testis. The incision is closed in layers by suturing.

54640
Orchiopexy is the surgical fixation of an undescended testicle into the scrotum. An incision is made in the scrotum or the inguinal area from the pubic bone to the upper lateral pelvic area in the skin crease made by the thigh and the lower abdomen. The physician searches for a testis that failed to descend in to the scrotum during development. The tissues are separated by dissection to find the testis in the inguinal canal area. The spermatic cord is mobilized to allow positioning of the testis in the scrotum. In the scrotum, a small pouch is created for the testis where the testis is sutured in place to prevent retraction back in to the inguinal canal. If there is a concomitant hernia it is often repaired at the same time through the same incision. The hernia present in the inguinal canal is repaired by folding and suturing of tissues to strengthen the abdominal wall and correct the weakness responsible for the hernia. The incision is closed in layers by suturing.

54650
Orchiopexy is the surgical fixation of an undescended testicle into the scrotum. An incision is made in the inguinal area from the pubic bone to the upper lateral pelvic area in the skin fold made by the thigh and the lower abdomen. The physician searches the abdominal cavity for a testis that failed to descend in to the scrotum during development. The tissues are separated by dissection and the incision is extended into the abdominal cavity to find the testis in the abdominal area. The tissues are separated by dissection to find the testis in the area. At this point several surgical options are available. The one chosen will depend on the mobility of the testis and how far it can be brought down through the inguinal canal and into the scrotum. The procedure may take two stages approximately six to 12 months apart. Eventually, the spermatic cord is mobilized sufficiently to allow positioning of the testis in the scrotum. In the scrotum a small pouch is created for the testis where the testis is sutured in place to prevent retraction back in to the inguinal canal or into the abdominal cavity. The incision is closed in layers by suturing.

54660
For cosmetic reasons, the physician places an artificial testis in the scrotum of a patient. After adequate local anesthesia, an incision is made in the inguinal area and the empty scrotal sac is dilated by passing a dissecting finger or a moist gauze sponge through the inguinal canal into the scrotum. A prosthetic testis is inserted into the scrotal sac and the neck of the scrotum is closed by suturing. The inguinal incision is closed in layers by suturing.

54670
The physician repairs injury (laceration or traumatic rupture) to the testis that occurs as a result of a blunt or penetrating injury. Often a laceration is present in the scrotum and the testis is explored and repaired through the open wound. Otherwise, an incision is made in the scrotum to expose the testis. Any devitalized testicular tissue is removed by sharp dissection and the thick tough fibrous tissue encasing the testis is closed by suturing. The scrotum is closed in layers by suturing. Often a rubber drain is placed to prevent the accumulation of fluid and blood in the scrotum.

54680
The physician transplants the testis(es) under the skin of the thigh to preserve function and viability following massive injury or surgical loss of the scrotal skin. The thigh is chosen because the temperature just under the skin is approximately the same as in the scrotum, a condition to normal testicular function. Incisions are made in the skin of the thigh adjacent to the scrotum and the testis is sutured in place with attention to preserving blood flow to the organ. The thigh incisions are closed in layers over a rubber drain brought out through the skin. In four to six weeks scrotal reconstruction is begun.

54690
The physician removes one or both testicles, which may be undescended, injured or diseased using a

laparoscope. The physician places a trocar at the umbilicus into the abdominal or retroperitoneal space and insufflates the abdominal cavity. The physician places a laparoscope through the umbilical incision and additional trocars are placed into the abdomen. The testis and all its associated structures are pushed up from the scrotum or freed from their undescended intra-abdominal location and removed through the abdominal or retroperitoneal space via the trocar port. Packing may be placed in the empty scrotum. Care is taken to avoid important nerves and vessels in the area. A prosthetic testis may be placed in the scrotum before the incision is closed in layers by suturing. The trocars are removed and the incisions are closed with sutures.

54692
The physician performs an orchiopexy (the surgical fixation of an undescended testicle into the scrotum) with the assistance of a fiberoptic laparoscope. A para-umbilical port is created by placing a trocar at the level of the umbilicus. The abdominal wall is insufflated. The laparoscope is placed through the umbilical port and additional trocars are placed into the abdominal cavity. The physician uses the laparoscope fitted with a fiberoptic camera and/or an operating instrument to search the abdominal cavity for the undescended testes. The physician may have several surgical options depending on the mobility of the testis and how far it can be brought down through the inguinal canal and into the scrotum. The procedure may take two stages approximately three to 12 months apart. Once, the spermatic cord is mobilized sufficiently to allow positioning of the testis in the scrotum (which often occurs during the first and perhaps only operative session). A small pouch is created for the testis where the testis is sutured in place to prevent retraction back in to the inguinal canal or into the abdominal cavity. The small abdominal incisions are closed by staple or suture in the usual fashion.

54700
The physician drains a collection of blood or an abscess within the scrotum. If the testis is the target of the drainage, it is held firmly with the scrotal skin stretched tightly over the testis and the epididymis positioned away from the site. A small incision is made through the skin of the scrotum. The underlying tissues are incised and dissected to expose the testis and the site to be drained. The testis may be stabilized by two sutures as an incision is made into the abscess or hematoma and fluid is expressed. Packing or a rubber drain may be placed to promote drainage. The incisions are usually not closed by suturing. Similar procedures are followed if the target is the epididymis or the scrotal space.

54800
The physician obtains a sample of epididymal tissues by needle biopsy. While the testis is held firmly with the scrotal skin stretched tightly over the testis and the epididymis positioned just under the taut skin, a biopsy needle is inserted into the area of concern in the epididymis. The needle biopsy sheath is advanced over the needle and twisted to shear off the enclosed sample and withdrawn containing the sample. The scrotal wound may be closed by suturing.

54830
The physician removes a local lesion of the epididymis by direct incision. The procedure is done under local or regional anesthesia. While the testis is held firmly with the scrotal skin stretched tightly over the testis and the epididymis positioned just under the taut skin, a small incision is made through the skin of the scrotum. The underlying tissues are incised and dissected to expose the epididymis and the area of concern. The epididymis may be stabilized by two sutures placed on each side of the lesion and an ellipse of tissue is removed from the epididymis containing the lesion between the two sutures. The stabilizing sutures are tied across the excision site to close it. The scrotal incision is closed by suturing.

54840
The physician removes a spermatocele, which is a small cyst, filled with fluid and spermatozoa, between the body of the testis and the epididymis. After adequate local anesthesia, an incision is made in the scrotum and the testis with its attached epididymis is brought out of the wound. The cyst is dissected free of the testis and excised. The involved area of the epididymis is sutured to the underlying testis and the scrotal wound is closed by suturing. Alternately the epididymis may be dissected free of all of its attachments to the testis. The blood vessels involved are tied and cut and/or cauterized to control bleeding. The freed epididymis is thus removed, a rubber drain is placed in the scrotum and the incision is closed by suturing.

54860-54861
The physician removes the epididymis. After adequate local anesthesia, an incision is made in the scrotum and the testis with its attached epididymis is brought out of the wound. The epididymis is dissected free of all of its attachments to the testis. The blood vessels involved are tied and cut and/or cauterized to control bleeding. The freed epididymis is thus removed, a rubber drain is left in the scrotum and the incision is closed by suturing. The epididymectomy is performed on one side in 54860, or both sides in 54861.

54865
The physician explores the epididymis by making an incision in the scrotum. The procedure is done under local or regional anesthesia. While the testis is held firmly with the scrotal skin stretched tightly over the testis and the epididymis positioned just under the taught skin, a small incision is made through the skin of the scrotum. The underlying tissues are incised and

dissected to expose the epididymis. The epididymis may be biopsied by placing two sutures on each side of the area of concern and an ellipse of tissue is removed from the epididymis containing the lesion between the two sutures. The stabilizing sutures are tied across the excision site to close it. The scrotal incision is closed by suturing. Alternatively, a biopsy may be done by needle puncture under direct vision.

54900-54901
The physician treats obstruction of the flow of spermatozoa from the epididymis to vas deferens, the tube that carries the semen. After adequate anesthesia, an incision is made in the scrotum and the testis with its attached epididymis and the vas deferens is brought out of the wound. The vas deferens is transected and the selected area of the epididymis is opened and the appropriate tubule in the area is brought out of the surrounding tissues and transected. The cut ends of these two tubes are sutured together and the vas deferens is sutured to the epididymis. A rubber drain is often placed in the scrotum and the incision is closed by suturing. In 54900, the procedure is performed on one side; in 54901, the procedure is bilateral.

55000
A hydrocele is a sac of fluid in the tunica vaginalis or along the spermatic cord. The physician treats a hydrocele by aspirating the fluid. After injecting a small area with local anesthetic, the physician inserts a needle on an aspirating syringe into the fluid filled hydrocele sac and withdraws the fluid into the syringe. After the aspiration and with the needle still in place, the sac may be injected with sclerosing medication to prevent accumulation of new fluid by stimulating scarring and hardening of the empty sac.

55040-55041
A hydrocele is a sac of fluid in the tunica vaginalis or along the spermatic cord. The physician treats a hydrocele by removing it. After injecting an area with local anesthetic and using aseptic techniques, the physician makes an incision in the scrotum or in the inguinal area. Care is taken to keep the hydrocele intact while it is dissected free of its attachments to the testis and other structures. The sac is opened, drained and partially excised leaving a remnant of tissue. The remaining tissue is swung back behind the epididymis and the spermatic cord and closed by suturing the edges together. The testis is anchored to the inside of the scrotum with three sutures to prevent later torsion or twisting of the testis. A rubber drain may be left in the scrotum and the incision closed in layers by suturing. The hydrocele is on one side in 55040. In 55041, each side is treated for hydrocele.

55060
The physician treats a hydrocele by removing the abnormal fluid filled sac in the scrotum or in the inguinal canal. After injecting an area with local anesthetic and using aseptic techniques, the physician makes an incision in the scrotum or in the inguinal area. Care is taken to keep the hydrocele intact while it is dissected free of its attachments to the testis and other structures. The sac is opened high along its front surface and the testis is pushed up through the sac and out through the incision. This inverts the hydrocele sac which is tacked by suturing to the spermatic cord structures behind the testis. The testis is returned to the scrotum and is anchored to the inside of the scrotum with three sutures to prevent later torsion or twisting of the testis. A rubber drain may be left in the scrotum and the incision closed in layers by suturing.

55100
After adequate local anesthesia, the physician makes an incision directly into the abscess of the scrotal wall. Pus is expressed and a drain or medicated gauze packing placed in the abscess cavity.

55110
The physician makes an incision in the scrotum for the purpose of direct visual inspection of the contents of the scrotum. This may involve one or both sides of the scrotum and may be done through one or two incisions and require incisions through the various layers of tissues to expose the testis and other structures. A drain may be left in the scrotum and the incisions closed in successive layers of sutures.

55120
The physician makes an incision in the scrotum for the purpose of foreign body removal. This may involve one or both sides of the scrotum and may be done through one or two incisions and may require incisions through the various layers of tissues to expose and locate the object. The foreign body is identified and isolated and removed with care to avoid damaging tissues in the scrotum. A drain may be placed in the scrotum and the incisions closed in successive layers of sutures.

55150
The physician removes excessive or diseased scrotal skin by excision. The extent of the procedure is dependent upon the disease process and the degree of involvement. The physician makes incisions in the scrotal skin, taking care to avoid injury to the underlying scrotal contents. In the simple case, the excess skin is removed and the defects closed in layers by suturing. In the more involved cases the testes and spermatic cords must be mobilized and removed from the scrotum and swung out of the way by making incisions in the inguinal areas. The affected scrotal skin is excised and the testes and cord structures returned to their anatomic positions. If not enough scrotal skin remains, flaps of skin are raised from the adjacent thighs and rotated to cover the testes. These grafts or flaps are separately reported. Rubber drains may be left in the scrotum and the operative site closed in layers by suturing.

55175-55180
The physician repairs defects and developmental abnormalities of the scrotum by wound revisions or the creation and suturing of simple scrotal skin flaps in 55175. In 55180, the reconstruction is more complex and the physician uses free skin grafts, mesh grafts, and/or the extensive use of rotational pedicle grafts from adjacent skin. These flaps or grafts are separately reported.

55200
The physician enters the vas deferens (the tube that carries spermatozoa from the testis) for purpose of obtaining a sample of semen or testing the patency of the tubes. Under local anesthesia, an incision is made in the upper outer scrotum overlying the spermatic cord. The tissues are dissected to expose the vas deferens. The tube is entered by puncturing with a small needle and fluid samples removed or solution injected to check for blockages. An alternate method involves the tube being cut open with a scalpel. A blunt needle is placed in the tube under direct vision and fluid samples removed or the tube checked for patency. If an incision is made in the tube, the tube must be repaired using microsurgical techniques before the scrotal incisions are closed in layers by suturing.

55250
The physician grasps the upper scrotum near the inguinal area and holds the spermatic cord between the thumb and the index finger. The skin overlying the immobilized cord is injected with local anesthetic and an incision is made through the scrotal wall to expose the tubular structures. Another incision is made to expose the vas deferens (spermatic tube) and the tissues dissected to free it from the adjacent vessels and supporting tissues. The isolated vas deferens is cut in two places and the intervening section of tube is removed. The cut ends of the vas deferens are cauterized and tied with suture material. The incisions are closed in layers by suturing. The procedure is usually repeated on the opposite side.

55300
The physician enters the vas deferens (the tube that carries spermatozoa from the testis) for purpose of testing the patency of the spermatozoa collecting system. An incision is made in the upper outer scrotum overlying the spermatic cord and the tissues dissected to expose the vas deferens.

55400
The physician treats a blockage in the vas deferens, the tube that carries semen. After anesthesia, an incision is made in the scrotum. The testis with its attached epididymis and the vas deferens are brought out of the wound. Dye injection studies and semen sampling is often done during the operation to determine the site of the blockage and to accurately choose the segment of tube for excision. The vas deferens is transected in two places, one on each side of the blocked area and the abnormal segment removed. The created cut ends are sutured together in one or two layers with care to align accurately the lumens of the tubes. The testis and associated structures are returned to the scrotum. A rubber drain is often placed in the scrotum and the incisions closed by suturing.

55450
The physician performs a ligation of the vas deferens (vasectomy) without cutting an incision in the skin. The procedure is done under local anesthesia. With thumb and index finger the surgeon grasps the spermatic cord beneath the skin, high in the scrotum near the inguinal area. The skin is pulled taught with the spermatic cord just underneath the skin. An instrument is pressed against the structures and activated sequentially. The instrument punctures the skin and cuts the spermatic cord, then clips the cord on each side of the cut area. The procedure may be repeated on the opposite side. The resulting puncture wounds are bandaged.

55500
A hydrocele is an abnormal fluid-filled sac. The physician treats a hydrocele of the spermatic cord by removing from the spermatic cord above the testis in the scrotum or in the inguinal canal. After injecting the area with local anesthetic, the physician makes an incision in the scrotum or in the inguinal area. The hydrocele is kept intact while it is freed of its attachments to the spermatic cord. The sac is opened, drained, and excised all the way to the internal inguinal ring in the upper groin area. The remaining tissues are repaired and closed by suturing. The testis is anchored to the inside of the scrotum with three sutures to prevent later torsion or twisting of the testis. A rubber drain may be placed in the scrotum and the incision closed in layers by suturing.

55520
The physician removes a lesion of the spermatic cord by dissection and excision. After injecting the area with local anesthetic, the physician makes an incision in the scrotum or in the inguinal area and dissects the tissues to expose the lesion. Care is taken to keep the lesion intact while it is dissected free of its attachments to the spermatic cord. This may involve mobilization of the testis. The lesion is removed by cutting all of its attachments. The tissues damaged during the dissection are repaired and closed by suturing. If the testis has been mobilized, it is anchored to the inside of the scrotum with three sutures to prevent later torsion or twisting. A drain may be placed in the scrotum and the incision is closed in layers by suturing.

55530
A varicocele is an abnormal dilation of the veins of the spermatic cord in the scrotum. The physician ligates the spermatic veins and/or excises a varicocele. An incision is made in the pubic area on the affected side and carried down to the spermatic cord as passes

through the inguinal canal. The cord is brought up into the incision and the structures of the cord are dissected, the veins identified, and ligated with suture material. Alternately, an incision is made in the scrotum and the dilated veins ligated separately may be removed. The incision is closed in layers by suturing.

55535
The physician ligates the spermatic veins and/or excises a varicocele which is an abnormal dilation of the veins of the spermatic cord in the scrotum. An incision is made in lateral lower abdomen just medial to the bony prominence of the pelvic bone on the affected side and carried down through the abdominal musculature to the spermatic vein and artery. The vein is identified and ligated (tied off) with suture material. The abdominal incision is closed in layers by suturing.

55540
The physician repairs an inguinal hernia and ligates the spermatic veins or excises a varicocele (an abnormal dilation of the veins of the spermatic cord in the scrotum). An incision is made in the pubic area on the affected side to expose the spermatic cord as it passes through the inguinal canal. The cord is brought into the incision, the structures of the cord are dissected, and the veins identified and ligated. The hernia is repaired through the same incision by folding and suturing of tissues to strengthen the abdominal wall and correct the weakness responsible for the hernia. Alternately, an incision is made in the scrotum and the dilated veins ligated separately and may be removed (excision) and a second incision made for hernia repair. All incisions are closed in layers by suturing.

55550
The physician ligates (ties or binds with suture) the spermatic veins and/or excises a varicocele which is an abnormal dilation of the veins of the spermatic cord in the scrotum. An umbilical port is created by placing a trocar at the level of the umbilicus. The abdominal wall is insufflated. The laparoscope is placed through the umbilical port and additional trocars are placed into the abdominal or pelvic cavity. The physician uses the laparoscope fitted with a fiberoptic camera and/or an operating instrument to explore and surgically ligate the spermatic veins to repair or remove the varicocele. The structures of the cord are dissected, the veins identified, and ligated with suture. The abdomen is deflated, the trocars removed, and the incisions are closed with sutures.

55600-55605
The physician incises or punctures one of the seminal vesicles, paired glands that lie behind the urinary bladder and produce fluid that is mixed with the semen produced in the testis. The seminal vesicle is approached through an incision in the lower abdomen or an incision in the perineum (area between the base of the scrotum and the anus). In the abdominal method, the physician retracts the bladder forward toward the pubic bone to expose the back of the bladder where the seminal vesicles are positioned, or the surgeon cuts through the front and back walls to gain access to the gland. The operative wounds are closed in layers by suturing. If the procedure does not require extensive dissection, report 55600; if extensive, report 55605.

55650
The physician removes one of the seminal vesicles, paired glands that lie behind the urinary bladder and produce a fluid that is mixed with semen from the testis. Through an incision in the lower abdomen or an incision in the perineum (area between the base of the scrotum and the anus) the seminal vesicle is approached. If the abdominal method is used the surgeon retracts the bladder forward toward the pubic bone to expose the back of the bladder where the seminal vesicles are positioned or the surgeon cuts through the front and back walls to gain access to the glands. The surgeon dissects the gland free of its attachments and clips it at its joint with the ejaculatory duct and removes it. The operative wounds are closed in layers by suturing.

55680
The physician excises a Mullerian duct cyst, a remnant of the prenatal development of the seminal vesicle. The seminal vesicles are paired glands that lie behind the urinary bladder and produce a fluid that is mixed with the semen from the testis. Through an incision in the lower abdomen or an incision in the perineum (area between the base of the scrotum and the anus) the seminal vesicle is approached. If the abdominal method is used, the surgeon retracts the bladder forward toward the pubic bone to expose the back of the bladder where the seminal vesicles are positioned or the surgeon cuts through the front and back walls to gain access to the glands. The surgeon dissects the cyst free of its attachments and clips it at the attachment to the seminal vesicle and removes it. The operative wounds are closed in layers by suturing.

55700
The physician obtains tissue from the prostate for analysis by needle or punch biopsy through one or more of three approaches. The biopsy needle is passed into the suspect area of the prostate by puncturing through skin of the perineum (the area between the base of the scrotum and the anus), by advancing the needle into the rectum by guidance with the index finger and puncturing through the rectal mucosa, or by advancing a biopsy instrument through the urethra. The biopsy needle is inserted into the prostate guided by an index finger or by ultrasound and the needle biopsy sheath is advanced over the needle and twisted to shear off the enclosed sample. The needle is withdrawn, containing the sample. This may be repeated two or more times to assure adequate sampling and the puncture site is bandaged.

55705
The physician obtains tissue from the prostate for analysis by direct incisional sampling. The prostate is usually approached in one of three ways: through skin of the perineum (the area between the base of the scrotum and the anus), through the rectal mucosa, or by advancing a biopsy instrument through the urethra. In any case, an incision is made and the tissues dissected to expose the prostate. The area of concern is identified and an excision is performed to remove tissue for analysis. Bleeding is controlled and the dissected tissues and skin incision are closed in layers by suturing.

55706
The physician uses stereotactic template-guided saturation sampling biopsies to map prostate cancer in high-risk patients. Transrectal ultrasound is used to visualize the prostate. Zones or reference planes of the prostate are determined, and a brachytherapy grid is placed against the perineum and rectum. Using the transperineal route under ultrasonic guidance, multiple biopsies are taken of the prostate. Typically, from 20 to 40 biopsies are taken using the grid as a guide, beginning at the highest point in the prostate and moving right to left in a row, down row by row until the grid is complete. In deeper planes, both a proximal and distal biopsy may be obtained. Each biopsy sample is marked for its coordinates, and all are mapped in 3D to determine the extent and exact position of malignant cells.

55720-55725
The physician performs a simple prostatotomy (cutting or puncturing the prostate) through one of two usual approaches. An aspirating needle is passed into the abscessed area of the prostate by puncturing through skin of the perineum (the area between the base of the scrotum and the anus), or by advancing the needle into the rectum by guidance with the index finger and puncturing through the rectal mucosa. The needle is inserted into the abscess in the prostate guided by an index finger or by ultrasound and the contents of the abscess removed by aspiration. The needle is withdrawn and the puncture site bandaged. Report 55720 for simple drainage, or 55725 if the procedure is complicated by excessive bleeding, infection, or other problem.

55801
The physician performs a prostatectomy (removal of the prostate gland) through an incision made in the perineum. The caliber (internal diameter) of the urethra is measured and if it is not adequate, the opening of the urethra is enlarged (meatotomy) and the diameter of the penile urethra is enlarged with an instrument (internal urethrotomy). A curved instrument (Lowery Tractor) is advanced into the urethra to the prostate to help to identify the structures and aid in the dissection. Through the perineal incision and with manipulation of the tractor, the tissues are dissected to expose the prostate. The curved tractor instrument in the urethra is replaced with a straight tractor. A portion of the prostate or the entire gland is removed with care to preserve the seminal vesicles. The operation is "subtotal" because the seminal vesicles remain intact. The bladder outlet is revised and the vas deferens is ligated and may be partially removed (vasectomy). Bleeding is controlled by ligation or cautery. A Foley catheter is placed in the bladder. A rubber drain may be placed in the site of the operative wound and brought out through a separate stab wound. The dissected tissues and the skin incision are closed in layers by suturing.

55810-55812
The physician performs a radical prostatectomy through an incision made in the skin between the base of the scrotum and the anus. If the internal diameter of the urethra is not adequate, the opening of the urethra is enlarged (meatotomy) and the diameter of the penile urethra is enlarged with an instrument (internal urethrotomy). A curved instrument (Lowery Tractor) is advanced into the urethra to the prostate to aid in the dissection. Through the perineal incision and with manipulation of the tractor, the tissues are dissected to expose the prostate. The curved tractor instrument in the urethra is replaced with a straight tractor. The entire gland is removed along with the seminal vesicles and the vas deferens. The bladder outlet is revised and bleeding controlled by ligation or cautery. In 55812, local lymph nodes are also removed for analysis. A Foley catheter is placed and left in the bladder. A rubber drain may be placed in the site of the operative wound and brought out through a separate stab wound. The dissected tissues and the skin incision are closed in layers by suturing.

55815
The physician removes the prostate gland through an incision made in the perineum and also a pelvic lymphadenectomy through a separate lower abdominal incision. A midline abdominal incision is made from the upper to the lower abdomen and the back wall of the abdomen is exposed. All lymph nodes along back wall of the pelvic and abdominal cavities are removed. The abdominal wound is closed in layers by suturing. In preparation for removal of the prostate, the caliber (internal diameter) of the urethra is measured and if it is not adequate the opening of the urethra is enlarged (meatotomy) and the diameter of the penile urethra is enlarged with an instrument (internal urethrotomy). A curved instrument (Lowery Tractor) is advanced into the urethra to aid in the dissection. Through the perineal incision and with manipulation of the tractor, the tissues are dissected to expose the prostate. The curved tractor instrument in the urethra is replaced with a straight tractor. The gland is removed along with the seminal vesicles and the vas deferens. The bladder outlet is revised and bleeding controlled by ligation or

cautery. A Foley catheter is placed and left in the bladder. A rubber drain may be placed in the site of the operative wound and brought out through a separate stab wound. The dissected tissues and the skin incision are closed in layers by suturing.

55821
The physician removes the prostate gland through an incision made in the lower abdomen just above the pubic area. In preparation for removal of the prostate, the caliber (internal diameter) of the urethra is measured and if it is not adequate the opening of the urethra is enlarged (meatotomy) and the diameter of the penile urethra is enlarged with an instrument (internal urethrotomy) and a catheter is passed into the urethra into the bladder. Through the lower abdominal incision the urinary bladder is exposed and opened by an incision in the region just above the bladder neck. During the dissection to expose the bladder a vasectomy may be performed. The bladder mucosa over the prostate is removed by excision to expose the prostate. The gland is removed by "shelling it out" by blunt dissection with the surgeon's index finger. The bladder outlet and the bladder wall are revised and bleeding controlled by packing with rolls of gauze, by ligation or cautery of bleeding vessels. A second catheter is placed and left in the bladder through the incision in the lower abdomen. A rubber drain is placed in the space between the pubic bone and the bladder and brought out through a separate stab wound. The dissected tissues and the skin incision are closed in layers by suturing.

55831
The physician removes the prostate gland through an incision made in the lower abdomen just above the pubic area. In preparation for removal of the prostate, the caliber (internal diameter) of the urethra is measured and if it is not adequate the opening of the urethra is enlarged (meatotomy) and the diameter of the penile urethra is enlarged with an instrument (internal urethrotomy) and a catheter is passed into the urethra into the bladder. Through the lower abdominal incision the urinary bladder is exposed and opened by an incision in the region just above the bladder neck. During the dissection to expose the bladder a vasectomy may be performed. The bladder mucosa over the prostate is removed by excision to expose the prostate. The gland is removed by "shelling it out" by blunt dissection with the surgeon's index finger. The bladder outlet and the bladder wall are revised and bleeding controlled by packing with rolls of gauze, by ligation or cautery of bleeding vessels. A second catheter is placed and left in the bladder through the incision in the lower abdomen. A rubber drain is placed between the pubic bone and the bladder and brought out through a separate stab wound. The dissected tissues and the skin incision are closed in layers by suturing.

55840
The physician performs a radical prostatectomy (removal of the prostate gland) through an incision made in the lower abdomen just above the pubic area. In preparation for removal of the prostate, a catheter is passed into the urethra into the bladder. Through a lower abdominal incision, with or without care to spare the nerves in the area, the urinary bladder is exposed and displaced backwards to enter the space behind the pubic bone and expose the area of the prostate. The gland with the capsule intact and the seminal vesicles and the portions of the vas deferens in the area are removed by freeing the prostate by blunt dissection and by transecting the urethra and cutting through the bladder outlet. The urinary catheter is brought into the operative site and used to create traction for the dissection. A second catheter is placed in the bladder after the first one is removed along with the prostate. The transected urethra is repaired by suturing to the newly created bladder outlet. A rubber drain is placed in the space between the pubic bone and the bladder and brought out through a separate stab wound. The dissected tissues and the skin incision are closed in layers by suturing.

55842
The physician performs a radical prostatectomy and a pelvic lymph node biopsy through a midline abdominal incision (this may be done in two stages within seven to 10 days). A midline incision is made from the upper to the lower abdomen and the abdominal cavity is entered. The back wall of the abdomen is exposed and the lymph nodes are checked for spread of tumor. Some may be removed and/or biopsied. Through the abdominal incision, with or without sparing the nerves in the area, the urinary bladder is exposed and displaced backwards to enter the space behind the pubic bone and expose the area of the prostate. The gland with the capsule intact, the seminal vesicles, and portions of the vas deferens in the area are removed by freeing the prostate by blunt dissection and by transecting the urethra and cutting through the bladder outlet. The urinary catheter is brought into the operative site and used to create traction for the dissection. A second catheter is placed in the bladder after the first one is removed along with the prostate. The transected urethra is repaired by suturing it to the newly created bladder outlet. A rubber drain is placed between the pubic bone and the bladder and brought out through a separate stab wound.

55845
The physician performs a radical prostatectomy and a pelvic lymph node biopsy through a midline abdominal incision (this may be done in two stages within seven to 10 days). A midline incision is made from the upper to the lower abdomen and the abdominal cavity is entered. The back wall of the abdomen is exposed and all of the lymph nodes along

the back wall of the pelvic and abdominal cavities are removed. In preparation for removal of the prostate, a catheter is passed into the urethra and into the bladder. Through the abdominal incision, with or without care to spare the nerves in the area, the urinary bladder is exposed and displaced backwards to enter the space behind the pubic bone and expose the area of the prostate. The gland with the capsule intact, the seminal vesicles, and the portions of the vas deferens in the area are removed by freeing the prostate by blunt dissection and by transecting the urethra and cutting through the bladder outlet. The urinary catheter is brought into the operative site and used to create traction for the dissection. A second catheter is placed in the bladder after the first one is removed along with the prostate. The dissected tissues and the skin incision are closed in layers by suturing.

55860

Through an incision made in the lower abdomen just above the pubic area, the physician inserts radioactive materials in the prostate. In preparation for the radiation treatment, a catheter is passed into the urethra into the bladder and a sheath is inserted into the rectum. Through the lower abdominal incision the urinary bladder is exposed and displaced backwards to enter the space behind the pubic bone and expose the prostate gland. With a finger in the rectum to guide the placement, the physician passes a hollow needle into the prostate through the abdominal incision. The needle is positioned in the prostate tumor and radioactive seeds are introduced into the needle and implanted in the prostate using an applicator. The needle is withdrawn a few millimeters and another seed is placed. This is repeated several times through multiple needle insertions. A rubber drain(s) is placed in the space between the pubic bone and the bladder and brought out through the incision wound. The dissected tissues and the skin incision are closed in layers by suturing. Alternatively, other approaches may be used in a similar fashion.

55862

Through an incision made in the abdomen, the physician inserts radioactive materials in the prostate and examines the pelvic and abdominal lymph nodes. A midline incision is made from the upper to the lower abdomen and the abdominal cavity is entered. The back wall of the abdomen is exposed and the lymph nodes are checked for spread of tumor. Some may be removed and/or biopsied. In preparation for the radiation treatment, a catheter is passed into the urethra into the bladder and a sheath is inserted into the rectum. Through the lower abdominal incision the urinary bladder is exposed and displaced backwards to enter the space behind the pubic bone and expose the prostate gland. With a finger in the rectum to guide the placement, the physician passes a hollow needle into the prostate through the abdominal incision. The needle is positioned in the prostate tumor and radioactive seeds are introduced into the needle and implanted in the prostate using an applicator. The needle is withdrawn a few millimeters and another seed is placed. This is repeated several times through multiple needle insertions. A rubber drain(s) is placed between the pubic bone and the bladder and brought out through the incision wound. The dissected tissues and the skin incision are closed in layers by suturing. Alternatively, other approaches may be used in a similar fashion.

55865

Through an incision made in the abdomen, the physician inserts radioactive materials in the prostate and examines the pelvic and abdominal lymph nodes. A midline incision is made from the upper to the lower abdomen and the abdominal cavity is entered. The back wall of the abdomen is exposed and all the lymph nodes along back wall of the pelvic and abdominal cavities are removed. In preparation for the radiation treatment, a catheter is passed into the urethra into the bladder and a sheath is inserted into the rectum. Through the lower abdominal incision the urinary bladder is exposed and displaced backwards to enter the space behind the pubic bone and expose the prostate gland. With a finger in the rectum to guide the placement, the physician passes a hollow needle into the prostate through the abdominal incision. The needle is positioned in the prostate tumor and radioactive seeds are introduced into the needle and implanted in the prostate using an applicator. The needle is withdrawn a few millimeters and another seed is placed. This is repeated several times through multiple needle insertions. A rubber drain(s) is placed between the pubic bone and the bladder and brought out through the incision wound. The dissected tissues and the skin incision are closed in layers by suturing. Alternatively, other approaches may be used in a similar fashion.

55866

The surgeon performs a laparoscopic radial prostatectomy. This cannot be done on a patient with prior open prostate surgery. The patient is positioned for laparoscopic surgery with the legs in low lithotomy position for rectal access. Five trocars are placed and the cavity is insufflated with gas. The vas deferens is divided, the seminal vesicles are mobilized, and the prostate is dissected off the rectum. The space of Retzius is developed by dividing the urachus medial to the umbilical ligaments. The endopelvic fascia is incised on both sides and the prostatic levator muscle attachments are bluntly removed. A suture is passed between the urethra and dorsal venous complex and tied. A second suture is passed through the anterior prostate. The bladder neck is opened anteriorly, the posterior margin is separated from the prostate, and the underlying seminal vesicles are exposed. The two prostatic pedicles are divided close to the prostate with the involved seminal vesicle retracted. The back surface of the prostate on each side is dissected from the neurovascular bundles until the prostate remains attached only at the apex. Between the two previously placed sutures, the dorsal vein is divided, the urethra is exposed, and the catheter is removed. The urethra is completely divided. The surgeon places a finger in the rectum for guidance and divides the muscles and remaining attachments to free the prostate completely. The vesicourethral anastomosis is done next with polyglycolic acid suture in running or interrupted simple sutures. A Foley catheter is placed and the anastomosis of the bladder to the urethra is tested. A suction drain is placed through a trocar site and the prostate is removed through a small port site incision.

55870

The physician uses an electrovibratory device that stimulates ejaculation. The electrostimulator probe is placed in the rectum and positioned adjacent to the prostate gland and a current of electricity is passed into the region of the prostate, seminal vesicles and the vas deferens. The stimulation excites the nerves of the area, causing ejaculation. The semen is collected and used for artificial insemination.

55873

The physician performs cryosurgical ablation of the prostate with ultrasonic guidance and monitoring. The physician places a suprapubic catheter into the bladder through a stab incision just above the pubic hairline. Next, the physician inserts a warming catheter through the urethra and into the bladder. The scrotum is elevated out of the operative field using a gauze sling. An ultrasound probe is inserted into the rectum to monitor the freezing process, and to view in real-time the probe placement during the procedure. Under ultrasonic guidance, the surgeon inserts from three to eight needles into the perineum and advances the needles into the prostate. Into each needle the surgeon advances a guidewire used to facilitate instrumentation. The skin is incised and a dilator is inserted over each guidewire to dilate the channels. Saline is injected to aid visibility of the ultrasound, the guidewire is removed, and a cryoprobe (3 mm diameter) is inserted through each dilator for direct contact with the prostate tissue. The cryoprobes, which deliver super-cooled liquid nitrogen or argon gas (both inert materials) to the prostate, are turned on at -70°C. Up to five cryoprobes can be running simultaneously at any one time. The five cryoprobes are turned on, taking the temperature down to -190°C, while the warming catheter guards against freezing the ureter. If the prostate thaws, the probes may be repositioned, and a second freeze may be performed. Once the prostate gland is completely frozen (resembling an ice ball) and all of the visible prostate tissue is destroyed, the surgeon removes the probes and applies pressure to the perineum to prevent hematoma formation. The punctures are sutured shut and the urethral warming catheter is removed.

55875

Transperineal placement of needles or catheters into the prostate gland for interstitial radioelement application is a form of brachytherapy. Brachytherapy is the application of radioactive isotopes for internal radiation. Radioactive material is encapsulated for interstitial implantation into the prostate tissue. Using separately reportable ultrasound or fluoroscopic guidance, the physician inserts the encapsulated radioactive seeds directly into the prostate tissue transperineally, using appropriate applicators (thin catheter tubes or needles). A previous transrectal ultrasound has been done on the volume of the prostate to map out the precise locations of the radioactive seeds. The radioactive isotopes, such as Iodine-125 or Palladium-103, contained within the tiny seeds are left in place and deliver their dose of radiation over a period of months. They do not cause any harm after they have become inert. This method provides radiation to the prescribed body area while minimizing exposure to normal tissue.

55876

The physician places interstitial devices for radiation therapy guidance into the prostate using a percutaneous technique. In one method, the patient is placed in the lithotomy position. Under guidance from a transrectal ultrasound wand, the physician injects a small capsule into the tissue of the prostate using a percutaneous needle injection device. The capsule allows for precision in targeting radiation and/or for measuring the radiation doses received. An injected capsule fiducial marker is visible by ultrasound and fluoroscopy, allowing for an accurate triangulation of the tissue to be treated. An injected capsule dosimeter relays radiation dose information so that the clinical team can monitor for any deviation between the radiation plan and the actual radiation received by the patient. The inserted capsule may act as a fiducial marker or dosimeter, or in many cases, will serve in both roles. This code reports the insertion of one or more of these capsules into the patient's prostate during a single surgical session.

55920

The physician places needles or catheters into the pelvic organs and/or genitalia, excluding the prostate, for subsequent interstitial radioelement application. The radioactive isotopes that are introduced subsequently, such as iodine-125 or palladium-103, are contained within tiny seeds that are left in place to deliver radiation over a period of months. They do not cause any harm after becoming inert. This method provides radiation to the prescribed body area while minimizing exposure to normal tissue.

55970

In a series of staged procedures, the physician removes portions of the male genitalia and forms female external genitals. The penis is dissected and portions are removed with care to preserve vital nerves and vessels in order to fashion a clitoris-like structure. The urethral opening is moved to a position similar to that of a normal female. A vagina is made by dissecting and opening the perineum. This opening is lined using pedicle or split thickness grafts. Labia are created out of skin from the scrotum and adjacent tissue. A stent or obturator is usually left in place in the newly created vagina for three weeks or longer.

55980
In a series of staged procedures, the physician forms a penis and scrotum using pedicle flap grafts and free skin grafts. Portions of the clitoris are used as well as the adjacent skin. Prostheses are often placed in the penis in order to have a sexually functional organ. Prosthetic testicles are fixed in the scrotum. The vagina is closed or removed.

56405
The vulva includes the labia majora, labia minora, mons pubis, bulb of the vestibule, vestibule of the vagina, greater and lesser vestibular glands, and vaginal orifice. The perineum is the area between the vulva and the anus. The physician makes an incision into the abscess at its softest point and drains the purulent contents. The cavity of the abscess is flushed and often packed with medicated gauze to facilitate drainage.

56420
The physician incises and drains a Bartholin's gland abscess. Bartholin's gland is at the end of the bulb of the vestibule of the vagina and is connected by a duct to the mucosa at the opening of the vagina. The physician makes an incision just inside the opening of the vagina through the mucosal surface into the cavity of the abscess to flush and drain it. A small wick or catheter may be left in the cavity to facilitate drainage.

56440
The physician treats a Bartholin's gland cyst with marsupialization. Bartholin's gland is at the end of the bulb of the vestibule of the vagina and is connected by a duct to the mucosa at the opening of the vagina. The physician makes an elliptical excision over the center of the Bartholin's gland cyst and drains it. The lining of the cyst is everted and approximated to the vaginal mucosa with sutures creating a pouch. Marsupialization prevents recurrent cysts and infections.

56441
The labia majora and minora are the greater and lesser folds of skin on the pudendum on either side of the vagina. The physician separates the labia majora from the labia minora, which are fused by fibrous bands of scar tissue. Using a blunt instrument and/or scissors, the labia are separated by breaking or cutting the fibrous tissue. The procedure is accomplished using general or local anesthesia.

56442
The physician performs a hymenotomy. A hymen is a membrane that partially or wholly occludes the vaginal opening. Following local injection of an anesthetic, the physician incises the hymenal membrane with a stellate (star-shaped) incision. This procedure is sometimes preceded by aspiration of the intact membrane with a needle and syringe.

56501-56515
The vulva includes the labia majora, labia minora, mons pubis, bulb of the vestibule, vestibule of the vagina, greater and lesser vestibular glands, and vaginal orifice. The physician destroys one or more lesions of the vulva, After examining the lower genital tract and perianal area with a colposcope, the physician destroys any lesions of the vulva by laser surgery, electrosurgery, chemosurgery, cryosurgery, or excision. Use 56501 to report single, simple lesion destruction, or 56515 to report multiple or complicated destruction of extensive vulvar lesions.

56605-56606
The vulva includes the labia majora, labia minora, mons pubis, bulb of the vestibule, vestibule of the vagina, greater and lesser vestibular glands, and vaginal orifice. The perineum is the area between the vulva and the anus. The physician removes a sample of tissue from the vulva or perineum. After injecting a local anesthetic around the suspect tissue, the physician obtains a sample using a skin punch or sharp scalpel. A clip or suture can be used to control bleeding if pressure is not successful. Use 56605 for the biopsy of one lesion and 56606 for each additional lesion.

56620-56625
The physician removes part or all of the vulva to treat premalignant or malignant lesions. A simple complete vulvectomy includes removal of all of the labia majora, labia minora, and clitoris, while a simple, partial vulvectomy may include removal of part or all of the labia majora and labia minora on one side and the clitoris. The physician examines the lower genital tract and the perianal skin through a colposcope. In 56620, a wide semi-elliptical incision that contains the diseased area is made. In 56625, two wide elliptical incisions encompassing the vulvar area are made. One elliptical incision extends from well above the clitoris around both labia majora to a point just in front of the anus. The second elliptical incision starts at a point between the clitoris and the opening of the urethra and is carried around both sides of the opening of the vagina. The underlying subcutaneous fatty tissue is removed along with the large portion of excised skin. Vessels are clamped and tied off with sutures or are electrocoagulated to control bleeding. The considerable defect is usually closed in layers using separately reportable plastic techniques. Vaginal gauze packing may be placed in the vagina.

56630
The physician removes part of the vulva to treat malignancy. A partial radical vulvectomy includes partial or complete removal of a large, deep segment of skin from the following structures: abdomen and groin, labia majora, labia minora, clitoris, mons veneris, and terminal portions of the urethra, vagina, and other vulvar organs. Through incisions in the lower abdomen, thighs, and vulvar area, the physician removes skin, subcutaneous fatty tissue, and deeper tissue. Also included in the en bloc removal of tissue are portions of the saphenous veins and ligaments and the target lesion. The resulting large and disfiguring defect is usually closed using separately reported plastic surgical techniques, which may include pedicle flaps or free skin grafts. Subcutaneous rubber drains may be left in the surgical site, and vaginal gauze packing may be placed in the vagina.

56631-56632
The physician removes part of the vulva to treat malignancy. A partial radical vulvectomy includes the partial or complete removal of a large, deep segment of skin and tissue from the abdomen and groin, labia majora and minora, clitoris, mons veneris, and terminal portions of the urethra, vagina, and other vulvar organs. Through incisions in the lower abdomen, thighs, and vulvar area, the physician removes skin, subcutaneous fatty tissue, and deeper tissue. The physician also removes superficial and deep inguinal lymph nodes and adjacent femoral lymph nodes on one side in 56631 and on both sides in 56632. Also included in the en bloc removal of tissue are portions of the saphenous veins and ligaments and the target lesion. The resulting large and disfiguring defect is usually closed in layers using plastic surgical techniques, which may include pedicle flaps or free skin grafts. Subcutaneous rubber drains may be left in the surgical site, and vaginal gauze packing may be placed in the vagina.

56633
The physician removes the vulva to treat malignancy. A complete radical vulvectomy includes the removal of a large, deep segment of skin and tissue from the following structures: abdomen and groin, labia majora, labia minora, clitoris, mons veneris, and terminal portions of the urethra, vagina, and other vulvar organs. Deep tissue from more than 80 percent of the vulva is excised. Through incisions in the lower abdomen, thighs, and vulvar area, the physician removes skin, subcutaneous fatty tissue, and deeper tissues. Also included in the en bloc removal of tissue are portions of the saphenous veins and ligaments and the target lesion. The resulting large and disfiguring defect is usually closed in layers using separately reported plastic surgical techniques, which may include pedicle flaps or free skin grafts. Subcutaneous rubber drains may be used, and vaginal gauze packing may be placed in the vagina.

56634-56637
The physician removes the vulva to treat malignancy. A complete radical vulvectomy includes the removal of a large, deep segment of skin and tissue from the lower abdomen and groin, labia majora and minora, clitoris, mons veneris, and terminal portions of the urethra, vagina, and other vulvar organs. Deep tissue from more than 80 percent of the vulva is removed. Through incisions in the lower abdomen, thighs, and vulvar area, the physician removes skin, subcutaneous fatty tissue, and deeper tissues. The physician also removes the inguinal and femoral lymph nodes on one side in 56634 and on both sides in 56637. Also included in the en bloc removal of tissue are portions of the saphenous veins and ligaments and the target lesion. The resulting large and disfiguring defect is usually closed in layers using plastic surgical techniques, which may include pedicle flaps or free skin grafts. Subcutaneous rubber drains may be used, and vaginal gauze packing may be placed in the vagina.

56640
The physician removes the vulva to treat malignancy. A complete radical vulvectomy includes the removal of a large, deep segment of skin and tissue from the following structures: lower abdomen and groin, labia majora, labia minora, clitoris, mons veneris, and terminal portions of the urethra, vagina, and other vulvar organs. Deep tissue from more than 80 percent of the vulva is removed. Through incisions in the lower abdomen, thighs, and vulvar area, the physician removes skin, subcutaneous fatty tissue, and deeper tissue. The physician also removes the inguinal and femoral lymph nodes on both sides as well as the iliac and pelvic lymph nodes in the pelvic cavity, which is entered through an abdominal incision. Also included in the en bloc removal of tissue are portions of the saphenous veins and ligaments and the target lesion. The resulting large and disfiguring defect is usually closed in layers using separately reported plastic surgical techniques, which may include pedicle flaps or free skin grafts. Subcutaneous rubber drains may be used, and vaginal gauze packing may be placed in the vagina.

56700
A hymen is a membrane that partially or wholly occludes the vaginal opening. Following local injection of an anesthetic, the physician excises a portion of the hymenal membrane. Using a scalpel or scissors, the physician removes the membrane at its junction with the opening of the vagina. The cut margins of the vaginal mucosa are sutured with fine, absorbable material.

56740
The physician removes a cystic Bartholin's gland, which lies at the tail end of the bulb of the vestibular opening just inside of the vagina. The physician makes an incision through the vaginal mucosa. The cyst is

isolated through the vaginal incision by dissecting the deeper fatty tissues and excised. The remaining cavity and skin are closed in layers using absorbable material.

56800
The physician repairs and restores the anatomy of the opening of the vagina by excising scar tissue and strengthening the supporting tissues using tissue flaps and suturing techniques. This procedure varies greatly from patient to patient, depending on the defect to be corrected.

56805
The physician reduces the size of an enlarged clitoris, which has been masculinized by the production of male hormones from an abnormal adrenal gland. A portion of the body of the clitoris is resected with care to ensure preservation of vital nerves and blood vessels to the glans of the clitoris. The incisions are closed using plastic surgical techniques.

56810
With upward traction on the vagina, the physician makes an incision from the lower vaginal opening to a point just in front of the anus. The underlying weakened tissues are dissected and repaired and tightened by suturing. This restores strength to the pelvic floor, closes tissue defects, and improves function of the perineal muscles.

56820-56821
The physician performs a colposcopy of the vulva, the external genitalia region of the female that includes the labia, clitoris, mons pubis, vaginal vestibule, bulb and glands, and the vaginal orifice. The patient is placed in the lithotomy position and the vulva is inspected through the colposcope, a binocular microscope used for direct visualization of the vagina and cervix. The bright light of the colposcope is directed so as to inspect the vulva and perianal area for any lesions or ulceration. In 56821, a biopsy is taken of any vulvar tissue in question under direct vision. The number and size of the biopsy will depend on the lesions. Pressure is applied and hemostasis of the biopsy site is achieved.

57000
Colpotomy is an incision in the wall of the vagina, usually to access a recess between the rectum and uterus formed by a fold in the peritoneum (cul-de-sac). Through a speculum inserted in the vagina, the physician grasps the posterior lip of the cervix with a toothed instrument called a tenaculum. The cervix is lifted, exposing the posterior vaginal pouch. An incision is made through the back wall of the vagina into the posterior pelvic cavity. Through this opening, the pelvic cavity can be explored using instruments. After exploration, the physician closes the incision with absorbable sutures.

57010
Colpotomy is an incision in the wall of the vagina, usually to access a recess between the rectum and uterus formed by a fold in the peritoneum (cul de sac). Through a speculum inserted in the vagina, the physician grasps the posterior lip of the cervix with a toothed instrument called a tenaculum. The cervix is lifted, exposing the posterior vaginal pouch. An incision is made through the back wall of the vagina into the posterior pelvic cavity. Through this opening, the pelvic cavity can be explored. The abscess in the cavity is located, entered, and drained through the vaginal incision. Rubber drains are often inserted and left in place for several days. The physician closes the incision with absorbable sutures.

57020
Colpocentesis is the aspiration of fluid in the peritoneum through the wall of the vagina. Through a speculum inserted in the vagina, the physician grasps the posterior lip of the cervix with a toothed instrument called a tenaculum. The cervix is lifted, exposing the posterior vaginal pouch and deep back wall of the vagina. A long needle attached to a syringe is inserted through the exposed vaginal wall and the posterior pelvic cavity is entered. Fluid is aspirated through the needle into the syringe.

57022-57023
The physician incises and drains a vaginal hematoma in an obstetrical or postpartum patient. The patient is placed in a dorso-lithotomy position. The physician inserts a speculum into the vagina. The hematoma is visualized, and incised. Blood and clot are drained from the hematoma. Electrocautery or suture is used to control bleeding. When needed, a Hemovac drain is placed. The vagina is irrigated, and the area of hematoma is sponged with dressings. When hemostasis is achieved, the speculum is removed. Report 57022 when the procedure is performed on an obstetrical patient and 57023 when the procedure is performed on a non-obstetrical patient. Hemovac drains may be placed if the hematoma bed is still oozing.

57061-57065
Using a colposcope, a binocular microscope used for direct visualization of the vagina and cervix, the physician identifies lesion(s) in and/or around the vagina. The physician destroys the abnormal tissue by chemosurgery, electrosurgery, laser surgery, or cryotherapy. Use 57061 if the lesions are few in number, small, or simple. Use 57065 if the lesions are numerous, large, or difficult.

57100-57105
The physician takes a sample of vaginal mucosa for examination. After injecting a local anesthetic into the suspect area, the physician obtains a sample with a skin punch or sharp scalpel. In 57100, the biopsy is simple and no sutures are required. In 57105, sutures are required as the excision site is extensive and bleeding may need to be controlled.

57106-57109

The physician excises part of the vagina. This is sometimes preceded by injection of medication to constrict blood vessels to control bleeding. The vagina is everted and sizeable sections are removed by sharp and blunt dissection. In 57107, the physician removes surrounding diseased and/or damaged tissue. In 57109, the physician removes surrounding diseased and/or damaged tissue, in addition to removing the pelvic lymph nodes, and performing biopsy of the lymph nodes of the aorta to check for the extent of disease. Remaining vaginal and/or support tissue is inverted and sutured in place to obliterate some or all of the space formerly occupied by the vagina. The perineum is closed over the former vaginal opening.

57110-57112

The physician performs a complete removal of the vaginal wall. This is sometimes proceeded by injection of medication to constrict blood vessels to control bleeding. The vagina is everted. An incision circumscribes the hymen, and the vagina is marked into four quadrants. Each quadrant of vaginal wall is removed by sharp and blunt dissection. In 57111, the physician removes surrounding diseased and/or damaged tissue. In 57112, the physician removes surrounding diseased and/or damaged tissue, in addition to removing the pelvic lymph nodes, and performs biopsy of the lymph nodes of the aorta to check for the extent of disease. The remaining support tissues are inverted and sutured in place obliterating the space formerly occupied by the vagina. The perineum is closed over the former vaginal opening.

57120

The physician grasps the deepest portion of the vaginal vault and everts the vagina. Two large flaps of vaginal wall are removed from opposite sides of the prolapsed vagina. The vaginal walls are sutured to one another and this structure is inverted back inside the body. The former vaginal opening is closed with sutures obliterating the vagina and preventing uterine prolapse.

57130

The physician excises a vaginal septum, an anomaly that separates the vagina into two portions. The septum can be longitudinal, creating two vaginal canals, or transverse, blocking the vagina and preventing menstrual flow. For a small, thin septum, the procedure is often done by injecting a local anesthetic in the tissues around the septum and making an incision through the narrowest portion of the septum. The divided tissue is tied off with suture material and the tissue is excised. For a thicker and more extensive septum, the procedure may be done under general anesthesia. The tissue is excised, and the resulting vaginal lining defects are closed. The vagina is packed with medicated gauze or a support device.

57135

Through a speculum inserted in the vagina, the physician uses a forceps or hemostat clamp to grasp and elongate the vaginal tissue containing the cyst or tumor, causing the mucosa to tent. With a scalpel or scissors, the physician excises an ellipse of tissue containing the lesion. The defect is closed with absorbable sutures.

57150

The physician passes a catheter or similar tube high into the vaginal canal and flushes the canal with medicated solution from a large syringe. The physician also paints infected areas with medication using a cotton-tipped applicator or similar device.

57155

Preoperative radiation may be prescribed for patients who have endometrial cancer with major cervical involvement that precludes initial hysterectomy. Vaginal brachytherapy is administered using low-dose rate (LDR) or high-dose rate (HDR) radiotherapy. The upper half to two-thirds of the vagina is treated. HDR vaginal brachytherapy is delivered using intracavitary vaginal insertion with a Fletcher applicator, consisting of a uterine tandem and vaginal cylinders. HDR treatments require multiple insertions, generally with one insertion done every week for three to six weeks; hospitalization is not required, and each insertion takes only a brief amount of time. LDR treatments are delivered once but do require hospitalization for two to three days. Hysterectomy follows in four to six weeks.

57160

The physician fits a pessary to a patient, provides instructions for its use, and inserts it into the vagina. A pessary is a prosthesis that comes in different shapes and styles and is used to support the uterus, cervical stump, or hernias of the pelvic floor. The pessary selection and fitting will depend on the patient's symptoms and anatomy.

57170

The physician fits a diaphragm or cervical cap and provides instructions for use. A diaphragm is a device that acts as a mechanical barrier between the vagina and the cervical canal. Cervical caps are larger, cup-like diaphragms placed over the cervix and held in place by suction. Either device can be used to prevent pregnancy.

57180

The physician pushes gauze packing into the vagina to put pressure on bleeding that is not related to childbirth or pregnancy. The packing may be coated with a chemical to make the blood clot and stop hemorrhaging.

57200-57210

The physician inserts a speculum into the vagina and identifies the extent of the vaginal laceration or wound that is not related to childbirth or pregnancy. Usually a local anesthetic is used; however, some instances may require general anesthesia. The wound is closed with absorbable sutures. In 57210, after the speculum is removed, the perineal laceration is closed in layers with sutures.

57220
The physician accesses the urethral sphincter from the vagina. With a catheter in the urethra, the physician dissects the midline vaginal wall separating it from the bladder and the proximal urethra. Sutures are placed at the junction of the bladder and urethra on each side of the urethra. This supports the area. Excess vaginal tissue is excised and the vaginal wall is closed.

57230
The physician repairs a urethrocele, which is a sagging or prolapse of the urethra through its opening or a bulging of the posterior wall of the urethra against the vaginal canal. The prolapsed urethral tissue is excised from the meatus in a circular manner. The cut edges of urethral mucosa and vaginal mucosa are sutured.

57240
The physician repairs a cystocele, which is a herniation of the bladder through its support tissues and against the anterior vaginal wall causing it to bulge downward. The physician may also repair a urethrocele, which is a prolapse of the urethra. An incision is made from the apex of the vagina to within 1 cm of the urethral meatus. Plication sutures are placed along the urethral course from the meatus to the bladder neck. A suture is placed through the pubourethral ligament to the posterior symphysis pubis on each side of the urethra. The sutures are tied (ligated) and the posterior urethra is pulled upward to a retropubic position. If a cystocele is repaired, mattress sutures are placed in the mobilized paravesical tissue. The vaginal mucosa is closed.

57250
The physician repairs a rectocele by colporrhaphy. A rectocele is a protrusion of part of the rectum through its supporting tissues against the vagina causing a bulging in the vagina. Colporrhaphy involves a plastic repair of the vagina and the fibrous tissue separating the vagina and rectum. The physician makes a posterior midline incision that includes the perineum and posterior vaginal wall. In order to strengthen the area, the rectovaginal fascia is plicated by folding and tacking, and it is closed with layered sutures. The physician may also perform a perineorrhaphy, which is a plastic repair of the perineum, including midline approximation of the levator and perineal muscles. Excess fascia in the posterior vaginal wall is excised. The incisions are closed with sutures.

57260
The physician repairs both a cystocele and rectocele by colporrhaphy. Colporrhaphy involves a plastic repair of the vagina and the fibrous tissue separating the bladder, vagina, and rectum. A cystocele is a herniation of the bladder through its support tissues causing the anterior vaginal wall to bulge downward. A rectocele is a protrusion of part of the rectum through its support tissues causing the posterior vaginal wall to bulge. Using a combined vaginal approach and a posterior midline incision that includes the perineum and posterior vaginal wall, the physician dissects the tissues between the bladder, urethra, vagina, and rectum. The specific tissue weaknesses are repaired and strengthened using tissue transfer techniques and layered and plication suturing. The physician may also repair a urethrocele, which is a prolapse of the urethra, and perform a perineorrhaphy, which is a plastic repair of the perineum, including midline approximation of the levator and perineal muscles. The incisions are closed with sutures.

57265
The physician repairs both a cystocele and rectocele by colporrhaphy. Colporrhaphy involves a plastic repair of the vagina and the fibrous tissue separating the bladder, vagina, and rectum. A cystocele is a herniation of the bladder through its support tissues causing the anterior vaginal wall to bulge downward. A rectocele is a protrusion of part of the rectum through its support tissues causing the posterior vaginal wall to bulge. Using a combined vaginal approach and a posterior midline incision that includes the perineum and posterior vaginal wall, the physician dissects the tissue between the bladder, urethra, vagina, and rectum. The specific tissue weaknesses are repaired and strengthened using tissue transfer techniques and layered and plication suturing. The physician also repairs an enterocele, which is a herniation of the bowel contents of the rectouterine pouch that protrudes into the septum of tissue between the bladder and vagina or between the vagina and rectum. Through the vagina, the enterocele sac is incised and ligated and the uterosacral ligaments and endopelvic fascia anterior to the rectum are approximated. The physician may also repair a urethrocele, which is a prolapse of the urethra, and perform a perineorrhaphy, which is a plastic repair of the perineum, including midline approximation of the levator and perineal muscles. The incisions are closed with sutures.

57267
The physician inserts mesh or other prosthetic support material to repair a pelvic floor defect using a vaginal approach. Pelvic floor defects resulting in prolapse of the pelvic viscera occur when the pelvic fascia weakens or is damaged. The physician selects the appropriate type of prosthetic support material. Some mesh supports, such as horseshoe shaped mesh, are purchased preformed in the desired configuration. Other types of mesh supports, such as tension free tapes, are cut and fashioned by the physician during surgery into the required shapes and sizes. The mesh is inserted through the vagina and placed at the site

requiring support. The exact placement of the mesh is determined by the type of pelvic floor defect being repaired. For example, horseshoe mesh is placed between the pubis and sacrum to close the area between the pelvic viscera and the inferior pelvic hiatus. Report 57267 in addition to the primary procedure for each site requiring insertion of mesh or other prosthesis, such as an anterior repair for cystocele or a posterior repair for a rectocele.

57268-57270

The physician repairs an enterocele, which is a herniation of the bowel contents of the rectouterine pouch that protrudes into the septum of tissue between the bladder and vagina or between the vagina and rectum. Through the vaginal approach in 57268, the physician incises and ligates the enterocele sac and approximates the uterosacral ligaments and endopelvic fascia anterior to the rectum. In 57270, the approach is made through an incision in the lower abdominal wall. A vaginal hysterectomy, anterior (cystocele) and posterior (rectocele) colporrhaphy, and perineorrhaphy may also be performed to augment the support.

57280

Through a lower abdominal incision, the physician attaches the vault of the vagina to the prominent point of the sacrum. This is accomplished by suturing surgical fabric or a strip of abdominal wall fascia to the tissue in front of the internal sacral wall inside the pelvic cavity forming a bridge. The apex of the vagina is firmly sutured to this bridge. This stabilizes the vaginal vault and prevents prolapse of the vagina. The abdominal incision is closed with sutures.

57282

Colpopexy is performed by transvaginal, extraperitoneal approach to restore the apex or vault of the vagina to its anatomic position in cases of prolapse. Extraperitoneal transvaginal approach is used to perform a sacrospinous ligament fixation or iliococcygeus fascial suspension. Sacrospinous ligament fixation is performed using an anterior transvaginal approach through the paravaginal space or a posterior transvaginal approach by perforation of the rectal pillar. A pair of sutures are placed approximately 1 to 2 cm apart in the sacrospinous ligaments. After placing the sutures in the sacrospinous ligaments, the apex of the vagina is identified and the sutures in the sacrospinal ligaments are incorporated into the apex of the vagina allowing for maximal suspension of the vaginal vault. Iliococcygeus fascial suspension is performed by extraperitoneal transvaginal approach. The rectum is first retracted medially. The iliococcygeus muscle is located lateral to the rectum and anterior to the ischial spine. A single suture is placed in both sides of the apex of the vaginal vault to provide bilateral fixation of the vault to the iliococcygeus fascia.

57283

Colpopexy is performed by transvaginal, intraperitoneal approach to restore the apex or vault of the vagina to its anatomic position in cases of prolapse. Intraperitoneal technique is used to perform a uterosacral ligament suspension or a levator myorrhaphy, which are performed using a posterior transvaginal approach. Uterosacral ligament suspension is performed by first locating the uterosacral ligament remnant with the use of Allis clamps posterior and medial to the ischial spine. Prior to placement of sutures in the ligaments, the ureters are located by palpation. Two to three nonabsorbable sutures are placed in each ligament and tied together. The ligaments are placated and brought together in the midline. Sutures are placed in the apical portion of the anterior and posterior vaginal walls to secure and anchor the vaginal walls to the plicated uterosacral ligaments. Levator myorrhaphy uses the levator musculature to repair the vaginal vault prolapse. The levator musculature is brought together and a high levator shelf created. The shelf is created by tagging and tying together the levator muscles at a site slightly above the junction of the levator and rectum. The vaginal vault is anchored to the shelf.

57284-57285

The physician repairs a paravaginal defect, in which there is loss of the lateral vaginal attachment to the pelvic sidewall, by dissecting the tissues between the vagina and the bladder and urethra. The specific tissue weaknesses are found, repaired, and strengthened using tissue transfer techniques and plication suturing. The paravaginal repair may be performed alone or in conjunction with cystocele repair, in which a herniation of the bladder through its support tissues into the anterior vaginal wall causes it to bulge downward. These procedures help restore the normal anatomic relationships of the urethra, bladder, and vagina. Report 57284 if access is achieved via laparotomy (open abdominal approach) and 57285 if a vaginal approach is utilized.

57287

The physician removes or revises a fascial or synthetic sling previously placed to correct urinary stress incontinence. To remove a sling, the physician makes a small abdominal skin incision to the level of the rectus fascia and releases the arm of the sling from the rectus abdominis. The physician releases the sling's attachment to the junction of the urethra via canals or tunnels formed by an instrument or a finger placed through a vertical or flap incision in the vaginal wall. In revision of a sling the physician may remove and partially or completely replace the sling using fascia or a synthetic graft through an abdominal and vaginal approach. The sling may be revised by increasing the tension on the sling using suture at one or both of the attachment sites at the junction of the urethra and/or to the rectus abdominis muscle. At the end of the procedure the area is irrigated, and hemostasis is achieved. The abdominal and/or vaginal incisions are closed with layered sutures.

57288

Through vaginal and abdominal incisions, the physician places a sling under the junction of the urethra and bladder. The physician places a catheter in the bladder, makes an incision in the anterior wall of the vagina, and folds and tacks the tissues around the urethra. A sling is formed out of synthetic material or from fascia harvested from the sheath of the rectus abdominis muscle. The loop end of the sling is sutured around the junction of the urethra. An incision is made in the lower abdomen and the ends of the sling are grasped with a clamp and pulled into the incision and sutured to the rectus abdominis sheath. The abdominal and vaginal incisions are closed in layers by suturing.

57289

The physician makes an inverted U-shaped incision in the area between the vagina and the urethra. By blunt and sharp dissection, the physician creates an opening in the space on each side of the urethra as it passes into the bladder. Using a continuous suture for each side, the physician stitches the fascial tissues along the urethra to the urethrovesical junction. The physician makes an incision in the abdomen above the pubis and, doing each side in turn, drives a Pereyra ligature carrier through the tissues just lateral to the midline and takes it down to the sutured tissue. The sutures are threaded into the instrument and brought back through the abdominal incision. The urethrovesical junction is elevated by pulling on the sutures and fixing them around the rectus abdominis muscle. In addition, the physician performs an anterior colporrhaphy using a vaginal approach, which corrects a cystocele and repairs the tissues between the vagina, bladder, and urethra.

57291-57292

For construction of an artificial vagina without graft, the physician develops a vagina by a program of perineal pressure using progressively longer and wider firm obturators. Pressure is applied to the soft area between the urethra and rectum with an obturator. Over several months of consistent, daily use by the patient, a sexually functional vagina can be created. In 57292, the physician creates or enlarges the vagina using one or more skin grafts. Through a midline episiotomy incision, the physician creates a space between the urethra and rectum. Using split thickness or full thickness skin grafts, the space is lined and the vagina created. An obturator or mold is inserted into the vagina and a catheter is passed into the bladder and left for several days. The full thickness skin donor sites are closed using plastic surgical techniques. The split thickness sites are dressed with medicated gauze.

57295

The physician revises or removes a previously placed prosthetic vaginal graft via a vaginal approach. The patient is placed in the lithotomy position and a speculum is inserted. The physician visualizes the vagina. The apex of the vagina is accessed with deep retractors. Dissection is carried out to reach the affected graft material. Depending upon the type of complication (i.e., stricture or infection), the vaginal graft may be completely or partially excised to remove eroding mesh or revisions may be made in the graft and surrounding tissue. The vaginal epithelial layers and pelvic fascia are rearranged or reapproximated and closed. Vaginal packing is put in place.

57296

The physician revises or removes a previously placed prosthetic vaginal graft using an open abdominal approach in conjunction with a vaginal approach. A laparotomy incision is made and the physician dissects into the pelvis. The vagina is elevated with tools or with the physician's hand. The graft is located, the peritoneum is opened over it, and the graft is dissected free and removed. Depending upon the type of complication (i.e., stricture or infection), the vaginal graft may be completely or partially excised to remove eroding mesh or revisions may be made in the graft and surrounding tissue. Endopelvic fascia is reapproximated and the vaginal epithelial layers and pelvic fascia are rearranged or reapproximated and closed. The abdominal incision is repaired in layers. Vaginal packing is put in place.

57300

The physician closes a rectovaginal fistula, which is an abnormal passage between the rectum and the vagina. The physician also repairs the perineum, fascia, and muscle-supporting structures between the rectum and vagina. The scar tissue and tract between the rectum and vagina are excised and the clean edges sutured together. Often a flap of tissue is transplanted between the vagina and the rectum and the area is closed in layers. The rectal wall opening is closed by inverting the mucosa into the rectal canal. The vaginal wall opening is closed by inverting the mucosal layer into the vaginal wall. Sometimes the vaginal side is left open for drainage.

57305

Through a lower abdominal incision, the physician closes a rectovaginal fistula, which is an abnormal passage between the rectum and the vagina. The physician also repairs the perineum, fascia, and muscle-supporting structures between the rectum and vagina. The scar tissue and tract between the rectum and vagina are excised and the clean edges sutured together. Often a flap of tissue is transplanted between the vagina and the rectum and the area is closed in layers. The rectal wall opening is closed by inverting the mucosa into the rectal canal. The vaginal wall opening is closed by inverting the mucosal layer into the vaginal wall. Sometimes the vaginal side is left open for drainage. The abdominal incision is closed with sutures.

57307-57308
Through a lower abdominal incision, the physician closes a rectovaginal fistula, which is an abnormal passage between the rectum and vagina. The physician also repairs the perineum, fascia, and muscle-supporting structures between the rectum and vagina. The scar tissue and tract between the rectum and vagina are excised and the clean edges sutured together. Often a flap of tissue is transplanted between the vagina and rectum and the area is closed in layers. The rectal wall opening created during the excision is closed by inverting the mucosa into the rectal canal. The vaginal wall opening is closed by inverting the mucosal layer into the vaginal canal. The vaginal side may be left open for drainage. In 57307, a transverse colostomy is done to divert the flow of feces and to allow healing of the rectal colon repair. The abdominal incision is closed with sutures. Report 57308 if the physician takes a transperineal approach, reconstructing the perineal body, with or without a levator plication.

57310-57311
The physician closes a urethrovaginal fistula, which is an abnormal passage between the urethra and vagina. With a catheter in the urethra, the fistula tract is excised and the defect in the urethra is sutured closed. A pad of fatty tissue is sutured between the repaired urethral defect and the vaginal defect in 57310. In 57311, a pad of fatty tissue and a strip of the bulbocavernosus muscle are brought through a tunnel created between the vagina and one labium. The fat and muscle flap are sutured between the repaired urethral defect and the vaginal defect. In either case, the involved area in the vagina is excised and the defect is sutured closed. The catheter is left in place for several days to allow healing of the urethra.

57320
The physician closes a vesicovaginal fistula, which is an abnormal passage between the bladder and the vagina. This procedure is done through the vagina with catheters via the urethra into both ureters. The fistula and surrounding scar tissue of the vaginal wall are usually excised. Using a vaginal approach, the bladder wall is opened and the bladder explored. The fistula is excised along with the surrounding tissue. The resulting defect is closed with sutures in layers, starting with the bladder wall and ending with the vaginal mucosa. In some cases, a pedicle graft of tissue may be sutured between the bladder and the vagina. A urethral or suprapubic catheter is left in the bladder to prevent distension of the bladder and tension to the sutured areas.

57330
The physician closes a vesicovaginal fistula, which is an abnormal passage between the bladder and the vagina. The procedure is done through the vagina and through the lower abdomen, with catheters through the urethra into both ureters. The physician opens the bladder wall through the lower abdominal incision and excises the fistula. The resulting defect is closed with sutures in layers, starting with the bladder wall and ending with the abdominal wall. Through the vagina, the physician excises the fistula and surrounding scar tissue of the vaginal wall. In some cases, a pedicle graft of tissue may be sutured between the bladder and the vagina. A urethral or suprapubic catheter is left in the bladder to prevent distension of the bladder and tension to the sutured areas.

57335
The physician uses various plastic surgical techniques to correct a small, underdeveloped vagina due to the overproduction of male hormones. The physician constructs a larger and more functional vagina using carefully placed incisions and skin grafts.

57400
The physician enlarges the vagina by using a set of progressively longer and wider vaginal obturator dilators. The physician inserts the vaginal dilators sequentially from smaller to larger with firm and gentle pressure while the patient is under anesthesia (other than local).

57410
The physician performs a manual examination of the vagina, including the cervix, uterus, tubes, and ovaries. During the examination, the patient is under anesthesia (other than local) because of the patient's inability to tolerate the procedure while fully alert or awake.

57415
Using a vaginal speculum, the physician removes a foreign body lodged in the vagina. During the procedure, the patient is under anesthesia (other than local) because of the patient's inability to tolerate the procedure while fully alert or awake, as in the case of a young child or due to the type or size of the object being removed.

57420-57421
The physician performs a colposcopy of the vagina and the cervix, if present. The patient is placed in the lithotomy position and a speculum is inserted into the vagina. The vagina is inspected through the colposcope, a binocular microscope providing direct, magnified visualization of the vagina and cervix. The physician examines the tissue for discharge, inflammation, ulceration, and lesions. The cervix is exposed, cleansed, and inspected for any ulceration or lesions. Acetic acid may be applied to help enhance visualization of the columnar villi and any lesions. In 57241, the area is examined and questionable tissue is

removed from the vagina and/or cervix under direct visualization. The number and size of the biopsy(ies) is variable; multiple biopsies may be taken. Pressure is applied with a cotton swab as silver nitrate or other solution is applied with another applicator directly onto the biopsy site(s) for hemostasis. The instruments are removed.

57423
The physician performs laparoscopic repair of a paravaginal defect, in which there is loss of the lateral vaginal attachment to the pelvic sidewall. Through small stab incisions in the abdomen, a fiberoptic laparoscope and trocars are inserted into the abdominal/pelvic space and the abdomen is insufflated. The bladder may be filled with sterile water to allow the surgeon to identify the superior border of the bladder's edge and then drained to prevent injury after the space of Retzius has been entered and the pubic ramus visualized. Following identification of the defect, the surgeon inserts the nondominant hand into the vagina in order to elevate the anterior vaginal wall and pubocervical fascia to their normal positions. Nonabsorbable sutures with attached needles are introduced through the laparoscopy port and grasped using a laparoscopic needle driver. A series of four to six sutures are placed and tied sequentially along the defects from the ischial spine toward the urethra. The procedure is repeated on the opposite side if a bilateral defect is present. The paravaginal defect repair may be performed alone or in conjunction with cystocele repair, in which a herniation of the bladder through its support tissues into the anterior vaginal wall causes it to bulge downward. These procedures help restore the normal anatomic relationships of the urethra, bladder, and vagina. At completion of the procedure, laparoscopic tools are removed, excess gas expelled, and fascial defects and skin edges are sutured.

57425
The physician performs a laparoscopic colpopexy and suspends or reattaches the apex of the vagina to the uterosacral ligaments to correct a uterovaginal prolapse and restore the vaginal apex to its normal anatomic position, often post-hysterectomy. Through small stab incisions in the abdomen, a fiberoptic laparoscope and trocars are inserted into the abdominal/pelvic space. The bowel is mobilized or moved aside to provide a better view and easier access to the uterosacral ligaments. A vaginal probe is placed for manipulation and to help ensure the cul-de-sac is properly closed. The peritoneum is incised over the vaginal apex. After the vaginal vault is elevated into its normal position, and the cul-de-sac is obliterated, if necessary, a suture is placed through the base of the right uterosacral ligament and through the apex of the vagina-securing it posteriorly to the top of the rectovaginal fascia and anteriorly to the pubocervical fascia (to a dermal or mesh graft, if placed) and secured. Four total sutures are used to elevate the vagina, this being done twice through each ligament and the vaginal apex on each side.

57426
The physician revises or removes a previously placed prosthetic vaginal graft via a laparoscopic approach. Through small stab incisions in the umbilicus and/or abdomen, a fiberoptic laparoscope and trocars are inserted into the peritoneal cavity. Depending upon the type of complication (e.g., mesh erosion into the bladder or persistent vaginal/pelvic pain), the vaginal graft may be completely or partially excised to remove eroding mesh or revisions may be made in the graft and surrounding tissue.

57452
The physician examines the cervix, including the upper/adjacent portion of the vagina through a colposcope, a binocular microscope used for direct visualization of the vagina, ectocervix, and endocervix. The physician may insert a speculum into the vagina to fully expose the cervix as part of this procedure.

57454-57456
The physician views the cervix, including the upper/adjacent portion of the vagina through a colposcope, a binocular microscope used for direct visualization of the vagina, ectocervix, and endocervix. The physician may insert a speculum into the vagina to fully expose the cervix as part of this procedure. The physician removes tissue for a biopsy of the cervix in 57455, performs endocervical curettage in 57456, and does both a biopsy and endocervical curettage in 57454. For biopsy, an instrument is inserted in the vagina and used to take one or more small tissue samples of the cervix. For endocervical curettage, a small curette is passed into the endocervical canal, which is the passage between the external cervical os and the uterine cavity. A specimen is obtained by scraping in the canal with the curette. The instrument is removed.

57460
The physician views the cervix, including the upper/adjacent portion of the vagina through a colposcope, a binocular microscope used for direct visualization of the vagina, ectocervix, and endocervix. The physician inserts a speculum into the vagina to fully expose the cervix. A biopsy specimen of cervical tissue is removed by the loop electrode excision procedure (LEEP). LEEP uses a hot cautery wire containing an electrical cutting current as a cutting instrument. Due to the electrical current, a grounding pad is attached to the patient's leg during the procedure.

57461
The physician views the cervix, including the upper/adjacent portion of the vagina, through a colposcope, a binocular microscope used for direct visualization of the vagina, ectocervix, and endocervix, and performs a loop electrode excision procedure (LEEP). The physician inserts a speculum into the vagina to fully

expose the cervix. The electric grounding pad is placed on the patient's leg and safety checks are run. The cutting current is set. Using a loop, the lesion is removed as one specimen. If the lesion is large and another pass is required, two equal specimens are removed and labeled for the axis of orientation. The same procedure is done again with a smaller loop if an endocervical excision is necessary. The bleeding vessels are cauterized, the vagina is inspected for any accidental injury, and the instruments are removed.

57500
The physician inserts a speculum into the vagina to view the cervix. A small cut is made in the cervix and biopsy forceps are used to remove a piece or multiple pieces of tissue, or to completely remove a lesion. Bleeding, usually minimal, may be stopped by electric current (fulguration).

57505
The physician inserts a speculum into the vagina to view the cervix. A small curette is used to scrape tissue from the endocervix, which is the region of the opening of the cervix into the uterine cavity.

57510-57513
The physician inserts a speculum into the vagina to view the cervix. In 57510, electric current or heat is used to destroy the outer layers of the cervix causing them to slough off. In 57511, the outer layers of the cervix are destroyed by freezing using a liquid such as carbon dioxide, freon, nitrous oxide, or nitrogen, or a low temperature instrument. The outer layers of the cervix slough off. This code can be used for a first-time or repeat procedure. In 57513, a laser is directed at the cervix to vaporize the outer cells.

57520
The physician performs a conization of the cervix, with or without fulguration, with or without dilation and curettage, with or without repair by using the cold knife or laser technique. The physician inserts a speculum into the vagina to view and fully expose the cervix. For most cases, the appropriate local anesthesia is administered as opposed to forms of premedication. Using a scalpel or laser instrument, a cone or slice of tissue including about 1 to 2 cm of the endocervix as well as exocervical cells is cut from the end of the cervix with the axis of the cone parallel to the axis of the cervix. Bleeding may be stopped by electric current. The cervix may need to be dilated and a curette used directly after conization to scrape tissue that is to be taken from further inside the uterus. The physician also may need to place interrupted figure-of-eight sutures to incorporate the bleeding site if direct cautery does not achieve hemostasis. The speculum is removed.

57522
The physician performs a conization of the cervix, with or without fulguration, with or without dilation and curettage, with or without repair by using the loop electrode excision procedure (LEEP). The physician inserts a speculum into the vagina to view and fully expose the cervix. For most cases, the appropriate local anesthesia is administered as opposed to forms of premedication. The electric grounding pad is placed and safety checks are run. The cutting current is set. Using a loop that encompasses the lesion, an excision of the ectocervix is done with every effort made to remove the lesion in one specimen. If the lesion is large and another pass is required, two equal specimens are removed and labeled for the axis of orientation. The same procedure is done again with a smaller loop if an endocervical excision is necessary. The cervix may be dilated and an endocervical curettage collected. When all specimens have been collected, the bleeding vessels are cauterized, the vagina is inspected for any accidental injury, and the speculum is removed. No colposcope is used in this procedure.

57530
The physician inserts a speculum into the vagina to view the cervix and perform an amputation of the cervix. A tool is used to pull down the cervix. A scalpel is used to divide the cervix from the uterus just after it enters the vagina. The physician removes the cervix through the vagina and stops the bleeding with cautery and sutures.

57531
The physician inserts a speculum into the vagina to view the cervix and perform a radical excision of the cervix, including removal of local lymph nodes. A tool is used to pull down the cervix. A scalpel is used to divide the cervix from the uterus just after it enters the vagina. The physician removes the cervix through the vagina, stops the bleeding with cautery, and also removes the pelvic lymph nodes bilaterally, performs a para-aortic lymph node biopsy, and may remove one or both tubes and/or ovaries.

57540-57545
The physician makes an incision horizontally just within the pubic hairline. In 57540, the physician removes the cervical stump, which is the part of the cervix left after the supracervical uterus has been removed. The incision is closed by suturing. In 57545, the physician removes the cervical stump and repairs the muscular floor of the pelvis where the cervix rests using suture plication. This involves folding the tissues on top of each other and suturing. The incision is sutured.

57550
Through an incision at the apex of the vagina, the physician removes the cervical stump, which is the part of the cervix left after the supracervical uterus has been removed. The vaginal incision is closed with sutures.

57555-57556
Through an incision in the apex of the vagina, the physician removes the cervical stump. In 57555, the physician also repairs the relaxed or herniated tissues in the front or back wall of the vagina. Through the vaginal incision, the physician dissects the tissues between the bladder, urethra, vagina, and rectum. The specific tissue weaknesses are repaired and strengthened using tissue transfer techniques and layered and plication suturing. The incisions are closed with sutures. In 57556, the physician also repairs an enterocele, which is a herniation of the bowel against the rectouterine pouch. Through the vaginal incision, the physician incises and ligates the enterocele sac and approximates the uterosacral ligaments and endopelvic fascia anterior to the rectum. The incisions are closed with sutures.

57558
The physician performs a dilation and curettage of the cervical stump. The physician inserts a speculum into the vagina to view the cervix. The physician enlarges the cervix using a dilator and scrapes tissue from the lining of the cervical stump, which is the part of the cervix left after removal of the uterus.

57700
The physician inserts a speculum into the vagina to view the cervix of a nonpregnant patient. Suture or wire is threaded around the cervix and pulled in pursestring fashion to make the opening smaller.

57720
The physician inserts a speculum into the vagina to view the cervix. The physician performs a plastic suture repair of a laceration or wound on the cervix. A plastic repair also can encompass excising scar tissue or tightening an incompetent cervix.

57800
The physician inserts a speculum into the vagina to view the cervix. A tool is used to grasp the cervix and pull it down. A dilator or series of dilators is inserted into the endocervix and passed through the cervical canal.

58100
The physician inserts a speculum into the vagina to view the cervix. A tool is used to grasp the cervix and pull it down. The physician places a curette in the endocervical canal and passes it into the uterus. The endometrial lining of the uterus is scraped on all sides to obtain tissue for diagnosis. Biopsy(ies) may also be taken from the endocervix. Cervical dilation is not required.

58110
A tool is used to grasp the cervix and pull it down. The physician places a curette in the endocervical canal and passes it into the uterus. The endometrial lining of the uterus is scraped in several places to obtain tissue for a biopsy sample. The endometrial sampling is performed in conjunction with direct visualization of the vagina and cervix and is reported in addition to the separately reportable primary colposcopy.

58120
The physician inserts a speculum into the vagina to view the cervix. A tool is used to grasp the cervix and pull it down. A dilator is inserted into the endocervix and through the cervical canal to enlarge the opening. The physician places a curette in the endocervical canal and passes it into the uterus. The endometrial lining of the uterus is scraped on all sides for diagnostic or therapeutic purposes.

58140
The physician removes one to four fibroid tumors from the wall of the uterus (intramural myomas) with a total weight of 250 gm or less and/or removes surface myomas by abdominal approach. A transverse incision is made in the abdomen, the anterior sheath of the rectus abdominis muscle is dissected, and muscles are retracted. Vasoconstrictors are injected and a tourniquet is applied to encompass the uterine mass and the adnexa to limit blood flow. A scalpel, electrocautery, and/or laser may be used to remove small surface myomas. The physician incises the uterus through the myometrium to expose the myoma, which is grasped with a clamp and dissected free from the surrounding myometrium with sharp and blunt dissection. The pedicle is isolated, clamped, and ligated and the myoma is dissected down to the pedicular blood supply. Other myomas are identified by palpating the uterine wall through the defect created by the already excised myoma. Adjacent myomas are reached and removed by tunneling further through the initial incision to avoid additional uterine trauma. The uterine wall defects are repaired by approximating the tissues to restore previous anatomy. The serosa is closed so as to minimize adhesion formation. Antiadhesion prophylaxis may be instilled in the abdominal cavity and the wound is closed.

58145
The physician removes one to four fibroid tumors from the wall of the uterus (intramural myomas) with a total weight of 250 gm or less and/or removes surface myomas by vaginal approach. This approach is used for pedunculated myomas protruding through the cervix and for prolapsed myomas. The cervix is dilated with laminaria to facilitate exposure and a tonsil snare or other appropriate device is passed through to reach the myoma. Prolapsed myomas are usually attached to the cervical or endometrial cavity by a stalk. The tumor is removed by ligating or twisting the stalk or a tonsil snare is employed to encircle the tumor, cut it from its stalk, and remove it. The instruments are removed.

58146
The physician removes five or more fibroid tumors from the wall of the uterus and/or intramural myomas with a total weight greater than 250 gm by abdominal

approach. A transverse incision is made in the abdomen (a midline incision is made for large myomas) and the anterior sheath of the rectus abdominis muscle is dissected and muscles are retracted. Vasoconstrictors are injected and a tourniquet is applied to encompass the uterine mass and the adnexa to limit blood flow. The physician incises the uterus down through the myometrium to expose the myoma, which is grasped with a clamp and dissected free from the surrounding myometrium with sharp and blunt dissection. For deep intramural myomas, the endometrial cavity may be exposed. The pedicle is isolated, clamped, and ligated and the myoma is dissected down to the pedicular blood supply. Other myomas are identified by palpating the uterine wall through the defect created by the already excised myoma. Adjacent myomas are reached and removed by tunneling further through the initial incision to avoid additional uterine trauma. The uterine wall defects are repaired by approximating the tissues to restore previous anatomy. The serosa is closed so as to minimize adhesion formation. Antiadhesion prophylaxis may be instilled in the abdominal cavity and the wound is closed.

58150
Through a horizontal incision just within the pubic hairline, the physician removes the uterus including the cervix and may elect to remove one or both of the ovaries and one or both of the fallopian tubes (salpingo-oophorectomy). The supporting pedicles containing the tubes, ligaments, and arteries are clamped and cut free. The uterus and cervix are removed along with a narrow rim or cuff of vaginal lining. The vaginal defect may be left open for drainage. The abdominal incision is closed by suturing.

58152
Through a horizontal incision just within the pubic hairline, the physician removes the uterus including the cervix and may elect to remove one or both of the ovaries and one or both of the fallopian tubes (salpingo-oophorectomy). The supporting pedicles containing the tubes, ligaments, and arteries are clamped and cut free. The uterus and cervix are removed. The bladder neck is suspended by placing sutures through the tissue surrounding the urethra and into the back of the symphysis pubis, which is the midline junction of the pubic bones in the front (Marshall-Marchetti-Krantz). The sutures are pulled tight so that the tissues are tacked to the symphysis pubis and the urethra is moved forward. The abdominal incision is closed by suturing.

58180
Through a horizontal incision just within the pubic hairline, the physician removes the uterus above the cervix and may elect to remove one or both of the ovaries and one or both of the fallopian tubes (salpingo-oophorectomy). The supporting pedicles containing the tubes, ligaments, and arteries are clamped and cut free. The uterus is cut free from the cervix leaving the cervix still attached to the vagina. The abdominal incision is closed by suturing.

58200
Through a horizontal incision just within the pubic hairline, the physician removes the uterus, including the cervix and part of the vagina. The supporting pedicles containing the tubes, ligaments and arteries are clamped and cut free and the uterus, cervix, and part of the vagina are removed. A biopsy is taken of the para-aortic and pelvic lymph nodes. The physician may elect to remove one or both of the ovaries and one or both of the fallopian tubes (salpingo-oophorectomy). The abdominal incision is closed by suturing.

58210
Through a horizontal incision just within the pubic hairline, the physician removes the uterus, including the cervix and the pelvic lymph nodes on both sides and takes a biopsy of the para-aortic lymph nodes. The supporting pedicles containing the tubes, ligaments, and arteries are clamped and cut free and the uterus, cervix, all or part of the vagina, and all pelvic lymph nodes are removed. The physician may elect to remove one or both of the ovaries and one or both of the fallopian tubes (salpingo-oophorectomy). The abdominal incision is closed by suturing.

58240
Through a horizontal incision just within the pubic hairline, the physician removes all of the organs and adjacent structures of the pelvis including the cervix, uterus, and all or part of the vagina. The supporting pedicles containing the tubes, ligaments, and arteries are clamped and cut free and the uterus, cervix, and all or part of the vagina are removed. The physician may remove one or both of the ovaries and one or both of the fallopian tubes (salpingo-oophorectomy). The physician removes the bladder and diverts urine flow by transplanting the ureters to the skin or colon. The rectum and part of the colon may be removed and an artificial abdominal opening in the skin surface created for waste (colostomy). The abdominal incision is closed by suturing.

58260
The physician performs a vaginal hysterectomy for a uterus 250 gm or less. An incision is made around the cervix through the full thickness of the vaginal membrane. The cut vaginal edge is pulled toward the lower cervix and vaginal dissection is continued with countertraction. The posterior peritoneum is opened to admit a finger examination of the pelvis. The uterosacral ligaments are clamped and possibly shortened, cut from the uterus, and secured to the vagina. The vesicovaginal space is entered. The connective tissue fusing the bladder and vagina is dissected and the bladder is separated from the cervix.

The bladder pillars are clamped, cut, and ligated near their cervical attachments, as well as the cardinal ligament tissue on each side of the cervix and the left and right uterine vessels. The physician clamps, cuts, and ligates the upper cardinal and lower broad ligament complex. Traction applied to the cervix moves the uterus down until the fundus is low in the pelvis. Hemostats are applied to the angle of the uterus on each side and the uterus is removed. The peritoneum is closed with purse-string sutures that incorporate the proximal part of the uterosacral ligaments.

58262-58263

The physician performs a vaginal hysterectomy for a uterus 250 gm or less and removes the tubes and/or ovaries. An incision is made around the cervix through the full thickness of the vaginal membrane. The cut vaginal edge is pulled toward the lower cervix and vaginal dissection is continued with countertraction. The posterior peritoneum is opened to admit a finger examination of the pelvis. The uterosacral ligaments are clamped and possibly shortened, cut from the uterus, and secured to the vagina. The vesicovaginal space is entered. The connective tissue fusing the bladder and vagina is dissected and the bladder is separated from the cervix. The bladder pillars are clamped, cut, and ligated near their cervical attachments, as well as the cardinal ligament tissue on each side of the cervix and the left and right uterine vessels. The physician clamps, cuts, and ligates the upper cardinal and lower broad ligament complex. Traction applied to the cervix moves the uterus down until the fundus is low in the pelvis. Hemostats are applied to the angle of the uterus on each side and the uterus is removed. After the uterus is exteriorized, care is taken to ensure ligation of the ovarian vessels. The ovary is excised under direct vision. For removal of both tubes and ovaries, the round ligament on one side at a time is clamped and divided. A tunnel is made through the layers of the uterine broad ligament that enclose the tube and the tube and ovary are clamped together. The structure is pulled forward, the two sheets of the broad ligament are each cut, and the broad ligament is opened completely. The whole specimen is separated from its attaching ligament, which is clamped, and the tube and ovary on that side are removed. Report 58263 if an enterocele is repaired in addition to removing the tube and/or ovary. An enterocele is a hernia of the intestine protruding against the vaginal wall. The hernia sac is bluntly and sharply dissected from the surrounding connective tissue, excised and ligated, and the surrounding tissues are strengthened and sutured. The peritoneal and vaginal wall incisions of the hysterectomy procedure are closed.

58267

The physician performs a vaginal hysterectomy, for a uterus 250 gm or less with colpo-urethrocystopexy, with or without endoscopic control. An incision is made around the cervix through the full thickness of the vaginal membrane. The cut vaginal edge is pulled toward the lower cervix and vaginal dissection is continued with countertraction. The posterior peritoneum is opened to admit a finger examination of the pelvis. The uterosacral ligaments are clamped and possibly shortened, cut from the uterus, and secured to the vagina. The vesicovaginal space is entered. The connective tissue fusing the bladder and vagina is dissected and the bladder is separated from the cervix. The bladder pillars are clamped, cut, and ligated near their cervical attachments, as well as the cardinal ligament tissue on each side of the cervix and the left and right uterine vessels. The physician clamps, cuts, and ligates the upper cardinal and lower broad ligament complex. Traction applied to the cervix moves the uterus down until the fundus is low in the pelvis. Hemostats are applied to the angle of the uterus on each side and the uterus is removed.
Colpo-urethrocystopexy is done in cases of urinary incontinence to elevate the lower part of the bladder that connects to the urethra (bladder neck) and the urethra to a new position higher in the pelvis so the muscles of the pelvic floor can help control urination. After the uterus has been exteriorized and the bladder and urethra separated from surrounding structures, the physician lifts the vagina upward, suspends the bladder neck and urethra by placing sutures through the fibromuscular wall of the vagina lateral to the tissue surrounding the urethra, and sutures the tissue to the symphysis pubis—the midline junction of the pubic bones at the front. An endoscope may be placed to ensure no sutures pass through the lining of the bladder and to evaluate ureteral patency. The sutures are pulled tight to tack the structures to the pubic bone and provide support.

58270

The physician performs a vaginal hysterectomy, for a uterus 250 gm or less with repair of an enterocele. An incision is made around the cervix through the full thickness of the vaginal membrane. The cut vaginal edge is pulled toward the lower cervix and vaginal dissection is continued with countertraction. The posterior peritoneum is opened to admit a finger examination of the pelvis. The uterosacral ligaments are clamped and possibly shortened, cut from the uterus, and secured to the vagina. The vesicovaginal space is entered. The connective tissue fusing the bladder and vagina is dissected and the bladder is separated from the cervix. The bladder pillars are clamped, cut, and ligated near their cervical attachments as well as the cardinal ligament tissue on each side of the cervix and the left and right uterine vessels. The anterior peritoneum is opened under direct vision to avoid damaging the bladder and admit finger exploration. The physician clamps, cuts, and ligates the upper cardinal and lower broad ligament complex now that the peritoneum is open both anterior and posterior to the uterine fundus. Hemostats are applied to the angle of the uterus on each side and the uterus is removed, usually posteriorly. The physician also repairs an enterocele, a herniation of intestine that protrudes against the vaginal wall, discovered during finger exploration. The hernia sac is bluntly and sharply dissected from the surrounding connective tissue, excised and ligated, and the surrounding tissues are strengthened and sutured. The peritoneum is closed with purse-string sutures that incorporate the proximal part of the uterosacral ligaments.

58275-58280

The physician performs a vaginal hysterectomy with total or partial vaginectomy in 58275-58280 and with enterocele repair in 58280. An incision is made around the cervix through the full thickness of the vaginal membrane. The cut vaginal edge is pulled toward the lower cervix and vaginal dissection is continued with countertraction. The posterior peritoneum is opened to admit a finger examination of the pelvis. The uterosacral ligaments are clamped and possibly shortened, cut from the uterus, and secured to the vagina. The vesicovaginal space is entered. The connective tissue fusing the bladder and vagina is dissected and the bladder is separated from the cervix. The bladder pillars are clamped, cut, and ligated near their cervical attachments, as well as the cardinal ligament tissue on each side of the cervix and the left and right uterine vessels. The anterior peritoneum is opened under direct vision to avoid damaging the bladder and admit finger exploration. The physician clamps, cuts, and ligates the upper cardinal and lower broad ligament complex now that the peritoneum is open both anterior and posterior to the uterine fundus. Traction applied to the cervix moves the uterus down until the fundus is low in the pelvis. Hemostats are applied to the angle of the uterus on each side and the uterus is removed, usually posteriorly. The vagina is everted out through its opening and totally or partially removed in sections by blunt and sharp dissection. Any remaining vaginal tissue and the supporting tissues are inverted back into the resulting defect and are sutured in place with total vaginectomy obliterating the space. Report 58280 if the physician also repairs an enterocele, a herniation of intestine protruding through the vaginal wall. The hernia sac is bluntly and sharply dissected from the surrounding connective tissue, excised and ligated, and the surrounding tissues are strengthened and sutured. The peritoneum is closed with purse-string sutures that incorporate the proximal part of the uterosacral ligaments.

58285

The physician performs a radical vaginal hysterectomy. This includes the uterus, its surrounding tissues, and the pelvic lymph nodes. An incision is made around the cervix through the full thickness of the vaginal membrane. The cut vaginal edge is pulled toward the lower cervix and vaginal dissection is continued with countertraction. The posterior peritoneum is opened to admit a finger examination of the pelvis. The uterosacral ligaments are clamped and possibly shortened, cut from the uterus, and secured to the vagina. The vesicovaginal space is entered. The connective tissue fusing the bladder and vagina is dissected and the bladder is separated from the cervix. The bladder pillars are clamped, cut, and ligated near their cervical attachments, as well as the cardinal ligament tissue on each side of the cervix and the left and right uterine vessels. The anterior peritoneum is opened under direct vision to avoid damaging the bladder and admit finger exploration. The physician clamps, cuts, and ligates the upper cardinal and lower broad ligament complex now that the peritoneum is open both anterior and posterior to the uterine fundus. Traction applied to the cervix moves the uterus down until the fundus is low in the pelvis. Hemostats are applied to the angle of the uterus on each side and the uterus is removed, usually posteriorly. The physician also removes the surrounding tissues, including part or all of the vagina and the pelvic lymph nodes. Any incisions are closed by suturing.

58290

The physician performs a vaginal hysterectomy, for a uterus greater than 250 gm. An incision is made around the cervix through the full thickness of the vaginal membrane. The cut vaginal edge is pulled toward the lower cervix and vaginal dissection is continued with countertraction. The posterior peritoneum is opened to admit a finger examination of the pelvis. The uterosacral ligaments are clamped and possibly shortened, cut from the uterus, and secured to the vagina. The vesicovaginal space is entered. The connective tissue fusing the bladder and vagina is dissected and the bladder is separated from the cervix. The bladder pillars are clamped, cut, and ligated near their cervical attachments as well as the cardinal ligament tissue on each side of the cervix and the left and right uterine vessels. The anterior peritoneum is opened under direct vision to avoid damaging the bladder and admit finger exploration. The physician clamps, cuts, and ligates the upper cardinal and lower broad ligament complex now that the peritoneum is open both anterior and posterior to the uterine fundus. Traction applied to the cervix moves the uterus down until the fundus is low in the pelvis. Hemostats are applied to the angle of the uterus on each side and the uterus is removed, usually posteriorly. When the uterus is too large to permit delivery through the anterior or posterior peritoneal opening, the myometrium may be incised circumferentially parallel to the uterine cavity axis and removed or the uterus can be dissected and removed one half at a time. The peritoneum is closed with purse-string sutures that incorporate the proximal part of the uterosacral ligaments. Colporrhaphy may be performed before the vaginal wall is closed by running or interrupted sutures placed side to side longitudinally.

58291-58292

The physician performs a vaginal hysterectomy, for a uterus greater than 250 gm and removes the tubes and/or ovaries. An incision is made around the cervix through the full thickness of the vaginal membrane. The cut vaginal edge is pulled toward the lower cervix and vaginal dissection is continued with countertraction. The posterior peritoneum is opened to admit a finger examination of the pelvis. The uterosacral ligaments are clamped and possibly shortened, cut from the uterus, and secured to the vagina. The vesicovaginal space is entered. The connective tissue fusing the bladder and vagina is dissected and the bladder is separated from the cervix. The bladder pillars are clamped, cut, and ligated near their cervical attachments, as well as the cardinal ligament tissue on each side of the cervix and the left and right uterine vessels. The anterior peritoneum is opened under direct vision to avoid damaging the bladder and admit finger exploration. The physician clamps, cuts, and ligates the upper cardinal and lower broad ligament complex now that the peritoneum is open both anterior and posterior to the uterine fundus. Traction applied to the cervix moves the uterus down until the fundus is low in the pelvis. Hemostats are applied to the angle of the uterus on each side and the uterus is removed, usually posteriorly. After the uterus is exteriorized, care is taken to ensure ligation of the ovarian vessels. The ovary is excised under direct vision. For removal of both tubes and ovaries, the round ligament on one side at a time is clamped and divided. A tunnel is made through the layers of the uterine broad ligament that enclose the tube and the tube and ovary are clamped together. The structure is pulled forward, the two sheets of the broad ligament are each cut, and the broad ligament is opened completely. The whole specimen is separated from its attaching ligament, which is clamped, and the tube and ovary on that side are removed. Report 58292 if an enterocele is repaired in addition to removing the tube and/or ovary. An enterocele is a hernia of the intestine protruding against the vaginal wall. The hernia sac is bluntly and sharply dissected from the surrounding connective tissue, excised and ligated, and the surrounding tissues are strengthened and sutured. The peritoneal and vaginal wall incisions of the hysterectomy procedure are closed.

58293

The physician performs a vaginal hysterectomy, for a uterus greater than 250 gm with colpo-urethrocystopexy, with or without endoscopic control. Colpo-urethrocystopexy is done after vaginal hysterectomy in cases of urinary incontinence to elevate the lower part of the bladder that connects to the urethra (bladder neck) and the urethra to a new position higher in the pelvis so the muscles of the pelvic floor can help control urination. An incision is made around the cervix through the full thickness of the vaginal membrane. The cut vaginal edge is pulled toward the lower cervix and vaginal dissection is continued with countertraction. The posterior peritoneum is opened to admit a finger examination of the pelvis. The uterosacral ligaments are clamped and possibly shortened, cut from the uterus, and secured to the vagina. The vesicovaginal space is entered. The connective tissue fusing the bladder and vagina is dissected and the bladder is separated from the cervix. The bladder pillars are clamped, cut, and ligated near their cervical attachments, as well as the cardinal ligament tissue on each side of the cervix and the left and right uterine vessels. The anterior peritoneum is opened under direct vision to avoid damaging the bladder and admit finger exploration. The physician clamps, cuts, and ligates the upper cardinal and lower broad ligament complex now that the peritoneum is open both anterior and posterior to the uterine fundus. Traction applied to the cervix moves the uterus down until the fundus is low in the pelvis. Hemostats are applied to the angle of the uterus on each side and the uterus is removed, usually posteriorly. When the uterus is too large to permit delivery through the anterior or posterior peritoneal opening, the myometrium may be incised circumferentially parallel to the uterine cavity axis and removed or the uterus can be dissected and removed one half at a time. After the uterus has been exteriorized and the bladder and urethra separated from surrounding structures, the physician lifts the vagina upward, suspends the bladder neck and urethra by placing sutures through the fibromuscular wall of the vagina lateral to the tissue surrounding the urethra, and sutures the tissue to the symphysis pubis—the midline junction of the pubic bones at the front. An endoscope may be placed to ensure no sutures pass through the lining of the bladder and to evaluate ureteral patency. The sutures are pulled tight to tack the structures to the pubic bone and provide support. Packing may be placed in the vagina to be removed later and urine is drained by a catheter placed intraoperatively.

58294

The physician performs a vaginal hysterectomy, for a uterus greater than 250 gm, with repair of an enterocele. An incision is made around the cervix through the full thickness of the vaginal membrane. The cut vaginal edge is pulled toward the lower cervix and vaginal dissection is continued with countertraction. The posterior peritoneum is opened to admit a finger examination of the pelvis. The uterosacral ligaments are clamped and possibly shortened, cut from the uterus, and secured to the vagina. The vesicovaginal space is entered. The connective tissue fusing the bladder and vagina is dissected and the bladder is separated from the cervix. The bladder pillars are clamped, cut, and ligated near their cervical attachments, as well as the cardinal ligament tissue on each side of the cervix and the left and right uterine vessels. The anterior peritoneum is opened under direct vision. The physician clamps, cuts, and ligates the upper cardinal and lower broad ligament complex now that the peritoneum is open both anterior and posterior to the uterine fundus. Traction applied to the cervix moves the uterus down until the fundus is low in the pelvis. Hemostats are applied to the angle of the uterus on each side and the uterus is removed, usually posteriorly. The physician also repairs an enterocele, a herniation of intestine that protrudes against the vaginal wall, discovered during finger exploration. The hernia sac is bluntly and sharply dissected from the surrounding connective tissue, excised and ligated, and the surrounding tissues are strengthened and sutured. The peritoneum is closed with purse-string sutures that incorporate the proximal part of the uterosacral ligaments.

58300-58301
The physician inserts a speculum into the vagina to visualize the cervix. A tool is used to gently pull down the cervix; it is dilated. In 58300, an intrauterine device (IUD), any of a variety of shapes (coil, loop, T, 7), is guided into the uterus through an insertion tube placed in the cervical os. In 58301, to remove a previously placed IUD from the uterus, a device is inserted through the cervical os and used to grasp and remove the IUD.

58321-58322
In 58321, the physician performs artificial insemination by injecting semen into the endocervical canal by applying the blunt tip of a plastic syringe to the external os (opening) of the cervix. Sometimes a cervical cap is used to keep the semen in and around the cervix for eight to 16 hours. In 58322, the physician dilates the cervix and inserts a long flexible tube into the cavity of the uterus. Semen is injected into the uterus by a syringe connected to the tube.

58323
Sperm are spun in a centrifuge that removes the superficial antibodies on the sperm in order to facilitate fertilization. The sperm are first washed in a medium three times the volume of the collected semen. This mixture is spun in a centrifuge and the layer of liquid is discarded. The sperm are resuspended in a fresh medium. This method removes debris, bacteria, antibodies, and abnormal spermatozoa.

58340
A small catheter is introduced into the cervical opening and a saline solution (for saline infusion sonohysterography [SIS]) or liquid radiographic contrast material (for hysterosalpingography) is injected into the endometrial cavity with mild pressure to force the material into the fallopian tubes. The shadow of the contrast material appears on separately reported x-ray films, permitting examination of the uterus and fallopian tubes for any abnormalities or blockages. When sonohysterography is performed, a thin catheter is inserted into the uterus and one to two teaspoons of saline solution is injected into the uterine cavity. Separately reported, fluid enhanced endovaginal ultrasound is performed with the saline solution acting as a contrast medium to view any abnormal anatomic findings in the uterus.

58345
The physician introduces a catheter into the cervix, and takes it into the uterus and through the fallopian tube. The catheter must be made of a material that will show on x-ray film so that any blockages or abnormalities in the tube can be seen. The physician may inject radiographic contrast material into the endometrial cavity with mild pressure to force the material into the tubes. The shadow of this material on separately reported x-ray film permits examination of the uterus and tubes for any abnormalities or blockages.

58346
The physician inserts radioactive Heyman capsules into the uterus to treat endometrial cancer. Radiotherapy is often the prescribed treatment for patients who are medically inoperable for endometrial carcinoma. Brachytherapy is administered via low dose radiation (LDR) or high dose radiation (HDR) technique, with the goal of achieving coverage of all uterine tissue. This is achieved with the placement of multiple Heyman capsules, inserted through the cervical os and placed in the uterus with consideration of appropriate radiation field. For low-dose treatment, Heyman capsules are used for patients with a large uterus to help expand the uterine cavity and cover the uterus. Heyman capsules also may be prescribed for patients with early-stage disease and low-grade histology, when radiation alone is the preferred therapy. Use this code once to report multiple capsules inserted during the same session.

58350
The physician injects a liquid dye or solution into the uterine cavity or directly into the fallopian tubes. This procedure is frequently performed during a separately reported surgery, open or laparoscopic, to verify patency of tubes.

58353
The physician performs an endometrial ablation, using heat without hysteroscopic guidance. The physician inserts a soft, flexible balloon attached to a thin catheter into the vagina through the cervix and into the uterus. The balloon is inflated with fluid, which expands to fit the size and shape of the patient's uterus. The fluid in the balloon is heated to 87°C or 188°F and maintained for eight to nine minutes while the uterine lining is treated. When the treatment cycle is complete, all the fluid is withdrawn from the balloon and the balloon and catheter are removed.

58356
The physician performs endometrial cryoablation with any required endometrial curettage using ultrasound guidance. The physician inserts a speculum for visualization of the cervix. A numbing block is placed in the cervix. A thin cryoablation device is inserted through the cervix into the uterus. The cryoablation device freezes targeted uterine endometrial tissue. The instrument is withdrawn following completion of the procedure. Ultrasound provides visualization of probe placement and real-time monitoring of the ice ball growth. If endometrial curettage is required, the physician passes a curette into the uterus through the endocervical canal. The lining of the uterus is scraped.

58400
The physician plicates stretched uterine broad ligaments, bringing the uterus back into place. Plication shortens the ligament by folding and tacking it. The physician may elect to plicate the round and sacrouterine ligaments as well. This procedure may be done through a small abdominal incision or through an incision in the vagina.

58410
The physician plicates stretched uterine broad ligaments, bringing the uterus back into place. Plication shortens the ligament by folding and tacking it. The physician may elect to plicate the round and sacrouterine ligaments as well. A portion of the presacral sympathetic nerve is removed or destroyed to alleviate pelvic pain. The procedure may be done through a small abdominal incision or through an incision in the vagina.

58520
The physician repairs a uterus that became lacerated or ruptured by nonobstetrical means. A large incision is made in the abdomen and the uterus is repaired with layered suturing of torn, crushed, or deeply lacerated tissue. The physician debrides the wound by removing foreign material or damaged tissue. Irrigation of the wound is performed and antimicrobial solutions are used to decontaminate and cleanse the wound. The physician may trim skin margins with a scalpel or scissors to allow for proper closure. The abdominal incision is closed.

58540
Through a small incision in the lower abdomen, the physician performs a plastic repair of a malformed uterus. This often is an extensive procedure that involves removing abnormal tissues, rearranging the uterine walls, and suturing.

58541-58542
The physician performs a laparoscopic hysterectomy, removing a uterus with a total weight of 250 gm or less while preserving the cervix. The patient is placed in the dorsal lithotomy position. After the insertion of a speculum in the vagina, the physician grasps the cervix with an instrument to manipulate the uterus during the surgery. A trocar is inserted periumbilically and the abdomen is insufflated with gas. Additional trocars are placed in the right and left lower quadrants. The uterus is dissected free from the bladder and surrounding tissue and its body is separated from the cervix. Coagulation is achieved with the aid of electrocautery instruments. Alternatively, some vessels may be ligated. The uterus is morcellized and removed using endoscopic tools. In 58542, one or both ovaries and/or one or both fallopian tubes are removed in similar fashion. Once the excisions are complete, the abdominal cavity is deflated and instruments and trocars removed. The fascia and skin are closed with sutures.

58543-58544
The physician performs a laparoscopic hysterectomy, removing a uterus with a total weight of more than 250 gm while preserving the cervix. The patient is placed in the dorsal lithotomy position. After the insertion of a speculum in the vagina, the physician grasps the cervix with an instrument to manipulate the uterus during the surgery. A trocar is inserted periumbilically and the abdomen is insufflated with gas. Additional trocars are placed in the right and left lower quadrants. The uterus is dissected free from the bladder and surrounding tissue and its body is separated from the cervix. Coagulation is achieved with the aid of electrocautery instruments. Alternatively, some vessels may be ligated. The uterus is morcellized and removed using endoscopic tools. In 58544, one or both ovaries and/or one or both fallopian tubes are removed in similar fashion. Once the excisions are complete, the abdominal cavity is deflated and instruments and trocars removed. The fascia and skin are closed with sutures.

58545
The physician performs a laparoscopic myomectomy, removing one to four fibroid tumors from the wall of the uterus (intramural myomas) with a total weight of 250 gm or less and/or removes surface myomas. The patient is placed in the dorsal lithotomy position. A trocar is inserted periumbilically and the abdomen is insufflated with gas. Additional trocars are placed in the right and left lower quadrants. Electrocautery instruments and/or laser may be used to remove small surface myomas. Pedunculated myomas are removed by ligating, twisting, or snaring the stalk. The physician incises the uterus through the myometrium to expose the myoma, which is dissected free from the surrounding myometrium. The pedicle is isolated, clamped, and ligated and the myoma is dissected down to the pedicular blood supply. The adjacent myomas may be reached and removed by tunneling further through the initial incision. The uterine wall defects are sutured laparoscopically, the trocars are removed, and the wounds are closed.

58546

The physician performs a laparoscopic myomectomy, removing five or more fibroid tumors from the wall of the uterus (intramural myomas) and/or intramural myomas with a total weight greater than 250 gm. The patient is placed in the dorsal lithotomy position. A trocar is inserted periumbilically and the abdomen is insufflated with gas. Additional trocars are placed in the right and left lower quadrants. The physician incises the uterus through the myometrium to expose the myoma, which is dissected free from the surrounding myometrium. The pedicle is isolated, clamped, and ligated and the myoma is dissected to the pedicular blood supply. The adjacent myomas may be reached and removed by tunneling further through the initial incision. After resecting large intramural myomas, removing them from the abdominal cavity may require making a culdotomy incision or using morcellation techniques. A minilaparotomy may be done with laparoscopic myomectomy as myomas are brought to the abdominal wall for removal and the uterus may be closed with some layered suturing. The laparoscopic instruments are removed and the wounds are closed.

58548

The physician performs a laparoscopic hysterectomy, bilateral total pelvic lymphadenectomy, and para-aortic lymph node sampling, and may remove all or portions of the fallopian tubes and ovaries. The patient is placed in the dorsal lithotomy position. After the insertion of a speculum in the vagina, the physician grasps the cervix with an instrument to manipulate the uterus during the surgery. A trocar is inserted periumbilically and the abdomen is insufflated with gas. Additional trocars are placed in the right and left lower quadrants. The uterus is dissected free from the bladder and surrounding tissue and its body with the cervix is dissected from the vagina. Alternately, the vagina may also be excised. Coagulation is achieved with the aid of electrocautery instruments. Some vessels may be ligated. The uterus is morcellized and removed using endoscopic tools. One or both ovaries and/or one or both fallopian tubes are removed in similar fashion. The physician removes the pelvic lymph nodes on both sides and takes samples or biopsies of the para-aortic lymph nodes. Once the excisions are complete, the abdominal cavity is deflated and instruments and trocars removed. The fascia and skin of the abdomen and vagina are closed with sutures.

58550-58552

The physician performs surgical laparoscopy with vaginal hysterectomy for a uterus 250 gm or less. The laparoscope is used to perform the initial operative portion of the hysterectomy. The patient is placed in the dorsal lithotomy position for the endoscopic portion. For the vaginal portion, the patient is positioned in stirrups. A trocar is inserted periumbilically and the abdomen is insufflated with gas. Additional trocars are placed in the right and left lower quadrants. An intra-abdominal and pelvic survey is done and any adhesions are lysed. The round ligaments are ligated and incised. Starting on the left round ligament, the vesicouterine peritoneal fold is incised and the peritoneal vessels are dissected and desiccated. The physician continues the incision across the lower uterine segment to the round ligament on the other side and dissects the bladder off the uterus and cervix. Staples are inserted through one port on the side to be stapled or a bipolar coagulation unit is inserted for electrocautery. At this point, if tubes and/or ovaries are to be removed, the infundibulopelvic ligament is now ligated lateral to the ovary. If not, the ligation is done medial to the ovary. Staple-ligation or electrodesiccation of the uterine vasculature is accomplished on both sides, followed by that of the cardinal ligaments. An anterior colpotomy incision is made to enter the vagina and the vaginal portion of the procedure is begun. The vaginal hysterectomy proceeds through a posterior cul-de-sac incision. The uterus is removed, the vagina is closed, and hemostasis is confirmed before the trocars are removed and the skin incisions are closed. Report 58550 for removal of uterus or 58552 if uterus, tubes, and/or ovaries are removed.

58553-58554

The physician performs surgical laparoscopy with vaginal hysterectomy for a uterus greater than 250 gm. The laparoscope is used to perform the initial operative portion of the hysterectomy. The patient is placed in the dorsal lithotomy position for the endoscopic portion. For the vaginal portion, the patient is positioned in stirrups. A trocar is inserted periumbilically and the abdomen is insufflated with gas. Additional trocars are placed in the right and left lower quadrants. An intra-abdominal and pelvic survey is done and any adhesions are lysed. The round ligaments are ligated and incised. Starting on the left round ligament, the vesicouterine peritoneal fold is incised and the peritoneal vessels are dissected and desiccated. The physician continues the incision across the lower uterine segment to the round ligament on the other side and dissects the bladder off the uterus and cervix. Staples are inserted through one port on the side to be stapled or a bipolar coagulation unit is inserted for electrocautery. At this point, if tubes and/or ovaries are to be removed, the infundibulopelvic ligament is now ligated lateral to the ovary. If not, the ligation is done medial to the ovary. Staple-ligation or electrodesiccation of the uterine vasculature is accomplished next on both sides, followed by that of the cardinal ligaments. An anterior colpotomy incision is made to enter the vagina and the vaginal portion of the procedure is begun. The vaginal hysterectomy proceeds with a posterior cul-de-sac incision made during the vaginal portion. When the uterus is too large to permit delivery through the anterior or posterior opening, extra incisions and/or manipulations may be necessary to remove the uterus. The vagina is closed, and hemostasis is confirmed before the trocars are removed and the skin incisions are closed. Report 58554 if tubes and/or ovaries are also removed.

58555
The physician performs a diagnostic inspection of the uterus using a hysteroscope. The physician advances the hysteroscope through the vagina and into the cervical os to gain entry into the uterine cavity. The physician inspects the uterine cavity with the fiberoptic scope for diagnostic purposes.

58558
The physician performs a diagnostic inspection of the uterus using a hysteroscope and removes a uterine polyp, removes uterine tissue for biopsy, and may perform cervical dilation and uterine curettage (D&C). The physician advances the hysteroscope through the vagina and into the cervical os to gain entry into the uterine cavity. The physician inspects the uterine cavity with the fiberoptic scope and removes a sample of the uterine lining and/or removes a growth (polypectomy) within the uterus and may perform a cervical dilation and uterine curettage, scraping (D&C) to take a complete sampling of the uterine lining.

58559
The physician removes scar tissue (adhesions) from within the uterus using a fiberoptic hysteroscope. The physician advances the hysteroscope through the vagina and into the cervical os to gain entry into the uterine cavity. The physician inspects the uterine cavity with the fiberoptic scope and removes or divides adhesions (fibrous scar tissue) that are artificially connecting the walls of the uterus.

58560
The physician removes tissue abnormally dividing the intrauterine cavity using a fiberoptic hysteroscope. The physician advances the hysteroscope through the vagina and into the cervical os to gain entry into the uterine cavity. The physician inspects the uterine cavity with the fiberoptic scope and resects an intrauterine septum (tissue creating an abnormal partition in the uterus).

58561
The physician surgically removes a leiomyomata (uterine fibroid tumor) with the assistance of a fiberoptic hysteroscope. The physician advances the hysteroscope through the vagina and into the cervical os to gain entry into the uterine cavity. The physician inspects the uterine cavity with the fiberoptic scope and removes uterine leiomyomata with the assistance of the fiberoptic scope.

58562
The physician surgically removes an impacted foreign body with the assistance of a fiberoptic hysteroscope. The physician advances the hysteroscope through the vagina and into the cervical os to gain entry into the uterine cavity. The physician inspects the uterine cavity with the fiberoptic scope and removes an impacted foreign body from the uterine wall with the assistance of the hysteroscope.

58563
The physician surgically removes (ablates) the inner lining of the uterus with the assistance of a fiberoptic hysteroscope. The physician advances the hysteroscope through the vagina and into the cervical os to gain entry into the uterine cavity. The physician inspects the uterine cavity with the fiberoptic scope and ablates the endometrium by various methods, such as resection, electrosurgical ablation, or thermoablation.

58565
The physician performs a hysteroscopy with bilateral fallopian tube cannulation and placement of permanent implants to occlude the fallopian tubes. The physician advances the hysteroscope through the vagina and into the cervical os to gain entry into the uterine cavity. The physician inserts a catheter into each fallopian tube. The catheter delivers a small metallic implant into each fallopian tube. The presence of the obstructive implant causes scar tissue to form, completely blocking the fallopian tube as a means of birth control.

58570-58571
The physician performs a laparoscopic total hysterectomy, removing a uterus with a total weight of 250 gm or less. Following appropriate anesthesia, the patient is placed in the dorsal lithotomy position. A Foley catheter ensures that the bladder is emptied during the procedure. A trocar is inserted periumbilically and the abdomen is insufflated with gas. Ancillary trocars are also placed suprapubically. Following abdominal pelvic inspection and lysis of any adhesions present, the uterus is mobilized. The uterine ligaments are sectioned, and the uterus and cervix are dissected free from the bladder and surrounding tissues. Coagulation is achieved with the aid of electrocautery instruments. Alternately, some vessels may be ligated. The uterus and cervix are morcellized and removed using endoscopic tools. In 58571, one or both ovaries and/or one or both fallopian tubes are removed in similar fashion. Once the excisions are complete, the abdominal cavity is deflated and instruments and trocars are removed. The fascia and skin are closed with sutures.

58572-58573
The physician performs a laparoscopic total hysterectomy, removing a uterus with a total weight of more than 250 gm. The cervix is also removed. Following appropriate anesthesia, the patient is placed in the dorsal lithotomy position. A Foley catheter ensures that the bladder is emptied during the procedure. A trocar is inserted periumbilically and the abdomen is insufflated with gas. Ancillary trocars are

also placed suprapubically. Following abdominal pelvic inspection and lysis of any adhesions present, the uterus is mobilized. The uterine ligaments are sectioned, and the uterus and cervix are dissected free from the bladder and surrounding tissues. Coagulation is achieved with the aid of electrocautery instruments. Alternately, some vessels may be ligated. The uterus and cervix are morcellized and removed using endoscopic tools. In 58573, one or both ovaries and/or one or both fallopian tubes are removed in similar fashion. Once the excisions are complete, the abdominal cavity is deflated and instruments and trocars are removed. The fascia and skin are closed with sutures.

58600
The physician ties off the fallopian tube or removes a portion of it on one side or both. The procedure may be done through the vagina or through a small incision just above the pubic hairline.

58605
The physician ties off the fallopian tube or removes a portion of it on one side or both. This procedure is done through a small incision just above the pubic hairline or vaginally during the same hospital stay as the delivery of a baby.

58611
The physician ties off the fallopian tube or removes a portion of it on one side or both. This procedure is done at the time of a cesarean section or during intra-abdominal surgery.

58615
The physician blocks one or both of the fallopian tubes with a band, clip, or Falope ring. The physician may elect to do the procedure through the vagina or through a small incision just above the pubic hairline.

58660
The physician performs a laparoscopic surgical cutting/releasing (lysis) of scar tissue (adhesions) surrounding the ovaries and/or fallopian tubes with the assistance of a fiberoptic laparoscope. The physician may first insert an instrument through the vagina to grasp the cervix and manipulate the uterus during surgery. Next, the physician makes a small incision just below the umbilicus through which a fiberoptic laparoscope is inserted. A second incision is made in the abdomen with additional instruments being placed through these incisions into the abdomen or pelvis. The physician manipulates the tools so that the pelvic organs can be observed, manipulated and lysis of adhesions can be performed. The abdomen is deflated, the trocars removed, and the incisions are closed with sutures.

58661
The physician performs a laparoscopic surgical removal of one or both ovaries and their accompanying fallopian tubes with the assistance of a fiberoptic laparoscope. The physician may first insert an instrument through the vagina to grasp the cervix and manipulate the uterus during surgery. Next, the physician makes a small incision just below the umbilicus through which a fiberoptic laparoscope is inserted. A second incision is made on the left or right side of the abdomen with additional instruments being placed through these incisions into the abdomen or pelvis. The physician manipulates the tools so that the pelvic organs can be observed, manipulated and removal of one or both ovaries and fallopian tubes can be performed with the laparoscope. The abdomen is deflated, the trocars removed and the incisions are closed with sutures.

58662
The physician performs a laparoscopic electrical cautery destruction of an ovarian, pelvic or peritoneal lesion with the assistance of a fiberoptic laparoscope. The physician may first insert an instrument through the vagina to grasp the cervix and manipulate the uterus during surgery. Next, the physician makes a small incision just below the umbilicus through which a fiberoptic laparoscope is inserted. A second incision is made on the left or right side of the abdomen with additional instruments being placed through these incisions into the abdomen or pelvis. The physician manipulates the tools so that the pelvic organs can be observed, manipulated and operated upon with the laparoscope. Once lesions are identified with the laparoscope, a third incision is typically made adjacent to the lesion through which an electric cautery tool, knife, or laser is inserted for lesion fulguration. The abdomen is deflated, the trocars removed and the incisions are closed with sutures.

58670
The physician performs a laparoscopic electrical cautery destruction of an oviduct (the uterine tube) with or without complete cutting through the fallopian tubes (transection) with the assistance of a fiberoptic laparoscope. The physician may first insert an instrument through the vagina to grasp the cervix and manipulate the uterus during surgery. Next, the physician makes a small incision just below the umbilicus through which a fiberoptic laparoscope is inserted. A second incision is made on the left or right side of the abdomen with additional instruments being placed through these incisions into the abdomen or pelvis. The physician manipulates the tools so that the pelvic organs can be observed, manipulated and operated upon with the laparoscope. A third incision is typically made adjacent to the fallopian tubes. To fulgurate the fallopian tube the physician inserts an electric cautery tool or a laser. The physician may cut the tubes and fulgurate or burn the ends. Additionally, the physician may transect (cut through) the fallopian tubes. The abdomen is deflated, the trocars removed and the incisions are closed with sutures.

58671
The physician performs a laparoscopic occlusion of the oviduct (the uterine tube) with the assistance of a fiberoptic laparoscope. The physician may first insert an instrument through the vagina to grasp the cervix and manipulate the uterus during surgery. Next, the physician makes a small incision just below the umbilicus through which a fiberoptic laparoscope is inserted. A second incision is made on the left or right side of the abdomen with additional instruments being placed through these incisions into the abdomen or pelvis. The physician manipulates the tools so that the pelvic organs can be observed, manipulated and operated upon with the laparoscope. A third incision is typically made adjacent to the fallopian tubes. To occlude the fallopian tubes, the physician places silicone rings or clips around the tubes through this incision. The abdomen is deflated, the trocars removed and the incisions are closed with sutures.

58672
The physician performs a laparoscopic surgical repair of the ovarian fimbria (fingerlike processes on the distal part of the infundibulum of the uterine tube) with the assistance of a fiberoptic laparoscope. The physician may first insert an instrument through the vagina to grasp the cervix and manipulate the uterus during surgery. Next, the physician makes a small incision just below the umbilicus through which a fiberoptic laparoscope is inserted. A second incision is made on the left or right side of the abdomen with additional instruments being placed through these incisions into the abdomen or pelvis. The physician manipulates the tools so that the pelvic organs can be observed, manipulated and operated upon with the laparoscope. A third incision is typically made adjacent to the fallopian tubes. The physician performs surgical repair of the ovarian fimbria using instruments placed through the abdomen and pelvic trocars. The abdomen is deflated, the trocars removed and the incisions are closed with sutures.

58673
The physician performs a laparoscopic surgical restoration of the patency of the uterine tube damaged typically by infection, tumor or endometriosis. The physician may first insert an instrument through the vagina to grasp the cervix and manipulate the uterus during surgery. Next, the physician makes a small incision just below the umbilicus through which a fiberoptic laparoscope is inserted. A second incision is made on the left or right side of the abdomen with additional instruments being placed through these incisions into the abdomen or pelvis. The physician manipulates the tools so that the pelvic organs can be observed, manipulated and operated upon with the laparoscope. A third incision is typically made adjacent to the fallopian tubes. The physician performs surgical restoration of the fallopian tube (salpingostomy) using instruments placed through the abdomen and pelvic trocars. The abdomen is deflated, the trocars removed and the incisions are closed with sutures.

58700
Through a small incision in the lower abdomen just above the pubic hairline, the physician removes part or all of the fallopian tube on one or both sides. The incision is closed by suturing.

58720
Through a small incision in the abdomen just above the pubic hairline, the physician removes part or all of the ovary and part or all of its fallopian tube on one or both sides. The incision is closed by suturing.

58740
The physician cuts free any fibrous tissue adhering to the ovaries or tubes through a small incision just above the pubic hairline.

58750
Through a small incision just above the pubic hairline, the physician excises the closed or blocked portion of the tube and sutures the clean edges together. The procedure is generally performed microsurgically in order to do an accurate repair.

58752
Through a small incision just above the pubic hairline, the physician removes a blocked portion of the tube near its junction with the uterus and reimplants the tube into the uterus in the same place.

58760
Through a small incision just above the pubic hairline, the physician reconstructs the existing fimbriae in a partially or totally obstructed (occluded) or closed off oviduct. Fimbriae are the hairlike fringes at the end of the fallopian tubes. Depending on the nature of the blockage, the physician may separate the fimbriae by gentle dilation or by electrosurgical dissection. The procedure is generally performed microsurgically in order to do an accurate repair.

58770
Through a small incision just above the pubic hairline, the physician creates a new opening in the fallopian tube where the fimbrial end has been closed by inflammation, infection, or injury. The procedure is generally performed microsurgically in order to do an accurate repair.

58800
The physician drains a cyst or cysts on one or both ovaries through an incision in the vagina. A cyst is a sac containing fluid or semisolid material. The cyst is ruptured with a surgical instrument, electrocautery, or a laser, and the fluid is removed.

58805
Through a small incision just above the pubic hairline, the physician drains a cyst or cysts on one or both ovaries. A cyst is a sac containing fluid or semisolid

material. The cyst is ruptured with a surgical instrument, electrocautery, or a laser, and the fluid is removed.

58820
The physician drains an abscess (infection) on the ovary through an incision in the vagina. The abscess is drained, cleaned out, and irrigated with antibiotics. Temporary catheters and tubes are often left in place to help drainage.

58822
Through a small abdominal incision just above the pubic hairline, the physician drains an abscess (infection) on the ovary. The abscess is drained, cleaned out, and irrigated with antibiotics. Temporary catheters and tubes are often left in place to help drainage.

58823
The physician drains an abscess (infection) in the pelvis percutaneously. The abscess is drained, cleaned out, and irrigated with antibiotics. Temporary catheters and tubes are often left in place to help drainage.

58825
The ovaries are placed behind the uterus and sutured in place prior to radiation therapy of the pelvis. The uterus acts as a shield protecting the ovaries from the radiation. The procedure is done through a small abdominal incision just above the pubic hairline.

58900
The physician takes a tissue sample from one or both ovaries for diagnosis. This procedure may be done through the vagina or abdominally through a small incision just above the pubic hairline.

58920
Through a small abdominal incision just above the pubic hairline, the physician takes a pie-shaped section or half of one or both of the ovaries to reduce the size and repairs each ovary with sutures.

58925
Through a small abdominal incision just above the pubic hairline, the physician removes a cyst or cysts on one or both of the ovaries.

58940
Through a small abdominal incision just above the top of the pubic hairline, the physician removes part or all of one or both of the ovaries.

58943
Through an abdominal incision extending from the top of the pubic hairline to the rib cage, the physician removes part or all of one or both ovaries depending on the extent of the malignancy. The physician takes a sampling of the lymph nodes surrounding the lower aorta within the pelvis and flushes the peritoneum, which is the lining of the abdominal cavity, with saline. The saline solution is suctioned from the peritoneum for separately reportable examination. Multiple tissue samples are excised. The physician also examines and takes tissue samples of the diaphragm. The physician may elect to remove one or both fallopian tubes and the omentum. The abdominal incision is closed with layered sutures.

58950
The physician performs the initial resection of an ovarian, tubal, or primary peritoneal malignancy. Through a full abdominal incision, the physician removes both tubes, both ovaries, and the omentum, which is a membrane of lymph nodes, blood vessels, and fat that forms a protective layer extending from the stomach to the transverse colon. The abdominal incision is closed with layered sutures.

58951
Through a full abdominal incision extending from just above the pubic hairline to the rib cage, the physician treats an ovarian, tubal, or peritoneal malignancy by taking out both tubes, both ovaries, and the omentum, which is a membrane of lymph nodes, blood vessels, and fat that forms a protective layer extending from the stomach to the transverse colon. The physician also removes the uterus, the pelvic lymph nodes, and a portion of the lymph nodes surrounding the lower aorta. The abdominal incision is closed with layered sutures. This code is to be used only for the initial surgical resection of the malignancy.

58952
Through a full abdominal incision extending from just above the pubic hairline to the rib cage, the physician treats an ovarian, tubal, or peritoneal malignancy by excising both tubes, both ovaries, and the omentum, which is a membrane containing fat, lymph, and blood vessels that acts as a protective layer extending from the stomach to the transverse colon. The physician also reduces the size of a tumor that has grown large enough to cause discomfort or problems. Due to the size and location, it may not be possible to remove the tumor. The abdominal incision is closed with layered sutures. This code is to be used only for the initial surgical resection of the malignancy.

58953-58954
Through a full abdominal incision extending from just above the pubic hairline to the rib cage, the physician treats an ovarian malignancy. Additionally, the physician may excise pelvic lymph nodes and partially remove para-aortic lymph nodes. In either procedure, the physician makes a full abdominal incision and carries dissection down to the abdominal cavity. The physician excises the fallopian tubes, both ovaries, the uterus, and the omentum, which is a membrane containing lymph, blood vessels, and fat in a protective layer that extends from the stomach to the transverse colon. The physician removes or reduces metastatic ovarian cancer implants from the abdominal cavity. In 58954, the physician additionally removes pelvic

lymph nodes and a portion of the lymph nodes that surrounds the lower aorta within the pelvis. The abdominal incision is closed with layered sutures.

58956

The physician performs a bilateral salpingo-oophorectomy with total omentectomy and total abdominal hysterectomy to treat a malignancy. A full abdominal incision is made extending from just above the pubic hairline to the rib cage. Dissection is carried down to the abdominal cavity. The physician excises the fallopian tubes, ovaries, the uterus, and the omentum. The supporting pedicles containing the tubes, ligaments, and arteries are clamped and cut free. The uterus and cervix are removed along with a narrow rim or cuff of the vaginal lining. The vaginal defect is often left open for drainage. Attention is directed to the omentum, a membrane of lymph, blood vessels, and fat that forms a protective layer that extends from the stomach to the transverse colon. The omentum is mobilized from the stomach and colon, divided from its blood supply, and removed. The physician inspects the abdominal cavity and removes any metastatic lesions. The abdominal incision is closed with layered sutures.

58957-58958

These codes report tumor debulking in recurrent ovarian, uterine, tubal, or peritoneal malignancies. Through a full abdominal incision extending from just above the pubic hairline to the rib cage, the physician explores the abdomen, pelvis, and viscera. In addition to debulking recurrent malignancy, the physician releases intestinal adhesions or excises all or portions of the omentum, ovaries, or fallopian tubes. The physician may remove all visible tumors or only reduce their size, depending on the nature of the malignancy and the structures involved. The abdominal incision is closed with layered sutures. Report 58958 when pelvic and para-aortic lymph nodes are also removed.

58960

This procedure is the second operation to check for a recurrence of the ovarian malignancy. Through a full abdominal incision extending from just above the pubic hairline to the rib cage, the physician may elect to remove the omentum, a membrane of lymph, blood vessels, and fat that forms a protective layer that extends from the stomach to the transverse colon. The physician may flush the lining of the abdominal cavity (peritoneum) and remove the liquid to check for cancerous cells. A tissue sample of the abdominal and pelvic peritoneum may be taken. The physician also may examine and take tissue samples of the diaphragm. The pelvic lymph nodes are removed and a portion of the lymph nodes that surrounds the lower aorta within the pelvis is removed. The abdominal incision is closed with layered sutures.

58970

The physician aspirates a mature or nearly mature egg from its follicle for in vitro fertilization. Visualization of the aspiration may be done laparoscopically or by ultrasound. The laparoscopic method uses three puncture sites in the lower abdomen—one for the laparoscope, one for the holding forceps, and one for the aspirating needle. The ultrasound guided technique involves using a transabdominal ultrasound transducer for guidance. The aspirating needle is passed through the bladder wall to the ovary or through the urethra and into the pelvic cavity. Another ultrasound method uses transvaginal ultrasound and transvaginal needle aspiration of the ovary. In all methods, the ovary and preovulatory follicle are visualized and punctured with a needle to withdraw the follicular fluid containing the egg.

58974

The physician places fertilized eggs in the uterus after the eggs have undergone 48 to 72 hours of laboratory culture. The embryos are aspirated into a small catheter. The catheter is passed through the cervical os and into the uterus. The eggs are injected into the uterus.

58976

In gamete intrafallopian transfer (GIFT), the physician mixes previously captured eggs with sperm and draws the mixture into a catheter. The catheter is passed through the cervix and uterus and into the tubes or passed through an abdominal incision and directly into the fimbrial end of the fallopian tube. The physician deposits the eggs and sperm in the tubes, permitting fertilization. In a zygote intrafallopian transfer (ZIFT), a physician draws an already fertilized egg into a catheter. The catheter is passed through the cervix and uterus and into the tube where the egg is deposited. GIFT is a one-step procedure while ZIFT is a two-step process. In ZIFT, the egg is collected and fertilized and transferred to the fallopian tube at a later time. GIFT and ZIFT can be done laparoscopically or hysteroscopically.

Maternity Care and Delivery

59000

The physician aspirates fluid from the amniotic sac for diagnostic purposes. Using separately reportable ultrasonic guidance, the physician inserts an amniocentesis needle through the abdominal wall into the interior of the pregnant uterus and directly into the amniotic sac to collect amniotic fluid for separately reportable analysis.

59001

The physician performs a therapeutic amniotic fluid reduction. Using separately reportable ultrasonic guidance, the physician inserts an 18- or 20-guage amniocentesis needle through the abdominal wall into the interior of the pregnant uterus and directly into the amniotic sac to remove excess levels of amniotic fluid (amnioreduction). Serial amniotic fluid volume reduction may be accomplished on an ongoing basis by repeating the procedure.

59012

The physician removes blood from the fetal umbilical cord for diagnostic purposes. Using separately reportable ultrasonic guidance, the physician inserts an amniocentesis needle through the abdominal wall into the cavity of the pregnant uterus and into the umbilical vessels to obtain fetal blood. This may be accomplished with a transplacental or transamniotic approach.

59015

The physician samples tissue from the placenta for diagnostic purposes. This procedure uses ultrasonic guidance and can be done by any one of three methods. In the transcervical method, the physician inserts a catheter through the cervix and into the uterine cavity toward the placental site. A sample of the placenta (chorionic villus) is aspirated to obtain placental cells for analysis for chromosomal abnormalities. The procedure may also be performed transvaginally or transabdominally.

59020

The physician evaluates fetal response to induced contractions in the mother. The physician applies external fetal monitors to the maternal abdominal wall. Pitocin is given intravenously to the mother to cause uterine contractions. The fetal heart rate and uterine contractions are monitored and recorded for 20 minutes to determine the effect of contractions on the fetus. This procedure is usually performed during the third trimester.

59025

The physician evaluates fetal heart rate response to its own activity. The patient reports fetal movements as an external monitor records fetal heart rate changes. The procedure is noninvasive and takes 20 to 40 minutes to perform. If the fetus is not active, an acoustic device may be used to stimulate activity.

59030

The physician samples fetal scalp blood during active labor for diagnostic purposes. This test, which assesses fetal distress during labor, must be done when the cervix is dilated more than 2 cm and the fetal vertex is low in the pelvis. The physician breaks the amniotic sac in patients whose water has not broken spontaneously and inserts an amnioscope through the vagina. An incision is made in the scalp with a narrow blade that penetrates no more than 2 mm. Blood is aspirated into a tube.

59050-59051

In 59050, a consultant other than the attending physician attaches an electrode directly to the presenting fetus' scalp via the cervix. The electrocardiographic impulses are transmitted to a cardiotachometer which converts the fetal electrocardiographic pattern into recorded electronic impulses. A catheter is inserted through the dilated cervix into the amniotic sac to measure and record the intervals between contractions. The procedure is supervised during labor until delivery. The recordings are analyzed and accompanied by an interpretive written report. In 59051, the consultant initiates the monitoring, provides the analysis and interpretive report, but does not supervise the patient during labor.

59070

The physician infuses an abnormally underhydrated amniotic sac with fluid. This may be done as a prophylactic measure for the fetus or to enhance sonographic imaging. An amniocentesis needle is placed through the mother's abdomen and advanced between extremities of the fetus under separately reportable ultrasound guidance. Normal sterile saline is infused into the uterus until the fetal anatomy is adequately visualized. The needle is removed and a detailed ultrasound is carried out.

59072

Fetal umbilical cord occlusion is carried out in cases of complicated monochorionic multiple gestation pregnancies or in cases to terminate a pregnancy due to a birth defect. Ultrasound is used to locate access to the umbilical cord, avoiding the placenta. Using ultrasound guidance, small forceps are advanced into the uterus and the cord of the affected fetus is identified and grasped. The umbilical cord may be ligated, occluded, or compressed. Complete absence of flow through the cord is confirmed and the instruments are removed.

59074

Fetal fluid drainage is done in cases of pleural effusions or pulmonary cysts, and especially in fetal megavesica, a rare syndrome caused by functional obstruction of the fetal urethra. The fetus' bladder is enlarged. Oligohydramnios, dilation of the lower and upper urinary tract, and hydronephrosis may also be present. Pulmonary hypoplasia can result from this and lead to hypoplastic abdominal musculature, urinary tract anomalies, and cryptorchidism. The fetal urinary bladder is emptied by transabdominal intrauterine vesicocentesis. Under continual ultrasound guidance, a 20-22 gauge needle is inserted through the mother's abdomen and advanced into the fetus' bladder. Fetal urine is aspirated and sent to the lab for analysis of urinary electrolytes and to determine renal function. The needle is removed and the patient kept for monitoring for up to another hour to check for refilling in the bladder. Similar fluid drainage is done by transabdominal intrauterine thoracocentesis for fetal pleural effusion.

59076

Fetal shunt placement is performed for pleural or vesical amniotic shunting in cases of pleural effusion, pulmonary cysts, or fetal megavesica, where the bladder is enlarged because of urethra blockage. Shunting is done to supply continuous drainage when reaccumulation of fluid is not successfully treated by isolated vesicocentesis or thoracocentesis. Fluids can be drained into the amniotic cavity through a double pigtailed catheter. The entry site on the mother's abdomen is cleaned with antiseptic solution and local anesthetic is infiltrated down to the myometrium. Under ultrasound guidance, a metal cannula with a trocar is introduced transabdominally into the amniotic cavity and inserted through the fetal chest wall in the midthoracic region, into the effusion or cyst (if megavesical fluid accumulation is the problem, the shunt is placed into the bladder). The trocar is removed and the catheter is inserted into the cannula. A short introducer rod is used to place the proximal half of the catheter into the effusion or cyst. The cannula is gradually removed into the amniotic cavity where the other half of the catheter is pushed by a longer introducer. There is now a conduit for fluid drainage into the amniotic space. Placement of the shunt is confirmed, the instruments are removed, and the patient is monitored for one to two hours. Follow-up ultrasound scans are performed at weekly intervals to check drainage and determine if the effusions reaccumulate, in which case another shunt may be inserted. The drains are immediately clamped and removed after delivery.

59100

The physician removes an embryo or hydatidiform mole through an incision in the abdominal wall and uterus. The surgery is similar to a cesarean section but the abdominal and uterine incisions are smaller. The lower abdominal wall is opened with a vertical or horizontal incision and the uterus is entered through the lower uterine segment. The physician removes the embryo or hydatidiform mole and may also remove any remaining membranes and placenta from the uterine cavity. Curettage of the uterine cavity may also be performed. The abdominal and uterine incisions are closed by suturing.

59120

The physician treats a tubal or ovarian ectopic pregnancy by removing the fallopian tube and/or ovary. Through the vagina or through an incision in the lower abdomen, the physician explores the pelvic cavity, inspects the gestation site for bleeding, and removes all products of conception, clots, and free blood. If the tube is affected, it may be excised by cutting a small wedge of the uterine wall at the junction of the fallopian tube and body of the uterus. If the ovary is affected, it may be removed. Lysis of adhesions may be indicated and the pelvis lavaged with saline solution. If an abdominal approach is used, the incision is closed with sutures.

59121

The physician treats a tubal or ovarian ectopic pregnancy by removing the embryo from the tube or ovary. Through an incision in the lower abdomen, the physician explores the pelvic cavity, inspects the gestation site for bleeding, and removes all products of conception, clots, and free blood. If the embryo is implanted in the fallopian tube, the physician may do one of the following: manually remove the embryo from the tube, make an incision to remove the embryo, or excise the section of the tube containing the embryo. If the embryo is implanted in the ovary, the physician resects the ovary to remove the embryo. Lysis of adhesions may be indicated and the pelvis lavaged with saline solution. The incision is closed with sutures.

59130

The physician removes an embryo or fetus implanted in the abdomen. The fertilized ovum may have implanted directly in the abdomen (primary) or it may have implanted after escaping from the tube through a rupture or through the fimbriated end (secondary). After making an abdominal incision, the physician surgically removes the fetus from the abdomen. The membranes are also removed and the cord is ligated near the placenta. The placenta is usually not removed unless attached to the fallopian tube, ovary, or uterine broad ligament. Abdominal lavage may also be indicated. The abdominal incision is closed with sutures. Although this procedure is rare, it can be done any time during gestation, even at or near term.

59135

The physician treats an interstitial pregnancy where the fertilized ovum has implanted in the portion of the tube that transverses the uterine wall by removing the uterus and cervix. Through an incision extending from just above the pubic hairline to the rib cage, the physician clamps and cuts free the supporting pedicles containing the tubes, ligaments, and arteries. The physician removes the uterus and cervix and may elect to remove the tubes and/or ovaries. Abdominal or pelvic lavage may also be indicated. The abdominal incision is closed with sutures.

59136
The physician treats an interstitial ectopic pregnancy where the fertilized ovum has implanted in the portion of the tube that transverses the uterine wall by partially resecting the uterus. Through an incision extending from just above the pubic hairline to the rib cage, the physician resects and reconstructs the uterine wall. The physician may also remove a portion or all of the fallopian tube. Abdominal or pelvic lavage may be indicated. The abdominal incision is closed with sutures.

59140
The physician treats an ectopic pregnancy where the embryo has implanted in the cervix. If the pregnancy is less than 12 weeks gestation, the physician usually removes the embryo through the vagina. The physician ligates the hypogastric arteries or the cervical branches of the uterus to control bleeding. Curettage of the endocervix and endometrium may stop heavy bleeding. Sutures and gauze packing may also be necessary. If later than 12 weeks gestation, the physician may treat the cervical pregnancy by performing an abdominal hysterectomy. Through a horizontal incision just within the pubic hairline, the physician clamps and cuts free the supporting pedicles containing the tubes, ligaments, and arteries. The uterus is removed above the cervix, and the incision is closed by suturing.

59150
The physician treats an ectopic pregnancy by laparoscopy without salpingectomy and/or oophorectomy. The physician inserts an instrument through the vagina to grasp the cervix while passing another instrument through the cervix and into the uterus to manipulate the uterus. Next, the physician makes a 1 cm incision in the umbilicus through which the abdomen is inflated and a fiberoptic laparoscope is inserted. A second incision is made on the left or right side of the abdomen. After locating the site of the gestation, another small incision is made above the site. Instruments are passed into the abdomen through the incisions. The physician removes the ectopic pregnancy by making an incision in the tube or ovary or by segmental excision. The abdominal incisions are closed with sutures.

59151
The physician treats an ectopic pregnancy by laparoscopy with salpingectomy and/or oophorectomy. The physician inserts an instrument through the vagina to grasp the cervix while passing another instrument through the cervix and into the uterus to manipulate the uterus. Next, the physician makes a 1 cm incision in the umbilicus through which the abdomen is inflated and a fiberoptic laparoscope is inserted. A second incision is made on the left or right side of the abdomen. After locating the site of the gestation, another small incision is made above the site. Instruments are passed into the abdomen through the incisions. The physician removes the tube and/or ovary containing the embryo and closes the abdominal incisions with sutures.

59160
The physician scrapes the endometrial lining of the uterus following childbirth. The physician passes a curette through the cervix and endocervical canal, and into the uterus. Due to the large, soft postpartum uterus that is especially susceptible to perforation, a large blunt curette, also known as a "banjo" curette, is preferable to the suction curette. The physician gently scrapes the endometrial lining of the uterus to control bleeding, treat obstetric lacerations, or remove any remaining placental tissue.

59200
The physician inserts a cervical dilator, such as a laminaria or prostaglandin, into the endocervix to chemically stimulate and dilate the cervical canal. Using a speculum, the physician views the cervix and uses a tool to grasp it and pull it down. A laminaria, which is a sterile applicator made of kelp or synthetic material, may be placed in the cervical canal where it absorbs moisture, swells, and gradually dilates the cervix prior to inducing labor. Or the physician may insert prostaglandin in the form of gel or suppositories into the cervix in order to prime it six to 12 hours before induction.

59300
A physician other than the physician who performed the delivery repairs an episiotomy or a vaginal tear or laceration. To repair an episiotomy, the physician sutures an incision made in the external genital area to widen the vulvar opening, avoid tearing, and permit easier passage of the fetus. To repair a vaginal tear, the physician approximates and sutures any vaginal tears or lacerations resulting from delivery.

59320
The physician threads suture material or wraps banding around the cervix to close an incompetent cervix. An incompetent cervix is one that dilates during the second trimester and will eventually allow the pregnancy to fall out. After inserting a speculum into the vagina to view the cervix, heavy suture material or wire is threaded around the cervix using purse-string sutures. The sutures are pulled tight to make the opening smaller and prevent spontaneous abortion.

59325
Through a small abdominal incision just above the pubic hairline, the physician places a band around the cervix at the level of the internal os (opening) to make the cervical opening smaller and prevent spontaneous abortion from an incompetent cervix. An incompetent cervix is one that dilates during the second trimester and will eventually allow the pregnancy to fall out. The abdominal incision is closed with sutures.

59350
The physician repairs a uterus that is lacerated or ruptured during pregnancy. A large incision is made in the abdomen and the uterus is sutured in layers. The abdominal incision is closed with sutures.

59400
The physician delivers an infant and placenta through the uterus and vagina. The physician may elect to assist the delivery with the use of forceps, vacuum extraction, or rupture of membranes. The physician may also elect to do an episiotomy, which is an incision in the perineum to widen the external opening. Episiotomy and laceration repair are included as well. This procedure covers both antepartum and postpartum care. Antepartum or prenatal care includes the initial and subsequent histories, physical examinations, recording of weight, blood pressures, fetal heart tones, and routine chemical urinalysis. It includes monthly visits up to 28 weeks gestation, biweekly visits to 36 weeks gestation, and weekly visits until delivery. Postpartum care includes hospital and office visits following delivery.

59409-59410
The physician delivers an infant and placenta through the uterus and vagina. The physician may elect to assist the delivery with the use of forceps, vacuum extraction, or rupture of membranes. The physician may also elect to do an episiotomy, which is an incision in the perineum to widen the external opening. Episiotomy and laceration repair are included as well. Code 59409 represents the vaginal delivery only and does not include antepartum or postpartum care. Code 59410 covers the vaginal delivery with postpartum care, which includes hospital and office visits following delivery.

59412
The physician turns the fetus from a breech presenting position to a cephalic presenting position. External cephalic version is performed by manipulating the fetus from the outside of the abdominal wall. The physician places both hands on the patient's abdomen and locates each pole of the fetus by palpation. The fetus is shifted so that the breech or rear end of the fetus is moved upward and the head downward. The physician may elect to use tocolytic drug therapy to suppress uterine contractions during the manipulation.

59414
The physician removes a retained placenta following delivery of the fetus, usually unattended, and after separation of the placenta from its intrauterine attachment. The physician places abdominal pressure just above the symphysis to elevate the uterus into the abdomen and prevent inversion of the uterus. This also helps move the placenta downward into the vagina. The umbilical cord is very gently pulled to help guide the placenta out of the birth canal. If the placenta cannot be removed by this technique or there is brisk bleeding, manual removal of the placenta may be indicated. Manual removal requires adequate analgesia or anesthesia. It is accomplished by grasping the fundus of the uterus with a hand on the abdomen. The other hand, wearing an elbow-length glove, is passed through the vagina into the uterus to separate the placenta and remove it.

59425-59426
Antepartum or prenatal care includes the initial and subsequent histories, physical examinations, recording of weight, blood pressures, fetal heart tones, and routine chemical urinalysis. It includes monthly visits up to 28 weeks gestation, biweekly visits to 36 weeks gestation, and weekly visits until delivery. 59425 includes four to six visits. 59426 covers seven or more visits.

59430
Postpartum care includes hospital and office visits following vaginal or cesarean section delivery.

59510
The physician delivers an infant through a horizontal or vertical incision in the abdomen and uterus. Once the incisions are made, the infant is delivered and the placenta separated and removed. The uterine and abdominal incisions are closed with sutures. This procedure includes both antepartum and postpartum care. Antepartum or prenatal care includes the initial and subsequent histories, physical examinations, recording of weight, blood pressures, fetal heart tones, and routine chemical urinalysis. It includes monthly visits up to 28 weeks gestation, biweekly visits to 36 weeks gestation, and weekly visits until delivery. Postpartum care includes hospital and office visits following delivery.

59514-59515
The physician delivers an infant through a horizontal or vertical incision in the abdomen and uterus. Once the incisions are made, the infant is delivered and the placenta separated and removed. The uterine and abdominal incisions are closed with sutures. Code 59514 represents the cesarean delivery only and does not include antepartum or postpartum care. Code 59515 covers the cesarean delivery with postpartum care, which includes hospital and office visits following delivery.

59525
The physician performs a hysterectomy immediately following cesarean delivery. Through the abdominal incision, the physician clamps and cuts free the supporting pedicles containing the tubes, ligaments, and arteries. The uterus is removed and the physician may elect to remove the cervix as well. In a subtotal hysterectomy, just the uterus is removed. In a total hysterectomy, both the uterus and cervix are removed. The abdominal incision is closed with sutures.

59610
The physician delivers an infant and placenta through the vagina. The patient has previously delivered by cesarean section. The physician may elect to assist the delivery with the use of forceps, vacuum extraction, or rupture of membranes. The physician may also elect to do an episiotomy, which is an incision in the perineum to widen the external opening. Episiotomy and laceration repair are included as well. This procedure covers both antepartum and postpartum care. Antepartum or prenatal care includes the initial and subsequent histories, physical examinations, recording of weight, blood pressures, fetal heart tones, and routine chemical urinalysis. It includes monthly visits up to 28 weeks gestation, biweekly visits to 36 weeks gestation, and weekly visits until delivery (approximately 12-15 visits). Because of the previous cesarean delivery, the physician monitors the patient during labor and delivery. Postpartum care includes hospital and office visits following delivery.

59612-59614
The physician delivers an infant and placenta through the vagina. The patient has previously delivered by cesarean section. The physician may elect to assist the delivery with the use of forceps. The physician may also elect to do an episiotomy, which is an incision in the perineum to widen the external opening. Episiotomy and laceration repair are included. Because of the previous cesarean delivery, the physician monitors the patient during labor and delivery. Code 59614 includes postpartum care, hospital office visits following delivery.

59618
After first attempting a vaginal delivery, the physician delivers an infant through a horizontal or vertical incision in the abdomen and uterus. The patient has previously delivered by cesarean section. Once the incisions are made, the infant is delivered and the placenta separated and removed. The uterine and abdominal incisions are closed with layered sutures. This procedure includes both antepartum and postpartum care. Antepartum or prenatal care includes the initial and subsequent histories, physical examinations, recording of weight, blood pressures, fetal heart tones, and routine chemical urinalysis. It includes monthly visits up to 28 weeks gestation, biweekly visits to 36 weeks gestation, and weekly visits until delivery (approximately 13-15 visits). Because of the previous cesarean delivery and the attempted vaginal delivery, the physician monitors the patient during labor and delivery. Postpartum care includes hospital and office visits following delivery.

59620-59622
After first attempting a vaginal delivery, the physician delivers an infant through a horizontal or vertical incision in the abdomen and uterus. The patient has previously delivered by cesarean section. Once the incisions are made, the infant is delivered and the placenta separated and removed. The uterine and abdominal incisions are closed with layered sutures because of the previous cesarean delivery and the attempted vaginal delivery, the physician monitors the patient during labor and delivery. Only delivery is included in 59620. Postpartum care is included in 59622. Postpartum care includes hospital and office visits following delivery.

59812
The physician removes the products of conception remaining after an incomplete spontaneous abortion in any trimester. To evacuate the uterus, the physician performs a dilation and suction curettage. The physician inserts a speculum into the vagina to view the cervix. A tenaculum is used to grasp the cervix, pull it down, and exert traction. If the cervix is not sufficiently dilated, a dilator is inserted into the endocervix and through the cervical canal to enlarge the opening. The physician places a cannula in the endocervical canal and passes it into the uterus. The suction machine is activated and the uterine contents are evacuated by rotation of the cannula. After suction curettage, a sharp curette may be used to gently scrape the uterus to ensure that it is empty.

59820-59821
The physician treats a missed abortion by suction curettage in the first trimester for 59820, and in the second trimester for 59821. In missed abortion, the fetus remains in the uterus four to eight weeks following its death. Ultrasonography may be needed to determine the size of the fetus prior to the procedure. The physician inserts a speculum into the vagina to view the cervix. A tenaculum is used to grasp the cervix, pull it down, and exert traction. A dilator is inserted into the endocervix and through the cervical canal to enlarge the opening. The physician places a cannula in the endocervical canal and passes it into the uterus. The suction machine is activated and the uterine contents are evacuated by rotation of the cannula. After suction curettage, a sharp curette may be used to gently scrape the uterus to ensure that it is empty.

59830
The physician treats a septic abortion with prompt evacuation of the uterus and vigorous medical treatment of the patient. A septic abortion is one complicated by generalized fever and infection. There is also inflammation and infection of the endometrium and in the cellular tissue around the uterus. The physician treats the infection with intravenous antibiotics and blood transfusions as necessary. To evacuate the uterus, the physician inserts a speculum into the vagina to view the cervix. A tenaculum is used to grasp the cervix, pull it down, and exert traction. A dilator is inserted into the endocervix and through the cervical canal to enlarge the opening. The physician

places a cannula in the endocervical canal and passes it into the uterus. The suction machine is activated and the uterine contents are evacuated by rotation of the cannula. After suction curettage, a sharp curette may be used to gently scrape the uterus to ensure that it is empty.

59840
The physician terminates a pregnancy by dilation and curettage. The physician inserts a speculum into the vagina to view the cervix. A tenaculum is used to grasp the cervix, pull it down, and exert traction. A dilator is inserted into the endocervix and through the cervical canal to enlarge the opening. The physician places a curette in the endocervical canal and passes it into the uterus. The uterine contents are removed by rotating the curette and gently scraping the uterus until all the products of conception are removed.

59841
The physician terminates a pregnancy by dilation and evacuation (D&E). Because D&E requires wider cervical dilation than curettage, the physician may dilate the cervix with a laminaria several hours to several days before the procedure. At the time of the procedure, the physician inserts a speculum into the vagina to view the cervix. A tenaculum is used to grasp the cervix, pull it down, and exert traction. The physician places a cannula in the dilated endocervical canal and passes it into the uterus. The suction machine is activated and the uterine contents are evacuated by rotation of the cannula. For pregnancies through 16 weeks, the cannula will usually evacuate the pregnancy. For later pregnancies, the cannula is used to drain amniotic fluid and to draw tissue into the lower uterus for extraction by forceps. In either case, a sharp curette may be used to gently scrape the uterus to ensure that it is empty.

59850
The physician terminates a pregnancy by inducing labor with amniocentesis and intra-amniotic injections. This method is usually used after the first trimester (13 weeks or more). The physician inserts an amniocentesis needle into the abdomen to obtain a free flow of clear amniotic fluid. A hypertonic solution is administered by gravity drip. The hypertonic solution results in fetal death and labor usually results. The fetus and placenta are delivered through the vagina.

59851
The physician begins the termination of a pregnancy by inducing labor with amniocentesis and intra-amniotic injections. This method is usually used after the first trimester (13 weeks or more). The physician inserts an amniocentesis needle into the abdomen to obtain a free flow of clear amniotic fluid. A hypertonic solution is administered by gravity drip. The hypertonic solution results in fetal death and labor usually results. Code 59851 is used when this method fails to expel all products of conception, and a dilation and curettage and/or evacuation is used to remove the remaining tissue.

59852
The physician begins the termination of a pregnancy by inducing labor with amniocentesis and intra-amniotic injections. This method is usually used after the first trimester (13 weeks or more). The physician inserts an amniocentesis needle into the abdomen to obtain a free flow of clear amniotic fluid. A hypertonic solution is administered by gravity drip. The hypertonic solution results in fetal death and labor usually results. Code 59852 is used when this method fails to expel all products of conception, and a hysterotomy, through an incision in the abdominal wall and uterus, is used to remove the remaining tissue. Following removal, the incision is closed with sutures.

59855
The physician terminates a pregnancy by inducing labor with vaginal suppositories. Before using the suppositories, a laminaria, which is an applicator made of kelp or synthetic material, may be inserted in the cervix to soften and expand the cervical canal. Once the cervix is ready, the physician inserts the vaginal suppositories and labor usually results. The fetus and placenta are delivered through the vagina.

59856
The physician begins the termination of a pregnancy by inducing labor with vaginal suppositories. Before using the suppositories, a laminaria, which is an applicator made of kelp or synthetic material, may be inserted in the cervix to soften and expand the cervical canal. Once the cervix is ready, the physician inserts the vaginal suppositories and labor usually results. 59856 is used when this method fails to expel all products of conception, and a dilation and curettage and/or evacuation is used to remove the remaining tissue.

59857
The physician begins the termination of a pregnancy by inducing labor with vaginal suppositories. Before using the suppositories, a laminaria, which is an applicator made of kelp or synthetic material, may be inserted in the cervix to soften and expand the cervical canal. Once the cervix is ready, the physician inserts the vaginal suppositories and labor usually results. 59857 is used when this method fails to expel all products of conception, and a hysterotomy, through an incision in the abdominal wall and uterus, is used to remove the remaining tissue. Following removal, the incision is closed with sutures.

59866
Selective reduction is performed to eliminate one or more fetuses of a multiple pregnancy in an attempt to increase the viability of the remaining fetuses. Fetuses are usually eliminated in this procedure until only a twin or triplet pregnancy remains. Physicians most

often use ultrasound guided intracardiac injection of potassium chloride to reduce the number of fetuses, although injection of potassium chloride in any part of the fetal body accomplishes the same result. When an intracardiac injection is performed, a 22 gauge spinal needle is advanced through the abdominal and uterine walls toward a cardiac echo using high-resolution ultrasound as a guide. With the needle position in the heart, a solution of potassium chloride is injected at intervals until prolonged cardiac standstill is observed. The physician withdraws the needle and redirects it into another gestational sac, as needed. The embryo(s) or fetus(es) that have been injected shrivel and decompose, leaving the remaining fetuses in utero an increased chance of surviving to term. Any sacs that remain intact are removed during delivery of the surviving fetus(es).

59870
The physician treats a hydatidiform mole (molar pregnancy) by evacuation and curettage of the uterus. The physician inserts a speculum into the vagina to view the cervix. A tenaculum is used to grasp the cervix, pull it down, and exert traction. A dilator is inserted into the endocervix and through the cervical canal to enlarge the opening. The physician places a cannula in the endocervical canal and passes it into the uterus. The suction machine is activated and the hydatidiform mole is evacuated by rotation of the cannula. After suction curettage, a sharp curette may be used to scrape the uterus and confirm that it is empty.

59871
The physician removes a cervical cerclage, a suture that had been placed to hold the cervix closed. A cerclage is most often placed when a cervix dilates too early during pregnancy and risks a miscarriage. The physician severs the sutures and removes them. This code includes anesthesia other than local.

Endocrine

60000
The physician incises and drains an infected thyroglossal (also called thyrolingual) cyst in the neck caused by incomplete closure or persistence of the embryonic thyroglossal duct between the developing thyroid and the back of the tongue. After the physician incises the cyst and drains the infected fluid, the wound may be irrigated with normal saline and a drainage system inserted. The drainage tubes may be stitched in place. A collection unit applies gentle suction to collect fluid from the incision site.

60100
The physician removes tissue from the thyroid for examination. The physician localizes the area to be biopsied by palpation or separately reportable ultrasound. A large, hollow, bore needle is passed through skin and muscle, into the thyroid. The tissue is removed and sent for separately reportable analysis.

60200
The physician removes a cyst or adenoma from a thyroid, or transects the isthmus. The physician exposes the thyroid via a transverse cervical incision in the skin line. The platysmas is divided and the strap muscles separated in the midline. The thyroid mass is identified. Blood supply to and from the lesion is controlled and the mass is locally excised. The skin and platysmas are closed.

60210
The physician removes part of a thyroid lobe, with or without an isthmusectomy. The physician exposes the thyroid via a transverse cervical incision in the skin line. The platysmas is divided and the strap muscles separated in the midline. The superior and inferior thyroid vessels are divided in the area for resection. The thyroid parenchyma is divided and dissected with cautery dissection. The skin and platysmas are closed.

60212
The physician removes part of a thyroid lobe, with contralateral subtotal lobectomy, including isthmusectomy. The physician exposes the thyroid via a transverse cervical incision in the skin line. The platysmas is divided and the strap muscles separated in the midline. The superior and inferior thyroid vessels are divided in the area for resection. The thyroid is divided and dissected with cautery dissection. The isthmus is dissected. The lobe is removed The skin and platysmas are closed. Report 60212 if with contralateral subtotal lobectomy, including isthmusectomy.

60220
The physician removes all of a thyroid lobe, with or without isthmusectomy. The physician exposes the thyroid via a transverse cervical incision in the skin line. The platysmas is divided and the strap muscles separated in the midline. The thyroid lobe to be excised is isolated and superior and inferior thyroid vessels serving that lobe are ligated. Parathyroid glands are preserved. The thyroid gland is divided in the midline of the isthmus over the anterior trachea. The thyroid lobe is resected. The platysmas and skin are closed.

60225
The physician removes all of a thyroid lobe with contralateral subtotal lobectomy, including isthmusectomy. The physician exposes the thyroid via a transverse cervical incision in the skin line. The platysmas is divided and the strap muscles separated in the midline. The thyroid lobe to be excised is isolated and superior and inferior thyroid vessels serving that lobe are ligated. The isthmus is severed. Parathyroid glands are preserved. The thyroid gland is divided in the midline of the isthmus over the anterior trachea.

The thyroid lobe is resected. The platysmas and skin are closed. Report 60225 if performed with contralateral subtotal lobectomy, including isthmusectomy.

60240
The physician removes all of the thyroid. The physician exposes the thyroid via a transverse cervical incision in the skin line. The platysmas is divided and the strap muscles separated in the midline. The thyroid gland is mobilized and the superior and inferior thyroid vessels are ligated. The parathyroid glands are preserved and the thyroid is resected free of the trachea and removed. The platysmas and skin are closed.

60252-60254
The physician removes a malignant thyroid and some lymph nodes. The physician exposes the thyroid via a transverse cervical incision in the skin line. The platysmas is divided and the strap muscles separated in the midline. The thyroid gland is mobilized and the superior and inferior thyroid vessels are ligated. The parathyroid glands are preserved and the thyroid is resected free of the trachea and removed. All enlarged lymph nodes are identified and excised. The platysmas and skin are closed. Report 60254 if a radical neck dissection is included in the procedure.

60260
The physician removes thyroid tissue remaining following a partial thyroidectomy. The physician enters through the previous incision scar. The platysmas and scar tissue are divided and the strap muscles are divided in the midline. While preserving the parathyroid glands, all the remaining scar tissue is resected. The platysmas and skin are closed.

60270-60271
The physician removes the thyroid, including the substernal thyroid gland. The physician exposes the thyroid via sternal split/transthoracic approach in 60270 or via a transverse cervical incision in the skin line in 60271. The platysmas is divided and the strap muscles separated in the midline. The thyroid gland is mobilized and the superior and inferior thyroid vessels are ligated. The parathyroid glands are preserved and the thyroid is resected free of the trachea and removed. Any substernal thyroid is bluntly dissected. Upper sternal incision may be necessary for complete excision of substernal thyroid. The platysmas and skin are closed. Report 60271 if with cervical approach.

60280-60281
The physician excises a thyroglossal duct cyst or sinus. The physician circumferentially incises the skin around the cyst or sinus and extends the incision along the tract to its origin. The midpart of the hyoid bone is excised. The wound is packed and allowed to heal by secondary intention. Report 60281 if thyroglossal duct cyst or sinus is recurrent.

60300
The physician aspirates or injects a thyroid cyst. The physician localizes the thyroid cyst by palpation or separately reportable ultrasound. A needle is passed through the skin into the cyst. The cyst is aspirated and tissue captured is sent for separately reportable analysis, or the cyst is injected with therapeutic or diagnostic matter.

60500
The physician removes or explores the parathyroids, glands adjacent to the thyroids. The physician exposes the thyroid via a transverse cervical incision in the skin line. The platysmas is divided and the strap muscles separated in the midline. The parathyroid glands are identified and tissue is excised for separately reportable pathological examination. The parathyroid may be removed; usually a port remains following excision. The platysmas and skin are closed.

60502
The physician re-explores the parathyroids, glands adjacent to the thyroids. The physician exposes the thyroid via the previous incision. The parathyroid glands are identified and tissue is excised for separately reportable pathological examination. The parathyroid may be removed; usually a port remains following excision. The platysmas and skin are closed.

60505
The physician removes or explores the parathyroids, glands adjacent to the thyroids with mediastinal exploration, sternal split or transthoracic approach. The physician exposes the thyroid via a sternal split or transthoracic approach. The parathyroid glands are identified and tissue is excised for separately reportable pathological examination. The mediastinum is explored. The parathyroid may be removed; usually a port remains following excision. The platysmas and skin are closed.

60512
The physician excises and reimplants a portion of the parathyroid. The physician exposes the thyroid via a transverse cervical incision in the skin line. The platysmas is divided and the strap muscles separated in the midline. Tissue is excised for separately reportable pathological examination. All four parathyroid glands are completely removed. One half of one gland is secured to the muscle of the sternocleidomastoid or upper arm. The platysmas and skin of the neck and transplant site are closed.

60520-60522
The physician removes part or all of the thymus gland. The physician exposes the thymus via a cervical incision in the skin line in 60520. The sternum is retracted and strap muscles separated. The superior lobe of the thymus is separated from the inferior aspect of the thyroid. The blood supply to the thymus is divided and the thymus is dissected free from the

pericardium and removed. The incision is closed. Report 60521 if performed with a sternal split or transthoracic approach without radical mediastinal dissection; report 60522 if performed with a sternal split or transthoracic approach, with radical mediastinal dissection.

60540-60545
The physician removes part or all of the adrenal gland with or without biopsy. The physician exposes the adrenal gland via an upper anterior midline abdominal or posterior incision. The retroperitoneal space is explored. The capsule of the kidney is incised and the adrenal capsule is opened. Blood supply to the adrenal gland is ligated and the gland is removed. The physician may remove tissue from the site for separately reportable pathological study. The physician closes the incision with sutures. Report 60545 if this procedure is performed with excision of an adjacent retroperitoneal tumor.

60600-60605
This physician removes a tumor from a small epithelioid structure (carotid body) just above the bifurcation of the carotid. The physician exposes the carotid body via an incision anterior to the sternocleidomastoid. After dissection down to the carotid sheath, the vein is retracted and the carotid bifurcation exposed. The blood supply to the tumor is ligated and the tumor resected. The incision is closed. Report 60605 if the carotid body tumor excision is performed with excision of the carotid artery.

60650
The physician performs a laparoscopic excision (removal) of the adrenal gland, or performs and laparoscopic exploration of the adrenal gland through the abdomen or back. In the abdominal approach, a trocar is placed at the level of the umbilicus and the abdomen is insufflated. The laparoscope is placed through the umbilical port and additional trocars are placed into the abdominal cavity as needed. In the back approach, the trocar is placed at the back proximal to the retroperitoneal space superior to the kidney, adjacent to the adrenal gland. The physician uses the laparoscope fitted with a fiberoptic camera and/or an operating tool to explore, biopsy, or removal of all or part of the adrenal gland. The abdomen is the deflated, the trocars are removed and the incisions are closed with sutures.

Nervous

61000-61001
The physician draws off cerebral spinal fluid through a cranial or fontanel suture in an infant in response to hydrocephalus or diagnosed meningitis. The physician places a needle through the fontanel at the suture line until cerebral spinal fluid is obtained. The needle is withdrawn and the area is bandaged. Report 61001 for subsequent taps for cerebral spinal fluid.

61020-61026
The physician withdraws cerebral spinal fluid for study, or injects it with a therapeutic or diagnostic substance. In 61020, The physician places a ventricular catheter through a previously formed burr hole or fontanel suture and withdraws fluid for study. In 61026, the catheter is used to inject a medication or other substance for diagnosis or treatment.

61050-61055
The physician performs a spinal puncture in the high cervical region (C1-C2) or at the base of the skull in the cisterna magna (cerebellomedullary cistern). For lateral cervical puncture, the physician uses a paramedian approach. For cisternal punctures, the needle is placed at the base of the skull. In 61050, the physician inserts a needle through the tissues to obtain fluid from the spine or cisterna magna. In 61055, a diagnostic or therapeutic injection occurs.

61070
The physician injects or aspirates the shunt tubing or reservoir with a needle to determine function. Shunt tubing eliminates excess cerebral spinal fluid in cases of hydrocephalus. The tubing runs behind the ear, through neck tissue, and into the gut. The physician places a needle into the tube or reservoir and injects radiologic dye, or aspirates to check for effective drainage.

61105-61108
The physician uses a manually operated twist drill to create an opening in the skull. The physician incises the scalp and peels it away from the area to be drilled. The physician places the drill over the affected area of the skull and twists until the drill pierces the periosteum and the dura is exposed. Fluid may be drawn off from the subdural space or from the ventricles. In 61105, the hole is made to alleviate pressure, and is used for subsequent surgery. In 61107, the hole is used to implant a ventricular drainage catheter, a fluid pressure recording device, or other intracerebral monitoring device. In 61108, the hole is used to access and evacuate or drain a subdural hematoma.

61120
The physician uses an electric burr drill to create a ventricular puncture to inject diagnostic fluid. The physician incises the scalp and peels it away from the area to be drilled. The physician places the drill over the area to be injected, and drills until the periosteum is reached. A ventricular puncture is made. The ventricles may be injected with gas, contrast media, dye, or radioactive material for diagnostic purposes.

61140-61151
The physician uses a burr drill or trephine to create a hole in the cranium through which a brain or

intracranial lesion or abscess is located. An abscess or cyst may be drained. The physician incises the scalp and peels it away from the area to be drilled. In 61140, a lesion biopsy is obtained using a forceps or curette. In 61150, a catheter is placed through the hole and into a brain abscess or cyst for drainage. Report 61151 for subsequent drainage of the abscess or cyst through the original burr hole.

61154
The physician drills a burr hole in the cranium to drain a hematoma. The hematoma is identified using separately reportable computed tomography (CT) scan. The physician incises the scalp and peels it away from the area to be drilled. The physician uses a burr drill to access the hematoma. An extradural (epidural) hematoma is located outside the dura, just under the periosteum. A subdural hematoma is located under the dura mater, which must be incised to reach the hematoma. The hematoma is decompressed and bleeding is controlled. For subdural hematomas, the dura is sutured closed. The scalp is repositioned and sutured into place.

61156-61210
The physician drills a burr hole in the cranium to aspirate a hematoma or cyst located in the brain. The hematoma or cyst is identified using a CT scan. The physician incises the scalp and peels it away from the area to be drilled. The physician drills through the cranium to the dura mater, which is incised. The brain is dissected and retracted until the hematoma or cyst is located. The hematoma or cyst is aspirated using a syringe if the fluid is to be sent to pathology. Otherwise, the fluid is irrigated and suctioned. The dura mater is sutured closed and the scalp is repositioned and sutured into place. In 61210, a ventricular catheter, reservoir, EEG electrodes, pressure recording device, or other cerebral monitoring device is placed through the burr hole following aspiration of the hematoma. These devices or monitors are used to follow intracranial pressure and cerebral function following surgery.

61215
The physician places a device for administering chemotherapy or other medication into the cerebral spinal fluid. The physician makes a skin incision at the level at which the catheter will be inserted into the reservoir. A dermal or subdermal pocket is created with blunt dissection. The reservoir is connected to the catheter and tested to ensure function. The pocket is sutured in layers.

61250-61253
The physician drills a burr hole or trephine. In 61250 the hole is made to access the supratentorial area of the brain. In 61253, the infratentorial, unilateral, or bilateral area of the brain is accessed. The physician makes an incision in the scalp over the area to be drilled, and uses a burr hole drill or a trephine to create an opening to the brain. The physician explores the area and closes the wound. No other procedures are reported at this time.

61304-61305
The physician performs an exploratory craniectomy or craniotomy. In 61304, the supratentorial area of the brain (above the tentorium of the cerebellum) is accessed. In 61305, the infratentorial (below the tentorium of the cerebellum) area of the brain is accessed. A craniectomy involves removal of skull bone. A craniotomy involves incision without bone removal. The physician incises the scalp and retracts it. The physician drills or cuts the cranium to access the area to be explored. Bone is removed and the area of the brain is explored. If performing a craniotomy, the bone is replaced. The skull pieces are screwed together and the scalp is sutured in layers.

61312-61315
The physician performs craniectomy or craniotomy to drain a hematoma. In 61312, the supratentorial hematoma is located in the epidural or subdural space. In 61313, the supratentorial hematoma is located within the brain. In 61314, the infratentorial hematoma is located in the epidural or subdural space. In 61315, the infratentorial hematoma is located within the cerebellum. The hematoma is identified using a CT scan. The physician incises the scalp and retracts it. The physician drills or cuts the cranium to access the hematoma. Bone is removed. Epidural and subdural hematomas are identified and evacuated under direct visualization. Hematomas within the brain are located using CT verified coordinates and directed dissection. After locating the hematoma, the physician evacuates it with suction and irrigates the area while monitoring for hemorrhage. The dura is sutured closed. The skull pieces are screwed together and the scalp is sutured in layers.

61316
A cranial bone graft is placed onto a part of the skull for repair following craniectomy, craniotomy, or other intracranial surgery. The donor site is already exposed for the primary procedure. The cranial bone graft harvested may be split- or full-thickness, a shaving graft, or bone dust. When a full-thickness graft is required, the dura around the edge of the graft is exposed with a burr or neurosurgical craniotomy technique. A split graft requires removing lateral bone from a contoured area, which leaves it exposed like an island, and an osteotome is correctly placed and tapped through to produce the bone graft. Shaving grafts are acquired similar to wood shaving and bone dust is produced by using a craniotome. The graft is placed to repair the defect and rigidly fixed, if necessary. Bone dust is placed and packed to fill the skull defect. Report this code in addition to the code for the primary procedure.

61320-61321
The physician performs craniectomy or craniotomy to drain an abscess. In 61320, the abscess is located in the supratentorial region. In 61321, the abscess is located infratentorial region. The abscess is identified using separately reportable CT scan. The physician incises the scalp and retracts it. The physician drills or cuts the cranium to access the abscess. Bone is removed. Epidural and subdural abscesses are identified and evacuated under direct visualization. Abscesses within the brain are located using CT verified coordinates and directed dissection. After locating the abscess, the physician evacuates it with suction and irrigates the area while monitoring for hemorrhage. The dura is sutured closed. The skull pieces are screwed together and the scalp is sutured in layers.

61322-61323
The neurosurgeon performs a decompressive craniotomy or craniectomy, with or without duraplasty, to treat intracranial hypertension usually caused by severe closed-head injury. A scalp frontotemporoparietal incision is made from the side of the head curving over the ear and extending posteriorly, continuing in a big question mark shape back to the frontal midline. When necessary, a temporal end craniectomy site is opened first and contused brain or hematoma removed for immediate decompression of hypertension before the scalp incision is finished. A bone flap is next elevated by a series of burr holes made with a trephine connected to a saw or with a high-speed drill and footplate tool for protecting the dura matter used to make cuts around the flap margin. For subdural hematoma described here (the most common result of closed-head trauma causing hypertension), a dural opening is made over the area of greatest clot size and contused brain tissue and blood clots are removed. When the brain is swollen, instead of a large dural opening, multiple slit openings are made in the dura, through which the clot is irrigated to prevent the brain tissue from herniating through the opening. In 61323, a lobectomy is done to remove severely contused frontal or temporal brain tissue. Bipolar cautery and hemostatic agents are applied to attain meticulous hemostasis, absolutely necessary for preventing recurrent hematomas. The dura is closed primarily or duraplasty may be done with a pericranial or fascia lata graft. The dura is tacked around the craniotomy margin and to the bone flap and a drain may be placed and brought out through a separate incision. The scalp is closed in layers.

61330
The physician decompresses an orbital roof fracture. The physician incises the frontal scalp area and retracts the scalp posteriorly and the forehead anteriorly. The frontal bone is cut and removed. The forebrain is retracted until the superior margins of the orbit are visualized. The roof of the orbit is decompressed after ensuring freedom of movement of extraocular eye muscles. The dura is closed, and the bone is replaced. The forehead and scalp are reanastomosed and sutured in layers.

61332-61334
The physician explores the orbit, and removes lesions or foreign bodies. The physician incises the frontal scalp area and retracts the scalp posteriorly and the forehead anteriorly. The frontal bone is cut and removed. The forebrain is retracted until the superior margins of the orbit are visualized. In 61332, suspect tissue is biopsied. In 61333, a lesion is excised. In 61334, a foreign body is removed. The roof of the orbit is reconstructed and freedom of movement of extraocular eye muscles is ensured. The dura is closed, and the skull is replaced. The forehead and scalp are reanastomosed and sutured in layers.

61340
The physician performs a subtemporal cranial decompression for benign intracranial hypertension (pseudotumor cerebri) or slit ventricle syndrome. Slit ventricle syndrome is a complication following shunting for hydrocephalus. The physician incises and retracts the scalp over the temporal area to be decompressed. A bone flap is next elevated by a series of burr holes made with a trephine connected to a saw or with a high-speed drill and footplate tool for protecting the dura mater used to make cuts around the bone flap margin. When intracranial access is gained, the pressure within the skull is relieved and the bone is replaced and secured to neighboring bone. The scalp is sutured in layers.

61343
The physician removes the posterior inferior occipital scalp and the posterior aspects of the cervical vertebrae to decompress the brain stem. A dural graft may be necessary. The physician makes a longitudinal incision from the occipital through the cervical spine and retracts laterally. Decompression is achieved when the inferior occiput is cut and removed and the posterior elements of the upper cervical vertebrae are removed. If a dural graft is needed to cover the resulting defect, fascia is harvested from the thigh or a cadaveric dural graft is used. The graft is positioned over the defect and sutured to the surrounding dura. The incision is sutured in layers.

61345
The physician lowers pressure in the brain caused by excess fluid. The patient is placed in a seated position or prone. The physician makes an incision in the midline extending from the posterior mid-scalp to the midcervical region. Dissection is continued to the skull. Drills and saws are used to open the occipital bone to enter the posterior fossa of the skull. The brain is decompressed by removal of blood and pathological tissue. The occipital bone is secured with sutures, wires, or plates and screws. The scalp and neck are sutured closed in layers.

61440

The physician cuts the tentorium. The tentorium supports the occipital lobes and covers the cerebellum. The physician incises and retracts the scalp and removes bone from the occiput. The tentorium is identified. The tissue that supports the occipital lobes is incised to loosen the tissue, releasing tension in the posterior brain.

61450

The physician applies or releases pressure on the sensory root of the gasserian ganglion. The gasserian ganglion supplies sensory innervation to the face via the trigeminal nerve. The physician makes a periauricular incision and retracts the scalp and raises a bone flap. The gasserian ganglion is located and decompressed or stimulated. If indicated, the nerve or a nerve branch is sectioned. The bone flap is replaced and fastened. The scalp is reanastomosed and sutured in layers.

61458-61480

The physician performs a suboccipital craniectomy to explore or release pressure from the cranial nerves or tracts in the brain stem. In 61458, the physician explores and frees affected cranial nerves from the surrounding tissue. In 61460, the physician, resects one or more cranial nerves. The nerves are freed before resection. In 61470, the physician resects a nerve tract as it passes through the medulla. In 61480, the physician resects a nerve tract as it passes through the mesencephalon or the cerebellar or cerebral peduncle. The physician incises and retracts the scalp and removes bone from the occiput. The brain is retracted to reveal the brain stem. The affected nerve tract is explored, decompressed, or resected. The bone is replaced and stabilized. The scalp is anastomosed and sutured in layers.

61490

The physician performs a lobotomy and a cingulotomy. The physician incises and retracts the scalp and removes bone in the frontal or parietal region. For a midline lobotomy, the physician dissects between the two cerebral hemispheres and creates a lesion through the gyrus cinguli. The bone is replaced and stabilized. The scalp is anastomosed and sutured in layers.

61500-61501

The physician removes a portion of the skull bone invaded by tumor or infection. In 61500, the physician removes a tumor or bony lesion. In 61501, the physician removes infected bone. The physician incises and retracts the scalp and removes bone from the affected area. A bone graft or plastic replacement may be used to reconstruct the skull. The scalp is anastomosed and sutured in layers.

61510-61516

The physician removes a supratentorial abscess or cyst. Supratentorial structures are those located above the tentorium cerebelli, the membrane that separates the cerebellum from the basal surface of the occipital and temporal lobes of the cerebrum. The physician incises and retracts the scalp and removes bone over the area of the tumor, meningioma, abscess, or cyst. The tumor, meningioma, abscess or cyst is identified and excised. The bone is replaced and stabilized. The scalp is anastomosed and sutured in layers. In 61510, the physician removes a brain tumor. In 61512, a meningioma is removed. A meningioma is a tumor of the lining of the brain. In 61514, an abscess is excised. In 61516, a cyst is excised or fenestrated. Fenestration is the surgical creation of an opening or window in the cyst to allow it to drain.

61517

A chemotherapeutic agent is implanted into a brain cavity at the time craniectomy or craniotomy is done to excise the brain tumor. The surgeon places the chemotherapeutic agent into a cavity of the brain that has already been directly accessed during surgery for excision of the tumor. This code includes cancer therapy agents other than brachytherapy radioelement ribbons or sources. This is an add-on code to be reported with the appropriate primary procedure for the brain tumor removal and cannot stand alone.

61518-61519

The physician removes an infratentorial or posterior fossa brain tumor or meningioma. Infratentorial structures are those located below the tentorium cerebelli, the membrane that separates the cerebellum from the basal surface of the occipital and temporal lobes of the cerebrum. The physician incises and retracts the scalp and removes bone from the affected area. The tumor is identified and excised. The bone is replaced and stabilized. The scalp is anastomosed and sutured in layers. In 61518, the physician removes a brain tumor other than a meningioma, cerebellopontine angle tumor, or midline tumor of skull base. In 61519, a meningioma is removed.

61520

The physician removes a brain tumor at the cerebellopontine angle. The physician makes a lateral posterior incision and removes an occipital bone flap. The cerebellum is retracted and brain stem is examined. The tumor at the cerebellopontine angle is resected. The bone is replaced and stabilized. The scalp is anastomosed and sutured in layers.

61521

The physician removes a midline brain tumor at the base of the skull. The physician uses a posterior auricular or transmastoid approach. The physician incises and retracts the scalp and removes a bone flap. The lateral cerebellum is retracted and the tumor, located near the brain stem, is identified and resected. The bone is replaced and stabilized. The scalp is anastomosed and sutured in layers.

Nervous

61522-61524
The physician removes an abscess or cyst located in the infratentorium or posterior fossa. Infratentorial structures are those located below the tentorium cerebelli, the membrane that separates the cerebellum from basal surface of the occipital and temporal lobes of the cerebrum. The physician incises and retracts the scalp and removes bone over the area of the abscess or cyst. The abscess or cyst is identified and excised the bone is replaced and stabilized. The scalp is anastomosed and sutured in layers. In 61522, an abscess is excised. In 61524 the cyst is excised or fenestrated. Fenestration is the surgical creation of an opening or window in the cyst to allow it to drain.

61526-61530
The physician excises a tumor at the cerebellopontine angle. Cerebellopontine angle tumors are benign neoplasms of the 8th cranial nerve and are more often referred to as acoustic neuromas. Other terms include: acoustic tumor, vestibular schwannoma, or angle tumor. Using a transmastoid approach, the physician incises the scalp and removes a bone flap. The tumor is identified and excised. The bone is replaced and stabilized. The scalp is anastomosed and sutured in layers. In 61530, a multiple approach technique is used with the tumor being accessed from both a transtemporal and a middle or posterior fossa approach.

61531
The physician implants electrodes in the subdural layer for long term seizure monitoring. The physician uses a burr drill or trephine to reach the subdural layer and implants linear strip electrodes in each hole. Subdural electrodes are placed just below the dura and do not penetrate the cerebral tissue. The scalp is sutured to close the incisions.

61533-61534
The physician implants electrodes in the subdural layer for long term seizure monitoring. A bone flap is elevated to implant a subdural electrode array along the cerebral hemispheres. The bone is replaced and stabilized. The scalp is anastomosed and sutured in layers. Report 61534 if the epileptogenic focus (the seizure center) is excised.

61535-61536
The physician removes an electrode array located in the subdural layer. The bone flap covering the electrode array is elevated and the array is removed. The bone is replaced and stabilized. The scalp is anastomosed and sutured in layers. Report 61536 if the array is removed in addition to excision of the epileptogenic focus (the seizure center).

61537
A temporal lobectomy is done for intractable epileptic seizures when the focal point of the seizures has been identified by previous exams to originate in that lobe. An access incision is made through the scalp and overlying muscle to reach the skull. Burr holes are drilled around the periphery of the bone flap area to be raised. Using a craniotome, the bone flap is freed and lifted to expose the dura, which is dissected and retracted out of the operative field. Incisions are made into the cortex and dissection is carried down deep into the cortex. The temporal horn of the lateral ventricle and the hippocampus are identified. The pia is next encountered and is incised and opened and the temporal lobe is removed, including any part of the hippocampus, amygdala, and uncus that are to be removed with the temporal lobe. Arteries are transected and coagulated, while preserving the main cerebral/choroidal arteries and the pia-arachnoid. With the temporal lobe removed, closure is begun by suturing the dura and replacing the bone flap into position. Screws or plates are placed to secure the bone flap to surrounding skull bone. The divided muscles are sutured and the galea and the scalp are closed.

61538
A temporal lobectomy with electrocorticography is done for intractable epileptic seizures when the focal point of the seizures has been identified by previous exams to originate in that lobe. An access incision is made through the scalp and overlying muscle to reach the skull. Burr holes are drilled around the periphery of the bone flap area to be raised. Using a craniotome, the bone flap is freed and lifted to expose the dura, which is dissected and retracted out of the operative field. Electrodes are prepared and placed on the brain. The electrical activity of the brain is recorded and mapped while the cortex is kept irrigated. The recording grids may be moved a few times to gain enough information about various sites. After the electrocorticography, the electrodes are removed and markers are placed. Incisions are made into the cortex and dissection is carried down deep into the cortex. The temporal horn of the lateral ventricle and the hippocampus are identified. The pia is next encountered and is incised and opened and the temporal lobe is removed, including any part of the hippocampus, amygdala, and uncus that are to be removed with the temporal lobe. Arteries are transected and coagulated, while preserving the main cerebral/choroidal arteries and the pia-arachnoid. With the temporal lobe removed, closure is done by suturing the dura and replacing the bone flap into position. Screws or plates are placed to secure the bone flap to surrounding skull bone. The divided muscles are sutured and the galea and the scalp are closed.

61539
A partial or total lobectomy with electrocorticography is done on a lobe other than the temporal lobe for intractable epileptic seizures after the focal point of the seizures has been identified by previous exams to originate there, often the frontal lobe. An access incision is made through the scalp and overlying

muscle to reach the skull. Burr holes are drilled around the periphery of the bone flap area to be raised. Using a craniotome, the bone flap is freed and lifted to expose the dura, which is dissected and retracted out of the operative field. Electrodes are prepared and placed on the brain. The electrical activity of the brain is recorded and mapped while the cortex is kept irrigated. The recording grids may be moved a few times to gain enough information about various sites. After the electrocorticography, the electrodes are removed and markers are placed. Incisions are made into the cortex and dissection is carried down deep into the cortex. The pia is next encountered and is incised and opened to gain access to the frontal lobe. The predetermined amount of frontal lobe is removed. Arteries are transected and coagulated, while preserving the main cerebral/choroidal arteries and the pia-arachnoid. With the frontal lobe removed, closure is done by suturing the dura and replacing the bone flap into position. Screws or plates are placed to secure the bone flap to surrounding skull bone. The divided muscles are sutured and the galea and the scalp are closed.

61540

A partial or total lobectomy is done on a lobe other than the temporal lobe for intractable epileptic seizures after the focal point of the seizures has been identified by previous exams to originate there, often the frontal lobe. An access incision is made through the scalp and overlying muscle to reach the skull. Burr holes are drilled around the periphery of the bone flap area to be raised. Using a craniotome, the bone flap is freed and lifted to expose the dura, which is dissected and retracted out of the operative field. Incisions are made into the cortex and dissection is carried down deep into the cortex. The pia is next encountered and is incised and opened to gain access to the frontal lobe. The predetermined amount of frontal lobe is removed. Arteries are transected and coagulated, while preserving the main cerebral/choroidal arteries and the pia-arachnoid. With the frontal lobe removed, closure is begun by suturing the dura and replacing the bone flap into position. Screws or plates are placed to secure the bone flap to surrounding skull bone. The divided muscles are sutured and the galea and the scalp are closed.

61541-61543

The physician cuts the fibers within the corpus callosum or removes all or part of a brain hemisphere. An electrode array is used to monitor brain function during surgery. In 61541, the physician transects the corpus callosum. In 61542, a hemisphere is removed. Report 61543 if a partial or subtotal (functional) hemispherectomy is performed. The dura is sutured around the remaining brain tissue. The bone flap is replaced and stabilized. The scalp is anastomosed and sutured in layers.

61544

The physician excises or destroys the choroid plexus. The choroid plexus produces spinal fluid. The physician cuts and retracts the scalp in the affected region. A bone flap is raised and tissues are dissected to the ventricle where the affected choroid plexus is located. The choroid plexus is resected, or destroyed using electrocautery. The bone is replaced and stabilized. The scalp is anastomosed and sutured in layers.

61545

The physician excises a craniopharyngioma through a craniotomy. The physician cuts and retracts the frontal scalp and raises a bone flap. The tissues are dissected to the sella turcica, and the craniopharyngioma is resected. The bone is replaced and fastened. The scalp is anastomosed and sutured in layers.

61546

The physician uses a craniotomy to remove a pituitary tumor or resect a portion of the gland. The physician cuts and retracts the frontal scalp and raises a bone flap. The tissues are dissected to the sella turcica, and the pituitary is identified. The tumor or hypertrophic gland is resected. The bone is replaced and fastened. The scalp is anastomosed and sutured in layers.

61548

The physician uses a transnasal or transseptal approach to remove a pituitary tumor or resect a portion of the gland. The physician accesses the base of the sella turcica through the nose. The incision may be made in the mouth underneath the upper lip to avoid facial scarring (transseptal approach). A small hole is drilled in the skull base through the inferior aspect of the sella turcica. The pituitary is identified and the tumor or hypertrophic gland is resected. The hole is packed with Gelfoam, with or without bone chips. The nasal and oral mucosa are sutured closed.

61550-61552

The physician performs a craniectomy for craniosynostosis. Craniosynostosis is a premature closure of the sutures of the skull. The physician incises and retracts the scalp over the fused suture line. The bones are cut to reshape the skull into an anatomically correct position. The recreated suture line is left open and the scalp is reanastomosed and sutured in layers. Report 61550 if a single suture is reformed. Report 61552 for multiple suture lines.

61556-61557

The physician performs a craniotomy for craniosynostosis. Craniosynostosis is a premature closure of the sutures of the skull. The physician incises and retracts the scalp over the fused suture lines. In 61556, the frontal or parietal bones are removed. In 61557, bifrontal bone flaps are raised. The bones are reshaped and a bone flap is created from the harvested bones to enlarge and reshape the skull. If the dura mater was damaged during bone harvest, it is sutured closed. The reshaped bone flap is positioned and secured to neighboring bone. The scalp is reanastomosed and sutured in layers.

61558-61559

The physician performs an extensive craniectomy for craniosynostosis affecting many suture lines. Craniosynostosis is a premature closure of the sutures of the skull. In 61558, no bone grafts are used to reshape the skull. In 61559, the physician harvests bone grafts to aid in reshaping. The physician retracts most or all of the scalp to expose the skull. The cranium is removed as a single unit. The physician breaks the skull and restores correct anatomical shape. If the cranium will not supply bone necessary to provide adequate room for brain growth, bone grafts are obtained and used for skull reshaping. If the dura mater was damaged during cranium harvest, it is primarily closed, or closed with a dural graft. The reshaped cranium pieces are replaced and secured to neighboring bone. The scalp is reapproximated and sutured in layers.

61563-61564

The physician removes an intra and extracranial bone tumor. In 61563, the optic nerve is not decompressed. In 61564, the optic nerve is decompressed. The physician cuts and retracts the scalp overlying the affected bone. The affected bone is resected and removed. Grafts may be necessary for reconstruction. The bone is fastened into place and the scalp is reanastomosed and sutured in layers.

61566

Amygdalohippocampectomy (AH) is done to treat intractable mesial temporal lobe epilepsy. This surgical procedure describes AH in which excision is limited to the anterior hippocampus, amygdala, and parahippocampal gyrus and preserves the fusiform gyrus and the lateral temporal lobe. MRI is done before surgery to map the margins of the involved brain structures. The patient is prepped with a general anesthetic and placement of a lumbar drain. With the patient's head in position, the scalp is incised and the underlying temporalis muscle is dissected to expose the skull. Burr holes are drilled around the periphery of the bone flap area to be raised. Using a craniotome, the bone flap is freed and lifted to expose the dura, which is dissected and retracted out of the operative field. An operating microscope is used. A brain retractor is inserted and cerebrospinal fluid is suctioned from the ambient cistern. The uncus is elevated with the retractor and the anatomical positioning of the related structures (fusiform and parahippocampal gyri, uncus, ambient cistern, and tentorium) is examined. Landmarks for cortical incisions are identified, such as the oculomotor nerve. Cortical incisions are made and the temporal horn of the lateral ventricle is exposed, using careful suction dissection of the cortex and white matter. The horn is opened and the amygdala and hippocampus are identified. The parahippocampal gyrus is now incised, exposing the posterior aspect of the temporal horn and anterior hippocampus. The thin layer of neural tissue connecting the hippocampus and the amygdala is divided with subpial aspiration. The parahippocampal gyrus is removed subpially, the hippocampus is divided transversely, and anterior choroidal and posterior cerebral arteries are coagulated and divided. The hippocampus is completely separated from the arachnoid membrane and removed. The amygdala facing the temporal horn is excised with an ultrasonic aspirator. Closure is done by suturing the dura and replacing the bone flap into position. Screws or plates are placed to secure the bone flap to surrounding skull bone. The divided muscles are sutured and the galea and the scalp are closed.

61567

The surgeon performs a craniotomy for multiple subpial transections, with electrocorticography during surgery. This procedure is done for chronic, intractable, complex partial seizures. The multiple subpial transections are done to reach the areas in the cortex where a focal point of the seizures is identified, as in the frontal, central, or temporal region, and cut the horizontal fibers responsible for the seizure while preserving the vertical fibers responsible for motor and speech. The patient is prepped with general anesthetic and placement of a lumbar drain. With the patient's head in position, the scalp is incised and the underlying temporalis muscle is dissected to expose the skull. Burr holes are drilled around the periphery of the bone flap area to be raised. Using a craniotome, the bone flap is freed and lifted to expose the dura, which is dissected and retracted out of the operative field. Electrodes are prepared and placed on the brain. The electrical activity of the brain is recorded and mapped while the cortex is kept irrigated. The recording grids may be moved a few times to gain enough information about various sites. After the electrocorticography, the electrodes are removed and markers are placed. The cortex is pierced or incised with a curved probe at the adjacent sulcus of the gyrus identified as the focal point of the seizures. The pia is also entered and the grey matter underneath is transected in that area. The probe is removed and the same thing is repeated approximately a centimeter further along the identified gyrus for the extent of the seizure focus. Closure is done by suturing the dura and replacing the bone flap into position. Screws or plates are placed to secure the bone flap to surrounding skull bone. The divided muscles are sutured and the galea and the scalp are closed.

61570-61571

The physician removes a foreign body from the brain. The physician incises the scalp and cuts the bone or creates a bone flap as necessary to reach the foreign body. The object is identified and removed. In 61571, the brain tissue damaged by the foreign object is debrided and irrigated. The dura is sutured closed and the bone is fastened into place.

61575-61576
The physician approaches the skull base, brain stem, or upper spinal cord and obtains a biopsy, decompresses the brain stem or spinal cord, or excises a lesion. In 61575, the physician access the affected area through the patient's mouth. In 61576, the physician performs a tracheostomy and cuts through the mandible and tongue to reach an extensive defect. The physician places a gag retractor in the patient's mouth and makes a posterior pharyngeal wall incision. The mucosa is retracted to the deep muscle layers which are dissected to reach the skull base or superior spinal cord. The bone is removed to expose the area of interest. A lesion may be biopsied or excised. Decompression is accomplished by removing bone from around the structure. If incised, the dura is closed and the posterior pharyngeal wall is reapproximated and sutured in layers.

61580
In this approach procedure, the physician exposes the anterior cranial fossa using a craniofacial approach to an extradural (outside the dura) lesion or defect at the skull base. To adequately expose the lesion or defect, the physician performs a lateral rhinotomy, ethmoidectomy, and sphenoidectomy all of which are included in the approach procedure. For full exposure of the lesion, the brain may need to be retracted from the skull base.

61581
In this approach procedure, the physician exposes the anterior cranial fossa using a craniofacial approach to an extradural (outside the dura) lesion or defect at the skull base. To adequately expose the lesion or defect, the physician performs an orbital exenteration, a lateral rhinotomy, ethmoidectomy, sphenoidectomy and/or maxillectomy all of which are included in the approach procedure. For full exposure of the lesion, the brain may need to be retracted from the skull base.

61582
In this approach procedure, the physician exposes the anterior cranial fossa using a craniofacial approach to an extradural (outside the dura) lesion or defect at the skull base. To adequately expose the lesion or defect, the physician performs a unilateral or bilateral craniotomy which is included in the approach procedure. For full exposure of the lesion, the frontal lobe is elevated and retracted from the skull base. If skull base lesions extend into the bones of the face, an osteotomy of the anterior cranial fossa may be required.

61583
In this approach procedure, the physician exposes the anterior cranial fossa using a craniofacial approach to an intradural (inside the dura) lesion or defect at the skull base. To adequately expose the lesion or defect, the physician performs a unilateral or bilateral craniotomy which is included in the approach procedure. For full exposure of the lesion, the frontal lobe is elevated and retracted from the skull base. If skull base lesions extend into the bones of the face, an osteotomy of the anterior cranial fossa may be required.

61584
In this approach procedure, the physician exposes the anterior cranial fossa using an orbitocranial (transorbital) approach to an extradural (outside the dura) lesion or defect at the skull base. To adequately expose the lesion or defect, the physician performs a supraorbital ridge osteotomy which is included in the approach procedure. For full exposure of the lesion, the frontal and/or temporal lobes are elevated and retracted from the skull base.

61585
In this approach procedure, the physician exposes the anterior cranial fossa using an orbitocranial (transorbital) approach to an extradural (outside the dura) lesion or defect at the skull base. To adequately expose the lesion or defect, the physician performs a supraorbital ridge osteotomy which is included in the approach procedure. The orbital contents are completely removed. For full exposure of the lesion, the frontal and/or temporal lobes are elevated and retracted from the skull base.

61586
In this approach procedure, the physician exposes the anterior cranial fossa using a bicoronal, transzygomatic and/or LeFort I osteotomy approach to a lesion or defect at the skull base. To enter the anterior cranial fossa, the surgeon may use a bicoronal scalp incision to expose the zygoma bone. The zygoma is removed with burrs and saws to enter the anterior skull. If visualization is inadequate, the surgeon may use an intraoral approach to fracture the maxilla and enter the skull. Once the lesion is adequately exposed, a separately reportable surgical procedure is performed which may include biopsy, excision, or other treatment of the lesion. At the conclusion, of this separately reportable procedure, the surgeon responsible for the approach will replace and secure the bony structures using wires, plates or screws as needed.

61590
In this approach procedure, the physician exposes the middle cranial fossa using an infratemporal (below the temporal fossa) pre-auricular (in front of the external ear) approach to a lesion at the skull base. This is also sometimes referred to as a transparotid approach. The transparotid approach allows access to the parapharyngeal space. First, the parotid gland is mobilized. This is followed by identification and dissection of the facial nerve. Parotidectomy with facial

Nervous

nerve preservation is performed. If adequate exposure has not been accomplished, the muscle overlying the mandible is divided and the mandible is displaced anteriorly. This approach may be combined with a transtemporal approach to improve exposure to lesions which extend posteriorly to involve the temporal bone.

61591
In this approach, the physician exposes the middle cranial fossa using an infratemporal (below the temporal fossa), post-auricular (behind the external ear) approach. To adequately expose the lesion or defect, it may be necessary to perform a mastoidectomy, resect the sigmoid sinus and/or decompress/mobilize the contents of the auditory canal or petrous carotid artery.

61592
In this approach procedure, an orbitocranial approach to the middle cranial fossa is performed. Skin incisions are made over the zygoma, and the frontal branches of the facial nerve and infraorbital nerve are identified, tagged, and divided. Soft tissue flaps are raised from the maxilla and zygoma, and osteotomies are performed with removal of the orbitozygomaticomaxillary complex. The temporalis muscle is displaced inferiorly exposing the skull base. If intracranial access is required a subtemporal craniectomy, or frontal or temporal craniotomy is performed. Following separately reportable lesion removal, bone segments are replaced and neurorrhaphy is performed along with meticulous reconstruction and closure.

61595
In this approach code, a transtemporal approach to the posterior cranial fossa, jugular foramen, or midline skull base is used. To obtain adequate exposure of the lesion or defect, the physician performs a mastoidectomy, decompression of sigmoid sinus and/or facial nerve, with or without mobilization. The temple, anterior and posterior ear, orbits, mandible, and mastoid may be resected to reach the affected area of the posterior cranial fossa.

61596
In this approach code, a transcochlear approach is used to expose the posterior cranial fossa, jugular foramen, or midline skull base. A postauricular incision is made and the ear is reflected anteriorly. A labyrinthectomy is performed and the internal auditory canal is skeletonized. The incus is removed, the facial nerve is completely decompressed, and opened widely into the hypotympanum. The greater superficial petrosal nerve is transected and the facial nerve is completely removed from the stylomastoid foramen to the internal auditory canal and rerouted posteriorly. The fallopian canal, stapedius muscle, and the turns of the cochlea are completely exenterated, carrying the dissection forward until the internal carotid artery wall is identified.

61597
In this approach, a transcondylar approach is used to expose the posterior cranial fossa, jugular foramen, or midline skull base. This far lateral suboccipital approach is used to expose the vertebral artery and lower cranial nerve complex in the posterior fossa. A post-auricular incision is made approximately 3 cm lateral to the midline, curving back toward the mastoid eminence. The skin flap created by the incision is retracted laterally exposing the greater occipital nerve and the greater occipital artery and vein. The sternocleidomastoid is incised parallel to its attachment. The suboccipital musculature is also incised and retracted. A suboccipital craniectomy is performed. The C1-C3 vertebral bodies are resected to further expose the cerebellum and a portion of the occipital condyle is removed. The vertebral artery is identified, decompressed and mobilized.

61598
In this approach code, a transpetrosal approach is used to expose the posterior cranial fossa, jugular foramen, or midline skull base. A craniotomy is performed posterior to the sigmoid sinus. The cerebellum is retracted posteriorly, allowing access to the petrosal and sigmoid sinuses which are ligated.

61600-61601
The physician uses a separately reportable anterior cranial fossa approach to resect a neoplastic, vascular, or infectious lesion at the base of the anterior cranial fossa. The physician incises and retracts the scalp or nasal mucosa and removes a bone flap to access the anterior cranial fossa. In 61600, the extradural lesion is identified and resected. Unaffected bone is replaced and fastened to neighboring bone. Bone defects are replaced with bone grafts. In 61601, the intradural lesion is identified and resected. The dura is primarily closed, with or without a dural graft. The bone flap is replaced and fastened to neighboring bone. The scalp is reapproximated and sutured in layers.

61605-61606
The physician uses a middle cranial fossa approach to resect a neoplastic, vascular, or infectious lesion located at the base of the middle cranial fossa (infratemporal fossa, parapharyngeal space, petrous apex). The approach is reported separately. The physician makes a pre- or post-auricular incision or an orbital zygomatic incision to access the middle cranial fossa. The physician retracts the tissues and performs an osteotomy to access the lesion. In 61605, the extradural lesion is identified and resected. Unaffected bone is replaced and fastened to neighboring bone. Bone defects are replaced with bone grafts. In 61606, the intradural lesion is identified and resected. The dura is primarily closed, with or without a dural graft. The bone flap is replaced and fastened to neighboring bone. The scalp is reapproximated and sutured in layers.

61607-61608
The physician uses a middle cranial fossa approach to resect a neoplastic, vascular, or infectious lesion located at the base of the middle cranial fossa (parasellar area, cavernous sinus, clivus, or midline skull base). The approach is reported separately. The physician makes a pre- or post auricular incision or an orbital zygomatic incision to access the middle cranial fossa. The physician retracts the tissues and performs an osteotomy to access the lesion. In 61607, the extradural lesion is identified and resected. Unaffected bone is replaced and fastened to neighboring bone. Bone defects are replaced with bone grafts. In 61608, the intradural lesion is identified and resected. The dura is primarily closed, with or without a dural graft. The bone flap is replaced and fastened to neighboring bone. The scalp is reapproximated and sutured in layers.

61609-61612
The physician transects or ligates a carotid artery in the cavernous sinus or petrous canal. Report 61609 for transection or ligation without repair in the cavernous sinus. Report 61610 if the carotid artery in the cavernous sinus is repaired by reanastomosis or graft placement. Report 61611 for transection or ligation without repair in the petrous canal. Report 61612 if the carotid artery in the petrous canal is repaired by reanastomosis or graft placement. These procedures are reported in addition to 61605 through 61608 (the primary definitive procedure).

61613
The physician uses a middle cranial fossa approach to access and obliterate a carotid aneurysm, arteriovenous malformation, or carotid-cavernous fistula. The approach is reported separately. Using an orbitocranial zygomatic approach, the physician incises and retracts the skin over the zygoma. The zygoma and the base of the skull are osteotomized to reach the cavernous sinus. The aneurysm, defect, or fistula is dissected and ligated. The skull and zygoma are packed with Gelfoam or bone pieces. The skin is reanastomosed and sutured in layers.

61615-61616
The physician uses a separately reportable skull base approach to resect or excise a neoplastic, vascular, or infectious lesion in the posterior cranial fossa, jugular foramen, foramen magnum, or C1-C3 vertebral bodies. The physician incises and retracts the scalp overlying the posterior cranial fossa and uses a transtemporal, transcochlear, transcondylar, or transpetrosal approach to reach the lesion. In 61615, the extradural lesion is identified and resected. Unaffected bone is replaced and fastened to neighboring bone. Bone defects are replaced with bone grafts. In 61616, the intradural lesion is identified and resected. The dura is primarily closed, with or without a dural graft. The bone flap is replaced and fastened to neighboring bone. The scalp is reapproximated and sutured in layers.

61618-61619
The physician repairs a cerebrospinal fluid leak in the dura following a craniotomy of the skull base. The approach is dependent on the location of the dural leak. In 61618, the physician uses a dural graft obtained from fascia, tensor fascia lata, or pericranium. In 61619, a vascularized pedicle flap is rotated over the dural defect. The temporalis, frontalis, or occipitalis muscle is used. The dural leak is closed by suturing the flap to the dura. Following anastomosis, intracranial pressure may be increased to test repair success under direct visualization. The bone flap is replaced and the scalp incision is sutured in layers.

61623
Temporary balloon occlusion (TBO) controls blood flow in arteries of the neck during procedures such as intracranial or extracranial aneurysm surgery. The balloon catheter, such as a double lumen Swan-Ganz, is placed in the artery and positioned at the point where occlusion is to occur. Selective catheterization is done first. The access artery is percutaneously punctured with a needle and a guidewire is fed through the artery into the target vessel, such as the cerebral carotid. A catheter is threaded over the guidewire to the point where it is to be occluded and the guidewire is removed. The balloon is inflated under fluoroscopy and occlusion is confirmed with small amounts of contrast material injected through the catheter and checked for stasis in the contrast column. The patient is monitored for change in neurologic status. The TBO is maintained only for about 20 to 30 minutes and angiographic studies may be done after occlusion of rule out post procedure vascular injury.

61624
The physician accesses an artery of the central nervous system percutaneously to permanently occlude or embolize a vascular malformation, destroy a tumor, or achieve hemostasis for a bleeding aneurysm. The access artery is percutaneously punctured with a needle and a guidewire is fed through the artery into the target vessel of the central nervous system. A catheter is threaded over the guidewire to the point where it is to be occluded and the guidewire is removed. When the catheter is in position, the defect is occluded or embolized with materials placed through the catheter to achieve clotting. Radiographic methods are used to position the catheter and test for successful occlusion.

61626
The physician uses a percutaneous catheter to access an arterial venous malformation, tumor, or bleeding aneurysm. The defect lies outside the central nervous system, in the head or neck regions (common carotid, external carotid, vertebral and their branches). The physician places a catheter in a peripheral artery (e.g.,

femoral artery). Using separately reportable fluoroscopic guidance, the physician locates the lesion with the catheter. The defect is occluded or embolized with materials placed through the catheter to aid clotting.

61630

The physician performs a percutaneous balloon angioplasty of an intracranial vessel, most often as an alternative to surgical carotid endarterectomy for carotid stenosis in high-risk patients. The patient undergoes an appropriate neurological and vascular work up preoperatively. A standard percutaneous transfemoral approach is most frequently used. Light intravenous sedation is administered. Standard diagnostic carotid and cerebral angiography is performed to confirm the suspected lesion and evaluate the cerebral circulation. The patient is anticoagulated and an antiplatelet agent is given. Using the femoral approach, the balloon is introduced on the tip of an angiographic catheter passed through the circulatory tree until it reaches the stenotic lesion. Once in place, the balloon is inflated, dilating the vessel and improving blood flow to the brain.

61635

The physician places an intravascular intracranial stent most often as an alternative to surgical carotid endarterectomy for carotid stenosis in high-risk patients. A percutaneous balloon angioplasty may also be performed. The patient undergoes an appropriate neurological and vascular work up preoperatively. A standard percutaneous transfemoral approach is most frequently used. Light intravenous sedation is administered. Standard diagnostic carotid and cerebral angiography is performed to confirm the suspected lesion and evaluate the cerebral circulation. The patient is anticoagulated and an antiplatelet agent is given. Using the femoral approach, a guiding catheter is placed from the groin into the common carotid artery. A microwire is passed through the guiding catheter and crosses the stenotic lesion in the artery. In the event that the stenosis is too tight to pass a stent primarily, an angioplasty balloon is used to predilate the stenosis prior to the stent placement. The microwire is left across the dilated segment, the balloon is removed, and the stent delivery device is placed. Once positioned, the stent is deployed across the region of the stenosis. If necessary, an additional balloon can be placed inside the deployed stent for post-dilation to make sure the struts of the stent are pressed firmly against the inner surface of the wall of the vessel.

61640-61642

The physician treats intracranial vasospasm via an endovascular approach most often performed under general anesthesia. Angioplasty is performed using a percutaneous transfemoral approach, usually with a six or seven French sheath. Heparin is administered to minimize the risk of thromboembolic events. Prior to the procedure, diagnostic angiography is performed to confirm the clinical suspicion of vasospasm and to correlate the findings with the clinical symptoms, since treatment is directed only at the areas of vasospasm correlating with symptoms. The custom-designed silicone microballoon, which conforms to the shape of the vessel, is guided through the intracranial vessels, and inflated to dilate the spastic vessel. This procedure is useful in improving blood flow to ischemic cerebral tissue by treating focal, as well as diffuse, areas of spasm involving more than one vascular territory. Report 61640 for balloon dilation of the first vessel; 61641 for each additional vessel in the same vascular family; and 61642 for vessels in different vascular families.

61680-61692

The physician resects an arteriovenous malformation (AVM) in the brain. This AVM is a tumor-like growth of blood vessels. After using angiography to locate the AVM, the physician performs a craniotomy in the affected area. The AVM is located and the blood vessels feeding the tumor are ligated. The tumor is resected and bleeding is controlled. The bone flap is repositioned and secured; the scalp is reanastomosed and sutured in layers. Report according to AVM location and ease of access: Report 61680 if the AVM is located in the supratentorial region and is easily accessible; 61682 if the supratentorial AVM is more difficult to access and remove; 61684 if the AVM is located in the infratentorial region and is easily accessible; 61686 if the infratentorial AVM is more difficult to access and remove; 61690 if the AVM is located in the dural layer and is easily accessible; and 61692 if the dural AVM is more difficult to access and remove.

61697

An open middle cranial fossa approach is used to locate a complex aneurysm of the internal carotid circulation. Complex aneurysms include those that are larger than 15 millimeters as well as those that contain calcifications or incorporate normal vessels at the aneurysm neck. The surgical technique used is dependent on the specific anatomic characteristics of the aneurysm. One technique involves direct treatment of the aneurysm with clipping and resection of the mass lesion. However, clipping of the aneurysm neck may not be possible if a thick, calcified wall is present. In this instance, incision of the aneurysmal sac and aneurysmorrhaphy (suturing of the aneurysm) may be necessary. When critical perforating vessels arise from the aneurysm, the patient may not be able to tolerate occlusion of the parent vessel. If this is the case, an extracranial or intracranial bypass procedure must first be performed with subsequent trapping or proximal occlusion of the vessel. In some instances, adjunctive techniques are utilized to aid in direct surgery. Techniques include cardiopulmonary bypass with cardiac arrest to allow for a slack aneurysm, which can be dissected from surrounding cerebral tissue. Another adjunctive technique is temporary occlusion of the parent vessel to allow decompression of the aneurysm. Once the aneurysm has been occluded, resected, and/or bypassed, the physician checks to make sure that the repairs are secure and that there is no bleeding. The dura is closed and the bone flap repositioned and secured. The scalp is sutured in layers.

61698
An open posterior cranial fossa approach is used to locate a complex aneurysm of the vertebrobasilar circulation. Complex aneurysms include those that are larger than 15 millimeters as well as those that contain calcifications or incorporate normal vessels at the aneurysm neck. The surgical technique used is dependent on the specific anatomic characteristics of the aneurysm. One technique involves direct treatment of the aneurysm with clipping and resection of the mass lesion. However, clipping of the aneurysm neck may not be possible if a thick, calcified wall is present. In this instance, incision of the aneurysmal sac and aneurysmorrhaphy (suturing of the aneurysm) may be necessary. When critical perforating vessels arise from the aneurysm, the patient may not be able to tolerate occlusion of the parent vessel. If this is the case, an extracranial or intracranial bypass procedure must first be performed with subsequent trapping or proximal occlusion of the vessel. In some instances, adjunctive techniques are utilized to aid in direct surgery. Techniques include cardiopulmonary bypass with cardiac arrest to allow for a slack aneurysm, which can be dissected from surrounding cerebral tissue. Another adjunctive technique is temporary occlusion of the parent vessel to allow decompression of the aneurysm. Once the aneurysm has been occluded, resected, and/or bypassed, the physician checks to make sure that the repairs are secure and that there is no bleeding. The dura is closed and the bone flap repositioned and secured. The scalp is sutured in layers.

61700
The physician resects a simple carotid aneurysm. Simple aneurysms include those that are 15 millimeters or less in size and contain no anatomical features that will complicate the surgery such as calcifications or critical perforating vessels at the aneurysm neck. After using angiography to locate the aneurysm, the physician uses a middle cranial fossa approach for access. The aneurysm is located and clipped under direct visualization. After making sure the clip is secure and there is no bleeding, the physician closes the dura. The bone flap is repositioned and secured and the scalp is sutured in layers.

61702
The physician resects a simple vertebrobasilar aneurysm. Simple aneurysms include those that are 15 millimeters or less in size and contain no anatomical features that will complicate the surgery such as calcifications or critical perforating vessels at the aneurysm neck. After using angiography to locate the aneurysm, the physician uses a posterior cranial fossa approach for access. The aneurysm is located and clipped under direct visualization. After making sure the clip is secure and there is no bleeding, the physician closes the dura. The bone flap is repositioned and secured and the scalp is sutured in layers.

61703
The physician resects an aneurysm after clamping the carotid artery to control bleeding. The physician makes a high neck incision and locates the ipsilateral carotid artery. Next, the physician performs a craniotomy to access the intracranial aneurysm. When the aneurysm is located, the carotid artery is occluded with a clamp. The physician places a clip on the aneurysm under direct visualization. Once the aneurysm has been clipped and bleeding is controlled, the carotid clamp is released. The aneurysm site is reexamined for bleeding. The physician closes the dura. The bone flap is repositioned and secured; the scalp is reanastomosed and sutured in layers. The neck incision is sutured in layers.

61705-61710
The physician clips an aneurysm, vascular malformation, or carotid-cavernous fistula. The physician makes a high neck incision and locates the ipsilateral carotid artery. Next, the physician performs a craniotomy to access the defect. In 61705, the physician performs a craniotomy to access the intracranial aneurysm, vascular malformation or carotid-cavernous fistula. Once the lesion is located, the cervical carotid is clamped and the carotid artery proximal and distal to the lesion is ligated to prevent blood flow to the lesion. The cervical carotid is unclamped while monitoring for bleeding in the craniotomy site. In 61708, the lesion is obliterated using electrothrombosis. In 61710, the physician embolizes the lesion with an intra-arterial balloon catheter or injects material to form a regional clot to obliterate the blood supply to the lesion. After the lesion has been obliterated, the dura is closed. The bone flap is repositioned and secured; the scalp is reanastomosed and sutured in layers.

61711
The physician anastomoses the arterial and extracranial-intracranial arteries. The physician performs a craniotomy in the affected area and locates the arteries to be anastomosed and dissects them from the surrounding tissue. The feeding artery is clamped and ligated and the proximal limb is sutured to the receiving artery. After verifying successful anastomosis and adequate blood flow, the dura is closed. The bone flap is repositioned and secured; the scalp is reanastomosed and sutured in layers.

Nervous

61720-61735
The physician creates a lesion of the brain through stereotactic methods. The tissue to be lesioned is mapped by using a CT or MRI scanning technique. The physician uses the coordinates obtained from the scans to locate the area of interest. The physician incises and retracts the scalp. A burr hole is drilled. An electrocautery unit or surgical knife is directed to the area of interest. When the precise location is reached and confirmed by the coordinates, the lesion is made. In 61720, a lesion is made in the globus pallidus or in the thalamus. In 61735, a lesion is made in subcortical structures other than the globus pallidus or the thalamus. After the lesion is made, the dura is sutured and the scalp is reapproximated and sutured in layers.

61750-61751
The physician biopsies, aspirates, or excises an intracranial lesion stereotactically. The lesion is mapped using a CT or MRI scanning technique. The physician uses the coordinates obtained from the scans to locate the area of interest. The physician incises and retracts the scalp. A burr hole is drilled. The physician inserts a biopsy needle into the area of interest to aspirate or biopsy the tissue. If the lesion is to be destroyed the physician inserts an electrocautery unit, knife or curette into the lesion. In 61751, the physician utilizes CT or MRI scanning intraoperatively to confirm lesion location and accurate placement of surgical instruments. The physician closes the dura and reapproximates the scalp and closes it in sutured layers.

61760
The physician implants depth electrodes into the cerebrum for long-term monitoring of seizures. After the desired locations of the electrodes have been mapped by CT or MRI scanning techniques, the physician incises and retracts the scalp. The physician drills a burr hole(s) and the electrodes are placed into the desired area of the brain by following the coordinates established by the scans. The dura is sutured closed and the scalp is reapproximated and sutured in layers.

61770
The physician implants catheters or probes into a lesion of the brain for radiation therapy. After using CT or MRI scanning techniques to map the desired locations of the catheters or probes, the physician incises and retracts the scalp. The physician drills a burr hole and the catheters or probes are placed into the desired area of the brain by following the coordinates established by the scans. The dura is sutured closed and the scalp is reapproximated and sutured in layers.

61790-61791
The physician under stereotactic guidance percutaneously creates a neurolytic lesion in the gasserian ganglion or the medullary trigeminal tract. The area of interest is located and mapped by CT or MRI scanning techniques. The physician guides a needle into the region to be destroyed. After reaffirming position by checking the coordinates of the needle, the physician injects, or electrically destroys the tissue. In 61790, the physician destroys the gasserian ganglion. In 61791, the physician destroys the medullary trigeminal tracts.

61795
Use this code in addition to the procedure code when the physician uses a computer to assist with coordinate determination established with a CT or MRI scan.

61796-61800
Before imaging, patients undergo application of a separately reportable stereotactic head frame (61800). Using high-resolution stereotactic imaging, a precise three-dimensional location of the brain lesion is identified. The physician uses the coordinates obtained from the images to focus linear accelerator, gamma ray, or particle beam energy onto the lesion, thereby destroying or inactivating it. This is a noninvasive procedure that does not require incision of the scalp or drilling into the skull. Report 61796 (no more than once per course of treatment) for stereotactic radiosurgery on a simple cranial lesion. Simple lesions include those that are less than 3.5 cm in maximum dimension and those that do not meet the criteria for a complex lesion. Report 61797 for each additional simple cranial lesion. Report code 61798 (no more than once per course of treatment) for stereotactic radiosurgery on a complex cranial lesion. Complex lesions include those that are 3.5 cm or greater in maximum dimension; those that are within the brainstem or adjacent (5 mm or less) to the optic nerve, optic chasm, or optic tract; schwannomas; arteriovenous malformations; cavernous sinus tumors; glomus tumors; parasellar or petroclival tumors; pineal region tumors; and pituitary tumors. Code 61798 is also reported for procedures such as thalamotomy or pallidotomy that create therapeutic lesions. If multiple lesions are treated and any single lesion is complex, report 61798. Report 61799 for each additional complex cranial lesion; however, codes 61797 and 61799 may not be reported more than four times for the entire course of treatment regardless of the number of lesions treated. Codes for cranial stereotactic radiosurgery include any required computer-assisted planning, dosimetry, targeting, positioning, or blocking by the neurosurgeon.

61850
The physician uses a twist or burr drill to reach the cortex or subcortex and implant neurostimulator electrodes. The physician incises the scalp and uses a twist or burr drill to expose the cortex for neurostimulator electrode placement. The physician places an electrode through an introducer needle into

the tissue to be stimulated. The electrodes are tested to verify placement and the incision is sutured in layers.

61860
The physician performs a craniectomy or craniotomy to reach the cortex and implant neurostimulator electrodes to affect the cerebrum. The cerebrum occupies the frontal portion of the cranial cavity. Its two hemispheres joined by the corpus callosum supply the majority of brain function. The physician incises the scalp and retracts it. The physician drills or cuts the cranium to expose the cortex for neurostimulator electrode placement. Bone is removed. The physician places an electrode through an introducer needle into the tissue to be stimulated, and the electrodes are tested to verify placement.

61863-61864
The surgeon performs a twist drill, burr hole, craniotomy, or craniectomy for stereotactic implantation of a deep-brain neurostimulator electrode array. This procedure is done for Parkinsonism, uncontrolled tremors, multiple sclerosis, and intractable dystonias. MRI or CT imaging (reported separately) may be done before surgery to map out the involved brain structures. Before surgery is begun, the patient has a stereotactic head frame applied and anchored to the skull. The surgery is planned with computer assistance, using the previously acquired CT or MRI images, and the target point trajectories for placing electrodes are discussed. The entry point is calculated. The patient is prepped, the head frame is assembled, and the coordinates are entered into the stereotactic system. The entry point is marked, the scalp is incised, and the skull is exposed. A twist drill or burr hole is made with a cranial drill and the dura is exposed and punctured for access. A cannula and electrode guide connected to the computer system is next inserted and the deep-brain stimulation neuroelectrode array is placed at the target point. Testing is done. Reposition and testing may be repeated several times before optimal results in tremor suppression mobility and decreased limb rigidity are observed. When the electrode array is in the best position, the guide cannula is removed. The array is fastened into position under radiographic imaging to monitor its placement. The lead has to be coiled in a pocket under the galea, which is sutured closed, followed by skin closure. Report 61864 when more than one array is placed into a target site. This also requires additional presurgical computerized trajectory planning and other entry site access through the skull to reach the additional target area.

61867-61868
The surgeon performs a twist drill, burr hole, craniotomy, or craniectomy for stereotactic implantation of a deep-brain neurostimulator electrode array with intraoperative use of microelectrode recording. This procedure is done for Parkinsonism, uncontrolled tremors, multiple sclerosis, and intractable dystonias. MRI or CT imaging (reported separately) may be done before surgery to map out the involved brain structures. Before surgery is begun, the patient has a stereotactic head frame applied and anchored to the skull. The surgery is planned with computer assistance, using the previously acquired CT or MRI images, and the target point trajectories for placing electrodes are discussed. The entry point is calculated. The patient is prepped, the head frame is assembled, and the coordinates are entered into the stereotactic system. The entry point is marked, the scalp is incised, and the skull is exposed. A twist drill or burr hole is made with a cranial drill and the dura is exposed and punctured for access. A cannula and electrode guide connected to the computer system is next inserted. The microelectrode is put into another cannula and also attached to the computer system. The cannula protecting the microelectrode is placed within the guide cannula and advanced. Microelectrode recording (MER) and stimulation is done during targeting and repositioning of the electrodes to determine the best placement. MER records the response of individual neurons and maps out the results to define the optimal target area. The microelectrode is removed from the cannula and the deep-brain stimulation neuroelectrode array is placed at the target point. Testing is carried out and the guide cannula is removed. The array is fastened into position with radiographic imaging monitoring its placement. The lead has to be coiled in a pocket under the galea, which is sutured closed, followed by skin closure. Report 61868 when more than one array is placed into a target site in the same manner. This requires additional presurgical computerized trajectory planning and other entry site access through the skull to reach the additional target area.

61870-61875
The physician performs a craniectomy to reach the cortex or subcortex and implant neurostimulator electrodes to affect the cerebellum. The cerebellum is located behind the brain stem and supplies coordination of movements. The physician incises the scalp and retracts it. The physician drills or cuts the cranium to expose the area for neurostimulator electrode placement. Bone is removed. The physician places an electrode through an introducer needle into the tissue to be stimulated, and the electrodes are tested to verify placement. In 61870, the electrodes are placed in the cortex. In 61875, the electrodes are placed in the subcortex (the area near the cortex). The dura is sutured closed. The skull stabilized and the scalp is sutured in layers.

61880
The physician removes or revises neurostimulator electrodes. The physician incises and retracts the scalp and drills a burr hole in the cranium to locate the electrode. The electrode is removed or revised. If

Nervous

necessary, the electrode is replaced. The dura is closed and the scalp is reapproximated and sutured in layers.

61885-61886

The physician inserts or replaces a cranial neurostimulator pulse generator or receiver into a subcutaneous pocket. The physician selects a location site, usually the infraclavicular area, and incises the skin. Using blunt dissection, the physician creates a pocket for the generator or receiver. The unit is connected to a previously positioned single electrode array. After ensuring that the device is functioning, the generator or receiver is sutured into place within its subcutaneous pocket. In 61886, the pulse generator or receiver is inserted or replaced and connected to two or more electrode arrays.

61888

The physician removes or revises a pulse generator or receiver within the subcutaneous pocket. The physician incises the skin above the unit. After locating the generator or receiver, the physician removes it or makes any necessary revisions to it and closes the incision.

62000-62010

The physician elevates a depressed skull fracture to restore anatomical position. The physician incises and retracts the scalp to expose the skull depression. In 62000, the physician drills a burr hole and pulls on the skull to elevate the bone. In 62005, there are multiple fracture lines. The bony pieces are stabilized in anatomic position. In 62010, the fracture has damaged the dura and brain. The physician removes the bony fragments and debrides the brain and dura. The dura is sutured closed and the bony fragments are approximated and stabilized in anatomic position. The scalp is reapproximated and sutured in layers.

62100

The physician repairs a dural/cerebrospinal fluid leak. The physician determines the location of the skull fracture using an MRI scan. The skin over the damaged area is incised. A bone flap is removed to access the dura which is sutured closed. The bone flap is replaced and stabilized. The scalp is reapproximated and sutured in layers.

62115-62117

The physician reduces an enlarged skull (e.g., secondary to hydrocephalus). The physician incises and retracts the scalp to expose the cranium. In 62115, the skull is cut and the bone is reshaped. In 62116, bone flaps are raised. After reshaping, the bony fragments are replaced and stabilized. In 62117, bone flaps are cut and raised. The bones are removed and reshaped; bone grafts may be used to shape the cranium. This code includes bone harvest.

62120-62121

The physician corrects an encephalocele. An encephalocele is a herniation in the brain into or through a defect in the cranium. In 62120, the defect is located in the skull vault. In 62121, the defect is in the skull base. The physician incises and retracts the scalp and raises a bone flap. The bone is reshaped to increase skull size. The skull is stabilized and the scalp is reapproximated and sutured in layers.

62140-62141

The physician corrects a defect in the cranium. In 62140, the defect is less than 5 cm. In 62141, the defect is greater than 5 cm. The physician incises and retracts the scalp. The bone flaps are lifted and remodeled. A prosthesis may be used to reapproximate the bony edges. The skull is stabilized and the scalp is reapproximated and sutured in layers.

62142

The physician removes a bone flap or prosthetic plate of the skull. The physician incises the scalp above the area to be resected and retracts it. The stabilizers are removed and the bone flap lifted. The scalp is reapproximated over the dura and sutured in layers.

62143

The physician replaces a bone flap or prosthetic plate of the skull. The physician incises the scalp and retracts it to expose the dura. The bone graft or prosthetic plate is placed over dura to correct the defect. The bone or prosthetic plate is stabilized and the scalp is reapproximated and sutured in layers.

62145

The physician reshapes or reconstructs the cranium in addition to reparative brain surgery. The physician incises the scalp above the defect area. A bone flap is raised and the physician inspects the dura and the underlying brain. Any dural defects are corrected. The bone flaps are reshaped, reapproximated and stabilized. The scalp is sutured in layers.

62146-62148

The physician reshapes or reconstructs the cranium using bone grafts obtained from the patient. The physician incises the scalp above the defect area. The scalp is retracted and the defect is located. The physician incises the cranium and reshapes available skull bone. The physician obtains bone grafts from the patient. The harvested bone is reshaped to supplement the cranium. The bones are approximated and stabilized. The scalp is reanastomosed and sutured in layers. Report 62146 if the defect is 5 cm or less in size; 62147 if the defect is greater than 5 cm; and 62148 if the surgeon reaccesses the surgical site of the cranioplasty and retrieves the bone graft used whether autologous or from another source.

62160

This code reports the use of intracranial neuroendoscopic techniques when placing or replacing a ventricular catheter of a shunt or external drainage system of the brain to divert the flow and drain obstructed cerebrospinal fluid (CSF). The physician inserts the neuroendoscope into the ventricular compartment of the brain through a burr hole in the skull just big enough to allow passage of the instrument. The scope works within the fluid-filled spaces of the ventricles and gives a much better visualization of the intracranial anatomy to allow the choroid plexus to be seen at the time of shunt placement. After the choroid plexus and ventricular anatomy are identified, the neuroendoscope is removed and the ventricular catheter is placed at a specific distance in front of and above the choroid plexus. The positioning above this potentially obstructive tissue improves shunt success since catheters placed in this position using the neuroendoscope require fewer shunt revisions and there is no need for a second pass through the brain parenchyma. This is an add-on code to be listed in conjunction with the code for the primary procedure.

62161
The physician uses a neuroendoscope for intracranial dissection of adhesions, fenestration of septum pellucidum, or intraventricular cysts. A small incision is made in the scalp based on the location of the cyst and a small burr hole is made in the skull just big enough to allow passage of the instrument. From this point, the scope is inserted into the cyst within the ventricle and the wall of the cyst is fenestrated, or opened, to drain the cystic fluid into one of the natural fluid chambers of the brain where it can be absorbed naturally. This is done by the use of a laser micro contact fiber inserted through the endoscope within the ventricular cannula. In this way, cystic adhesions within the ventricles can also be dissected as well as fenestration of the septum pellucidum, the membrane separating the horns of the lateral ventricles, for cyst drainage. This code includes placement, replacement, or removal of a ventricular catheter.

62162-62163
The physician uses a neuroendoscope for intracranial fenestration or excision of a colloid cyst. A colloid cyst is a benign tumor in the third ventricle that contains a fluid of jelly-like substance. A small incision is made in the scalp behind the hairline and a small burr hole is made in the skull just big enough to allow passage of the instrument. From this point, the scope is inserted within the third ventricle and navigated to the tumor. The wall of the tumor is coagulated with electrical current and fenestrated, or opened, with sharp dissection. Suction catheters are used to empty the contents and the wall is excised. Any remaining tissue is destroyed with electrical current and the endoscope is removed. This code includes the placement of an external ventricular catheter for drainage. Report 62163 if the neuroendoscope is inserted in a similar procedure and used to locate and retrieve an intracranial foreign body.

62164
The physician uses a neuroendoscope for the intracranial excision of a brain tumor. A small incision is made in the scalp based on the location of the tumor and a small burr hole is made in the skull just big enough to allow passage of the instrument. The scope is inserted into the ventricular compartment and moved to the tumor site. Many brain tumors occur situated deep within the brain in the ventricles. The neuroendoscope works with clarity within the fluid-filled spaces of the ventricles. The tumor is easily identified because of the different tissue appearance and is resected and removed completely through the endoscope under direct vision. Using the neuroendoscope allows bleeding vessels to be seen and other important tissue within the ventricle to be avoided and eliminates the need for long scalp incisions, skull flaps, and dissection through brain tissue. This code includes the placement of an external ventricular catheter for drainage.

62165
The physician excises a pituitary tumor using neuroendoscopic techniques employed transnasally or transsphenoidally. The face and nostrils are prepped as well as the abdomen, in case a fat graft must be harvested. Vasoconstriction is achieved in the nasal mucosa and blunt dissection is used on the middle turbinate to view the uncinate process, which is removed with rongeurs. A complete ethmoidectomy is done with removal of the posterior half of the middle turbinate. A Freer elevator is used to identify the sphenoid sinus ostia behind the posterior ethmoid wall and the ostium is enlarged with pituitary rongeurs. The sphenoid anterior wall is removed for insertion of the endoscope. The sinus mucosa is removed with rongeurs and blunt dissection to expose the posterior sphenoid sinus wall and the sella floor. The pituitary fossa is entered and the sella floor is opened with an osteotome, if possible, or small, high-speed drills. The dura is coagulated with bipolar cautery and an incision is made. The tumor can now be removed with suction and angled curettes. The scope is advanced into the empty pituitary fossa as the tumor is removed to check for complete resection with the assistance of angled telescopes. Hemostasis is ensured after tumor removal. If cerebrospinal fluid is seen, the sella is packed with a fat graft harvested from the abdomen. The instruments are removed and no nasal packing is required.

62180
The physician performs a ventriculocisternostomy to form a communicating duct from the lateral ventricles to the cisterna magna to drain excess CSF into the spinal cord where it can be absorbed. The scalp is incised and retracted posterior to the ear. The physician drills a burr hole and inserts the proximal portion of the shunt toward the lateral ventricles, with or without the aid of an endoscope until CSF flows through the shunt. The distal end of the shunt is

directed toward the cisterna magna until CSF flows through the shunt. The two ends are connected and tested. The dura is sutured closed and the scalp is reapproximated and sutured in layers.

62190-62192

The physician creates a shunt to form a communicating duct from the subdural or subarachnoid to the atria, jugular veins, auricular processes, pleural space, peritoneal space, or another area to drain excess CSF. The scalp is incised over the affected area. The physician drills a burr hole and inserts the proximal portion of the shunt into the subdural or subarachnoid space. The distal end of the shunt is directed and tunneled subcutaneously toward the selected drain site. The two ends are connected and tested. The dura is sutured closed and the scalp is reapproximated and sutured in layers. In an incision is required at the distal end, the incision is sutured in layers. Report 62190 if the distal end is located at the atria, jugular veins, or auricular processes. Report 62192 if it is located at the pleural space, peritoneal space, or another area.

62194

The physician irrigates or replaces a subarachnoid or subdural shunt system catheter. The physician incises and retracts the scalp over the placement origin. The dura is incised, and the catheter is irrigated to verify function. If the catheter is inoperative, it is replaced. The dura is sutured closed and the scalp is reapproximated and sutured in layers.

62200

The physician performs a ventriculocisternostomy to form a communicating duct from the third ventricle to the cisterna magna to drain excess CSF into the spinal cord where it can be absorbed. The scalp is incised and retracted posterior to the ear. The physician drills a burr hole and inserts the proximal portion of the shunt toward the third ventricle until CSF flows through the shunt. The distal end of the shunt is directed toward the cisterna magna until CSF flows through the shunt. The two ends are connected and tested. The dura is sutured closed and the scalp is reapproximated and sutured in layers.

62201

The physician performs a ventriculocisternostomy of the third ventricle (third ventriculostomy) using stereotactic, neuroendoscopic techniques. Third ventriculostomy is done in hydrocephalus cases to create a pathway for obstructed cerebrospinal fluid (CSF) by opening a communication between the third ventricle and the subarachnoid space to allow the fluid to drain internally. This method prevents the need for shunt placement in many cases. A small incision is made in the scalp and a small burr hole is made in the skull just big enough to allow passage of the endoscopic instrument. Computerized tomography (CT) guidance for stereotactic positioning is used. The neuroendoscope is inserted through the burr hole into the third ventricle. A contact laser fiber is inserted through the endoscope onto the floor of the third ventricle and the contact tip perforates the intracranial tissue at different points, avoiding arteries. The newly opened communication is verified when the circulation of CSF is unobstructed. Hemostasis is achieved, the instruments are removed, and the incision is closed.

62220-62223

The physician creates a shunt to form a communicating duct from the lateral ventricles to the atria, jugular veins, auricular processes, pleural space, peritoneal space, or another area, to drain excess CSF. The scalp is incised and retracted posterior to the ear. The physician drills a burr hole and inserts the proximal portion of the shunt toward the lateral ventricles, with or without the aid of an endoscope, until CSF flows through the shunt. The distal end of the shunt is directed and tunneled subcutaneously toward the selected drain site. The two ends are connected and tested. The dura is sutured closed and the scalp is reapproximated and sutured in layers. If an incision is required at the distal end, the incision is sutured in layers. Report 62220 if the distal end is located at the atria, jugular veins, or auricular processes. Report 62223 if it is located at the pleural space, peritoneal space, or another area. A neuroendoscope may be used to aid in placing the ventricular catheter and connecting it to the shunt system drainage site terminus, but is not an inclusive component of these codes.

62225-62230

The physician replaces or revises a previously placed, inoperative cerebrospinal fluid shunt system or component. The physician incises and retracts the scalp over the placement origin and drills a burr hole to gain access. The dura is incised, and the inoperative portion of the shunt system is located and replaced or revised. In 62225, the ventricular catheter is irrigated or replaced. In 62230, a cerebrospinal fluid shunt, obstructed valve, or distal catheter is revised or replaced. The shunt system is reconnected and tested. The dura is sutured closed; the scalp is reapproximated and sutured in layers. A neuroendoscope may be used to aid in placing the ventricular catheter and connecting it to the shunt system drainage site terminus, but is not an inclusive component of these codes.

62252

An adjustable cerebrospinal fluid (CSF) shunt is reprogrammed. Adjustable shunts have a pressure differential valve that alters resistance using a magnetic field transmitted through the skin. During a routine office visit, the valve setting is changed using an antenna whose emitted magnetic field rotates the stepper valve to the desired position. The stepper adjusts the tension of the spring, which in turn imposes resistance on the ball valve altering the flow of CSF fluid from the ventricles.

62256-62258
The physician removes a complete cerebrospinal fluid shunt system without replacement in 62256, and with replacement by a similar or other shunt in 62258. The physician incises and retracts the scalp over the placement origin. The dura is incised, and the shunt is located and removed. The dura is sutured closed; the scalp is reapproximated and sutured in layers. Report 62256 if the shunt system is only removed. Report 62258 if the shunt system is replaced during the same operation.

62263-62264
Epidural adhesions are lysed percutaneously by an injection, such as hypertonic saline or an enzyme solution, or by mechanical means. The patient is placed in the sitting or lateral decubitus position for insertion of a needle into a vertebral interspace. The site to be entered is sterilized, local anesthesia is administered, and the needle is inserted. Separately reportable contrast media with fluoroscopy may be injected to confirm proper needle placement and to identify epidural adhesions. The physician injects the adhesiolytic solution or performs mechanical adhesion destruction, such as with a catheter, to lyse epidural adhesions. The needle and/or catheter is removed and the wound is dressed. Report 62263 for multiple adhesiolysis sessions on two or more days and 62264 for multiple adhesiolysis sessions occurring only on one day.

62267
The physician removes contents within the intervertebral disc, nucleus pulposus, or paravertebral tissue with a needle for diagnostic purposes. Separately reportable computed tomography or fluoroscopic guidance verifies placement of the needle. A spinal needle is inserted, the contents of the targeted location are aspirated, and the needle is removed. The wound is dressed. If this procedure is performed under fluoroscopic guidance, injection of the contrast is an inclusive component and is not reported separately.

62268
The physician removes the contents of a cyst or syrinx with a needle. An x-ray verifies placement of the needle (separately reportable). A spinal needle is inserted once the cyst or syrinx is located. The contents of the cyst are aspirated and the needle is removed. The wound is dressed.

62269
This procedure is performed to determine the nature and extent of a suspected lesion. The patient is placed in a spinal tap position. The affected vertebrae are located and local anesthesia is administered. A biopsy needle is inserted. In some cases, blood is drawn through the needle for testing. Separately reportable imaging confirms placement, and samples are drawn from the lesion for inspection. When the procedure is completed, the needle is removed and the wound is dressed.

62270
The patient is placed in a spinal tap position. The biopsy needle is inserted. Fluid is drawn through the needle for separately reportable testing. When the procedure is completed, the needle is removed and the wound is dressed.

62272
This procedure is performed to lessen cerebrospinal fluid pressure. The patient is placed in a spinal tap position. The L3 and L4 vertebrae are located and local anesthesia is administered. The lumbar puncture needle is inserted. In some cases, spinal fluid is drawn through the needle as in a lumbar puncture test. In other cases, a catheter is inserted and the fluid empties into a reservoir. Pressure reading is performed with a manometer. When the procedure is completed, the needle is removed and the wound is dressed. In many cases, the patient lies prone to prevent fluid leakage.

62273
This procedure is performed following a spinal puncture to prevent spinal fluid leakage. The patient remains in a spinal tap position. The patient's blood is injected outside the dura to clot and plug the wound, preventing spinal fluid leakage. The wound is dressed and monitored.

62280-62282
This procedure is performed to destroy nerve tissue or adhesions. The patient is placed in a spinal tap position. The site is sterilized, and the needle is inserted under fluoroscopic guidance. The needle is placed at the proper level and the neurolytic substance is administered. Once the injection/infusion is completed, the needle is removed and the wound dressed. Report 62280 if the substance is administered to the subarachnoid level. Report 62281 if the needle is inserted in the epidural region of a cervical or thoracic level. Report 62282 if the needle is inserted in the epidural region of a lumbar or sacral (caudal) level.

62284
The physician injects dye into the epidural or intrathecal space for myelography and/or computed tomography (CT scan), reported separately. The patient is placed in a spinal tap position. The site is sterilized and the needle is inserted. The needle is placed to the proper level and the dye is administered. The needle is removed and the wound dressed.

62287
This decompression procedure corrects a bulge in an intervertebral disc. It is commonly referred to as percutaneous discectomy and may be accomplished by several techniques including nonautomated (manual), automated, or laser. For all techniques, the patient is

placed in a spinal tap position on the left side. In a separately reportable procedure, a C-arm x-ray verifies placement of the needle in the disc. Once the disc is located, local anesthesia is injected and a small stab wound is made. A spinal needle is inserted with additional monitoring of placement and injection of anesthesia. Using a manual technique, the physician inserts one or two needles into the disc without puncturing the dura. The patient is placed on pure oxygen, and the nucleus pulposus is suctioned out until the desired decompression is accomplished. The needle(s) are removed, and the wound is dressed. The automated technique makes use of a probe that can simultaneously dissect the disc and suck it into the probe. Laser discectomy accomplishes the decompression by vaporizing the protruding disc.

62290
This procedure is performed to gauge the amount of damage suffered by an intervertebral disc. The patient is placed on an image intensification table in a left lateral decubitus position with hips and knees are flexed. The injection site is determined and marked on the sterilized surface, and local anesthesia is injected. A small stab wound is made in the tissue overlying the vertebrae. The physician directs a needle at a 45 degree angle to the center line toward the spine. In a separately reported procedure, the needle is monitored radiographically. A small needle is inserted through original needle once the needle reaches the lamina. The physician pushes this needle to the disc and injects 1 ml to 2 ml of contrast medium. In separately reported procedures, radiographs are made and the procedure may be performed again on another level. The wound is dressed.

62291
This procedure is performed to gauge the amount of damage suffered by an intervertebral disc. The patient is placed on an image intensification table in a supine position with the head extended. The proper injection site is determined and marked on the sterilized surface, and local anesthesia is injected. A small stab wound is made in the tissue overlying the vertebrae. The physician directs a needle at a 35 degree angle to the sagittal plane toward the spine. In a separately reported procedure, the needle is monitored radiographically. A small needle is inserted through original needle once the needle reaches the lamina. The physician pushes this needle to the disc and injects 1 ml to 2 ml of contrast medium. In separately reported procedures, radiographs are made and the procedure may be performed again on another level. The wound is dressed.

62292
This procedure introduces a corrective chemical enzyme into a herniated disc. The patient is placed in a spinal tap position on the left side. In a separately reported procedure, an x-ray verifies location of the disc. Once the disc is located, local anesthesia is injected and a small stab wound is made. A spinal needle is inserted with additional monitoring of placement and injection of anesthesia. Without puncturing the dura, the physician inserts the needle into the disc. This procedure can be performed with one or two needles. A separately reportable saline acceptance test is performed to verify correct placement. Discography is performed with an opaque substance to verify location of the herniated disc. A reparative enzyme is injected. The needles are removed and the wound is dressed.

62294
This procedure is performed to locate and occlude an arteriovenous malformation (AVM) in the spinal cord. A separately reportable x-ray is used to position the patient and identify the artery to be injected. The physician directs a needle at the feeder arteries of the AVM and causes an occlusion by embolization. The needle is monitored radiographically. Once the occlusion of the AVM is completed and needle is removed, the wound is dressed.

62310
The patient is placed in a sitting or lateral decubitus position for the physician to insert a needle into the vertebral interspace of the thoracic or cervical region. The site to be entered is sterilized, local anesthesia is administered and the needle is inserted. Contrast media with fluoroscopy may be injected to confirm proper needle placement. The physician injects a solution to provide a therapeutic or diagnostic outcome. The solution is injected into the epidural or subarachnoid space. With the procedure complete the needle is removed and the wound is dressed.

62311
The patient is placed in a sitting or lateral decubitus position for the physician to insert a needle into the vertebral interspace of the lumbar or sacral region. The site to be entered is sterilized, local anesthesia is administered and the needle is inserted. Contrast media may be injected to confirm proper needle placement under fluoroscopy. The physician injects a solution to provide a therapeutic or diagnostic outcome. The solution is injected into the epidural or subarachnoid space. With the procedure complete the needle is removed and the wound is dressed.

62318
The patient is placed in the sitting or lateral decubitus position for the physician to insert a catheter into the vertebral interspace of the cervical or thoracic region for continuous or intermittent infusion of material. The site to be entered is sterilized, local anesthesia is administered and the infusion catheter is inserted. Contrast media with fluoroscopy may be injected to confirm proper catheter placement. The physician provides continuous infusion or intermittent bolus injection of solution to provide a therapeutic or

diagnostic outcome. The solution is injected into the epidural or subarachnoid space. With the procedure complete the needle is removed and the wound is dressed.

62319
The patient is placed in the sitting or lateral decubitus position for the physician to insert a catheter into the vertebral interspace of the lumbar or sacral region for continuous or intermittent infusion of material. The site to be entered is sterilized, local anesthesia is administered and the infusion catheter is inserted. Contrast media may be injected to confirm proper catheter placement. The physician provides continuous infusion or intermittent bolus injection of solution to provide a therapeutic or diagnostic outcome. The solution is injected into the epidural or subarachnoid space. With the procedure complete the needle is removed and the wound is dressed.

62350-62355
This procedure is performed to allow direct instillation of medication via the cerebrospinal fluid. If the catheter is to be implanted the patient is placed in a spinal tap position and the fascia, paravertebral muscles, and ligaments are incised and separated. The physician inserts the catheter tip into the epidural space (the space outside the dura) or through the dura placing the catheter tip into the subarachnoid space. Tissue around the catheter may be sutured to hold the catheter in place. The catheter end is tunneled to the site where an implantable reservoir or implantable infusion pump has been previously placed or where a pump or reservoir is to be placed (subcutaneously) in a separately reportable procedure. This procedure also includes the revision of an intrathecal or epidural catheter, which may include replacing or repositioning a catheter. In 62351, the physician performs a laminectomy, making an incision and removing the lamina of the vertebra to access the dura through which the catheter is inserted. In 62355, the catheter is removed.

62360-62365
This procedure is performed to allow medication (e.g., cancer chemotherapy, pain management drugs) to be placed into a subcutaneous reservoir for intrathecal or epidural drug infusion. The physician makes a midline incision overlying the placement site. The reservoir is placed in the subcutaneous tissues and attached to a previously placed catheter. Layered sutures are used to close the incision. Report 62360 for subcutaneous reservoir implantation or replacement, 62361 for non-programmable pump implantation or replacement, 62362 for a programmable pump implantation or replacement, and 62365 for removal of the reservoir or pump.

62367-62368
The physician, physician's assistant, nurse, or physical therapist places electrodes over the site of the programmable pump and reviews performance of the generator on a computer. Report 62637 if the pump is not reprogrammed; report 62368 if it is reprogrammed.

63001-63011
The physician makes a posterior midline incision overlying the vertebrae. The paravertebral muscles are retracted. The physician removes the appropriate spinous process and interspinous ligament with a rongeur. The physician excises the lamina and the attached ligamentum flavum may be removed. Decompression is continued by removal of bony overgrowths or tissue until the dural sac and nerve roots are free from any compression. Free-fat grafts or Gelfoam may be placed over the exposed nerve roots. If the ligamentum flavum has not been removed or if only portions of it were removed, it may be closed over the fat graft. A drain is placed superficial to the fat graft; the fascia, subcutaneous tissue, and skin are closed in layers. Report 63003 if vertebrae are thoracic; report 63005 if vertebrae are lumbar, except in the case of spondylolisthesis; and report 63011 if vertebrae are sacral.

63012
The physician performs the laminectomy to correct spondylolisthesis, the slipping of the lumbar vertebrae forward where they join the sacral vertebrae. The physician makes a midline incision overlying the lumbar vertebrae to facilitate repair of the spondylolisthesis. The fascia are incised and the paravertebral muscles are retracted. The physician resects the spinous processes of all three vertebrae and the middle part of the loose fifth lumbar neural arch. The ligamentum flavum is freed or excised at various levels of vertebrae. The fifth lumbar nerve root is retracted. Decompression is carried out to include the facets as well as other bony or soft tissue structures that may be applying pressure to the spinal cord, nerve roots, or cauda equina. The procedure is repeated on the opposite side. The incision is closed with layered sutures.

63015-63017
The patient is face down and the physician makes a posterior midline incision overlying the vertebrae. The paravertebral muscles are retracted. A rongeur removes the appropriate spinous processes and interspinous ligaments. The physician excises the affected laminae and the attached ligamentum flavum may be removed. Decompression is continued by removal of bony overgrowths or tissue until the dural sac and nerve roots are free from compression. Free-fat grafts or Gelfoam may be placed over the exposed nerve roots. If the ligamentum flavum has not been removed or if only portions of it were removed it may be closed over the fat graft. A drain is placed superficial to the fat graft; the fascia, subcutaneous tissue, and skin are closed in layers. Report 63015 if vertebrae are cervical;

report 63016 if the laminae are thoracic; report 63017 if lumbar.

63020-63035
In one method, a midline incision is made through a posterior (back) approach overlying the vertebrae. The incision is carried down through the tissue to the paravertebral muscles, which are retracted. The ligamentum flavum, which attaches the lamina from one vertebra to the lamina of another may be partially or completely removed. Part of the lamina is removed on one side to allow access to the spinal cord. If a disc has ruptured, fragments or the part of the disc compressing the nerves are removed. A partial removal of a facet (facetectomy) or removal of bone around the foramen (foraminotomy) may also be performed to relieve pressure on the nerve. When decompression is complete, a free-fat graft may be placed to protect the nerve root. If the ligamentum flavum was not removed, it is placed over the fat graft. Paravertebral muscles are repositioned and the tissue is closed in layers. Report 63020 if the discs are cervical. Report 63030 if lumbar. Note that approaches may be open as described above or endoscopically assisted. In an endoscopically assisted approach, a small guide probe is inserted under fluoroscopic guidance. Using magnified video as well as fluoroscopic guidance, the endoscope is manipulated through the foramen and into the spinal canal. Once the guide probe has been advanced to the surgical site, a slightly larger tube is manipulated over the guide probe. Surgical instruments are advanced through the hollow center of the tube. Herniated disc fragments are removed, and the disc is reconfigured to eliminate pressure on the nerve root(s). The endoscope is withdrawn. The incision is sutured or simply dressed with an adhesive bandage. Report 63035 for additional interspaces, cervical or lumbar.

63040-63044
Through a posterior approach, a midline incision is made overlying the vertebrae. The incision is carried through the tissue to the paravertebral muscles, which are retracted. If the ligamentum flavum (which attaches lamina from one vertebrae to the lamina of another) is still present, it may be partially or completely removed. The lamina may be removed on the opposite side or more of the lamina may be removed from the previous site to allow access to the spinal cord. If ruptured intervertebral disc fragments or part of the disc continues to compress the nerve, they are removed. A partial removal of a facet or removal of bone around the foramen may also be performed if they are causing pressure on the nerve. When decompression is complete, a previously placed free-fat graft may be replaced over the nerve root. If the ligamentum flavum was not removed in the first surgery or in the exploration it is placed over the fat graft. Paravertebral muscles are repositioned and the tissue is closed in layers. Report 63040 if performed on a single cervical interspace; report 63042 if performed on a single lumbar interspace; report 63043 for each additional cervical interspace; report 63044 for each additional lumbar interspace.

63045-63048
The patient is face down. Magnification may be used during the procedure. The physician makes a midline incision overlying the affected vertebrae. Fascia is incised. Paravertebral muscles are retracted. The physician removes the spinous processes with rongeurs. If the stenosis is central, the physician removes the lamina out to the articular facets using a burr. If the compression is in the lateral recess, only half of the lamina is removed. A Penfield elevator peels the ligamentum flavum away from the dura. Nerve root canals are freed by additional resection of the facet, and compression is relieved by removal of any bony or tissue overgrowth around the foramen. Removal of the lamina, facets, and bony tissue or overgrowths may be performed bilaterally when indicated. The rongeur, retractor, and microscope are removed. A free-fat graft may be placed over the nerve root(s) for protection. If the ligamentum flavum was spared, it is placed over the free-fat graft. Paravertebral muscles are repositioned and the deeper tissues and skin are closed with layered sutures. Report 63046 if the procedure affects a thoracic vertebra; report 63047 if the procedure affects a lumbar vertebra; and 63048 for procedures affecting each additional vertebra.

63050-63051
Cervical laminoplasty with decompression of the spinal cord is performed to treat cases of myelopathy related to severe spinal stenosis that will not respond to conservative treatment. Intraoperative neurologic monitoring is used during the procedure. The head is immobilized. The surgeon makes an incision in the back of the neck over the target spinal area and dissects down through the soft tissues to access the spine. The spinous processes are exposed. A subperiosteal dissection is done to mobilize the muscles, taking care to preserve the ligaments. Foraminotomies may be done when foraminal stenosis or lateral disc herniation is present. A high-speed drill burr creates a gutter in the lamina on both an opening and closing side so the spinous processes may be opened like a door on a hinge. The cancellous bone and outer cortex are removed. An osteotomy is performed by lifting up on the opening side with a hook while displacing the processes to the opposite side. The laminae are opened like a door on a hinge to the side that displays the worst compression or signs of myeloradiculopathy. This opens the restriction and decompresses the previously pinched spinal cord. The hinge is held in place by small pieces of bone struts. Report 63051 when reconstruction of the posterior bony elements is performed. Fibular or tricortical iliac crest allografts are used. The prepared graft is notched and fitted into place in the "open door" position of the lamina. Titanium miniplates (or other fixation device) may be

Nervous

used to stabilize each level. The tissues are sutured back into place and a suction drain is placed.

63055-63057
This procedure is performed to relieve pressure on the spinal cord, equina, and nerve roots caused by a herniated disc. The physician approaches the herniated disc through the pedicle on the side of the disc's bulge. Additional exposure is made by removing the lamina and facet joint. The physician removes the disc fragments and closes the wound in layers. Report 63055 if the segment is thoracic. Report 63056 if the segment is lumbar. A far lateral herniated lumbar intervertebral disc may require an alternative approach through the facet joint (transfacet) or foramina (transforaminal). Report 63057 for each additional segment, thoracic or lumbar.

63064-63066
The physician makes an incision two inches to three inches lateral to the spine through fascia, muscles, and a section of a rib. The physician enters anterior to the transverse process and the pedicle using a Kerrington rongeur or burr. Exposure may be increased by removal of the transverse process. The spinal cord or nerve root is decompressed by removing the herniated disc. The wound is filled with saline and radiographs (separately reported) are made to assure no air is leading into the lungs. The muscles fall over a drain and the tissue is closed with layered sutures. Report 63064 if a single segment is repaired. Report 63066 for additional segments.

63075-63076
The physician performs a cervical discectomy to remove all or part of a herniated intervertebral disc. The patient is placed supine with a head halter on the jawbone (mandible). The physician makes a transverse incision overlying the intervertebral disc. The sternocleidomastoid muscle and the carotid artery are retracted. The physician excises the anterior anulus of the disc and uses pituitary forceps to remove as much disc material as possible. A spreader and microscope are used to enhance the evacuation. A drill is used to remove the transverse bar above and below. Graft material is obtained from the ilium and fashioned into a T-shape. The graft is placed into the disc space and traction is released. The muscles fall back into place and the incision is closed with layered sutures. Report 63075 if the discectomy is in a single interspace. Report 63076 for each additional cervical interspace.

63077-63078
The physician makes an incision along the rib corresponding to the second thoracic vertebra above the involved intervertebral disc, except in cases involving the top five discs. The rib is removed for access and eventually used in the graft, which is obtained through an extrapleural or transpleural approach. Vessels are tied away from the spine. The disc is removed to the posterior ligament using a microscope and nibbling instruments. The end plates are stripped of their cartilage. The physician makes a slot in one vertebral body and a hole in the other to accept the graft, which is made of several sections of rib. The physician ties the grafts together with heavy suture material and closes the tissue with layered sutures. A chest drain may be inserted. Report 63077 for a single thoracic interspace. Report 63078 for each additional thoracic interspace.

63081-63082
The patient is placed supine with traction-producing tongs. The physician makes a right transverse incision at mid-position of the planned surgical procedure, and longitudinally between the thyroid gland and the carotid sheath. The discs above and below the vertebrae are excised using a curette. Cartilaginous endplates are removed using a high-speed burr. The crushed part of the vertebral body is partially or completely removed, and the section is prepared for the graft. The anterior surfaces of the vertebrae above and below the fusion are debrided. The physician prepares a separately reportable, tricortical iliac graft and inserts it into the site, tapping it into place with a Moe impacter. Traction is released. Bone chips are packed in and, if needed, a metal plate is screwed to the spine over the graft. The muscles fall back into place and the wound is closed with layered sutures. Report 63081 if one segment is involved; report 63082 for each additional cervical segment.

63085-63088
This procedure corrects compression on the spinal cord resulting from an anterior fracture of the vertebra. The patient is placed in a swimmer's position. The physician makes an incision through the fascia, muscles, and moves aside any organs. The discs above and below the vertebrae are excised using a curette. Cartilaginous endplates are removed using a high-speed burr. The crushed part of the vertebral body is partially or completely removed, and the section is prepared for the graft. The anterior surfaces of adjacent vertebrae are debrided. The physician prepares a tricortical iliac graft and inserts it into the site, tapping it into place with a Moe impacter. Traction is released. Bone chips are packed in and, if needed, a metal plate is screwed to the spine over the graft. The muscles fall back into place and the wound is closed with layered sutures. Report 63085 if one thoracic segment is involved; report 63086 if more than one is involved; report 63087 if caudal equina, lower thoracic, or lumbar, single segment is involved; report 63088 for each additional segment.

63090-63091
The physician makes a transperitoneal or retroperitoneal approach through skin, fascia, muscles, and ligaments. The physician incises the anterior longitudinal ligament above and below the vertebral body. Using magnification, the physician removes the

disc to the posterior longitudinal ligament using nipper instruments. The physician may use dowel or tricortical iliac grafts and prepares the site as appropriate using an osteotome. Usually three grafts can be inserted. They are tapped into place and surrounded with bone chips. The physician sutures the anterior longitudinal ligament. The peritoneum and abdomen are closed in the usual manner. Report 63090 for a single segment. Report 63091 for each additional segment.

63101-63103

A vertebral corpectomy with correction of spinal cord or nerve root compression is done for fractures or tumors of the vertebrae. The body of the vertebra may be partially or completely resected. The lateral extracavitary approach is done with a midline incision made in the area of the fractured segment and inferiorly curved out to the lateral plane. The paraspinous muscles are exposed, lifted off the spinous processes, and divided and lifted off the ribs. The targeted vertebral body is identified. The corresponding ribs are dissected from the intercostal muscles and the pleura and resected in one piece from the posterior curve to the costovertebral connection. The appropriate transverse process and part of the facet and pedicle are removed with a drill from the lateral aspect. The dura and the vertebral body are now exposed from the dorsolateral view. Further posterior and lateral access to the vertebral body is gained by gently retracting the nerve root and surrounding structures. The central portion of the vertebral body is removed with a drill, exposing more area, and any bone fragments or tumor masses are removed away from the spinal cord or nerve roots. Curettes and rongeurs are used to remove disc material. At this point, any necessary fusion, intervertebral reconstruction, or grafting is undertaken and reported separately. Cartilage is scraped, bone is decorticated, and an arthrodesis or reconstruction is accomplished by tapping bone graft material into the vertebral endplates. A drain is placed and closure is done in layers. Report 63101 for vertebral corpectomy by lateral extracavitary approach on a single thoracic segment, 63102 for a single lumbar segment, and 63103 for each additional thoracic or lumbar segment.

63170

This procedure is performed to alleviate peripheral pain caused by avulsion of parts of the spinal cord's white matter. The patient is face down. The physician makes a midline incision. The fascia are incised. The paravertebral muscles and ligaments are retracted. Following a laminectomy, the physician incises the dura to gain access to the spinal cord. Without disturbing the central grey matter, the physician incises the outer white matter of the spinal cord, using a laser or a radio frequency electrode to thermally coagulate the white matter. Fascia, muscles, and ligaments are allowed to fall back into place. The physician closes the incision with layered sutures.

63172-63173

This procedure is performed to alleviate the effects of a spinal cyst or syrinx. The patient is face down. The physician makes a midline incision overlying the affected vertebrae. The fascia are incised. The paravertebral muscles are retracted. Laminectomy is performed. The spinal needle is placed in the intramedullary cyst or syrinx, and the cyst or syrinx is drained to the subarachnoid space. Fascia, muscles, and ligaments are allowed to fall back into place. The incision is closed with layered sutures. Report 63172 if the drainage is to the subarachnoid space. Report 63173 if the drainage is to the peritoneal or pleural space.

63180-63182

The patient is face down. The physician makes a midline incision overlying the affected vertebrae. The fascia are incised. The paravertebral muscles are retracted. The physician incises the dura and locates the dentate ligaments. With the aid of magnification, the physician sections the affected ligaments. The dura is closed with sutures or a graft to assure competency. The incision is closed with layered sutures. Report 63180 if the one or two vertebra is affected; report 63182 if more than two vertebrae are affected.

63185-63190

A rhizotomy is performed on the anterior nerve roots to stop involuntary spasmodic movements associated with paraplegia or torticollis. It is also performed on the posterior nerve roots to eliminate pain in a restricted area. The patient is face down. The physician makes a midline incision overlying the affected vertebrae. The fascia are incised. The paravertebral muscles are retracted. Laminectomy is performed. The physician identifies the anterior or posterior nerve roots to be divided. Each is lifted with a nerve hook and severed. Fascia, muscles, and ligaments are allowed to fall back into place. The incision is closed with layered sutures. Report 63185 if the procedure includes one or two segments; report 63190 if the procedure includes two or more segments.

63191

This procedure is performed to alleviate chronic pain. The patient is face down. The physician makes a midline incision overlying the affected vertebrae. The fascia are incised. The paravertebral muscles are retracted. The physician removes the lamina. The physician identifies and incises the spinal accessory nerve. The lesion is removed and sutures are placed in the perineurium of the nerves. The sutures are approximated and tied. Fascia, muscles, and ligaments are allowed to fall back into place. The incision is closed with layered sutures.

63194-63195
This procedure is performed to alleviate pain. The patient is face down. The physician makes a midline incision overlying the affected vertebrae. The fascia are incised. The paravertebral muscles are retracted. A laminectomy is performed. The physician identifies the anterolateral tracts in the appropriate level on the side opposite the pain. The dentate ligament is divided at the level of the cordotomy. The ligament is drawn posteriorly toward the midline to expose the anterolateral part of the cord. A cordotomy knife is introduced into the spinal cord anterior to the dentate ligament and directed toward the anterior spinal artery. The tissue in front of this artery is divided with the knife. The incision is closed with layered sutures. Report 63194 if the affected vertebrae are cervical; report 63195 if the affected vertebrae are thoracic.

63196-63197
This procedure is performed to alleviate pain. The patient is face down. The physician makes a midline incision overlying the site of the cordotomy. The fascia are incised. The paravertebral muscles are retracted. A laminectomy is performed. The physician identifies the spinothalamic tracts in the appropriate levels. The dentate ligament is divided at the level of the cordotomy. The ligament is drawn posteriorly toward the midline to expose the anterolateral part of the cord. A cordotomy knife is introduced into the spinal cord anterior to the dentate ligament and directed toward the anterior spinal artery. The tissue in front of this artery is divided with the knife. The incision is closed with layered sutures. Report 63196 if the affected vertebrae are cervical; report 63197 if the affected vertebrae are thoracic.

63198-63199
This procedure is performed to stop chronic pain or spasms. The patient is face down. The physician makes a midline incision overlying the affected vertebrae. The fascia are incised. The paravertebral muscles are retracted. The physician identifies the spinothalamic tracts in the appropriate level. The dentate ligament is divided at the level of the cordotomy. The ligament is drawn posteriorly toward the midline to expose the anterolateral part of the cord. A cordotomy knife is introduced into the spinal cord anterior to the dentate ligament and directed toward the anterior spinal artery. The tissue in front of this artery is divided with the knife. Muscles, fascia, and ligaments are allowed to fall back into place. The incision is closed with layered sutures. The procedure is performed on the opposite side of the spinal cord within 14 days. Report 63198 if the cervical vertebrae are affected; report 63199 if the thoracic vertebrae are affected.

63200
This procedure is performed to correct neurological deficits in the lower extremities and sphincter dysfunctions caused by a spinal cord shortened by adhesions to the dura. The patient is face down. The physician makes a midline incision over the lumbar vertebrae. The fascia are incised. The paravertebral muscles are retracted. A laminectomy is performed. The physician may choose from a number of techniques, but generally requires a dural opening. A surgical microscope is used to dissect the adhesions and fibrous bands. The filum is identified and transected. Care is taken to avoid severing the nerves tangled with the adhesions. If no spina bifida or myelomeningocele is present, the dura is closed to make a "sac." Muscles, fascia, and ligaments are closed. The incision is closed with a layered sutures.

63250-63252
This procedure is performed for excision or purposeful occlusion of an arteriovenous malformation (AVM) of the spinal cord. The patient is face down. The physician makes an incision overlying the cervical vertebra in the area of the AVM. The fascia and paraspinal muscles are retracted and a laminectomy is performed to access the spinal cord. Microsurgical techniques are used to excise or occlude the AVM. After muscles, fascia, and ligaments are repaired, the incision is closed with layered sutures. Report 63251 if thoracic; report 63252 if thoracolumbar.

63265-63268
This procedure removes a growth in the spine. The patient is face down. The physician makes a midline incision. Fascia are incised. Paravertebral muscles are retracted. The physician removes the laminae and the spinous processes of the vertebrae to expose the outside of the dura. The extradural intraspinal lesion is excised or evacuated. The incision is closed with layered sutures. Report 63265 if the lesion is in the cervical region; report 63266 if the lesion is in the thoracic region; report 63267 if the lesion is in the lumbar region. Report 63268 if the lesion is in the sacral region.

63270-63273
This procedure removes a growth in the spine. The patient is face down. The physician makes a midline incision. The fascia are incised. The paravertebral muscles are retracted. The physician removes the laminae and the spinous processes of the vertebrae to be exposed. The dura is exposed and incised. The pia-arachnoid is incised as necessary. The lesion is removed. The incision is closed with layered sutures. Report 63270 if the lesion is located in the cervical region; report 63271 if the lesion is in the thoracic region; report 63272 if the lesion is in the lumbar region; report 63273 if the lesion is in the sacral region.

63275-63278
The patient is face down. The physician makes a midline incision. Fascia are incised. Paravertebral muscles are retracted. The physician removes the laminae and the spinous processes of the vertebrae to the dura. A biopsy is taken of the neoplasm and the

neoplasm is removed. Muscles, fascia, and ligaments are repaired. The incision is closed with layered sutures. Report 63275 if the neoplasm is in the cervical area; report 63276 if it is in the thoracic area; report 63277 if it is in the lumbar area; and report 63278 if it is in the sacral area.

63280
This procedure is performed to remove a growth in the spine. The patient is face down. The physician makes a midline incision. Fascia are incised. Paravertebral muscles are retracted. The physician removes the laminae and the spinous processes of the vertebrae to be exposed. The dura is exposed and incised. The neoplasm is identified and a biopsy is taken. The neoplasm is removed. The dura is sutured with silk sutures, and the incision is closed with layered sutures.

63281
The patient is face down. The physician makes a midline incision. Fascia are incised. Paravertebral muscles are retracted. The physician removes the laminae and the spinous processes of the vertebrae to be exposed. The dura is exposed and incised. The neoplasm is identified and a biopsy is taken. The neoplasm is removed. The dura is sutured with silk sutures, and the incision is closed with layered sutures.

63282
This procedure is performed to remove a growth in the spine. The patient is face down. The physician makes a midline incision. Fascia are incised. Paravertebral muscles are retracted. The physician removes the laminae and the spinous processes of the vertebrae to be exposed. The dura is exposed and incised. The neoplasm is identified and a biopsy is taken. The neoplasm is removed. The dura is sutured with silk sutures, and the incision is closed with layered sutures.

63283
This procedure is performed to remove a growth in the spine. The patient is face down. The physician makes a midline incision. Fascia are incised. Paravertebral muscles are retracted. The physician removes the laminae and the spinous processes of the vertebrae to be exposed. The dura is exposed and incised. The neoplasm is identified and a biopsy is taken. The neoplasm is removed. The dura is sutured with silk sutures, and the incision is closed with layered sutures.

63285
This procedure is performed to remove a growth in the spine. The patient is face down. The physician makes a midline incision. Fascia are incised. Paravertebral muscles are retracted. The physician removes the laminae and the spinous processes of the vertebrae to be exposed. The dura is exposed and incised. The neoplasm is identified and a biopsy is taken. The neoplasm is removed. The dura is sutured with silk sutures, and the incision is closed with layered sutures.

63286
This procedure is performed to remove a growth in the spine. The patient is face down. The physician makes a midline incision. Fascia are incised. Paravertebral muscles are retracted. The physician removes the laminae and the spinous processes of the vertebrae to be exposed. The dura is exposed and incised. The neoplasm is identified and a biopsy is taken. The neoplasm is removed. The dura is sutured with silk sutures, and the incision is closed with layered sutures.

63287
This procedure is performed to remove a growth in the spine. The patient is face down. The physician makes a midline incision. Fascia are incised. Paravertebral muscles are retracted. The physician removes the laminae and the spinous processes of the vertebrae to be exposed. The dura is exposed and incised. The neoplasm is identified and a biopsy is taken. The neoplasm is removed. The dura is sutured with silk sutures, and the incision is closed with layered sutures.

63290
This procedure is performed to remove a growth in the spine. The patient is face down. The physician makes a midline incision. Fascia are incised. Paravertebral muscles are retracted. The physician removes the laminae and the spinous processes of the vertebrae to be exposed. The dura is exposed and incised. The neoplasm is identified and a biopsy is taken. The neoplasm is removed. The dura is sutured with silk sutures, and the incision is closed with layered sutures.

63295
The physician performs an osteoplastic reconstruction of the dorsal spine elements at the time of a separate intraspinal procedure. Osteoplastic reconstruction is performed to stabilize elements in the spine that have been damaged by benign or malignant lesions or by disease processes. Following the intraspinal procedure, the dura is closed. Dorsal spinal elements including laminae, spinous processes and supporting ligaments are replaced in anatomic position in the spine. Holes are drilled into the lateral aspect of each lamina and the dorsal spine elements are secured in place using sutures, wires, or miniplates.

63300
This procedure is performed to remove an intraspinal lesion in the extradural space of the spinal canal. The patient is placed supine with the head extended by tongs and traction. A right transverse incision or right vertical incision is made in the lateral neck. The muscles and fascia are incised and retracted. Entering between the trachea and the carotid sheath, the physician resects the vertebral body and the intraspinal lesion is excised by the physician. After repair of the muscles, fascia, and ligaments, the wound closed with layered sutures.

63301
This procedure is performed to remove a lesion from a vertebra. The patient is placed in a lateral decubitus position and the physician makes a transthoracic approach overlying the rib corresponding to the affected vertebrae. The physician removes the rib and retracts muscles, fascia, and organs to expose the spine. The tumor mass is completely excised. Following repair of the muscles, fascia, and ligaments, the wound is closed in a routine fashion over suction drains.

63302
This procedure is performed to remove a lesion of the vertebral body, which compresses the spinal cord. The patient is placed in a lateral decubitus position with supports under the buttocks and shoulder, and the muscle, fascia, ribs, and organs are incised or retracted. An incision is made in the diaphragm to purchase access to the spine. The tumor mass is completely excised. After muscles, fascia, and ligaments are repaired, the wound is closed in a routine fashion over suction drains.

63303
This procedure is performed to remove a lesion of the vertebral body, which compresses the spinal cord. The patient is placed in a lateral decubitus position with approach from the left side, and the muscle, fascia, ribs, and organs are incised or retracted. The physician makes a groove in the vertebral bodies above and below the crushed vertebra and removes the discs above and below. Tricortical iliac crest grafts are obtained, prepared, and tapped into the grooves with a Moe impactor. An AO plate is screwed to the vertebra above and below the injured level to maintain fusion. A separately reported radiograph is obtained to assure proper placement, and the wound closed with layered sutures.

63304
This procedure is performed to correct a fracture or growth of the vertebral body, which compresses the spinal cord. The patient is placed supine with the head extended by tongs and traction. A right transverse incision or right vertical incision is made in the lateral neck. The muscles and fascia are incised and retracted. The dura may be incised. Entering between the trachea and the carotid sheath, the physician makes a groove in the vertebral bodies above and below the crushed vertebra and removes the discs above and below. Tricortical iliac crest grafts are obtained, prepared, and tapped into the grooves with a Moe impactor. Traction is removed. An AO plate is screwed to the vertebra above and below the injured level to maintain fusion. A separately reported radiograph is obtained to assure proper placement, and the wound closed with layered sutures.

63305
This procedure is performed to correct a fracture or growth of the vertebral body, which compresses the spinal cord. The patient is placed in a lateral decubitus position and the muscle, fascia, ribs, and organs are incised or retracted. The dura may be incised. The physician makes a groove in the vertebral bodies above and below the crushed vertebra and removes the discs above and below. Tricortical iliac crest grafts are obtained, prepared, and tapped into the grooves with a Moe impactor. An AO plate is screwed to the vertebra above and below the injured level to maintain fusion. A separately reported radiograph is obtained to assure proper placement, and the wound closed with layered sutures.

63306
This procedure is performed to remove a lesion of the vertebral body, which compresses the spinal cord. The patient is placed in a lateral decubitus position with supports under the buttocks and shoulder, and the muscle, fascia, ribs, and organs are incised or retracted. The dura may be incised. An incision is made in the diaphragm to purchase access to the spine. The physician makes a groove in the vertebral bodies above and below the crushed vertebra and removes the discs above and below. Tricortical iliac crest grafts are obtained, prepared, and tapped into the grooves with a Moe impactor. An AO plate is screwed to the vertebra above and below the injured level to maintain fusion. A separately reported radiograph is obtained to assure proper placement, and the wound closed with layered sutures.

63307
This procedure is performed to remove a lesion of the vertebral body, which compresses the spinal cord. The patient is placed in a lateral decubitus position with approach from the left side, and the muscle, fascia, ribs, and organs are incised or retracted. The dura may be incised. The physician makes a groove in the vertebral bodies above and below the crushed vertebra and removes the discs above and below. Tricortical iliac crest grafts are obtained, prepared, and tapped into the grooves with a Moe impactor. An AO plate is screwed to the vertebra above and below the injured level to maintain fusion. A separately reported radiograph is obtained to assure proper placement, and the wound closed with layered sutures.

63308
This procedure is performed to remove a lesion of the vertebral body, which compresses the spinal cord. The patient is placed in a lateral decubitus position with approach from the left side, and the muscle, fascia, ribs, and organs are incised or retracted. The physician makes a groove in the vertebral bodies above and below the crushed vertebra and removes the discs above and below. Tricortical iliac crest grafts are obtained, prepared, and tapped into the grooves with a Moe impactor. An AO plate is screwed to the vertebra above and below the injured level to maintain fusion. A separately reported radiograph is obtained to assure

proper placement, and the wound closed with layered sutures.

63600-63615

Lesions in the spinal cord are produced to alleviate chronic pain in a particular area of the body. A common surgery involves creating a lesion in the spinothalamic tracts for pain relief. In this procedure, a stereotactic guidance system is used to enable a physician to conceptualize a position in three-dimensional space. The stereotactic frame is applied to the head with full neck flexion and fixed to the operating table with the patient in the sitting position. Following previously determined coordinates, needles are placed through the C1-C2 interspace. Electrical stimulation and other methods are applied to create a lesion that will block the pain. The needles and the frame are removed. Wounds are dressed. Report 63610 if the stereotactic method is used for a procedure not followed by another; report 63615 if the stereotactic method is used to biopsy, aspirate, or excise a lesion from the spinal cord.

63620-63621

High-resolution stereotactic imaging identifies a precise, three-dimensional location of the spinal lesion. The physician uses the coordinates obtained from the images to focus linear accelerator, gamma ray, or particle beam energy onto the lesion, thereby destroying or inactivating it. This is a noninvasive procedure that does not require incision into the spine. Report 63620 (no more than once per course of treatment) for stereotactic radiosurgery on a single spinal lesion. Report 63621 for each additional spinal lesion; however, 63621 should not be reported more than two times for the entire course of treatment regardless of the number of lesions treated and may be reported only once per lesion. Codes for spinal stereotactic radiosurgery are reported by the surgeon and include any required computer-assisted planning, dosimetry, targeting, positioning, or blocking. These codes are assigned only when the treated tumors affect spinal neural tissue or lie alongside the dura mater.

63650

This procedure is performed to alleviate pain or control spasms. The patient is face down. A standard epidural puncture is made. A thin-walled needle is placed at the appropriate segment. A flexible wire electrode is threaded through the needle under fluoroscopic control. Intraoperative testing is carried out to assure correct electrode positioning creating maximum paresthesia in the pain region. The needle is removed and a dressing applied. A transmitter (pulse generator or receiver) is inserted in a separately reportable procedure. Stimulation may be applied as soon as four days following the procedure.

63655

This procedure is performed to alleviate pain or control spasms. The patient is face down. The physician makes a midline incision overlying the affected vertebrae. The fascia are incised. The paravertebral muscles are retracted. The lamina is removed to expose the epidural space. The physician places passive electrodes or plates or paddles in the epidural space proximate to the desired spine segment. Paravertebral muscles are reapproximated and the incision is closed with layered sutures. A transmitter (pulse generator or receiver) is inserted in a separately reportable procedure. Stimulation may be applied as soon as four days following the procedures.

63661-63662

The physician removes spinal neurostimulator electrode percutaneous arrays (63661) or spinal neurostimulator plates or paddles that were placed via laminotomy or laminectomy (62662). The patient is face down (prone). The physician makes a midline incision overlying the affected vertebrae. The fascia is incised. The paravertebral muscles are retracted. The physician removes the electrode plates or paddles in the epidural space proximate to the spine segment. Stimulation is applied. These codes include the use of fluoroscopic guidance, when performed.

63663-63664

The physician revises neurostimulator electrode percutaneous arrays or neurostimulator electrode plates or paddles that were placed via laminotomy or laminectomy. Replacement of these devices may also be performed. The patient is face down (prone). The physician makes a midline incision overlying the affected vertebrae. The fascia is incised. The paravertebral muscles are retracted. The physician revises the electrodes or plates or paddles in the epidural space proximate to the spine segment or moves them to a new vertebral segment. Stimulation is applied. These codes include fluoroscopic guidance, when performed. Report 63663 when the original electrodes were placed percutaneously. Report 63664 when the electrodes were originally placed via laminotomy or laminectomy or if a laminectomy is performed to gain access to the epidural space in the event of movement to a new segment.

63685

The physician inserts or replaces a spinal neurostimulator pulse generator or receiver into a subcutaneous pocket. Placing a spinal neurostimulator is often done to treat cases of intractable pain. The physician selects a location site, usually the abdominal area, and incises the skin. Using blunt dissection, the physician creates a pocket for the generator or receiver. The unit is connected to a previously placed electrode, which is separately implanted and normally positioned in a dural/epidural pocket over the spinal cord of the affected vertebral area. After ensuring that the device is functioning, the generator or receiver is sutured into place within its subcutaneous pocket.

63688
This procedure is performed to promote nerve regeneration. The patient is placed in a prone. The physician makes a midline incision overlying the affected vertebrae. The fascia is incised. The paravertebral muscles are retracted. The physician moves or removes the direct electrode needles or inductive electrode pads in or on the epidural space proximate to the damaged spine segment, placing them in the right plane. The generator or receiver is moved or removed over sutured muscles but below the skin. Layered sutures are used to close the incision.

63700-63702
The physician corrects a defect in which the outer coverings of the spinal cord, meninges, and (sometimes) nervous tissue bulge through a bony defect. The patient is face down, and the physician makes a midline incision and retraction through the skin, muscles, and paravertebral ligaments. The dura is incised to avoid herniated neural tissue. The physician places the neural tissue in the spinal canal. In the lumbar region, filum terminale are often identified tethering the cord and divided. The dural defect, subcutaneous tissues, and skin are closed with layered sutures. Report 63700 for meningoceles less than 5 cm diameter; report 63702 for meningoceles greater than 5 cm.

63704-63706
The physician corrects a defect in which the spinal cord, malformed nerve roots, and meninges all protrude through the defect, often directly exposed to the outside of the body. Surgery can be performed in one of many ways, though most require fusion from the thoracic region to the sacrum. The physician places the patient prone and incises the defect to the subarachnoid space. Using a microscope, the edges of the neural placode are trimmed of skin, dural remnants, and fat. The lateral edges of the placode are sutured together to form a tube. The dura is incised and closed. Skin is closed with sutures. Report 63704 if the myelomeningocele is less than 5 cm in diameter; report 63706 if the defect is more than 5 cm in diameter.

63707-63709
This procedure is performed to mend an opening in the dura, preventing a dangerous infection. The patient is face down, and the physician makes a midline incision, retracting the skin, muscles, and paravertebral ligaments. The physician removes and prepares a graft of subcutaneous fat, freeze-dried dura, fascia, or muscle. Suction is used to keep the incision free of cerebrospinal fluid. Single dural stitches are used to achieve closure. A second needle is attached to the free suture ends and the needles are passed through the graft, which is tied down over the outside of the repaired tear to achieve watertight closure. If the dural defect is small and difficult to access, the graft can be placed inside the dura. After verifying that the repair is watertight, the physician proceeds with closure. Report 63709 if a laminectomy is required to correct a dural/ cerebrospinal fluid leak or pseudomeningocele.

63710
At the end of a procedure where the dura has been incised, the physician sometimes prepares a graft of subcutaneous fat, freeze-dried dura, fascia, or muscle. Suction is used to keep the incision free of cerebral spinal fluid. Single dural stitches are used to achieve closure. A second needle is attached to the free suture ends and the needles are passed through the graft, which is tied down outside of the repaired tear to achieve watertight closure. If the dural defect is small and difficult to access, the graft can be placed inside the dura. After verifying that the repair is watertight, the physician proceeds with closure.

63740-63741
This procedure drains excess cerebral spinal fluid that may cause hydrocephalus. The patient is placed in a spinal tap position and the fascia, paravertebral muscles, and ligaments are incised and separated. The physician removes the lamina, inserting the shunt through the dura into the subarachnoid space. The shunt is passed around the flank to the peritoneal, pleural, or other space for drainage. The incisions are closed with layered sutures. Report 63740 if a laminectomy is needed to place the shunt. Report 63741 if the shunt is placed without excising the lamina.

63744
The physician makes an incision at the site of the original incision. Scar tissue, colloidal tissues, and adhesions are removed. The physician may irrigate the shunt with saline or other substances. If it is malfunctioning, the shunt is freed and replaced. A new shunt is placed in the site. Incisions are closed using layered sutures.

63746
The physician makes an incision at the site of the original incision. Scar tissue, colloidal tissues, and adhesions are removed. The shunt is freed and removed. Incisions are closed using layered sutures.

64400-64405
The physician anesthetizes a branch of the trigeminal nerve in 64400, the facial nerve in 64402, or the greater occipital nerve in 64405. The trigeminal nerve supplies sensory and motor fibers to the face, and is usually blocked superficially. The facial nerve supplies motor fibers to the muscles of facial expression. The greater occipital nerve supplies sensory fibers to the scalp. The physician draws a local anesthetic into a syringe and injects it into the branch of the nerve to be anesthetized.

64408
The physician anesthetizes the vagus nerve. The vagus nerve supplies sensory fibers to the pharynx and glottis, and carries parasympathetic fibers to the digestive system and heart. The physician draws a local anesthetic into a syringe and injects it in the branch of the nerve proximal to the area to be anesthetized.

64410
The physician anesthetizes the phrenic nerve to limit motor control of the diaphragm. The physician draws a local anesthetic into a syringe and injects it in the nerve. This anesthesia would be supplied in cases of unending hiccups, or diagnostically to predict the effect of nerve loss.

64412
The physician anesthetizes the spinal accessory nerve to limit sensation in the trapezius and lower neck. The physician draws a local anesthetic into the syringe and injects it into the branch of the nerve proximal to the area to be anesthetized.

64413
The physician anesthetizes the cervical plexus for sympathetically mediated pain and anesthesia to the back of the neck and head. The physician draws a local anesthetic into three syringes and injects near the transverse processes of C2 to C4, avoiding vascular injection.

64415-64416
The physician anesthetizes the brachial plexus with a single injection to provide anesthesia and pain control to the arm in 64415. The physician draws a local anesthetic into the syringe and injects it into the brachial plexus, approached in one of three locations: intrascalene, supraclavicular, or axillary. In 64416, continuous infusion of local anesthetic through a catheter is done to provide a nerve block lasting longer than the block effect achieved through a single injection. An indwelling catheter is placed and positioned so as to provide anesthesia to the brachial plexus. An infusion pump is connected to the catheter to supply a continuous flow of infused anesthetic agent at a set rate. The infusion system may be used for regional surgical anesthesia when general anesthesia is not required and for postoperative pain management. Catheter placement is included in 64416 and is not reported separately.

64417
The physician anesthetizes the axillary nerve to provide anesthesia to the shoulder. The physician draws a local anesthetic into a syringe and injects the nerve blocking agent into the axillary nerve.

64418
The physician anesthetizes the suprascapular nerve to relax the supraspinatus and infraspinatus muscles and differentiate between brachial plexus mediated or C5 or C6 mediated pain. The physician draws a local anesthetic into the syringe and injects it into the suprascapular nerve.

64420-64421
The physician anesthetizes the intercostal nerve to block chest wall pain. In 64420, a single injection is performed. In 64421, multiple nerves are injected to provide pain relief to a larger area (regional block).

64425
The physician anesthetizes the ilioinguinal and iliohypogastric nerves to block the inguinal and lower abdomen for pain control. The physician draws a local anesthetic into the syringe and injects it in a fan-like manner medial to the hip bone toward the umbilicus.

64430-64435
The physician anesthetizes the pudendal nerve for anesthesia of the perineum, rectum, and parts of the bladder and genitals. In 64430, the pudendal nerve is blocked, typically for perineal pain control, for example, during vaginal delivery. Code 64435 is a female-only procedure in which the area around the cervix is injected with a local anesthetic to supply pain control for the first stage of labor.

64445-64446
The physician anesthetizes the sciatic nerve with a single injection to provide anesthesia and pain control for the distal lower extremity in 64445. The physician draws a local anesthetic into the syringe and injects it into the sciatic nerve. In 64446, continuous infusion of local anesthetic through a catheter is done to provide a nerve block lasting longer than a single injection. An indwelling catheter is placed and positioned so as to provide anesthesia to the sciatic nerve. An infusion pump is connected to the catheter to supply a continuous flow of infused anesthetic agent at a set rate. The infusion system may be used for regional surgical anesthesia when general anesthesia is not required and for postoperative pain management.

64447-64448
The physician anesthetizes the femoral nerve with a single injection to provide anesthesia and pain control for the lower extremity in 64447. The physician draws a local anesthetic into the syringe and injects it into the femoral nerve. In 64448, continuous infusion of local anesthetic through a catheter is done to provide a nerve block lasting longer than a single injection. An indwelling catheter is placed and positioned so as to provide anesthesia to the femoral nerve. An infusion pump is connected to the catheter to supply a continuous flow of infused anesthetic agent at a set rate. The infusion system may be used for regional surgical anesthesia when general anesthesia is not required and for postoperative pain management.

64449
The physician performs a nerve block, posterior approach, on the lumbar plexus by infusing an anesthetic agent through a catheter placed for daily

management of pain and administration of anesthesia. The lumbar plexus is formed from the nerve branches in the psoas major muscle: the ilioinguinal, obturator, iliohypogastric, lateral femoral cutaneous, genito-femoral, and the femoral nerves. IV sedatives and analgesics are set up. With the patient in the right lateral decubitus position, the insertion point for the needle is marked. Local anesthetic is also given. The needle is advanced toward the lumbar plexus, avoiding any transverse processes of the lumbar vertebrae until it is in proper position within the compartment of the psoas muscle, and stimulation of the plexus is seen by the contraction of certain muscles. Blood and cerebral spinal fluid is aspirated. After determining that the needle is in the correct position and that the injection will not go intravenously or intrathecally, local anesthesia is injected through the needle, and an infusion catheter is fed through the needle past the tip. Catheter placement is also checked, the catheter is secured in place, and continuous infusion is begun.

64450
The physician anesthetizes a nerve to provide pain control or blockage. The physician draws a local anesthetic into the syringe and injects it into the branch of the nerve to be anesthetized. This code is used to report nerve blocks of other nerves not specifically listed in this section.

64455
The physician injects a local anesthetic agent and/or steroid into a plantar common digital nerve from the dorsal direction. This procedure is often performed to treat Morton's neuroma, a frequently occurring injury of the forefoot that affects the third web space of the toes.

64479-64480
The physician injects anesthetic and/or steroid into the epidural space using a transforaminal approach. This approach is used primarily in the treatment of herniated discs and requires separately reportable fluoroscopic direction. The injection may be performed on a single or multiple cervical or thoracic level. Report 64479 for a single level; report 64480 for each additional level.

64483-64484
The physician injects anesthetic and/or steroid into the epidural space using a transforaminal approach. This approach is used primarily in the treatment of herniated discs and requires separately reportable fluoroscopic direction. The injection may be performed on a single or multiple lumbar or sacral level. Report 64483 for a single level, report 64484 for each additional level.

64490-64492
The physician injects a diagnostic or therapeutic agent into a cervical or thoracic paravertebral facet joint or into the nerves that innervate the joint using fluoroscopic or CT guidance. The paravertebral facet joints, also called zygapophyseal or "Z" joints, consist of the bony surfaces between the vertebrae that articulate with each other. The injection may be performed on a single level or on multiple levels. Report 64490 for a single level, 64491 for a second level, and 64492 for the third and any additional levels.

64493-64495
The physician injects a diagnostic or therapeutic agent into a lumbar or sacral paravertebral facet joint or into the nerves that innervate the joint using fluoroscopic or CT guidance. The paravertebral facet joints, also called zygapophyseal or "Z" joints, consist of the bony surfaces between the vertebrae that articulate with each other. The injection may be performed on a single level or on multiple levels. Report 64493 for a single level, 64494 for a second level, and 64495 for the third and any additional levels.

64505
The physician injects the sphenopalatine ganglion nerve with an anesthetic agent to provide anesthesia to the nasal mucosa. The anesthesia is applied by entering through the nares and injecting cocaine posterior to the middle turbinate.

64508
The physician injects the carotid sinus nerve with an anesthetic agent to block sympathetically mediated pain or cardiovascular responses.

64510
The physician performs a nerve block on the stellate ganglion, (also known as the cervicothoracic ganglion) by injecting an anesthetic agent to block sympathetically mediated pain. The stellate ganglion is located at the C7/T1 level vertebrae; its fibers distribute to the head, neck, heart, and upper limb. This block is used to provide anesthetic relief for pain in the face, neck, and upper extremity. Using separately reportable fluoroscopic imaging, the physician guides the needle into correct placement in the ganglion and injects the nerve block agent.

64517
The physician performs a nerve block on the superior hypogastric plexus by injecting an anesthetic agent through a needle inserted in the L5/S1 interspace. The superior hypogastric plexus, also called the presacral nerve, is located in front of the upper part of the sacrum and is formed by lower lumbar nerves responsible for pain sensation in the pelvic area. This nerve block is done in such cases as severe, intractable menstrual pain and pain due to pelvic area metastases from cancer such as prostatic malignancy. The patient is placed in the prone position and prepped. A 6-inch needle is guided under radiological imaging, such as fluoroscopy (reported separately), into the ventral lateral spine and through the L5/S1 interspace. Needle position is checked by injecting contrast material and

Nervous

aspirating for the return of any blood, urine, or cerebral spinal fluid. With negative aspiration results and imaging verifying that the needle position is in the prevertebral space and not within a blood vessel, a ureter, or spinal nerves, local anesthetic is injected on both sides.

64520
The physician performs a nerve block on lumbar or thoracic paravertebral sympathetic nerves by injecting an anesthetic agent to block sympathetically mediated pain. The lumbar or thoracic block provides anesthetic relief for pain in the torso, pelvis, and lower extremities. Using separately reportable fluoroscopic imaging, the physician guides the needle into correct placement into the paravertebral sympathetic nerve fibers and injects the nerve block agent.

64530
The physician injects the celiac plexus with an anesthetic to block sympathetically mediated or visceral pain. Anesthesia is provided with or without radiologic monitoring.

64550
A transcutaneous neurostimulator is applied to the patient. The provider places electrode pads over the area to be stimulated and connects a transmitter box to the electrodes (e.g., TENS unit). Current is transmitted through the skin to sensory fibers which helps decrease the pain sensation along the nerve distribution.

64553-64565
The physician places an electrode percutaneously (through the skin) through an introducer needle into the tissue to be stimulated. Electrodes placed over sensory nerves decrease pain sensation in the distribution of the nerve. Electrodes placed over motor nerves stimulate paralyzed muscles to prevent atrophy. In 64553, the electrodes are placed over the motor or sensory points of cranial nerves. In 64555, the electrodes are placed over peripheral motor or sensory nerves, excluding sacral nerves. In 64560, the electrodes are placed over the autonomic nerves contributing to sympathetically mediated pain. Report 64561 when stimulators are placed near sacral nerves, which control the behavior of the bladder, sphincter, and pelvic floor muscles. In 64565, the electrodes are placed at the neuromuscular junction to stimulate a specific area of muscle tissue.

64573-64581
The physician makes an incision to place the electrode. The physician uses a scalpel to incise the skin and dissects the to the anatomical location. The incision aides the physician in accurately placing and testing the electrode while visualizing results. After stimulating the area, the incision is closed with layered sutures. Electrodes placed over sensory nerves decrease pain sensation in the distribution of the nerve. Electrodes placed over motor nerves stimulate paralyzed muscles to prevent atrophy. In 64573, the incision is placed in the region of a specific sensory or motor cranial nerve. In 64575, the electrodes are placed over peripheral motor or sensory nerves. In 64577, the electrodes are placed over autonomic nerves contributing to sympathetically mediated pain. In 64580, the electrodes are placed at the neuromuscular junction to stimulate a specific area of muscle tissue. In 64581, the electrodes are placed at the sacral nerve for urinary control.

64585
The physician revises or removes previously placed neurostimulator electrodes. The physician makes an incision overlying the electrodes. If the initial placement has not resulted in optimal pain control or motor stimulation, the electrodes are moved to optimize results. If the neurostimulator device is no longer required, the electrodes are removed. The incision is closed with layered sutures.

64590
The physician inserts or replaces a peripheral or gastric neurostimulator pulse generator or receiver into a subcutaneous pocket. Peripheral neurostimulators are used to transmit electrical impulses to nerves outside of the brain or spinal cord, such as the sacral nerve to help the bladder muscles contract and treat cases of urinary incontinence or retention, or for pain relief. Gastric neurostimulators transmit electrical impulses in the same way, to treat nausea and vomiting in patients with gastroparesis. The physician selects a location site, usually the abdominal area, and incises the skin. Using blunt dissection, the physician creates a pocket for the generator or receiver. The unit is connected to a previously placed electrode, which is separately implanted to stimulate the target nerve. After ensuring that the device is functioning, the generator or receiver is sutured into place within its subcutaneous pocket.

64595
The physician revises or removes a peripheral or gastric neurostimulator pulse generator or receiver with or without replacement. The placement incision is reopened and tissues are dissected to the transmitter pocket. If the procedure is performed because the device is malfunctioning, the unit is checked and repairs made or a new unit is inserted. If the device is no longer required, it is removed. The incision is closed in layered sutures.

64600-64610
The physician destroys a portion of the trigeminal nerve to block pain or motor control to the face or scalp. Destruction is accomplished by injecting the nerve with alcohol or phenol. In 64600, a supraorbital, infraorbital, mental, or inferior alveolar branch of the trigeminal nerve is destroyed. In 64605, the second and third division branches at the foramen ovale are destroyed. Report 64610 if the second and third

division branches at the foramen ovale are destroyed under radiologic monitoring.

64612
The physician administers a neurotoxin to paralyze dysfunctional muscle tissue innervated by the facial nerve. Chemodenervation works by introducing a substance used to block the transfer of chemicals at the presynaptic membrane. Botulinum toxin type A (BTX-A, Botox®) is the substance most commonly used for chemodenervation of muscle tissue innervated by the facial nerve. The physician identifies the nerve(s) or muscle endplate(s) by direct surgical exposure or through the insertion of an electromyographic needle into the muscle. A small amount of BTX-A is injected into the muscle belly, inducing muscle paralysis within 24 to 48 hours. The duration of the effect can vary, but typically is three to four months. Gradually, blocked nerves form new neuromuscular junctions resulting in the return of muscle function. BTX-A is dose-dependent and reversible secondary to the regeneration process. BTX-A injections are an effective treatment for a variety of disorders of abnormal muscle tone, including muscle overactivity or spasticity.

64613
The physician administers a neurotoxin to paralyze dysfunctional muscle tissue of the neck. Chemodenervation works by introducing a substance used to block the transfer of chemicals at the presynaptic membrane. Botulinum toxin type A (BTX-A, Botox®), phenol (sometimes combined with botulinum toxin type A), and/or ethyl alcohol may be used. The physician identifies the nerve(s) or muscle endplate(s) by direct surgical exposure or through the insertion of an electromyographic needle into the muscle. A small amount of the selected agent is injected into nerve(s) or muscle endplate(s), inducing muscle paralysis. The duration of the effect is variable, usually one to 12 months when phenol or alcohol is used, and three to four months when BTX-A is used. BTX-A is dose-dependent and reversible secondary to the regeneration process. Gradually, blocked nerves form new neuromuscular junctions resulting in the return of muscle function.

64614
The physician administers a neurotoxin to paralyze dysfunctional muscle tissue in the extremities or trunk. Chemodenervation works by introducing a substance used to block the transfer of chemicals at the presynaptic membrane. Botulinum toxin type A (BTX-A, Botox®), phenol (sometimes combined with botulinum toxin type A), and/or ethyl alcohol may be used. The physician identifies the nerve(s) or muscle endplate(s) by direct surgical exposure or through the insertion of an electromyographic needle into the muscle. A small amount of the selected agent is injected into nerve(s) or muscle endplate(s), inducing muscle paralysis. The duration of the effect is variable, usually one to 12 months when phenol or alcohol is used, and three to four months when BTX-A is used. BTX-A is dose-dependent and reversible secondary to the regeneration process. Gradually, blocked nerves form new neuromuscular junctions resulting in the return of muscle function.

64620-64640
These procedures are performed to treat chronic pain. The affected nerve is destroyed using chemical, thermal, electrical, or radiofrequency techniques, which may be used independently or in combination. These procedures are designed to destroy the specific site(s) in the nerve root that produce(s) the pain while leaving sensation intact. Generally intravenous conscious sedation is used during the initial phase of the procedure so that the patient can assist the physician in identifying the site of pain and the correct placement of the neurolytic agent, and local anesthesia is administered during the destruction phase of the procedure. Using separately reportable fluoroscopic guidance, a needle is inserted into the affected nerve root. An electrode is inserted through the needle and a mild electrical current is passed through the electrode. The current produces a tingling sensation at a site on the nerve. The electrode is manipulated until the tingling sensation is felt at the same site as the pain. Once the physician has determined that the electrode is positioned at the site responsible for the pain, a local anesthetic is administered and a neurolytic agent applied. Chemical destruction involves injection of a neurolytic substance (e.g., alcohol, phenol, glycerol) into the affected nerve root. Thermal techniques use heat. Electrical techniques use an electrical current. Radiofrequency, also referred to as radiofrequency rhizotomy, uses a solar or microwave current. Report 64620 when the site is the intercostal nerve. Report 64622–64623 when one or more lumbar/sacral paravertebral facet joint nerve is treated and 64626–64627 when the treatment is at the cervical/thoracic facet joint level. Report 64630 for the pudendal nerve, 64632 for the plantar common digital nerve, and 64640 for other peripheral nerves or branches.

64650-64653
The physician administers a neurotoxin to the eccrine glands to reduce hyperhydrosis (excessive sweating). The skin area to be injected is identified by applying iodine to the skin followed by a light dusting with cornstarch. The resulting chemical change caused by the patient's perspiration turns the area black. Botulinum toxin type A (BTX-A, Botox®) is injected intradermally into the site with a series of injections, usually 10 to 15 injections per axilla, via a Teflon-coated 23- to 26-gauge electromyogram (EMG) needle with syringe. Since the sweat glands are between the dermis and the dermal fat tissue, the injections must be precise. BTX-A must be injected

deep enough to reach the nerve endings but not so deep as to go into the fat. Report 64650 for eccrine glands of both axillae. Report 64653 for eccrine glands of other body areas.

64680
The physician destroys the celiac plexus by applying a neurolytic agent to the celiac plexus. The celiac plexus is a network of nervous tissue that mediates sympathetic pain from the abdomen. This neurolytic block is often performed for pain relief of unresectable cancer in the upper abdomen. The celiac plexus is destroyed usually by chemodenervation, injecting phenol or alcohol to paralyze the network of nervous tissue. This procedure may be performed with or without radiologic monitoring, but is normally performed under CT guidance.

64681
The physician performs a neurolysis on the superior hypogastric plexus by injecting a chemical, thermal, or electrical agent through a needle inserted in the L5/S1 interspace. The superior hypogastric plexus, also called the presacral nerve, is located in front of the upper part of the sacrum and is formed by lower lumbar nerves responsible for pain sensation in the pelvic area. Nerve destruction is done in such cases as severe, intractable menstrual pain and pain due to pelvic area metastases from cancer such as prostatic malignancy when an anesthetic nerve block does not offer sufficient relief. The patient is placed in the prone position and prepped. A 6-inch needle is guided under radiological imaging, such as fluoroscopy (reported separately), into the ventral lateral spine and through the L5/S1 interspace. Needle position is checked by injecting contrast material and aspirating for the return of any blood, urine, or cerebral spinal fluid. With negative aspiration results and imaging verifying that the needle position is in the prevertebral space and not within a blood vessel, a ureter, or spinal nerves, the neurolytic agent is injected, or delivered, to both sides.

64702-64704
In 64702, the physician releases a compressed nerve in a digit of the hand or foot. The physician makes an incision overlying the nerve. Surrounding tissues are dissected from the nerve freeing it from scar tissue or adhesions. The incision is repaired in layers. One or both of the digital nerves in a single finger or toe are decompressed. In 64704, a nerve in the hand or foot is decompressed.

64708-64714
The physician repairs a compressed major peripheral nerve in the arm or leg. Repair is accomplished by decompressing the nerve from the surrounding tissue. Report 64708 if repair was done on a nerve other than the following: if sciatic nerve, report 64712; if brachial plexus, report 64713; and lumbar plexus, report 64714.

64716
The physician frees an intact cranial nerve from scar tissue (neuroplasty) or moves an intact nerve to a new position (transposition). The physician makes an incision overlying the nerve, dissects it free of the surrounding tissue and, if necessary, moves the nerve to a new position. If the nerve is in bone and must be decompressed, freed, or moved, the overlying bone is first removed using drills and/or osteotomes.

64718
The physician decompresses a stressed ulnar nerve by freeing the nerve and the tissue surrounding the nerve. The physician makes an incision at the medial epicondyle and locates the nerve. Surrounding tissues are dissected from the nerve and the nerve is freed from the underlying bed. The nerve is moved over the epicondyle and stabilized with sutures in the surrounding tissue. The incision is sutured in layers.

64719-64721
The physician decompresses or transposes a portion of the ulnar or median nerve to restore feeling to the hand. The physician makes a horizontal incision in the wrist at the metacarpal joints and locates the nerve. In 64719, the ulnar nerve is located and freed. In 64721, the median nerve is decompressed by freeing the nerve inside the carpal tunnel. Soft tissues are resected and the nerve is freed from the underlying bed. Care is taken to ensure tension is released and the incision is sutured in layers.

64722-64726
The physician decompresses a nerve. In 64722, the nerve is unspecified. In 64726 the nerve is located at the base of the foot and supplies sensory fibers to one of the toes. The physician makes an incision in the area of nerve tension and locates the nerve. Surrounding soft tissues are dissected from the nerve to release pressure on the nerve.

64727
The physician makes an incision over the affected nerve and locates the nerve. The physician resects the nerve sheath parallel to the fibers and releases scar tissue within the nerve.

64732-64736
The physician transects or removes a nerve that supplies motor or sensory innervation to the affected head and neck area to eliminate pain. For supraorbital nerve, report 64732, for infraorbital nerve report 64734, for the mental nerve report 64736.

64738
The physician transects or removes a nerve that supplies sensory innervation to the lower jaw and teeth. The physician makes a small osteotomy into the bone and locates the nerve. The nerve is transected to eliminate pain.

64740-64744
The physician transects or removes a nerve that supplies motor or sensory innervation to the affected head and neck area to eliminate pain. For lingual nerve, report 64740. For facial nerve (complete or any branches) report 64742. For the greater occipital nerve, report 64744. The physician incises the area at the most proximal portion of the nerve innervating the problem area. The nerve is located, and transected and the proximal portion of the nerve is buried in the surrounding tissue or bone to prevent neuroma formation.

64746
The physician transects or removes a portion of the phrenic nerve. The phrenic nerve supplies innervation to the diaphragm. The physician makes a horizontal neck incision and dissects the surrounding tissue and locates the nerve. The nerve is transected and the proximal portion of the nerve is buried in the surrounding tissue to prevent neuroma formation.

64752-64760
The physician transects or removes a portion of the vagus nerve. The vagus nerves supplies parasympathetic fibers to the heart and gastrointestinal tract. In 64752, the physician performs a left thoracotomy and locates the vagus nerve inferior to the cardiac branches. The nerve is transected to decrease gut motility and acid production in the stomach. In 64755, the physician makes a vertical midline epigastric incision and locates specific branches of the vagus nerve responsible for acid production in the stomach. In 64760, the physician makes a vertical midline epigastric incision and locates the vagus nerve. After locating the nerve or nerve branches, the physician transects them. The incision is sutured in layers.

64761
The physician transects or removes a portion of the pudendal nerve. The pudendal nerve supplies sensory innervation to the groin. The physician makes an incision over the ischial spine and dissects the tissues to locate the nerve. The nerve is transected and the proximal portion of the nerve is buried in the surrounding tissue to prevent neuroma formation. This block may be performed for chronic pelvic pain or cancer pain. The incision is sutured in layers.

64763-64766
The physician transects (cuts) or avulses (pulls out) the obturator nerve. The physician makes an incision overlying the adductor muscles. The adductor muscles are separated from each other and the obturator nerve is located. The physician accesses the nerve by an extrapelvic approach in 64763 or by an intrapelvic approach in 64766. The nerve is transected or avulsed and the incision repaired in layers.

64771
The physician cuts or avulses another cranial nerve, such as branch nerves of major nerves not listed in previous codes. The physician makes an incision on the face or neck overlying the extradural portion of the other cranial nerve. The tissues are dissected and the nerve is exposed. The nerve is destroyed. The incision is sutured in layers.

64772
The physician cuts or avulses another spinal nerve, such as branch nerves of major nerves not listed in other codes. The physician incises the skin overlying the nerve from C1 to S4. The tissues are dissected and the nerve is exposed. The nerve is destroyed. The incision is sutured in layers.

64774-64778
The physician excises a neuroma of a peripheral nerve. A neuroma is a tumor formed secondarily by trauma to the nerve. In 64774, the physician incises the skin and locates and excises the neuroma in the subcutaneous tissue. In 64776, the physician incises the skin over the digital nerve and excises the neuroma. Report 64778 for each additional neuroma of a separate digit.

64782-64783
The physician excises a neuroma of a peripheral nerve (except digital nerve) of the hand or foot. A neuroma is a benign tumor formed secondarily by trauma to the nerve. The physician incises the affected area in a hand or foot. After locating the nerve with the symptomatic neuroma, the physician excises the tumor. The incision is sutured in layers. Report 64783 for additional neuromas of the hand or foot.

64784-64786
The physician excises a neuroma of a major peripheral nerve. A neuroma is a benign tumor formed secondarily by trauma to the nerve. In 64784, the physician incises the area over the affected major peripheral nerve except sciatic. After locating the nerve with the symptomatic neuroma, the physician excises the tumor. The incision is sutured in layers. In 64786, the physician incises the skin at the back of the upper leg or buttocks near the symptomatic neuroma and locates the tumor on the sciatic nerve. After locating the nerve with the symptomatic neuroma, the physician excises the tumor. The incision is sutured in layers.

64787
The physician implants a nerve into a bone or muscle to prevent neuroma formation after excision of a neuroma. In bony implantation, the physician drills a small hole in the bone to implant the nerve. The surrounding tissue is brought together around the nerve to secure the nerve to the bone. In muscle implantation the nerve is sutured into muscle bed. The surrounding tissue is brought together and sutured to secure the nerve in the muscle.

64788-64792
The physician excises a neurofibroma or a neurolemmoma. A neurofibroma is a tumor of peripheral nerves caused by abnormal proliferation of Schwann cells. A neurolemmoma is a tumor of a peripheral nerve sheath. To remove the tumor, the physician incises the skin over the tumor and dissects the surrounding tissue. The tumor is freed and excised from the nerve, without damaging the nerve when possible. The incision is sutured in layers. In 64788, the tumor is located on a cutaneous nerve. In 64790, the tumor lies on a major peripheral nerve. In 64792, an extensive excision is required due to size or malignancy.

64795
The physician biopsies a nerve. The physician makes an incision overlying the suspect nerve. The tissues are dissected to locate the nerve, and a biopsy specimen is obtained. The incision is sutured in layers.

64802-64804
The physician performs a cervical sympathectomy or cervical thoracic sympathectomy. The cervical sympathetic chain supplies sympathetic innervation to the head, neck, and upper extremities. The thoracic chain supplies sympathetic innervation to the chest and its contents. In 64802, the physician makes a midlateral incision of the neck and dissects the tissues to locate the sympathetic chain. In 64804, the physician makes a thoracotomy and dissects the tissues to locate the sympathetic chain along the vertebral bodies. The ganglia (nerve cell bodies which lay outside the spinal cord) are identified and resected. The incision is sutured in layers.

64809
The physician performs a sympathectomy on the thoracolumbar sympathetic nerves. The physician makes a lateral incision through the thoracic area to reach the sympathetic ganglia, which lie on the lateral border of the vertebral column. The physician determines at which level to remove the ganglia, and dissects to the vertebral bodies. The sympathetic plexus is located and resected. The wound is sutured in layers.

64818
The physician performs a sympathectomy on the lumbar sympathetic nerves. The physician makes a lateral incision through the lumbar area to reach the sympathetic ganglia, which lie on the lateral border of the vertebral column. The physician determines at which level to remove the ganglia, and dissects to the vertebral bodies. The sympathetic plexus is located and resected. The wound is sutured in layers.

64820-64823
In 64820, the physician performs a digital sympathectomy using a microscope for visualization. The physician makes an incision along the digital artery in the medial and lateral aspects of the digit. The artery is identified and the adventitia is stripped from the blood vessel. Peripherally, the sympathetic nerves follow the arteries and lie in the adventitia layer. The incision is closed in layers. Report 64821 when the procedure is performed on the radial artery. Report 64822 when the procedure is performed on the ulnar artery. Report 64823 when the procedure is performed on the superficial palmar arch.

64831-64832
The physician repairs a digital (finger or toe) nerve. The physician locates the damaged nerve in a previously opened incision or wound of a finger or toe. The nerve is sutured to restore sensory or motor function. Report 64831 for a single nerve, report 64832 for each additional nerve repaired.

64834-64840
The physician repairs a sensory or motor nerve in the hand or foot. The physician locates the damaged nerve in a previously opened incision or wound of the hand or foot. The nerve is sutured to restore sensory function. In 64834, a common sensory nerve is repaired. In 64835, the median motor thenar nerve is repaired. This nerve supplies motor innervation to the thenar eminence (proximal thumb). In 64836, the ulnar motor nerve is repaired. This nerve supplies motor innervation to the extensor muscles of the forearm and hand. Report 64837 for repair of additional nerves in the hand or foot. In 64840, the tibial nerve is repaired. The tibial nerve supplies sensory innervation to the sole of the foot. Closure or reconstruction is separately reported.

64856-64859
The physician repairs a major peripheral nerve in the arm or leg, except for the sciatic nerve. The physician locates the damaged nerve in a previously opened incision or wound of the arm or leg. The nerve is sutured to restore sensory and/or motor innervation. The nerve may be moved (transposed) to decrease tension on the nerve. 64856 covers all peripheral nerves of the arm or leg except the sciatic nerve. Report 64857 if no transposition is necessary for repair. Report 64858 for repair of the sciatic nerve. When repairing more than one nerve, report 64859 for each addition nerve. Closure or reconstruction is separately reported.

64861-64862
The physician repairs the brachial plexus nerve or the lumbar plexus nerve. The brachial plexus supplies sensory and motor innervation to the arm. The lumbar plexus supplies sensory and motor innervation to the lower back, buttocks, and legs. The physician locates the damaged nerve in a previously opened incision or wound. In 64861, the nerve damage is in the neck or axilla. In 64862, the nerve damage is in the pelvis. The nerve is sutured to restore sensory and/or motor innervation. Closure or reconstruction is separately reported.

64864-64865
The physician repairs a nerve of the face or exterior head. The physician locates the damaged nerve in a previously opened incision or wound. In 64864, the damaged nerve is located on the face or the external cranium. In 64865, the damaged nerve is located in the temple area and grafting may be required. If a nerve is grafted, the sural nerve is often the donor nerve. Graft harvest is separately reported. The nerve is sutured to restore sensory and/or motor innervation. Closure or reconstruction is separately reported.

64866-64870
The physician creates an anastomosis (connection of two nerves that are not normally connected) to restore motor innervation to the face. In 64866, the facial nerve is anastomosed with the spinal accessory nerve. The physician makes a horizontal incision in the posterior lateral neck and isolates the spinal accessory nerve. The nerve is isolated and brought forward and sutured to the facial nerve. In 64868, the physician makes a horizontal lateral neck incision and isolates the hypoglossal nerve. The nerve is brought forward and sutured to the facial nerve. In 64870, the physician makes a horizontal anterior neck incision and isolates the phrenic nerve. The nerve is rotated toward the facial nerve and sutured into place.

64872-64876
The physician repairs a nerve where repair was delayed because the initial wound was contaminated. The wound is explored to locate the distal portion of the nerve. In 64872, the proximal and distal nerves are sutured together to restore innervation. In 64874, the nerve was shortened during damage. To reanastomose the nerve, the distal and proximal portions of the nerve are freed from surrounding tissues, approximated, and sutured to restore innervation. Report 64876 if excessive trauma caused loss of a significant section of a major nerve. For this procedure, a portion of the parallel bone is resected in order to approximate the distal and proximal ends of the nerve.

64885-64886
The physician obtains and places a nerve graft to restore innervation to the head or neck. In 64885, the graft is less than 4 cm long, in 64886, the graft is greater than 4 cm. A typical graft harvest is obtained from the sural nerve. To harvest the graft, the physician makes a lateral incision of the lateral malleolus of the ankle. The nerve is identified and freed. The physician cuts the nerve to obtain the length needed for the graft, elongating the incision as necessary. The proximal and distal sural nerve endings are anastomosed. The physician makes an incision over the damaged nerve and dissects the tissues to locate the nerve. The damaged area of the nerve is resected and removed. Innervation is restored by suturing the graft is sutured to the proximal and distal ends of the damaged nerve.

64890-64891
The physician obtains and places a nerve graft to restore innervation to the hand or foot. In 64890, the graft is up to 4 cm long; in 64891, the graft is greater than 4 cm. A typical graft harvest is obtained from the sural nerve. To harvest the graft, the physician makes a lateral incision of the lateral malleolus of the ankle. The nerve is identified and freed. The physician cuts the nerve to obtain the length needed for the graft, elongating the incision as necessary. The proximal and distal sural nerve endings are anastomosed. The physician makes an incision over the damaged nerve and dissects the tissues to locate the nerve. The damaged area of the nerve is resected and removed. Innervation is restored by suturing the graft to the proximal and distal ends of the damaged nerve.

64892-64893
The physician obtains and places a nerve graft to restore innervation to the arm or leg. In 64892, the graft is up to 4 cm long; in 64893, the graft is greater than 4 cm. A typical graft harvest is obtained from the sural nerve. To harvest the graft, the physician makes a lateral incision of the lateral malleolus of the ankle. The nerve is identified and freed. The physician cuts the nerve to obtain the length needed for the graft, elongating the incision as necessary. The proximal and distal sural nerve endings are anastomosed. The physician makes an incision over the damaged nerve and dissects the tissues to locate the nerve. The damaged area of the nerve is resected and removed. Innervation is restored by suturing the graft to the proximal and distal ends of the damaged nerve.

64895-64896
The physician obtains and places a nerve graft to restore innervation where a cable nerve of the hand or foot is damaged. In 64895, the graft is up to 4 cm long, and in 64896, the graft is greater than 4 cm. A typical graft harvest is obtained by taking multiple sections of the sural nerve. To harvest the graft, the physician makes an incision near the lateral malleolus of the ankle. The nerve is identified and freed. The physician cuts the nerve to obtain the length needed for the graft, elongating the incision as necessary. The proximal and distal sural nerve endings are anastomosed. The physician makes an incision over the damaged nerve and dissects the tissues to locate the nerve. The damaged area of the nerve is resected and removed. Innervation is restored by suturing graft strands to multiple proximal and distal ends of the damaged nerve cable.

64897-64898
The physician obtains and places a nerve graft to restore innervation where a cable nerve of the arm or leg is damaged (e.g., sciatic nerve or lumbar plexus nerve). In 64897, the graft is less than 4 cm long, and in 64898, the graft is greater than 4 cm. A typical graft harvest is obtained by taking multiple sections of the

sural nerve. To harvest the graft, the physician makes an incision near the lateral malleolus of the ankle. The nerve is identified and freed. The physician cuts the nerve to obtain the length needed for the graft, elongating the incision as necessary. The proximal and distal sural nerve endings are anastomosed. The physician makes an incision over the damaged nerve and dissects the tissues to locate the nerve. The damaged area of the nerve is resected and removed. Innervation is restored by suturing graft strands to multiple proximal and distal ends of the damaged nerve cable.

64901-64902

The physician grafts additional nerves. This code is used in addition to initial nerve graft codes, and includes graft harvest. Report 64901 for each additional single strand graft, report 64902 for each additional multiple strand graft.

64905-64907

The physician transfers a nerve pedicle from an intact nerve to a damaged nerve. A pedicle is an intact nerve used as a donor for regeneration of axons in the damaged nerve. In 64905, the first stage is completed. The physician makes an incision over the donor nerve site and locates the nerve. The nerve is freed from surrounding tissues and cut. The proximal portion of the donor nerve is transferred to the distal portion of the recipient nerve. The incision is sutured in layers. In 64907, the second stage is completed. The physician reopens the surgical incision and locates the donor and recipient nerves. The donor nerve is resected from the recipient nerve and primarily reanastomosed to its distal end. The distal end of the recipient nerve is reanastomosed to its proximal end. The nerves may be freed from surrounding tissues if necessary to complete anastomosis. The incision is sutured in layers.

64910

The physician repairs a nerve and uses a graft to restore innervation. The physician makes an incision over the damaged nerve and dissects tissues to locate the nerve. The damaged area of the nerve is resected and removed. Innervation is restored by building a bridge to each end of the resected nerve and suturing the proximal and distal ends of the bridge into place around each severed nerve end. This technique is usually limited to nerve gaps of 3 cm or less. The bridge is usually 1 cm longer than the defect so that it covers the distal and proximal ends of the resected nerve. The bridge is composed of a bioabsorbable, corrugated synthetic conduit of polyglycolic acid. Once the bridge is sutured into place, the artificial nerve conduit is infused with a solution of heparin and saline to prevent clot formation. The operative wound is repaired in layers. Over time, the nerve conduit is restored and the tube is resorbed by surrounding tissue.

64911

The physician repairs a nerve and uses a vein graft to restore innervation. The physician obtains the venous graft by making an incision over the donor site and locating the vein. The vein is freed from surrounding tissues and excised, and vessels are tied or cauterized. The incision is sutured in layers. The physician makes an incision over the damaged nerve and dissects tissues to locate the nerve. The damaged area of the nerve is resected and removed. Innervation is restored by building a bridge of vein to each end of the resected nerve and suturing the proximal and distal ends of the bridge into place around each severed nerve end. This technique is usually limited to nerve gaps of 3 cm or less. The bridge is usually 1 cm longer than the defect so that it covers the distal and proximal ends of the resected nerve. Once the bridge is sutured into place, it is infused with a solution of heparin and saline to prevent clot formation. The operative wound is repaired in layers. Over time, the nerve conduit is restored.

Eye and Ocular Adnexa

65091-65093

The physician removes the contents of the eyeball: the vitreous, retina, choroid, lens, iris, and ciliary muscles. Retained is the tough, white outer shell (the sclera). After an ocular speculum has been inserted, the physician dissects the conjunctiva free from the sclera. An elliptical incision is made in the sclera surrounding the cornea, and the contents of the anterior chamber are removed. The physician uses a spoon to remove the contents of the posterior chamber, and scrapes the inside of the sclera with gauze on a curette. Only the scleral shell remains. The conjunctiva may be removed. A temporary (e.g., for 65091) or permanent (e.g., for 65093) implant is inserted into the scleral shell at this time. The sclera is attached to the implant, usually with sutures.

65101-65105

The physician severs the eyeball from the extraorbital muscles and optic nerve and removes it. After an ocular speculum has been inserted, the physician dissects the conjunctiva free at the corneal-scleral juncture (the limbus). The physician cuts each extraocular muscle at its juncture to the eyeball and severs the optic nerve. The eyeball, and sometimes the conjunctiva, is removed but the extraocular muscles remain attached at the back of the eye socket. A spherical implant is placed in the eye socket. This implant, if unattached to the extraocular muscles, may be temporary (e.g., 65101) or permanent (e.g., 65103). The extraocular muscles may be attached to the permanent implant to allow normal movement of the prosthesis (e.g., 65105).

65110-65112
The physician sutures the eyelids closed. An elliptical incision is cut through the skin, subcutaneous tissue, muscle and periosteum to the bone beginning at the upper nasal orbital rim and is carried below the brow to the lateral canthus. The incision is extended from the upper nasal quadrant along the nasal and inferior orbit rim to the lateral canthus, terminating in a wide canthotomy. The periosteum is freed around the orbital rim with a periosteum elevator, beginning in the upper temporal quadrant. The trochlea is detached with a sharp dissection. In the upper temporal quadrant, the lacrimal gland is removed. The lacrimal sac is separated from its attachments and removed. The medial and lateral canthal ligaments are cut with a blunt dissection. A blunt dissection is also used to separate the periorbital to the apex, and the firm attachment of the periosteum is cut from the bone with scissors. The orbital contents are removed. Pieces of orbital bone may be excised (e.g., for 65112). The orbit is packed with dry gauze and pressure is applied to control bleeding.

65114
The physician splits the upper and lower eyelids at the gray line throughout their length, leaving the cilia and the skin anteriorly, and the tarsus, the orbicularis muscle, the conjunctiva, the palpebral muscle and the fascial planes posteriorly. The margins of the posterior halves of the lids are sutured together. The lateral bony wall and the temporal fossa are exposed by lateral canthotomy and dissection of the skin, continuous with both lids. The orbital septum is incised. The trochlea is detached with a sharp dissection. The lacrimal gland and lacrimal sac are removed. The medial and lateral canthal ligaments are cut with a blunt dissection. A blunt dissection is also used to separate the periorbital to the apex. The firm attachment of the periosteum is cut from the bone with scissors. The orbital contents are removed. An incision is made in the fascia at the origin of the temporalis muscle. Fascia and muscle are reflected from the temporal fossa. Adherent fascia is excised from the upper margin of the zygomatic process. The muscle is dissected beneath the process. The temporalis muscle and its fascia are taken through the opening into the orbit. After the muscle and the fascia are spread to fill the orbit, they are sutured to the periosteum.

65125
The physician modifies an ocular implant that has been created elsewhere. The modifications may include the addition of screws or other prosthetic appendages to alter the shape of the prosthesis so that it better fits the patient's eye. The physician may drill holes to accommodate the screws.

65130-65140
The physician inserts a permanent ocular prosthesis into a patient's orbit. In each case, an ocular speculum is placed in the eye, any conjunctiva is retracted, and any temporary prosthesis is removed. In a patient whose eye has been eviscerated, the implant is attached to the remaining sclera (e.g., 65130). In a patient following enucleation, the implant is otherwise secured (e.g., 65135). In some cases, eye muscles are attached to corresponding niches in the prosthesis to provide for more natural movement of the artificial eye following enucleation (e.g., 65140).

65150-65155
The physician returns an ocular prosthesis to the patient's eye socket. After an ocular speculum is inserted, the physician places the ocular prosthesis back into an eye from which it had been previously removed. The prosthesis is attached to the sclera in an eviscerated eye, or otherwise secured in an enucleated eye (e.g., 65150). In 65155, foreign material may be required to better secure the prosthesis and/or the prosthesis may be reattached to extraocular muscles. In either procedure, conjunctival tissue may be grafted over the prosthesis once it is secured.

65175
The physician removes the ocular implant from the eye socket. After placing an ocular speculum, the physician cuts and retracts any conjunctival tissue or Tenon's capsule overlying the prosthesis. Any connection between the implant and extraocular muscle or sclera is severed and the ocular implant is removed.

65205-65210
The physician picks the foreign body or mineral deposit from the conjunctiva with the side of the beveled edge of a needle (e.g., 65205). A small incision may be required to remove an embedded foreign body (e.g., 65210). In this case, the physician may cut a V-shaped incision to access the defect through a flap, or a straight incision may be made. The incision may penetrate the conjunctiva, but it does not penetrate the sclera. Generally, a slit lamp is used when removing any embedded foreign body. After the removal, the physician may apply a broad spectrum antibiotic and a moderate pressure patch over the closed lid for 24-48 hours.

65220-65222
The physician may remove a superficial foreign body or mineral deposit from the cornea with the side of the beveled edge of a needle (e.g., 65220). An incision may be required to remove an embedded foreign body (e.g., 65222). If so, the physician may cut a V-shaped incision to access the defect through a flap, or a straight incision may be made. The incision does not penetrate the cornea. Generally, a slit lamp is used with any embedded foreign body. After the removal, the physician may apply a broad spectrum antibiotic and a moderate pressure patch over the closed lid for 24-48 hours.

65235
The physician removes a foreign body, intraocular, from the anterior chamber of the eye or lens. The physician makes a small incision in the connective tissue between the cornea and the sclera (the limbus) and retrieves the foreign body through the opening with intraocular forceps or another small instrument. Generally, foreign bodies that pierce the lens are self-sealing and removal is not attempted. The incision is sutured. The physician applies an antibiotic ointment. Sometimes a pressure patch is placed on the eye for 24-48 hours.

65260
Diagnostic tests locate the foreign body before surgery is attempted. The physician will use an electromagnetic or magnetic probe to retrieve a metallic foreign body from the area behind the lens (the posterior segment). In the anterior route, the physician first dilates the patient's pupil. In a series of moves aligning the magnet to the metallic foreign body, the physician draws the foreign body to the front of the eye and around the lens into the anterior chamber. The physician makes an incision in the connective tissue between the cornea and the sclera (the limbus) and retrieves the foreign body. In the posterior route, the physician makes a small incision in the conjunctiva over the site of the foreign body. A magnet is applied and the foreign body removed. The incision from either is repaired, and an injection may be required to reestablish proper fluid levels in the anterior and/or posterior chamber of the eye. A broad spectrum antibiotic or a pressure patch may be applied. Among the tools common to this procedure are Gruning's, Haab's, or Hirschberg's magnets.

65265
Diagnostic tests locate the foreign body before surgery is attempted. The physician will use intraocular forceps to retrieve the nonmetallic foreign body from the area behind the lens (the posterior segment). The physician makes an incision through the conjunctiva overlying the site of the foreign body. The foreign body is retrieved with intraocular forceps. Nonmetallic foreign bodies in the vitreous or retina may be removed through a pars plana approach. Either incision is repaired with a layered closure, and an injection may be required to reestablish proper fluid levels in the anterior or posterior chambers of eye. A broad spectrum antibiotic or a pressure patch may be applied.

65270-65273
An ocular speculum may be placed in the patient's eye. The physician irrigates the laceration and sutures the conjunctival wound (e.g., 65270). In mobilization and rearrangement (e.g., 65272), an extensive conjunctival laceration requires the creation of a flap or graft sutured over the wound, and the eyes are patched to limit their movement while the injury heals. A graft may be obtained from conjunctival tissue of the upper eyelid or from a sliding flap formed following a circumcorneal incision. Extensive repair or repair of the eye of a child may require hospitalization to further limit eye movement (e.g., 65273).

65275-65285
The physician removes any foreign body from the cornea with a hollow needle or forceps and the wound is irrigated. The nonperforating tear in the cornea (e.g., 65275) is repaired with sutures. In 65280 and 65285, the perforating tear in the cornea and any tear in the sclera may be sutured. The cornea may be splinted using a soft contact lens bandage. An air or saline injection may be required to reestablish proper ocular pressure in the anterior chamber. If the laceration involves the uveal tissue (the vascular layer beneath the sclera), injured tissue may be cut out or repositioned before the uvea is sutured (e.g., 65285), and the sclera and conjunctiva may each require separate closure. In any of the three procedures, topical antibiotic or a pressure patch may be applied.

65286
Tissue glue, also called medical adhesive or cyanoacrylate tissue adhesive, acts as a suture in laceration repairs of the cornea and/or sclera. If the cornea is perforated, the physician may seal the perforation with tissue adhesive after debriding the outermost layer of cornea (the epithelium) to enhance adhesion. The patient may be fitted with a soft contact lens to be worn during the healing process. Antibiotic ointment is applied. A pressure patch may be used.

65290
The physician repairs a deep laceration to the orbital complex. This laceration extends through the extraocular muscles that aid the eye in directional movement. The laceration extends through tendinous attachment of the muscles to the bony orbit and may include the deep connective tissue envelope encasing the eyeball. Each anatomic structure is identified and reapproximated with sutures. The wound is closed in layers.

65400-65410
The physician removes the corneal lesion (e.g., 65400) using a blade and forceps or scleral scissors. The edges of the lesion are undermined following a superficial incision in the cornea. Sutures are not required. Antibiotic ointment and possibly a 24-hour pressure patch is applied. The lesion is superficial; the cornea is not perforated by the excision. Sometimes, only a portion of the lesion is removed for diagnostic purposes (e.g., 65410).

65420-65426
A pterygium is a fleshy, wedge of the bulbar conjunctiva covering a portion of the medial cornea. The physician excises the pterygium with a blade and forceps or scleral scissors. The edges of the pterygium

are undermined following a superficial incision in the clear cornea. Forceps retract the freed pterygium and it is excised as gentle pressure pulls it away from the corneal tissue and across the limbus and sclera. The physician applies sutures to the sclera and conjunctiva as needed. Often, no graft or tissue rearrangement is needed (e.g., 65420). However, the physician may transpose the pterygium with normal conjunctival tissue to move it out of the field of vision in what is sometimes called McReynold's operation, or may make a circumcorneal incision and use a conjunctival flap to repair the pterygium site (e.g., 65426). A topical antibiotic and a pressure patch may be applied in either procedure.

65430

In the office, the physician scrapes the surface of the corneal defect with a spatula. The scrapings will be cultured to determine a diagnosis.

65435-65436

In cases of corneal erosion or degeneration, the physician may attempt to stimulate new growth of the cornea's outermost layer by essentially "wounding" it. The physician removes the outermost layer of the cornea (epithelium) by scraping or cutting it with a spatula or curette (e.g., 65435). Chemical cauterization may be applied. An alternative to cutting or scraping is the application by swab of EDTA (ethylenediaminetetraacetic acid), an acid that destroys the corneal epithelium. (e.g., 65436). In either case, an antibiotic ointment or pressure patch may be applied once the procedure is complete.

65450

The physician applies a freezing probe, a laser beam, or a heat probe directly to a corneal defect to destroy it. Freezing is the most common method used for this procedure. The physician applies antibiotic ointment and sometimes, a pressure patch.

65600

In cases of corneal erosion or degeneration, the physician may attempt to stimulate new growth of the cornea's outermost layer by essentially "wounding" it. The physician places a speculum in the eye and uses a fine needle to create hundreds of tiny pricks in the surface of the outermost layer of the cornea (the epithelium). A topical antibiotic and patch may be applied. This procedure is sometimes called a corneal "tattoo."

65710

The physician performs an anterior lamellar corneal transplant (keratoplasty). "Lamellar" means thin layer and refers to the outermost layers of the cornea. The physician measures the patient's cornea to select the size of trephine that will be used to excise corneal tissue. The physician punches a circular hole in the outermost layers of the cornea of a donor eye, using the trephine. The physician removes the round layer of corneal tissue, threads it with sutures, and sets it aside. The trephine is used to repeat this process in the cornea of the patient, removing the defective corneal tissue. The donor cornea is of similar diameter and thickness as the removed tissue. The donor cornea is positioned with the preplaced sutures; additional sutures secure it to the cornea. The physician may use a saline or air injection into the anterior chamber during the procedure. When the procedure is completed, the speculum is removed. Antibiotic ointment and a pressure patch may be applied. This code includes preparation of the donor material.

65730-65755

Penetrating refers to the thickness of the donor cornea, indicating its full thickness. The physician measures the patient's cornea to select the size of trephine that will be used to excise corneal tissue. The physician punches a circular hole in the cornea of the donor eye using the trephine. The physician removes the disc of corneal tissue, threads it with preplaced sutures, and sets it aside. In aphakic patients, vitreous and/or aqueous may be withdrawn from the eye before the cornea is removed. A metal ring may be sutured to the sclera of an aphakic patient to stabilize the operative field. The defective cornea of the patient is removed with the trephine. The donor cornea is positioned with sutures; additional sutures secure it to the cornea. The physician may use a saline or air injection to restore proper intraocular pressure. Report 65730 for those patients who still have a natural lens or are phakic—with lens. Report 65750 for those patients who have had cataract extraction surgery or are aphakic—without lens. Code 65755 is for patients who have an artificial lens or are pseudophakic—without natural lens.

65756-65757

Endothelial cells line the cornea's inner surface and constantly produce fluid to keep the cornea clear. There are a limited number of these cells, and they do not increase in number (proliferate). If they become diseased or damaged or if there are not enough cells, the cornea may become cloudy. The physician performs an endothelial corneal transplant (keratoplasty) using a fresh or preserved graft in 65756. Preparation of the donor material is reported separately with code 65757. Deep lamellar endothelial keratoplasty (DLEK) is a form of keratoplasty in which the physician removes a disc of endothelial cell tissue from the patient's cornea and replaces it with a disc of endothelial cell tissue of the same size that has been removed from the donor cornea. The disc may be created with a mechanical device or with a laser microkeratome. The physician approaches from the front side of the patient's cornea and creates a lamellar incision just anterior to Descement's membrane (the basement membrane found between the cornea's stromal and endothelial layers). After making this circular incision, the physician then makes side incisions from the level of the lamellar incision back through the bottom of the cornea, creating a disc consisting only of Descement's and endothelium. An identical disc from donor tissue is then created using the same process. The physician rolls the recipient's disc up and removes it through a tiny incision at the edge of the cornea. The donor disc is also rolled and is placed inside the eye through the same incision. The physician unfolds the disc and fits it into the site created by removal of the recipient's disc. Antibiotic ointment and a pressure patch may be applied.

65760
The cornea is one of several structures in the eye that contributes to refraction. Altering the shape of the cornea therefore alters visual acuity. The physician retracts the patient's eyelids with an ocular speculum. Using a planing device, the physician removes a partial-thickness central portion of the patient's cornea, freezes it and reshapes it on an electronic lathe. The revised cornea is positioned and secured with sutures. This is done to correct optical error. The physician may use a saline or air injection into the anterior chamber during the procedure. The speculum is removed. Antibiotic ointment and a pressure patch may be applied.

65765
The cornea is one of several structures in the eye that contributes to refraction. Altering the shape of the cornea therefore alters visual acuity. The physician retracts the patient's eyelids with an ocular speculum and measures the patient's cornea to select the size of trephine that will be used to excise corneal tissue. The physician punches a circular hole in the cornea of the donor eye using the trephine. The physician removes the disk of corneal tissue and sets it aside. An incision is made at the juncture of the cornea and the sclera (the limbus) and the patient's cornea is separated into two layers. The physician inserts the donor cornea between layers of the recipient's cornea. The resulting change in the corneal curvature alters the refractive properties of the cornea to correct the preexisting refractive error. The speculum is removed. Antibiotic ointment and a pressure patch may be applied.

65767
The cornea is one of several structures in the eye that contributes to refraction. Altering the shape of the cornea therefore alters visual acuity. The physician retracts the patient's eyelids with an ocular speculum and measures the patient's cornea to select the size of trephine that will be used to excise corneal tissue. The physician punches a circular hole in the cornea of the donor eye using the trephine. The physician removes the disk of corneal tissue and sets it aside. On a lathe, the physician shapes a lens made of two layers from a donor cornea, the stroma and Bowman's membrane. The physician sutures this donor cornea to the surface of the patient's cornea. The resulting change in the corneal curvature alters the refractive properties of the cornea to correct the preexisting refractive error. The speculum is removed. Antibiotic ointment and a pressure patch may be applied.

65770
The physician creates a new anterior chamber with a plastic optical implant that replaces a severely damaged cornea that cannot be repaired. Sometimes the corneal prosthesis is sutured to the sclera; other times, extensive damage to the eye requires the implant be sutured to the closed and incised eyelid.

65771
The cornea is one of several structures in the eye that contributes to refraction. Altering the shape of the cornea therefore alters visual acuity. The physician retracts the patient's eyelids with an ocular speculum and measures the patient's cornea. The physician places multiple, nonpenetrating cuts in the cornea in a bicycle spoke pattern to reduce myopia, or a variety of peripheral cornea tangential cuts for astigmatic correction. There are two basic surgical approaches: Russian, in which the incisions are made from the edges to the center of the cornea; and American, in which the incisions are made from the center to the periphery. The number and length of the incisions depend upon the patient's age and degree of myopia. The resulting change in the corneal curvature alters the refractive properties of the cornea to correct the preexisting refractive error. The speculum is removed. Antibiotic ointment and a pressure patch may be applied.

65772-65775
The cornea is one of several structures in the eye that contributes to refraction. Altering the shape of the cornea therefore alters visual acuity. When a previous surgery (e.g., for insertion of an intraocular lens or a corneal procedure) results in astigmatism, the physician at a later date returns the patient to the operating room to correct the problem. The physician retracts the patient's eyelids with an ocular speculum. In corneal relaxing (65772), an "X" cut is made on the cornea to repair the error. Slices along the "X" are removed and its edges are sutured. In the corneal wedge resection (65775), a wedge is cut from the cornea and the edges sutured. The resulting change in the corneal curvature alters the refractive properties of the cornea to correct the preexisting refractive error. The speculum is removed. Antibiotic ointment and a pressure patch may be applied.

65780
Amniotic membrane transplantation for ocular surface reconstruction is done for corneal defects such as burns, scarring, thinning, ulcer, and perforation. Human amniotic membrane that is obtained from cesarean deliveries is used. The tissue is prepared and cryopreserved. Use of this tissue induces rapid re-epithelialization of corneal epithelium to a good

surface for successful reconstruction. The eye is properly draped before incision. A lid speculum is used to keep the lids and lashes from the operative field. Using an operative microscope, any necrotic corneal epithelium is debrided. The preserved amniotic membrane tissue is trimmed to fit the defect area. The membrane must be placed a certain side up and down. The surface of basement membrane cells faces upward and the stromal cell surface is down. The membrane is sutured into place and the sutures are trimmed and made flush or even below the surface of the corneal epithelium. This process is repeated until all of the thinning areas or defect areas are repaired in line with the surrounding normal-thickness of corneal tissue. The instruments are removed and a topical antibiotic/ steroid treated bandage contact lens is placed.

65781

Limbal/conjunctival stem cell allografting for ocular surface reconstruction is done for corneal defects or damage resulting in a total loss of stem cell function. Corneal tissue relies on stem cells located in the limbal epithelium (the zone where corneal and conjunctival epithelia meet) to regenerate. The graft is taken from a cadaver or another living donor, not the patient. When harvesting grafts from a cadaver, they are taken from the corneoscleral rim, which is too deep and cannot be done when harvesting from a living donor. The central part of the cornea is excised and the remaining rim of cornea and sclera is sectioned into two halves, leaving a tiny rim of sclera around the limbus. The posterior part of each half is removed with a crescent blade and the donor tissue is placed with the epithelial layer upwards into a preparation solution until placement. The recipient eye of the patient is prepped and draped. Any adherent conjunctiva is excised along with any subconjunctival scar tissue. The conjunctiva is resected from the limbus in 360 degrees. The recipient beds are prepared by removing conjunctival tissue to expose the sclera. Abnormal corneal epithelium is dissected so as to leave a smooth surface. The eye is kept moist to await the graft transplantation. The previously removed corneoscleral pieces of limbal grafting tissue are centered over the damaged recipient eye and sutured into place with the corneal donor edges overlying the limbus of the damaged eye. A graft harvested from a living donor (see 68371) will be a conjunctival limbal graft and is placed with the limbal edge of the graft at the recipient limbus. The instruments are removed, the eye is patched, applying antibiotic and steroid cream, and a shield is placed.

65782

Limbal conjunctival autograft or autograft limbal transplantation (ALT) for ocular surface reconstruction is done for corneal defects or damage resulting in a total loss of stem cell function. Corneal tissue relies on stem cells located in the limbal epithelium (the zone where corneal and conjunctival epithelia meet) to regenerate. The graft is taken from the patient's other healthy eye to replace the lost stem cell population in the diseased eye. Both eyes are draped for surgery. The recipient eye is done first. Any adherent conjunctiva is excised along with any subconjunctival scar tissue. The conjunctiva is resected from the limbus in 360 degrees. The recipient beds are prepared by removing conjunctival tissue to expose the sclera. Abnormal corneal epithelium is dissected to leave a smooth surface. The eye is kept moist and attention is turned to the donor eye. The borders of the graft are marked to match the recipient beds. Saline solution is injected to raise the conjunctiva from the Tenon's layer. Incisions are made on the lateral borders of the graft first, undermining is done between, the posterior ridge is incised, and the graft is reflected. Dissection is carried to the conjunctival/limbal junction and anterior dissection is finished. The epitheliectomy removes tissue only at a superficial level and does not include sclera or corneal stroma. The free graft is removed and prepared in an appropriate storage medium. The posterior conjunctiva is advanced and anchored to the episclera. Topical antibiotics and steroids are instilled and the lids closed. The speculum is inserted again into the recipient eye, the graft is sutured into position, and the ends are cut at the knot and flushed with the corneal surface. The instruments are removed and the eyes are patched and protected.

65800-65805

Though constantly flushed and renewed, the overall pressure of aqueous is constant in a healthy eye's anterior chamber. Too little or too much fluid can cause permanent damage. The physician aspirates aqueous from between the iris and the cornea (the anterior chamber) with a needle in what is typically called an "anterior chamber tap." The needle usually enters the anterior chamber through the corneal-scleral juncture (the limbus). In some cases, the removal of the fluid is diagnostic (e.g., 65800). The physician may inject air to normalize eye pressure after fluid has been removed. If ocular pressure is high, a therapeutic removal of aqueous may be performed (e.g., 65805).

65810

The physician aspirates the gel-like vitreous that has pushed forward into the space between the iris and the cornea (the anterior chamber). Using a needle that enters the eye through the corneal-scleral juncture (the limbus), the prolapsed vitreous is removed. A laser might be used to destroy part of the membrane between the lens and the vitreous (the anterior hyaloid membrane). The physician may inject air to normalize eye pressure after fluid has been removed.

65815

Blood in the anterior chamber can coagulate and block the flow of aqueous. It can also cause cornea staining. The physician aspirates blood from between the iris and the cornea (the anterior chamber) with a needle that enters the eye through the corneal-scleral juncture (the limbus). In some cases, the physician may inject saline to flush the blood and make its removal easier. The physician may inject air to normalize eye pressure after fluid has been removed.

65820
To improve drainage of fluids in the eye, the physician enters the anterior chamber through an incision in the scleral-corneal juncture (the limbus) and cuts with a gonioknife. The blade passes across the anterior to the opposite limbus and a sweep is made to open the angle of the ring of meshlike tissue at the iris-scleral junction (the trabecular meshwork) of the opposite portion of the eye. De Vincentiis operation and Barkan's operation are both goniotomy procedures.

65850
To improve drainage of fluids in the eye, the physician inserts a trabeculotome into Schlemm's canal and rotates it into the anterior chamber to open the ring of meshlike tissue (the trabecular meshwork). The name (ab) externo, meaning outside the eye, refers to the surgical approach from outside the eye cutting toward the anterior chamber.

65855
The physician uses an argon laser to selectively burn the ring of meshlike tissue at the iris-scleral junction (the trabecular meshwork) to improve the drainage of fluids in the anterior segment. The physician begins by placing a special contact on the eye to be treated. This lens allows the physician to view the angle structures of the eye and the trabecular network while using the laser. Though the trabecular network runs along the circumference of the iris, the physician burns holes in only a portion of that circumference during a single treatment session. In this way, the physician can measure the effects of each treatment upon the eye's fluid, and suspend treatment once the proper intraocular fluid pressure is reached. No incision is made during this procedure.

65860
Sometimes scar tissue or adhesions bind structures within the eye, interfering with vision or with intraocular pressure. The physician uses a YAG laser to selectively sever vitreal, corneal, or ciliary strands or adhesions binding the iris to adjunct structures and interfering with vision. The physician begins by placing a special contact on the eye to be treated. This lens allows the physician to view the angle structures of the eye and the trabecular network while using the laser. The strands or adhesions are not removed; they simply fall out of the visual field.

65865
Sometimes scar tissue or adhesions bind structures within the eye, interfering with vision or with intraocular pressure. Through an incision in the corneal-scleral juncture (the limbus) the physician enters the anterior segment to sever vitreal, corneal, or ciliary strands or adhesions binding the iris to adjunct structures interfering with vision. The strands or adhesions are not removed; they simply fall out of the visual field.

65870-65875
The physician enters the anterior segment through the limbus to sever strands or adhesions binding the iris to adjunct structures interfering with vision. In the anterior synechiae (e.g., for 65870) the physician severs adhesions of the base of the iris to the cornea. For posterior synechiae (e.g., for 65875), the adhesions between the iris to the capsule of the lens or to the surface of the vitreous body are severed. Once the adhesions have been severed, the intraocular pressure may be restored with an injection of fluid or air. The incision is closed and an antibiotic and pressure patch may be applied.

65880
The physician enters the anterior segment through the limbus to sever strands or adhesions binding the cornea to the gel-like vitreous that has prolapsed into the anterior chamber. Once the adhesions have been severed, the intraocular pressure may be restored with an injection of fluid or air. The incision is closed and an antibiotic and pressure patch may be applied.

65900
Epithelial downgrowth describes the improper healing of surgical or traumatic wound to the cornea. The outer lining of the cornea (the epithelium) fails to close properly over the wound, instead growing around to the inner side of the cornea, sometimes continuing its growth to other structures of the eye. Disturbances in intraocular pressure and vision can result. The physician retracts the patient's eyelids with an ocular speculum. The physician locates and excises the extraneous epithelial tissue from where it has spread into the anterior chamber. The original wound may be trimmed and revised. Injections may be required to restore pressure in the anterior or posterior chambers. The procedure may require sutures or tissue glue, antibiotic ointment or a pressure patch.

65920
The clouding of the lens capsule (cataract) causes visual loss. To correct this problem, a bad lens is replaced with an artificial one. Sometimes complications require the removal of the artificial lens. The physician retracts the patient's eyelids with an ocular speculum. The physician cuts and retracts the conjunctiva and makes an incision at the juncture of the cornea and sclera (the limbus). The physician removes from the anterior segment the previously placed artificial lens (called an intraocular lens or IOL). It is not replaced. The limbus and the conjunctiva are closed with sutures. Antibiotic or a pressure patch may be applied.

65930
A blood clot in the anterior segment can block the flow of aqueous, thereby elevating intraocular pressure. It can also stain the cornea. Either condition can lead to permanent visual loss. The physician retracts the patient's eyelids with an ocular speculum. The physician uses a needle to aspirate a blood clot which has pooled in the anterior section between the iris and the cornea. The needle may enter the anterior segment through the cornea or through the limbus (the juncture of the cornea and sclera). Topical antibiotic or a patch may be applied when the procedure is complete.

66020-66030
Though constantly flushed and renewed, the overall pressure of aqueous is constant in a healthy eye's anterior chamber. Too little or too much fluid can cause permanent damage. The physician administers a needle injection of air or liquid (e.g., 66020) or medication (e.g., 66030) to the anterior of the eye. The needle may enter the anterior segment through the cornea or through the limbus (the juncture of the cornea and sclera).

66130
The sclera, coming from the Greek word for "hard," is the tough, white, outer coat of the eye. To remove a scleral lesion, the physician cuts through the thin, transparent conjunctiva and snips the lesion with scleral scissors. The scleral and conjunctival wounds may not require sutures. The physician applies antibiotic ointment and possibly a 24-hour pressure patch.

66150-66155
To create a new pathway for fluids in the eye, the physician makes an incision in the conjunctiva near the limbus (the corneal-scleral juncture). Using a trephine to remove a circular portion of sclera and iris (e.g., 66150) or by destroying a portion of the sclera and iris by burning it with a hot probe (e.g., 66155), the physician creates a collection area to improve the flow of aqueous. One method of this procedure is called Elliot's operation. The physician closes the incision with sutures and may restore the intraocular pressure with an injection of water or saline. A topical antibiotic or pressure patch may be applied.

66160
To improve the flow of aqueous, the physician makes an incision in the conjunctiva near the limbus (the corneal-scleral juncture). By using a punch or scleral scissors, the physician removes a portion of sclera and iris, creating a collection area for fluids in the anterior chamber. Various methods of sclerectomy include Lindner's, LaGrange, Knapp's, Holth's and Herbert's operations. The physician closes the incision with sutures and may restore the intraocular pressure with an injection of water or saline. A topical antibiotic or pressure patch may be applied.

66165
To improve the flow of fluids in the eye, the physician places an ocular speculum in the patient's eye, and accesses the anterior chamber through an incision through the limbus (the corneal-scleral juncture). The physician creates a permanent drainage route through the anterior chamber by taking a piece of iris tissue clipped with scleral scissors from the edge of the iris and wedging it into an incision in the iris so that it will act as a wick to draw aqueous from one side of the iris to the other. The physician closes the incision with sutures and may restore the intraocular pressure with an injection of water or saline. A topical antibiotic or pressure patch may be applied.

66170-66172
Though constantly flushed and renewed, the overall pressure of aqueous is constant in a healthy eye's anterior chamber. Too little or too much fluid can cause permanent damage. The physician places an ocular speculum in the patient's eye, and accesses the anterior chamber through an incision through the limbus (the corneal-scleral juncture). To promote better drainage of fluid, the physician removes a partial thickness portion of the ring of meshlike tissue at the iris-scleral junction (the trabecular meshwork), and a scleral trap door is left open so that aqueous may flow through the new channel into the space between the conjunctival and the sclera or cornea (bleb). The physician closes the incision with sutures and may restore the intraocular pressure with an injection of water or saline. A topical antibiotic or pressure patch may be applied. This procedure is performed in absence of previous surgery (e.g., for 66170) or as a repeated surgery where adhesions are reduced (e.g., for 66172). The adhesions may also have been caused by trauma.

66180-66185
Though constantly flushed and renewed, the overall pressure of aqueous is constant in a healthy eye's anterior chamber. Too little or too much fluid can cause permanent damage. To enhance drainage, the physician places an ocular speculum in the patient's eye and makes an incision in the conjunctiva and sutures tubing to the sclera. The tubing enters the anterior portion of the eye at the juncture of the sclera and cornea (the limbus). This improves the aqueous flow in the anterior chamber. The tube implant connects to a reservoir plate (a bleb) sutured into place behind the pars plana between the extraocular muscles. The physician stretches conjunctival tissue over the shunt and reservoir and sutures it into place. The physician closes the incision with sutures and may restore the intraocular pressure with an injection of water or saline. A topical antibiotic or pressure patch may be applied. A revision is done and 66185 reported if the first procedure is unsuccessful and must be altered.

66220-66225
A staphyloma is a bulging protrusion of the vascular coating of the eyeball (uvea) into a thin, stretched portion of the sclera. To repair the staphyloma, the physician places an ocular speculum in the patient's eye, and makes an incision in the conjunctiva and sclera over the site of a staphyloma. The physician excises the full-thickness staphyloma. A piece of stretched sclera may also be removed. The physician uses sutures or tissue glue in the layered repair. Antibiotic ointment and a patch may be applied. A graft (e.g., 66225) usually indicates that size of the staphyloma required that donor sclera tissue be grafted across the wound.

66250
The physician reexplores an eye wound that is the site of previous surgery to revise post-operative defects. The physician uses a number of techniques, based on the wound and previous surgery. Surgery may be major or minor.

66500-66505
Though constantly flushed and renewed, the overall pressure of aqueous is constant in a healthy eye's anterior chamber. Too little or too much fluid can cause permanent damage. To enhance the flow of fluids in the anterior chamber, the physician makes an incision in the corneal-scleral juncture (the limbus). The physician slices through the iris in a side-to-side motion in an effort to increase the flow of aqueous hampered by a pupillary block (e.g., 66500). No tissue is removed. In the iris bombe, where the iris balloons forward blocking aqueous outflow channels, the surgeon pierces the iris in two places (e.g., 66505). The physician closes the incision with sutures and may restore intraocular pressure with an injection of water or saline. A topical antibiotic or pressure patch may be applied.

66600-66605
The physician places a contact lens on the patient's eye to direct the laser's beam. The excision of a full-thickness piece of the iris is usually accomplished with an argon laser. The physician uses the "chipping away technique" until the iris is penetrated for the excision. With cyclectomy (e.g., 66605), the burn is deeper, going through the iris into the ciliary body.

66625
After placing an ocular speculum in the patient's eye, the physician makes an incision at the juncture of the cornea and sclera (the limbus). The physician removes a piece of iris, providing a direct passageway for aqueous. This causes the intraocular pressure to fall as aqueous from behind the iris can flow forward and drain from the eye. This procedure is also called basal, buttonhole, or stenopeic iridectomy. The physician may close the incision with sutures and may restore the intraocular pressure with an injection of water or saline. A topical antibiotic or pressure patch may be applied.

66630
Though constantly flushed and renewed, the overall pressure of aqueous is constant in a healthy eye's anterior chamber. Too little or too much fluid can cause permanent damage. To enhance the flow of fluids in the eye, the physician makes an incision at the juncture of the cornea and sclera (the limbus). The physician removes a wedge piece from the iris leaving what is often referred to as a keyhole pupil. This causes the intraocular pressure to fall as aqueous from behind the iris can flow forward and drain from the eye. The physician may close the incision with sutures and may restore the intraocular pressure with an injection of water or saline. A topical antibiotic or pressure patch may be applied.

66635
After placing an ocular speculum in the patient's eye, the physician makes an incision at the juncture of the cornea and sclera (the limbus). The physician trims an inner ring of iris as a means of widening an abnormally small pupil and improving vision. The physician may close the incision with sutures and may restore the intraocular pressure with an injection of water or saline. A topical antibiotic or pressure patch may be applied.

66680-66682
After placing an ocular speculum in the patient's eye, the physician makes an incision at the juncture of the cornea and sclera (the limbus) to approach and repair a trauma-caused tear of the iris from the ciliary body. The wedge shaped tear is affixed to the ciliary body with dissolving sutures, or with stitches that can be removed through an incision prepared for that retrieval. This procedure includes the later removal of the McCannel suture. The physician may close the incision with sutures and may restore the intraocular pressure with an injection of water or saline. A topical antibiotic or pressure patch may be applied. Report 66682 for a suture of the iris or ciliary body.

66700-66710
The ciliary body supplies the anterior chamber with aqueous humor. In cases where high intraocular pressure cannot otherwise be controlled, portions of the ciliary body are destroyed to reduce the production of aqueous humor. The physician makes an incision in the conjunctiva and through the sclera in the pars plana opposite the site of the ciliary body to be treated. The physician uses a heat probe (diathermy) or laser (cyclophotocoagulation) to burn holes in the ciliary body. The physician closes the incision with layered sutures and may restore the intraocular pressure with an anterior and/or posterior injection. A topical antibiotic or pressure patch may be applied. Report 66700 when diathermy is used and 66710 if transscleral cyclophotocoagulation is used.

66711
The ciliary body supplies the anterior chamber with aqueous humor. In cases where high intraocular pressure cannot otherwise be controlled, portions of the ciliary body are destroyed to reduce the production of aqueous humor. Endoscopic cyclophotocoagulation is done on the ciliary body. This may be accomplished by different methods. With the pupil dilated, a limbal incision is made and any posterior synechiae are lysed. Viscoelastic material is injected under the iris to partially fill and expand the ciliary sulcus. The endoscopic cyclophotocoagulation probe is inserted under the iris. The probe allows simultaneous visualization with the photocoagulation. Approximately half the circumference of the ciliary body is treated through the first limbal incision. Another incision is made 180 degrees from the first and the other half of the ciliary body circumference is treated. The viscoelastic material is removed by irrigation and aspiration and the wounds are closed. For aphakic or pseudoaphakic eyes, the procedure is done from a posterior pars plana approach to reach the ciliary body and a limited vitrectomy is also performed.

66720
The ciliary body supplies the anterior chamber with aqueous humor. In cases where high intraocular pressure cannot otherwise be controlled, portions of the ciliary body are destroyed to reduce the production of aqueous humor. The physician applies a freezing probe to the sclera over the ciliary body with the purpose of destroying the ciliary process. This is especially useful in aphakic patients.

66740
The ciliary body supplies the anterior chamber with aqueous humor. In cases where high intraocular pressure cannot otherwise be controlled, portions of the ciliary body are destroyed to reduce the production of aqueous humor. The physician makes an incision in the conjunctiva and sclera in the pars plana adjacent to the portion of ciliary body to be treated. The physician passes a spatula through the incision and into the suprachoroidal space of the anterior chamber. The spatula separates the ciliary body from the scleral spur. This may result in a lowering of intraocular pressure by a decrease in aqueous humor formation from the now detached ciliary body or by increasing uveovascular scleral outflow of aqueous. The physician closes the incision with layered sutures and may restore the intraocular pressure with an anterior and/or posterior injection. A topical antibiotic or pressure patch may be applied.

66761
After applying a topical anesthetic, the physician places a special contact lens on the eye of the patient. The argon or YAG laser is focused on the iris and multiple short bursts of laser light create holes in the iris. This procedure allows fluids in the eye to pass from behind the iris through the openings into the space between the iris and the cornea (the anterior chamber). This lowers intraocular pressure.

66762
The physician places a special contact lens on the eye of the patient and uses multiple bursts of light from an argon laser to create an additional hole in the iris.

66770
The physician places a special contact lens on the eye of the patient. The YAG or Argon laser is focused on the cyst or lesion and multiple short bursts of light destroy the abnormal tissue.

66820
The patient initially had extracapsular cataract surgery in which the posterior shell of the lens was not removed from the eye. But the capsule and/or the membrane adjacent to it (the anterior hyaloid) has since become opaque and must be opened in this new surgery. After placing an ocular speculum in the patient's eye, the pupil is dilated. The physician inserts a small needle, a Ziegler or Wheeler knife or special scissors into the corneal-scleral juncture (the limbus) and advances it to the edge of the capsule and through to the membrane, cutting a flap in the opaque membrane in the field of vision. The physician maneuvers the instrument around any artificial lens. No tissue is removed from the eye; the flap simply opens a window of vision. The physician may close the incision with sutures and may restore the intraocular pressure with an injection of water or saline. A topical antibiotic or pressure patch may be applied.

66821
The patient initially had extracapsular cataract surgery in which the posterior shell of the lens was not removed from the eye. But the capsule and/or the membrane adjacent to it (the anterior hyaloid) has since become opaque and must be destroyed in this new surgery. After a topical anesthetic is applied to the eye, the pupil is dilated. A number of YAG laser shots are focused to a point on the capsule, cutting it. Bursts from the YAG open a flap in the capsule, resulting in immediate improvement in vision. Multiple sessions may be needed to create an adequate opening in the lens capsule.

66825
The physician inserts a lid speculum between the patient's eyelids and the eye is secured by a suture. The physician cuts an opening at the juncture of the cornea and sclera (limbus) to access the artificial lens. The physician adjusts the artificial lens so that the attachments (haptics) of the implant are secured. The physician may close the incision with sutures and may restore the intraocular pressure with an injection of water or saline. A topical antibiotic or pressure patch may be applied.

66830
The patient initially had extracapsular cataract surgery, in which the posterior shell of the lens was not removed from the eye. But the capsule and/or the membrane adjacent to it (the anterior hyaloid) has since become opaque and must be removed in this new surgery. The physician inserts an ocular speculum into the patient's orbit, and makes an incision at the juncture of the cornea and sclera (the limbus). A small cutting needle and suction device (an irrigating cystotome) is inserted to chip away the posterior lens capsule. In some cases, the iris must be cut or a piece of iris removed to access the lens capsule. The adjacent membrane (the anterior hyaloid) may also removed. The physician irrigates the area during aspiration. The physician may close the incision with sutures and may restore the intraocular pressure with an injection of water or saline. A topical antibiotic or pressure patch may be applied.

66840
The physician makes an incision at the juncture of the cornea and sclera (the limbus). The anterior wall of the lens is incised. A probe attached to an irrigating/aspirating machine is inserted into the lens and the lens is destroyed and sucked away. The physician may close the incision with sutures and may restore the intraocular pressure with an injection of water or saline. A topical antibiotic or pressure patch may be applied.

66850
The physician makes an incision in the cornea or the pars plana. The anterior wall of the lens is cut out. The same type of irrigating/aspirating machine used for extracapsular surgery is used for phacofragmentation, but this time the probe is a needle that vibrates 40,000 times per second (phacofragmentation), or sound waves (phacoemulsification, ultrasound) that break up the lens. The physician uses irrigation and suction to remove the once hard nucleus, now liquefied by mechanical or sound vibrations. The physician may close the incision with sutures or may design a sutureless "self-sealing" incision. The physician may restore the intraocular pressure with an injection of water or saline. A topical antibiotic or pressure patch may be applied.

66852
To remove a cataract obstructing the view of the retina during retinal surgery, or to remove a piece of natural lens retained following cataract surgery, the physician makes an incision in the conjunctiva, sclera, and choroid of the pars plana. The physician approaches the lens capsule from behind. If the lens is being removed, the wall of the posterior lens capsule is removed and a small suction device is inserted into the lens. The lens material is sucked out. The physician irrigates the area during aspiration. If a retained portion of the lens is removed, a portion of the clear gel in the back of the eye may be removed as well (vitrectomy). The incision is closed with layered sutures. The physician may restore anterior or posterior intraocular pressure with an injection of water or saline. A topical antibiotic or pressure patch may be applied.

66920-66930
Intracapsular cataract extraction (ICCE) is when the lens and capsule are removed intact. The physician inserts an ocular speculum. An incision is made in the corneal-scleral juncture (the limbus). To enhance the flow of fluids in the eye, the physician may punch a hole in the iris before inserting a surgical instrument filled with coolant (cryoprobe) into the anterior chamber. The lens adheres to the cryoprobe as it freezes, and when the cryoprobe is removed, the lens comes with it (e.g., for 66920). The same technique is used to removed a dislocated lens (e.g., for 66930). The physician may close the incision with sutures and may restore intraocular pressure with an injection of water or saline. A topical antibiotic or pressure patch may be applied.

66940
Extracapsular cataract extraction (ECCE) is when the anterior shell and the nucleus of the lens capsule are both removed, leaving the posterior shell of the lens capsule in place. The physician inserts a lid speculum between the patient's eyelids and makes an incision in the corneal-scleral juncture (the limbus). To enhance the flow of fluids in the eye, the physician may punch a hole in the iris. Using a method other than aspiration or phacofragmentation, the physician removes the lens in parts: first the anterior lens, then the inner, hard nucleus. The clear, posterior capsule remains. The physician may close the incision with sutures and may restore the intraocular pressure with an injection of water or saline. A topical antibiotic or pressure patch may be applied.

66982
The physician performs a complex extracapsular cataract removal with insertion of an intraocular lens prosthesis in a one-stage procedure. A local anesthetic is injected into the periorbital area. The physician makes a small horizontal incision where the cornea and sclera meet and, upon entering the eye through the incision, gently opens the front of the capsule and removes the hard center, or nucleus, of the lens. Using a microscope, the ophthalmologist suctions out the soft lens cortex, leaving the capsule in place. The area is irrigated and aspirated and an intraocular lens (IOL) (plastic disc that replaces the natural lens) is inserted. The ophthalmologist sutures the incision and instills antibiotic ointment and applies an eye patch. A metal shield is secured over the eye with tape. Standard phacoemulsification may be performed if the lens capsule is intact and sufficient zonular support remains. In capsulorrhexis, the ophthalmologist shatters the cataract nucleus with an ultrasonic

oscillating probe. After fragmentation, the phaco probe is inserted into the eye and the cataract is suctioned out through an irrigation-aspiration probe. An IOL is inserted once all of the material is removed. Suture fixation is chosen if both capsular and zonular supports are insufficient and the angle is minimally damaged.

66983

Intracapsular cataract extraction (ICCE) is when the lens and capsule are removed intact. The physician inserts an ocular speculum. An incision is made in the corneal-scleral juncture (the limbus). To enhance the flow of fluids in the eye, the physician may punch a hole in the iris before inserting a surgical instrument filled with coolant (cryoprobe) into the anterior chamber. The lens adheres to the cryoprobe as it freezes, and when the cryoprobe is removed, the lens comes with it. The physician injects a bubble of air into the anterior chamber to protect the cornea. The physician places an intraocular lens in the anterior chamber. The optic, or center, of the implant lies centered at the pupil and the haptics (securing attachments) of the implant are wedged in the anterior chamber, fixating the implant so it cannot move. The physician may close the incision with sutures and may restore the intraocular pressure with an injection of water or saline. A topical antibiotic or pressure patch may be applied.

66984

Extracapsular cataract extraction (ECCE) is when the anterior shell and the nucleus of the lens capsule are both removed, leaving the posterior shell of the lens capsule in place. The physician inserts a lid speculum between the patient's eyelids and makes an incision in the corneal-scleral juncture (the limbus). To enhance the flow of fluids in the eye, the physician may punch a hole in the iris. Using a cutting and suction or ultrasonic device, the physician removes the lens in parts: first the anterior lens, then the inner, hard nucleus. The clear, posterior capsule remains. The physician injects a bubble of air into the anterior chamber to protect the cornea. The physician guides the intraocular implant into the eye. The haptics (securing attachments) lodge into the ciliary sulcus or the lens capsule, occupying the exact position of the original cataract. The physician may close the incision with sutures and may restore the intraocular pressure with an injection of water or saline. A topical antibiotic or pressure patch may be applied.

66985

The physician inserts an ocular speculum. An incision is made in the corneal-scleral juncture (the limbus). For an anterior lens, the physician places an intraocular lens in the fluid-filled space between the iris and cornea (the anterior chamber). The optic, or center, of the implant lies just in front of the pupil and the haptics (securing attachments) of the implant are wedged between the iris and cornea, fixating the implant so it cannot move. For a posterior lens, the physician injects a bubble of air into the anterior chamber to protect the cornea. The physician guides the intraocular implant into the eye. The haptics lodge into the ciliary sulcus or the lens capsule. The physician may close the incision with sutures and may restore the intraocular pressure with an injection of water or saline. A topical antibiotic or pressure patch may be applied.

66986

Early models of intraocular lens (IOL) implants sometimes cause irritation in the patient's eye. They can also become dislocated. Here, the physician exchanges the problematic lens for a newer one. For anterior IOL, the physician replaces an intraocular lens in the fluid-filled space between the iris and cornea (the anterior chamber). The optic, or center, of the implant lies just in front of the pupil and the haptics (securing attachments) of the implant are lodged between the iris and cornea, fixating the implant so it cannot move. For posterior IOL, the physician injects a bubble of air into the anterior chamber through a syringe to protect the cornea. The physician replaces the intraocular implant in the eye. The haptics lodge into the ciliary sulcus or the lens capsule. The physician may close the incision with sutures and may restore the intraocular pressure with an injection of water or saline. A topical antibiotic or pressure patch may be applied.

66990

The ophthalmic endoscope is used for diagnostic purposes or in conjunction with another procedure. The endoscope is properly focused prior to the procedure. Once prepared, an 18- to 20-gauge endoscopic probe tip is inserted through a sclerotomy site. The physician maintains a working distance of 2 to 10 mm to allow visualization of the internal eye structures. It is commonly used when visualization is impaired by pathological changes or poor pupillary dilatation. Once the procedure is complete, the endoscope is removed and the physician may close the incision with sutures. A topical antibiotic or pressure patch maybe applied. This code is used in addition to the primary procedure.

67005-67010

The physician inserts a needle at the limbus or through the cornea (open sky technique) and passes the needle to the back of the anterior segment where a portion of displaced vitreous humor is aspirated (e.g., 67005). If most or all of the vitreous is extracted, mechanical tools are used (e.g., 67010). When this is done, the physician extracts the vitreous, using a mechanical cutting and suctioning process that may involve a rotoextractor or vitreous infusion suction cutter (VICS). In either case, the aspirated vitreous is usually replaced by an injection of a vitreous substitute or aqueous. Any incision is closed with sutures.

67015
The physician inserts a needle into the posterior chamber through the pars plana to aspirate vitreous. Sometimes a posterior sclerotomy is made to release the fluid. When this is done, the physician extracts the vitreous, using a mechanical cutting and suctioning process that may involve a rotoextractor or vitreous infusion suction cutter (VICS). This is often called a vitreous chamber tap in operative reports. Once completed, the incision is repaired with sutures. Intraocular pressure may be adjusted with an injection. A pressure patch may be applied.

67025
The physician inserts a syringe in the pars plana to inject a material like healon or silicone. The injection may be required to replace vitreous that has been aspirated as part of this procedure, to restore intraocular pressure lost in another manner.

67027-67028
The physician implants an intravitreal drug delivery system to provide consistent delivery of a drug to an area of the eye affect by disease. Implants are capable of releasing a controlled amount of a specific drug for months, avoiding drug toxicity and other problems associated with prolonged intravenous therapies. Using a scalpel the physician makes an inferotemporal pars plana incision. Approximately 0.5 milliliter of vitreous is removed. The implant (e.g., ganciclovir or fluocinolone acetonide) in the form of a small pellet is placed through the wound, implanted into the vitreous, and sutured to the sclera. In 67028, the physician introduces medication into the posterior segment. The wound is closed and intraocular pressure is restored.

67030
The physician makes a small incision in the conjunctiva, sclera, and choroid in the pars plana. A narrow knife is inserted to cut vitreous strands that obstruct the patient's vision (e.g., 67030). The strands generally fall away from the visual field and are not retrieved. The physician repairs the pars plana incision with a layered closure and may restore the intraocular pressure with an injection of aqueous or vitreal substitute. A cataract specialist might approach the dissection through a limbal incision (at the corneal-scleral juncture), instead of through the pars plana. A topical antibiotic or pressure patch may be applied after either approach.

67031
The vitreous is the clear gel filling the posterior cavity of the eyeball. After applying a topical anesthetic and dilating the patient's pupil, the physician applies a special contact lens to the cornea of the patient. The physician uses a YAG laser to cut vitreous strands, adhesions, or opacities that obstruct the patient's vision. No tissue is removed and no incision is made. More than one treatment may be required.

67036
The physician performs a mechanical vitrectomy, utilizing a pars plana approach. The physician applies a special contact lens to the cornea to better visualize the back of the eye. Three small incisions are made in the eyeball, each about 4 mm from the juncture of the cornea and sclera. One incision is for a light cannula, one for an infusion cannula, and one for the cutting or suction instruments. The physician extracts the vitreous, using a mechanical cutting and suctioning process that may involve a rotoextractor or vitreous infusion suction cutter (VISC). This is often called a posterior sclerotomy in operative reports. The cannulas are extracted and the incisions repaired with layered closures. Injections may be required to reestablish intraocular pressure. A topical antibiotic or pressure patch may be applied.

67039-67040
The vitreous is the clear gel filling the posterior cavity of the eyeball. The physician applies a special contact lens to the cornea to better visualize the back of the eye. Three small incisions are made in the eyeball, each about 4 mm from the juncture of the cornea and sclera. (This is the pars plana approach.) One incision is for a light cannula, one for an infusion cannula and one for the laser. The physician extracts the vitreous, using a mechanical cutting and suctioning process that may involve a rotoextractor or vitreous infusion suction cutter (VICS). With focal endolaser photocoagulation (e.g., 67039), the physician uses a laser to treat minor retinal disorders. If the physician performs endolaser panretinal photocoagulation (e.g., 67040), a stronger laser treats larger retinal problems, like retinal detachments, diabetic retinopathy, or retinal holes. The cannulas are extracted and the incisions repaired with layered closures. Injections may be required to reestablish the intraocular pressure. A topical antibiotic or pressure patch may be applied.

67041
In macular pucker, or cellophane retinopathy, scar tissue forms a membrane across the central retina of the eye (the macula) and interferes with central vision. The vitreous is the clear gel filling the posterior cavity of the eyeball. The physician applies a special contact lens to the cornea to better visualize the back of the eye. Three small incisions are made in the eyeball, each about 4 mm from the juncture of the cornea and sclera. (This is the pars plana approach.) One incision is for a light cannula, one for an infusion cannula, and one for the cutting or suction instruments. The physician extracts the vitreous, using a mechanical cutting and suctioning process that may involve a rotoextractor or vitreous infusion suction cutter (VISC). This is often called a posterior sclerotomy in operative reports. To

repair a macular pucker, the physician uses specialized microsurgical instruments to gently peel and remove the scar tissue from the surface of the retina in order to alleviate the traction and lessen the retinal surface distortion. The cannulas are extracted and the incisions repaired with layered closures. Injections may be required to reestablish intraocular pressure. A topical antibiotic or pressure patch may be applied.

67042
The vitreous is the clear gel filling the posterior cavity of the eyeball. The physician applies a special contact lens to the cornea to better visualize the back of the eye. Three small incisions are made in the eyeball, each about 4 mm from the juncture of the cornea and sclera. (This is the pars plana approach.) One incision is for a light cannula, one for an infusion cannula, and one for the cutting or suction instruments. To repair a macular hole or treat diabetic macular edema, the physician uses specialized microsurgical instruments to grasp and peel the internal limiting membrane of the retina. The cannulas are extracted and the incisions repaired with layered closures. Injections of air, gas, or silicone oil may be required to stabilize the retina. A topical antibiotic or pressure patch may be applied.

67043
The vitreous is the clear gel filling the posterior cavity of the eyeball. The physician applies a special contact lens to the cornea to better visualize the back of the eye. Three small incisions are made in the eyeball, each about 4 mm from the juncture of the cornea and sclera. (This is the pars plana approach.) One incision is for a light cannula, one for an infusion cannula, and one for the cutting or suction instruments. Using a subretinal pick or infusion cannula, the physician performs a retinotomy to access the subretinal membrane. The membrane is carefully elevated and grasped with subretinal forceps, then gently peeled and removed through the retinotomy site. Focal endolaser coagulation may also be performed to treat minor retinal disorders, or the physician may perform endolaser panretinal photocoagulation using a stronger laser to treat larger retinal problems such as retinal detachments, diabetic retinopathy, or retinal holes. Injections of air, gas, or silicone oil may be required to stabilize the retina. The cannulas are extracted and the incisions repaired with layered closures.

67101
When the retina detaches, it separates from its nourishing blood supply and falls into the posterior cavity of the eye. Loss of vision results. The physician reattaches the retina by freezing (cryotherapy) and thus sealing the retinal tissue to the back of the eye, or by diathermy, where heat is used for the same purpose. The physician explores the sclera and stay sutures are placed under the involved rectus muscles so the eye can be rotated to expose the area to be treated. Sometimes, a rectus muscle is temporarily detached to permit adequate exposure. Cryotherapy and diathermy are performed without entering the posterior chamber; either probe is pressed against the sclera overlying the site of the retinal defect, sealing it against the choroid. If subretinal fluid must be drained, the physician makes an incision in the sclera (sclerotomy) to permit access to the middle layer of the eye's shell (the choroid), which is perforated so that fluid drains out. Any incisions are repaired with layered closures. Injections may be required to reestablish proper intraocular pressure. A topical antibiotic or pressure patch may be applied.

67105
When the retina detaches, it separates from its nourishing blood supply and falls into the posterior cavity of the eye. Loss of vision results. Using a laser light or xenon arc that goes through a dilated pupil without an incision, the physician burns spots at the site of the retinal detachment or retinal tear to seal the retina back into place against the choroid (vascular, middle layer of the eye's shell). If subretinal fluid must be drained, the physician cuts through the conjunctiva and into the sclera (sclerotomy) to access to the choroid, which is perforated so that fluid drains out. Any incisions are repaired with layered closures. Injections may be required to reestablish the intraocular pressure. A topical antibiotic or pressure patch may be applied.

67107
The physician explores the sclera to locate the site overlying a retinal detachment. Stay sutures are placed under involves rectus muscles so the eye may be exposed to area that will be treated. The physician treats the retinal tear externally, by placing a cold or hot probe over the scleral and depressing it. The burn seals the choroid to the retina at the site of the tear. The physician cuts a groove in the sclera and mattress sutures are places across this incision. Any subretinal fluid is drained. A Silastic band is laid in the scleral bed and sutured in place. Sometimes, a silicone sponge is placed under the band. Additional cryotherapy or photocoagulation may be accomplished at this time. When the tear has been adequately repaired and supported, the rectus muscle sutures are removed.

67108
When the retina detaches, it separates from its nourishing blood supply and falls into the posterior cavity of the eye. Loss of vision results. The physician reattaches the retina by freezing (cryotherapy), heat application (diathermy), or laser light to seal the retinal tissue to the back of the eye. Cryotherapy and diathermy are performed without entering the posterior chamber; either probe is pressed against the sclera overlying the site of the retinal defect, sealing it against the choroid. If a laser is used, the light goes through a dilated pupil without an incision to burn spots at the site of the retinal detachment or retinal tear

and seal the retina back into place against the choroid (vascular, middle layer of the eye's shell). A scleral buckle may be placed by suturing a silicone band around the scleral bed and securing it. The buckle supports the healing retinal tear and holds the retina against the choroid by increasing the pressure within the eye. Expendable gas may also be injected into the eye to flatten out the retinal detachment against the choroid. The physician also removes any vitreous opacity or vitreous traction. The lens may also be removed if it interferes with the physician's view of the retina or if the lens is in the way of the removal of scar tissue. Any incisions may be repaired with sutures. Antibiotic ointment and a pressure patch may be applied.

67110
When the retina detaches, it separates from its nourishing blood supply and falls into the posterior cavity of the eye. Loss of vision results. The physician uses a needle to inject expandable gas into the eye to flatten the retinal tear and applies laser or cryotherapy to seal the retinal tear. The physician explores the sclera to locate the site overlying a retinal detachment. Stay sutures are placed under involved rectus muscles so the eye may be exposed to area that will be treated. Air or other gas is injected through the sclera into the posterior segment of the eye to flatten the retinal detachment against the choroid. The patient is instructed to maintain a posture that will position the bubble against the detachment. The physician treats the retinal tear externally, by placing a cold (cryotherapy) or hot (diathermy) probe over the sclera and depressing it. The burn seals the choroid to the retina at the site of the tear. This procedure is often called pneumatic retinopexy.

67112
The physician performs a reoperative procedure to correct retinal detachment following failed surgery. Making an incision, the physician isolates the site of retinal detachment. The physician reseals the retinal tissues to the back of the eye with diathermy or cryotherapy, and uses alloplastic materials to buckle and reinforce the sclera. Any vitreous opacities and retractions are removed. Incisions are closed with sutures.

67113
When the retina detaches, it separates from its nourishing blood supply and falls into the posterior cavity of the eye. Loss of vision results. To repair a complex retinal detachment, the physician first extracts the vitreous, using a mechanical cutting and suctioning process that may involve a rotoextractor or vitreous infusion suction cutter (VISC). This is often called a posterior sclerotomy. To strip the epiretinal membrane, the physician uses a retinal cutting instrument to peel membrane or scar tissue creating tension on the retinal surface. To reattach the retina, the physician may also use freezing (cryotherapy) or laser light to seal the retinal tissue to the back of the eye. Cryotherapy is performed without entering the posterior chamber; a probe is pressed against the sclera overlying the site of the retinal defect, sealing it against the choroid. If a laser is used, the light goes through a dilated pupil without an incision to burn spots at the site of the retinal detachment or retinal tear and seals the retina back into place against the choroid (vascular, middle layer of the eye's shell). A scleral buckle may be placed by suturing a silicone band around the scleral bed and securing it. The buckle supports the healing retinal tear and holds the retina against the choroid by increasing the pressure within the eye. Expendable gas, air, or silicone oil may also be injected into the eye to flatten out the retinal detachment against the choroid. If subretinal fluid must be drained, the physician cuts through the conjunctiva and into the sclera (sclerotomy) to access the choroid, which is perforated so that fluid drains out. The physician also removes any vitreous opacity or vitreous traction. The lens may also be removed if it interferes with the physician's view of the retina or if the lens is in the way of the removal of scar tissue. Any incisions may be repaired with sutures. Antibiotic ointment and a pressure patch may be applied.

67115
The physician inserts an ocular speculum. To release the tension in a previously placed scleral buckle, the physician makes an incision in the conjunctiva and sclera, adjusts the buckle, and repairs the surgical wound with sutures.

67120
The physician inserts an ocular speculum. The physician removes a previously implanted extraocular tube, reservoir, buckle, or other prosthetic device from the eye. The physician may close the incision with sutures and may restore the intraocular pressure with an injection of water or saline. A topical antibiotic or pressure patch may be applied.

67121
An incision is made in the pars plana near the site of an intraocular lens that has fallen into the posterior segment of the eye. The physician removes the extracapsular IOL from the eye. The physician closes the incision with sutures and may restore the intraocular pressure with an injection of vitreous substitute. A topical antibiotic or pressure patch may be applied.

67141
When the retina detaches, it separates from its nourishing blood supply and falls into the posterior cavity of the eye. Loss of vision results. The physician secures a degenerating retina by freezing (cryotherapy) and thus sealing the retinal tissue to the back of the eye, or by diathermy, where heat is used for the same purpose. The physician explores the sclera and stay

sutures are placed under the involved rectus muscles so the eye can be rotated to expose the area to be treated. Sometimes, a rectus muscle is temporarily detached to permit adequate exposure. Cryotherapy and diathermy are performed without entering the posterior chamber; either probe is pressed against the sclera overlying the site of the retinal defect, sealing it against the choroid.

67145
Using a laser light or xenon arc that goes through a dilated pupil without an incision, the physician burns spots at the site of the retinal weakness to seal the retina into place against the choroid (vascular, middle layer of the eye's shell). No incision is made. Multiple sessions may be required.

67208
The physician destroys a lesion of the retina by freezing (cryotherapy), or by heat (diathermy). The physician explores the sclera and stay sutures are placed under the involves rectus muscles so the eye can be rotated to expose the area to be treated. Sometimes, a rectus muscle is temporarily detached to permit adequate exposure. Cryotherapy and diathermy are performed without entering the posterior chamber; either probe is pressed against the sclera overlying the site of the retinal lesion until it is destroyed or until the session is completed. Any muscle incision is repaired and any stay sutures removed. A topical antibiotic or pressure patch may be applied.

67210
The physician destroys a lesion of the retina using a laser or xenon arc. After the patient's eye has been dilated, the physician places a special contact on the eye of the patient. Photocoagulation by laser or xenon arc is performed without entering the posterior chamber; the destructive light beam is guided through the contact and to the retinal lesion, which is destroyed in one session or in a series of sessions. A topical antibiotic or pressure patch may be applied.

67218
The physician treats a malignancy, tumor, growth, or edema by exposing it to a radioactive implant. The plaque-like implant is secured with sutures to the sclera overlying the site of a malignancy. At a future time, the physician recovers the implant. The incision is repaired. An antibiotic ointment and pressure patch may be applied.

67220
The physician destroys a lesion of the choroid using photocoagulation. In one or more sessions the physician directs short spots of a laser's beam at new blood vessels that have grown beneath the macula to seal leaking blood or fluid that can damage vision. Or, the physician may scatter the laser spots through the sides of the retina to reduce abnormal blood vessel growth (choroidal neovascularization) and seal the retina to the back of the eye.

67221-67225
The physician performs photodynamic therapy. This is a two-step procedure used for wet type macular degeneration to treat the abnormal blood vessels that grow under the retina. The fluid and blood present from the new blood vessel growth causes scar formation that destroys vision. Photodynamic therapy closes the abnormal blood vessels to stop or stabilize leakage and improve vision. First, the physician injects the drug Visudyne (verteporfin) intravenously into the patient's arm. This is a dye that marks the abnormal blood vessels under the retina by binding to them. A few minutes after the injection, the ophthalmologist shines a non-thermal 689-nanometer laser light into the patient's eye to activate the drug. The light reacts with the photosensitive chemical in verteporfin, and releases active oxygen molecules that cause cell death in the leaking blood vessels but not healthy ones. When the dye interacts with the light, the abnormal vessels are destroyed and closed off but the normal ones are spared. Report 67221 when photodynamic therapy is performed on one eye and 67225 when photodynamic therapy is performed on the second eye during the same session.

67227-67228
The physician destroys small vessels that are leaking blood on the retina by freezing (cryotherapy), by heat (diathermy) (e.g., 67227), or treats them with photocoagulation (e.g., 67228). Cryotherapy and diathermy may be performed without entering the posterior chamber; either probe is pressed against the sclera overlying the site of the retinopathy until it is destroyed. With a laser light or xenon arc aimed through a dilated pupil without an incision, the physician may burn spots at the site of diabetic retinopathy to seal vessels that have been leaking into the retina. At least 500 Xenon arc burns or 2000 burns from an argon laser are applied. This procedure is often referred to as "scattered destruction." Multiple sessions may be required, although these codes should be reported only once during a defined treatment period.

67229
The physician treats extensive or progressive retinopathy by freezing (cryotherapy) or by laser (photocoagulation) in a preterm infant (less than 37 weeks gestation at birth), performed from birth up to 1 year of age. Performed under topical or general anesthesia, cryotherapy may be performed without entering the posterior chamber. Under direct visualization, the physician applies a freezing probe to the avascular retina; approximately 50 applications may be required. Alternately, the physician may ablate the targeted area using a laser photocoagulation device. Multiple sessions may be required, although this code

should be reported only once during a defined treatment period.

67250-67255
To repair a thin, weakened sclera, the physician places an ocular speculum in the patient's eye, and makes an incision in the conjunctiva and sclera over the site of the defect. The sclera may be cinched and overlapped for reinforcement (e.g., for 67250) or a patch of donor sclera may be sutured over the weakened area (e.g., 67255). A piece of stretched sclera may also be removed. The physician uses sutures or tissue glue in the layered repair. Antibiotic ointment and a patch may be applied.

67311-67312
Strabismus is an imbalance in the muscles of the eyeball that control eyeball movement. Surgery can sometimes correct this imbalance. A speculum is placed in the patient's eye (no previous surgery). The physician makes incisions in the conjunctiva at the juncture of the sclera and cornea (the limbus) or in the cul-de-sac (Parks incision). Radial relaxing incisions in the conjunctiva are made and the muscle (either medial or lateral rectus) is isolated with a muscle hook. The muscle is strengthened by resection (removal of a measured segment) or weakened by recession (retroplacement of the muscle attachment). The muscles are secured with sutures. The operative wound is closed with sutures. In 67311, one horizontal muscle is treated; in 67312 two horizontal muscles in the same eye are treated.

67314-67316
Strabismus is an imbalance in the muscles of the eyeball that control eyeball movement. Surgery can sometimes correct this imbalance. A speculum is placed in the patient's eye, the physician makes incisions in the conjunctiva at the juncture of the sclera and cornea (the limbus) or in the cul-de-sac (Parks incision). Radial relaxing incisions in the conjunctiva are made and the muscle (either superior or inferior rectus) is isolated with a muscle hook. The muscle is strengthened by resection (removal of a measured segment) or weakened by recession (retroplacement of the muscle attachment). The muscles are secured with sutures. The operative wound is closed with sutures. In 67314, one vertical muscle is treated; in 67316 two vertical muscles in the same eye are treated.

67318
Strabismus is an imbalance in the muscles of the eyeball that control eyeball movement. Surgery can sometimes correct this imbalance. A speculum is placed in the patient's eye (no previous surgery). The physician makes incisions in the conjunctiva about 7 mm posterior to the juncture of the sclera and cornea (the limbus) in the superior nasal quadrant of the globe. An incision is made to expose the sclera and a muscle hook is used to engage the superior rectus muscle initially. The tendon of the superior oblique may be located about 12 mm behind the medial or nasal edge of the insertion of the superior rectus. The physician repairs, recesses, or resects the superior oblique muscle. The operative would is closed with layered sutures.

67320
A speculum is placed in the patient's eye, the physician makes incisions in the conjunctiva at the juncture of the sclera and cornea (the limbus) to expose the muscle. The extraocular muscle or muscles to be transposed are isolated, and the physician exposes the area of sclera to which the transposed muscles are to be attached. The insertions of the transposed muscles are relocated generally adjacent to the paretic or weak muscle. They are attached to the sclera with sutures, and the surgical wound is closed with sutures. Occasionally, the transposed muscle may be split and one-half of the muscle relocated.

67331
Strabismus is an imbalance in the muscles of the eyeball that control eyeball movement. Surgery can sometimes correct this imbalance. A speculum is placed in the patient's eye, the physician makes incisions in the conjunctiva at the juncture of the sclera and cornea (the limbus) to expose the muscle. The extraocular muscle or muscles involved are isolated, and the appropriate definitive primary strabismus surgery (any of those reported with codes 67311-67318) is performed: recession or resection on horizontal or vertical muscles, or any procedure on oblique extraocular muscles. This is an add-on code used in conjunction with any strabismus surgery to denote the increased level of difficulty involved in both the planning and performance of the chosen strabismus surgery on an eye that has had previous surgery or injury, but not involving the extraocular muscles.

67332
Strabismus is an imbalance in the muscles of the eyeball that control eyeball movement. Surgery can sometimes correct this imbalance. A speculum is placed in the eye of a patient and the physician makes incisions in the conjunctiva at the juncture of the sclera and cornea (the limbus) to expose the muscle. The extraocular muscle is isolated, and the physician performs the appropriate definitive primary strabismus surgery after freeing the muscle from surrounding fibrotic or scarred tissues. The muscle or muscles are dissected posteriorly to ensure lack of incarceration and repositioned if necessary. The surgical wound is closed with sutures. This is an add-on code used in conjunction with the appropriate strabismus surgery to denote the increased level of difficulty involved in surgery on extraocular muscles that have scarring due to previous strabismus or retinal detachment surgery, injury, or myopathy.

67334
Strabismus is an imbalance in the muscles of the eyeball that control eyeball movement. Surgery can sometimes correct this imbalance. A speculum is placed in the patient's eye, the physician makes incisions in the conjunctiva and sclera to expose the muscle. During strabismus surgery, the extraocular muscle is isolated far posterior to its insertion. The borders or edges of the muscle are sutured to the eye far back of the insertion in what is commonly called the Faden procedure. The surgical wound is closed with sutures. This is an add-on code used in conjunction with the appropriate strabismus surgery to denote that the posterior fixation suturing technique was employed on an extraocular muscle.

67335
Strabismus is an imbalance in the muscles of the eyeball that control eyeball movement. Surgery can sometimes correct this imbalance. The muscle or muscles to be placed on an adjustable suture are isolated in the usual fashion during separately reportable strabismus surgery. Instead of permanently suturing the muscle to the eyeball by tying and cutting the suture distal to the knot, the sutures are tied and brought out through the overlying conjunctiva. Tension on the muscle is adjusted later when the anesthetic is no longer affecting the position of the globe.

67340
Strabismus is an imbalance in the muscles of the eyeball that control eyeball movement. Surgery can sometimes correct this imbalance. The physician makes an extensive incision of the conjunctiva at the juncture of the cornea and the sclera (the limbus). This is called a peritomy. In the plane of the detached muscle, retractors afford increased visibility. Extensive posterior dissection may be necessary in an effort to locate the severed, lost, or detached muscle and reapproximate it to the eyeball with sutures. Once the repair is completed, the incision is repaired. This is an add-on code used in conjunction with the definitive strabismus surgery to report the exploration and/or repair required when an extraocular muscle was detached.

67343
During the performance of separately reported horizontal muscle surgery, scar tissue from a vertical muscle is excised. Or, during the performance of separately reported vertical muscle surgery, horizontal muscle scar tissue is excised. The scar tissue of the extraocular muscle is isolated, and the physician uses a scalpel to dissect the scars and fibrotic tissue from the muscle affecting the muscle itself. The surgical wound is closed with sutures.

67345
The extraocular muscle is identified through direct surgical exposure or through the insertion of an electromyographic needle into the muscle. A small quantity of botulin toxin is injected into the belly of the muscle. Onset of paralysis takes 24 to 48 hours and lasts from four to eight weeks.

67346
A speculum is placed in the patient's eye and the physician makes incisions in the conjunctiva and sclera to expose the muscle. The extraocular muscle to be tested is isolated and the physician uses a scalpel to remove a small portion of the muscle. The excision will not affect overall action of the eye muscle. The surgical wound is closed with sutures.

67400-67405
The physician accesses the orbit through a subciliary, extraperiosteal, or transconjunctival incision. In the subciliary incision, an incision is made in the upper eyelid. In the extraperiosteal incision, the approach is through an incision anterior, superior, interior, or medial to the eye allowing access to the bone beneath the periosteum. In the transconjunctival approach, the lower lid is everted and an incision is made over the infraorbital rim through the inferior cul-de-sac. In 67400, soft tissue or bone may be excised for examination, but no other tissue is removed or repaired. In 67405, fluid is drained from the orbit. In either case, the incision is closed with layered sutures.

67412-67413
The physician removes a lesion or a foreign body from the orbit through a subciliary, frontal, or transconjunctival incision. In the subciliary incision, an incision is made in the lower eyelid. In the frontal approach, an incision is made in the lid crease with a further postseptal dissection for removal of a lesion or foreign body in this portion of the orbit. In the transconjunctival approach, the lower lid is everted and an incision is made over the infraorbital rim through the inferior cul-de-sac. In 67412, the lesion is excised. In 67413, the foreign body is removed. In either case, the incision is closed with layered sutures.

67414
The physician removes bone from the orbit through a subciliary or transconjunctival incision. In the subciliary incision, an incision is made in the lower eyelid. In the transconjunctival approach, the lower lid is everted and an incision is made over the infraorbital rim through the inferior cul-de-sac. Bone is excised for decompression. The incision is closed with layered sutures.

67415
With the aid of a separately reported fluoroscope or x-ray visualization, the physician directs the needle toward the targeted area and aspirates a small amount. No incision is made and no repair is required.

67420-67430
The physician makes an incision in the lateral aspect of the orbit. A C-shaped incision is made down to the

periosteum overlying the lateral orbital rim. The periosteum is incised posterior to the rim itself. The temporalis muscle is moved aside and the globe is protected with pliable retractors. A vibrating saw removes the bone of the lateral orbital rim. In 67420 the lesion is excised from the orbit. In 67430, a foreign body is removed. In either case, the bone is replaced and wired into position and the operative wound is closed in layers.

67440
The physician makes an incision in the lateral aspect of the orbit. A C-shaped incision is made down to the periosteum overlying the lateral orbital rim. The periosteum is incised posterior to the rim itself. The temporalis muscle is moved aside and the globe is protected with pliable retractors. A vibrating saw is used to remove the bone from the lateral orbital rim. Fluid is excised from the orbit and the bone is replaced and wired into position. The operative wound is closed in layers.

67445
The physician makes an incision in the lateral aspect of the orbit. A C-shaped incision is made down to the periosteum overlying the lateral orbital rim. The periosteum is incised posterior to the rim itself. The temporalis muscle is moved aside and the globe is protected with pliable retractors. A vibrating saw removes the bone of the lateral orbital rim. A piece of orbital bone is removed for decompression. The bone flap is replaced and wired into position. The operative wound is closed in layers.

67450
The physician makes an incision in the lateral aspect of the orbit. A C-shaped incision is made down to the periosteum overlying the lateral orbital rim. The periosteum is incised posterior to the rim itself. The temporalis muscle is moved aside and the globe is protected with pliable retractors. A vibrating saw removes the bone of the lateral orbital rim. The physician explores the orbit and may remove tissue for examination. No other procedure is performed. The bone is replaced and wired into position. The operative wound is closed in layers.

67500-67505
The physician injects a therapeutic or anesthetic medication (e.g., for 67500) or alcohol (e.g., for 67505) into the orbit through the lower eyelid or in a transconjunctival method.

67515
A blunt or sharp-tipped needle is guided along the surface of the globe beneath the conjunctiva and between the sclera and Tenon's capsule. When the tip of the needle is in the appropriate location, medication or other substance is injected into the Tenon's capsule.

67550-67560
The physician inserts a prosthesis in the eye in 67550 or revises or removes an orbital implant in 67560. An orbital implant lies outside the muscle cone and is usually secured with sutures.

67570
The physician makes an incision in the lateral or medial aspect of the fornix. In a lateral approach, a C-shaped incision is made down to the periosteum overlying the lateral orbital rim. The periosteum is incised posterior to the rim itself. The temporalis muscle is moved aside and the globe is protected with pliable retractors. The bone is removed to access the optic nerve. In a medial approach, the conjunctiva is incised and the medial rectus muscle is temporarily disinserted. Sutures are passed through the terminal portion of the medial rectus muscle and its insertion into the globe is noted. The eye is rotated laterally to gain access to the optic nerve medially. In either case, once the nerve has been identified, several small fenestrations are made. A dissection is carried down through the outer meningeal layer covering the optic nerve until the subarachnoid space is reached. An egress of cerebral spinal fluid indicates decompression of the nerve sheath. The operative wound is closed in layers.

67700
The eyelid is prepped and draped and local anesthetic is applied. A transverse incision is made to drain the abscess in the lid. The wound is irrigated and may be closed with sutures.

67710
This procedure generally follows a previously performed tarsorrhaphy (closure of the eyelid), usually attempted to protect the cornea. The eyelid is prepped and draped, and local anesthetic is applied. The previously formed seam or union between the upper and lower lid is delineated and divided using sharp scissors.

67715
Under local anesthesia, the face and eyelids are draped and prepped. Scissors cut the lateral canthus to further divide the upper and lower lid to extend the division.

67800-67808
A chalazion is a small mass in the eyelid that results in chronic inflammation. The face and eye are prepped and draped and local anesthesia (e.g., for 67800, 67801 and 67805) or general anesthesia (e.g., for 67808) is administered. Usually, general anesthesia is reserved for very young or otherwise uncooperative patients. The physician applies a chalazion clamp to expose the posterior surface of the eyelid. The chalazion is incised with a blade and a curette is used to explore the lid after the incision has been drained. Any pockets of infection are drained. The lips of the

Eye and Ocular Adnexa

wound are generally cauterized to prevent excessive bleeding. The clamp is released.

67810
A local anesthetic is applied and the face and eyelid are prepped and draped. A small amount of tissue is excised from the suspect portion of the eyelid. Sutures may be required to repair the incision.

67820
Trichiasis is a condition wherein eyelashes are ingrown or misdirected in their growth so that they irritate the tissues of the eye. Using a biomicroscope, the physician plucks the offending eyelashes with forceps. The lash follicles are not treated.

67825
Trichiasis is a condition wherein eyelashes are ingrown or misdirected in their growth so that they irritate the tissues of the eye. The physician treats the area of trichiasis with local anesthetic. In cryotherapy, the freezing probe is applied to the area of trichiasis. After a period of repeated freezing and thawing, the lash follicles are usually destroyed. In electrosurgery, electrolysis directed at the follicles destroys them.

67830-67835
Trichiasis is a condition wherein eyelashes are ingrown or misdirected in their growth so that they irritate the tissues of the eye. The physician treats the area of trichiasis with a local anesthetic and preps and drapes the face and eye. The physician uses a scalpel to split the eyelid margin at the gray line (the junction of the palpebral mucosa and skin). The area of abnormal eyelash growth is excised in both 67830 and 67835. Additionally in 67835, tissue for a split-thickness graft is harvested from the buccal mucosa inside the patient's mouth. No repair is required at the graft harvest site. The graft is inlaid between the palpebral conjunctiva and the skin. In either case, sutures may be required.

67840
The physician administers a local anesthetic and the face and eyelid are draped and prepped for surgery. The eyelid lesion is outlined in a marking pen. The lesion is incised and the surgical wound is repaired with sutures if necessary.

67850
The physician administers a local anesthetic and the face and eyelid are draped and prepped for surgery. An electrocautery tool or photocoagulation is used to destroy the small eyelid lesion.

67875
The constant action of the eyelid opening and closing against the cornea can cause problems in patients with chronic corneal conditions. Temporary closure of the eyelid may provide relief for an eroded or painful cornea. The physician administers local anesthetic to the eyelids. A permanent suture is passed through the skin and eyelid margin at the gray line of the upper lid and corresponding portion of the lower lid. This process is repeated several times in each eye, creating a permanent marginal adhesion. The sutures are usually tied over a bolster to prevent erosion of the suture through the lid.

67880
The constant action of the eyelid opening and closing against the cornea can cause problems in patients with chronic corneal conditions. Temporary closure of the eyelid may provide relief for an eroded or painful cornea. The physician administers a local anesthetic and preps and drapes the face and eyelids for surgery. Tissue along the mucocutaneous junction at the margins of the eyelids is excised. A suture is passed through the skin and eyelid margin at the gray line of the upper lid and corresponding portion of the lower lid. This process is repeated several times in each eye, creating a permanent marginal adhesion. The sutures are usually tied over a bolster to prevent erosion of the suture through the lid. The sutures are removed a week to 10 days later, after the lid margins have adhered.

67882
The constant action of the eyelid opening and closing against the cornea can cause problems in patients with chronic corneal conditions. Temporary closure of the eyelid may provide relief for an eroded or painful cornea. The physician administers a local anesthetic and preps and drapes the face and eyelids for surgery. Tissue along the mucocutaneous junction at the margins of the eyelids is excised. A tongue of tarsal plate is isolated from above the upper or lower lid. The tarsal plate is sutured into a corresponding area of the opposite lid. The physician passes a suture through the skin and eyelid margin at the gray line of the upper lid and corresponding portion of the lower lid. This process is repeated several times in each eye, creating a permanent marginal adhesion. The sutures are usually tied over a bolster to prevent erosion of the suture through the lid. The sutures are removed a week to 10 days later, after the lid margins have adhered.

67900
Ptosis refers to a droop or displacement resulting from paralysis. The physician makes an incision directly above the brow (supraciliary), through the mid-forehead or near the hairline (coronal). A dissection is carried down to the area of the brow. The skin is pulled superiorly and the brow approximated to its proper position above the supraorbital rim. The incision is repaired with sutures.

67901
The physician performs a repair of blepharoptosis by frontalis muscle technique using suture or other material. Blepharoptosis is a droop or displacement of the upper eyelid resulting from paralysis. The physician makes an incision directly above the brow (supraciliary). The frontalis fixation technique is a

mechanical suspension that transfers the movement of the upper lid to the frontalis muscle above the eyelid. Banked fascia from a cadaver donor or other material such as Mersilene mesh may be used to create a sling to the frontalis muscle. It is sutured in place. The incision is repaired with sutures.

67902
The physician performs a repair of blepharoptosis by frontalis muscle technique using an autologous fascia to create a sling. The fascia is harvested, usually from the knee, in a separately reportable procedure. Blepharoptosis is a droop or displacement of the upper eyelid resulting from paralysis. The physician makes an incision directly above the brow (supraciliary). The frontalis fixation technique is a mechanical suspension that transfers the movement of the upper lid to the frontalis muscle above the eyelid. It is sutured in place. The physician obtains fascia from the patient's thigh and uses this fascia to create a sling to the frontalis muscle. This sling helps suspend the lid. The incisions are repaired with sutures.

67903
Blepharoptosis is a droop or displacement of the upper eyelid resulting from paralysis. The physician administers local anesthetic and the patient's face and eyelid are draped and prepped for surgery. The eyelid is everted and the physician makes an incision along the upper posterior edge of the tarsus. The levator complex, including Mueller's muscle, is isolated for a distance superiorly to correspond with the amount of ptosis to be corrected. The levator aponeurosis is advanced onto the tarsal plate internally until the eyelid margin falls at the appropriate location below the limbus. The incision is repaired.

67904
Blepharoptosis is a droop or displacement of the upper eyelid resulting from paralysis. The physician administers local anesthetic and the patient's face and eyelid are draped and prepped for surgery. An incision line is outlined along the crease of the upper eyelid. A dissection is carried down the normal insertion point of the distal point of the levator tendon. The levator tendon is isolated. The physician uses sutures to advance the levator tendon onto the tarsal plate in an adjustable fashion. If the patient is old enough to undergo the procedure under local anesthetic, the patient is placed in a sitting position and eyelid height and contour are evaluated under the effect of gravity. The amount that the levator tendon is advanced corresponds to the degree of preoperative ptosis. If the patient is not able to undergo the procedure under local anesthetic, general anesthesia is used and a predetermined amount of advancement is performed. In either case, the incision is repaired with sutures once the tendon has been secured in its new location.

67906
Blepharoptosis is a droop or displacement of the upper eyelid resulting from paralysis. The physician administers local anesthetic and the patient's face and eyelid are draped and prepped for surgery. The physician performs a repair that provides a mechanical suspension of the upper lid, transferring the movement of the upper lid to the frontalis muscle action of the eyebrow. The most common technique involves the creation of three horizontal incisions extending to the level of the tarsal plate approximately 3 mm above the upper eyelid margin in the midline, nasal, and lateral quarters. Three corresponding incisions are made just above the brow down to the periosteum of the bone. The lid is suspended in a double rhomboid configuration as the physician passes the suspending material deep in the lid tissue at the depth of the anterior surface of the levator aponeurosis through the orbital septum in front of the bone and out through the medial and lateral brow incisions. The knots are pulled up and tied to elevate the eyelid margin to the level of the superior limbus. The ends of the sutures are burned in the wound. The incisions are repaired with sutures.

67908
The physician administers local anesthetic and the patient's face and eyelid are draped and prepped for surgery. The physician everts the upper eyelid and a series of curved clamps are placed across the everted undersurface of the upper lid. All of the tissue distal to the clamps is removed or resected. This includes conjunctiva, tarsus, Muller's muscle, and the distal insertion of the levator aponeurosis. A running suture or purse string suture is used to consolidate the remaining tissues.

67909
The physician administers local anesthetic and the patient's face and eyelid are draped and prepped for surgery. With an incision usually at the previous incision line, the physician attempts to reduce a previous overcorrection of ptosis. The levator aponeurosis is cut free of disinserted from its attachment to the levator aponeurosis, and the incision is repaired with sutures.

67911
The physician administers local anesthetic and the patient's face and eyelid are draped and prepped for surgery. The physician outlines the incision line, usually in the crease of the upper lid. The distal portion of the tendon responsible for elevating the lid (levator aponeurosis) is isolated from its attachment to the tarsal plate. The levator aponeurosis is allowed to retract itself posteriorly or autogenous graft materials are inserted between the levator aponeurosis and the tarsal plate. The patient is generally placed in a sitting position and the amount of the retraction of the levator aponeurosis is judged by the position of the eyelid

while the patient is sitting on the table. Alternatively, the eyelid margin may be placed approximately 2 mm below the limbus. When the lid is positioned satisfactorily, it is affixed. The incision is closed with sutures.

67912
Lagophthalmos is a condition in which the upper eyelid is not providing complete closure to the eye, causing dryness and other complications. This code reports lagophthalmos correction using the insertion of a gold weight or other lid load into the upper eyelid for gravity-assisted closure. The surgical field is prepared around the eye and a traction suture is placed into the lid margin. An incision is made in the lid crease and dissection is carried out on the upper lid structures to expose the anterior surface of the tarsus. The weight to be used has been predetermined; it is centered over the exposed upper tarsal surface and sutured into place. After irrigation, the orbicularis oculi muscle must be closed over the inserted weight and the crease in the eyelid is restored through suturing. Antibiotics are applied and the eye is patched.

67914
An ectropion is a turning outward of the margin of the eyelid. The physician administers local anesthetic and the patient's face and eyelid are draped and prepped for surgery. The physician uses absorbable sutures to foreshorten the posterior tissues of the eyelid in an effort to redirect the rotation of the eyelid posteriorly. No incisions are required for this treatment of ectropion.

67915
An ectropion is a turning outward of the margin of the eyelid. The physician administers local anesthetic and the patient's face and eyelid are draped and prepped for surgery. Bipolar or unipolar cautery is employed to shrink the posterior tissues of the eyelid margin in an effort to rotate the lid margin posteriorly toward the globe. No incision is made.

67916
An ectropion is a turning outward of the margin of the eyelid. The physician administers local anesthetic and the patient's face and eyelid are draped and prepped for surgery. A section of tarsus and conjunctiva in the configuration of a diamond or rhomboid is taken from the posterior or back surface of the lower lid. Incisions are closed with interrupted absorbable sutures to rotate the eyelid margin posteriorly toward the globe.

67917
An ectropion is a turning outward of the margin of the eyelid. The physician administers local anesthetic and the patient's face and eyelid are draped and prepped for surgery. The physician makes an incision in the lower lid and isolates a tongue or strip of tarsus in the lateral one third of the lower lid. Nonabsorbable sutures are passed through the tarsal strip. The periosteum of tough fibrous tissue that lines the bone of the lateral orbital rim is isolated. The sutures from the tarsal strip are passed through the periosteum overlying the bone of the lateral orbital rim. The physician tightens the sutures. Eyelid margin tension and contour are evaluated and adjusted. The incision or incisions are repaired with sutures.

67921
An entropion is an inversion of the margin of the eyelid. The physician administers local anesthetic and the patient's face and eyelid are draped and prepped for surgery. The physician threads sutures through the inferior fornix or inferior cul-de-sac externally to the lash line. The sutures are placed in the medial, middle, and lateral third of the eyelid in a mattress fashion. These absorbable sutures are tied on the skin side. The sutures act to evert the eyelid margin anteriorly, correcting the malposition of the eyelid. No incision is made in this procedure.

67922
An entropion is an inversion of the margin of the eyelid. The physician administers local anesthetic and the patient's face and eyelid are draped and prepped for surgery. The physician uses bipolar or monopolar cautery to create a central tissue shrinkage to rotate the eyelid margin anteriorly. This corrects the malposition of the eyelid. No incisions are made in this procedure.

67923
An entropion is an inversion of the margin of the eyelid. The physician administers local anesthetic and the patient's face and eyelid are draped and prepped for surgery. A triangular section of tarsus is excised from the eyelid. A large chalazion clamp may be used to evert the lid and excise the triangle of tarsus, which usually measures 8 mm to 10 mm at the base. A piece of exposed orbicularis muscle is removed with the wedge. The edges of the excision site are approximated and repaired with sutures.

67924
An entropion is an inversion of the margin of the eyelid. The physician administers local anesthetic and the patient's face and eyelid are draped and prepped for surgery. The physician makes the incision along approximately 80 percent of the width of the eyelid for extensive repair. The physician uses deep sutures to sever the eyelid margin outwardly. Strips of tarsus may also be excised from the eyelid. All incisions are repaired with sutures. This procedure is sometimes performed under general anesthesia.

67930-67935
The physician administers local anesthetic and the patient's face and eyelid is draped and prepped for surgery. The physician irrigates the wound and approximates its edges. The wound is repaired in layered sutures. In 67930, the wound is through a

Eye and Ocular Adnexa

partial thickness of eyelid; in 67935, the wound is through the full thickness of the eyelid.

67938
The physician administers local anesthetic and the patient's face and eyelid are draped and prepped for surgery. The physician locates the foreign body through palpation. An incision is made through the anterior surface if the foreign body is principally on the anterior of the lid; the lid is everted if the foreign body is near the posterior surface. An attempt is made to conceal the incision line in the crease of the upper lid, or through a subciliary incision, when possible. The foreign body is removed and the wound is irrigated. The wound is repaired with layered sutures.

67950
The physician administers local anesthetic and the patient's face and eyelid are draped and prepped for surgery. The physician increases the lid margin by cutting the medial or lateral canthus (juncture of upper and lower eyelid). The physician rearranges the anterior tissues of the lids to prevent adherence.

67961-67966
The physician administers local anesthetic and the patient's face and eyelid are draped and prepped for surgery. A section of full-thickness eyelid is excised from the upper or lower eyelid. The section includes the defect and a margin of normal tissue. The edges of the excision site are approximated to reconstitute the eyelid contour and the wound is closed with layered sutures. Sometimes, a separately reported skin graft or pedicle flap is required to achieve proper cosmetic results. In 67961, up to one-fourth of the lid margin is removed; in 67966, more than one-fourth is removed.

67971
The patient's face and eyelid are draped and prepped for surgery. Local or general anesthesia may be administered. The patient has already undergone a separately reported excision that has created a significant eyelid defect requiring reconstruction of up to two-thirds of the eyelid. Because the defect is too large for direct closure, portions of the opposing eyelid are excised and grafted to reconstruct the eyelid. The opposite lid is everted and a horizontal incision through the tarsus and conjunctival approximately 4 mm from the eyelid margin is performed. Vertical incisions are made through the conjunctiva to match the width of the flap. The dissection is carried down through Muller's muscle toward the fornix or cul-de-sac. The advancing tarsal conjunctival flap is grafted to the opposing lid and secured with sutures. A separately reportable free, full-thickness skin graft may be applied to complete the reconstruction.

67973-67974
The patient's face and eyelid are draped and prepped for surgery. Local or general anesthesia may be administered. The patient has already undergone a separately reported excision that has created a significant eyelid defect requiring reconstruction. Because the defect is too large (e.g., total lower lid for 67973 and total upper lid for 67974), portions of the opposing eyelid are excised and grafted to reconstruct the eyelid. The opposite lid is everted and a horizontal incision through the tarsus and conjunctival approximately 4 mm from the eyelid margin is performed. Vertical incisions are made through the conjunctiva to match the width of the flap. The dissection is carried down through Muller's muscle toward the fornix or cul-de-sac. The advancing tarsal conjunctival flap is grafted to the opposing lid and secured with sutures. A separately reported free, full-thickness skin graft may be applied to complete the reconstruction.

67975
The patient's face and eyelid are draped and prepped for surgery. Local or general anesthesia may be administered. Approximately six weeks after a separately reported reconstruction of the eyelid, the tissue is divided to create an upper and lower lid. Any redundant tissue is trimmed.

68020
The patient's face and eyelid are draped and prepped for surgery. Local anesthesia is administered. A vertical or horizontal incision is made in the posterior surface of the eyelid margin. The incision does not extend to the eyelid margin itself. The contents of the cyst are drained with a cotton-tipped probe or a curette.

68040
Trachoma is a chronic inflammation of the eye causing granulations to form on conjunctival tissue. The patient's face and eyelid are draped and prepped for surgery. Local anesthesia may be administered. Under biomicroscopic guidance, the physician everts the eyelid margin and removes the conjunctival follicles with a cotton-tipped swab or a curette. No incision is required.

68100
The patient's face and eyelid are draped and prepped for surgery. Local anesthesia may be administered. A portion of the bulbar or palpebral conjunctival is excised with a curette. Sutures may be required to repair the wound.

68110-68115
The patient's face and eyelid are draped and prepped for surgery. Local anesthesia is administered. A lesion on the bulbar or palpebral conjunctival is excised with a curette. Sutures may be required to repair the wound. The lesion is up to 1 cm in size in 68110 and larger than 1 cm in 68115.

68130
The patient's face and eyelid are draped and prepped for surgery. Local anesthesia is administered and a lid speculum is inserted. A lesion on the conjunctiva and

adjacent superficial sclera is excised with a curette. No sutures usually are required.

68135
The patient's face and eyelid are draped and prepped for surgery. Local anesthesia is administered and a lid speculum is inserted. A freezing probe (cryotherapy) is applied to a lesion on the conjunctiva. No repair is required.

68200
The physician applies a drop of topical anesthetic to the eye. A small gauge needle is inserted to deliver a medication such as a cortical steroid or antibiotic into the subconjunctival space.

68320
The patient's face and eyelid are draped and prepped for surgery. Local anesthesia is administered. With the aid of an operating microscope, the physician separates the conjunctival epithelial tissue from the underlying Tenon's capsule. The site to which the harvested tissue is to be grafted is prepared to accept the tissue. Its margins are freshened and the conjunctival graft is arranged and sutured into place. The tissue for graft can be a free graft or extensive rearrangement of existing tissue.

68325
The patient's face and eyelid are draped and prepped for surgery. Local anesthesia is administered. The physician separates the buccal mucous membrane that will be used for the graft from its location within the patient's mouth. The site to which the donor tissue is to be grafted is prepared to accept the tissue. Its margins are freshened and the conjunctival graft is arranged and sutured into place. The donor graft site does not usually require a repair.

68326
The patient's face and eyelid are draped and prepped for surgery. Local anesthesia is administered. With the aid of an operating microscope, the physician separates the conjunctival epithelial tissue from the underlying Tenon's capsule. The tissue for graft can be a free graft or extensive rearrangement of existing tissue. The site to which the donor tissue is to be grafted is prepared to accept the tissue. Its margins are freshened and the conjunctival graft is sutured into a foreshortened, or scarred inferior cul-de-sac or fornix. The fornix can be reformed with the use of a cul-de-sac suture fixation or with the use of a silicon stent attached to the orbital rim. The stent is used to mold the fornix and is sutured into place securely and left for up to two weeks.

68328
The patient's face and eyelid are draped and prepped for surgery. Local anesthesia is administered. The physician separates the buccal mucous membrane that will be used for the graft from its location within the patient's mouth. The donor graft site does not usually require a repair. The site to which the donor tissue is to be grafted is prepared to accept the tissue. Its margins are freshened and the conjunctival graft is sutured into a foreshortened, or scarred inferior cul-de-sac or fornix. The fornix can be reformed with the use of a cul-de-sac suture fixation or with the use of a silicon stent attached to the orbital rim. The stent is used to mold the fornix and is sutured into place securely and left for up to two weeks.

68330
A symblepharon is an adhesion between the conjunctiva on the eyeball (bulbar conjunctiva) and the conjunctiva on the inner eyelid (tarsal conjunctiva). The patient's face and eyelid are draped and prepped for surgery. Local anesthesia is administered. The physician divides the adhesions between the globe and palpebral conjunctiva and repairs the conjunctival wound with adjacent tissue transfer. Sutures are required, and a silicon stent may be placed in the eye to prevent the development of further adhesions during the healing process.

68335
A symblepharon is an adhesion between the conjunctiva on the eyeball (bulbar conjunctiva) and the conjunctiva on the inner eyelid (tarsal conjunctiva). The patient's face and eyelid are draped and prepped for surgery. Local anesthesia is administered. The physician separates the conjunctival adhesions and grafts replacement tissue over the site of the symblepharon. The tissue for graft can be a free graft of conjunctival tissue from the same or other eye, or buccal mucosa obtained from inside the patient's mouth. The site to which the donor tissue is to be grafted is prepared to accept the tissue. Its margins are freshened and the conjunctival graft is sutured in place. A silicon stent or contact lens may be placed in the eye to prevent the development of further adhesions during the healing process.

68340
A symblepharon is an adhesion between the conjunctiva on the eyeball (bulbar conjunctiva) and the conjunctiva on the inner eyelid (tarsal conjunctiva). The patient's face and eyelid are draped and prepped for surgery. Local anesthesia is administered. The physician divides the adhesions between the globe and palpebral conjunctiva. No other repair is usually needed, although a conformer or contact lens may be placed in the eye to prevent the development of further adhesions during the healing process.

68360
The patient's face and eyelid are draped and prepped for surgery. Local anesthesia is administered. The physician elevates the conjunctiva from the Tenon's capsule and a small tongue of free conjunctiva is advanced via a flap to another site where it is secured with sutures.

68362
The patient's face and eyelid are draped and prepped for surgery. Local anesthesia is administered. The physician elevates the conjunctiva from the Tenon's capsule and the conjunctiva is advanced cover the de-epithelialized cornea. The leading edge of the conjunctival flap is sutured along the medial extent of the corneal defect.

68371
A conjunctival allograft is harvested from a living donor for transplantation to another recipient to help the process of re-epithelialization in cases of corneal epithelial damage and disease when the normal population of conjunctival/limbal stem cells has been depleted. The donor eye is prepped and draped. The lid speculum is inserted to maintain the lids and lashed from the operative field. The conjunctival borders of the graft to be removed are marked with a surgical marking pen to approximate the recipient bed dimensions. Saline solution is injected subconjunctivally to raise the conjunctiva from the Tenon's layer. Incisions are made on the lateral borders of the graft first, with undermining done between those borders. The posterior ridge is incised and the graft is reflected. Dissection is carried to the conjunctival/ limbal junction and anterior dissection is finished, moving into the peripheral cornea. The epitheliectomy from a living donor is kept at a superficial level like that of a keratectomy with limbal and peripheral corneal tissue, no sclera or corneal stroma. The free graft is removed and prepared in an appropriate storage medium. The wound is closed. Topical antibiotics and steroids are instilled and the lids are closed and patches applied.

68400
The lacrimal system serves to keep the conjunctiva and cornea moist through the production, distribution, and elimination of tears. The physician administers a local anesthetic along the edge of the supratemporal portion of the orbital rim over the lacrimal gland. An incision is made beneath the superior orbital rim or in the lid crease of the upper lid. The incision is extended to the lacrimal fossa where the abscess is drained. The wound is irrigated and repaired with layered sutures.

68420
The lacrimal system serves to keep the conjunctiva and cornea moist through the production, distribution, and elimination of tears. The lacrimal sac is an enlarged portion of the lacrimal duct that drains these tears. The physician administers a local anesthetic along the medical canthal tendon. A stab incision is made directly into the lacrimal sac and the pressure created by the sequestered abscess is relieved. The wound may be irrigated and repaired with layered sutures.

68440
The lacrimal system serves to keep the conjunctiva and cornea moist through the production, distribution, and elimination of tears. Tears produced by the lacrimal gland are eliminated through the lacrimal punctum, a small openings in the inner canthus. The physician administers a local anesthetic at the lacrimal punctum and uses sharp scissors to snip the lacrimal punctum, usually posteriorly. A dilating probe is introduced to ensure that enlargement of the punctum has been achieved.

68500-68505
The lacrimal system serves to keep the conjunctiva and cornea moist through the production, distribution, and elimination of tears. The tears are produced in the lacrimal gland. The physician makes an incision beneath the superior orbital rim or in the lid crease of the upper lid. The incision is extended to the periosteum overlying the bone of the supraorbital rim. A periosteal elevator is used to isolate and dissect the lacrimal gland from its position in the lacrimal fossa. The gland is removed in total in 68500 and a part of the gland is removed in 68505. In either case, the wound is repaired with layered sutures.

68510
The lacrimal system serves to keep the conjunctiva and cornea moist through the production, distribution, and elimination of tears. The tears are produced in the lacrimal gland. The physician makes an incision beneath the superior orbital rim or in the lid crease of the upper lid. The incision is extended to lacrimal fossa. A previously determined portion of the lacrimal gland is excised for analysis. The wound is repaired with layered sutures.

68520
The lacrimal system serves to keep the conjunctiva and cornea moist through the production, distribution, and elimination of tears. The lacrimal sac is an enlarged portion of the lacrimal duct that eliminates these tears. The physician administers a local anesthetic along the medial canthal tendon. An incision is made midway between the bridge of the nose and the medial canthal tendon. The dissection is carried down to the periosteum overlying the bone of the superior lacrimal crest. A periosteal elevator is used to separate the lacrimal sac from its normal location. The sac is removed. The wound is repaired with layered sutures.

68525
The lacrimal system serves to keep the conjunctiva and cornea moist through the production, distribution, and elimination of tears. The lacrimal sac is an enlarged portion of the lacrimal duct that eliminates these tears. The physician administers a local anesthetic along the medial canthal tendon. An incision is made midway between the bridge of the nose and the medial canthal tendon. The dissection is carried down to the periosteum overlying the bone of the superior lacrimal crest. A portion of the lacrimal sac is removed. The wound is repaired with layered sutures.

68530
The lacrimal system serves to keep the conjunctiva and cornea moist through the production, distribution, and elimination of tears. Ducts distribute the tears to the eye and nose. The physician administers a local anesthetic along the medial canthal tendon. An incision is made midway between the bride of the nose and the medial canthal tendon. The dissection is carried down to the foreign body or lacrimal stone. It is removed, and the wound is repaired with layered sutures.

68540
The lacrimal system serves to keep the conjunctiva and cornea moist through the production, distribution, and elimination of tears. The tears are produced in the lacrimal gland. The physician makes an incision beneath the superior orbital rim or in the lid crease of the upper lid. The incision is extended to the periosteum overlying the bone of the supraorbital rim or to the lacrimal fossa. The tumor is isolated and removed with a rim of normal lacrimal gland tissue. The wound is repaired with layered sutures.

68550
The lacrimal system serves to keep the conjunctiva and cornea moist through the production, distribution, and elimination of tears. The tears are produced in the lacrimal gland. The physician makes an incision beneath the superior orbital rim or in the lid crease of the upper lid. The incision is extended to the periosteum overlying the bone of the supraorbital rim or to the lacrimal fossa. The tumor has invaded the lacrimal fossa, so an osteotome is used to remove the portion of affected bone. The wound is repaired with layered sutures.

68700
The lacrimal system serves to keep the conjunctiva and cornea moist through the production, distribution, and elimination of tears. Lacrimal canaliculi are the ducts that carry the tears from the lacrimal gland where they are produced to the nose. The physician uses a probe to locate the distal and proximal ends of the canaliculi in the injured eye of patient. The ends are freshened and reattached with sutures. The wound is closed with layered sutures.

68705
The lacrimal system serves to keep the conjunctiva and cornea moist through the production, distribution, and elimination of tears. Tears produced by the lacrimal gland are released into the eye through the lacrimal punctum, a small opening in the inner canthus. The physician administers a local anesthetic at the lacrimal punctum and applies bipolar or monopolar cautery to the palpebral conjunctiva just below the level of the inferior punctum. The result is a repositioning of the punctum itself. No incisions are made and no repairs required in this procedure.

68720
The lacrimal system serves to keep the conjunctiva and cornea moist through the production and distribution of tears. The lacrimal sac is an enlarged portion of the lacrimal duct that distributes these tears. The physician administers a local anesthetic along the medial canthal tendon. A 1 cm incision is made in the skin midway between the bridge of the nose and the medial canthal tendon. The dissection is carried down to the periosteum overlying the bone of the superior lacrimal crest. The lacrimal sac is opened and a communication is established been the lacrimal sac and underlying bone and nasal mucosa. The lacrimal mucosa is exposed and a connection between the medial portion of the lacrimal sac and the nasal mucosa is created and secured with sutures. The incision is repaired with layered sutures.

68745-68750
The lacrimal system serves to keep the conjunctiva and cornea moist through the production and distribution of tears. The lacrimal sac is an enlarged portion of the lacrimal duct that distributes these tears. The physician administers a local anesthetic along the medial canthal tendon. A 1 cm incision is made in the skin midway between the bridge of the nose and the medial canthal tendon. The dissection is carried down to the periosteum overlying the bone of the superior lacrimal crest. The lateral portion of lacrimal sac is connected by a series of interrupted sutures to the nasal mucosa. A glass tube is inserted to create a connection from the lacrimal system to the nasal mucosa in 68750. The incision is repaired with layered sutures.

68760
The lacrimal system serves to keep the conjunctiva and cornea moist through the production, distribution, and elimination of tears. Tears produced by the lacrimal gland are drained from the eye through the lacrimal punctum, a small opening in the inner canthus. The physician administers a local anesthetic at the lacrimal punctum and uses a heat source such as cautery or argon laser to close the proximal portion of the canalicular and lacrimal system including the lacrimal punctum.

68761
The lacrimal system serves to keep the conjunctiva and cornea moist through the production, distribution, and elimination of tears. Tears produced by the lacrimal gland are drained from the eye through the lacrimal punctum, a small opening in the inner canthus. The physician administers a local anesthetic at the lacrimal punctum and closes the punctum by inserting a plug. The plug may be a permanent silicone plug or a temporary collagen plug.

68770
The lacrimal system serves to keep the conjunctiva and cornea moist through the production, distribution, and elimination of tears. Tears produced by the lacrimal

gland are drained from the eye through the lacrimal punctum, a small opening in the inner canthus. The physician administers a local anesthetic at the lacrimal punctum and uses a probe to locate the lacrimal fistula. The fistula is dissected and its core is removed. The incision is repaired with layered sutures.

68801
The physician treats a suspected injury or blockage of the lacrimal punctum, the opening on the medial eyelids, to assist in drainage of secretions. The physician inserts a plastic probe, catheter, or large suture. The physician may irrigate the punctum to evaluate the patency of lacrimal drainage system.

68810-68811
The lacrimal system keeps the conjunctiva and cornea moist through the production, distribution, and elimination of the watery lacrimal secretion, called tears. Tears produced by the lacrimal gland are drained from the eye through the lacrimal punctum, a small opening near the margin of each eyelid. The physician dilates the proximal portion of the lacrimal system and threads a probe along the canaliculus to the lacrimal sac. No incisions are made and no repairs are necessary. This is performed with the patient under local anesthetic in 68810. In 68811, less patent ducts or a less cooperative patient requires general anesthesia.

68815
The lacrimal system keeps the conjunctiva and cornea moist through the production, distribution, and elimination of the watery lacrimal secretion, called tears. Ducts distribute the tears to the eye and nose. The physician dilates the proximal portion of the lacrimal system and threads a probe along the canaliculus to the lacrimal sac. Canalicular stents are passed through the duct and placed in the distal portion of the lacrimal system. The tubes remain in place for three to six months before they are removed. No incisions are made and no repairs are necessary.

68816
The lacrimal system keeps the conjunctiva and cornea moist through the production, distribution, and elimination of the watery lacrimal secretion, called tears. Ducts distribute the tears to the eye and nose. Using topical anesthesia, the physician treats an obstructed nasolacrimal duct by dilating the puncta and canaliculi and threading a probe into the lacrimal system. The probe is removed and the balloon catheter is advanced through the superior punctum, canaliculus, lacrimal sac, and into the nasolacrimal duct down to the nasal floor. An inflation device filled with sterile water is attached to the balloon catheter and used to inflate the balloon. The balloon is deflated and the inflation procedure is repeated. The physician pulls the balloon proximally and positions it within the lacrimal sac and nasolacrimal duct junction, where the inflation procedure is again repeated. The balloon is then fully deflated and the catheter withdrawn from the lacrimal system.

68840
The lacrimal system serves to keep the conjunctiva and cornea moist through the production, distribution, and elimination of tears. Ducts distribute the tears to the eye and nose. The physician threads a probe along the canaliculi. No incisions are made and no repairs are necessary. The canaliculi may be irrigated during the procedure.

68850
The lacrimal system serves to keep the conjunctiva and cornea moist through the production, distribution, and elimination of tears. A cannula is inserted into the lacrimal duct. Under radiographic guidance, radiopaque dye is introduced into the lacrimal system through the cannula. The supervision and interpretation of the radiographic results of the injection are reported separately; this code reports only the injection of the contrast medium.

Auditory

69000-69005
Through a small incision in the skin or at times into the perichondrium external ear at the site of the abscess or hematoma (collection of blood), the physician drains the contents of the abscess in a simple procedure (e.g., 69000). Occasionally, a small drain tube is inserted and packing is placed to facilitate healing. A bolster with through-and-through sutures is placed to prevent accumulation of fluid. In a complicated procedure (e.g., 69005), the physician also devotes more time to cleaning the abscess cavity, and a soft sponge is placed in the canal after antibiotic ear drops have been applied.

69020
The physician makes an incision in the skin and drains an abscess in the external auditory canal. Occasionally, packing is inserted to absorb the drainage and facilitate healing. Usually no further treatment is needed and no closure is required.

69090
The physician or technician uses a sharp instrument such as a sterile needle or a piercing gun to form an opening in the ear lobe. After the puncture is complete, the area is cleaned with a disinfectant and an earring is inserted to keep the opening patent. No further treatment is usually necessary.

69100
The physician uses a scalpel or punch forceps to excise a portion of a lesion on the external ear for diagnostic purposes. Unless the incision is large, a sutured closure is usually unnecessary.

69105
The physician uses a scalpel, curette, or small biopsy forceps to excise a portion of a lesion on the external ear for diagnostic purposes. Ear canal packing may be required.

69110
The physician removes a full-thickness section of the external ear, often as a triangular wedge. The portion of the ear removed will vary from case to case, but most frequently it is in the curved upper portion of the ear. A small portion of normal tissue surrounding the defect is also removed. The wound is closed with layered sutures.

69120
Using a scalpel or electric knife, the physician amputates the external ear. The wound is closed during a second procedure involving a skin graft or flap.

69140
Entering through the external opening of the ear, the physician makes an incision in the skin covering the exostosis to expose the bone beneath it. The bony growth is removed with a curette or drill. The skin is replaced over the site and the canal is packed to provide hemostasis and to hold the skin in position.

69145
Through the external opening of the ear, the physician uses a knife to excise a soft tissue lesion with surrounding margin or normal tissue. Some limited drilling of the ear canal may be done. The external ear canal may be packed. If extensive skin is removed, a separate grafting procedure may be required at this time.

69150
Through a postauricular incision, the physician uses a scalpel to remove an extensive lesion in the ear canal. Depending upon whether the lesion involves bone, a section of supporting hard tissue may be excised. The tympanic membrane, parotid gland, facial nerve, and portions of the mandible and mastoid may also be removed. A separately reported graft or flap may be performed at this time, or the surgical wound may be repaired with a layered closure.

69155
Through a postauricular incision, the physician uses a scalpel to remove an extensive lesion of the ear canal. A section of supporting hard tissue may be excised as well as the tympanic membrane, parotid gland, facial nerve, and portions of the mandible and mastoid. The physician performs a neck dissection, removing the lymph nodes from that side of the neck. The jugular vein, spinal accessory nerve, or sternocleidomastoid muscle may be removed as well. The carotid artery, vagus, sympathetic, phrenic, brachial plexus, hypoglossal and lingual nerves are spared. A separately reported graft or flap may be performed at this time, or the surgical wound may be repaired with a layered closure.

69200-69205
Under direct visualization, the physician or technician removes a foreign body from the external auditory canal using delicate forceps, a cerumen spoon, or suction. In the case of a live insect, oil is dropped into the ear to immobilize it before it is removed. No anesthetic or local anesthetic is used in 69200. If a child or an adult cannot tolerate the procedure while awake, it is performed under general anesthesia in 69205. Code 69205 is also reported in cases where the foreign body is so large, an incision is made in the external meatus to enlarge the opening before the foreign body can be extracted.

69210
Under direct visualization, the physician removes impacted cerumen (ear wax) using suction, a cerumen spoon or delicate forceps. If no infection is present, the ear canal may be irrigated.

69220-69222
Routine mastoid cavity debridement is required every three to six months in patients who have undergone a radical or modified radical mastoidectomy. Under direct visualization, the physician uses suction, a cerumen spoon, and delicate forceps to remove skin debris and drainage from the mastoid cavity, a bony extension of the ear canal. The cavity is cleaned simply in 69220. The cavity may require more extensive cleaning, as in the case of infection or extensive debris, in 69222. Sometimes this extensive cleaning requires general anesthesia or the use of a laser to remove granulation tissue.

69300
The physician corrects a protruding ear. The physician makes an incision on the posterior auricle and raises the posterior skin off the cartilage. A new antihelical fold is created with multiple sutures through the cartilage. Some techniques employ limited cartilage cutting. A small ellipse of posterior skin is removed and the skin is closed with sutures. Packing corresponding to the anterior ear contours is placed. The size of the auricle may be reduced.

69310
The physician makes a postauricular incision and removes the thick, stenotic plug of soft tissue from the external auditory canal. Some drilling of the bony canal may be needed to enlarge the bony canal. Thin skin grafts are used to reline the canal and are held in place by packing. The posterior incision is repaired with sutures.

69320
The physician makes a postauricular incision and drills just behind and above the temporomandibular joint region. Drilling is continued until the ossicles are identified. The new bony canal is enlarged. The

eardrum is reconstructed and split thickness skin grafts are used to line the new canal. A large canal opening is made by removing skin and soft tissue. The canal is packed and the incision is repaired with sutures.

69400
The physician topically decongests and anesthetizes the nose and nasopharynx. The Eustachian tube is cannulated with a small catheter through the nose, often with the aid of a nasopharyngoscope. Air is forced into the catheter to inflate the Eustachian tube. The catheter is removed.

69401
The physician inflates a blocked or collapsed Eustachian tube by increasing the air pressure in the nasopharynx. One method is to blow air against the resistance of the closed mouth and nose. Another method is to close one side of the nose and force air into the other nostril with a Politzer bag as the patient swallows.

69405
The physician makes an incision in the posterior ear canal skin and raises the eardrum. The Eustachian tube opening in the middle ear is visualized and a small catheter is inserted into the Eustachian tube to stent it open. This can be left in place indefinitely. No repair is made.

69420-69421
After the application of a local anesthetic (e.g., for 69420) or a general anesthetic (e.g., for 69421) and using a microscope for guidance, the physician makes an incision in the patient's tympanic membrane. Fluid is suctioned from the middle ear space and may be reserved for analysis. The Eustachian tube may be inflated. No closure is required.

69424
Assisted by microscopic visualization and using delicate forceps or hook, the physician removes from the tympanic membrane a previously placed ventilating tube with the patient under general anesthesia. No other treatment is required.

69433-69436
In a patient who has received a local or topical anesthetic (e.g., for 69433) or a general anesthetic (e.g., for 69436), the physician inserts a ventilating tube. Under direct visualization with a microscope, the physician makes a small incision in the tympanum (eardrum). Any middle ear fluid is suctioned and may be reserved for analysis. The physician inserts a ventilating tube into the opening in the tympanum. No other treatment is required.

69440
Entering through the external ear canal opening or through a postauricular incision (behind the ear) and into the ear canal, the physician performs exploratory surgery of the middle ear. The eardrum is lifted posteriorly and the middle ear is explored including testing the mobility of the ossicular chain. No major treatment is rendered at this time. The eardrum and canal skin are repositioned and the canal is packed. Any postauricular incision is sutured.

69450
Through the external ear canal opening, the physician treats a lesion or other irritation to the tympanic membrane. The physician makes an incision in the posterior canal skin and reflects the eardrum forward. Under microscopic guidance, the physician removes adhesions from the tympanic membrane (tympanolysis). When tympanolysis is complete, the eardrum and canal skin are repositioned and packing is placed in the ear canal.

69501
Through a postaural or endaural incision, the physician removes the mastoid cortex (outer bone) and drills out some of the mastoid air cells to enter the mastoid antrum. This is usually done as a drainage procedure for mastoid disease limited to the antrum region. A myringotomy with or without tube placement may be performed. A temporary drain may be placed and the incision is sutured.

69502
Through a postaural or endaural incision, the physician drills out the mastoid cavity. The mastoid sinus is exposed posteriorly. The tegmen (bony plate separating the mastoid and middle cranial fossa) is exposed superiorly. The posterior ear canal wall remains intact. The horizontal semicircular canal and part of the incus are visualized. Cholesteatoma or diseased mastoid mucosa is removed. The incision is sutured. A temporary drain may be placed a dressing is applied.

69505
The physician makes incisions in the ear canal to develop a posterior tympanomeatal flap that is reflected forward. Through a postaural or endaural incision, the physician drills out the mastoid cortex. The mastoid antrum is identified. Granulations and any cholesteatoma are removed. The posterior bony canal wall is taken down to the level of the facial nerve. If cholesteatoma involves the ossicles, they are removed. The posterior skin flap and eardrum are repositioned to cover the facial ridge and part of the mastoid cavity. A meatoplasty is performed. The mastoid cavity and ear canal are packed, the incision sutured, and a dressing placed.

69511
The physician makes incisions in the ear canal to develop a posterior tympanomeatal flap that is reflected forward. Through a postaural or endaural incision, the physician drills out the mastoid cells. The posterior and superior bony canal walls are taken down to the level of the facial nerve. The ossicles, except for the stapes if possible, are removed as well as the

Eustachian tube orifice mucosa, middle ear mucosa, granulations, and cholesteatoma. The middle ear and mastoid are exposed to the exterior through the ear canal. A large meatoplasty is performed. Packing is placed, the incision is sutured, and a dressing is applied.

69530
Through a postaural or endaural incision, the physician drills out the mastoid cavity. The mastoid sinus is exposed posteriorly. The tegmen (bony plate separating the mastoid and middle cranial fossa) is exposed superiorly. The posterior ear canal wall remains intact. The horizontal semicircular canal and part of the incus are visualized. Various cell tracts around the semicircular canals are explored to drain the petrous apex. If this is unsuccessful, the posterior and superior bony canal walls are taken down to the level of the facial nerve. The ossicles, except for the stapes if possible, are removed as well as the Eustachian tube orifice mucosa, middle ear mucosa, granulations, and cholesteatoma. Cell tracts between the carotid artery and cochlea or the jugular bulb and cochlea are followed to open the petrous apex and drain any infection. A meatoplasty is performed. A temporary drain may be placed. The incision is sutured and a dressing is applied.

69535
The physician elevates the auricle with a superior flap. If the auricle and surrounding skin is involved, a wide excision of the skin and subcutaneous tissues is performed. The sternocleidomastoid muscle is separated from the mastoid tip, exposing the internal jugular vein. The seventh nerve is sacrificed. The zygomatic arch is divided. The middle fossa dura is exposed and elevated from the temporal bone. The head of the mandible is removed to expose the internal carotid artery. With a drill and chisel, the carotid canal is opened. The sigmoid sinus is skeletonized and a chisel is used to make the final bony cuts through the medial temporal bone. Hemostasis is obtained with cautery and packing. A parotidectomy and/or neck dissection may also be required. A separately reportable reconstructive procedure may be performed at this time. Otherwise, the incisions are repaired with a layered closure.

69540
Through the external ear canal opening, the physician removes the aural polyp with a cup forceps or an ear snare. Bleeding is controlled with packing or epinephrine on a cotton ball. Antibiotic drops may be instilled.

69550
Through the external auditory canal, the physician makes an incision in the posterior canal skin and reflects the skin flap and eardrum forward. Under microscopic visualization, the small vascular tumor is grasped with a cup forceps and gently removed. Hemostasis is obtained with packing soaked in epinephrine. Once bleeding is controlled, the middle ear is packed with absorbable material. The eardrum and skin flap are repositioned and the ear canal is packed.

69552
Through a postaural incision, the physician drills out the mastoid cavity. The mastoid sinus is exposed posteriorly. The tegmen (bony plate separating the mastoid and middle cranial fossa) is exposed superiorly. The posterior ear canal wall remains intact. An extended facial recess is sometimes needed to completely visualize the tumor. The vascular tumor is grasped and removed with cup forceps. Hemostasis is obtained using absorbable packing. Usually, the ossicles can be left undisturbed. For larger tumors, the posterior canal wall and ossicles may be removed. The incision is repaired with sutures and a dressing is applied.

69554
The surgeon makes an incision in front of the ear. The facial nerve, hypoglossal nerve, spinal accessory nerve, internal jugular vein, and carotid artery are identified in the neck. A complete mastoidectomy with extended facial recess is performed. The tip of the mastoid is removed and the jugular bulb is exposed and ligated inferiorly. The mastoid sinus is skeletonized, opened, and packed. Hemostasis is obtained with packing. If the tumor extends intracranially, a craniotomy may be necessary. A parotidectomy may also be needed if further mobilization of the facial nerve is required. The ear canal and ossicles may be removed. The incision is repair with a layered closure. Dressings are applied.

69601
Using a postaural incision, the physician revises a previously performed simple mastoidectomy with a complete mastoidectomy. The physician drills out the mastoid cavity. The mastoid sinus is exposed posteriorly. The tegmen (bony plate separating the mastoid and middle cranial fossa) is exposed superiorly. The posterior ear canal wall remains intact. The horizontal semicircular canal and part of the incus are visualized. Cholesteatoma or diseased mastoid mucosa are removed. The incision is sutured. A temporary drain may be placed and a dressing is applied.

69602
Using a postaural incision, the physician revises a previously performed simple or complete mastoidectomy with a modified radical mastoidectomy by removing all the mastoid cells, granulations, pus, and the bony partitions of the mastoid cavity. A tympanomeatal flap is developed and reflected anteriorly. The posterior and superior bony canal walls are taken down to the level of the facial nerve. If cholesteatoma is present around the ossicles, the ossicles are removed. The tympanomeatal flap is

Auditory

repositioned over the facial ridge and into the mastoid cavity. Some middle ear space is thus maintained. A large meatoplasty is performed. The ear canal and mastoid cavity are packed and the incision is closed with sutures.

69603
Using an endaural or postauricular incision, the physician revises a previously performed complete or modified radical mastoidectomy with a radical mastoidectomy. The posterior and superior bony canal walls are taken down to the level of the facial nerve. The ossicles, except for the stapes if possible, are removed as well as the Eustachian tube orifice mucosa, middle ear mucosa, granulations, and cholesteatoma. The middle ear and mastoid are exposed to the exterior through the ear canal. A large meatoplasty is performed. Packing is placed, the incision is sutured, and a dressing is applied.

69604
Through a postauricular or endaural incision, the physician revises the site of a previous mastoidectomy. The posterior canal may be taken down. Ossicles may be removed. The physician performs a tympanoplasty in conjunction with the revision mastoidectomy. The edges of the tympanic membrane perforation are roughened ("rimming the perforation") and a fascia graft is placed under or over the tympanic membrane remnant. No ossicular reconstruction is done. Absorbable packing may be placed in the middle ear. The canal and mastoid cavity are packed, and the incision is sutured. A dressing is applied.

69605
The physician revises a previously performed mastoidectomy with an apicectomy. Through a postural or endaural incision, the physician drills out the remaining mastoid cavity. The mastoid sinus is exposed posteriorly. The tegmen (bony plate separating the mastoid and middle cranial fossa) is exposed superiorly. The posterior ear canal wall remains intact. The horizontal semicircular canal and part of the incus are visualized. Various cell tracts around the semicircular canals are explored to drain the petrous apex. If this is unsuccessful, the posterior and superior bony canal walls are taken down to the level of the facial nerve. The ossicles, except for the stapes if possible, are removed as well as the Eustachian tube orifice mucosa, middle ear mucosa, granulations, and cholesteatoma. Cell tracts between the carotid artery and cochlea or the jugular bulb and cochlea are followed to open the petrous apex and drain any infection. A meatoplasty is performed. A temporary drain may be placed. The incision is sutured and a dressing is applied.

69610
Under microscopic visualization, the tympanic membrane is repaired. The physician may roughen the tympanic membrane perforation ("rimming the perforation") to prepare the site before closure and may apply a paper patch. In some cases, the edges of a traumatic perforation of the eardrum may need to be elevated from the middle ear with a delicate hook.

69620
Through the external ear canal, the physician visualizes the tympanic membrane and the eardrum defect. The edges of the eardrum perforation are roughened ("rimming the perforation"). Some dissolvable packing may be placed through the perforation into the middle ear space. A fat graft plug may be placed in the perforation or a piece of fascia may be placed medial to the eardrum over the dissolvable packing. A tympanomeatal flap may be raised. Any incisions are sutured and a dressing is applied.

69631
The physician makes an incision in the ear canal skin through a postauricular or transcanal approach. The edges of the tympanic membrane are roughened ("rimming the perforation"). The physician reflects the eardrum forward. The middle ear is explored, and lysis of any adhesions is performed. Any squamous debris or middle ear cholesteatoma is removed and the physician inspects and palpates the ossicles. No ossicular reconstruction is done at this time. Some drilling or curetting of the canal wall may be necessary. Some fascia from the temporalis muscle or other tissues is harvested as a graft to repair the tympanic membrane perforation. Some packing may be placed in the middle ear to support the graft. The graft may be placed under (underlay or medial graft technique) or on top of the remaining eardrum (overlay or lateral graft technique). The canal skin is repositioned and the canal is packed. Any external incisions are sutured, and a dressing is applied.

69632
The physician makes an incision in the ear canal skin through a postauricular or transcanal approach. The edges of the tympanic membrane are roughened ("rimming the perforation"). The physician reflects the eardrum forward. The middle ear is explored, and lysis of any adhesions is performed. Any squamous debris or middle ear cholesteatoma is removed and the physician inspects and palpates the ossicles. The ossicular chain can also be reconstructed by sculpting and repositioning the patient's own ossicles. The natural ossicle may be replaced with a donor cadaver ossicle, or a sculpted bone strut or piece of cartilage. Some packing may be placed in the middle ear to support the reconstructed ossicle prior to final positioning of the eardrum graft. Some drilling or curetting of the canal wall may be necessary. Some fascia from the temporalis muscle or other tissues is harvested as a graft to repair the tympanic membrane perforation. The graft may be placed under (underlay or medial graft technique) or on top of the remaining eardrum (overlay or lateral graft technique). The canal

Auditory

skin is repositioned and the canal is packed. Any external incisions are sutured, and a dressing is applied.

69633
The physician makes an incision in the ear canal skin through a postauricular or transcanal approach. The edges of the tympanic membrane are roughened ("rimming the perforation"). The physician reflects the eardrum forward. The middle ear is explored, and lysis of any adhesions is performed. Any squamous debris or middle ear cholesteatoma is removed and the physician inspects and palpates the ossicles. The ossicular chain is reconstructed using a synthetic reconstructive prosthesis. A partial ossicular prosthesis (PORP) is used when the stapes suprastructure is present. If the stapes suprastructure is absent, a total ossicular replacement prosthesis (TORP) is used. A piece of cartilage may be placed between the eardrum and prosthesis. Some packing may be placed in the middle ear to support the reconstructed ossicle prior to final positioning of the eardrum graft. Some drilling or curetting of the canal wall may be necessary. Some fascia from the temporalis muscle or other tissues is harvested as a graft to repair the tympanic membrane perforation. The graft may be placed under (underlay or medial graft technique) or on top of the remaining eardrum (overlay or lateral graft technique). The canal skin is repositioned and the canal is packed.

69635
Through a postauricular incision, the physician removes the mastoid cortex (outer bone) and drills out some of the mastoid air cells to enter the mastoid antrum. The edges of the tympanic membrane are roughened ("rimming the perforation"). The physician reflects the eardrum forward. The middle ear is explored, and lysis of any adhesions is performed. Any squamous debris or middle ear cholesteatoma is removed and the physician inspects and palpates the ossicles. No ossicular reconstruction is done at this time. Some drilling or curetting of the canal wall may be necessary. Some fascia from the temporalis muscle or other tissues is harvested as a graft to repair the tympanic membrane perforation. Some packing may be placed in the middle ear to support the graft. The graft may be placed under (underlay or medial graft technique) or on top of the remaining eardrum (overlay or lateral graft technique). The canal skin is repositioned and the canal is packed. Any external incisions are sutured, and a dressing is applied.

69636
Through a postauricular incision, the physician removes the mastoid cortex (outer bone) and drills out some of the mastoid air cells to enter the mastoid antrum. The edges of the tympanic membrane are roughened ("rimming the perforation"). The physician reflects the eardrum forward. The middle ear is explored, and lysis of any adhesions is performed. Any squamous debris or middle ear cholesteatoma is removed and the physician inspects and palpates the ossicles. The ossicular chain can be reconstructed by sculpting and repositioning the patient's own ossicles. The natural ossicle may also be replaced with a donor cadaver ossicle, or a sculpted bone strut or piece of cartilage. Some packing may be placed in the middle ear to support the reconstructed ossicle prior to final positioning of the eardrum graft. Some drilling or curetting of the canal wall may be necessary. Some fascia from the temporalis muscle or other tissues is harvested as a graft to repair the tympanic membrane perforation. The graft may be placed under (underlay or medial graft technique) or on top of the remaining eardrum (overlay or lateral graft technique). The canal skin is repositioned and the canal is packed. Any external incisions are sutured, and a dressing is applied.

69637
Through a postauricular incision, the physician removes the mastoid cortex (outer bone) and drills out some of the mastoid air cells to enter the mastoid antrum. The edges of the tympanic membrane are roughened ("rimming the perforation"). The physician reflects the eardrum forward. The middle ear is explored, and lysis of any adhesions is performed. Any squamous debris or middle ear cholesteatoma is removed and the physician inspects and palpates the ossicles. The ossicular chain is reconstructed using a synthetic reconstructive prosthesis. A partial ossicular prosthesis (PORP) is used when the stapes suprastructure is present. If the stapes suprastructure is absent, a total ossicular replacement prosthesis (TORP) is used. A piece of cartilage may be placed between the eardrum and prosthesis. Some packing may be placed to support the reconstructed ossicle prior to positioning of the eardrum graft. Some drilling or curetting of the canal wall may be necessary. Some fascia from the temporalis muscle or other tissues is harvested as a graft to repair the perforation. The graft may be placed under (underlay or medial graft technique) or on top of the remaining eardrum (overlay or lateral graft technique). The canal skin is repositioned and the canal is packed.

69641
The physician makes incisions in the ear canal to develop a posterior tympanomeatal flap that is reflected forward. Through a postaural or endaural incision, the physician drills out the mastoid cortex. The mastoid antrum is identified. Granulations and any cholesteatoma are removed. The posterior bony canal wall is taken down to the level of the facial nerve. The middle ear is explored, and lysis of any adhesions is performed. Any squamous debris or middle ear cholesteatoma is removed and the physician inspects and palpates the ossicles. No ossicular reconstruction is done at this time. Some fascia from the temporalis muscle or other tissues is harvested as a graft to repair

Auditory

the tympanic membrane perforation. Some packing may be placed in the middle ear to support the graft. The graft may be placed under (underlay or medial graft technique) or on top of the remaining eardrum (overlay or lateral graft technique). The posterior skin flap and reconstructed eardrum are repositioned to cover the facial ridge and part of the mastoid cavity. A meatoplasty is performed. The mastoid cavity and ear canal are packed, the incision sutured, and a dressing placed.

69642
The physician makes incisions in the ear canal to develop a posterior tympanomeatal flap that is reflected forward. Through a postaural or endaural incision, the physician drills out the mastoid cortex. The mastoid antrum is identified. Granulations and any cholesteatoma are removed. The posterior bony canal wall is taken down to the level of the facial nerve. The middle ear is explored, and lysis of any adhesions is performed. Any squamous debris or middle ear cholesteatoma is removed and the physician inspects and palpates the ossicles. The ossicular chain can be reconstructed by sculpting and repositioning the patient's own ossicles. The natural ossicle also may be replaced with a donor cadaver ossicle, or a sculpted bone strut or piece of cartilage. Some packing may be placed in the middle ear to support the reconstructed ossicle prior to final positioning of the eardrum graft. Some fascia from the temporalis muscle or other tissues is harvested as a graft to repair the tympanic membrane perforation. Some packing may be placed in the middle ear to support the graft. The graft may be placed under (underlay or medial graft technique) or on top of the remaining eardrum (overlay or lateral graft technique). The posterior skin flap and reconstructed eardrum are repositioned to cover the facial ridge and part of the mastoid cavity. A meatoplasty is performed. The mastoid cavity and ear canal are packed, the incision sutured, and a dressing placed.

69643
Through a postauricular incision, the physician removes the mastoid cortex (outer bone) and drills out the mastoid air cells. The edges of the tympanic membrane are roughened ("rimming the perforation"). The physician reflects the eardrum forward. The middle ear is explored, and lysis of any adhesions is performed. Any squamous debris or middle ear cholesteatoma is removed and the physician inspects and palpates the ossicles. No ossicular reconstruction is done at this time. If the posterior canal wall is taken down, it is reconstructed with cartilage, bone, or hydroxyapatite (i.e., Wehr's canal wall reconstruction). Some fascia from the temporalis muscle or other tissues is harvested as a graft to repair the tympanic membrane perforation. Some packing may be placed in the middle ear to support the graft. The graft may be placed under (underlay or medial graft technique) or on top of the remaining eardrum (overlay or lateral graft technique). The canal skin is repositioned and the canal and mastoid cavity are packed. Any external incisions are sutured, and a dressing is applied.

69644
Through a postauricular incision, the physician removes the mastoid cortex (outer bone) and drills out the mastoid air cells. The edges of the tympanic membrane are roughened ("rimming the perforation"). The physician reflects the eardrum forward. The middle ear is explored, and lysis of any adhesions is performed. Any squamous debris or middle ear cholesteatoma is removed and the physician inspects and palpates the ossicles. The ossicular chain may be reconstructed by sculpting and repositioning the patient's own ossicles. The natural ossicle also may be replaced with a donor cadaver ossicle, or a sculpted bone strut or piece of cartilage. Some packing may be placed in the middle ear to support the reconstructed ossicle prior to final positioning of the eardrum graft. If the posterior canal wall is taken down, it is reconstructed with cartilage, bone, or hydroxyapatite (i.e., Wehr's canal wall reconstruction). Some fascia from the temporalis muscle or other tissues is harvested as a graft to repair the tympanic membrane perforation. Some packing may be placed in the middle ear to support the graft. The graft may be placed under (underlay or medial graft technique) or on top of the remaining eardrum (overlay or lateral graft technique). The canal skin is repositioned and the canal and mastoid cavity are packed. Any external incisions are sutured, and a dressing is applied.

69645
Through a postauricular incision, the physician removes the mastoid cortex (outer bone) and drills out the mastoid air cells. A posterior canal skin flap and remaining eardrum are preserved and reflected forward. The middle ear is explored, and lysis of any adhesions is performed. Any squamous debris or middle ear cholesteatoma is removed and the physician inspects and palpates the ossicles. The posterior canal wall is taken down to the level of the facial nerve. All or part of the ossicles are removed in addition to the middle ear mucosa. No ossicular reconstruction is attempted. Some fascia from the temporalis muscle or other tissues is harvested as a graft to repair the tympanic membrane perforation. Some packing may be placed in the middle ear to support the graft. The graft may be placed under (underlay or medial graft technique) or on top of the remaining eardrum (overlay or lateral graft technique). A piece of Silastic may be placed in the middle ear to develop an air-containing space. The canal skin is repositioned and the canal and mastoid cavity are packed. Any external incisions are sutured, and a dressing is applied.

69646
Through a postauricular incision, the physician removes the mastoid cortex (outer bone) and drills out

the mastoid air cells. A posterior canal skin flap and remaining eardrum are preserved and reflected forward. The middle ear is explored, and lysis of any adhesions is performed. Any squamous debris or middle ear cholesteatoma is removed and the physician inspects and palpates the ossicles. The posterior canal wall is taken down to the level of the facial nerve. All or part of the ossicles are removed in addition to the middle ear mucosa. Reconstruction is accomplished with the sculpting of the patient's own ossicle, or through the placement of a donor cadaver ossicle, cartilage, or bone graft, or prosthetic device. A reconstructed eardrum is positioned over the reconstructed ossicular chain. Some packing may be placed in the middle ear to support the graft. The graft may be placed under (underlay or medial graft technique) or on top of the remaining eardrum (overlay or lateral graft technique). Some fascia from the temporalis muscle or other tissues is harvested as a graft to repair the tympanic membrane perforation. Some packing may be placed in the middle ear to support the graft. The graft may be placed under (underlay or medial graft technique) or on top of the remaining eardrum (overlay or lateral graft technique). The canal skin is repositioned and the canal and mastoid cavity are packed. Any external incisions are sutured, and a dressing is applied. The canal skin is repositioned and the canal and mastoid cavity are packed. Any external incisions are sutured, and a dressing is applied.

69650
The physician makes an incision in the posterior canal skin through the external ear canal opening. Under microscopic visualization, the physician reflects the skin flap and posterior eardrum forward. A small amount of the posterior bony canal may need to be removed with a curette or drill. The incus and stapes are visualized and palpated. If the stapes is fixated it can be mobilized by applying pressure to it with delicate instruments. The canal skin and eardrum are repositioned and the ear canal is packed.

69660
The surgeon makes an incision in the posterior canal skin through the external canal opening. Occasionally, a postauricular incision may be substituted. Under microscopic guidance, the physician reflects the canal skin flap and posterior eardrum forward. Some posterior canal bone may be removed with a curette or drill. The ossicular chain is palpated. If the stapes is fixed, it is separated from the incus. The stapes can be removed (stapedectomy) or an opening can be made in the stapes footplate with a laser or drill (stapedotomy). A prosthesis is placed on the incus to replace the stapes. A piece of fascia, vein, perichondrium, or fat might be applied around or under the prosthesis. The skin and eardrum are repositioned, and the ear canal is packed.

69661
The surgeon makes an incision in the posterior canal skin through the external canal opening. Occasionally, a postauricular incision may be substituted. Under microscopic guidance, the physician reflects the canal skin flap and posterior eardrum forward. Some posterior canal bone may be removed with a curette or drill. The ossicular chain is palpated. If the stapes is fixed, it is separated from the incus. The stapes is removed (stapedectomy). The physician drills an opening in the markedly thickened footplate through which the prosthesis is inserted and attached to the incus. A piece of fascia, vein, perichondrium, or fat might be applied around or under the prosthesis. The skin and eardrum are repositioned, and the ear canal is packed.

69662
The physician revises a stapedectomy or stapedotomy. The physician makes an incision over the previous incision site in the posterior canal or through the external canal opening. Alternately a previous postauricular incision may be reincised. Under microscopic guidance, the physician reflects the canal skin flap and posterior eardrum forward. Some posterior canal bone may be removed with a curette or drill. The ossicular chain is palpated. If the stapes has become fixed since the previous surgery it is separated from the incus. The footplate may be opened with a laser or drilled out. The prosthesis may be repositioned, revised, or removed and replaced. A piece of fascia, vein, perichondrium, or fat previously placed may be removed and replaced around or under the prosthesis. The skin and eardrum are repositioned, and the ear canal is packed.

69666
The physician makes a posterior canal incision through the external ear canal opening. Sometimes, a postauricular incision is performed instead. Under microscopic guidance, the physician reflects the skin flap and posterior eardrum forward. The oval window area is inspected for fluid leak from the inner ear. The lining around the oval window is gently roughened. The area is packed with fat, fascia or muscle tissue. The eardrum and skin flap are replaced and the canal is packed. If a postauricular incision is made, it is sutured.

69667
The physician makes a posterior canal incision through the external ear canal opening. Sometimes, a postauricular incision is performed instead. Under microscopic guidance, the physician reflects the skin flap and posterior eardrum forward. The round window area is inspected for fluid leak from the inner ear. The lining around the round window is gently roughened. The area is packed with fat, fascia or muscle tissue. The eardrum and skin flap are replaced

and the canal is packed. If a postauricular incision is made, it is sutured.

69670
Through a postauricular incision, the physician accesses the mastoid cavity of a previous mastoidectomy. Any remaining mastoid disease is removed. To lessen the size of a large mastoid cavity or to stop a cerebrospinal leak, the cavity is obliterated with a rotation flap of fascia or muscle and/or free fat graft and skin. The flap is sutured into place, and the incision is sutured.

69676
The physician makes an incision in the posterior canal wall skin and raises a skin flap and the eardrum forward. Jacobson's nerve is identified in the middle ear and is divided. The eardrum and canal skin are repositioned and packing is placed in the ear canal.

69700
The physician makes an incision around the postauricular fistula, a skin-lined tunnel. The fistula tract is excised, and the incision site is repaired with sutures.

69710
Through a postauricular incision, the physician drills a circular depression in the outer skull cortex behind the mastoid cavity. The internal coil is seated in the circular depression and secured to the skull with titanium screws. The subcutaneous tissue over the internal coil may be thinned. The wound is irrigated and repaired with sutures. A dressing is applied.

69711
Through a postauricular incision, the physician accesses a previously implanted electromagnetic bone conduction hearing device. The device is repaired or removed. The wound is irrigated and repaired with sutures. A dressing is applied.

69714-69715
The physician uses a percutaneous connector system based on a skin penetrating bone anchored titanium pedestal, housing a multichannel electrode array to implant a cochlear stimulating system. The physician makes a small break in the skin at the temporal bone and angles and places the stem of a titanium pedestal toward the cochlea, leaving a bridge of bone between it and the cortical mastoid. A tunnel is drilled to create a passage for the electrode array and the stem of the titanium pedestal is tapped into a tapered hole in the mastoid. The soft tissue surrounding the pedestal is thinned to prevent local movement and minimize the incidence of infection at the site. The internal collector plate of the pedestal holds platinum-iridium pins for the electrode array. The external collector plate, attached by a spring latching mechanism to the internal plate, contains a multielectrode array that provides a number of independent channels of stimulation. Report 69714 when the procedure is performed without mastoidectomy. Report 69715 when the physician drills out the mastoid cavity to remove diseased tissue.

69717-69718
Generally, titanium fixation plates are not removed after osteosynthesis because they have high biocompatibility and high corrosion resistance characteristics. However, various problems (i.e., improper electrode insertion or migration, device failure, serious flap complication) may require removal and replacement surgery of the osseointegrated implant. To remove the implant, the physician opens the skin at the temporal bone at the site of the original implant and removes any fibrous tissue sheathing the implant. The existing pedestal and electrode array are removed and replaced. Report 69717 when the procedure is performed without mastoidectomy. Report 69718 when the physician drills out the mastoid cavity to remove diseased tissue.

69720
Through a postauricular incision, the physician drills out the mastoid cavity. The sigmoid sinus is exposed posteriorly. The posterior ear canal wall remains intact. The horizontal semicircular canal and part of the incus are visualized. The vertical portion of the facial nerve is exposed. The facial recess is opened and the bone over the horizontal portion (middle ear) of the facial nerve is removed. The incus may be separated from the stapes. The incus and part of the malleus may be removed. The facial nerve sheath is incised from the stylomastoid foramen to the geniculate ganglion. The postauricular wound is sutured and a dressing is applied.

69725
Through a postauricular incision, the physician drills out the mastoid cavity. The sigmoid sinus is exposed posteriorly. The posterior ear canal wall remains intact. The horizontal semicircular canal and part of the incus are visualized. The vertical portion of the facial nerve is exposed. The facial recess is opened and the bone over the horizontal portion (middle ear) of the facial nerve is removed. Decompression continues medial to the geniculate ganglion. The incus and part of the malleus are usually removed. Sometimes, a combined transmastoid and middle fossa approach is required to access the nerve adequately, in which case, a piece of temporal bone is excised to access the middle cranial fossa.

69740
Through a postauricular incision, the physician drills out the mastoid cavity. The posterior ear canal wall remains intact. The horizontal semicircular canal and part of the incus are visualized. The vertical portion of the facial nerve is exposed. The facial recess is opened and the bone over the horizontal portion (middle ear) of the facial nerve is removed. The incus may be separated from the stapes. The incus and part of the malleus may be removed. The nerve defect is

identified, and the nerve is decompressed. Cut ends of the facial nerve are sutured to each other, or grafted to a harvested nerve in an end-to-end fashion. The postauricular wound is sutured and a dressing is applied.

69745
Through a postauricular incision, the physician drills out the mastoid cavity. The posterior ear canal wall remains intact. The horizontal semicircular canal and part of the incus are visualized. The vertical portion of the facial nerve is exposed. The facial recess is opened and the bone over the horizontal portion (middle ear) of the facial nerve is removed. The incus and part of the malleus are usually removed. The nerve defect is identified, and the nerve is decompressed. Cut ends of the facial nerve are sutured to each other, or grafted to a harvested nerve in an end-to-end fashion. Sometimes, a combined transmastoid and middle fossa approach is required to access the nerve adequately, in which case, a piece of temporal bone is excised to access the middle cranial fossa.

69801-69802
In a transcanal approach (69801), the physician makes an incision in the posterior ear canal skin through the external ear opening and reflects the skin flap and posterior tympanic membrane forward. For a mastoid approach (69802), the physician drills out the mastoid cavity. In either case, the posterior ear canal wall remains intact. The horizontal semicircular canal is visualized. Under microscopic guidance, a variety of procedures may be performed, including placement of a small, temporary or permanent tack through the stapes footplate; placement of a hook through the round window or ultrasonography or cryotherapy of the round window. In 69801, the canal is packed. In 69802, the mastoid cavity is packed and the incision is closed with sutures.

69805-69806
Through a postauricular incision, the physician drills out the mastoid cavity. The posterior ear canal wall remains intact. The horizontal and posterior semicircular canals are visualized. Drilling is continued until the endolymphatic sac is identified. The physician uses a diamond burr and fine picks to remove the bone around the sack (decompression) in 69805. A shunt is inserted into the sac in 69806. In either case, the mastoid cavity is packed with absorbable packing and the outer incision is sutured and a pressure dressing is applied.

69820
Through an endaural incision, the physical performs a partial mastoidectomy. The mastoid antrum and horizontal semicircular canal are identified. The posterior ear canal wall is removed down to the level of the facial nerve after elevating and protecting the posterior canal wall and eardrum. The incus and head of the malleus are removed. A small opening is created in the horizontal canal. The eardrum and canal skin are repositioned to cover the opening (fenestration). The mastoid is packed, the incision is repaired, and a dressing is placed.

69840
Through an endaural incision, the physician revises a previous fenestration of the lateral semicircular canal. The physician drills through the mastoid bone to reach the lateral semicircular canal. Additional canal bone is removed, leaving the inner membrane intact. The eardrum and canal skin are repositioned to cover the opening (fenestration). The mastoid is packed, the incision is repaired, and a dressing is placed.

69905
The physician makes an incision in the posterior canal skin and reflects the skin flap and posterior eardrum forward. Under microscopic visualization through the external ear opening, the incus and stapes are removed. A right angle hook is fed through the oval window to remove the contents of the vestibule. The physician may drill a connection between the oval and round windows. The middle ear is packed with gelatin foam. The eardrum and canal skin are repositioned, and the ear canal is packed.

69910
Through a postauricular incision, the physician drills out the mastoid cavity. The posterior ear canal wall remains intact. The horizontal, posterior, and superior semicircular canals are removed along with the lining of the labyrinth. The incision is repaired with sutures and a dressing is applied.

69915
Through a postauricular incision, the physician drills out the mastoid cavity. The posterior ear canal wall remains intact. The horizontal, posterior, and superior semicircular canals are removed along with the lining of the labyrinth. The internal auditory canal is identified. The bone over the internal auditory canal is removed, exposing the dura. The dura is opened and the vestibular nerve is identified and cut. The facial nerve is preserved. The dura is closed and the mastoid cavity is packed. The incision is repaired with sutures and a dressing is applied.

69930
The physician makes a U-shaped incision, creating a skin flap well behind the mastoid, and drills a circular depression in the squamous portion of the temporal bone in which the internal coil will be housed. The mastoid air cells are removed with a drill, and a facial recess approach is used. The bony ear canal is preserved. The internal coil is secured in the depressed area of the temporal bone, and the electrode is introduced through the facial recess and the round window into the cochlea. The ground wire attached to the internal coil is introduced into the temporalis muscle. The incision is sutured.

69950
A vertical incision is made just anterior to the auricle and is extended superiorly to expose the temporalis muscle. The muscle is divided. A section of the skull (craniotomy) is removed to expose the dura over the temporal lobe of the brain. The dura is elevated off the floor of the middle fossa. The physician drills to thin the bone over the floor of the middle fossa to identify the facial nerve. The facial nerve is followed to the internal auditory canal. The canal is decompressed with the drill and the dura covering the vestibular nerves is opened. The vestibular nerves are cut while preserving the facial and cochlear nerves. A muscle graft is placed over the internal auditory canal, and the bone is replaced in the skull defect. The incision is sutured and a dressing is applied.

69955
A vertical incision is made just anterior to the auricle and is extended superiorly to expose the temporalis muscle. The muscle is divided. A section of the skull (craniotomy) is removed to expose the dura over the temporal lobe of the brain. The dura is elevated off the floor of the middle fossa. The bone over the facial nerve is removed with the drill. If there is a tumor of the facial nerve, it is resected. If the nerve has been transected because of trauma, it is repaired with sutures. A nerve graft may be needed. A transmastoid approach may also be needed if extensive decompression is required. A muscle graft is placed over the floor of the middle cranial fossa. The bone plug is replaced in the skull defect. The incision is sutured and a dressing is applied.

69960
A vertical incision is made just anterior to the auricle and is extended superiorly to expose the temporalis muscle. The muscle is divided. A section of the skull (craniotomy) is removed to expose the dura over the temporal lobe of the brain. The dura is elevated off the floor of the middle fossa. The physician identifies the internal auditory canal. A drill is used to remove bone to open the canal (decompression). A muscle graft is placed over the internal auditory canal and the bone is replaced in the skull defect. The incision is sutured and a dressing is applied.

69970
A vertical incision is made just anterior to the auricle and is extended superiorly to expose the temporalis muscle. The muscle is divided. A section of the skull (craniotomy) is removed to expose the dura over the temporal lobe of the brain. The dura is elevated off the floor of the middle fossa. The physician isolates and dissects a tumor of the temporal bone. The internal auditory canal may be decompressed. A muscle graft is placed over the internal auditory canal. The bone plug is returned to the skull, the incision is sutured, and a dressing is applied.

69990
The physician uses a surgical microscope when the services are performed using the techniques of microsurgery, except when the microscopy is part of the procedure (such as in 15756). This code is reported in addition to the primary procedure.

Radiology

70010
A radiographic study using fluoroscopy is performed on the posterior fossa when a lesion is suspected, or to detect cerebrospinal fluid (CSF) leaks or normal pressure hydrocephalus (NPH). Contrast medium, usually barium sulfate, may be used to enhance visibility and is instilled in the patient through a lumbar area puncture into the subarachnoid space. The radiologist takes a series of pictures by sending an x-ray beam through the body, using fluoroscopy to view the enhanced structure on a television camera. The patient is angled from an erect position through a recumbent position with the body tilted so as to maintain feet higher than the head to help the flow of contrast into the study area.

70015
A radiographic study is performed that maps the tumor pathology of a mass within the posterior fossa. The brainstem and cerebellum are contained within the posterior fossa and the cerebellopontine angle cistern is often the location of a mass, such as a schwannoma or meningioma. Images are taken sequentially over a period of hours and days after introducing a radiotracer intrathecally by lumbar puncture. Cisternography may also be used to detect cerebrospinal fluid (CSF) leaks or normal pressure hydrocephalus (NPH).

70030
X-rays of the eyes are obtained to determine the location of a foreign body in the eye. After positioning the patient, a one- or two-view x-ray is obtained. Transparent objects such as glass may not be good candidates for x-ray visualization. The physician supervises the procedure and interprets and reports the findings.

70100-70110
The lower jaw bone is x-rayed. In 70100, three or less projections are taken for a partial view of the bone structure and in 70110, four or more projections are taken for a complete view of the bone structure.

70120
Films are taken of the mastoid processes, or lower portion of the temporal bone of the skull, which protrudes just behind the ear. Both mastoid processes are always examined for comparison purposes, and it is essential that the radiographs be exact duplicates in both positioning of the site and technical quality. Several varying views may be taken, but the key

element of this procedure is that it reports less than three views per side.

70130
Films are taken of the mastoid processes, or lower portion of the temporal bone of the skull, which protrudes just behind the ear. Both mastoid processes are always examined for comparison purposes, and it is essential that the radiographs be exact duplicates in both positioning of the site and technical quality. Several varying views may be taken, but the key element of this procedure is that it reports a complete exam, or minimum of three views per side.

70134
Films are taken of the petrous portions of the skull to demonstrate internal auditory meati, or organs of hearing. Several different views may be taken, both with varying angulation of the x-ray beam, as well as varying the position of the patient's skull.

70140
X-rays of the facial bones are obtained to determine an injury, fracture, or neoplasm. After positioning the patient, less than three views of the facial bones are obtained. The physician supervises the procedure and interprets and reports the findings.

70150
X-rays of the facial bones are obtained to determine an injury, fracture, or neoplasm. After positioning the patient, a complete series of x-rays of the facial bones, with a minimum of three views, is obtained. The physician supervises the procedure and interprets and reports the findings.

70160
Films are taken of the nasal bones to include a complete exam, or minimum of three views. Typically, this exam would consist of both right and left lateral (side to side) for comparison, as well as a tangential projection in which the x-ray beam is directed from a position above the patient's head down through the nose. This view is primarily used to demonstrate the medial or lateral (side to side) displacement of nasal fractures.

70170
Dacryocystography is the radiographic evaluation of the lacrimal system to localize the site of an obstruction. One cc of a water-soluble contrast medium is injected through the lower canaliculus and x-rays of the excretory system are obtained. The physician supervises the procedure and interprets and reports the findings.

70190
Radiological examination of the optic foramina is useful in the evaluation of trauma, tumors, or foreign bodies. After positioning the patient, the radiologist obtains x-rays of the optic foramina. The physician supervises the procedure and interprets and reports the findings.

70200
Radiological examination of the orbits is useful in the evaluation of trauma, tumors, or foreign bodies. After positioning the patient, the radiologist obtains a minimum of four x-ray views of the orbits. Standard methods include posteroanterior (PA) exposures from two different positions, lateral views, optic canal projections, and oblique views of each side for comparison. The physician supervises the procedure and interprets and reports the findings.

70210
Films are taken of the paranasal sinuses in one or two views. Although there are several sinus projections, each serving a specific purpose, many of them are used only when required to visualize a specific lesion. Typically, but not necessarily, this code would call for a side to side (lateral) view and a back to front (PA) view, depending on the specific sinus in question. The projections are routinely taken with the patient in an erect position to demonstrate presence or absence of fluid.

70220
Films are taken of the paranasal sinuses for a complete study, with a minimum of three views. There are several sinus projections used when required to visualize a specific lesion. Projections routinely taken consist of four to five standard views of the skull, which adequately demonstrate all of the paranasal sinuses on a majority of patients. Specific exams may be included to test a particular sinus, e.g., frontal sinus, maxillary sinus, and sphenoid or ethmoid sinuses. These projections are routinely taken with the patient in an erect position to demonstrate presence or absence of fluid.

70240
Films are taken of the sella turcica, the depression within the sphenoid bone that houses the pituitary gland. The patient is placed in the prone semioblique position and the x-ray beam is directed to a spot slightly anterior and superior to the external auditory meatus while the patient's head is maintained in a lateral position.

70250-70260
Films are taken of the skull bones. In 70250, three or less views are taken, and in 70260, a complete exam with a four view minimum is performed. The most common projections for routine skull series are AP axial (front to back), lateral, and PA axial (back to front). X-rays may be taken with the patient placed erect, prone, or supine and either code may include stereoradiography, which is a technique that produces three-dimensional images.

70300-70320
Films are taken of the mouth to show teeth and/or surrounding bone. In dental radiography, the film may be placed inside or outside the mouth. Code 70300 reports a single view only, 70310 reports a partial examination, and 70320 reports a complete full mouth exam.

70328-70330
The temporomandibular joint is x-rayed in two projections on one side only in 70328 and in two projections on both sides in 70330. One film is taken with the mouth open and one with the mouth closed.

70332
A radiographic contrast study is performed on the temporomandibular joint. A contrast material is injected into the joint spaces, followed by x-ray examination of the joint. This allows the physician to see the position of the structures not normally seen on conventional x-rays.

70336
Magnetic resonance imaging (MRI) is a radiation-free, noninvasive, technique to produce high quality sectional images of the inside of the body in multiple planes. MRI uses the natural magnetic properties of the hydrogen atoms in our bodies that emit radiofrequency signals when exposed to radio waves within a strong electro-magnetic field. These signals are processed and converted by the computer into high-resolution, three-dimensional, tomographic images. Patients with metallic or electronic implants or foreign bodies cannot be exposed to MRI. The patient must remain still while lying on a motorized table within the large, circular MRI tunnel. A sedative may be administered as well as contrast material for image enhancement. This code reports an exam of the temporomandibular joint(s).

70350
A lateral or frontal x-ray projection is taken to examine the skull, jaw, and related tooth positions. The machine holds the patient's head in the same position each time so that a series of cephalograms can be directly compared for growth and development over time.

70355
A panoramic radiographic study is performed on the mandibular arch and its supporting structures. A single image is produced of the mandible for diagnostic purposes. The physician evaluates trauma, third molar, and other unique disease conditions. Tooth development and anomalies may also be studied.

70360
The technologist uses x-rays to obtain soft tissue images of the patient's neck rather than bone. The radiologist obtains two views, typically front to back (AP), and side to side (lateral). This procedure is performed to visualize abnormal air patterns or suspected foreign bodies or obstructions within the throat or neck.

70370
A radiologic examination is performed to visualize the pharynx, which serves as passage for both food and air, and larynx, or the organ of voice. Films are typically taken to show soft tissues of the neck. The films are often taken while the patient inhales or makes phonetic sounds. The key element of this code is that it includes x-ray fluoroscopy and/or magnification technique in addition to the radiologic exam.

70371
A radiologic study is performed for pharyngeal and speech evaluation. Cineradiography, or video recording, is employed, as the physiologic event of speech and swallowing occur too rapidly for normal fluoroscopic viewing. High-speed frame rates are used to evaluate speech and swallowing, and later reviewed and interpreted by the radiologist.

70373
A radiographic contrast study is performed of the larynx, or organ of voice. Iodized oil is given in conjunction with the examination via tubing, which allows oil to drip down the patient's throat at the radiologist's discretion. The radiologist, via x-ray fluoroscopy, simultaneously watches the image amplified and displayed on a TV monitor. Rapid film sequencing must be used to record the image, which may be studied and interpreted by the radiologist.

70380
Films are taken to visualize a salivary gland for possible calculus (calcium deposit). Typically, a front to back (AP) or back to front (PA) view is taken of the side in question. The patient is asked to fill his cheek with air, if possible, to enhance detail of the x-ray, particularly for demonstration of calcific deposits. A lateral, or side to side view, as well as an intra-oral projection, may also be taken.

70390
A radiographic contrast study is performed to visualize the salivary glands and ducts, typically to demonstrate possible lesions or tumors, salivary fistulae, or to localize calcium deposits within the gland. The radiologist injects the main salivary duct with radiopaque dye (contrast), after which it flows into the duct system and is examined with x-ray fluoroscopy. The projected image is amplified and displayed on a TV monitor for the radiologist to review and interpret.

70450-70470
Computed tomography directs multiple narrow beams of x-rays around the body structure being studied and uses computer imaging to produce thin cross-sectional views of various layers (or slices) of the body. It is useful for the evaluation of trauma, tumor, and foreign bodies as CT is able to visualize soft tissue as well as bones. Patients are required to remain motionless during the study and sedation may need to be administered as well as a contrast medium for image

enhancement. These codes report an exam of the head or brain. Report 70450 if no contrast is used. Report 70460 if performed with contrast and 70470 if performed first without contrast and again following the injection of contrast.

70480-70482
Computed tomography directs multiple narrow beams of x-rays around the body structure being studied and uses computer imaging to produce thin cross-sectional views of various layers (or slices) of the body. It is useful for the evaluation of trauma, tumor, and foreign bodies as CT is able to visualize soft tissue as well as bones. Patients are required to remain motionless during the study and sedation may need to be administered as well as a contrast medium for image enhancement. These codes report an exam of the orbit, sella, posterior fossa, or outer, middle, or inner ear. Report 70480 if no contrast is used. Report 70481 if performed with contrast and 70482 if performed first without contrast and again following the injection of contrast.

70486-70488
Computed tomography directs multiple narrow beams of x-rays around the body structure being studied and uses computer imaging to produce thin cross-sectional views of various layers (or slices) of the body. It is useful for the evaluation of trauma, tumor, and foreign bodies as CT is able to visualize soft tissue as well as bones. Patients are required to remain motionless during the study and sedation may need to be administered as well as a contrast medium for image enhancement. These codes report an exam of the maxillofacial area. Report 70486 if no contrast is used. Report 70487 if performed with contrast and 70488 if performed first without contrast and again following the injection of contrast.

70490-70492
Computed tomography directs multiple narrow beams of x-rays around the body structure being studied and uses computer imaging to produce thin cross-sectional views of various layers (or slices) of the body. It is useful for the evaluation of trauma, tumor, and foreign bodies as CT is able to visualize soft tissue as well as bones. Patients are required to remain motionless during the study and sedation may need to be administered as well as a contrast medium for image enhancement. These codes report an exam of the soft tissue of the neck. Report 70490 if no contrast is used. Report 70491 if performed with contrast and 70492 if performed first without contrast and again following the injection of contrast.

70496-70498
Computed tomographic angiography (CTA) is a procedure used for the imaging of vessels to detect aneurysms, blood clots, and other vascular irregularities. Contrast medium is rapidly infused intravenously, at intervals, usually with an automatic injector, and the patient is scanned with thin section axial or spiral mode x-ray beams. The images obtained are acquired with narrower collimation and reconstructed at shorter intervals than standard CT images. Three-dimensional images are generated and postprocessing reconstruction is done at a workstation on the scanner. CTA also provides information unavailable with conventional angiography, such as vessel wall thickness (mural thrombus) and the venous anatomy of a target organ and/or associated organs within the scan range. Report 70496 for an exam of the head and 70498 for an exam of the neck. These codes report exams with contrast materials and image postprocessing. Noncontrast images, if performed, are also included in these procedures.

70540-70543
Magnetic resonance imaging (MRI) is a radiation-free, noninvasive technique to produce high-quality sectional images of the inside of the body in multiple planes. MRI uses the natural magnetic properties of the hydrogen atoms in our bodies that emit radiofrequency signals when exposed to radio waves within a strong electromagnetic field. These signals are processed and converted by the computer into high-resolution, three-dimensional, tomographic images. Patients with metallic or electronic implants or foreign bodies cannot be exposed to MRI. The patient must remain still while lying on a motorized table within the large, circular MRI tunnel. A sedative may be administered, as well as contrast material for image enhancement. These codes report an exam of the orbit, face, or neck, or any combination of these. Report 70540 if no contrast is used; 70542 if performed with contrast; and 70543 if performed first without contrast and again following the injection of contrast.

70544-70546
Magnetic resonance angiography (MRA) is magnetic resonance imaging (MRI) that specifically visualizes blood vessels and blood flow to evaluate vascular disorders within the structure being studied. Unlike CT, it does not rely on the absorption of x-ray energy. Magnetic resonance imaging uses the natural magnetic properties of the hydrogen atoms in our bodies that emit radiofrequency signals when exposed to radio waves within a strong electro-magnetic field. These signals are processed and converted by the computer into high-resolution, three-dimensional tomographic images. Patients with metallic or electronic implants or foreign bodies cannot be exposed to MRI. The patient must remain still while lying on a motorized table within the large, circular MRI tunnel. A sedative may be administered as well as contrast material for image enhancement. These codes report an exam of the head. Report 70544 if no contrast is used. Report 70545 if performed with contrast and 70546 if performed first without contrast and again following the injection of contrast.

70547-70549
Magnetic resonance angiography (MRA) is a special type of magnetic resonance imaging (MRI) that specifically visualizes blood vessels and blood flow to evaluate vascular disorders within the structure being studied. Unlike CT, it does not rely on the absorption of x-ray energy. Magnetic resonance imaging uses the natural magnetic properties of the hydrogen atoms in our bodies that emit radiofrequency signals when exposed to radio waves within a strong electro-magnetic field. These signals are processed and converted by the computer into high-resolution, three-dimensional tomographic images. Patients with metallic or electronic implants or foreign bodies cannot be exposed to MRI. The patient must remain still while lying on a motorized table within the large, circular MRI tunnel. A sedative may be administered as well as contrast material for image enhancement. These codes report and exam of the neck. Report 70547 if no contrast is used. Report 70548 if performed with contrast and 70549 if performed first without contrast and again following the injection of contrast.

70551-70553
Magnetic resonance imaging (MRI) is a radiation-free, noninvasive, technique to produce high quality sectional images of the inside of the body in multiple planes. MRI uses the natural magnetic properties of the hydrogen atoms in our bodies that emit radiofrequency signals when exposed to radio waves within a strong electro-magnetic field. These signals are processed and converted by the computer into high-resolution, three-dimensional, tomographic images. Patients with metallic or electronic implants or foreign bodies cannot be exposed to MRI. The patient must remain still while lying on a motorized table within the large, circular MRI tunnel. A sedative may be administered as well as contrast material for image enhancement. These codes report an exam of the brain, including the brain stem. Report 70551 if no contrast is used. Report 70552 if performed with contrast and 70553 if performed first without contrast and again following the injection of contrast.

70554-70555
Functional magnetic resonance imaging (fMRI) captures metabolic changes in the working brain using progressive magnetic resonance imaging (MRI). MRI is a radiation-free, noninvasive technique to produce high-quality sectional images of the inside of the body in multiple planes. MRI uses the natural magnetic properties of the hydrogen atoms in our bodies that emit radiofrequency signals when exposed to radio waves within a strong electromagnetic field. These signals are processed and converted by the computer into high-resolution, three-dimensional, tomographic images. In fMRI, the patient's head is immobilized by a brace and the patient's table is placed in the MRI machine. The clinician asks the patient to perform small tasks that can be accomplished in the confined setting of the MRI equipment. Images are recorded while the patient is at rest and a series of progressive images is taken when a task is being performed. These images are analyzed to determine the effect of the task upon brain function. Report 70554 for repetitive testing without a physician or psychologist and 70555 when the entire test is performed by a physician or psychologist.

70557-70559
Magnetic resonance imaging (MRI) is a radiation-free, noninvasive technique to produce high quality sectional images of the inside of the body in multiple planes. MRI uses the natural magnetic properties of the hydrogen atoms in our bodies that emit radiofrequency signals when exposed to radio waves within a strong electro-magnetic field. These signals are processed and converted by the computer into high-resolution, three-dimensional, tomographic images. Patients with metallic or electronic implants or foreign bodies cannot be exposed to MRI. These codes report an exam of the brain, including the brain stem and skull base, performed during an open intracranial procedure to look for residual tumor tissue or vascular malformation. Report 70557 if no contrast is used; 70558 if the MRI imaging is performed with contrast; and 70559 if during surgery, the MRI is performed first without contrast and again following the injection of contrast.

71010
A radiograph is taken of the patient's chest from front to back (AP). Typically, this is done when the patient is too ill to stand or be turned to the prone position. The key element of this code is that it reports a single, frontal view.

71015
A stereoradiograph is taken of the patient's chest from the frontal view. Stereoradiography is a technique that produces the image in three dimensions for viewing.

71020
Films are taken of the patient's chest to include a frontal and side to side (lateral) view. This code specifically reports these two views.

71021
Films are taken of the patient's chest with the patient placed in a side to side (lateral) position, as well as a standard front to back position (AP). Another front to back (AP) film is also taken with the patient leaning back resting shoulders against the wall/film tray in a lordotic (arched back) position. This projection produces x-rays that demonstrate the top, or apices, of the lungs.

71022
Radiographs are taken of the patient's chest with the patient in a standard front to back (AP) position, as well as side to side (laterally). In addition, right and left obliques, or angled views, are taken. The key element

of this code is that it reports specifically frontal, lateral, and oblique views.

71023
Films are taken of the patient's chest, which include a frontal and side to side (lateral) view, using fluoroscopy to follow an opaque medium as it is swallowed. The patient holds the cup of contrast medium and swallows as directed, during or immediately before exposure. Frontal and lateral views are taken, both of which require the patient to be erect or recumbent. For the lateral view, the arms must be placed over the head.

71030
Films are taken of the patient's chest, specifically a complete exam, with a minimum of four views. Typically, this would include a back to front (PA), side to side (lateral), and right and left obliques, but may include any number of specialized projections, e.g., axial (angulated) views or lateral decubitus views for fluid levels.

71034
Films are taken of the patient's chest to make a complete exam with four or more views, using fluoroscopy to follow an opaque medium as it is swallowed. The patient holds the cup of contrast medium and swallows as directed, during or immediately before exposure. Contrast medium, usually barium sulfate, enhances visibility of internal organs, such as the esophagus and stomach. The radiologist takes a series of pictures by sending an x-ray beam through the body, using fluoroscopy to view the enhanced structures on a television camera.

71035
Radiographs are taken of the patient's chest. This code reports special views, but does not specify number of films allowed. Specific examples may include Bucky studies and/or lateral decubitus studies, wherein the patient is prone or supine and the x-ray beam is directed through the side of the chest. This lateral projection shows change in position of fluid and reveals areas that are obscured by the fluid in standard, upright projections.

71040-71060
In bronchography, x-rays are taken of the bronchial tree and the trachea to locate obstructions. The patient is place supine and administered a local anesthetic. A catheter is threaded down the windpipe after being introduced through the nose or mouth. More anesthesia and the contrast medium are administered through the catheter and the x-rays are taken. In 71040, unilateral pictures are taken and in 71060, both right and left sides are viewed.

71090
A pacemaker is inserted in the chest under fluoroscopy and radiography. An incision is made in the chest below the collarbone to create a pocket under the skin. The wire(s), called lead(s), of the pacemaker are threaded through a vein and placed in the right atrium or right ventricle, using fluoroscopy to visually guide the wires for correct placement. The lead(s) is attached to the heart chamber on the inside surface (endocardial) and the generator is inserted into the pocket created under the collarbone. Leads may also be implanted on the outer heart surface (epicardial) and the generator inserted in a pocket created in the upper abdomen in cases of congenital heart disease. This code reports the fluoroscopy, radiography, radiological supervision and interpretation for a pacemaker insertion.

71100
Films are taken unilaterally of the affected side of the ribs with two views in AP (front to back) or PA (back to front) views.

71101
Films are taken unilaterally of the affected side of the ribs for a minimum of three views, including the posterior ribs.

71110
Films are taken bilaterally of the ribs for three views of the ribcage, with the patient placed supine and the x-ray directed at the thorax midpoint, above or below the xiphoid process for a bilateral view.

71111
A minimum of four films are taken bilaterally of the ribcage, including the posterior ribs, with the patient placed supine for AP and PA views and the x-ray directed at the thorax midpoint, above or below the xiphoid process for a bilateral view.

71120
Films are taken of the sternum with a minimum of two views from an anterior oblique and lateral position.

71130
Films are taken of the sternoclavicular joint or joints with a minimum of three views from posteroanterior and oblique projections.

71250-71270
Computed tomography directs multiple narrow beams of x-rays around the body structure being studied and uses computer imaging to produce thin cross-sectional views of various layers (or slices) of the body. It is useful for the evaluation of trauma, tumor, and foreign bodies as CT is able to visualize soft tissue as well as bones. Patients are required to remain motionless during the study and sedation may need to be administered as well as a contrast medium for image enhancement. These codes report an exam of the thorax. Report 71250 if no contrast is used. Report 71260 if performed with contrast and 71270 if performed first without contrast and again following the injection of contrast.

71275
Computed tomographic angiography (CTA) is a procedure used for the imaging of vessels to detect aneurysms, blood clots, and other vascular irregularities, excluding the heart. Contrast medium is rapidly infused intravenously, at intervals, usually with an automatic injector, and the patient is scanned with thin section axial or spiral mode x-ray beams. The images obtained are acquired with narrower collimation and reconstructed at shorter intervals than standard CT images. Three-dimensional images are generated and postprocessing reconstruction is done at a workstation on the scanner. CTA provides information unavailable with conventional angiography, such as vessel wall thickness (mural thrombus) and the venous anatomy of the target organ. This code reports an exam of the chest with contrast materials and image postprocessing. Noncontrast images, if performed, are also included in this procedure.

71550-71552
Magnetic resonance imaging (MRI) is a radiation-free, noninvasive, technique to produce high quality sectional images of the inside of the body in multiple planes. MRI uses the natural magnetic properties of the hydrogen atoms in our bodies that emit radiofrequency signals when exposed to radio waves within a strong electro-magnetic field. These signals are processed and converted by the computer into high-resolution, three-dimensional, tomographic images. Patients with metallic or electronic implants or foreign bodies cannot be exposed to MRI. The patient must remain still while lying on a motorized table within the large, circular MRI tunnel. A sedative may be administered as well as contrast material for image enhancement. These codes report an exam of the chest. Report 71550 if no contrast is used. Report 71551 if performed with contrast and 71552 if performed first without contrast and again following the injection of contrast.

71555
Magnetic resonance angiography (MRA) is magnetic resonance imaging (MRI) that specifically visualizes blood vessels and blood flow to evaluate vascular disorders within the structure being studied. Unlike CT, it does not rely on the absorption of x-ray energy. Magnetic resonance imaging uses the natural magnetic properties of the hydrogen atoms in our bodies that emit radiofrequency signals when exposed to radio waves within a strong electro-magnetic field. These signals are processed and converted by the computer into high-resolution, three-dimensional tomographic images. Patients with metallic or electronic implants or foreign bodies cannot be exposed to MRI. The patient must remain still while lying on a motorized table within the large, circular MRI tunnel. A sedative may be administered as well as contrast material for image enhancement. This code reports an exam of the chest.

72010
The entire spine is surveyed in a radiologic exam that includes anteroposterior views, with the patient supine, knees flexed, and feet flat on the table; and lateral views, recumbent or erect. Right and left posterior obliques may be performed with the patient in the semi-supine position with the spine at a 45 degree angle to the table.

72020
One film is taken of the spine that requires specification of the level examined.

72040-72052
A radiologic examination of the cervical spine is performed that includes a minimum of two views in 72040, a minimum of four views in 72050, and a complete study in 72052. The complete study includes films taken in oblique (angled) positions and in flexion and/or extension positioning.

72069
Typically a film is taken of the thoracolumbar spine from front to back (AP) while the patient is standing erect. This film is used to detect any curvature of the spine when scoliosis or other pathology may be present.

72070-72074
A radiologic examination of the thoracic spine is performed that includes two views in 72070, three views in 72072, and a minimum of four views in 72074. These procedures do not specify that a certain view must be performed.

72080
Films are taken of the thoracolumbar area of the spine in two views not specifically stated.

72090
A typical scoliosis series consists of four views of the thoracic and lumbar spine: one from front to back (AP) with the patient standing; one from front to back (AP) with the patient supine, or lying down; and finally, two views with alternate right and left flexion in the supine position. In addition, a lateral, or side to side projection made with the patient standing to show spondylolisthesis or to demonstrate exaggerated degrees of kyphosis or lordosis is often recommended. The key element to this code is that it includes supine and erect studies. The number of films allowed is not specified.

72100-72110
A radiologic examination of the lumbosacral spine is performed that includes two or three views in 72100, and a minimum of four views in 72110. These procedures do not specify that a certain view must be performed.

72114
Films are taken of the lumbosacral spine, or lower back, for a complete radiologic study. A complete

lumbar spine series typically includes x-rays taken from front to back (AP), side to side (lateral), and oblique, or angled right and left views. In addition, this code includes bending views, films taken with the patient bending to the left and right to demonstrate mobility of the intervertebral joints, and/or films taken with the patient in both flexion and extension, typically in cases of disc protrusion to localize the involved joint.

72120

Films are taken of the lumbar spine, or lower back, with the patient bending to the left and right to demonstrate the mobility of the intervertebral joints and/or films with the patient in both flexion and extension, typically in cases of disc protrusion to localize the involved joint. The key element to this code is that a minimum of four films in bending views only are taken.

72125-72127

Computed tomography directs multiple narrow beams of x-rays around the body structure being studied and uses computer imaging to produce thin cross-sectional views of various layers (or slices) of the body. It is useful for the evaluation of trauma, tumor, and foreign bodies as CT is able to visualize soft tissue as well as bones. Patients are required to remain motionless during the study and sedation may need to be administered. These codes report an exam of the cervical spine. For CT of the spine, contrast material may be administered intravenously (part of the procedure)or intrathecally (reported separately). These codes report and exam of the cervical spine. Report 72125 if no contrast is used. Report 72126 if performed with contrast and 72127 if performed first without contrast and again following the injection of contrast.

72128-72130

Computed tomography directs multiple narrow beams of x-rays around the body structure being studied and uses computer imaging to produce thin cross-sectional views of various layers (or slices) of the body. It is useful for the evaluation of trauma, tumor, and foreign bodies as CT is able to visualize soft tissue as well as bones. Patients are required to remain motionless during the study and sedation may need to be administered. These codes report an exam of the thoracic spine. For CT of the spine, contrast material may be administered intravenously (part of the procedure)or intrathecally (reported separately). These codes report an exam of the thoracic spine. Report 72128 if no contrast is used. Report 72129 if performed with contrast and 72130 if performed first without contrast and again following the injection of contrast.

72131-72133

Computed tomography directs multiple thin beams of x-rays at the body structure being studied and uses computer imaging to produce thin cross-sectional views of various layers (or slices) of the body. It is useful for the evaluation of trauma, tumor, and foreign bodies as CT is able to visualize soft tissue as well as bones. Patients are required to remain motionless during the study and sedation may need to be administered. These codes report an exam of the lumbar spine. For CT of the spine, contrast material may be administered intravenously (part of the procedure)or intrathecally (reported separately). These codes report an exam of the lumbar spine. Report 72131 if no contrast is used. Report 72132 if performed with contrast and 72133 if performed first without contrast and again following the injection of contrast.

72141-72142, 72156

Magnetic resonance imaging (MRI) is a radiation-free, noninvasive, technique to produce high quality sectional images of the inside of the body in multiple planes. MRI uses the natural magnetic properties of the hydrogen atoms in our bodies that emit radiofrequency signals when exposed to radio waves within a strong electro-magnetic field. These signals are processed and converted by the computer into high-resolution, three-dimensional, tomographic images. Patients with metallic or electronic implants or foreign bodies cannot be exposed to MRI. The patient must remain still while lying on a motorized table within the large, circular MRI tunnel. A sedative may be administered as well as contrast material for image enhancement. For cervical spinal canal and contents, report 72141 if no contrast is used; report 72142 if performed with contrast and 72156 if performed first without contrast and again following the injection of contrast.

72146-72147, 72157

Magnetic resonance imaging (MRI) is a radiation-free, noninvasive, technique to produce high quality sectional images of the inside of the body in multiple planes. MRI uses the natural magnetic properties of the hydrogen atoms in our bodies that emit radiofrequency signals when exposed to radio waves within a strong electro-magnetic field. These signals are processed and converted by the computer into high-resolution, three-dimensional, tomographic images. Patients with metallic or electronic implants or foreign bodies cannot be exposed to MRI. The patient must remain still while lying on a motorized table within the large, circular MRI tunnel. A sedative may be administered as well as contrast material for image enhancement. For thoracic spinal canal and contents, report 72146 if no contrast is used; report 72147 if performed with contrast and 72157 if performed first without contrast and again following the injection of contrast.

72148-72149, 72158

Magnetic resonance imaging (MRI) is a radiation-free, noninvasive, technique to produce high quality sectional images of the inside of the body in multiple planes. MRI uses the natural magnetic properties of the hydrogen atoms in our bodies that emit radiofrequency signals when exposed to radio waves within a strong electro-magnetic field. These signals are processed and converted by the computer into high-resolution, three-dimensional, tomographic images. Patients with metallic or electronic implants or foreign bodies cannot be exposed to MRI. The patient must remain still while lying on a motorized table within the large, circular MRI tunnel. A sedative may be administered as well as contrast material for image enhancement. For lumbar spinal canal and contents, report 72148 if no contrast is used; report 72149 if performed with contrast and 72158 if performed first without contrast and again following the injection of contrast.

72159
Magnetic resonance angiography (MRA) is magnetic resonance imaging (MRI) that specifically visualizes blood vessels and blood flow to evaluate vascular disorders within the structure being studied. Unlike CT, it does not rely on the absorption of x-ray energy. Magnetic resonance imaging uses the natural magnetic properties of the hydrogen atoms in our bodies that emit radiofrequency signals when exposed to radio waves within a strong electro-magnetic field. These signals are processed and converted by the computer into high-resolution, three-dimensional tomographic images. Patients with metallic or electronic implants or foreign bodies cannot be exposed to MRI. The patient must remain still while lying on a motorized table within the large, circular MRI tunnel. A sedative may be administered as well as contrast material for image enhancement. This code reports an exam of the spinal canal and contents.

72170
One or two views are taken of the pelvis. The most common view is from front to back (AP) with the patient lying supine with feet inverted 15 degrees to overcome the anteversion (or rotation) of the femoral necks. The pelvic girdle, femoral head, neck, trochanters, and upper femurs are also shown.

72190
A minimum of three films are taken of the pelvis, typically front to back (AP) with the patient lying supine. The patient's legs are placed in what is termed a "frogleg" lateral position, wherein the patient's feet are drawn up toward the buttocks, at which point the knees are allowed to drop down to the table with feet together. A third film may be taken with the patient lying on his or her side for a lateral view of the pelvis, as well as unilateral views of the hips, if necessary.

72191
Computed tomographic angiography (CTA) of the pelvis is performed with contrast materials and image postprocessing. CTA produces images of vessels to detect aneurysms, blood clots, and other vascular irregularities. Contrast medium is rapidly infused intravenously, at intervals, usually with an automatic injector, and the patient is scanned with thin section axial or spiral mode x-ray beams. The images are acquired with narrower collimation and reconstructed at shorter intervals than standard CT images. Three-dimensional images are generated and postprocessing reconstruction is done at a workstation on the scanner. CTA also provides information unavailable with conventional angiography, such as vessel wall thickness (mural thrombus) and the venous anatomy of a target organ and/or associated organs within the scan range. Noncontrast images, if performed, are also included in this procedure.

72192-72194
Computed tomography directs multiple narrow beams of x-rays around the body structure being studied and uses computer imaging to produce thin cross-sectional views of various layers (or slices) of the body. It is useful for the evaluation of trauma, tumor, and foreign bodies as CT is able to visualize soft tissue as well as bones. Patients are required to remain motionless during the study and sedation may need to be administered as well as a contrast medium for image enhancement. These codes report an exam of the pelvis. Report 72192 if no contrast is used. Report 72193 if performed with contrast and 72194 if performed first without contrast and again following the injection of contrast.

72195-72197
Magnetic resonance imaging (MRI) is a radiation-free, noninvasive, technique to produce high quality sectional images of the inside of the body in multiple planes. MRI uses the natural magnetic properties of the hydrogen atoms in our bodies that emit radiofrequency signals when exposed to radio waves within a strong electro-magnetic field. These signals are processed and converted by the computer into high-resolution, three-dimensional, tomographic images. Patients with metallic or electronic implants or foreign bodies cannot be exposed to MRI. The patient must remain still while lying on a motorized table within the large, circular MRI tunnel. A sedative may be administered as well as contrast material for image enhancement. These codes report an exam of the pelvis. Report 72195 if no contrast is used. Report 72196 if performed with contrast and 72197 if performed first without contrast and again following the injection of contrast.

72198
Magnetic resonance angiography (MRA) is magnetic resonance imaging (MRI) that specifically visualizes blood vessels and blood flow to evaluate vascular disorders within the structure being studied. Unlike CT, it does not rely on the absorption of x-ray energy. Magnetic resonance imaging uses the natural magnetic properties of the hydrogen atoms in our bodies that emit radiofrequency signals when exposed to radio waves within a strong electro-magnetic field. These

signals are processed and converted by the computer into high-resolution, three-dimensional tomographic images. Patients with metallic or electronic implants or foreign bodies cannot be exposed to MRI. The patient must remain still while lying on a motorized table within the large, circular MRI tunnel. A sedative may be administered as well as contrast material for image enhancement. This code reports an exam of the pelvis.

72200-72202
Films are taken of the articulation between the sacrum, the triangular bone beneath the lumbar vertebrae, and the ilium, or upper portion of the hip bone. The exam may be performed in both anteroposterior and right and left posterior oblique views. Code 72200 reports one or two views and 72202 reports three or more views.

72220
Films are taken (minimum of two views) of the sacrum and the coccyx. The sacrum is a triangular bone located between the fifth lumbar vertebra and the coccyx. It is formed by five connected vertebrae and is wedged between the two innominate bones. The coccyx is the small bone at the very base of the spinal column, and is formed by the fusion of four vertebrae. The sacrum and the coccyx form the posterior (back) boundary of the pelvis. While anteroposterior (AP; front to back) and lateral (side) views are the most common views taken, this procedure is used for any two or more views reported.

72240-72270
In myelography, a radiographic study using fluoroscopy is performed on the spinal cord and nerve root branches when a lesion is suspected. A nonionic water-soluble radiopaque contrast media is used to enhance visibility and is instilled in the patient through a lumbar or cervical area puncture into the subarachnoid space. The radiologist takes a series of pictures by sending an x-ray beam through the body, using fluoroscopy to view the enhanced structure on a television camera. The patient is angled from an erect position through a recumbent position with the body tilted so as to maintain feet higher than the head to help the flow of contrast into the study area. Code 72240 reports a cervical myelogram; 72255 reports a thoracic myelogram; 72265 reports lumbosacral myelogram; and 72270 reports a myelogram of two or more regions, such as lumbar/thoracic, cervical/ thoracic or lumbar/thoracic/cervical.

72275
A radiologic imaging examination is performed on the veins lining the spinal canal. Contrast is injected into the epidural space under direct fluoroscopy. Examining the flow of contrast in the epidural space around the nerves to be studied aids in the diagnosis of intervertebral disc herniations, narrowing and swelling around the nerve and/or nerve roots, and compressive lesions.

72285,72295
Individual intervertebral discs are imaged and examined in discography, also known as nucleography. Iodinated contrast medium is injected into the center of the disc. A series of images is taken by the radiologist and interpreted and reported. This technique is used to determine the extent of the target disc(s) disease. Report 72285 for the cervical or thoracic discs and 72295 for the lumbar discs.

72291-72292
These codes report the radiological supervision and interpretation for percutaneous vertebroplasty, vertebral augmentation, or sacroplasty (sacral augmentation), per vertebral body or sacrum. Percutaneous vertebroplasty is the injection of polymethyl methacrylate into collapsed or diseased vertebra. The polymethyl methacrylate acts as a bone cement to relieve debilitating pain resulting from osteoporosis, bone metastases, and hemangiomas. Vertebral augmentation is a similar procedure that, in addition, involves the introduction of inflatable balloon catheters (tamps) into the vertebral body to restore height and to create a cavity into which the polymethyl methacrylate can be injected. In a sacroplasty procedure, the polymethyl methacrylate cement is injected into the sacrum and the sacral defect or insufficiency fracture rather than the vertebral body, using CT or fluoroscopic guidance. Report 72291 if fluoroscopic guidance was provided and 72292 if CT guidance was provided.

73000
Films are taken of the clavicle for a complete radiologic examination. The number of films is not specified. The patient is placed supine for a front to back (AP) view and the x-ray is directed to the midpoint and perpendicular to the clavicle.

73010
Films are taken of the scapula for a complete examination. The number of films is not specified. Anteroposterior (AP) and lateral views may be taken. The patient is placed supine for a front to back (AP) view and may be erect or recumbent for a lateral view. The arm is abducted to make a 90 degree angle to the body with the elbow flexed.

73020-73030
Films are taken of the shoulder. The patient is supine with the arm extended to a 90 degree angle from the body and externally rotated while the head is turned to face opposite the affected side. Code 73020 is for reporting one view only and 73030 specifies a minimum of two views.

73040
The synovial joint of the shoulder is visualized internally through arthrography, the direct injection of air and/or contrast material into the joint for radiological examination. Local anesthesia in injected

into the joint followed by the contrast material and/or air. A series of images are taken and interpreted. Fluoroscopic films and guidance for needle localization is included. Arthrography helps diagnose conditions of cartilage abnormalities, arthritis and bursitis, rotator cuff tear, and frozen joint. AP (front to back) views are taken with the affected arm rotated externally and internally and with the arm in a neutral, flexed position lying over the abdomen.

73050
A radiologic examination is made of the acromioclavicular joints bilaterally, with no specified amount of views. The patient is placed in a sitting or standing upright position with arms at the side for an anteroposterior view. The patient may also be given weights to hold in each hand for weighted distraction radiographs of each joint.

73060
Two or more films are taken of the humerus with the x-ray beam aimed midshaft. The patient is supine with the hand also supinated for an AP view and with the hand rotated internally for an oblique view.

73070-73080
A radiologic examination of the elbow joint is made. Films of the elbow may be taken in the AP position with the hand supinated, oblique positioning with the hand pronated and/or externally rotated, and in the lateral position with the wrist lateral and the elbow flexed at 90 degrees. Code 73070 reports two views and 73080 reports a complete exam with a minimum of three views.

73085
The synovial joint of the elbow is visualized internally through arthrography, the direct injection of air and/or contrast material into the joint for radiological examination. Local anesthesia in injected into the joint followed by the contrast material and/or air. A series of images are taken by the radiologist and interpreted. Fluoroscopic films and guidance for needle localization is included. Arthrography helps diagnose conditions of cartilage abnormalities, arthritis and bursitis, and frozen joint.

73090
Two films of the forearm are taken with the x-ray beam aimed at the midforearm. Films may be taken in the AP position with the hand supinated, in the true lateral position and in oblique positioning.

73092
A minimum of two films of an infant's forearm are taken with the x-ray beam aimed at the midforearm. The infant or child must first be immobilized to prevent movement during the film taking. Films may be taken in the AP position with the hand supinated, in the true lateral position and in oblique positioning.

73100-73110
A radiologic examination of the wrist is made in posteroanterior, oblique, or lateral views. Code 73100 reports two views only and 73110 reports three or more views.

73115
The wrist is visualized internally through arthrography, the direct injection of air and/or contrast material into the joint for radiological examination. Local anesthesia in injected into the joint followed by the contrast material and/or air. A series of images are taken and interpreted. Fluoroscopic films and guidance for needle localization is included. Arthrography helps diagnose conditions of cartilage abnormalities, arthritis and bursitis, and frozen joint. The hand and wrist is placed in the posteroanterior (PA) position with the hand rotated outward and the x-ray beam aimed vertically at the wrist or with the hand and wrist in PA position with the beam aimed at the wrist from a few degrees below the elbow.

73120-73130
A radiologic exam of the hand is made with films being taken in the PA (posteroanterior), internal or external oblique, or lateral positions. Code 73120 reports two views only. Code 73130 reports three or more views.

73140
Two or more views of the fingers (second through fifth digits, not thumb) are taken. The x-ray beam is aimed at the proximal interphalangeal joint for all positions, back to front, external or internal oblique, or lateral views.

73200-73202
Computed tomography directs multiple narrow beams of x-rays around the body structure being studied and uses computer imaging to produce thin cross-sectional views of various layers (or slices) of the body. It is useful for the evaluation of trauma, tumor, and foreign bodies as CT is able to visualize soft tissue as well as bones. Patients are required to remain motionless during the study and sedation may need to be administered as well as a contrast medium for image enhancement. These codes report an exam of the upper extremity. Report 73200 if no contrast is used. Report 73201 if performed with contrast and 73202 if performed first without contrast and again following the injection of contrast.

73206
Computed tomographic angiography (CTA) is a procedure used for the imaging of vessels to detect aneurysms, blood clots, and other vascular irregularities. Contrast medium is rapidly infused intravenously, at intervals, usually with an automatic injector, and the patient is scanned with thin section axial or spiral mode x-ray beams. The images obtained are acquired with narrower collimation and reconstructed at shorter intervals than standard CT

images. Three-dimensional images are generated and postprocessing reconstruction is done at a workstation on the scanner. CTA also provides information unavailable with conventional angiography, such as vessel wall thickness (mural thrombus) and the venous anatomy of a target organ and/or associated organs within the scan range. This code reports an exam of the upper extremity with contrast materials and image postprocessing. Noncontrast images, if performed, are also included in this procedure.

73218-73220

Magnetic resonance imaging (MRI) is a radiation-free, noninvasive, technique to produce high quality sectional images of the inside of the body in multiple planes. MRI uses the natural magnetic properties of the hydrogen atoms in our bodies that emit radiofrequency signals when exposed to radio waves within a strong electro-magnetic field. These signals are processed and converted by the computer into high-resolution, three-dimensional, tomographic images. Patients with metallic or electronic implants or foreign bodies cannot be exposed to MRI. The patient must remain still while lying on a motorized table within the large, circular MRI tunnel. A sedative may be administered as well as contrast material for image enhancement. For upper extremity other than joint, report 73218 if no contrast is used; 73219 if performed with contrast; and 73220 if performed first without contrast and again following the injection of contrast.

73221-73223

Magnetic resonance imaging (MRI) is a radiation-free, noninvasive, technique to produce high quality sectional images of the inside of the body in multiple planes. MRI uses the natural magnetic properties of the hydrogen atoms in our bodies that emit radiofrequency signals when exposed to radio waves within a strong electro-magnetic field. These signals are processed and converted by the computer into high-resolution, three-dimensional, tomographic images. Patients with metallic or electronic implants or foreign bodies cannot be exposed to MRI. The patient must remain still while lying on a motorized table within the large, circular MRI tunnel. A sedative may be administered as well as contrast material for image enhancement. For any joint of the upper extremity. Report 73221 if no contrast is used; 73222 if performed with contrast; and 73223 if performed first without contrast and again following the injection of contrast.

73225

Magnetic resonance angiography (MRA) is magnetic resonance imaging (MRI) that specifically visualizes blood vessels and blood flow to evaluate vascular disorders within the structure being studied. Unlike CT, it does not rely on the absorption of x-ray energy. Magnetic resonance imaging uses the natural magnetic properties of the hydrogen atoms in our bodies that emit radiofrequency signals when exposed to radio waves within a strong electro-magnetic field. These signals are processed and converted by the computer into high-resolution, three-dimensional tomographic images. Patients with metallic or electronic implants or foreign bodies cannot be exposed to MRI. The patient must remain still while lying on a motorized table within the large, circular MRI tunnel. A sedative may be administered as well as contrast material for image enhancement. This code reports an exam of the upper extremity.

73500-73510

One film only is taken of the right or the left hip in 73500. Two or more films are taken for a complete study of the right or the left hip in 73510. For a front to back (AP) view, the patient is placed supine with the toes on the affected side inverted. For a frogleg view, the affected hip is flexed with the knee bent.

73520

A minimum of two views are taken of each hip that includes a front to back view of the pelvic area. For a front to back (AP) view, the patient is placed supine with toes inverted. For a frogleg view, the knees are bent as much as possible with the soles of the feet touching each other.

73525

This code reports the radiological supervision and interpretation for hip arthrography. Using a fluoroscope, the physician marks the point of the femoral neck on the skin with ink. The femoral artery is palpated and marked as well to avoid inadvertent puncture. Skin traction may be applied to increase the space between the femoral head and acetabulum. The physician inserts a needle into the capsule (located by fluoroscope) and aspirates the synovial fluid for a culture check. After aspiration, a contrast agent is injected into the hip joint and the needle is removed. X-rays are taken with the hip in neutral, external, and internal rotation. A second set of x-rays may be taken following the hip movements.

73530

An x-ray is taken of the hip while on the operating table. The patient is supine with the knee on the unaffected side flexed and abducted away from the side to be studied.

73540

Two or more films are taken of an infant or child's pelvis and hips. The infant or child must first be immobilized to prevent movement during the film taking.

73542

Films are taken of the sacroiliac joint for arthrography, which involves injecting gas into the joint to visualize the cartilage and ligaments. This code reports only the radiological supervision and interpretation. If formal arthrography is not performed, recorded, and a formal radiologic report is not issued, use 77003 for fluoroscopic guidance for sacroiliac joint injections.

73550
Two films only are taken of the femur, or thigh bone, the longest and largest in the body. In the front to back or lateral views, the x-ray beam is aimed at the midshaft. For the AP (front to back) view, the patient is supine with the foot turned inward a few degrees. For a lateral view, the patient is placed laterally with the knee flexed and the affected side down.

73560-73564
A radiologic examination of the knee is done. The patient is positioned for the desired view(s) of the knee and x-ray films are taken. These codes do not specify which views must be taken. Code 73560 reports one or two views only. Use 73562 to report three views and 73564 for a complete exam of the knee with a minimum of four views.

73565
An x-ray is taken of the knees bilaterally in a front to back (anteroposterior) projection while the patient is standing.

73580
The patient is placed supine (lying on the back) on an x-ray table with the knee flexed over a small pillow. The knee is cleansed with Betadine and covered with a drape. A skin anesthetic may be applied. The physician passes a 20-gauge needle into the femoropatellar space. Air and a contrast agent is injected. After the injection, the patient is asked to move the knee to produce an even coating of the joint structures. Multiple x-rays are taken of the knee. This code reports the radiological supervision and interpretation only. Use a separately reportable code for the arthrography.

73590
Two films of the lower leg bones are taken. The physician interprets and reports the findings.

73592
Two or more films are taken of an infant's right or left lower extremity. The infant or child must first be immobilized to prevent movement during the film taking. The physician interprets and reports the findings.

73600-73610
Two films are taken of the ankle in 73600 and a complete radiologic exam of the ankle is performed in 73610 with three or more films taken. The codes do not specify that a specific view must be performed. The physician interprets and reports the findings.

73615
The physician injects radiopaque fluid into the ankle for arthrography. The physician inserts a needle into the joint and aspirates if necessary. Opaque contrast solution is injected into the ankle and the needle is removed. Films are taken of the ankle. This code reports the radiological supervision and interpretation only. Use a separately reportable code for the injection.

73620-73630
Two films are taken of the foot in 73620 and a complete radiologic exam of the foot is performed in 73630 with three or more films taken. The codes do not specify that a specific view must be performed. The physician interprets and reports the findings.

73650
Two or more films are taken of the calcaneus or heel bone. The physician interprets and reports the findings.

73660
Two or more films are taken of the toes. The physician interprets and reports the findings.

73700-73702
Computed tomography (CT) directs multiple narrow beams of x-rays around the body structure being studied and uses computer imaging to produce thin cross-sectional views of various layers (or slices) of the body. CT is useful for the evaluation of trauma, tumor, and foreign bodies as CT is able to visualize soft tissue as well as bones. Patients are required to remain motionless during the study and sedation may need to be administered as well as a contrast medium for image enhancement. These codes report an exam of the lower extremity. Report 73700 if no contrast is used. Report 73701 if performed with contrast and 73702 if performed first without contrast and again following the injection of contrast.

73706
Computed tomographic angiography (CTA) is a procedure used for the imaging of vessels to detect aneurysms, blood clots, and other vascular irregularities. Contrast medium is rapidly infused intravenously, at intervals, usually with an automatic injector, and the patient is scanned with thin section axial or spiral mode x-ray beams. The images obtained are acquired with narrower collimation and reconstructed at shorter intervals than standard CT images. Three-dimensional images are generated and postprocessing reconstruction is done at a workstation on the scanner. CTA also provides information unavailable with conventional angiography such as vessel wall thickness (mural thrombus) and the venous anatomy of a target organ and/or associated organs within the scan range. This code reports an exam of the lower extremity with contrast materials and image postprocessing. Noncontrast images, if performed, are also included in this procedure.

73718-73720
Magnetic resonance imaging (MRI) is a radiation-free, noninvasive, technique to produce high quality sectional images of the inside of the body in multiple planes. MRI uses the natural magnetic properties of the hydrogen atoms in our bodies that emit radiofrequency

signals when exposed to radio waves within a strong electro-magnetic field. These signals are processed and converted by the computer into high-resolution, three-dimensional, tomographic images. Patients with metallic or electronic implants or foreign bodies cannot be exposed to MRI. The patient must remain still while lying on a motorized table within the large, circular MRI tunnel. A sedative may be administered as well as contrast material for image enhancement. For lower extremity other than joint, report 73718 if no contrast is used; 73719 if performed with contrast; and 73720 if performed first without contrast and again following the injection of contrast.

73721-73723

Magnetic resonance imaging (MRI) is a radiation-free, noninvasive, technique to produce high quality sectional images of the inside of the body in multiple planes. MRI uses the natural magnetic properties of the hydrogen atoms in our bodies that emit radiofrequency signals when exposed to radio waves within a strong electro-magnetic field. These signals are processed and converted by the computer into high-resolution, three-dimensional, tomographic images. Patients with metallic or electronic implants or foreign bodies cannot be exposed to MRI. The patient must remain still while lying on a motorized table within the large, circular MRI tunnel. A sedative may be administered as well as contrast material for image enhancement. For any joint of the lower extremity, report 73721 if no contrast is used; 73722 if performed with contrast; and 73723 if performed first without contrast and again following the injection of contrast.

73725

Magnetic resonance angiography (MRA) is magnetic resonance imaging (MRI) that specifically visualizes blood vessels and blood flow to evaluate vascular disorders within the structure being studied. Unlike CT, it does not rely on the absorption of x-ray energy. Magnetic resonance imaging uses the natural magnetic properties of the hydrogen atoms in our bodies that emit radiofrequency signals when exposed to radio waves within a strong electro-magnetic field. These signals are processed and converted by the computer into high-resolution, three-dimensional tomographic images. Patients with metallic or electronic implants or foreign bodies cannot be exposed to MRI. The patient must remain still while lying on a motorized table within the large, circular MRI tunnel. A sedative may be administered as well as contrast material for image enhancement. This code reports an exam of the lower extremity.

74000

Films are taken of the abdominal cavity in one view from front to back. Because an abdominal x-ray usually precedes another diagnostic imaging procedure, it is not coded separately unless performed as a separately identifiable examination.

74010

Films are taken of the abdominal cavity from front to back, with an oblique view and a focused (coned down or spot) view. Because an abdominal x-ray usually precedes another diagnostic imaging procedure, it is not coded separately unless performed as a separately identifiable examination.

74020

Films are taken of the abdominal cavity from front to back, back to front, or front to back with the patient lying on the side and/or standing. Because an abdominal x-ray usually precedes another diagnostic imaging procedure, it is not coded separately unless performed as a separately identifiable examination.

74022

Films are taken of the abdominal cavity with the patient lying flat, standing, and/or lying on the side. This procedure includes a single view chest x-ray. Because an abdominal x-ray usually precedes another diagnostic imaging procedure, it is not coded separately unless performed as a separately identifiable examination.

74150-74170

Computed tomography directs multiple thin beams of x-rays at the body structure being studied and uses computer imaging to produce thin cross-sectional views of various layers (or slices) of the body. It is useful for the evaluation of trauma, tumor, and foreign bodies as CT is able to visualize soft tissue as well as bones. Patients are required to remain motionless during the study and sedation may need to be administered as well as a contrast medium for image enhancement. These codes report an exam of the abdomen. Report 74150 if no contrast is used. Report 74160 if performed with contrast and 74170 if performed first without contrast and again following the injection of contrast.

74175

Computed tomographic angiography (CTA) of the abdomen is performed with contrast material and image postprocessing. CTA is a procedure used for the imaging of vessels. CTA of the abdomen may detect aneurysms, thrombosis, and ischemia in the arteries supplying blood to the digestive system, as well as locate gastrointestinal bleeding. Contrast medium is rapidly infused at intervals, usually with an automatic injector, and the patient is scanned with thin section axial or spiral mode x-ray beams. The images obtained are acquired with narrower collimation and reconstructed at shorter intervals than standard CT images. Three-dimensional images are generated and postprocessing reconstruction is done at a workstation on the scanner. Noncontrast images, if performed, are also included in this procedure.

74181-74183

Magnetic resonance imaging (MRI) is a radiation-free, noninvasive, technique to produce high quality sectional images of the inside of the body in multiple planes. MRI uses the natural magnetic properties of the hydrogen atoms in our bodies that emit radiofrequency signals when exposed to radio waves within a strong electro-magnetic field. These signals are processed and converted by the computer into high-resolution, three-dimensional, tomographic images. Patients with metallic or electronic implants or foreign bodies cannot be exposed to MRI. The patient must remain still while lying on a motorized table within the large, circular MRI tunnel. A sedative may be administered as well as contrast material for image enhancement. These codes report an exam of the abdomen. Report 74181 if no contrast is used; 74182 if performed with contrast; and 74183 if performed first without contrast and again following the injection of contrast.

74185

Magnetic resonance angiography (MRA) is magnetic resonance imaging (MRI) that specifically visualizes blood vessels and blood flow to evaluate vascular disorders within the structure being studied. Unlike CT, it does not rely on the absorption of x-ray energy. Magnetic resonance imaging uses the natural magnetic properties of the hydrogen atoms in our bodies that emit radiofrequency signals when exposed to radio waves within a strong electro-magnetic field. These signals are processed and converted by the computer into high-resolution, three-dimensional tomographic images. Patients with metallic or electronic implants or foreign bodies cannot be exposed to MRI. The patient must remain still while lying on a motorized table within the large, circular MRI tunnel. A sedative may be administered as well as contrast material for image enhancement. This code reports an exam of the abdomen.

74190

A radiographic exam is done on the peritoneal cavity to define the pattern of air in the cavity after injection of air or contrast. The physician inserts a needle or catheter in to the peritoneal cavity and injects air or contrast as a diagnostic procedure. X-rays are taken. The needle or catheter is removed. This code reports the radiological supervision and interpretation for a peritoneogram. Use a separately reportable code for the procedure.

74210

Films are taken of the pharynx, which is a muscular, membrane-type tube that extends from the base of the skull to the level of the sixth cervical vertebra, where it becomes one with the esophagus. It is the passageway for air from the nasal cavity to the larynx or voice box, and for food from the mouth to the esophagus. The pharynx is also referred to as the cervical esophagus. There are no number or type of views associated with this procedure.

74220

Films are taken of the esophagus, which is the muscular tube, about nine inches long, that carries swallowed foods and liquids from the pharynx to the stomach. Films are taken both before and after introduction of a contrast material consisting of barium sulfate. Hence, this study is also commonly referred to as a "barium swallow." Structural abnormalities of the esophagus and vessels, such as esophageal varices, may be diagnosed by use of this study. There are no number or type of views associated with this procedure.

74230

This study is also known as a modified barium swallow. The patient is seated and positioned upright or in a semi-reclining position. Foods and liquids of different quantities and textures are soaked in or mixed with barium and given to the patient for the study. The patient is fluoroscoped while he/she swallows the various test items, and the fluoroscopic image is recorded on videotape for later review. This procedure includes observation of the food/liquid while in the mouth and during chewing, the tongue's mobility, movement of the hyoid bone and larynx, closing of the larynx and contraction of the pharynx, the extent of the pharyngoesophageal opening, and any aspiration or penetration of the swallowed bolus into the upper airway. Muscle strength may also be measured.

74235

The physician uses an esophagoscope to locate and remove a foreign body from the esophagus. The physician passes a rigid or flexible esophagoscope through the patient's mouth and into the esophagus. The foreign body is located. It may be suctioned, or grasped with forceps ad retracted through the scope. An alternative technique that may be used for objects too large to grasp is to pass a deflated balloon beyond the foreign body. The balloon is inflated and withdrawn simultaneously with the scope and the foreign body. This code reports the radiological supervision and interpretation. Use a separately reportable code for the procedure.

74240-74245

Films are taken of the upper gastrointestinal tract in an anterior oblique or lateral view. Breath is held during the film taking for either view positioning. This radiological exam helps diagnose neoplasms, ulcers, obstructions, and other diseases. 74240 is performed with or without delayed films and with or without KUB. 74241 is performed with KUB (kidneys, ureter, and bladder), which is a general x-ray of the midabdominal section. 74245 includes a radiologic exam of the small intestine in addition to the upper GI tract and multiple films taken in a series. The patient is face down for the small intestine films.

74246-74249
A radiologic exam is made of the upper gastrointestinal tract using fluoroscopy with a contrast material, known as barium swallow or barium "milkshake." This exam aids in diagnosing neoplasms, ulcers, obstructions, hiatal hernias and enteritis. The patient is strapped to the table and swallows the barium while standing upright. Throughout the exam, the table is tilted at various angles for differing views from the fluoroscope. 74246 is done without KUB and 74247 is done with KUB, which is a general x-ray of the midabdominal section. For the small intestine follow-through reported in 74249, several hours must go by before the contrast medium reaches the point of study in the intestine. All codes may be performed with or without glucagon, which relaxes smooth muscle found in the GI tract and inhibits the muscle motility, thereby making better quality of images.

74250
A radiologic exam of the small intestine is done for which the patient is face down and x-rays are taken in a series of multiple films. The patient holds his or her breath during film taking.

74251
A radiologic exam of the small bowel is done by enteroclysis and taken in a series of multiple films. For enteroclysis, the physician inserts a tube through the patient's mouth and passes it down into the stomach and the small intestine. The tube is connected to a pump that sends barium through the tube for visualizing the GI tract and small bowel.

74260
X-ray films are taken of the duodenum and the pancreas to help diagnose tumors or lesions. A tube is passed through the nose, into the stomach, and on into the duodenum with guidance from fluoroscopy. A drug for relaxing the duodenum is given and a contrast medium is pumped through the tube. Air may also be injected. X-rays are taken and the tube removed.

74261-74263
Computed tomographic (CT) colonography, also referred to as virtual colonoscopy (VC), provides detailed, cross-sectional views of the colon by use of an x-ray machine linked to a computer. The aim of screening (74263) is to detect and remove precancerous polyps in asymptomatic patients. Diagnostic CT colonography (74261, 74262) is a noninvasive technique that is being investigated for use in symptomatic patients to diagnose and stage colon cancer. The patient is prepared for CT colonoscopy with bowel cleansing. Intravenous contrast and a spasmolytic agent may be administered via a rectal tube, but neither is required. An enema tip is inserted and the colon is distended with air or CO2. Once patient preparation is complete, one of several CT techniques can be used. One of the more common techniques uses thin collimation and three-dimensional (3-D), endoluminal computerized reconstructed images. A variation of this technique is CT pneumocolon that uses thicker collimation and intravenous contrast without 3-D reconstruction. Report 74261 for diagnostic CT colonography without contrast material and 74262 for that with contrast materials (including noncontrast images when performed). Report 74263 for screening CT colonography. All codes include image postprocessing.

74270
A radiological exam of the large intestine is carried out after the administration of a barium enema to instill contrast into the colon. Fluoroscopy and x-rays are used to observe the image as the contrast fills the colon. This test helps to diagnose cancer, colitis, and other diseases. After the patient has emptied the colon, more films are taken. A general x-ray of the abdomen, known as KUB, may be done.

74280
A radiological exam of the colon is carried out. The morning of the exam, a rectal bisacodyl suppository is given. One mg of glucagon may be administered through IV. Glucagon relaxes smooth muscle found in the GI tract and inhibits muscle motility, thereby making better quality of images. The rectal tip of the enema kit is inserted and a high-density barium suspension (85% w/v) is administered undiluted. The colon is distended with air and the barium, which coats the colon walls and acts as a contrast agent to enable the physician to identify any abnormalities. Fluoroscopy is used to take images of the colon.

74283
An enema of air or barium contrast is administered to reduce an intussusception or obstruction. An intussusception is a section of bowel that has slipped into another loop of bowel and can cause necrosis of the tissue, perforation and infection, even death. With the patient in position, the air or contrast is instilled into the colon through the anus to reduce the intussusception or clear the intraluminal obstruction.

74290
Oral cholecystography provides radiographic visualization of the gallbladder after the oral ingestion of a radiopaque, iodinated dye that comes in the form of pills. Adequate visualization of the gallbladder requires concentration of this dye within the gallbladder. On x-ray film, the biliary calculi (gallstones) are visualized as radiolucent shadows within a dye-filled gallbladder. Gallbladder polyps and tumors occasionally also can be seen as filling defects.

74291
Oral cholecystography provides radiographic visualization of the gallbladder after the oral ingestion of a radiopaque, iodinated dye that comes in the form of pills. Adequate visualization of the gallbladder requires concentration of this dye within the

gallbladder. Occasionally, the gallbladder will not visualize after a single dose of dye tablets is ingested. In this case, the test should be repeated using a double dose, on the same day or on another day. Should this situation occur, report this procedure for the additional or repeat study.

74300-74301

In intraoperative cholangiography, the common bile duct is directly injected with radiopaque material. The surgeon removes the gallbladder. Stones appear as radiolucent shadows. Gallstones, tumors, or strictures cause partial or total obstruction of the flow of dye into the duodenum. This code reports only the radiological supervision and interpretation. Since the surgeon performs the dye injection in an intraoperative cholangiogram, this is the only code that the radiologist can report for this procedure. 74301 is an add-on code and cannot stand-alone. This code is used in conjunction with 74300, in the event that the surgeon would request another set of plain x-ray films to be taken during the operative session.

74305

Postoperative cholangiography is done through an existing catheter and is used to detect retained common bile duct stones after the gallbladder has been removed, and to demonstrate good flow of bile contrast into the duodenum. Radiopaque dye is injected through a T-tube, which is a device inserted into the biliary duct and brought out through the abdominal wall after bile duct exploration and removal of the gallbladder. It allows for drainage of the bile duct and for introduction of contrast medium for postoperative radiological study of the bile duct. This code reports only the radiological supervision and interpretation. The injection of the dye through the T-tube is reported separately.

74320

In percutaneous cholangiography, a radiographic medium is injected into the common bile duct for diagnostic purposes. The physician inserts a needle between the ribs into the lumen of the common bile duct and checks positioning by aspiration. This code reports only the radiological supervision and interpretation required in performing this procedure.

74327

The physician removes a stone from the biliary duct after previous surgery. The common bile duct is approached by placing a scope into the tract through a previously placed drainage tube (T-tube). Manipulating basket or snare tools through the scope, the physician removes the stone(s). This code reports only the radiological supervision and interpretation required in performing this procedure.

74328-74330

The physician performs an endoscopic retrograde cholangiopancreatography (ERCP) for diagnostic or therapeutic reasons. The physician passes the endoscope through the patient's oropharynx, esophagus, stomach, and into the small intestine. A smaller subscope may be inserted through the sphincter of Oddi into the system of ducts that drain the pancreas (74329) or into the biliary ductal system that drains the gallbladder (74328), or both (74330). These codes report only the radiological supervision and interpretation required in performing this procedure to the respective extent of catheterization.

74340

A long, Miller-Abbott gastrointestinal tube with a mercury-filled balloon at the bottom is introduced, usually nasally, and used to clear gastrointestinal strictures. The patient is seated lower than the person performing the procedure and the dilator is placed in the posterior pharynx. The patient swallows and the tube and balloon are carried into the small intestine. The balloon is inflated and withdrawn until resistance is encountered. The balloon is partially deflated, withdrawn a little more and re-inflated. This process is repeated several times to achieve dilation of the stricture. This procedure may be done without fluoroscopy or with fluoroscopy by instilling a diluted contrast into the balloon. This code includes the fluoroscopies, films, and radiological supervision and interpretation. Use a separately reportable code for the tube placement.

74355

The physician places a tube in the jejunum for feeding through an abdominal incision. A section of proximal jejunum is selected and a tube is placed in the jejunum and brought out through the abdominal wall. This segment of jejunum is securely tacked to the inside of the abdominal wall. This code reports only the radiological supervision and interpretation required in performing this procedure.

74360

The physician passes a balloon dilator into the patient's mouth and uses a fluoroscope to place the dilator at the point of constriction. The balloon is briefly inflated several times until the area of narrowing is sufficiently enlarged. It is possible to use a guide wire to place the balloon. This code reports only the radiological supervision and interpretation required in performing this procedure.

74363

The physician advances an endoscope through an incision in the abdominal wall or an existing T-tube into the common bile duct. The biliary tract may be filled with contrast medium for identifying areas of abnormality, stricture, or obstruction in the common bile duct, biliary tree, and gallbladder. The physician advances a balloon-tipped catheter through the tract or T-tube so that it is above the site of the duct stricture, inflates the balloon, and draws it back through the stricture to achieve dilation. This may be repeated until optimum dilation is achieved. The physician may place a stent to prevent future stricture. This code reports only the radiological supervision and interpretation required in performing this procedure.

74400

Radiographic imaging of the kidneys and ureters is done before and after the administration of an intravenous contrast material to identify abnormalities of the kidneys and urinary tract. Abdominal films are obtained and contrast medium is injected into a vein. Radiographs are again obtained while the contrast material is being excreted. This is also known as intravenous pyelography or IVP. This procedure may be done with or without KUB, a general abdominal x-ray, or with or without tomography, x-rays taken onto film moving opposite the beams to yield a single plane shadowless image.

74410-74415

Radiographic imaging of the kidneys and ureters is done immediately following an infused intravenous drip or a rapid bolus injection of contrast agent. A front to back film of the abdomen is taken after contrast administration. Report 74415 if done with nephrotomography, x-rays taken onto film moving opposite the beams to yield a single plane shadowless image. This can be used to check the patency of a nephrostomy tube.

74420

Radiographic imaging of the kidneys and ureters is done following retrograde (against the normal flow) administration of a radiopaque contrast material, usually barium sulfate. A catheter is passed into the bladder and on through a ureter into the kidney. The contrast material in injected through the catheter or tube. Films are taken to show the flow of contrast as it moves through the urethra and into the upper urinary tract. This may be performed with KUB, a general x-ray of the abdomen.

74425

A radiographic exam of the urinary tract is performed with injection or instillation of a contrast medium. This test is done to follow the normal flow of urine through the tract (antegrade) and may identify obstructions, abnormalities in the urinary tract, or assess function following surgery. Contrast medium is introduced percutaneously with a needle or through an existing tube, catheter, or stoma. For percutaneous needle injection, the skin is anesthetized and the needle inserted under fluoroscopic guidance into a calyx of the kidney. Contrast medium is injected and radiographs are taken. This code reports the radiological supervision and interpretation. Use a separately reportable code for the surgical procedure.

74430

A radiographic exam of the bladder with a minimum of three views is performed using contrast material to diagnose rupture, injury, or stress incontinence. A catheter is inserted into the bladder and contrast medium is instilled using mild pressure injection. The catheter is clamped after the contrast medium has filled the bladder and the bladder is fully expanded. Films are taken to observe any medium that is outside the bladder. The bladder is next drained and more films may be taken to look for other evidence of rupture following the flow of contrast outside the bladder. This code reports the radiological supervision and interpretation. Use a separately reportable code for the surgical procedure.

74440

A radiographic exam is done to determine obstruction in the epididymis, seminal vesicle duct, or vas deferens. Methylene blue is injected into the vas to test for obstruction of the ejaculatory duct. If during cystoscopy, dye is seen, the ducts are patent and vesiculography may be obtained to further determine obstruction. The vas is approached through an incision in the scrotum. The testis is freed and the vas separated. After a catheter is threaded into the vas, saline or lactated Ringers are instilled to determine patency or blockage. Flow resistance may require more formal vasography, with water-soluble contrast media instilled through a ureteral catheter fed to the seminal vesicles through a dilated vas. Epididymography requires taking images of the coiled tube connecting the testis to the vas deferens. This code reports the radiological supervision and interpretation for epididymography, vesiculography, or vasography.

74445

Corpora cavernosography is performed to determine the area and degree of a venous leakage. The penis is anesthetized and prepped with tubing attached to a pressure transducer that is connected to an infusion pump. Needles are inserted into the cavernosa and contrast material injected at a rate that will maintain a certain pressure so the penis can remain erect while the x-rays are taken. Fluoroscopy locates the leakage, which is determined to be minimal, moderate, or diffuse. This code reports the radiological supervision and interpretation for the procedure.

74450

A radiographic exam of the urethra and bladder is performed using contrast material to diagnose strictures, obstructions and abnormalities, or as postoperative function assessments. It is most often performed on males. A balloon catheter is threaded into the urethra and the balloon is inflated. Fluoroscopy is used to aid in injecting the contrast medium through the catheter. Films are taken to show the flow of contrast as it moves retrograde (against the normal flow) through the urethra and into certain parts of the bladder. The bladder is next drained and more images may be taken of the urethra. This code reports the radiological supervision and interpretation. Use a separately reportable code for the surgical procedure.

74455
A radiographic exam of the urethra and bladder is performed using contrast material to evaluate voiding function. The patient first empties the bladder. A catheter is inserted through the urethra into the bladder and any excess fluid is drained. Contrast medium is slowly instilled until it fills the bladder while the flow is observed via fluoroscopy. Films may be taken if reflux of medium is seen backing into the ureters. Once voiding commences, the catheter is removed and the voiding function is imaged on films or video. This code reports the radiological supervision and interpretation. Use a separately reportable code for the surgical procedure.

74470
A renal cyst is studied using contrast medium by inserting a spinal needle into the affected kidney. With the patient face down, the site for the puncture is identified with separate radiographic localization of the cyst and kidney. The skin of the puncture site is anesthetized and the needle is inserted and advanced to the kidney, while being observed on a fluoroscopic video monitor. Some of the cyst's contents are removed and a small amount of contrast is injected. This is repeated with films being taken intermittently throughout the process. When the cyst is filled with the contrast medium, more images are taken with the patient in various positions. This code reports the radiological supervision and interpretation. Use a separately reportable code for the surgical procedure.

74475
The physician inserts a catheter or intracatheter percutaneously into the renal pelvis for drainage and/or contrast injection for radiographic studies. With the patient face down and the puncture site having been identified by separately reportable means, a local anesthetic is injected. A needle with a guidewire is slowly advanced into the kidney under fluoroscopic guidance. The needle is removed and the tract may be dilated to accommodate the catheter or nephrostomy tube which is fixed in place and secured also under fluoroscopic control. This code reports the radiological supervision and interpretation. Use a separately reportable code for the surgical procedure.

74480
The physician inserts a ureteral catheter or stent percutaneously into the ureter through the renal pelvis for drainage and/or contrast injection for radiographic studies. With the patient face down and the puncture site having been identified by separately reportable means, a local anesthetic is injected. A needle with a guidewire is slowly advanced into the kidney under fluoroscopic guidance. The needle is removed and the tract may be dilated to accommodate the ureteral catheter, which is inserted into the kidney pelvis and manipulated into and down the ureter until it reaches the bladder also under fluoroscopic monitoring. An internal stent will reside in the ureter and an external stent will have one end that remains outside the body. This code reports the radiological supervision and interpretation. Use a separately reportable code for the surgical procedure.

74485
A previously existing nephrostomy tract to the kidney and/or ureters, or urethra is dilated under fluoroscopic control. A series of dilators in increasing size are inserted into the nephrostomy opening, usually over a guidewire. A balloon may also be used. The ureters may be dilated by advancing the dilators through the nephrostomy tract or inserting them into the ureters from the bladder. For urethral dilation, a guidewire may be advanced through the urethral stricture and one or more catheters of increasing size placed over the guidewire. A balloon is inserted and inflated until the stricture is dilated. This code reports the radiological supervision and interpretation. Use a separately reportable code for the surgical procedure.

74710
Although most abnormalities of the female pelvis can be suspected by using clinical measurements, x-ray pelvimetry is the most accurate means of determining adequacy of the pelvic bony structures for a normal vaginal delivery. With pelvimetry, comparison is made with the capacity of the pelvis to the size of the infant's head, in order to discover any disproportion. However, radiographic pelvimetry is not used often in modern obstetrics because of the risks associated with radiation. This code is reported with or without locating the placenta.

74740
In hysterosalpingography, the uterine cavity and fallopian tubes are visualized radiographically after the injection of contrast material through the cervix. Uterine tumors, intrauterine adhesions, and developmental anomalies can be seen. Tubal obstruction caused by internal scarring, tumor, or kinking can also be detected. This code reports only the radiological supervision and interpretation. The injection portion of this study is reported separately.

74742
The physician introduces a catheter into the cervix and takes it into the uterus and through the fallopian tube to diagnose any blockages or to re-establish patency. The physician may elect to inject liquid radiographic contrast material into the endometrial cavity with mild pressure to force the material into the tubes (hysterosalpingogram). The shadow of this material on x-ray film permits examination of the uterus and tubes for any abnormalities or blockages. This code reports only the radiological supervision and interpretation. The introduction of the catheter into the fallopian tube is reported separately.

74775
The perineum, which is the area between the vulva and the anus in the female, is viewed to determine the sex of the patient. It is used mainly in cases where an infant is born with ambiguous genitalia. The procedure also may be used to check for an abnormal opening (fistula) between the vagina and bladder or the vagina and rectum. When locating a fistula, the use of contrast material is included.

75557-75559
Cardiac magnetic resonance imaging (MRI) is a radiation-free, noninvasive technique that produces high quality, detailed, three-dimensional imaging of complex congenital heart defects, as well as functional cardiac analysis. MRI uses the natural magnetic properties of the hydrogen atoms in our bodies that emit radiofrequency signals when exposed to radio waves within a strong electromagnetic field. These signals are processed and converted by the computer into high-resolution images. Patients with metallic or electronic implants or foreign bodies cannot be exposed to MRI. The patient must remain still while lying on a motorized table within the large, circular MRI tunnel. A sedative may be administered. Imaging is performed by obtaining tomographic cuts from the base to the apex and/or the interior to the posterior in order to interrogate the entire heart. Function studies may include observation of the atria and/or ventricles, qualitative and quantitative assessment of ventricular function, and obtaining numerical values for ejection fraction (EF) ventricular volumes, ventricular mass, and cardiac output. Report 75557 for observation of the cardiac function and morphology without administration of a contrast agent. Report 75559 if stress imaging is included. Following dobutamine injection, which mimics the effects of exercise on the heart and induces ischemia, the physician evaluates the left ventricular wall's ability to move during physical stress.

75561-75565
Cardiac magnetic resonance imaging (MRI) is a radiation-free, noninvasive technique that produces high quality, detailed, three-dimensional imaging of complex congenital heart defects, as well as functional cardiac analysis. MRI uses the natural magnetic properties of the hydrogen atoms in our bodies that emit radiofrequency signals when exposed to radio waves within a strong electromagnetic field. These signals are processed and converted by the computer into high-resolution images. Patients with metallic or electronic implants or foreign bodies cannot be exposed to MRI. The patient must remain still while lying on a motorized table within the large, circular MRI tunnel. A sedative may be administered. Images are first obtained without contrast materials, followed by administration of contrast materials and further sequences. Imaging is performed by obtaining tomographic cuts from the base to the apex and/or the interior to the posterior in order to interrogate the entire heart. Function studies may include observation of the atria and/or ventricles, qualitative and quantitative assessment of ventricular function, and obtaining numerical values for ejection fraction (EF) ventricular volumes, ventricular mass, and cardiac output. Report 75561 for observation of cardiac function and morphology. Report 75563 if stress imaging is included. Following dobutamine injection, which mimics the effects of exercise on the heart and induces ischemia, the physician evaluates the left ventricular wall's ability to move during physical stress. If velocity flow mapping is performed, report 75565 in addition to the code for the primary procedure.

75571
Computed tomography directs multiple narrow beams of x-rays around the body structure being studied and uses computer imaging to produce thin, cross-sectional views of various layers (or slices) of the body. It is useful for the evaluation of calcium deposits on the coronary tree. Patients are required to remain motionless during the study. This code reports the CT of the heart and quantitative evaluation of calcium deposits in the coronary tree. High levels of calcium deposits in the heart triple a person's likelihood of suffering an adverse coronary event (e.g., myocardial infarct, cardiac arrest, etc.).

75572-75574
The physician performs computed tomography (CT) of the heart utilizing contrast materials to evaluate cardiac structure and morphology. CT directs multiple, thin beams of x-rays at the body and uses computer imaging to produce thin, cross-sectional views of various layers of the body. It is useful in the evaluation of soft tissue. Because patients are required to be motionless during CT, this creates issues when producing CT images of the heart, which is continually moving rhythmically. In a cardiac gating technique, the patient is undergoing CT while attached to ECG leads. CT image acquisition is triggered by the ECG, allowing for coordination of imaging with periods of movement and rest within the heart. Code 75572 includes 3D image postprocessing, assessment of cardiac function, and evaluation of venous structures, if performed. Code 75573 reports CT of a heart with congenital anomalies, also performed utilizing contrast materials to evaluate cardiac structure and morphology. This code includes 3D image postprocessing, assessment of left ventricular (LV) cardiac function, right ventricular (RV) structure and function, and evaluation of venous structures, if performed. Report 75574 for CT of the heart utilizing contrast materials in conjunction with computerized tomographic angiography (CTA) to evaluate the heart, coronary arteries, and any bypass grafts that are present. In addition to the CT imaging of the heart as described previously, a CTA of native and anomalous coronary arteries and coronary bypass grafts is obtained. CTA is a procedure used for imaging

of vessels to detect aneurysms, blood clots, and other vascular irregularities. Contrast media is rapidly infused intravenously, at intervals, usually with an automatic injector. The patient's heart is scanned with thin section axial or spiral mode x-ray beams. Three-dimensional images are generated and postprocessing reconstruction is done at a workstation on the scanner. Vessel wall thickness and the venous anatomy of the heart are evaluated. This code also includes 3D image postprocessing (including evaluation of cardiac structure and morphology, assessment of cardiac function, and evaluation of venous structures, if performed).

75600
A local anesthetic is applied over the common femoral artery. The artery is percutaneously punctured with a needle and a guidewire is fed through the artery into the thoracic aorta. A catheter is threaded over the guidewire to the point of study and the guidewire removed. Contrast medium is injected and films are taken. This code reports the radiological supervision and interpretation. Use separately reportable code for the catheterization.

75605
A local anesthetic is applied over the common femoral artery. The artery is percutaneously punctured with a needle and a guidewire is fed through the artery into the thoracic aorta. A catheter is threaded over the guidewire to the point of study and the guidewire is removed. Contrast medium is injected and films are taken by serialography, producing a series of individual x-ray films. This code reports the radiological supervision and interpretation. Use a separately reportable code for the catheterization.

75625
A local anesthetic is applied over the common femoral artery. The artery is percutaneously punctured with a needle and a guidewire is fed through the artery into the abdominal aorta. A catheter is threaded over the guidewire to the point of study and the guidewire is removed. Contrast medium is injected and films are taken by serialography, producing a series of individual x-ray films. This code reports the radiological supervision and interpretation. Use a separately reportable code for the catheterization.

75630
A local anesthetic is applied over the common femoral artery. The artery is percutaneously punctured with a needle and a guidewire is fed through the artery into the abdominal aorta. A catheter is threaded over the guidewire to the point of study and the guidewire is removed. Contrast medium is injected into the abdominal aorta and a series of continuous films are taken of the contrast flow through the aorta and its runoff into the arteries of both legs. This code reports the radiological supervision and interpretation. Use a separately reportable code for the catheterization.

75635
Computed tomographic angiography (CTA) is a procedure used for the imaging of vessels to detect aneurysms, blood clots, and other vascular irregularities. Contrast medium is rapidly and regularly infused at intervals, usually with an automatic injector, and the patient is scanned by CT for images of the abdominal aorta and both lower extremities as the contrast runs down through the iliofemoral pathway. The images obtained are acquired with narrower collimation and reconstructed at shorter intervals than standard CT images. Three-dimensional images are generated and postprocessing reconstruction is done at a workstation on the scanner. This code reports an exam of the abdominal aorta with bilateral iliofemoral lower extremity runoff with contrast materials and image postprocessing. Noncontrast images, if performed, are also included in this procedure.

75650
A local anesthetic is applied over the common femoral artery, although other approaches may be used. The artery is percutaneously punctured with a needle and a guidewire is fed through the artery into the aortic arch near the great vessels branching from it. A catheter is threaded over the guidewire to the point of study and the guidewire removed. Contrast medium is injected using a power injector into the aortic arch and a very rapid sequence of films are taken during the injection of the contrast flow through the arch and the origin of the cervicocerebral arteries (left common carotid and common carotid and brachiocephalic on the right). This code reports the radiological supervision and interpretation. Use separately reportable code for the catheterization.

75658
A local anesthetic is applied over the puncture site. The artery is percutaneously punctured with a needle and a guidewire inserted and fed into the brachial artery. A catheter is threaded over the guidewire to the point of study and the guidewire removed. A retrograde (against normal flow) injection of contrast medium is done into the brachial artery and films are obtained. This code reports the radiological supervision and interpretation. Use separately reportable code for the catheterization.

75660
A local anesthetic is applied over the femoral, brachial, subclavian, or axillary artery. The artery is percutaneously punctured with a needle and a guidewire is inserted and selectively fed through the artery into the right or left external carotid. A catheter is threaded over the guidewire to the point of study and the guidewire removed. Contrast medium is injected and a series of x-rays is performed to visualize the vessels and evaluate any abnormalities. This code reports the radiological supervision and interpretation

only. Use a separately reportable code for the catheterization.

75662
A local anesthetic is applied over the femoral, brachial, subclavian, or axillary artery. The artery is percutaneously punctured with a needle and a guidewire is inserted and selectively fed through the artery into the external carotid. A catheter is threaded over the guidewire to the point of study and the guidewire removed. Contrast medium is injected and a series of x-rays performed bilaterally to visualize the vessels and evaluate any abnormalities. This code reports the radiological supervision and interpretation only. Use a separately reportable code for the catheterization.

75665
A local anesthetic is applied over the femoral, brachial, subclavian, or axillary artery. The artery is percutaneously punctured with a needle and a guidewire is fed through the artery into the right or left (cerebral) carotid. A catheter is threaded over the guidewire to the point of study and the guidewire removed. Contrast medium is injected into the cerebral arterial system and a series of x-rays is performed to visualize the vessels and evaluate any abnormalities. This code reports the radiological supervision and interpretation only. Use a separately reportable code for the catheterization.

75671
A local anesthetic is applied over the femoral, brachial, subclavian, or axillary artery. The artery is percutaneously punctured with a needle and a guidewire is fed through the artery into the (cerebral) carotid. A catheter is threaded over the guidewire to the point of study and the guidewire removed. Contrast medium is injected into the cerebral arterial system and a series of x-rays performed bilaterally to visualize the vessels and evaluate any abnormalities. This code reports the radiological supervision and interpretation only. Use a separately reportable code for the catheterization.

75676
A local anesthetic is applied over the femoral, brachial, subclavian, or axillary artery. The artery is percutaneously punctured with a needle and a guidewire is fed through the artery into the right or left (cervical) carotid. A catheter is threaded over the guidewire to the point of study and the guidewire removed. Contrast medium is injected and a series of x-rays is performed to visualize the vessels and evaluate any abnormalities. This code reports the radiological supervision and interpretation only. Use a separately reportable code for the catheterization.

75680
A local anesthetic is applied over the femoral, brachial, subclavian, or axillary artery. The artery is percutaneously punctured with a needle and a guidewire is fed through the artery into the (cervical) carotid. A catheter is threaded over the guidewire to the point of study and the guidewire removed. Contrast medium is injected and a series of x-rays performed bilaterally to visualize the vessels and evaluate any abnormalities. This code reports the radiological supervision and interpretation only. Use a separately reportable code for the catheterization.

75685
A local anesthetic is applied over the femoral, brachial, subclavian, or axillary artery. The artery is percutaneously punctured with a needle and a guidewire is fed through the artery to the point of study suitable for imaging vertebral, cervical, and/or intracranial arteries. A catheter is threaded over the guidewire until it, too, reaches the point of study and the guidewire is removed. Contrast medium is injected and a series of x-rays performed to visualize the vessels and evaluate any abnormalities. This code reports the radiological supervision and interpretation only. Use a separately reportable code for the catheterization.

75705
A local anesthetic is applied over the artery of access, usually the common femoral artery. The artery is percutaneously punctured with a needle and a guidewire is fed through the artery into the aorta. Under fluoroscopic guidance, a catheter is threaded over the guidewire to the aorta and advanced directly into a spinal artery suitable for viewing the study area. The guidewire is removed. Contrast medium is injected in the lowest level first and just above that in sequence and films are taken until the study has covered the area of interest. This code reports the radiological supervision and interpretation only. Use a separately reportable code for the catheterization.

75710
The arteries of one arm, leg, hand, or foot that are not normally seen in an x-ray are examined radiologically by injecting contrast material. A local anesthetic is applied over the area of access which could be femoral, brachial, subclavian, or axillary artery. The artery is percutaneously punctured with a needle and a guidewire is fed through the artery to the point of study. A catheter is threaded over the guidewire until it, too, reaches the point of study and the guidewire is removed. Contrast medium is injected through the catheter and a series of x-rays or fluoroscopic images taken to visualize the vessels and evaluate any abnormalities. The catheter is removed and pressure applied to the site. This code reports the radiological supervision and interpretation. Use a separately reportable code for the catheterization.

75716
The arteries of bilateral extremities such as both arms or legs, that are not normally seen in an x-ray are examined radiologically by injecting contrast material.

A local anesthetic is applied over the area of access which could be femoral, brachial, subclavian, or axillary artery. The artery is percutaneously punctured with a needle and a guidewire is fed through the artery to the point of study. A catheter is threaded over the guidewire until it, too, reaches the point of study and the guidewire is removed. Contrast medium is injected through the catheter and a series of x-rays or fluoroscopic images taken to visualize the vessels and evaluate any abnormalities. The catheter is removed and pressure applied to the site. This code reports the radiological supervision and interpretation. Use a separately reportable code for the catheterization.

75722-75724

The renal artery on the right or left side is radiologically examined using contrast material in 75722 and both renal arteries are examined in 75724. Patients with a renal complication are first well hydrated with a drip and given medications to protect the kidney from further damage by the contrast agent. A local anesthetic is applied over the access artery, usually the common femoral artery, which is percutaneously punctured with a needle. A guidewire is fed through until it reaches the renal artery. A catheter is threaded over the guidewire and the guidewire is removed. Contrast medium is injected and a series of x-rays or fluoroscopic images are taken to visualize the vessels and evaluate any abnormalities. If a flush aortogram is performed, the catheter is directed to the aorta and dye is injected as x-rays are taken to look for plaque build-up. The catheter is removed and pressure applied to the site. These codes report only the radiological supervision and interpretation for the procedure.

75726

An artery supplying the abdominal organ of concern is examined radiologically by injecting contrast material. A local anesthetic is applied over the area of access, usually the common femoral artery. The artery is percutaneously punctured with a needle and a guidewire is fed through the artery to the point of study. A catheter is threaded over the guidewire until it, too, reaches the point of study and the guidewire is removed. Contrast medium is injected through the catheter and a series of x-rays or fluoroscopic images taken to visualize the vessels and evaluate any abnormalities. If an aortogram is performed, the catheter is directed to the origin of the coronary arteries and dye is injected into them as x-rays are taken to look for plaque build-up. The catheter is removed and pressure applied to the site. This code reports the radiological supervision and interpretation. Use separately reportable code for the catheterization.

75731

The left or right adrenal gland, located on top of the upper end of each kidney is examined radiologically by injecting contrast material. A local anesthetic is applied over the common femoral artery. The artery is percutaneously punctured with a needle and a guidewire is fed through the artery, the aorta, and further into the renal artery. A catheter is threaded over the guidewire until it, too, reaches the point of study and the guidewire is removed. Contrast medium is injected through the catheter and a series of x-rays or fluoroscopic images taken to visualize the vessels and evaluate any abnormalities. The catheter is removed and pressure applied to the site. This code reports the radiological supervision and interpretation. Use separately reportable code for the catheterization.

75733

The adrenal glands located on top of the upper end of each kidney are examined radiologically by injecting contrast material. A local anesthetic is applied over the common femoral artery. The artery is percutaneously punctured with a needle and a guidewire is fed through the artery, the aorta, and further into the renal arteries. A catheter is threaded over the guidewire until it, too, reaches the point of study and the guidewire is removed. Contrast medium is injected through the catheter and a series of x-rays or fluoroscopic images taken to visualize the vessels and evaluate any abnormalities. The catheter is removed and pressure applied to the site. This code reports the radiological supervision and interpretation. Use separately reportable code for the catheterization.

75736

An angiogram is done on operative candidates for pelvic fixation to rule out retroperitoneal arterial bleeding. A local anesthetic is applied over the common femoral artery. The artery is percutaneously punctured with a needle and a guidewire is fed through the artery into the study area in the pelvic region. A catheter is threaded over the guidewire until it, too, reaches the point of study and the guidewire is removed. Contrast medium is injected through the catheter and a series of x-rays or fluoroscopic images taken to visualize the vessels and evaluate for any transected or bleeding arteries. Embolization may be dictated by angiography results to hemorrhaging for definitive stabilization treatment. The catheter is removed and pressure applied to the site. This code reports the radiological supervision and interpretation. Use separately reportable code for the catheterization.

75741

A local anesthetic is applied over the site where the catheter is to be introduced; this is most often the common femoral or internal jugular vein. The vein is percutaneously punctured and the catheter selectively manipulated through the vena cava, right atrium, and right ventricle into the left or right pulmonary artery. Contrast medium is injected and films are taken to visualize the vessels and evaluate any abnormalities. This code reports the radiological supervision and interpretation only. Use a separately reportable code for the catheterization.

75743
A local anesthetic is applied over the site where the catheter is to be introduced; this is most often the common femoral or internal jugular vein. The vein is percutaneously punctured and the catheter selectively manipulated through the vena cava, right atrium, and right ventricle into the pulmonary arteries. Contrast medium is injected and films taken bilaterally to visualize the vessels and evaluate any abnormalities. This code reports the radiological supervision and interpretation only. Use a separately reportable code for the catheterization.

75746
A local anesthetic is applied over the site where the catheter is to be introduced; this is most often either the common femoral or internal jugular vein. The vein is percutaneously punctured and the catheter manipulated through to the main pulmonary artery or the right atrium. Contrast medium is injected and films are taken to visualize the vessels and evaluate any abnormalities such as blockages, narrowing, or aneurysms. This code reports the radiological supervision and interpretation only. Use a separately reportable code for the catheterization.</p>

75756
A local anesthetic is applied over the site where the catheter is to be introduced; this is most often the common femoral or brachial artery. The artery is percutaneously punctured with a needle and a guidewire is fed through the artery to the internal mammary. A catheter is threaded over the guidewire to the point of study and the guidewire is removed. Contrast medium is injected and a series of x-rays performed to visualize the vessels and evaluate any abnormalities. This code reports the radiological supervision and interpretation only. Use a separately reportable code for the catheterization.

75774
This procedure reports each additional vessel studied after the basic, initial study. It involves manipulating the catheter into additional second, third, or higher order vessels within a vascular family and performing injection of contrast and taking additional films. This code is an add-on code and cannot stand alone.

75791
A local anesthetic is applied over the site where the catheter is to be introduced; this is most often the common femoral or brachial artery. The artery is percutaneously punctured with a needle and a guidewire is fed through the artery until it reaches the arteriovenous shunt created in the dialysis patient, usually in the upper extremity. A catheter is threaded over the guidewire to the point of study and the guidewire is removed. Contrast medium is injected and a series of x-rays are taken to visualize the shunt and evaluate its function, including all radiographic imaging deemed necessary from the arterial anastomosis and adjacent artery through the entire venous outflow (inferior and superior vena cava included). This code reports only the radiological supervision and interpretation portion of this procedure.

75801-75803
Vital blue dye is injected into the subcutaneous tissues for outlining of skin lymphatics. As soon as the lymphatic vessels are visualized by their blue color, the physician makes a small incision to gain access. The lymph vessel is cannulated with a needle and a fine catheter is attached. A small amount of dye is injected to ensure correct placement and the needle is advanced a few millimeters into the vessel. The needle and catheter are secured and dye is injected with a syringe. X-rays are made. Code 75801 reports the radiological supervision and interpretation for lymphangiography of an extremity on one side only; 75803 reports the radiological supervision and interpretation for lymphangiography of extremities on both sides. Use a separately reportable code for the injection procedure.

75805-75807
Vital blue dye is injected into the subcutaneous tissues for outlining of skin lymphatics. As soon as the lymphatic vessels are visualized by their blue color, the physician makes a small incision to gain access. The lymph vessel is cannulated with a needle and a fine catheter is attached. A small amount of dye is injected to ensure correct placement and the needle is advanced a few millimeters into the vessel. The needle and catheter are secured and dye is injected with a syringe. X-rays are made. Code 75805 reports the radiological supervision and interpretation for lymphangiography on one side only of the pelvic/abdominal region. Code 75807 reports the radiological supervision and interpretation for lymphangiography on both sides of the pelvic/abdominal region. Use a separately reportable code for the injection procedure.

75809
The physician injects contrast material through the skin into the reservoir of a peritoneal-venous shunt or directly into shunt tubing or reservoir with a needle. Shunt tubing is a drain to eliminate excess cerebral spinal fluid in cases of hydrocephalus. The tubing of a peritoneal-venous shunt drains the accumulation of fluids in cases of ascites into a major vein. The physician places the needle and injects radiologic dye. Pictures are taken to visualize the flow of contrast and check for effective drainage. This code reports the radiological supervision and interpretation only. Use a separately reportable code for the shuntogram injection procedure.

75810

The physician makes an incision in the lower left axilla. An 18 or 20-gauge sheath catheter is inserted into the middle of the soft, sponge-like tissue of the spleen. The splenic vein is visualized and the catheter is placed. 2.0-3 cc of radiopaque dye is injected per second, totaling about 15.0-20 cc of dye. X-rays are taken every second for about 12 seconds. The catheter is removed and the incision covered with a dressing. This code reports the radiological supervision and interpretation only. Use a separately reportable code for the splenoportography injection procedure.

75820-75822

The physician performs a radiographic study on the veins of a left or right extremity, upper or lower, in 75820 and both the left and right legs or arms in 75822. This type of study is most often performed on the lower extremities as opposed to the arms and commonly involves the femoral vein, described here. A local anesthetic is applied over the site where the catheter is to be introduced. The vein is percutaneously punctured with a needle and a guidewire is fed through the vein to the point where dye will be injected. A catheter is threaded over the guidewire and the guidewire is removed. Contrast medium is injected and a series of x-rays performed to visualize the vessels and evaluate any abnormalities. In venography, contrast medium is injected into the catheter that has traveled to an area upstream of the site under investigation. These codes report the radiological supervision and interpretation only. Use a separately reportable code for the catheterization.

75825-75827

A local anesthetic is applied over a distal vein (typically antecubital, internal jugular, subclavian, or femoral) and the vein is percutaneously punctured with a needle. A guidewire is fed through the vein to the inferior vena cava in 75825 and the superior vena cava in 75827. The physician may slide an introducer sheath over the guidewire into the venous lumen before inserting a catheter. The catheter is inserted into the vein and threaded over the guidewire to the inferior (75825) or superior (75827) vena cava. The guidewire is removed. Contrast medium is injected and a series of x-rays performed to visualize and evaluate any abnormalities. In venography, contrast medium is injected into the catheter that has traveled to an area upstream of the site under investigation. These codes report the radiological supervision and interpretation only. Use a separately reportable code for the catheterization.

75831-75833

A local anesthetic is applied over the site where the catheter is to be introduced; this is most often the common femoral vein. The vein is percutaneously punctured with a needle and a guidewire is inserted and selectively fed through the vein until it reaches the desired location in the venous system. A catheter is threaded over the guidewire into the selected point in the vein and the wire is removed. Contrast medium for venography is injected through the catheter that has traveled to an area upstream of the site under investigation. X-rays are taken. Code 75831 reports the radiological supervision and interpretation only for venography of the left or right renal vein and 75833 is used for both renal veins. Use a separately reportable code for the catheterization.

75840-75842

A local anesthetic is applied over the site where the catheter is to be introduced; this is most often the common femoral vein. The vein is percutaneously punctured with a needle and a guidewire is inserted and selectively fed through the vein until it reaches the desired location in the venous system. A catheter is threaded over the guidewire into the selected point in the vein and the wire is removed. Contrast medium for venography is injected through the catheter that has traveled to an area upstream of the site under investigation. X-rays are taken. Code 75840 reports the radiological supervision and interpretation only for venography of the left or right adrenal vein and 75842 is used for both adrenal veins. Use a separately reportable code for the catheterization.

75860

A local anesthetic is applied over the site where the catheter is to be introduced and the access vein is percutaneously punctured with a needle. A guidewire is inserted and advanced through the vein until it reaches the desired location in the venous system for imaging the sinus (petrosal, inferior sagittal) or jugular vein. A catheter is threaded over the guidewire to the selected point and the wire is removed. Non-ionic diluted contrast medium is injected over approximately 30 seconds through the catheter that has traveled to an area upstream of the site under investigation. Images are acquired. This code reports the radiological supervision and interpretation only. Use a separately reportable code for the catheterization.

75870

A local anesthetic is applied over the site where the catheter is to be introduced and the access vein is percutaneously punctured with a needle. A guidewire is inserted and advanced through the dominant jugular vein until it reaches the desired location for studying the superior sagittal sinus, which is the primary venous drainage for the cranial vasculature. A catheter is threaded over the guidewire into the selected point in the vein and the wire is removed. Non-ionic diluted contrast medium is injected through the catheter that has traveled to an area upstream of the site under investigation. Images are acquired. This code reports the radiological supervision and interpretation only. Use a separately reportable code for the catheterization.

75872
In epidural venography, a needle is inserted into the epidural space of the spine while the patient is sitting in a position with the chin on the chest and the knees pulled up or positioned on the left side. A catheter is threaded over the needle until it reaches the epidural space around the spinal cord and the needle is removed. Contrast is injected into the catheter and radiographic pictures are taken. This is done on patients with a penetrating trauma to the area, or subarachnoid or parenchymal hemorrhage. This code reports the radiological supervision and interpretation only. Use a separately reportable code for the catheterization.

75880
The physician introduces a needle or catheter through a puncture site in the skin into a peripheral vein. A guidewire is inserted and selectively fed through the vein until it reaches the desired location in the venous system for imaging the orbital veins. A catheter is threaded over the guidewire into the selected point in the vein and the wire is removed. Radiopaque dye is administered into the facial or frontal veins, and x-rays are taken to visualize the orbital veins and cavernous sinuses. This code reports the radiological supervision and interpretation only. Use a separately reportable code for the catheterization.

75885
A radiographic exam of the portal vein of the liver is done by inserting a needle through the abdomen. The patient's right side is cleansed and a local anesthetic given at the puncture site. A needle is inserted into the skin just under the ribs and diaphragm and advanced to the liver under fluoroscopic guidance. The needle is aimed at the portal vein and when blood returns from the needle, a small amount of contrast is injected to confirm placement into the portal vein. When in place, a guidewire is inserted and a catheter follows. More contrast is injected, radiographs taken and intravenous, hemodynamic pressures in the portal vein are recorded. This code reports the radiological supervision and interpretation only. Use a separately reportable code for the catheterization.

75887
A radiographic exam of the portal vein of the liver is done by inserting a needle through the abdomen. The patient's right side is cleansed and a local anesthetic given at the puncture site. A needle is inserted into the skin just under the ribs and diaphragm and advanced to the liver under fluoroscopic guidance. The needle is aimed at the portal vein and when blood returns from the needle, a small amount of contrast is injected to confirm placement into the portal vein. When in place, a guidewire is inserted and a catheter follows. More contrast is injected and radiographs are taken. This code reports the radiological supervision and interpretation only. Use a separately reportable code for the catheterization.

75889-75891
A local anesthetic is applied over the common femoral vein and a guidewire is fed through until it reaches the hepatic vein. A catheter is threaded over the guidewire and the guidewire is removed. For wedged hepatic venography, the catheter is wedged into a small hepatic vein branch to approximate the portal pressure occurring in liver disease. For free hepatic venography, the catheter tip lies free in the hepatic vein. Correct positioning of the catheter is monitored by fluoroscopy. Contrast medium is injected into the vein and x-rays are taken. Report 75889 if this is done together with hemodynamic evaluation in which blood movement through the liver is monitored by indwelling catheters connected to transducers. The pressure forces within the arteries and veins are converted to electrical signals and displayed on screen. Report 75891 if hepatic venography is performed without the hemodynamic evaluation. These codes report the radiological supervision and interpretation only.

75893
Venous sampling involves withdrawing blood from a patient's vein into a vacuum tube. For parathyroid hormone or renin testing, a catheter is used for sampling. The catheter must be advanced through the abdominal aorta and into the renal arteries from an outside access point, usually the common femoral vein. When the catheter is correctly placed, several samples are withdrawn. This code reports the radiological supervision and interpretation only.

75894
A blood vessel is blocked by inserting an occlusive agent under fluoroscopic monitoring to stop or restrict the blood flow. This is done to restrict blood supply to a tumor, treat vascular malformations, or control hemorrhaging. A local anesthetic is given at the puncture site and a needle is inserted into the selected vessel followed by a guidewire. The needle is removed. A catheter is inserted over the guidewire and advanced to the vessel requiring treatment. A blocking agent is injected or inserted and monitored. The effect may remain permanent or require another transcatheter embolization with time. This code reports the radiological supervision and interpretation only. Use a separately reportable code for the catheterization.

75896
Blood flow in a vessel clogged by an obstruction such as a blood clot is re-established by transcatheter infusion. A local anesthetic is given at the puncture site and a needle is inserted into the selected vessel followed by a catheter advanced within the blocked artery until its tip lies within the clot. A thrombolytic substance is infused continuously over intervals and the progress monitored using fluoroscopic images. Additional separate angiography may be done to assess

vessel patency. This code reports the radiological supervision and interpretation only. Use a separately reportable code for the catheterization.

75898
Angiography is performed during or following transcatheter infusion or embolization through the existing catheter to reassess the therapy's effectiveness. A radiopaque contrast medium is injected through the catheter and by fluoroscopic images recorded of the vessel, the radiologist interprets the status of the blood vessel and the effectiveness of treatment rendered.

75900
During thrombolytic infusion therapy, the existing intravascular catheter is removed and replaced under fluoroscopic control. Contrast medium is injected for guidance. A guidewire is inserted over which the existing catheter is removed and the replacement catheter is threaded. The guidewire may be removed or left in place. This code reports the radiological supervision and interpretation only.

75901
Pericatheter obstructive material, such as a fibrin sheath, is removed from around a central venous device via separate venous access. Central venous catheters often fail because of the accumulation of an obstructing thrombus or fibrin sheath around the tip of the catheter. The catheter is first checked that it can aspirate and flush forward. The pericatheter material is identified by contrast material injection. Generally, a right femoral vein access is used. A guidewire followed by an angiographic catheter are advanced into the superior vena cava and exchanged for a loop snare with its catheter, which are advanced cephalad along the length of the central venous catheter beyond the ports. The loop snare is tightly closed about the CV catheter to encircle it and slowly pulled down and off the tip of the catheter, stripping off the pericatheter obstructive material. This is repeated a few times and the catheter is rechecked for infusion and injection ability of the ports. A contrast study is done again to identify any fibrin and the process may be repeated until the fibrin sheath is completely removed. This code reports only the radiological supervision and interpretation required for this procedure.

75902
Intraluminal obstructive material, such as a thrombus or fibrin sheath, is removed from inside a central venous device through the lumen of the device. This does not require a separate access incision. The central venous catheter is first checked that it can aspirate and flush forward. The obstructing material is disrupted and removed mechanically by using an angioplasty balloon or other catheter introduced into the central venous catheter through its entry site on the skin. The catheter is checked for unimpeded, restored flow and the process may be repeated until the CV catheter is cleared. This code reports the radiological supervision and interpretation only required for this procedure.

75940
A filter is placed into the inferior vena cava percutaneously, usually through the right internal jugular vein. Fluoroscopy is used to monitor and guide the process. An incision is made just above the clavicle and another small incision is made into the vein once it is identified. A catheter loaded with the filter is inserted into the vein and threaded through until it reaches the inferior vena cava. The filter is released from the catheter and opens to fill the diameter and grip the walls of the vena cava. The filter-loaded catheter may also be advanced over a guidewire to the vena cava after needle puncture of the internal jugular vein. This code reports the radiological supervision and interpretation only for this procedure.

75945-75946
An ultrasound is performed on the inside of a blood vessel previously treated for an obstruction or stricture. The ultrasound may be done during or after a therapeutic procedure such as dilation, stent deployment, or atherectomy. An intravascular ultrasound catheter is threaded over an already placed guidewire to the study area and its external end is connected to the display monitor. Ultrasonic images of the vessel are displayed on the monitor and if satisfactory, the catheter is removed and the therapeutic procedure completed. Report 75945 for ultrasound on the initial, non-coronary vessel and 75946 for each additional (non-coronary) vessel studied beyond the initial. These codes report the radiological supervision and interpretation only.

75952
An infrarenal abdominal aortic aneurysm is repaired endovascularly using the skills of both a vascular surgeon and a radiologist. A small incision is made in the groin over one or both femoral arteries. Under separately reportable fluoroscopy, a synthetic stent graft contained inside a long plastic holding capsule is threaded over a guidewire to the infrarenal aneurysm. Once the stent is in place, the holding capsule is released and the stent graft expands like a spring and anchors itself to the artery wall. A balloon catheter may be threaded to the graft site and inflated to fully expand the prosthesis. The catheter is removed and the site closed. The aneurysm, excluded from the blood flow, typically shrinks over time. This code reports the radiological supervision and interpretation only for this procedure.

75953
A leak, called an endoleak, may occur at fixation sites of a grafted aneurysm through the body of the graft or from patent arteries within the aneurysm sac and may require additional endovascular reparation. A proper extension prosthesis, contained within a long plastic holding capsule is threaded through the arteries over a

guidewire to the site of the leak. Once the extension prosthesis is in place, the holding capsule is released and the extension prosthesis expands like a spring and anchors itself to the artery wall. A balloon catheter may be threaded to the graft site and inflated to fully expand the prosthesis. The catheter is removed and the site closed. This code reports the radiological supervision and interpretation only for this procedure.

75954
An iliac artery aneurysm, pseudoaneurysm, vascular malformation, or trauma injury is repaired by placing a graft from within the artery. A leak, called an endoleak, may occur at fixation sites of a grafted aneurysm through the body of the graft or from patent arteries within the aneurysm sac and may require endovascular reparation. The aneurysm is identified using angiography. The endograft, contained inside a holding device, is introduced into the artery under fluoroscopy and positioned at the target zone area of repair. This may need to be done by open access exposure of the artery or by threading guidewires and catheters through to the site. Once the endograft is in place, it is deployed within the artery at the aneurysm site. Balloon angioplasties and other stent deployments necessary to position the graft or ensure proper functioning are part of this procedure. The graft position is confirmed, any endoleaks are identified, and the status of runoff vessels is evaluated for any related stenosis, dissection, thrombosis, or embolism. This code reports only the radiological supervision and interpretation required for this procedure.

75956-75957
The physician repairs the descending thoracic aorta by placing an endoprosthesis from within the artery. Endovascular repair may be performed for an aneurysm, pseudoaneurysm, dissection, penetrating ulcer, intramural hematoma, or traumatic disruption. The defect in the descending thoracic aorta is identified using aortography. The endoprosthesis, contained inside a holding device, is introduced into the artery under fluoroscopy and positioned at the target zone area of repair. Extension prostheses may be required to the level of the celiac artery origin. In 75956, when the endoprosthesis is in position, it is deployed within the artery at the target site in the descending thoracic aorta, covering the origin of the left subclavian artery. A balloon angioplasty may be necessary to achieve proper positioning and functioning of the endoprosthesis. The placement position is confirmed, the catheter is removed, and the arteriotomy site is closed. These codes report only the radiological supervision and interpretation required for this procedure. Report 75956 when the repair covers the left subclavian artery origin and 75957 when the repair does not cover the left subclavian artery origin.

75958
A leak, called an endoleak, may occur at the proximal fixation sites of a grafted descending thoracic aorta defect through the body of the graft or from patent arteries within the defect and may require endovascular reparation. A proximal extension prosthesis is placed endovascularly to repair an endoleak in a grafted descending thoracic aortic aneurysm, pseudoaneurysm, dissection, penetrating ulcer, intramural hematoma, or traumatic disruption. The target site is identified by aortography and the proper extension prosthesis is selected. Under fluoroscopy, the extension prosthesis, contained inside a long plastic holding capsule, is threaded through the arteries to the site of the leak. Once the extension prosthesis is in place, the holding capsule is removed. The extension prosthesis, activated by heat, expands like a spring and becomes anchored to the artery wall at the site of the endoleak. If full expansion of the prosthesis does not occur automatically, a balloon catheter is threaded to the graft site and inflated within the endovascular prosthesis until full expansion is achieved. The placement position is confirmed, the catheter is removed, and the arteriotomy site is closed. This code reports only the radiological supervision and interpretation required for this procedure.

75959
A leak, called an endoleak, may occur at the distal fixation sites of a previously grafted descending thoracic aorta defect through the body of the graft or from patent arteries within the defect and may require endovascular reparation. One or more distal extension prosthesis modules are placed endovascularly to the level of the celiac artery to repair an endoleak in a previously grafted descending thoracic aortic aneurysm, pseudoaneurysm, dissection, penetrating ulcer, intramural hematoma, or traumatic disruption. The target site is identified by aortography and the proper extension prosthesis is selected. Under fluoroscopy, the extension prosthesis, contained inside a long plastic holding capsule, is threaded through the arteries to the site of the leak. Once the extension prosthesis is in place, the holding capsule is removed. The extension prosthesis, activated by heat, expands like a spring and becomes anchored to the artery wall at the site of the endoleak. If full expansion of the prosthesis does not occur automatically, a balloon catheter is threaded to the graft site and inflated within the endovascular prosthesis until full expansion is achieved. The placement position is confirmed, the catheter is removed, and the arteriotomy site is closed. This code reports only the radiological supervision and interpretation required for this procedure and is reported only once regardless of the number of extension modules deployed.

75960
A stent(s) is introduced into a blood vessel (other than a coronary, carotid, or vertebral vessel) requiring

endovascular support percutaneously or openly. In a percutaneous approach, the skin is punctured with a needle inserted into the access blood vessel. A guidewire is threaded through the needle into the blood vessel. The needle is removed. A catheter with a stent-transporting tip is advanced over the guidewire into the vessel, and the wire is extracted. The catheter travels to the point where the vessel needs additional support. The compressed stent(s) is passed from the catheter out into the vessel, where it deploys, expanding to support the vessel walls. The catheter is removed and pressure is applied over the puncture site. In an open approach, the skin overlying the vessel is incised and the stent-transporting tipped catheter is inserted into the vessel after it has been dissected and opened with a knife. After the stent(s) is deployed and the catheter is removed, the skin is closed in layers. This code reports the radiological supervision and interpretation only. This code is reported per vessel, not per stent.

75961
A foreign body such as the broken tip of a catheter within a blood vessel is retrieved. A local anesthetic is applied over the puncture site and the skin is percutaneously punctured with a needle. A guidewire is fed through the blood vessel and the needle is removed. A catheter with a grasping instrument (e.g., hook, loop, basket) is advanced over the guidewire to the site of the foreign body. The instrument grasps the foreign body and it is withdrawn with the catheter. Pressure is applied over the puncture site. This code reports the radiological supervision and interpretation only for this procedure.

75962-75964
A narrowing or stricture of a peripheral artery is stretched to allow a normal flow of blood. A local anesthetic is applied over the access site, usually the femoral artery, and the skin is percutaneously punctured with a needle. A guidewire is fed through the blood vessel and the needle is removed. A catheter with a deflated balloon is advanced over the guidewire to the narrowed portion of the vessel. The balloon is inflated to stretch the vessel to a larger diameter allowing a more normal flow of blood. Several inflations may be performed along the narrowed area. Transluminal angioplasty may be done through an incision in the skin overlying the artery of access. Vessel clamps are applied and the artery is nicked to create an opening for the balloon catheter. Report 75962 for transluminal balloon angioplasty on one peripheral artery and 75964 for each additional peripheral artery treated after the first artery. These codes report the radiological supervision and interpretation only.

75966-75968
A narrowing or stricture of a renal or visceral artery (supplying organs in the abdominal/pelvic area) is stretched to allow a normal flow of blood. A local anesthetic is applied over the access site, usually the femoral artery, and the skin is percutaneously punctured with a needle. A guidewire is fed through the blood vessel and the needle removed. A catheter with a deflated balloon is advanced over the guidewire to the narrowed portion of the vessel. The balloon is inflated to stretch the vessel to a larger diameter allowing a more normal flow of blood. Several inflations may be performed along the narrowed area. Transluminal angioplasty may be done through an incision in the skin overlying the artery of access. Vessel clamps are applied and the artery is nicked to create an opening for the balloon catheter. Report 75966 for transluminal balloon angioplasty on a renal or other visceral artery and 75968 for each additional renal or visceral artery treated after the first artery. These codes report the radiological supervision and interpretation only.

75970
A biopsy specimen is obtained through a catheter. The biopsy catheter may be inserted through an already existing drainage tube or catheter, through a tract or pathway, such as the urethra during cystourethroscopy, or through the skin and into the access artery. Fluoroscopy is used to guide the catheter through its course from entry to the point of study to be biopsied. A biopsy brush, fine biopsy needle, or biting forceps may be inserted through the catheter to obtain the cells or tissue for examination. This code reports the radiological supervision and interpretation only.

75978
A narrowing or stricture of a vein is stretched to allow a normal flow of blood. A local anesthetic is applied over the access site and the skin is percutaneously punctured with a needle. A guidewire is fed through the blood vessel and the needle is removed. A catheter with a deflated balloon is advanced over the guidewire to the narrowed portion of the vessel. The balloon is inflated to stretch the vessel to a larger diameter allowing a more normal flow of blood. Several inflations may be performed along the narrowed area. Transluminal angioplasty may be done through an incision in the skin overlying the access vein. Vessel clamps are applied and the vein is nicked to create an opening for the balloon catheter. This code reports the radiological supervision and interpretation only for venous transluminal balloon angioplasty.

75980
The physician introduces a catheter into the liver to drain fluid using fluoroscopy and contrast to guide the process. The puncture site on the right side of the body is incised, the needle inserted between the ribs, advanced into the liver, and into the bile duct. Contrast medium is injected to visualize the intrahepatic bile ducts. A guidewire is inserted and advanced to the point of obstruction through an optimal duct

permitting access and drainage. A catheter is threaded over the guidewire and dilators may be used to enlarge both the opening and the tract from the skin to the bile duct. The drainage catheter is inserted and positioned at the obstruction and secured to the skin. This code reports the radiological supervision and interpretation only for this procedure.

75982
The physician introduces a catheter into the liver to drain fluid both internally and externally, usually on patients with inoperable bile duct obstruction. The puncture site on the right side of the body is incised. A needle is inserted between the ribs, advanced into the liver, and into the bile duct. Contrast medium is injected to visualize the intrahepatic bile ducts by fluoroscopy. A guidewire is inserted and advanced into the duodenum to bypass the inoperable obstruction. A catheter is threaded over the guidewire and dilators may be used to enlarge both the opening and the tract from the skin to the bile duct. The drainage catheter is inserted and positioned so that openings for drainage are both above and below the obstruction and secured in place. This allows bile to flow to an external drainage system as well as into the duodenum. This code reports the radiological supervision and interpretation only for this procedure.

75984
An existing percutaneous drainage tube or catheter (e.g., genitourinary system or abscess) is replaced with contrast monitoring. A guidewire is usually inserted into the existing catheter to guide the new one. The old catheter is removed and the replacement catheter is threaded back over the guidewire. Contrast injection allows for correct positioning to be visualized with fluoroscopic images displayed on a screen. This code reports the radiological supervision and interpretation only.

75989
Fluoroscopic, ultrasonic, or CT guidance may be used for percutaneous drainage of an abscess or to obtain a specimen and place a tube or catheter. Once the abscess is located, the skin is punctured with a needle to begin draining. A catheter may be advanced over a guidewire inserted through the needle and into the abscess cavity. The tract to the outside is dilated to facilitate placing a percutaneous drainage tube. The cavity is aspirated and the drainage tube placed at the lowest point to ensure complete drainage. The drainage tube is secured to suction drainage. This code reports the radiological supervision and interpretation only for this procedure.

75992-75993
A stenosed peripheral artery is treated intraluminally to relieve blockage. A needle punctures the skin at the access site and is followed by a guidewire and an introducer sheath to protect and enclose the opening. A series of catheters and guidewires are inserted until the narrowed, stenosed area has been transversed. Finally an atherectomy catheter is manipulated to the study area and activated to cut or drill a channel through the plaque lesion and reopen the artery. Contrast medium is injected to fluoroscopically visualize the degree of luminal opening. The process may be repeated with a larger diameter catheter. Use 75992 to report transluminal atherectomy on one peripheral artery and 75993 for each additional peripheral artery treated. These codes report the radiological supervision and interpretation only.

75994
A stenosed renal artery is treated intraluminally to relieve blockage. A needle punctures the skin at the access site and is followed by a guidewire and an introducer sheath to protect and enclose the opening. A series of catheters and guidewires are inserted until the narrowed, stenosed area has been transversed. Finally an atherectomy catheter is manipulated to the renal artery and activated to cut or drill a channel through the plaque lesion and reopen the artery. Contrast medium is injected to fluoroscopically visualize the degree of luminal opening. The process may be repeated with a larger diameter catheter. This code reports the radiological supervision and interpretation only for this procedure.

75995-75996
A stenosed visceral artery (supplying abdominal organs) is treated intraluminally to relieve blockage. A needle punctures the skin at the access site and is followed by a guidewire and an introducer sheath to protect and enclose the opening. A series of catheters and guidewires are inserted until the narrowed, stenosed area has been transversed. Finally an atherectomy catheter is manipulated to the study area and activated to cut or drill a channel through the plaque lesion and reopen the artery. Contrast medium is injected to fluoroscopically visualize the degree of luminal opening. The process may be repeated with a larger diameter catheter. Use 75995 to report transluminal atherectomy of one visceral artery and 75996 for each additional visceral artery treated. These codes report the radiological supervision and interpretation only.

76000
A radiologist provides separate fluoroscopic monitoring of the body for up to one hour for procedures that do not always include fluoroscopy as an integral component of the procedure. This is reported separately to describe the physician work entailed in providing fluoroscopic monitoring. If formal contrast x-ray studies are done and included as a part of the procedure to produce films with written interpretation and report, fluoroscopy is already included and cannot be separately reported.

76001
A radiologist provides fluoroscopic monitoring of the body for more than one hour while assisting a non-radiologic physician (e.g., nephrologist, pulmonologist). This code is reported to describe the physician work entailed in providing fluoroscopic during procedures such as nephrostolithotomy and bronchoscopy. If formal contrast x-ray studies are done and included as a part of the procedure to produce films with written interpretation and report, fluoroscopy is already included and cannot be separately reported.

76010
Children frequently ingest foreign objects that can be diagnosed by plain film radiography. A single view is taken of the gastrointestinal pathway from nose to rectum to locate a foreign body.

76080
An injection of radiopaque material is made directly into a sinus tract (a canal or passage leading to an abscess) or through a previously placed catheter, to determine the existence, nature, or size of an abscess or fistula (an abnormal tube-like passage from a normal body cavity to a free surface or to another body cavity). This code reports the radiological supervision and interpretation only.

76098
Immediately after removal of the suspected breast lesion and the localization wire, the specimen is sent to be examined so the surgeon may complete the operative procedure. The sample is compressed and an x-ray taken to identify that it is the suspected lesion and the information is immediately returned to the surgeon.

76100
A radiological exam is done on a body section in a single plane by scanning an x-ray beam across the body in one direction to take pictures of the structures under study in the selected plane. The films show detailed images of the structures within the single selected plane by blurring out the images above and below. Use this code for a single plane radiological exam of a single body section other than urography.

76101-76102
Tomography is a radiographic technique that uses conventional, film-based picture taking to create images of a structure that remains in the focal plane while blurring out images that appear superficial or deep to the focal structure. When an exposure is made, the x-ray tube and the film move in opposite directions at the same time. Polytomographic examinations are often performed for viewing dental structures or the temporomandibular joint. There are machines designed especially for taking these polytomographic pictures and most are computer-aided. The complex motion tomographic x-rays are done in circular, spiral, elliptical, or hypercycloidal multidirectional motions. Report 76101 for a unilateral complex motion radiologic exam and 76102 for a bilateral.

76120-76125
Cineradiography uses high speed x-ray films to take a series of images of an organ or system in motion such as the vocal cords or heart. These images taken in exposure ranges of nanoseconds to milliseconds are like the individual frames of a motion picture. This allows the movement to be frozen and tracked very minutely to gather information about time-varying characteristics. Use 76120 when performed alone and not specifically included as part of the procedure. Use 76125 when cineradiography is performed in conjunction with a routine exam.

76140
A radiologist provides a consultation and a written report after reviewing an x-ray exam that was performed elsewhere.

76150
A diagnostic image is produced on paper instead of on film. An electrically charged photosensitive plate is placed on one side of the patient and the x-ray beam is directed from the other. After exposure, charge patterns of tissue density and absorption are left on the plate, which is dusted with a colored, negatively-charged powdered toner. A blue-on-white picture is able to be transferred to a sheet of paper covered with plastic. This test aids in detecting foreign bodies within soft tissue.

76350
Subtraction in conjunction with contrast studies is a technique whereby any subsequent images visualized after introduction of a contrast material are taken out or subtracted from the main picture or data to be studied, such as subtracting out bone in order to enhance the vasculature in angiogram studies.

76376-76377
The physician provides concurrent supervision for processing of computerized tomography (CT), magnetic resonance imaging (MRI), ultrasound, or other tomographic modality with 3D manipulation of volumetric data sets and image rendering. The exact nature of the 3D manipulation is dependent upon the type of study being performed and the purpose of the diagnostic imaging. Image manipulation can include 3D image segmentation (i.e., removing skeletal structure to better visualize vascular structure followed by identifying and segmenting vessels for individual analysis and review), 3D volume and surface rendering, and 3D image restoration by deconvolution (i.e., unfolding the colon or straightening tortuous blood vessels). Work can include diagnostic imaging and surgical planning with 3D images, scientific modeling and simulation, and other work involving volumetric data. Report 76376 for 3D rendering not requiring

image postprocessing on an independent workstation. Report 76377 when image postprocessing on an independent workstation is required.

76380

Computed tomography (CT) scanning directs multiple narrow beams of x-rays around the body structure(s) being studied and uses computer imaging to produce thin cross-sectional views of various layers (or slices) of the body. It is able to visualize soft tissue as well as bones. This code reports a limited or a localized follow-up study.

76390

Magnetic resonance spectroscopy (MRS) is used to determine chemical and metabolic properties of a particular region, organ, or structure within the body. MRS can be done at the same time as standard MRI, which yields cross-sectional, anatomic information about the spatial properties of a region relative to its surrounding areas; MRS however, provides rich information about the biochemical composition or metabolite concentration levels of the localized region, identifying very subtle changes. In vivo spectroscopy is a noninvasive method that relies on nuclear magnetic resonance principles: MRS requires the patient to be placed in a strong magnetic field with a radiowave transmit pulse set at a very particular frequency in order to observe the signal produced by the nuclei specific to the type of atom chosen for the study, such as hydrogen or phosphorus. The spectrum results are in the form of a frequency axis in parts per million and a signal amplitude axis. The specific nuclei within a chosen metabolite will give rise to peaks uniquely positioned along the frequency axis; the position of the peak is called the chemical shift. The signal amplitude of a peak is quantified and correlates directly to the concentration of the assigned metabolite.

76506

Echoencephalography is done to determine ventricular size, investigate suspected fluid masses or other intracranial abnormalities, and define cerebral contents. During the test, the radiation technician guides the transducer over the area of the brain to be examined. The transducer sends an ultrasound beam through the tissue. The reflected sound waves are converted into electrical impulses and displayed on a video screen for interpretation or photographing for later interpretation. Abnormal results may indicate cerebral edema, lesions, or subdural and extradural hemorrhage. The gray (Gy) scale refers to the amount of energy absorbed by the tissue. Real-time scan is a two-dimensional scanning procedure with display of both two-dimensional structure and motion with time. A-mode is a one-dimensional measurement procedure. This code includes A-mode encephalography as a secondary component where indicated.

76510

Diagnostic ophthalmic ultrasound, also called echography, is performed to image intraocular anatomy or to differentiate orbital lesions or disease. A-scan is a one-dimensional measurement procedure using high-frequency sound waves introduced into the eye in a straight line. B-scan utilizes sound waves in a two-dimensional scanning procedure to display a two-dimensional image of the internal ocular structures. Through a transducer placed on the eye, high-frequency sound waves are sent through the eye, which reflect back to a receiver, are converted into electrical pulses, and displayed on screen. In quantitative A scan, the resulting single-dimensional image provides information about tissue structure and reflective/sound absorptive properties. B-scan can locate structures in the eye that may be obscured by cataract, hemorrhages, or opacities and provides information as to a lesion's shape, mobility, insertion, or relationship to neighboring structures. This code reports both types of scanning performed in the same patient encounter.

76511

Diagnostic ophthalmic ultrasound, also called echography, is done to image intraocular anatomy or to differentiate orbital lesions or disease. A-scan is a one-dimensional measurement procedure using high-frequency sound waves introduced into the eye in a straight line by a transducer placed on the eye. As the waves reflect off the eye tissue, they are picked up by the same transducer, converted to electrical pulses, and displayed on screen. The resulting single-dimensional image is composed of vertical spikes that vary according to the tissue density. Quantitative A-scan only is applied for this code. Quantitative A-scan provides information about a lesion's tissue structure, and reflective/sound absorptive properties.

76512

Diagnostic ophthalmic ultrasound, also called echography, is done to image intraocular anatomy or to differentiate orbital lesions or disease. B-scan utilizes sound waves in a two-dimensional scanning procedure to display a two-dimensional image of the internal ocular structures. A transducer placed on the eye sends high-frequency sound waves into the eye, which reflect back to a receiver, are converted into electrical pulses, and displayed on screen. B-scan can locate structures in the eye that may be obscured by cataract, hemorrhages, or opacities and provides information as to a lesion's shape, mobility, insertion, or relationship to neighboring structures. Diagnostic B-scan is applied for this code with or without superimposed non-quantitative A-scan. Superimposed non-quantitative A-scan may be topographical and can give more precise measurements along one parallel sound beam, and identify the borders or maximum height of the tumor.

76513

Diagnostic ophthalmic ultrasound, also called echography, is done to image intraocular anatomy or to differentiate orbital lesions or disease. Anterior eye segment ultrasound is accomplished using B-scan of 20-50 MHz. This high-frequency ultrasound imaging produces pictures of the eye that approach microscopic resolution (50 microns). B-scan utilizes sound waves in a two-dimensional scanning procedure to display a two-dimensional image of the internal ocular structures. A transducer sends high-frequency sound waves into the eye, which reflect back to a receiver, are converted into electrical pulses, and displayed on screen. In the immersion (water bath) method, the eye is maintained in direct contact with a water bath, through the use of a special cup filled with saline solution inserted between the eyelids. The tip of the transducer is not in direct contact with the eye.

76514

Diagnostic ophthalmic ultrasound is done to determine corneal thickness on one or both eyes by using corneal pachymetry, which is non-invasive and painless. Measuring the cornea is done by administrating a topical anesthetic into the eye and placing a plastic ultrasonic probe onto the central cornea. A pachymeter uses ultrasound to determine the thickness of the cornea in any given location. A short wave burst of sound is generated by a transmitter and sent through the eye tissue. The detector positioned close to the transmitter detects the echo. The echo reflected from near the surface reaches the detector faster than echoes reflected at lower-lying levels. The structure of the tissue, the thickness of the corneal structure at any given location, is determined on the basis of the echo's time distribution. Pachymetry is an essential measurement prior to certain surgical procedures, such as LASIK, that require removing tissue from the cornea. These measurements ascertain whether the cornea will retain enough thickness to prevent complications.

76516-76519

A-scan uses ultrasonography, or echography, to image intraocular anatomy to determine the axial length of the eye (from the cornea to the retina) for calculating the power required for an intraocular lens implant. High-frequency sound waves are introduced into the eye in a straight line by a transducer placed on the eye. As the waves reflect off the eye tissue, they are also picked up by the same transducer, converted to electrical pulses and displayed on screen. The resulting single-dimensional image is composed of vertical spikes that vary according to the tissue density. Report 76516 for ophthalmic measurements by ultrasound echography and 76519 if intraocular power lens calculation is done.

76529

B-scan utilizes sound waves in a two-dimensional scanning procedure to display a two-dimensional image of the internal ocular structures and ultrasonically locate a foreign body in the eye. A transducer placed on the eye sends high-frequency sound waves into the eye which reflect back to a receiver, are converted into electrical pulses, and displayed on screen. B-scan can also locate structures or objects in the eye that may be obscured by cataract, hemorrhages, or opacities.

76536

Diagnostic ultrasound is an imaging technique bouncing sound waves far above the level of human perception through interior body structures. The sound waves pass through different densities of tissue and reflect back to a receiving unit at varying speeds. The unit converts the waves to electrical pulses that are immediately displayed in picture form on screen. Real time scanning displays structure images and movement with time. This code reports ultrasound, real time with image documentation, for the soft tissues of the head and neck (e.g., thyroid, parathyroid).

76604

Diagnostic ultrasound is an imaging technique bouncing sound waves far above the level of human perception through interior body structures. The sound waves pass through different densities of tissue and reflect back to a receiving unit at varying speeds. The unit converts the waves to electrical pulses that are immediately displayed in picture form on screen. Real time scanning displays structure images and movement with time. This code reports ultrasound and real time for the chest, including the mediastinum.

76645

Diagnostic ultrasound is an imaging technique bouncing sound waves far above the level of human perception through interior body structures. The sound waves pass through different densities of tissue and reflect back to a receiving unit at varying speeds. The unit converts the waves to electrical pulses that are immediately displayed in picture form on screen. Real time scanning displays structure images and movement with time. This code reports ultrasound and real time for one or both breasts.

76700-76705

Diagnostic ultrasound is an imaging technique bouncing sound waves far above the level of human perception through interior body structures. The sound waves pass through different densities of tissue and reflect back to a receiving unit at varying speeds. The unit converts the waves to electrical pulses that are immediately displayed in picture form on screen. Real time scanning displays structure images and movement with time. Report 76700 for ultrasound and real time of the entire abdomen and 76705 for a single quadrant or organ of the abdomen.

76770-76775
Diagnostic ultrasound is an imaging technique bouncing sound waves far above the level of human perception through interior body structures. The sound waves pass through different densities of tissue and reflect back to a receiving unit at varying speeds. The unit converts the waves to electrical pulses that are immediately displayed in picture form on screen. Real time scanning displays structure images and movement with time. Report 76770 for ultrasound and real time for a complete retroperitoneal exam that includes renal, aortic, and lymphatic structures and 76775 for a limited retroperitoneal exam.

76776
This code reports ultrasound of a transplanted kidney, with duplex Doppler studies. Diagnostic ultrasound is an imaging technique bouncing sound waves far above the level of human perception through interior body structures. The sound waves pass through different densities of tissue and reflect back to a receiving unit at varying speeds. The unit converts the waves to electrical pulses that are immediately displayed in picture form on screen. Duplex studies combine real time with Doppler, which uses the frequency shifts of the emitted waves against their echoes to measure velocity, such as for blood flow.

76800
Diagnostic ultrasound is an imaging technique bouncing sound waves far above the level of human perception through interior body structures. The sound waves pass through different densities of tissue and reflect back to a receiving unit at varying speeds. The unit converts the waves to electrical pulses that are immediately displayed in picture form on screen. Ultrasonography of the spinal canal and its contents includes imaging of the spinal cord, the vertebrae, and the intervertebral discs.

76801-76802
Diagnostic ultrasound is an imaging technique bouncing sound waves far above the level of human perception through interior body structures. The sound waves pass through different densities of tissue and reflect back to a receiving unit at varying speeds. The unit converts the waves to electrical pulses that are immediately displayed in picture form on screen. Real time scanning displays both two-dimensional structure images and movement with time. Use 76801 to report real time ultrasound, transabdominal, with image documentation on a pregnant uterus for fetal and maternal evaluation in the first trimester of a single or first gestation. This includes determining the number of fetuses and gestational sacs and taking their measurements, surveying the visible fetal and placental structure, assessing amniotic fluid volume and sac shape, and examining the maternal uterus and adnexa. Report 76802 for each additional gestation evaluation.

76805-76810
Diagnostic ultrasound is an imaging technique bouncing sound waves far above the level of human perception through interior body structures. The sound waves pass through different densities of tissue and reflect back to a receiving unit at varying speeds. The unit converts the waves to electrical pulses that are immediately displayed in picture form on screen. Real time scanning displays both two-dimensional structure images and movement with time. Use 76805 to report real time ultrasound, transabdominal, with image documentation on a pregnant uterus for fetal and maternal evaluation after the first trimester of a single or first gestation. This includes determining the number of fetuses and amniotic/chorionic sacs, taking measurements appropriate for gestational age, surveying intracranial, spinal, abdominal, and heart chamber anatomy as well as the insertion site of the umbilical cord and the location of the placenta, and assessing amniotic fluid and maternal adnexa. Report 76810 for each additional gestation evaluation.

76811-76812
Diagnostic ultrasound is an imaging technique bouncing sound waves far above the level of human perception through interior body structures. The sound waves pass through different densities of tissue and reflect back to a receiving unit at varying speeds. The unit converts the waves to electrical pulses that are immediately displayed in picture form on screen. Real time scanning displays both two-dimensional structure images and movement with time. Use 76811 to report real time ultrasound, transabdominal, with image documentation on a pregnant uterus for fetal and maternal evaluation plus detailed fetal anatomic examination of a single or first gestation. This includes determining the number of fetuses and amniotic/chorionic sacs, taking measurements appropriate for gestational age, and surveying intracranial, spinal, abdominal, and heart chamber anatomy plus a detailed evaluation of the brain and ventricles, face, heart and outflow tracts, chest, abdominal organs, and number, length, and structure of the limbs. Assessing amniotic fluid, maternal adnexa, and any other fetal anatomy is also done with a detailed evaluation of the umbilical cord and the placenta. Report 76812 for each additional gestation evaluation.

76813-76814
Fetal nuchal translucency provides a noninvasive method to screen for chromosomal abnormalities or heart defects in the first trimester. Nuchal pertains to the back of the neck. Until the lymphatic system of the fetus develops, the back of the neck is a good predictor of fetal health, because the fetus will lie on its back and edema will form in the neck if circulatory problems are present. In a fetal nuchal translucency test, ultrasound transducers on the maternal abdomen or vagina focus on the fetal neck, and the depth of tissue there is measured. The examination includes a calculation of

fetal length, and the two measurements are correlated. Fetal nuchal edema does not provide a definitive diagnosis, but would warrant further testing (e.g., chorionic villus sampling). Report 76813 for fetal nuchal translucency testing of one fetus and 76814 for each additional fetus.

76815
Diagnostic ultrasound is an imaging technique bouncing sound waves far above the level of human perception through interior body structures. The sound waves pass through different densities of tissue and reflect back to a receiving unit at varying speeds. The unit converts the waves to electrical pulses that are immediately displayed in picture form on screen. Real time scanning displays both two-dimensional structure images and movement with time. Use 76815 to report real time ultrasound with image documentation on a pregnant uterus for a limited evaluation focused on the assessment of one or more of the following: fetal heartbeat, placental location, fetal position, and/or qualitative amniotic fluid volume for one or more fetuses.

76816
Diagnostic ultrasound is an imaging technique bouncing sound waves far above the level of human perception through interior body structures. The sound waves pass through different densities of tissue and reflect back to a receiving unit at varying speeds. The unit converts the waves to electrical pulses that are immediately displayed in picture form on screen. Real time scanning displays both two-dimensional structure images and movement with time. Use 76816 to report real time ultrasound, transabdominal, with image documentation on a pregnant uterus for a follow-up to reassess fetal size by measuring standard growth parameters and amniotic fluid volume, and to re-evaluate an organ system suspected or confirmed to be abnormal on a previous scan. Report 76816 per fetus evaluated.

76817
Diagnostic ultrasound is an imaging technique bouncing sound waves far above the level of human perception through interior body structures. The sound waves pass through different densities of tissue and reflect back to a receiving unit at varying speeds. The unit converts the waves to electrical pulses that are immediately displayed in picture form on screen. Real time scanning displays both two-dimensional structure images and movement with time. Use 76817 to report real time ultrasound on a pregnant uterus done transvaginally, with image documentation.

76818-76819
The health of a term or near-term fetus is assessed using ultrasound to monitor the fetus' movements, tone, and breathing, as well as to check amniotic fluid volume. The fetal heart rate is also monitored electronically in a biophysical profile. The physician conducts a non-stress test which monitors the baby's heart rate over a period of 20 minutes or more to look for accelerations with the baby's movement. Report 76819 if the fetal profile is done without non-stress testing.

76820-76821
Doppler ultrasonography, or echography, is performed for fetal surveillance to determine the velocity of blood flow through the umbilical artery (76820) or the middle cerebral artery (76821). Doppler works off the principle that when emitted sound waves reflect back off a moving object, the frequency of the reflected waves will vary in relation to the speed of the moving object. The frequency of sound waves bouncing back off moving blood cells is converted to the velocity of blood flow through the vessel and is seen on screen as a wave with peak, systole, and diastole. Velocity waveforms through the umbilical artery of a normally growing fetus are different from those of a growth-retarded fetus. The peak systolic velocity through the middle cerebral artery is inversely related to the amount of hematocrit in fetal blood. These tests determine the timing of labor induction and when fetal anemia is severe enough to require a transfusion. The ultrasound is carried out transabdominally or endovaginally.

76825-76826
Diagnostic ultrasound is an imaging technique bouncing sound waves far above the level of human perception through interior body structures. The sound waves pass through different densities of tissue and reflect back to a receiving unit at varying speeds. The unit converts the waves to electrical pulses that are immediately displayed in picture form on screen. These codes report fetal echocardiography, real time, with or without M-mode recording. Real time scanning displays both two-dimensional structure images and movement with time. M-mode is a single dimension method of recording amplitude and velocity of a moving structure producing the echoes being studied. Report 76825 for a complete evaluation of a fetal cardiovascular system and 76826 for a follow-up or repeat study.

76827-76828
Diagnostic ultrasound is an imaging technique bouncing sound waves far above the level of human perception through interior body structures. The sound waves pass through different densities of tissue and reflect back to a receiving unit at varying speeds. The unit converts the waves to electrical pulses that are immediately displayed in picture form on screen. These codes report fetal doppler echocardiography by pulsed or continuous sound wave. Fetal echocardiography is done to study the unborn baby's heart in much greater detail than is possible with a routine pregnancy ultrasound when the mother is at risk for giving birth to a baby with heart defects.

Doppler echography uses the frequency shifts of the emitted waves against their echoes to measure velocity, such as for blood flow through the heart. Pulsed wave transmits and records from a single source to determine a precise site of signal origin but not high velocity. Continuous wave uses two transducers: one to continually transmit and the other to record. This scan determines high velocities. Report 76827 for a complete fetal echocardiographic evaluation and 76828 for a follow-up or repeat study.

76830
Diagnostic ultrasound is an imaging technique bouncing sound waves far above the level of human perception through interior body structures. The sound waves pass through different densities of tissue and reflect back to a receiving unit at varying speeds. The unit converts the waves to electrical pulses that are immediately displayed in picture form on screen. This code reports transvaginal ultrasonography.

76831
Diagnostic ultrasound is an imaging technique bouncing sound waves far above the level of human perception through interior body structures. The sound waves pass through different densities of tissue and reflect back to a receiving unit at varying speeds. The unit converts the waves to electrical pulses that are immediately displayed in picture form on screen. This code reports saline infusion sonohysterography, with or without color flow Doppler. The addition of color flow Doppler monitors the behavior of a moving structure, such as flowing blood. The color image that is produced depicts the various levels of fluid concentration within a given area. In the case of saline infusion sonohysterography, a thin catheter, the size of uncooked spaghetti, is introduced into the cervical opening and into the uterus and one to two teaspoons of saline solution is injected into the uterine cavity. Fluid enhanced endovaginal ultrasound is done with the saline solution acting as a contrast medium to view any abnormal anatomic findings in the uterus that needs to be further evaluated. This code reports only the radiological supervision and interpretation.

76856-76857
Diagnostic ultrasound is an imaging technique bouncing sound waves far above the level of human perception through interior body structures. The sound waves pass through different densities of tissue and reflect back to a receiving unit at varying speeds. The unit converts the waves to electrical pulses that are immediately displayed in picture form on screen. Real time scanning displays both structure images and movement with time. Report 76856 for a complete pelvic evaluation in a patient who is not pregnant and 76857 for a limited or follow-up pelvic evaluation, for example, to monitor real time follicle development on the ovary to evaluate gonadotrophin therapy.

76870
Diagnostic ultrasound is an imaging technique bouncing sound waves far above the level of human perception through interior body structures. The sound waves pass through different densities of tissue and reflect back to a receiving unit at varying speeds. The unit converts the waves to electrical pulses that are immediately displayed in picture form on screen. This code reports ultrasonography of the scrotum and scrotal contents.

76872-76873
Diagnostic ultrasound is an imaging technique bouncing sound waves far above the level of human perception through interior body structures. The sound waves pass through different densities of tissue and reflect back to a receiving unit at varying speeds. The unit converts the waves to electrical pulses that are immediately displayed in picture form on screen. Report 76872 for transrectal ultrasound or echography for either sex; Report 76873 for a prostate volume evaluation for planning brachytherapy treatment, which involves planting tiny radioactive elements into a treatment area.

76880
Diagnostic ultrasound is an imaging technique bouncing sound waves far above the level of human perception through interior body structures. The sound waves pass through different densities of tissue and reflect back to a receiving unit at varying speeds. The unit converts the waves to electrical pulses that are immediately displayed in picture form on screen. Real time scanning displays structure images and movement with time. This code reports ultrasonography of structures other than veins and arteries of an arm, leg, hand, or foot.

76885-76886
Diagnostic ultrasound is an imaging technique bouncing sound waves far above the level of human perception through interior body structures. The sound waves pass through different densities of tissue and reflect back to a receiving unit at varying speeds. The unit converts the waves to electrical pulses that are immediately displayed in picture form on screen. Real time imaging displays both two-dimensional structure images and movement with time. Report 76885 for dynamic ultrasonography of an infant's hips requiring physician manipulation involving compressing the leg at the knee and prying the hip outward as the sound wave transducer is applied to the hip area. Report 76886 for static ultrasonography of an infant's hips requiring the legs to be still while the sound wave transducer is applied to the hip area.

76930
The physician drains fluid from the pericardial space around the heart guided by ultrasound. Ultrasound is an imaging technique bouncing sound waves far above the level of human perception through interior body

structures. The sound waves pass through different densities of tissue and reflect back to a receiving unit, which converts the waves to electrical pulses that are immediately displayed in picture form on screen. The physician places a long needle below the sternum and directs it into the pericardial space. When fluid is aspirated, the physician may advance a guidewire through the needle into the pericardial space and exchange the needle over the guidewire for a drainage catheter. The physician removes as much pericardial fluid as is required. This code reports the imaging supervision and interpretation only for this procedure.

76932

The physician takes a biopsy of muscle tissue from within the heart guided by ultrasound. Ultrasound is an imaging technique bouncing sound waves far above the level of human perception through interior body structures. The sound waves pass through different densities of tissue and reflect back to a receiving unit, which converts the waves to electrical pulses that are immediately displayed in picture form on screen. The physician threads a biopsy catheter to the heart through a central intravenous line often inserted into the femoral vein and takes tissue samples of the heart's septum. This code reports the imaging supervision and interpretation only for this procedure.

76936

After sedation, the pseudoaneurysm or arteriovenous fistula is examined with a duplex scanner. The physician assesses the feasibility of compression repair by compressing the neck of the pseudoaneurysm. If the pseudoaneurysm can be completely ablated visually, therapeutic compression therapy is attempted. The physician applies directed pressure to ablate the pseudoaneurysm while blood flow is maintained. Continuous compression is maintained for 10-minute intervals (20-minute intervals if the patient is anticoagulated) until the pseudoaneurysm is thrombosed. If thrombosis has not occurred after four intervals, further attempts to noninvasively thrombose the aneurysm are usually abandoned. If successful ablation has occurred, the patient is kept flat in bed for 6-8 hours with a sandbag on the groin. At 24 hours, the patient is reexamined for evidence of pseudoaneurysm recurrence. At the completion of ablation, the arteries and veins are assessed for patency with the duplex scanner.

76937

This is an add-on code to report ultrasound guidance used in conjunction with procedures requiring vascular access. For example: a tunneled, centrally inserted CVAD is inserted without subcutaneous port or pump. The site over the access vein (e.g., subclavian, jugular) is injected with local anesthesia and punctured with a needle or accessed by cutdown approach. A guidewire is inserted. A subcutaneous tunnel is created using a blunt pair of forceps or sharp tunneling tools, over the clavicle from the anterior chest wall to the venotomy site, which is dilated to the right size. The catheter is passed through this tunnel over the guidewire and into the target vein. Report 76937 for the ultrasound guidance used for this procedure, including the evaluation of potential vascular access sites or the patency of selected vessels; guidance during needle entry and catheter manipulation; and verification of final catheter positioning. This code includes permanent recording and reporting.

76940

Ultrasound guidance is used during tissue ablation of a vital organ. Diagnostic ultrasound is an imaging technique bouncing sound waves far above the level of human perception through interior body structures. The sound waves pass through different densities of tissue and reflect back to a receiving unit at varying speeds. The unit converts the waves to electrical pulses that are immediately displayed in picture form on screen. Report this code when intraoperative ultrasound guidance and monitoring is done with laparoscopic or open ablation.

76941

The physician performs a blood transfusion to a fetus or inserts an amniocentesis needle through the abdominal wall into the umbilical vessels of the pregnant uterus and obtains fetal blood guided by ultrasound. Ultrasound is an imaging technique bouncing sound waves far above the level of human perception through interior body structures. The sound waves pass through different densities of tissue and reflect back to a receiving unit, which converts the waves to electrical pulses that are immediately displayed in picture form on screen. For fetal blood transfusion, the physician locates the umbilical vein. A needle is directed through the abdominal wall into the amniotic cavity. The umbilical vein is pierced and fetal blood is exchanged with transfused blood. This code reports the imaging supervision and interpretation only for this procedure.

76942

Ultrasonic guidance is used for guiding needle placement required for procedures such as breast biopsies, needle aspirations, injections, or placing localizing devices. Ultrasound is the process of bouncing sound waves far above the level of human perception through interior body structures. The sound waves pass through different densities of tissue and reflect back to a receiving unit at varying speeds. The unit converts the waves to electrical pulses that are immediately displayed in picture form on screen. Once the exact needle entry site is determined along with the depth of the lesion, the optimal route from the skin to the lesion is decided. The needle is inserted and advanced to the lesion under ultrasonic guidance. This code reports the imaging supervision and interpretation only for this procedure.

76945
The physician aspirates cells from the chorionic villus (early stage of the placenta) under ultrasonic guidance. Ultrasound is an imaging technique bouncing sound waves far above the level of human perception through interior body structures. The sound waves pass through different densities of tissue and reflect back to a receiving unit, which converts the waves to electrical pulses that are immediately displayed in picture form on screen. In the transcervical method, a catheter is inserted through the cervix and into the uterine cavity toward the chorionic villus or early placenta. Aspirated cells are obtained for abnormal chromosome analysis. The procedure may also be done transvaginally or transabdominally. The transabdominal approach can be done throughout pregnancy while the other approaches are usually done between 9 and 12 weeks gestation. This code reports the imaging supervision and interpretation only for this procedure.

76946
The physician withdraws fluid from the amniotic sac under ultrasonic guidance. Ultrasound is an imaging technique bouncing sound waves far above the level of human perception through interior body structures. The sound waves pass through different densities of tissue and reflect back to a receiving unit, which converts the waves to electrical pulses that are immediately displayed in picture form on screen. Following preparation of the skin and administration of a local anesthetic, a small gauge needle is introduced into the amniotic sac and fluid aspirated. This code reports the imaging supervision and interpretation only for this procedure.

76948
The physician aspirates ova under ultrasonic guidance. Ultrasound is an imaging technique bouncing sound waves far above the level of human perception through interior body structures. The sound waves pass through different densities of tissue and reflect back to a receiving unit, which converts the waves to electrical pulses that are immediately displayed in picture form on screen. Following preparation of the skin and administration of a local anesthetic, a small gauge needle is introduced into the ovary and the ova are aspirated. This code reports the imaging supervision and interpretation only for this procedure.

76950
Ultrasound is used for placing radiation therapy fields. Ultrasound is an imaging technique bouncing sound waves far above the level of human perception through interior body structures. The sound waves pass through different densities of tissue and reflect back to a receiving unit, which converts the waves to electrical pulses that are immediately displayed in picture form on screen. Images of both normal and abnormal tissue structures are obtained and the treatment field area volume is determined. The normal tissues surrounding the treatment area are also defined. Acquiring this data is an important step in planning the patient's radiation treatment.

76965
Ultrasonic guidance is used for the accurate guiding and placement of an interstitial radioactive implant into a tumor during the course of brachytherapy for malignant neoplasms, such as in the prostate. Ultrasound is an imaging technique bouncing sound waves far above the level of human perception through interior body structures. The sound waves pass through different densities of tissue and reflect back to a receiving unit, which converts the waves to electrical pulses that are immediately displayed in picture form on screen. Radioactive implants may be enclosed in various apparatus modes such as tubes, needles, wires, or seeds. Common materials used are radium, cobalt-60, cesium-137, gold-198, and iridium-192.

76970
A follow-up study is performed after a previous ultrasonic study has been completed. The follow-up study may include a repeat A-scan, B-scan, or both. A-scan utilizes sound waves introduced in a straight line to display a single dimension image of vertical peaks and B-scan utilizes sound waves in a two-dimensional scanning procedure to display a two-dimensional image.

76975
The physician uses endoscopic ultrasound to examine the esophageal and gastric wall. Ultrasound is an imaging technique bouncing sound waves far above the level of human perception through interior body structures. The sound waves pass through different densities of tissue and reflect back to a receiving unit, which converts the waves to electrical pulses that are immediately displayed in picture form on screen. The physician passes an endoscope equipped with the ultrasound transducer through the patient's mouth into the esophagus. The esophagus, stomach, duodenum, and sometimes jejunum are viewed through ultrasonic images to determine the extent of cancerous tissue. This code reports the imaging supervision and interpretation only for this process.

76977
Bone mineral density studies are used to evaluate diseases of bone and/or the responses of bone disease to treatment. Densities are measured at the wrist, hip, spine, or calcaneus. The studies assess bone mass or density associated with such diseases as osteoporosis, osteomalacia, and renal osteodystrophy. This code reports using low level ultrasound for measuring bone density instead of ionizing radiation.

76998
Ultrasonography is used during a procedure to guide the physician in successfully accomplishing the surgery. Ultrasonic guidance may be used by the

physician intraoperatively during many different types of operations on various areas of the body. Examples of intraoperative ultrasonic guidance include evaluating tissue removal in anatomical structures such as the breast, brain, abdominal organs, etc. This procedure may also be used to determine the location and depth of incisions to be made. This code is not to be used for ultrasound guidance for open or laparoscopic radiofrequency tissue ablation.

77001
This code reports the fluoroscopic guidance for placement, replacement, or removal of a central venous access device (CVAD) to be used in conjunction with the code for the procedure. For example, a tunneled, centrally inserted CVAD is inserted without subcutaneous port or pump. The site over the access vein (e.g., subclavian, jugular) is injected with local anesthesia and punctured with a needle or accessed by cutdown approach. A guidewire is inserted. A subcutaneous tunnel is created using a blunt pair of forceps or sharp tunneling tools over the clavicle from the anterior chest wall to the venotomy site, which is dilated to the right size. The catheter is passed through this tunnel over the guidewire and into the target vein. Fluoroscopy is used throughout the procedure to guide catheter placement and to check the positioning of the catheter tip. This code includes any contrast injections done through the access site or through the catheter with the necessary corresponding radiological supervision and interpretation of the venography, and the radiographic check of final catheter position.

77002
Needle biopsy or fine needle aspiration is guided by fluoroscopic visualization. A cutting biopsy or fine needle is inserted into the target area and the position reaffirmed by fluoroscopy. This is done for an internal mass or lesion that has been positively identified by other diagnostic imaging performed earlier.

77003
Spinal and certain paraspinal diagnostic or therapeutic nerve injection procedures (e.g., epidural, transforaminal epidural, subarachnoid, or sacroiliac joint injections) are guided by fluoroscopy before and during catheter or needle insertion. The target structure is localized, the needle is placed and advanced, and the contrast injection is visualized under fluoroscopic monitoring.

77011
For stereotactic localization, a movable arm holding a needle is guided by computerized tomography (CT) to locate the lesion from different angles at different fixed points. The CT images tell the computer where the coordinates are to correctly align the needle.

77012
Computed tomography (CT) is used for guiding needle biopsies. CT scanning directs multiple narrow beams of x-rays around the body structure being studied and uses computer imaging to produce thin cross-sectional views of various layers (or slices) of the body. It is able to visualize soft tissue, as well as bones. Patients are required to remain motionless during the study. Once the exact needle entry site is determined, along with the depth of the lesion, the optimal route from the skin to the lesion is decided. The needle is inserted and advanced to the lesion and another CT scan image is done to confirm placement for the biopsy. This code reports the radiological supervision and interpretation only for this procedure.

77013
Computed tomographic guidance is used for the ablation of parenchymal (vital organ) tissue. The patient receives intravenous pain medication and sedation. Grounding pads are placed on the patient's thigh. A needle-electrode with an insulated shaft and a noninsulated distal tip is inserted through the skin and directly into the tissue to be ablated. Computed tomography (CT) is used to guide the needle to the correct spot and to monitor treatment. Each treatment session has about 10 to 15 minutes of active ablation. The energy at the needle tip causes ionic agitation and frictional heat in the surrounding tissue, which leads to cell death and coagulative necrosis. This results in a 3 to 5 cm sphere of dead tissue per treatment session. In large tumors, the physician may create more than one sphere next to each other to try to turn the tumor edges in three dimensions. A small margin of normal tissue next to tumors is also burned. The dead tumor cells are not removed, but are gradually replaced by fibrosis and scar tissue. This code reports the CT guidance and monitoring of the ablation procedure.

77014
Computed tomography (CT) is used in guiding the placement of radiation therapy fields. CT scanning directs multiple narrow beams of x-rays around the body structure being studied and uses computer imaging to produce thin cross-sectional views of various layers (or slices) of the body. It is able to visualize soft tissue, as well as bones. Patients are required to remain motionless during the study. Cross-sectional images of both normal and abnormal tissue structures are obtained and the treatment field area volume is determined. The normal tissues surrounding the treatment area are also defined. Acquiring this data is an important step in planning the patient's radiation treatment.

77021
Magnetic resonance is used for guiding needle placement required for procedures such as breast biopsies, needle aspirations, injections, or placing localizing devices. Magnetic resonance imaging (MRI) is a radiation-free, noninvasive technique that produces high-quality images. MRI uses the natural magnetic properties of the hydrogen atoms in our bodies that

emit radiofrequency signals when exposed to radio waves within a strong electromagnetic field. These signals are processed and converted by the computer into high-resolution, three-dimensional, tomographic images. Some methods for magnetic resonance needle placement include coating the needle with contrast material, placing metallic ringlets along the needle, or using a receiving coil in the tip of the needle. This code reports the radiological supervision and interpretation only for this procedure.

77022
A needle-electrode with an insulated shaft and a noninsulated distal tip is inserted through the skin and directly into the tissue to be ablated. Magnetic resonance imaging (MRI) is used to guide the needle to the correct spot and to monitor treatment. Each treatment session has about 10 to 15 minutes of active ablation of parenchymal (vital organ) tissue. The energy at the needle tip causes ionic agitation and frictional heat in the surrounding tissue, which leads to cell death and coagulative necrosis. This results in a 3 to 5 cm sphere of dead tissue per treatment session. In large tumors, the physician may create more than one sphere next to each other to try to turn the tumor edges in three dimensions. A small margin of normal tissue next to tumors is also burned. The dead tumor cells are not removed, but are gradually replaced by fibrosis and scar tissue. This code reports the magnetic resonance guidance and monitoring of the ablation procedure.

77031
A lesion in the breast is localized for biopsy. In the localization process, a movable arm holding the needle works together with the mammography unit that images the lesion from different angles at different fixed points. The mammogram information tells a computer where the coordinates are to correctly align the biopsy needle. Needle position is confirmed with more views taken and a stab incision made in the skin. The needle is advanced to the lesion and additional stereotactic views confirm needle placement. This code reports the radiological supervision and interpretation only for this procedure.

77032
A needle localization wire is inserted into a breast lesion preoperatively under radiologic visualization in preparation for biopsy or removal. The skin is marked over the area of the lesion and mammograms performed. A needle with a hooked wire is inserted into the lesion from a perpendicular angle and advanced deep enough to remain within the lesion when the patient moves. X-rays are again taken to confirm needle placement within the lesion. Adjustments may need to be made. The needle is withdrawn while the hooked wire remains anchored. A short length of wire extends beyond the skin surface of the breast, which is taped and covered. This code reports the radiological supervision and interpretation only for this procedure.

77051-77052
These add-on codes are to be used only in conjunction with the primary procedures for diagnostic and screening mammography. These additional procedures report computer-aided detection of lesions, with further physician interpretive review of those films obtained in the mammogram. Computer aided detection (CAD) utilizes the x-ray taken of the breast and scans the analog mammography film with a laser beam and analyzes the video display for suspicious areas, most often converting it into digital data for the computer first. The patient does not need to be present for the CAD process. Report 77051 when the test is diagnostic and 77052 when the test is a screening mammography.

77053-77054
The physician performs an injection procedure for mammary ductogram or galactogram. A needle and cannula are inserted into the duct of the breast. Contrast medium is introduced into the breast duct for the radiographic visualization. A dissecting microscope may be used to aid in placing the cannula. The needle and cannula are removed when the study is complete. Report 77053 for a single duct studied and 77054 for multiple ducts. These codes report the radiological supervision and interpretation only for this procedure.

77055-77057
Mammography is a radiographic technique used to diagnose breast cysts or tumors in women with symptoms of breast disease or to detect them before they are palpable in women who are asymptomatic. Mammography is done using a different type of x-ray than is used for routine exams that do not penetrate tissue as easily. The breast is compressed firmly between two planes and pictures are taken. This spreads the tissue and allows for a lower x-ray dose. Use 77055 for a single breast and 77056 for both breasts. Report 77057 for both breasts done in an asymptomatic screening with two views taken of each breast.

77058-77059
Magnetic resonance imaging (MRI) is a radiation-free, noninvasive technique to produce high-quality sectional images of the inside of the body in multiple planes. MRI uses the natural magnetic properties of the hydrogen atoms in our bodies that emit radiofrequency signals when exposed to radio waves within a strong electromagnetic field. These signals are processed and converted by the computer into high-resolution, three-dimensional, tomographic images. Patients with metallic or electronic implants or foreign bodies cannot be exposed to MRI. The patient must remain still while lying on a motorized table within the large, circular MRI tunnel. A sedative may be administered, as well as an IV injected contrast material for image

enhancement. Report 77058 for magnetic resonance imaging of the left or right breast and 77059 for both breasts.

77071
Joint radiography is done under manual stress application conditions performed by the physician to visualize characteristics of the joint that would not normally be seen on films taken in routine positioning. The physician puts on lead-lined gloves and forcibly holds the body part in the desired position to maintain stress on the joint while x-rays are taken. This code includes radiography of the contralateral joint, if indicated.

77072
Bone age studies are a way of estimating the stage of development or skeletal decline of a child based on an x-ray, usually of the nondominant hand and wrist. The x-ray is compared to the bone structure standards equal to the child's chronological age. This allows for identifying growth failure and the need for treatment before the child's bones fuse, after which additional growth is not possible. For children younger than age 3, films of multiple areas (e.g., wrist, knee, and foot) lead to greater accuracy.

77073
Bone length studies accurately measure the length of the long bones in the skeleton. Typically, four film exposures are performed during a scanogram, as it is usually called. Views of the hip, leg, knee, and ankle are usually taken. However, there is no number or type of views specified for this code.

77074
Various bones in the body are x-rayed. A limited study is reported when specific symptomatic sites are examined. This procedure is rarely performed to determine any spread of cancer, having been replaced by nuclear bone scanning, a more precise study for diagnosing metastases.

77075
A radiologic exam is performed in which the axial (head and trunk) and appendicular (extremities) skeleton is surveyed for evidence of metastatic disease. It may also be performed on children to identify current and/or old healed fractures in the case of suspected child abuse. This procedure is rarely performed for metastatic disease, having been replaced by nuclear bone scanning, a more precise study for diagnosing metastases.

77076
A radiologic exam is performed in which an infant's axial (head and trunk) and appendicular (extremities) skeleton is surveyed for evidence of current and/or old healed fractures in the case of suspected child abuse or to identify signs of lesions due to leukemic infiltrates.

77077
A radiologic exam is done in which two or more joints are surveyed. A single view only is taken of the joints being examined. The joints surveyed require specification and are not delineated in the code.

77078-77079
A CT density study is performed to measure the patient's bone mass. Bone mineral density is evaluated as a screening test for osteoporosis, to evaluate diseases of bone, and to review the responses of bone disease to treatment. Densities can be measured at the wrist, hip, spine, or calcaneus. The studies assess bone mass or density associated with such diseases as osteoporosis, osteomalacia, and renal osteodystrophy. This particular bone density study uses computerized tomography (CT) for the imaging modality. CT directs multiple, narrow beams of x-rays around the body structure being studied and uses computer imaging to produce thin cross-sectional views of various layers (or slices) of the body. Report 77078 for a bone density study by CT of the hips, pelvis, or spine (axial skeleton) and 77079 for a bone density study by CT of peripheral bones, such as the wrist or heel bone (appendicular skeleton).

77080-77082
An x-ray density study is performed to measure the patient's bone mass. Bone mineral density is evaluated as a screening test for osteoporosis, to evaluate diseases of bone, and to review the responses of bone disease to treatment. Densities can be measured at the wrist, radius, hip, pelvis, spine, or heel. Dual energy x-ray absorptiometry (DEXA) is a two-dimensional projection system that involves two x-ray beams with different levels of energy being pulsed alternately. The results are given in two scores reported as standard deviations from bone density of a person 30 years of age, which is the age of peak bone mass. Report 77080 for DEXA of the hips, pelvis, or spine (axial skeleton); 77081 for DEXA of peripheral bones, such as the wrist or heel bone (appendicular skeleton); and 77082 for one or more vertebral sites to assess a fracture.

77083
Bone mineral density studies are used to evaluate diseases of bone and/or the responses of bone disease to treatment. Densities are measured at the wrist, hip, spine, or calcaneus. The studies assess bone mass or density associated with such diseases as osteoporosis, osteomalacia, and renal osteodystrophy. Photodensitometry, or radiographic absorptiometry, provides a quantitative measurement of the bone mineral density of the cortical bone (outer layer) by taking two radiographs with direct exposure film at different settings. This procedure is done to monitor for gross bone changes as occurs with osteoporosis.

77084
Magnetic resonance imaging (MRI) is a radiation-free, noninvasive technique to produce high-quality sectional images of the inside of the body in multiple

planes. MRI uses the natural magnetic properties of the hydrogen atoms in our bodies that emit radiofrequency signals when exposed to radio waves within a strong electromagnetic field. The signals are transformed into images based on the differing densities of tissues. Bone marrow contains fat cells, with high water content, and nonfat cells. MRI can give information about early changes in the marrow of the bone and the medullary cavity's composition and distribution of red and yellow marrow cells to evaluate for avascular necrosis of bone. Metastatic tumors are visualized directly because of the differences in signal intensity between normal bone marrow and tumor tissue.

77261-77263

Treatment planning is conducted for radiation therapy. Treatment planning for oncology patients is the process of developing a complete plan for the course of radiation therapy. The best way to deliver the treatment to the malignancy while blocking the dose received by normal tissues must be determined. This requires localizing the tumor, determining its extent of malignancy and the volume to be treated, choosing the best method of treatment, the number and size of treatment ports, and calculating time and dosage among other procedures. A port is the site where the treatment beam will enter the skin and concentrate upon the malignant area(s). Simple planning, reported in 77261, consists of a single area of malignancy with a single port or opposing ports parallel to each other and basic or no blocking. Intermediate planning, reported in 77262, consists of two separate areas of malignancy with three or more ports that converge, multiple blocks, or time or dosage considerations. Complex planning, reported in 77263, consists of three or more separate areas of malignancy with tangential ports, wedges or compensators, complex blocking, a combination of two or more modes of treatment, or rotating or other beam considerations.

77280-77290

Simulation-aided field setting is done prior to beginning the course of radiation treatment. This is done to determine the size and location of the ports to be used so that they surround the tumor. A port is the site where the treatment beam will enter the skin and concentrate upon the malignant area(s). Simulation can be done on a dedicated simulator, a radiation therapy treatment unit, an x-ray machine, or CT scanner. Simulation allows visualization and definition of the exact treatment area(s). Simple simulation, reported in 77280, is done for a single area of malignancy with a single port or opposing ports parallel to each other and basic or no blocking. Intermediate simulation, reported in 77285, is done for two separate areas of malignancy with three or more ports and multiple blocks. Complex simulation, reported in 77290, is done for three or more areas of malignancy with tangential ports and complex blocking that may require customized shielding blocks, rotation or arc therapy, brachytherapy source and hyperthermia probe verification, and use of contrast materials.

77295

Three dimensional simulation-aided field setting is done prior to beginning the course of radiation treatment. This is done to determine the size and location of the ports to be used so that they surround the tumor. A port is the site where the treatment beam will enter the skin and concentrate upon the malignant area(s). Simulation can be done on a dedicated simulator, a radiation therapy treatment unit, an x-ray machine, or CT scanner. Simulation allows visualization and definition of the exact treatment area(s). Three dimensional simulation involves using CT and/or MRI data to have computer-generated reconstructions of tumor volume and dose distribution of multiple or moving beams in three dimensional displays.

77300

Dosimetry is the calculation of the radiation dose to be delivered to the tumor. The physician chooses the energy level and modality of photon or electron beams to be used for each simulated port, even if only one treatment area is concerned. Once the tentative treatment fields have been determined, the dosimetry of the treatment portals can be calculated. A basic radiation dosimetry calculation is a photon calculation that includes central axis depth dose, time dose factor (TDF), nominal standard dose (NSD), gap calculation, off-axis and tissue inhomogeneity factors, as well as calculation of nonionizing radiation surface and depth dose. Dosimetry may be repeated during the course of treatment as required.

77301

Intensity modulated radiotherapy (IMRT) is capable of varying the intensity of radiation exposure in a portion of a field depending on whether tumor or critical normal structures are present in the beam pathway. The radiation therapy consists of multiple pencil thin beams or beamlets, calculated to hit tumors with high dose radiation beams and sensitive normal tissues with modulated lower intensity beams, leaving them mostly unaffected. Planning for IMRT uses powerful computer programs that calculate the optimal arrangement of beam angle configurations and dosage intensities to deliver the best treatment. If the isodose distribution for target and critical structure partial tolerance specification and dose-volume histograms are not satisfactory, the optimization is repeated with modifications to clinical parameters, until an acceptable solution is reached.

77305-77315

For the initial setting of the treatment portals, an isodose distribution of the beams is required. Usually done by computer, a teletherapy isodose plan plots the lines of the same dosage levels to be delivered within the treatment field, usually from a combination of beams converging upon the treatment field. Only one plan may be reported per any therapy course to a specific treatment field. A simple teletherapy isodose plan, reported in 77305, consists of one or two parallel opposed ports directed to a single area of interest. An intermediate teletherapy isodose plan, reported in 77310, consists of three or more treatment ports directed to a single area of interest. A complex teletherapy isodose plan, reported in 77315, consists of tangential ports, the use of wedges, compensators, complex blocking, and rotating or beam considerations.

77321

Special teletherapy port plans are usually done in connection with a complex level of treatment. These are electron calculations and cannot be submitted for the same field with a basic radiation dosimetry calculation, which is photon. Electron beams require attention because of their characteristics in interacting with living tissue. A special teletherapy port plan calculates the dosage level of the treatment portal for the use of electrons or heavy particles when used in a portion of or as the main mode of treatment for the field of interest.

77326-77328

Brachytherapy is the application of radioactive isotopes for internal radiation. Some radioactive material is encapsulated in metal seeds, wires, tubes, or needles for intracavitary or interstitial implantation and some are prepared in solutions for instillation or oral administration. Sealed sources are inserted by the physician in or around the tumor. Sources are intracavitary or permanent interstitial placements and ribbons are temporary interstitial placements. Brachytherapy gives greater control over localized malignancy while preserving function and reducing damage to surrounding tissue. Brachytherapy isodose plans are necessary to determine the amount of radiation that the tumor will absorb and the distribution of radiation around the sources. Report 77326 for simple plan with calculation made from a single plane, application of 1 to 4 sources/ribbons, remote afterloading, 1 to 8 sources. Report 77327 for intermediate calculation from multiplane doses, application of 5 to 10 sources/ribbons, remote afterloading, 9 to 12 sources. Report 77328 for complex calculation from multiplane doses, volume implant calculations, application of over 10 sources/ ribbons, remote afterloading, over 12 sources, and spatial reconstruction.

77331

Dosimetry is the calculation of the radiation dose to be delivered to the tumor. The physician chooses the energy level and modality of photon or electron beams to be used for each simulated port, even if only one treatment area is concerned. Once the tentative treatment fields have been determined, the dosimetry of the treatment portals can be calculated. Special dosimetry uses measuring and monitoring devices when the physician deems it necessary to calculate the total amount of radiation that a patient has received at any given point. The results determine whether to uphold or alter the current treatment plan.

77332-77334

Treatment devices used in radiation oncology are customized blocks or shields to protect healthy tissue surrounding the treatment area and are made from energy-absorbing material such as cerrobend. Treatment device services contain a professional and technical component. The professional component is based upon the physician's participation in the actual design of the block. The technical component is based on each individual block requiring time and materials to be fabricated. 77332 reports a simple block; 77333 reports intermediate device services for multiple blocks; 77334 reports complex, irregular blocks, shields, compensators, wedges, molds, or casts.

77336

This code reports ongoing medical physics consultation services to benefit patients undergoing radiation therapy. It includes quality assurance of dose delivery such as verification of dose calculation data, measuring for safe and effective use of software and equipment such as simulators, linear accelerators, and block devices. It also includes assessment of treatment parameters and review of treatment documentation, reported weekly during therapy.

77338

A multi-leaf collimator (MLC) device is used in conjunction with the delivery of intensity modulated radiation therapy (IMRP). Multi-leaf collimators are devices that are composed of individual 'leaves" of a material, often tungsten, that can block a particle beam by moving independently in and out of the beam's path. Used on linear accelerators, MLCs provide conformal shaping of the radiotherapy treatment beams. Code 77338 reports the design and construction of the MLC device based upon the IMRT plan and should be reported only once per IMRT plan.

77370

A special medical radiation physics consultation requires a written analysis on the course of treatment and is done at direct request of the radiation oncologist when the complexity of the treatment plan is great. Problems analyzed may include photon and electron treatment plans and their consequences, complex dosage calculations because of interactions between multiple treatment fields, intensity modulating radiation, total body irradiation, blocking procedures, or stereotactic or brachytherapy services.

77371-77372

Stereotactic radiosurgery (SRS) is a radiation therapy technique designed to deliver a large radiation dose to discrete tumor sites in the brain, while minimizing damage to healthy tissue. First, computers map the exact location of the malignancy. Next, the patient is fitted with a plastic mold or cast to keep the body part still so that the radiation can be aimed accurately from several directions. Radiation is delivered to one or more tumor sites. Report 77371 for a single session that is multi-source Cobalt 60 based and 77372 for a single session that is linear accelerator based. These codes report a complete course of treatment for one or more cranial lesions.

77373

Stereotactic body radiation therapy (SBRT) is a radiation therapy technique designed to deliver a large radiation dose to discrete tumor sites in the lungs, liver, or elsewhere, while minimizing damage to healthy tissue. This code covers SBRT in any location except the brain. First, computers map the exact location of the malignancy. Next, the patient is fitted with a plastic mold or cast to keep the body part still and radiation beams are delivered accurately from several directions.

77401

Radiation treatment delivery involves the delivery of a beam of radioactive electromagnetic energy from a treatment machine distanced from the treatment area. External radiation is very often delivered by linear accelerator which can deliver x-rays (photons) or electrons to a targeted area. Cobalt teletherapy units and cesium teletherapy units are also used to direct gamma rays from a distance to the targeted area. Photons can target deeper lying tumor tissue, while electrons are used for the maximum dose of radiation near the skin surface, making the method suitable to treat skin, superficial lesions, and shallow tumor volumes where underlying tissues need to be protected. Radiation treatment delivery codes are dependent upon the number and complexity of treatment areas as well as the energy level. Use this code to report superficial and/or orthovoltage energy levels, which are kilovoltage doses and usually treat superficial skin lesions.

77402-77406

Radiation treatment delivery involves the delivery of a beam of radioactive electromagnetic energy from a treatment machine distanced from the treatment area. External radiation is very often delivered by linear accelerator which can deliver x-rays (photons) or electrons to a targeted area. Cobalt teletherapy units and cesium teletherapy units are also used to direct gamma rays from a distance to the targeted area. Photons can target deeper lying tumor tissue, while electrons are used for the maximum dose of radiation near the skin surface, making the method suitable to treat skin, superficial lesions, and shallow tumor volumes where underlying tissues need to be protected. These codes are dependent upon the number and complexity of treatment areas as well as the energy level, measured in megavolts (MeV). Use 77402 to report a single treatment area, single port or parallel opposed ports, simple or no blocks; up to 5 MeV. Use 77403 for 6-10 MeV; use 77404 for 11-19 MeV; and use 77406 for 20 MeV or greater.

77407-77411

Radiation treatment delivery involves the delivery of a beam of radioactive electromagnetic energy from a treatment machine distanced from the treatment area. External radiation is very often delivered by linear accelerator which can deliver x-rays (photons) or electrons to a targeted area. Cobalt teletherapy units and cesium teletherapy units are also used to direct gamma rays from a distance to the targeted area. Photons can target deeper lying tumor tissue, while electrons are used for the maximum dose of radiation near the skin surface, making the method suitable to treat skin, superficial lesions, and shallow tumor volumes where underlying tissues need to be protected. These codes are dependent upon the number and complexity of treatment areas as well as the energy level, measured in megavolts (MeV). Use 77407 to report two separate treatment areas, three or more ports on a single treatment area, use of multiple blocks; up to 5 MeV. Use 77408 for 6-10 MeV; use 77409 for 11-19 MeV; and use 77411 for 20 MeV or greater.

77412-77416

Radiation treatment delivery involves the delivery of a beam of radioactive electromagnetic energy from a treatment machine distanced from the treatment area. External radiation is very often delivered by linear accelerator which can deliver x-rays (photons) or electrons to a targeted area. Cobalt teletherapy units and cesium teletherapy units are also used to direct gamma rays from a distance to the targeted area. Photons can target deeper lying tumor tissue, while electrons are used for the maximum dose of radiation near the skin surface, making the method suitable to treat skin, superficial lesions, and shallow tumor volumes where underlying tissues need to be protected. These codes are dependent upon the number and complexity of treatment areas as well as the energy level, measured in megavolts (MeV). Use 77412 to report three or more separate treatment areas, custom blocking, tangential ports, wedges, rotational beams, compensators, or electron beams; up to 5 MeV. Use 77413 for 6-10 MeV; use 77414 for 11-19 MeV; and use 77416 for 20 MeV or greater.

77417

Therapeutic radiology port films are taken at regular intervals to verify correct positioning of all treatment portals on patients undergoing external beam radiation therapy, since discrepancies in the field placements can happen frequently and this negatively effects the treatment outcomes. The beam of the radiation treatment machine is used to make radiographic portal films. Portal images like a snapshot are taken for localization with a partial dose or recorded for the treatment for verification. Port film charges are a technical service only.

77418

Intensity modulated radiotherapy (IMRT) treatment is capable of varying the intensity of radiation exposure in a portion of a field depending on whether tumor or critical normal structures are present in the beam pathway. The radiation therapy consists of multiple pencil thin beams or beamlets, calculated to hit tumors with high dose radiation and sensitive normal tissues with modulated, lower-intensity beams, leaving them mostly unaffected. By dividing the radiation beam into multiple slices, the intensity of the beam in any slice can be varied by computer-controlled dynamic multileaf collimation (MLC) during the radiation exposure. MLC systems consist of multiple narrow leaves that are modulated under computer control and allow custom-shaped beam apertures without fabricated blocks. During IMRT delivery, the leaves of the MLC are adjusted while the beam is on to modify the delivery of radiation across the portal.

77421

Radiation treatment delivery involves the transfer of a beam of radioactive electromagnetic energy from a treatment machine distanced from the treatment area. Stereotactic body radiation therapy is a radiation therapy technique designed to deliver a large radiation dose to discrete tumor sites in the lungs, liver, brain, or elsewhere while minimizing damage to healthy tissue. Stereoscopic x-ray guidance utilizes infrared and/or camera technology to precisely localize targets in conjunction with intensity modulated radiation therapy and stereotactic radiotherapy. This code reports the stereoscopic x-ray guidance only.

77422-77423

External beam radiotherapy is radiation delivered from a distant source outside the body and directed at the patient's cancer site. High-energy neutron radiotherapy destroys the cells ability to divide and grow by damaging the cells through nuclear interactions, which decreases the damaged cells chances of repairing themselves. Since high-energy neutron radiotherapy works in the absence of oxygen, unlike conventional radiation therapy, it is used to treat larger tumors and is particularly effective in treating inoperable salivary gland tumors, bone cancers, and certain types of advanced malignancies of the pancreas, bladder, lung, prostate, and uterus. Due to the high potency of neutron radiation, the required dose is much less than with conventional radiotherapy, and a full course may be delivered in 10 to 12 treatments rather than the usual 30 to 40. Report 77422 for a single treatment area using a single port or parallel-opposed ports with no blocks or simple blocking. Report 77423 for treatment of one or more isocenters with coplanar or non-coplanar geometry with blocking and/or wedge, and/or compensator(s).

77427

The physician reviews the port films. The dosimetry, dose delivery, and treatment parameters are reviewed. Treatment setup and positioning of the patient is evaluated including the assessment of immobilization devices, blocks, wedges, or other devices. The physician also provides care of infected skin, prescribes necessary medications, and manages fluid and electrolytes as well as pain management. Nutritional counseling may be provided as necessary. This radiation treatment management code is accurately reported using units of five fractions or treatment sessions. This code is reported at the completion of each five sessions with the exception of the completion of the treatment course when it may be used for three or more sessions.

77431

The physician reviews the port films. The dosimetry, dose delivery, and treatment parameters are reviewed. The treatment setup and positioning of the patient is evaluated including the assessment of immobilization devices, blocks, wedges, or other devices. The physician also provides care of infected skin, prescribes necessary medications, manages fluid and electrolytes as well as pain management. Nutritional counseling may be provided as necessary. This radiation treatment management code is used when the course of therapy consists of only one or two fractions (treatment sessions), excepting single application brachytherapy which does not require management.

77432

This service involves using multiple megavoltage treatment ports that are directed to a specific area within the brain. When a linear accelerator is used, the extremely narrow x-ray beam from the machine remains focused on the tumor volume of the cranial lesion while the movement of the machine is coordinated to distribute the beam entry points over a wider radius. Stereotactic treatment delivery requires three-dimensional simulation for accuracy. This code is for a complete course of treatment consisting of one session and reports the radiation oncology services performed as part of the stereotactic radiosurgery procedure.

77435

Stereotactic body radiation therapy (SBRT) is a radiation therapy technique designed to deliver a large radiation dose to discrete tumor sites within the body (excluding brain) while minimizing damage to healthy tissue. This code reports treatment management for a course of SBRT. Treatment management includes review of port films; review of dosimetry, dose delivery, and treatment parameters; treatment set up; positioning of the patient; assessment of immobilization devices, blocks or wedges; ongoing evaluation of the patient's response to treatment; coordination of care; and ordering and review of laboratory or other tests.

77470

This service covers the extra planning and monitoring effort involved in the use of special radiation therapy procedures such as total or hemibody irradiation or intraoperative cone irradiation.

77520-77525

Protons are positively charged particles that are particularly beneficial in treating malignancies and other neoplastic abnormalities near sensitive structures such as the optic nerve and spinal cord. Proton beam treatment delivers higher doses of radiation to tumors than photon beams and at the same time does not exceed radiation tolerance of normal, healthy tissue next to the targeted area. Because of the physical properties of the positively-charged protons, they stop short just at the target and do not deposit a dose beyond that boundary, making proton beam treatment advantageous for deep seated and solid tumors in any body site. Report 77520 for simple proton treatment delivery to a single treatment area utilizing a single non-tangential/oblique port and custom blocking without compensation and 77522 with compensation (custom-made devices attached to the treatment unit for manipulating the radiation dose). Report 77523 for intermediate proton delivery to one or more treatment areas utilizing two or more ports or one or more tangential/oblique ports, with custom blocks and compensators; and report 77525 for complex proton treatment delivery to one or more treatment areas utilizing two or more ports per treatment area with matching or patching fields and/or multiple isocenters, with custom blocks and compensators.

77600-77620

Hyperthermia uses heat in an attempt to speed cell metabolism. This is performed to increase potential cell destruction in the treatment of a malignancy by making tumors more susceptible to the therapy. The heat can be generated by a variety of sources, including microwave, ultrasound and radio frequency conduction. Report 77600 for hyperthermia, externally generated, superficial (i.e., heating to a depth of 4 cm or less) and 77605 for deep (i.e., heating to depths greater than 4 cm). For heat generated by interstitial probes acting like small antennae or microwave radiators placed directly into the tumor area, report 77610 for 5 or fewer interstitial applicators and 77615 for more than 5 interstitial applicators. For hyperthermia generated by intracavitary probes placed into a body cavity, report 77620.

77750

The physician infuses or instills a radioactive solution to kill cancerous cells. Brachytherapy is the application of radioactive isotopes for internal radiation. Radioactive material is encapsulated for intracavitary or interstitial implantation or prepared in solutions for instillation or oral administration. For this brachytherapy procedure, the physician intravenously injects a radioactive substance (e.g., Strontium -89) in solution into a vein or the physician may instill a radioactive substance in solution into a body cavity. This type of brachytherapy may be referred to as unsealed internal radiation therapy. This code includes three months of follow-up care.

77761-77763

Brachytherapy is the application of radioactive isotopes for internal radiation. Radioactive material is encapsulated for intracavitary or interstitial implantation or prepared in solutions for instillation or oral administration. For intracavitary application, the physician inserts encapsulated radioactive elements (e.g., metal seeds, wires, tubes, or needles) into the affected body cavity using appropriate applicators, surgically inserted under ultrasound or fluoroscopic guidance. The physician may suture the applicator into or near the tumor. A radioactive isotope, usually Cesium, Iridium, or Cobalt, is placed in the applicator. The isotopes are left in place for two to three days, but may be left longer. This method provides radiation to a limited body area while minimizing exposure to normal tissue. Report 77761 for simple intracavitary application of 1 to 4 sources/ribbons; 77762 for intermediate intracavitary application of 5 to 10 sources/ribbons; and 77763 for complex intracavitary application of more than 10 sources/ribbons.

77776-77778

Brachytherapy is the application of radioactive isotopes for internal radiation. Radioactive material is encapsulated for intracavitary or interstitial implantation or prepared in solutions for instillation or oral administration. For interstitial application, the physician inserts encapsulated radioactive elements (e.g., metal seeds, wires, tubes, or needles) directly into the affected tissue using appropriate applicators, surgically inserted under ultrasound or fluoroscopic guidance. The physician may suture the applicator into or near the tumor. A radioactive isotope, usually Cesium, Iridium, or Cobalt, is placed in the applicator. The isotopes are left in place for two to three days, but may be left longer. Tiny seeds of radioactive material may be inserted directly into the tumor area and left there permanently. This method provides radiation to a limited body area while minimizing exposure to normal tissue. Report 77776 for simple interstitial application of 1 to 4 sources/ribbons; 77777 for intermediate interstitial application of 5 to 10 sources/ribbons; and 77778 for complex interstitial application of more than 10 sources/ribbons.

77785-77787

Brachytherapy is the application of radioactive isotopes for internal radiation. For remote afterloading high-dose rate radionuclide brachytherapy, tiny catheters are used together with a single, high-intensity radioactive material to produce the desired radiation distribution pattern around the tumor area. Extremely tiny catheters are fixed in place around the tumor and connected to the treatment machine. These catheters, or applicators, usually do not require surgical manipulation to set them in place. Once in position, the machine loads its radioactive source into each catheter, set at predetermined positions along each catheter for previously calculated dwelling times. The radioactive isotopes are left in place for a short period, usually only three to five minutes, due to the high radioactivity of the source that makes it thousands of times more powerful than normal brachytherapy sources. Report 77785 for one channel; 77786 for two to 12 channels; and 77787 for more than 12 channels.

77789

The physician performs a surface application of a radiation source. The physician places the radioactive source sealed in a small holder against a tumor. When surface application is used for treating pterygium, radioactive seeds are placed into a soft, plastic template, which is inserted into an eye plaque that is implanted during surgery for a specified duration and removed.

77790

The use of radiation sources for therapy requires attention and preparations for proper and safe handling of the radioelement. This code reports the supervision, handling, and loading of the radiation source used for conventional brachytherapy, not depending on the number of sources or complexity of the source used. The care of instruments involved in radioelement usage is also included.

78000-78001

The uptake test is a measure of thyroid function to determine how much iodine the thyroid will take up and is expressed as the percentage of the administered radioiodine present in the thyroid gland at a given time after administration. A standard count must be taken of the Iodide-123 capsule before giving it to the patient by using an uptake probe, a sodium iodide counter within a lead shield. For a single, two-hour uptake exam, the neck is extended with the patient supine and the probe placed over the gland. A background count is also taken over the thigh by placing a probe over one leg. Net counts are obtained by subtracting background counts. Report 78001 if multiple determinations at six- and 24-hour intervals are done.

78003

A suppression test involves administration of thyroid hormone to check if a nodule is acting autonomously or if it can be suppressed. A baseline radioiodide uptake and scan must first be obtained. The procedure requires giving the patient T3 hormone three times a day for eight days with radioiodide given orally on the seventh day. The determining uptake and scan are taken on the eighth day. Normal thyroid tissue that functions dependent on thyroid stimulating hormone will be suppressed by the T3. The stimulation test involves administering thyroid stimulating hormone (TSH) to check if a nonvisualized thyroid is present and active. A baseline radioiodide uptake and scan must first be obtained. The procedure requires giving the patient intramuscular injections of thyroid stimulating hormone (TSH) for three days along with a radioiodide tracer. A comparison uptake and scan are taken. Normal functioning thyroid tissue should show more than fifty percent increase in uptake following the simulation. This code does not include the initial uptake studies.

78006-78007

The thyroid imaging scan is performed for anatomical size and physiological evaluation. A radioactive tracer that will focus in the thyroid, such as an Iodide-123 capsule or a 99m-technetium injection is administered. With the patient supine, the neck is extended and the head immobilized. Images are scanned by a scintillation or gamma camera that detects the radiation from the tracer in the target tissue. The uptake test is a measure of thyroid function to determine how much iodine the thyroid will take up and is expressed as the percentage of the administered radioactivity present in the thyroid gland at a given time after administration. For a single, two-hour uptake exam, the neck is extended with the patient supine and the probe placed over the gland. A background count is also taken over the thigh by placing a probe over one leg. Net counts are obtained by subtracting background counts. Multiple determinations at six- and 24-hour intervals may be done in addition to the two-hour test. Report 78006 for imaging with single determination uptake and 78007 for imaging with multiple determination uptake.

78010-78011

The thyroid imaging scan is performed for anatomical size and physiological evaluation. A radioactive tracer that will focus in the thyroid, such as an Iodide-123 capsule or a 99m-technietium injection is administered. The physician palpates the patient's neck and outlines areas to be marked. With the patient supine, the neck is extended and the head immobilized. Images are scanned by a scintillation or gamma camera that detects the radiation from the tracer in the target tissue. Thyroid carcinoma functions much less than normal thyroid tissue and appears as a cold lesion with little or no accumulation of the radioiodide. Report 78011 for a vascular flow exam when a radioactive tracer is administered that will allow the blood flow and vascularity of the thyroid to be monitored by imaging at different intervals.

78015-78018
An imaging scan for thyroid cancer metastases is done only after ablation of normal thyroid tissue, six to 12 months after therapy treatment. Post-thyroidectomy patients with thyroid cancer are referred for whole body and area scanning to evaluate the thyroidectomy and demonstrate the presence and location of metastatic disease. Radioactive sodium iodide is given to the patient orally. The patient is placed supine with the neck extended and the head immobilized. Images are acquired of the neck, chest, or other clinically suspect areas with a scintillation or gamma camera that detects the radiation from the tracer in the target tissue. 78016 reports additional studies, such as a urinary recovery test in which urine is collected at intervals for radioactivity counts. Report 78018 for a whole body imaging scan.

78020
The uptake test is a measure of thyroid function to determine how much iodine the thyroid will take up and is expressed as the percentage of the administered radioactivity present in the thyroid gland at a given time after administration. An uptake for thyroid cancer metastases is done only after ablation of normal thyroid tissue. This is an add-on code. Radioactive iodine is given to the patient orally. The neck is extended with the patient supine and the probe placed over the gland. Since total thyroidectomy has been done to treat the cancer, and any remaining thyroid tissue would not be functioning, the radioactive iodine uptake noted to occur in the neck would be concentrated by metastatic lesions.

78070
Parathyroid imaging is a diagnostic tool for localizing parathyroid adenomas and hyperplastic glands by using dual radiotracer imaging and obtaining two sets of pictures. Thallium-210, which is taken up by the thyroid gland, is injected and the patient is placed supine with the neck extended and the camera centered over the neck. 60-second images are taken from 5 to 20 minutes following the injection. 99m-technetium is also injected and thyroid images taken from 5 to 10 minutes after injection. The images are normalized to each other and the technetium images are subtracted, distinguishing normal tissue from the parathyroid tissue. A thyroid image may be obtained 16 to 24 hours after oral administration of Iodine-123 and subtracted from thallium images to yield a more optimal subtraction image due to a better thyroid-to-background ratio.

78075
Nuclear adrenal imaging is used to evaluate biochemical evidence of adrenal cortical functioning. The adrenal cortex is responsible for steroid hormone production which is dependent on the availability and movement of cholesterol. Radiolabeled cholesterol is therefore the logical choice for adrenal cortex imaging. Depending on the underlying diagnosis, additional medications to aid in imaging are given at prescribed intervals and lengths of time in preparation for the study. After patients are injected with the radiocholesterol NP-59, they return for imaging a few days later. Optimal imaging intervals have also been empirically determined for different underlying diagnoses. All patients are given a solution to block thyroid uptake and a laxative to hasten excretion of the radiocholesterol metabolites. The patient is placed in the prone position for imaging and the gamma camera is centered to detect the radioactivity in the adrenal region.

78102-78104
Radiolabeled sulphur colloid is the most commonly used radiopharmaceutical for bone marrow imaging. The radiotracer is injected into the patient and images are obtained after a two or three-hour delay for optimal evaluation. A scintillation or gamma camera takes planar images of the study area on computer screen or film by detecting the gamma radiation from the radionuclide that has traveled to the bone marrow as it "scintillates" or gives off energy in a flash of light when coming in contact with the camera's detector. The bone marrow scan provides information about the distribution of functioning bone marrow and any irregular pattern of marrow tissue expansion occurring in different clinical states such as malignancy or infection. Report 78102 for bone marrow imaging of a limited area; 78103 for multiple areas; and 78104 for whole body imaging.

78110-78111
The radiopharmaceutical volume-dilution technique is performed to determine the patient's plasma volume by using a radiolabeled protein tracer such as iodinated serum albumin. The tracer is injected intravenously into one arm and a blood sample is withdrawn from the opposite arm 15 minutes after the injection. A standard solution is prepared by diluting a known volume of the injected radiopharmaceutical with water to a known volume. The dilution factor is figured. The blood sample is centrifuged and divided into 5-ml aliquots for plasma calculation using a formula involving the dilution factor from the standard sample. Report 78110 for a single sampling and 78111 if multiple samplings are collected at 15, 25, and 35 minutes after the injection.

78120-78121
The red cell volume determination test is done by using radioactive chromium to label red blood cells (RBCs). One or two vials of blood are withdrawn from the patient, the RBCs are separated out of the sample, and mixed with the radioisotope. One sample is saved to prepare the standard sample by diluting the known volume of radiolabeled RBCs with water to a known volume. Another sample is injected back into the patient's arm and after a 15 minute delay, blood is

withdrawn from the opposite arm. The red cell volume is calculated using a formula that applies the dilution factor from the standard. Report 78121 if multiple samplings are collected at 15, 25, and 35 minutes after the injection.

78122

The radiopharmaceutical volume-dilution technique is performed to determine the patient's plasma volume and red cell volume simultaneously by using a radiolabeled protein tracer such as iodinated serum albumin and autologous radiolabeled red blood cells. The procedure involves collecting blood and recording the blood counts to calculate the volumes using respective formulas that apply the dilution factor from a standard sample of each radiotracer. The radioactive protein tracer is injected intravenously into the arm as well as the radiolabeled autologous red blood cells and blood samples are withdrawn at 15, 25, and 35 minute intervals after the injection. Standard samples are prepared of each radiotracer by diluting a known volume with water until a known volume is reached. The blood samples are centrifuged and divided into 5-ml aliquots for separate red blood cell volume and plasma volume calculations which require different formulas.

78130-78135

A red cell survival study uses radioactive chromium to tag autologous red blood cells (RBCs) to evaluate the rate of red blood cell destruction, or lifespan, in patients with suspected hemolytic anemia. Prior to the procedure, the RBC volume is measured. Blood is withdrawn from the patient, the red blood cells are separated out, mixed with the radioisotope, and injected back into the patient. The initial blood sample is taken on the first day and repeated at intervals for the next two to three weeks or until half of the initial radioactive chromium labeled RBCs are present. Whole blood samples are withdrawn and the hematocrit levels recorded. If a sequestration study is also performed (78135), an aliquot of initial labeled RBCs is saved and the patient's skin is marked over the liver and spleen for detector placement. Each day that the patient returns for the survival study, surface counting is performed over the desired locations with a probe, or scintillation counter, and the different ratios (organ-to-standard, liver-spleen) are compared.

78140

Red blood cell (RBC) sequestration if a test using Chromium-51 labeled autologous red blood cells to determine if the liver or spleen is the major site of sequestration. An aliquot of the patient's own radiolabeled RBCs is saved for a standard measurement and another is re-injected. The patient's skin is marked over the liver and spleen for detector placement. Over the following weeks, surface counting is performed at the desired locations with a probe, or scintillation counter, and the different ratios (organ-to-standard, liver-spleen) are compared. Since extravascular RBC destruction occurs mainly in the liver and spleen, the sequestration counts of radiolabeled RBC accumulation in the liver or spleen over time indicate the organs' related roles in RBC destruction.

78185

Radiolabeled sulphur colloid is the most commonly used radiopharmaceutical for spleen imaging. The radiotracer is injected into the patient and images are obtained after a 15-20 minute delay. A scintillation or gamma camera takes planar images of the study area on computer screen or film by detecting the gamma radiation from the radionuclide that has traveled to the spleen as it "scintillates" or gives off energy in a flash of light when coming in contact with the camera's detector. The imaging is done first with a lead strip placed on the left costal margin and again after the strip is removed. If the imaging is done with a vascular flow study, radiolabeled damaged red blood cells are injected and their flow is followed in the spleen visualization. Splenic imaging is an indirect way of evaluation for liver disease since the disease will shunt the radiocolloid away from the liver.

78190

Once released from the bone marrow, platelets normally circulate in the blood for 8 to 10 days. In patients with certain types of chronic disease such as immune thrombocytopenic purpura (chronic ITP), an autoimmune disorder in which patients produce platelet autoantibodies that destroy blood platelets, the platelet survival time is shortened due to their destruction by the autoantibodies. The patient develops a low platelet count (thrombocytopenia). Platelet destruction occurs mainly in the spleen and to some extent in the liver and bone marrow. The tracer kinetic method involves using a radiolabeled biologically active compound to build a mathematical model for calculating the rate of platelet destruction. For this procedure, the tracer, radiolabeled plasma, is injected intravenously and a scintillation counter that detects the radiation from the plasma is used to follow the movement and destruction of platelets, and measure their concentration in specific organs or tissues.

78191

Once released from the bone marrow, platelets normally circulate in the blood for 8 to 10 days. In patients with certain types of chronic disease such as immune thrombocytopenic purpura (chronic ITP), an autoimmune disorder in which patients produce platelet autoantibodies that destroy blood platelets, the platelet survival time is shortened due to their destruction by the autoantibodies. The patient develops a low platelet count (thrombocytopenia). For the procedure, blood is withdrawn from the patient, the platelets are separated and labeled with Indium-111, and reinjected intravenously. Samples are withdrawn at intervals and the platelet levels recorded until a certain level of tagged platelets are left in circulation.

78195

Diagnostic nuclear lymphatic and lymph node imaging is a tool for studying diseases involving nodal tissue and evaluating lymphatic transport. The patient is placed in a supine position and radioactive antimony sulfide colloid is injected according to the lymph node to be visualized. For axillary and apical lymph nodes, for example, the injection is into the medial two interdigital webs of the hand and imaging is done two to four hours later. For the internal mammary lymph nodes, the injection is into the posterior rectus sheath below the rib cage and imaging is dependent upon the study. For the iliopelvic nodes, injection is into the perianal region with the patient in a knee to chest position. A scintillation or gamma camera takes planar images of the study area on computer screen or film by detecting the gamma radiation from the radiopharmaceutical in the lymphatic tissue as it "scintillates" or gives off energy when coming in contact with the camera's detector.

78201

Diagnostic nuclear medicine uses small amounts of gamma-emitting radioactive materials, or tracers, to determine the cause of the medical problem based on the function, or chemistry, of the organ or tissue. In a static test, the radionuclide travels to the intended organ. Radiolabeled sulphur colloid is the most commonly used radiopharmaceutical for liver imaging. The radioisotope is injected into a peripheral vein and extracted by the liver. A scintillation or gamma camera takes planar images of the study area on computer screen or film by detecting the gamma radiation from the radiopharmaceutical in the body tissue as it "scintillates" or gives off energy in a flash of light when coming in contact with the camera's detector, usually a sodium iodide crystal. Uniform distribution throughout the liver is normal; but an uneven distribution may indicate a tumor.

78202

Radiolabeled sulphur colloid is the most commonly used radiopharmaceutical for diagnostic nuclear imaging of the liver because it is taken up by the reticuloendothelial cells. The radioisotope is injected into a peripheral vein and extracted by the liver. For imaging done with a vascular flow test, red blood cells are labeled to image the blood flow. A scintillation or gamma camera takes images of the liver on computer screen or film by detecting the gamma radiation from the radiopharmaceutical in the tissue and the blood as it flows through the liver. This helps characterize lesions or tumors and determine vascular complications in the liver. Impaired blood flow and reticuloendothelial function can show up as patchy colloid uptake in the liver with preferential bone marrow and spleen uptake.

78205-78206

Tomographic SPECT (single photon emission computed tomography) imaging permits an in-depth evaluation of the complex anatomy and functional activity of the liver by introducing a radiolabeled sulphur colloid through an injection into a peripheral vein and detecting the distribution of gamma radiation emitted from the radiopharmaceutical taken up by the reticuloendothelial cells of the liver. SPECT imaging differs from the usual planar scans of the gamma camera by rotating a single or multiple-head camera mounted on a gantry around the patient to give three-dimensional computer reconstructed views of cross-sectional slices of the liver. For imaging done with a vascular flow test, red blood cells are labeled to enable imaging of the blood flow through the liver. Report 78205 for SPECT imaging of the liver without vascular flow and 78206 for SPECT imaging with vascular flow.

78215-78216

Radiolabeled sulphur colloid is the most commonly used radiopharmaceutical for diagnostic nuclear imaging of the liver. Radiolabeled heat-denatured red blood cells are used for detecting asplenia and polysplenia. The radioisotope is injected into a peripheral vein and extracted by the liver and spleen. For imaging done with a vascular flow test, red blood cells are labeled to image the blood flow through the liver and spleen. A scintillation or gamma camera takes images of the liver and spleen on computer screen or film by detecting the gamma radiation from the radiopharmaceutical in the tissue and/or the blood as it flows through the study organs. This helps characterize lesions or tumors and determine vascular complications. Report 78215 for static liver and spleen imaging without vascular flow and 78216 for liver and spleen imaging with vascular flow.

78220

Special radiolabeled aminoacetic acids that are rapidly cleared by hepatocytes and excreted in the bile are used in a nuclear liver function study. The radiotracer is injected into a peripheral vein and followed by serial imaging with a scintillation, or gamma camera, on computer screen or film by detecting the gamma radiation from the radiopharmaceutical in the liver and throughout the biliary tract as it is expelled. Biliary function scanning is used in diagnosing acute cholecystitis, cholestasis, obstructions, leaks, biliary-enteric fistulas, and cysts.

78223

For nuclear imaging of the hepatobiliary ductal system with gall bladder, special radiolabeled aminoacetic acids that are rapidly cleared by hepatocytes and excreted in the bile are injected into a peripheral vein. A scintillation or gamma camera takes planar images of the ductal system on computer screen or film by detecting the gamma radiation from the radiopharmaceutical in the body tissue as it "scintillates" or gives off energy in a flash of light when coming in contact with the camera's detector. This imaging may be done with or without pharmacologic intervention to aid in visualizing the gallbladder and/or measuring its function. An oral agent is administered that concentrates in the gallbladder after being absorbed in the intestine and excreted by the liver. The resulting opacification or even nonvisualization of the gallbladder can diagnose disease such as stones, polyps, and cholesterolosis. This code also includes calculations for a quantitative measurement of gallbladder function.

78230-78231
Diagnostic nuclear medicine uses small amounts of gamma-emitting radioactive materials, or tracers, to determine the cause of the medical problem based on the function, or chemistry, of the organ or tissue. In a static test, the radionuclide travels to the intended organ. For salivary gland imaging, the patient is injected with a low-level radiotracer and immediately imaged with a scintillation or gamma camera that takes planar images of the salivary, or parotid, gland by detecting the gamma radiation from the radiopharmaceutical in the body tissue. Report 78231 if the imaging is done by serial imaging and another set for comparison is taken after the patient has been given lemon candy to stimulate the salivary glands.

78232
In a nuclear imaging salivary gland function study, the patient is given a radiolabeled sulfur colloid mixture under the tongue that allows the visualization of the flow of saliva from the oral cavity through to the esophagus and the stomach. A gamma camera takes planar images by detecting the gamma radiation from the radiopharmaceutical in the saliva as it moves through the body. The test usually is conducted for an hour after the administration of the radiotracer to follow the saliva pathway.

78258
Diagnostic nuclear medicine uses small amounts of gamma-emitting radioactive materials, or tracers, to determine the cause of the medical problem based on the function, or chemistry, of the organ or tissue. For esophageal motility imaging, a radioactive sulfur colloid in water is administered orally and followed by a scintillation, or gamma camera, that takes planar images by detecting the gamma radiation from the radiopharmaceutical as it gives off energy while being swallowed down the esophagus. This test is done to diagnose motility and neurodegenerative disorders, reverse peristalsis, and dysphagia.

78261
Radiolabeled pertechnetate is administered intravenously for a nuclear imaging study of gastric mucosa, especially in children. A scintillation, or gamma camera, scans a wide vision field from the xiphoid to the symphysis pubis and takes planar images by detecting the gamma radiation from the radiopharmaceutical. Gastric mucosa surfaces of the stomach will selectively collect and secrete the pertechnetate. Gastric mucosa in an ectopic site, such as Meckel's diverticulum, will accumulate the radiotracer the same as in the stomach, and allow visualization of the ectopic area as long as there is sufficient mucosa to focally concentrate the tracer.

78262
Diagnostic nuclear medicine uses small amounts of gamma-emitting radioactive materials, or tracers, to determine the cause of the medical problem based on the function, or chemistry, of the organ or tissue. For a gastroesophageal reflux study, a sulfur colloid radioisotope in liquid form such as milk is given to the patient to drink. A scintillation, or gamma camera, takes images on camera or film by detecting the gamma radiation from the radiotracer in the liquid in the stomach to visualize any gastroesophageal reflux. The test is usually done for an hour following ingestion of the material.

78264
Diagnostic nuclear medicine uses small amounts of gamma-emitting radioactive materials, or tracers, to determine the cause of the medical problem based on the function, or chemistry, of the organ or tissue. For a gastric emptying study, a sulfur colloid radioisotope in liquid form such as milk is given to the patient to drink. A scintillation, or gamma camera, takes images on camera or film by detecting the gamma radiation from the radiopharmaceutical in the liquid as it moves through the stomach to measure the gastric emptying time. The test is usually done for an hour following ingestion of the material.

78267-78268
Diagnostic nuclear medicine uses small amounts of gamma-emitting radioactive materials, or tracers, to determine the cause of the medical problem based on the function, or chemistry, of the organ or tissue. The urea breath test is a noninvasive method of diagnosing a Helicobacter pylori infection of the stomach. The patient swallows a pill or drinks a solution containing the chemical urea, labeled with the radioactive isotope C-14. The bacteria will produce an enzyme that breaks down the urea into ammonia and carbon dioxide gas, if they are present. The gas contains the tagged carbon and is quickly absorbed into the bloodstream and expelled in the breath. Breath samples are taken six, 12, and 20 minutes after swallowing the pill. Urease activity produced by the bacteria, when present, will be made manifest in the breath samples collected by the presence of exhaled tagged carbon molecules. Analysis is done using a scintillation counter in a nuclear medicine or radiology department. Report 78267 for

the isotope administration and sample collection and 78268 for the breath test analysis.

78270-78272
The Schilling test checks for vitamin B12 deficiency. The patient swallows a capsule that contains radioactive vitamin B12 and an hour later is given an injection of vitamin B12 that is not radioactively labeled. All urine excreted in the following 24 hours is collected and checked for radioactive B12 which will be present if it was absorbed. If the first test shows that it was not absorbed, the same test is done again except that this time the patient also takes a capsule containing intrinsic factor. If there is now radioactive vitamin B12 in the urine, an intrinsic factor deficiency is likely the cause of the vitamin B12 deficiency. Report 78270 for the Schilling test without intrinsic factor; 78271 for the Schilling test with intrinsic factor; and 78272 for combined vitamin B12 absorption studies both with and without intrinsic factor.

78278
Diagnostic nuclear medicine uses small amounts of gamma-emitting radioactive materials, or tracers, to determine the cause of the medical problem based on the function, or chemistry, of the organ or tissue. For acute gastrointestinal blood loss imaging, a radioactive colloid is injected intravenously and images are scanned over a large field of vision including the abdomen and pelvis by a camera that detects the gamma radiation from the radioactive tracer introduced into the patient. Detection of a hemorrhage depends on the localization of radiotracer that has filtered out of the blood vessel and into the surrounding bowel lumen. Different angle images may be necessary to rule out bleeding that may be obstructed by other organs, such as the liver and spleen.

78282
A diagnostic gastrointestinal protein loss study is done through nuclear medicine to quantitate the amount of protein loss that is occurring through the GI tract. Two equal doses of chromic chloride are prepared-one for the patient and one to be used as the standard measurement. The patient is injected intravenously via a stopcock and the port of the stopcock is flushed with saline. The stools are collected for the next 4 days in containers with lids to be returned to nuclear medicine. The standard dose is dispensed into a gallon bucket filled with water. When the stool samples return, they are filled with water to the top and mixed. The counts of both the standard and stool samples are taken and compared for diagnosis.

78290
Intestine imaging done with nuclear scintigraphy involves injecting the patient with radioactive sodium pertechnetate. With the patient supine, the scintillation, or gamma camera, scans a wide field of view covering the abdominal area and takes images on camera or film by detecting the gamma radiation from the radioactive tracer introduced into the patient. Structural abnormalities, such as ectopic gastric mucosa, diverticula, or twisting of the bowel causing obstruction may be detected and localized. Gastric mucosa surfaces in an ectopic site will selectively collect and secrete the pertechnetate. Patients suspected of Meckel's diverticulum are given a medication to increase gastric uptake of the pertechnetate. When scanning for inflammatory disorders of the bowel, such as Crohn's disease and ulcerative colitis, autologous radiolabeled white blood cells, which focus at inflammation sites, are used as the radiotracer for imaging purposes.

78291
Diagnostic nuclear medicine imaging can test peritoneovenous shunt patency in patients with intractable ascites. The shunt is plastic tubing equipped with a pressure valve that is inserted to connect the peritoneal cavity to the internal jugular or subclavian vein and permit the return of ascites fluid and proteins to the venous system. Normal inspiration creates the necessary intra-abdominal versus intrathoracic pressure change that allows the pressure valve to open and drain the ascites fluid. The ascites fluid is radiolabeled and followed by imaging with a camera that detects the gamma radiation from the radiotracer introduced into the patient. If the fluid is circulating into the systemic system correctly through a patent shunt, the radiotracer will appear in the cells of the liver.

78300-78315
Various radiopharmaceutical agents are used for diagnostic nuclear imaging of bones and/or joints. Gallium, a calcium analogue, is the radiopharmaceutical of choice when scanning for an inflammatory process because it accumulates in areas of bone mineral turnover, such as fractures, and localizes to infected or inflamed areas like inflammatory arthritis. Combining gallium with radiolabeled white blood cells, which also localize at infection sites, adds more diagnostic specificity when searching for acute osteomyelitis or osteoarthropathy. Radioactive diphosphonates are used for bony metastatic disease screening. A camera scans the area of study and detects the gamma radiation from the radiotracer introduced into the patient to detect and localize the disease process. Report 78300 for bone and/or joint imaging of a limited area; 78305 for multiple areas; 78306 for a whole body scan; and 78315 for a three-phase scan.

78320
Tomographic SPECT (single photon emission computed tomography) imaging permits an in-depth evaluation of complex anatomy within body structures such as the bones and joints by introducing a radionuclide and detecting the distribution of gamma

radiation emitted from the radiotracer with a single or multiple-head camera mounted on a gantry to rotate around the patient. SPECT images give three-dimensional computer reconstructed views of cross-sectional slices of the body. Gallium, a calcium analogue, is the radiopharmaceutical of choice when scanning for an inflammatory process in the bones or joints because it accumulates in areas of bone mineral turnover, such as fractures, and localizes to infected or inflamed areas like inflammatory arthritis. Combining gallium with radiolabeled white blood cells, which also localize at infection sites, adds more diagnostic specificity when searching for acute osteomyelitis or osteoarthropathy. Radioactive diphosphonates are used for bony metastatic disease screening.

78350-78351

Single and dual photon absorptiometry are both noninvasive techniques to measure the absorption of the mono or dichromatic photon beam by bone material. The painless study device is placed directly on the patient and uses a small amount of radionuclide to measure the bone mass absorption efficiency of the energy used. This provides a quantitative measurement of the bone mineral density of cortical bone in diseases like osteoporosis and can be used to assess an individual's response to treatment at different intervals. Report 78350 for single photon energy and 78351 for dual photon energy.

78428

For detecting right to left cardiac shunts, radiolabeled macroaggregated albumin is used, which is trapped by the lungs and will be identified in the systemic circulation if a right to left shunt is present. For left to right shunts, the first pass technique is used. A bolus of radionuclide is injected and rapid image frames are acquired as it moves in the venous system through the chambers of the heart. Early recirculation detected would identify a left to right shunt.

78445

Nuclear imaging for non-cardiac vascular flow studies may be performed to test for arterial or venous peripheral vascular diseases or injuries, graft patency, and even catheter malfunctions. In radionuclide angiography, for example, red blood cells from the patient are tagged with radioactivity and injected intravenously. A scintillation camera positioned over the arterial area of interest detects the radioactivity in the blood and takes a series of dynamic images every 2 to 3 seconds immediately after injection, followed by static images. These are recorded on computer and/or film to be studied at different frame rates, times, and intensities. Normal flow is demonstrated as swift and unimpeded. Luminal narrowing or widening, blood flow obstructions and occlusions, and extraluminal accumulation of the radioactive cells can be visualized for diagnostic purposes.

78451-78452

For tomographic myocardial perfusion imaging, the patient receives an intravenous injection of a radionuclide, usually thallium or technetium-99m, which localizes only in nonischemic tissue. SPECT (single photon emission computed tomographic) images of the heart are taken immediately to identify areas of perfusion vs. infarction. SPECT imaging differs from planar imaging by using a single or multiple-head camera that rotates around the patient to give three-dimensional tomographic imaging of the heart displayed in thin slices. In the nonstress version of the procedure, radionuclide is injected and images are taken without stress induction. In 78451, a single study is performed at rest or stress. If the test is to be done at a stress condition, it is induced with the standard treadmill exercise test or pharmacologically with the infusion of a vasodilator. In 78452, multiple studies are done at rest and/or stress with a second injection of radionuclide given again in the redistribution and/or resting phase just prior to resting images being taken. These codes also include attenuation correction (AC), which provides a more accurate diagnostic image for diagnosing defects or infarcted areas by raising the importance of radioactivity distribution counts arising from certain areas. For instance, counts from the anterior wall may be reduced or impeded by the presence of the breast. These codes also include qualitative or quantitative wall motion, ejection fraction (EF) by first pass or gated technique, and additional quantification, when performed.

78453-78454

For planar myocardial perfusion imaging, stress is induced with the standard treadmill exercise test or pharmacologically with the infusion of a vasodilator, if the test is to be done at stress conditions. The patient receives an intravenous injection of a radionuclide, usually thallium or technetium-99m, which localizes only in nonischemic tissue. Planar images of the heart are scanned immediately with a gamma camera that detects the radiation in the heart tissue to identify areas of infarction. In the nonstress version of the procedure, radionuclide is injected and images taken without stress induction. In 78453, a single study is performed at rest or stress. In 78454, multiple procedures are done at rest and/or at stress with a second injection of radionuclide given again in the redistribution or resting phase just prior to resting images being taken. For tests performed during pharmacological or exercise-induced stress, report the appropriate stress testing code. These codes also include qualitative or quantitative wall motion, ejection fraction (EF) by first pass or gated technique, and additional quantification, when performed.

78456

Diagnostic nuclear imaging for acute venous thrombosis imaging uses radiolabeled peptides.

Peptides are short-string proteins that attach to platelets, which are essential in blood clotting, and localize at sites where clots are present or beginning to form. Images from a scintillation, or gamma camera, are taken by detecting the gamma radiation from the radiotracer in the peptides attached to the blood component and these images can identify clots as soon as 10 minutes after the injection. Usually another set of images is done after 60 to 90 minutes following the injection as the image quality tends to improve with time after the injection. If a scan showed significantly increased uptake in any region of one leg compared to the other, or more intense uptake on delayed imaging, deep venous thrombosis is suspected.

78457-78458

A diagnostic nuclear venogram is done to identify the presence and location of thrombi (blood clots) within the venous system. An intravenous injection of a radiopharmaceutical into one or both extremities, most often the legs, is first performed. This is followed by rapid sequence imaging as the radiopharmaceutical passes through the venous system. Unilateral imaging for venous thrombosis is reported with 78457; bilateral imaging is reported with 78458. Bilateral studies may be performed even when only one leg is symptomatic for deep-vein thrombus as the normal extremity if used for comparison purposes.

78459

The cardiac muscle is imaged using data received from positron-emitting radionuclides administered to the patient. The collision of the positrons emitted by the radionuclide with the negatively-charged electrons normally present in tissue is computer synthesized to produce an image, usually in color. This image will show the presence or absence of ischemic or fibrotic cardiac tissue and allow evaluation of metabolic functioning of cardiac tissue.

78466-78469

A radionuclide is injected intravenously that localizes in recently (under 72-hours) infarcted myocardial tissue. Multiple cardiac images are obtained between one and four hours after injection of the isotope. The location and extent of infarct can be determined by the presence of the radionuclide in the heart tissue. In 78468, first-pass technique is utilized. In first-pass technique, a bolus of Technetium-99m or other radionuclide is injected and visualized as it moves through the venous system into the right atrium, right ventricle, pulmonary artery, lungs, left atrium, left ventricle, and aorta. Several cardia cycles are generally observed. Ejection fraction measurements from both the right and left ventricle are calculated by determining the change in radioactivity over time. In 78469, SPECT images are obtained. SPECT images are tomographic reconstructions derived from a single- or multiple-head gamma camera that rotates around the patient. Tomographic imaging displays the heart in thin slices allowing better separation of myocardial and nonmyocardial structures. SPECT imaging is helpful in identifying small infarcts that are sometimes missed using planar imaging alone.

78472-78473

Radionuclide, which will adhere to the patient's red blood cells, is injected intravenously for cardiac blood pool imaging. Multiple images of the heart, synchronized with the electrocardiographic RR interval (ECG gated), are taken several minutes later, after the radionuclide has spread through the blood pool. These images are computer synthesized and data is generated to produce a video display of cardiac wall motion, calculation of left ventricular ejection fractions, and images based on computer manipulation of the data received. In 78472, the procedure is performed as a single study at rest or stress, not both; in 78473, the procedure is performed at both rest and stress. For tests performed during pharmacological or exercise-induced stress, report the appropriate stress testing code also.

78481-78483

A bolus of radionuclide is injected intravenously for cardiac blood pool imaging, first pass technique. As the radioisotope passes through the cardiac chambers, rapid sequence imaging and computer generation of data and images is done to produce a video display of cardiac wall motion, calculation of ventricular ejection fractions, and images based on computer manipulation of the data received. This technique provides information about the functional status of the heart at rest or in response to stress. In 78481, the procedure is performed as a single study at rest or stress, not both; in 78483, the procedure is performed at rest and stress. For tests performed during pharmacological or exercise-induced stress, report the appropriate stress testing code also.

78491-78492

The cardiac muscle is imaged using data received from positron-emitting radionuclides administered to the patient. The collision of the positrons emitted by the radionuclide with the negatively-charged electrons normally present in tissue is computer synthesized to produce an image, usually in color, which will show the presence or absence of perfusion into normal or ischemic cardiac tissue. In 78491, the procedure is performed as a single study at rest or stress, not both; in 78492, the procedure is performed at rest and stress. For tests performed during pharmacological or exercise-induced stress, report the appropriate stress testing code also.

78494

Radionuclide, which will adhere to the patient's red blood cells, is injected intravenously for cardiac blood pool imaging, gated equilibrium. Multiple SPECT (single photon emission computed tomography) images of the heart, synchronized with the electrocardiographic RR interval (ECG gated), are taken several minutes later, after the radionuclide has spread through the blood pool. These SPECT images are taken by a rotating single or multiple-head camera for three-dimensional views of cross-sectional slices and provide better contrast in imaging and greater accuracy than planar scans. The SPECT images are computer synthesized and data is generated to produce a video display of cardiac wall motion, calculation of ventricular ejection fractions, and images based on computer manipulation of the data received.

78496
A bolus of radionuclide is injected intravenously for cardiac blood pool imaging with right ventricular ejection fraction by first pass technique. As the radioisotope in the venous system passes through the cardiac chambers, rapid sequence imaging, synchronized with the electrocardiographic RR interval (ECG gated), is done. This first pass technique provides information for right ventricular ejection fraction calculation not possible with static gated images which do not show right ventricular count in isolation. This test for functional status of the heart is done as a single study at rest in addition to the primary procedure.

78580
Nuclear pulmonary perfusion imaging uses a venous injection of radioactive macroaggregated albumin particles which are too large to pass through the pulmonary capillary bed and accumulate there as they are strained out. A scintillation or gamma camera takes planar images on computer screen or film by detecting the gamma radiation from the radiopharmaceutical in the lungs as it "scintillates" or gives off energy in a flash of light when coming in contact with the camera's detector. Localization of the radioactive particles is proportional to the blood flow and thereby maps lung perfusion. Standard perfusion imaging usually consists of 8 planar images from different projections with the posterior oblique views being most important since they image the lower lobes, the most common site for pulmonary embolism.

78584
Ventilation and perfusion imaging of the lungs is used to detect pulmonary embolism and the percentage of total perfusion and ventilation attributable to each lung. Perfusion imaging is done after a venous injection of radioactive macroaggregated albumin is given to the patient. The albumin particles are too large to pass through the pulmonary capillary bed and accumulate there as they are strained out. This localization of particles is proportional to the blood flow and thereby maps lung perfusion. A nuclear ventilation image is obtained to complement the perfusion image. For a single breath image, a posterior view of the thorax is taken as the patient inhales radiolabeled Xenon gas in a single breath and holds it as long as possible. This image obtained from the gamma camera that detects the radioactivity from the gas in the lungs will show well-ventilated areas having uniform activity and poorly ventilated areas with decreased or absent radioactivity.

78585
Ventilation and perfusion imaging of the lungs is used to detect pulmonary embolism and the percentage of total perfusion and ventilation attributable to each lung. For perfusion imaging, a venous injection of radioactive macroaggregated albumin is given to the patient. The albumin particles are too large to pass through the pulmonary capillary bed and accumulate there as they are strained out. This localization of particles is proportional to the blood flow and thereby maps lung perfusion. For complementary ventilation rebreathing and washout imaging, the patient breathes in a mixture of radioactive xenon gas and oxygen for a few minutes, allowing equilibration of the xenon in the airways. After rebreathing, single or multiple wash-in images are taken to reflect the total ventilated lung volume. Next, the patient breathes the room air and exhales the xenon gas while serial washout images are taken to visualize any focal retention of the radioactive particles that would demonstrate obstructive airway disease. This is done with or without single breath imaging upon initial inhalation of the radiolabeled gas.

78586-78587
Nuclear ventilation imaging of the lungs is designed to show the regional distribution of inspired air throughout the lung tissue and the uptake and clearance dynamics of the lungs. The patient is usually placed supine and breathes in a radioaerosol through a tube that is attached to a nebulizer. Once the aerosol is inhaled, the radioactivity stays in the area where it was deposited long enough to take images with a camera that detects the gamma radiation being given off from the aerosol in the air spaces. Increased central deposition occurs in severe obstructive airway disorders. Very rapid clearance from the lungs reflects interstitial lung disease, such as in smokers, where systemic absorption rises due to increased alveolar capillary permeability. Report 78586 for ventilation imaging from a single projection and 78587 for multiple projections such as anterior, posterior, and lateral views.

78588
Ventilation and perfusion imaging of the lungs is used to detect pulmonary embolism and the percentage of total perfusion and ventilation attributable to each lung. For perfusion imaging, an injection of radioactive macroaggregated albumin is given to the patient. The albumin particles are too large to pass through the pulmonary capillary bed and accumulate there as they are strained out. This localization of particles is proportional to the blood flow and thereby maps lung perfusion. For ventilation images, a series of single or

multiple projection views, comparable to the perfusion views, are taken after the patient has inhaled a radiolabeled aerosol. The radioactivity stays in the area where it was deposited long enough to take images. If there is no obstruction, consistent appearance and disappearance of the radioactive gas in the air spaces of the lungs is shown.

78591

Nuclear ventilation imaging of the lungs is designed to show the regional distribution of inspired air throughout the lung tissue and the uptake and clearance dynamics of the lungs. For a single breath, single projection ventilation image, a posterior view of the thorax is taken as the patient inhales radiolabeled Xenon gas in a single breath and holds it as long as possible. This image obtained from the gamma camera that detects the radioactivity from the gas in the lungs will show well-ventilated areas having uniform activity and poorly ventilated areas with decreased or absent radioactivity.

78593-78594

Nuclear ventilation imaging of the lungs is designed to show the regional distribution of inspired air throughout the lung tissue and the uptake and clearance dynamics of the lungs. For rebreathing and washout imaging, the patient breathes in a mixture of radioactive xenon gas and oxygen for a few minutes, allowing equilibration of the xenon in the airways. After rebreathing, single or multiple posterior wash-in images are taken to reflect the total ventilated lung volume. Next, the patient breathes the room air and exhales the xenon gas while serial washout images are taken to visualize any focal retention of the radioactive particles that would demonstrate obstructive airway disease. This is done with or without single breath imaging upon initial inhalation of the radiolabeled gas. Report 78593 if images are taken from a single projection only, usually posterior; and report 78594 if images include anterior, posterior, and/or lateral views.

78596

Ventilation and perfusion imaging of the lungs is used to detect pulmonary embolism and the percentage of total perfusion and ventilation attributable to each lung. Ventilation imaging of the lungs shows the regional distribution of inspired air throughout the lung tissue and the uptake and clearance dynamics of the lungs by having the patient inhale a radioaerosol or gas. Perfusion imaging uses an injection of radioactive albumin which are particles too big to pass through the pulmonary capillary bed and accumulate there, mapping blood perfusion as they are strained out. The two types of images complement each other for diagnosis purposes. When the data for these studies is acquired on a digital computer, lung ventilation and perfusion can be quantitated for gradient comparisons and function differential calculations.

78600, 78605

Diagnostic nuclear medicine uses small amounts of gamma-emitting radioactive materials, or tracers, to determine the cause of the medical problem based on the function, or chemistry, of the organ or tissue. This is in contrast to diagnostic tests that determine disease presence based on structural appearance. In a static test, the radionuclide travels to the intended organ. The organ, tissue, or bone under study determines the type of radioactive material used and it is introduced by injection, swallowing, or inhalation. A scintillation or gamma camera takes planar images of the study area on computer screen or film by detecting the gamma radiation from the radiopharmaceutical in the body tissue as it "scintillates" or gives off energy in a flash of light when coming in contact with the camera's detector. Report less than four static views of the brain with 78600 and four or more with 78605.

78601, 78606

Diagnostic nuclear medicine uses small amounts of gamma-emitting radioactive materials, or tracers, to determine the cause of the medical problem based on the function, or chemistry, of the organ or tissue. This is in contrast to diagnostic tests that determine disease presence based on structural appearance. In a static test, the radionuclide travels to the intended organ. The organ, tissue, or bone under study determines the type of radioactive material used and it is introduced by injection, swallowing, or inhalation. A scintillation or gamma camera takes planar images of the study area on computer screen or film by detecting the gamma radiation from the radiopharmaceutical in the body tissue as it "scintillates" or gives off energy in a flash of light when coming in contact with the camera's detector. Report less than four static views of the brain with 78600 and four or more with 78605.

78607

Tomographic SPECT (single photon emission computed tomography) imaging permits an in-depth evaluation of the complex anatomy and functional activity of the brain by introducing a radionuclide and detecting the distribution of gamma radiation emitted from the radiopharmaceutical introduced into the brain tissue. SPECT images differ from the usual planar scans of the gamma camera by rotating a single- or multiple-head camera mounted on a gantry (frame) around the patient to give three-dimensional computer reconstructed views of cross-sectional slices of the brain.

78608

Positron emission tomography (PET) produces thin slice images of the body that can be reassembled into three-dimensional representations by detecting positron-emitting radionuclides from a radiopharmaceutical introduced into the body. These radionuclides must be produced in a cyclotron or generator that can bombard chemicals with neutrons to produce unstable, short-lived radioisotopes, such as carbon-11, nitrogen-13, and oxygen-15. These can be readily incorporated into common and important, biological body compounds for administration. Data from the imaging yields metabolic or biochemical function information depending on the type of molecule tagged. In PET imaging of the brain with metabolic evaluation, the radionuclide in injected intravenously and carried to the brain where the scanner detects the radioactivity as the compound accumulates in different regions of the brain. By using specifically tagged compounds, information on glucose, oxygen, or drug metabolism in the brain is obtained.

78609

Positron emission tomography (PET) produces thin slice images of the body that can be reassembled into three-dimensional representations by detecting positron-emitting radionuclides from a radiopharmaceutical introduced into the body. These radionuclides must be produced in a cyclotron or generator that can bombard chemicals with neutrons to produce unstable, short-lived radioisotopes, such as carbon-11, nitrogen-13, and oxygen-15. These can be readily incorporated into common and important, biological body compounds for administration. Data from the imaging yields metabolic or biochemical function information depending on the type of molecule tagged. In PET imaging of the brain with perfusion evaluation, the radionuclide in injected intravenously and carried to the brain where the scanner detects the radioactivity as the tracer accumulates in different areas of the brain proportional to the rate of delivery of blood to that volume of brain tissue.

78610

Diagnostic nuclear medicine uses small amounts of gamma-emitting radioactive materials, or tracers, to determine the cause of the medical problem based on the function, or chemistry, of the organ or tissue. In a vascular flow test, the radionuclide labels red blood cells and therefore goes wherever the blood flows. The radionuclide is administered to the patient and a scintillation or gamma camera takes time-delayed, dynamic images of the study area on computer screen or film by detecting the gamma radiation from the radiopharmaceutical in the blood as it flows through the study area. This helps characterize lesions or tumors and determine vascular complications in an organ. Use this code for a vascular flow study only of the brain.

78630

Diagnostic nuclear medicine uses small amounts of gamma-emitting radioactive materials, or tracers, to determine the cause of the medical problem based on the function, or chemistry, of the organ or tissue. Cisternography is done to determine if there is any abnormal cerebral spinal fluid flow occurring in or around the brain. A lumbar puncture is necessary to inject the radiotracer into the lower spinal canal region. A scintillation or gamma camera takes planar images of the study area on computer screen or film by detecting the gamma radiation from the radiopharmaceutical in the body tissue as it "scintillates" or gives off energy when coming in contact with the camera's detector. Cisternography is a multiple-day procedure requiring 6-hour, 24-hour, and 48-hour scan sessions.

78635

Diagnostic nuclear ventriculography is done to measure ventricular size in the brain, especially for patients with hydrocephalus who have shunts to drain abnormal accumulations of cerebrospinal fluid (CSF) in the brain due to ventricular obstruction of the normal cerebrospinal fluid pathways. A lumbar puncture may be necessary to inject the radiotracer into the lower spinal canal region or it may be injected into a reservoir or valve of the shunt. A scintillation or gamma camera takes images of the study area on computer screen or film by detecting the gamma radiation from the injected radiopharmaceutical.

78645

A shunt is a tube placed in the interior ventricles of the brain that drains fluid by a pressure controlled valve away from the brain to another part of the body, usually the abdominal cavity, where it is reabsorbed. In order to detect any malfunction and assess the shunt's patency in a noninvasive manner, a radiotracer is injected into a reservoir or valve of the shunt. A scintillation or gamma camera takes images of the head, chest, and abdomen by detecting the radiation from the injected radiopharmaceutical to determine the movement of the tracer from the shunt in the brain to the peritoneal cavity.

78647

Tomographic SPECT (single photon emission computed tomography) imaging permits an in-depth evaluation of complex anatomy or functional activity in the body by injecting a radionuclide and detecting the distribution of gamma radiation emitted from the radiopharmaceutical introduced into the body tissues being studied. Cerebrospinal fluid (CSF) flow imaging will detect any abnormalities or injury occurring in the normal pathways of CSF. A lumbar puncture is necessary to inject the radiotracer into the lower spinal canal region. SPECT images differ from the usual planar scans of the gamma camera by rotating a single or multiple-head camera mounted on a gantry around the patient to give three-dimensional, computer-reconstructed views of cross-sectional slices of the body.

78650

Diagnostic nuclear medicine uses small amounts of gamma-emitting radioactive materials, or tracers, to determine the cause of the medical problem based on the function, or chemistry, of the organ or tissue. Intracranial trauma, surgery, infection, malformation, or disease such as hydrocephalus or neoplasms can cause cerebrospinal fluid (CSF) to leak into and drain from nasal or oral cavities. A lumbar puncture may be necessary to inject the radiotracer into the lower spinal canal region. A scintillation or gamma camera takes images of the study area on computer screen or film by detecting the gamma radiation from the radiopharmaceutical to detect fluid levels in sinuses that suggest leakage and determine the leakage location.

78660
Dacryocystography is the radiographic evaluation of the lacrimal system to localize the site of an obstruction. In diagnostic nuclear medicine, a drop of a radiotracer is instilled in the eye and subsequent imaging by a scintillation or gamma camera is performed to follow the passage of the radioactivity and the rate at which it disappears into the lacrimal system to assess if there is a stone or other blockage that interferes with normal tearing function.

78700
Diagnostic nuclear medicine uses small amounts of gamma-emitting radioactive materials, or tracers, to determine a structural cause of the medical problem in the kidney. For kidney imaging, a radionuclide such as 99mTc-DMSA is chosen because it will travel to the kidney and remain in the functional tissue there. It is injected into the patient and a scintillation or gamma camera takes planar images of the kidney on computer screen or film by detecting the gamma radiation from the radiopharmaceutical in the renal tissue as it "scintillates" or gives off energy in a flash of light when coming in contact with the camera's detector. Supply and injection of the radionuclide are reported separately.

78701
For diagnostic nuclear imaging of the kidney with a vascular flow test, the radionuclide 99mTc-DTPA is commonly chosen because it will follow the blood as it flows through the kidney and also identify any obstruction in the collecting system to determine the rate at which the kidney's are filtering. It is injected into the patient and a special scintillation or gamma camera takes planar images of the study area on computer screen or film by detecting the gamma radiation from the radiopharmaceutical as it flows through the kidney.

78707-78709
For a diagnostic nuclear imaging study of kidney structure with vascular flow and function test, a radiopharmaceutical is injected that follows the blood flow through the kidneys in the normal pathway for urine production. Obstructions in the collecting system are identified, along with the rate at which the kidneys are filtering the blood, and how well the tubules and ducts are functioning. A scintillation or gamma camera scans the study area and takes images on computer screen or film by detecting the gamma radiation from the radiopharmaceutical as it flows through the kidney. If pharmacological intervention is used, a diuretic may also be injected that will increase urine flow during the exam. If the radiotracer accumulates and the kidney fails to clear it after diuretic administration, surgery may be necessary to correct the obstruction. Report 78707 for a single study without pharmacological intervention; 78708 for a single study with intervention; and 78709 for multiple studies, done with and without intervention.

78710
Tomographic SPECT (single photon emission computed tomography) imaging permits an in-depth evaluation of the complex anatomy and functional activity of the kidney by injecting a radionuclide and detecting the distribution of gamma radiation emitted from the radiopharmaceutical introduced into the renal tissue. SPECT images differ from the usual planar scans of the gamma camera by rotating a single or multiple-head camera mounted on a gantry around the patient to give three-dimensional computer reconstructed views of cross-sectional slices of the kidney.

78725
A non-imaging radioisotopic study of kidney function requires a radioisotope that is cleared from the body only by the glomerular filtration action of the kidneys. Measuring the glomerular filtration rate (GFR) is the best assessment of total renal function. The radioisotope is injected and blood samples are taken at two, three, and four hours for radioactive concentration counts. The filtration rate of the kidneys is proportional to the clearance rate of the radioisotope from the blood and is calculated using this information together with the distribution volume. The GFR can also be calculated by using urine collections but this method has more intrinsic complications than blood sampling.

78730
For a urinary bladder residual study, the patient is injected with 99mTc-DTPA to evaluate for obstructions or noncompliant bladder. Images are obtained with a gamma camera to record bladder activity for a set amount of time before voiding. The bladder is emptied and the volume that was discharged is measured. Bladder activity is re-imaged for the same length of time after voiding. The residual urine volume is calculated using the amount of urine passed and the bladder counts both before and after voiding. Introduction and supply of the radionuclide are reported separately.

78740
A nuclear urethral reflex study is a voiding cystogram recorded with the use of a radiopharmaceutical that has

been injected into the patient. Fluids are given into the bladder for half an hour through a Foley catheter and posterior images of activity are taken. According to the patient's need, the bladder is emptied while digital recordings are taken to the end of voiding and continued for another few minutes. Images are reconstructed from the digital data system to detect the presence and identify the grade of ureteric or intrarenal reflux which can lead to severe kidney damage. Time-activity curves may also by calculated to show increased renal activity during voiding due to the reflux.

78761
For testicular diagnostic nuclear imaging, 99mTc-pertechnetate is injected into a vein in the arm and travels to the testicle where it accumulates. In a vascular flow test, the radionuclide labels red blood cells and therefore goes wherever the blood flows. A scintillation or gamma camera takes images of the study area on computer screen or film by detecting the gamma radiation from the radiotracer concentrated in the testicle or the blood as it flows through the testicle. This test determines whether the blood supply to the testis is compromised. Administration and supply of the radionuclide are reported separately.

78800-78802
Diagnostic nuclear medicine uses small amounts of gamma-emitting radioactive materials, or tracers, to determine the cause of the medical problem based on the function, or chemistry, of the organ or tissue. Monoclonal antibodies used for diagnosing certain cancers are developed from tumor-associated antigens and radiolabeled. This becomes the radiopharmaceutical used for tumor localization. After administration of the specialized radiotracer, a camera, called a scintillation or gamma camera, takes planar images of the study area on computer screen or film by detecting the gamma radiation from the radiopharmaceutical focused in the body tissue. Report 78800 for tumor localization or distribution of the radiopharmaceutical within a limited area; 78801 for multiple areas; and 78802 for scanning over the whole body done on a single day.

78803
Tomographic SPECT (single photon emission computed tomography) imaging permits an in-depth evaluation of complex anatomy and can localize tumors within organs and body structures by introducing a radionuclide and detecting the distribution of gamma radiation emitted from the radiotracer introduced into the tissue being studied. Monoclonal antibodies used for diagnosing certain cancers are developed from tumor-associated antigens and radiolabeled for use as the radiopharmaceutical in tumor localization. Tomographic SPECT images differ from the usual planar scans of the gamma camera by rotating a single or multiple-head camera mounted on a gantry around the patient to give three-dimensional computer reconstructed views of cross-sectional slices of the body.

78804
Diagnostic nuclear medicine uses small amounts of gamma-emitting radioactive materials, or tracers, to determine the cause of the medical problem based on the function, or chemistry, of the organ or tissue. Monoclonal antibodies used for diagnosing certain cancers are developed from tumor-associated antigens and radiolabeled. This becomes the radiopharmaceutical used for tumor localization. After administration of the specialized radiotracer, a camera, called a scintillation or gamma camera, takes planar images of the study area on computer screen or film by detecting the gamma radiation from the radiopharmaceutical focused in the body tissue. Report this code for scanning over the whole body requiring two or more days of imaging.

78805-78806
Gallium, a calcium analogue, is the radiopharmaceutical of choice when scanning for an inflammatory process because it localizes to infected areas by attaching to plasma proteins found at infection sites and accumulating in areas of bone mineral turnover, such as fractures and inflammatory arthritis. Gallium is often combined with radiolabeled white blood cells, which also accumulate at infection sites but not at areas of increased bone replenishing, to augment accuracy in inflammatory localization. After administration of the specialized radiotracer, a camera, called a scintillation or gamma camera, takes planar images of the study area on computer screen or film by detecting the gamma radiation from the radiopharmaceutical in the body tissue as it "scintillates" or gives off energy when coming in contact with the camera's detector. Report 78805 for inflammatory process localization within a limited area and 78806 for scanning over the whole body.

78807
Tomographic SPECT (single photon emission computed tomography) imaging permits an in-depth evaluation of complex anatomy and can localize an inflammatory process within body structures by introducing a radionuclide and detecting the distribution of gamma radiation emitted from the radiotracer with a single or multiple-head camera mounted on a gantry to rotate around the patient and give three-dimensional computer reconstructed views of cross-sectional slices of the body. Gallium, a calcium analogue, is the radiopharmaceutical of choice when scanning for an inflammatory process because it localizes to infected areas by attaching to plasma proteins found at infection sites and accumulating in areas of bone mineral turnover, such as fractures and inflammatory arthritis. When combined with labeled white blood cells, which also accumulate at infection

sites but not at areas of increased bone replenishing, accuracy in localizing an inflammatory process is increased.

78808
This code reports the injection procedure for radiopharmaceutical localization of structures such as a parathyroid adenoma prior to gamma probe localization.

78811-78813
Positron emission tomography (PET) produces thin slice images of the body that can be reassembled into three-dimensional representations by detecting positron-emitting radionuclides from a radiopharmaceutical introduced into the body. These radionuclides must be produced in a cyclotron or generator that can bombard chemicals with neutrons to produce unstable, short-lived radioisotopes, such as carbon-11, nitrogen-13, and oxygen-15. These can be readily incorporated into common and important, biological body compounds for administration. Data from this kind of imaging yields metabolic or biochemical function information depending on the type of molecule tagged. In PET tumor imaging, information about the tumor's glucose and oxygen utilization is obtained, which reveals the tumor's behavior compared to normal tissue or benign tumors. Report 78811 for PET imaging of a limited area such as the chest alone; 78812 for imaging from the skull base to the mid-thigh; and 78813 for imaging of the whole body.

78814-78816
Positron emission tomography (PET) produces thin slice images of the body that can be reassembled into three-dimensional representations by detecting positron-emitting radionuclides from a radiopharmaceutical introduced into the body. Computed tomography (CT) directs multiple narrow beams of x-rays around a body structure to produce thin, cross-sectional views of anatomical layers (or slices) of the body. The PET scan is highly sensitive to metabolic activity of the tumor while CT provides a detailed internal picture of the size, shape, and location of the tumor. PET, alone, has a definite limitation with respect to spatial resolution and physiological uptake of the radiopharmaceutical tracer, in some areas, can be underestimated or misinterpreted without accurate, anatomical correlations. Scanners that concurrently utilize PET with CT imaging correct for this limitation of PET, by fusing the data for precise anatomical location together with highly sensitive metabolic imaging. Report 78814 for concurrently acquired PET/CT imaging of a limited area, such as the head and neck alone; 78815 for imaging from the skull base to the mid-thigh; and 78816 for whole body scanning.

79005
Radiopharmaceutical therapy is given to the patient via oral administration. The patient swallows the radiolabeled substance prepared in a form to be given by mouth. The strategy for using radiopharmaceutical therapy is to combine radioactive, beta-particle emitters with relatively short half-lives to specific tissue-seeking molecules that can be administered to the patient. The treatment is designed to target certain types of cancers or malfunctioning tissue. An example is radioactive iodine, I-131, given to the patient orally, to treat thyroid cancers and hormone overproduction (hyperthyroidism) since iodine is specifically taken up by thyroid cells.

79101
Radiopharmaceutical therapy is given to the patient via intravenous administration. The patient is given a radiolabeled substance prepared in a form to be injected or instilled directly into a vein. The strategy for using radiopharmaceutical therapy is to combine radioactive, beta-particle emitters with relatively short half-lives to specific tissue-seeking molecules that can be administered to the patient. The treatment is designed to target certain types of cancers or malfunctioning tissue. An example is radioactive phosphorous, P-32, as sodium phosphate administered by intravenous injection. Since phosphorus-32 has a high bone marrow toxicity, it is used for treating polycythemia vera and chronic leukemia to slow the rate at which bone marrow produces cells and induce a state of remission.

79200
Radiopharmaceutical therapy is given to the patient via intracavitary administration. Intracavitary radiotherapy refers to the placement of radioactive sources within a body space or cavity, such as the bladder, esophagus, lung, vagina, or uterus, to give high doses of radiation to the cancer, while giving only low doses to the surrounding tissues. An applicator designed for placing the radioactive source within the specific body cavity is inserted and the radiotherapy is administered through the applicator.

79300
Colloids are a mixture in which one substance divided into minute, insoluble particles (called colloidal particles) is dispersed uniformly throughout a second substance, the suspension medium. Radioactive colloidal solutions that contain natural or synthetic molecules are relatively impermeable to the vascular membrane and are useful for interstitial radioactive therapy. Interstitial radiopharmaceutical therapy by radioactive colloid administration refers to the placement of this type of radioactive source directly into the affected tissue to give high doses of radiation to the cancer, while giving only low doses to the surrounding tissues. An applicator designed for placing the radioactive source within the specific body tissue is inserted and the radiotherapy is administered through the applicator. An example is inserting plastic tubes

into prostate tissue and placing rapid dose radioactive colloid solutions within the tubes.

79403
Radiopharmaceutical therapy using radiolabeled monoclonal antibodies infused intravenously is given to the patient as a method of cancer treatment. Monoclonal antibodies are developed from tumor-specific associated antigens and radiolabeled to form a highly stable metal complex. This type of therapy is often called radioimmunotherapy because it combines the very specific targeting capability of a single antibody with the cancer killing power of a radioisotope. The radiolabeled monoclonal antibodies are infused intravenously where they circulate systemically, seeking out the targeted cancer cells, such as in cases of non-Hodgkin's lymphoma, in which this type of radioimmunotherapy has been found effective. This treatment may be done on an outpatient basis, but the patient is observed for immune reaction before discharge.

79440
Each episode of joint bleeding causes inflammation and swelling of the synovial membrane. If bleeding occurs often or is not treated adequately, the inflammation may become chronic and can lead to thickening of the synovial membrane and the release of substances that can destroy cartilage and bone. The administration of intraarticular radiopharmaceutical therapy is done to destroy the membrane through radiation, rather than performing a surgical procedure to remove the damaged membrane. A radioactive substance, such as phosphorus-32, is injected into the joint at a time when the patient has not been bleeding, and after a period of prophylactic therapy has already been done to reduce swelling of the membrane as much as possible.

79445
Radiopharmaceutical therapy is given to the patient via intra-arterial particulate administration. The patient is given a radiolabeled substance prepared in a form to be introduced directly into an artery. The treatment is designed to target certain types of cancers or malfunctioning tissue by blocking blood supply to the tumor while increasing the concentration of local radioactive drug therapy. An example is transcatheter selective hepatic chemoembolization using a suspension of cisplatin and particulate polyvinyl alcohol for liver metastases or carcinomas. After a catheter is selectively placed within the target hepatic artery and the distribution of arteries feeding the tumor is determined, a microcatheter is inserted and nonabsorbable polyvinyl alcohol particles are injected to obstruct blood flow to the tumor, along with an injection of intra-arterial cisplatin suspension. The intra-arterial particulate administration increases the drug concentration in the area of the hypoxic tumor.

Pathology and Laboratory

80047
A basic metabolic panel with ionized calcium includes the following tests: calcium (ionized) (82330), carbon dioxide (82374), chloride (82435), creatinine (82565), glucose (82947), potassium (84132), sodium (84295), and urea nitrogen (BUN) (84520). Blood specimen is obtained by venipuncture. See the specific codes for additional information about the listed tests.

80048
A basic metabolic panel with total calcium includes the following tests: total calcium (82310), carbon dioxide (82374), chloride (82435), creatinine (82565), glucose (82947), potassium (84132), sodium (84295), and urea nitrogen (BUN) (84520). The blood specimen is obtained by venipuncture. See the specific codes for additional information about the listed tests.

80050
A general health panel includes the following tests: albumin (82040), total bilirubin (82247), calcium (82310), carbon dioxide (bicarbonate) (82374), chloride (82435), creatinine (82565), glucose (82947), alkaline phosphatase (84075), potassium (84132), total protein (84155), sodium (84295), alanine amino transferase (ALT) (SGPT) (84460), aspartate amino transferase (AST) (SGOT) (84450), urea nitrogen (BUN) (84520), and thyroid stimulating hormone (84443). In addition, this panel includes a hemogram with automated differential (85025 or 85027 and 85004) or hemogram (85027) with manual differential (85007 or 85009). Blood specimen is obtained by venipuncture. See specific codes for additional information about the listed tests.

80051
An electrolyte panel includes the following tests: carbon dioxide (82374), chloride (82435), potassium (84132), and sodium (84295). Blood specimen is obtained by venipuncture. See specific codes for additional information about the listed tests.

80053
A comprehensive metabolic panel includes the following tests: albumin (82040), total bilirubin (82247), total calcium (82310), carbon dioxide (bicarbonate) (82374), chloride (82435), creatinine (82565), glucose (82947), alkaline phosphatase (84075), potassium (84132), total protein (84155), sodium (84295), alanine amino transferase (ALT) (SGPT) (84460), aspartate amino transferase (AST) (SGOT) (84450), and urea nitrogen (BUN) (84520). Blood specimen is obtained by venipuncture. See the specific codes for additional information about the listed tests.

80055
An obstetric panel includes the following tests: hepatitis B surface antigen (HBsAg) (87340), rubella antibody (86762), qualitative non-treponemal

antibody syphilis test (VDRL, RPR, ART) (86592), RBC antibody screen (86850), ABO blood typing (86900), and Rh (D) blood typing (86901). In addition, this panel includes either an automated complete blood count (CBC) and automated differential white blood count (WBC) as described by 85025 or 85027 and 85004 OR automated CBC (85027) and appropriate manual differential WBC count (85007 or 85009). Blood specimen is obtained by venipuncture. See specific codes for additional information about the listed tests.

80061
A lipid panel includes the following tests: total serum cholesterol (82465), high-density cholesterol (HDL cholesterol) by direct measurement (83718), and triglycerides (84478). Blood specimen is obtained by venipuncture. See specific codes for additional information about the listed tests.

80069
A renal function panel includes the following tests: albumin (82040), total calcium (82310), carbon dioxide (bicarbonate) (82374), chloride (82435), creatinine (82565), glucose (82947), inorganic phosphorus (phosphate) (84100), potassium (84132), sodium (84295), and urea nitrogen (BUN) (84520).

80074
An acute hepatitis panel includes the following tests: hepatitis A antibody (HAAb), IgM antibody (86709), hepatitis B core antibody (HbcAb), IgM antibody (86705), hepatitis B surface antigen (HbsAg) (87340), and hepatitis C antibody (86803).

80076
A hepatic function panel includes the following tests: albumin (82040), total bilirubin (82247), direct bilirubin (82248), alkaline phosphatase (84075), protein, total (84155), alanine amino transferase (ALT) (SGPT) (84460), and aspartate amino transferase (AST) (SGOT) (84450). Blood specimen is obtained by venipuncture. See the specific codes for additional information about the listed tests.

80100
This test may be requested as a drug screen for multiple drug classes. The screening test must be performed by a chromatographic technique that has good sensitivity, although it may not be as specific as a confirmatory test. Thin-layer chromatography is a common chromatographic technique for drug screening tests. It is performed by applying a thin layer adsorbent to a rectangular plate in the stationary phase. The specimen is applied to the plate and the end of the plate is placed in a solvent. As the solvent rises along the adsorbent on the plate, the different components of the specimen are carried along at varying rates and deposited along the plate. The different components can be separately visualized and analyzed. Positive tests are always confirmed with a second method. Specimen type varies.

80101
This test may be requested as a drug screen for a single drug class. The screening test should be performed by a technique that has good sensitivity, although it may not be as specific as a confirmatory test. A number of different methods are available to screen for single drugs or drug classes, including simple drug screening kits that rely on immunoassay for detection of a single specific drug or drug class. For example, Placidyl (aka ethchlorvynol) can be screened in urine with a very simple colorimetric test where equal parts of urine and a single reagent are mixed and observed for a visual color change. This would be reported with 80101. Positive tests are always confirmed with a second method.

80102
This test may be requested as drug screen confirmation. It is performed when the initial drug screen (80100-80101) is positive. Confirmatory tests must be both sensitive and specific and involve a different technique than the initial screen. For example, if the initial screen is performed by thin layer chromatography identifying a spot on the chromatogram that is the right color and in the right place to be consistent with a particular drug, it is confirmed with a more specific method, like high performance liquid chromatography (HPLC), gas chromatography-mass spectrometry (GC-MS), or immunoassay. If the drug suspected is a barbiturate, for example, a confirmatory HPLC method might be done to prove that the compound had the correct retention time, etc., and to identify it exactly as a particular barbiturate. This would be reported with 80102.

80103
Tissue is sometimes tested for the presence of drugs. This code reports the tissue preparation only.

80150
Amikacin is a type of antibiotic. Test specimens are frequently collected at peak and trough periods, which is shortly after administration of amikacin and again just before the next administration when serum concentration is at its lowest. This is an effective approach to determine a therapeutic level of drug. Method is radioimmunoassay (RIA) or high performance liquid chromatography (HPLC).

80152
Amitriptyline is a tricyclic antidepressant and the prototype brand name is Elavil. Test specimens are frequently collected at the trough period, which is about 12 hours after the last dose when serum concentration is at its lowest. This is an effective approach to determine a therapeutic level of drug. Drug overdose may be reason for the test as well. Method is typically high performance liquid

chromatography (HPLC) or gas liquid chromatography (GLC). This drug may be prescribed for disorders outside of depressive states, such as chronic pain.

80154
Benzodiazepines encompass a family of mild sedatives, including diazepam (Valium) and Ativan. These drugs may be assayed to determine therapeutic levels, or sometimes to determine levels in the system following overdose. Test specimens are frequently collected at the trough period, which is about 12 hours after the last dose when serum concentration is at its lowest. Method is high performance liquid chromatography (HPLC), gas liquid chromatography (GLC), or radioimmunoassay (RIA). This family of drugs may be prescribed for numerous conditions and disorders. Alcohol withdrawal is a common use for diazepam, as are muscle spasms.

80156
This drug, also known as Tegretol, is an enzyme inducer. Blood specimen collection is by venipuncture. CSF is obtained by spinal puncture, which is reported separately. Test specimens for total levels are frequently collected at the trough period, which is about 12 hours after the last dose when serum concentration is at its lowest. This is an effective approach to determine a therapeutic level of drug. This drug is absorbed slowly and erratically by the GI tract and a total concentration may be required, depending on the treatment underway. Methods include high performance liquid chromatography (HPLC) or gas liquid chromatography (GLC). Tegretol may be administered for such conditions as trigeminal neuralgia, epilepsy, and manic disorders. It is known for its anticonvulsant and pain management properties.

80157
This drug, also known as Tegretol, is an enzyme inducer. Specimen collection is by venipuncture. Test specimens for free drug concentrations may be collected near peak levels about two to eight hours after ingestion. Methods include high performance liquid chromatography (HPLC) or gas liquid chromatography (GLC). This drug is absorbed slowly and erratically by the gastrointestinal (GI) tract and a free plasma concentration may be assayed, depending on the type of treatment underway. Tegretol may be administered for such conditions as trigeminal neuralgia, epilepsy, and manic disorders. It is known for its anticonvulsant and pain management properties.

80158
This drug is also known as Sandimmune. It is an immunosuppressant and is often monitored. Test specimens are frequently collected at the trough period, which is typically about 12 hours after the last dose when serum concentration is at its lowest. Method is high performance liquid chromatography (HPLC) or fluorescence polarization immunoassay (FPIA).

80160
This drug is also known as Norpramin and is among the tricyclic antidepressants. Steady state test specimens are frequently collected at the trough period, which is about 12 hours after the last dose when serum concentration is at its lowest. This is an effective approach to determine a therapeutic level of drug. Overdose is also a reason to run this test. Method is high performance liquid chromatography (HPLC) or gas liquid chromatography (GLC).

80162
This digitalis glycoside has numerous trade names: Crystodigin, Purodigin, Lanoxin, etc. The drugs are used principally to treat conditions surrounding congestive heart failure, such as arrhythmias, atrial fibrillation, and tachycardia. Test specimens may be drawn during peak and trough periods, which is shortly after administration of digitalis and again just before the next administration when serum concentration is at its lowest. Method is high performance liquid chromatography (HPLC) or gas liquid chromatography (GLC).

80164
This drug is also known as Depakene. This drug is often used to treat seizures. Test specimens are frequently collected at the trough period, which is about 12 hours after the last dose when serum concentration is at its lowest. This is an effective approach to determine a therapeutic level of drug. Method is gas liquid chromatography (GLC), gas chromatography-mass spectrometry (GC-MS), and enzyme immunoassay (EIA).

80166
This drug is also known as Sinequan or Adapin. This drug is classified as a tricyclic antidepressant (TCA). Steady state test specimens are frequently collected at the trough period, which is about 12 hours after the last dose when serum concentration is at its lowest. This is an effective approach to determine a therapeutic level of drug. Overdose may also prompt this test. Method is high performance liquid chromatography (HPLC), gas liquid chromatography (GLC), gas chromatography-mass spectrometry (GC-MS), and radioimmunoassay (RIA).

80168
This drug may also be known as Zarontin. This is an anticonvulsant medication. Test specimens may be drawn during peak and trough periods, which is shortly after administration of Zarontin and again just before the next administration when serum concentration is at its lowest. Methods include high performance liquid chromatography (HPLC), radioimmunoassay (RIA), and microbiology assay.

80170
This drug is classified as an aminoglycoside, an antibiotic. In its injectable form, the drug may be

prescribed for gram-negative infections, septicemia, and other serious infections, as well as unknown causative organisms. Common trade names include Garamycin and Gentacidin. A typical course will run seven to 10 days. Monitoring may be initiated to measure drug clearance via the kidneys. Patients with impaired renal function may accumulate the drug. Peak serum concentrations can be expected about 30 to 60 minutes following an intramuscular injection though concentrations occur just before the next dose. Dosage is highly dependent on the severity of infection. Methodology varies.

80172
This test may include the abbreviation for gold, Au, or the name Myochrysine. Gold salts are sometimes used in the treatment of rheumatoid arthritis. Therapeutic levels may be difficult to determine. Method is atomic absorption spectrophotometry (AAS).

80173
This drug, also known as Haldol, is a well-established tranquilizer with antipsychotic and other properties. Blood concentrations of haloperidol do not correspond well with therapeutic dosages; therefore, assays may be performed to establish compliance or to measure the body's ability to metabolize the drug. Methods may include high performance liquid chromatography (HPLC), gas liquid chromatography (GLC), and radioimmunoassay (RIA).

80174
This drug may also be known as Tofranil. The drug is classified as a tricyclic antidepressant (TCA). Steady state test specimens are frequently collected at the trough period, which is about 12 hours after the last dose when serum concentration is at its lowest. This is an effective approach to determine a therapeutic level of drug. Overdose may also prompt this test. Method is high performance liquid chromatography (HPLC), gas liquid chromatography (GLC), gas chromatography-mass spectrometry (GC-MS), and radioimmunoassay (RIA).

80176
This drug may also be known as Xylocaine, Dilocaine, L-caine, etc. Lidocaine is widely used in its various forms, including nonprescription ointments. However, lidocaine may be injected as an intravenous bolus as a treatment for ventricular arrhythmias and for cardiac manipulation. Any of a number of methods may be used, including high performance liquid chromatography (HPLC), gas liquid chromatography (GLC), gas chromatography-mass spectrometry (GC-MS), and fluorescence polarization immunoassay (FPIA).

80178
This drug may also be known as Eskalith. Lithium is a naturally occurring mineral and its salts may be used in the treatment of mental disorders, in particular bipolar depression. Steady state test specimens are frequently collected at the trough period, which is about 12 hours after the last dose when serum concentration is at its lowest. This is an effective approach to determine a therapeutic level of drug. Methods may include flame emission spectroscopy (FES), atomic absorption spectrophotometry (AAS), and ion-specific electrode (ISE).

80182
This drug may also be known as Aventyl or Pamelor. This drug is classified as a tricyclic antidepressant (TCA). Steady state test specimens are frequently collected at the trough period, which is about 12 hours after the last dose when serum concentration is at its lowest. This is an effective approach to determine a therapeutic level of drug. Overdose may also prompt this test. Any of a number of methods may be used, including high performance liquid chromatography (HPLC), gas liquid chromatography (GLC), and gas chromatography-mass spectrometry (GC-MS).

80184
This drug may also be known as Luminal. This drug may be administered to control seizures. Test specimens are frequently collected at the trough period, which is about 12 hours after the last dose when serum concentration is at its lowest. This is an effective approach to determine a therapeutic level of drug. Methodology may include gas liquid chromatography (GLC) and high performance liquid chromatography (HPLC).

80185-80186
This drug may also be known as Dilantin. This drug may be administered to control seizures. Steady state test specimens are frequently collected at the trough period, which is about 12 hours after the last dose when serum concentration is at its lowest. This is an effective approach to determine a therapeutic level of drug. Report 80185 for total serum levels and 80186 when free phenytoin is assayed. Methodology may include high performance liquid chromatography (HPLC), gas liquid chromatography (GLC), radioimmunoassay (RIA), and fluorescence polarization immunoassay (FPIA). Free phenytoin is assayed by ultracentrifugation. Phenytoin is a known teratogen (cause of birth defects) and lowest therapeutic levels possible are often sought.

80188
This drug may also be known as Mysoline. This drug may be administered to control seizures. Test specimens are frequently collected at the trough period, which is about 12 hours after the last dose when serum concentration is at its lowest. This is an effective approach to determine a therapeutic level of drug. Methodology may include high performance liquid chromatography (HPLC), gas liquid chromatography (GLC), or enzyme immunoassay (EIA).

80190
This drug may also be known as Procan, Promine, or Pronestyl. This drug may be administered as an antiarrhythmic. Test specimens are frequently collected at the trough period, which is about 12 hours after the last dose when serum concentration is at its lowest. This is an effective approach to determine a therapeutic level of drug. Methodology may include high performance liquid chromatography (HPLC), gas liquid chromatography (GLC), and enzyme immunoassay (EIA).

80192
This procedure tests for Procan as well as metabolites, known as NAPA (n-acetyl procainamide).

80194
This drug may also be known as Duraquin, Quinate, Quinora, or Cardioquin. This drug is often administered as an antiarrhythmic. Test specimens are frequently collected at the trough period, which is about 12 hours after the last dose when serum concentration is at its lowest. This is an effective approach to determine a therapeutic level of drug. Methodology may include high performance liquid chromatography (HPLC) and gas liquid chromatography (GLC).

80195
This procedure tests for the level of sirolimus (rapamycin), a potent immunosuppressant in the blood. Sirolimus blood levels may be affected by cytochrome P450 3A4 inducers or inhibitors or by patient liver function (hepatic insufficiency). Therapeutic drug monitoring (TDM) of sirolimus concentrations are frequently performed to monitor blood concentration levels and evaluate dosage.

80196
This drug is known universally as aspirin and may also be referred to as a nonsteroidal antiinflammatory drug (NSAID). Specimen collection is at trough, which is the time just before the next dose of the drug when blood concentration is at its lowest. Overdose may also prompt this test. Methodology may include high performance liquid chromatography (HPLC) or gas liquid chromatography (GLC). Colorimetry and fluorometry may also be used.

80197
This drug is also known as Prograf. It is an immunosuppressant and may be prescribed for a number of conditions, including post-transplant therapies. Blood concentration monitoring may be ordered with this drug, particularly when delivered by IV. In this event, specimen collection may be random. Methodology may include high performance liquid chromatography (HPLC).

80198
This drug may also be known by numerous names, such as Aerolate, Bronkodyl, Sustaire, and Theophyl. This drug is available in several different forms, which may affect the type of assay run. Samples may be drawn about 30 minutes after oral administration. When delivered by IV, specimen collection may be random. The drug is widely used as a bronchodilator and to relieve bronchospasms. Methodology may include high performance liquid chromatography (HPLC) or gas liquid chromatography (GLC).

80200
This drug is also known as Nebcin. This drug has bactericidal properties and is usually injected. Specimen collection is at peak and trough. Peak will occur about one hour after an intramuscular injection and trough will occur about 12 hours after that. Method will often be by radioimmunoassay (RIA), microbiological assay, or high performance liquid chromatography (HPLC).

80201
This drug may also be known as Topamax. It is currently classified as an orphan drug, a designation for certain drugs and biologicals used principally for very rare diseases. The product is kept in supply only in limited quantities for the limited number of patients requiring therapy. Distribution is not general. This particular drug is used primarily in the treatment of Lennox-Gastaut syndrome.

80202
This drug may also be known as Vancocin. Specimen collection may be drawn during the trough period. This occurs around 30 minutes prior to the next dose. It is sometimes also drawn at peak. Toxic and therapeutic dosages for vancomycin can be difficult to determine due to the way the drug is metabolized. Methods include radioimmunoassay (RIA), high performance liquid chromatography (HPLC), and microbiological assay.

80400
This test is sometimes ordered as corticotropin-releasing factor stimulation (or CRF) test, adrenocorticotropic hormone (ACTH) infusion test, rapid ACTH test, or cosyntropin test. Method is immunoassay. A chemistry test must be performed to determine baseline serum cortisol (serum ACTH may also be ordered). Shortly thereafter, cosyntropin, an ACTH-like drug, is administered to the patient, typically by IV bolus. Blood is again drawn and assayed for a change in serum cortisol. Variations are seen in administering a 24-hour test and a three-day test. This code reports the test for adrenal insufficiency (Addison's disease), which is an ordinary reason for the test. See 82533 for serum cortisol testing specifics.

80402
This test may be ordered as an enzyme deficiency ACTH stimulation test. This code specifically cites 21-hydroxylase deficiency. The classic 21-hydroxylase deficiency is noted in ambiguous genitalia in neonates,

but a later onset is also found. Cosyntropin, an ACTH-like drug, is administered to the patient, typically by IV bolus. Overproduction of the metabolite 17-hydroxyprogesterone is often associated with this condition and it is tested for as a baseline and following the ACTH stimulation injection. Cortisol levels are tested in a similar fashion in this panel.

80406
This test may be ordered as a 3B-HSD panel. The official description for the code is for 3 beta-hydroxydehydrogenase deficiency or congenital adrenal hyperplasia. The panel may often be performed on infants and small children, but adult patients are also tested. The condition involves defects in steroid synthesis. A bolus infusion of ACTH is given to the patient after baseline cortisol and 17-hydroxypregnenolone have been drawn. Cortisol and 17-hydroxypregnenolone are drawn again and the results interpreted.

80408
This panel may be ordered as a saline infusion test. Specimen is drawn from the patient while in an upright position and the product saved for baseline aldosterone and renin testing. The patient is administered saline, usually intravenously, while in a recumbent position. Specimen is again drawn for aldosterone and renin levels. In healthy individuals, aldosterone output is suppressed when the volume of blood is expanded. The test is useful in the evaluation of kidney function.

80410
This test may be ordered as human calcitonin test (HCT) or thyrocalcitonin panel. Calcitonin is a hormone secreted by the thyroid gland in response to elevated serum calcium levels. Calcitonin secretion causes the calcium to be excreted by the kidneys. A baseline calcitonin level is drawn. Stimulation of the thyroid for this panel is typically pentagastrin delivered by IV. Blood is again drawn at five and 10 minutes from stimulation. The patient should be fasting.

80412
This test may be ordered as CRH "Stim" panel. This panel allows for multiple specimens to be drawn before administration of CRH. Orders may call for blood draws from both petrous sinus veins as well as from a peripheral source. Note the high number of cortisol and ACTH tests to be run. The timing of specimen draws for cortisol and ACTH may differ somewhat. The panel is useful to differentiate Cushing's disease and certain ACTH-secreting tumors, among other disorders.

80414
This test may be ordered as a HCG "Stim" or human chorionic gonadotropin panel. Blood specimens may be drawn on two separate mornings before HCG is administered, usually by intramuscular injection. Injections may be repeated on two following days. Blood collection times may vary following HCG administration. The test is useful in diagnosis of certain cases of hypogonadotrophism as well as certain steroid deficiencies.

80415
This test may be ordered as a HCG "Stim" or human chorionic gonadotropin panel. Blood specimens may be drawn on two separate mornings before HCG is administered, usually by intramuscular injection and sometimes in several sessions. Timing of blood draws may vary, but just prior to the first administration of HCG and four hours after is common for women. Estradiol is among the more active endogenous estrogens. The panel is useful in the diagnosis of certain menstrual disorders, fertility problems, and estrogen-producing tumors.

80416-80417
These tests may be ordered as renin "Stim" panel, renin activity panel, or plasma renin activity (PRA) panel. Baseline samples may be drawn from the renal vein (80416) or peripheral vein (80417) and tested for renin. Renin is an enzyme synthesized in the kidney. A renin-stimulating agent, such as the diuretics captopril and furosemide, is administered, usually orally and usually in several stages. The patient remains upright for several hours before again testing for renin, once again, usually in stages. The panel is a useful screen and diagnostic tool for various forms of hypertension, renal artery disorders, and other disorders of the renal/ circulatory system.

80418
This series of tests may also be ordered as a pituitary panel and many large facilities will have an internal code name for this panel. This is a complex panel with numerous tests. Facilities with proper capabilities can offer a rapid, combined series where stimulation agents (i.e., insulin, thyrotropin-releasing hormone, and luteinizing hormone-releasing hormone) are administered simultaneously on a single day. This panel may be used most often for a suspected pituitary tumor. See individual code listings for specifics about portions of the panel.

80420
Baseline samples are usually drawn. Dexamethasone is the suppression agent and it is usually administered orally at night. The next morning a fasting blood sample is drawn and rendered to serum. The cortisol level is measured as described in 82533. The free cortisol is a urine test as described in 82530. This panel is a 48-hour work up to differentiate diagnoses, such as Cushing's syndrome from alcoholism, obesity, and depression.

80422
Arginine is a powerful stimulator of glucagon in healthy patients and may be administered as the stimulating agent for this panel. Baseline blood work is

typically performed prior to stimulating glucagon. This glucagon tolerance panel tests for insulinoma, a type of benign tumor of cells in the islets of Langerhans portion of the pancreas. Insulinoma is a prime cause of the condition known as hypoglycemia. Glucagon is a hormone secreted in the pancreas in response to hypoglycemic conditions.

80424
Arginine is a powerful stimulator of glucagon in healthy patients and may be administered as the stimulating agent for this panel. Baseline blood work is typically performed prior to stimulating glucagon. Pheochromocytoma is usually a benign tumor of the adrenal gland. Glucagon is a hormone secreted in the pancreas in response to hypoglycemic conditions. Abnormally high levels of glucagon have been linked to pheochromocytomas. The panel includes a test for fractionated catecholamines, as described by 82384. This test further differentiates a diagnosis of adrenal tumor from hypothymia and hypertension.

80426
This panel may be ordered as a GnRH "Stim." The panel tests for a variety of disorders, including pituitary disorders and premature sexual development in children. Baseline blood work is usually drawn. The gonadotropin-releasing hormone (GnRH) is typically administered by intravenous bolus. The peak response for follicle stimulating hormone (FSH) will be somewhat different than for luteinizing hormone (LH). Blood is often drawn at 30 minutes, 60 minutes, and 120 minutes.

80428
This panel may be ordered as a GH provocation test, insulin tolerance test (ITT), and as the Arginine test. Baseline blood work is typically drawn. Stimulation of growth hormone is often achieved through an intravenous infusion of arginine hydrochloride, L-dopa, or clonidine. This may be administered over about 30 minutes. Blood specimens are collected at 15 minutes, 30 minutes, and 45 minutes. These samples will be tested for HCG as specified in 83003.

80430
This panel may be ordered as a GH suppression test. Blood work is typically drawn before the test as a baseline. Glucose is the suppression agent for GH and administration may be orally. Blood is again drawn, often at 60 and 120 minutes for glucose, with one more specimen drawn for HCG.

80432
This panel may be ordered as connecting peptide insulin, insulin C-peptide, or proinsulin C-peptide. C-peptide is formed in the islets of Langerhans in the pancreas along with insulin. Both are released into the portal vein. C-peptide levels generally correlate to insulin levels and may reflect pancreatic function. Blood work is usually performed prior to the test to establish a baseline. Insulin is injected intravenously and blood is drawn at intervals for C-peptide and glucose; insulin is tested for only once.

80434
The insulin tolerance panel for ACTH insufficiency typically involves baseline blood work before testing. The insulin is administered following a fasting period, typically by an indwelling needle. The panel is specifically for adrenocorticosteroid hormone (ACTH). The cortisol test is an indirect but accurate measure of ACTH. The panel is useful to assess hypothalamic/pituitary/adrenal interaction.

80435
The insulin tolerance panel for growth hormone insufficiency typically involves baseline blood work before testing. The insulin is administered following a fasting period, typically orally. The panel is specifically for growth hormone or human growth hormone (GH or HGH). Glucose is administered, typically by IV bolus, and specimens are drawn at regular intervals following dosage. Note the number of times each component is drawn.

80436
The metyrapone panel typically involves baseline blood work before testing. The metyrapone is typically administered orally with the cortisol and 11 deoxycortisol tested for again the following morning. The test is sometimes administered outpatient and is useful in determining secondary adrenal insufficiencies, among other disorders.

80438-80439
These tests are also known as TRH test or thyrotropin releasing factor (TRF) test. The thyrotropin-releasing hormone is typically administered by IV bolus shortly after collecting a sample to baseline for thyroid stimulating hormone. Report 80438 for a one-hour version of the test and 80439 for a two-hour version. Either test is useful in testing the anterior pituitary gland's ability to secrete TSH (normal response is for a rise in secretion following administration of TRH).

80440
This test may be called prolactin stimulation after TRH or simply prolactin "Stim." Baseline blood work is performed before administration of thyrotropin releasing hormone. IV usually administers the TRH and blood is again drawn at 15 minutes and 30 minutes. The test is for hyperprolactinemia, or high levels of prolactin in the blood. This condition is sometimes linked to renal, thyroid, or liver problems.

80500-80502
A clinical pathology consultation is a service performed by a physician (pathologist) in response to a request from the attending physician regarding test results requiring additional medical interpretive judgment. Pharmacokinetic consultations regarding therapeutic drug levels may be reported with this code. Code

80500 reports a limited consultation not requiring review of the patient's history and medical records. Code 80502 reports a comprehensive consultation related to more complex diagnostic problems and requires review of the patient's history and medical records.

81000
This type of test may be ordered by the brand name product and the analytes tested. Although screens are considered to show the presence of an analyte (qualitative), some newer products are semi-quantitative. Many are plastic strips that contain sites impregnated with chemicals that react with urine when the strip is dipped into a specimen. The result is a color change that is compared against a standardized chart. Most strips will test for numerous analytes, as well as for pH and specific gravity. Tablets work in a similar fashion. A drop of urine is placed on the tablet and a chemical reaction causes a color change that is compared to a standard chart. Usually only a single analyte is under consideration, per tablet. Code 81000 involves a manual (nonautomated) test and includes a microscopic examination. Microscopy involves examination of the urine sediments or solids. The urine is first centrifuged in a graduated tube to concentrate the sediments. Samples (either wet or dry) are examined, usually under both high and low power, and abnormal constituents are noted. These may include a wide range of biological abnormalities, such as blood cells, casts, and bacteria, as well as chemical anomalies, such as crystals.

81001
This type of test may be ordered by the type of processor used and the analytes tested. The testing methodology is similar to the manual strips, except that the color change caused by the chemical reaction with urine is processed and read mechanically. The strip is exposed to the urine sample and is mechanically fed through a processor that reads the colors emitted by the reaction. The unit will be calibrated according to international standards and readings have a high degree of accuracy. The result may be displayed on a monitor, but is always printed or recorded in some form. Code 81001 also includes a microscopy. Microscopy involves examination of the urine sediments or solids. The urine is first centrifuged in a graduated tube to concentrate the sediments. Samples (either wet or dry) are examined, usually under both high and low power, and abnormal constituents are noted. These may include a wide range of biological abnormalities, such as blood cells, casts, and bacteria, as well as chemical anomalies, such as crystals.

81002
This type of test may be ordered by the brand name product and the analytes tested. Although usually considered screens to show the presence of an analyte (qualitative), some newer products are semi-quantitative. Many are plastic strips that contain sites impregnated with chemicals that react with urine when the strip is dipped into a specimen. The result is a color change that is compared against a standardized chart. Most strips will test for numerous analytes, as well as for pH and specific gravity. Tablets work in a similar fashion. A drop of urine is placed on the tablet and a chemical reaction causes a color change that is compared to a standard chart. Usually only a single analyte is under consideration per tablet, however. Code 81002 does not include a microscopic examination of the urine sample or its components.

81003
This type of test may be ordered by the type of processor used and the analytes tested. The testing methodology is similar to the manual strips, except that the color change caused by the chemical reaction with urine is processed and read mechanically. The strip is exposed to the urine sample and is mechanically fed through a processor that reads the colors emitted by the reaction. The unit will be calibrated according to international standards and readings have a high degree of accuracy. The result may be displayed on a monitor, but is always printed or recorded in some form. Code 81003 does not include a microscopic examination of the urine sample or its components.

81005
This test may be ordered by the type of processor used and the analytes under examination. The method will be any type of automated analyzer, usually colorimetry. The results of a semi-quantitative test indicate the presence or absence of an analyte and may be expressed as simply positive or negative. A qualitative result may be indicated as trace, 1+, 2+, etc.

81007
This type of test may be ordered by the brand name of the commercial kit used and the bacteria that the kit screens for. Human urine is normally free of bacteria. However, bacteria can easily be introduced upon voiding. In addition, specimens containing any amount of pathological bacteria can have the organisms rapidly multiply after collection. For this reason, specimens are often examined shortly after collection. Method includes any method except culture or dipstick. The test is often performed by commercial kit. The type of kit used should be specified in the report.

81015
This test may be ordered as a microscopic analysis. Human urine is normally free of bacteria. However, bacteria can easily be introduced upon voiding. In addition, specimens containing any amount of pathological bacteria can have the organisms rapidly multiply after collection. For this reason, specimens are often examined shortly after collection. The sample may first be centrifuged into a graduated tube to

concentrate the sediments, or solid matter, held in suspension. The concentration of bacteria as well as cell types, crystals, and other elements seen is reported.

81020
This test may be ordered as a two-glass or three-glass test, a MacConkey-blood agar test, an MC-blood agar test, or any of the previous with a gram-positive plate. This is a culture for bacteria and will typically involve a culture plate of 5 percent sheep's blood agar and a MacConkey plate (a medium containing differentiate for lactose and nonlactose fermenters). A third plate of gram-positive media may offer further discrimination of bacteria cultured. The test is useful in determining the types and prevalence of bacteria in the urine.

81025
This test may be ordered by any of the brand name kits available. The tests typically involve a dipstick impregnated with reagents that chemically react upon contact with urine. A change in color indicates positive or negative for the presence of hormones found in the urine of women in early pregnancy.

81050
This test may be ordered as simply a volume measurement, a flow study, uroflowmetry, or urodynamic study. Timed collections are typically collected over a given period (24 hours is common). This test may be performed as a preliminary study to determine the volume of urine voided per second. A flowmeter device may be used or a simple timing of the flow into a graduated container may be employed. The test is sometimes also administered as a baseline or otherwise in conjunction with urinary tract procedures that might affect flow.

82000
This test is commonly ordered as acetaldehyde level. It is used to measure ethanol exposure/ingestion as ethanol is converted to acetaldehyde by alcohol dehydrogenase. Methodology is gas-liquid chromatography (GLC).

82003
This test is commonly ordered as acetaminophen or Tylenol level. Method is immunoassay or UV spectrophotometry. Acetaminophen levels may be seen in overdose situations and measurement is useful to determine toxicity and potential liver damage. The expected half-life of acetaminophen is one to three hours.

82009-82010
These tests are also referred to as blood ketone analysis or blood nitroprusside reaction. Method is nitroprusside reaction (colorimetry). These tests may be performed to assess suspected metabolic disorders or to determine absolute or relative starvation, especially in children. Qualitative analysis (82009) tests for the presence of acetone or other ketone bodies while quantitative analysis (82010) measures the amount of acetone or other ketone bodies.

82013
This test is also referred to as red blood cell (RBC) acetylcholinesterase, erythrocytic cholinesterase, or true cholinesterase. Method is colorimetric or spectrophotometric rate of hydrolysis determination. This test may be performed to determine certain RBC disorders such as thalassemias, spherocytosis, and other anemias. It may also be used to determine toxicity or exposure to certain insecticides. For amniotic fluid specimen, a separately reportable amniocentesis is performed. The presence of acetylcholinesterase activity and increased alpha-fetoprotein in amniotic fluid are presumptive evidence of an open neural tube defect in the fetus.

82016-82017
These tests may be requested as qualitative acylcarnitine (carnitine esters) and quantitative acylcarnitine (carnitine esters). Acylcarnitine is a condensation product formed from carboxylic acid and carnitine. It has a variety of metabolic roles and may be an indicator of inborn errors of metabolism, chronic disease, or acute and critical illness. Methods include enzymatic, chromatography, and mass-spectrometry. Qualitative analysis (82016) tests for the presence of acylcarnitine while quantitative analysis (82017) measures the amount of acylcarnitine.

82024
This test is also referred to as adrenocorticotropic hormone (ACTH) or corticotropin. Method is radioimmunoassay. This test may be performed to determine the presence of Cushing's disease, depression, or pheochromocytoma, among other conditions.

82030
This test is also referred to as cyclic adenosine monophosphate (AMP) or cAMP. Methodology is radioimmunoassay (RIA). This test may be performed in the presence of hypercalcemia for determination of hyperparathyroidism.

82040
This test measures the concentration of albumin in serum, plasma, or whole blood. It is often used to determine nutritional status, renal disease, and other chronic diseases, particularly those involving the kidneys or liver. A blood sample is typically drawn from a vein in the hand or forearm. The skin over the vein is cleaned with an antiseptic, and a tourniquet is wrapped around the upper arm to enlarge the lower arm veins by restricting the blood flow. A thin needle is inserted into the vein, the tourniquet is removed, and blood flows from the vein through the needle and is collected into a vial or syringe. The needle is withdrawn and the puncture site covered to prevent

bleeding. The blood sample is sent to the laboratory for testing.

82042
This code reports quantitative analysis for albumin on urine, CSF, or amniotic fluid. Urine tests are usually performed on a 24-hour urine specimen to measure protein loss of patients with hypoalbuminemia. Patients typically perform specimen collection over a 24-hour period. Method is colorimetry. CSF analysis requires separately reportable spinal puncture and the test is performed using nephelometry. Amniotic fluid analysis requires separately reportable ultrasound guidance and amniocentesis and test is usually performed by autoanalyzer.

82043-82044
"Microalbuminuria" is defined as albuminuria of 30 to 300 mg/24 hours and is requested to determine early increase of proteinuria, usually in diabetes and in pre-eclampsia before protein becomes evident by conventional urinalysis. Patients commonly perform specimen collection over a 24-hour period. Methods include radioimmunoassay (RIA) or enzyme-linked immunosorbent assay (ELISA). Report 82043 for quantitative microalbumin and 82044 for semi-quantitative or reagent strip microalbumin.

82045
Ischemia modified albumin (IMA) is a blood assay that measures cobalt albumin binding. In the presence of myocardial ischemia, there is decreased ability of the N-terminal region of human albumin to bind cobalt. This test may also be requested as Co(II)-albumin binding assay. Method is colorimetric assay with results recorded in absorbance units (ABSU). The test is used to detect early onset unstable angina and myocardial infarction.

82055
This test may also be requested as ethanol, ethyl alcohol, or ETOH. If the specimen is blood (serum), collection is typically by venipuncture. Method is commonly enzymatic rate analysis (alcohol dehydrogenase). This test is typically performed to determine alcohol level for medical or legal purposes, to screen unconscious patients, to diagnose alcohol intoxication to determine appropriate therapy, and to monitor ethanol treatment for methanol intoxication.

82075
This test may be used primarily in screening for ethanol levels above the legal limit for driving. The legal limit varies from state to state with levels above 0.08-0.1 g/dL usually being defined as legally intoxicated.

82085
This test may also be requested as aldolase (ALD) or fructose biphosphate aldolase. Methods may include ultraviolet, kinetic, coupled enzymatic and colorimetric. This test can be useful in the identification of a variety of degenerative diseases, myopathies, and inflammations.

82088
For serum aldosterone, blood is obtained by post-fasting venipuncture. Extreme care must be taken in preparing the patient before specimen collection and handling the specimen in order to obtain an accurate measurement. Blood specimens are usually taken early in the morning and a notation is made as to whether the patient was sitting or supine. A second test may be performed approximately four hours later. A radioimmunoassay (RIA) is typically employed for analysis of the specimen. This test is most commonly used in the diagnosis of specific types of adrenal adenomas, or secondary aldosteronism caused by cirrhosis, congestive heart failure, nephrosis, potassium loading, toxemia of pregnancy, and other states of contraction of plasma volume. Urine aldosterone requires a 24-hour non-fasting urine specimen. The patient flushes the first urine of the day. All voided urine for the next 24 hours is collected. Method is radioimmunoassay.

82101
Alkaloids are nitrogenous substances found in plants, many of which are pharmacologically active. Common alkaloids include morphine, quinine, atropine, and strychnine. This test may be is used to measure (quantitate) the amount of a specific alkaloid present in a random urine specimen.

82103
This test may also be requested as A1 AT, AAT, Acute Phase Proteins, or -1-Antitrypsin. Method is by radial immunodiffusion (RID), or nephelometry. This test is used to detect hereditary decreases in the production of alpha1-antitrypsin, chronic obstructive lung disease, or liver disease.

82104
This test may also be requested as A1AT phenotype, AAT phenotype, and Pi phenotype. This test is used to detect hereditary decreases in the production of alpha1-antitrypsin by specific phenotype. There are more than 75 inherited variants of AAT. Two variants, Pi ZZ and Pi SZ phenotypes, represent severe deficiencies and are associated with chronic obstructive lung disease, liver disease, and hepatoma. Method is by radial immunodiffusion (RID).

82105
This test may be abbreviated as AFP. It may also be referred to as fetal alpha globulin. While this test is most often associated with pregnancy, it is also used to diagnose a variety of other conditions. During pregnancy, the test is normally performed between the 16th and 18th week of gestation. If levels are abnormal, it may be repeated approximately one week after the first test. Analysis is normally performed by radioimmunoassay (RIA).

82106
The test may be abbreviated as AFP. The test is normally performed on pregnant women initially between the 16th and 18th week of gestation. An amniotic AFP may be performed when serum AFP (82105) results are abnormal to confirm a diagnosis. An ultrasound is performed to determine the exact location of the fetus. AFP levels are measured, generally by radioimmunoassay (RIA).

82107
This test may also be ordered as an AFP-L3. The test is a measure of the L3 form of alpha fetoprotein in a patient with chronic liver disease. The specimen is blood. Using a special fluorescent reagent, the L3 form of AFP is separated from other forms of alpha fetoprotein and tagged with a special fluorescent reagent. L3 is then measured as a percentage of total AFP. The calculations occur within an instrument developed for this test. The test is primarily used in the clinical evaluation of patient risk, as elevated levels of AFP-L3 in a patient with chronic liver disease are associated with hepatocellular carcinoma.

82108
This test may be abbreviated as Al. The test is used to monitor patients at risk for aluminum toxicity due to exposure or disease states, which cause aluminum accumulation (e.g., chronic renal failure). Blood specimen is obtained by venipuncture. A random urine sample is obtained. Method is atomic absorption spectrophotometry (AAS).

82120
This test is administered to determine the specific cause of vaginitis and may be performed following negative testing for yeasts or trichomonas. Disturbances in normal anaerobic flora are usually the etiological source. A saline wet slide is prepared and characteristic cells are identified microscopically, namely epithelial cells with bacilli clinging to the surfaces. A solution of potassium hydroxide (KOH) is added to the mount to activate amines. A characteristic odor is released when amines are present and become volatile.

82127-82128
These tests may also be referred to as a metabolic screen for amino acids. Several methods may be used including thin layer chromatography (TLC), gas chromatography (GC), and ion-exchange chromatography. These tests determine whether an amino acid is or is not present (qualitative analysis). Code 82127 tests for the presence of single amino acids while 82128 tests for the presence of multiple amino acids.

82131
This test may be requested as specific amino acid (e.g., cystine, tyrosine, methionine, propionic acid). Method is ion-exchange chromatography. This test measures (quantifies) amounts of single specified amino acids.

82135
This test may be requested as aminolevulinic acid (ALA), delta ALA or DALA. Aminolevulinic acid is a precursor of heme, produced from glycine and succinyl-CoA. This test is used to diagnose genetic disorders that allow porphyrin products, specifically aminolevulinic acid, to accumulate in the liver or red blood cells. Methodology includes spectrophotometry or ion exchange resin columns.

82136-82139
These tests may be requested as specific amino acids (e.g., cystine, tyrosine, methionine, propionic acid). Method is ion-exchange chromatography. This test measures (quantifies) amounts of multiple specified amino acids. Report 82136 for two to five amino acids. Report 82139 for six or more.

82140
This test may be requested as NH3. Elevated levels may indicate that the liver is not able to detoxify ammonia from the blood due to severe liver disease. A number of methods are used including enzymatic, resin enzymatic, and ion-selective electrode (ISE).

82143
This prenatal procedure may be requested as an amniotic fluid spectral analysis, Lily test, and amniotic fluid OD 450 spectral analysis. Amniotic fluid is collected by amniocentesis and the specimen is protected from exposure to light. A separately reported ultrasound is performed to determine the exact location of the fetus prior to the amniocentesis. Method of testing is spectrophotometry. This test measures the amount of free bilirubin in the amniotic fluid.

82145
This test may be requested as a quantitative analysis of amphetamine/methamphetamine. A number of methods are used. Methods used for blood include gas-liquid chromatography (GLC), gas chromatometry/mass spectrometry (GC/MS), and radioimmunoassay (RIA). Methods used for urine include enzyme immunoassay (EIA), high performance liquid chromatography (HPLC), fluorescence polarization immunoassay (FPIA), and RIA. This test measures (quantifies) the amount of amphetamine or methamphetamine in the urine.

82150
Serum amylase is elevated in acute pancreatitis and is, therefore, a common test when abdominal pain, epigastric tenderness, nausea, and vomiting are present. There are multiple methods of testing for amylase.

82154
This test may be requested as 3-Alpha-diol G. Androstanediol glucuronide is an androgen formed in

the peripheral tissues. Elevated levels are frequently seen in females with hirsutism (excessive body hair). When androstanediol glucuronide is elevated, treatment of hirsutism is directed at the peripheral tissue sites rather than at other sites that are sometimes responsible for overproduction of androgens (adrenal cortex, ovary). Method is radioimmunoassay (RIA).

82157
An androgenic steroid secreted by the testes, adrenal cortex, and ovaries. This test is used primarily to evaluate androgen production in females with hirsutism. Blood is obtained by venipuncture. Method is radioimmunoassay (RIA).

82160
Androsterone is a steroid hormone metabolite in the androgen series that is measured for evaluation of syndromes of androgen excess such as hirsutism and polycystic ovary syndrome. It has been measured typically by methods involving extraction and chromatography, followed by detection and quantification by colorimetric or immunometric techniques. Measurement of this compound has largely been replaced by determination of other specific plasma androgens (e.g., testosterone) by modern, sensitive assays.

82163
This hormone acts as a powerful vasopressor, raising blood pressure and reducing fluid loss in the kidney by restricting blood flow. It also stimulates aldosterone secretion. Blood is obtained by venipuncture. The patient must remain in a recumbent position for 30 minutes prior to obtaining the blood specimen. Angiotensin II is difficult to measure accurately and great care must be taken in both collection and storage of the specimen. Method is radioimmunoassay (RIA). Degradation products and interfering peptides must be removed from the specimen prior to RIA.

82164
This test may be requested as ACE or peptidyl-dipeptidase A. ACE converts angiotensin I to angiotensin II. Method is spectrofluorometric combined with various synthetic substrates or radioimmunoassay (RIA).

82172
This test may be requested as Apolipoprotein A, Apolipoprotein A-1, Apolipoprotein B, Apolipoprotein E, Apo-A, Apo-A1, Apo-B, or Apo-E. Apolipoproteins are the components of lipoprotein complexes found in high-density lipoprotein (HDL), low-density lipoprotein (LDL), and very low-density lipoprotein (VLDL). There are numerous variables that are designated as A, B, C, D, and E with some further subdivided (e.g., A1, A2, B48, B100, C1). Those of primary interest for laboratory testing are Apo-A1, Apo-B, and Apo-E. Multiple methods are used, including radioimmunoassay (RIA), radial immunodiffusion (RID), and enzyme-linked immunosorbent assay (ELISA).

82175
Arsenic is a toxic metallic element with exposure occurring by inhalation or ingestion. Urine is the preferred specimen for acute exposure and when the patient is symptomatic. A 24-hour urine specimen is required. Method is colorimetry, atomic absorption spectrophotometry (AAS), or neutron activation analysis (NAA). This test measures (quantifies) the amount of arsenic present.

82180
This test is used to evaluate vitamin C deficiency. It may be performed with or without vitamin C saturation. When performed as a saturation test, megadoses of vitamin C are given over a three-to-four day period. The amount of vitamin C is measured (quantified).

82190
AAS is a method for detecting the absorption of specific wavelengths of light by analyte that have been vaporized in a flame. The analysis is performed using an instrument known as an atomic absorption spectrometer. Analytes are typically pure elements, since each element has a specific absorption spectrum.

82205
This test may be requested as a quantitative analysis of barbiturates. A number of methods are used. Methods used for blood include gas-liquid chromatography (GLC), gas chromatometry/mass spectrometry (GC/MS), and radioimmunoassay (RIA). Methods used for urine include enzyme immunoassay (EIA) and high performance liquid chromatography (HPLC). This test measures (quantifies) the amount of barbiturate.

82232
This test may be requested as Beta2M. Beta2M is a small (micro) nonpolymorphic protein. CSF is obtained by spinal puncture, which is reported separately. Method is by radioimmunoassay (RIA), enzyme immunoassay (EIA), or immunoradiometric assay (IRMA).

82239-82240
This is sometimes referred to as glycocholic acid. Bile acids are steroid acids derived from cholesterol. Cholylglycine is a bile salt formed by glycine and cholic acid. Method is enzymatic or gas-liquid chromatography (GLC). Code 82239 reports total concentration of all bile acids. Code 82240 reports total concentration of cholylglycine only.

82247-82248
Bilirubin is a bile pigment formed by the breakdown of hemoglobin during both normal and abnormal erythrocyte destruction. Direct (conjugated) bilirubin is that portion of the bilirubin that has been taken up by the liver cells to form bilirubin diglucuronide.

Indirect (unconjugated) bilirubin is that portion of the bilirubin that has not been taken up by the liver cells. Total bilirubin is the sum of direct and indirect bilirubin present in the specimen. Method is diazotization. Spectrophotometry may be used in neonates six weeks or younger. Report 82247 for total bilirubin. Report 82248 for direct bilirubin.

82252
Bilirubin is not normally present in feces, appearing only in cases of rapid peristaltic movement of the gut or disturbances in normal intestinal flora. Detection may be useful in evaluation of some types of diarrhea. It can be detected with the dipstick or tablet tests commonly used for urine, by testing the supernatant fluid from watery feces, or adding water to solid feces.

82261
This test may be requested as an indirect test for biotin. Biotinidase is an enzyme required for the recycling of biotin. Biotinidase deficiency is a genetic condition. Newborn screening tests may include testing for deficiency of this enzyme. Method is colorimetry or enzymatic.

82270
This test may be requested as a screening guaiac, screening stool guaiac, or by a variety of brand names. The patient is instructed to obtain three consecutive stool specimens and send the kit to a lab or physician office for performance of the test. The method is peroxidase activity. This test reports the presence (qualitative analysis) of blood in the stool, but does not quantify the amount. This code is used to report the service when performed as colorectal neoplasm screening.

82271
A specimen, other than stool, is obtained for detection of blood. The method is peroxidase activity. This test reports the presence (qualitative analysis) of blood in a specimen other than stool, but does not quantify the amount.

82272
This test may be requested as a screening guaiac or screening stool guaiac, or by a variety of brand names. The patient is instructed to obtain three consecutive stool specimens and send the kit to a lab or physician office for performance of the test. The method is peroxidase activity. This test detects the presence (qualitative analysis) of blood in the stool, but does not quantify the amount. This code is used to report the service when performed for reasons other than colorectal neoplasm screening.

82274
Fecal sample is dispersed in a diluent with antibodies for hemoglobin antigen to form a complex of antibody and antigen. A complex of antibody and antigen is separated from the specimen and exposed to a second antibody for the hemoglobin antigen. A sample from the first complex is bound to a solid carrier, and a sample from the second antibody exposure is labeled with a detection agent to determine the presence of hemoglobin antigen in the original fecal specimen. This code requires three samples, which must be obtained from separate bowel movements, and each sample must be placed in a sterile leakproof container with a screw-cap lid for transport to the laboratory.

82286
Bradykinin is a biologically active peptide, found in plasma and many other tissues and fluids, important in the inflammatory response. A pathogenic role for Bradykinin has been suggested in diseases ranging from asthma to hereditary angioedema, as well as other kinds of swelling disorders and allergic-type diseases. It is measured in body fluids by techniques including immunoassay, capillary electrophoresis, chromatography and mass-spectrometry.

82300
Cadmium may be abbreviated as Cd. Cadmium is a bivalent metal. This test is used to evaluate toxic levels of cadmium after industrial exposure to cadmium fumes or ingestion of cadmium. A 24-hour urine specimen is recommended and must be collected in a plastic container. The patient flushes the first urine of the day and discards it. All voided urine for the next 24 hours is collected. Method is atomic absorption spectroscopy (AAS).

82306
This test may be requested as 25-OHD3, 25(OH) Calciferol, Vitamin D 25-Hydroxy, Vitamin D3 25-OH, or Calciferol 25-Hydroxy. Specimen is serum or plasma and method is high performance liquid chromatography (HPLC), competitive protein binding (CPB), or radioimmunoassay (RIA). This code includes fractions, if performed.

82308
This test may be requested as thyrocalcitonin. This test may be used to screen for specific malignant neoplasms. A fasting blood specimen should be taken. The specimen is collected in a chilled tube and the test performed within 10 minutes of collection. Serum (plasma) is separated in a refrigerated centrifuge and frozen. The test is performed by assay or radioimmunoassay (RIA).

82310
This test may be abbreviated Ca. Blood is obtained by venipuncture or heel stick. Specimen is obtained in the morning and a fasting sample is preferable. Postural changes and venous stasis may provide misleading results. Accurate diagnosis may require obtaining additional specimens on subsequent days. Method is spectrophotometry or atomic absorption spectroscopy (AAS). The test may be used to assess thyroid and parathyroid function.

82330
This test may also be referred to as free calcium. It may be abbreviated iCa, Ca++ or Ca+2. Ionized or free calcium refers to calcium that is not bound to proteins in the blood. It is the metabolically active portion of the calcium in the blood. Blood is obtained by venipuncture and collected anaerobically. Method is by ion-selective electrode (ISE). The test may be used to assess thyroid and parathyroid function.

82331
The calcium infusion test is a provocative test for evaluation of medullary thyroid carcinoma (MTC). Calcitonin levels are measured following an IV infusion of calcium solution, and sometimes calcium levels are also measured to evaluate calcium incorporation or monitor hypercalcemia.

82340
This test may be abbreviated Ca urine, Ca++ or Ca+2. A 24-hour urine specimen is generally required. The patient flushes the first urine of the day and discards it. All voided urine for the next 24 hours is collected and refrigerated. Method is spectrophotometry or atomic absorption spectrometry (AAS).

82355-82360
These tests may be requested as a stone analysis or nephrolithiasis analysis. The specimen should be rinsed to remove any tissue or blood. Chemical analysis generally includes testing for the presence of calcium, carbonate, cystine, magnesium, oxalate, phosphates and urates. The analysis may be qualitative (82355), identifying only the chemicals that are present, or it may be quantitative (82360) measuring the amounts of each of the chemicals identified.

82365
This test may be requested as a stone analysis or nephrolithiasis analysis. The specimen should be rinsed to remove any tissue or blood. The stone is analyzed for the presence of calcium, carbonate, cystine, magnesium, oxalate, phosphates, and urates. This code is specific for analysis by infrared spectroscopy, which is generally performed only by reference laboratories.

82370
This test may be requested as a stone analysis or nephrolithiasis analysis. The specimen should be rinsed to remove any tissue or blood. The stone is analyzed for the presence of calcium, carbonate, cystine, magnesium, oxalate, phosphates, and urates. This code is specific for analysis by x-ray diffraction, which is generally performed only by reference laboratories. X-ray diffraction can separately analyze the nidus (center), which often differs chemically from the cortex (external layer).

82373
This test may be ordered as a CDT or CDT percentage. Blood specimen is obtained by venipuncture. The specimen is clotted and separated. Method is nephelometry or turbidimetric immunoassay. Carbohydrate deficient transferrin is a protein formed in the liver and abnormally high elevations are linked to a prolonged period of high alcohol use. The test may be ordered to confirm diagnosis of alcoholism or to measure compliance with an abstinence program.

82374
This test may be requested as CO2, HCO3, or bicarbonate. Bicarbonate (carbon dioxide) is an indicator of electrolyte and acid-base status (alkalosis, acidosis). It is elevated in metabolic alkalosis, compensated respiratory acidosis, and hypokalemia. It is decreased in metabolic acidosis, compensated respiratory alkalosis, and in diabetic ketoacidosis. Blood specimen is normally obtained by arterial puncture, but venipuncture may also be used. Bicarbonate is usually calculated using the Henderson-Hasselbalch equation (HCO3 = Total CO2 – H2CO3). However, it can also be determined by titration.

82375-82376
These tests may be requested as carboxyhemoglobin, CO, or COHb. Carbon monoxide is a colorless, odorless, tasteless, poisonous gas formed by burning fuels, including natural gas, wood, and gasoline. These tests are used to identify the level of carbon monoxide poisoning in individuals with known or suspected exposure to the toxic gas. Method is colorimetry, spectrophotometry, or gas-liquid chromatography (GLC). Report 82375 when testing for the amount (quantitative analysis) of carbon monoxide. Report 82376 when testing (qualifying) the presence of carbon monoxide.

82378
This test may be abbreviated as CEA. While CEA occurs normally in the gastrointestinal tract, it may be elevated for certain benign and malignant neoplasms and other diseases. CEA is used primarily to monitor patients with colorectal cancer and to a lesser extent advanced breast cancer. Method is immunofluorescence, enzyme immunoassay (EIA), and radioimmunoassay (RIA).

82379
Carnitine has a variety of metabolic roles and may be an indicator of inborn errors of metabolism, chronic disease, or acute and critical illness. Method is enzymatic. This test measures (quantifies) the amount of both total and free carnitine present.

82380
This test may also be requested as beta-carotene. Carotene is an isomeric pigment found in a number of vegetables and fruits. In the liver, carotene is converted to Vitamin A, which, in turn, is converted to retinal, the major molecule that enables vision. Method is high

performance liquid chromatography (HPLC), colorimetry.

82382
Catecholamines are biogenic amines that include epinephrine, norepinephrine, and dopamine. This test is used to diagnose hypertension caused by increased levels of catecholamines secreted by specific types of tumors. A 24-hour urine specimen is preferred but shorter timed collections may also be used. The patient flushes the first urine of the day and discards it. All voided urine for the next 24 hours is collected and refrigerated. Method is fluorometry. Code 82382 reports total catecholamines and therefore does not differentiate between epinephrine, norepinephrine, and dopamine.

82383
Catecholamines are biogenic amines that include epinephrine, norepinephrine, and dopamine. This test is used to diagnose hypertension caused by increased levels of catecholamines secreted by specific types of tumors. Blood specimen is obtained by venipuncture. Preferred method is high performance liquid chromatography (HPLC), but radioimmunoassay (RIA) or radiochemical assay may also be used. Code 82383 tests for total catecholamines and does not differentiate between epinephrine, norepinephrine, and dopamine.

82384
Catecholamines are biogenic amines that include epinephrine, norepinephrine, and dopamine. This test is used to diagnose hypertension caused by increased levels of catecholamines secreted by specific types of tumors. Preferred method is high performance liquid chromatography (HPLC), but radioimmunoassay (RIA) or radiochemical assay may also be used. Code 82384 reports fractionated catecholamines and quantifies total epinephrine, norepinephrine, and dopamine separately. Most assays measure only free catecholamines, but some measure both free and conjugated types.

82387
Cathepsin D is an indicator of metastatic breast cancer. Neoplastic tissue must be dissected free of fat and normal breast tissue, sliced into small pieces, placed in a tube, and quick frozen in liquid nitrogen. The tissue is analyzed by means of enzymatic immunoassay (EIA) or immunoradiometric assay (IRMA).

82390
This test may be requested as Cp, copper oxidase, or ferroxidase. Ceruloplasmin is a copper oxidase enzyme found in plasma. Decreased levels of ceruloplasmin are found in Wilson's disease, a disorder of copper metabolism. Several methods may be used, including spectrophotometry, nephelometry, or radial immunodiffusion (RID) for blood specimens. RID is the method for urine.

82397
Chemiluminescent assay refers to a detection method, whereby a chemiluminogenic substrate is converted to a chemiluminescent (light emitting) product.

82415
This test may be requested as a chloramphenicol, Chloromycetin, or Mychel-S level. Chloramphenicol is a broad spectrum antibiotic. This test is used to monitor therapeutic and toxic levels. Several methods may be used, including high performance liquid chromatography (HPLC), gas-liquid chromatography (GLC), microbiological assay (MB), colorimetry, or enzymatic immunoassay (EIA).

82435
This test may be requested as Cl, blood. Chloride is a salt of hydrochloric acid and is important in maintaining electrolyte balance. Methods include colorimetry, coulometry, and ion-selective electrode (ISE).

82436
This test may be requested as Cl, urine. Chloride is important in maintaining proper electrolyte balance. A 24-hour urine test is preferred, but shorter timed collections and random specimens may also be used. If a timed specimen is used, the patient flushes the first urine of the day and discards it. All voided urine for the next 24 hours (or shorter time increment) is collected and refrigerated. Methods include colorimetry, coulometry, and ion-selective electrode (ISE).

82438
This test may be requested as a cystic fibrosis sweat test or Cl, sweat. Saliva is sometimes used for cystic fibrosis evaluation, but is not as reliable as sweat. Sweat is obtained from the forearm by pilocarpine iontophoresis, which is reported separately. Method is usually ion-selective electrode (ISE), but colorimetry, coulometry, Schales and Schales method, and Cotlove titration are also used.

82441
Chlorinated hydrocarbons are contained in solvents and are absorbed cutaneously and by inhalation. While they vary in toxicity, all are CNS depressants and can cause liver and kidney damage with prolonged exposure. This test is used to screen for toxic levels. Levels of one or more of the following substances are screened: carbon tetrachloride, chloroform, dichloromethane, trichloroethylene, and tetrachloroethylene. Testing methods include gas chromatography flame ionization detection (GC-FID) and gas chromatography electron capture detector (GC-ECD). Colorimetry measurement of metabolites may also be used but is nonspecific.

82465
Cholesterol level is a risk indicator for atherosclerosis and myocardial infarction. Blood specimen is obtained

by venipuncture. Method is enzymatic. This test reports total cholesterol in serum or whole blood.

82480
This test may be requested as acylcholine acylhydrolase, cholinesterase II, EC, PchE, pseudocholinesterase, SChE, or S-Pseudocholine Esterase. Cholinesterase is an enzyme of the hydrolase class with serum cholinesterase being specific to choline esters. Serum cholinesterase is requested primarily for diagnosis of an inherited hypersensitivity to the certain anesthetics or when organophosphate or carbamate insecticide poisoning is suspected. Methods are colorimetry, kinetic enzyme with substrates, and fluorometry. This procedure is specific to serum cholinesterase.

82482
This test may be requested as acetylcholinesterase, cholinesterase I, erythrocytic cholinesterase, or true cholinesterase. Cholinesterase is an enzyme of the hydrolase class with RBC cholinesterase being specific to the substrate acetylcholine. RBC cholinesterase is requested when organophosphate or carbamate insecticide poisoning is suspected. Blood specimen is obtained by venipuncture. Methods include colorimetry, fluorometry, and spectrophotometry. This procedure is specific to RBC cholinesterase.

82485
The test may be called dermatan sulfate. It is a glycosaminoglycan (formerly called a mucopolysaccharide) found mostly in skin, but also in blood vessels, heart valves, tendons, and lungs. It accumulates abnormally in several of the mucopolysaccharidosis disorders and plays a role in coagulation, cardiovascular disease, carcinogenesis, infection, wound repair, and fibrosis. The specimen is a 24 hour or timed urine. Chondroitin B Sulfate has been measured using chromatographic techniques such as high performance liquid chromatography (HPLC).

82486
This code reports a specific chromatography technique for analyzing substances that are not specifically listed elsewhere in the chemistry section. Chromatography, itself, uses a number of different techniques to separate and analyze the specimen components. Code 82486 reports column chromatography, which uses a sorbent packed in a column. The specimen is dissolved in a solvent and poured into the column. Some of the specimen components bind to the sorbent and are retained in the column, while others escape. Subsequent washings with the same or different solvents cause more strongly bound components to escape. These components can be individually analyzed. This code tests for the presence (qualitative analysis) of a single analyte.

82487-82488
These codes report specific chromatography techniques for analyzing substances that are not specifically listed elsewhere in the chemistry section. Chromatography uses a number of different techniques to separate and analyze the specimen components. Codes 82487 and 82488 report paper chromatography, which uses a special-grade filter paper in the stationary phase. The specimen is applied to the paper and the end of the paper is placed in a solvent. The solvent rises along the paper, carrying and depositing the different components of the specimen along the filter paper. The different components can be separately visualized and analyzed. These codes test for the presence (qualitative analysis) of a single analyte. Report 82487 for 1-dimensional and 82488 for 2-dimensional.

82489
This code reports a specific chromatography technique for analyzing substances that are not specifically listed elsewhere in the chemistry section. Chromatography uses a number of different techniques to separate and analyze the specimen components. Code 82489 reports thin-layer chromatography, which uses a thin layer adsorbent applied to a rectangular plate in the stationary phase. The specimen is applied to the plate and the end of the plate is placed in a solvent. As the solvent rises along the adsorbent on the plate, the different components of the specimen are carried along at varying rates and deposited along the plate. The different components can be separately visualized and analyzed. This code tests for the presence (qualitative analysis) of a single analyte.

82491-82492
These codes report specific chromatography techniques for analyzing substances that are not specifically listed elsewhere in the chemistry section. Chromatography uses a number of different techniques to separate and analyze the specimen components. Codes 82491-82492 report column chromatography, which uses a sorbent packed in a column. The specimen is dissolved in a solvent and poured into the column. Some of the specimen components bind to the sorbent and are retained in the column, while others escape. Subsequent washings with the same or different solvents cause more strongly bound components to escape. These components can be individually analyzed. Code 82491 measures (quantifies) the amount of a single analyte, while 82492 measures (quantifies) the amount of multiple analytes.

82495
Chromium is an essential nutrient that is toxic in large doses. The test monitors for environmental or occupational chromium toxicity that is associated with skin respiratory and other diseases such as lung cancer. Blood, urine or hair may be tested. Methods used

include atomic absorption spectrometry (AAS) and neutron activation analysis (NAA).

82507
Citrate determinations in urine are useful in evaluating nephrolithiasis. A 24-hour urine specimen is required. The patient flushes the first urine of the day and discards it. All voided urine for the next 24 hours is collected and refrigerated. Citrate may be measured using enzymatic/spectrophotometric methods or chromatography.

82520
Cocaine is a refined derivative of the coca plant and is a frequently abused drug. Blood specimen is obtained by venipuncture. Multiple methods may be used including enzyme immunoassay (EIA), fluorescence polarization immunoassay (FPIA), radioimmunoassay (RIA), gas-liquid chromatography (GLC), high performance liquid chromatography (HPLC), and gas chromatography/mass spectrometry (GC-MS). The procedure measures (quantifies) the amount of cocaine or its metabolites in the sample.

82523
This test may be ordered as collagen crosslink N-telopeptide or pyridinium collagen crosslinks. Pyridinium includes pyrinoline and deoxypyridinoline. Collagen cross-links are markers for bone resorption and are useful in evaluating and managing osteoporosis. A timed urine specimen is required. When testing for N-telopeptide, a two-hour specimen is usually obtained. Pyridinium, including pyrinoline and deoxypyridinoline, requires a 24-hour specimen. When a timed specimen is used, the patient flushes the first urine of the day and discards it. All voided urine for the next 24 hours (or shorter time increment) is collected and refrigerated. Method is enzyme-linked immunosorbent assay (ELISA) for N-telopeptide and high performance liquid chromatography (HPLC) for pyridinium.

82525
This test may be abbreviated as Cu. Copper is an essential trace mineral. Copper deficiency is rare, however, copper may accumulate to excessive levels in patients with Wilson's disease (a disorder of copper metabolism), primary biliary cirrhosis, and chronic extrahepatic biliary obstruction. Liver specimen is obtained by separately reportable liver biopsy. Methods include colorimetry and atomic absorption spectrometry (AAS) and specimen types vary.

82528
This test may be requested as Compound B. Corticosterone is a natural corticosteroid, similar to cortisol except that it does not possess anti-inflammatory qualities. Blood specimen is obtained by venipuncture. Method is radioimmunoassay.

82530
Cortisol is a naturally occurring glucocorticoid responsible for metabolism of glucose, protein, and fats and is important in immune system function. Urinary free cortisol is used in initial screening for Cushing's syndrome. Amniotic fluid levels of free cortisol are useful in evaluating fetal lung maturation. To obtain an amniotic fluid specimen, an ultrasound is performed to determine the exact location of the fetus. Methods include high performance liquid chromatography (HPLC) for urine and radioimmunoassay (RIA) for amniotic fluid. This test measures free (unbound) cortisol only.

82533
Cortisol is a naturally occurring glucocorticoid responsible for metabolism of glucose, protein, and fats and is important in immune system function. To obtain an amniotic fluid specimen, an ultrasound is performed to determine the exact location of the fetus. The fluid is sent to the lab for analysis. Method is radioimmunoassay (RIA), competitive protein binding (CPB), or fluorescent assay. This test measures total cortisol (both free and bound) in various specimen types.

82540
Creatine is measured in urine or serum to evaluate certain conditions involving increased muscle tissue breakdown. It has been measured in erythrocytes as an indicator of erythrocyte survival time in the evaluation of hemolytic disorders. It can be measured by colorimetric or enzymatic/spectrophotometric methods.

82541-82542
These codes report specific chromatography techniques combined with mass spectrometry for analyzing substances that are not specifically listed elsewhere in the chemistry section. Chromatography uses different techniques to separate and analyze the specimen components. Codes 82541-82542 report column chromatography combined with mass spectrometry. Column chromatography uses a sorbent packed in a column. The specimen is dissolved in a solvent and poured into the column. Some of the specimen components bind to the sorbent and are retained in the column, while others escape. Subsequent washings with the same or different solvents cause more strongly bound components to escape. These components can be individually analyzed. Mass spectrometry represents one of the most powerful new tools available for studying complex substances. Mass spectrometry isolates specific substances by sorting a stream of electrified particles (ions) based on their mass. Code 82541 screens for the presence (qualitative analysis) of an analyte using a single stationary and mobile phase, while 82542 measures (quantifies) the amount of an analyte using a single stationary and mobile phase.

82543-82544
These codes report specific chromatography techniques combined with mass spectrometry for analyzing substances that are not specifically listed elsewhere in the chemistry section. Chromatography uses different techniques to separate and analyze the specimen components. Codes 82543-82544 report column chromatography combined with mass spectrometry. Column chromatography uses a sorbent packed in a column. The specimen is dissolved in a solvent and poured into the column. Some of the specimen components bind to the sorbent and are retained in the column, while others escape. Subsequent washings with the same or different solvents cause more strongly bound components to escape. These components can be individually analyzed. Mass spectrometry represents one of the most powerful new tools available for studying complex substances. Mass spectrometry isolates specific substances by sorting a stream of electrified particles (ions) based on their mass. These two tests are also performed with a stable isotope dilution. Code 82543 measures (quantifies) a single analyte using a single stationary and mobile phase, while 82544 measures (quantifies) the amount of multiple analytes using a single stationary and mobile phase.

82550
This test may be requested as creatine kinase (CK) or creatine phosphokinase (CPK). Blood specimen is obtained by venipuncture. Method is enzymatic, kinetic, or spectrophotometry. This code reports total CK. Creatine kinase is an enzyme found in striated muscle and it is released following injury. Elevated CK levels are primarily associated with myocardial infarction, trauma and surgery, but CK levels may be elevated with a number of other conditions as well.

82552
This test may be requested as creatine kinase (CK) isoenzymes or creatine phosphokinase (CPK) isoenzymes. Method is electrophoresis (EP), column ion-exchange chromatography. Creatine kinase consists of three isoenzymes, each of which is composed of two units, muscle (MM), brain (BB), or muscle and brain (MB). CK1 (BB) is found primarily in the brain and smooth muscle, CK2 (MB) in cardiac muscle, and CK3 (MM) in skeletal muscle. Because elevated CK levels are indicative of injury to the cells, quantifying the levels of each isoenzyme may assist in pinpointing the injured site.

82553
This test may be requested as creatine kinase (CK) MB fraction, creatine phosphokinase (CPK) MB fraction, or CK2. Methods include immunochemical, fluorometric radial partition, microparticle enzyme immunoassay, immunoenzymetric, or chemiluminometric. Creatine kinase consists of three isoenzymes, which are each composed of two units, muscle (MM), brain (BB), or muscle and brain (MB). CK1 (BB) is found primarily in the brain and smooth muscle, CK2 (MB) in cardiac muscle, and CK3 (MM) in skeletal muscle. This code tests for the MB or CK2 fraction only.

82554
This test may be requested as CK isoforms or CPK isoforms. Blood specimen is obtained by venipuncture. Methods include electrophoresis (EP), high performance liquid chromatography (HPLC), and isoelectric focusing (IEF). Creatine kinase consists of three isoenzymes, which are each composed of two units, muscle (MM), brain (BB), or muscle and brain (MB). CK1 (BB) is found primarily in the brain and smooth muscle, CK2 (MB) in cardiac muscle, and CK3 (MM) in skeletal muscle. These isoenzymes can be further subdivided into isoforms which are designated by the isoenzyme (MM, MB, BB) followed by a number (e.g., 1, 2, 3) Examples include CK-MB1, CK-MB2.

82565
Serum creatinine is the most common laboratory test for evaluating renal function. Method is enzymatic or colorimetry.

82570
Urine creatinine levels are not normally used to evaluate disease processes except as part of a creatinine clearance test, but they are a good indicator of the adequacy of timed urine specimens. Amniotic fluid creatinine is used to evaluate fetal maturity. For amniotic fluid specimen, a separately reportable amniocentesis is performed. Method is enzymatic, Jaffe reaction, or manual.

82575
This test may be requested as urea clearance or urea nitrogen clearance. Both blood and urine specimens are required. Blood specimen is obtained by venipuncture. A 24-hour urine specimen is preferred, but timed shorter increments may also be acceptable. Method is enzymatic or Jaffe reaction, or alkaline picrate. Creatinine clearance is a calculation of urine and serum creatinine content adjusted by urine volume and body size. The test is a general indicator of glomerular filtration function of the kidneys.

82585
Fibrinogen with an abnormal physical property causing it to precipitate in the cold (4¡ C) and dissolve again when warmed to 37¡ C is known as cryofibrinogen. This test is performed to evaluate cold intolerance. Blood specimen is obtained by venipuncture in a prewarmed tube and must be kept warmed. Method is cold precipitation.

82595
Cryoglobulin is a serum globulin with an abnormal physical property causing it to precipitate at cold temperatures (4 degrees C) and dissolve again when warmed to 37degrees C. It is indicative of lymphoproliferative disorders, collagen vascular

disease, and a variety of infections and other diseases. Blood specimen is obtained by venipuncture in a prewarmed tube and must be kept warmed. Method is cold precipitation.

82600
This test may be requested as CN, hydrocyanic acid, or potassium or sodium cyanide. Cyanide is poisonous, both as a gas (inhaled) and as a salt (ingested). It binds to cytochrome oxidase, preventing cellular respiration. Multiple methods may be used, including colorimetry, spectrophotometry, microdiffusion, gas chromatography-mass spectrometry (GC-MS), and high performance liquid chromatography (HPLC).

82607
This test may be requested as antipernicious anemia factor, true cyanocobalamin, or Vitamin B12. It is essential for red blood cell maturation and for gastrointestinal and neurologic health. Decreased levels may be indicative of certain anemias. Method is chemiluminescence, competitive protein binding (CPB) radioassay, or radioimmunoassay (RIA).

82608
This test may be requested as unsaturated Vitamin B12 binding capacity (UBBC) and Vitamin B12. It is essential for red blood cell maturation and for gastrointestinal and neurologic health. This test may be used to evaluate for certain anemias, myeloproliferative disorders, and the congenital absence of transcobalamin II or cobalophilin. Method is radioimmunoassay (RIA).

82610
Code 82610 reports the quantitative determination of Cystatin C, which is used to diagnose impaired kidney function. Serum Cystatin C is a useful indicator of glomerular filtration rate (GFR), particularly in elderly, very obese, and malnourished patients whose serum creatinine can be misleading. It is also used in renal function assessment in patients suspected of having renal disease, and for monitoring the response to treatment in those with kidney disease. The method of testing varies by laboratory.

82615
Cystine and homocystine are amino acids indicative of disease when found in the urine. Method is ion exchange chromatography or spectrophotometry.

82626
This test may be requested as unconjugated DHEA. Serum DHEA levels may be used to evaluate delayed puberty and hirsutism. Elevations may be indicative of ovarian disorders, neoplasm of the adrenal gland, Cushing's disease, or ectopic ACTH-producing neoplasm. Decreased levels in amniotic fluid may be indicative of congenital adrenal hypoplasia. For amniotic fluid specimen, a separately reportable amniocentesis is performed. Method is radioimmunoassay (RIA) or gas-liquid chromatography (GLC).

82627
This test may be requested as DHEA-S or DHEAS. Serum DHEA-S levels may be used to evaluate hirsutism. Elevations may be indicative of ovarian or adrenal disorders, neoplasm of the adrenal cortex, Cushing's disease, or ectopic ACTH-producing neoplasm. Decreased levels in amniotic fluid may be indicative of anencephaly. For amniotic fluid specimen, an amniocentesis is performed. Method is typically radioimmunoassay (RIA).

82633
This test may be requested as DOC. Deoxycorticosterone is a hormone produced in small quantities by the adrenal cortex. A normal circadian rise and fall in levels is noted. Method is radioimmunoassay (RIA). The test may be ordered during pregnancy for a variety of reasons, including preeclampsia.

82634
This test may be requested as Compound S. This test may be ordered to evaluate adrenocortical function. Do not confuse with metyrapone stimulation panel (see comments). Blood specimen is obtained by venipuncture. Methods include radioimmunoassay (RIA) and chromatography.

82638
This test may be requested as cholinesterase or pseudocholinesterase inhibition test. Dibucaine is used in this test as an inhibitor of cholinesterase to evaluate for unusual phenotypes with hypersensitivity to certain drugs. Individuals with these phenotypes experience apnea (cessation of breathing) when certain drugs are administered. Method is enzymatic.

82646
This test may be requested as hydrocodone quantitative analysis. Dihydrocodeinone is an opioid having sedative and analgesic effects. Methods include radioimmunoassay (RIA), gas-liquid chromatography (GLC), enzyme immunoassay (EIA), high-performance liquid chromatography (HPLC) for blood, and fluorescence polarization immunoassay (FPIA) for urine. This test measures (quantifies) the amount of dihydrocodeinone present.

82649
This test may be requested as hydromorphone or Dilaudid quantitative analysis. Dihydromorphinone is an opioid. Methods include radioimmunoassay (RIA), gas-liquid chromatography (GLC), and enzyme immunoassay (EIA).

82651
This test may be requested as DHT. Dihydroxytestosterone is a powerful androgenic hormone formed in the peripheral tissues. It is believed

to be responsible for the development of most male secondary characteristics at puberty. Method is radioimmunoassay (RIA).

82652
This test may be requested as 1,25 (OH) Vitamin D, 1,25-Dihydroxy Vitamin D, 1,25-Dihydroxycholecalciferal, and Vitamin D, 1,25-Dihydroxy. This is the most active form of Vitamin D. It is formed by the renal cells and is essential for calcium absorption. Specimen is serum or plasma, and method is radioimmunoassay (RIA) or column chromatography. This code includes fractions, if performed.

82654
This test may be requested as Methadone or Dolophine quantitative analysis. Dimethadione is an opioid. Methods include radioimmunoassay (RIA), gas-liquid chromatography (GLC), enzyme immunoassay (EIA), and high-performance liquid chromatography (HPLC).

82656
Pancreatic elastase (EL-1) is a marker for exocrine pancreatic function. The test identifies pancreatic exocrine insufficiency due to conditions such as chronic pancreatitis, gallstones, cystic fibrosis, and other conditions. A random stool sample is obtained. Method is enzyme linked immunosorbent assay (ELISA).

82657-82658
These codes report enzyme assays using a variety of different methods, some established and some relatively new. Code 82657 reports enzyme assay with nonradioactive substrate (substance upon which an enzyme acts), while 82658 reports enzyme assay with radioactive substrate.

82664
This code reports various electrophoretic techniques. Electrophoresis is a test method that uses an electrical field to move particles toward electrical poles. It separates ionic substances based on differences in their rates of migration toward the poles. Some types of electrophoresis include disc, gel, isoenzyme, and thin layer.

82666
Epiandrosterone is a steroid hormone metabolite in the androgen series that is measured for evaluation of syndromes of androgen excess such as hirsutism and polycystic ovary syndrome. It has been measured typically by methods involving extraction and chromatography, followed by detection and quantification by colorimetric or immunometric techniques. Measurement of this compound has largely been replaced by determination of other specific plasma androgens (e.g., testosterone) by modern, sensitive assays.

82668
This test may be requested as EPO or S-EPO. Erythropoietin is a hormone that regulates the production of erythrocytes (red blood cells). Method is radioimmunoassay (RIA) or chemoluminescent immunoassay.

82670
This test may be requested as unconjugated estradiol (E2). Estradiol is derived from ovaries, testes, and the placenta and is the most active endogenous estrogen. Method is radioimmunoassay (RIA).

82671
This test may be requested as fractionated estrogens. Estrogens are the female sex hormones and include estradiol, estrone, and estriol. Blood specimen is obtained by venipuncture. Method is radioimmunoassay. Fractionation involves separating total estrogen into its components.

82672
This test may be requested as total estrogen in serum or urine. Because the serum assay does not measure estriol levels, urine assay is perhaps more commonly ordered. Estrogens are the female sex hormones and include estradiol, estrone, and estriol. Method is spectroscopy or fluorometry.

82677
This test may be requested as estriol (E3). Estriol is a relatively weak estrogen, present in high concentrations during pregnancy. Low levels may be indicative of maternal complications (e.g., diabetes, preeclampsia), fetal growth retardation, or fetal anomaly (e.g., anencephaly). For amniotic fluid specimen, a separately reportable amniocentesis is performed. Method is radioimmunoassay (RIA) for serum or urine and gas-liquid chromatography (GLC) for amniotic fluid.

82679
This test may be requested as estrone (E1). Estrone is a moderately potent estrogen, derived primarily from oxidation of estradiol, but also secreted by the ovaries. For amniotic fluid specimen, a separately reportable amniocentesis is performed. Method is radioimmunoassay (RIA) for serum or urine and gas-liquid chromatography-mass spectrometry (GLC-MC) for amniotic fluid.

82690
This test may be requested as Placidyl quantitative analysis. Ethchlorvynol is a non-barbiturate sedative and hypnotic. Method is gas-liquid chromatography (GLC) or colorimetry. This test measures (quantitates) the amount of the drug present.

82693
This test may be requested as 1,2-ethanediol. Ethylene glycol is toxic substance and a component of common automotive antifreeze. The substance has a natural

sweet odor and exposure is by accidental or intentional ingestion. Methods include gas chromatography-flame ionization detection (GC-FID), liquid chromatography (LC), enzymatic assay, photometry, and fluorometry.

82696
Etiocholanolone is a steroid hormone metabolite in the androgen series that is measured for evaluation of syndromes of androgen excess such as hirsutism and polycystic ovary syndrome. It has been measured typically by methods involving extraction and chromatography, followed by detection and quantification by colorimetric or immunometric techniques. Measurement of this compound has largely been replaced by determination of other specific plasma androgens (e.g., testosterone) by modern, sensitive assays.

82705
This test is used to evaluate steatorrhea, which is an abnormal amount of fat in the stool sometimes found with celiac disease and malabsorption syndromes. This is a qualitative test that assesses the presence of fat in the stool. A random stool specimen is obtained. Method is microscopic screen.

82710
This test is used to evaluate malabsorption and steatorrhea, which is an abnormal amount of fat in the stool. This test may be requested as 24-hour, 48-hour, or 72-hour stool collection for fat analysis. A 72-hour collection period is preferred. The patient is placed on a diet containing 50-150 grams of fat/day beginning at least two days prior to testing. All stool is collected in a plastic container for the designated time period. Method is gravimetry or titrimetry.

82715
Quantitative fecal fat analysis is used in the evaluation of diarrhea and malabsorption. Differentiation of the types of fat excreted can be useful in identifying the cause of steatorrhea, such as differentiating pancreatic insufficiency from other causes of malabsorption. Generally, fecal fat is differentiated as neutral fat (triglycerides) and nonesterified fat (free fatty acids), but it may be more specifically differentiated as long or short chain fatty acids, and may include cholesterol analysis. Methods used for analysis include differential extraction with gravimetric quantification, enzymatic analysis of fecal extracts, or chromatography.

82725
This test may be requested as nonesterified fatty acids (NEFA) or free fatty acids (FFA). Method is colorimetry, spectrophotometry, or enzymatic.

82726
Very long chain fatty acid levels are elevated in certain demyelinating diseases such as adrenoleukodystrophy and adrenomyeloneuropathy, and in several paroxysmal disorders including Zellweger syndrome and infantile Refsum's disease. Skin fibroblasts may be obtained by scraping. Methods include new techniques such as capillary gas chromatography, mass spectrometry, and stable isotope dilution.

82728
Serum ferritin level measures available iron stores and is a reliable indicator of normal, as well as deficient, levels. Blood specimen is obtained by venipuncture. Method is radioimmunoassay (RIA), immunoradiometric assay (IRMA), enzyme immunoassay (EIA), or enzyme linked immunosorbent assay (ELISA).

82731
Fibronectin is an adhesive glycoprotein. The presence of fetal fibronectin in cervicovaginal secretions is an indicator that a pregnant woman will soon go into labor, and it is tested for the purpose of predicting premature labor. Rapid enzyme-linked immunosorbent assay (ELISA) tests are available to perform the assay on cervical swab specimens. The test is a semi-quantitative (positive or negative) test.

82735
Fluoride is available as hydrogen fluoride and its organic salts. These salts are used in industry and as components of insecticides. Fluoride is also given as a dietary supplement in areas where it is not available in drinking water. However, fluoride is toxic in excessive quantities. This test is performed to evaluate fluoride toxicity. Method is fluoride specific electrode, ion-selective potentiometry, or gas-liquid chromatography (GLC).

82742
This test may be requested as Dalmane, quantitative analysis. Flurazepam is a benzodiazepine with sedative and hypnotic effects. Method is gas chromatography (GC), gas chromatography-mass spectrometry (GC-MS), high performance liquid chromatography (HPLC), or thin layer chromatography (TLC). This test measures (quantitates) the amount of the drug present.

82746
This test may be requested as serum folate. This test is used to detect folic acid deficiency. Folic acid is a B vitamin necessary for normal red blood cell production. It is stored in the body as folates. Folic acid deficiency results in a form of megaloblastic anemia. Method is competitive binding protein (CPB) radioimmunoassay, chemiluminescence, or microbiological assay.

82747
This test may be requested as RBC folate or red cell folate. It is used to detect folic acid deficiency. Folic acid is a B vitamin necessary for normal red blood cell production. It is stored in the body as folates. Folic acid deficiency results in a form of megaloblastic anemia. Method is radioimmunoassay (RIA), competitive binding protein (CPB) radioimmunoassay, or chemiluminescence.

82757
This test may be requested as levulose analysis. Fructose is normally present in semen, but may be absent with some congenital anomalies of the male genital tract. A semen specimen is obtained. Method is colorimetry.

82759
Galactokinase is an enzyme necessary for galactose utilization. This test evaluates galactosemia resulting from galactokinase deficiency. Method is radioisotope.

82760
Galactose levels are normally measured shortly after a galactose-rich meal or a glass of milk. Galactose is derived from dietary lactose. It appears in urine when lactose is not converted to glucose due to an inherited enzyme deficiency. This test is performed on blood or urine after ingestion of a galactose-rich meal. Multiple specimens may be required for a galactose tolerance test. Method is enzymatic.

82775-82776
These tests may be requested as UDP-G-1-P. Galactose-1-phosphate uridyl transferase is an enzyme necessary for utilization of galactose. This test is performed to identify deficiency in this enzyme. Method is radiometric or uridine diphosphoglucose (UDPG) consumption assay. Report 82775 when enzyme levels are measured (quantitated). Report 82776 when screening only for the presence (qualitative analysis) of the enzyme.

82784
This test may be requested as immunoglobulin, IgA, IgD, IgG, or IgM. Immunoglobulins are in the group of proteins classified as antibodies. Immunoglobulins are produced in response to foreign proteins referred to antigens. IgG is the most abundant immunoglobulin. It is produced in response to secondary exposure to viral and bacterial antigens. IgA is found primarily in the respiratory, gastrointestinal, and genitourinary tracts, as well as in tears and saliva. It is responsible for protecting the mucous membranes from viral and bacterial antigens. Congenital IgA deficiency is also associated with autoimmune disease. IgM is produced following primary exposure to an antigen and is active against rheumatoid factors, gram-negative organisms, and the ABO blood group. IgD properties are not well understood but increases with chronic infection, connective tissue disorders, and some liver disease. Serum immunoglobulins may be tested for the four types (IgA, IgD, IgG, and IgM) reported with this code. Saliva may be tested for IgA. CSF may be tested for IgA, IgD, IgG, and IgM. CSF is obtained by spinal puncture, which is reported separately. Method is dependent on specimen source and specific immunoglobulins being tested. Serum is usually analyzed using radial immunodiffusion (RID), enzyme linked immunosorbent assay (ELISA), nephelometry, or turbidimetry. Urine uses electroimmunodiffusion (EID). Saliva uses radial immunodiffusion (RID). CSF is analyzed with radioimmunoassay (RIA).

82785
This test may be requested as immunoglobulin, IgE. Immunoglobulins are in the group of proteins classified as antibodies. Immunoglobulins are produced in response to foreign proteins referred to as antigens. IgE is produced in response to allergic reactions and anaphylaxis. CSF is obtained by spinal puncture, which is reported separately. Method is radioimmunoassay (RIA). Paper radioimmunosorbent test may also be used for serum specimen only.

82787
This test may be requested as immunoglobulin subclasses or IgG subclasses. There are four IgG subclasses, which are designated as IgG1, IgG2, IgG3, and IgG4. IgG is part of the body's defense system against infection. Deficiencies of single subclasses, particularly IgG1, can significantly impair this defense. Blood specimen is obtained by venipuncture. Method is radial immunodiffusion (RID), enzyme linked immunosorbent assay (ELISA), nephelometry, or turbidimetry.

82800
This test may be requested as blood pH. Blood pH is tested to identify acidemia or alkalemia. Arterial puncture is preferred, but venipuncture may also be performed. Method is glass pH electrode or potentiometry.

82803-82805
These tests may be requested as arterial blood gases (ABGs). Blood gases are usually requested to evaluate disturbances of acid-base balance, which may be caused by respiratory or metabolic disorders. Blood specimen is obtained by arterial puncture. Code 82803 reports any combination of pH, pCO2, pO2, CO2, and HCO3, including calculated O2 saturation. Code 82805 reports any combination of the same gases, but O2 saturation is performed by direct measurement. Method is selective electrode, potentiometry, or spectrophotometry (O2 saturation).

82810
This test may be requested as O2. Oxygen saturation is the percent of the oxygen in the blood that combines with hemoglobin. Blood specimen is obtained by arterial puncture. Method is spectrophotometry.

82820
This test may be requested as oxygen, P50 or as pO2, P50. This test is performed to measure the affinity of hemoglobin for oxygen, which allows evaluation of oxygen delivery to body tissues. Blood specimen is obtained by arterial puncture. Method is spectrophotometry or potentiometry.

82926-82928
These tests may be requested as hydrochloric acid (HCl) analysis. This code reports chemical analysis of gastric acid obtained by gastric intubation and aspiration. Chemical analysis evaluates free (unbound) HCl and total (bound and unbound) HCl. Report 82926 for analysis of free AND total gastric acid. Report 82928 for analysis of free OR total gastric acid.

82938
Gastrin stimulation test with secretin may be performed to evaluate patients with suspected gastrinoma and Zollinger-Ellison syndrome. Blood specimen is obtained prior to secretin injection and at five-minute to 15-minute intervals over the next 30 to 60 minutes. Method is radioimmunoassay (RIA).

82941
Gastrin, produced by G cells in the antrum of the stomach, stimulates production of gastric acid. Gastrin may be measured to evaluate patients with suspected gastrinoma and Zollinger-Ellison syndrome. Method is radioimmunoassay (RIA).

82943
Glucagon is a hormone secreted by the pancreas. It stimulates the conversion of glycogen stored in the liver to glucose. Glucagon levels may be requested to evaluate suspected diabetes mellitus or glucagonoma. Method is radioimmunoassay (RIA).

82945
Glucose is the end product of carbohydrate metabolism, providing energy for living organisms. It is found in body fluids including joint fluid and CSF. Both elevated and decreased levels of glucose may be indicative of disease processes. Joint fluid specimen is obtained by separately reportable arthrocentesis. CSF specimen is obtained by separately reportable spinal puncture. Method is enzymatic.

82946
Glucagon is a hormone secreted by the pancreas. It stimulates the conversion of glycogen stored in the liver to glucose. Glucagon tolerance test may be requested to evaluate suspected diabetes mellitus or glucagonoma. A fasting glucagon level is obtained. A high carbohydrate meal or an oral dose of glucose is given. Glucagon levels are tested at 30, 60, and 120-minute intervals. Method is radioimmunoassay (RIA).

82947
This test may be requested as a fasting blood sugar (FBS). This quantitative test is used to evaluate disorders of carbohydrate metabolism. The patient has ordinarily fasted for eight hours. Method is enzymatic.

82948
This test is used to monitor disorders of carbohydrate metabolism. Blood specimen is obtained by finger stick. A drop of blood is placed on the reagent strip for a specified amount of time. When the prescribed amount of time has elapsed, the strip is blotted and the reagent strip is compared to a color chart. Method is reagent strip with visual comparison.

82950
This test may also be requested as glucose, postprandial (PP). This test is used to monitor disorders of carbohydrate metabolism. The patient consumes a high carbohydrate meal or an oral glucose solution. Blood glucose levels are checked two hours after the meal or glucose solution. A one-hour postprandial screen may be used to evaluate pregnant women for gestational diabetes mellitus. Method of testing varies.

82951-82952
These tests may be requested as GTT, oral GTT, OGTT, intravenous GTT, or IVGTT. This test is used to monitor disorders of carbohydrate metabolism. This test is normally performed using an oral dose of glucose, but may also be performed using intravenous glucose. A blood specimen is obtained prior to glucose administration and at intervals following glucose administration. Code 82951 reports three specimens. Each additional specimen beyond three is reported with 82952. Method of testing varies.

82953
This test may be requested as a tolbutamide tolerance test. It is used to evaluate pancreatic tumor and functional hypoglycemia. Baseline glucose and insulin levels are obtained. Tolbutamide is administered intravenously. Glucose and insulin levels are obtained at 3, 30, 60, 90, 120, and 180 minutes following the tolbutamide administration.

82955-82960
These tests may be requested as G6PD quantitative or G6PD screen. This test is used to identify genetic G6PD deficiency, which causes hemolytic anemia after ingestion of certain drugs and foods and may also cause hemolytic disease of the newborn (HDN). Blood specimen is obtained by venipuncture. Method is methemoglobin reduction (Brewer's test), modified Bishop (ultraviolet), dye reduction, or ascorbic or fluorescent spot tests. Code 82955 is used to report measurement of amount (quantitation) of G6PD in erythrocytes, while 82960 reports screening (qualitative analysis) for the presence of G6PD only.

82962
This test is used to monitor disorders of carbohydrate metabolism. This test reports blood glucose monitoring by an FDA-approved device. While the code states that it is for home use, these devices may also be used in the physician office. Blood is obtained by finger stick. Method is enzymatic, electrochemical, or spectrophotometry by small portable device designed for home glucose testing.

82963
Deficiencies of this enzyme occur in metabolic disorders, particularly Gaucher disease. The enzyme is increased following liver ischemic injury, making it favorable to monitor serum levels for this condition. Blood specimen is obtained by venipuncture. Tissue is obtained by surgical excision or biopsy, reported separately. It can be measured by enzymatic methods using spectrophotometry.

82965
This test may be abbreviated as GLD or GLDH. GLD is an enzyme found primarily in the liver, but also in erythrocytes. GLD may be requested to evaluate liver and biliary disease as well as Reye's syndrome. Blood specimen is obtained by venipuncture. Method is spectrophotometry.

82975
This test may be abbreviated as Gln. Glutamine is an amino acid and is the most abundant amino acid found in CSF. This test may used to evaluate hepatic encephalopathy, Reye's syndrome, meningitis, rheumatoid arthritis, and other conditions. Specimen types vary. CSF obtained by spinal puncture is reported separately. Method is ion-exchange chromatography or colorimetry.

82977
This test may be requested as GGT or glutamyl transpeptidase. GGT is an enzyme. This test may be used to evaluate liver disease in children or as a screening test for alcoholism. Method is radioimmunoassay (RIA).

82978
Glutathione is a red blood cell tripeptide whose synthesis is generated by two enzymes. It is normally present in blood and serves an important role in protecting red blood cells against oxidant stress produced during infections and by certain drugs. A deficiency of glutathione is commonly associated with hemolytic anemia. Literature on methodology is somewhat unclear, but cyanide-ascorbate may be among the approaches.

82979
Glutathione reductase is an enzyme. This test may be performed to evaluate riboflavin deficiency or G6PD deficiency. Method is enzymatic or spectrophotometry.

82980
This test may be requested as Doriden level. Glutethimide is a nonbarbiturate similar to phenobarbital and used as a sedative and hypnotic. Method is gas-liquid chromatography (GLC), high performance liquid chromatography (HPLC), or gas chromatography-mass spectrometry (GC-MS). The test measures (quantifies) the amount of the drug.

82985
This test may be requested as serum fructosamine test. It is used to assess the level of blood glucose control in the recent past. It is useful in evaluating patient compliance and the accuracy of the patient's blood glucose self-monitoring. Blood specimen is obtained by venipuncture. Method is colorimetry, nitroblue tetrazolium (NBT).

83001
This test may be requested as FSH or follitropin. FSH is a gonadotropic hormone produced by the pituitary gland. It stimulates growth and maturation of the ovarian follicle in females and promotes spermatogenesis in males. This test may be requested in an infertility work-up. Method is immunoassay.

83002
This test may be requested as LH, lutropin, or interstitial cell-stimulating hormone (ICSH). LH is a gonadotropic hormone secreted by the pituitary gland. LH required for ovulation in females and stimulates testosterone production in males. LH may be ordered as part of an infertility work-up. Method is immunoassay.

83003
This test may be requested as GH, HGH, or somatotropin. This test may be used to evaluate pituitary gigantism or dwarfism, acromegaly, hypopituitarism, adrenocortical hyperfunction, fetal anencephaly (amniotic fluid analysis), as well as other conditions. Amniotic fluid sample is obtained by amniocentesis, which is reported separately. Method is radioimmunoassay.

83008
Cyclic guanosine monophosphate (cGMP) is a so-called "messenger" nucleotide, important in cell function. Levels have been measured in the evaluation of calcium metabolism disorders, including pseudohypoparathyroidism, and in certain other endocrine disorders. The most common method reported in the literature is radioimmunoassay.

83009
The urease activity blood test is a noninvasive method of diagnosing a *Helicobacter pylori* infection of the stomach. The patient swallows a pill or drinks a solution containing the chemical urea, labeled with the nonradioactive isotope C-13. The bacteria will produce an enzyme that breaks down the urea into ammonia and carbon dioxide gas, if they are present. The gas contains the tagged carbon and is quickly absorbed into the bloodstream and later expelled in the breath. A blood sample is taken 30 minutes after ingesting the radiolabeled urea. Urease activity produced by the bacteria, when present, will be made manifest in the blood sample by the presence of tagged carbon molecules. Analysis is done by gas isotope ratio mass spectrometry.

83010
This test may be requested as Hp, HPT, hemoglobin-binding protein. Method is turbidimetry or nephelometry. This procedure measures (quantifies) the amount of haptoglobin present in serum. Haptoglobin is a plasma glycoprotein. Haptoglobin prevents loss of free hemoglobin in the blood by binding with it and removing it to the liver. This test may be indicated to evaluate anemia or other indicators of hemolysis, pregnancy induced hypertension, transfusion reactions, as well as other conditions.

83012
This test may be requested as Hp phenotype, HPT phenotype, or hemoglobin-binding protein phenotype. Haptoglobin is a plasma glycoprotein. Method is turbidimetry or nephelometry. Haptoglobin prevents loss of free hemoglobin in the blood by binding with it and removing it to the liver. There are three common phenotypes, Hp 1-1, Hp 2-1, Hp 2-2. Hp 1-1 is a monomer, while Hp 2-1 and Hp 2-2 are polymers with much greater molecular weights. This is important in evaluating nephritic syndrome because Hp 1-1 is excreted resulting in a decreased haptoglobin level, while Hp 2-1 and Hp 2-2 are retained resulting in an increase. Method is turbidimetry or nephelometry.

83013-83014
Helicobacter pylori (H. pylori), formerly referred to as Campylobacter pylori, is a gram-negative microaerophilic bacteria that causes gastritis and pyloric ulcers. Testing for H. pylori used to require a gastric or duodenal biopsy; however, these bacteria can now be identified using a simple breath test. The patient swallows a pill or drinks a solution containing the chemical, urea, labeled with a stable, nonradioactive isotope, C-13. The bacteria will produce an enzyme that breaks down the urea into ammonia and carbon dioxide gas if they are present. The gas contains the tagged carbon and is quickly absorbed into the bloodstream and expelled in the breath. Breath samples are taken six, 12, and 20 minutes after swallowing the pill. Urease activity produced by the bacteria is detected in the breath samples collected by the presence of exhaled tagged carbon molecules. Analysis is done in a pathology laboratory using a mass spectrometer. Report 83013 for the breath test analysis and 83014 for the isotope administration and sample collection.

83015
This test may be requested as a toxic metal or poisonous metal screen. Method is atomic absorption spectrometry (AAS), colorimetry, or neutron activation analysis (NAA). This test reports screening only (qualitative analysis) to detect and identify the presence of heavy metals.

83018
This test may be requested as a toxic metal or poisonous metal quantitation. Method is atomic absorption spectrometry (AAS), colorimetry, or neutron activation analysis (NAA). This test measures (quantifies) of the amount of each single metal present. Each metal quantified is reported separately.

83020
This test may be requested as Hb electrophoresis. This test uses electrophoresis to test for several hemoglobin variants. It is used to identify the different types of hemoglobin present in the blood and measure (quantify) the amounts of each. The normal types of hemoglobin are Hb A1, Hb A2, and Hb F (fetal). When Hb F exceeds five percent of total hemoglobin after age 6 months, it may be an indicator of thalassemia. Increased amounts of Hb A2 may also indicate thalassemia. Abnormal variants, which can be identified by electrophoresis, include Hb S and Hb C. Hb S is the most common hemoglobin variant and is indicative of sickle cell anemia. Hb C is indicative of hemolytic anemia.

83021
This test may be requested as Hb chromatography. This test uses chromatography to test for several hemoglobin variants. It is used to identify the different types of hemoglobin present in the blood and measure (quantify) the amounts of each. The normal types of hemoglobin are Hb A1, Hb A2, and Hb F (fetal). When Hb F exceeds five percent of total hemoglobin after age 6 months, it may be an indicator of thalassemia. Increased amounts of Hb A2 may also indicate thalassemia. Abnormal variants, which can be identified by electrophoresis, include Hb S and Hb C. Hb S is the most common hemoglobin variant and is indicative of sickle cell anemia. Hb C is indicative of hemolytic anemia.

83026
The copper sulfate method for measuring hemoglobin is performed by placing a drop of blood into each of a series of containers containing copper sulfate solutions of varying specific gravity. If the drop sinks, the blood has greater specific gravity than the copper sulfate solution. The specific gravity of whole blood strongly correlates to the hemoglobin concentration, so the hemoglobin concentration may be accurately estimated. Specimen collection is by venipuncture.

83030
This is also known as Hb F. Hemoglobin F is the normal hemoglobin of the fetus. Most Hb F is replaced by hemoglobin A in the first days after birth. Hb F has an increased capacity to carry oxygen and is present in increased amounts in some pathologic conditions, including sickle cell anemia, aplastic anemia, and leukemia. Small amounts are produced throughout life.

83033
Hemoglobin F (Hb F) is the normal hemoglobin of the term fetus. Most Hb F is replaced by hemoglobin A in the first days after birth. Elevated levels after age 6

months may be indicative of a blood disorder. Hb F has an increased capacity to carry oxygen and the test is also useful in determining whether bleeding disorders may have occurred preterm. Method for blood specimen is electrophoresis. Method for stool specimen may be by alkali denaturation visual screening. Hemoglobin F is alkali resistant. The procedure is used to examine fresh "red" blood taken from a fresh stool sample.

83036-83037
These tests may also be known as HbA1C. A blood specimen is collected. Glycosylated hemoglobin levels reflect the average level of glucose in the blood over a three-month period. Methods may include high-performance liquid chromatography and ion exchange chromatography (83036) or FDA approved home monitoring device (83037).

83045
This test is performed after the onset of symptoms to detect the presence of the derivative methemoglobin in hemoglobin. This derivative occurs when the iron in hemoglobin is changed to different state due to certain compounds introduced into the blood stream (e.g., sulfonamides, chlorates, nitrates, nitrites, aniline). This is a qualitative test to determine the presence of methemoglobin. Method is typically co-oximetry (spectrophotometry).

83050
This test is performed after the onset of symptoms to detect and measure (quantitative) the percentage of total hemoglobin containing the derivative methemoglobin. This derivative occurs when the iron in hemoglobin is changed to a different state due to certain compounds introduced into the blood stream (e.g., sulfonamides, chlorates, nitrates, nitrites, aniline, and phenacetin). Methods may include co-oximetry (spectrophotometry).

83051
This test evaluates hemolytic anemia, especially intravascular hemolysis. Plasma hemoglobin is increased with intravascular hemolysis, ABO incompatible transfusion, traumatic hemolysis, falciparum malaria, burns, and other conditions. Increase may occur in some cases of extravascular hemolysis, delayed transfusion reaction, slight increase in sickle cell anemia, and ß-thalassemia. One method of testing is spectrophotometry.

83055
This test is performed after the onset of symptoms to detect the presence of the derivative sulfhemoglobin in hemoglobin. Method is co-oximetry (spectrophotometry). The derivative occurs when certain compounds (e.g., phenacetin or sulfonamides) bind with hemoglobin. The hemoglobin is no longer able to transport oxygen. The condition is untreatable, except to wait until the affected red bloods are destroyed in their normal life cycle.

83060
This test is performed after the onset of symptoms to measure (quantitative) the percentage of total hemoglobin containing the derivative sulfhemoglobin. Method is co-oximetry (spectrophotometry). The derivative occurs when certain compounds (e.g., phenacetin or sulfonamides) bind with hemoglobin.

83065
This is also known as the unstable hemoglobin heat denaturation test. Unstable hemoglobin is a chronic fall in the stable baseline of hemoglobin. Method is by heat denaturation. This test changes the physical properties of the globin (the protein constituent of hemoglobin) and the results in the subsequent loss of its biological activity.

83068
This test screens for unstable hemoglobin (a fall in the stable baseline of hemoglobin). Method is to test the stability of the hemoglobin is checked against isopropanol hemoglobin prep solubility. Falling—or unstable hemoglobin—levels may indicate viral or bacterial infections or, in severe cases, there may be evidence of hepatic dysfunction and renal insufficiency due to anemia. Evaluation and treatment depends on changes in the hematologic levels from baseline and symptoms, rather than absolute values that are stable.

83069
Method is spectrophotometry. It tests the presence of hemoglobin in the urine without the concurrent presence of red blood cells. Hemoglobin appears in urine only when levels in the blood are higher than the amount that can be reclaimed by the protein haptoglobin. Hemoglobin detected in the urine may indicate hemolytic anemia, or the hemolysis that can result from a transfusion reaction or other process.

83070
This test is performed to detect the presence (qualitative) of hemosiderin. Methods may include slide preparation and stain for microscopic examination. A sample from a morning collection of urine is preferable. Hemosiderin is an iron containing pigment derived from hemoglobin. The presence of hemosiderin may indicate immune hemolytic anemia secondary to drugs (e.g., penicillins, cephalosporins, levodopa, methyldopa, quinidine, and sulfonamides).

83071
This test is performed to quantify the presence of hemosiderin. Specimen collection is by random urine sample. A sample from a morning collection of urine is preferred. Hemosiderin is an iron containing pigment derived from hemoglobin. The presence of hemosiderin may indicate immune hemolytic anemia secondary to drugs (e.g., penicillins, cephalosporins, levodopa, methyldopa, quinidine, and sulfonamides).

83080
The test may be performed to detect the deficiency of hexosaminidase. Specimen collection is by venipuncture; if female, patient should not be pregnant. Methods may include chromatography, and automated heat inactivation/fluorometry. Levels of hexosaminidase can identify patients and carriers of Tay-Sachs disease. This genetic disorder results in degeneration of the central nervous system.

83088
This test detects the presence and measures the levels of histamine. Method may be radioimmunoassay for blood or urine. Histamine is stored in mast cells and basophils and is released from cells in the tissues upon injury, causing local inflammation. Histamine also plays a part in controlling gastric secretions, smooth muscle control, cardiac stimulation, stimulation of sensory nerve endings and alertness. Certain medications may result in an excess of histamine in the blood stream, producing sedation, weight gain, and hypotension.

83090
This test may be requested as total homocysteine (tHcy). The presence of homocysteine in urine or blood may be indicative of metabolic disorders. More recently, plasma homocysteine has been identified as a possible predictor for cardiovascular disease with risk increasing progressively with homocystine concentration. This code reports quantitative analysis of homocysteine levels. Method is high performance liquid chromatography (HPLC), ion exchange chromatography, or spectrophotometry.

83150
This test is performed for the analysis of catecholamines or catecholamine metabolites homovanillic acid (HVA). Specimen collection is random or 24-hour urine test. Method may be high performance liquid chromatography. The test is performed to assist in diagnosing and monitoring pheochromocytoma or neuroblastoma. Catecholamines are produced by a part of the adrenal gland and metabolized to inactive substances excreted in the urine. They are also the main metabolites of neuroblastomas.

83491
This test is used to measure the cortisol metabolites (17-OCHS) for assessing adrenocortical function. Specimen collection is by 24-hour urine sample. A 24-hour test is necessary due to variations in cortisol metabolite excretion. Method is commonly Porter-Silber. Low levels of 17-OCHS indicate hyposecretion of glucocorticoids that can result in Addison's disease (primary adrenal insufficiency). Elevated levels of 17-OCHS indicate hypersecretion of glucocorticoids, especially cortisol and cortisone, which can result in a condition called Cushing's syndrome.

83497
This test may be performed to measure the levels of 5-HIAA for detecting and following the clinical course of patients with carcinoid tumors. Specimen collection is urine, collected over a 24-hour period. Method is high performance liquid chromatography. These tumors contain enteroendocrine cells that secrete stomach gastrin, a secretory hormone released upon nerve impulse. Neurohormones, such as gastrin, are metabolized by the liver and excreted in the urine. Rising levels of 5-HIAA may indicate a tumor is progressing; falling levels of 5-HIAA may indicate that a tumor is responding to antineoplastic therapy. This test measures (quantifies) the level of 5-HIAA present in the specimen.

83498
This test may also be known as 17-OHP. Methodology may involve radioimmunoassay. This test is performed to diagnose and manage certain metabolic diseases. Insufficient amounts of hydroxyprogesterone can block the synthesis of cortisol, resulting in conditions such as adrenal hyperplasia, hirsutism (excessive body and facial hair, especially in women), and infertility.

83499
20-hydroxyprogesterone is a weakly active metabolite of progesterone with progestational activity. Levels have been measured in evaluation of ovulation, and gestagenic activity during the menstrual cycle and pregnancy. Typical methodology is column separation (chromatography) with radioimmunoassay detection.

83500
This test may also be known by the abbreviation Hyp. Specimen collection is by venipuncture for serum or plasma; separately reportable lumbar puncture for CSF; or a 24-hour urine specimen. Methods may include high performance liquid chromatography, ion-exchange chromatography, and colorimetry. This test detects the presence of free hydroxyproline, due to a defect in the enzyme hydroxyproline oxidase. A defect in the enzyme carried by both parent results in hyperhydroxyprolinemia. This condition has no effect on collagen metabolism.

83505
This test is performed to detect the percentage of total hydroxyproline. Methods may include high performance liquid chromatography and colorimetry. This test may be useful in measuring response to therapy in Paget's disease.

83516-83518
Immunoassay uses highly specific antigen to antibody binding to identify specific chemical substances. This code reports a number of immunoassay techniques for identifying analytes (chemical substances) that are not specifically identified elsewhere, excluding infectious agent antibody or infectious agent antigen. More specific methods reported with these codes include

enzyme immunoassay (EIA) and fluoroimmunoassay (FIA). This test identifies (qualitative analysis) the substance or roughly measures (semi-quantitative analysis) the amount of the substance. Code 83516 reports multiple step method, while 83518 reports single step method.

83519
Immunoassay uses highly specific antigen to antibody binding to identify specific chemical substances. This code reports measurement (quantitative analysis) using radioimmunoassay (RIA) technique for identifying analytes (chemical substances) that are not specifically identified elsewhere, excluding infectious agent antibody or infectious agent antigen.

83520
Immunoassay uses highly specific antigen to antibody binding to identify specific chemical substances. This code reports measurement (quantitative analysis) using a technique other than radioimmunoassay (RIA) for identifying analytes (chemical substances) that are not specifically identified elsewhere, excluding infectious agent antibody or infectious agent antigen.

83525
This test measures total insulin, which includes both the protein bound and free hormone present in the blood. Method is radioimmunoassay (RIA). This test is used to evaluate hypoglycemia, which may be caused by insulin producing neoplasm or islet cell hyperplasia.

83527
This test measures free insulin. Free insulin may also be referred to as active or unbound insulin. A fasting blood specimen is obtained by venipuncture. Method is radioimmunoassay. In rare instances, the level of total insulin (protein bound and unbound) may be normal or elevated when free insulin is actually low.

83528
Intrinsic factor (IF) is a glycoprotein secreted by the gastric glands and necessary for the absorption of vitamin B12. Method is guinea pig intestinal mucosal homogenate (GPIMH) or radioassay. Indications are that this test is not frequently performed.

83540
This test may be requested as Fe. Iron is an essential constituent of hemoglobin, which is present in foods and absorbed through the small bowel (duodenum and jejunum). Method is colorimetry or atomic absorption spectrophotometry. This test is often used in combination with other tests to evaluate anemia, acute leukemia, lead poisoning, acute hepatitis, and vitamin B6 deficiency. It is also used to evaluate iron poisoning caused by accidental overdose (children) or excessive use of supplements.

83550
This test may be abbreviated as TIBC. Iron is an essential constituent of hemoglobin, which is present in foods and absorbed through the small bowel (duodenum and jejunum). Method is colorimetry or atomic absorption spectrophotometry. TIBC measures the total amount of iron capable of binding to the protein transferrin. This test is often used in combination with other tests to evaluate anemia, various neoplasms, acute hepatitis and other liver disease, hemochromatosis, thalassemia, and renal disease.

83570
This test may be abbreviated as ICD or IDH. CSF is obtained by spinal puncture, which is reported separately. Method is enzymatic or colorimetry. Isocitrate dehydrogenase is an enzyme. Elevated serum or plasma levels may indicate hepatitis, malignant neoplasm metastatic to liver, or other liver disease. Elevated CSF levels may indicate acute bacterial meningitis, vascular lesions of the brain, or malignant neoplasms of the cerebrospinal system.

83582
This test is may be referred to as a 17-KGS. Urine specimen collection is performed over a 24-hour period. Method is Norymberski reaction, which is the Zimmerman color reaction after treatment with a strong oxidizing agent (e.g., periodate, bismuthite). This test is used to assess for increased adrenal function as in Cushing's Syndrome, stress, and some cases of adrenogenital syndrome, or decreased adrenal function as with Addison's disease and hypopituitarism. It measures 17-ketosteroids (KS) after cortols, cortolones, pregnanetriol, and 17-OHCS are oxidized to 17-KS. 17-KS are metabolites of the androgenic sex hormones (i.e., testosterone) that are secreted from the adrenal cortex and testes.

83586
This test is may be ordered as 17-KS. Urine specimen collection is performed over a 24-hour period. Method is Zimmerman reaction, which is colorimetry after extractions. This test is used to assess for adrenal androgens. The 17-ketosteroids (KS) may be elevated in Cushing's Syndrome, some adrenal and gonadal tumors, pregnancy, and female pseudohermaphrodism. The 17-KS are metabolites of the androgenic sex hormones (i.e., testosterone) secreted from the adrenal cortex and testes. This test does not detect major androgens, testosterone, and dihydrotestosterone.

83593
This test may be ordered as 17-KS fractionation. Urine specimen collection is performed over a 24-hour period. Method is column chromatography or gas-liquid chromatography (GLC). This test is for the quantitation of androsterone, etiocholanolone, and dehydroepiandrosterone (DHEA), the three major metabolites in the urine. It evaluates the presence of adrenal and gonadal abnormalities.

83605
This test is used to assess lactic blood levels to document the presence of tissue hypoxia, determine the degree of hypoxia, and monitor the effect of therapy in blood, plasma, or cerebrospinal fluid (CSF). Specimen collection is CSF from a spinal puncture or arterial or venous blood. Hand clenching and the use of a tourniquet should be avoided to prevent the build-up of potassium and lactic acid. Method is enzymatic or gas chromatography (GS). This test may be used to determine lactic acidosis when unaccountable anion gap metabolic acidosis is detected.

83615
This test may also be ordered as LD or LDH. The test is a measure of LD or LDH, which is found in many body tissues, particularly the heart, liver, red blood cells, and kidneys. Methods used are lactate to pyruvate or pyruvate to lactate. This test may be ordered for a wide variety of disorders, including renal diseases and congestive heart failure.

83625
This test may be ordered as LDH isoenzymes or LD isoenzymes. Three serial blood specimens are collected at 6-8 hour intervals to detect changes in the LD isoenzymes. Shifts in the values of five clinically significant LD fractions monitored over time create diagnostic patterns that correlate with diseases such as myocardial infarction, renal infarction and hepatic congestion. This allows for the differential diagnosis of numerous conditions. Method is by electrophoresis or immunochemical methods, including immunoprecipitation. This test may be ordered for a wide variety of reasons, and results may point to numerous diagnoses.

83630-83631
Lactoferrin in feces is a marker for intestinal inflammation in patients with abdominal pain and/or diarrhea. It aids in discrimination and monitoring progression of inflammatory bowel disease. Lactoferrin is produced by white blood cells in the intestines. A random stool sample is obtained and preserved in enteric transport media. Method is enzyme-linked immunosorbent assay (ELISA). Report 83630 for a qualitative study and 83631 for a quantitative study.

83632
This test may be called maternal serum hPL. Specimen collection is obtained by venipuncture. Method used is radioimmunoassay (RIA) or turbidimetric latex immunoassay. This test may be used to evaluate antepartum placental function and fetal health. It is also used as an indicator of intrauterine growth retardation in twin pregnancy, evaluation of placental function, and may be used to assess gestational age. Other uses are in detecting non-germ cell neoplasms.

83633
This is a diagnostic urine test to identify the presence of lactase in the small intestine. When there are high levels of lactose in the gut, lactose is absorbed and excreted in the urine. It is an indicator of lactose intolerance or intestinal disease. Method is gas chromatography. The absence of lactose implies a decrease in calcium absorption.

83634
This is a diagnostic urine test to extract and quantify (measure) the presence of lactose. Specimen collection is by random urine sample. Method may be by gas chromatography. The absence of lactose implies a decrease in calcium absorption.

83655
This test may be ordered using Pb, the chemical abbreviation for lead. A whole blood test may be used to identify more recent lead exposures; the urine test is used to determine lead body burden, rather than to diagnose lead poisoning. In some instances, serum, hair samples, or bronchoalveolar lavage fluids may be tested. Specimen collection for urine is usually a 24-hour collection. Method used is source dependent, but commonly electrothermal atomic absorption spectrometry (AAS). Bronchoalveolar lavage specimens may be tested by x-ray fluorescence spectrometry.

83661
Specimen collection is by amniocentesis, but amniotic fluid may be collected vaginally after rupture of the amniotic membrane. This test determines fetal pulmonary maturation and may be an indicator for the possibility of development of respiratory distress syndrome (RDS). Method used is thin-layer chromatography (TLC) and a 1D or 2D approach may be specified.

83662
This test may also be ordered as pulmonary surfactant or the "shake test." Specimen collection is by amniocentesis. Method involves diluting amniotic fluid with ethanol and shaking the specimen. This test indicates fetal pulmonary maturation and newborn risk for respiratory distress syndrome. The test may also be useful in managing other conditions in both mother and fetus during late stages of pregnancy.

83663
Specimen collection is by amniocentesis. The amniotic fluid is analyzed by fluorescent polarization (FPOL). A fluorescent phospholipid analogue is added to amniotic fluid and its fluorescence polarization is measured using a fluorescence polarimeter. The presence of increased amounts of surfactant indicating increased lung maturity result in lower polarization levels. Therefore, polarization values decrease during gestation in conjunction with maturation of the pulmonary surfactant system. This test indicates fetal

pulmonary maturation and newborn risk for respiratory distress syndrome.

83664
Specimen collection is by amniocentesis. Lamellar body density is calculated by measuring the number of surfactant containing particles per microliter of amniotic fluid. Method is automated cell count. This test indicates fetal pulmonary maturation and newborn risk for respiratory distress syndrome.

83670
This test may also be ordered as LAP or leucyl aminopeptidase. Methods are commonly colorimetry, fluorometry, and enzyme assay. The test is commonly used to measure biliary excretory function for differential diagnoses of liver and pancreatic disorders.

83690
This test may also be called triacylglycerol acylhydrolase. Method is often by turbidimetric, a specialized processor. The test is used generally to indicate pancreatic, hepatic duct, and renal disorders.

83695
This test may also be requested as Lp (a). Lipoprotein (a) is a low-density lipoprotein associated with clot formation, hardening and narrowing of the arteries. The patient is instructed to fast for 12 hours prior to this test. A blood specimen is obtained through venipuncture. Lipoprotein (a) is measured using an enzyme-linked immunosorbent assay (ELISA).

83698
This test is also ordered as a PLAC. The test measures an enzyme called lipoprotein-associated phospholipase A2. Persons at risk for heart disease or stroke may have higher levels of this enzyme. The specimen is blood serum or plasma. The PLAC test is typically a microplate-based enzyme-linked sandwich immunosorbent assay. The test is a component of clinical risk assessment for coronary artery disease and ischemic stroke associated with atherosclerosis.

83700
Lipoproteins are comprised of subclasses of lipoprotein particles. These subclasses are of different sizes, lipid and apolipoprotein composition, and function. Elevated levels of lipoproteins serve as a marker for premature coronary heart disease. The patient is fasting. Venipuncture is performed to obtain a blood sample. The test is performed using electrophoretic methods on plasma using a homogeneous gel to separate particles based on size.

83701
This test may be referred to as Type III fractionation. Type III hyperlipoproteinemia is an inherited disorder whereby both the cholesterol and triglycerides show high plasma concentrations. This particular test is usually performed following previous tests to further isolate abnormal beta-lipoproteins. The patient is told to fast. Blood is drawn by venipuncture. The test may be performed by various methods including ultracentrifugation or electrophoresis. Ultracentrifugation is more common and is considered the traditional standard for accuracy in high-density lipoproteins (HDL) subclass quantitation.

83704
This test is used to measure the subclasses of lipoprotein contained in plasma by measurement of the plasma nuclear magnetic resonance (NMR) spectrum followed by computerized reversal of the optical distortion creating a clearer image (deconvolution) of the spectral data and calculation of the subclass concentrations. Each lipoprotein particle in plasma "broadcasts" a distinctive lipid NMR signal that is graphed. The deconvolution and calculation steps are computed by using analysis software. The test is performed on plasma, acquired by venipuncture. The patient is requested to fast prior to this test.

83718
This test may be requested as HDL, HDLC, or HDL cholesterol. Lipoproteins are compounds composed of lipids bound to proteins, which are transported through the blood. High-density lipoprotein (HDL) is frequently referred to as "good cholesterol," or "friendly lipid," as it is responsible for decreasing plaque deposits in blood vessels. High levels of HDL decrease the risk of premature coronary artery disease. This code reports direct measurement only, normally performed using an enzymatic or precipitation method.

83719
This test measures VLDL, the lipoprotein that carries triglycerides in the blood. The test is useful to determine a patient's risk of arteriosclerotic occlusive disease, as well as other cholesterol-related disorders. The method used is electrophoresis and may first involve ultracentrifugation.

83721
This test may also be referred to as LDL-C. It measures the amount of low-density lipoprotein (LDL), also known as "bad cholesterol." The test is useful to determine the patient's risk of coronary heart disease (CHD), among other disorders. Method may be by precipitation procedure with results derived by the Friedewald formula.

83727
This test may also be referred to as the LH-RH test. Natural bursts of LH-RH govern the release of luteinizing hormone and follicular stimulating hormone, both essential to ovulation. The test is useful in diagnosing problems in LH-RH transport or production, as well as associated fertility problems. Methodology may entail administration of a stimulation agent with a baseline blood sample drawn

before the injection and several after. Samples may be tested by immunoassay.

83735
Magnesium, abbreviated Mg, is an inorganic cation essential for many physiochemical processes. It is an enzyme activator found in body fluids and cells. Magnesium depletion is clinically associated with weakness and neuromuscular disorders including cardiac arrhythmias and seizures. IV therapy, malabsorption, dialysis, pregnancy, toxicity and conditions such as hyperparathyroidism and hyperaldosteronism deplete magnesium. Specimen types and methods of testing vary. Colorimetry or spectrophotometry are methods frequently used.

83775
This test may also be known as MDH, or MD. This enzyme is widely distributed in the system's cellular makeup and levels follow lactate dehydrogenase activity. The test is probably considered of general usefulness and indications are that it is not frequently run. Specimen collection is by venipuncture for blood; surgical excision or biopsy for tissue. Methodology may be by electrophoresis.

83785
This test is usually performed to determine manganese toxicity, exposure, or poisoning. Specimen collection may be venipuncture, 24-hour urine collection, or random or spot urine samples. Hair is sometimes analyzed as is fluid from bronchoalveolar lavage. Methods are source dependent and include neutron activation and atomic absorption spectrophotometry (AAS) with Zeeman background correction for blood and urine. Hair may be processed with acetone and nitric acid before testing with AAS as well. Fluids are likely to be x-ray fluorescence spectrum.

83788
This test identifies the presence (qualitative) of specific analytes in protein. The specimen varies. Method is mass spectrometry. The test is used for identifying the chemical makeup and structure of a substance. Tandem MS (MS/MS) is a method using sequential analysis to provide structural information by establishing relationships between substances. This test assists in analyzing viruses, sequencing and analyzing peptides and proteins, and providing information on such life-threatening diseases as AIDS and various types of skin cancers.

83789
This test is used for identifying the chemical makeup and structure of a substance. The specimen type varies. Method is mass spectrometry (MS). This test is used to analyze viruses, sequence and analyze peptides and proteins, and to provide information on such life-threatening diseases as AIDS and various types of skin cancers. This test quantifies (measures) the amount of analyte in the specimen.

83805
This test is performed to provide therapeutic monitoring and toxicity evaluation of this antianxiety agent (numerous trade names exist, including Equanil and Meprospan). Method used is gas-liquid chromatography or high performance liquid chromatography. Quantitative measurement may be taken for numerous reasons.

83825
This test may also be ordered as Hg. The specimen is whole blood, a 24 hour urine sample or hair cut close to the scalp. Methods are electrothermal atomic absorption, gold electrode deposition, or gas chromatography. Mercury toxicity may cause neurological defects, pneumonitis, and other problems depending on mode of entry into the body (e.g., vapor, ingestion) and which form it enters as: elemental, inorganic, and organic.

83835
The test is performed to determine metanephrine or normetanephrine concentrations. The specimen is urine collected over a 24-hour period. Method is high performance liquid chromatography (HPLC). Metanephrine or normetanephrine concentrations may be associated with neuroendocrine tumors or even associated with intense physical activity, life threatening illness and drug interferences.

83840
This test is used to measure toxicity and the determination of methadone in the system in cases of drug abuse. The specimen is a random urine sample. Methods for screening purposes are thin-layer chromatography and enzyme immunoassay; for confirmation, gas chromatography/mass spectrometry. This agent is widely used in the detoxification of opiate addicts.

83857
This test measures methemalbumin. It is representative of intravascular hemolysis. The specimen is serum or amniotic fluid. Methods may include Schumm test, ether, ammonium sulfide, EP for serum, and spectrophotometry for serum or plasma.

83858
This test is also known as methsuximide/ normethsuximide and celontin. The specimen is serum or plasma. Methods may include gas-liquid chromatography and high-performance liquid chromatography. This test may be ordered to measure the amount of methsuximide, which is an anticonvulsant used in treating petit mal and psychomotor epilepsy.

83864-83866
These tests may also be known as glycosaminoglycans, Keratosulfate, AMPS, and GAGS. Methods may include turbidimetry, paper spot test, and colorimetry. This test may be used to detect the presence of

mucopolysaccharides in solution.
Mucopolysaccharides are important in the diagnosis of certain genetic metabolic disorders, such as Scheie's syndrome (also called a-L-iduronidase deficiency, Scheie type, and mucopolysaccharidosis IS).

83872
This test may also be referred to as a mucin coagulation test or joint fluid test, in addition to Rope's test. This test analyzes the hyaluronic acid in synovial fluid. Specimen collection is by arthrocentesis. Method involves adding a few drops of synovial fluid into a weak solution of acetic acid. The mixture is evaluated for clumping and change of fluid opacity. Test results may be a general guide to numerous rheumatological disorders.

83873
This test may be ordered as an MBP assay. The specimen is spinal fluid. . In rare instances, serum may be tested for myelin basic protein from patients with recent head injuries. Ordinarily, the CSF sample is taken when a patient is experiencing certain symptoms characteristic of disease activity, typically multiple sclerosis. Test methods include radial immunodiffusion (RIA), electroimmunodiffusion, immunofluorometry, immunoprecipitation, or immunonephelometry. This test is typically used as an evaluation of disease activity, rather than for diagnostic purposes.

83874
Myoglobin is a principle protein of skeletal and cardiac muscle tissue. Elevated serum levels may be found in severe muscle conditions, such as polymyositis and crushing traumas to muscle and bone. This test may be used in association with other disorders as well, such as acute myocardial infarct and infections. Methods include radioimmunoassay (RIA), fluorometric immunoassay, and immunoturbidimetry for blood. Urine specimens may be processed by antigen-antibody reaction nephelometry.

83876
Myeloperoxidase (MPO) is a quantitative cardiac marker for ischemic heart disease. Plasma MPO levels help to identify patients who are at risk for myocardial infarction, particularly when used in addition to existing markers for cardiovascular disease. Code 83876 reports a myeloperoxidase enzyme immunoassay for use in identifying troponin-negative patients without EKG changes presenting with chest pain who are at higher risk, and may also be used in myeloproliferative disorders.

83880
Plasma levels of natriuretic peptides, particularly B-type, help predict left ventricular hypertrophy and systolic dysfunction, determine CHF in asymptomatic patients, and provide risk assessment after ischemic symptoms in coronary syndromes. The specimen is plasma. Radioimmunoassay (RIA) may be used.

83883
Nephelometry is a method to measure the concentration of a suspension using an instrument (nephelometer) for assessing turbidity of a solution. For example, this code can be used to measure the concentration of albumin in body fluid. Albumins make up about 60 percent of plasma proteins, and exert considerable pressure in maintaining water balance between blood and tissues. Report this nephelometry test when the analyte is not specifically cited elsewhere in this section.

83885
This test may also be known as Nickel U or as Ni. Specimen types vary. Methods may include atomic absorption spectrophotometry and x-ray fluorescence spectrometry. Measurement of nickel is useful to determine chronic environmental exposure of manufactured products containing nickel.

83887
Cotinine, a metabolite of nicotine, also may be detected by this test. The specimen is serum, plasma or whole blood. Random or times urine samples may also be used. Methods may include gas chromatography, high performance liquid chromatography, and colorimetry.

83890
Molecular diagnostic assays can determine whether an individual carries a genetic mutation associated with specific diseases (without manifestation of the disease symptoms) and can be used to interpret, diagnose, and monitor disease states, and in screening and preventive medicine to detect carriers or those predisposed to specific diseases. Molecular biology studies involve the isolation or extraction of the molecular sequence to be studied. Gene isolation may be used to study neurodegenerative diseases such as ataxia and Alzheimer's disease. Assign 83890 for each nucleic acid type.

83891
Molecular diagnostic assays can determine whether an individual carries a genetic mutation associated with specific diseases (without manifestation of the disease symptoms) and can be used to interpret, diagnose, and monitor disease states, and in screening and preventive medicine to detect carriers or those predisposed to specific diseases. The techniques may include extraction/precipitation, chromatography, centrifugation, and electrophoresis. Report 83891 for each nucleic acid type.

83892
Molecular diagnostic assays can determine whether an individual carries a genetic mutation associated with specific diseases (without manifestation of the disease symptoms) and can be used to interpret, diagnose, and monitor disease states, and in screening and preventive medicine to detect carriers or those predisposed to specific diseases. Enzymatic digestion is a technique to

degrade or modify DNA to hybridize a test strand of DNA against a reference. Report 83892 for each enzyme treatment.

83893
Molecular diagnostic assays can determine whether an individual carries a genetic mutation associated with specific diseases (without manifestation of the disease symptoms) and can be used to interpret, diagnose, and monitor disease states, and in screening and preventive medicine to detect carriers or those predisposed to specific diseases. Dot/slot blot production involves detection methods in proteins. Report 83893 for each nucleic acid preparation.

83894
Molecular diagnostic assays can determine whether an individual carries a genetic mutation associated with specific diseases (without manifestation of the disease symptoms) and can be used to interpret, diagnose, and monitor disease states, and in screening and preventive medicine to detect carriers or those predisposed to specific diseases. Electrophoresis separates and determines the size and purity of the nucleic acid. Report 83894 for each nucleic acid preparation.

83896
Molecular diagnostic assays can determine whether an individual carries a genetic mutation associated with specific diseases (without manifestation of the disease symptoms), used to interpret, diagnose and monitor disease states, and in screening and in preventive medicine to detect carriers or those predisposed to specific diseases. Nucleic acid probes are used to locate, diagnose, and monitor inherited and infectious diseases.

83897
Molecular diagnostic assays can determine whether an individual carries a genetic mutation associated with specific diseases (without manifestation of the disease symptoms), used to interpret, diagnose, and monitor disease states, and in screening and in preventive medicine to detect carriers or those predisposed to specific diseases. Fresh, frozen, or ethanol-fixed tissue may be used in Southern blot tests for possible diagnosis of immunoglobulin heavy chain and T-cell receptor beta or to identify the presence of DNA sequences in totally isolated DNA (DNA isolated from tissue or cells). Report 83897 for each nucleic acid preparation.

83898
This procedure is a component of a molecular diagnostic test protocol. Molecular diagnostic assays can determine whether an individual carries a genetic mutation associated with a specific disease. They may also be used to interpret, diagnose, and monitor disease states, or in screening and in preventive medicine to detect carriers or those predisposed to specific diseases. Target amplification is one of the predominant technologies used in molecular diagnostics, increasing the target molecules to levels that can be easily detected using a variety of reporter systems. The method used for amplification is polymerase chain reaction (PCR). Nucleic acids in fresh, frozen, ethanol-fixed, or paraffin-embedded tissues may be amplified by PCR. This code may be reported for each DNA sequence target amplified.

83900-83901
Multiplex target amplification is performed using multiple primer pairs, one pair specific for each targeted sequence. These procedures are components of a molecular diagnostic test protocol. Molecular diagnostic assays can determine whether an individual carries a genetic mutation associated with a specific disease through analysis of one or more nucleic acid sequences. Target amplification is one of the predominant technologies used in molecular diagnostics, increasing the target molecules to levels that can be easily detected using a variety of reporter systems. Report 83900 for the first two nucleic acid sequences and 83901 for each additional sequence beyond two.

83902
Molecular diagnostic assays can determine whether an individual carries a genetic mutation associated with specific diseases (without manifestation of the disease symptoms), used to interpret, diagnose and monitor disease states, and in screening and in preventive medicine to detect carriers or those predisposed to specific diseases. Transcription involves the transfer of information from a DNA molecule into an RNA molecule.

83903
Molecular diagnostic assays can determine whether an individual carries a genetic mutation associated with specific diseases (without manifestation of the disease symptoms), used to interpret, diagnose and monitor disease states, and in screening and in preventive medicine to detect carriers or those predisposed to specific diseases. Various methods of mutation scanning are used to detect any mutation within a region of DNA. This code involves scanning of a single strand by physical properties.

83904
This method is a diagnostic test to detect alterations in DNA sequence that are known to be found in high frequency among individuals affected by the specific disorder. They may also be used to interpret, diagnose and monitor disease states, and in screening and in preventive medicine to detect carriers or those predisposed to specific diseases. Various methods of mutation scanning are used to detect any mutation within a region of DNA. This code is used for methods used in DNA sequence alterations, such as point mutations, deletions, insertions, and inversions.

83905
Molecular diagnostic assays can determine whether an individual carries a genetic mutation associated with specific diseases (without manifestation of the disease symptoms), used to interpret, diagnose and monitor disease states, and in screening and in preventive medicine to detect carriers or those predisposed to specific diseases. An allele is one of a pair of genes that control the same characteristic but have a different effect. This code identifies certain genetic mutations by allele transcription on a single segment of nucleic acid.

83906
Molecular diagnostic assays can determine whether an individual carries a genetic mutation associated with specific diseases (without manifestation of the disease symptoms), used to interpret, diagnose and monitor disease states, and in screening and in preventive medicine to detect carriers or those predisposed to specific diseases. An allele is one of a pair of genes that control the same characteristic but have a different effect. This code identifies certain genetic mutations by allele translation on a single segment of nucleic acid.

83907
This procedure is a component of a molecular diagnostic test protocol. Tissues for molecular diagnostic testing must be processed prior to amplification to release nucleic acids and remove inhibitory substances. Lysis is the process of destroying cells by breaking cell membranes or cell walls with chemicals to obtain an optimal specimen of nucleic acid for testing. Report 83907 for each specimen.

83908
This procedure is a component of a molecular diagnostic testing protocol. Nonradioactive, synthetic probes have been developed that target or detect specific nucleic acid sequences for analysis through molecular diagnostic testing. The probes signal the presence of specific nucleic acid sequences within a cell sample submitted for analysis. Signal amplification methods enhance the signal without changing the number of target molecules and are available in a variety of molecular detection formats. This code may be reported for each DNA sequence prepared for analysis using signal amplification.

83909
This procedure is a component of a molecular diagnostic test referred to as capillary zone electrophoresis (CZE). CZE is performed on clinically significant DNA obtained by polymerase chain reaction (PCR) in the course of a molecular diagnostic assay. It is a highly sensitive method that detects and identifies DNA point mutants associated with specific diseases. Report 83909 for each nucleic acid preparation.

83912
Molecular diagnostic assays can determine whether an individual carries a genetic mutation associated with specific diseases (without manifestation of the disease symptoms), used to interpret, diagnose and monitor disease states, and in screening and in preventive medicine to detect carriers or those predisposed to specific diseases.

83913
A specimen of ribonucleic acid (RNA) is mixed with a reagent to stabilize it in order to minimize processing urgency and to ensure target integrity in molecular testing. RNA stabilization will extend the sample's shelf, refrigerator, and freezer life. This code reports any method which employs a device or a chemical to prevent degradation of the RNA specimen.

83914
This procedure describes alternative methods of post-amplification mutation identification performed by some laboratories during molecular diagnostic testing. These methods detect and identify DNA point mutants associated with specific diseases.

83915
This test is also known as 5'-N'TASE, and 5'-NT. The specimen is serum or synovial fluid. Methods vary greatly, and may include molybdate color reaction, high performance liquid chromatography, and colorimetry. The test may be ordered to assist in identifying the cause of increased 5'-nucleotidase, a liver-related enzyme.

83916
The specimen is cerebrospinal fluid (CFS) and serum. Methods may include thin-gel agarose high-resolution electrophoresis and isoelectric focusing. This test may be used to identify diagnoses of inflammatory and autoimmune diseases of the CNS and other degenerative states.

83918
This test also may involve analyzing patterns of excretion for specific diagnosis. Urine is the preferred specimen due to concentration of the metabolites excreted by the kidney. Urine collection is typically over a 24-hour period. Methods may include gas chromatography, followed by mass spectroscopy. There are many sources for organic acids, though most come from the metabolism of amino acids, fatty acids, carbohydrates, and cholesterol, and hormones such as steroids. Abnormal patterns of organic acids in excretion may be due to genetic metabolic disorders, vitamin deficiencies, and certain drugs.

83919
This test may involve analyzing patterns of excretion for specific diagnosis. Urine is the preferred specimen due to concentration of the metabolites excreted by the kidney, but blood testing may also be performed. There are many sources for organic acids, though most come from the metabolism of amino acids, fatty acids, carbohydrates, and cholesterol, and hormones such as steroids. Abnormal patterns of organic acids in

excretion may be due to genetic metabolic disorders, vitamin deficiencies, certain drugs, and identification of inborn errors of metabolism. Qualitative screening tests are typically performed by thin layer chromatography, but may involve other chemical or chromatographic techniques.

83921
This test is a quantitative test for organic acids and the preferred specimen is urine due to concentration of metabolites excreted by the kidney. Methods may include gas chromatography, followed by mass spectroscopy. The test may be performed on acutely ill neonates, suspected cases of Reye's syndrome, or failure-to-thrive syndrome, and patients with metabolic acidosis, (associated with severe infections).

83925
Test methods include thin-layer chromatography, enzyme immunoassay, gas chromatography, and high performance liquid chromatography. This test measures the amount of a given opiate present and may be ordered to measure toxicity or possible drug abuse of opiates, such as morphine and meperidine (Demerol). Report 83925 for each test procedure for drugs and metabolites.

83930
This test is also known as osmolal gap and serum osmolality. The specimen is serum or plasma. Methodology may involve freezing point depression or vapor pressure techniques. The test measures the amount of molecules or ions (particles) in a solution of water or the presence of osmotically active molecules in serum. The test may be used to determine liver disease and disorders, electrolyte and water balance.

83935
This test may also be known as osmolal gap. The specimen is a random urine sample. Method may be by freezing point depression. The test may be used to determine renal disease and disorders, electrolyte and water balance. The results may be high or low urine osmolality, depending on the differential diagnosis.

83937
Osteocalcin is a test developed to measure bone formation and for monitoring therapy of preexisting bone conditions. An imbalance between the two (formation and reabsorption) may account for many of the metabolic bone diseases, such as Paget's disease and osteomalacia. The specimen is serum or plasma. Methods may include enzyme-linked immunosorbent assay (ELISA).

83945
This test is also known as oxalic acid. Urine collection is over a 24-hour period, or a first morning. The specimen may be taken as an estimate of daily output. Methods of testing may include colorimetry and high performance liquid chromatography. The test may be performed to determine patients at risk of forming oxalate calculi (stones), which are common in the urinary tract.

83950-83951
Proteins that are involved in tumor growth (oncoproteins) are coded for by a gene with a DNA sequence that causes cancer (oncogene). The human epidermal growth factor receptor 2 gene, a proto-oncogene, encodes for the HER-2/neu protein, a cell surface growth factor receptor that is expressed on the cytoplasmic membrane of some epithelial cells and regulates normal cell growth and division. Gene amplification causes overexpression of the HER-2/neu oncoprotein, which correlates to higher cell growth rates and oncogenic transformation. Immunohistochemical methods are often used to measure the overexpression of HER-2/neu protein. Code 83950 reports the evaluation of the staining pattern for intensity and the degree to which the cytoplasmic membrane is encircled with stain, indicating overexpression of the protein. Des-gamma-carboxy-prothrombin (DCP) is an oncoprotein whose levels are used to detect liver cancer at an early stage and to monitor its progression. Increased levels may also indicate the development of portal vein invasion (PVI), making it a valuable tool in the prediction of disease progression and worsening prognosis. When used in combination with AFP-L3%, DCP can help identify patients at risk of developing hepatocellular cancer. The test is by enzyme immunoassay; the sample is serum. Report DCP testing with 83951..

83970
This test may also be ordered as a PTH or parathyrin. The specimen is post-fasting serum requiring special handling. Methods may include immunochemiluminometric assay (ICMA), radioimmunoassay (RIA), and immunoradiometric assay (IRMA). Testing determines the PTH levels and may be used to differentiate between primary or secondary causes of parathyroid disorders.

83986
This test may also be called fecal pH, pleural fluid pH, or thoracentesis pH. The specimen for pleural fluid is by thoracentesis; for stool, fresh random sample; for urine, random sample; or ascitic fluid by paracentesis, etc. Methods may include a pH meter for pleural fluid; aqueous stool suspension with pH paper for stool; dipstick double indicator principal or pH meter for urine. The test may be ordered to differentiate among numerous diagnoses, depending on the sample taken and the method used.

83987
Exhaled breath condensate pH is used to ascertain the underlying cause of chronic cough and airway irritation (e.g., acid reflux disease). The patient uses a specialized breath collection/condensation device to collect breath condensate. The breath condensate is

then degassed and analyzed using a special pH electrode in order to obtain accurate results.

83992
This test is performed to evaluate the presence of phencyclidine (also known as PCP, or angel dust), an illegal street drug. Methodology may include immunoassay, thin-layer chromatography (TLC), gas chromatography (GC), and gas chromatography/mass spectrometry (GC/TC), which quantifies the amount of drug.

83993
This test is used to diagnose and monitor inflammatory bowel disease (IBD). Calprotectin is a calcium-binding protein produced primarily by neutrophils. Elevated fecal calprotectin levels may be indicative of IBD or gastrointestinal (GI) tract infections, and often signal an upcoming clinical relapse in patients with inactive IBD. The test employs a quantitative enzyme immunoassay methodology to detect calprotectin in a fecal sample.

84022
Derivatives of phenothiazine are numerous and most are classified as antipsychotics. A common one is Chlorpromazine. Methods may include high performance liquid chromatography (HPLC), thin-layer chromatography (TLC), gas chromatography (GC) or fluorometry for blood; thin-layer chromatography (TLC), gas-liquid chromatography (GLC), or radioimmunoassay (RIA) for urine. The test is performed to evaluate the amount of phenothiazine present.

84030
This test is used to screen for phenylketonuria (PKU), a condition resulting in the inability of the body to break down the amino acid phenylalanine. Untreated PKU may lead to increased phenylalanine levels resulting in mental retardation. A blood sample is placed on special paper and is usually collected within 48 to 72 hours after birth. This test may be ordered as a Guthrie, Phenylketonuria, PKU test, or phenylalanine screen. Additional testing is needed to confirm the diagnosis of PKU if this screening test is positive.

84035

This test detects the presence of phenylketone, a metabolite created in the breakdown of the amino acid phenylamine. Methods may include gas chromatography. The amino acid is essential to developing infants and normal protein metabolism throughout life. This is a qualitative screening test for the presence of phenylketones.

84060
This is also known as phosphoric monoester phosphohydrolase and ACP. This test is often performed on individuals with diagnoses such as skeletal metastasis, myelocytic leukemia, and is useful in staging prostatic cancer rather than initial diagnosis of prostate cancer. The specimen is post-fasting serum. Methods may include radioimmunoassay (RIA), enzyme immunoassay (EIA),and spectrophotometry.

84061
This test is performed to detect acid phosphatase, a constituent of semen, as part of evidence collection following a sex crime. The specimen is vaginal fluid. Some specimens may be placed in transport tubes; others may be submitted on slides as smears. This test does not detect the presence of spermatozoa. Levels of phosphatase may be elevated due to vaginal infection, which may confuse test results.

84066
This test may also be known as PAP and prostatic phosphatase. The specimen is post-fasting serum. Methods may include radioimmunoassay (RIA), enzyme monophosphate, alpha naphthylphosphate, and titrate inhibition. This test may be used to stage prostate cancer, to diagnose metastatic prostate adenocarcinoma and to monitor treatment of those diagnosed with prostatic carcinoma.

84075
This test may be requested as ALP. ALP is an enzyme. It is an indicator of liver cell damage. Amniotic fluid ALP may be screened for cystic fibrosis in mothers who have had a child affected with the disease. Methods include a number of kinetic spectrophotometry and fluorescent techniques, as well as 4-nitrylphenophosphate (4-NPP) and diethanolamine (DEA).

84078
This test may be performed to identify general liver and bone diseases. Methodology involves heat inhibition at 56 degrees Celsius.

84080
This test may also be known as ALP isoenzymes. This test may be ordered for patients with increased serum total alkaline phosphatase, or to compare total alkaline phosphatase to placental, liver, bone, and Regan isoenzymes. Methods may include electrophoresis or enzymatic.

84081
These tests together are frequently ordered as LS/PG. Testing is performed in conjunction with an L/S (lecithin/sphingomyelin) ratio for assessment of fetal maturity based on pulmonary surfactant. This test may be performed to determine fetal lung maturity and to establish the possibility of the development of respiratory distress syndrome in the fetus. The specimen is by amniocentesis, a separately reportable procedure Methods may include thin-layer chromatography (TLC) and immunologic and enzymatic assays.

84085
This test may also be known as 6-PGD. The specimen is whole blood. Methodology may involve spectrophotometry. The test may be performed to detect the presence and measure the levels of phosphogluconate, 6-, dehydrogenase, RBC, an enzyme present in the metabolic breakdown of sugars.

84087
This is also known as glucose-6-phosphate isomerase. The specimen is whole blood. Methods may include spectrophotometry and colorimetric. The test may be performed to detect the presence and measure the levels in serum of phosphohexose isomerase, an enzyme present in the breakdown of fructose.

84100
This test may be ordered as PO4. Methods may include phosphomolybdate-colorimetric and modified molybdate-enzymatic, and colorimetric. The testing may be performed to measure high or low levels of phosphorus to determine a variety of differential diagnoses. Potassium supplements increase phosphate levels. Also, phosphate levels may increase during the last trimester of pregnancy.

84105
This test is performed to identify the calcium/ phosphorus balance. High values may be associated with primary hyperparathyroidism, vitamin D deficiency, and renal tubular acidosis; low values may be due to hypoparathyroidism, pseudohypoparathyroidism, and vitamin D toxicity. The test may also be used for nephrolithiasis assessment.

84106
This test may also be known as Watson-Schwartz, PCG and Hoesch tests. The specimen is random urine which requires special handling. Methods are the Watson-Schwartz and Hoesch tests, and Ehrlich's reagent. The Hoesch test does not respond to urobilirubin. The test may be used to screen for acute intermittent porphyria and for acute attacks of abdominal and extremity pain.

84110
This test may also be known as Porphobilinogen (PBG), urine. The specimen is a 24-hour or a random urine sample, requiring special handling. Urine colored amber-red or burgundy, which darkens in light, indicates the presence of abnormally high levels. This test may be used to detect levels of porphobilinogen associated in the diagnosis of genetic or drug-induced abnormal porphyrin metabolism. Methods may involve gas chromatography, colorimetry, and spectrophotometry. This test measures (quantifies) porphobilinogen present in the specimen.

84119
This test may be used to detect the presence (qualitative) of porphyria cutanea tarda (PCT). The patient typically collects a 24-hour urine Methods may include high performance liquid chromatography. Urine porphyrins are useful for evaluating photosensitivity due to abnormal metabolism of the protein used in the synthesis of the iron (heme) in hemoglobin.

84120
This test is performed for the quantitative evaluation (measurement) of porphyrias, which may include enzyme deficiencies that are necessary for heme synthesis and chemical porphyrias. Specimen is urine collected by the patient over a 24-hour period. Methods may include chromatography, fluorometry, and high performance liquid chromatography (HPLC).

84126-84127
Results may be used to measure the levels of coproporphyrin (a nitrogen-containing substance excreted in the feces from the breakdown of bilirubin from hemoglobin decomposition) and protoporphyrin (a form of porphyrin that combines with iron and protein to form organic molecules such as hemoglobin). The specimen is feces which may be a random or timed collection. Method is high performance liquid chromatography and fluorometry.

84132
This test may be requested as K or K+. Potassium is the major electrolyte found in intracellular fluids. Potassium influences skeletal and cardiac muscle activity. Very small fluctuations outside the normal range may cause significant health risk, including muscle weakness and cardiac arrhythmias. Blood specimen is serum, plasma, or whole blood. Methods include atomic absorption spectrometry (AAS), ion-selective electrode (ISE), and flame emission spectroscopy (FES).

84133
This test may be ordered as urine K+. The specimen is collected by the patient over a 24-hour period or is random urine sample. Methods may include flame emission photometry and ion-selective electrode (ISE). The test may be ordered to determine elevated levels for the differential diagnoses of chronic renal failure, renal tubular acidosis, and for diuretic therapy.

84134
The test may also be known as PAB, thyroxine-binding prealbumin (TBPA), thyretin, and transthyretin. The specimen may be serum, a random or a 24-hour urine specimen or spinal fluid. . A separately reportable lumbar puncture is performed to obtain cerebrospinal fluid (CSF). Methods may include electrophoresis and nephelometry (serum). The test may be used as an indicator of nutrition, liver injury, chronic kidney disease, and in the diagnosis of Hodgkin's disease.

84135
This test measures pregnanediol to evaluate progesterone production by the ovaries and placenta.

Methods may involve gas-liquid chromatography and radioimmunoassay. Progesterone initiates the phase in ovulation that prepares the endometrium for implantation of a fertilized ovum. The serum and urine level of the progesterone metabolite pregnanediol increases rapidly during this phase, making it a useful measure in documenting and charting ovulation.

84138
This test is also known as 17-Hydroxyprogesterone or 17-OH-Progesterone. Methods may include extraction/gas-liquid chromatography (GLC) and spectrophotometry. This test may be performed to determine differential diagnoses of adrenogenital syndrome, tumors of ovary and adrenal cortices, Stein-Leventhal syndrome, and congenital adrenal hyperplasia, among others.

84140
This test is used for detecting and measuring the levels of pregnenolone, a steroid involved in the synthesis of numerous hormones. The specimen is blood (to include cord blood) or a 24 hour timed urine collection. Method is typically radioimmunoassay.

84143
Serum or urine from a female patient may be examined using radioimmunoassay in this test for detecting and measuring the levels of 17-hydroxypregnenolone, a hormonal metabolite.

84144
This test is performed to determine corpus luteum function, confirm ovulation, and to diagnose incompetent luteal phase and insufficient progesterone production, which may be the cause of habitual abortions. The specimen is serum. Methods may include radioimmunoassay (RIA) and direct time-resolved fluorescence immunoassay.

84145
Procalcitonin (PCT) is produced in the thyroid cells of healthy individuals as a precursor for the hormone calcitonin and is not normally found in human blood. However, bacterial infections may cause many of the body's organs to produce PCT, resulting in a rapid elevation of PCT blood levels. This increase is not caused by viral infections. PCT blood levels reflect the severity of bacterial infection, making it a useful biomarker in the diagnosis of bacterial infection and sepsis. Specimen is serum or plasma; test method is by various assays.

84146
Prolactin is a hormone secreted by the anterior pituitary gland. This test may be performed for the differential diagnoses of prolactinemia, galactorrhea (lactation disorder), pituitary adenomas, pituitary prolactinoma, and other pituitary tumors. The specimen is post-fasting serum. Methods may include immunoassay and radioimmunoassay (RIA).

84150
Method is enzyme immunoassay. Prostaglandin (PG) is a potent unsaturated fatty acid that can act against organs in exceedingly low concentrations, and in their pharmaceutical form may be used for terminating pregnancy or treating asthma. This test may also be known as PG.

84152-84154
The specimen is serum. Methods may include radioimmunoassay (RIA) and monoclonal two-site immunoradiometric assay. These tests may be performed to determine the presence of cancer of the prostate, benign prostatic hypertrophy (BPH), prostatitis, post prostatectomy to detect residual cancer, and to monitor therapy. There are several forms of PSA present in serum. PSA may be complexed with the protease inhibitor alpha-1 antichymotrypsin (PSA-ACT). Complexed PSA is the most measurable form. PSA is also found in a free form. Free PSA is not complexed to a protease inhibitor. Higher levels of free PSA are more often associated with benign conditions of the prostate than with prostate cancer. Total PSA measures both complexed and free levels to provide a total amount present in the serum. A percentage of each form is sometimes calculated to distinguish benign from malignant conditions. Code 84152 reports complexed PSA; 84153 is for total serum PSA; 84154 is for free (not complexed) PSA.

84155-84157
A total protein test may be performed to assess nutritional status. Serum, plasma, or whole blood is tested for protein in 84155. Synovial, cerebrospinal, or other fluid is obtained in 84157. A urine specimen is required for 84156. For amniotic fluid specimen (84157), a separately reportable amniocentesis is performed. Aspiration of other body fluids (CSF, bronchial fluid, exudates) may also require separately reportable procedures. The method is biuret for blood (serum) and amniotic fluid. The method is turbidimetry or nephelometry for urine and CSF. For other body fluids, the method is turbidimetry or biuret.

84160
A total protein test may be performed to assess nutritional status. This code reports any source of specimen. Collection/aspiration of other body fluids (CSF, amniotic fluid, exudates) may require separately reportable procedures. This code reports protein tested for by refractometry. The method determines the velocity of light through a refractive material (plasma).

84163
Pregnancy associated plasma protein-A (PAPP-A, PAPPA) is a large zinc binding protein that acts as an enzyme. The test is used as a marker for Down's syndrome in the fetus. It can also be used as a marker for acute coronary syndromes such as angina and acute myocardial infarction. Blood specimen is obtained by venipuncture. Testing for Down's syndrome requires a

maternal blood sample. Purified human PAPP-A is used as the immunogen (antigen). Methods include enzyme linked immunosorbent assay (ELISA) and Western blot.

84165-84166
Serum protein electrophoretic fractionation and quantitation is performed primarily to evaluate for multiple myeloma or to test for hypogammaglobulinemia. The specimen is serum. Methods may be cellulose acetate and agarose electrophoresis. The value of this testing lies in the proportion of these proteins and the patterns they create on the graph, giving diagnostic clues for some diseases. Report 84165 when serum is tested and 84166 when another fluid such as urine or cerebral spinal fluid is tested.

84181-84182
Western blot is an immunoassay technique that detects and confirms certain antibody proteins in blood or other body fluid. Combining an electrophoresis process with a process that blots or transfers the separated proteins onto a membrane, the western blot is frequently utilized as a follow-up confirmatory test to assist in diagnosing a specific disease. Examples of confirmatory testing include that for HIV and Lyme disease. Report 84182 for each immunological probe that is utilized for band identification. These codes include interpretation and report.

84202-84203
This test is performed to diagnose various anemias and lead toxicity. Code 84203 is a qualitative test used as a screen to determine if protoporphyrin is present in the specimen. Code 84202 measures (quantifies) the level of protoporphyrin present. The specimen is whole blood. Methods may include hematofluorometry methods and high performance liquid chromatography.

84206
This test may be performed for the differential diagnoses of insulinoma, renal failure, factitious hypoglycemia, and diabetes mellitus. The specimen is post-fasting serum, requiring special handling. Method is radioimmunoassay.

84207
This test may also be known as PLP. Vitamin B6 is also known as pyridoxine and pyridoxal 5-phosphate. The specimen is plasma, requiring special handling. Methods may include enzyme assay, high performance liquid chromatography (HPLC) with fluorometric detection, and immunoradiometric assay. This test may be performed to identify vitamin B6 deficiency (i.e., nutritional deficiencies as a result of other diseases including chronic alcoholism).

84210
This test is also known as pyruvic acid test. The specimen is blood. Methods are usually enzymatic and colorimetry. This test measures the level of pyruvate in whole blood. The abnormal breakdown of red blood cells and subsequent release of hemoglobin characterize a congenital deficiency of pyruvate.

84220
The specimen is washed red blood cells. Method is spectrophotometric kinetic assay. This test may be performed to identify pyruvate kinase deficiency and hemolytic anemia in newborns.

84228
Quinine is used in the treatment of malaria, atrial fibrillation, and other disorders of muscular tissues. Urine is collected by a patient over a 24-hour period. Method is thin-layer chromatography.

84233
This test may be ordered to assist in identifying a breast cancer patient's ability to respond to chemotherapy and endocrine therapy. The specimen is surgical tissue. The surgical procedure is separately billable. Methods may include biochemical measurement in cytosol fractions of tumor homogenate, dextranestradiol conjugate, immunoperoxidase using tissue sections, enzyme immunoassay (EIA), and in situ hybridization.

84234
This test assists in identifying a patient's ability to respond to treatment in breast and other cancers and may be ordered as a PgR assay. The specimen is surgical tissue. Methods may include sucrose density gradient, steroid binding assay, and enzyme immunoassay.

84235
The test may be used to predict or monitor patient response to hormonal therapy. The specimen is whole blood or plasma; separately reportable biopsy or surgical excision for tumor tissue. Methods are radioimmunoassay (most commonly used technique), gas-liquid and liquid chromatography or electrophoresis.

84238
This test may be used to predict or monitor patient response to therapy, including AChR. Methods include radioimmunoassay (most commonly used technique), gas-liquid and liquid chromatography, or electrophoresis. The test is performed to determine the concentration of the target substance.

84244
This test may be ordered as plasma renin activity, or PRA. The specimen is plasma. Certain medications such as beta-blockers, may affect testing outcome. Methodology may include radioimmunoassay.

84252
This test may be used primarily to determine nutritional deficiency of this vitamin. The specimen is plasma which requires special handling or a 24-hour urine specimen. Methods may include high performance liquid chromatography (HPLC) or fluorometry.

84255
This test may also be known by the abbreviation Se. The specimen is serum or urine collected over a 24-hour period. Methods may include fluorometry and atomic absorption. The blood and the urine test may be performed simultaneously. This test may be ordered to monitor nutritional therapy and for possible toxic exposure.

84260
This test may also be called 5-HT or 5-Hydroxytryptamine. The specimen is whole blood or serum or spinal fluid. A separately reportable lumbar puncture is performed to collect cerebrospinal fluid (CSF). Methods may include fluorometry, radioimmunoassay (RIA), and gas or liquid chromatography spinal puncture to obtain specimen is reported separately, see 62270. This test may be performed to diagnose carcinoid syndrome and severe depression.

84270
The test may be used to predict or monitor patient response to hormonal therapy and to assist in certain diagnoses, including hypothyroidism and hyperthyroidism. This test may also be ordered as SHBG. The specimen is serum which requires special handling or amniotic fluid. Methods include CMA or radioimmunoassay.

84275
This test may also be known by Lipid Associated Sialic Acid or LASA. The specimen is serum. The term "sialic acids" comprises a group of natural neuraminic acid derivatives. The activity of the enzyme, neuraminidase, is also referred to as sialidase. Deficiency of the enzyme may result in the clinical disease sialidosis, a syndrome that may involve involuntary twitching of the muscular group affected and cherry-red spots on the skin. Methods include enzyme assay and spectrometry.

84285
Silica is a naturally occurring and common mineral found in sands, clays, and quartz deposits. Exposure is commonly by inhalation of dusts during rock mining and certain manufacturing. Deposition on the eyes and mucosal surfaces may also be a pathway of exposure. Most commonly, however, phagocytic cells may distribute the silica along lymph channels once the particles are inhaled and collect in lung alveoli. Long-term exposure is linked to numerous illnesses, including silicosis. Sputum induction is performed and silica is detected using light microscopy, electron microscopy, or polarized light.

84295-84302
Sodium is an electrolyte found in extracellular fluid. Blood specimen for serum, plasma, or whole blood sodium (Na) in 84295 is obtained by venipuncture. Methods include atomic absorption spectrometry (AAS), flame emission photometry, and ion-selective electrode (ISE). The specimen for urine Na in 84300 is collected over a 24-hour period or by random urine sample. Methods may include flame emission photometry and ISE. This test is used to identify increased (hypernatremia) and decreased (hyponatremia) levels of sodium due to various conditions or disease states. Report 84302 for a sodium level test done on another source of specimen other than blood serum or urine.

84305
Somatomedin is a protein mainly produced in the liver. It is a peptide dependent on growth hormone for its actions. This test may be used to diagnose and evaluate response to therapy for a variety of growth disorders. The test may be performed to diagnose acromegaly, dwarfism, pituitary disease and disorders, nutritional deficiencies, and to monitor response to therapies. The specimen is plasma, which requires special handling. Methodology may use a process of dissociation from binding protein and chromatography, followed by radioimmunoassay (RIA).

84307
This test may be performed to measure somatostatin, a hormone found in the pancreas and in the gut. Specimen is plasma, requiring special handling. Method is usually radioimmunoassay. This hormone regulates the body's production of insulin, glucagon, gastrin, secretin, and renin. Somatostatin also may control how the body secretes insulin and glucagon.

84311
Specimen types include blood, random urine, or a 24-hour timed urine collection. Method is typically spectrophotometry, which provides a quantitative measure of the amount of a material in a solution absorbing applied light. Report this test for an analyte not elsewhere specified. Measuring the absorption of visible, ultraviolet or infrared light makes quantitative measurements of concentrations of reagents. The specimen is by the bodily fluid chosen as a sample (e.g., gastric secretions). Method is by specific gravity, which measures the concentration or the weight of a substance as compared to an equal volume of water. For laboratory testing, specific gravity shows the density of a specific material.

84315
Specific gravity is a measure of concentration. It is the weight of a substance, as compared with that of an equal volume of water. Body fluids are typically collected by needle aspiration or lavage. The method of testing is refractometer.

84375
Fructose, galactose, lactose, maltose and l-xyulose are sugars found in urine of patients with inherited metabolic disorders. Thin layer chromatography or paper chromatography is a method to separate and

identify sugars in urine when a metabolic order is suspected.

84376-84379
These tests may be used for infants who are failing to thrive due to lactose, sucrose, or fructose imbalances. Methods include gas chromatography and mass spectrometry to test for sugars, mono-, di-, and oligosaccharides in body fluids.

84392
This test may be ordered to determine kidney stone risk and in the investigation of sulfur metabolism studies. Sulfates may be measured for the diagnosis of metachromatic leukodystrophy (sulfatide lipidosis), an inherited lipid metabolism that results in the accumulation of metachromatic lipids in the tissues of the central nervous system, leading to paralysis and often death in early adolescence. The specimen is a random or timed urine collection. Method is spectrophotometry.

84402-84403
These tests may be used to evaluate testosterone levels. Testosterone is an androgenic hormone responsible for, among other biological activities, secondary male characteristics in women. Increased testosterone levels in women may be linked to a variety of conditions, including hirsutism. Code 84403 reports total testosterone, which includes both protein bound and free testosterone. Code 84402 reports testosterone as a free unbound protein. This test may be ordered to assist in diagnosis of hypogonadism, hypopituitarism, and Klinefelter's syndrome, among other disorders. The specimen is serum. Method may be by radioimmunoassay (RIA) and immunoassay (non-isotopic).

84425
This is also known as Vitamin B1. The specimen is whole blood. Methods are high performance liquid chromatography and thiochrome-fluorometry. Mild thiamine deficiency occurs during pregnancy, in alcoholics, the elderly and in cases of persistent vomiting and fasting. Severe thiamine deficiency, called beriberi, is characterized by peripheral neuritis or cardiac failure. The quantitation of thiamine provides the sensitivity and specificity necessary for clinical evaluation of thiamine nutritional status.

84430
This drug may also be known as Nipride, Nitroprusside, Thanite, Lithane, or KCN. The specimen is serum or plasma or random urine sample. Methods may include photometry or chromatography. The test may be ordered to evaluate thiocyanate toxicity, nitroprusside therapy and poisoning, or cigarette use.

84431
This immunoassay is used to measure thromboxane metabolites, including thromboxane, if performed. The specimen is urine. Determination of the total level of thromboxane production is useful in identifying patients who remain at risk of a cardiovascular event despite being on aspirin therapy.

84432
This test is also known as Tg. The specimen is serum. This test is performed to determine thyroglobulin levels to identify thyroid disorders and tumors.

84436
This test may be ordered as a T4. The specimen is serum. Methods may include radioimmunoassay (RIA), enzyme-linked immunosorbent assay (ELISA), fluorescence polarization immunoassay (FPIA), and chemiluminescence assay (CIA). The test is performed to determine thyroid function as screening test; total thyroxine makes up approximately 99 percent of the thyroid hormone.

84437
This test may be ordered as a neonatal T4. The specimen is whole blood. The specimen may be taken at the same time as a PKU (Phenylalanine) test. Method is typically radioimmunoassay (RIA). The test may be performed to determine hypothyroidism in newborns (performed in all 50 states) to prevent mental retardation and to monitor suppressive and replacement therapy.

84439
This test may be ordered as a FT4, free T4, FTI or FT4 index. The specimen is serum, requiring special handling. Methods may include radioimmunoassay and equilibrium dialysis for reference method. Free thyroxine is a minimal amount of the total T4 level (approximately one percent). This test is not influenced by thyroid-binding abnormalities and perhaps correlates more closely with the true hormonal status. It may be effective in the diagnosis of hyperthyroidism and hypothyroidism.

84442
Thyroxin binding globulin is a plasma protein that binds with thyroxine and transports it in the blood. Elevated levels may be associated with pregnancy and newborn states, hepatitis, and other disorders. Decreased levels may be associated with liver diseases and acromegaly, among other disorders. The specimen is serum. Methods may include chemiluminescent immunoassay, equilibrium dialysis, ultrafiltration, and solid phase enzyme immunoassay (EIA) technology.

84443
TSH is produced in the pituitary gland and stimulates the secretion of thyrotropin (T3) and thyroxine (T4); these secretory products monitor TSH. The specimen is serum, requiring special handling. Heel stick or umbilical cord sample is drawn from newborns and may be collected on a special paper. Methods may include radioimmunoassay (RIA), sandwich immunoradiometric assay (IRMA), fluorometric

enzyme immunoassay with use of monoclonal antibodies, or microparticle enzyme immunoassay on IMx (MEIA). This test may be performed to determine thyroid function, to differentiate from various types of hypothyroidism (e.g., primary, and pituitary/ hypothalamic), or to diagnose hyperthyroidism. The test may be ordered to evaluate therapy in patients receiving hypothyroid treatment, and to detect congenital hypothyroidism.

84445
This test may also be ordered as TSI. This serum test measures the amount of thyroid stimulating antibody, which stimulates the thyroid to produce excessive amounts of thyroid hormone. Methods may include vitro bioassay and radioimmunoassay. The test may be useful in diagnosis of Grave's disease (hyperthyroidism).

84446
This test may also be known as a-tocopherol. The specimen is serum or plasma, requiring special handling. Methods may include high performance liquid chromatography (HPLC), fluorometry after solvent extraction, and colorimetry. The test may be performed to determine vitamin E deficiency, to evaluate patients on long-term parenteral nutrition, and to evaluate numerous disorders.

84449
Cortisol-binding globulin (Transcortin) is a type of glycoprotein. This test is performed to evaluate adrenal activity. It plays a role in fat and water metabolism. The specimen is serum. Method may include chemiluminescent. Levels of cortisol help in the diagnosis of Cushing's syndrome, and Addison's disease.

84450
This test is usually referred to as aspartate aminotransferase (AST) or as serum glutamic oxaloacetic transaminase (SGOT). AST is an enzyme found primarily in heart muscle and the liver. Serum levels are low unless there is cellular damage, at which time large amounts are released into circulation. AST levels are increased following acute myocardial infarction (MI). Liver disease may also cause elevated levels of AST. Blood specimen is serum or plasma. Method is spectrophotometry, kinetic assay, and enzymatic.

84460
This test is usually referred to as alanine aminotransferase (ALT) or as serum glutamic pyruvic transaminase (SGPT). ALT is an enzyme found primarily in liver cells and elevations may be indicative of liver disease. Blood specimen is serum or plasma. Method is spectrophotometry or enzymatic.

84466
An alternative name for this test is siderophilin. The specimen is serum. Measurement of transferrin levels in serum aids in the diagnosis of malnutrition, acute inflammation, infection and red blood cell disorders, such as iron deficiency anemia. Methods of testing vary to include immunologic or turbidometric assay.

84478
This test may be requested as trig. Triglycerides are blood lipids that are transported through the circulatory system by lipoproteins. Triglycerides contribute to atherosclerosis and other arterial diseases. Blood specimen is serum or plasma. Method is enzymatic or colorimetry.

84479
This test may be requested as T3 uptake and T4 uptake or THBR. The specimen is serum. Method is chemiluminescent immunoassay.

84480
This test may be ordered as a T3 (RIA) or total T3. The specimen is serum. Methods may include radioimmunoassay (RIA), immunochemiluminometric assay, and fluorometric immunoassay. Abnormal results may be diseases and disorders related to the thyroid.

84481
This test may also be known as FT3, or free T3. The specimen is serum. Method may involve equilibrium dialysis (tracer). This test may be used to identify thyroid dysfunction, such as hyperthyroidism and hypothyroidism.

84482
Reverse T3 (rT3) is an inactive form of the thyroid hormone T3, and is found in the blood of normal people. The specimen is serum. Measurement of rT3 has been suggested in differentiating euthyroid sick syndrome from true hypothyroidism, and in identifying factitious hyperthyroidism. RT3 is typically measured by radioimmunoassay.

84484
This test may also be known as troponin regulatory complex. The specimen is serum. Methods may include radioimmunoassay, enzyme-linked immunosorbent assay, and immunoenzymatic assay. This quantitative test measures the levels of troponin, found in muscle tissues. Elevated levels of troponin may be related to myocardial infarction and ischemic heart disease.

84485
This test may also be referred to as duodenal trypsinogen. Trypsin in duodenal aspirate has been measured by both radioimmunoassay and enzymatic methods. Measurement is useful in evaluation of pancreatic disease, such as primary biliary cirrhosis and cystic fibrosis, and malabsorption syndromes.

84488-84490
These tests may be called fecal tryptic activity or immunoreactive trypsin. The specimen is fresh random

stool sample. Methods may be kinetic and potentiometric, and x-ray film method. Trypsin is an enzyme that acts to degrade protein and it may be referred to as proteolytic enzyme, or proteinase. This test is performed to screen for pancreatic exocrine function and malabsorption syndromes in children under the age of four. Three specimens may be taken for an accurate assessment of pancreatic function. For qualitative screening, report 84488; for quantitative measurement, see 84490.

84510
This test may also be known by the abbreviation Tyr. Measurement of tyrosine is useful in the evaluation of certain amino-acidopathies or inborn errors of metabolism, and to determine possible thyroid disorders and various other diseases Tyrosine has been measured by chromatographic techniques such as HPLC or gas chromatography combined with a variety of detection/evaluation technologies, including mass-spectrometry. Specimen types vary.

84512
This may also be known as troponin regulatory complex. The specimen is plasma. Cardiac troponins are markers for myocardial muscle damage. Qualitative tests (positive/negative results) are primarily used to rule-in or rule-out myocardial infarction. Several bedside, point-of-care type assays are available. Methods are radioimmunoassay, enzyme-linked immunosorbent assay, and immunoenzymatic assay may also be seen.

84520
This test may be requested as blood urea nitrogen (BUN). Urea is an end product of protein metabolism. BUN may be requested to evaluate dehydration or renal function. Blood specimen is serum or plasma. Method is colorimetry, enzymatic, or rate conductivity. This test measures (quantitates) the amount of urea in the blood.

84525
This test may also be ordered as a BUN. This test may provide useful information regarding carbohydrate metabolism (diabetes), kidney function, and acid-base balance. The specimen type is plasma. Method is reagent strip.

84540
This test may provide useful information regarding carbohydrate metabolism (diabetes), kidney function, and acid-base balance, in addition to dietary protein. Urea is a measure of protein breakdown in the body. Urine urea excretion can be measured to obtain a ratio between the plasma (blood) urea and the urine urea; this ratio is an indicator of kidney function. Urine collection over a 24-hour period. Methods may include enzymatic assay, colorimetry, and conductometric.

84545
This test is also known as BUN-blood urea nitrogen. The specimen is taken over a 24-hour period. Urea nitrogen is formed in the liver as an end product of protein metabolism. Increased or decreased levels of urea nitrogen can indicate renal disease, dehydration, congestive heart failure, and gastrointestinal bleeding, starvation, shock or urinary tract obstruction (by tumor or prostate gland).

84550
This test may be requested as urate. Uric acid may be ordered to evaluate gout, renal function and a number of other disorders. Blood specimen is serum or plasma. Method is enzymatic or high performance liquid chromatography (HPLC).

84560
Uric acid is also known as urate. Methods may include high performance liquid chromatography, uricase, and phosphotungstate. The test may be ordered to determine the possible occurrence of calculus formation, evaluate uric acid in gout, and to identify genetic defects and some malignancies in body fluids other than blood.

84577
This also is known as the urobilinogen 48-hour feces test. The specimen is by random stool sample. Method is colorimetry. It is used to detect the presence of the yellow substance called urobilin that develops from the chemical breakdown of urobilinogen, which is excreted in the feces.

84578
This test is used to detect the presence of urobilinogen in urine. The specimen is random urine sample. Urobilinogen determination in urine is a useful liver function test, and can be helpful in evaluating some hemolytic anemias. Urobilinogen can be detected qualitatively by a simple, visual colorimetric test or by urine dipstick. Methods may include Ehrlich's aldehyde reagent, para-dimethylaminobenzaldehyde reacts with urobilinogen with a color enhancer.

84580-84583
These tests are used to report quantitative or semi-quantitative measurement of urobilinogen present in the urine. The specimen may be performed over a two-hour period. Elevated levels of urobilinogen can be early indicators of various types of liver disorders. Methods may include Ehrlich's aldehyde reagent, Watson's method, and Urobilistix. This test identifies some cases of liver diseases and hemolytic anemias. Report 84580 for a timed quantitative measurement urobilinogen; report 84583 for a semi-quantitative measurement of urobilinogen.

84585
This test is also called 3-methoxy-4-hydroxymandelic acid test, and also as VMA. Urine collection is over a 24-hour period and requires special handling. Methods

may include colorimetry, spectrophotometry, gas chromatography, and high performance liquid chromatography (HPLC). The test may be performed to evaluate hypertensive states and to diagnose certain tumors and to monitor the efficacy of treatment modalities.

84586
VIP (vasoactive intestinal peptide) is found in and released from the central nervous system. It is found in the gut and affects the cells of the immune system. The specimen is plasma. Method is radioimmunoassay. The test may be used to determine the concentration of vasoactive intestinal peptide (VIP) in serum.

84588
This test is also known as Arginine Vasopressin Hormone and Antidiuretic Hormone (ADH). The specimen is plasma. Method is radioimmunoassay. Vasopressin, secreted by the hypothalamus and stored and released by the posterior pituitary gland, increases blood pressure and the rate at which the kidneys absorb water.

84590
This vitamin is also known as retinol. The specimen is serum, and requires special handling. Methods are electrochemical, high performance liquid chromatography (HPLC), and fluorescence or UV/VIS spectroscopy. Levels of vitamin A can be increased in specific diseases and toxic states, and decreased levels are seen in other conditions, such as, nutritional deficiency.

84591
This test is used to analyze vitamin levels that are not specified elsewhere such as biotin and niacin. Methods are dependent on the specific vitamin level being analyzed and on the type of specimen, but include microbiological assay (urine biotin levels), high performance liquid chromatography (HPLC) (urine niacin levels) solid phase (cellulose) binding assay (plasma biotin levels), chemiluminescence (serum biotin levels).

84597
This test is used to analyze vitamin K, a fat-soluble vitamin that plays an important role in blood clotting. The specimen is serum which requires special handling. Method is high-performance liquid chromatography A. A deficiency in vitamin K is characterized by the increased tendency to bleed, including internal bleeding. Such bleeding episodes may be severe in newborn infants.

84600
This is also known as volatile toxicology, which would include acetone, ethanol, isopropanol, and methanol. The specimen is serum or plasma, random urine, or gastric samples (collected by gastric lavage). Method may be gas-liquid chromatography (GLC). This test is performed to determine systemic alcohol levels and possibly as surveillance for drug abuse and to evaluate methanol and isopropanol toxicity due to ingestion, inhalation, or contact.

84620
This test may also be ordered as a xylose tolerance test. The test measures the intestines' ability to absorb D-xylose, a simple sugar, as an indicator of whether nutrients are being properly absorbed. Multiple blood and/or urine specimens are collected at timed intervals after dosing with a standardized dose of D-Xylose. Samples and sampling collection times are physician specified based on patient age and other parameters.

84630
This test is also known as Serum Zn. The specimen is serum or whole blood or a 24-hour urine sample. . Methods may include atomic absorption spectrometry (AAS). Zinc is a trace mineral in the body, linked to thyroid hormone function and blood clotting. The test may be performed to determine nutrient levels for patients on total parenteral nutrition (TPN) and for burn victims and critically ill patients. The test may also be ordered to evaluate possible zinc toxicity.

84681
This test may also be known as a connecting peptide insulin test or a pro-insulin c-peptide. The specimen is post-fasting serum or urine is over a 24-hour period. Methods may include radioimmunoassay (RIA). The test is primarily performed to determine hypoglycemia and to measure pancreatic beta cell secretory function. It may also be used to determine residual beta cell function in insulin-dependent diabetes, and to differentiate between insulin and non-insulin diabetics.

84702
This test may be ordered as hCG or as a serum pregnancy test. The specimen is serum. Method may be radioimmunoassay (RIA), two-site immunoradiometric assay (IRMA), two-site enzyme-linked immunosorbent assay (ELISA), and radioreceptor assay (RRA). This test is quantitative and measures the amount of hCG present, a determinate of pregnancy and certain tumors.

84703
This test is also known as a beta-subunit human chorionic gonadotropin. The specimen is serum or random urine sample. Methods may include radioimmunoassay (RIA), immunoradiometric (IRMA), and enzyme immunoassay. The test may be ordered to determine pregnancy, ectopic pregnancy, and hCG tumors, and as a screening prior to select medical care (e.g., sterilization).

84704
Free beta human chorionic gonadotropin (hCG) is a biochemical marker used in early (first trimester) screening to detect such abnormalities as Down syndrome, Trisomy 18, and neural tube defects. Maternal serum levels of free beta hCG are elevated in

Down syndrome pregnancies and markedly reduced in Trisomy 18. This test is quantitative and identifies the free beta chain of human chorionic gonadotropin using an enzyme immunoassay methodology.

84830
This test is used for the qualitative detection of the luteinizing hormone (LH) in urine. The specimen is urine. Method is rapid chromatographic immunoassay. LH is always present in the blood and urine, though its levels are higher in urine during ovulation. The LH surge and actual release of the egg is considered as the most fertile time of the cycle, and the most likely time for becoming pregnant.

85002
This test may be ordered as a bleeding time or as an Ivy bleeding time. A small, superficial wound is nicked in the patient's forearm. Essentially, the amount of time it takes for the wound to stop bleeding is recorded at bedside. The Ivy bleeding time test is one standardized method. All methods are manual or point of care. A bleeding time is a rough measure of platelet (thrombocyte) function. The test is often performed on a pre-operative patient.

85004
This test may be ordered as a blood count with automated differential. The specimen is whole blood. Method is automated cell counter. The blood count typically includes a measurement of normal cell constituents including white blood cells or leukocytes, red blood cells, and platelets. In addition, this test includes a differential count of the white blood cells or "diff" in which the following leukocytes are differentiated and counted automatically: neutrophils or granulocytes, lymphocytes, monocytes, eosinophils, and basophils.

85007-85008
This test may be ordered as a manual blood smear examination, RBC smear, peripheral blood smear, or RBC morphology without differential parameters in 85008 and with manual WBC differential in 85007. The specimen is whole blood. The method is manual testing. A blood smear is prepared and microscopically examined for the presence of normal cell constituents, including white blood cells, red blood cells, and platelets. In 85008, the white blood cell and platelet or thrombocyte counts are estimated and red cell morphology is commented on if abnormal. In 85007, a manual differential of white blood cells is included in which the following leukocytes are differentiated: neutrophils or granulocytes, lymphocytes, monocytes, eosinophils, and basophils.

85009
This test may be ordered as a buffy coat differential or as a differential WBC count, buffy coat. Blood is whole blood. Other collection types (e.g., finger stick or heel stick) do not yield the volume of blood required for this test. Method is manual testing. The whole blood is centrifuged to concentrate the white blood cells, and a manual WBC differential is performed in which the following leukocytes are differentiated: neutrophils or granulocytes, lymphocytes, monocytes, eosinophils, and basophils. This test is usually performed when the number of WBCs or leukocytes is abnormally low and the presence of abnormal white cells (e.g., blasts or cancer cells) is suspected clinically.

85013
This test may be ordered as a microhematocrit, a spun microhematocrit, or a "spun crit." The specimen (whole blood) is by finger stick or heel stick in infants. The sample is placed in a tube and into a microcentrifuge device. The vials can be read manually against a chart for the volume of packed red cells or a digital reader in the centrifuge device. A spun microhematocrit only reports the volume of packed red cells. It is typically performed at sites where limited testing is available, the patient is a very difficult blood draw, or on infants.

85014
This test may be ordered as a hematocrit, Hmt, or Hct. The specimen is whole blood. Method is automated cell counter. The hematocrit or volume of packed red cells (VPRC) in the blood sample is calculated by multiplying the red blood cell count or RBC times the mean corpuscular volume or MCV.

85018
This test may be ordered as hemoglobin, Hgb, or hemoglobin concentration. The specimen is whole blood. Method is usually automated cell counter but a manual method is seen in labs with a limited test menu and blood bank drawing stations. Hemoglobin is an index of the oxygen-carrying capacity of the blood.

85025-85027
This test may be ordered as a complete automated blood count (CBC). The specimen is whole blood. Method is automated cell counter. This code includes the measurement of erythrocytes (red blood cells or RBC), leukocytes (white blood cells or WBC), hemoglobin, hematocrit (volume of packed red blood cells or VPRC), platelet or thrombocyte count, and indices (mean corpuscular hemoglobin or MCH, mean corpuscular hemoglobin concentration or MCHC, mean corpuscular volume or MCV, and red cell distribution width or RDW). Code 85025 includes an automated differential of the white blood cells or "diff" in which the following leukocytes are differentiated: neutrophils or granulocytes, lymphocytes, monocytes, eosinophils, and basophils. Report 85027 if the complete CBC, or automated blood count, is done without the differential WBC count.

85032
This code reports a manual cell count done for red blood cells (erythrocytes), white blood cells

(leukocytes), or platelets (thrombocytes), each. The specimen is whole blood. The method is manual examination and counting.

85041
This test may be ordered as red blood cell count or RBC. The specimen is by whole blood. Method is automated cell counter.

85044
This test may be ordered as a manual reticulocyte count or as a manual "retic." The specimen is whole blood. Method is manual. A blood smear is prepared and stained with a dye that highlights the reticulum in the immature red blood cells, or the reticulocytes. The reticulocytes reported as a percentage of total red blood cells.

85045
This test may be ordered as an automated reticulocyte count, an "auto retic," or a reticulocyte by flow cytometry. The specimen is whole blood. Method is automated cell counter or flow cytometer. Reticulocytes are immature red blood cells that still contain mitochondria and ribosomes. The reticulocytes are reported as a percentage of total red blood cells.

85046
This test may be ordered as a reticulocyte count and hemoglobin concentration, "retics" and Hgb, or as an "auto retic" and hemoglobin. The specimen is whole blood. Method is automated cell counter. The blood is stained with a dye that marks the reticulum in immature red blood cells, or reticulocytes. The reticulocytes are reported as a percentage of total red blood cells. The automated reticulocyte blood count also includes one or more cellular parameters, such as the hemoglobin content of the reticulocytes (CHr), the fraction of immature reticulocytes (IRF), the RNA content, or the volume of reticulocytes.

85048-85049
This test may be ordered as an automated white blood cell or WBC count, white cell count, or leukocyte count for 85048 and as an automated platelet count in 85049. The specimen is whole blood. Method is automated cell counter. In 85048, the population of white blood cells, or WBCs in the blood sample, is counted by machine. Only the number of white blood cells or leukocytes is reported. In 85049, the population of platelets or thrombocytes in the blood sample is counted by machine. Only the number of platelets is reported.

85055
Reticulated platelets (RP) are the newly released, or most recently produced, platelets in circulation that contain some residual RNA in their cytoplasm. The specimen is whole blood. The measurement of reticulated platelets is used in thrombocytopenic patients to estimate the thrombocytopoietic status of bone marrow, and evaluate whether the pathophysiology is due to increased peripheral platelet destruction or decreased platelet production. RP counts are also used to monitor the state of megakaryopoiesis in patients with post-chemo or post-transplant status. The method is flow cytometry.

85060
This test may be ordered as a peripheral blood smear with interpretation by a physician, with a written report. It would usually be ordered following a hemogram with WBC differential where the technologist noted the presence of significant abnormalities and requested a pathology review. Although lacking specificity, peripheral smears also provide a quick and cost-effective screening for the presence of bacteremia. The specimen is whole blood. The method is manual. A blood smear is prepared and reviewed by a physician/pathologist, who submits a written interpretation of the findings.

85097
This test may be ordered as a bone marrow smear interpretation with or without differential cell count. The specimen is by aspiration with a syringe. The bone marrow aspirate may be collected from a variety of sites, including the posterior iliac crest (preferred) and the sternum. The method is manual. Slides or smears are prepared from the aspirate and stained. The slides are reviewed by a physician/pathologist and a written interpretation of the findings is submitted. This report may include a differential count of the white blood cells present.

85130
This test may be ordered as a chromogenic substrate assay but would more likely be ordered as a specific clotting factor assay (e.g., factor V, fibrinogen, or antithrombin III) by chromogenic analysis. The specimen is plasma. The method is usually automated coagulation instrument but may be manual.

85170
This test may be ordered as a clot retraction or a clot retraction study. The specimen whole blood. The method is manual. Clot retraction time is a measurement of blood platelet function. Normal blood begins to retract 30 to 60 minutes after collection. The test is an older method to measure platelet or thrombocyte function.

85175
This test may be ordered as a whole blood dilution clot lysis time. The specimen is whole blood. The method is manual. This is a non-specific test of fibrinolytic or clot-lysing activity. The tubes are examined at 24 and 48-hour intervals to assess degeneration of the clots. The test is rarely used today, as there are other specific assays that provide more useable information to the physician.

85210
This test may be ordered as a factor II, clotting factor II, or a prothrombin factor assay. The specimen is plasma. The method is usually automated coagulation instrument but may be manual. This factor is one of several essential to clot formation. A decreased amount of this factor may be associated with clotting impairment.

85220
This test may be ordered as a factor V, clotting factor V, or labile factor assay. It may be ordered as a proaccelerin assay or an AcG factor assay. The specimen is plasma. The method is usually automated coagulation instrument, but may be manual. This factor is one of several essential to clot formation. A decreased amount of this factor may be associated with blood clotting disorders.

85230
This test may be ordered as a factor VII assay, stable factor assay, or clotting factor VII assay. It may also be ordered as a proconvertin assay. The specimen is plasma. The method is usually automated coagulation instrument, but may be manual. This factor is one of several essential to clot formation. A decreased amount of this factor may be associated with blood clotting disorders.

85240
This test may be ordered as a factor VIII assay, AHF, or an anti-hemophilic globulin or AHG assay. The specimen is plasma. The method is automated coagulation instrument, but may be manual. This factor is one of a number of factors essential for clot formation. A decreased amount or absence may be associated with blood clotting disorders (i.e., hemophilia A). This test is essentially an assay for the presence and quantity of the AHG.

85244
This test may be ordered as factor VIII related antigen or VIIIR: Ag. The specimen is plasma. The method is automated coagulation instrument, but may be manual. The presence of Factor VIII related antigen is associated with carriers of the bleeding disorder hemophilia. The test may be useful for the detection of carriers of hemophilia A and in prenatal diagnoses.

85245
This test may be ordered as a ristocetin cofactor, VIIR:Rco, or Von Willebrand factor ristocetin cofactor. The specimen is plasma. The method is automated coagulation instrument, but may be manual. This test measures platelet aggregation in response to introduction of ristocetin into the tube. The resulting level of ristocetin cofactor may be interpreted to assess the function of the Von Willebrand Factor, which may be indicative of the presence of Von Willebrand's disease and the variant or type of the disorder.

85246
This test may be ordered as factor VIII related antigen, VIIR:Ag, Von Willebrand factor or vWF, or Von Willebrand factor antigen vWF:Ag. The specimen is plasma. The method is automated coagulation instrument, but may be manual. A deficiency or low level of Von Willebrand factor antigen is associated with Von Willebrand's disease (a bleeding disorder). A diminished VW factor antigen with reduced function of VW factor can lead to a diagnosis of a variant of Von Willebrand's known as Type I. An absence of VW factor antigen, with undetectable function of VW factor, can lead to a diagnosis of a variant of Von Willebrand's known as Type III.

85247
This test may be ordered as factor VIII assay with multimeric analysis of Von Willebrand factor, agarose gel electrophoresis of Von Willebrand factor, or vWF:Ag multimeric analysis. The specimen is plasma. The method is agarose gel electrophoresis. This test provides a differential diagnosis for variants of Von Willebrand's disease. The absence of multimeric VW factor may be indicative of a variant of Von Willebrand's known as Type II.

85250
This test may be ordered as a factor IX assay, a PTC assay, or a Christmas disease assay. The specimen is plasma. The method is automated coagulation instrument, but may be manual. This factor is one of a number of factors essential to clot formation. A decreased amount of this factor may be associated with a form of homeostasis disorder. A factor IX deficiency is the second most common clotting factor deficiency that results in a variant of hemophilia known by the suffix B or simply Christmas disease.

85260
This test may be ordered as a factor X assay or rarely as a Stuart-Prower assay. The specimen is plasma. The method is automated coagulation instrument but may be manual. This factor is one of a number of factors essential for clot formation. A decreased amount of this factor may be associated with a systemic coagulation disorder known as Factor X deficiency.

85270
This test may be ordered as a factor XI assay or as a PTA assay or antihemophilic C assay. The specimen is plasma. The method is automated coagulation instrument, but may be manual. This factor is one of a number of factors essential for clot formation. A decreased amount of this factor XI may be associated with systemic blood clotting disorder known as Hemophilia C.

85280
This test may be ordered as a factor XII assay or as a Hageman factor assay. The specimen is plasma. The method is automated coagulation instrument, but may

be manual. This factor is one of a number of factors involved in clot formation. A decreased amount of this factor may be associated with blood clotting problems.

85290
This test may be ordered as a factor XIII assay or as a fibrin stabilizing factor assay. The specimen is plasma. The method is automated coagulation instrument but may be manual. This factor is one of a number of factors involved in clot formation. A decreased amount of this factor may be associated with clot dissolution and bleeding problems.

85291
This test may be ordered as a factor XIII solubility screen or a fibrin stabilizing factor solubility screen. The specimen is plasma. The method is manual. This factor is one of a number of factors involved in clot formation. A decreased amount of this factor may be associated with clot dissolution and bleeding problems. This code does not measure the amount of factor XIII antigen but is a measure of factor XIII function.

85292
This test may be ordered as a prekallikrein assay. The method is usually automated coagulation instrument but may be manual. A prekallikrein deficiency results in a prolonged clotting time but is not associated with abnormal bleeding.

85293
This test may be ordered as a high molecular weight kininogen or HMWK assay, a HMW kininogen assay, a Fitzgerald factor assay, or rarely as a Williams factor assay or a Flaujeac factor assay. The specimen is plasma. The method is automated coagulation instrument, but may be manual. A Fitzgerald or HMWK factor deficiency results in a prolonged clotting time but is not associated with abnormal bleeding.

85300
This test may be ordered as an antithrombin III activity assay, an AT-III functional assay, or as a functional antithrombin III assay. The specimen is plasma. The method is automated coagulation instrument, but may be manual. A decrease in antithrombin III function or activity is associated with thrombosis or episodes of abnormal clot formation.

85301
This test may be ordered as an antithrombin III antigen assay, an immunological antithrombin III assay, or an AT-III antigen assay. The specimen is plasma. The method is automated coagulation instrument but may be manual. Levels of antithrombin III antigen may be normal even though the antithrombin III activity is decreased, see 85300. Deficiencies of this antigen are associated with thrombosis or episodes of abnormal clot formation.

85302
This test may be ordered as a protein C antigen assay or an immunological protein C assay. The specimen is plasma. The method is enzyme immunoassay. A decrease in protein C antigen levels is associated with thrombosis or episodes of abnormal clot formation.

85303
This test may be ordered as a protein C activity assay, or as a functional protein C assay. The specimen is plasma. The method is enzyme immunoassay. A decrease in protein C activity or functional levels is associated with thrombosis or episodes of abnormal clot formation.

85305
This test may be ordered as a total protein S assay, protein S antigen assay, or immunological protein S antigen assay. The specimen is plasma. The method is enzyme immunoassay. A decrease in protein S antigen levels is associated with thrombosis or episodes of abnormal clot formation.

85306
This test may be ordered as a free protein S assay, a protein S functional assay, or a protein S activity assay. The specimen is plasma. The method is enzyme immunoassay. A decrease in protein S activity or functional levels is associated with thrombosis or episodes of abnormal clot formation.

85307
This test may be requested as activated protein C (APC) resistance test. Blood specimen is plasma. Method is clotting assay. This test is used to evaluate patients with thrombosis. APC is an important natural anticoagulant present in the blood which functions by inactivating the coagulation factors FVa and FVIIIa. The APC resistance test consists of a standard activated partial thromboplastin time (APTT) test performed both in the absence and presence of commercially available activated protein C. In the normal response, the presence of APC will prolong the clotting time due to the anticoagulant action of this protein. Failure to prolong the clotting time in the presence of APC is an abnormality resulting from resistance to this protein. The results are reported as a ratio of the APC-APTT/APTT.

85335
This test may be ordered as a factor inhibitor test or a Bethesda qualitative test. The specific factor will be ordered (i.e., factor VIII). The specimen plasma. The method is automated coagulation instrument, but may be manual. This test is used to detect the presence of inhibitors or inactivators against a coagulation factor. It is rare but not impossible to exhibit inhibitors against more than one coagulation factor. This assay may be ordered several times before the inhibitor's target factor is identified.

85337
This test may be ordered as a thrombomodulin assay. The specimen is plasma. The method is usually automated coagulation instrument but may be manual. Thrombomodulin is a protein involved in activation of the clot dissolution or lysis process.

85345
This test may be ordered as a clotting time, a whole blood clotting time, or a Lee-White clotting time. The specimen is whole blood. The method is manual. The Lee-White clotting time measures the ability of blood to clot and is performed at the patient's bedside to monitor anticoagulant therapy such as heparin, warfarin, or coumadin.

85347
This test may be ordered as an activated clotting time, an activated whole blood clotting time, or an activated Lee-White clotting time. The specimen is whole blood. The method is manual. The activated clotting time measures the ability of blood to clot and is a precursor to the activated partial thromboplastin time (85730), or PTT.

85348
This test may be ordered as a clotting time. The specimen is whole blood finger stick or, in infants, heel stick. Methods vary, as the formal description implies. Point-of-care testing often involves a hand held instrument that gives some measurement of whole blood clotting time.

85360
This test may be ordered as euglobulin lysis time, euglobulin clot lysis time, or an EGT. The specimen is plasma. The method is manual. This test is a measure of fibrinolytic or clot dissolving activity and is useful in the diagnostic workup for numerous disorders.

85362
This test may be ordered as fibrin (or fibrinogen) degradation products (FDP) or fibrin (or fibrinogen) split products (FSP). Specimen is blood or urine. The test method is latex agglutination. The degradation products of fibrinogen have characteristic biological properties, including the inhibition of clotting. This test measures the products of fibrinolytic or clot dissolving activity. FDP tests on urine are performed primarily post kidney transplant and are helpful as a predictor of rejection.

85366
This test may be ordered as a protamine paracoagulation, fibrin monomer, ethanol gelation or ethanol gel, protamine sulfate, or protamine gelation test. The specimen is blood. The degradation products of fibrinogen have characteristic biological properties, including the inhibition of clotting. This test measures the products of fibrinolytic or clot dissolving activity. The test is not in common usage.

85370
This test may be ordered as quantitative fibrin (or fibrinogen) degradation products (FDP) or quantitative FDP, quantitative fibrin (or fibrinogen) split products (FSP). The specimen is blood. The method is radioimmunoassay (RIA). The degradation products of fibrinogen have characteristic biological properties, including the inhibition of clotting. This test measures the products of fibrinolytic or clot dissolving activity. The degradation products are quantitated.

85378-85379
These tests may be ordered as D-dimer, latex agglutination, or slide D-dimer, semi-quantitative or qualitative. The specimen is plasma. The degradation products of fibrinogen have characteristic biological properties, including the inhibition of clotting. Code 85378 is a semi-quantitative or qualitative measure of two degradation fragments known as the D-dimer. The method typically includes latex agglutination, specific antisera. Code 85379 is a quantitative measure using enzyme-linked immunosorbent assay (ELISA).

85380
The ultrasensitive test for fibrin-degradation products, specifically D-dimer, is a simple and rapid qualitative or semiquantitative in vitro whole blood agglutination assay test that relies on an antibody specific for D-dimer. A small amount of venous (non-clotted) whole blood is required. D-dimer is a specific fibrin degradation product that is produced in the body by the activation of the plasmin enzyme, which breaks down clots and fibrinogen, such as when deep venous thrombosis or pulmonary embolism is present. Elevated levels of D-dimer indicate that active fibrinolysis is occurring. Positive results are not as specific as negative results, which can rule out active fibrin breakdown and, therefore, the diagnosis of embolism accurately.

85384
This test may be ordered as, Factor I, clotting Factor I, fibrinogen, or fibrinogen activity. The specimen is plasma. The method is usually by automated coagulation instrument but may be done manually. This factor is one of a number essential to clot formation. A decreased amount of this factor may be associated bleeding disorders.

85385
This test may be ordered as Factor I, clotting Factor I, or fibrinogen antigen. The specimen is plasma. The method is usually automated coagulation instrument but may be manual. This factor is one of a number essential to clot formation. A decreased amount of this factor may be associated with bleeding disorders.

85390
This test may be ordered as a fibrinolysin screen, as a coagulopathy screen, or as a disseminated intravascular coagulopathy (DIC) screen. The specimen is blood.

The method combines automated coagulation instrument, latex agglutination, and automated cell counter. This test typically screens for intravascular coagulation disorders. A pathology interpretation and report is included with the screen.

85396
A coagulation/fibrinolysis assay is done on whole blood to assess the viscoelastic properties of blood as it clots. Information about the kinetics of clot formation and growth and the strength and stability of the formed clot provides a more global assessment about hemostatic function as a whole dynamic process. The interaction between fibrinogen, platelets, and the protein coagulation process are measured in viscoelastic assays as clotting happens, and followed through to clot lysis. This is invaluable in surgical circumstances for patients who have been treated with anticoagulants, or are suspected of thromboembolic disease.

85397
This test is used to measure the functional activity of ADAMTS-13, an enzyme whose malfunction may lead to thrombotic thrombocytopenic purpura (TTP) or other thrombocytopenic conditions. It also measures the functional activity of other proteases and proteins involved in coagulation and fibrinolysis for which there are no more specific codes. Specimen is plasma and test method is enzyme-linked immunosorbent assay (ELISA) or fluorescence energy transfer (FRET). Report 85397 for each analyte tested.

85400
This test may be ordered as euglobulin lysis time, plasmin level, or plasmin activity. The specimen is plasma. The method is chromogenic substrate. Plasmin is an important agent in the dissolution of clots. Increased plasmin levels are present during fibrinolytic or clot dissolving activity.

85410
This test may be ordered as alpha-2-antiplasmin. The specimen is plasma. The method is typically radial immunodiffusion. Increased alpha-2-antiplasmin levels are present during fibrinolytic or clot dissolving activity.

85415
This test may be ordered as plasminogen activator, plasminogen activator inhibitor (PAI). The specimen is plasma. The method is chromogenic substrate or enzyme linked immunosorbent assay. Increased plasminogen activator levels are present during fibrinolytic or clot dissolving activity.

85420
This test may be ordered as plasminogen level, functional plasminogen, or plasminogen activity. The specimen is plasma. The method is chromogenic substrate. Increased plasminogen levels are present during fibrinolytic or clot dissolving activity, intrauterine death, and some metastatic cancers.

85421
This test may be ordered as plasminogen antigen level. The specimen is plasma. The method is radial immunodiffusion. Increased plasminogen antigen levels may be present during fibrinolytic or clot dissolving activity, intrauterine death, and some metastatic cancers.

85441
This test may be ordered as a Heinz body stain, or a direct Heinz body stain. Heinz bodies are anomalous intracellular erythrocytic (red blood cell) inclusions, composed of denatured hemoglobin that attach to the cell membrane. The specimen is whole blood or finger stick in adults, or heel stick in infants. The method is phase contrast microscopy or supravital stain (e.g., methyl violet, crystal violet, and brilliant cresyl blue, new methylene blue). Elevated numbers of Heinz bodies are found following exposure to certain drugs and toxic chemicals, some enzyme deficiencies, and as a result of inherited disorders of blood hemoglobin.

85445
This test may be ordered as an induced Heinz body stain. Heinz bodies are anomalous intracellular erythrocytic (red blood cell) inclusions, composed of denatured hemoglobin that attach to the cell membrane. The specimen is whole blood or finger stick in adults, or heel stick in infants. The method is phase microscopy or supravital stain (e.g., methyl violet, crystal violet, and brilliant cresyl blue, new methylene blue). A blood sample is treated with a chemical (usually acetyl phenylhydrazine) and a blood smear is prepared and examined for the presence of Heinz bodies in the red blood cells. This test may be necessary to identify patients with certain types of unstable blood hemoglobin disorders.

85460
This test may be ordered as a Kleihauer-Betke stain or K-B stain, a Kleihauer-Betke stain for fetal hemoglobin, a Kleihauer-Betke stain for fetomaternal hemorrhage, acid-resistant fetal cells, or a differential lysis stain. The specimen is whole blood or finger stick. This test is not performed on infants. The method is semi-quantitative stain following acid elution. The blood smear is stained and examined microscopically. The number of red cells containing fetal hemoglobin or acid-resistant hemoglobin red cells are counted and reported as a percentage of the normal adult hemoglobin-containing red cells. This test is usually performed on post-partum mothers to determine if the newborn bled during delivery. The number of acid-resistant, or fetal cells, present is useful in developing postpartum treatment plans, especially with Rh-negative mothers.

85461
This test may be ordered as a fetal hemoglobin screening test, a fetal red cell rosette, a FetalDex screen, or a fetal screen. The specimen is whole blood or finger stick. This test is not appropriate for infants. The blood

is treated with a chemical (anti-D) that causes fetal cells to form a rosette, or circle, of cells. This test is a screen usually performed on Rh-negative post-partum mothers to determine if the newborn bled during delivery.

85475
This test may be ordered as an acid hemolysin test, positive acidified serum test, or as a Ham test. The specimen is whole blood or finger stick in adults, or heel stick in infants. The method is manual. The patient's red blood cells are incubated with a mildly acidic solution and observed for hemolysis. Patients with paroxysmal nocturnal hemoglobinuria (PNH) have a positive acid hemolysin test.

85520
This test may be ordered as a heparin assay, a quantitative heparin analysis, or as a heparin level. The specimen is plasma. The method is chromogenic assay. This test measures the amount of heparin in a patient's blood and is usually ordered when the patient is on low-dose heparin therapy.

85525
This test may be ordered as a heparin neutralization test, a heparin-thrombin coagulation time test, or as protamine neutralization test. The specimen is plasma. The method is manual. This test is used to determine the dose of protamine needed to neutralize heparin-induced bleeding.

85530
This test may be ordered as a heparin-protamine tolerance test. Protamine is given as an antidote to heparin overdose. However, some patients develop hypersensitivity to protamine and may go into anaphylactic shock if they receive a dosage. Method is point of care testing. This test is used to assess hypersensitivity to protamine and measures the amount of protamine that can be safely administered.

85536
This test may also be ordered as a Prussian blue stain, hemosiderin stain, or red cell iron stain. The test is performed to identify abnormal iron accumulations in peripheral red blood cells. The specimen is blood stored unclotted. Method is slide preparation with Perl's Prussian blue stain and visual microscopy. The stain binds to iron in the blood cell and the test may be used to classify anemias as well as other disorders.

85540
This test may be ordered as a leukocyte alkaline phosphatase test (LAP), LAP score. The specimen is whole blood. The method is enzyme reaction with leukocyte alkaline phosphatase liberating naphthol, which is manually stained. Smears from freshly collected whole blood are prepared, stained, and examined microscopically. One hundred cells are counted and phosphatase activity scores (0 to 4+) totaled. The amount of leukocyte alkaline phosphatase present aids in the differential diagnosis of various leukemias.

85547
This test may be ordered as a red blood cell mechanical fragility test, or as a mechanical red cell fragility. The specimen is whole blood or finger stick in adults, or heel stick in infants. The method is manual. Some disorders of red blood cells cause variations in the cell membrane, which may be demonstrated by stressing the red cells.

85549
This test may be ordered as a muramidase test, a myelomonocytic lysozyme test, or as a malignant lymphoma lysozyme test. The specimen is serum, bone marrow aspirate or 24-hour urine specimen. The method is flow cytometry, gel diffusion assay, radioimmunoassay or enzymatic. The presence of this protein aids in the differential diagnosis of certain leukemias and lymphomas.

85555
This test may be ordered as an osmotic fragility test, a red blood cell fragility, an uninucleated osmotic fragility, or as a red blood cell osmotic fragility. The specimen is whole blood. The method is manual. Certain diseases cause red cells to change from their normal shape, which may increase or decrease their ability to take up water without lysing. The red cells are diluted with increasing concentrations of sodium chloride. The concentration that demonstrates hemolysis, or bursting, of the red cells, is compared to a normal patient's red cells.

85557
This test may be ordered as an incubated osmotic fragility test, an incubated red blood cell fragility, or as an incubated red blood cell osmotic fragility. The specimen is whole blood. The method is manual. Certain diseases cause red cells that have been incubated at 37 degrees for 24 hours to change from their normal shape, which may increase or decrease their ability to take up water without lysing. The red cells are diluted with increasing concentrations of sodium chloride. The concentration that demonstrates hemolysis or bursting of the red cells is compared to a normal patient's red cells.

85576
This test may be ordered as a platelet aggregation study, or as an in vitro platelet aggregation study. Specimen is plasma. The method may be platelet aggregometer. Platelet function is measured by observing the amount of platelet clumping that occurs when certain chemicals are added to a solution of platelets. The test is an in vitro enactment of the platelet aggregation that occurs naturally at the site of vascular injury. The test may be used to detect von Willebrand's disease or other inherited platelet disjunction diseases.

85597
This test may be ordered as a PNP, a platelet neutralization test, or as a platelet neutralization test for lupus anticoagulant. The specimen is by venipuncture. Some patients with systemic lupus develop an anticoagulant that reacts with platelets. This test is very sensitive to this anticoagulant.

85610
This test may be ordered as a prothrombin time (PT), a prothrombin, or as simply PT. The specimen is plasma. Method is one-stage using an automated device. The prothrombin time is prolonged when deficiencies of coagulation factors II, V, VII, or X are present. More commonly, this test monitors the effectiveness of the anticoagulant drug Coumadin or warfarin, prescribed to patients who have had blood clots or myocardial infarction.

85611
This test may be ordered as a diluted prothrombin time (PT), a prothrombin 1:1, or as plasma diluted PT. The specimen is plasma. Addition or dilution with normal plasma differentiates between a clotting factor deficiency and a circulating anticoagulant. Prolonged prothrombin times due to a clotting factor deficiency will shorten to normal with the addition of normal plasma while a prolonged prothrombin time due to a circulating anticoagulant may increase with the addition of normal plasma.

85612
This test may be ordered as a Stypven time, Russell viper venom time, or as an undiluted Russell viper venom time. The specimen is plasma. Method is automated with a phospholipid being added to the test system to neutralize platelet activity. This test is used to confirm fibrinogen deficiency, deficiencies of Factors II and V, and some types of Factor X deficiency.

85613
This test may be ordered as a diluted Russell viper venom time. The specimen is plasma. Method is automated. This test is used to confirm the presence of a lupus anticoagulant.

85635
This test may be ordered as a reptilase test or, more commonly, reptilase time (RT). The specimen is plasma. Method involves adding venom of pit viper to a sample of the patient's plasma and recording the clotting time. This test is most often used to monitor the effectiveness of thrombolytic or clot-lysing drugs such as streptokinase or urokinase. It may also be used to detect the presence of coagulation disorders such as dysfibrinogenemias (non-functional or abnormal fibrinogen) and clotting disorders such as disseminated intravascular coagulation (DIC).

85651
This test may be ordered as an erythrocyte sedimentation rate (ESR), a Westergren sedimentation rate, Wintrobe sedimentation rate, or simply as a "sed rate." The specimen is whole blood. This test is a non-specific screening test for a number of diseases including anemia, disorders of protein production such as multiple myeloma, other conditions that alter the size and/or shape of red cells or erythrocytes, and to screen diseases that cause an increase or decrease in the amount of protein in the plasma. Further studies are often launched by ESR results. The method is manual. A variety of procedures have been used over time to study sedimentation rate. A common one performed manually is the Westergren tube.

85652
This test may be ordered as a Zeta sedimentation rate or as a Zeta sed rate. Specimen is whole blood. Method is centrifugation; this is an automated test. This test is a non-specific screening test for a number of diseases including anemia, disorders of protein production such as multiple myeloma, and other conditions that alter the size and/or shape of red cells or erythrocytes. This test may also be used to screen diseases that cause an increase or decrease in the amount of protein in the plasma or liquid portion of the blood.

85660
This test may be ordered as a sickle cell metabisulfite test, a sickle cell reduction test, an erythrocyte (RBC) sickling test, or as an RBC reduction sickle cell test. Specimen is whole blood. The method is manual. Whole blood is mixed with a reducing agent that causes erythrocytes that contain abnormal amounts of hemoglobin S to sickle or change their shape to an elongated 'sickle' cell. The solution is examined microscopically and the numbers of sickle cells are reported as a percentage of normal erythrocytes or RBCs.

85670
This test may be ordered as a thrombin time or as a TT. The specimen is plasma. The method is manual clotting. This test is used to measure the last stage of clotting which is the conversion of fibrinogen to fibrin following the addition of thrombin. This test is prolonged during heparin therapy, in the presence of fibrin split products, and other circulating anticoagulants, and in disorders of fibrinogen.

85675
This test may be ordered as a thrombin time titer or as a diluted thrombin time. The specimen is plasma. The method is manual clotting. This test is used to detect the presence of clotting inhibitors other than heparin. Dilutions of thrombin are used in 85675.

85705
This test may be ordered as a tissue thromboplastin inhibition test (TTI), or as a lupus anticoagulant (LA) test. Extravascular tissue requires a biopsy, which is reported separately. The method is manual clotting. This test is used when the patient has prolonged

prothrombin time (85610) and/or partial thromboplastin time (85730) not due to coagulation factor deficiencies or drug therapy, such as heparin or Coumadin. Some patients with suspected or diagnosed diseases such as lupus erythematosus and AIDS may be candidates for this test.

85730
This test may be ordered as a partial thromboplastin time or PTT, or as an activated partial thromboplastin time or APTT. The specimen is plasma. The method is automated coagulation instrument. The partial thromboplastin time is prolonged when deficiencies of coagulation factors VIII, IX, XI, and XII are present. This test is used to monitor the effectiveness of the anticoagulant drug heparin, which is prescribed for patients who have had blood clots or heart attacks.

85732
This test may be ordered as a diluted partial thromboplastin time, a PTT or APTT 1:1, or as a plasma diluted PTT or APTT. The specimen is plasma. The method is automated coagulation instrument. Addition of or dilution with normal plasma differentiates between a clotting factor deficiency and a circulating anticoagulant. Prolonged partial thromboplastin times due to a clotting factor deficiency will shorten to normal with the addition of normal plasma while a prolonged PTT due to a circulating anticoagulant may increase with the addition of normal plasma.

85810
This test may be ordered as a serum viscosity test or as a viscosity. The specimen is serum. Finger stick or heel stick is not acceptable. The method is viscometer. This test measures the viscosity or thickness of serum as compared to saline. Increased viscosity may be found in disorders such as Waldenström macroglobulinemia.

86000
This test may be ordered as febrile agglutinins or febrile agglute; or separately as Brucella antibody titers, Francisella Murine typhus antibody titers, Q fever antibody titers, Rocky Mountain spotted fever titers. Method is agglutination. If positive at a screening dilution, quantitation may be performed. Serologic agglutination may be used to identify and measure an antigen/antibody response to an infectious disease.

86001
IgG is an immunoglobulin that may be a factor in some allergic reactions. Allergen IgG testing may be performed by RAST (radioallergosorbent) methodology or FETA.

86003
Method may be by agar gel diffusion, ELISA, or Western blot. Immunoglobulin E (IgE) testing may be used when skin testing is unreliable due to generalized dermatitis or severe dermatographism, or when the patient is unable to discontinue use of antihistamines.

86005
This test may be ordered as a RAST (radioallergosorbent test) or by any of the several brand name products available. Blood specimen is serum. The test is essentially a contact reagent method. A dipstick or a disk is exposed to the patient's blood. A change in color indicates the presence of antibodies, indicating an "allergic" status.

86021
This test may also be ordered as alloantibody identification, or alloagglutinin identification (the term "isoantibodies" is archaic). The term autoantibody may also be used. Leukocyte antibodies correlate closely to human leukocyte antigens, a complex genetic code for the immune system. The leukocyte antibody side of the equation may be referred to as alloagglutinins. This type of test is usually ordered to predict for one of several disorders: severe immune reactions from fetomaternal leukocyte incompatibility and/or neonatal incompatibilities, post-blood transfusion reactions, and poor blood component viability following transfusion. Alloantibodies arising from previous pregnancies and transfusions may be evident years after antigen exposure. Autoantibodies are usually identified with autoimmune disorders and infectious diseases. Methods may include agglutination and flow cytometry.

86022
This test may also be requested as serotonin release test. Platelets are small irregularly shaped cells, lacking a nucleus. Platelets serve a variety of functions, including providing a surface area for a variety of reactions. Autoantibodies develop in response to the body's own platelets as a result of idiopathic thrombocytopenia. Alloantibodies develop following exposure to outside antigens, often from blood transfusions. Certain drugs may also induce platelet antibodies. Blood specimen is serum, requiring special handling. Methods include indirect immunofluorescence (IIF), flow cytometry, enzyme linked immunosorbent assay (ELISA).

86023
This test may be ordered as a platelet-associated IgG. Platelets are small irregularly shaped cells, lacking a nucleus. Platelets serve a variety of functions, including providing a surface area for a variety of reactions. This test may be associated with idiopathic thrombocytopenia purpurea (ITP), a serious disorder involving low platelet counts. Method may commonly be by immunofluorescence (IF) or radial immunodiffusion (RID). IgG may also be detected by indirect assay involving interaction between patient blood product and normal platelets.

86038
This test may be ordered as antinuclear antibodies (ANA) test or, less commonly, nuclear binding antibody (NBA). The specimen is serum. Methods

include indirect immunofluorescent methodology and enzyme-linked immunoassay (ELISA). This test is used to measure autoantibodies to the nucleus of human cells and may be used as a screening test for autoimmune diseases such as systemic lupus erythematosus (SLE) and the family of diseases commonly known as scleroderma.

86039
This test may be ordered as antinuclear antibodies (ANA) titer or, less commonly, nuclear binding antibody (NBA) titer. The specimen is serum. Methods include indirect immunofluorescent methodology and enzyme-linked immunoassay (ELISA). The test is used to measure autoantibodies in the nucleus of human cells and may be used as a screening test for autoimmune diseases such as systemic lupus erythematosus (SLE) and the family of diseases known as scleroderma.

86060
The test is ordered as antistreptolysin O (ASO) titer. The specimen is serum. Method is hemagglutination. The test is used for serological documentation of a group A streptococcal infection and may be used as a screening test for acute rheumatic fever, or glomerulonephritis.

86063
This test may be ordered as antistreptolysin O (ASO) screen. The specimen is serum. Methods include hemagglutination and slide agglutination. The test is used for serological documentation of a group A streptococcal infection and may be used as a screening test for acute rheumatic fever or glomerulonephritis.

86077
This physician service is an assessment of crossmatch blood work and/or evaluation of irregular antibody prior to transfusion. This type of physician review may be called for when anomalies arise in the antibody evaluation. An interpretation and written report are specifically required in the code description.

86078
This physician service is an assessment of transfusion reaction, including suspicion of transmissible disease. This type of assessment occurs following transfusion and an interpretation and written report are specifically required in the code description. Common reactions include fever and hives. Of greater concern are anaphylactic shock, graft-versus-host disease, and pulmonary edema.

86079
This physician service involves a written authorization to deviate from standard blood banking procedures. Many facilities maintain rare antigen variants well beyond recommended storage life simply to ensure availability. The code reports the authorization to transfuse this type of blood product, as well as product with incompatible Rh to the recipient. A written report is required.

86140
This test may be ordered as a C-reactive protein (CRP). The specimen is serum. The test may be performed by one of several methods, including latex agglutination and enzyme-linked immunoassay (ELISA). Elevated levels of C-reactive protein may be used as a measure for nonspecific inflammatory response. High levels of CRP may be present in bacterial infection, some tumors and various types of tissue damage, but more commonly in acute rheumatic fever and rheumatoid arthritis.

86141
C-reactive protein is released into the bloodstream when the blood vessels leading to the heart are damaged, which qualifies it is a nonspecific marker of inflammation. Measurement of C-reactive protein by high sensitivity CRP (hsCRP) assays adds to the predictive value of other markers used to assess a variety of conditions which can lead to elevated serum concentration of CRP, including inflammation, infection, and malignancy. C-reactive protein, hsCRP is also used to assess cardiovascular and peripheral vascular disease. Serum or plasma is the specimen. CRP assay involves the coating of artificially produced particles (i.e., Latex) with an antibody specific to human CRP aggregate in the presence of CRP from the patient sample of formed immune complex. The immune complex causes an increase in light scattering that is proportional to the concentration of CRP in the sample. The light scattering is quantified optically by measuring turbidity.

86146
Beta 2 glycoprotein 1 antibody actually refers to a group of autoantibodies used as serological markers for antiphospholipid syndrome (APS). APS is characterized by recurrent arterial and venous thrombosis as well as recurrent fetal loss. These autoantibodies are natural regulators of the blood coagulation cascade. Blood specimen is serum or citrated plasma. Method is enzyme-linked immunoassay (ELISA). The test may be repeated at regular intervals.

86147
This test may also be ordered as antiphospholipid antibody or anticardiolipin antibodies (ACA). The specimen is serum. Method is enzyme-linked immunoassay (ELISA). The test may be used to classify patients with recurrent venous or arterial thrombosis, thrombocytopenia (low platelet count), recurrent fetal loss, and acquired valvular heart disease, and systemic lupus erythematosus (SLE).

86148
Testing for antiphosphatidylserine antibodies, a class of phospholipid antibodies, identifies various

autoimmune disorders and antiphospholipid syndrome in patients that are negative for anticardiolipin antibodies. Antiphospholipid syndrome (APS) is an autoimmune condition that may manifest with fetal loss, thrombosis, or autoimmune thrombocytopenia. The specimen is serum. The method of testing is enzyme immunoassay.

86155
This test may be ordered as phagocytic cell function evaluation, NBT slide assay, or DCF assay. The specimen is whole blood. The method is gel agar diffusion. Live neutrophils are required for a successful test. This test may be used for screening infections, perinatal abscesses, multiple episodes of pneumonia, or delayed wound healing may be tested. Patients under treatment for malignancy or those treated with immunosuppressive antiviral therapies may also be candidates.

86156
This test may be ordered as cold agglute or thermal amplitude assay. The specimen is serum. Method is hemagglutination. The test may be used to provide an early detection of an immunoglobulin M (IgM) class antibody, which may be present in acute primary atypical pneumonia (Mycoplasma pneumoniae) and certain hemolytic anemias. Low levels of cold agglutinins have been demonstrated in malaria, peripheral vascular disease, and common respiratory diseases.

86157
This test may be ordered as cold agglute titer or thermal amplitude assay. The specimen is serum The method is hemagglutination. This test may be used to screen immunoglobulin M (IgM) class antibody, which may be present in acute primary atypical pneumonia (Mycoplasma pneumoniae) and certain hemolytic anemias. Low levels of cold agglutinins have been demonstrated in malaria, peripheral vascular disease, and common respiratory diseases.

86160
This test may be ordered as individual complement components 2-5 or Factor B. The specimen is serum. Methodology is radial immunodiffusion or nephelometry. Complement activation is a multi-component biological response function of the immune system present in inflammatory conditions; the degree of complement activation may be used to indicate the intensity of the inflammatory process. Syndromes associated with complement activation include rheumatoid arthritis, systemic lupus erythematosus (SLE), gram negative sepsis, and chronic hepatitis.

86161
This test may be ordered as individual complement component The specimen is serum Methodology is radial immunodiffusion or nephelometry. Complement activation is a multi-component biological response function of the immune system present in inflammatory conditions; the degree of complement activation may be used to indicate the intensity of the inflammatory process. Syndromes associated with complement activation include rheumatoid arthritis, systemic lupus erythematosus (SLE), gram negative sepsis, and chronic hepatitis.

86162
This test may be ordered as complement CH50, total. The specimen is serum. Methodology involves an indicator system using predetermined amounts of sheep red blood cells coated with antibody and is measured by spectrophotometry. Complement activation is a multi-component biological response function of the immune system present in inflammatory conditions; the degree of complement activation may be used to indicate the intensity of the inflammatory process. Syndromes associated with complement activation include rheumatoid arthritis, systemic lupus erythematosus (SLE) gram negative sepsis and chronic hepatitis.

86171
This test may be ordered as a complement assay. The complementary system involves enzymes and regulatory proteins synthesized in the liver. Activation of the system triggers a cascading, or sequential, response that may lead to histamine release, inflammation, and other normal activities of the immune system. Blood specimen is serum. Complement fixation is widely used test that relies on these principles. The test may be used for a wide variety of suspected illnesses, including viral infections.

86185
This test may also be referred to as countercurrent immunoelectrophoresis or counterelectrophoresis. A cerebrospinal fluid specimen is the most common, as it is used in cases of suspected bacterial meningitis, but other sources may also be used. CSF specimen is obtained by separately reportable spinal puncture. Pleural fluid is obtained by separately reportable thoracentesis. The test methodology is similar to crossed immunoelectrophoresis (86327), since it involves a double electroimmunodiffusion.

86200
This test may also be known as anti-CCP or CCP antibodies. The test is used to diagnose rheumatoid arthritis (RA) in the earliest stages. The specimen is serum and the method of testing is by enzyme linked immunosorbent assay. (ELISA).

86225
This test may be ordered as anti-DNA, anti-ds-DNA, dsDNA antibody, or anti-native DNA. The specimen is serum. Methods include indirect immunofluorescent assay and enzyme-linked immunosorbent assay (ELISA). This test may be performed for patients

previously diagnosed with systemic lupus erythematous (SLE). These patients may exhibit a high level of antibody against their own native double-stranded DNA, and results of the test may indicate renal involvement. This test for the double-stranded DNA. Low levels of the antibody may be found in other autoimmune disorders such as Sjögren's syndrome, mixed connective tissue disease, and progressive systemic sclerosis.

86226
This test may be ordered as ssDNA, antibody IgG, or anti-single stranded DNA. The specimen is serum. Method is enzyme-linked immunosorbent assay (ELISA). Single stranded DNA antibodies are found in 20 to 30 percent of all cases of systemic lupus erythematosus (SLE), and less specific in the diagnosis of SLE compared to double-stranded DNA antibodies. Lower levels of double-stranded DNA antibodies are associated with chronic inflammatory processes, malignancy, drug-induced lupus, or cardiolipin antibodies (cross-reaction).

86235
Examples of antibodies covered by this code are listed in the CPT(r) description; however, other antibodies may also be reported with this code. This test is performed to detect antibodies associated with system lupus erythematosis (SLE) and mixed connective tissue disease. Anti-Sm is highly specific for SLE. Anti-RNP is found with a variety of rheumatoid diseases. The specimen is serum. The most common method of testing is flow cytometry.

86243
Cell surfaces feature complex molecular structures to regulate activities with other cells. The Fc receptor is a site on certain cells (i.e., macrophages, eosinophils, etc.) to accommodate specific antigen/antibody activities. The Fc receptors may work in connection with specific immunoglobulins or classes. Three types are sometimes referred to: FcRI, FcRII, and FcRIII. A key function is to trigger phagocytes to feed and ingest antigens. Method of testing varies.

86255-86256
These codes report detection of noninfectious agents using fluorescent agent antibody technique. A number of noninfectious agents are reported with codes 86255 and 86256. Some antibodies reported with these codes include: acetylcholine receptor antibody (anti-AChR); adrenal cortex antibodies; anti D. S., DNA, IFA using C. Luciliae; mitochondrial antibody, liver; smooth muscle antibody; antineutrophil antibody; endomysial antibody; parietal cell antibody; and myositis-specific auto antibody. Code 86255 is a screen and reports the presence of the antibody only. Code 86256 is a titer and reports the level of antibody present.

86277
This test may also be ordered as somatotropin antibody, GH antibody test, or IGF (insulin-like growth factor) antibody. Portions of the pituitary gland secrete growth hormone. Serum levels normally rise and fall throughout the day. Radioimmunoassay (RIA) is the method of choice.

86280
This is a general methodology code for any test that measures the ability of soluble antigen to inhibit the agglutination of antigen-coated red blood cells by antibodies. In this test, a fixed amount of antibodies to the antigen in question is mixed with a fixed amount of red blood cells coated with the antigen (see passive hemagglutination above). Also included in the mixture are the sample to be analyzed for the presence of the antigen. If the sample contains the antigen, the soluble antigen will compete with the antigen coated on the red blood cells for binding to the antibodies, thereby inhibiting the agglutination of the red blood cells. The sample varies. This test is useful in identifying secretor status of an individual in saliva and used for antibody identification workups.

86294
This code is may be requested as single step qualitative or semi-quantitative immunoassay to identify the presence of a specific tumor antigen. The specimen is serum. Method is immunoassay.

86300
This test may also be requested as CEA carbohydrate antigen 15-3. Method is immunoassay or ICMA. Quantitative analysis for CA 15-3 is used primarily to monitor patients for recurrence of breast cancer after diagnosis and initial treatment or to evaluate response to therapy. Elevated levels are often indicative of a recurrence or a failed treatment.

86301
This test may also be requested as carbohydrate antigen 19-9. The specimen is serum. Method is immunoassay. Quantitative analysis for CA 19-9 is used primarily as a marker for pancreatic cancer. It identifies recurrence and monitors patients. It is also used to monitor gastrointestinal, head/neck, and gynecological cancer. It may identify recurrence of stomach, colorectal, liver, gallbladder, and urothelial malignancies.

86304
This test may also be requested as cancer antigen 125. The specimen is serum. Method is immunoassay. CA 125 is found in ovarian cancers, and some endometrium and fallopian tube cancers. Testing for CA 125 is performed primarily to detect residual tumor in women who have been previously diagnosed with ovarian malignancy.

86305
The gene for human epididymis protein 4 (HE4) is among those most often identified in gene expression

profiles of epithelial ovarian carcinomas and has been shown to be elevated in a high percentage of women with ovarian cancer. This test is used as an aid in monitoring disease progression or recurrence; the specimen is blood.

86308-86310
These tests may be requested as a heterophile antibody screen and/or titer. Common brand names include Monospot, Monosticon, Dri-Dot. Heterophile antibodies are commonly tested to diagnose infectious mononucleosis. Blood specimen is serum or plasma. Method is agglutination. Code 86308 is a screen that identifies the presence of the antibody only; while 86309 is a titer that identifies the level of antibody present. Code 86310 reports a more specific methodology for testing heterophile titers using both beef cells and guinea pig kidneys.

86316
This test is an immunoassay for tumor antigen and may be requested by the specific antigen. Some of the more common tumor antigens include carbohydrate antigen 549 (CA 549), carbohydrate antigen 72-4 (CA 72-4, TAG 72), and carbohydrate antigen 50 (CA 50). Each of these antigens is specific for certain types of cancer. CA 549 is found in Stage IV metastatic breast cancer and is used primarily to evaluate response to therapy.

86317
This code may be requested to measure the amount of specific infectious disease antibodies in the blood that are not otherwise specified. It would normally be obtained subsequent to qualitative or semi-quantitative immunoassays (86318, 86602-86804), which identify the presence of specific antibodies but do not measure the amount of antibody present. Method is immunoassay.

86318
This code may be requested as single step qualitative or semi-quantitative immunoassay to identify the presence of a specific infectious agent antibodies. Specimen is serum. Method is immunoassay. Single step methods frequently use a reagent strip for the specific antibody.

86320
This code may be abbreviated as serum IEP. Blood specimen is serum. This code is used to report a technique most often used to identify monoclonal gammopathy or lymphoproliferative processes, specifically myelomas. It combines electrophoresis and immunodiffusion. This test is qualitative only.

86325
This code may be abbreviated as IEP. A random urine specimen is obtained. CSF is obtained by separately reportable spinal puncture. This code is used to report a technique most often used to identify monoclonal gammopathy or lymphoproliferative processes, specifically myelomas. It combines electrophoresis and immunodiffusion. This test is qualitative only.

86327
Two-dimensional or crossed immunoelectrophoresis (IEP) is similar to standard IEP as described in 86320 and 86325; however, following immunodiffusion, electrophoresis is performed a second time at right angles to the original separation.

86329-86331
These tests may be abbreviated as ID. Immunodiffusion (86329) involves an antibody-antigen reaction that causes a visible precipitate to form. It is a technique used in identifying immunoglobulin. Ouchterlony gel diffusion (86331) involves evaluation of the precipitin reaction in a clear gel. Immune complex assays were once thought to be a promising diagnostic technique. However, they have generally been replaced with tests that are more specific, more standardized, and less expensive. Blood specimen is serum which requires special handling. Method is a complement binding (CP) technique.

86332
Immune complex assays were once thought to be a promising diagnostic technique. However, they have generally been replaced with tests that are more specific, more standardized, and less expensive. Blood specimen is obtained by venipuncture. Method is a complement binding (CP) technique.

86334-86335
Immunofixation electrophoresis (IFE) is a method or technique used to detect the presence of aberrant proteins, especially monoclonal proteins, and to identify when certain protein groups are being increased or decreased in blood serum or urine, particularly. This test can help diagnose and monitor the progression of diseases like multiple myeloma, monoclonal gammopathies, and kidney-damaging diseases. The specimen is serum. For urine testing, a 24-hour urine specimen is required. IFE involves high-resolution electrophoresis combined with immunoprecipitation The value in performing immunofixation electrophoresis is identifying the presence of a particular type of protein, or immunoglobulin. Report 86334 for a serum test and 86335 for another fluid, such as urine or cerebral spinal fluid.

86336
Inhibin A is a protein hormone related to pregnancy which is a screening marker of Down Syndrome. Testing for high levels of Inhibin A may be considered as a fourth hormone check that increases the accuracy of screening for Down Syndrome in addition to alpha-fetoprotein (AFP), human chorionic gonadotropin (HCG or hCG), and estriol levels. In Down Syndrome, Inhibin A and HCG protein hormone levels tend to be high while the other two tend to be

low. The Inhibin A pregnancy hormone level is tested from maternal serum in the 16th to 18th week of gestation. A serum sample is from the mother and radioimmunoassay (RIA) may be used to analyze the sample.

86337
This test may be requested as insulin antibody or anti-insulin Ab. It usually includes testing for antibodies to both beef and pork insulin. Insulin dependent diabetics sometimes develop IgG antibodies to insulin, which can cause insulin resistance making larger doses of insulin necessary to achieve the same level of control. However, they may also develop IgA, IgM, IgD, and IgE antibodies. Most of these antibodies do not cause clinical problems. The specimen is serum. Method is radioimmunoassay (RIA), radiobinding assay, or enzyme linked immunosorbent assay (ELISA).

86340
This test may be requested as intrinsic factor (IF) antibody. There are two types of IF antibody. Type I, blocking antibody, is the more common of the two. It prevents binding of B12 with intrinsic factor but will not react with complex intrinsic factor. Type II antibody, binding antibody, reacts with either free of complex IF. The specimen is serum. Method is radioimmunoassay (RIA).

86341
This test detects the formation of antibodies to the pancreatic islet cell, which causes destruction of those cells and, therefore, loss of an individual's ability to produce insulin. The presence of islet cell antibodies are helpful in establishing an initial diagnosis of Type I, insulin-dependent diabetes mellitus (IDDM) and in identifying those individuals at high risk of developing IDDM. It is also useful in identifying potential transplant donors for pancreatic islet cells. The specimen is serum. Various methods are used.

86343
This test is performed to quantify the levels of histamine. The specimen is plasma. Urine is collected over a 24-hour period. Methods are fluorometric, radioenzymatic, and immunoassay. Allergic and non-allergic intolerance to drugs, insect venom, paints or cosmetics, as well as heat or cold, or stress may induce histamine release. By using the histamine release test it is possible to identify a broad spectrum of allergies.

86344
Abnormalities in leukocyte phagocytosis may be used as a screen for a variety of disorders. The specimen is whole blood. Method is flow cytometry or fluorescence microscopy. Leukocytes protect against infection and immunological disease in a process called phagocytosis. It involves ingesting and killing invading microbes inside biological compartments called phagolysosomes.

86352
The human immune system consists of two separate yet interrelated forms of immunity: humoral immunity and cell-mediated immunity (CMI). The measurement of CMI is useful in many applications, including clinical management of organ transplant recipients, management of infectious diseases such as HIV or HCV, cancer, autoimmunity, and development of drugs and vaccines. This cellular function assay detects CMI in whole blood in immunosuppressed patients by measuring their early response to immune system stimulation and detection of adenosine triphosphate (ATP), a biomarker.

86353
This test may also be requested as lymphocyte mitogen response test or phytohemagglutinin (PHA) stimulation. Lymphocytes are normally produced early in an immune response. This test is used to determine the adequacy of early immune response using nonspecific mitogens or specific antigens as transforming agents capable of inducing blastogenesis. This process involves isolation of lymphocytes in peripheral blood and culture of the isolated lymphocytes in microtiter plates for three to seven days. Prior to harvest of cultured cells, the lymphocytes are pulsed with triturated thymidine. Incorporated thymidine is measured. Control values are used to calculate a stimulation index.

86355
This test may also be referred to as a B lymphocyte assay. B cells, also known as B lymphocytes, are responsible for making antibodies. B cells develop and mature in the bone marrow. An increased B cell count may be indicative of such diseases as chronic lymphocytic leukemia, multiple myeloma, Waldenström's macroglobulinemia, and DiGeorge syndrome. Decreased B cell count may indicate such conditions as acute lymphoblastic leukemia and congenital and acquired immunoglobulin deficiency disorders. The specimen is whole blood. The quantitative number of B lymphocytes is determined using flow cytometry.

86356
Using specific antibody labeling with flow cytometry measurement, this test detects the amount of specific antigens on mononuclear cells (lymphocytes, dendritic cells, monocytes, macrophages). This test distinguishes cellular disorders such as cancer and autoimmune diseases that have different antigen markers. This code is reported for each antigen.

86357
This is a blood test that provides a total count of target cells that are killed by natural killer (NK) cells. The total count of cells killed by NK cells is compared to total live cells to determine NK activity. NK cells are lymphocytes that have many functions, one of which is to produce a cytoxic chemical called tumor necrosis

factor (TNF). This is a chemical that kills malignant (cancer) cells in the body. However, in some women NK cells attack the embryo in early pregnancy causing spontaneous abortion. The specimen is whole blood. NK cells are separated from the blood and are cultured at different dilutions with target cells from an embryonic cancer cell line. These target cells have been tagged with cytoplasmic dye. Flow cytometry is used to identify the target cells that have been killed by the NK cells. Flow cytometry is used to precisely count the percentage of dead to live cells at the different dilutions.

86359
This test may also be referred to as T-cell assay, T-cell analysis, or T-cell study. It is used to quantitate total T-cell lymphocytes without providing absolute counts of the different types of lymphocytes. Examples of different types of lymphocytes included in the total count are CD3, CD4, CD8, CD20, CD38, etc. The specimen is whole blood. Whole blood is added to fluorochrome-labeled antibodies, also referred to as monoclonal antibodies, which bind specifically to cell surface antigens on lymphocytes. This is used in conjunction with flow cytometry to obtain the total T-cell count. This test is used to type and classify different types of lymphomas and lymphocytic leukemias as well as to monitor immunodeficiency states, including HIV infections.

86360
This test may also be requested as T4/T8 ratio, CD4/CD8 ratio, T-cell assay for CD4/CD8. It is used to quantitate CD4 and CD8 specifically, and from those counts to obtain a CD4 to CD8 ratio. Whole blood is added to fluorochrome-labeled antibodies, also referred to as monoclonal antibodies, which bind specifically to cell surface antigens on lymphocytes. This is used in conjunction with flow cytometry to obtain the CD4 and CD8 cell counts. This test is used primarily in staging HIV infection and monitoring the effects of treatment. It may also be useful in diagnosing and monitoring congenital immunodeficiencies.

86361
This test may also be requested as T-cell assay for CD4. The specimen. Whole blood is added to fluorochrome-labeled antibodies, also referred to as monoclonal antibodies, which bind specifically to cell surface antigens on lymphocytes. This is used in conjunction with flow cytometry to obtain the CD4 cell count. This test is used primarily in staging HIV infection and monitoring the effects of treatment. It may also be useful in diagnosing and monitoring congenital immunodeficiencies.

86367
Many different subsets of stem cells are present in the blood and bone marrow. Some stem cell subtypes are able to differentiate into several cell types. These are called multipotent or multilineage stem cells. Multipotent stem cells have the capacity to differentiate into myeloid, lymphoid, erythroid, and megakaryocytic lineages. Other stem cell subtypes are lineage specific and differentiate only to a single cell type. While there is no test to specifically identify the multipotent stem cells, it has been discovered that high counts of progenitor cells with surface antigen CD34+ enhance engraftment in stem cell transplant recipients. This test quantifies the total number of specific stem cells subtypes in the body, such as stem cells with surface antigen CD34+ cells. Periodic blood samples are obtained to determine total amounts of circulating CD34+ cells. Flow cytometry is used to identify specific stem cell subtypes and to determine total counts of CD34+ cells. Using this test the physician can determine when the total number of circulating stem cells containing CD34+ is sufficient to begin harvesting stem cells for subsequent transplant.

86376
This test is performed to determine the presence of antithyroid microsomal antibodies. The specimen is serum. A hemagglutination test for thyroid antigens is used and, if that test is positive, it is followed by a fluorescent scan to show a decrease or absence of thyroid-stable iodine. Other methods include ELISA (enzyme linked immunosorbent assay) or particle agglutination (PA). The anti-microsomal antibody or microsomal antibody test may be used to diagnose conditions such as Hashimoto's thyroiditis and other autoimmune disorders. Hashimoto's disease is an autoimmune thyroid disorder characterized by the production of antibodies in response to thyroid antigens. Normal thyroid structures are replaced by lymphocytes and lymphoid germinal centers.

86378
This test may be ordered as glycosylation-inhibiting factor (GLIF), macrophage migration inhibiting factor (MIF) test and the macrophage inhibition factor (MIF) test. Specimen collection is by venipuncture. Binding assay and immunocytochemical analysis have been used to detect the release and activation of MIF in inflammatory response. MIF is released by the pituitary and by macrophages during inflammatory response and has become an important immunotherapy target to treat a variety of inflammatory diseases and condition, such as rheumatoid polyarthritis and Crohn's disease.

86382
Tissue samples may be collected by biopsy. Fluorescent dye may be used to identify the target virus directly from clinical specimens or tissue. Neutralization tests are used in various serological tests to identify antibodies to the target virus in serum (i.e., Herpes simplex virus). The identification aids in the diagnosis of diseases caused by the virus. Specimen type varies.

86384
This code also may be ordered as Nitroblue Tetrazolium (NBT). The specimen is whole blood. A

biochemical assay and simple laboratory equipment (microscope, incubator and centrifuge) are used to detect phagocytosis and intracellular killing of microorganisms by normal polymorphonuclear neutrophils. The test has been found to have several applications, including the detection of certain immunodeficiency disorders (i.e., AIDS), Hodgkin's disease, and chronic lymphocytic leukemia.

86403-86406
These tests may be ordered as PA. The specimen is serum. There are several methods used in tandem with PA tests, such as fluorescence enzyme assay and scattered light flow cytometry. Particle agglutination (PA) tests may be performed to evaluate immune status to and diagnosis certain viruses (i.e., measles virus infection Use 86403 to report each separate antibody screen, and 86406 to report each antibody tested according to titer.

86430
This test may be ordered as rheumatoid antibody (RA), arthritis screen, or rheumatoid factor (RF). The specimen is serum,. The test is most significantly used as a qualitative measurement in evaluating patients with inflammatory polyarthritis. The presence of RF is not by itself usually considered sufficient to establish a diagnosis of rheumatoid arthritis, but as a contributing factor or a prognostic marker to a diagnosis. Testing methodology is by latex agglutination, ELISA, or nephelometry.

86431
This test may be ordered as rheumatoid antibody (RA) titer, arthritis screen, or rheumatoid factor (RF) titer. The specimen is serum. The test is most significantly used as a quantitative measurement in evaluating patients with inflammatory polyarthritis. The presence or quantity of RF is not by itself usually considered sufficient to establish a diagnosis of rheumatoid arthritis, but as a contributing factor or a prognostic marker to a diagnosis. Testing methodology is by latex agglutination, ELISA, or nephelometry.

86480
This blood test is used to diagnose latent (non-active) infection with tuberculosis (TB) and may be performed instead of a skin test. The blood test can be accomplished in a single patient visit and unlike the skin test, its results do not require subjective interpretation of a health worker.

86485
This test may be ordered as candida delayed hypersensitivity testing (DHT or DHR). The methods are: the intradermal test and the prick test. Candida albicans is a common environmental yeast, and this testing is usually a control for anergy or immunocompetence. A standardized concentration of the yeast is introduced into the skin of the arm, usually by needle or skin prick. The test site is examined within 30 minutes and again at 24, 48, and 72-hour intervals. Evidence of a reaction is recorded.

86486
This code reports skin tests for antigens other than those for which a more specific code exists. Testing methods may consist of the intradermal test and the prick test. A standardized concentration of the antigen is introduced into the skin of the arm, usually by needle or skin prick. The test site is examined within specified time frames and evidence of a reaction is recorded.

86490
This test may be ordered as coccidioides delayed hypersensitivity testing (DHT or DHR). It may also be ordered as cocci skin test. Two testing methods are: the intradermal test and the prick test. A standardized concentration of the antigen is introduced into the skin of the arm, usually by needle or skin prick. The test site is examined within 30 minutes and again at 24, 48, and 72-hour intervals. Evidence of a reaction is recorded. This test has limited value diagnostically and usually provides supporting information only.

86510
This test may be ordered as histoplasma skin test. Two testing methods are: the intradermal test and the prick test. A standardized concentration of antigen is introduced into the skin of the arm, usually be needle or skin prick. The site is examined within 30 minutes and again at 24, 48, and 72- hour intervals. Evidence of a reaction is recorded. This test has limited value diagnostically.

86580
This test may be ordered as TB skin test, TB delayed hypersensitivity testing (DHT or DHR), Tuberculin skin test, Mantoux test, or purified protein derivative test (PPD). A standardized concentration of tuberculin PPD is introduced into the skin of the arm. The method is intradermal. The test may screen individuals in high-risk circumstances, or as routine surveillance among certain populations regularly exposed (i.e., health care workers). Patients showing certain signs or symptoms are also tested. Culture extracts of tuberculin proteins in a test dosage is injected intradermally (forearm). The test site is examined at 24, 48, and 72-hour intervals for evidence of induration. Evidence of a reaction is recorded.

86590
This test is commonly ordered as ASO. The specimen is serum. The test is useful for detection of antibody to an extracellular antigenic product of group A streptococci and commonly used to detect previous exposure to group A strep. The test may be performed by latex agglutination or enzyme-linked immunosorbent assay (ELISA).

86592
This nontreponemal (screening) antibody test is commonly ordered as RPR (rapid plasma reagin), STS (serologic test for syphilis), VDRL (venereal disease research laboratory), or ART (automated reagin test). It may also be ordered as standard test for syphilis. The specimen is serum. The test is commonly used to provide a diagnosis (screening test) for syphilis. The method is by nontreponemal rapid plasma reagin (RPR)-particle agglutination test. More recently, it is being performed by automated methodology, such as enzyme-linked immunosorbent assay (ELISA).

86593
This nontreponemal (screening) test is commonly ordered as quantitative RPR (rapid plasma reagin), STS (serologic test for syphilis), VDRL (venereal disease research laboratory), or ART (automated reagin test). This test may also be ordered as a standard test for syphilis. The specimen is serum. It is most commonly used to provide a monitor for treatment, or to establish a diagnosis of reinfection with syphilis. The method is nontreponemal rapid plasma reagin-particle agglutination test or anticardiolipin antibodies. More recently, it is being performed by automated methodology, such as by enzyme-linked immunosorbent assay (ELISA).

86602
This test is commonly ordered as anti-actinomyces or actinomyces antibody titer. The specimen is serum. The test is used as a rapid serological method to diagnose for nocardial infections (infections caused by *Nocardia*, a *genus* of gram-positive bacteria). The methods are: complement fixation (CF), immunodiffusion, agglutination assay, and Western blot (immunoblot).

86603
This test is commonly ordered as anti-adenovirus titer or adenovirus antibody titer. The specimen is serum. The test is traditionally used as a rapid serological method to diagnose for adenovirus infections. The methods are: complement fixation (CF), immunofluorescent, and enzyme-linked immunosorbent assay (ELISA).

86606
This test is commonly ordered as anti-aspergillus titer or aspergillus antibody titer. The specimen serum. The test is used as a rapid serological method to diagnose for aspergillus infection. The methods are: complement fixation (CF), counterimmunoelectrophoresis, radioimmunoassay, immunofluorescence, enzyme-linked immunosorbent assay (ELISA), and immunodiffusion.

86609
This test is commonly ordered as a generic test for any bacterium that has not otherwise been specified. This test will usually utilize the words anti, titer, or antibody. The specimen is serum. The test is traditionally used as a rapid serological method to diagnose bacterial infections. The methods are: complement fixation (CF), immunofluorescence, and enzyme-linked immunosorbent assay (ELISA).

86611
This test may also be known as bacillary angiomatosis (BA) or bacillary peliosis (BP) antibody. IgG testing may be used to identify current or past infection whereas IgM is more specific for current infection. The specimen is serum. Methods include enzyme immunoassay (EIA) and indirect fluorescence antibody test. The *Bartonella genus* of bacteria is implicated in a variety of life threatening infections. Exposure to the bacillus and presence of antibodies may remain asymptomatic. An opportunistic infection arising in some AIDS patients is linked to the Bartonella genus and is noted for vascular lesions.

86612
This test is commonly ordered as anti-Blastomyces or Blastomyces antibody titer. It may occasionally be ordered as "blasto" titer. The specimen is serum. The test is used as a rapid serological method to diagnose for Blastomyces infections. The methods are: complement fixation (CF), immunodiffusion, agglutination assay, immunofluorescence, enzyme-linked immunosorbent assay (ELISA), and Western blot (immunoblot).

86615
This test is may be ordered as pertussis or whooping cough antibody. Bordetella pertussis is the causative agent of whooping cough. This test demonstrates antibodies, which is not a common approach to developing a clinical diagnosis due to the time required for seroconversion. However, it may be used to evaluate immunity following immunization. Blood specimen is serum. Methods include enzyme-linked immunosorbent assay (ELISA), microhemagglutination, complement fixation (CF), and toxin neutralization.

86617
This test may be ordered as a Lyme disease confirmation test. Borrelia burgdorferi is the causative agent of Lyme disease, (the vector being a tick). Antibodies usually build up in patients several weeks or longer into an infection. This test is confirmatory, meaning previous diagnostic work has been performed. Blood specimen is serum. CSF specimen is obtained by spinal puncture that is reported separately. This test reports a second test for confirmation by immunoblot or Western blot. It may also be used to establish a diagnosis following indeterminate ELISA results.

86618
This test may be ordered simply as a Lyme disease antibody test. Borrelia burgdorferi is the causative

agent of Lyme disease,(the vector being a tick). Antibodies usually build up in patients several weeks or longer into an infection. Blood specimen is serum. CSF specimen is obtained by spinal puncture, which is reported separately. Methods include enzyme-linked immunosorbent assay (ELISA), enzyme immunoassay (EIA), indirect fluorescent antibody (IFA), or specific IgG, IgM, and IgA by antibody capture.

86619
This test may be ordered as a relapsing fever antibody. Relapsing fever is caused by spirochetes of the genus Borrelia, and those infected suffer alternating fevers and chills. Ticks and body lice are the vectors to humans. Blood specimen is serum. Literature is unclear about methods and reasons to order such testing. Indications are that this test is rarely performed.

86622
Brucellosis is a rare illness caused by bacteria from the genus Brucella. Humans contract the disease by ingesting meat or dairy products of infected cattle, sheep, or wild game animals. Direct infection from animals to humans may also occur and is found predominantly in workers in the livestock and meat processing industries. Blood specimen is serum. Standard tube agglutination method is common. Other methods used include complement fixation (CF) and enzyme linked immunosorbent assay (ELISA). Because this disease is almost eliminated from United States and Canadian cattle and sheep populations, this test is not commonly performed.

86625
Campylobacter is a genus of bacteria, some of which are responsible for a wide variety of illnesses in humans. Enteritis is among the more common illnesses. Campylobacter is also implicated in Guillain-Barré syndrome, a form of peripheral neuropathy. Blood specimen is obtained by venipuncture. The literature is unclear about methods and reasons to order such testing. Most clinical cases of Campylobacter infection resolve themselves spontaneously or following drug therapy.

86628
Candida is a ubiquitous genus of fungi, some species of which are pathogenic to humans. The range of illnesses is quite large. This test is performed primarily to evaluate suspected systemic invasions by Candida. If confirmed, tests may be obtained at biweekly intervals to assess effectiveness of drug therapy. Blood specimen is serum. Methods include: latex agglutination (LA), immunodiffusion (ID), crossed (2-dimensional) immunoelectrophoresis, and enzyme-linked immunosorbent assay (ELISA).

86631
This test may be ordered as Chlamydia psittaci or LVG titer. The specimen is serum or finger stick in adults, or heel stick in infants. Methods are complement fixation (CF), enzyme-linked immunosorbent assay (ELISA), and immunofluorescent antibody (IFA). This test may be used to determine exposure to Chlamydia, though the test should not be used as a specific type. Chlamydomonas is a genus of algae that can cause nongonococcal urethritis, among other infections.

86632
This test may be ordered as Chlamydia IgM titer. The specimen is serum or finger stick in adults, or heel stick in infants. Complement fixation (CF), enzyme-linked immunosorbent assay (ELISA) and immunofluorescent antibody (IFA) are methods commonly used to determine previous exposure to Chlamydia or a current infection. Chlamydomonas is a genus of algae that can cause nongonococcal urethritis, among other infections.

86635
This test may be ordered as Coccidioides titer, Coccidioides antibody titer, Cocci titer or Cocci precipitins. The specimen is serum or finger stick in adults, or heel stick in infants. Methods include complement fixation (CF), enzyme-linked immunosorbent assay (ELISA), immunofluorescent antibody (IFA), immunodiffusion, and precipitin test. The test may be performed to determine current infection or assess prognosis of Coccidioides immitis, a fungus that causes coccidioidomycosis.

86638
This test may be ordered as Q fever titer, Q fever antibody titer, or C. brunetti titer. The specimen is serum. Methods are complement fixation (CF), enzyme-linked immunosorbent assay (ELISA), immunofluorescent antibody (IFA), immunodiffusion, or indirect hemagglutination (IHA). The test may be performed to determine Q fever due to Coxiella brunetti.

86641
This test may be ordered as AB cryptococcus antibody titer, or cryptococcosis. The specimen is serum. Methods are complement fixation (CF), enzyme-linked immunosorbent assay (ELISA), and immunofluorescent antibody (IFA). This test may be performed to determine exposure and prognosis of cryptococcosis, an infectious disease caused by the fungus Cryptococcus neoformans characterized by nodular lesions or abscesses in the lungs, subcutaneous tissues, joints, and the brain and meninges.

86644
This test may be ordered as CMV-IFA, CMV titers, Cytomegalic inclusion titers, or CMV IgG. The specimen is serum. Methods are complement fixation (CF), enzyme-linked immunosorbent assay (ELISA), immunofluorescent antibody (IFA), and latex agglutination. This test may be performed to determine current cytomegalovirus (CMV) infection. CMV is any of several viruses that can cause severe disease

especially in newborns by infecting the salivary glands, brain, kidneys, liver, and lungs.

86645
This test is commonly ordered as CMV IgM antibody titer, CMV IgM titer, cytomegalovirus IGM antibody titer, or CMV IgM. The specimen is serum or finger stick in adults, or heel stick in infants. Methods are complement fixation (CF), enzyme-linked immunosorbent assay (ELISA), immunofluorescent antibody (IFA), and latex agglutination. This may be performed to determine previous exposure to cytomegalovirus (CMV) or an acute CMV infection. CMV is any of several viruses that can cause severe disease especially in newborns by infecting the salivary glands, brain, kidneys, liver, and lungs.

86648
This test may be ordered as Diphtheria antibody titer, or DPT titer. The specimen is serum. Methods are complement fixation (CF), enzyme-linked immunosorbent assay (ELISA), immunofluorescent antibody (IFA), and latex agglutination. The test may be performed to determine exposure to Diphtheria, a bacterial disease that can cause inflammation to the heart and nervous system.

86651
This test may be ordered as La Crosse virus titer, California encephalitis titer, or bunyavirus titer. The specimen is serum. Methods are complement fixation (CF), or enzyme-linked immunosorbent assay (ELISA). This test may be performed to confirm the presence of the California encephalitis viral infection. There are several strains of the encephalitis virus that can cause inflammatory conditions, especially in the tissues of the brain.

86652
This test may be ordered as Eastern equine encephalitis titer. The specimen is serum. Methods are complement fixation (CF), or enzyme-linked immunosorbent assay (ELISA). This test may be performed to confirm the presence of Eastern equine encephalitis. There are several strains of the encephalitis virus that can cause inflammatory conditions, especially in the tissues of the brain.

86653
This test may be ordered as St. Louis virus titer or St. Louis encephalitis titer. The specimen is serum. Methods are complement fixation (CF), or enzyme-linked immunosorbent assay (ELISA). This test may be performed to confirm the presence of St. Louis encephalitis. There are several strains of the encephalitis virus that can cause inflammatory conditions, especially in the tissues of the brain.

86654
This test may be ordered as Western equine encephalitis titer. The specimen is serum. Methods are complement fixation (CF), or enzyme-linked immunosorbent assay (ELISA). This test may be performed to determine the presence of the Western equine encephalitis virus. There are several strains of the encephalitis virus that can cause inflammatory conditions, especially in the tissues of the brain.

86658
This test may be ordered as enterovirus antibody panel (IgG or IgM), coxsackie A titer, or poliovirus titer. The panel includes coxsackie, A and B, echovirus, and poliovirus. The specimen is serum. Methods are complement fixation (CF), viral neutralization, or enzyme-linked immunosorbent assay (ELISA). This test may be performed to determine presence of the coxsackie A virus, poliovirus, or other enteroviruses that typically occur in the gastrointestinal tract, but may also cause respiratory ailments, meningitis, and neurological disorders.

86663-86665
These tests may be ordered as EBV-EA titer, EBNA (IgG or IgM) titer, or EBV.VCA (IgG or IgM), or EB-VCA (IgG or IgM) titer. The specimen is serum. The test has been used as a serological method to detect previous exposure to EBV or acute EBV disease. Methods are complement fixation (CF) or enzyme-linked immunosorbent assay (ELISA), indirect fluorescent antibody, or immunofluorescent antibody (IFA). Code 86663 identifies an early antigen (short-lived); 86664 is reported for nuclear antigen; 86665 is used for viral capsid antigen (VCA). The VCA test may be the most effectual of the three tests for determining EB viral infection, which is the main cause of infectious mononucleosis.

86666
This test may also be ordered as Ehrlichia IgM or IgG. The specimen is serum. Methods include indirect fluorescent antibody (IFA) and immunofluorescent antibody (IFA). The Ehrlichia genus of rickettsia bacteria is implicated in a form of tick fever similar to Rocky Mountain Spotted Fever sometimes referred to as "spotless" fever. Testing may occur during acute or convalescent phases of illness.

86668
This test is also known as Tularemia antibody titer, rabbit fever antibodies, and Francisella tularensis antibodies. The specimen is serum. Methods include complement fixation (CF), enzyme-linked immunosorbent assay (ELISA), or immunofluorescent antibody (IFA) agglutination, and hemagglutination. The test may be performed to determine the presence of the bacteria F. tularensis, a bacterium transmitted by insect bite that causes tularemia marked by toxemia.

86671
This code should be used to report antibody testing for fungi, which do not have a more specific genus or species code listed in this section. For example, antibody testing for sporotrichosis would be reported

with this code. Blood specimen is serum. Methods are varied and may include: complement fixation (CF), immunodiffusion, latex agglutination (LA), immunofluorescence, Western blot (immunoblot), crossed (2-dimensional) immunoelectrophoresis, and enzyme-linked immunosorbent assay (ELISA).

86674
This test may be requested as Giardia antibody or Giardia titer. Giardia lamblia is the causative protozoal organism of the intestinal disorder known as Giardia. Blood specimen is serum. Methods such as commercial kit, enzyme immunoassay (EIA), and indirect immunofluorescence may be employed.

86677
This test may be ordered as a H. Pylori antibody titer or Campylobacter pylori serology. The specimen is serum. Method is enzyme-linked immunosorbent assay (ELISA) or chemiluminescence. The test may be performed to determine the presence of Helicobacter Pylori, a common cause of intestinal disease and suspected as a cause of ulcerated stomach tissue.

86682
This code reports antibody testing for any of species of helminths not elsewhere classified in this section. Helminths are parasitic worms and many are further classified as nematodes. Helminthic infections may be intestinal or of tissues. Blood specimen is serum. Test methodologies will vary according to the suspected parasite. Methods may include enzyme immunoassay (EIA) and bentonite flocculation. Tissue parasites are easier to assay for antibodies than are those affecting the GI tract.

86684
This test may be ordered as a H. Influenza (type A or B) antibody titer. The specimen is serum. Method is complement fixation, EIA, or enzyme-linked immunosorbent assay (ELISA). This test is performed to determine the presence of H. Influenza, a common cause of chronic intestinal disease.

86687
This test is commonly ordered as HTLV-I antibody titer or Human T Cell Leukemia I Virus titer. The specimen is by venipuncture or finger stick in adults, or heel stick in infants. Methods are Western blot, radioimmunoprecipitation, and screen enzyme immunoassay. This test may be performed to determine the presence of HTLV-I virus and to screen blood and blood products used for transfusions.

86688
This test is commonly ordered as HTLV-II antibody titer or human T cell leukemia II virus titer. The specimen is serum. Methods are Western blot, radioimmunoprecipitation, and screen enzyme immunoassay. This test may be performed to determine the presence of HTLV-II virus and to screen blood and blood products used for transfusions.

86689
This test is commonly ordered as HTLV or HIV by Western blot. The specimen is serum. This test may be performed as a confirmation of a positive test for human T cell leukemia II virus or human immunodeficiency virus (HIV), often by a previous enzyme-linked immunoassay (ELISA).

86692
This test may be ordered as hepatitis D antibody, hepatitis delta antibody, or superinfection antibody. Hepatitis D occurs concurrently with hepatitis B and may lead to more severe clinical symptoms than hepatitis B alone, a condition known as superinfection. Specimen is serum. Methodology may involve enzyme immunoassay (EIA).

86694-86696
These tests may be ordered as HSV antibody titer, HSV titer, herpes simplex antibody titer, or HSV IgG/IGM. The specimen is serum or finger stick in adults, or heel stick in infants. A number of methodologies have been employed, such as complement fixation (CF), enzyme-linked immunosorbent assay (ELISA), indirect fluorescent antibody (IFA), enzyme immunoassay, and latex agglutination. This test has been used as a serologic method to detect previous or recent exposure to herpes simplex. To report non-specific type testing, see 86694; testing for type 1, see 86695; testing for type 2, see 86696.

86698
This test may be requested as histoplasma antibody. Histoplasma capsulatum is a fungus that may be infectious in humans. Incidence seems tied to certain regions. Many infections are asymptomatic or feature mild symptoms. Blood specimen is serum. Complement fixation (CF) is quantifiable and is considered one of the best methods. Immunodiffusion (ID), agar diffusion, latex agglutination (LA), radioimmunoassay (RIA), or enzyme immunoassay (EIA) may also be used.

86701
This test may be ordered as an HIV-1 serological test, an HIV-1 antibody, or by an internal code. HIV is a retrovirus and the causative agent of acquired immunodeficiency syndrome (AIDS). Specimen is serum. Numerous kits are now available that use a variety of viral proteins and serumsynthetic peptides as antigens. Methodology is enzyme immunoassay (EIA), enzyme-linked immunosorbent assay (ELISA), radioimmunoprecipitation assay (RIPA), or indirect fluorescent antibody (IFA). A negative test does not guarantee negative status and the test is often repeated several times.

86702
This test may be ordered as an HIV-2 serological antibody. This is an antibody test for HIV-2, a retrovirus closely related to simian AIDS and found

initially in West African nations and Portugal, but with cases also being reported in the United States since 1987. Blood specimen is serum. Specific kits are now available that use a variety of viral proteins and synthetic peptides as antigens to test for HIV-2. Methodology is enzyme immunoassay (EIA), enzyme-linked immunosorbent assay (ELISA), radioimmunoprecipitation assay (RIPA), or indirect fluorescent antibody (IFA). A negative test does not guarantee negative status and the test is often repeated several times.

86703
This test may be ordered as a combined HIV-1 and -2 serological, a combined HIV-1 and-2 antibody. This is an antibody test that tests for both HIV-1 and HIV-2 in a single assay. Both are retroviruses. HIV-1 is the causative agent of acquired immunodeficiency syndrome (AIDS) while HIV-2 is closely related to simian AIDS. Blood specimen is serum. Specific kits are now available that use a variety of viral proteins and synthetic peptides as antigens to test for both HIV-1 and HIV-2. Methodology is enzyme immunoassay (EIA), enzyme-linked immunosorbent assay (ELISA), radioimmunoprecipitation assay (RIPA), or indirect fluorescent antibody (IFA). A negative test does not guarantee negative status and the test is often repeated several times.

86704
This test may be ordered as hepatitis Bc Ab (HBcAb), total. It may also be ordered as HBcAb, anti-HBc, HBVc Ab, anti-HBVc. This test identifies Hepatitis B core total antibodies (IgG and IgM), which are markers available to identify individuals with acute, chronic, or past infection of hepatitis B. The presence of high-titered IgM specific HBcAb is always indicative of an acute infection. The presence of IgG may indicate acute or chronic infection. Blood specimen is serum. Methods include radioimmunoassay (RIA) and enzyme-linked immunosorbent assay (ELISA).

86705
This test may be ordered as hepatitis Bc Ab (HBcAb), IgM. It may also be ordered as HBcAb, anti-HBc, HBVc Ab, anti-HBVc. This test identifies Hepatitis B core IgM antibodies, the presence of which always indicates an acute infection. Blood specimen is serum. Methods include radioimmunoassay (RIA) and enzyme-linked immunosorbent assay (ELISA).

86706
This test may be requested as Hepatitis B surface antibody (HBsAb), Hepatitis Bs Ab, HBV surface antibody, or anti-HBs. The presence of HBsAb is indicative of a previous resolved infection or vaccination against hepatitis B. Blood specimen is serum. Methods include radioimmunoassay (RIA), enzyme immunoassay (EIA), immunoradiometric assay (IRMA), and immunoenzymatic assay (IEMA).

86707
This test may be ordered as hepatitis Be antibody (HBeAb) as Hepatitis Be Ab, HBVe, or anti-HBe. The presence of HBeAb usually indicates a high likelihood of a lesser infectivity and usually points to a benign outcome, although some individuals with HBeAb have chronic hepatitis. Blood specimen is serum. Methods include immunoradiometric assay (IRMA) and enzyme immunoassay (EIA).

86708
This test may be ordered as Hepatitis A Antibody (HAAb), HAV antibody, anti-Hep A or anti-HAV total (IgG and IgM). The presence of HAV IgG antibody may indicate acute infection or previous resolved infection, while IgM antibody always indicates acute infectious disease. Blood specimen is serum. Methods include radioimmunoassay (RIA), enzyme immunoassay (EIA), immunoradiometric assay (IRMA), immunoenzymatic assay (IEMA), and microparticle enzyme immunoassay (MEIA).

86709
This test may be ordered as Hepatitis A Antibody (Haas), HAV IgM antibody, anti-Hep A IgM, or anti-HAV IgM. The presence of IgM antibody indicates acute infectious disease. Blood specimen is serum. Methods include radioimmunoassay (RIA), enzyme immunoassay (EIA), immunoradiometric assay (IRMA), immunoenzymatic assay (IEMA), and microparticle enzyme immunoassay (MEIA).

86710
This test may be ordered as Flu A or Flu B, or Influenza A/B antibody titers. It may also be ordered as anti-Influenza A/B. The presence of IgG antibody usually indicates previous exposure, while IgM indicates a current acute infection. Blood specimen is serum. Methods vary with hemagglutination inhibition (HI) (HAI) being preferred for influenza A and complement fixation (CF) for influenza B. Other methods currently in use are immunofluorescent assay (IFA), enzyme-linked immunosorbent assay (ELISA), radial immunodiffusion (RID), and enzyme immunoassay (EIA).

86713
This test may be ordered as Legionella antibody titers or as anti-Legionella. Both IgG and IgM antibodies should be tested. IgA testing may also be indicated. The presence of IgG antibody usually indicates previous exposure. The demonstration of IgM or IgA antibodies may establish the diagnosis of a current acute or recent Legionella infection. Blood specimen is serum. Methods include: immunofluorescent assay (IFA) and enzyme-linked immunosorbent assay (ELISA).

86717
This test is ordered as Leishmania antibody titers or anti-Leishmania. This protozoan infection may also be

referred to as kala-azar. The presence of IgG antibody usually indicates previous exposure. The demonstration of IgM or IgA antibodies may establish the diagnosis of a current acute or recent Leishmania infection. Blood specimen is serum,. Preferred methods are complement fixation (CF) and enzyme-linked immunosorbent assay (ELISA). However, a number of other methods are employed including indirect hemagglutination (IHA), immunofluorescent assay (IFA), immunoblot, and enzyme immunoassay (EIA).

86720
This test may be ordered as Leptospira antibody titers or anti-Leptospira. Blood specimen is serum. The presence of IgG antibody usually indicates previous exposure. The demonstration of IgM or IgA antibodies may establish the diagnosis of a current acute or recent Leptospira infection. Methods include complement fixation (CF); hemagglutination, immunofluorescent assay (IFA) and enzyme-linked immunosorbent assay (ELISA).

86723
This test may be ordered as Listeria antibody titers or anti-Listeria. Blood specimen is serum. The presence of IgG antibody usually indicates previous exposure. The demonstration of IgM or IgA antibodies may establish the diagnosis of an acute or recent Listeria infection. Methods include immunofluorescent assay (IFA) and enzyme-linked immunosorbent assay (ELISA).

86727
This test is ordered as LCM or LCMC antibody titers. It may also be ordered as anti-LCM. The presence of IgG antibody usually indicates previous exposure. The demonstration of IgM or IgA antibodies may establish the diagnosis of a current acute or recent LCM infection. Blood specimen is serum. A separately reportable spinal puncture is used to collect CSF. Immunofluorescent assay (IFA), direct fluorescent antibody (DFA), and enzyme-linked immunosorbent assay (ELISA) methods are among those employed in identifying antibody response to the specific LCMC. A positive direct examination by electromicroscopy or direct fluorescent microscopy is indicative of active disease.

86729
This test is ordered as Chlamydia trachomatis antibody titers or LGV antibody titers. It may also be ordered as anti-LGV or anti-Chlamydia trachomatis. Lymphogranuloma Venereum is a sexually transmitted infection caused by C. trachomatis L1, L2, and L3 serovars(rarely reported in the United States). The presence of antibodies alone cannot positively differentiate LGV from other chlamydial infections. Testing must be correlated with clinical evidence of LGV. Blood specimen is serum. Immunofluorescent assay (IFA) and complement fixation (CF) methods are employed in identifying an antibody response.

86732
This test may be ordered as Rhizopus antibody titer, Rhizomucor antibody titer, or Cunninghamella antibody titer. These are the common species of molds that cause mucormycosis, a rare opportunistic infection usually found in patients with pre-existing conditions. Blood specimen is serum or finger stick. Literature is unclear, but immunofluorescent assay (IFA) is a common method to detect antibody responses.

86735
This test may be ordered as mumps antibody titers or anti-mumps titers. Testing may be performed to diagnose an acute infection or to evaluate immune status. The presence of IgG antibody alone usually indicates previous exposure and immunity. IgM antibodies in combination with IgG establish the diagnosis of a current acute or recent mumps infection. Blood specimen is serum. Preferred methods include enzyme immunoassay (EIA) and virus neutralization test (NT). Other methods that may be employed include hemagglutination inhibition (HAI), complement fixation (CF), indirect fluorescent antibody (IFA), and hemolysis in gel.

86738
This test is ordered as Mycoplasma antibody titers. It may also be ordered as anti-walking pneumonia, primary atypical pneumonia (PAP), pleuropneumonia-like organism (PPLO), or anti-Mycoplasma titers. The presence of IgG antibody usually indicates previous exposure to Mycoplasma. The demonstration of IgM antibodies is required to establish the diagnosis of a current acute or recent Mycoplasma infection. Blood specimen is serum. Methods include immunofluorescent assay (IFA), complement fixation (CF), and enzyme immunoassay (EIA), and IgM antibody agglutination.

86741
This test is ordered as N. meningitidis antibody titers. It may also be ordered as anti-Neisseria meningitidis. This is the causative agent of meningococcal meningitis. The presence of IgG antibody usually indicates previous exposure to N. meningitidis. The demonstration of IgM or IgA antibodies may establish the diagnosis of a current acute or recent meningitidis infection. Blood specimen is serum. CSF is obtained by spinal puncture that is reported separately. Method is enzyme-linked immunosorbent assay (ELISA).

86744
This test is ordered as Nocardia antibody titers. It may also be ordered as anti-Nocardia titers. Pathogenic species of Nocardia include N. asteroides, N. brasiliensis, N. caviae, N. farcinica, N. transvalensis, and N. nova. Nocardiosis generally occurs only in immunosuppressed individuals and presents as suppurative or cavitary pneumonia, cutaneous abscesses, or mycetoma formation on an extremity. The

presence of IgG antibody usually indicates previous exposure to Nocardia. The demonstration of IgM or IgA antibodies may establish the diagnosis of a current acute or recent Nocardia infection. Blood specimen is serum. Method is enzyme-linked immunosorbent assay (ELISA) or Western blot.

86747
This test may be ordered as Parvovirus antibody titers, anti-Parvovirus titers, or Parvo B19 antibody titers. The presence of IgG antibody usually indicates previous exposure to Parvovirus B19. The demonstration of IgM antibodies may establish the diagnosis of a current acute or recent Parvovirus B19 infection. Blood specimen is serum,. Enzyme-linked immunosorbent assay (ELISA), radioimmunoassay (RIA), and Western blot are among methods employed in identifying an antibody response to Parvovirus B19.

86750
This test is ordered as malaria antibody titers. This test is used primarily to screen blood donors. Specimen is whole blood. Method is indirect immunofluorescence (IIF).

86753
This test is for antibodies to any of the clinically significant simple, single-celled organisms within the subkingdom of protozoa not specified by a more specific code in this section of CPT(r). For example, detection of Entamoeba histolytica antibodies would be reported 86753. The specimen is serum. Enzyme-linked immunosorbent assay (ELISA), radioimmunoassay (RIA) complement fixation, Western Blot, indirect hemagglutination (IHA) are among the methods employed in identifying an antibody response to the specific protozoa.

86756
This test is ordered as RSV antibody titers. It may also be ordered as anti-respiratory syncytial viral titers, and anti-RSV titers. The presence of IgG antibody usually indicates previous exposure to respiratory syncytial virus. The demonstration of IgM antibodies may establish the diagnosis of a current acute or recent infection. Blood specimen is serum Enzyme-linked immunosorbent assay (ELISA), enzyme immunoassay (EIA), and complement fixation (CF) are among methodologies employed in identifying an antibody response.

86757
This test may also be ordered by the name of the suspected rickettsial pathogen (e.g., Rocky Mountain Spotted Fever, typhus). Blood specimen is serum. Methods include enzyme-linked immunoassay (ELISA) with indirect fluorescent antibody (IFA) confirmation.

86759
This test is ordered as rotavirus antibody titer. It may also be ordered as anti-rotavirus titer, Adenovirus 40-41 antibody titer, and anti-rotavirus titer. The presence of IgG antibody usually indicates previous exposure to rotavirus. The demonstration of IgM antibodies may establish the diagnosis of a recent or current rotavirus infection. Blood specimen is serum Enzyme-linked immunosorbent assay (ELISA) and radioimmunoassays (RIA) are among methods employed in identifying antibody response to the specific to rotavirus.

86762
This test is ordered as rubella antibody titers. It may also be ordered as German measles antibody titers, and anti-rubella titers. The test is used primarily to evaluate immune status. The presence of rubella IgG and IgM antibodies may indicate previous exposure, vaccination, or current acute infection. Blood specimen is serum. Enzyme-linked immunosorbent assay (ELISA), enzyme immunoassay (EIA), and latex agglutination (LA) are among methods used in identifying antibody response, with ELISA being more common in larger, high volume laboratories.

86765
This test is ordered as rubeola antibody titers. It may also be ordered as measles antibody titers, anti-measles titers and anti-rubeola titers. This test is used primarily to evaluate immune status as clinical symptoms related to acute infection make laboratory testing unnecessary. CSF specimen is used for diagnosis of subacute sclerosing panencephalitis (SSPE). The presence of rubeola IgG antibody alone usually indicates previous exposure to rubeola. Both IgG and IgM antibodies are present with a current acute or recent rubeola infection. Blood specimen is serum. CSF specimen is reported separately. Hemagglutination inhibition test (HAI) is the preferred method of testing for immune status. Enzyme-linked immunosorbent assay (ELISA), enzyme immunoassay (EIA), complement fixation (CF), and neutralization test (NT) are other methods commonly employed in identifying an antibody response.

86768
This test is ordered as Salmonella antibody titers. It may also be ordered as anti-Salmonella titers, S. typhi antibody titers or Salmonella typhi antibody titers. The presence of Salmonella IgG antibody usually indicates previous exposure to salmonella. The demonstration of Salmonella IgM antibodies may establish the diagnosis of a recent or current salmonella infection. The specimen is serum, Enzyme-linked immunosorbent assay (ELISA) principles are most commonly employed in identifying an antibody response to the specific Salmonella. Agglutination principles may be utilized for the identification of S. typhi antibody.

86771
This test is ordered as Shigella antibody titers. It may also be ordered as anti-Salmonella titers. The presence of Shigella IgG antibody usually indicates previous exposure to Shigella. The demonstration of Shigella

IgM antibodies may establish the diagnosis of a recent or current Shigella infection. Blood specimen is serum. Enzyme-linked immunosorbent assay (ELISA) principles are most commonly employed in identifying an antibody response to the specific to Shigella. Agglutination principles may also be utilized for the identification of Shigella.

86774
This test is ordered as tetanus antibody titers. It may also be ordered as anti-tetanus titers, or Clostridium tetani antibody titers. This test is not commonly used as a diagnostic test for acute infection. It may be used to evaluate immune status. Blood specimen is serum,. Titration of tetanus antitoxin neutralization principles is the most common method. Agglutination, passive hemagglutination, or enzyme-linked immunosorbent assay (ELISA) principles may also be utilized.

86777
This test is ordered as Toxoplasma IgG antibody titers. It may also be ordered as anti-Toxoplasma IgG titers, or toxo IgG titers. The presence of Toxoplasma IgG antibody may indicate current or past infection. Blood specimen is serum,. Amniotic fluid is collected by amniocentesis that is reported separately. Enzyme-linked immunosorbent assay (ELISA) or immunofluorescent assay (IFA) principles may be used for the identification of Toxoplasma antibody.

86778
This test is ordered as Toxoplasma IgM antibody titers. It may also be ordered as anti-Toxoplasma IgM titers, or toxo IgM titers. The demonstration of Toxoplasma IgM antibodies may establish the diagnosis of a recent or current infection. Blood specimen is serum amniotic fluid collected by amniocentesis that is reported separately. Enzyme-linked immunosorbent assay (ELISA) or immunofluorescent assay (IFA) principles may be used for the identification of toxoplasma IgM antibody.

86780
Treponema pallidum antibody tests are used to screen and confirm syphilis. This test may be ordered as a screening or confirmatory test for syphilis or as a screening or confirmatory test for a positive venereal disease research lab test (VDRL), rapid plasma reagent (RPR), or serologic test (STS) for syphilis. Blood specimen is serum. Fluorescent antibody (FA) or FTA principles are most commonly employed in identifying an antibody response to the specific syphilis. Agglutination or flocculation of cardiolipin principles may also be used for the identification of syphilis antibody.

86784
This test is ordered as trichinella antibody titers. It may also be ordered as trichinosis antibody titers. Trichinella antibody titers are to diagnosis infestation with the parasitic roundworm Trichinella spiralis that is transmitted by eating undercooked pork or bear meat. Blood specimen is serum. Methods include bentonite flocculation test (BFT); indirect immunofluorescence (IIF), complement fixation (CF), latex agglutination (LA), enzyme immunoassay (EIA), and enzyme-linked immunosorbent assay (ELISA).

86787
This test may be requested as VZV antibody titers, chicken pox antibody titers, or herpes zoster antibody titers. This test is performed primarily to evaluate immune status. Blood specimen is serum. Methods may include enzyme immunoassay (EIA), enzyme-linked immunosorbent assay (ELISA), complement fixation, and fluorescent antibody against membrane antigen (FAMA).

86788
This code is commonly ordered as WNV IgM. Specimen is cerebrospinal fluid or blood serum. Method used is an antibody capture enzyme-linked immunosorbent assay. WNV IgM of cerebrospinal fluid is the most definitive test for WNV of the central nervous system, as antibodies may persist in the blood for more than a year following a resolved infection. WNV IgM will be positive only if a WNV infection has been active for at least eight days. West Nile virus usually causes a mild infection, but in some cases, leads to life-threatening encephalitis or meningitis.

86789
This code is commonly ordered as WNV IgG. Specimen is cerebrospinal fluid or blood serum. Method used is enzyme immunoassay, plaque reduction neutralization, or hemagglutination inhibition. WNV IgG will be positive only if a WNV infection has been active for at least three weeks. West Nile virus usually causes a mild infection, but in some cases, leads to life-threatening encephalitis or meningitis.

86790
This test is ordered as viral antibody titers not elsewhere specified. The specimen is serum The presence of viral IgG antibody usually indicates previous exposure, while viral IgM antibodies may establish the diagnosis of a recent or current infection. Methods include enzyme-linked immunosorbent assay (ELISA), indirect fluorescent antibody (IFA), and agglutination.

86793
This test is ordered as Yersinia antibody titers or by species name including Y. enterocolitica antibody and Y. pestis (bubonic plague) antibody. Blood specimen is serum. A common method used is agglutination. However, newer techniques are also used that include an immunoblot, enzyme-linked immunosorbent assay (ELISA), indirect fluorescent antibody (IFA).

86800
This test is ordered as thyroglobulin antibody titers or anti-thyroglobulin. The presence of thyroglobulin antibody usually indicates presence of circulating autoantibodies in patients with endocrine disease (i.e., thyroiditis, Graves' disease). The specimen is serum. Methods may include enzyme-linked immunosorbent assay (ELISA), tanned RBC agglutination test, radiobinding assay, and immunoradiometric assay (IRMA).

86803
This test may be ordered as hepatitis C antibody titers. It may also be ordered as anti-hepatitis C titers, HCV Ab titers, and anti-HCV titers. This test is normally used for an initial hepatitis C screen. Positive or unequivocal tests are repeated using different techniques that are reported separately. Blood specimen is serum,. Methods may include enzyme-linked immunosorbent assay (ELISA) or enzyme immunoassay (EIA).

86804
These tests may be ordered as hepatitis C antibody titers, anti-hepatitis C titers, HCV Ab titers, or anti-HCV titers. The specimen is serum. Recombinant immunoblot assay (RIBA) principles may be employed in identifying an antibody response to the specific hepatitis C virus. The presence of IgG antibody by RIBA is a confirmatory test.

86805-86806
These tests may also be referred to as compatibility tests or major histocompatibility complex (MHC) tests. These tests pertain primarily to matching potential donor tissues to transplant patients, but uses may also include bench research. Methodology involves mixing purified donor lymphocytes with recipient sera or known antibodies. Cytotoxic reaction (cell death) is visually monitored, usually by incubation method. Indicator dyes may be used to identify dead cells. Titration involves methodology to determine quantities. Report 86805 for testing with titration; 86806 for testing without titration.

86807-86808
These tests may be requested as PRA screen. This test is a preliminary screen to measure cytotoxicity, or cell death, when blood product is mixed. The standard method involves culturing and monitoring cytotoxicity, using marker dyes, and the corresponding buildup of antibodies, through replication and DNA. Code 86807 reports standard testing methods. Code 86808 reports a rapid method, where antibody growth and cytotoxicity are more immediately evident.

86812
This test may also be ordered as a histocompatibility antigen test, Class I (or Class III) antigen test, or according to a specific antigen (e.g., A10). This test pertains primarily to matching potential donor tissues to transplant patients. This test determines HLA compatibility of specific antigens. Method involves mixing purified donor lymphocytes with a known sera and complement. A culture is prepared and cytotoxic reaction (cell death) is monitored.

86813
This test may also be ordered as histocompatibility antigens test, Class I (or Class III) antigens test, or according to specific multiple antigens (e.g., A10-B-7). This test pertains primarily to matching potential donor tissues to transplant patients This test determines HLA compatibility of multiple antigens. Method involves mixing purified donor lymphocytes with a known sera and complement. A culture is prepared and cytotoxic reaction (cell death) is monitored.

86816
This test may also be ordered as a Class II antigen test, or simply HLA-D antigen. This test pertains primarily to matching potential donor tissues to transplant patients. The D human lymphocyte antigens (HLA) are located separately from the Class I and Class III antigens on the chromosome. Subregion names DR, DQ, and DP are described. This test determines HLA compatibility of a single Class II antigen. Method involves mixing purified donor lymphocytes with the sera and complement. A culture is prepared and cytotoxic reaction (cell death) is monitored.

86817
This test may also be ordered as a Class II antigens test, or simply HLA-D antigens. This test pertains primarily to matching potential donor tissues to transplant patients. The D human leukocyte antigens (HLA) are located separately from the Class I and Class III antigens on the chromosome. Subregion names DR, DQ, and DP are described. This test determines HLA compatibility for multiple Class II antigens. Method involves mixing purified donor lymphocytes with the sera and complement. A culture is prepared and cytotoxic reaction (cell death) is monitored.

86821
This test may also be ordered as a mixed lymphocyte culture (MLC) reaction, Class II antigen test, or simply HLA-D antigen. Donor and recipient blood samples are often collected at the same time. This test pertains primarily to matching potential donor tissues to transplant patients. The D human leukocyte antigens (HLA) are located separately from the Class I and Class III antigens on the chromosome and the MLC method is particularly good at identifying them. This test determines HLA compatibility of Class II antigens. The method is described in literature as mixing purified donor lymphocytes with the recipient's lymphocytes. A culture is prepared and the recipient's lymphocytic response is monitored. The greater the response, the greater the degree of antigen disparity.

86822
This test may also be ordered as a secondary mixed lymphocyte culture , a primed reaction Class II antigen test (PLC), or simply HLA-D primed. Donor and recipient blood samples are often collected at the same time. This test methodology is a rapid test and may take 24 to 36 hours to complete, rather than the seven to 10 days for an MLC (86821). The test is specific to certain Class II antigens.

86825-86826
This test describes non-cytotoxic crossmatches, such as flow cytometry, and identifies a subgroup of potential organ transplant recipients whose risk of graft failure or post-transplant complications may be elevated because of low levels of an antibody that is undetected by lymphocytoxic crossmatch procedures. When used as part of a pre-transplant risk assessment, cytoxic and flow cytometry crossmatches provide differing, but complementary, information. Using three color fluorescent tests with CD3 and CD19 monoclonals and conjugated anti-human immunoglobulin, histocompatibility crossmatching is performed to optimize allocation of organs to the most compatible donor/recipient pairs. Report 86825 for the first serum sample or dilution and 86826 for each additional sample or dilution.

86850
This test may be ordered as an RBC antibody detection. The test is a screen for particular antibodies to red cell antigens that may present problems during a blood transfusion or childbirth. Blood specimen is whole blood. The test may be performed using tubes, microtiter plates, or gel cards. Another method is agglutination.

86860
Elution is a technique for removing antibody from antibody/antigen complex on RBCs for identification purposes. Blood specimen is whole blood. The process is usually part of a workup to aid in diagnosis of certain autoimmune disorders such as autoimmune hemolytic anemia, and for resolution of incompatible crossmatches due to unidentified antibodies, and to identify the antibody causing hemolytic disease of a newborn (HDN).

86870
This test is also known as an antibody panel. Blood specimen is whole blood. The test identifies an antibody isolated by techniques reported by 86850 and/or 86860 above. The test may be performed using tubes, microtiter plates, or gel cards. This code can be reported up to four times during the same session for differences in technique necessary for identification (i.e., regular panel, cold-panel, pre-warmed panel, and enzyme treated panel).

86880
This test is also known as a direct Coombs or sometimes as a direct antiglobulin test (DAT). Blood specimen is whole blood. The test is used to detect coating of the RBCs by antibody or complement. It is useful in diagnosis of hemolytic disease of the newborn (HDN), detection of autoimmune hemolytic anemia, investigation of transfusion reactions, and detection of red cell sensitization reactions caused by medication. Method may be by gel test, flow cytometry, or enzyme-linked immunosorbent assay (ELISA) or hemagglutination.

86885
This test is also known as an indirect Coombs, IAT, or sometimes as selective antibody screen. The indirect antiglobulin test indicates whether there is antibody in the serum, which will react to combine with antigen on the red cell. Uses for the IAT include determining if there are IgG antibodies (coating antibodies) in the patient's serum; investigating the ability to sensitize red blood cells; crossmatching, detection of Du (weak D) antigen; and investigation of transfusion reactions. The specimen is whole blood. Methodology includes agglutination, hemolysis of Type 0 test cells, flow cytometry, or enzyme-linked immunosorbent assay (ELISA). Report this code for each reagent red cell.

86886
This test is also known as an antibody titer. The test determines the strength of antibody identified through test described in 86870. The specimen is whole blood. Method is serial dilution with saline, enzyme, or low ionic strength saline followed by antiglobulin. Report this code for each antibody titer.

86890
This reports the donation of blood for one's own use. This procedure is used for patients requiring surgery who pre-deposit their own blood for use during the surgery. The procedure is most useful for patients with complex antibody production or extremely rare antibodies that make location of compatible blood difficult.

86891
This procedure may also be known as a cell-saver. This is a device used in surgeries where large blood losses are inherent to the procedure (i.e., total hip, certain heart and lung procedures, liver and spleen operations). The device aspirates spilled blood in the surgical cavity, washes it, and returns the RBCs to the patient. This reduces the need for stored blood. In postoperative patients, there may be major seepage and the patient is not physically up to additional surgery to correct the problem. The cell-saver washes the seepage and transfuses it back to the patient.

86900
This test may also be known as blood group. The test determines whether a patient is O, A, B, or AB by

testing for the presence or absence of these antigens on the RBC surface. This typing of blood is the oldest and most widely recognized. Blood specimen is whole blood. The classic test method is by agglutination but gel testing is common.

86901
This test is known as Rh type. The test determines whether a patient is "positive" or "negative" by identifying the presence (Rh positive) or absence (Rh negative) of Rh antigens on the RBC surface. Blood specimen is whole blood. Method is enzyme-linked immunosorbent assay (ELISA), but may be performed by agglutination or gel test.

86903
This test is used to screen donated units of blood prior to a transfusion using reagent serum. The test confirms the absence of the antigen associated with the antibody identified by the test reported by 86870.

86904
This test is used to screen for compatible blood using patient serum when there is insufficient time to identify an antibody and screen units for the associated antigen prior to transfusion. The test is also helpful when commercial antiserum to the antigen is not available.

86905
This test is used to confirm the absence of antigens corresponding to antibodies identified by the antibody identification test (86870).

86906
Rh phenotyping may be required to assist in confirming the identity of an Rh antibody detected during screening, or when a family study is being undertaken for any number of reasons. Some donor centers maintain limited supplies of phenotyped blood to issue patients who have corresponding antibodies.

86910-86911
These tests are a method to determine percentages of whether a particular male is the biological father of a particular child. These codes essentially group elements of 86900, 86901, and 86905 (MN refers to M antigen and N antigen, important in phenotyping). Code 86911 is reported when calculations using the antigen system in 86910 are indeterminate and additional systems must be analyzed. These codes also report all mathematical calculations of probability. These tests result in only a statistical probability of paternity. 86920 This test is one of the crossmatch components of tests ordered as "type and crossmatch." This step checks mainly for ABO compatibility of the unit being transfused. It may be the only step in the compatibility phase of the crossmatch when the patient has no demonstrated antibodies, or after a massive transfusion where very little of the patient's blood volume is his/her own. DNA testing is more commonly done.

86920
This test is one of the crossmatch components of tests ordered as "type and crossmatch." This step checks mainly for ABO compatibility of the unit being transfused. It may be the only step in the compatibility phase of the crossmatch when the patient has no demonstrated antibodies, or after a massive transfusion where very little of the patient's blood volume is his/her own.

86921
This test is one of the crossmatch components of tests ordered as "type and crossmatch." This test is an intermediate step using incubation technique, in a full major compatibility test (86920, 86921, and 86922). It is a crucial step in sensitization of IgG antigens.

86922
This test is the final step in a major crossmatch. A full, major crossmatch will always be performed when antibodies are present in the patient's serum, unless more than 10 units have been given in a 24-hour period.

86923
This computer check is referred to as an electronic crossmatch, computer-assisted crossmatch, or E-XM. Some labs match donor blood for transfusions to specific patients based on patient test results previously performed and stored in the blood bank computer system. The sole purpose of the electronic crossmatch is to confirm ABO compatibility between patient and donor. Do not use 86923 in conjunction with 86920-86922 for same unit crossmatch.

86927
Fresh frozen plasma (FFP) is frozen within six hours of donation. It maintains clotting factors in the frozen state and for this reason is used to treat certain clotting disorders, such as over-medication with Coumadin, liver diseases (i.e., parenchymal liver disease), and disseminated intravascular coagulation (DIC). It may also be used for plasma exchanges to treat diseases like thrombotic thrombocytopenic purpura (TTP), Raynaud's disease, and glomerulonephritis. This code reports only the thawing process.

86930-86932
The preparation for freezing is also known as glycerolization. Freezing allows reasonably long-term storage of pre-deposited blood. The preparation of frozen blood with thawing is also known as deglycerolization. The product is thawed and washed to remove preservative. Certain cold-insoluble proteins, such as factor VIII and fibrinogen, may be removed when the blood is close to thawing. Report 86930 for freezing, including preparation, each unit of blood. Report 86931 for thawing, each unit of blood and 86932 for freezing (including preparation) and thawing, each unit of blood.

86940-86941
These tests are used for screening (86940) or incubation (86941) of hemolysins and cold agglutinins. Cold agglutinins may mask antibodies that are not expected to be present in the blood and hemolysins are substances that lyse or dissolve red blood cells. In these tests red cells subject to incubation with and without various additives, such as glucose to determine the degree that red blood cells will lyse or clump. Irradiation is used primarily to prevent graft versus host disease (GVHD) in certain immunosuppressed patients, newborns, and patients that share the same human lymphocyte antigen (HLA) haplotype as the donor. The process inactivates the lymphocytes. Irradiation is also required when the donor is a blood relation of the recipient (GVHD).

86945
Irradiation is used primarily to prevent graft versus host disease (GVHD) in certain immunosuppressed patients, newborns, and patients that share the same human lymphocyte antigen (HLA) haplotype as the donor. The process inactivates the lymphocytes. Irradiation is also required when the donor is a blood relation of the recipient (GVHD).

86950
Granulocyte transfusion is indicated in patients on chemotherapy for leukemia or those with severe infection whose absolute granulocyte count is less than 500/cu mm.

86960
Volume reduction of blood is usually performed by an extra centrifugation step that removes plasma during processing of a blood product. Removal of excess donor plasma is indicated in patients who cannot tolerate the full volume or when ABO incompatible single donor platelets are transfused. Volume reduction may be helpful in patients with febrile transfusion reactions that persist despite leukocyte reduction.

86965
Pooling in this sense means to blend blood product from a variety of sources. Platelets and cryoprecipitate units are pooled in order to provide an adequate amount of product for the transfusion to be therapeutic. Cryoprecipitate is the fraction of blood which contains cold-insoluble proteins, such as factor VIII and fibrinogen. Cryoprecipitate is collected from frozen blood that is brought to thawing temperature.

86970
The incubation of red blood cells with certain chemical agents or drugs is performed to enhance the agglutination reaction of red blood cells during antibody identification. IgM antibodies are easily detected in saline at room temperature as IgM antibodies are able to bridge between RBC's owing to their large size, efficiently creating what is seen as agglutination. IgG antibodies are smaller and require assistance to bridge well enough to form a visual agglutination reaction

86971
The enzyme pretreatment of red blood cells is undertaken when there are multiple antibodies or one that is too weak to demonstrate without pre-treatment of the reagent RBCs. The enzyme used depends on the suspected antibody. Certain enzymes enhance particular antibodies while destroying others.

86972
In some red cell typing and antibody detection procedures it is desirable to exclude other cellular components of whole blood, such as white blood cells or platelets. Isolation of RBCs from whole blood may be accomplished by centrifugation in a density gradient.

86975
This method removes antibodies to certain drugs by using pre-treated red blood cells and the patient's serum. Serum is incubated with the treated RBCs (to attach the drug antibody) and centrifuged. The serum is removed and used in further testing.

86976
This is code is similar to 86975. There are times when the amount of antibody exceeds the amount of antigen attached to the RBCs. In these cases, the serum is diluted prior to adsorption or re-adsorption.

86977
In some instances, cell adsorption of the interfering substance will not work, and inhibitor is incubated with the patient's serum to "neutralize" the substance. The antibody to Sda is one of these substances.

86978
Incubation of the patient's cells and patient's serum together prior to testing can remove some autoimmune complexes. This can be done refrigerated for cold autoantibodies or warm for warm autoantibodies. In cases of multiple antibodies, each antibody may be absorbed out in turn by using reagent RBCs of known antigenicity.

86985
In transfusion cases where the patient is a child or where transfusion of a full unit of product will overload the circulatory system, a unit will be split into multiple smaller units.

87001
Animal inoculation with infected tissue, blood, or other specimen source is used in the diagnosis of several diseases, including rabies, Colorado tick fever, and infantile botulism. There are different specimen types for the different tests. Contact the reference lab that is performing the test for type of specimen and transport. There are, however, more rapid tests to diagnose these diseases.

87003

Animal inoculation with infected tissue, blood, or other specimen source is used in the diagnosis of several diseases, including rabies, Colorado tick fever, and infantile botulism. There are different specimen types for the different tests. Contact the reference lab that is performing the test for type of specimen and transport. This test is used to observe signs of illness in inoculated mice for as long as three weeks and for the dissection of mice and preparation of tissue for microscopy to confirm diagnosis when mice become ill or die.

87015

Concentration may also be referred to as thick smear preparation. The source samples are treated to concentrate the presence of suspect organisms, usually through sedimentation or flotation. There are two common methods of concentration for ova and parasite exams: formalin concentration and zinc sulfate flotation. The most common concentration methods for AFB stains or cultures are the N-acetyl-L cysteine method, cytocentrifugation, and the Zephiran-trisodium phosphate method. Do not report 87015 in conjunction with 87177.

87040

Samples for bacterial blood culture are drawn by venipuncture and usually consist of a set of bottles, an aerobic and an anaerobic bottle. Drawing at least two sets of cultures increases the effectiveness of the test. This code includes anaerobic culture along with aerobic, if appropriate. Presumptive identification of aerobic pathogens or microorganisms in the blood sample is by means of identifying colony morphology. The test includes gram staining and subculturing to selective media for the detection of bacterial growth. There are several automated systems that detect the presence of bacteria using colorimetric, radiometric, or spectrophotometric means. The purpose of blood culture tests is to detect the presence of aerobic and anaerobic bacteria in blood and to identify the bacteria, but not to the specific level of genus or species requiring additional testing, such as slide cultures.

87045

This test may be called a stool culture, culture for Salmonella and Shigella, or routine culture when stool or rectal swab is the specimen. The testing method includes gram staining and subculturing to selective media for the detection of bacterial growth. This test cultures specifically for the initial identification of enteric pathogens Salmonella and Shigella.

87046

This test may be requested by the name of the suspected pathogenic organism. Presumptive identification of aerobic pathogens or microorganisms in the stool sample is by means of identifying colony morphology. The test includes gram staining and subculturing to selective media for the detection of bacterial growth. There are several automated systems that detect the presence of bacteria using colorimetric, radiometric, or spectrophotometric means. The purpose of this stool culture test is to detect the presence of enteric pathogens in the form of aerobic bacteria and to identify the micro-organism(s), but not to the specific level of genus or species requiring additional testing, such as slide cultures. Report this code once for each plate prepared. Stool or rectal swab is the specimen.

87070-87071

Common names for this test are numerous and may include routine culture, aerobic culture, or, using a body or source site, may be referred to as vaginal culture, cerebral spinal fluid culture, etc. Presumptive identification of aerobic pathogens or microorganisms in the sample is by means of identifying colony morphology. The test includes gram staining and subculturing to selective media for the detection of bacterial growth. There are several automated systems that detect the presence of bacteria using colorimetric, radiometric, or spectrophotometric means. The purpose of this culture test is to detect the presence of any or multiple aerobic bacteria from a body source or site, except urine, blood, or stool samples, and to identify the micro-organism(s), but not to the specific level of genus or species requiring additional testing, such as slide cultures. The collection and transport of specimen is varied and specimen dependent. Report 87071 when the identified aerobic isolate(s) is quantified in growth numbers.

87073

The most common name for this procedure is anaerobic culture. Presumptive identification of anaerobic pathogens or microorganisms in the sample is by means of identifying colony morphology. The test includes gram staining and subculturing to selective media for the detection of bacterial growth. There are several automated systems that detect the presence of bacteria using colorimetric, radiometric, or spectrophotometric means. This culture test detects the presence of anaerobic bacteria in a body site or source, except blood, urine, or stool, and identifies the micro-organism(s), but not to the specific level of genus or species requiring additional testing, such as slide cultures. The isolate(s) identified is quantified in growth numbers. Tissues, fluids, and aspirations, except from blood, urine, or stool samples, are collected in anaerobic vials or with anaerobic transport swabs and transported immediately. Anaerobic bacteria are sensitive to oxygen and cold.

87075

The most common name for this procedure is anaerobic culture. Presumptive identification of anaerobic pathogens or microorganisms in the sample is by means of identifying colony morphology. The test includes gram staining and subculturing to selective media for the detection of bacterial growth. There are several automated systems that detect the presence of bacteria using colorimetric, radiometric, or spectrophotometric means. The purpose of this culture test is to detect the presence of any or multiple anaerobic bacteria from any body source or site, except blood, and to identify the micro-organism(s), but not to the specific level of genus or species requiring additional testing, such as slide cultures. Tissues, fluids, and aspirations, except blood samples, are collected in anaerobic vials or with anaerobic transport swabs and transported immediately. Anaerobic bacteria are sensitive to oxygen and cold.

87076-87077

This code reports definitive anaerobic (87076) or aerobic (87077) organism identification of an already-isolated anaerobic or aerobic bacterium. The pathogen has already been presumptively identified, but additional testing is required to identify the specific genus or species. The additional definitive testing methods include biochemical panels and slide cultures. Studies using chromatography, molecular probes, or specific immunological techniques may be employed for definitive testing, but are not included in this code and are reported separately.

87081-87084

This is a presumptive screening culture for one or more pathogenic organisms. The methodology is by culture and the culture should be identified by type (e.g., anaerobic, aerobic) and specimen source (e.g., pleural, peritoneal, bronchial aspirates). If a specific organism is suspected, the person ordering the test will typically use common names, such as strep screen, staph screen, etc., to specify the organism for screening. Presumptive identification includes gram staining as well as up to three tests, such as a catalase, oxidase, or urease test. Screenings included in this code are nonmotile, catalase-positive, gram-positive rod bacteria. Report 87084 when an estimation of the number of organisms is also made, based on a density chart.

87086-87088

These codes report the performance of a urine bacterial culture with a calibrated inoculating device so that a colony count accurately correlates with the number of organisms in the urine. In 87088, isolation and presumptive identification of bacteria recovered from the sample is done by means of identifying colony morphology, subculturing organisms to selective media and the performance of a gram stain or other simple test to identify bacteria to the genus level. There are several automated systems that detect the presence of bacteria using colorimetric, radiometric, or spectrophotometric means. In 87086, quantified colony count numbers within the urine sample are measured.

87101

Dermatophyte culture and fungal culture are common names for this test. Fungi are divided into two broad categories, yeasts and molds. Skin, hair or nail scrapings from infected site are transferred to appropriate agar. Growth and confirmation by microscopic methods identify, or confirm, a presumptive identification of fungus isolated. Alternately, the scrapings are dropped onto dermatophyte test media (DMT) at the time of collection. The media changes color to indicate dermatophyte growth.

87102

Fungal culture, yeast culture, and mold culture are common names for this procedure. Collection is as varied as the sources and the same specimen may be used for other tests. This test is to culture and isolate fungi (yeast or mold) with presumptive identification. Presumptive identification may include fungi (yeast or mold) present or a genus name with no species (e.g., Aspergillus).

87103

Fungal blood culture and blood culture for yeast are common names for this procedure. Blood is subcultured to fungal media. This test procedure is a culture to isolate fungi (yeast or mold) with presumptive identification. Presumptive identification may include fungi (yeast or mold) present or a genus name with no species (e.g., Aspergillus).

87106

This test is commonly known as a fungal yeast identification. Yeast isolates from fungal cultures are further tested for definitive identification. This code reports testing only for yeast pathogens. Various identification procedures, including growth patterns, and macroscopic and microscopic characteristics, are employed. Examples of fungal yeast pathogens that might require definitive identification include: Histoplasma, Coccidioides and Blastomyces.

87107

This test is commonly known as a mold identification. Molds are filamentous fungi that can cause severe, life-threatening infections in immunocompromised individuals. Mold isolates from fungal cultures are further tested for definitive identification. Various identification procedures, including growth patterns, and macroscopic and microscopic characteristics, are employed. Examples of conidium-forming filamentous fungi species that might require definitive identification include: Aspergillus sp., Fusarium sp., Rhizopus arrhizus, Scedosporium apiospermum and Sporothrix schenckii.

87109

A common name for this test is Mycoplasma culture. Specimens are typically transported in viral transport media (VTM). Mycoplasma culture methods are employed. This procedure is for the isolation and identification of Mycoplasma.

87110
This test is commonly known as a Chlamydia culture. A swab of the infected site is placed in a vial of sucrose transport media containing antibiotics and glass beads. The specimen is generally kept refrigerated. The test method is by cell culture, fluorescent stain. The cell culture technique is to isolate for Chlamydia.

87116
Common names include AFB culture, TB culture, mycobacterium culture, and acid-fast culture. Collection methods are source dependent. The methodology is by culture for the isolation and presumptive identification of mycobacterium. An acid-fast smear should be done at the time the specimen is cultured. Media for isolation should include both solid and liquid types.

87118
This procedure is a definitive identification of mycobacterial organisms isolated by procedure 87116. This procedure may be performed by a reference laboratory after isolation by a primary lab. Methodology is traditional biochemical tests for identification of mycobacterium.

87140
Specific antisera are combined with a fluorescent dye and used to stain slides of organisms. Stained slides are scanned with a fluorescent microscope to look for fluorescing organisms. Typing of organisms by immunofluorescent technique is usually to determine whether an organism is of a more pathogenic strain, to determine a treatment, or for epidemiological purposes.

87143
This procedure is performed to provide more specific typing of cultured pathogenic organisms. The methodology is gas liquid chromatography (GLC) or high pressure liquid chromatography (HPLC) to analyze byproducts of rapidly growing organisms. GLC is an automated technique in which the culture specimen is dissolved in a solvent, vaporized, and transported by an inert gas through an adsorbent gas-liquid column containing detectors that analyze and graph the components of the specimen. HPLC is similar to GLC except that the liquid is forced under high pressure through a column packed with sorbent and separated by various methods including adsorption, gel filtration, ion-exchange, or partition. This procedure is performed on an isolated organism as in the definitive identification of mycobacterium.

87147
This test is used for more specifically identifying cultured specimens using an immunologic method other than immunofluorescence. For example, agglutination technique may be used to more specifically identify Salmonella usually to a group level since there are more than 2,000 serovar of Salmonella. The different species have been grouped by common antigens and are tested with polyvalent antisera and reported by group (e.g., Salmonella Group D).

87149-87150
Organisms from any type of culture are identified by nucleic acid probes. Nucleic acid (DNA or RNA) probes may be used to diagnose and monitor infectious diseases. These probes can be used to detect fungi and other organisms after they have been grown in culture. Culturing is required for many organisms because direct staining does not produce accurate results. Specificity using this culture technique is nearly 100 percent for many organisms. Report 87149 for direct probe technique and 87150 for amplified probe technique.

87152
This test may also be known by the acronym PFGE (pulsed field gel electrophoresis), or CHEF (contour-clamped homogeneous electronic), or a combination of the two. A bacterial culture and nucleic acid isolation precedes the test and cells are harvested by centrifugation and washing. The PGFE method resolves and separates very large DNA molecules for cloning and direct visualization of small chromosomes (among other genetic analysis This emerging method provides information about macromolecular structure and function and has been used to detect in vivo chromosome breakage and degradation, the number and size of chromosomes, and to identify invasive infection in humans.

87153
This code describes the identification of organisms from any type of culture using the nucleic acid sequencing method. Isolation and identification of the genetic material of organisms known to be the infectious agent in certain diseases are helpful in determining the most precise therapy and antimicrobials for treatment of the patient. For example, identification of bacterial isolates by 16S rRNA gene sequencing identifies uncommon bacteria that cannot be identified using conventional methods. Report 87153 for each isolate. If additional studies involving molecular probes, chromatography, or immunologic techniques are performed, these should be reported separately.

87158
Any methodology that would identify a microbial organism to the species level or a type level that does not involve the use of biochemical substrates (traditional bacteriology), antigen specific fluorescent stain, gas chromatography, phage testing, or agglutination or precipitation from antigen-antibody reactions. Lectin assays and bacteriocin typing are two tests that fit in this procedure description.

87164-87166
Names commonly used include dark field for syphilis and dark field exam. Dark field microscopic exams have generally been limited to the bacteria called spirochetes. Treponema pallidum, the agent of syphilis, Borrelia burgdorferi, the agent of Lyme disease; and Leptospira are among the better known spirochetes. Specimens for dark field exam are typically examined within 30 minutes of collection. Certain immunological tests have rendered this method to be somewhat outdated. The term "dark field" refers to the staining method. If the lab is responsible for specimen collection, report 87164. If the lab is not responsible for collection of the specimen, report 87166.

87168
This test is performed to identify arthropods that might be vectors of disease causing organisms in man. Arthropods are small animals having a hard, jointed exoskeleton and paired legs. This group of animals includes lice and ticks. Method is visual examination (macroscopic) of the source specimen.

87169
This test is performed to identify parasites other than arthropods that might be vectors of disease causing organisms in man. Method is visual examination (macroscopic) of the source specimen.

87172
This test may be requested as pinworm examination. Clear tape is applied to the perianal area. The tape is removed and submitted to the laboratory on a clean slide. Method is microscopic examination.

87176
This test may be called grinding or homogenization of tissue. The methodology is mechanical disruption of the tissue to enhance extraction of endotoxin. It may involve the use of sterile equipment, such as scissors, mortar and pestle, or disposable grinders.

87177
Common names for this procedure are ova and parasite exam, or O & P. Stool is collected in a clean, leak-proof container (when processed within one hour) or the specimen is added to formalin or fixative (both available in commercial kits). The methodology of an ova and parasite exam for stools includes a direct smear, and smear of concentrated material, such as formalin concentration technique or zinc flotation method. Identification is by observing parasites with the aid of a microscope. Do not report 87177 in conjunction with 87015.

87181
A susceptibility study is performed to determine the susceptibility of a bacterium to an antibiotic. The methodology is agar diffusion (the E test is a method of agar diffusion). The specific antibiotics could be chosen and limited. The test is reported per antibiotic tested. The agar dilution is reported as minimum inhibitory concentration (MIC), which is a method of measuring the exact amount of antibiotic needed to inhibit an organism.

87184
This is commonly called a Kirby-Bauer or Bauer-Kirby sensitivity test. It is a sensitivity test to determine the susceptibility of a bacterium to an antibiotic. The methodology is disk diffusion and results are reported as sensitive, intermediate, or resistant. As many as 12 antibiotic disks may be used per plate and the procedure is billed per plate not per antibiotic disk.

87185
Bacteria produce enzymes that can inactivate some types of antibiotics. This susceptibility test identifies those bacteria that will be resistant to certain types of antibiotics by detecting the presence of these enzymes.

87186
This procedure may be called an MIC, or a sensitivity test. It is a sensitivity test to determine the susceptibility of a bacterium to an antibiotic. The methodology is microtiter dilution (several commercial panels use this method). Results are given as a minimum inhibitory concentration (MIC) with an interpretation of sensitive, intermediate, or resistant. The antibiotics on commercial plates are numerous, but predetermined. The procedure is charged by plate not by antibiotic.

87187
This test may be called an MBC (minimum bactericidal concentration). MBC is the dilution of antibiotic needed to kill the bacteria. MICs are tube dilutions read visually. Tubes that may visually appear to have no growth are cultured to solid media to detect a concentration of antibiotic where no organisms grow (MBC).

87188
This test may be referred to as an MIC (minimum inhibitory concentration). It is a susceptibility test to determine the sensitivity of a bacterium to an antibiotic. The methodology is macrobroth dilution. Results are given as a minimum inhibitory concentration (MIC) with an interpretation of sensitive, intermediate, or resistant. The procedure is charged per antibiotic tested.

87190
Mycobacterium susceptibility test is a procedure done only on mycobacterium (e.g., M. tuberculosis, M. marinum, etc.). Proportion method is used and involves testing of a panel of antibiotics used only for the treatment of mycobacterium. Results are given as sensitive or resistant.

87197
This procedure is called a serum cidal level, a serum bactericidal titer, or a Schlichter test. This test cannot be performed without a bacterial organism that has

been previously isolated from the same patient. The killing power of the patient's serum against the isolated pathogen is measured. Blood is usually drawn and tested at peak and trough level of the antibiotic.

87205
Any smear done on a primary source (e.g., sputum, CSF, etc.) to identify bacteria, fungi, and cell types. An interpretation of findings is provided. Bacteria, fungi, WBCs, and epithelial cells may be estimated in quantity with an interpretation as to the possibility of contamination by normal flora. A gram stain may be the most commonly performed smear of this type.

87206
A fluorescent or acid-fast stain for bacteria, fungi, parasites, viruses or cell types. These are stains usually for specific groups of organisms (e.g., mycobacterium and Nocardia). Identification of Cryptosporidium and related parasites are examples of parasites that can be identified by fluorescent or acid fast stain. An interpretation is included.

87207
This is a stain to look for inclusion bodies or parasites (e.g., malaria inside red cells). Its use to detect herpes has been outdated by amplification and immunological methods. An interpretation is included.

87209
This is a stain to look for the inclusion of trichome or iron hematoxylin indicating the presence of parasites or their eggs. An interpretation is included.

87210
This test may be requested as a KOH prep. A wet mount is prepared from a primary source to detect bacteria, fungi, or ova and parasites. Motility of organisms is visible on wet mounts and the addition of a simple stain, such as iodine, India ink, or simple dyes, may aid detection of bacteria, fungi, and parasites. An interpretation of findings is included.

87220
Potassium hydroxide (KOH) prep and calcofluor stains are the most common methods of looking for hyphal elements and/ or yeast in tissue. The KOH causes a clearing of the specimen to make fungus more visible. The preparation is enhanced for microscopic observation by adding a drop of calcofluor, a type of fluorescent dye, to the slide and reading the preparation with a fluorescent microscope.

87230
This procedure is a toxin assay for diagnosis of toxin producing organisms, such as Clostridium difficile, E. coli 0157, enterotoxigenic E. coli, and Vibrio cholerae. Stool is collected for testing. Filtrates of the stool are inoculated into cell cultures and observed for CPE (cytopathic effect) microscopically. Confirmation of toxin production may be done by toxin neutralization. Different cell cultures are used to test for different toxins, so organism must be specified.

87250
Embryonated egg or small animal inoculation with specimen source is used in the diagnosis of some viruses. There are different specimen types for the different viruses. Contact the reference lab that is performing the test for type of specimen and transport. There are, however, more rapid tests to diagnosis for most viral infections. This code includes observation for signs of illness in inoculated mice for as long as three weeks and dissection of mice and preparation of tissue for microscopy to confirm diagnosis when mice become ill or die.

87252
Cell culture is a procedure used particularly for viral detection. There is a general viral culture which can detect most viruses, but when a specific agent is suspected such as CMV, HSV, Influenzae A or B, mumps, or varicella zoster, more specific and rapid culture techniques can be used. This procedure provides presumptive identification by cytopathic effect only. Specimens may be collected by swab, washings and fluids, and blood draw.

87253
This code reports additional tissue culture studies required for specific virus identification and is reported for each isolate.

87254
This test may also be ordered as a shell vial (SV) culture, a rapid shell assay, or an immediate early antigen test. Specimen collection is by separately reportable appropriate procedure. Shell vial isolation cultures offer more immediate results (often 48-hours) than conventional cultures. The technique is particularly useful in identification of respiratory organisms. Immunofluorescence is a technique in which antibody reacts with an antigen on a fixed slide. The antibody in turn reacts with antihuman globulins for the diagnosis of infectious diseases. The fluorescence is best viewed with a laser-scanning confocal microscope.

87255
A peptide substrate specific for a viral enzyme proteolytic activity is used for detection of viral infection in primary source biological samples, such as serum and whole cells. Enzyme proteolytic activity is the splitting of protein peptide bonds with the formation of smaller polypeptides. This peptide cleavage, catalyzed by the specific enzyme, causes an increase in fluorescence, which allows determination of the specific enzymatic activity by visualizing the protease activity with a fluorescence microscope.

87260
This test may be requested as adenovirus by DFA or by immunofluorescence. It is most commonly used to

diagnose serotypes that cause infantile gastroenteritis. A random stool sample is obtained. Infectious agent antigen detection by immunofluorescence includes direct and indirect fluorescent antibody technique and involves using monoclonal antibodies and immunofluorescence microscopy. Cellular material must be obtained from the site for immunofluorescence to be an effective diagnostic technique.

87265
This test may be requested as Bordetella pertussis or parapertussis by DFA or by immunofluorescence. Bordetella pertussis is the causative agent of whooping cough. Infectious agent antigen detection by immunofluorescence includes direct and indirect fluorescent antibody technique and involves using monoclonal antibodies and immunofluorescence microscopy. Cellular material must be obtained from the site for immunofluorescence to be an effective diagnostic technique.

87267
An enterovirus is detected by direct fluorescent antibody (DFA) staining technique. Molecules of a fluorescent dye are chemically linked to antibodies that are introduced into the specimen sample and bind with their specific antigen (e.g., the enterovirus) to form an antibody-antigen complex. The presence of the infectious agent microorganism is detected indirectly when the fluorescent reaction of the dye is seen under a special microscope. The enterovirus is isolated in cell culture for the test. Specimens include throat swabs, CSF, and blood samples. An enterovirus includes polio, Coxsackie, and echovirus.

87269
This procedure may be requested as Giardia by direct fluorescent antibody (DFA) stain or by immunofluorescence. The Giardia lamblia parasite causes severe diarrhea, cramps, and stomach-ache, and can lead to weight loss and dehydration. Contamination occurs in soil, food, water, or surfaces in contact with infected feces. Giardia is a very common cause of waterborne disease in humans in the United States. Infectious agent antigen detection by immunofluorescence includes direct and indirect fluorescent antibody technique and involves using monoclonal antibodies and immunofluorescence microscopy. Cellular material must be obtained from the site for immunofluorescence to be an effective diagnostic technique.

87270
This test may be requested as Chlamydia trachomatis or C. trachomatis by DFA or by immunofluorescence. C. trachomatis is a frequently occurring sexually transmitted disease. It may cause nonspecific urethritis or pelvic inflammatory disease (PID), although it is frequently asymptomatic in women. Another serotype also causes conjunctivitis. Infectious agent antigen detection by immunofluorescence includes direct and indirect fluorescent antibody technique and involves using monoclonal antibodies and immunofluorescence microscopy. Cellular material must be obtained from the site for immunofluorescence to be an effective diagnostic technique.

87271
A cytomegalovirus is detected by direct fluorescent antibody (DFA) staining technique. The presence of the infectious agent microorganism is detected indirectly when the fluorescent reaction of the dye is seen under a special microscope. The cytomegalovirus is isolated in cell culture for the test. Specimens include throat swabs, CSF, and blood samples. A cytomegalovirus is any virus in the Betaherpesvirinae subfamily.

87272
This procedure may be referred to as a direct fluorescent antibody (DFA) or immunofluorescent stain for cryptosporidium. This parasite infects the gastrointestinal tract causing symptoms such as diarrhea, weight loss, fever, and abdominal pain. Infectious agent antigen detection by immunofluorescence includes direct and indirect fluorescent antibody technique and involves using monoclonal antibodies and immunofluorescence microscopy.

87273
This test may be requested as HSV 2 by DFA or HSV 2 by immunofluorescence. HSV 2 is a sexually transmitted disease with lesions occurring primarily in the genitourinary tract. Infectious agent antigen detection by immunofluorescence includes direct and indirect fluorescent antibody technique and involves using monoclonal antibodies and immunofluorescence microscopy. Cellular material must be obtained from the site for immunofluorescence to be an effective diagnostic technique.

87274
This test may be requested as HSV 1 by DFA or HSV 1 by immunofluorescence. HSV 1 is primarily responsible for oral lesions frequently referred to as fever blisters or cold sores. Infectious agent antigen detection by immunofluorescence includes direct and indirect fluorescent antibody technique and involves using monoclonal antibodies and immunofluorescence microscopy. Cellular material must be obtained from the site for immunofluorescence to be an effective diagnostic technique.

87275

This test may be requested as influenza B (less common strain) by DFA or by immunofluorescence. Infectious agent antigen detection by immunofluorescence includes direct and indirect fluorescent antibody technique and involves using monoclonal antibodies and immunofluorescence microscopy. Cellular material must be obtained from the site for immunofluorescence to be an effective diagnostic technique.

87276

This test may be requested as influenza A (most common strain) by DFA or by immunofluorescence. The causative agent is subject to wide variation in antigenic type. This is referred to as antigen shift and causes new variations of the Type A virus to appear at two to three year intervals. Infectious agent antigen detection by immunofluorescence includes direct and indirect fluorescent antibody technique and involves using monoclonal antibodies and immunofluorescence microscopy. Cellular material must be obtained from the site for immunofluorescence to be an effective diagnostic technique.

87277

This procedure may be requested as Legionella micdadei by direct fluorescent antibody (DFA) stain or by immunofluorescence. L. micdadei is the second most commonly isolated member of Legionella. Infectious agent antigen detection by immunofluorescence includes direct and indirect fluorescent antibody technique and involves nonculture (primary source) detection of infected cells using monoclonal antibodies and immunofluorescence microscopy. Cellular material must be obtained from the site for immunofluorescence to be an effective diagnostic technique. For DFA procedure it is acceptable to prepare and send two air-dried smears. This method may be a rapid diagnosis, but is not as accurate as cultured tests.

87278

This procedure may be requested as Legionella pneumophila by direct fluorescent antibody (DFA) stain or by immunofluorescence. L. pneumophila is the bacterium associated with Legionnaires' disease and Pontiac fever. Infectious agent antigen detection by immunofluorescence includes direct and indirect fluorescent antibody technique and involves nonculture (primary source) detection of infected cells using monoclonal antibodies and immunofluorescence microscopy. Cellular material must be obtained from the site for immunofluorescence to be an effective diagnostic technique. For DFA procedure it is acceptable to prepare and send two air-dried smears. This method may be a rapid diagnosis, but is not as accurate as cultured tests.

87279

This test may be requested as parainfluenza virus by DFA or by immunofluorescence. Parainfluenza is a group of viruses that cause upper respiratory infections that are often the causative agents in croup, bronchitis and bronchiolitis. Infectious agent antigen detection by immunofluorescence includes direct and indirect fluorescent antibody technique and involves using monoclonal antibodies and immunofluorescence microscopy. Cellular material must be obtained from the site for immunofluorescence to be an effective diagnostic technique.

87280

This test may be requested as DFA or immunofluorescent stain for respiratory syncytial virus (RSV). RSV causes respiratory disease that can be particularly severe in infants. Infectious agent antigen detection by immunofluorescence includes direct and indirect fluorescent antibody technique and involves using monoclonal antibodies and immunofluorescence microscopy. Cellular material must be obtained from the site for immunofluorescence to be an effective diagnostic technique.

87281

This test may be requested as pneumocystis carinii or PCP by DFA or by immunofluorescence. Pneumocystis carinii causes lung infection or pneumonia in premature infants, cancer patients, patients being treated with immunosuppressive medications for the management of organ transplantation or cancer, and AIDS patients. Infectious agent antigen detection by immunofluorescence includes direct and indirect fluorescent antibody technique and involves using monoclonal antibodies and immunofluorescence microscopy. Cellular material must be obtained from the site for immunofluorescence to be an effective diagnostic technique.

87283

This test may be requested as rubeola stain or rubeola IFA. Rubeola, more commonly referred to as measles, is characterized by fever, coryza, cough, and conjunctivitis after which Koplik's spots appear in the mouth with pharyngitis and inflammation of the laryngeal and tracheobronchial mucosa. Infectious agent antigen detection by immunofluorescence includes direct and indirect fluorescent antibody technique and involves using monoclonal antibodies and immunofluorescence microscopy. Cellular material must be obtained from the site for immunofluorescence to be an effective diagnostic technique.

87285
The spirochete Treponema pallidum is the causative agent of syphilis. Infectious agent antigen detection by immunofluorescence includes direct and indirect fluorescent antibody technique and involves using monoclonal antibodies and immunofluorescence microscopy. Cellular material must be obtained from the site for immunofluorescence to be an effective diagnostic technique.

87290
This test may be requested as direct fluorescent stain for varicella zoster virus. This is the causative agent of chickenpox. Infectious agent antigen detection by immunofluorescence includes direct and indirect fluorescent antibody technique and involves using monoclonal antibodies and immunofluorescence microscopy. Cellular material must be obtained from the site for immunofluorescence to be an effective diagnostic technique. This test has a high specificity, but sensitivity is dependent on adequacy of the sample collected. A negative sample should be cultured.

87299
This code reports immunofluorescent technique of specific infectious agents not identified by more specific codes. Infectious agent antigen detection by immunofluorescence includes direct and indirect fluorescent antibody technique and involves using monoclonal antibodies and immunofluorescence microscopy. Cellular material must be obtained from the site for immunofluorescence to be an effective diagnostic technique.

87300
This code reports immunofluorescent technique to identify multiple strains of bacteria or other infectious organisms in a single test. Infectious agent antigen detection by immunofluorescence includes direct and indirect fluorescent antibody technique and involves using monoclonal antibodies and immunofluorescence microscopy. Cellular material must be obtained from the site for immunofluorescence to be an effective diagnostic technique.

87301
This test may be requested as adenovirus enteric types 40/41 by enzyme immunoassay (EIA). These serotypes cause infantile gastroenteritis. A random stool sample is the specimen.

87305
This test may be requested as enzyme immunoassay (EIA) for the detection of Aspergillus or Aspergillus galactomannan antigen. The specimen is blood serum. Aspergillus is a life-threatening infection in patients with immune systems compromised by leukemia, organ or bone marrow transplant, or chemotherapy.

87320
This test may be requested as Chlamydia trachomatis or C. trachomatis by enzyme immunoassay (EIA). C. trachomatis is a frequently occurring sexually transmitted disease. It may cause nonspecific urethritis or pelvic inflammatory disease (PID), although it is frequently asymptomatic in women. Another serotype also causes conjunctivitis. Enzyme immunoassay refers to a technique that utilizes a chemical bond between an enzyme and an antigen or antibody as a label to identify specific chemical or infectious agents. Special reagents and equipment are required for C. trachomatis EIA. Sensitivity of EIA is approximately 75 to 85 percent.

87324
This test may be requested as enzyme immunoassay (EIA) for the detection of Clostridium difficile toxin or more simply referred to as a C. difficile toxin test. A random stool sample is obtained. Fresh stool should be kept refrigerated and transported in clean leak proof container.

87327
This test may be requested as enzyme immunoassay (EIA) for the detection of Cryptococcus neoformans. Blood is obtained by venipuncture. CSF is obtained by separately reportable lumbar puncture. Cryptococcosis is a life threatening infection of the meninges in patients with compromised immune systems due to diseases such as acquired immune deficiency syndrome (AIDS). This test is most effective when performed on CSF of patients with symptoms of cryptococcal meningitis; however, serum may also contain detectable levels of antigen.

87328
This procedure is for the detection of cryptosporidium by EIA (Enzyme Immunoassay). This parasite infects the gastrointestinal tract causing symptoms such as diarrhea, weight loss, fever, and abdominal pain. A random stool sample is obtained. Transport fresh or preserved stool in clean leak proof container.

87329
This procedure is for the qualitative or semiquantitative detection of Giardia lamblia by EIA (enzyme immunoassay). The Giardia lamblia parasite causes severe diarrhea, cramps, and stomachache, and can lead to weight loss and dehydration. Contamination occurs in soil, food, water, or surfaces in contact with infected feces. Giardia is a very common cause of waterborne disease in humans in the United States. The specimen is a random stool specimen.

87332

This test may be requested as cytomegalovirus (CMV) by enzyme immunoassay (EIA). CMV is part of the viral family that includes herpes zoster, Epstein-Barr, and Varicella zoster infections. CMV usually causes only mild symptoms except in fetal infection or immunosuppressed patients, including AIDS and transplant patients. Blood specimen is obtained by venipuncture. Enzyme immunoassay refers to a technique that utilizes a chemical bond between an enzyme and an antigen or antibody as a label to identify specific chemical or infectious agents. EIA is often used in conjunction with culture.

87335

This test may be requested enzyme immunoassay (EIA) for the detection of Escherichia Coli (E. Coli) 0157. E. Coli 0157 is the causative agent of hemorrhagic colitis in food borne epidemics. A random stool sample is obtained. Stool or rectal swabs may be transported in Carey-Blair transport media. Fresh stool can be sent in clean leak proof container, but if transport time exceeds two hours the specimen should be frozen at -70 C.

87336

This test may be requested as enzyme immunoassay (EIA) for the detection of Entamoeba histolytica dispar group. E histolytica is an enteric protozoan that exists in trophozoite or cyst form. Three to six stool examinations are recommended, each permanently stained using a trichrome stain. Biopsies may be obtained by separately reportable open or endoscopic procedure.

87337

This test may be requested as enzyme immunoassay (EIA) for the detection of Entamoeba histolytica group. E. histolytica is an enteric protozoan that exists in trophozoite or cyst form. Three to six stool examinations are recommended. Each is stained permanently using a trichrome stain. This test is used to identify all genera but the dispar group. See code 87336 for identification of E. hystolytica dispar.

87338

This test may be ordered as an H. pylori antibody titer, stool. Specimen collection is from a stool sample, particularly drawn from mucous in the specimen. Method is multiple step, qualitative or semiquantitative, enzyme immunoassay (EIA) or enzyme-linked immunosorbent assay (ELISA). H. pylori may be found along the gastric mucosa and on the mucosal cells of the GI tract and its presence is linked to several serious disorders of the stomach.

87339

This test may be ordered as an H. pylori antibody titer. Method is multiple step, qualitative or semiquantitative, enzyme immunoassay (EIA) or enzyme-linked immunosorbent assay (ELISA). H. pylori may be found along the gastric mucosa and on the mucosal cells of the GI tract and its presence is linked to several serious disorders of the stomach.

87340

This test may be requested as HBsAg by enzyme immunoassay (EIA). Hepatitis B is a retrovirus that can cause persistent infection leading to cirrhosis and hepatocellular carcinoma. HBsAg is a lipoprotein that coats the surface of the hepatitis B virus. Blood specimen is serum.

87341

This test may be requested as HBsAg by enzyme immunoassay (EIA) confirmation. This assay is performed only when a specimen is repeatedly reactive for Hepatitis B surface antigen. Elevated HBsAg levels beyond 6 months may indicate a chronic carrier (i.e., chronic hepatitis). The HBsAg neutralization test is performed to identify false positives. False positives on a standard HBsAg test will not neutralize with anti-HBs in the confirmatory assay. Hepatitis B is a retrovirus that can cause persistent infection leading to cirrhosis and hepatocellular carcinoma. HBsAg is a lipoprotein that coats the surface of the hepatitis B virus. Blood specimen is obtained by venipuncture. Enzyme immunoassay refers to a technique that utilizes a chemical bond between an enzyme and an antigen or antibody as a label to identify specific chemical or infectious agents.

87350

This test may be requested as HBeAg by enzyme immunoassay (EIA). Hepatitis B is a retrovirus that can cause persistent infection leading to cirrhosis and hepatocellular carcinoma. HBeAg is normally tested only on individuals who are chronically HBsAg positive. Blood specimen is serum.

87380

This test may be requested as hepatitis delta agent (HDAg) by enzyme immunoassay (EIA). Hepatitis delta agent is normally tested only on individuals who are chronically HBsAg positive or have an exacerbation of their hepatitis as HDAg requires the presence of HBsAg to become an infectious virus. Blood specimen is serum.

87385
This test may be requested as Histoplasma capsulatum by enzyme immunoassay (EIA). Histoplasma capsulatum infection results from inhalation or ingestion of spores and is common in the Midwestern United States. It is usually asymptomatic, but on occasion causes acute pneumonia, disseminated reticuloendothelial hyperplasia with hepatosplenomegaly and anemia, or influenza-like symptoms with joint effusion and erythema nodosum. Reactivated infection is common in immunocompromised individuals affecting lungs, meninges, heart, peritoneum and adrenal glands. Blood specimen is serum.

87390
This test may be requested as human immunodeficiency virus Type 1 (HIV-1) by EIA. HIV-1 is the causative agent of acquired immunodeficiency syndrome (AIDS). Blood specimen is obtained by venipuncture. Enzyme immunoassay refers to a technique that utilizes a chemical bond between an enzyme and an antigen or antibody as a label to identify specific chemical or infectious agents. If EIA is positive, it is repeated. Two out of three tests must be positive before the test is reported as positive. All positive EIA tests are confirmed with an additional test using a different technique, usually Western blot, which is reported separately.

87391
This test may be requested as human immunodeficiency virus Type 2 (HIV-2) by EIA. HIV-2 is a retrovirus closely related to simian AIDS and found initially in West African nations and Portugal, but with cases also being reported in the United States since 1987. Blood specimen is serum. If EIA is positive, it is repeated. Two out of three tests must be positive before the test is reported as positive. All positive EIA tests are confirmed with an additional test using a different technique, usually Western blot, which is reported separately.

87400
This test may be requested as Influenza A EIA or Influenza B EIA. Blood specimen is serum. Other specimens may be collected by separately reportable procedures. Influenza A and B are a genus of the virus that causes the acute respiratory illness known as influenza. The designation is based on antigenic testing. Testing may occur during the acute phase of illness and again 10 to 14 days after onset of symptoms.

87420
This test may be requested as respiratory syncytial virus (RSV) by enzyme immunoassay (EIA). RSV causes respiratory disease that can be particularly severe in infants. Blood specimen is serum.

87425
This test may be requested as rotavirus by enzyme immunoassay (EIA). Rotavirus causes sometimes severe infectious gastroenteritis in infants and young children. Adults may contract a milder infection. Blood specimen is serum.

87427
This test may be ordered as a Shigella Type 1 by EIA or S. dysenteriae test by EIA. Blood specimen is serum. Shigella is an enteric pathogen known for its ability to produce protein toxins that cause acute gut inflammation and dysentery. Serology tests are usually conducted during the acute phase of illness.

87430
This test may be requested as Streptococcus A by enzyme immunoassay (EIA). Streptococcus A is a form of beta hemolytic streptococcus that causes pharyngitis. Untreated infection may lead to rheumatic fever or glomerulonephritis.

87449-87451
These codes report enzyme immunoassay (EIA) of infectious agents that are not specifically identified elsewhere. Code 87449 reports testing for a single organism using a multiple step method; 87450 reports testing for a single organism using a single step method; and 87451 reports testing for multiple organisms using a multiple step method and a polyvalent antiserum. The term polyvalent when used in reference to microbiology denotes an antibody molecule with multiple antigen binding sites.

87470
This test may be requested as B. henselae or B. quintana. These organisms are gram-negative bacilli that infect the red blood cells and epithelial cells of the lymph nodes, liver, and spleen. Blood specimen is serum. Tissue specimen requires a separately reportable biopsy. The specimen is treated to isolate the nucleic acid. Nucleic acid is analyzed using direct probe technique.

87471
This test may be requested as B. henselae or B. quintana. These organisms are gram-negative bacilli that infect the red blood cells and epithelial cells of the lymph nodes, liver, and spleen. Blood specimen is serum. Tissue specimen requires a separately reportable biopsy. The specimen is treated to isolate the nucleic acid (DNA, RNA) and eliminate substances that inhibit amplification. The nucleic acid is amplified using specific primers for B. henselae and B. quintana sequences.

87472
This test may be requested as B. henselae or B. quintana. These organisms are gram-negative bacilli that infect the red blood cells and epithelial cells of the lymph nodes, liver, and spleen. Blood specimen is serum. Tissue specimen requires a separately reportable biopsy. The specimen is treated to isolate the nucleic acid (DNA, RNA). This code reports quantification only and is used primarily to assess extent of disease or disease progression.

87475
This test may be requested as DNA direct probe for Lyme disease. Borrelia burgdorferi is bacteria transmitted by tick bite and the causative agent of Lyme disease, acrodermatitis chronica atrophicans, and erythema chronicum migrans. Blood specimen is serum. CSF requires a spinal puncture, which is reported separately. Synovial fluid is obtained by arthrocentesis and is reported separately. A random urine specimen is obtained. DNA from spirochete Borrelia burgdorferi is analyzed using direct probe technique.

87476
This test may be requested as DNA amplified probe for Lyme disease. Borrelia burgdorferi is bacteria transmitted by tick bite and the causative agent of Lyme disease, acrodermatitis chronica atrophicans, and erythema chronicum migrans. Blood specimen is serum. CSF requires a spinal puncture, which is reported separately. Synovial fluid is obtained by arthrocentesis and is reported separately. A random urine specimen is obtained. DNA from spirochete Borrelia burgdorferi is analyzed using amplified probe technique. The DNA is amplified using specific primers for Borrelia burgdorferi sequences.

87477
This test may be requested as Lyme disease quantification using DNA. Borrelia burgdorferi is bacteria transmitted by tick bite and the causative agent of Lyme disease, acrodermatitis chronica atrophicans, and erythema chronicum migrans. Blood specimen is serum. CSF requires a spinal puncture, which is reported separately. Synovial fluid is obtained by arthrocentesis and is reported separately. A random urine specimen is obtained.

87480
This test is used to diagnosis an infection by any species of Candida, but usually C. albicans. This test would normally be performed to diagnosis systemic (invasive) candidiasis. Blood is serum. The specimen is treated to isolate nucleic acid (DNA, RNA). Nucleic acid is analyzed using direct probe technique.

87481
This test is used to diagnosis an infection by any species of Candida, but usually C. albicans. This test would normally be performed to diagnosis systemic (invasive) candidiasis. Blood is serum. The specimen is treated to isolate the nucleic acid (DNA, RNA) and eliminate substances that inhibit amplification. The nucleic acid is amplified using specific primers for Candida sequences.

87482
This test is used to diagnosis an infection by any species of Candida, but usually C. albicans. This test would normally be performed to diagnosis systemic (invasive) candidiasis. Blood is serum. The specimen is treated to isolate the nucleic acid (DNA, RNA). This code reports quantification only and is used primarily to assess extent of disease or disease progression.

87485
Chlamydia pneumoniae causes both upper and lower respiratory tract infections and is a causative agent in many community acquired pneumonia. Blood is serum. Sputum may be obtained by deep coughing or aerosol induced technique. The specimen is treated to isolate nucleic acid (DNA, RNA). Nucleic acid is analyzed using direct probe technique.

87486
Chlamydia pneumoniae causes both upper and lower respiratory tract infections and is a causative agent in many community acquired pneumonia. Blood is serum. Sputum may be obtained by deep coughing or aerosol induced technique. The DNA is amplified using a technique such as polymerase chain reaction (PCR).

87487
Chlamydia pneumoniae causes both upper and lower respiratory tract infections and is a causative agent in many community acquired pneumonia. Blood is serum. Sputum may be obtained by deep coughing or aerosol induced technique. The specimen is treated to isolate the nucleic acid (DNA, RNA). This code reports quantification only and is used primarily to assess extent of disease or disease progression.

87490
This test may be requested as Chlamydia trachomatis or C. trachomatis by direct DNA probe. C. trachomatis is a frequently occurring sexually transmitted disease. It may cause nonspecific urethritis or pelvic inflammatory disease (PID), frequently asymptomatic in women. Another serotype also causes conjunctivitis. The specimen is treated to isolate the DNA using direct probe.

87491
This test may be requested as Chlamydia trachomatis or C. trachomatis by polymerase chain reaction. C. trachomatis is a frequently occurring sexually transmitted disease. It may cause nonspecific urethritis or pelvic inflammatory disease (PID), frequently

asymptomatic in women. Another serotype also causes conjunctivitis. The DNA is amplified using a technique such as polymerase chain reaction (PCR).

87492
This test may be requested as Chlamydia trachomatis or C. trachomatis DNA quantification. C. trachomatis is a frequently occurring sexually transmitted disease. It may cause nonspecific urethritis or pelvic inflammatory disease (PID), frequently asymptomatic in women. Another serotype also causes conjunctivitis. This code reports quantification only.

87493
This code reports infectious agent detection by nucleic acid (DNA, RNA) amplified probe for clostridium difficile toxin B (tcdB). This test is used to diagnose patients whose symptoms include persistent non-bloody diarrhea, decreased appetite, abdominal discomfort, and elevated temperature following antibiotic therapy. Nucleic acid detection, also referred to as molecular pathology, is a rapidly developing diagnostic technique that is especially useful in identifying microorganisms that require tedious isolation and incubation and/or those which cannot be cultured. Another advantage of molecular methods is that they are able to detect infectious agents at much lower levels than required using other techniques. Amplified probe involves isolating and identifying the infectious agent DNA or RNA. This involves cell lysis and extraction of the DNA using phenol or chloroform. The nucleic acids are amplified using one of several techniques. Polymerase chain reaction (PCR) is the most frequently used amplification technique.

87495
This test may be requested as cytomegalovirus (CMV) direct DNA probe technique. CMV is part of the viral family that includes herpes zoster, Epstein-Barr, and varicella zoster infections. CMV usually causes only mild symptoms except in fetal infection or immunosuppressed patients, including AIDS and transplant patients. Blood specimen is serum. A random urine specimen is obtained. A separately reportable tissue biopsy is obtained. The specimen is treated to isolate the DNA using direct probe.

87496
This test may be requested as cytomegalovirus (CMV) by polymerase chain reaction (PCR). CMV is part of the viral family that includes herpes zoster, Epstein-Barr, and varicella zoster infections. CMV usually causes only mild symptoms except in fetal infection or immunosuppressed patients, including AIDS and transplant patients. Blood specimen is serum. A random urine specimen is obtained. A separately reportable tissue biopsy is obtained. The DNA is amplified using a technique such as polymerase chain reaction (PCR).

87497
This test may be requested as cytomegalovirus (CMV) quantification. CMV is part of the viral family that includes herpes zoster, Epstein-Barr, and varicella zoster infections. CMV usually causes only mild symptoms except in fetal infection or immunosuppressed patients, including AIDS and transplant patients. Blood specimen is serum. A random urine specimen is obtained. A separately reportable tissue biopsy is obtained. This code reports quantification only and is usually performed following amplification that is reported separately.

87498
This test may be requested as enterovirus by polymerase chain reaction (PCR). Detection of enterovirus nucleic acid provides a differential diagnosis of meningitis. Specimen is usually cerebrospinal fluid or throat swab. This test typically uses a real time reverse transcription polymerase chain reaction (RT-RTP) methodology in the collected clinical samples. The test results are usually available significantly faster than viral culture results.

87500
Vancomycin is an antibiotic. The ability of certain microorganisms to withstand vancomycin treatment is called vancomycin resistance (VR). VR resistance is increasingly problematic in hospitals, nursing homes, and other health care facilities where vancomycin has been used as the drug of "last resort" to treat urinary tract, wound infections, and other serious disease processes resistant to other antibiotics. Testing organisms from clinical specimens with DNA amplified probe tests can identify vancomycin resistance genes, such as vanA and vanB genes of the Enterococcus that have a particularly high resistance to vancomycin, so other treatment options can be initiated.

87510
This test may also be requested as haemophilus vaginalis by direct nucleic acid probe. Gardnerella vaginalis is a gram-negative bacterium which causes an infection of the female genital tract producing a gray or yellow discharge. The specimen is treated to isolate nucleic acid (DNA, RNA). Nucleic acid is analyzed using direct probe technique.

87511
This test may also be requested as haemophilus vaginalis by amplified nucleic acid probe. Gardnerella vaginalis is a gram-negative bacterium which causes an infection of the female genital tract producing a gray or yellow discharge. The nucleic acid is amplified using specific primers for Gardnerella vaginalis sequences.

87512
This test may also be requested as haemophilus vaginalis. Gardnerella vaginalis is a gram-negative bacterium which causes an infection of the female genital tract producing a gray or yellow discharge. The

specimen is treated to isolate the nucleic acid (DNA, RNA). This code reports quantification only and is used primarily to assess extent of disease or disease progression.

87515
This test may be requested as HBV DNA direct probe. Hepatitis B is a retrovirus that can cause persistent infection leading to cirrhosis and hepatocellular carcinoma. Molecular (DNA) tests are useful in identifying potentially infectious individuals as well as chronic progression of the disease. Blood specimen is serum. A liver biopsy is required for analysis of liver tissue and is reported separately. The specimen is treated to isolate the DNA using direct probe.

87516
This test may be requested as HBV DNA by polymerase chain reaction (PCR). Hepatitis B is a retrovirus that can cause persistent infection leading to cirrhosis and hepatocellular carcinoma. Molecular (DNA) tests are useful in identifying potentially infectious individuals as well as chronic progression of the disease. Blood specimen is serum. A liver biopsy is required for analysis of liver tissue and is reported separately The DNA is amplified using a technique such as polymerase chain reaction (PCR).

87517
This test may be requested as HBV DNA quantification. Hepatitis B is a retrovirus that can cause persistent infection leading to cirrhosis and hepatocellular carcinoma. Blood specimen is serum. A liver biopsy is required for analysis of liver tissue and is reported separately. Quantification is used primarily to monitor response to therapy in chronic hepatitis B. This code reports quantification only.

87520
This test may be requested as HCV RNA direct probe. Hepatitis C is also referred to as non-A non-B (NANB) hepatitis. Blood specimen is serum. A liver biopsy is required for analysis of liver tissue and is reported separately. The specimen is treated to isolate the RNA using direct probe. This test is used primarily by research facilities.

87521
This test may be requested as HCV RNA amplified probe or as HCV RNA RT-PCR. Hepatitis C is also referred to as non-A non-B (NANB) hepatitis. Blood specimen is serum. A liver biopsy is required for analysis of liver tissue and is reported separately. Testing for HCV by amplified probe requires a molecular method referred to as reverse transcription polymerase chain reaction (RT-PCR). This test is used primarily by research facilities.

87522
This test may be requested as HCV RNA quantification using molecular technique. Hepatitis C is also referred to as non-A non-B (NANB) hepatitis. Blood specimen is serum. A liver biopsy is required for analysis of liver tissue and is reported separately. This code reports quantification only.

87525
This test may be requested as HGV-RNA direct probe. Blood specimen is serum. A liver biopsy is required for analysis of liver tissue and is reported separately. The specimen is treated to isolate the RNA using direct probe. This test is used primarily by research facilities. HGV is associated with acute and chronic hepatitis and active infection has been observed to persist for up to nine years. HGV is transmissible via blood transfusion and also can be acquired by exposure to blood and blood products.

87526
This test may be requested as HGV RNA amplified probe or as HCGV RNA RT-PCR. Blood specimen is serum. A liver biopsy is required for analysis of liver tissue and is reported separately. Testing for HGV by amplified probe requires a molecular method referred to as reverse transcription polymerase chain reaction (RT-PCR). This test is used primarily by research facilities. HGV is associated with acute and chronic hepatitis and active infection has been observed to persist for up to nine years. HGV is transmissible via blood transfusion and also can be acquired by exposure to blood and blood products.

87527
This test may be requested as HGV RNA quantification using molecular technique. Blood specimen is serum. A liver biopsy is required for analysis of liver tissue and is reported separately. This code reports quantification only. HGV is associated with acute and chronic hepatitis and active infection has been observed to persist for up to nine years. HGV is transmissible via blood transfusion and also can be acquired by exposure to blood and blood products.

87528
This test may be requested as HSV by direct DNA probe. Herpes simplex may be classified as HSV type 1 (HSV 1) or HSV type 2 (HSV 2). HSV 1 is primarily responsible for oral lesions frequently referred to as fever blisters or cold sores. HSV 2 is a sexually transmitted disease with lesions occurring primarily in the genitourinary tract. Lesion swab/scrapings are obtained. CSF is obtained by spinal puncture. Blood specimen is serum. The specimen is treated to isolate the DNA using direct probe. Detection and typing (HSV1, HSV2) by direct DNA probe is superior to culture methods.

87529
This test may be requested as HSV by amplified DNA probe. Herpes simplex may be classified is HSV type 1 (HSV 1) or HSV type 2 (HSV 2). HSV 1 is primarily responsible for oral lesions frequently referred to as fever blisters or cold sores. HSV 2 is a sexually

transmitted disease with lesions occurring primarily in the genitourinary tract. Lesion swab/scrapings are obtained. CSF is obtained by spinal puncture. Blood specimen is serum. The DNA is amplified using a technique such as polymerase chain reaction (PCR). Detection and typing (HSV 1, HSV 2) by amplified DNA probe is superior to culture methods.

87530
This test may be requested as HSV quantification by molecular technique. Herpes simplex may be classified is HSV type 1 (HSV 1) or HSV type 2 (HSV 2). HSV 1 is primarily responsible for oral lesions frequently referred to as fever blisters or cold sores. HSV 2 is a sexually transmitted disease with lesions occurring primarily in the genitourinary tract. Lesion swab/ scrapings are obtained. CSF is obtained by spinal puncture. Blood specimen is serum. This code reports quantification only.

87531
This test may be requested as HHV-6 direct DNA probe. Human herpes virus-6 is most commonly associated with roseola in children, but also causes pneumonitis, encephalitis, and hepatitis in immunosuppressed individuals. Sputum is obtained by deep coughing or by separately reportable aerosol induced technique. Respiratory fluids may also be obtained endoscopically using bronchial alveolar lavage and reported separately. CSF is obtained by spinal puncture and reported separately. Blood specimen is serum. Liver tissue is obtained by biopsy, also reported separately. The cells are lysed and DNA is extracted. HHV-6 DNA is identified by direct probe.

87532
This test may be requested as HHV-6 amplified DNA probe. Human herpes virus-6 is most commonly associated with roseola in children, but also causes pneumonitis, encephalitis, and hepatitis in immunosuppressed individuals. Sputum is obtained by deep coughing or by separately reportable aerosol induced technique. Respiratory fluids may also be obtained endoscopically using bronchial alveolar lavage and reported separately. CSF is obtained by spinal puncture, which is reported separately. Blood specimen is serum. Liver tissue is obtained by biopsy, also reported separately. The cells are lysed and DNA is extracted. HHV-6 DNA is amplified using specific primers.

87533
This test may be requested as HHV-6 quantification using nucleic acid technique. Human herpes virus-6 is most commonly associated with roseola in children, but also causes pneumonitis, encephalitis, and hepatitis in immunosuppressed individuals. Sputum is obtained by deep coughing or by separately reportable aerosol induced technique. Respiratory fluids may also be obtained endoscopically using bronchial alveolar lavage, which is reported separately. CSF is obtained by spinal puncture and reported separately. Blood specimen is serum. Liver tissue is obtained by biopsy, also reported separately. The cells are lysed and DNA is extracted. This code reports quantification only.

87534
This test may be requested as human immunodeficiency virus Type 1 (HIV-1) by direct nucleic acid (DNA, RNA) probe. HIV is the causative agent of acquired immunodeficiency syndrome (AIDS). Blood specimen is serum. A random urine sample is obtained. Tissue is obtained by separately reportable biopsy procedure. The specimen is treated to isolate the DNA using direct probe.

87535
This test may be requested as human immunodeficiency virus Type 1 (HIV-1) by amplified nucleic acid (DNA, RNA) probe or HIV-1 by PCR. HIV is the causative agent of acquired immunodeficiency syndrome (AIDS). Blood specimen is serum. A random urine sample is obtained. Tissue is obtained by separately reportable biopsy procedure. The DNA is amplified using a technique such as polymerase chain reaction (PCR).

87536
This test may be requested as human immunodeficiency virus Type 1 (HIV-1) nucleic acid (DNA, RNA) quantification. HIV is the causative agent of acquired immunodeficiency syndrome (AIDS). Blood specimen is serum. A random urine sample is obtained. Tissue is obtained by separately reportable biopsy procedure. This code reports quantification only.

87537
This test may be requested as human immunodeficiency virus Type 2 (HIV-2) by EIA. HIV-2 is a retrovirus closely related to simian AIDS and found initially in West African nations and Portugal, but with cases also being reported in the United States since 1987. Blood specimen is serum. The specimen is treated to isolate the DNA using direct probe.

87538
This test may be requested as human immunodeficiency virus Type 2 (HIV-2) by EIA. HIV-2 is a retrovirus closely related to simian AIDS and found initially in West African nations and Portugal, but with cases also being reported in the United States since 1987. Blood specimen is serum. Infectious agent antigen detection by amplified DNA probe technique involves nonculture detection of infected cells. The DNA is amplified using a technique such as polymerase chain reaction (PCR).

87539
This test may be requested as human immunodeficiency virus Type 2 (HIV-2) by EIA. HIV-2 is a retrovirus closely related to simian AIDS and found initially in West African nations and Portugal, but with

cases also being reported in the United States since 1987. Blood specimen is serum. This code reports quantification only.

87540
This test may also be requested as nucleic acid probe for Legionnaire's disease. The bacteria responsible for the disease, Legionella pneumophila, cause a fulminating pneumonia. It can also cause an influenza-like illness known as Pontiac fever. Sputum is obtained by deep coughing or by separately reportable aerosol induced technique. The specimen is treated to isolate nucleic acid using direct probe.

87541
This test may also be requested as nucleic acid probe for Legionnaire's disease. The bacteria responsible for the disease, Legionella pneumophila, cause a fulminating pneumonia. It can also cause an influenza-like illness known as Pontiac fever. Sputum is obtained by deep coughing or by separately reportable aerosol induced technique. The specimen is treated to isolate nucleic acids, which are then amplified using a technique such as polymerase chain reaction (PCR).

87542
This test may also be requested as nucleic acid quantification for Legionnaire's disease. The bacteria responsible for the disease, Legionella pneumophila, cause a fulminating pneumonia. It can also cause an influenza-like illness known as Pontiac fever. Sputum is obtained by deep coughing or by separately reportable aerosol induced technique. This code reports quantification only.

87550
This test may be requested as Mycobacterial direct DNA probe. Blood specimen is serum. A random urine sample is obtained. Sputum is obtained by deep coughing or by separately reportable aerosol induced technique. Tissue is obtained in a separately reportable biopsy procedure. DNA is isolated directly from the specimen or following culture. The specimen is treated to isolate the Mycobacterial species. The DNA probe is hybridized and the excess probe removed. The bound probe is analyzed using chemiluminescence, color detection, or autoradiography.

87551
This test may be requested as Mycobacterial amplified DNA probe or Mycobacterial polymerase chain reaction (PCR). Blood specimen is serum. A random urine sample is obtained. Sputum is obtained by deep coughing or by separately reportable aerosol induced technique. Tissue is obtained in a separately reportable biopsy procedure. DNA is isolated directly from the specimen or following culture. DNA amplification is performed using PCR or transcription-based techniques. DNA amplification assay provides increased accuracy in diagnosis.

87552
This test may be requested as Mycobacterial nucleic acid quantification. Blood specimen is serum. A random urine sample is obtained. Sputum is obtained by deep coughing or by separately reportable aerosol induced technique. Tissue is obtained in a separately reportable biopsy procedure. DNA is isolated directly from the specimen or following culture. The specimen is treated to isolate the Mycobacterial species. This code reports quantification only.

87555
This test may be requested as tuberculosis (TB) test by direct nucleic acid probe. Tuberculosis was once diagnosed only by conventional culture techniques, which required four to six weeks for identification of mycobacteria tuberculosis. Nucleic acid probes allow for accurate identification in as little as 36-48 hours. Sputum is obtained by deep coughing or by separately reportable aerosol induced technique. The specimen is treated to isolate nucleic acid using direct probe.

87556
This test may be requested as tuberculosis (TB) test by amplified nucleic acid probe. Tuberculosis was once diagnosed only by conventional culture techniques, which required four to six weeks for identification of mycobacteria tuberculosis. Nucleic acid probes allow for accurate identification in as little as 36-48 hours. Sputum is obtained by deep coughing or by separately reportable aerosol induced technique. The specimen is treated to isolate nucleic acid using an amplified probe technique such as polymerase chain reaction (PCR). To enhance sensitivity PCR may be followed by oligonucleotide hybridization or nested PCR studies.

87557
This test may be requested as tuberculosis (TB) quantification by nucleic acid technique. Tuberculosis was once diagnosed only by conventional culture techniques, which required four to six weeks for identification of mycobacteria tuberculosis. Nucleic acid probes allow for accurate identification in as little as 36-48 hours. Sputum is obtained by deep coughing or by separately reportable aerosol induced technique. This code reports quantification only.

87560
This test may be requested as Mycobacterial avium-intracellulare direct DNA probe. Blood specimen is serum. A random urine sample is obtained. Sputum is obtained by deep coughing or by separately reportable aerosol induced technique. Tissue is obtained in a separately reportable biopsy procedure. DNA is isolated directly from the specimen or following culture. The DNA probe is hybridized and the excess probe removed. The bound probe is analyzed using chemiluminescence, color detection, or autoradiography.

87561
This test may be requested as Mycobacterial avium-intracellulare amplified DNA probe or Mycobacterial avium-intracellulare polymerase chain reaction (PCR). Blood specimen is serum. A random urine sample is obtained. Sputum is obtained by deep coughing or by separately reportable aerosol induced technique. Tissue is obtained in a separately reportable biopsy procedure. DNA is isolated directly from the specimen or following culture. DNA amplification is performed using PCR or transcription-based techniques. DNA amplification assay provides increased accuracy in diagnosis.

87562
This test may be requested as Mycobacterial avium-intracellulare nucleic acid quantification. Blood specimen is serum. A random urine sample is obtained. Sputum is obtained by deep coughing or by separately reportable aerosol induced technique. Tissue is obtained in a separately reportable biopsy procedure. DNA is isolated directly from the specimen or following culture. The specimen is treated to isolate the Mycobacterial avium-intracellulare. This code reports quantification only.

87580
This test may be requested as Mycoplasma pneumoniae direct DNA probe. Mycoplasma pneumoniae is responsible for anywhere from one to eight percent of all community acquired pneumonias diagnosed each year. Sputum is obtained by deep coughing or by separately reportable aerosol induced technique. Specimen may also be obtained endoscopically using bronchial alveolar lavage, reported separately. Direct nucleic acid probe is a rapid and sensitive test for Mycoplasma pneumoniae nucleic acids, specifically rRNA, in respiratory fluids. Cells must be lysed to release the Mycoplasma pneumoniae specific rRNA.

87581
This test may be requested as Mycoplasma pneumoniae amplified DNA probe. Mycoplasma pneumoniae is responsible for anywhere from one to eight percent of all community acquired pneumonias diagnosed each year. Sputum is obtained by deep coughing or by separately reportable aerosol induced technique. Specimen may also be obtained endoscopically using bronchial alveolar lavage, reported separately. Nucleic acid probe is a rapid and sensitive test for Mycoplasma pneumoniae nucleic acids, specifically rRNA, in respiratory fluids. Cells must be lysed to release the Mycoplasma pneumoniae specific rRNA. They are amplified using polymerase chain reaction (PCR).

87582
This test may be requested as Mycoplasma pneumoniae nucleic acid quantification. Mycoplasma pneumoniae is responsible for anywhere from 1 to 8 percent of all community acquired pneumonias diagnosed each year. Sputum is obtained by deep coughing or by separately reportable aerosol induced technique. Specimen may also be obtained endoscopically using bronchial alveolar lavage, reported separately. Nucleic acid probe is a rapid and sensitive test for Mycoplasma pneumoniae nucleic acids, specifically rRNA, in respiratory fluids. Cells must be lysed to release the Mycoplasma pneumoniae specific rRNA. This code reports quantification only.

87590
This test may be requested as gonorrhea direct DNA probe, gonorrhea molecular probe assay, or DNA detection of gonorrhea. Neisseria gonorrhea is one of the most common sexually transmitted infections. Molecular (nucleic acid probe) techniques offer rapid, accurate identification of Neisseria gonorrhea. While a cervical or urethral swab is preferred, molecular techniques are sensitive enough to detect the organism in urine also. Neisseria gonorrhea can be detected by DNA, RNA, or rRNA probes.

87591
This test may be requested as gonorrhea amplified DNA probe, gonorrhea molecular probe assay, or DNA detection of gonorrhea. Neisseria gonorrhea is one of the most common sexually transmitted infections. Molecular (nucleic acid probe) techniques offer rapid, accurate identification of Neisseria gonorrhea. While a cervical or urethral swab is preferred, molecular techniques are sensitive enough to detect the organism in urine also. Neisseria gonorrhea can be detected by DNA or rRNA probes. Amplification can be performed using a number of techniques. Polymerase chain reaction (PCR) and ligase chain reaction (LCR) detect gonorrhea DNA. An assay is also available which detects gonorrhea ribosomal RNA (rRNA)

87592
This test may be requested as gonorrhea nucleic acid quantification. Neisseria gonorrhea is one of the most common sexually transmitted infections. Molecular (nucleic acid probe) techniques offer rapid, accurate identification of Neisseria gonorrhea. While a cervical or urethral swab is preferred, molecular techniques are sensitive enough to detect the organism in urine also. Neisseria gonorrhea can be detected by DNA or rRNA probes. This code reports quantification only.

87620
This test may be requested as human papillomavirus (HPV) direct DNA probe. Human papillomaviruses are a genus of viruses that causes warts (benign neoplasms of skin and mucous membranes). There are at least 58 known types. HPV is commonly associated with both plantar and genital warts. HPV infection of the cervix is of particular concern as it may be associated with cervical cancer. The specimen is probed with commercially available DNA probes for specific HPV types. DNA probes are specific for HPV types 6, 11, 16, 18, 31, 33, and 35.

87621
This test may be requested as human papillomavirus (HPV) amplified DNA probe. Human papillomaviruses are a genus of viruses that causes warts (benign neoplasms of skin and mucous membranes). There are at least 58 known types. HPV is commonly associated with both plantar and genital warts. HPV infection of the cervix is of particular concern as it may be associated with cervical cancer. The specimen is amplified by polymerase chain reaction (PCR) and probed for specific HPV types. DNA probes are only able to detect a limited number of HPV types, including types 6, 11, 16, 18, 31, 33, and 35.

87622
This test may be requested as human papillomavirus (HPV) amplified DNA probe. Human papillomaviruses are a genus of viruses that causes warts (benign neoplasms of skin and mucous membranes). There are at least 58 known types. HPV is commonly associated with both plantar and genital warts. HPV infection of the cervix is of particular concern as it may be associated with cervical cancer. The specimen is treated to encourage attachment of HPV DNA to filters. This code reports quantification only.

87640
This test may be requested as *Staphylococcus aureus* by amplified probe assay. Specimen is blood or other body fluid. This test uses amplified probe assay to detect DNA or RNA sequences (usually DNA) specific for *S. aureus*. The specimen is treated to isolate the DNA or RNA and eliminate substances that inhibit amplification. The *S. aureus* DNA or RNA is amplified using specific primers.

87641
This test may be requested as MRSA by amplified probe assay. Specimen is blood or other body fluid. This test uses amplified probe assay to detect DNA or RNA sequences (usually DNA) specific for methicillin-resistant *Staphylococcus aureus*. The specimen is treated to isolate the DNA or RNA and eliminate substances that inhibit amplification. The MRSA DNA or RNA is amplified using specific primers. This assay establishes the presence of both *S. aureus* and methicillin resistance. MRSA is resistant to not only methicillin, but also common antibiotics including oxacillin, penicillin, and amoxicillin.

87650
This test may be requested as Streptococcus A by direct nucleic acid probe. Streptococcus A is a form of beta hemolytic streptococcus, which causes pharyngitis. Untreated infection can cause rheumatic fever or glomerulonephritis. The specimen is treated to isolate the DNA using a direct probe.

87651
This test may be requested as Streptococcus A by amplified nucleic acid probe. Streptococcus A is a form of beta hemolytic streptococcus, which causes pharyngitis. Untreated infection can cause rheumatic fever or glomerulonephritis. The specimen is treated to isolate the DNA and eliminate substances that inhibit amplification. The Streptococcus A DNA is amplified using specific primers.

87652
This test may be requested as Streptococcus A nucleic acid quantification. Streptococcus A is a form of beta hemolytic streptococcus, which causes pharyngitis. Untreated infection can cause rheumatic fever or glomerulonephritis. This code reports quantification only.

87653
This test may be requested as GBS by direct nucleic acid probe. Group B Streptococcus is generally performed on pregnant women in labor or at any time during their pregnancy. The specimen is vaginal or rectal swab. The specimen is treated to isolate the DNA using an amplified probe assay to detect nucleic acid sequences specific to GBS. Results can be obtained in an hour, allowing for neonatal intervention or antibiotic treatment of the pregnant mother.

87660
A microbiology test for trichomonas vaginalis, by direct probe technique, may be requested as trichomonas vaginalis direct DNA probe, molecular probe assay, or DNA detection of trichomonas vaginalis. Direct probe is a method to detect DNA of a target microorganism. This technique uses DNA probes that hybridize to whole chromosomes or specific target sequences for detection. The target DNA in the sample is fixed onto a slide and denatured from double-stranded DNA to single-stranded DNA. The target DNA is hybridized with that of the probe, reassociating into double-stranded nucleic acid. The unbound DNA is removed and the remaining DNA is counterstained and placed under fluoroscopy to visualize the hybridized probe attached to the target material.

87797
This code reports infectious agent detection by nucleic acid (DNA, RNA) direct probe for microorganisms that are not identified with a more specific code in range 87470-87652. Nucleic acid detection, also referred to as molecular pathology, is a rapidly developing diagnostic technique that is especially useful in identifying microorganisms which require tedious isolation and incubation and/or those which cannot be cultured. Another advantage of molecular methods is that they are able to detect infectious agents at much lower levels than required using other techniques. Direct probe involves isolating and identifying the infectious agent DNA or RNA. This involves cell lysis and extraction of the DNA using phenol or chloroform.

87798
This code reports infectious agent detection by nucleic acid (DNA, RNA) amplified probe for microorganisms that are not identified with a more specific code in range 87470-87652. Nucleic acid detection, also referred to as molecular pathology, is a rapidly developing diagnostic technique that is especially useful in identifying microorganisms which require tedious isolation and incubation and/or those which cannot be cultured. Another advantage of molecular methods is that they are able to detect infectious agents at much lower levels than required using other techniques. Amplified probe involves isolating and identifying the infectious agent DNA or RNA. This involves cell lysis and extraction of the DNA using phenol or chloroform. The nucleic acids are amplified using one of several techniques. Polymerase chain reaction (PCR) is the most frequently used amplification technique. Other techniques include ligase chain reaction (LCR) and the signal detection method (bDNA).

87799
This code reports infectious agent quantification using nucleic acid (DNA, RNA) technique for microorganisms that are not identified with a more specific code in range 87470-87652. Nucleic acid detection, also referred to as molecular pathology, is a rapidly developing diagnostic technique that is especially useful in identifying microorganisms which require tedious isolation and incubation and/or those which cannot be cultured. Another advantage of molecular methods is that they are able to detect infectious agents at much lower levels than required using other techniques. Quantification may be performed following direct or amplified probe. It measures the amount of the microorganism DNA/RNA present.

87800-87801
Code 87800 reports multiple infectious agent detection by nucleic acid (DNA or RNA) using direct probe technique. Nucleic acid detection, also referred to as molecular pathology, is a rapidly developing diagnostic technique that is especially useful in identifying microorganisms that require tedious isolation and incubation and/or those that cannot be cultured. Another advantage of molecular methods is that they are able to detect infectious agents at much lower levels than required using other techniques. The test is useful in that absolute specificity of hard-to-identify organisms can be attained. Report 87801 when the multiple DNA target sequences are amplified using any of several techniques, such as polymerase chain reaction (PCR), or ligase chain reaction (LCR), or signal detection (bDNA).

87802
Enzyme immunoassay (EIA) is a method for identifying organisms, extracellular toxins, and viral agents that use an enzyme bound antibody to detect antigen. The test may be performed directly on clinical samples or on organisms recovered from bacterial or viral culture. Direct optical observation, or optical immunoassay, allows for direct visual interpretation of any antibody-antigen reaction in the presence of low level light. This code reports the detection of Streptococcus, group B.

87803
Clostridium difficile is the major cause of antibiotic-associated diarrhea and colitis and is the cause for virtually all cases of pseudo-membranous colitis (PMC). The organism is found in stools of most patients with these diseases. One gram of stool is collected and sent to the laboratory unpreserved. The fecal sample is dispersed in a diluent with antibodies for Clostridium difficile antigen to form a complex of antibody and antigen. A complex of antibody and antigen is separated from the specimen and exposed to a second antibody for the antigen, and a portion of the antibody. A sample from the first complex is bound to a solid carrier and a sample from the second antibody exposure is labeled with a detection agent to determine the presence of Clostridium difficile antigen in the original fecal specimen.

87804
Influenza, a highly contagious, acute viral infection of the respiratory tract, is caused by a single-strand RNA virus known as an influenza virus. An infection may be identified by direct detection of the virus in respiratory secretions (usually, collected within one week of onset of symptoms) using enzyme immunoassay with monoclonal antibodies to detect viral antigen in the sample.

87807
Enzyme immunoassays (EIA) are methods for identifying organisms, extracellular toxins, and viral agents using protein and polysaccharide antigens. The test may be performed directly on clinical samples, after growth on agar plates, or in viral cell cultures. The basis of detection is antigen-antibody binding. Cultures and impression smears for both aerobic and anaerobic infectious agents are commonly taken from involved lymph nodes, sputum, pleural fluid, cerebrospinal fluid (CSF), and spleen. Direct optical microscopic observation allows for continuous direct observation of low-light or low-contrast samples in the presence of fluorescence. This code reports the detection of respiratory syncytial virus.

87808
Enzyme immunoassays (EIA) are methods for identifying organisms, extracellular toxins, and viral agents using protein and polysaccharide antigens. The specimen is vaginal secretions. The basis of detection is antigen-antibody binding. Direct optical microscopic observation allows for continuous direct observation of low-light or low-contrast samples in the presence of

fluorescence. This code reports the detection of Trichomonas vaginalis.

87809
Human adenoviruses (HAdV) are significant sources of eye and respiratory tract disease, and are some of the most commonly isolated viruses. Pharyngoconjunctival fever (PCF) is a well known adenoviral disease, and certain types of HAdVs (7 and 3) may cause pneumonia. Viral conjunctivitis is often difficult to distinguish, since the presence of an upper respiratory infection (URI), conjunctival follicles, preauricular nodes, or watery discharge provides no definitive differentiation from bacterial conjunctivitis. This test is performed on a conjunctival sample and is used to detect adenovirus group antigen in order to distinguish viral vs. bacterial infections. Test is by enzyme immunoassay and includes direct optical observation of results on a solid matrix.

87810
This test may be requested as an optical immunoassay for Chlamydia trachomatis. C. trachomatis is a frequently occurring sexually transmitted disease. It may cause nonspecific urethritis or pelvic inflammatory disease (PID), although it is frequently asymptomatic in women. Another serotype also causes conjunctivitis. This test reports antigen detection using a competitive protein-binding assay, where an antigen binds to an antibody, which is fixed to a reflecting surface. This change in reflection can be observed directly as a color change.

87850
This test may be requested as an optical immunoassay for Neisseria gonorrhea. N. Gonorrhea is one of the most common sexually transmitted infections. This test reports detection using a competitive protein-binding assay where an antigen binds to an antibody, which is fixed to a reflecting surface. This change in reflection can be observed directly as a color change.

87880
This test may be requested as an optical immunoassay for Streptococcus A. Streptococcus A is a form of beta hemolytic streptococcus, which causes pharyngitis. Untreated infection can cause rheumatic fever or glomerulonephritis. This test reports detection using a competitive protein-binding assay where an antigen binds to an antibody, which is fixed to a reflecting surface. This change in reflection can be observed directly as a color change.

87899
This test may be requested as an optical immunoassay. This test reports detection using a competitive protein-binding assay where an antigen binds to an antibody, which is fixed to a reflecting surface. This change in reflection can be observed directly as a color change. This code should be reported when the infectious agent being tested does not have a more specific code.

87900
This test directly and quantitatively measures resistance of a patients viral infection to drugs in order to help the physician select appropriate drugs. The test uses nucleic acid application to derive protease (PR) and reverse transcriptase (RT) sequences from a patients plasma sample. A resistance test vector (RTV) is constructed by incorporating the patient-derived segment into a viral vector with an indicator gene, firefly luciferase, inserted within a portion of the viral envelope gene. The completion of a single round of viral replication results in the production of luciferase. Drug susceptibility is measured by comparing luciferase activity produced in the presence and absence of drugs. Susceptible viruses produce low levels of luciferase activity in the presence of PR and/or RT inhibitors, whereas viruses with reduced susceptibility to these drugs produce higher levels of luciferase.

87901-87904
Treatment of human immunodeficiency virus (HIV) requires multiple antiviral drugs administered in combination to suppress virus replication. However, over time, HIV can become resistant to one or more of these. Resistance can be recognized by identifying increases in the viral load and declines in the CD4 counts. These codes are used to report assays that help identify HIV antiviral drug resistance. A genotype assay that can predict expected HIV drug resistance for most individuals is reported with 87901. In 87902, hepatitis C virus (HCV) DNA is isolated for the patient specimens and amplified by polymerase chain reaction; one distinct gene segment shows amplification if HCV DNA is present. Anti-HBc IgM can be detected at about the same time clinical symptoms appear. Report 87903 for a phenotype assay that may be required when newer drugs are being considered for treatment of HIV, as newer drugs sometimes do not have sufficient data to predict expected outcomes based on genotype studies alone. Phenotype analysis reported by 87903 includes drug resistance tissue culture analysis of up to 10 drugs. Report 87904 for each additional drug tested.

87905
This code is used to report the enzymatic activity of an infectious agent, other than a virus, using an immunologic technique.

88000
This code reports the examination of a body after death. The body is dissected. The organs and tissues (excluding the brain and central nervous system) are systematically examined and described. This is usually done to determine the cause of death, to improve diagnosis and treatment of diseases, or to benefit family members in cases of heritable illnesses.

88005
This code reports the examination of a body after death. The body is dissected. The organs and tissues are systematically examined and described, including the brain. This is usually done to determine the cause of death, to improve diagnosis and treatment of diseases, or to benefit family members in cases of heritable illnesses.

88007
This code reports the examination of a body after death. The body is dissected. The organs and tissues are systematically examined and described, including the brain and spinal cord. This is usually done to determine the cause of death, to improve diagnosis and treatment of diseases, or to benefit family members in cases of heritable illnesses.

88012
This code reports the examination of an infant's body after death (birth through 12th month). The body is dissected. The organs and tissues are systematically examined and described, including the brain. This is usually done to determine the cause of death, to improve diagnosis and treatment of diseases, or to benefit family members in cases of heritable illnesses.

88014
This code reports the examination of a newborn's body after death (birth through 28th day), or the examination of a stillborn fetus. The body is dissected. The organs and tissues are systematically examined and described, including the brain. This is usually done to determine the cause of death, to improve diagnosis and treatment of diseases, or to benefit family members in cases of heritable illnesses.

88016
This code reports the examination of a stillborn fetus whose body tissues have become softened, as happens when there is a delay from the time of death in utero to the delivery. The body is dissected. The organs and tissues are systematically examined and described, including the brain. This is usually done to determine the cause of death, to improve diagnosis and treatment of diseases, or to benefit family members in cases of heritable illnesses.

88020
This code reports the examination of a body after death. The body is dissected. The organs and tissues are systematically examined (gross and microscopic) and described (except the brain and central nervous system). Representative samples from the organs are taken and microscopically examined and described. Laboratory tests may also be performed on tissue samples. This is usually done to determine the cause of death, to improve diagnosis and treatment of diseases, or to benefit family members in cases of heritable illnesses.

88025
This code reports the examination of a body after death. The body is dissected. The organs and tissues are systematically examined (gross and microscopic) and described (including the brain). Representative samples from the organs are taken and microscopically examined and described. Laboratory tests may also be performed on tissue samples. This is usually done to determine the cause of death, to improve diagnosis and treatment of diseases, or to benefit family members in cases of heritable illnesses.

88027
This code reports the examination of a body after death. The body is dissected. The organs and tissues are systematically examined (gross and microscopic) and described (including the brain and spinal cord). Representative samples from the organs are taken and microscopically examined and described. Laboratory tests may also be performed on tissue samples. This is usually done to determine the cause of death, to improve diagnosis and treatment of diseases, or to benefit family members in cases of heritable illnesses.

88028
This code reports the examination of an infant's body after death (birth through 12th month). The body is dissected. The organs and tissues are systematically examined (gross and microscopic) and described (including the brain). Representative samples from the organs are taken and microscopically examined and described. Laboratory tests may also be performed on tissue samples. This is usually done to determine the cause of death, to improve diagnosis and treatment of diseases, or to benefit family members in cases of heritable illnesses.

88029
This code reports the examination of a newborn's body after death (birth through 28th day), or the examination of a stillborn fetus. The body is dissected. The organs and tissues are systematically examined (gross and microscopic) and described (including the brain). Representative samples from the organs are taken and microscopically examined and described. Laboratory tests may also be performed on tissue samples. This is usually done to determine the cause of death, to improve diagnosis and treatment of diseases, or to benefit family members in cases of heritable illnesses.

88036
This code reports the examination of a body after death. The body is dissected. Certain organs and tissues within a system or region of the body are systematically examined (gross and microscopic) and described. Representative samples from the organs are taken and microscopically examined and described. Laboratory tests may also be performed on tissue samples. This is usually done to determine the cause of death, to improve diagnosis and treatment of diseases,

or to benefit family members in cases of heritable illnesses.

88037
This code reports the examination of a body after death. The body is dissected. A single organ and its related tissues are systematically examined (gross and microscopic) and described. Representative samples from the organ are taken and microscopically examined and described. Laboratory tests may also be performed on organ tissue samples. This is usually done to determine the cause of death, to improve diagnosis and treatment of diseases, or to benefit family members in cases of heritable illnesses.

88040
This code reports the examination of a body after death. The body is dissected. The organs and tissues are systematically examined (gross and microscopic) and described. Representative samples from the organs are taken and microscopically examined and described. Laboratory tests may also be performed on tissue samples. This is usually done for the purpose of gathering and preserving evidence for presentation in a court of law.

88045
A coroner is a public official, elected or appointed, who investigates the causes and circumstances of deaths from unnatural causes that occur within a specific legal jurisdiction (i.e., county). In many jurisdictions, coroners must present themselves and sign death certificates of all persons who die while not under the care of a physician. In some instances, a preliminary gross exam is performed on-site and procedural arrangements are made for a more thorough examination under laboratory conditions. As with all codes in the postmortem examination range, 88045 reports physician services. Only four states require coroners to be physicians. A medical examiner is a physician.

88104-88107
These tests have many different names, depending on the type of specimen obtained for analysis (e.g., bronchial cytology, esophageal cytology, etc.). Specimen is obtained by separately reportable washing or brushing procedure. Code 88104 reports cytopathology evaluation of smear specimens, including alcohol fixed, Papanicolaou, direct smear with 95 percent ethanol, or liquid fixative; 88106 is for filter method only and 88107 reports cytopathology evaluation of specimen using both smear and filtration techniques.

88108
Cytopathology, concentration technique, (e.g., Saccomanno, cytocentrifugation, and cytospins) may be done on many different types of specimen samples like bronchial, cervicovaginal, and conjunctival brushings, nipple discharge, sputum, and gastrointestinal epithelial cell specimens. Cellular smear preparations (cervicovaginal, conjunctival, bronchial brushings, nipple discharge) are immediately fixated in 95 percent ethanol or pap fixative to eliminate drying. GI, urologic, and sputum samples are collected with a Saccomanno fixative added. Following preparation, the sample is centrifuged to yield a pellet at the bottom of the tube and overlying supernatant. The clear fluid supernatant is decanted completely and the pellet is used to make direct smears of the concentrated sample for cytopathology and cell counts. Cytocentrifugation, cytospins, smears and interpretations are then preformed.

88112
Selective cellular enhancement for cytopathology, such as liquid based slide preparation method, is reported when both concentration and enrichment of cytology specimens is done beyond a concentration technique alone reported with 88108 (e.g., Saccomanno, cytocentrifugation, and cytospins). Enhancement technologies allow not only for concentration of the diagnostic material, but also for removing of background debris on complicated specimens that cannot be evaluated with typical concentration techniques alone (see 88108). One liquid based slide preparation method uses a filtration system with a disposable filter, support, and means of drawing fluid where cells are caught within a large enough area to provide a high-quality, high-yield monolayer slide that has good quantity, distribution, and clarity for diagnostic purposes. When a sample is prepared using enhanced cytopathology, the slide preparation is examined and compared to previous studies. Report this for any specimen except cervical or vaginal.

88125
For this cytopathology code, biological samples from crime scenes are studied using techniques common to DNA testing, such as fluorescent staining. Forensic cytopathology is the application of this type of testing for legal purposes. Forensic scientists study biological evidence and samples collected at crime scenes, such as hair, blood, and sperm for DNA testing to assist in the inclusion or the exclusion of an individual in the crime.

88130
This screening test will identify the presence or lack of sex chromatin. Specimen collection is by buccal mucosa scraping, Specimen should be chemically preserved with a fixative such as 95 percent ethanol. Method is by smear and microscopy. Examination of cells obtained by amniocentesis for the presence or absence of sex chromatin is a technique used to determine the infant's sex prior to birth.

88140
Fluorescent staining techniques are used to identify a Barr body in a polymorphonuclear leukocyte. In females one of the two X chromosomes remains tightly coiled. In some nuclei the coiled chromosome is visible

as a small dense mass known as a Barr body. In the lobulated nucleus of the polymorphonuclear leukocyte it can be seen as a protrusion, often in the shape of a drumstick.

88141
This test is for the interpretation by a physician of a Papanicolaou (Pap) smear. This code is used in addition to the code for the technical service.

88142-88143
These tests may be identified by the name "thin prep." Specimen collection is by cervical or endocervical scraping or aspiration of vaginal fluid. The physician obtaining the specimen places the specimen in a preservative suspension. At the laboratory, special instruments take the cells in the preservative suspension and "plate-out" a monolayer for screening-the careful review of the specimen for abnormal cells. Report 88142 for manual screening done under physician supervision and 88143 for manual screening followed by manual rescreening, done under physician supervision. System of reporting may be Bethesda or non-Bethesda.

88147-88148
These tests may be identified as a cervical smear, Pap smear, or vaginal cytology. Specimen collection is by cervical or endocervical scraping or aspiration of vaginal fluid. Method is microscopy examination of a spray or liquid fixated smear. Code 88147 should be used to report smears screened by automated system under physician supervision, while 88148 reports automated screening with manual rescreening under physician supervision. System of reporting may be Bethesda or non-Bethesda.

88150-88154
These tests may also be identified as a cervical smear, Pap smear, or vaginal cytology. The Specimen is cells collected by scraping or brushing the cervix or endocervix, or aspiration of vaginal fluid. The specimen is then smeared onto a slide and chemically treated with a preservative. These codes should be reported when the any system other than the Bethesda System of evaluating and describing cervical/vaginal cytopathology slides is used. Code selection is based on the screening process used, with manual screening under physician supervision being reported with 88150, manual screening and computer-assisted rescreening under physician supervision with 88152, manual screening and rescreening under physician supervision with 88153, manual screening and computer-assisted rescreening using cell selection and review under physician supervision with 88154.

88155
This test may also be identified as the maturation index, cytologic estrogen effect, karyopyknotic index, or estrogenic index. Specimen collection is by tongue depressor or wooden spatula of the lateral vaginal wall. Method is microscopy examination of a spray or liquid fixated smear. The test may be used to determine the balance of estrogen and progesterone of the vaginal squamous epithelium.

88160-88162
Specimen collection is by separately reportable percutaneous needle biopsy. Methods include microscopy examination of smears or a centrifuge specimen. These codes report the pathology examination portion of the procedure only. Code 88160 reports screening and interpretation only. Code 88161 reports preparation, screening and interpretation. Code 88162 reports an extended study involving more than five slides and/or multiple stains.

88164-88167
These tests may be identified as a cervical smear, Pap smear, or vaginal cytology. Specimen collection is by scraping or brushing the cervix or endocervix, or aspiration of vaginal fluid. Method is microscopy examination of a spray or liquid coated smear. These codes should be reported when the Bethesda System of evaluating and describing cervical/vaginal cytopathology slides is used. Code selection is based on the screening process used, with manual screening under physician supervision being reported with 88164, manual screening and rescreening under physician supervision with 88165, manual screening and computer-assisted rescreening under physician supervision with 88166, manual screening and computer-assisted rescreening using cell selection and review under physician supervision with 88167.

88172-88173
These codes are used to report the pathology examination portion of the fine needle aspirate procedure only. Code 88172 reports the immediate cytohistologic evaluation to determine the adequacy of the specimen. Code 88173 reports the final interpretation and report.

88174-88175
These tests may be identified by the brand name ThinPrep. Specimen collection is by cervical or endocervical scraping or aspiration of vaginal fluid. Report 88174 for automated screening done under physician supervision and 88175 when automated screening is followed by manual rescreening or review under physician supervision.

88182
Flow cytometry allows a single cell to be measured for a variety of characteristics that are determined as the cell flows in a liquid. Information about the cells is gathered by measuring visible and fluorescent light emissions. Specimen collection is by biopsy or needle biopsy for tissue and bone marrow; blood is drawn by venipuncture. To perform DNA or cell cycle analysis, the cells are first stained with a fluorescent dye. Flow analysis is performed to determine a cell's DNA

content. Cell cycle analysis performed by cell cytometry can determine a cells position in the cell cycle based on its DNA content.

88184-88185
These codes report the technical component for flow cytometry tests performed to identify specific cell surface, cytoplasmic or nuclear markers. To identify cell surface markers, a fluorescent dye is attached to antibodies or receptor ligands. The cells are subjected to flow cytometry and the amount of the receptor on the surface is detected by the level of fluorescence. Flow cytometry can also be used to detect multiple cell-surface markers simultaneously. Antibodies used in flow cytometry are determined by the presumptive diagnosis. Detection of antigens by flow cytometry allows identification and quantification of cells with specific characteristics that may be indicative of immune deficiencies, malignancies, or other disease processes. Report 88184 for the first marker, and 88185 for each additional marker.

88187-88189
These codes report the interpretation of flow cytometry tests. Flow cytometry results as measured by the detector are typically displayed as dot plots or histograms. The physician must interpret these dot plots and histograms. The physician reports interpretation services based on the number of markers being analyzed. Report 88187 for two to eight markers, 88188 for nine to 15 markers, and 88189 for 16 or more markers.

88230
This code is used to report lymphocyte culture for non-neoplastic disorders, which would include chromosome analysis as well as other cytogenetic studies. Cytogenetics is the branch of genetics that studies cellular (cyto) structure and function as it relates to heredity (genetics). White blood cells, specifically T-lymphocytes, are the most commonly used specimen for chromosome analysis. A peripheral blood specimen is obtained by venipuncture. The blood is separated into its cellular constituents and the white blood cells are extracted. The white blood cells are placed in a tissue culture medium. White blood cells, specifically T-lymphocytes, are stimulated with phytohemagglutinin (PHA) and grown in the tissue culture.

88233
This code is used to report culturing of skin cells or other solid tissue cells for evaluation of nonneoplastic disorders (i.e., chromosome analysis and other cytogenetic studies). Cytogenetics is the branch of genetics that studies cellular (cyto) structure and function as it relates to heredity (genetics). Skin cells may be obtained by buccal smear or separately reportable biopsy. Solid tissue specimen requires separately reportable biopsy. Skin or other solid tissue cells are placed in a tissue culture medium. The cells are stimulated and grown in the tissue culture.

88235
This code is used to report culturing of fetal cells for evaluation of nonneoplastic disorders (i.e., chromosome analysis and other cytogenetic studies). Cytogenetics is the branch of genetics that studies cellular (cyto) structure and function as it relates to heredity (genetics). Fetal cells are normally cultured to detect chromosome abnormalities and sex-linked disorders. A separately reportable amniocentesis or chorionic villus sampling is performed. Culture and growth of an adequate number of fetal cells for analysis may require two to three weeks.

88237
This code is used to report tissue culture only of bone marrow or blood cells for the purpose of evaluating neoplastic, usually malignant, disorders. Many neoplastic disorders have a genetic origin and therefore cytogenetic studies aid in diagnosis and are prognostic indicators. In addition, they may identify individuals at high risk for developing certain cancers. Bone marrow is obtained by separately reportable biopsy. Blood specimen is whole blood. The marrow and blood cells may be separated by cell type. The cells are placed in a tissue culture medium, which stimulates cell growth.

88239
This code is used to report tissue culture only of solid tumor cells for the purpose of evaluating neoplastic, usually malignant, disorders. Many neoplastic disorders have a genetic origin and therefore cytogenetic studies aid in diagnosis and are prognostic indicators. Translocations and deletions of nuclear DNA are especially common in the chromosomes of tumor cells, which makeup is different from that of normal somatic cells. This code reports cell culture prepared from a biopsied or resected solid tumor. The cells are placed in a tissue culture medium, which stimulates cell growth.

88240
Cryopreservation is a technique of freezing and maintaining cells at extremely low temperatures to preserve the genetic and metabolic properties of the cell. Cryopreservation is performed to allow storage of cells for subsequent culture and analysis at a reference laboratory. Report this code for each cell line. A cell line is considered one that holds the potential for indefinite subculture in a lab setting.

88241
Cells frozen by cryopreservation are thawed and expanded (amplified) for study. Report each aliquot separately. An aliquot refers to the equal division of a sample of a substance, with each part related quantitatively to each other and to the sample as a whole.

88245
This cytogenetic study may be requested as a chromosome breakage analysis, sister chromatid exchange (SCE) study, or a chromosome instability test. This test involves evaluation for increased sister chromatid exchange (SCE) of 20 to 25 cells. This exchange refers to the crossing over of genetic information between the sister chromatids. This analysis is specifically for chromosome breakage syndromes, which are characterized by an increased rate of SCE during cell division where exact duplication of the genetic information in each chromatid fails to occur. Instead, genetic information is rearranged between the sister chromatids during cell division. This test would normally use more traditional techniques, such as direct microscopic analysis of cells arrested in metaphase.

88248
This test may be requested by the name of the specific breakage syndrome being evaluated. Examples include Ataxia-telangiectasia (A-T) breakage study, Fanconi anemia (FA) breakage study, Fragile X breakage study, and Xeroderma pigmentosum (XP) chromosome breakage study. It may also be requested simply as a chromosome breakage study or chromosome instability study. Fragile sites along the chromosome that may appear as bent or partially detached fragments characterize chromosome breakage syndromes. The specific location of the fragile site determines the characteristics of the specific syndrome. The syndrome is associated with a moderate degree of intellectual delay. The procedure includes collecting 50 to 100 cells, counting 20, and performing two karyotypes. A karyotype is a visual exam of each chromosome pair from cells arrested in metaphase.

88249
This code reports a specific technique for analysis of breakage syndromes involving clastogen stress. Clastogen is a substance (e.g., chemical or radiation) that causes chromosome breakage when applied to the cell. Some substances that can be used as clastogens include diepoxybutane, mitomycin C, ionizing radiation, and UV radiation. When applied to the cells, these clastogens will identify fragile sites on the chromosome. The location of the fragile site is used to diagnose the specific breakage syndrome. The code includes the scoring of 100 cells.

88261-88262
These codes are reported for chromosome analysis to detect certain inherited disorders or syndromes, excluding breakage syndromes. The chromosomes of individuals with suspected genetic anomalies and neoplastic disorders are analyzed to provide definitive diagnosis. In addition, suspected carriers may be analyzed for recessive traits that may affect, or have affected, their offspring. Code 88261 should be reported for a five-cell count and one karyotype, with banding. Code 88262 should be reported for a 15 to 20-cell count and two karyotypes, with banding. Karyotype is the full chromosome set that genetically defines an individual. Banding refers to the appearance of stripes on stained paired bundles of chromosomes. This test would normally use more traditional techniques, such as direct microscopic analysis of cells arrested in metaphase.

88263
This code is reported for chromosome analysis of 45 cells for the presence of mosaicism. It includes two karyotypes with banding. Mosaicism refers to alterations in chromosomes that do not affect every somatic (non-sex cell) chromosome, but are manifested during embryonic development. The individual is said to have two or more cell lines of different genetic or chromosomal make-up. Karyotype is the full chromosome set that genetically defines an individual. Banding refers to the appearance of stripes on stained paired bundles of chromosomes. This test would normally use more traditional techniques, such as direct microscopic analysis of cells arrested in metaphase.

88264
This test reports chromosome analysis related to malignant neoplasms (cancer). Cancer cytogenetics requires complete analysis (not just counting) of 20-25 cells. Chromosome analysis is performed to identify specific chromosomal anomalies, which can aid in diagnosis and provide prognostic indicators for certain cancers. In addition, identification of aberrant chromosomal bands provides information on the specific genes affected in certain malignancies. Individuals with family histories indicating a high risk for certain types of cancer can be tested to determine whether they carry the aberrant bands.

88267
This is a prenatal technique used to analyze chromosomes from cells of extracted amniotic fluid or chorionic villus for possible genetic abnormalities that can be detected during embryonic development. The code includes a 15-cell count, one karyotype, with banding. Karyotype is the full chromosome set that genetically defines an individual. Banding refers to the appearance of stripes on stained paired bundles of chromosomes. This test would normally use more traditional techniques, such as direct microscopic analysis of cells arrested in metaphase with Giemsa or quinacrine banding techniques.

88269
This is a prenatal technique used to analyze intact chromosomes within the cells of amniotic fluid for possible genetic abnormalities that can be detected during embryonic development. The code includes a cell count from six to 12 colonies, one karyotype, with banding. Karyotype is the full chromosome set that genetically defines an individual. Banding refers to the

appearance of stripes on stained paired bundles of chromosomes. By studying the occurrence of different DNA bands in the population, one can calculate the probability of two DNA samples matching one another. Any number of methods may be used, including polymerase chain reaction (PCR), restriction fragment length polymorphism (RFLP), and Northern or Southern blot.

88271
Molecular cytogenetics represents relatively new techniques capable of detecting changes in chromosomes that cannot be detected by traditional microscopic techniques. This code reports the use of a DNA probe to identify chromosomal abnormalities. Fluorescent in situ hybridization (FISH) is one type of DNA probe. It allows chromosomes and genes to be analyzed simultaneously. In situ hybridization involves treating native double-stranded DNA to render it single-stranded. The strand is incubated to allow the strand to recognize complementary bases and to reform as a double-strand (hybridization). When a strand is radioactively marked, it is the "probe." The specificity to which the hybridization takes place is analyzed.

88272-88273
Molecular cytogenetics represent relatively new techniques capable of detecting changes in chromosomes that cannot be detected by traditional microscopic techniques. In situ hybridization is the base pairing of a sequence of DNA to chromosomes on a microscope slide. The technique involves printing thousands of protein-coded DNA (cDNA) clones on a single microscope slide. Fluorescent cDNA probes prepared from any cell or tissue source of interest are paired to provide a large-scale view of gene expression. In situ hybridization is used to determine the consequences of a given genetic alteration on gene expression. Report 88272 when three to five cells are analyzed usually to identify derivatives and markers. Report 88273 when 10 to 30 cells are analyzed usually for the purpose of identifying microdeletions. A microdeletion involves the removal or acquired absence of one or more nucleotides from a gene or chromosome.

88274-88275
Molecular cytogenetics represent relatively new techniques capable of detecting changes in chromosomes that cannot be detected by traditional microscopic techniques. In situ hybridization is the base pairing of a sequence of DNA to chromosomes on a microscope slide. In situ hybridization is used to determine the consequences of a given genetic alteration on gene expression. Report 88274 for in situ hybridization techniques used during interphase (resting phase) of cell division, for analyzing 25 to 99 cells. When 100 to 300 cells are analyzed report 88275.

88280
This code is reported for chromosome analysis to detect certain disorders or syndromes that may be inherited. The chromosomes of individuals with suspected genetic anomalies and neoplastic disorders are analyzed to provide definitive diagnosis. In addition, suspected carriers may be analyzed for recessive traits that may affect, or have affected, their offspring. This code is used for each additional karyotype beyond the number stipulated in other chromosome analysis codes in this same section of CPT 1999. Karyotype is the full chromosome set that genetically defines an individual. The term is also used for the standardized visual maps of chromosomal makeup, a technique used in identifying and organizing abnormalities. This test would usually involve more traditional microscopic techniques.

88283-88285
These codes are used for chromosome analysis to detect certain disorders or syndromes that may be inherited. The chromosomes of individuals with suspected genetic anomalies and neoplastic disorders are analyzed to provide definitive diagnosis. In addition, suspected carriers may be analyzed for recessive traits that may affect, or have affected, their offspring. Code 88283 is used for each additional karyotype specialized banding technique, such as NOR and C-banding. C-banding is a method of identifying banding patterns based on nucleic acid content and staining. Report 88285 for additional cells counted, each study. This test would usually involve more traditional microscopic techniques.

88289
This code is used for chromosome analysis to detect certain disorders or syndromes that may be inherited. The chromosomes of individuals with suspected genetic anomalies and neoplastic disorders are analyzed to provide definitive diagnosis. In addition, suspected carriers may be analyzed for recessive traits that may affect, or have affected, their offspring. This code is used for each additional high resolution study.

88291
This code is used to report physician interpretation and report of complex cytogenetic and molecular cytogenetic tests or when abnormal cytogenetic tests require complex interpretations.

88300
This procedure may be called a gross pathology exam or gross exam of tissue. The exam may not be specifically ordered ahead of time; rather, the tissue is harvested in the course of a surgery and sent for routine lab evaluation. Tissue is submitted in a container labeled with the source, preoperative diagnosis, and patient identification information. Specimens from separate sites must be submitted in separate containers, each labeled with the tissue source.

88302
This examination may be ordered as a gross and microscopic pathology exam or a gross and microscopic tissue exam. The exam may not be specifically ordered ahead of time; rather, the tissue is harvested in the course of a surgery and sent for routine lab evaluation. Tissue is submitted in a container labeled with the tissue source, preoperative diagnosis, and patient identification information. Specimens from separate sites must be submitted in separate containers, each labeled with the tissue source. This procedure is used to describe examination of tissues presumed normal. It includes both a gross and microscopic examination with the microscopic exam mainly to confirm the tissue is free of disease. Examples of its use might include tissues from a fallopian tube or vas deferens performed in the course of sterilization procedures, newborn foreskin following circumcision, hernia sac, hydrocele sac, etc.

88304-88309
These examinations would be ordered as a gross and microscopic pathology exam or a gross and microscopic tissue exam. Tissue is submitted in a container labeled with the tissue source, preoperative diagnosis, and patient identification information. Specimens from separate sites must be submitted in separate containers, each labeled with the tissue source. Codes 88304-88309 describe levels of service for specimens requiring additional levels of work due to a presumed presence of disease. Code 88304 describes the lowest level of complexity for diseased or abnormal tissue with each subsequent code (88305, 88307, and 88309) describing in ascending order higher levels of complexity and physician work. Specific types of disease and tissue sites are listed for each code in the CPT(r) description.

88311
This procedure is performed in addition to the basic surgical pathology examination (88302-88309) on specimens requiring decalcification for accurate evaluation. When calcium is present in the tissue, the specimen is too hard to be properly sectioned for microscopic evaluation. Using an acid solution, calcareous matter is removed from bone and other tissue (decalcification). The specimen is bathed in a solution to remove calcium ions via an ion exchange. This process may take hours or days depending on the specimen. Decalcification is commonly performed in bone marrow biopsy.

88312-88314
These codes report stains used in the evaluation of some tissue specimens. Depending on the type of specimen and the reason for the pathology examination, different stains may be required to highlight or outline cells for identification. Code 88312 reports Group I stains for microorganisms; 88313 reports Group II stains for all other conditions excluding immunocytochemistry and immunoperoxidase. Examples of Group II stains include Ziehl-Neelsen, acid phosphatase stain with and without tartrate, alpha-naphthyl esterase stain with and without fluoride, amyloid, ASD chloroacetate esterase stain, nonspecific esterase, PAS stain, and Sudan black stain. Code 88314 reports histochemical staining with frozen sections, and is reported in addition to the code for the primary procedure. All codes within this range include interpretation and report.

88318-88319
These codes report additional histochemistry services performed with basic pathology services. Code 88318 reports determinative tests for chemical components (e.g., copper, zinc), while 88319 reports determinative tests for enzyme constituents, each constituent. An example of a specimen that might require histochemistry for enzyme constituents (88319) is a muscle biopsy.

88321-88325
A pathology consultation involves an opinion or advice on the presence or absence of diseased or abnormal tissue provided at the request of another physician. These three codes report consultations and written interpretations on slide or material referred from another facility or source. Code 88321 reports a consultation and written report on slide prepared by another source; 88323 reports a consultation and written report on material referred from another source requiring routine preparation of slides by the consultant; and 88325 reports a comprehensive consultation with review of records, evaluation of specimens requiring more complex slide preparation, and a written report.

88329
The procedure may also be referred to as an intraoperative pathology exam. A pathology consultation involves an opinion or advice on the presence or absence of diseased or abnormal tissue provided at the request of another physician. This code describes a pathology consultation during the course of a surgery, and includes only a gross examination of tissue without concurrent microscopic examination. Intraoperative consultations are performed to assist the surgeon in determining immediate surgical course.

88331-88332
These procedures may also be referred to as an intraoperative pathology exam with frozen section (FS). A pathology consultation involves an opinion or advice on the presence or absence of diseased or abnormal tissue provided at the request of another physician. These codes describe such a pathology consultation during the course of a surgery. The codes include a gross examination of tissue and frozen sections, including a written interpretation of findings. The specimen is immediately frozen in a cold liquid or cold environment (-20 to -70 C) to facilitate sectioning

with a microtome. The specimen is sectioned using a cryostat which is a refrigerated box containing a microtome. Once sectioned, the tissues are placed on a slide, stained and examined microscopically. Code 88331 reports examination of a single block of tissue; 88332 reports each additional block of tissue from the same specimen. Intraoperative consultations are performed to assist the surgeon in determining immediate surgical course.

88333-88334

These procedures may also be referred to as intraoperative pathology consultation or intraoperative cytologic examination. During the course of an operation, a specimen is examined cytologically by touch prep where suspicious cells are scraped and smeared onto glass slides for staining and examination, or squash prep where the specimen is .minced,. placed on a slide and examined after staining. Report 88333 for first site examination and 88334 for each additional site examined.

88342

This immunohistochemistry procedure is also referred to as immunostain or peroxidase-antiperoxidase (PAP). It is a technique used to identify specific antigens found in tumor cells. It is used primarily for the diagnosis of poorly differentiated neoplasms. There are several methods of performing immunocytochemistry tests; however, all involve treating the specimen with a tumor specific antibody, incubation, and subsequent washing of the specimen to remove unbound antibody and counterstaining with secondary antibodies to determine the antibody location. The specimen is examined for positive and negative responses. Multiple immunostains are normally performed on each specimen to more specifically identify the suspect neoplasm by providing known positive and negative responses specific to that neoplasm. Report this code once for each antibody used.

88346-88347

Immunofluorescent studies may be performed using a direct or indirect technique. The direct method, also referred to as a direct fluorescent antibody (DFA), uses biopsied tissues. The indirect method, also referred to as indirect fluorescent antibody (IFA), uses serum. Both involve introduction of fluorescein-tagged antibodies. Antibodies used are dependent upon tissue being examined and the suspected diagnosis, but may include IgG, IgM, IgA, C3, C4, C1q, properdin, fibrin, fibrinogen, and albumin. The specimen is examined under fluorescent microscopy for intensity, pattern, and distribution of immunoglobulins.

88348-88349

These procedures are also referred to as electron microscopy (EM), transmission electron microscopy, or ultrastructural study. They are used primarily for the diagnosis of neoplasms when other techniques have failed to provide a definitive diagnosis. Tissues are prepared and fixed in a plastic polymer. Initially, thick sections (1 micron) are cut and stained to identify best specimen sites for further study. Subsequently, thin sections are cut and prepared with electron dense stain. The specimens are examined using electron microscopy. Code 88348 reports diagnostic EM. Code 88349 reports scanning EM.

88355-88358

These procedures may also be referred to as histomorphometry. Methodology is by flow cytometry or quantitative image analysis system. Cells are stained and the histologic organization, including structure, composition, and function, is evaluated.

88360-88361

Morphometric analysis may also be referred to as histomorphometry. A quantitative or semiquantitative test is done for tumor immunohistochemistry, such as the Her-2/neu receptor. The HER-2/neu protein is a cell surface growth factor receptor expressed on the cytoplasmic membrane of some epithelial cells. This protein regulates normal cell growth and division. An increased number of HER-2/neu genes in the cell nucleus causes over expression of the HER-2/neu oncoprotein, which in turn produces growth signals leading to cell transformation and cancer development. Microthin sections of the fixed, paraffin-embedded tissue are mounted on glass slides. Antigen retrieval with citrate buffers or microwaving is done to inhibit peroxidase activity and background staining. Immunostaining is done by adding a dilution containing the primary antibody to the receptor protein and incubating. Counterstaining with secondary antibodies is done to visualize antibody location. Further analysis is done to determine the histologic organization of the tumor and measure its structure, form and composition, quantitatively or semiquantitatively, either manually for 88360 or using computer-assisted technology for 88361. These codes are reported once for each antibody used to test for a specific protein receptor, such as Her-2/neu, estrogen, or progesterone receptor.

88362

Teased fiber evaluation is a technique used in specialty neuropathology labs. Peripheral nerves are often encased in a myelin sheath. This lipid-like substance is important to nerve function and can be an element in diagnostic evaluation. The technique involves biopsy collection, usually under local anesthetic. Light and electron microscopy are usually employed. Individual nerve fibers are "teased" from surrounding tissues to analyze myelinated nerve fiber size, distribution, and density.

88365

This test is also known as DNA-to-DNA homology, or simply ISH. In situ hybridization involves isolating and detecting specific nucleotide (mRNA) sequences within morphologically preserved cells and tissues by hybridizing a complementary nucleic acid strand, called a probe, to the sequence of interest within the prepared cells. The cells of interest may be snap-frozen and fixed in paraformaldehyde, spun out of suspension onto glass slides and fixed with methanol, or fixed in formalin and embedded in paraffin. The probe is first labeled with an easily detectable substance, such as a radioactive isotope, before hybridization. Types of probes used are oligonucleotides, single-stranded DNA, double-stranded DNA, and RNA, or riboprobes. The labeled probe strand is added to the prepared cells. The pairing or bonding (hybridization) that occurs between the complementary sequences of nucleotide bases in the probe to the specific mRNA sequences allows the expression of the type of sequence being detected to be seen on the target gene. This code is reported once for each type of probe used.

88367-88368
Morphometric analysis may also be referred to as histomorphometry. A quantitative or semiquantitative analysis is done with in situ hybridization. In situ hybridization involves isolating and detecting specific nucleotide (mRNA) sequences within morphologically preserved cells and tissues by hybridizing a complementary nucleic acid strand, called a probe, to the sequence of interest within the prepared cells. The cells of interest may be snap frozen and fixed in paraformaldehyde, spun out of suspension onto glass slides and fixed with methanol, or formalin fixed embedded in paraffin. The probe is first labeled with an easily detectable substance, such as a radioactive isotope, before hybridization. Types of probes used are oligonucleotides, single-stranded DNA, double-stranded DNA, and RNA, or riboprobes. The labeled probe strand is added to the prepared cells. The pairing or bonding (hybridization) that occurs between the complementary sequences of nucleotide bases in the probe to the specific mRA sequences allows the expression of the type of sequence being detected to be seen on the target gene. Analysis is done to determine the organization, structure, form and composition within the morphologically preserved cells being studied, either manually in 88668 or using computer-assisted technology in 88367. These codes are reported once for each type of probe used.

88371-88372
Western blot is an immunoassay technique that detects and confirms certain viral antibodies. Protein analysis of tissue involves separation of protein and glycoprotein components by electrophoresis. For certain diagnoses, polyacrylamide gel electrophoresis is used to create substrate bands that are transferred by electrophoretic blotting to a membrane. Patient serum is placed on the substrate strips and any of the targeted antibodies present will bind to the viral antigens. Report 88372 when the protein analysis of tissue by Western blot includes an immunological probe for band identification. The band patterns are visualized by immunohistochemical methods. Either service requires interpretation and written report.

88380-88381
Laser capture microdissection (LCM) (88380) is a method for procuring pure cells from specific microscopic regions of tissue sections to study developing disease lesions in actual tissue. A transfer film is applied to the surface of the tissue section. Under the microscope, the diagnostic pathologist or researcher views the thin tissue section and chooses microscopic clusters of cells to study. When the cells of choice are in the center of the field of view, a pulsed laser beam activates a spot on the transfer film immediately above the cells of interest. At this location the film melts and fuses with the underlying cells. When the film is removed, the chosen cells are held, while the rest of the tissue is left behind. This allows multiple homogeneous samples within the tissue section to be targeted for analysis. If microdissection is performed utilizing a manual technique (using hand-held tools such as needles or mechanical micromanipulator-based approaches), report 88381.

88384-88386
Molecular diagnostic assays can determine whether an individual carries a genetic mutation associated with a specific disease, without manifestation of the symptoms. They may also be used to interpret, diagnose, and monitor disease states, and in screening and in preventive medicine to detect carriers or those predisposed to specific diseases. Report 88384 for the evaluation of 11-50 array-based molecular probes, 88385 for evaluation of 51-250 probes, and 88386 when 251-500 probes are evaluated.

88387-88388
The physician performs a macroscopic (visual) examination, dissection, and preparation of tissues for analytical studies that are non-microscopic, such as nucleic acid-based molecular studies. Report 88387 for each tissue preparation (e.g., a single lymph node). Report 88388 when this procedure is performed in conjunction with a touch imprint, intraoperative consultation, or frozen section.

88720
Bilirubin is a bile pigment produced through the breakdown of blood components. High bilirubin concentrations in the blood is known as jaundice. Transcutaneous bilirubinometry uses subcutaneous tissue photometry to measure bilirubin concentration, particularly in newborns. The optic head of the photometric analyzer is pressed against the infant's skin and takes several seconds to obtain a measurement.

88738
This test is a quantitative measurement of hemoglobin. One indication is the diagnosis of anemia or polycythemia in order to evaluate the severity of these

conditions and to observe the patient's response to treatment. Measurement of hemoglobin by the transcutaneous method eliminates the need to draw blood. Instead, a visible and near-infrared spectroscopic device is used and measurements are obtained by a handheld probe, typically on the forearm.

88740-88741
Carboxyhemoglobin is hemoglobin with carbon monoxide bound to it instead of the normal oxygen. Methemoglobin is hemoglobin that has been altered so that it is unable to carry oxygen. Methemoglobin may be acquired by exposure to certain chemical agents, or it may be due a genetic condition. In vivo measures are noninvasive using visible and near-infrared optical bands.

89049
The Caffeine Halothane Contracture Test (CHCT) is performed on freshly biopsied muscle for diagnosis of malignant hyperthermia (MH) susceptibility. MH is a life-threatening condition resulting from a genetic sensitivity of the skeletal muscles to volatile anesthetics. A muscle biopsy is obtained, usually from the thigh. The specimen is exposed to caffeine and halothane separately and the sustained muscle tension responses are recorded. Comparison of the strength of contracture (sustained muscle tension) for each exposure with previously established standards allows determination of MH susceptibility.

89050-89051
CSF cell count may also be referred to as a CSF analysis or spinal fluid analysis; joint fluid cell count may also be referred to as synovial fluid analysis. In 89050, a manual nucleated blood cell count using a hemacytometer is performed on fluids obtained during a separately reportable spinal puncture or arthrocentesis. In 89051, a differential cell study using manually prepared smears or a cytocentrifuge is performed in addition to the cell count. Depending on the suspected condition, a number of separately reportable additional tests may be performed.

89055
A fecal material leukocyte count is done on a stool sample by direct smear and stain to detect the presence of WBCs and aid in the differential diagnosis of diarrheal disease. Certain conditions are associated with marked fecal leukocyte presence, moderate numbers present, and the absence of fecal leukocytes. Fecal leukocyte absence indicates invasive toxic bacterial infection, giardiasis, or viral infection. Moderate and marked leukocytes indicate antibiotic-associated colitis, shigellosis, amebiasis, and salmonellosis. The methylene blue stain test for fecal polymorphonuclear leukocytes has a high sensitivity for bacterial diarrhea detection but this test does not preempt the use of a culture.

89060
A fluid sample is obtained. A variety of different methods may be used to process the specimen depending on the source. The fluid is analyzed for the presence of crystals using direct light or polarized light microscopy. A newer technique using atomic force microscopy (AFM) may be available in some laboratories.

89100-89105
A tube is inserted orally or nasally and positioned in the duodenum. When a single specimen is obtained (89100), the duodenal contents are simply aspirated. When multiple specimens are obtained (89105), pancreatic or gallbladder stimulation is required and the following procedure is used. Intravenous administration of synthetic C-terminal octapeptide of cholecystokinin or cholecystokinin pancreozymin is performed. Duodenal fluid is collected over a period of 20-30 minutes. Specimens are usually collected in multiple containers with the bile from each source being identified as common duct origin (yellow in color), gallbladder origin (viscous, green or green brown color), and hepatic duct origin (lighter in color than the other two sources). Alternately, the bile may be pooled into a single specimen.

89125
Prior to obtaining the stool specimen the patient is placed on a diet containing at least 60 gm of fat/day. A random stool specimen is obtained. A small amount of stool is prepared with Sudan III stain and examined microscopically. A random urine sample is obtained. Urine sediment is stained with Sudan III or IV and analyzed using light and polarized microscopy. Respiratory secretions may be obtained by separately reportable bronchoscopy and are stained and analyzed using techniques similar to those for other types of specimens.

89130-89132
The patient is not allowed to take anything by mouth except water after the evening meal on the day prior to the study. A tube is inserted orally or nasally and positioned in the stomach. Correct placement is verified using separately reportable fluoroscopy or x-ray. Gentle suction is applied and gastric contents aspirated. The contents are sent to the lab where chemical and/or cytopathology analysis is performed. When the procedure is performed without stimulation report 89130, with stimulation report 89132.

89135-89141
The patient is not allowed to take anything by mouth except water after the evening meal on the day prior to the study. A tube is inserted orally or nasally and positioned in the stomach. Correct placement is verified using separately reportable fluoroscopy or x-ray. Gentle, constant suction is applied and gastric contents aspirated. Secretions acquired during the first 15-30 minutes of suction are discarded. A Toomey

syringe is used to aspirate all contents for the next 60-120 minutes. The specimens are obtained over 15-minute increments and placed into four to eight separate containers. These constitute the basal acid output (BAO). When only a BAO is obtained report 89135 for a one-hour study or 89136 for a two-hour study. Codes 89140 and 89141 include all services in a BAO. However, in addition to BAO, gastric stimulation is accomplished using pentagastrin or Histalog. Post-stimulation contents are aspirated for a minimum of 60 minutes. These specimens are also collected in 15-minute increments and stored in separate specimen containers. For gastric secretory study including stimulation, report 89140 if total duration of study is two hours, or 89141 if total duration is three hours.

89160

An adequate intake of red meat is required for 24-72 hours prior to testing. A stool specimen is obtained. The specimen is mixed with 10 percent solution of eosin in ethanol and stained on a slide for three minutes and cover-slipped. It is analyzed microscopically for rectangular striated muscle fibers.

89190

Two slides are normally obtained. Wright's stain is applied and the specimens are examined microscopically for the presence of eosinophils.

89220

Sputum is obtained for a specimen by using an aerosol-induced technique. This is a separate procedure from the testing of the sputum sample, which is used to study airway inflammation in asthma and other respiratory disorders. Sputum induction is done to collect an adequate sample of secretions from the lower respiratory tract in patients who do not produce sputum spontaneously. This is done by having the patient inhale an aerosol of normal or hypertonic saline. Oral secretions or saliva are not a sputum sample and different protocols have the patient rinse and dry the mouth, spit into a separate cup, or brush his/her teeth and rinse before sample collection to avoid contamination. A nebulizer that provides sufficient output of saline aerosol is used. With patient cooperation, inhalation is done at regular intervals until enough sputum for a sample is expectorated or until the patient feels the urge to cough.

89225

A random stool sample is collected. It is examined microscopically for the presence of starch granules.

89230

An iontophoresis sweat collection test, also called a chloride sweat test, is done to diagnose cystic fibrosis (CF) in children. Iontophoresis is the topical introduction of ionized drugs into the skin using direct current / positive current is applied to drive positively charged drug molecules into the tissues. Sweat production is stimulated to obtain the sweat sample by placing pads or filter paper soaked in pilocarpine onto clean skin on the arm or neck. Positive electrodes are strapped over the pads. The circuit is completed by likewise placing negative electrodes over water-soaked pads. Low-voltage electrical current is left on for about five minutes to repel small amounts of pilocarpine into the skin. The electrodes are removed and the skin under the positive electrode is cleansed and dried. Pre-weighed filter paper is placed over the area and secured firmly with cling wrap. The filter paper is removed again after about 30 minutes, placed back in its bottle, and weighed again to calculate the amount of sweat collected. Iontophoresis may be repeated until enough sample is collected; it is then analyzed for chloride and sodium content. People with CF have an increased amount of sodium and chloride (salt) in their sweat. Concentrations greater than 60 mmol/L are consistent with the diagnosis of CF.

89235

This procedure is also referred to as the antidiuretic hormone (ADH) suppression test or vasopressin suppression test. The water load test is done to diagnose inappropriate antidiuretic hormone syndrome. Patients with this syndrome do not respond to increasing their fluid intake and will have little or no change in output. The patient is given a water load of 20-25 mL/ per kg of body weight. Urine output and plasma and urine osmolality are measured over the next few hours to determine whether the water load is being excreted. Normal values will increase output with a decrease in plasma and urine osmolality.

89250-89251

Eggs (oocytes) are aspirated transvaginally using ultrasound guidance in a separately reportable procedure. Eggs or previously fertilized embryos are kept in an incubator in a Petri dish culture for less than four days in 89250. Code 89251 is reserved for those instances when co-culture techniques over and above those normally required are performed.

89253

Assisted embryo hatching is performed in selected cases on the day of embryo transfer. A pipette is placed on one side of the embryo to keep it from moving. A very delicate, hollow needle called a hatching needle is placed on the other side of the embryo. An acidic solution is expelled from the needle against the outer shell (zona pellucida) of the embryo. The acidic solution digests a small area of the outer shell. The embryo is washed and replaced in the culture solution in the incubator.

89254

Because the egg (oocyte) is microscopic, only the follicle (fluid filled structure surrounding the egg) can be seen during the ultrasound-guided retrieval. Upon aspiration of the follicle, specially trained personnel use a microscope to search for the oocyte-cumulus complex, which includes the egg and surrounding cumulus cells from the ovary. This is accomplished by pouring the collected fluid into flat dishes and using a microscope to search for eggs.

89255
After the embryos have been cultured for two to six days, three to four healthy embryos are selected for transfer. Selected embryos are loaded into a transfer catheter. In a separately reportable procedure, the catheter is placed in the cervical canal and the embryos are transferred into the uterine cavity.

89257
A separately reportable testicular biopsy with aspiration is performed to obtain sperm. This may be required in cases where azoospermia is due to suspected obstruction to the spermatic ducts or in instances where the patient has had a failed reversal of a vasectomy. This procedure reports microscopic examination of aspirated fluid for the presence of sperm. If sperm are identified, further evaluation services may be performed and would be reported separately.

89258
Embryos not required for current uterine transfer are frozen using a process referred to as cryopreservation. Pre-implantation embryo preservation is a relatively new procedure as compared to sperm preservation (see 89259), but more than two-thirds of the embryos survive the cryopreservation process and can be preserved for an indefinite period of time.

89259
A cryoprotectant, usually glycerol or Dimethyl Sulfoxide (DMSO), is mixed with the semen to reduce damage to sperm during the freezing process. The semen specimen is placed in a vial and frozen in liquid nitrogen at -196 C. This halts all biologic and metabolic processes allowing the sperm to be preserved for many years.

89260
Prior to insemination or further diagnostic studies, the sperm go through a spinning and washing process in a series of solutions. The purpose of this is to separate sperm from seminal fluids, allowing the sperm to go through a process referred to as capacitation. Capacitation is an invisible change mature spermatozoa must undergo to acquire accelerated movement, allowing them to navigate through the uterus and fallopian tube. In addition, this procedure checks the ability of the sperm to swim in a forward progressive fashion. This procedure includes a semen analysis (count, motility, volume and differential).

89261
Prior to insemination or further diagnostic studies, the sperm go through a spinning and washing process in a series of solutions. The purpose of this is to separate sperm from seminal fluids, allowing the sperm to go through a process referred to as capacitation. Capacitation is an invisible change mature spermatozoa must undergo to acquire accelerated movement, allowing them to navigate through the uterus and fallopian tube. This complex prep includes a Percoll gradient and albumin gradient. This procedure includes a semen analysis (count, motility, volume and differential).

89264
A separately reportable testicular biopsy is performed to obtain sperm. A small amount of testicular tissue is taken for microscopic evaluation for the presence of sperm. This test is used only when no other means is available of obtaining a sperm sample because of the possibility of causing further testicular damage.

89268
Insemination requires a sperm cell to be introduced to an egg (oocyte) for fertilization procedures. The sperm is prepared through a washing method, which separates the sperm cells from the seminal fluid. The washing filters out white blood cells, prostaglandins, and other debris, as well as cells with less motility, to provide the highest concentration of viable sperm. Once the concentrated spermatozoa have been prepared, they are placed in a culture medium with the eggs. If injection is required for fertilization, the protective coating of cells is removed from the egg and the sperm cell is directly injected.

89272
Culture of eggs (oocytes) or embryos usually occurs for 48 to 72 hours. This code describes an extended period of time for the cells to incubate in a culture medium, which will improve the identification of the most viable embryos. It is sometimes necessary to wait up to five days for the embryo to become a blastocyte before implantation due to high risk of multiple gestation or repeated IVF failures.

89280-89281
Assisted oocyte fertilization is done with microtechnique. A single sperm is injected into the egg (oocyte) to enable fertilization when sperm counts are very low or when sperm are non-motile. It requires micromanipulation of the sperm, which is also referred to as microtechnique. The usual method involves intracytoplasmic sperm injection (ICSI). Using ICSI technique, the mature egg is held in place with a holding pipette. A very delicate, sharp, hollow needle is used to immobilize and pick up a single sperm. This needle is inserted through the egg's outer shell (zona pellucida) into the cytoplasm of the egg. The sperm is injected into the cytoplasm and the needle removed. The eggs are checked the next day for evidence of fertilization. Report 89280 for 10 oocytes or less and 89281 for more than 10 oocytes.

89290-89291
Biopsy of an egg (oocyte) polar body or embryo blastomere (an embryo with six to eight cells) is

indicated for patients who carry genetic disorders such as Sickle cell anemia, hemophilia, Fragile X syndrome, and others, and for those experiencing difficulty with a successful IVF or ICSI. The process of a biopsy includes inserting a microneedle into a fertilized egg to extract polar bodies of the oocyte, or to extract a single cell from a six to eight cell embryo. Screenings are performed through the process of FISH (fluorescent in-situ hybridization) and PCR (polymerase chain reaction). During FISH, a small amount of DNA is analyzed through staining of fluorochromes. PCR is able to detect gene-sequences or single genes, which may have abnormal mutations. Report 89290 for a biopsy of five or less embryos and 89291 for six or more embryos.

89300-89322

Semen analysis is generally performed in specialized infertility/andrology laboratories. Sexual activity culminating in ejaculation should be avoided for a minimum of 48 hours prior to testing. In 89300, a post coital specimen is obtained using a cervical swab. The test is timed to coincide with ovulation. Semen is tested for the presence (quantity) and/or motility of sperm. In 89310-89322, semen is collected using a condom-like seminal fluid collection device or by masturbation into a sterile container. In 89310, only sperm movement (motility) and number (concentration or count that measures how many million sperm are in each milliliter of fluid) are performed. Code 89320 reports a semen analysis that includes measurement of the ejaculate's volume, number, structure (shape) of sperm, sperm movement (motility), and direction of movement (forward motility). In addition, fluid thickness, acidity, and sugar content may be evaluated. Code 89321 tests only for the presence (quantity) and/or motility of sperm. In 89322, a detailed evaluation of the shape (morphology) is performed utilizing specially stained slides and microscopic examination of the sperm under high power magnification. In order to be considered normal, the sperm must meet a strict set of criteria regarding the shape and size of the head, mid-piece, and tail. A Kruger test is helpful in determining which reproductive techniques and methodologies may be most appropriate and successful. Tests reported with 89300-89322 may be accomplished using a variety of methods including semen function tests and computer-assisted sperm morphology/motility studies.

89325

This procedure tests for antisperm antibodies in both the male and female. Semen and cervical mucus are placed together in a medium. Antisperm antibodies bind with the sperm inhibiting movement and their ability to fertilize. The sperm will appear clumped together on microscopic examination.

89329

This test is also called sperm penetration assay (SPA) or hamster zona free ovum (HZFO) and tests the ability of the sperm to penetrate a hamster egg, which has been stripped of the zona pellucida (outer membrane). The patient should abstain from sexual activity culminating in ejaculation for a minimum of 48 hours. Semen is collected postcoitus using a condom-like seminal fluid collection device or by masturbation into a sterile container. Upon receiving the specimen in the laboratory, the sperm is washed and placed in a culture medium along with a single hamster egg. It is examined periodically using phase contrast microscopy. The test measures the ability of sperm to capacitate (invisible change which allows sperm to navigate rapidly forward), acrosome react (structural change fusing the outer membrane of the acrosome with the plasma membrane of the sperm head freeing enzymes in the acrosome which facilitate entry into the ovum), and fuse with the ovum.

89330

Sperm mucus interaction is assessed in vitro. Human or bovine ovulatory mucus is placed in a capillary tube. Sperm penetration is measured over a period of 90 minutes. Sperm progression defined as those sperm that have progressed the farthest down the tube is measured. Patient sperm penetration can be compared with fertile sperm specimens using in vitro methods.

89331

Retrograde ejaculation, in which the seminal fluid travels backward into the bladder following ejaculation, is often seen in patients with diabetes, or in men following transurethral surgery at or near the bladder neck, dissection of the retroperitoneal lymph nodes, or spinal cord injuries. The patient may present with low semen volume, motility (movement), and sperm concentration (count). In a urinalysis performed immediately after ejaculation, the specimen is examined under the microscope for the presence of sperm. If detected, the specimen is further processed to evaluate the concentration, motility, and morphology (shape).

89335

Storage of reproductive tissues is cryogenically maintained at an appropriate facility. A cryoprotectant is added to reduce cellular damage and the tissue is placed in vials, straws, or test tubes. The tissue is gradually frozen in the vapor of liquid nitrogen. Once frozen, the tissue is stored in liquid nitrogen at -196 degrees centigrade. Report 89335 for testicular reproductive tissue cryopreservation.

89342-89346

These codes report the long-term maintenance of preserved reproductive tissue samples and fertilized embryos in an appropriate storage facility per year. Report 89342 for embryo(s), 89343 for sperm/semen,

89344 for testicular or ovarian tissue, and 89346 for oocyte(s).

89352-89356
Thawing of cryopreserved tissue requires thawing in different substances for set lengths of time so as to maintain the integrity of the specimen and prevent damage by thawing too quickly. The cryovial is removed from the liquid nitrogen and placed at room temperature until ice crystals have dissolved. A waterbath is prepared at the desired temperature in which the specimen is placed. After the water bath, each specimen is placed in a series of solutions to complete the thawing process. Report 89352 for embryos, 89353 for sperm/semen, 89354 for reproductive testicular/ovarian tissue, and 89356 for oocytes.

Medicine

90281
This code identifies the immune globulin (Ig), human, for intramuscular use. An immune globulin is a passive immunization agent obtained from donated, pooled human plasma. Passive immunity is achieved for a short period as the antibodies received through the immune globulin are circulated through the body. The recipient's immune system is not stimulated to build its own antibodies. Report this code with the appropriate administration code.

90283
This code identifies the immune globulin (IgIV), human, for intravenous administration. An immune globulin is a passive immunization agent obtained from donated, pooled human plasma. Passive immunity is achieved for a short period as the antibodies received through the immune globulin are circulated through the body. The recipient's immune system is not stimulated to build its own antibodies. Report this code with the appropriate administration code.

90284
This code identifies the human immune globulin for use in subcutaneous infusions (SCIg). An immune globulin is a passive immunization agent obtained from donated pooled human plasma. Passive immunity is achieved for a short period as the antibodies received through the immune globulin are circulated through the body. The recipient's immune system is not stimulated to build its own antibodies. Some patients have insufficient venous access or adverse reactions to intravenous treatments, making them unsuitable candidates for traditional IVIg therapy. Controlled doses of immune globulin are administered over a period of several hours through a small needle placed just under the skin. Report this code with the appropriate administration code.

90287
This code identifies the Botulinum antitoxin, equine, administered by any route. The antitoxin is a passive immunizing agent derived from purified serum from previously immunized horses. The antibodies received through the antiserum are circulated through the body and neutralize toxins produced by strains of the Botulinum bacteria. Report this code with the appropriate administration code.

90288
This code identifies the botulism immune globulin, human, for intravenous use. This immune globulin is a passive immunization agent that gives protection against Botulism and is obtained from donated, pooled human plasma. Passive immunity is achieved for a short period as the antibodies received through the immune globulin are circulated through the body. The recipient's immune system is not stimulated to build its own antibodies. Report this code with the appropriate administration code.

90291
This code identifies the cytomegalovirus immune globulin (CMV-IgIV), human, for intravenous use. This immune globulin is a passive immunization agent that gives protection against the Cytomegalovirus and is obtained from donated, pooled human plasma. Passive immunity is achieved for a short period as the antibodies received through the immune globulin are circulated through the body. The recipient's immune system is not stimulated to build its own antibodies. Report this code with the appropriate administration code.

90296
This code identifies the diphtheria antitoxin, equine, administered by any route. The antitoxin is a passive immunizing agent derived from purified serum from previously immunized horses. The antibodies received through the antiserum are circulated through the body and neutralize toxins produced by Corynebacterium diphtheriae. Report this code with the appropriate administration code.

90371
This code identifies the hepatitis B immune globulin (HBIg), human, for intramuscular use. This immune globulin is a passive immunization agent that gives protection against Hepatitis B and is obtained from donated, pooled human plasma. Passive immunity is achieved for a short period as the antibodies received through the immune globulin are circulated through the body. The recipient's immune system is not stimulated to build its own antibodies. Report this code with the appropriate administration code.

90375-90376
Code 90375 identifies the rabies immune globulin (RIg), human, for intramuscular and/or subcutaneous use and 90376 identifies the heat-treated Rabies

immune globulin (RIg-HT), also for intramuscular and/ or subcutaneous use. This immune globulin is a passive immunization agent that gives protection against Rabies and is obtained from donated, pooled human plasma. Passive immunity is achieved for a short period as the antibodies received through the immune globulin are circulated through the body. The recipient's immune system is not stimulated to build its own antibodies. Report these codes with the appropriate administration code.

90378

Code 90378 identifies the respiratory syncytial virus (RSV) recombinant monoclonal antibody for intramuscular use, 50 mg, each. This humanized monoclonal antibody (IgG) gives protection against the respiratory syncytial virus and is injected once a month during the RSV season. Passive immunity is achieved for a short period as the antibodies received are circulated through the body. The recipient's immune system is not stimulated to build its own antibodies. Report this code with the appropriate administration code.

90384-90386

Code 90384 identifies the human Rho(D) immune globulin (RhIg) for intramuscular use, full-dose; 90385 is for a mini-dose. Code 90386 identifies the human Rho(D) immune globulin (RhIgIV) for intravenous use. This immune globulin is a passive immunization agent that gives protection against reactions between blood that is negative for the presence of Rh antigens on the surface of red blood cells to blood that is positive for the presence of Rh antigens on the RBC. Report these codes with the appropriate administration code.

90389

This code identifies a tetanus immune globulin (TIg), human, for intramuscular use. This immune globulin is a passive immunization agent that gives protection against tetanus and is obtained from donated, pooled human plasma. Passive immunity is achieved for a short period as the antibodies received through the immune globulin are circulated through the body. The recipient's immune system is not stimulated to build its own antibodies. Report this code with the appropriate administration code.

90393

This code identifies the vaccinia immune globulin, human, for intramuscular use. This immune globulin is a passive immunization agent that gives protection against vaccinia and is obtained from donated, pooled human plasma. The vaccinia virus causes cutaneous and systemic reactions occurring as a complication of smallpox vaccination. Passive immunity is achieved for a short period as the antibodies received through the immune globulin are circulated through the body. The recipient's immune system is not stimulated to build its own antibodies. Report this code with the appropriate administration code.

90396

This code identifies varicella-zoster immune globulin, human, for intramuscular use. This immune globulin is a passive immunization agent that gives protection against varicella-zoster and is obtained from donated, pooled human plasma. Passive immunity is achieved for a short period as the antibodies received through the immune globulin are circulated through the body. The recipient's immune system is not stimulated to build its own antibodies. Report this code with the appropriate administration code.

90465-90466

The physician instructs the patient or family on the benefits and risks related to the vaccine or toxoid. The physician counsels the patient or family regarding signs and symptoms of adverse effects and when to seek medical care for any adverse effects. A physician, nurse, or medical assistant administers an injectable (percutaneous, intradermal, subcutaneous, or intramuscular) immunization to the patient. It may be a single vaccine or a combination vaccine/toxoid in one immunization administration (e.g., diphtheria, pertussis, and tetanus toxoids are in a single DPT immunization). Report 90465 for one vaccine and 90466 for each additional vaccine (single or combination vaccine/toxoid) provided on the same day to a child younger than eight years of age.

90467-90468

The physician instructs the patient or family on the benefits and risks related to the vaccine or toxoid. The physician counsels the patient or family regarding signs and symptoms of adverse effects and when to seek medical care for any adverse effects. A physician, nurse, or medical assistant administers an immunization to a patient via an intranasal (e.g., nasal spray) or an oral route (e.g., a liquid that is swallowed). It may be a single vaccine or a combination vaccine/toxoid in one immunization administration (e.g., adenovirus, Rotavirus, typhoid, poliovirus). Report 90467 for one vaccine and 90468 for each additional vaccine (single or combination vaccine/toxoid) provided on the same day to a child younger than eight years of age.

90470

This code reports administration of the H1N1 influenza immunization and includes counseling, when performed. The patient or family are instructed on the benefits and risks related to the vaccine. A physician, nurse, or medical assistant administers the immunization to a patient via intramuscular injection or intranasal spray.

90471-90472

A physician, nurse, or medical assistant administers an injectable (percutaneous, intradermal, subcutaneous, or intramuscular) immunization to the patient. It may be a single vaccine or a combination vaccine/toxoid in one immunization administration (e.g., diphtheria, pertussis, and tetanus toxoids are in a single DPT immunization). Report 90471 for one vaccine and 90472 for each additional vaccine (single or combination vaccine/toxoid).

90473-90474
A physician, nurse, or medical assistant administers an immunization to a patient via an intranasal (e.g., nasal spray) or an oral route (e.g., a liquid that is swallowed). It may be a single vaccine or a combination vaccine/ toxoid in one immunization administration (e.g., adenovirus, Rotavirus, typhoid, poliovirus). Report 90473 for one vaccine and 90474 for each additional vaccine (single or combination vaccine/toxoid).

90476-90477
A vaccine produces active immunization by inducing the immune system to build its own antibodies against specific microorganisms/viruses. The body retains memory of the antibody production pattern for long-term protection. These vaccine codes are for a live, oral preparation against an adenovirus and contain the actual virus. An adenovirus causes diseases of the upper respiratory tract and conjunctivae and is also present in latent infections in normal persons. Types 3, 4, 7, 14, and 21 have been isolated from patients with acute respiratory disease. Use 90476 to report a type 4-adenovirus vaccine and 90477 for a type 7. Report these codes with the appropriate administration code.

90581
A vaccine produces active immunization by inducing the immune system to build its own antibodies against specific microorganisms/viruses. The body retains memory of the antibody production pattern for long-term protection. This vaccine is prepared for subcutaneous use against anthrax. Cutaneous anthrax is the most common among humans and is caused by the bacteria Bacillus anthracis or its spores. It is usually acquired from contact with infected animals or their waste material. The most fatal form of anthrax is inhaled and can cause pneumonia. Report this code with the appropriate administration code.

90585
A vaccine produces active immunization by inducing the immune system to build its own antibodies against specific microorganisms/viruses. The body retains memory of the antibody production pattern for long-term protection. This live vaccine is prepared for percutaneous use against tuberculosis using Bacillus Calmette-Guerin (BCG) and contains the actual pathogen, a strain of Mycobacterium bovis. Report this code with the appropriate administration code.

90586
A vaccine produces active immunization by inducing the immune system to build its own antibodies against specific microorganisms/viruses. The body retains memory of the antibody production pattern for long-term protection. This live vaccine is prepared for intravesical use against bladder cancer using Bacillus Calmette-Guerin (BCG) and contains the actual pathogen, a strain of Mycobacterium bovis. Report this code with the appropriate administration code.

90632-90634
These codes are used to report a hepatitis A vaccine for intramuscular use, prepared in various dosages. The vaccine is prepared from the blood plasma of asymptomatic human carriers of hepatitis caused by the hepatitis A virus or through recombinant DNA technology. Report 90632 for an adult dosage; report 90633 for a 2-dose schedule for a pediatric/adolescent dosage, and 90634 for a 3-dose schedule for pediatric/ adolescent dosage. Report these codes with the appropriate administration code.

90636
This code reports a hepatitis A and hepatitis B vaccine (HepA-HepB) for intramuscular use in an adult dosage. The vaccine is prepared from the blood plasma of asymptomatic human carriers of hepatitis caused by the hepatitis A and the hepatitis B virus (HepA-HepB) or through recombinant DNA technology. Report this code with the appropriate administration code.

90644
A vaccine produces active immunization by inducing the immune system to build its own antibodies against specific microorganisms/viruses. The body retains memory of these antibody production patterns for long-term protection. This code reports a meningococcal conjugate vaccine (serogroups C & Y), hemophilus influenza b vaccine, and tetanus toxoid conjugate (Hib-MenCY-TT) prepared for intramuscular use in a four-dose schedule for children 2 to 15 months of age. Report this code with the appropriate administration code.

90645
A vaccine produces active immunization by inducing the immune system to build its own antibodies against specific microorganisms/viruses. The body retains memory of the antibody production pattern for long-term protection. The Hemophilus influenza b vaccine (Hib), HbOC conjugate, is prepared for intramuscular use, in a 4-dose schedule, to immunize a patient against influenza, caused by the bacteria species of the same name, Haemophilus influenzae. Report this code with the appropriate administration code.

90646
A vaccine produces active immunization by inducing the immune system to build its own antibodies against specific microorganisms/viruses. The body retains memory of the antibody production pattern for long-term protection. The Hemophilus influenza b vaccine (Hib), PRP-D conjugate, is prepared for intramuscular use, booster only, to immunize a patient against influenza, caused by the bacteria species of the

same name, Haemophilus influenzae. Report this code with the appropriate administration code.

90647
A vaccine produces active immunization by inducing the immune system to build its own antibodies against specific microorganisms/viruses. The body retains memory of the antibody production pattern for long-term protection. A Hemophilus influenza b vaccine (Hib), PRP-OMP conjugate, is prepared for intramuscular use, in a 3-dose schedule, to immunize a patient against influenza, caused by the bacteria species of the same name, Haemophilus influenzae. Report this code with the appropriate administration code.

90648
A vaccine produces active immunization by inducing the immune system to build its own antibodies against specific microorganisms/viruses. The body retains memory of the antibody production pattern for long-term protection. A Hemophilus influenza b vaccine (Hib), PRP-T conjugate, is prepared for intramuscular use, in a 4-dose schedule, to immunize a patient against influenza, caused by the bacteria species of the same name, Haemophilus influenzae. Report this code with the appropriate administration code.

90649-90650
A vaccine produces active immunization by inducing the immune system to manufacture its own antibodies against specific microorganisms/viruses. The body retains memory of the antibody production pattern for long-term protection. A human papilloma virus (HPV) vaccine is prepared in a three-dose schedule for intramuscular use. The vaccine may be bivalent (types 16 and 18) or quadrivalent (types 6, 11, 16, and 18). The vaccine immunizes a patient against HPV or assists in producing an immune reaction to the E6 and E7 viral proteins to prevent or destroy the growth of abnormal or cancerous cells. Report the bivalent vaccine with 90650 and the quadrivalent vaccine with 90649. Report these codes with the appropriate administration code.

90655-90656
These codes report the supply of the vaccine only. A vaccine produces active immunization by inducing the immune system to build its own antibodies against specific microorganisms/viruses. The body retains memory of the antibody production pattern for long-term protection. A split virus suspension of the prevalent strains of influenza is prepared for intramuscular injection. Report 90655 for a preservative free, split virus influenza vaccine to be administered to children six to 35 months of age and 90656 if the vaccine is administered to individuals three years of age or older. Report these codes with the appropriate administration code.

90657-90658
These codes report the supply of the vaccine only. A vaccine produces active immunization by inducing the immune system to build its own antibodies against specific microorganisms/viruses. The body retains memory of the antibody production pattern for long-term protection. A split virus suspension of the prevalent strains of influenza is prepared for intramuscular use. Report 90657 for the vaccine supply when administered to children ages six to 35 months and 90658 for vaccines administered to individuals three years of age or older. The vaccine induces active immunity to the highly contagious infection of the respiratory tract caused by a myxovirus and transmitted by airborne droplet infection. Report these codes with the appropriate administration code.

90660
A vaccine produces active immunization by inducing the immune system to build its own antibodies against specific microorganisms/viruses. The body retains memory of the antibody production pattern for long-term protection. A suspension of the prevalent strain of influenza virus is prepared for intranasal use. The vaccine provides active immunity to the highly contagious infection of the respiratory tract caused by a myxovirus and transmitted by airborne droplet infection. This live vaccination contains the actual pathogen. Report this code with the appropriate administration code.

90661
A vaccine produces active immunization by inducing the immune system to build its own antibodies against specific microorganisms/viruses. The body retains memory of the antibody production pattern for long-term protection. A suspension of the prevalent strain of influenza virus that has been derived from cell cultures is prepared for intramuscular use. Cell culture-derived vaccines are those in which the virus is grown in mammalian cells rather than egg-derived. The vaccine provides active immunity to the highly contagious infection of the respiratory tract caused by a myxovirus and transmitted by airborne droplet infection. This vaccine is preservative and antibiotic-free. This code reports a subunit, and should be reported with the appropriate administration code.

90662
A vaccine produces active immunization by inducing the immune system to build its own antibodies against specific microorganisms/viruses. The body retains memory of the antibody production pattern for long-term protection. Subvirion (split virus) vaccines do not contain the entire virus; rather, they contain purified portions. Split virus vaccines are believed to cause fewer adverse effects in children and young adults, while maintaining its ability to stimulate an immune response (immunogenicity) comparable to that of whole virus preparations. Due to their

decreased rates of side effects, only split virus preparations are recommended for children younger than 13 years of age. A suspension of the prevalent strain of influenza virus is prepared for intramuscular use. This code reports a preservative-free split virus vaccine whose immunogenicity has been enhanced with increased antigens. Report this code with the appropriate administration code.

90663
This code reports a pandemic formulation of the H1N1 influenza virus vaccine. An influenza pandemic is a large-scale eruption of disease that takes place when a new influenza virus emerges in the human population, spreading easily between individuals and resulting in serious illness. A pandemic can rapidly travel across a whole region, a continent, or the world. Unlike seasonal influenza, individuals have little immunity to this virus. This code identifies the vaccine product only and must be reported in addition to the appropriate immunization administration code.

90665
A vaccine produces active immunization by inducing the immune system to build its own antibodies against specific microorganisms/viruses. The body retains memory of the antibody production pattern for long-term protection. This code reports an adult dose vaccine against Lyme disease, for intramuscular use. Lyme disease is an acute inflammatory infection transmitted by the tick-borne bacteria, Borrelia burgdorferi. Report this code with the appropriate administration code.

90669-90670
Pneumococcal vaccines provide protection against infections of the lungs, blood, and brain. These codes report supply of the vaccine only. A vaccine produces active immunization by inducing the immune system to build its own antibodies against specific microorganisms/viruses. The body retains memory of the antibody production pattern for long-term protection. These codes report active suspension conjugate vaccine for intramuscular use. Report 90669 for supply of the 7 valent pneumococcal conjugate vaccine and 90670 for supply of the 13 valent variety. Report these codes with the appropriate administration code.

90675-90676
A vaccine produces active immunization by inducing the immune system to build its own antibodies against specific microorganisms/viruses. The body retains memory of the antibody production pattern for long-term protection. Code 90675 reports a vaccine for immunization against rabies, and protection against postexposure spread, for intramuscular use; 90676 is for intradermal use. The vaccine is prepared from a suspension of killed rabies virus prepared from duck embryo. Report these codes with the appropriate administration code.

90680-90681
A rotavirus replicates in the cells of the intestine and causes acute diarrhea, particularly in infants. A vaccine produces active immunization by inducing the immune system to build its own antibodies against specific microorganisms/viruses. The body retains memory of the antibody production pattern for long-term protection. A vaccine for immunization against a rotavirus is prepared for oral use in a three-dose schedule in 90680. This live pentavalent vaccine contains the actual virus. Code 90681 reports a two-dose oral live attenuated human rotavirus vaccine. Report these codes with the appropriate administration code.

90690
A vaccine produces active immunization by inducing the immune system to build its own antibodies against specific microorganisms/viruses. The body retains memory of the antibody production pattern for long-term protection. A typhoid vaccine for immunization against the bacterial infection usually caused by Salmonella typhi is prepared for oral use. This live vaccine contains the actual pathogen. The bacterial infection is transmitted by contaminated milk, water, and food and causes high fever, diarrhea, and rash. Report this code with the appropriate administration code.

90691
A vaccine produces active immunization by inducing the immune system to build its own antibodies against specific microorganisms/viruses. The body retains memory of the antibody production pattern for long-term protection. A typhoid vaccine, Vi capsular polysaccharide form (ViCPs), for immunization against the bacterial infection usually caused by Salmonella typhi, is prepared for intramuscular use. The bacterial infection is transmitted by contaminated milk, water, and food and causes high fever, diarrhea, and rash. Report this code with the appropriate administration code.

90692
A vaccine produces active immunization by inducing the immune system to build its own antibodies against specific microorganisms/viruses. The body retains memory of the antibody production pattern for long-term protection. A typhoid vaccine, heat- and phenol-inactivated (H-P), for immunization against the bacterial infection usually caused by Salmonella typhi, is prepared for subcutaneous or intradermal use. The bacterial infection is transmitted by contaminated milk, water, and food and causes high fever, diarrhea, and rash. Report this code with the appropriate administration code.

90693
A vaccine produces active immunization by inducing the immune system to build its own antibodies against specific microorganisms/viruses. The body retains

memory of the antibody production pattern for long-term protection. A typhoid vaccine, acetone-killed, dried (AKD), for immunization against the bacterial infection usually caused by Salmonella typhi, is prepared for subcutaneous use (U.S. military). The bacterial infection is transmitted by contaminated milk, water, and food and causes high fever, diarrhea, and rash. Report this code with the appropriate administration code.

90696-90701
These codes report supply of the vaccine only. A toxoid stimulates the body's own immune system to produce specific antitoxin antibodies that destroy the toxins secreted by bacteria. This provides immunity that is effective and long lasting. A vaccine produces active immunization by inducing the immune system to build its own antibodies against specific microorganisms/viruses. The body retains memory of these antibody production patterns for long-term protection. Code 90696 describes an intramuscular vaccine for diphtheria, tetanus toxoids, and acellular pertussis (synthetic form) combined with inactivated poliovirus vaccine, or DTaP-IPV, for administration to children four through six years of age. Code 90698 reports the immunization supply of diphtheria, tetanus toxoids, and acellular pertussis (synthetic form) vaccine, combined with haemophilus influenza Type B, and inactivated poliovirus vaccine, or DTaP-Hib-IPV, for intramuscular use. Code 90700 describes a vaccine for intramuscular use against diphtheria, tetanus, and pertussis (in acellular form—synthetic) for administration to children younger than seven years of age. It is commonly called DTaP. Code 90701 describes a vaccine for intramuscular use against diphtheria, tetanus, and pertussis (in whole cell form), commonly called DTP. The DTaP/DTP vaccinations are routine immunizations for children. Report these codes with the appropriate administration code.

90702-90703
These codes report supply of the toxoid only. A toxoid stimulates the body's own immune system to produce specific antitoxin antibodies that destroy the toxins secreted by bacteria. This provides immunity that is effective and long lasting. Code 90702 reports toxoids against diphtheria and tetanus (DT), adsorbed for intramuscular use, for administration to individuals younger than age seven. Code 90703 reports a tetanus toxoid alone for intramuscular use. Report these codes with the appropriate administration code.

90704-90706
A vaccine produces active immunization by inducing the immune system to build its own antibodies against specific microorganisms/viruses. The body retains memory of these antibody production patterns for long-term protection. These codes all report a live vaccine for subcutaneous use. Code 90704 is for a mumps virus vaccine, 90705 reports a measles vaccine, and 90706 is for rubella. A live vaccine contains the actual pathogen. Report these codes with the appropriate administration code.

90707-90708
A vaccine produces active immunization by inducing the immune system to build its own antibodies against specific microorganisms/viruses. The body retains memory of these antibody production patterns for long-term protection. Code 90707 reports the combined measles, mumps, and rubella (MMR) vaccine, live, for subcutaneous use. Code 90708 reports the measles and rubella virus vaccine, live, for subcutaneous use. A live vaccine contains the actual pathogens. Report these codes with the appropriate administration code.

90710
A vaccine produces active immunization by inducing the immune system to build its own antibodies against specific microorganisms/viruses. The body retains memory of these antibody production patterns for long-term protection. This vaccine combines measles, mumps, rubella, and varicella (MMRV) for subcutaneous use. This live vaccine contains the actual pathogens. Report this code with the appropriate administration code.

90712
A vaccine produces active immunization by inducing the immune system to build its own antibodies against specific microorganisms/viruses. The body retains memory of these antibody production patterns for long-term protection. This code describes the poliovirus vaccine, (OPV)(any type), for oral use. This live vaccine contains the actual pathogen. Report this code with the appropriate administration code.

90713
A vaccine produces active immunization by inducing the immune system to manufacture its own antibodies against specific microorganisms/viruses. The body retains memory of these antibody production patterns for long-term protection. This code describes the inactivated poliovirus vaccine (IPV) for subcutaneous or intramuscular use. Report this code with the appropriate administration code.

90714
This code reports supply of the toxoid only. A toxoid stimulates the body's own immune system to produce specific antitoxin antibodies that destroy the toxins secreted by bacteria. This provides immunity that is effective and long lasting. This code reports the immunization supply of tetanus and diphtheria toxoids (Td), adsorbed, preservative free, for intramuscular administration to patients seven years of age or older. Report this code with the appropriate administration code.

Medicine

90715
This code reports the vaccine/toxoid product supply only. A toxoid stimulates the body's own immune system to produce specific antitoxin antibodies that destroy the toxins secreted by bacteria. This provides immunity that is effective and long lasting. A vaccine produces active immunization by inducing the immune system to build its own antibodies against specific microorganisms/viruses. The body retains memory of these antibody production patterns for long-term protection. This code reports the immunization supply of tetanus, diphtheria toxoids, and acellular pertussis (synthetic form) vaccine (DTaP) for intramuscular administration to patients seven years of age or older. Report this code with the appropriate administration code.

90716
A vaccine produces active immunization by inducing the immune system to build its own antibodies against specific microorganisms/viruses. The body retains memory of these antibody production patterns for long-term protection. This code describes a live varicella virus vaccine for subcutaneous use. This vaccine contains the actual pathogen. Report this code with the appropriate administration code.

90717
A vaccine produces active immunization by inducing the immune system to build its own antibodies against specific microorganisms/viruses. The body retains memory of these antibody production patterns for long-term protection. This code reports the live vaccine against yellow fever for subcutaneous use. A live vaccine contains the actual pathogen. Report this code with the appropriate administration code.

90718-90719
This code reports supply of a toxoid only. A toxoid stimulates the body's own immune system to produce specific antitoxin antibodies that destroy the toxins secreted by bacteria. This provides active immunity that is effective and long lasting. Code 90718 describes toxoids against tetanus and diphtheria (Td), adsorbed for intramuscular use, for administration to patients seven years of age or older. Code 90719 reports a diphtheria toxoid alone for intramuscular use. Report these codes with the appropriate administration code.

90720
A toxoid stimulates the body's own immune system to produce specific antitoxin antibodies that destroy the toxins secreted by bacteria. This provides immunity that is effective and long lasting. A vaccine produces active immunization by inducing the immune system to build its own antibodies against specific microorganisms/viruses. The body retains memory of these antibody production patterns for long-term protection. Code 90720 describes a vaccine combining diphtheria and tetanus toxoids, whole cell pertussis vaccine, and Hemophilus influenza B vaccine, (DTP-Hib), for intramuscular use. Report this code with the appropriate administration code.

90721
A toxoid stimulates the body's own immune system to produce specific antitoxin antibodies that destroy the toxins secreted by bacteria. This provides immunity that is effective and long lasting. A vaccine produces active immunization by inducing the immune system to build its own antibodies against specific microorganisms/viruses. The body retains memory of these antibody production patterns for long-term protection. Code 90721 reports a combination vaccine/toxoid of diphtheria and tetanus toxoids, acellular pertussis vaccine, and Hemophilus influenza B vaccine for intramuscular use (DtaP-Hib). Report this code with the appropriate administration code.

90723
A toxoid stimulates the body's own immune system to produce specific antitoxin antibodies that destroy the toxins secreted by bacteria. This provides immunity that is effective and long lasting. A vaccine produces active immunization by inducing the immune system to build its own antibodies against specific microorganisms/viruses. The body retains memory of these antibody production patterns for long-term protection. Code 90723 describes an immunization combining diphtheria and tetanus toxoids, acellular pertussis vaccine, Hepatitis B, and poliovirus vaccine, inactivated (DtaP-HepB-IPV), for intramuscular use. Report this code with the appropriate administration code.

90725
A vaccine produces active immunization by inducing the immune system to build its own antibodies against specific microorganisms/viruses. The body retains memory of these antibody production patterns for long-term protection. This code reports the supply of a cholera vaccine prepared for injectable use. Report this code with the appropriate administration code.

90727
A vaccine produces active immunization by inducing the immune system to build its own antibodies against specific microorganisms/viruses. The body retains memory of these antibody production patterns for long-term protection. This code reports the supply of a vaccine against plague for intramuscular use. Report this code with the appropriate administration code.

90732
This code reports supply of a vaccine only. A vaccine produces active immunization by inducing the immune system to build its own antibodies against specific microorganisms/viruses. The body retains memory of these antibody production patterns for long-term protection. This code reports a pneumococcal polysaccharide vaccine, 23-valent, adult or immunosuppressed patient dosage, for

subcutaneous or intramuscular administration to patients two years of age or older. Report this code with the appropriate administration code.

90733
A vaccine produces active immunization by inducing the immune system to build its own antibodies against specific microorganisms/viruses. The body retains memory of these antibody production patterns for long-term protection. This code reports a meningococcal polysaccharide vaccine (any group), for subcutaneous use. Report this code with the appropriate administration code.

90734
This code reports the supply of a tetravalent (serogroups A, C, Y, and W-135) meningococcal polysaccharide vaccine conjugated to diphtheria toxoid, for intramuscular use. A vaccine produces active immunization by inducing the immune system to build its own antibodies against specific microorganisms/viruses. The body retains memory of these antibody production patterns for long-term protection. Report 90734 for this particular vaccine product only. Report this code with the appropriate administration code.

90735
A vaccine produces active immunization by inducing the immune system to build its own antibodies against specific microorganisms/viruses. The body retains memory of these antibody production patterns for long-term protection. This code describes a Japanese encephalitis virus vaccine for subcutaneous use. Report this code with the appropriate administration code.

90736
A vaccine produces active immunization by inducing the immune system to manufacture its own antibodies against specific microorganisms/viruses. The body retains memory of these antibody production patterns for long-term protection. This code reports a live herpes zoster (shingles) vaccine for subcutaneous injection. Shingles is a reactivation of the herpes zoster virus that causes chickenpox. The virus persists in a dormant state and may reactivate with certain conditions or advancing age that cause or is associated with immune system compromise. This vaccine prevents herpes zoster and postherpetic neuralgia as a result of the dormant virus in sensory nerve cells. Report this code with the appropriate administration code.

90738
Japanese encephalitis is a mosquito-borne viral infection and is the foremost cause of viral encephalitis in Asia. A vaccine produces active immunization by inducing the immune system to build its own antibodies against specific microorganisms/viruses. The body retains memory of these antibody production patterns for long-term protection. This code describes an inactivated Japanese encephalitis virus vaccine for intramuscular use. Report this code with the appropriate administration code.

90740-90747
A vaccine produces active immunization by inducing the immune system to build its own antibodies against specific microorganisms/viruses. The body retains memory of these antibody production patterns for long-term protection. These codes are used to report the supply of a hepatitis B vaccine for intramuscular use, prepared in various dosages. Report 90740 for a 3-dose schedule for a dialysis or immunosuppressed patient; 90743 for an adolescent 2-dose schedule; 90744 for a pediatric/adolescent 3-dose schedule; 90746 for an adult dosage; and 90747 for a 4-dose schedule for a dialysis or immunosuppressed patient. Report these codes with the appropriate administration code.

90748
A vaccine produces active immunization by inducing the immune system to build its own antibodies against specific microorganisms/viruses. The body retains memory of these antibody production patterns for long-term protection. This code describes a combined hepatitis B and Hemophilus influenza B (HepB-Hib)) vaccine for intramuscular use. Report this code with the appropriate administration code.

90801
The clinician interviews the patient in an initial diagnostic examination, which includes taking the patient's history and assessing his/her mental status, as well as disposition. The psychiatrist may spend time communicating with family, friends, coworkers, or other sources as part of this examination and may even perform the diagnostic interview on the patient through other informative sources. Laboratory or other medical studies and their interpretation are also included.

90802
The clinician performs a psychiatric diagnostic examination on the patient using interactive methods of interviewing. This is most often the method used with individuals who are too young or incapable of developing expressive communication skills, or individuals who have lost that ability. This type of diagnostic interview is often done with children. Toys, physical aids, and non-verbal interaction and interpretation skills are employed to gain communication with a patient not capable of engaging with the clinician by using adult language skills.

90804-90805
The therapist provides individual psychotherapy in an office or outpatient facility using supportive interactions, suggestion, persuasion, reality discussions, re-education, behavior modification techniques, reassurance, and the occasional aid of

Medicine

medication. These interactions are done with the goal of gaining further insight and affecting behavior change or support through understanding. Individual psychotherapy is performed face to face with the patient for 20-30 minutes. Report 90804 if the patient received psychotherapy only and 90805 if medical evaluation and management services were also furnished.

90806-90807
The therapist provides individual psychotherapy in an office or outpatient facility using supportive interactions, suggestion, persuasion, reality discussions, re-education, behavior modification techniques, reassurance, and the occasional aid of medication. These interactions are done with the goal of gaining further insight and affecting behavior change or support through understanding. Individual psychotherapy is performed face to face with the patient for 45-50 minutes. Report 90806 if the patient received psychotherapy only and 90807 if medical evaluation and management services were also furnished.

90808-90809
The therapist provides individual psychotherapy in an office or outpatient facility using supportive interactions, suggestion, persuasion, reality discussions, re-education, behavior modification techniques, reassurance, and the occasional aid of medication. These interactions are done with the goal of gaining further insight and affecting behavior change or support through understanding. Individual psychotherapy is performed face to face with the patient for 75-80 minutes. Report 90808 if the patient received psychotherapy only and 90809 if medical evaluation and management services were also furnished.

90810-90811
The therapist provides interactive psychiatric services in an office or outpatient facility for therapeutic purposes. The interactive method is most often used with individuals who are too young, or incapable, of developing expressive communication skills, or individuals who have lost that ability. This type of psychotherapy is often done with children. Toys, physical aids, and non-verbal play and interaction, including the use of interpreter skills, are employed to gain communication with a patient not capable of engaging with the clinician by using adult language skills. Individual psychotherapy is performed face to face with the patient for 20-30 minutes. Report 90810 if the patient received psychotherapy only and 90811 if medical evaluation and management services were also furnished.

90812-90813
The psychotherapist provides interactive psychiatric services in an office or outpatient facility for therapeutic purposes. The interactive method is most often used with individuals who are too young, or incapable, of developing expressive communication skills, or individuals who have lost that ability. This type of psychotherapy is often done with children. Toys, physical aids, and non-verbal play and interaction, including the use of interpreter skills, are employed to gain communication with a patient not capable of engaging with the clinician by using adult language skills. Individual psychotherapy is performed face to face with the patient for 45-50 minutes. Report 90812 if the patient received psychotherapy only and 90813 if medical evaluation and management services were also furnished.

90814-90815
The therapist provides interactive psychiatric services in an office or outpatient facility for therapeutic purposes. The interactive method is most often used with individuals who are too young, or incapable, of developing expressive communication skills, or individuals who have lost that ability. This type of psychotherapy is often done with children. Toys, physical aids, and non-verbal play and interaction, including the use of interpreter skills, are employed to gain communication with a patient not capable of engaging with the clinician by using adult language skills. Individual psychotherapy is performed face to face with the patient for 75-80 min. Report 90814 if the patient received psychotherapy only and 90815 if medical evaluation and management services were also furnished.

90816-90817
The therapist provides individual psychotherapy in an inpatient hospital, partial hospital, or residential care setting using supportive interactions, suggestion, persuasion, reality discussions, re-education, behavior modification techniques, reassurance, and the occasional aid of medication. These interactions are done with the goal of gaining further insight and affecting behavior change or support through understanding. Individual psychotherapy is performed face to face with the patient for 20-30 minutes. Report 90816 if the patient received psychotherapy only and 90817 if medical evaluation and management services were also furnished.

90818-90819
The therapist provides individual psychotherapy in an inpatient hospital, partial hospital, or residential care setting using supportive interactions, suggestion, persuasion, reality discussions, reeducation, behavior modification techniques, reassurance, and the occasional aid of medication. These interactions are done with the goal of gaining further insight and affecting behavior change or support through understanding. Individual psychotherapy is performed face to face with the patient for 45-50 minutes. Report 90818 if the patient received psychotherapy only and

90819 if medical evaluation and management services were also furnished.

90821-90822
The therapist provides individual psychotherapy in an inpatient hospital, partial hospital, or residential care setting using supportive interactions, suggestion, persuasion, reality discussions, reeducation, behavior modification techniques, reassurance, and the occasional aid of medication. These interactions are done with the goal of gaining further insight and affecting behavior change or support through understanding. Individual psychotherapy is performed face to face with the patient for 75-80 minutes. Report 90821 if the patient received psychotherapy only and 90822 if medical evaluation and management services were also furnished.

90823-90824
The therapist provides interactive psychiatric services in an inpatient hospital, partial hospital, or residential care setting for therapeutic purposes. The interactive method is most often used with individuals who are too young, or incapable, of developing expressive communication skills, or individuals who have lost that ability. This type of psychotherapy is often done with children. Toys, physical aids, and non-verbal play and interaction, including the use of interpreter skills, are employed to gain communication with a patient not capable of engaging with the clinician by using adult language skills. Individual psychotherapy is performed face to face with the patient for 20-30 minutes. Report 90823 if the patient received psychotherapy only and 90824 if medical evaluation and management services were also furnished.

90826-90827
The therapist provides interactive psychiatric services in an inpatient hospital, partial hospital, or residential care setting for therapeutic purposes. The interactive method is most often used with individuals who are too young, or incapable, of developing expressive communication skills, or individuals who have lost that ability. This type of psychotherapy is often done with children. Toys, physical aids, and non-verbal play and interaction, including the use of interpreter skills, are employed to gain communication with a patient not capable of engaging with the clinician by using adult language skills. Individual psychotherapy is performed face to face with the patient for 45-50 minutes. Report 90826 if the patient received psychotherapy only and 90827 if medical evaluation and management services were also furnished.

90828-90829
The therapist provides interactive psychiatric services in an inpatient hospital, partial hospital, or residential care setting for therapeutic purposes. The interactive method is most often used with individuals who are too young, or incapable, of developing expressive communication skills, or individuals who have lost that ability. This type of psychotherapy is often done with children. Toys, physical aids, and non-verbal play and interaction, including the use of interpreter skills, are employed to gain communication with a patient not capable of engaging with the clinician by using adult language skills. Individual psychotherapy is performed face to face with the patient for 75-80 minutes. Report 90828 if the patient received psychotherapy only and 90829 if medical evaluation and management services were also furnished.

90845
The therapist performs psychoanalysis by utilizing methods of intense observation and analytical skills to investigate the patient's past experiences, unconscious motivations, and internal conflicts, as well as contributing medical conditions, to discover how these pilot the patient's current behavior and emotions. The psychiatrist seeks to produce change in maladapted behavior. Psychoanalysis includes reviewing medical notes and making clinical setting arrangements, assisting the patient in further self-awareness, working through barriers, understanding self-observations, and modifying mental behavior and status while continuing to elicit more information and personal exploration. This code also includes follow-up work of documentation, content review, and peer consultation.

90846
The therapist provides family psychotherapy in a setting where the care provider meets with the patient's family without the patient present. The family is part of the patient evaluation and treatment process. Family dynamics as they relate to the patient's mental status and behavior are a main focus of the sessions. Attention is also given to the impact the patient's condition has on the family, with therapy aimed at improving the interaction between the patient and family members.

90847
The therapist provides family psychotherapy in a setting where the care provider meets with the patient's family jointly with the patient. The family is part of the patient evaluation and treatment process. Family dynamics as they relate to the patient's mental status and behavior are a main focus of the sessions. Attention is also given to the impact the patient's condition has on the family, with therapy aimed at improving the interaction between the patient and family members. Reviewing records, communicating with other providers, observing and interpreting patterns of behavior and communication between the patient and family members, and decision making regarding treatment, including medication management or any physical exam related to the medication, is included.

90849
The therapist provides multiple family group psychotherapy by meeting with several patients'

Medicine

families together. This is usually done in cases involving similar issues and often in settings of group homes, drug treatment facilities, or hospital rehabilitation centers. The session may focus on the issues of the patient's hospitalization or substance abuse problems. Attention is also given to the impact the patient's condition has on the family. This code is reported once for each family group present.

90853
The psychiatric treatment provider conducts psychotherapy for a group of several patients in one session. Group dynamics are explored. Emotional and rational cognitive interactions between individual persons in the group are facilitated and observed. Personal dynamics of any individual patient may be discussed within the group setting. Processes that help patients move toward emotional healing and modification of thought and behavior are used, such as facilitating improved interpersonal exchanges, group support, and reminiscing. The group may be composed of patients with separate and distinct maladaptive disorders or persons sharing some facet of a disorder. This code should be used for group psychotherapy with other patients, and not members of the patients' families.

90857
The therapist provides interactive group psychotherapy, usually to patients who are too young, or incapable, of engaging with the clinician through expressive language communication skills, or individuals who have lost that ability. This type of psychotherapy is often done with children. Toys, physical aids, and non-verbal play and interaction, including the use of interpreter skills, are employed to help the patient and clinician work through the issues being treated. Reviewing patient records, including medication and lab tests, making observations and assessments and interpreting reactions and interactions within the group, arranging group and individual follow-up services, and record dictation are included.

90862
This code describes the psychiatric services of managing the patient's medications, including the patient's current use of the medicines, a medical review of the benefits and treatment progression, management of side effects, and review or change of prescription. This is pharmacologically related and involves only minimal medical psychotherapy.

90865
A hypnotic drug known as Amytal or sodium amobarbital is infused into the patient via an intravenous drip for psychiatric diagnostic or psychotherapeutic treatment purposes. Amytal is a hypnotic sedative used for diagnosing dissociative disorders and to treat trauma victims by accessing repressed memories, emotions, or events to facilitate healing. This is often used after other measures have failed and/or when gaining a definitive diagnosis is medically essential. A sodium Amytal interview is often conducted in an inpatient setting, to monitor the effects of the drug. The patient is in a hypnotic state, where memories, as the patient perceives them, are more confidently reviewed. These interviews are often videotaped for later discussion.

90870
The treating clinician initiates a seizure using electroconvulsive therapy (ECT), most often to combat chronic or profound depression, especially psychotic or intractable manic forms and used for people who cannot take antidepressants. The clinician anesthetizes the patient with a barbiturate and a muscle relaxant. Electrodes are placed on the patient's temples and/or forehead and a measured electrical dose is applied for about a second to commence the seizure, typically lasting 30 seconds to a minute. EEG and EKG monitors follow the seizure activity and heart rhythm while the patient sleeps through the therapy. The patient awakens a few minutes later.

90875-90876
The treating clinician gives individual psychophysiological therapy by utilizing biofeedback training together with psychotherapy to modify behavior. The clinician prepares the patient with sensors that read and display skin temperature, blood pressure, muscle tension, or brain wave activity. The patient is taught how certain thought processes, stimuli, and actions affect these physiological responses. The treating clinician works with the patient to learn to recognize and manipulate these responses, to control maladapted physiological functions, through relaxation and awareness techniques. Psychotherapy is also rendered using supportive interactions, suggestion, persuasion, reality discussions, re-education, behavior modification techniques, reassurance, and the occasional aid of medication. Individual psychophysiological therapy is performed face to face with the patient. Report 90875 for sessions of 20-30 minutes and 90876 for sessions of approximately 45-50 minutes.

90880
Hypnosis is used as a modality for psychotherapy. The therapist induces an altered state of consciousness, or focused attention, in the patient. While patients are in this relaxed state of heightened awareness and suggestibility, they can experience changes in the way they feel, think, and behave in response to suggestions directed to them by the hypnotherapist. This modality for psychiatric services helps the therapist to achieve an alteration in the patient's thought and behavior patterns.

90882
The clinician uses this code to report work done with agencies, employers, or institutions on a psychiatric patient's behalf in order to achieve environmental

changes and interventions for managing the patient's medical condition.

90885
The clinician reviews and evaluates the patient's hospital records, other psychiatric reports such as psychometric and projective tests, and other pertinent data for the purpose of gaining a medical diagnosis and insight into the patient's present condition.

90887
The clinician interprets the results of a patient's psychiatric and medical examinations and procedures, as well as any other pertinent recorded data, and spends time explaining the patient's condition to family members and other responsible parties involved with the patient's care and well-being. Advice is also given as to how family members can best assist the patient.

90889
The clinician prepares a report on a patient's mental condition, current psychiatric status, history, treatment regimen, and progress for other physicians, agencies, or insurance carriers involved with the patient's care, except for legal or consultative purposes.

90901
Biofeedback trains patients to control their autonomic or involuntary nervous system responses to regulate vital signs such as heart rate, blood pressure, temperature, and muscle tension. Monitors of various types are used to indicate body responses, which the patient learns to associate with related stimuli and also control in serial sessions. This code applies to any of several modalities of biofeedback training. Biofeedback is used for treatment of conditions including high blood pressure, incontinence, Raynaud's syndrome, and anticipatory nausea due to chemotherapy.

90911
Biofeedback trains patients to control their autonomic or involuntary nervous system responses to regulate vital signs like heart rate, blood pressure, temperature, and muscle tension. This code applies to biofeedback training for monitoring muscles specifically of the anus and/or rectum, perineum, and urethral sphincter. Electromyography, which measures muscle contractions, and/or manometry to measure pressure are included. This particular biofeedback training is done to help the incontinent patient gain control of the related muscles.

90935-90937
Hemodialysis is a process to remove toxins from the blood and to maintain fluid and electrolyte balance when the kidneys no longer function. The procedure involves using a previously placed catheter in an artery or a vein to withdraw the patient's blood, mechanically circulating the blood through a dialysis machine to remove the toxins and wastes, and transfusing the blood back to the patient. Code 90935 applies to one hemodialysis treatment that includes a single physician evaluation of the patient and 90937 is for a hemodialysis procedure when patient re-evaluation(s) must be done during the procedure, with or without substantial revision of the dialysis prescription.

90940
A hemodialysis access flow study is performed to determine blood flow in a graft or arteriovenous fistula. The health care provider performs the test after approximately 30 minutes of treatment and after turning off ultrafiltration. In the direct dilution method, also known as the urea-based measurement of recirculation, arterial and venous line samples are drawn and the blood rate is reduced to 120 mL/minute. The blood pumped is turned off 10 seconds after reducing the blood flow rate and an arterial line is clamped above the sampling port. Systemic arterial samples are drawn, the line is disconnected, and dialysis is resumed. Measurements of BUN in the arterial, venous, and arterial sample are taken and the percent recirculation is calculated. This code includes the hook-up, measurement, and disconnection.

90945-90947
Dialysis is a process to remove toxins from the blood and to maintain fluid and electrolytes balance when the kidneys no longer function. In peritoneal dialysis, a fluid is introduced into the peritoneal cavity that removes toxins and electrolytes, which passively leach into the fluid. Hemofiltration, similar to hemodialysis, employs passing large volumes of blood over extracorporeal, adsorbent filters that remove waste products from the blood. Other continuous renal replacement therapies may be employed, such as continuous arteriovenous hemofiltration that uses small-volume, low-resistance blood filters that are powered by the patient's own arterial pressure, thus eliminating the need for a mechanical pump. Code 90945 applies to one dialysis procedure, other than hemodialysis, with a single physician evaluation of the patient. Code 90947 applies to a dialysis procedure, other than hemodialysis, that requires repeated physician evaluations, with or without substantial revision of a dialysis prescription.

90951-90953
These codes apply to all outpatient, ESRD-related physician services provided during a one-month period for patients younger than two years of age. These codes include establishing the dialyzing cycle, all outpatient management for each dialysis visit, patient management during the dialysis treatment, any telephone calls, and physician evaluation and management related to the ESRD such as assessing the patient's nutritional status, growth and development, and providing parental counseling. Dialysis treatment is not included. Code assignment is based on the number of face-to-face physician visits per month.

Report 90951 for four or more visits, 90952 for two or three, and 90953 for one.

90954-90956
These codes apply to all outpatient, ESRD-related physician services provided during a one-month period for patients two through 11 years of age. These codes include establishing the dialyzing cycle, all outpatient management for each dialysis visit, patient management during the dialysis treatment, any telephone calls, and physician evaluation and management related to the ESRD such as assessing the patient's nutritional status, growth and development, and providing parental counseling. Dialysis treatment is not included. Code assignment is based on the number of face-to-face physician visits per month. Report 90954 for four or more visits, 90955 for two or three, and 90956 for one.

90957-90959
These codes apply to all outpatient, ESRD-related physician services provided during a one-month period for patients 12 through 19 years of age. These codes include establishing the dialyzing cycle, all outpatient management for each dialysis visit, patient management during the dialysis treatment, any telephone calls, and physician evaluation and management related to the ESRD such as assessing the patient's nutritional status, growth and development, and providing parental counseling. Dialysis treatment is not included. Code assignment is based on the number of face-to-face physician visits per month. Report 90957 for four or more visits, 90958 for two or three, and 90959 for one.

90960-90962
These codes apply to all outpatient, ESRD-related physician services provided during a one-month period for patients 20 years of age or older. These codes include establishing the dialyzing cycle, all outpatient management for each dialysis visit, patient management during the dialysis treatment, any telephone calls, and physician evaluation and management related to the ESRD. Dialysis treatment is not included. Code assignment is based on the number of face-to-face physician visits per month. Report 90960 for four or more visits, 90961 for two or three, and 90962 for one.

90963-90966
These codes apply to all ESRD-related physician services provided during a one-month period to home dialysis patients of specified ages. These codes include establishing the dialyzing cycle as well as physician evaluation and management related to the ESRD. Codes 90963–90965 also include assessment of the patient's nutritional status, growth and development, and provision of parental counseling. Code assignment is based on age. Report 90963 for patients younger than 2 years of age, 90964 for patients 2 to 11 years of age, 90965 for patients 12 to 19 years of age, and 90966 for patients over the age of 20.

90967-90970
This code range applies to all ESRD-related services provided to dialysis patients of specified ages who receive dialysis services for less than a full month. These codes are reported per day and are appropriate for use in the following circumstances: home dialysis patients who receive less than a full month of services; patients who are transient; a partial month in which one or more face-to-face visits occurred without a complete assessment; hospitalization of the patient prior to a complete assessment being made; and discontinuance of dialysis due to patient's recovery, receipt of a kidney transplant, or death. For reporting purposes, a month is considered 30 days. Code assignment is based on age. Report 90967 for patients younger than 2 years of age, 90968 for patients 2 to 11 years of age, 90969 for patients 12 to 19 years of age, and 90970 for patients over the age of 20.

90989-90993
The physician or health care provider trains the patient and/or the patient's caregiving helper to perform the dialysis procedure, any mode. Report 90989 when the course is completed; 90993 is reported per training session of the course when it is not completed.

90997
Hemoperfusion is a technique to remove toxins from the blood and to maintain fluid and electrolyte balance when the kidneys no longer function. The physician draws the patient's blood, perfuses the blood through activated charcoal or resin, and transfuses the blood back into the patient using a needle and catheter.

91000
The physician performs esophageal intubation and collection of cytology washings by inserting a tube through the patient's nose or mouth into the esophagus. Fluid and cell samples, are taken by washing the esophagus with a fluid such as saline to increase the sample yield. The sample is preserved and mounted on a slide for microscopic viewing.

91010
The physician inserts a tube with sensors into the patient's nose or mouth and down into the stomach to perform an esophageal motility study. The muscles of the esophagus and/or the gastroesophageal junction, which propel food and water into the stomach, are studied to measure the pressure of the contraction waves and diagnose abnormalities in the esophageal muscle that affect swallowing. The tube is slowly withdrawn and stopped at different points along the esophagus. The patient is directed to swallow a little amount of water at each stopping point and the contraction wave pressure and swallowing action are measured and graphed.

91011
The physician inserts a tube with sensors into the patient's nose or mouth and down into the stomach to perform an esophageal motility study. The muscles of the esophagus and/or the gastroesophageal junction, which propel food and water into the stomach, are studied to measure the pressure of the contraction waves and diagnose abnormalities in the esophageal muscle that affect swallowing. The tube is slowly withdrawn and stopped at different points along the esophagus. The patient is directed to swallow a little amount of water at each stopping point and the contraction wave pressure and swallowing action are measured and graphed. This motility study is combined with a Mecholyl Provocation test, also called a Methacholine Provocation or Challenge test, or Histamine or Bronchial Challenge Test. This determines the severity of bronchial hypersensitivity, and determine the cause and effectiveness of treatment for bronchospasm. Varied doses of methacholine chloride solution are administered to the patient, following a scheduled protocol of gradually increasing concentration, through a nebulizer with constant output compressor, or a dosimeter-driven nebulizer. The patient performs breathing as instructed, and test measurements are taken by spirometry, both before and 3 minutes after the inhalation challenge of gradually increasing, aerosolized methacholine chloride/diluent solution.

91012
The physician inserts a tube with sensors through the patient's nose or mouth and down into the stomach to perform an esophageal motility study. The muscles of the esophagus and/or the gastroesophageal junction, which propel food and water into the stomach, are studied to measure the pressure of the contraction waves and diagnose abnormalities in the esophageal muscle that affect swallowing. The tube is slowly withdrawn and stopped at different points along the esophagus. The patient is directed to swallow a little amount of water at each stopping point and the contraction wave pressure and swallowing action are measured and graphed. This motility study is combined with a provocative acid perfusion study, also called a Bernstein test, to try and replicate the type of chest pain the patient has been experiencing. This aids in diagnosing the pain as non-cardiac, due to esophageal reflux. Both hydrochloric acid and an alternate saline control solution are infused one after the other via the nasogastric tube, without the patient being aware of the identity of the solution. The symptoms of chest pain are recorded as the patient identifies them.

91020
The physician inserts a tube with sensors into the patient's nose or mouth and down into the stomach to perform a gastric motility study. The muscles of the stomach and the gastroduodenal junction, which propel food and water into the first part of the small intestines, are studied to measure the pressure of the contraction waves and diagnose abnormalities in the muscle that affect digestion. Sensors on the tube measure the amount of pressure generated by the stomach muscles as food is moved into the small intestine. The tighter the muscles contract around the tube, the greater pressure that is sensed. The data is recorded for computer analysis.

91022
The physician inserts a tube with sensors into the patient's nose or mouth and down into the duodenum to perform a duodenal motility study. The muscles of the duodenum and the gastroduodenal junction, which propel food and water into the first part of the small intestines, are studied to measure the pressure of the contraction waves and diagnose abnormalities in the muscle that affect digestion. Sensors on the tube measure the amount of pressure generated by the duodenal muscles as food is moved into the small intestine. The tighter the muscles contract around the tube, the greater pressure that is sensed. The data is recorded for computer analysis.

91030
This code reports a provocative acid perfusion study, also called a Bernstein test, performed on the esophagus, not in conjunction with a motility test. The acid perfusion test is done to try and replicate atypical chest pain the patient has been experiencing and aid in diagnosing the pain as non-cardiac, or due to esophageal reflux/esophagitis. Both hydrochloric acid and an alternate saline control solution are infused one after the other via a nasogastric tube, without the patient being aware of the identity of the solution. The symptoms of chest pain are recorded as the patient identifies them.

91034
The physician performs a gastroesophageal reflux test using esophageal pH electrode placement and recording. This procedure evaluates the proper functioning of the lower esophageal sphincter, the strong muscular ring located at the entrance to the stomach. When this specialized muscle opens at the wrong time, stomach acid will flow back up into the esophagus, causing gastroesophageal reflux. A small, thin probe, or electrode, that measures the pH (acidity) level within the esophagus is affixed at the end of flexible nasal catheter tubing. The catheter is inserted through the nose down to the target area in the esophagus, usually determined by manometry, and connected to a data recorder. The probe records the pH level within the esophagus. Neutral pH is 7. The lower the number, the more acidic the environment. The stomach has a normal pH around 2. The pH recording may be done over the course of a day. The catheter/tubing is taped behind the ear and out of the way under clothing, and connected to a small data recorder

that is worn around the waist. This code includes the analysis and interpretation of the recorded results.

91035
The physician performs a gastroesophageal reflux test using mucosal attached telemetry pH electrode placement and recording. A small capsule containing a radiotelemetry pH sensor is inserted endoscopically in the esophagus and temporarily attached to the esophageal wall. The capsule monitors esophageal pH levels over a 48-hour period. This information is transmitted to an external pager-sized receiver worn by the patient that records pH levels. After the 48-hour testing period, the data is downloaded from the receiver to a computer that contains software for analyzing pH levels. The physician provides a written interpretation of the computer analysis. The capsule does not need to be removed as it spontaneously detaches within seven to 10 days and passes through the digestive tract.

91037-91038
The physician performs an esophageal function test with gastroesophageal reflux testing using nasal catheter intraluminal impedance electrode placement and recording. The patient fasts for a minimum of six hours. An impedance probe affixed to flexible nasal catheter tubing is inserted through the nose down to the lower esophageal sphincter following location of the lower sphincter by manometry. The impedance probe contains several electrodes that make up multiple measuring segments each 2 cm in length. The measuring segments are located at intervals above the proximal border of the lower esophageal sphincter. The patient is given a liquid or solid bolus to swallow. As the bolus passes through the esophagus, the average electrical resistance between two adjacent electrodes (impedance) is measured. The electrodes detect esophageal contraction and expansion and movement of the bolus through the esophagus in real time, as well as any gastroesophageal reflux. Esophageal function is evaluated by calculating the bolus transport time (BTT), which is the time it takes the bolus to pass from the proximal measuring segment and exit through the distal measuring segment. Contraction wave velocity (CWV), which is the speed of the contraction wave from the proximal measuring segment to the distal measuring segment, is also evaluated. This test is also referred to as multichannel intraluminal impedance testing or MII. Report 91037 for a recording of one hour or less. Report 91038 for prolonged recording of greater than one hour, up to 24 hours.

91040
The physician performs esophageal balloon distension provocation study to evaluate chest pain of undetermined etiology that is suspected to be noncardiac in origin. The patient fasts for a minimum of six hours. A local anesthetic is sprayed into the patient's throat. With the patient in an upright position, a probe is passed through the mouth into the esophagus. The subject is placed supine with the head of the exam table elevated approximately 30 degrees. Manometric pressure recordings are obtained to identify the upper and lower esophageal sphincters. The probe is removed and the physician inserts a balloon into the esophagus. The balloon is moved along the esophagus and inflated multiple times to increasing diameters at selected sites in the esophagus in an attempt to provoke chest pain in the patient. Pain is measured by conscious perception or objective responses to the stimuli. Perception of moderate to severe chest pain with low levels of balloon distension is considered to be positive for noncardiac chest pain.

91052
The physician performs a gastric analysis test, also known as a Hollander Test, to determine the acidity of stomach secretions, the effectiveness of a vagotomy, or the possibility or ulcer recurrence. The physician inserts a tube through the patient's nose or mouth and down into the stomach. Gastric contents are suctioned out for collection to determine basal acid output (BAO). Insulin, or other gastric secretion stimulant, such as histamine, pentagastrin, calcium, or secretin, is given to the patient. Blood glucose is monitored while continued collection of gastric contents is done. Following sample collection, gastric contents undergo volume, pH, acid concentration, and volume measurements. BAO is calculated in mmol of acid secreted/hour and compared to the stimulant induced peak acid output.

91055
The physician performs gastric intubation, collection of washings, and slide preparation with specimen for cytology. A tube is inserted through the patient's nose or mouth and down into the stomach. Fluid and cell samples are taken by washing the stomach with a fluid such as saline to increase the sample yield. The sample is preserved and mounted on a slide for microscopic viewing.

91065
The hydrogen breath test uses a measurement of hydrogen in the breath to test for a number of conditions that cause gastrointestinal symptoms. It can be used to diagnose lactase deficiency, fructose intolerance, bacterial overgrowth, or oro-cecal gastrointestinal (rapid) transit. Only anaerobic bacteria in the colon are capable of producing hydrogen. The bacteria produce hydrogen when they are exposed to unabsorbed food. Excessive amounts of hydrogen also may be produced in a condition called bacterial overgrowth. Bacterial overgrowth occurs when the bacteria in the colon move back into the small intestine. The bacteria are exposed to food in the small intestine that has not been fully digested and absorbed. Regardless of the condition causing the excessive production of hydrogen, the end result is the same.

Some of the hydrogen produced by the bacteria is absorbed into the blood flowing through the wall of the intestine and colon. The blood travels to the lungs where the hydrogen is released and exhaled in the breath where it can be measured. Prior to hydrogen breath testing, a special diet may be required and individuals must fast for at least 12 hours. At the start of the test, a sample breath is taken. The individual blows into and fills a balloon with a breath of air. The concentration of hydrogen from the sample breath is removed from the balloon and measured. The individual ingests a small amount of the test sugar (lactose, fructose, lactulose). Samples of breath are collected and analyzed for hydrogen every 15 minutes for three to five hours. After ingestion of test doses of the dietary sugars lactose and sucrose, any production of hydrogen is an indication that an intolerance condition is present. When oro-cecal gastrointestinal (rapid) transit is present, the test dose of undigested lactulose reaches the colon more quickly than normal, and, therefore, hydrogen is produced by bacteria in the colon. With bacterial overgrowth, ingestion of lactulose results in two separate periods in which hydrogen is produced: the first period produces excessive hydrogen caused by the bacteria in the small intestine and the second period produces excessive hydrogen caused by the bacteria in the colon.

91105

The physician performs gastric lavage, also known as stomach pumping. This code applies to evacuating stomach contents for therapeutic treatment, such as for ingested poisons or decompression for intestinal obstruction. A nasogastric or orogastric tube is inserted down into the patient's stomach and the stomach's contents are suctioned out with the aid of an irrigating fluid, such as saline. The physician removes the tube.

91110

Gastrointestinal (GI) tract imaging from inside the lumen of the intestinal tract is done in a non-invasive manner by capsule endoscopy, allowing the doctor to directly view the small intestine. The patient is required to fast for 10 hours before the procedure. The patient swallows the endoscopic capsule with a glass of water. Color video images from inside the GI tract are recorded as the natural peristaltic movement passes the capsule smoothly and painlessly through the system. The data is transmitted by sensors, secured to the patient's abdomen, from the capsule to a data recorder, worn like a belt around the patient's waist, while the patient goes about daily ambulatory activities. After eight hours, the patient returns the equipment for processing at the computer workstation. The physician views and interprets the images and prepares a report.

91111

Sensors are placed on the patient's chest. The patient swallows a camera capsule while reclining in a prone position. The capsule is the size of a vitamin capsule and is equipped with a camera in each end. The cameras capture hundreds of images each minute as the capsule moves down the esophagus. These images are transmitted to the sensors and are visualized and reviewed by the physician, who evaluates and reports upon the patient's condition and determines appropriate treatment as necessary. The capsule is for one-time use and will be excreted by the patient sometime after the procedure is complete.

91120

The physician performs a rectal sensation tone and compliance test using graded balloon distention to evaluate anorectal pathology. Tone tests for relaxation or rigidity in the rectum. Compliance tests the distensibility of the rectum. Sensation tests for fullness and discomfort upon distention. The patient is asked to empty his or her bowels. The patient is placed in left lateral decubitus position with the head lowered 20 degrees. The physician inserts a two-lumen catheter containing a cylindrical bag into the rectum. One lumen is used to inflate the bag; the other is used to measure pressure within the bag. With the distal end of the bag 5 cm from the anal verge, the bag is inflated with air. Inflation is slowly increased and sensation, tone, and compliance monitored. The balloon is deflated when the patient experiences discomfort and urgency lasting more than 30 seconds.

91122

The physician performs anorectal manometry to help in diagnosing constipation and/or incontinence due to myotonic dysfunction or suspected cases of Hirschsprung's Disease. Hirschsprung's Disease is a congenital absence of ganglion nerve cells in the plexus that innervates the colon and/or rectum to relax the internal anorectal sphincter in response to rectal distension. A manometry probe is advanced into the rectum after a digital exam. The probe is slowly withdrawn, taking continuous pressure measurements until the high pressure area of the anal sphincters is located. With the patient relaxed, the "basal anal pressure" is recorded, and highest pressures are recorded as the patient performs a maximum squeeze. The manometry catheter is inserted again with a rectal balloon that is slowly inflated to the patient's first sensation of fullness and the volume is recorded. The anal sphincter response to the rectal distention is also recorded. Another manometry technique using a 3 balloon apparatus may also be employed in which pressure measurements are taken as the external, middle, and internal rectal balloons are inflated and deflated to note threshold levels and sphincter responses.

91123

Abnormalities in the rectal emptying can lead to disorders of defecation and severe cases of impaction. Pulsed Irrigation Evacuation (PIE) of fecal impaction is an automated enema that is also used for bowel

Medicine

management of chronic constipation patients without voluntary bowel control (e.g., quadriplegics, paraplegics, and spina bifida). The PIE system consists of a speculum, tubing, a disposable collection container, and an electrical unit that delivers positive and negative air pressure through the tubing. During the procedure, small pulses of warm tap water are delivered into the rectum, serving to rehydrate feces and promote peristalsis.

91132-91133
In electrogastrography (EGG), electrodes are placed on the skin over the stomach at a specific distance from each other and attached to a recording computer. The electrical activity initiated by the distal two-thirds of the stomach (gastric electrical activity—GEA) is recorded and analyzed by the computer. Report 91132 when diagnostic electrogastrography is performed alone. Report 91133 when diagnostic EGG is performed in conjunction with the administration of a drug in an attempt to manipulate conditions and provoke a measurable abnormality.

92002
The physician sees a new patient, one who has not been seen within that group practice for at least three years, for intermediate ophthalmological services. The patient's medical history is reviewed, or interval history if more than three years have passed since the patient was seen within that group practice. General medical observations, an external ocular and adnexal examination, and other diagnostic procedures like ophthalmoscopy, biomicroscopy, or tonometry are done. The visit may include mydriasis (the dilation of the patient's pupils). Generally, the patient has an acute condition that does not require a comprehensive service or the patient is being examined for a chronic, but stable, condition (i.e., known cataract).

92004
The physician sees a new patient, one who has not been seen within that group practice for at least three years, for comprehensive ophthalmological services. The physician performs a complete visual system examination, reviews the patient's medical history, or interval history if more than three years have passed since the patient was seen, and performs a general medical observation in addition to external and ophthalmoscopic examinations. Gross visual fields and basic sensorimotor examinations are also done, including biomicroscopy, examination with cycloplegia (temporary immobilization of the ciliary body) or mydriasis (the dilation of pupils), and tonometry. Other examination techniques such as retinoscopy, keratometry, slit lamp viewing, tear testing, corneal staining, corneal sensitivity, fundus examination, and exophthalmometry may also be employed and are included in the comprehensive exam when initiation of diagnostic or treatment programs is dependent upon the examining techniques. It may take more than one patient encounter to complete this service.

92012
The physician sees an established patient for intermediate ophthalmological services. The patient's medical history is reviewed. General medical observations, an external ocular and adnexal examination, and other diagnostic procedures like ophthalmoscopy, biomicroscopy, or tonometry are done when required to continue the diagnostic and treatment regimen. The visit may include mydriasis (the dilation of the patient's pupils). Generally, the patient has an acute condition that does not require a comprehensive service or the patient is being examined for a chronic, but stable, condition (i.e., known cataract).

92014
The physician sees an established patient, one who has been seen by a doctor in that group practice within the last three years, for comprehensive ophthalmological services. The physician performs a complete visual system examination, reviews the patient's medical history, and performs a general medical observation in addition to external and ophthalmoscopic examinations. Gross visual fields and basic sensorimotor examinations are also done, including biomicroscopy, examination with cycloplegia (temporary immobilization of the ciliary body) or mydriasis (the dilation of pupils), and tonometry. Other examination techniques such as retinoscopy, keratometry, slit lamp viewing, tear testing, corneal staining, corneal sensitivity, fundus examination, and exophthalmometry may also be employed and are included in the comprehensive exam when initiation or continuation of diagnostic or treatment programs is dependent upon the examining techniques. It may take more than one patient encounter to complete the service.

92015
The examiner determines the prescription required for the patient's eyeglasses or contact lenses by evaluating the effectiveness of a series of lenses through which the patient is asked to view an eye chart. This is usually accomplished with a refractor, a device that contains a range of lens powers that can be quickly changed, allowing the patient to compare various combinations when viewing the eye chart. A prescription is issued; no fitting for eyeglasses or contact lenses occurs at this time.

92018-92019
The physician performs an eye exam and evaluation under general anesthesia. The patient may have significant injury or cannot otherwise tolerate the examination while conscious. This exam may include manipulation of the globe to establishing the passive range of motion or another manipulation to help in diagnosing the condition. Report 92018 for a complete

examination, such as when gonioscopy (see 92020) is done under anesthesia; and 92019 for a limited examination.

92020

The angle of the anterior chamber of the eye is examined in a gonioscopy to assess for angle closure glaucoma, iris neovascularization, or other injury or disease process in the anterior chamber. Since the cornea's curvature creates internal reflection when the anterior angle structures are viewed directly, a gonioscopic lens is used to observe the angle. Corneal integrity is first determined using fluorescein. The patient is given anesthesia, the goniolens is prepared, and the physician places it on the patient's cornea. The lens puts a concave surface against the cornea, eliminating its refracting surface and allowing the angle to be observed with oblique mirrors. With the illumination lamp and microscope set and the beam oriented parallel to the axis of the mirror, the gonioscopy is accomplished and the angle of the anterior chamber of the eye is examined. The lens is removed, the eye is irrigated, and the cornea is checked again.

92025

This procedure is also known as computer-assisted keratography or videokeratography. A computer images and analyzes the shape of the patient's cornea. The patient is placed facing a light-filled bowl shape. A digital camera resides at the base of the bowl, and the light pattern reflected from the bowl to the cornea is recorded by the camera. The topology of the cornea is then analyzed by the computer software, and reports are produced for physician evaluation.

92060

The examiner utilizes a series of vertical and horizontal prism bars or individual handheld prisms to measure ocular deviation in a sensorimotor examination. Ocular deviations, such as strabismus, are seen when the eyes position themselves to each other on axes different from what is needed. Ocular deviations can occur in the horizontal or vertical plane. The eyes may move in toward each other (convergent) or away from each other (divergent). One eye (monocular) or both eyes (binocular) may be affected. The deviation may be observed to be the same no matter what direction the eyes are looking (concomitant) or to vary depending on where the eyes are looking (nonconcomitant). These deviations can be caused by ocular muscle anomalies, trauma or disease, or neuromuscular damage. The patient is asked to focus on a distant or near object in varying locations. An occluder may be alternately used to cover one eye while testing the other. Multiple measurements are taken and interpreted and a report is prepared.

92065

The physician prescribes exercises to correct ocular problems, most frequently caused by ocular muscle imbalances. The patient is trained to perform these therapeutic exercises to improve vision by gaining the proper binocular cooperation of the eyes one with the other, such as when one eye's vision and movement is neglected to avoid seeing double. These exercises frequently include repetitive tasks with prisms, color cards, or rods and moving objects progressively closer or further away in different planes. This includes continuing medical direction and evaluation.

92070

The physician measures the patient's cornea for the fitting of a soft contact lens that has no refractive properties or, in the case of keratoconus, with refractive properties. This soft contact lens, often called a collagen shield, is placed over the cornea as a bandage to protect a damaged eye, to cushion a painful cornea, or to reshape the cornea in keratoconus. This code includes the supply of the lens.

92081

A visual field test measures the extent of the field of vision as an eye fixates straight ahead, with standard illumination. Any peripheral vision loss or blind spots are documented. The blind spots are plotted on visual field charts. This code reports a limited examination, such as a tangent screen, Autoplot, arc perimeter, or a single stimulus level automated test, such as Octopus 3 or 7. A tangent screen, for example, is a black screen made of felt mounted on the wall that has meridians, blind spot, and degrees from fixation stitched into it. Fixation is the direction of gaze that allows the object's visual image to fall on the central fovea of the retina—the area of most acute vision. With one eye occluded and full distance correction worn, white spots are introduced and the patient is tested at one and/or two meters. The points are transferred from screen to a chart.

92082

A visual field test measures the extent of the field of vision as an eye fixates straight ahead, with standard illumination. Any peripheral vision loss or blind spots are documented. This code describes an intermediate procedure and may involve the use of specialized methods. For example, the Goldmann perimeter may be used with at least two isopters plotted. An isopter is the outer margins of a visual field within which any particular object or stimulus should be seen. A hollow white spherical bowl device is positioned a set distance from the patient and luminous targets that differ in size and intensity are projected onto standardized background illumination, statically or kinetically. The stimulus check is usually static, not moving, when testing inside 30 degrees. This method can test the full limit of peripheral vision and uses internationally standardized testing conditions with fixation always monitored. Fixation is the direction of gaze that allows the object's visual image to fall on the central fovea of the retina—the area of most acute vision.

Medicine

Medicine

92083
A visual field test measures the extent of the field of vision as an eye fixates straight ahead, with standard illumination. Any peripheral vision loss or blind spots are documented. This code describes an extended procedure and may involve the use of specialized methods. The Goldmann perimeter may be used with at least three isopters plotted, plus a static check done within the central 30 degrees. An isopter is the outer margins of a visual field within which any particular object or stimulus should be seen. A hollow white spherical bowl device is positioned a set distance from the patient and luminous targets that differ in size and intensity are projected onto standardized background illumination, statically or kinetically. This method can test the full limit of peripheral vision and uses internationally standardized testing conditions with fixation always monitored. Fixation is the direction of gaze that allows the object's visual image to fall on the central fovea of the retina—the area of most acute vision.

92100
In a healthy eye's anterior chamber, aqueous humor is continually drained and renewed to maintain a constant overall pressure. Increased pressure from this fluid causes glaucoma and can lead to blindness. Serial tonometry involves multiple pressure checks over the course of a day to monitor significant peaks and acute elevations in intraocular pressure within a 24-hour period (diurnal curve). Different tonography testing equipment and techniques may be used. In Goldmann's applanation tonometry, or the blue-light glaucoma-screening test, the patient is given a drop of fluorescein staining dye and anesthetic. The forehead and chin are supported on a headrest. A slit lamp is positioned until the tonometer probe just touches the cornea and the physician can view a limbal glow, or blue light circle. This applanation method measures the force required to flatten a certain area of the cornea, which is dependent upon the pressure in the eye. The force per area is converted to the intraocular pressure measurement. A portable TonoPen is a device that gives an instant digital measurement when touched to the eye.

92120
In a healthy eye's anterior chamber, aqueous humor is continually drained and renewed to maintain a constant overall pressure. Increased pressure from this fluid causes glaucoma and can lead to blindness. Indentation tonometry is a method of measuring and recording intraocular pressure. This technique uses an instrument such as a flat or weighted plunger centered within a footplate or a probe. When the probe/footplate is placed on the cornea, the plunger force required to cause a lateral movement (indentation change) or displacement of the plunger on the flattened area of the cornea is measured based on the instrument weight used or the calibrated displacement sensitivity of the plunger. The measurements convert to the intraocular pressure within the eye. The findings are recorded on a scaled strip of paper or digitally. Interpretation and report are included.

92130
In a healthy eye's anterior chamber, aqueous humor is continually drained and renewed to maintain a constant overall pressure. Increased pressure from this fluid causes glaucoma and can lead to blindness. In tonographic water provocation testing, the patient drinks one quart of water after fasting and the intraocular pressure changes are measured and recorded using a tonometric device. Tonography indirectly measures the intraocular pressure by determining the amount of force required to cause an indentation or displacement on the eye. This force is relational to the resistance, hence pressure, within the eye.

92135
This procedure involves using a laser for computerized scanning ophthalmic diagnostic imaging of the posterior segment. One type of scanning laser currently in use for early detection of glaucoma is known as a scanning laser glaucoma test (SLGT). The SLGT analyzes the nerve fiber layer in the posterior portion of the eye using a confocal scanning laser ophthalmoscope and/or polarimetry. During the examination, the patient fixates on a light. A technician aligns and focuses the scanning instrument. The retinal nerve fiber layer (RNFL), which is the only part of the retina that can alter the state of polarized light, is scanned with a low power laser beam that double-passes the RNFL. The instrument measures the change in polarization (retardation) that is directly related to the thickness of the tissue. A computer analyzes the measurements compared to standardized norms. Results are displayed and the data is stored in the computer for use as a comparison for future testing. This code reports a unilateral procedure; interpretation and report are included.

92136
Optical Coherence Biometry (OCB) is an ophthalmic diagnostic test that measures the curvature of the cornea and the depth of the anterior chamber in addition to the axial length of the eye, without ultrasound. This is done to calculate the correct intraocular lens (IOL) power for implantation in order to come as close as possible to the target refraction after surgery. The procedure is non-invasive and uses partial coherence interferometry or birefringent light, as opposed to sound, to perform the imaging. The patient focuses on a small fixation point and the imaging of the eye is achieved with an instrument using light sources at certain wavelengths. When the highest quality axial length display has been found, subsequent measurements are taken and stored in a computer, as well as automatically transferred to an IOL calculator

program. This allows immediate and individualized computation of IOL implant options for the patient.

92140
In a healthy eye's anterior chamber, aqueous humor is continually drained and renewed to maintain a constant overall pressure. Increased pressure from this fluid causes glaucoma and can lead to blindness. In a provocative test for glaucoma, the patient is given drops to dilate the pupil, or may also be placed in a dark room, to cause the iris to fall forward in an attempt to close off the drainage angle. When the angle closes, pressure in the eye is measured for the increase in intraocular pressure since the fluid cannot drain. Increases at 10 mmHg or above are said to be indicative of risk for angle-closure glaucoma. The physician interprets the results and prepares a report. These tests are not commonly performed today and should be coded with care.

92225-92226
Ophthalmoscopy allows a complete view of the back of the eye. After the pupils have been dilated, views of the retina are seen with the indirect ophthalmoscope. The exam is extended. The direct ophthalmoscope allows the highly magnified view of the posterior portion of the retina; an indirect ophthalmoscope gives a broader view that includes the posterior and anterior retina and vitreous. An extended ophthalmoscopy can also be performed with a contact lens, three-mirror lens, or 90-diopter lens. One or both eyes are viewed and the physician sketches views of the patient's retinas and their defects. The initial exam (92225) may be insufficient for diagnosis. The follow-up is reported with 92226.

92230
Ophthalmoscopy allows a complete view of the back of the eye. This procedure is for detection of abnormalities of retinal blood vessels. The patient's eyes are dilated. The angioscopy begins when a small amount of fluorescein dye is injected into the arm. The dye is transported to the eye through the blood vessels. As the dye traverses the retinal vessels, the retina is viewed through the ophthalmoscope using filters that enhance the fluorescence of the eye.

92235
Ophthalmoscopy allows a complete view of the back of the eye. This procedure is for detection of abnormalities of retinal blood vessels. The patient's eyes are dilated. The angioscopy begins when a small amount of fluorescein dye is injected into the arm. The dye is transported to the eye through the blood vessels. As the dye traverses the retinal vessels, a motorized camera attached to an ophthalmoscope photographs a sequence, documenting the dye's progress through the vessels of the retina. Both eyes are photographed. The photographs are black and white. The circulation takes seconds, but photography continues in 10- to 30-minute intervals to check for late leakage of recirculating dye. The physician reviews the film and makes a diagnostic evaluation of the patient's retina.

92240
Ophthalmoscopy allows viewing of the eyeball's interior through the pupil. Indocyanine-green (ICG) dye fluoresces through blood and pigment and is used for detecting abnormalities in the vascular choroid, which lies between the retina and sclera. The patient's eyes are dilated. The angioscopy begins when a small amount of ICG is injected into the arm, and transported to the eye through the blood vessels. Rapid injection is essential. As the dye transverses the choroid, a motorized camera attached to an ophthalmoscope photographs a sequence, documenting the dye's progress through the choroidal vessels. The photography is generally performed bilaterally, but may be performed unilaterally. Photographs are in black and white. Timing for photography is determined by arm to retinal time. This is estimated at about 10 seconds in young patients and 12 to 18 seconds in older patients.

92250
Ophthalmoscopy allows a complete view of the back of the eye. The physician or technician aligns the fundus camera, which is attached to an ophthalmoscope, along the patient's optical axis after the patient's pupil has been dilated. The 35 mm camera is, in effect, a large ophthalmoscope that allows viewing of the retina and a light flash system for producing color photographs of the retina. Both eyes are photographed. The results are interpreted by the physician.

92260
The physician exerts pressure on the sclera with a spring plunger while observing with an ophthalmoscope the vessels of the optic disc. Ophthalmodynamometry gives a measurement of the relative pressures in the central retinal arteries. It is also an indirect means of assessing carotid artery flow on either side.

92265
The physician or technician applies concentric needle electrodes to the patient's extraocular muscles to record muscle actions. This procedure is mostly applied for research into eye movement.

92270
A normal retina has a predictable electrical response to light. The EOG records metabolic changes in the retinal pigment epithelium by evaluating the retina's response to light. The physician or technician places electrodes on the skin around the eye so that eye movements of both eyes can be recorded separately or together. The EOG is often used in cases where the electroretinography isn't sensitive enough to pick up macular degeneration. The physician interprets the results of the test.

92275
A normal retina has a predictable electrical response to light. To determine if the retina is damaged, the physician places an ocular fitted contact lens electrode on the patient's eye and another electrode on the forehead so that the retina's electrical responses to external stimuli can be recorded under light-adapted conditions. This procedure, often abbreviated ERG, is repeated in dark-adapted conditions. The ERG waves are analyzed by the physician.

92283
This test describes an extended color vision examination involving an anomaloscope or equivalent, which is an instrument used to diagnose abnormalities of color perception in which one-half of a field of color is matched by mixing two other colors.

92284
This exam tests the function of the two photoreceptors: the rods and the cones. Rods are most sensitive in dim illumination and are responsible for night vision. The cones are more sensitive in bright luminations and are responsible for day vision. The eye to be tested is exposed to a bright light and the room is darkened. At 30-second intervals, the light is increased and the effect of the stimulus on the retina is measured by a adaptometer machine.

92285
These photos are often referred to as anterior segment photography and are used to document abnormalities of the anterior segment that do not require magnification to be seen in the lids, cornea, anterior chamber, lens, and iris. The physician photographs the eye using a freestanding camera, a camera affixed to a slit lamp, goniophotography, or stereo-photography.

92286
The physician performs this microscopy, often called endothelial cell count or specular microscopy, to check the integrity and density of the endothelial cells that comprise the innermost layer of the cornea.

92287
The physician performs this microscopy to examine the iris. This procedure includes fluorescein angiography, which is for detection of abnormalities of retinal blood vessels. The angioscopy begins when a small amount of fluorescein dye is injected into the arm. The dye is transported to the eye through the blood vessels. As the dye traverses the vessels in the iris, the iris is viewed through the scope using filters that enhance the fluorescence of the eye. This test most often is used to delineate fine neovascularization of tumors in the anterior segment.

92310
Using a keratometer, the technician determines the patient's corneal curvatures. The lenses are fitted for power, size, curvature, flexibility, and lens type. The fitting includes instruction and training of the wearer and incidental revision of the lens during the training period. This code is to be used for both eyes and for non-aphakic patients.

92311-92312
Using a keratometer, the technician determines the patient's corneal curvature. The lens is fitted for power, size, curvature, flexibility, and lens type. The fitting includes instruction and training of the wearer and incidental revision of the lens during the training period. These codes are to be used for aphakic patients. Report 92311 if one eye is fitted or 92312 for both eyes.

92313
Using a keratometer, the technician determines the patient's corneal curvature. The corneoscleral lens is fitted for power, size, curvature, flexibility, and lens type. The fitting includes instruction and training of the wearer and incidental revision of the lens during the training period.

92314
Using a keratometer, the independent technician determines the patient's corneal curvature. The lens is fitted for power, size, curvature, flexibility, and lens type. The fitting includes instruction and training of the wearer and incidental revision of the lens during the training period. This code is to be used for both eyes and for non-aphakic patients.

92315-92316
Using a keratometer, the independent technician determines the patient's corneal curvature. The lens is fitted for power, size, curvature, flexibility, and lens type. The fitting includes instruction and training of the wearer and incidental revision of the lens during the training period. These codes are to be used for aphakic patients. Report 92315 if one eye is fitted or 92316 for both eyes.

92317
Using a keratometer, the independent technician determines the patient's corneal curvature. The corneoscleral lens is fitted for power, size, curvature, flexibility, and lens type. The fitting includes instruction and training of the wearer and incidental revision of the lens during the training period.

92325
The physician or technician uses a grinder to flatten or polish the contact lens or lens edge to provide a more comfortable fit.

92326
The ophthalmologist meets with the patient to discuss replacement of contact lenses, which may be due to wear and tear of the existing pair, loss, or discomfort. A new prescription is a separately reported service.

92340-92342
The physician or technician measures the patient's anatomical facial characteristics, records the laboratory

specifications, and performs the final adjustment of the monofocal (92340), bifocal (92341), or multifocal (92342) spectacles to the visual axes and anatomical topography.

92352-92353
The physician or technician measures the aphakic patient's anatomical facial characteristics, records the laboratory specifications, and performs the final adjustment of the monofocal (92352) or multifocal (92353) spectacles to the visual axes and anatomical topography.

92354
Some low vision aids are simply a convex lens mounted to spectacles. The physician or technician measures the patient's anatomical facial characteristics, records the laboratory specifications, and performs the final adjustment of the monofocal spectacles to the visual axes and anatomical topography.

92355
A focusable Galilean or Keplarian (internal prism) system in a spectacle frame is a popular choice. The fitting of the spectacles is separate from the prescription of the spectacles, which is considered part of the eye exam. The physician measures the anatomical facial characteristics, writes laboratory specifications, and makes the final adjustment of the spectacles to the visual axes and anatomical topography. The supply of materials is a separate component, as is the prescription.

92358
The physician or technician procures or provides a temporary, ready-made contact lens to a patient, whose natural intraocular lens had been previously removed surgically.

92370-92371
The physician or technician repairs or refits a pair of spectacles. Adjustments may be made to the ear or nosepieces or plastic frames may be heated and bent to better fit the patient, who has natural or artificial intraocular lenses. Report 92370 if the patient is not aphakic and 92371 if the patient is aphakic.

92502
Occasionally, a child or an adult is uncooperative and an otolaryngologic examination cannot be performed until the patient is placed under general anesthesia. At other times, as in the case of a trauma victim, the patient is already anesthetized. At this time a thorough examination of the ear, including otoscopy, nose, and larynx, is completed.

92504
The physician uses an operating binocular microscope to examine the ear and occasionally the nose for direct, detailed visualization.

92506
The physician takes a history of the patient, including speech and language development, hearing loss, and physical and mental development. A physical examination is performed. Hearing tests and speech/language evaluations are performed. Assessment of deficits and a plan for the patient are made. These plans may involve speech therapy, hearing aids, etc. In auditory processing disorders, the patient (usually children) cannot process the information heard due to lack of integration between the ears and the brain, even though hearing may be normal. Central auditory processing disorder (CAPD) is often confused with or functions as an underlying factor to a number of learning disabilities.

92507-92508
Under direction of a physician, the patient undergoes developmental programs such as speech therapy, sign language, or lip reading instruction or hearing rehabilitation. In auditory processing disorders, the patient (usually a child) cannot process the information heard due to lack of integration between the ears and the brain, even though hearing may be normal. Central auditory processing disorder (CAPD) is often confused with or functions as an underlying factor to a number of learning disabilities. The treatment program is for the individual in 92507 or in a group setting in 92508.

92511
The examination is performed with the patient lying on his back and under a local anesthetic with topical Lidocaine that is sprayed onto the back of the throat and into the nasal passages. The physician introduces the flexible fiberoptic endoscope through the nose and advances it into the pharynx to determine whether there are any fixed blockages such as a deviated septum, nasal polyps, or enlarged adenoids and tonsils. The physician may position the tip of the endoscope at the level of the hard palate and instruct the patient to perform simple maneuvers that demonstrate airway activity under conditions that promote or prevent collapse. The test may be performed to identify anatomic factors contributing to sleep disorder, stability of the upper airway, and determining treatments.

92512
Nasal function studies are performed for analyzing nasal resistance during breathing. In rhinomanometry, the physician uses a tubular probe to generate and transmit an audible sound signal into the patient's nasal cavity through an anatomically fitted nosepiece. A microphone picks up the sound from the nasal cavity and the data is analyzed by computer to determine area distance in the nasal cavity.

92516
Facial nerve functions studies, such as electroneuronography (EnoG), are used to diagnose facial paralysis disorders, such as Bell's palsy (a

Medicine

unilateral or bilateral facial paralysis due to a viral attack on the facial nerve). These tests include an ENoG or an electromyogram that measure nerve conduction to diagnose degenerative disorders. In an electromyogram, the physician attaches small disc electrodes to the skin surface over the muscle or nerve by inserting small metal needles into the areas. The needle or electrode may be changed as needed for a complete study. An oscilloscope displays and records the data.

92520
The physician inserts a laryngoscope through the mouth or nose to examine the larynx. An indirect laryngoscope uses mirrors to view the larynx, while a direct laryngoscope is done with a fiberoptic scope. The function studies are used to diagnose the reason for laryngeal dysfunction such as swallowing disorders, chronic hoarseness, or an obstruction.

92526
The treatment of swallowing disorders is aimed at finding the specific cause of the dysfunction to treat the problem, such as anti-reflux medications to decrease stomach acidity or improve esophageal motility. Patients who have had strokes and cannot be treated surgically or by drugs for swallowing dysfunctions may require assistance from a rehabilitation specialist. In severe cases, the physician may elect to insert a feeding tube through the nose or in the stomach through the abdomen.

92531
Nystagmus is uncontrolled rapid movement of the eyeball in a horizontal, vertical, or rotary motion. It can be a symptom of a disturbance in the patient's vestibular system and can be induced to measure the difference between the patient's right and left vestibular functions. The patient's eyes are observed for spontaneous nystagmus as the patient is asked to look straight ahead, 30 degrees to 45 degrees to the right, and 30 degrees to 45 degrees to the left. No electrodes are used and no recording made.

92532
A positional nystagmus test measures whether the eyes can maintain a static position when the head is in different position, which helps in documenting and quantifying patient complaints of dizziness in certain positions. The test also may be performed as a diagnostic tool to determine if an abnormality is associated with the central nervous system or the peripheral nervous system. The patient is placed in a variety of positions including supine with head extended dorsally, left and right, and sitting in an attempt to induce nystagmus. This is done with the patient's eye open so that eye movements can be observed directly. No recording electrodes are used to record the nystagmus.

92533
Nystagmus is uncontrolled rapid movement of the eyeball in a horizontal, vertical, or rotary motion. It can be a symptom of a disturbance in the patient's vestibular system and can be induced to measure the difference between the patient's right and left vestibular functions. In this test, each ear is separately irrigated with cold water and warm water to create nystagmus in the patient. The physician or audiologist observes the patient to detect any difference between the reaction of the right side and the left side. Four irrigations occur: a warm and cold irrigation for both the right and the left ear.

92534
A rotating drum made of alternating light and dark vertical stripes is placed in front of the patient and the patient is instructed to stare at the drum without focusing on any one stripe. The eyes are observed for nystagmus while the drum is rotated in one direction. The direction of the drum is reversed. No electrodes are used.

92540
The physician performs a basic vestibular evaluation with recordings, often to evaluate a patient complaint of dizziness. Nystagmus is uncontrolled rapid movement of the eyeball in a horizontal, vertical, or rotary motion. It can be a symptom of a disturbance in the patient's vestibular system and can be induced to measure the difference between the patient's right and left vestibular functions. ENG (electronystagmography) electrodes are placed and the patient is asked to look straight ahead, 30 degrees to 45 degrees to the right, and 30 degrees to 45 degrees to the left. Recordings are made to detect spontaneous nystagmus. In the positional nystagmus test, an ENG recording is made of the rapid eye movements occurring with the patient's head placed in a minimum of four positions (e.g., supine with head extended dorsally, left, right, and sitting). This is often done using infrared video recording systems. An optokinetic nystagmus test is usually done with a rotating drum of alternating light and dark vertical stripes. The drum is placed in front of the patient and the patient is instructed to stare at the drum without focusing on any one stripe. The drum is rotated in one direction and reversed and rotated in the opposite direction. ENG electrodes are used to record nystagmus. In an oscillating tracking test, the patient is asked to follow a swinging object such as a ball on a string. ENG electrodes are in place and a recording is made of the eye tracking the motion. The recording is analyzed for smoothness.

92541
Nystagmus is uncontrolled rapid movement of the eyeball in a horizontal, vertical, or rotary motion. It can be a symptom of a disturbance in the patient's vestibular system and can be induced to measure the difference between the patient's right and left vestibular

functions. ENG (electronystagmography) electrodes are placed and the patient is asked to look straight ahead, 30 degrees to 45 degrees to the right, and 30 degrees to 45 degrees to the left. Recordings are made to detect spontaneous nystagmus.

92542

Nystagmus is uncontrolled rapid movement of the eyeball in a horizontal, vertical, or rotary motion and can appear as a symptom of a disturbance in the patient's vestibular system. Nystagmus is measured to determine whether dizziness is due to a disease of the inner ear and whether it affects one or both sides. In the positional nystagmus test, an electronystagmography (ENG) recording is made of the rapid eye movements occurring with the patient's head placed in a variety of positions, e.g., supine with head extended dorsally, left, right, and sitting. This is often done using infrared video recording systems.

92543

Nystagmus is uncontrolled rapid movement of the eyeball in a horizontal, vertical, or rotary motion. It can be a symptom of a disturbance in the patient's vestibular system and can be induced to measure the difference between the patient's right and left vestibular functions. In this test, each ear is separately irrigated with cold water and warm water to create nystagmus in the patient. ENG recordings are evaluated to detect any difference between the nystagmus of the right side and the left side. Four irrigations occur: a warm and cold irrigation for both the right and the left ear.

92544

Nystagmus is uncontrolled rapid movement of the eyeball in a horizontal, vertical, or rotary motion. It can be a symptom of a disturbance in the patient's vestibular system and can be induced to measure the difference between the patient's right and left vestibular functions. This test is usually done with a rotating drum of alternating light and dark vertical stripes. The drum is placed in front of the patient and the patient is instructed to stare at the drum without focusing on any one stripe. The drum is rotated in one direction and reversed and rotated in the opposite direction. ENG electrodes are used to record nystagmus.

92545

Nystagmus is uncontrolled rapid movement of the eyeball in a horizontal, vertical, or rotary motion. It can be a symptom of a disturbance in the patient's vestibular system and can be induced to measure the difference between the patient's right and left vestibular functions. With ENG electrodes in place, the patient is asked to follow a swinging object such as a ball on a string. A recording is made of the eye tracking the motion. The recording is analyzed for smoothness.

92546

Nystagmus is uncontrolled rapid movement of the eyeball in a horizontal, vertical, or rotary motion. It can be a symptom of a disturbance in the patient's vestibular system and can be induced to measure the difference between the patient's right and left vestibular functions. The patient is seated in a rotary chair with the head bent forward 30 degrees. ENG electrodes are placed to measure nystagmus while the chair is rotated with the patient's eyes closed. A recording is made and studied to determine an abnormal labyrinthine response on one side or the other.

92547

ENG electrodes are placed to measure vertical and rotary nystagmus. List 92547 separately in addition to the code for the primary procedure, and use 92547 in conjunction with 92541-92546.

92548

Computerized dynamic posturography tests a patient's sensory organization, motor control, evoked postural responses (EMG), and sway patterns to assess balance and postural instability by systematic manipulation of somatosensory and visual information. The patient is placed in the posturography system. The system is made up of a force plate that controls foot support and a visual surround reference that can be controlled. Force transducers measure the vertical and horizontal force output of the patient's feet. The patient's center-of-force is used as an estimate of body sway during testing. A sway bar and potentiometer is placed at the pelvis and shoulder, which measures anterior-posterior position. Displacement of the visual surround is changed as the ankle angle is changed. In the posture portion of posturography, the support surface rotates faster than the body can move, producing a sway and ankle rotation that is opposite of what normally occurs in a standing position on a fixed surface. This exaggerated sway produces a stretching of the ankle joint, which is recorded as three surface EMG signals from the gastrocnemius and tibialis anterior muscles of the legs to a computer that records the data. Patients with normal function will maintain balance while patients with a disturbance of balance will elicit abnormal results. The EMG portion of posturography along with the sensory organization and motor control tests differentiate between the possible diagnoses causing the patient's imbalance and postural instability.

92550

The audiologist performs tympanometry and reflex threshold measurements. Tympanometry varies the pressure in the external ear canal and identifies the pressure at which maximum sound transmission occurs. This corresponds to current middle ear pressure status. Using an ear probe, the eardrum's resistance to sound transmission is measured in response to pressure changes. The pressures are recorded and compared to normal values. For reflex threshold measurements, the audiologist places a probe in one ear (ipsilateral ear) to measure the impedance of the middle ear and places an earphone on the patient's opposite ear (contralateral ear). A loud sound is presented in the contralateral or ipsilateral ear and the change in impedance caused by the contraction of the stapedius muscle is measured. The acoustic stapedial reflex threshold test (ASRT) measures response to acoustic stimuli (threshold) using the lowest intensity stimulus to obtain a reliable positive stapedial reflex with an acoustic meter. Among other applications, these measurements are used to diagnose neuro-otological conditions and/or determine the appropriate treatment or rehabilitation modalities.

92551
Earphones are placed and the patient is asked to respond to tones of different pitches and intensities. This is a limited study using a few different pitches and intensities. If a patient fails to respond appropriately, additional testing is indicated.

92552-92553
Often physicians or technicians can diagnose a cause of hearing loss through tests using an audiometer. Many causes of hearing loss have characteristic threshold curves. In pure tone audiometry, earphones are placed and the patient is asked to respond to tones of different pitches (frequencies) and intensities. The threshold, which is the lowest intensity of the tone that the patient can hear 50 percent of the time, is recorded for a number of frequencies on each ear. Bone thresholds (92553) are obtained in a similar manner except a bone oscillator is used on the mastoid or forehead to conduct the sound instead of tones through earphones. The air and bone thresholds are compared to differentiate between conductive, sensorineural, or mixed hearing losses.

92555-92556
Often physicians or technicians can diagnose a cause of hearing loss through tests using an audiometer. Many causes of hearing loss have characteristic threshold curves unique to that specific diagnosis. In speech audiometry, earphones are placed and the patient is asked to repeat bisyllabic (spondee) words. The softest level at which the patient can correctly repeat 50 percent of the spondee words is called the speech reception threshold. The threshold is recorded for each ear in 92555. This process occurs in 92556, in addition to a discrimination test. There, the word discrimination score is the percentage of spondee words that a patient can repeat correctly at a given intensity level above his or her speech reception threshold. This is also measured for each ear.

92557
Often physicians or technicians can diagnose a cause of hearing loss through tests using an audiometer. Many causes of hearing loss have characteristic threshold curves. In comprehensive audiometry, earphones are placed and the patient is asked to respond to tones of different pitches (frequencies) and intensities. The threshold, which is the lowest intensity of the tone that the patient can hear 50 percent of the time, is recorded for a number of frequencies on each ear. Bone thresholds are obtained in a similar manner except a bone oscillator is used on the mastoid or forehead to conduct the sound instead of tones through earphones. The air and bone thresholds are compared to differentiate between conductive, sensorineural, or mixed hearing losses. With the earphones in place, the patient is also asked to repeat bisyllabic (spondee) words. The softest level at which the patient can correctly repeat 50 percent of the spondee words is called the speech reception threshold. The threshold is recorded for each ear. The word discrimination score is the percentage of spondee words that a patient can repeat correctly at a given intensity level above his or her speech reception threshold. This is also measured for each ear.

92559
Often physicians or technicians can diagnose a cause of hearing loss through tests using an audiometer. Many causes of hearing loss have characteristic threshold curves. In audiometric testing of groups, many people are tested concurrently usually by pure tone screening. Earphones are placed and the patient is asked to respond to tones of different pitches and intensities. This is a limited study using a few different pitches and intensities.

92560-92561
Often physicians or technicians can diagnose a cause of hearing loss through tests using an audiometer. Bekesy audiometry is a complex and rarely used diagnostic test. A special audiometer is used to deliver pulsing and continuous tones to the patient through earphones. The patient makes an audiogram by pushing and relaxing a button to indicate whether or not the tone was heard at changing intensity levels. In 92560, the audiograms are used as a screening tool to determine hearing thresholds. In 92561, the tracings are analyzed and categorized into several different hearing patterns.

92562
Earphones are placed and tones of the same pitch but different intensities are presented to each ear (binaural) or tones of different intensities and pitches are presented to the same ear (monaural). The patient is asked to compare the loudness of the tones. Differences in intensities that are perceived by the patient as the same are measured.

92563
Earphones are placed and a tone is presented to the patient at a volume above the patient's lowest hearing level for that tone. Measurements are made of the time the tone is audible or the increase in volume needed to maintain an audible tone over time. These measurements are compared to established norms and can be reported at different tone frequencies.

92564

Earphones are placed and tones are presented to the patient. The loudness of the tones is increased in small increments. The patient is tested on the ability to detect slight changes in loudness. A percentage of the correctly identified loudness changes is recorded.

92565

This test is for unilateral pseudohypacusis (malingering). It is based on the principle that if two sounds of the same frequency but different intensities are presented simultaneously to both ears, only the louder tone will be heard. Tones are presented to the good ear at a level above that ear's threshold to obtain a response. Tones are presented to the poor ear simultaneously. The intensity of the sound in the poor ear is increased while the intensity presented to the good ear remains the same. The patient will respond until the intensity of the tones in the poor ear exceeds that of the good ear. At that point, the patient will not respond because the patient is not supposed to hear out of the poor ear. However, the patient should still respond, as the intensity of presentation to the good ear has not changed.

92567

Using an ear probe, the eardrum's resistance to sound transmission is measured in response to pressure changes. Tympanometry varies the pressure in the external ear canal and identifies the pressure at which maximum sound transmission occurs. This corresponds to current middle ear pressure status. The pressures are recorded and compared to normal values.

92568

The audiologist places a probe in one ear (ipsilateral ear) to measure the impedance of the middle ear and places an earphone on the patient's opposite ear (contralateral ear). A loud sound is presented in the contralateral or ipsilateral ear and the change in impedance caused by the contraction of the stapedius muscle is measured. The acoustic stapedial reflex threshold test (ASRT) measures response to acoustic stimuli (threshold) using the lowest intensity stimulus to obtain a reliable positive stapedial reflex with an acoustic meter. Among other applications, these measurements are used to diagnose neuro-otological conditions and/or determine the appropriate treatment or rehabilitation modalities.

92570

The audiologist performs acoustic immittance testing. Using an ear probe, the eardrum's resistance to sound transmission is measured in response to pressure changes. Tympanometry varies the pressure in the external ear canal and identifies the pressure at which maximum sound transmission occurs. This corresponds to current middle ear pressure status. The pressures are recorded and compared to normal values. To measure acoustic reflex threshold testing, the audiologist places a probe in one ear (ipsilateral ear) to measure the impedance of the middle ear and places an earphone on the patient's opposite ear (contralateral ear). A loud sound is presented in the contralateral or ipsilateral ear and the change in impedance caused by the contraction of the stapedius muscle is measured. The acoustic stapedial reflex threshold test (ASRT) measures response to acoustic stimuli (threshold) using the lowest intensity stimulus to obtain a reliable positive stapedial reflex with an acoustic meter. Among other applications, these measurements are used to diagnose neuro-otological conditions and/or determine the appropriate treatment or rehabilitation modalities. In the acoustic reflex decay test, the audiologist again places a probe to measure impedance in one ear and places an earphone on the other ear. A loud tone is presented to one of the ears and maintained for 10 seconds. The impedance change (acoustic reflex) is measured by the probe. In a normal ear, the reflex persists for 10 seconds. In an abnormal ear, the reflex diminishes at least 50 percent in the first five seconds. The presence or absence of this reflex is important in the diagnosis of middle ear dysfunctions. In neural hearing loss, this reflex adapts or decays. Determining whether it adapts or decays aids in differential diagnosis of sensory and neural hearing loss.

92571

The patient is presented monosyllabic words, which are low pass filtered, allowing only the parts of each word below a certain frequency (pitch) to be presented. A score is given on the number of correct responses. This test is most commonly used to identify central auditory dysfunction.

92572

With the patient wearing earphones, the audiologist presents bisyllabic (spondee) words in groups of two words. The first syllable of the first word is given to one ear (first word ear) and the last syllable of the first word is given to the same ear at the same time the first syllable of the second word is given to the opposite ear (second word ear). The second syllable of the second word is presented alone to the second word ear. The patient is asked to identify the words presented to each ear and a score is given for each ear.

92575

The audiologist places earphones on the patient and presents tones to the patient at different volumes and different frequencies (pitches). The volume at each frequency where the patient responds correctly 50 percent of the time is the threshold at that frequency. The sounds presented through the earphones are air-conduction. The air-conduction thresholds are measured in the presence of noise (masking) through a bone vibrator on the side of the head (bone-conducted masking). The masked and unmasked air-conduction thresholds are compared.

Medicine

92576
Using earphones, seven-word sentences that do not follow normal rules of grammar are presented to one ear while a taped story is presented to the other ear simultaneously (competition). The patient is scored on the ability to correctly identify the seven-word sentences. This test is principally used for central hearing disorders.

92577
This is a test for unilateral pseudohypacusis (malingering). It is based on the principle that if two sounds of the same frequency and different intensities are presented simultaneously to both ears, only the louder will be heard. Bisyllabic (spondee) words are presented to the good ear at a level above that ear's threshold to respond. Words are presented simultaneously to the poor ear. The intensity of the sound in the poor ear is increased while the intensity presented to the good ear remains the same. The patient will respond until the intensity of the words in the poor ear exceeds that of the good ear. At that point, the patient will not respond because the patient is not supposed to hear out of the poor ear. However, the patient should still respond, as the intensity of presentation to the good ear has not changed.

92579
Visual reinforcement audiometry (VRA) is used to test hearing in infants and in both difficult-to-test children and adults. The process includes case history and otologic examination, typically conducted in a sound booth. Lighted toys are used as reinforcement for response to auditory stimuli. Stimuli may include frequency-specific signals, calibrated noises, or live voice. The results are usually recorded on an audiogram. The interpretation of the testing addresses the type and the severity of hearing loss and any recommendations.

92582
Often physicians or technicians can diagnose a cause of hearing loss through tests using an audiometer. Many causes of hearing loss have characteristic threshold curves. Conditioning play audiometry tests pure tone air and bone conduction and speech thresholds in children. Test sounds can be presented with earphones or sound field testing (pure tone air conduction only). The child is conditioned to perform a simple task (i.e., drop a block in a bucket) when the test sound is heard.

92583
Often physicians or technicians can diagnose a cause of hearing loss through tests using an audiometer. Many causes of hearing loss have characteristic threshold curves. In select picture audiometry, the patient is placed in a booth with or without earphones. The patient is asked to identify different pictures with the instructions given at different intensity levels. A threshold level for speech, which is the intensity level at which the patient responds correctly 50 percent of the time, is obtained.

92584
An electrode is placed through the tympanic membrane into the promontory of the inner ear. The ear is stimulated and recordings are made of the electrical response of the cochlear nerve. This can be done under local, topical, or general anesthesia.

92585-92586
Electrodes are placed in various locations on the scalp and electrical recordings are made in response to auditory stimulations. The origin of the electrical response is believed to be from the auditor nerve and brain stem. The physician interprets the results of the tests. Report 92585 if the procedure is comprehensive. Report 92586 if the test is limited.

92587-92588
A probe tip is placed in the ear canal. The probe tip emits a repeated clicking sound. The clicking sound passes through the tympanic membrane, middle ear, and to the inner ear. In the inner ear, the sound is picked up by the hair cells in the cochlea. Computerized equipment is able to record an echo off the hair cell in the cochlea. Report 92587 if the test is limited to a single stimulus level. Report 92588 if the test is comprehensive or a diagnostic evaluation.

92590-92591
The physician takes a history of hearing loss. The patient's ears are examined. Medical or surgical treatment is offered if possible. The appropriate type of hearing aid is selected to fit the patient's pattern of hearing loss. Report 92590 if one ear is fitted with a hearing aid and 92591 if both ears receive aids.

92592-92593
The audiologist inspects the hearing aid and checks the battery. The aid is cleaned and the power and clarity are checked using a special stethoscope, which attaches to the hearing aid. Report 92592 if a monaural hearing aid is checked and 92593 if both hearing aids are checked.

92594-92595
A printout from a hearing aid analyzer is used to compare the electroacoustical characteristics of a monaural hearing aid with the specifications for that aid in 92594 or a binaural hearing aid with specifications for that aid in 92595.

92596
This test can be performed in one of several ways. One method is to check the speech or pure tone threshold, which is the intensity at which the patient responds correctly 50 percent of the time, with and without ear protection (ear plugs or earphones) while the patient is in a soundproof booth.

92597
A voice prosthetic device, such as an amplifier, is used to augment speech for a patient with complete or partial speech loss. This code applies to evaluating the patient for use of and/or fitting the device often by a speech therapist or physician.

92601-92602
A diagnostic analysis of a cochlear implant, including programming, is done post-operatively to fit the previously placed external devices, connect to the implant, and program the stimulator. Cochlear implants are equipped with software that allows for different programming specific to the patient's daily activities. Threshold levels, volume, pulse widths, live-voice speech adjustments, input dynamic range, and frequency shaping templates are evaluated and set according to individual needs. This is done for patients 7 years of age and younger in 92601. For children 7 years of age and younger, speech stimuli are used more frequently to determine the optimal setting. Report 92602 for subsequent modifications or reprogramming.

92603-92604
A diagnostic analysis of a cochlear implant, including programming, is done post-operatively to fit the previously placed external devices, connect to the implant, and program the stimulator. Cochlear implants are equipped with software that allows for different programming specific to the patient's daily activities. Threshold levels, volume, pulse widths, live-voice speech adjustments, input dynamic range, and frequency shaping templates are evaluated and set according to the individual needs. This is done for patients older than 7 years of age in 92603. Patients older than 7 years of age are able to provide significant feedback for fine-tuning adjustment. Report 92604 for subsequent modifications or reprogramming.

92605
The assessment for the appropriate non-speech-generating augmentative and alternative communication (AAC) device is highly variable and dependent on the patient's age, ability, and motivation. Motor skills, hearing, vision, cognitive abilities, language comprehension, and general health are evaluated to determine the suitability of a high-tech or low-tech device. Once these are evaluated, an appropriate AAC device is prescribed.

92606
This code includes therapeutic services associated with the use of non-speech generating devices. Services differ according to the device used. Electronic equipment may require routine maintenance, programming, and mounting systems. Other equipment may require customization (e.g., symbol boards). Non-speech generating devices may require some patient therapeutic, rehabilitation, or occupational training.

92607-92608
The patient is evaluated face to face by a specialist to determine the motor skills, hearing, cognitive abilities, comprehension, natural speech, esophageal and pharyngeal air flow, general health, and patient motivation for prescription of speech-generating augmentative and alternative communication (AAC) device. Once these are evaluated, an appropriate speech-generating device is prescribed. Report 92607 for the first hour and 92608 for each additional 30 minutes.

92609
This code includes therapeutic services associated with the use of speech generating devices. Services differ according to the device used. Electronic equipment may require routine maintenance, programming, or modification. Speech generating devices may require some patient therapeutic, rehabilitation, or occupational training.

92610
The patient is evaluated to determine the oral and pharyngeal swallowing function. Assessment of the oral cavity includes the size, position, resting tone, range of motion and development of the tongue, lips, and palate. Palpation of the thyroid notch or cricoid arch with swallowing is used to determine elevation of the pharynx. Using a curved probe, sensation of the oral cavity may be assessed. An inventory of cranial nerves must also be included.

92611
Motion fluoroscopic examinations are done of the swallowing function by cine or video recording. The patient is seated upright in a normal eating posture. Small amounts of liquid barium and barium-coated foods of varying consistencies, textures, and flavors are administered allowing visualization of the swallowing function by fluoroscopy. The patient is given liquids, pastes, and solid foods that are visually followed from the oral cavity to the pharynx and the cervical esophagus. A portion of this test is usually repeated with the patient in a horizontal position.

92612-92613
A flexible fiberoptic nasopharyngoscope is positioned posterior to the soft palate to allow visualization during swallowing. The patient is given foods of varying consistencies dyed with food coloring to aid visualization of the swallowing function. Liquids, pastes, and solid food are ingested separately and visualized. The procedure is recorded by cine or video. Report 92613 for physician interpretation and report only.

92614-92615
A flexible fiberoptic laryngoscope is inserted into the nasal passage and advanced just proximal to the test site for laryngeal sensory evaluation. Air pulses of varying degrees in intensity are administered. Vocal

fold adduction of the laryngeal adductor reflex is evaluated for vocal fold movement, absence of movement, or swallow initiation and visualized on a video monitor. The procedure is recorded by cine or video. Report 92615 for physician interpretation and report only.

92616-92617
A flexible fiberoptic nasopharyngoscope is positioned posterior to the soft palate to allow visualization during swallowing. The patient is given foods of varying consistencies dyed with food coloring to aid visualization of the swallowing function. Liquids, pastes, and solid food are ingested separately and visualized. After this portion is complete, laryngeal sensory testing is initiated. A flexible fiberoptic laryngoscope is inserted into the nasal passage and advanced just proximal to the test site. Air pulses of varying degrees in intensity are administered. Vocal fold adduction of the laryngeal adductor reflex is evaluated for vocal fold movement, absence of movement, or swallow initiation and visualized on a video monitor. The procedure is recorded by cine or video. Report 92617 for physician interpretation and report only.

92620-92621
The audiologist evaluates central auditory function. Central auditory processes are the auditory mechanisms that are responsible for what the brain does with what the ears hear. Many individuals have no difficulty detecting the presence of sound but have other auditory difficulties related to central auditory processes such as understanding conversation in noisy environments, following complex directions, and learning new vocabulary words. There are two major categories of tests: behavioral tests and electrophysiologic tests. The behavioral tests can be monotic or dichotic. Monotic tests use a single stimulus presented to one ear at a time or tests in which two stimuli are presented to one ear. Dichotic tests use the same stimulus applied to both ears. Testing may be performed on only one ear (monaural) or both ears simultaneously (binaural). Specific types of tests that can be given include monaural low-redundancy speech tests, dichotic speech tests, temporal patterning tests, and binaural interaction tests. The audiologist selects the appropriate battery of central auditory function tests after evaluating the patient using routine hearing tests. Central auditory function tests are used to differentiate central from peripheral hearing loss and occasionally to identify the site of a lesion in the central nervous system. Report 92620 for the first 60 minutes of the evaluation and 92621 for each additional 15 minutes.

92625
The audiologist performs a tinnitus assessment including pitch, loudness, matching, and masking. Subjective tinnitus is an acoustic like sensation, often described as a ringing sound located within the head, for which there is no external cause. Other descriptions of the sound include roaring, hissing, music, crickets, and static-like. A tinnitus assessment is performed to determine the exact nature of the acoustic sensation or sound. First the pitch or frequency of the tinnitus is determined and then the loudness of the sensation or sound. The audiologist tries to reproduce or match the pitch and loudness using sound generators designed for this purpose. The masking process also uses sound generators to identify external sound stimuli that mask the tinnitus. Masking is a procedure that makes the tinnitus less distracting to the patient by use of a controlled noise that covers the noise of the tinnitus.

92626-92627
The patient is evaluated face to face by a physician or speech and language therapist to evaluate the status of auditory rehabilitation therapies that includes listening inventories and phonetic discrimination testing to determine the patient's level of sound perception and sound discrimination ability. Rehabilitation goals include maximizing auditory skills and communication abilities. These rehabilitation goals progress from awareness of environmental sound to increasingly higher levels of speech discrimination. Report 92626 for the first hour and 92627 for each additional 15 minutes.

92630-92633
Auditory rehabilitation is auditory training or therapy conducted by a physician, speech and language therapist, or teacher of the hearing impaired. Pre-lingual hearing loss therapies (92630) remedy hearing impairments that are acquired before the child has acquired language (usually due to trauma or disease) or are congenital in etiology. Post-lingual hearing loss therapies (92633) remedy hearing impairments that occur after the acquisition of speech and language and can be due to disease, medication side effects, or trauma. Post-lingual hearing usually progresses gradually. Rehabilitation goals include maximizing auditory skills and communication abilities. These rehabilitation goals progress from awareness of environmental sound to increasingly higher levels of speech discrimination.

92640
A diagnostic analysis of an auditory brainstem implant, including programming, is done post-operatively to fit the previously placed external devices, connect to the implant, and program the stimulator. Auditory brainstem implants are equipped with software that allows for different programming specific to the patient's daily activities. Threshold levels, volume, pulse widths, live-voice speech adjustments, input dynamic range, and frequency shaping templates are evaluated and set according to individual needs.

92950
Cardiopulmonary arrest occurs when the patient's heart and lungs suddenly stop. In a clinical setting, cardiopulmonary resuscitation, the attempt at restarting the heart and lungs, is usually directed by a physician or another health care provider who is certified in Advanced Cardiac Life Support (ACLS). The patient's lungs are ventilated by mouth-to-mouth breathing or by a bag and mask. The patient's circulation is assisted using external chest compression. An electronic defibrillator may be used to shock the heart into restarting. Medications used to restart the heart include epinephrine and lidocaine.

92953
A temporary pacemaker is placed on the patient's heart to regulate heartbeats considered dangerously irregular. The physician applies electrodes to the chest wall. The electrodes give small electronic shocks through the chest to pace the heart as controlled by the physician.

92960-92961
The physician may administer an electronic shock to the patient's chest to regulate heartbeats considered dangerously irregular. The physician uses a defibrillator machine and places two paddles on the patient's chest and/or back. A measured electric shock is delivered through the chest to the heart to convert the heartbeat to a regular rhythm. Report 92960 for external cardioversion and 92961 when the procedure is performed internally.

92970
In internal circulatory assist, the femoral artery is cannulated and a catheter with balloon or other device is inserted into the aorta. Various devices may be used to assist circulation. This code should be reported for the internal insertion of such a device, but should not be used to report intra-aortic balloon pump (IABP) or implantation of ventricular assist devices that are reported elsewhere.

92971
Devices are placed at the outside of the body to assist circulation. One example of external circulatory assist is Military Anti-Shock Trousers (MAST), which apply counterpressure around the legs and abdomen. The artificial peripheral resistance helps coronary perfusion. In a related procedure, pressure cuffs are used to assist circulation. The patient is placed on a treatment table where their lower extremities are wrapped in a series of three compressive air cuffs, which inflate and deflate in synchronization with the patient's cardiac cycle. During diastole the three sets of air cuffs are inflated sequentially (distal to proximal) compressing the vascular beds within the muscles of the calves, lower thighs, and upper thighs. This action results in an increase in diastolic pressure, generation of retrograde arterial blood flow, and an increase in venous return. The cuffs are deflated simultaneously just prior to systole, which produces a rapid drop in vascular impedance, a decrease in ventricular workload, and an increase in cardiac output. The augmented diastolic pressure and retrograde aortic flow appear to improve myocardial perfusion, while systolic unloading appears to reduce cardiac workload and oxygen requirements. The increased venous return coupled with enhanced systolic flow appears to increase cardiac output.

92973
The physician percutaneously removes a blood clot from a native or grafted coronary artery. A double lumen catheter is passed to the area of the clot. A high-pressure saline stream (via a pump) is introduced through a lumen that has multiple jet orifices located at the distal tip. The low-pressure zone created by the jets causes the clot to break-up into small pieces and be pushed through the catheter with a force that drives debris from the thrombus through the other lumen (exhaust) and out of the body. The procedure is useful to clear fatty and degenerated arteries and to modify plaques in preparation for more definitive treatment with adjunctive balloon angioplasty or stenting.

92974
Using an X-ray machine in a cardiac catheterization laboratory, the physician places the delivery catheter in the coronary artery at the site of the in-stent restenosis (re-blockage in the artery). The transfer delivery device is connected to the delivery catheter; the transfer delivery device is used to deliver the radioactive seeds to the location. There are various methods for transcatheter placement, but commonly the methods involve the use of a guiding catheter. The radioactive seeds are positioned at the location for an appropriate length of time to administer radiation to the artery. At the completion of the radiation treatment, the radioactive seeds are returned to the transfer device.

92975-92977
In 92975 the physician places a hollow catheter in the aorta from the arm or leg via a small incision. Using fluoroscopic guidance, the physician advances the catheter tip to the coronary artery to be treated and confirms the presence of thrombus (blood clot) in the artery by injecting contrast material through the catheter into the artery. In 92977 a catheter equipped with an infusion tip is threaded into the vessel. The physician infuses a thrombolytic agent (urokinase, for example) into the affected artery in order to dissolve the thrombus. The physician may perform contrast injections to assess the size and extent of the thrombus after infusion of the thrombolytic agent. The catheter is removed from the patient's body. Pressure is placed over the incision to stem bleeding. The patient is observed for a period afterward.

92978-92979
Intravascular ultrasound may be used during diagnostic evaluation of a coronary vessel or graft. It may also be used both before and after a therapeutic

Medicine

intervention upon a coronary vessel or graft to assess patency and integrity of the vessel or graft. A needle is inserted through the skin and into a blood vessel. A guide wire is threaded through the needle into a coronary blood vessel or graft. The needle is removed. An intravascular ultrasound catheter is placed over the guide wire. The ultrasound probe is used to obtain images from inside the vessel to assess area and extent of disease prior to interventional therapy as well as adequacy of therapy after interventional therapy. The ultrasound probe provides a two-dimensional, cross-sectional view of the vessel or graft as the probe is advanced and withdrawn along the area of interest. When the ultrasound examination is complete, the catheter is removed. Report 92978 for the initial vessel or graft. In 92979, the physician advances the ultrasound catheter into additional vessels or grafts to assess patency and structure. The catheter and guide wire are removed and pressure is applied over the puncture site to stop bleeding.

92980-92981
A stent is used to hold open a blocked or collapsed blood vessel in the heart. The physician makes a small incision in the arm or leg. Two catheters are placed. A central venous catheter is inserted through the femoral or brachial artery and a second catheter is threaded up to the heart. Any obstruction is first treated by inflating a balloon at the tip of the second catheter (PTCA) and/or by using a rotary cutter (atherectomy) to flatten or remove the obstruction. A stent is introduced through a catheter and placed under radiographic guidance. Pressure is placed over the incision for 20 to 30 minutes to stem bleeding. The patient is observed for a period afterward. Report 92980 for one coronary vessel. Report 92981 for each additional vessel.

92982-92984
The physician makes a small incision in the arm or leg. Two catheters are placed. A central venous catheter is inserted through the femoral or brachial artery and a second catheter with a balloon tip is threaded up to the heart. The physician inflates the balloon at the tip of the second catheter to flatten plaque obstructing the artery against the walls of the artery. If sufficient results are not obtained after the first inflation, the physician may reinflate the balloon for a longer period of time or at greater pressure. The catheter is removed. Pressure is placed over the incision for 20 to 30 minutes to stem bleeding. The patient is observed for a period afterward. Report 92982 for the balloon catheterization of one blocked vessel. Report 92984 for each additional vessel treated.

92986-92990
Valvuloplasty is a procedure for opening a blocked valve. The physician makes a small incision in the arm or leg. Two catheters are placed—a central venous catheter and a second catheter threaded up to the heart. The physician inflates a balloon at the tip of the second catheter to open the blocked valve. The catheter is removed. Pressure is placed over the incision for 20 to 30 minutes to stem bleeding. The patient is observed for a period afterward. Report 92985 if the procedure is performed on the aortic valve; 92987 if the procedure is performed on the mitral valve; and 92990 if the procedure is performed on the pulmonary valve.

92992
Certain congenital heart defects, particularly those involving transposition of the great vessels, require surgical creation or enlargement of an opening in the interatrial septum (wall) that separates the upper right and left chambers of the heart. The physician makes a small incision in the arm or leg. Two catheters are placed—a central venous catheter and a second catheter threaded up to the heart. When the foramen ovale has not closed, a deflated balloon (Rashkind-type) is passed through the foramen ovale, inflated, and pulled through the atrial septum, enlarging the opening and improving oxygenation of the blood. When the septum is intact, the deflated balloon (Rashkind-type) is passed from the right atrium through the septum to the left atrium, inflated, and withdrawn, creating an interatrial septal defect and improving oxygenation of the blood. The catheters are removed. Pressure is placed over the incision for 20 to 30 minutes to stem bleeding. A cardiac catheterization may be included. The patient is observed for a period afterward.

92993
The purpose of this procedure is to increase blood flow across the atrial septum in children with certain forms of cyanotic congenital heart disease. This procedure is used as an alternative to the Rashkind procedure (balloon method of atrial septostomy), typically in infants older than 1 month of age. The physician makes a small incision in the femoral vein. The physician places a transseptal sheath in the right femoral vein using standard methods, advancing the sheath to the superior vena cava under fluoroscopic or echocardiographic guidance. The physician uses a transseptal needle to cross the atrial septum, entering the left atrium. The physician introduces a guidewire into the left atrium and removes the transseptal catheter while leaving the wire in place. The physician advances a septostomy catheter over the wire into the left atrium. This catheter has a retracted blade, which the physician extends. The physician pulls the blade slowly across the atrial septum from the left into the right atrium, under fluoroscopic or echocardiographic guidance. The physician may make several passes with the blade catheter in this fashion. The physician removes the septostomy catheter and venous sheath. Pressure is placed over the incision for 20 to 30 minutes to stem bleeding. The patient is observed for a period afterward.

92995-92996
The physician removes the atherosclerotic plaque blocking the coronary artery. The physician makes a small incision in the arm or leg. Two catheters are placed. A central venous catheter is inserted through the femoral or brachial artery and a second catheter threaded up to the heart blockage. The blockage is removed using a rotary cutter introduced through a catheter under radiographic guidance. The blockage may also require subsequent inflation of the balloon on the tip of the second catheter to flatten any remaining plaque. The catheters are removed. Pressure is placed over the incision for 20 to 30 minutes to stem bleeding. The patient is observed for a period afterward. Report 92995 for the first vessel. Report 92996 for each additional vessel.

92997
The purpose of this procedure is to use a balloon to expand a narrowed pulmonary artery. The physician places an introducer sheath in the femoral vein, using percutaneous puncture. The physician places an angioplasty catheter through the introducer sheath into the femoral vein and advances it under fluoroscopic guidance to the right ventricle and out into the main pulmonary artery. The physician advances the angioplasty balloon into the narrowed pulmonary artery, using injections of x-ray contrast material to guide the way. The physician inflates the balloon to expand the pulmonary artery, sometimes using several balloon inflations. The physician removes the catheter and sheath from the femoral vein. Vessel hemostasis is achieved using manual pressure. Pressure is placed on the wound for 20 to 30 minutes to stem bleeding.

92998
Following single vessel percutaneous transluminal pulmonary artery balloon angioplasty (92997), the physician redirects the balloon angioplasty catheter to an additional pulmonary artery. The physician may change to a different sized balloon catheter if the additional pulmonary artery is of different size. The physician inflates the balloon to expand the pulmonary artery, sometimes using several balloon inflations. The physician removes the catheter and sheath from the femoral vein. Pressure is placed on the wound for 20 to 30 minutes to stem bleeding.

93000
Twelve electrodes are placed on a patient's chest to record the electrical activity of the heart. A physician interprets the findings. This code is used to report the combined technical and professional components of an ECG.

93005
Twelve electrodes are placed on a patient's chest in a standard pattern to record the electrical activity of the heart. This code is used to report the technical component only.

93010
A physician interprets a previously acquired recording of the heart's electrical activity acquired by placing 12 electrodes on the patient's chest. This code is used to report only the professional component.

93012
A patient uses a portable unit to record the electrical activity of the heart. Following a symptomatic episode, the electrocardiogram rhythm strips recording is transmitted by telephone to the physician for printing. This code is reported one time per every 30 days of 24-hour attended monitoring. This code is used to report the technical component only.

93014
A patient uses a portable unit to record the electrical activity of the heart. The recording is transmitted by telephone to the physician for printing. This code applies to the physician's interpretation of the printed report.

93015
A continuous recording of electrical activity of the heart is acquired by an assistant supervised by a physician while the patient is exercising on a treadmill or bicycle and/or given medicines. The stress on the heart during the test is monitored. This code includes the test, physician supervision, and physician interpretation of the report.

93016
An assistant supervised by a physician makes a continuous recording of the electrical activity of a patient's heart while the patient is exercising on a treadmill or stationary bicycle with or without medication. This code applies only to the physician's supervision of the test.

93017
An assistant supervised by a physician makes a continuous recording of the electrical activity of a patient's heart while the patient is exercising on a treadmill or stationary bicycle with or without medication. This code applies only to acquiring the test.

93018
An assistant supervised by a physician records the electrical activity of a patient's heart while the patient is exercising on a treadmill or stationary bicycle with or without medication. This code applies to the physician's interpretation of a previously acquired report.

93024
The purpose of the study is to evaluate for coronary artery spasm. If ergonovine is not available, certain other ergot medications may be infused for the same purpose. Following baseline coronary angiography (coded elsewhere), the physician infuses gradually escalating doses of ergonovine into a peripheral vein,

Medicine

while monitoring for chest discomfort and electrocardiographic changes. Repeat angiography is performed during ergonovine infusion to assess the size of the coronary lumen. If the patient develops symptomatic coronary spasm, the physician may directly infuse vasodilating medications through the intracoronary catheter to relieve the problem.

93025
T-Wave Alternans testing is an electrocardiographic method of measuring the alternating electrical amplitude from beat to beat on an electrocardiogram and is used as a method of evaluating ventricular arrhythmia risk. Microvolt T-wave alternans can be measured during exercise or pharmacologic stress, or during cardiac pacing, using a spectral analytic method with equipment that is able to detect as little as one microvolt of T-wave alternans. In electrode placement for a 12-lead ECG, the health care provider positions the leads on the wrists and ankles or shoulders and groins. Left leg electrodes are placed below the heart (but not on the chest), preferably below the umbilicus. The sensing electrodes look at the inferior surface of the heart, the left or lateral side of the heart, and at the right side of the heart.

93040
One to three electrodes placed on a patient's chest are used to record electrical activity of the heart. The physician interprets the report.

93041
An assistant records the electrical activity of the heart by placing one to three electrodes on a patient's chest in a predetermined pattern. This code describes the tracing only.

93042
A physician interprets a recording of electrical activities of a patient's heart acquired by placing one to three electrodes on the patient's chest.

93224-93227
The purpose of this study is to evaluate the patient's ambient heart rhythm during a full daily cycle. The physician instructs the patient in the use of a wearable electrocardiographic (ECG) recorder (also known as a Holter monitor). A technician places ECG leads on the patient's chest, and the patient wears the recorder for 24 hours. The patient returns the device, and the recorded heart rhythm is played back into digital format by a technician. The technician uses visual superimposition scanning to classify different ECG waveforms and to generate a report. The generated report describes the overall rhythm and significant arrhythmias. Rhythm strips are also generated. Code 93224 reports the recording, scanning analysis with report, physician review of the data, and the provision of a final interpretation in a report. Code 93225 reports the recording only, which includes connection, recording of data, and disconnection; code 93226 reports only the scanning analysis with report; code 93227 reports only the physician review and interpretation.

93228-93229
Mobile cardiovascular telemetry (MCT) uses external electrodes placed on the patient's body to continuously record electrocardiographic rhythm. Data segments are transmitted to a remote surveillance location by phone signal (cellular or landline); this is accomplished automatically and does not require patient intervention. Selected rhythm segments may be triggered for transmission automatically by rapid and slow heart rates or by the patient during a symptomatic episode. Data are analyzed continuously in real time. A remote technician responds to the alerts from the wearable device, reviewing the data and notifying the physician depending on the stipulated criteria. Report code 93228 for physician review and interpretation with report, and 93229 for technical support to include connection, instructions to the patient for use, attended surveillance, analysis, and transmission of daily and emergent data reports per physician protocol. These codes may be reported only once per 30-day period.

93230-93233
The purpose of this study is to evaluate the patient's ambient heart rhythm during a full daily cycle. The physician instructs the patient in the use of a wearable electrocardiographic (ECG) recorder (also known as a Holter monitor). A technician places ECG leads on the patient's chest, and the patient wears the recorder for 24 hours. The patient returns with the device, which is disconnected. Code 93231 includes hook-up, recording, and disconnection. Analysis/report is coded separately (93232), as is physician review and interpretation (93233). If all of these services are to be billed together, use 93230. This range of codes does not include superimposition scanning.

93235-93237
The purpose of this study is to evaluate the patient's ambient heart rhythm using wearable electrocardiographic rhythm-derived monitoring. A technician places ECG leads on the patient's chest, and the electrocardiographic signals are monitored for 24 hours. A computer classifies different ECG waveforms in real time. Intermittent full-sized waveform tracings are generated when the computer flags an abnormal rhythm or possibly when the patient activates the device. A report is generated by the computer, often with the help of a technician. If this is done without physician review and interpretation, report 93236. If physician review and interpretation are billed separately, report 93237. If monitoring and data analysis with report are to be billed together with physician review and interpretation, report 93235.

93268-93272
The purpose of this study is to evaluate the patient's ambient heart rhythm during symptoms. The physician instructs the patient in the use of a wearable rhythm monitor. A technician places ECG leads on the patient's chest, and the monitor uses a continuous loop mechanism to constantly record the patient's rhythm. During symptoms, the patient activates the monitor by pressing a button. The resulting recording includes ECG activity prior to and during symptoms. The patient uses the device to transmit the recording over the telephone line, allowing a rhythm printout to be generated. The physician reviews and interprets this rhythm strip. Code 93268 reports transmission and physician review and interpretation; code 93270 reports the recording only (including connection, recording, and disconnection); code 93271 reports monitoring, receipt of transmissions, and analysis; and code 93272 reports only the physician review and interpretation. These codes are reported only one time per 30-day time period of 24-hour attended monitoring.

93278
Electrodes placed on a patient's chest record the heart's electrical activity. This technique uses signal-averaged electrocardiography (SAECG) and may include a standard electrocardiogram.

93279-93281
A programming device evaluation is performed in person in order to test the device's function and select the most favorable permanent programmed values. Patients with previously implanted pacemakers require periodic programming device evaluations. This diagnostic procedure includes a face-to-face assessment of all device functions. Components that must be evaluated in order to assign a code from this range include the battery, leads, capture and sensing function, heart rhythm, and programmed parameters. Stored and measured data regarding these components are retrieved using an office, hospital, or emergency room instrument. This information is assessed to discern battery voltage, lead impedance, and settings for rhythm treatment and tachycardia detection, as well as to determine the pacemaker's current programming. If necessary, the sensing value and rate response, upper and lower heart rates, AV intervals, pacing voltage and pulse duration, and diagnostics are adjusted. These codes include physician review and interpretation and report, and are assigned per procedure. Report 93279 for evaluation of a single-lead pacemaker system (one in which there is pacing and sensing function in only one chamber of the heart). Report 93280 for evaluation of a dual-lead device (one with pacing and sensing function in only two chambers). Report 93281 for evaluation of a multiple-lead device (one with pacing and sensing function in three or more chambers).

93282-93284
A programming device evaluation is performed in person in order to test the device's function and select the most favorable permanent programmed values. Patients with previously implanted cardioverter-defibrillator (ICD) systems require periodic programming device evaluations. This diagnostic procedure includes a face-to-face assessment of all device functions. Components that must be evaluated in order to assign a code from this range include the battery, leads, programmed parameters, presence or absence of therapy for ventricular tachyarrhythmias, and heart rhythm. Stored and measured data regarding these components are retrieved using an office, hospital, or emergency room instrument. This information is assessed to discern battery voltage, lead impedance, and settings for rhythm treatment and tachycardia detection, as well as to determine the ICD's current programming. If necessary, the sensing value and sensor rate response, upper and lower heart rates, AV intervals, pacing voltage and pulse duration, and diagnostics are adjusted. Ventricular tachycardia detection and therapies may also be altered. These codes include physician review, interpretation, and report, and are assigned per procedure. Report 93282 for evaluation of a single-lead ICD system (one in which there is pacing and sensing function in only one chamber of the heart). Report 93283 for evaluation of a dual-lead device (one with pacing and sensing function in only two chambers). Report 93284 for evaluation of a multiple-lead device (one with pacing and sensing function in three or more chambers).

93285
A programming device evaluation is performed in person in order to test the device's function and select the most favorable permanent programmed values. Patients with previously placed implantable loop recorder (ILR) systems require periodic programming device evaluations. This diagnostic procedure includes a face-to-face assessment of all device functions. Components that must be evaluated include heart rate and rhythm during recorded episodes (both patient-initiated and device algorithm detected events), as well as programmed parameters. Stored and measured data are retrieved using an office, hospital, or emergency room instrument. This information is assessed to discern current programming and to evaluate specific aspects of the device's function. If necessary, the bradycardia and tachycardia detection criteria will be adjusted. This code includes physician review, interpretation, and report, and is assigned per procedure.

93286-93287
A programming device evaluation is performed in person in order to test the device's function and select the most favorable permanent programmed values. Patients with previously implanted pacemaker or

Medicine

cardioverter-defibrillator (ICD) systems may require adjustment of the device to patient-specific settings prior to a surgery, test, or procedure. The device system data is interrogated to evaluate the battery, leads, and sensors, as well as the stored patient and system measurements. If necessary, the device is programmed to settings appropriate for the surgery, test, or procedure. A postprocedure evaluation and programming is also performed, with adjustments as required. Report 93286 for evaluation and programming of a single-, dual-, or multiple-lead pacemaker system. Report 93287 for evaluation of a single-, dual-, or multiple-lead ICD system. Both codes include physician analysis, review, and report.

93288-93292

Patients with a previously implanted device, such as a cardiac pacemaker, implantable cardioverter-defibrillator (ICD), implantable cardiovascular monitor (ICM), or implantable loop recorder (ILR), require periodic interrogation device evaluations. This diagnostic procedure includes a face-to-face assessment of all device functions. Components that must be evaluated in order to assign code 93288 include the battery, lead(s), capture and sensing function, heart rhythm, and programmed parameters of a single-, dual-, or multiple-lead pacemaker system. Code 93289 requires evaluation of the battery, lead(s), capture and sensing function, heart rhythm derived elements, presence or absence of therapy for ventricular tachyarrhythmias, and programmed parameters of a single-, dual-, or multiple-lead ICD system. Code 93290 requires analysis of at least one recorded physiologic cardiovascular data element obtained from internal or external sensors and evaluation of programmed parameters of an ICM. Code 93291 requires evaluation of heart rate and rhythm during recorded episodes (from both patient-initiated and device algorithm detected events), as well as evaluation of programmed parameters, of an ILR. Code 93292 reports an interrogation device evaluation of a wearable defibrillation system. These codes include physician analysis, review, and report. They also include connection, recording, and disconnection, and are assigned per procedure.

93293

Patients with previously implanted pacemakers require periodic analysis of pacemaker function. A pacemaker may be implanted to control a patient's irregular heartbeat. This code applies to transtelephonic pacemaker monitoring, a form of evaluation in which the patient sends a rhythm strip over the telephone using a transmitter. This transmission is recorded by a receiving location using a receiver/recorder. The rhythm strip is recorded both with and without a magnet being applied over the pacemaker and is assessed for heart rate and rhythm as well as atrial and ventricular capture and sensing (if observed). The pacemaker's battery status is also determined. Code 93293 may be reported for a single, dual, or multiple lead pacemaker system, and includes physician analysis, review, and report. This code should be reported only once per 90-day period.

93294-93296

Patients with a previously implanted device, such as a cardiac pacemaker or implantable cardioverter-defibrillator (ICD), require periodic interrogation device evaluations. These codes report remote evaluations only and apply to single-, dual-, or multiple-lead devices. Code 93294 reports the remote evaluation of a pacemaker system with interim physician analysis, review, and report. Components that must be evaluated in order to assign this code include the battery, lead(s), capture and sensing function, heart rhythm, and programmed parameters. Code 93295 reports the remote evaluation of an ICD system with interim physician analysis, review, and report; required evaluation components include the battery, lead(s), capture and sensing function, heart rhythm derived elements, presence or absence of therapy for ventricular tachyarrhythmias, and programmed parameters. Code 93296 reports the acquisition of remote data, transmission receipt and technician review, technical support, and result distribution and applies to both pacemaker and ICD systems. Codes from this range may be reported only once per 90-day period.

93297-93299

Patients with a previously implanted device, such as an implantable cardiovascular monitor (ICM) or implantable loop recorder (ILR), require periodic interrogation device evaluations. These codes report remote evaluations only and may be reported only once per 30-day period. Code 93297 reports the remote evaluation of an ICM and includes the analysis of at least one recorded physiologic cardiovascular data element obtained from internal or external sensors. Physician analysis, review, and report are also included. Code 93298 requires the analysis of recorded heart rhythm data and also includes the physician's review and report. Code 93299 reports remote data acquisition, transmission receipt and review by a technician, technical support, and distribution of results, and applies to both ICM and ILR devices.

93303

Transducers are placed on the patient's chest to record an echocardiograph, which uses ultrasound to visualize the heart's function, blood flow, valves, and chambers. This code applies to an evaluation for congenital defects.

93304

Transducers are placed on a patient's chest to record an echocardiograph, which uses ultrasound to visualize the heart's function, blood flow, valves, and chambers.

This code applies to a follow-up or a limited evaluation for congenital defects.

93306-93308
This is a noninvasive study that uses ultrasound to visualize the heart's function, blood flow, valves, and chambers. Two-dimensional echocardiography, also referred to as real-time imaging, is performed using multiple transducers or a rotating transducer, and these images are recorded on videotape. Computer reconstruction provides the two-dimensional image of specific planes of the heart. M-mode, when performed, provides additional detail of specific portions of the heart. A stationary ultrasound beam is directed at the area of the heart requiring additional study. Report 93306 for a complete evaluation that includes spectral and color flow Doppler, which provide information regarding intracardiac blood flow and hemodynamics. Report 93307 for a complete evaluation but without spectral or color flow Doppler. Report 93308 for a follow-up or limited study.

93312-93314
Transesophageal echocardiography (TEE) is an invasive technique whereby the transducer is placed at the tip of an endoscope and introduced into the patient's esophagus to record a two-dimensional echocardiograph. This set of codes should be used for TEE used to diagnose cardiac sources of emboli, prosthetic heart valve malfunction, endocarditis, aortic dissection, cardiac tumors, and valvular heart disease excluding congenital heart disease. Code 93312 applies to a complete evaluation including probe placement, image acquisition, and the physician's interpretation. Report 93313 for probe placement only. Report 93314 for image acquisition, physician interpretation, and report only.

93315-93317
Transesophageal echocardiography (TEE) is an invasive technique whereby the transducer is placed at the tip of an endoscope and introduced into the patient's esophagus to record a two-dimensional echocardiograph. This set of codes should be used for TEE used to diagnose cardiac sources of emboli, prosthetic heart valve malfunction, endocarditis, aortic dissection, cardiac tumors, and valvular heart disease excluding congenital heart disease. The set of codes is specific to evaluations for congenital defects. Report 93315 for a complete evaluation of congenital defects, including probe placement, image acquisition, and the physician's interpretation. Report 93316 for probe placement only. Report 93317 for image acquisition, physician interpretation, and report only.

93318
Transesophageal echocardiography (TEE) is an invasive technique whereby the transducer is placed at the tip of an endoscope and introduced into the patient's esophagus to record a two-dimensional echocardiograph. TEE provides high-quality, real-time images of the beating heart and mediastinal structures. This code reports ongoing hemodynamic monitoring using TEE. TEE may be used to monitor critically ill patients in the intensive care unit as well as patients in certain operative settings. In both the intensive care unit and the operating room, it is used to monitor cardiac function including cardiac preload, contractility, and valve function in patients with acute hemodynamic decompensation. In addition, TEE may also be used to assess and monitor mediastinal, heart, lung, and aortic injury resulting from blunt chest trauma even in patients undergoing other life-saving procedures.

93320-93321
Transducers are placed on a patient's chest to record a Doppler echocardiograph, which uses ultrasound to visualize blood flow velocity, direction, and type of flow in different locations in the heart. Doppler studies can be displayed on a strip chart or video recorder. Report 93320 for a complete evaluation and 93321 for limited or follow-up studies.

93325
The technique for Doppler color flow velocity mapping is similar to that of other echocardiographs with transducers being placed on the patient's chest to record cardiac activity. Color Doppler is two-dimensional Doppler in which the signal is encoded with color to more clearly identify flow direction. List 93325 separately in addition to the code for echocardiography (76825, 76826, 76827, 76828, 93303, 93304, 93308, 93312, 93314, 93315, 93317, 93350, and 93351).

93350-93352
In this range of codes, transducers are placed on a patient's chest to record a two-dimensional echocardiograph, which uses ultrasound to visualize the heart's function, blood flow, valves, and chambers. Code 93350 applies to the echocardiography completed while the patient is at rest and exercising on a treadmill or stationary bicycle with or without medication and includes M-mode recording, when performed. Code 93351 also includes the performance of continuous electrocardiographic monitoring with supervision by the physician. Code 93352 is assigned as an additional code to report the use of an echocardiographic contrast agent during the stress test and should not be reported more than once per stress echocardiogram. Supply of the contrast agent and/or the drugs used in pharmacologic stress are reported separately in addition to these procedure codes.

93501
The physician threads a catheter to the heart, most frequently through an introducing sheath placed percutaneously into the femoral vein. However, the physician may elect to use the subclavian, internal jugular, or antecubital vein instead. The catheter is threaded into the right atrium, through the tricuspid

valve into the right ventricle, and across the pulmonary valve into the pulmonary arteries. ECG monitoring for the entirety of the procedure is included. Blood samples, pressure and electrical recordings, and/or other tests are performed through the catheter. This code applies to catheterizing the heart's right side only.

93503
The physician threads a catheter to the right heart through a central intravenous line often inserted up the femoral vein to take blood samples, pressure and electrical recordings, and/or other tests. This code applies to the insertion of a flow directed catheter, such as the Swan-Ganz device, used for measuring pressure and related parameters.

93505
The physician threads a catheter to the heart through a central intravenous line often inserted up the femoral vein to take tissue samples of the heart's septum.

93508
The physicians performs a catheter placement in coronary arteries, arterial coronary conduits, and/or venous coronary bypass grafts for coronary angiography without concomitant left heart catheterization. The physician places an introducer sheath in an artery, typically the femoral artery, using percutaneous puncture. The physician advances an angiography catheter through the introducer sheath into the ascending aorta and advances it, under fluoroscopic guidance, to the opening of the coronary artery, arterial coronary conduit, or venous coronary bypass graft. The physician injects radiopaque contrast material through the catheter into the vessel while recording a cineangiogram. The physician removes the catheter and sheath from the femoral artery. Pressure is placed on the wound for 20 to 30 minutes to stem bleeding.

93510-93511
The physician threads a catheter to the heart, most frequently through an introducing sheath placed percutaneously into the femoral, brachial, or axillary artery using retrograde technique. Using this technique, the catheter passes through the aortic valve into the left ventricle. Blood samples, pressure and electrical recordings, and/or other tests are performed. ECG monitoring for the entirety of the procedure is included. Report 93510 for percutaneous catheter placement. Report 93511 when surgical dissection or a cutdown is required to locate the artery.

93514
The physician performs left heart catheterization by left ventricular puncture. The physician uses this approach to the left heart when standard approaches cannot be performed, usually due to abnormal anatomy or the presence of prosthetic heart valves. The physician locates the left ventricular apex using palpation, fluoroscopy, and possibly echocardiography. The physician anesthetizes the skin overlying the ventricle, using local anesthetic. The physician punctures the skin and chest wall with a large bore needle, aimed into the left ventricular cavity. The physician introduces a guidewire through the needle into the left ventricle and removes the needle backwards over the guidewire. The physician advances a catheter over the needle and into the left ventricular cavity. The physician manipulates the catheter to record left heart pressures and may inject radiographic contrast through the catheter to obtain a left ventriculogram.

93524
The physician threads a catheter to the heart using combined retrograde and transseptal techniques to evaluate left heart function. The retrograde portion is performed through an introducing sheath placed percutaneously into the femoral, brachial, or axillary artery. The catheter is passed through the aortic valve into the left ventricle. Transseptal catheterization involves passing a catheter from the right femoral vein to the right atrium. The interatrial wall or septum is punctured and the catheter is passed into the left atrium through the mitral valve and into the left ventricle. Blood samples, pressure, electrical recordings, and/or other measurements are obtained.

93526
This procedure is performed to evaluate both right and left heart function. To accomplish right heart catheterization, the physician threads a catheter through an introducing sheath placed percutaneously into the femoral, subclavian, internal jugular, or antecubital vein. The catheter is threaded into the right atrium, through the tricuspid valve into the right ventricle, and across the pulmonary valve into the pulmonary arteries. Left heart catheterization is also performed, in this case using retrograde technique. The catheter is inserted through an introducing sheath placed percutaneously into the femoral, brachial, or axillary artery. The catheter is passed through the aortic valve into the left ventricle. ECG monitoring for the entirety of the procedure is included. Blood samples, pressure and electrical recordings, and/or other tests are performed through the catheter.

93527
This procedure is performed to evaluate both right and left heart function. To accomplish right heart catheterization, the physician threads a catheter through an introducing sheath placed percutaneously into the femoral, subclavian, internal jugular, or antecubital vein. The catheter is threaded into the right atrium, through the tricuspid valve into the right ventricle, and across the pulmonary valve into the pulmonary arteries. Left heart catheterization is also performed using transseptal technique. A catheter is threaded into the right atrium where the interatrial septum (wall) is punctured and the catheter is inserted into the left atrium and passed through the mitral valve

and into the left ventricle. Retrograde left heart catheterization may also be performed. When retrograde technique is used, a catheter is inserted through an introducing sheath placed percutaneously into the femoral, brachial, or axillary artery. The catheter is passed through the aortic valve into the left ventricle. ECG monitoring for the entirety of the procedure is included. Blood samples, pressure and electrical recordings, and/or other tests are performed through the catheter.

93528
This procedure is performed to evaluate both right and left heart function. To accomplish right heart catheterization, the physician threads a catheter through an introducing sheath placed percutaneously into the femoral, subclavian, internal jugular, or antecubital vein. The catheter is threaded into the right atrium, through the tricuspid valve into the right ventricle, and across the pulmonary valve into the pulmonary arteries. To evaluate left heart function, a direct percutaneous puncture into the left ventricle is performed. Retrograde left heart catheterization may also be performed. When retrograde technique is used, a catheter is inserted through an introducing sheath placed percutaneously into the femoral, brachial, or axillary artery. The catheter is passed through the aortic valve into the left ventricle. ECG monitoring for the entirety of the procedure is included. Blood samples, pressure, electrical recordings, and/or other measurements are made.

93529
This procedure is performed to evaluate both right and left heart function. To accomplish right heart catheterization, the physician threads a catheter through an introducing sheath placed percutaneously into the femoral, subclavian, internal jugular, or antecubital vein. The catheter is threaded into the right atrium, through the tricuspid valve into the right ventricle, and across the pulmonary valve into the pulmonary arteries. Left heart catheterization is also performed using transseptal technique. In this case, a catheter is threaded into the right atrium and passed through an existing septal opening into the left atrium. It is passed through the mitral valve and into the left ventricle. Retrograde left heart catheterization may also be performed. When retrograde technique is used, a catheter is inserted through an introducing sheath placed percutaneously into the femoral, brachial, or axillary artery. The catheter is passed through the aortic valve into the left ventricle. ECG monitoring for the entirety of the procedure is included. Blood samples, pressure and electrical recordings, and/or other tests are performed through the catheter.

93530
The physician performs a right heart catheterization for congenital cardiac anomalies. The physician investigates congenital cardiac anomalies by measuring pressures, taking blood samples for oximetry, and/or injecting contrast to assess chamber size and function. The physician places an introducer sheath in a vein (typically, the femoral vein) using percutaneous puncture. The physician places a lumen catheter through the introducer sheath into the femoral vein and advances it, under fluoroscopic guidance, to the heart chamber receiving venous circulation. The physician may use the fluid filled catheter to record intracardiac pressures, withdraw blood samples, or inject radiopaque contrast material. The physician removes the catheter and sheath from the femoral vein. Pressure is placed on the wound for 20 to 30 minutes to stem bleeding.

93531
The physician performs combined right heart catheterization and retrograde left heart catheterization to investigate congenital cardiac anomalies. The physician places an introducer sheath in a vein (typically, the femoral vein) using percutaneous puncture. The physician places a lumen catheter through the introducer sheath into the femoral vein and advances it, under fluoroscopic guidance, to the heart chamber receiving venous circulation. The physician places an introducer sheath in an artery (typically, the femoral artery) using percutaneous puncture. The physician places a lumen catheter through the introducer sheath into the femoral artery and advances it, under fluoroscopic guidance, through the aorta to the heart chamber providing arterial circulation. The physician may use the fluid filled catheters to record intracardiac pressures, withdraw blood samples, or inject radiopaque contrast material. The physician removes the catheters and sheaths from the femoral vessels. Pressure is placed on the wound for 20 to 30 minutes to stem bleeding.

93532
The purpose of this procedure is to investigate congenital cardiac anomalies by measuring pressures, taking blood samples for oximetry, and/or injecting contrast to assess chamber size and function. The physician places an introducer sheath in a vein (typically, the femoral vein) using percutaneous puncture. The physician places a lumen catheter through the introducer sheath into the femoral vein and advances it, under fluoroscopic guidance, to the heart chamber receiving venous circulation. The physician exchanges this catheter over a wire for a transseptal puncture needle, dilator, and sheath. The physician advances the transseptal puncture apparatus to the right atrium and punctures the intraatrial septum with the needle. The physician advances the needle, dilator, and transseptal sheath into the left atrium. The physician may also perform retrograde left heart catheterization as follows. The physician places an introducer sheath and lumen catheter in an artery (typically, the femoral artery) using percutaneous puncture. The physician advances the lumen catheter,

under fluoroscopic guidance, through the aorta to the heart chamber providing arterial circulation. The physician may use the fluid filled catheters to record intracardiac pressures, withdraw blood samples, or inject radiopaque contrast material. The physician removes the catheters and sheaths from the femoral vessels. Pressure is placed on the wound for 20 to 30 minutes to stem bleeding.

93533
The purpose of this procedure is to investigate congenital cardiac anomalies by measuring pressures, taking blood samples for oximetry, and/or injecting contrast to assess chamber size and function. The physician places an introducer sheath in a vein (typically, the femoral vein) using percutaneous puncture. The physician places a lumen catheter through the introducer sheath into the femoral vein and advances it, under fluoroscopic guidance, to the heart chamber receiving venous circulation. The physician directs this catheter through an existing septal opening into the left atrium. The physician may also perform retrograde left heart catheterization as follows. The physician places an introducer sheath and lumen catheter in an artery (typically, the femoral artery) using percutaneous puncture. The physician advances the lumen catheter, under fluoroscopic guidance, through the aorta to the heart chamber providing arterial circulation. The physician may use the fluid filled catheters to record intracardiac pressures, withdraw blood samples, or inject radiopaque contrast material. The physician removes the catheters and sheaths from the femoral vessels. Pressure is placed on the wound for 20 to 30 minutes to stem bleeding.

93539
The physician injects dye through a previously placed and separately reportable catheter threaded through a central line. This code applies to injecting dye into arterial conduits to check patency with fluoroscopy. Any required repositioning of catheters or use of automatic power injectors is included in this procedure.

93540
The physician injects dye through a previously placed and separately reportable catheter threaded through a central line. This code applies to injecting dye into bypass grafts of coronary arteries to check patency with fluoroscopy. The catheter is removed and pressure applied to the wound. Any required repositioning of catheters or use of automatic power injectors is included in this procedure.

93541
The physician injects dye through a previously placed catheter threaded through a central line. This code applies to injecting dye into the pulmonary artery to evaluate function with fluoroscopy. The catheter is removed and pressure applied to the wound. Any required repositioning of catheters or use of automatic power injectors is included in this procedure.

93542
The physician injects dye through a previously placed catheter threaded through a central line. This code applies to injecting dye into the right ventricle or atrium to evaluate function with fluoroscopy. The catheter is removed and pressure applied to the wound. Any required repositioning of catheters or use of automatic power injectors is included in this procedure.

93543
The physician injects dye through a previously placed catheter threaded through a central line. This code applies to injecting dye into the left ventricle or atrium to evaluate function with fluoroscopy. Any required repositioning of catheters or use of automatic power injectors is included in this procedure.

93544
The physician injects dye through a previously placed and separately reportable catheter threaded through a central line. This code applies to injecting dye into the aorta to evaluate function with fluoroscopy. Any required repositioning of catheters or use of automatic power injectors is included in this procedure.

93545
The physician injects dye through a previously placed and separately reportable catheter threaded through a central line. This code applies to injecting dye into the coronary arteries to evaluate function with fluoroscopy. Any required repositioning of catheters or use of automatic power injectors is included in this procedure.

93555
During separately reportable cardiac catheterization and injection procedures, the physician supervises imaging and interprets the findings in a written report. This code applies to imaging supervision for injection procedures of atrial and ventricular spaces.

93556
During separately reportable cardiac catheterization and injection procedures, the physician supervises imaging and interprets the findings in a written report. This code applies to imaging supervision for injection procedures of the pulmonary vessels, aorta, and heart blood vessels, including venous bypass grafts and arterial conduits.

93561-93562
Indicator dilution studies use a technique based on the principle that the volume of a fluid within a container can be determined by adding a known quantity of an indicator to the fluid and measuring the concentration of the indicator after it has completely mixed with the fluid. A time-concentration curve arises and the area of the inscribed curve is calculated. The physician threads

a catheter through a central line leading to the heart and dye, such as nontoxic, water-soluble indocyanine green, or a thermal indicator, usually iced saline, is injected. In the thermodilution method, cardiac output is measured by a computer using an equation that incorporates body temperature, injection volume and temperature, time, and other calculated ratios over a denominator of the integral of the change in blood temperature during the cold injection, reflected by the area of the inscribed curve. Report 93562 if a subsequent cardiac output measurement is taken.

93571-93572
A diagnostic angiography is the x-ray visualization of the heart and blood vessels after the introduction of a radiopaque contrast medium. Testing for patient hypersensitivity to the iodine content of the medium is advised before the radiopaque substance is used. The physician injects the contrast medium into a catheter inserted into a peripheral artery and threaded through the vessel to the visceral site. A Doppler ultrasound records blood velocity and pressure by measuring the frequency of ultrasonic waves reflected from moving surface. This code reports the Doppler measurements of the initial vessel; a second code reports the primary coronary angiography procedure. Report 93572 for each additional vessel beyond the initial vessel.

93580
A congenital atrial septal defect is closed percutaneously by catheter. This procedure may be performed on infants or adults, usually under moderate sedation. After heparinization in induced, a combined right and left heart catheterization is first undertaken through the existing septal opening. Contrast material is injected for atrial and ventricular angiograms to map the anatomy. Using a specialized catheter, the atrial defect is crossed from the right atrium into the left. The catheter is threaded into the upper left pulmonary vein. A guidewire is inserted, the catheter is removed, and a balloon is threaded over the guidewire into position across the defect and inflated with low pressure. The "stretched" diameter of the defect is measured. Testing is carried out to ensure that the repair will remain hemodynamically stable by occluding the defect temporarily with the balloon while taking right-side pressures and saturation measurements. A dilator and sheath holding the device are advanced over the guidewire and positioned in the left atrium. Positioning is checked using echocardiography or fluoroscopy before releasing the device. The implant is deployed across the atrial opening and positioning is checked again. Any leaks, abnormal placement, or an improperly sized device may require removal of the implant and placement of a second device. The catheters and guidewires are removed.

93581
A congenital ventricular septal defect is closed percutaneously by catheter. The patient is given local anesthesia and the femoral artery and vein are cannulated. A guidewire and catheter are inserted and advanced through the ventricular septum, into the right ventricle, and across the tricuspid valve into the right atrium. A separate venous sheath is placed in the jugular vein to allow passage of a snare catheter. The snare is advanced into the atrium and grasps the free wire or catheter that was threaded through the ventricular septal defect. This provides a through-and-through from the femoral vein to the ventricular septal defect and out the jugular. The jugular end is used to pass a dilator and sheath over the defect for the positioning of the occlusive device into the left ventricle. The sheath must be in the exact position with its tip in the left ventricle for delivery of the occlusive device. If necessary, traction is used at the opposite end to secure the sheath as the dilator is removed. If the sheath is displaced during removal of the dilator, the dilator is reinserted for correct positioning. Once the sheath is in place and the dilator removed, the delivery catheter loaded with an occlusive device is advanced to the center of the right atrium. The device is advanced out of the delivery catheter and into the tip of the sheath. It is gently advanced so that the distal legs are in the left ventricle and the center of the device is in the defect. A slight withdrawing of the sheath causes the distal legs to open within the left ventricle. Further withdrawal of the sheath allows the proximal legs to open in the right ventricle. The occlusion is confirmed with angiography and the delivery system and catheters are removed.

93600
The physician places a venous sheath, usually in a femoral vein, using standard techniques. The physician advances an electrical catheter through the venous sheath and into the right heart under fluoroscopic guidance. The physician attaches the catheter to an electrical recording device to allow depiction of the intracardiac electrograms obtained from electrodes on the catheter tip. The physician moves the catheter tip to the bundle of His, on the anteroseptal tricuspid annulus, and obtains recordings. Alternatively, the physician may obtain similar recordings by placing a catheter into the left ventricular outflow tract via the aorta.

93602
The physician places a venous sheath, usually in a femoral vein, using standard techniques. The physician advances an electrical catheter through the venous sheath and into the right heart under fluoroscopic guidance. The physician attaches the catheter to an electrical recording device to allow depiction of the intracardiac electrograms obtained from electrodes on the catheter tip. The physician moves the catheter tip to the right atrium and obtains recordings. The

Medicine

physician may obtain left atrial recordings by crossing the interatrial septum. Alternatively, the physician may obtain left atrial recordings by placing an arterial catheter into the aorta and crossing both the aortic and mitral valves in a retrograde fashion.

93603
The physician places a venous sheath, usually in a femoral vein, using standard techniques. The physician advances an electrical catheter through the venous sheath and into the right heart under fluoroscopic guidance. The physician attaches the catheter to an electrical recording device to allow depiction of the intracardiac electrograms obtained from electrodes on the catheter tip. The physician moves the catheter tip to the right ventricle and obtains recordings.

93609
The physician places an appropriate arterial or venous sheath, usually femoral, to allow access to the chamber to be mapped. The physician advances an electrical catheter through the sheath and into the appropriate chamber under fluoroscopic guidance. The physician attaches the catheter to an electrical recording device to allow depiction of the intracardiac electrograms obtained from electrodes on the catheter tip. The physician moves the catheter tip throughout the chamber to be mapped and obtains recordings. The physician compares activation times from different sites in order to identify the origin of the tachycardia.

93610
The physician places a venous sheath, usually in a femoral vein, using standard techniques. The physician advances an electrical catheter through the venous sheath and into the right heart under fluoroscopic guidance. The physician attaches the catheter to an electrical pacing device to allow transmission of pacing impulses through the catheter to the right atrium. The physician may pace the left atrium by placing the catheter in the coronary sinus or by crossing the interatrial septum. Alternatively, the physician may pace the left atrium by placing an arterial catheter into the aorta and crossing both the aortic and mitral valves in a retrograde fashion.

93612
The physician places a venous sheath using standard techniques. The physician advances an electrical catheter through the venous sheath and into the right ventricle under fluoroscopic guidance. The physician attaches the catheter to an electrical pacing device to allow transmission of pacing impulses through the catheter to the right ventricle. Alternatively, the physician may pace the left ventricle by placing the catheter in the right atrium, crossing the intraatrial septum and mitral valve. Finally, the physician may pace the left ventricle by advancing a catheter through an arterial sheath, via the aorta, across the aortic valve into the left ventricle.

93613
Electrophysiologic studies use electric stimulation and monitoring in the diagnosis of conduction abnormalities that predispose patients to bradyarrhythmias and to determine a patient's chance of developing ventricular and supraventricular tachyarrhythmias. The physician inserts an electrode catheter percutaneously into the right subclavian vein and, under fluoroscopic guidance, positions the electrode catheter at the right ventricular apex, both for recording and stimulating the right atrium and the right ventricle. A second electrode catheter is inserted percutaneously into the right femoral vein and positioned across the tricuspid valve for recording the His bundle electrogram. For mapping, a third electrode catheter is inserted percutaneously from the right femoral artery and advanced into the left ventricle. Ventricular tachycardia is induced by programmed ventricular stimulation from both the right and left ventricular apexes. The earliest activation site is determined and the diastolic pressure is recorded on the endocardial activation map during the ventricular tachycardia. Intracardiac electrograms with surface electrocardiograms are simultaneously displayed and recorded on a multichannel oscilloscopic photographic recorder.

93615
The physician places electrodes into the esophagus via an oropharyngeal or nasopharyngeal route. The physician attaches the catheter to an electrical recording device to allow depiction of the esophageal electrograms obtained from electrodes on the catheter tip. The physician moves the catheter tip to the esophageal site that provides the optimal signal and obtains recordings. The physician compares the esophageal and surface electrograms to identify the mechanism of the arrhythmia.

93616
The physician measures the heart's electrical function using a catheter placed into the patient's esophagus. The recording electrode at the end of the probe measures electrical activity of the atrium by pacing with or without recording activity of the ventricle.

93618
The physician places an appropriate arterial or venous sheath, usually femoral, to allow access to the chamber to be studied. The physician advances an electrical catheter through the sheath and into the appropriate chamber under fluoroscopic guidance. The physician attaches the catheter to an electrical pacing device to allow transmission of pacing impulses through the catheter to the heart chamber of interest. The physician stimulates the heart with rapid pacing or programmed electrical stimulation until the arrhythmia is induced.

93619
The physician places three venous sheaths, usually in one or both femoral veins, using standard techniques.

The physician advances three electrical catheters through the venous sheaths and into the right heart under fluoroscopic guidance. The physician attaches the three catheters to an electrical recording device to allow depiction of the intracardiac electrograms obtained from electrodes on the catheter tips. The physician moves the tips of the three catheters to the right atrium, the bundle of His, and the right ventricle and obtains recordings.

93620
The physician places three venous sheaths, usually in one or both femoral veins, using standard techniques. The physician advances three electrical catheters through the venous sheaths and into the right heart under fluoroscopic guidance. The physician attaches the three catheters to an electrical recording device to allow depiction of the intracardiac electrograms obtained from electrodes on the catheter tips. The physician moves the tips of the three catheters to the right atrium, the bundle of His, and the right ventricle and obtains recordings. The physician attaches the catheters to an electrical pacing device to allow transmission of pacing impulses through the catheters to the different heart chambers. The physician stimulates the heart with rapid pacing or programmed electrical stimulation in an attempt to induce an arrhythmia.

93621
The physician places four central venous sheaths using standard techniques. The physician advances four electrical catheters through the venous sheaths and into the right heart under fluoroscopic guidance. The physician attaches the four catheters to an electrical recording device to allow depiction of the intracardiac electrograms obtained from electrodes on the catheter tips. The physician moves the tips of the four catheters to the right atrium, the bundle of His, the coronary sinus, and the right ventricle and obtains recordings. The physician may attach the catheters to an electrical pacing device to allow transmission of pacing impulses through the catheters to the different heart chambers. The physician may stimulate the heart with rapid pacing or programmed electrical stimulation in an attempt to induce an arrhythmia.

93622
The physician places three central venous sheaths and an arterial sheath using standard techniques. The physician advances four electrical catheters through these sheaths and into the heart under fluoroscopic guidance. The physician attaches the four catheters to an electrical recording device to allow depiction of the intracardiac electrograms obtained from electrodes on the catheter tips. The physician moves the tips of the four catheters to the right atrium, the bundle of His, the right ventricle, and the left ventricle and obtains recordings. The physician may attach the catheters to an electrical pacing device to allow transmission of pacing impulses through the catheters to the different heart chambers. The physician may stimulate the heart with rapid pacing or programmed electrical stimulation in an attempt to induce an arrhythmia.

93623
The physician places an appropriate arterial or venous sheath, usually femoral, to allow access to the chamber to be studied. The physician advances an electrical catheter through the sheath and into the appropriate chamber under fluoroscopic guidance. An intravenous drug, such as isoproterenol, is infused. The physician attaches the catheter to an electrical pacing device to allow transmission of pacing impulses through the catheter to the heart chamber of interest. The physician stimulates the heart with rapid pacing or programmed electrical stimulation in an attempt to induce an arrhythmia. Use this code with 93620, 93621, and 93622.

93624
Following administration of therapy (antiarrhythmic drugs, surgery, ablation, etc.), the physician places an appropriate arterial or venous sheath, usually femoral, to allow access to the chamber to be studied. Under fluoroscopic guidance, the physician advances an electrical catheter through the sheath and into the appropriate chamber. An intravenous drug, such as isoproterenol, is infused. The physician attaches the catheter to an electrical pacing device to allow transmission of pacing impulses through the catheter to the heart chamber of interest. The physician stimulates the heart with rapid pacing or programmed electrical stimulation in an attempt to induce an arrhythmia.

93631
The purpose of this procedure is to localize the site of tachycardia during open-heart surgery to allow surgical correction of the tachycardia. The physician may place pacing or mapping catheters inside the heart prior to or during surgery using a standard transvenous approach. Additionally, the surgeon will place electrical probes on the outside (epicardium) of the heart in order to allow additional mapping. The physician attaches the catheters and probes to an electrical recording device to allow depiction of the electrograms obtained from electrodes on the catheter and probe tips. The surgeon's electrical probe can be moved around the outside of the heart to allow comparison of electrical activation times from different regions. The physician may attach the catheters to an electrical pacing device to allow transmission of pacing impulses through the catheters to the different heart chambers. The physician may stimulate the heart with rapid pacing or programmed electrical stimulation in an attempt to induce an arrhythmia.

93640
The purpose of this study is to ensure that the cardioverter-defibrillator (ICD) leads are positioned

Medicine

well and working properly, to guarantee proper function of this device in the future. Leads are typically placed in the heart via the subclavian vein, but occasionally defibrillation patches are placed on the epicardium or under the skin. To test the leads, the physician records cardiac electrical signals from the leads and paces the heart through the leads. The physician may test the leads using the actual ICD or by hooking the leads to an external device. The physician uses the leads to pace the heart into an arrhythmia, such as ventricular tachycardia or fibrillation. The ICD or external device detects the arrhythmia and shocks the heart through the ICD leads. The physician may perform this test with several different levels of shock to ensure the ICD can reliably terminate the arrhythmia.

93641

The purpose of this study is to ensure that the cardioverter-defibrillator (ICD) and ICD leads are positioned well and working properly, to guarantee proper function of this device in the future. Leads are typically placed in the heart via the subclavian vein, but occasionally defibrillation patches are placed on the epicardium or under the skin. To test the leads, the physician records cardiac electrical signals from the leads and paces the heart through the leads. The physician attaches the leads to the ICD generator. The physician uses the ICD pulse generator to pace the heart into an arrhythmia, such as ventricular tachycardia or fibrillation. The ICD detects the arrhythmia and shocks the heart through the ICD leads. The physician may perform this test with several different levels of shock to ensure the ICD can reliably terminate the arrhythmia.

93642

The purpose of this study is to ensure that the cardioverter-defibrillator (ICD) and ICD leads are positioned well and working properly, to guarantee proper function of this device in the future. The physician records cardiac electrical signals from the leads and paces the heart through the leads to determine pacing threshold. The physician uses the ICD pulse generator to pace the heart into an arrhythmia, such as ventricular tachycardia or fibrillation. The ICD detects and terminates the arrhythmia using pacing or shocking the heart through the ICD lead. The physician may reprogram the ICD's treatment parameters to optimize the device function to best treat the patient's arrhythmia.

93650

The purpose of this procedure is to create complete heart block, usually for control of the ventricular rate during atrial arrhythmias. The physician places a venous sheath, usually in a femoral vein, using standard techniques. The physician advances an electrical catheter through the venous sheath and into the right heart using fluoroscopic guidance. The physician attaches the catheter to an electrical recording device to allow depiction of the intracardiac electrograms obtained from electrodes on the catheter tip. The physician moves the catheter tip to the bundle of His, on the anteroseptal tricuspid annulus, and obtains recordings. Alternatively, the physician may obtain similar recordings by placing a catheter into the left ventricular outflow tract via the aorta. The physician maps the His bundle area and ablates the His bundle by sending cautery (radiofrequency) current through the catheter. The physician may also place a temporary pacing catheter in the right ventricle for this procedure.

93651

The purpose of this procedure is to ablate an arrhythmogenic focus or pathway to cure supraventricular arrhythmias. The ablation is typically done following a more complex electrophysiologic study, coded elsewhere. The physician places an introducer sheath, typically in a femoral vein, using standard techniques. The physician advances an electrical catheter through the sheath and into the heart using fluoroscopic guidance. The physician attaches the catheter to an electrical recording device to allow depiction of the intracardiac electrograms obtained from electrodes on the catheter tip. The physician moves the catheter tip to the arrhythmogenic focus or pathway while guided by electrical recordings and fluoroscopic views. The physician ablates the focus or pathway by sending cautery (radiofrequency) current through the catheter.

93652

The physician ablates an arrhythmogenic focus or pathway in the right or left ventricle to cure ventricular tachycardia. The ablation is typically done following a more complex electrophysiologic study, coded elsewhere. The physician places an introducer sheath, typically in a femoral artery or vein, using standard techniques. The physician advances an electrical catheter through the sheath and into the right or left ventricle using fluoroscopic guidance. The physician attaches the catheter to an electrical recording device to allow depiction of the intracardiac electrograms obtained from electrodes on the catheter tip. The physician moves the catheter tip to the arrhythmogenic focus or pathway while guided by electrical recordings and fluoroscopic views. The physician ablates the focus or pathway by sending cautery (radiofrequency) current through the catheter.

93660

The purpose of this procedure is to evaluate the patient's susceptibility to neurocardiogenic syncope. The physician secures the patient to the tilt table and attaches ECG leads to the chest. The physician also attaches an intermittent blood pressure monitor. The physician tilts the table, with the patient on it, and monitors the patient's symptoms, heart rhythm, and blood pressure. The physician may infuse medication, such as isoproterenol, through a standard intravenous catheter and repeat the tilt test.

93662
During separately reportable electrophysiologic evaluation or intracardiac catheter ablation of arrhythmogenic focus, intracardiac echocardiography (ICE) is performed. ICE uses intravascular ultrasound imaging systems in the cardiac chambers providing direct endocardial visualization. A single rotating transducer that provides a 360-degree field of view in a plane transverse to the long axis of the catheter is introduced through a long vascular sheath. Access is typically via the femoral vein. The transducer is directed to various sites within the heart. During electrophysiologic evaluation, ICE is used to guide placement of mapping and stimulating catheters. During intracardiac ablation procedures, ICE allows for precise anatomic localization of the ablation catheter tip in relation to endocardial structures. Since the focus of some arrhythmias can be anatomically determined, it also allows the ablative procedure to be performed using anatomic landmarks.

93668
An exercise physiologist or nurse supervises rehabilitation exercises in a patient diagnosed with peripheral arterial disease (PAD). Rehabilitation for PAD is provided using a motorized treadmill or a track. The patient is supervised during physical exercise sessions lasting between 45 to 60 minutes in order to achieve symptom-limited claudication. The supervising provider monitors the patient's claudication threshold and other cardiovascular limitations and adjusts the level of activity in order to reduce claudication symptoms and increase exercise tolerance.

93701
Bioimpedance is a noninvasive, continuous measurement of blood flow, respiration, and other cardiopulmonary dynamics, using a patient's thorax as an impedance transducer. The health care provider attaches the patient to the bioimpedance system with solid-gel electrodes placed along the widest dimension of the thorax. The electrical bioimpedance measurement current is passed through the thorax in a direction parallel with the spine between a pair of electrodes placed on the upper neck and a pair of electrodes placed on the upper abdomen. On its way through the thorax, the measurement current seeks the shortest and the most conductive pathway. As a result, the majority of the thoracic electrical bioimpedance (TEB) measurement current flows through the thoracic aorta and superior and inferior vena. The measurement current produces a high-frequency voltage across the impedance of the thorax, sensed by two other pairs of electrodes placed at the beginning of the thorax and the end of the thorax. The sensing electrodes also detect the ECG signal. The heart rate is derived from the R-R intervals of the ECG signal.

93720-93722
Plethysmography measures and records changes in the volume of a body part in response to variations in the amount of blood passing through or contained in that body part. Total body plethysmography uses a chamber enclosing the body and is used primarily to assess respiratory function. Report 93720 for the complete procedure, including physician interpretation and report; 93721 for the tracing or technical component only; and 93722 for the physician interpretation and report only.

93724
Patients with previously implanted pacemakers require periodic analysis of pacemaker function. This code applies to routine electronic analysis of pacemakers used to control irregularly fast heartbeats (antitachycardial) and includes electrocardiogram, programming, tests, and physician interpretation of the tests.

93740
Temperature gradient studies assess heart or circulatory functions by contrasting temperatures of certain vessels via an intravenous catheter.

93745
The physician performs initial set-up and programming of a wearable cardioverter-defibrillator. A wearable cardioverter-defibrillator is an external device that includes a monitor, electrodes, and an alarm contained in a vest-like garment that is worn 24 hours a day by the patient. The wearable cardioverter-defibrillator is used to detect, monitor, and treat life-threatening tachycardia and fibrillation that can lead to sudden cardiac arrest and death. The wearable cardioverter-defibrillator works by restoring a normal rhythm using low frequency shocks (cardioversion) or by returning a fast, disordered rhythm to normal rhythm by means of high-energy shock(s) (defibrillation). This code reports the initial programming of the system by the physician that includes establishing a baseline ECG. The initial set-up also includes verifying data transmission to a data repository, patient instruction on wearing the device, and patient reporting of events or problems with the device.

93750
Patients with a previously implanted ventricular assist device (VAD) require periodic interrogation of the device. Code 93750 reports a diagnostic procedure that is performed in person, and includes a face-to-face assessment of all device functions. Components that must be evaluated include device parameters (alarms, drivelines, and power surges) and a review of the device function (flow/volume status, septum status, and recovery). This code includes the physician

analysis, review, and report. It also includes device programming, if performed.

93770
Venous blood pressure is measured to assess heart and circulatory system functions. This code applies to the peripheral measurement.

93784
Blood pressure is monitored and recorded over a 24-hour period on an outpatient basis for the physician's analysis and interpretation. Code 93784 should be used for the complete procedure including physician interpretation and report.

93786
The purpose of this study is to evaluate the patient's ambient blood pressure during a 24-hour period. A technician attaches the blood pressure monitor to the patient, who wears the monitor for 24 hours. During this period, the device obtains blood pressure measurements and records them on magnetic tape or computer disk. This code does not include scanning analysis with report (coded 93788) or physician review with interpretation and report (coded 93790).

93788
The purpose of this study is to evaluate the patient's ambient blood pressure during a 24-hour period. A technician attaches the blood pressure monitor to the patient, who wears the monitor for 24 hours. During this period, the device obtains blood pressure measurements and records them on magnetic tape or computer disk. A technician scans the data and generates a data summary. This code does not include recording (coded 93786).

93790
The purpose of this study is to evaluate the patient's ambient blood pressure during a 24-hour period. A technician attaches the blood pressure monitor to the patient, who wears the monitor for 24 hours. During this period, the device obtains blood pressure measurements and records them on magnetic tape or computer disk. A technician scans the data and generates a data summary. The physician reviews and interprets the data and generates a report. This code does not include recording (coded 93786) or scanning analysis with report (coded 93788).

93797
Patients with severe cardiac disease, particularly those who have had myocardial infarctions, surgery on the coronary vessels, and other occlusive coronary artery diseases, often require outpatient rehabilitation. A physician supervises outpatient cardiac rehabilitation in areas of exercise, diet, and related modalities. This code excludes continuous electrocardiogram monitoring.

93798
Patients with severe cardiac disease, particularly those who have had myocardial infarctions, surgery on the coronary vessels, and other occlusive coronary artery diseases, often require outpatient rehabilitation. A physician supervises outpatient cardiac rehabilitation in areas of exercise, diet, and related modalities. This code includes continuous electrocardiogram monitoring.

93875
The physician or an assistant performs an ultrasound scan of the extracranial arteries in the head and neck to evaluate vascular blood flow in relation to blockage. Ultrasound uses high frequency sound waves to provide an image. This code applies to a bilateral evaluation using multiple noninvasive modalities to include blood flow, pneumoplethysmography, and ultrasound.

93880
The physician or an assistant performs a Duplex ultrasound scan, which is a combination of real-time and Doppler studies, of the extracranial arteries in the head and neck to evaluate vascular blood flow in relation to blockage. Ultrasound uses high frequency sound waves to provide an image. This code applies to both sides of the head and neck.

93882
The physician or an assistant performs a Duplex ultrasound scan, which is a combination of real-time and Doppler studies, of the extracranial arteries in the head and neck to evaluate vascular blood flow in relation to blockage. Ultrasound uses high frequency sound waves to provide an image. This code applies to a unilateral (one side of the head or neck) or limited study.

93886
The physician or an assistant performs a Doppler ultrasound scan of the extracranial arteries in the head and neck to evaluate vascular blood flow in relation to blockage. This code applies to a complete study of the intracranial arteries.

93888
The physician or an assistant performs a Doppler ultrasound scan of the extracranial arteries in the head and neck to evaluate vascular blood flow in relation to blockage. This code applies to a limited study of the intracranial arteries.

93890
The physician performs a vasoreactivity transcranial Doppler study of the intracranial arteries to identify cerebrovascular disease. Transcranial Doppler is a noninvasive ultrasound technology used to evaluate blood flow in the major intracranial arteries. Vasoreactivity, also referred to as vasomotor reactivity, measures changes in blood flow velocity in response to pharmacologic or other agent. A Doppler ultrasound

scan of the intracranial arteries is performed and flow velocity measured. A pharmacologic or other agent is administered and Doppler ultrasound scan is again performed and flow velocity measured. Changes in blood flow velocity in the intracranial arteries are compared and analyzed.

93892-93893
The physician performs a transcranial Doppler study of the intracranial arteries for detection of emboli. Transcranial Doppler is a noninvasive ultrasound technology used to evaluate blood flow in the major intracranial arteries. A new application of transcranial Doppler includes the classification and quantification of intracranial emboli. Intracranial circulating microemboli appear as high intensity transient signals in the transcranial Doppler waveform. Report 93892 if the study is performed without intravenous microbubble injection. Report 93893 if the study is performed with intravenous microbubble injection. Transcranial Doppler studies described as "with contrast" are performed with intravenous microbubble injection. The bubbles serve to enhance ultrasound signals thus enabling better visualization of the intracranial arteries.

93922-93923
The physician or assistant evaluates the arteries of the arms or legs to check blood flow in relation to blockage. In one example, the physician places a transducer on each leg at a prescribed level and measures the change in blood-handling characteristics during constriction by pneumatic cuffs. Technique is similar—the constriction and measuring of tension in the vascular system—but the medium may change. Code 93922 applies to ultrasound, plethysmography, and oxygen tension measurements in a bilateral evaluation limited to one level. Code 93923 includes multiple levels and provocative functional maneuvers.

93924
The physician or assistant evaluates the arteries of the arms or legs to check blood flow in relation to blockage. This code applies to ultrasound and oxygen tension measurements in a bilateral evaluation that occurs before and after a treadmill stress test.

93925-93926
The physician or assistant evaluates the arteries of the legs bilaterally to check blood flow in relation to blockage by use of Duplex ultrasonography, which is a combination of real-time and Doppler studies. Code 93925 refers to a complete bilateral study. Code 93926 applies to studies of one leg or limited areas of both legs.

93930
A diagnostic study is performed on the upper extremity arteries or arterial bypass grafts. A duplex scan involves a two-dimensional ultrasonic scan, which provides a two-dimensional display of the structure. This procedure is a complete bilateral study and is not intended to report unilateral procedures.

93931
A diagnostic study is performed on a specific site or area of the upper extremity arteries. A duplex scan involves a two-dimensional ultrasonic scan, which provides a two-dimensional display of the structure. This reports limited or follow-up ultrasounds.

93965
The physician or assistant evaluates the veins in the arms and legs. This code applies to a complete bilateral evaluation including blood flow, plethysmography, and ultrasound.

93970
The physician or assistant performs a Duplex ultrasound scan, which is a combination of real-time and Doppler studies, of the veins in the arms or legs to evaluate vascular blood flow in relation to blockage. This code applies to complete responses to compression and other tests and includes both sides.

93971
The physician or assistant performs a Duplex ultrasound scan, which is a combination of real-time and Doppler studies, of the veins in the arms or legs to evaluate vascular blood flow in relation to blockage. This code applies to complete responses to compression and other tests and includes one side or limited areas of both sides.

93975
The physician or assistant performs a Duplex ultrasound scan, which is a combination of real-time and Doppler studies, of the arteries and veins in the abdominal, pelvic, or genitorectal areas to evaluate vascular blood flow in relation to blockage. This code applies to a complete bilateral evaluation.

93976
The physician or assistant performs a Duplex ultrasound scan, which is a combination of real-time and Doppler studies, of the arteries and veins in the abdominal, pelvic, or genitorectal areas to evaluate vascular blood flow in relation to blockage. This code applies to a limited evaluation.

93978
The physician or assistant performs a Duplex ultrasound scan, which is a combination of real-time and Doppler studies, of the arteries and veins in the aorta, inferior vena cava, or iliac areas to evaluate vascular blood flow in relation to blockage. This code applies to a complete bilateral evaluation.

93979
The physician or assistant performs a Duplex ultrasound scan, which is a combination of real-time and Doppler studies, of the arteries and veins in the aorta, inferior vena cava, or iliac areas to evaluate

vascular blood flow in relation to blockage. This code applies to one side or limited areas of the sides.

93980-93981
The physician performs a Duplex ultrasound scan, producing real-time images integrating B-mode two-dimensional structure with Doppler mapping or imaging of motion with time, of the arteries and veins in the penis to evaluate vascular blood flow in and out of the penis in relation to blockages. Report 93980 for a complete evaluation and 93981 for a follow-up or a limited study.

93982
The physician performs a noninvasive, physiologic study of a patient with an implanted, wireless pressure sensor in the aneurysmal sac following endovascular repair of an aortic aneurysm. The physician places a receiver near the abdomen of the patient and the receiver picks up transmissions from the implanted sensor. A realtime, high-resolution pressure waveform is displayed on the integrated system's monitor and the measurements are recorded. This code reports a complete study including recording, analysis, and interpretation and report.

93990
The physician performs a Duplex ultrasound scan, producing real-time images integrating B-mode two-dimensional structure with Doppler mapping or imaging of motion with time, of a hemodialysis access site, including the arterial inflow, body of the access site or device, and venous outflow, to evaluate vascular blood flow in relation to blockage.

94002-94004
A mechanical ventilator is applied with a mask over the nose and mouth or through a tube placed into the trachea for patients requiring help breathing due to a lung disorder. Intermittent positive pressure breathing uses positive pressure during the inspiration phase of breathing. Code 94002 applies to ventilation assistance using adjustments in volume and pressure on the initial day of treatment in a hospital to an inpatient or observation patient and 94003 is reported for ventilation assistance to a hospital inpatient observation patient provided on subsequent days. Ventilation assistance and management provided to a nursing facility patient is reported with 94004 on a per day basis.

94005
A mechanical ventilator is applied with a mask over the nose and mouth or through a tube placed into the trachea for patients requiring help breathing due to a lung disorder. Intermittent positive pressure breathing uses positive pressure during the inspiration phase of breathing. Code 94005 reports at least 30 minutes of care plan oversight for ventilation assist and management occurring within a calendar month for a patient at home or in assisted living (domiciliary or rest home). The physician reviews lab work and other studies and orders revisions in the care plan as appropriate.

94010
A spirometer in a pulmonary lab is used to measure functions of the lungs including the amount of air contained in the lungs, the rate of expiration, and the volume of air a patient respires. The physician interprets the results of the spirometry and a graphic record is obtained.

94011-94012
A spirometer is an instrument that measures and records the volume of inhaled and exhaled air and is used to assess pulmonary function. This range of codes reports the measurement of spirometric forced expiratory flow in a patient 2 years of age or younger. Patients of this age often require sedation for testing in order to retain relaxed breathing. In one method, the child is positioned on a specialized bed. A technician places a mask over the child's mouth and nose. A loose jacket-type bag is fitted around the chest and upper abdomen. After the child takes a few breaths, the jacket bag inflates, giving the chest a gentle squeeze and forcing the air from the child's lungs. In order to measure lung size, the technician closes the upper portion of the bed and air flow through the mask is briefly discontinued. The resultant change in air pressure allows the computer to measure lung size. Report 94011 for measurements obtained without the use of bronchodilators and 94012 for those obtained before and after the use of a bronchodilator. These codes include laboratory procedures and the interpretation of test results.

94013
This code reports the measurement of lung volumes in children 2 years of age or younger. These measurements are useful in the evaluation of patients with respiratory symptoms and are typically limited to periods of sleep so that maneuvers such as face mask positioning, short occlusions of the airway, and application of an inflatable jacket can be more easily tolerated. Functional residual capacity (FRC) refers to the volume of air contained in the lung at end-tidal expiration and can be determined by gas dilution techniques or whole body plethysmography. Forced vital capacity (FVC) measures the total volume of air exhaled, and expiratory reserve volume (ERV) is the amount of additional air that can be exhaled following normal expiration. This code includes laboratory procedures and interpretation of test results.

94014-94016
A spirometer is an instrument that measures and records the volume of inhaled and exhaled air and is used to assess pulmonary function. This range of codes is used to report a patient initiated spirometric recording up to a 30-day period. Report 94014 when the procedure includes teaching the patient how to use

Medicine

a spirometer, recording the volume of air exhaled and inhaled, analyzing the data, recalibrating the unit, and the physician's analysis of the pulmonary function. Report 94015 when the procedure involves recording the data (hook-up, continued education, data transmission and capture, trend analysis, and periodic recalibration) without the physician's analysis of the pulmonary function. Report 94016 when the physician reviews and interprets the information only.

94060
A spirometer in a pulmonary lab is used to measure functions of the lungs including the amount of air contained in the lungs, the rate of expiration, and the volume of air a patient respires. The physician performs a bronchodilation responsiveness test by using spirometry completed both before and after administering a bronchodilating medicine to the patient.

94070
A spirometer in a pulmonary lab is used to measure functions of the lungs including the amount of air contained in the lungs, the rate of expiration, and the volume of air a patient respires. This code applies to spirometry conducted multiple times to evaluate bronchospasm provocation after exposing the patient to an agent, such as antigen(s), exercise, cold air, or methacholine. This test usually follows performance of 94010 where reduced airflow is indicated.

94150
This procedure measures the largest volume of air a patient can expire from his lungs. The patient amount of air inhaled and exhaled is measured and calculated with body size to determine the capacity of the lungs. This test is important for determining the threshold of capacity needed for vitality in patients with compromised respiration. For men, this is typically four to five liters; for women, this is normally three to four liters. It is normally performed as a part of a larger procedure and should only be billed separately when performed alone.

94200
This code applies to measuring maximum breathing capacity or maximal voluntary ventilation (the largest volume of air that a patient can inhale and exhale in 60 seconds). The patient inhales to the maximum vital capacity and exhales into a spirometer. The physician measures the maximal expiratory flow at 50 percent of expired vital capacity and at 75 percent of expired vital capacity.

94240
Pulmonary function testing is performed in a pulmonary lab using helium, nitrogen open circuit, or another method to check lung functions to include residual capacity or residual volume, the volume of air remaining in the lung after a patient exhales. The physician interprets the report.

94250
Pulmonary function testing is performed in a pulmonary lab using helium, nitrogen open circuit, or another method to check lung functions to include residual capacity or residual volume, the volume of air remaining in the lung after a patient exhales. The physician interprets results. This code applies to collecting and, in a separately reportable procedure, evaluating expired air.

94260
Pulmonary function testing is performed in a pulmonary lab using helium, nitrogen open circuit, or another method to check lung functions to include residual capacity or residual volume, the volume of air remaining in the lung after a patient exhales. The physician interprets results. This code applies to the total volume of thoracic gas.

94350
Pulmonary function testing is performed in a pulmonary lab using helium, nitrogen open circuit, or another method to check lung functions to include residual capacity or residual volume, the volume of air remaining in the lung after a patient exhales. The physician interprets results. This code applies to the distribution of inspired gas using multiple breath nitrogen washout curves and including alveolar nitrogen or helium equilibration time.

94360
Pulmonary function testing is performed in a pulmonary lab using helium, nitrogen open circuit, or another method to check lung functions to include residual capacity or residual volume, the volume of air remaining in the lung after a patient exhales. The physician interprets results. This code applies to measuring the resistance to airflow using oscillatory or plethysmographic methods.

94370
Pulmonary function testing is performed in a pulmonary lab using helium, nitrogen open circuit, or another method to check lung functions to include residual capacity or residual volume, the volume of air remaining in the lung after a patient exhales. The physician interprets results. This code applies to measuring the total airway closing volume in a single breath.

94375
Pulmonary function testing is performed in a pulmonary lab using helium, nitrogen open circuit, or another method to check lung functions to include residual capacity or residual volume, the volume of air remaining in the lung after a patient exhales. The physician interprets results. This code applies to measuring the respiratory flow volume loop.

94400
Pulmonary function testing is performed in a pulmonary lab using helium, nitrogen open circuit, or

another method to check lung functions to include residual capacity or residual volume, the volume of air remaining in the lung after a patient exhales. The physician interprets results. This code applies to the patient breathing in carbon dioxide and measuring the resultant lung response.

94450
Pulmonary function testing is performed in a pulmonary lab using helium, nitrogen open circuit, or another method to check lung functions to include residual capacity or residual volume, the volume of air remaining in the lung after a patient exhales. The physician interprets results. This code applies to a patient's response to low amounts of oxygen.

94452-94453
The physician performs a high altitude simulation test (HAST). This is a specialized type of oxygenation study performed on individuals with pulmonary disease who have marginal oxygenation and are considering traveling by airplane and/or an excursion to a higher altitude. The test is performed to determine the patient's pulmonary function at higher altitudes and to determine the quantity of supplemental oxygen that will be required for a safe trip at various altitudes. The test is performed at rest and with gradients of activity. The test includes interpretation and written report. Report 94452 if the high altitude simulation test is performed alone. Report 94453 if it is performed with supplemental oxygen titration.

94610
A catheter is inserted into a separately reported endotracheal tube placed in a newborn. The physician administers surfactant in a single bolus or in divided doses through the catheter into the lungs of the patient. Surfactant is usually administered within minutes of birth. Surfactant is formed relatively late in the development of a fetus and is administered to premature infants to prevent or mitigate pulmonary complications.

94620-94621
A pulmonary exercise stress test is done to test how much air moves in and out of the lungs during exercise and to determine where breathing problems are occurring, since they may be in the lungs, heart, or circulation. A simple exercise stress test is done with the patient riding a stationary bike (ergometer) or walking on a treadmill. Heart rate, breathing, and blood pressure are monitored before beginning the exercise. Basic ventilation studies are performed with a spirometer and recording device in a simple exercise test (94620) as the patient breathes through a mouthpiece and connecting tube while a nose clip prevents nasal breathing. The patient's oxygen level is monitored with pulse oximetry. Complex testing (94621) uses electrodes placed on the upper body to monitor the heart. Throughout the process, blood samples may be taken to measure oxygen uptake and carbon dioxide waste products in the blood during exercise.

94640
A pressurized or nonpressurized inhalation treatment is applied for an acute obstruction of the airway, preventing the patient from taking in sufficient air on his or her own, or for sputum induction for diagnostic purposes. This is done with an aerosol generator, nebulizer, metered dose inhaler or intermittent positive pressure breathing (IPPB) device.

94642
An antimicrobial medication called pentamidine is given in cases of pneumocystis carinii pneumonia treatment or prophylaxis in high risk groups. The patient breathes the aerosolized medication into the lungs.

94644-94645
This treatment is often called a nebulized wet aerosol (NWA). A continuous aerosol inhalation treatment is applied for an acute obstruction of the airway that prevents the patient from taking in sufficient air on his or her own. This is done employing an aerosol generator. Report 94644 for the first hour of treatment and 94645 for each additional hour.

94660
A mechanical ventilator is applied with a mask over the nose and mouth or through a tube placed into the trachea for patients requiring help breathing due to a lung disorder. Intermittent positive pressure breathing uses positive pressure during the inspiration phase of breathing. This code applies to initial evaluation or application of continuous positive airway pressure for ventilation assistance with positive pressure during inspiration and exhalation.

94662
A mechanical ventilator is applied with a mask over the nose and mouth or through a tube placed into the trachea for patients requiring help breathing due to a lung disorder. Intermittent negative pressure breathing uses negative pressure during the inspiration phase of breathing. This code applies to subsequent evaluation or application of continuous negative airway pressure for ventilation assistance with negative pressure during inspiration and exhalation.

94664
A demonstration is done for the patient on how to use an aerosol generator, nebulizer, metered dose inhaler, or intermittent positive pressure breathing device (IPPB) and/or the patient's utilization is evaluated.

94667
A respiratory therapist supervised by a physician manipulates the chest wall—cupping, vibration, and percussion—to mobilize secretions and improve breathing for some lung disorders. This code applies to initial evaluation and treatment.

94668
A respiratory therapist supervised by a physician manipulates the chest wall—cupping, vibration, and percussion—to mobilize secretions and improve breathing for some lung disorders. This code applies to subsequent evaluation and treatment.

94680
Pulmonary testing supervised by a physician in a lab measures functions of the lungs. This code applies to collecting expired air and evaluating oxygen uptake using direct methods during rest and exercise.

94681
Pulmonary testing supervised by a physician in a lab measures functions of the lungs. This code applies to collecting expired air and evaluating oxygen uptake, carbon dioxide output, and percentage oxygen extracted.

94690
Pulmonary testing supervised by a physician in a lab measures functions of the lungs. This code applies to collecting expired air and evaluating oxygen uptake using indirect methods during rest.

94720
Pulmonary testing supervised by a physician in a lab measures functions of the lungs. This code applies to measuring carbon monoxide diffusing capacity when the patient inhales carbon dioxide and the physician compares the inhaled and exhaled amounts.

94725
Pulmonary testing supervised by a physician in a lab measures functions of the lungs. This code applies to measuring membrane diffusing capacity when the patient inhales a gas such as carbon monoxide and the physician compares the inhaled and exhaled amounts.

94750
Pulmonary testing supervised by a physician in a lab measures functions of the lungs. This code applies to measuring compliance of the lungs using various methods.

94760
A sensor is placed on the ear lobe or finger to measure oxygen levels in the blood for a pulse oximetry. A light shines through the capillary bed for the measurement. This code applies to a single measurement

94761
A sensor is placed on the ear lobe or finger to measure oxygen levels in the blood for a pulse oximetry. A light shines through the capillary bed for the measurement. This code applies to multiple measurements.

94762
A sensor is placed on the ear lobe or finger to measure oxygen levels in the blood for a pulse oximetry. A light shines through the capillary bed for the measurement. This code applies to continuous overnight measurement.

94770
A pulmonary lab assistant performs pulmonary function testing to measure various aspects of the lungs. A physician interprets the report. This code applies to using an infrared light device to measure the carbon dioxide amounts in expired air.

94772
A pulmonary lab assistant performs pulmonary function testing to measure various aspects of the lungs. A physician interprets the report. This code applies to measuring the circadian respiratory pattern of an infant over a 12- to 24-hour period (pediatric pneumogram).

94774-94777
These codes report clinical services provided for a 30-day period to a pediatric patient who is using an apnea monitor. An apnea monitor is a device designed to detect cessation of breathing, either directly through measurement of respiration and/or indirectly through monitoring of physiological signs such as heart rate, pulse, or blood oxygen concentration. Devices typically feature both visual and audio alarm systems. Some may provide remote alarm systems, programmed software, or a monitor. An internal and/or hard copy recording system may also be featured. Report 94774 when the service includes hookup, initiation of recording, and disconnection in addition to a report by the physician who reviews the accumulated data; 94775 when the service includes only hookup, initiation of recording, and disconnection; 94776 when the data is transmitted, downloaded, and analyzed by computer; and 94777 when the physician reviews and reports upon the accumulated data.

95004
A physician scratches, punctures, or pricks the skin to introduce specific allergy extracts to determine a patient's allergies. The immediate skin reaction is documented. This code includes test interpretation and physician report.

95010
A physician scratches, punctures, or pricks the skin to introduce drugs, venoms, or other biological agents to determine a patient's allergies. The immediate skin reaction is documented. This code includes the physician's test interpretation and report. The number of tests should be specified.

95012
A patient's nitric oxide (NO) level is measured using specialized equipment and under the direct supervision of a clinician. The patient is instructed to exhale, place the testing device in the mouth, and inhale to lung capacity. The clinician monitors the patient to ensure that a steady compliance inhalation and exhalation are performed. The process is repeated

Medicine

and the patient's NO level is determined by the device, which uses the sensitivity of a chemiluminescence gas analyzer and integrated software to measure NO molecules at very low concentrations. This test is commonly used for patients with asthma or other respiratory disorders.

95015
A physician injects drugs, venoms, or other biological substances into the skin to determine the patient's allergies. The immediate reaction is documented. This code includes the physician's test interpretation and report. The number of tests should be specified.

95024
The physician injects suspected allergenic substances into the skin to determine the patient's specific allergies. The immediate skin reaction is documented. This code includes test interpretation and physician report.

95027
The physician uses intracutaneous tests, sequential and incremental, with allergenic extracts for airborne allergens, immediate type reaction, to determine a patient's specific allergies. The number of tests must be specified. This code includes test interpretation and physician report.

95028
A physician injects suspected allergenic substances into a patient to determine the patient's specific allergies. The delayed skin reaction is documented.

95044
A physician applies a patch containing specific allergenic substances to a patient's arm to determine the patient's specific allergies. The reaction is documented.

95052
A physician applies a patch containing specific allergenic substances to a patient's arm and exposes the area to ultraviolet light to determine a patient's specific allergies. The reaction is documented.

95056
A physician exposes an area of the patient's skin to ultraviolet light to determine the patient's allergic reactions. The reaction is documented.

95060
A physician introduces specific allergy extracts to the patient's eye mucus membranes to determine the patient's specific allergic reactions. The reaction is documented.

95065
A physician introduces specific allergy extracts to the patient's mucus membrane in the nose to determine the patient's specific allergic reactions. The reaction is documented.

95070
A physician has the patient inhale histamines, methacholamines, or other medications to determine the patient's specific allergies. The reaction is documented.

95071
A physician has the patient inhale specific allergenic substances to determine the patient's specific allergies. The reaction is documented.

95075
A physician has the patient ingest specific substances such as food or drugs to determine the patient's specific allergies. The reaction is documented.

95115
A physician injects small but increasing dosages of a substance to which the patient is allergic for desensitization. This code applies to a single injection of the allergen and does not include the provision of the substance.

95117
A physician injects small but increasing dosages of a substance to which the patient is allergic for desensitization. This code applies to two or more injections of the allergen and does not include the provision of the substance.

95120
A physician injects small but increasing dosages of a substance to which the patient is allergic for desensitization. This code applies to a single injection of the allergen and includes the provision of the substance.

95125
A physician injects small but increasing dosages of a substance to which the patient is allergic for desensitization. This code applies to two or more injections of the allergen and does include the provision of the substance.

95130
A physician injects small but increasing dosages of insect venom to which the patient is allergic for desensitization. This code applies to the injection of one venom and includes the provision of the venom.

95131
A physician injects small but increasing dosages of insect venom to which the patient is allergic for desensitization. This code applies to the injection of two venoms and includes the provision of the venoms.

95132
A physician injects small but increasing dosages of insect venom to which the patient is allergic for desensitization. This code applies to the injection of three venoms and includes the provision of the venoms.

95133
A physician injects small but increasing dosages of insect venom to which the patient is allergic for desensitization. This code applies to the injection of four venoms and includes the provision of the venoms.

95134
A physician injects small but increasing dosages of insect venom to which the patient is allergic for desensitization. This code applies to the injection of five venoms and includes the provision of the venoms.

95144
This code reports the allergist's preparation and supply of an antigen extract for allergen immunotherapy in a single dosage vial. The antigen is to be administered by another physician. Single dose vials contain one dose to be administered in a single injection.

95145-95170
These codes report the physician's preparation of an antigen for allergen immunotherapy and the provision of the antigen extract itself. These codes also include the providing physician's calculations for the concentration and volume to be used in the dosage based upon the patient's previous skin test results and personal history. These codes do not, however, include the administration of the allergen therapy. The number of doses must be specified and the vial(s) (series of vials from a treatment board or one multiple dose vial) from which the dose may be drawn is irrelevant. Report the code based on the type of preparation, i.e., the number of different venoms contained in a single administered injection of the extract. Report 95145 for a dose containing one single stinging insect venom, 95146 for an extract containing two single stinging insect venoms, 95147 for three, 95148 for four, and 95149 for five single stinging insect venoms in one dose extract. Code 95165 reports single or multiple antigens (not stinging insect), and 95170 is for a whole body extract of a biting insect or other arthropod.

95180
The physician administers small but increasing dosages of a substance that causes the patient's allergic reaction to become less sensitized and thereby develop the patient's tolerance to the substance. This code applies to each hour spent in performing a rapid desensitization procedure to a medication such as insulin, penicillin, or horse serum.

95250-95251
The physician monitors glucose levels by continuous recording and storage of glucose values. Monitoring may be performed with an invasive device or a noninvasive device. The invasive device monitors glucose levels by insertion of a sensor in the subcutaneous tissue in the lower abdomen or other area. The sensor measures the change in intracellular fluid (ICF) and sends the information from the sensor to a small monitor that stores the data for a minimum of 72 hours. The noninvasive device is worn like a wristwatch and measures glucose with an electric current and biometric sensor. The time intervals at which interstitial glucose is measured range from every five minutes with the invasive devices to every 20 minutes with the noninvasive device. After the patient has worn the sensor for a minimum of 72 hours, it is removed and the data from the monitor are downloaded into a computer. Specialized software interprets the data, and a technical report is generated. The interpretation and report of the data are reported with 95251.

95803
Actigraphy testing is done continuously for a minimum of three days, including recording, analysis, and interpretation, to study sleep/wake patterns and circadian rhythms. An actigraph device is attached to the patient's wrist, ankle, or trunk. The device contains a movement detector. Movement is sampled several times every second and transduced into an analog electrical form, digitized, and stored for analysis. The data are downloaded to a computer for sleep/wake analysis.

95805
Physiological parameters of a patient asleep in a lab setting are monitored for at least six hours. A physician interprets the results. This code applies to multiple sleep latency testing during periods of napping to assess sleepiness.

95806
An unattended sleep study is performed. Physiological parameters of a patient asleep in a lab setting or home are monitored for at least six hours. Oxygen saturation and cardiorespiratory measurements, including heart rate, respiratory airflow, and respiratory effort (thoracoabdominal movement) are made during the test. A physician interprets the results.

95807
Physiological parameters of a patient asleep in a lab setting are monitored for at least six hours. A physician interprets the results. This code applies to testing of several parameters, including ventilation, respiratory effort, ECG or heart rate, oxygen saturation, by a technologist.

95808
Physiological parameters of a patient asleep in a lab setting are monitored for at least six hours for polysomnography studies. In contrast to sleep studies, polysomnography details measurements such as sleep staging with electroencephalogram (EEG), electro-oculogram, and submental electromyogram. This code applies to sleep staging with one to three additional measurements such as respiration, airflow, oximetry, muscle activity, vital signs, and snoring.

Medicine

95810-95811
Physiological parameters of a patient asleep in a lab setting are monitored for at least six hours for polysomnography studies. In contrast to sleep studies, polysomnography details measurements such as sleep staging with electroencephalogram (EEG), electro-oculogram, and submental electromyogram. This code applies to sleep staging with four or more additional measurements such as respiration, airflow, oximetry, muscle activity, vital signs, and snoring. Report 95811 if the procedure includes initiation of continuous positive airway pressure therapy or bi-level ventilation, attended by a technologist.

95812
Sensors are placed on a patient's head in an electroencephalogram (EEG) to measure and record the brain's electrical activity. Brain waves are captured on paper or electronic medium for study. This code applies to EEG monitoring for 41-60 minutes.

95813
Sensors are placed on a patient's head in an electroencephalogram (EEG) to measure and record the brain's electrical activity. Brain waves are captured on paper or electronic medium for study. This code applies to an EEG acquired in more than one hour.

95816
Sensors are placed on a patient's head in an electroencephalogram (EEG) to measure and record the brain's electrical activity. Brain waves are captured on paper or electronic medium for study. This code applies to a patient awake and drowsy during the EEG.

95819
Sensors are placed on a patient's head in an electroencephalogram (EEG) to measure and record the brain's electrical activity. Brain waves are captured on paper or electronic medium for study. This code applies to a patient intermittently awake and asleep during the EEG.

95822
Sensors are placed on a patient's head in an electroencephalogram (EEG) to measure and record the brain's electrical activity. Brain waves are captured on paper or electronic medium for study. This code applies to a patient recorded in coma or sleeping during the EEG.

95824
Sensors are placed on a patient's head in an electroencephalogram (EEG) to measure and record the brain's electrical activity. Brain waves are captured on paper or electronic medium for study. This code applies to checking a patient for brain activity and determining whether the patient is brain dead. This involves evaluation by isoelectric encephalogram for a minimum of 30 minutes with no EEG change in response to sound or pain.

95827
Sensors are placed on a patient's head in an electroencephalogram (EEG) to measure and record the brain's electrical activity. Brain waves are captured on paper or electronic medium for study. This code applies to all night recording of a patient.

95829
Sensors are placed directly on the brain's surface during surgery in an electrocorticogram to measure and record the brain's electrical activity. Brain waves are captured on paper or electronic medium for study in a separately reported procedure.

95830
The physician places sensors in or near the sphenoid process. Any electroencephalographic (EEG) recording is separately reportable.

95831
Muscles or muscle groups are tested for strength. This code applies to manually testing the arm, leg, or trunk.

95832
Muscles or muscle groups are tested for strength. This code applies to manually testing the hands.

95833
Muscles or muscle groups are tested for strength. This code applies to manually testing the body exclusive of the hands.

95834
Muscles or muscle groups are tested for strength. This code applies to manually testing the body inclusive of the hands.

95851
Testing determines active and passive range of motion for extremities and joints. This code applies to manually testing each arm or leg or sections of the spine in a separately reported procedure.

95852
Testing determines active and passive range of motion for joints of the hand. This code applies to manually testing the hands.

95857
This test for myasthenia gravis involves injecting Tensilon (edrophonium chloride) intravascularly. After administration by a physician, eye muscle abnormalities will markedly decrease within two minutes after injection in individuals with myasthenia gravis.

95860-95864
Needle electromyography (EMG) records the electrical properties of muscle using an oscilloscope. Recordings, which may be amplified and heard through a loudspeaker, are made during needle insertion, with the muscle at rest, and during contraction. Report 95860 when one extremity (arm or leg) is tested; 95861 for tests of two extremities; 95863 for tests of

three extremities; and 95864 for tests of four extremities.

95865-95866
Needle electromyography (EMG) records the electrical properties of muscle using an oscilloscope. Recordings, which may be amplified and heard through a loudspeaker, are made during needle insertion with the muscle at rest and during contraction. Internal smooth muscle tissue in the larynx (95865) and hemidiaphragm (95866) are measured by needle placement in muscular organ tissue.

95867-95868
Needle electromyography (EMG) records the electrical properties of muscle using an oscilloscope. Recordings, which may be amplified and heard through a loudspeaker, are made during needle insertion, with the muscle at rest, and during contraction. These codes are specific to the 12 nerves that emerge from or enter the cranium. Report 95867 for unilateral studies and 95868 for bilateral studies.

95869-95870
Needle electromyography (EMG) records the electrical properties of thoracic paraspinal muscles, excluding T1 or T12 (95869) using an oscilloscope. Recordings, which may be amplified and heard through a loudspeaker, are made during needle insertion, with the muscle at rest, and during contraction. Report 95870 for a limited study of muscles in one extremity or non-limb (axial) muscles other than thoracic paraspinal or cranial supplied muscles or sphincters.

95872
Needle electromyography (EMG) records the electrical properties of muscle using an oscilloscope. Recordings, which may be amplified and heard through a loudspeaker, are made during needle insertion, with the muscle at rest, and during contraction. This procedure uses a single fiber electrode to obtain additional information on specific muscles, including quantitative measurement of jitter, blocking, and/or fiber density.

95873
Chemodenervation procedures often require not only electromyographic guidance but also an electrical stimulation of the neuromuscular sites to be injected. This stimulation, coupled with the guidance procedures, increases the efficacy of the primary chemodenervation procedure by ensuring precise delivery.

95874
Needle electromyography (EMG) guidance is a component of chemodenervation procedures performed to treat spasticity and myoclonus and dystonia disorders by injection of denervation agents that block the transmission of nerve impulses to muscle tissue. The EMG guidance provides maximum efficiency in delivery of the agents to the affected neuromuscular sites.

95875
Needle electromyography (EMG) records the electrical properties of muscle using an oscilloscope. Recordings, which may be amplified and heard through a loudspeaker, are made during needle insertion, with the muscle at rest, and during contraction. This procedure tests electrical properties of ischemic limb during exercise and includes lactic acid determination.

95900-95904
Nerve testing uses sensors to measure and record nerve functions including conduction, amplitude, and latency/velocity. Nerves are stimulated with electric shocks along the course of the muscle. The time required to initiate contraction is measured and recorded. Measurements of distal latency, the time required to traverse the segment nearest the muscle, and conduction velocity, the time required for an impulse to travel a measured length of nerve, are also recorded. Report 95900 for motor testing without F-wave studies; 95903 for motor testing with F-wave studies; and 95904 if the test is of sensory response. Each nerve tested can be billed separately.

95905
Nerve testing uses sensors to measure and record nerve functions including conduction, amplitude, and latency/velocity. Nerves are stimulated with electric shocks along the course of the muscle. The time required to initiate contraction is measured and recorded. Measurements of distal latency (the time required to traverse the segment nearest the muscle) and conduction velocity (the time required for an impulse to travel a measured length of nerve) are also recorded. Code 95905 reports motor and/or sensory nerve conduction tests performed using preconfigured electrode arrays. It includes F-wave study, when performed, as well as interpretation and report. Report 95905 only once for each limb studied.

95920
This code is used when an evoked potential study is required during surgery. This is often necessary to determine what effect a surgery is having on specific nerve functions. In some cases, continuous monitoring is necessary. Report this code per hour.

95921
Utilizing ECG monitoring the patient's autonomic nervous system function is evaluated by performance of at least two of the following tests; deep breathing while timing the inhalation and exhalation with recording and calculation of the longest R-R intervals of each respiration cycle for at least six cycles; recording of ECG during at least three performances of the valsalva strain including a 30-45 second interval after the strain; or after laying supine for a period of

Medicine

time the patient stands and R-R interval at 15 and 30 seconds is recorded.

95922
To test the sympathetic nervous system's ability to regulate blood pressure, the physician places an electronic blood pressure monitor on the patient. The patient is placed supine and asked to perform the Valsalva maneuver (expelling air against a closed glottis) while blood pressure is checked between heartbeats. The patient is asked to cease the maneuver and is tilted using the table for at least five minutes. Beat by beat blood pressure measurements are taken and evaluated to determine the nervous system's ability to respond to the test.

95923
This test is performed to gauge the damage to the autonomic nerves serving the skin. In the Silastic sweat imprint (method of Minor), the patient lies on the stomach or back. An iodine/castor oil mixture is painted on the area to be tested and left to dry. The area is dusted with powdered starch. The physician injects pilocarpine to stimulate sweating, and remains for 20 to 30 minutes to evaluate the sweating, its amount, and distribution. As the patient sweats, the starch dissolves and reacts with the iodine to produce a dark purple color. Areas not stained indicate impaired sympathetic reactions. The patient is cleaned after the test.

95925-95927
The physician uses somatosensory-evoked potential to provide information about the integrity of the peripheral nerves, spinal cord, brain stem, and the cortex. Evoked potentials require low voltages and the placement of electrodes on the scalp near the parts of the nervous system where the signals are generated. The physician may place electrical stimulation at the median nerve of the wrist or the posterior tibial nerve at the ankle, or the physician may stimulate points between these and the central nervous system. Many applications may be necessary to screen background noise to measure the interval between stimulation and generated response. Report 95925 if the upper limbs are being tested; 95926 for tests of the lower limbs; and 95927 for tests of the trunk or head.

95928-95929
The physician uses transcranial central motor evoked potential to provide information about the integrity of the peripheral nerves, spinal cord, brain stem, and the cortex. Evoked potentials require low voltages and the placement of electrodes on the scalp near the parts of the nervous system where the signals are generated. Following skin preparation with acetone, the physician places electrodes that provide electrical stimulation at selected sites on the scalp. Cutaneous electrodes are also placed at target sites. Common target sites are the finger, forearm, biceps, and/or leg. The physician uses transcranial motor stimulation to test motor response in target muscles. Responses are recorded in target muscles with surface or coaxial electrodes. Transcranial stimulation cannot target specific muscles; however, it does allow stimulation of specific muscle groups. Report 95928 if the upper limbs are being tested; 92929 for tests of the lower limbs.

95930
The physician uses sensors to measure and record nerve functions such as conduction and amplitude and, in this code, for using visual evoked potentials (VEP) to test the central nervous system. This code applies to the checkerboard or flash technique.

95933
The physician uses sensors to measure and record nerve functions such as conduction and amplitude. This code applies to testing the blink reflex.

95934
The physician uses sensors to measure and record nerve functions such as conduction and amplitude. This code applies to testing the amplitude and latency (H-reflex) of the lower leg muscles.

95936
The physician uses sensors to measure and record nerve functions such as conduction and amplitude. This code applies to testing the amplitude and latency (H-reflex) of muscles other than the lower leg muscles.

95937
The physician uses sensors to measure and record nerve functions such as conduction and amplitude. This code applies to measure the junction between nerves and muscles for one nerve.

95950
The physician places sensors on a patient's head in an electroencephalogram (EEG) to measure and record the brain's electrical activity. This code applies to an eight-channel EEG to evaluate a cerebral seizure for each 24-hour period of monitoring.

95951
The physician places sensors on a patient's head in an electroencephalogram (EEG) to measure and record the brain's electrical activity. This code applies to a 16 or more channel telemetry EEG, combined with video recording and interpretation, to evaluate and monitor presurgical localization of the specific area where the cerebral seizure emanates and applies to each 24-hour period of monitoring.

95953
The physician places sensors on a patient's head in an electroencephalogram (EEG) to measure and record the brain's electrical activity. This code applies to a computerized portable 16 or more channel EEG, with recording and interpretation, to evaluate a cerebral seizure for each 24-hour period of monitoring.

95954
The physician places sensors on a patient's head in an electroencephalogram (EEG) to measure and record the brain's electrical activity. This code applies to a patient stimulated by medications or physical activity.

95955
The physician places sensors on a patient's head in an electroencephalogram (EEG) to measure and record the brain's electrical activity. This code applies to an EEG during surgery exclusive of surgery to the brain.

95956
The physician places sensors on a patient's head in an electroencephalogram (EEG) to measure and record the brain's electrical activity. This code applies to a 16-channel telemetry EEG to evaluate a cerebral seizure over each 24-hour period of monitoring.

95957
The physician places sensors on a patient's head in an electroencephalogram (EEG) to measure and record the brain's electrical activity. This code applies to computer digital analysis of an EEG as in cases of epilepsy.

95958
The physician places sensors on a patient's head in an electroencephalogram (EEG) to measure and record the brain's electrical activity. This code applies to a Wada activation test to evaluate function of the brain hemispheres.

95961
Sensors record the response of electrodes placed on the brain and stimulated during surgery. The procedure maps the brain's surface to determine the focus of a seizure or other abnormality. This code applies to the first hour of physician attendance.

95962
Sensors record the response of electrodes placed on the brain and stimulated during surgery. The procedure maps the brain's surface to determine the focus of a seizure or other abnormality. This code applies to every hour of physician attendance after the first.

95965-95967
Magnetoencephalography (MEG) provides functional mapping information about how the brain processes sensory stimulation by measuring the associated magnetic fields emanating from the outer surface of the brain. MEG can be used both as a tool for fundamental study of the brain and for assessing patients with specific neurological disorders. The biomagnetometer is commonly housed in a shielded room; the recording device contains magnetic detection coils continuously bathed in liquid helium to superconducting temperatures of -269 degrees Celsius. The spontaneous (95965) or evoked (95966-95967) magnetic fields emanating from the brain induce a current in these coils, which in turn produce a magnetic field in a device called a superconducting quantum interference device (SQUID), which makes images every 1/1000 of a second. MEG identifies where in the brain the electrical current is flowing in response to the stimulus. For example, MEG can be used to determine the millimeters of the brain responsible for fingertip sensation and movement, which can be crucial in surgeries involving neuroresection.

95970
A previously placed neurostimulator pulse generator is tested to verify that is it functioning properly. The neurostimulator may be a simple or complex brain, spinal cord, or peripheral device. Functions that may be tested include rate, pulse amplitude and duration, configuration of waveform, battery status, electrode selectability, output modulation, cycling, impedance, and patient compliance. This code reports testing without reprogramming of the device.

95971
A previously placed neurostimulator pulse generator is tested to verify that it is functioning properly. In this case, a simple spinal cord or peripheral device is tested. A simple device affects only three or fewer of the following: pulse amplitude, pulse duration, pulse frequency, eight or more electrode contacts, cycling, stimulation train duration, train spacing, number of programs, number of channels, phase angle, alternating electrode polarities, configuration of wave form, or more than one clinical feature. All of the functions that apply may be tested intraoperatively or on subsequent occasions. This code reports testing with reprogramming of the device.

95972-95973
A previously placed neurostimulator pulse generator is tested to verify that it is functioning properly. In this case, a complex spinal cord or peripheral device is tested. A complex device affects more than three of the following: pulse amplitude, pulse duration, pulse frequency, eight or more electrode contacts, cycling, stimulation train duration, train spacing, number of programs, number of channels, phase angle, alternating electrode polarities, configuration of wave form, or more than one clinical feature. All of the functions that apply may be tested intraoperatively or on subsequent occasions. Report 95972 for the first hour of testing and reprogramming of the device. Report 95973 for each additional 30 minutes of testing and reprogramming.

95974-95975
This range of codes involves a complex neurostimulator, a device that provides chronic electrical stimulation to the nerves of the central or peripheral nervous system and, for these two codes, implanted in the cranial nerve. The stimulation affects the pulse (amplitude, duration, frequency) to treat, for example, the tremors characteristic of Parkinson's disease. Report 95974 for electronic analysis of a

complex cranial nerve neurostimulator pulse generator/transmitter with intraoperative or subsequent programming. The procedure may include nerve interface testing and the code is used for the first hour, while 95975 is reported for each additional 30 minutes beyond the first hour.

95978-95979

A previously placed neurostimulator pulse generator is tested to verify that it is functioning properly. In this case, a complex brain device is tested. A complex device affects more than three of the following: pulse amplitude, pulse duration, pulse frequency, eight or more electrode contacts, cycling, stimulation train duration, train spacing, number of programs, number of channels, phase angle, alternating electrode polarities, configuration of wave form, or more than one clinical feature. All of the functions that apply may be tested initially or on subsequent occasions. Report 95978 for the first hour of testing and reprogramming of the device. Report 95979 for each additional 30 minutes of testing and reprogramming.

95980

The physician tests a gastric neurostimulator pulse generator to verify that it is functioning properly. Functions that may be tested include rate, pulse amplitude and duration, configuration of waveform, battery status, electrode selectability, output modulation, cycling, impedance, and patient measurement. This code reports intraoperative testing with programming of the device.

95981

The physician tests a previously placed gastric neurostimulator pulse generator to verify that it is functioning properly. Functions that may be tested include rate, pulse amplitude and duration, configuration of waveform, battery status, electrode selectability, output modulation, cycling, impedance, and patient measurement. This code reports subsequent testing without reprogramming of the device.

95982

The physician tests a previously placed gastric neurostimulator pulse generator to verify that it is functioning properly. Functions that may be tested include rate, pulse amplitude and duration, configuration of waveform, battery status, electrode selectability, output modulation, cycling, impedance, and patient measurement. This code reports subsequent testing with reprogramming of the device.

95990-95991

Refilling and maintenance of an implantable spinal (intrathecal, epidural) or intraventricular (brain) pump or reservoir is done. Implantable pumps or reservoirs are placed in subcutaneous pockets at appropriate sites on the body and hold a long-term supply of the drug or medication being infused into the patient. They are refilled through the skin by a needle placed into the pump device. The patient's specific pump is identified and the required volume amount is checked. The site of the implant is prepped. The refill kit is assembled and a template is positioned over the site. A needle is inserted through the template center hole and into the pump/reservoir, which is filled with more drug infusate. Report 95991 when a physician administers the drug refill.

95992

Benign positional vertigo is an inner ear problem caused by crystals (canaliths) floating in the fluid of the inner ear. With a change in position, these crystals may stimulate a portion of the inner ear, resulting in short periods of dizziness. The physician treats benign positional vertigo with a series of repositioning movements known as Epley or Semont maneuvers. The patient is placed in various positions during the maneuver, which may cause temporary dizziness. A neck collar may be worn overnight to assist in keeping the head and neck in the correct position. Report code 95992 once for each day of treatment.

96000-96001

Human motion analysis has several applications including biomedical and athletic performance. To conduct a biomedical analysis, patient movements are recorded, digitized, copied on computer, and processed. For example, when calculating net joint moments, the joint center is calculated using a local coordinate system created from body markers. When tracking markers in 3D using video, two or more cameras are used to identify the markers. After all parameters are found (e.g., linear acceleration, angular acceleration, ground reaction forces) and gathered using stereo X-rays or MRI techniques, the resultant net joint forces and moments can be calculated. In 3-D kinematics, joint centers are digitized for the first few frames of the sequence recorded. Linear parameters of movement can be measured to assess horizontal and vertical motion. Also, angular parameters can measure the degrees of movement of the joints to analyze specific joint motion. In 96001, while taking dynamic plantar pressure measurements, data is collected using a pressure sensor platform positioned on a walkway. The patient walks along the walkway so pressure data can be analyzed in areas of the foot (i.e., the heel, metatarsal heads, and the hallux). The peak pressure is determined in all areas and the highest pressure of all sites (i.e., peak pressure foot) is measured. Report 96004 in addition to each of these codes for physician review and interpretation of results, which includes the physician's written report.

96002

Electrodes placed on the muscle belly, parallel to the grain of the muscle fiber, detects an electrical signal that comes from active muscles (the patient is in motion during the test). The strength and pattern of the signal is seen on a computer screen and the data is collected in a software program that is able to run various analyses of the data to create useful reports regarding muscle function. For example, gait analysis allows the clinician to analyze time normal activation patterns separately for stance and swing phases between conditions or against data base values. Report 96002 for a study of one to 12 muscles. Report 96004 in addition to this code for physician review and interpretation of results, which includes the physician's written report.

96003
Electrodes placed on the muscle belly, parallel to the grain of the muscle fiber, detect an electrical signal that comes from active muscles (the patient is in motion during the test). The strength and pattern of the signal is seen on a computer screen and the data is collected in a software program that is able to run various analyses of the data to create useful reports regarding muscle function. For example, gait analysis allows the clinician to analyze time normal activation patterns separately for stance and swing phases between conditions or against database values. Use 96003 to report dynamic fine wire electromyography for one muscle. Report 96004 in addition to this code for physician review and interpretation of results, which includes the physician's written report.

96004
The physician reviews and interprets computer-based motion analysis, dynamic plantar pressure measurements, dynamic surface electromyography during walking or other functional activities, and dynamic fine wire electromyography performed using codes 96000, 96001, 96002, and 96003 to report the service.

96020
During a separately reported functional MRI (fMRI), the physician or psychologist administers a series of tests involving language, memory, cognition, movement, and sensation, and reviews the results and reports upon them in a process called functional brain mapping. These reports identify the expected versus observed locations of brain activity documented by the fMRI as the patient performs specific tasks.

96040
The trained genetic counselor meets with an individual, couple, or family to investigate family genetic history and assess the risks associated with genetic defects in offspring. This code covers 30 minutes of face-to-face counseling, review of medical data, or data collection (interviews).

96101-96103
The physician or psychologist administers and interprets the results of psychological testing. The testing in written, oral, computer, or combined formats measures personality, emotions, intellectual functioning, and psychopathology. Code 96101 applies to each hour of testing and includes both face-to-face time administering tests to the patient, as well as interpretation and preparation of the report; however, it is not used to report the interpretation of technician- or computer-administered tests. In 96102, a technician administers the test, which is interpreted and reported by a qualified health care professional. In 96103, the test is administered by computer, which is interpreted and reported by a qualified health care professional.

96105
The physician or other health care professional administers tests to measure communication problems such as speech and writing in an aphasic patient. This code applies to each hour of testing.

96110
The physician or other health care professional measures cognitive, psychomotor, and other abilities characteristic to development through written, oral, or combined format testing. This code applies to limited testing.

96111
The physician or other health care professional measures cognitive, motor, social, language, and other abilities characteristic of development through written, oral, or combined format testing. This code applies to extended testing.

96116
The physician or psychologist evaluates aspects of thinking, reasoning, and judgment to evaluate a patient's neurocognitive abilities. This code applies to each hour of examination time and includes both face-to-face time with the patient and time spent interpreting test results and preparing a report.

96118-96120
The physician or psychologist administers a series of tests in thinking, reasoning, judgment, and memory to evaluate the patient's neurocognitive abilities. Code 96118 applies to each hour of testing and includes face-to-face time administering tests to the patient, as well as interpretation and preparation of the report; however, it is not used to report the interpretation of technician- or computer-administered tests. In 96119, a technician administers the test, which is interpreted and reported by a qualified health care professional. In 96120, the test is administered by computer, which is interpreted and reported by a qualified health care professional.

96125
A qualified health care professional administers standardized cognitive performance testing to evaluate such factors as the patient's immediate, recent, and remote memory; temporal and spatial orientation; general information recall; problem-solving and abstract reasoning abilities; organizational skills; and auditory processing and retention. This code applies to

each hour of testing and includes face-to-face time administering tests to the patient, as well as interpretation and preparation of the report.

96150-96151
These codes report assessment of psychological, behavioral, emotional, cognitive, and relevant social factors that can prevent, treat, or manage physical health problems. The assessment must be associated with an acute or chronic illness, the prevention of a physical illness or disability, and the maintenance of health. The initial assessment (96150) and re-assessment (96151) apply to each 15-minute direct, face-to-face session with the patient. A reassessment (96151) is reported to obtain objective measures of goals formulated in the initial assessment and to modify plans as is indicated to support the goals.

96152-96155
These are interventional services prescribed to modify the psychological, behavioral, emotional, cognitive, and social factors relevant to and affecting the patient's physical health problems. Each code applies to a 15-minute session of direct face-to-face intervention. Report 96152 for the initial assessment with the individual/patient only. Report 96153 for intervention attended by a group (two or more patients). Report 96154 for intervention that includes the family with the patient present. Report 96155 for intervention with the family without the patient's presence.

96360-96361
A physician or an assistant under direct physician supervision infuses a hydration solution (prepackaged fluid and electrolytes) for 31 minutes to one hour through an intravenous catheter inserted by needle into a patient's vein or by infusion through an existing indwelling intravascular access catheter or port. Report 96361 for each additional hour beyond the first hour. Intravenous infusion for hydration lasting 30 minutes or less is not reported.

96365-96368
A physician or an assistant under direct physician supervision injects or infuses a therapeutic, prophylactic (preventive), or diagnostic medication other than chemotherapy or other highly complex drugs or biologic agents via intravenous route. Infusions are administered through an intravenous catheter inserted by needle into a patient's vein or by injection or infusion through an existing indwelling intravascular access catheter or port. Report 96365 for the initial hour and 96366 for each additional hour. Report 96367 for each additional sequential infusion, up to one hour, and 96368 for each concurrent infusion of substances other than chemotherapy or other highly complex drugs or biologic agents.

96369-96371
A physician or an assistant under direct physician supervision infuses a therapeutic or prophylactic (preventive) medication other than chemotherapy or other highly complex drug or biologic agent via a subcutaneous route. Indications for subcutaneous infusion may include coma, dysphagia, nausea/vomiting, intestinal obstruction, malabsorption, or extreme weakness. Infusions are administered through a needle inserted beneath the skin; common infusion sites include the upper arm, shoulder, abdomen, and thigh. Report 96369 for infusions lasting longer than 15 minutes and up to one hour. This code includes pump set-up and the establishment of subcutaneous infusion sites. Report 96370 for each additional hour and 96371 for an additional pump set-up with the establishment of new subcutaneous infusion sites. Codes 96369 and 96371 should be reported only once per encounter.

96372-96376
The physician or an assistant under direct physician supervision administers a therapeutic, prophylactic, or diagnostic substance by subcutaneous or intramuscular injection (96372), intra-arterial injection (96373), or by push into an intravenous catheter or intravascular access device (96374 for a single or initial substance, 96375 for each additional sequential IV push of a new substance, and 96376 for each additional sequential IV push of the same substance after 30 minutes have elapsed). The push technique involves an infusion of less than 15 minutes. Code 96376 may be reported only by facilities.

96401-96402
The physician or supervised assistant prepares and administers non-hormonal medication to combat diseases such as malignant neoplasms or microorganisms. These codes apply to medication injected under the skin (subcutaneous) or into a muscle (intramuscular) often in the arm or leg. Report 96402 for a hormonal medication administered to combat diseases such as malignant neoplasms or microorganisms.

96405-96406
The physician or supervised assistant prepares and administers medication to combat diseases such as malignant neoplasms or microorganisms. Report 96405 when medication is injected directly into the lesion, up to and including seven lesions. Report 96406 when more than seven lesions are treated.

96409-96411
The physician or supervised assistant prepares and administers a chemotherapeutic medication to combat malignant neoplasms or microorganisms. The drug is administered through intravenous (IV) push technique in which the physician or supervised assistant is continuously present to administer the injection and observe the patient or for an infusion of less than 15 minutes. Report 96409 for a single or the initial substance or drug given. Report 96411 for each additional substance or drug given.

96413-96415
The physician or supervised assistant prepares and administers a chemotherapeutic medication to combat malignant neoplasms or microorganisms. These codes describe infusions through catheter tubing placed in a vein. Report 96413 for a single or the initial substance given for up to one hour of service. Report 96415 for each additional hour of service beyond the initial hour.

96416
The physician or supervised assistant prepares and administers a chemotherapeutic medication to combat malignant neoplasms or microorganisms. This code applies to initiating an infusion that will take more than eight hours and requires using an implanted pump or a portable pump to infuse the medication slowly through catheter tubing placed in a vein.

96417
The physician or supervised assistant prepares and administers a chemotherapeutic medication to combat malignant neoplasms or microorganisms. This code applies to initiating a separate additional substance for infusion that is adjunct to the primary chemotherapy infusion service reported by 96413.

96420
The physician or supervised assistant prepares and administers a chemotherapeutic medication to combat malignant neoplasms or microorganisms. The drug is administered by intra-arterial push technique, in which the medication is injected in a timed fashion into the nearest port of a catheter already placed in an artery. Placement of the intra-arterial catheter itself is not included.

96422-96423
The physician or supervised assistant prepares and administers a chemotherapeutic medication to combat malignant neoplasms or microorganisms. The drug is administered through infusion technique, in which the medication is allowed to slowly enter the body through a catheter already in place within an artery. Report 96422 for the first hour of intra-arterial infusion and 96423 for each additional hour.

96425
The physician or supervised assistant prepares and administers a chemotherapeutic medication to combat malignant neoplasms or microorganisms. This code applies to initiating an infusion that will take more than eight hours and requires using an implanted pump or a portable pump to infuse the medication very slowly through catheter tubing placed in an artery.

96440
The physician or supervised assistant prepares and administers a chemotherapeutic medication to combat malignant neoplasms or microorganisms. This code applies to medication injected into the lung cavity through a catheter placed into the pleura.

96445
The physician or supervised assistant prepares and administers a chemotherapeutic medication to combat malignant neoplasms or microorganisms. This code applies to medication injected into the abdominal cavity through a catheter placed in the peritoneum.

96450
The physician or supervised assistant prepares and administers a chemotherapeutic medication to combat malignant neoplasms or microorganisms. This code applies to medication injected into the spinal cord through a catheter placed through the space between the lower back bones (lumbar puncture).

96521
The physician or supervised assistant prepares and administers medication to combat diseases such as malignant neoplasms or microorganisms. This code applies to maintaining or refilling portable pumps used for prolonged infusions.

96522
Refilling and maintenance of an implantable pump or reservoir for systemic drug delivery is done. The implantable pump or reservoir is identified and the required volume amount checked. The site of the implant is prepped. The refill kit is assembled and a template is placed over the appropriate site. A needle is inserted through a template center hole and into the pump/reservoir, which is filled with more drug infusate.

96523
The venous access device is irrigated with an anticoagulant to prevent coagulation at the catheter tip. The venous access device is prepped with alcohol. The anticoagulant in the tubing is withdrawn. The tubing is flushed with normal saline. A measured amount of anticoagulant is instilled into the tubing.

96542
The physician or supervised assistant prepares and administers a chemotherapeutic medication to combat malignant neoplasms or microorganisms. This code applies to medication infused into the central nervous system through a catheter leading from a subcutaneous reservoir of medication in the brain's subarachnoid or intraventricular space.

96567
In photodynamic therapy (PDT), the physician applies a photosensitizing agent, such as 20 percent topical aminolevulinic acid HCl, directly onto the patient's lesions to treat premalignant cells, such as non-hyperkeratotic actinic keratosis, and malignant cells. The patient is sent home and scheduled to return within the time frame required for the light treatment to activate the photosensitive drug. The lesions are irradiated with a photodynamic therapy illuminator for a predetermined amount of minutes. The exposure time does not depend on the number of lesions. The

blue light exposure causes a cytotoxic reaction with the topical agent that was applied to the lesions, killing the existing cells and preventing the spread of the suspect or malignant cells. The code is reported per exposure session, not for each lesion treated.

96570-96571
In photodynamic therapy (PDT), the physician injects the photosensitizing agent, such as a porphyrin, into the patient's bloodstream where it is absorbed by cells all over the body. The agent remains in cancer cells for a longer time than it does in normal cells. When the treated cancer cells are exposed to laser light, the photosensitizing agent absorbs the energy from light particles called photons and transfers this energy to surrounding oxygen molecules. This produces an active form of oxygen, toxic free radicals, that destroy the treated cancer cells. Light exposure must be timed so that it occurs when most of the photosensitizing agent has left healthy cells but is still present in the cancer cells. The light source used in the procedure is directed for internal application through a bronchoscope into the lungs for the treatment of lung cancer or through an endoscope into the gastrointestinal tract for the treatment of gastrointestinal tract cancer. Report 96570 for the first 30 minutes and 96571 for each additional 15 minutes. The bronchoscopy and endoscopy procedures for the lung and gastrointestinal tract are reported separately.

96900
The physician uses ultraviolet light to treat skin ailments.

96902
The physician examines by microscope hairs plucked or clipped from a patient's scalp to determine telogen and anagen counts. The physician also looks for structural hair shaft deformities. Results of the test determine if hair loss is result of short-term biological changes, malnutrition, medication, or hereditary.

96904
Whole body integumentary photography, also known as dermatoscopy, epiluminescence microscopy, and skin surface microscopy, is a noninvasive technique of collecting images of skin lesions for identifying features of malignant vs. benign skin changes. Immersion oil is first applied to the skin to remove the natural reflection of light from the skin surface and to render the outermost skin layer transparent. A stereomicroscope is used to visualize the epidermis and the dermal junction. Dermatoscopic images are also recorded, and may be reviewed with the aid of standard or digitized photographs. Digitized images allow computer-aided diagnosis as well as image enhancement for viewing a lesion's distinguishing features. Digitizing also allows the images to be stored and retrieved when following a lesion's progression over time.

96910
The physician uses photosensitive chemicals and light rays to treat skin ailments. This code applies to tar and ultraviolet B rays (Goeckerman treatment) or petrolatum and ultraviolet B rays.

96912
The physician uses photosensitive chemicals and light rays to treat skin ailments. This code applies to psoralens and ultraviolet A rays (PUVA).

96913
The physician uses photosensitive chemicals and light rays to treat skin ailments. This code applies to tar and ultraviolet B rays (Goeckerman treatment) and/or psoralens and ultraviolet A rays (PUVA) used for severe skin problems requiring between four to eight hours of care under a physician's direct supervision.

96920-96922
The physician uses a fiberoptic handpiece to deliver short pulses from a 308-nm UV-B laser for the treatment of psoriatic skin lesions. Prior to the start of treatment, the optimal dose is determined by exposing uninvolved skin to the minimal effective amount of UV-B. Once this dose is established, mineral oil is applied on the lesion to enhance penetration and reduce scattering. The physician uses the fiberoptic handpiece to irradiate the lesions by using a "painting" motion. The treatment is usually painless and does not require anesthesia. Report 96920 for a total treated area less that 250 sq cm, 96921 for a total area of 250 sq cm to 500 sq cm, and 96922 for an area larger than 500 sq cm.

97001
The health care provider examines the patient/client. This includes taking a comprehensive history, systems review, and tests and measures. Tests and measures may include but are not limited to tests of range of motion, motor function, muscle performance, joint integrity, neuromuscular status, and review of orthotic or prosthetic devices. The PT formulates an assessment, prognosis, and notes an anticipated intervention.

97002
The health care provider re-examines the patient/client to obtain objective measures of progress toward stated goals. Tests and measures include but are not limited to those noted in 97001. The PT modifies the treatment plan as is indicated to support medical necessity of skilled intervention.

97003
The health care provider evaluates the patient. Various movements required for activities of daily living are examined. Dexterity, range of movement, and other elements may also be studied.

97004
The health care provider re-evaluates the patient to gauge progress of therapy. Various movements required for activities of daily living are examined. Dexterity, range of movement, and other elements may also be studied.

97005
The health care provider examines the patient, which includes taking a comprehensive history, systems review, and obtaining tests of range of motion, motor function, muscle performance, joint integrity, and neuromuscular status. The healthcare provider formulates an assessment, prognosis, and notes the anticipated intervention.

97006
The health care provider re-examines the patient to obtain objective measures of progress toward stated goals. Tests include, but are not limited to, range of motion, motor function, muscle performance, joint integrity, and neuromuscular status. The healthcare provider modifies the treatment plan as is indicated to support medical necessity of skilled intervention.

97010
The health care provider applies heat (dry or moist) or cold to one or more body parts with appropriate padding to prevent skin irritation. The patient is given necessary safety instructions. The treatment requires supervision only and typically only one unit is billed per day. However, when multiple separate treatment sessions are performed per day, it is appropriate to report one unit for each treatment session.

97012
The health care provider applies sustained or intermittent mechanical traction to the cervical and/or lumbar spine. The mechanical force produces distraction between the vertebrae thereby relieving pain and increasing tissue flexibility. The treatment requires supervision and typically only one unit is billed per day. However, when multiple separate treatment sessions are performed per day, it is appropriate to report one unit for each treatment session.

97014
The health care provider applies electrical stimulation to one or more areas in order to stimulate muscle function, enhance healing, and alleviate pain and/or edema. The clinician chooses which type of electrical stimulation is appropriate. The treatment requires supervision and typically only one unit is billed per day. However, when multiple separate treatment sessions are performed per day, it is appropriate to report one unit for each treatment session.

97016
The health care provider applies a vasopneumatic device to treat extremity edema (usually lymphedema). A pressurized sleeve is applied. Girth measurements are taken pre- and posttreatment. Typically only one unit is billed per day. However, when multiple separate treatment sessions are performed per day, it is appropriate to report one unit for each treatment session.

97018
The health care provider uses a paraffin bath to apply superficial heat to a hand or foot. The part is repeatedly dipped into the paraffin forming a glove. Use of paraffin facilitates treatment of arthritis and other conditions that cause limitations in joint flexibility. The treatment requires supervision and typically only one unit is billed per day. However, when multiple separate treatment sessions are performed per day, it is appropriate to report one unit for each treatment session.

97022
The provider uses a whirlpool to provide superficial heat and cold in an environment that facilitates range of motion and/or exercise. The provider decides the appropriate water temperature and provides safety instruction. The treatment requires supervision and typically only one unit is billed per day. However, when multiple separate treatment sessions are performed per day, it is appropriate to report one unit for each treatment session.

97024
The health care provider uses diathermy or microwave as a form of superficial heat for one or more body areas. After application and safety instructions have been provided, the clinician supervises the treatment. The treatment typically includes only one unit is billed per day. However, when multiple separate treatment sessions are performed per day, it is appropriate to report one unit for each treatment session.

97026
The health care provider uses infrared light as a form of superficial heat that will increase circulation to one or more localized areas. The treatment requires supervision and typically only one unit is billed per day. However, when multiple separate treatment sessions are performed per day, it is appropriate to report one unit for each treatment session.

97028
The health care provider applies ultraviolet light to treat dermatological problems. Once applied and safety instructions have been provided, the treatment is supervised. Typically only one unit is billed per day. However, when multiple separate treatment sessions are performed per day, it is appropriate to report one unit for each treatment session.

97032
The health care provider applies electrical stimulation to one or more areas to promote muscle function and/or pain control. This treatment requires direct contact

Medicine

by the provider and can be billed in multiple 15-minute units.

97033
The health care provider uses electrical current to administer medication to one or more areas. Iontophoresis is usually prescribed for soft tissue inflammatory conditions and pain control. This code requires constant attendance by the clinician and can be billed in 15-minute units.

97034
The health care provider uses hot and cold baths in a repeated, alternating fashion to stimulate the vasomotor response of a localized body part. This code requires constant attendance and can be billed in 15-minute units.

97035
The health care provider applies ultrasound to increase circulation to one or more areas. A water bath or some form of ultrasound lotion must be used as a coupling agent to facilitate the procedure. The delivery of corticosteroid medication via ultrasound is called phonophoresis and is reported using this code. The medication as a supply may or may not be paid by the payer. Ultrasound or phonophoresis requires constant attendance and can be billed in 15-minute units.

97036
Hubbard tank is used when it is necessary to immerse the full body into water. Care of wounds and burns may require use of the Hubbard tank to facilitate tissue cleansing and debridement. This code requires constant attendance of a health care provider and can be billed in 15-minute units.

97110
The health care provider and/or patient perform therapeutic exercises to one or more body areas to develop strength, endurance, and flexibility. This code requires direct contact with a health care provider and may be billed in 15-minute units.

97112
The health care provider and/or patient perform activities to one or more body areas that facilitate reeducation of movement, balance, coordination, kinesthetic sense, posture, and proprioception. This code requires direct contact with a health care provider and may be billed in 15-minute units.

97113
The health care provider directs and/or performs therapeutic exercises with the patient/client in the aquatic environment. This code requires skilled intervention by the health care provider and documentation must support medical necessity of the aquatic environment. This code can be billed in 15-minute units.

97116
The health care provider instructs the patient in specific activities that will facilitate ambulation and stair climbing with or without an assistive device. Proper gait sequencing and safety instructions are included when appropriate. This code requires direct contact with the health care provider and may be billed in 15-minute units.

97124
The health care provider uses massage to provide muscle relaxation, increase localized circulation, soften scar tissue, or mobilize mucous secretions in the lung via tapotement and/or percussion. This code requires direct with the health care provider contact and can be billed in 15-minute units, regardless of number of body parts treated.

97139
This code may be used if a health care provider performs a therapeutic procedure to one or more body areas that is not listed under the current codes. A narrative descriptor should be noted on the claim and documentation in the medical record should clearly support the procedure. This code is reported for each 15-minute unit.

97140
The health care provider performs manual therapy techniques including soft tissue and joint mobilization, manipulation, manual traction, and/or manual lymphatic drainage to one or more areas. This code requires direct contact of the health care provider with the patient and can be billed in 15-minute units.

97150
The health care provider supervises group activities (two or more patients/clients) during therapeutic procedures on land or in the aquatic environment. The patients/clients do not have to be performing the same activity simultaneously; however, the need for skilled intervention must be documented. This code can be reported once for each group participant.

97530
The health care provider uses dynamic therapeutic activities designed to achieve improved functional performance (e.g., lifting, pulling, bending). This code requires direct contact with the health care provider and can be billed in 15-minute units.

97532
The health care provider works one-on-one with an individual to assist in the development of cognitive skills in individuals with inherited learning disabilities or in individuals who have lost these skills as a result of illness or brain injury. The individual often needs to develop compensatory methods of processing and retrieving information when disability, illness, or injury has affected these cognitive processes. Cognitive skill development includes mental exercises that assist the patient in areas such as attention, memory, perception,

language, reasoning, planning, problem-solving, and related skills.

97533
Sensory experiences include touch, movement, body awareness, sight, sound, and the pull of gravity. The process of the brain organizing and interpreting this information is called sensory integration. Sensory integration provides a crucial foundation for later, more complex learning and behavior. The health care provider works one-on-one with individuals with sensory integration disorders to provide techniques for enhancing sensory processing and adapting to environmental demands. Sensory integration disorders may be the result of a learning disability, illness, or brain injury.

97535
The health care provider instructs and trains the patients in self-care and home management activities (e.g., ADL and use of adaptive equipment in the kitchen, bath, and/or car). Direct contact with the health care provider is required. This code can be billed in 15-minute units.

97537
The health care provider instructs and trains the patient/client in community/work re-integration activities (e.g., work task analysis, money management, shopping, work environment modification, safe accessing of transportation, and the use of available assistive technology devices or adaptive equipment). This requires direct one-on-one contact with the patient by the health care provider and is billed in 15-minute increments.

97542
The health care provider assesses the patient for the type and size of a wheelchair or trains the patient in the proper wheelchair skills (e.g., propulsion, safety techniques).

97545-97546
This code is used for a procedure where the injured worker is put through a series of conditioning exercises and job simulation tasks in preparation for return to work. Endurance, strength, and proper body mechanics are emphasized. The patient is also educated in problem solving skills related to job task performance and employing correct lifting and positioning techniques. Report 97546 for each additional hour after the initial two hours.

97597-97598
The health care provider performs wound care management by using selective debridement techniques to remove devitalized tissue without anesthesia. Selective techniques are those in which the physician has complete control over which tissue is removed and which is left behind. Selective techniques include high-pressure waterjet with or without suction, and sharp debridement techniques using scissors, a scalpel, or forceps. Another newer method of selective debridement is autolysis, which uses the body's own enzymes and moisture to re-hydrate, soften, and finally liquefy hard eschar and slough. Autolytic debridement is accomplished using occlusive or semi-occlusive dressings that keep wound fluid in contact with the necrotic tissue. Types of dressing applications used in autolytic debridement include hydrocolloids, hydrogels, and transparent films. Wound assessment, topical applications, instructions regarding ongoing care of the wound, and the possible use of a whirlpool for treatment are included in these codes. Report 97597 for a total wound surface area less than or equal to 20 sq. cm and 97598 for a total wound surface area greater than 20 sq. cm. Report the appropriate code per session.

97602
The health care provider performs wound care management to promote healing using non-selective debridement techniques to remove devitalized tissue. Non-selective debridement techniques are those in which both necrotic and healthy tissue are removed. Non-selective techniques, sometimes referred to as mechanical debridement, include wet-to-moist dressings, enzymatic chemicals, and abrasion. Wet-to-moist debridement involves allowing a dressing to proceed from wet to moist, and manually removing the dressing, which removes both the necrotic and healthy tissue. Chemical enzymes are fast acting products that produce slough of necrotic tissue. Abrasion involves scraping the wound surface with a tongue blade or similar blunt instrument.

97605-97606
The health care provider performs negative pressure wound therapy (NPWT) with vacuum assisted drainage collection to promote healing of a chronic non-healing wound, including diabetic or pressure (decubitus) ulcer. This procedure includes topical applications to the wound, wound assessment, and patient or caregiver instruction related to on-going care per session. Negative pressure wound therapy uses controlled application of subatmospheric pressure to a wound. The subatmospheric pressure is generated using an electrical pump. The electrical pump conveys intermittent or continuous subatmospheric pressure through connecting tubing to a specialized wound dressing. The specialized wound dressing includes a porous foam dressing that covers the wound surface and an airtight adhesive dressing that seals the wound and contains the subatmospheric pressure at the wound site. Negative pressure wound therapy promotes healing by increasing local vascularity and oxygenation of the wound bed, evacuating wound fluid thereby reducing edema, and removing exudates and bacteria. Drainage from the wound is collected in a canister. Report 97605 for a wound(s) with a total surface area less than or equal to 50 sq. cm. Report

97606 for a wound(s) with a total surface area greater than 50 sq. cm.

97750
The health care provider performs a test of physical performance evaluating function of one or more body areas and evaluates functional capacity. A written report is included. This is in addition to a routine evaluation or re-evaluation (97001-97004). This code can be billed in 15-minute increments.

97755
Use this code to report one-on-one patient contact time, per 15 minutes, with a health care provider who performs an assessment for the suitability and benefits of acquiring any assistive technology device or equipment that will restore, augment, or compensate for existing functional ability in the patient; or that will optimize functional tasks and/or maximize the patient's environmental accessibility. This includes the preparation of a written report.

97760
The health care provider fits and/or trains the patient in the use of an orthotic device for one or more body parts. This includes assessment as to type of orthotic when appropriate. This does not include fabrication time, if appropriate, or cost of materials.

97761
The health care provider fits and/or trains the patient in the use of a prosthetic device for one or more body parts. This includes assessment for the appropriate type of prosthetic device. This does not include fabrication time, if applicable, or cost of materials.

97762
The health care provider evaluates the effectiveness of an existing orthotic or prosthetic device and makes recommendations for changes, as appropriate.

97802-97804
A dietetic professional provides medical nutrition therapy assessment or re-assessment and intervention in a face-to-face or group patient setting. After nutritional screening identifies patients at risk, preventive or therapeutic dietary therapy is initiated to induce a positive result in the role nutrition plays in improving health outcomes. Report 97802 for the initial assessment and intervention face-to-face with an individual patient for each 15 minutes of medical nutrition therapy. Report 97803 for re-assessment and intervention with an individual patient for each 15 minutes of medical nutrition therapy. Report 97804 for group medical nutrition therapy provided for two or more individuals, each 30 minutes.

97810-97811
The health care provider applies acupuncture therapy by inserting one or more fine needles into the patient as dictated by acupuncture meridians for the relief of pain. The needles are twirled or manipulated by hand to generate therapeutic stimulation. No electrical stimulation is employed with this procedure. Report 97810 for the initial 15 minutes of personal one-on-one contact with the patient and 97811 for each additional 15 minutes of personal one-on-one contact with the patient, with re-insertion of the needle.

97813-97814
The health care provider applies acupuncture therapy by inserting one or more fine needles into the patient as dictated by acupuncture meridians for the relief of pain. The needles are energized by employing a micro-current for electrical stimulation. Report 97813 for the initial 15 minutes of personal one-on-one contact with the patient and 97814 for each additional 15 minutes of personal one-on-one contact with the patient, with reinsertion of the needle.

98925-98929
The physician uses these codes to report osteopathic manipulation, unique manual treatments that are used to treat somatic dysfunction and related disorders. Several techniques exist. Body regions included are head, cervical thoracic, lumbar, sacral, pelvic, extremities, rib cage, abdomen, and viscera. Report 98925 if one to two body regions are involved; 98926 if three to four body regions are involved; 98927 if five to six body regions are involved; 98928 if seven to eight body regions are involved; and 98929 if nine body regions are involved.

98940-98943
The chiropractor uses these codes to report the unique manual treatments used to influence joint and neurophysiological function. Several modalities exist. Report 98940 if treatment is spinal, one to two regions; 98941 if treatment is spinal, three to four regions; 98942 if treatment is spinal, five regions; and 98943 if treatment is extraspinal (head, extremities, rib cage, and abdomen), one or more regions.

98960-98962
The qualified, nonphysician health care professional provides education and training using a standard curriculum. This training is prescribed by a physician to enable the patient to concurrently self-manage established illnesses or diseases with health care providers. Report 98960 for education and training provided for an individual patient for each 30 minutes of service. Report 98961 for a group of two to four patients and 98962 for a group of five to eight patients.

98966-98968
A qualified health care professional (nonphysician) provides telephone assessment and management services to a patient in a non-face-to-face encounter. These episodes of care may be initiated by an established patient or by the patient's guardian. These codes are not reported if the telephone service results in a decision to see the patient within 24 hours or at

the next available urgent visit appointment; instead, the phone encounter is regarded as part of the pre-service work of the subsequent face-to-face encounter. These codes are also not reported if the telephone call is in reference to a service performed and reported by the qualified health care professional that occurred within the past seven days or within the postoperative period of a previously completed procedure. This applies both to unsolicited patient follow-up or that requested by the health care professional. Report 98966 for telephone services requiring five to 10 minutes of medical discussion, 98967 for telephone services requiring 11 to 20 minutes of medical discussion, and 98968 for telephone services requiring 21 to 30 minutes of medical discussion. Do not report 98966-98968 if these codes have been reported within the previous seven days.

98969
On-line medical assessment and management services are those provided to an established patient, guardian, or health care provider in response to a patient's on-line inquiry utilizing Internet resources in a non-face-to-face encounter. Code 98969 reports services provided by a qualified health care professional (nonphysician). In order for these services to be reportable, the health care professional must provide a personal, timely response to the inquiry and the encounter must be permanently stored via electronic means or hard copy. A reportable service includes all communication related to the on-line encounter, such as phone calls, provision of prescriptions, and orders for laboratory services. This code is not reported if the on-line evaluation is in reference to a service performed and reported by the same health care professional within the past seven days or within the postoperative period of a previously completed procedure. Rather, the on-line service is considered to be part of the previous service or procedure. This applies both to unsolicited patient follow-up or that requested by the health care professional. Report 98969 only once for the same episode of care during a seven-day period.

99000
This code is adjunct to basic services rendered. The physician reports this for the handling and/or conveyance of a specimen from the physician's office to a laboratory.

99001
This code is adjunct to basic services rendered. The physician reports this code for the handling and/or conveyance of a specimen from the patient in other than the physician's office to the laboratory.

99002
This code is adjunct to basic services rendered. The physician reports this code regarding handling, conveyance, and/or any other service in connection with implementation of devices such as orthotic, protective, and prosthetic fabricated by an outside laboratory and fitted by the attending physician.

99024
The physician reports this code to indicate a postoperative follow-up visit, normally included in the surgical package when the physician performs an evaluation and management service for reason(s) that are related to the original procedure.

99026-99027
The code reports the time for hospital mandated on call service provided by the physician. This code does not include prolonged physician attendance time for standby services or the time spent performing other reportable procedures or services. Report 99026 for each hour of hospital mandated on call service spent in the hospital and 99027 for each hour of hospital mandated on call service spent outside the hospital.

99050
This code is adjunct to basic services rendered. The physician reports this code to indicate services after posted office hours in addition to basic services.

99051
This code is adjunct to basic services rendered. The physician reports this code to indicate services provided during posted evening, weekend, or holiday office hours in addition to basic services.

99053
This code is adjunct to basic services rendered. The physician reports this code to indicate services provided between 10 p.m. and 8 a.m. at a 24-hour facility in addition to basic services.

99056
This code is adjunct to basic services rendered. The physician reports this code to indicate services typically provided in the office that are provided in a different location at the request of a patient.

99058
This code is adjunct to basic services rendered. The physician reports this code to indicate services provided in the office on an emergency basis that disrupt other scheduled office services.

99060
This code is adjunct to basic services rendered. The physician reports this code to indicate services provided on an emergency basis in a location other than the physician's office that disrupt other scheduled office services.

99070
This code is adjunct to basic services rendered. The physician reports this code to indicate supplies and materials provided by the physician over and above those usually included with the office visit or other services rendered. This code does not include

eyeglasses; report the appropriate supply code if eyeglasses are provided. List drugs, trays, supplies, and other materials provided when using this code.

99071
This code is adjunct to basic services rendered. The physician reports this code to indicate educational supplies provided by the physician for the patient's education.

99075
This code is adjunct to basic services rendered. The physician reports this code to indicate medical testimony.

99078
The physician provides educational services to patients in a group setting. The topics vary according to the group but can include prenatal care, diet, diabetic instruction, and smoke cessation.

99080
This code is adjunct to basic services rendered. The physician reports this code to indicate reports such as insurance forms, more than the information in standard communications methods or forms.

99082
This code is adjunct to basic services rendered. The physician reports this code to indicate unusual travel for the purpose of transportation or accompanying the patient.

99090
This code is adjunct to basic services rendered. The physician reports this code to indicate analysis of clinical data stored in computers.

99091
This is the collection and interpretation of physiologic data by the physician or other qualified health care professional. The data (e.g., blood pressure) is stored digitally and may be transmitted by the patient and/or the caregiver to the physician. The report should contain the time it took the provider to acquire the physiologic data, review and interpret the data, and modify any care plan due to the additional data acquisition. A minimum of 30 minutes of time must be spent in the collection and interpretation of data to report this service.

99100
This code is adjunct to basic services rendered. The physician reports this code to indicate qualifying circumstances regarding anesthesia for a patient younger than 1 year or older than 70 years of age.

99116
This code is adjunct to basic services rendered. The physician reports this code to indicate qualifying circumstances regarding anesthesia complicated by utilization of total body hypothermia.

99135
This code is adjunct to basic services rendered. The physician reports this code to indicate qualifying circumstances regarding anesthesia complicated by utilization of controlled hypotension.

99140
This code is adjunct to basic services rendered. The physician reports this code to indicate qualifying circumstances regarding anesthesia complicated by emergency conditions. Specify emergency conditions encountered when submitting a claim.

99143-99145
A physician or trained health care professional administers medication that allows a decreased level of consciousness but does not put the patient completely asleep inducing a state called moderate (conscious) sedation. This allows the patient to breathe without assistance and respond to commands. This is used for less invasive procedures and/or as a second medication for pain. This code reports sedation services provided by the same physician performing the primary procedure with the assistance of an independent trained health care professional to assist in monitoring the patient. Report 99143 for the first 30 minutes of intra-service time for sedation services rendered to a patient younger than five years of age. Report 99144 for the first 30 minutes of intra-service time for sedation services rendered to a patient age five years of age or older. Report 99145 for each additional 15 minutes of service.

99148-99150
A physician or trained health care professional administers medication that allows a decreased level of consciousness but does not put the patient completely asleep, inducing a state called moderate (conscious) sedation. This allows the patient to breathe without assistance and respond to commands. This is used for less invasive procedures and/or as a second medication for pain. These codes report services provided by a physician other than the health care professional performing the diagnostic or therapeutic service that the sedation supports. Report 99148 for the first 30 minutes of intra-service time for sedation services rendered to a patient younger than five years of age. Report 99149 for the first 30 minutes of intra-service time for sedation services rendered to a patient age five years of age or older. Report 99150 for each additional 15 minutes of service.

99170
The physician focuses the colposcope on the anogenital area of a child to magnify and directly observe the condition of living tissues in cases of suspected trauma. This examination allows a more complete examination than a normal physical exam since the colposcope magnifies from six to 40 times.

99172
The patient's visual function is evaluated in this exam with several parts. For visual acuity, the physician asks the patient to stand at a specified distance (20 feet for Snellen eye chart) away from the chart. The patient is instructed to cover the left eye with the left hand or hold a card in front of the lens for those patients wearing eyeglasses. The patient reads the letters on the chart to test the visual acuity of the right eye. The process is repeated for the other eye. Ocular alignment is checked by determining whether the eyes work together in the same direction. The patient is positioned in front of a screen, looking ahead, and the non-tested eye is covered in a field of vision screening. The health care provider flashes objects in various areas in the field of vision and the patient is asked to respond. The patient's response creates a map of the visual field. To test color vision, the patient looks at cards with many different colored dots that make specific shapes. The patient with normal color vision will be able to discern the shapes within the colors. This exam identifies possible vision problems. It does not replace the examination by an ophthalmologist or optometrist and is used as a screening test only.

99173
The physician asks the patient to stand at a specified distance (20 feet for Snellen eye chart) from the chart. The patient is instructed to cover the left eye with the left hand or hold a card in front of the lens for those patients wearing eyeglasses. The patient reads the letters on the screen to test the visual acuity of the right eye. The process is repeated for the other eye. This exam identifies possible vision problems; it does not replace the examination by an ophthalmologist or optometrist and is used as a screening test only.

99174
Ocular photoscreening is a diagnostic tool that may prove effective in testing preverbal children and children with developmental disorders for amblyogenic factors such as strabismus, media opacities, and severe refractive disorders. It can be used more effectively than standard techniques in preverbal children and children with developmental disorders because it only requires that the patient be able to focus on the target long enough for photoscreening. Photoscreening is performed with a specialized camera or video system that obtains images of the pupillary reflexes and red reflexes. Currently there are two types of photoscreening systems available. One type uses a trained evaluator to analyze the data. The second uses a computerized system to interpret the images. Code 99174 reports a bilateral screening with interpretation and report.

99175
The physician administers ipecac or a similar substance to induce vomiting and observes the patient until the stomach is adequately emptied of poison.

99183
The physician attends and supervises hyperbaric oxygen therapy. Report per session. Report hyperbaric oxygen therapy procedures separately.

99190-99192
The health care provider assembles and operates a pump with an oxygenator or heat exchanger. Report 99190 to identify each hour; 99191 to report 45 minutes; and 99192 to report 30 minutes.

99195
The health care provider draws blood from the patient to right dramatically imbalanced blood levels (i.e., hemoglobin, potassium salts). The procedure is similar to drawing blood from a donor, but a number of pints may be taken to reduce the imbalance. Blood removal is performed under a physician's direction.

99500
The home health provider may visit patients with prenatal complications from the first month until the birth of the baby in 99500. The home nurse may obtain vaginal-anorectal/cervical cultures, perform a non-stress test and uterine and fetal heart rate monitoring, draw blood for serology (including offering of AFP/HIV testing), and other tests such as glucose screening to check for gestational diabetes.

99501
A home visit for postnatal assessment may include a review of plans for future health maintenance and care, including routine infant immunizations, identification of illness and periodic health evaluations, and linking the family with other sources of support such as social services, parenting classes, and lactation consultants as necessary.

99502
The home health care provider measures vital signs, does a physical examination, and assesses developmental norms in the newborn and discusses feeding and care with the mother. The home health care provider teaches and answers questions regarding childcare and determines if there are any problems requiring a physician's intervention. Postpartum early discharge is defined as six hours to 36 hours after uncomplicated vaginal delivery or 72 hours after uncomplicated cesarean delivery. Specialized nursing helps the family make the transition from hospital to home.

99503
A trained respiratory therapist or other health care professional provides care for patients with temporary or chronic respiratory conditions. The health care professional may provide pulmonary evaluations, patient and family education and counseling, and instruction in self-care. The visit is designed to assist the physician in caring for the patient by avoiding complications, infections, disease progression, and to ultimately reduce hospitalizations. The visit may also

include evaluation and monitoring of the equipment used, including diagnostics and calibration of the equipment; changes in medications (e.g., bronchodilator); and/or advice and education about dosage and the use of a particular medication.

99504
A respiratory therapist or other home health care professional visits a patient's home to give mechanical ventilation care. The health care professional instructs the patient and family members on the ventilator equipment, including checking the machine and the settings. During the home health visit, related equipment or issues, such as oxygen and tracheostomy care (when present), is discussed.

99505
The home health care provider measures vital signs, inspects incisions, assesses mobility and appetite, and determines if there are problems or situations that could require a surgeon's intervention. The provider checks the stoma site and the stoma's function. The home health provider teaches and answers questions the patient may have about the care and maintenance of the colostomy and/or cystostomy. The home health provider also administers medications or draws blood so that the surgeon can continue to monitor the patient's condition. Most patients who have had a colostomy or cystostomy will be seen by a home health provider one or more times after discharge.

99506
The home health provider visits a patient's home to perform an intermuscular injection of medication per a physician's or another valid order. The home health provider brings supplies and medications that are necessary to accomplish the injection to the patient's home, including a syringe, needle, liquid disinfectant, cotton ball, and adhesive tape. The procedure involves inserting the needle, aspiration and slow injection, and at the end of the procedure a cotton ball is placed over the injection site. Adhesive tape is applied over the cotton ball.

99507
The home health provider visits the patient at home for care and maintenance of catheter, such as urinary catheters, and catheters placed for drainage or enteral feeding. Skilled procedures required for the home visit include Foley catheter and suprapubic catheter insertion and management; gastrostomy tube/catheter maintenance and enteral feeding; dressing changes and assessment of catheter-related wounds; management of open or draining wounds, ulcers, or fistulae and drainage tube/catheter management; related suture/ staple removal; and urinary incontinence catheter management.

99509
In order to qualify for home assistance with activities of daily living and personal care, the patient must be unable to perform two or more activities of daily living, such as eating, toileting, transferring, bathing, dressing, and continence. When a referral is made, a health care provider visits the home to conduct a comprehensive assessment of the patient's needs. The plan of care is developed in conjunction with the client, physician, and family. Acting as a liaison with the client's physician and other community programs, the case manager responds to all client requests, questions, and concerns and reports frequently on the client's status and progress.

99510
A home health professional makes an initial visit to the home to evaluate specific needs. If home health care would be of benefit, a plan of care is developed based on medical orders from the patient's provider. For example, a plan might specify one or more visits from a therapist. The provider regularly reviews progress reports.

99511
A home health visit includes assistance with dietary management and bowel management/retraining (i.e., use of prescribed medication as well as establishing a habit regimen to treat constipation). The home health caregiver may manually remove the impaction or administer an enema. The amount of fluid administered depends on the age and size of the person receiving the enema. If necessary, a specimen is collected for diagnostic evaluation.

99512
This code reports a home visit for hemodialysis. A home health nurse commonly visits the patient three times a week to provide hemodialysis. Each treatment lasts from two to four hours. Before treatment, access is made to the bloodstream to provide a way for blood to be carried from the patient to the dialysis machine, which filters out wastes and extra fluids and returns the blood back to the patient. The access may be under the skin or outside the body. During treatment, the patient can read, write, sleep, talk, or watch television.

99601-99602
A home health professional visits the patient at home to perform the infusion of a specialty drug per a physician's order. The home health provider brings the supplies and medication required and administers and oversees the infusion. Each infusion takes up to two hours per visit for 99601. Report 99602 for each additional hour.

99605-99607
A pharmacist provides individual management of medication therapy with assessment and intervention. This patient-specific service includes review of pertinent history and profiling of prescription and non-prescription medications. The pharmacist evaluates the medication profile for under- or over-dosing, duplications, and possible drug

interactions, and makes recommendations based on the assessment, including communication with the prescriber. Report 99605 for the initial 15-minute individual new patient encounter provided face-to-face by the pharmacist; 99606 for the initial 15-minute individual established patient encounter; and 99607 for each additional 15 minutes spent with the patient.

A local anesthetic is applied over the site where the catheter is to be introduced; this is most often the common femoral or brachial artery. The artery is percutaneously punctured with a needle and a guidewire is fed through the artery until it reaches the arteriovenous shunt created in the patient, usually in the upper extremity. A catheter is threaded over the guidewire to the point of study and the guidewire is removed. Contrast medium is injected and a series of x-rays taken to visualize the shunt and evaluate its function. This code reports the radiological supervision and interpretation only. Use a separately reportable code for the catheterization.

Category III

0016T

Transpupillary thermotherapy is a sub-threshold laser photocoagulation technique that can result in closure of choroidal neovascularization (CNV) while sparing the neurosensory retina. Treatment is typically done without retrobulbar anesthesia, though topical anesthesia may be applied. The laser HeNe aiming beam is set at low to moderate intensity and the ophthalmologist bisects the retina by a moderate-to-high slit beam to visualize the retina and the RPE. Treatment is stopped at the first sign of retinal color change.

0017T

Laser treatment in patients with dry age-related macular degeneration (AMD) has been shown to cause resorption of drusen, which may benefit the natural course of the disease. There are ongoing clinical trials that utilize sub-threshold diode laser treatment that minimizes damage to the retina and is not perceptible to the patient or to the clinician. The method consists of placing a grid of 48 ophthalmoscopically invisible diode laser spots around the macula. The ophthalmologist administers photocoagulation as a grid in four concentric rings that spares the fovea.

0019T

Low-energy extracorporeal shock wave therapy (ESWT) delivers pulses of low-pressure sound waves that travel through fluid and soft tissue, affecting sites of impedance change, such as the bone-soft tissue interface. Extracorporeal shock wave therapy is used to treat painful orthopedic conditions such as plantar fasciitis, calcaneal spurs, and lateral epicondylitis because of the therapy's stimulatory effect on soft tissue and bone, which often heal back stronger after exposure to ESWT. The painful area is identified and marked. Coupling gel is applied to the treatment area and the shock head of the device is coupled to the patient and positioned for good contact. The technician increases the delivery rate incrementally to the maximum power and number of shocks. The main difference between low and high-energy shock wave therapy is the amount of anesthesia or sedation required. Low-energy can often be done in an office setting and does not require heavy sedation or general anesthesia as does high-energy therapy.

0030T

A test for detecting the presence of antibodies directed at prothrombin is done by ELISA method, using prothrombin coated on irradiated plates and phosphatidylserine/prothrombin complex as antigen. ELISA method is an Enzyme-linked Immunosorbent Assay that basically functions using antigens or antibodies linked to an easily-assayed enzyme. The capturing antibody is purified and bound to a solid phase and the antigen is added and allowed to complex with the bound antibody. The unbound products are removed with washing. A labeled second antibody, the detection antibody, is added and allowed to bind with the antigen present in the antigen/antibody complex, forming a sandwich matrix. The amount of labeled second antibody found in the matrix is measured with the use of a colored substrate. Different immunoglobulin class antibodies within the family of antiphospholipid antibodies are screened to detect those that will classify a patient with ABS, or antiphospholipid syndrome. The antibodies are directed against plasma proteins bound to phospholipids. Prothrombin is one of the best-known phospholipid binding proteins.

0042T

Cerebral perfusion analysis is performed to evaluate the blood supply to the brain utilizing computed tomography (CT). A contrast enhancement agent known as a tracer is administered. The blood transports the tracer to the brain, where the tracer perfuses, or fills, the tissue. This perfused tissue appears brighter in the CT image. The rate at which the tissue becomes brighter is proportional to the perfusion rate. A perfusion-weighted image is displayed by the software for the CT scanner, which measures the rate of change.

0048T-0050T

A ventricular assist device (VAD) is a temporary measure used to support the heart by substituting for left and/or right heart function when a patient has had a heart attack, is in acute heart failure, has a damaged or weakened heart wall, or is awaiting transplantation. VADs can replace the work of the left ventricle, right ventricle, or both. A left VAD helps the heart pump blood through the rest of the body, and a right VAD helps the heart pump blood to the lungs to become oxygenated again. This is done by inserting catheters to circulate the blood through external tubing to a pump machine located outside the body and back to the correct artery. VADs inserted by percutaneous transseptal access do not require open chest surgery and can be inserted in a cath lab. The access site is through the femoral artery or vein. Using a needle, the interatrial septum is punctured and the catheter position within the left atrium is verified by injecting dye. The catheter is exchanged for a stiff guidewire and the interatrial puncture site is dilated, followed by insertion of a venous inflow cannula into the left atrium, which is sutured to the skin on the thigh. Next, an arterial perfusion catheter is inserted percutaneously into the right femoral artery and advanced into the lower abdominal aorta. Heparin-coated tubing is attached to connect the catheters to the pump. The arterial clamp is removed and the pump speed is set. The left ventricle is now unloaded by diverting blood from the left atrium to the systemic circulation. Report 0048T for percutaneous transseptal insertion of the VAD. Report 0050T for removal of the device.

0051T

Total replacement heart systems, or artificial hearts, are implanted as a temporary measure until transplantation, or to prolong life for those not eligible for transplant. One artificial heart system, described here, is a self-contained, electrohydraulic action heart, charged from a battery source through the skin. Once attached, the natural atria pump blood into the artificial ventricles of the replacement heart and the hydraulic pump moves the blood into circulation. The patient is prepared for open heart surgery, and an extended median sternotomy is made. A subcutaneous/ submuscular pocket is created in the patient's abdominal area for the internal battery and the heart's pumping controller unit, and these internal components are placed between muscle layers. A separate incision is made over the chest wall for placement of the internal transcutaneous energy transmission coil, which is sutured into an appropriate position where the external coil may lie flat over it without much interposing tissue. Cardiopulmonary bypass is initiated, the aorta is cross-clamped, and cardiectomy is undertaken to remove the native ventricles and transect the great vessels. Outflow grafts are anastomosed to the pulmonary artery and the aorta. The artificial ventricles are anastomosed to the native atrial cuffs and all air is removed from the system. The aortic cross-clamp is released and cardiopulmonary bypass weaned onto the artificial heart support. The internal components are connected to the artificial heart and energy is transferred through the transcutaneous coils, where external battery packs transmit power across the skin to keep the internal battery charged.

0052T

This code reports repair or removal and replacement of the thoracic unit of a total replacement heart system or artificial heart. The thoracic unit is the pump that consists of the artificial ventricles, which are attached to the natural atria, containing their corresponding valves, and the motor-driven hydraulic pumping system, or the pneumatic air pressure valves, depending on the system. Repair or removal and replacement of this component requires open chest access in a procedure following the same kind of steps for implantation (see 0051T), except that the other internal components are already in position and must be reconnected after repair or replacement is complete.

0053T

This code reports repair or removal and replacement of an internal component of a total replacement heart system or artificial heart, excluding the thoracic unit. Internal components include the implanted rechargeable battery, which is continually charged by external battery packs, the internal transcutaneous coil for receiving the battery charge across the skin, or the control unit, which monitors and controls the pumping speed of the artificial heart. These components are repaired or removed and replaced back in their prepared subcutaneous/submuscular pockets, and tunneled back to their connection with the thoracic unit, which is not replaced or repaired in this code.

0054T-0055T

Computer-assisted musculoskeletal navigation techniques are used with many orthopedic procedures, especially for accurate placement of the acetabular component during hip replacement surgery. Preoperative images of patient-specific bone geometry are first obtained for the surgical plan in whatever imaging modality is to be used. The patient-specific surgical plan and images are used during surgery to guide the surgeon by combining these with intraoperative navigation capabilities. Optical targets, or trackers, such as digitizing or LED-equipped probes, are attached to points on the bone anatomy or to surgical tools. An optical camera tracks the position of these for accurate navigation and measurement in relation to any bone or instrument movement as the surgery is performed. The software in these navigational systems matches or "registers" the position of the patient on the operating table to the geometric description of the bony surface derived from the images already used to plan the surgery. Multiple images are simultaneously displayed on the monitor. The "virtual" tool trajectory that corresponds to the tracked tool movements is displayed over the previously saved views in real-time as the surgeon operates. These are add-on codes to be used in addition to the primary procedure. Report 0054T for image-guidance based on fluoroscopic imaging and

0055T for CT/MRI imaging. If CT and MRI are both performed, 0055T is reported only once.

0071T-0072T
Focused ultrasound ablation is a noninvasive surgical technique that uses thermal ablation to destroy uterine leiomyomata. In focused ultrasound ablation the ultrasound beam penetrates through soft tissues causing localized high temperatures for a few seconds at the targeted site, in this case the uterine leiomyomata. This produces thermocoagulation and necrosis of the uterine leiomyomata without damage to overlaying and surrounding tissues. Magnetic resonance (MR) guidance is used in conjunction with focused ultrasound ablation to provide more precise target definition. Since certain MR parameters are also temperature sensitive, MR guidance also allows estimation of optimal thermal doses to the uterine leiomyomata and detection of relatively small temperature elevations in surrounding tissues thereby preventing any irreversible damage to surrounding tissues. Report 0071T for total leiomyomata tissue volume less than 200 cc. Report 0072T for leiomyomata tissue volume equal to or greater than 200 cc.

0073T
Compensator-based beam modulation treatment delivery of inversed planned treatment using three or more high-resolution (milled or cast) compensator convergent beam modulated fields is a method of delivering intensity modulated radiation therapy (IMRT). Prior to treatment delivery, a computerized planning system is used to calculate dose by inverse treatment planning method for IMRT optimization. The planner chooses beam angles and writes a prescription for targets identifying critical structures. The computerized planning system optimizes beam weights and modulation patterns and generates files for milling or casting of the required high resolution compensators that are fabricated as prescribed and planned. During treatment delivery solid filters modulate the beams. Code 0073T reports only the treatment delivery component and is reported for each treatment session.

0075T-0076T
Placing stents into extracranial vertebral and intrathoracic carotid arteries percutaneously (through a catheter) is a less invasive alternative to open endarterectomy. The procedure is carried out by making a small incision in the leg to access an artery and threading a catheter through the artery to the target. A stent delivery system that may also include an embolic capturing device is loaded into a delivery pod and advanced to the blocked or narrowed artery through the catheter. The embolic protection device is deployed first, distal to the lesion so that any emboli are collected as the blood passes through the device. The stent is advanced out of the pod until it expands to open the narrowing. The procedure is performed under radiologic supervision. Report 0075T for the placement of the stent(s) into the initial artery and 0076T for stent placement into each additional vessel. Both codes include radiologic supervision and interpretation.

0078T-0081T
Endovascular repair of an abdominal aortic aneurysm, pseudoaneurysm, or dissection, using a prosthesis, and involving visceral branches (superior mesenteric, celiac, and/or renal artery) requires the skills of both a vascular surgeon and a radiologist. Although different types of prostheses may be used, when visceral branches are involved, a fenestrated modular bifurcated graft is often placed, described here, which requires that a small incision be made in the groin over both femoral arteries through which the endovascular devices are inserted. If a modular bifurcated graft is used, it incorporates two or more components, which are assembled intravascularly to form the graft and completely exclude an aneurysm. Under fluoroscopic guidance, the physician inserts the aortic component and one iliac limb through one femoral artery. These are contained inside a plastic holding capsule that is threaded through the arteries to the site of the aneurysm. Next, the physician inserts the opposite iliac limb by contralateral femoral artery access. The physician mates the aortic and iliac limb inserted into the first femoral artery to the opposite iliac limb inserted by contralateral femoral artery access. Since this repair extends above the visceral vessels, a visceral extension prosthesis is required. The physician places the extension prosthesis and cuts fenestrations (holes) at each visceral artery orifice to allow side branch perfusion of these vessels. Next, catheters are used to place overlapping stents at each fenestration and vessel orifice to secure the junction. Once the graft components and stents are in place, the holding capsule and catheters are removed and the arteriotomy site is closed. Report 0078T for the endovascular repair of the abdominal aortic aneurysm. Placement of the visceral extension prosthesis is reported separately with 0079T. Radiological supervision and interpretation of the endovascular repair and the placement of the visceral extension prosthesis are also reported separately with 0080T and 0081T respectively.

0085T
A marker for heart transplant rejection, the breath methylated alkane contour (BMAC) is administered as a lab test. Heart transplant rejection is accompanied by oxidative stress that degrades membrane polyunsaturated fatty acids, evolving alkanes, and methylalkanes. These are excreted in the form of volatile organic compounds (VOC). To evaluate VOC, a breath sample is taken. Breath VOCs are analyzed using gas chromatography and mass spectrometry. The BMAC is derived based on the abundance of C4-C20 alkanes and monomethylalkanes.

Category III

0092T

Total disc arthroplasty is done to replace a severely damaged or diseased intervertebral cervical disc, most often caused by degenerative disc disease. The physician uses an anterior approach to reach multiple damaged cervical vertebrae by making an incision through the neck, avoiding the esophagus, trachea, and thyroid. Retractors separate the intervertebral muscles. The affected intervertebral location is confirmed by separately reportable x-ray. The physician cleans out the intervertebral disc space with a rongeur, removing the cartilaginous material to be replaced in preparation for inserting the implants. This may include osteophytectomy for nerve root or spinal cord decompression, as well as microdissection. One type of implant for total disc replacement has two endplates made of a metal alloy and a convex weight-bearing surface made of ultra high molecular weight polyethylene. The endplates are inserted in a collapsed form and seated into the vertebral bodies above and below the interspaces. Minimal distraction is applied to open the intervertebral spaces, and the polyethylene disc material is snap-fit into the lower endplates. With the disc assemblies complete, the wound is closed and a drain may be placed. Report 0092T for each additional cervical interspace treated with total disc arthroplasty in conjunction with 22856.

0095T

The physician removes an artificial disc prosthesis placed during a previous disc arthroplasty by anterior approach. The physician approaches the cervical vertebrae by making an incision through the neck, avoiding the esophagus, trachea, and thyroid. Retractors separate the intervertebral muscles. The implant is located and any adhesions are freed. Distraction is applied to open the intervertebral space and the implant is removed. The area is explored and debrided. When the procedure is complete, the fascia and vertebral muscles are repaired and returned to their anatomical positions, drains are placed, and the wound is closed. Code 0095T must be reported in conjunction with 22864; assign once for each additional cervical interspace.

0098T

The physician revises an artificial disc prosthesis placed during a previous disc arthroplasty through anterior approach. The prosthesis may be migrating from a lack of fixation and require components to be replaced or adjusted. The physician approaches the cervical vertebrae by making an incision through the neck, avoiding the esophagus, trachea, and thyroid. Retractors separate the intervertebral muscles. The implant is located, the area is explored, and any adhesions are freed. Distraction is applied to open the intervertebral space. The arthroplastic disc is removed, and the endplates of the vertebral body are reshaped and prepped for reinsertion. New height, depth, and width dimensions may also be taken with the vertebral body distracted in cases where another, more appropriately sized disc prosthesis is required. The components are reinserted, and the fascia and vertebral muscles are repaired and returned to their anatomical positions. The incision is closed. Code 0098T must be reported in conjunction with 22861; assign once for each additional cervical interspace.

0099T

Intrastromal corneal ring segments are prescription corneal inserts implanted for surgical treatment of mild myopia. The rings are made of ultra-thin, biocompatible polymethylmethacrylate. The corneal ring is inserted between layers of the outer edge of the cornea, causing flattening of the center of the cornea to gently reshape the contour of the eye. Insertion is done under topical anesthesia and only takes about 15 minutes. The incision positions and segment placement are marked on the cornea and a radial incision is made with a diamond blade on the marked zone. Micro fine nylon interrupted sutures are placed to close the initial incision.

0100T

An electronic retinal prosthesis is implanted to restore some lost vision and create visual perception by electronically stimulating the retina. Diseases such as retinitis pigmentosa and age-related macular degeneration destroy vision by degenerating the rod and cone photoreceptors in the eye. These electronically conducting devices help patients detect light or distinguish between objects such as a cup or plate. The retinal prosthesis is a sliver, or tiny chip, of silicone and platinum attached to and sitting on top of the retina.

0101T-0102T

High-energy extracorporeal shock wave delivery involves the application of pressure waves that travel through fluid and soft tissue, with effects of the shock wave occurring at sites where there is a change in impedance, such as the bone-soft tissue interface. Extracorporeal shock wave therapy is used to treat common orthopedic conditions (i.e., plantar calcaneal spurs, epicondylopathic humeri radialis) because of the therapy's stimulatory effect on bone formation. Other potential uses of extracorporeal shock wave therapy include treating bone marrow hypoxia and subperiosteal hemorrhage, increasing regional blood flow, and activating osteogenic factors such as bone morphogenic protein, direct cellular effects, and mechanical effects as a result of strain gradients. Code 0101T reports high energy extracorporeal shock wave application to the musculoskeletal system, other than plantar fascia or lateral humeral epicondyle, and 0102T requires anesthesia other than local for high energy shock wave application performed by a physician on the lateral humeral epicondyle.

0103T

Holotranscobalamin (HoloTC) is the sum total of cobalamin (Cbl), known as vitamin B12, bound to transcobalamin (TC), the plasma protein responsible for transporting vitamin B12 to all cells of the body. Since only the minor fraction of Cbl bound to TC is actually available to cells, laboratory quantification of HoloTC is evaluated as a marker for Vitamin B12 deficiency. The commercially available technique involves adding a capturing reagent comprised of magnetic particles coated with monoclonal anti-human TC to the sample of blood serum or EDTA plasma. A reducing reagent is added to the separated transcobalamin, followed by a denaturing reagent, and a tracer. The vitamin B12 released from TC and the tracer compete to bind to the B12 binder, intrinsic factor. The unbound tracer is next removed by centrifuging. The measured amount of bound radioactivity is inversely proportional to the amount of vitamin B12 bound to transcobalamin in the sample. The concentration of B12 on TC is determined.

0104T-0105T

The provider measures cardiac output non-invasively using an infrared photoacoustic gas analyzing system. The patient's nose is clipped closed to maintain rebreathing into the closed system with the inert gas mixture. Rebreathing technique is performed through the mouthpiece and gas is sampled continuously from the mouthpiece for analysis. The patient breathes synchronously with a graph tachymeter on the computer screen and completely empties the rebreathing bag with each breath to maintain a constant ventilation rate and volume. The analyzer interfaces with a computer and software that controls the respiratory valve and analyzer settings, and stores the retrieved gas concentration data. Report 0104T for inert gas rebreathing during rest and 0105T for inert gas rebreathing during exercise.

0106T-0107T

Quantitative sensory testing (QST) done with pressure touch or vibration stimuli assesses nerve fiber sensation in a larger diameter and detects sensory loss in cases of diabetes, alcoholism, and drug therapy or evaluates nerve recovery after surgery. When applying vibration stimuli (0107T), described here, a small controller unit with two separate vibrator rods is used. The rods apply the vibration stimulus to the skin while the vibration amplitude is adjusted through the control unit. Report 0106T when similar quantitative sensory testing is done using a device designed to apply touch pressure stimuli at different thresholds to the area being tested.

0108T-0110T

Quantitative sensory testing (QST) done as thermal sensory analysis can diagnose early diabetic neuropathy. A small thermode device capable of heating or cooling is attached to the patient's skin and the extremity is tested with heat or cooling stimuli to assess sensation. The patient's thresholds for warmth, cold, heat-induced pain, or cold-induced pain are quantitatively measured and compared with reference values that are age-matched for the normal population. The test may take up to an hour, depending on the number of sites to be tested. Report 0108T for QST testing and interpretation per extremity using cold stimuli and 0109T for heat-pain stimuli. Use 0110T for QST testing and interpretation per extremity using stimuli other than heat, cold, vibration, or pressure.

0111T

Long chain (C20-22) omega-3 fatty acids in red blood cell (RBC) membranes are measured. Long chain fatty acid levels have been associated with insulin resistance, coronary heart disease, and cardiac risk factors. A blood sample is obtained by venipuncture. Method is chromatography.

0123T

The physician creates a new tract or pathway for filtering aqueous fluid from the posterior chamber of the eye. Using an operating microscope, a small conjunctival flap is first created. An electromagnetic plasma ablation device creates a tiny pit through the sclera above the ciliary body and behind the iris. The metal tip creates a pore or a tract through the ciliary body into the posterior chamber of the eye beginning at the base of the scleral pit created above. The conjunctival flap is reattached.

0124T

The physician performs a conjunctival incision and places medication into the posterior segment of the eye for treatment of conditions of the choroid and retina, such as macular degeneration. After placing a lid speculum and administering lidocaine, the physician makes a small 2 to 3 mm conjunctival incision into the Tenon's capsule in the upper, outer quadrant a few millimeters from the limbus. A blunt tipped, curved cannula is inserted into the posterior area of the globe through the Tenon's space and positioned with the tip near the macula. The medication is injected, and the cannula is removed. Pressure is applied, and the speculum is removed. Sutures are not usually required to close the conjunctiva. This code does not include supply of the medication itself.

0126T

An intima-media thickness (IMT) study is performed on the common carotid artery. The measurements of the inner two artery layers, the intima and the media, are used as risk factor indicators for atherosclerosis and coronary heart disease. This non-invasive test is performed by scanning with high-resolution B mode ultrasonography and using computer enhancement and analysis to determine the thickness of the intima and media of the carotid artery. The results evaluate for any thickening or signs of anatomical changes from early atherosclerotic disease.

0130T

The pharmacist performs a validated, statistically reliable, randomized, controlled, single-patient clinical investigational review of FDA approved drugs used to treat chronic conditions and supplies interpretation and report to the prescribing professional. These single-patient trials compare medications that may be prescribed for the same condition, to help determine the optimal treatment and promote compliance and cost-effective drug use. In this trial design, the patient normally receives two treatments, one at a time, in random order. The patient receives each treatment for at least two multiple-day periods so that replication can be achieved. In the majority of single-patient trials, the consecutive periods are paired and the treatment order is independently randomized for each pair so that variability due to temporal trends can be reduced. The physician sends a prescription to a properly equipped and trained pharmacist. A standard test protocol is specified, as well as the two test agents to be utilized. In the majority of cases, the pharmacist will manage patient registration and eligibility screening. A trial test kit is prepared to capture data on effectiveness and adverse effects from the patient in diary form. Various methods are utilized for daily data capture, including Web-based data entry screens, interactive voice recognition systems, and mark-sense readable paper diaries. Upon completion of the trial, a statistical analysis is performed and the physician is provided a summary, as well as a detailed report of the results, which is used to direct the patient's ongoing therapy.

0140T

The pH level from exhaled breath condensation is used to evaluate the severity of respiratory conditions, such as asthma or chronic cough. The patient exhales into a disposable breath condensate collector. A chilled metal condenser or an electric breath-cooling device is used with the collector. The patient puts the mouthpiece into her mouth and breathes normally for up to 10 minutes. The condenser or cooling device is removed from the collector and the condensate is placed in a microcentrifuge tube and de-aerated with argon. The pH level is measured with a microelectrode.

0141T

Islet cells are insulin-producing cell clusters found only in the pancreas. In islet cell transplants, insulin-producing islet cells are infused into the liver by portal vein embolization. Islet cell transplant is considered a less invasive alternative to pancreatic transplant. The physician uses ultrasonic guidance to insert a catheter through a skin incision in the upper abdomen and into the portal vein of the liver. Islet cells are slowly infused through the catheter. The pressure within the portal vein is monitored during the procedure to ensure that the vessel is not occluded. The catheter is removed and the incision closed. The islet cells will attach to the vessel walls in the portal vein and begin releasing insulin within a month. This procedure is limited to persons with type 1 diabetes.

0142T

Islet cells are insulin-producing cell clusters found only in the pancreas. In islet cell transplants, insulin-producing islet cells are infused into the liver by portal vein embolization. Islet cell transplant is considered a less invasive alternative to pancreatic transplant. In an open procedure, the surgeon makes an incision in the skin overlying the liver and inserts a catheter into the portal vein. Islet cells are slowly infused through the catheter. The pressure within the portal vein is monitored during the procedure to ensure that the vessel is not occluded. The catheter is removed, and the incision closed. The islet cells will attach to the vessel walls in the portal vein and begin releasing insulin within a month. This procedure is limited to persons with type 1 diabetes.

0143T

Islet cells are insulin-producing cell clusters found only in the pancreas. In islet cell transplants, insulin-producing islet cells are infused into the liver by portal vein embolization. Islet cell transplant is considered a less invasive alternative to pancreatic transplant. The physician places a laparoscope via a small periumbilical port or through a small incision in the right upper quadrant, and an additional port is placed in the right upper quadrant under direct vision. The physician inserts a catheter into the portal vein of the liver. Islet cells are slowly infused through the catheter. The pressure within the portal vein is monitored during the procedure to ensure that the vessel is not occluded. The catheter is removed along with the laparoscope tools, and the incision closed. The islet cells will attach to the vessel walls in the portal vein and begin releasing insulin within a month. This procedure is limited to persons with type 1 diabetes.

0155T

The physician performs laparoscopic placement of gastric neurostimulator electrodes. The electrodes are placed for the purpose of weight loss in the morbidly obese patient. The physician makes an incision and places a trocar at the umbilicus to insufflate the abdomen. The laparoscope is placed through the umbilical port and additional trocars are placed into the abdominal cavity. The lesser curvature of the stomach is identified and the physician secures electrodes into the muscle. The electrodes are connected to a neurostimulator. The physician removes the laparoscope and tools from the abdomen, which is deflated and repaired with sutures. Report 0155T for initial placement or replacement of the gastric electrodes.

0156T

The physician performs a laparoscopic revision or removal of gastric neurostimulator electrodes. The electrodes initially were placed for the purpose of weight loss in the morbidly obese patient. The physician makes an incision and places a trocar at the umbilicus to insufflate the abdomen. The laparoscope is placed through the umbilical port and additional trocars are placed into the abdominal cavity. The lesser curvature of the stomach and the electrodes are identified and revised or dissected free of the stomach musculature and removed. The physician removes the laparoscope and tools from the abdomen, which is deflated and repaired with sutures.

0157T
The physician performs an open procedure to place gastric neurostimulator electrodes on the stomach. The electrodes are implanted for the purpose of weight loss in the morbidly obese patient. The physician makes a laparotomy incision and dissects down to the stomach. The lesser curvature of the stomach is identified and the physician secures electrodes into the muscle. The electrodes are connected to a neurostimulator. The surgical incision is repaired with layered sutures. Report 0157T for initial placement or replacement of the gastric electrodes.

0158T
The physician performs an open procedure to revise or remove gastric neurostimulator electrodes on the stomach. The electrodes were initially implanted for the purpose of weight loss in the morbidly obese patient. The physician makes a laparotomy incision and dissects down to the stomach. The lesser curvature of the stomach and the electrodes secured in the stomach muscle are identified and the physician revises or removes the electrodes. The surgical incision is repaired with layered sutures.

0159T
The physician uses dynamic contrast-enhanced MRI (DCE-MRI) to evaluate lesions of the breast. Pharmacokinetic analysis describes a process in which the data is calibrated by a computer to the patient's specific physiology. The physician reviews for interpretation the test results. This procedure is performed secondary to the primary MRI procedure.

0160T-0161T
Transcranial magnetic stimulation (TMS) is a technique to stimulate the brain by electromagnetic induction with a coil placed on the scalp. For direct stimulation to cortical neurons, a strong magnetic field pulse is generated over the patient's scalp to activate cortical neurons in the brain. This procedure has been applied to activate neuronal processes and to disturb the normal operation of the brain. Treatment planning is reported with 0160T and each TMS session is reported with 0161T.

0163T
Total disc arthroplasty is done to replace a severely damaged or diseased intervertebral disc, most often caused by degenerative disc disease. The physician uses an anterior approach to reach damaged lumbar vertebrae by making an incision through the abdomen. Some implants require only minimal access, approximately 7 cm long, for a mini-retroperitoneal approach. Retractors separate the intervertebral muscles. The affected intervertebral disc locations are confirmed by separately reportable x-ray. The physician cleans out the intervertebral disc spaces with a rongeur, removing the cartilaginous material to be replaced in preparation for inserting implants. One type of implant for total disc replacement has two endplates made of a metal alloy and a convex weight-bearing surface made of ultra high molecular weight polyethylene. The endplates are inserted in a collapsed form and seated into the vertebral bodies above and below the interspace. Minimal distraction is applied to open the intervertebral spaces, and the polyethylene disc material is snap-fit into the lower endplate. With the disc assemblies complete, the wound is closed and a drain may be placed. Report this code for each additional lumbar disc replacement after the first, which is reported with 22857.

0164T
The physician removes an artificial disc prosthesis placed during a previous disc arthroplasty by anterior approach. The physician uses an anterior approach to reach the implant in the lumbar vertebrae by making an incision through the abdomen. Some implants require only minimal access, approximately 7 cm long, for a mini-retroperitoneal approach. Retractors separate the intervertebral muscles. The affected intervertebral implant location is confirmed by separately reportable x-ray. The physician cleans out the intervertebral disc space with a rongeur, removing the cartilaginous material to be replaced in preparation for removing an implant, and removes the implant. With the disc assembly removal complete, the wound is closed and a drain may be placed. Report 0164T for each additional lumbar artificial disc removal after the first, which is reported with 22865.

0165T
The physician revises an artificial disc prosthesis placed during a previous disc arthroplasty through an anterior approach. The prosthesis may be migrating from a lack of fixation and require components to be replaced or adjusted. The lumbar vertebrae are approached by making an incision through the abdomen. Retractors separate the intervertebral muscles. The implant is located, the area is explored, and any adhesions are freed. Distraction is applied to open the intervertebral space. The arthroplastic disc is removed, and the endplates of the vertebral body are reshaped and prepped for reinsertion. New height, depth, and width dimensions may also be taken with the vertebral body distracted in cases where another, more appropriately sized disc prosthesis is required. The components are reinserted, and the fascia and vertebral muscles are repaired and returned to their anatomical positions.

The incision is closed. This code reports each additional lumbar interspace and must be reported in conjunction with 22862.

0166T
The physician performs endoscopic operative repair of a ventricular septal defect using an implant. Through multiple endoscopic incisions in the chest, the physician accesses and visualizes the outer (epicardial) surface of the heart. The myocardium is incised, and the endoscopic tool carrying the septal plug implant is advanced to the site of the ventricular defect. The defect is closed with the implant, and the endoscope is removed and access incisions are sutured in layers.

0167T
The physician performs endoscopic operative repair of a ventricular septal defect using an implant. Cardiopulmonary bypass is initiated. Through multiple endoscopic incisions in the chest, the physician accesses and visualizes the outer (epicardial) surface of the heart. The myocardium is incised and the endoscopic tool carrying the septal plug implant is advanced to the site of the ventricular defect. The defect is closed with the implant and the endoscope is removed and access incisions are sutured in layers. Cardiopulmonary bypass is discontinued when heart function returns.

0168T
The physician treats allergic rhinitis by exposing nasal tissue to ultraviolet and visible light. A light wand connected to a specialized light source is fitted with a disposable nasal tip and inserted into the nasal cavity of the patient for three minutes or less. During the treatment, the physician rotates the light source to continually pan the nasal cavity to ensure the treatment reaches all nasal tissue. The light inhibits histamine release from mast cells and induces apoptosis in T cells and eosinophils. The process is repeated in the contralateral nostril. The patient is instructed to use vitamin B oil as a salve after the treatment. This code reports one treatment course of rhinophototherapy.

0169T
An infusion catheter is implanted in the brain for convection enhanced delivery of an antineoplastic drug. Following a computerized stereotactic plan, the physician creates a burr hole in the patient's skull. Using stereotactic guidance, the physician places a catheter system into the area of the brain in which a tumor has been resected. This area will be treated with cintredekin besudotox to stop or slow the growth of the malignancy. The drug infusion typically occurs slowly over several days. When the infusion is completed, the catheter is withdrawn.

0171T-0172T
The physician inserts spinous process distraction devices, also known as interspinous process decompression devices (IPD), in the posterior column of the lumbar spine to enable spinal stabilization without the restrictions in motion that are created by spinal fusion. With the patient under appropriate anesthesia (often local anesthesia with light IV sedation) and in the lateral decubitus position (on the side), the physician makes a posterior 2 to 4 inch midline incision. Removal of bone or ligament may be necessary for device insertion. The spinous processes are exposed at the appropriate level and confirmed radiographically. While preserving the supraspinous ligament, the physician dilates the interspinous ligament and inserts and secures the IPD implant. Report 0171T if the device is inserted at a single level and 0172T for each additional level.

0173T
The physician monitors intraocular pressure (IOP) during vitrectomy surgery. IOP monitoring may be accomplished indirectly by placing disposable blood pressure transducers into the line tubing utilized for vitrectomy infusion. It may also be monitored by inserting a catheter pressure transducer directly into the vitreous via an extra pars plana incision. In either approach, pressure measurements are obtained simultaneously during the various stages of the vitrectomy, including air-fluid exchange and gas-forced fusion.

0174T-0175T
Computer-aided detection (CAD) systems are diagnostic tools that assist radiologists in the detection of subtle findings to facilitate early cancer detection. Used as an adjunct to radiographic images of the chest, it analyzes and highlights areas in the image that appear to be solid nodules, alerting the radiologist to the need for additional analysis. The CAD system consists of dedicated computer software and a review workstation. After initial images are obtained, copies are sent to the workstation for user review and also to the processing server for CAD analysis. Areas of irregularity are analyzed and a report generated that points out suspicious areas the radiologist can reassess. Code 0174T reports CAD of chest radiographs with further physician review for interpretation and report performed concurrently with primary interpretation. It is reported in addition to the primary radiology procedure. Code 0175T reports CAD that is performed remotely from the primary interpretation and is not reported in conjunction with the primary procedure.

0176T-0177T
The physician dilates the aqueous outflow canal (canaloplasty) for the treatment of glaucoma. Via scleral cutdown, the physician dilates the circular canal in the eye that drains aqueous humor from the anterior chamber into the anterior ciliary veins (Schlemm's canal) using a flexible microcatheter and viscoelastic. Intraoperative ultrasound imaging guidance is frequently used to ensure proper catheterization. Report 0177T if a polypropylene suture is placed

within the canal to improve aqueous outflow and preserve canal patency.

0178T-0180T

The physician performs an electrocardiogram. Electrocardiographic signals are used as indicators of cardiac pathology. Multichannel electrocardiography, also known as body surface mapping, utilizes multiple leads in order to collect as much information as possible about the heart's electrical behavior. A minimum of 64 electrodes are placed, strategically, to record the electrical activity of the heart, including graphic presentation and analysis. Report 0178T for the combined technical and professional components, 0179T for the tracing and graphics only, and 0180T for the interpretation and report only.

0181T

The physician determines corneal hysteresis (CH) by air impulse stimulation. The physician applies force to the cornea by rapid air pulse. The cornea moves inward, reaches the point of being flat (applanation), and then continues in to form a slight concavity. Milliseconds after applanation, the air pump is turned off and the pressure to the eye decreases. As this pressure decreases, the cornea returns to its natural shape while passing through the applanated state. Utilizing an advanced electro-optical system, two intraocular pressure (IOP) measurements are obtained during this process, the first as the cornea moves inward and the second as it returns to its baseline. The difference between these two values is corneal hysteresis.

0182T

The physician delivers high dose rate electronic brachytherapy, a type of radiation therapy indicated for the treatment of early stage breast cancer following breast-conserving surgery. A form of accelerated partial breast irradiation (APBI), it is designed to precisely target the portion of the tissue surrounding the tumor as opposed to the entire breast. This form of brachytherapy is delivered in fewer fractions and at larger doses per fraction, resulting in a treatment duration of four to five days as opposed to the standard five to seven weeks of whole-breast irradiation. Under local anesthesia and utilizing ultrasound guidance, the surgeon makes a small incision in the skin over the lumpectomy cavity and inserts a trocar through which a balloon applicator is inserted. The balloon is inflated with sterile water until ultrasound reveals that the cavity is filled and the surgical margin conforms to the applicator. The surgeon dresses the entrance wound and tapes the applicator shaft to the patient's skin. Details of the treatment plan, formulated using standard treatment planning software, are downloaded into a controller. The x-ray source, which is encased in a sheath, is inserted into the applicator shaft and connected to the controller. The source travels to the distant point of the shaft inside the saline-filled balloon and stops. Radiation treatment is delivered according to the preset treatment plan. Treatments are typically broken down into two fractions per day for five days, for a total of 10 fractions. Following each treatment, the source is removed. The applicator remains inside the breast until the entire treatment regimen is complete, after which it is removed.

0183T

The physician performs wound treatment utilizing a device that produces low-frequency, ultrasound-generated mist. This non-contact, non-thermal modality promotes wound healing through cellular stimulation. Indicated for acute, chronic, and colonized wounds, as well as burns and ulcers, it provides wound cleansing, bacteria removal, and maintenance debridement of fibrin and tissue exudates. The device uses ultrasound technology to atomize saline, delivering a continuous mist to the treatment site. Multiple passes over the wound are made with the treatment head of the device for a predetermined treatment session. This code includes assessment of the wound, topical applications when performed, and ongoing care instructions. Report this code once per day for the duration of treatment.

0184T

The physician excises a rectal tumor using the transanal endoscopic microsurgical (TEMS) approach. Following administration of appropriate anesthesia, the patient is placed in a lithotomy position. Dilation of the rectum is achieved and maintained with constant-flow carbon dioxide insufflation. Using specially designed instruments inserted via a resectoscope, full-thickness excision of the tumor is usually achieved. Dissection and suturing are performed within the rectal cavity.

0185T

This code reports the analysis of data pertaining to patient-specific findings, using more than one variable. This allows tracking of probability assessments and may decrease unnecessary diagnostic imaging or other tests. A measurable computer probability assessment and report is included.

0186T

The physician performs suprachoroidal delivery of a pharmacologic agent. In one method, the physician uses a microcannulation system. Under appropriate sedation, the physician makes a pars plana incision and exposes the suprachoroidal space. The microcannula is inserted, threaded through the suprachoroidal space, and directed toward the targeted posterior segment tissues under direct visualization. After confirmation of catheter location, the pharmacologic agent can be delivered. Code 0186T reports delivery of the pharmacologic agents only; it does not include the medication supply.

0187T
Scanning computerized ophthalmic diagnostic imaging (SCODI) of the anterior segment, which consists of the cornea, iris, ciliary body, and lens, is performed. In one form of SCODI, a camera generates images from the anterior corneal surface to the posterior surface of the lens. Software extracts elevation points from these images and generates a three-dimensional model. Interpretation and report are included in this procedure.

0188T-0189T
The physician delivers direct medical care from an off-site location for a patient who is critically ill or critically injured. Using real-time interactive videoconferencing, this method of critical care is used in addition to on-site critical care services in situations where the patient requires more resources than are available on-site. The physician must have real-time access to the patient's medical record (medication record, nursing and progress notes, vital signs, laboratory and other diagnostic test results, and x-rays), as well as the ability to enter orders electronically, document the services provided, communicate by videoconference with on-site personnel, thoroughly assess the patient and equipment, and communicate with patients and family members on a real-time basis. Report 0188T for the first 30–74 minutes of remote real-time interactive video-conferenced critical care on a given date. This code should be reported only once per day, even though the time spent by the physician on that day may not be continuous. Report 0189T in conjunction with 0188T for each additional 30-minute period in excess of the first 74 minutes.

0190T
Epiretinal radiation is used to treat the wet form of age-related macular degeneration, which is characterized by the formation of new blood vessels that grow into the subretinal space (choroidal neovascularization or CNV). Focal intraocular radiation is delivered to a subfoveal choroidal neovascular lesion. The physician, using a standard vitrectomy procedure, inserts the cannula tip of a handheld surgical device into the vitreous cavity and places it over the lesion. The tip is held in place over the lesion, the radiation source (strontium-90) advances down the cannula, and focused radiation is delivered for a prescribed period of time. Code 0190T reports placement of the intraocular radiation source applicator and is reported in addition to the primary procedure (67036).

0191T-0192T
The physician treats refractory primary open-angle glaucoma by draining aqueous humor from the anterior chamber directly into Schlemm's canal by shunting or stenting, lowering intraocular pressure (IOP) without the formation of a filtering bleb. In one method, the physician uses an internal approach through the cornea and anterior chamber. A 1 mm to 2 mm clear corneal incision is made, through which a stent is inserted into Schlemm's canal using a microdelivery system. In an alternate method, an external approach is made through the subconjunctiva. An extraocular reservoir (subconjunctival space) is not used in either approach. Report 0191T if an internal approach is used and 0192T if the approach is external.

0193T
The physician uses radiofrequency energy to treat female stress urinary incontinence, the involuntary loss of urine from the urethra due to increased intra-abdominal pressure. Using a small transurethral probe, the physician applies low temperature radiofrequency energy to targeted submucosal areas of the bladder neck and urethra. This results in minute structural alterations to the collagen which, upon healing, make the tissues firmer and increase their resistance to involuntary leakage.

0195T-0196T
The physician performs lumbar spinal fusion using a presacral interbody technique. In one method, the intervertebral space is accessed over the presacral fat pad, typically under fluoroscopic guidance. The physician makes a small incision in the midline over the tail bone (coccyx), incises the adjacent fascia, and enters the presacral space. A blunt instrument is advanced along the sacrum's anterior surface to a point at which the center of the disc can be accessed. When the correct position is confirmed, a 3 mm sharp wire is advanced up to the disc space. Dilator tubes are inserted over this wire in order to create an opening in the sacrum that will accommodate a 10 mm working channel. The disc space is cleared through this channel using appropriate surgical instruments, the bone plates are scraped clean, and a mixture of bone, bone substitute, and bone marrow is inserted into the disc space. A hole is then created in the fifth lumbar vertebra, and the working channel is exchanged to allow for passage of the larger instrumentation rod. Report 0195T for a single lumbar interspace and 0196T for each additional interspace.

0197T
Image-guided radiation therapy is a technique in which frequent imaging occurs during the course of a radiation therapy session (intra-fraction) in order to ensure that the radiation is delivered to the correct target location but spares surrounding tissues. Decisions regarding administration adjustments are made on the basis of the imaging results. Various methods of localization and tracking of patient or tumor motion may be used, including gating or 3D positional or surface tracking technology. In one method, an electromagnetic transponder is implanted into the prostate prior to external beam therapy for

prostate cancer. This transponder transmits radiofrequency waves to a computerized system, which provides information regarding position and movement of the prostate. This motion data is used by clinicians to assist in radiation therapy setup and as a positional monitor during delivery of treatment, alerting the clinician if the tumor moves outside the pathway of the radiation beam. Report 0197T for each fraction of treatment.

0198T

The physician tests for glaucoma, a multi-factorial disease that is affected by both intraocular pressure (IOP) and ocular blood flow (OBF). Each time the heart beats, a bolus of blood flows through the ocular choroid, causing IOP to rise and fall with each pulse. Greatest risk to the eye occurs when IOP is high and pulsatile OBF is low, resulting in stress on the retinal neurons near the disc. The physician uses an ocular blood flow tonometer that repeatedly measures the IOP during the cardiac pulse cycle. The tonometer takes multiple readings per second and analyzes the changes in IOP. A computer analyzes the data, calculates the pulsatile OBF, and provides a report of the minimum, average, and maximum values. Code 0198T includes interpretation and report.

0199T

This code reports a type of tremor analysis device that consists of an accelerometer and/or a gyroscope. Attached to the patient's arm or finger, these devices measure tremor. After attachment of the device(s), the patient is instructed to perform several tasks, such as placing the hands in the lap for several seconds, extending the arms straight in front of the body for several seconds, and extending the arm to touch the nose. An EMG testing component may be included in some models. In addition to their use in diagnosing tremors, these devices may also be used for patients receiving deep brain stimulation to direct adjustments to the settings of the neurostimulator. This code includes interpretation and report.

0200T-0201T

Percutaneous sacroplasty (sacral augmentation) is performed by a one- or two-sided injection into a sacral insufficiency fracture. A local anesthetic is administered. In a separately reportable procedure, the radiologist uses imaging techniques, such as CT scanning and fluoroscopy, to guide percutaneous placement of the needle during the procedure and to monitor the injection procedure. Sterile biomaterial such as polymethyl methacrylate is injected from one side or both sides into the sacrum and sacral insufficiency fracture and acts as a bone cement. Report 0200T for unilateral percutaneous sacroplasty using one or more needles and 0201T for a bilateral procedure using two or more needles. These codes include the use of a balloon or mechanical device, if utilized.

0202T

The physician performs facet joint replacement (facet arthroplasty) of a posterior vertebral joint at a single level of the lumbar spine using fluoroscopic guidance. The paravertebral facet joint consists of the bony surfaces between the vertebrae that articulate with each other. A facet replacement device is inserted in the posterior column of the lumbar spine to restore structure and function. The device replaces all or a portion of a facet joint on a vertebral body. In one method, the physician removes, by partial resection, a posterior vertebral component (facet) and inserts a facet prosthesis. The patient is placed prone and an incision is made overlying the affected vertebra and taken down to the level of the fascia. The fascia is incised and the paravertebral muscles are retracted. The physician removes the affected facet and replaces it with the prosthesis. Facetectomy, laminectomy, foraminotomy, and vertebral column fixation (with or without bone cement injection) may also be performed and are included in this code. Paravertebral muscles are repositioned and the tissue and skin are closed with layered sutures.

0203T-0204T

Unattended sleep studies are used by physicians in the diagnosis of certain patients with suspected sleep disorders. Without the attendance of a technologist, the test is performed with a portable recording device that simultaneously measures heart rate, oxygen saturation, respiratory analysis by airflow or peripheral arterial tone, and sleep time (0203T). Report 0204T for an unattended sleep study that measures a minimum of heart rate, oxygen saturation, and respiratory analysis by airflow or peripheral arterial tone. A physician interprets the results.

0205T

During diagnostic or therapeutic cardiac catheterization procedures, such as angiography, intracoronary stent insertion, coronary atherectomy, and heart catheterization, the interventional cardiologist uses an intravascular spectroscopy system consisting of a laser light source, a small fiberoptic catheter, and a console to assess coronary plaque. The ability to identify the chemical composition of coronary artery plaques in a patient undergoing a percutaneous coronary intervention can assist in determining the most appropriate type of stent (drug-eluting vs. bare metal). For example, lipid rich plaques may cause secondary events such as thrombosis after stenting; this determination can guide the choice of stent selected. This code reports intravascular catheter-based spectroscopy of a native or graft coronary vessel and includes imaging supervision, interpretation, and report. Report this code once for each vessel.

0206T
The physician performs an electrocardiogram. Electrocardiographic signals are used as indicators of cardiac pathology. Multichannel electrocardiography, also known as body surface mapping, utilizes multiple leads in order to collect as much information as possible about the heart's electrical behavior. A minimum of 64 electrodes are placed, strategically, to record the electrical activity of the heart, including graphic presentation and analysis. Code 0206T reports remote algorithmic analysis with computer probability assessment of data derived from an electrocardiogram. This code includes a report of the analysis.

0207T
The physician performs an automated evacuation of the meibomian glands using heat and intermittent pressure in order to remove obstruction and restore the natural flow of meibomian gland secretions. The outermost layer of the eye is a thin layer made up of many lipids (meibum) that are secreted by the meibomian glands located on the upper and lower eyelids. These glands may become occluded or obstructed, resulting in dry eye symptoms. The physician delivers heat to the lids via an infrared device or eye steamer device. Once secretions are in a more liquid state, the physician uses lid massage and compression of the meibomian gland body to evacuate the contents.

0208T-0209T
Pure tone audiometry is performed using a computer-assisted audiometer. Many causes of hearing loss have characteristic threshold curves. In pure tone audiometry, earphones are placed and the patient is asked to respond to tones of different pitches (frequencies) and intensities. The threshold, which is the lowest intensity of the tone that the patient can hear 50 percent of the time, is recorded for a number of frequencies on each ear. For pure tone signals, which are single-frequency tones that are produced electronically and transferred through an earphone or bone conduction vibrator, hearing sensitivity is measured separately in each ear. In one method, masking noise is provided to the non-test ear when it is determined by the computer that masking is necessary. Through touch-screen operation, the patient self-administers the tests while following verbal and onscreen instructions. Report 0208T for automated audiometry including the air conduction mode only and 0209T for automated audiometry including air and bone conduction modes. The air and bone thresholds are compared to differentiate between conductive, sensorineural, or mixed hearing losses.

0210T-0211T
Automated speech audiometry thresholds are performed using a computer-assisted device. Causes of hearing loss may often be diagnosed through the use of tests using an audiometer. Many causes of hearing loss have characteristic threshold curves unique to that specific diagnosis. In speech audiometry, earphones are placed and the patient is asked to repeat bisyllabic (spondee) words. The softest level at which the patient can correctly repeat 50 percent of the spondee words is called the speech reception threshold. The threshold is recorded for each ear in 0210T. This process occurs in 0211T, in addition to a discrimination test. The word discrimination score is the percentage of spondee words that a patient can repeat correctly at a given intensity level above his or her speech reception threshold. This is also measured for each ear.

0212T
Automated comprehensive audiometry threshold evaluation and speech recognition is performed with the use of a computer-assisted device. Causes of hearing loss can often be diagnosed through tests using an audiometer. Many causes of hearing loss have characteristic threshold curves. In comprehensive audiometry, earphones are placed and the patient is asked to respond to tones of different pitches (frequencies) and intensities. The threshold, which is the lowest intensity of the tone that the patient can hear 50 percent of the time, is recorded for a number of frequencies on each ear. Bone thresholds are obtained in a similar manner except a bone oscillator is used on the mastoid or forehead to conduct the sound instead of tones through earphones. The air and bone thresholds are compared to differentiate between conductive, sensorineural, or mixed hearing losses. With the earphones in place, the patient is also asked to repeat bisyllabic (spondee) words. The softest level at which the patient can correctly repeat 50 percent of the spondee words is called the speech reception threshold. The threshold is recorded for each ear. The word discrimination score is the percentage of spondee words that a patient can repeat correctly at a given intensity level above his or her speech reception threshold. This is also measured for each ear.

0213T-0215T
The physician injects a diagnostic or therapeutic agent into a cervical or thoracic paravertebral facet joint or into the nerves that innervate the joint using ultrasound guidance. The paravertebral facet joints, also called zygapophyseal or "Z" joints, consist of the bony surfaces between the vertebrae that articulate with each other. The injection may be performed on a single level or on multiple levels. Report 0213T for a single level, 0214T for a second level, and 0215T for the third and any additional levels.

0216T-0218T
The physician injects a diagnostic or therapeutic agent into a lumbar or sacral paravertebral facet joint or into the nerves that innervate the joint using ultrasound guidance. The paravertebral facet joints, also called zygapophyseal "Z" joints, consist of the bony surfaces between the vertebrae that articulate with each other.

The injection may be performed on a single level or on multiple levels. Report 0216T for a single level, 0217T for a second level, and 0218T for the third and any additional levels.

0219T-0222T

The physician places unilateral or bilateral posterior intrafacet implants in the cervical (0219T), thoracic (0220T), or lumbar (0221T) vertebral segments using imaging guidance. Bone grafts or synthetic devices may also be used and are included in these codes. Report 0222T for each additional vertebral segment.